Literature
The Evolving Canon

SECOND EDITION

Sven P. Birkerts
EMERSON COLLEGE

Allyn and Bacon
Boston London Toronto Sydney Tokyo Singapore

For my wife, Lynn Focht, and my children, Mara and Liam

Vice President, Humanities: Joseph Opiela
Developmental Editor: Allen Workman
Series Editorial Assistant: Susannah Davidson
Marketing Manager: Lisa Kimball
Editorial-Production Administrator: Rowena Dores
Editorial-Production Service: Lauren Green Shafer
Cover Administrator: Linda Knowles
Composition Buyer: Linda Cox
Manufacturing Buyer: Megan Cochran
Text Designer: Deborah Schneck
Cover Designer: Studio Nine
Photo Researcher: Laurie Frankenthaler/F & F Associates

Library of Congress Cataloging-in-Publication Data

Birkerts, Sven.
    Literature: the evolving canon / Sven P. Birkerts.—2nd ed.
      p.   cm.
    Includes bibliographical references and indexes.
    ISBN 0-205-17515-5
    1. Canon (Literature)   2. Literature—History and criticism—
Theory, etc.   I. Title.
PN81.B542   1996
808—dc20   95–19938
                                                 CIP

Credits continued on page 1674, which constitutes a continuation of the copyright page.

Printed in the United States of America
10 9 8 7 6 5 4 3   99

Brief Contents

Contents

10 Writing about Fiction 140

11 A Fiction Writer's Career: Alice Munro 163

12 A Fiction Writer's Career: James Baldwin 194

13 A Fiction Anthology 230

14 Responding to Stories   458

Poetry 533

18   Rhythm and Meter in Poetry   590

19   Fixed Forms in Poetry   615

20 Imagery in Poetry   638

24 Writing about Poetry   704

28 Responding to Poems   944

Drama   997

Casebook   1613

The Evolving Canon in a Video Age   1614

Appendices   1637

A: Critical Perspectives   1638

B: Researching and Documenting a Paper about Literature   1653

C: Glossary   1663

Credits   1674

Index of First Lines of Poetry   1685

Index of Authors and Titles   1689

Preface

The Preface to the first edition of *Literature: The Evolving Canon* sounded the theme of a rapidly changing world, and proposed a fresh approach to reading and responding to literature. The passing of three years has only underscored my sense that the renovation of the old order is the new constant we must live with. The spread of electronic communications continues to advance the cause of global awareness and emphasizes the need for supple and adaptable reflexes. For the teacher and student of literature this means developing a cosmopolitan set of perspectives *and* keeping a grasp on the accumulated legacy of many centuries. This book has been written—and revised—to meet these needs.

The Teaching Environment for Literature.   Change is, of course, a wind that blows in many directions at once. The negative effects of the transformation—the wholesale shift to a global electronic circuitry—are worrisome. On the largest scale there is a sense that we are becoming uncentered, wandering forth without our traditional sources of wisdom. Teachers routinely lament that their students are no longer interested in the tried and true ways of print culture, further loosening the grasp on traditional contexts. On an institutional level, meanwhile, those traditional contexts themselves are under fire. In colleges and universities all over the country teachers and administrators are locked in fierce struggles over the canon. To ask what texts are essential for the curriculum is really to ask about the purpose of education. The old maps no longer give us the lay of the land.

But there is a positive side to this transformation. Electronic globalization (among many other factors) has made possible great new infusions of energy. It is the kind of energy that is released when old forms and perspectives are shattered. What looks like a battle over the canon—a battle charted in the Casebook at the end of this text—can be seen from another angle as the first growing pains of a multicultural liberation movement. The people are clamoring at the gates; urgent voices insist on getting a hearing. In the long run this can only enrich us.

Nor is the multicultural pressure confined to the domestic front. The world has become the global village that Marshall McLuhan prophesied, and the result is not just a polyglot confusion but a thrilling diversity as well. This cultural variety can no longer go unrepresented or unexamined. To teach any of the humanities in a context that ignores our global culture is to be willfully parochial. It just won't wash. The reader of the second edition of *Literature: The Evolving Canon* will therefore find that the emphasis on domestic as well as global diversity is undiminished. Indeed, changes and new selections have been made with an eye to keeping the mixture fresh—more voices have been included in this continually evolving canon.

Goals and New Features for This Revision

The changes in this new edition derive from a single imperative: to make the text a more supple and useful teaching tool. All of the new selections are here to add depth to the presentation of the tradition—for example, Melville's "Bartleby the Scrivener"—or to expand diversity by showcasing new talent, such as fiction by Reginald McKnight.

To engage students more fully—to provoke the kinds of responses that lead to thoughtful writing—I have not only expanded the chapters that deal with writing about fiction, poetry, and drama, but I have also developed new "Responding to" applications for each genre (Chapters 14, 28, and 37). These offer students a chance to work with critical responses as secondary sources, while at the same time demonstrating how students can integrate these materials into their own interpretations. In addition, new questions now accompany every selection in the "elements" chapters in fiction and poetry, as well as every play.

Finally, expanded appendices present not only more detail on incorporating secondary sources in an interpretative paper—reflecting applicable material in the chapters on "Responding to"—but also they enrich discussions of various critical approaches by modeling ways that a student might apply these perspectives in writing. Another new addition, a full Glossary of definitions of literary terms and concepts, rounds out the volume.

Continuing Goals for This Book. This text continues to have a two-fold mission. First, it aims not only to represent but also to *celebrate* diversity. I have not set out to design a representative canon. Rather, I have worked in reverse. I have assumed from the outset the richness and variety of a world culture, and I have sought to reflect some part of it in these pages. I have followed my enthusiasms as well as a strong sense, based on my own teaching experience, of works that students would find both interesting and relevant to their own lives.

My second purpose, no less important, has been to assert at every turn the rootedness of all reading experiences in language. Just as line and color are the soul of painting, so are the word, the sentence, the poetic line the heart of literary art. And it is precisely this—the grasp and appreciation of language—that is put under threat in an electronic culture. If this text proclaims a new world in its selections, it also fights a campaign on behalf of language in its approach.

This campaign is carried out on all fronts. The selections, which I've already discussed, were made on the basis of literary excellence. I looked for texts in which the language is vivid and the perspectives are challenging. Second, the discussions of elements and instructional examples all insist upon the importance of close-focus reading. Skimming over a work of literature is like listening to music with wax plugs in your ears—it makes no sense.

Finally, I have tried to underscore the importance of this attentiveness by building a strong link between reading and writing. My own belief is that writing completes what reading begins. It not only teaches the skills of coherent and graceful expression, but also marks the truest path to the meaning of a work. There is no better way to think about a text—or maybe anything—than to write about it. In this edition, even more than in its predecessor, I have tried to make the necessary bridges between reading, response, and written expression. There is more discussion of writing strategies in the three "Writing about" chapters; questions designed to quicken reflection and response have been added throughout; and "Responding to" chapters now emphasize continuity between reading and writing using specific text groupings and assignment suggestions.

One final observation. Literature is not, to crib from the political speechwriters, a business of smoke and mirrors. It functions according to very specific principles. These may undergo modification from one era to another, but they do not disappear. They are the artistic laws that guide and constrain the imagination and we discover them in every culture and every genre, whether in the stories of Toni Cade Bambara or William Faulkner, the poems of Thomas Hardy or Lorna Dee Cervantes. We are not moved to laughter, outrage, sorrow, or enlightenment by accident. This should become increasingly clear as you work through this text. Canons are nothing but groupings of works that come alive for us. If I have a single hope for this particular grouping it is that it will help students see just how it is that words on the page can interact to make a dance in the mind.

A Focus on "Reading into Writing"

To carry out a major objective of the book and to further the idea that "writing completes what reading begins," the text stresses the importance of a written response from the very first chapter. The many discussions and samples of writing in response all emphasize the link between close and careful reading and the formulation of ideas and arguments.

Each genre unit includes its own "Writing about" chapter (Chapters 10, 24, 36)—a detailed "case study" presentation of how a typical student might go about the process of reading, responding, formulating, and then writing to communicate ideas to peers or instructors. These chapters offer step-by-step models that illuminate the complete writing encounter. First sketches and early drafts are shown, as are examples of student-peer critiques. New discussions in each section focus on strategies for incorporating text summaries into the larger presentation of the student's own original ideas. The final version is included to illustrate how suggestions and new insights can be incorporated.

The questions that accompany the various selections have all been designed not only to encourage close reading, but also to provoke the kind of thinking that leads to the formulation of ideas for writing. There are now questions for all of the works in the elements chapters, a major addition that enforces my insistence on the link between attentiveness and response.

Users will notice, too, an amplification of critical contexts. An array of new essays in the "Responding to" chapters (14, 28, and 37) encourages students to find a deeper engagement with the selected works, not only developing their insights, but also testing them against those of various critics. Writing examples show how other students have made use of critics and outside sources in building their arguments. The expansion of Appendix B, "Researching and Documenting a Paper about Literature," will help the writer make proper use of quotations and source materials; materials on attribution as well as the avoidance of plagiarism have likewise been added.

Appendix A, "Critical Perspectives," offers compact but informative discussions of the major approaches to literary criticism that have evolved in recent decades. These context-rich presentations will help the student to understand the fundamental assumptions underlying these approaches. Critical Perspectives are linked to illustrative materials throughout the book (explanations of New Critical close-reading, for example, are keyed to appropriate applications of close-reading technique in the text). Each discussion is now accompanied by a short writing sample that suggests how that approach might be used in a student essay. Also, for students who are especially interested in exploring some of these perspectives, brief reading lists are included.

The Organization of the Literature Chapters

Literature: The Evolving Canon is built around the three traditional genres: fiction, poetry, and drama. A unit for each includes some introductory chapters, literary texts in various groupings, and a separate "Responding to" chapter providing critical material on key works from that genre. In addition, the text includes a comprehensive Casebook on the evolving canon. Added to the selections that assess this core issue from various vantages is an essay of my own that explores some of the implications of computers and CD-ROM packages on traditional learning procedures.

Literature Selected for Breadth and Depth. The Fiction and Poetry units both begin with elements-based chapters that investigate the key components of the genre (Character, Plot, Sound and Sense in Poetry, Voice in Poetry, etc.) and make extensive use of examples. Questions are posed to involve the student more deeply in an array of works and to pave the way toward the writing response. Both units offer comprehensive anthologies of additional readings. In Fiction as in Poetry, the selections have been made to reflect global and multicultural perspectives, as well as to provide an appealing mix of traditional and contemporary readings. New selections for this edition have followed the same principle, adding, for instance, Melville's classic story, "Bartleby the Scrivener" and Ralph Lombreglia's postmodern humoresque "Men under Water." The sections of additional readings continue to be arranged chronologically to provide the student with a sense of historical context.

The plays in the Drama unit are arranged in chronological sequence with interspersed discussions of key historical developments. These discussions emphasize the diverse social contexts out of which the plays have emerged. The text provides a generous selection of full-length plays as well as several shorter works that can be compactly examined (or perhaps even staged) in one class sitting.

Since a major feature of this text is its global and multicultural vantage, a number of works originally written in other languages are featured. The translation issue is addressed head-on in a chapter (23) in the Poetry unit. Not only are students introduced to the problem of translatability, but they are challenged to examine several translated versions of poems originally written in foreign languages (one Spanish, one French, one Italian, and one German). A more thorough "case study"—this of a Chinese poem by Wang Wei—shows how the small decisions made by translators can change the overall effect of the translation.

Each of the three units showcases two authors, giving the student a chance to experience a literary sensibility (and the genre) at greater depth. The Fiction unit has special sections on the careers of Alice Munro and James Baldwin. Poetry, similarly, explores the developing styles of Adrienne Rich and Gary Snyder. Pairs of plays by Sophocles and Shakespeare bring added dimension to the Drama unit.

Comparisons and Perspectives. Although the formal arrangement of the literature selections is by element or according to chronology, the readings have been chosen to encourage the making of comparisons and contrasts in terms of theme, style, the handling of literary devices, and so forth. The "Responding to" chapters implement this directly—allowing students to compare, say, Nabokov's reading of a Chekhov story with Joyce Carol Oates's contemporary re-imagining of the same story—but selections throughout have been made on the basis of how they might be taught alongside other selections. The "Instructor's Resource Manual" offers many suggestions about interesting or instructive comparisons and contrasts. Linkages are further enhanced by the inclusion of critical perspectives in Appendix A. The student can not only establish a web of textual connections, but also interpret these connections according to one or another of the dominant critical traditions (Formalism, Reader-Response Theory, Psychoanalytical criticism, etc.).

Teaching Aids for the Texts. All the literary texts have been carefully glossed, a boon to the many students who need help with historical references or obscure terms. Depending on need, glosses are placed either at the foot of the page or in the margin. To facilitate quick reference, prose paragraphs are numbered at every fifth paragraph, while poems and plays in verse form are numbered at five-line intervals.

The new questions that have been added for all works in the various elements sections are meant to focus discussion and give the student a stronger understanding of the complex engagement that reading represents.

Chapter Discussions and Study Apparatus

The chapter texts in the Fiction and Poetry units are arranged to call attention to the key concepts and elements that form the basis of any understanding of these genres. The chapter texts in Drama are rooted in an extensive discussion of the origins of Greek drama. Subsequent changes and departures are examined in a historical context, with close attention paid to the connections between social realities and expressive styles. Contemporary drama selections (including a new play by Maria Irene Fornes) are especially focused on issues of race and gender.

The text supplies biographical information about each author in the Fiction and Drama units. Dates of birth and death are provided for the poets. In addition, drawings or photographs of selected authors are included to satisfy student curiosity.

Key terms and concepts are italicized in chapter text. These concepts are treated in brief summary form in the Glossary, which is indexed to provide locations and cross-references separately from the other indexes of first lines of poetry and authors and titles.

Instructor's Resource Manual

A comprehensive Instructor's Resource Manual offers extensive teaching suggestions and supplemental information. Every story, poem, and play is discussed, usually in terms of useful areas of analysis and writing suggestions. Works are consistently cross-referenced with other works to promote stylistic and other kinds of comparisons, and to permit reading assignments to be made in thematic clusters. All of the questions in the text are addressed in the Manual, along with suggested lines of discussion and ideas for collaborative work in groups. Another new feature is the inclusion of relevant contextual material from the previous edition and some biographical notes on selected poets. A media resource listing at the end of the Manual provides all sorts of suggested options for enhanced presentation of materials, and teaching notes are included for key videotapes available to adopters of this text. The Manual also includes my essay on the experience of teaching students who are alienated from literary texts. "Teaching in a Video Age" outlines a number of strategies to intensify links between reading, responding, and writing.

Acknowledgments

Several reviewers have commented on the previous edition and provided guidance and suggestions for this revision. Especially helpful has been detailed commentary and notes from Mark Rollins of Ohio University. Also very useful were reviews and suggestions from Bonnie Flaig of Kalamazoo Community College, Charlotte Hoffmann of Nassau Community College, Emory Maiden of Appalachian State University, Jeff Nelms of Tarrant County Junior College, and Michael Schwartz of Bucks County Community College. In addition, some very helpful comments and suggestions have come to our attention from Beverly Carmo of Allegheny County Community College, Ruth Lepson and Kristine Woolover of Northeastern University, Alma McCurdich of Salt Lake Community College, Barbara Pearson of the University of Miami–Coral Gables, and Marty Schictman and Tom Hennings of Eastern Michigan University.

The reviewers who commented on early drafts have given reactions and suggestions that have been most helpful to shaping this book's teaching focus. Our thanks to the reviewers of the first edition manuscript: Ellin Carter, The Ohio State University; James Egan, The University of Akron; James A. Grimshaw, East Texas State University; Robert D. Habich, Ball State University; Iris Rose Hart, Santa Fe Community College; Vicki Hendricks, Broward Community College; David K. Himber, St. Petersburg Junior College; Douglas Krienke, Sam Houston State University; Marjorie D. Lewis, Texas Christian University; Barry Maid, University of Arkansas–Little Rock; Paul Mariani, the University of Massachusetts–Amherst; Thomas E. Martinez, Villanova University; Judith K. Powers, University of Wyoming; and Charles Workman, Samford University.

I am grateful to others who have helped me with this book: at Allyn and Bacon, my editor, Joe Opiela; my Developmental Editor, Allen Workman; Editorial Assistant Susannah Davidson; and Production Administrator Rowena Dores. I also thank the following people who have influenced my work in teaching and writing about literature as well as in making this book:

Askold Melnyczuk, Boston University; Tom Sleigh, Dartmouth College; Stuart Dischell, Boston University; George Scialabba; Sue Standing, Wheaton College; Fred Marchant, Suffolk University; William Corbett; Alex Johnson; Suzanne Berne, Harvard University; George Packer, Harvard University; Stratis Haviaras, Harvard University; DeWitt Henry, Emerson College; Alfred Alcorn, Harvard University; Douglas Bauer; Sue Miller; Jim Kelly; and Thomas Frick. And many thanks go to my wife, Lynn Focht.

S. P. B.

1 Literature: Reading into Writing

We seem to be entering a new historical period, one that is bent upon questioning the status of all definitions and former certainties. On the global scale we see the rapid and radical alteration of national boundaries and allegiances. The once monolithic Soviet Union was falling to pieces even as I wrote these words. The European countries have begun a cooperative alliance that is bound to change the social and economic life of hundreds of millions of people. Words like *socialism*, *communism*, and *European* will soon no longer mean what they once did.

A similar spirit of transformation has gripped our cultural life as well. We see controversies over funding for the arts, at the root of which are serious questions about what should be called art and who should make the call. And our colleges and universities are embroiled in tense shouting matches over curricula. At issue is the "canon," that body of works that many believe form the necessary basis for an education. Upholders of the traditional canon argue that certain texts are uncontestably great and must be the central pillars of all liberal schooling, never mind that most of them have been authored by white males. The critics, on the other hand, contend that curricula need to adapt to changes in the larger social fabric; that the vital presence of women, gays, and diverse racial groups in academia—and society—makes a thorough revision of teaching goals essential.

WHAT IS LITERATURE?

Literature sits right in the middle of the crossfire. Battles are fought not only over which texts form the core of the Western inheritance, but also over which approaches best serve to foster comprehension. Marxist? Feminist? Deconstructionist? And behind these disputes is yet another—the dispute over what constitutes literature. Where are the boundary lines to be drawn? What do we include and exclude, and why? Do women's diaries from the nineteenth century count as worthy objects of literary study? How about African American slave narratives? Who will decide?

Critics have wrestled with these questions at length in recent years. English critic Terry Eagleton, for instance, looks back at the history of English literature and finds that there are no consistent guidelines for inclusion, and never have been. In some periods, memoirs and works of history or speculation were accepted as literature; in others, not. Moreover, works dismissed as inferior in one epoch may be crowned as masterpieces in another. Poet John Donne was cursed with obscurity for centuries; poet and critic T. S. Eliot had to argue in favor of his greatness. Seen from the longer vantage of history, every attainment is to some degree temporary. What is "literary" and what is "great" are both to a large degree the products of consensus. That is, they are what people at any one time agree they are.

This agreement, of course, is no simple thing, and the opinions of the man or woman in the street do not have much to do with it. What finally matters is institutional consensus, which really means a series of tug-o'-war matches fought out in conference rooms and in the pages of academic journals. Back-room votes determine policy; policy shapes curricula; and curricula decide, to a significant extent, what we learn and carry about as our picture of the world.

The student is not generally aware of this chain of influence. He or she opens the textbook and finds set out, in bold lettering, the principal genres, authors, and approaches to study. *This* is literature. *Here* are the elements of fiction, poetry, and drama. And participation in reading and writing about these texts makes it so—the ideas and valuations crystallize in millions of separate sensibilities.

I am not suggesting that we call a strike and refuse to play the game. That would be preposterous. The genre divisions and selections of representative works may not be givens from on high, but neither are they an arbitrary mélange of notions and preferences. Fiction, poetry, drama, and the essay are always shifting their boundaries, true, but their roots remain strong. Indeed, the genres exist as they do because they mark out necessary expressive options: Writers tend to think in fictional, poetic, dramatic, and essayistic terms. Maybe they do so because the genres are there; but quite possibly the genres exist because they meet specific artistic needs—and have done so for millennia.

The point of all this is that literature is not governed by absolutes. The student needs to recognize that nothing is God-given about the way literature gets written, read, or studied. Rather, the literary encounter always takes place in a historical context. We are products of our society, and we read with needs and expectations that are considerably different from those shared by students of a century ago. At the same time, certain constants remain. Stories get written in the same basic forms because those forms seem to work on readers. The basic human emotions continue to drive the subjects, no matter how much those subjects have changed. Relativism and recurrence—both are true. We should try to enter these diverse literary worlds with open minds.

What is literature? I have described a contested terrain, where there is no unanimity about what is to be included, but I have said nothing about criteria. On what basis are decisions made? How does a work pass the test? How serious or formal or innovative does it have to be? For example, we would probably agree that a literary text should have some content or meaning to project, but how much? And are there more and less appropriate kinds of contents? The same holds for form. Are there more and less suitable forms for certain kinds of expression? The distinctions to be made are endless. In fact, we find as many versions of the literary as there are people offering versions. Some believe that art must be morally uplifting; others insist that it stare without flinching into the darkest places of the heart. Some uphold the usefulness and vitality of traditional forms, while others regard them as confining cages.

Who will choose, and on what grounds? Again, consensus is not to be disregarded. If certain works and approaches are favored by a majority of readers, we ought to consider the reasons. One does not have to bow low before the dominant view, but acknowledgment is good manners, if nothing more. By the same token, to ignore the voices from outside the sanctioned tradition is to be closed-minded. Progress in the arts has seldom originated in the safety of the center. What we think of as classics today are works that were often seen as affronts to good taste when they first appeared. James Joyce and D. H. Lawrence were both widely banned; now they are cornerstones of the literature curriculum. Diversity challenges us to be vigilant and flexible. We should approach our reading without preconceptions so far as that is possible. If this advice sounds like trying to have things both ways, so be it. The face-off between traditionalists and innovators is not about to be resolved soon. A compromise that looks for virtues in both positions seems sensible.

CONTEXTS IN READING

Uncertainty rears its head again as soon as we look at literature from the perspective of the individual reader. We find no hard-and-fast rules about framing the proper interpretation of a work or determining whether it is good or bad. People are different, and their responses to the same work will vary tremendously. What is for one reader a work of genius will be obscure or irrelevant to another reader. Does this mean that there are no standards or criteria of value? Of course not. What the variability of responses underscores is the importance of private contexts to the reading process. Only after these have been identified and understood can we work toward some consensus about the meaning and artistic value of a story, poem, or play.

We therefore need to look at the relation between the work—its language, setting, themes, and so on—and the world of the reader. A story by John Cheever about well-to-do advertising executives living in Connecticut will mean one thing to a first-generation Asian American living in Tucson, and something quite different to a student from an affluent New England milieu. The first student may insist that the story is meaningless, while the second may argue that it is a perfect portrait of upper-middle-class culture. The discussion cannot proceed until the terms—the social codes and assumptions—of the story have been articulated. One student needs to make the effort to grasp the codes; the other has to accept that they are not universal or inevitable. The same flexibility would be required if the class were to read a poem about life in the barrio, or on an Indian reservation in New Mexico. The enrichment finally comes not just from the work, but also from the experience of internalizing new perspectives.

We see another example of the importance of identifying contexts in cases in which students are asked to make sense of some literary work from the past, possibly from the past of another culture. While we are always free to like or dislike a given work—Sophocles' *Oedipus Rex*, say—we cannot dismiss its value just because it doesn't immediately "speak" to us. We owe it to the play, no less than to ourselves, to try to understand what we can about the Greek culture in which the drama originated. We need to know how Sophocles and his contemporaries saw the world— the place of fate, the attitudes toward tragedy—before we judge. If we do choose to argue that the play is a failure, and it is our right to do so, we have to present our case from an informed context. Otherwise, it is we who have failed, not Sophocles.

This matter of understanding other contexts and of enlarging upon our own is one of the main reasons for studying literature, especially in a classroom. To be sure, anyone who knows how to read can acquire an education independently. And such an approach has its uses—the reader decides what to study, at what pace, and for what purpose. But the classroom structure is in other ways invaluable. Group discussions create a forum in which opinions can be tested, reactions refined, and contexts of evaluation compared. The free exchange of reactions to a given work seldom results in unanimity, but it reveals as nothing else can the kinds of judgments that underlie interpretation. One student says, "I thought he despised his wife," while another counters with, "No, he loved her but he just couldn't admit it." The discussion hits a standoff. The obvious next step is for each student to present evidence, to back up the assertions made: *"Here is why I think he despised her." "I believe he loved her because. . . ."* Usually one line of argument is more persuasive, one interpretation is more inclusive. Other class members become a kind of jury.

Once we have engaged in this process of debate with a group of our peers, or any other community of readers, we begin to understand the literary work itself differently. The text becomes less sacred, more available to inspection and exploration, than we might have allowed at first. We also learn that interpretation is a process that moves through stages. We don't just say, "I give it two thumbs up," and be done with it. Rather, we unpack layers, deepening and refining our reactions as we go. The first impression is only the starting point.

We start to see, then, that consensus is not a state or a static condition, but the unattainable goal of a complex and dynamic process. Just as the public and institutional perceptions about the value of artistic works are always in flux, so too are our private responses open to modification. You may start with one set of understandings, only to find that further exploration and discussion with others begins to change your assumptions. Indeed, a vigorous in-class debate about a given work can become the occasion for examining your whole system of expectations and preconceptions. If nothing else, such interchanges serve as a reminder that how we read has everything to do with our individuality. True consensus would be universal agreement, and that will never come about. What we strive for instead is a public explication of interpretations and the thought processes that underlie them. These can be usefully compared.

In some cases you may find that your arguments and understandings are challenged—even overpowered—by those of others. But you may just as readily find that a difference of opinion strengthens your conviction about your own reading. Whatever the outcome, however, the exchange of views deepens your involvement with the work and paves the way for writing. It stands as a reminder that responses and interpretations are not absolutes and that the assertions ventured on the page must be not only coherent but persuasive as well.

FROM READING INTO WRITING

Though we tend to speak of reading and writing as two distinct processes—the one a kind of taking in, the other a putting out—the two in fact belong together. They are not only side by side on a continuum, but connected. Reading *is* a taking in of information and impressions, but it is also an active engagement that generates a continual stream of responses. When we read we interact. We turn strings of words into images and thoughts as we work to establish clarity. We translate words into thoughts and then react to the thoughts. In a very real sense we collaborate with the author to create the text. (The literary theorists would say that we *actualize,* or *concretize,* the text.)

This response aspect of reading can also be seen as the first step of the writing process. To write about anything we must have something to say. Our initial act when we set out to write about a literary work is to take a step back and sift through our reactions—the ideas and emotions we had while reading. Thus, there is no clear line between the taking in and the putting out. Writing finishes what reading begins. Writing brings coherence and depth to the unstructured chaos of our reading-thoughts. The more sustained and disciplined activity of shaping these thoughts allows us to discover what we really think about a work.

The value of writing as a technology—we often forget that writing was invented to fill a set of human needs—is that it arrests and externalizes our thoughts. We plant our idea on the page, fixing it in place with words, and it stays there, allowing us to examine it. We are free to add to it, or to qualify it, or to rid it of vagueness and redundancy; we can manipulate a single statement until it takes on the complexity we desire. We might begin by writing the obvious: "Homer's Odysseus was a brave man." Then, recognizing that our words do not do full justice to the hero or the nature of his trials, we might ponder the nature of bravery and look for ways to make a less obvious assertion. "Odysseus's bravery," we might decide, "was more than just a willingness to face danger. It revealed the character of a man willing to act on his code of honor even when he was frightened." Writing forces us to make our response explicit and workable. While the second recognition may have been part of our reading experience all along, it took the deliberation of the writing process to bring it out.

Writing, then, is a way into thinking. It *is* thinking. Searching for the right words and the right sequence of ideas, we make a map of our response; when we go back to clarify, amplify, and prune, we improve the map. Similarly, the writing process sharpens our reading. It is one thing to read through an author's text simply for the pleasure or instruction of reading, and quite another to read it in order to write about it. Reading to write intensifies our attentiveness dramatically. We become alert to important passages and study the fine points of the writer's style. Like practiced mechanics, we get in under the hood and check out the moving parts. We also find ourselves moving rapidly back and forth from the ideas we are shaping to the words on the page. We check and double-check meanings. In this way the writing and reading become facets of a single act of responsive exploration. And what we learn from the process has applications that ultimately matter far more than the immediate assignment.

We come now to some practical considerations. The basic fact is that reading and writing—focusing upon a text, formulating ideas, and organizing those ideas into coherent written form—are the very core of the academic process. We don't have far to search to find out the reasons for this. Simply, the comprehension and communication skills that reading and writing foster are prized above all others in the professional world. The people who succeed in that world are the ones who can read information, textual and other, to find what is important and what is not; they can interpret that information and communicate their interpretation sensibly and concisely. The aptitudes and reflexes that you sharpen in responding to a short story or a poem are the same ones you will call upon in preparing a presentation to a prospective client or devising a smart courtroom defense.

Reading and writing about literary works thus serves a double function. Ideally, the process brings insights about the self and about the universal complexities of living. In addition, the process also teaches mastery of a set of operations that are vital in almost any field of practical endeavor.

Reading and Responding—An Example

I stated earlier that reading and writing were, in a sense, side by side on a continuum. What this means is that the steps that lead from the first encounter with a text to the final written product unfold in a natural sequence. These steps can be isolated and discussed, at least to some degree, and in the "Writing about" and "Responding to" chapters that accompany the Fiction, Poetry, and Drama sections of this book, specific applications will be illustrated. As a more general introduction, I offer a breakdown of some of the basic procedures that link the reading responses to a written interpretation. Here is a short text.

Louis Jenkins (1942–   )

FISH OUT OF WATER

When he finally landed the fish it seemed so strange, so unlike other fishes he'd caught, so much bigger, more silvery, more important, that he half expected it to talk, to grant his wishes if he returned it to the water. But the fish said nothing, made no pleas, gave no promises. His fishing partner said, "Nice fish, you ought to have it mounted." Other people who saw it said the same thing, "Nice fish . . . " So he took it to the taxidermy shop but when it came back it didn't look quite the same. Still, it was an impressive trophy. Mounted on a big board the way it was, it was too big to fit in the car. In those days he could fit everything he owned into the back of his Volkswagen but the fish changed all that. After he married, a year or so later, nothing would fit in the car. He got a bigger car. Then a new job, children. . . . The fish moved with them from house to house, state to state. All that moving around took its toll on the fish, it began to look worn, a fin was broken off. It went into the attic of the new house. Just before the divorce became final, when he was moving to an apartment, his wife said "Take your goddamn fish." He hung the fish on the wall before he'd unpacked anything else. The fish seemed huge, too big for this little apartment. Boy, it was big. He couldn't imagine he'd ever caught a fish that big.

Jenkins's text belongs to a genre called the *prose poem*. There are no hard-and-fast rules for the form—the writer can sketch a narrative or simply gather images and impressions into a suggestive expression. Prose poems are usually short; while they may make use of the verbal compression that we associate with poetry, they follow the basic conventions of prose presentation.

We begin, as always, by reading. Once, twice, a third time, and maybe more. Because "Fish Out of Water" is short, we can give it a more intense inspection than we might give to the longer works we are apt to encounter. I know of no rationale for rereading except the obvious: the more you read a text, the better you know it, and the more likely you are to grasp its subtleties. Some teachers will insist on three or more readings of a work; others will leave the decision up to the student. The point, of course, is not how often, but how well. How long should you brush your teeth? Until they are clean—what else is to be said?

One thing is safe to say, however. A single reading of a work is not likely to suffice, no matter how intelligent and attentive the reader. Comprehension comes in stages. The first reading gives us the general feel. We assess the tone, the general progress of the narrative (or, if it is a lyric poem, the sequence of the images), and we get a sense of the thematic direction. We read through once to know where we should linger to focus; we leave mental markers at places that may be confusing or that we suspect may hold special significance. The second time through we hold a picture of the whole in mind and we determine the relative importance of the parts.

Two readings may be sufficient for comprehension. But if we plan to write about a work, we will probably zero in again, this time perhaps armed with a pencil or marker. And even then we are not finished. When the writing begins and we start to wrestle our ideas and intuitions into words, we may well find ourselves staring again and again at certain passages.

Reading Jenkins's prose poem for the very first time, we probably take in the main lines of the narrative. A man has caught a very large fish, has had it mounted, and has carried it around with him as a memento. As his life has changed, with marriage, children and different jobs, the trophy has gradually become another piece of clutter. Then, with divorce and the onset of new changes, the fish is once again out on display. And now, for whatever reason, it strikes the man as remarkable—he cannot believe that he had ever caught such a thing.

Though in our first reading we tend to be mainly concerned with getting the story straight, we are doubtless aware that Jenkins intends the fish to have some particular significance, both for the man and for his reader. We may be thinking that it stands for something, that it possesses some symbolic value. But what? Clearly it has something to do with the man's youth and his way of seeing the world. But this interpretation is very general, and if we intend to write about the text, we realize that these notions are not sufficient basis.

A second reading will deepen our involvement, bringing forward new ideas and possibly new perplexities. We might notice, for instance, that Jenkins has taken some pains to emphasize qualities other than the size. The fish is "strange" and "important"; there is some mystery about it. He tells us that the man "half expected it to talk" and brings up the idea of wishes being granted. Perhaps this brings to mind the old fairy tale about the fisherman who was granted three wishes—wishes that inspired his wife with greed and ultimately backfired. But no, the fish "said nothing." The only useful connection to be made is with the divorce and the man's wife telling him to take his "goddamn fish." But it is not clear whether anything could be made of the fairy tale link.

The next thing we might pause over is Jenkins's observation that when the man got his fish back from the taxidermist's "it didn't look quite the same." The author does not specify what had changed. Did the fish look smaller? Had it lost some of its strangeness? We can only wonder, and hope that some later detail will explain what had happened to the fish, or the man's perception of it.

Two sentences later, we encounter a peculiar turn of phrase. Jenkins reveals that the fish, presumably an ocean fish—a marlin?—was too big to fit in the car when mounted, then adds: "In those days he could fit everything he owned into the back of his Volkswagen but the fish changed all that." What he means, of course, is that for the first time the man owns something that is too big for the back of his car. But the phrasing—and we must assume it is deliberate—makes it sound as though the fish *acted* to change "all that." That, in other words, it did have some uncanny power to change his life. It is almost as if the fish brought on the life-changes that ensued: marriage, children, and so on. Jenkins wants his reader to at least suspect that there is something special about the creature, even if it does not speak or grant wishes.

As the man's life becomes more domesticated, the importance of the fish seems to diminish. It is relegated to the attic and is all but forgotten. But then, it suddenly acquires importance again. Reading the piece a second time, we pay more attention to the wife's words: "Take your goddamn fish." Jenkins makes it appear that she was singling the fish out, paying it special mind. And once again the possibility of a greater significance comes to mind. She focused on the fish because *she* associated it with something about her husband. Indeed, his first act upon moving to his own apartment was to hang the fish on the wall. More than anything else, this last gesture underscores the idea that the fish had become an important token. The last lines—"Boy, it was big. He couldn't imagine he'd ever caught a fish that big"—support the interpretation that the fish represented the sense of wonder that had accompanied the man's innocence, the wonder he'd lost in his years of marriage and was possibly ready to recover now that he was alone again.

The second reading, then, gives us a sense of having entered the text. We may not be ready to sit down and write an interpretation, but we are probably ready to begin thinking toward a thesis. We have discovered several possible points of departure.

It is, naturally, foolish to try to prescribe fixed procedures for writing. Different people have different thought rhythms and different strategies for writing. Some writers make copious notes and diagrams; others are able to structure things without putting a mark on the page. But there has to be a certain basic common direction—a movement from generality to specificity—that can best be illustrated using written notations.

Here, to begin, are the kinds of margin comments that a third reading might yield:

FISH OUT OF WATER

title maybe refers to the man, too

Key word—this will be no ordinary story

maybe its importance has to do more with his state of mind than with the fish

diminishes importance

makes it seem like the fish does have powers

process of adulthood/domesticity begins

sudden turn

fish regains former importance—shows how much his life has changed

refers to old fairy tale

What has changed?

fish loses special status—maybe because he is changing

wife shown to be unsympathetic, as in fairy tale

When he finally landed the fish it seemed so strange, so unlike other fishes he'd caught, so much bigger, more silvery, more important, that he half expected it to talk, to grant his wishes if he returned it to the water. But the fish said nothing, made no pleas, gave no promises. His fishing partner said, "Nice fish, you ought to have it mounted." Other people who saw it said the same thing, "Nice fish . . ." So he took it to the taxidermy shop but when it came back it didn't look quite the same. Still, it was an impressive trophy. Mounted on a big board the way it was, it was too big to fit in the car. In those days he could fit everything he owned into the back of his Volkswagen but the fish changed all that. After he married, a year or so later, nothing would fit in the car. He got a bigger car. Then a new job, children. . . . The fish moved with them from house to house, state to state. All that moving around took its toll on the fish, it began to look worn, a fin was broken off. It went into the attic of the new house. Just before the divorce became final, when he was moving to an apartment, his wife said "Take your goddamn fish." He hung the fish on the wall before he'd unpacked anything else. The fish seemed huge, too big for this little apartment. Boy, it was big. He couldn't imagine he'd ever caught a fish that big.

The third reading may not produce any great revelations, but we might make some potentially useful discoveries. First, we should consider that the title might have to do with the man as well as the fish. If so, then the implication would be that he was not meant to tread the predictable path of adult responsibility. We might also be struck this time by the different degrees of importance that were accorded to the fish itself. It was strange and important; then it was a "Nice fish," an "impressive trophy"; then a "worn" old artifact; and finally "huge." It seems more likely that the appearance, or presence, of the fish is directly related to the man's perception—that it is, therefore, a kind of barometer of his inner state. If this is true, then the prose poem can be read as a kind of lesson about the place of wonder in our lives. The fish changes from being something miraculous to being a worn old object to being once again a marvel. We may notice, however, that at the end the man is less taken with the fish itself than with the fact that *he* had once caught it.

I stated earlier that the reading and writing processes were closely linked. These stages of interpretation should suggest not only how the focus changes with increased exposure to the text, but also how reading responses naturally begin to generate clusters of ideas—ideas that very often take on a momentum and shape that are the prelude to writing. The step from an annotated response like the one shown above to the formation of a "tentative thesis" is a short one.

The tentative thesis is the first rough formation of a governing concept. It marks the end of the more receptive act of reading (though one does return to the text over and over to test and confirm ideas and intuitions) and the beginning of the more productive act of writing. From the tentative thesis will crystallize the more concrete thesis, which then becomes the basis for writing.

Writing as a Reflection on Reading

From our repeated readings of Jenkins's piece we may arrive at a general interpretation, which could be expressed in writing more or less as follows: Louis Jenkins's prose poem "Fish Out of Water" uses a man's changing responses to an enormous fish he has caught to suggest the sacrifice of wonder that comes with the passage from youth to the responsibilities of adulthood.

The tentative thesis is fairly straightforward and offers nothing surprising, but it has the advantage of supplying a basic framework within which the various turns of the story can be understood. But we might also realize that it does not quite capture the dynamic of Jenkins's piece; it lacks precision and elaboration. The phrase "changing responses" does not convey the true nature of his experience, which was, as we noted, a shift from confronting the wondrousness of the big fish to the realization years later that he had once caught it himself. The focus, in other words, moves from the marvel of the fish to the marvel of his own youth, and in the process a sad message is passed along about the diminishing of one person's response toward life.

With these considerations before us, we are ready to try to refine the tentative thesis into a more explicit version. Here is one revised thesis: Louis Jenkins's prose poem "Fish Out of Water" discloses the process of sacrifice by which we move from youth to responsible adulthood. A young man begins by catching a great fish and mounting it as a trophy. Years later, after his marriage has failed, he looks at his prize again, but what he now sees is the lost wonder that was his own youth.

This may not be the best possible distillation of Jenkins's prose poem, but it feels like a thesis strong enough to support a draft. I don't intend to work through the whole sequence of first and final drafts here (examples of student essays—drafts and revision—can be found in the "Writing about" and "Responding to" chapters), but some comments on the process may be helpful.

The main thing to be emphasized is that writing about a work of literature is not an arbitrary hit-or-miss operation. The writing originates in, and fulfills, the reading. The two are connected. In a sense, the processes even mirror each other, for just as each new reading brings about a narrowing of focus and a concentration upon points of significance, so each formulation of response gets more specific.

Finding a workable thesis is essential. When you have set out your overall idea with sufficient clarity, you should be able to map out the basic contours of your paper. The approaches, naturally, vary with the writer and the task at hand. Some writers need to work out a rigorous outline with every step calculated; others find it sufficient to scratch out a short list of cues and reminders. Few of us have the gift of being able to see the whole line of an argument or interpretation clearly in our minds. The bottom-line wisdom is that you should stay with whatever best serves your writing habits and your temperament.

Years of trial and error have shown many writers that they need to begin with a coherent and supportable thesis and that they have to have a clear idea of how they will finally conclude. In this case, the rewritten thesis might suffice, provided we know our direction. We may decide to conclude by finding a way to reflect on Jenkins's title, perhaps incorporating the idea that the fish out of water also refers to the man's failure at fulfilling the husband/father/breadwinner role he had assumed for himself.

As for the rest of the essay, perhaps the most reasonable approach would be to work through the prose poem sequentially, identifying the various ways in which the man's perception of the fish changed. We might point out the fairy tale connection (remarking, too, on the unsympathetic portrayal of the wife), and zero in on the paradoxical statement about how "the fish changed all that," meaning his simple life. The rest could be worked out sentence by sentence in the act of composition. There is no escaping it. No outline, even the most detailed, can save you from the task of stitching sense out of strings of words.

Some people find the act of writing easy and natural; they turn on the tap and the sentences and paragraphs flow forth. Most of the rest of us find it more or less excruciating—at least at times. Writing is difficult for various reasons. Our ideas are not clear to us, the right words won't come, the underlying organization eludes us. . . . And then, of course, there is the matter of what we expect of ourselves. We usually have enough of a sense of what we want to say to know when we are not getting our meaning into words. The frustration of not making the sense we want to be making can be intolerable.

While no one has discovered a foolproof solution for this dilemma, the drafting process can be very useful. A draft is by definition incomplete—it is a trial, an approach. Writing out a paper in rough form allows us a certain ease. We don't have to linger over every word, and we can make mistakes. We can try to capture our basic ideas in a looser prose, for we know that we will return later to make our points with greater precision. Best of all, the rough draft fixes our ideas to the page, where they can be seen. We are free to circle around them, drawing arrows, adding words, striking clumsy turns of phrase. Because our assertions are there on the page, we can test the logic of the connections; we can move things around to fit.

Obviously a great deal can be written about the steps by which the writer transforms the rough draft into the finished product. The thesis, written out in preliminary form, needs to be reexamined.

- Does it effectively introduce the paragraphs that follow?
- Does it give the reader the necessary overview?
- If the thesis does hold water, then what about the body of the paper?
- Have the points been made in coherent order?
- Is the argument logical? Or, if the paper is an interpretation, are the basic assumptions clearly set out?
- Are there examples in the text to support the assertions that have been made?
- Has the reader been directed to the evidence in the smoothest possible way?

- Are transitions used effectively?
- Do the paragraphs hook together naturally, the end of one suggesting a link to the beginning of the next?

Finally, there is the matter of the conclusion. To restate the thesis is not enough. The writer must in some way reflect upon it, add to it, show the reader that there was a purpose and direction to the presentation in the body of the paper. The final paragraph or paragraphs should leave a memorable impression. As the thesis is a signpost guiding the reader to what will follow, so the conclusion is a concise reminder of what has been ventured.

Students often have one advantage that other writers cannot always claim—a direct and immediate response. Not only does the teacher evaluate papers in written comments and possibly in conference as well, but many classes use peer group evaluations. In both cases, the feedback helps to isolate problem areas and encourages new formulations. No less important, the student comes to realize what is so often forgotten during the solitary hours of composition: that the process that began in reading and was carried on in writing ends only when that writing reaches another reader. The purpose of writing is not simply expression, it is communication.

Fiction

2 Reading Fiction

There is a well-known cartoon showing five men in blindfolds, each trying to describe a creature based upon the part he has encountered. One, feeling the leg, calls out that it is rounded and solid; another, pulling on the tail, reports that the animal is long, thin, and flexible. We see all five men and the creature—an elephant. The joke has to do with how radically people misperceive things from their limited perspectives.

Fiction is a bit like that elephant, with many people examining some part and insisting that they know the whole. What do we talk about when we talk about fiction? Do we mean the so-called classics of serious literature, works like *Huckleberry Finn* and *Moby-Dick*? Can we include *Love's Flaming Passion* from the drugstore rack? or the latest experimental word-collage from a literary magazine? or the books that were read to us at bedtime when we were children? All of these are, strictly speaking, examples of kinds of fiction. Obviously, however, we will not get far if we try to pursue a discussion that includes all of the above.

WHAT IS FICTION?

In the interests of clarity, then, and because we are talking of works to be read within an academic context, we will use the general term *fiction* as a shorthand for what is sometimes called *serious*, or *literary* fiction. And how are we to define this, aside from making the circular observation that it is the kind of work likely to be found in a text like this? A definition requires a brief discussion of background.

Fiction comes from the Latin root *fingere*, which means "to feign," or pretend. Rooted in the oral storytelling tradition, which is nearly as old as language itself, fiction has to do with the invented accounts of the deeds and fates of people, most of them likewise invented. Though animals and various kinds of mythic creatures are also fictional subjects, they are invariably endowed with human attributes and speech abilities.

The art is universal and its origins are readily imagined. Long ago, in the days of tribal culture, people lived and worked in close proximity; they must have whiled away long nights with the telling of stories. The best of these—the most spellbinding, the most entertaining—were repeated over and over, until their details and structural turns reached a high level of refinement and were memorized. Some, we know, survived into written literature. When the Greeks developed their writing arts in the fifth century B.C., for instance, the great oral epics of Homer were finally preserved on the page—we know them now as the *Iliad* and *Odyssey*. In the same way, centuries of stories passed along by word of mouth in the Near East were eventually gathered into the legendary *Arabian Nights* collections. Later still, the Brothers Grimm collected tales that had circulated throughout Europe from the time of the Middle Ages. Every culture has its own tradition of folklore based on preserved oral narratives.

Does Fiction Bring Us Imagination or Reality?

Fiction, even the most verbally sophisticated fiction, has its roots deep in these storytelling traditions, and it shares their original purpose, which was to amaze and delight an audience of listeners. Of course, the public event of storytelling has become, for most of us, the private encounter with the printed page. But the fundamental character of the art survives. Fiction is still the imagination's response to the enormous human appetite for entertainment. But entertainment must be construed in far-reaching terms. It is not just a matter of lightness and frivolity; it has its serious side, too. Heroic exploits and amazing coincidences cannot by themselves gratify our complex desires. The early tellers of tales doubtless found that while their listeners enjoyed shipwrecks and battles and fabulous romances, they also wanted stories that would be about people like themselves, narratives that could help them with the problems of daily living. Thus, alongside the tales of adventure arose what are sometimes called *moral tales*; their object was, in addition to providing diversion, to give the listener a dose of moral instruction.

From the start, then, fiction has been a weaving together of two very different strands—one pulling the listener *away* from the world of daily cares, the other pulling him *toward* that world. The two are not, of course, mutually exclusive. A great many works of fiction have successfully fused the fantastic or improbable with treatments of theme and character that can teach us things that are useful in our own lives. Herman Melville's *Moby-Dick*, Jonathan Swift's *Gulliver's Travels*, and Gabriel García Márquez's *One Hundred Years of Solitude* are just a few examples of serious works of fiction that rouse all the senses even as they look searchingly at the mysteries of the human heart.

We have not yet answered the question "What is fiction?" but we have made a start. Fiction entertains, and it also, to different degrees, explores what has been grandly called "the human condition." Indeed, the exploration is often part of the entertainment. We are all to some extent fascinated by other lives and curious to learn how others make sense of grief, betrayal, unexpected success, and so on. We may feel pangs of desolation at a given character's death or fall from fortune, but insofar as we are engaged by the plight we are also entertained. We are at the same time removed from our daily concerns and brought into contact with our deeper emotions. This paradoxical split is at the core of the experience of fiction.

Does Fiction Carry a Social Message?

So far these observations have focused on the more subjective, or reader-based, meaning of fiction. However, another way to look at the question is from a public, or institutional, vantage: in certain practical terms, fiction is whatever our institutions—our teachers and textbooks—say it is. To understand this is to understand what is at stake in the battle over the "canon" that was discussed in Chapter 1. One side argues in terms of absolutes, contending that there is a body of established great works; the opposition claims that many of these works are accepted as masterpieces because they embody the value systems of the ruling elite, and that literary values are in fact relative. The critics would revise definitions and curricula in ways that are responsive to the needs of readers with diverse cultural backgrounds.

If we try to define fiction by referring to the terms of the canon debate, we will end up facing a stark either/or choice. Either the art is to be understood in a fairly tradition-bound way, with repeated bows to what Victorian critic Matthew Arnold called the "touch-stones"—the certified attainments of greatness—or else everything is to be judged in the societal context, with questions of quality and value seen as relative. There is not much common ground between the two.

The debate is likely to continue for a good long time, and we would be foolish to leave all questions about fiction and literature hanging until a winner is declared (which, of course, is not going to happen). We should have some basis for making evaluations without feeling that we have to swear a blood oath to one or the other embattled party. And we do: common sense.

The commonsense position skirts the horns of the dilemma, asserting simply that both positions have validity so long as they are not taken to extremes. Literature—*fiction*—is, like all art, created for human beings by human beings. We may be different from one another in our particular identities, but we are similar in our basic psychological structure—similar enough that we can communicate using language and trust to the possibility of understanding each other. Can we not be trusted to find the value in works from the canon as well as works from new sources? To say that we cannot take meaning from Charles Dickens as well as from an African slave narrative is to hold a limited view of the human potential. And to hold, further, that we need to be shown that one is superior to the other adds further insult. We know when we are moved, challenged, entertained, and instructed. Of course, we don't always have the background or context to appreciate a given work fully. But this is as much at issue in reading a novel set in a Zuni Indian pueblo in the present as in reading a novel from the eighteenth century. What is learning if not the process of acquiring contexts? And how are we to acquire contexts if not through exposure?

Our personal reactions to a work of fiction are not, however, the last word. Reactions will vary tremendously based on the experiences and values of the reader. This is why we need to test consensus, to use a situation like that offered by the classroom to discuss and compare responses. *Not* because there is such a thing as a right response, but because in the act of comparing perspectives, we each see things we had overlooked. Other readers' interpretations have a way of sending us back for a second look at the evidence. Invariably we start to modify our understanding of the work in question. We emerge with a more complex reading—one that we carry alongside our original primary experience. Significantly, interpretability is one of the qualities that distinguish the kind of fiction that we are trying to define.

MAKING CONTACT WITH
A FICTIONAL WORLD

The reading of fiction is at once simpler and more demanding than many other kinds of reading. This statement may sound self-cancelling, but it actually points toward the complexity of the act.

Reading fiction—as opposed, say, to reading works of history or social science—is simpler because the work itself often has a natural appeal: involvement in the subject brings absorption. Fiction is rooted in the writer's deep desire to seduce, compel, or enchant the reader. The work's natural terrain is human nature, a subject in which we all have some stake, and its aim is, among other things, to shed some new light on our shared experience. A story or novel may pose difficulties and require our closest attention, but it seldom forces us against the grain of our natural curiosity. If we can open ourselves up, strike a receptive posture, the work will carry us forward. We will read on because we want to know what happens next, or because we sense that we are learning something that may help us to understand our own experience.

But reading fiction can also be more challenging, and call for more concentration, than other kinds of reading. The language is often used differently; it asks more of us. We have to pay heed not only to the *what* of the story but also to the *how*. Most of the time—when we race through a report in the daily newspaper or work through a chapter in a textbook—we turn the pages for the sake of information. We read words for their *denotative* value, what might be called their dictionary meaning; we strip off the facts and ideas and move on. We do not expect an article in a news magazine to use ambiguous language or significant kinds of rhythmic variation.

But as soon as we look at a more imaginative piece of writing, we meet a new set of requirements. To read literature we must be ready to understand language in both its denotative and *connotative*—or suggestive—uses. And reading becomes necessarily more demanding. Suddenly we pay attention not only to the meanings of words, but to their associations as well. Moreover, we have to read the author's tone, looking for clues about how to interpret the actions and speeches of the characters. We watch out for images that might signal deeper thematic meanings. And we listen to the sentences themselves, hearing cues in rhythms and changes of rhythm. Silence and concentration are essential.

Reading and Rereading a Work of Fiction

Any work of literature worth reading at all is probably worth reading at least twice. Certainly any work that you hope to be able to discuss or write about deserves this kind of focus. Of course, we don't always find ourselves in ideal circumstances. During a busy semester you may need to put out superhuman effort just to keep up with required reading for classes; rereading is a luxury you can scarcely afford. Still, there are very good reasons why you should try whenever possible to experience a work twice. The difference in comprehension and depth of penetration is significant.

When you begin a story or a novel you are plunged into an alien world, a place with characters, situations, and assumptions that have to be figured out. As often as not, the language itself asks for maximum attention; the writer is trying to tell and suggest as much as possible in a limited space. Sometimes the intensity is enough to make your mind reel and you have to take a break.

Think of the fictional world as an unknown terrain. As you begin to read you walk forward slowly, not knowing what to expect, following the path that has been set down. In time you will find that your patience and attentiveness bring rewards. The characters begin to stir to life and seem to move of their own volition; situations sort themselves out; and your desire to find out what happens next wins out over your natural uncertainty. By the end of the reading you usually have the scenario clear in your mind. You are able to say with some confidence, "I've read the story."

But what a revealing experience it is to then read the work a second time. The element of surprise is missing, true, but your mind is suddenly free to observe and explore. As a traveler you no longer expend most of your energy in following the path and looking for direction markers; you are free to examine your surroundings. The energy that in the first reading went into fleshing out and tracking the characters and holding the turns of plot in mind can now be used elsewhere. Now that you know that the romance between X and Y will fizzle out, you can monitor their actions and interchanges to get further insights into the failure. No less important, you can begin to enjoy the language for its own sake, lingering over images, descriptions, and more subtle turns of phrase.

When people talk about the reading process, they all too often assume that it is continuous, as if the reader starts in with the first word and progresses steadily until the final period is reached. A more accurate depiction would show a jaggedly discontinuous motion: short forward jerks, pauses, countless backtrackings, sudden rushes, more pauses. Not only are you working to comprehend or pausing to savor, but you are also constantly fending off the thoughts, memories, and associations that the writing evokes. How many times have you finished a page only to realize that you looked at all the words without absorbing a bit of the sense? The only remedy for this is to exert yourself to enter the fictional world fully—let the language claim you and the page will come to life.

Listening to the Fiction We Read

Connection with the words—their pace and texture and suggestiveness—is vital for the true reading experience. Just as painters love color, writers love language. They use its sounds and rhythms as visual artists use shape and pigment. The prose of newspapers and advertising brochures may be written for rapid visual consumption, but fiction is written for the ear. This does not mean that you need to read stories out loud to get their full effect, but you should try to hear the words and sentences clearly in your auditory imagination. Indeed, one of our remarkable linguistic abilities is to hear words in our thoughts almost as if they have been spoken.

The operation is a natural one. As you read this sentence you are most likely sounding it out to yourself silently. You do the same thing when you read a story, but with more care, making sure that you hear the words clearly and completely. You want more than their sense—you want the movement of their sense, the meaning of the rhythm. In writing no less than in daily conversation, the way that something is said is half the message.

Attentive reading takes time and energy, but if you want the full experience you have to exert the effort. If you speed-read, you create the effect of a sound-blur. You may get through the story more quickly, but you will have little sense about what the story has to say. Speed reading might be compared to racing through an art gallery, throwing a quick glance at paintings that the artist struggled with for months. True appreciation begins with a simple gesture of respect.

CLOSE READING

Close reading is an operation required of all serious students of literature. The term is self-explanatory. Such reading calls for heightened attentiveness, a vigilance that goes beyond what we practice in merely careful reading. To close read is to slow down the textual encounter to focus upon the contribution that diction (or word choice), sentence construction, imagery, and rhythm make to the meaning of the work or passage in question. To read closely is to treat every element of the prose as significant; the scrutiny can be as intense as that given to poetry. Of course, not every writer stands up under the pressure. A close reading of a passage from a dime-store romance will not yield up many wonders. But among serious practitioners of fiction, we find a number of stylists who reveal their finest insights only when closely interpreted.

Close reading requires patience and stamina. It is essentially the same process as *explication* (see Appendix A, "Critical Perspectives") except that explication presents the fruits of attentive reading in written form. Unless you are writing a doctoral dissertation on a given work, you are not likely to bring such scrutiny to bear upon an entire story or novel. But even the examination of a passage from a work of fiction generally brings insights that can be useful in understanding the whole.

An Example of Close Reading

Let me give an instance of what such attentiveness in reading involves. Here is the opening paragraph from John Updike's story "Separating" (which appears in Chapter 13):

> The day was fair. Brilliant. All that June the weather had mocked the Maples' internal misery with solid sunlight—golden shafts and cascades of green in which their conversations had wormed unseeing, their sad murmuring selves the only stain in Nature. Usually by this time of the year they had acquired tans; but when they met their elder daughter's plane on her return from a year in England they were almost as pale as she, though Judith was too dazzled by the sunny opulent jumble of her native land to notice. They did not spoil her homecoming by telling her immediately. Wait a few days, let her recover from jet lag, had been one of their formulations, in that string of gray dialogues—over coffee, over cocktails, over Cointreau—that had shaped the strategy of their dissolution, while the earth performed its annual stunt of renewal unnoticed beyond their closed windows.

Richard had thought to leave at Easter; Joan had insisted they wait until the four children were at last assembled, with all exams passed and ceremonies attended, and the bauble of summer to console them. So he had drudged away, in love, in dread, repairing screens, getting the mowers sharpened, rolling and patching their new tennis court.

Updike is reknowned for his stylistic skills, his ability to put the full resources of language to work. There is much to be gained from a careful inspection of his opening. The title, "Separating," tells you what to expect, and a preliminary reading of the paragraph provides the basic information: Richard and Joan, the parents of four children, have decided to separate. They have done so with some planning and intend to wait until all their children have finished their school obligations before breaking the news. In the meantime, life must go on with some appearance of normalcy.

If you were reading quickly, you would absorb this information and move along. But by close reading, by going back and working through the paragraph slowly, heeding the language and drawing inferences from the details provided, you can learn a good deal more. You can deduce, for instance, that the Maples are probably quite well-off—certainly well-off enough to send their daughter to England for a year and to have a tennis court. You can also get the impression that they follow the rituals of the upper-middle class: drinking cocktails and Cointreau, acquiring tans, and so on. The fact that their "formulations" had been made gradually, "over coffee, over cocktails, over Cointreau," suggests that they are, at least in most obvious respects, reasonable people—you don't hear of drunken fights or sudden desertions. Indeed, the fact that they can wait for the right moment, carrying on as always, tells a good deal about their marriage. Appearances and codes of behavior are all-important in this world.

But if you now listen to the diction and monitor Updike's use of images, the other part of the story emerges. Right from the start he opposes the outer and inner, appearances and realities. The sunny weather, as he describes it, "had mocked the Maples' internal misery." Exteriors and interiors are set into opposition, as are darkness and light. Conversations "had wormed," and their "sad murmuring selves" are seen as "the only stain in Nature," as if the Maples alone were going against some universal system of laws. Against the bright sunlight, he tells of their "gray dialogues."

Updike then finds a very subtle way to accentuate the growing seriousness of the situation. He achieves his desired effect by suddenly trivializing Nature, by describing the coming of Spring as an "annual stunt" that passes "unnoticed." The Maples are so absorbed in their private melodrama that they disregard the changing of the seasons: they disregard it because in view of their situation, the renewal is unwelcome—it would make the deterioration of the family even more unbearable.

One could continue in this vein, questioning the significance of Richard's desire to leave at Easter, the day of resurrection, commenting upon the condescension implied by the parent's thinking of summer as a "bauble" that might "console" the children, focusing upon the ambivalence of Richard's drudging away, "in love, in dread," but the point is probably clear. Artistic prose not only repays close reading, but demands it.

Which Kind of Interpretation Is Best?

A reading like this raises the interesting and vexing question of interpretation. Basically, no two individuals reading a work will discover the same significance or supply the same explanations. (I touched upon this earlier.) What I have presented are one reader's comments on Updike's opening paragraph, and another reader may well have different reactions based upon different discoveries. Indeed, Updike himself, if he made himself available for interrogation, might assert that he had an entirely different set of stylistic intentions. Which interpretation is best? Who should we listen to?

These questions have been taken up in great detail by literary theoreticians and their responses span a considerable gamut. Some would argue, for example, that the meaning of a literary work is absolute, conforming exactly to the author's intention, and that any other stance opens the door to the chaotic forces of uncertainty. Others might insist that there is no right reading, only different readings. In other words, if a reader chooses to understand *King Lear* not as a tragedy but as a satire, he or she is entitled to do so. Who is to judge otherwise?

Most readers and critics, however, incline to a commonsense compromise. Language is, after all, a public medium; the meanings and associations can be established with at least approximate accuracy. Interpretations can be compared and tested; they can, like any other idea or opinion, be measured against consensus. This is not to say that the consensus view is always the best, but we cannot deny the implications of the fact that it exists. The reader who would declare *King Lear* a satiric work is entitled to that view, but must be willing to reply to the generations of readers who have deemed the play a tragedy. Interpretation is not constrained, except by a certain responsibility to the considered views of other readers.

When you approach a work of fiction, then, you should be willing to read attentively, to respond openly, and to explore possible interpretations independently. One of the great values of a course in literature is that it allows for discussion; you can test your ideas and intuitions in a public context and then refine your insights in written work. What you need to keep in mind—for it is easy to forget in an academic setting—is that every work, every *word,* was originally composed by an individual who sat in a room, alone, bent upon passing along some vision of human experience. If you keep that in mind, you will realize that the final goal of any interpretation is not to produce an impressive paper but to add to the store of your understanding of life itself.

3 Character

The various elements of fiction are, like the ingredients of a sauce, all essential. But some are more essential than others. We can conceive of a story without a setting—it may take the form of a conversation—or lacking in symbols or prominent themes. We would have a very hard time, however, imagining a story without any characters, human or other. (Franz Kafka's celebrated story "The Metamorphosis" is narrated by a man who has been turned into a giant beetle—but his perceptions are those of a human.) The reason is simple. A story is not likely to work if our basic human impulses, our curiosity and empathy, have not been engaged. For engagement to happen there must be psychological complications. This is the age-old truth about fiction and it is not likely to change.

There are, of course, exceptions. Some contemporary works achieve their effects by subverting our expectations. Characters are portrayed as deliberately flat; their psychological blankness makes a point about dehumanizing forces in our society. But by and large the traditional view still prevails: that plot is a function of character, rather than vice versa. As the Greek philosopher Heraclitus said, "Character is destiny." Events are determined by the character structure of the participants—hence our perennial fascination with the lives of powerful figures and the way those lives contribute to the unfolding of public events. One person will face circumstance in a way that brings triumph; another, in the same situation, will make decisions that lead to tragedy. And what applies to public figures applies to us as well. What we do and how we act are determined by who we are.

While the novelist works on a large canvas and has a greater range of options, the short story writer must economize, using fewer characters and situations. Most stories feature a central figure, or *protagonist* (from the Greek for "first actor"), and one or more secondary figures. Depending upon the author's choice of *point of view* (see Chapter 7), the protagonist can be presented either in the third person—in which case we see the person from the outside—or else in the first person, as the narrator. In Guy de Maupassant's "The String," which we will discuss shortly, the protagonist is set before us in the third person: "Maître Hauchecorne, of Bréauté," writes Maupassant, "had just arrived at Goderville, and was directing his steps toward the square, when he perceived upon the ground a little piece of string." Olive Schreiner, meanwhile, in her story "The Woman's Rose" (see Chapter 9) has her protagonist tell her tale directly: "I have an old, brown, carved box; the lid is broken and tied with a string."

There are also other options. A story can be told in the first person but be centered upon a third-person protagonist. Mark Twain makes use of a complex variation of this in "The Notorious Jumping Frog of Calaveras County" (see Chapter 8), in which his narrator meets a man named Simon Wheeler who begins telling a story about a man with a compulsion for betting. It is the story within a story that engages our interest, and the betting man is the true protagonist.

Character and Psychological Depth

As a rule of thumb, the greater the impression of psychological depth a writer can create, the greater the chances for reader involvement. Character depth in fiction is like perspective in painting—it is what creates the illusion of life. The author can achieve this in several ways. First, obviously, a character must be shown to be consistent. It will not do to have the protagonist (or any other character) appear suspicious and narrow-minded in one scene, and relaxed and easygoing in another, unless the circumstances can account for the difference.

Second, the character can be presented as growing or changing on account of experience. Part of the reason we find a story like Anton Chekhov's "The Lady with the Little Dog" (see Chapter 14) convincing is that we see the protagonist, Gurov, change from being a somewhat heedless seducer to a man capable of empathy. Third, the writer can enhance the sense of depth and complexity by using different kinds of characters. A protagonist will seem all the more complex and real if set beside simpler, *flatter* figures.

This leads us to some basic definitions. Characters in fiction are customarily divided into several types. *Rounded* and *dynamic* characters are more lifelike. They exhibit greater subtlety in terms of behavior and motivation; they emerge from the background and give the impression of living and moving in time. They have dimension—hence "round." Strictly speaking, a dynamic character is one who undergoes some significant change during the course of the events related. He or she is generally rounded. However, not every rounded character is dynamic. The test is whether the character is fundamentally the same at the end of the story as at the beginning. Most protagonists, and Chekhov's Gurov is a fine example, are both rounded and dynamic; the change, or development, from start to finish is the psychological glue that holds the story together.

Writers also make use of *flat*, or *static*, characters. This is not because they lack the inclination to develop a full roster of rounded individuals. Usually it is a matter of artistic need. The story writer knows that the impression of believability is heightened through the interplay of foreground and background. Roundedness and dynamism stand out better if they are contrasted to flatness. Or very possibly the writer is using a character for a limited function. In Sarah Orne Jewett's "A White Heron" (see Chapter 5), for example, the protagonist is a young girl named Sylvia, but the balance of the story, as well as the necessary sequence of events, requires that she have a guardian. For this reason, Jewett creates Mrs. Tilley. The woman is both flat and static—nothing in her character changes—but the story could not move forward naturally without her.

It is worth noting, however, that not all flat characters are *stereotypes*. A stereotyped character generally exhibits standardized attributes, often for comic effect. Literature abounds in greedy landlords, dashing officers, and so on. Jewett's Mrs. Tilley may be undeveloped as a character, but she is not a type.

Characters in Opposition and Interaction

A different kind of character, somewhat more common in folk tales and early short stories, is the *antagonist*. This figure, flat or rounded, is set up in opposition to the protagonist. An antagonist is generally bent upon blocking or frustrating the protagonist's aims, or else is intent upon causing harm. In Maupassant's "The String," as we shall see, Hauchecorne's predicament is the direct result of an accusation by his long-time enemy, Malandain. Malandain (his name even contains the Latin root *mal*—or "bad") is scarcely developed, but his antagonist's role is vital to the story's outcome. For a more obvious antagonist we might look to the well-known "Cinderella" story from the Brothers Grimm collection. Cinderella's wicked stepmother is as evil as the young girl is good, and the full resolution of the story comes only when she is defeated. Protagonist and antagonist in this instance create the tension that drives the narrative forward.

Fictional characters are finally as diverse as people themselves, and there is little point in trying to devise other type categories. We might note, however, that the place of character, if not the function, has changed along with the development of literature through the centuries. What we see is a growing psychological complexity and a gradual displacement of plot. While authors are still interested in telling what happened, they are even more interested in exploring the impact of different kinds of events on the human psyche. In much twentieth-century fiction, the real action is internal, while the external crisis need not be dramatic at all.

A Classic Story That Reveals Character

Guy de Maupassant (1850–1893) is one of the writers who represent the short story at a turning point. Though he was still very much concerned with plot and with creating vividly dramatic situations, he was also aware that the true center of all conflict—and interest—is the human heart. In his story "The String," he takes on a very large challenge: to see how great an effect he can derive from the seemingly smallest of causes. Here we can see, in bold relief, the truth of Heraclitus's dictum, "Character is fate."

Guy de Maupassant (1850–1893)

Guy de Maupassant was fortunate enough to have as his teacher the greatest prose writer of his age, Gustave Flaubert. Flaubert taught his young apprentice to go in quest of the unrepeatable, defining detail: "You must make me see, with a single word, in what way one cab-horse is totally unlike fifty others that go before and after it." The instruction bore abundant fruit. Beginning with the publication of his story "*Boule de Suif*" ("Ball of Fat") in 1880, Maupassant built a career as one of the shrewdest and most readable writers ever to have worked in the genre. His clear gaze, his keen sense of human motivation and action, and his unencumbered style continue to exert an influence on practitioners of the short story form.

Maupassant's life was, like those of so many other gifted writers (Poe, Gogol), short and—at least at the end—wretched. He had contracted syphilis while a young man, most likely while serving in the French army. The disease erupted again when he was at the height of his productivity, driving him into total insanity before his death of paresis. If he left a monument to himself, it was an image of the full range of the life of his times refracted through hundreds of imagined destinies.

THE STRING

Along all the roads around Goderville the peasants and their wives were coming toward the little town, for it was market-day. The men walked with slow steps, their whole bodies bent forward at each movement of their long twisted legs, deformed by their hard work, by the weight on the plough which, at the same time, raises the left shoulder and distorts the figure, by the reaping of the wheat which forces the knees apart to get a firm stand, by all the slow and painful labors of the country. Their blouses, blue, starched, shining as if varnished, ornamented with a little design in white at the neck and wrists, puffed about their bony bodies, seemed like balloons ready to carry them off. From each of them a head, two arms, and two feet protruded.

Some led a cow or a calf at the end of a rope, and their wives, walking behind the animal, whipped its haunches with a leafy branch to hasten its progress. They carried on their arms large wicker-baskets, out of which a chicken here, a duck there, thrust out its head. And they walked with a quicker, livelier step than their husbands. Their spare, straight figures were wrapped in a scanty little shawl, pinned over their flat bosoms, and their heads were enveloped in a piece of white linen tightly pressed on the hair and surmounted by a cap.

Then a wagon passed, its nag's jerky trot shaking up and down two men seated side by side and a woman in the bottom of the vehicle, the latter holding on to the sides to lessen the hard jolts.

In the square of Goderville there was a crowd, a throng of human beings and animals mixed together. The horns of the cattle, the rough-napped top-hats of the rich peasants, and the head-gear of the peasant women rose above the surface of the crowd. And the clamorous, shrill, screaming voices made a continuous and savage din which sometimes was dominated by the robust lungs of some countryman's laugh, of the long lowing of a cow tied to the wall of a house.

It all smacked of the stable, the dairy, and the dung-heap, of hay and sweat, giving forth that sharp, unpleasant odor, human and animal, peculiar to the people of the fields.

Maître Hauchecorne, of Bréauté, had just arrived at Goderville, and was directing his steps toward the square, when he perceived upon the ground a little piece

5

of string. Maître Hauchecorne, economical like a true Norman, thought that everything useful ought to be picked up, and he stooped painfully, for he suffered from rheumatism. He took the bit of thin cord from the ground and was beginning to roll it carefully when he noticed Maître Malandain, the harness-maker, on the threshold of his door, looking at him. They had once had a quarrel together on the subject of a halter, and they had remained on bad terms, being both good haters. Maître Hauchecorne was seized with a sort of shame to be seen thus by his enemy, picking a bit of string out of the dirt. He concealed his find quickly under his blouse, then in his trousers pocket; then he pretended to be still looking on the ground for something which he did not find, and he went towards the market, his head thrust forward, bent double by his pains.

He was soon lost in the noisy and slowly moving crowd, which was busy with interminable bargainings. The peasants looked at cows, went away, came back, perplexed, always in fear of being cheated, not daring to decide, watching the vendor's eye, ever trying to find the trick in the man and the flaw in the beast.

The women, having placed their great baskets at their feet, had taken out the poultry, which lay upon the ground, tied together by the feet, with terrified eyes and scarlet crests.

They heard offers, stated their prices with a dry air and impassive face, or perhaps, suddenly deciding on some proposed reduction, shouted to the customer who was slowly going away: "All right, Maître Anthime, I'll give it to you for that."

Then little by little the square was deserted, the Angelus rang for noon, and those who lived too far away went to the different inns.

At Jourdain's the great room was full of people eating, as the big yard was full of vehicles of all kinds, carts, gigs, wagons, nondescript carts, yellow with dirt, mended and patched, raising their shafts to the sky like two arms, or perhaps with their shafts on the ground and their backs in the air.

Right against the diners seated at the table, the immense fireplace, filled with bright flames, cast a lively heat on the backs of the row on the right. Three spits were turning on which were chickens, pigeons, and legs of mutton; and an appetizing odor of roast meat and gravy dripping over the nicely browned skin rose from the hearth, lightened hearts, and made mouths water.

All the aristocracy of the plough ate there, at Maître Jourdain's, tavern keeper and horse dealer, a clever fellow who had money.

The dishes were passed and emptied, as were the jugs of yellow cider. Everyone told his affairs, his purchases, and sales. They discussed the crops. The weather was favorable for the greens but rather damp for the wheat.

Suddenly the drum began to beat in the yard, before the house. Everybody rose, except a few indifferent persons, and ran to the door, or to the windows, their mouths still full, their napkins in their hands.

After the public crier had stopped beating his drum, he called out in a jerky voice, speaking his phrases irregularly:

"It is hereby made known to the inhabitants of Goderville, and in general to all persons present at the market, that there was lost this morning, on the road to Benzeville, between nine and ten o'clock, a black leather pocket-book containing five hundred francs and some business papers. The finder is requested to return same to the Mayor's office or to Maître Fortuné Houlbrèque of Manneville. There will be twenty francs reward."

10

15

Then the man went away. The heavy roll of the drum and the crier's voice were again heard at a distance.

Then they began to talk of this event discussing the chances that Maître Houlbrèque had of finding or not finding his pocket-book.

And the meal concluded. They were finishing their coffee when the chief of the gendarmes appeared upon the threshold.

He inquired:

"Is Maître Hauchecorne, of Bréauté, here?"

Maître Hauchecorne, seated at the other end of the table, replied:

"Here I am."

And the officer resumed:

"Maître Hauchecorne, will you have the goodness to accompany me to the Mayor's office? The Mayor would like to talk to you."

The peasant, surprised and disturbed, swallowed at a draught his tiny glass of brandy, rose, even more bent than in the morning, for the first steps after each rest were specially difficult, and set out, repeating: "Here I am, here I am."

The Mayor was awaiting him, seated in an armchair. He was the local lawyer, a stout, serious man, fond of pompous phrases.

"Maître Hauchecorne," said he, "you were seen this morning picking up, on the road to Benzeville, the pocket-book lost by Maître Houlbrèque, of Manneville."

The countryman looked at the Mayor in astonishment, already terrified by this suspicion resting on him without his knowing why.

"Me? Me? I picked up the pocket-book?"

"Yes, you, yourself."

"On my word of honor, I never heard of it."

"But you were seen."

"I was seen, me? Who says he saw me?"

"Monsieur Malandain, the harness-maker."

The old man remembered, understood, and flushed with anger.

"Ah, he saw me, the clodhopper, he saw me pick up this string, here, Mayor." And rummaging in his pocket he drew out the little piece of string.

But the Mayor, incredulous, shook his head.

"You will not make me believe, Maître Hauchecorne, that Monsieur Malandain, who is a man we can believe, mistook this cord for a pocket-book."

The peasant, furious, lifted his hand, spat at one side to attest his honor, repeating:

"It is nevertheless God's own truth, the sacred truth. I repeat it on my soul and my salvation."

The Mayor resumed:

"After picking up the object, you stood like a stilt, looking a long while in the mud to see if any piece of money had fallen out."

The old fellow choked with indignation and fear.

"How anyone can tell—how anyone can tell—such lies to take away an honest man's reputation! How can anyone—"

There was no use in his protesting, nobody believed him. He was confronted with Monsieur Malandain, who repeated and maintained his affirmation. They abused each other for an hour. At his own request, Maître Hauchecorne was searched. Nothing was found on him.

Finally the Mayor, very much perplexed, discharged him with the warning that he would consult the Public Prosecutor and ask for further orders.

The news had spread. As he left the Mayor's office, the old man was surrounded and questioned with a serious or bantering curiosity, in which there was no indignation. He began to tell the story of the string. No one believed him. They laughed at him.

He went along, stopping his friends, beginning endlessly his statement and his protestations showing his pockets turned inside out, to prove that he had nothing. 50

They said:

"Ah, you old devil!"

And he grew angry, becoming exasperated, hot, and distressed at not being believed, not knowing what to do and always repeating himself.

Night came. He had to leave. He started on his way with three neighbors to whom he pointed out the place where he had picked up the bit of string; and all along the road he spoke of his adventure.

In the evening he took a turn in the village of Bréauté, in order to tell it to everybody. He only met with incredulity. 55

It made him ill all night.

The next day about one o'clock in the afternoon, Marius Paumelle, a hired man in the employ of Maître Breton, husbandman at Ymauville, returned the pocketbook and its contents to Maître Houlbrèque of Manneville.

This man claimed to have found the object in the road; but not knowing how to read, he had carried it to the house and given it to his employer.

The news spread through the neighborhood. Maître Hauchecorne was informed of it. He immediately went the circuit and began to recount his story completed by the happy climax. He triumphed.

"What grieved me so much was not the thing itself, as the lying. There is nothing so shameful as to be placed under a cloud on account of a lie." 60

He talked of his adventure all day long, he told it on the highway to people who were passing by, in the inn to people who were drinking there, and to persons coming out of church the following Sunday. He stopped strangers to tell them about it. He was calm now, and yet something disturbed him without his knowing exactly what it was. People had the air of joking while they listened. They did not seem convinced. He seemed to feel that remarks were being made behind his back.

On Tuesday of the next week he went to the market at Goderville, urged solely by the necessity he felt of discussing the case.

Malandain, standing at his door, began to laugh on seeing him pass. Why?

He approached a farmer from Criquetot, who did not let him finish and giving him a thump in the stomach said to his face:

"You clever rogue." 65

Then he turned his back on him.

Maître Hauchecorne was confused, why was he called a clever rogue?

When he was seated at the table, in Jourdain's tavern he commenced to explain "the affair."

A horse dealer from Monvilliers called to him:

"Come, come, old sharper, that's an old trick; I know all about your piece of string!" 70

Hauchecorne stammered:

"But the pocket-book was found."

But the other man replied:

"Shut up, papa, there is one that finds, and there is one that brings back. No one is any the wiser, so you get out of it."

The peasant stood choking. He understood. They accused him of having had the pocket-book returned by a confederate, by an accomplice. 75

He tried to protest. All the table began to laugh.

He could not finish his dinner and went away, in the midst of jeers.

He went home ashamed and indignant, choking with anger and confusion, the more dejected that he was capable with his Norman cunning of doing what they had accused him of, and even of boasting of it as a good trick. His innocence seemed to him, in a confused way, impossible to prove, as his sharpness was known. And he was stricken to the heart by the injustice of the suspicion.

Then he began to recount the adventure again, enlarging his story every day, adding each time new reasons, more energetic protestations, more solemn oaths which he imagined and prepared in his hours of solitude, his whole mind given up to the story of the string. He was believed so much the less as his defense was more complicated and his arguing more subtle.

"Those are lying excuses," they said behind his back. 80

He felt it, consumed his heart over it, and wore himself out with useless efforts. He was visibly wasting away.

The wags now made him tell about the string to amuse them, as they make a soldier who has been on a campaign tell about his battles. His mind, seriously affected, began to weaken.

Towards the end of December he took to his bed.

He died in the first days of January, and in the delirium of his death struggles he kept claiming his innocence, reiterating:

"A piece of string, a piece of string—look—here it is." 85

[1884]
Translated by Ernest Boyd

[1884]
Translated by Ernest Boyd

As you read the following discussion, consider these questions:

1. How does Maupassant establish the character of Hauchecorne? Cite specific examples of observed behavior that suggest what kind of a man he is.

2. In what ways is Hauchecorne seen as being typical of his peasant class?

3. How does Maupassant set up Hauchecorne and Malandain as rivals? Where do your sympathies as a reader lie? Why?

4. Do your responses to Hauchecorne change as you read the story? How does Maupassant flesh out his depiction of Hauchecorne? At what point does Hauchecorne defy your expectations? How does this change your reaction to him?

5. Is Hauchecorne finally a comic or tragic figure, or both? Explain your answer.

Discussion: Action as a Revelation of Character. Maupassant's "The String" is a masterpiece of compression. It is straightforward and balanced, carrying no extra baggage. Indeed, the story unfolds effortlessly from the slightest of premises—almost as if Maupassant had been presented with a challenge: Take a piece of string and use it to reveal the character of a man.

Maupassant begins the tale from the distance. Before we ever meet Hauchecorne, we are given a portrait of the peasants arriving at the town of Goderville on market-day. The reason for beginning thus is simple. Not only does the author want to establish the setting and the human milieu, but he also wants to make it clear that Hauchecorne is but another member of this undifferentiated throng. This is a deliberate set-up, for what Maupassant is really asserting is that even though the peasants all seem like variations on a basic type when seen from a distance, they are all unique individuals when seen up close. This is, incidentally, a favorite device of movie-makers, who often establish the impression of a busy city crowd before zooming in to single out the protagonist.

Hauchecorne is not named until the sixth paragraph. But no sooner does he claim our attention than he makes his decisive move, stooping to pick up the piece of string. We learn a great deal about the man in the course of the paragraph: that he is "economical like a true Norman," that he has rheumatism and is therefore probably an older man, that he is quarrelsome and a "good hater," and that while he is frugal enough to pick up the string, he is also aware that there is something shameful about being observed in the act. The shame is all the keener because it is his old adversary, Malandain, who has spotted him.

Maupassant is a subtle psychologist, and he has told us a good deal through these observations. Most tellingly, he has, in pinpointing Hauchecorne's shame, revealed a core ambivalence in the man. And as the story proceeds, we see that it is the part of Hauchecorne that is ashamed that leads him to go to extremes in protesting his innocence. The figure of Malandain is also important here. That he is Hauchecorne's enemy and that he has seen his guilty expression leads to the next important turn. By reporting that Hauchecorne was picking up and concealing a wallet, Malandain takes the antagonist's role, bringing the story to its early climax, which is his accusation through the mayor. The rest of the story, including the report of the found wallet, is part of the *falling action* (see Chapter 4).

By placing the climax as early as he does, Maupassant shifts the reader's attention away from the plot (there is really no more suspense about what will happen) and focuses it upon character. If Hauchecorne were a different kind of man, the story would end—it would not be a story so much as a report of an event. In most cases, with most people, the discovery of the wallet would close the case: let bygones be bygones, and the less said the better.

But what interests Maupassant, and the reader, is that Hauchecorne cannot let the matter drop, that he feels that his character has been falsely judged and that he must set matters to right. He thinks that if he can make a convincing enough argument for his innocence, he will succeed in erasing the false impression that people have formed of him. This is his mistake, and this is where Maupassant discloses his keen understanding of the human psyche. For the more Hauchecorne protests his innocence, the more his listeners incline toward suspicion. It is a fundamental human reflex to mistrust this kind of insistence. Hauchecorne does not realize that he is calling attention to some uncertainty, some flaw, in his being. The others pick up on this and exploit it—teasing him, pretending not to believe him, making out that he perpetrated some even more cunning deception.

Maupassant has his eye on a psychologic truth here, which is that something in human nature enjoys the discomfort of others. But what the local peasants perceive as Hauchecorne's discomfort is really something deeper. It is a wound at the very root of his character. Hauchecorne does not believe in himself. He depends all too much on his image in the eyes of those around him. He was, it would seem, happy enough to be thought clever and cunning before—for these are attributes prized by his fellows—but when that perception becomes a perception of dishonesty, he crumbles. He cannot stop thinking about the incident, and his obsession torments him and weakens him until he dies. His last words—"A piece of string, a piece of string—look—here it is"—reveal a man undone by his own nature.

The causes of the drama are laughably trivial, but the effects are very nearly tragic. Maupaussant's art is to offer the reader a glimpse not only into the uncertain heart of the old man, but also into the peasant culture to which he belongs. Maupassant's view of human nature is cynical, but it is not altogether heartless. Though we may agree with Hauchecorne's tormentors that he is a ridiculous figure, we may also finish the story feeling a certain compassion for his suffering.

A Story That Reveals Character Indirectly

Maupassant's story presents its protagonist and its other characters in the third person so that we follow their actions—and grasp the consequences of those actions—from a distance. Egyptian writer Naguib Mahfouz, by contrast, presents his unnamed protagonist in the first person. We take part in the boy's adventure from within, shuttling back and forth between fear and dreamy pleasure. Although the Egyptian setting may seem exotic, and the customs unfamiliar, the narrative itself has an immediacy that transcends all cultural boundaries. The questions that follow the story will highlight certain aspects of Mahfouz's treatment of character.

Naguib Mahfouz (1911–   )

Naguib Mahfouz was born in Cairo, Egypt. He studied philosophy at Cairo University, graduating in 1934. He worked as a civil servant and a university administrator as well as in the government film broadcasting organization, all the while writing the works that have made him the leading Arab novelist. Mahfouz's early work reflects a preoccupation with history, while in recent decades he has sought to capture life in modern-day Egypt. Mahfouz is known to be a recluse, and even receiving the 1988 Nobel prize for literature did not encourage him to step into the public eye.

Mahfouz's best-known works in English are *Midaq Alley* and *Miramar.*

THE CONJURER MADE
OFF WITH THE DISH

'The time has come for you to be useful,'
said my mother to me, and she slipped her hand into her pocket, saying:

'Take this piastre° and go off and buy some beans. Don't play on the way and
keep away from the cars.'

I took the dish, put on my clogs and went out, humming a tune. Finding a crowd
in front of the bean-seller, I waited until I discovered a way through to the marble
table.

'A piastre's worth of beans, mister,' I called out in my shrill voice.

He asked me impatiently: 5

'Beans alone? With oil? With cooking butter?'

I didn't answer and he said to me roughly:

'Make way for someone else.'

I withdrew, overcome by embarrassment and returned home defeated.

'Returning with an empty dish?' my mother shouted at me. 'What did you do—
spill the beans or lose the piastre, you naughty boy?'   10

'Beans alone? With oil? With cooking butter—? you didn't tell me,' I protested.

'You stupid, what do you eat every morning?'

'I don't know.'

'You good-for-nothing, ask him for beans with oil.'

I went off to the man and said: 15

'A piastre's worth of beans with oil, mister.'

With a frown of impatience he asked:

'Linseed oil? Nut oil? Olive oil?'

I was taken aback and again made no answer:

'Make way for someone else,' he shouted at me.   20

I returned in a rage to my mother, who called out in astonishment:

'You've come back empty-handed—no beans and no oil.'

'Linseed oil? Nut oil? Olive oil?—you didn't tell me,' I said angrily.

'Beans with oil means beans with linseed oil.'

'How should I know?'   25

'You're a good-for-nothing and he's a tiresome man—tell him beans with linseed oil.'

'How should I know?'

I went off quickly and called out to the man while still some yards from his shop:

'Beans with linseed oil, mister.'

'Put the piastre on the counter,' he said, plunging the ladle into the pot.   30

I put my hand into my pocket but didn't find the piastre. I searched round for
it anxiously. I turned my pocket inside out but found no trace of it. The man withdrew the ladle empty, saying with disgust:

'You've lost the piastre—you're not a boy to be depended on.'

'I haven't lost it,' I said, looking under my feet and round about me. 'It's been
in my pocket all the time.'

---

piastre: coin.

'Make way for someone else and don't make trouble.'
I returned to my mother with an empty dish.
'Good grief, you idiot boy!'
'The piastre. . . .'
'What of it?'
'It wasn't in my pocket.'
'Did you buy sweets with it?'
'I swear I didn't.'
'How did you lose it?'
'I don't know.'
'Do you swear by the Koran° you didn't buy anything with it?'
'I swear.'
'There's a hole in your pocket.'
'No there isn't.'
'Maybe you gave it to the man the first time or the second.'
'Maybe.'
'Are you sure of nothing?'
'I'm hungry.'
She clapped her hands together in a gesture of resignation.

'Never mind,' she said. 'I'll give you another piastre but I'll take it out of your money-box, and if you come back with an empty dish I'll break your head.'

I went off at a run, dreaming of a delicious breakfast. At the turning leading to the alleyway where the bean-seller was I saw a crowd of children and heard merry, festive sounds. My feet dragged as my heart was pulled towards them. At least let me have a fleeting glance. I slipped in amongst them and found the conjurer looking straight at me. A stupefying joy overwhelmed me; I was completely taken out of myself. With the whole of my being I became involved in the tricks of the rabbits and the eggs, and the snakes and the ropes. When the man came up to collect money, I drew back mumbling, 'I haven't got any money.'

He rushed at me savagely and I escaped only with difficulty. I ran off, my back almost broken by his blow, and yet I was utterly happy as I made my way to the seller of beans.

'Beans with linseed oil for a piastre, mister,' I said.
He went on looking at me without moving, so I repeated my request.
'Give me the dish,' he demanded angrily.

The dish! Where was the dish? Had I dropped it while running? Had the conjurer made off with it?

'Boy, you're out of your mind.'

I turned back, searching along the way for the lost dish. The place where the conjurer had been I found empty, but the voices of children led me to him in a nearby lane. I moved round the circle; when the conjurer spotted me he shouted out threateningly:

'Pay up or you'd better scram.'
'The dish!' I called out despairingly.
'What dish, you little devil?'
'Give me back the dish.'
'Scram or I'll make you into food for snakes.'

Koran: sacred text of Islam.

He had stolen the dish, yet fearfully I moved away out of sight and wept. Whenever a passer-by asked me why I was crying I would reply:

'The conjurer made off with the dish.'

Through my misery I became aware of a voice saying:

'Come along and watch.'

I looked behind me and saw a peep-show had been set up. I saw dozens of children hurrying towards it and taking it in turns to stand in front of the peepholes, while the man began making his commentary on the pictures:

'There you've got the gallant knight and the most beautiful of all ladies, Zainat al-Banat.'

Drying my tears, I gazed up in fascination at the box, completely forgetting the conjurer and the dish. Unable to overcome the temptation, I paid over the piastre and stood in front of the peep-hole next to a girl who was standing in front of the other one, and there flowed across our vision enchanting picture stories. When I came back to my own world I realized I had lost both the piastre and the dish, and there was no sign of the conjurer. However, I gave no thought to the loss, so taken up was I with the pictures of chivalry, love and deeds of daring. I forgot my hunger; I forgot the fear of what threatened me back home. I took a few paces back so as to lean against an ancient wall of what had once been a Treasury and the seat of office of the Cadi,° and gave myself up wholly to my reveries. For a long while I dreamt of chivalry, of Zainat al-Banat and the ghoul. In my dream I spoke aloud, giving meaning to my words with gestures. Thrusting home the imaginary lance, I said:

'Take that, O ghoul, right in the heart!'

'And he raised Zainat al-Banat up behind him on his horse,' came back a gentle voice.

I looked to my right and saw the young girl who had been beside me at the performance. She was wearing a dirty dress and coloured clogs and was playing with her long plait of hair; in her other hand were the red and white sweets called 'Lady's fleas,' which she was leisurely sucking. We exchanged glances and I lost my heart to her.

'Let's sit down and rest,' I said to her.

She appeared to be agreeable to my suggestion, so I took her by the arm and we went through the gateway of the ancient wall and sat down on the step of a stairway that went nowhere, a stairway that rose up until it ended in a platform behind which there could be seen a blue sky and minarets. We sat in silence, side by side. I pressed her hand and we sat on in silence, not knowing what to say. I experienced feelings that were new, strange and obscure. Putting my face close to hers, I breathed in the natural smell of her hair, mingled with an odour of earth, and the fragrance of breath mixed with the aroma of sweets. I kissed her lips. I swallowed my saliva which had taken on a sweetness from the dissolved 'Lady's fleas'. I put my arm around her, without her uttering a word, kissing her cheek and lips. Her lips grew still as they received the kiss, then went back to sucking at the sweets. At last she decided we should get up. I seized her arm anxiously.

'Sit down,' I said.

'I'm going,' she said simply.

'Where to?' I asked irritably.

Cadi: administrator.

Character

'To the midwife Umm Ali,' and she pointed to a house at the bottom of which was a small ironing shop.

'Why?'

'To tell her to come quickly.'

'Why?'

'My mother's crying in pain at home. She told me to go to the midwife Umm Ali and to take her along quickly.'

'And you'll come back after that?'

She nodded her head in assent. Her mentioning her mother reminded me of my own and my heart missed a beat. Getting up from the ancient stairway, I made my way back home. I wept out loud, a tried method by which I would defend myself. I expected she would come to me but she did not. I wandered from the kitchen to the bedroom but found no trace of her. Where had my mother gone? When would she return? I was bored with being in the empty house. An idea occurred to me: I took a dish from the kitchen and a piastre from my savings and went off immediately to the seller of beans. I found him asleep on a bench outside the shop, his face covered over by his arm. The pots of beans had vanished and the long-necked bottles of oil had been put back on the shelf and the marble top washed down.

'Mister,' I whispered, approaching.

Hearing nothing but his snoring, I touched his shoulder. He raised his arm in alarm and looked at me through reddened eyes.

'Mister.'

'What do you want?' he asked roughly, becoming aware of my presence and recognizing me.

'A piastre's worth of beans with linseed oil.'

'Eh?'

'I've got the piastre and I've got the dish.'

'You're crazy, boy,' he shouted at me. 'Get out or I'll bash your brains in.'

When I didn't move he pushed me so violently I went sprawling on to my back. I got up painfully, struggling to hold back the crying that was twisting my lips. My hands were clenched, one on the dish and the other on the piastre. I threw him an angry look. I thought about returning with my hopes dashed, but dreams of heroism and valour altered my plan of action. Resolutely, I made a quick decision and with all my strength threw the dish at him. It flew through the air and struck him on the head, while I took to my heels, heedless of everything. I was convinced I'd killed him, just as the knight had killed the ghoul. I didn't stop running till I was near the ancient wall. Panting, I looked behind me but saw no signs of any pursuit. I stopped to get my breath back, then asked myself what I should do now that the second dish was lost? Something warned me not to return home directly, and soon I had given myself over to a wave of indifference that bore me off where it willed. It meant a beating, neither more nor less, on my return, so let me put it off for a time. Here was the piastre in my hand and I could have some sort of enjoyment with it before being punished. I decided to pretend I had forgotten my having done wrong—but where was the conjurer, where was the peep-show? I looked everywhere for them but to no avail.

Worn out by this fruitless searching, I went off to the ancient stairway to keep my appointment. I sat down to wait, imagining to myself the meeting. I yearned for another kiss redolent with the fragrance of sweets. I admitted to myself that the little girl had given me sensations I had never experienced before. As I waited and dreamed, a whispering sound came to me from faraway behind me. I climbed the stairs cautiously and at the final landing I lay down flat on my face in order to see what was behind it, without anyone being able to spot me. I saw some ruins surrounded by a high wall, the last of what remained of the Treasury and the Chief Cadi's house. Directly under the stairs sat a man and a woman, and it was from them that the whispering came. The man looked like a tramp; the woman like one of those gypsies that tend sheep. An inner voice told me that their meeting was similar to the one I had had. Their lips and eyes revealed this, but they showed astonishing expertise in the extraordinary things they did. My gaze became rooted upon them with curiosity, surprise, pleasure, and a certain amount of disquiet. At last they sat down side by side, neither of them taking any notice of the other. After quite a while the man said:

'The money!'

'You're never satisfied,' she said irritably.

Spitting on the ground, he said: 'You're crazy.'

100

'You're a thief.'

He slapped her hard with the back of his hand, and she gathered up a handful of earth and threw it in his face. Then he sprang at her, fastening his fingers on her windpipe. In vain she gathered all her strength to escape from his grip. Her voice failed her, her eyes bulged out of their sockets, while her feet struck out at the air. In dumb terror I stared at the scene till I saw a thread of blood trickling down from her nose. A scream escaped from my mouth. Before the man raised his head, I had crawled backwards; descending the stairs at a jump, I raced off like mad to wherever my legs might carry me. I didn't stop running till I was out of breath. Gasping for breath, I was quite unaware of my whereabouts, but when I came to myself I found I was under a raised vault at the middle of a crossroads. I had never set foot there before and had no idea of where I was in relation to our quarter. On both sides sat sightless beggars, and crossing it from all directions were people who paid attention to no one. In terror I realized I had lost my way and that countless difficulties lay in wait for me before I would find my way home. Should I resort to asking one of the passers-by to direct me? What, though, would happen if chance should lead me to a man like the vendor of beans or the tramp of the waste plot? Would a miracle come about whereby I'd see my mother approaching so that I could eagerly hurry towards her? Should I try to make my own way, wandering about till I came across some familiar landmark that would indicate the direction I should take? I told myself that I should be resolute and take a quick decision: the day was passing and soon mysterious darkness would descend.

Translated from the Arabic by Denys Johnson-Davis

QUESTIONS

1. What is your first impression of the narrator's age, and what is this impression based upon? Do you change your estimate as the story unfolds? If so, explain why.

2. Though the story begins on a comic note, it later changes its tone. Find the place, or places, where the narrative seems to shift and comment upon the ways that your sense of the boy's character is altered.

3. How would you characterize the narrator? Is he as stupid as the adults make him out to be? What indications do you get of his inner life? In what ways has your impression of the boy changed by the end of the story?

4. Does Mahfouz want his reader to like the boy? Analyze your own feelings and try to account for them.

5. How does the episode of the peep-show change the direction of the story? Describe the role of the girl. In what way is she shown to be similar to the narrator?

6. Is there a way in which the style of the narration is suited to the narrator? What do the sudden shifts of attention and the constant focus upon the immediate present tell us about the boy's perception of the world?

7. What does the boy see while he is waiting for the girl to return? Is it significant that he should see the couple from the same platform where he had kissed the girl? Explain.

8. How does the tone of the story change after this episode? Does the boy see the world differently than he did before? If so, how?

9. How does Mahfouz use symbolic elements in the last paragraph of the story and how do these contribute to your final impression of the boy's situation? In what sense could this story be said to express a universal statement about coming of age? Can you imagine a comparable narrative being written about a period in your own youth?

4 Plot

If it is true, as I have suggested, that there is no short story without character, then it is no less true that there is no reason for the story—or character—to exist without plot. Plot is what arises the moment the character, or characters, are set into motion. This brings us to the very source of the storyteller's art: to involve a listener or reader in the unfolding of a chain of events, creating an active curiosity about what has happened or will happen and then gratifying that curiosity. Characters are the pieces on the chessboard, and plot is the strategic moving of those pieces.

A DEFINITION OF PLOT

Any discussion of plot must begin with the drawing of a crucial distinction between *plot* and *narrative*. E. M. Forster formulated the difference most memorably. He observed that if we write "The king died and the queen died," we have a narrative, but if we write, instead, "The king died, and the queen died of grief," then we have a plot. The second assertion has established a link of cause between the two events. And this, the making of connections, or designs, is the essence of storytelling. Narrative is simply a record of what happened. For narrative to become plot it must reveal its meaning in human terms. Events only become interesting, which is to say *relevant* to our understanding of life, when we see their effect upon people, or, in the case of fiction, upon characters.

This is not to say, however, that the writer always explains the connection of events to lives. That task is quite often left to the reader; it is the puzzle that we try to solve as we read and that draws us more deeply into the world of the story. The writer may, indeed, deliberately present a narrative sequence in such a way that it falls to the reader to assemble it into a plot. In Olive Schreiner's story "The Woman's Rose" (see Chapter 9), we are told by the narrator that she has for many years kept a rose in her box of mementos. She later reveals how it happened that another woman, a rival, presented her with the flower. Schreiner leaves it to her reader to determine that the rose was bestowed as one beautiful woman's tribute to another's beauty, and that the recipient kept it because it taught her something about human generosity. The plot, in other words, depends upon our willingness to draw the necessary inferences, to make the human connections. If we read the story without thinking about the link between the elements, then we have only absorbed its narrative component.

Narrative is *what* is told; plot is *how* the material is shaped to affect the reader. Events unfold in sequence: one thing happens, then another. But stories are very often told in different order. A writer may choose to tell us right away that two men had a fight and that one of the men was killed, and only then step back in time to show what circumstances provoked the incident. How the story gets told depends upon the effect the writer desires. It may be that in this case the writer is less interested in the drama of physical combat, and more concerned with the changing relationship between two old friends. By revealing the fight and the death at the outset, the writer has determined the way we will experience the story of the relationship. We will understand the whole pattern of their relations as marking out a path toward betrayal and confrontation. Another writer, looking to create a different response, might narrate the events in sequence, possibly even trying to surprise the reader with the outcome. The basic elements are more or less the same, but how they are used, or plotted, makes a tremendous difference.

Changing the natural sequence of events is only one of the writer's plot options. The use of multiple narrators is another. Suppose that the writer is less interested in what happened than in the different ways that people perceive events. Why not tell the same story twice, or three times, allowing variations to emerge in each person's telling? This is precisely what the Japanese writer Ryunosuke Akutagawa did in his novella *Rashomon*, in which no fewer than seven versions of a violent rape are recounted.

The writer may also choose to tell several stories at once, making use of parallel plots or subplots. A *parallel plot* generally tells two stories of equal importance, moving from one to the other and back again; a *subplot* tends to be secondary, often taking the form of a story told by a character within the story. Both of these strategies are common within novels (reading Dickens, for example, we often find ourselves holding three or four plotlines in mind at any time), but they are less often encountered in the short story. The reason is simple. Two or more plots can only resonate off each other where there is ample narrative space. Building a short story around two plots is like having two large families living together in a small apartment—it's possible, but it's not easy.

PATTERNS OF PLOT DEVELOPMENT

The short story, by and large, tends to move toward what Edgar Allan Poe called "the single effect," a culmination that pulls together and resolves the tensions created by the characters and their circumstances. And what is quite remarkable is that for all of the diverse technical options open to the writer, most stories still conform to what we might think of as the classic short story form. It would seem that there is a time-tested way to engage and hold a reader, and that an author takes a certain risk in disregarding it.

The classic pattern, from which our fundamental descriptive terms are derived, is linear, with beginning, middle, and end coming in natural sequence. There is a set-up, or *exposition*, in which the characters and their situations are introduced. This is followed by the *rising action*, which poses and then intensifies the complications, building toward a *climax*. The climax is the moment of maximum tension, the point after which the circumstances must change. After the climax comes the *resolution*, also known as the *falling action*, which shows the consequences. The resolution tells the reader how things turned out, answering the inevitable question "What finally happened?" Sometimes an author will attach a further explanation so that the reader makes no mistake about the meaning of the outcome. This is the *denouement*, which is a French term that literally means "unraveling." Most authors, though, especially modern authors, prefer to leave the meanings and implications for the reader. They favor a policy of *indirection; that is, they would rather suggest than tell.

In 1863, German author Gustav Freytag proposed the simple pyramid shape—often called *Freytag's triangle*—as a model for the ideal structure of a play. The scheme has since been used in many analyses of the short story as well:

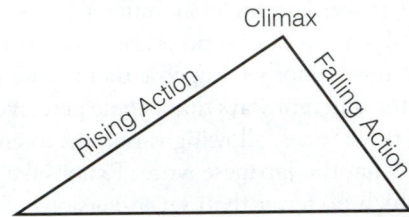

Climax

Rising Action

Falling Action

Streamlined and elegant though it is, Freytag's triangle simplifies as much as it clarifies. It cannot accommodate stories that begin at the climax and work in reverse, or stories that bypass dramatic resolution in favor of quieter revelations, or *epiphanies* (moments of illumination or understanding experienced by a character). Nor does it adequately map the difference between the exposition and rising action, or the falling action and the resolution. A more accurate rendering of the classic short story might be as follows:

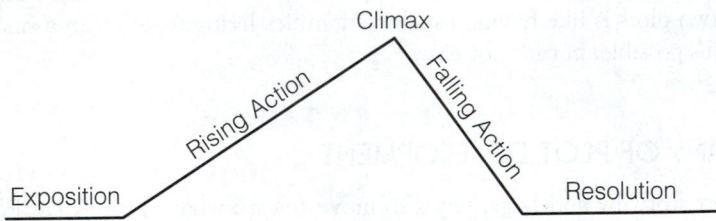

Climax

Rising Action

Falling Action

Exposition

Resolution

Washington Irving's "The Legend of Sleepy Hollow" (see Chapter 13), which might be called America's first great short story, is a perfect example of the classic form. The exposition introduces the protagonist, Ichabod Crane, showing his character and hinting at his particular weaknesses. (Irving portrays a somewhat foolish and self-satisfied bookworm who imagines himself—wrongly—to be attractive to women.) The rising action brings all the main characters together at a party. Irving builds tension and expectation in the reader, who knows that Ichabod will have to ride home along the lonely, and supposedly haunted, road. The climax comes when Ichabod, riding, is attacked by what he believes is the legendary Headless Horseman (it is his rival, Brom Bones, in disguise). The resolution then tells us what the villagers found the next morning (a broken pumpkin, a riderless horse) and gives a few surmises about the fate of the schoolmaster, Ichabod.

Irving's plot might be diagrammed thus:

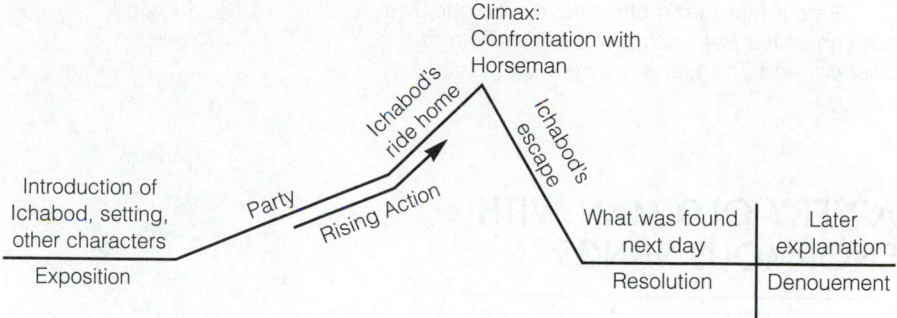

Climax:
Confrontation with
Horseman

Ichabod's
ride home

Ichabod's
escape

Party

Rising Action

Introduction of
Ichabod, setting,
other characters

What was found
next day

Later
explanation

Exposition

Resolution

Denouement

Varieties of Suspense and Expectation

Stories like Irving's hold our attention by creating an atmosphere of suspense around the characters and events. We turn the pages because we want to learn what happens next. Suspense creates expectation through the holding back of information; there is a promise of revelation to come. Sometimes the promise is implicit in the situation: the two men are fighting to the death and we read on to see who will win. In other cases, the author may subtly prepare the ground for us through *foreshadowing*—that is, passing along cues and hints about what will happen. Thus, in "The Legend of Sleepy Hollow," Irving devotes several long passages early on to descriptions of the spooky countryside and to the retelling of old rumors about ghosts and headless riders. When Ichabod finally sets out on his homeward ride, we remember this lore and our pulses quicken.

Of course, not every story is structured according to the classic pattern. But it is safe to say that most story writers have absorbed the pattern, and when they make their choices and departures they do so for good reasons.

Here is a story that both follows and plays against the classic pattern.

Gabriel García Márquez (1928–   )

Gabriel García Márquez was born in Aracataca, near the coast of Colombia. He was raised by his maternal grandparents and recalls a childhood filled with stories and legends, many of which later surfaced in his fiction. García Márquez worked for many years as a reporter, in Colombia and later in Paris. But his real love from the first was storytelling. In 1955 he published his first book, *Leaf Storm and Other Stories,* and three years later a short novel entitled *No One Writes to the Colonel.* But his masterpiece, the book that changed the complexion of Latin American writing, was *One Hundred Years of Solitude* (1967), written while the author lived in Mexico City.

García Márquez's other novels include *The Autumn of the Patriarch, Love in the Time of Cholera,* and *The General in His Labyrinth.*

A VERY OLD MAN WITH ENORMOUS WINGS

On the third day of rain they had killed so many crabs inside the house that Pelayo had to cross his drenched courtyard and throw them into the sea, because the newborn child had a temperature all night and they thought it was due to the stench. The world had been sad since Tuesday. Sea and sky were a single ash-gray thing and the sands of the beach, which on March nights glimmered like powdered light, had become a stew of mud and rotten shell-fish. The light was so weak at noon that when Pelayo was coming back to the house after throwing away the crabs, it was hard for him to see what it was that was moving and groaning in the rear of the courtyard. He had to go very close to see that it was an old man, a very old man, lying face down in the mud, who, in spite of his tremendous efforts, couldn't get up, impeded by his enormous wings.

Frightened by that nightmare, Pelayo ran to get Elisenda, his wife, who was putting compresses on the sick child, and he took her to the rear of the courtyard. They both looked at the fallen body with mute stupor. He was dressed like a rag-picker. There were only a few faded hairs left on his bald skull and very few teeth in his mouth, and his pitiful condition of a drenched great-grandfather had taken away any sense of grandeur he might have had. His huge buzzard wings, dirty and half-plucked, were forever entangled in the mud. They looked at him so long and so closely that Pelayo and Elisenda very soon overcame their surprise and in the end found him familiar. Then they dared speak to him, and he answered in an incomprehensible dialect with a strong sailor's voice. That was how they skipped over the inconvenience of the wings and quite intelligently concluded that he was a lonely castaway from some foreign ship wrecked by the storm. And yet, they called in a neighbor woman who knew everything about life and death to see him, and all she needed was one look to show them their mistake.

"He's an angel," she told them. "He must have been coming for the child, but the poor fellow is so old that the rain knocked him down."

On the following day everyone knew that a flesh-and-blood angel was held captive in Pelayo's house. Against the judgment of the wise neighbor woman, for whom angels in those times were the fugitive survivors of a celestial conspiracy, they did not have the heart to club him to death. Pelayo watched over him all afternoon from the kitchen, armed with his bailiff's club, and before going to bed he dragged him out of the mud and locked him up with the hens in the wire chicken coop. In the middle of the night, when the rain stopped, Pelayo and Elisenda were still killing crabs. A short time afterward the child woke up without a fever and with a desire to eat. Then they felt magnanimous and decided to put the angel on a raft with fresh water and provisions for three days and leave him to his fate on the high seas. But when they went out into the courtyard with the first light of dawn, they found the whole neighborhood in front of the chicken coop having fun with the angel, without the slightest reverence, tossing him things to eat through the openings in the wire as if he weren't a supernatural creature but a circus animal.

Father Gonzaga arrived before seven o'clock, alarmed at the strange news. By that time onlookers less frivolous than those at dawn had already arrived and they were making all kinds of conjectures concerning the captive's future. The simplest among them thought that he should be named mayor of the world. Others of sterner mind felt that he should be promoted to the rank of five-star general in order to win all wars. Some visionaries hoped that he could be put to stud in order to implant on earth a race of winged wise men who could take charge of the universe. But Father Gonzaga, before becoming a priest, had been a robust woodcutter. Standing by the wire, he reviewed his catechism in an instant and asked them to open the door so that he could take a close look at that pitiful man who looked more like a huge decrepit hen among the fascinated chickens. He was lying in a corner drying his open wings in the sunlight among the fruit peels and breakfast leftovers that the early risers had thrown him. Alien to the impertinences of the world, he only lifted his antiquarian eyes and murmured something in his dialect when Father Gonzaga went into the chicken coop and said good morning to him in Latin. The parish priest had his first suspicion of an imposter when he saw that he did not understand the language of God or know how to greet His ministers. Then he noticed that seen close up he was much too human: he had an unbearable smell of the outdoors, the back side of his wings was strewn with parasites and his main feathers had been mistreated by terrestrial winds, and nothing about him measured up to the proud dignity of angels. Then he came out of the chicken coop and in a brief sermon warned the curious against the risks of being ingenuous. He reminded them that the devil had the bad habit of making use of carnival tricks in order to confuse the unwary. He argued that if wings were not the essential element in determining the difference between a hawk and an airplane, they were even less so in the recognition of angels. Nevertheless, he promised to write a letter to his bishop so that the latter would write to his primate so that the latter would write to the Supreme Pontiff in order to get the final verdict from the highest courts.

His prudence fell on sterile hearts. The news of the captive angel spread with such rapidity that after a few hours the courtyard had the bustle of a marketplace and they had to call in troops with fixed bayonets to disperse the mob that was about to knock the house down. Elisenda, her spine all twisted from sweeping up so much marketplace trash, then got the idea of fencing in the yard and charging five cents admission to see the angel.

The curious came from far away. A traveling carnival arrived with a flying acrobat who buzzed over the crowd several times, but no one paid any attention to him because his wings were not those of an angel but, rather, those of a sidereal° bat. The most unfortunate invalids on earth came in search of health: a poor woman who since childhood had been counting her heartbeats and had run out of numbers; a Portuguese man who couldn't sleep because the noise of the stars disturbed him; a sleepwalker who got up at night to undo the things he had done while awake; and many others with less serious ailments. In the midst of that shipwreck disorder that

5

---

sidereal: coming from the stars.

made the earth tremble, Pelayo and Elisenda were happy with fatigue, for in less than a week they had crammed their rooms with money and the line of pilgrims waiting their turn to enter still reached beyond the horizon.

The angel was the only one who took no part in his own act. He spent his time trying to get comfortable in his borrowed nest, befuddled by the hellish heat of the oil lamps and sacramental candles that had been placed along the wire. At first they tried to make him eat some mothballs, which, according to the wisdom of the wise neighbor woman, were the food prescribed for angels. But he turned them down, just as he turned down the papal lunches that the penitents brought him, and they never found out whether it was because he was an angel or because he was an old man that in the end he ate nothing but eggplant mush. His only super-natural virtue seemed to be patience. Especially during the first days, when the hens pecked at him, searching for the stellar parasites that proliferated in his wings, and the cripples pulled out feathers to touch their defective parts with, and even the most merciful threw stones at him, trying to get him to rise so they could see him standing. The only time they succeeded in arousing him was when they burned his side with an iron for branding steers, for he had been motionless for so many hours that they thought he was dead. He awoke with a start, ranting in his her-metic language and with tears in his eyes, and he flapped his wings a couple of times, which brought on a whirlwind of chicken dung and lunar dust and a gale of panic that did not seem to be of this world. Although many thought that his reac-tion had been one not of rage but of pain, from then on they were careful not to annoy him, because the majority understood that his passivity was not that of a hero taking his ease but that of a cataclysm in repose.

Father Gonzaga held back the crowd's frivolity with formulas of maidservant in-spiration while awaiting the arrival of a final judgment on the nature of the captive. But the mail from Rome showed no sense of urgency. They spent their time finding out if the prisoner had a navel, if his dialect had any connection with Aramaic, how many times he could fit on the head of a pin, or whether he wasn't just a Norwe-gian with wings. Those meager letters might have come and gone until the end of time if a providential event had not put an end to the priest's tribulations.

It so happened that during those days, among so many other carnival attrac-tions, there arrived in town the traveling show of the woman who had been changed into a spider for having disobeyed her parents. The admission to see her was not only less than the admission to see the angel, but people were permitted to ask her all manner of questions about her absurd state and to examine her up and down so that no one would ever doubt the truth of her horror. She was a frightful tarantula the size of a ram and with the head of a sad maiden. What was most heart-rending, how-ever, was not her outlandish shape but the sincere affliction with which she re-counted the details of her misfortune. While still practically a child she had sneaked out of her parents' house to go to a dance, and while she was coming back through the woods after having danced all night without permission, a fearful thunderclap rent the sky in two and through the crack came the lightning bolt of brimstone that changed her into a spider. Her only nourishment came from the meatballs that char-itable souls chose to toss into her mouth. A spectacle like that, full of so much human truth and with such a fearful lesson, was bound to defeat without even try-ing that of a haughty angel who scarcely deigned to look at mortals. Besides, the few miracles attributed to the angel showed a certain mental disorder, like the blind man who didn't recover his sight but grew three new teeth, or the paralytic who didn't get to walk but almost won the lottery, and the leper whose sores sprouted sunflowers. Those consolation miracles, which were more like mocking fun, had already ruined the angel's reputation when the woman who had been changed into a spider finally crushed him completely. That was how Father Gonzaga was cured forever of his insomnia and Pelayo's courtyard went back to being as empty as during the time it had rained for three days and crabs walked through the bedrooms.

10

The owners of the house had no reason to lament. With the money they saved they built a two-story mansion with balconies and gardens and high netting so that crabs wouldn't get in during the winter, and with iron bars on the windows so that angels wouldn't get in. Pelayo also set up a rabbit warren close to town and gave up his job as bailiff for good, and Elisenda bought some satin pumps with high heels and many dresses of iridescent silk, the kind worn on Sunday by the most desirable women in those times. The chicken coop was the only thing that didn't receive any attention. If they washed it down with creolin and burned tears of myrrh inside it every so often, it was not in homage to the angel but to drive away the dungheap stench that still hung everywhere like a ghost and was turning the new house into an old one. At first, when the child learned to walk, they were careful that he not get too close to the chicken coop. But then they began to lose their fears and got used to the smell, and before the child got his second teeth he'd gone inside the chicken coop to play, where the wires were falling apart. The angel was no less standoffish with him than with other mortals, but he tolerated the most ingenious infamies with the patience of a dog who had no illusions. They both came down with chicken pox at the same time. The doctor who took care of the child couldn't resist the temptation to listen to the angel's heart, and he found so much whistling in the heart and so many sounds in his kidneys that it seemed impossible for him to be alive. What surprised him most, however, was the logic of his wings. They seemed so natural on that completely human organism that he couldn't understand why other men didn't have them too.

When the child began school it had been some time since the sun and rain had caused the collapse of the chicken coop. The angel went dragging himself about here and there like a stray dying man. They would drive him out of the bedroom with a broom and a moment later find him in the kitchen. He seemed to be in so many places at the same time that they grew to think that he'd been duplicated, that he was reproducing himself all through the house, and the exasperated and unhinged Elisenda shouted that it was awful living in that hell full of angels. He could scarcely eat and his antiquarian eyes had also become so foggy that he went about bumping into posts. All he had left were the bare cannulae° of his last feathers. Pelayo threw a blanket over him and extended him the charity of letting him sleep in the shed, and only then did they notice that he had a temperature at night, and was delirious with the tongue twisters of an old Norwegian. That was one of the few times they became alarmed, for they thought he was going to die and not even the wise neighbor woman had been able to tell them what to do with dead angels.

And yet he not only survived his worst winter, but seemed improved with the first sunny days. He remained motionless for several days in the farthest corner of the courtyard, where no one would see him, and at the beginning of December some large, stiff feathers began to grow on his wings, the feathers of a scarecrow, which

_____

cannulae: tubular sockets holding feathers to a body.

looked more like another misfortune of decrepitude. But he must have known the reason for those changes, for he was quite careful that no one should notice them, that no one should hear the sea chanteys that he sometimes sang under the stars. One morning Elisenda was cutting some bunches of onions for lunch when a wind that seemed to come from the high seas blew into the kitchen. Then she went to the window and caught the angel in his first attempts at flight. They were so clumsy that his fingernails opened a furrow in the vegetable patch and he was on the point of knocking the shed down with the ungainly flapping that slipped on the light and couldn't get a grip on the air. But he did manage to gain altitude. Elisenda let out a sigh of relief, for herself and for him, when she saw him pass over the last houses, holding himself up in some way with the risky flapping of a senile vulture. She kept watching him even when she was through cutting the onions and she kept on watching until it was no longer possible for her to see him, because then he was no longer an annoyance in her life but an imaginary dot on the horizon of the sea.

[1955]

Translated by Gabriel García Márquez

As you read the following discussion, consider these questions:

1. Use specific examples to show how García Márquez creates expectations in the beginning of his story. Explain how these expectations are either met or defeated.

2. What is the atmosphere of the story, and how is it established? How does the atmosphere affect the presentation of events?

3. García Márquez likes to juxtapose probable and improbable elements in his narratives. Find two instances where the ordinary and the seemingly impossible coexist. Describe the effect on the reader.

4. What is the climax of the story? Has García Márquez done anything to prepare the reader? How is his handling of this crucial moment different from that of other authors you might have read? Cite a specific contrast.

5. How are the story's plot elements related to the presentation of character? How do the angel's behavior and attitude determine the turns of the narrative?

6. What is the final effect of García Márquez's ending? Is it uplifting, miraculous, or anticlimactic? Explain your answer.

Discussion. García Márquez is here writing in a mode that has come to be known as *magical realism*, which simply means that the author brings together the ordinary and the fantastic in startling ways. But García Márquez puts an interesting spin on the material, presenting the miraculous in such a way that it comes to seem dreary and unremarkable. To achieve this effect, he deliberately subverts the classic structure.

It is a simple but effective tactic. The whole point of the traditional form is to build suspense through the rising action, then to release tension through a climax and resolution. García Márquez keeps the form, but he refuses to play the game.

The author lures us in with the promise of remarkable revelations. To begin with, there is the unusual atmosphere. Everything is slightly exaggerated: that the rain would have killed so many crabs that Pelayo had to carry them to the sea, that the light was so weak that it was hard to see even at noon. . . .Then comes the final sentence of the paragraph, holding its surprise for the last: ". . . it was an old man, a very old man, lying face down in the mud, who, in spite of his tremendous efforts, couldn't get up, impeded by his enormous wings."

Here are the first touches of the exposition. The reader, confronted with the marvelous, cannot wait to continue, to find out what surprises lie in store. But García Márquez slyly refuses gratification. Instead of building tension through the rising action, he deflates it. We wait for the old man—angel or freak—to stir himself and perform some miracle. He does nothing. He waits in his cage like some flea-ridden zoo animal. People come from faraway places to see him, but he does nothing: "The angel was the only one who took no part in his own act. He spent his time trying to get comfortable in his borrowed nest, befuddled by the hellish heat of the oil lamps and sacramental candles that had been placed along the wire."

The habit of expectation is a hard one to break, however. Even when it seems quite clear that no eruption of wonders is imminent, we keep our hopes alive. It is as if a voice were saying: "We have a man with wings—possibly an angel—in a cage. Something has to happen." Suspense is inherent in the very idea of a story. We assume that there is a point to the narration, that the writer would not bother if there were not. We read on.

García Márquez is well aware of the reader's itch for dramatic action, and he plays to it most skillfully. He stretches his anticlimactic narration to the very limit and then teases the reader into a renewed expectancy. The switch comes near the midpoint of the story. García Márquez describes Father Gonzaga's correspondence with church authorities in Rome and then rekindles our interest with a simple storyteller's twist: "Those meager letters might have come and gone until the end of time if a providential event had not put an end to the priest's tribulations." We sit up, ready to hear about this "providential event," which is sure to bring the story to its moment of climax.

But once again the writer has thrown us a red herring. While it is an astonishing thing that he sets before us—a woman who has been turned into a tarantula the size of a ram—nothing comes of it. That is, the spider-woman does not become an antagonist; there is no struggle, no particular tension, and no sense of climax. The people who had taken an interest in the man with wings simply turn away to new spectacles.

Strictly speaking, this nonclimax *does* function as a climax. It marks the turning point. Whatever expectations we had of the man with wings are pushed to the side. His story proved to be a false alarm, an absence of story. The only question now is how García Márquez is going to conclude what he has begun.

But one should always trust a master storyteller. García Márquez knows the reader's heart; he knows that the best time to inject surprise is when the reader has given up on surprise. And so, in the last paragraph, against all indications, the old man recovers. His feathers begin to grow back, and he starts to sing his sea chanteys under the stars. Then: "One morning Elisenda was cutting some bunches of onions for lunch when a wind that seemed to come from the high seas blew into the kitchen." This burst of freshness is the very reverse of the murky rain that brought the old man to the town. All the despondency and gloom that have gathered through the story are dispelled. The last paragraph, which is a resolution, and technically part of the falling action, functions as a climax would. It could not have this effect if García Márquez had not prepared us from the start with a series of fizzles. Now we feel release. We are with Elisenda, watching as the long-delayed miracle takes place: "She kept watching him even when she was through cutting the onions and she kept on watching until it was no longer possible for her to see him, because then he was no longer an annoyance in her life but an imaginary dot on the horizon of the sea."

Defying the Expectations of Plot

The short story has evolved considerably from its origins in the spoken tale. Writers from Anton Chekhov to James Joyce and beyond have worked in defiance of conventional expectations, producing stories that replace dramatic plot structure with episode as well as building suspense with private revelations or epiphanies. Readers of many contemporary stories are hard put to find evidence of what were formerly the staple goods of the genre. But while many of the fundamental premises have been altered anarchy does not rule. There are still certain basic requirements: action has to reveal character, and some psychological change has to be effected; the reader needs to feel movement from point A to point B, however those points might be defined.

We tend to think of the drift toward plotlessness as a modernist development, but writers have long been interested in testing the elasticity of the short story form. Herman Melville's "Bartleby the Scrivener" (see Chapter 13) turns a character's refusal to act into its central premise. Melville's contemporary, Nathaniel Hawthorne (1804–1864), takes on a no less revolutionary idea in "Wakefield." In this story we see another kind of nonevent becoming the basis of a literary tale. The first sentence gives us much of the plot—that a man who will be called "Wakefield" once "absented himself for a long time from his wife"—and by the end of the opening paragraph we know the whole story. Yet the narrative goes on for several pages, and for what purpose? How does Hawthorne fill the rest of the container? Mainly, he fills it by playing relentlessly upon the reader's desire for explanation, for comprehensible narrative. The author gives us the barest suppositions and speculations—but he does so knowing that our appetite for coherence will have us filling in the blanks, inserting our imaginings and interpretations wherever they are needed. By the time we are finished reading we find that we have collaborated with Hawthorne to create a haunting emblem of absence. We have taken part in an unsolved mystery and we are somehow the wiser for it.

Nathaniel Hawthorne (1804–1864)

Nathaniel Hawthorne might be considered the conscience of American literature. The passions and phantasmagoric imaginings that ran riot in the works of Poe, his near-contemporary, are in Hawthorne bridled by the stern hand of the moralist. His family background, one might argue, had some part to play in the shaping of his disposition. His Salem, Massachusetts, forebears included a great-grandfather who had persecuted Quakers from the judicial bench; his grandfather, another judge, had been one of the presiding figures at the Salem witch trials.

Hawthorne decided early upon the writer's vocation. He attended Bowdoin College in Maine for four years, then returned to Salem to work at his craft. He began selling his dark, allegorical writings to periodicals, publishing his first collection, *Twice-Told Tales,* in 1837. He lived for a while at Brook Farm, a communal experiment in West Roxbury, Massachusetts; his novel *The Blithedale Romance* (1852) draws some of its background from that period. Hawthorne similarly made use of his experience of working at the Boston Customs House, incorporating it into the introduction of *The Scarlet Letter.* This novel, published in 1850, is regarded as his masterpiece.

In 1853 President Franklin Pierce, whom Hawthorne had befriended at Bowdoin, appointed the writer to the post of Consul to Liverpool. Hawthorne lived in England and later traveled in Italy, returning to the United States only four years before his death.

Hawthorne wrote voluminously. His writings include the novels *The House of the Seven Gables* (1851) and *The Marble Faun* (1860) and the stories of *Mosses from an Old Manse* (1846).

WAKEFIELD

In some old magazine or newspaper I recollect a story, told as truth, of a man—let us call him Wakefield—who absented himself for a long time from his wife. The fact, thus abstractedly stated, is not very uncommon, nor—without a proper distinction of circumstances—to be condemned either as naughty or nonsensical. Howbeit, this, though far from the most aggravated, is perhaps the strangest, instance on record, of marital delinquency; and, moreover, as remarkable a freak as may be found in the whole list of human oddities. The wedded couple lived in London. The man, under pretence of going a journey, took lodgings in the next street to his own house, and there, unheard of by his wife or friends, and without the shadow of a reason for such self-banishment, dwelt upwards of twenty years. During that period, he beheld his home every day, and frequently the forlorn Mrs. Wakefield. And after so great a gap in his matrimonial felicity—when his death was reckoned certain, his estate settled, his name dismissed from memory, and his wife, long, long ago, resigned to her autumnal widowhood—he entered the door one evening, quietly, as from a day's absence, and became a loving spouse till death.

This outline is all that I remember. But the incident, though of the purest originality, unexampled, and probably never to be repeated, is one, I think, which appeals to the generous sympathies of mankind. We know, each for himself, that none of us would perpetrate such a folly, yet feel as if some other might. To my own contemplations, at least, it has often recurred, always exciting wonder, but with a sense that the story must be true, and a conception of its hero's character. Whenever any subject so forcibly affects the mind, time is well spent in thinking of it. If the reader choose, let him do his own meditation; or if he prefer to ramble with me through the twenty years of Wakefield's vagary, I bid him welcome; trusting that there will be a pervading spirit and a moral, even should we fail to find them, done up neatly, and condensed into the final sentence. Thought has always its efficacy, and every striking incident its moral.

What sort of a man was Wakefield? We are free to shape out our own idea, and call it by his name. He was now in the meridian of life; his matrimonial affections, never violent, were sobered into a calm, habitual sentiment; of all husbands, he was likely to be the most constant, because a certain sluggishness would keep his heart at rest, wherever it might be placed. He was intellectual, but not actively so; his mind occupied itself in long and lazy musings, that ended to no purpose, or had not vigor to attain it; his thoughts were seldom so energetic as to seize hold of words. Imagination, in the proper meaning of the term, made no part of Wakefield's gifts. With a cold but not depraved nor wandering heart, and a mind never feverish with riotous thoughts, nor perplexed with originality, who could have anticipated that our friend would entitle himself to a foremost place among the doers of eccentric deeds? Had his acquaintances been asked, who was the man in London the surest to perform nothing to-day which should be remembered on the morrow, they would have thought of Wakefield. Only the wife of his bosom might have hesitated. She, without having analyzed his character, was partly aware of a quiet selfishness, that had rusted into his inactive mind; of a peculiar sort of vanity, the most uneasy attribute about him; of a disposition to craft, which had seldom produced more positive effects than the keeping of petty secrets, hardly worth revealing; and, lastly, of what she called a little strangeness, sometimes, in the good man. This latter quality is indefinable, and perhaps non-existent.

Let us now imagine Wakefield bidding adieu to his wife. It is the dusk of an October evening. His equipment is a drab greatcoat, a hat covered with an oilcloth, top-boots, an umbrella in one hand and a small portmanteau in the other. He has informed Mrs. Wakefield that he is to take the night coach into the country. She would fain inquire the length of his journey, its object, and the probable time of his return; but, indulgent to his harmless love of mystery, interrogates him only by a look. He tells her not to expect him positively by the return coach, nor to be alarmed should he tarry three or four days; but, at all events, to look for him at supper on Friday evening. Wakefield himself, be it considered, has no suspicion of what is before him. He holds out his hand, she gives her own, and meets his parting kiss in the matter-of-course way of a ten years' matrimony; and forth goes the middle-aged Mr. Wakefield, almost resolved to perplex his good lady by a whole week's absence. After the door has closed behind him, she perceives it thrust partly open, and a vision of her husband's face, through the aperture, smiling on her, and gone in a moment. For the time, this little incident is dismissed without a thought. But, long afterwards, when she has been more years a widow than a wife, that smile recurs, and flickers across all her reminiscences of Wakefield's visage. In her many musings, she surrounds the original smile with a multitude of fantasies, which make it strange and awful: as, for instance, if she imagines him in a coffin, that parting look is frozen on his pale features; or, if she dreams of him in heaven, still his blessed spirit wears a quiet and crafty smile. Yet, for its sake, when all others have given him up for dead, she sometimes doubts whether she is a widow.

But our business is with the husband. We must hurry after him along the street, ere he lose his individuality, and melt into the great mass of London life. It would be vain searching for him there. Let us follow close at his heels, therefore, until, after several superfluous turns and doublings, we find him comfortably established by the fireside of a small apartment, previously bespoken. He is in the next street to his own, and at his journey's end. He can scarcely trust his good fortune, in having got thither unperceived—recollecting that, at one time, he was delayed by the throng, in the very focus of a lighted lantern; and, again, there were footsteps that seemed to tread behind his own, distinct from the multitudinous tramp around him; and, anon, he heard a voice shouting afar, and fancied that it called his name. Doubtless, a dozen busybodies had been watching him, and told his wife the whole affair. Poor Wakefield! Little knowest thou thine own insignificance in this great world! No mortal eye but mine has traced thee. Go quietly to thy bed, foolish man; and, on the morrow, if thou wilt be wise, get thee home to good Mrs. Wakefield, and tell her the truth. Remove not thyself, even for a little week, from thy place in her chaste bosom. Were she, for a single moment, to deem thee dead, or lost, or lastingly divided from her, thou wouldst be wofully conscious of a change in thy true wife forever after. It is perilous to make a chasm in human affections; not that they gape so long and wide—but so quickly close again!

Almost repenting of his frolic, or whatever it may be termed, Wakefield lies down betimes, and starting from his first nap, spreads forth his arms into the wide and solitary waste of the unaccustomed bed. "No,"—thinks he, gathering the bedclothes about him,—"I will not sleep alone another night."

In the morning he rises earlier than usual, and sets himself to consider what he really means to do. Such are his loose and rambling modes of thought that he has taken this very singular step with the consciousness of a purpose, indeed, but without being able to define it sufficiently for his own contemplation. The vagueness of the project, and the convulsive effort with which he plunges into the execution of it, are equally characteristic of a feeble-minded man. Wakefield sifts his ideas, however, as minutely as he may, and finds himself curious to know the progress of matters at home—how his exemplary wife will endure her widowhood of a week; and briefly, how the little sphere of creatures and circumstances, in which he was a central object, will be affected by his removal. A morbid vanity, therefore, lies nearest the bottom of the affair. But, how is he to attain his ends? Not, certainly, by keeping close in this comfortable lodging, where, though he slept and awoke in the next street to his home, he is as effectually abroad as if the stage-coach had been whirling him away all night. Yet, should he reappear, the whole project is knocked in the head. His poor brains being hopelessly puzzled with this dilemma, he at length ventures out, partly resolving to cross the head of the street, and send one hasty glance towards his forsaken domicile. Habit—for he is a man of habits—takes him by the hand, and guides him, wholly unaware, to his own door, where, just at the critical moment, he is aroused by the scraping of his foot upon the step. Wakefield! whither are you going?

At that instant his fate was turning on the pivot. Little dreaming of the doom to which his first backward step devotes him, he hurries away, breathless with agitation hitherto unfelt, and hardly dares turn his head at the distant corner. Can it be that nobody caught sight of him? Will not the whole household—the decent Mrs. Wakefield, the smart maid servant, and the dirty little footboy—raise a hue and cry, through London streets, in pursuit of their fugitive lord and master? Wonderful escape! He gathers courage to pause and look homeward, but is perplexed with a sense of change about the familiar edifice, such as affects us all, when, after a separation of months or years, we again see some hill or lake, or work of art, with which we were friends of old. In ordinary cases, this indescribable impression is caused by the comparison and contrast between our imperfect reminiscences and the reality. In Wakefield, the magic of a single night has wrought a similar transformation, because, in that brief period, a great moral change has been effected. But this is a secret from himself. Before leaving the spot, he catches a far and momentary glimpse of his wife, passing athwart the front window, with her face turned towards the head of the street. The crafty nincompoop takes to his heels, scared with the idea that, among a thousand such atoms of mortality, her eye must have detected him. Right glad is his heart, though his brain be somewhat dizzy, when he finds himself by the coal fire of his lodgings.

So much for the commencement of this long whim-wham. After the initial conception, and the stirring up of the man's sluggish temperament to put it in practice, the whole matter evolves itself in a natural train. We may suppose him, as the result of deep deliberation, buying a new wig, of reddish hair, and selecting sundry garments, in a fashion unlike his customary suit of brown, from a Jew's old-clothes bag. It is accomplished. Wakefield is another man. The new system being now established, a retrograde movement to the old would be almost as difficult as the step that placed him in his unparalleled position. Furthermore, he is rendered obstinate by a sulkiness occasionally incident to his temper, and brought on at present by the inadequate sensation which he conceives to have been produced in the bosom of Mrs. Wakefield. He will not go back until she be frightened half to death. Well; twice or thrice has she passed before his sight, each time with a heavier step, a paler cheek, and more anxious brow; and in the third week of his non-appearance he detects a portent of evil entering the house, in the guise of an apothecary. Next day the knocker is muffled. Towards nightfall comes the chariot of a physician, and deposits its big-wigged and solemn burden at Wakefield's door, whence, after a quarter of an hour's visit, he emerges, perchance the herald of a funeral. Dear woman! Will she die? By this time, Wakefield is excited to something like energy of feeling, but still lingers away from his wife's bedside, pleading with his conscience that she must not be disturbed at such a juncture. If aught else restrains him, he does not know it. In the course of a few weeks she gradually recovers; the crisis is over; her heart is sad, perhaps, but quiet; and, let him return soon or late, it will never be feverish for him again. Such ideas glimmer through the mist of Wakefield's mind, and render him indistinctly conscious that an almost impassable gulf divides his hired apartment from his former home. "It is but in the next street!" he sometimes says. Fool! it is in another world. Hitherto, he has put off his return from one particular day to another; henceforward, he leaves the precise time undetermined. Not to-morrow—

probably next week—pretty soon. Poor man! The dead have nearly as much chance of revisiting their earthly homes as the self-banished Wakefield.

Would that I had a folio to write, instead of an article of a dozen pages! Then might I exemplify how an influence beyond our control lays its strong hand on every deed which we do, and weaves its consequences into an iron tissue of necessity. Wakefield is spell-bound. We must leave him, for ten years or so, to haunt around his house, without once crossing the threshold, and to be faithful to his wife, with all the affection of which his heart is capable, while he is slowly fading out of hers. Long since, it must be remarked, he had lost the perception of singularity in his conduct.

10

Now for a scene! Amid the throng of a London street we distinguish a man, now waxing elderly, with few characteristics to attract careless observers, yet bearing, in his whole aspect, the handwriting of no common fate, for such as have the skill to read it. He is meagre; his low and narrow forehead is deeply wrinkled; his eyes, small and lustreless, sometimes wander apprehensively about him, but oftener seem to look inward. He bends his head, and moves with an indescribable obliquity of gait, as if unwilling to display his full front to the world. Watch him long enough to see what we have described, and you will allow that circumstances—which often produce remarkable men from nature's ordinary handiwork—have produced one such here. Next, leaving him to sidle along the footwalk, cast your eyes in the opposite direction, where a portly female, considerably in the wane of life, with a prayer-book in her hand, is proceeding to yonder church. She has the placid mien of settled widowhood. Her regrets have either died away, or have become so essential to her heart, that they would be poorly exchanged for joy. Just as the lean man and well-conditioned woman are passing, a slight obstruction occurs, and brings these two figures directly in contact. Their hands touch; the pressure of the crowd forces her bosom against his shoulder; they stand, face to face, staring into each other's eyes. After a ten years' separation, thus Wakefield meets his wife!

The throng eddies away, and carries them asunder. The sober widow, resuming her former pace, proceeds to church, but pauses in the portal, and throws a perplexed glance along the street. She passes in, however, opening her prayer-book as she goes. And the man! with so wild a face that busy and selfish London stands to gaze after him, he hurries to his lodgings, bolts the door, and throws himself upon the bed. The latent feelings of years break out; his feeble mind acquires a brief energy from their strength; all the miserable strangeness of his life is revealed to him at a glance: and he cries out, passionately, "Wakefield! Wakefield! You are mad!"

Perhaps he was so. The singularity of his situation must have so moulded him to himself, that, considered in regard to his fellow-creatures and the business of life, he could not be said to possess his right mind. He had contrived, or rather he had happened, to dissever himself from the world—to vanish—to give up his place and privileges with living men, without being admitted among the dead. The life of a hermit is nowise parallel to his. He was in the bustle of the city, as of old; but the crowd swept by and saw him not; he was, we may figuratively say, always beside his wife and at his hearth, yet must never feel the warmth of the one nor the affection of the other. It was Wakefield's unprecedented fate to retain his original share of human sympathies, and to be still involved in human interests, while he had lost his reciprocal influence on them. It would be a most curious speculation to trace out the effect of such circumstances on his heart and intellect, separately, and in unison. Yet, changed as he was, he would seldom be conscious of it, but deem himself the same man as ever; glimpses of the truth, indeed, would come, but only for the moment; and still he would keep saying,"I shall soon go back!"—nor reflect that he had been saying so for twenty years.

I conceive, also, that these twenty years would appear, in the retrospect, scarcely longer than the week to which Wakefield had at first limited his absence. He would look on the affair as no more than an interlude in the main business of his life. When, after a little while more, he should deem it time to reenter his parlor, his wife would clap her hands for joy, on beholding the middle-aged Mr. Wakefield. Alas, what a mistake! Would Time but await the close of our favorite follies, we should be young men, all of us, and till Doomsday.

One evening, in the twentieth year since he vanished, Wakefield is taking his customary walk towards the dwelling which he still calls his own. It is a gusty night of autumn, with frequent showers that patter down upon the pavement, and are gone before a man can put up his umbrella. Pausing near the house, Wakefield discerns, through the parlor windows of the second floor, the red glow and the glimmer and fitful flash of a comfortable fire. On the ceiling appears a grotesque shadow of good Mrs. Wakefield. The cap, the nose and chin, and the broad waist, form an admirable caricature, which dances, moreover, with the up-flickering and down-sinking blaze, almost too merrily for the shade of an elderly widow. At this instant a shower chances to fall, and is driven, by the unmannerly gust, full into Wakefield's face and bosom. He is quite penetrated with its autumnal chill. Shall he stand, wet and shivering here, when his own hearth has a good fire to warm him, and his own wife will run to fetch the gray coat and small-clothes, which, doubtless, she has kept carefully in the closet of their bed chamber? No! Wakefield is no such fool. He ascends the steps—heavily!—for twenty years have stiffened his legs since he came down—but he knows it not. Stay, Wakefield! Would you go to the sole home that is left you? Then step into your grave! The door opens. As he passes in, we have a parting glimpse of his visage, and recognize the crafty smile, which was the precursor of the little joke that he has ever since been playing off at his wife's expense. How unmercifully has he quizzed the poor woman! Well, a good night's rest to Wakefield! 15

This happy event—supposing it to be such—could only have occurred at an unpremeditated moment. We will not follow our friend across the threshold. He has left us much food for thought, a portion of which shall lend its wisdom to a moral, and be shaped into a figure. Amid the seeming confusion of our mysterious world, individuals are so nicely adjusted to a system, and systems to one another and to a whole, that, by stepping aside for a moment, a man exposes himself to a fearful risk of losing his place forever. Like Wakefield, he may become, as it were, the Outcast of the Universe.

[1835]

QUESTIONS

1. Look carefully at the first paragraph of the story. Why do you suppose Hawthorne summarizes the plot as he does? What is the effect of this strategy? Once you know the basic plot, why do you keep reading?

2. What information and perspectives does Hawthorne add after the first paragraph? How is your reading shaped by your knowledge of the outcome?

3. How does Hawthorne invite the reader into the story? Give examples showing the author engaging the reader directly.

4. Do we learn any more about Wakefield from getting a closer view of his actions during his absence? If so, give specific examples.

5. How believable is Hawthorne's tale? Can you imagine similar events happening today?

6. Imagine what happens once Wakefield crosses the threshold and enters his home—and his old life—again. What do you suppose Hawthorne wants us to imagine?

7. What is the point of "Wakefield"? Is Hawthorne ultimately more concerned with his character or his theme? Explain your answer.

8. Compare "Wakefield" with Melville's "Bartleby the Scrivener" (Chapter 13). Are Wakefield and Bartleby in any way kindred spirits?

5 Setting

In fiction, *setting* refers both to the physical location of the events and to the time in which they happen. And just as *where* and *when* are the two vital coordinates of our own lives (indeed, they are so vital and familiar that we often look past them), so they hold a central place in the lives and worlds projected in fiction. How the author makes use of the setting, of course, depends entirely upon the desired effect. One of the first things we do as readers is attempt to situate the events, to place them within a context. Setting has everything to do with this context, even when it appears to be unimportant. Old legends and folktales, for example, often begin in the haziest manner: "Once upon a time in a faraway place. . . ." But who would deny that the impression of dreamy universality that they evoke arises, at least in part, from our inability to fix the particulars of when and where?

THE FUNCTIONS OF SETTING

Setting fulfills several obvious functions in a work of fiction. First, it can give the reader the impression of verisimilitude—that *this really happened*. Consider Maupassant's story "The String," discussed earlier (Chapter 3). The credibility of the events, all of which unfold from Hauchecorne's action of stooping down for a piece of string, depends to a large degree on the reader's ability to picture the whole milieu of the Norman peasant. Note how effectively Maupassant shows us the people in their native place:

> Along all the roads around Goderville the peasants and their wives were coming toward the little town, for it was market-day. The men walked with slow steps, their whole bodies bent forward at each movement of their long twisted legs, deformed by their hard work, by the weight on the plough which, at the same time, raises the left shoulder and distorts the figure, by the reaping of the wheat which forces the knees apart to get a firm stand, by all the slow and painful labors of the country.

When people think of setting, they very often think of passages of pure description. But as the Maupassant passage suggests, the establishment of place is often done less directly. If we look carefully at these few sentences, we will find that the author has told us a great deal: this is a rural district, which holds a weekly market-day, and the principal work of the local peasants involves ploughing and reaping wheat. As we read, we draw these inferences more or less consciously, and the process involves us more deeply in the story.

Like Maupassant, García Márquez, in "A Very Old Man with Enormous Wings" (Chapter 4), conveys the essentials of place without resorting to overt description. And while his rendering of place is not given in a conspicuous descriptive chunk, few readers would deny the important role that place—and atmosphere of place—hold in this work:

> On the third day of rain they had killed so many crabs inside the house that Pelayo had to cross his drenched courtyard and throw them into the sea, because the newborn child had a temperature all night and they thought it was due to the stench. The world had been sad since Tuesday. Sea and sky were a single ash-gray thing and the sands of the beach, which on March nights glimmered like powdered light, had become a stew of mud and rotten shellfish.

The reader works like a detective, building up an impression from scattered details. The intensity of the rain and the proliferation of crabs, the Spanish-sounding name of "Pelayo," and the proximity of the sea all combine to conjure a tropical setting (possibly García Márquez's own Colombia). In a sense, though, the precise geographic region matters much less than the atmospheric setting. We are in a rainy, murky, dispiriting place. This is not an idle embellishment, but an essential aspect of the story, for it is only against the reader's sense of dank confinement that the fresh gusts of wind at the story's end have their impact.

The second function of setting, no less important than the creation of a believable impression, is to situate us in space and time so that we can understand the events of the story as shaped by specific factors. In fiction, as in life, people behave differently—and in some ways *are* different—in different places and at different times. Maupassant's story asks that we believe certain things about the character of the French peasant, more specifically the inhabitant of Normandy during some part of the late eighteenth or early nineteenth century. Maupassant characterizes the whole of that peasant culture as hardworking, frugal, and shrewd—all attributes that can be seen as adaptive to the specific realities of place and time. He would not grant the same characteristics to a group of idle nobles gambling in the casinos at Monte Carlo.

The placing of events in time functions in the same way. It is essential that we know when reading Nathaniel Hawthorne's stories that most of them are set in New England villages in the seventeenth and early eighteenth centuries. His investigations of human morality take on their full meaning only when we understand the intense religiosity of the early Puritans and the strictness of their public codes. The same situations—that is, the same moral tensions—would be difficult to generate in a story about present-day Salem. Time and place make context, and context creates the conditions for meaning.

The third significant use of setting has to do with the enhancement of theme, either through suggestion or through more direct symbolism. Here the *where* generally matters more than the *when*, though of course the striking of the midnight hour or the coming of the dawn can certainly be used to highlight meanings and significances. The author has many more such options with place. Simply stated: Every situation happens within a setting, and that setting can be treated in such a way as to give particular focus to the meaning of what is taking place. Thus, in Naguib Mahfouz's "The Conjurer Made Off with the Dish" (Chapter 3), the narrator, who has been presented as a young man just verging on the sexual and psychological awakenings of puberty, is shown as arriving at the crossing of two roads.

It is, on the one hand, a *literal* crossroads—meant to be just what it is—for roads inevitably cross everywhere around us. But it is also, clearly, a symbolic crossroads as well, supplying the reader with a striking visual equivalent of the dividedness inside the young man.

THE SUGGESTIVE POWERS OF SETTING IN A STORY

A set of important distinctions must be made between the literal, suggestive, and symbolic uses of setting. The lines of interpretation are not always easy to draw. Indeed, the difficulty is one of the challenges that literature poses to the attentive reader. When we read of a character standing in a dark wood, are we to understand it as just a dark wood or as a dark wood suggesting something more (a moral confusion in that character's life, an impending act of violence)? Are we to go still further to find, as we do when we read Dante's *Inferno*, that the dark wood symbolizes a sinfulness that is the result of having lost sight of God? No satisfying answer can be given, but the reader is urged to be aware of the different interpretive possibilities. They allow, as a discussion of Sarah Orne Jewett's "A White Heron" may demonstrate, various points of access to the deeper psychological layers of the work.

Sarah Orne Jewett (1849–1909)

Sarah Orne Jewett was born in South Berwick, in southern Maine, the daughter of a country doctor. For sixty years she kept her attentive eye fastened upon the lives of her fellow New Englanders. Under the influence first of Harriet Beecher Stowe, later of Flaubert, Tolstoy, and James, she forged a serene naturalistic style that was wonderfully suited for capturing the rural and small-town lives that so intrigued her. Jewett published her first collection of stories, *Deerhaven,* in 1877. *A White Heron and Other Stories* followed nine years later. And in 1896 Jewett published her best-known work *The Country of the Pointed Firs,* a series of linked sketches detailing the entwined lives in a Maine seacoast village.

But Jewett, as the reader will see, is more than just a dispassionate observer and recorder of simple lives. Her work is also haunted by intense dreams and longings. The private passions of her characters flash like heat lightning. At moments, as in "A White Heron," Jewett's prose almost resembles D. H. Lawrence's.

A WHITE HERON

I

The woods were already filled with shadows one June evening, just before eight o'clock, though a bright sunset still glimmered faintly among the trunks of the trees. A little girl was driving home her cow, a plodding, dilatory, provoking creature in her behavior, but a valued companion for all that. They were going away from the western light, and striking deep into the dark woods, but their feet were familiar with the path, and it was no matter whether their eyes could see it or not.

There was hardly a night the summer through when the old cow could be found waiting at the pasture bars; on the contrary, it was her greatest pleasure to hide herself away among the high huckleberry bushes, and though she wore a loud bell she had made the discovery that if one stood perfectly still it would not ring. So Sylvia had to hunt for her until she found her, and call Co'! Co'! with never an answering Moo, until her childish patience was quite spent. If the creature had not given good milk and plenty of it, the case would have seemed very different to her owners. Besides, Sylvia had all the time there was, and very little use to make of it. Sometimes in pleasant weather it was a consolation to look upon the cow's pranks as an intelligent attempt to play hide and seek, and as the child had no playmates she lent herself to this amusement with a good deal of zest. Though this chase had been so long that the wary animal herself had given an unusual signal of her whereabouts, Sylvia had only laughed when she came upon Mistress Moolly at the swamp-side, and urged her affectionately homeward with a twig of birch leaves. The old cow was not inclined to wander farther, she even turned in the right direction for once as they left the pasture, and stepped along the road at a good pace. She was quite ready to be milked now, and seldom stopped to browse. Sylvia wondered what her grandmother would say because they were so late. It was a great while since she had left home at half past five o'clock, but everybody knew the difficulty of making this errand a short one. Mrs. Tilley had chased the horned torment too many summer evenings herself to blame any one else for lingering, and was only thankful as she waited that she had Sylvia, nowadays, to give such valuable assistance. The good woman suspected that Sylvia loitered occasionally on her own account; there never was such a child for straying about out-of-doors since the world was made! Everybody said that it was a good change for a little maid who had tried to grow for eight years in a crowded manufacturing town, but, as for Sylvia herself, it seemed as if she never had been alive at all before she came to live at the farm. She thought often with wistful compassion of a wretched dry geranium that belonged to a town neighbor.

" 'Afraid of folks,' " old Mrs. Tilley said to herself, with a smile, after she had made the unlikely choice of Sylvia from her daughter's houseful of children, and was returning to the farm. " 'Afraid of folks,' they said! I guess she won't be troubled no great with 'em up to the old place!" When they reached the door of the lonely house and stopped to unlock it, and the cat came to purr loudly, and rub against them, a deserted pussy, indeed, but fat with young robins, Sylvia whispered that this was a beautiful place to live in, and she never should wish to go home.

The companions followed the shady wood-road, the cow taking slow steps, and the child very fast ones. The cow stopped long at the brook to drink, as if the pasture were not half a swamp, and Sylvia stood still and waited, letting her bare feet cool themselves in the shoal water, while the great twilight moths struck softly against her. She waded on through the brook as the cow moved away, and listened to the thrushes with a heart that beat fast with pleasure. There was a stirring in the great boughs overhead. They were full of little birds and beasts that seemed to be wide-awake, and going about their world, or else saying good-night to each other in sleepy twitters. Sylvia herself felt sleepy as she walked along. However, it was not much farther to the house, and the air was soft and sweet. She was not often in the woods so late as this, and it made her feel as if she were a part of the gray shadows and the moving leaves. She was just thinking how long it seemed since she first came to the farm a year ago, and wondering if everything went on in the noisy town just the same as when she was there; the thought of the great red-faced boy who used to chase and frighten her made her hurry along the path to escape from the shadow of the trees.

Suddenly this little woods-girl is horror-stricken to hear a clear whistle not very far away. Not a bird's whistle, which would have a sort of friendliness, but a boy's whistle, determined, and somewhat aggressive. Sylvia left the cow to whatever sad fate might await her, and stepped discreetly aside into the bushes, but she was just too late. The enemy had discovered her, and called out in a very cheerful and persuasive tone, "Halloa, little girl, how far is it to the road?" and trembling Sylvia answered almost inaudibly, "A good ways." 5

She did not dare to look boldly at the tall young man, who carried a gun over his shoulder, but she came out of her bush and again followed the cow, while he walked alongside.

"I have been hunting for some birds," the stranger said kindly, "and I have lost my way, and need a friend very much. Don't be afraid," he added gallantly. "Speak up and tell me what your name is, and whether you think I can spend the night at your house, and go out gunning early in the morning."

Sylvia was more alarmed than before. Would not her grandmother consider her much to blame? But who could have foreseen such an accident as this? It did not appear to be her fault, and she hung her head as if the stem of it were broken, but managed to answer, "Sylvy," with much effort when her companion again asked her name.

Mrs. Tilley was standing in the doorway when the trio came into view. The cow gave a loud moo by way of explanation.

"Yes, you'd better speak up for yourself, you old trial! Where'd she tucked herself away this time, Sylvy?" Sylvia kept an awed silence; she knew by instinct that her grandmother did not comprehend the gravity of the situation. She must be mistaking the stranger for one of the farmer-lads of the region. 10

The young man stood his gun beside the door, and dropped a heavy game-bag beside it; then he bade Mrs. Tilley good-evening, and repeated his wayfarer's story, and asked if he could have a night's lodging.

"Put me anywhere you like," he said. "I must be off early in the morning, before day; but I am very hungry, indeed. You can give me some milk at any rate, that's plain."

"Dear sakes, yes," responded the hostess, whose long slumbering hospitality seemed to be easily awakened. "You might fare better if you went out on the main road a mile or so, but you're welcome to what we've got. I'll milk right off, and you make yourself at home. You can sleep on husks or feathers," she proffered graciously. "I raised them all myself. There's good pasturing for geese just below here

60   Setting

towards the ma'sh. Now step round and set a plate for the gentleman, Sylvy!" And Sylvia promptly stepped. She was glad to have something to do, and she was hungry herself.

It was a surprise to find so clean and comfortable a little dwelling in this New England wilderness. The young man had known the horrors of its most primitive housekeeping, and the dreary squalor of that level of society which does not rebel at the companionship of hens. This was the best thrift of an old-fashioned farmstead, though on such a small scale that it seemed like a hermitage. He listened eagerly to the old woman's quaint talk, he watched Sylvia's pale face and shining gray eyes with ever growing enthusiasm, and insisted that this was the best supper he had eaten for a month; then, afterward, the new-made friends sat down in the doorway together while the moon came up.

Soon it would be berry-time, and Sylvia was a great help at picking. The cow was a good milker, though a plaguy thing to keep track of, the hostess gossiped frankly, adding presently that she had buried four children, so that Sylvia's mother, and a son (who might be dead) in California were all the children she had left. "Dan, my boy, was a great hand to go gunning," she explained sadly. "I never wanted for pa'tridges or gray squer'ls while he was to home. He's been a great wand'rer, I expect, and he's no hand to write letters. There, I don't blame him, I'd ha' seen the world myself if it had been so I could. 15

"Sylvia takes after him," the grandmother continued affectionately, after a minute's pause. "There ain't a foot o' ground she don't know her way over, and the wild creatur's counts her one o' themselves. Squer'ls she'll tame to come an' feed right out o' her hands, and all sorts o' birds. Last winter she got the jay-birds to bangeing here, and I believe she'd 'a' scanted herself of her own meals to have plenty to throw out amongst 'em, if I hadn't kep' watch. Anything but crows, I tell her, I'm willin' to help support,—though Dan he went an' tamed one o' them that did seem to have reason same as folks. It was round here a good spell after he went away. Dan an' his father they didn't hitch,—but he never held up his head ag'in after Dan had dared him an' gone off."

The guest did not notice this hint of family sorrows in his eager interest in something else.

"So Sylvy knows all about birds, does she?" he exclaimed, as he looked round at the little girl who sat, very demure but increasingly sleepy, in the moonlight. "I am making a collection of birds myself. I have been at it ever since I was a boy." (Mrs. Tilley smiled.) "There are two or three very rare ones I have been hunting for these five years. I mean to get them on my own ground if they can be found."

"'Do you cage 'em up?" asked Mrs. Tilley doubtfully, in response to this enthusiastic announcement.

"Oh, no, they're stuffed and preserved, dozens and dozens of them," said the ornithologist, "and I have shot or snared every one myself. I caught a glimpse of a white heron three miles from here on Saturday, and I have followed it in this direction. They have never been found in this district at all. The little white heron, it is," and he turned again to look at Sylvia with the hope of discovering that the rare bird was one of her acquaintances. 20

But Sylvia was watching a hop-toad in the narrow footpath.

"You would know the heron if you saw it," the stranger continued eagerly. "A queer tall white bird with soft feathers and long thin legs. And it would have a nest perhaps in the top of a high tree, made of sticks, something like a hawk's nest."

Sylvia's heart gave a wild beat; she knew that strange white bird, and had once stolen softly near where it stood in some bright green swamp grass away over at the other side of the woods. There was an open place where the sunshine always seemed strangely yellow and hot, where tall, nodding rushes grew, and her grandmother had warned her that she might sink in the soft black mud underneath and never be heard of more. Not far beyond were the salt marshes and beyond those was the sea, the sea which Sylvia wondered and dreamed about, but never had looked upon, though its great voice could often be heard above the noise of the woods on stormy nights.

"I can't think of anything I should like so much as to find that heron's nest," the handsome stranger was saying. "I would give ten dollars to anybody who could show it to me," he added desperately, "and I mean to spend my whole vacation hunting for it if need be. Perhaps it was only migrating, or had been chased out of its own region by some bird of prey."

Mrs. Tilley gave amazed attention to all this, but Sylvia still watched the toad, not divining, as she might have done at some calmer time, that the creature wished to get to its hole under the doorstep, and was much hindered by the unusual spectators at that hour of the evening. No amount of thought, that night, could decide how many wished-for treasures the ten dollars, so lightly spoken of, would buy.

The next day the young sportsman hovered about the woods, and Sylvia kept him company, having lost her first fear of the friendly lad, who proved to be most kind and sympathetic. He told her many things about the birds and what they knew and where they lived and what they did with themselves. And he gave her a jackknife, which she thought as great a treasure as if she were a desert-islander. All day long he did not once make her troubled or afraid except when he brought down some unsuspecting singing creature from its bough. Sylvia would have liked him vastly better without his gun; she could not understand why he killed the very birds he seemed to like so much. But as the day waned, Sylvia still watched the young man with loving admiration. She had never seen anybody so charming and delightful; the woman's heart, asleep in the child, was vaguely thrilled by a dream of love. Some premonition of that great power stirred and swayed these young foresters who traversed the solemn woodlands with soft-footed silent care. They stopped to listen to a bird's song; they pressed forward again eagerly, parting the branches—speaking to each other rarely and in whispers; the young man going first and Sylvia following, fascinated, a few steps behind, with her gray eyes dark with excitement.

She grieved because the longed-for white heron was elusive, but she did not lead the guest, she only followed, and there was no such thing as speaking first. The sound of her own unquestioned voice would have terrified her—it was hard enough to answer yes or no when there was need of that. At last evening began to fall, and they drove the cow home together, and Sylvia smiled with pleasure when they came to the place where she heard the whistle and was afraid only the night before.

II

Half a mile from home, at the farther edge of the woods, where the land was highest, a great pine-tree stood, the last of its generation. Whether it was left for a boundary mark, or for what reason, no one could say; the woodchoppers who had felled its mates were dead and gone long ago, and a whole forest of sturdy trees, pines and oaks and maples, had grown again. But the stately head of this old pine towered above them all and made a landmark for sea and shore miles and miles away. Sylvia knew it well. She had always believed that whoever climbed to the top of it could see the ocean; and the little girl had often laid her hand on the great rough trunk and looked up wistfully at those dark boughs that the wind always stirred, no matter how hot and still the air might be below. Now she thought of the tree with a new excitement, for why, if one climbed it at break of day, could not one see all the world, and easily discover whence the white heron flew, and mark the place, and find the hidden nest?

What a spirit of adventure, what wild ambition! What fancied triumph and delight and glory for the later morning when she could make known the secret! It was almost too real and too great for the childish heart to bear.

All night the door of the little house stood open, and the whippoorwills came and sang upon the very step. The young sportsman and his old hostess were sound asleep, but Sylvia's great design kept her broad awake and watching. She forgot to think of sleep. The short summer night seemed as long as the winter darkness, and at last when the whippoorwills ceased, and she was afraid the morning would after all come too soon, she stole out of the house and followed the pasture path through the woods, hastening toward the open ground beyond, listening with a sense of comfort and companionship to the drowsy twitter of a half-awakened bird, whose perch she had jarred in passing. Alas, if the great wave of human interest which flooded for the first time this dull little life should sweep away the satisfactions of an existence heart to heart with nature and the dumb life of the forest!

There was the huge tree asleep yet in the paling moonlight, and small and hopeful Sylvia began with utmost bravery to mount to the top of it, with tingling, eager blood coursing the channels of her whole frame, with her bare feet and fingers, that pinched and held like bird's claws to the monstrous ladder reaching up, up, almost to the sky itself. First she must mount the white oak tree that grew alongside, where she was almost lost among the dark branches and the green leaves heavy and wet with dew; a bird fluttered off its nest, and a red squirrel ran to and fro and scolded pettishly at the harmless housebreaker. Sylvia felt her way easily. She had often climbed there, and knew that higher still one of the oak's upper branches chafed against the pine trunk, just where its lower boughs were set close together. There, when she made the dangerous pass from one tree to the other, the great enterprise would really begin.

She crept out along the swaying oak limb at last, and took the daring step across into the old pine-tree. The way was harder than she thought; she must reach far and hold fast, the sharp dry twigs caught and held her and scratched her like angry talons, the pitch made her thin little fingers clumsy and stiff as she went round and round the tree's great stem, higher and higher upward. The sparrows and robins in the woods below were beginning to wake and twitter to the dawn, yet it seemed much lighter there aloft in the pine-tree, and the child knew that she must hurry if her project were to be of any use.

The tree seemed to lengthen itself out as she went up, and to reach farther and farther upward. It was like a great main-mast to the voyaging earth; it must truly have been amazed that morning through all its ponderous frame as it felt this determined spark of human spirit creeping and climbing from higher branch to branch. Who knows how steadily the least twigs held themselves to advantage this light, weak creature on her way! The old pine must have loved his new dependent. More than all the hawks, and bats, and moths, and even the sweet-voiced thrushes, was the brave, beating heart of the solitary gray-eyed child. And the tree stood still and held away the winds that June morning while the dawn grew bright in the east.

Sylvia's face was like a pale star, if one had seen it from the ground, when the last thorny bough was past, and she stood trembling and tired but wholly triumphant, high in the tree-top. Yes, there was the sea with the dawning sun making a golden dazzle over it, and toward that glorious east flew two hawks with slow-moving pinions. How low they looked in the air from that height when before one had only seen them far up, and dark against the blue sky. Their gray feathers were as soft as moths; they seemed only a little way from the tree, and Sylvia felt as if she too could go flying away among the clouds. Westward, the woodlands and farms reached miles and miles into the distance; here and there were church steeples, and white villages; truly it was a vast and awesome world.

The birds sang louder and louder. At last the sun came up bewilderingly bright. Sylvia could see the white sails of ships out at sea, and the clouds that were purple and rose-colored and yellow at first began to fade away. Where was the white heron's nest in the sea of green branches, and was this wonderful sight and pageant of the world the only reward for having climbed to such a giddy height? Now look down again, Sylvia, where the green marsh is set among the shining birches and dark hemlocks; there where you saw the white heron once you will see him again; look, look! a white spot of him like a single floating feather comes up from the dead hemlock and grows larger, and rises, and comes close at last, and goes by the landmark pine with steady sweep of wing and outstretched slender neck and crested head. And wait! wait! do not move a foot or a finger, little girl, do not send an arrow of light and consciousness from your two eager eyes, for the heron has perched on a pine bough not far beyond yours, and cries back to his mate on the nest, and plumes his feathers for the new day!

35

The child gives a long sigh a minute later when a company of shouting cat-birds comes also to the tree, and vexed by their fluttering and lawlessness the solemn heron goes away. She knows his secret now, the wild, light, slender bird that floats and wavers, and goes back like an arrow presently to his home in the green world beneath. Then Sylvia, well satisfied, makes her perilous way down again, not daring to look far below the branch she stands on, ready to cry sometimes because her fingers ache and her lamed feet slip. Wondering over and over again what the stranger would say to her, and what he would think when she told him how to find his way straight to the heron's nest.

"Sylvy, Sylvy!" called the busy old grandmother again and again, but nobody answered, and the small husk bed was empty, and Sylvia had disappeared.

The guest waked from a dream, and remembering his day's pleasure hurried to dress himself that it might sooner begin. He was sure from the way the shy little girl looked once or twice yesterday that she had at least seen the white heron, and now she must really be persuaded to tell. Here she comes now, paler than ever, and her worn old frock is torn and tattered and smeared with pine pitch. The grandmother and the sportsman stand in the door together and question her, and the splendid moment has come to speak of the dead hemlock-tree by the green marsh.

But Sylvia does not speak after all, though the old grandmother fretfully rebukes her, and the young man's kind appealing eyes are looking straight in her own. He can make them rich with money; he has promised it, and they are poor now. He is so well worth making happy, and he waits to hear the story she can tell.

No, she must keep silence! What is it that suddenly forbids her and makes her dumb? Has she been nine years growing, and now, when the great world for the first time puts out a hand to her, must she thrust it aside for a bird's sake? The murmur of the pine's green branches is in her ears, she remembers how the white heron came flying through the golden air and how they watched the sea and the morning together, and Sylvia cannot speak; she cannot tell the heron's secret and give its life away.

40

Dear loyalty, that suffered a sharp pang as the guest went away disappointed later in the day, that could have served and followed him and loved him as a dog loves! Many a night Sylvia heard the echo of his whistle haunting the pasture path as she came home with the loitering cow. She forgot even her sorrow at the sharp report of his gun and the piteous sight of thrushes and sparrows dropping silent to the ground, their songs hushed and their pretty feathers stained and wet with blood. Were the birds better friends than their hunter might have been,—who can tell? Whatever treasures were lost to her, woodlands and summer-time, remember! Bring your gifts and graces and tell your secrets to this lonely country child!

[1886]

As you read the following discussion, consider these questions:

1. Use specific examples to show how Jewett creates a mood through the accumulation of descriptive detail.

2. How does the atmosphere of the opening passage contribute to the development of the story? Could Jewett have achieved the same effect if the story had begun in the morning? Why or why not?

3. Where is Sylvy from, and why is she living with her grandmother? Does this information add anything to our understanding of her character or her relation to her surroundings?

4. What is the young man's relation to the setting? Cite passages that suggest he might be different from Sylvy.

5. How does Jewett use natural detail to give a sense of nighttime in the forest? How does Sylvy fit into those surroundings?

6. What specific details does Jewett use to evoke the coming of dawn? What is the effect of Sylvy's new vantage? How does it change our perspective on events in the story?

7. Could this story be transposed to another setting yet retain the same effect? Imagine one such transposition.

Discussion: The Functions of Setting in "A White Heron." Jewett's story provides a very clear illustration of the various functions of setting in a work of fiction. The work is, to begin with, entirely rooted in place—without the setting there would be no story. Jewett draws deeply on the specific elements of her native terrain (she was born and raised in Maine, where "A White Heron" presumably takes place) not only to give her tale a literal grounding, but also to impart suggestive and symbolic resonances.

The story begins with an evocation of place: "The woods were already filled with shadows one June evening, just before eight o'clock, though a bright sunset still glimmered faintly among the trunks of the trees." In a single sentence Jewett has told us where we are (woods), located us in time (just before eight o'clock on a June evening), and given us the precise atmospheric image of a sunset still glimmering on the trunks of trees. We hold this impression in mind through the following paragraphs as Sylvia, the protagonist, is introduced, and as we follow her on her homeward walk.

Jewett briefly gives us the facts about Sylvia (she is eight years old, and her grandmother, Mrs. Tilley, has taken her from the city to live with Mrs. Tilley on the farm) and adds Mrs. Tilley's observation: "there never was such a child for straying about out-of-doors since the world was made!" This last characterization is important because it establishes a close identification between Sylvia and the natural world around her—an identification that will have significant bearing on the theme of the story.

Sylvia is out late, but even though the woods are growing darker and darker, she does not mind. She knows her way. Indeed, she quite loves wandering with the cow, Mistress Moolly. "She was not often in the woods so late as this, and it made her feel as if she were part of the gray shadows and the moving leaves." Her immersion in nature is both easy and profound, but it is broken by the whistle, and then the appearance of a young man. In a sense, this moment of encounter prefigures the whole story. Sylvia's happy absorption in the nature around her is interrupted by a stranger. She will not be able to recover that innocent state of mind until she has been forced to make a very difficult choice about whether to preserve or destroy. And even after she has chosen on behalf of nature, she will not be able to return to the same condition of innocence. She will have taken an important step in her coming-of-age, and the world will no longer look the same to her.

The young man is a hunter—he collects birds, stuffing and mounting them. Jewett does not present him as an evil figure. To the contrary, he is cheerful and easygoing. But he may represent another, perhaps masculine, relation to nature. Nature is something to be used, conquered, and analyzed. Sylvia does not simply turn from him, however. She is drawn by his friendliness, and though she is too young to form a genuine sexual attraction, she is stirred to some confusion by his masculine presence. Jewett conveys her state beautifully, using a specific detail from the surroundings. As the young man, Mrs. Tilley, and Sylvia all sit on the front step after their supper, the girl watches a hop-toad on the footpath. She is distracted, listening to the hunter's description of the white heron, and she stares at the toad, "not divining, as she might have done at some calmer time, that the creature wished to get to its hole under the doorstep, and was much hindered by the unusual spectators at that hour of the evening." The young man, his stories, and her own keen desire to earn the ten-dollar bounty for finding the heron, all combine to cut Sylvia away from her customary sensitivity to the natural surroundings.

Sylvia decides to find the heron for the man, and her solitary trek into the woods, where she climbs the immense pine tree, leads to the story's climax. Again, setting is absolutely essential. Using deft descriptive touches, Jewett evokes the atmosphere of the woods in the hours before dawn: "The short summer night seemed as long as the winter darkness, and at last when the whippoorwills ceased, and she was afraid the morning would come after all too soon, she stole out of the house and followed the pasture path through the woods, hastening toward the open ground beyond, listening with a sense of comfort and companionship to the drowsy twitter of a half-awakened bird, whose perch she had jarred in passing."

But as we approach the climax of the story, as Sylvia hoists herself up the great tree to look for the heron, the setting takes on suggestive and symbolic attributes. The tree is a natural object, but it also becomes a psychological testing ground. She has come to a point in her life where she must face her fears and surpass herself, and the tree is the means. And it is the ordeal of the climb—the passing of the test—that allows her to glimpse the true magnificence of nature, a glimpse that will convince her, later, not to disclose the heron's whereabouts to the man.

The heron itself, which can be considered a part of the natural setting, is similarly both literal—a bird found in the area—and symbolic. It is rare, and it is noble in appearance. Like the white dove, the traditional symbol of peace, the white heron seems to stand for purity and innocence (and, if we see the story as manifesting sexual tensions, virginity). When Sylvia makes the decision to keep silent, she is siding not only with the bird, but with the values and associations she ascribes to it. She is casting her lot with nature.

In "A White Heron," then, the specific details of setting are linked to the larger order of nature itself, a link Jewett achieves by using symbol and suggestion. We should also note her striking use of light and darkness, not only in establishing context and atmosphere, but also in creating thematic emphasis. It is hardly incidental that the story—which is fundamentally the story of Sylvia's first coming-of-age, or "enlightenment"—should begin on the ground, amid deepening shadows, and should reach its climax high in the tree, with the sun rising over the horizon.

An Example of Setting as a Force in the Story

The author's focus upon setting is likely to vary according to the needs of the story. Stories in which plot is paramount are often reliant upon particulars of place and time. Stories concerned with character psychology and interaction, on the other hand, may make do with just the sketchiest indications of setting. Readers are not likely to find many stories like Bessie Head's "Looking for a Rain God," in which setting and climate are every bit as important as the characters.

Bessie Head (1937–1986)

Bessie Head was born in South Africa. She spent many years working as an educator in her adopted country of Botswana. She also worked for a time as a journalist in Johannesburg. Head published three novels and a collection of stories, *The Collector of Treasures,* before her death from hepatitis.

LOOKING FOR
A RAIN GOD

It is lonely at the lands where the people go to plough. These lands are vast clearings in the bush, and the wild bush is lonely too. Nearly all the lands are within walking distance from the village. In some parts of the bush where the underground water is very near the surface, people made little rest camps for themselves and dug shallow wells to quench their thirst while on their journey to their own lands. They experienced all kinds of things once they left the village. They could rest at shady watering places full of lush, tangled trees with delicate pale-gold and purple wildflowers springing up between soft green moss and the children could hunt around for wild figs and any berries that might be in season. But from 1958, a seven-year drought fell upon the land and even the watering places began to look as dismal as the dry open thornbush country; the leaves of the trees curled up and withered; the moss became dry and hard and, under the shade of the tangled trees, the ground turned a powdery black and white, because there was no rain. People said rather humorously that if you tried to catch the rain in a cup it would only fill a teaspoon. Toward the beginning of the seventh year of drought, the summer had become an anguish to live through. The air was so dry and moisture-free that it burned the skin. No one knew what to do to escape the heat and tragedy was in the air. At the beginning of that summer, a number of men just went out of their homes and hung themselves to death from trees. The majority of the people had lived off crops, but for two years past they had all returned from the lands with only their rolled-up skin blankets and cooking utensils. Only the charlatans, incanters, and witch doctors made a pile of money during this time because people were always turning to them in desperation for little talismans and herbs to rub on the plough for the crops to grow and the rain to fall.

The rains were late that year. They came in early November, with a promise of good rain. It wasn't the full, steady downpour of the years of good rain but thin, scanty, misty rain. It softened the earth and a rich growth of green things sprang up everywhere for the animals to eat. People were called to the center of the village to hear the proclamation of the beginning of the ploughing season; they stirred themselves and whole families began to move off to the lands to plough.

The family of the old man, Mokgobja, were among those who left early for the lands. They had a donkey cart and piled everything onto it, Mokgobja—who was over seventy years old; two girls, Neo and Boseyong; their mother Tiro and an unmarried sister, Nesta; and the father and supporter of the family, Ramadi, who drove the donkey cart. In the rush of the first hope of rain, the man, Ramadi, and the two women, cleared the land of thornbush and then hedged their vast ploughing area with this same thornbush to protect the future crop from the goats they brought along for milk. They had cleared out and deepened the old well with its pool of muddy water and still in this light, misty rain, Ramadi inspanned two oxen and turned the earth over with a hand plough.

The land was ready and ploughed, waiting for the crops. At night, the earth was alive with insects singing and rustling about in search of food. But suddenly, by mid-November, the rain flew away; the rain clouds fled away and left the sky bare. The sun danced dizzily in the sky, with a strange cruelty. Each day the land was covered

Setting

in a haze of mist as the sun sucked up the last drop of moisture out of the earth. The family sat down in despair, waiting and waiting. Their hopes had run so high; the goats had started producing milk, which they had eagerly poured on their porridge, now they ate plain porridge with no milk. It was impossible to plant the corn, maize, pumpkin, and watermelon seeds in the dry earth. They sat the whole day in the shadow of the huts and even stopped thinking, for the rain had fled away. Only the children, Neo and Boseyong, were quite happy in their little-girl world. They carried on with their game of making house like their mother and chattered to each other in light, soft tones. They made children from sticks around which they tied rags, and scolded them severely in an exact imitation of their own mother. Their voices could be heard scolding the day long: "You stupid thing, when I send you to draw water, why do you spill half of it out of the bucket!" "You stupid thing! Can't you mind the porridge pot without letting the porridge burn!" And then they would beat the rag dolls on their bottoms with severe expressions.

The adults paid no attention to this; they did not even hear the funny chatter; they sat waiting for rain; their nerves were stretched to breaking-point willing the rain to fall out of the sky. Nothing was important, beyond that. All their animals had been sold during the bad years to purchase food, and of all their herd only two goats were left. It was the women of the family who finally broke down under the strain of waiting for rain. It was really the two women who caused the death of the little girls. Each night they started a weird, high-pitched wailing that began on a low, mournful note and whipped up to a frenzy. Then they would stamp their feet and shout as though they had lost their heads. The men sat quiet and self-controlled; it was important for men to maintain their self control at all times but their nerve was breaking too. They knew the women were haunted by the starvation of the coming year.   5

Finally, an ancient memory stirred in the old man, Mokgobja. When he was very young and the customs of the ancestors still ruled the land, he had been witness to a rain-making ceremony. And he came alive a little, struggling to recall the details which had been buried by years and years of prayer in a Christian church. As soon as the mists cleared a little, he began consulting in whispers with his youngest son, Ramadi. There was, he said, a certain rain god who accepted only the sacrifice of the bodies of children. Then the rain would fall; then the crops would grow, he said. He explained the ritual and as he talked, his memory became a conviction and he began to talk with unshakable authority. Ramadi's nerves were smashed by the nightly wailing of the two women and soon the two men began whispering with the two women. The children continued their game: "You stupid thing! How could you have lost the money on the way to the shop! You must have been playing again!"

After it was all over and the bodies of the two little girls had been spread across the land, the rain did not fall. Instead, there was a deathly silence at night and the devouring heat of the sun by day. A terror, extreme and deep, overwhelmed the whole family. They packed, rolling up their skin blankets and pots, and fled back to the village.

People in the village soon noted the absence of the two little girls. They had died at the lands and were buried there, the family said. But people noted their ashen, terror-stricken faces and a murmur arose. What had killed the children, they wanted to know? And the family replied that they just died. And people said amongst themselves that it was strange that the two deaths had occurred at the same time. And there was a feeling of great unease at the unnatural looks of the family.

Soon the police came around. The family told them the same story of death and burial at the lands. They did not know what the children had died of. So the police asked to see the graves. At this, the mother of the children broke down and told everything.

Throughout that terrible summer the story of the children hung like a dark cloud of sorrow over the village, and the sorrow was not assuaged when the old man and Ramadi were sentenced to death for ritual murder. All they had on the statute books was that ritual murder was against the law and must be stamped out with the death penalty. The subtle story of strain and starvation and breakdown was inadmissible evidence at court; but all the people who lived off crops knew in their hearts that only a hair's breadth had saved them from sharing a fate similar to that of the Mokgobja family. They could have killed something to make the rain fall.

QUESTIONS

1. How do Bessie Head's descriptions of the setting—including climate—change during the course of the opening paragraph?

2. How does she use specific details to convey the worsening drought? Give examples, and comment on the sensory effectiveness.

3. How do the slight November rains set the plot into motion? Why does the "false alarm" make the return of drought even harder to bear?

4. How do Head's descriptions of the children's games intensify the tension?

5. Do you believe that Mokgobja and his family are evil? If not, how do you explain the murders?

6. What is the role of ancient tribal lore in the story? Would your reaction to this tale be any different if the sacrifice had brought on the desired rainfall? Explain.

6 Theme

Taken together, the characters, plot, and setting of a work of fiction can be said to make up its body. The theme, by analogy, is the heart, or soul. To talk about theme is to talk about the essential subject of the story or novel, its dominant idea or ideas, what the work is about. We may read literature for many reasons, but most often we do so to experience meaning—to find out truths about human nature and to enrich our understanding of the psychological and moral bases of our lives. And, indeed, the expression of themes—or meanings—is a good part of what drives an author to write in the first place. Fiction, however fanciful or entertaining it might be, almost always arises from the writer's desire to communicate some particular insight or feeling about the business of living.

DISCOVERING THE THEME

Though theme is central to fiction, it can also prove elusive. As readers, we have to recognize that thematic elements are often complex and shaded around with ambiguity. In many cases they are woven deeply into the fabric of the whole work and cannot be plucked free with a single motion. This embeddedness may prove to be an obstacle to the reader who would grab the message and move on, but in fact it is part of what makes the reading of fiction worthwhile. There is a great difference between reading a story that explores the difficulty of love and reading the message LOVE IS DIFFICULT in a fortune cookie. The encapsulated message does not allow us to experience its truth—we either accept it or we don't. The same truth, expressed in a story, has everything to do with specific characters and situations. The meaning arises from the turns of the narration. We live it in stages, and we are provided with a context for understanding. Usually, too, the presentation is such that we have to draw connections and inferences for ourselves—we earn what we learn.

As readers concerned with theme, we need to cultivate both patience and a taste for ambiguities and shades of meaning. A writer like D. H. Lawrence (Chapter 13), for example, has many stories that explore the complex relations between men and women. But unless we are willing to do away with all subtleties and gray areas, we can never reduce any of these works to a simple formulation: that men are like this and women like that, or that the nature of love is such and such. Lawrence's intent is to guide the reader toward new ways of considering different kinds of human encounters. We finish reading his stories—like "Odour of Chrysanthemums"—with a strong sense of forces in collision. We do not recognize one theme, usually, but several, entwined in the story as they are in life. That one story suggests several significant ideas at once: that the needs of the body and the emotional self are not only different, but also at odds; that affection and aggression—love and hate—can live side by side; and that death can bring understanding into the lives of the survivors. These *are* some of Lawrence's themes, and they can be isolated and discussed. But it would be a mistake to think that the value of his fiction rested upon a cluster of extractable meaning. The value lies in our process of confrontation and recognition. We make these ideas real by applying them to our own lives.

Literary meanings, then, are often diffuse and multiple. We may be daunted at first, but we should not let ourselves be overwhelmed. Rather, we should approach the question of theme with care and openness and be willing at times to navigate among shadows. It may help us as readers to realize that there is no such thing as a "right answer." Works of literature are not puzzles to be solved, and they should not be approached that way. They are expressions awaiting our interpretations, and the process of inquiry is very often as meaningful as the conclusions we finally reach.

Granted, the cookie-cutter approach is tempting—we identify a theme and tell ourselves we have solved the story. Some people even use the laundry-list approach, as if there were only so many themes to be spotted and tagged—themes such as "man's inhumanity to man" and "the human struggle against Nature" and "the place of value in a soulless age." But such tagging accomplishes nothing. It usually raises more questions than it answers. What do we mean when we say that a certain story depicts the human struggle against Nature? What have we clarified or understood? Not much, really. Such designations begin to become interesting only when we begin to assess their specific relevance to the story. And as soon as we do this, we have left the slotting process behind and have begun the more uncertain task of interpretation.

Themes do not come in categories, or if they do the categories are so general as to be useless. Themes are the understandings we reach when we look searchingly at the most important parts of the human experience. They are, for this simple reason, universal, covering the primary emotions and relations: love, hate, friendship, betrayal, loss, fear, idealism, and on and on. We find them in stories and novels because we find them in our lives. They cannot be taken care of once and for all; they can only be explored.

The best way to approach any work of literature is with a mind free of expectations. We should try to let the work have its say before we set about to figure its meanings. Of course we can never escape our own values and biases, nor the subtle influences of our race, class, and gender. But we should hold back on judgments until we have finished reading the work. In the same way, to start in with one eye open for thematic clues is a mistake—we may find the trail but miss out on the countryside that surrounds it. And finally, when we have finished reading and have begun the interpretive process, we should be ready to hover among hunches and guesses; we should not feel that we have failed if we cannot stamp CASE CLOSED on the file.

The following story, Delmore Schwartz's "In Dreams Begin Responsibilities," was not chosen because it was especially difficult or ambiguous (though it does have its murky areas). Rather, it can be viewed as fairly representative of the ways in which stories tend to hold their meanings in layers.

Delmore Schwartz (1913-1966)

Delmore Schwartz was one of the saddest of many sad American success stories. Born in New York City to Jewish immigrant parents, Schwartz early revealed his passion for books and writing. He had already styled himself a poet and man of letters when he attended the University of Wisconsin in the early 1930s. In 1938 he made good on his promise, publishing *In Dreams Begin Responsibilities,* a collection of poems that won the praise of the masters of the age, including T. S. Eliot, Ezra Pound, Wallace Stevens, and William Carlos Williams. Soon after, Schwartz was publishing poems, stories, and essays in the most prestigious publications of the day. His ambition was boundless, and he had the talent to match it—and then he crashed. In the last decades of his life, Schwartz suffered ever more debilitating bouts of depressive illness; he felt his inspiration had deserted him. Schwartz's reputation has declined somewhat in recent years, but the best of his poems and stories have a secure place in our literature. They crackle with what might be called a first-generation electricity, which the passing of years has not diminished.

IN DREAMS BEGIN RESPONSIBILITIES

I

I think it is the year 1909. I feel as if I were in a motion picture theatre, the long arm of light crossing the darkness and spinning, my eyes fixed on the screen. This is a silent picture as if an old Biograph one, in which the actors are dressed in ridiculously old-fashioned clothes, and one flash succeeds another with sudden jumps. The actors too seem to jump about and walk too fast. The shots themselves are full of dots and rays, as if it were raining when the picture was photographed. The light is bad.

It is Sunday afternoon, June 12th, 1909, and my father is walking down the quiet streets of Brooklyn on his way to visit my mother. His clothes are newly pressed and his tie is too tight in his high collar. He jingles the coins in his pockets, thinking of the witty things he will say. I feel as if I had by now relaxed entirely in the soft darkness of the theatre; the organist peals out the obvious and approximate emotions on which the audience rocks unknowingly. I am anonymous, and I have forgotten myself. It is always so when one goes to the movies, it is, as they say, a drug.

My father walks from street to street of trees, lawns and houses, once in a while coming to an avenue on which a streetcar skates and gnaws, slowly progressing. The conductor, who has a handle-bar mustache, helps a young lady wearing a hat like a bowl with feathers on to the car. She lifts her long skirts slightly as she mounts the steps. He leisurely makes change and rings his bell. It is obviously Sunday, for everyone is wearing Sunday clothes, and the street-car's noises emphasize the quiet of the holiday. Is not Brooklyn the City of Churches? The shops are closed and their shades drawn, but for an occasional stationery store or drug-store with great green balls in the window.

My father has chosen to take this long walk because he likes to walk and think. He thinks about himself in the future and so arrives at the place he is to visit in a state of mild exaltation. He pays no attention to the houses he is passing, in which the Sunday dinner is being eaten, nor to the many trees which patrol each street, now coming to their full leafage and the time when they will room the whole street in cool shadow. An occasional carriage passes, the horse's hooves falling like stones in the quiet afternoon, and once in a while an automobile, looking like an enormous upholstered sofa, puffs and passes.

My father thinks of my mother, of how nice it will be to introduce her to his family. But he is not yet sure that he wants to marry her, and once in a while he becomes panicky about the bond already established. He reassures himself by thinking of the big men he admires who are married: William Randolph Hearst,° and William Howard Taft, who has just become President of the United States.   5

My father arrives at my mother's house. He has come too early and so is suddenly embarrassed. My aunt, my mother's sister, answers the loud bell with her napkin in her hand, for the family is still at dinner. As my father enters, my grandfather rises from the table and shakes hands with him. My mother has run upstairs to tidy herself. My grandmother asks my father if he has had dinner, and tells him that Rose will be downstairs soon. My grandfather opens the conversation by remarking on the mild June weather. My father sits uncomfortably near the table, holding his hat in his hand. My grandmother tells my aunt to take my father's hat. My uncle, twelve years old, runs into the house, his hair tousled. He shouts a greeting to my father, who has often given him a nickel, and then runs upstairs. It is evident that the respect in which my father is held in this household is tempered by a good deal of mirth. He is impressive, yet he is very awkward.

II

Finally my mother comes downstairs, all dressed up, and my father being engaged in conversation with my grandfather becomes uneasy, not knowing whether to greet my mother or continue the conversation. He gets up from the chair clumsily and says "hello" gruffly. My grandfather watches, examining their congruence, such as it is, with a critical eye, and meanwhile rubbing his bearded cheek roughly, as he always does when he reflects. He is worried; he is afraid that my father will not make a good husband for his oldest daughter. At this point something happens to the film, just as my father is saying something funny to my mother; I am awakened

---

William Randolph Hearst: Hearst (1863–1951) was an American publishing tycoon.

to myself and my unhappiness just as my interest was rising. The audience begins to clap impatiently. Then the trouble is cared for but the film has been returned to a portion just shown, and once more I see my grandfather rubbing his bearded cheek and pondering my father's character. It is difficult to get back into the picture once more and forget myself, but as my mother giggles at my father's words, the darkness drowns me.

My father and mother depart from the house, my father shaking hands with my mother once more, out of some unknown uneasiness. I stir uneasily also, slouched in the hard chair of the theatre. Where is the older uncle, my mother's older brother? He is studying in his bedroom upstairs, studying for his final examination at the College of the City of New York, having been dead of rapid pneumonia for the last twenty-one years. My mother and father walk down the same quiet streets once more. My mother is holding my father's arm and telling him of the novel which she has been reading; and my father utters judgments of the characters as the plot is made clear to him. This is a habit which he very much enjoys, for he feels the utmost superiority and confidence when he approves and condemns the behavior of other people. At times he feels moved to utter a brief "Ugh"—whenever the story becomes what he would call sugary. This tribute is paid to his manliness. My mother feels satisfied by the interest which she has awakened; she is showing my father how intelligent she is, and how interesting.

They reach the avenue, and the street-car leisurely arrives. They are going to Coney Island this afternoon, although my mother considers that such pleasures are inferior. She has made up her mind to indulge only in a walk on the boardwalk and a pleasant dinner, avoiding the riotous amusements as being beneath the dignity of so dignified a couple.

My father tells my mother how much money he has made in the past week, exaggerating an amount which need not have been exaggerated. But my father has always felt that actualities somehow fall short. Suddenly I begin to weep. The determined old lady who sits next to me in the theatre is annoyed and looks at me with an angry face, and being intimidated, I stop. I drag out my handkerchief and dry my face, licking the drop which has fallen near my lips. Meanwhile I have missed something, for here are my mother and father alighting at the last stop, Coney Island.

10

III

They walk toward the boardwalk, and my father commands my mother to inhale the pungent air from the sea. They both breathe in deeply, both of them laughing as they do so. They have in common a great interest in health, although my father is strong and husky, my mother frail. Their minds are full of theories of what is good to eat and not good to eat, and sometimes they engage in heated discussions of the subject, the whole matter ending in my father's announcement, made with a scornful bluster, that you have to die sooner or later anyway. On the boardwalk's flagpole, the American flag is pulsing in an intermittent wind from the sea.

My father and mother go to the rail of the boardwalk and look down on the beach where a good many bathers are casually walking about. A few are in the surf. A peanut whistle pierces the air with its pleasant and active whine, and my father goes to buy peanuts. My mother remains at the rail and stares at the ocean. The ocean seems merry to her; it pointedly sparkles and again and again the pony waves are released. She notices the children digging in the wet sand, and the bathing costumes of the girls who are her own age. My father returns with the peanuts. Overhead the sun's lightning strikes and strikes, but neither of them are at all aware of it. The boardwalk is full of people dressed in their Sunday clothes and idly strolling. The tide does not reach as far as the boardwalk, and the strollers would feel no danger if it did. My mother and father lean on the rail of the boardwalk and absently stare at the ocean. The ocean is becoming rough; the waves come in slowly, tugging strength from far back. The moment before they somersault, the moment when they arch their backs so beautifully, showing green and white veins amid the black, that moment is intolerable. They finally crack, dashing fiercely upon the sand, actually driving, full force downward, against the sand, bouncing upward and forward, and at last petering out into a small stream which races up the beach and then is recalled. My parents gaze absentmindedly at the ocean, scarcely interested in its harshness. The sun overhead does not disturb them. But I stare at the terrible sun which breaks up sight, and the fatal, merciless, passionate ocean, I forget my parents. I stare fascinated and finally, shocked by the indifference of my father and mother, I burst out weeping once more. The old lady next to me pats me on the shoulder and says "There, there, all of this is only a movie, young man, only a movie," but I look up once more at the terrifying sun and the terrifying ocean, and being unable to control my tears, I get up and go to the men's room, stumbling over the feet of the other people seated in my row.

IV

When I return, feeling as if I had awakened in the morning sick for lack of sleep, several hours have apparently passed and my parents are riding on the merry-go-round. My father is on a black horse, my mother on a white one, and they seem to be making an eternal circuit for the single purpose of snatching the nickel rings which are attached to the arm of one of the posts. A hand-organ is playing; it is one with the ceaseless circling of the merry-go-round.

For a moment it seems that they will never get off the merry-go-round because it will never stop. I feel like one who looks down on the avenue from the 50th story of a building. But at length they do get off; even the music of the hand-organ has ceased for a moment. My father has acquired ten rings, my mother only two, although it was my mother who really wanted them.

They walk on along the boardwalk as the afternoon descends by imperceptible degrees into the incredible violet of dusk. Everything fades into a relaxed glow, even the ceaseless murmuring from the beach, and the revolutions of the merry-go-round. They look for a place to have dinner. My father suggests the best one on the boardwalk and my mother demurs, in accordance with her principles.

However they do go to the best place, asking for a table near the window, so that they can look out on the boardwalk and the mobile ocean. My father feels omnipotent as he places a quarter in the waiter's hand as he asks for a table. The place is crowded and here too there is music, this time from a kind of string trio. My father orders dinner with a fine confidence.

As the dinner is eaten, my father tells of his plans for the future, and my mother shows with expressive face how interested she is, and how impressed. My father becomes exultant. He is lifted up by the waltz that is being played, and his own future begins to intoxicate him. My father tells my mother that he is going to expand his business, for there is a great deal of money to be made. He wants to settle down. After all, he is twenty-nine, he has lived by himself since he was thirteen, he is making more and more money, and he is envious of his married friends when he visits them in the cozy security of their homes, surrounded, it seems, by the calm domestic pleasures, and by delightful children, and then, as the waltz reaches the moment when all the dancers swing madly, then, then with awful daring, then he asks my mother to marry him, although awkwardly enough and puzzled, even in his excitement, at how he had arrived at the proposal, and she, to make the whole business worse, begins to cry, and my father looks nervously about, not knowing at all what to do now, and my mother says: "It's all I've wanted from the moment I saw you," sobbing, and he finds all of this very difficult, scarcely to his taste, scarcely as he had thought it would be, on his long walks over Brooklyn Bridge in the revery of a fine cigar, and it was then that I stood up in the theatre and shouted: "Don't do it. It's not too late to change your minds, both of you. Nothing good will come of it, only remorse, hatred, scandal, and two children whose characters are monstrous." The whole audience turned to look at me, annoyed, the usher came hurrying down the aisle flashing his searchlight, and the old lady next to me tugged me down into my seat, saying: "Be quiet. You'll be put out, and you paid thirty-five cents to come in." And so I shut my eyes because I could not bear to see what was happening. I sat there quietly.

V

But after awhile I begin to take brief glimpses, and at length I watch again with thirsty interest, like a child who wants to maintain his sulk although offered the bribe of candy. My parents are now having their picture taken in a photographer's booth along the boardwalk. The place is shadowed in the mauve light which is apparently necessary. The camera is set to the side on its tripod and looks like a Martian man. The photographer is instructing my parents in how to pose. My father has his arm over my mother's shoulder, and both of them smile emphatically. The photographer brings my mother a bouquet of flowers to hold in her hand but she holds it at the wrong angle. Then the photographer covers himself with the black cloth which drapes the camera and all that one sees of him is one protruding arm and his hand which clutches the rubber ball which he will squeeze when the picture is finally taken. But he is not satisfied with their appearance. He feels with certainty that somehow there is something wrong in their pose. Again and again he issues from his hidden place with new directions. Each suggestion merely makes matters worse. My father is becoming impatient. They try a seated pose. The photographer explains that he has pride, he is not interested in all of this for the money, he wants to make beautiful pictures. My father says: "Hurry up, will you? We haven't got all night." But the photographer only scurries about apologetically, and issues new directions. The photographer charms me. I approve of him with all my heart, for I know just how he feels, and as he criticizes each revised pose according to some unknown idea of rightness, I become quite hopeful. But then my father says angrily: "Come on, you've had enough time, we're not going to wait any longer." And the photographer, sighing unhappily, goes back under his black covering, holds out his hand, says: "One, two, three, Now!", and the picture is taken, with my father's smile turned to a grimace and my mother's bright and false. It takes a few minutes for the picture to be developed and as my parents sit in the curious light they become quite depressed.

VI

They have passed a fortune-teller's booth, and my mother wishes to go in, but my father does not. They begin to argue about it. My mother becomes stubborn, my father once more impatient, and then they begin to quarrel, and what my father would like to do is walk off and leave my mother there, but he knows that that would never do. My mother refuses to budge. She is near to tears, but she feels an uncontrollable desire to hear what the palm-reader will say. My father consents angrily, and they both go into a booth which is in a way like the photographer's, since it is draped in black cloth and its light is shadowed. The place is too warm, and my father keeps saying this is all nonsense, pointing to the crystal ball on the table. The fortune-teller, a fat, short woman, garbed in what is supposed to be Oriental robes, comes into the room from the back and greets them, speaking with an accent. But suddenly my father feels that the whole thing is intolerable; he tugs at my mother's arm, but my mother refuses to budge. And then, in terrible anger, my father lets go of my mother's arm and strides out, leaving my mother stunned. She moves to go after my father, but the fortune-teller holds her arm tightly and begs her not to do so, and I in my seat am shocked more than can ever be said, for I feel as if I were walking a tight-rope a hundred feet over a circus-audience and suddenly the rope is showing signs of breaking, and I get up from my seat and begin to shout once more the first words I can think of to communicate my terrible fear and once more the usher comes hurrying down the aisle flashing his searchlight, and the old lady pleads with me, and the shocked audience has turned to stare at me, and I keep shouting: "What are they doing? Don't they know what they are doing? Why doesn't my mother go after my father? If she does not do that, what will she do? Doesn't my father know what he is doing?"—But the usher has seized my arm and is dragging me away, and as he does so, he says: "What are *you* doing? Don't you know that you can't do whatever you want to do? Why should a young man like you, with your whole life before you, get hysterical like this? Why don't you *think* of what you're doing? You can't act like this even if other people aren't around! You will be sorry if you do not do what you should do, you can't carry on like this, it is not right, you will find that out soon enough, everything you do matters too much," and he said that dragging me through the lobby of the theatre into the cold light, and I woke up into the bleak winter morning of my 21st birthday, the windowsill shining with its lip of snow, and the morning already begun.

As you read the following discussion, consider these questions:

1. What strategies does Schwartz use to establish distance between the narrator and his parents in the opening passages of the story?

2. What is the narrator's reaction to his young parents and their courtship? How does that reaction change as the story progresses?

3. Identify the climactic scene between the narrator's parents-to-be. In what way is it significant that his mother wants to peer into the future?

4. How does Schwartz convey the narrator's building anxiety? Have you, as a reader, come to believe that he *is* in a movie theater?

5. What does the narrator shout to the screen in section VI? Explain what prompts his reaction.

6. What does the usher tell the narrator? What does he mean, in the larger sense?

7. What is the effect of the last sentence? How does the narrator's awakening relate to the rest of the story?

Discussion. We can see right away that we will not be able to dispense with the question of theme—or meaning—in a few quick sentences. Schwartz has presented us with a situation that carries strong and tangled emotional materials. The narrator dreams the dream of his parents' courtship as if it were a movie being shown in a theater. As he views the images, he experiences distress, anxiety, and anger. But he is also concerned—the outcome of the situation matters greatly to him. How, then, do we begin to determine what Schwartz is trying to communicate?

Sometimes the best place to begin is right at the top—with the title. "In Dreams Begin Responsibilities" (though Schwartz does not tell us this) is a phrase drawn from a poem by William Butler Yeats. Yeats was writing about the origins of national loyalty in the Irish people, but Schwartz is clearly giving the phrase a private and nonpolitical application. For our purposes, it is enough to focus upon the word *dreams*, at least for now. Though it is not made fully clear until the end, the story related the contents of the narrator's dream. Schwartz is deceptive, however, letting us believe, or almost believe, that we are in a darkened movie theater. "I feel as if I were in a motion picture theater," says the narrator, but he then returns to the theater setting so often that we forget the *as if*.

Why doesn't Schwartz just present the narrative as a dream and be done with it? Why does he need the movie pretense? It's hard to say. Maybe he wanted the extra distancing, the added sense of objectification. But maybe he also wanted a set-up that would leave some actual space between the narrator and what he sees, and that would allow him to express his reactions to the material he views. After all, the reactions are at the heart of the work; they cannot be dispensed with.

What we have, then, is a dream in the form of a movie—a movie that comes complete with an attentive audience and projector problems. The subject, dull enough to anyone but the narrator, is an afternoon and evening in the lives of his parents-to-be. The courting couple go to Coney Island, then to a restaurant, where his father proposes (and his mother accepts); then they have a fight over going to see a fortune-teller, a fight that we must assume was resolved. The narrator is made so anxious by the fight, and the threat of the couple not coming together, that he creates a disturbance and is escorted from the theater. He wakes to find it is his twenty-first birthday; there is a fresh snowfall.

The picture we are given of the parents is conventional enough—they are shy with each other, they observe proprieties—and by itself could not sustain a story. The tension element and the central interest arise both from the idea that one could view a crucial time in the past as a film and from the responses that certain actions evoke in the narrator. These responses are of several kinds. Early on, when the father exaggerates his income to his wife-to-be, the narrator inexplicably weeps. Soon after, he expresses shock at his parents' indifference to the beauties of sun and ocean. Then, when his father has proposed, when his mother says "It's all I've ever wanted from the moment I saw you," he stands up and shouts, "Don't do it. . . . Nothing good will come of it, only remorse, hatred, scandal, and two children whose characters are monstrous."

THE SEARCH FOR INSIGHT AND UNDERSTANDING THROUGH THE THEME

At this point we might well conclude that we have found the *point* of the story: that the narrator is miserable in his life and is expressing a wish to undo the chain of events that brought him into existence. But this would be jumping to conclusions. For what do we then make of his extreme agitation when the fortune-teller holds his mother's arm, keeping her from going after his father? It would seem that he is afraid that their disagreement will separate them permanently; that they will not marry and that he will not be born.

Which is it? Does the narrator fear the marriage or desire it? Since his distress is the last thing we participate in, we assume that the desire is stronger than the fear. But this is not quite satisfactory either, for throughout the recounting of the movie/dream the narrator is shown as knowing how things come out. He knows, for example, when his uncle will die. Why is he so worried about the outcome of the argument?

The explanation seems to lie in the fact that this is a dream, and that the logic of dreams is not bound to daytime logic. How often have we not had the experience of dreaming something that is perfectly implausible and having the awareness, even as we dream, that such a scenario could not happen? Schwartz is doing something similar. Moreover, he is taking as his premise the idea, familiar to psychologists, that our dreams are often our way of expressing emotions and fantasies that we do not admit to our waking selves. The story, then, might be read as an account of the narrator's true feelings about his parents and himself. And if this is the case, then it would seem that his real inner state is one of great ambivalence—that he feels strongly both ways, hating his life and also desiring it.

The story makes a certain sense if we read it not as the expression of a single sentiment or emotion, but rather as a dramatization of competing voices. The young man who stands up in the theater and shouts "Don't do it" is shushed by the people sitting around him. They are also part of the dream—and, hence, part of the dreamer—and represent his other, more guarded self. He not only acts out different emotions in his own person, but also dreams up a crowd that will silence him. If there is a single truth in this story, it is the truth that tells of many-sidedness. Emotions are neither simple nor obvious, and they are usually opposed by opposite emotions.

A final thematic consideration (though of course one could keep going and find many layers of significance in the story) arises from the narrator's awakening. In the very last sentence we are informed that this is the morning of his twenty-first birthday. We can interpret this either as a simple statement of fact or as a clue to interpretation. The latter seems more likely. In our culture the age twenty-one means something. It marks the individual's full coming-of-age, the entry into societal maturity. And coming-of-age, almost by definition, requires that the struggles of youth be resolved. At twenty-one the individual is expected to leave the family behind and go forth to make a life. Clearly this expectation has some bearing on the story. Indeed, it allows us to situate the dream, understanding it as the symbolic arena for the working-out and mastering of confused emotions.

In this light, the final moments of the dream signal that the struggle is *not* over, that the narrator has not yet made peace with his own past. And if this is so, then the descriptive mention of the snow in the final sentence, along with the phrase "bleak winter morning," is a forecast of hard times to come.

If this discussion has made anything clear, it is that thematic meaning is not a prize inside a box; it is, instead, at every turn a function of interpretation. Themes and meanings exist, but in fiction as in life, they are deeply embedded in the fabric of the work. The patient search for understanding is every bit as valuable as the insights that reward the search.

Indian writer R. K. Narayan's story "House Opposite" is somewhat shorter, and simpler in structure, than "In Dreams Begin Responsibilities." Nevertheless, it presents its own thematic challenges. The questions at the end offer some approaches to theme and meaning in the work.

R. K. Narayan (1906–   )

R. K. Narayan was born in India, and he is widely regarded as that country's premier writer. Narayan has published numerous novels, including *Swami and Friends and The Vendor of Sweets,* and story collections, among them the celebrated *Under the Banyan Tree.* His work includes essays and travel books as well as modern prose versions of the great Indian epics, the *Mahabharata* and the *Ramayana.*

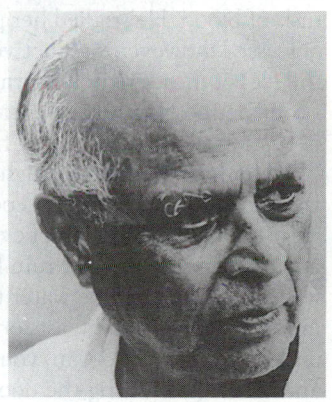

HOUSE OPPOSITE

The hermit invariably shuddered when he looked out of his window. The house across the street was occupied by a shameless woman. Late in the evening, men kept coming and knocking on her door—afternoons, too, if there was a festival or holiday. Sometimes they lounged on the pyol of her house, smoking, chewing tobacco, and spitting into the gutter—committing all the sins of the world, according to the hermit who was striving to pursue a life of austerity, forswearing family, possessions, and all the comforts of life. He found this single-room tenement with a couple of coconut trees and a well at the backyard adequate, and the narrow street swarmed with children: sometimes he called in the children, seated them around, and taught them simple moral lessons and sacred verse. On the walls he had nailed a few pictures of gods cut out of old calendars, and made the children prostrate themselves in front of them before sending them away with a piece of sugar candy each.

His daily life followed an unvarying pattern. Birdlike, he retired at dusk, lying on the bare floor with a wooden block under his head for a pillow. He woke up at four, ahead of the rooster at the street corner, bathed at the well, and sat down on a piece of deerskin to meditate. Later he lit the charcoal stove and baked a few chapattis for breakfast and lunch and cooked certain restricted vegetables and greens, avoiding potato, onion, okra, and such as might stimulate the baser impulses.

Even in the deepest state of meditation, he could not help hearing the creaking of the door across the street when a client left after a night of debauchery. He rigorously suppressed all cravings of the palate, and punished his body in a dozen ways. If you asked him why, he would have been at a loss to explain. He was the antithesis of the athlete who flexed his muscles and watched his expanding chest before a mirror. Our hermit, on the contrary, kept a minute check of his emaciation and felt a peculiar thrill out of such an achievement. He was only following without questioning his ancient guru's instructions, and hoped thus to attain spiritual liberation.

One afternoon, opening the window to sweep the dust on the sill, he noticed her standing on her doorstep, watching the street. His temples throbbed with the rush of blood. He studied her person—chiseled features, but sunk in fatty folds. She possessed, however, a seductive outline; her forearms were cushion-like and perhaps the feel of those encircling arms attracted men. His gaze, once it had begun to hover about her body, would not return to its anchor—which should normally be the tip of one's nose, as enjoined by his guru and the yoga shastras.

Her hips were large, thighs stout like banana stalks, on the whole a mattresslike creature on which a patron could loll all night without a scrap of covering—"Awful monster! Personification of evil." He felt suddenly angry. Why on earth should that creature stand there and ruin his tapas: all the merit he had so laboriously acquired was draining away like water through a sieve. Difficult to say whether it was those monstrous arms and breasts or thighs which tempted and ruined men . . . He hissed under his breath, "Get in, you devil, don't stand there!" She abruptly turned round and went in, shutting the door behind her. He felt triumphant, although his command and her compliance were coincidental. He bolted the window tight and retreated to the farthest corner of the room, settled down on the deerskin, and kept repeating, "Om,° Om, Rama,° Jayarama": the sound "Rama" had a potency all its own—and was reputed to check wandering thoughts and distractions. He had a profound knowledge of mantras and their efficacy. "Sri Rama . . . ," he repeated, but it was like a dilute and weak medicine for high fever. It didn't work. "Sri Rama, Jayarama . . . ," he repeated with a desperate fervor, but the effect lasted not even a second. Unnoticed, his thoughts strayed, questioning: Who was that fellow in a

---

Om: Hindu prayer invocation.
Rama: Hindu deity.

Theme

check shirt and silk upper cloth over his shoulder descending the steps last evening when I went out to the market? Seen him somewhere . . . where? when? . . . ah, he was the big tailor on Market Road . . . with fashionable men and women clustering round him! Master-cutter who was a member of two or three clubs . . . Hobnobbed with officers and businessmen—and this was how he spent his evening, lounging on the human mattress! And yet fashionable persons allowed him to touch them with his measuring tape! Contamination, nothing but contamination; sinful life. He cried out in the lonely room, "Rama! Rama!" as if hailing someone hard of hearing. Presently he realized it was a futile exercise. Rama was a perfect incarnation, of course, but he was mild and gentle until provoked beyond limit, when he would storm and annihilate the evildoer without a trace, even if he was a monster like Ravana. Normally, however, he had forbearance, hence the repetition of his name only resulted in calmness and peace, but the present occasion demanded stern measures. God Siva's° mantra should help. Did he not open his Third Eye and reduce the God of Love to ashes, when the latter slyly aimed his arrow at him while he was meditating? Our hermit pictured the god of matted locks and fiery eyes and recited aloud: "Om Namasivaya," that lonely hall resounding with his hoarse voice. His rambling, unwholesome thoughts were halted for a while, but presently regained their vigor and raced after the woman. She opened her door at least six times on an evening. Did she sleep with them all together at the same time? He paused to laugh at this notion, and also realized that his meditation on the austere god was gone. He banged his fist on his temples, which pained but improved his concentration. "Om Namasivaya . . ." Part of his mind noted the creaking of the door of the opposite house. She was a serpent in whose coils everyone was caught and destroyed—old and young and the middle-aged, tailors and students (he had noticed a couple of days ago a young B.Sc. student from Albert Mission Hostel at her door), lawyers and magistrates (why not?) . . . No wonder the world was getting overpopulated—with such pressure of the elemental urge within every individual! O God Siva, this woman must be eliminated. He would confront her some day and tell her to get out. He would tell her, "Oh, sinful wretch, who is spreading disease and filth like an open sewer: think of the contamination you have spread around—from middle-aged tailor to B.Sc. student. You are out to destroy mankind. Repent your sins, shave your head, cover your ample loins with sackcloth, sit at the temple gate and beg or drown yourself in sarayu after praying for a cleaner life at least in the next birth . . ." 5

Thus went his dialogue, the thought of the woman never leaving his mind, during all the wretched, ill-spent night; he lay tossing on the bare floor. He rose before dawn, his mind made up. He would clear out immediately, cross Nallappa's Grove, and reach the other side of the river. He did not need a permanent roof; he would drift and rest in any temple or mantap or in the shade of a banyan tree: he recollected an ancient tale he had heard from his guru long ago . . . A harlot was sent to heaven when she died, while her detractor, a self-righteous reformer, found himself in hell. It was explained that while the harlot sinned only with her body, her detractor was corrupt mentally, as he was obsessed with the harlot and her activities, and could meditate on nothing else.

Our hermit packed his wicker box with his sparse possessions—a god's image in copper, a rosary, the deerskin, and a little brass bowl. Carrying his box in one hand,

---

Siva: Hindu deity.

he stepped out of the house, closing the door gently behind him. In the dim hour of the dusk, shadowy figures were moving—a milkman driving his cow ahead, laborers bearing crowbars and spades, women with baskets on their way to the market. While he paused to take a final look at the shelter he was abandoning, he heard a plaintive cry, "Swamiji,"° from the opposite house, and saw the woman approach him with a tray, heaped with fruits and flowers. She placed it at his feet and said in a low reverential whisper: "Please accept my offering. This is a day of remembrance of my mother. On this day I pray and seek a saint's blessing. Forgive me . . ." All the lines he had rehearsed for a confrontation deserted him at this moment; looking at her flabby figure, the dark rings under her eyes, he felt pity. As she bent down to prostrate, he noticed that her hair was indifferently dyed and that the parting in the middle widened into a bald patch over which a string of jasmine dangled loosely. He touched her tray with the tip of his finger as a token of acceptance, and went down the street without a word.

QUESTIONS

1. How do the hermit and the woman in the house opposite represent opposing values?

2. What details does Narayan use to characterize the hermit's life and the woman's?

3. The hermit is depicted as striving for absolute purity. Is there anything in Narayan's presentation that suggest that he may have trouble realizing his aim?

4. How does the hermit see the woman? Is there anything about his focus that hints that his disgust may not be absolute?

5. What does Narayan's own attitude to his character seem to be? Does he admire him or regard him critically, or is he neutral? Find a passage that supports your contention.

6. How does Narayan convey the struggle in the hermit's mind? Why do the hermit's strategies seem to fail?

7. What is the message of the ancient tale that the hermit recollects?

8. Look closely at the encounter at the end of the story. What does the woman communicate to the hermit and what is his reaction? What is Narayan saying about preconceptions and about human compassion? Do you believe that his recognition is likely to change his character?

9. Is Narayan finally passing judgment upon either austerity or so-called sinfulness?

10. Is there a single theme that you could extract from the story? Does it do justice to the situation as it is presented?

11. Would this story be any different if set in this country? Write a brief description of a contemporary American version.

Swamiji: term of reverent address to a holy man.

7 Point of View

The story writer has a number of options to consider when deciding how to present events. The final effect of a story is generally achieved through specific manipulations of character and plot. For this reason, the writer's most important technical decision may be what *point of view* to use. Point of view is determined by who is telling the story—an unidentified author, the protagonist, a minor character—and the degree of knowledge possessed by the teller. To decide what point of view to use, an author needs to ask certain questions. For example: How involved do I want the reader to be in the thoughts and actions of my characters? How much should be revealed? What vantage will allow the strongest climax and the most effective resolution of tensions? The basic possibilities are worth examining carefully.

VARIETIES IN THE USE OF NARRATIVE VIEWPOINT

First Person. First person means that the story is told from the point of view of a participant—is, indeed, seen through that person's eyes. The narrator, or teller, uses the first-person "I," and access to information is determined by the role of the character. That is, the reader will only know what that "I" reports. However, the writer can exercise a good deal of control by deciding how to place that "I." The speaking voice can belong to a minor character who sees key events from a distance, thus giving an appearance of objectivity. Or, at the other extreme, the teller can be positioned at—and *be*—the center of interest. Both Delmore Schwartz's "In Dreams Begin Responsibilities" (Chapter 6) and Naguib Mahfouz's "The Conjurer Made Off with the Dish" (Chapter 3) are stories told in the first person by the protagonist. Behind them, invisible to the reader, is the controlling presence of the author, who can be said to don the mask of the character. We should never assume that the author is speaking about his or her own experience. This is fiction, after all, and the story belongs to the invented teller.

Second Person. We rarely encounter fiction written in the voice of the second person, or "you," but it does exist. Mexican writer Carlos Fuentes has written a powerful short story, "Aura," using the "you" address. More recently, Jay McInerney adopted this point of view for his highly popular novel *Bright Lights, Big City*. But there are not many other instances, and for good reason. The use of "you" creates a fundamental problem with character identification. "You" is by definition an object of address, and its use implies the necessary presence of another. The sentence "You wake up and get dressed" suggests either an all-seeing onlooker, an author adopting an intimate relation to the character, or a personality capable of commenting upon its every movement with a self-conscious detachment. Either possibility raises great problems for a writer with a story to tell, and most writers therefore avoid this mode of address altogether.

Third person. Third person is the most widely used vantage in fiction, probably because it is the most adaptable. The third-person address assumes a neutral, or objective, presentation. It is the lens of the camera trained upon the action. The narrator is presumed to be the author, standing outside the events of the narration. Occasionally, especially in early novels like Henry Fielding's *Tom Jones* or Laurence Sterne's *Tristram Shandy*, the author would take the liberty of intruding a first-person voice into the third-person action, commenting or philosophizing, something like, "I will now leave my hero in the arms of his beloved. . . ." The effect is intimate, and often humorous, but such intrusions also break the reader's spell. We are awakened, however briefly, from our immersion in events and reminded that this is a book we are reading. Most fiction, however—and certainly most modern fiction—observes a strict separation between the author and the narrative.

The possible variations of the third-person narration are endless, for the author can choose the degree of involvement as well as the extent of knowledge. He or she can be *omniscient* (from the Greek for "all-knowing"), with access to every thought and emotion of the characters. Or the author can elect to be partially informed (the mode is called, somewhat self-contradictorily, the *limited omniscient*), assuming insight only into certain characters—or else assuming only partial insight. Or the author can restrict himself or herself to the position of pure observer, taking in exteriors and noting actions and conversations, but with no pretense to access to the characters' inner workings. French writer Alain Robbe-Grillet takes this approach to extremes, reducing his narratives to nothing more than the minutely rendered reports of what is available to the eye.

In his long story "The Dead," James Joyce shows how a writer can shift from one vantage to another, achieving, in this case, a texture of great complexity and mounting psychological force. Joyce begins the story (Chapter 13) with a straightforward objective use of the third person: "Lily, the caretaker's daughter, was literally run off her feet. Hardly had she brought one gentleman into the little pantry behind the office on the ground floor and helped him off with his overcoat than the wheezy hall-door bell clanged again and she had to scamper along the bare hallway to let in another guest." And when he introduces his protagonist, Gabriel, one of the guests, the treatment is likewise objective.

Very soon, though, we are let in on what might be called Gabriel's uppermost, or most immediate, thoughts and emotions. Joyce describes his reaction to a remark made by Lily thus: "He was still discomposed by the girl's bitter and sudden retort. It had cast a gloom over him which he tried to dispel by arranging his cuffs and the bows of his tie." By the end of the story, however, we have been brought into the deepest reaches of his self. Joyce skillfully slides us over the barrier that lies between objective and subjective views, and we feel that we have come to inhabit Gabriel's mind: "He stretched himself cautiously along under the sheets and lay down beside his wife. One by one, they were all becoming shades. Better pass boldly into that other world, in the full glory of some passion, than fade and wither dismally with age." Some part of the story's power surely has to do with the distance we have traveled from the very first third-person mention of Lily.

In the last passage quoted, Joyce switches from the third-person objective to the omniscient mode. In giving us Gabriel's thoughts (notice that he dispenses with the customary "he thought" attribution), he makes use of the *interior monologue*. This is yet another technique. Used in the first person or, as here, the third person, the interior monologue gives the reader direct access to the inner life of a character. Gabriel's thoughts are here composed into orderly sentences and give a stylized transcription of his thought process. Interior monologue is in this way distinct from *stream-of-consciousness* presentation. Stream-of-consciousness, used by Joyce in his novel *Ulysses*, attempts to express the inner process directly, incorporating unedited the characters' incidental thoughts and stray observations. Here is Leopold Bloom, Joyce's protagonist from *Ulysses*, shown in the full rambling chaos of his thoughts: "Where is my hat, by the way? Must have put it back on the peg. Or hanging up on the floor. Funny, I don't remember that. Hallstand too full. Four umbrellas, her raincloak."

It is vital to note that not only do writers use different vantages to tell their stories, but they may also grant their narrators varying degrees of intelligence and reliability. Indeed, one of the staples of modern fiction is the story told by the *unreliable narrator*, a figure whose own personality in some way colors the telling of the events. The story is always filtered through the voice that tells it. That voice may belong to a liar, a fool, or a person so taken up with appearances that he misses the real point of what he is reporting. The reader should always be alert for clues about the narrator's own personality and strive to measure the truth of what is told accordingly. As the old saying goes: "Trust the tale, not the teller."

CONTRASTING VIEWPOINTS AND IRONY

A perfect instance of a story that needs to be carefully filtered by the reader is Frank O'Connor's "My Oedipus Complex," which tells of events in the faraway world of adults as they are experienced by a watchful, but also naive, boy.

Frank O'Connor (1903–1966)

Frank O'Connor was born Michael O'Donovan in Cork, Ireland. His family's impoverished circumstances prevented him from finishing even his early schooling, but his tremendous love for books stood him in good stead—he achieved a place as one of the greatest short story writers of all time.

During the Irish struggle for independence. O'Connor was a member of the Irish Republican Army. Afterward, when he supported himself working as a librarian in Cork and Dublin, he began to work at short fiction. O'Connor's first important publication came in 1931 when the *Atlantic Monthly* printed "Guests of the Nation,"

which has remained one of his most popular
pieces. His first collection saw print that same
year, and from that time on he lived by his pen.
O'Connor spent many years in the United States,
teaching and writing. By the time of his death he
had published close to fifty books—including
works of translation and several studies of the
fiction writer's art—fourteen of them story
collections.

MY OEDIPUS COMPLEX

Father was in the army all through the
war—the first war, I mean—so, up to the age of five, I never saw much of him, and
what I saw did not worry me. Sometimes I woke and there was a big figure in khaki
peering down at me in the candlelight. Sometimes in the early morning I heard the
slamming of the front door and the clatter of nailed boots down the cobbles of the
lane. These were Father's entrances and exits. Like Santa Claus he came and went
mysteriously.

In fact, I rather liked his visits, though it was an uncomfortable squeeze between
Mother and him when I got into the big bed in the early morning. He smoked,
which gave him a pleasant musty smell, and shaved, an operation of astounding interest. Each time he left a trail of souvenirs—model tanks and Gurkha° knives with
handles made of bullet cases, and German helmets and cap badges and button-
sticks, and all sorts of military equipment—carefully stowed away in a long box on
top of the wardrobe, in case they ever came in handy. There was a bit of the magpie about Father; he expected everything to come in handy. When his back was
turned, Mother let me get a chair and rummage through his treasures. She didn't
seem to think so highly of them as he did.

The war was the most peaceful period of my life. The window of my attic faced
southeast. My mother had curtained it, but that had small effect. I always woke with
the first light and, with all the responsibilities of the previous day melted, feeling
myself rather like the sun, ready to illumine and rejoice. Life never seemed so simple and clear and full of possibilities as then. I put my feet out from under the
clothes—I called them Mrs. Left and Mrs. Right—and invented dramatic situations
for them in which they discussed the problems of the day. At least Mrs. Right did;
she was very demonstrative, but I hadn't the same control of Mrs. Left, so she mostly
contented herself with nodding agreement.

They discussed what Mother and I should do during the day, what Santa Claus
should give a fellow for Christmas, and what steps should be taken to brighten the
home. There was that little matter of the baby, for instance. Mother and I could
never agree about that. Ours was the only house in the terrace without a new baby,
and Mother said we couldn't afford one till Father came back from the war because

---

Gurkha: Nepalese soldier in the British army.

they cost seventeen and six. That showed how simple she was. The Geneys up the road had a baby, and everyone knew they couldn't afford seventeen and six. It was probably a cheap baby, and Mother wanted something really good, but I felt she was too exclusive. The Geneys' baby would have done us fine.

Having settled my plans for the day, I got up, put a chair under the attic window, and lifted the frame high enough to stick out my head. The window overlooked the front gardens of the terrace behind ours, and beyond these it looked over a deep valley to the tall, red-brick houses terraced up the opposite hillside, which were all still in shadow, while those at our side of the valley were all lit up, though with long strange shadows that made them seem unfamiliar; rigid and painted.   5

After that I went into Mother's room and climbed into the big bed. She woke and I began to tell her of my schemes. By this time, though I never seem to have noticed it, I was petrified in my nightshirt, and I thawed as I talked until, the last frost melted, I fell asleep beside her and woke again only when I heard her below in the kitchen, making the breakfast.

After breakfast we went into town; heard Mass at St. Augustine's and said a prayer for Father, and did the shopping. If the afternoon was fine we either went for a walk in the country or a visit to Mother's great friend in the convent, Mother St. Dominic. Mother had them all praying for Father, and every night, going to bed, I asked God to send him back safe from the war to us. Little, indeed, did I know what I was praying for!

One morning, I got into the big bed, and there, sure enough, was Father in his usual Santa Claus manner, but later, instead of uniform, he put on his best blue suit, and Mother was as pleased as anything. I saw nothing to be pleased about, because, out of uniform, Father was altogether less interesting, but she only beamed, and explained that our prayers had been answered, and off we went to Mass to thank God for having brought Father safely home.

The irony of it! That very day when he came in to dinner he took off his boots and put on his slippers, donned the dirty old cap he wore about the house to save him from colds, crossed his legs, and began to talk gravely to Mother, who looked anxious. Naturally, I disliked her looking anxious, because it destroyed her good looks, so I interrupted him.

"Just a moment, Larry!" she said gently.   10

This was only what she said when we had boring visitors, so I attached no importance to it and went on talking.

"Do be quiet, Larry!" she said impatiently. "Don't you hear me talking to Daddy?"

This was the first time I had heard those ominous words, "talking to Daddy," and I couldn't help feeling that if this was how God answered prayers, he couldn't listen to them very attentively.

"Why are you talking to Daddy?" I asked with as great a show of indifference as I could muster.

"Because Daddy and I have business to discuss. Now, don't interrupt again!"   15

In the afternoon, at Mother's request, Father took me for a walk. This time we went into town instead of out the country, and I thought at first, in my usual optimistic way, that it might be an improvement. It was nothing of the sort. Father and I had quite different notions of a walk in town. He had no proper interest in trams, ships, and horses, and the only thing that seemed to divert him was talking to fellows as old as himself. When I wanted to stop he simply went on, dragging me behind him by the hand; when he wanted to stop I had no alternative but to do the same. I noticed that it seemed to be a sign that he wanted to stop for a long time whenever he leaned against a wall. The second time I saw him do it I got wild. He seemed to be settling himself forever. I pulled him by the coat and trousers, but, unlike Mother who, if you were too persistent, got into a wax and said: "Larry, if you don't behave yourself, I'll give you a good slap," Father had an extraordinary capacity for amiable inattention. I sized him up and wondered would I cry, but he seemed to be too remote to be annoyed even by that. Really, it was like going for a walk with a mountain! He either ignored the wrenching and pummelling entirely, or else glanced down with a grin of amusement from his peak. I had never met anyone so absorbed in himself as he seemed.

At teatime, "talking to Daddy" began again, complicated this time by the fact that he had an evening paper, and every few minutes he put it down and told Mother something new out of it. I felt this was foul play.

Man for man, I was prepared to compete with him any time for Mother's attention, but when he had it all made up for him by other people it left me no chance. Several times I tried to change the subject without success.

"You must be quiet while Daddy is reading, Larry," Mother said impatiently.

It was clear that she either genuinely liked talking to Father better than talking to me, or else that he had some terrible hold on her which made her afraid to admit the truth.

"Mummy," I said that night when she was tucking me up, "do you think if I prayed hard God would send Daddy back to the war?"   20

She seemed to think about that for a moment.

"No, dear," she said with a smile. "I don't think he would."

"Why wouldn't he, Mummy?"

"Because there isn't a war any longer, dear."

"But, Mummy, couldn't God make another war, if He liked?"   25

"He wouldn't like to, dear. It's not God who makes wars, but bad people."

"Oh!" I said.

I was disappointed about that. I began to think that God wasn't quite what he was cracked up to be.

Next morning I woke at my usual hour, feeling like a bottle of champagne. I put out my feet and invented a long conversation in which Mrs. Right talked of the trouble she had with her own father till she put him in the Home. I didn't quite know what the Home was but it sounded the right place for Father. Then I got my chair and stuck my head out of the attic window. Dawn was just breaking, with a guilty air that made me feel I had caught it in the act. My head bursting with stories and schemes, I stumbled in next door, and in the half-darkness scrambled into the big bed. There was no room at Mother's side so I had to get between her and Father. For the time being I had forgotten about him, and for several minutes I sat bolt upright, racking my brains to know what I could do with him. He was taking up more than his fair share of the bed, and I couldn't get comfortable, so I gave him several kicks that made him grunt and stretch. He made room all right, though. Mother waked and felt for me.

I settled back comfortably in the warmth of the bed with my thumb in my mouth.

"Mummy!" I hummed, loudly and contentedly.   30

"Sssh! dear," she whispered. "Don't wake Daddy!"

This was a new development, which threatened to be even more serious than "talking to Daddy." Life without my early-morning conferences was unthinkable.

"Why?" I asked severely.

"Because poor Daddy is tired."

This seemed to me a quite inadequate reason, and I was sickened by the sentimentality of her "poor Daddy." I never liked that sort of gush; it always struck me as insincere.

"Oh!" I said lightly. Then in my most winning tone: "Do you know where I want to go with you today, Mummy?"

"No, dear," she sighed.

"I want to go down the Glen and fish for thornybacks with my new net, and then I want to go out to the Fox and Hounds, and—"

"Don't-wake-Daddy!" she hissed angrily, clapping her hand across my mouth.

But it was too late. He was awake, or nearly so. He grunted and reached for the matches. Then he stared incredulously at his watch.

"Like a cup of tea, dear?" asked Mother in a meek, hushed voice I had never heard her use before. It sounded almost as though she were afraid.

"Tea?" he exclaimed indignantly. "Do you know what the time is?"

"And after that I want to go up the Rathcooney Road," I said loudly, afraid I'd forget something in all those interruptions.

"Go to sleep at once, Larry!" she said sharply.

I began to snivel. I couldn't concentrate, the way that pair went on, and smothering my early-morning schemes was like burying a family from the cradle.

Father said nothing, but lit his pipe and sucked it, looking out into the shadows without minding Mother or me. I knew he was mad. Every time I made a remark Mother hushed me irritably. I was mortified. I felt it wasn't fair; there was even something sinister in it. Every time I had pointed out to her the waste of making two beds when we could both sleep in one, she had told me it was healthier like that, and now here was this man, this stranger, sleeping with her without the least regard for her health! He got up early and made tea, but though he brought Mother a cup he brought none for me.

"Mummy," I shouted, "I want a cup of tea, too."

"Yes, dear," she said patiently. "You can drink from Mummy's saucer."

That settled it. Either Father or I would have to leave the house. I didn't want to drink from Mother's saucer; I wanted to be treated as an equal in my own home, so, just to spite her, I drank it all and left none for her. She took that quietly, too.

But that night when she was putting me to bed she said gently:

"Larry, I want you to promise me something."

"What is it?" I asked.

"Not to come in and disturb poor Daddy in the morning. Promise?"

"Poor Daddy" again! I was becoming suspicious of everything involving that quite impossible man.

"Why?" I asked.

"Because poor Daddy is worried and tired and he doesn't sleep well."

"Why doesn't he, Mummy?"

"Well, you know, don't you, that while he was at the war Mummy got the pennies from the Post Office?"

"From Miss MacCarthy?"

"That's right. But now, you see, Miss MacCarthy hasn't any more pennies, so Daddy must go out and find us some. You know what would happen if he couldn't?" 60

"No," I said, "tell us."

"Well, I think we might have to go out and beg for them like the poor old woman on Fridays. We wouldn't like that, would we?"

"No," I agreed. "We wouldn't."

"So you'll promise not to come in and wake him?"

"Promise." 65

Mind you, I meant that. I knew pennies were a serious matter, and I was all against having to go out and beg like the old woman on Fridays. Mother laid out all my toys in a complete ring round the bed so that, whatever way I got out, I was bound to fall over one of them.

When I woke I remembered my promise all right. I got up and sat on the floor and played—for hours, it seemed to me. Then I got my chair and looked out the attic window for more hours. I wished it was time for Father to wake; I wished someone would make me a cup of tea. I didn't feel in the least like the sun; instead, I was bored and so very, very cold! I simply longed for the warmth and depth of the big featherbed.

At last I could stand it no longer. I went into the next room. As there was still no room at Mother's side I climbed over her and she woke with a start.

"Larry," she whispered, gripping my arm very tightly, "what did you promise?"

"But I did, Mummy," I wailed, caught in the very act. "I was quiet for ever so long." 70

"Oh, dear, and you're perished!" she said sadly, feeling me all over. "Now, if I let you stay will you promise not to talk?"

"But I want to talk, Mummy," I wailed.

"That has nothing to do with it," she said with a firmness that was new to me. "Daddy wants to sleep. Now, do you understand that?"

I understood it only too well. I wanted to talk, he wanted to sleep—whose house was it, anyway?

"Mummy," I said with equal firmness, "I think it would be healthier for Daddy to sleep in his own bed." 75

That seemed to stagger her, because she said nothing for a while.

"Now, once for all," she went on, "you're to be perfectly quiet or go back to your own bed. Which is it to be?"

The injustice of it got me down. I had convicted her out of her own mouth of inconsistency and unreasonableness, and she hadn't even attempted to reply. Full of spite, I gave Father a kick, which she didn't notice but which made him grunt and open his eyes in alarm.

"What time is it?" he asked in a panic-stricken voice, not looking at Mother but at the door, as if he saw someone there.

"It's early yet," she replied soothingly. "It's only the child. Go to sleep again. . . . Now, Larry," she added, getting out of bed, "you've wakened Daddy and you must go back." 80

This time, for all her quiet air, I knew she meant it, and knew that my principal rights and privileges were as good as lost unless I asserted them at once. As she lifted me, I gave a screech, enough to wake the dead, not to mind Father. He groaned.

"That damn child! Doesn't he ever sleep?"

"It's only a habit, dear," she said quietly, though I could see she was vexed.

"Well, it's time he got out of it," shouted Father, beginning to heave in the bed. He suddenly gathered all the bedclothes about him, turned to the wall, and then looked back over his shoulder with nothing showing only two small, spiteful, dark eyes. The man looked very wicked.

To open the bedroom door, Mother had to let me down, and I broke free and dashed for the farthest corner, screeching. Father sat bolt upright in bed.

"Shut up, you little puppy!" he said in a choking voice.

I was so astonished that I stopped screeching. Never, never had anyone spoken to me in that tone before. I looked at him incredulously and saw his face convulsed with rage. It was only then that I fully realized how God had codded me, listening to my prayers for the safe return of this monster.

"Shut up, you!" I bawled, beside myself.

"What's that you said?" shouted Father, making a wild leap out of the bed.

"Mick, Mick!" cried Mother. "Don't you see the child isn't used to you?"

"I see he's better fed than taught," snarled Father, waving his arms wildly. "He wants his bottom smacked."

All his previous shouting was as nothing to these obscene words referring to my person. They really made my blood boil.

"Smack your own!" I screamed hysterically. "Smack your own! Shut up! Shut up!"

At this he lost his patience and let fly at me. He did it with the lack of conviction you'd expect of a man under Mother's horrified eyes, and it ended up as a mere tap, but the sheer indignity of being struck at all by a stranger, a total stranger who had cajoled his way back from the war into our big bed as a result of my innocent intercession, made me completely dotty. I shrieked and shrieked, and danced in my bare feet, and Father, looking awkward and hairy in nothing but a short gray army shirt, glared down at me like a mountain out for murder. I think it must have been then that I realized he was jealous too. And there stood Mother in her nightdress, looking as if her heart was broken between us. I hoped she felt as she looked. It seemed to me that she deserved it all.

From that morning out my life was a hell. Father and I were enemies, open and avowed. We conducted a series of skirmishes against one another, he trying to steal my time with Mother and I his. When she was sitting on my bed, telling me a story, he took to looking for some pair of old boots which he alleged he had left behind him at the beginning of the war. While he talked to Mother I played loudly with my toys to show my total lack of concern. He created a terrible scene one evening when he came in from work and found me at his box, playing with his regimental badges, Gurkha knives and button-sticks. Mother got up and took the box from me.

"You mustn't play with Daddy's toys unless he lets you, Larry," she said severely. "Daddy doesn't play with yours."

For some reason Father looked at her as if she had struck him and then turned away with a scowl.

"Those are not toys," he growled, taking down the box again to see had I lifted anything. "Some of those curios are very rare and valuable."

But as time went on I saw more and more how he managed to alienate Mother and me. What made it worse was that I couldn't grasp his method or see what attraction he had for Mother. In every possible way he was less winning than I. He had a common accent and made noises at his tea. I thought for a while that it might be the newspapers she was interested in, so I made up bits of news of my own to read to her. Then I thought it might be the smoking, which I personally thought attractive, and took his pipes and went round the house dribbling into them till he caught me. I even made noises at my tea, but Mother only told me I was disgusting. It all seemed to hinge round that unhealthy habit of sleeping together, so I made a point of dropping into their bedroom and nosing round, talking to myself, so that they wouldn't know I was watching them, but they were never up to anything that I could see. In the end it beat me. It seemed to depend on being grown-up and giving people rings, and I realized I'd have to wait.

But at the same time I wanted him to see that I was only waiting, not giving up the fight. One evening when he was being particularly obnoxious, chattering away well above my head, I let him have it.   100

"Mummy," I said, "do you know what I'm going to do when I grow up?"

"No, dear," she replied. "What?"

"I'm going to marry you," I said quietly.

Father gave a great guffaw out of him, but he didn't take me in. I knew it must only be pretense. And Mother, in spite of everything, was pleased. I felt she was probably relieved to know that one day Father's hold on her would be broken.

"Won't that be nice?" she said with a smile.   105

"It'll be very nice," I said confidently. "Because we're going to have lots and lots of babies."

"That's right, dear," she said placidly. "I think we'll have one soon, and then you'll have plenty of company."

I was no end pleased about that because it showed that in spite of the way she gave in to Father she still considered my wishes. Besides, it would put the Geneys in their place.

It didn't turn out like that, though. To begin with, she was very preoccupied—I supposed about where she would get the seventeen and six—and though Father took to staying out late in the evenings it did me no particular good. She stopped taking me for walks, became as touchy as blazes, and smacked me for nothing at all. Sometimes I wished I'd never mentioned the confounded baby—I seemed to have genius for bringing calamity on myself.

And calamity it was! Sonny arrived in the most appalling hullabaloo—even that much he couldn't do without a fuss—and from the first moment I disliked him. He was a difficult child—so far as I was concerned he was always difficult—and demanded far too much attention. Mother was simply silly about him, and couldn't see when he was only showing off. As company he was worse than useless. He slept all day, and I had to go round the house on tiptoe to avoid waking him. It wasn't any longer a question of not waking Father. The slogan now was "Don't-wake-Sonny!" I couldn't understand why the child wouldn't sleep at the proper time, so whenever Mother's back was turned I woke him. Sometimes to keep him awake I pinched him as well. Mother caught me at it one day and gave me a most unmerciful flaking.   110

One evening, when Father was coming in from work, I was playing trains in the front garden. I let on not to notice him; instead, I pretended to be talking to myself, and said in a loud voice: "If another bloody baby comes into this house, I'm going out."

Father stopped dead and looked at me over his shoulder.

"What's that you said?" he asked sternly.

"I was only talking to myself," I replied, trying to conceal my panic. "It's private."

He turned and went in without a word. Mind you, I intended it as a solemn warning, but its effect was quite different. Father started being quite nice to me. I could understand that, of course. Mother was quite sickening about Sonny. Even at mealtimes she'd get up and gawk at him in the cradle with an idiotic smile, and tell Father to do the same. He was always polite about it, but he looked so puzzled you could see he didn't know what she was talking about. He complained of the way Sonny cried at night, but she only got cross and said that Sonny never cried except when there was something up with him—which was a flaming lie, because Sonny never had anything up with him, and only cried for attention. It was really painful to see how simpleminded she was. Father wasn't attractive, but he had a fine intelligence. He saw through Sonny, and now he knew that I saw through him as well.

115

One night I woke with a start. There was someone beside me in the bed. For one wild moment I felt sure it must be Mother, having come to her senses and left Father for good, but then I heard Sonny in convulsions in the next room, and Mother saying: "There! There! There!" and I knew it wasn't she. It was Father. He was lying beside me, wide awake, breathing hard and apparently as mad as hell.

After a while it came to me what he was mad about. It was his turn now. After turning me out of the big bed, he had been turned out himself. Mother had no consideration now for anyone but that poisonous pup, Sonny. I couldn't help feeling sorry for Father. I had been through it all myself, and even at that age I was magnanimous. I began to stroke him down and say: "There! There!" He wasn't exactly responsive.

"Aren't you asleep either?" he snarled.

"Ah, come on and put your arm around us, can't you?" I said, and he did, in a sort of way. Gingerly, I suppose, is how you'd describe it. He was very bony but better than nothing.

At Christmas he went out of his way to buy me a really nice model railway. 120

As you read the following discussion, consider these questions:

1. Looking closely at the first paragraph of his story, discuss how O'Connor establishes point of view. What sorts of descriptive details does he use, and how do they help us to create the persona of the narrator?

2. Explain briefly what is meant by the Oedipus complex, and then relate this to the narrator's situation.

3. Cite instances where O'Connor uses the clash between the boy's point of view and that of the reader's to create humor.

4. How does the father's return affect the boy? How does O'Connor manipulate point of view to establish the distance between the two characters?

5. What is the boy's understanding of his mother's pregnancy? How does the arrival of the new baby bring the father and son together?

6. Imagine how the story would be different if told in the third person or through the eyes of another character. Discuss.

7. Write a short episode in which a child narrator misunderstands an encounter with an adult.

Discussion. Frank O'Connor's story depends almost entirely on point of view for its memorable presentation of family tensions and its humor. The author has orchestrated his narrative in such a way that we can be said to be reading two stories at the same time. The first is told by the young boy, Larry. We learn about his life—his close relationship with his mother, the changes wrought by his father's return from war, and the reconciliation of the boy and his father that comes only when his mother has another baby. The second story is the one that was put together by reading between the lines as we apply our adult understanding to the information that Larry gives us. The richness of the reading experience comes about through the overlapping of the two stories and is very much a product of O'Connor's artistry.

We will get a better grasp of O'Connor's strategy if we reflect for a moment upon the title and its implications. "My Oedipus Complex" is a direct reference to Sigmund Freud's well-known theory about a crucial stage in the psychological development of a young boy. (He proposed a similar theory, called the Electra complex, to explain a maturation phase in young girls.) Oedipus (see Sophocles' play *Oedipus Rex* in Chapter 30) was the figure in Greek mythology of whom it was prophesied that he would kill his father and marry his own mother. He sought to avoid this fate, but owing to several instances of mistaken identity, ended up killing his father, Laius, and marrying his widowed mother, Jocasta. When he realized what he had done, he put out his eyes and wandered forth from his land as an exile.

Freud's theory, while not so dramatic, recognizes a basic conflict in the young boy's psyche, a desire to replace the father in the mother's affections, which may also include murderous fantasies. The boy successfully outgrows the phase when he accepts reality, deciding that instead of *being* the father, he will be *like* the father.

O'Connor, as we can see from the story, has followed the basic Freudian pattern of conflict and resolution, even going so far as to have the boy announce to his mother that he will one day marry her. But his ability to get inside his character and to create the specific details of his circumstance is such that we never get the sense that we are being led along through anything like a case study. Moreover, where Freud saw a struggle of primal forces, O'Connor finds an opportunity for fond humor.

From start to finish, the whole story is told through the eyes of Larry. He is nearly five at the beginning and cannot be much more than seven at the end. We should be aware, however, that O'Connor is not narrating the events as if Larry were that young. Rather, as the explanatory tone of the first sentence indicates (especially the aside, "the first war, I mean"), the voice probably belongs to an adult looking back. Indeed, the title confirms it, for the young Larry would not know what an Oedipus complex was.

But even though the story is told by an adult who is looking back, that adult—the grown-up Larry—never allows his wisdom or insight to color his presentation. The events are set down just as they might have been experienced by the boy.

The reader is planted inside the child's perceptions by the third sentence: "Sometimes I woke and there was a big figure in khaki peering down at me in the candlelight." We not only glimpse the difference in size between boy and father, but also grasp the distance between them. The father is a stranger—a "big figure." Not until the very end of the story will Larry accept that figure as his father. Significantly, the story ends where it begins, but Larry's last words show how much their relationship has changed: "Ah, come on and put your arm around us, can't you?"

O'Connor plays the tension between the child's point of view and the reader's matured understanding throughout. Our response to what Larry is telling us is by and large a feeling of irony, though that feeling takes on different shades depending upon the context. (*Irony*, simply defined, is the incongruity we register between what is stated and the manner of the stating. Ironic effects may be intentional or unintentional.) When Larry states that "The war was the most peaceful period of my life," we may feel a prick of discomfort, for of course we know something of the terrible realities of trench warfare. But when Larry remarks that his family couldn't afford a baby "because they cost seventeen and six," we smile wryly at the extent of a child's innocence.

These are isolated ironies and we register them whenever Larry makes a statement that reveals his misinterpretation of what we know to be the facts of the case. But O'Connor also makes use of what is sometimes called *situational irony*; that is, he makes his readers feel the larger discrepancy between Larry's whole situation as he imagines it and the situation as we believe it to exist. This is best illustrated by Larry's serious, but also laughable, attempt to claim the full rights of an adult—his making up bits of news to amuse his mother and walking around the house with his father's pipes. O'Connor adds a clever twist when he has Larry's mother chide the boy for looking in his father's souvenir box. "You mustn't play with Daddy's toys unless he lets you," she says. "Daddy doesn't play with yours." This is not just the mother trying to speak the child's language—she really does see her husband's collecting of war memorabilia as juvenile.

We could work through this story and find innumerable instances of the discrepancy between Larry's point of view and that of the adults, but these few examples should suffice. The main point is that the writer has a great many choices to make when trying to figure out how best to tell a story. In some cases the tension within the plot itself is sufficient, and there is no need to use the reader as a foil. The writer can just work to create the fictional illusion, just like the filmmaker who wants us to forget that what is on the screen is not reality but a series of scripted scenes played by actors. But at other times, as with "My Oedipus Complex," the writer will exploit any opportunity, reminding the reader at every turn that this is a tale told by a teller and that the teller's version may not represent the only interpretation of events.

The Unreliable Narrative Filter

Just as Frank O'Connor assumes the point of view of a young boy to tell a story that in many ways exceeds his comprehension, so does another O'Connor (Flannery) employ a similar technique to achieve a very different effect.

Unlike Frank O'Connor, Flannery O'Connor chooses to tell her story not in the first- but rather in the more conventionally neutral third-person voice. But as is made clear right away, the narrative will be filtered through its protagonist. "Her doctor had told Julian's mother that she must lose twenty pounds on account of her blood pressure. . . ." The designation "Julian's mother" tells us straight off that the central figure in this story will not be the woman, but her son, and even though Julian's mother dominates the opening passage, we feel that the dominance is temporary. And we are right. With the appearance of Julian in the second paragraph, the narrative is handed over: everything that follows will be refracted through his exasperated sensibility.

O'Connor allows Julian's rage to dictate everything about her presentation. Though we are seeing Julian through the third-person lens, we feel that we are there in his thoughts. We observe as, step by step, he mounts his case against the one person he is most dependent on, refusing to see her world or agree to her terms. O'Connor is shrewd—she portrays Julian's attitudes in such a way that we can grasp what he cannot. We see his outbursts as signs of his enmeshment with his mother. Indeed, it is for us to establish a more realistic and sympathetic picture of the mother.

What is O'Connor's intent in engineering this particular approach? In part it is to bring Julian to a crisis of self-recognition and to involve us in the drama of his awakening. Her use of the third-person filter allows us to perceive—and feel—the conflict between his critical intellect and the buried but undeniable needs of his emotional life. The mother's stroke allows her to bring Julian's angry rationalizations crashing down, and in the process O'Connor reveals a good deal about the deep nature of intolerance. This becomes a delicious irony, for it is precisely his mother's racism that triggers Julian's anger the most.

Flannery O'Connor
(1925–1964)

Flannery O'Connor was born in Savannah, Georgia, and attended the Georgia State College for Women. Winning a fellowship to the Writers' Workshop of the University of Iowa, she went on to take an MFA and become one of the most illustrious graduates of that prestigious program. After living for a short time in New York City, O'Connor felt the first ravages of a serious illness and moved back to Georgia to live with her mother on a farm. Despite suffering from lupus, she produced the novels *Wise Blood* (1952) and *The Violent Bear It Away* (1960), and several collections of short stories. *The Complete Stories* (1971), published posthumously, won her the National Book Award.

O'Connor was a devout Christian who used her work to probe and test her religious insights. O'Connor's scenarios are often violent and grotesque, but discerning readers have looked beyond into the serious moral interrogation they represent.

Point of View

EVERYTHING THAT RISES MUST CONVERGE

Her doctor had told Julian's mother that she must lose twenty pounds on account of her blood pressure, so on Wednesday nights Julian had to take her downtown on the bus for a reducing class at the Y. The reducing class was designed for working girls over fifty, who weighed from 165 to 200 pounds. His mother was one of the slimmer ones, but she said ladies did not tell their age or weight. She would not ride the buses by herself at night since they had been integrated, and because the reducing class was one of her few pleasures, necessary for her health, and *free*, she said Julian could at least put himself out to take her, considering all she did for him. Julian did not like to consider all she did for him, but every Wednesday night he braced himself and took her.

She was almost ready to go, standing before the hall mirror, putting on her hat, while he, his hands behind him, appeared pinned to the door frame, waiting like Saint Sebastian for the arrows to begin piercing him. The hat was new and had cost her seven dollars and a half. She kept saying, "Maybe I shouldn't have paid that for it. No, I shouldn't have. I'll take it off and return it tomorrow. I shouldn't have bought it."

Julian raised his eyes to heaven. "Yes, you should have bought it," he said. "Put it on and let's go." It was a hideous hat. A purple velvet flap came down on one side of it and stood up on the other; the rest of it was green and looked like a cushion with the stuffing out. He decided it was less comical than jaunty and pathetic. Everything that gave her pleasure was small and depressed him.

She lifted the hat one more time and set it down slowly on top of her head. Two wings of gray hair protruded on either side of her florid face, but her eyes, sky-blue, were as innocent and untouched by experience as they must have been when she was ten. Were it not that she was a widow who had struggled fiercely to feed and clothe and put him through school and who was supporting him still, "until he got on his feet," she might have been a little girl that he had to take to town.

"It's all right, it's all right," he said. "Let's go." He opened the door himself and started down the walk to get her going. The sky was a dying violet and the houses stood out darkly against it, bulbous liver-colored monstrosities of a uniform ugliness though no two were alike. Since this had been a fashionable neighborhood forty years ago, his mother persisted in thinking they did well to have an apartment in it. Each house had a narrow collar of dirt around it in which sat, usually, a grubby child. Julian walked with his hands in his pockets, his head down and thrust forward and his eyes glazed with the determination to make himself completely numb during the time he would be sacrificed to her pleasure.   5

The door closed and he turned to find the dumpy figure, surmounted by the atrocious hat, coming toward him. "Well," she said, "you only live once and paying a little more for it, I at least won't meet myself coming and going."

"Some day I'll start making money," Julian said gloomily—he knew he never would—"and you can have one of those jokes whenever you take the fit." But first they would move. He visualized a place where the nearest neighbors would be three miles away on either side.

"I think you're doing fine," she said, drawing on her gloves. "You've only been out of school a year. Rome wasn't built in a day."

She was one of the few members of the Y reducing class who arrived in hat and gloves and who had a son who had been to college. "It takes time," she said, "and the world is in such a mess. This hat looked better on me than any of the others, though when she brought it out I said, 'Take that thing back. I wouldn't have it on my head,' and she said, 'Now wait till you see it on,' and when she put it on me, I said, 'We-ull,' and she said, 'If you ask me, that hat does something for you and you do something for the hat, and besides,' she said, 'with that hat, you won't meet yourself coming and going.' "

Julian thought he could have stood his lot better if she had been selfish, if she had been an old hag who drank and screamed at him. He walked along, saturated in depression, as if in the midst of his martyrdom he had lost his faith. Catching sight of his long, hopeless, irritated face, she stopped suddenly with a grief-stricken look, and pulled back on his arm. "Wait on me," she said. "I'm going back to the house and take this thing off and tomorrow I'm going to return it. I was out of my head. I can pay the gas bill with that seven-fifty." 10

He caught her arm in a vicious grip. "You are not going to take it back," he said. "I like it."

"Well," she said, "I don't think I ought . . . "

"Shut up and enjoy it," he muttered, more depressed than ever.

"With the world in the mess it's in," she said, "it's a wonder we can enjoy anything. I tell you, the bottom rail is on the top."

Julian sighed. 15

"Of course," she said, "if you know who you are, you can go anywhere." She said this every time he took her to the reducing class. "Most of them in it are not our kind of people," she said, "but I can be gracious to anybody. I know who I am."

"They don't give a damn for your graciousness," Julian said savagely. "Knowing who you are is good for one generation only. You haven't the foggiest idea where you stand now or who you are."

She stopped and allowed her eyes to flash at him. "I most certainly do know who I am." she said, "and if you don't know who you are, I'm ashamed of you."

"Oh hell," Julian said.

"Your great-grandfather was a former governor of this state," she said. "Your grandfather was a prosperous landowner. Your grandmother was a Godhigh." 20

"Will you look around you," he said tensely, "and see where you are now?" and he swept his arm jerkily out to indicate the neighborhood, which the growing darkness at least made less dingy.

"You remain what you are," she said. "Your great-grandfather had a plantation and two hundred slaves."

"There are no more slaves," he said irritably.

"They were better off when they were," she said. He groaned to see that she was off on that topic. She rolled onto it every few days like a train on an open track. He knew every stop, every junction, every swamp along the way, and knew the exact point at which her conclusion would roll majestically into the station: "It's ridiculous. It's simply not realistic. They should rise, yes, but on their own side of the fence."

"Let's skip it," Julian said. 25

"The ones I feel sorry for," she said, "are the ones that are half white. They're tragic."

"Will you skip it?"

"Suppose we were half white. We would certainly have mixed feelings."

"I have mixed feelings now," he groaned.

"Well let's talk about something pleasant," she said. "I remember going to Grandpa's when I was a little girl. Then the house had double stairways that went up to what was really the second floor—all the cooking was done on the first. I used to like to stay down in the kitchen on account of the way the walls smelled. I would sit with my nose pressed against the plaster and take deep breaths. Actually the place belonged to the Godhighs but your grandfather Chestny paid the mortgage and saved it for them. They were in reduced circumstances," she said, "but reduced or not, they never forgot who they were."

"Doubtless that decayed mansion reminded them," Julian muttered. He never spoke of it without contempt or thought of it without longing. He had seen it once when he was a child before it had been sold. The double stairways had rotted and been torn down. Negroes were living in it. But it remained in his mind as his mother had known it. It appeared in his dreams regularly. He would stand on the wide porch, listening to the rustle of oak leaves, then wander through the high-ceilinged hall into the parlor that opened onto it and gaze at the worn rugs and faded draperies. It occurred to him that it was he, not she, who could have appreciated it. He preferred its threadbare elegance to anything he could name and it was because of it that all the neighborhoods they had lived in had been a torment to him— whereas she had hardly known the difference. She called her insensitivity "being adjustable."

"And I remember the old darky who was my nurse, Caroline. There was no better person in the world. I've always had a great respect for my colored friends," she said. "I'd do anything in the world for them and they'd . . . "

"Will you for God's sake get off that subject?" Julian said. When he got on a bus by himself, he made it a point to sit down beside a Negro, in reparation as it were for his mother's sins.

"You're mighty touchy tonight," she said. "Do you feel all right?"

"Yes I feel all right," he said. "Now lay off."

She pursed her lips. "Well, you certainly are in a vile humor," she observed. "I just won't speak to you at all."

They had reached the bus stop. There was no bus in sight and Julian, his hands still jammed in his pockets and his head thrust forward, scowled down the empty street. The frustration of having to wait on the bus as well as ride on it began to creep up his neck like a hot hand. The presence of his mother was borne in upon him as she gave a pained sigh. He looked at her bleakly. She was holding herself very erect under the preposterous hat, wearing it like a banner of her imaginary dignity. There was in him an evil urge to break her spirit. He suddenly unloosened his tie and pulled it off and put it in his pocket.

She stiffened. "Why must you look like *that* when you take me to town?" she said. "Why must you deliberately embarrass me?"

"If you'll never learn where you are," he said, "you can at least learn where I am."

"You look like a—thug," she said.

"Then I must be one," he murmured.

"I'll just go home," she said. "I will not bother you. If you can't do a little thing like that for me . . . "

Rolling his eyes upward, he put his tie back on. "Restored to my class," he muttered. He thrust his face toward her and hissed, "True culture is in the mind, the *mind*," he said, and tapped his head, "the mind."

"It's in the heart," she said, "and in how you do things and how you do things is because of who you *are*."

"Nobody in the damn bus cares who you are." 45

"I care who I am," she said icily.

The lighted bus appeared on top of the next hill and as it approached, they moved out into the street to meet it. He put his hand under her elbow and hoisted her up on the creaking step. She entered with a little smile, as if she were going into a drawing room where everyone had been waiting for her. While he put in the tokens, she sat down on one of the broad front seats for three which faced the aisle. A thin woman with protruding teeth and long yellow hair was sitting on the end of it. His mother moved up beside her and left room for Julian beside herself. He sat down and looked at the floor across the aisle where a pair of thin feet in red and white canvas sandals were planted.

His mother immediately began a general conversation meant to attract anyone who felt like talking. "Can it get any hotter?" she said and removed from her purse a folding fan, black with a Japanese scene on it, which she began to flutter before her.

"I reckon it might could," the woman with the protruding teeth said, "but I know for a fact my apartment couldn't get no hotter."

"It must get the afternoon sun," his mother said. She sat forward and looked up and down the bus. It was half filled. Everybody was white. "I see we have the bus to ourselves," she said. Julian cringed. 50

"For a change," said the woman across the aisle, the owner of the red and white canvas sandals. "I come on one the other day and they were thick as fleas—up front and all through."

"The world is in a mess everywhere," his mother said. "I don't know how we've let it get in this fix."

"What gets my goat is all those boys from good families stealing automobile tires," the woman with the protruding teeth said. "I told my boy, I said you may not be rich but you been raised right and if I ever catch you in any such mess, they can send you on to the reformatory. Be exactly where you belong."

"Training tells," his mother said. "Is your boy in high school?"

"Ninth grade," the woman said. 55

"My son just finished college last year. He wants to write but he's selling typewriters until he gets started," his mother said.

The woman leaned forward and peered at Julian. He threw her such a malevolent look that she subsided against the seat. On the floor across the aisle there was an abandoned newspaper. He got up and got it and opened it out in front of him. His mother discreetly continued the conversation in a lower tone but the woman across the aisle said in a loud voice, "Well that's nice. Selling typewriters is close to writing. He can go right from one to the other."

"I tell him," his mother said, "that Rome wasn't built in a day."

Behind the newspaper Julian was withdrawing into the inner compartment of his mind where he spent most of his time. This was a kind of mental bubble in which he established himself when he could not bear to be a part of what was going on around him. From it he could see out and judge but in it he was safe from any kind of penetration from without. It was the only place where he felt free of the general idiocy of his fellows. His mother had never entered it but from it he could see her with absolute clarity.

The old lady was clever enough and he thought that if she had started from any of the right premises, more might have been expected of her. She lived according to the laws of her own fantasy world, outside of which he had never seen her set foot. The law of it was to sacrifice herself for him after she had first created the necessity to do so by making a mess of things. If he had permitted her sacrifices, it was only because her lack of foresight had made them necessary. All of her life had been a struggle to act like a Chestny without the Chestny goods, and to give him everything she thought a Chestny ought to have; but since, said she, it was fun to struggle, why complain? And when you had won, as she had won, what fun to look back on the hard times! He could not forgive her that she had enjoyed the struggle and that she thought *she* had won.

What she meant when she said she had won was that she had brought him up successfully and had sent him to college and that he had turned out so well—good looking (her teeth had gone unfilled so that his could be straightened), intelligent (he realized he was too intelligent to be a success), and with a future ahead of him (there was of course no future ahead of him). She excused his gloominess on the grounds that he was still growing up and his radical ideas on his lack of practical experience. She said he didn't yet know a thing about "life," that he hadn't even entered the real world—when already he was as disenchanted with it as a man of fifty.

The further irony of all this was that in spite of her, he had turned out so well. In spite of going to only a third-rate college, he had, on his own initiative, come out with a first-rate education; in spite of growing up dominated by a small mind, he had ended up with a large one; in spite of all her foolish views, he was free of prejudice and unafraid to face facts. Most miraculous of all, instead of being blinded by love for her as she was for him, he had cut himself emotionally free of her and could see her with complete objectivity. He was not dominated by his mother.

The bus stopped with a sudden jerk and shook him from his meditation. A woman from the back lurched forward with little steps and barely escaped falling in his newspaper as she righted herself. She got off and a large Negro got on. Julian kept his paper lowered to watch. It gave him a certain satisfaction to see injustice in daily operation. It confirmed his view that with a few exceptions there was no one worth knowing within a radius of three hundred miles. The Negro was well dressed and carried a briefcase. He looked around and then sat down on the other end of the seat where the woman with the red and white canvas sandals was sitting. He immediately unfolded a newspaper and obscured himself behind it. Julian's mother's elbow at once prodded insistently into his ribs. "Now you see why I won't ride on these buses by myself," she whispered.

The woman with the red and white canvas sandals had risen at the same time the Negro sat down and had gone further back in the bus and taken the seat of the woman who had got off. His mother leaned forward and cast her an approving look.

Julian rose, crossed the aisle, and sat down in the place of the woman with the canvas sandals. From this position, he looked serenely across at his mother. Her face had turned an angry red. He stared at her, making his eyes the eyes of a stranger. He felt his tension suddenly lift as if he had openly declared war on her.

60

65

He would have liked to get in conversation with the Negro and to talk with him about art or politics or any subject that would be above the comprehension of those around them, but the man remained entrenched behind his paper. He was either ignoring the change of seating or had never noticed it. There was no way for Julian to convey his sympathy.

His mother kept her eyes fixed reproachfully on his face. The woman with the protruding teeth was looking at him avidly as if he were a type of monster new to her.

"Do you have a light?" he asked the Negro.

Without looking away from his paper, the man reached in his pocket and handed him a packet of matches.

"Thanks," Julian said. For a moment he held the matches foolishly. A NO SMOKING sign looked down upon him from over the door. This alone would not have deterred him; he had no cigarettes. He had quit smoking some months before because he could not afford it. "Sorry," he muttered and handed back the matches. The Negro lowered the paper and gave him an annoyed look. He took the matches and raised the paper again.

70

His mother continued to gaze at him but she did not take advantage of his momentary discomfort. Her eyes retained their battered look. Her face seemed to be unnaturally red, as if her blood pressure had risen. Julian allowed no glimmer of sympathy to show on his face. Having got the advantage, he wanted desperately to keep it and carry it through. He would have liked to teach her a lesson that would last her a while, but there seemed no way to continue the point. The Negro refused to come out from behind his paper.

Julian folded his arms and looked stolidly before him, facing her but as if he did not see her, as if he had ceased to recognize her existence. He visualized a scene in which, the bus having reached their stop, he would remain in his seat and when she said, "Aren't you going to get off?" he would look at her as at a stranger who had rashly addressed him. The corner they got off on was usually deserted, but it was well lighted and it would not hurt her to walk by herself the four blocks to the Y. He decided to wait until the time came and then decide whether or not he would let her get off by herself. He would have to be at the Y at ten to bring her back, but he could leave her wondering if he was going to show up. There was no reason for her to think she could always depend on him.

He retired again into the high-ceilinged room sparsely settled with large pieces of antique furniture. His soul expanded momentarily but then he became aware of his mother across from him and the vision shriveled. He studied her coldly. Her feet in little pumps dangled like a child's and did not quite reach the floor. She was training on him an exaggerated look of reproach. He felt completely detached from her. At that moment he could with pleasure have slapped her as he would have slapped a particularly obnoxious child in his charge.

He began to imagine various unlikely ways by which he could teach her a lesson. He might make friends with some distinguished Negro professor or lawyer and bring him home to spend the evening. He would be entirely justified but her blood pressure would rise to 300. He could not push her to the extent of making her have a stroke, and moreover, he had never been successful at making any Negro friends. He had tried to strike up an acquaintance on the bus with some of the better types, with ones that looked like professors or ministers or lawyers. One morning he had sat down next to a distinguished-looking dark brown man who had answered his

Point of View

questions with a sonorous solemnity but who had turned out to be an undertaker. Another day he had sat down beside a cigar-smoking Negro with a diamond ring on his finger, but after a few stilted pleasantries, the Negro had rung the buzzer and risen, slipping two lottery tickets into Julian's hand as he climbed over him to leave.

He imagined his mother lying desperately ill and his being able to secure only a Negro doctor for her. He toyed with that idea for a few minutes and then dropped it for a momentary vision of himself participating as a sympathizer in a sit-in demonstration. This was possible but he did not linger with it. Instead, he approached the ultimate horror. He brought home a beautiful suspiciously Negroid woman. Prepare yourself, he said. There is nothing you can do about it. This is the woman I've chosen. She's intelligent, dignified, even good, and she's suffered and she hasn't thought it *fun*. Now persecute us, go ahead and persecute us. Drive her out of here, but remember, you're driving me too. His eyes were narrowed and through the indignation he had generated, he saw his mother across the aisle, purple-faced, shrunken to the dwarf-like proportions of her moral nature, sitting like a mummy beneath the ridiculous banner of her hat.

75

He was tilted out of his fantasy again as the bus stopped. The door opened with a sucking hiss and out of the dark a large, gaily dressed, sullen-looking colored woman got on with a little boy. The child, who might have been four, had on a short plaid suit and a Tyrolean hat with a blue feather in it. Julian hoped that he would sit down beside him and that the woman would push in beside his mother. He could think of no better arrangement.

As she waited for her tokens, the woman was surveying the seating possibilities—he hoped with the idea of sitting where she was least wanted. There was something familiar-looking about her but Julian could not place what it was. She was a giant of a woman. Her face was set not only to meet opposition but to seek it out. The downward tilt of her large lower lip was like a warning sign: DON'T TAMPER WITH ME. Her bulging figure was encased in a green crepe dress and her feet overflowed in red shoes. She had on a hideous hat. A purple velvet flap came down on one side of it and stood up on the other; the rest of it was green and looked like a cushion with the stuffing out. She carried a mammoth red pocketbook that bulged throughout as if it were stuffed with rocks.

To Julian's disappointment, the little boy climbed up on the empty seat beside his mother. His mother lumped all children, black and white, into the common category, "cute," and she thought little Negroes were on the whole cuter than little white children. She smiled at the little boy as he climbed on the seat.

Meanwhile the woman was bearing down upon the empty seat beside Julian. To his annoyance, she squeezed herself into it. He saw his mother's face change as the woman settled herself next to him and he realized with satisfaction that this was more objectionable to her than it was to him. Her face seemed almost gray and there was a look of dull recognition in her eyes, as if suddenly she had sickened at some awful confrontation. Julian saw that it was because she and the woman had, in a sense, swapped sons. Though his mother would not realize the symbolic significance of this, she would feel it. His amusement showed plainly on his face.

The woman next to him muttered something unintelligible to herself. He was conscious of a kind of bristling next to him, a muted growling like that of an angry cat. He could not see anything but the red pocketbook upright on the bulging green thighs. He visualized the woman as she had stood waiting for her tokens—the ponderous figure, rising from the red shoes upward over the solid hips, the mammoth bosom, the haughty face, to the green and purple hat.

His eyes widened.

The vision of the two hats, identical, broke upon him with the radiance of a brilliant sunrise. His face was suddenly lit with joy. He could not believe that Fate had thrust upon his mother such a lesson. He gave a loud chuckle so that she would look at him and see that he saw. She turned her eyes on him slowly. The blue in them seemed to have turned a bruised purple. For a moment he had an uncomfortable sense of her innocence, but it lasted only a second before principle rescued him. Justice entitled him to laugh. His grin hardened until it said to her as plainly as if he were saying aloud: Your punishment exactly fits your pettiness. This should teach you a permanent lesson.

Her eyes shifted to the woman. She seemed unable to bear looking at him and to find the woman preferable. He became conscious again of the bristling presence at his side. The woman was rumbling like a volcano about to become active. His mother's mouth began to twitch slightly at one corner. With a sinking heart, he saw incipient signs of recovery on her face and realized that this was going to strike her suddenly as funny and was going to be no lesson at all. She kept her eyes on the woman and an amused smile came over her face as if the woman were a monkey that had stolen her hat. The little Negro was looking up at her with large fascinated eyes. He had been trying to attract her attention for some time.

"Carver!" the woman said suddenly. "Come heah!"

When he saw that the spotlight was on him at last, Carver drew his feet up and turned himself toward Julian's mother and giggled.

"Carver!" the woman said. "You heah me? Come heah!"

Carver slid down from the seat but remained squatting with his back against the base of it, his head turned slyly around toward Julian's mother, who was smiling at him. The woman reached a hand across the aisle and snatched him to her. He righted himself and hung backwards on her knees, grinning at Julian's mother. "Isn't he cute?" Julian's mother said to the woman with the protruding teeth.

"I reckon he is," the woman said without conviction.

The Negress yanked him upright but he eased out of her grip and shot across the aisle and scrambled, giggling wildly, onto the seat beside his love.

"I think he likes me," Julian's mother said, and smiled at the woman. It was the smile she used when she was being particularly gracious to an inferior. Julian saw everything lost. The lesson had rolled off her like rain on a roof.

The woman stood up and yanked the little boy off the seat as if she were snatching him from contagion. Julian could feel the rage in her at having no weapon like his mother's smile. She gave the child a sharp slap across his leg. He howled once and then thrust his head into her stomach and kicked his feet against her shins. "Behave," she said vehemently.

The bus stopped and the Negro who had been reading the newspaper got off. The woman moved over and set the little boy down with a thump between herself and Julian. She held him firmly by the knee. In a moment he put his hands in front of his face and peeped at Julian's mother through his fingers.

"I see yoooooooo!" she said and put her hand in front of her face and peeped at him.

The woman slapped his hand down. "Quit yo' foolishness," she said, "before I knock the living Jesus out of you!"

Julian was thankful that the next stop was theirs. He reached up and pulled the cord. The woman reached up and pulled it at the same time. Oh my God, he thought. He had the terrible intuition that when they got off the bus together, his mother would open her purse and give the little boy a nickel. The gesture would be as natural to her as breathing. The bus stopped and the woman got up and lunged to the front, dragging the child, who wished to stay on, after her. Julian and his mother got up and followed. As they neared the door, Julian tried to relieve her of her pocketbook.

"No," she murmured, "I want to give the little boy a nickel."

"No!" Julian hissed. "No!"

She smiled down at the child and opened her bag. The bus door opened and the woman picked him up by the arm and descended with him, hanging at her hip. Once in the street she set him down and shook him.

Julian's mother had to close her purse while she got down the bus step but as soon as her feet were on the ground, she opened it again and began to rummage inside. "I can't find but a penny," she whispered, "but it looks like a new one."

"Don't do it!" Julian said fiercely between his teeth. There was a streetlight on the corner and she hurried to get under it so that she could better see into her pocketbook. The woman was heading off rapidly down the street with the child still hanging backward on her hand.

"Oh little boy!" Julian's mother called and took a few quick steps and caught up with them just beyond the lamppost. "Here's a bright new penny for you," and she held out the coin, which shone bronze in the dim light.

The huge woman turned and for a moment stood, her shoulders lifted and her face frozen with frustrated rage, and stared at Julian's mother. Then all at once she seemed to explode like a piece of machinery that had been given one ounce of pressure too much. Julian saw the black fist swing out with the red pocketbook. He shut his eyes and cringed as he heard the woman shout, "He don't take nobody's pennies!" When he opened his eyes, the woman was disappearing down the street with the little boy staring wide-eyed over her shoulder. Julian's mother was sitting on the sidewalk.

"I told you not to do that," Julian said angrily. "I told you not to do that!"

He stood over her for a minute, gritting his teeth. Her legs were stretched out in front of her and her hat was on her lap. He squatted down and looked her in the face. It was totally expressionless. "You got exactly what you deserved," he said. "Now get up."

He picked up her pocketbook and put what had fallen out back in it. He picked the hat up off her lap. The penny caught his eye on the sidewalk and he picked that up and let it drop before her eyes into the purse. Then he stood up and leaned over and held his hands out to pull her up. She remained immobile. He sighed. Rising above them on either side were black apartment buildings, marked with irregular rectangles of light. At the end of the block a man came out of a door and walked off in the opposite direction. "All right," he said, "suppose somebody happens by and wants to know why you're sitting on the sidewalk?"

She took the hand and, breathing hard, pulled heavily up on it and then stood for a moment, swaying slightly as if the spots of light in the darkness were circling around her. Her eyes, shadowed and confused, finally settled on his face. He did not try to conceal his irritation. "I hope this teaches you a lesson," he said. She leaned forward and her eyes raked his face. She seemed trying to determine his identity. Then, as if she found nothing familiar about him, she started off with a headlong movement in the wrong direction.

"Aren't you going on to the Y?" he asked.

"Home," she muttered.

"Well, are we walking?"

For answer she kept going. Julian followed along, his hands behind him. He saw no reason to let the lesson she had had go without backing it up with an explanation of its meaning. She might as well be made to understand what had happened to her. "Don't think that was just an uppity Negro woman," he said. "That was the whole colored race which will no longer take your condescending pennies. That was your black double. She can wear the same hat as you, and to be sure," he added gratuitously (because he thought it was funny), "it looked better on her than it did on you. What all this means," he said, "is that the old world is gone. The old manners are obsolete and your graciousness is not worth a damn." He thought bitterly of the house that had been lost for him. "You aren't who you think you are," he said.   110

She continued to plow ahead, paying no attention to him. Her hair had come undone on one side. She dropped her pocketbook and took no notice. He stooped and picked it up and handed it to her but she did not take it.

"You needn't act as if the world had come to an end," he said, "because it hasn't. From now on you've got to live in a new world and face a few realities for a change. Buck up," he said, "it won't kill you."

She was breathing fast.

"Let's wait on the bus," he said.

"Home," she said thickly.   115

"I hate to see you behave like this," he said. "Just like a child. I should be able to expect more of you." He decided to stop where he was and make her stop and wait for a bus. "I'm not going any farther," he said, stopping. "We're going on the bus."

She continued to go on as if she had not heard him. He took a few steps and caught her arm and stopped her. He looked into her face and caught his breath. He was looking into a face he had never seen before. "Tell Grandpa to come get me," she said.

He stared, stricken.

"Tell Caroline to come get me," she said.

Stunned, he let her go and she lurched forward again, walking as if one leg were shorter than the other. A tide of darkness seemed to be sweeping her from him. "Mother!" he cried. "Darling, sweetheart, wait!" Crumpling, she fell to the pavement. He dashed forward and fell at her side, crying, "Mamma, Mamma!" He turned her over. Her face was fiercely distorted. One eye, large and staring, moved slightly to the left as if it had become unmoored. The other remained fixed on him, raked his face again, found nothing and closed.   120

"Wait here, wait here!" he cried and jumped up and began to run for help toward a cluster of lights he saw in the distance ahead of him. "Help, help!" he shouted, but his voice was thin, scarcely a thread of sound. The lights drifted farther away the faster he ran and his feet moved numbly as if they carried him nowhere.

The tide of darkness seemed to sweep him back to her, postponing from moment to moment his entry into the world of guilt and sorrow.

QUESTIONS

1. Though O'Connor writes her story in the third person, how does she establish that the point of view belongs to Julian?
2. How does the author depict relations between mother and son? Where do your sympathies as a reader lie, and to what extent is this attributed to point of view?
3. Give examples showing how O'Connor intensifies our sense of Julian's feelings through his observations of external details.
4. What do you perceive to be the limitations of Julian's character? How much do you trust his perceptions of his mother? Explain.
5. What brings about Julian's awakening? How has O'Connor manipulated point of view to intensify our sense of the shock he feels at his mother's collapse?
6. Compare "Everything That Rises Must Converge" to Frank O'Connor's "My Oedipus Complex." Explain how each story depends on the distorted perceptions of its main character and how these perceptions are controlled by point of view.

8 Tone

The *tone* of a work of fiction might be defined as *how* the *what* gets told. What are the properties of the voice and telling style of the author or the author's chosen narrator? Is the story told in a neutral, straightforward manner or humorously? Is the narrator calm and reflective or anxious or excited? Is the address colloquial—that is, casual and true to actual conversational speech—or formal? What does the diction, or word-choice, tell us? We answer these kinds of questions automatically as we read, and they shape our response significantly.

Tone is directly related to point of view. How the story is told depends on who is telling it and has everything to do with the narrator's relation to the events. Different points of view allow for very different tonal possibilities.

VARIETIES OF TONE AND VIEWPOINT

Third-person narration, for instance, automatically presumes a certain degree of objectivity. It is the camera lens that we are supposed to forget about. We rarely find third-person narration that is not neutral and straightforward. Indeed, any deviation away from matter-of-factness tends to call attention to the teller, and this tends to undermine the effectiveness of the third-person vantage. At times, of course, such undermining is part of the author's purpose. Writers of what is sometimes called "metafiction" make it part of their program to remind the reader that a given story is construction. Like those filmmakers who pull the camera back to reveal the set and the hanging microphones, they try to break the illusion, and one of their favorite techniques is to violate the natural neutrality of the third person. Most fiction writers, however, stay with the traditional repertoire of techniques.

The opening of Sarah Orne Jewett's "A White Heron" (Chapter 5) is an excellent example of the tone we have come to expect when we read a story written in the third person:

> The woods were already filled with shadows one June evening, just before eight o'clock, though a bright sunset still glimmered faintly among the trunks of the trees. A little girl was driving home her cow, a plodding, dilatory, provoking creature in her behavior, but a valued companion for all that. They were going away from the western light, and striking deep into the dark woods, but their feet were familiar with the path, and it was no matter whether their eyes could see it or not.

The narrative voice is calm and detached; there is nothing in the tone to call attention to the state of the narrator. Quite the reverse: the presentation is such that we forget about the narrator altogether and focus on the setting in front of us.

For comparison's sake, take a look at the first few sentences of D. H. Lawrence's "Odour of Chrysanthemums" (Chapter 13):

> The small locomotive engine, Number 4, came clanking, stumbling down from Selston with seven full wagons. It appeared round the corner with loud threats of speed, but the colt that it startled from among the gorse, which still flickered indistinctly in the raw afternoon, out-distanced it at a canter. A woman, walking up the railway line to Underwood, drew back into the hedge, held her basket aside, and watched the footplate of the engine advancing.

The subjects of Jewett's and Lawrence's stories are as different as can be, but the similarities in the narrative tone are great—so great that we can perceive no difference between the unseen narrators. They are quite simply lenses, objective and all-seeing eyes of witness.

When a story is told in the first person, however, the speaker's personality and involvement have everything to do with how we as readers perceive the situation. We might go so far as to say that once a writer has decided to tell a story in the first person, the next most important decision is to settle on the attitude of the teller to the tale. This, in turn, determines the story's tone.

In "My Oedipus Complex" (Chapter 7), the point of view (that of a young boy telling about his own life) and the tone (absolute sincerity coupled with self-importance) were instrumental in creating the ironic and often humorous effects. The reader kept having to weigh the boy's earnest conviction against his or her more mature—and more cynical—view of the world. Interestingly, Naguib Mahfouz's story "The Conjurer Made Off with the Dish" (Chapter 3), which is also narrated by a young boy, elicits a very different reaction from the reader. Mahfouz controls his tone and point of view in such a way that we are not constantly measuring the boy's statements against our adult understanding of things. Though we may laugh at some of his misadventures, we feel the poignance of his coming of age sharply at the story's end. Our vastly divergent responses to the experiences of the two boys have everything to do with the tone with which they tell their stories.

As we saw in the discussion of Frank O'Connor's story (see Chapter 7), one of the main tonal options of the first person is *irony*. The narrator can tell the story in such a way that the reader finds another meaning behind the literal sense of the words. In "My Oedipus Complex" that second meaning derives from the adult understandings that we bring to the boy's words. The irony is intended by the author but not by the narrator. But we can imagine instances in which the irony is intended by the narrator as well. Deliberate understatement is probably the most common use of tonal irony. We find it, for example, in Mark Twain's "The Notorious Jumping Frog of Calaveras County," which follows shortly. The narrator has just listened to an involved yarn spun by one Simon Wheeler. He is at the point of escaping when Wheeler proposes to tell him more. Says the narrator, using decorum to mask his impatience, "I did not think that a continuation of the history of the enterprising vagabond *Jim* Smiley would be likely to afford me much information concerning the Rev. *Leonidas* W. Smiley and so I started away." He is being sublimely ironic.

With first-person narratives, then, the relation between the teller and the tale, which is expressed through the tone, is all-important. And while in many cases the writer will try to exploit some possibility of tension—having the tone be at odds with the subject, using an unreliable narrator, and so on—this is not always the case. In some instances, the first-person narrator adopts a neutral tone, and the reader is asked to regard the events at face value. This happens most commonly when the narrator is telling a story that took place a long time ago. The assumption is that the teller has made peace with the emotions and is now in a position to give a clear account of what took place. Olive Schreiner's story "The Woman's Rose" (Chapter 9) is a case in point. The rose that gives the story its title has been locked away in a box of mementos. As the woman explains its meaning, the circumstances of its being there, she must gaze deep into the past. Like the dried and pressed flower, the events of years past are embalmed; they have lost their power, except insofar as they move her to remember.

TONE AND DICTION

The key to assessing tone, especially in first-person narratives, is diction. We take our cues from the style of the teller, looking not only at word choice and attitude—the two are obviously closely related—but also at the level of the diction. From this we learn a good deal about how the narrator sees himself, and also how he wants to be seen. In "The Notorious Jumping Frog of Calaveras County," Mark Twain makes wonderful play with the possibilities of tone. He encloses one yarn within another and lets two very different levels of diction collide on the page. In most stories, however, the tone and diction are set right away and remain within the given limits. Our involvement as readers depends upon our accepting the character and the style of narration.

Here are several opening passages, chosen to give some indication of the gamut of tonal possibilities open to the first-person narrative. The first is from Raymond Carver's "Intimacy":

> I have some business out west anyway, so I stop off in this little town where my former wife lives. We haven't seen each other in four years. But from time to time, when something of mine appeared, or was written about me in the magazines or papers—a profile or an interview—I sent her these things. I don't know what I had in mind except I thought she might be interested. In any case, she never responded.

The diction tells us right away who the narrator is and how to begin reading the story. It is the voice of the common man telling of his life in a matter-of-fact and casual tone. We are alerted to this in the very first sentence by three specific usages: "anyway," "so," and "this." All three are indicators of colloquial speech and would not be found in more formal utterance. Even before we've begun to hear about what happened to Carver's narrator, we have begun to make certain assumptions.

Compare the casual diction of Carver's narrator with the highly formalized idiom of Henry James's narrator in his short story "Brooksmith," which begins as follows:

We are scattered now, the friends of the late Mr. Oliver Offord; but whenever we chance to meet I think we are conscious of a certain esoteric respect for each other. "Yes, you too have been in Arcadia," we seem not too grumpily to allow. When I pass the house in Mansfield Street I remember that Arcadia was there. I don't know who has it now, and I don't want to know; it's enough to be sure that if I should ring the bell there would be no such luck for me as that Brooksmith should open the door.

We are greeted immediately by hints of the class and attitude of the narrator. The tone is careful, measured, in every way civilized. The word choice and the elaborate syntax suggest the usages of the British upper class. The phrasing of "we seem not too grumpily to allow" speaks volumes; it carries indirect pronouncement almost to the point of parody. We can be sure that the speaker in this story will never slap us on the back and say, "Listen, pal—." One could argue, of course, that James published "Brooksmith" in 1891, nearly a century before Carver wrote his story, and that usages and styles change. But even allowing for the historical difference, we can clearly determine that these are two very different individuals, who would tell their stories in very different ways no matter what period they were writing in.

The function of tone and diction is starkly revealed in Twain's "The Jumping Frog of Calaveras County," a story that not only delights in using different levels of diction, but also manages to play the conventions of colloquial conversation against the conventions of the written.

Mark Twain (1835–1910)

Mark Twain, born Samuel Langhorne Clemens in Missouri, hardly needs an introduction. As author of *The Adventures of Tom Sawyer* (1876), *The Prince and the Pauper* (1882), *A Connecticut Yankee in King Arthur's Court* (1889), *The Adventures of Huckleberry Finn* (1884), and innumerable other works, he is one of the towering figures of American literature. In his day, he worked as a newspaper reporter, editor, printer, steamboat pilot, stand-up humorist, and gold prospector—jobs that all added grist to the tirelessly inventive mill of his writing. Twain, as do very few other writers, conveys the flavor of a crucial epoch in American life—the opening of the great frontier. "The Notorious Jumping Frog of Calaveras County" is one of Twain's best-loved short stories. Written in 1865, it preserves, folded up in its easy rambling humor, a glimmer of life in the American West in the days of the Gold Rush.

THE NOTORIOUS JUMPING FROG OF CALAVERAS COUNTY

In compliance with the request of a friend of mine who wrote me from the East, I called on good-natured, garrulous old Simon Wheeler and inquired after my friend's friend, Leonidas W. Smiley, as requested to do, and I hereunto append the result. I have a lurking suspicion that *Leonidas W. Smiley* is a myth, that my friend never knew such a personage, and that he only conjectured that if I asked old Wheeler about him, it would remind him of his infamous *Jim* Smiley and he would go to work and bore me to death with some exasperating reminiscence of him as long and as tedious as it should be useless to me. If that was the design, it succeeded.

I found Simon Wheeler dozing comfortably by the barroom stove of the dilapidated tavern in the decayed mining camp of Angel's, and I noticed that he was fat and bald-headed and had an expression of winning gentleness and simplicity upon his tranquil countenance. He roused up and gave me good day. I told him that a friend of mine had commissioned me to make some inquiries about a cherished companion of his boyhood named *Leonidas W. Smiley—Rev. Leonidas W. Smiley*, a young minister of the Gospel, who he had heard was at one time a resident of Angel's Camp. I added that if Mr. Wheeler could tell me anything about this Rev. Leonidas W. Smiley, I would feel under many obligations to him.

Simon Wheeler backed me into a corner and blockaded me there with his chair, and then sat down and reeled off the monotonous narrative which follows this paragraph. He never smiled, he never frowned, he never changed his voice from the gentle-flowing key to which he tuned his initial sentence, he never betrayed the slightest suspicion of enthusiasm, but all through the interminable narrative there ran a vein of impressive earnestness and sincerity which showed me plainly that, so far from his imagining that there was anything ridiculous or funny about his story, he regarded it as a really important matter and admired its two heroes as men of transcendent genius in *finesse*. I let him go on in his own way and never interrupted him once.

"Rev. Leonidas W. H'm, Reverend Le——Well, there was a feller here once by the name of *Jim* Smiley, in the winter of '49—or maybe it was the spring of '50—I don't recollect exactly, somehow, though what makes me think it was one or the other is because I remember the big flume° warn't finished when he first come to the camp; but anyway, he was the curiousest man about always betting on anything that turned up you ever see, if he could get anybody to bet on the other side, and if he couldn't he'd change sides. Any way that suited the other man would suit *him*—any way just so's he got a bet, *he* was satisfied. But still he was lucky, uncommon lucky; he most always come out winner. He was always ready and laying for a chance; there couldn't be no solit'ry thing mentioned but that feller'd offer to bet on it and take ary side you please, as I was just telling you. If there was a horse-race, you'd find him flush or you'd find him busted at the end of it; if there was a dog-

---

flume: an artificial water channel used in gold mining.

fight, he'd bet on it; if there was a cat-fight, he'd bet on it; if there was a chicken-fight, he'd bet on it; why, if there was two birds setting on a fence, he would bet you which one would fly first; or if there was a camp-meeting, he would be there reg'lar to bet on Parson Walker, which he judged to be the best exhorter about here, and so he was too, and a good man. If he even see a straddle-bug start to go any-wheres, he would bet you how long it would take him to get to—to wherever he was going to, and if you took him up, he would foller that straddle-bug to Mexico but what he would find out where he was bound for and how long he was on the road. Lots of the boys here has seen that Smiley and can tell you about him. Why, it never made no difference to *him*—he'd bet on *any* thing—the dangdest feller. Parson Walker's wife laid very sick once for a good while, and it seemed as if they warn't going to save her; but one morning he come in and Smiley up and asked him how she was, and he said she was considerable better—thank the Lord for his in-f'nite mercy—and coming on so smart that with the blessing of Prov'dence she'd get well yet; and Smiley, before he thought, says, 'Well, I'll resk two-and-a-half she don't anyway.'

"Thish-yer Smiley had a mare—the boys called her the fifteen-minute nag but that was only in fun, you know, because of course she was faster than that—and he used to win money on that horse, for all she was so slow and always had the asthma, or the distemper, or the consumption, or something of that kind. They used to give her two or three hundred yards' start and then pass her under way, but always at the fag end of the race she'd get excited and desperate like, and come cavorting and straddling up and scattering her legs around limber, sometimes in the air and some-times out to one side among the fences, and kicking up m-o-r-e dust and raising m-o-r-e racket with her coughing and sneezing and blowing her nose—and *always* fetch up at the stand just about a neck ahead, as near as you could cipher it down.   5

"And he had a little small bull-pup, that to look at him you'd think he warn't worth a cent but to set around and look ornery and lay for a chance to steal some-thing. But as soon as money was up on him he was a different dog; his under-jaw'd begin to stick out like the fo'castle of a steamboat and his teeth would uncover and shine like the furnaces. And a dog might tackle him and bully-rag him, and bite him and throw him over his shoulder two or three times, and Andrew Jack-son—which was the name of the pup—Andrew Jackson would never let on but what *he* was satisfied and hadn't expected nothing else—and the bets being dou-bled and doubled on the other side all the time, till the money was all up; and then all of a sudden he would grab that other dog jest by the j'int of his hind leg and freeze to it—not chaw, you understand, but only just grip and hang on till they throwed up the sponge, if it was a year. Smiley always come out winner on that pup till he harnessed a dog once that didn't have no hind legs, because they'd been sawed off in a circular saw, and when the thing had gone along far enough and the money was all up and he come to make a snatch for his pet holt, he see in a minute how he'd been imposed on and how the other dog had him in the door, so to speak, and he 'peared surprised, and then he looked sorter discouraged-like and didn't try no more to win the fight, and so he got shucked out bad. He give Smiley a look, as much as to say his heart was broke, and it was *his* fault for putting up a dog that hadn't no hind legs for him to take holt of, which was his main dependence in a fight, and then he limped off a piece and laid down and died. It was a good pup, was that Andrew Jackson, and would have made a name for hisself if he'd lived, for the stuff was in him and he had genius—I know it, because he hadn't no opportunities to speak of, and it don't stand to reason that a dog could make such a fight as he could under them circumstances if he hadn't no talent. It always makes me feel sorry when I think of that last fight of his'n and the way it turned out.

"Well, thish-yer Smiley had rat-tarriers, and chicken cocks, and tomcats and all them kind of things till you couldn't rest, and you couldn't fetch nothing for him to bet on but he'd match you. He ketched a frog one day and took him home, and said he cal'lated to educate him; and so he never done nothing for three months but set in his back yard and learn that frog to jump. And you bet you he *did* learn him, too. He'd give him a little punch behind, and the next minute you'd see that frog whirling in the air like a doughnut—see him turn one summerset, or maybe a couple if he got a good start, and come down flat-footed and all right, like a cat. He got him up so in the matter of ketching flies, and kep' him in practice so constant, that he'd nail a fly every time as fur as he could see him. Smiley said all a frog wanted was education and he could do 'most anything—and I believe him. Why, I've seen him set Dan'l Webster° down here on this floor—Dan'l Webster was the name of the frog—and sing out, 'Flies, Dan'l, flies!' and quicker'n you could wink he'd spring straight up and snake a fly off'n the counter there, and flop down on the floor ag'in as solid as a gob of mud, and fall to scratching the side of his head with his hind foot as indifferent as if he hadn't no idea he'd been doin' any more'n any frog might do. You never see a frog so modest and straight-for'ard as he was, for all he was so gifted. And when it come to fair and square jumping on a dead level, he could get over more ground at one straddle than any animal of his breed you ever see. Jumping on a dead level was his strong suit, you understand; and when it come to that, Smiley would ante up money on him as long as he had a red. Smiley was monstrous proud of his frog, and well he might be for fellers that had traveled and been everywheres all said he laid over any frog that ever *they* see.

"Well, Smiley kep' the beast in a little lattice box, and he used to fetch him down-town sometimes and lay for a bet. One day a feller—a stranger in the camp, he was—come acrost him with his box and says:

"'What might it be that you've got in the box?'

"And Smiley says, sorter indifferent-like, 'It might be a parrot, or it might be a canary, maybe, but it ain't—it's only just a frog.'

"And the feller took it and looked at it careful, and turned it round this way and that, and says, 'H'm—so 'tis. Well, what's *he* good for?'

"'Well,' Smiley says, easy and careless, 'he's good enough for *one* thing, I should judge—he can outjump any frog in Calaveras County.'

"The feller took the box again and took another long, particular look, and give it back to Smiley and says, very deliberate, 'Well,' he says, 'I don't see no p'ints about that frog that's any better'n any other frog.'

"'Maybe you don't,' Smiley says. 'Maybe you understand frogs and maybe you don't understand 'em; maybe you've had experience and maybe you ain't only a amature, as it were. Anyways, I've got *my* opinion, and I'll resk forty dollars that he can outjump any frog in Calaveras County.'

"And the feller studied a minute and then says, kinder sad-like, 'Well, I'm only a stranger here and I ain't got no frog; but if I had a frog, I'd bet you.'

10

15

Dan'l Webster: Daniel Webster (1782–1852) was a famed congressman and a thundering orator.

"And then Smiley says, 'That's all right—that's all right—if you'll hold my box a minute, I'll go and get you a frog.' And so the feller took the box and put up his forty dollars along with Smiley's, and set down to wait.

"So he set there a good while thinking and thinking to himself, and then he got the frog out and prized his mouth open and took a teaspoon and filled him full of quail-shot—filled him pretty near up to his chin—and set him on the floor. Smiley he went to the swamp and slopped around in the mud for a long time, and finally he ketched a frog and fetched him in and give him to this feller, and says:

"'Now, if you're ready, set him alongside of Dan'l, with his forepaws just even with Dan'l's, and I'll give the word.' Then he says, 'One—two—three—git!' and him and the feller touched up the frogs from behind, and the new frog hopped off lively, but Dan'l give a heave and hysted up his shoulders—so—like a Frenchman, but it warn't no use—he couldn't budge; he was planted as solid as a church, and he couldn't no more stir than if he was anchored out. Smiley was a good deal surprised, and he was disgusted too, but he didn't have no idea what the matter was, of course.

"The feller took the money and started away, and when he was going out at the door, he sorter jerked his thumb over his shoulder—so—at Dan'l and says again, very deliberate, 'Well,' he says, 'I don't see no p'ints about that frog that's any better'n any other frog.'

"Smiley he stood scratching his head and looking down at Dan'l a long time, and at last he says, 'I do wonder what in the nation that frog throw'd off for—I wonder if there ain't something the matter with him—he 'pears to look mighty baggy, somehow.' And he ketched Dan'l by the nap of the neck and hefted him, and says, 'Why, blame my cats if he don't weigh five pound!' and turned him upside down and he belched out a double handful of shot. And then he see how it was, and he was the maddest man—he set the frog down and took out after that feller, but he never ketched him. And—" 20

[Here Simon Wheeler heard his name called from the front yard and got up to see what was wanted.] And turning to me as he moved away, he said: "Just set where you are, stranger, and rest easy—I ain't going to be gone a second."

But, by your leave, I did not think that a continuation of the history of the enterprising vagabond *Jim* Smiley would be likely to afford me much information concerning the Rev. *Leonidas W.* Smiley and so I started away.

At the door I met the sociable Wheeler returning, and he buttonholed me and recommenced:

"Well, this-yer Smiley had a yaller one-eyed cow that didn't have no tail, only just a short stump like a bannanner, and—"

However, lacking both time and inclination, I did not wait to hear about the afflicted cow but took my leave. 25

As you read the following discussion, consider these questions:

1. Picking out specific phrases from the opening paragraphs, characterize the personality and attitude of the narrator.

2. How does the narrator regard Simon Wheeler? What does the narrator prepare the reader to expect from Wheeler?

3. In what way does Wheeler's speech differ from the narrator's? Find three examples of colorful regional figures of speech.

4. How does Wheeler use dialogue to characterize Smiley and the stranger? How does their speech differ from his own?

5. How does Twain use different speech idioms—a clash of tones—to generate humor? Find several examples of humor and try to explain what makes each instance funny.

6. What is your attitude toward the narrator when he returns to finish the story? If a popularity contest were held, who would win—the narrator or Wheeler?

Discussion. Our first response after reading "The Notorious Jumping Frog of Calaveras County" is likely to be that this is no story at all—or, rather, that if it is, it is a shaggy dog story of the sort that people tell during sleepless nights at summer camp. There seems to be no real point. And indeed, given Twain's own penchant for pulling his readers' legs, that *is* the point. We read on because we believe that something extraordinary will happen. Simon Wheeler sets up his tale as though it will come to a climax, and when it does not, we may feel cheated. But it is also possible that we accept the tall tale on its own terms, overlooking its inconclusiveness and taking pleasure in the telling itself.

Twain's strategy is simple enough. He encloses the lively conversational meanderings of Simon Wheeler within the far more formal narration of the first-person narrator. The juxtaposition of two very different tones has the effect of calling greater attention to Simon Wheeler's salty colloquial speaking style. Our first impulse, given the narrator's description of a fat old bald-headed man dozing by a stove in a tavern, is to find him a figure of fun and to regard his monologue skeptically, much as we imagine the narrator regards it. But Twain draws us in. We start paying attention to Wheeler's offbeat anecdotes, and by the time he is interrupted, we may feel that he is a far more interesting character than the somewhat stodgy narrator.

The story begins on an off-putting note. The narrator adopts a stiff and humorless tone—a tone more suited to legal briefs than to storytelling. The diction is of the kind we associate with wills and deeds: "In compliance with the request of a friend of mine . . ." and "I hereunto append the result." And while the narrator expresses the fear that Simon Wheeler will bore him to death with his tales, we may have the same reaction to his own formal recitation.

The narrator's attitude to the story he is about to transcribe is likewise not calculated to win the reader. After he confesses his skepticism about the truth of the story—his own suspicion is that "*Leonidas W.* Smiley is a myth"—he openly states that Wheeler's reminiscence was not only "long" and "tedious," but "useless." This is hardly an enticing advertisement for the reader who wants either amusement or enlightenment. But Twain, who was well-known for his skills as a storyteller, has his purpose clearly in mind. Moreover, he understands exactly how far he can play the reader; he will carry us right to the threshold of boredom before unleashing his charms.

Twain needs only three paragraphs in the narrator's voice to explain the circumstance, provide some impressions of Wheeler, and get the old man ready to talk. And again, lest we missed it the first time, he gives us advance warning, telling how Wheeler sat down and "reeled off the monotonous narrative which follows this paragraph." At this point the only thing that keeps the reader going is the hope that the narrator's judgment is wrong, and that the story will in fact be interesting.

The first few sentences of Wheeler's monologue are not promising. In manner and diction he strikes us as the very essence of the talkative old bore. He sputters and stalls, unable to get the story going: ". . . in the winter of '49—or maybe it was the spring of '50—I don't recollect exactly, somehow, though what makes me think it was one or the other . . ." We twitch impatiently. With little else to pay attention to, we very likely become aware of what are for us the odd colloquial turns of his speech—his use of words like "feller," "warn't," and "curiousest." These establish for us the image of the rural codger that will remain with us throughout.

But even though the tone itself does not change, Wheeler's delivery suddenly picks up speed. He is done with his fumbling and ready to engage his tale. The switch comes in the middle of the first long sentence, when he interrupts his own meanderings and sets himself on track: ". . . but anyway, he was the curiousest man about always betting on anything that turned up you ever see . . ." And from this point on, the chat becomes lively. Wheeler does his best to characterize Jim Smiley by giving examples of his yen for betting. The loose—one might even say slack—rhythms of his beginning tighten up: "If there was a horse-race, you'd find him flush or you'd find him busted at the end of it; if there was a dog-fight, he's bet on it; if there was a cat-fight, he'd bet on it; if there was a chicken-fight, he'd bet on it; why, if there was two birds setting on a fence, he would bet you which one would fly first. . . ." We realize that while Wheeler may be talkative, he can also be amusing. The repetitions and exaggerations help to fill in the picture: The old geezer is also a sly storyteller who knows how to pitch his wares for effect.

This quality of Wheeler's, which draws us in to his narrative, also creates in us the expectation that there will be some outrageous climax. There isn't. Jim Smiley trains a frog to jump, bets, and gets outwitted by a stranger. We wait in vain for a further payoff. And just when it seems that Wheeler might fill us in, he is called away. Twain has worked his trick. He has aroused our appetites; and having done so, he perversely abandons us to the narrator. The latter makes a few excuses and takes his leave. And as we shake our heads, we get it: It was the going, not the getting there, that mattered. We either lost ourselves in Wheeler's tale, or we didn't. If we did, it was probably because of Twain's skillful manipulation of voice and the subtle and humorous possibilities of tone.

Like "The Notorious Jumping Frog of Calaveras County," Toni Cade Bambara's "The Hammer Man" depends on the tone of the first-person narration for its particular effects. Read the story closely, paying special attention to the narrator's relation to the events described and how that relation is signaled by the tone.

Toni Cade Bambara (1939–   )

Toni Cade Bambara was born in New York City and grew up in Harlem. She discovered her passion for writing at an early age and began to publish her stories while in her early twenties. She was greatly influenced by a trip to Cuba in 1973. Writing, she discovered, was a vital form of political participation. Bambara has been active ever since on behalf of Black causes. Her stories were collected in *Gorilla, My Love* in 1972. Her 1980 novel, *The Salt Eaters,* was given the American Book Award.

THE HAMMER MAN

I was glad to hear that Manny had fallen off the roof. I had put out the tale that I was down with yellow fever, but nobody paid me no mind, least of all Dirty Red who stomped right in to announce that Manny had fallen off the roof and that I could come out of hiding now. My mother dropped what she was doing, which was the laundry, and got the whole story out of Red. "Bad enough you gots to hang around with boys," she said. "But fight with them too. And you would pick the craziest one at that."

Manny was supposed to be crazy. That was his story. To say you were bad put some people off. But to say you were crazy, well, you were officially not to be messed with. So that was his story. On the other hand, after I called him what I called him and said a few choice things about his mother, his face did go through some piercing changes. And I did kind of wonder if maybe he sure was nuts. I didn't wait to find out. I got in the wind. And then he waited for me on my stoop all day and all night, not hardly speaking to the people going in and out. And he was there all day Saturday, with his sister bringing him peanut-butter sandwiches and cream sodas. He must've gone to the bathroom right there cause every time I looked out the kitchen window, there he was. And Sunday, too. I got to thinking the boy was mad.

"You got no sense of humor, that's your trouble," I told him. He looked up, but he didn't say nothing. All at once I was real sorry about the whole thing. I should've settled for hitting off the little girls in the school yard, or waiting for Frankie to come in so we could raise some kind of hell. This way I had to play sick when my mother was around cause my father had already taken away my BB gun and hid it.

I don't know how they got Manny on the roof finally. Maybe the Wakefield kids, the ones who keep the pigeons, called him up. Manny was a sucker for sick animals and things like that. Or maybe Frankie got some nasty girls to go up on the roof with him and got Manny to join him. I don't know. Anyway, the catwalk had lost all its cement and the roof always did kind of slant downward. So Manny fell off the roof. I got over my yellow fever right quick, needless to say, and ventured outside. But by this time I had already told Miss Rose that Crazy Manny was after me. And Miss Rose, being who she was, quite naturally went over to Manny's house and said a few harsh words to his mother, who, being who she was, chased Miss Rose out into the street and they commenced to get with it, snatching bottles out of the garbage cans and breaking them on the johnny pumps and stuff like that.

Dirty Red didn't have to tell us about this. Everybody could see and hear all. I never figured the garbage cans for an arsenal, but Miss Rose came up with sticks and table legs and things, and Manny's mother had her share of scissor blades and bicycle chains. They got to rolling in the streets and all you could see was pink drawers and fat legs. It was something else. Miss Rose is nutty but Manny's mother's crazier than Manny. They were at it a couple of times during my sick spell. Everyone would congregate on the window sills or the fire escape, commenting that it was still much too cold for this kind of nonsense. But they watched anyway. And then Manny fell off the roof. And that was that. Miss Rose went back to her dream books and Manny's mother went back to her tumbled-down kitchen of dirty clothes and bundles of rags and children. [5]

My father got in on it too, cause he happened to ask Manny one night why he was sitting on the stoop like that every night. Manny told him right off that he was going to kill me first chance he got. Quite naturally this made my father a little warm, me being his only daughter and planning to become a doctor and take care of him in his old age. So he had a few words with Manny first, and then he got hold of the older brother, Bernard, who was more his size. Bernard didn't see how any of it was his business or my father's business, so my father got mad and jammed Bernard's head into the mailbox. Then my father started getting messages from Bernard's uncle about where to meet him for a showdown and all. My father didn't say a word to my mother all this time; just sat around mumbling and picking up the phone and putting it down, or grabbing my stickball bat and putting it back. He carried on like this for days till I thought I would scream if the yellow fever didn't have me so weak. And then Manny fell off the roof, and my father went back to his beer-drinking buddies.

I was in the school yard, pitching pennies with the little boys from the elementary school, when my friend Violet hits my brand new Spaudeen over the wall. She came running back to tell me that Manny was coming down the block. I peeked beyond the fence and there he was all right. He had his head all wound up like a mummy and his arm in a sling and his leg in a cast. It looked phony to me, especially that walking cane. I figured Dirty Red had told me a tale just to get me out there so Manny could stomp me, and Manny was playing it up with his costume and all till he could get me.

"What happened to him?" Violet's sisters whispered. But I was too busy trying to figure out how this act was supposed to work. Then Manny passed real close to the fence and gave me a look.

"You had enough, Hammer Head," I yelled. "Just bring your crummy self in this yard and I'll pick up where I left off." Violet was knocked out and the other kids went into a huddle. I didn't have to say anything else. And when they all pressed me later, I just said, "You know that hammer he always carries in his fatigues?" And they'd all nod waiting for the rest of a long story. "Well, I took it away from him." And I walked off nonchalantly.

Manny stayed indoors for a long time. I almost forgot about him. New kids moved into the block and I got all caught up with that. And then Miss Rose finally hit the numbers° and started ordering a whole lot of stuff through the mail and we would sit on the curb and watch these weird-looking packages being carried in, trying to figure out what simpleminded thing she had thrown her money away on when she might as well wait for the warm weather and throw a block party for all her godchildren.

After a while a center opened up and my mother said she'd increase my allowance if I went and joined because I'd have to get out of my pants and stay in skirts, on account of that's the way things were at the center. So I joined and got to thinking about everything else but old Hammer Head. It was a rough place to get along in, the center, but my mother said that I needed to be be'd with and she needed to not be with me, so I went. And that time I sneaked into the office, that's when I really got turned on. I looked into one of those not-quite-white folders and saw that I was from a deviant family in a deviant neighborhood. I showed my mother

10

---

numbers: the lucky combination in an illegal betting operation.

the word in the dictionary, but she didn't pay me no mind. It was my favorite word after that. I ran it in the ground till one day my father got the strap just to show how deviant he could get. So I gave up trying to improve my vocabulary. And I almost gave up my dungarees.

Then one night I'm walking past the Douglas Street park cause I got thrown out of the center for playing pool when I should've been sewing, even though I had already decided that this was going to be my last fling with boy things, and starting tomorrow I was going to fix my hair right and wear skirts all the time just so my mother would stop talking about her gray hairs, and Miss Rose would stop calling me by my brother's name by mistake. So I'm walking past the park and there's ole Manny on the basketball court, perfecting his lay-ups and talking with himself. Being me, I quite naturally walk right up and ask what the hell he's doing playing in the dark, and he looks up and all around like the dark had crept up on him when he wasn't looking. So I knew right away that he'd been out there for a long time with his eyes just going along with the program.

"There was two seconds to go and we were one point behind," he said, shaking his head and staring at his sneakers like they was somebody. "And I was in the clear. I'd left the man in the backcourt and there I was, smiling; you dig, cause it was in the bag. They passed the ball and I slid the ball up nice and easy cause there was nothing to worry about. And . . ." He shook his head. "I muffed the goddamn shot. Ball bounced off the rim . . ." He stared at his hands. "The game of the season. Last game." And then he ignored me altogether, though he wasn't talking to me in the first place. He went back to the lay-ups, always from the same spot with his arms crooked in the same way, over and over. I must've gotten hypnotized cause I probably stood there for at least an hour watching like a fool till I couldn't even see the damn ball, much less the basket. But I stood there anyway for no reason I know of. He never missed. But he cursed himself away. It was torture. And then a squad car pulled up and a short cop with hair like one of the Marx Brothers came out hitching up his pants. He looked real hard at me and then at Manny.

"What are you two doing?"

"He's doing a lay-up. I'm watching." I said with my smart self.   15

Then the cop just stood there and finally turned to the other one who was just getting out of the car.

"Who unlocked the gate?" the big one said.

"It's always unlocked," I said. Then we three just stood there like a bunch of penguins watching Manny go at it.

"This on the level?" the big guy asked, tilting his hat back with the thumb the way big guys do in hot weather. "Hey you," he said, walking over to Manny. "I'm talking to you." He finally grabbed the ball to get Manny's attention. But that didn't work. Manny just stood there with his arms out waiting for the pass so he could save the game. He wasn't paying no mind to the cop. So, quite naturally, when the cop slapped him upside his head it was a surprise. And when the cop started counting three to go, Manny had already recovered from the slap and was just ticking off the seconds before the buzzer sounded and all was lost.

"Gimme the ball, man." Manny's face was all tightened up and ready to pop.   20

"Did you hear what I said, black boy?"

Now, when somebody says that word like that, I gets warm. And crazy or no crazy, Manny was my brother at that moment and the cop was the enemy.

"You better give him back his ball," I said. "Manny don't take no mess from no cops. He ain't bothering nobody. He's gonna be Mister Basketball when he grows up. Just trying to get a little practice in before the softball season starts."

"Look here, sister, we'll run you in too," Harpo° said.

"I damn sure can't be your sister seeing how I'm a black girl. Boy, I sure will be glad when you run me in so I can tell everybody about that. You must think you're in the South, mister."

The big guy screwed his mouth up and let one of them hard-day sighs. "The park's closed, little girl, so why don't you and your boyfriend go on home."

That really got me. The "little girl" was bad enough but that "boyfriend" was too much. But I kept cool, mostly because Manny looked so pitiful waiting there with his hands in a time-out and there being no one to stop the clock. But I kept my cool mostly cause of that hammer in Manny's pocket and no telling how frantic things can get what with a big-mouth like me, a couple of wise cops, and a crazy boy too.

"The gates are open," I said real quiet-like, "and this here's a free country. So why don't you give him back his ball?"

The big cop did another one of those sighs, his specialty I guess, and then he bounced the ball to Manny who went right into his gliding thing clear up to the backboard, damn near like he was some kind of very beautiful bird. And then he swooshed that ball in, even if there was no net, and you couldn't really hear the swoosh. Something happened to the bones in my chest. It was something.

"Crazy kids anyhow," the one with the wig said and turned to go. But the big guy watched Manny for a while and I guess something must've snapped in his head, cause all of a sudden he was hot for taking Manny to jail or court or somewhere and started yelling at him and everything, which is a bad thing to do to Manny, I can tell you. And I'm standing there thinking that none of my teachers, from kindergarten right on up, none of them knew what they were talking about. I'll be damned if I ever knew one of them rosy-cheeked cops that smiled and helped you get to school without neither you or your little raggedy dog getting hit by a truck that had a smile on its face, too. Not that I ever believed it. I knew Dick and Jane was full of crap from the get-go, especially them cops. Like this dude, for example, pulling on Manny's clothes like that when obviously he had just done about the most beautiful thing a man can do and not be a fag. No cop could swoosh without a net.

"Look out, man," was all Manny said, but it was the way he pushed the cop that started the real yelling and threats. And I thought to myself, Oh God here I am trying to change my ways, and not talk back in school, and do like my mother wants, but just have this last fling, and now this—getting shot in the stomach and bleeding to death in Douglas Street park and poor Manny getting pistol-whipped by those bastards and whatnot. I could see it all, practically crying too. And it just wasn't no kind of thing to happen to a small child like me with my confirmation picture in the paper next to my weeping parents and schoolmates. I could feel the blood sticking to my shirt and my eyeballs slipping away, and then that confirmation picture again; and my mother and her gray hair; and Miss Rose heading for the precinct with a shotgun; and my father getting old and feeble with no one to doctor him up and all.

25

30

Harpo: one of the Marx Brothers comedy team. Harpo was known for his frizzy mop of hair and his ability as a harpist.

And I wished Manny had fallen off the damn roof and died right then and there and saved me all this aggravation of being killed with him by these cops who surely didn't come out of no fifth-grade reader. But it didn't happen. They just took the ball and Manny followed them real quiet-like right out of the park into the dark, and then into the squad car with his head dropping and his arms in a crook. And I went on home cause what the hell am I going to do on a basketball court, and it getting to be nearly midnight?

I didn't see Manny no more after he got into that squad car. But they didn't kill him after all cause Miss Rose heard he was in some kind of big house for people who lose their marbles. And then it was spring finally, and me and Violet was in this very boss fashion show at the center. And Miss Rose bought me my first corsage—yellow roses to match my shoes.

[1966]

QUESTIONS

1. Who is the narrator? How does the reader determine her age and her situation? What is her background?

2. What do you find out from her tone about her relationship with Manny? How do you interpret the first sentence, and how does that interpretation determine your reading of her story?

3. How does the narrator's tone express her attitudes toward her family, her school, and the "white" world represented by the police? Find examples that illustrate your points.

4. Does the narrator's relationship with Manny change over the course of the story? How so? Can you find corresponding changes in the tone of her narration?

5. Find several instances where the narrator's diction informs the reader of her emotions.

6. Evaluate the narrator's tone at the end of the story, and compare it with that of the opening passage. How is the reader to understand the girl's feeling about what happened to Manny? Is Bambara using deliberate understatement? If so, why?

7. How does the girl's tone express her growing allegiance to Manny during the confrontation scene? Is there any difference between the tone of what she thinks and the tone of her speech?

8. Find three instances where Bambara uses street-diction to create a believable atmosphere.

9. Would this story be significantly different if Bambara had written it in a more formal prose style? How so?

9 Symbolism

One of the many distinguishing peculiarities of our species is that we carry on a great deal of our business of living by way of signs and symbols. We talk and write (language is a sign system), we raise flags, gather in churches and synagogues to perform rituals in front of meaningful emblems, and so on. The idea that one thing can stand for or suggest another is almost second nature to us.

Much of our traffic is with *conventional symbols*: the cross as a symbol of crucifixion and therefore of salvation; a raised fist as a symbol of solidarity; spring as a symbol for new beginnings. . . . Our participation in society is, to some degree, dependent on our willingness to recognize and use these tokens of shared meaning. We usually do this so automatically that we are not even aware of participating in acts of symbolic behavior. A short definition may be useful.

A symbol is any object, action, person, place, or idea that carries additional—and recognizable—meaning for one or more people. The conventional symbols described above have meanings that are understood by large numbers of people. But we can also set up private symbols. Indeed, we do so constantly. A particular bench in the park becomes a symbol because it was the site of our first kiss; we save a ticket stub from a special evening until it becomes a personal memento.

SYMBOLS IN LITERATURE AND FICTION

Literary symbols work in a similar way. That is, they may be conventional, with the author making use of a traditional emblem—a character cast as a Christ-figure, a flying bird signifying freedom. Or they may be private, intrinsic to the work, and revealing their symbolic character only gradually through repetition or strategic placement. Determining symbols of the latter kind is, as we shall see, a matter of interpretation; the reader has to do some guesswork.

Because symbols are so various and so universally used, they are hard to discuss in cut-and-dried terms. Many readers believe, mistakenly, that they are planted in a work like radishes and that one simply finds them and plucks them free. This may be true on rare occasions, but usually it is not. Usually a symbol functions as a kind of force field, sending out waves of suggestion that penetrate many layers of the work and add to its meaning. They are not to be extracted so much as probed and questioned.

Symbols carry powerful condensed meanings—that is their function. Though they are often concrete emblems—a watch, a rose, a knife—they do not generally reduce to a simple abstract concept. A gun may symbolize destruction and violence, but it is also associated, at least in Freudian psychology, with sexual potency. Symbols tend to point outward; they do not so much mean as suggest.

But even in cases where a symbol may seem fairly obvious, we need to be careful. That is, a gun may sometimes stand for destruction or sexual potency, but not always. There are times—in a crime novel or a war story, say—when a gun is just itself, when it symbolizes nothing. The larger relevance—the symbolism—requires an appropriate context. We need some reason for thinking that the author intended A to represent B.

The question of the author's intention is important in the study of literature, and it raises vital issues. For instance, how do we ever know whether an author intended the reader to find a certain meaning or suggestion? Are we to see the fact that a character lost her wedding ring as symbolic of the impending ruin of the marriage, or is it just one of life's unfortunate mishaps? Unless the author has gone on record explaining his or her intentions, there is no reliable answer. Indeed, some would argue that even the author's testimony will not clinch the matter—that authors are often as much in the dark about why they write something as any reader.

But this view seems extreme, proposing a picture of a world in which nothing can ever be known and where all meanings are up for grabs. We should be able to trust common sense and intuition to carry us a long way in the interpretive process. If we, as readers, are naturally moved to make an association, then we have reason to think that the author wanted us to do so. Moreover, symbols, if they are used effectively, should allow us to feel their power—we shouldn't have to go hunting for them. If we find ourselves searching too hard, the odds are that there is no symbol, or that the author's attempt to introduce one has fizzled.

How Do Literary Symbols Send Messages?

We need to remember that symbols are not artificially contrived entities—at least not usually. Rather, they are manifestations of a universal human tendency to read higher significance into things and events. Symbolism may well be a holdover from the religious animism that was at the heart of all early cultures. People believed that their gods communicated by way of signs and that the way to survive and prosper was to know how to interpret those signs. The habit of treating things as signs and signifiers has survived into our far more secular age. We are forever avoiding ladders, riding elevators in buildings that have no thirteenth floor, and choosing our clothing to send one or another set of messages. Authors are no different. They are symbol-making and symbol-reading creatures like the rest of us, and it stands to reason that they would make significant use of this capacity in their art.

Symbols function in different ways within a work of fiction. In some instances the character is aware of the symbolic nature of a given thing or situation. The narrator of Olive Schreiner's story "The Woman's Rose" (which appears shortly) preserved the rose given to her by another woman. The flower was presented as a symbolic token and was accepted as such. The symbolism itself was both public and private. That is, the rose is a conventional symbol for love, and those overtones are not entirely absent from the story. But the woman sees it more as an emblem of respect and of selflessness.

In Isak Dinesen's story "The Blue Jar" (Chapter 10), on the other hand, we read of a woman's lifelong quest for a jar of a particular color of blue. The symbolic value of this blue jar is utterly private, and it is for us as readers to try to understand its meaning from the nature of the woman's obsession.

In these two cases, both the reader and the fictional characters acknowledge some symbolic value in a given object. But in many cases the symbol is apparent only to the reader, for only the reader can see enough about the situation to warrant attributing significance. In Sarah Orne Jewett's "A White Heron" (Chapter 5), for example, the young girl, Sylvia, knows the beauty and rarity of the lone white heron, but she does not draw the connection that is so obvious to the reader—the bird is a figure for her own youthful innocence.

A certain ambiguity is necessary for the symbol-making process to succeed. An object or a situation can be charged with significance, but it must also be convincingly itself. That is, we must believe in the actual reality of the white heron in the story if its symbolism is to affect us. Otherwise, we are too conscious of the fact that the author has tried to inject meaning deliberately, and our reading response is contaminated.

When it is used effectively in a work of fiction, a symbol deepens the thematic resonance and involves the reader more deeply in the discovering and making of meanings. While the associations tend to radiate outward and extend the reach of the work, the symbol itself often works like a magnet, pulling the stray bits of metal—the more incidental elements—into a pattern. When we encounter the symbol and feel its power, we often feel that we have touched an archetypal, or universal, layer of the human soul. We experience a sense of resonance and uplift that cannot be fully explained or analyzed.

Symbol versus Allegory

In addition to symbolism, we sometimes—albeit rarely—find an author using *allegory*. If symbols tend toward multiplicity, allegories are reductive. They are symbolic systems in which each element represents a specific abstract concept. Allegory was a favored mode for conveying religious messages, as we see in John Bunyan's well-known *Pilgrim's Progress*, in which the hero, named Christian, undertakes a great journey to the Heavenly City. Along the way—each stage of his journey is of course exemplary—he meets characters named Prudence, Piety, and Mr. Worldly Wiseman. Every action and interchange is a cipher in a larger code, the purpose of which is to show the universalized spiritual pilgrimage that every Christian must undergo to attain salvation.

While many contemporary writers use symbolic elements in their work, few attempt to devise a complete and self-consistent allegorical structure. Possibly the last successful attempt was made by George Orwell in his novella *Animal Farm*, which depicted Europe's postwar political alignments by using the figures of barnyard animals. The allegorist must be careful, as Orwell was, that the equivalences be very clear to the reader.

A STORY WITH A CENTRAL SYMBOL

Japanese writer Junichiro Tanizaki has placed a symbol directly at the center of his haunting story "Tattoo." We see with disturbing clarity how a symbolic image exerts its power over both possessor and beholder. We see, too, how destruction and eroticism can become bound until they are inextricable.

Junichiro Tanizaki (1886–1965)

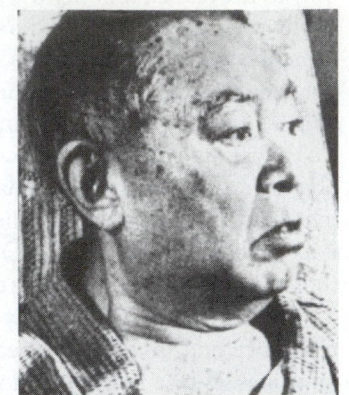

Tanizaki was born into an old Japanese merchant family. At the outset of his long literary career he proclaimed a devotion to the innovative writings of his Western masters, among them Poe, Baudelaire, and Oscar Wilde. His early works reveal an obsession with themes of cruelty and sexual power. In time, Tanizaki modified his approach, turning more and more to reflection upon the Japanese cultural heritage. His celebrated novel *Some Prefer Nettles* (1928) portrayed the deep conflict within the Japanese psyche between the traditional ways and the lure of the West. His massive novel *The Makioka Sisters* (1934–1938) is a faithfully realistic chronicle of family life in prewar Osaka. In later years, however, as in the short novel *The Key* (1958), Tanizaki returned to some of the preoccupations of his younger years. The novel presents the inside story of a marriage with a special view to the sexual interactions of the couple.

"Tattoo" was first published in 1910.

TATTOO

These things happened at a time when the noble virtue of frivolity still flourished, when today's relentless struggle for existence was yet unknown. The faces of the young aristocrats and squires were darkened by no cloud; at court the maids of honor and the great courtesans° always wore smiles on their lips; the occupations of clown and professional teahouse wit were held in high esteem; life was peaceful and full of joy. In the theater and in the writings of the time, beauty and power were portrayed as inseparable.

Physical beauty, indeed, was the chief aim of life, and in its pursuit people went so far as to have themselves tattooed. On their bodies, brilliant lines and colors were raveled in a sort of dance. When visiting the gay quarters, they would choose as bearers for their palanquins° men whose bodies were skillfully tattooed, and the

---

courtesans: women hired for pleasure by the well-to-do.
palanquin: a covered litter, or seat for gentry, carried on horizontal poles by bearers.

courtesans of Yoshiwara and Tatsumi gave their love to men whose bodies boasted beautiful tattoos. Frequenters of the gambling dens, firemen, merchants, and even samurai all had recourse to the tattooer's art. Tattoo exhibitions were frequently arranged where the participants, fingering the tattoo marks on each other's bodies, would praise the original design of one and criticize the shortcomings of another.

There was a young tattooer of outstanding talent. He was much in fashion and his reputation rivaled even those of the great masters of old, Charibun of Asakusa, Yakkohei of Matsushimachō, and Konkonjirō. His works were greatly prized at the tattoo exhibitions and most admirers of the art aspired to become his clients. While the artist Darumakin was known for his fine drawings and Karakusa Gonta was the master of the vermilion tattoo, this man Seikichi was famous for the originality of his compositions and for their voluptuous quality.

Previously he had achieved a certain reputation as a painter, belonging to the school of Toyokuni and Kunisada and specializing in genre paintings. In descending to the rank of tattooer, he still preserved the true spirit of an artist and a great sensitivity. He declined to execute his work on people whose skin or general physique did not appeal to him, and such customers as he did accept had to agree implicitly to the design of his choosing and also to his price. Moreover, they had to endure for as long as one or two months the excruciating pain of his needles.

Within this young tattooer's heart lurked unsuspected passions and pleasures. When the pricking of his needles caused the flesh to swell and the crimson blood to flow, his patients, unable to endure the agony, would emit groans of pain. The more they groaned, the greater was the artist's strange pleasure. He took particular delight in vermilion designs, which are known to be the most painful of tattoos. When his clients had received five or six hundred pricks of the needle and then taken a scalding hot bath the more vividly to bring out the colors, they would often collapse half dead at Seikichi's feet. As they lay there unable to move, he would ask 5 with a satisfied smile: "So it really hurts?"

When he had to deal with a fainthearted customer whose teeth would grind or who gave out shrieks of pain, Seikichi would say: "Really, I thought you were a native of Kyoto where people are supposed to be courageous. Please try to be patient. My needles are unusually painful." And glancing from the corner of his eyes at the victim's face, now moist with tears, he would continue his work with utter unconcern. If, on the contrary, his patient bore the agony without flinching, he would say: "Ah, you are much braver than you look. But wait a while. Soon you will be unable to endure it in silence, try as you may." And he would laugh, showing his white teeth.

* * *

For many years now, Seikichi's great ambition had been to have under his needle the lustrous skin of some beautiful girl, on which he dreamed of tattooing, as it were, his very soul. This imaginary woman had to meet many conditions as to both physique and character; a lovely face and a fine skin would not in themselves satisfy Seikichi. In vain had he searched among the well-known courtesans for a woman who would measure up to his ideal. Her image was constantly in his mind, and although three years had now elapsed since he started this quest, his desire had only grown with time.

It was on a summer's evening while walking in the Fukagawa district that his attention was caught by a feminine foot of dazzling whiteness disappearing behind the curtains of a palanquin. A foot can convey as many variations of expression as a face, and this white foot seemed to Seikichi like the rarest of jewels. The perfectly shaped toes, the iridescent nails, the rounded heel, the skin, as lustrous as if it had been washed for ages by the limpid waters of some mountain brook—all combined to make a foot of absolute perfection designed to stir the heart of a man and to trample upon his soul. Seikichi knew at once that this was the foot of the woman for whom he had searched these many years. Joyously he hurried after the palanquin, hoping to catch a glimpse of its occupant, but after following it for several streets, he lost sight of it around a corner. From then on what had been a vague yearning was transformed into the most violent of passions.

One morning a year later Seikichi received a visit at his house in the Fukagawa district. It was a young girl sent on an errand by a friend of his, a certain geisha° from the Tatsumi quarter.

"Excuse me, sir," the girl said timidly. "My mistress has asked me to deliver this coat to you personally and to request you to be so good as to make a design on the lining." 10

She handed him a letter and a woman's coat, the latter wrapped in a paper bearing the portrait of the actor Iwai Tojaku. In her letter the geisha informed Seikichi that the young messenger was her newly adopted ward and was soon to make her debut as a geisha in the restaurants of the capital. She asked him to do what he could to launch the girl on her new career.

Seikichi looked closely at the visitor who, though no more than sixteen or seventeen, had in her face something strangely mature. In her eyes were reflected the dreams of all the handsome men and beautiful women who had lived in this city, where the virtues and vices of the whole country converged. Then Seikichi's glance went to her delicate feet, shod in street clogs covered with plaits of straw.

"Could it have been you who left the Hirasei restaurant last June in a palanquin?"

"Yes, sir, it was I," she said, laughing at his strange question. "My father was still alive then and he used to take me occasionally to the Hirasei restaurant."

"I have been waiting for you now for five years," said Seikichi. "This is the first time that I have seen your face but I know you by your feet. . . .There is something that I should like you to see. Please come inside, and do not be afraid." 15

So saying, he took the hand of the reluctant girl and led her upstairs into a room which looked out on the great river. He fetched two large picture scrolls and spread one of them before her.

It was a painting of Mo Hsi, the favorite princess of the ancient Chinese emperor, Chou the Cruel. Languidly she leaned against a balustrade, and the bottom of her richly brocaded gown rested on the steps of the staircase leading to a garden. Her tiny head seemed almost too delicate to support the weight of her crown, which

---

geisha: a woman trained to provide entertainment for pay.

was encrusted with lapis lazuli and coral. In her right hand she held a cup, slightly tilted, and with an indolent expression she watched a prisoner who was about to be beheaded in the garden below. Secured hand and foot to a stake, he stood there awaiting his last moment; his eyes were closed, his head bent down. Pictures of such scenes tend to vulgarity, but so skillfully had the painter portrayed the expressions of the princess and of the condemned man that this picture scroll was a work of consummate art.

For a while the young girl fixed her gaze on the strange painting. Unconsciously her eyes began to shine and her lips trembled; gradually her face took on a resemblance to that of the young Chinese princess.

"Your spirit is reflected in that painting," said Seikichi, smiling with pleasure as he gazed at her.

"Why have you shown me such a terrible picture?" asked the girl, passing her hand over her pale forehead. 20

"The woman depicted here is yourself. Her blood flows through your veins."

Seikichi then unrolled the other scroll, which was entitled "The Victims." In the center of the picture a young woman leaned against a cherry tree, gazing at a group of men's corpses which lay about her feet; pride and satisfaction were to be discerned in her pale face. Hopping about among the corpses, a swarm of little birds chirped happily. Impossible to tell whether the picture represented a battlefield or a spring garden!

"This painting symbolizes your future," said Seikichi, indicating the face of the young woman, which again strangely resembled that of his visitor. "The men fallen on the ground are those who will lose their lives because of you."

"Oh, I beg you," she cried, "put that picture away." And as if to escape its terrifying fascination, she turned her back to the scroll and threw herself on the straw matting. There she lay with lips trembling and her whole body shuddering. "Master, I will confess to you. . . . As you have guessed, I have in me the nature of that woman. Take pity on me and hide the picture."

"Do not talk like a coward! On the contrary, you should study the painting more carefully and then you will soon stop being frightened of it." 25

The girl could not bring herself to raise her head, which remained hidden in the sleeve of her kimono. She lay prostrate on the floor saying over and over: "Master, let me go home. I am frightened to be with you."

"You shall stay for a while," said Seikichi imperiously. "I alone have the power to make of you a beautiful woman."

From among the bottles and needles on his shelf Seikichi selected a vial containing a powerful narcotic.

* * *

The sun shone brightly on the river. Its reflected rays threw a pattern like golden waves on the sliding doors and on the face of the young sleeping woman. Seikichi closed the doors and sat down beside her. Now for the first time he was able to relish her strange beauty fully, and he thought that he could have spent years sitting there gazing at that perfect, immobile face.

But the urge to accomplish his design overcame him before many moments. Having fetched his tattooing instruments from the shelf, Seikichi uncovered the girl's body and began to apply to her back the point of his pen, held between the thumb, ring finger, and little finger of his left hand. With the needle, held in his right hand, he pricked along the lines as they were drawn. As the people of Memphis° once embellished with sphinxes and pyramids the fine land of Egypt, so Seikichi now adorned the pure skin of this young girl. It was as if the tattooer's very spirit entered into the design, and each injected drop of vermilion was like a drop of his own blood penetrating the girl's body.

He was quite unconscious of the passage of time. Noon came and went, and the quiet spring day moved gradually toward its close. Indefatigably Seikichi's hand pursued its work without ever waking the girl from her slumber. Presently the moon hung in the sky, pouring its dreamy light over the rooftops on the other side of the river. The tattoo was not yet half done. Seikichi interrupted his work to turn up the lamp, then sat down again and reached for his needle.

Now each stroke demanded an effort, and the artist would let out a sigh, as if his own heart had felt the prick. Little by little there began to appear the outline of an enormous spider. As the pale glow of dawn entered the room, this animal of diabolic mien spread its eight legs over the girl's back.

The spring night was almost over. Already one could hear the dip of the oars as the rowboats passed up and down the river; above the sails of the fishing smacks, swollen with the morning breeze, one could see the mists lifting. And at last Seikichi brought himself to put down his needle. Standing aside, he studied the enormous female spider tattooed on the girl's back, and as he gazed at it, he realized that in this work he had expressed the essence of his whole life. Now that it was completed, the artist was aware of a great emptiness.

"To give you beauty I have poured my whole soul into this tattoo," Seikichi murmured. "From now on there is not a woman in Japan to rival you! Never again will you know fear. All men, all men will be your victims. . . ."

Did she hear his words? A moan rose to her lips, her limbs moved. Gradually she began to regain consciousness, and as she lay breathing heavily in and out, the spider's legs moved on her back like those of a living animal.

"You must be suffering," said Seikichi. "That is because the spider is embracing your body so closely."

She half opened her eyes. At first they had a vacant look, then the pupils began to shine with a brightness that matched the moonlight reflected on Seikichi's face.

"Master, let me see the tattoo on my back! If you have given me your soul, I must indeed have become beautiful."

She spoke as in a dream, and yet in her voice there was a new note of confidence, of power.

"First you must take a bath to brighten the colors," Seikichi answered her. And he added with unwonted solicitude: "It will be painful, most painful. Have courage!"

"I will bear anything to become beautiful," said the girl.

She followed Seikichi down some stairs into the bathroom, and as she stepped into the steaming water her eyes glistened with pain.

"Ah, ah, how it burns!" she groaned. "Master, leave me and wait upstairs. I shall join you when I am ready. I do not want any man to see me suffer."

Memphis: an ancient Egyptian city.

Symbolism

But when she stepped out of the bath, she did not even have strength to dry herself. She pushed aside Seikichi's helping hand and collapsed on the floor. Groaning, she lay with her long hair flowing across the floor. The mirror behind her reflected the soles of two feet, iridescent as mother-of-pearl.

Seikichi went upstairs to wait for her, and when at last she joined him she was dressed with care. Her damp hair had been combed out and hung about her shoulders. Her delicate mouth and curving eyebrows no longer betrayed her ordeal, and as she gazed out at the river there was a cold glint in her eyes. Despite her youth she had the mien of a woman who had spent years in teahouses and acquired the art of mastering men's hearts. Amazed, Seikichi reflected on the change in the timid girl since the day before. Going to the other room, he fetched the two picture scrolls which he had shown her.

"I offer you these paintings," he said. "And also, of course, the tattoo. They are yours to take away."

"Master," she answered, "my heart is now free from all fear. And you . . . you shall be my first victim!"

She threw him a look, piercing as a newly sharpened sword blade. It was the look of the young Chinese princess, and of that other woman who leaned against a cherry tree surrounded by singing birds and dead bodies. A feeling of triumph raced through Seikichi.

"Let me see your tattoo," he said to her. "Show me your tattoo."

Without a word, she inclined her head and unfastened her dress. The rays of the morning sun fell on the young girl's back and its golden gleam seemed to set fire to the spider.

Translated by Ivan Morris

As you read the following discussion, consider these questions:	1. Reflect upon the customs of tattooing and the purposes of making a permanent design on the skin. What symbols are often tattooed on a willing customer?

As you read the following discussion, consider these questions:

1. Reflect upon the customs of tattooing and the purposes of making a permanent design on the skin. What symbols are often tattooed on a willing customer?

2. What is Seikichi's attitude toward his art? How is he different from other practitioners?

3. Why does Seikichi get so excited by the young geisha? What does he see in her?

4. How does Seikichi convince the geisha to allow him to tattoo her?

5. What symbolic suggestions do you find in the pictures that Seikichi shows the girl?

6. What is the reader's first indication that the girl might not be as innocent as she appears?

7. What does Seikichi tattoo on the girl's body, and what does the design symbolize?

8. How does the symbol change the girl? How do you interpret the final scene? Has Seikichi knowingly created a "monster"?

Discussion. Tanizaki's unusual and disturbing story allows us a special glimpse of the use of symbol in fiction, for in this case the work is actually *about* the power that symbols can exert over human destinies. The particular focus in "Tattoo" is upon the cruel way that power can dominate relations between men and women. There are strong overtones of violence and sexuality, and these, as we shall see, are expressed in the frightening symbolic image of the spider tattooed upon the young woman's back.

Before discussing the story, we should step back for a moment to assess the context. The reader's first response is very likely a feeling of shock at the sexism of the characterization of the young woman. Seikichi, if not Tanizaki himself, invests her with a vanity and heartlessness that are deeper than character flaws; they signal the presence of evil itself. But we should not therefore be in a hurry to dismiss the work, for a closer look at the dynamics of the plot, as well as a more careful reading of the symbolism, reveals the seriousness of the author's intent. Tanizaki devises an extreme situation in order to explore the roots of human sexuality and the power that images have to imprison their makers.

His portrayal of the young woman is sexist, certainly, but the author is very much aware of that fact. Indeed, one might argue that a criticism of the drastic inequality of the sexes in the Japanese culture of the time is part of the weave of the story.

How we decide on this matter depends to some extent upon how we choose to interpret the tone of the story (see Chapter 8).

The very first sentence raises the issue. "These things happened at a time when the noble virtue of frivolity still flourished," begins Tanizaki, and already we must decide how to take his words. Frivolity and nobility are contradictory terms. Should we strain against common sense and accept the statement at face value, or should we grant that the words might be tinged with a bitter irony?

Reading further in the first few paragraphs, we may begin to suspect that Tanizaki despises this culture—a culture in which "the occupations of clown and professional teahouse wit were held in high esteem" and "Physical beauty . . . was the chief aim of life." It would follow, then, that he in no way means us to approve of his characters or their actions. It may well be that he wants us to study the depravity of the situation as a doctor might study a malignant tissue culture.

The story itself is simple in structure and ambiguous in its resonances. Tanizaki uses the plot to create a frame for his symbol and then lets the symbol carry the thematic weight. And symbols, as mentioned earlier, are seldom straightforward; they usually are dense with multiple meanings.

Seikichi is a tattoo artist—and a strong emphasis should fall on the word "artist." He does not merely decorate the bodies of his clients; he seeks to inscribe on them his own unique vision. Like any artist—any artist, that is, in the old romantic conception—he dreams of creating a masterpiece. And when he finally meets the young woman he has been searching for, he seizes the opportunity.

Tattoos, of course, are symbols, but the tattoo-maker's art has symbolic suggestion as well. It presupposes an ideal of artificiality: that the beauty of the natural body is not enough, but must be improved upon. Moreover, the new beauty—the work of art grafted upon the skin—can only be attained at the cost of great physical pain. The art, then, has a deep link to suffering. This idea too belongs to the romantic mythology of art. The work, in this case the tattoo, acquires part of its power and meaning because it has taken a certain human toll.

The young girl has been sent to Seikichi on an errand. She is the servant of a geisha and is about to make her debut as a geisha herself. A geisha is a professional entertainer trained to serve the needs of wealthy men—needs that can include, but are not limited to, sex. We may assume that the young woman is still a virgin, that she has not yet tested her own sexual nature. A strong part of Seikichi's attraction has to do with her youth and innocence.

Seikichi's first impression of his visitor is crucial. Though she was but sixteen or seventeen, she "had in her face something strangely mature." And: "In her eyes were reflected the dreams of all the handsome men and beautiful women who had lived in this city, where the virtues and vices of the whole country converged." Already we see that Seikichi does not see the young woman as a person, but rather as a kind of screen for the dreams of others, including his own. The strange maturity that he discerns in her face suggests, further, that she is in some way a divided being; underneath her innocence, very likely unknown even to herself, lies something else.

Seikichi then seeks to discover that hidden side, to draw it forth. He leads his visitor into a room and shows her two picture scrolls, both of which depict a beautiful woman's heartlessness before a scene of cruelty. In one instance a prisoner is about to be beheaded; in the other the woman is surrounded by "a group of men's corpses," while her expression shows "pride and satisfaction." Seikichi watches the young woman closely. "Unconsciously her eyes began to shine and her lips trembled," writes Tanizaki. She is clearly fascinated. It is as if the hidden side of her nature were stepping forth.

In each case, however, Seikichi also finds that her face has taken on a resemblance to the woman in the painting. We should not interpret this as meaning that her features actually transform. Rather, it seems to indicate the power of Seikichi's obsession. He looks at the young woman's face and sees what he wants to see. In the language of modern psychology, he "projects" upon her his own attitudes about women.

The visitor herself reacts to the paintings with great ambivalence. On the one hand, she is horrified and asks Seikichi to put the pictures away; on the other, she shudders and confesses: "I have in me the nature of that woman." She asks again that he hide the pictures, this time so that she will not have to face the truth about herself.

After he has drugged the young woman, Seikichi sets to work tattooing her. Again, the process itself has a kind of symbolic meaning. The artist is succumbing to inspiration, to the desire to create a haunting image; he is also consciously inflicting pain. It is as if he is avenging himself upon all women through this deed.

The image that he creates—the symbol—is that of a gigantic female spider. Seikichi exclaims: "To give you beauty I have poured my whole soul into this tattoo," adding that "All men, all men will be your victims. . . ." The whole business is perverse: Seikichi's obsession, his way of testing his visitor, his drugging her, and the image itself. That he should now declare that image to be a source of beauty strains our credulity. Yet within the context that Tanizaki has set out, this outlandish statement makes a certain sense. Seikichi is taking cruel pleasure in his accomplishment; he believes that he has captured the truth of her inner nature and thereby released a hidden power. What he does not perhaps understand is that he will be the first victim of that power.

Seikichi's choice of the symbol of the female spider is entirely in keeping with his vision of women. The spider itself is a traditional symbol of entrapment. The female spider, however, is said to devour the male after mating, thus yoking together love and death. In a manner of speaking, then, Seikichi has devised his own web and has walked into it. Acting out of cruel fascination, as well as possible desire for vengeance, he has found and brought forth a hidden evil. Once he has given it a symbolic form, thereby releasing it, he must be destroyed. The young woman wakens from her stupor, and as soon as she sees the symbol on her back, she releases her darker nature. She becomes what Seikichi has wished upon her—a female spider—and as she unfastens her dress, we know that she will give herself to the artist, then kill him.

"Tattoo" is saturated with the brooding darkness that Tanizaki so much admired in Edgar Allan Poe. It is a disturbing tale of psychological terror, but it is also a parable about images and symbols. Tanizaki is well aware of the human tendency to conform to the expectations of those around us. We possess a frightening plasticity, and it sometimes allows us to become what others think we are. We don't need to share Seikichi's warped beliefs about the female nature to experience certain shudders of recognition.

A SYMBOL AS FOCAL POINT FOR EMOTION

Olive Schreiner's brief story "The Woman's Rose" uses symbolism to make a less extreme statement. She is less interested in transmitting a vision than in registering a moment of recognition in a woman's life.

Olive Schreiner (1855–1920)

Olive Schreiner was born on the Eastern Cape frontier of Southern Africa, daughter of a German missionary and an English mother. She received little in the way of formal education but taught herself out of books while serving as a governess on various remote farmsteads. Her novel *The Story of an African Farm* (1883) won wide acclaim—it is one of the first works in English by a colonial to have broken through to a larger readership. During the 1890s Schreiner wrote a large number of short stories, many of them a kind of impressionistic play with her own memories. ("The Woman's Rose" dates from this period.) Schreiner was one of a great many women writers rediscovered after the advent of the women's movement. Her own feminist manifesto, *Woman and Labour* (1911), found new readers in the 1970s and 1980s. *From Man to Man,* a novel treating of feminist and racial issues, was published posthumously in 1926.

THE WOMAN'S ROSE

I have an old, brown, carved box; the lid is broken and tied with a string. In it I keep little squares of paper, with hair inside, and a little picture which hung over my brother's bed when we were children, and other things as small. I have in it a rose. Other women also have such boxes where they keep such trifles, but no one has my rose.

When my eye is dim, and my heart grows faint, and my faith in woman flickers, and her present is an agony to me, and her future a despair, the scent of that dead rose, withered for twelve years, comes back to me. I know there will be spring; as surely as the birds know it when they see above the snow two tiny, quivering green leaves. Spring cannot fail us.

There were other flowers in the box once: a bunch of white acacia flowers, gathered by the strong hand of a man, as we passed down a village street on a sultry afternoon, when it had rained, and the drops fell on us from the leaves of the acacia trees. The flowers were damp; they made mildew marks on the paper I folded them in. After many years I threw them away. There is nothing of them left in the box now, but a faint, strong smell of dried acacia, that recalls that sultry summer afternoon; but the rose is in the box still.

It is many years ago now; I was a girl of fifteen, and I went to visit in a small up-country town. It was young in those days, and two days' journey from the nearest village; the population consisted mainly of men. A few were married, and had their wives and children, but most were single. There was only one young girl there when I came. She was about seventeen, fair, and rather fully-fleshed; she had large dreamy blue eyes, and wavy light hair; full, rather heavy lips, until she smiled; then her face broke into dimples, and all her white teeth shone. The hotel-keeper may have had a daughter, and the farmer in the outskirts had two, but we never saw them. She reigned alone. All the men worshipped her. She was the only woman they had to think of. They talked of her on the 'stoep', at the market, at the hotel; they watched for her at street corners; they hated the man she bowed to or walked with down the street. They brought flowers to the front door; they offered her their horses; they begged her to marry them when they dared. Partly, there was something noble and heroic in this devotion of men to the best woman they knew; partly there was something natural in it, that these men, shut off from the world, should pour at the feet of one woman the worship that otherwise would have been given to twenty; and partly there was something mean in their envy of one another. If she had raised her little finger, I suppose, she might have married any one out of twenty of them.

Then I came. I do not think I was prettier; I do not think I was so pretty as she was. I was certainly not as handsome. But I was vital, and I was new, and she was old—they all forsook her and followed me. They worshipped me. It was to my door that the flowers came; it was I had twenty horses offered me when I could only ride one; it was for me they waited at street corners; it was what I said and did that they talked of. Partly I liked it. I had lived alone all my life; no one ever had told me I was beautiful and a woman. I believed them. I did not know it was simply a fashion, which one man had set and the rest followed unreasoningly. I liked them to ask me to marry them, and to say, No. I despised them. The mother heart had not swelled in me yet; I did not know all men were my children, as the large woman knows when her heart is grown. I was too small to be tender. I liked my power. I was like a child with a new whip, which it goes about cracking everywhere, not caring against what. I could not wind it up and put it away. Men were curious creatures, who liked me, I could never tell why. Only one thing took from my pleasure; I could not bear that they had deserted her for me. I liked her great dreamy blue eyes, I liked her slow walk and drawl; when I saw her sitting among men, she seemed to me much too good to be among them; I would have given all their compliments if she would once have smiled at me as she smiled at them, with all her face breaking into radiance, with her dimples and flashing teeth. But I knew it never could be; I felt sure she hated me; that she wished I was dead; that she wished I had never come to the village. She did not know, when we went out riding, and a man who had always ridden beside her came to ride beside me, that I sent him away; that once when a man thought to win my favour by ridiculing her slow drawl before me I turned on him so fiercely that he never dared come before me again. I knew she knew that at the hotel men had made a bet as to which was the prettier, she or I, and had asked each man who came in, and that the one who had staked on me won. I hated them for it, but I would not let her see that I cared about what she felt towards me.

She and I never spoke to each other.

If we met in the village street we bowed and passed on; when we shook hands we did so silently, and did not look at each other. But I thought she felt my presence in a room just as I felt hers.

At last the time for my going came. I was to leave the next day. Someone I knew gave a party in my honour, to which all the village was invited.

It was midwinter. There was nothing in the gardens but a few dahlias and chrysanthemums, and I suppose that for two hundred miles round there was not a rose to be bought for love or money. Only in the garden of a friend of mine, in a sunny corner between the oven and the brick wall, there was a rose tree growing which had on it one bud. It was white, and it had been promised to the fair-haired girl to wear at the party.

The evening came; when I arrived and went to the waiting-room, to take off my mantle, I found the girl there already. She was dressed in pure white, with her great white arms and shoulders showing, and her bright hair glittering in the candlelight, and the white rose fastened at her breast. She looked like a queen. I said 'Good-evening,' and turned away quickly to the glass to arrange my old black scarf across my old black dress.

Then I felt a hand touch my hair.

'Stand still,' she said.

I looked in the glass. She had taken the white rose from her breast, and was fastening it in my hair.

'How nice dark hair is; it sets off flowers so.' She stepped back and looked at me. 'It looks much better there!'

I turned round.

'You are so beautiful to me,' I said.

'Y-e-s,' she said, with her slow Colonial drawl; 'I'm so glad.'

We stood looking at each other.

Then they came in and swept us away to dance. All the evening we did not come near to each other. Only once, as she passed, she smiled at me.

The next morning I left the town.

I never saw her again.

Years afterwards I heard she had married and gone to America; it may or may not be so—but the rose—the rose is in the box still! When my faith in woman grows dim, and it seems that for want of love and magnanimity she can play no part in any future heaven; then the scent of that small withered thing comes back—spring cannot fail us.

QUESTIONS

1. The narrator has preserved various mementos in her carved box. How does the reader come to understand that the rose is the most important? What had the acacia flowers signified to her? Is it significant that she threw them away, leaving only the rose?

2. What are the narrator's feelings toward the other young woman? Why should she resent the attention that she herself is getting from the men?

3. What is the difference in Schreiner's presentation of men and women in the story? What is the view of male-female relations expressed? How does this view connect with the thematic statement in the last paragraph?

4. How does Schreiner dramatize the scene at the party through her use of color? Does the white rose have different symbolic overtones than a red rose?

5. So much passes unstated between the two women. What does the woman in white intend to communicate by giving away the rose? What does her gesture—and the flower—come to mean in later years?

6. Discuss how "The Woman's Rose" can be said to reflect feminist conceptions of male and female relationships. Is this a story with a message? If so, what is the message?

7. What does Schreiner mean when she writes that "spring cannot fail us"?

10 Writing about Fiction

To write about fiction is to set out upon a path that very soon branches off in many different directions. Choices abound. There is no one right, or best, way to do it. Different teachers have different requirements, based in part upon their own preferences and their expectations of their students. And the works themselves, the stories or novels that are to be written about, are so diverse that no tidy pattern or set of patterns can be applied. One teacher wants a close analysis of a crucial scene, another wants you to explore symbols and themes, and so on. Finally, you, as students, each have your own aptitudes and favored ways of working. Who is going to step forward to lay down the law that *this* is the way to do it?

The observations that follow, therefore, are not meant as prescriptions. They are suggestions—ideas and approaches you might think about before you sit down to write about fiction. But while they are not in any sense ironclad, they are not completely arbitrary, either; for among practicing writers a certain degree of consensus exists. If you read enough guides and "how to" books, you will see that there is a basic agreement about approach and execution. This agreement seems to affirm that the human brain digests, processes, and spins out information in fairly predictable sequences. And some knowledge of these sequences will very likely help you with your own writing.

Naturally there are always exceptions. We have all heard of writers who have but to pick up a pen—or turn on the word-processor—to start generating perfect prose. They scribble no notes, make no outlines, and never seem to suffer over faulty drafts. If you are one of the lucky few, then read no further. These reflections are meant for those of us who are not so fortunate, who have to sweat and groan (at least a little) before producing anything fit for a reader's eye.

WHY WRITE ABOUT FICTION?

Why indeed? Most of you write about fiction because you have no other choice—the course-work requires it. But there are other, somewhat less matter-of-fact, reasons for doing it. First, writing automatically puts you into a more intense and demanding relation to a work of art. Writing is, as I argued in Chapter 1, a highly charged form of reading; it is an active and productive engagement. To write about a work of fiction requires a kind of reading-attentiveness that goes far beyond the usual ways that we engage a text. And this attentiveness opens doors. It carries you into the work, allowing you to grapple with its deeper messages and test its meanings. To write about a story—to write *well*—you have to approach it as though it truly matters. Address a serious work seriously and you will be surprised at the pay-off. Not only will you find ideas to write about, but you will very likely find that those ideas are not sealed in a vacuum. They refer to the world and the perplexing business of living in it. In other words, they refer to you. Writing—which is thus not only intensified reading, but intensified *thinking*—is one of the best ways to touch the deeper layers of your own experience.

No less important, writing about fiction—or any other literary genre—helps you to develop an array of skills that will stand you in good stead in any number of careers. To write a good paper about a story by Eudora Welty or Ernest Hemingway (or anyone else), you need to be able to read attentively, analyze components, and focus on particulars; you then need to find a thesis, gather support for your inter-pretation, and present your points in an organized and persuasive format. These req-uisites may explain why law schools look at the applications of English majors with special interest. Admissions officers know that these basic cognitive abilities can easily be retooled to different specifications. Needless to say, the same abilities are highly prized in all parts of the professional world.

WRITING BEGINS WITH READING

No matter who the writer, and no matter how short the interval between assign-ment and submission, the process of writing a literary essay—or paper—can be bro-ken down into several distinct stages. Of course, there are different kinds of writing. One may be called upon to present an *analysis*, breaking the whole down into its constituent parts and focusing upon some particular aspect; or an *explication*, in which a single passage is given the most intense scrutiny; or an essay that *compares and contrasts* elements from separate works. Or the point of the paper may be a the-matic exploration, in which the central meanings are assessed and explored. But whatever the writing assignment has as its goal, it will nearly always have its roots in a reading of one or more works.

As I have suggested elsewhere, reading takes many forms, depending on the pur-pose. Whatever it is that you do with the Sunday paper is not to be compared with the sustained attentiveness that you bring to a work of literature. But even when the reading is serious, there are levels and degrees of focus. If you are reading a book of stories purely for pleasure, you tend to approach the words on the page with differ-ent attitudes and expectations than if you are reading to write. This is not to say that when you read to write you are turning your back on pleasure. But you cannot really help being alert in different ways. You are, after all, reading in order to re-spond. You have to fix your sights not only on the *what* of the story, but also on the *how* and the *why*.

Switching from one mode of reading to another is not always easy. You can't just put on your "serious" glasses and get to work. If you are going to write about an author's work, no matter what the assignment, you should be willing to read it sev-eral times. The first reading, however careful, is a preliminary. You need to get through the story once just to find out how to approach it best the second time. And even though you have probably not picked up a pencil to make a single note, the writing process has begun; for as soon as you adjust your expectations to make a second approach, you have started the sifting and sorting process that will ultimately lead to putting words on the page.

The matter of adjusting expectations is fairly automatic—you don't really have to "do" anything. Your first reading gives you a sense of the terrain; you know who does what to whom, and how. You may even feel that you understand the story quite well. Nevertheless, the second time through you will be reading a different story. Once you know how things develop, the mainspring of suspense slackens. You are free to slow down, to look at other features, and to inspect details. And you know, in the most basic sense, where you need to look more closely. Your first reading has given you a set of cues: this story is about a man's crisis of faith, or about a woman's suppressed love; the author expends a great deal of energy—or none—in describing the surroundings; there is an obvious use of water imagery, and so on. You have strewn the work with your own marking flags, and now you can go back to them for a second look.

The first reading gives you the more obvious kinds of information. But a response will naturally be more interesting, and will stand a better chance of holding a reader, if it goes beyond the obvious. Who wants to read—or write—another paper that simply announces that Hemingway was concerned with codes of manhood in his fiction, or that D. H. Lawrence built narrative tension around a struggle between the sexes? These are observations, necessary but obvious, that anyone can derive from a first reading. The second (and maybe third and fourth) reading will likely lead you to a more specific set of responses. Knowing that there is a struggle between the sexes, say, you would pick up a more powerful lens. You would work your way back through the story looking for subtleties of motivation, symbolic suggestions, and significant turning points in the action. You would be ready to start planning your paper.

PLANNING AND PONDERING

Of all the stages of the writing process, the hardest to account for is the passage from the reading to the first notation of ideas. So much depends upon who the reader is and what kinds of things he or she notices and responds to. Still, some observations about the sifting operations of the mind can be made.

To begin with, when you prepare to write you are not faced, as some might suppose, with moving from no thought to thought—from blankness to idea. We all think with greater or lesser intensity all of the time (studies in neuropsychology bear this out). You may try to suppress your thought process while reading in order to concentrate, but success is only partial. As you move from sentence to sentence, following the trail of the story, you are constantly reacting, sending out feelers, and making connections. The thoughts are often fairly basic, taking the form of response or surmise: "She is going to leave him," "A life like that would be depressing," "He acts just like John," and so on. Indeed, in the first reading it is especially hard to discriminate between more and less relevant reactions, for until you know how things will turn out, nearly everything has potential application.

The second reading is crucial because it allows the responses to take on a sharper relief. Scattered impressions tend to come together into clusters, and rough thematic outlines begin to emerge. You find out, for instance, that you were wrong; she is *not* going to leave him. Therefore, in your second reading you will be looking more closely at *her*, her character; you will be trying to pin down why your supposition was wrong. You will be ready to start generating the ideas that lead to writing.

How, then, do you begin? Assuming that you have some choice in the matter—that is, that your teacher has not assigned you an analysis of the snow imagery in James Joyce's "The Dead"—you begin by interrogating your own reading. "Was I affected in any way by this story? How so? What caused my reaction? Was there a scene, a character, a description, or an image that most struck me? What *about* it struck me?" The more securely you can ground yourself in your own reading experience, the better are your chances for finding a topic that seems worth pursuing. The best possible point of departure is a puzzle or a question, for the sincere attempt to answer it can bring a powerful momentum into writing a paper.

TAKING NOTES

Most students have developed some system of annotation or note-taking that they use as a kind of foundation toward coming up with an interpretation and, eventually, a thesis. These notes can be anything from privately encoded shorthand to extensive commentary; they may be scrawled in the margins of the text or set out neatly on separate pages. Whatever form notes take, their purpose is specific. They mark the first necessary transition from thought to reaction to writing. They may be—and usually are—a long way from the finished product, but these notes are a way of filling the emptiness of a blank page that many find to be the first impediment to writing.

For many, note-taking is a way of recording thoughts, inklings of thoughts, questions, and so on. When you underline or highlight a passage you are, in effect, starting the process. You are saying, "This is important," or, "I may want to come back to this." Just by touching the pen or pencil to the text page you are beginning to grapple with issues. Some students grapple so vigorously that the author's words are nearly obliterated by markings. Words get circled, phrases are linked with connecting lines, arrows shoot out to the margins where key words are inscribed: "Conflict!" or "Irony." And as connections are formed in the reader's mind, these abbreviated markings often give way to more detailed responses: "Red used symbolically to indicate anger."

Note-taking is spontaneous and is not to be legislated. There is no right way to mark a text. Everyone is different. Indeed, some people cannot bear to mark a book, even the lowliest of textbooks, but however you decide to proceed—even if it means writing out complete sentences in a separate notebook—you will find the process to be liberating. Taking notes breaks the ice; it allows you to see at a glance what parts of the text have struck you so that you can return to inspect them again. For most writers—student or professional—private notations are a path toward the formulation of interpretation.

INTERPRETING A STORY

Interpretation is the core activity of literary study. Before you can find a thesis and write about a work you must interpret. You must arrive at an explanation. There is nothing unnatural or forbidding about this—it is an inevitable part of the reading process. The focused reader automatically questions the text, asking not just "What does it mean?" but also "What does it mean *to me?*" Arriving at an interpretation means coming up with explicit answers to these questions.

Of course, this is often harder to do than my breezy assertion might suggest. Literary works are often confusing or ambiguous; or else they seem to allow for many different kinds of explanations. Then there is the tyranny of "rightness." How do you know whether or not your interpretation is way off base? On some level you don't—this is both the beauty and the horror of the business. If the author had a single specific message to communicate he wouldn't need the elaborate transport system of the work. But meanings are shadowy entities, complex tissues of suggestion. They are not so much inserted into the work by the author as they are constructed from the work by the reader. To understand this is to make a great stride toward understanding literature.

To interpret a story is to explain what *you* think it is about. Subjectivity—trusting your own reaction—is a big part of the interpretive enterprise. There is no right or wrong answer, provided you can match your explanation to the work in a way that makes sense. It is perfectly possible for two highly intelligent and trained readers to arrive at two very different interpretations. This artistic ambiguity is what makes literary criticism possible; otherwise it would just be a matter of establishing the correct readings. But that would spell the end of literature, which continues to live precisely to the extent that its meanings can be contested by readers from generation to generation.

But where does this leave the student who needs to write a paper about a work of fiction? In a condition of great freedom, and at the mercy of her instincts, intuitions, and basic common sense. Out of this freedom she must venture forward by asking questions: How did I react to this story? What caused my reaction? Is this what the author may have wanted? Why do I think so? What are the elements that work together to create this impression? and so on. You are free to interpret as you wish, keeping in mind that the account you give must make sense and correspond to what the author has put on the page. If you want to argue, for example, that Kate Chopin's "The Story of an Hour" (Chapter 13) is an indictment of female passivity, you have to make your case by pointing to and quoting parts of the story that support your theory. You would do the same if you wished to interpret the story as an early voicing of the feminist credo.

The interpretation is accountable to the work. It therefore should take the whole work into consideration, not just the parts that lend themselves to the argument. It should also be self-consistent, assuming a unity of purpose and execution on the author's part. In other words, *not:* "Kate Chopin not only deals with the struggle of women who are dependent upon men, but also shows the male perspective to be beside the point." A self-consistent interpretation cannot contradict itself. It is, rather, a kind of contour map that can be laid over the text and made to fit.

Just as there is no sure-fire recipe for writing, there is no proven way to make an interpretation. You arrive at it by thinking, second-guessing the author, asking the kinds of questions cited earlier; you get there by making notes and building them slowly into an explanatory statement. You do *not* get there by summarizing or retelling the story in simplified form. (See the section on Summarizing.) Interpretation requires that you map your own responses and make use of them. You cannot interpret without some degree of engagement in the work.

The most common mistake that unpracticed writers make after the first inklings of an insight is to rush to the typewriter or computer. Resist if you can. Interpretations are seldom arrived at with a finger-snap; more generally they ripen. Make notes and sit with them. Allow your notes to generate other notes. Specific ideas—the kinds that tend to pop up in margin notations—are steps in a larger thinking process. They are links in a chain and cannot be hurried. Your insights may not be ready to be rushed to print; they may be part of something larger. There is every chance that a hasty assault will paralyze the development. Similarly, if you lock a single idea or response into concrete expression too soon, you seal it off from the possibility of further transformation. You grow wedded to your one formula and more exploratory kinds of thinking can get short-circuited. Keep yourself open for surprises and discoveries. If note-taking is not enough—for many it is too restrictive, too analytical—you may wish to try your hand at associative freewriting.

FREEWRITING

Freewriting is not to be confused with *sprinting*, the process in which a writer puts down words as quickly as possible with the hope that the preconscious mind will release some unexpected, and useful, strand of association. Freewriting is more like the process of doodling. The writer notes down ideas and responses as they naturally occur, exercising no restraint or discipline. There is no attempt at this stage to devise a sequence; outlining will come later. What often happens, however, is that the writer begins to glimpse connections between various ideas and starts making linkages.

Freewriting ought to be relaxed, even playful. The purpose, as with sprinting, is to trigger associations. There is a natural tendency—and a few trial attempts will probably confirm this for you—for ideas to get sharper and more concrete. The general gives way to the particular. Let's say you have just read a story about the breakup of a marriage. A first freewritten response, *tension in relationship*, may fairly quickly lead you to specific refinements, like *woman frustrated by lack of emotional contact* and *man feels misunderstood, has violent outbursts*, and so on. Once the words are on the page, the mind can freely reflect on them and make further distinctions.

At first, your freewritten notations are likely to be descriptive—you begin with what you feel sure about, staking the terrain of the story. As in the short examples above, there may be no idea as yet. But suppose that you now note another aspect of the relationship in this hypothetical story: *the woman fears the husband's rage, but also seems to welcome it*. This, too, is descriptive. But it also contains the germ of an idea. For the statement contains a paradox, a tension of opposition, that may prove useful for building a *thesis*, or central argument. The underlying idea might be something like this: There is a cycle in the relationship; the husband's expression of rage brings the couple closer together by providing a basis for emotional contact. In other words, that which poses the greatest threat may also, in a curious way, open the way toward the salvation of the relationship.

Though you are, with this, not quite ready to begin writing, you have taken a major step forward. You have found an idea that could, with some fitting and elaborating, form the backbone of the paper. You have an angle that might prove to be a worthy thesis, in which case your writing process has a clear direction. Your job now is to test your idea, to search out specific instances in the story that support the assertion, and to check to see whether there might not be some strong arguments against it.

LOCATING A THESIS

One of the main functions of the freewriting process is to lead you to a thesis. Writers who don't freewrite usually evolve their own strategies—making notes in the margins, highlighting passages, and so on. What all modes share in common is that they not only attempt to make a bridge between thinking and writing, but also have as their goal the discovery of a governing concept that works: a thesis, the main point of the paper. Insights, however brilliant, need a frame that can hold them. And the reader, to whom the paper is finally addressed, needs to know that the words on the page have a purpose.

Though you will probably begin writing a draft before you know all the fine points of your presentation (a big part of writing is, after all, discovery), you should never set out before your thesis is clear to you—so clear, in fact, that you could write it out on one side of an index card. The thesis of an essay on the story of the failing relationship might be something like this: "The tensions in the marriage between Adam and Eve are part of a larger cycle. Emotional distance creates the conditions for confrontation, and confrontation allows for contact. The eventual collapse of the marriage shows that contact is not enough." You might then go on to write a paper that explores, with examples and analysis, how the cycle works itself out over the course of the story. You can then take up the larger question of whether such a relationship falsifies the ideals of marriage, or whether it illustrates the pitfalls common to most human relationships. Any number of variations are possible.

The thesis should be specific enough to be interesting and at the same time general enough to allow you room for speculation. If you were to propose as your main argument that *relationships often have problems,* the reader would naturally yawn. But beware of going too far in the other direction, asserting for example that "In the course of her marriage to Adam, Eve often found that Adam would start to show anger after he had been drinking, and that he would then start to criticize their marriage." A statement like this is really part of the discussion of the thesis—by itself it lacks the breadth or interest to support a whole paper. In deciding whether your idea for a thesis is right, therefore, you need judgment. You also need to be able to picture to yourself how you might build an argument or presentation. Finally, you need to ask yourself whether you, as a reader, would have any interest in reading a paper on the chosen idea.

Usually—not always—the thesis is set out early in the paper. (Some would even specify that it be placed at the end of the first paragraph, directly following the general lead-in sentences.) Placing the thesis right up front gives you, as the writer, a clear directive about how the supporting material will be organized. It also gives the reader a ready frame within which to hold that material.

Once you have settled upon your thesis, you are ready to move from the more reflective work of formulation to the more hands-on tasks of structuring. The freewriting pages are put aside so that the outlining process can begin.

OUTLINING

Not all writers use outlines—at least formal outlines—and those who do have generally adapted the traditional format to their own needs. An outline is really nothing more than a map of logical procedures. Most of you were probably taught the standard form—the narrowing columns of numerals and letters—in high school. The odds are, however, that few of you start organizing your papers in so formal a manner. What's more, such outlining requires that you know what you are going to say from start to finish. Some writers like that security; many others prefer some element of surprise and trust that they will find the right arguments and examples as they go along. But very few (certainly very few professionals) begin work without notations of one sort or another. A basic grasp of structure is indispensable.

Even if you refuse the rigors of the formal outline, you will probably need to develop some sort of intelligible shorthand for yourself. You should never just begin at the beginning and trust that your native intelligence will get you where you need to go. It very well may, but you will find that in the process you have expended a great deal of energy, checking and rechecking what you have written to make sure that it all hangs together. Even the sketchiest outline can help you avoid this. A few key words and arrows may even do the job. Use whatever will serve your memory best. The whole idea of an outline is to allow you to hold the complete sequence of your paper in mind. The step-by-step development of an idea is much easier if you can take in the trajectory of the essay at a glance.

As important as it is to reach the right level of readiness before writing, it will not do to wait too long. The writer never knows everything in advance. Indeed, a too-detailed map can take the pleasure out of the journey. While many will not want to go as far as novelist E. M. Forster, who once stated that he wrote to find out what he was thinking, you probably should be ready to take the plunge while there are still a few blanks in your conception. But you should study your outline, or idea-sketch, closely to make sure that you can account for the major steps of the argument and to assure yourself that they follow logically.

One useful thing to do while you are working through the outline phase is to gather up the specific quotations you plan to use in your paper. Nothing so disrupts the actual writing process as having to pause for long periods while you hunt through your text for the best passage to cite. In addition, gathering the material in advance helps to sharpen your focus. If you know that you will be quoting a specific passage, then you will be more likely to pave the way for it in your discussion; the quotation won't feel as though it has been jimmied into place. If, on the other hand, you find yourself thinking, "How do I know which quotation to use if I don't know what I'm going to be arguing?" then you may not yet be ready to launch your essay. By the same token, once you have a clear sense of what examples you will cite, you are probably ready to start writing your draft.

SUMMARIZING

Before we look at the drafting process, it may be useful to look at the art of summarizing. I say "art" because summarizing is not, as some believe, a simple matter of restating the plot. Rather, it is a kind of condensation that already assumes a certain understanding of the text; that is, before you summarize you already need to have a clear sense of what is important and what is not. You also need to know when it is necessary and when it is to be avoided. Teachers often caution *against* giving summaries for one very obvious reason: a great many students summarize indiscriminately. Indeed, they sometimes act as if to write about a literary work is to retell it from start to finish.

Summary is not the main point of the literary essay, but it is very often an essential part of it. To summarize is to supply context. It is to lend a hand to the reader, telling her what she needs to know in order to follow your argument or analysis. As you will see in the student essay that follows, a writer must situate a reader. It is no use beginning a paper, "When Lady Helena finally finds the blue jar she has been looking for. . . ." Even the reader who has just finished Isak Dinesen's story "The Blue Jar" is likely to feel overwhelmed. Far better to write:

> In her story "The Blue Jar," author Isak Dinesen tells of a woman's lifelong quest for a jar of a particular blue color, a color that might be said to symbolize perfect love. Lady Helena begins her quest when she is still quite young—indeed, not long after a fated disaster that threw her into the company of a young sailor for nine days. Her search appears to be a search for the pure happiness she had experienced. Years pass and Lady Helena grows old. When she finally finds the blue jar she has been looking for . . .

There is no hard and fast rule about when to summarize or how much to summarize. Generally summaries are given early; they are part of the process of zeroing in on the thesis of the paper. You should, however, avoid the unnecessarily mechanical tactic of beginning the paper with summary. It is far more effective—usually—to capture the reader's interest with some telling observation, something that will alert him or her to the fact that this will be an essay of ideas. Compare the openings of the first and final drafts of the student paper (pp. 153 and 158) on Dinesen's "The Blue Jar." The revised version can be seen to hold out a promise that the draft does not. While not completely summary, the opening of the draft can be said to suffer from the summarizing impulse. Summary should come in a container labeled with a warning: USE SPARINGLY.

How much is enough? The ideal summary gives the reader what he needs to know to grasp the point being made; it supplies essential context, but does not overwhelm the incidentals. There is an elasticity factor. Depending on the need, a summary can be compressed into a single sentence or it can swell into a retelling almost as long as the work in question. Think carefully about how much you need to prove your theory and act accordingly.

By and large, summaries avoid detail and description. They confine themselves to the main thrusts of the action and render these in general terms. Where it is important, they include emotional and psychological information. In summarizing one story it may be enough to write: "The woman waited for her husband for many years." But make sure you account for what is important to the story. You may need to add: "She fell deeper into despair every day." To do a work justice you must have some understanding of what it is trying to communicate, and this is where the art of summarizing comes in.

DRAFTING

A draft is a trial run, a full presentation that is still open to changes, insertions, and countless fine-tunings. No matter how accomplished you are as a writer, it is folly to believe that you will get your thoughts—and prose—into final form right away. To suppose such a thing not only sets you up for disappointment but inhibits the entire writing process. A draft is a pencil sketch, and it leaves you the freedom of using your eraser. In the lucky event that your first venture is nearly perfect, you have only to follow over the contours with ink.

Long ago, before the advent of the word-processor, rewriting necessitated complete retyping. Most writers now have the option of making selective changes. The option brings ease, but it also carries certain dangers. You can make changes and additions in the body of a paragraph without rewriting the whole. And you can shift paragraphs around with the push of a button. But don't forget that language is always in context. Make sure that you read closely the materials that precede and follow your alteration to confirm that you have not upset the balance of the presentation.

There is something to be said for the painstaking process of typing and retyping. Mainly, a full retyping encourages secondary—or stylistic—revision. In going over what you thought was a perfectly satisfactory sentence you often find a better, more evocative way to phrase the idea. If you use a word-processor, you should at least give yourself that option. When you have written your first draft, print out a clean copy and read it through slowly, first word to last, with a pencil in your hand. Make changes and incorporate them. Don't succumb to the temptation to leave well enough alone.

AN ESSAY ABOUT A STORY: A CASE STUDY

What follows now is a more specific account of the essay writing procedure. Here, as a sample text, is Isak Dinesen's very short story "The Blue Jar." You will see how one student worked through the stages of freewriting, locating a thesis, outlining, drafting, and rewriting.

Isak Dinesen (1885–1962)

Isak Dinesen was born Karen Blixen near Elsinore, Denmark. A member of an old and distinguished Danish family, Blixen married a cousin and in 1914 traveled with him to British East Africa. Her celebrated book of reminiscences, *Out of Africa* (1937), chronicles her years of living on a struggling plantation. After divorcing her husband, she returned to Denmark and began to write the stories that made her reputation. Her books include *Seven Gothic Tales* (1934), *Winter's Tales* (1942), *Last Tales* (1957), and *Anecdotes of Destiny* (1958).

THE BLUE JAR

There was once an immensely rich old Englishman who had been a courtier and councillor to the Queen and who now, in his old age, cared for nothing but collecting ancient blue china. To that end he travelled to Persia, Japan and China, and he was everywhere accompanied by his daughter, the Lady Helena. It happened, as they sailed in the Chinese Sea, that the ship caught fire on a still night, and everybody went into the lifeboats and left her. In the dark and the confusion the old peer was separated from his daughter. Lady Helena got up on deck late, and found the ship quite deserted. In the last moment a young English sailor carried her down into a lifeboat that had been forgotten. To the two fugitives it seemed as if fire was following them from all sides, for the phosphorescence played in the dark sea, and, as they looked up, a falling star ran across the sky, as if it was going to drop into the boat. They sailed for nine days, till they were picked up by a Dutch merchantman, and came home to England.

The old lord had believed his daughter to be dead. He now wept with joy, and at once took her off to a fashionable watering-place so that she might recover from the hardships she had gone through. And as he thought it must be unpleasant to her that a young sailor, who made his bread in the merchant service, should tell the world that he has sailed for nine days alone with a peer's daughter, he paid the boy a fine sum, and made him promise to go shipping in the other hemisphere and never come back. "For what," said the old nobleman, "would be the good of that?"

When Lady Helena recovered, and they gave her the news of the Court and of her family, and in the end also told her how the young sailor had been sent away never to come back, they found that her mind had suffered from her trials, and that she cared for nothing in all the world. She would not go back to her father's castle in its park, nor go to Court, nor travel to any gay town of the continent. The only thing which she now wanted to do was to go, like her father before her, to collect rare blue china. So she began to sail, from one country to the other, and her father went with her.

In her search she told the people, with whom she dealt, that she was looking for a particular blue color, and would pay any price for it. But although she bought many hundred blue jars and bowls, she would always after a time put them aside and say: "Alas, alas, it is not the right blue." Her father, when they had sailed for many years, suggested to her that perhaps the color which she sought did not exist. "O God, Papa," said she, "how can you speak so wickedly? Surely there must be some of it left from the time when all the world was blue."

Her two old aunts in England implored her to come back, still to make a great match. But she answered them: "Nay, I have got to sail. For you must know, dear aunts, that it is all nonsense when learned people tell you that the seas have got a bottom to them. On the contrary, the water, which is noblest of the elements, does, of course, go all through the earth, so that our planet really floats in the ether, like a soap bubble. And there, on the other hemisphere, a ship sails, with which I have got to keep pace. We two are like the reflection of one another, in the deep sea, and the ship of which I speak is always exactly beneath my own ship, upon the opposite side of the globe. You have never seen a big fish swimming underneath a boat, following it like a dark-blue shade in the water. But in that way this ship goes, like the shadow of my ship, and I draw it to and fro wherever I go, as the moon draws the tides, all through the bulk of the earth. If I stopped sailing, what would those poor sailors who made their bread in the merchant service do? But I shall tell you a secret," she said. "In the end my ship will go down, to the centre of the globe, and at the very same hour the other ship will sink as well—for people call it sinking, although I can assure you that there is no up and down in the sea—and there, in the midst of the world, we two shall meet."

5

Many years passed, the old lord died and Lady Helena became old and deaf, but she still sailed. Then it happened, after the plunder of the summer palace of the Emperor of China, that a merchant brought her a very old blue jar. The moment she set eyes on it she gave a terrible shriek. "There it is!" she cried. "I have found it at last. This is the true blue. Oh, how light it makes one. Oh, it is as fresh as a breeze, as deep as a deep secret, as full as I say not what." With trembling hands she held the jar to her bosom, and sat for six hours sunk in contemplation of it. Then she said to her doctor and her lady-companion: "Now I can die. And when I am dead you will cut out my heart and lay it in the blue jar. For then everything will be as it was then. All shall be blue round me, and in the midst of the blue world my heart will be innocent and free, and will beat gently, like a wake that sings, like the drops that fall from an oar blade." A little later she asked them: "Is it not a sweet thing to think that, if only you have patience, all that has ever been, will come back to you?" Shortly afterwards the old lady died.

The assignment given in this class asked the student to pick one short story from the anthology and to write either an explication of one passage or an analysis of one of the central elements. *Explication*, as the teacher explained, is a highly magnified inspection of one crucial portion of the work, usually no longer than several paragraphs. The point of the exercise is to isolate specific components—turns of phrase, images, instances of significant diction—to show how they contribute to the purpose of the whole work. The process, he explained, is like taking a tissue culture: by looking closely enough at an isolated group of cells, a doctor is very often able to make discoveries about the functioning of the larger organism.

The second option, *analysis*, allows for a larger perspective. An essay in analysis singles out one of the various elements in the work—for example, the presentation of character or setting, the use of point of view, or the placement of symbols—in order to explore its function in the text. Unlike explication, analysis can range freely through the work, focusing on relevant materials. Each approach has its own advantages, of course. And the differences between them are not absolute. A paper explicating a part of a story may use some techniques of analysis, separating out aspects of the passage and studying their contribution. In the same way, an analysis—of setting or character, say—might zero in on a particular description, subjecting it to careful explication. In other words, the boundaries between kinds of writing are by no means absolute.

Rereading, Freewriting, and a Preliminary Thesis

One student chose Isak Dinesen's story "The Blue Jar" and decided that she would probably write an essay analyzing the significance of the jar that gives the story its name. Her initial reading had convinced her that there was probably enough symbolism to support an analysis paper.

The student—Kyla—began by reading the story over again several times (she patted herself on the back for choosing a short text). On the third reading she made marks in the margin of the page and underlined several passages. She was trying to find an angle on her subject, some insight that might lead her to a thesis. What she found to be most interesting as she reread the story was that the blue jar seemed to have layers of significance. It was, on the one hand, an object to be collected for its beauty and workmanship. But it was also suggestive in other ways. Lady Helena not only connected the color blue with innocence, speaking of "the time when all the world was blue," but also linked the color with her memory of being rescued at sea by the young sailor. As Kyla underlined different passages, she grew more secure about her general topic. She believed that she could write a strong paper that would show how the jar gradually became a symbol for everything that was important to Lady Helena.

Kyla's next step was to try to develop her ideas through freewriting. Setting the story aside, she took out a sheet of paper and began writing down her random impressions, some of which are shown here.

> A love story, finally, but a strange one. The rela-
> tionship is never shown and we don't know what hap-
> pened. Does it matter what happened? In a way what
> matters is what Lady H. believed. If she believed it
> was true love, or perfection, then maybe it was. Maybe
> she was crazy. Maybe Dinesen is talking about how being
> forced to live against your instincts and desires
> drives you mad (the father sent away the sailor cuz he
> was the wrong sort of person). Sounds like Romeo and
> Juliet or something. Other evidence that she's crazy:
> her theory about the boat on the opposite side of the
> world. Are we supposed to think this is profound or
> mystical, or insane? Not clear. Maybe it's not supposed
> to be clear. Maybe we're supposed to put aside our
> usual ideas. The ending definitely has a "love conquers
> all" feel to it--very romantic. The blue jar is defi-
> nitely a symbol for her. Of innocence and all, but also
> of the perfection of those days at sea . . .

Kyla went on in this vein for several pages. When she reread her freewritten notes, she drew a big circle around part of this passage. She found something promising in the fundamental uncertainty about whether Lady Helena was fulfilling a dream of true love or losing her mind. She didn't know just how she would connect this idea to her analysis of the blue jar motif, but she trusted that some connection would come.

When Kyla sat down at her desk later in the day, she felt ready to think her way through to a thesis. She wrote down her two main ideas as follows:

```
Isak Dinesen uses a woman's obsession with a blue
jar to reveal how love can affect a person's life.
```

And:

```
The reader is never entirely sure whether Lady
Helena has lost her mind, or whether her belief in
love has allowed her a final happiness.
```

Kyla spent a long time staring at the two sentences, trying to figure out if there was a way in which they could be joined together to make a convincing thesis statement. At last she thought she saw a way. She wrote:

```
In her story "The Blue Jar," Isak Dinesen uses one
woman's obsession with the symbolic meanings of a piece
of rare blue china as a way to ask about the differ-
ences between love and madness.
```

For Kyla, arriving at a thesis quickly clarified her overall approach for her. She did not feel that she needed to write an elaborate outline, but she did make a simple list. With a longer story she might have copied out passages to use in her presentation, but in this case she did not feel that was necessary. Here is her outline sketch.

```
1. Introduction--set out basic thesis
2. General plot summary (simple)
3. Introduce blue jar as symbol and discuss layers
   of significance
4. Closer look at final scene--quote
5. Conclusion--what is D. saying about love and
   madness?
```

A First Draft

Having set out her plan, Kyla began to work on her first draft. She knew enough about her writing habits to know that a rough version, however clumsy and incomplete, would give her something concrete to work with. She wrote as follows (my own annotations have been added):

```
"The Blue Jar"--A Search for True Love
                                              introduce
    In "The Blue Jar," Danish story writer Isak        thesis more
Dinesen uses one woman's obsession with the            smoothly
```

symbolic meanings of a piece of rare blue
china as a way to question the difference between love and madness. Her characters are simple and never really come to life, but that
does not matter to the reader. We are, like
Dinesen, interested in the question, for it is
universal.

loose
connection
between 1st
and 2nd
sentences

A young woman, Lady Helena, is stranded in
a lifeboat with an English sailor. They are
together for a long time. When they are saved,
the girl's father, "a rich old Englishman,"
sends the sailor away.

no reason for
quoting brief
identification

Why is sailor
sent away?

Lady Helena falls ill for a time. When she
recovers she is changed. She has no interest
in news of the court. Instead, she joins
her father in his search for rare blue
china, sailing the world to find the perfect
shade. When he suggests that the color might
not exist, she says, "Surely there must be
some of it left from the time when all the
world was blue." We see she views it symbolically.

avoid strings
of short
sentences

more comment
on suggestive
quotations

Lady Helena also imagines that there is a
ship on the other side of the world, following
hers, and that one day the two ships will sink
and meet in the middle of the world. She grows
old, still sailing.

One day a merchant brings her a blue jar,
the very one she has been looking for. "There
it is!" she cries. She tells her doctor that
when she dies her heart should be placed in
the jar. "For then everything will be as it
was then," she explains. Before she dies, she
asks: "Is it not a sweet thing to think that,
if only you have patience, all that has ever
been, will come back to you?"

mysterious
idea needs
more context

Dinesen is obviously using blue as a symbol. When Lady Helena speaks of the time "when
all the world was blue," we associate the
color with innocence, a Garden of Eden kind of

thing. Her idea about the other ship suggests that she still thinks of the sailor. Though we are not told what happened while Lady Helena and the sailor were in the boat together, we assume that they fell in love. This would explain why she never married.

"kind of thing" is too casual

When the perfect jar is found, Lady Helena knows that her death is near. But she is not afraid. She believes that she has recovered her long-ago happiness and that if her heart is placed in the jar she will experience a kind of eternal bliss. She dies happily--or so we are to think.

In the final scene, Dinesen clarifies her use of the symbol. Thinking of her heart in the jar, Lady Helena says, "All shall be blue round me, and in the midst of the blue world my heart will be innocent and free, and will beat gently, like a wake that sings, like the drops that fall from an oar blade." These two similes, about the wake and the drops, make it clear that her fantasy is connected to a memory--that the wake and the drops are from her days with the sailor.

good use of specific evidence

Lady Helena never meets her sailor again, and yet when she dies it is as if she has fulfilled her love. Dinesen says a great deal here about the power of love. That it can be as real in memory as in the present. "The Blue Jar" shows how belief affects a life. Some people may say that Lady Helena is crazy, but what is crazy and who is to say? If she believes that she has fulfilled her life, then maybe she has.

not a sentence

too general needs elaboration

Rethinking, Discussing, and Rewriting

Reading over her draft, Kyla was not completely satisfied. She felt that she had gotten the main points down, but that she had not really explored the implications with any depth. She did not feel that she was finally saying that much—the story seemed to her more profound and interesting than her treatment revealed. She also thought that she had spent too much time simply retelling the plot. She decided that when she sat down to rewrite the draft she would try to compress the summary and to devote correspondingly more space to the discussion of Dinesen's use of symbols to convey a philosophy about love.

First, however, she would have another chance to test out her views. At the next class meeting her teacher divided the students into small discussion groups. Kyla found herself sitting with three of her peers, all of whom had written about the Dinesen story. The purpose of the small-group exercise was to encourage students to compare ideas and insights. After a few minutes of banter they started in. Each group member summarized his or her basic approach, making a case for a particular interpretation of the story.

Kyla was surprised to find out how different the readings were from one another. Larry, the first to speak, saw the story as chronicling Lady Helena's disintegration. "It's about what happens when you are not allowed to love," he said. He saw the work as Dinesen's way of passing judgment upon the artificial and exclusive ways of the aristocracy. Larry was convinced that Lady Helena had lost her mind and that her instructions to have her heart removed were proof positive of that fact.

Dierdre, the next to speak, said that she saw how Larry had arrived at his interpretation, but she admitted that she herself had viewed the story less as an attack upon aristocracy than as a questioning of sexist assumptions. "The girl never took power over her life," said Dierdre. "She gave in to her father's wishes, she took up his hobby, and she let herself drift passively from place to place, unable to act on her feelings. I don't think she went crazy so much as she escaped into the only kind of fantasy that could give her life meaning."

Kyla nodded to signal her interest. She told the group that she, too, had explored the madness question, but that she was not sure that Dinesen wanted to present Lady Helena as either a failure or a madwoman. "Those were different times," she said. "She may not have been thinking in terms of women's rights. And I think that it's too easy to say she's just crazy. Doesn't her craziness have something mysterious and noble about it?"

"You think there's any way she's sane?" Greg, the last member of the group, spoke up. "She thinks that there's a hole in the middle of the world. She orders her doctor to cut out her heart and put it in a jar. . . ."

Kyla laughed. "When you put it like that, sure—she's nuts. But don't you agree that there are some different laws for stories of this kind? This is a romantic legend. There's a long tradition of lovers drinking poison and stabbing themselves. We don't write all these people off as simple lunatics. What about Romeo, and Juliet, and Anna Karenina, who threw herself in front of a train?"

The group members went back and forth on the question. Interestingly, the debate divided along gender lines. Larry and Greg saw no way around the insanity verdict, while both Kyla and Dierdre were prepared to allow a more romantically lenient interpretation. By the end of the class period the four were in a friendly standoff. "So much for your ideas about consensus," said Greg as the teacher came by.

"I didn't suggest that you were going to *reach* consensus, Greg. I said we would *test* consensus." He moved up to the front of the room to address the whole class.

"Ladies and gentlemen—a word of reminder. The point of these group discussions is not to get you all to be writing the same paper. The point is to sharpen your thinking and to make you aware of the fact that different interpretations are possible. My hope is that when you sit down to do your rewrites you will hear other voices in your heads—critical, questioning voices. You are not only giving an interpretation, but also defending an interpretation. You are making the strongest possible case for your views."

Kyla remembered her teacher's words later, and she began to understand the value of the small-group discussion. She had not, it's true, changed her view about the story. But she realized that the point about love and lunacy would have to be made with some care. What's more, she already knew that as she advanced her argument she would, at some level, be carrying on her debate with Larry and Greg. The best way to break through the standoff, at least as far as she was concerned, was to write a convincing essay. Rising to the challenge, Kyla took out her draft. This time she read with a sharpened pencil in her hand.

The more she thought about it, the more Kyla realized that her opening was weak. She had used her thesis as the first sentence but had done little to follow it up. The statement seemed abrupt, and the following sentence, about the flatness of the characters, did not connect. She knew that she wanted something more elegant and suggestive to draw her reader in. She then remembered that in her freewriting she had mentioned *Romeo and Juliet*. That brought to mind a discussion in her high-school English class about lovers being driven beyond all bounds of accepted behavior. She dug out her old notebook, and there she found a passage copied from another Shakespeare play, *A Midsummer Night's Dream*. It was just what she needed:

Lovers and madmen have such seething brains,
Such shaping fantasies, that apprehend
More than cool reason ever comprehends.

Writers speak reverently of what they sometimes call "gift moments"—unexpected discoveries or realizations that solve a problem. Kyla felt that she had made a lucky find, though in fact she had been following an inward trail of association. Thinking about the connection between love and madness, she recalled her Shakespeare class, then her notebook. The luck was in finding the very quotation she needed. She knew right away that the Shakespeare passage would set up the love/madness concept in a more interesting and authoritative way. The rest would follow, provided that she took care to compress the plot summary and to expand upon the different meanings of the color blue.

Here is Kyla's final version, the one that she submitted to her teacher. She spent several hours hunched in front of her computer screen, trying to get the sentences to flow smoothly and making sure that her transitions were logical. Naturally, there is no way to account for the countless alterations, except to say that from sentence to sentence Kyla would read over what she had written and ask herself if her interpretation made sense. She tried her best to think her way into the story and to avoid making obvious points. Her final version was, as she expected, longer than the draft.

A Final Draft

"The Blue Jar"--Love's Shaping Fantasies

good
incorporation
of quotation in
title

The idea that love and madness are somehow linked is as old as literature. "Lovers and madmen have such seething brains," wrote Shakespeare in A Midsummer Night's Dream. "Such shaping fantasies, that apprehend/ More than cool reason ever comprehends." There are no rules for lovers. True passion will throw itself at every obstacle. But even though the behavior is very much like madness, we insist on thinking that love makes it noble. We think of the suicides of Romeo and Juliet as tragic, not crazy.

quotation introduces theme nicely

useful comparison

The Danish writer Isak Dinesen (1885-1962) has another variation on the theme of doomed love. Though her story "The Blue Jar" is full of romantic ideas about perfect love, the lovers meeting after death, and so on, it differs from the usual pattern. There are no love scenes, no violent climaxes (unless putting a heart in a jar counts), and the ending is happy. But in spite of this, Dinesen makes her reader think about the meaning of true love.

dates help the reader place the story

a smart move—to characterize story by how it differs from pattern

"The Blue Jar" is as simple as a fairy tale. The main characters--a rich old councillor and his daughter--are two-dimensional. The plot is written like a summary. But the story works, because against this flatness the mysterious symbol of blue stands out and works on the imagination.

clear statement of key idea

repetitious —avoid restating points

The plot, like the characters, is simple. A rich man's daughter is rescued from a burning ship by a young English sailor. The two spend nine days together in a small boat. When Lady Helena returns to her father, he finds the sailor a post in the other hemisphere. We never learn what took place between Lady Helena and the sailor.

Lady Helena's family, writes Dinesen, "found that her mind had suffered from her trials, and that she cared for nothing in all the world." The young woman refuses all suit-ors. Like her father, she devotes herself to searching for rare blue china.

It is permissible to speak of a dead author in present tense when discussing a work

One day, when she is old, she finds what she has been searching for: the perfect blue jar. She knows that her mysterious mission has been accomplished and that she will soon die. She then gives instructions to her doctor and traveling companion that after her death her heart is to be removed and placed in the jar. She dies soon after.

passage lacking in emphasis does not convey the extraordinary quality of this plot development

Dinesen is not interested in plot or char-acter, but in showing how strong the power of love can be. After her father sends the sailor away, Lady Helena is obviously depressed. But she does not go against his wishes as Shake-speare's Juliet did. Instead, she creates a world of her own--a world of true love where the limits of reality have no place. She hunts for her blue jar, the color symbolic of inno-cence. Some of it must be left over, she tells her father, "from the time when all the world was blue." She also believes that there is an-other ship following hers on the opposite side of the world.

needs smoother paragraph transition

a good way to reestablish opening comparison

writer assumes color symbolic of innocence without giving reason

comment on quotation

better to quote full sentence

The image of the two ships is also a kind of symbol. Lady Helena believes that the sailor shares her love and that they are together in their love even though they are a world apart. "In the end," she tells her aunts, "my ship will go down to the centre of the globe, and at the very same hour the other ship will sink as well . . . and there, in the midst of the world, we two shall meet."

avoid "also" constructions

comma missing from quotation

use of ellipses to avoid quoting unnecessary material

Just as Lady Helena goes against all scien-tific knowledge when she insists that the oceans

a strong transitional idea, but needs to be expressed more fully to make a paragraph are joined in the middle of the earth, so she rejects common sense in her final fantasy.

In the last scene, Dinesen clarifies her use of the symbolic blue color. Thinking of her heart inside that jar, Lady Helena visualizes innocence and freedom. Her heart, she says, "will beat gently, like a wake that sings, like the drops that fall from an oar blade." These two similes, about the wake and the drops, make it clear that her lifelong fantasy is connected to a specific memory. Those are the images that she remembers from her days with the sailor, and the perfect shade of blue must be the one that lives in her memory.

writer wisely retained strong passage from rough draft

overstated— writer does not know this for certain; phrase it as a surmise

The reader of "The Blue Jar" is finally left to hover between Lady Helena's absolute conviction and the more commonsense view that lovers are not reunited after death and that hearts do not go on beating after they are removed from the body. This strain is probably what Dinesen wanted us to feel. She plays on the fact that death is a mystery and that we don't really know what comes after. For Lady Helena, believing may have made it so. People can argue that she is just crazy, but who will say for sure? There is a small chance that her happiness was complete, that true love <u>did</u> conquer all. That small chance is just what Dinesen needed to bring her puzzling story to a close.

nicely suggestive ending— captures the mysteriousness of the story

The discovery of a new way to lead into her thesis allowed Kyla to rewrite her paper, and it allowed her a broader scope for her discussion. When she reread the final draft, however, she was still not completely satisfied. She felt that she had not succeeded in compressing the plot as she had hoped. She also noted that her explication of the final scene was anything but thorough. In trying to get her basic points across, she had not left herself room for more focused questioning. She would have liked to pick apart the images with more care. And she had other ideas that she could have worked in, especially the idea that the heart in the blue jar was in some way a symbol for the two lovers together in their boat. But time had run out. She was happy enough with her work, especially her opening, to hand the paper in.

Writing about Fiction

COMPARISON AND CONTRAST

One of the most effective ways to engage a work of literature is to set it alongside another and to search out comparisons and contrasts. (It is possible, but difficult, to do one without doing the other.) The options are various. You can look at two works by a single author, checking for similarities and differences in approach, treatment of character, and so on. Or you can pick works by two authors who are contemporaries, or authors from different periods. The selections can be made on the basis of general similarity or obvious divergence—or anything in between. Strictly speaking, anything can be compared with anything else. Write a paper comparing a grapefruit and a tractor—it's possible. But the point, at least when talking about works of fiction, is to compare and contrast in order to gain specific insights. If you look at Hemingway's treatment of women in his fiction in isolation, you get one picture. A larger, more suggestive, picture emerges when you compare his treatment with Virginia Woolf's (the two were more or less contemporaries). Both approaches have their uses. One of the main uses of comparison/contrast is to create a wider context for the works in question. But the process also underlines the tremendous differences between one artistic vision and another.

There is a general procedure for writing this kind of essay. To begin with, you will almost never find yourself comparing or contrasting one complete work with another. Most stories are just too complex to permit point-by-point comparisons. Each has its own characters, plot designs, settings, points of view, and so on. The first step is to determine *what* is to be considered. Do you want to explore similarities and differences between Virginia Woolf's and James Joyce's use of interior monologue? or D. H. Lawrence's and Katherine Mansfield's portrayals of death? or do you want to look at two stories by Raymond Carver to compare the depictions of male-female relationships? There is no dearth of rich topics.

You may want to begin, then, by isolating some particular element from the stories you have chosen. The basic elements of fiction, as discussed elsewhere, are character, plot, setting, theme, point of view, symbol (or figurative language in general), and tone. Almost every story makes some use of each, and once you have determined which seems most fruitful you can get to work. With your two stories before you, you can start charting an approach.

How you build your essay will depend upon several things. Like the analytic essay, a comparison/contrast essay needs to be organized around some thesis, some main point. Your key to finding this lies in the basic nature of your approach. If you have picked two stories that exhibit a strong similarity—in theme, say—then you must ask yourself what is the strongest assertion you can make. For example: "Though the stories are vastly different in plot, setting, and point of view, Sarah Orne Jewett's 'A White Heron' and Kate Chopin's 'The Story of an Hour' both depict their protagonists finding self-recognition in solitary struggles." Having made such an assertion early on in your essay, you might then go on to explain how those struggles came about and to inquire into their specific similarities and differences.

The same basic tactic holds true for approaches stressing contrast, though here you might take a common attribute as your pivot: "While James Joyce's 'The Dead' and D. H. Lawrence's 'Odour of Chrysanthemums' both dissect the failures of communication in marriages, the stories use very different approaches to achieve their end." Of course, not every thesis needs to be set up in such a fashion—how boring it would be if they were! You might try out some such formulation simply to clarify your topic to yourself.

As you set about writing the main part of your essay, you might keep several suggestions in mind. First, it is much easier to feature one story and to use the other as an examining tool. Though your democratic instinct might favor giving each work equal time, the practical result is a loss of center. It becomes very hard to avoid the "on the one hand . . . on the other hand" effect. By putting one story in the foreground you automatically create a focus, thus: "Of the two stories, Joyce's makes subtler use of characterization, and while his approach is not nearly as dramatic as Lawrence's, his conclusion reflects a deeper despair." You would then set the stage with a preliminary discussion of "The Dead," clarifying Joyce's approach, before bringing Lawrence forward.

There is no one right way to structure a comparison/contrast paper. Some writers favor the two-part approach, in which, to stay with the example, Joyce's story would be examined in its entirety, then Lawrence's would be introduced and discussed with reference to points made about "The Dead." Others are more comfortable switching back and forth several times. They might compare Joyce's and Lawrence's presentation of husband and wife, then look at their treatment of the climactic scene, then assess the darkness of their respective visions. What you want to avoid is an uncentered fidgeting from one work to the other: "Lawrence uses obvious symbols; Joyce does not. But Joyce's way of setting nearly all of his scenes in rooms and corridors makes for an atmosphere every bit as constricting as Lawrence's. Lawrence, though. . . ." If you go on like this for more than a paragraph you will very likely lose the good will of your reader, not to mention the main thread of your argument.

As I suggested earlier, analysis, explication, and comparison/contrast are the main ways to approach literary works. Each has something to teach, and thus each is worth practicing independently. But in fact the best literary writing makes use of all three modes. Analysis is often most effective when it builds upon the careful sifting that is explication; and the strongest insights are often found when one thing is related to another. The final version of the student paper showed this clearly. While the essay was written as an analysis of the thematic use of symbol, it scored points early by making a comparison with Shakespeare's lovers. And though space did not permit, the student could have strengthened her final paragraphs by explicating Lady Helena's last words.

Every writer refines his or her approach over years of writing, mastering different tools, learning what works best in any given situation, and learning the quirks of the process. Some find that they need to be painstaking about making outlines; others trust themselves to inspiration and then revise innumerable times. What is the formula? Whatever works. I once heard an interviewer ask the writer Susan Sontag how many times she generally revised a given essay. She said—without a pause—"seventeen or eighteen, usually." This is not meant to intimidate the would-be essayist so much as to suggest the lengths to which a writer will go to get it right. Implicit, but less immediately obvious, is the fact that the reward must finally outweigh the struggle. Otherwise Sontag, or any writer, would not persist.

11 A Fiction Writer's Career: Alice Munro

Canadian writer Alice Munro is widely acknowledged as one of the living masters of the short
story. Readers and critics alike have testified to
her ability to pack her stories with a near-novelistic density. Her characters are
complex and unpredictable, and her settings and atmospheres have an authenticity that suggests that they have not so much been invented as excavated from the
memory cells. Munro herself must be counted as one of the more reticent of contemporary authors, volunteering little in the way of biographical information. She
has not made it a practice to draw the connecting lines between her experience
and her work. This reticence may be due to a natural instinct toward privacy, but
it may also have something to do with a fear commonly expressed by writers of fiction—that readers will try to interpret the work in the light of what is known
about the life.

The fear is not unjustified. Literary biography is a major industry, and a great
many critics occupy themselves in reading an author's work through the lens of
the life. Critical interpretation of writers like Ernest Hemingway, Thomas Wolfe,
Anne Sexton, Sylvia Plath, and dozens of others has been greatly influenced by
such readings. The insights to be gained are considerable. After all, the art does
not grow up in a vacuum. But by the same token, too great a zealousness about
finding correspondences between the life and the work can easily skew the understanding of the work. Perhaps the fear of just such misinterpretation explains
Munro's attitude.

Certainly the information available on this writer does not give the critic
grounds for any speculative theorizing. We know just the bare facts. Munro was born
in 1931 in Wingham, Ontario, and attended the local public schools. From 1949 to
1951 she studied at the University of Western Ontario. She married in 1951, had
three children, and divorced in 1976. She married for a second time that same year.
The rest of her history is the history of the work.

Munro has been fairly prolific. Her first collection of stories, *Dance of the Happy
Shades,* was published in 1968. It was followed by a novel, *Lives of Girls and Women,*
in 1971. Since then she has published five collections of stories: *Something I've Been
Meaning to Tell You* (1974); *The Beggar Maid: Stories of Flo and Rose* (1978); *The
Moons of Jupiter* (1982); *The Progress of Love* (1986); and, most recently, *Friend of
My Youth* (1990).

Of course, we never *really* know, even with the most forthcoming of writers, just
how the fiction draws upon the life. The most obvious way, the direct transposition

of an actual event, is less common than one might think. Even the most obviously autobiographical circumstances are generally transformed, with some elements heightened and others suppressed. Do we say, then, that the "improved" version of the actual is truer than another writer's invention? On what grounds?

The fact is that there are a thousand and one ways in which writers mine the contents of their own experience, even when the outward situation has been altered. And these fictional projections have no less bearing on the truth than the more circumstantially faithful account. Some would even argue that all writing is nothing else than fictional projection, and that all impulses to set words on paper derive from psychological losses experienced early in life. The writing, according to this view, is a more-or-less direct attempt to understand the injuries and set them right.

How much this may or may not explain Alice Munro's art is impossible to gauge. Certainly in reading the stories we get a strong sense of a writer eavesdropping on her own experience. The particulars may be different, and certain characters may have been spun out of the imagination, but the observed detail and the play of emotion and memory feel as though they are coming directly from the self. This may be the quality that so many readers have responded to in Munro's fiction: every one of her stories feels lit up by the flame of the actual. Their special quality, while hard to explain, is readily discerned.

Munro, like Chekhov and Frank O'Connor, among others, writes stories that center on the lives of ordinary people. She explores the private trials and disappointments that have shaped her characters, but she also searches out moments of realization and revelation. These very often come about through the unexpected discovery of love or affection, or else through the illumination that memory can bring. Indeed, one of the distinctive attributes of Munro's fiction is her vivid presentation of the patterns that memories weave through our waking lives. She has the gift for finding—or creating—those moments in which the surfacing memory brings a new understanding to bear upon some long-familiar situation.

Though Munro is adept at setting her stories in a wide variety of locales, the true country of her imagination is the small-town Canada of her own origins. Many of her best stories return to the places and atmospheres she knows best, and they feature characters (often women) so deeply known through their quirks and eccentricities that they cannot have been invented out of whole cloth. As James Joyce drew upon a Dublin of the mind, and William Faulkner a Mississippi, so Munro, working on a smaller scale, has steadily populated a corner of Ontario.

The two stories included here are drawn from Munro's collection *The Beggar Maid: Stories of Flo and Rose*. I took two stories from one volume not only because they showed her procedure clearly, but also because their juxtaposition may allow the reader a deeper sense of how Munro looks at people and places through a lens of time. These happen to be the first and last stories in the book. The intervening stories follow the girl, Rose, through her coming-of-age, her love affairs, marriage, and divorce, but as "Who Do You Think You Are?", the second of the stories, makes clear, there is a way in which time—the time that matters—seems to stand still. Rose has grown up and gone away; in another sense, however, she has not budged, and all that has happened since the coming of adulthood vanishes before the power of the past.

ROYAL BEATINGS

Royal Beating. That was Flo's promise. You are going to get one Royal Beating.

The word Royal lolled on Flo's tongue, took on trappings. Rose had a need to picture things, to pursue absurdities, that was stronger than the need to stay out of trouble, and instead of taking this threat to heart she pondered: how is a beating royal? She came up with a tree-lined avenue, a crowd of formal spectators, some white horses and black slaves. Someone knelt, and the blood came leaping out like banners. An occasion both savage and splendid. In real life they didn't approach such dignity, and it was only Flo who tried to supply the event with some high air of necessity and regret. Rose and her father soon got beyond anything presentable.

Her father was king of the royal beatings. Those Flo gave never amounted to much; they were quick cuffs and slaps dashed off while her attention remained elsewhere. You get out of my road, she would say. You mind your own business. You take that look off your face.

They lived behind a store in Hanratty, Ontario. There were four of them: Rose, her father, Flo, Rose's young half brother Brian. The store was really a house, bought by Rose's father and mother when they married and set up here in the furniture and upholstery repair business. Her mother could do upholstery. From both parents Rose should have inherited clever hands, a quick sympathy with materials, an eye for the nicest turns of mending, but she hadn't. She was clumsy, and when something broke she couldn't wait to sweep it up and throw it away.

Her mother had died. She said to Rose's father during the afternoon, "I have a feeling that is so hard to describe. It's like a boiled egg in my chest, with the shell left on." She died before night, she had a blood clot on her lung. Rose was a baby in a basket at the time, so of course could not remember any of this. She heard it from Flo, who must have heard it from her father. Flo came along soon afterward, to take over Rose in the basket, marry her father, open up the front room to make a grocery store. Rose, who had known the house only as a store, who had known only Flo for a mother, looked back on the sixteen or so months her parents spent here as an orderly, far gentler and more ceremonious time, with little touches of affluence. She had nothing to go on but some egg cups her mother had bought, with a pattern of vines and birds on them, delicately drawn as if with red ink; the pattern was beginning to wear away. No books or clothes or pictures of her mother remained. Her father must have got rid of them, or else Flo would. Flo's only story about her mother, the one about her death, was oddly grudging. Flo liked the details of a death: the things people said, the way they protested or tried to get out of bed or swore or laughed (some did those things), but when she said that Rose's mother mentioned a hard-boiled egg in her chest she made the comparison sound slightly foolish, as if her mother really was the kind of person who might think you could swallow an egg whole.

Her father had a shed out behind the store, where he worked at his furniture repairing and restoring. He caned chair seats and backs, mended wickerwork, filled cracks, put legs back on, all most admirably and skillfully and cheaply. That was his pride: to startle people with such fine work, such moderate, even ridiculous charges. During the Depression people could not afford to pay more, perhaps, but he continued the practice through the war, through the years of prosperity after the war, until he died. He never discussed with Flo what he charged or what was owing. After he died she had to go out and unlock the shed and take all sorts of scraps of paper and torn envelopes from the big wicked-looking hooks that were his files. Many of these she found were not accounts or receipts at all but records of the weather, bits of information about the garden, things he had been moved to write down.

Ate new potatoes 25th June. Record.
Dark Day, 1880's, nothing supernatural. Clouds of ash from forest fires.
Aug. 16, 1938. Giant thunderstorm in evng. Lightning str. Pres. Church,
Turberry Twp. Will of God?
Scald strawberries to remove acid.
All things are alive. Spinoza.

Flo thought Spinoza° must be some new vegetable he planned to grow, like broccoli or eggplant. He would often try some new thing. She showed the scrap of paper to Rose and asked, did she know what Spinoza was? Rose did know, or had an idea— she was in her teens by that time—but she replied that she did not. She had reached an age where she thought she could not stand to know any more, about her father, or about Flo; she pushed any discovery aside with embarrassment and dread.

There was a stove in the shed, and many rough shelves covered with cans of paint and varnish, shellac and turpentine, jars of soaking brushes and also some dark sticky bottles of cough medicine. Why should a man who coughed constantly, whose lungs took in a whiff of gas in the War (called, in Rose's earliest childhood, not the First, but the Last, War) spend all his days breathing fumes of paint and turpentine? At the time, such questions were not asked as often as they are now. On the bench outside Flo's store several old men from the neighborhood sat gossiping, drowsing, in the warm weather, and some of these old men coughed all the time too. The fact is they were dying, slowly and discreetly, of what was called, without any particular sense of grievance, "the foundry disease." They had worked all their lives at the foundry in town, and now they sat still, with their wasted yellow faces, coughing, chuckling, drifting into aimless obscenity on the subject of women walking by, or any young girl on a bicycle.

From the shed came not only coughing, but speech, a continual muttering, reproachful or encouraging, usually just below the level at which separate words could be made out. Slowing down when her father was at a tricky piece of work, taking on a cheerful speed when he was doing something less demanding, sandpapering or painting. Now and then some words would break through and hang clear and nonsensical on the air. When he realized they were out, there would be a quick bit of cover-up coughing, a swallowing, an alert, unusual silence.

"Macaroni, pepperoni, Botticelli, beans—"

What could that mean? Rose used to repeat such things to herself. She could never ask him. The person who spoke these words and the person who spoke to her as her father were not the same, though they seemed to occupy the same space. It would be the worst sort of taste to acknowledge the person who was not supposed to be there; it would not be forgiven. Just the same, she loitered and listened. 10

Spinoza: Benedict Spinoza (1632–1677), a Dutch philosopher.

The cloud-capped towers, she heard him say once.

"The cloud-capped towers, the gorgeous palaces."

That was like a hand clapped against Rose's chest, not to hurt, but astonish her, to take her breath away. She had to run then, she had to get away. She knew that was enough to hear, and besides, what if he caught her? It would be terrible.

This was something the same as bathroom noises. Flo had saved up, and had a bathroom put in, but there was no place to put it except in a corner of the kitchen. The door did not fit, the walls were only beaverboard. The result was that even the tearing of a piece of toilet paper, the shifting of a haunch, was audible to those working or talking or eating in the kitchen. They were all familiar with each other's nether voices, not only in their more explosive moments but in their intimate sighs and growls and pleas and statements. And they were all most prudish people. So no one ever seemed to hear, or be listening, and no reference was made. The person creating the noises in the bathroom was not connected with the person who walked out.

They lived in a poor part of town. There was Hanratty and West Hanratty, with the river flowing between them. This was West Hanratty. In Hanratty the social structure ran from doctors and dentists and lawyers down to foundry workers and factory workers and draymen; in West Hanratty it ran from factory workers and foundry workers down to large improvident families of casual bootleggers and prostitutes and unsuccessful thieves. Rose thought of her own family as straddling the river, belonging nowhere, but that was not true. West Hanratty was where the store was and they were, on the straggling tail end of the main street. Across the road from them was a blacksmith shop, boarded up about the time the war started, and a house that had been another store at one time. The Salada Tea sign had never been taken out of the front window; it remained as a proud and interesting decoration though there was no Salada Tea for sale inside. There was just a bit of sidewalk, too cracked and tilted for rollerskating, though Rose longed for roller skates and often pictured herself whizzing along in a plaid skirt, agile and fashionable. There was one street light, a tin flower; then the amenities gave up and there were dirt roads and boggy places, front-yard dumps and strange-looking houses. What made the houses strange-looking were the attempts to keep them from going completely to ruin. With some the attempt had never been made. These were gray and rotted and leaning over, falling into a landscape of scrub hollows, frog ponds, cattails and nettles. Most houses, however, had been patched up with tarpaper, a few fresh shingles, sheets of tin, hammered-out stovepipes, even cardboard. This was, of course, in the days before the war, days of what would later be legendary poverty, from which Rose would remember mostly low-down things—serious-looking anthills and wooden steps, and a cloudy, interesting, problematical light on the world.

15

There was a long truce between Flo and Rose in the beginning. Rose's nature was growing like a prickly pineapple, but slowly, and secretly, hard pride and skepticism overlapping, to make something surprising even to herself. Before she was old enough to go to school, and while Brian was still in the baby carriage, Rose stayed in the store with both of them—Flo sitting on the high stool behind the counter, Brian asleep by the window; Rose knelt or lay on the wide creaky floorboards working with crayons on pieces of brown paper too torn or irregular to be used for wrapping.

People who came to the store were mostly from the houses around. Some country people came too, on their way home from town, and a few people from Hanratty, who walked across the bridge. Some people were always on the main street, in and out of stores, as if it was their duty to be always on display and their right to be welcomed. For instance, Becky Tyde.

Becky Tyde climbed up on Flo's counter, made room for herself beside an open tin of crumbly jam-filled cookies.

"Are these any good?" she said to Flo, and boldly began to eat one. "When are you going to give us a job, Flo?"

"You could go and work in the butcher shop," said Flo innocently. "You could go and work for your brother." 20

"Roberta?" said Becky with a stagey sort of contempt. "You think I'd work for him?" Her brother who ran the butcher shop was named Robert but often called Roberta, because of his meek and nervous ways. Becky Tyde laughed. Her laugh was loud and noisy like an engine bearing down on you.

She was a big-headed loud-voiced dwarf, with a mascot's sexless swagger, a red velvet tam, a twisted neck that forced her to hold her head on one side, always looking up and sideways. She wore little polished high-heeled shoes, real lady's shoes. Rose watched her shoes, being scared of the rest of her, of her laugh and her neck. She knew from Flo that Becky Tyde had been sick with polio as a child, that was why her neck was twisted and why she had not grown any taller. It was hard to believe that she had started out differently, that she had ever been normal. Flo said she was not cracked, she had as much brains as anybody, but she knew she could get away with anything.

"You know I used to live out here?" Becky said, noticing Rose. "Hey! What's-your-name! Didn't I used to live out here, Flo?"

"If you did it was before my time," said Flo, as if she didn't know anything.

"That was before the neighborhood got so downhill. Excuse me saying so. My father built his house out here and he built his slaughterhouse and we had half an acre of orchard." 25

"Is that so?" said Flo, using her humoring voice, full of false geniality, humility even. "Then why did you ever move away?"

"I told you, it got to be such a downhill neighborhood," said Becky. She would put a whole cookie in her mouth if she felt like it, let her cheeks puff out like a frog's. She never told any more.

Flo knew anyway, and who didn't. Everyone knew the house, red brick with the veranda pulled off and the orchard, what was left of it, full of the usual outflow—car seats and washing machines and bedsprings and junk. The house would never look sinister, in spite of what had happened in it, because there was so much wreckage and confusion all around.

Becky's old father was a different kind of butcher from her brother according to Flo. A bad-tempered Englishman. And different from Becky in the matter of mouthiness. His was never open. A skinflint, a family tyrant. After Becky had polio he wouldn't let her go back to school. She was seldom seen outside the house, never outside the yard. He didn't want people gloating. That was what Becky said, at the trial. Her mother was dead by that time and her sisters married. Just Becky and Robert at home. People would stop Robert on the road and ask him, "How about your sister, Robert? Is she altogether better now?"

"Yes." 30

"Does she do the housework? Does she get your supper?"

"Yes."

"And is your father good to her, Robert?"

The story being that the father beat them, had beaten all his children and beaten his wife as well, beat Becky more now because of her deformity, which some people believed he had caused (they did not understand about polio). The stories persisted and got added to. The reason that Becky was kept out of sight was now supposed to be her pregnancy, and the father of the child was supposed to be her own father. Then people said it had been born, and disposed of.

"What?"

"Disposed of," Flo said. "They used to say go and get your lamb chops at Tydes's, get them nice and tender! It was all lies in all probability," she said regretfully.

Rose could be drawn back—from watching the wind shiver along the old torn awning, catch in the tear—by this tone of regret, caution, in Flo's voice. Flo telling a story—and this was not the only one, or even the most lurid one, she knew—would incline her head and let her face go soft and thoughtful, tantalizing, warning.

"I shouldn't even be telling you this stuff."

More was to follow.

Three useless young men, who hung around the livery stable, got together—or were got together, by more influential and respectable men in town—and prepared to give old man Tyde a horsewhipping, in the interests of public morality. They blacked their faces. They were provided with whips and a quart of whiskey apiece, for courage. They were: Jelly Smith, a horse-racer and a drinker; Bob Temple, a ball-player and strongman; and Hat Nettleton, who worked on the town dray, and had his nickname from a bowler hat he wore, out of vanity as much as for the comic effect. He still worked on the dray, in fact; he had kept the name if not the hat, and could often be seen in public—almost as often as Becky Tyde—delivering sacks of coal, which blackened his face and arms. That should have brought to mind his story, but didn't. Present time and past, the shady melodramatic past of Flo's stories, were quite separate, at least for Rose. Present people could not be fitted into the past. Becky herself, town oddity and public pet, harmless and malicious, could never match the butcher's prisoner, the cripple daughter, a white streak at the window: mute, beaten, impregnated. As with the house, only a formal connection could be made.

The young men primed to do the horsewhipping showed up late, outside Tyde's house, after everybody had gone to bed. They had a gun, but they used up their ammunition firing it off in the yard. They yelled for the butcher and beat on the door; finally they broke it down. Tyde concluded they were after his money, so he put some bills in a handkerchief and sent Becky down with them, maybe thinking those men would be touched or scared by the sight of a little wry-necked girl, a dwarf. But that didn't content them. They came upstairs and dragged the butcher out from under his bed, in his nightgown. They dragged him outside and stood him in the snow. The temperature was four below zero, a fact noted later in court. They meant to hold a mock trial but they could not remember how it was done. So they began to beat him and kept beating him until he fell. They yelled at him, *Butcher's meat!* and continued beating him while his nightgown and the snow he was lying in turned red. His son Robert said in court that he had not watched the beating. Becky said that Robert had watched at first but had run away and hid. She herself had watched all the way through. She watched the men leave at last and her father made his delayed bloody progress through the snow and up the steps of the veranda. She did not go out to help him, or open the door until he got to it. Why not? she was asked in court, and she said she did not open the door because she did not want to let the cold into the house.

Old man Tyde then appeared to have recovered his strength. He sent Robert to harness the horse, and made Becky heat water so that he could wash. He dressed and took all the money and with no explanation to his children got into the cutter and drove to Belgrave where he left the horse tied in the cold and took the early morning train to Toronto. On the train he behaved oddly, groaning and cursing as if he was drunk. He was picked up on the streets of Toronto a day later, out of his mind with fever, and was taken to a hospital, where he died. He still had all the money. The cause of death was given as pneumonia.

But the authorities got wind, Flo said. The case came to trial. The three men who did it all received long prison sentences. A farce, said Flo. Within a year they were all free, had all been pardoned, had jobs waiting for them. And why was that? It was because too many higher-ups were in on it. And it seemed as if Becky and Robert had no interest in seeing justice done. They were left well-off. They bought a house in Hanratty. Robert went into the store. Becky after her long seclusion started on a career of public sociability and display.

That was all. Flo put the lid down on the story as if she was sick of it. It reflected no good on anybody.

"Imagine," Flo said.

Flo at this time must have been in her early thirties. A young woman. She wore exactly the same clothes that a woman of fifty, or sixty, or seventy, might wear: print housedresses loose at the neck and sleeves as well as the waist; bib aprons, also of print, which she took off when she came from the kitchen into the store. This was not a common costume at the time, for a poor though not absolutely poverty-stricken woman; it was also, in a way, a scornful deliberate choice. Flo scorned slacks, she scorned the outfits of people trying to be in style, she scorned lipstick and permanents. She wore her own black hair cut straight across, just long enough to push behind her ears. She was tall but fine-boned, with narrow wrists and shoulders, a small head, a pale, freckled, monkeyish face. If she had thought it worthwhile, and had the resources, she might have had a black-and-pale, fragile, nurtured sort of prettiness; Rose realized that later. But she would have to have been a different person altogether; she would have to have learned to resist making faces, at herself and others.

Rose's earliest memories of Flo were of extraordinary softness and hardness. The soft hair, the long, soft, pale cheeks, soft almost invisible fuzz in front of her ears and above her mouth. The sharpness of her knees, hardness of her lap, flatness of her front.

When Flo sang:

> Oh the buzzin' of the bees in the cigarette trees
> And the soda-water fountain . . .

Rose thought of Flo's old life before she married her father, when she worked as a waitress in the coffee shop in Union Station, and went with her girl friends Mavis and Irene to Centre Island, and was followed by men on dark streets and knew how pay phones and elevators worked. Rose heard in her voice the reckless dangerous life of cities, the gum-chewing sharp answers.

And when she sang:

> Then slowly, slowly, she got up
> And slowly she came nigh him
> And all she said, that she ever did say,
> Was young man I think, you're dyin'!

Rose thought of a life Flo seemed to have had beyond that, earlier than that, crowded and legendary, with Barbara Allen and Becky Tyde's father and all kinds of outrages and sorrows jumbled up together in it.

The royal beatings. What got them started?   50

Suppose a Saturday, in spring. Leaves not out yet but the doors open to the sunlight. Crows. Ditches full of running water. Hopeful weather. Often on Saturdays Flo left Rose in charge of the store—it's a few years now, these are the years when Rose was nine, ten, eleven, twelve—while she herself went across the bridge to Hanratty (going uptown they called it) to shop and see people, and listen to them. Among the people she listened to were Mrs. Lawyer Davies, Mrs. Anglican Rector Henley-Smith, and Mrs. Horse-Doctor McKay. She came home and imitated their flibberty voices. Monsters, she made them seem; of foolishness, and showiness, and self-approbation.

When she finished shopping she went into the coffee shop of the Queen's Hotel and had a sundae. What kind? Rose and Brian wanted to know when she got home, and they would be disappointed if it was only pineapple or butterscotch, pleased if it was a Tin Roof, or Black and White. Then she smoked a cigarette. She had some ready-rolled, that she carried with her, so that she wouldn't have to roll one in public. Smoking was the one thing she did that she would have called showing off in anybody else. It was a habit left over from her working days, from Toronto. She knew it was asking for trouble. Once the Catholic priest came over to her right in the Queen's Hotel, and flashed his lighter at her before she could get her matches out. She thanked him but did not enter into conversation, lest he should try to convert her.

Another time, on the way home, she saw at the town end of the bridge a boy in a blue jacket, apparently looking at the water. Eighteen, nineteen years old. Nobody she knew. Skinny, weakly looking, something the matter with him, she saw at once. Was he thinking of something? Just as she came up even with him, what does he do but turn and display himself, holding his jacket open, also his pants. What he must have suffered from the cold, on a day that had Flo holding her coat collar tight around her throat.

When she first saw what he had in his hand, Flo said, all she could think of was, what is he doing out here with a baloney sausage?

She could say that. It was offered as truth; no joke. She maintained that she despised dirty talk. She would go out and yell at the old men sitting in front of her store.   55

"If you want to stay where you are you better clean your mouths out!"

Saturday, then. For some reason Flo is not going uptown, has decided to stay home and scrub the kitchen floor. Perhaps this has put her in a bad mood. Perhaps she was in a bad mood anyway, due to people not paying their bills, or the stirring-up of feelings in spring. The wrangle with Rose has already commenced, has been going on forever, like a dream that goes back and back into other dreams, over hills and through doorways, maddeningly dim and populous and familiar and elusive.

They are carting all the chairs out of the kitchen preparatory to the scrubbing, and they have also got to move some extra provisions for the store, some cartons of canned goods, tins of maple syrup, coal-oil cans, jars of vinegar. They take these things out to the woodshed. Brian who is five or six by this time is helping drag the tins.

"Yes," says Flo, carrying on from our lost starting point. "Yes, and that filth you taught to Brian."

"What filth?"

"And he doesn't know any better."   60

There is one step down from the kitchen to the woodshed, a bit of carpet on it so worn Rose can't even remember seeing the pattern. Brian loosens it, dragging a tin.

"Two Vancouvers," she says softly.

Flo is back in the kitchen. Brian looks from Flo to Rose and Rose says again in a slightly louder voice, an encouraging sing-song, "Two Vancouvers—"

"Fried in snot!" finishes Brian, not able to control himself any longer.

"Two pickled arseholes—"   65

"—tied in a knot!"

There it is. The filth.

> Two Vancouvers fried in snot!
> Two pickled arseholes tied in a knot!

Rose has known that for years, learned it when she first went to school. She came home and asked Flo, what is a Vancouver?

"It's a city. It's a long ways away."

"What else besides a city?"

Flo said, what did she mean, what else? How could it be fried, Rose said, approaching the dangerous moment, the delightful moment, when she would have to come out with the whole thing.   70

"Two Vancouvers fried in snot!/Two pickled arseholes tied in a knot!"

"You're going to get it!" cried Flo in a predictable rage. "Say that again and you'll get a good clout!"

Rose couldn't stop herself. She hummed it tenderly, tried saying the innocent words aloud, humming through the others. It was not just the words snot and arsehole that gave her pleasure, though of course they did. It was the pickling and tying and the unimaginable Vancouvers. She saw them in her mind shaped rather like octopuses, twitching in the pan. The tumble of reason; the spark and spit of craziness.

Lately she has remembered it again and taught it to Brian, to see if it has the same effect on him, and of course it has.

"Oh, I heard you!" says Flo. "I heard that! And I'm warning you!"   75

So she is. Brian takes the warning. He runs away, out the woodshed door, to do as he likes. Being a boy, free to help or not, involve himself or not. Not committed to the household struggle. They don't need him anyway, except to use against each other, they hardly notice his going. They continue, can't help continuing, can't leave each other alone. When they seem to have given up they really are just waiting and building up steam.

Flo gets out the scrub pail and the brush and the rag and the pad for her knees, a dirty red rubber pad. She starts to work on the floor. Rose sits on the kitchen table, the only place left to sit, swinging her legs. She can feel the cool oilcloth, because she is wearing shorts, last summer's tight faded shorts dug out of the summer-clothes bag. They smell a bit moldy from winter storage.

Flo crawls underneath, scrubbing with the brush, wiping with the rag. Her legs are long, white and muscular, marked all over with blue veins as if somebody had been drawing rivers on them with an indelible pencil. An abnormal energy, a violent disgust, is expressed in the chewing of the brush at the linoleum, the swish of the rag.

What do they have to say to each other? It doesn't really matter. Flo speaks of Rose's smart-aleck behavior, rudeness and sloppiness and conceit. Her willingness to make work for others, her lack of gratitude. She mentions Brian's innocence, Rose's corruption. Oh, don't you think you're somebody, says Flo, and a moment later, Who do you think you are? Rose contradicts and objects with such poisonous reasonableness and mildness, displays theatrical unconcern. Flo goes beyond her ordinary scorn and self-possession and becomes amazingly theatrical herself, saying it was for Rose that she sacrificed her life. She saw her father saddled with a baby daughter and she thought, what is that man going to do? So she married him, and here she is, on her knees.

At that moment the bell rings, to announce a customer in the store. Because the fight is on, Rose is not permitted to go into the store and wait on whoever it is. Flo gets up and throws off her apron, groaning—but not communicatively, it is not a groan whose exasperation Rose is allowed to share—and goes in and serves. Rose hears her using her normal voice.   80

"About time! Sure is!"

She comes back and ties on her apron and is ready to resume.

"You never have a thought for anybody but your ownself! You never have a thought for what I'm doing."

"I never asked you to do anything. I wish you never had. I would have been a lot better off."

Rose says this smiling directly at Flo, who has not yet gone down on her knees. Flo sees the smile, grabs the scrub rag that is hanging on the side of the pail, and throws it at her. It may be meant to hit her in the face but instead it falls against Rose's leg and she raises her foot and catches it, swinging negligently against her ankle.   85

"All right," says Flo. "You've done it this time. All right."

Rose watches her go to the woodshed door, hears her tramp through the woodshed, pause in the doorway, where the screen door hasn't yet been hung, and the storm door is standing open, propped with a brick. She calls Rose's father. She calls him in a warning, summoning voice, as if against her will preparing him for bad news. He will know what this is about.

The kitchen floor has five or six different patterns of linoleum on it. Ends, which Flo got for nothing and ingeniously trimmed and fitted together, bordering them with tin strips and tacks. While Rose sits on the table waiting, she looks at the floor, at this satisfying arrangement of rectangles, triangles, some other shape whose name she is trying to remember. She hears Flo coming back through the woodshed, on the creaky plank walk laid over the dirt floor. She is loitering, waiting, too. She and Rose can carry this no further, by themselves.

Rose hears her father come in. She stiffens, a tremor runs through her legs, she feels them shiver on the oilcloth. Called away from some peaceful, absorbing task, away from the words running in his head, called out of himself, her father has to say something. He says, "Well? What's wrong?"

Now comes another voice of Flo's. Enriched, hurt, apologetic, it seems to have been manufactured on the spot. She is sorry to have called him from his work. Would never have done it, if Rose was not driving her to distraction. How to distraction? With her back talk and impudence and her terrible tongue. The things Rose has said to Flo are such that, if Flo had said them to her mother, she knows her father would have thrashed her into the ground.

Rose tries to butt in, to say this isn't true.

What isn't true?

Her father raises a hand, doesn't look at her, says, "Be quiet."

When she says it isn't true, Rose means that she herself didn't start this, only responded, that she was goaded by Flo, who is now, she believes, telling the grossest sort of lies, twisting everything to suit herself. Rose puts aside her other knowledge that whatever Flo has said or done, whatever she herself has said or done, does not really matter at all. It is the struggle itself that counts, and that can't be stopped, can never be stopped, short of where it has got to, now.

Flo's knees are dirty, in spite of the pad. The scrub rag is still hanging over Rose's foot.

Her father wipes his hands, listening to Flo. He takes his time. He is slow at getting into the spirit of things, tired in advance, maybe, on the verge of rejecting the role he has to play. He won't look at Rose, but at any sound or stirring from Rose, he holds up his hand.

"Well we don't need the public in on this, that's for sure," Flo says, and she goes to lock the door of the store, putting in the store window the sign that says BACK SOON, a sign Rose made for her with a great deal of fancy curving and shading of letters in black and red crayon. When she comes back she shuts the door to the store, then the door to the stairs, then the door to the woodshed.

Her shoes have left marks on the clean wet part of the floor.

"Oh, I don't know," she says now, in a voice worn down from its emotional peak. "I don't know what to do about her." She looks down and sees her dirty knees (following Rose's eyes) and rubs at them viciously with her bare hands, smearing the dirt around.

"She humiliates me," she says, straightening up. There it is, the explanation. "She humiliates me," she repeats with satisfaction. "She has no respect."

"I do not!"

"Quiet, you!" says her father.

"If I hadn't called your father you'd still be sitting there with that grin on your face! What other way is there to manage you?"

Rose detects in her father some objections to Flo's rhetoric, some embarrassment and reluctance. She is wrong, and ought to know she is wrong, in thinking that she can count on this. The fact that she knows about it, and he knows she knows, will not make things any better. He is beginning to warm up. He gives her a look. This look is at first cold and challenging. It informs her of his judgment, of the hopelessness of her position. Then it clears, it begins to fill up with something else, the way a spring fills up when you clear the leaves away. It fills with hatred and pleasure. Rose sees that and knows it. Is that just a description of anger, should she see his eyes filling up with anger? No. Hatred is right. Pleasure is right. His face loosens and changes and grows younger, and he holds up his hand this time to silence Flo.

"All right," he says, meaning that's enough, more than enough, this part is over, things can proceed. He starts to loosen his belt.

Flo has stopped anyway. She has the same difficulty Rose does, a difficulty in believing that what you know must happen really will happen, that there comes a time when you can't draw back.

"Oh, I don't know, don't be too hard on her." She is moving around nervously as if she has thoughts of opening some escape route. "Oh, you don't have to use the belt on her. Do you have to use the belt?"

He doesn't answer. The belt is coming off, not hastily. It is being grasped at the necessary point. *All right you.* He is coming over to Rose. He pushes her off the table. His face, like his voice, is quite out of character. He is like a bad actor, who turns a part grotesque. As if he must savor and insist on just what is shameful and terrible about this. That is not to say he is pretending, that he is acting, and does not mean it. He is acting, and he means it. Rose knows that, she knows everything about him.

She has since wondered about murders, and murderers. Does the thing have to be carried through, in the end, partly for the effect, to prove to the audience of one—who won't be able to report, only register, the lesson—that such a thing can happen, that there is nothing that can't happen, that the most dreadful antic is justified, feelings can be found to match it?

She tries again looking at the kitchen floor, that clever and comfortable geometrical arrangement, instead of looking at him or his belt. How can this go on in front of such daily witnesses—the linoleum, the calendar with the mill and creek and autumn trees, the old accommodating pots and pans?

Hold out your hand!

Those things aren't going to help her, none of them can rescue her. They turn bland and useless, even unfriendly. Pots can show malice, the patterns of linoleum can leer up at you, treachery is the other side of dailiness.

At the first, or maybe the second, crack of pain, she draws back. She will not accept it. She runs around the room, she tries to get to the doors. Her father blocks her off. Not an ounce of courage or stoicism in her, it would seem. She runs, she screams, she implores. Her father is after her, cracking the belt at her when he can, then abandoning it and using his hands. Bang over the ear, then bang over the other ear. Back and forth, her head ringing. Bang in the face. Up against the wall and bang in the face again. He shakes her and hits her against the wall, he kicks her legs. She is incoherent, insane, shrieking. *Forgive me! Oh please, forgive me!*

Flo is shrieking too. *Stop, stop!*

Not yet. He throws Rose down. Or perhaps she throws herself down. He kicks her legs again. She has given up on words but is letting out a noise, the sort of noise that makes Flo cry, *Oh, what if people can hear her?* The very last-ditch willing sound of humiliation and defeat it is, for it seems Rose must play her part in this with the same grossness, the same exaggeration, that her father displays, playing his. She plays his victim with a self-indulgence that arouses, and maybe hopes to arouse, his final, sickened contempt.

They will give this anything that is necessary, it seems, they will go to any lengths.

Not quite. He has never managed really to injure her, though there are times, of course, when she prays that he will. He hits her with an open hand, there is some restraint in his kicks.

Now he stops, he is out of breath. He allows Flo to move in, he grabs Rose up and gives her a push in Flo's direction, making a sound of disgust. Flo retrieves her, opens the stair door, shoves her up the stairs.

"Go on up to your room now! Hurry!"

Rose goes up the stairs, stumbling, letting herself stumble, letting herself fall against the steps. She doesn't bang her door because a gesture like that could still bring him after her, and anyway, she is weak. She lies on the bed. She can hear through the stovepipe hole Flo snuffling and remonstrating, her father saying angrily that Flo should have kept quiet then, if she did not want Rose punished she should not have recommended it. Flo says she never recommended a hiding like that.

120

They argue back and forth on this. Flo's frightened voice is growing stronger, getting its confidence back. By stages, by arguing, they are being drawn back into themselves. Soon it's only Flo talking; he will not talk anymore. Rose has had to fight down her noisy sobbing, so as to listen to them, and when she loses interest in listening, and wants to sob some more, she finds she can't work herself up to it. She has passed into a state of calm, in which outrage is perceived as complete and final. In this state events and possibilities take on a lovely simplicity. Choices are mercifully clear. The words that come to mind are not the quibbling, seldom the conditional. Never is a word to which the right is suddenly established. She will never speak to him, she will never look at them with anything but loathing, she will never forgive them. She will punish them; she will finish them. Encased in these finalities, and in her bodily pain, she floats in curious comfort, beyond herself, beyond responsibility.

Suppose she dies now? Suppose she commits suicide? Suppose she runs away? Any of these things would be appropriate. It is only a matter of choosing, of figuring out the way. She floats in her pure superior state as if kindly drugged.

And just as there is a moment, when you are drugged, in which you feel perfectly safe, sure, unreachable, and then without warning and right next to it a moment in which you know the whole protection has fatally cracked, though it is still pretending to hold soundly together, so there is a moment now—the moment, in fact, when Rose hears Flo step on the stairs—that contains for her both present peace and freedom and a sure knowledge of the whole down-spiralling course of events from now on.

Flo comes into the room without knocking, but with a hesitation that shows it might have occurred to her. She brings a jar of cold cream. Rose is hanging on to advantage as long as she can, lying face down on the bed, refusing to acknowledge or answer.

"Oh come on," Flo says uneasily. "You aren't so bad off, are you? You put some of this on and you'll feel better."

125

She is bluffing. She doesn't know for sure what damage has been done. She has the lid off the cold cream. Rose can smell it. The intimate, babyish, humiliating smell. She won't allow it near her. But in order to avoid it, the big ready clot of it in Flo's hand, she has to move. She scuffles, resists, loses dignity, and lets Flo see there is not really much the matter.

"All right," Flo says. "You win. I'll leave it here and you can put it on when you like."

Later still a tray will appear. Flo will put it down without a word and go away. A large glass of chocolate milk on it, made with Vita-Malt from the store. Some rich streaks of Vita-Malt around the bottom of the glass. Little sandwiches, neat and appetizing. Canned salmon of the first quality and reddest color, plenty of mayonnaise. A couple of butter tarts from a bakery package, chocolate biscuits with a peppermint filling. Rose's favorites, in the sandwich, tart and cookie line. She will turn away, refuse to look, but left alone with these eatables will be miserably tempted, roused and troubled and drawn back from thoughts of suicide or flight by the smell of salmon, the anticipation of crisp chocolate, she will reach out a finger, just to run it around the edge of one of the sandwiches (crusts cut off!) to get the overflow, get a taste. Then she will decide to eat one, for strength to refuse the rest. One will not be noticed. Soon, in helpless corruption, she will eat them all. She will drink the chocolate milk, eat the tarts, eat the cookies. She will get the malty syrup out of the bottom of the glass with her finger, though she sniffles with shame. Too late.

Flo will come up and get the tray. She may say, "I see you got your appetite still," or, "Did you like the chocolate milk, was it enough syrup in it?" depending on how chastened she is feeling, herself. At any rate, all advantage will be lost. Rose will understand that life has started up again, that they will all sit around the table eating again, listening to the radio news. Tomorrow morning, maybe even tonight. Unseemly and unlikely as that may be. They will be embarrassed, but rather less than you might expect considering how they have behaved. They will feel a queer lassitude, a convalescent indolence, not far off satisfaction.

One night after a scene like this they were all in the kitchen. It must have been summer, or at least warm weather, because her father spoke of the old men who sat on the bench in front of the store.

"Do you know what they're talking about now?" he said, and nodded his head toward the store to show who he meant, though of course they were not there now, they went home at dark.

"Those old coots," said Flo. "What?"

There was about them both a geniality not exactly false but a bit more emphatic than was normal, without company.

Rose's father told them then that the old men had picked up the idea somewhere that what looked like a star in the western sky, the first star that came out after sunset, the evening star, was in reality an airship hovering over Bay City, Michigan, on the other side of Lake Huron. An American invention, sent up to rival the heavenly bodies. They were all in agreement about this, the idea was congenial to them. They believed it to be lit by ten thousand electric light bulbs. Her father had ruthlessly disagreed with them, pointing out that it was the planet Venus they saw, which had appeared in the sky long before the invention of an electric light bulb. They had never heard of the planet Venus.

"Ignoramuses," said Flo. At which Rose knew, and knew her father knew, that Flo had never heard of the planet Venus either. To distract them from this, or even apologize for it, Flo put down her teacup, stretched out with her head resting on the chair she had been sitting on and her feet on another chair (somehow she managed to tuck her dress modestly between her legs at the same time), and lay stiff as a board, so that Brian cried out in delight, "Do that! Do that!"

Flo was double-jointed and very strong. In moments of celebration or emergency she would do tricks.

They were silent while she turned herself around, not using her arms at all but just her strong legs and feet. Then they all cried out in triumph, though they had seen it before.

Just as Flo turned herself Rose got a picture in her mind of that airship, an elongated transparent bubble, with its strings of diamond lights, floating in the miraculous American sky.

"The planet Venus!" her father said, applauding Flo. "Ten thousand electric lights!"

There was a feeling of permission, relaxation, even a current of happiness, in the room.   140

Years later, many years later, on a Sunday morning, Rose turned on the radio. This was when she was living by herself in Toronto.

Well sir.

It was a different kind of place in our day. Yes it was.

It was all horses then. Horses and buggies. Buggy races up and down the main street on the Saturday nights.

"Just like the chariot races," says the announcer's, or interviewer's, smooth encouraging voice.   145

I never seen a one of them.

"No sir, that was the old Roman chariot races I was referring to. That was before your time."

Musta been before my time. I'm a hunerd and two years old.

"That's a wonderful age, sir."

It is so.   150

She left it on, as she went around the apartment kitchen, making coffee for herself. It seemed to her that this must be a staged interview, a scene from some play, and she wanted to find out what it was. The old man's voice was so vain and belligerent, the interviewer's quite hopeless and alarmed, under its practiced gentleness and ease. You were surely meant to see him holding the microphone up to some toothless, reckless, preening centenarian, wondering what in God's name he was doing here, and what he would say next?

"They must have been fairly dangerous."

What was dangerous?

"Those buggy races."

They was. Dangerous. Used to be the runaway horses. Used to be a-plenty of accidents. Fellows was dragged along on the gravel and cut their face open. Wouldna matter so much if they was dead. Heh.   155

Some of them horses was the high-steppers. Some, they had to have the mustard under their tail. Some wouldn step out for nothin. That's the thing it is with the horses. Some'll work and pull till they drop down dead and some wouldn pull your cock out of a pail of lard. Hehe.

It must be a real interview after all. Otherwise they wouldn't have put that in, wouldn't have risked it. It's all right if the old man says it. Local color. Anything rendered harmless and delightful by his hundred years.

Accidents all the time then. In the mill. Foundry. Wasn't the precautions.

"You didn't have so many strikes then, I don't suppose? You didn't have so many unions?"

Everybody taking it easy nowadays. We worked and we was glad to get it. Worked and was glad to get it.

"You didn't have television."

Didn't have no TV. Didn't have no radio. No picture show.

"You made your own entertainment."

That's the way we did.

"You had a lot of experiences young men growing up today will never have."

Experiences.

"Can you recall any of them for us?"

I eaten groundhog meat one time. One winter. You wouldna cared for it. Heh.

There was a pause, of appreciation, it would seem, then the announcer's voice saying that the foregoing had been an interview with Mr. Wilfred Nettleton of Hanratty, Ontario, made on his hundred and second birthday, two weeks before his death, last spring. A living link with our past. Mr. Nettleton had been interviewed in the Wawanash County Home for the Aged.

Hat Nettleton.

Horsewhipper into centenarian. Photographed on his birthday, fussed over by nurses, kissed no doubt by a girl reporter. Flash bulbs popping at him. Tape recorder drinking in the sound of his voice. Oldest resident. Oldest horsewhipper. Living link with our past.

Looking out from her kitchen window at the cold lake, Rose was longing to tell somebody. It was Flo who would enjoy hearing. She thought of her saying *Imagine!* in a way that meant she was having her worst suspicions gorgeously confirmed. But Flo was in the same place Hat Nettleton had died in, and there wasn't any way Rose could reach her. She had been there even when that interview was recorded, though she would not have heard it, would not have known about it. After Rose put her in the Home, a couple of years earlier, she had stopped talking. She had removed herself, and spent most of her time sitting in a corner of her crib, looking crafty and disagreeable, not answering anybody, though she occasionally showed her feelings by biting a nurse.

QUESTIONS

1. How does Munro use specific detail to evoke the setting? Give examples. What is the reader to surmise about the social situation of Rose's family? How is the awareness of class important to the reader's understanding of the family and the town?

2. How does Munro establish the characters of Flo and Rose? Do you think she means us to remain neutral as readers? If not, then who wins our sympathy, and why? How does the fact that Flo is Rose's stepmother enter into their relationship? How do both characters use this fact for their own purposes?

3. How does the argument begin? How does it fit into the larger pattern of their relations? How does Munro convey a sense of inevitability about the tensions and their escalation?

4. What is the role of the father in the story? Do you sense that he is putting on an act? Why? How does Munro let us know that all of the participants are acting?

5. How does your view of the characters change over the full course of the argument? Does Flo become more sympathetic or more treacherous? Is there a sense in which the family welcomes these fights—needs them? Explain.

6. What function is served by the second plot involving Becky Tyde and her father? Do you think Munro means us to draw a comparison between one beating and the other? In what ways are the circumstances different? What is the reader to conclude from the difference?

7. Munro ends her story with a long view into the past. What does Rose feel when she hears Hat on the radio? Is the reader to conclude that time washes away all sins? Comment.

8. What are Rose's feelings toward Flo at the end of the story? Does the new time perspective change your view of Flo, of Rose's childhood?

9. Comment on the significance of the title. Is Munro being ironic when she calls the beatings "royal"?

WHO DO YOU THINK YOU ARE?

There were some things Rose and her brother Brian could safely talk about, without running aground on principles or statements of position, and one of them was Milton Homer. They both remembered that when they had measles and there was a quarantine notice put up on the door—this was long ago, before their father died and before Brian went to school—Milton Homer came along the street and read it. They heard him coming over the bridge and as usual he was complaining loudly. His progress through town was not silent unless his mouth was full of candy; otherwise he would be yelling at dogs and bullying the trees and telephone poles, mulling over old grievances.

"And I did not and I did not and I did not!" he yelled, and hit the bridge railing.

Rose and Brian pulled back the quilt that was hung over the window to keep the light out, so they would not go blind.

"Milton Homer," said Brian appreciatively.

Milton Homer then saw the notice on the door. He turned and mounted the steps and read it. He could read. He would go along the main street reading all the signs out loud.

Rose and Brian remembered this and they agreed that it was the side door, where Flo later stuck on the glassed-in porch; before that there was only a slanting wooden platform, and they remembered Milton Homer standing on it. If the quarantine notice was there and not on the front door, which led into Flo's store, then the store must have been open; that seemed odd, and could only be explained by Flo's having bullied the Health Officer. Rose couldn't remember; she could only remember Milton Homer on the platform with his big head on one side and his fist raised to knock.

"Measles, huh?" said Milton Homer. He didn't knock, after all; he stuck his head close to the door and shouted, "Can't scare me!" Then he turned around but did not leave the yard. He walked over to the swing, sat down, took hold of the ropes and began moodily, then with mounting and ferocious glee, to give himself a ride.

"Milton Homer's on the swing, Milton Homer's on the swing!" Rose shouted. She had run from the window to the stairwell.

Flo came from wherever she was to look out the side window.

　A Fiction Writer's Career: Alice Munro

"He won't hurt it," said Flo surprisingly. Rose had thought she would chase him with the broom. Afterward she wondered: could Flo have been frightened? Not likely. It would be a matter of Milton Homer's privileges.

"I can't sit on the seat after Milton Homer's sat on it!"

"You! You go on back to bed."

Rose went back into the dark smelly measles room and began to tell Brian a story she thought he wouldn't like.

"When you were a baby, Milton Homer came and picked you up."

"He did not."

"He came and held you and asked what your name was. I remember."

Brian went out to the stairwell.

"Did Milton Homer come and pick me up and ask what my name was? Did he? When I was a baby?"

"You tell Rose he did the same for her."

Rose knew that was likely, though she hadn't been going to mention it. She didn't really know if she remembered Milton Homer holding Brian, or had been told about it. Whenever there was a new baby in a house, in that recent past when babies were still being born at home, Milton Homer came as soon as possible and asked to see the baby, then asked its name, and delivered a set speech. The speech was to the effect that if the baby lived, it was to be hoped it would lead a Christian life, and if it died, it was to be hoped it would go straight to Heaven. The same idea as baptism, but Milton did not call on the Father or the Son or do any business with water. He did all this on his own authority. He seemed to be overcome by a stammer he did not have at other times, or else he stammered on purpose in order to give his pronouncements more weight. He opened his mouth wide and rocked back and forth, taking up each phrase with a deep grunt.

"And *if* the Baby—*if* the Baby—*if* the Baby—*lives*—"

Rose would do this years later, in her brother's living room, rocking back and forth, chanting, each *if* coming out like an explosion, leading up to the major explosion of *lives*.

"He will live a—good life—and he will—and he will—and he will—*not* sin. He will lead a *good life—a good life*—and he will *not sin*. He will *not sin!*"

"And if the baby—if the baby—if the baby—*dies*—"

"Now that's enough. That's enough, Rose," said Brian, but he laughed. He could put up with Rose's theatrics when they were about Hanratty.

"How can you remember?" said Brian's wife Phoebe, hoping to stop Rose before she went on too long and roused Brian's impatience. "Did you see him do it? That often?"

"Oh no," said Rose, with some surprise. "I didn't see him do it. What I saw was Ralph Gillespie *doing* Milton Homer. He was a boy in school. Ralph."

Milton Homer's other public function, as Rose and Brian remembered it, was to march in parades. There used to be plenty of parades in Hanratty. The Orange Walk, on the Twelfth of July; the High School Cadet Parade, in May; the schoolchildren's Empire Day Parade; the Legion's Church Parade; the Santa Claus Parade; the Lions Club Old-Timers' Parade. One of the most derogatory things that could be said about anyone in Hanratty was that he or she was fond of parading around, but almost every soul in town—in the town proper, not West Hanratty, that goes without saying—would get a chance to march in public in some organized and approved affair. The only thing was that you must never look as if you were enjoying it; you had to give the impression of being called forth out of preferred obscurity, ready to do your duty and gravely preoccupied with whatever notions the parade celebrated.

The Orange Walk was the most splendid of all the parades. King Billy at the head of it rode a horse as near pure white as could be found, and the Black Knights at the rear, the noblest rank of Orangemen°—usually thin, and poor, and proud and fanatical old farmers—rode dark horses and wore the ancient father-to-son top hats and swallowtail coats. The banners were all gorgeous silks and embroideries, blue and gold, orange and white, scenes of Protestant triumph, lilies and open Bibles, mottoes of godliness and honor and flaming bigotry. The ladies came beneath their sunshades, Orangemen's wives and daughters all wearing white for purity. Then the bands, the fifes and drums, and gifted step-dancers performing on a clean hay wagon as a movable stage.

Also, there came Milton Homer. He could show up anywhere in the parade and he varied his place in it from time to time, stepping out behind King Billy or the Black Knights or the step-dancers or the shy orange-sashed children who carried the banners. Behind the Black Knights he would pull a dour face, and hold his head as if a top hat was riding on it; behind the ladies he wiggled his hips and diddled an imaginary sunshade. He was a mimic of ferocious gifts and terrible energy. He could take the step-dancers' tidy show and turn it into an idiot's prance, and still keep the beat.

The Orange Walk was his best opportunity, in parades, but he was conspicuous in all of them. Head in the air, arms whipping out, snootily in step, he marched behind the commanding officer of the Legion. On Empire Day he provided himself with a Red Ensign and a Union Jack, and kept them going like whirligigs above his head. In the Santa Claus parade he snatched candy meant for children; he did not do it for a joke.

You would think that somebody in authority in Hanratty would have put an end to this. Milton Homer's contribution to any parade was wholly negative, designed, if Milton Homer could have designed anything, just to make the parade look foolish. Why didn't the organizers and the paraders make an effort to keep him out? They must have decided that was easier said than done. Milton lived with his two old-maid aunts, his parents being dead, and nobody would have liked to ask the two old ladies to keep him home. It must have seemed as if they had enough on their hands already. How could they keep him in, once he had heard the band? They would have to lock him up, tie him down. And nobody wanted to haul him out and drag him away once things began. His protests would have ruined everything. There wasn't any doubt that he would protest. He had a strong, deep voice and he was a strong man, though not very tall. He was about the size of Napoleon. He had kicked through gates and fences when people tried to shut him out of their yards. Once he had smashed a child's wagon on the sidewalk, simply because it was in his way. Letting him participate must have seemed the best choice, under the circumstances.

Not that it was done as the best of bad choices. Nobody looked askance at Milton in a parade; everybody was used to him. Even the Commanding Officer would

30

Orangemen: a militantly Protestant group named after a society founded in Northern Ireland.

A Fiction Writer's Career: Alice Munro

let himself be mocked, and the Black Knights with their old black grievances took no notice. People just said, "Oh, there's Milton," from the sidewalk. There wasn't much laughing at him, though strangers in town, city relatives invited to watch the parade, might point him out and laugh themselves silly, thinking he was there officially and for purposes of comic relief, like the clowns who were actually young businessmen, unsuccessfully turning cartwheels.

"Who is that?" the visitors said, and were answered with nonchalance and a particularly obscure sort of pride.

"That's just Milton Homer. It wouldn't be a parade without Milton Homer." 35

"The village idiot," said Phoebe, trying to comprehend these things, with her inexhaustible unappreciated politeness, and both Rose and Brian said that they had never heard him described that way. They had never thought of Hanratty as a village. A village was a cluster of picturesque houses around a steepled church on a Christmas card. Villagers were the costumed chorus in the high school operetta. If it was necessary to describe Milton Homer to an outsider, people would say that he was "not all there." Rose had wondered, even at that time, what was the part that wasn't there? She still wondered. Brains, would be the easiest answer. Milton Homer must surely have had a low I.Q. Yes; but so did plenty of people, in Hanratty and out of it, and they did not distinguish themselves as he did. He could read without difficulty, as shown in the case of the quarantine sign; he knew how to count his change, as evidence in many stories about how people had tried to cheat him. What was missing was a sense of precaution, Rose thought now. Social inhibition, though there was no such name for it at that time. Whatever it is that ordinary people lose when they are drunk, Milton Homer never had, or might have chosen not to have— and this is what interests Rose—at some point early in life. Even his expressions, his everyday looks, were those that drunks wear in theatrical extremity—goggling, leering, drooping looks that seemed boldly calculated, and at the same time helpless, involuntary; is such a thing possible?

The two ladies Milton Homer lived with were his mother's sisters. They were twins; their names were Hattie and Mattie Milton, and they were usually called Miss Hattie and Miss Mattie, perhaps to detract from any silly sound their names might have had otherwise. Milton had been named after his mother's family. That was a common practice, and there was probably no thought of linking together the names of two great poets. That coincidence was never mentioned and was perhaps not noticed. Rose did not notice it until one day in high school when the boy who sat behind her tapped her on the shoulder and showed her what he had written in his English book. He had stroked out the word *Chapman's*° in the title of a poem and inked in the word *Milton*, so that the title now read: *On First Looking into Milton Homer.*

Any mention of Milton Homer was a joke, but this changed title was also a joke because it referred, rather weakly, to Milton Homer's more scandalous behavior. The story was that when he got behind somebody in a line-up at the Post Office or a movie theater, he would open his coat and present himself, then lunge and commence rubbing. Though of course he wouldn't get that far; the object of his passion

---

Chapman's: refers to the sonnet by John Keats (1795–1821) entitled *On First Looking into Chapman's Homer* (see Chapter 19).

would have ducked out of his way. Boys were said to dare each other to get him into position, and stay close ahead of him until the very last moment, then jump aside and reveal him in dire importunity.

It was in honor of this story—whether it was true or not, had happened once under provocation, or kept happening all the time—that ladies crossed the street when they saw Milton coming, that children were warned to stay clear of him. *Just don't let him monkey around* was what Flo said. He was allowed into houses on those ritual occasions when there was a new baby—with hospital births getting commoner, those occasions diminished—but at other times the doors were locked against him. He would come and knock, and kick the door panels, and go away. But he was let have his way in yards, because he didn't take things, and could do so much damage if offended.

Of course, it was another story altogether when he appeared with one of his aunts. At those times he was hangdog-looking, well-behaved; his powers and his passions, whatever they were, all banked and hidden. He would be eating candy the aunt had bought him, out of a paper bag. He offered it when told to, though nobody but the most greedy person alive would touch what might have been touched by Milton Homer's fingers or blessed by his spittle. The aunts saw that he got his hair cut; they did their best to keep him presentable. They washed and ironed and mended his clothes, sent him out in his raincoat and rubbers, or knitted cap and muffler, as the weather indicated. Did they know how he conducted himself when out of their sight? They must have heard, and if they heard they must have suffered, being people of pride and Methodist morals. It was their grandfather who had started the flax mill in Hanratty and compelled all his employees to spend their Saturday nights at a Bible Class he himself conducted. The Homers, too, were decent people. Some of the Homers were supposed to be in favor of putting Milton away but the Milton ladies wouldn't do it. Nobody suggested they refused out of tender-heartedness.   40

"They won't put him in the Asylum, they're too proud."

Miss Hattie Milton taught at the high school. She had been teaching there longer than all the other teachers combined and was more important than the Principal. She taught English—the alteration in the poem was the more daring and satisfying because it occurred under her nose—and the thing she was famous for was keeping order. She did this without apparent effort, through the force of her large-bosomed, talcumed, spectacled, innocent and powerful presence, and her refusal to see that there was any difference between teenagers (she did not use the word) and students in Grade Four. She assigned a lot of memory work. One day she wrote a long poem on the board and said that everyone was to copy it out, then learn it off by heart, and the next day recite it. This was when Rose was in her third or fourth year at high school and she did not believe these instructions were to be taken literally. She learned poetry with ease; it seemed reasonable to her to skip the first step. She read the poem and learned it, verse by verse, then said it over a couple of times in her head. While she was doing this Miss Hattie asked her why she wasn't copying.

Rose replied that she knew the poem already, though she was not perfectly sure that this was true.

"Do you really?" said Miss Hattie. "Stand up and face the back of the room."

Rose did so, trembling for her boast.   45

"Now recite the poem to the class."

A Fiction Writer's Career: Alice Munro

Rose's confidence was not mistaken. She recited without a hitch. What did she expect to follow? Astonishment and compliments, and unaccustomed respect?

"Well, you may know the poem," Miss Hattie said, "but that is no excuse for not doing what you were told. Sit down and write it in your book. I want you to write every line three times. If you don't get finished you can stay after four."

Rose did have to stay after four, of course, raging and writing while Miss Hattie got out her crocheting. When Rose took the copy to her desk Miss Hattie said mildly enough but with finality, "You can't go thinking you are better than other people just because you can learn poems. Who do you think you are?"

This was not the first time in her life Rose had been asked who she thought she was; in fact the question had often struck her like a monotonous gong and she paid no attention to it. But she understood, afterward, that Miss Hattie was not a sadistic teacher; she had refrained from saying what she now said in front of the class. And she was not vindictive; she was not taking revenge because she had not believed Rose had been proved wrong. The lesson she was trying to teach here was more important to her than any poem, and one she truly believed Rose needed. It seemed that many other people believed she needed it, too.   50

The whole class was invited, at the end of the senior year, to a lantern slide show at the Miltons' house. The lantern slides were of China, where Miss Mattie, the stay-at-home twin, had been a missionary in her youth. Miss Mattie was very shy, and she stayed in the background, working the slides, while Miss Hattie commented. The lantern slides showed a yellow country, much as expected. Yellow hills and sky, yellow people, rickshaws, parasols, all dry and papery-looking, fragile, unlikely, with black zigzags where the paint had cracked, on the temples, the roads and faces. At this very time, the one and only time Rose sat in the Miltons' parlor, Mao° was in power in China and the Korean War was under way, but Miss Hattie made no concessions to history, any more than she made concessions to the fact that the members of her audience were eighteen and nineteen years old.

"The Chinese are heathens," Miss Hattie said. "That is why they have beggars."

There was a beggar, kneeling in the street, arms outstretched to a rich lady in a rickshaw,° who was not paying any attention to him.

"They do eat things we wouldn't touch," Miss Hattie said. Some Chinese were pictured poking sticks into bowls. "But they eat a better diet when they become Christians. The first generation of Christians is an inch and a half taller."

Christians of the first generation were standing in a row with their mouths open, possibly singing. They wore black and white clothes.   55

After the slides, plates of sandwiches, cookies, tarts were served. All were homemade and very good. A punch of grape juice and ginger ale was poured into paper cups. Milton sat in a corner in his thick tweed suit, a white shirt and a tie, on which punch and crumbs had already been spilled.

"Some day it will just blow up in their faces," Flo had said darkly, meaning Milton. Could that be the reason people came, year after year, to see the lantern slides and drink the punch that all the jokes were about? To see Milton with his jowls and

---

Mao: Mao Tse-tung (1893–1976), leader of Communist China.
rickshaw: a hand-drawn two-wheel passenger cart in China.

stomach swollen as if with bad intentions, ready to blow? All he did was stuff himself at an unbelievable rate. It seemed as if he downed date squares, hermits, Nanaimo bars and fruit drops, butter tarts and brownies, whole, the way a snake will swallow frogs. Milton was similarly distended.

Methodists were people whose power in Hanratty was passing, but slowly. The days of the compulsory Bible Class were over. Perhaps the Miltons didn't know that. Perhaps they knew it but put a heroic face on their decline. They behaved as if the requirements of piety hadn't changed and as if its connection with prosperity was unaltered. Their brick house, with its overstuffed comfort, their coats with collars of snug dull fur, seemed proclaimed as a Methodist house, Methodist clothing, inelegant on purpose, heavy, satisfactory. Everything about them seemed to say that they had applied themselves to the world's work for God's sake, and God had not let them down. For God's sake the hall floor shone with wax around the runner, the lines were drawn perfectly with a straight pen in the account book, the begonias flourished, the money went into the bank.

But mistakes were made, nowadays. The mistake the Milton ladies made was in drawing up a petition to be sent to the Canadian Broadcasting Corporation, asking for the removal from the air of the programs that interfered with churchgoing on Sunday nights: Edgar Bergen and Charlie McCarthy; Jack Benny; Fred Allen.° They got the minister to speak about their petition in church—this was in the United Church, where Methodists had been outnumbered by Presbyterians and Congregationalists, and it was not a scene Rose witnessed, but had described to her by Flo—and afterward they waited, Miss Hattie and Miss Mattie, one on each side of the outgoing stream, intending to deflect people and make them sign the petition, which was set up on a little table in the church vestibule. Behind the table Milton Homer was sitting. He had to be there; they never let him get out of going to church on Sunday. They had given him a job to keep him busy; he was to be in charge of the fountain pens, making sure they were full and handing them to signers.

That was the obvious part of the mistake. Milton had got the idea of drawing whiskers on himself, and had done so, without the help of a mirror. Whiskers curled out over his big sad cheeks, up toward his bloodshot foreboding eyes. He had put the pen in his mouth, too, so that ink had blotched his lips. In short, he had made himself so comical a sight that the petition which nobody really wanted could be treated as a comedy, too, and the power of the Milton sisters, the flaxmill Methodists, could be seen as a leftover dribble. People smiled and slid past; nothing could be done. Of course the Milton ladies didn't scold Milton or put on any show for the public, they just bundled him up with their petition and took him home.   60

"That was the end of them thinking they could run things," Flo said. It was hard to tell, as always, what particular defeat—was it that of religion or pretension?—she was so glad to see.

The boy who showed Rose the poem in Miss Hattie's own English class in Hanratty High School was Ralph Gillespie, the same boy who specialized in Milton

---

Edgar . . . Allen: Edgar Bergen, Charlie McCarthy, Jack Benny, and Fred Allen, popular entertainers on American radio shows of the 1940s.

A Fiction Writer's Career: Alice Munro

Homer imitations. As Rose remembered it, he hadn't started on the imitations at the time he showed her the poem. They came later, during the last few months he was in school. In most classes he sat ahead of Rose or behind her, due to the alphabetical closeness of their names. Beyond this alphabetical closeness they did have something like a family similarity, not in looks but in habits or tendencies. Instead of embarrassing them, as it would have done if they had really been brother or sister, this drew them together in helpful conspiracy. Both of them lost or mislaid, or never adequately provided themselves with, all the pencils, rulers, erasers, pen nibs, ruled paper, graph paper, the compass, dividers, protractor, necessary for a successful school life; both of them were sloppy with ink, subject to spilling and blotting mishaps; both of them were negligent about doing homework but panicky about not having done it. So they did their best to help each other out, sharing whatever supplies they had, begging from their more provident neighbors, finding someone's homework to copy. They developed the comradeship of captives, of soldiers who have no heart for the campaign, wishing only to survive and avoid action.

That wasn't quite all. Their shoes and boots became well acquainted, scuffling and pushing in friendly and private encounter, sometimes resting together a moment in tentative encouragement; this mutual kindness particularly helped them through those moments when people were being selected to do mathematics problems on the blackboard.

Once Ralph came in after noon hour with his hair full of snow. He leaned over and shook snow onto Rose's desk, saying, "Do you have those dandruff blues?"

"No. Mine's white."

65

This seemed to Rose a moment of some intimacy, with its physical frankness, its remembered childhood joke. Another day at noon hour, before the bell rang, she came into the classroom and found him, in a ring of onlookers, doing his Milton Homer imitation. She was surprised and worried; surprised because his shyness in class had always equalled hers and had been one of the things that united them; worried that he might not be able to bring it off, might not make them laugh. But he was very good; his large, pale, good-natured face took on the lumpy desperation of Milton's; his eyes goggled and his jowls shook and his words came out in a hoarse hypnotized singsong. He was so successful that Rose was amazed, and so was everybody else. From that time on Ralph began to do imitations; he had several, but Milton Homer was his trademark. Rose never quite got over a comradely sort of apprehension on his behalf. She had another feeling as well, not envy but a shaky sort of longing. She wanted to do the same. Not Milton Homer; she did not want to do Milton Homer. She wanted to fill up in that magical, releasing way, transform herself; she wanted the courage and the power.

Not long after he started publicly developing these talents he had, Ralph Gillespie dropped out of school. Rose missed his feet and his breathing and his finger tapping her shoulder. She met him sometimes on the street but he did not seem to be quite the same person. They never stopped to talk, just said hello and hurried past. They had been close and conspiring for years, it seemed, maintaining their spurious domesticity, but they had never talked outside of school, never gone beyond the most formal recognition of each other, and it seemed they could not, now. Rose never asked him why he had dropped out; she did not even know if he had found a job. They knew each other's necks and shoulders, heads and feet, but were not able to confront each other as full-length presences.

After a while Rose didn't see him on the street anymore. She head that he had joined the Navy. He must have been just waiting till he was old enough to do that. He had joined the Navy and gone to Halifax. The war was over, it was only the peacetime Navy. Just the same it was odd to think of Ralph Gillespie, in uniform, on the deck of a destroyer, maybe firing off guns. Rose was just beginning to understand that the boys she knew, however incompetent they might seem, were going to turn into men, and be allowed to do things that you would think required a lot more talent and authority than they could have.

There was a time, after she gave up the store and before her arthritis became too crippling, during which Flo went out to Bingo games and sometimes played cards with her neighbors at the Legion Hall. When Rose was home on a visit conversation was difficult, so she would ask Flo about the people she saw at the Legion. She would ask for news of her own contemporaries, Horse Nicholson, Runt Chesterton, whom she could not really imagine as grown men; did Flo ever see them?

"There's one I see and he's around there all the time. Ralph Gillespie." 70

Rose said that she had thought Ralph Gillespie was in the Navy.

"He was, but he's back home now. He was in an accident."

"What kind of accident?"

"I don't know. It was in the Navy. He was in a Navy hospital three solid years. They had to rebuild him from scratch. He's all right now except he walks with a limp, he sort of drags the one leg."

"That's too bad." 75

"Well, yes. That's what I say. I don't hold any grudge against him but there's some up there at the Legion that do."

"Hold a grudge?"

"Because of the pension," said Flo, surprised and rather contemptuous of Rose for not taking into account so basic a fact of life, and so natural an attitude, in Hanratty. "They think, well, he's set for life. I say he must've suffered for it. Some people say he gets a lot but I don't believe it. He doesn't need much, he's all on his own. One thing, if he suffers pain he don't let on. Like me. I don't let on. Weep and you weep alone. He's a good darts player. He'll play anything that's going. And he can imitate people to the life."

"Does he still do Milton Homer? He used to do Milton Homer at school."

"He does him. Milton Homer. He's comical at that. He does some others too." 80

"Is Milton Homer still alive? Is he still marching in parades?"

"Sure he's still alive. He's quietened down a lot, though. He's out there at the County Home and you can see him on a sunny day down by the highway keeping an eye on the traffic and licking up an ice cream cone. Both the old ladies is dead."

"So he isn't in the parades anymore?"

"There isn't the parades to be in. Parades have fallen off a lot. All the Orangemen are dying out and you wouldn't get the turnout, anyway, people'd rather stay home and watch TV."

On later visits Rose found that Flo had turned against the Legion. 85

"I don't want to be one of those old crackpots," she said.

"What old crackpots?"

"Sit around up there telling the same stupid yarns and drinking beer. They make me sick."

A Fiction Writer's Career: Alice Munro

This was very much in Flo's usual pattern. People, places, amusements, went abruptly in and out of favor. The turnabouts had become more drastic and frequent with age.

"Don't you like any of them anymore? Is Ralph Gillespie still going there?" ₉₀

"He still is. He likes it so well he tried to get himself a job there. He tried to get the part-time bar job. Some people say he got turned down because he already has the pension, but I think it was because of the way he carries on."

"How? Does he get drunk?"

"You couldn't tell if he was, he carries on just the same, imitating, and half the time he's imitating somebody that the newer people that's come to town, they don't know even who the person was, they just think it's Ralph being idiotic."

"Like Milton Homer?"

"That's right. How do they know it's supposed to be Milton Homer and what was Milton Homer like? They don't know. Ralph don't know when to stop. He Milton Homer'd himself right out of a job." ₉₅

After Rose had taken Flo to the County Home—she had not seen Milton Homer there, though she had seen other people she had long believed dead—and was staying to clean up the house and get it ready for sale, she herself was taken to the Legion by Flo's neighbors, who thought she must be lonely on a Saturday night. She did not know how to refuse, so she found herself sitting at a long table in the basement of the hall, where the bar was, just at the time the last sunlight was coming across the fields of beans and corn, across the gravel parking lot and through the high windows, staining the plywood walls. All around the walls were photographs, with names lettered by hand and taped to the frames. Rose got up to have a look at them. The Hundred and Sixth, just before embarkation, 1915. Various heroes of that war, whose names were carried on by sons and nephews, but whose existence had not been known to her before. When she came back to the table a card game had started. She wondered if it had been a disruptive thing to do, getting up to look at the pictures. Probably nobody ever looked at them; they were not for looking at; they were just there, like the plywood on the walls. Visitors, outsiders, are always looking at things, always taking an interest, asking who was this, when was that, trying to liven up the conversation. They put too much in; they want too much out. Also, it could have looked as if she was parading around the room, asking for attention.

A woman sat down and introduced herself. She was the wife of one of the men playing cards. "I've seen you on television," she said. Rose was always a bit apologetic when somebody said this; that is, she had to control what she recognized in herself as an absurd impulse to apologize. Here in Hanratty the impulse was stronger than usual. She was aware of having done things that must seem high-handed. She remembered her days as a television interviewer, her beguiling confidence and charm; here as nowhere else they must understand how that was a sham. Her acting was another matter. The things she was ashamed of were not what they must think she was ashamed of; not a flopping bare breast, but a failure she couldn't seize upon or explain.

This woman who was talking to her did not belong to Hanratty. She said she had come from Sarnia° when she was married, fifteen years ago.

_____

Sarnia: a city in Ontario.

"I still find it hard to get used to. Frankly I do. After the city. You look better in person than you do in that series."

"I should hope so," said Rose, and told about how they made her up. People were interested in things like that and Rose was more comfortable, once the conversation got on to technical details.

"Well, here's old Ralph," the woman said. She moved over, making room for this thin, gray-haired man holding a mug of beer. This was Ralph Gillespie. If Rose had met him on the street she would not have recognized him, he would have been a stranger to her, but after she had looked at him for a moment he seemed quite unchanged to her, unchanged from himself at seventeen or fifteen, his gray hair which had been light brown still falling over his forehead, his face still pale and calm and rather large for his body, the same diffident, watchful, withholding look. But his body was thinner and his shoulders seemed to have shrunk together. He wore a short-sleeved sweater with a little collar and three ornamental buttons; it was light blue with beige and yellow stripes. This sweater seemed to Rose to speak of aging jauntiness, a kind of petrified adolescence. She noticed that his arms were old and skinny and that his hands shook so badly that he used both of them to raise the glass of beer to his mouth.

"You're not staying around here long, are you?" said the woman who had come from Sarnia.

Rose said that she was going to Toronto tomorrow, Sunday, night.

"You must have a busy life," the woman said, with a large sigh, an honest envy that in itself would have declared out-of-town origins.

Rose was thinking that on Monday at noon she was to meet a man for lunch and to go to bed. This man was Tom Shepherd, whom she had known for a long time. At one time he had been in love with her, he had written love letters to her. The last time she had been with him, in Toronto, when they were sitting up in bed afterward drinking gin and tonic—they always drank a good deal when they were together—Rose suddenly thought, or knew, that there was somebody now, some woman he was in love with and was courting from a distance, probably writing letters to, and that there must have been another woman he was robustly bedding, at the time he was writing letters to her. Also, and all the time, there was his wife. Rose wanted to ask him about this; the necessity, the difficulties, the satisfactions. Her interest was friendly and uncritical but she knew, she had just enough sense to know, that the question would not do.

The conversation at the Legion had turned on lottery tickets, Bingo games, winnings. The men playing cards—Flo's neighbors among them—were talking about a man who was supposed to have won ten thousand dollars, and never publicized the fact, because he had gone bankrupt a few years before and owed so many people money.

One of them said that if he had declared himself bankrupt, he didn't owe the money anymore.

"Maybe he didn't owe it then," another said. "But he owes it now. The reason is, he's got it now."

This opinion was generally favored.

Rose and Ralph Gillespie looked at each other. There was the same silent joke, the same conspiracy, comfort; the same, the same.

"I hear you're quite a mimic," Rose said.

That was wrong; she shouldn't have said anything. He laughed and shook his head.

"Oh, come on. I hear you do a sensational Milton Homer."

"I don't know about that."

"Is he still around?"

"Far as I know he's out at the County Home."

"Remember Miss Hattie and Miss Mattie? They had the lantern slide show at their house."

"Sure."

"My mental picture of China is still pretty well based on those slides."

Rose went on talking like this, though she wished she could stop. She was talking in what elsewhere might have been considered an amusing, confidential, recognizably and meaninglessly flirtatious style. She did not get much response from Ralph Gillespie, though he seemed attentive, even welcoming. All the time she talked, she was wondering what he wanted her to say. He did want something. But he would not make any move to get it. Her first impression of him, as boyishly shy and ingratiating, had to change. That was his surface. Underneath he was self-sufficient, resigned to living in bafflement, perhaps proud. She wished that he would speak to her from that level, and she thought he wished it, too, but they were prevented.

But when Rose remembered this unsatisfactory conversation she seemed to recall a wave a kindness, of sympathy and forgiveness, though certainly no words of that kind had been spoken. That peculiar shame she carried around with her seemed to have been eased. The thing she was ashamed of, in acting, was that she might have been paying attention to the wrong things, reporting antics, when there was always something further, a tone, a depth, a light, that she couldn't get and wouldn't get. And it wasn't just about acting she suspected this. Everything she had done could sometimes be seen as a mistake. She had never felt this more strongly than when she was talking to Ralph Gillespie, but when she thought about him afterward her mistakes appeared unimportant. She was enough a child of her time to wonder if what she felt about him was simply sexual warmth, sexual curiosity; she did not think it was. There seemed to be feelings which could only be spoken of in translation; perhaps they could only be acted on in translation; not speaking of them and not acting on them is the right course to take because translation is dubious. Dangerous, as well.

For these reasons Rose did not explain anything further about Ralph Gillespie to Brian and Phoebe when she recalled Milton Homer's ceremony with babies or his expression of diabolical happiness on the swing. She did not even mention that he was dead. She knew he was dead because she still had a subscription to the Hanratty paper. Flo had given Rose a seven-year subscription on the last Christmas when she felt obliged to give Christmas presents; characteristically, Flo said that the paper was just for people to get their names in and hadn't anything in it worth reading. Usually Rose turned the pages quickly and put the paper in the firebox. But she did see the story about Ralph which was on the front page.

FORMER NAVY MAN DIES

Mr. Ralph Gillespie, Naval Petty Officer, retired, sustained fatal head injuries at the Legion Hall on Saturday night last. No other person was implicated in the fall and unfortunately several hours passed before Mr. Gillespie's body was discovered.

It is thought that he mistook the basement door for the exit door and lost his balance, which was precarious due to an old injury suffered in his naval career which left him partly disabled.

The paper went on to give the names of Ralph's parents, who were apparently still alive, and of his married sister. The Legion was taking charge of the funeral services.

Rose didn't tell this to anybody, glad that there was one thing at least she wouldn't spoil by telling, though she knew it was lack of material as much as honorable restraint that kept her quiet. What could she say about herself and Ralph Gillespie, except that she felt his life, close, closer than the lives of men she'd loved, one slot over from her own?

QUESTIONS

1. Who is Milton Homer? How does Munro give us a sense of his appearance and character using detail?

2. What is Milton's role in the life of the town? Why do people put up with his behavior? How much of the tolerance has to do with his aunts? Explain.

3. How does your view of Milton change over the course of the story? What happens to him, and to the town, with the passage of time?

4. How does Munro portray Rose in this story? Is her character consistent with the depiction in "Royal Beatings"? What has become of Rose? What is her career, and how has it affected the way she is viewed by others?

5. Why does Munro choose to tell the story as she does, with Rose visiting her brother and his wife? Would the story be any different if its events were simply narrated directly?

6. What is the original basis of Ralph Gillespie's relationship with Rose? How does she react to his imitations of Milton? Why? What happens to their relationship after Ralph quits school? What happens to him?

7. What is the role of Flo in the story? How has she changed from the Flo of "Royal Beatings"?

8. What does the information about Rose's adult life contribute to the story?

9. How does Rose come to encounter Ralph again? What is their conversation like? Why does Rose find it "unsatisfactory"?

10. What does Munro mean when she talks about Rose's feelings toward Ralph—that they could only be spoken of and acted on "in translation"?

11. Comment on the title. Where do these words appear in the story? Can you find the same words in "Royal Beatings"? What do they tell us about Rose's character and the responses she seems to elicit in others?

SUGGESTIONS FOR WRITING

1. Look at the depictions of Rose in both stories. Are they similar or different? Do they reveal different sides of her nature? Is there a pattern of consistency? What about the fact that Rose was shown as acting in "Royal Beatings" and that she has grown up to be an actress? What is her own sense about her choice of profession?

2. Write a short character analysis of Rose based upon the information given in the two stories.

3. Discuss Munro's use of subplots. Compare the Becky Tyde story with that of Milton Homer. Is it significant that both are seen as town "characters"? How do their stories reflect upon the narrative of Rose's own life?

A Fiction Writer's Career: Alice Munro

4. Look carefully at Munro's use of time in both stories. How and why does she switch vantages, moving from past to near-present? How does she indicate the passage of large chunks of time, and to what effect? Give special consideration to Munro's sudden telescoping of time at the ends of both stories.

5. How does Munro use descriptions and depiction of character interactions to create a sense of small-town life? Focus on one scene in each story where the evocations seem particularly strong and discuss how she achieves her effects.

6. Look at specific scenes in both stories to discuss how Munro creates a picture of the world as seen by a child. Compare the view through the eyes of the younger Rose in "Royal Beatings" with that of the older schoolgirl in "Who Do You Think You Are?"

12 A Fiction Writer's Career: James Baldwin

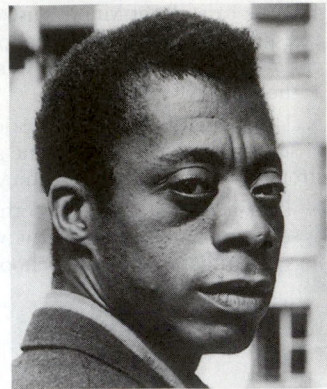

James Baldwin, who by the time of his death in
1987 had secured a place alongside Richard Wright and Ralph Ellison as the leading African American writer, was born in New York City in 1924. He grew up in
Harlem, in a large family, and attended DeWitt Clinton High School in the Bronx.

Baldwin was, by all accounts, an intelligent and solitary youth. He felt tyrannized by his stepfather, David Baldwin, a bitter man who held a factory job during
the week and preached the gospel from Harlem storefronts on weekends. Baldwin
escaped his presence by going to the local library. Indeed, in later years he told an
interviewer: "I read books like they were some weird kind of food." And reading led,
as it so often does, to his own attempts at writing.

When he was fourteen years old, Baldwin experienced an intense religious crisis. "I became for the first time in my life afraid," he said, "afraid of the evil within
me and afraid of the evil without." So strong was the religious impulse—it would die
out a few years later—that Baldwin took to preaching on Sundays at the local Pen-
tecostal assembly. This did not, however, bring him any closer to his stepfather, who
had already begun to experience debilitating bouts of mental illness.

Baldwin graduated from high school, but he did not go on to college. He
worked at a number of jobs and before long left the family home in Harlem to live
in New York City's Greenwich Village. It was there that he applied himself to writing in earnest, working on stories, book reviews, articles, and a first novel, *In My
Father's House*. Through the novel he tried to come to terms with his experiences,
especially his troubled relationship with his stepfather. He eventually abandoned
the book.

Baldwin faced another struggle in the years of his young manhood—the struggle to face his homosexuality. He was not able to come fully to terms with his sexual preference until he moved to the Village. Once he did come out, however,
Baldwin was candid and unashamed. He went further still, making homosexuality
the subject of some of his fiction in a time when such forthrightness was very rare.

In 1948, Baldwin made a move to free himself from the racial oppression of U.S.
culture. He sailed to Paris, where he lived for the next eight years. The change of
environment was evidently liberating for Baldwin as a writer, as a steady stream of
novels and essays testifies. During this period, Baldwin produced the books that secured his reputation as one of the leading African American writers. These include
the novels *Go Tell It on the Mountain* (1953) and *Giovanni's Room* (1956) and the
nonfictional *Notes of a Native Son* (1955).

Baldwin continued his productivity after his return to New York in 1956. By that time he had achieved enough of a reputation to be cast as a black spokesman, and throughout the years of the Civil Rights movement he lent his prestige, and his pen, to the cause. Increasing involvement led to increasing militancy, and by the mid-1960s Baldwin was declaring that unless the black people were granted full equality the country would be torn apart by violence. Baldwin's books from this period, including the novel *Another Country* (1962) and the polemical essays in *Nobody Knows My Name* (1963), reflect his obsession with questions of race and violence.

By the late 1960s, Baldwin saw his gravest fears realized. Both Robert Kennedy, in his eyes an advocate of the black cause, and Martin Luther King were assassinated in 1968. The country seemed poised for violent revolution. Baldwin, dispirited and deeply saddened by the death of King, moved back to Europe. He traveled first to Istanbul, Turkey, and later settled in southern France. Heavy drinking and chain-smoking had begun to take their toll on his health, but he remained prolific for some years. Before his death in 1987, Baldwin made several prolonged visits to this country to teach and lecture. Though critics felt that his writing had begun to fall off in quality, his reputation was not greatly affected; his best novels, stories, and essays have a permanent place in our literature.

Baldwin gave most of his fiction-producing energies to the novel. He published only one collection of stories, *Going to Meet the Man* (1965), but as that collection showed, he knew how to turn a powerful story. And indeed, *Going to Meet the Man*, which gathers work from nearly twenty years, allows us to sample some of the fictional range reflected in the novels. Of the two stories presented here, "Sonny's Blues" (1957) examines the effects of an oppressive environment on the lives of two estranged brothers, and the title story, written in the 1960s, is a terrifying statement about the twisted roots of racial hatred (it may, in fact, be more than some readers can stomach).

In "Sonny's Blues," Baldwin traces the tensions between two brothers, but he also gives a sense of the larger picture. We see how the difficulties within the family are connected to the tensions in the society and to the particular despair of the black people. "Going to Meet the Man" releases those tensions in what may feel to some a prolonged assault upon the senses. It is a harsh, painful, and in many ways ugly story. But for those very reasons it is also a necessary story. If it is not a statement about where we are at the present, it is certainly a dark reminder of where we have been.

SONNY'S BLUES

I read about it in the paper, in the subway, on my way to work. I read it, and I couldn't believe it, and I read it again. Then perhaps I just stared at it, at the newsprint spelling out his name, spelling out the story. I stared at it in the swinging lights of the subway car, and in the faces and bodies of the people, and in my own face, trapped in the darkness which roared outside.

It was not to be believed and I kept telling myself that, as I walked from the subway station to the high school. And at the same time I couldn't doubt it. I was scared, scared for Sonny. He became real to me again. A great block of ice got settled in my belly and kept melting there slowly all day long, while I taught my classes algebra. It was a special kind of ice. It kept melting, sending trickles of ice water all up and down my veins, but it never got less. Sometimes it hardened and seemed to expand until I felt my guts were going to come spilling out or that I was going to choke or scream. This would always be at a moment when I was remembering some specific thing Sonny had once said or done.

When he was about as old as the boys in my classes his face had been bright and open, there was a lot of copper in it; and he'd had wonderfully direct brown eyes, and great gentleness and privacy. I wondered what he looked like now. He had been picked up, the evening before, in a raid on an apartment downtown, for peddling and using heroin.

I couldn't believe it: but what I mean by that is that I couldn't find any room for it anywhere inside me. I had kept it outside me for a long time. I hadn't wanted to know. I had had suspicions, but I didn't name them, I kept putting them away. I told myself that Sonny was wild, but he wasn't crazy. And he'd always been a good boy, he hadn't ever turned hard or evil or disrespectful, the way kids can, so quick, so quick, especially in Harlem. I didn't want to believe that I'd ever see my brother going down, coming to nothing, all that light in his face gone out, in the condition I'd already seen so many others. Yet it had happened and here I was, talking about algebra to a lot of boys who might, every one of them for all I knew, be popping off needles every time they went to the head.° Maybe it did more for them than algebra could.

I was sure that the first time Sonny had ever had horse,° he couldn't have been much older than these boys were now. These boys, now, were living as we'd been living then, they were growing up with a rush and their heads bumped abruptly against the low ceiling of their actual possibilities. They were filled with rage. All they really knew were two darknesses, the darkness of their lives, which was now closing in on them, and the darkness of the movies, which had blinded them to that other darkness, and in which they now, vindictively, dreamed, at once more together than they were at any other time, and more alone.

When the last bell rang, the last class ended, I let out my breath. It seemed I'd been holding it for all that time. My clothes were wet—I may have looked as though I'd been sitting in a steam bath, all dressed up, all afternoon. I sat alone in the classroom a long time. I listened to the boys outside, downstairs, shouting and cursing and laughing. Their laughter struck me for perhaps the first time. It was not the joyous laughter which—God knows why—one associates with children. It was mocking and insular, its intent was to denigrate. It was disenchanted, and in this, also, lay the authority of their curses. Perhaps I was listening to them because I was thinking about my brother and in them I heard my brother. And myself.

One boy was whistling a tune, at once very complicated and very simple, it seemed to be pouring out of him as though he were a bird, and it sounded very cool and moving through all that harsh, bright air, only just holding its own through all those other sounds.

I stood up and walked over to the window and looked down into the courtyard. It was the beginning of the spring and the sap was rising in the boys. A teacher

head: toilet.
horse: heroin.

passed through them every now and again, quickly, as though he or she couldn't wait to get out of that courtyard, to get those boys out of their sight and off their minds. I started collecting my stuff. I thought I'd better get home and talk to Isabel.

The courtyard was almost deserted by the time I got downstairs. I saw this boy standing in the shadow of a doorway, looking just like Sonny. I almost called his name. Then I saw that it wasn't Sonny, but somebody we used to know, a boy from around our block. He'd been Sonny's friend. He'd never been mine, having been too young for me, and, anyway, I'd never liked him. And now, even though he was a grown-up man, he still hung around that block, still spent hours on the street corners, was always high and raggy. I used to run into him from time to time and he'd often work around to asking me for a quarter or fifty cents. He always had some real good excuse, too, and I always gave it to him. I don't know why.

But now, abruptly, I hated him. I couldn't stand the way he looked at me, partly like a dog, partly like a cunning child. I wanted to ask him what the hell he was doing in the school courtyard. 10

He sort of shuffled over to me, and he said, "I see you got the papers. So you already know about it."

"You mean about Sonny? Yes, I already know about it. How come they didn't get you?"

He grinned. It made him repulsive and it also brought to mind what he'd looked like as a kid. "I wasn't there. I stay away from them people."

"Good for you." I offered him a cigarette and I watched him through the smoke. "You come all the way down here just to tell me about Sonny?"

"That's right." He was sort of shaking his head and his eyes looked strange, as though they were about to cross. The bright sun deadened his damp dark brown skin and it made his eyes look yellow and showed up the dirt in his kinked hair. He smelled funky.° I moved a little away from him and I said, "Well, thanks. But I already know about it and I got to get home." 15

"I'll walk you a little ways," he said. We started walking. There were a couple of kids still loitering in the courtyard and one of them said goodnight to me and looked strangely at the boy beside me.

"What're you going to do?" he asked me. "I mean, about Sonny?"

"Look. I haven't seen Sonny for over a year, I'm not sure I'm going to do anything. Anyway, what the hell *can* I do?"

"That's right," he said quickly, "ain't nothing you can do. Can't much help old Sonny no more, I guess."

It was what I was thinking and so it seemed to me he had no right to say it. 20

"I'm surprised at Sonny, though," he went on—he had a funny way of talking, he looked straight ahead as though he were talking to himself—"I thought Sonny was a smart boy, I thought he was too smart to get hung."

"I guess he thought so too," I said sharply, "and that's how he got hung. And how about you? You're pretty goddamn smart, I bet."

Then he looked directly at me, just for a minute. "I ain't smart," he said. "If I was smart, I'd have reached for a pistol a long time ago."

"Look. Don't tell *me* your sad story, if it was up to me, I'd give you one." Then I felt guilty—guilty, probably, for never having supposed that the poor bastard *had* a

---

funky: unwashed.

story of his own, much less a sad one, and I asked, quickly, "What's going to happen to him now?"

He didn't answer this. He was off by himself some place. "Funny thing," he said, and from his tone we might have been discussing the quickest way to get to Brooklyn, "when I saw the papers this morning, the first thing I asked myself was if I had anything to do with it. I felt sort of responsible."

I began to listen more carefully. The subway station was on the corner, just before us, and I stopped. He stopped, too. We were in front of a bar and he ducked slightly, peering in, but whoever he was looking for didn't seem to be there. The juke box was blasting away with something black and bouncy and I half watched the barmaid as she danced her way from the juke box to her place behind the bar. And I watched her face as she laughingly responded to something someone said to her, still keeping time to the music. When she smiled one saw the little girl, one sensed the doomed, still-struggling woman beneath the battered face of the semi-whore.

"I never *give* Sonny nothing," the boy said finally, "but a long time ago I come to school high and Sonny asked me how it felt." He paused, I couldn't bear to watch him, I watched the barmaid, and I listened to the music which seemed to be causing the pavement to shake. "I told him it felt great." The music stopped, the barmaid paused and watched the juke box until the music began again. "It did."

All this was carrying me some place I didn't want to go. I certainly didn't want to know how it felt. It filled everything, the people, the houses, the music, the dark, quicksilver barmaid, with menace; and this menace was their reality.

"What's going to happen to him now?" I asked again.

"They'll send him away some place and they'll try to cure him." He shook his head. "Maybe he'll even think he's kicked the habit. Then they'll let him loose"— he gestured, throwing his cigarette into the gutter. "That's all."

"What do you mean, that's *all*?"

But I knew what he meant.

"I *mean*, that's *all*." He turned his head and looked at me, pulling down the corners of his mouth. "Don't you know what I mean?" he asked, softly.

"How the hell *would* I know what you mean?" I almost whispered it, I don't know why.

"That's right," he said to the air, "how would *he* know what I mean?" He turned toward me again, patient and calm, and yet I somehow felt him shaking, shaking as though he were going to fall apart. I felt that ice in my guts again, the dread I'd felt all afternoon; and again I watched the barmaid, moving about the bar, washing glasses, and singing. "Listen. They'll let him out and then it'll just start all over again. That's what I mean."

"You mean—they'll let him out. And then he'll just start working his way back in again. You mean he'll never kick the habit. Is that what you mean?"

"That's right," he said, cheerfully. "*You* see what I mean."

"Tell me," I said at last, "why does he want to die? He must want to die, he's killing himself, why does he want to die?"

He looked at me in surprise. He licked his lips. "He don't want to die. He wants to live. Don't nobody want to die, ever."

Then I wanted to ask him—too many things. He could not have answered, or if he had, I could not have borne the answers. I started walking. "Well, I guess it's none of my business."

"It's going to be rough on old Sonny," he said. We reached the subway station. "This is your station?" he asked. I nodded. I took one step down. "Damn!" he said, suddenly. I looked up at him. He grinned again. "Damn it if I didn't leave all my money home. You ain't got a dollar on you, have you? Just for a couple of days, is all."

All at once something inside gave and threatened to come pouring out of me. I didn't hate him any more. I felt that in another moment I'd start crying like a child.

"Sure," I said. "Don't sweat." I looked in my wallet and didn't have a dollar, I only had a five. "Here," I said. "That hold you?"

He didn't look at it—he didn't want to look at it. A terrible, closed look came over his face, as though he were keeping the number on the bill a secret from him and me. "Thanks," he said, and now he was dying to see me go. "Don't worry about Sonny. Maybe I'll write him or something."

"Sure," I said. "You do that. So long."

"Be seeing you," he said. I went on down the steps.

And I didn't write Sonny or send him anything for a long time. When I finally did, it was just after my little girl died, and he wrote me back a letter which made me feel like a bastard.

Here's what he said:

> Dear brother,
> You don't know how much I needed to hear from you. I wanted to write you many a time but I dug how much I must have hurt you and so I didn't write. But now I feel like a man who's been trying to climb up out of some deep, real deep and funky hole and just saw the sun up there, outside. I got to get outside.
> I can't tell you much about how I got here. I mean I don't know how to tell you. I guess I was afraid of something or I was trying to escape from something and you know I have never been very strong in the head (smile). I'm glad Mama and Daddy are dead and can't see what's happened to their son and I swear if I'd known what I was doing I would never have hurt you so, you and a lot of other fine people who were nice to me and who believed in me.
> I don't want you to think it had anything to do with me being a musician. It's more than that. Or maybe less than that. I can't get anything straight in my head down here and I try not to think about what's going to happen to me when I get outside again. Sometime I think I'm going to flip and *never* get outside and sometime I think I'll come straight back. I tell you one thing, though, I'd rather blow my brains out than go through this again. But that's what they all say, so they tell me. If I tell you when I'm coming to New York and if you could meet me, I sure would appreciate it. Give my love to Isabel and the kids and I was sure sorry to hear about little Gracie. I wish I could be like Mama and say the Lord's will be done, but I don't know it seems to me that trouble is the one thing that never does get stopped and I don't know what good it does to blame it on the Lord. But maybe it does some good if you believe it.
>
> Your brother,
Sonny

Then I kept in constant touch with him and I sent him whatever I could and I went to meet him when he came back to New York. When I saw him many things I thought I had forgotten came flooding back to me. This was because I had begun, fi-

45

nally, to wonder about Sonny, about the life that Sonny lived inside. This life, what-ever it was, had made him older and thinner and it had deepened the distant still-ness in which he had always moved. He looked very unlike my baby brother. Yet, when he smiled, when we shook hands, the baby brother I'd never known looked out from the depths of his private life, like an animal waiting to be coaxed into the light.

"How you been keeping?" he asked me. 50

"All right. And you?"

"Just fine." He was smiling all over his face. "It's good to see you again."

"It's good to see you."

The seven years' difference in our ages lay between us like a chasm: I wondered if these years would ever operate between us as a bridge. I was remembering, and it made it hard to catch my breath, that I had been there when he was born; and I had heard the first words he had ever spoken. When he started to walk, he walked from our mother straight to me. I caught him just before he fell when he took the first steps he ever took in this world.

"How's Isabel?" 55

"Just fine. She's dying to see you."

"And the boys?"

"They're fine, too. They're anxious to see their uncle."

"Oh, come on. You know they don't remember me."

"Are you kidding? Of course they remember you." 60

He grinned again. We got into a taxi. We had a lot to say to each other, far too much to know how to begin.

As the taxi began to move, I asked, "You still want to go to India?"

He laughed. "You still remember that. Hell, no. This place is Indian enough for me."

"It used to belong to them," I said.

And he laughed again. "They damn sure knew what they were doing when they got rid of it." 65

Years ago, when he was around fourteen, he'd been all hipped on the idea of going to India. He read books about people sitting on rocks, naked, in all kinds of weather, but mostly bad, naturally, and walking barefoot through hot coals and ar-riving at wisdom. I used to say that it sounded to me as though they were getting away from wisdom as fast as they could. I think he sort of looked down on me for that.

"Do you mind," he asked, "if we have the driver drive alongside the park? On the west side—I haven't seen the city in so long."

"Of course not," I said. I was afraid that I might sound as though I were hu-moring him, but I hoped he wouldn't take it that way.

So we drove along, between the green of the park and the stony, lifeless elegance of hotels and apartment buildings, toward the vivid, killing streets of our childhood. These streets hadn't changed, though housing projects jutted up out of them now like rocks in the middle of a boiling sea. Most of the houses in which we had grown up had vanished, as had the stores from which we had stolen, the basements in which we had first tried sex, the rooftops from which we had hurled tin cans and bricks. But houses exactly like the house of our past yet dominated the landscape, boys ex-actly like the boys we once had been found themselves smothering in these houses, came down into the streets for light and air and found themselves encircled by disaster. Some escaped the trap, most didn't. Those who got out always left something of themselves behind, as some animals amputate a leg and leave it in the trap. It might be said, perhaps, that I had escaped, after all, I was a school teacher; or that Sonny had, he hadn't lived in Harlem for years. Yet, as the cab moved uptown through streets which seemed, with a rush, to darken with dark people, and as I covertly studied Sonny's face, it came to me that what we both were seeking through our separate cab windows was that part of ourselves which had been left behind. It's always at the hour of trouble and confrontation that the missing member aches.

We hit 110th Street and started rolling up Lenox Avenue. And I'd known this avenue all my life, but it seemed to me again, as it had seemed on the day I'd first heard about Sonny's trouble, filled with a hidden menace which was its very breath of life. 70

"We almost there," said Sonny.

"Almost." We were both too nervous to say anything more.

We live in a housing project. It hasn't been up long. A few days after it was up it seemed uninhabitably new, now, of course, it's already rundown. It looks like a parody of the good, clean, faceless life—God knows the people who live in it do their best to make it a parody. The beat-looking grass lying around isn't enough to make their lives green, the hedges will never hold out the streets, and they know it. The big windows fool no one, they aren't big enough to make space out of no space. They don't bother with the windows, they watch the TV screen instead. The playground is most popular with the children who don't play at jacks, or skip rope, or roller skate, or swing, and they can be found in it after dark. We moved in partly because it's not too far from where I teach, and partly for the kids; but it's really just like the houses in which Sonny and I grew up. The same things happen, they'll have the same things to remember. The moment Sonny and I started into the house I had the feeling that I was simply bringing him back into the danger he had almost died trying to escape.

Sonny has never been talkative. So I don't know why I was sure he'd be dying to talk to me when supper was over the first night. Everything went fine, the oldest boy remembered him, and the youngest boy liked him, and Sonny had remembered to bring something for each of them; and Isabel, who is really much nicer than I am, more open and giving, had gone to a lot of trouble about dinner and was genuinely glad to see him. And she's always been able to tease Sonny in a way that I haven't. It was nice to see her face so vivid again and to hear her laugh and watch her make Sonny laugh. She wasn't, or, anyway, she didn't seem to be, at all uneasy or embarrassed. She chatted as though there were no subject which had to be avoided and she got Sonny past his first, faint stiffness. And thank God she was there, for I was filled with that icy dread again. Everything I did seemed awkward to me, and everything I said sounded freighted with hidden meaning. I was trying to remember everything I'd heard about dope addiction and I couldn't help watching Sonny for signs. I wasn't doing it out of malice. I was trying to find out something about my brother. I was dying to hear him tell me he was safe.

"Safe!" my father grunted, whenever Mama suggested trying to move to a neighborhood which might be safer for children. "Safe, hell! Ain't no place safe for kids, 75 nor nobody."

He always went on like this, but he wasn't, ever, really as bad as he sounded, not even on weekends, when he got drunk. As a matter of fact, he was always on the lookout for "something a little better," but he died before he found it. He died suddenly, during a drunken weekend in the middle of the war, when Sonny was fifteen. He and Sonny hadn't ever got on too well. And this was partly because Sonny was the apple of his father's eye. It was because he loved Sonny so much and was frightened for him, that he was always fighting with him. It doesn't do any good to fight with Sonny. Sonny just moves back, inside himself, where he can't be reached. But the principal reason that they never hit it off is that they were so much alike. Daddy was big and rough and loud-talking, just the opposite of Sonny, but they both had—that same privacy.

Mama tried to tell me something about this, just after Daddy died. I was home on leave from the army.

This was the last time I ever saw my mother alive. Just the same, this picture gets all mixed up in my mind with pictures I had of her when she was younger. The way I always see her is the way she used to be on a Sunday afternoon, say, when the old folks were talking after the big Sunday dinner. I always see her wearing pale blue. She'd be sitting on the sofa. And my father would be sitting in the easy chair, not far from her. And the living room would be full of church folks and relatives. There they sit, in chairs all around the living room, and the night is creeping up outside, but nobody knows it yet. You can see the darkness growing against the windowpanes and you hear the street noises every now and again, or maybe the jangling beat of a tambourine from one of the churches close by, but it's real quiet in the room. For a moment nobody's talking, but every face looks darkening, like the sky outside. And my mother rocks a little from the waist, and my father's eyes are closed. Everyone is looking at something a child can't see. For a minute they've forgotten the children. Maybe a kid is lying on the rug, half asleep. Maybe somebody's got a kid in his lap and is absent-mindedly stroking the kid's head. Maybe there's a kid, quiet and big-eyed, curled up in a big chair in the corner. The silence, the darkness coming, and the darkness in the faces frighten the child obscurely. He hopes that the hand which strokes his forehead will never stop—will never die. He hopes that there will never come a time when the old folks won't be sitting around the living room, talking about where they've come from, and what they've seen, and what's happened to them and their kinfolk.

But something deep and watchful in the child knows that this is bound to end, is already ending. In a moment someone will get up and turn on the light. Then the old folks will remember the children and they won't talk any more that day. And when light fills the room, the child is filled with darkness. He knows that every time this happens he's moved just a little closer to that darkness outside. The darkness outside is what the old folks have been talking about. It's what they've come from. It's what they endure. The child knows that they won't talk any more because if he knows too much about what's happened to *them*, he'll know too much too soon, about what's going to happen to *him*.

The last time I talked to my mother, I remember I was restless. I wanted to get out and see Isabel. We weren't married then and we had a lot to straighten out between us. 80

There Mama sat, in black, by the window. She was humming an old church song, *Lord, you brought me from a long ways off*. Sonny was out somewhere. Mama kept watching the streets.

"I don't know," she said, "if I'll ever see you again, after you go off from here. But I hope you'll remember the things I tried to teach you."

"Don't talk like that," I said, and smiled. "You'll be here a long time yet."

She smiled, too, but she said nothing. She was quiet for a long time. And I said, "Mama, don't you worry about nothing. I'll be writing all the time, and you be getting the checks. . . ."

"I want to talk to you about your brother," she said, suddenly. "If anything happens to me he ain't going to have nobody to look out for him."

"Mama," I said, "ain't nothing going to happen to you *or* Sonny. Sonny's all right. He's a good boy and he's got good sense."

"It ain't a question of his being a good boy," Mama said, "nor of his having good sense. It ain't only the bad ones, nor yet the dumb ones that gets sucked under." She stopped, looking at me. "Your Daddy once had a brother," she said, and she smiled in a way that made me feel she was in pain. "You didn't never know that, did you?"

"No," I said, "I never knew that," and I watched her face.

"Oh, yes," she said, "your Daddy had a brother." She looked out of the window again. "I know you never saw your Daddy cry. But *I* did—many a time, through all these years."

I asked her, "What happened to his brother? How come nobody's ever talked about him?"

This was the first time I ever saw my mother look old.

"His brother got killed," she said, "when he was just a little younger than you are now. I knew him. He was a fine boy. He was maybe a little full of the devil, but he didn't mean nobody no harm."

Then she stopped and the room was silent, exactly as it had sometimes been on those Sunday afternoons. Mama kept looking out into the streets.

"He used to have a job in the mill," she said, "and, like all young folks, he just liked to perform on Saturday nights. Saturday nights, him and your father would drift around to different places, go to dances and things like that, or just sit around with people they knew, and your father's brother would sing, he had a fine voice, and play along with himself on his guitar. Well, this particular Saturday night, him and your father was coming home from some place, and they were both a little drunk and there was a moon that night, it was bright like day. Your father's brother was feeling kind of good, and he was whistling to himself, and he had his guitar slung over his shoulder. They was coming down a hill and beneath them was a road that turned off from the highway. Well, your father's brother, being always kind of frisky, decided to run down this hill, and he did, with that guitar banging and clanging behind him, and he ran across the road, and he was making water behind a tree. And your father was sort of amused at him and he was still coming down the hill, kind of slow. Then he heard a car motor and that same minute his brother stepped from behind the tree, into the road, in the moonlight. And he started to cross the road. And your father started to run down the hill, he says he don't know why. This car was full of white men. They was all drunk, and when they seen your father's brother they let out a great whoop and holler and they aimed the car straight at him. They was having fun, they just wanted to scare him, the way they do sometimes, you know. But they was drunk. And I guess the boy, being drunk, too, and scared, kind of lost his head. By the time he jumped it was too late. Your father says he heard his brother scream when the car rolled over him, and he heard the wood of that guitar when it give, and he heard them strings go flying, and he heard them white men shouting, and the car kept on a-going and it ain't stopped till this day. And, time your father got down the hill, his brother weren't nothing but blood and pulp."

Tears were gleaming on my mother's face. There wasn't anything I could say.   95

"He never mentioned it," she said, "because I never let him mention it before you children. Your Daddy was like a crazy man that night and for many a night thereafter. He says he never in his life seen anything as dark as that road after the lights of that car had gone away. Weren't nothing, weren't nobody on that road, just your Daddy and his brother and that busted guitar. Oh, yes. Your Daddy never did really get right again. Till the day he died he weren't sure but that every white man he saw was the man that killed his brother."

She stopped and took out her handkerchief and dried her eyes and looked at me.

"I ain't telling you all this," she said, "to make you scared or bitter or to make you hate nobody. I'm telling you this because you got a brother. And the world ain't changed."

I guess I didn't want to believe this. I guess she saw this in my face. She turned away from me, toward the window again, searching those streets.

"But I praise my Redeemer," she said at last, "that He called your Daddy home before me. I ain't saying it to throw no flowers at myself, but, I declare, it keeps me from feeling too cast down to know I helped your father get safely through this world. Your father always acted like he was the roughest, strongest man on earth. And every-body took him to be like that. But if he hadn't had *me* there—to see his tears!"   100

She was crying again. Still, I couldn't move. I said, "Lord, Lord, Mama, I didn't know it was like that."

"Oh, honey," she said, "there's a lot that you don't know. But you are going to find it out." She stood up from the window and came over to me. "You got to hold on to your brother," she said, "and don't let him fall, no matter what it looks like is happening to him and no matter how evil you gets with him. You going to be evil with him many a time. But don't you forget what I told you, you hear?"

"I won't forget," I said. "Don't you worry, I won't forget. I won't let nothing hap-pen to Sonny."

My mother smiled as though she was amused at something she saw in my face. Then, "You may not be able to stop nothing from happening. But you got to let him know you's *there*."

Two days later I was married, and then I was gone. And I had a lot of things on my mind and I pretty well forgot my promise to Mama until I got shipped home on a special furlough for her funeral.   105

And, after the funeral, with just Sonny and me alone in the empty kitchen, I tried to find out something about him.

"What do you want to do?" I asked him.

"I'm going to be a musician," he said.

For he had graduated, in the time I had been away, from dancing to the juke box to finding out who was playing what, and what they were doing with it, and he had bought himself a set of drums.

"You mean, you want to be a drummer?" I somehow had the feeling that being a drummer might be all right for other people but not for my brother Sonny.   110

"I don't think," he said, looking at me very gravely, "that I'll ever be a good drummer. But I think I can play a piano."

I frowned. I'd never played the role of the older brother quite so seriously before, had scarcely ever, in fact, *asked* Sonny a damn thing. I sensed myself in the presence of something I didn't really know how to handle, didn't understand. So I made my frown a little deeper as I asked: "What kind of musician do you want to be?"

He grinned. "How many kinds do you think there are?"

"Be *serious*," I said.

He laughed, throwing his head back, and then looked at me. "I *am* serious."

"Well, then, for Christ's sake, stop kidding around and answer a serious question. I mean, do you want to be a concert pianist, you want to play classical music and all that, or—or what?" Long before I finished he was laughing again. "For Christ's *sake*, Sonny!"

He sobered, but with difficulty. "I'm sorry. But you sound so—*scared!*" and he was off again.

"Well, you may think it's funny now, baby, but it's not going to be so funny when you have to make your living at it, let me tell you *that*." I was furious because I knew he was laughing at me and I didn't know why.

"No," he said, very sober now, and afraid, perhaps, that he'd hurt me, "I don't want to be a classical pianist. That isn't what interests me. I mean"—he paused, looking hard at me, as though his eyes would help me to understand, and then gestured helplessly, as though perhaps his hand would help—"I mean, I'll have a lot of studying to do, and I'll have to study *everything*, but, I mean, I want to play *with*—jazz musicians." He stopped. "I want to play jazz," he said.

Well, the word had never before sounded as heavy, as real, as it sounded that afternoon in Sonny's mouth. I just looked at him and I was probably frowning a real frown by this time. I simply couldn't see why on earth he'd want to spend his time hanging around nightclubs, clowning around on bandstands, while people pushed each other around a dance floor. It seemed—beneath him, somehow. I had never thought about it before, had never been forced to, but I suppose I had always put jazz musicians in a class with what Daddy called "good-time people."

"Are you *serious?*"

"Hell, *yes*, I'm serious."

He looked more helpless than ever, and annoyed, and deeply hurt.

I suggested, helpfully: "You mean—like Louis Armstrong?"

His face closed as though I'd struck him. "No. I'm not talking about none of that old-time, down home crap."

"Well, look, Sonny, I'm sorry, don't get mad. I just don't altogether get it, that's all. Name somebody—you know, a jazz musician you admire."

"Bird."°

"Who?"

"Bird! Charlie Parker! Don't they teach you nothing in the goddamn army?"

I lit a cigarette. I was surprised and then a little amused to discover that I was trembling. "I've been out of touch," I said. "You'll have to be patient with me. Now. Who's this Parker character?"

"He's just one of the greatest jazz musicians alive," said Sonny, sullenly, his hands in his pockets, his back to me. "Maybe *the* greatest," he added, bitterly, "that's probably why *you* never heard of him."

°*Bird*: Charlie "Bird" Parker (1920–1955), legendary jazz saxophone player of the 1940s.

115

120

125

130

"All right," I said, "I'm ignorant. I'm sorry. I'll go out and buy all the cat's records right away, all right?"

"It don't," said Sonny, with dignity, "make any difference to me. I don't care what you listen to. Don't do me no favors."

I was beginning to realize that I'd never seen him so upset before. With another part of my mind I was thinking that this would probably turn out to be one of those things kids go through and that I shouldn't make it seem important by pushing it too hard. Still, I didn't think it would do any harm to ask: "Doesn't all this take a lot of time? Can you make a living at it?"

He turned back to me and half leaned, half sat, on the kitchen table. "Everything takes time," he said, "and—well, yes, sure, I can make a living at it. But what I don't seem to be able to make you understand is that it's the only thing I want to do."

"Well, Sonny," I said gently, "you know people can't always do exactly what they *want* to do—"

"*No*, I don't know that," said Sonny, surprising me. "I think people *ought* to do what they want to do, what else are they alive for?"

"You getting to be a big boy," I said desperately, "it's time you started thinking about your future."

"I'm thinking about my future," said Sonny, grimly. "I think about it all the time."

I gave up. I decided, if he didn't change his mind, that we could always talk about it later. "In the meantime," I said, "you got to finish school." We had already decided that he'd have to move in with Isabel and her folks. I knew this wasn't the ideal arrangement because Isabel's folks are inclined to be dicty° and they hadn't especially wanted Isabel to marry me. But I didn't know what else to do. "And we have to get you fixed up at Isabel's."

There was a long silence. He moved from the kitchen table to the window. "That's a terrible idea. You know it yourself."

"Do you have a *better* idea?"

He just walked up and down the kitchen for a minute. He was as tall as I was. He had started to shave. I suddenly had the feeling that I didn't know him at all.

He stopped at the kitchen table and picked up my cigarettes. Looking at me with a kind of mocking, amused defiance, he put one between his lips. "You mind?"

"You smoking already?"

He lit the cigarette and nodded, watching me through the smoke. "I just wanted to see if I'd have the courage to smoke in front of you." He grinned and blew a great cloud of smoke to the ceiling. "It was easy." He looked at my face. "Come on, now. I bet you was smoking at my age, tell the truth."

I didn't say anything but the truth was on my face, and he laughed. But now there was something very strained in his laugh. "Sure. And I bet that ain't all you was doing."

He was frightening me a little. "Cut the crap," I said. "We already decided that you was going to go and live at Isabel's. Now what's got into you all of a sudden?"

"*You* decided it," he pointed out. "*I* didn't decide nothing." He stopped in front of me, leaning against the stove, arms loosely folded. "Look, brother. I don't want

135

140

145

---

dicty: dictatorial, bossy.

A Fiction Writer's Career: James Baldwin

to stay in Harlem no more, I really don't." He was very earnest. He looked at me, then over toward the kitchen window. There was something in his eyes I'd never seen before, some thoughtfulness, some worry all his own. He rubbed the muscle of one arm. "It's time I was getting out of here."

"Where do you want to go, Sonny?"

"I want to join the army. Or the navy, I don't care. If I say I'm old enough, they'll believe me."

Then I got mad. It was because I was so scared. "You must be crazy. You goddamn fool, what the hell do you want to go and join the *army* for?"

"I just told you. To get out of Harlem."

"Sonny, you haven't even finished *school*. And if you really want to be a musician, how do you expect to study if you're in the *army?*"

He looked at me, trapped, and in anguish. "There's ways. I might be able to work out some kind of deal. Anyway, I'll have the G.I. Bill when I come out."

"*If* you come out." We stared at each other. "Sonny, please. Be reasonable. I know the setup is far from perfect. But we got to do the best we can."

"I ain't learning nothing in school," he said. "Even when I go." He turned away from me and opened the window and threw his cigarette out into the narrow alley. I watched his back. "At least, I ain't learning nothing you'd want me to learn." He slammed the window so hard I thought the glass would fly out, and turned back to me. "And I'm sick of the stink of these garbage cans!"

"Sonny," I said, "I know how you feel. But if you don't finish school now, you're going to be sorry later that you didn't." I grabbed him by the shoulders. "And you only got another year. It ain't so bad. And I'll come back and I swear I'll help you do *whatever* you want to do. Just try to put up with it till I come back. Will you please do that? For me?"

He didn't answer and he wouldn't look at me.

"Sonny. You hear me?"

He pulled away. "I hear you. But you never hear anything *I* say."

I didn't know what to say to that. He looked out of the window and then back at me. "OK," he said, and sighed. "I'll try."

Then I said, trying to cheer him up a little, "They got a piano at Isabel's. You can practice on it."

And as a matter of fact, it did cheer him up for a minute. "That's right," he said to himself. "I forgot that." His face relaxed a little. But the worry, the thoughtfulness, played on it still, the way shadows play on a face which is staring into the fire.

But I thought I'd never hear the end of that piano. At first, Isabel would write me, saying how nice it was that Sonny was so serious about his music and how, as soon as he came in from school, or wherever he had been when he was supposed to be at school, he went straight to that piano and stayed there until suppertime. And, after supper, he went back to that piano and stayed there until everybody went to bed. He was at the piano all day Saturday and all day Sunday. Then he bought a record player and started playing records. He'd play one record over and over again, all day long sometimes, and he'd improvise along with it on the piano. Or he'd play one section of the record, one chord, one change, one progression, then he'd do it on the piano. Then back to the record. Then back to the piano.

Well, I really don't know how they stood it. Isabel finally confessed that it wasn't like living with a person at all, it was like living with sound. And the sound didn't make any sense to her, didn't make any sense to any of them—naturally. They began, in a way, to be afflicted by this presence that was living in their home. It was as though Sonny were some sort of god, or monster. He moved in an atmosphere which wasn't like theirs at all. They fed him and he ate, he washed himself, he walked in and out of their door; he certainly wasn't nasty or unpleasant or rude, Sonny isn't any of those things; but it was as though he were all wrapped up in some cloud, some fire, some vision all his own; and there wasn't any way to reach him.

At the same time, he wasn't really a man yet, he was still a child, and they had to watch out for him in all kinds of ways. They certainly couldn't throw him out. Neither did they dare to make a great scene about that piano because even they dimly sensed, as I sensed, from so many thousands of miles away, that Sonny was at that piano playing for his life.

But he hadn't been going to school. One day a letter came from the school board and Isabel's mother got it—there had, apparently, been other letters but Sonny had torn them up. This day, when Sonny came in, Isabel's mother showed him the letter and asked where he'd been spending his time. And she finally got it out of him that he'd been down in Greenwich Village, with musicians and other characters, in a white girl's apartment. And this scared her and she started to scream at him and what came up, once she began—though she denies it to this day—was what sacrifices they were making to give Sonny a decent home and how little he appreciated it.

Sonny didn't play the piano that day. By evening, Isabel's mother had calmed down but then there was the old man to deal with, and Isabel herself. Isabel says she did her best to be calm but she broke down and started crying. She says she just watched Sonny's face. She could tell, by watching him, what was happening with him. And what was happening was that they penetrated his cloud, they had reached him. Even if their fingers had been a thousand times more gentle than human fingers ever are, he could hardly help feeling that they had stripped him naked and were spitting on that nakedness. For he also had to see that his presence, that music, which was life or death to him, had been torture for them and that they had endured it, not at all for his sake, but only for mine. And Sonny couldn't take that. He can take it a little better today than he could then but he's still not very good at it and, frankly, I don't know anybody who is.

The silence of the next few days must have been louder than the sound of all the music ever played since time began. One morning, before she went to work, Isabel was in his room for something and she suddenly realized that all of his records were gone. And she knew for certain that he was gone. And he was. He went as far as the navy would carry him. He finally sent me a postcard from some place in Greece and that was the first I knew that Sonny was still alive. I didn't see him any more until we were both back in New York and the war had long been over.

170

He was a man by then, of course, but I wasn't willing to see it. He came by the house from time to time, but we fought almost every time we met. I didn't like the way he carried himself, loose and dreamlike all the time, and I didn't like his friends, and his music seemed to be merely an excuse for the life he led. It sounded just that weird and disordered.

A Fiction Writer's Career: James Baldwin

Then we had a fight, a pretty awful fight, and I didn't see him for months. By and by I looked him up, where he was living, in a furnished room in the Village, and I tried to make it up. But there were lots of other people in the room and Sonny just lay on his bed, and he wouldn't come downstairs with me, and he treated these other people as though they were his family and I weren't. So I got mad and then he got mad, and then I told him that he might just as well be dead as live the way he was living. Then he stood up and he told me not to worry about him any more in life, that he *was* dead as far as I was concerned. Then he pushed me to the door and the other people looked on as though nothing were happening, and he slammed the door behind me. I stood in the hallway, staring at the door. I heard somebody laugh in the room and then the tears came to my eyes. I started down the steps, whistling to keep from crying, I kept whistling to myself, *You going to need me, baby, one of these cold, rainy days.*

I read about Sonny's trouble in the spring. Little Grace died in the fall. She was a beautiful little girl. But she only lived a little over two years. She died of polio and she suffered. She had a slight fever for a couple of days, but it didn't seem like anything and we just kept her in bed. And we would certainly have called the doctor, but the fever dropped, she seemed to be all right. So we thought it had just been a cold. Then, one day, she was up, playing, Isabel was in the kitchen fixing lunch for the two boys when they'd come in from school, and she heard Grace fall down in the living room. When you have a lot of children you don't always start running when one of them falls, unless they start screaming or something. And, this time, Gracie was quiet. Yet, Isabel says that when she heard that *thump* and then that silence, something happened to her to make her afraid. And she ran to the living room and there was little Grace on the floor, all twisted up, and the reason she hadn't screamed was that she couldn't get her breath. And when she did scream, it was the worst sound, Isabel says, that she'd ever heard in all her life, and she still hears it sometimes in her dreams. Isabel will sometimes wake me up with a low, moaning, strangling sound and I have to be quick to awaken her and hold her to me and where Isabel is weeping against me seems a mortal wound.

I think I may have written Sonny the very day that little Grace was buried. I was sitting in the living room in the dark, by myself, and I suddenly thought of Sonny. My trouble made his real.

One Saturday afternoon, when Sonny had been living with us, or anyway, been in our house, for nearly two weeks, I found myself wandering aimlessly about the living room, drinking from a can of beer, and trying to work up courage to search Sonny's room. He was out, he was usually out whenever I was home, and Isabel had taken the children to see their grandparents. Suddenly I was standing still in front of the living room window, watching Seventh Avenue. The idea of searching Sonny's room made me still. I scarcely dared to admit to myself what I'd be searching for. I didn't know what I'd do if I found it. Or if I didn't.

On the sidewalk across from me, near the entrance to a barbecue joint, some people were holding an old-fashioned revival meeting. The barbecue cook, wearing a dirty white apron, his conked° hair reddish and metallic in the pale sun, and a cigarette between his lips, stood in the doorway, watching them. Kids and older

175

_____

conked: straightened, greased.

people paused in their errands and stood there, along with some older men and a couple of very tough-looking women who watched everything that happened on the avenue, as though they owned it, or were maybe owned by it. Well, they were watching this, too. The revival was being carried on by three sisters in black, and a brother. All they had were their voices and their Bibles and a tambourine. The brother was testifying and while he testified two of the sisters stood together, seeming to say, amen, and the third sister walked around with the tambourine outstretched and a couple of people dropped coins into it. Then the brother's testimony ended and the sister who had been taking up the collection dumped the coins into her palm and transferred them to the pocket of her long black robe. Then she raised both hands, striking the tambourine against the air, and then against one hand, and she started to sing. And the two other sisters and the brother joined in.

It was strange, suddenly, to watch, though I had been seeing these meetings all my life. So, of course, had everybody else down there. Yet, they paused and watched and listened and I stood still at the window. *"Tis the old ship of Zion,"* they sang, and the sister with the tambourine kept a steady, jangling beat, *"it has rescued many a thousand!"* Not a soul under the sound of their voices was hearing this song for the first time, not one of them had been rescued. Nor had they seen much in the way of rescue work being done around them. Neither did they especially believe in the holiness of the three sisters and the brother, they knew too much about them, knew where they lived, and how. The woman with the tambourine, whose voice dominated the air, whose face was bright with joy, was divided by very little from the woman who stood watching her, a cigarette between her heavy, chapped lips, her hair a cuckoo's nest, her face scarred and swollen from many beatings, and her black eyes glittering like coal. Perhaps they both knew this, which was why, when, as rarely, they addressed each other, they addressed each other as Sister. As the singing filled the air the watching, listening faces underwent a change, the eyes focusing on something within; the music seemed to soothe a poison out of them; and time seemed, nearly, to fall away from the sullen, belligerent, battered faces, as though they were fleeing back to their first condition, while dreaming of their last. The barbecue cook half shook his head and smiled, and dropped his cigarette and disappeared into his joint. A man fumbled in his pockets for change and stood holding it in his hand impatiently, as though he had just remembered a pressing appointment further up the avenue. He looked furious. Then I saw Sonny, standing on the edge of the crowd. He was carrying a wide, flat notebook with a green cover, and it made him look, from where I was standing, almost like a schoolboy. The coppery sun brought out the copper in his skin, he was very faintly smiling, standing very still. Then the singing stopped, the tambourine turned into a collection plate again. The furious man dropped in his coins and vanished, so did a couple of the women, and Sonny dropped some change in the plate, looking directly at the woman with a little smile. He started across the avenue, toward the house. He has a slow, loping walk, something like the way Harlem hipsters walk, only he's imposed on this his own half-beat. I had never really noticed it before.

I stayed at the window, both relieved and apprehensive. As Sonny disappeared from my sight, they began singing again. And they were still singing when his key turned in the lock.

"Hey," he said.

"Hey, yourself. You want some beer?"   180

"No. Well, maybe." But he came up to the window and stood beside me, look-ing out. "What a warm voice," he said.

They were singing *If I could only hear my mother pray again!*

"Yes," I said, "and she can sure beat that tambourine."

"But what a terrible song," he said, and laughed. He dropped his notebook on the sofa and disappeared into the kitchen. "Where's Isabel and the kids?"

"I think they went to see their grandparents. You hungry?"

"No." He came back into the living room with his can of beer. "You want to come some place with me tonight?"

I sensed, I don't know how, that I couldn't possibly say no. "Sure. Where?"

He sat down on the sofa and picked up his notebook and started leafing through it. "I'm going to sit in with some fellows in a joint in the Village."

"You mean, you're going to play, tonight?"

"That's right." He took a swallow of his beer and moved back to the window. He gave me a sidelong look. "If you can stand it."

"I'll try," I said.

He smiled to himself and we both watched as the meeting across the way broke up. The three sisters and the brother, heads bowed, were singing *God be with you till we meet again.* The faces around them were very quiet. Then the song ended. The small crowd dispersed. We watched the three women and the lone man walk slowly up the avenue.

"When she was singing before," said Sonny, abruptly, "her voice reminded me for a minute of what heroin feels like sometimes—when it's in your veins. It makes you feel sort of warm and cool at the same time. And distant. And—and sure." He sipped his beer, very deliberately not looking at me. I watched his face. "It makes you feel—in control. Sometimes you've got to have that feeling."

"Do you?" I sat down slowly in the easy chair.

"Sometimes." He went to the sofa and picked up his notebook again. "Some people do."

"In order," I asked, "to play?" And my voice was very ugly, full of contempt and anger.

"Well"—he looked at me with great, troubled eyes, as though, in fact, he hoped his eyes would tell me things he could never otherwise say—"they *think* so. And *if* they think so—!"

"And what do *you* think?" I asked.

He sat on the sofa and put his can of beer on the floor. "I don't know," he said, and I couldn't be sure if he were answering my question or pursuing his thoughts. His face didn't tell me. "It's not so much to *play*. It's to *stand* it, to be able to make it at all. On any level." He frowned and smiled: "In order to keep from shaking to pieces."

"But these friends of yours," I said, "they seem to shake themselves to pieces pretty goddamn fast."

"Maybe." He played with the notebook. And something told me that I should curb my tongue, that Sonny was doing his best to talk, that I should listen. "But of course you only know the ones that've gone to pieces. Some don't—or at least they haven't *yet* and that's just about all *any* of us can say." He paused. "And then there are some who just live, really, in hell, and they know it and they see what's hap-pening and they go right on. I don't know." He sighed, dropped the notebook, folded his arms. "Some guys, you can tell from the way they play, they on something *all* the time. And you can see that, well, it makes something real for them. But of course," he picked up his beer from the floor and sipped it and put the can down again, "they *want* to, too, you've got to see that. Even some of them that say they don't—*some*, not all."

"And what about you?" I asked—I couldn't help it. "What about you? Do *you* want to?"

He stood up and walked to the window and remained silent for a long time. Then he sighed. "Me," he said. Then: "While I was downstairs before, on my way here, listening to that woman sing, it struck me all of a sudden how much suffering she must have had to go through—to sing like that. It's *repulsive* to think you have to suffer that much."

I said: "But there's no way not to suffer—is there, Sonny?"

"I believe not," he said and smiled, "but that's never stopped anyone from trying." He looked at me. "Has it?" I realized, with this mocking look, that there stood between us, forever, beyond the power of time or forgiveness, the fact that I had held silence—so long!—when he had needed human speech to help him. He turned back to the window. "No, there's no way not to suffer. But you try all kinds of ways to keep from drowning in it, to keep on top of it, and to make it seem—well, like *you*. Like you did something, all right, and now you're suffering for it. You know?" I said nothing. "Well you know," he said, impatiently, "why *do* people suffer? Maybe it's better to do something to give it a reason, *any* reason." 205

"But we just agreed," I said, "that there's no way not to suffer. Isn't it better, then, just to—take it?"

"But nobody just takes it," Sonny cried, "that's what I'm telling you! *Everybody* tries not to. You're just hung up on the *way* some people try—it's not *your* way!"

The hair on my face began to itch, my face felt wet. "That's not true," I said, "that's not true. I don't give a damn what other people do, I don't even care how they suffer. I just care how *you* suffer." And he looked at me. "Please believe me," I said, "I don't want to see you—die—trying not to suffer."

"I won't," he said flatly, "die trying not to suffer. At least, not any faster than anybody else."

"But there's no need," I said, trying to laugh, "is there? in killing yourself." 210

I wanted to say more, but I couldn't. I wanted to talk about will power and how life could be—well, beautiful. I wanted to say that it was all within; but was it? or, rather, wasn't that exactly the trouble? And I wanted to promise that I would never fail him again. But it would all have sounded—empty words and lies.

So I made the promise to myself and prayed that I would keep it.

"It's terrible sometimes, inside," he said, "that's what's the trouble. You walk these streets, black and funky and cold, and there's not really a living ass to talk to, and there's nothing shaking, and there's no way of getting it out—that storm inside. You can't talk it and you can't make love with it, and when you finally try to get with it and play it, you realize *nobody's* listening. So you've got to listen. You got to find a way to listen."

And then he walked away from the window and sat on the sofa again, as though all the wind had suddenly been knocked out of him. "Sometimes you'll do *anything* to play, even cut your mother's throat." He laughed and looked at me. "Or your brother's." Then he sobered. "Or your own." Then: "Don't worry. I'm all right now and I think I'll be all right. But I can't forget—where I've been. I don't mean just the physical place I've been, I mean where I've *been*. And *what* I've been."

"What have you been, Sonny?" I asked.

He smiled—but sat sideways on the sofa, his elbow resting on the back, his fingers playing with his mouth and chin, not looking at me. "I've been something I didn't recognize, didn't know I could be. Didn't know anybody could be." He stopped, looking inward, looking helplessly young, looking old. "I'm not talking about it now because I feel *guilty* or anything like that—maybe it would be better if I did, I don't know. Anyway, I can't really talk about it. Not to you, not to anybody," and now he turned and faced me. "Sometimes, you know, and it was actually when I was most *out* of the world, I felt that I was in it, that I was *with* it, really, and I could play or I didn't really have to *play*, it just came out of me, it was there. And I don't know how I played, thinking about it now, but I know I did awful things, those times, sometimes, to people. Or it wasn't that I *did* anything to them—it was that they weren't real." He picked up the beer can; it was empty; he rolled it between his palms: "And other times—well, I needed a fix, I needed to find a place to lean, I needed to clear a space to *listen*—and I couldn't find it, and I—went crazy, I did terrible things to *me*, I was terrible *for* me." He began pressing the beer can between his hands, I watched the metal begin to give. It glittered, as he played with it like a knife, and I was afraid he would cut himself, but I said nothing. "Oh well. I can never tell you. I was all by myself at the bottom of something, stinking and sweating and crying and shaking, and I smelled it, you know? my stink, and I thought I'd die if I couldn't get away from it and yet, all the same, I knew that everything I was doing was just locking me in with it. And I didn't know," he paused, still flattening the beer can, "I didn't know, I still *don't* know, something kept telling me that maybe it was good to smell your own stink, but I didn't think that *that* was what I'd been trying to do—and—who can stand it?" and he abruptly dropped the ruined beer can, looking at me with a small, still smile, and then rose, walking to the window as though it were the lodestone rock. I watched his face, he watched the avenue. "I couldn't tell you when Mama died—but the reason I wanted to leave Harlem so bad was to get away from drugs. And then, when I ran away, that's what I was running from—really. When I came back, nothing had changed, *I* hadn't changed, I was just—older." And he stopped, drumming with his fingers on the windowpane. The sun had vanished, soon darkness would fall. I watched his face. "It can come again," he said, almost as though speaking to himself. Then he turned to me. "It can come again," he repeated. "I just want you to know that."

"All right," I said, at last. "So it can come again. All right."

He smiled, but the smile was sorrowful. "I had to try to tell you," he said.

"Yes," I said. "I understand that."

"You're my brother," he said, looking straight at me, and not smiling at all. 220

"Yes," I repeated, "yes. I understand that."

He turned back to the window, looking out. "All that hatred down there," he said, "all that hatred and misery and love. It's a wonder it doesn't blow the avenue apart."

We went to the only nightclub on a short, dark street, downtown. We squeezed through the narrow, chattering, jam-packed bar to the entrance of the big room, where the bandstand was. And we stood there for a moment, for the lights were very dim in this room and we couldn't see. Then, "Hello, boy," said the voice and an enormous black man, much older than Sonny or myself, erupted out of all that atmospheric lighting and put an arm around Sonny's shoulder. "I been sitting right here," he said, "waiting for you."

He had a big voice, too, and heads in the darkness turned toward us.

Sonny grinned and pulled a little away, and said, "Creole, this is my brother. I told you about him."

Creole shook my hand. "I'm glad to meet you, son," he said, and it was clear that he was glad to meet me *there*, for Sonny's sake. And he smiled, "You got a real musician in *your* family," and he took his arm from Sonny's shoulder and slapped him, lightly, affectionately, with the back of his hand.

"Well. Now I've heard it all," said a voice behind us. This was another musician, and a friend of Sonny's, a coal-black, cheerful-looking man, built close to the ground. He immediately began confiding to me, at the top of his lungs, the most terrible things about Sonny, his teeth gleaming like a lighthouse and his laugh coming up out of him like the beginning of an earthquake. And it turned out that everyone at the bar knew Sonny, or almost everyone; some were musicians, working there, or nearby, or not working, some were simply hangers-on, and some were there to hear Sonny play. I was introduced to all of them and they were all very polite to me. Yet, it was clear that, for them, I was only Sonny's brother. Here, I was in Sonny's world. Or, rather: his kingdom. Here, it was not even a question that his veins bore royal blood.

They were going to play soon and Creole installed me, by myself, at a table in a dark corner. Then I watched them, Creole, and the little black man, and Sonny, and the others, while they horsed around, standing just below the bandstand. The light from the bandstand spilled just a little short of them and, watching them laughing and gesturing and moving about, I had the feeling that they, nevertheless, were being most careful not to step into that circle of light too suddenly; that if they moved into the light too suddenly, without thinking, they would perish in flame. Then, while I watched, one of them, the small, black man, moved into the light and crossed the bandstand and started fooling around with his drums. Then— being funny and being, also, extremely ceremonious—Creole took Sonny by the arm and led him to the piano. A woman's voice called Sonny's name and a few hands started clapping. And Sonny, also being funny and being ceremonious, and so touched, I think, that he could have cried, but neither hiding it nor showing it, riding it like a man, grinned, and put both hands to his heart and bowed from the waist.

Creole then went to the bass fiddle and a lean, very bright-skinned brown man jumped up on the bandstand and picked up his horn. So there they were, and the atmosphere on the bandstand and in the room began to change and tighten. Someone stepped up to the microphone and announced them. Then there were all kinds of murmurs. Some people at the bar shushed others. The waitress ran around, frantically getting in the last orders, guys and chicks got closer to each other, and the lights on the bandstand, on the quartet, turned to a kind of indigo. Then they all looked different there. Creole looked about him for the last time, as though he were making certain that all his chickens were in the coop, and then he—jumped and struck the fiddle. And there they were.

All I know about music is that not many people ever really hear it. And even then, on the rare occasions when something opens within, and the music enters, what we mainly hear, or hear corroborated, are personal, private, vanishing evocations. But the man who creates the music is hearing something else, is dealing with the roar rising from the void and imposing order on it as it hits the air. What is evoked in him, then, is of another order, more terrible because it has no words, and triumphant, too, for that same reason. And his triumph, when he triumphs, is ours. I just watched Sonny's face. His face was troubled, he was working hard, but he wasn't with it. And I had the feeling that, in a way, everyone on the bandstand was waiting for him, both waiting for him and pushing him along. But as I began to watch Creole, I realized that it was Creole who held them all back. He had them on a short rein. Up there, keeping the beat with his whole body, wailing on the fiddle, with his eyes half closed, he was listening to everything, but he was listening to Sonny. He was having a dialogue with Sonny. He wanted Sonny to leave the shoreline and strike out for the deep water. He was Sonny's witness that deep water and drowning were not the same thing—he had been there, and he knew. And he wanted Sonny to know. He was waiting for Sonny to do the things on the keys which would let Creole know that Sonny was in the water. 230

And, while Creole listened, Sonny moved, deep within, exactly like someone in torment. I had never before thought of how awful the relationship must be between the musician and his instrument. He has to fill it, this instrument, with the breath of life, his own. He has to make it do what he wants it to do. And a piano is just a piano. It's made out of so much wood and wires and little hammers and big ones, and ivory. While there's only so much you can do with it, the only way to find this out is to try; to try and make it do everything.

And Sonny hadn't been near a piano for over a year. And he wasn't on much better terms with his life, not the life that stretched before him now. He and the piano stammered, started one way, got scared, stopped; started another way, panicked, marked time, started again; then seemed to have found a direction, panicked again, got stuck. And the face I saw on Sonny I'd never seen before. Everything had been burned out of it, and at the same time, things usually hidden were being burned in, by the fire and fury of the battle which was occurring in him up there.

Yet, watching Creole's face as they neared the end of the first set, I had the feeling that something had happened, something I hadn't heard. Then they finished, there was scattered applause, and then, without an instant's warning, Creole started into something else, it was almost sardonic, it was *Am I Blue*. And, as though he commanded, Sonny began to play. Something began to happen. And Creole let out the reins. The dry, low, black man said something awful on the drums, Creole answered, and the drums talked back. Then the horn insisted, sweet and high, slightly detached perhaps, and Creole listened, commenting now and then, dry, and driving, beautiful and calm and old. Then they all came together again, and Sonny was part of the family again. I could tell this from his face. He seemed to have found, right there beneath his fingers, a damn brand-new piano. It seemed that he couldn't get over it. Then, for a while, just being happy with Sonny, they seemed to be agreeing with him that brand-new pianos certainly were a gas.

Then Creole stepped forward to remind them that what they were playing was the blues. He hit something in all of them, he hit something in me, myself, and the music tightened and deepened, apprehension began to beat the air. Creole began to tell us what the blues were all about. They were not about anything very new. He and his boys up there were keeping it new, at the risk of ruin, destruction, madness, and death, in order to find new ways to make us listen. For, while the tale of how we suffer, and how we are delighted, and how we may triumph is never new, it always must be heard. There isn't any other tale to tell, it's the only light we've got in all this darkness.

And this tale, according to that face, that body, those strong hands on those strings, has another aspect in every country, and a new depth in every generation. Listen, Creole seemed to be saying, listen. Now these are Sonny's blues. He made the little black man on the drums know it, and the bright, brown man on the horn. Creole wasn't trying any longer to get Sonny in the water. He was wishing him Godspeed. Then he stepped back, very slowly, filling the air with the immense suggestion that Sonny speak for himself. ²³⁵

Then they all gathered around Sonny and Sonny played. Every now and again one of them seemed to say, amen. Sonny's fingers filled the air with life, his life. But that life contained so many others. And Sonny went all the way back, he really began with the spare, flat statement of the opening phrase of the song. Then he began to make it his. It was very beautiful because it wasn't hurried and it was no longer a lament. I seemed to hear with what burning he had made it his, and what burning we had yet to make it ours, how we could cease lamenting. Freedom lurked around us and I understood, at last, that he could help us to be free if we would listen, that he would never be free until we did. Yet, there was no battle in his face now, I heard what he had gone through, and would continue to go through until he came to rest in earth. He had made it his: that long line, of which we knew only Mama and Daddy. And he was giving it back, as everything must be given back, so that, passing through death, it can live forever. I saw my mother's face again, and felt, for the first time, how the stones of the road she had walked on must have bruised her feet. I saw the moonlit road where my father's brother died. And it brought something else back to me, and carried me past it, I saw my little girl again and felt Isabel's tears again, and I felt my own tears begin to rise. And I was yet aware that this was only a moment, that the world waited outside, as hungry as a tiger, and that trouble stretched above us, longer than the sky.

Then it was over. Creole and Sonny let out their breath, both soaking wet, and grinning. There was a lot of applause and some of it was real. In the dark, the girl came by and I asked her to take drinks to the bandstand. There was a long pause, while they talked up there in the indigo light and after awhile I saw the girl put a Scotch and milk on top of the piano for Sonny. He didn't seem to notice it, but just before they started playing again, he sipped from it and looked toward me, and nodded. Then he put it back on top of the piano. For me, then, as they began to play again, it glowed and shook above my brother's head like the very cup of trembling.°

QUESTIONS

1. What is the narrator's reaction when he reads in the paper of his brother's arrest? What role is played in the story by Sonny's old school friend? How is it that the narrator despises him but also gives him money?

2. Why does the narrator finally write to Sonny? How does Sonny's response reveal his character? Why does the narrator take Sonny in when he is released from prison?

---

cup of trembling: Isaiah 51:22, ". . . I have taken out of thine hand the cup of trembling . . . thou shalt no more drink it again . . ."

3. Discuss what you see as the difference in personalities between Sonny and his brother. Are there ways in which the narrator shows himself to be a failure, and ways in which Sonny is shown to have admirable qualities?

4. What is the story that the narrator's mother tells about the boys' uncle? How does it connect to the larger picture that Baldwin paints of life in Harlem? What does the narrator learn that changes his view about his father?

5. How is Sonny's self-esteem injured while he is living at Isabel's? What does he do? Why do you think he turned to drugs? Is there any relation suggested between the drugs and the jazz? What is the essential difference between the two?

6. Look carefully at the street meeting scene. What role is Baldwin ascribing to religion in the life of the community? Does he see it as another escape, like heroin? Or is there a fundamental difference? And what does the narrator understand about the singing? What is Sonny's comment on the singer and how does it connect with the final scene of the story?

7. Why is Sonny inhibited when he first sits down to the piano? How does Creole draw him out? What is Creole trying to tell him?

8. Reread the last passage (Sonny's solo). What is Baldwin saying about the importance of art, its place in our lives? Do you believe that Sonny has conquered his demons? Explain.

GOING TO MEET
THE MAN

"What's the matter?" she asked.

"I don't know," he said, trying to laugh, "I guess I'm tired."

"You've been working too hard," she said. "I keep telling you."

"Well, goddammit, woman," he said, "it's not my fault!" He tried again; he wretchedly failed again. Then he just lay there, silent, angry, and helpless. Excitement filled him just like a toothache, but it refused to enter his flesh. He stroked her breast. This was his wife. He could not ask her to do just a little thing for him, just to help him out, just for a little while, the way he could ask a nigger girl to do it. He lay there, and he sighed. The image of a black girl caused a distant excitement in him, like a far-away light; but, again, the excitement was more like pain; instead of forcing him to act, it made action impossible.

"Go to sleep," she said, gently, "you got a hard day tomorrow."

"Yeah," he said, and rolled over on his side, facing her, one hand still on one breast. "Goddamn the niggers. The black stinking coons. You'd think they'd learn. Wouldn't you think they'd learn? I mean, *wouldn't* you?"

"They going to be out there tomorrow," she said, and took his hand away, "get some sleep."

He lay there, one hand between his legs, staring at the frail sanctuary of his wife. A faint light came from the shutters; the moon was full. Two dogs, far away, were barking at each other, back and forth, insistently, as though they were agreeing to make an appointment. He heard a car coming north on the road and he half sat up, his hand reaching for his holster, which was on a chair near the bed, on top of his pants. The lights hit the shutters and seemed to travel across the room and then went out. The sound of the car slipped away, he heard it hit gravel, then heard it no more. Some liverlipped students, probably, heading back to that college—but coming from where? His watch said it was two in the morning. They

5

could be coming from anywhere, from out of state most likely, and they would be at the court-house tomorrow. The niggers were getting ready. Well, they would be ready, too.

He moaned. He wanted to let whatever was in him out; but it wouldn't come out. Goddamn! he said aloud, and turned again, on his side, away from Grace, staring at the shutters. He was a big, healthy man and he had never had any trouble sleeping. And he wasn't old enough yet to have any trouble getting it up—he was only forty-two. And he was a good man, a God-fearing man, he had tried to do his duty all his life, and he had been a deputy sheriff for several years. Nothing had ever bothered him before, certainly not getting it up. Sometimes, sure, like any other man, he knew that he wanted a little more spice than Grace could give him and he would drive over yonder and pick up a black piece or arrest her, it came to the same thing, but he couldn't do that now, no more. There was no telling what might happen once your ass was in the air. And they were low enough to kill a man then, too, everyone of them, or the girl herself might do it, right while she was making believe you made her feel so good. The niggers. What had the good Lord Almighty had in mind when he made the niggers? Well. They were pretty good at that, all right. Damn. Damn. Goddamn.

This wasn't helping him to sleep. He turned again, toward Grace again, and moved close to her warm body. He felt something he had never felt before. He felt that he would like to hold her, hold her, hold her, and he buried in her like a child and never have to get up in the morning again and go downtown to face those faces, good Christ, they were ugly! and never have to enter that jail house again and smell that smell and hear that singing; never again feel that filthy, kinky, greasy hair under his hand, never again watch those black breasts leap against the leaping cattle prod, never hear those moans again or watch that blood run down or the fat lips split or the sealed eyes struggle open. They were animals, they were no better than animals, what could be done with people like that? Here they had been in a civilized country for years and they still lived like animals. Their houses were dark, with oil cloth or cardboard in the windows, the smell was enough to make you puke your guts out, and there they sat, a whole tribe, pumping out kids, it looked like, every damn five minutes, and laughing and talking and playing music like they didn't have a care in the world, and he reckoned they didn't, neither, and coming to the door, into the sunlight, just standing there, just looking foolish, not thinking of anything but just getting back to what they were doing, saying, Yes suh, Mr. Jesse. I surely will, Mr. Jesse. Fine weather, Mr. Jesse. Why, I thank you, Mr. Jesse. He had worked for a mail-order house for a while and it had been his job to collect the payments for the stuff they bought. They were too dumb to know that they were being cheated blind, but that was no skin off his ass—he was just supposed to do his job. They would be late—they didn't have the sense to put money aside; but it was easy to scare them, and he never really had any trouble. Hell, they all liked him, the kids used to smile when he came to the door. He gave them candy, sometimes, or chewing gum, and rubbed their rough bullet heads—maybe the candy should have been poisoned. Those kids were grown now. He had had trouble with one of them today.

"There was this nigger today," he said; and stopped; his voice sounded peculiar. He touched Grace. "You awake?" he asked. She mumbled something, impatiently, she was probably telling him to go to sleep. It was all right. He knew that he was not alone.

A Fiction Writer's Career: James Baldwin

"What a funny time," he said, "to be thinking about a thing like that—you listening?" She mumbled something again. He rolled over on his back. "This nigger's one of the ringleaders. We had trouble with him before. We must have had him out there at the work farm three or four times. Well, Big Jim C. and some of the boys really had to whip that nigger's ass today." He looked over at Grace; he could not tell whether she was listening or not; and he was afraid to ask again. "They had this line you know, to register"—he laughed, but she did not—"and they wouldn't stay where Big Jim C. wanted them, no, they had to start blocking traffic all around the court house so couldn't nothing or nobody get through, and Big Jim C. told them to disperse and they wouldn't move, they just kept up that singing, and Big Jim C. figured that the others would move if this nigger would move, him being the ringleader, but he wouldn't move and he wouldn't let the others move, so they had to beat him and a couple of the others and they threw them in the wagon—but *I* didn't see this nigger till I got to the jail. They were still singing and I was supposed to make them stop. Well, I couldn't make them stop for me but I knew he could make them stop. He was lying on the ground jerking and moaning, they had threw him in a cell by himself, and blood was coming out of his ears from where Big Jim C. and his boys had whipped him. Wouldn't you think they'd learn? I put the prod to him and he jerked some more and he kind of screamed—but he didn't have much voice left. "You make them stop that singing," I said to him, "you hear me? You make them stop that singing." He acted like he didn't hear me and I put it to him again, under his arms, and he just rolled around on the floor and blood started coming from his mouth. He'd pissed his pants already." He paused. His mouth felt dry and his throat was as rough as sandpaper; as he talked, he began to hurt all over with that peculiar excitement which refused to be released. "You all are going to stop your singing, I said to him, and you are going to stop coming down to the court house and disrupting traffic and molesting the people and keeping us from our duties and keeping doctors from getting to sick white women and getting all them Northerners in this town to give our town a bad name—!" As he said this, he kept prodding the boy, sweat pouring from beneath the helmet he had not yet taken off. The boy rolled around in his own dirt and water and blood and tried to scream again as the prod hit his testicles, but the scream did not come out, only a kind of rattle and moan. He stopped. He was not supposed to kill the nigger. The cell was filled with a terrible odor. The boy was still. "You hear me?" he called. "You had enough?" The singing went on. "You had enough?" His foot leapt out, he had not known it was going to, and caught the boy flush on the jaw. *Jesus,* he thought, *this ain't no nigger, this is a goddamn bull,* and he screamed again, "You had enough? You going to make them stop that singing now?"

But the boy was out. And now he was shaking worse than the boy had been shaking. He was glad no one could see him. At the same time, he felt very close to a very peculiar, particular joy; something deep in him and deep in his memory was stirred, but whatever was in his memory eluded him. He took off his helmet. He walked to the cell door.

"White man," said the boy, from the floor, behind him.

He stopped. For some reason, he grabbed his privates.

"You remember Old Julia?"

The boy said, from the floor, with his mouth full of blood, and one eye, barely open, glaring like the eye of a cat in the dark, "My grandmother's name was Mrs. Julia Blossom. *Mrs.* Julia Blossom. You going to call our women by their right names yet.—And those kids ain't going to stop singing. We going to keep on singing until every one of you miserable white mothers go stark raving out of your minds." Then he closed the one eye; he spat blood; his head fell back against the floor.

He looked down at the boy, whom he had been seeing off and on, for more than a year, and suddenly remembered him: Old Julia had been one of his mail-order customers, a nice old woman. He had not seen her for years, he supposed that she must be dead.

He had walked into the yard, the boy had been sitting in a swing. He had smiled at the boy, and asked "Old Julia home?"

The boy had looked at him for a long time before he answered. "Don't no Old Julia live here." ₂₀

"This is her house. I know her. She's lived here for years."

The boy shook his head. "You might know a Old Julia someplace else, white man. But don't nobody by that name live here."

He watched the boy; the boy watched him. The boy certainly wasn't more than ten. *White man*. He didn't have time to be fooling around with some crazy kid. He yelled, "Hey! Old Julia!"

But only silence answered him. The expression on the boy's face did not change. The sun beat down on them both, still and silent; he had the feeling that he had been caught up in a nightmare, a nightmare dreamed by a child; perhaps one of the nightmares he himself had dreamed as a child. It had that feeling—everything familiar, without undergoing any other change, had been subtly and hideously displaced: the trees, the sun, the patches of grass in the yard, the leaning porch and the weary porch steps and the cardboard in the windows and the black hole of the door which looked like the entrance to a cave, and the eyes of the pickaninny, all, all, were charged with malevolence. *White man*. He looked at the boy. "She's gone out?"

The boy said nothing. ₂₅

"Well," he said, "tell her I passed by and I'll pass by next week." He started to go; he stopped. "You want some chewing gum?"

The boy got down from the swing and started for the house. He said, "I don't want nothing you got, white man." He walked into the house and closed the door behind him.

Now the boy looked as though he were dead. Jesse wanted to go over to him and pick him up and pistol whip him until the boy's head burst open like a melon. He began to tremble with what he believed was rage, sweat, both cold and hot, raced down his body, the singing filled him as though it were a weird, uncontrollable, monstrous howling rumbling up from the depths of his own belly, he felt an icy fear rise in him and raise him up, and he shouted, he howled, "You lucky we *pump* some white blood into you every once in a while—your women! Here's what I got for all the black bitches in the world—!" Then he was, abruptly, almost too weak to stand; to his bewilderment, his horror, beneath his own fingers, he felt himself violently stiffen—with no warning at all; he dropped his hands and stared at the boy and he left the cell.

"All that singing they do," he said. "All that singing." He could not remember the first time he had heard it; he had been hearing it all his life. It was the sound with which he was most familiar—though it was also the sound of which he had been least conscious—and it had always contained an obscure comfort. They were singing to God. They were singing for mercy and they hoped to go to heaven, and he had even sometimes felt, when looking into the eyes of some of the old women, a few of the very old men, that they were singing for mercy for his soul, too. Of course he had never thought of their heaven or of what God was, or could be, for them; God was the same for everyone, he supposed, and heaven was where good people went—he supposed. He had never thought much about what it meant to be a good person. He tried to be a good person and treat everybody right: it wasn't his fault if the niggers had taken it into their heads to fight against God and go against the rules laid down in the Bible for everyone to read! Any preacher would tell you that. He was only doing his duty: protecting white people from the niggers and the niggers from themselves. And there were still lots of good niggers around—he had to remember that; they weren't all like that boy this afternoon; and the good niggers must be mighty sad to see what was happening to their people. They would thank him when this was over. In that way they had, the best of them, not quite looking him in the eye, in a low voice, with a little smile: We surely thanks you, Mr. Jesse. From the bottom of out hearts, we thanks you. He smiled. They hadn't all gone crazy. This trouble would pass.—He knew that the young people had changed some of the words to the songs. He had scarcely listened to the words before and he did not listen to them now; but he knew that the words were different; he could hear that much. He did not know if the faces were different, he had never, before this trouble began, watched them as they sang, but he certainly did not like what he saw now. They hated him, and this hatred was blacker than their hearts, blacker than their skins, redder than their blood, and harder, by far, than his club. Each day, each night, he felt worn out, aching, with their smell in his nostrils and filling his lungs, as though he were drowning—drowning in niggers; and it was all to be done again when he awoke. It would never end. It would never end. Perhaps this was what the singing had meant all along. They had not been singing black folks into heaven, they had been singing white folks into hell.

Everyone felt this black suspicion in many ways, but no one knew how to express it. Men much older than he, who had been responsible for law and order much longer than he, were now much quieter than they had been, and the tone of their jokes, in a way that he could not quite put his finger on, had changed. These men were his models, they had been friends to his father, and they had taught him what it meant to be a man. He looked to them for courage now. It wasn't that he didn't know that what he was doing was right—he knew that, nobody had to tell him that; it was only that he missed the ease of former years. But they didn't have much time to hang out with each other these days. They tended to stay close to their families every free minute because nobody knew what might happen next. Explosions rocked the night of their tranquil town. Each time each man wondered silently if perhaps this time the dynamite had not fallen into the wrong hands. They thought that they knew where all the guns were; but they could not possibly know every move that was made in that secret place where the darkies lived. From time to time it was suggested that they form a posse and search the home of every nigger, but they hadn't done it yet. For one thing, this might have brought the bastards from the North down on their backs; for another, although the niggers were scattered throughout the town—down in the hollow near the railroad tracks, way west near the mills, up on the hill, the well-off ones, and some out near the college—nothing seemed to happen in one part of town without the niggers immediately knowing it in the other. This meant that they could not take them by surprise. They rarely mentioned it, but they *knew* that some of the niggers had guns. It stood to reason, as they said, since, after all, some of them had been in the Army. There were niggers in the Army right now and God knows they wouldn't have had any trouble stealing this half-assed government blind—the whole world was doing it, look at the European countries and all those countries in Africa. They made jokes about it—bitter jokes; and they cursed the government in Washington, which had betrayed them; but they had not yet formed a posse. Now, if their town had been laid out like some towns in the North, where all the niggers lived together in one locality, they could have gone down and set fire to the houses and brought about peace that way. If the niggers had all lived in one place, they could have kept the fire in one place. But the way this town was laid out, the fire could hardly be controlled. It would spread all over town—and the niggers would probably be helping it to spread. Still, from time to time, they spoke of doing it, anyway; so that now there was a real fear among them that somebody might go crazy and light the match. 30

They rarely mentioned anything not directly related to the war that they were fighting, but this had failed to establish between them the unspoken communication of soldiers during a war. Each man, in the thrilling silence which sped outward from their exchanges, their laughter, and their anecdotes, seemed wrestling, in various degrees of darkness, with a secret which he could not articulate to himself, and which, however directly it related to the war, related yet more surely to his privacy and his past. They could no longer be sure, after all, that they had all done the same things. They had never dreamed that their privacy could contain any element of terror, could threaten, that is, to reveal itself, to the scrutiny of a judgment day, while remaining unreadable and inaccessible to themselves; nor had they dreamed that the past, while certainly refusing to be forgotten, could yet so stubbornly refuse to be remembered. They felt themselves mysteriously set at naught, as no longer entering into the real concerns of other people—while here they were, outnumbered, fighting to save the civilized world. They had thought that people would care—people didn't care; not enough, anyway, to help them. It would have been a help, really, or at least a relief, even to have been forced to surrender. Thus they had lost, probably forever, their old and easy connection with each other. They were forced to depend on each other more and, at the same time, to trust each other less. Who could tell when one of them might betray them all, for money, or for the ease of confession? But no one dared imagine what there might be to confess. They were soldiers fighting a war, but their relationship to each other was that of accomplices in a crime. They all had to keep their mouths shut.

I stepped in the river at Jordan.

Out of the darkness of the room, out of nowhere, the line came flying up at him, with the melody and the beat. He turned wordlessly toward his sleeping wife. *I stepped in the river at Jordan.* Where had he learned that song?

"Grace," he whispered. "You awake?"

She did not answer. If she was awake, she wanted him to sleep. Her breathing was slow and easy, her body slowly rose and fell.

I stepped in the river at Jordan
The water came to my knees.

He began to sweat. He felt an overwhelming fear, which yet contained a curious and dreadful pleasure.

I stepped in the river at Jordan
The water came to my waist.

It had been night, as it was now, he was in the car between his mother and his father, sleepy, his head in his mother's lap, sleepy, and yet full of excitement. The singing came from far away, across the dark fields. There were no lights anywhere. They had said goodbye to all the others and turned off on this dark dirt road. They were almost home.

I stepped in the river at Jordan,
The water came over my head,
I looked way over to the other side,
He was making up my dying bed!

"I guess they singing for him," his father said, seeming very weary and subdued now. "Even when they're sad, they sound like they just about to go and tear off a piece." He yawned and leaned across the boy and slapped his wife lightly on the shoulder, allowing his hand to rest there for a moment. "Don't they?"

"Don't talk that way," she said.

"Well, that's what we going to do," he said, "you can make up your mind to that." He started whistling. "You see? When I begin to feel it, I gets kind of musical, too."

Oh, Lord! Come on and ease my troubling mind!   40

He had a black friend, his age, eight, who lived nearby. His name was Otis. They wrestled together in the dirt. Now the thought of Otis made him sick. He began to shiver. His mother put her arm around him.

"He's tired," she said.

"We'll be home soon," said his father. He began to whistle again.

"We didn't see Otis this morning," Jesse said. He did not know why he said this. His voice, in the darkness of the car, sounded small and accusing.

"You haven't seen Otis for a couple of mornings," his mother said.   45

That was true. But he was only concerned about *this* morning.

"No," said his father, "I reckon Otis's folks was afraid to let him show himself this morning."

"But Otis didn't do nothing!" Now his voice sounded questioning.

"Otis *can't* do nothing," said his father, "he's too little." The car lights picked up their wooden house, which now solemnly approached them, the lights falling around it like yellow dust. Their dog, chained to a tree, began to bark.

"We just want to make sure Otis *don't* do nothing," said his father, and stopped the car. He looked down at Jesse. "And you tell him what your Daddy said, you hear?"   50

"Yes sir," he said.

His father switched off the lights. The dog moaned and pranced, but they ignored him and went inside. He could not sleep. He lay awake, hearing the night sounds, the dog yawning and moaning outside, the sawing of the crickets, the cry of the owl, dogs barking far away, then no sounds at all, just the heavy, endless buzzing of the night. The darkness pressed on his eyelids like a scratchy blanket. He turned, he turned again. He wanted to call his mother, but he knew his father would not like this. He was terribly afraid. Then he heard his father's voice in the other room, low, with a joke in it; but this did not help him, it frightened him more, he knew what was going to happen. He put his head under the blanket, then pushed his head out again, for fear, staring at the dark window. He heard his mother's moan, his father's sigh; he gritted his teeth. Then their bed began to rock. His father's breathing seemed to fill the world.

That morning, before the sun had gathered all its strength, men and women, some flushed and some pale with excitement, came with news. Jesse's father seemed to know what the news was before the first jalopy stopped in the yard, and he ran out, crying, "They got him, then? They got him?"

The first jalopy held eight people, three men and two women and three children. The children were sitting on the laps of the grown-ups. Jesse knew two of them, the two boys; they shyly and uncomfortably greeted each other. He did not know the girl.

"Yes, they got him," said one of the women, the older one, who wore a wide hat and a fancy, faded blue dress. "They found him early this morning."

"How far had he got?" Jesse's father asked.

"He hadn't got no further than Harkness," one of the men said. "Look like he got lost up there in all them trees—or maybe he just got so scared he couldn't move." They all laughed.

"Yes, and you know it's near a graveyard, too," said the younger woman, and they laughed again.

"Is that where they got him now?" asked Jesse's father.

By this time there were three cars piled behind the first one, with everyone looking excited and shining, and Jesse noticed that they were carrying food. It was like a Fourth of July picnic.

"Yeah, that's where he is," said one of the men, "declare, Jesse, you going to keep us here all day long, answering your damn fool questions. Come on, we ain't got no time to waste."

"Don't bother putting up no food," cried a woman from one of the cars, "we got enough. Just come on."

"Why, thank you," said Jesse's father, "we be right along, then."

"I better get a sweater for the boy," said his mother, "in case it turns cold."

Jesse watched his mother's thin legs cross the yard. He knew that she also wanted to comb her hair a little and maybe put on a better dress, the dress she wore to church. His father guessed this, too, for he yelled behind her, "Now don't you go trying to turn yourself into no movie star. You just come on." But he laughed as he said this, and winked at the men; his wife was younger and prettier than most of the other women. He clapped Jesse on the head and started pulling him toward the car. "You all go on," he said, "I'll be right behind you. Jesse, you go tie up that there dog while I get this car started."

The cars sputtered and coughed and shook; the caravan began to move; bright dust filled the air. As soon as he was tied up, the dog began to bark. Jesse's mother came out of the house, carrying a jacket for his father and a sweater for Jesse. She had put a ribbon in her hair and had an old shawl around her shoulders.

"Put these in the car, son," she said, and handed everything to him. She bent down and stroked the dog, looked to see if there was water in his bowl, then went back up the three porch steps and closed the door.

"Come on," said his father, "ain't nothing in there for nobody to steal." He was sitting in the car, which trembled and belched. The last car of the caravan had disappeared, but the sound of singing floated behind them.

224

Jesse got into the car, sitting close to his father, loving the smell of the car, and the trembling, and the bright day, and the sense of going on a great and unexpected journey. His mother got in and closed the door and the car began to move. Not until then did he ask, "Where are we going? Are we going on a picnic?"

He had a feeling that he knew where they were going, but he was not sure. 70

"That's right," his father said, "we're going on a picnic. You won't ever forget *this* picnic—!"

"Are we," he asked, after a moment, "going to see the bad nigger—the one that knocked down old Miss Standish?"

"Well, I reckon," said his mother, "that we *might* see him."

He started to ask, *Will a lot of niggers be there? Will Otis be there?*—but he did not ask his question, to which, in a strange and uncomfortable way, he already knew the answer. Their friends, in the other cars, stretched up the road as far as he could see; other cars had joined them; there were cars behind them. They were singing. The sun seemed, suddenly very hot, and he was, at once very happy and a little afraid. He did not quite understand what was happening, and he did not know what to ask—he had no one to ask. He had grown accustomed, for the solution of such mysteries, to go to Otis. He felt that Otis knew everything. But he could not ask Otis about this. Anyway, he had not seen Otis for two days; he had not seen a black face anywhere for more than two days; and he now realized, as they began chugging up the long hill which eventually led to Harkness, that there were no black people anywhere. From the houses in which they lived, all along the road, no smoke curled, no life stirred—maybe one or two chickens were to be seen, that was all. There was no one at the windows, no one in the yard, no one sitting on the porches, and the doors were closed. He had come this road many a time and seen women washing in the yard (there were no clothes on the clotheslines) men working in the fields, children playing in the dust; black men passed them on the road other mornings, other days, on foot, or in wagons, sometimes in cars, tipping their hats, smiling, joking, their teeth a solid white against their skin, their eyes as warm as the sun, the blackness of their skin like dull fire against the white of the blue or the grey of their torn clothes. They passed the nigger church—dead-white, desolate, locked up; and the graveyard, where no one knelt or walked, and he saw no flowers. He wanted to ask, *Where are they? Where are they all?* But he did not dare. As the hill grew steeper, the sun grew colder. He looked at his mother and his father. They looked straight ahead, seeming to be listening to singing which echoed and echoed in this graveyard silence. They were strangers to him now. They were looking at something he could not see. His father's lips had a strange, cruel curve, he wet his lips from time to time, and swallowed. He was terribly aware of his father's tongue, it was as though he had never seen it before. His mother patted her hair and adjusted the ribbon, leaning forward to look into the car mirror. "You look all right," said his father, and laughed. "When that nigger looks at you, he's going to swear he threw away his life for nothing. Wouldn't be surprised if he don't come back to haunt you." And he laughed again.

The singing now slowly began to cease; and he realized that they were nearing their destination. They had reached a straight, narrow, pebbly road, with trees on either side. The sunlight filtered down on them from a great height, as though they were under-water; and the branches of the trees scraped against the cars with a tearing sound. To the right of them, and beneath them, invisible now, lay the town; and to the left, miles of trees which led to the high mountain range which his ancestors had crossed in order to settle in this valley. Now, all was silent, except for the bumping of tires against the rocky road, the sputtering of motors, and the sound of a crying child. And they seemed to move more slowly. They were beginning to climb again. He watched the cars ahead as they toiled patiently upward, disappearing into the sunlight of the clearing. Presently, he felt their vehicle also rise, heard his father's changed breathing, the sunlight hit his face, the trees moved away from them, and they were there. As their car crossed the clearing, he looked around. There seemed to be millions, there were certainly hundreds of people in the clearing, staring toward something he could not see. There was a fire. He could not see the flames, but he smelled the smoke. Then they were on the other side of the clearing, among the trees again. His father drove off the road, and parked the car behind a great many other cars. He looked down at Jesse.

75

"You all right?" he asked.

"Yes sir," he said.

"Well, come on, then," his father said. He reached over and opened the door on his mother's side. His mother stepped out first. They followed her into the clearing. At first he was aware only of confusion, of his mother and father greeting and being greeted, himself being handled, hugged, and patted, and told how much he had grown. The wind blew the smoke from the fire across the clearing into his eyes and nose. He could not see over the backs of the people in front of him. The sounds of laughing and cursing and wrath—and something else—rolled in waves from the front of the mob to the back. Those in front expressed their delight at what they saw, and this delight rolled backward, wave upon wave, across the clearing, more acrid than the smoke. His father reached down suddenly and sat Jesse on his shoulders.

Now he saw the fire—of twigs and boxes, piled high; flames made pale orange and yellow and thin as a veil under the steadier light of the sun; grey-blue smoke rolled upward and poured over their heads. Beyond the shifting curtain of fire and smoke, he made out first only a length of gleaming chain, attached to a great limb of the tree; then he saw that this chain bound two black hands together at the wrist, dirty yellow palm facing dirty yellow palm. The smoke poured up; the hands dropped out of sight; a cry went up from the crowd. Then the hands slowly came into view again, pulled upward by the chain. This time he saw the kinky, sweating, bloody head—he had never before seen a head with so much hair on it, hair so black and tangled that it seemed like another jungle. The head was hanging. He saw the forehead, flat and high, with a kind of arrow of hair in the center, like he had, like his father had; they called it a widow's peak; and the mangled eye brows, the wide nose, the closed eyes, and the glinting eye lashes and the hanging lips, all streaming with blood and sweat. His hands were straight above his head. All his weight pulled downward from his hands; and he was a big man, a bigger man than his father, and black as an African jungle Cat, and naked. Jesse pulled upward; his father's hands held him firmly by the ankles. He wanted to say something, he did not know what, but nothing he said could have been heard, for now the crowd roared again as a man stepped forward and put more wood on the fire. The flames leapt up. He thought he heard the hanging man scream, but he was not sure. Sweat was pouring from the hair in his armpits, poured down his sides, over his chest, into his navel and his groin. He was lowered again; he was raised again. Now Jesse knew that he heard him scream. The head went back, the mouth wide open, blood bubbling from the mouth; the veins of the neck jumped out; Jesse clung to his fa-

A Fiction Writer's Career: James Baldwin

ther's neck in terror as the cry rolled over the crowd. The cry of all the people rose to answer the dying man's cry. He wanted death to come quickly. They wanted to make death wait: and it was they who held death, now, on a leash which they lengthened little by little. *What did he do?* Jesse wondered. *What did the man do? What did he do?*—but he could not ask his father. He was seated on his father's shoulders, but his father was far away. There were two older men, friends of his father's, raising and lowering the chain; everyone, indiscriminately, seemed to be responsible for the fire. There was no hair left on the nigger's privates, and the eyes, now, were wide open, as white as the eyes of a clown or a doll. The smoke now carried a terrible odor across the clearing, the odor of something burning which was both sweet and rotten.

He turned his head a little and saw the field of faces. He watched his mother's face. Her eyes were very bright, her mouth was open: she was more beautiful than he had ever seen her, and more strange. He began to feel a joy he had never felt before. He watched the hanging, gleaming body, the most beautiful and terrible object he had ever seen till then. One of his father's friends reached up and in his hands he held a knife: and Jesse wished that he had been that man. It was a long, bright knife and the sun seemed to catch it, to play with it, to caress it—it was brighter than the fire. And a wave of laughter swept the crowd. Jesse felt his father's hands on his ankles slip and tighten. The man with the knife walked toward the crowd, smiling slightly; as though this were a signal, silence fell; he heard his mother cough. Then the man with the knife walked up to the hanging body. He turned and smiled again. Now there was silence all over the field. The hanging head looked up. It seemed fully conscious now, as though the fire had burned out terror and pain. The man with the knife took the nigger's privates in his hand, one hand, still smiling, as though he were weighing them. In the cradle of the one white hand, the nigger's privates seemed as remote as meat being weighed on the scales; but seemed heavier, too, much heavier, and Jesse felt his scrotum tighten; and huge, huge, much bigger than his father's, flaccid, hairless, the largest thing he had ever seen till then, and the blackest. The white hand stretched them, cradled them, caressed them. Then the dying man's eyes looked straight into Jesse's eyes—it could not have been as long as a second, but it seemed longer than a year. Then Jesse screamed, and the crowd screamed as the knife flashed, first up, then down, cutting the dreadful thing away, and the blood came roaring out. Then the crowd rushed forward tearing at the body with their hands, with knives, with rocks, with stones, howling and cursing. Jesse's head, of its own weight, fell downward toward his father's head. Someone stepped forward and drenched the body with kerosene. Where the man had been, a great sheet of flame appeared. Jesse's father lowered him to the ground.

80

"Well, I told you," said his father, "you wasn't never going to forget *this* picnic." His father's face was full of sweat, his eyes were very peaceful. At that moment Jesse loved his father more than he had ever loved him. He felt that his father had carried him through a mighty test, had revealed to him a great secret which would be the key to his life forever.

"I reckon," he said. "I reckon."

Jesse's father took him by the hand and, with his mother a little behind them, talking and laughing with the other women, they walked through the crowd, across the clearing. The black body was on the ground, the chain which had held it was being rolled up by one of his father's friends. Whatever the fire had left undone, the hands and the knives and the stones of the people had accomplished. The head was caved in, one eye was torn out, one ear was hanging. But one had to look carefully to realize this, for it was, now, merely, a black charred object on the black, charred ground. He lay spread-eagled with what had been a wound between what had been his legs.

"They going to leave him here, then?" Jesse whispered.

"Yeah," said his father, "they'll come and get him by and by. I reckon we better get over there and get some of that food before it's all gone." 85

"I reckon," he muttered now to himself, "I reckon." Grace stirred and touched him on the thigh: the moonlight covered her like glory. Something bubbled up in him, his nature again returned to him. He thought of the boy in the cell; he thought of the man in the fire; he thought of the knife and grabbed himself and stroked himself and a terrible sound, something between a high laugh and a howl, came out of him and dragged his sleeping wife up on one elbow. She stared at him in a moonlight which had now grown cold as ice. He thought of the morning and grabbed her, laughing and crying, crying and laughing, and he whispered, as he stroked her, as he took her, "Come on, sugar, I'm going to do you like a nigger, just like a nigger, come on, sugar, and love me just like you'd love a nigger." He thought of the morning as he labored and she moaned, thought of morning as he labored harder than he ever had before, and before his labors had ended, he heard the first cock crow and the dogs begin to bark, and the sound of tires on the gravel road.

QUESTIONS

1. What is the situation of the story, the literal time-frame? What is it, at least outwardly, that has Jesse preoccupied? What is to happen the following day?

2. How does Baldwin bring in memories from the near and the distant past? How do these memories help to clarify your understanding of Jesse's state in the present?

3. Baldwin makes many links between violence, power, and sexuality in the story. Isolate several instances and comment upon the connections that Baldwin wants us to be making.

4. How is it possible that Jesse sees himself as a "good man"? What are the views of blacks he holds that allow him to believe this about himself?

5. What is Jesse's reaction when he believes he killed the prisoner? Who is the prisoner and what happened when he and Jesse encountered each other years ago?

6. How have things changed for Jesse and his white friends since the beginnings of the Civil Rights movement?

7. How does Baldwin show attitudes and prejudices being passed between generations? Do you sense that Jesse would have been different if his parents had been different?

8. How does Baldwin create horror in the "picnic" scene? How does the reader's reaction of disgust add to the story's power?

9. What do you make of the fact that Jesse needs these memories of cruelty and violence to get aroused? In what ways might Baldwin be making symbolic suggestions about relations between the races?

10. What does the ending represent? Do you think Baldwin believes that change is coming? Or is the white man beyond redemption?

SUGGESTIONS FOR WRITING

1. "Sonny's Blues" and "Going to Meet the Man" give us considerably different views of black life in the United States. Read both carefully and speculate in what ways they might have

A Fiction Writer's Career: James Baldwin

been written by the same man. Is there some continuity to the vision? What, based on just the evidence of Baldwin's stories, was it like to be a black man in the middle of the twentieth century?

2. Looking at "Sonny's Blues" and "Going to Meet the Man," comment on the differences in Baldwin's presentation of black and white consciousness.

3. Both of these stories make use of certain symbolic elements. Isolate one scene in each story in which symbolic suggestion plays a part and note similarities and differences.

4. If Baldwin were alive today, what do you imagine he would say about the state of black-white relations? Which of the stories seems to you more relevant to the situation at present? Why?

13 A Fiction Anthology

Washington Irving (1783–1859)

It is fitting that Washington Irving was named for
the first president of the United States, for he is
this country's first great man of letters. Born and
raised in Manhattan, Irving received most of his
education through his own voluminous reading.
Though he studied law as a young man, frail
health threw him off the track of a legal
career. When his family sent him to Europe
early in 1804, he was already trying his hand
at literary ventures. Two years after his return,
in 1808, he published *Knickerbocker's History
of New York.*

Irving quickly perceived the difficulty that a
writer would have in making a living strictly with
his pen. The young nation, he wrote, was too
busy building itself to care for the more
meditative enterprises of literature. Consequently,
in 1815, Irving set sail for England, ostensibly to
work in the family import-export business. But
after the family company went bankrupt in 1818,
he stayed on to pursue his artistic career. He did
not return to New York until 1832. In the interval
he published his celebrated *The Sketch Book*
(1819), *Bracebridge Hall* (1822), and a number
of other works. Following his return, Irving took
up the immense task of a five-volume life of
George Washington. He died shortly after the
final volume was published.

> NOTE: *Because of his shyness, as well as his desire
> to add a resonance of the legendary to his work, Irv-
> ing often made use of invented personae. That "The
> Legend of Sleepy Hollow" is supposedly found
> among the papers of one Diedrich Knickerbocker is
> part of the fiction.*

THE LEGEND OF SLEEPY HOLLOW

> A pleasing land of drowsy head it was,
>   Of dreams that wave before the half-shut eye,
> And of gay castles in the clouds that pass,
>   For ever flushing round a summer sky.
>
>   CASTLE OF INDOLENCE

In the bosom of one of those spacious coves which indent the eastern shore of the Hudson, at that broad expansion of the river denominated by the ancient Dutch navigators the Tappan Zee,° and where they always prudently shortened sail, and implored the protection of St. Nicholas when they crossed, there lies a small markettown or rural port, which by some is called Greensburgh, but which is more generally and properly known by the name of Tarry Town. This name was given, we are told, in former days, by the good house-wives of the adjacent country, from the inveterate propensity of their husbands to linger about the village tavern on market-days. Be that as it may, I do not vouch for the fact, but merely advert to it for the sake of being precise and authentic. Not far from this village, perhaps about two miles, there is a little valley, or rather lap of land, among high hills, which is one of the quietest places in the whole world. A small brook glides through it, with just murmur enough to lull one to repose; and the occasional whistle of a quail, or tapping of a woodpecker, is almost the only sound that ever breaks in upon the uniform tranquillity.

I recollect that, when a stripling, my first exploit in squirrel-shooting was in a grove of tall walnut-trees that shades one side of the valley. I had wandered into it at noon-time, when all nature is particularly quiet, and was startled by the roar of my own gun, as it broke the Sabbath stillness around, and was prolonged and re-verberated by the angry echoes. If ever I should wish for a retreat, whither I might steal from the world and its distractions, and dream quietly away the remnant of a troubled life, I know of none more promising than this little valley.

From the listless repose of the place, and the peculiar character of its inhabi-tants, who are descendants from the original Dutch settlers, this sequestered glen has long been known by the name of SLEEPY HOLLOW, and its rustic lads are called the Sleepy Hollow Boys throughout all the neighboring country. A drowsy, dreamy influence seems to hang over the land, and to pervade the very atmosphere. Some say that the place was bewitched by a high German doctor, during the early days of the settlement; others, that an old Indian chief, the prophet or wizard of his tribe, held his pow-wows there before the country was discovered by Master Hendrick Hudson. Certain it is, the place still continues under the sway of some bewitching

---

Tappan Zee: a broad lake on New York's upper Hudson River (on the shore of which Irving had his home).

power, that holds a spell over the minds of the good people, causing them to walk in a continual reverie. They are given to all kinds of marvellous beliefs; are subject to trances and visions; and frequently see strange sights, and hear music and voices in the air. The whole neighborhood abounds with local tales, haunted spots, and twilight superstitions; stars shoot and meteors glare oftener across the valley than in any other part of the country, and the nightmare, with her whole ninefold, seems to make it the favorite scene of her gambols.

The dominant spirit, however, that haunts this enchanted region, and seems to be commander-in-chief of all the powers of the air, is the apparition of a figure on horseback without a head. It is said by some to be the ghost of a Hessian° trooper, whose head had been carried away by a cannonball, in some nameless battle during the Revolutionary War, and who is ever and anon seen by the country folk, hurrying along in the gloom of night, as if on the wings of the wind. His haunts are not confined to the valley, but extend at times to the adjacent roads, and especially to the vicinity of a church at no great distance. Indeed, certain of the most authentic historians of those parts, who have been careful in collecting and collating the floating facts concerning this spectre, allege that the body of the trooper, having been buried in the churchyard, the ghost rides forth to the scene of battle in nightly quest of his head; and that the rushing speed with which he sometimes passes along the Hollow, like a midnight blast, is owing to his being belated, and in a hurry to get back to the churchyard before daybreak.

Such is the general purport of this legendary superstition, which has furnished materials for many a wild story in that region of shadows; and the spectre is known, at all the country firesides, by the name of the Headless Horseman of Sleepy Hollow.

It is remarkable that the visionary propensity I have mentioned is not confined to the native inhabitants of the valley, but is unconsciously imbibed by every one who resides there for a time. However wide awake they may have been before they entered that sleepy region, they are sure, in a little time, to inhale the witching influence of the air, and begin to grow imaginative, to dream dreams, and see apparitions.

I mention this peaceful spot with all possible laud; for it is in such little retired Dutch valleys, found here and there embosomed in the great State of New York, that population, manners, and customs remain fixed; while the great torrent of migration and improvement, which is making such incessant changes in other parts of this restless country, sweeps by them unobserved. They are like those little nooks of still water which border a rapid stream; where we may see the straw and bubble riding quietly at anchor, or slowly revolving in their mimic harbor, undisturbed by the rush of the passing current. Though many years have elapsed since I trod the drowsy shades of Sleepy Hollow, yet I question whether I should not still find the same trees and the same families vegetating in its sheltered bosom.

In this by-place of nature, there abode, in a remote period of American history, that is to say, some thirty years since, a worthy wight of the name of Ichabod Crane; who sojourned, or, as he expressed it, "tarried," in Sleepy Hollow, for the purpose of instructing the children of the vicinity. He was a native of Connecticut, a State which supplies the Union with pioneers for the mind as well as for the forest, and sends forth yearly its legions of frontier woodsmen and country schoolmasters. The

5

Hessian: a German mercenary fighting in the British Army during the Revolutionary War.

A Fiction Anthology

cognomen of Crane was not inapplicable to his person. He was tall, but exceedingly lank, with narrow shoulders, long arms and legs, hands that dangled a mile out of his sleeves, feet that might have served for shovels, and his whole frame most loosely hung together. His head was small, and flat at top, with huge ears, large green glassy eyes, and a long snipe nose, so that it looked like a weathercock perched upon his spindle neck, to tell which way the wind blew. To see him striding along the profile of a hill on a windy day, with his clothes bagging and fluttering about him, one might have mistaken him for the genius of famine descending upon the earth, or some scarecrow eloped from a corn-field.

His school-house was a low building of one large room, rudely constructed of logs; the windows partly glazed, and partly patched with leaves of old copy-books. It was most ingeniously secured at vacant hours by a withe twisted in the handle of the door, and stakes set against the window-shutters; so that, though a thief might get in with perfect ease, he would find some embarrassment in getting out: an idea most probably borrowed by the architect, Yost Van Houten, from the mystery of an eel-pot. The school-house stood in a rather lonely but pleasant situation, just at the foot of a woody hill, with a brook running close by, and a formidable birch-tree growing at one end of it. From hence the low murmur of his pupils' voices, conning over their lessons, might be heard on a drowsy summer's day, like the hum of a bee-hive; interrupted now and then by the authoritative voice of the master, in the tone of menace or command; or, peradventure, by the appalling sound of the birch, as he urged some tardy loiterer along the flowery path of knowledge. Truth to say, he was a conscientious man, and ever bore in mind the golden maxim, "Spare the rod and spoil the child."—Ichabod Crane's scholars certainly were not spoiled.

I would not have it imagined, however, that he was one of those cruel poten-tates of the school, who joy in the smart of their subjects; on the contrary, he ad-ministered justice with discrimination rather than severity, taking the burden off the backs of the weak, and laying it on those of the strong. Your mere puny stripling, that winced at the least flourish of the rod, was passed by with indulgence; but the claims of justice were satisfied by inflicting a double portion on some little, tough, wrong-headed, broad-skirted Dutch urchin, who sulked and swelled and grew dogged and sullen beneath the birch. All this he called "doing his duty" by their par-ents; and he never inflicted a chastisement without following it by the assurance, so consolatory to the smarting urchin, that "he would remember it, and thank him for it the longest day he had to live."   10

When school-hours were over, he was even the companion and playmate of the larger boys; and on holiday afternoons would convoy some of the smaller ones home, who happened to have pretty sisters, or good housewives for mothers, noted for the comforts of the cupboard. Indeed it behooved him to keep on good terms with his pupils. The revenue arising from his school was small, and would have been scarcely sufficient to furnish him with daily bread, for he was a huge feeder, and, though lank, had the dilating powers of an anaconda; but to help out his maintenance, he was, according to country custom in those parts, boarded and lodged at the houses of the farmers, whose children he instructed. With these he lived successively a week at a time; thus going the rounds of the neighborhood, with all his worldly effects tied up in a cotton handkerchief.

That all this might not be too onerous on the purses of his rustic patrons, who are apt to consider the costs of schooling a grievous burden, and schoolmasters as mere drones, he had various ways of rendering himself both useful and agreeable. He assisted the farmers occasionally in the lighter labors of their farms; helped to make hay; mended the fences; took the horses to water; drove the cows from pasture; and cut wood for the winter fire. He laid aside, too, all the dominant dignity and absolute sway with which he lorded it in his little empire, the school, and became wonderfully gentle and ingratiating. He found favor in the eyes of the mothers, by petting the children, particularly the youngest; and like the lion bold, which whilom so magnanimously the lamb did hold, he would sit with a child on one knee, and rock a cradle with his foot for whole hours together.

In addition to his other vocations, he was the singing-master of the neighborhood, and picked up many bright shillings by instructing the young folks in psalmody.° It was a matter of no little vanity to him, on Sundays, to take his station in front of the church-gallery, with a band of chosen singers; where, in his own mind, he completely carried away the palm from the parson. Certain it is, his voice resounded far above all the rest of the congregation; and there are peculiar quavers still to be heard in that church, and which may even be heard half a mile off, quite to the opposite side of the mill-pond, on a still Sunday morning, which are said to be legitimately descended from the nose of Ichabod Crane. Thus, by divers little makeshifts in that ingenious way which is commonly denominated "by hook and by crook," the worthy pedagogue got on tolerably enough, and was thought, by all who understood nothing of the labor of headwork, to have a wonderfully easy life of it.

The schoolmaster is generally a man of some importance in the female circle of a rural neighborhood; being considered a kind of idle, gentleman-like personage, of vastly superior taste and accomplishments to the rough country swains, and, indeed, inferior in learning only to the parson. His appearance, therefore, is apt to occasion some little stir at the tea-table of a farm-house, and the addition of a supernumerary dish of cakes or sweetmeats, or, peradventure, the parade of a silver tea-pot. Our man of letters, therefore, was peculiarly happy in the smiles of all the country damsels. How he would figure among them in the churchyard, between services on Sundays! gathering grapes for them from the wild vines that overrun the surrounding trees; reciting for their amusement all the epitaphs on the tombstones; or sauntering, with a whole bevy of them, along the banks of the adjacent mill-pond; while the more bashful country bumpkins hung sheepishly back, envying his superior elegance and address.

From his half itinerant life, also, he was a kind of travelling gazette, carrying the whole budget of local gossip from house to house: so that his appearance was always greeted with satisfaction. He was, moreover, esteemed by the women as a man of great erudition, for he had read several books quite through, and was a perfect master of Cotton Mather's° *History of New England Witchcraft*, in which, by the way, he most firmly and potently believed.

He was, in fact, an odd mixture of small shrewdness and simple credulity. His appetite for the marvellous, and his powers of digesting it, were equally extraordinary; and both had been increased by his residence in this spellbound region. No tale was too gross or monstrous for his capacious swallow. It was often his delight, after his school was dismissed in the afternoon, to stretch himself on the rich bed of clover

---

psalmody: psalm-singing.

Mather: Cotton Mather (1663–1728), an American Puritan clergyman who presided at witchcraft trials in Salem, Mass., in 1692.

bordering the little brook that whimpered by his school-house, and there con over old Mather's direful tales, until the gathering dusk of the evening made the printed page a mere mist before his eyes. Then, as he wended his way, by swamp and stream, and awful woodland, to the farm-house where he happened to be quartered, every sound of nature, at that witching hour, fluttered his excited imagination; the moan of the whippoorwill from the hill-side, the boding cry of the tree-toad, that harbinger of storm; the dreary hooting of the screech-owl, or the sudden rustling in the thicket of birds frightened from their roost. The fire-flies, too, which sparkled most vividly in the darkest places, now and then startled him, as one of uncommon brightness would stream across his path; and if, by chance, a huge blockhead of a beetle came winging his blundering flight against him, the poor varlet was ready to give up the ghost, with the idea that he was struck with a witch's token. His only resource on such occasions, either to drown thought or drive away evil spirits, was to sing psalm-tunes; and the good people of Sleepy Hollow, as they sat by their doors of an evening, were often filled with awe, at hearing his nasal melody, "in linked sweetness long drawn out," floating from the distant hill, or along the dusky road.

Another of his sources of fearful pleasure was, to pass long winter evenings with the old Dutch wives, as they sat spinning by the fire, with a row of apples roasting and spluttering along the hearth, and listen to their marvellous tales of ghosts and goblins, and haunted fields, and haunted brooks, and haunted bridges, and haunted houses, and particularly of the headless horseman, or Galloping Hessian of the Hollow, as they sometimes called him. He would delight them equally by his anecdotes of witchcraft, and the direful omens and portentous sights and sounds in the air, which prevailed in the earlier times of Connecticut; and would frighten them woefully with speculations upon comets and shooting-stars, and with the alarming fact that the world did absolutely turn round, and that they were half the time topsy-turvy!

But if there was a pleasure in all this, while snugly cuddling in the chimney-corner of a chamber that was all of a ruddy glow from the crackling wood-fire, and where, of course, no spectre dared to show his face, it was dearly purchased by the terrors of his subsequent walk homewards. What fearful shapes and shadows beset his path amidst the dim and ghastly glare of a snowy night!—With what wistful look did he eye every trembling ray of light streaming across the waste fields from some distant window!—How often was he appalled by some shrub covered with snow, which, like a sheeted spectre, beset his very path!—How often did he shrink with curdling awe at the sound of his own steps on a frosty crust beneath his feet; and dread to look over his shoulder, lest he should behold some uncouth being tramping close behind him!—and how often was he thrown into complete dismay by some rushing blast, howling among the trees, in the idea that it was the Galloping Hessian on one of his nightly scourings!

All these, however, were mere terrors of the night, phantoms of the mind that walk in darkness; and though he had seen many spectres in his time, and been more than once beset by Satan in divers shapes, in his lonely perambulations, yet daylight put an end to all these evils; and he would have passed a pleasant life of it, in despite of the devil and all his works, if his path had not been crossed by a being that causes more perplexity to mortal man than ghosts, goblins, and the whole race of witches put together, and that was—a woman.

Among the musical disciples who assembled, one evening in each week, to receive his instructions in psalmody, was Katrina Van Tassel, the daughter and only child of a substantial Dutch farmer. She was a blooming lass of fresh eighteen; plump as a partridge; ripe and melting and rosy-cheeked as one of her father's peaches, and universally famed, not merely for her beauty, but her vast expectations. She was withal a little of a coquette, as might be perceived even in her dress, which was a mixture of ancient and modern fashions, as most suited to set off her charms. She wore the ornaments of pure yellow gold, which her great-great-grandmother had brought over from Saardam°; the tempting stomacher° of the olden time; and withal a provokingly short petticoat, to display the prettiest foot and ankle in the country round.

20

Ichabod Crane had a soft and foolish heart towards the sex; and it is not to be wondered at that so tempting a morsel soon found favor in his eyes; more especially after he had visited her in her paternal mansion. Old Baltus Van Tassel was a perfect picture of a thriving, contented, liberal-hearted farmer. He seldom, it is true, sent either his eyes or his thoughts beyond the boundaries of his own farm; but within those everything was snug, happy, and well-conditioned. He was satisfied with his wealth, but not proud of it; and piqued himself upon the hearty abundance rather than the style in which he lived. His stronghold was situated on the banks of the Hudson, in one of those green, sheltered, fertile nooks in which the Dutch farmers are so fond of nestling. A great elm-tree spread its broad branches over it; at the foot of which bubbled up a spring of the softest and sweetest water, in a little well, formed of a barrel; and then stole sparkling away through the grass, to a neighboring brook, that bubbled along among alders and dwarf willows. Hard by the farm-house was a vast barn, that might have served for a church; every window and crevice of which seemed bursting forth with the treasures of the farm; the flail was busily resounding within it from morning till night; swallows and martins skimmed twittering about the eaves; and rows of pigeons, some with one eye turned up, as if watching the weather, some with their heads under their wings, or buried in their bosoms, and others swelling, and cooing, and bowing about their dames, were enjoying the sunshine on the roof. Sleek unwieldly porkers were grunting in the repose and abundance of their pens; whence sallied forth, now and then, troops of sucking pigs, as if to snuff the air. A stately squadron of snowy geese were riding in an adjoining pond, convoying whole fleets of ducks; regiments of turkeys were gobbling through the farm-yard, and guinea fowls fretting about it, like ill-tempered housewives, with their peevish discontented cry. Before the barn-door strutted the gallant cock, that pattern of a husband, a warrior, and a fine gentleman, clapping his burnished wings, and crowing in the ride and gladness of his heart—sometimes tearing up the earth with his feet, and then generously calling his ever-hungry family of wives and children to enjoy the rich morsel which he had discovered.

The pedagogue's mouth watered, as he looked upon this sumptuous promise of luxurious winter fare. In his devouring mind's eye he pictured to himself every roasting-pig running about with a pudding in his belly, and an apple in his mouth; the pigeons were snugly put to bed in a comfortable pie, and tucked in with a coverlet of crust; the geese were swimming in their own gravy; and the ducks pairing cosily in dishes, like snug married couples, with a decent competency of

---

Saardam: a Dutch city.
stomacher: a decorative bodice worn tightly over the stomach and waist.

onion-sauce. In the porkers he saw carved out the future sleek side of bacon, and juicy relishing ham; not a turkey but he beheld daintily trussed up, with its gizzard under its wing, and, peradventure, a necklace of savory sausages; and even bright chanticleer himself lay sprawling on his back, in a side-dish, with uplifted claws, as if craving that quarter which his chivalrous spirit disdained to ask while living.

As the enraptured Ichabod fancied all this, and as he rolled his great green eyes over the fat meadow-lands, the rich fields of wheat, of rye, of buckwheat, and Indian corn, and the orchard burdened with ruddy fruit, which surrounded the warm tenement of Van Tassel, his heart yearned after the damsel who was to inherit these domains, and his imagination expanded with the idea how they might be readily turned into cash, and the money invested in immense tracts of wild land, and shingle palaces in the wilderness. Nay, his busy fancy already realized his hopes, and presented to him the blooming Katrina, with a whole family of children, mounted on the top of a wagon loaded with household trumpery, with pots and kettles dangling beneath; and he beheld himself bestriding a pacing mare, with a colt at her heels, setting out for Kentucky, Tennessee, or the Lord knows where.

When he entered the house, the conquest of his heart was complete. It was one of those spacious farm-houses, with high-ridged, but lowly-sloping roofs, built in the style handed down from the first Dutch settlers; the low projecting eaves forming a piazza along the front, capable of being closed up in bad weather. Under this were hung flails, harness, various utensils of husbandry, and nets for fishing in the neighboring river. Benches were built along the sides for summer use; and a great spinning-wheel at one end, and a churn at the other, showed the various uses to which this important porch might be devoted. From this piazza the wandering Ichabod entered the hall, which formed the centre of the mansion and the place of usual residence. Here, rows of resplendent pewter, ranged on a long dresser, dazzled his eyes. In one corner stood a huge bag of wool ready to be spun; in another a quantity of linsey-woolsey° just from the loom; ears of Indian corn, and strings of dried apples and peaches, hung in gay festoons along the walls, mingled with the gaud of red peppers; and a door left ajar gave him a peep into the best parlor, where the claw-footed chairs and dark mahogany tables shone like mirrors; and irons, with their accompanying shovel and tongs, glistened from their covert of asparagus tops; mock-oranges and conch-shells decorated the mantel-piece; strings of various colored birds' eggs were suspended above it, a great ostrich egg was hung from the centre of the room, and a corner-cupboard, knowingly left open, displayed immense treasures of old silver and well-mended china.

From the moment Ichabod laid his eyes upon these regions of delight, the peace of his mind was at an end, and his only study was how to gain the affections of the peerless daughter of Van Tassel. In this enterprise, however, he had more real difficulties than generally fell to the lot of a knight-errant of yore, who seldom had anything but giants, enchanters, fiery dragons, and such like easily conquered adversaries, to contend with; and had to make his way merely through gates of iron and brass, and walls of adamant, to the castle-keep, where the lady of his heart was confined; all which he achieved as easily as a man would carve his way to the cen-

---

°linsey-woolsey: fabric of cotton or linen woven with wool.

tre of a Christmas pie; and then the lady gave him her hand as a matter of course. Ichabod, on the contrary, had to win his way to the heart of a country coquette, beset with a labyrinth of whims and caprices, which were forever presenting new difficulties and impediments; and he had to encounter a host of fearful adversaries of real flesh and blood, the numerous rustic admirers, who beset every portal to her heart; keeping a watchful and angry eye upon each other, but ready to fly out in the common cause against any new competitor.

Among these the most formidable was a burly, roaring, roistering blade, of the name of Abraham, or, according to the Dutch abbreviation, Brom Van Brunt, the hero of the country round, which rang with his feats of strength and hardihood. He was broad-shouldered and double-jointed, with short, curly black hair, and a bluff but not unpleasant countenance, having a mingled air of fun and arrogance. From his Herculean° frame and great powers of limb, he had received the nickname of BROM BONES, by which he was universally known. He was famed for great knowledge and skill in horsemanship, being as dexterous on horseback as a Tartar. He was foremost at all races and cockfights; and, with the ascendency which bodily strength acquires in rustic life, was the umpire in all disputes, setting his hat on one side, and giving his decisions with an air and tone admitting of no gainsay or appeal. He was always ready for either a fight or a frolic; but had more mischief than ill-will in his composition; and, with all his overbearing roughness, there was a strong dash of waggish good-humor at the bottom. He had three or four boon companions, who regarded him as their model, and at the head of whom he scoured the country, attending every scene of feud or merriment for miles round. In cold weather he was distinguished by a fur cap, surmounted with a flaunting fox's tail; and when the folks at a country gathering descried this well-known crest at a distance, whisking about among a squad of hard riders, they always stood by for a squall. Sometimes his crew would be heard dashing along past the farm-houses at midnight, with whoop and halloo, like a troop of Don Cossacks; and the old dames, startled out of their sleep, would listen for a moment till the hurry-scurry had clattered by, and then exclaim, "Ay, there goes Brom Bones and his gang!" The neighbors looked upon him with a mixture of awe, admiration, and good-will; and when any madcap prank, or rustic brawl, occurred in the vicinity, always shook their heads, and warranted Brom Bones was at the bottom of it.

This rantipole hero had for some time singled out the blooming Katrina for the object of his uncouth gallantries; and though his amorous toyings were something like the gentle caresses and endearments of a bear, yet it was whispered that she did not altogether discourage his hopes. Certain it is, his advances were signals for rival candidates to retire, who felt no inclination to cross a line in his amours; insomuch, that, when his horse was seen tied to Van Tassel's paling on a Sunday night, a sure sign that his master was courting, or, as it is termed, "sparking," within, all other suitors passed by in despair, and carried the war into other quarters.

Such was the formidable rival with whom Ichabod Crane had to contend, and, considering all things, a stouter man than he would have shrunk from the competition, and a wiser man would have despaired. He had, however, a happy mixture of pliability and perseverance in his nature; he was in form and spirit like a supple-jack—yielding, but tough; though he bent, he never broke; and though he bowed

---

Herculean: like the mythic hero Hercules; a body of heroic proportions.

A Fiction Anthology

beneath the slightest pressure yet, the moment it was away—jerk! he was as erect, and carried his head as high as ever.

To have taken the field openly against his rival would have been madness; for he was not a man to be thwarted in his amours, any more than that stormy lover, Achilles. Ichabod, therefore, made his advances in a quiet and gently insinuating manner. Under cover of his character of singing-master, he had made frequent visits at the farm-house; not that he had anything to apprehend from the meddlesome interference of parents, which is so often a stumbling-block in the path of lovers. Balt Van Tassel was an easy, indulgent soul; he loved his daughter better even than his pipe, and, like a reasonable man and an excellent father, let her have her way in everything. His notable little wife, too, had enough to do to attend to her house-keeping and manage her poultry; for, as she sagely observed, ducks and geese are foolish things, and must be looked after, but girls can take care of themselves. Thus while the busy dame bustled about the house, or plied her spinning-wheel at one end of the piazza, honest Balt would sit smoking his evening pipe at the other, watching the achievements of a little wooden warrior, who, armed with a sword in each hand, was most valiantly fighting the wind on the pinnacle of the barn. In the meantime, Ichabod would carry on his suit with the daughter by the side of the spring under the great elm, or sauntering along in the twilight,—that hour so favorable to the lover's eloquence.

I profess not to know how women's hearts are wooed and won. To me they have always been matters of riddle and admiration. Some seem to have but one vulnerable point or door of access, while others have a thousand avenues, and may be captured in a thousand different ways. It is a great triumph of skill to gain the former, but a still greater proof of generalship to maintain possession of the latter, for the man must battle for his fortress at every door and window. He who wins a thousand common hearts is therefore entitled to some renown; but he who keeps undisputed sway over the heart of a coquette, is indeed a hero. Certain it is, this was not the case with the redoubtable Brom Bones; and from the moment Ichabod Crane made his advances, the interests of the former evidently declined; his horse was no longer seen tied at the palings on Sunday nights, and a deadly feud gradually arose between him and the preceptor of Sleepy Hollow.

Brom, who had a degree of rough chivalry in his nature, would fain have carried matters to open warfare, and have settled their pretensions to the lady according to the mode of those most concise and simple reasoners, the knights-errant of yore—by single combat; but Ichabod was too conscious of the superior might of his adversary to enter the lists against him: he had overheard a boast of Bones, that he would "double the schoolmaster up, and lay him on a shelf of his own school-house;" and he was too wary to give him an opportunity. There was something extremely provoking in this obstinately pacific system; it left Brom no alternative but to draw upon the funds of rustic waggery in his disposition, and to play off boorish practical jokes upon his rival. Ichabod became the object of whimsical persecution to Bones and his gang of rough riders. They harried his hitherto peaceful domains; smoked out his singing-school, by stopping up the chimney; broke into the school-house at night, in spite of its formidable fastenings of withe and window-stakes, and turned everything topsy-turvy: so that the poor schoolmaster began to think all the witches in the country held their meetings there. But what was still more annoying, Brom took opportunities of turning him into ridicule in presence of his mistress, and had a scoundrel dog

30

whom he taught to whine in the most ludicrous manner, and introduced as a rival of Ichabod's to instruct her in psalmody.

In this way matters went on for some time, without producing any material effect on the relative situation of the contending powers. On a fine autumnal afternoon, Ichabod, in pensive mood, sat enthroned on the lofty stool whence he usually watched all the concerns of his little literary realm. In his hand he swayed a ferule, that sceptre of despotic power; the birch of justice reposed on three nails, behind the throne, a constant terror to evil-doers; while on the desk before him might be seen sundry contraband articles and prohibited weapons, detected upon the persons of idle urchins; such as half-munched apples, pop-guns, whirligigs, fly-cages, and whole legions of rampant little paper game-cocks. Apparently there had been some appalling act of justice recently inflicted, for his scholars were all busily intent upon their books, or slyly whispering behind them with one eye kept upon the master; and a kind of buzzing stillness reigned throughout the school-room. It was suddenly interrupted by the appearance of a negro, in tow-cloth jacket and trousers, a round-crowned fragment of a hat, like the cap of Mercury,° and mounted on the back of a ragged, wild, half-broken colt, which he managed with a rope by way of halter. He came clattering up to the school-door with an invitation to Ichabod to attend a merry-making or "quilting frolic," to be held that evening at Mynheer Van Tassel's; and having delivered his message with that air of importance, and effort at fine language, which a negro is apt to display on petty embassies of the kind, he dashed over the brook, and was seen scampering away up the Hollow, full of the importance and hurry of his mission.

All was now bustle and hubbub in the late quiet school-room. The scholars were hurried through their lessons, without stopping at trifles; those who were nimble skipped over half with impunity, and those who were tardy had a smart application now and then in the rear, to quicken their speed, or help them over a tall word. Books were flung aside without being put away on the shelves, inkstands were overturned, benches thrown down, and the whole school was turned loose an hour before the usual time, bursting forth like a legion of young imps, yelping and racketing about the green, in joy at their early emancipation.

The gallant Ichabod now spent at least an extra half-hour at his toilet, brushing and furbishing up his best and indeed only suit of rusty black, and arranging his locks by a bit of broken looking-glass, that hung up in the school-house. That he might make his appearance before his mistress in the true style of a cavalier, he borrowed a horse from the farmer with whom he was domiciliated, a choleric old Dutchman, of the name of Hans Van Ripper, and, thus gallantly mounted, issued forth, like a knight-errant in quest of adventures. But it is meet I should, in the true spirit of romantic story, give some account of the looks and equipments of my hero and his steed. The animal he bestrode was a broken-down plough-horse, that had outlived almost everything but his viciousness. He was gaunt and shagged, with a ewe neck and a head like a hammer; his rusty mane and tail were tangled and knotted with burrs; one eye had lost its pupil, and was glaring and spectral; but the other had the gleam of a genuine devil in it. Still he must have had fire and mettle in his day, if we may judge from the name he bore of Gunpowder. He had, in fact, been a favorite steed of his master's, the choleric Van Ripper, who was a furious rider,

---

Mercury: a messenger of the gods, depicted with a round winged cap.

A Fiction Anthology

and had infused, very probably, some of his own spirit into the animal; for, old and broken-down as he looked, there was more of the lurking devil in him than in any young filly in the country.

Ichabod was a suitable figure for such a steed. He rode with short stirrups, which brought his knees nearly up to the pommel of the saddle; his sharp elbows stuck out like grasshoppers'; he carried his whip perpendicularly in his hand, like a sceptre, and, as his horse jogged on, the motion of his arms was not unlike the flapping of a pair of wings. A small wool hat rested on the top of his nose, for so his scanty strip of forehead might be called; and the skirts of his black coat fluttered out almost to the horse's tail. Such was the appearance of Ichabod and his steed, as they shambled out of the gate of Hans Van Ripper, and it was altogether such an apparition as is seldom to be met with in broad daylight. 35

It was, as I have said, a fine autumnal day, the sky was clear and nature wore that rich and golden livery which we always associate with the idea of abundance. The forests had put on their sober brown and yellow, while some trees of the tenderer kind had been nipped by the frosts into brilliant dyes of orange, purple, and scarlet. Streaming files of wild ducks began to make their appearance high in the air; the bark of the squirrel might be heard from the groves of beech and hickory nuts, and the pensive whistle of the quail at intervals from the neighboring stubble-field.

The small birds were taking their farewell banquets. In the fulness of their revelry, they fluttered, chirping and frolicking, from bush to bush, and tree to tree, capricious from the very profusion and variety around them. There was the honest cockrobin, the favorite game of stripling sportsmen, with its loud querulous notes; and the twittering blackbirds flying in sable clouds; and the golden-winged woodpecker, with his crimson crest, his broad black gorget, and splendid plumage; and the cedar-bird, with its red-tipt wings and yellow-tipt tail, and its little monteiro cap of feathers; and the blue jay, that noisy coxcomb, in his gay light-blue coat and white under-clothes, screaming and chattering, nodding and bobbing and bowing, and pretending to be on good terms with every songster of the grove.

As Ichabod jogged slowly on his way, his eye, ever open to every symptom of culinary abundance, ranged with delight over the treasures of jolly autumn. On all sides he beheld vast store of apples; some hanging in oppressive opulence on the trees; some gathered into baskets and barrels for the market; others heaped up in rich piles for the cider-press. Farther on he beheld great fields of Indian corn, with its golden ears peeping from their leafy coverts, and holding out the promise of cakes and hasty-pudding; and the yellow pumpkins lying beneath them, turning up their fair round bellies to the sun, and giving ample prospects of the most luxurious of pies; and anon he passed the fragrant buckwheat fields, breathing the odor of the bee-hive, and as he beheld them, soft anticipations stole over his mind of dainty slapjacks, well buttered, and garnished with honey or treacle, by the delicate little dimpled hand of Katrina Van Tassel.

Thus feeding his mind with many sweet thoughts, and "sugared suppositions," he journeyed along the sides of a range of hills which look out upon some of the goodliest scenes of the mighty Hudson. The sun gradually wheeled his broad disk down into the west. The wide bosom of the Tappan Zee lay motionless and glossy, excepting that here and there a gentle undulation waved and prolonged the blue shadow of the distant mountain. A few amber clouds floated in the sky, without a breath of air to move them. The horizon was of a fine golden tint, changing gradually into a pure apple-green, and from that into the deep blue of the mid-heaven. A slanting ray lingered on the woody crests of the precipices that overhung some parts of the river, giving greater depth to the dark-gray and purple of their rocky sides. A sloop was loitering in the distance, dropping slowly down with the tide, her sail hanging uselessly against the mast; and as the reflection of the sky gleamed along the still water, it seemed as if the vessel was suspended in the air.

It was toward evening that Ichabod arrived at the castle of the Heer Van Tassel, which he found thronged with the pride and flower of the adjacent country. Old farmers, a spare leathern-faced race, in homespun coats and breeches, blue stockings, huge shoes, and magnificent pewter buckles. Their brisk withered little dames, in close crimped caps, long-waisted shortgowns, homespun petticoats, with scissors and pin-cushions, and gay calico pockets hanging on the outside. Buxom lasses, almost as antiquated as their mothers, excepting where a straw hat, a fine ribbon, or perhaps a white frock, gave symptoms of city innovation. The sons, in short square-skirted coats with rows of stupendous brass buttons, and their hair generally queued in the fashion of the times, especially if they could procure an eel-skin for the purpose, it being esteemed, throughout the country, as a potent nourisher and strengthener of the hair.

Brom Bones, however, was the hero of the scene, having come to the gathering on his favorite steed, Daredevil, a creature, like himself, full of mettle and mischief, and which no one but himself could manage. He was, in fact, noted for preferring vicious animals, given to all kinds of tricks, which kept the rider in constant risk of his neck, for he held a tractable well-broken horse as unworthy of a lad of spirit.

Fain would I pause to dwell upon the world of charms that burst upon the enraptured gaze of my hero, as he entered the state parlor of Van Tassel's mansion. Not those of the bevy of buxom lasses, with their luxurious display of red and white; but the ample charms of a genuine Dutch country tea-table, in the sumptuous time of autumn. Such heaped-up platters of cakes of various and almost indescribable kinds, known only to experienced Dutch housewives! There was the doughty doughnut, the tenderer oly koek, and the crisp and crumbling cruller; sweet cakes and short cakes, ginger-cakes and honey-cakes, and the whole family of cakes. And then there were apple-pies and peach-pies and pumpkin-pies; besides slices of ham and smoked beef; and moreover delectable dishes of preserved plums, and peaches, and pears, and quinces; not to mention broiled shad and roasted chickens; together with bowls of milk and cream, all mingled higgledy-piggledy, pretty much as I have enumerated them, with the motherly tea-pot sending up its clouds of vapor from the midst— Heaven bless the mark! I want breath and time to discuss this banquet as it deserves, and am too eager to get on with my story. Happily, Ichabod Crane was not in so great a hurry as his historian, but did ample justice to every dainty.

He was a kind and thankful creature, whose heart dilated in proportion as his skin was filled with good cheer; and whose spirits rose with eating as some men's do with drink. He could not help, too, rolling his large eyes round him as he ate, and chuckling with the possibility that he might one day be lord of all this scene of almost unimaginable luxury and splendor. Then, he thought, how soon he'd turn his back upon the old school-house; snap his fingers in the face of Hans Van Ripper, and every other niggardly patron, and kick any itinerant pedagogue out-of-doors that should dare to call him comrade!

Old Baltus Van Tassel moved about among his guests with a face dilated with content and good-humor, round and jolly as the harvest-moon. His hospitable attentions were brief, but expressive, being confined to a shake of the hand, a slap on the shoulder, a loud laugh, and a pressing invitation to "fall to, and help themselves."

And now the sound of the music from the common room, or hall, summoned to the dance. The musician was an old gray-headed negro, who had been the itinerant orchestra of the neighborhood for more than half a century. His instrument was as old and battered as himself. The greater part of the time he scraped on two or three strings, accompanying every movement of the bow with a motion of the head; bowing almost to the ground, and stamping with his foot whenever a fresh couple were to start.

45

Ichabod prided himself upon his dancing as much as upon his vocal powers. Not a limb, not a fibre about him was idle; and to have seen his loosely hung frame in full motion, and clattering about the room, you would have thought Saint Vitus° himself, that blessed patron of the dance, was figuring before you in person. He was the admiration of all the negroes; who, having gathered, of all ages and sizes, from the farm and the neighborhood, stood forming a pyramid of shining black faces at every door and window, gazing with delight at the scene, rolling their white eyeballs, and showing grinning rows of ivory from ear to ear. How could the flogger of urchins be otherwise than animated and joyous? The lady of his heart was his partner in the dance, and smiling graciously in reply to all his amorous oglings; while Brom Bones, sorely smitten with love and jealousy, sat brooding by himself in one corner.

When the dance was at an end, Ichabod was attracted to a knot of the sager folks, who, with old Van Tassel, sat smoking at one end of the piazza, gossiping over former times, and drawing out long stories about the war.

This neighborhood, at the time of which I am speaking, was one of those highly favored places which abound with chronicle and great men. The British and American line had run near it during the war; it had, therefore, been the scene of marauding, and infested with refugees, cowboys, and all kinds of border chivalry. Just sufficient time has elapsed to enable each story-teller to dress up his tale with a little becoming fiction, and, in the indistinctness of his recollection, to make himself the hero of every exploit.

There was the story of Doffue Martling, a large blue-bearded Dutchman, who had nearly taken a British frigate with an old iron nine-pounder from a mud breastwork, only that his gun burst at the sixth discharge. And there was an old gentleman who shall be nameless, being too rich a mynheer to be lightly mentioned, who, in the battle of White Plains, being an excellent master of defence, parried a musketball with a small sword, insomuch that he absolutely felt it whiz round the blade, and glance off at the hilt; in proof of which he was ready at any time to show the sword, with the hilt a little bent. There were several more that had been equally great in the field, not one of whom but was persuaded that he had a considerable hand in bringing the war to a happy termination.

But all these were nothing to the tales of ghosts and apparitions that succeeded. The neighborhood is rich in legendary treasures of the kind. Local tales and super-

---

Saint Vitus: "Saint Vitus dance" was the name once given to a neurological disorder that causes uncontrolled twitching of the body.

stitions thrive best in these sheltered long-settled retreats; but are trampled underfoot by the shifting throng that forms the population of most of our country places. Besides, there is no encouragement for ghosts in most of our villages, for they have scarcely had time to finish their first nap, and turn themselves in their graves before their surviving friends have travelled away from the neighborhood; so that when they turn out at night to walk their rounds, they have no acquaintance left to call upon. This is perhaps the reason why we so seldom hear of ghosts, except in our long-established Dutch communities. ₅₀

The immediate cause, however, of the prevalence of supernatural stories in these parts was doubtless owing to the vicinity of Sleepy Hollow. There was a contagion in the very air that blew from the haunted region; it breathed forth an atmosphere of dreams and fancies infecting all the land. Several of the Sleepy Hollow people were present at Van Tassel's and, as usual, were doling out their wild and wonderful legends. Many dismal tales were told about funeral trains, and mourning cries and wailings heard and seen about the great tree where the unfortunate Major André was taken, and which stood in the neighborhood. Some mention was made also of the woman in white, that haunted the dark glen at Raven Rock, and was often heard to shriek on winter nights before a storm, having perished there in the snow. The chief part of the stories, however, turned upon the favorite spectre of Sleepy Hollow, the headless horseman, who had been heard several times of late, patrolling the country; and, it was said, tethered his horse nightly among the graves in the churchyard.

The sequestered situation of this church seems always to have made it a favorite haunt of troubled spirits. It stands on a knoll, surrounded by locust-trees and lofty elms, from among which its decent white-washed walls shine modestly forth, like Christian purity beaming through the shades of retirement. A gentle slope descends from it to a silver sheet of water, bordered by high trees, between which, peeps may be caught at the blue hills of the Hudson. To look upon its grass-grown yard, where the sunbeams seem to sleep so quietly, one would think that there at least the dead might rest in peace. On one side of the church extends a wide woody dell, along which raves a large brook among broken rocks and trunks of fallen trees. Over a deep black part of the stream, not far from the church, was formerly thrown a wooden bridge; the road that led to it, and the bridge itself, were thickly shaded by overhanging trees, which cast a gloom about it, even in the daytime, but occasioned a fearful darkness at night. This was one of the favorite haunts of the headless horseman; and the place where he was most frequently encountered. The tale was told of old Brouwer, a most heretical disbeliever in ghosts, how he met the horseman returning from his foray into Sleepy Hollow, and was obliged to get up behind him; how they galloped over bush and brake, over hill and swamp, until they reached the bridge; when the horseman suddenly turned into a skeleton, threw old Brouwer into the brook, and sprang away over the tree-tops with a clap of thunder.

This story was immediately matched by a thrice marvellous adventure of Brom Bones, who made light of the galloping Hessian as an arrant jockey. He affirmed that, on returning one night from the neighboring village of Sing Sing, he had been overtaken by this midnight trooper; that he had offered to race with him for a bowl of punch, and should have won it too, for Daredevil beat the goblin horse all hollow, but, just as they came to the church bridge, the Hessian bolted, and vanished in a flash of fire.

All these tales, told in that drowsy undertone with which men talk in the dark, the countenances of the listeners only now and then receiving a casual gleam from the glare of a pipe, sank deep in the mind of Ichabod. He repaid them in kind with large extracts from his invaluable author, Cotton Mather, and added many marvellous events that had taken place in his native State of Connecticut, and fearful sights which he had seen in his nightly walks about the Sleepy Hollow.

The revel now gradually broke up. The old farmers gathered together their families in their wagons, and were heard for some time rattling along the hollow roads, and over the distant hills. Some of the damsels mounted on pillions behind their favorite swains, and their light-hearted laughter, mingling with the clatter of hoofs, echoed along the silent woodlands, sounding fainter and fainter until they gradually died away—and the late scene of noise and frolic was all silent and deserted. Ichabod only lingered behind, according to the custom of country lovers, to have a *tête-à-tête* with the heiress, fully convinced that he was now on the high road to success. What passed at this interview I will not pretend to say, for in fact I do not know. Something, however, I fear me, must have gone wrong, for he certainly sallied forth, after no very great interval, with an air quite desolate and chop-fallen.—Oh, these women! these women! Could that girl have been playing off any of her coquettish tricks?—Was her encouragement of the poor pedagogue all a mere sham to secure her conquest of his rival?—Heaven only knows, not I!—Let it suffice to say, Ichabod stole forth with the air of one who had been sacking a hen-roost, rather than a fair lady's heart. Without looking to the right or left to notice the scene of rural wealth on which he had so often gloated, he went straight to the stable, and with several hearty cuffs and kicks, roused his steed most uncourteously from the comfortable quarters in which he was soundly sleeping, dreaming of mountains of corn and oats, and whole valleys of timothy and clover.

It was the very witching time of night that Ichabod, heavy-hearted and crest-fallen, pursued his travel homewards, along the sides of the lofty hills which rise above Tarry Town, and which he had traversed so cheerily in the afternoon. The hour was as dismal as himself. Far below him, the Tappan Zee spread its dusky and indistinct waste of waters, with here and there the tall mast of a sloop riding quietly at anchor under the land. In the dead hush of midnight he could even hear the barking of the watchdog from the opposite shore of the Hudson; but it was so vague and faint as only to give an idea of his distance from this faithful companion of man. Now and then, too, the long-drawn crowing of a cock, accidentally awakened, would sound far, far off, from some farm-house away among the hills—but it was like a dreaming sound in his ear. No signs of life occurred near him, but occasionally the melancholy chirp of a cricket, or perhaps the gutteral twang of a bull-frog, from a neighboring marsh, as if sleeping uncomfortably, and turning suddenly in his bed.

All the stories of ghosts and goblins that he had heard in the afternoon, now came crowding upon his recollection. The night grew darker and darker; the stars seemed to sink deeper in the sky, and driving clouds occasionally hid them from his sight. He had never felt so lonely and dismal. He was, moreover, approaching the very place where many of the scenes of the ghost-stories had been laid. In the centre of the road stood an enormous tulip-tree, which towered like a giant above all the other trees of the neighborhood, and formed a kind of landmark. Its limbs were gnarled, and fantastic, large enough to form trunks for ordinary trees, twisting down almost to the earth, and rising again into the air. It was connected with the tragical story of the unfortunate André, who had been taken prisoner hard by; and was uni-

55

versally known by the name of Major André's tree. The common people regarded it with a mixture of respect and superstition, partly out of sympathy for the fate of its ill-starred namesake, and partly from the tales of strange sights and doleful lamentations told concerning it.

As Ichabod approached this fearful tree, he began to whistle: he thought his whistle was answered,—it was but a blast sweeping sharply through the dry branches. As he approached a little nearer, he thought he saw something white, hanging in the midst of the tree,—he paused and ceased whistling; but on looking more narrowly, perceived that it was a place where the tree had been scathed by lightning, and the white wood laid bare. Suddenly he heard a groan,—his teeth chattered and his knees smote against the saddle: it was but the rubbing of one huge bough upon another, as they were swayed about by the breeze. He passed the tree in safety; but new perils lay before him.

About two hundred yards from the tree a small brook crossed the road, and ran into a marshy and thickly wooded glen, known by the name of Wiley's swamp. A few rough logs, laid side by side, served for a bridge over this stream. On that side of the road where the brook entered the wood, a group of oaks and chestnuts, matted thick with wild grape-vines, threw a cavernous gloom over it. To pass this bridge was the severest trial. It was at this identical spot that the unfortunate André was captured, and under the covert of those chestnuts and vines were the sturdy yeomen concealed who surprised him. This has ever since been considered a haunted stream, and fearful are the feelings of the school boy who has to pass it alone after dark.

As he approached the stream, his heart began to thump; he summoned up, however, all his resolution, gave his horse half a score of kicks in the ribs, and attempted to dash briskly across the bridge; but instead of starting forward, the perverse old animal made a lateral movement, and ran broadside against the fence. Ichabod, whose fears increased with the delay, jerked the reins on the other side, and kicked lustily with the contrary foot: it was all in vain; his steed started, it is true, but it was only to plunge to the opposite side of the road into a thicket of brambles and alder bushes. The schoolmaster now bestowed both whip and heel upon the starveling ribs of old Gunpowder, who dashed forward, snuffling and snorting, but came to a stand just by the bridge, with a suddenness that had nearly sent his rider sprawling over his head. Just at this moment a plashy tramp by the side of the bridge caught the sensitive ear of Ichabod. In the dark shadow of the grove, on the margin of the brook, he beheld something huge, misshapen, black, and towering. It stirred not, but seemed gathered up in the gloom, like some gigantic monster ready to spring upon the traveller.

60

The hair of the affrighted pedagogue rose upon his head with terror. What was to be done? To turn and fly was now too late; and besides, what chance was there of escaping ghost or goblin, if such it was, which could ride upon the wings of the wind? Summoning up, therefore, a show of courage, he demanded in stammering accents—"Who are you?" He received no reply. He repeated his demand in a still more agitated voice. Still there was no answer. Once more he cudgelled the sides of the inflexible Gunpowder, and, shutting his eyes, broke forth with involuntary fervor into a psalm-tune. Just then the shadowy object of alarm put itself in motion, and, with a scramble and a bound, stood at once in the middle of the road. Though the night was dark and dismal, yet the form of the unknown might now in some degree be ascertained. He appeared to be a horseman of large dimensions, and mounted on a black horse of powerful frame. He made no offer of molestation or sociability, but kept aloof on one side of the road, jogging along on the blind side of old Gunpowder, who had now got over his fright and waywardness.

Ichabod, who had no relish for this strange midnight companion, and bethought himself of the adventure of Brom Bones with the Galloping Hessian, now quickened his steed, in hopes of leaving him behind. The stranger, however, quickened his horse to an equal pace. Ichabod pulled up, and fell into a walk, thinking to lag behind,—the other did the same. His heart began to sink within him; he endeavored to resume his psalm-tune, but his parched tongue clove to the roof of his mouth, and he could not utter a stave. There was something in the moody and dogged silence of this pertinacious companion, that was mysterious and appalling. It was soon fearfully accounted for. On mounting a rising ground, which brought the figure of his fellow-traveller in relief against the sky, gigantic in height, and muffled in a cloak, Ichabod was horror-struck, on perceiving that he was headless!— but his horror was still more increased, on observing that the head, which should have rested on his shoulders, was carried before him on the pommel of the saddle: his terror rose to desperation; he rained a shower of kicks and blows upon Gunpowder, hoping, by a sudden movement, to give his companion the slip,—but the spectre started full jump with him. Away then they dashed, through thick and thin; stones flying, and sparks flashing at every bound. Ichabod's flimsy garments fluttered in the air, as he stretched his long lank body away over his horse's head, in the eagerness of his flight.

They had now reached the road which turns off to Sleepy Hollow; but Gunpowder, who seemed possessed with a demon, instead of keeping up it, made an opposite turn, and plunged headlong downhill to the left. This road leads through a sandy hollow, shaded by trees for about a quarter of a mile, where it crosses the bridge famous in goblin story, and just beyond swells the green knoll on which stands the white-washed church.

As yet the panic of the steed had given his unskilful rider an apparent advantage in the chase; but just as he had got half-way through the hollow, the girths of the saddle gave way, and he felt it slipping from under him. He seized it by the pommel, and endeavored to hold it firm, but in vain; and had just time to save himself by clasping old Gunpowder round the neck, when the saddle fell to the earth, and he heard it trampled underfoot by his pursuer. For a moment, the terror of Hans Van Ripper's wrath passed across his mind—for it was his Sunday saddle; but this was no time for petty fears; the goblin was hard on his haunches; and (unskilful rider that he was!) he had much ado to maintain his seat; sometimes slipping on one side, sometimes on another, and sometimes jolted on the high ridge of his horse's backbone, with a violence that he verily feared would cleave him asunder.

An opening in the trees now cheered him with the hopes that the church-bridge was at hand. The wavering reflection of a silver star in the bosom of the brook told him that he was not mistaken. He saw the walls of the church dimly glaring under the trees beyond. He recollected the place where Brom Bones' ghostly competitor had disappeared. "If I can but reach that bridge," thought Ichabod, "I am safe." Just then he heard the black steed panting and blowing close behind him; he even fancied that he felt his hot breath. Another convulsive kick in the ribs, and old Gunpowder sprang upon the bridge; he thundered over the resounding planks; he gained the opposite side; and now Ichabod cast a look behind to see if his pursuer should vanish, according to rule, in a flash of fire and brimstone. Just then he saw the goblin rising in his stirrups, and in the very act of hurling his head at him. Ichabod endeavored to dodge the horrible missile, but too late. It encountered his cranium with a tremendous crash,—he was tumbled headlong into the dust, and Gunpowder, the black steed, and the goblin rider, passed by like a whirlwind.

The next morning the old horse was found without his saddle, and with the bridle under his feet, soberly cropping the grass at his master's gate. Ichabod did not make his appearance at breakfast;—dinner-hour came, but no Ichabod. The boys assembled at the school-house, and strolled idly about the banks of the brook; but no schoolmaster. Hans Van Ripper now began to feel some uneasiness about the fate of poor Ichabod, and his saddle. An inquiry was set on foot, and after diligent investigation they came upon his traces. In one part of the road leading to the church was found the saddle trampled in the dirt; the tracks of horses' hoofs deeply dented in the road, and evidently at furious speed, were traced to the bridge, beyond which, on the bank of a broad part of the brook, where the water ran deep and black, was found the hat of the unfortunate Ichabod, and close beside it a shattered pumpkin.

The brook was searched, but the body of the schoolmaster was not to be discovered. Hans Van Ripper, as executor of his estate, examined the bundle which contained all his worldly effects. They consisted of two shirts and a half; two stocks for the neck; a pair or two of worsted stockings, an old pair of corduroy small-clothes; a rusty razor; a book of psalm-tunes, full of dogs' ears; and a broken pitch-pipe. As to the books and furniture of the school-house, they belonged to the community, excepting Cotton Mather's *History of Witchcraft*, a *New England Almanac*, and a book of dreams and fortune-telling; in which last was a sheet of foolscap much scribbled and blotted in several fruitless attempts to make a copy of verses in honor of the heiress of Van Tassel. These magic books and the poetic scrawl were forthwith consigned to the flames by Hans Van Ripper; who from that time forward determined to send his children no more to school; observing, that he never knew any good come of this same reading and writing. Whatever money the schoolmaster possessed, and he had received his quarter's pay but a day or two before, he must have had about his person at the time of his disappearance.

The mysterious event caused much speculation at the church on the following Sunday. Knots of gazers and gossips were collected in the churchyard, at the bridge, and at the spot where the hat and pumpkin had been found. The stories of Brouwer, of Bones, and a whole budget of others, were called to mind; and when they had diligently considered them all, and compared them with the symptoms of the present case, they shook their heads, and came to the conclusion that Ichabod had been carried off by the Galloping Hessian. As he was a bachelor, and in nobody's debt, nobody troubled his head any more about him. The school was removed to a different quarter of the Hollow, and another pedagogue reigned in his stead.

It is true, an old farmer, who had been down to New York on a visit several years after, and from whom this account of the ghastly adventure was received, brought home the intelligence that Ichabod Crane was still alive; that he had left the neighborhood, partly through fear of the goblin and Hans Van Ripper, and partly in mortification at having been suddenly dismissed by the heiress; that he had changed his quarters to a distant part of the country; had kept school and studied law at the same time, had been admitted to the bar, turned politician, electioneered, written for the newspapers, and finally had been made a justice of the Ten Pound Court. Brom Bones too, who shortly after his rival's disappearance conducted the blooming Katrina in triumph to the altar, was observed to look exceedingly know-ing whenever the story of Ichabod was related, and always burst into a hearty laugh at the mention of the pumpkin; which led some to suspect that he knew more about the matter than he chose to tell.

The old country wives, however, who are the best judges of these matters, maintain to this day that Ichabod was spirited away by supernatural means; and it is a favorite story often told about the neighborhood round the winter evening fire. The bridge became more than ever an object of superstitious awe, and that may be the reason why the road has been altered of late years, so as to approach the church by the border of the millpond. The school-house, being deserted, soon fell to decay, and was reported to be haunted by the ghost of the unfortunate pedagogue; and the ploughboy, loitering homeward of a still summer evening, has often fancied his voice at a distance, chanting a melancholy psalm-tune, among the tranquil soli-tudes of Sleepy Hollow.

70

POSTSCRIPT, *found in the handwriting of Mr. Knickerbocker.*

The preceding Tale is given, almost in the precise words in which I heard it re-lated at a Corporation meeting of the ancient city of Manhattoes,° at which were present many of its sagest and most illustrious burghers. The narrator was a pleas-ant, shabby, gentlemanly old fellow, in pepper-and-salt clothes, with a sadly hu-morous face; and one whom I strongly suspected of being poor,—he made such efforts to be entertaining. When his story was concluded, there was much laugh-ter and approbation, particularly from two or three deputy aldermen, who had been asleep the greater part of the time. There was, however, one tall, dry-looking old gentleman, with beetling eyebrows, who maintained a grave and rather severe face throughout; now and then folding his arms, inclining his head, and looking down upon the floor, as if turning a doubt over in his mind. He was one of your wary men, who never laugh, but on good grounds—when they have reason and the law on their side. When the mirth of the rest of the company had subsided and silence was restored, he leaned one arm on the elbow of his chair, and sticking the other akimbo, demanded, with a slight but exceedingly sage mo-tion of the head, and contraction of the brow, what was the moral of the story, and what it went to prove?

The story-teller, who was just putting a glass of wine to his lips, as a refreshment after his toils, paused for a moment, looked at his inquirer with an air of infinite def-erence, and, lowering the glass slowly to the table, observed, that the story was in-tended most logically to prove:

"There is no situation in life but has its advantages and pleasures—provided we will but take a joke as we find it;

"That, therefore, he that runs races with goblin troopers is likely to have rough riding of it.

Manhattoes: the Dutch version of the Indian name for what is now Manhattan.

"*Ergo,*° for a country schoolmaster to be refused the hand of a Dutch heiress, is a certain step to high preferment in the state."

The cautious old gentleman knit his brows tenfold closer after this explanation, being sorely puzzled by ratiocination of the syllogism; while, methought, the one in pepper-and-salt eyed him with something of a triumphant leer. At length he observed, that all this was very well, but still he thought the story a little on the extravagant—there were one or two points on which he had his doubts.

"Faith, sir," replied the story-teller, "as to that matter, I don't believe one half of it myself."

Herman Melville (1819–1891)

Herman Melville represents a classic example of the great writer who is undervalued in his own lifetime and who must await changes in literary sensibility before he can get his due. The son of a New England merchant, Melville worked a number of jobs as a young man before he shipped out to the South Seas on a whaling ship. After several years of adventures on various vessels, he returned to America. He enjoyed an astonishing period of literary productivity, publishing seven novels in six years. *Moby-Dick,* considered by most to be his masterpiece, was published in 1851. But the author did not find much of a market for his works, which included *Typee* (1846), *Omoo* (1847), and *Pierre* (1852). Melville spent nineteen years working as a customs inspector in his native New York. His last important work, *Billy Budd,* was not published until some thirty years after his death. He never knew he would later be viewed as one of the major writers of his era.

BARTLEBY THE SCRIVENER

A Story of Wall Street

I am a rather elderly man. The nature of my avocations for the last thirty years has brought me into more than ordinary contact with what would seem an interesting and somewhat singular set of men,

---

ergo: Latin for "therefore."

A Fiction Anthology

of whom as yet nothing that I know of has ever been written:—I mean the law-copyists or scriveners. I have known very many of them, professionally and privately, and if I pleased, could relate divers histories, at which good-natured gentlemen might smile, and sentimental souls might weep. But I waive the biographies of all other scriveners for a few passages in the life of Bartleby, who was a scrivener the strangest I ever saw or heard of. While of other law-copyists I might write the complete life, of Bartleby nothing of that sort can be done. I believe that no materials exist for a full and satisfactory biography of this man. It is an irreparable loss to literature. Bartleby was one of those beings of whom nothing is ascertainable, except from the original sources, and in his case those are very small. What my own astonished eyes saw of Bartleby, *that* is all I know of him, except, indeed, one vague report which will appear in the sequel.

Ere introducing the scrivener, as he first appeared to me, it is fit I make some mention of myself, my *employés*, my business, my chambers, and general surroundings; because some such description is indispensable to an adequate understanding of the chief character about to be presented.

Imprimis:° I am a man who, from his youth upward, has been filled with a profound conviction that the easiest way of life is the best. Hence, though I belong to a profession proverbially energetic and nervous, even to turbulence, at times, yet nothing of that sort have I ever suffered to invade my peace. I am one of those unambitious lawyers who never addresses a jury, or in any way draws down public applause; but in the cool tranquillity of a snug retreat, do a snug business among rich men's bonds and mortgages and title-deeds. All who know me, consider me an eminently *safe* man. The late John Jacob Astor,° a personage little given to poetic enthusiasm, had no hesitation in pronouncing my first grand point to be prudence; my next, method. I do not speak it in vanity, but simply record the fact, that I was not unemployed in my profession by the late John Jacob Astor; a name which, I admit, I love to repeat, for it hath a rounded and orbicular sound to it, and rings like unto bullion. I will freely add, that I was not insensible to the late John Jacob Astor's good opinion.

Some time prior to the period at which this little history begins, my avocations had been largely increased. The good old office, now extinct in the State of New-York, of a Master in Chancery, had been conferred upon me. It was not a very arduous office, but very pleasantly remunerative. I seldom lose my temper; much more seldom indulge in dangerous indignation at wrongs and outrages; but I must be permitted to be rash here and declare, that I consider the sudden and violent abrogation of the office of Master in Chancery, by the new Constitution, as a —— premature act; inasmuch as I had counted upon a life-lease of the profits, whereas I only received those of a few short years. But this is by the way.

My chambers were upstairs at No. _____ Wall-street. At one end they looked upon the white wall of the interior of a spacious skylight shaft, penetrating the building from top to bottom. This view might have been considered rather tame than otherwise, deficient in what landscape painters call "life." But if so, the view from the other end of my chambers offered, at least, a contrast, if nothing more. In that direction my windows commanded an unobstructed view of a lofty brick wall, black

---

Imprimis: first; to begin with.
Astor: a New York millionaire, entrepreneur, and developer.

by age and everlasting shade; which wall required no spyglass to bring out its lurking beauties, but for the benefit of all nearsighted spectators, was pushed up to within ten feet of my window panes. Owing to the great height of the surrounding buildings, and my chambers being on the second floor, the interval between this wall and mine not a little resembled a huge square cistern.

At the period just preceding the advent of Bartleby, I had two persons as copyists in my employment, and a promising lad as an officeboy. First, Turkey; second, Nippers; third, Ginger Nut. These may seem names, the like of which are not usually found in the Directory.° In truth they were nicknames, mutually conferred upon each other by my three clerks, and were deemed expressive of their respective persons or characters. Turkey was a short, pursy Englishman of about my own age, that is, somewhere not far from sixty. In the morning, one might say, his face was of a fine florid hue, but after twelve o'clock, meridian—his dinner hour—it blazed like a grate full of Christmas coals; and continued blazing—but, as it were, with a gradual wane—till 6 o'clock P.M. or thereabouts, after which I saw no more of the proprietor of the face, which, gaining its meridian with the sun, seemed to set with it, to rise, culminate, and decline the following day, with the like regularity and undiminished glory. There are many singular coincidences I have known in the course of my life, not the least among which was the fact, that exactly when Turkey displayed his fullest beams from his red and radiant countenance, just then, too, at that critical moment, began the daily period when I considered his business capacities as seriously disturbed for the remainder of the twenty-four hours. Not that he was absolutely idle, or averse to business then; far from it. The difficulty was, he was apt to be altogether too energetic. There was a strange, inflamed, flurried, flighty recklessness of activity about him. He would be incautious in dipping his pen into his inkstand. All his blots upon my documents, were dropped there after twelve o'clock, meridian. Indeed, not only would he be reckless and sadly given to making blots in the afternoon, but some days he went further, and was rather noisy. At such times, too, his face flamed with augmented blazonry, as if cannel coal had been heaped on anthracite. He made an unpleasant racket with his chair; spilled his sand-box; in mending his pens, impatiently split them all to pieces, and threw them on the floor in a sudden passion; stood up and leaned over his table, boxing his papers about in a most indecorous manner, very sad to behold in an elderly man like him. Nevertheless, as he was in many ways a most valuable person to me, and all the time before twelve o'clock, meridian, was the quickest, steadiest creature, too, accomplishing a great deal of work in a style not easy to be matched—for these reasons, I was willing to overlook his eccentricities, though indeed, occasionally, I remonstrated with him. I did this very gently, however, because, though the civilest, nay, the blandest and most reverential of men in the morning, yet in the afternoon he was disposed, upon provocation, to be slightly rash with his tongue, in fact, insolent. Now, valuing his morning services as I did, and resolved not to lose them—yet, at the same time made uncomfortable by his inflamed ways after twelve o'clock; and being a man of peace, unwilling by my admonitions to call forth unseemly retorts from him—I took upon me, one Saturday noon (he was always worse on Saturdays), to hint to him, very kindly, that perhaps now that he was growing old, it might be well to abridge his labors; in short, he need not come to my chambers after twelve

---

in the Directory: in the personnel records.

o'clock, but, dinner over, had best go home to his lodgings and rest himself till tea-time. But no; he insisted upon his afternoon devotions. His countenance became intolerably fervid, as he oratorically assured me—gesticulating with a long ruler at the other end of the room—that if his services in the morning were useful, how indispensable, then, in the afternoon?

"With submission, sir," said Turkey on this occasion, "I consider myself your right-hand man. In the morning I but marshal and deploy my columns; but in the afternoon I put myself at their head, and gallantly charge the foe, thus!"—and he made a violent thrust with the ruler.

"But the blots, Turkey," intimated I.

"True,—but, with submission, sir, behold these hairs! I am getting old. Surely, sir, a blot or two of a warm afternoon is not to be severely urged against gray hairs. Old age—even if it blot the page—is honorable. With submission, sir, we *both* are getting old."

This appeal to my fellow-feeling was hardly to be resisted. At all events, I saw that go he would not. So I made up my mind to let him stay, resolving, nevertheless, to see to it, that during the afternoon he had to do with my less important papers.   10

Nippers, the second on my list, was a whiskered, sallow, and, upon the whole, rather piratical-looking young man of about five and twenty. I always deemed him the victim of two evil powers—ambition and indigestion. The ambition was evinced by a certain impatience of the duties of a mere copyist—an unwarrantable usurpation of strictly professional affairs, such as the original drawing up of legal documents. The indigestion seemed betokened in an occasional nervous testiness and grinning irritability, causing the teeth to audibly grind together over mistakes committed in copying; unnecessary maledictions, hissed, rather than spoken, in the heat of business; and especially by a continual discontent with the height of the table where he worked. Though of a very ingenious mechanical turn, Nippers could never get this table to suit him. He put chips under it, blocks of various sorts, bits of pasteboard, and at last went so far as to attempt an exquisite adjustment by final pieces of folded blotting-paper. But no invention would answer. If, for the sake of easing his back, he brought the table lid at a sharp angle well up towards his chin, and wrote there like a man using the steep roof of a Dutch house for his desk—then he declared that it stopped the circulation in his arms. If now he lowered the table to his waistbands, and stooped over it in writing, then there was a sore aching in his back. In short, the truth of the matter was, Nippers knew not what he wanted. Or, if he wanted anything, it was to be rid of a scrivener's table altogether. Among the manifestations of his diseased ambition was a fondness he had for receiving visits from certain ambiguous-looking fellows in seedy coats, whom he called his clients. Indeed I was aware that not only was he, at times, considerable of a ward-politician, but he occasionally did a little business at the Justices' courts, and was not unknown on the steps of the Tombs.° I have good reason to believe, however, that one individual who called upon him at my chambers, and who, with a grand air, he insisted was his client, was no other than a dun,° and the alleged title-deed, a bill. But with all his failings, and the annoyances he caused me, Nippers, like his compatriot Turkey, was a very useful man to me; wrote a neat, swift hand; and when he chose, was not defi-

---

Tombs: New York City jail; also, a place to post bail.
dun: a bill collector.

cient in a gentlemanly sort of deportment. Added to this, he always dressed in a gentlemanly sort of way; and so, incidentally, reflected credit upon my chambers. Whereas with respect to Turkey, I had much ado to keep him from being a reproach to me. His clothes were apt to look oily and smell of eating-houses. He wore his pantaloons very loose and baggy in summer. His coats were execrable; his hat not to be handled. But while the hat was a thing of indifference to me, inasmuch as his natural civility and deference, as a dependent Englishman, always led him to doff it the moment he entered the room, yet his coat was another matter. Concerning his coats, I reasoned with him; but with no effect. The truth was, I suppose, that a man with so small an income, could not afford to sport such a lustrous face and a lustrous coat at one and the same time. As Nippers once observed, Turkey's money went chiefly for red ink. One winter day I presented Turkey with a highly-respectable looking coat of my own, a padded gray coat, of a most comfortable warmth, and which buttoned straight up from the knee to the neck. I thought Turkey would appreciate the favour, and abate his rashness and obstreperousness of afternoons. But no. I verily believe that buttoning himself up in so downy and blanket-like a coat had a pernicious effect upon him; upon the same principle that too much oats are bad for horses. In fact, precisely as a rash, restive horse is said to feel his oats, so Turkey felt his coat. It made him insolent. He was a man whom prosperity harmed.

Though concerning the self-indulgent habits of Turkey I had my own private surmises, yet touching Nippers I was well persuaded that whatever might be his faults in other respects, he was, at least, a temperate young man. But, indeed, nature herself seemed to have been his vintner, and at his birth charged him so thoroughly with an irritable, brandy-like disposition, that all subsequent potations were needless. When I consider how, amid the stillness of my chambers, Nippers would sometimes impatiently rise from his seat, and stooping over his table, spread his arms wide apart, seize the whole desk, and move it, and jerk it, with a grim, grinding motion on the floor, as if the table were a perverse voluntary agent, intent on thwarting and vexing him; I plainly perceive that for Nippers, brandy and water were altogether superfluous.

It was fortunate for me that, owing to its peculiar cause—indigestion—the irritability and consequent nervousness of Nippers, were mainly observable in the morning, while in the afternoon he was comparatively mild. So that Turkey's paroxysms only coming on about twelve o'clock, I never had to do with their eccentricities at one time. Their fits relieved each other like guards. When Nippers' was on, Turkey's was off; and *vice versa*. This was a good natural arrangement under the circumstances.

Ginger Nut, the third on my list, was a lad some twelve years old. His father was a carman, ambitious of seeing his son on the bench instead of a cart, before he died. So he sent him to my office as student at law, errand boy, and cleaner and sweeper, at the rate of one dollar a week. He had a little desk to himself, but he did not use it much. Upon inspection, the drawer exhibited a great array of the shells of various sorts of nuts. Indeed, to this quick-witted youth the whole noble science of the law was contained in a nut-shell. Not the least among the employments of Ginger Nut, as well as one which he discharged with the most alacrity, was his duty as cake and apple purveyor for Turkey and Nippers. Copying law papers being proverbially a dry, husky sort of business, my two scriveners were fain to moisten their mouths very often with Spitzenbergs° to be had at the numerous stalls nigh the

---

Spitzenbergs: a kind of apple.

Custom House and Post Office. Also, they sent Ginger Nut very frequently for that peculiar cake—small, flat, round, and very spicy—after which he had been named by them. Of a cold morning when business was but dull, Turkey would gobble up scores of these cakes, as if they were mere wafers—indeed they sell them at the rate of six or eight for a penny—the scrape of his pen blending with the crunching of the crisp particles in his mouth. Of all the fiery afternoon blunders and flurried rashnesses of Turkey, was his once moistening a ginger-cake between his lips, and clapping it on to a mortgage for a seal. I came within an ace of dismissing him then. But he mollified me by making an oriental bow, and saying—"With submission, sir, it was generous of me to find you in° stationery on my own account."

Now my original business—that of a conveyancer and title hunter, and drawer-up of recondite documents of all sorts—was considerably increased by receiving the master's office. There was now great work for scriveners. Not only must I push the clerks already with me, but I must have additional help. In answer to my advertisement, a motionless young man one morning stood upon my office threshold, the door being open, for it was summer. I can see that figure now—pallidly neat, pitiably respectable, incurably forlorn! It was Bartleby.   15

After a few words touching his qualifications, I engaged him, glad to have among my corps of copyists a man of so singularly sedate an aspect, which I thought might operate beneficially upon the flighty temper of Turkey, and the fiery one of Nippers.

I should have stated before that ground glass folding-doors divided my premises into two parts, one of which was occupied by my scriveners, the other by myself. According to my humour I threw open these doors, or closed them. I resolved to assign Bartleby a corner by the folding-doors, but on my side of them, so as to have this quiet man within easy call, in case any trifling thing was to be done. I placed his desk close up to a small side-window in that part of the room, a window which originally had afforded a lateral view of certain grimy back-yards and bricks, but which, owing to subsequent erections, commanded at present no view at all, though it gave some light. Within three feet of the panes was a wall, and the light came down from far above, between two lofty buildings, as from a very small opening in a dome. Still further to a satisfactory arrangement, I procured a high green folding screen, which might entirely isolate Bartleby from my sight, though not remove him from my voice. And thus, in a manner, privacy and society were conjoined.

At first Bartleby did an extraordinary quantity of writing. As if long famishing for something to copy, he seemed to gorge himself on my documents. There was no pause for digestion. He ran a day and night line, copying by sun-light and by candle-light. I should have been quite delighted with his application, had he been cheerfully industrious. But he wrote on silently, palely, mechanically.

It is, of course, an indispensable part of a scrivener's business to verify the accuracy of his copy, word by word. Where there are two or more scriveners in an office, they assist each other in this examination, one reading from the copy, the other holding the original. It is a very dull, wearisome, and lethargic affair. I can readily imagine that to some sanguine temperaments it would be altogether intolerable. For example, I cannot credit that the mettlesome poet Byron would have contentedly sat down with Bartleby to examine a law document of, say five hundred pages, closely written in a crimpy hand.

_____

find you in: supply you with.

Now and then, in the haste of business, it had been my habit to assist in comparing some brief document myself, calling Turkey or Nippers for this purpose. One object I had in placing Bartleby so handy to me behind the screen, was to avail myself of his services on such trivial occasions. It was on the third day, I think, of his being with me, and before any necessity had arisen for having his own writing examined, that, being much hurried to complete a small affair I had in hand, I abruptly called to Bartleby. In my haste and natural expectancy of instant compliance, I sat with my head bent over the original on my desk, and my right hand sideways, and somewhat nervously extended with the copy, so that immediately upon emerging from his retreat, Bartleby might snatch it and proceed to business without the least delay.   20

In this very attitude did I sit when I called to him, rapidly stating what it was I wanted him to do—namely, to examine a small paper with me. Imagine my surprise, nay, my consternation, when without moving from his privacy, Bartleby in a singularly mild, firm voice, replied, "I would prefer not to."

I sat awhile in perfect silence, rallying my stunned faculties. Immediately it occurred to me that my ears had deceived me, or Bartleby had entirely misunderstood my meaning. I repeated my request in the clearest tone I could assume. But in quite as clear a one came the previous reply, "I would prefer not to."

"Prefer not to," echoed I, rising in high excitement, and crossing the room with a stride. "What do you mean? Are you moon-struck? I want you to help me compare this sheet here—take it," and I thrust it toward him.

"I would prefer not to," said he.

I looked at him steadfastly. His face was leanly composed; his gray eye dimly calm. Not a wrinkle of agitation rippled him. Had there been the least uneasiness, anger, impatience or impertinence in his manner; in other words, had there been anything ordinarily human about him, doubtless I should have violently dismissed him from the premises. But as it was, I should have as soon thought of turning my pale plaster-of-paris bust of Cicero out of doors. I stood gazing at him awhile, as he went on with his own writing, and then reseated myself at my desk. This is very strange, thought I. What had one best do? But my business hurried me. I concluded to forget the matter for the present, reserving it for my future leisure. So calling Nippers from the other room, the paper was speedily examined.   25

A few days after this, Bartleby concluded four lengthy documents, being quadruplicates of a week's testimony taken before me in my High Court of Chancery. It became necessary to examine them. It was an important suit, and great accuracy was imperative. Having all things arranged, I called Turkey, Nippers and Ginger Nut from the next room, meaning to place the four copies in the hands of my four clerks, while I should read from the original. Accordingly Turkey, Nippers and Ginger Nut had taken their seats in a row, each with his document in hand, when I called to Bartleby to join this interesting group.

"Bartleby! quick, I am waiting."

I heard a slow scrape of his chair legs on the uncarpeted floor, and soon he appeared standing at the entrance of his hermitage.

"What is wanted?" said he mildly.

"The copies, the copies," said I hurriedly. "We are going to examine them. There"—and I held towards him the fourth quadruplicate.   30

"I would prefer not to," he said, and gently disappeared behind the screen.

For a few moments I was turned into a pillar of salt,° standing at the head of my seated column of clerks. Recovering myself, I advanced toward the screen, and demanded the reason for such extraordinary conduct.

"*Why* do you refuse?"

"I would prefer not to."

With any other man I should have flown outright into a dreadful passion, scorned all further words, and thrust him ignominiously from my presence. But there was something about Bartleby that not only strangely disarmed me, but in a wonderful manner touched and disconcerted me. I began to reason with him. 35

"These are your own copies we are about to examine. It is labour saving to you, because one examination will answer for your four papers. It is common usage. Every copyist is bound to help examine his copy. Is it not so? Will you not speak? Answer!"

"I prefer not to," he replied in a flute-like tone. It seemed to me that while I had been addressing him, he carefully revolved every statement that I made; fully comprehended the meaning; could not gainsay the irresistible conclusion; but, at the same time, some paramount consideration prevailed with him to reply as he did.

"You are decided, then, not to comply with my request—a request made according to common usage and common sense?"

He briefly gave me to understand that on that point my judgment was sound. Yes: his decision was irreversible.

It is not seldom the case that when a man is browbeaten in some unprecedented and violently unreasonable way, he begins to stagger in his own plainest faith. He begins, as it were, vaguely to surmise that, wonderful as it may be, all the justice and all the reason are on the other side. Accordingly, if any disinterested persons are present, he turns to them for some reinforcement for his own faltering mind. 40

"Turkey," said I, "what do you think of this? Am I not right?"

"With submission, sir," said Turkey, with his blandest tone, "I think that you are."

"Nippers," said I, "what do *you* think of it?"

"I think I should kick him out of the office."

(The reader of nice perceptions will here perceive that, it being morning, Turkey's answer is couched in polite and tranquil terms, but Nippers' reply in ill-tempered ones. Or, to repeat a previous sentence, Nippers' ugly mood was on duty, and Turkey's off.) 45

"Ginger Nut," said I, willing to enlist the smallest suffrage in my behalf, "what do *you* think of it?"

"I think, sir, he's a little *luny*,"° replied Ginger Nut, with a grin.

"You hear what they say," said I, turning towards the screen, "come forth and do your duty."

But he vouchsafed no reply. I pondered a moment in sore perplexity. But once more business hurried me. I determined again to postpone the consideration of this dilemma to my future leisure. With a little trouble we made out to examine the papers without Bartleby, though at every page or two, Turkey deferentially dropped his opinion that this proceeding was quite out of the common; while Nippers, twitch-

---

turned into . . . salt: paralyzed, dumbfounded; refers to Lot's wife in Genesis.
luny: loony.

ing in his chair with a dyspeptic nervousness, ground out between his set teeth occasional hissing maledictions against the stubborn oaf behind the screen. And for his (Nippers') part, this was the first and the last time he would do another man's business without pay.

Meanwhile Bartleby sat in his hermitage, oblivious to everything but his own peculiar business there.

Some days passed, the scrivener being employed upon another lengthy work. His late remarkable conduct led me to regard his ways narrowly. I observed that he never went to dinner; indeed that he never went any where. As yet I had never of my personal knowledge known him to be outside of my office. He was a perpetual sentry in the corner. At about eleven o'clock though, in the morning, I noticed that Ginger Nut would advance toward the opening in Bartleby's screen, as if silently beckoned thither by a gesture invisible to me where I sat. The boy would then leave the office jingling a few pence, and reappear with a handful of ginger-nuts which he delivered in the hermitage, receiving two of the cakes for his trouble.

He lives, then, on ginger-nuts, thought I; never eats a dinner, properly speaking; he must be a vegetarian then; but no; he never eats even vegetables, he eats nothing but ginger-nuts. My mind then ran on in reveries concerning the probable effects upon the human constitution of living entirely on ginger-nuts. Ginger-nuts are so called because they contain ginger as one of their peculiar constituents, and the final flavoring one. Now what was ginger? A hot, spicy thing. Was Bartleby hot and spicy? Not at all. Ginger, then, had no effect upon Bartleby. Probably he preferred it should have none.

Nothing so aggravates an earnest person as a passive resistance. If the individual so resisted be of a not inhumane temper, and the resisting one perfectly harmless in his passivity; then, in the better moods of the former, he will endeavor charitably to construe to his imagination what proves impossible to be solved by his judgment. Even so, for the most part, I regarded Bartleby and his ways. Poor fellow! thought I, he means no mischief; it is plain he intends no insolence; his aspect sufficiently evinces that his eccentricities are involuntary. He is useful to me. I can get along with him. If I turn him away, the chances are he will fall in with some less indulgent employer, and then he will be rudely treated, and perhaps driven forth miserably to starve. Yes. Here I can cheaply purchase a delicious self-approval. To befriend Bartleby; to humour him in his strange wilfulness, will cost me little or nothing, while I lay up in my soul what will eventually prove a sweet morsel for my conscience. But this mood was not invariable with me. The passiveness of Bartleby sometimes irritated me. I felt strangely goaded on to encounter him in new opposition, to elicit some angry spark from him answerable to my own. But indeed I might as well have essayed to strike fire with my knuckles against a bit of Windsor soap. But one afternoon the evil impulse in me mastered me, and the following little scene ensued:

"Bartleby," said I, "when those papers are all copied, I will compare them with you."

"I would prefer not to."

"How? Surely you do not mean to persist in that mulish vagary?"

No answer.

I threw open the folding-doors near by, and turning upon Turkey and Nippers, exclaimed in an excited manner:

"He says, a second time, he won't examine his papers. What do you think of it, Turkey?"

It was afternoon, be it remembered. Turkey sat glowing like a brass boiler, his bald head steaming, his hands reeling among his blotted papers. 60

"Think of it?" roared Turkey; "I think I'll just step behind his screen, and black his eyes for him!"

So saying, Turkey rose to his feet and threw his arms into a pugilistic position. He was hurrying away to make good his promise, when I detained him, alarmed at the effect of incautiously rousing Turkey's combativeness after dinner.

"Sit down, Turkey," said I, "and hear what Nippers has to say. What do you think of it, Nippers? Would I not be justified in immediately dismissing Bartleby?"

"Excuse me, that is for you to decide, sir. I think his conduct quite unusual, and indeed unjust, as regards Turkey and myself. But it may only be a passing whim."

"Ah," exclaimed I, "You have strangely changed your mind then—you speak very gently of him now." 65

"All beer," cried Turkey; "gentleness is effects of beer—Nippers and I dined together to-day. You see how gentle *I* am, sir. Shall I go and black his eyes?"

"You refer to Bartleby, I suppose. No, not to-day, Turkey," I replied; "pray, put up your fists."

I closed the doors, and again advanced towards Bartleby. I felt additional incentives tempting me to my fate. I burned to be rebelled against again. I remembered that Bartleby never left the office.

"Bartleby," said I, "Ginger Nut is away; just step round to the Post Office, won't you? (it was but a three minutes' walk), and see if there is any thing for me."

"I would prefer not to." 70

"You *will* not?"

"I *prefer* not."

I staggered to my desk, and sat there in a deep study. My blind inveteracy returned. Was there any other thing in which I could procure myself to be ignominiously repulsed by this lean, penniless wight?—my hired clerk? What added thing is there, perfectly reasonable, that he will be sure to refuse to do?

"Bartleby!"

No answer. 75

"Bartleby," in a louder tone.

No answer.

"Bartleby," I roared.

Like a very ghost, agreeably to the laws of magical invocation, at the third summons, he appeared at the entrance of his hermitage.

"Go to the next room, and tell Nippers to come to me." 80

"I prefer not to," he respectfully and slowly said, and mildly disappeared.

"Very good, Bartleby," said I, in a quiet sort of serenely severe self-possessed tone, intimating the unalterable purpose of some terrible retribution very close at hand. At the moment I half intended something of the kind. But upon the whole, as it was drawing towards my dinner-hour, I thought it best to put on my hat and walk home for the day, suffering much from perplexity and distress of mind.

Shall I acknowledge it? The conclusion of this whole business was, that it soon became a fixed fact of my chambers, that a pale young scrivener, by the name of Bartleby, had a desk there; that he copied for me at the usual rate of four cents a folio (one hundred words); but he was permanently exempt from examining the work done by him, that duty being transferred to Turkey and Nippers, out of compliment doubtless to their superior acuteness; moreover, said Bartleby was never on any account to be despatched on the most trivial errand of any sort; and that even if entreated to take upon him such a matter, it was generally understood that he would prefer not to—in other words, that he would refuse point-blank.

As days passed on, I became considerably reconciled to Bartleby. His steadiness, his freedom from all dissipation, his incessant industry (except when he chose to throw himself into a standing revery behind his screen), his great stillness, his unalterableness of demeanor under all circumstances, made him a valuable acquisition. One prime thing was this,—*he was always there*;—first in the morning, continually through the day, and the last at night. I had a singular confidence in his honesty. I felt my most precious papers perfectly safe in his hands. Sometimes to be sure I could not, for the very soul of me, avoid falling into sudden spasmodic passions with him. For it was exceeding difficult to bear in mind all the time those strange peculiarities, privileges, and unheard of exemptions, forming the tacit stipulations on Bartleby's part under which he remained in my office. Now and then, in the eagerness of despatching pressing business, I would inadvertently summon Bartleby, in a short, rapid tone, to put his finger, say, on the incipient tie of a bit of red tape with which I was about compressing some papers. Of course, from behind the screen the usual answer, "I prefer not to," was sure to come; and then, how could a human creature with common infirmities of our nature, refrain from bitterly exclaiming upon such perverseness—such unreasonableness. However, every added repulse of this sort which I received only tended to lessen the probability of my repeating the inadvertence.

Here it must be said, that according to the customs of most legal gentlemen occupying chambers in densely-populated law buildings, there were several keys to my door. One was kept by a woman residing in the attic, which person weekly scrubbed and daily swept and dusted my apartments. Another was kept by Turkey for convenience sake. The third I sometimes carried in my own pocket. The fourth I knew not who had.

Now, one Sunday morning I happened to go to Trinity Church, to hear a celebrated preacher, and finding myself rather early on the ground, I thought I would walk round to my chambers for awhile. Luckily I had my key with me; but upon applying it to the lock, I found it resisted by something inserted from the inside. Quite surprised, I called out; when to my consternation a key was turned from within; and thrusting his lean visage at me, and holding the door ajar, the apparition of Bartleby appeared, in his shirt sleeves, and otherwise in a strangely tattered dishabille, saying quietly that he was sorry, but he was deeply engaged just then, and—preferred not admitting me at present. In a brief word or two, he moreover added, that perhaps I had better walk round the block two or three times, and by that time he would probably have concluded his affairs.

Now, the utterly unsurmised appearance of Bartleby, tenanting my law-chambers of a Sunday morning, with his cadaverously gentlemanly *nonchalance*, yet withal firm and self-possessed, had such a strange effect upon me, that incontinently I slunk away from my own door, and did as desired. But not without sundry twinges of impotent rebellion against the mild effrontery of this unaccountable scrivener. Indeed, it was his wonderful mildness chiefly, which not only disarmed me, but unmanned me, as it were. For I consider that one, for the time, is in a way unmanned when he tranquilly permits his hired clerk to dictate to him, and order him away from his own premises. Furthermore, I was full of uneasiness as to what Bartleby could possibly be doing in my office in his shirt sleeves, and in an other-

A Fiction Anthology

wise dismantled condition of a Sunday morning. Was any thing amiss going on? Nay, that was out of the question. It was not to be thought of for a moment that Bartleby was an immoral person. But what could he be doing there—copying? Nay again, whatever might be his eccentricities, Bartleby was an eminently decorous person. He would be the last man to sit down to his desk in any state approaching to nudity. Besides, it was Sunday; and there was something about Bartleby that forbade the supposition that he would by any secular occupation violate the proprieties of the day.

Nevertheless, my mind was not pacified; and full of a restless curiosity, at last I returned to the door. Without hindrance I inserted my key, opened it, and entered. Bartleby was not to be seen. I looked round anxiously, peeped behind his screen; but it was very plain that he was gone. Upon more closely examining the place, I surmised that for an indefinite period Bartleby must have ate, dressed, and slept in my office, and that too without plate, mirror, or bed. The cushioned seat of a ricketty old sofa in one corner bore the faint impress of a lean, reclining form. Rolled away under his desk, I found a blanket; under the empty grate, a blacking° box and brush; on a chair, a tin basin, with soap and a ragged towel; in a newspaper a few crumbs of gingernuts and a morsel of cheese. Yes, thought I, it is evident enough that Bartleby has been making his home here, keeping bachelor's hall all by himself. Immediately then the thought came sweeping across me, What miserable friendlessness and loneliness are here revealed! His poverty is great; but his solitude, how horrible! Think of it. Of a Sunday, Wall street is deserted as Petra,° and every night of every day it is an emptiness. This building too, which of week-days hums with industry and life, at nightfall echoes with sheer vacancy, and all through Sunday is forlorn. And here Bartleby makes his home; sole spectator of a solitude which he has seen all populous—a sort of innocent and transformed Marius brooding among the ruins of Carthage!°

For the first time in my life a feeling of overpowering stinging melancholy seized me. Before, I had never experienced aught but a not-unpleasing sadness. The bond of a common humanity now drew me irresistibly to gloom. A fraternal melancholy! For both I and Bartleby were sons of Adam. I remembered the bright silks and sparkling faces I had seen that day, in gala trim, swan-like sailing down the Mississippi of Broadway; and I contrasted them with the pallid copyist, and thought to myself, Ah, happiness courts the light, so we deem the world is gay; but misery hides aloof, so we deem that misery there is none. These sad fancyings–chimeras, doubtless, of a sick and silly brain—led on to other and more special thoughts, concerning the eccentricities of Bartleby. Presentiments of strange discoveries hovered round me. The scrivener's pale form appeared to me laid out, among uncaring strangers, in its shivering winding sheet.

Suddenly I was attracted by Bartleby's closed desk, the key in open sight left in the lock.

I mean no mischief, seek the gratification of no heartless curiosity, thought I; besides, the desk is mine, and its contents too, so I will make bold to look within. Everything was methodically arranged, the papers smoothly placed. The pigeon

90

blacking: shoe polish.
Petra: an abandoned Roman ghost city in modern Jordan.
Marius . . . Carthage: Roman exile who fled to an abandoned, ruined city.

holes were deep, and, removing the files of documents, I groped into their recesses. Presently I felt something there, and dragged it out. It was an old bandanna handkerchief, heavy and knotted. I opened it, and saw it was a savings' bank.

I now recalled all the quiet mysteries which I had noted in the man. I remembered that he never spoke but to answer; that though at intervals he had considerable time to himself, yet I had never seen him reading—no, not even a newspaper; that for long periods he would stand looking out, at his pale window behind the screen, upon the dead brick wall; I was quite sure he never visited any refectory or eatinghouse; while his pale face clearly indicated that he never drank beer like Turkey, or tea and coffee even, like other men; that he never went anywhere in particular that I could learn; never went out for a walk, unless indeed that was the case at present; that he had declined telling who he was, or whence he came, or whether he had any relatives in the world; that though so thin and pale, he never complained of ill health. And more than all, I remembered a certain unconscious air of pallid— how shall I call it?—of pallid haughtiness, say, or rather an austere reserve about him, which had positively awed me into my tame compliance with his eccentricities, when I had feared to ask him to do the slightest incidental thing for me, even though I might know, from his long-continued motionlessness, that behind his screen he must be standing in one of those dead-wall reveries of his.

Revolving all these things, and coupling them with the recently discovered fact that he made my office his constant abiding place and home, and not forgetful of his morbid moodiness; revolving all these things, a prudential feeling began to steal over me. My first emotions had been those of pure melancholy and sincerest pity; but just in proportion as the forlornness of Bartleby grew and grew to my imagination, did that same melancholy merge into fear, that pity into repulsion. So true it is, and so terrible too, that up to a certain point the thought or sight of misery enlists our best affections; but, in certain special cases, beyond that point it does not. They err who would assert that invariably this is owing to the inherent selfishness of the human heart. It rather proceeds from a certain hopelessness of remedying excessive and organic ill. To a sensitive being, pity is not seldom pain. And when at last it is perceived that such pity cannot lead to effectual succor, common sense bids the soul be rid of it. What I saw that morning persuaded me that the scrivener was the victim of innate and incurable disorder. I might give alms to his body; but his body did not pain him; it was his soul that suffered, and his soul I could not reach.

I did not accomplish the purpose of going to Trinity Church that morning. Somehow, the things I had seen disqualified me for the time from church-going. I walked homeward, thinking what I would do with Bartleby. Finally, I resolved upon this:—I would put certain calm questions to him the next morning, touching his history, &c., and if he declined to answer them openly and unreservedly (and I supposed he would prefer not), then to give him a twenty dollar bill over and above whatever I might owe him, and tell him his services were no longer required; but that if in any other way I could assist him, I would be happy to do so, especially if he desired to return to his native place, wherever that might be, I would willingly help to defray the expenses. Moreover, if, after reaching home, he found himself at any time in want of aid, a letter from him would be sure of a reply.

The next morning came. 95

"Bartleby," said I, gently calling to him behind his screen.

No reply.

"Bartleby," said I, in a still gentler tone, "come here; I am not going to ask you to do anything you would prefer not to do—I simply wish to speak to you."

Upon this he noiselessly slid into view.

"Will you tell me, Bartleby, where you were born?"

"I would prefer not to."

"Will you tell me *anything* about yourself?"

"I would prefer not to."

"But what reasonable objection can you have to speak to me? I feel friendly towards you."

He did not look at me while I spoke, but kept his glance fixed upon my bust of Cicero, which, as I then sat, was directly behind me, some six inches above my head.

"What is your answer, Bartleby?" said I, after waiting a considerable time for a reply, during which his countenance remained immovable, only there was the faintest conceivable tremor of the white attenuated mouth.

"At present I prefer to give no answer," he said, and retired into his hermitage.

It was rather weak in me I confess, but his manner on this occasion nettled me. Not only did there seem to lurk in it a certain calm disdain, but his perverseness seemed ungrateful, considering the undeniable good usage and indulgence he had received from me.

Again I sat ruminating what I should do. Mortified as I was at his behavior, and resolved as I had been to dismiss him when I entered my office, nevertheless I strangely felt something superstitious knocking at my heart, and forbidding me to carry out my purpose, and denouncing me for a villain if I dared to breathe one bitter word against this forlornest of mankind. At last, familiarly drawing my chair behind his screen, I sat down and said: "Bartleby, never mind then about revealing your history; but let me entreat you, as a friend, to comply as far as may be with the usages of this office. Say now you will help to examine papers to-morrow or next day: in short, say now that in a day or two you will begin to be a little reasonable:— say so, Bartleby."

"At present I would prefer not to be a little reasonable," was his mildly cadaverous reply.

Just then the folding-doors opened, and Nippers approached. He seemed suffering from an unusually bad night's rest, induced by severer indigestion than common. He overheard those final words of Bartleby.

"*Prefer not*, eh?" gritted Nippers—"I'd *prefer* him, if I were you, sir," addressing me—"I'd *prefer* him; I'd give him preferences, the stubborn mule! What is it, sir, pray, that he *prefers* not to do now?"

Bartleby moved not a limb.

"Mr. Nippers," said I, "I'd prefer that you would withdraw for the present."

Somehow, of late I had got into the way of involuntarily using this word "prefer" upon all sorts of not exactly suitable occasions. And I trembled to think that my contact with the scrivener had already and seriously affected me in a mental way. And what further and deeper aberration might it not yet produce? This apprehension had not been without efficacy in determining me to summary means.

As Nippers, looking very sour and sulky, was departing, Turkey blandly and deferentially approached.

"With submission, sir," said he, "yesterday I was thinking about Bartleby here, and I think that if he would but prefer to take a quart of good ale every day, it would do much towards mending him, and enabling him to assist in examining his papers."

"So you have got the word too," said I, slightly excited.

"With submission, what word, sir," asked Turkey, respectfully crowding himself into the contracted space behind the screen, and by so doing, making me jostle the scrivener. "What word, sir?"

"I would prefer to be left alone here," said Bartleby, as if offended at being mobbed in his privacy.

"*That's* the word, Turkey," said I—"*that's* it."

"Oh, *prefer?* oh, yes—queer word. I never use it myself. But, sir, as I was saying, if he would but prefer—"

"Turkey," interrupted I, "you will please withdraw."

"Oh certainly, sir, if you prefer that I should."

As he opened the folding-door to retire, Nippers at his desk caught a glimpse of me, and asked whether I would prefer to have a certain paper copied on blue paper or white. He did not in the least roguishly accent the word prefer. It was plain that it involuntarily rolled from his tongue. I thought to myself, surely I must get rid of a demented man, who already has in some degree turned the tongues, if not the heads, of myself and clerks. But I thought it prudent not to break the dismission at once.

The next day I noticed that Bartleby did nothing but stand at his window in his dead-wall revery. Upon asking him why he did not write, he said that he had decided upon doing no more writing.

"Why, how now? what next?" exclaimed I, "do no more writing?"

"No more."

"And what is the reason?"

"Do you not see the reason for yourself," he indifferently replied.

I looked steadfastly at him, and perceived that his eyes looked dull and glazed. Instantly it occurred to me, that his unexampled diligence in copying by his dim window for the first few weeks of his stay with me might have temporarily impaired his vision.

I was touched. I said something in condolence with him. I hinted that of course he did wisely in abstaining from writing for a while, and urged him to embrace that opportunity of taking wholesome exercise in the open air. This, however, he did not do. A few days after this, my other clerks being absent, and being in a great hurry to dispatch certain letters by the mail, I thought that, having nothing else earthly to do, Bartleby would surely be less inflexible than usual, and carry these letters to the Post Office. But he blankly declined. So, much to my inconvenience, I went myself.

Still added days went by. Whether Bartleby's eyes improved or not, I could not say. To all appearance, I thought they did. But when I asked him if they did, he vouchsafed no answer. At all events, he would do no copying. At last, in reply to my urgings, he informed me that he had permanently given up copying.

"What!" exclaimed I; "suppose your eyes should get entirely well—better than ever before—would you not copy then?"

"I have given up copying," he answered and slid aside.

He remained as ever, a fixture in my chamber. Nay—if that were possible—he became still more of a fixture than before. What was to be done? He would do nothing in the office: why should he stay there? In plain fact, he had now become a millstone° to me, not only useless as a necklace, but afflictive to bear. Yet I was sorry for

----

millstone: figuratively, an unshakable stone around the neck; a burden.

him. I speak less than truth when I say that, on his own account, he occasioned me uneasiness. If he would but have named a single relative or friend, I would instantly have written, and urged their taking the poor fellow away to some convenient retreat. But he seemed alone, absolutely alone in the universe. A bit of wreckage in the mid-Atlantic. At length, necessities connected with my business tyrannized over all other considerations. Decently as I could, I told Bartleby that in six days' time he must unconditionally leave the office. I warned him to take measures, in the interval, for procuring some other abode. I offered to assist him in this endeavor, if he himself would but take the first step towards a removal. "And when you finally quit me, Bartleby," added I, "I shall see that you go away not entirely unprovided. Six days from this hour, remember."

At the expiration of that period, I peeped behind the screen, and lo! Bartleby was there.

I buttoned up my coat, balanced myself; advanced slowly towards him, touched his shoulder, and said, "The time has come; you must quit this place; I am sorry for you; here is money; but you must go."

"I would prefer not," he replied, with his back still towards me.

"You *must*."   140

He remained silent.

Now I had an unbounded confidence in this man's common honesty. He had frequently restored to me sixpences and shillings carelessly dropped upon the floor, for I am apt to be very reckless in such shirt-button affairs. The proceeding then which followed will not be deemed extraordinary.

"Bartleby," said I, "I owe you twelve dollars on account; here are thirty-two; the odd twenty are yours.—Will you take it?" and I handed the bills towards him.

But he made no motion.

"I will leave them here then," putting them under a weight on the table. Then taking my hat and cane and going to the door, I tranquilly turned and added—"After you have removed your things from these offices, Bartleby, you will of course lock the door—since every one is now gone for the day but you—and if you please, slip your key underneath the mat, so that I may have it in the morning. I shall not see you again; so good-bye to you. If hereafter in your new place of abode I can be of any service to you, do not fail to advise me by letter. Good-bye, Bartleby, and fare you well."   145

But he answered not a word; like the last column of some ruined temple, he remained standing mute and solitary in the middle of the otherwise deserted room.

As I walked home in a pensive mood, my vanity got the better of my pity. I could not but highly plume myself on my masterly management in getting rid of Bartleby. Masterly I call it, and such it must appear to any dispassionate thinker. The beauty of my procedure seemed to consist in its perfect quietness. There was no vulgar bullying, no bravado of any sort, no choleric hectoring, no striding to and fro across the apartment, jerking out vehement commands for Bartleby to bundle himself off with his beggarly traps.° Nothing of the kind. Without loudly bidding Bartleby depart—as an inferior genius might have done—I *assumed* the ground that depart he must; and upon that assumption built all I had to say. The more I thought over my procedure, the more I was charmed with it. Nevertheless, next morning, upon awakening, I had

---

traps: trappings, baggage.

my doubts,—I had somehow slept off the fumes of vanity. One of the coolest and wisest hours a man has, is just after he awakes in the morning. My procedure seemed as sagacious as ever,—but only in theory. How it would prove in practice—there was the rub. It was truly a beautiful thought to have assumed Bartleby's departure; but, after all, that assumption was simply my own, and none of Bartleby's. The great point was, not whether I had assumed that he would quit me, but whether he would prefer so to do. He was more a man of preferences than assumptions.

After breakfast, I walked down town, arguing the probabilities *pro* and *con*. One moment I thought it would prove a miserable failure, and Bartleby would be found all alive at my office as usual; the next moment it seemed certain that I should see his chair empty. And so I kept veering about. At the corner of Broadway and Canal Street, I saw quite an excited group of people standing in earnest conversation.

"I'll take odds he doesn't," said a voice as I passed.

"Doesn't go?—done!" said I, "put up your money." 150

I was instinctively putting my hand in my pocket to produce my own, when I remembered that this was an election day. The words I had overheard bore no reference to Bartleby, but to the success or non-success of some candidate for the mayoralty. In my intent frame of mind, I had, as it were, imagined that all Broadway shared in my excitement, and were debating the same question with me. I passed on, very thankful that the uproar of the street screened my momentary absent-mindedness.

As I had intended, I was earlier than usual at my office door. I stood listening for a moment. All was still. He must be gone. I tried the knob. The door was locked. Yes, my procedure had worked to a charm; he indeed must be vanished. Yet a certain melancholy mixed with this: I was almost sorry for my brilliant success. I was fumbling under the door mat for the key, which Bartleby was to have left there for me, when accidentally my knee knocked against a panel, producing a summoning sound, and in response a voice came to me from within—"Not yet; I am occupied."

It was Bartleby.

I was thunderstruck. For an instant I stood like the man who, pipe in month, was killed one cloudless afternoon long ago in Virginia, by summer lightning; at his own warm open window he was killed, and remained leaning out there upon the dreamy afternoon, till some one touched him, and he fell.

"Not gone!" I murmured at last. But again obeying that wondrous ascendancy which the inscrutable scrivener had over me—and from which ascendancy, for all my chafing, I could not completely escape—I slowly went down stairs and out into the street, and while walking round the block, considered what I should next do in this unheard-of perplexity. Turn the man out by an actual thrusting I could not; to drive him away by calling him hard names would not do; calling in the police was an unpleasant idea; and yet, permit him to enjoy his cadaverous triumph over me,—this too I could not think of. What was to be done? or, if nothing could be done, was there anything further that I could *assume* in the matter? Yes, as before I had prospectively assumed that Bartleby would depart, so now I might retrospectively assume that departed he was. In the legitimate carrying out of this assumption, I might enter my office in a great hurry, and pretending not to see Bartleby at all, walk straight against him as if he were air. Such a proceeding would in a singular degree have the appearance of a home-thrust.° It was hardly possible that

---

home-thrust: fatal or devastating blow.

Bartleby could withstand such an application of the doctrine of assumptions. But, upon second thought, the success of the plan seemed rather dubious. I resolved to argue the matter over with him again. 155

"Bartleby," said I, entering the office, with a quietly severe expression, "I am seriously displeased. I am pained, Bartleby. I had thought better of you. I had imagined you of such a gentlemanly organization, that in any delicate dilemma a slight hint would suffice—in short, an assumption. But it appears I am deceived. Why," I added, unaffectedly starting, "you have not even touched that money yet," pointing to it, just where I had left it the evening previous.

He answered nothing.

"Will you, or will you not, quit me?" I now demanded in a sudden passion, advancing close to him.

"I would prefer *not* to quit you," he replied, gently emphasizing the *not*.

"What earthly right have you to stay here? Do you pay any rent? Do you pay my taxes? Or is this property yours?" 160

He answered nothing.

"Are you ready to go on and write now? Are your eyes recovered? Could you copy a small paper for me this morning? or help examine a few lines? or step round to the Post Office? In a word, will you do any thing at all, to give a colouring to your refusal to depart the premises?"

He silently retired into his hermitage.

I was now in such a state of nervous resentment that I thought it but prudent to check myself, at present, from further demonstrations. Bartleby and I were alone. I remembered the tragedy of the unfortunate Adams and the still more unfortunate Colt° in the solitary office of the latter; and how poor Colt, being dreadfully incensed by Adams, and imprudently permitting himself to get wildly excited, was at unawares hurried into his fatal act—an act which certainly no man could possibly deplore more than the actor himself. Often it had occurred to me in my ponderings upon the subject, that had that altercation taken place in the public street, or at a private residence, it would not have terminated as it did. It was the circumstance of being alone in a solitary office, upstairs, of a building entirely unhallowed by humanizing domestic associations—an uncarpeted office, doubtless, of a dusty, haggard sort of appearance;—this it must have been, which greatly helped to enhance the irritable desperation of the hapless Colt.

But when this old Adam° of resentment rose in me and tempted me concerning Bartleby, I grappled him and threw him. How? Why, simply by recalling the divine injunction: "A new commandment give I unto you, that ye love one another." Yes, this it was that saved me. Aside from higher considerations, charity often operates as a vastly wise and prudent principle—a great safeguard to its possessor. Men have committed murder for jealousy's sake, and anger's sake, and hatred's sake, and selfishness' sake, and spiritual pride's sake; but no man that ever I heard of, ever committed a diabolical murder for sweet charity's sake. Mere self-interest, then, if no better motive can be enlisted, should, especially with high-tempered men, prompt all beings to charity and philanthropy. At any rate, upon the occasion in question, I strove to drown my exasperated feelings towards the scrivener by benev-

---

Adams . . . Colt: in a newsworthy brawl of the 1840s, Colt inadvertently killed Adams with a blow to the head.
Adam: Biblical originator of sinful temptation.

olently constructing his conduct. Poor fellow, poor fellow! thought I, he doesn't mean any thing; and besides, he has seen hard times, and ought to be indulged.

I endeavored also immediately to occupy myself, and at the same time to comfort my despondency. I tried to fancy that in the course of the morning, at such time as might prove agreeable to him, Bartleby, of his own free accord, would emerge from his hermitage, and take up some decided line of march in the direction of the door. But no. Half-past twelve o'clock came; Turkey began to glow in the face, overturn his inkstand, and become generally obstreperous; Nippers abated down into quietude and courtesy; Ginger Nut munched his noon apple; and Bartleby remained standing at his window in one of his profoundest dead-wall reveries. Will it be credited? Ought I to acknowledge it? That afternoon I left the office without saying one further word to him.

Some days now passed, during which, at leisure intervals I looked a little into "Edwards on the Will," and "Priestley on Necessity."° Under the circumstances, those books induced a salutary feeling. Gradually I slid into the persuasion that these troubles of mine, touching the scrivener, had been all predestinated from eternity, and Bartleby was billeted upon me for some mysterious purpose of an all-wise Providence, which it was not for a mere mortal like me to fathom. Yes, Bartleby, stay there behind your screen, thought I; I shall persecute you no more; you are harmless and noiseless as any of these old chairs; in short, I never feel so private as when I know you are here. At least I see it, I feel it; I penetrate to the predestinated purpose of my life. I am content. Others may have loftier parts to enact; but my mission in this world, Bartleby, is to furnish you with office-room for such period as you may see fit to remain.

I believe that this wise and blessed frame of mind would have continued with me, had it not been for the unsolicited and uncharitable remarks obtruded upon me by my professional friends who visited the rooms. But thus it often is, that the constant friction of illiberal minds wears out at last the best resolves of the more generous. Though to be sure, when I reflected upon it, it was not strange that people entering my office should be struck by the peculiar aspect of the unaccountable Bartleby, and so be tempted to throw out some sinister observations concerning him. Sometimes an attorney having business with me, and calling at my office, and finding no one but the scrivener there, would undertake to obtain some sort of precise information from him touching my whereabouts; but without heeding his idle talk, Bartleby would remain standing immovable in the middle of the room. So, after contemplating him in that position for a time, the attorney would depart, no wiser than he came.

Also, when a Reference° was going on, and the room full of lawyers and witnesses and business was driving fast, some deeply occupied legal gentleman present, seeing Bartleby wholly unemployed, would request him to run round to his (the legal gentleman's) office and fetch some papers for him. Thereupon, Bartleby would tranquilly decline, and yet remain idle as before. Then the lawyer would give a great stare, and turn to me. And what could I say? At last I was made aware that all through the circle of my professional acquaintance, a whisper of wonder was running round, having reference to the strange creature I kept at my office. This wor-

---

Edwards . . . Priestley: early sermonizers on predestination and God's will.
Reference: lawyers' conference.

ried me very much. And as the idea came upon me of his possibly turning out a long-lived man, and keep occupying my chambers, and denying my authority; and perplexing my visitors; and scandalizing my professional reputation; and casting a general gloom over the premises; keeping soul and body together to the last upon his savings (for doubtless he spent but half a dime a day), and in the end perhaps outlive me, and claim possession of my office by right of his perpetual occupancy: as all these dark anticipations crowded upon me more and more, and my friends continually intruded their relentless remarks upon the apparition in my room, a great change was wrought in me. I resolved to gather all my faculties together, and for ever rid me of this intolerable incubus.°

Ere revolving any complicated project, however, adapted to this end, I first simply suggested to Bartleby the propriety of his permanent departure. In a calm and serious tone, I commended the idea to his careful and mature consideration. But having taken three days to meditate upon it, he apprised me that his original determination remained the same; in short, that he still preferred to abide with me.　170

What shall I do? I now said to myself, buttoning up my coat to the last button. What shall I do? what ought I to do? what does conscience say I *should* do with this man, or rather ghost? Rid myself of him, I must; go, he shall. But how? You will not thrust him, the poor, pale, passive mortal—you will not thrust such a helpless creature out of your door? you will not dishonour yourself by such cruelty? No, I will not, I cannot do that. Rather would I let him live and die here, and then mason up his remains in the wall. What then will you do? For all your coaxing, he will not budge. Bribes he leaves under your own paper-weight on your table; in short, it is quite plain that he prefers to cling to you.

Then something severe, something unusual must be done. What! surely you will not have him collared by a constable, and commit his innocent pallor to the common jail? And upon what ground could you procure such a thing to be done?—a vagrant, is he? What! he a vagrant, a wanderer, who refuses to budge? It is because he will *not* be a vagrant, then, that you seek to count him *as* a vagrant. That is too absurd. No visible means of support: there I have him. Wrong again: for indubitably he *does* support himself, and that is the only unanswerable proof that any man can show of his possessing the means so to do. No more then. Since he will not quit me, I must quit him. I will change my offices; I will move elsewhere; and give him fair notice, that if I find him on my new premises I will then proceed against him as a common trespasser.

Acting accordingly, next day I thus addressed him: "I find these chambers too far from the City Hall; the air is unwholesome. In a word, I propose to remove my offices next week, and shall no longer require your services. I tell you this now, in order that you may seek another place."

He made no reply, and nothing more was said.

On the appointed day I engaged carts and men, proceeded to my chambers, and having but little furniture, every thing was removed in a few hours. Throughout all, the scrivener remained standing behind the screen, which I directed to be removed the last thing. It was withdrawn; and being folded up like a huge folio, left him the motionless occupant of a naked room. I stood in the entry watching him a moment, while something from within me upbraided me.　175

---

incubus: parasitic monster.

I re-entered, with my hand in my pocket—and—and my heart in my mouth.

"Good-bye, Bartleby; I am going—good-bye, and God some way bless you; and take that," slipping something in his hand. But it dropped upon the floor, and then—strange to say—I tore myself from him whom I had so longed to be rid of.

Established in my new quarters, for a day or two I kept the door locked, and started at every footfall in the passages. When I returned to my rooms after any little absence, I would pause at the threshold for an instant, and attentively listen, ere applying my key. But these fears were needless. Bartleby never came nigh me.

I thought all was going well, when a perturbed looking stranger visited me, inquiring whether I was the person who had recently occupied rooms at No. ____ Wall-street.

Full of forebodings, I replied that I was.   180

"Then sir," said the stranger, who proved a lawyer, "you are responsible for the man you left there. He refuses to do any copying, he refuses to do any thing; he says he prefers not to; and he refuses to quit the premises."

"I am very sorry, sir," said I, with assumed tranquillity, but an inward tremor, "but, really, the man you allude to is nothing to me—he is no relation or apprentice of mine, that you should hold me responsible for him."

"In mercy's name, who is he?"

"I certainly cannot inform you. I know nothing about him. Formerly I employed him as a copyist; but he has done nothing for me now for some time past."

"I shall settle him then,—good morning, sir."   185

Several days passed, and I heard nothing more; and though I often felt a charitable prompting to call at the place and see poor Bartleby, yet a certain squeamishness of I know not what withheld me.

All is over with him, by this time, thought I at last, when through another week no further intelligence reached me. But coming to my room the day after, I found several persons waiting at my door in a high state of nervous excitement.

"That's the man—here he comes," cried the foremost one, whom I recognized as the lawyer who had previously called upon me alone.

"You must take him away, sir, at once," cried a portly person among them, advancing upon me, and whom I knew to be the landlord of No. ____ Wall-street. "These gentlemen, my tenants, cannot stand it any longer; Mr. B ____," pointing to the lawyer, "has turned him out of his room, and he now persists in haunting the building generally, sitting upon the banisters of the stairs by day, and sleeping in the entry by night. Everybody is concerned; clients are leaving the offices; some fears are entertained of a mob; something you must do, and that without delay."

Aghast at this torrent, I fell back before it, and would fain have locked myself in my new quarters. In vain I persisted that Bartleby was nothing to me—no more than to any one else. In vain:—I was the last person known to have anything to do with him, and they held me to the terrible account. Fearful then of being exposed in the papers (as one person present obscurely threatened) I considered the matter, and at length said, that if the lawyer would give me a confidential interview with the scrivener, in his (the lawyer's) own room, I would that afternoon strive my best to rid them of the nuisance they complained of.   190

Going up stairs to my old haunt, there was Bartleby silently sitting upon the banister at the landing.

"What are you doing here, Bartleby?" said I.

"Sitting upon the banister," he mildly replied.

I motioned him into the lawyer's room, who then left us.

"Bartleby," said I, "are you aware that you are the cause of great tribulation to me, by persisting in occupying the entry after being dismissed from the office?" 195

No answer.

"Now one of two things must take place. Either you must do something, or something must be done to you. Now what sort of business would you like to engage in? Would you like to re-engage in copying for some one?"

"No; I would prefer not to make any change."

"Would you like a clerkship in a dry-goods store?"

"There is too much confinement about that. No, I would not like a clerkship; but I am not particular." 200

"Too much confinement," I cried, "why you keep yourself confined all the time!"

"I would prefer not to take a clerkship," he rejoined, as if to settle that little item at once.

"How would a bar tender's business suit you? There is no trying of the eyesight in that."

"I would not like it at all; though, as I said before, I am not particular."

His unwonted wordiness inspirited me. I returned to the charge. 205

"Well then, would you like to travel through the country collecting bills for the merchants? That would improve your health."

"No, I would prefer to be doing something else."

"How then would going as a companion to Europe to entertain some young gentleman with your conversation,—how would that suit you?"

"Not at all. It does not strike me that there is anything definite about that. I like to be stationary. But I am not particular."

"Stationary you shall be then," I cried, now losing all patience, and for the first time in all my exasperating connection with him fairly flying into a passion. "If you do not go away from these premises before night, I shall feel bound—indeed I *am* bound—to—to—to quit the premises myself!" I rather absurdly concluded, knowing not with what possible threat to try to frighten his immobility into compliance. Despairing of all further efforts, I was precipitately leaving him, when a final thought occurred to me—one which had not been wholly unindulged before. 210

"Bartleby," said I, in the kindest tone I could assume under such exciting circumstances, "will you go home with me now—not to my office, but my dwelling—and remain there till we can conclude upon some convenient arrangement for you at our leisure? Come, let us start now, right away."

"No: at present I would prefer not to make any change at all."

I answered nothing; but effectually dodging every one by the suddenness and rapidity of my flight, rushed from the building, ran up Wall street towards Broadway, and jumping into the first omnibus was soon removed from pursuit. As soon as tranquillity returned I distinctly perceived that I had now done all that I possibly could, both in respect to the demands of the landlord and his tenants, and with regard to my own desire and sense of duty, to benefit Bartleby, and shield him from rude persecution. I now strove to be entirely care-free and quiescent; and my conscience justified me in the attempt; though indeed it was not so successful as I could have wished. So fearful was I of being again hunted out by the incensed landlord and his exasperated tenants, that, surrendering my business to Nippers, for a few days I drove about the upper part of the town and through the suburbs, in my rockaway;° crossed over to Jersey City and Hoboken, and paid fugitive visits to Manhattanville and Astoria. In fact I almost lived in my rockaway for the time.

When again I entered my office, lo, a note from the landlord lay upon the desk. I opened it with trembling hands. It informed me that the writer had sent to the police, and had Bartleby removed to the Tombs° as a vagrant. Moreover, since I knew more about him than any one else, he wished me to appear at that place, and make a suitable statement of the facts. These tidings had a conflicting effect upon me. At first I was indignant; but at last almost approved. The landlord's energetic, summary disposition had led him to adopt a procedure which I do not think I would have decided upon myself; and yet as a last resort, under such peculiar circumstances, it seemed the only plan.

As I afterwards learned, the poor scrivener, when told that he must be conducted to the Tombs, offered not the slightest obstacle, but in his pale, unmoving way silently acquiesced. 215

Some of the compassionate and curious bystanders joined the party; and headed by one of the constables, arm in arm with Bartleby the silent procession filed its way through all the noise, and heat, and joy of the roaring thoroughfares at noon.

The same day I received the note I went to the Tombs, or, to speak more properly, the Halls of Justice. Seeking the right officer, I stated the purpose of my call, and was informed that the individual I described was indeed within. I then assured the functionary that Bartleby was a perfectly honest man, and greatly to be a compassionated, (however unaccountable) eccentric. I narrated all I knew, and closed by suggesting the idea of letting him remain in as indulgent confinement as possible till something less harsh might be done—though indeed I hardly knew what. At all events, if nothing else could be decided upon, the alms-house must receive him. I then begged to have an interview.

Being under no disgraceful charge, and quite serene and harmless in all his ways, they had permitted him freely to wander about the prison, and especially in the inclosed grass-platted yards thereof. And so I found him there, standing all alone in the quietest of the yards, his face towards a high wall—while all around, from the narrow slits of the jail windows, I thought I saw peering out upon him the eyes of murderers and thieves.

"Bartleby!"

"I know you," he said, without looking round,—"and I want nothing to say to you." 220

"It was not I that brought you here, Bartleby," said I, keenly pained at his implied suspicion. "And to you, this should not be so vile a place. Nothing reproachful attaches to you by being here. And see, it is not so sad a place as one might think. Look, there is the sky and here is the grass."

"I know where I am," he replied, but would say nothing more, and so I left him.

As I entered the corridor again, a broad, meat-like man, in an apron, accosted me, and jerking his thumb over his shoulder said—"Is that your friend?"

"Yes."

_____

rockaway: small carriage.
Tombs: New York jail.

"Does he want to starve? If he does, let him live on the prison fare, that's all." 225

"Who are you?" asked I, not knowing what to make of such an unofficially speaking person in such a place.

"I am the grub-man. Such gentlemen as have friends here, hire me to provide them with something good to eat."

"Is this so?" said I, turning to the turnkey.

He said it was.

"Well then," said I, slipping some silver into the grub-man's hands (for so they called him), "I want you to give particular attention to my friend there; let him have the best dinner you can get. And you must be as polite to him as possible." 230

"Introduce me, will you?" said the grub-man, looking at me with an expression which seemed to say he was all impatience for an opportunity to give a specimen of his breeding.

Thinking it would prove of benefit to the scrivener, I acquiesced; and asking the grub-man his name, went up with him to Bartleby.

"Bartleby, this is Mr. Cutlets; you will find him very useful to you."

"Your sarvant, sir, your sarvant," said the grub-man, making a low salutation behind his apron. "Hope you find it pleasant here, sir;—spacious grounds—cool apartments, sir—hope you'll stay with us some time—try to make it agreeable. May Mrs. Cutlets and I have the pleasure of your company to dinner, sir, in Mrs. Cutlets' private room?"

"I prefer not to dine to-day," said Bartleby, turning away. "It would disagree with me; I am unused to dinners." So saying, he slowly moved to the other side of the inclosure and took up a position fronting the dead-wall. 235

"How's this?" said the grub-man, addressing me with a stare of astonishment. "He's odd, aint he?"

"I think he is a little deranged," said I, sadly.

"Deranged? deranged is it? Well now, upon my word, I thought that friend of yourn was a gentleman forger; they are always pale and genteel-like, them forgers. I can't help pity 'em—can't help it, sir. Did you know Monroe Edwards?" he added touchingly, and paused. Then, laying his hand pityingly on my shoulder, sighed, "he died of consumption at Sing-Sing.° So you weren't acquainted with Monroe?"

"No, I was never socially acquainted with any forgers. But I cannot stop longer. Look to my friend yonder. You will not lose by it. I will see you again."

Some few days after this, I again obtained admission to the Tombs, and went through the corridors in quest of Bartleby; but without finding him. 240

"I saw him coming from his cell not long ago," said a turnkey, "maybe he's gone to loiter in the yards."

So I went in that direction.

"Are you looking for the silent man?" said another turnkey passing me. "Yonder he lies—sleeping in the yard there. 'Tis not twenty minutes since I saw him lie down."

The yard was entirely quiet. It was not accessible to the common prisoners. The surrounding walls, of amazing thickness, kept off all sounds behind them. The Egyptian character of the masonry weighed upon me with its gloom. But a soft imprisoned turf grew under foot. The heart of the eternal pyramids, it seemed, wherein, by some strange magic, through the clefts grass-seed, dropped by birds, had sprung.

Sing-Sing: a state prison.

Strangely huddled at the base of the wall—his knees drawn up, and lying on his side, his head touching the cold stones—I saw the wasted Bartleby. But nothing stirred. I paused; then went close up to him; stooped over, and saw that his dim eyes were open; otherwise he seemed profoundly sleeping. Something prompted me to touch him. I felt his hand, when a tingling shiver ran up my arm and down my spine to my feet. 245

The round face of the grub-man peered upon me now. "His dinner is ready. Won't he dine to-day, either? Or does he live without dining?"

"Lives without dining," said I, and closed the eyes.

"Eh!—He's asleep, ain't he?"

"With kings and counsellors," murmured I.

There would seem little need for proceeding further in this history. Imagination will readily supply the meagre recital of poor Bartleby's interment. But ere parting with the reader, let me say, that if this little narrative has sufficiently interested him, to awaken curiosity as to who Bartleby was, and what manner of life he led prior to the present narrator's making his acquaintance, I can only reply, that in such curiosity I fully share—but am wholly unable to gratify it. Yet here I hardly know whether I should divulge one little item of rumour, which came to my ear a few months after the scrivener's decease. Upon what basis it rested, I could never ascertain; and hence, how true it is I cannot now tell. But inasmuch as this vague report has not been without a certain strange suggestive interest to me, however sad, it may prove the same with some others; and so I will briefly mention it. The report was this: that Bartleby had been a subordinate clerk in the Dead Letter Office° at Washington, from which he had been suddenly removed by a change in the administration. When I think over this rumor I cannot adequately express the emotions which seize me. Dead letters! Does it not sound like dead men? Conceive a man by nature and misfortune prone to a pallid hopelessness: can any business seem more fitted to heighten it than that of continually handling these dead letters, and assorting them for the flames? For by the cart-load they are annually burned. Sometimes from out the folded paper the pale clerk takes a ring:—the finger it was meant for, perhaps, moulders in the grave; a bank-note sent in swiftest charity:—he whom it would relieve, nor eats nor hungers any more; pardon for those who died despairing; hope for those who died unhoping; good tidings for those who died stifled by unrelieved calamities. On errands of life, these letters speed to death.

Ah Bartleby! Ah humanity! 250

Kate Chopin (1851–1904)

Kate Chopin has come to be revered in recent years as an important early champion of feminist consciousness. While her avowed master was Maupassant, whose work she translated, she was able to inflect his more neutral clearsightedness with a decidedly critical slant. As "The Story of an Hour" demonstrates with such economy, Chopin's primary interest was in tracing a woman's emotional

---

Dead Letter Office: depot for unclaimed U.S. mail

life. Her best-known work, the novel *The Awakening* (1899), was seen as shocking in its day. Few writers—certainly no women—had treated the theme of adultery with such candor. Chopin's other works include *Bayou Folk* (1894) and *A Night in Arcadie* (1897), both story collections.

Though born in St. Louis, Chopin spent many years in Louisiana. After her husband, a cotton broker, died in 1882, she moved back to St. Louis with her six children. The public outcry surrounding *The Awakening* embittered her and all but silenced her writing for the last years of her life.

THE STORY OF AN HOUR

Knowing that Mrs. Mallard was afflicted with a heart trouble, great care was taken to break to her as gently as possible the news of her husband's death.

It was her sister Josephine who told her, in broken sentences; veiled hints that revealed in half concealing. Her husband's friend Richards was there, too, near her. It was he who had been in the newspaper office when intelligence of the railroad disaster was received, with Brently Mallard's name leading the list of "killed." He had only taken the time to assure himself of its truth by a second telegram, and had hastened to forestall any less careful, less tender friend in bearing the sad message.

She did not hear the story as many women have heard the same, with a paralyzed inability to accept its significance. She wept at once, with sudden, wild abandonment, in her sister's arms. When the storm of grief had spent itself she went away to her room alone. She would have no one follow her.

There stood, facing the open window, a comfortable, roomy armchair. Into this she sank, pressed down by a physical exhaustion that haunted her body and seemed to reach into her soul.

She could see in the open square before her house the tops of trees that were all aquiver with the new spring life. The delicious breath of rain was in the air. In the street below a peddler was crying his wares. The notes of a distant song which some one was singing reached her faintly, and countless sparrows were twittering in the eaves.

5

There were patches of blue sky showing here and there through the clouds that had met and piled one above the other in the west facing her window.

She sat with her head thrown back upon the cushion of the chair, quite motionless, except when a sob came up into her throat and shook her, as a child who had cried itself to sleep continues to sob in its dreams.

She was young, with a fair, calm face, whose lines bespoke repression and even a certain strength. But now there was a dull stare in her eyes, whose gaze was fixed away off yonder on one of those patches of blue sky. It was not a glance of reflection, but rather indicated a suspension of intelligent thought.

There was something coming to her and she was waiting for it, fearfully. What was it? She did not know; it was too subtle and elusive to name. But she felt it, creeping out of the sky, reaching toward her through the sounds, the scents, the color that filled the air.

Now her bosom rose and fell tumultuously. She was beginning to recognize this thing that was approaching to possess her, and she was striving to beat it back with her will—as powerless as her two white slender hands would have been.   10

When she abandoned herself a little whispered word escaped her slightly parted lips. She said it over and over under her breath: "free, free, free!" The vacant stare and the look of terror that had followed it went from her eyes. They stayed keen and bright. Her pulses beat fast, and the coursing blood warmed and relaxed every inch of her body.

She did not stop to ask if it were or were not a monstrous joy that held her. A clear and exalted perception enabled her to dismiss the suggestion as trivial.

She knew that she would weep again when she saw the kind, tender hands folded in death; the face that had never looked save with love upon her, fixed and gray and dead. But she saw beyond that bitter moment a long procession of years to come that would belong to her absolutely. And she opened and spread her arms out to them in welcome.

There would be no one to live for her during those coming years: she would live for herself. There would be no powerful will bending hers in that blind persistence with which men and women believe they have a right to impose a private will upon a fellow-creature. A kind intention or a cruel intention made the act seem no less a crime as she looked upon it in that brief moment of illumination.

And yet she had loved him—sometimes. Often she had not. What did it matter! What could love, the unsolved mystery, count for in face of this possession of self-assertion which she suddenly recognized as the strongest impulse of her being!   15

"Free! Body and soul free!" she kept whispering.

Josephine was kneeling before the closed door with her lips to the keyhole, imploring for admission. "Louise, open the door! I beg; open the door—you will make yourself ill. What are you doing, Louise? For heaven's sake open the door."

"Go away. I am not making myself ill." No; she was drinking in a very elixir of life through that open window.

Her fancy was running riot along those days ahead of her. Spring days, and summer days, and all sorts of days that would be her own. She breathed a quick prayer that life might be long. It was only yesterday she had thought with a shudder that life might be long.

She arose at length and opened the door to her sister's importunities. There was a feverish triumph in her eyes, and she carried herself unwittingly like a goddess of Victory. She clasped her sister's waist, and together they descended the stairs. Richards stood waiting for them at the bottom.   20

Some one was opening the front door with a latchkey. It was Brently Mallard who entered, a little travel-stained, composedly carrying his gripsack and umbrella. He had been far from the scene of accident, and did not even know there had been one. He stood amazed at Josephine's piercing cry; at Richards' quick motion to screen him from the view of his wife.

But Richards was too late.

When the doctors came they said she had died of heart disease—of joy that kills.

Charlotte Perkins Gilman
(1860–1935)

Charlotte Perkins Gilman was born in Hartford, Connecticut. A grandniece of the author Harriet Beecher Stowe, she attended the Rhode Island School of Design and later worked as a commercial artist. Married in 1884, Gilman left her husband four years later. During this period, Gilman had a severe nervous breakdown, which forms the partial subject of her best-known work, "The Yellow Wallpaper."

Gilman wrote voluminously in various genres, producing poetry, autobiography, and political and feminist tracts, which include *Concerning Children* (1900) and *Human Work* (1904). She also lectured widely and, from 1909 to 1917, published her own journal, the *Forerunner*, to which she contributed many articles exploring the problematic relations between the sexes. In 1935, suffering from cancer, Gilman took her own life.

THE YELLOW WALLPAPER

It is very seldom that mere ordinary people like John and myself secure ancestral halls for the summer.

A colonial mansion, a hereditary estate, I would say a haunted house and reach the height of romantic felicity—but that would be asking too much of fate!

Still, I will proudly declare that there is something queer about it.

Else, why should it be let so cheaply? And why have stood so long untenanted?

John laughs at me, of course, but one expects that. 5

John is practical in the extreme. He has no patience with faith, an intense horror of superstition, and he scoffs openly at any talk of things not to be felt and seen and put down in figures.

John is a physician, and *perhaps*—(I would not say it to a living soul, of course, but this is dead paper and a great relief to my mind)—*perhaps* that is one reason I do not get well faster.

You see, he does not believe I am sick! And what can one do?

If a physician of high standing, and one's own husband, assures friends and relatives that there is really nothing the matter with one but temporary nervous depression—a slight hysterical tendency—what is one to do?

My brother is also a physician, and also of high standing, and he says the same thing. 10

So I take phosphates or phosphites—whichever it is—and tonics, and air and exercise, and journeys, and am absolutely forbidden to "work" until I am well again.

Personally, I disagree with their ideas.

Personally, I believe that congenial work, with excitement and change, would do me good.

But what is one to do?

I did write for a while in spite of them; but it *does* exhaust me a good deal—having to be so sly about it, or else meet with heavy opposition.

I sometimes fancy that in my condition, if I had less opposition and more society and stimulus—but John says the very worst thing I can do is to think about my condition, and I confess it always makes me feel bad.

So I will let it alone and talk about the house.

The most beautiful place! It is quite alone, standing well back from the road, quite three miles from the village. It makes me think of English places that you read about, for there are hedges and walls and gates that lock, and lots of separate little houses for the gardeners and people.

There is a *delicious* garden! I never saw such a garden—large and shady, full of box-bordered paths, and lined with long grape-covered arbors with seats under them.

There were greenhouses, but they are all broken now.

There was some legal trouble, I believe, something about the heirs and co-heirs; anyhow, the place has been empty for years.

That spoils my ghostliness, I am afraid, but I don't care—there is something strange about the house—I can feel it.

I even said so to John one midnight evening, but he said what I felt was a draught, and shut the window.

I get so unreasonably angry with John sometimes. I'm sure I never used to be so sensitive. I think it is due to this nervous condition.

But John says if I feel so I shall neglect proper self-control; so I take pains to control myself—before him, at least, and that makes me very tired.

I don't like our room a bit. I wanted one downstairs that opened into the piazza and had roses all over the window, and such pretty old-fashioned chintz hangings! But John would not hear of it.

He said there was only one window and not room for two beds, and no near room for him if he took another.

He is very careful and loving, and hardly lets me stir without special direction.

I have a schedule prescription of each hour in the day; he takes all care from me, and so I feel basely ungrateful not to value it more.

He said he came here solely on my account, that I was to have perfect rest and all the air I could get. "Your exercise depends on your strength, my dear," said he, "and your food somewhat on your appetite; but air you can absorb all the time." So we took the nursery at the top of the house.

It is a big, airy room, the whole floor nearly, with windows that look all ways, and air and sunshine galore. It was nursery first, and then play-room and gymnasium, I should judge, for the windows are barred for little children, and there are rings and things in the walls.

The paint and paper look as if a boys' school had used it. It is stripped off—the paper—in great patches all around the head of my bed, about as far as I can reach, and in a great place on the other side of the room low down. I never saw a worse paper in my life. One of those sprawling, flamboyant patterns committing every artistic sin.

It is dull enough to confuse the eye in following, pronounced enough constantly to irritate and provoke study, and when you follow the lame uncertain curves for a

15

20

25

30

little distance they suddenly commit suicide—plunge off at outrageous angles, destroy themselves in unheard-of contradictions.

The color is repellent, almost revolting: a smoldering unclean yellow, strangely faded by the slow-turning sunlight. It is a dull yet lurid orange in some places, a sickly sulphur tint in others.

No wonder the children hated it! I should hate it myself if I had to live in this room long. 35

There comes John, and I must put this away—he hates to have me write a word.

We have been here two weeks, and I haven't felt like writing before, since that first day.

I am sitting by the window now, up in this atrocious nursery, and there is nothing to hinder my writing as much as I please, save lack of strength.

John is away all day, and even some nights when his cases are serious.

I am glad my case is not serious! 40

But these nervous troubles are dreadfully depressing.

John does not know how much I really suffer. He knows there is no reason to suffer, and that satisfies him.

Of course it is only nervousness. It does weigh on me so not to do my duty in any way!

I meant to be such a help to John, such a real rest and comfort, and here I am a comparative burden already!

Nobody would believe what an effort it is to do what little I am able—to dress and entertain, and order things. 45

It is fortunate Mary is so good with the baby. Such a dear baby!

And yet I *cannot* be with him, it makes me so nervous.

I suppose John never was nervous in his life. He laughs at me so about this wallpaper!

At first he meant to repaper the room, but afterward he said that I was letting it get the better of me, and that nothing was worse for a nervous patient than to give way to such fancies.

He said that after the wallpaper was changed it would be the heavy bedstead, and then the barred windows, and then that gate at the head of the stairs, and so on. 50

"You know the place is doing you good," he said, "and really, dear, I don't care to renovate the house just for a three months' rental."

"Then do let us go downstairs," I said. "There are such pretty rooms there."

Then he took me in his arms and called me a blessed little goose, and said he would go down cellar, if I wished, and have it whitewashed into the bargain.

But he is right enough about the beds and windows and things.

It is as airy and comfortable a room as anyone need wish, and, of course, I would not be so silly as to make him uncomfortable just for a whim. 55

I'm really getting fond of the big room, all but that horrid paper.

Out of one window I can see the garden—those mysterious deep-shaded arbors, the riotous old-fashioned flowers, and bushes and gnarly trees.

Out of another I get a lovely view of the bay and a little private wharf belonging to the estate. There is a beautiful shaded lane that runs down there from the house. I always fancy I see people walking in these numerous paths and arbors, but

John has cautioned me not to give way to fancy in the least. He says that with my imaginative power and habit of story-making, a nervous weakness like mine is sure to lead to all manner of excited fancies, and that I ought to use my will and good sense to check the tendency. So I try.

I think sometimes that if I were only well enough to write a little it would relieve the press of ideas and rest me.

But I find I get pretty tired when I try. 60

It is so discouraging not to have any advice and companionship about my work. When I get really well, John says we will ask Cousin Henry and Julia down for a long visit; but he says he would as soon put fireworks in my pillow-case as to let me have those stimulating people about now.

I wish I could get well faster.

But I must not think about that. This paper looks to me as if it *knew* what a vicious influence it had!

There is a recurrent spot where the pattern lolls like a broken neck and two bulbous eyes stare at you upside down.

I get positively angry with the impertinence of it and the everlastingness. Up and down and sideways they crawl, and those absurd unblinking eyes are everywhere. There is one place where two breadths didn't match, and the eyes go all up and down the line, one a little higher than the other. 65

I never saw so much expression in an inanimate thing before, and we all know how much expression they have! I used to lie awake as a child and get more entertainment and terror out of blank walls and plain furniture than most children could find in a toy-store.

I remember what a kindly wink the knobs of our big old bureau used to have, and there was one chair that always seemed like a strong friend.

I used to feel that if any of the other things looked too fierce I could always hop into that chair and be safe.

The furniture in this room is no worse than inharmonious, however, for we had to bring it all from downstairs. I suppose when this was used as a playroom they had to take the nursery things out, and no wonder! I never saw such ravages as the children have made here.

The wallpaper, as I said before, is torn off in spots, and it sticketh closer than a brother—they must have had perseverance as well as hatred. 70

Then the floor is scratched and gouged and splintered, the plaster itself is dug out here and there, and this great heavy bed, which is all we found in the room, looks as if it had been through the wars.

But I don't mind it a bit—only the paper.

There comes John's sister. Such a dear girl as she is, and so careful of me! I must not let her find me writing.

She is a perfect and enthusiastic housekeeper, and hopes for no better profession. I verily believe she thinks it is the writing which makes me sick!

But I can write when she is out, and see her a long way off from these windows. 75

There is one that commands the road, a lovely shaded winding road, and one that just looks off over the country. A lovely country, too, full of great elms and velvet meadows.

This wallpaper has a kind of subpattern in a different shade, a particularly irritating one, for you can only see it in certain lights, and not clearly then.

A Fiction Anthology

But in the places where it isn't faded and where the sun is just so—I can see a strange, provoking, formless sort of figure that seems to skulk behind that silly and contemptuous front design.

There's sister on the stairs!

Well, the Fourth of July is over! The people are all gone, and I am tired out. John thought it might do me good to see a little company, so we just had Mother and Nellie and the children down for a week.

Of course I didn't do a thing. Jennie sees to everything now.

But it tired me all the same.

John says if I don't pick up faster he shall send me to Weir Mitchell[1] in the fall.

But I don't want to go there at all. I had a friend who was in his hands once, and she says he is just like John and my brother, only more so!

Besides, it is such an undertaking to go so far.

I don't feel as if it was worthwhile to turn my hand over for anything, and I'm getting dreadfully fretful and querulous.

I cry at nothing, and cry most of the time.

Of course I don't when John is here, or anybody else, but when I am alone.

And I am alone a good deal just now. John is kept in town very often by serious cases, and Jennie is good and lets me alone when I want her to.

So I walk a little in the garden or down that lovely lane, sit on the porch under the roses, and lie down up here a good deal.

I'm getting really fond of the room in spite of the wallpaper. Perhaps *because* of the wallpaper.

It dwells in my mind so!

I lie here on this great immovable bed—it is nailed down, I believe—and follow that pattern about by the hour. It is as good as gymnastics, I assure you. I start, we'll say, at the bottom, down in the corner over there where it has not been touched, and I determine for the thousandth time that I *will* follow that pointless pattern to some sort of a conclusion.

I know a little of the principle of design, and I know this thing was not arranged on any laws of radiation, or alternation, or repetition, or symmetry, or anything else that I ever heard of.

It is repeated, of course, by the breadths, but not otherwise.

Looked at in one way, each breadth stands alone; the bloated curves and flourishes—a kind of "debased Romanesque" with delirium tremens go waddling up and down in isolated columns of fatuity.

But, on the other hand, they connect diagonally, and the sprawling outlines run off in great slanting waves of optic horror, like a lot of wallowing sea-weeds in full chase.

The whole thing goes horizontally, too, at least it seems so, and I exhaust myself trying to distinguish the order of its going in that direction.

They have used a horizontal breadth for a frieze, and that adds wonderfully to the confusion.

---

[1]Dr. S. Weir Mitchell (1829–1914) was an eminent neurologist who advocated "rest cures" for nervous disorders. He was the author of *Diseases of the Nervous System, Especially of Women* (1881).

There is one end of the room where it is almost intact, and there, when the crosslights fade and the low sun shines directly upon it, I can almost fancy radiation after all—the interminable grotesque seems to form around a common center and rush off in headlong plunges of equal distraction.

It makes me tired to follow it. I will take a nap, I guess.

I don't know why I should write this.

I don't want to.

I don't feel able.

And I know John would think it absurd. But I *must* say what I feel and think in some way—it is such a relief!

But the effort is getting to be greater than the relief.

Half the time now I am awfully lazy, and lie down ever so much. John says I mustn't lose my strength, and has me take cod liver oil and lots of tonics and things, to say nothing of ale and wines and rare meat.

Dear John! He loves me very dearly, and hates to have me sick. I tried to have a real earnest reasonable talk with him the other day, and tell him how I wish he would let me go and make a visit to Cousin Henry and Julia.

But he said I wasn't able to go, nor able to stand it after I got there; and I did not make out a very good case for myself, for I was crying before I had finished.

It is getting to be a great effort for me to think straight. Just this nervous weakness, I suppose.

And dear John gathered me up in his arms, and just carried me up stairs and laid me on the bed, and sat by me and read to me till it tired my head.

He said I was his darling and his comfort and all he had, and that I must take care of myself for his sake, and keep well.

He says no one but myself can help me out of it, that I must use my will and self-control and not let any silly fancies run away with me.

There's one comfort—the baby is well and happy, and does not have to occupy this nursery with the horrid wallpaper.

If we had not used it, that blessed child would have! What a fortunate escape! Why, I wouldn't have a child of mine, an impressionable little thing, live in such a room for worlds.

I never thought of it before, but it is lucky that John kept me here after all; I can stand it so much easier than a baby, you see.

Of course I never mention it to them anymore—I am too wise—but I keep watch for it all the same.

There are things in the wallpaper that nobody knows about but me, or ever will.

Behind that outside pattern the dim shapes get clearer every day.

It is always the same shape, only very numerous.

And it is like a woman stooping down and creeping about behind that pattern. I don't like it a bit. I wonder—I begin to think—I wish John would take me away from here!

It is so hard to talk with John about my case, because he is so wise, and because he loves me so.

But I tried it last night.

It was moonlight. The moon shines in all around just as the sun does.

I hate to see it sometimes, it creeps so slowly, and always comes in by one window or another.

John was asleep and I hated to waken him, so I kept still and watched the moonlight on that undulating wallpaper till I felt creepy.

The faint figure behind seemed to shake the pattern, just as if she wanted to get out.

I got up softly and went to feel and see if the paper *did* move, and when I came back John was awake.

"What is it, little girl?" he said. "Don't go walking about like that—you'll get cold."

I thought it was a good time to talk, so I told him that I really was not gaining here, and that I wished he would take me away.

"Why darling!" said he. "Our lease will be up in three weeks, and I can't see how to leave before.

"The repairs are not done at home, and I cannot possibly leave town just now. Of course, if you were in any danger, I could and would, but you really are better, dear, whether you can see it or not. I am a doctor, dear and I know. You are gaining flesh and color, your appetite is better, I feel really much easier about you."

"I don't weigh a bit more," said I, "nor as much; and my appetite may be better in the evening when you are here but it is worse in the morning when you are away!"

"Bless her little heart," said he with a big hug, "She shall be as sick as she pleases! But now let's improve the shining hours by going to sleep, and talk about it in the morning!"

"And you won't go away?" I asked gloomily.

"Why, how can I, dear? It is only three weeks more and then we will take a nice little trip for a few days while Jennie is getting the house ready. Really, dear, you are better!"

"Better in body perhaps—" I began, and stopped short, for he sat up straight and looked at me with such a stern, reproachful look that I could not say another word.

"My darling," said he, "I beg you, for my sake and for our child's sake, as well as for your own, that you will never for one instant let that idea enter your mind! There is nothing so dangerous, so fascinating, to a temperament like yours. It is a false and foolish fancy. Can you trust me as a physician when I tell you so?"

So of course I said no more on that score, and we went to sleep before long. He thought I was asleep first, but I wasn't, and lay there for hours trying to decide whether that front pattern and the back pattern really did move together or separately.

On a pattern like this, by daylight, there is a lack of sequence, a defiance of law, that is a constant irritant to a normal mind.

The color is hideous enough, and unreliable enough, and infuriating enough, but the pattern is torturing.

You think you have mastered it, but just as you get well under way in following, it turns a back-somersault and there you are. It slaps you in the face, knocks you down, and tramples upon you. It is like a bad dream.

The outside pattern is a florid arabesque, reminding one of a fungus. If you can imagine a toadstool in joints, an interminable string of toadstools, budding and sprouting in endless convolutions—why, that is something like it.

That is, sometimes!

There is one marked peculiarity about this paper, a thing nobody seems to notice but myself, and that is that it changes as the light changes.

When the sun shoots in through the east window—I always watch for that first long, straight ray—it changes so quickly that I never can quite believe it.

That is why I watch it always.

By moonlight—the moon shines in all night when there is a moon—I wouldn't know it was the same paper.

At night in any kind of light, in twilight, candlelight, lamplight, and worst of all by moonlight, it becomes bars! The outside pattern, I mean, and the woman behind it is as plain as can be.

I didn't realize for a long time what the thing was that showed behind, that dim subpattern, but now I am quite sure that it is a woman.

By daylight she is subdued, quiet. I fancy it is the pattern that keeps her so still. It is so puzzling. It keeps me quiet by the hour.

I lie down ever so much now. John says it is good for me, and to sleep all I can.

Indeed he started the habit by making me lie down for an hour after each meal.

It is a very bad habit, I am convinced, for you see, I don't sleep.

And that cultivates deceit, for I don't tell them I'm awake—oh, no!

The fact is I am getting a little afraid of John.

He seems very queer sometimes, and even Jennie has an inexplicable look.

It strikes me occasionally, just as a scientific hypothesis, that perhaps it is the paper!

I have watched John when he did not know I was looking, and come into the room suddenly on the most innocent excuses, and I've caught him several times *looking at the paper!* And Jennie too. I caught Jennie with her hand on it once.

She didn't know I was in the room, and when I asked her in a quiet, a very quiet voice, with the most restrained manner possible, what she was doing with the paper, she turned around as if she had been caught stealing, and looked quite angry—asked me why I should frighten her so!

Then she said that the paper stained everything it touched, that she had found yellow smooches on all my clothes and John's and she wished we would be more careful!

Did not that sound innocent? But I know she was studying that pattern, and I am determined that nobody shall find it out but myself!

Life is very much more exciting now than it used to be. You see, I have something more to expect, to look forward to, to watch. I really do eat better, and am more quiet than I was.

John is so pleased to see me improve! He laughed a little the other day, and said I seemed to be flourishing in spite of my wallpaper.

I turned it off with a laugh. I had no intention of telling him it was *because* of the wallpaper—he would make fun of me. He might even want to take me away.

I don't want to leave now until I have found it out. There is a week more, and I think that will be enough.

I'm feeling so much better!

I don't sleep much at night, for it is so interesting to watch developments; but I sleep a good deal during the daytime.

In the daytime it is tiresome and perplexing.

There are always new shoots on the fungus, and new shades of yellow all over it. I cannot keep count of them, though I have tried conscientiously.

It is the strangest yellow, that wallpaper! It makes me think of all the yellow things I saw—not beautiful ones like buttercups, but old, foul, bad yellow things.

But there is something else about that paper—the smell! I noticed it the moment we came into the room, but with so much air and sun it was not bad. Now we have had a week of fog and rain, and whether the windows are open or not, the smell is here.

It creeps all over the house.

I find it hovering in the dining-room, skulking in the parlor, hiding in the hall, lying in wait for me on the stairs.

It gets into my hair.

Even when I go to ride, if I turn my head suddenly and surprise it—there is that smell!

Such a peculiar odor, too! I have spent hours in trying to analyze it, to find what it smelled like.

It is not bad—at first—and very gentle, but quite the subtlest, most enduring odor I ever met.

In this damp weather it is awful. I wake up in the night and find it hanging over me.

It used to disturb me at first. I thought seriously of burning the house—to reach the smell.

But now I am used to it. The only thing I can think of that it is like is the *color* of the paper! A yellow smell.

There is a very funny mark on this wall, low down, near the mopboard. A streak that runs around the room. It goes behind every piece of furniture, except the bed, a long straight, even *smooch*, as if it had been rubbed over and over.

I wonder how it was done and who did it, and what they did it for. Round and round and round—round and round and round—it makes me dizzy!

I really have discovered something at last.

Through watching so much at night, when it changes so, I have finally found out.

The front pattern *does* move—and no wonder! The woman behind shakes it!

Sometimes I think there are a great many women behind, and sometimes only one, and she crawls around fast, and her crawling shakes it all over.

Then in the very bright spots she keeps still, and in the very shady spots she just takes hold of the bars and shakes them hard.

And she is all the time trying to climb through. But nobody could climb through that pattern—it strangles so; I think that is why it has so many heads.

They get through and then the pattern strangles them off and turns them upside down, and makes their eyes white!

If those heads were covered or taken off it would not be half so bad.

I think that woman gets out in the daytime!

And I'll tell you why—privately—I've seen her!

I can see her out of every one of my windows!

It is the same woman, I know, for she is always creeping, and most women do not creep by daylight.

I see her in that long shaded lane, creeping up and down. I see her in those dark grape arbors, creeping all round the garden.

I see her on that long road under the trees, creeping along, and when a carriage comes she hides under the blackberry vines.

I don't blame her a bit. It must be very humiliating to be caught creeping by daylight!

I always lock the door when I creep by daylight. I can't do it at night, for I know John would suspect something at once.

And John is so queer now that I don't want to irritate him. I wish he would take another room! Besides, I don't want anybody to get that woman out at night but myself.

I often wonder if I could see her out of all the windows at once.

But, turn as fast as I can, I can only see out of one at one time.

And though I always see her, she *may* be able to creep faster than I can turn! I have watched her sometimes away off in the open country, creeping as fast as a cloud shadow in a wind.

If only that top pattern could be gotten off from the under one! I mean to try it, little by little.

I have found out another funny thing, but I shan't tell it this time! It does not do to trust people too much.

There are only two more days to get this paper off, and I believe John is beginning to notice. I don't like the look in his eyes.

And I heard him ask Jennie a lot of professional questions about me. She had a very good report to give.

She said I slept a good deal in the daytime.

John knows I don't sleep very well at night, for all I'm so quiet!

He asked me all sorts of questions too, and pretended to be very loving and kind.

As if I couldn't see through him!

Still, I don't wonder he acts so, sleeping under this paper for three months.

It only interests me, but I feel sure John and Jennie are affected by it.

Hurrah! This is the last day, but it is enough. John is to stay in town over night, and won't be out until this evening.

Jennie wanted to sleep with me—the sly thing; but I told her I should undoubtedly rest better for a night all alone.

That was clever, for really I wasn't alone a bit! As soon as it was moonlight and that poor thing began to crawl and shake the pattern, I got up and ran to help her.

I pulled and she shook. I shook and she pulled, and before morning we had peeled off yards of that paper.

A strip about as high as my head and half around the room.

And then when the sun came and that awful pattern began to laugh at me, I declared I would finish it today!

We go away tomorrow, and they are moving all my furniture down again to leave things as they were before.

Jennie looked at the wall in amazement, but I told her merrily that I did it out of pure spite at the vicious thing.

She laughed and said she wouldn't mind doing it herself, but I must not get tired.

How she betrayed herself that time!

But I am here, and no person touches this paper but me—not *alive!*

She tried to get me out of the room—it was too patent! But I said it was so quiet and empty and clean now that I believed I would lie down again and sleep all I could, and not to wake me even for dinner—I would call when I woke.

So now she is gone, and the servants are gone, and the things are gone, and there is nothing left but that great bedstead nailed down, with the canvas mattress we found on it.

We shall sleep downstairs tonight, and take the boat home tomorrow.

I quite enjoy the room, now it is bare again.

How those children did tear about here!

This bedstead is fairly gnawed!

But I must get to work.

I have locked the door and thrown the key down into the front path.

I don't want to go out, and I don't want to have anybody come in, till John comes.

I want to astonish him.

I've got a rope up here that even Jennie did not find. If that woman does get out, and tries to get away, I can tie her!

But I forgot I could not reach far without anything to stand on!

This bed will *not* move!

I tried to lift and push it until I was lame, and then I got so angry I bit off a little piece at one corner—but it hurt my teeth.

Then I peeled off all the paper I could reach standing on the floor. It sticks horribly and the pattern just enjoys it! All those strangled heads and bulbous eyes and waddling fungus growths just shriek with derision!

I am getting angry enough to do something desperate. To jump out of the window would be admirable exercise, but the bars are too strong even to try.

Besides I wouldn't do it. Of course not. I know well enough that a step like that is improper and might be misconstrued.

I don't like to *look* out of the windows even—there are so many of those creeping women, and they creep so fast.

I wonder if they all come out of that wallpaper as I did!

But I am securely fastened now by my well-hidden rope—you don't get *me* out in the road there!

I suppose I shall have to get back behind the pattern when it comes night, and that is hard!

It is so pleasant to be out in this great room and creep around as I please!

I don't want to go outside. I won't, even if Jennie asks me to.

For outside you have to creep on the ground, and everything is green instead of yellow.

But here I can creep smoothly on the floor, and my shoulder just fits in that long smooch around the wall, so I cannot lose my way.

Why, there's John at the door!

It is no use, young man, you can't open it!

How he does call and pound!

Now he's crying to Jennie for an axe.

It would be a shame to break down that beautiful door!

"John, dear!" said I in the gentlest voice. "The key is down by the front steps, under a plantain leaf!"

That silenced him for a few moments.

Then he said, very quietly indeed, "Open the door, my darling!"

"I can't," said I. "The key is down by the front door under a plantain leaf!" And then I said it again, several times, very gently and slowly, and said it so often that he had to go and see, and he got it of course, and came in. He stopped short by the door.

"What is the matter?" he cried. "For God's sake, what are you doing!"

I kept on creeping just the same, but I looked at him over my shoulder.

"I've got out at last," said I, "in spite of you and Jennie. And I've pulled off most of the paper, so you can't put me back!"

Now why should that man have fainted? But he did, and right across my path by the wall, so that I had to creep over him every time!

James Joyce (1882–1941)

It was said after the publication of James Joyce's *Ulysses* (1922) that if the city of Dublin were to vanish from the face of the earth, it would be possible to restore every brick and nail of it by referring to that novel. Similarly, one could argue that if all evidence of literary modernism were destroyed, the works of Joyce would allow us to reconstruct the full development. For in the course of his restless career Joyce recapitulated the entire literary tradition.

Born in a suburb of Dublin, Joyce received an excellent but erratic education. He studied first with the Jesuit fathers but after a collapse of the family's fortunes spent some years fending for himself. He took a degree from University College in Dublin in 1902.

Joyce's intellectual independence and brilliance were evident from the start. Discovering his facility for languages, he taught himself a dozen. When he conceived an interest in Henrik Ibsen, he quickly mastered Norwegian so that he could read his works in the original.

After graduating from University College, Joyce flirted briefly with the idea of studying medicine. He moved to Paris to attend the College de Médicine but dropped out after one class. (He made excellent use of his medical background, slight though it may have been, in his creation of the character of Buck Mulligan in *Ulysses*.)

Joyce had begun writing while still an adolescent. During his brief sojourn in Paris he worked at a series of sketches based upon overheard conversations and observed encounters. These he called "Epiphanies," and many were artfully threaded into the stories of *Dubliners* (1914) and the novel *A Portrait of the Artist as a Young Man* (1916).

Returning to Dublin to be with his dying mother, Joyce discovered that despite his Irish heritage he could not work freely in the midst of his people. Like Stephen Dedalus, the protagonist in *Portrait,* he decided that he had to escape the nets of place "to forge in the smithy of my soul the uncreated conscience of my race."

Joyce left Ireland in 1904 and never lived there again. Until his death he supported himself and his family in various European cities—Trieste, Zurich, Paris—on a patchwork of financial arrangements. He translated, taught languages, and accepted generous donations from his brother Stanislaus and from the fundraising activities of his great admirer Ezra Pound.

THE DEAD

Lily, the caretaker's daughter, was literally run off her feet. Hardly had she brought one gentleman into the little pantry behind the office on the ground floor and helped him off with his overcoat than the wheezy hall-door bell clanged again and she had to scamper along the bare hallway to let in another guest. It was well for her she had not to attend to the ladies also. But Miss Kate and Miss Julia had thought of that and had converted the bathroom upstairs into a ladies' dressing-room. Miss Kate and Miss Julia were there, gossiping and laughing and fussing, walking after each other to the head of the stairs, peering down over the banisters and calling down to Lily to ask her who had come.

It was always a great affair, the Misses Morkan's annual dance. Everybody who knew them came to it, members of the family, old friends of the family, the members of Julia's choir, any of Kate's pupils that were grown up enough, and even some of Mary Jane's pupils too. Never once had it fallen flat. For years and years it had gone off in splendid style, as long as anyone could remember; ever since Kate and Julia, after the death of their brother Pat, had left the house in Stoney Batter° and taken Mary Jane, their only niece, to live with them in the dark, gaunt house on Usher's Island, the upper part of which they had rented from Mr. Fulham, the corn-factor on the ground floor. That was a good thirty years ago if it was a day. Mary Jane, who was then a little girl in short clothes, was now the main prop of the household, for she had the organ in Haddington Road. She had been through the Academy and gave a pupils' concert every year in the upper room of the Antient Concert Rooms. Many of her pupils belonged to the better-class families on the Kingstown and Dalkey line. Old as they were, her aunts also did their share. Julia, though she was quite grey, was still the leading soprano in Adam and Eve's, and Kate, being too feeble to go about much, gave music lessons to beginners on the old square piano in

---

Stoney Batter; etc.: settings in and around Dublin.

the back room. Lily, the caretaker's daughter, did housemaid's work for them. Though their life was modest, they believed in eating well; the best of everything: diamond-bone sirloins, three-shilling tea and the best bottled stout. But Lily seldom made a mistake in the orders, so that she got on well with her three mistresses. They were fussy, that was all. But the only thing they would not stand was back answers.

Of course, they had good reason to be fussy on such a night. And then it was long after ten o'clock and yet there was no sign of Gabriel and his wife. Besides they were dreadfully afraid that Freddy Malins might turn up screwed. They would not wish for worlds that any of Mary Jane's pupils should see him under the influence; and when he was like that it was sometimes very hard to manage him. Freddy Malins always came late, but they wondered what could be keeping Gabriel: and that was what brought them every two minutes to the banisters to ask Lily had Gabriel or Freddy come.

"O, Mr. Conroy," said Lily to Gabriel when she opened the door for him, "Miss Kate and Miss Julia thought you were never coming. Goodnight, Mrs. Conroy."

"I'll engage they did," said Gabriel, "but they forget that my wife here takes three mortal hours to dress herself."   5

He stood on the mat, scraping the snow from his goloshes, while Lily led his wife to the foot of the stairs and called out:

"Miss Kate, here's Mrs. Conroy."

Kate and Julia came toddling down the dark stairs at once. Both of them kissed Gabriel's wife, said she must be perished alive, and asked was Gabriel with her.

"Here I am as right as the mail, Aunt Kate! Go on up. I'll follow," called out Gabriel from the dark.

He continued scraping his feet vigorously while the three women went upstairs, laughing, to the ladies' dressing-room. A light fringe of snow lay like a cape on the shoulders of his overcoat and like toecaps on the toes of his goloshes; and, as the buttons of his overcoat slipped with a squeaking noise through the snow-stiffened frieze, a cold, fragrant air from out-of-doors escaped from crevices and folds.   10

"Is it snowing again, Mr. Conroy?" asked Lily.

She had preceded him into the pantry to help him off with his overcoat. Gabriel smiled at the three syllables she had given his surname and glanced at her. She was a slim, growing girl, pale in complexion and with hay-coloured hair. The gas in the pantry made her look still paler. Gabriel had known her when she was a child and used to sit on the lowest step nursing a rag doll.

"Yes, Lily," he answered, "and I think we're in for a night of it."

He looked up at the pantry ceiling, which was shaking with the stamping and shuffling of feet on the floor above, listened for a moment to the piano and then glanced at the girl, who was folding his overcoat carefully at the end of a shelf.

"Tell me, Lily," he said in a friendly tone, "do you still go to school?"   15

"O no, sir," she answered. "I'm done schooling this year and more."

"O, then," said Gabriel gaily, "I suppose we'll be going to your wedding one of these fine days with your young man, eh?"

The girl glanced back at him over her shoulder and said with great bitterness:

"The men that is now is only all palaver and what they can get out of you."

Gabriel coloured, as if he felt he had made a mistake and, without looking at her, kicked off his goloshes and flicked actively with his muffler at his patent-leather shoes.   20

He was a stout, tallish young man. The high colour of his cheeks pushed upwards even to his forehead, where it scattered itself in a few formless patches of pale
red; and on his hairless face there scintillated restlessly the polished lenses and the
bright gilt rims of the glasses which screened his delicate and restless eyes. His glossy
black hair was parted in the middle and brushed in a long curve behind his ears
where it curled slightly beneath the groove left by his hat.

When he had flicked lustre into his shoes he stood up and pulled his waistcoat
down more tightly on his plump body. Then he took a coin rapidly from his pocket.

"O Lily," he said, thrusting it into her hands, "it's Christmas-time, isn't it?
Just . . . here's a little. . . ."

He walked rapidly towards the door.

"O no, sir!" cried the girl, following him. "Really, sir, I wouldn't take it." 25

"Christmas-time! Christmas-time!" said Gabriel, almost trotting to the stairs
and waving his hand to her in deprecation.

The girl, seeing that he had gained the stairs, called out after him:

"Well, thank you, sir."

He waited outside the drawing-room door until the waltz should finish, listening to the skirts that swept against it and to the shuffling of feet. He was still discomposed by the girl's bitter and sudden retort. It had cast a gloom over him which
he tried to dispel by arranging his cuffs and the bows of his tie. He then took from
his waistcoat pocket a little paper and glanced at the headings he had made for his
speech. He was undecided about the lines from Robert Browning, for he feared they
would be above the heads of his hearers. Some quotation that they would recognise
from Shakespeare or from the Melodies would be better. The indelicate clacking of
the men's heels and the shuffling of their soles reminded him that their grade of culture differed from his. He would only make himself ridiculous by quoting poetry to
them which they could not understand. They would think that he was airing his superior education. He would fail with them just as he had failed with the girl in the
pantry. He had taken up a wrong tone. His whole speech was a mistake from first to
last, an utter failure.

Just then his aunts and his wife came out of the ladies' dressing-room. His aunts
were two small, plainly dressed old women. Aunt Julia was an inch or so the taller.
Her hair, drawn low over the tops of her ears, was grey; and grey also, with darker
shadows, was her large flaccid face. Though she was stout in build and stood erect,
her slow eyes and parted lips gave her the appearance of a woman who did not
know where she was or where she was going. Aunt Kate was more vivacious. Her
face, healthier than her sister's, was all puckers and creases, like a shrivelled red
apple, and her hair, braided in the same old-fashioned way, had not lost its ripe nut
colour. 30

They both kissed Gabriel frankly. He was their favourite nephew, the son of
their dead elder sister, Ellen, who had married T. J. Conroy of the Port and Docks.

"Gretta tells me you're not going to take a cab back to Monkstown tonight,
Gabriel," said Aunt Kate.

"No," said Gabriel, turning to his wife, "we had quite enough of that last year,
hadn't we? Don't you remember, Aunt Kate, what a cold Gretta got out of it? Cab
windows rattling all the way, and the east wind blowing in after we passed Merrion.
Very jolly it was. Gretta caught a dreadful cold."

Aunt Kate frowned severely and nodded her head at every word.

"Quite right, Gabriel, quite right," she said. "You can't be too careful."

"But as for Gretta there," said Gabriel, "she'd walk home in the snow if she were let."

Mrs. Conroy laughed.

"Don't mind him, Aunt Kate," she said. "He's really an awful bother, what with green shades for Tom's eyes at night and making him do the dumb-bells, and forcing Eva to eat the stirabout. The poor child! And she simply hates the sight of it! . . . O, but you'll never guess what he makes me wear now!"

She broke out into a peal of laughter and glanced at her husband, whose admiring and happy eyes had been wandering from her dress to her face and hair. The two aunts laughed heartily, too, for Gabriel's solicitude was a standing joke with them.

"Goloshes!" said Mrs. Conroy. "That's the latest. Whenever it's wet underfoot I must put on my goloshes. To-night even, he wanted me to put them on, but I wouldn't. The next thing he'll buy me will be a diving suit."

Gabriel laughed nervously and patted his tie reassuringly, while Aunt Kate nearly doubled herself, so heartily did she enjoy the joke. The smile soon faded from Aunt Julia's face and her mirthless eyes were directed towards her nephew's face. After a pause she asked:

"And what are goloshes, Gabriel?"

"Goloshes, Julia!" exclaimed her sister. "Goodness me, don't you know what goloshes are? You wear them over your . . . over your boots, Gretta, isn't it?"

"Yes," said Mrs. Conroy. "Guttapercha° things. We both have a pair now. Gabriel says everyone wears them on the continent."

"O, on the continent," murmured Aunt Julia, nodding her head slowly.

Gabriel knitted his brows and said, as if he were slightly angered:

"It's nothing very wonderful, but Gretta thinks it very funny because she says the word reminds her of Christy Minstrels."

"But tell me, Gabriel," said Aunt Kate, with brisk tact. "Of course, you've seen about the room. Gretta was saying . . ."

"O, the room is all right," replied Gabriel. "I've taken one in the Gresham."

"To be sure," said Aunt Kate, "by far the best thing to do. And the children, Gretta, you're not anxious about them?"

"O, for one night," said Mrs. Conroy. "Besides, Bessie will look after them."

"To be sure," said Aunt Kate again. "What a comfort it is to have a girl like that, one you can depend on! There's that Lily, I'm sure I don't know what has come over her lately. She's not the girl she was at all."

Gabriel was about to ask his aunt some questions on this point, but she broke off suddenly to gaze after her sister, who had wandered down the stairs and was craning her neck over the banisters.

"Now, I ask you," she said almost testily, "where is Julia going? Julia! Julia! Where are you going?"

Julia, who had gone half way down one flight, came back and announced blandly:

"Here's Freddy."

At the same moment a clapping of hands and a final flourish of the pianist told that the waltz had ended. The drawing-room door was opened from within and

---

guttapercha: rubber-like material for boots.

some couples came out. Aunt Kate drew Gabriel aside hurriedly and whispered into his ear:

"Slip down, Gabriel, like a good fellow and see if he's all right, and don't let him up if he's screwed. I'm sure he's screwed. I'm sure he is."

Gabriel went to the stairs and listened over the banisters. He could hear two persons talking in the pantry. Then he recognised Freddy Malins' laugh. He went down the stairs noisily.

"It's such a relief," said Aunt Kate to Mrs. Conroy, "that Gabriel is here. I always feel easier in my mind when he's here. . . . Julia, there's Miss Daly and Miss Power will take some refreshment. Thanks for your beautiful waltz, Miss Daly. It made lovely time." ⟨60⟩

A tall wizen-faced man, with a stiff grizzled moustache and swarthy skin, who was passing out with his partner, said:

"And may we have some refreshment, too, Miss Morkan?"

"Julia," said Aunt Kate summarily, "and here's Mr. Browne and Miss Furlong. Take them in, Julia, with Miss Daly and Miss Power."

"I'm the man for the ladies," said Mr. Browne, pursing his lips until his moustache bristled and smiling in all his wrinkles. "You know, Miss Morkan, the reason they are so fond of me is——"

He did not finish his sentence, but, seeing that Aunt Kate was out of earshot, at once led the three young ladies into the back room. The middle of the room was occupied by two square tables placed end to end, and on these Aunt Julia and the caretaker were straightening and smoothing a large cloth. On the sideboard were arrayed dishes and plates, and glasses and bundles of knives and forks and spoons. The top of the closed square piano served also as a sideboard for viands and sweets. At a smaller sideboard in one corner two young men were standing, drinking hop-bitters.° ⟨65⟩

Mr. Browne led his charges thither and invited them all, in jest, to some ladies' punch, hot, strong and sweet. As they said they never took anything strong, he opened three bottles of lemonade for them. Then he asked one of the young men to move aside, and, taking hold of the decanter, filled out for himself a goodly measure of whisky. The young men eyed him respectfully while he took a trial sip.

"God help me," he said, smiling, "it's the doctor's orders."

His wizened face broke into a broader smile, and the three young ladies laughed in musical echo to his pleasantry, swaying their bodies to and fro, with nervous jerks of their shoulders. The boldest said:

"O, now, Mr. Browne, I'm sure the doctor never ordered anything of the kind."

Mr. Browne took another sip of his whisky and said, with sidling mimicry: ⟨70⟩

"Well, you see, I'm like the famous Mrs. Cassidy, who is reported to have said: 'Now, Mary Grimes, if I don't take it, make me take it, for I feel I want it.'"

His hot face had leaned forward a little too confidentially and he had assumed a very low Dublin accent so that the young ladies, with one instinct, received his speech in silence. Miss Furlong, who was one of Mary Jane's pupils, asked Miss Daly what was the name of the pretty waltz she had played; and Mr. Browne, seeing that he was ignored, turned promptly to the two young men who were more appreciative.

---

hop-bitters: strongly flavored ale.

A red-faced young woman, dressed in pansy, came into the room, excitedly clapping her hands and crying:

"Quadrilles! Quadrilles!"°

Close on her heels came Aunt Kate, crying:

"Two gentlemen and three ladies, Mary Jane!"

"O, here's Mr. Bergin and Mr. Kerrigan," said Mary Jane. "Mr. Kerrigan, will you take Miss Power? Miss Furlong, may I get you a partner, Mr. Bergin. O, that'll just do now."

"Three ladies, Mary Jane," said Aunt Kate.

The two young gentlemen asked the ladies if they might have the pleasure, and Mary Jane turned to Miss Daly.

"O, Miss Daly, you're really awfully good, after playing for the last two dances, but really we're so short of ladies to-night."

"I don't mind in the least, Miss Morkan."

"But I've a nice partner for you, Mr. Bartell D'Arcy, the tenor. I'll get him to sing later on. All Dublin is raving about him."

"Lovely voice, lovely voice!" said Aunt Kate.

As the piano had twice begun to prelude to the first figure Mary Jane led her recruits quickly from the room. They had hardly gone when Aunt Julia wandered slowly into the room, looking behind her at something.

"What is the matter, Julia?" asked Aunt Kate anxiously. "Who is it?"

Julia, who was carrying in a column of table-napkins, turned to her sister and said, simply, as if the question had surprised her:

"It's only Freddy, Kate, and Gabriel with him."

In fact right behind her Gabriel could be seen piloting Freddy Malins across the landing. The latter, a young man of about forty, was of Gabriel's size and build, with very round shoulders. His face was fleshy and pallid, touched with colour only at the thick hanging lobes of his ears and at the wide wings of his nose. He had coarse features, a blunt nose, a convex and receding brow, tumid and protruded lips. His heavy-lidded eyes and the disorder of his scanty hair made him look sleepy. He was laughing heartily in a high key at a story which he had been telling Gabriel on the stairs and at the same time rubbing the knuckles of his left fist backwards and forwards into his left eye.

"Good-evening, Freddy," said Aunt Julia.

Freddy Malins bade the Misses Morkan good-evening in what seemed an off-hand fashion by reason of the habitual catch in his voice and then, seeing that Mr. Browne was grinning at him from the sideboard, crossed the room on rather shaky legs and began to repeat in an undertone the story he had just told to Gabriel.

"He's not so bad, is he?" said Aunt Kate to Gabriel.

Gabriel's brows were dark but he raised them quickly and answered:

"O, no, hardly noticeable."

"Now, isn't he a terrible fellow!" she said. "And his poor mother made him take the pledge° on New Year's Eve. But come on, Gabriel, into the drawing-room."

Before leaving the room with Gabriel she signalled to Mr. Browne by frowning and shaking her forefinger in warning to and fro. Mr. Browne nodded in answer and, when she had gone, said to Freddy Malins:

---

quadrilles: a group dance for four.
take the pledge: swear off alcohol.

A Fiction Anthology

"Now, then, Teddy, I'm going to fill you out a good glass of lemonade just to buck you up."

Freddy Malins, who was nearing the climax of his story, waved the offer aside impatiently but Mr. Browne, having first called Freddy Malins' attention to a disarray in his dress, filled out and handed him a full glass of lemonade. Freddy Malins' left hand accepted the glass mechanically, his right hand being engaged in the mechanical readjustment of his dress. Mr. Browne, whose face was once more wrinkling with mirth, poured out for himself a glass of whisky while Freddy Malins exploded, before he had well reached the climax of his story, in a kink of high-pitched bronchitic laughter and, setting down his untasted and overflowing glass, began to rub the knuckles of his left fist backwards and forwards into his left eye, repeating words of his last phrase as well as his fit of laughter would allow him.

Gabriel could not listen while Mary Jane was playing her Academy piece, full of runs and difficult passages, to the hushed drawing-room. He liked music but the piece she was playing had no melody for him and he doubted whether it had any melody for the other listeners, though they had begged Mary Jane to play something. Four young men, who had come from the refreshment-room to stand in the doorway at the sound of the piano, had gone away quietly in couples after a few minutes. The only persons who seemed to follow the music were Mary Jane herself, her hands racing along the key-board or lifted from it at the pauses like those of a priestess in momentary imprecation, and Aunt Kate standing at her elbow to turn the page.

Gabriel's eyes, irritated by the floor, which glittered with beeswax under the heavy chandelier, wandered to the wall above the piano. A picture of the balcony scene in *Romeo and Juliet* hung there and beside it was a picture of the two murdered princes in the Tower which Aunt Julia had worked in red, blue and brown wools when she was a girl. Probably in the school they had gone to as girls that kind of work had been taught for one year. His mother had worked for him as a birthday present a waistcoat of purple tabinet, with little foxes' heads upon it, lined with brown satin and having round mulberry buttons. It was strange that his mother had had no musical talent though Aunt Kate used to call her the brains carrier of the Morkan family. Both she and Julia had always seemed a little proud of their serious and matronly sister. Her photograph stood before the pierglass.° She held an open book on her knees and was pointing out something in it to Constantine who, dressed in a man-o'-war suit,° lay at her feet. It was she who had chosen the names of her sons for she was very sensible of the dignity of family life. Thanks to her, Constantine was now senior curate in Balbriggan and, thanks to her, Gabriel himself had taken his degree in the Royal University. A shadow passed over his face as he remembered her sullen opposition to his marriage. Some slighting phrases she had used still rankled in his memory; she had once spoken of Gretta as being country cute and that was not true of Gretta at all. It was Gretta who had nursed her during all her last long illness in their house at Monkstown.

He knew that Mary Jane must be near the end of her piece for she was playing again the opening melody with runs of scales after every bar and while he waited for the end the resentment died down in his heart. The piece ended with a trill of oc-

---

pierglass: mirror.
man-o'-war suit: sailor suit.

taves in the treble and a final deep octave in the bass. Great applause greeted Mary Jane as, blushing and rolling up her music nervously, she escaped from the room. The most vigorous clapping came from the four young men in the doorway who had gone away to the refreshment-room at the beginning of the piece but had come back when the piano had stopped. 100

Lancers° were arranged. Gabriel found himself partnered with Miss Ivors. She was a frank-mannered talkative young lady, with a freckled face and prominent brown eyes. She did not wear a low-cut bodice and the large broach which was fixed in the front of her collar bore on it an Irish device and motto.

When they had taken their places she said abruptly:

"I have a crow to pluck with you."

"With me?" said Gabriel.

She nodded her head gravely. 105

"What is it?" asked Gabriel, smiling at her solemn manner.

"Who is G. C.?" answered Miss Ivors, turning her eyes upon him.

Gabriel coloured and was about to knit his brows, as if he did not understand, when she said bluntly:

"O, innocent Amy! I have found out that you write for *The Daily Express*. Now, aren't you ashamed of yourself?"

"Why should I be ashamed of myself?" asked Gabriel, blinking his eyes and trying to smile. 110

"Well, I'm ashamed of you," said Miss Ivors frankly. "To say you'd write for a paper like that. I didn't think you were a West Briton."

A look of perplexity appeared on Gabriel's face. It was true that he wrote a literary column every Wednesday in *The Daily Express*, for which he was paid fifteen shillings. But that did not make him a West Briton surely. The books he received for review were almost more welcome than the paltry cheque. He loved to feel the covers and turn over the pages of newly printed books. Nearly every day when his teaching in the college was ended he used to wander down the quays to the second-hand booksellers, to Hickey's on Bachelor's Walk, to Webb's or Massey's on Aston's Quay, or to O'Clohissey's in the by-street. He did not know how to meet her charge. He wanted to say that literature was above politics. But they were friends of many years' standing and their careers had been parallel, first at the University and then as teachers: he could not risk a grandiose phrase with her. He continued blinking his eyes and trying to smile and murmured lamely that he saw nothing political in writing reviews of books.

When their turn to cross had come he was still perplexed and inattentive. Miss Ivors promptly took his hand in a warm grasp and said in a soft friendly tone:

"Of course, I was only joking. Come, we cross now."

When they were together again she spoke of the University question and Gabriel felt more at ease. A friend of hers had shown her his review of Browning's poems. That was how she had found out the secret: but she liked the review immensely. Then she said suddenly: 115

"O, Mr. Conroy, will you come for an excursion to the Aran Isles° this summer? We're going to stay there a whole month. It will be splendid out in the Atlantic.

_____

Lancers: a kind of dance.

Aran Isles: islands off the Irish-speaking west coast of Ireland.

You ought to come. Mr. Clancy is coming, and Mr. Kilkelly and Kathleen Kearney. It would be splendid for Gretta too if she'd come. She's from Connacht,° isn't she?"

"Her people are," said Gabriel shortly.

"But you will come, won't you?" said Miss Ivors, laying her warm hand eagerly on his arm.

"The fact is," said Gabriel, "I have just arranged to go——"

"Go where?" asked Miss Ivors. 120

"Well, you know, every year I go for a cycling tour with some fellows and so——"

"But where?" asked Miss Ivors.

"Well, we usually go to France or Belgium or perhaps Germany," said Gabriel awkwardly.

"And why do you go to France and Belgium," said Miss Ivors, "instead of visiting your own land?"

"Well," said Gabriel, "it's partly to keep in touch with the languages and partly for a change." 125

"And haven't you your own language to keep in touch with—Irish?" asked Miss Ivors.

"Well," said Gabriel, "if it comes to that, you know, Irish is not my language."

Their neighbours had turned to listen to the cross-examination. Gabriel glanced right and left nervously and tried to keep his good humour under the ordeal which was making a blush invade his forehead.

"And haven't you your own land to visit," continued Miss Ivors, "that you know nothing of, your own people, and your own country?"

"O, to tell you the truth," retorted Gabriel suddenly, "I'm sick of my own country, sick of it!" 130

"Why?" asked Miss Ivors.

Gabriel did not answer for his retort had heated him.

"Why?" repeated Miss Ivors.

They had to go visiting together and, as he had not answered her, Miss Ivors said warmly:

"Of course, you've no answer." 135

Gabriel tried to cover his agitation by taking part in the dance with great energy. He avoided her eyes for he had seen a sour expression on her face. But when they met in the long chain he was surprised to feel his hand firmly pressed. She looked at him from under her brows for a moment quizzically until he smiled. Then, just as the chain was about to start again, she stood on tiptoe and whispered into his ear:

"West Briton!"

When the lancers were over Gabriel went away to a remote corner of the room where Freddy Malins' mother was sitting. She was a stout feeble old woman with white hair. Her voice had a catch in it like her son's and she stuttered slightly. She had been told that Freddy had come and that he was nearly all right. Gabriel asked her whether she had had a good crossing. She lived with her married daughter in Glasgow° and came to Dublin on a visit once a year. She answered placidly that she had had a beautiful crossing and that the captain had been most attentive to her.

Connacht: a county in western Ireland.
Glasgow: an industrial city in Scotland.

She spoke also of the beautiful house her daughter kept in Glasgow, and of all the friends they had there. While her tongue rambled on Gabriel tried to banish from his mind all memory of the unpleasant incident with Miss Ivors. Of course the girl or woman, or whatever she was, was an enthusiast but there was a time for all things. Perhaps he ought not to have answered her like that. But she had no right to call him a West Briton before people, even in joke. She had tried to make him ridiculous before people, heckling him and staring at him with her rabbit's eyes.

He saw his wife making her way towards him through the waltzing couples. When she reached him she said into his ear:

"Gabriel, Aunt Kate wants to know won't you carve the goose as usual. Miss Daly will carve the ham and I'll do the pudding."   140

"All right," said Gabriel.

"She's sending in the younger ones first as soon as this waltz is over so that we'll have the table to ourselves."

"Were you dancing?" asked Gabriel.

"Of course I was. Didn't you see me? What row had you with Molly Ivors?"

"No row. Why? Did she say so?"   145

"Something like that. I'm trying to get that Mr. D'Arcy to sing. He's full of conceit, I think."

"There was no row," said Gabriel moodily, "only she wanted me to go for a trip to the west of Ireland and I said I wouldn't."

His wife clasped her hands excitedly and gave a little jump.

"O, do go, Gabriel," she cried. "I'd love to see Galway° again."

"You can go if you like," said Gabriel coldly.   150

She looked at him for a moment, then turned to Mrs. Malins and said:

"There's a nice husband for you, Mrs. Malins."

While she was threading her way back across the room Mrs. Malins, without adverting to the interruption, went on to tell Gabriel what beautiful places there were in Scotland and beautiful scenery. Her son-in-law brought them every year to the lakes and they used to go fishing. Her son-in-law was a splendid fisher. One day he caught a beautiful big fish and the man in the hotel cooked it for their dinner.

Gabriel hardly heard what she said. Now that supper was coming near he began to think again about his speech and about the quotation. When he saw Freddy Malins coming across the room to visit his mother Gabriel left the chair free for him and retired into the embrasure of the window. The room had already cleared and from the back room came the clatter of plates and knives. Those who still remained in the drawing-room seemed tired of dancing and were conversing quietly in little groups. Gabriel's warm trembling fingers tapped the cold pane of the window. How cool it must be outside! How pleasant it would be to walk out alone, first along by the river and then through the park! The snow would be lying on the branches of the trees and forming a bright cap on the top of the Wellington Monument. How much more pleasant it would be there than at the supper-table!

He ran over the headings of his speech: Irish hospitality, sad memories, the Three Graces, Paris, the quotation from Browning. He repeated to himself a phrase he had written in his review: "One feels that one is listening to a thought-tormented music." Miss Ivors had praised the review. Was she sincere? Had she really any life

---

Galway: a port city in western Ireland.

of her own behind all her propagandism? There had never been any ill-feeling between them until that night. It unnerved him to think that she would be at the supper-table, looking up at him while he spoke with her critical quizzing eyes. Perhaps she would not be sorry to see him fail in his speech. An idea came into his mind and gave him courage. He would say, alluding to Aunt Kate and Aunt Julia: "Ladies and Gentlemen, the generation which is now on the wane among us may have had its faults but for my part I think it had certain qualities of hospitality, of humour, of humanity, which the new and very serious and hypereducated generation that is growing up around us seems to me to lack." Very good: that was one for Miss Ivors. What did he care that his aunts were only two ignorant old women?   155

A murmur in the room attracted his attention. Mr. Browne was advancing from the door, gallantly escorting Aunt Julia, who leaned upon his arm, smiling and hanging her head. An irregular musketry of applause escorted her also as far as the piano and then, as Mary Jane seated herself on the stool, and Aunt Julia, no longer smiling, half turned so as to pitch her voice fairly into the room, gradually ceased. Gabriel recognised the prelude. It was that of an old song of Aunt Julia's—*Arrayed for the Bridal*. Her voice, strong and clear in tone, attacked with great spirit the runs which embellish the air and though she sang very rapidly she did not miss even the smallest of the grace notes. To follow the voice, without looking at the singer's face, was to feel and share the excitement of swift and secure flight. Gabriel applauded loudly with all the others at the close of the song and loud applause was borne in from the invisible supper table. It sounded so genuine that a little colour struggled into Aunt Julia's face as she bent to replace in the music-stand the old leather-bound song-book that had her initials on the cover. Freddy Malins, who had listened with his head perched sideways to hear her better, was still applauding when everyone else had ceased and talking animatedly to his mother who nodded her head gravely and slowly in acquiescence. At last, when he could clap no more, he stood up suddenly and hurried across the room to Aunt Julia whose hand he seized and held in both his hands, shaking it when words failed him or the catch in his voice proved too much for him.

"I was just telling my mother," he said, "I never heard you sing so well, never. No, I never heard your voice so good as it is to-night. Now! Would you believe that now? That's the truth. Upon my word and honour that's the truth. I never heard your voice sound so fresh and so . . . so clear and fresh, never."

Aunt Julia smiled broadly and murmured something about compliments as she released her hand from his grasp. Mr. Browne extended his open hand towards her and said to those who were near him in the manner of a showman introducing a prodigy to an audience:

"Miss Julia Morkan, my latest discovery!"

He was laughing very heartily at this himself when Freddy Malins turned to him and said: 160

"Well, Browne, if you're serious you might make a worse discovery. All I can say is I never heard her sing half so well as long as I am coming here. And that's the honest truth."

"Neither did I," said Mr. Browne. "I think her voice has greatly improved."

Aunt Julia shrugged her shoulders and said with meek pride:

"Thirty years ago I hadn't a bad voice as voices go."

"I often told Julia," said Aunt Kate emphatically, "that she was simply thrown away in that choir. But she never would be said by me."   165

She turned as if to appeal to the good sense of the others against a refractory child while Aunt Julia gazed in front of her, a vague smile of reminiscence playing on her face.

"No," continued Aunt Kate, "she wouldn't be said or led by anyone, slaving there in that choir night and day, night and day. Six o'clock on Christmas morning! And all for what?"

"Well, isn't it for the honour of God, Aunt Kate?" asked Mary Jane, twisting round on the piano-stool and smiling.

Aunt Kate turned fiercely on her niece and said:

"I know all about the honour of God, Mary Jane, but I think it's not at all honourable for the pope to turn out the women out of the choirs that have slaved there all their lives and put little whipper-snappers of boys over their heads. I suppose it is for the good of the Church if the pope does it. But it's not just, Mary Jane, and it's not right." 170

She had worked herself into a passion and would have continued in defence of her sister for it was a sore subject with her but Mary Jane, seeing that all the dancers had come back, intervened pacifically:

"Now, Aunt Kate, you're giving scandal to Mr. Browne who is of the other persuasion."

Aunt Kate turned to Mr. Browne, who was grinning at this allusion to his religion, and said hastily:

"O, I don't question the pope's being right. I'm only a stupid old woman and I wouldn't presume to do such a thing. But there's such a thing as common everyday politeness and gratitude. And if I were in Julia's place I'd tell that Father Healey straight up to his face . . . "

"And besides, Aunt Kate," said Mary Jane, "we really are all hungry and when we are hungry we are all very quarrelsome." 175

"And when we are thirsty we are also quarrelsome," added Mr. Browne.

"So that we had better go to supper," said Mary Jane, "and finish the discussion afterwards."

On the landing outside the drawing-room Gabriel found his wife and Mary Jane trying to persuade Miss Ivors to stay for supper. But Miss Ivors, who had put on her hat and was buttoning her cloak, would not stay. She did not feel in the least hungry and she had already overstayed her time.

"But only for ten minutes, Molly," said Mrs. Conroy. "That won't delay you."

"To take a pick itself," said Mary Jane, "after all your dancing." 180

"I really couldn't," said Miss Ivors.

"I am afraid you didn't enjoy yourself at all," said Mary Jane hopelessly.

"Ever so much, I assure you," said Miss Ivors, "but you really must let me run off now."

"But how can you get home?" asked Mrs. Conroy.

"O, it's only two steps up the quay." 185

Gabriel hesitated a moment and said:

"If you will allow me, Miss Ivors, I'll see you home if you are really obliged to go."

But Miss Ivors broke away from them.

"I won't hear of it," she cried. "For goodness' sake go in to your suppers and don't mind me. I'm quite well able to take care of myself."

"Well, you're the comical girl, Molly," said Mrs. Conroy frankly. 190

"*Beannachl libh*," cried Miss Ivors, with a laugh, as she ran down the staircase.

Mary Jane gazed after her, a moody puzzled expression on her face, while Mrs. Conroy leaned over the banisters to listen for the hall-door. Gabriel asked himself was he the cause of her abrupt departure. But she did not seem to be in ill humour: she had gone away laughing. He stared blankly down the staircase.

At the moment Aunt Kate came toddling out of the supper-room, almost wringing her hands in despair.

"Where is Gabriel?" she cried. "Where on earth is Gabriel? There's everyone waiting in there, stage to let, and nobody to carve the goose!"

"Here I am, Aunt Kate!" cried Gabriel, with sudden animation, "ready to carve a flock of geese, if necessary."

A fat brown goose lay at one end of the table and at the other end, on a bed of creased paper strewn with sprigs of parsley, lay a great ham, stripped of its outer skin and peppered over with crust crumbs, a neat paper frill round its ship and beside this was a round of spiced beef. Between these rival ends ran parallel lines of side-dishes: two little minsters of jelly, red and yellow; a shallow dish full of blocks of blanc-mange° and red jam, a large green leaf-shaped dish with a stalk-shaped handle, on which lay bunches of purple raisins and peeled almonds, a companion dish on which lay a solid rectangle of Smyrna figs, a dish of custard topped with grated nutmeg, a small bowl full of chocolates and sweets wrapped in gold and silver papers and a glass vase in which stood some tall celery stalks. In the centre of the table there stood, as sentries to a fruit-stand which upheld a pyramid of oranges and American apples, two squat old-fashioned decanters of cut glass, one containing port and the other dark sherry. On the closed square piano a pudding in a huge yellow dish lay in waiting and behind it were three squads of bottles of stout and ale and minerals, drawn up according to the colours of their uniforms, the first two black, with brown and red labels, the third and smallest squad white, with transverse green sashes.

Gabriel took his seat boldly at the head of the table and, having looked to the edge of the carver, plunged his fork firmly into the goose. He felt quite at ease now for he was an expert carver and liked nothing better than to find himself at the head of a well-laden table.

"Miss Furlong, what shall I send you?" he asked. "A wing or a slice of the breast?"

"Just a small slice of the breast."

"Miss Higgins, what for you?"

"O, anything at all, Mr. Conroy."

While Gabriel and Miss Daly exchanged plates of goose and plates of ham and spiced beef Lily went from guest to guest with a dish of hot floury potatoes wrapped in a white napkin. This was Mary Jane's idea and she had also suggested apple sauce for the goose but Aunt Kate had said that plain roast goose without any apple sauce had always been good enough for her and she hoped she might never eat worse. Mary Jane waited on her pupils and saw that they got the best slices and Aunt Kate and Aunt Julia opened and carried across from the piano bottles of stout and ale for the gentlemen and bottles of minerals for the ladies. There was a great deal of confusion and laughter and noise, the noise of orders and counter-orders, of knives and forks, of corks and glass-stoppers. Gabriel began to carve second helpings as soon as he had finished the first round without serving himself. Everyone protested loudly so that he compromised by taking a long draught of stout for he had found the carv-

195

200

blancmange: a milk pudding.

ing hot work. Mary Jane settled down quietly to her supper but Aunt Kate and Aunt Julia were still toddling round the table, walking on each other's heels, getting in each other's way and giving each other unheeded orders. Mr. Browne begged of them to sit down and eat their suppers and so did Gabriel but they said there was time enough, so that, at last, Freddy Malins stood up and, capturing Aunt Kate, plumped her down on her chair amid general laughter.

When everyone had been well served Gabriel said, smiling:

"Now, if anyone wants a little more of what vulgar people call stuffing let him or her speak."

A chorus of voices invited him to begin his own supper and Lily came forward with three potatoes which she had reserved for him.

"Very well," said Gabriel amiably, as he took another preparatory draught, "kindly forget my existence, ladies and gentlemen, for a few minutes."

He set to his supper and took no part in the conversation with which the table covered Lily's removal of the plates. The subject of talk was the opera company which was then at the Theatre Royal. Mr. Bartell D'Arcy, the tenor, a dark-complexioned young man with a smart moustache, praised very highly the leading contralto of the company but Miss Furlong thought she had a rather vulgar style of production. Freddy Malins said there was a negro chieftain singing in the second part of the Gaiety pantomime who had one of the finest tenor voices he had ever heard.

"Have you heard him?" he asked Mr. Bartell D'Arcy across the table.

"No," answered Mr. Bartell D'Arcy carelessly.

"Because," Freddy Malins explained, "now I'd be curious to hear your opinion of him. I think he has a grand voice."

"It takes Teddy to find out the really good things," said Mr. Browne familiarly to the table.

"And why couldn't he have a voice too?" asked Freddy Malins sharply. "Is it because he's only a black?"

Nobody answered this question and Mary Jane led the table back to the legitimate opera. One of her pupils had given her a pass for *Mignon*. Of course it was very fine, she said, but it made her think of poor Georgina Burns. Mr. Browne could go back farther still to the old Italian companies that used to come to Dublin—Tietjens, Ilma de Murzka, Campanini, the great Trebelli Giuglini, Ravelli, Aramburo. Those were the days, he said, when there was something like singing to be heard in Dublin. He told too of how the top gallery of the old Royal used to be packed night after night, of how one night an Italian tenor had sung five encores to *Let me like a Soldier fall*, introducing a high C every time and of how the gallery boys would sometimes in their enthusiasm unyoke the horses from the carriage of some great *prima donna* and pull her themselves through the streets to her hotel. Why did they never play the grand old operas now, he asked, *Dinorah, Lucrezia Borgia?* Because they could not get the voices to sing them: that was why.

"O, well," said Mr. Bartell D'Arcy, "I presume there are as good singers to-day as there were then."

"Where are they?" asked Mr. Browne defiantly.

"In London, Paris, Milan," said Mr. Bartell D'Arcy warmly. "I suppose Caruso,° for example, is quite as good, if not better than any of the men you have mentioned."

Caruso: Enrico Caruso (1873–1921), the legendary Italian-born tenor.

"Maybe so," said Mr. Browne. "But I may tell you I doubt it strongly."

"O, I'd give anything to hear Caruso sing," said Mary Jane.

"For me," said Aunt Kate, who had been picking a bone, "there was only one tenor. To please me, I mean. But I suppose none of you ever heard of him."

"Who was he, Miss Morkan?" asked Mr. Bartell D'Arcy politely.

"His name," said Aunt Kate, "was Parkinson. I heard him when he was in his prime and I think he had then the purest tenor voice that was ever put into a man's throat."

"Strange," said Mr. Bartell D'Arcy. "I never even heard of him."

"Yes, yes, Miss Morkan is right," said Mr. Browne. "I remember hearing of old Parkinson but he's too far back for me."

"A beautiful, pure, sweet, mellow English tenor," said Aunt Kate with enthusiasm.

Gabriel having finished, the huge pudding was transferred to the table. The clatter of forks and spoons began again. Gabriel's wife served out spoonfuls of the pudding and passed the plates down the table. Midway down they were held up by Mary Jane, who replenished them with raspberry or orange jelly or with blancmange and jam. The pudding was of Aunt Julia's making and she received praises for it from all quarters. She herself said that it was not quite brown enough.

"Well, I hope, Miss Morkan," said Mr. Browne, "that I'm brown enough for you because, you know, I'm all brown."

All the gentlemen, except Gabriel, ate some of the pudding out of compliment to Aunt Julia. As Gabriel never ate sweets the celery had been left for him. Freddy Malins also took a stalk of celery and ate it with his pudding. He had been told that celery was a capital thing for the blood and he was just then under doctor's care. Mrs. Malins, who had been silent all through the supper, said that her son was going down to Mount Melleray in a week or so. The table then spoke of Mount Melleray, how bracing the air was down there, how hospitable the monks were and how they never asked for a penny-piece from their guests.

"And do you mean to say," asked Mr. Browne incredulously, "that a chap can go down there and put up there as if it were a hotel and live on the fat of the land and then come away without paying anything?"

"O, most people give some donation to the monastery when they leave," said Mary Jane.

"I wish we had an institution like that in our Church," said Mr. Browne candidly.

He was astonished to hear that the monks never spoke, got up at two in the morning and slept in their coffins. He asked what they did it for.

"That's the rule of the order," said Aunt Kate firmly.

"Yes, but why?" asked Mr. Browne.

Aunt Kate repeated that it was the rule, that was all. Mr. Browne still seemed not to understand. Freddy Malins explained to him, as best he could, that the monks were trying to make up for the sins committed by all the sinners in the outside world. The explanation was not very clear for Mr. Browne grinned and said:

"I like that idea very much but wouldn't a comfortable spring bed do them as well as a coffin?"

"The coffin," said Mary Jane, "is to remind them of their last end."

As the subject had grown lugubrious it was buried in a silence of the table during which Mrs. Malins could be heard saying to her neighbour in an indistinct undertone:

"They are very good men, the monks, very pious men."

220

225

230

235

The raisins and almonds and figs and apples and oranges and chocolates and sweets were now passed about the table and Aunt Julia invited all the guests to have either port or sherry. At first Mr. Bartell D'Arcy refused to take either but one of his neighbours nudged him and whispered something to him upon which he allowed his glass to be filled. Gradually as the last glasses were being filled the conversation ceased. A pause followed, broken only by the noise of the wine and by unsettlings of chairs. The Misses Morkan, all three, looked down at the tablecloth. Someone coughed once or twice and then a few gentlemen patted the table gently as a signal for silence. The silence came and Gabriel pushed back his chair and stood up.

The patting at once grew louder in encouragement and then ceased altogether. Gabriel leaned his ten trembling fingers on the tablecloth and smiled nervously at the company. Meeting a row of upturned faces he raised his eyes to the chandelier. The piano was playing a waltz tune and he could hear the skirts sweeping against the drawing-room door. People, perhaps, were standing in the snow on the quay out-side, gazing up at the lighted windows and listening to the waltz music. The air was pure there. In the distance lay the park where the trees were weighted with snow. The Wellington Monument wore a gleaming cap of snow that flashed westward over the white field of Fifteen Acres.   240

He began:

"Ladies and Gentlemen,

"It has fallen to my lot this evening, as in years past, to perform a very pleas-ing task but a task for which I am afraid my poor powers as a speaker are all too in-adequate."

"No, no!" said Mr. Browne.

"But, however that may be, I can only ask you to-night to take the will for the deed and to lend me your attention for a few moments while I endeavour to express to you in words what my feelings are on this occasion.   245

"Ladies and Gentlemen, it is not the first time that we have gathered together under this hospitable roof, around this hospitable board. It is not the first time that we have been the recipients—or perhaps, I had better say, the victims—of the hos-pitality of certain good ladies."

He made a circle in the air with his arm and paused. Everyone laughed or smiled at Aunt Kate and Aunt Julia and Mary Jane who all turned crimson with pleasure. Gabriel went on more boldly:

"I feel more strongly with every recurring year that our country has no tradition which does it so much honour and which it should guard so jealously as that of its hospitality. It is a tradition that is unique as far as my experience goes (and I have visited not a few places abroad) among the modern nations. Some would say, per-haps, that with us it is rather a failing than anything to be boasted of. But granted even that, it is, to my mind, a princely failing, and one that I trust will long be cul-tivated among us. Of one thing, at least, I am sure. As long as this one roof shelters the good ladies aforesaid—and I wish from my heart it may do so for many and many a long year to come—the tradition of genuine warm-hearted courteous Irish hospi-tality, which our forefathers have handed down to us and which we in turn must hand down to our descendants, is still alive among us."

A hearty murmur of assent ran round the table. It shot through Gabriel's mind that Miss Ivors was not there and that she had gone away discourteously: and he said with confidence in himself:

"Ladies and Gentlemen,   250

"A new generation is growing up in our midst, a generation actuated by new ideas and new principles. It is serious and enthusiastic for these new ideas and its enthusiasm, even when it is misdirected is, I believe, in the main sincere. But we are living in a sceptical and, if I may use the phrase, a thought-tormented age: and sometimes I fear that this new generation, educated or hypereducated as it is, will lack those qualities of humanity, of hospitality, of kindly humour which belonged to an older day. Listening to-night to the names of all those great singers of the past it seemed to me, I must confess, that we were living in a less spacious age. Those days might, without exaggeration, be called spacious days: and if they are gone beyond recall let us hope, at least, that in gatherings such as this we shall still speak of them with pride and affection, still cherish in our hearts the memory of those dead and gone great ones whose fame the world will not willingly let die."

"Hear, hear!" said Mr. Browne loudly.

"But yet," continued Gabriel, his voice falling into a softer inflection, "there are always in gatherings such as this sadder thoughts that will recur to our minds: thoughts of the past, of youth, of changes, of absent faces that we miss here to-night. Our path through life is strewn with many such sad memories: and were we to brood upon them always we could not find the heart to go on bravely with our work among the living. We have all of us living duties and living affections which claim, and rightly claim, our strenuous endeavours.

"Therefore, I will not linger on the past. I will not let any gloomy moralising intrude upon us here to-night. Here we are gathered together for a brief moment from the bustle and rush of our everyday routine. We are met here as friends, in the spirit of good-fellowship, as colleagues, also to a certain extent, in the true spirit of camaraderie, and as the guests of—what shall I call them?—the Three Graces of the Dublin musical world."

The table burst into applause and laughter at this allusion. Aunt Julia vainly asked each of her neighbours in turn to tell her what Gabriel had said. 255

"He says we are the Three Graces, Aunt Julia," said Mary Jane.

Aunt Julia did not understand but she looked up, smiling, at Gabriel, who continued in the same vein:

"Ladies and Gentlemen,

"I will not attempt to play to-night the part that Paris° played on another occasion. I will not attempt to choose between them. The task would be an invidious one and one beyond my poor powers. For when I view them in turn, whether it be our chief hostess herself, whose good heart, whose too good heart, has become a byword with all who know her, or her sister, who seems to be gifted with perennial youth and whose singing must have been a surprise and a revelation to us all to-night, or, last but not least when I consider our youngest hostess, talented, cheerful, hard-working and the best of nieces, I confess, Ladies and Gentlemen, that I do not know to which of them I should award the prize."

Gabriel glanced down at his aunts and, seeing the large smile on Aunt Julia's face and the tears which had risen to Aunt Kate's eyes, hastened to his close. He raised his glass of port gallantly, while every member of the company fingered a glass expectantly, and said loudly: 260

Paris: Trojan prince required by Zeus to judge whether Hera, Athena, or Aphrodite was the fairest.

"Let us toast them all three together. Let us drink to their health, wealth, long life, happiness and prosperity and may they long continue to hold the proud and self-won position which they hold in their profession and the position of honour and affection which they hold in our hearts."

All the guests stood up, glass in hand, and turning towards the three seated ladies, sang in unison, with Mr. Browne as leader:

> For they are jolly gay fellows,
> For they are jolly gay fellows,
> For they are jolly gay fellows,
> Which nobody can deny.

Aunt Kate was making frank use of her handkerchief and even Aunt Julia seemed moved. Freddy Malins beat time with his pudding-fork and the singers turned towards one another, as if in melodious conference, while they sang with emphasis:

> Unless he tells a lie,
> Unless he tells a lie,

Then, turning once more towards their hostesses, they sang:

> For they are jolly gay fellows,
> For they are jolly gay fellows,
> For they are jolly gay fellows,
> Which nobody can deny.

The acclamation which followed was taken up beyond the door of the supper-room by many of the other guests and renewed time after time, Freddy Malins acting as officer with his fork on high. 265

The piercing morning air came into the hall where they were standing so that Aunt Kate said:

"Close the door, somebody. Mrs. Malins will get her death of cold."

"Browne is out there, Aunt Kate," said Mary Jane.

"Browne is everywhere," said Aunt Kate, lowering her voice.

Mary Jane laughed at her tone. 270

"Really," she said archly, "he is very attentive."

"He has been laid on here like the gas," said Aunt Kate in the same tone, "all during the Christmas."

She laughed herself this time good-humouredly and then added quickly: "But tell him to come in, Mary Jane, and close the door. I hope to goodness he didn't hear me."

At that moment the hall-door was opened and Mr. Browne came in from the doorstep, laughing as if his heart would break. He was dressed in a long green overcoat with mock astrakhan cuffs and collar and wore on his head an oval fur cap. He pointed down the snow-covered quay from where the sound of shrill prolonged whistling was borne in.

"Teddy will have all the cabs in Dublin out," he said. 275

Gabriel advanced from the little pantry behind the office, struggling into his overcoat and, looking round the hall, said:

"Gretta not down yet?"

"She's getting on her things, Gabriel," said Aunt Kate.

"Who's playing up there?" asked Gabriel.

"Nobody. They're all gone."

"O no, Aunt Kate," said Mary Jane. "Bartell D'Arcy and Miss O'Callaghan aren't gone yet."

"Someone is fooling at the piano anyhow," said Gabriel.

Mary Jane glanced at Gabriel and Mr. Browne and said with a shiver:

"It makes me feel cold to look at you two gentlemen muffled up like that. I wouldn't like to face your journey home at this hour."

"I'd like nothing better this minute," said Mr. Browne stoutly, "than a rattling fine walk in the country or a fast drive with a good spanking goer between the shafts."

"We used to have a very good horse and trap at home," said Aunt Julia sadly.

"The never-to-be-forgotten Johnny," said Mary Jane, laughing.

Aunt Kate and Gabriel laughed too.

"Why, what was wonderful about Johnny?" asked Mr. Browne.

"The late lamented Patrick Morkan, our grandfather, that is," explained Gabriel, "commonly known in his later years as the old gentleman, was a glue-boiler."

"O, now, Gabriel," said Aunt Kate, laughing, "he had a starch mill."

"Well, glue or starch," said Gabriel, "the old gentleman had a horse by the name of Johnny. And Johnny used to work in the old gentleman's mill, walking round and round in order to drive the mill. That was all very well; but now comes the tragic part about Johnny. One fine day the old gentleman thought he'd like to drive out with the quality to a military review in the park."

"The Lord have mercy on his soul," said Aunt Kate compassionately.

"Amen," said Gabriel. "So the old gentleman, as I said, harnessed Johnny and put on his very best tall hat and his very best stock collar and drove out in grand style from his ancestral mansion somewhere near Back Lane, I think."

Everyone laughed, even Mrs. Malins, at Gabriel's manner and Aunt Kate said:

"O, now, Gabriel, he didn't live in Back Lane, really. Only the mill was there."

"Out from the mansion of his forefathers," continued Gabriel, "he drove with Johnny. And everything went on beautifully until Johnny came in sight of King Billy's statue: and whether he fell in love with the horse King Billy sits on or whether he thought he was back again in the mill, anyhow he began to walk round the statue."

Gabriel paced in a circle round the hall in his goloshes amid the laughter of the others.

"Round and round he went," said Gabriel, "and the old gentleman, who was a very pompous old gentleman, was highly indignant. 'Go on, sir! What do you mean, sir? Johnny! Johnny! Most extraordinary conduct! Can't understand the horse!' "

The peal of laughter which followed Gabriel's imitation of the incident was interrupted by a resounding knock at the hall door. Mary Jane ran to open it and let in Freddy Malins. Freddy Malins, with his hat well back on his head and his shoulders humped with cold, was puffing and steaming after his exertions.

"I could only get one cab," he said.

"O, we'll find another along the quay," said Gabriel.

"Yes," said Aunt Kate. "Better not keep Mrs. Malins standing in the draught."

Mrs. Malins was helped down the front steps by her son and Mr. Browne and, after many manoeuvres, hoisted into the cab. Freddy Malins clambered in after her and spent a long time settling her on the seat, Mr. Browne helping him with advice. At last she was settled comfortably and Freddy Malins invited Mr. Browne into the cab.

There was a good deal of confused talk, and then Mr. Browne got into the cab. The cabman settled his rug over his knees, and bent down for the address. The confusion grew greater and the cabman was directed differently by Freddy Malins and Mr. Browne, each of whom had his head out through a window of the cab. The difficulty was to know where to drop Mr. Browne along the route, and Aunt Kate, Aunt Julia and Mary Jane helped the discussion from the doorstep with cross-directions and contradictions and abundance of laughter. As for Freddy Malins he was speechless with laughter. He popped his head in and out of the window every moment to the great danger of his hat, and told his mother how the discussion was progressing, till at last Mr. Browne shouted to the bewildered cabman above the din of everybody's laughter:

"Do you know Trinity College?"

"Yes, sir," said the cabman.

"Well, drive bang up against Trinity College gates," said Mr. Browne, "and then we'll tell you where to go. You understand now?"

"Yes, sir," said the cabman.

"Make like a bird for Trinity College."

"Right, sir," said the cabman. 310

The horse was whipped up and the cab rattled off along the quay amid a chorus of laughter and adieus.

Gabriel had not gone to the door with the others. He was in a dark part of the hall gazing up the staircase. A woman was standing near the top of the first flight, in the shadow also. He could not see her face but he could see the terracotta and salmon-pink panels of her skirt which the shadow made appear black and white. It was his wife. She was leaning on the banisters, listening to something. Gabriel was surprised at her stillness and strained his ear to listen also. But he could hear little save the noise of laughter and dispute on the front steps, a few chords struck on the piano and a few notes of a man's voice singing.

He stood still in the gloom of the hall, trying to catch the air that the voice was singing and gazing up at his wife. There was grace and mystery in her attitude as if she were a symbol of something. He asked himself what is a woman standing on the stairs in the shadow, listening to distant music, a symbol of. If he were a painter he would paint her in that attitude. Her blue felt hat would show off the bronze of her hair against the darkness and the dark panels of her skirt would show off the light ones. *Distant Music* he would call the picture if he were a painter.

The hall-door was closed; and Aunt Kate, Aunt Julia and Mary Jane came down the hall, still laughing.

"Well, isn't Freddy terrible?" said Mary Jane. "He's really terrible." 315

Gabriel said nothing but pointed up the stairs towards where his wife was standing. Now that the hall-door was closed the voice and the piano could be heard more clearly. Gabriel held up his hand for them to be silent. The song seemed to be in the old Irish tonality and the singer seemed uncertain both of his words and of his voice. The voice, made plaintive by distance and by the singer's hoarseness, faintly illuminated the cadence of the air with words expressing grief:

> O, the rain falls on my heavy locks
> And the dew wets my skin,
> My babe lies cold . . .

"O," exclaimed Mary Jane. "It's Bartell D'Arcy singing and he wouldn't sing all the night. O, I'll get him to sing a song before he goes."

"O, do, Mary Jane," said Aunt Kate.

Mary Jane brushed past the others and ran to the staircase, but before she reached it the singing stopped and the piano was closed abruptly.

"O, what a pity!" she cried. "Is he coming down, Gretta?"

Gabriel heard his wife answer yes and saw her come down towards them. A few steps behind her were Mr. Bartell D'Arcy and Miss O'Callaghan.

"O, Mr. D'Arcy," cried Mary Jane, "It's downright mean of you to break off like that when we were all in raptures listening to you."

"I have been at him all the evening," said Miss O'Callaghan, "and Mrs. Conroy, too, and he told us he had a dreadful cold and couldn't sing."

"O, Mr. D'Arcy," said Aunt Kate, "now that was a great fib to tell."

"Can't you see that I'm as hoarse as a crow?" said Mr. D'Arcy roughly.

He went into the pantry hastily and put on his overcoat. The others, taken aback by his rude speech, could find nothing to say. Aunt Kate wrinkled her brows and made signs to the others to drop the subject. Mr. D'Arcy stood swathing his neck carefully and frowning.

"It's the weather," said Aunt Julia, after a pause.

"Yes, everybody has colds," said Aunt Kate readily, "everybody."

"They say," said Mary Jane, "we haven't had snow like it for thirty years; and I read this morning in the newspapers that the snow is general all over Ireland."

"I love the look of snow," said Aunt Julia sadly.

"So do I," said Miss O'Callaghan. "I think Christmas is never really Christmas unless we have the snow on the ground."

"But poor Mr. D'Arcy doesn't like the snow," said Aunt Kate, smiling.

Mr. D'Arcy came from the pantry, fully swathed and buttoned, and in a repentant tone told them the history of his cold. Everyone gave him advice and said it was a great pity and urged him to be very careful of his throat in the night air. Gabriel watched his wife, who did not join in the conversation. She was standing right under the dusty fanlight and the flame of the gas lit up the rich bronze of her hair, which he had seen her drying at the fire a few days before. She was in the same attitude and seemed unaware of the talk about her. At last she turned towards them and Gabriel saw that there was colour on her cheeks and that her eyes were shining. A sudden tide of joy went leaping out of his heart.

"Mr. D'Arcy," she said, "what is the name of that song you were singing?"

"It's called *The Lass of Aughrim*," said Mr. D'Arcy, "but I couldn't remember it properly. Why? Do you know it?"

"*The Lass of Aughrim*," she repeated. "I couldn't think of the name."

"It's a very nice air,"° said Mary Jane. "I'm sorry you were not in voice to-night."

"Now, Mary Jane," said Aunt Kate, "don't annoy Mr. D'Arcy. I won't have him annoyed."

Seeing that all were ready to start she shepherded them to the door, where good-night was said:

"Well, good-night, Aunt Kate, and thanks for the pleasant evening."

"Good-night, Gabriel. Good-night, Gretta!"

"Good-night, Aunt Kate, and thanks ever so much. Good-night, Aunt Julia."

"O, good-night, Gretta, I didn't see you."

320

325

330

335

340

---

air: melody.

"Good-night, Mr. D'Arcy. Good-night, Miss O'Callaghan."

"Good-night, Miss Morkan."

"Good-night, again."

"Good-night, all. Safe home."

"Good-night. Good-night."

The morning was still dark. A dull, yellow light brooded over the houses and the river; and the sky seemed to be descending. It was slushy underfoot; and only streaks and patches of snow lay on the roofs, on the parapets of the quay and on the area railings. The lamps were still burning redly in the murky air and, across the river, the palace of the Four Courts stood out menacingly against the heavy sky.

She was walking on before him with Mr. Bartell D'Arcy, her shoes in a brown parcel tucked under one arm and her hands holding her skirt up from the slush. She had no longer any grace of attitude, but Gabriel's eyes were still bright with happiness. The blood went bounding along his veins; and the thoughts went rioting through his brain, proud, joyful, tender, valorous.

She was walking on before him so lightly and so erect that he longed to run after her noiselessly, catch her by the shoulders and say something foolish and affectionate into her ear. She seemed to him so frail that he longed to defend her against something and then to be alone with her. Moments of their secret life together burst like stars upon his memory. A heliotrope envelope was lying beside his breakfast-cup and he was caressing it with his hand. Birds were twittering in the ivy and the sunny web of the curtain was shimmering along the floor: he could not eat for happiness. They were standing on the crowded platform and he was placing a ticket inside the warm palm of her glove. He was standing with her in the cold, looking in through a grated window at a man making bottles in a roaring furnace. It was very cold. Her face, fragrant in the cold air, was quite close to his; and suddenly he called out to the man at the furnace:

"Is the fire hot, sir?"

But the man could not hear with the noise of the furnace. It was just as well. He might have answered rudely.

A wave of yet more tender joy escaped from his heart and went coursing in warm flood along his arteries. Like the tender fire of stars moments of their life together, that no one knew of or would ever know of, broke upon and illumined his memory. He longed to recall to her those moments, to make her forget the years of their dull existence together and remember only their moments of ecstasy. For the years, he felt, had not quenched his soul or hers. Their children, his writing, her household cares had not quenched all their souls' tender fire. In one letter that he had written to her then he had said: "Why is it that words like these seem to me so dull and cold? Is it because there is no word tender enough to be your name?"

Like distant music these words that he had written years before were borne towards him from the past. He longed to be alone with her. When the others had gone away, when he and she were in the room in the hotel, then they would be alone together. He would call her softly:

"Gretta!"

Perhaps she would not hear at once: she would be undressing. Then something in his voice would strike her. She would turn and look at him. . . .

At the corner of Winetavern Street they met a cab. He was glad of its rattling noise as it saved him from conversation. She was looking out of the window and seemed tired. The others spoke only a few words, pointing out some building or street. The horse galloped along wearily under the murky morning sky, dragging his old rattling box after his heels, and Gabriel was again in a cab with her, galloping to catch the boat, galloping to their honeymoon.

As the cab drove across O'Connell Bridge Miss O'Callaghan said:

"They say you never cross O'Connell Bridge without seeing a white horse." 360

"I see a white man this time," said Gabriel.

"Where?" asked Mr. Bartell D'Arcy.

Gabriel pointed to the statue, on which lay patches of snow. Then he nodded familiarly to it and waved his hand.

"Good-night, Dan," he said gaily.

When the cab drew up before the hotel, Gabriel jumped out and, and in spite of Mr. Bartell D'Arcy's protest, paid the driver. He gave the man a shilling over his fare. The man saluted and said: 365

"A prosperous New Year to you, sir."

"The same to you," said Gabriel cordially.

She leaned for a moment on his arm in getting out of the cab and while standing at the curbstone, bidding the others good-night. She leaned lightly on his arm, as lightly as when she had danced with him a few hours before. He had felt proud and happy then, happy that she was his, proud of her grace and wifely carriage. But now, after the kindling again of so many memories, the first touch of her body, musical and strange and perfumed, sent through him a keen pang of lust. Under cover of her silence he pressed her arm closely to his side; and, as they stood at the hotel door, he felt that they had escaped from their lives and duties, escaped from home and friends and run away together with wild and radiant hearts to a new adventure.

An old man was dozing in a great hooded chair in the hall. He lit a candle in the office and went before them to the stairs. They followed him in silence, their feet falling in soft thuds on the thickly carpeted stairs. She mounted the stairs behind the porter, her head bowed in the ascent, her frail shoulders curved as with a burden, her skirt girt tightly about her. He could have flung his arms about her hips and held her still, for his arms were trembling with desire to seize her and only the stress of his nails against the palms of his hands held the wild impulse of his body in check. The porter halted on the stairs to settle his guttering candle. They halted, too, on the steps below him. In the silence Gabriel could hear the falling of the molten wax into the tray and the thumping of his own heart against his ribs.

The porter led them along a corridor and opened a door. Then he set his unstable candle down on a toilet-table and asked at what hour they were to be called in the morning. 370

"Eight," said Gabriel.

The porter pointed to the tap of the electric light and began a muttered apology, but Gabriel cut him short.

"We don't want any light. We have light enough from the street. And I say," he added, pointing to the candle, "you might remove that handsome article, like a good man."

The porter took up his candle again, but slowly, for he was surprised by such a novel idea. Then he mumbled good-night and went out. Gabriel shot the lock to.

A ghastly light from the street lamp lay in a long shaft from one window to the door. Gabriel threw his overcoat and hat on a couch and crossed the room towards the window. He looked down into the street in order that his emotion might calm a little. Then he turned and leaned against a chest of drawers with his back to the light. She had taken off her hat and cloak and was standing before a large swinging mirror, unhooking her waist.° Gabriel paused for a few moments, watching her, and then said:

375

"Gretta!"

She turned away from the mirror slowly and walked along the shaft of light towards him. Her face looked so serious and weary that the words would not pass Gabriel's lips. No, it was not the moment yet.

"You looked tired," he said.

"I am a little," she answered.

"You don't feel ill or weak?"

380

"No, tired: that's all."

She went on to the window and stood there, looking out. Gabriel waited again and then fearing that diffidence was about to conquer him, he said abruptly:

"By the way, Gretta!"

"What is it?"

"You know that poor fellow Malins?" he said quickly.

385

"Yes. What about him?"

"Well, poor fellow, he's a decent sort of chap, after all," continued Gabriel in a false voice. "He gave me back that sovereign I lent him, and I didn't expect it, really. It's a pity he wouldn't keep away from that Browne, because he's not a bad fellow, really."

He was trembling now with annoyance. Why did she seem so abstracted? He did not know how he could begin. Was she annoyed, too, about something? If she would only turn to him or come to him of her own accord! To take her as she was would be brutal. No, he must see some ardour in her eyes first. He longed to be master of her strange mood.

"When did you lend him the pound?" she asked, after a pause.

Gabriel strove to restrain himself from breaking out into brutal language about the sottish Malins and his pound. He longed to cry to her from his soul, to crush her body against his, to overmaster her. But he said:

390

"O, at Christmas, when he opened that little Christmas-card shop in Henry Street."

He was in such a fever of rage and desire that he did not hear her come from the window. She stood before him for an instant, looking at him strangely. Then, suddenly raising herself on tiptoe and resting her hands lightly on his shoulders, she kissed him.

"You are a very generous person, Gabriel," she said.

Gabriel, trembling with delight at her sudden kiss and at the quaintness of her phrase, put his hands on her hair and began smoothing it back, scarcely touching it with his fingers. The washing had made it fine and brilliant. His heart was brimming over with happiness. Just when he was wishing for it she had come to him of her own accord. Perhaps her thoughts had been running with his. Perhaps she had felt the impetuous desire that was in him, and then the yielding mood had come upon her. Now that she had fallen to him so easily, he wondered why he had been so diffident.

He stood, holding her head between his hands. Then, slipping one arm swiftly about her body and drawing her towards him, he said softly:

395

---

waist: a garment encircling the body's middle.

A Fiction Anthology

"Gretta, dear, what are you thinking about?"

She did not answer nor yield wholly to his arm. He said again, softly:

"Tell me what it is, Gretta. I think I know what is the matter. Do I know?"

She did not answer at once. Then she said in an outburst of tears:

"O, I am thinking about that song, *The Lass of Aughrim*."

She broke loose from him and ran to the bed and, throwing her arms across the bed-rail, hid her face. Gabriel stood stock-still for a moment in astonishment and then followed her. As he passed in the way of the cheval-glass he caught sight of himself in full length, his broad, well-filled shirtfront, the face whose expression always puzzled him when he saw it in a mirror, and his glimmering gilt-rimmed eye-glasses. He halted a few paces from her and said:

"What about the song? Why does that make you cry?"

She raised her head from her arms and dried her eyes with the back of her hand like a child. A kinder note than he had intended went into his voice.

"Why, Gretta?" he asked.

"I am thinking about a person long ago who used to sing that song."

"And who was the person long ago?" asked Gabriel, smiling.

"It was a person I used to know in Galway when I was living with my grand-mother," she said.

The smile passed away from Gabriel's face. A dull anger began to gather again at the back of his mind and the dull fires of his lust began to glow angrily in his veins.

"Someone you were in love with?" he asked ironically.

"It was a young boy I used to know," she answered, "named Michael Furey. He used to sing that song, *The Lass of Aughrim*. He was very delicate."

Gabriel was silent. He did not wish her to think that he was interested in this delicate boy.

"I can see him so plainly," she said, after a moment. "Such eyes as he had: big, dark eyes! And such an expression in them—an expression!"

"O, then, you are in love with him?" said Gabriel.

"I used to go out walking with him," she said, "when I was in Galway."

A thought flew across Gabriel's mind.

"Perhaps that was why you wanted to go to Galway with that Ivors girl?" he said coldly.

She looked at him and asked in surprise:

"What for?"

Her eyes made Gabriel feel awkward. He shrugged his shoulders and said:

"How do I know? To see him, perhaps."

She looked away from him along the shaft of light towards the window in silence.

"He is dead," she said at length. "He died when he was only seventeen. Isn't it a terrible thing to die so young as that?"

"What was he?" asked Gabriel, still ironically.

"He was in the gasworks," she said.

Gabriel felt humiliated by the failure of his irony and by the evocation of this figure from the dead, a boy in the gasworks. While he had been full of memories of their secret life together, full of tenderness and joy and desire, she had been com-paring him in her mind with another. A shameful consciousness of his own person assailed him. He saw himself as a ludicrous figure, acting as a pennyboy for his aunts, a nervous, well-meaning sentimentalist, orating to vulgarians and idealising his own clownish lusts, the pitiable fatuous fellow he had caught a glimpse of in the mirror. Instinctively he turned his back more to the light lest she might see the shame that burned upon his forehead. ₄₂₅

He tried to keep up his tone of cold interrogation, but his voice when he spoke was humble and indifferent.

"I suppose you were in love with this Michael Furey, Gretta," he said.

"I was great with him at that time," she said.

Her voice was veiled and sad. Gabriel, feeling now how vain it would be to try to lead her whither he had purposed, caressed one of her hands and said, also sadly:

"And what did he die of so young, Gretta? Consumption, was it?" ₄₃₀

"I think he died for me," she answered.

A vague terror seized Gabriel at this answer, as if, at that hour when he had hoped to triumph, some impalpable and vindictive being was coming against him, gathering forces against him in its vague world. But he shook himself free of it with an effort of reason and continued to caress her hand. He did not question her again, for he felt that she would tell him of herself. Her hand was warm and moist: it did not respond to his touch, but he continued to caress it just as he had caressed her first letter to him that spring morning.

"It was in the winter," she said, "about the beginning of the winter when I was going to leave my grandmother's and come up here to the convent. And he was ill at the time in his lodgings in Galway and wouldn't be let out, and his people in Oughterard were written to. He was in decline, they said, or something like that. I never knew rightly."

She paused for a moment and sighed.

"Poor fellow," she said. "He was very fond of me and he was such a gentle boy. We used to go out together, walking, you know, Gabriel, like the way they do in the country. He was going to study singing only for his health. He had a very good voice, poor Michael Furey." ₄₃₅

"Well; and then?" asked Gabriel.

"And then when it came to the time for me to leave Galway and come up to the convent he was much worse and I wouldn't be let see him so I wrote him a letter saying I was going up to Dublin and would be back in the summer, and hoping he would be better then."

She paused for a moment to get her voice under control, and then went on:

"Then the night before I left, I was in my grandmother's house in Nuns' Island, packing up, and I heard gravel thrown up against the window. The window was so wet I couldn't see, so I ran downstairs as I was and slipped out the back into the garden and there was the poor fellow at the end of the garden, shivering."

"And did you not tell him to go back?" asked Gabriel. ₄₄₀

"I implored of him to go home at once and told him he would get his death in the rain. But he said he did not want to live. I can see his eyes as well! He was standing at the end of the wall where there was a tree."

"And did he go home?" asked Gabriel.

"Yes, he went home. And when I was only a week in the convent he died and he was buried in Oughterard, where his people came from. O, the day I heard that, that he was dead!"

She stopped, choking with sobs, and, overcome by emotion, flung herself face downward on the bed, sobbing in the quilt. Gabriel held her hand for a moment

longer, irresolutely, and then, shy of intruding on her grief, let it fall gently and
walked quietly to the window.

She was fast asleep.

 Gabriel, leaning on his elbow, looked for a few moments unresentfully on her
tangled hair and half-open mouth, listening to her deep-drawn breath. So she had
had that romance in her life: a man had died for her sake. It hardly pained him now
to think how poor a part he, her husband, had played in her life. He watched her
while she slept, as though he and she had never lived together as man and wife. His
curious eyes rested long upon her face and on her hair: and, as he thought of what
she must have been then, in that time of her first girlish beauty, a strange, friendly
pity for her entered his soul. He did not like to say even to himself that her face was
no longer beautiful, but he knew that it was no longer the face for which Michael
Furey had braved death.

 Perhaps she had not told him all the story. His eyes moved to the chair over
which she had thrown some of her clothes. A petticoat string dangled to the floor.
One boot stood upright, its limp upper fallen down: the fellow of it lay upon its side.
He wondered at his riot of emotions of an hour before. From what had it proceeded?
From his aunt's supper, from his own foolish speech, from the wine and dancing, the
merry-making when saying good-night in the hall, the pleasure of the walk along
the river in the snow. Poor Aunt Julia! She, too, would soon be a shade with the
shade of Patrick Morkan and his horse. He had caught that haggard look upon her
face for a moment when she was singing *Arrayed for the Bridal*. Soon, perhaps, he
would be sitting in that same drawing-room, dressed in black, his silk hat on his
knees. The blinds would be drawn down and Aunt Kate would be sitting beside him,
crying and blowing her nose and telling him how Julia had died. He would cast
about in his mind for some words that might console her, and would find only lame
and useless ones. Yes, yes: that would happen very soon.

 The air of the room chilled his shoulders. He stretched himself cautiously along
under the sheets and lay down beside his wife. One by one, they were all becoming
shades. Better pass boldly into that other world, in the full glory of some passion,
than fade and wither dismally with age. He thought of how she who lay beside him
had locked in her heart for so many years that image of her lover's eyes when he had
told her that he did not wish to live.

 Generous tears filled Gabriel's eyes. He had never felt like that himself towards
any woman but he knew that such a feeling must be love. The tears gathered more
thickly in his eyes and in the partial darkness he imagined he saw the form of a
young man standing under a dripping tree. Other forms were near. His soul had approached that region where dwell the vast hosts of the dead. He was conscious of,
but could not apprehend, their wayward and flickering existence. His own identity
was fading out into a grey impalpable world: the solid world itself, which these dead
had one time reared and lived in, was dissolving and dwindling.

 A few light taps upon the pane made him turn to the window. It had begun to
snow again. He watched sleepily the flakes, silver and dark, falling obliquely against
the lamplight. The time had come for him to set out on his journey westward. Yes,
the newspapers were right snow was general all over Ireland. It was falling on every
part of the dark central plain, on the treeless hills, falling softly upon the Bog of
Allen and, farther westward, softly falling into the dark mutinous Shannon waves.

It was falling, too, upon every part of the lonely churchyard on the hill where Michael Furey lay buried. It lay thickly drifted on the crooked crosses and head-stones, on the spears of the little gate, on the barren thorns. His soul swooned slowly as he heard the snow falling faintly through the universe and faintly falling, like the descent of their last end, upon all the living and the dead.   450

D. H. Lawrence (1885–1930)

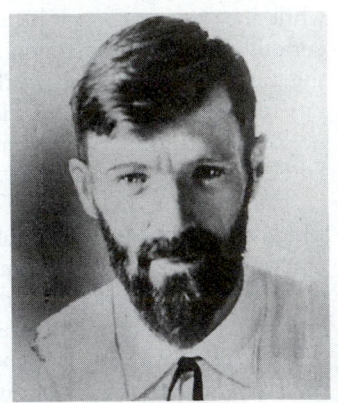

David Herbert Lawrence was a miner's son from the English coal-mining district of Nottinghamshire. He had studied to be a teacher, but he began to publish prose and poetry very soon after taking a post in South London. His first novel, *The White Peacock,* appeared in 1909. Lawrence was so prolific that he was soon able to devote himself strictly to literature.

For the twenty years of his career, Lawrence was a highly controversial figure because of his strongly worded, emancipated views on love and sexuality—expressed in his novels *The Rainbow* (1915), *Women in Love* (1920), and *Lady Chatterley's Lover* (1928)—not to mention his own scandalous elopement with Frieda Weekley, wife of a well-known scholar. He and Frieda traveled from Italy to Australia to Mexico to the American Southwest, looking to ease the tuberculosis that finally killed him.

ODOUR OF CHRYSANTHEMUMS

I

The small locomotive engine, Number 4, came clanking, stumbling down from Selston with seven full wagons. It appeared round the corner with loud threats of speed, but the colt that it startled from among the gorse, which still flickered indistinctly in the raw afternoon, out-distanced it at a canter. A woman, walking up the railway line to Underwood, drew back into the hedge, held her basket aside, and watched the footplate° of the engine advancing. The trucks thumped heavily past, one by one, with slow inevitable movement, as she stood insignificantly trapped between the jolting black wagons and the hedge; then they curved away

---

footplate: the locomotive platform where an engineer stands.

towards the coppice° where the withered oak leaves dropped noiselessly, while the birds, pulling at the scarlet hips beside the track, made off into the dusk that had already crept into the spinney.° In the open, the smoke from the engine sank and cleaved to the rough grass. The fields were dreary and forsaken, and in the marshy strip that led to the whimsey, a reedy pit-pond, the fowls had already abandoned their run among the alders, to roost in the tarred fowlhouse. The pit-bank loomed up beyond the pond, flames like red sores licking its ashy sides, in the afternoon's stagnant light. Just beyond rose the tapering chimneys and the clumsy black headstocks of Brinsley Colliery.° The two wheels were spinning fast up against the sky, and the winding engine rapped out its little spasms. The miners were being turned up.

The engine whistled as it came into the wide bay of railway lines beside the colliery, where rows of trucks stood in harbour.

Miners, single, trailing and in groups, passed like shadows diverging home. At the edge of the ribbed level of sidings squat a low cottage, three steps down from the cinder track. A large bony vine clutched at the house, as if to claw down the tiled roof. Round the bricked yard grew a few wintry primroses. Beyond, the long garden sloped down to a bush-covered brook course. There were some twiggy apple trees, winter-crack trees, and ragged cabbages. Beside the path hung dishevelled pink chrysanthemums, like pink cloths hung on bushes. A woman came stooping out of the felt-covered fowl-house, half-way down the garden. She closed and padlocked the door, then drew herself erect, having brushed some bits from her white apron.

She was a tall woman of imperious mien, handsome, with definite black eyebrows. Her smooth black hair was parted exactly. For a few moments she stood steadily watching the miners as they passed along the railway: then she turned towards the brook course. Her face was calm and set, her mouth was closed with disillusionment. After a moment she called:

"John!" There was no answer. She waited, and then said distinctly: 5

"Where are you?"

"Here!" replied a child's sulky voice from among the bushes. The woman looked piercingly through the dusk.

"Are you at that brook?" she asked sternly.

For answer the child showed himself before the raspberry-canes that rose like whips. He was a small, sturdy boy of five. He stood quite still, defiantly.

"Oh!" said the mother, conciliated. "I thought you were down at that wet brook—and you remember what I told you—"   10

The boy did not move or answer.

"Come, come on in," she said more gently, "It's getting dark. There's your grandfather's engine coming down the line!"

The lad advanced slowly, with resentful, taciturn movement. He was dressed in trousers and waistcoat of cloth that was too thick and hard for the size of the garments. They were evidently cut down from a man's clothes.

As they went slowly towards the house he tore at the ragged wisps of chrysanthemums and dropped the petals in handfuls among the path.

"Don't do that—it does look nasty," said his mother. He refrained, and she, suddenly pitiful, broke off a twig with three or four wan flowers and held them against

---

coppice: thicket.
spinney: small grove.
colliery: coal mine.

her face. When mother and son reached the yard her hand hesitated, and instead of laying the flower aside, she pushed it in her apron-band. The mother and son stood at the foot of the three steps looking across the bay of lines at the passing home of the miners. The trundle of the small train was imminent. Suddenly the engine loomed past the house and came to a stop opposite the gate. 15

The engine-driver, a short man with round grey beard, leaned out of the cab high above the woman.

"Have you got a cup of tea?" he said in a cheery, hearty fashion.

It was her father. She went in, saying she would mash. Directly, she returned.

"I didn't come to see you on Sunday," began the little grey-bearded man.

"I didn't expect you," said his daughter. 20

The engine-driver winced; then, reassuming his cheery, airy manner, he said:

"Oh, have you heard then? Well, and what do you think—?"

"I think it is soon enough," she replied.

At her brief censure the little man made an impatient gesture, and said coaxingly, yet with dangerous coldness:

"Well, what's a man to do? It's no sort of life for a man of my years, to sit at my own hearth like a stranger. And if I'm going to marry again it may as well be soon as late—what does it matter to anybody?" 25

The woman did not reply, but turned and went into the house. The man in the engine-cab stood assertive, till she returned with a cup of tea and a piece of bread and butter on a plate. She went up the steps and stood near the footplate of the hissing engine.

"You needn't 'a' brought me bread an' butter," said her father. "But a cup of tea"—he sipped appreciatively—"it's very nice." He sipped for a moment or two, then: "I hear as Walter's got another bout on," he said.

"When hasn't he?" said the woman bitterly.

"I heerd tell of him in the 'Lord Nelson' braggin' as he was going to spend that b——afore he went: half a sovereign that was."

"When?" asked the woman. 30

"A' Sat'day night—I know that's true."

"Very likely," she laughed bitterly. "He gives me twenty-three shillings."

"Aye, it's a nice thing, when a man can do nothing with his money but make a beast of himself!" said the grey-whiskered man. The woman turned her head away. Her father swallowed the last of his tea and handed her the cup.

"Aye," he sighed, wiping his mouth. "It's a settler, it is——"

He put his hand on the lever. The little engine strained and groaned, and the train rumbled towards the crossing. The woman again looked across the metals. Darkness was settling over the spaces of the railway and trucks: the miners, in grey sombre groups, were still passing home. The winding engine pulsed hurriedly, with brief pauses. Elizabeth Bates looked at the dreary flow of men, then she went indoors. Her husband did not come. 35

The kitchen was small and full of firelight; red coals piled glowing up the chimney mouth. All the life of the room seemed in the white, warm hearth and the steel fender° reflecting the red fire. The cloth was laid for tea; cups glinted in the shadows. At the back, where the lowest stairs protruded into the room, the boy sat strug-

---

fender: fireplace screen.

A Fiction Anthology

gling with a knife and a piece of white wood. He was almost hidden in the shadow. It was half-past four. They had but to await the father's coming to begin tea. As the mother watched her son's sullen little struggle with the wood, she saw herself in his silence and pertinacity; she saw the father in her child's indifference to all but himself. She seemed to be occupied by her husband. He had probably gone past his home, slunk past his own door, to drink before he came in, while his dinner spoiled and wasted in waiting. She glanced at the clock, then took the potatoes to strain them in the yard. The garden and fields beyond the brook were closed in uncertain darkness. When she rose with the saucepan, leaving the drain steaming into the night behind her, she saw the yellow lamps were lit along the high road that went up the hill away beyond the space of the railway lines and the field.

Then again she watched the men trooping home, fewer now and fewer.

Indoors the fire was sinking and the room was dark red. The woman put her saucepan on the hob, and set a batter-pudding near the mouth of the oven. Then she stood unmoving. Directly, gratefully, came quick young steps to the door. Someone hung on the latch a moment, then a little girl entered and began pulling off her outdoor things, dragging a mass of curls, just ripening from gold to brown, over her eyes with her hat.

Her mother chid her for coming late from school, and said she would have to keep her at home the dark winter days.

"Why, mother, it's hardly a bit dark yet. The lamp's not lighted, and my father's not home."

"No, he isn't. But it's a quarter to five! Did you see anything of him?"

The child became serious. She looked at her mother with large, wistful blue eyes.

"No, mother, I've never seen him. Why? Has he come up an' gone past, to Old Brinsley? He hasn't, mother, 'cos I never saw him."

"He'd watch that," said the mother bitterly, "he'd take care as you didn't see him. But you may depend upon it, he's seated in the 'Prince o' Wales.' He wouldn't be this late."

The girl looked at her mother piteously.

"Let's have our teas, mother, should we?" said she.

The mother called John to table. She opened the door once more and looked out across the darkness of the lines. All was deserted: she could not hear the winding-engines.

"Perhaps," she said to herself, "he's stopped to get some ripping done."

They sat down to tea. John, at the end of the table near the door, was almost lost in the darkness. Their faces were hidden from each other. The girl crouched against the fender slowly moving a thick piece of bread before the fire. The lad, his face a dusky mark on the shadow, sat watching her who was transfigured in the red glow.

"I do think it's beautiful to look in the fire," said the child.

"Do you?" said her mother. "Why?"

"It's so red, and full of little caves—and it feels so nice, and you can fair smell it."

"It'll want mending directly," replied her mother, "and then if your father comes he'll carry on and say there never is a fire when a man comes home sweating from the pit. A public house is always warm enough."

There was silence till the boy said complainingly: "Make haste, our Annie."

"Well, I am doing! I can't make the fire do it no faster, can I?"

"She keeps wafflin' it about so's to make 'er slow," grumbled the boy.

"Don't have such an evil imagination, child," replied the mother.

Soon the room was busy in the darkness with the crisp sound of crunching. The mother ate very little. She drank her tea determinedly, and sat thinking. When she rose her anger was evident in the stern unbending of her head. She looked at the pudding in the fender and broke out:

"It is a scandalous thing as a man can't even come home to his dinner! If it's crozzled° up to a cinder I don't see why I should care. Past his very door he goes to get to a public-house, and here I sit with his dinner waiting for him—"

She went out. As she dropped piece after piece of coal on the red fire, the shadows fell on the walls, till the room was almost in total darkness. 60

"I canna see," grumbled the invisible John. In spite of herself, the mother laughed.

"You know the way to your mouth," she said. She set the dust-pan outside the door. When she came again like a shadow on the hearth, the lad repeated, complaining sulkily:

"I canna see."

"Good gracious!" cried the mother irritably, "you're as bad as your father if it's a bit dusk!"

Nevertheless, she took a paper spill from a sheaf on the mantelpiece and proceeded to light the lamp that hung from the ceiling in the middle of the room. As she reached up, her figure displayed itself just rounding with maternity. 65

"Oh, mother——!" exclaimed the girl.

"What?" said the woman, suspended in the act of putting the lampglass over the flame. The copper reflector shone handsomely on her, as she stood with uplifted arm, turning to face her daughter.

"You've got a flower in your apron!" said the child, in a little rapture at this unusual event.

"Goodness me!" exclaimed the woman, relieved. "One would think the house was afire." She replaced the glass and waited a moment before turning up the wick. A pale shadow was seen floating vaguely on the floor.

"Let me smell!" said the child, still rapturously, coming forward and putting her face to her mother's waist. 70

"Go along, silly!" said the mother, turning up the lamp. The light revealed their suspense so that the woman felt it almost unbearable. Annie was still bending at her waist. Irritably, the mother took the flowers out from her apron-band.

"Oh, mother—don't take them out!" Annie cried, catching her hand and trying to replace the sprig.

"Such nonsense!" said the mother, turning away. The child put the pale chrysanthemums to her lips, murmuring:

"Don't they smell beautiful!"

Her mother gave a short laugh. 75

"No," she said, "not to me. It was chrysanthemums when I married him, and chrysanthemums when you were born, and the first time they ever brought him home drunk, he'd got brown chrysanthemums in his buttonhole."

She looked at the children. Their eyes and their parted lips were wondering. The mother sat rocking in silence for some time. Then she looked at the clock.

"Twenty minutes to six!" In a tone of fine bitter carelessness she continued: "Eh, he'll not come now till they bring him. There he'll stick! But he needn't come rolling

---

crozzled: burnt.

in here in his pit-dirt, for I won't wash him. He can lie on the floor——Eh, what a fool I've been, what a fool! And this is what I came here for, to this dirty hole, rats and all, for him to slink past his very door. Twice last week—he's begun now——"

She silenced herself, and rose to clear the table.

While for an hour or more the children played, subduedly intent, fertile of imagination, united in fear of the mother's wrath, and in dread of their father's home-coming, Mrs. Bates sat in her rocking-chair making a "singlet"° of thick cream-coloured flannel, which gave a dull wounded sound as she tore off the grey edge. She worked at her sewing with energy, listening to the children, and her anger wearied itself, lay down to rest, opening its eyes from time to time and steadily watching, its ears raised to listen. Sometimes even her anger quailed and shrank, and the mother suspended her sewing, tracing the footsteps that thudded along the sleepers outside: she would lift her head sharply to bid the children "hush," but she recovered herself in time, and the footsteps went past the gate, and the children were not flung out of their play-world. 80

But at last Annie sighed, and gave in. She glanced at her wagon of slippers, and loathed the game. She turned plaintively to her mother.

"Mother!"—but she was inarticulate.

John crept out like a frog from under the sofa. His mother glanced up. "Yes," she said, "just look at those shirt-sleeves!"

The boy held them out to survey them, saying nothing. Then somebody called in a hoarse voice away down the line, and suspense bristled in the room, till two people had gone by outside, talking.

"It is time for bed," said the mother. 85

"My father hasn't come," wailed Annie plaintively. But her mother was primed with courage.

"Never mind. They'll bring him when he does come—like a log." She meant there would be no scene. "And he may sleep on the floor till he wakes himself. I know he'll not go to work to-morrow after this!"

The children had their hands and faces wiped with a flannel. They were very quiet. When they had put on their night-dresses, they said their prayers, the boy mumbling. The mother looked down at them, at the brown silken bush of inter-twining curls in the nape of the girl's neck, at the little black head of the lad, and her heart burst with anger at their father, who caused all three such distress. The children hid their faces in her skirts for comfort.

When Mrs. Bates came down, the room was strangely empty, with a tension of expectancy. She took up her sewing and stitched for some time without raising her head. Meantime her anger was tinged with fear.

II

The clock struck eight and she rose suddenly, dropping her sewing on her chair. She went to the stair-foot door, opened it, listening. Then she went out, locking the door behind her. 90

Something scuffled in the yard, and she started, though she knew it was only the rats with which the place was over-run. The night was very dark. In the great bay of railway lines, bulked with trucks, there was no trace of light, only away back

---

singlet: a man's jersey undershirt.

she could see a few yellow lamps at the pit-top, and the red smear of the burning pit-bank on the night. She hurried along the edge of the track, then, crossing the converging lines, came to the stile by the white gates, whence she emerged on the road. Then the fear which had led her shrank. People were walking up to New Brinsley; she saw the lights in the houses; twenty yards farther on were the broad windows of the "Prince of Wales," very warm and bright, and the loud voices of men could be heard distinctly. What a fool she had been to imagine that anything had happened to him! He was merely drinking over there at the "Prince of Wales." She faltered. She had never yet been to fetch him, and she never would go. So she continued her walk towards the long straggling line of houses, standing back on the highway. She entered a passage between the dwellings.

"Mr. Rigley?—Yes! Did you want him? No, he's not in at this minute."

The raw-boned woman leaned forward from her dark scullery and peered at the other, upon whom fell a dim light through the blind of the kitchen window.

"Is it Mrs. Bates?" she asked in a tone tinged with respect.

"Yes. I wondered if your Master was at home. Mine hasn't come yet."

" 'Asn't 'e! Oh, Jack's been 'ome an' 'ad 'is dinner an' gone out. 'E's just gone for 'alf an hour afore bed-time. Did you call at the 'Prince of Wales'?"

"No——"

"No, you didn't like——! It's not very nice." The other woman was indulgent. There was an awkward pause. "Jack never said nothink about—about your Master," she said.

"No!—I expect he's stuck in there!"

Elizabeth Bates said this bitterly, and with recklessness. She knew that the woman across the yard was standing at her door listening, but she did not care. As she turned:

"Stop a minute! I'll just go an' ask Jack if 'e knows anythink," said Mrs. Rigley.

"Oh no—I wouldn't like to put——!"

"Yes, I will, if you'll just step inside an' see as th' childer doesn't come downstairs and set theirselves afire."

Elizabeth Bates, murmuring a remonstrance, stepped inside. The other woman apologised for the state of the room.

The kitchen needed apology. There were little frocks and trousers and childish undergarments on the squab and on the floor, and a litter of playthings everywhere. On the black American cloth of the table were pieces of bread and cake, crusts, slops, and a teapot with cold tea.

"Eh, ours is just as bad," said Elizabeth Bates, looking at the woman, not at the house. Mrs. Rigley put a shawl over her head and hurried out, saying:

"I shanna be a minute."

The other sat, noting with faint disapproval the general untidiness of the room. Then she fell to counting the shoes of various sizes scattered over the floor. There were twelve. She sighed and said to herself: "No wonder!"—glancing at the litter. There came the scratching of two pairs of feet on the yard, and the Rigleys entered. Elizabeth Bates rose. Rigley was a big man, with very large bones. His head looked particularly bony. Across his temple was a blue scar, caused by a wound got in the pit, a wound in which the coal-dust remained blue like tattooing.

" 'Asna 'e come whoam yit?" asked the man, without any form of greeting, but with deference and sympathy. "I couldna say wheer he is—'e's non ower theer!"— he jerked his head to signify the "Prince of Wales."

95

100

105

322

" 'E's 'appen gone up to th' 'Yew,' " said Mrs. Rigley.

There was another pause. Rigley had evidently something to get off his mind: "Ah left 'im finishin' a stint,' he began. "Loose-all' 'ad bin gone about ten minutes when we com'n away, an' I shouted: 'Are ter comin', Walt?' an' 'e said: 'Go on, Ah shanna be but a'ef a minnit,' so we com'n ter th' bottom, me an' Bowers, thinkin' as 'e wor just behint, an' 'ud come up i' th' next bantle——"

He stood perplexed, as if answering a charge of deserting his mate. Elizabeth Bates, now again certain of disaster, hastened to reassure him:

"I expect 'e's gone up to th' 'Yew Tree,' as you say. It' not the first time. I've fretted myself into a fever before now. He'll come home when they carry him."

"Ay, isn't it too bad!" deplored the other woman.

"I'll just step up to Dick's an' see if 'e *is* theer," offered the man, afraid of appearing alarmed, afraid of taking liberties.

"Oh, I wouldn't think of bothering you that far," said Elizabeth Bates, with emphasis, but he knew she was glad of his offer.

As they stumbled up the entry, Elizabeth Bates heard Rigley's wife run across the yard and open her neighbour's door. At this, suddenly all the blood in her body seemed to switch away from her heart.

"Mind!" warned Rigley. "Ah've said many a time as Ah'd fill up them ruts in this entry, sumb'dy'll be breakin' their legs yit."

She recovered herself and walked quickly along with the miner.

"I don't like leaving the children in bed, and nobody in the house," she said.

"No, you dunna!" he replied courteously. They were soon at the gate of the cottage.

"Well, I shanna be many minnits. Dunna you be frettin' now, 'e'll be all right," said the butty.°

"Thank you very much, Mr. Rigley," she replied.

"You're welcome!" he stammered, moving away. "I shanna be many minnits."

The house was quiet. Elizabeth Bates took off her hat and shawl, and rolled back the rug. When she had finished, she sat down. It was a few minutes past nine. She was startled by the rapid chuff of the winding-engine at the pit, and the sharp whirr of the brakes on the rope as it descended. Again she felt the painful sweep of her blood, and she put her hand to her side, saying aloud: "Good gracious!—it's only the nine o'clock deputy going down," rebuking herself.

She sat still listening. Half an hour of this, and she was wearied out.

"What am I working myself up like this for?" she said pitiably to herself, "I s'll only be doing myself some damage."

She took out her sewing again.

At a quarter to ten there were footsteps. One person! She watched for the door to open. It was an elderly woman, in a black bonnet and a black woollen shawl— his mother. She was about sixty years old, pale, with blue eyes, and her face all wrinkled and lamentable. She shut the door and turned to her daughter-in-law peevishly.

"Eh, Lizzie, whatever shall we do, whatever shall we do!" she cried.

Elizabeth drew back a little, sharply.

"What is it, mother?" she said.

---

butty: chum; mining partner.

The elder woman seated herself on the sofa. "I don't know, child, I can't tell you!"—she shook her head slowly. Elizabeth sat watching her, anxious and vexed.

"I don't know," replied the grandmother, sighing very deeply. "There's no end to my troubles, there isn't. The things I've gone through, I'm sure it's enough——!" She wept without wiping her eyes, the tears running. 135

"But, mother," interrupted Elizabeth, "what do you mean? What is it?"

The grandmother slowly wiped her eyes. The fountains of her tears were stopped by Elizabeth's directness. She wiped her eyes slowly.

"Poor child! Eh, you poor thing!" she moaned. "I don't know what we're going to do, I don't—and you as you are—it's a thing, it is indeed!"

Elizabeth waited.

"Is he dead?" she asked, and at the words her heart swung violently, though she felt a slight flush of shame at the ultimate extravagance of the question. Her words sufficiently frightened the old lady, almost brought her to herself. 140

"Don't say so, Elizabeth! We'll hope it's not as bad as that; no, may the Lord spare us that, Elizabeth. Jack Rigley came just as I was sittin' down to a glass afore going to bed, an' 'e said: ' 'Appen you'll go down th' line, Mrs. Bates. Walt's had an accident. 'Appen you'll go an' sit wi' 'er till we can get him home.' I hadn't time to ask him a word afore he was gone. An' I put my bonnet on an' come straight down, Lizzie. I thought to myself: 'Eh, that poor blessed child, if anybody should come an' tell her of a sudden, there's no knowing' what'll 'appen to 'er.' You mustn't let it upset you, Lizzie—or you know what to expect. How long is it, six months—or is it five, Lizzie? Ay!"—the old woman shook her head—"time slips on, it slips on! Ay!"

Elizabeth's thoughts were busy elsewhere. If he was killed—would she be able to manage on the little pension and what she could earn?—she counted up rapidly. If he was hurt—they wouldn't take him to the hospital—how tiresome he would be to nurse!—but perhaps she'd be able to get him away from the drink and his hateful ways. She would—while he was ill. The tears offered to come to her eyes at the picture. But what sentimental luxury was this she was beginning? She turned to consider the children. At any rate she was absolutely necessary for them. They were her business.

"Ay!" repeated the old woman, "it seems but a week or two since he brought me his first wages. Ay—he was a good lad, Elizabeth, he was, in his way. I don't know why he got to be such a trouble, I don't. He was a happy lad at home, only full of spirits. But there's no mistake he's been a handful of trouble, he has! I hope the Lord'll spare him to mend his ways. I hope so, I hope so. You've had a sight o' trouble with him, Elizabeth, you have indeed. But he was a jolly enough lad wi' me, he was, I can assure you. I don't know how it is. . . ."

The old woman continued to muse aloud, a monotonous irritating sound, while Elizabeth thought concentratedly, startled once, when she heard the winding-engine chuff quickly, and the brakes skirr with a shriek. Then she heard the engine more slowly, and the brakes made no sound. The old woman did not notice. Elizabeth waited in suspense. The mother-in-law talked, with lapses into silence.

"But he wasn't your son, Lizzie, an' it makes a difference. Whatever he was, I remember him when he was little, an' I learned to understand him and to make allowances. You've got to make allowances for them——" 145

It was half-past ten, and the old woman was saying: "But it's trouble from beginning to end; you're never too old for trouble, never too old for that——" when the gate banged back, and there were heavy feet on the steps.

"I'll go, Lizzie, let me go," cried the old woman, rising. But Elizabeth was at the door. It was a man in pit-clothes.

"They're bringin' 'im, Missis," he said. Elizabeth's heart halted a moment. Then it surged on again, almost suffocating her.

"Is he—is it bad?" she asked.

The man turned away, looking at the darkness: 150

"The doctor says 'e'd been dead hours. 'E saw 'im i' th' lamp-cabin."

The old woman, who stood just behind Elizabeth, dropped into a chair, and folded her hands, crying: "Oh, my boy, my boy!"

"Hush!" said Elizabeth, with a sharp twitch of a frown. "Be still, mother, don't waken th' children: I wouldn't have them down for anything!"

The old woman moaned softly, rocking herself. The man was drawing away. Elizabeth took a step forward.

"How was it?" she asked.   155

"Well, I couldn't say for sure," the man replied, very ill at ease. " 'E wor finishin' a stint an' th' butties 'ad gone, an' a lot o' stuff come down atop 'n 'im."

"And crushed him?" cried the widow, with a shudder.

"No," said the man, "it fell at th' back of 'im. 'E wor under th' face, an' it niver touched 'im. It shut 'im in. It seems 'e wor smothered."

Elizabeth shrank back. She heard the old woman behind her cry:

"What?—what did 'e say it was?"   160

The man replied, more loudly: " 'E wor smothered!"

Then the old woman wailed aloud, and this relieved Elizabeth.

"Oh, mother," she said, putting her hand on the old woman, "don't waken th' children, don't waken th' children."

She wept a little, unknowing, while the old mother rocked herself and moaned. Elizabeth remembered that they were bringing him home, and she must be ready. "They'll lay him in the parlour," she said to herself, standing a moment pale and perplexed.

Then she lighted a candle and went into the tiny room. The air was cold and damp, but she could not make a fire, there was no fireplace. She set down the candle and looked round. The candlelight glittered on the lustre-glasses, on the two vases that held some of the pink chrysanthemums, and on the dark mahogany. There was a cold, deathly smell of chrysanthemums in the room. Elizabeth stood looking at the flowers. She turned away, and calculated whether there would be room to lay him on the floor, between the couch and the chiffonier. She pushed the chairs aside. There would be room to lay him down and to step round him. Then she fetched the old red tablecloth, and another old cloth, spreading them down to save her bit of carpet. She shivered on leaving the parlour; so, from the dresser drawer she took a clean shirt and put it at the fire to air. All the time her mother-in-law was rocking herself in the chair and moaning.   165

"You'll have to move from there, mother," said Elizabeth. "They'll be bringing him in. Come in the rocker."

The old mother rose mechanically, and seated herself by the fire, continuing to lament. Elizabeth went into the pantry for another candle, and there, in the little pent-house under the naked tiles, she heard them coming. She stood still in the pantry doorway, listening. She heard them pass the end of the house, and come awkwardly down the three steps, a jumble of shuffling footsteps and muttering voices. The old woman was silent. The men were in the yard.

Then Elizabeth heard Matthews, the manager of the pit, say: "You go in first, Jim. Mind!"

The door came open, and the two women saw a collier backing into the room, holding one end of a stretcher, on which they could see the nailed pit-boots of the dead man. The two carriers halted, the man at the head stooping to the lintel° of the door.

"Wheer will you have him?" asked the manager, a short, white-bearded man.   170

Elizabeth roused herself and came from the pantry carrying the unlighted candle.

"In the parlour," she said.

"In there, Jim!" pointed the manager, and the carriers backed round into the tiny room. The coat with which they had covered the body fell off as they awkwardly turned through the two doorways, and the women saw their man, naked to the waist, lying stripped for work. The old woman began to moan in a low voice of horror.

"Lay th' stretcher at th' side," snapped the manager, "an' put 'im on th' cloths. Mind now, mind! Look you now——!"

One of the men had knocked off a vase of chrysanthemums. He stared awkwardly, then they set down the stretcher. Elizabeth did not look at her husband. As soon as she could get in the room, she went and picked up the broken vase and the flowers.   175

"Wait a minute!" she said.

The three men waited in silence while she mopped up the water with a duster.

"Eh, what a job, what a job, to be sure!" the manager was saying, rubbing his brow with trouble and perplexity. "Never knew such a thing in my life, never! He'd no business to ha' been left. I never knew such a thing in my life! Fell over him clean as a whistle, an' shut him in. Not four foot of space, there wasn't—yet it scarce bruised him."

He looked down at the dead man, lying prone, half naked, all grimed with coal-dust.

"'Sphyxiated,' the doctor said. It *is* the most terrible job I've ever known. Seems as if it was done o' purpose. Clean over him, an' shut 'im in, like a mousetrap"—he made a sharp, descending gesture with his hand.   180

The colliers standing by jerked aside their heads in hopeless comment.

The horror of the thing bristled upon them all.

Then they heard the girl's voice upstairs calling shrilly: "Mother, mother—who is it? Mother, who is it?"

Elizabeth hurried to the foot of the stairs and opened the door:

"Go to sleep!" she commanded sharply. "What are you shouting about? Go to sleep at once—there's nothing——"   185

Then she began to mount the stairs. They could hear her on the boards, and on the plaster floor of the little bedroom. They could hear her distinctly:

"What's the matter now?—what's the matter with you, silly thing?"—her voice was much agitated, with an unreal gentleness.

"I thought it was some men come," said the plaintive voice of the child. "Has he come?"

"Yes, they've brought him. There's nothing to make a fuss about. Go to sleep now, like a good child."

---

lintel: horizontal crosspiece over a doorway.

They could hear her voice in the bedroom, they waited whilst she covered the children under the bedclothes.

"Is he drunk?" asked the girl, timidly, faintly.

"No! No—he's not! He—he's asleep."

"Is he asleep downstairs?"

"Yes—and don't make a noise."

There was silence for a moment, then the men heard the frightened child again:

"What's that noise?"

"It's nothing, I tell you, what are you bothering for?"

The noise was the grandmother moaning. She was oblivious of everything, sitting on her chair rocking and moaning. The manager put his hand on her arm and bade her "Sh—sh!!"

The old woman opened her eyes and looked at him. She was shocked by this interruption, and seemed to wonder.

"What time is it?" the plaintive thin voice of the child, sinking back unhappily into sleep, asked this last question.

"Ten o'clock," answered the mother more softly. Then she must have bent down and kissed the children.

Matthews beckoned to the men to come away. They put on their caps and took up the stretcher. Stepping over the body, they tiptoed out of the house. None of them spoke till they were far from the wakeful children.

When Elizabeth came down she found the mother alone on the parlour floor, leaning over the dead man, the tears dropping on him.

"We must lay him out," the wife said. She put on the kettle, then returning knelt at the feet, and began to unfasten the knotted leather laces. The room was clammy and dim with only one candle, so that she had to bend her face almost to the floor. At last she got off the heavy boots and put them away.

"You must help me now," she whispered to the old woman. Together they stripped the man.

When they arose, saw him lying in the naïve dignity of death, the women stood arrested in fear and respect. For a few moments they remained still, looking down, the old mother whimpering. Elizabeth felt countermanded. She saw him, how utterly inviolable he lay in himself. She had nothing to do with him. She could not accept it. Stooping, she laid her hand on him, in claim. He was still warm, for the mine was hot where he had died. His mother had his face between her hands, and was murmuring incoherently. The old tears fell in succession as drops from wet leaves; the mother was not weeping, merely her tears flowed. Elizabeth embraced the body of her husband, with cheek and lips. She seemed to be listening, inquiring, trying to get some connection. But she could not. She was driven away. He was impregnable.

She rose, went into the kitchen, where she poured warm water into a bowl, brought soap and flannel and a soft towel.

"I must wash him," she said.

Then the old mother rose stiffly, and watched Elizabeth as she carefully washed his face, carefully brushing the big blond moustache from his mouth with the flannel. She was afraid with a bottomless fear, so she ministered to him. The old woman, jealous, said:

"Let me wipe him!"—and she kneeled on the other side drying slowly as Elizabeth washed, her big black bonnet sometimes brushing the dark head of her daughter-in-law. They worked thus in silence for a long time. They never forgot it

Odour of Chrysanthemums   **327**

was death, and the touch of the man's dead body gave them strange emotions, different in each of the women; a great dread possessed them both, the mother felt the lie was given to her womb, she was denied; the wife felt the utter isolation of the human soul, the child within her was a weight apart from her. 210

At last it was finished. He was a man of handsome body, and his face showed no traces of drink. He was blond, full-fleshed, with fine limbs. But he was dead.

"Bless him," whispered his mother, looking always at his face, and speaking out of sheer terror. "Dear lad—bless him!" She spoke in a faint, sibilant ecstasy of fear and mother love.

Elizabeth sank down again to the floor, and put her face against his neck, and trembled and shuddered. But she had to draw away again. He was dead, and her living flesh had no place against his. A great dread and weariness held her: she was so unavailing. Her life was gone like this.

"White as milk he is, clear as a twelve-month baby, bless him, the darling!" the old mother murmured to herself. "Not a mark on him, clear and clean and white, beautiful as ever a child was made," she murmured with pride. Elizabeth kept her face hidden.

"He went peaceful, Lizzie—peaceful as sleep. Isn't he beautiful, the lamb? Ay—he must ha' made his peace, Lizzie. 'Appen he made it all right, Lizzie, shut in there. He'd have time. He wouldn't look like this if he hadn't made his peace. The lamb, the dear lamb. 'Eh, but he had a hearty laugh. I loved to hear it. He had the heartiest laugh, Lizzie, as a lad——" 215

Elizabeth looked up. The man's mouth was fallen back, slightly open under the cover of the moustache. The eyes, half shut, did not show glazed in the obscurity. Life with its smoky burning gone from him, had left him apart and utterly alien to her. And she knew what a stranger he was to her. In her womb was ice of fear, because of this separate stranger with whom she had been living as one flesh. Was this what it all meant—utter, intact separateness, obscured by heat of living? In dread she turned her face away. The fact was too deadly. There had been nothing between them, and yet they had come together, exchanging their nakedness repeatedly. Each time he had taken her, they had been two isolated beings, far apart as now. He was no more responsible than she. The child was like ice in her womb. For as she looked at the dead man, her mind, cold and detached said clearly: "Who am I? What have I been doing? I have been fighting a husband who did not exist. *He* existed all the time. What wrong have I done? What was that I have been living with? There lies the reality, this man." And her soul died in her for fear: she knew she had never seen him, he had never seen her, they had met in the dark and had fought in the dark, not knowing whom they met nor whom they fought. And now she saw, and turned silent in seeing. For she had been wrong. She had said he was something he was not; she had felt familiar with him. Whereas he was apart all the while, living as she never lived, feeling as she never felt.

In fear and shame she looked at his naked body, that she had known falsely. And he was the father of her children. Her soul was torn from her body and stood apart. She looked at his naked body and was ashamed, as if she had denied it. After all, it was itself. It seemed awful to her. She looked at his face, and she turned her own face to the wall. For his look was other than hers, his way was not her way. She had denied him what he was—she saw it now. She had refused him as himself. And this had been her life, and his life. She was grateful to death, which restored the truth. And she knew she was not dead.

And all the while her heart was bursting with grief and pity for him. What had he suffered? What stretch of horror for this helpless man! She was rigid with agony. She had not been able to help him. He had been cruelly injured, this naked man, this other being, and she could make no reparation. There were the children—but the children belonged to life. This dead man had nothing to do with them. He and she were only channels through which life had flowed to issue in the children. She was a mother—but how awful she knew it now to have been a wife. And he, dead now, how awful he must have felt it to be a husband. She felt that in the next world he would be a stranger to her. If they met there, in the beyond, they would only be ashamed of what had been before. The children had come, for some mysterious reason, out of both of them. But the children did not unite them. Now he was dead, she knew how eternally he was apart from her, how eternally he had nothing more to do with her. She saw this episode of her life closed. They had denied each other in life. Now he had withdrawn. An anguish came over her. It was finished then: it had become hopeless between them long before he died. Yet he had been her husband. But how little!

"Have you got his shirt, 'Lizabeth?"

Elizabeth turned without answering, though she strove to weep and behave as her mother-in-law expected. But she could not, she was silenced. She went into the kitchen and returned with the garment.

"It is aired," she said, grasping the cotton shirt here and there to try. She was almost ashamed to handle him; what right had she or anyone to lay hands on him; but her touch was humble on his body. It was hard work to clothe him. He was so heavy and inert. A terrible dread gripped her all the while: that he could be so heavy and utterly inert, unresponsive, apart. The horror of the distance between them was almost too much for her—it was so infinite a gap she must look across.

At last it was finished. They covered him with a sheet and left him lying, with his face bound. And she fastened the door of the little parlour, lest the children should see what was lying there. Then, with peace sunk heavy on her heart, she went about making tidy the kitchen. She knew she submitted to life, which was her immediate master. But from death, her ultimate master, she winced with fear and shame.

William Faulkner (1897–1962)

Although William Faulkner is abundantly represented in anthologies of short fiction, he was not in any real sense a short story writer. His interest was less in the contained dramas that take place in the life of the individual, far more in trying to capture the destinies of families and groups over time. To achieve his aim, Faulkner more or less invented and populated an entire county in his native Mississippi. He called it Yoknapatawpha County, and a substantial portion of his highly productive career was devoted to the chronicling of its citizens and their doings. Many of his short stories—he published four collections in his lifetime—can be seen as threads extracted from the larger fabric of that place. "Wash" is a case in point.

Faulkner began his literary apprenticeship as a newspaper writer in New Orleans. He met writer Sherwood Anderson there, and Anderson helped him to publish his first novel, *Soldier's Pay* (1926). Soon after that he conceived the scheme that would become his life's work, and in a period spanning just over a decade, he published the novels that made his name famous: *The Sound and the Fury* (1929), *As I Lay Dying* (1930), *Sanctuary* (1931), *Light in August* (1932), *Absalom, Absalom!* (1936), and *The Hamlet* (1940). Ten years later, in 1950, he was awarded the Nobel Prize for literature.

WASH

Sutpen stood above the pallet bed on which the mother and child lay. Between the shrunken planking of the wall the early sunlight fell in long pencil strokes, breaking upon his straddled legs and upon the riding whip in his hand, and lay across the still shape of the mother, who lay looking up at him from still, inscrutable, sullen eyes, the child at her side wrapped in a piece of dingy though clean cloth. Behind them an old Negro woman squatted beside the rough hearth where a meager fire smoldered.

"Well, Milly," Sutpen said, "too bad you're not a mare. Then I could give you a decent stall in the stable."

Still the girl on the pallet did not move. She merely continued to look up at him without expression, with a young, sullen, inscrutable face still pale from recent travail. Sutpen moved, bringing into the splintered pencils of sunlight the face of a man of sixty. He said quietly to the squatting Negress, "Griselda foaled this morning."

"Horse or mare?" the Negress said.

"A horse. A damned fine colt. . . . What's this?" He indicated the pallet with the hand which held the whip.

5

"That un's a mare, I reckon."

"Hah," Sutpen said. "A damned fine colt. Going to be the spit and image of old Rob Roy when I rode him North in '61. Do you remember?"

"Yes, Master."

"Hah." He glanced back towards the pallet. None could have said if the girl still watched him or not. Again his whip hand indicated the pallet. "Do whatever they need with whatever we've got to do it with." He went out, passing out the crazy doorway and stepping down into the rank weeds (there yet leaned rusting against the corner of the porch the scythe which Wash had borrowed from him three months ago to cut them with) where his horse waited, where Wash stood holding the reins.

When Colonel Sutpen rode away to fight the Yankees, Wash did not go. "I'm looking after the Kernel's place and niggers," he would tell all who asked him and some who had not asked—a gaunt, malaria-ridden man with pale, questioning eyes, who looked about thirty-five, though it was known that he had not only a daughter but an eight-year-old granddaughter as well. This was a lie, as most of them—the few remaining men between eighteen and fifty—to whom he told it, knew, though there were some who believed that he himself really believed it, though even these believed that he had better sense than to put it to the test with Mrs. Sutpen or the Sutpen slaves. Knew better or was just too lazy and shiftless to try it, they said, knowing that his sole connection with the Sutpen plantation lay in the fact that for years now Colonel Sutpen had allowed him to squat in a crazy shack on a slough in the river bottom on the Sutpen place, which Sutpen had built for a fishing lodge in his bachelor days and which had since fallen in dilapidation from disuse, so that now it looked like an aged or sick wild beast crawled terrifically there to drink in the act of dying.

The Sutpen slaves themselves heard of his statement. They laughed. It was not the first time they had laughed at him, calling him white trash behind his back. They began to ask him themselves, in groups, meeting him in the faint road which led up from the slough and the old fish camp, "Why ain't you at de war, white man?"

Pausing, he would look about the ring of black faces and white eyes and teeth behind which derision lurked. "Because I got a daughter and a family to keep," he said. "Git out of my road, niggers."

"Niggers?" they repeated; "niggers?" laughing now. "Who him, calling us niggers?"

"Yes," he said. "I ain't got no niggers to look after my folks if I was gone."

"Nor nothing else but dat shack down yon dat Cunnel wouldn't *let* none of us live in."

Now he cursed them; sometimes he rushed at them, snatching up a stick from the ground while they scattered before him, yet seeming to surround him still with that black laughing, derisive, evasive, inescapable, leaving him panting and impotent and raging. Once it happened in the very back yard of the big house itself. This was after bitter news had come down from the Tennessee mountains and from Vicksburg, and Sherman had passed through the plantation, and most of the Negroes had followed him. Almost everything else had gone with the Federal troops, and Mrs. Sutpen had sent word to Wash that he could have the scuppernongs° ripening in the arbor in the back yard. This time it was a house servant, one of the few Negroes who remained; this time the Negress had to retreat up the kitchen steps, where she turned. "Stop right dar, white man. Stop right whar you is. You ain't never crossed dese steps whilst Cunnel here, and you ain't ghy' do hit now."

This was true. But there was this of a kind of pride: he had never tried to enter the big house, even though he believed that if he had, Sutpen would have received him, permitted him. "But I ain't going to give no black nigger the chance to tell me I can't go nowhere," he said to himself. "I ain't even going to give Kernel the chance to have to cuss a nigger on my account." This, though he and Sutpen had spent more than one afternoon together on those rare Sundays when there would be no company in the house. Perhaps his mind knew that it was because Sutpen had nothing else to do, being a man who could not bear his own company. Yet the fact remained

10

15

---

scuppernong: a kind of grape.

that the two of them would spend whole afternoons in the scuppernong arbor, Sutpen in the hammock and Wash squatting against a post, a pail of cistern water between them, taking drink for drink from the same demijohn. Meanwhile on weekdays he would see the fine figure of the man—they were the same age almost to a day, though neither of them (perhaps because Wash had a grandchild while Sutpen's son was a youth in school) ever thought of himself as being so—on the fine figure of the black stallion, galloping about the plantation. For that moment his heart would be quiet and proud. It would seem to him that that world in which Negroes, whom the Bible told him had been created and cursed by God to be brute and vassal° to all men of white skin, were better found and housed and even clothed than he and his; that world in which he sensed always about him mocking echoes of black laughter was but a dream and an illusion, and that the actual world was this one across which his own lonely apotheosis seemed to gallop on the black thoroughbred, thinking how the Book said also that all men were created in the image of God and hence all men made the same image in God's eyes at least; so that he could say, as though speaking of himself, "A fine proud man. If God Himself was to come down and ride the natural earth, that's what He would aim to look like."

Sutpen returned in 1865, on the black stallion. He seemed to have aged ten years. His son had vanished the same winter in which his wife had died. He returned with his citation for gallantry from the hand of General Lee to a ruined plantation, where for a year now his daughter had subsisted partially on the meager bounty of the man to whom fifteen years ago he had granted permission to live in that tumbledown fishing camp whose very existence he had at the time forgotten. Wash was there to meet him, unchanged: still gaunt, still ageless, with his pale, questioning gaze, his air diffident, a little servile, a little familiar. "Well, Kernel," Wash said, "they kilt us but they ain't whupped us yit, air they?"

That was the tenor of their conversation for the next five years. It was inferior whiskey which they drank now together from a stoneware jug, and it was not in the scuppernong arbor. It was in the rear of the little store which Sutpen managed to set up on the highroad: a frame shelved room where, with Wash for clerk and porter, he dispensed kerosene and staple foodstuffs and stale gaudy candy and cheap beads and ribbons to Negroes or poor whites of Wash's own kind, who came afoot or on gaunt mules to haggle tediously for dimes and quarters with a man who at one time could gallop (the black stallion was still alive; the stable in which his jealous get lived was in better repair than the house where the master himself lived) for ten miles across his own fertile land and who had led troops gallantly in battle; until Sutpen in fury would empty the store, close and lock the doors from the inside. Then he and Wash would repair to the rear and the jug. But the talk would not be quiet now, as when Sutpen lay in the hammock, delivering an arrogant monologue while Wash squatted guffawing against his post. They both sat now, though Sutpen had the single chair while Wash used whatever box or keg was handy, and even this for just a little while, because soon Sutpen would reach that stage of impotent and furious undefeat in which he would rise, swaying and plunging, and declare again that he would take his pistol and the black stallion and ride single-handed into Washington and kill Lincoln, dead now, and Sherman, now a private citizen. "Kill them!" he would shout. "Shoot them down like the dogs they are—"

---

vassal: servant; serf.

"Sho, Kernel; sho, Kernel," Wash would say, catching Sutpen as he fell. Then he would commandeer the first passing wagon or, lacking that, he would walk the mile to the nearest neighbor and borrow one and return and carry Sutpen home. He entered the house now. He had been doing so for a long time, taking Sutpen home in whatever borrowed wagon might be, talking him into locomotion with cajoling murmurs as though he were a horse, a stallion himself. The daughter would meet them and hold open the door without a word. He would carry his burden through the once white formal entrance, surmounted by a fanlight° imported piece by piece from Europe and with a board now nailed over a missing pane, across a velvet carpet from which all nap was now gone, and up a formal stairs, now but a fading ghost of bare boards between two strips of fading paint, and into the bedroom. It would be dusk by now, and he would let his burden sprawl onto the bed and undress it and then he would sit quietly in a chair beside. After a time the daughter would come to the door. "We're all right now," he would tell her. "Don't you worry none, Miss Judith."   20

Then it would become dark, and after a while he would lie down on the floor beside the bed, though not to sleep, because after a time—sometimes before midnight—the man on the bed would stir and groan and then speak. "Wash?"

"Hyer I am, Kernel. You go back to sleep. We ain't whupped yit, air we? Me and you kin do hit."

Even then he had already seen the ribbon about his granddaughter's waist. She was now fifteen, already mature, after the early way of her kind. He knew where the ribbon came from; he had been seeing it and its kind daily for three years, even if she had lied about where she got it, which she did not, at once bold, sullen, and fearful.

"Sho now," he said. "Ef Kernel wants to give hit to you, I hope you minded to thank him."

His heart was quiet, even when he saw the dress, watching her secret, defiant, frightened face when she told him that Miss Judith, the daughter, had helped her to make it. But he was quite grave when he approached Sutpen after they closed the store that afternoon, following the other to the rear.   25

"Get the jug," Sutpen directed.

"Wait," Wash said. "Not yit for a minute."

Neither did Sutpen deny the dress. "What about it?" he said.

But Wash met his arrogant stare; he spoke quietly. "I've knowed you for going on twenty years. I ain't never yit denied to do what you told me to do. And I'm a man nigh sixty. And she ain't nothing but a fifteen-year-old gal."

"Meaning that I'd harm a girl? I, a man as old as you are?"   30

"If you was ara other man, I'd say you was as old as me. And old or no old, I wouldn't let her keep that dress nor nothing else that come from your hand. But you are different."

"How different?" But Wash merely looked at him with his pale, questioning, sober eyes. "So that's why you are afraid of me?"

Now Wash's gaze no longer questioned. It was tranquil, serene. "I ain't afraid. Because you air brave. It ain't that you were a brave man at one minute or day of your life and got a paper to show hit from General Lee. But you air brave, the same

---

fanlight: a fancy half-circle window over a doorway.

as you air alive and breathing. That's where hit's different. Hit don't need no ticket from nobody to tell me that. And I know that whatever you handle or tech, whether hit's a regiment of men or a ignorant gal or just a hound dog, that you will make hit right."

Now it was Sutpen who looked away, turning suddenly, brusquely. "Get the jug," he said sharply.

"Sho, Kernel," Wash said.

So on that Sunday dawn two years later, having watched the Negro midwife, whom he had walked three miles to fetch, enter the crazy door beyond which his granddaughter lay wailing, his heart was still quiet though concerned. He knew what they had been saying—the Negroes in cabins about the land, the white men who loafed all day long about the store, watching quietly the three of them: Sutpen, himself, his granddaughter with her air of brazen and shrinking defiance as her condition became daily more and more obvious, like three actors that came and went upon a stage. "I know what they say to one another," he thought. "I can almost hyear them: *Wash Jones has fixed old Sutpen at last. Hit taken him twenty years, but he has done hit at last.*"

It would be dawn after a while, though not yet. From the house, where the lamp shone dim beyond the warped door frame, his granddaughter's voice came steadily as though run by a clock, while thinking went slowly and terrifically, fumbling, involved somehow with a sound of galloping hooves, until there broke suddenly free in mid-gallop the fine proud figure of the man on the fine proud stallion, galloping; and then that at which thinking fumbled, broke free too and quite clear, not in justification nor even explanation, but as the apotheosis, lonely, explicable, beyond all fouling by human touch: "He is bigger than all them Yankees that kilt his son and his wife and taken his niggers and ruined his land, bigger than this hyer durn country that he fit for and that has denied him into keeping a little country store; bigger than the denial which hit helt to his lips like the bitter cup in the Book. And how could I have lived this nigh to him for twenty years without being teched and changed by him? Maybe I ain't as big as him and maybe I ain't done none of the galloping. But at least I done been drug along. Me and him kin do hit, if so be he will show me what he aims for me to do."

Then it was dawn. Suddenly he could see the house, and the old Negress in the door looking at him. Then he realized that his granddaughter's voice had ceased. "It's a girl," the Negress said. "You can go tell him if you want to." She reëntered the house.

"A girl," he repeated; "a girl"; in astonishment, hearing the galloping hooves, seeing the proud galloping figure emerge again. He seemed to watch it pass, galloping through avatars which marked the accumulation of years, time, to the climax where it galloped beneath a brandished sabre and a shot-torn flag rushing down a sky in color like thunderous sulphur, thinking for the first time in his life that perhaps Sutpen was an old man like himself. "Gittin a gal," he thought in that astonishment; then he thought with the pleased surprise of a child: "Yes, sir. Be dawg if I ain't lived to be a great-grandpaw after all."

He entered the house. He moved clumsily, on tiptoe, as if he no longer lived there, as if the infant which had just drawn breath and cried in light had dispossessed him, be it of his own blood too though it might. But even above the pallet he could see little save the blur of his granddaughter's exhausted face. Then the Negress squatting at the hearth spoke, "You better gawn tell him if you going to. Hit's daylight now." ⁴⁰

But this was not necessary. He had no more than turned the corner of the porch where the scythe leaned which he had borrowed three months ago to clear away the weeds through which he walked, when Sutpen himself rode up on the old stallion. He did not wonder how Sutpen had got the word. He took it for granted that this was what had brought the other out at this hour on Sunday morning, and he stood while the other dismounted, and he took the reins from Sutpen's hand, and expression on his gaunt face almost imbecile with a kind of weary triumph, saying, "Hit's a gal, Kernel. I be dawg if you ain't as old as I am—" until Sutpen passed him and entered the house. He stood there with the reins in his hand and heard Sutpen cross the floor to the pallet. He heard what Sutpen said, and something seemed to stop dead in him before going on.

The sun was now up, the swift sun of Mississippi latitudes, and it seemed to him that he stood beneath a strange sky, in a strange scene, familiar only as things are familiar in dream, like the dreams of falling to one who has never climbed. "I kain't have heard what I thought I heard," he thought quietly. "I know I kain't." Yet the voice, the familiar voice which had said the words was still speaking, talking now to the old Negress about a colt foaled that morning. "That's why he was up so early," he thought. "That was hit. Hit ain't me and mine. Hit ain't even hisn that got him outen bed."

Sutpen emerged. He descended into the weeds, moving with that heavy deliberation which would have been haste when he was younger. He had not yet looked full at Wash. He said, "Dicey will stay and tend to her. You better—" Then he seemed to see Wash facing him and paused. "What?" he said.

"You said—" To his own ears Wash's voice sounded flat and ducklike, like a deaf man's. "You said if she was a mare, you could give her a good stall in the stable."

"Well?" Sutpen said. His eyes widened and narrowed, almost like a man's fists flexing and shutting, as Wash began to advance towards him, stooping a little. Very astonishment kept Sutpen still for the moment, watching that man whom in twenty years he had no more known to make any motion save at command than he had the horse which he rode. Again his eyes narrowed and widened; without moving he seemed to rear suddenly upright. "Stand back," he said suddenly and sharply. "Don't you touch me." ⁴⁵

"I'm going to tech you, Kernel," Wash said in that flat, quiet, almost soft voice, advancing.

Sutpen raised the hand which held the riding whip; the old Negress peered around the crazy door with her black gargoyle face of a worn gnome. "Stand back, Wash," Sutpen said. Then he struck. The old Negress leaped down into the weeds with the agility of a goat and fled. Sutpen slashed Wash again across the face with the whip, striking him to his knees. When Wash rose and advanced once more he held in his hands the scythe which he had borrowed from Sutpen three months ago and which Sutpen would never need again.

When he reëntered the house his granddaughter stirred on the pallet bed and called his name fretfully. "What was that?" she said.

"What was what, honey?"

"That ere racket out there." ⁵⁰

"'Twarn't nothing," he said gently. He knelt and touched her hot forehead clumsily. "Do you want ara thing?"

"I want a sup of water," she said querulously. "I been laying here wanting a sup of water a long time, but don't nobody care enough to pay me no mind."

"Sho now," he said soothingly. He rose stiffly and fetched the dipper of water and raised her head to drink and laid her back and watched her turn to the child with an absolutely stonelike face. But a moment later he saw that she was crying quietly. "Now, now," he said, "I wouldn't do that. Old Dicey says hit's a right fine gal. Hit's all right now. Hit's all over now. Hit ain't no need to cry now."

But she continued to cry quietly, almost sullenly, and he rose again and stood uncomfortably above the pallet for a time, thinking as he had thought when his own wife lay so and then his daughter in turn: "Women. Hit's a mystry to me. They seem to want em, and yit when they git em they cry about hit. Hit's a mystry to me. To ara man." Then he moved away and drew a chair up to the window and sat down.

Through all that long, bright, sunny forenoon he sat at the window, waiting. Now and then he rose and tiptoed to the pallet. But his granddaughter slept now, her face sullen and calm and weary, the child in the crook of her arm. Then he returned to the chair and sat again, waiting, wondering why it took them so long, until he remembered that it was Sunday. He was sitting there at mid-afternoon when a half-grown white boy came around the corner of the house upon the body and gave a choked cry and looked up and glared for a mesmerized instant at Wash in the window before he turned and fled. Then Wash rose and tiptoed again to the pallet.

The granddaughter was awake now, wakened perhaps by the boy's cry without hearing it. "Milly," he said, "air you hungry?" She didn't answer, turning her face away. He built up the fire on the hearth and cooked the food which he had brought home the day before: fatback° it was, and cold corn pone°; he poured water into the stale coffee pot and heated it. But she would not eat when he carried the plate to her, so he ate himself, quietly, alone, and left the dishes as they were and returned to the window.

Now he seemed to sense, feel, the men who would be gathering with horses and guns and dogs—the curious, and the vengeful: men of Sutpen's own kind, who had made the company about Sutpen's table in the time when Wash himself had yet to approach nearer to the house than the scuppernong arbor—men who had also shown the lesser ones how to fight in battle, who maybe also had signed papers from the generals saying that they were among the first of the brave; who had also galloped in the old days arrogant and proud on the fine horses across the fine plantations—symbols also of admiration and hope; instruments too of despair and grief.

That was who they would expect him to run from. It seemed to him that he had no more to run from than he had to run to. If he ran, he would merely be fleeing one set of bragging and evil shadows for another just like them, since they were all of a kind throughout all the earth which he knew, and he was old, too old to flee far even if he were to flee. He could never escape them, no matter how much or how

---

fatback: a strip of fat taken from a side of pork.
corn pone: cornbread made without milk or eggs.

A Fiction Anthology

far he ran: a man going on sixty could not run that far. Not far enough to escape beyond the boundaries of earth where such men lived, set the order and the rule of living. It seemed to him that he now saw for the first time, after five years, how it was that Yankees or any other living armies had managed to whip them: the gallant, the proud, the brave; the acknowledged and chosen best among them all to carry courage and honor and pride. Maybe if he had gone to the war with them he would have discovered them sooner. But if he had discovered them sooner, what would he have done with his life since? How could he have borne to remember for five years what his life had been before?

Now it was getting toward sunset. The child had been crying; when he went to the pallet he saw his granddaughter nursing it, her face still bemused, sullen, inscrutable. "Air you hungry yit?" he said.

"I don't want nothing."

"You ought to eat."   60

This time she did not answer at all, looking down at the child. He returned to his chair and found that the sun had set. "Hit kain't be much longer," he thought. He could feel them quite near now, the curious and the vengeful. He could even seem to hear what they were saying about him, the undercurrent of believing beyond the immediate fury: *Old Wash Jones he come a tumble at last. He thought he had Sutpen, but Sutpen fooled him. He thought he had Kernel where he would have to marry the gal or pay up. And Kernel refused.* "But I never expected that, Kernel!" he cried aloud, catching himself at the sound of his own voice, glancing quickly back to find his granddaughter watching him.

"Who you talking to now?" she said.

"Hit ain't nothing. I was just thinking and talked out before I knowed hit."

Her face was becoming indistinct again, again a sullen blur in the twilight. "I reckon so. I reckon you'll have to holler louder than that before he'll hear you, up yonder at that house. And I reckon you'll need to do more than holler before you get him down here too."   65

"Sho now," he said. "Don't you worry none." But already thinking was going smoothly on: "You know I never. You know how I ain't never expected or asked nothing from ara living man but what I expected from you. And I never asked that. I didn't think hit would need. I said, *I don't need to. What need has a fellow like Wash Jones to question or doubt the man that General Lee himself says in a handwrote ticket that he was brave?* Brave," he thought. "Better if nara one of them had never rid back home in '65"; thinking *Better if his kind and mine too had never drawn the breath of life on this earth. Better that all who remain of us be blasted from the face of the earth than that another Wash Jones should see his whole life shredded from him and shrivel away like a dried shuck thrown onto the fire.*

He ceased, became still. He heard the horses, suddenly and plainly; presently he saw the lantern and the movement of men, the glint of gun barrels, in its moving light. Yet he did not stir. It was quite dark now, and he listened to the voices and the sounds of underbrush as they surrounded the house. The lantern itself came on; its light fell upon the quiet body in the weeds and stopped, the horses tall and shadowy. A man descended and stooped in the lantern light, above the body. He held a pistol; he rose and faced the house. "Jones," he said.

"I'm here," Wash said quietly from the window. "That you, Major?"

"Come out."

"Sho," he said quietly. "I just want to see to my granddaughter."   70

"We'll see to her. Come on out."

"Sho, Major. Just a minute."

"Show a light. Light your lamp."

"Sho. In just a minute." They could hear his voice retreat into the house, though they could not see him as he went swiftly to the crack in the chimney where he kept the butcher knife: the one thing in his slovenly life and house in which he took pride, since it was razor sharp. He approached the pallet, his granddaughter's voice:

"Who is it? Light the lamp, grandpaw." 75

"Hit won't need no light, honey. Hit won't take but a minute," he said, kneeling, fumbling toward her voice, whispering now. "Where air you?"

"Right here," she said fretfully. "Where would I be? What is. . . ." His hand touched her face. "What is. . . . Grandpaw! Grand. . . ."

"Jones!" the sheriff said. "Come out of there!"

"In just a minute, Major," he said. Now he rose and moved swiftly. He knew where in the dark the can of kerosene was, just as he knew that it was full, since it was not two days ago that he had filled it at the store and held it there until he got a ride home with it, since the five gallons were heavy. There were still coals on the hearth; besides the crazy building itself was like tinder: the coals, the hearth, the walls exploding in a single blue glare. Against it the waiting men saw him in a wild instant springing toward them with the lifted scythe before the horses reared and whirled. They checked the horses and turned them back toward the glare, yet still in wild relief against it the gaunt figure ran toward them with the lifted scythe.

"Jones!" the sheriff shouted. "Stop! Stop, or I'll shoot. Jones! Jones!" Yet still the gaunt, furious figure came on against the glare and roar of the flames. With the scythe lifted, it bore down upon them, upon the wild glaring eyes of the horses and the swinging glints of gun barrels, without any cry, any sound. 80

Yasunari Kawabata (1899–1972)

Yasunari Kawabata was born in Osaka, Japan. He lost his family while he was still a child, a fact that accounts in some part for the loneliness and melancholy that tinge many of his writings. Kawabata graduated from the Tokyo Imperial University in 1924, and the following year published his first novel, *The Izu Dancer*. Many novels and short stories followed, and by the 1940s he was recognized as Japan's leading writer. Readers found much to admire both in his exploration of the deep struggle between the traditional and modern in Japanese society and in his delicate way of suggesting nuance through detail. He was awarded the Nobel prize for literature in 1968, the first Japanese thus honored. He committed suicide four years later.

A SMILE OUTSIDE THE
NIGHT STALL

I stopped short. It must have been two hours since the Hakuhin, a building that always closes at the same time in the evening, had tightly shut its doors. My back to those doors on the thoroughfare in Ueno, I had stopped in front of a firecracker stand and an optician's stall. I had been looking at the crowds on the pavement from evening into night, and, to my eyes, the dirt sidewalk, whose breadth was the space between the Hakuhin and the night stalls, seemed curiously wide, so that I felt shy about walking down the middle of it. Each time a belated pedestrian went by, the color of the packed, water-sprinkled dirt sank all the more blackly into itself, and the scraps of wastepaper floated up all the more whitely. It was late at night. The wagon of a vendor who had closed shop moved off. At the firecracker stand, unwrapped firecracker sticks; Azuma Peonies; Flower Wheels; Land Mines wrapped in colored paper bags; Snow, Moon, and Flowers; and Three-Colored Pine Needles in colored paper boxes were lined up in red-ochre rows. At the optician's stall, old-age glasses; glasses for the nearsighted; tinted glasses; glasses for show with frames of gold (probably gilt), silver, gold and copper alloy, steel, or tortoiseshell; binoculars; dust goggles; swimming goggles; magnifying glasses; and the like were ranged in rows. But I wasn't looking at the firecrackers or the eyeglasses.

The firecracker stand and the optician's stall were about three feet apart. Since no one was looking at their goods, the two vendors had come out of their stalls and seemed to be doing something together in that three-foot space. If the glasses vendor had moved two feet into the space and the firecracker vendor one foot, it was only because the firecracker girl had shifted her shop bench, too, while the glasses vendor had left his bench behind his stall. He didn't seem to miss it.

Floating up on his toes, his legs slightly spread, the man pressed down hard on his left knee with the elbow to which he entrusted the weight of his bent-over upper body. With a girl's short bamboo clog, which he dangled between his legs from his right hand, he was busy writing characters in the black dirt.

The girl was intently reading, from the top down, the column of characters being written by the man. The bench on which she sat was low and her clogs had teeth so that her knees were raised and slightly parted. Her shop apron dangling between her legs, she bent over so that her small breasts pressed against her knees; her arms hung down around them, her hands resting lightly, palms upward, on her insteps. Her crudely patterned summer kimono was somewhat sweat-stained, and her "cleft-peach" coiffure had come slightly undone. Because of her breasts pressing against the slightly parted knees, the collar of her kimono clung to her nape and, in front, revealed a little of her bosom.

Observing these two and the ground being written on, I loitered nearby. Although I could take the pair in at a glance, I wasn't able to make out the characters inscribed by the clog. The man, not erasing a character once he had written it but simply writing over it, kept doing one after the other. Even so, the firecracker girl could probably read them. When some meaning had been completed there on the ground, without thinking to or knowing it, the two would suddenly raise their faces and glance at each other. But, before they could smile at each other or say something with their eyes or lips, the girl would drop her eyes to the ground and the man would start to write again. The girl had the slender fingers and waist of a child born to a poor family in old down-town Tokyo, but she seemed to have shot up ahead of her years.

When the man had written three or four new characters, the girl abruptly leaned forward off the bench. Reaching out her left hand that had rested on her instep, she tried to snatch the clog away from the man. The man nimbly withdrew his hand. They exchanged glances. But neither said a word, and neither showed any change of expression. It was strange. The girl docilely brought her hand back to her instep. The man planted himself solidly on his heels, spread his knees farther apart, and began to write another character. This time, before he had finished the character, the girl shot out her left hand like lightning. But the man's hand was even quicker. Giving up, the firecracker girl again drew back her hand docilely. As she was returning her hand to her instep, she suddenly turned her face to the side and met my eye. I wasn't ready for such an encounter. Involuntarily, she flashed me a little smile. I, also involuntarily, gave her a little smile in return.

The firecracker girl's smile passed straight into my heart. As I watched the postures and actions of the couple, the smile that was in my heart was lured to the surface in all its purity by the girl. It was an innocent smile.

The man, drawn by the direction of the girl's gaze, also looked at me. Giving me a sly grin, he then immediately put on a stern face. Suddenly I felt chilled. The girl, blushing slightly, raised her left hand to her cleft-peach hairdo as if to tidy it. Her face was hidden by her sleeve. All of this had taken place in the short space of time after the girl had stretched out her hand to snatch the bamboo clog from the man. Although I lightly parried the ill will of the look he threw at me, I felt ashamed of having stolen other people's secrets. I walked away.

Glasses vendor! Your displeasure is understandable. Probably you did not know it, but the girl's blushing and hiding her face with her sleeve must have been on your account. Because a little smile that bloomed fleetingly outside the night stall was stolen from you by me. Of course, even though you glanced at each other, you were so intent on what you were doing that your faces were almost expressionless. So the girl's smile ought to have been given to you. If only I hadn't been looking, you probably would have given the girl the same smile in return. However, if I stole a glimpse and a moment of that time before the girl's father or older brother came for her, if my innocent smile at that instant mirrored the girl's own smile, didn't you in turn give me a hard look along with your sly smile? If I may use the terms of your trade, the spectacles of your heart are slightly clouded and out of focus. But there is to-morrow evening, and the evening after. Write down thousands, hundreds of thousands of characters in the dirt until you reach the center of the earth!

Firecracker girl! Left-handed girl! For you, it's probably all the same, but I worry that, as you peer down into the well that the glasses dealer, by writing thousands and hundreds of millions of characters, will carve into the earth with the bamboo clog, you may have a dizzy spell and fall down that well. I cannot tell whether it is better to fall down such a well or to guard against falling. Probably it would be best for you to follow behind the wagon that your father or older brother, who has come for you, draws behind him, thinking of the glasses dealer as you walk along the deserted streets of the neighborhood. . . . But how would it be if you were to set off all at once all of the firecrackers lined up in your stall—the Azuma Peonies, the Flower Wheels, the Land Mines, the Snow, Moon, and Flowers, the Three-Colored Pine Needles—making a flower of fire bloom in the lonely night? If you did that, even the glasses vendor might jump up in absolute astonishment and run away.

10

Translated by Lane Dunlop and J. Martin Holman

Zora Neale Hurston (1901–1960)

Zora Neale Hurston was born in the all-Black town of Eatonville, Florida. Her mother died when she was eleven, and her father sent her to live with various relatives. Although she never finished grade school, she eventually attended Howard University in Washington, D.C. Her writing career began with a story published in a university literary magazine in 1921.

For a period in the 1920s, Hurston lived in New York City and took an active role in what has come to be known as "the Harlem Renaissance"—it was a time of tremendous cultural ferment not only in literary arts but in music and painting. With the onset of the Great Depression in the 1930s, Hurston devoted herself to writing fiction and to gathering up tales and legends from her Florida community. Although she had some success in seeing her work published, financial rewards did not follow. She died as she had begun, impoverished, in her home state. Hurston's works include the stories of *The Eatonville Anthology* (1927), the lore and reportage of *Mules and Men* (1935), and her celebrated novel *Their Eyes Were Watching God* (1937).

SPUNK

I

A giant of a brown-skinned man sauntered up the one street of the village and out into the palmetto thickets with a small pretty woman clinging lovingly to his arm.

"Looka theah, folkses!" cried Elijah Mosley, slapping his leg gleefully.

"Theah they go, big as life an' brassy as tacks."

All the loungers in the store tried to walk to the door with an air of nonchalance but with small success.

"Now pee-eople!" Walter Thomas gasped. "Will you look at'em!"

"But that's one thing Ah likes about Spunk Banks—he ain't skeered of nothin' on God's green footstool—*nothin*'! He rides that log down at saw-mill jus' like he struts 'round wid another man's wife—us' don't give a kitty. When Tes' Miller got cut to giblets on that circle-saw, Spunk steps right up and starts ridin'. The rest of us was skeered to go near it."

A round-shouldered figure in overalls much too large came nervously in the door and the talking ceased. The men looked at each other and winked.

"Gimme some soda-water. Sass'prilla° Ah reckon," the newcomer ordered, and stood far down the counter near the open pickled pig-feet tub to drink it.

Elijah nudged Walter and turned with mock gravity to the new-comer.

"Say, Joe, how's everything up yo' way? How's yo' wife?"

Joe started and all but dropped the bottle he was holding. He swallowed several times painfully and his lips trembled.

"Aw' Lige, you oughtn't to do nothin' like that," Walter grumbled. Elijah ignored him.

"She jus' passed heah a few minutes ago goin' thata way," with a wave of his hand in the direction of the woods.

Now Joe knew his wife had passed that way. He knew that the men lounging in the general store had seen her, moreover, he knew that the men knew *he* knew. He stood there silent for a long moment staring blankly with his Adam's apple twitching nervously up and down his throat. One could actually see the pain he was suffering, his eyes, his face, his hands, and even the dejected slump of his shoulders. He set the bottle down upon the counter. He didn't bang it, just eased it out of his hand silently and fiddled with his suspender buckle.

"Well, Ah'm goin' after her to-day. Ah'm goin' an' fetch her back. Spunk's done gone too fur."

He reached deep down into his trouser pocket and drew out a hollow ground razor, large and shiny, and passed his moistened thumb back and forth over the edge.

"Talkin' like a man, Joe. 'Course that's yo' fambly affairs, but Ah like to see grit in anybody."

Joe Kanty laid down a nickel and stumbled out into the street.

Dusk crept in from the woods. Ike Clarke lit the swinging oil lamp that was almost immediately surrounded by candle-flies. The men laughed boisterously behind Joe's back as they watched him shamble woodward.

"You oughtn't to said whut you said to him, 'Lige—look how it worked him up," Walter chided.

"And Ah hope it did work him up. Tain't even decent for a man to take and take like he do."

"Spunk will sho' kill him."

"Aw, Ah doan know. You never kin tell. He might turn him up an' spank him fur gettin' in the way, but Spunk wouldn't shoot no unarmed man. Dat razor he carried outa heah ain't gonna run Spunk down an' cut him, an' Joe ain't got the nerve to go to Spunk with it knowing he totes that Army .45. He makes that break outa heah to bluff us. He's gonna hide that razor behind the first palmetto root an' sneak back home to bed. Don't tell me nothin' 'bout that rabbit-foot colored man. Didn't

---

sass'prilla: A sweet soft drink flavored with sarsaparilla, a tropical root.

A Fiction Anthology

he meet Spunk an' Lena face to face one day las' week an' mumble sumthin' to Spunk 'bout lettin' his wife alone?"

"What did Spunk say?" Walter broke in. "Ah like him fine but tain't right the way he carries on wid Lena Kanty, jus' 'cause Joe's timid 'bout fightin'."

"You wrong theah, Walter. Tain't 'cause Joe's timid at all, it's 'cause Spunk wants Lena. If Joe was a passle of wile cats Spunk would tackle the job just the same. He'd go after *anything* he wanted the same way. As Ah wuz sayin' a minute ago, he tole Joe right to his face that Lena was his. 'Call her and see if she'll come. A woman knows her boss an' she answers when he calls.' 'Lena, ain't I yo' husband?' Joe sorter whines out. Lena looked at him real disgusted but she don't answer and she don't move outa her tracks. Then Spunk reaches out an' takes hold of her arm an' says: 'Lena, youse mine. From now on Ah works for you an' fights for you an' Ah never wants you to look to nobody for a crumb of bread, a stitch of close or a shingle to go over yo' head, but *me* long as Ah live. Ah'll git the lumber foh owah house tomorrow. Go home an' git yo' things together!'

" 'Thass mah house,' Lena speaks up. 'Papa gimme that.'

" 'Well,' says Spunk, 'doan give up whut's yours, but when youse inside doan forgit youse mine, an' let no other man git outa his place wid you!'

"Lena looked up at him with her eyes so full of love that they wuz runnin' over, an' Spunk seen it an' Joe seen it too, and his lip started to tremblin' and his Adam's apple was galloping up and down his neck like a race horse. Ah bet he's wore out half a dozen Adam's apples since Spunk's been on the job with Lena. That's all he'll do. He'll be back heah after while swallowin' an' workin' his lips like he wants to say somethin' an' can't."

"But didn't he do *nothin'* to stop 'em?"

"Nope, not a frazzlin' thing—jus' stood there. Spunk took Lena's arm and walked off jus' like nothin' ain't happened and he stood there gazin' after them till they was outa sight. Now you know a woman don't want no man like that. I'm jus' waitin' to see whut he's goin' to say when he gits back." 30

II

But Joe Kanty never came back, never. The men in the store heard the sharp report of a pistol somewhere distant in the palmetto thicket and soon Spunk came walking leisurely, with his big black Stetson set at the same rakish angle and Lena clinging to his arm, came walking right into the general store. Lena wept in a frightened manner.

"Well," Spunk announced calmly, "Joe came out there wid a meat axe an' made me kill him."

He sent Lena home and led the men back to Joe—crumpled and limp with his right hand still clutching his razor.

"See mah back? Mah close cut clear through. He sneaked up an' tried to kill me from the back, but Ah got him, an' got him good, first shot," Spunk said.

The men glared at Elijah, accusingly. 35

"Take him up an' plant him in Stony Lonesome,"° Spunk said in a careless voice. "Ah didn't wanna shoot him but he made me do it. He's a dirty coward, jumpin' on a man from behind."

Stony Lonesome: a cemetery.

Spunk turned on his heel and sauntered away to where he knew his love wept in fear for him and no man stopped him. At the general store later on, they all talked of locking him up until the sheriff should come from Orlando, but no one did anything but talk.

A clear case of self-defense, the trial was a short one, and Spunk walked out of the court house to freedom again. He could work again, ride the dangerous log-carriage that fed the singing, snarling, biting circle-saw; he could stroll the soft dark lanes with his guitar. He was free to roam the woods again; he was free to return to Lena. He did all of these things.

III

"Whut you reckon, Walt?" Elijah asked one night later. "Spunk's gittin' ready to marry Lena!"

"Naw! Why, Joe ain't had time to git cold yit. Nohow Ah didn't figger Spunk was the marryin' kind."

"Well, he is," rejoined Elijah. "He done moved most of Lena's things—and her along wid 'em—over to the Bradley house. He's buying it. Jus' like Ah told yo' all right in heah the night Joe was kilt. Spunk's crazy 'bout Lena. He don't want folks to keep on talkin' 'bout her—thass reason he's rushin' so. Funny thing 'bout that bob-cat, wan't it?"

"What bob-cat, 'Lige? Ah ain't heered 'bout none."

"Ain't cher? Well, night befo' las' as they was goin' to bed, a big black bob-cat, black all over, you hear me, *black,* walked round and round that house and howled like forty, an' when Spunk got his gun an' went to the winder to shoot it, he says it stood right still an' looked him in the eye, an' howled right at him. The thing got Spunk so nervoused up he couldn't shoot. But Spunk says twan't no bob-cat nohow. He says it was Joe done sneaked back from Hell!"

"Humph!" sniffed Walter, "he oughter be nervous after what he done. Ah reckon Joe come back to dare him to marry Lena, or to come out an' fight. Ah bet he'll be back time and again, too. Know what Ah think? Joe wuz a braver man than Spunk."

There was a general shout of derision from the group.

"Thass a fact," went on Walter. "Lookit whut he done; took a razor an' went out to fight a man he knowed toted a gun an' wuz a crack shot, too; 'nother thing Joe wuz skeered of Spunk, skeered plumb stiff! But he went jes' the same. It took him a long time to get his nerve up. Tain't nothin' for Spunk to fight when he ain't skeered of nothin'. Now, Joe's done come back to have it out wid the man that's got all he ever had. Y'all know Joe ain't never had nothin' nor wanted nothin' besides Lena. It musta been a h'ant cause ain't nobody never seen no black bob-cat."

"'Nother thing," cut in one of the men, "Spunk was cussin' a blue streak to-day 'cause he 'lowed dat saw wuz wobblin'—almos' got 'im once. The machinist come, looked it over an said it wuz alright. Spunk musta been leanin' t'wards it some. Den he claimed somebody pushed 'im but twan't nobody close to 'im. Ah wuz glad when knockin' off time came. I'm skeered of dat man when he gits hot. He'd beat you full of button holes as quick as he's look atcher."

IV

The men gathered the next evening in a different mood, no laughter. No badinage this time.

"Look, 'Lige, you goin' to set up wid Spunk?"

"Naw, Ah reckon not, Walter. Tell yuh the truth, Ah'm a li'l bit skittish. Spunk died too wicket—died cussin' he did. You know he thought he was done outa life." 50

"Good Lawd, who'd he think done it?"

"Joe."

"Joe Kanty? How come?"

"Walter, Ah b'leeve Ah will walk up thata way an' set. Lena would like it Ah reckon."

"But whut did he say, 'Lige?" 55

Elijah did not answer until they had left the lighted store and were strolling down the dark street.

"Ah wuz loadin' a wagon wid scantlin' right near the saw when Spunk fell on the carriage but 'fore Ah could git to him the saw got him in the body—awful sight. Me an' Skint Miller got him off but it was too late. Anybody could see that. The fust thing he said wuz: 'He pushed me, 'Lige—the dirty hound pushed me in the back!'—he was spittin' blood at ev'ry breath. We laid him on the sawdust pile with his face to the East so's he could die easy. He helt mah han' till the last, Walter, and said: 'It was Joe, 'Lige . . . the dirty sneak shoved me . . . he didn't dare come to mah face . . . but Ah'll git the son-of-a-wood louse soon's Ah get there an' make hell too hot for him . . . Ah felt him shove me . . . !' Thass how he died."

"If spirits kin fight, there's a powerful tussle goin' on somewhere ovah Jordan 'cause Ah b'leeve Joe's ready for Spunk an' ain't skeered any more—yas, Ah b'leeve Joe pushed 'im mahself.' "

They had arrived at the house. Lena's lamentations were deep and loud. She had filled the room with magnolia blossoms that gave off a heavy sweet odor. The keepers of the wake tipped about whispering in frightened tones. Everyone in the village was there, even old Jeff Kanty, Joe's father, who a few hours before would have been afraid to come within ten feet of him, stood leering triumphantly down upon the fallen giant as if his fingers had been the teeth of steel that laid him low.

The cooling board consisted of three sixteen-inch boards on saw horses, a dingy sheet was his shroud. 60

The women ate heartily of the funeral baked meats and wondered who would be Lena's next. The men whispered coarse conjectures between guzzles of whiskey.

[1927]

Eudora Welty (1909–   )

Eudora Welty was born in Jackson, Mississippi, where she still lives in her family house. She has pursued what might be called the Henry James career path; that is, she has more or less consecrated her life to her art. She has not moved from her place of birth, nor has she married. But whereas James wrote prose attuned to the complex indirections of the social realm, Welty has gone in the opposite direction. Her stories are seen, heard, and known with the fingertips down to the least real-life cobweb. Her settings may be limited, but what she reveals within those settings about human nature is without limit.

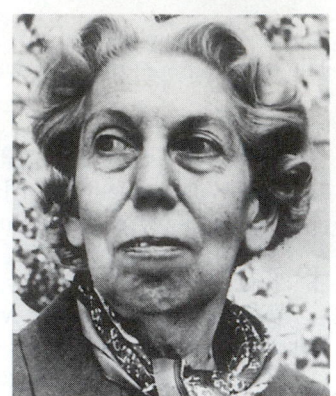

Welty's books include *A Curtain of Green* (1941), *The Wide Net and Other Stories* (1943), *The Golden Apples* (1949), *The Bride of the Innisfallen and Other Stories* (1955), and the novels *Delta Wedding* (1946) and *The Optimist's Daughter* (1972).

Welty writes of her approach: "What I do in the writing of any character is to try to enter into the mind, heart, and skin of a human being who is not myself. Whether this happens to be a man or a woman, young or old, with skin Black or White, the challenge lies in making the jump itself."

A WORN PATH

It was December—a bright frozen day in the early morning. Far out in the country there was an old Negro woman with her head tied in a red rag, coming along a path through the pinewoods. Her name was Phoenix Jackson. She was very old and small and she walked slowly in the dark pine shadows, moving a little from side to side in her steps, with the balanced heaviness and lightness of a pendulum in a grandfather clock. She carried a thin, small cane made from an umbrella, and with this she kept tapping the frozen earth in front of her. This made a grave and persistent noise in the still air, that seemed meditative like the chirping of a solitary little bird.

She wore a dark striped dress reaching down to her shoe tops, and an equally long apron of bleached sugar sacks, with a full pocket: all neat and tidy, but every time she took a step she might have fallen over her shoelaces, which dragged from her unlaced shoes. She looked straight ahead. Her eyes were blue with age. Her skin had a pattern all its own of numberless branching wrinkles and as though a whole little tree stood in the middle of her forehead, but a golden color ran underneath, and the two knobs of her cheeks were illumined by a yellow burning under the dark. Under the red rag her hair came down on her neck in the frailest of ringlets, still black, and with an odor like copper.

Now and then there was a quivering in the thicket. Old Phoenix said, "Out of my way, all you foxes, owls, beetles, jack rabbits, coons and wild animals! . . . Keep out from under these feet, little bob-whites. . . . Keep the big wild hogs out of my path. Don't let none of those come running my direction. I got a long way." Under her small black-freckled hand her cane, limber as a buggy whip, would switch at the brush as if to rouse up any hiding things.

On she went. The woods were deep and still. The sun made the pine needles almost too bright to look at, up where the wind rocked. The cones dropped as light as feathers. Down in the hollow was the mourning dove—it was not too late for him.

The path ran up a hill. "Seem like there is chains about my feet, time I get this far," she said, in the voice of argument old people keep to use with themselves. "Something always take a hold of me on this hill—pleads I should stay."

After she got to the top she turned and gave a full, severe look behind her where she had come. "Up through pines," she said at length. "Now down through oaks."

Her eyes opened their widest, and she started down gently. But before she got to the bottom of the hill a bush caught her dress.

Her fingers were busy and intent, but her skirts were full and long, so that before she could pull them free in one place they were caught in another. It was not possible to allow the dress to tear. "I in the thorny bush," she said. "Thorns, you doing your appointed work. Never want to let folks pass, no sir. Old eyes thought you was a pretty little *green* bush."

Finally, trembling all over, she stood free, and after a moment dared to stoop for her cane.

"Sun so high!" she cried, leaning back and looking, while the thick tears went over her eyes. "The time getting all gone here."

At the foot of this hill was a place where a log was laid across the creek.

"Now comes the trial," said Phoenix.

Putting her right foot out, she mounted the log and shut her eyes. Lifting her skirt, leveling her cane fiercely before her, like a festival figure in some parade, she began to march across. Then she opened her eyes and she was safe on the other side.

"I wasn't as old as I thought," she said.

But she sat down to rest. She spread her skirts on the bank around her and folded her hands over her knees. Up above her was a tree in a pearly cloud of mistletoe. She did not dare to close her eyes, and when a little boy brought her a plate with a slice of marble-cake on it she spoke to him. "That would be acceptable," she said. But when she went to take it there was just her own hand in the air.

So she left that tree, and had to go through a barbed-wire fence. There she had to creep and crawl, spreading her knees and stretching her fingers like a baby trying to climb the steps. But she talked loudly to herself: she could not let her dress be torn now, so late in the day, and she could not pay for having her arm or her leg sawed off if she got caught fast where she was.

At last she was safe through the fence and risen up out in the clearing. Big dead trees, like black men with one arm, were standing in the purple stalks of the withered cotton field. There sat a buzzard.

"Who you watching?"

In the furrow she made her way along.

"Glad this not the season for bulls," she said, looking sideways, "and the good Lord made his snakes to curl up and sleep in the winter. A pleasure I don't see no two-headed snake coming around that tree, where it come once. It took a while to get by him, back in the summer."

She passed through the old cotton and went into a field of dead corn. It whispered and shook and was taller than her head. "Through the maze now," she said, for there was no path.

Then there was something tall, black, and skinny there, moving before her.

At first she took it for a man. It could have been a man dancing in the field. But she stood still and listened, and it did not make a sound. It was as silent as a ghost.

"Ghost," she said sharply, "who be you the ghost of? For I have heard of nary death close by."

But there was no answer—only the ragged dancing in the wind. 25

She shut her eyes, reached out her hand, and touched a sleeve. She found a coat and inside that an emptiness, cold as ice.

"You scarecrow," she said. Her face lighted. "I ought to be shut up for good," she said with laughter. "My senses is gone. I too old. I the oldest people I ever know. Dance, old scarecrow," she said, "while I dancing with you."

She kicked her foot over the furrow, and with mouth drawn down, shook her head once or twice in a little strutting way. Some husks blew down and whirled in streamers about her skirts.

Then she went on, parting her way from side to side with the cane, through the whispering field. At last she came to the end, to a wagon track where the silver grass blew between the red ruts. The quail were walking around like pullets, seeming all dainty and unseen.

"Walk pretty," she said. "This the easy place. This the easy going." 30

She followed the track, swaying through the quiet bare fields, through the little strings of trees silver in their dead leaves, past cabins silver from weather, with the doors and windows boarded shut, all like old women under a spell sitting there. "I walking in their sleep," she said, nodding her head vigorously.

In a ravine she went where a spring was silently flowing through a hollow log. Old Phoenix bent and drank. "Sweet-gum makes the water sweet," she said, and drank more. "Nobody know who made this well, for it was here when I was born."

The track crossed a swampy part where the moss hung as white as lace from every limb. "Sleep on, alligators, and blow your bubbles." Then the track went into the road.

Deep, deep the road went down between the high green-colored banks. Overhead the live-oaks met, and it was as dark as a cave.

A black dog with a lolling tongue came up out of the weeds by the ditch. She was meditating, and not ready, and when he came at her she only hit him a little with her cane. Over she went in the ditch, like a little puff of milkweed. 35

Down there, her senses drifted away. A dream visited her, and she reached her hand up, but nothing reached down and gave her a pull. So she lay there and presently went to talking. "Old woman," she said to herself, "that black dog come up out of the weeds to stall you off, and now there he sitting on his fine tail, smiling at you."

A white man finally came along and found her—a hunter, a young man, with his dog on a chain.

"Well, Granny!" he laughed. "What are you doing there?"

"Lying on my back like a June-bug waiting to be turned over, mister," she said, reaching up her hand.

He lifted her up, gave her a swing in the air, and set her down. "Anything broken, Granny?" 40

"No sir, them old dead weeds is springy enough," said Phoenix, when she had got her breath. "I thank you for your trouble."

"Where do you live, Granny?" he asked, while the two dogs were growling at each other.

"Away back yonder, sir, behind the ridge. You can't even see it from here."

"On your way home?"

"No sir, I going to town." 45

"Why, that's too far! That's as far as I walk when I come out myself, and I get something for my trouble." He patted the stuffed bag he carried, and there hung down a little closed claw. It was one of the bob-whites, with its beak hooked bitterly to show it was dead. "Now you go on home, Granny!"

"I bound to go to town, mister," said Phoenix. "The time come around."

He gave another laugh, filling the whole landscape. "I know you old colored people! Wouldn't miss going to town to see Santa Claus!"

But something held old Phoenix very still. The deep lines in her face went into a fierce and different radiation. Without warning, she had seen with her own eyes a flashing nickel fall out of the man's pocket onto the ground.

"How old are you, Granny?" he was saying.   50

"There's no telling, mister," she said, "no telling."

Then she gave a little cry and clapped her hands and said, "Git on away from here, dog! Look! Look at that dog!" She laughed as if in admiration. "He ain't scared of nobody. He a big black dog." She whispered, "Sic him!"

"Watch me get rid of that cur," said the man. "Sic him, Pete! Sic him!"

Phoenix heard the dogs fighting, and heard the man running and throwing sticks. She even heard a gunshot. But she was slowly bending forward by that time, further and further forward, the lid stretched down over her eyes, as if she were doing this in her sleep. Her chin was lowered almost to her knees. The yellow palm of her hand came out from the fold of her apron. Her fingers slid down and along the ground under the piece of money with the grace and care they would have in lifting an egg from under a setting hen. Then she slowly straightened up, she stood erect, and the nickel was in her apron pocket. A bird flew by. Her lips moved. "God watching me the whole time. I come to stealing."

The man came back, and his own dog panted about them. "Well, I scared him off that time," he said, and then he laughed and lifted his gun and pointed it at Phoenix. 55

She stood straight and faced him.

"Doesn't the gun scare you?" he said, still pointing it.

"No, sir, I seen plenty go off closer by, in my day, and for less than what I done," she said, holding utterly still.

He smiled, and shouldered the gun. "Well, Granny," he said, "you must be a hundred years old, and scared of nothing. I'd give you a dime if I had any money with me. But you take my advice and stay home, and nothing will happen to you."

"I bound to go on my way, mister," said Phoenix. She inclined her head in the red rag. Then they went in different directions, but she could hear the gun shooting again and again over the hill.   60

She walked on. The shadows hung from the oak trees to the road like curtains. Then she smelled wood-smoke, and smelled the river, and she saw a steeple and the cabins on their steep steps. Dozens of little black children whirled around her. There ahead was Natchez shining. Bells were ringing. She walked on.

In the paved city it was Christmas time. There were red and green electric lights strung and crisscrossed everywhere, and all turned on in the daytime. Old Phoenix would have been lost if she had not distrusted her eyesight and depended on her feet to know where to take her.

She paused quietly on the sidewalk where people were passing by. A lady came along in the crowd, carrying an armful of red-, green- and silver-wrapped presents; she gave off perfume like the red roses in hot summer, and Phoenix stopped her.

"Please, missy, will you lace up my shoe?" She held up her foot.

"What do you want, Grandma?"   65

"See my shoe," said Phoenix. "Do all right for out in the country, but wouldn't look right to go in a big building."

"Stand still then, Grandma," said the lady. She put her packages down on the sidewalk beside her and laced and tied both shoes tightly.

"Can't lace 'em with a cane," said Phoenix. "Thank you, missy. I doesn't mind asking a nice lady to tie up my shoe, when I gets out on the street."

Moving slowly and from side to side, she went into the big building, and into the tower of steps, where she walked up and around and around until her feet knew to stop.

She entered a door, and there she saw nailed up on the wall the document that had been stamped with the gold seal and framed in the gold frame, which matched the dream that was hung up in her head. 70

"Here I be," she said. There was a fixed and ceremonial stiffness over her body.

"A charity case, I suppose," said an attendant who sat at the desk before her.

But Phoenix only looked above her head. There was sweat on her face, the wrinkles in her skin shone like a bright net.

"Speak up, Grandma," the woman said. "What's your name? We must have your history, you know. Have you been here before? What seems to be the trouble with you?"

Old Phoenix only gave a twitch to her face as if a fly were bothering her. 75

"Are you deaf?" cried the attendant.

But then the nurse came in.

"Oh, that's just old Aunt Phoenix," she said. "She doesn't come for herself— she has a little grandson. She makes these trips just as regular as clockwork. She lives away back off the Old Natchez Trace." She bent down. "Well, Aunt Phoenix, why don't you just take a seat? We won't keep you standing after your long trip." She pointed.

The old woman sat down, bolt upright in the chair.

"Now, how is the boy?" asked the nurse. 80

Old Phoenix did not speak.

"I said, how is the boy?"

But Phoenix only waited and stared straight ahead, her face very solemn and withdrawn into rigidity.

"Is his throat any better?" asked the nurse. "Aunt Phoenix, don't you hear me? Is your grandson's throat any better since the last time you came for the medicine?"

With her hands on her knees, the old woman waited, silent, erect and motion-less, just as if she were in armor. 85

"You mustn't take up our time this way, Aunt Phoenix," the nurse said. "Tell us quickly about your grandson, and get it over. He isn't dead, is he?"

At last there came a flicker and then a flame of comprehension across her face, and she spoke.

"My grandson. It was my memory had left me. There I sat and forgot why I made my long trip."

"Forgot?" The nurse frowned. "After you came so far?"

Then Phoenix was like an old woman begging a dignified forgiveness for waking up frightened in the night. "I never did go to school, I was too old at the Surrender,"° she said in a soft voice. "I'm an old woman without an education. It was my memory fail me. My little grandson, he is just the same, and I forgot it in the coming." 90

Surrender: the surrender of the Confederacy that ended the Civil War.

"Throat never heals, does it?" said the nurse, speaking in a loud, sure voice to old Phoenix. By now she had a card with something written on it, a little list. "Yes. Swallowed lye. When was it?—January—two-three years ago—"

Phoenix spoke unmasked now. "No, missy, he not dead, he just the same. Every little while his throat begin to close up again, and he not able to swallow. He not get his breath. He not able to help himself. So the time come around, and I go on another trip for the soothing medicine."

"All right. The doctor said as long as you came to get it, you could have it," said the nurse. "But it's an obstinate case."

"My little grandson, he sit up there in the house all wrapped up, waiting by himself," Phoenix went on. "We is the only two left in the world. He suffer and it don't seem to put him back at all. He got a sweet look. He going to last. He wear a little patch quilt and peep out holding his month open like a little bird. I remembers so plain now. I not going to forget him again, no, the whole enduring time. I could tell him from all the others in creation."

"All right." The nurse was trying to hush her now. She brought her a bottle of medicine. "Charity," she said, making a check mark in a book.   95

Old Phoenix held the bottle close to her eyes, and then carefully put it into her pocket.

"I thank you," she said.

"It's Christmas time, Grandma," said the attendant. "Could I give you a few pennies out of my purse?"

"Five pennies is a nickel," said Phoenix stiffly.

"Here's a nickel," said the attendant.   100

Phoenix rose carefully and held out her hand. She received the nickel and then fished the other nickel out of her pocket and laid it beside the new one. She stared at her palm closely, with her head on one side.

Then she gave a tap with her cane on the floor.

"This is what come to me to do," she said. "I going to the store and buy my child a little windmill they sells, made out of paper. He going to find it hard to believe there such a thing in the world. I'll march myself back where he waiting, holding it straight up in this hand."

She lifted her free hand, gave a little nod, turned around, and walked out of the doctor's office. Then her slow step began on the stairs, going down.

Amos Tutuola (1920–)

Amos Tutuola was born in a Nigerian village and was erratically educated in British colonial and missionary schools in Lagos and in provincial towns. His education ended early as he searched desperately for work in the wake of World War II, but he began writing and publishing shortly after Nigerian independence, and he has long been recognized as a major author for that country.

FEATHER WOMAN OF THE JUNGLE

From the Town of Famine
to the Town of the Water People
The entertainment of the fifth night
(My Fourth Journey)

In the fourth night, when the people gathered in the front of my house and the drinks were served as they were dancing and singing with great joy. Then I stopped them and I addressed them first as follows: "I am very happy indeed to see all of you again in front of me and I thank every one of you for the true affection you have on me, although I am the head of the village. And I wonder greatly, too, to see that you are increased again this night more than 90 per cent. But (all sat quietly and paid great attention to me) when I first saw the whole of you, I was afraid, but after I thought it over again my fear was expelled. Because I first thought within myself that where to get sufficient planks to make coffins for every one of you when you die because you are too many. But when I thought it over again, I remembered that not the whole of you would need coffins to bury you when you die. Because many of you would be killed and eaten up by the wild animals. Many would die in the rivers, many would be burnt into ashes by the fire, many would be kidnapped and so many of you would be fallen into the wells. So, therefore, coffins would not be required for those who died such death, and so many would not die in their homes but where their people would not see their bodies to bury with coffins." But the people were greatly annoyed when they heard like that from me. All were snapping their fingers on heads and saying that they would not die in the rivers or in the fire or in the wells or eaten up by the wild animals, but they would die in their homes, villages, etc., and they would be buried with coffins. But after a while, when their noises went down, I explained to them that they must not misunderstand me, because there was nobody on earth who could know the real place and real time he or she is going to die, or if anyone knew, let him or her tell me. And if anyone knew it, it meant I was guilty of what I had said. Having said so, I hesitated to hear the reply, but there was none of the people who could reply but they admitted at last.

After they danced and drank some of their palm-wine, I started to tell them the story as follows:

One fine morning, after six months that I had returned from my third journey, I took my usual gun, hunting-bag and matchet. I bade good-bye to my father, mother, sister and brother and all my friends and my neighbours. Some of the people cautioned me very seriously not to go for any treasure again. They said that all I had brought were enough. But I told them that I must try more for we knew of today but we did not know of tomorrow.

Then I left my village that bright day and I was going to the north this time. Having travelled for several days, I came to a town. This town was very big and famous. It was near a very wide and deep river. Immediately I entered the town I was greatly shocked first with fear when I saw the terrible appearances of the people or the inhabitants. Every one of them was so leaned that he had no more muscle on his body. Every one of them was as thin as a dried stick. The legs and arms were just like sticks. The eyes were seeing faintly in the skull except the head, which was so big that the thin neck could not even carry it. Both upper and lower jaws had already dried up like a roasted meat. The stomach was no more seen except the breast and exposed ribs.

When I first saw them in that appearances, I thought within myself and cried out unnoticed: "Ah, how people were created so terribly like this?" Because in the first instance I did not know that they were in famine and that they were starved until when they had leaned to that state. And they were so starved that the breasts of the women had dried up. The king, too, was so bitterly starved that he was unable to put on his crown whenever he went out. And it was a great pity that the hunger had forced the people of the town not to respect the king or chiefs again except one who brought food to them.

But, according to the custom of that town, I was first taken to the king and when he approved of my staying there, then I lodged in the house of the paramount chief which was almost next to the palace of the king. When it was night I tried to sleep but I was unable to fall asleep because of hunger. So hardly in the morning when I went to the king and told him: "Please, King, I am badly hungry, will you give me something to eat now?" But he said at the same time: "Is that so? Sorry, we are in great famine since past few years, therefore, I have no food to give you except cold water which is our main food in this town at present!"

Then I went back to my room, I sat and I was expecting that the paramount chief would soon send food to me as the king had failed to give it to me. Having waited for many hours and yet he did not send anything to me. Then I sold my shame and I went to him. Without shame, I told him that I wanted to eat. But he said that their main food was cold water. He said furthermore, that the famine was so serious they they had money but it was useless. They had plenty of costly clothes but the hunger did not let them wear them and even the clothes were oversized them because they had leaned too much. And again, this paramount chief advised me that I should be drinking the cold water.

Having heard like that as well from him, then without hesitation I started to drink the cold water. But when it was not yet daybreak when I was woken by hunger in the following morning. I hardly got up when I went to the king's attendants, I complained to them again that since I had come to the town I had nothing to eat except cold water which I was drinking. I complained to them perhaps they might help me. But I was very surprised that they did not allow me to tell them all of my complaints when they interrupted immediately they heard the word "hunger" from me. They naked themselves and told me to look how every one of them was leaned. They told me further that I, too, would soon become bones if I kept longer in that town.

Having failed again to get food from the attendants, I shook my head with surprise before I left them. When I returned to my room, I sat down quietly and I began to think how to get food by all means. I first thought to go back to my village to be bringing the foodstuffs to this town for sale. But I remembered that my village was too far travelled always.

As I was still suggesting within myself of what to do, it came to my mind to go to the big river which was near this town, perhaps I might get fishes from there. And without hesitation, I went to that river. Luckily, I found many canoes tied up to the trees on the bank and I loosened one. I put my matchet in it and then I pushed it on the river. I started to find fishes about to kill. But there was none to be found. But, of course, as I was still paddling along, I came to the swampy bush at about twelve o'clock p.m. In that swampy bush there were many palm-trees. When I stopped the canoe I climbed one palm-tree but unfortunately, there was no fruits on it. But when I climbed the third one, I found two ripen bunches of palm-fruits on top of it. So I drove all the birds which were eating them away first and then I cut both down.

After I had put them in the canoe, I first ate of them to my satisfaction and then I took the rest to the town. But I was nearly torn into pieces by the hungry people as I was carrying them along in the town to the king. However, I carried them to the king at last. With great wonder and admiration, he took them from me and thanked me greatly. Having eaten as many fruits as he could then he distributed the rest to his people.

After the people had gone back to their houses the king invited me to one of his property rooms. He showed me all his money and many other property as gold, silver, costly beads and diamonds. He promised me that when the famine was finished, he would give me a lot of money, gold, silver, diamond and beads as rewards. Having promised me like that, I replied with a smile that I would try my best to be supplying him the fruits till when the famine was finished and then I went back to my room, in the paramount chief's house.

In the following morning I went to the river again. I tried all my efforts in climbing so many palm-trees. Luckily after a while, I got one bunch of palm-fruits and I brought it to the king. After he had eaten of the fruits to his satisfaction he distributed the rest to his people. It was so I brought the fruits to the king and his people for the period of five months. But unfortunately, as the famine was not stopped in time and the season of the palm-fruits came to an end, therefore, I could not get anything for the king any more. I tried all my best to get the fruits, but it was in vain.

When it was the third day that I had not eaten except to drink the cold water from morning till night, I was so weak that I thought that I would die soon. I thought of going back to my village that time, but I could not trek the distance of about one mile when I would fall down. This, my fourth journey, was so bad and hopeless that I said within myself that if I returned to my village this time I would never attempt to go for any treasure again.

Having failed in all my efforts to get food, then I went back to the palm-trees perhaps I might get some fruits which probably had fallen to the bottoms of the palm-trees during the season. So I started to search the bottom of every palm-tree and I found only one over-ripen fruit when it was about three o'clock in the afternoon. I hastily picked it up. But as I held it, I said to myself sorrowfully that what a single palm-fruit could do for me. It could not satisfy my hunger.

Anyhow, I went in the canoe. But as I was paddling it along on the river and when I came to the deepest part of it, this palm-fruit was mistakenly fallen into the water. And this affected me so badly that I threw the paddle in the canoe and then jumped in the water without hesitation. But as I was swimming here and there just to pick up the fruit, someone held my both feet and was pulling me down into the bottom of the river. Having tried all my best to take my feet from him and failed, then I left myself to him. After a while he pulled me into the water and it was then

10

15

I saw who was pulling me. He held one coffin, with left hand. The lid of that coffin was glass and he hardly pushed that lid to one side when he pushed me in it and he entered it as well and then covered it with that glass lid at the same time. As I was inside the coffin with him, I was breathing in and out quite easily and I saw plainly that this man covered his body from the knee to the waist with the leather of big fish. He had no hair on head but small scales instead, his arms were very short and were as strong as iron, but there were fingers on each arm and they were resembled that of human being. Although he had two eyes like myself but each was as round as full moon.

But to my fear, he had fins on shoulders, elbows, knees and ankles and there were a number of moustache on his upper jaw, which was that of a big fish. His mouth was flat but his nose was round. As the coffin was taking us deeply into the river, this man began to treat me badly. Sometime, he would scratch my face with his sharp nails, sometime he would slap me on the ear and sometime he would be frightening by pointing a sharp iron on my eyes. It was like that he was ill-treating me until the coffin took us to the bottom of the river. Then he pushed the lid of the coffin to one side, he came down and then pulled me out. When I came down, I noticed that we were on the land and not in the water as before. The river was seen no more. Then he pushed me in front of him and told me to be going along on one road which led to a very beautiful house. As I was going along it so he was following me as fast as he could.

On both sides of that road there were beautiful trees and flowers. Having travelled on that road for a while I was seeing several men similar to this one, they lined up on both sides of the road as if they were policemen or soldiers. Having travelled farther, we came to the front of that beautiful house. And it was then I saw it clearly that it was a mighty palace. As he was escorting me along in it and as we were going from one place to another, I was seeing the costly decorations which were hung on every corner. Again, I noticed that the sun was so dull that there was only little difference from the full moon of the dry season. The air was a little thicker than my village's air and the sands on the ground were as white as white cloth. The sky was almost cloudy throughout the day.

After a while, that man escorted me to the beautiful sitting-room in which one beautiful lady sat in royal state. Without hesitation I stood before her and bowed down as the man who had escorted me in stood at back. But when I stood for a few minutes, I simply walked to one of the seats and then sat on it. Hardly crossed my legs when I started to glance at every decorations which were on the walls and on the floor. Now it was revealed to me that the inhabitants of this town were the water people and that beautiful lady was the nymph of the river, so they were belonged to the fish race. The nymph and her attendants and guardsmen were very surprised as I was not afraid of them at all, but they did not know that I had surrendered myself to all what might happened to me that time.

The decorations on the walls were stuffed goldfishes, polished large sea shells, skulls of the sea animals, etc., and every part of that walls was twinkling like stars. The seats were also stuffed fishes and were as fresh as if they were still alive. The ruler or the nymph herself was dressed in the skins of beautiful fishes. The skins were so highly refined that they were as smooth as very costly clothes. Some were shining like gold, some were twinkling like the bright stars and the top ones were shining steadily like diamonds. She sat on an armchair which had many carved sea creatures on top. She stretched feet on a well-polished skull of a big whale. Many big sea tortoises were walking about on the floor and the crown on her head was full of small beautiful sea shells.

As far as I saw her, she was about thirty years old. Her eyes were very clear and the face was very fresh as the face of a fifteen-year-old girl. There were no scars or pimples on her cheeks or face and the hair of her head was not so much dark but, of course, probably the climate of that town had turned the hair to be like that. Her teeth were very white and very closely to each other. Her nose was quite pointed like that of an image, the slippers on her feet were made from the soft leather of crocodile. She had clear and lovely voice and her face always seemed as if she was kind and merciful.

As I was still noticing these things, a number of another set of guardsmen walked in and those whom I met in there walked out and those who were just come in took over the duty. Again, I noticed these new set of the guardsmen that every-one of them was a man of strong body, stout and fearful to see. The skull of shark was on everyone's head, and wore the apron which was the skin of fish, but the scaly skins of fishes were their purtises and gloves. Many of them held the tails of big fishes. Each of that tails was about four feet long and the width was about six inches and very thick indeed and sharp thorns were lined up on both edges. Some of those who held the long spears were shielded their breasts with the very big tor-toise back shells. All of these were their uniforms. Every one of them was a giant-like and cynical.

As I sat on the chair facing the nymph or the queen of the river, and I was still looking at the decorations and thinking also in mind that no doubt I would leave this town with much wealths, the man who had brought me in there started to complain to the nymph that he brought me before her for punishment because I struck his head when I jumped on the river when the only palm-fruit which I could find had fallen into the river. That man hardly complained to the nymph when all her guardsmen gathered at my back and ready to hold me. But the nymph hastily rang the bell on her side, to them to leave me. Then with a very cool voice, she asked from me: "Why did you strike him on the head?" So before I started to reply, I first crossed my feet and seated very easy as if I was in my house and then I said: "In fact, I jumped on the river when the only palm-fruit that I could get, had fallen in the water. But I did not know whether I had struck him on the head, but if it was so then it was by a mistake." She asked again: "Why did you jump into the river in respect of one palm-fruit?" And as those guardsmen were in attention and got ready to hold me if the nymph gave them the order to do so. So I replied: "My work was to find the palm-fruits to the people of the town of famine because they had nothing to eat since the famine had started in their town and they had already leaned to the bones." But when she heard like that from me, she was so wondered that she sat up and then asked again: "The famine was so serious that only the palm-fruits the people eat?" I said: "Yes. Even the palm-fruits were not easily to get." Then she and her guardsmen breathed out with wonder and as she hesitated and was looking at me the guardsmen looked at each other's eyes with great won-der and then stood easy and that showed me that they were in sympathy with me. So the nymph said suddenly: "Oh, no wonder, your appearance even shows that you are in a great famine because you are too lean." But I hastily interrupted: "That town is not mine but I went there to find the treasure."

But as she was about to ask me another question, one beautiful lady walked in that moment. She put one big basin in front of her and then she bowed down for her and walked out. When she removed the lid of that basin, it was roasted fish and then she started to eat it as a refreshment. But as I was very hungry even before I was brought before her, so I stood up, I walked to her and without excuse, I took some slices and then I walked back to me seat and there I started to eat the fish bit by bit with greediness. But as the nymph was kind and merciful, she rang the bell on her side and after a few seconds, one attendant walked in. Then she told her to take me to the dining-room and give me food. So I walked out with that attendant. She (attendant) gave me the nice food which I ate to my entire satisfaction. After that I went back to the nymph. Having discussed with me about the famine for a while, she stood up and walked into one room opposite that sitting-room. After a while she came back with one round box. It was very big but one man could carry it from one place to another. It was sealed round. She gave it to me and then explained to me that, "This sealed box (she pointed finger to it) will supply food and drinks of all kinds to you and the people of the town of famine throughout the period of the famine. But you and the people must be very careful not to break the delicate box. If you break it it will not be able to supply anything to you any more and all of you will be punished for it. Furthermore, if it is stolen from you, all of you will be punished as well. And again, you must put in your mind always that you must not come back to me for anything as from today!"

Having warned me like that she rang the bell and the man (the water-man) who had brought me to her, walked in. As he stood before her, she told him to take me back to where he had caught me. Then I put the box on head, I thanked her greatly before I followed the water-man and some of the guardsmen led us to a short distance before they went back. After a while we came to where that coffin was. Having put that box in it and I went inside it, the water-man pushed it on to the river and then he entered it. But to my surprise, he hardly covered it with its lid when the coffin started to run furiously on the water and within a few seconds it floated on the very part of that river from which he had caught me before.

As my canoe was still driven here and there by the tides. Then as soon as the coffin stopped closely to it, I put that box in it and then I started to paddle it along to the town of famine. But the water-man did not talk to me until when he had brought me back to the river and returned to the nymph.

When I paddled the canoe for about two hours I reached the bank of that river. Having tied up the canoe, I carried the box direct to the king. In the presence of the paramount chief the king removed the lid of it. To their surprise, they met several basins of variety of food and one small spoon in it. But they did not believe me when I told them that the food would be sufficient to feed the whole people till whenever the famine was finished.

Anyhow, the king put the box in his strong-room and he choose me to be serving the food to the people and to himself. Then I first served him and the paramount chief and they had first satisfied their hunger, then the whole people in the town were invited to the palace. The king told them that everyone of them should go back to his or her house and bring the plate and spoon. Then the people ran back to their houses and they returned with all these things after a few minutes. Then I began to serve each of them. But the people ate and drank to their satisfaction and yet the food and the drinks remained in that box as if I had not served from them.

It was so the people and the king were eating and drinking to their satisfaction for three times daily for three months and yet the food and the drinks remained as if nothing had touched them. And within a few weeks more, the people had for-

25

gotten the famine. They had enough muscles on bodies, they became as powerful as before the famine had started. They were able to walk about easily in the town, singing, dancing, and laughing with great joy. They were so satisfied that they determined not to work again for their living.

But as the news of that wonderful box had spread to many towns and villages and many people from those towns and villages had come to witness that box. So one midnight, a gang of night marauders came from one of those towns to the palace. When they came in and as they were trying to break and enter into the strong-room to steal the box away to their town. The king's bugle-blowers who were keeping watch of the gate of the palace, started to blow the bugles just to wake the king and the rest people in the palace. When the people and the king woke, they took clubs, cudgels, matchets, axes, bows and arrows, etc. They rushed to the marauders and I followed them with my matchet in my hand. Then all of us started to beat them, but they beat us so mercilessly in return that everyone got wounds all over the body. They beat me until I fell down unconsciously. Every part of my body was bleeding continuously. But at last, when the arrows were shot to them continuously for a few minutes then they ran away for their lives.

After the marauders had escaped, the king and some of the rest people took from the floor to one room. The king started to treat my wounds with medicine and all were healed within a few days. And the marauders did not attempt to come to the palace for some weeks, but one of them whom we did not recognize at all, came to the bugle-blowers. He tried all his possible best and made friends with them. He was so kind to them that they did not suspect him as one of the marauders. He was sitting with them from morning till the evening. He was just spying the easiest way to get into the strong-room in which the wonderful box was kept always.

Having satisfied himself, then he went back to his members and told them to be ready for another attempt to steal the box. In the very night that they were leaving, he had come to the bugle-blowers before his members. He was playing with them as he was usually doing. But he hid one bottle of thick honey under his dress. When he noticed that the bugle-blowers went to the palace to take their supper, he hastily filled their bugles with that thick honey and then hung them back on their usual rack before they came back.

When they returned he ate and drank with them, after that he told them that he was going to visit another man in the next house. But not knowing that immediately he had left them, he went direct to the rest marauders. He told them that it was time to go and burgle the strong-room. Then all of them came to the town and entered the palace through the other gate. As they were splitting the door of the strong-room with axes, the bugle-blowers woke and hastily took their bugles from the rack. But when they put them in the mouths just to be blowing as a warning to the king and the people in the palace that the night marauders came again. The thick honey started to run from their bugles into their mouths. Therefore, they were unable to blow the bugles, but they were licking the honey and enjoying it as it was running into their mouths and it was so the marauders were breaking the strong-room as hastily as they could.

It was like that the room was broken into and the wonderful box together with the king's property was taken and then they left the town as quickly as possible. And they had gone far away before the bugle-blowers were able to blow their bugles after they had licked the honey in their bugles. Anyhow, the king and the rest people took up the fighting weapons. Then we chased the marauders to catch and then to take the box back from them. But they had gone too far away, we did not see any trace of them.

Then we came back to the palace. The king cast down on his throne and was thinking sorrowfully of what to eat in the morning. In the morning, when the people gathered in the front of the palace and were waiting for their breakfast, the king and his paramount chief told me to go back to the nymph for another wonderful box. But when I explained to the king that the nymph had warned me already not to come back to her for anything and she had warned me as well that if the box was split or stolen away, we would be punished for it. The hungry people shouted at a time: "Don't tell us a lie! But you must go back to her and if you explain to her how the box was stolen from the strong-room, she would not refuse to give you another one!" Again, I insisted to go back, but that time the king and the paramount chief said that if I refused to go back to the nymph it meant I disobeyed their order and therefore, they would punish me and the punishment was to behead me.

Anyhow, I went back to that river and as I was paddling the canoe along, I came to the same spot from where the water-man had taken me to the nymph the other day. Then I willfully threw the paddle in the water with the hope that it would sink like that palm-fruit. But when the paddle did not sink, I jumped into the water and I hardly dived when the same water-man held my both feet and pulled me deeply into the water before he put me inside the same coffin and within a few minutes it took us to the town of the nymph. Then the water-man took me before her like the first time. He complained to her that he caught me again when I struck his head with my feet.

But the nymph grew annoyed when she saw me there again. Instead to say anything to the complaint of the water-man, she asked me: "Had I not told you last time not to come here again?" I replied with trembling voice: "In fact you had told me not to come to you again. But I come back to take another wonderful box in which everlasting food and drinks are kept!" Having heard like that from me, she became more anger and asked: "By the way, what has happened to the one which I had given to you the other day?" I replied that the night marauders had stolen it away from the king's strong-room a few days ago. Then she remarked with fearful voice: "Is that how you people are careless? I had warned you that you should keep the box so safely that it might not be stolen. All right, I shall send another thing to the king which will teach all of you sense!"

Then she stood up and entered the same room opposite the sitting-room and I was very happy when she told me that she would send another thing to us which would teach us sense. After a while, she returned with one huge sealed pot. When gave it to me, she told me that I should open it when the whole people and the king gathered into one place. Then I thanked her greatly for I believed that this pot was going to supply the food and drinks like that box. So when I was ready to leave, she rang the bell to the same water-man and he walked in at the same time. As he bowed down for her, she told him to take me back with the same coffin. Having taken me back to where he had caught me, then I put the pot in my canoe and I paddled it to the bank and from there I carried the pot to the town.

The hungry people and the king who had already gathered in the front of the palace and were waiting for my return, shouted greatly with joy when they saw the pot on my head. But when I gave it to the king and he put it in the middle of the people, then I told him how he would open it. So he first told the people to bring their plates nearer and then he forced it open. But uncountable of bees, wasps and all kinds of the stinging insects rushed out from it instead of food and drinks. Without hesitation, these insects started to sting all of us. Within a few minutes many people were stung to death, that place was disordered at the same time. Everyone was running helter-skelter for his or her life. And at last, as the king was running away for his life, the crown fell off from his head but he was unable to wait and take it back. So almost all the people of the town of famine had run away for their lives and when the town was empty, then I took my gun, hunting bag and matchet, and I started to go back to my village at the same time. I could not wait to tell the king to fulfill his promise but, of course, he too was nowhere to be found.

After a few days' travel, I reached my village and I entered my father's house very quietly, but not as joyfully as my last three journeys which had profited me greatly. Then the people rushed to my house to honour my return, but they were greatly shocked when they noticed that I did not bring anything this time. Having told them all what had happened to me in the town of famine, some cautioned me not to go any journey again and some advised me not to give up my adventures because time was not always as straight as a straight line and that one who was finding goodness about must endanger his life and must be able to endure all hardships as well. Then I thanked them greatly. After that I sent for drinks and all of us drank together till the midnight.

"That was the end of my fourth journey. It was so many journeys were not profitable in those days. One journey might prove to be a better one from beginning but might be the worst towards the end. But I was not discouraged at all as my fourth journey was vanity at last. I thank you for your listening. Good night to you all." Then after the people of my village had danced, sung and drunken for a few minutes they went back to their houses.

Nadine Gordimer (1923–   )

Nadine Gordimer was born in a small town near Johannesburg, South Africa. Uninspired by her education at a convent school, she turned to books at an early age. Then, following the pattern so common among writers, she sought to create fictional worlds of her own. Gordimer was greatly influenced by the work of D. H. Lawrence, Henry James, and Ernest Hemingway. From their prose, as well as from her own highly developed skills as an observer, she honed a realistic style that has allowed her to fashion psychologically complex assessments of life in her native land. Gordimer has returned repeatedly in novels and stories to the subject of racial relations, exploring not only the conflicts between black and white cultures but also the many strategies of compromise and coexistence. Not content with exploring the situation through fiction, Gordimer has written a great many essays and polemics that reflect her anger at apartheid policies. Her novels include *The*

Conservationist, Burger's Daughter, A Guest of Honour, and July's People, while her stories have been collected in Soft Voice of the Serpent, Something Out There, A Soldier's Embrace, and other volumes.

TOWN AND COUNTRY LOVERS

I

Dr Franz-Josef von Leinsdorf is a geologist absorbed in his work; wrapped up in it, as the saying goes—year after year the experience of this work enfolds him, swaddling him away from the landscapes, the cities and the people, wherever he lives: Peru, New Zealand, the United States. He's always been like that, his mother could confirm from their native Austria. There, even as a handsome small boy he presented only his profile to her: turned away to his bits of rock and stone. His few relaxations have not changed much since then. An occasional skiing trip, listening to music, reading poetry—Rainer Maria Rilke° once stayed in his grandmother's hunting lodge in the forests of Styria and the boy was introduced to Rilke's poems while very young.

Layer upon layer, country after country, wherever his work takes him—and now he has been almost seven years in Africa. First the Côte d'Ivoire,° and for the past five years, South Africa. The shortage of skilled manpower brought about his recruitment here. He has no interest in the politics of the countries he works in. His private preoccupation-within-the-preoccupation of his work has been research into underground watercourses, but the mining company that employs him in a senior though not executive capacity is interested only in mineral discovery. So he is much out in the field—which is the veld, here—seeking new gold, copper, platinum and uranium deposits. When he is at home—on this particular job, in this particular country, this city—he lives in a two-roomed flat in a suburban block with a landscaped garden, and does his shopping at a supermarket conveniently across the street. He is not married—yet. That is how his colleagues, and the typists and secretaries at the mining company's head office, would define his situation. Both men and women would describe him as a good-looking man, in a foreign way, with the lower half of the face dark and middle-aged (his mouth is thin and curving, and no matter how close-shaven his beard shows like fine shot embedded in the skin round mouth and chin) and the upper half contradictorily young, with deep-set eyes (some would say grey, some black), thick eyelashes and brows. A tangled gaze: through which concentration and gleaming thoughtfulness perhaps appear as fire and languor. It is this that the women in the office mean when they remark he's not unattractive. Although the gaze seems to promise, he has never invited any one of them

---

Rainer Maria Rilke: a famous German-Austrian poet (see Chapters 23 and 27).
Côte d'Ivoire: Africa's Ivory Coast.

to go out with him. There is the general assumption he probably has a girl who's been picked for him, he's bespoken by one of his own kind, back home in Europe where he comes from. Many of these well-educated Europeans have no intention of becoming permanent immigrants; neither the remnant of white colonial life nor idealistic involvement with Black Africa appeals to them.

One advantage, at least, of living in underdeveloped or half-developed countries is that flats are serviced. All Dr von Leinsdorf has to do for himself is buy his own supplies and cook an evening meal if he doesn't want to go to a restaurant. It is simply a matter of dropping in to the supermarket on his way from his car to his flat after work in the afternoon. He wheels a trolley up and down the shelves, and his simple needs are presented to him in the form of tins, packages, plastic-wrapped meat, cheeses, fruit and vegetables, tubes, bottles . . . At the cashiers' counters where customers must converge and queue there are racks of small items uncategorized, for last-minute purchase. Here, as the coloured girl cashier punches the adding machine, he picks up cigarettes and perhaps a packet of salted nuts or a bar of nougat. Or razor-blades, when he remembers he's running short. One evening in winter he saw that the cardboard display was empty of the brand of blades he preferred, and he drew the cashier's attention to this. These young coloured girls are usually pretty unhelpful, taking money and punching their machines in a manner that asserts with the time-serving obstinacy of the half-literate the limit of any responsibility towards customers, but this one ran an alert glance over the selection of razor-blades, apologized that she was not allowed to leave her post, and said she would see that the stock was replenished 'next time'. A day or two later she recognized him, gravely, as he took his turn before her counter—'I ahssed them, but it's out of stock. You can't get it. I did ahss about it.' He said this didn't matter. 'When it comes in, I can keep a few packets for you.' He thanked her.

He was away with the prospectors the whole of the next week. He arrived back in town just before nightfall on Friday, and was on his way from car to flat with his arms full of briefcase, suitcase and canvas bags when someone stopped him by standing timidly in his path. He was about to dodge round unseeingly on the crowded pavement but she spoke. 'We got the blades in now. I didn't see you in the shop this week, but I kept some for when you come. So . . . '

He recognized her. He had never seen her standing before, and she was wearing a coat. She was rather small and finely-made, for one of them. The coat was skimpy but no big backside jutted. The cold brought an apricot-graining of warm colour to her cheekbones, beneath which a very small face was quite delicately hollowed, and the skin was smooth, the subdued satiny colour of certain yellow wood. That crêpey hair, but worn drawn back flat and in a little knot pushed into one of the cheap wool chignons that (he recognized also) hung in the miscellany of small goods along with the razor-blades, at the supermarket. He said thanks, he was in a hurry, he'd only just got back from a trip—shifting the burdens he carried, to demonstrate. 'Oh shame.' She acknowledged his load. 'But if you want I can run in and get it for you quickly. If you want.'

He saw at once it was perfectly clear that all the girl meant was that she would go back to the supermarket, buy the blades and bring the packet to him there where he stood, on the pavement. And it seemed that it was this certainty that made him say, in the kindly tone of assumption used for an obliging underling, 'I live just across there—*Atlantis*—that flat building. Could you drop them by, for me—number seven-hundred-and-eighteen, seventh floor—'

5

She had not before been inside one of these big flat buildings near where she worked. She lived a bus- and train-ride away to the West of the city, but this side of the black townships, in a township for people her tint. There was a pool with ferns, not plastic, and even a little waterfall pumped electrically over rocks, in the entrance of the building *Atlantis;* she didn't wait for the lift marked GOODS but took the one meant for whites and a white woman with one of those sausage-dogs on a lead got in with her but did not pay her any attention. The corridors leading to the flats were nicely glassed-in, not draughty.

He wondered if he should give her a twenty-cent piece for her trouble—ten cents would be right for a black; but she said, 'Oh no—please, here—' standing outside his open door and awkwardly pushing back at his hand the change from the money he'd given her for the razor-blades. She was smiling, for the first time, in the dignity of refusing a tip. It was difficult to know how to treat these people, in this country; to know what they expected. In spite of her embarrassing refusal of the coin, she stood there, completely unassuming, fists thrust down the pockets of her cheap coat against the cold she'd come in from, rather pretty thin legs neatly aligned, knee to knee, ankle to ankle.

'Would you like a cup of coffee or something?'

He couldn't very well take her into his study-cum-living-room and offer her a drink. She followed him to his kitchen, but at the sight of her pulling out the single chair to drink her cup of coffee at the kitchen table, he said, 'No—bring it in here—' and led the way into the big room where, among his books and his papers, his files of scientific correspondence (and the cigar boxes of stamps from the envelopes) his racks of records, his specimens of minerals and rocks, he lived alone.

It was no trouble to her; she saved him the trips to the supermarket and brought him his groceries two or three times a week. All he had to do was to leave a list and the key under the doormat, and she would come up in her lunch-hour to collect them, returning to put his supplies in the flat after work. Sometimes he was home and sometimes not. He bought a box of chocolates and left it, with a note, for her to find; and that was acceptable, apparently, as a gratuity.

Her eyes went over everything in the flat although her body tried to conceal its sense of being out of place by remaining as still as possible, holding its contours in the chair offered her as a stranger's coat is set aside and remains exactly as left until the owner takes it up to go. 'You collect?'

'Well, these are specimens—connected with my work.'

'My brother used to collect. Miniatures. With brandy and whisky and that, in them. From all over. Different countries.'

The second time she watched him grinding coffee for the cup he had offered her she said, 'You always do that? Always when you make coffee?'

'But of course. Is it no good, for you? Do I make it too strong?'

'Oh it's just I'm not used to it. We buy it ready—you know, it's in a bottle, you just add a bit to the milk or water.'

He laughed, instructive: 'That's not coffee, that's a synthetic flavouring. In my country we drink only real coffee, fresh, from the beans—you smell how good it is as it's being ground?'

She was stopped by the caretaker and asked what she wanted in the building? Heavy with the *bona fides* of groceries clutched to her body, she said she was work-

10

15

ing at number 718, on the seventh floor. The caretaker did not tell her not to use the whites' lift; after all, she was not black; her family was very light-skinned.

There was the item 'grey button for trousers' on one of his shopping lists. She said as she unpacked the supermarket carrier, 'Give me the pants, so long, then,' and sat on his sofa that was always gritty with fragments of pipe tobacco, sewing in and out through the four holes of the button with firm, fluent movements of the right hand, gestures supplying the articulacy missing from her talk. She had a little yokel's, peasant's (he thought of it) gap between her two front teeth when she smiled that he didn't much like, but, face ellipsed to three-quarter angle, eyes cast down in concentration with soft lips almost closed, this didn't matter. He said, watching her sew, 'You're a good girl'; and touched her. 20

She remade the bed every late afternoon when they left it and she dressed again before she went home. After a week there was a day when late afternoon became evening, and they were still in the bed.

'Can't you stay the night?'

'My mother,' she said.

'Phone her. Make an excuse.' He was a foreigner. He had been in the country five years, but he didn't understand that people don't usually have telephones in their houses, where she lived. She got up to dress. He didn't want that tender body to go out in the night cold and kept hindering her with the interruption of his hands; saying nothing. Before she put on her coat, when the body had already disappeared, he spoke. 'But you must make some arrangement.'

'Oh my mother!' Her face opened to fear and vacancy he could not read. 25

He was not entirely convinced the woman would think of her daughter as some pure and unsullied virgin . . . 'Why?'

The girl said, 'S'e'll be scared. S'e'll be scared we get caught.'

'Don't tell her anything. Say I'm employing you.' In this country he was working in now there were generally rooms on the roofs of flat buildings for tenants' servants.

She said: 'That's what I told the caretaker.'

She ground fresh coffee beans every time he wanted a cup while he was working at night. She never attempted to cook anything until she had watched in silence while he did it the way he liked, and she learned to reproduce exactly the simple dishes he preferred. She handled his pieces of rock and stone, at first admiring the colours—'It'd make a beautiful ring or a necklace, ay.' Then he showed her the striations, the formation of each piece, and explained what each was, and how, in the long life of the earth, it had been formed. He named the mineral it yielded, and what that was used for. He worked at his papers, writing, writing, every night, so it did not matter that they could not go out together to public places. On Sundays she got into his car in the basement garage and they drove to the country and picnicked away up in the Magaliesberg, where there was no one. He read or poked about among the rocks; they climbed together, to the mountain pools. He taught her to swim. She had never seen the sea. She squealed and shrieked in the water, showing the gap between her teeth, as—it crossed his mind—she must do when among her own people. Occasionally he had to go out to dinner at the houses of colleagues from the mining company; she sewed and listened to the radio in the flat and he found her in the bed, warm and already asleep, by the time he came in.

He made his way into her body without speaking; she made him welcome without a word. Once he put on evening dress for a dinner at his country's consulate; watching him brush one or two fallen hairs from the shoulders of the dark jacket that sat so well on him, she saw a huge room, all chandeliers and people dancing some dance from a costume film—stately, hand-to-hand. She supposed he was going to fetch, in her place in the car, a partner for the evening. They never kissed when either left the flat; he said, suddenly, kindly, pausing as he picked up cigarettes and keys, 'Don't be lonely.' And added, 'Wouldn't you like to visit your family sometimes, when I have to go out?'

30

He had told her he was going home to his mother in the forests and mountains of his country near the Italian border (he showed her on the map) after Christmas. She had not told him how her mother, not knowing there was any other variety, assumed he was a medical doctor, so she had talked to her about the doctor's children and the doctor's wife who was a very kind lady, glad to have someone who could help out in the surgery as well as the flat.

She remarked wonderingly on his ability to work until midnight or later, after a day at work. She was so tired when she came home from her cash register at the supermarket that once dinner was eaten she could scarcely keep awake. He explained in a way she could understand that while the work she did was repetitive, undemanding of any real response from her intelligence, requiring little mental or physical effort and therefore unrewarding, his work was his greatest interest, it taxed his mental capacities to their limit, exercised all his concentration, and rewarded him constantly as much with the excitement of a problem presented as with the satisfaction of a problem solved. He said later, putting away his papers, speaking out of a silence: 'Have you done other kinds of work?' She said, 'I was in a clothing factory before. Sportbeau shirts; you know? But the pay's better in the shop.'

Of course. Being a conscientious newspaper-reader in every country he lived in, he was aware that it was only recently that the retail consumer trade in this one had been allowed to employ coloureds as shop assistants; even punching a cash register represented advancement. With the continuing shortage of semi-skilled whites a girl like this might be able to edge a little farther into the white-collar category. He began to teach her to type. He was aware that her English was poor, even though, as a foreigner, in his ears her pronunciation did not offend, nor categorize her as it would in those of someone of his education whose mother tongue was English. He corrected her grammatical mistakes but missed the less obvious ones because of his own sometimes exotic English usage—she continued to use the singular pronoun 'it' when what was required was the plural 'they'. Because he was a foreigner (although so clever, as she saw) she was less inhibited than she might have been by the words she knew she misspelled in her typing. While she sat at the typewriter she thought how one day she would type notes for him, as well as making coffee the way he liked it, and taking him inside her body without saying anything, and sitting (even if only through the empty streets of quiet Sundays) beside him in his car, like a wife.

On a summer night near Christmas—he had already bought and hidden a slightly showy but nevertheless good watch he thought she would like—there was a knocking at the door that brought her out of the bathroom and him to his feet, at his worktable. No one ever came to the flat at night; he had no friends intimate enough to drop in without warning. The summons was an imperious banging that did not pause and clearly would not stop until the door was opened.

She stood in the open bathroom doorway gazing at him across the passage into the living-room; her bare feet and shoulders were free of a big bath-towel. She said nothing, did not even whisper. The flat seemed to shake with the strong unhurried blows.

35

He made as if to go to the door, at last, but now she ran and clutched him by both arms. She shook her head wildly; her lips drew back but her teeth were clenched, she didn't speak. She pulled him into the bedroom, snatched some clothes from the clean laundry laid out on the bed and got into the wall-cupboard, thrusting the key at his hand. Although his arms and calves felt weakly cold he was horrified, distastefully embarrassed at the sight of her pressed back crouching there under his suits and coat; it was horrible and ridiculous. *Come out!* he whispered. *No! Come out!* She hissed: *Where? Where can I go?*

Never mind! Get out of there!

He put out his hand to grasp her. At bay, she said with all the force of her terrible whisper, baring the gap in her teeth: *I'll throw myself out the window.*

She forced the key into his hand like the handle of a knife. He closed the door on her face and drove the key home in the lock, then dropped it among coins in his trouser pocket.

He unslotted the chain that was looped across the flat door. He turned the serrated knob of the Yale lock. The three policemen, two in plain clothes, stood there without impatience although they had been banging on the door for several minutes. The big dark one with an elaborate moustache held out in a hand wearing a plaited gilt ring some sort of identity card.

40

Dr von Leinsdorf said quietly, the blood coming strangely back to legs and arms, 'What is it?'

The sergeant told him they knew there was a coloured girl in the flat. They had had information; 'I been watching this flat three months, I know.'

'I am alone here.' Dr von Leinsdorf did not raise his voice.

'I know, I know who is here. Come—' And the sergeant and his two assistants went into the living-room, the kitchen, the bathroom (the sergeant picked up a bottle of after-shave cologne, seemed to study the French label) and the bedroom. The assistants removed the clean laundry that was laid upon the bed and then turned back the bedding, carrying the sheets over to be examined by the sergeant under the lamp. They talked to one another in Afrikaans,° which the Doctor did not understand. The sergeant himself looked under the bed, and lifted the long curtains at the window. The wall cupboard was of the kind that has no knobs; he saw that it was locked and began to ask in Afrikaans, then politely changed to English, 'Give us the key.'

Dr von Leinsdorf said, 'I'm sorry, I left it at my office—I always lock and take my keys with me in the mornings.'

45

'It's no good, man, you better give me the key.'

He smiled a little, reasonably. 'It's on my office desk.'

The assistants produced a screwdriver and he watched while they inserted it where the cupboard doors met, gave it quick, firm but not forceful leverage. He heard the lock give.

Afrikaans: the language of Dutch settlers in South Africa.

A Fiction Anthology

She had been naked, it was true, when they knocked. But now she was wearing a long-sleeved T-shirt with an appliquiéd butterfly motif on one breast, and a pair of jeans. Her feet were still bare; she had managed, by feel, in the dark, to get into some of the clothing she had snatched from the bed, but she had no shoes. She had perhaps been weeping behind the cupboard door (her cheeks looked stained) but now her face was sullen and she was breathing heavily, her diaphragm contracting and expanding exaggeratedly and her breasts pushing against the cloth. It made her appear angry; it might simply have been that she was half-suffocated in the cupboard and needed oxygen. She did not look at Dr von Leinsdorf. She would not reply to the sergeant's questions.

They were taken to the police station where they were at once separated and in turn led for examination by the district surgeon. The man's underwear was taken away and examined, as the sheets had been, for signs of his seed. When the girl was undressed, it was discovered that beneath her jeans she was wearing a pair of men's briefs with his name on the neatly-sewn laundry tag; in her haste, she had taken the wrong garment to her hiding-place.

Now she cried, standing there before the district surgeon in a man's underwear. He courteously pretended not to notice. He handed briefs, jeans and T-shirt round the door, and motioned her to lie on a white-sheeted high table where he placed her legs apart, resting in stirrups, and put into her where the other had made his way so warmly a cold hard instrument that expanded wider and wider. Her thighs and knees trembled uncontrollably while the doctor looked into her and touched her deep inside with more hard instruments, carrying wafers of gauze.

When she came out of the examining room back to the charge office, Dr von Leinsdorf was not there; they must have taken him somewhere else. She spent what was left of the night in a cell, as he must be doing; but early in the morning she was released and taken home to her mother's house in the coloured township by a white man who explained he was the clerk of the lawyer who had been engaged for her by Dr von Leinsdorf. Dr von Leinsdorf, the clerk said, had also been bailed out that morning. He did not say when, or if she would see him again.

A statement made by the girl to the police was handed in to Court when she and the man appeared to meet charges of contravening the Immorality Act in a Johannesburg flat on the night of—December, 19—. *I lived with the white man in his flat. He had intercourse with me sometimes. He gave me tablets to take to prevent me becoming pregnant.*

Interviewed by the Sunday papers, the girl said, 'I'm sorry for the sadness brought to my mother.' She said she was one of nine children of a female laundry worker. She had left school in Standard Three because there was no money at home for gym clothes or a school blazer. She had worked as a machinist in a factory and a cashier in a supermarket. Dr von Leinsdorf taught her to type his notes.

Dr Franz-Josef von Leinsdorf, described as the grandson of a baroness, a cultured man engaged in international mineralogical research, said he accepted social distinctions between people but didn't think they should be legally imposed. 'Even in my own country it's difficult for a person from a higher class to marry one from a lower class.'

The two accused gave no evidence. They did not greet or speak to each other in Court. The Defence argued that the sergeant's evidence that they had been living together as man and wife was hearsay. (The woman with the dachshund, the caretaker?) The magistrate acquitted them because the State failed to prove carnal intercourse had taken place on the night of—December, 19—.

The girl's mother was quoted, with photograph, in the Sunday papers: 'I won't let my daughter work as a servant for a white man again.'

II

The farm children play together when they are small; but once the white children go away to school they soon don't play together any more, even in the holidays. Although most of the black children get some sort of schooling, they drop every year farther behind the grades passed by the white children; the childish vocabulary, the child's exploration of the adventurous possibilities of dam, koppies, mealie lands and veld°—there comes a time when the white children have surpassed these with the vocabulary of boarding-school and the possibilities of inter-school sports matches and the kind of adventures seen at the cinema. This usefully coincides with the age of twelve or thirteen; so that by the time early adolescence is reached, the black children are making, along with the bodily changes common to all, an easy transition to adult forms of address, beginning to call their old playmates *missus* and *baasie*—little master.

The trouble was Paulus Eysendyck did not seem to realize that Thebedi was now simply one of the crowd of farm children down at the kraal,° recognizable in his sisters' old clothes. The first Christmas holidays after he had gone to boarding-school he brought home for Thebedi a painted box he had made in his wood-work class. He had to give it to her secretly because he had nothing for the other children at the kraal. And she gave him, before he went back to school, a bracelet she had made of thin brass wire and the grey-and-white beans of the castor-oil crop his father cultivated. (When they used to play together, she was the one who had taught Paulus how to make clay oxen for their toy spans.) There was a craze, even in the *platteland*° towns like the one where he was at school, for boys to wear elephant-hair and other bracelets beside their watch-straps; his was admired, friends asked him to get similar ones for them. He said the natives made them on his father's farm and he would try. 60

When he was fifteen, six feet tall, and tramping round at school dances with the girls from the 'sister' school in the same town; when he had learnt how to tease and flirt and fondle quite intimately these girls who were the daughters of prosperous farmers like his father; when he had even met one who, at a wedding he had attended with his parents on a nearby farm, had let him do with her in a locked storeroom what people did when they made love—when he was as far from his childhood as all this, he still brought home from a shop in town a red plastic belt and gilt hoop ear-rings for the black girl, Thebedi. She told her father the missus had given these to her as a reward for some work she had done—it was true she sometimes was called to help out in the farmhouse. She told the girls in the kraal that she had a sweetheart nobody knew about, far away, away on another farm, and they giggled, and teased, and admired her. There was a boy in the kraal called Njabulo who said he wished he could have bought her a belt and ear-rings.

---

dam, koppies, mealie lands, veld: pond, hills, grain lands, plains.
kraal: village.
platteland: flat-land.

When the farmer's son was home for the holidays she wandered far from the kraal and her companions. He went for walks alone. They had not arranged this; it was an urge each followed independently. He knew it was she, from a long way off. She knew that his dog would not bark at her. Down at the dried-up river-bed where five or six years ago the children had caught a leguaan one great day—a creature that combined ideally the size and ferocious aspect of the crocodile with the harmlessness of the lizard—they squatted side by side on the earth bank. He told her traveller's tales: about school, about the punishments at school, particularly, exaggerating both their nature and his indifference to them. He told her about the town of Middleburg, which she had never seen. She had nothing to tell but she prompted with many questions, like any good listener. While he talked he twisted and tugged at the roots of white stinkwood and Cape willow trees that looped out of the eroded earth around them. It had always been a good spot for children's games, down there hidden by the mesh of old, ant-eaten trees held in place by vigorous ones, wild asparagus bushing up between the trunks, and here and there prickly-pear cactus sunken-skinned and bristly, like an old man's face, keeping alive sapless until the next rainy season. She punctured the dry hide of a prickly-pear again and again with a sharp stick while she listened. She laughed a lot at what he told her, sometimes dropping her face on her knees, sharing amusement with the cool shady earth beneath her bare feet. She put on her pair of shoes—white sandals, thickly Blanco-ed against the farm dust—when he was on the farm, but these were taken off and laid aside, at the river-bed.

One summer afternoon when there was water flowing there and it was very hot she waded in as they used to do when they were children, her dress bunched modestly and tucked into the legs of her pants. The schoolgirls he went swimming with at dams or pools on neighbouring farms wore bikinis but the sight of their dazzling bellies and thighs in the sunlight had never made him feel what he felt now, when the girl came up the bank and sat beside him, the drops of water beading off her dark legs the only points of light in the earth-smelling, deep shade. They were not afraid of one another, they had known one another always; he did with her what he had done that time in the storeroom at the wedding, and this time it was so lovely, so lovely, he was surprised . . . and she was surprised by it, too—he could see in her dark face that was part of the shade, with her big dark eyes, shiny as soft water, watching him attentively: as she had when they used to huddle over their teams of mud oxen, as she had when he told her about detention weekends at school.

They went to the river-bed often through those summer holidays. They met just before the light went, as it does quite quickly, and each returned home with the dark—she to her mother's hut, he to the farmhouse—in time for the evening meal. He did not tell her about school or town any more. She did not ask questions any longer. He told her, each time, when they would meet again. Once or twice it was very early in the morning; the lowing of the cows being driven to graze came to them where they lay, dividing them with unspoken recognition of the sound read in their two pairs of eyes, opening so close to each other.

He was a popular boy at school. He was in the second, then the first soccer team. The head girl of the 'sister' school was said to have a crush on him; he didn't particularly like her, but there was a pretty blonde who put up her long hair into a kind of doughnut with a black ribbon round it, whom he took to see films when the schoolboys and girls had a free Saturday afternoon. He had been driving tractors and other farm vehicles since he was ten years old, and as soon as he was eighteen he got a driver's licence and in the holidays, this last year of his school life, he took neighbours' daughters to dances and to the drive-in cinema that had just opened twenty kilometres from the farm. His sisters were married, by then; his parents often left him in charge of the farm over the weekend while they visited the young wives and grandchildren.

When Thebedi saw the farmer and his wife drive away on a Saturday afternoon, the boot° of their Mercedes filled with fresh-killed poultry and vegetables from the garden that it was part of her father's work to tend, she knew that she must come not to the river-bed but up to the house. The house was an old one, thick-walled, dark against the heat. The kitchen was its lively thorough-fare, with servants, food supplies, begging cats and dogs, pots boiling over, washing being damped for ironing, and the big deepfreeze the missus had ordered from town, bearing a crocheted mat and a vase of plastic irises. But the dining-room with the bulging-legged heavy table was shut up in its rich, old smell of soup and tomato sauce. The sitting-room curtains were drawn and the T.V. set silent. The door of the parents' bedroom was locked and the empty rooms where the girls had slept had sheets of plastic spread over the beds. It was in one of these that she and the farmer's son stayed together whole nights—almost: she had to get away before the house servants, who knew her, came in at dawn. There was a risk someone would discover her or traces of her presence if he took her to his own bedroom, although she had looked into it many times when she was helping out in the house and knew well, there, the row of silver cups he had won at school.

When she was eighteen and the farmer's son nineteen and working with his father on the farm before entering a veterinary college, the young man Njabulo asked her father for her. Njabulo's parents met with hers and the money he was to pay in place of the cows it is customary to give a prospective bride's parents was settled upon. He had no cows to offer; he was a labourer on the Eysendyck farm, like her father. A bright youngster; old Eysendyck had taught him brick-laying and was using him for odd jobs in construction, around the place. She did not tell the farmer's son that her parents had arranged for her to marry. She did not tell him, either, before he left for his first term at the veterinary college, that she thought she was going to have a baby. Two months after her marriage to Njabulo, she gave birth to a daughter. There was no disgrace in that; among her people it is customary for a young man to make sure, before marriage, that the chosen girl is not barren, and Njabulo had made love to her then. But the infant was very light and did not quickly grow darker as most African babies do. Already at birth there was on its head a quantity of straight, fine floss, like that which carries the seeds of certain weeds in the veld. The unfocused eyes it opened were grey flecked with yellow. Njabulo was the matt, opaque coffee-grounds colour that has always been called the black; the colour of Thebedi's legs on which beaded water looked oyster-shell blue, the same colour as Thebedi's face, where the black eyes, with their interested gaze and clear whites, were so dominant.

Njabulo made no complaint. Out of his farm labourer's earnings he bought from the Indian store a cellophane-windowed pack containing a pink plastic bath, six napkins, a card of safety pins, a knitted jacket, cap and bootees, a dress, and a tin of Johnson's Baby Powder, for Thebedi's baby.

When it was two weeks old Paulus Eysendyck arrived home from the veterinary college for the holidays. He drank a glass of fresh, still-warm milk in the childhood

---

boot: trunk.

familiarity of his mother's kitchen and heard her discussing with the old house-servant where they could get a reliable substitute to help out now that the girl Thebedi had had a baby. For the first time since he was a small boy he came right into the kraal. It was eleven o'clock in the morning. The men were at work in the lands. He looked about him, urgently; the women turned away, each not wanting to be the one approached to point out where Thebedi lived. Thebedi appeared, coming slowly from the hut Njabulo had built in white man's style, with a tin chimney, and a proper window with glass panes set in straight as walls made of unfired bricks would allow. She greeted him with hands brought together and a token movement representing the respectful bob with which she was accustomed to knowledge she was in the presence of his father or mother. He lowered his head under the doorway of her home and went in. He said, 'I want to see. Show me.'

She had taken the bundle off her back before she came out into the light to face him. She moved between the iron bedstead made up with Njabulo's checked blankets and the small wooden table where the pink plastic bath stood among food and kitchen pots, and picked up the bundle from the snugly-blanketed grocer's box where it lay. The infant was asleep; she revealed the closed, pale, plump tiny face, with a bubble of spit at the corner of the mouth, the spidery pink hands stirring. She took off the woollen cap and the straight fine hair flew up after it in static electricity, showing gilded strands here and there. He said nothing. She was watching him as she had done when they were little, and the gang of children had trodden down a crop in their games or transgressed in some other way for which he, as the farmer's son, the white one among them, must intercede with the farmer. She disturbed the sleeping face by scratching or tickling gently at a cheek with one finger, and slowly the eyes opened, saw nothing, were still asleep, and then, awake, no longer narrowed, looked out at them, grey with yellowish flecks, his own hazel eyes. 70

He struggled for a moment with a grimace of tears, anger and self-pity. She could not put out her hand to him. He said, 'You haven't been near the house with it?'

She shook her head.

'Never?'

Again she shook her head.

'Don't take it out. Stay inside. Can't you take it away somewhere. You must give it to someone—' 75

She moved to the door with him.

He said, 'I'll see what I will do. I don't know.' And then he said: 'I feel like killing myself.'

Her eyes began to glow, to thicken with tears. For a moment there was the feeling between them that used to come when they were alone down at the river-bed.

He walked out.

Two days later, when his mother and father had left the farm for the day, he appeared again. The women were away on the lands, weeding, as they were employed to do as casual labour in summer; only the very old remained, propped up on the ground outside the huts in the flies and the sun. Thebedi did not ask him in. The child had not been well; it had diarrhoea. He asked where its food was. She said, 'The milk comes from me.' He went into Njabulo's house, where the child lay; she did not follow but stayed outside the door and watched without seeing an old crone who had lost her mind, talking to herself, talking to the fowls who ignored her. 80

She thought she heard small grunts from the hut, the kind of infant grunt that indicates a full stomach, a deep sleep. After a time, long or short she did not know, he came out and walked away with plodding stride (his father's gait) out of sight, towards his father's house.

The baby was not fed during the night and although she kept telling Njabulo it was sleeping, he saw for himself in the morning that it was dead. He comforted her with words and caresses. She did not cry but simply sat, staring at the door. Her hands were cold as dead chickens' feet to his touch.

Njabulo buried the little baby where farm workers were buried, in the place in the veld the farmer had given them. Some of the mounds had been left to weather away unmarked, others were covered with stones and a few had fallen wooden crosses. He was going to make a cross but before it was finished the police came and dug up the grave and took away the dead baby: someone—one of the other labourers? their women?—had reported that the baby was almost white, that, strong and healthy, it had died suddenly after a visit by the farmer's son. Pathological tests on the infant corpse showed intestinal damage not always consistent with death by natural causes.

Thebedi went for the first time to the country town where Paulus had been to school, to give evidence at the preparatory examination into the charge of murder brought against him. She cried hysterically in the witness box, saying yes, yes (the gilt hoop ear-rings swung in her ears), she saw the accused pouring liquid into the baby's mouth. She said he had threatened to shoot her if she told anyone.

More than a year went by before, in that same town, the case was brought to trial. She came to Court with a new-born baby on her back. She wore gilt hoop ear-rings; she was calm; she said she had not seen what the white man did in the house.   85

Paulus Eysendyck said he had visited the hut but had not poisoned the child.

The Defence did not contest that there had been a love relationship between the accused and the girl, or that intercourse had taken place, but submitted there was no proof that the child was the accused's.

The judge told the accused there was strong suspicion against him but not enough proof that he had committed the crime. The Court could not accept the girl's evidence because it was clear she had committed perjury either at this trial or at the preparatory examination. There was the suggestion in the mind of the Court that she might be an accomplice in the crime; but, again, insufficient proof.

The judge commended the honourable behaviour of the husband (sitting in court in a brown-and-yellow-quartered golf cap bought for Sundays) who had not rejected his wife and had 'even provided clothes for the unfortunate infant out of his slender means'.

The verdict on the accused was 'not guilty'.   90

The young white man refused to accept the congratulations of press and public and left the Court with his mother's raincoat shielding his face from photographers. His father said to the press, 'I will try and carry on as best I can to hold up my head in the district.'

Interviewed by the Sunday papers, who spelled her name in a variety of ways, the black girl, speaking in her own language, was quoted beneath her photograph: 'It was a thing of our childhood, we don't see each other any more.'

Italo Calvino (1923–1985)

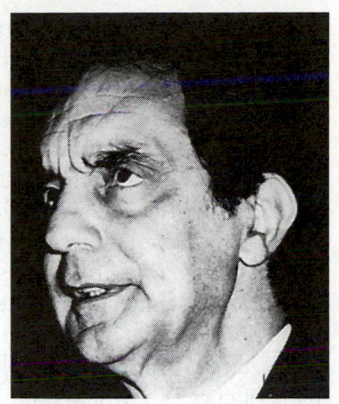

Italo Calvino was born in Cuba to Italian parents. He lived in Italy and France most of his life. Over the years his fiction (mainly stories) evolved from the neorealism of the postwar years to a fantastical, often whimsical, metafiction that challenged the assumptions of conventional forms. The narratives in *Cosmicomics* and *t-zero* adopt many of the techniques of science fiction and combine a scientist's exactitude with a daydreamer's relaxed inventiveness. Calvino's novel *If on a Winter's Night a Traveller* beguiles the reader with a series of suspenseful narratives, all of which are broken off before they can conclude. But the reader is cajoled by the promise of a new story—the cycle goes on and on. Calvino also assembled a highly popular collection, *Italian Folktales,* from which the reader learns that the charming profusion of this man's tales grew from an ancient heritage. Calvino's works include *Invisible Cities, Mr. Palomar, The Baron in the Trees,* and *The Castle of Crossed Destinies.*

THE DISTANCE OF
THE MOON

At one time, according to Sir George H. Darwin,° the Moon was very close to the Earth. Then the tides gradually pushed her far away: the tides that the Moon herself causes in the Earth's waters, where the Earth slowly loses energy.

How well I know!—*old Qfwfq cried,*—the rest of you can't remember, but I can. We had her on top of us all the time, that enormous Moon: when she was full—nights as bright as day, but with a butter-colored light—it looked as if she were going to crush us; when she was new, she rolled around the sky like a black umbrella blown by the wind; and when she was waxing, she came forward with her horns so low she seemed about to stick into the peak of a promontory and get caught there. But the whole business of the Moon's phases worked in a different way then: because the distances from the Sun were different, and the orbits, and the angle of something or other, I forget what; as for

---

Darwin: an invented name, as are all proper names in the story.

eclipses, with Earth and Moon stuck together the way they were, why, we had eclipses every minute: naturally, those two big monsters managed to put each other in the shade constantly, first one, then the other.

Orbit? Oh, elliptical, of course: for a while it would huddle against us and then it would take flight for a while. The tides, when the Moon swung closer, rose so high nobody could hold them back. There were nights when the Moon was full and very, very low, and the tide was so high that the Moon missed a ducking in the sea by a hair's-breadth; well, let's say a few yards anyway. Climb up on the Moon? Of course we did. All you had to do was row out to it in a boat and, when you were underneath, prop a ladder against her and scramble up.

The spot where the Moon was lowest, as she went by, was off the Zinc Cliffs. We used to go out with those little rowboats they had in those days, round and flat, made of cork. They held quite a few of us: me, Captain Vhd Vhd, his wife, my deaf cousin, and sometimes little Xlthlx—she was twelve or so at that time. On those nights the water was very calm, so silvery it looked like mercury, and the fish in it, violet-colored, unable to resist the Moon's attraction, rose to the surface, all of them, and so did the octopuses and the saffron medusas. There was always a flight of tiny creatures—little crabs, squid, and even some weeds, light and filmy, and coral plants—that broke from the sea and ended up on the Moon, hanging down from that lime-white ceiling, or else they stayed in midair, a phosphorescent swarm we had to drive off, waving banana leaves at them.

This is how we did the job: in the boat we had a ladder: one of us held it, another climbed to the top, and a third, at the oars, rowed until we were right under the Moon; that's why there had to be so many of us (I only mentioned the main ones). The man at the top of the ladder, as the boat approached the Moon, would become scared and start shouting: "Stop! Stop! I'm going to bang my head!" That was the impression you had, seeing her on top of you, immense, and all rough with sharp spikes and jagged, saw-tooth edges. It may be different now, but then the Moon, or rather the bottom, the underbelly of the Moon, the part that passed closest to the Earth and almost scraped it, was covered with a crust of sharp scales. It had come to resemble the belly of a fish, and the smell too, as I recall, if not downright fishy, was faintly similar, like smoked salmon.

In reality, from the top of the ladder, standing erect on the last rung, you could just touch the Moon if you held your arms up. We had taken the measurements carefully (we didn't yet suspect that she was moving away from us); the only thing you had to be very careful about was where you put your hands. I always chose a scale that seemed fast (we climbed up in groups of five or six at a time), then I would cling first with one hand, then with both, and immediately I would feel ladder and boat drifting away from below me, and the motion of the Moon would tear me from the Earth's attraction. Yes, the Moon was so strong that she pulled you up; you realized this the moment you passed from one to the other: you had to swing up abruptly, with a kind of somersault, grabbing the scales, throwing your legs over your head, until your feet were on the Moon's surface. Seen from the Earth, you looked as if you were hanging there with your head down, but for you, it was the normal position, and the only odd thing was that when you raised your eyes you saw the sea above you, glistening, with the boat and the others upside down, hanging like a bunch of grapes from the vine.

My cousin, the Deaf One, showed a special talent for making those leaps. His clumsy hands, as soon as they touched the lunar surface (he was always the first to jump up from the ladder), suddenly became deft and sensitive. They found immediately the spot where he could hoist himself up; in fact just the pressure of his palms seemed enough to make him stick to the satellite's crust. Once I even thought I saw the Moon come toward him, as he held out his hands.

He was just as dextrous in coming back down to Earth, an operation still more difficult. For us, it consisted in jumping, as high as we could, our arms upraised (seen from the Moon, that is, because seen from the Earth it looked more like a dive, or like swimming downwards, arms at our sides), like jumping up from the Earth in other words, only now we were without the ladder, because there was nothing to prop it against on the Moon. But instead of jumping with his arms out, my cousin bent toward the Moon's surface, his head down as if for a somersault, then made a leap, pushing with his hands. From the boat we watched him, erect in the air as if he were supporting the Moon's enormous ball and were tossing it, striking it with his palms; then, when his legs came within reach, we managed to grab his ankles and pull him down on board.

Now, you will ask me what in the world we went up on the Moon for; I'll explain it to you. We went to collect the milk, with a big spoon and a bucket. Moonmilk was very thick, like a kind of cream cheese. It formed in the crevices between one scale and the next, through the fermentation of various bodies and substances of terrestrial origin which had flown up from the prairies and forests and lakes, as the Moon sailed over them. It was composed chiefly of vegetal juices, tadpoles, bitumen, lentils, honey, starch crystals, sturgeon eggs, molds, pollens, gelatinous matter, worms, resins, pepper, mineral salts, combustion residue. You had only to dip the spoon under the scales that covered the Moon's scabby terrain, and you brought it out filled with that precious muck. Not in the pure state, obviously; there was a lot of refuse. In the fermentation (which took place as the Moon passed over the expanses of hot air above the deserts) not all the bodies melted; some remained stuck in it: fingernails and cartilage, bolts, sea horses, nuts and peduncles,° shards of crockery, fishhooks, at times even a comb. So this paste, after it was collected, had to be refined, filtered. But that wasn't the difficulty: the hard part was transporting it down to the Earth. This is how we did it: we hurled each spoonful into the air with both hands, using the spoon as a catapult. The cheese flew, and if we had thrown it hard enough, it stuck to the ceiling, I mean the surface of the sea. Once there, it floated, and it was easy enough to pull it into the boat. In this operation, too, my deaf cousin displayed a special gift; he had strength and a good aim; with a single, sharp throw, he could send the cheese straight into a bucket we held up to him from the boat. As for me, I occasionally misfired; the contents of the spoon would fail to overcome the Moon's attraction and they would fall back into my eye.

I still haven't told you everything, about the things my cousin was good at. That job of extracting lunar milk from the Moon's scales was child's play to him: instead of the spoon, at times he had only to thrust his bare hand under the scales, or even one finger. He didn't proceed in any orderly way, but went to isolated places, jumping from one to the other, as if he were playing tricks on the Moon, surprising her, or perhaps tickling her. And wherever he put his hand, the milk spurted out as if from a nanny goat's teats. So the rest of us had only to follow him and collect with our spoons the substance that he was pressing out, first here, then there, but always

---

peduncle: a stalk bearing a single flower.

as if by chance, since the Deaf One's movements seemed to have no clear, practical sense. There were places, for example, that he touched merely for the fun of touching them: gaps between two scales, naked and tender folds of lunar flesh. At times my cousin pressed not only his fingers but—in a carefully gauged leap—his big toe (he climbed onto the Moon barefoot) and this seemed to be the height of amusement for him, if we could judge by the chirping sounds that came from his throat as he went on leaping.

The soil of the Moon was not uniformly scaly, but revealed irregular bare patches of pale, slippery clay. These soft areas inspired the Deaf One to turn somersaults or to fly almost like a bird, as if he wanted to impress his whole body into the Moon's pulp. As he ventured farther in this way, we lost sight of him at one point. On the Moon there were vast areas we had never had any reason or curiosity to explore, and that was where my cousin vanished; I had suspected that all those somersaults and nudges he indulged in before our eyes were only a preparation, a prelude to something secret meant to take place in the hidden zones.

We fell into a special mood on those nights off the Zinc Cliffs: gay, but with a touch of suspense, as if inside our skulls, instead of the brain, we felt a fish, floating, attracted by the Moon. And so we navigated, playing and singing. The Captain's wife played the harp; she had very long arms, silvery as eels on those nights, and armpits as dark and mysterious as sea urchins; and the sound of the harp was sweet and piercing, so sweet and piercing it was almost unbearable, and we were forced to let out long cries, not so much to accompany the music as to protect our hearing from it.

Transparent medusas° rose to the sea's surface, throbbed there a moment, then flew off, swaying toward the Moon. Little Xlthlx amused herself by catching them in midair, though it wasn't easy. Once, as she stretched her little arms out to catch one, she jumped up slightly and was also set free. Thin as she was, she was an ounce or two short of the weight necessary for the Earth's gravity to overcome the Moon's attraction and bring her back: so she flew up among the medusas, suspended over the sea. She took fright, cried, then laughed and started playing, catching shellfish and minnows as they flew, sticking some into her mouth and chewing them. We rowed hard, to keep up with the child: the Moon ran off in her ellipse, dragging that swarm of marine fauna through the sky, and a train of long, entwined seaweeds, and Xlthlx hanging there in the midst. Her two wispy braids seemed to be flying on their own, outstretched toward the Moon; but all the while she kept wriggling and kicking at the air, as if she wanted to fight that influence, and her socks—she had lost her shoes in the flight—slipped off her feet and swayed, attracted by the Earth's force. On the ladder, we tried to grab them.

The idea of eating the little animals in the air had been a good one; the more weight Xlthlx gained, the more she sank toward the Earth; in fact, since among those hovering bodies hers was the largest, mollusks and seaweeds and plankton began to gravitate about her, and soon the child was covered with siliceous little shells, chitinous carapaces, and fibers of sea plants. And the farther she vanished into that tangle, the more she was freed of the Moon's influence, until she grazed the surface of the water and sank into the sea.

We rowed quickly, to pull her out and save her: her body had remained magnetized, and we had to work hard to scrape off all the things encrusted on her. Ten-

10

---

medusa: tentacled jellyfish.

der corals were wound about her head, and every time we ran the comb through her hair there was a shower of crayfish and sardines; her eyes were sealed shut by limpets° clinging to the lids with their suckers; squids' tentacles were coiled around her arms and her neck; and her little dress now seemed woven only of weeds and sponges. We got the worst of it off her, but for weeks afterwards she went on pulling out fins and shells, and her skin, dotted with little diatoms,° remained affected forever, looking—to someone who didn't observe her carefully—as if it were faintly dusted with freckles.

This should give you an idea of how the influences of Earth and Moon, practically equal, fought over the space between them. I'll tell you something else: a body that descended to the Earth from the satellite was still charged for a while with lunar force and rejected the attraction of our world. Even I, big and heavy as I was: every time I had been up there, I took a while to get used to the Earth's up and its down, and the others would have to grab my arms and hold me, clinging in a bunch in the swaying boat while I still had my head hanging and my legs stretching up toward the sky.

"Hold on! Hold on to us!" they shouted at me, and in all that groping, sometimes I ended up by seizing one of Mrs. Vhd Vhd's breasts, which were round and firm, and the contact was good and secure and had an attraction as strong as the Moon's or even stronger, especially if I managed, as I plunged down, to put my other arm around her hips, and with this I passed back into our world and fell with a thud into the bottom of the boat, where Captain Vhd Vhd brought me around, throwing a bucket of water in my face.

This is how the story of my love for the Captain's wife began, and my suffering. Because it didn't take me long to realize whom the lady kept looking at insistently: when my cousin's hands clasped the satellite, I watched Mrs. Vhd Vhd, and in her eyes I could read the thoughts that the deaf man's familiarity with the Moon were arousing in her; and when he disappeared in his mysterious lunar explorations, I saw her become restless, as if on pins and needles, and then it was all clear to me, how Mrs. Vhd Vhd was becoming jealous of the Moon and I was jealous of my cousin. Her eyes were made of diamonds, Mrs. Vhd Vhd's; they flared when she looked at the Moon, almost challengingly, as if she were saying: "You shan't have him!" And I felt like an outsider.

The one who least understood all of this was my deaf cousin. When we helped him down, pulling him—as I explained to you—by his legs, Mrs. Vhd Vhd lost all her self-control, doing everything she could to take his weight against her own body, folding her long silvery arms around him; I felt a pang in my heart (the times I clung to her, her body was soft and kind, but not thrust forward, the way it was with my cousin), while he was indifferent, still lost in his lunar bliss.

I looked at the Captain, wondering if he also noticed his wife's behavior; but there was never a trace of any expression on that face of his, eaten by brine, marked with tarry wrinkles. Since the Deaf One was always the last to break away from the Moon, his return was the signal for the boats to move off. Then, with an unusually polite gesture, Vhd Vhd picked up the harp from the bottom of the boat and handed it to his wife. She was obliged to take it and play a few notes. Nothing could sepa-

15

---

limpet: a kind of mollusc.
diatoms: unicellular algae.

rate her more from the Deaf One than the sound of the harp. I took to singing in a low voice that sad song that goes: "Every shiny fish is floating, floating; and every dark fish is at the bottom, at the bottom of the sea . . . " and all the others, except my cousin, echoed my words.

Every month, once the satellite had moved on, the Deaf One returned to his solitary detachment from the things of the world; only the approach of the full Moon aroused him again. That time I had arranged things so it wasn't my turn to go up, I could stay in the boat with the Captain's wife. But then, as soon as my cousin had climbed the ladder, Mrs. Vhd Vhd said: "This time I want to go up there, too!" 20

This had never happened before; the Captain's wife had never gone up on the Moon. But Vhd Vhd made no objection, in fact he almost pushed her up the ladder bodily, exclaiming: "Go ahead then!" and we all started helping her, and I held her from behind, felt her round and soft on my arms, and to hold her up I began to press my face and the palms of my hands against her, and when I felt her rising into the Moon's sphere I was heartsick at that lost contact, so I started to rush after her, saying: "I'm going to go up for a while, too, to help out!"

I was held back as if in a vise. "You stay here; you have work to do later," the Captain commanded, without raising his voice.

At that moment each one's intentions were already clear. And yet I couldn't figure things out; even now I'm not sure I've interpreted it all correctly. Certainly the Captain's wife had for a long time been cherishing the desire to go off privately with my cousin up there (or at least to prevent him from going off alone with the Moon), but probably she had a still more ambitious plan, one that would have to be carried out in agreement with the Deaf One: she wanted the two of them to hide up there together and stay on the Moon for a month. But perhaps my cousin, deaf as he was, hadn't understood anything of what she had tried to explain to him, or perhaps he hadn't even realized that he was the object of the lady's desires. And the Captain? He wanted nothing better than to be rid of his wife; in fact, as soon as she was confined up there, we saw him give free rein to his inclinations and plunge into vice, and then we understood why he had done nothing to hold her back. But had he known from the beginning that the Moon's orbit was widening?

None of us could have suspected it. The Deaf One perhaps, but only he: in the shadowy way he knew things, he may have had a presentiment that he would be forced to bid the Moon farewell that night. This is why he hid in his secret places and reappeared only when it was time to come back down on board. It was no use for the Captain's wife to try to follow him: we saw her cross the scaly zone various times, length and breadth, then suddenly she stopped, looking at us in the boat, as if about to ask us whether we had seen him.

Surely there was something strange about that night. The sea's surface, instead of being taut as it was during the full Moon, or even arched a bit toward the sky, now seemed limp, sagging, as if the lunar magnet no longer exercised its full power. And the light, too, wasn't the same as the light of other full Moons; the night's shadows seemed somehow to have thickened. Our friends up there must have realized what was happening; in fact, they looked up at us with frightened eyes. And from their mouths and ours, at the same moment, came a cry: "The Moon's going away!" 25

The cry hadn't died out when my cousin appeared on the Moon, running. He didn't seem frightened, or even amazed: he placed his hands on the terrain, flinging himself into his usual somersault, but this time after he had hurled himself into the air he remained suspended, as little Xlthlx had. He hovered a moment between

Moon and Earth, upside down, then laboriously moving his arms, like someone swimming against a current, he headed with unusual slowness toward our planet.

From the Moon the other sailors hastened to follow his example. Nobody gave a thought to getting the Moon-milk that had been collected into the boats, nor did the Captain scold them for this. They had already waited too long, the distance was difficult to cross by now; when they tried to imitate my cousin's leap or his swimming, they remained there groping, suspended in midair. "Cling together! Idiots! Cling together!" the Captain yelled. At this command, the sailors tried to form a group, a mass, to push all together until they reached the zone of the Earth's attraction: all of a sudden a cascade of bodies plunged into the sea with a loud splash.

The boats were now rowing to pick them up. "Wait! The Captain's wife is missing!" I shouted. The Captain's wife had also tried to jump, but she was still floating only a few yards from the Moon, slowly moving her long, silvery arms in the air. I climbed up the ladder, and in a vain attempt to give her something to grasp I held the harp out toward her. "I can't reach her! We have to go after her!" and I started to jump up, brandishing the harp. Above me the enormous lunar disk no longer seemed the same as before: it had become much smaller, it kept contracting, as if my gaze were driving it away, and the emptied sky gaped like an abyss where, at the bottom, the stars had begun multiplying, and the night poured a river of emptiness over me, drowned me in dizziness and alarm.

"I'm afraid," I thought. "I'm too afraid to jump. I'm a coward!" and at that moment I jumped. I swam furiously through the sky, and held the harp out to her, and instead of coming toward me she rolled over and over, showing me first her impassive face and then her backside.

"Hold tight to me!" I shouted, and I was already overtaking her, entwining my limbs with hers. "If we cling together we can go down!" and I was concentrating all my strength on uniting myself more closely with her, and I concentrated my sensations as I enjoyed the fullness of that embrace. I was so absorbed I didn't realize at first that I was, indeed, tearing her from her weightless condition, but was making her fall back on the Moon. Didn't I realize it? Or had that been my intention from the very beginning? Before I could think properly, a cry was already bursting from my throat. "I'll be the one to stay with you for a month!" Or rather, "On you!" I shouted, in my excitement: "On you for a month!" and at that moment our embrace was broken by our fall to the Moon's surface, where we rolled away from each other among those cold scales.

30

I raised my eyes as I did every time I touched the Moon's crust, sure that I would see above me the native sea like an endless ceiling, and I saw it, yes, I saw it this time, too, but much higher, and much more narrow, bound by its borders of coasts and cliffs and promontories, and how small the boats seemed, and how unfamiliar my friends' faces and how weak their cries! A sound reached me from nearby: Mrs. Vhd Vhd had discovered her harp and was caressing it, sketching out a chord as sad as weeping.

A long month began. The Moon turned slowly around the Earth. On the suspended globe we no longer saw our familiar shore, but the passage of oceans as deep as abysses and deserts of glowing lapilli, and continents of ice, and forests writhing with reptiles, and the rocky walls of mountain chains gashed by swift rivers, and swampy cities, and stone graveyards, and empires of clay and mud. The distance spread a uniform color over everything: the alien perspective made every image alien; herds of elephants and swarms of locusts ran over the plains, so evenly vast and dense and thickly grown that there was no difference among them.

I should have been happy: as I had dreamed, I was alone with her, that intimacy with the Moon I had so often envied my cousin and with Mrs. Vhd Vhd was now my exclusive prerogative, a month of days and lunar nights stretched uninterrupted before us, the crust of the satellite nourished us with its milk, whose tart flavor was familiar to us, we raised our eyes up, up to the world where we had been born, finally traversed in all its various expanse, explored landscapes no Earth-being had ever seen, or else we contemplated the stars beyond the Moon, big as pieces of fruit, made of light, ripened on the curved branches of the sky, and everything exceeded my most luminous hopes, and yet, and yet, it was, instead, exile.

I thought only of the Earth. It was the Earth that caused each of us to be that someone he was rather than someone else; up there, wrested from the Earth, it was as if I were no longer that I, nor she that She, for me. I was eager to return to the Earth, and I trembled at the fear of having lost it. The fulfillment of my dream of love had lasted only that instant when we had been united, spinning between Earth and Moon: torn from its earthly soil, my love now knew only the heart-rending nostalgia for what it lacked: a where, a surrounding, a before, an after.

This is what I was feeling. But she? As I asked myself, I was torn by my fears. Because if she also thought only of the Earth, this could be a good sign, a sign that she had finally come to understand me, but it could also mean that everything had been useless, that her longings were directed still and only toward my deaf cousin. Instead, she felt nothing. She never raised her eyes to the old planet, she went off, pale, among those wastelands, mumbling dirges and stroking her harp, as if completely identified with her temporary (as I thought) lunar state. Did this mean I had won out over my rival? No; I had lost: a hopeless defeat. Because she had finally realized that my cousin loved only the Moon, and the only thing she wanted now was to become the Moon, to be assimilated into the object of that extra-human love. 35

When the Moon had completed its circling of the planet, there we were again over the Zinc Cliffs. I recognized them with dismay: not even in my darkest previsions had I thought the distance would have made them so tiny. In that mud puddle of the sea, my friends had set forth again, without the now useless ladders; but from the boats rose a kind of forest of long poles; everybody was brandishing one, with a harpoon or a grappling hook at the end, perhaps in the hope of scraping off a last bit of Moon-milk or of lending some kind of help to us wretches up there. But it was soon clear that no pole was long enough to reach the Moon; and they dropped back, ridiculously short, humbled, floating on the sea; and in that confusion some of the boats were thrown off balance and overturned. But just then, from another vessel a longer pole, which till then they had dragged along on the water's surface, began to rise: it must have been made of bamboo, of many, many bamboo poles stuck one into the other, and to raise it they had to go slowly because—thin as it was—if they let it sway too much it might break. Therefore, they had to use it with great strength and skill, so that the wholly vertical weight wouldn't rock the boat.

Suddenly it was clear that the tip of that pole would touch the Moon, and we saw it graze, then press against the scaly terrain, rest there a moment, give a kind of little push, or rather a strong push that made it bounce off again, then come back and strike that same spot as if on the rebound, then move away once more. And I recognized, we both—the Captain's wife and I—recognized my cousin: it couldn't have been anyone else, he was playing his last game with the Moon, one of his tricks, with the Moon on the tip of his pole as if he were juggling with her. And we realized that his virtuosity had no purpose, aimed at no practical result, indeed you would have said he was driving the Moon away, that he was helping her departure, that he wanted to show her to her more distant orbit. And this, too, was just like him: he was unable to conceive desires that went against the Moon's nature, the Moon's course and destiny, and if the Moon now tended to go away from him, then he would take delight in this separation just as, till now, he had delighted in the Moon's nearness.

What could Mrs. Vhd Vhd do, in the face of this? It was only at this moment that she proved her passion for the deaf man hadn't been a frivolous whim but an irrevocable vow. If what my cousin now loved was the distant Moon, then she too would remain distant, on the Moon. I sensed this, seeing that she didn't take a step toward the bamboo pole, but simply turned her harp toward the Earth, high in the sky, and plucked the strings. I say I saw her, but to tell the truth I only caught a glimpse of her out of the corner of my eye, because the minute the pole had touched the lunar crust, I had sprung and grasped it, and now, fast as a snake, I was climbing up the bamboo knots, pushing myself along with jerks of my arms and knees, light in the rarefied space, driven by a natural power that ordered me to return to the Earth, oblivious of the motive that had brought me here, or perhaps more aware of it than ever and of its unfortunate outcome; and already my climb up the swaying pole had reached the point where I no longer had to make any effort but could just allow myself to slide, head-first, attracted by the Earth, until in my haste the pole broke into a thousand pieces and I fell into the sea, among the boats.

My return was sweet, my home refound, but my thoughts were filled only with grief at having lost her, and my eyes gazed at the Moon, forever beyond my reach, as I sought her. And I saw her. She was there where I had left her, lying on a beach directly over our heads, and she said nothing. She was the color of the Moon; she held the harp at her side and moved one hand now and then in slow arpeggios. I could distinguish the shape of her bosom, her arms, her thighs, just as I remember them now, just as now, when the Moon has become that flat, remote circle, I still look for her as soon as the first silver appears in the sky, and the more it waxes, the more clearly I imagine I can see her, her or something of her, but only her, in a hundred, a thousand different vistas, she who makes the Moon the Moon and, whenever she is full, sets the dogs to howling all night long, and me with them.

Translated by Jonathan Cape

Milan Kundera (1929–   )

Milan Kundera was born in Brno, Czechoslovakia. In 1948, after a long apprenticeship in music, Kundera decided to pursue a career in film. He studied at the Prague Academy of Music and Dramatic Arts and later joined the faculty there. But it was finally writing that proved to be his path to self-expression. Though he had written poetry since his early teens, Kundera tried his hand at short stories in the late 1950s. His first collection, *Laughable Loves,* won him great notoriety.

Kundera came into collision with the government authorities after the 1968 invasion of

Czechoslovakia by the Soviets. His calls for freedom of artistic expression branded him a troublemaker. In 1975 Kundera traveled to France to accept a teaching post at the University of Rennes. He has remained in France, although he has not given up his Czech citizenship.

Kundera has attained great success in Europe and the United States with his novels, which include *The Joke, Life Is Elsewhere, The Farewell Party, The Book of Laughter and Forgetting,* and *The Unbearable Lightness of Being.* This last novel was made into an acclaimed film.

THE HITCHHIKING GAME

I

The needle on the gas gauge suddenly dipped toward empty and the young driver of the sports car declared that it was maddening how much gas the car ate up. "See that we don't run out of gas again," protested the girl (about twenty-two), and reminded the driver of several places where this had already happened to them. The young man replied that he wasn't worried, because whatever he went through with her had the charm of adventure for him. The girl objected; whenever they had run out of gas on the highway it had, she said, always been an adventure only for her. The young man had hidden and she had had to make ill use of her charms by thumbing a ride and letting herself be driven to the nearest gas station, then thumbing a ride back with a can of gas. The young man asked the girl whether the drivers who had given her a ride had been unpleasant, since she spoke as if her task had been a hardship. She replied (with awkward flirtatiousness) that sometimes they had been *very* pleasant but that it hadn't done her any good as she had been burdened with the can and had had to leave them before she could get anything going. "Pig," said the young man. The girl protested that she wasn't a pig, but that he really was. God knows how many girls stopped him on the highway, when he was driving the car alone! Still driving, the young man put his arm around the girl's shoulders and kissed her gently on the forehead. He knew that she loved him and that she was jealous. Jealousy isn't a pleasant quality, but if it isn't overdone (and if it's combined with modesty), apart from its inconvenience there's even something touching about it. At least that's what the young man thought. Because he was only twenty-eight, it seemed to him that he was old and knew everything that a man could know about women. In the girl sitting beside him he valued precisely what, until now, he had met with least in women: purity.

The needle was already on empty, when to the right the young man caught sight of a sign, announcing that the station was a quarter of a mile ahead. The girl hardly had time to say how relieved she was before the young man was signaling left and driving into a space in front of the pumps. However, he had to stop a little way off, because beside the pumps was a huge gasoline truck with a large metal tank and a bulky hose, which was refilling the pumps. "We'll have to wait," said the young man to the girl and got out of the car. "How long will it take?" he shouted to the man in overalls. "Only a moment," replied the attendant, and the young man said: "I've heard that one before." He wanted to go back and sit in the car, but he saw that the girl had gotten out the other side. "I'll take a little walk in the meantime," she said. "Where to?" the young man asked on purpose, wanting to see the girl's embarrassment. He had known her for a year now but she would still get shy in front of him. He enjoyed her moments of shyness, partly because they distinguished her from the women he'd met before, partly because he was aware of the law of universal transience, which made even his girl's shyness a precious thing to him.

II

The girl really didn't like it when during the trip (the young man would drive for several hours without stopping) she had to ask him to stop for a moment somewhere near a clump of trees. She always got angry when, with feigned surprise, he asked her why he should stop. She knew that her shyness was ridiculous and old-fashioned. Many times at work she had noticed that they laughed at her on account of it and deliberately provoked her. She always got shy in advance at the thought of how she was going to get shy. She often longed to feel free and easy about her body, the way most of the women around her did. She had even invented a special course in self-persuasion: she would repeat to herself that at birth every human being received one out of the millions of available bodies, as one would receive an allotted room out of the millions of rooms in an enormous hotel. Consequently, the body was fortuitous and impersonal, it was only a ready-made, borrowed thing. She would repeat this to herself in different ways, but she could never manage to feel it. This mind-body dualism was alien to her. She was too much one with her body; that is why she always felt such anxiety about it.

She experienced this same anxiety even in her relations with the young man, whom she had known for a year and with whom she was happy, perhaps because he never separated her body from her soul and she could live with him *wholly*. In this unity there was happiness, but right behind the happiness lurked suspicion, and the girl was full of that. For instance, it often occurred to her that the other women (those who weren't anxious) were more attractive and more seductive and that the young man, who did not conceal the fact that he knew this kind of woman well, would someday leave her for a woman like that. (True, the young man declared that he'd had enough of them to last his whole life, but she knew that he was still much younger than he thought.) She wanted him to be completely hers and she to be completely his, but it often seemed to her that the more she tried to give him everything, the more she denied him something: the very thing that a light and superficial love or a flirtation gives to a person. It worried her that she was not able to combine seriousness with lightheartedness.

But now she wasn't worrying and any such thoughts were far from her mind. She felt good. It was the first day of their vacation (of their two-week vacation, about which she had been dreaming for a whole year), the sky was blue (the whole year she had been worrying about whether the sky would really be blue), and he was beside her. At his, "Where to?" she blushed, and left the car without a word. She walked around the gas station, which was situated beside the highway in total isolation, surrounded by fields. About a hundred yards away (in the direction in which they were traveling), a wood began. She set off for it, vanished behind a little bush, and gave herself up to her good mood. (In solitude it was possible for her to get the greatest enjoyment from the presence of the man she loved. If his presence had been continuous, it would have kept on disappearing. Only when alone was she able to *hold on* to it.)

When she came out of the wood onto the highway, the gas station was visible. The large gasoline truck was already pulling out and the sports car moved forward toward the red turret of the pump. The girl walked on along the highway and only at times looked back to see if the sports car was coming. At last she caught sight of it. She stopped and began to wave at it like a hitchhiker waving at a stranger's car. The sports car slowed down and stopped close to the girl. The young man leaned toward the window, rolled it down, smiled, and asked, "Where are you headed, miss?"

"Are you going to Bystritsa?" asked the girl, smiling flirtatiously at him.

"Yes, please get in," said the young man, opening the door. The girl got in and the car took off.

III

The young man was always glad when his girl friend was gay. This didn't happen too often; she had a quite tiresome job in an unpleasant environment, many hours of overtime without compensatory leisure and, at home, a sick mother. So she often felt tired. She didn't have either particularly good nerves or self-confidence and easily fell into a state of anxiety and fear. For this reason he welcomed every manifestation of her gaiety with the tender solicitude of a foster parent. He smiled at her and said: "I'm lucky today. I've been driving for five years, but I've never given a ride to such a pretty hitchhiker."

The girl was grateful to the young man for every bit of flattery; she wanted to linger for a moment in its warmth and so she said, "You're very good at lying."

"Do I look like a liar?"

"You look like you enjoy lying to women," said the girl, and into her words there crept unawares a touch of the old anxiety, because she really did believe that her young man enjoyed lying to women.

The girl's jealousy often irritated the young man, but this time he could easily overlook it for, after all, her words didn't apply to him but to the unknown driver. And so he just casually inquired, "Does it bother you?"

"If I were going with you, then it would bother me," said the girl and her words contained a subtle, instructive message for the young man; but the end of her sentence applied only to the unknown driver, "but I don't know you, so it doesn't bother me."

"Things about her own man always bother a woman more than things about a stranger" (this was now the young man's subtle, instructive message to the girl), "so seeing that we are strangers, we could get on well together."

The girl purposely didn't want to understand the implied meaning of his message, and so she now addressed the unknown driver exclusively:

"What does it matter, since we'll part company in a little while?"

"Why?" asked the young man.

"Well, I'm getting out at Bystritsa."

"And what if I get out with you?" 20

At these words the girl looked up at him and found that he looked exactly as she imagined him in her most agonizing hours of jealousy. She was alarmed at how he was flattering her and flirting with her (an unknown hitchhiker), and *how becoming it was to him*. Therefore she responded with defiant provocativeness, "What would *you* do with me, I wonder?"

"I wouldn't have to think too hard about what to do with such a beautiful woman," said the young man gallantly and at this moment he was once again speaking far more to his own girl than to the figure of the hitchhiker.

But this flattering sentence made the girl feel as if she had caught him at something, as if she had wheedled a confession out of him with a fraudulent trick. She felt toward him a brief flash of intense hatred and said, "Aren't you rather too sure of yourself?"

The young man looked at the girl. Her defiant face appeared to him to be completely convulsed. He felt sorry for her and longed for her usual, familiar expression (which he used to call childish and simple). He leaned toward her, put his arm around her shoulders, and softly spoke the name with which he usually addressed her and with which he now wanted to stop the game.

But the girl released herself and said: "You're going a bit too fast!" 25

At this rebuff the young man said: "Excuse me, miss," and looked silently in front of him at the highway.

IV

The girl's pitiful jealousy, however, left her as quickly as it had come over her. After all, she was sensible and knew perfectly well that all this was merely a game. Now it even struck her as a little ridiculous that she had repulsed her man out of jealous rage. It wouldn't be pleasant for her if he found out why she had done it. Fortunately women have the miraculous ability to change the meaning of their actions after the event. Using this ability, she decided that she had repulsed him not out of anger but so that she could go on with the game, which, with its whimsicality, so well suited the first day of their vacation.

So again she was the hitchhiker, who had just repulsed the overenterprising driver, but only so as to slow down his conquest and make it more exciting. She half turned toward the young man and said caressingly:

"I didn't mean to offend you, mister!"

"Excuse me, I won't touch you again," said the young man. 30

He was furious with the girl for not listening to him and refusing to be herself when that was what he wanted. And since the girl insisted on continuing in her role, he transferred his anger to the unknown hitchhiker whom she was portraying. And all at once he discovered the character of his own part: he stopped making the gallant remarks with which he had wanted to flatter his girl in a roundabout way, and began to play the tough guy who treats women to the coarser aspects of his masculinity: willfulness, sarcasm, self-assurance.

This role was a complete contradiction of the young man's habitually solicitous approach to the girl. True, before he had met her, he had in fact behaved roughly rather than gently toward women. But he had never resembled a heartless tough guy, because he had never demonstrated either a particularly strong will or ruthlessness. However, if he did not resemble such a man, nonetheless he had *longed* to at one time.

Of course it was a quite naive desire, but there it was. Childish desires withstand all the snares of the adult mind and often survive into ripe old age. And this childish desire quickly took advantage of the opportunity to embody itself in the proffered role.

The young man's sarcastic reserve suited the girl very well—it freed her from herself. For she herself was, above all, the epitome of jealousy. The moment she stopped seeing the gallantly seductive young man beside her and saw only his inaccessible face, her jealousy subsided. The girl could forget herself and give herself up to her role.

Her role? What was her role? It was a role out of trashy literature. The hitchhiker stopped the car not to get a ride, but to seduce the man who was driving the car. She was an artful seductress, cleverly knowing how to use her charms. The girl slipped into this silly, romantic part with an ease that astonished her and held her spellbound.

V

There was nothing the young man missed in his life more than lightheartedness. The main road of his life was drawn with implacable precision. His job didn't use up merely eight hours a day, it also infiltrated the remaining time with the compulsory boredom of meetings and home study, and, by means of the attentiveness of his countless male and female colleagues, it infiltrated the wretchedly little time he had left for his private life as well. This private life never remained secret and sometimes even became the subject of gossip and public discussion. Even two weeks' vacation didn't give him a feeling of liberation and adventure; the gray shadow of precise planning lay even here. The scarcity of summer accommodations in our country compelled him to book a room in the Tatras° six months in advance, and since for that he needed a recommendation from his office, its omnipresent brain thus did not cease knowing about him even for an instant. 35

He had become reconciled to all this, yet all the same from time to time the terrible thought of the straight road would overcome him—a road along which he was being pursued, where he was visible to everyone, and from which he could not turn aside. At this moment that thought returned to him. Through an odd and brief conjunction of ideas the figurative road became identified with the real highway along which he was driving—and this led him suddenly to do a crazy thing.

"Where did you say you wanted to go?" he asked the girl.

"To Banska Bystritsa," she replied.

"And what are you going to do there?"

"I have a date there." 40

"Who with?"

"With a certain gentleman."

The car was just coming to a large crossroads. The driver slowed down so he could read the road signs, then turned off to the right.

"What will happen if you don't arrive for that date?"

"It would be your fault and you would have to take care of me." 45

"You obviously didn't notice that I turned off in the direction of Nove Zamky."

"Is that true? You've gone crazy!"

Tatras: part of the Carpathian mountain range along the Czech-Polish border.

A Fiction Anthology

"Don't be afraid, I'll take care of you," said the young man.

So they drove and chatted thus—the driver and the hitchhiker who did not know each other.

The game all at once went into a higher gear. The sports car was moving away not only from the imaginary goal of Banska Bystritsa, but also from the real goal, toward which it had been heading in the morning: the Tatras and the room that had been booked. Fiction was suddenly making an assault upon real life. The young man was moving away from himself and from the implacable straight road, from which he had never strayed until now. 50

"But you said you were going to the Low Tatras!" The girl was surprised.

"I am going, miss, wherever I feel like going. I'm a free man and I do what I want and what it pleases me to do."

VI

When they drove into Nove Zamky it was already getting dark.

The young man had never been here before and it took him a while to orient himself. Several times he stopped the car and asked the passersby directions to the hotel. Several streets had been dug up, so that the drive to the hotel, even though it was quite close by (as all those who had been asked asserted), necessitated so many detours and roundabout routes that it was almost a quarter of an hour before they finally stopped in front of it. The hotel looked unprepossessing, but it was the only one in town and the young man didn't feel like driving on. So he said to the girl, "Wait here," and got out of the car.

Out of the car he was, of course, himself again. And it was upsetting for him to find himself in the evening somewhere completely different from his intended destination—the more so because no one had forced him to do it and as a matter of fact he hadn't even really wanted to. He blamed himself for this piece of folly, but then became reconciled to it. The room in the Tatras could wait until tomorrow and it wouldn't do any harm if they celebrated the first day of their vacation with something unexpected. 55

He walked through the restaurant—smoky, noisy, and crowded—and asked for the reception desk. They sent him to the back of the lobby near the staircase, where behind a glass panel a superannuated blonde was sitting beneath a board full of keys. With difficulty, he obtained the key to the only room left.

The girl, when she found herself alone, also threw off her role. She didn't feel ill-humored, though, at finding herself in an unexpected town. She was so devoted to the young man that she never had doubts about anything he did, and confidently entrusted every moment of her life to him. On the other hand the idea once again popped into her mind that perhaps—just as she was now doing—other women had waited for her man in his car, those women whom he met on business trips. But surprisingly enough this idea didn't upset her at all now. In fact, she smiled at the thought of how nice it was that today she was this other woman, this irresponsible, indecent other woman, one of those women of whom she was so jealous. It seemed to her that she was cutting them all out, that she had learned how to use their weapons; how to give the young man what until now she had not known how to give him: lightheartedness, shamelessness, and dissoluteness. A curious feeling of satisfaction filled her, because she alone had the ability to be all women and in this way (she alone) could completely captivate her lover and hold his interest.

The young man opened the car door and led the girl into the restaurant. Amid the din, the dirt, and the smoke he found a single, unoccupied table in a corner.

VII

"So how are you going to take care of me now?" asked the girl provocatively.

"What would you like for an aperitif?"

The girl wasn't too fond of alcohol, still she drank a little wine and liked vermouth fairly well. Now, however, she purposely said: "Vodka."

"Fine," said the young man. "I hope you won't get drunk on me."

"And if I do?" said the girl.

The young man did not reply but called over a waiter and ordered two vodkas and two steak dinners. In a moment the waiter brought a tray with two small glasses and placed it in front of them.

The man raised his glass, "To you!"

"Can't you think of a wittier toast?"

Something was beginning to irritate him about the girl's game. Now sitting face to face with her, he realized that it wasn't just the *words* which were turning her into a stranger, but that her *whole persona* had changed, the movements of her body and her facial expression, and that she unpalatably and faithfully resembled that type of woman whom he knew so well and for whom he felt some aversion.

And so (holding his glass in his raised hand), he corrected his toast: "O.K., then I won't drink to you, but to your kind, in which are combined so successfully the better qualities of the animal and the worse aspects of the human being."

"By 'kind' do you mean all women?" asked the girl.

"No, I mean only those who are like you."

"Anyway it doesn't seem very witty to me to compare a woman with an animal."

"O.K.," the young man was still holding his glass aloft, "then I won't drink to your kind, but to your soul. Agreed? To your soul, which lights up when it descends from your head into your belly, and which goes out when it rises back up to your head."

The girl raised her glass. "O.K., to my soul, which descends into my belly."

"I'll correct myself once more," said the young man. "To your belly, into which your soul descends."

"To my belly," said the girl, and her belly (now that they had named it specifically), as it were, responded to the call; she felt every inch of it.

Then the waiter brought their steaks and the young man ordered them another vodka and some soda water (this time they drank to the girl's breasts), and the conversation continued in this peculiar, frivolous tone. It irritated the young man more and more how *well able* the girl was to become the lascivious miss. If she was able to do it so well, he thought, it meant that she really was like that. After all, no alien soul had entered into her from somewhere in space. What she was acting now was she herself; perhaps it was that part of her being which had formerly been locked up and which the pretext of the game had let out of its cage. Perhaps the girl supposed that by means of the game she was *disowning* herself, but wasn't it the other way around? Wasn't she becoming herself only through the game? Wasn't she freeing herself through the game? No, opposite him was not sitting a strange woman in his girl's body; it was his girl, herself, no one else. He looked at her and felt growing aversion toward her.

However, it was not only aversion. The more the girl withdrew from him *psychically*, the more he longed for her *physically*. The alien quality of her soul drew attention to her body, yes, as a matter of fact it turned her body into a body for *him* as if until now it had existed for the young man hidden within clouds of compassion, tenderness, concern, love, and emotion, as if it had been lost in these clouds (yes, as if this body had been lost!). It seemed to the young man that today he was seeing his girl's body for the first time.

After her third vodka and soda the girl got up and said flirtatiously, "Excuse me."

The young man said, "May I ask you where you are going, miss?"

"To piss, if you'll permit me," said the girl and walked off between the tables back toward the plush screen.

80

VIII

She was pleased with the way she had astounded the young man with this word, which—in spite of all its innocence—he had never heard from her. Nothing seemed to her truer to the character of the woman she was playing than this flirtatious emphasis placed on the word in question. Yes, she was pleased, she was in the best of moods. The game captivated her. It allowed her to feel what she had not felt till now: *a feeling of happy-go-lucky irresponsibility.*

She, who was always uneasy in advance about her every next step, suddenly felt completely relaxed. The alien life in which she had become involved was a life without shame, without biographical specifications, without past or future, without obligations. It was a life that was extraordinarily free. The girl, as a hitchhiker, could do anything, *everything was permitted her.* She could say, do, and feel whatever she liked.

She walked through the room and was aware that people were watching her from all the tables. It was a new sensation, one she didn't recognize: *indecent joy caused by her body.* Until now she had never been able to get rid of the fourteen-year-old girl within herself who was ashamed of her breasts and had the disagreeable feeling that she was indecent, because they stuck out from her body and were visible. Even though she was proud of being pretty and having a good figure, this feeling of pride was always immediately curtailed by shame. She rightly suspected that feminine beauty functioned above all as sexual provocation and she found this distasteful. She longed for her body to relate only to the man she loved. When men stared at her breasts in the street it seemed to her that they were invading a piece of her most secret privacy which should belong only to herself and her lover. But now she was the hitchhiker, the woman without a destiny. In this role she was relieved of the tender bonds of her love and began to be intensely aware of her body. And her body became more aroused the more alien the eyes watching it.

She was walking past the last table when an intoxicated man, wanting to show off his worldliness, addressed her in French: "*Combien,°* *mademoiselle?*"

The girl understood. She thrust out her breasts and fully experienced every movement of her hips, then disappeared behind the screen.

85

IX

It was a curious game. This curiousness was evidenced, for example, in the fact that the young man, even though he himself was playing the unknown driver remarkably well, did not for a moment stop seeing his girl in the hitchhiker. And it was precisely this that was tormenting. He saw his girl seducing a strange man, and had the bitter privilege of being present, of seeing at close quarters how she looked and

---

Combien: French—how much?

of hearing what she said when she was cheating on him (when she had cheated on him, when she would cheat on him). He had the paradoxical honor of being himself the pretext for her unfaithfulness.

This was all the worse because he worshipped rather than loved her. It had always seemed to him that her inward nature was *real* only within the bounds of fidelity and purity, and that beyond these bounds it simply didn't exist. Beyond these bounds she would cease to be herself, as water ceases to be water beyond the boiling point. When he now saw her crossing this horrifying boundary with nonchalant elegance, he was filled with anger.

The girl came back from the rest room and complained: "A guy over there asked me: *Combien, mademoiselle?*"

"You shouldn't be surprised," said the young man, "after all, you look like a whore."

"Do you know that it doesn't bother me in the least?"   90

"Then you should go with the gentleman!"

"But I have you."

"You can go with him after me. Go and work out something with him."

"I don't find him attractive."

"But in principle you have nothing against it, having several men in one night."   95

"Why not, if they're good-looking."

"Do you prefer them one after the other or at the same time?"

"Either way," said the girl.

The conversation was proceeding to still greater extremes of rudeness; it shocked the girl slightly but she couldn't protest. Even in a game there lurks a lack of freedom; even a game is a trap for the players. If this had not been a game and they had really been two strangers, the hitchhiker could long ago have taken offense and left. But there's no escape from a game. A team cannot flee from the playing field before the end of the match, chess pieces cannot desert the chessboard: the boundaries of the playing field are fixed. The girl knew that she had to accept whatever form the game might take, just because it was a game. She knew that the more extreme the game became, the more it would be a game and the more obediently she would have to play it. And it was futile to evoke good sense and warn her dazed soul that she must keep her distance from the game and not take it seriously. Just because it was only a game her soul was not afraid, did not oppose the game, and narcotically sank deeper into it.

The young man called the waiter and paid. Then he got up and said to the girl, "We're going."   100

"Where to?" The girl feigned surprise.

"Don't ask, just come on," said the young man.

"What sort of way is that to talk to me?"

"The way I talk to whores," said the young man.

X

They went up the badly lit staircase. On the landing below the second floor a group of intoxicated men was standing near the rest room. The young man caught hold of the girl from behind so that he was holding her breast with his hand. The men by the rest room saw this and began to call out. The girl wanted to break away, but

A Fiction Anthology

the young man yelled at her: "Keep still!" The men greeted this with general rib-aldry and addressed several dirty remarks to the girl. The young man and the girl reached the second floor. He opened the door of their room and switched on the light. 105

It was a narrow room with two beds, a small table, a chair, and a washbasin. The young man locked the door and turned to the girl. She was standing facing him in a defiant pose with insolent sensuality in her eyes. He looked at her and tried to discover behind her lascivious expression the familiar features which he loved tenderly. It was as if he were looking at two images through the same lens, at two images superimposed one upon the other with the one showing through the other. These two images showing through each other were telling him that *every-thing* was in the girl, that her soul was terrifyingly amorphous, that it held faithful-ness and unfaithfulness, treachery and innocence, flirtatiousness and chastity. This disorderly jumble seemed disgusting to him, like the variety to be found in a pile of garbage. Both images continued to show through each other and the young man understood that the girl differed only on the surface from other women, but deep down was the same as they: full of all possible thoughts, feelings, and vices, which justified all his secret misgivings and fits of jealousy. The impression that certain outlines delineated her as an individual was only a delusion to which the other per-son, the one who was looking, was subject—namely himself. It seemed to him that the girl he loved was a creation of his desire, his thoughts, and his faith and that the real girl now standing in front of him was hopelessly alien, hopelessly *ambigu-ous*. He hated her.

"What are you waiting for? Strip," he said.

The girl flirtatiously bent her head and said, "Is it necessary?"

The tone in which she said this seemed to him very familiar; it seemed to him that once long ago some other woman had said this to him, only he no longer knew which one. He longed to humiliate her. Not the hitchhiker, but his own girl. The game merged with life. The game of humiliating the hitchhiker became only a pre-text for humiliating his girl. The young man had forgotten that he was playing a game. He simply hated the woman standing in front of him. He stared at her and took a fifty-crown bill from his wallet. He offered it to the girl. "Is that enough?"

The girl took the fifty crowns and said: "You don't think I'm worth much." 110

The young man said: "You aren't worth more."

The girl nestled up against the young man. "You can't get around me like that! You must try a different approach, you must work a little!"

She put her arms around him and moved her mouth toward his. He put his fin-gers on her mouth and gently pushed her away. He said: "I only kiss women I love."

"And you don't love me?"

"No." 115

"Whom do you love?"

"What's that got to do with you? Strip!"

XI

She had never undressed like this before. The shyness, the feeling of inner panic, the dizziness, all that she had always felt when undressing in front of the young man (and she couldn't hide in the darkness), all this was gone. She was standing in front

The Hitchhiking Game **391**

of him self-confident, insolent, bathed in light, and astonished at where she had all of a sudden discovered the gestures, heretofore unknown to her, of a slow, provocative striptease. She took in his glances, slipping off each piece of clothing with a caressing movement and enjoying each individual stage of this exposure.

But then suddenly she was standing in front of him completely naked and at this moment it flashed through her head that now the whole game would end, that, since she had stripped off her clothes, she had also stripped away her dissimulation, and that being naked meant that she was now herself and the young man ought to come up to her now and make a gesture with which he would wipe out everything and after which would follow only their most intimate love-making. So she stood naked in front of the young man and at this moment stopped playing the game. She felt embarrassed and on her face appeared the smile, which really belonged to her— a shy and confused smile.

But the young man didn't come to her and didn't end the game. He didn't notice the familiar smile. He saw before him only the beautiful, alien body of his own girl, whom he hated. Hatred cleansed his sensuality of any sentimental coating. She wanted to come to him, but he said: "Stay where you are, I want to have a good look at you." Now he longed only to treat her as a whore. But the young man had never had a whore and the ideas he had about them came from literature and hearsay. So he turned to these ideas and the first thing he recalled was the image of a woman in black underwear (and black stockings) dancing on the shiny top of a piano. In the little hotel room there was no piano, there was only a small table covered with a linen cloth leaning against the wall. He ordered the girl to climb up on it. The girl made a pleading gesture, but the young man said, "You've been paid." 120

When she saw the look of unshakable obsession in the young man's eyes, she tried to go on with the game, even though she no longer could and no longer knew how. With tears in her eyes she climbed onto the table. The top was scarcely three feet square and one leg was a little bit shorter than the others so that standing on it the girl felt unsteady.

But the young man was pleased with the naked figure, now towering above him, and the girl's shy insecurity merely inflamed his imperiousness. He wanted to see her body in all positions and from all sides, as he imagined other men had seen it and would see it. He was vulgar and lascivious. He used words that she had never heard from him in her life. She wanted to refuse, she wanted to be released from the game. She called him by his first name, but he immediately yelled at her that she had no right to address him so intimately. And so eventually in confusion and on the verge of tears, she obeyed, she bent forward and squatted according to the young man's wishes, saluted, and then wiggled her hips as she did the Twist for him. During a slightly more violent movement, when the cloth slipped beneath her feet and she nearly fell, the young man caught her and dragged her to the bed.

He had intercourse with her. She was glad that at least now finally the unfortunate game would end and they would again be the two people they had been before and would love each other. She wanted to press her mouth against his. But the young man pushed her head away and repeated that he only kissed women he loved. She burst into loud sobs. But she wasn't even allowed to cry, because the young man's furious passion gradually won over her body, which then silenced the complaint of her soul. On the bed there were soon two bodies in perfect harmony, two sensual bodies, alien to each other. This was exactly what the girl had most dreaded all her life and had scrupulously avoided till now: love-making without emotion or love. She knew that she had crossed the forbidden boundary, but she proceeded across it without objections and as a full participant—only somewhere, far off in a corner of her consciousness, did she feel horror at the thought that she had never known such pleasure, never so much pleasure as at this moment—beyond that boundary.

XII

Then it was all over. The young man got up off the girl and, reaching out for the long cord hanging over the bed, switched off the light. He didn't want to see the girl's face. He knew that the game was over, but didn't feel like returning to their customary relationship. He feared this return. He lay beside the girl in the dark in such a way that their bodies would not touch.

After a moment he heard her sobbing quietly. The girl's hand diffidently, childishly touched his. It touched, withdrew, then touched again, and then a pleading, sobbing voice broke the silence, calling him by his name and saying, "I am me, I am me . . ."

125

The young man was silent, he didn't move, and he was aware of the sad emptiness of the girl's assertion, in which the unknown was defined in terms of the same unknown quantity.

And the girl soon passed from sobbing to loud crying and went on endlessly repeating this pitiful tautology:° "I am me, I am me, I am me . . ."

The young man began to call compassion to his aid (he had to call it from afar, because it was nowhere near at hand), so as to be able to calm the girl. There were still thirteen days' vacation before them.

Translated by Suzanne Rappaport

Donald Barthelme (1931–1989)

Donald Barthelme was born in Philadelphia and grew up in Houston, where he attended the University of Houston. He took up writing early, winning high school awards and later working as a reporter. Barthelme's quirky, intelligent and darkly humorous short stories, many of them published in *The New Yorker*, established his reputation as an original contemporary stylist. He had a flair for composing striking narrative collages, mixing and matching materials from all parts of the cultural spectrum. The stories range from the dark and brooding to the brightly celebratory. Barthelme's collections include *Come Back, Dr. Caligari; Unspeakable Practices, Unnameable Acts;* and *Great Days.*

---

tautology: philosophical redundancy.

ME AND MISS MANDIBLE

Miss Mandible wants to make love to me but she hesitates because I am officially a child; I am, according to the records, according to the gradebook on her desk, according to the card index in the principal's office, eleven years old. There is a misconception here, one that I haven't quite managed to get cleared up yet. I am in fact thirty-five, I've been in the Army, I am six feet one, I have hair in the appropriate places, my voice is a baritone, I know very well what to do with Miss Mandible if she ever makes up her mind.

In the meantime we are studying common fractions. I could, of course, answer all the questions, or at least most of them (there are things I don't remember). But I prefer to sit in this too-small seat with the desktop cramping my thighs and examine the life around me. There are thirty-two in the class, which is launched every morning with the pledge of allegiance to the flag. My own allegiance, at the moment, is divided between Miss Mandible and Sue Ann Brownly, who sits across the aisle from me all day long and is, like Miss Mandible, a fool for love. Of the two I prefer, today, Sue Ann; although between eleven and eleven and a half (she refuses to reveal her exact age) she is clearly a woman, with a woman's disguised aggression and a woman's peculiar contradictions.

15 September

Happily our geography text, which contains maps of all the principal landmasses of the world, is large enough to conceal my clandestine journal-keeping, accomplished in an ordinary black composition book. Every day I must wait until Geography to put down such thoughts as I may have had during the morning about my situation and my fellows. I have tried writing at other times and it does not work. Either the teacher is walking up and down the aisles (during this period, luckily, she sticks close to the map rack in the front of the room) or Bobby Vanderbilt, who sits behind me, is punching me in the kidneys and wanting to know what I am doing. Vanderbilt, I have found out from certain desultory conversations on the playground, is hung up on sports cars, a veteran consumer of *Road & Track*. This explains the continual roaring sounds which seem to emanate from his desk; he is reproducing a record album called *Sounds of Sebring*.°

19 September

Only I, at times (only at times), understand that somehow a mistake has been made, that I am in a place where I don't belong. It may be that Miss Mandible also knows this, at some level, but for reasons not fully understood by me she is going along with the game. When I was first assigned to this room I wanted to protest, the error seemed obvious, the stupidest principal could have seen it; but I have come to believe it was deliberate, that I have been betrayed again.

Now it seems to make little difference. This life-role is as interesting as my former life-role, which was that of a claims adjuster for the Great Northern Insurance

---

Sounds of Sebring: a record of race-car track noises.

A Fiction Anthology

Company, a position which compelled me to spend my time amid the debris of our civilization: rumpled fenders, roofless sheds, gutted warehouses, smashed arms and legs. After ten years of this one has a tendency to see the world as a vast junkyard, looking at a man and seeing only his (potentially) mangled parts, entering a house only to trace the path of the inevitable fire. Therefore when I was installed here, although I knew an error had been made, I countenanced it, I was shrewd; I was aware that there might well be some kind of advantage to be gained from what seemed a disaster. The role of The Adjuster teaches one much.

5

22 September

I am being solicited for the volleyball team. I decline, refusing to take unfair profit from my height.

23 September

Every morning the roll is called: Bestvina, Bokenfohr, Broan, Brownly, Cone, Coyle, Crecelius, Darin, Durbin, Geiger, Guiswite, Heckler, Jacobs, Kleinschmidt, Lay, Logan, Masei, Mitgang, Pfeilsticker. It is like the litany chanted in the dim miserable dawns of Texas by the cadre sergeant of our basic training company.

In the Army, too, I was ever so slightly awry. It took me a fantastically long time to realize what the others grasped almost at once: that much of what we were doing was absolutely pointless, to no purpose. I kept wondering why. Then something happened that proposed a new question. One day we were commanded to white-wash, from the ground to the topmost leaves, all of the trees in our training area. The corporal who relayed the order was nervous and apologetic. Later an off-duty captain sauntered by and watched us, white-splashed and totally weary, strung out among the freakish shapes we had created. He walked away swearing. I understood the principle (orders are orders), but I wondered: Who decides?

29 September

Sue Ann is a wonder. Yesterday she viciously kicked my ankle for not paying attention when she was attempting to pass me a note during History. It is swollen still. But Miss Mandible was watching me, there was nothing I could do. Oddly enough Sue Ann reminds me of the wife I had in my former role, while Miss Mandible seems to be a child. She watches me constantly, trying to keep sexual significance out of her look; I am afraid the other children have noticed. I have already heard, on that ghostly frequency that is the medium of classroom communication, the words *"Teacher's pet!"*

2 October

Sometimes I speculate on the exact nature of the conspiracy which brought me here. At times I believe it was instigated by my wife of former days, whose name was . . . I am only pretending to forget. I know her name very well, as well as I know the name of my former motor oil (Quaker State) or my old Army serial number (US 54109268). Her name was Brenda.

10

7 October

Today I tiptoed up to Miss Mandible's desk (when there was no one else in the room) and examined its surface. Miss Mandible is a clean-desk teacher, I discovered. There was nothing except her gradebook (the one in which I exist as a sixth-grader) and a text, which was open at a page headed *Making the Processes Meaningful*. I read: "Many pupils enjoy working fractions when they understand what they are doing. They have confidence in their ability to take the right steps and to obtain correct answers. However, to give the subject full social significance, it is necessary that many realistic situations requiring the processes be found. Many interesting and life-like problems involving the use of fractions should be solved . . ."

8 October

I am not irritated by the feeling of having been through all this before. Things are done differently now. The children, moreover, are in some ways different from those who accompanied me on my first voyage through the elementary schools: *"They have confidence in their ability to take the right steps and to obtain correct answers."* This is surely true. When Bobby Vanderbilt, who sits behind me and has the great tactical advantage of being able to maneuver in my disproportionate shadow, wishes to bust a classmate in the mouth he first asks Miss Mandible to lower the blind, saying that the sun hurts his eyes. When she does so, *bip!* My generation would never have been able to con authority so easily.

13 October

I misread a clue. Do not misunderstand me: it was a tragedy only from the point of view of the authorities. I conceived that it was my duty to obtain satisfaction for the injured, for an elderly lady (not even one of our policyholders, but a claimant against Big Ben Transfer & Storage, Inc.) from the company. The settlement was $165,000; the claim, I still believe, was just. But without my encouragement Mrs. Bichek would never have had the self-love to prize her injury so highly. The company paid, but its faith in me, in my efficacy in the role, was broken. Henry Goodykind, the district manager, expressed this thought in a few not altogether un-sympathetic words, and told me at the same time that I was to have a new role. The next thing I knew I was here, at Horace Greeley Elementary, under the lubricious eye of Miss Mandible.

17 October

Today we are to have a fire drill. I know this because I am a Fire Marshal, not only for our room but for the entire right wing of the second floor. This distinction, which was awarded shortly after my arrival, is interpreted by some as another mark of my somewhat dubious relations with our teacher. My armband, which is red and decorated with white felt letters reading FIRE, sits on the little shelf under my desk, next to the brown bag containing the lunch I carefully make for myself each morning. One of the advantages of packing my own lunch (I have no one to pack it for me) is that I am able to fill it with things I enjoy. The peanut butter sandwiches that my mother made in my former existence, many years ago, have been banished in favor of ham and cheese. I have found that my diet has mysteriously adjusted to my new situation; I no longer drink, for instance, and when I smoke, it is in the boys' john, like everybody else. When school is out I hardly smoke at all. It is only in the matter of sex that I feel my own true age; this is apparently something that, once learned, can never be forgotten. I live in fear that Miss Mandible will one day keep me after school, and when we are alone, create a compromising situation. To avoid this I have become a model pupil: another reason for the pronounced dislike I have encountered in certain quarters. But I cannot deny that I am singed by those long glances from the vicinity of the chalkboard; Miss Mandible is in many ways, notably about the bust, a very tasty piece.

24 October

There are isolated challenges to my largeness, to my dimly realized position in the class as Gulliver.° Most of my classmates are polite about this matter, as they would be if I had only one eye, or wasted, metal-wrapped legs. I am viewed as a mutation of some sort but essentially a peer. However Harry Broan, whose father has made himself rich manufacturing the Broan Bathroom Vent (with which Harry is frequently reproached; he is always being asked how things are in Ventsville), today inquired if I wanted to fight. An interested group of his followers had gathered to observe this suicidal undertaking. I replied that I didn't feel quite up to it, for which he was obviously grateful. We are now friends forever. He has given me to understand privately that he can get me all the bathroom vents I will ever need, at a ridiculously modest figure.

15

25 October

"*Many interesting and lifelike problems involving the use of fractions should be solved . . .*" The theorists fail to realize that everything that is either interesting or lifelike in the classroom proceeds from what they would probably call interpersonal relations: Sue Ann Brownly kicking me in the ankle. How lifelike, how womanlike, is her tender solicitude after the deed! Her pride in my newly acquired limp is transparent; everyone knows that she has set her mark upon me, that it is a victory in her unequal struggle with Miss Mandible for my great, overgrown heart. Even Miss Mandible knows, and counters in perhaps the only way she can, with sarcasm. "Are you wounded, Joseph?" Conflagrations smolder behind her eyelids, yearning for the Fire Marshal clouds her eyes. I mumble that I have bumped my leg.

30 October

I return again and again to the problem of my future.

4 November

The underground circulating library has brought me a copy of *Movie-TV Secrets*, the multicolor cover blazoned with the headline "Debbie's Date Insults Liz!" It is a gift from Frankie Randolph, a rather plain girl who until today has had not one word for me, passed on via Bobby Vanderbilt. I nod and smile over my shoulder in acknowledgment; Frankie hides her head under her desk. I have seen these magazines being passed around among the girls (sometimes one of the boys will condescend to inspect a particularly lurid cover). Miss Mandible confiscates them whenever she finds one. I leaf through *Movie-TV Secrets* and get an eyeful. "The exclusive picture on these pages isn't what it seems. We know how it looks and we know what the gossipers will do. So in the interests of a nice guy, we're publishing the facts first. Here's what really happened!" The picture shows a rising young movie idol in bed, pajama-ed and bleary-eyed, while an equally blowzy young woman looks startled beside him. I am happy to know that the picture is not really what it seems; it seems to be nothing less than divorce evidence.

Gulliver: the gigantic hero of Swift's fantasy tale *Gulliver's Travels*.

What do these hipless eleven-year-olds think when they come across, in the same magazine, the full-page ad for Maurice de Paree, which features "Hip Helpers" or what appear to be padded rumps? ("A real undercover agent that adds appeal to those hips and derriere, both!") If they cannot decipher the language the illustrations leave nothing to the imagination. "Drive him frantic . . ." the copy continues. Perhaps this explains Bobby Vanderbilt's preoccupation with Lancias and Maseratis; it is a defense against being driven frantic.

Sue Ann has observed Frankie Randolph's overture, and catching my eye, she pulls from her satchel no less than seventeen of these magazines, thrusting them at me as if to prove that anything any of her rivals has to offer, she can top. I shuffle through them quickly, noting the broad editorial perspective: 20

> "Debbie's° Kids Are Crying"
> "Eddie° Asks Debbie: Will You . . . ?"
> "The Nightmares Liz° Has About Eddie!"
> "The Things Debbie Can Tell About Eddie"
> "The Private Life of Eddie and Liz"
> "Debbie Gets Her Man Back?"
> "A New Life for Liz"
> "Love Is a Tricky Affair"
> "Eddie's Taylor-Made Love Nest"
> "How Liz Made a Man of Eddie"
> "Are They Planning to Live Together?"
> "Isn't It Time to Stop Kicking Debbie Around?"
> "Debbie's Dilemma"
> "Eddie Becomes a Father Again"
> "Is Debbie Planning to Re-wed?"
> "Can Liz Fulfill Herself?"
> "Why Debbie Is Sick of Hollywood"

Who are these people, Debbie, Eddie, Liz, and how did they get themselves in such a terrible predicament? Sue Ann knows, I am sure; it is obvious that she has been studying their history as a guide to what she may expect when she is suddenly freed from this drab, flat classroom.

I am angry and I shove the magazines back at her with not even a whisper of thanks.

5 November

The sixth grade at Horace Greeley Elementary is a furnace of love, love, love. Today it is raining, but inside the air is heavy and tense with passion. Sue Ann is absent; I suspect that yesterday's exchange has driven her to her bed. Guilt hangs about me. She is not responsible, I know, for what she reads, for the models proposed to her by a venal publishing industry; I should not have been so harsh. Perhaps it is only the flu.

Nowhere have I encountered an atmosphere as charged with aborted sexuality as this. Miss Mandible is helpless; nothing goes right today. Amos Darin has been found drawing a dirty picture in the cloakroom. Sad and inaccurate, it was offered not as a sign of something else but as an act of love in itself. It has excited even those

---

Debbie, Eddie, Liz: actress Debbie Reynolds, singer Eddie Fisher, actress Elizabeth Taylor—favorite headliners of the scandal magazines of the 1950s and 1960s.

who have not seen it, even those who saw but understood only that it was dirty. The room buzzes with imperfectly comprehended titillation. Amos stands by the door, waiting to be taken to the principal's office. He wavers between fear and enjoyment of his temporary celebrity. From time to time Miss Mandible looks at me reproachfully, as if blaming me for the uproar. But I did not create this atmosphere, I am caught in it like all the others.   25

8 November

Everything is promised my classmates and me, most of all the future. We accept the outrageous assurances without blinking.

9 November

I have finally found the nerve to petition for a larger desk. At recess I can hardly walk; my legs do not wish to uncoil themselves. Miss Mandible says she will take it up with the custodian. She is worried about the excellence of my themes. Have I, she asks, been receiving help? For an instant I am on the brink of telling her my story. Something, however, warns me not to attempt it. Here I am safe, I have a place; I do not wish to entrust myself once more to the whimsy of authority. I resolve to make my themes less excellent in the future.

11 November

A ruined marriage, a ruined adjusting career, a grim interlude in the Army when I was almost not a person. This is the sum of my existence to date, a dismal total. Small wonder that re-education seemed my only hope. It is clear even to me that I need reworking in some fundamental way. How efficient is the society that provides thus for the salvage of its clinkers!

14 November

The distinction between children and adults, while probably useful for some purposes, is at bottom a specious one, I feel. There are only individual egos, crazy for love.

15 November

The custodian has informed Miss Mandible that our desks are all the correct size for sixth-graders, as specified by the Board of Estimate and furnished the schools by the Nu-Art Educational Supply Corporation of Englewood, California. He has pointed out that if the desk size is correct, then the pupil size must be incorrect. Miss Mandible, who has already arrived at this conclusion, refuses to press the matter further. I think I know why. An appeal to the administration might result in my removal from the class, in a transfer to some sort of setup for "exceptional children." This would be a disaster of the first magnitude. To sit in a room with child geniuses (or, more likely, children who are "retarded") would shrivel me in a week. Let my experience here be that of the common run, I say; let me be, please God, typical.   30

20 November

We read signs as promises. Miss Mandible understands by my great height, by my resonant vowels, that I will one day carry her off to bed. Sue Ann interprets these same signs to mean that I am unique among her male acquaintances, therefore most desirable, therefore her special property as is everything that is Most Desirable. If neither of these propositions works out then life has broken faith with them.

I myself, in my former existence, read the company motto ("Here to Help in Time of Need") as a description of the duty of the adjuster, drastically mislocating the company's deepest concerns. I believed that because I had obtained a wife who was made up of wife-signs (beauty, charm, softness, perfume, cookery) I had found love. Brenda, reading the same signs that have now misled Miss Mandible and Sue Ann Brownly, felt she had been promised that she would never be bored again. All of us, Miss Mandible, Sue Ann, myself, Brenda, Mr. Goodykind, still believe that the American flag betokens a kind of general righteousness.

But I say, looking about me in this incubator of future citizens, that signs are signs, and some of them are lies.

23 November

It may be that my experience as a child will save me after all. If only I can remain quietly in this classroom, making my notes while Napoleon plods through Russia in the droning voice of Harry Broan, reading aloud from our History text. All of the mysteries that perplexed me as an adult have their origins here. But Miss Mandible will not permit me to remain ungrown. Her hands rest on my shoulders too warmly, and for too long.

7 December

It is the pledges that this place makes to me, pledges that cannot be redeemed, that will confuse me later and make me feel I am not *getting anywhere*. Everything is presented as the result of some knowable process; if I wish to arrive at four I get there by way of two and two. If I wish to burn Moscow the route I must travel has already been marked out by another visitor. If, like Bobby Vanderbilt, I yearn for the wheel of the Lancia 2.4-liter coupé, I have only to go through the appropriate process, that is, get the money. And if it is money itself that I desire, I have only to *make* it. All of these goals are equally beautiful in the sight of the Board of Estimate; the proof is all around us, in the no-nonsense ugliness of this steel and glass building, in the straightline matter-of-factness with which Miss Mandible handles some of our less reputable wars. Who points out that arrangements sometimes slip, that errors are made, that signs are misread? *"They have confidence in their ability to take the right steps and to obtain correct answers."*

35

8 December

My enlightenment is proceeding wonderfully.

9 December

Disaster once again. Tomorrow I am to be sent to a doctor, for observation. Sue Ann Brownly caught Miss Mandible and me in the cloakroom, during recess, Miss Mandible's naked legs in a scissors around my waist. For a moment I thought Sue Ann was going to choke. She ran out of the room weeping, straight for the principal's office, certain now which of us was Debbie, which Eddie, which Liz. I am sorry to be the cause of her disillusionment, but I know that she will recover. Miss Mandible is ruined but fulfilled. Although she will be charged with contributing to the delinquency of a minor, she seems at peace, *her* promise has been kept. She knows now that everything she has been told about life, about America, is true.

I have tried to convince the school authorities that I am a minor only in a very special sense, that I am in fact mostly to blame—but it does no good. They are as dense as ever. My contemporaries are astounded that I present myself as anything other than an innocent victim. Like the Old Guard marching through the Russian drifts, the class marches to the conclusion that truth is punishment.

Bobby Vanderbilt has given me his copy of *Sounds of Sebring*, in farewell.

John Updike (1932–)

John Updike was born in Shillington, Pennsylvania. Although he originally aspired to a career as a visual artist, Updike early decided to make use of his literary gifts instead. Over the past three decades he has emerged as one of our most prolific and versatile men of letters, writing essays, stories and novels, poetry, art criticism, and speeches and addresses (which he views not as chores but further opportunities for literary expression). Updike's fiction holds up a mirror to our changing society, exploring the manners and morals of the upper-middle class. His work includes the novels *Of the Farm* and *The Centaur* and the volumes of his Rabbit tetralogy: *Rabbit Run, Rabbit Redux, Rabbit Is Rich,* and *Rabbit at Rest*.

SEPARATING

The day was fair. Brilliant. All that June the weather had mocked the Maples' internal misery with solid sunlight—golden shafts and cascades of green in which their conversations had wormed unseeing, their sad murmuring selves the only stain in Nature. Usually by this time of the year they had acquired tans; but when they met their elder daughter's plane on her return from a year in England they were almost as pale as she, though Judith was too dazzled by the sunny opulent jumble of her native land to notice. They did not spoil her homecoming by telling her immediately. Wait a few days, let her recover from jet lag, had been one of their formulations, in that string of gray dialogues—over coffee, over cocktails, over Cointreau°—that had shaped the strategy of their dissolution, while the earth performed its annual stunt of renewal unnoticed beyond their

---

Cointreau: an orange-flavored liqueur.

closed windows. Richard had thought to leave at Easter; Joan had insisted they wait until the four children were at last assembled, with all exams passed and ceremonies attended, and the bauble of summer to console them. So he had drudged away, in love, in dread, repairing screens, getting the mowers sharpened, rolling and patching their new tennis court.

The court, clay, had come through its first winter pitted and windswept bare of redcoat. Years ago the Maples had observed how often, among their friends, divorce followed a dramatic home improvement, as if the marriage were making one last effort to live; their own worst crisis had come amid the plaster dust and exposed plumbing of a kitchen renovation. Yet, a summer ago, as canary-yellow bulldozers gaily churned a grassy, daisy-dotted knoll into a muddy plateau, and a crew of pigtailed young men raked and tamped clay into a plane, this transformation did not strike them as ominous, but festive in its impudence; their marriage could rend the earth for fun. The next spring, waking each day at dawn to a sliding sensation as if the bed were being tipped, Richard found the barren tennis court—its net and tapes still rolled in the barn—an environment congruous with his mood of purposeful desolation, and the crumbling of handfuls of clay into cracks and holes (dogs had frolicked on the court in a thaw; rivulets had eroded trenches) an activity suitably elemental and interminable. In his sealed heart he hoped the day would never come.

Now it was here. A Friday. Judith was re-acclimated; all four children were assembled, before jobs and camps and visits again scattered them. Joan thought they should be told one by one. Richard was for making an announcement at the table. She said, "I think just making an announcement is a cop-out. They'll start quarrelling and playing to each other instead of focusing. They're each individuals, you know, not just some corporate obstacle to your freedom."

"O.K., O.K. I agree." Joan's plan was exact. That evening, they were giving Judith a belated welcome-home dinner, of lobster and champagne. Then, the party over, they, the two of them, who nineteen years before would push her in a baby carriage along Fifth Avenue to Washington Square, were to walk her out of the house, to the bridge across the salt creek, and tell her, swearing her to secrecy. Then Richard Jr., who was going directly from work to a rock concert in Boston, would be told, either late when he returned on the train or early Saturday morning before he went off to his job; he was seventeen and employed as one of a golf-course maintenance crew. Then the two younger children, John and Margaret, could, as the morning wore on, be informed.

"Mopped up, as it were," Richard said.

"Do you have any better plan? That leaves you the rest of Saturday to answer any questions, pack, and make your wonderful departure."

"No," he said, meaning he had no better plan, and agreed to hers, though to him it showed an edge of false order, a hidden plea for control, like Joan's long chore lists and financial accountings and, in the days when he first knew her, her too-copious lecture notes. Her plan turned one hurdle for him into four—four knife-sharp walls, each with a sheer blind drop on the other side.

All spring he had moved through a world of insides and outsides, of barriers and partitions. He and Joan stood as a thin barrier between the children and the truth. Each moment was a partition, with the past on one side and the future on the other, a future containing this unthinkable *now*. Beyond four knifelike walls a new life for him waited vaguely. His skull cupped a secret, a white face, a face both frightened and soothing, both strange and known, that he wanted to shield from tears, which

5

A Fiction Anthology

he felt all about him, solid as the sunlight. So haunted, he had become obsessed with battening down the house against his absence, replacing screens and sash cords, hinges and latches—a Houdini° making things snug before his escape.

The lock. He had still to replace a lock on one of the doors of the screened porch. The task, like most such, proved more difficult than he had imagined. The old lock, aluminum frozen by corrosion, had been deliberately rendered obsolete by manufacturers. Three hardware stores had nothing that even approximately matched the mortised hole its removal (surprisingly easy) left. Another hole had to be gouged, with bits too small and saws too big, and the old hole fitted with a block of wood—the chisels dull, the saw rusty, his fingers thick with lack of sleep. The sun poured down, beyond the porch, on a world of neglect. The bushes already needed pruning, the windward side of the house was shedding flakes of paint, rain would get in when he was gone, insects, rot, death. His family, all those he would lose, filtered through the edges of his awareness as he struggled with screw holes, splinters, opaque instructions, minutiae of metal.

Judith sat on the porch, a princess returned from exile. She regaled them with stories of fuel shortages, of bomb scares in the Underground, of Pakistani workmen loudly lusting after her as she walked past on her way to dance school. Joan came and went, in and out of the house, calmer than she should have been, praising his struggles with the lock as if this were one more and not the last of their long succession of shared chores. The younger of his sons for a few minutes held the rickety screen door while his father clumsily hammered and chiseled, each blow a kind of sob in Richard's ears. His younger daughter, having been at a slumber party, slept on the porch hammock through all the noise—heavy and pink, trusting and forsaken. Time, like the sunlight, continued relentlessly; the sunlight slowly slanted. Today was one of the longest days. The lock clicked, worked. He was through. He had a drink; he drank it on the porch, listening to his daughter. "It was so sweet," she was saying, "during the worst of it, how all the butchers and bakery shops kept open by candlelight. They're all so plucky and cute. From the papers, things sounded so much worse here—people shooting people in gas lines, and everybody freezing."   10

Richard asked her, "Do you still want to live in England forever?" *Forever*: the concept, now a reality upon him, pressed and scratched at the back of his throat.

"No," Judith confessed, turning her oval face to him, its eyes still childishly far apart, but the lips set as over something succulent and satisfactory. "I was anxious to come home. I'm an American." She was a woman. They had raised her; he and Joan had endured together to raise her, alone of the four. The others had still some raising left in them. Yet it was the thought of telling Judith—the image of her, their first baby, walking between them arm in arm to the bridge—that broke him. The partition between his face and the tears broke. Richard sat down to the celebratory meal with the back of his throat aching; the champagne, the lobster seemed phases of sunshine; he saw them and tasted them through tears. He blinked, swallowed, croakily joked about hay fever. The tears would not stop leaking through; they came not through a hole that could be plugged but through a permeable spot in a membrane, steadily, purely, endlessly, fruitfully. They became, his tears, a shield for himself against these others—their faces, the fact of their assembly, a last time as

---

Houdini: Harry Houdini (1874–1926), a legendary escape artist.

innocents, at a table where he sat the last time as head. Tears dropped from his nose as he broke the lobster's back; salt flavored his champagne as he sipped it; the raw clench at the back of his throat was delicious. He could not help himself.

His children tried to ignore his tears. Judith, on his right, lit a cigarette, gazed upward in the direction of her too energetic, too sophisticated exhalation; on her other side, John earnestly bent his face to the extraction of the last morsels—legs, tail segments—from the scarlet corpse. Joan, at the opposite end of the table, glanced at him surprised, her reproach displaced by a quick grimace, of forgiveness, or of salute to his superior gift of strategy. Between them, Margaret, no longer called Bean, thirteen and large for her age, gazed from the other side of his pane of tears as if into a shopwindow at something she coveted—at her father, a crystalline heap of splinters and memories. It was not she, however, but John who, in the kitchen, as they cleared the plates and carapaces away, asked Joan the question: *"Why is Daddy crying?"*

Richard heard the question but not the murmured answer. Then he heard Bean cry, "Oh, no-oh!"—the faintly dramatized exclamation of one who had long expected it.

John returned to the table carrying a bowl of salad. He nodded tersely at his father and his lips shaped the conspiratorial words "She told."   15

"Told what?" Richard asked aloud, insanely.

The boy sat down as if to rebuke his father's distraction with the example of his own good manners. He said quietly, "The separation."

Joan and Margaret returned; the child, in Richard's twisted vision, seemed diminished in size, and relieved, relieved to have had the bogieman at last proved real. He called out to her—the distances at the table had grown immense—"You knew, you always knew," but the clenching at the back of his throat prevented him from making sense of it. From afar he heard Joan talking, levelly, sensibly, reciting what they had prepared: it was a separation for the summer, an experiment. She and Daddy both agreed it would be good for them; they needed space and time to think; they liked each other but did not make each other happy enough, somehow.

Judith, imitating her mother's factual tone, but in her youth off-key, too cool, said, "I think it's silly. You should either live together or get divorced."

Richard's crying, like a wave that has crested and crashed, had become tumultuous; but it was overtopped by another tumult, for John, who had been so reserved, now grew larger and larger at the table. Perhaps his younger sister's being credited with knowing set him off. "Why didn't you *tell* us?" he asked, in a large round voice quite unlike his own. "You should have *told* us you weren't getting along."   20

Richard was startled into attempting to force words through his tears. "We *do* get along, that's the trouble, so it doesn't show even to us—" *That we do not love each other* was the rest of the sentence; he couldn't finish it.

Joan finished for him, in her style. "And we've always, *especially*, loved our children."

John was not mollified. "What do you care about *us*?" he boomed. "We're just little things you *had*." His sisters' laughing forced a laugh from him, which he turned hard and parodistic: "Ha ha *ha*." Richard and Joan realized simultaneously that the child was drunk, on Judith's homecoming champagne. Feeling bound to keep the center of the stage, John took a cigarette from Judith's pack, poked it into his mouth, let it hang from his lower lip, and squinted like a gangster.

"You're not little things we had," Richard called to him. "You're the whole point. But you're grown. Or almost."

The boy was lighting matches. Instead of holding them to his cigarette (for they had never seen him smoke; being "good" had been his way of setting himself apart), he held them to his mother's face, closer and closer, for her to blow out. Then he lit the whole folder—a hiss and then a torch, held against his mother's face. Prismed by tears, the flame filled Richard's vision; he didn't know how it was extinguished. He heard Margaret say, "Oh stop showing off," and saw John, in response, break the cigarette in two and put the halves entirely into his mouth and chew, sticking out his tongue to display the shreds to his sister.

Joan talked to him, reasoning—a fountain of reason, unintelligible. "Talked about it for years . . . our children must help us . . . Daddy and I both want . . ." As the boy listened, he carefully wadded a paper napkin into the leaves of his salad, fashioned a ball of paper and lettuce, and popped it into his mouth, looking around the table for the expected laughter. None came. Judith said, "Be mature," and dismissed a plume of smoke.

Richard got up from this stifling table and led the boy outside. Though the house was in twilight, the outdoors still brimmed with light, the lovely waste light of high summer. Both laughing, he supervised John's spitting out the lettuce and paper and tobacco into the pachysandra. He took him by the hand—a square gritty hand, but for its softness a man's. Yet, it held on. They ran together up into the field, past the tennis court. The raw banking left by the bulldozers was dotted with daisies. Past the court and a flat stretch where they used to play family baseball stood a soft green rise glorious in the sun, each weed and species of grass distinct as illumination on parchment. "I'm sorry, so sorry," Richard cried. "You were the only one who ever tried to help me with all the goddam jobs around this place."

Sobbing, safe within his tears and the champagne, John explained, "It's not just the separation, it's the whole crummy year, I *hate* that school, you can't make any friends, the history teacher's a scud."

They sat on the crest of the rise, shaking and warm from their tears but easier in their voices, and Richard tried to focus on the child's sad year—the weekdays long with homework, the weekends spent in his room with model airplanes, while his parents murmured down below, nursing their separation. How selfish, how blind, Richard thought; his eyes felt scoured. He told his son, "We'll think about getting you transferred. Life's too short to be miserable."

They had said what they could, but did not want the moment to heal, and talked on, about the school, about the tennis court, whether it would ever again be as good as it had been that first summer. They walked to inspect it and pressed a few more tapes more firmly down. A little stiltedly, perhaps trying now to make too much of the moment, Richard led the boy to the spot in the field where the view was best, of the metallic blue river, the emerald marsh, the scattered islands velvety with shadow in the low light, the white bits of beach far away. "See," he said. "It goes on being beautiful. It'll be here tomorrow."

"I know," John answered, impatiently. The moment had closed.

Back in the house, the others had opened some white wine, the champagne being drunk, and still sat at the table, the three females, gossiping. Where Joan sat had become the head. She turned, showing him a tearless face, and asked, "All right?"

"We're fine," he said, resenting it, though relieved, that the party went on without him.

In bed she explained, "I couldn't cry I guess because I cried so much all spring. It really wasn't fair. It's your idea, and you made it look as though I was kicking you out."

"I'm sorry," he said. "I couldn't stop. I wanted to but couldn't." 35

"You *didn't* want to. You loved it. You were having your way, making a general announcement."

"I love having it over," he admitted. "God, those kids were great. So brave and funny." John, returned to the house, had settled to a model airplane in his room, and kept shouting down to them, "I'm O.K. No sweat." "And the way," Richard went on, cozy in his relief, "they never questioned the reasons we gave. No thought of a third person. Not even Judith."

"That *was* touching," Joan said.

He gave her a hug. "You were great too. Very reassuring to everybody. Thank you." Guiltily, he realized he did not feel separated.

"You still have Dickie to do," she told him. These words set before him a black mountain in the darkness; its cold breath, its near weight affected his chest. Of the four children, his elder son was most nearly his conscience. Joan did not need to add, "That's one piece of your dirty work I won't do for you." 40

"I know. I'll do it. You go to sleep."

Within minutes, her breathing slowed, became oblivious and deep. It was quarter to midnight. Dickie's train from the concert would come in at one-fourteen. Richard set the alarm for one. He had slept atrociously for weeks. But whenever he closed his lids some glimpse of the last hours scorched them—Judith exhaling toward the ceiling in a kind of aversion, Bean's mute staring, the sunstruck growth in the field where he and John had rested. The mountain before him moved closer, moved within him; he was huge, momentous. The ache at the back of his throat felt stale. His wife slept as if slain beside him. When, exasperated by his hot lids, his crowded heart, he rose from bed and dressed, she awoke enough to turn over. He told her then, "Joan, if I could undo it all, I would."

"Where would you begin?" she asked. There was no place. Giving him courage, she was always giving him courage. He put on shoes without socks in the dark. The children were breathing in their rooms, the downstairs was hollow. In their confusion they had left lights burning. He turned off all but one, the kitchen overhead. The car started. He had hoped it wouldn't. He met only moonlight on the road; it seemed a diaphanous companion, flickering in the leaves along the roadside, haunting his rearview mirror like a pursuer, melting under his headlights. The center of town, not quite deserted, was eerie at this hour. A young cop in uniform kept company with a gang of T-shirted kids on the steps of the bank. Across from the railroad station, several bars kept open. Customers, mostly young, passed in and out of the warm night, savoring summer's novelty. Voices shouted from cars as they passed; an immense conversation seemed in progress. Richard parked and in his weariness put his head on the passenger seat, out of the commotion and wheeling lights. It was as when, in the movies, an assassin grimly carries his mission through the jostle of a carnival—except the movies cannot show the precipitous, palpable slope you cling to within. You cannot climb back down; you can only fall. The synthetic fabric of the car seat, warmed by his cheek, confided to him an ancient, distant scent of vanilla.

A train whistle caused him to lift his head. It was on time; he had hoped it would be late. The slender draw-gates descended. The bell of approach tingled happily. The great metal body, horizontally fluted, rocked to a stop, and sleepy teenagers disembarked, his son among them. Dickie did not show surprise that his father was meeting him at this terrible hour. He sauntered to the car with two friends, both taller than he. He said "Hi" to his father and took the passenger's seat with an exhausted promptness that expressed gratitude. The friends got in the back, and Richard was grateful; a few more minutes' postponement would be won by driving them home.

He asked, "How was the concert?" 45

"Groovy," one boy said from the back seat.

"It bit," the other said.

"It was O.K.," Dickie said, moderate by nature, so reasonable that in his childhood the unreason of the world had given him headaches, stomach aches, nausea. When the second friend had been dropped off at his dark house, the boy blurted, "Dad, my eyes are killing me with hay fever! I'm out there cutting that mothering grass all day!"

"Do we still have those drops?"

"They didn't do any good last summer." 50

"They might this." Richard swung a U-turn on the empty street. The drive home took a few minutes. The mountain was here, in his throat. "Richard," he said, and felt the boy, slumped and rubbing his eyes, go tense at his tone, "I didn't come to meet you just to make your life easier. I came because your mother and I have some news for you, and you're a hard man to get ahold of these days. It's sad news."

"That's O.K." The reassurance came out soft, but quick, as if released from the tip of a spring.

Richard had feared that his tears would return and choke him, but the boy's manliness set an example, and his voice issued forth steady and dry. "It's sad news, but it needn't be tragic news, at least for you. It should have no practical effect on your life, though it's bound to have an emotional effect. You'll work at your job, and go back to school in September. Your mother and I are really proud of what you're making of your life; we don't want that to change at all."

"Yeah," the boy said lightly, on the intake of his breath, holding himself up. They turned the corner; the church they went to loomed like a gutted fort. The home of the woman Richard hoped to marry stood across the green. Her bedroom light burned.

"Your mother and I," he said, "have decided to separate. For the summer. Nothing legal, no divorce yet. We want to see how it feels. For some years now, we haven't been doing enough for each other, making each other as happy as we should be. Have you sensed that?" 55

"No," the boy said. It was an honest, unemotional answer: true or false in a quiz.

Glad for the factual basis, Richard pursued, even garrulously, the details. His apartment across town, his utter accessibility, the split vacation arrangements, the advantages to the children, the added mobility and variety of the summer. Dickie listened, absorbing. "Do the others know?"

"Yes."

"How did they take it?"

"The girls pretty calmly. John flipped out; he shouted and ate a cigarette and made a salad out of his napkin and told us how much he hated school."

His brother chuckled. "He did?"

"Yeah. The school issue was more upsetting for him than Mom and me. He seemed to feel better for having exploded."

"He did?" The repetition was the first sign that he was stunned.

"Yes. Dickie, I want to tell you something. This last hour, waiting for your train to get in, has been about the worst of my life. I hate this. *Hate* it. My father would have died before doing it to me." He felt immensely lighter, saying this. He had dumped the mountain on the boy. They were home. Moving swiftly as a shadow, Dickie was out of the car, through the bright kitchen. Richard called after him, "Want a glass of milk or anything?"

"No thanks."

"Want us to call the course tomorrow and say you're too sick to work?"

"No, that's all right." The answer was faint, delivered at the door to his room; Richard listened for the slam that went with a tantrum. The door closed normally, gently. The sound was sickening.

Joan had sunk into that first deep trough of sleep and was slow to awake. Richard had to repeat, "I told him."

"What did he say?"

"Nothing much. Could you go say goodnight to him? Please."

She left their room, without putting on a bathrobe. He sluggishly changed back into his pajamas and walked down the hall. Dickie was already in bed, Joan was sitting beside him, and the boy's bedside clock radio was murmuring music. When she stood, an inexplicable light—the moon?—outlined her body through the nightie. Richard sat on the warm place she had indented on the child's narrow mattress. He asked him, "Do you want the radio on like that?"

"It always is."

"Doesn't it keep you awake? It would me."

"No."

"Are you sleepy?"

"Yeah."

"Good. Sure you want to get up and go to work? You've had a big night."

"I want to."

Away at school this winter he had learned for the first time that you can go short of sleep and live. As an infant he had slept with an immobile, sweating intensity that had alarmed his babysitters. In adolescence had often been the first of the four children to go to bed. Even now, he would go slack in the middle of a television show, his sprawled legs hairy and brown. "O.K. Good boy. Dickie, listen. I love you so much, I never knew how much until now. No matter how this works out, I'll always be with you. Really."

Richard bent to kiss an averted face but his son, sinewy, turned and with wet cheeks embraced him and gave him a kiss, on the lips, passionate as a woman's. In his father's ear he moaned one word, the crucial, intelligent word: "*Why?*"

Why. It was a whistle of wind in a crack, a knife thrust, a window thrown open on emptiness. The white face was gone, the darkness was featureless. Richard had forgotten why.

Susan Sontag (1933–   )

Susan Sontag was born in New York and raised in Tucson and Los Angeles. She realized early that books and writers mattered to her more than anything else. Though she studied philosophy at the University of Chicago and has taught and lectured widely, she often adopts a decidedly nonacademic stance. She has established herself as a leading intellectual, publishing criticism, screenplays, and fiction. Sontag's fiction, which includes the novels *Death Kit* and *The Benefactor* as well as the stories collected in *I, Etcetera,* reflects a sensibility attuned to the fragmenting forces of our culture but pledged to the possibilities of private integrity.

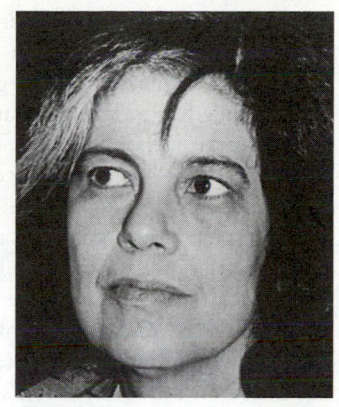

THE WAY WE LIVE NOW

At first he was just losing weight, he felt only a little ill, Max said to Ellen, and he didn't call for an appointment with his doctor, according to Greg, because he was managing to keep on working at more or less the same rhythm, but he did stop smoking, Tanya pointed out, which suggests he was frightened, but also that he wanted, even more than he knew, to be healthy, or healthier, or maybe just to gain back a few pounds, said Orson, for he told her, Tanya went on, that he expected to be climbing the walls (isn't that what people say?) and found, to his surprise, that he didn't miss cigarettes at all and reveled in the sensation of his lungs' being ache-free for the first time in years. But did he have a good doctor, Stephen wanted to know, since it would have been crazy not to go for a checkup after the pressure was off and he was back from the conference in Helsinki, even if by then he was feeling better. And he said, to Frank, that he would go, even though he was indeed frightened, as he admitted to Jan, but who wouldn't be frightened now, though, odd as that might seem, he hadn't been worrying until recently, he avowed to Quentin, it was only in the last six months that he had the metallic taste of panic in his mouth, because becoming seriously ill was something that happened to other people, a normal delusion, he observed to Paolo, if one was thirty-eight and had never had a serious illness; he wasn't, as Jan confirmed, a hypochondriac. Of course, it was hard not to worry, everyone was worried, but it wouldn't do to panic, because, as Max pointed out to Quentin, there wasn't anything one could do except wait and hope, wait and start being careful, be careful, and hope. And even if one did prove to be ill, one shouldn't give up, they had new treatments that promised an arrest of the disease's inexorable course, research was progressing. It seemed that everyone was in touch with everyone else several times a week, checking in, I've never spent so many hours at a time on the phone, Stephen said to Kate, and when I'm exhausted after the two or three calls made to me, giving me the latest, instead of switching off the phone to give myself a respite I tap out the number of another friend or acquaintance, to pass on the news. I'm not sure I can afford to think so much about it, Ellen said, and I suspect my own motives, there's something morbid I'm getting used to, getting excited by, this must be like what people felt in London during the Blitz.° As far as I know, I'm not at risk, but you never know, said Aileen. This thing is totally unprecedented, said Frank. But don't you think he ought to see a doctor, Stephen insisted. Listen, said Orson, you can't force people to take care of themselves, and what makes you think the worst, he could be just run down, people still do get ordinary illnesses, awful ones, why are you assuming it has to be *that*. But all I want to be sure, said Stephen, is that he understands the options, because most people don't, that's why they won't see a doctor or have the test, they think there's nothing one can do. But is there anything one can do, he said to Tanya (according to Greg), I mean what do I gain if I go to the doctor; if I'm really ill, he's reported to have said, I'll find out soon enough.

And when he was in the hospital, his spirits seemed to lighten, according to Donny. He seemed more cheerful than he had been in the last months, Ursula said, and the bad news seemed to come almost as a relief, according to Ira, as a truly unexpected blow, according to Quentin, but you'd hardly expect him to have said the same thing to all his friends, because his relation to Ira was so different from his relation to Quentin (this according to Quentin, who was proud of their friendship), and perhaps he thought Quentin wouldn't be undone by seeing him weep, but Ira insisted that couldn't be the reason he behaved so differently with each, and that maybe he was feeling less shocked, mobilizing his strength to fight for his life, at the moment he saw Ira but overcome by feelings of hopelessness when Quentin arrived with flowers, because anyway the flowers threw him into a bad mood, as Quentin told Kate, since the hospital room was choked with flowers, you couldn't have crammed another flower into that room, but surely you're exaggerating, Kate said, smiling, everybody likes flowers. Well, who wouldn't exaggerate at a time like this, Quentin said sharply Don't you think *this* is an exaggeration. Of course I do, said Kate gently, I was only teasing, I mean I didn't mean to tease. I know that, Quentin said, with tears in his eyes, and Kate hugged him and said well, when I go this evening I guess I won't bring flowers, what does he want, and Quentin said, according to Max, what he likes best is chocolate. Is there anything else, asked Kate, I mean like chocolate but not chocolate. Licorice, said Quentin, blowing his nose. And besides that. Aren't *you* exaggerating now, Quentin said, smiling. Right, said Kate, so if I want to bring him a whole raft of stuff, besides chocolate and licorice, what else. Jelly beans, Quentin said.

He didn't want to be alone, according to Paolo, and lots of people came in the first week, and the Jamaican nurse said there were other patients on the floor who would be glad to have the surplus flowers, and people weren't afraid to visit, it wasn't like the old days, as Kate pointed out to Aileen, they're not even segregated in the hospital anymore, as Hilda observed, there's nothing on the door of his room warning visitors of the possibility of contagion, as there was a few years ago; in fact, he's in a double room and, as he told Orson, the old guy on the far side of the curtain (who's clearly on the way out, said Stephen) doesn't even have the disease, so, as Kate went on, you really should go and see him, he'd be happy to see you, he likes having peo-

---

Blitz: German bombing assaults during World War II.

ple visit, you aren't not going because you're afraid, are you. Of course not, Aileen said, but I don't know what to say, I think I'll feel awkward, which he's bound to notice, and that will make him feel worse, so I won't be doing him any good, will I. But he won't notice anything, Kate said, patting Aileen's hand, it's not like that, it's not the way you imagine, he's not judging people or wondering about their motives, he's just happy to see his friends. But I never was really a friend of his, Aileen said, you're a friend, he's always liked you, you told me he talks about Nora with you, I know he likes me, he's even attracted to me, but he respects you. But, according to Wesley, the reason Aileen was so stingy with her visits was that she could never have him to herself, there were always others there already and by the time they left still others had arrived, she'd been in love with him for years, and I can understand, said Donny, that Aileen should feel bitter that if there could have been a woman friend he did more than occasionally bed, a woman he really loved, and my God, Victor said, who had known him in those years, he was crazy about Nora, what a heart-rending couple they were, two surly angels, then it couldn't have been she.

And when some of the friends, the ones who came every day, waylaid the doctor in the corridor, Stephen was the one who asked the most informed questions, who'd been keeping up not just with the stories that appeared several times a week in the *Times* (which Greg confessed to have stopped reading, unable to stand it anymore) but with articles in the medical journals published here and in England and France, and who knew socially one of the principal doctors in Paris who was doing some much-publicized research on the disease, but his doctor said little more than that the pneumonia was not life-threatening, the fever was subsiding, of course he was still weak but he was responding well to the antibiotics, that he'd have to complete his stay in the hospital, which entailed a minimum of twenty-one days on the IV, before she could start him on the new drug, for she was optimistic about the possibility of getting him into the protocol; and when Victor said that if he had so much trouble eating (he'd say to everyone when they coaxed him to eat some of the hospital meals, that food didn't taste right, that he had a funny metallic taste in his mouth) it couldn't be good that friends were bringing him all that chocolate, the doctor just smiled and said that in these cases the patient's morale was also an important factor, and if chocolate made him feel better she saw no harm in it, which worried Stephen, as Stephen said later to Donny, because they wanted to believe in the promises and taboos of today's high-tech medicine but here this reassuringly curt and silver-haired specialist in the disease, someone quoted frequently in the papers, was talking like some oldfangled country GP who tells the family that tea with honey or chicken soup may do as much for the patient as penicillin, which might mean, as Max said, that they were just going through the motions of treating him, that they were not sure about what to do, or rather, as Xavier interjected, that they didn't know what the hell they were doing, that the truth, the real truth, as Hilda said, upping the ante, was that they didn't, the doctors, really have any hope.

Oh, no, said Lewis, I can't stand it, wait a minute, I can't believe it, are you sure, I mean are they sure, have they done all the tests, it's getting so when the phone rings I'm scared to answer because I think it will be someone telling me someone else is ill; but did Lewis really not know until yesterday, Robert said testily, I find that hard to believe, everybody is talking about it, it seems impossible that someone wouldn't have called Lewis; and perhaps Lewis did know, was for some reason pretending not to know already, because, Jan recalled, didn't Lewis say something months ago to

Greg, and not only to Greg, about his not looking well, losing weight, and being worried about him and wishing he'd see a doctor, so it couldn't come as a total surprise. Well, everybody is worried about everybody now, said Betsy, that seems to be the way we live, the way we live now. And, after all, they were once very close, doesn't Lewis still have the keys to his apartment, you know the way you let someone keep the keys after you've broken up, only a little because you hope the person might just saunter in, drunk or high, late some evening, but mainly because it's wise to have a few sets of keys strewn around town, if you live alone, at the top of a former commercial building that, pretentious as it is, will never acquire a doorman or even a resident superintendent, someone whom you can call on for the keys late one night if you find you've lost yours or have locked yourself out. Who else has keys, Tanya inquired, I was thinking somebody might drop by tomorrow before coming to the hospital and bring some treasures, because the other day, Ira said, he was complaining about how dreary the hospital room was, and how it was like being locked up in a motel room, which got everybody started telling funny stories about motel rooms they'd known, and at Ursula's story, about the Luxury Budget Inn in Schenectady, there was an uproar of laughter around his bed, while he watched them in silence, eyes bright with fever, all the while, as Victor recalled, gobbling that damned chocolate. But, according to Jan, whom Lewis's keys enabled to tour the swank of his bachelor lair with an eye to bringing over some art consolation to brighten up the hospital room, the Byzantine icon wasn't on the wall over his bed, and that was a puzzle until Orson remembered that he'd recounted without seeming upset (this disputed by Greg) that the boy he'd recently gotten rid of had stolen it, along with four of the *maki-e* lacquer boxes, as if these were objects as easy to sell on the street as a TV or a stereo. But he's always been very generous, Kate said quietly, and though he loves beautiful things isn't really attached to them, to things, as Orson said, which is unusual in a collector, as Frank commented, and when Kate shuddered and tears sprang to her eyes and Orson inquired anxiously if he, Orson, had said something wrong, she pointed out that they'd begun talking about him in a retrospective mode, summing up what he was like, what made them fond of him, as if he were finished, completed, already a part of the past.   5

Perhaps he was getting tired of having so many visitors, said Robert, who was, as Ellen couldn't help mentioning, someone who had come only twice and was probably looking for a reason not to be in regular attendance, but there could be no doubt, according to Ursula, that his spirits had dipped, not that there was any discouraging news from the doctors, and he seemed now to prefer being alone a few hours of the day; and he told Donny that he'd begun keeping a diary for the first time in his life, because he wanted to record the course of his mental reactions to this astonishing turn of events, to do something parallel to what the doctors were doing, who came every morning and conferred at his bedside about his body, and that perhaps it wasn't so important what he wrote in it, which amounted, as he said wryly to Quentin, to little more than the usual banalities about terror and amazement that this was happening to him, to him also, plus the usual remorseful assessments of his past life, his pardonable superficialities, capped by resolves to live better, more deeply, more in touch with his work and his friends, and not to care so passionately about what people thought of him, interspersed with admonitions to himself that in this situation his will to live counted more than anything else and that if he really wanted to live, and trusted life, and liked himself well enough (down, ol'debbil Thanatos!°), he *would* live, he would be an exception; but perhaps all this, as Quentin ruminated, talking on the phone to Kate, wasn't the point, the point was that by the very keeping of the diary he was accumulating something to reread one day, slyly staking out his claim to a future time, in which the diary would be an object, a relic, in which he might not actually reread it, because he would want to have put this ordeal behind him, but the diary would be there in the drawer of his stupendous Majorelle desk, and he could already, he did actually say to Quentin one late sunny afternoon, propped up in the hospital bed, with the stain of chocolate framing one corner of a heartbreaking smile, see himself in the penthouse, the October sun streaming through those clear windows instead of this streaked one, and the diary, the pathetic diary, safe inside the drawer.

It doesn't matter about the treatment's side effects, Stephen said (when talking to Max), I don't know why you're so worried about that, every strong treatment has some dangerous side effects, it's inevitable, you mean otherwise the treatment wouldn't be effective, Hilda interjected, and anyway, Stephen went on doggedly, just because there *are* side effects it doesn't mean he has to get them, or all of them, each one, or even some of them. That's just a list of all the possible things that could go wrong, because the doctors have to cover themselves, so they make up a worst-case scenario, but isn't what's happening to him, and to so many other people, Tanya interrupted, a worst-case scenario, a catastrophe no one could have imagined, it's too cruel, and isn't everything a side effect, quipped Ira, even *we* are all side effects, but we're not bad side effects, Frank said, he likes having his friends around, and we're helping each other, too; because his illness sticks us all in the same glue, mused Xavier, and, whatever the jealousies and grievances from the past that have made us wary and cranky with each other, when something like this happens (the sky is falling, the sky is falling!) you understand what's really important. I agree, Chicken Little, he is reported to have said. But don't you think, Quentin observed to Max, that being as close to him as we are, making time to drop by the hospital every day, is a way of our trying to define ourselves more firmly and irrevocably as the well, those who aren't ill, who aren't going to fall ill, as if what's happened to him couldn't happen to us, when in fact the chances are that before long one of us will end up where he is, which is probably what he felt when he was one of the cohort visiting Zack in the spring (you never knew Zack, did you?), and, according to Clarice, Zack's widow, he didn't come very often, he said he hated hospitals, and didn't feel he was doing Zack any good, that Zack would see on his face how uncomfortable he was. Oh, he was one of those, Aileen said. A coward. Like me.

And after he was sent home from the hospital, and Quentin had volunteered to move in and was cooking meals and taking telephone messages and keeping the mother in Mississippi informed, well, mainly keeping her from flying to New York and heaping her grief on her son and confusing the household routine with her oppressive ministrations, he was able to work an hour or two in his study, on days he didn't insist on going out, for a meal or a movie, which tired him. He seemed optimistic, Kate thought, his appetite was good, and what he said, Orson reported, was

---

Thanatos: the personification of death, from the ancient Greek word for death.

that he agreed when Stephen advised him that the main thing was to keep in shape, he was a fighter, right, he wouldn't be who he was if he weren't, and was he ready for the big fight, Stephen asked rhetorically (as Max told it to Donny), and he said you bet, and Stephen added it could be a lot worse, you could have gotten the disease two years ago, but now so many scientists are working on it, the American team and the French team, everyone bucking for that Nobel Prize a few years down the road, that all you have to do is stay healthy for another year or two and then there will be good treatment, real treatment. Yes, he said, Stephen said, my timing is good. And Betsy, who had been climbing on and rolling off macrobiotic diets for a decade, came up with a Japanese specialist she wanted him to see but thank God, Donny reported, he'd had the sense to refuse, but he did agree to see Victor's visualization therapist, although what could one possibly visualize, said Hilda, when the point of visualizing disease was to see it as an entity with contours, borders, here rather than there, something limited, something you were the host of, in the sense that you could disinvite the disease, while this was so total; or would be, Max said. But the main thing, said Greg, was to see that he didn't go the macrobiotic route, which might be harmless for plump Betsy but could only be devastating for him, lean as he'd always been, with all the cigarettes and other appetite-suppressing chemicals he'd been welcoming into his body for years; and now was hardly the time, as Stephen pointed out, to be worried about cleaning up his act, and eliminating the chemical additives and other pollutants that we're all blithely or not so blithely feasting on, blithely since we're healthy, healthy as we can be; so far, Ira said. Meat and potatoes is what I'd be happy to see him eating, Ursula said wistfully. And spaghetti and clam sauce, Greg added. And thick cholesterol-rich omelets with smoked mozzarella, suggested Yvonne, who had flown from London for the weekend to see him. Chocolate cake, said Frank. Maybe not chocolate cake, Ursula said, he's already eating so much chocolate.

And when, not right away but still only three weeks later, he was accepted into the protocol for the new drug, which took considerable behind-the-scenes lobbying with the doctors, he talked less about being ill, according to Donny, which seemed like a good sign, Kate felt, a sign that he was not feeling like a victim, feeling not that he *had* a disease but, rather, was living *with* a disease (that was the right cliché, wasn't it?), a more hospitable arrangement, said Jan, a kind of cohabitation which implied that it was something temporary, that it could be terminated, but terminated how, said Hilda, and when you say hospitable, Jan, I hear hospital. And it was encouraging, Stephen insisted, that from the start, at least from the time he was finally persuaded to make the telephone call to his doctor, he was willing to say the name of the disease, pronounce it often and easily, as if it were just another word, like boy or gallery or cigarette or money or deal, as in no big deal, Paolo interjected, because, as Stephen continued, to utter the name is a sign of health, a sign that one has accepted being who one is, mortal, vulnerable, not exempt, not an exception after all, it's a sign that one is willing, truly willing, to fight for one's life. And we must say the name, too, and often, Tanya added, we mustn't lag behind him in honesty, or let him feel that, the effort of honesty having been made, it's something done with and he can go on to other things. One is so much better prepared to help him, Wesley replied. In a way he's fortunate, said Yvonne, who had taken care of a problem at the New York store and was flying back to London this evening, sure, fortunate, said

Wesley, no one is shunning him Yvonne went on, no one's afraid to hug him or kiss him lightly on the mouth, in London we are, as usual, a few years behind you, people I know, people who would seem to be not even remotely at risk, are just terrified, but I'm impressed by how cool and rational you all are; you find us cool, asked Quentin. But I have to say, he's reported to have said, I'm terrified, I find it very hard to read (and you know how he loves to read, said Greg; yes, reading is his television, said Paolo) or to think, but I don't feel hysterical. I feel quite hysterical, Lewis said to Yvonne. But you're able to *do* something for him, that's wonderful, how I wish I could stay longer, Yvonne answered, it's rather beautiful, I can't help thinking, this utopia of friendship you've assembled around him (this pathetic utopia, said Kate), so that the disease, Yvonne concluded, is not, anymore, out there. Yes, don't you think we're more at home here, with him, with the disease, said Tanya, because the imagined disease is so much worse than the reality of him, whom we all love, each in our fashion, having it. I know for me his getting it has quite demystified the disease, said Jan, I don't feel afraid, spooked, as I did before he became ill, when it was only news about remote acquaintances, whom I never saw again after they became ill. But you know you're not going to come down with the disease, Quentin said, to which Ellen replied, on her behalf, that's not the point, and possibly untrue, my gynecologist says that everyone is at risk, everyone who has a sexual life, because sexuality is a chain that links each of us to many others, unknown others, and now the great chain of being has become a chain of death as well. It's not the same for you, Quentin insisted, it's not the same for you as it is for me or Lewis or Frank or Paolo or Max, I'm more and more frightened, and I have every reason to be. I don't think about whether I'm at risk or not, said Hilda, I know that I was afraid to know someone with the disease, afraid of what I'd see, what I'd feel, and after the first day I came to the hospital I felt so relieved. I'll never feel that way, that fear, again; he doesn't seem different from me. He's not, Quentin said.

According to Lewis, he talked more often about those who visited more often, which is natural, said Betsy, I think he's even keeping a tally. And among those who came or checked in by phone every day, the inner circle as it were, those who were getting more points, there was still a further competition, which was what was getting on Betsy's nerves, she confessed to Jan; there's always that vulgar jockeying for position around the bedside of the gravely ill, and though we all feel suffused with virtue at our loyalty to him (speak for yourself, said Jan), to the extent that we're carving time out of every day, or almost every day, though some of us are dropping out, as Xavier pointed out, aren't we getting at least as much out of this as he is. Are we, said Jan. We're rivals for a sign from him of special pleasure over a visit, each stretching for the brass ring of his favor, wanting to feel the most wanted, the true nearest and dearest, which is inevitable with someone who doesn't have a spouse and children or an official in-house lover, hierarchies that no one would dare contest, Betsy went on, so we are the family he's founded, without meaning to, without official titles and ranks (we, we, snarled Quentin); and is it so clear, though some of us, Lewis and Quentin and Tanya and Paolo, among others, are ex-lovers and all of us more or less than friends, which one of us he prefers, Victor said (now it's us, raged Quentin), because sometimes I think he looks forward more to seeing Aileen, who has visited only three times, twice at the hospital and once since he's been home, than he does you or me; but, according to Tanya, after being very disappointed that Aileen hadn't come, now he was angry, while, according to Xavier, he was not really hurt but touchingly passive, accepting Aileen's absence as something he somehow deserved. But he's happy to have people around, said Lewis; he says when he doesn't have company he gets very sleepy, he sleeps (according to Quentin), and then perks up when someone arrives, it's important that he not feel ever alone. But, said Victor, there's one person he hasn't heard from, whom he'd probably like to hear from more than most of us; but she didn't just vanish, even right after she broke away from him, and he knows exactly where she lives now, said Kate, he told me he put in a call to her last Christmas Eve, and she said it's nice to hear from you and Merry Christmas, and he was shattered, according to Orson, and furious and disdainful, according to Ellen (what do you expect of her, said Wesley, she was burned out), but Kate wondered if maybe he hadn't phoned Nora in the middle of a sleepless night, what's the time difference, and Quentin said no, I don't think so, I think he wouldn't want her to know.

10

And when he was feeling even better and had regained the pounds he'd shed right away in the hospital, though the refrigerator started to fill up with organic wheat germ and grapefruit and skimmed milk (he's worried about his cholesterol count, Stephen lamented), and told Quentin he could manage by himself now, and did, he started asking everyone who visited how he looked, and everyone said he looked great, so much better than a few weeks ago, which didn't jibe with what anyone had told him at that time; but then it was getting harder and harder to know how he looked, to answer such a question honestly when among themselves they wanted to be honest, both for honesty's sake and (as Donny thought) to prepare for the worst, because he'd been looking like *this* for so long, at least it seemed so long, that it was as if he'd always been like this, how did he look before, but it was only a few months, and those words, pale and wan looking and fragile, hadn't they always applied? And one Thursday Ellen, meeting Lewis at the door of the building, said, as they rode up together in the elevator, how is he *really*? But you see how he is, Lewis said tartly, he's fine, he's perfectly healthy, and Ellen understood that of course Lewis didn't think he was perfectly healthy but that he wasn't worse, and that was true, but wasn't it, well, almost heartless to talk like that. Seems inoffensive to me, Quentin said, but I know what you mean, I remember once talking to Frank, somebody, after all, who has volunteered to do five hours a week of office work at the Crisis Center (I know, said Ellen), and Frank was going on about this guy, diagnosed almost a year ago, and so much further along, who'd been complaining to Frank on the phone about the indifference of some doctor, and had gotten quite abusive about the doctor, and Frank was saying there was no reason to be so upset, the implication being that *he*, Frank, wouldn't behave so irrationally, and I said, barely able to control my scorn, but Frank, Frank, he has every reason to be upset, he's dying, and Frank said, said according to Quentin, oh, I don't like to think about it that way.

And it was while he was still home, recuperating, getting his weekly treatment, still not able to do much work, he complained, but, according to Quentin, up and about most of the time and turning up at the office several days a week, that bad news came about two remote acquaintances, one in Houston and one in Paris, news that was intercepted by Quentin on the ground that it could only depress him, but Stephen contended that it was wrong to lie to him, it was so important for him to live in the truth; that had been one of his first victories, that he was candid, that he was even willing to crack jokes about the disease, but Ellen said it wasn't good to give him this end-of-the-world feeling, too many people were getting ill, it was becoming such a common destiny that maybe some of the will to fight for his life would be drained out of him if it seemed to be as natural as, well, death. Oh, Hilda said, who didn't know personally either the one in Houston or the one in Paris, but knew *of* the one in Paris, a pianist who specialized in twentieth-century Czech and Polish music, I have his records, he's such a valuable person, and, when Kate glared at her, continued defensively, I know every life is equally sacred, but that *is* a thought, another thought, I mean, all these valuable people who aren't going to have their normal four score as it is now, these people aren't going to be replaced, and it's such a loss to the culture. But this isn't going to go on forever, Wesley said, it can't, they're bound to come up with something (they, they, muttered Stephen), but did you ever think, Greg said, that if some people don't die, I mean even if they can keep them alive (they, they, muttered Kate), they continue to be carriers, and that means, if you have a conscience, that you can never make love, make love fully, as you'd been wont—wantonly, Ira said—to do. But it's better than dying, said Frank. And in all his talk about the future, when he allowed himself to be hopeful, according to Quentin, he never mentioned the prospect that even if he didn't die, if he were so fortunate as to be among the first generation of the disease's survivors, never mentioned, Kate confirmed, that whatever happened it was over, the way he had lived until now, but, according to Ira, he did think about it, the end of bravado, the end of folly, the end of trusting life, the end of taking life for granted, and of treating life as something that, samurai-like, he thought himself ready to throw away lightly, impudently; and Kate recalled, sighing, a brief exchange she'd insisted on having as long as two years ago, huddling on a banquette covered with steel-gray industrial carpet on an upper level of The Prophet and toking up for their next foray onto the dance floor: she'd said hesitantly, for it felt foolish asking a prince of debauchery to, well, take it easy, and she wasn't keen on playing big sister, a role, as Hilda confirmed, he inspired in many women, are you being careful, honey, you know what I mean. And he replied, Kate went on, no, I'm not, listen, I can't, I just can't, sex is too important to me, always has been (he started talking like that, according to Victor, after Nora left him), and if I get it, well, I get it. But he wouldn't talk like that now, would he, said Greg; he must feel awfully foolish now, said Betsy, like someone who went on smoking, saying I can't give up cigarettes, but when the bad X-ray is taken even the most besotted nicotine addict can stop on a dime. But sex isn't like cigarettes, is it, said Frank, and, besides, what good does it do to remember that he was reckless, said Lewis angrily, the appalling thing is that you just have to be unlucky once, and wouldn't he feel even worse if he'd stopped three years ago and had come down with it anyway, since one of the most terrifying features of the disease is that you don't know when you contracted it, it could have been ten years ago, because surely this disease has existed for years and years, long before it was recognized; that is, named. Who knows how long (I think a lot about that, said Max) and who knows (I know what you're going to say, Stephen interrupted) how many are going to get it.

I'm feeling fine, he's reported to have said whenever someone asked him how he was, which was almost always the first question anyone asked. Or: I'm feeling better, how are you? But he said other things, too. I'm playing leapfrog with myself, he is reported to have said, according to Victor. And: There must be a way to get something positive out of this situation, he's reported to have said to Kate. How American of him, said Paolo. Well, said Betsy, you know the old American adage: When you've got a lemon, make lemonade. The one thing I'm sure I couldn't take, Jan said he said to her, is becoming disfigured, but Stephen hastened to point out the disease doesn't take that form very often anymore, its profile is mutating, and, in conversation with Ellen, wheeled up words like blood-brain barrier; I never thought there was a barrier *there*, said Jan. But he mustn't know about Max, Ellen said, that would really depress him, please don't tell him, he'll have to know, Quentin said grimly, and he'll be furious not to have been told. But there's time for that, when they take Max off the respirator, said Ellen; but isn't it incredible, Frank said, Max was fine, not feeling ill at all, and then to wake up with a fever of a hundred and five, unable to breathe, but that's the way it often starts, with absolutely no warning, Stephen said, the disease has so many forms. And when, after another week had gone by, he asked Quentin where Max was, he didn't question Quentin's account of a spree in the Bahamas, but then the number of people who visited regularly was thinning out, partly because the old feuds that had been put aside through the first hospitalization and the return home had resurfaced, and the flickering enmity between Lewis and Frank exploded, even though Kate did her best to mediate between them, and also because he himself had done something to loosen the bonds of love that united the friends around him, by seeming to take them all for granted, as if it were perfectly normal for so many people to carve out so much time and attention for him, visit him every few days, talk about him incessantly on the phone with each other; but, according to Paolo, it wasn't that he was less grateful, it was just something he was getting used to, the visits. It had become, with time, a more ordinary kind of situation, a kind of ongoing party, first at the hospital and now since he was home, barely on his feet again, it being clear, said Robert, that I'm on the B list; but Kate said, that's absurd, there's no list; and Victor said, but there is, only it's not he, it's Quentin who's drawing it up. He wants to see us, we're helping him, we have to do it the way he wants, he fell down yesterday on the way to the bathroom, he mustn't be told about Max (but he already knew, according to Donny), it's getting worse.

When I was home, he is reported to have said, I was afraid to sleep, as I was dropping off each night it felt like just that, as if I were falling down a black hole, to sleep felt like giving in to death, I slept every night with the light on; but here, in the hospital, I'm less afraid. And to Quentin he said, one morning, the fear rips through me, it tears me open; and, to Ira, it presses me together, squeezes me toward myself. Fear gives everything its hue, its high. I feel so, I don't know how to say it, exalted, he said to Quentin. Calamity is an amazing high, too. Sometimes I feel *so* well, so powerful, it's as if I could jump out of my skin. Am I going crazy, or what? Is it all this attention and coddling I'm getting from everybody, like a child's dream of being loved? Is it the drugs? I know it sounds crazy but sometimes I think this is a *fantastic* experience, he said shyly; but there was also the bad taste in the mouth, the pressure in the head and at the back of the neck, the red, bleeding gums, the painful, if pink-lobed, breathing, and his ivory pallor, color of white chocolate. Among those who wept when told over the phone that he was back in the hospital were Kate and Stephen (who'd been called by Quentin), and Ellen, Victor, Aileen, and Lewis (who were called by Kate), and Xavier and Ursula (who were called by Stephen). Among those who didn't weep were Hilda, who said that she'd just learned that her seventy-five-year-old aunt was dying of the disease, which she'd contracted from a transfusion given during her successful double bypass of five years ago, and Frank and Donny and Betsy, but this didn't mean, according to Tanya, that they weren't moved and appalled, and Quentin thought they might not be coming soon to the hospital but would send presents; the room, he was in a private room this time, was filling up with flowers, and plants, and books, and tapes. The high tide of barely suppressed acrimony of the last weeks at home subsided into the routines of hospital visiting, though more than a few resented Quentin's having charge of the visiting book (but it was Quentin who had the idea, Lewis pointed out); now, to insure a steady stream of visitors, preferably no more than two at a time (this, the rule in all hospitals, wasn't enforced here, at least on this floor; whether out of kindness or inefficiency, no one could decide), Quentin had to be called first, to get one's time slot, there was no more casual dropping by. And his mother could no longer be prevented from taking a plane and installing herself in a hotel near the hospital; but he seemed to mind her daily presence less than expected, Quentin said; said Ellen it's we who mind, do you suppose she'll stay long. It was easier to be generous with each other visiting him here in the hospital, as Donny pointed out, than at home, where one minded never being alone with him; coming here, in our twos and twos, there's no doubt about what our role is, how we should be, collective, funny, distracting, undemanding, light, it's important to be light, for in all this dread there is gaiety, too, as the poet said, said Kate. (His eyes, his glittering eyes, said Lewis.) His eyes looked dull, extinguished, Wesley said to Xavier, but Betsy said his face, not just his eyes, looked soulful, warm; whatever is there, said Kate, I've never been so aware of his eyes; and Stephen said, I'm afraid of what my eyes show, the way I watch him, with too much intensity, or a phony kind of casualness, said Victor. And, unlike at home, he was clean-shaven each morning, at whatever hour they visited him; his curly hair was always combed; but he complained that the nurses had changed since he was here the last time, and that he didn't like the change, he wanted everyone to be the same. The room was furnished now with some of his personal effects (odd word for one's things, said Ellen), and Tanya brought drawings and a letter from her nine-year-old dyslexic son, who was writing now, since she'd purchased a computer; and Donny brought champagne and some helium balloons, which were anchored to the foot of his bed; tell me about something that's going on, he said, waking up from a nap to find Donny and Kate at the side of his bed, beaming at him; tell me a story, he said wistfully, said Donny, who couldn't think of anything to say; you're the story, Kate said. And Xavier brought an eighteenth-century Guatemalan wooden statue of Saint Sebastian° with upcast eyes and open mouth, and when Tanya said what's that, a tribute to eros past, Xavier said where I come from Sebastian is venerated as a protector against pestilence. Pestilence symbolized by arrows? Symbolized by arrows. All people remember is the body of a beautiful youth bound to a tree, pierced by arrows (of which he always seems oblivious, Tanya interjected), people forget that the story continues, Xavier continued, that when the Christian women came to bury the martyr they found him still alive and nursed him back to health. And he said, according to Stephen, I didn't know Saint Sebastian didn't die. It's undeniable, isn't it, said Kate on the phone to Stephen, the fascination of the dying. It makes me ashamed. We're learning how to die, said Hilda, I'm not ready to learn, said Aileen; and Lewis, who was coming straight

---

°*Saint Sebastian:* a saint traditionally depicted as shot full of arrows.

from the other hospital, the hospital where Max was still being kept in ICU, met Tanya getting out of the elevator on the tenth floor, and as they walked together down the shiny corridor past the open doors, averting their eyes from the other patients sunk in their beds, with tubes in their noses, irradiated by the the bluish light from the television sets, the thing I can't bear to think about, Tanya said to Lewis, is someone dying with the TV on.

He has that strange, unnerving detachment now, said Ellen, that's what upsets me, even though it makes it easier to be with him. Sometimes he was querulous. I can't stand them coming in here taking my blood every morning, what are they doing with all that blood, he is reported to have said; but where was his anger, Jan wondered. Mostly he was lovely to be with, always saying how are *you*, how are you feeling. He's so sweet now, said Aileen. He's so nice, said Tanya. (Nice, nice, groaned Paolo.) At first he was very ill, but he was rallying, according to Stephen's best information, there was no fear of his not recovering this time, and the doctor spoke of his being discharged from the hospital in another ten days if all went well, and the mother was persuaded to fly back to Mississippi, and Quentin was readying the penthouse for his return. And he was still writing his diary, not showing it to anyone, though Tanya, first to arrive one late-winter morning, and finding him dozing, peeked, and was horrified, according to Greg, not by anything she read but by a progressive change in his handwriting: in the recent pages, it was becoming spidery, less legible, and some lines of script wandered and tilted about the page. I was thinking, Ursula said to Quentin, that the difference between a story and a painting or photograph is that in a story you can write, He's still alive. But in a painting or a photo you can't show "still." You can just show him being alive. He's still alive, Stephen said.

15

Raymond Carver (1938–1988)

Raymond Carver was born in Clatskanie, Oregon. His early years were, as he often wrote, filled with struggle. Married at nineteen, Carver lived for years among the working poor, drifting from job to job. In 1958 he enrolled at a state college in California and studied with the writer John Gardner. Carver's hard living gradually found its way into his fiction. His first collection of stories, *Will You Please Be Quiet, Please,* was nominated for a National Book Award in 1976. Readers and critics alike recognized the power of his hard but compassionate narrative style. Carver discovered that he had lung cancer while he was still in his mid-forties. He died just as his greatness was being recognized by a larger reading public. Carver's story collections include *What We Talk About When We Talk About Love* and *Cathedral.* He also published several books of poetry.

WHERE I'M
CALLING FROM

J.P. and I are on the front porch at Frank Martin's drying-out facility. Like the rest of us at Frank Martin's, J.P. is first and foremost a drunk. But he's also a chimney sweep. It's his first time here, and he's scared. I've been here once before. What's to say? I'm back. J.P.'s real name is Joe Penny, but he says I should call him J.P. He's about thirty years old. Younger than I am. Not much younger, but a little. He's telling me how he decided to go into his line of work, and he wants to use his hands when he talks. But his hands tremble. I mean, they won't keep still. "This has never happened to me before," he says. He means the trembling. I tell him I sympathize. I tell him the shakes will idle down. And they will. But it takes time.

We've only been in here a couple of days. We're not out of the woods yet. J.P. has these shakes, and every so often a nerve—maybe it isn't a nerve, but it's something—begins to jerk in my shoulder. Sometimes it's at the side of my neck. When this happens, my mouth dries up. It's an effort just to swallow then. I know something's about to happen and I want to head it off. I want to hide from it, that's what I want to do. Just close my eyes and let it pass by, let it take the next man. J.P. can wait a minute.

I saw a seizure yesterday morning. A guy they call Tiny. A big fat guy, an electrician from Santa Rosa. They said he'd been in here for nearly two weeks and that he was over the hump. He was going home in a day or two and would spend New Year's Eve with his wife in front of the TV. On New Year's Eve, Tiny planned to drink hot chocolate and eat cookies. Yesterday morning he seemed just fine when he came down for breakfast. He was letting out with quacking noises, showing some guy how he called ducks right down onto his head. "Blam. Blam," said Tiny, picking off a couple. Tiny's hair was damp and was slicked back along the sides of his head. He'd just come out of the shower. He'd also nicked himself on the chin with his razor. But so what? Just about everybody at Frank Martin's has nicks on his face. It's something that happens. Tiny edged in at the head of the table and began telling about something that had happened on one of his drinking bouts. People at the table laughed and shook their heads as they shoveled up their eggs. Tiny would say something, grin, then look around the table for a sign of recognition. We'd all done things just as bad and crazy, so, sure, that's why we laughed. Tiny had scrambled eggs on his plate, and some biscuits and honey. I was at the table, but I wasn't hungry. I had some coffee in front of me. Suddenly, Tiny wasn't there anymore. He'd gone over in his chair with a big clatter. He was on his back on the floor with his eyes closed, his heels drumming the linoleum. People hollered for Frank Martin. But he was right there. A couple of guys got down on the floor beside Tiny. One of the guys put his fingers inside Tiny's mouth and tried to hold his tongue. Frank Martin yelled, "Everybody stand back!" Then I noticed that the bunch of us were leaning over Tiny, just looking at him, not able to take our eyes off him. "Give him air!" Frank Martin said. Then he ran into the office and called the ambulance.

Tiny is on board again today. Talk about bouncing back. This morning Frank Martin drove the station wagon to the hospital to get him. Tiny got back too late for his eggs, but he took some coffee into the dining room and sat down at the table anyway. Somebody in the kitchen made toast for him, but Tiny didn't eat it. He just sat with his coffee and looked into his cup. Every now and then he moved his cup back and forth in front of him.

I'd like to ask him if he had any signal just before it happened. I'd like to know if he felt his ticker skip a beat, or else begin to race. Did his eyelid twitch? But I'm not about to say anything. He doesn't look like he's hot to talk about it, anyway. But what happened to Tiny is something I won't ever forget. Old Tiny flat on the floor, kicking his heels. So every time this little flitter starts up anywhere, I draw some breath and wait to find myself on my back, looking up, somebody's fingers in my mouth.

5

In his chair on the front porch, J.P. keeps his hands in his lap. I smoke cigarettes and use an old coal bucket for an ashtray. I listen to J.P. ramble on. It's eleven o'clock in the morning—an hour and a half until lunch. Neither one of us is hungry. But just the same we look forward to going inside and sitting down at the table. Maybe we'll get hungry.

What's J.P. talking about, anyway? He's saying how when he was twelve years old he fell into a well in the vicinity of the farm he grew up on. It was a dry well, lucky for him. "Or unlucky," he says, looking around him and shaking his head. He says how late that afternoon, after he'd been located, his dad hauled him out with a rope. J.P. had wet his pants down there. He'd suffered all kinds of terror in that well, hollering for help, waiting, and then hollering some more. He hollered himself hoarse before it was over. But he told me that being at the bottom of that well had made a lasting impression. He'd sat there and looked up at the well mouth. Way up at the top, he could see a circle of blue sky. Every once in a while a white cloud passed over. A flock of birds flew across, and it seemed to J.P. their wingbeats set up this odd commotion. He heard other things. He heard tiny rustlings above him in the well, which made him wonder if things might fall down into his hair. He was thinking of insects. He heard wind blow over the well mouth, and that sound made an impression on him, too. In short, everything about his life was different for him at the bottom of that well. But nothing fell on him and nothing closed off that little circle of blue. Then his dad came along with the rope, and it wasn't long before J.P. was back in the world he'd always lived in.

"Keep talking, J.P. Then what?" I say.

When he was eighteen or nineteen years old and out of high school and had nothing whatsoever he wanted to do with his life, he went across town one afternoon to visit a friend. This friend lived in a house with a fireplace. J.P. and his friend sat around drinking beer and batting the breeze. They played some records. Then the doorbell rings. The friend goes to the door. This young woman chimney sweep is there with her cleaning things. She's wearing a top hat, the sight of which knocked J.P. for a loop. She tells J.P.'s friend that she has an appointment to clean the fireplace. The friend lets her in and bows. The young woman doesn't pay him any mind. She spreads a blanket on the hearth and lays out her gear. She's wearing these black pants, black shirt, black shoes and socks. Of course, by now she's taken her hat off. J.P. says it nearly drove him nuts to look at her. She does the work, she cleans the chimney, while J.P. and his friend play records and drink beer. But they watch her and they watch what she does. Now and then J.P. and his friend look at each other and grin, or else they wink. They raise their eyebrows when the upper half of the young woman disappears into the chimney. She was all-right-looking, too, J.P. said.

When she'd finished her work, she rolled her things up in the blanket. From J.P.'s friend, she took a check that had been made out to her by his parents. And then she asks the friend if he wants to kiss her. "It's supposed to bring good luck," she says. That does it for J.P. The friend rolls his eyes. He clowns some more. Then, probably blushing, he kisses her on the cheek. At this minute, J.P. made his mind up about something. He put his beer down. He got up from the sofa. He went over to the young woman as she was starting to go out the door.   10

"Me, too?" J.P. said to her.

She swept her eyes over him. J.P. says he could feel his heart knocking. The young woman's name, it turns out, was Roxy.

"Sure," Roxy says. "Why not? I've got some extra kisses." And she kissed him a good one right on the lips and then turned to go.

Like that, quick as a wink, J.P. followed her onto the porch. He held the porch screen door for her. He went down the steps with her and out to the drive, where she'd parked her panel truck. It was something that was out of his hands. Nothing else in the world counted for anything. He knew he'd met somebody who could set his legs atremble. He could feel her kiss still burning on his lips, etc. J.P. couldn't begin to sort anything out. He was filled with sensations that were carrying him every which way.

He opened the rear door of the panel truck for her. He helped her store her things inside. "Thanks," she told him. Then he blurted it out—that he'd like to see her again. Would she go to a movie with him sometime? He'd realized, too, what he wanted to do with his life. He wanted to do what she did. He wanted to be a chimney sweep. But he didn't tell her that then.   15

J.P. says she put her hands on her hips and looked him over. Then she found a business card in the front seat of her truck. She gave it to him. She said, "Call this number after ten tonight. We can talk. I have to go now." She put the top hat on and then took it off. She looked at J.P. once more. She must have liked what she saw, because this time she grinned. He told her there was a smudge near her mouth. Then she got into her truck, tooted the horn, and drove away.

"Then what?" I say. "Don't stop now, J.P."

I was interested. But I would have listened if he'd been going on about how one day he'd decided to start pitching horseshoes.

It rained last night. The clouds are banked up against the hills across the valley. J.P. clears his throat and looks at the hills and the clouds. He pulls his chin. Then he goes on with what he was saying.

Roxy starts going out with him on dates. And little by little he talks her into letting him go along on jobs with her. But Roxy's in business with her father and brother and they've got just the right amount of work. They don't need anybody else. Besides, who was this guy J.P.? J.P. what? Watch out, they warned her.   20

So she and J.P. saw some movies together. They went to a few dances. But mainly the courtship revolved around their cleaning chimneys together. Before you know it, J.P. says, they're talking about tying the knot. And after a while they do it, they get married. J.P.'s new father-in-law takes him in as a full partner. In a year or so, Roxy has a kid. She's quit being a chimney sweep. At any rate, she's quit doing the work. Pretty soon she has another kid. J.P.'s in his midtwenties by now. He's buying a house. He says he was happy with his life. "I was happy with the way things were going," he says. "I had everything I wanted. I had a wife and kids I loved, and I was doing what I wanted to do with my life." But for some reason—who knows why we do what we do?—his drinking picks up. For a long time he drinks beer and beer only. Any kind of beer—it didn't matter. He says he could drink beer twenty-four hours a day. He'd drink beer at night while he watched TV. Sure, once in a while he drank hard stuff. But that was only if they went out on the town, which was not often, or else when they had company over. Then a time comes, he doesn't know why, when he makes the switch from beer to gin-and-tonic. And he'd have more gin-and-tonic after dinner, sitting in front of the TV. There was always a glass of gin-and-tonic in his hand. He says he actually liked the taste of it. He began stopping off after work for drinks before he went home to have more drinks. Then he began missing some dinners. He just wouldn't show up. Or else he'd show up, but he wouldn't want anything to eat. He'd filled up on snacks at the bar. Sometimes he'd walk in the door and for no good reason throw his lunch pail across the living room. When Roxy yelled at him, he'd turn around and go out again. He moved his drinking time up to early afternoon, while he was still supposed to be working. He tells me that he was starting off the morning with a couple of drinks. He'd have a belt of the stuff before he brushed his teeth. Then he'd have his coffee. He'd go to work with a thermos bottle of vodka in his lunch pail.

J.P. quits talking. He just clams up. What's going on? I'm listening. It's helping me relax, for one thing. It's taking me away from my own situation. After a minute, I say, "What the hell? Go on, J.P." He's pulling his chin. But pretty soon he starts talking again.

J.P. and Roxy are having some real fights now. I mean *fights*. J.P. says that one time she hit him in the face with her fist and broke his nose, "Look at this," he says. "Right here." He shows me a line across the bridge of his nose. "That's a broken nose." He returned the favor. He dislocated her shoulder for her. Another time he split her lip. They beat on each other in front of the kids. Things got out of hand. But he kept on drinking. He couldn't stop. And nothing could make him stop. Not even with Roxy's dad and her brother threatening to beat the hell out of him. They told Roxy she should take the kids and clear out. But Roxy said it was her problem. She got herself into it, and she'd solve it.

Now J.P. gets real quiet again. He hunches his shoulders and pulls down in his chair. He watches a car driving down the road between this place and the hills.

I say, "I want to hear the rest of this, J.P. You better keep talking."   25

"I just don't know," he says. He shrugs.

"It's all right," I say. And I mean it's okay for him to tell it. "Go on, J.P."

One way she tried to fix things, J.P. says, was by finding a boyfriend. J.P. would like to know how she found the time with the house and kids.

I look at him and I'm surprised. He's a grown man. "If you want to do that," I say, "you find the time. You make the time."

J.P. shakes his head. "I guess so," he says.   30

Anyway, he found out about it—about Roxy's boyfriend—and he went wild. He manages to get Roxy's wedding ring off her finger. And when he does, he cuts it into several pieces with a pair of wire-cutters. Good, solid fun. They'd already gone a couple of rounds on this occasion. On his way to work the next morning, he gets arrested on a drunk charge. He loses his driver's license. He can't drive the truck to work anymore. Just as well, he says. He'd already fallen off a roof the week before and broken his thumb. It was just a matter of time until he broke his neck, he says.

He was here at Frank Martin's to dry out and to figure how to get his life back on track. But he wasn't here against his will, any more than I was. We weren't locked up. We could leave any time we wanted. But a minimum stay of a week was recommended, and two weeks or a month was, as they put it, "strongly advised."

As I said, this is my second time at Frank Martin's. When I was trying to sign a check to pay in advance for a week's stay, Frank Martin said, "The holidays are always bad. Maybe you should think of sticking around a little longer this time? Think in terms of a couple of weeks. Can you do a couple of weeks? Think about it, anyway. You don't have to decide anything right now," he said. He held his thumb on the check and I signed my name. Then I walked my girlfriend to the front door and said goodbye. "Goodbye," she said, and she lurched into the doorjamb and then onto the porch. It's late afternoon. It's raining. I go from the door to the window. I move the curtain and watch her drive away. She's in my car. She's drunk. But I'm drunk, too, and there's nothing I can do. I make it to a big chair that's close to the radiator, and I sit down. Some guys look up from their TV. Then they shift back to what they were watching. I just sit there. Now and then I look up at something that's happening on the screen.

Later that afternoon the front door banged open and J.P. was brought in between these two big guys—his father-in-law and brother-in-law, I find out afterward. They steered J.P. across the room. The old guy signed him in and gave Frank Martin a check. Then these two guys helped J.P. upstairs. I guess they put him to bed. Pretty soon the old guy and the other guy came downstairs and headed for the front door. They couldn't seem to get out of this place fast enough. It was like they couldn't wait to wash their hands of all this. I didn't blame them. Hell, no. I don't know how I'd act if I was in their shoes.

A day and a half later J.P. and I meet up on the front porch. We shake hands and comment on the weather. J.P. has a case of the shakes. We sit down and prop our feet up on the railing. We lean back in our chairs like we're just out there taking our ease, like we might be getting ready to talk about our bird dogs. That's when J.P. gets going with his story.   35

It's cold out, but not too cold. It's a little overcast. Frank Martin comes outside to finish his cigar. He has on a sweater buttoned all the way up. Frank Martin is short and heavy. He has curly gray hair and a small head. His head is too small for the rest of his body. Frank Martin puts the cigar in his mouth and stands with his arms crossed over his chest. He works that cigar in his mouth and looks across the valley. He stands there like a prizefighter, like somebody who knows the score.

J.P. gets quiet again. I mean, he's hardly breathing. I toss my cigarette into the coal bucket and look hard at J.P., who scoots farther down in his chair. J.P. pulls up his collar. What the hell's going on? I wonder. Frank Martin uncrosses his arms and takes a puff on the cigar. He lets the smoke carry out of his mouth. Then he raises his chin toward the hills and says, "Jack London used to have a big place on the other side of this valley. Right over there behind that green hill you're looking at. But alcohol killed him. Let that be a lesson to you. He was a better man than any of us. But he couldn't handle the stuff, either." Frank Martin looks at what's left of his cigar. It's gone out. He tosses it into the bucket. "You guys want to read something while you're here, read that book of his, *The Call of the Wild*. You know the one I'm talk-ing about? We have it inside if you want to read something. It's about this animal that's half dog and half wolf. End of sermon," he says, and then hitches his pants up and tugs his sweater down. "I'm going inside," he says. "See you at lunch."

"I feel like a bug when he's around," J.P. says. "He makes me feel like a bug." J.P. shakes his head. Then he says, "Jack London. What a name! I wish I had me a name like that. Instead of the name I got."

My wife brought me up here the first time. That's when we were still together, try-ing to make things work out. She brought me here and she stayed around for an hour or two, talking to Frank Martin in private. Then she left. The next morning Frank Martin got me aside and said, "We can help you. If you want help and want to lis-ten to what we say." But I didn't know if they could help me or not. Part of me wanted help. But there was another part.

This time around, it was my girlfriend who drove me here. She was driving my car. She drove us through a rainstorm. We drank champagne all the way. We were both drunk when she pulled up in the drive. She intended to drop me off, turn around, and drive home again. She had things to do. One thing she had to do was to go to work the next day. She was a secretary. She had an okay job with this electronic-parts firm. She also had this mouthy teenaged son. I wanted her to get a room in town, spend the night, and then drive home. I don't know if she got the room or not. I haven't heard from her since she led me up the front steps the other day and walked me into Frank Martin's office and said, "Guess who's here."   40

But I wasn't mad at her. In the first place, she didn't have any idea what she was letting herself in for when she said I could stay with her after my wife asked me to leave. I felt sorry for her. The reason I felt sorry for her was that on the day before Christmas her Pap smear came back, and the news was not cheery. She'd have to go back to the doctor, and real soon. That kind of news was reason enough for both of us to start drinking. So what we did was get ourselves good and drunk. And on Christmas Day we were still drunk. We had to go out to a restaurant to eat, because she didn't feel like cooking. The two of us and her mouthy teenaged son opened some presents, and then we went to this steakhouse near her apartment. I wasn't hungry. I had some soup and a hot roll. I drank a bottle of wine with the soup. She drank some wine, too. Then we started in on Bloody Marys. For the next couple of days, I didn't eat anything except salted nuts. But I drank a lot of bourbon. Then I said to her, "Sugar, I think I'd better pack up. I better go back to Frank Martin's."

She tried to explain to her son that she was going to be gone for a while and he'd have to get his own food. But right as we were going out the door, this mouthy kid screamed at us. He screamed, "The hell with you! I hope you never come back. I hope you kill yourselves!" Imagine this kid!

Before we left town, I had her stop at the package store, where I bought us the champagne. We stopped someplace else for plastic glasses. Then we picked up a bucket of fried chicken. We set out for Frank Martin's in this rainstorm, drinking and listening to music. She drove. I looked after the radio and poured. We tried to make a little party of it. But we were sad, too. There was that fried chicken, but we didn't eat any.

I guess she got home okay. I think I would have heard something if she didn't. But she hasn't called me, and I haven't called her. Maybe she's had some news about herself by now. Then again, maybe she hasn't heard anything. Maybe it was all a mistake. Maybe it was somebody else's smear. But she has my car, and I have things at her house. I know we'll be seeing each other again.

They clang an old farm bell here to call you for mealtime. J.P. and I get out of our chairs and we go inside. It's starting to get too cold on the porch, anyway. We can see our breath drifting out from us as we talk. 45

New Year's Eve morning I try to call my wife. There's no answer. It's okay. But even if it wasn't okay, what am I supposed to do? The last time we talked on the phone, a couple of weeks ago, we screamed at each other. I hung a few names on her. "Wet brain!" she said, and put the phone back where it belonged.

But I wanted to talk to her now. Something had to be done about my stuff. I still had things at her house, too.

One of the guys here is a guy who travels. He goes to Europe and places. That's what he says, anyway. Business, he says. He also says he has his drinking under control and he doesn't have any idea why he's here at Frank Martin's. But he doesn't remember getting here. He laughs about it, about his not remembering. "Anyone can have a blackout," he says. "That doesn't prove a thing." He's not a drunk—he tells us this and we listen. "That's a serious charge to make," he says. "That kind of talk can ruin a good man's prospects." He says that if he'd only stick to whiskey and water, no ice, he'd never have these blackouts. It's the ice they put into your drink that does it. "Who do you know in Egypt?" he asks me. "I can use a few names over there."

For New Year's Eve dinner Frank Martin serves steak and baked potato. My appetite's coming back. I clean up everything on my plate and I could eat more. I look over at Tiny's plate. Hell, he's hardly touched a thing. His steak is just sitting there. Tiny is not the same old Tiny. The poor bastard had planned to be at home tonight. He'd planned to be in his robe and slippers in front of the TV, holding hands with his wife. Now he's afraid to leave. I can understand. One seizure means you're ready for another. Tiny hasn't told any more nutty stories on himself since it happened. He's stayed quiet and kept to himself. I ask him if I can have his steak, and he pushes his plate over to me.

Some of us are still up, sitting around the TV, watching Times Square, when Frank Martin comes in to show us his cake. He brings it around and shows it to each of us. I know he didn't make it. It's just a bakery cake. But it's still a cake. It's a big white cake. Across the top there's writing in pink letters. The writing says, HAPPY NEW YEAR—ONE DAY AT A TIME. 50

"I don't want any fucking cake," says the guy who goes to Europe and places. "Where's the champagne?" he says, and laughs.

We all go into the dining room. Frank Martin cuts the cake. I sit next to J.P. He eats two pieces and drinks a Coke. I eat a piece and wrap another piece in a napkin, thinking of later.

J.P. lights a cigarette—his hands are steady now—and he tells me his wife is coming in the morning, the first day of the new year.

"That's great," I say. I nod. I lick the frosting off my finger. "That's good news, J.P."

"I'll introduce you," he says. 55

"I look forward to it," I say.

We say goodnight. We say Happy New Year. I use a napkin on my fingers. We shake hands.

I go to the phone, put in a dime, and call my wife collect. But nobody answers this time, either. I think about calling my girlfriend, and I'm dialing her number when

I realize I really don't want to talk to her. She's probably at home watching the same thing on TV that I've been watching. Anyway, I don't want to talk to her. I hope she's okay. But if she has something wrong with her, I don't want to know about it.

After breakfast, J.P. and I take coffee out to the porch. The sky is clear, but it's cold enough for sweaters and jackets.

"She asked me if she should bring the kids," J.P. says. "I told her she should keep the kids at home. Can you imagine? My God, I don't want my kids up here."   60

We use the coal bucket for an ashtray. We look across the valley to where Jack London used to live. We're drinking more coffee when this car turns off the road and comes down the drive.

"That's her!" J.P. says. He puts his cup next to his chair. He gets up and goes down the steps.

I see this woman stop the car and set the brake. I see J.P. open the door. I watch her get out, and I see them hug each other. I look away. Then I look back. J.P. takes her by the arm and they come up the stairs. This woman broke a man's nose once. She has had two kids, and much trouble, but she loves this man who has her by the arm. I get up from the chair.

"This is my friend," J.P. says to his wife. "Hey, this is Roxy."

Roxy takes my hand. She's a tall, good-looking woman in a knit cap. She has on a coat, a heavy sweater, and slacks. I recall what J.P. told me about the boyfriend and the wirecutters. I don't see any wedding ring. That's in pieces somewhere, I guess. Her hands are broad and the fingers have these big knuckles. This is a woman who can make fists if she has to.   65

"I've heard about you," I say. "J.P. told me how you got acquainted. Something about a chimney, J.P. said."

"Yes, a chimney," she says. "There's probably a lot else he didn't tell you," she says. "I bet he didn't tell you everything," she says, and laughs. Then—she can't wait any longer—she slips her arm around J.P. and kisses him on the check. They start to move to the door. "Nice meeting you," she says. "Hey, did he tell you he's the best sweep in the business?"

"Come on now, Roxy," J.P. says. He has his hand on the doorknob.

"He told me he learned everything he knew from you," I say.

"Well, that much is sure true," she says. She laughs again. But it's like she's thinking about something else. J.P. turns the doorknob. Roxy lays her hand over his. "Joe, can't we go into town for lunch? Can't I take you someplace?"   70

J.P. clears his throat. He says, "It hasn't been a week yet." He takes his hand off the doorknob and brings his fingers to his chin. "I think they'd like it if I didn't leave the place for a little while yet. We can have some coffee here," he says.

"That's fine," she says. Her eyes work over to me again. "I'm glad Joe's made a friend. Nice to meet you," she says.

They start to go inside. I know it's a dumb thing to do, but I do it anyway. "Roxy," I say. And they stop in the doorway and look at me. "I need some luck," I say. "No kidding. I could do with a kiss myself."

J.P. looks down. He's still holding the knob, even though the door is open. He turns the knob back and forth. But I keep looking at her. Roxy grins. "I'm not a sweep anymore," she says. "Not for years. Didn't Joe tell you that? But, sure, I'll kiss you, sure."

She moves over. She takes me by the shoulders—I'm a big man—and she plants this kiss on my lips. "How's that?" she says.   75

"That's fine," I say.

"Nothing to it," she says. She's still holding me by the shoulders. She's looking me right in the eyes. "Good luck," she says, and then she lets go of me.

"See you later, pal," J.P. says. He opens the door all the way, and they go in.

I sit down on the front steps and light a cigarette. I watch what my hand does, then I blow out the match. I've got the shakes. I started out with them this morning. This morning I wanted something to drink. It's depressing, but I didn't say anything about it to J.P. I try to put my mind on something else.

I'm thinking about chimney sweeps—all that stuff I heard from J.P.—when for some reason I start to think about a house my wife and I once lived in. That house didn't have a chimney, so I don't know what makes me remember it now. But I remember the house and how we'd only been in there a few weeks when I heard a noise outside one morning. It was Sunday morning and it was still dark in the bedroom. But there was this pale light coming in from the bedroom window. I listened. I could hear something scrape against the side of the house. I jumped out of bed and went to look.

"My God!" my wife says, sitting up in bed and shaking the hair away from her face. Then she starts to laugh. "It's Mr. Venturini," she says. "I forgot to tell you. He said he was coming to paint the house today. Early. Before it gets too hot. I forgot all about it," she says, and laughs. "Come on back to bed, honey. It's just him."

"In a minute," I say.

I push the curtain away from the window. Outside, this old guy in white coveralls is standing next to his ladder. The sun is just starting to break above the mountains. The old guy and I look each other over. It's the landlord, all right—this old guy in coveralls. But his coveralls are too big for him. He needs a shave, too. And he's wearing this baseball cap to cover his bald head. Goddamn it, I think, if he isn't a weird old fellow. And a wave of happiness comes over me that I'm not him—that I'm me and that I'm inside this bedroom with my wife.

He jerks his thumb toward the sun. He pretends to wipe his forehead. He's letting me know he doesn't have all that much time. He breaks into a grin. It's then I realize I'm naked. I look down at myself. I look at him again and shrug. What did he expect?

My wife laughs. "Come *on*," she says. "Get back in this bed. Right now. This minute. Come on back to bed."

I let go of the curtain. But I keep standing there at the window. I can see the old fellow nod to himself like he's saying, "Go on, sonny, go back to bed. I understand." He tugs on the bill of his cap. Then he sets about his business. He picks up his bucket. He starts climbing the ladder.

I lean back into the step behind me now and cross one leg over the other. Maybe later this afternoon I'll try calling my wife again. And then I'll call to see what's happening with my girlfriend. But I don't want to get her mouthy kid on the line. If I do call, I hope he'll be out somewhere doing whatever he does when he's not around the house. I try to remember if I ever read any Jack London books. I can't remember. But there was a story of his I read in high school. "To Build a Fire," it was called. This guy in the Yukon is freezing. Imagine it—he's actually going to freeze to death if he can't get a fire going. With a fire, he can dry his socks and things and warm himself.

He gets his fire going, but then something happens to it. A branchful of snow drops on it. It goes out. Meanwhile, it's getting colder. Night is coming on.

I bring some change out of my pocket. I'll try my wife first. If she answers, I'll wish her a Happy New Year. But that's it. I won't bring up business. I won't raise my voice. Not even if she starts something. She'll ask me where I'm calling from, and I'll have to tell her. I won't say anything about New Year's resolutions. There's no way to make a joke out of this. After I talk to her, I'll call my girlfriend. Maybe I'll call her first. I'll just have to hope I don't get her kid on the line. "Hello, sugar," I'll say when she answers. "It's me."

Luisa Valenzuela (1938–)

Luisa Valenzuela was born in Buenos Aires, Argentina. She has lived for many years in New York City, working as a journalist. Her translated works include *Clara, Strange Things Happen Here,* and *Other Weapons.*

I'M YOUR HORSE IN THE NIGHT

The doorbell rang: three short rings and one long one. That was the signal, and I got up, annoyed and a little frightened; it could be them, and then again, maybe not; at these ungodly hours of the night it could be a trap. I opened the door expecting anything except him, face to face, at last.

He came in quickly and locked the door behind him before embracing me. So much in character, so cautious, first and foremost checking his—our—rear guard. Then he took me in his arms without saying a word, not even holding me too tight but letting all the emotions of our new encounter overflow, telling me so much by merely holding me in his arms and kissing me slowly. I think he never had much faith in words, and there he was, as silent as ever, sending me messages in the form of caresses.

We finally stepped back to look at one another from head to foot, not eye to eye, out of focus. And I was able to say Hello showing scarcely any surprise despite all those months when I had no idea where he could have been, and I was able to say

I thought you were fighting up north
I thought you'd been caught
I thought you were in hiding
I thought you'd been tortured and killed
I thought you were theorizing about the revolution in another country

Just one of many ways to tell him I'd been thinking of him, I hadn't stopped thinking of him or felt as if I'd been betrayed. And there he was, always so god-damn cautious, so much the master of his actions.

430

"Quiet, Chiquita. You're much better off not knowing what I've been up to." 5

Then he pulled out his treasures, potential clues that at the time eluded me: a bottle of cachça and a Gal Costa record. What had he been up to in Brazil? What was he planning to do next? What had brought him back, risking his life, knowing they were after him? Then I stopped asking myself questions (quiet, Chiquita, he'd say). Come here, Chiquita, he was saying, and I chose to let myself sink into the joy of having him back again, trying not to worry. What would happen to us tomorrow, and the days that followed?

Cachça's a good drink. It goes down and up and down all the right tracks, and then stops to warm up the corners that need it most. Gal Costa's voice is hot, she envelops us in its sound and half-dancing, half-floating, we reach the bed. We lie down and keep on staring deep into each other's eyes, continue caressing each other without allowing ourselves to give into the pure senses just yet. We continue recognizing, rediscovering each other.

Beto, I say, looking at him. I know that isn't his real name, but it's the only one I can call him out loud. He replies:

"We'll make it someday, Chiquita, but let's not talk now."

It's better that way. Better if he doesn't start talking about how we'll make it someday and ruin the wonder of what we're about to attain right now, the two of us, all alone. 10

"A noite eu so teu cavalo," Gal Costa suddenly sings from the record player.

"I'm your horse in the night," I translate slowly. And so as to bind him in a spell and stop him from thinking about other things:

"It's a saint's song, like in the *macumba*. Someone who's in a trance says she's the horse of the spirit who's riding her, she's his mount."

"Chiquita, you're always getting carried away with esoteric meanings and witchcraft. You know perfectly well that she isn't talking about spirits. If you're my horse in the night it's because I ride you, like this, see? . . . Like this . . . That's all."

It was so long, so deep and so insistent, so charged with affection that we ended up exhausted. I fell asleep with him still on top of me. 15

I'm your horse in the night.

The goddamn phone pulled me out in waves from a deep well. Making an enormous effort to wake up, I walked over to the receiver, thinking it could be Beto, sure, who was no longer by my side, sure, following his inveterate habit of running away while I'm asleep without a word about where he's gone. To protect me, he says.

From the other end of the line, a voice I thought belonged to Andrés—the one we call Andrés—began to tell me:

"They found Beto dead, floating down the river near the other bank. It looks as if they threw him alive out of a chopper. He's all bloated and decomposed after six days in the water, but I'm almost sure it's him."

"No, it can't be Beto," I shouted carelessly. Suddenly the voice no longer sounded like Andrés: it felt foreign, impersonal. 20

"You think so?"

"Who is this?" Only then did I think to ask. But that very moment they hung up.

Ten, fifteen minutes? How long must I have stayed there staring at the phone like an idiot until the police arrived? I didn't expect them. But, then again, how could I not? Their hands feeling me, their voices insulting and threatening, the house searched, turned inside out. But I already knew. So what did I care if they broke every breakable object and tore apart my dresser?

They wouldn't find a thing. My only real possession was a dream and they can't deprive me of my dreams just like that. My dream the night before, when Beto was there with me and we loved each other. I'd dreamed it, dreamed every bit of it, I was deeply convinced that I'd dreamed it all in the richest detail, even in full color. And dreams are none of the cops' business.

They want reality, tangible facts, the kind I couldn't even begin to give them. 25

Where is he, you saw him, he was here with you, where did he go? Speak up, or you'll be sorry. Let's hear you sing, bitch, we know he came to see you, where is he, where is he holed up? He's in the city, come on, spill it, we know he came to get you.

I haven't heard a word from him in months. He abandoned me, I haven't heard from him in months. He ran away, went underground. What do I know, he ran off with someone else, he's in another country. What do I know, he abandoned me, I hate him, I know nothing.

(Go ahead, burn me with your cigarettes, kick me all you wish, threaten, go ahead, stick a mouse in me so it'll eat my insides out, pull my nails out, do as you please. Would I make something up for that? Would I tell you he was here when a thousand years ago he left me forever?)

I'm not about to tell them my dreams. Why should they care? I haven't seen that so-called Beto in more than six months, and I loved him. The man simply vanished. I only run into him in my dreams, and they're bad dreams that often become nightmares.

Beto, you know now, if it's true that they killed you, or wherever you may be, Beto, I'm your horse in the night and you can inhabit me whenever you wish, even if I'm behind bars. Beto, now that I'm in jail I know that I dreamed you that night; it was just a dream. And if by some wild chance there's a Gal Costa record and a half-empty bottle of cachça in my house, I hope they'll forgive me: I will them out of existence. 30

Translated by Deborah Bonner

Amy Hempel (1951–)

Amy Hempel was born in Chicago. She lived for a time on the West Coast, where many of the stories in her collection *Reasons to Live* are set. She now makes her home in New York.

Hempel's stories are aggressively contemporary. She favors sketchy plot lines and builds her narratives around snapshots of characters interacting. These features, combined with her penchant for details incorporated from the brand-name present, make her a good representative of the so-called minimalist camp. Her humor and keen ear for speech habits are some of Hempel's distinguishing features as a writer.

IN THE CEMETERY
WHERE AL JOLSON°
IS BURIED

"Tell me things I won't mind forgetting," she said. "Make it useless stuff or skip it."

I began. I told her insects fly through rain, missing every drop, never getting wet. I told her no one in America owned a tape recorder before Bing Crosby did. I told her the shape of the moon is like a banana—you see it looking full, you're seeing it end-on.

The camera made me self-conscious and I stopped. It was trained on us from a ceiling mount—the kind of camera banks use to photograph robbers. It played us to the nurses down the hall in Intensive Care.

"Go on, girl," she said. "You get used to it."

I had my audience. I went on. Did she know that Tammy Wynette° had changed her tune? Really. That now she sings "Stand by Your *Friends*"? That Paul Anka° did it too, I said. Does "You're Having *Our* Baby." That he got sick of all that feminist bitching. 5

"What else?" she said. "Have you got something else?"

Oh, yes.

For her I would always have something else.

"Did you know that when they taught the first chimp to talk, it lied? That when they asked her who did it on the desk, she signed back the name of the janitor. And that when they pressed her, she said she was sorry, that it was really the project director. But she was a mother, so I guess she had her reasons."

"Oh, that's good," she said. "A parable." 10

"There's more about the chimp," I said. "But it will break your heart."

"No, thanks," she says, and scratches at her mask.

We look like good-guy outlaws. Good or bad, I am not used to the mask yet. I keep touching the warm spot where my breath, thank God, comes out. She is used to hers. She only ties the strings on top. The other ones—a pro by now—she lets hang loose.

We call this place the Marcus Welby° Hospital. It's the white one with the palm trees under the opening credits of all those shows. A Hollywood hospital, though in fact it is several miles west. Off camera, there is a beach across the street.

She introduces me to a nurse as the Best Friend. The impersonal article is more intimate. It tells me that *they* are intimate, the nurse and my friend. 15

"I was telling her we used to drink Canada Dry ginger ale and pretend we were in Canada."

Al Jolson: (1886–1950) American entertainer; he starred in blackface in the first "talkie" film, *The Jazz Singer.*
Tammy Wynette: a country singer, known for her hit "Stand By Your Man."
Paul Anka: a popular singer in the late 1950s and early 1960s.
Marcus Welby: doctor in a hospital-based television drama in the 1960s.

"That's how dumb we were," I say.

"You could be sisters," the nurse says.

So how come, I'll bet they are wondering, it took me so long to get to such a glamorous place? But do they ask?

They do not ask.

Two months, and how long is the drive?

The best I can explain it is this—I have a friend who worked one summer in a mortuary. He used to tell me stories. The one that really got to me was not the grisliest, but it's the one that did. A man wrecked his car on 101 going south. He did not lose consciousness. But his arm was taken down to the wet bone—and when he looked at it—it scared him to death.

I mean, he died.

So I hadn't dared to look any closer. But now I'm doing it—and hoping that I will live through it.

She shakes out a summer-weight blanket, showing a leg you did not want to see. Except for that, you look at her and understand the law that requires *two* people to be with the body at all times.

"I thought of something," she says. "I thought of it last night. I think there is a real and present need here. You know," she says, "like for someone to do it for you when you can't do it yourself. You call them up whenever you want—like when push comes to shove."

She grabs the bedside phone and loops the cord around her neck.

"Hey," she says, "the end o' the line."

She keeps on, giddy with something. But I don't know with what.

"I can't remember," she says. "What does Kübler-Ross° say comes after Denial?"

It seems to me Anger must be next. Then Bargaining, Depression, and so on and so forth. But I keep my guesses to myself.

"The only thing is," she says, "is where's Resurrection? God knows, I want to do it by the book. But she left out Resurrection."

She laughs, and I cling to the sound the way someone dangling above a ravine holds fast to the thrown rope.

"Tell me," she says, "about that chimp with the talking hands. What do they do when the thing ends and the chimp says, 'I don't want to go back to the zoo'?"

When I don't say anything, she says, "Okay—then tell me another animal story. I like animal stories. But not a sick one—I don't want to know about all the seeing-eye dogs going blind."

No, I would not tell her a sick one.

"How about the hearing-ear dogs?" I say. "They're not going deaf, but they are getting very judgmental. For instance, there's this golden retriever in New Jersey, he wakes up the deaf mother and drags her into the daughter's room because the kid has got a flashlight and is reading under the covers."

Kübler-Ross: psychologist Elizabeth Kübler-Ross; her book *On Death and Dying* describes stages in a patient's acceptance of death.

"Oh, you're killing me," she says. "Yes, you're definitely killing me."

"They say the smart dog obeys, but the smarter dog knows when to disobey."

"Yes," she says, "the smarter anything knows when to disobey. Now, for example." 40

She is flirting with the Good Doctor, who has just appeared. Unlike the Bad Doctor, who checks the IV drip before saying good morning, the Good Doctor says things like "God didn't give epileptics a fair shake." The Good Doctor awards himself points for the cripples he could have hit in the parking lot. Because the Good Doctor is a little in love with her, he says maybe a year. He pulls a chair up to her bed and suggests I might like to spend an hour on the beach.

"Bring me something back," she says. "Anything from the beach. Or the gift shop. Taste is no object."

He draws the curtain around her bed.

"Wait!" she cries.

I look in at her. 45

"Anything," she says, "except a magazine subscription."

The doctor turns away.

I watch her mouth laugh.

What seems dangerous often is not—black snakes, for example, or clear-air turbulence. While things that just lie there, like this beach, are loaded with jeopardy. A yellow dust rising from the ground, the heat that ripens melons overnight—this is earthquake weather. You can sit here braiding the fringe on your towel and the sand will all of a sudden suck down like an hourglass. The air roars. In the cheap apartments on-shore, bathtubs fill themselves and gardens roll up and over like green waves. If nothing happens, the dust will drift and the heat deepen till fear turns to desire. Nerves like that are only bought off by catastrophe.

"It never happens when you're thinking about it," she once observed. "Earthquake, earthquake, earthquake," she said. 50

"Earthquake, earthquake, earthquake," I said.

Like the aviaphobe° who keeps the plane aloft with prayer, we kept it up until an aftershock cracked the ceiling.

That was after the big one in seventy-two. We were in college; our dormitory was five miles from the epi-center. When the ride was over and my jabbering pulse began to slow, she served five parts champagne to one part orange juice, and joked about living in Ocean View, Kansas. I offered to drive her to Hawaii on the new world psychics predicted would surface the next time, or the next.

I could not say that now—next.

Whose next? she could ask. 55

Was I the only one who noticed that the experts had stopped saying *if* and now spoke of *when*? Of course not; the fearful ran to thousands. We watched the traffic of Japanese beetles for deviation. Deviation might mean more natural violence.

---

aviaphobe: one who is afraid of flying.

I wanted her to be afraid with me. But she said, "I don't know. I'm just not."

She was afraid of nothing, not even of flying.

I have this dream before a flight where we buckle in and the plane moves down the runway. It takes off at thirty-five miles an hour, and then we're airborne, skimming the tree tops. Still, we arrive in New York on time.

It is so pleasant. 60

One night I flew to Moscow this way.

She flew with me once. That time she flew with me she ate macadamia nuts while the wings bounced. She knows the wing tips can bend thirty feet up and thirty feet down without coming off. She believes it. She trusts the law of aerodynamics. My mind stampedes. I can almost accept that a battleship floats when everybody knows steel sinks.

I see fear in her now, and am not going to try to talk her out of it. She is right to be afraid.

After a quake, the six o'clock news airs a film clip of first-graders yelling at the broken playground per their teacher's instructions.

"*Bad* earth!" they shout, because anger is stronger than fear. 65

But the beach is standing still today. Everyone on it is tranquilized, numb, or asleep. Teenaged girls rub coconut oil on each other's hard-to-reach places. They smell like macaroons. They pry open compacts like clam-shells; mirrors catch the sun and throw a spray of white rays across glazed shoulders. The girls arrange their wet hair with silk flowers the way they learned in *Seventeen*. They pose.

A formation of low-riders pulls over to watch with a six-pack. They get vocal when the girls check their tan lines. When the beer is gone, so are they—flexing their cars on up the boulevard.

Above this aggressive health are the twin wrought-iron terraces, painted flamingo pink, of the Palm Royale. Someone dies there every time the sheets are changed. There's an ambulance in the driveway, so the remaining residents line the balconies, rocking and not talking, one-upped.

The ocean they stare at is dangerous, and not just the undertow. You can almost see the slapping tails of sand sharks keeping cruising bodies alive.

If she looked, she could see this, some of it, from her window. She would be the first to say how little it takes to make a thing all wrong. 70

There was a second bed in the room when I got back to it!

For two beats I didn't get it. Then it hit me like an open coffin.

She wants every minute, I thought. She wants my life.

"You missed Gussie," she said.

Gussie is her parents' three-hundred-pound narcoleptic maid. Her attacks often come at the ironing board. The pillowcases in that family are all bordered with scorch. 75

"It's a hard trip for her," I said. "How is she?"

"Well, she didn't fall asleep, if that's what you mean. Gussie's great—you know what she said? She said, 'Darlin', stop this worriation. Just keep prayin', down on your knees'—me, who can't even get out of bed."

She shrugged. "What am I missing?"

"It's earthquake weather," I told her.

"The best thing to do about earthquakes," she said, "is not to live in California." 80

436 A Fiction Anthology

"That's useful," I said. "You sound like Reverend Ike°—'The best thing to do for the poor is not to be one of them.'

We're crazy about Reverend Ike.

I noticed her face was bloated.

"You know," she said, "I feel like hell. I'm about to stop having fun."

"The ancients have a saying," I said. " 'There are times when the wolves are silent; there are times when the moon howls.' "　　　　　　　　　　　85

"What's that, Navaho?"

"Palm Royale lobby graffiti," I said. "I bought a paper there. I'll read you something."

"Even though I care about nothing?"

I turned to the page with the trivia column. I said, "Did you know the more shrimp flamingo birds eat, the pinker their feathers get?" I said, "Did you know that Eskimos need refrigerators? Do you know *why* Eskimos need refrigerators? Did you know that Eskimos need refrigerators because how else would they keep their food from freezing?"

I turned to page three, to a UPI filler datelined Mexico City. I read her MAN ROBS BANK WITH CHICKEN, about a man who bought a barbecued chicken at a stand down the block from a bank. Passing the bank, he got the idea. He walked in and approached a teller. He pointed the brown paper bag at her and she handed over the day's receipts. It was the smell of barbecue sauce that eventually led to his capture.　　90

The story had made her hungry, she said—so I took the elevator down six floors to the cafeteria, and brought back all the ice cream she wanted. We lay side by side, adjustable beds cranked up for optimal TV-viewing, littering the sheets with Good Humor wrappers, picking toasted almonds out of the gauze. We were Lucy and Ethel, Mary and Rhoda° in extremis. The blinds were closed to keep light off the screen.

We watched a movie starring men we used to think we wanted to sleep with. Hers was a tough cop out to stop mine, a vicious rapist who went after cocktail waitresses.

"This is a good movie," she said when snipers felled them both.

I missed her already.

A Filipino nurse tiptoed in and gave her an injection. The nurse removed the pile of popsicle sticks from the nightstand—enough to splint a small animal.　　95

The injection made us both sleepy. We slept.

I dreamed she was a decorator, come to furnish my house. She worked in secret, singing to herself. When she finished, she guided me proudly to the door. "How do you like it?" she asked, easing me inside.

Every beam and sill and shelf and knob was draped in gay bunting, with streamers of pastel crepe looped around bright mirrors.

"I have to go home," I said when she woke up.

She thought I meant home to her house in the Canyon, and I had to say No, *home* home. I twisted my hands in the time-honored fashion of people in pain. I was supposed to offer something. The Best Friend. I could not even offer to come back.　　100

Reverend Ike: a broadcast preacher.

Lucy and Ethel; Mary and Rhoda: "best-friend" characters in the popular TV sitcoms "I Love Lucy" and "The Mary Tyler Moore Show."

I felt weak and small and failed.

Also exhilarated.

I had a convertible in the parking lot. Once out of that room, I would drive it too fast down the Coast high-way through the crab-smelling air. A stop in Malibu for sangria. The music in the place would be sexy and loud. They'd serve papaya and shrimp and watermelon ice. After dinner I would shimmer with lust, buzz with heat, vibrate with life, and stay up all night.

Without a word, she yanked off her mask and threw it on the floor. She kicked at the blankets and moved to the door. She must have hated having to pause for breath and balance before slamming out of Isolation, and out of the second room, the one where you scrub and tie on the white masks.

A voice shouted her name in alarm, and people ran down the corridor. The Good Doctor was paged over the intercom. I opened the door and the nurses at the station stared hard, as if this flight had been my idea.

"Where is she?" I asked, and they nodded to the supply closet.

I looked in. Two nurses were kneeling beside her on the floor, talking to her in low voices. One held a mask over her nose and mouth, the other rubbed her back in slow circles. The nurses glanced up to see if I was the doctor—and when I wasn't, they went back to what they were doing.

"There, there, honey," they cooed.

On the morning she was moved to the cemetery, the one where Al Jolson is buried, I enrolled in a "Fear of Flying" class. "What is your worst fear?" the instructor asked, and I answered, "That I will finish this course and still be afraid."

I sleep with a glass of water on the nightstand so I can see by its level if the coastal earth is trembling or if the shaking is still me.

What do I remember?

I remember only the useless things I hear—that Bob Dylan's mother invented Wite-Out, that twenty-three people must be in a room before there is a fifty-fifty chance two will have the same birthday. Who cares whether or not it's true? In my head there are bath towels swaddling this stuff. Nothing else seeps through.

I review those things that will figure in the retelling: a kiss through surgical gauze, the pale hand correcting the position of the wig. I noted these gestures as they happened, not in any retrospect—though I don't know why looking back should show us more than looking *at*.

It is just possible I will say I stayed the night.

And who is there that can say that I did not?

I think of the chimp, the one with the talking hands.

In the course of the experiment, that chimp had a baby. Imagine how her trainers must have thrilled when the mother, without prompting, began to sign to her newborn.

Baby, drink milk.

Baby, play ball.

And when the baby died, the mother stood over the body, her wrinkled hands moving with animal grace, forming again and again the words: Baby, come hug, Baby, come hug, fluent now in the language of grief.

A Fiction Anthology

Ralph Lombreglia (1951–)

Ralph Lombreglia grew up in a working-class family in New Jersey. He began publishing his inventive and idiosyncratic short stories in the 1980s, and he has seen several included in the prestigious *Best American Short Stories* series. His two collections are *Men Under Water* (1990) and *Make Me Work* (1994). Lombreglia is an amateur jazz guitarist and has an abiding interest in computer technologies. He recently co-produced a CD-ROM on the life and work of Jack Kerouac. Lombreglia lives and works in the Boston area.

MEN UNDER WATER

The Peter Pan Diner, 10:30 A.M. Breakfast with Gunther.

"You're depressed again," Gunther says to me. "I can tell." He has the catsup bottle in one fist like a chisel or a caulking gun, and with the heel of his other hand he's hammering catsup over his hash browns and scrambled eggs. He's getting some on the bacon and toast, too.

"I'm not depressed," I say.

"You're not eating."

"Gunther, I eat at home, remember? At breakfast time. I never eat here."

He slips into his pouting voice. "You used to," he says.   5

This is a bad sign. It means that Gunther is especially needy and delusional today. I haven't ordered anything but coffee in the Peter Pan since the first week I worked for him, more than six months ago.

I look at him, busying himself with breakfast on the other side of the booth. Lately I've spent more hours of each week with Gunther than I've spent with my wife, and still there are times—this moment is one of them—when I see him as I saw him the day we met, times when I cannot get beyond the amazing epidermal surface of the man. Gunther is one of the largest people I've ever known, but it's more than that, more than his general enormousness, the smooth expanse of his completely bald head, the perfect beardlessness of his broad face. Gunther has no eyebrows, no body hair whatsoever as far as I know; even the large nostrils of his great, wide nose are pink hairless tunnels running up into his skull. His velour pullover is open to his sternum, and the exposed chest is precisely the complexion of all the rest of him—the shrimplike color of new Play-Doh, the substance from which Gunther sometimes seems to be made. Under the movie lights he likes to muck around with, his skin goes translucent and you can watch the blood vessels keeping him alive.

"If you're not depressed," he says around a mouthful of catsup and eggs, "what are you?"

"Subdued," I say.   10

"Oh," he says. "Well, would you mind knocking off being subdued? You're not putting out any energy. I can't do it all by myself."

"Do what?"

"Write this goddam screenplay," he says.

"Oh. Which screenplay is this?"

"You know perfectly well which screenplay. The sci-fi one with the giant radioactive crayfish and the girl scientist who understands them, and who's also the love interest for the guy scientist. The one we've been working on all week."

"Oh, that one," I say. "I forgot. I thought maybe you meant the Kung Fu screenplay. I guess that was last week."

"You want to work on that one? Hey, we could even do a hybrid of the two. Say these huge radioactive crayfish attack mankind with a sort of lobster version of Kung Fu, bopping people with their big claws. The guy scientist also happens to be a martial-arts master. In the end, he conquers the lobsters by building robots programmed to hit them in their pressure points. But before that there's a scene where the lobsters grab the girl and he has to take a couple of them down with his bare hands."

"No, Gunther." I sip my coffee and stare out the window above the personal jukebox mounted on the wall of our booth. The jukebox is playing Roy Orbison's "Pretty Woman," Gunther's favorite song. He put it on to cheer me up.

Outside, a light gray ash is failing from the sky like rain. Cleveland has a lot of smokestack industry, and the Peter Pan is one of the venerable old smokestack-area diners. That's why we come here to eat. Not because we work in the plants ourselves—our work, like God, is everywhere and nowhere—but because this is where reality is, the life and labor of the folk, the source of all art. Someday, after he's made the two or three commercial pictures that will establish him as one of the major film forces of our time, Gunther wants to celebrate his native city in a cinematic tone poem about the ballet of heavy manufacture, the romance of rubber and steel.

I show him my wristwatch. "What about the Puerto Rican couple on Liberty Place with the gas leak in their stove? Or the nursing students on Meadow with no hot water? You told them today for sure. And your answering service. I'll bet you didn't call your answering service. You'll call it at three this afternoon, and then we'll have to work until nine tonight."

Gunther throws his fork onto his plate. People at the counter turn on their stools to look at us. "This is your whole problem," he says. He clangs his coffee cup with his spoon to get the attention of our waitress. It's Alice today, a good woman. If Gunther gets too abusive, she'll pour coffee in his lap. She's done it before. She comes over now and fills our cups.

"I try to foster a creative spirit," Gunther says to me. Alice flashes him a look, the coffeepot poised in the air. He stops talking and stares at the table until she's gone on her way. "I try to pay you for your imagination," he says, "not just for dumb monkey work I could get anybody to do. I try to treat you like an artist. And all you want to do is fix toilets." He picks up the cream and sugar and pours long streams of each into his cup. Then he starts the singsongy voice. "Yes, for a certain number of hours each week we have to do some essentially noncreative work, things that are not really what artists like us should be doing—painting apartments, replacing water heaters, fixing toilets. But it keeps us humble, I say. I try to be philosophical about it. I don't go into a mood just because I can't work on my movies every minute of every day."

"I left my house three hours ago, Gunther."

"Here we go again," he says.

He doesn't start paying my hourly wages until we leave the diner. But if I don't go over to Gunther's house each morning and wake him up and, while he takes a shower, watch parts of movies he's videotaped, and then listen to him rant about screenplays over breakfast at the Peter Pan, we won't go to work at all and I won't be paid anything. 25

He turns to the jukebox and speaks to Roy Orbison. "Roy," he says, "what am I going to do with this guy? Sensitive and gifted, yes, but he has real limitations. He actually wants to work for wages." He turns back to me. "You're not being flexible," he says. "That's a major character flaw; you should watch that. How many times have I explained this to you? You're working for—and will soon be the partner of— an important motion picture producer who happens at the moment to be trapped inside a landlord's body."

"That's not how it was advertised," I say. "It was advertised: 'Handyman and general helper, no experience necessary.' That's the ad I responded to. You changed it to scriptwriter after I was hired."

"After I discovered the talent I can't let you throw away, even if you want to. A good part of each week is ours to be talented together, you and me. We toss some ideas back and forth"—he slaps my shoulder—"and in a couple of weeks we have a screenplay. I round up some investors, we start shooting the movie, we're on our way. We could have made some progress on this movie right here at breakfast, but no, you're subdued. You think that just because we have to go fix a toilet today, that's all we are, two guys who have to fix a toilet, and you let it get you down."

"What toilet?" I say. "You're keeping something from me."

"Weren't you the one who wanted me to call my answering service?" 30

He stands up and tosses his wadded napkin onto his plate, smiling and bobbing his head from side to side like Hardy to Laurel. He leans toward me over the table as if to confide a great truth, a truth that will be true long after everything else is dust. "Rock band," he says, and strides away from the booth. Then he comes back, doing his wicked leer. "The horror, the horror," he adds.

We pay our bill and stroll out of the Peter Pan into the sunlight and ashes, me in my paint-spattered carpenter's pants and sweatshirt, Gunther swaggering in his red-and-yellow-striped velour pullover and racing shades. It's 11:30 A.M., almost time for lunch. The rest of the world has already accomplished much since waking, and laid down foundations for the accomplishment of much more. We have ac- complished nothing. But neither have we yet lost everything, I remind myself. We still have much of what we had when the day began. I have my job with Gunther— twenty dollars an hour under the table, starting now—and Gunther has his small real estate empire, his Ford Bronco, the ability to pay me twenty dollars for each hour I ride around in it with him, and an unflagging, magical belief in the rightness of his life and methods despite all evidence to the contrary.

And he has me. We have each other.

Tina, my wife, cannot believe I continue to hold this job. We need the money, but Tina has had enough. She can't take any more stories about Gunther. She can't take what working for Gunther is doing to me. I'm no longer the man she married, Tina says. My inability to leave Gunther has raised serious questions about the deep struc- ture of my personality, and now Tina wants us both to go in for counseling. She says she's become a kind of co-alcoholic, living through my experiences with this man.

She's had to go through it all with me, even though it's not her life, and now in some perverse way she feels that she works for Gunther too.

Every night when I get home I must drink for one full hour and rail to Tina about Gunther. I tell her what Gunther has done to me that day, what he's done to his tenants, the lies he's made me tell the tenants about those things, the movie-script ideas he's forced me to invent. After an hour I'm usually able to take a shower and have dinner. But it's growing longer now, up to two hours sometimes. At first it was exotic and Tina enjoyed it. Every night I would bring home amazing new stories. Tina would listen and shake her head in wonder, marveling over the character of Gunther, the shamelessness of the business world, the length and breadth of the illusions men can entertain about themselves.   35

But then late last winter I came home one night with the Pakistani-baby story. Tina teaches in a day-care center, and the Pakistani-baby story pushed her over the edge. I'd been shoveling snow at Gunther's garden-apartment buildings when a Pakistani woman came out into the parking lot in her flowing ocher robes, weeping and screaming because there was no heat and her baby was freezing. I went inside to have a look, something I'm not supposed to do on my own. I'm supposed to refer tenants to Gunther's answering service, nothing more. In the apartment I could see my breath more clearly than I could outside. The woman's baby was swaddled in many blankets; only its nose and lips were sticking out, and they were blue. Sitting at the dinette table in his overcoat was the woman's husband, a little brown man with mournful eyes, eating a bowl of curry and shivering. Something big snapped inside me when I saw their lives. I showed them how to call the tenants'-rights division of Legal Aid, and then I gave them Gunther's unlisted home number, the most forbidden thing there is. Gunther and I had our biggest fight over the Pakistani family. When I got home, Tina spent the whole evening trying to calm me down. I quit for two entire weeks that time, finally going back for three dollars more an hour.

But now I must quit this job forever, Tina says—really quit, not just quit the way I do every week.

Every Friday when Gunther pays me what I'm owed, I put the cash in my pocket and say Sayonara. After a full week of Gunther, I can't envision one more day. He shakes his head, looks at the ground, asks me what he's done wrong. Nothing, Gunther, I always say, not a thing, you're a prince. I just can't take the real estate life anymore.

You lack vision, he always says. You're turning your back on a brilliant future. The real estate is only a stop along the way, Reggie. Next stop, Hollywood!

No can do, Gunther, I say. We shake hands and go our separate ways forever. Sunday morning I buy the paper and read the ads. Again each week, in return for two thirds of a person's waking life, the free market offers enough money to rent a shed and eat a can of beans every day. "I'm presently holding the best job in Cleveland," I tell Tina. She puts her hands over her ears. Then Sunday afternoon Gunther calls to offer me an hourly increase of fifty cents over what I made the previous week. I accept his new offer. I started at four dollars an hour. I'm up to twenty now. In his big house on a hill above town, Gunther has shown me where he hides his gun. When I reach fifty dollars an hour, he wants me to kill him.   40

Gunther's real estate holdings consist of two three-story brick garden-apartment buildings down near the Projects, eight or nine rambling wooden Victorians scattered all over the rest of town, and miscellaneous. Miscellaneous includes some garages Gunther rents to people for their cars, and a couple of apartments he has the nerve to rent over the garages. Of the enormous Victorians, three are divided vertically into two-families, and another five or six—the ones in the better areas—have been partitioned into warrens of small studios and one-bedrooms for which Gunther charges outrageous rents. The massage parlor is in one of those; when Gunther's feeling uninspired, we go there and pretend we have to check on things. Only one of the Victorians—the biggest one, in the worst neighborhood—has its original structure and gets rented as one place, to one party.

Acid Rain, the rock band, lives there.

Now Gunther hits the gravel of Acid Rain's horseshoe drive going fast, and then jumps on the brake so we slide sideways the last thirty feet to the house. Three old Chevy vans are parked around the drive, all painted with the band's name and logo—a thundercloud with a skull and crossbones in it—and seven huge Harley-Davidsons. In the backyard is a big Doberman and an even bigger shepherd, both on frail-looking chains. They start howling at us. The washing machine and dryer are still out there, their doors torn off, birds and squirrels living in them, and enough old hibachi grills to build a rusty bridge to Barbecueland. Here and there stray concrete blocks and bricks are making dead rectangular voids in the two-foot-high crabgrass.

Gunther loads my arms with equipment from the back of the Bronco—coils of pipe, rolls of solder, garnet paper, a plumber's snake, a portable light, extension cords, a large toolbox. He leads the way with the propane torch, me following him to the house like a pack mule. Luke, the leader of Acid Rain, greets us.

"Why the fuck don't you call your answering service?" Luke says.   45

"Now, Luke," says Gunther, "I don't think you should be the one to start casting stones. I could say hurtful things to you too. I could say, for instance, why don't you stop trying to flush each other down the toilets? It clogs them up."

"Ha, ha," Luke says. Then he doesn't say anything else, because he doesn't know where Gunther's breaking point is. Luke is not dumb, but you can see in his face that he can't figure Gunther out. He understands that Gunther did not go from being a poor, snot-nosed son of a drunked-up electrician to owning a small real estate empire by taking unlimited abuse from people like him. But then sometimes Gunther seems a jolly fellow who doesn't always act in his own best interest. It's confusing for Luke. I sympathize.

And then there's the way Gunther looks, the massive pink presence of him.

Luke reports that all three toilets in the house are broken. I look at Gunther and narrow my eyes. He looks away, sheepish. On the ride over here, Gunther let slip that Acid Rain first called about their toilet a week ago. It was just the first-floor toilet then.

We make our way through the house. Acid Rain's place was an opulent Cleveland mansion once, and there are still great cut-glass chandeliers hanging in the downstairs rooms above the drums and amplifiers and dismantled motorcycles. The glass pendants are gray blobs now, coated with greasy dust. The residents have decorated the chandeliers with panty hose, pictures from motorcycle magazines, tennis balls, guitar strings. We head upstairs to begin with the topmost toilet. The law of gravity. Various tattooed men are wandering around with women in black leather. Catastrophic metal music is playing in all the rooms on the second floor.   50

I'd like to mention here that I'm a great lover of music, and so is Tina. We believe that music transcends all the differences between people, and we like to get out when we can to hear a band and dance and have fun. Even after all the things

I had witnessed here, we still had perfectly open minds the night we went to see Acid Rain play at the GloWorm, over on the other side of the beltway. That's all I can say. When Tina finds out I was here again today, she'll go crazy. Maybe I won't even go home tonight.

Otis, the keyboard player, appears in a doorway on the second floor. Otis is completely blind, and two of Acid Rain's roadies—all the roadies and many other people live in the house with the band—are blind in one eye apiece. People can be blind for many reasons, and you don't ordinarily think of blindness as caused by the blind person, the result of something he did to himself. But with Acid Rain, the thought leaps to mind. Over the months, I've watched to see if other ones become blind too—from drinking rubbing alcohol, say, or fighting among themselves over food or females, the way squirrels do. So far, it's only the same three.

"Is that my landlord?" Otis says. "Do I hear my landlord's voice?"

"My man Otis," says Gunther. "How you doing, Otis?"

"How am I doing? I'm going to the bathroom in the backyard, motherfucker. That's how I'm doing."   55

"It's under control now, Otis," Gunther says, sidestepping quietly around him and motioning for me to follow. But I'm draped with the coils of pipe, extension cords, the plumber's snake, and I clank when I move.

Otis grabs me. "The dude who mows the lawn, right?" he says. "The landlord's sidekick?"

"I just work for the guy, Otis," I say. "You think it's a picnic? You think he doesn't do the same to me? Every day's a nightmare with this bozo, Otis."

Otis smiles and holds out his palm. "Hey," he says.

I slap his hand. "Renters of the world unite. Death to landlords."   60

"Right on!" Otis says, slapping me back. "Let's do it now!"

"No, Otis," I say. "Let him fix the toilets first."

"Good point," Otis says. "OK. I'll be waiting right here,"

We head up the last flight of stairs. "You overdid it a little," Gunther says, "but I was still impressed. You were convincing, and I liked the way you improvised under pressure. I thought you were just a writer. Now I find out you have natural acting ability. I'm giving you a screen test when we get back home."

On the third floor, Gunther sees the toilet from the hallway. His face becomes an image of the human capacity for sadness. "I think I just got a blown mind gasket," he says. He lights up the propane torch and shoots little bursts of blue flame into the bathroom. "Firing retro rockets," he says. "Leaving doomed planet."   65

"Two words, Gunther," I say. "Just two little words."

"I know," he says. "You quit."

"No," I say. "Roto-Rooter."

"That's one word," he says. We back away from the bathroom. Gunther grips the banister and looks down into the spacious stairwell as though he might plunge himself into it. Then his head snaps up and he slaps me in the belly. "I just had an incredible idea," he says.

"No, Gunther," I say. "Whatever it is. Please, no."   70

"Everything just fell together for me," he says. "Oh, man, this is good."

Back down on the landing, Otis is waiting. "Otis," Gunther says. "It's bigger than we thought. We have to call Roto-Rooter."

"You lie," Otis says, producing a length of chain from his leather vest.

"No, Otis," I say. "He's telling the truth this one time. It was my idea to call Roto-Rooter. There's no way this clown can fix these toilets."

"OK," Otis says. "I believe you, brother. But if you lie, I kill you too." 75

"Don't worry, Otis," I say.

We head downstairs. In the kitchen we find Luke and some of the women swigging on bottles of Colt 45.

"Luke," Gunther says. "My man. I want to ask you a question. You like movies, Luke?"

"I like going to the bathroom," Luke says, slamming his bottle on the table.

"We're calling Roto-Rooter on that, Luke, OK? Roto-Rooter, like on TV? The guys in the big yellow truck with the little sissy uniforms? You'll be able to make poo-poo right here tonight. Now sit down. I want you to answer my question. You like movies?" 80

"Yeah, sure."

"OK. When was the last time you saw a really great movie about an American rock-and-roll band? I mean a movie that had it all—bar scenes, motorcycle scenes, dressing room scenes, rehearsal scenes, groupie love scenes, and the monster victory-concert scene at the end when the band comes back to its hometown after making it big. A movie that captured all the suffering and the glory, the whole incredible life of a great, semi-famous cult rock band in a medium-sized American city. Luke, when was the last time you saw a movie like that?"

"I never saw no such movie," Luke says.

"That's right!" Gunther says.

The Peter Pan Diner, 2:00 P.M. Alice comes over with the menus. "You guys really making a big day of it, huh?" she says. 85

"We're celebrating, Alice," Gunther says. "Two meatloaf specials, one for me and one for my lucky charm here. Gravy on everything. That's the password today, Alice. Gravy."

Alice flashes me a look—can I handle him by myself? I nod and she takes the menus away.

Gunther is on an inspirational roll. "This is it!" he says, gripping my shoulder. "My movie! Plot, characters, myth, fantasy! Commercial potential! It was right under my nose! But that's the way it always is in the art game, eh, Roscoe?" He pulls a legal pad out of his briefcase. "So what do you think? I say we start with the Luke character—let's call him Luke—we start with him as an inner-city kid, you know, getting his first guitar, getting beat on by his alcoholic father because he practices guitar instead of getting a job. Plays good pool and B-ball, but he's better on guitar. Everybody's against him. His fellow gang members think guitar is for queers. And we need the bad father, right? We've got to give Luke something big to rebel against. I mean, he can't *like* his father."

"Cliché, Gunther. Cliché, cliché, cliché."

"You always say that. Well, I say life's a cliché! I'm not letting that stop me!" 90

"Scratch the childhood," I say. "It begins with music, the band rehearsing in this tenement while the titles roll up the screen. Helicopter shot of the building, close in on the window of their apartment, music getting louder and louder until we're right in there with them. Then the landlord bursts in, demanding the rent. They don't have any money, so they beat the landlord to death with their guitars."

"Sounds like a cliché to me!" Gunther says, chortling and writing it all down. "But it's not bad! We might be able to use that! OK, no childhood. Maybe we can put it back later. Or maybe—how about this?—Luke can go back and see his old dad in the hospital after he's famous. The old dad has the big C in his liver now, but together they watch Luke in concert on the tube in his hospital room. Just before he dies he recognizes how wrong he always was."

"And he apologizes for the way things were. And it straightens Luke's head out about his life."

"Right!"

"Perfect."

"And the record biz, hey? We need a big scene with these parasitic record-producer types who want to tell Luke how to play, what kinds of clothes to wear. They want to make Luke like everybody else so they can use him to get all this money to put up their own noses. But Luke has a dream. He tells everybody to screw themselves. In the end they all want to kiss his ass."

"That's good," I say. "That's original." The meat-loaf specials arrive. We dive into gravy. "Gunther," I say after a few bites, "it takes millions of dollars to make a real movie. You realize that, right? Millions."

"I have a little surprise for you," he says in the nursery-rhyme voice.

"No, Gunther, please, whatever it is, no."

"We're going to my place after lunch," he says. "Hollywood's paying your salary for the rest of the day. Before, I was going to leave you with the toilets and do the heavy business on my own. And I was worried, I admit it, because I didn't have the killer idea to show the big boys. But it came to me when I needed it. We're partners now, Ricardo. I always said you wouldn't be sorry if you stuck with me."

"Big boys?" I say. "What big boys?"

At Gunther's house, a silver Mercedes with vanity plates is parked at the top of the drive. Gunther downshifts the Bronco and creeps toward the silver car as though he can't believe it's actually there. "This is really happening," he says.

For a year now he's been running an ad in the paper to attract investors to his film-production company. Every month a few cranks respond; that's all, nobody with money. But yesterday when he called his answering service he found a message from these guys. They've invested in movies before. He told me about it on the way over here.

He parks the Bronco and gets out. The two men getting out of the Mercedes look like they want to get back in when they see him. The driver is a thin young guy with a spiky haircut, blue-green iridescent jacket, Hawaiian shirt, black jeans, red shoes. The passenger is a small man in his early sixties, salt-and-pepper hair brushed back, business suit. Gunther introduces himself and shakes hands. He motions for me to come over. "Gentleman," he says, "this is my associate, Flip. Flip is the co-author of my new screenplay."

I shake hands too. The driver's name is Willie. He's into the whole sullen James Dean thing. The passenger is Joseph, kindly and soft-spoken, with an Eastern European accent. His voice makes me see scenes for a movie version of our horrible century—bombings and occupations, pogroms, refugee camps, a boy in shabby knickers calling out the prices of fruit on the streets of the New World.

Both men are looking at my clothes. I brush the front of myself, but none of the paint spatters come off. "We like to be comfortable," I say.

Willie licks his lips, dubious, but Joseph smiles and nods. We go inside. Willie and Joseph look around. Gunther's place looks good. It's a big old house that didn't look so good when I first saw it, but often, while his tenants suffer, Gunther has me work around here. I've painted every room, sanded and finished the floors. One week in the winter we tore out the whole kitchen and put in a new one. Sometimes Gunther even has me clean the bathrooms for MaryLou, his wife, while he sits on a hassock in the hall telling me about screenplay ideas.

"You're prospering, Gunther," Joseph says.

"I guess I'm doing all right," Gunther says. He's more nervous than I thought he was. He tries to wink at me but botches it and looks like he's just been poked in the eye. "Flip, would you show Joseph and Willie into the living room? Gin and tonics, gentlemen?"

"Very good," Joseph says.

110

"Flip? Or would you prefer one of those nice English ales?"

"Gin and tonic is fine, Gunther," I say. I take the men into the living room. The furnishings are trim and tasteful, vaguely Scandinavian. They were chosen by MaryLou. Gunther would have chosen a lot of chrome bars and Naugahyde. The living room makes me realize in a sudden sweet way just how completely MaryLou holds Gunther's life together for him, what an impossible piece of luck or inspiration it was that he married her. If she ever left him he'd have to die, but she never will. She's a loving soul, from people even poorer than his, her head not easily turned from grateful devotion. Gunther put her through college while he worked, and never made it to college himself. She teaches grammar school now and thinks his carryings-on are what you put up with when you're married to a genius.

We sit down. French doors open from the living room into the dining room, now the office of the production company, where the big, useless 16mm Movieola is poised like an old burro grazing among the bundles of screenplay drafts stacked everywhere. I've written whole scenes of them while Gunther's tenants acted out their martyrdom. Joseph and Willie are peering in there from the sofa. They don't know what to make of it all. I hear Gunther clinking glassware in the distant kitchen.

In a voice as soft as Joseph's I say, "Gunther is an unusual person." It's hardly an outlandish statement. They nod, meaning that they'd noticed, and wait for me to go on. "He's actually rather amazing. Four, five years ago he had nothing. Now he owns properties all over town. Everything he has he built up for himself, with no help from anyone. His drive to succeed is unstoppable. All his life he's dreamed of making movies. He works on screenplays in his sleep." I lean forward and lower my voice even further. "His father was an electrician who drank himself to death, beat the kids, and smashed up the house all the time when Gunther was growing up. Now Gunther supports his old mother, bought a nice little house for her to live in across town. He put his wife through college. You'll see him come in here with a Coke for himself. He never touches a drink, straight as an arrow. You understand what I'm saying. I'm talking about character, what motivates a man."

Everything I'm telling Willie and Joseph is true. Yes, I'm casting it in a certain light, even perceiving it as I say it, but I'm not telling a single lie.

115

"A lot of people have had it tough," Willie says.

But Joseph waves his hand. "I appreciate what you say," he says.

Gunther comes in with the drinks on a tray, three gin-and-tonics and a Coke for himself. He sits down in a big chair. "Well," he says. Then he's about to say something else, but nothing comes out. We sip our drinks, waiting.

"So, Gunther," Joseph says, "you want to make a movie."

Gunther nods without expression. To the untrained eye, he looks as enigmatic as Buddha, full of secret knowledge. But I've learned to read the fantastic face. He wants to speak, but his body has locked up on him. He never really believed that a man like Joseph would come to his house someday. His stage fright is as immense and immovable as himself.

"Joseph," I say. "Willie. Have you ever noticed that beyond the basic animal requirements there are very few things that all human beings must have, and that these few things are not physical but rather metaphysical, things of the spirit? Faith of some kind is the obvious example. Can you think of another?"

Willie looks at Joseph. "This is kind of a weird thing to be talking about," Willie says.

But Joseph thinks it over and says, "Love, of course."

"Oh, good," I say. "Right. The big one. And how about learning, some systematic acquisition of knowledge?"

"Yes," Joseph says, nodding his head.

"Now I'm thinking of one more," I say. "One more nonphysical thing that all people must have, a thing that is always present whenever human beings gather together in grief or in joy."

Willie looks at his watch. Part of his job is to protect Joseph's precious time. "This is kind of like Twenty Questions," he says. "This might be fun at a party."

"Party is a clue," I say.

Joseph straightens up on the sofa. "Music!" he says.

I nod my head and smile. "Yes, Joseph, music."

"The nonphysical part fooled me," Willie says.

"Now, friends," I say, "the movie we're going to make is about music. Joseph, I'll bet there's a tape machine in your car out there. I'm going to guess what's on it at this very moment. Mozart."

"Wrong!" Joseph says, clapping his hands. "Mozart is in the glove compartment, I'll grant you that! But on the machine is Prokofiev. We listened to it on the way over here." He wags his finger at me. "You were wrong, smart boy!"

"Ha-ha!" I say. "But still I've made my point. You take your favorite music with you wherever you go. *And*," I say, "the second part of my point—it's music that Willie doesn't like."

"Right!" Joseph says. "He complains every day. But that part was easy, smart boy. Look at Willie's clothes, look at his hair."

"Sure," I say. "But look further, Joseph. Look at Willie and see the American moviegoer. We practically have Mr. Entertainment sitting right here. And that, Joseph, is why—for the crucial question—we must now defer to Willie."

I sip my drink.

"Willie," I say. "I have a question for you. When was the last time you saw a really great movie about an American rock-and-roll band? I mean a movie that had it all—bar scenes, motorcycle scenes, dressing room scenes, rehearsal scenes, groupie love scenes, and the monster victory-concert scene at the end when the band comes back to its hometown after making it big. A movie that captured all the suffering and the glory, the whole incredible life of a great, semi-famous cult rock band in a medium-sized American city. Willie, when was the last time you saw a movie like that?"

"I never saw any such movie," Willie says. 140

"That's right," I say.

Gunther's kitchen, 5:00 P.M. Gunther on the floor on his hands and knees.

"Gunther, get up," I say, looking in the refrigerator for those good English ales he was talking about. "Stop doing that. Show some self-respect. Where are those ales, you charlatan, you complete fraud? What if I'd decided to have one?"

"There wouldn't have been any left," he says, continuing to do what he's been doing—crawling on all fours, nudging MaryLou's silver serving tray around the floor with his nose the way a dog nudges its bowl. Periodically he howls like a dog too, and when he does, tears spring from his eyes—which he takes care not to let drip upon the small slip of blue paper resting on the silver tray.

"I'm making a movie!" he keeps bawling between howls.

The slip of blue paper is the check Joseph wrote to Gunther before driving away in the silver Mercedes ten minutes ago. It's for an amount so large I can't bring myself to say it. When he wrote it, Joseph called it good-faith money. He has more, and he knows other investors. 145

I finish making another gin-and-tonic. "Gunther," I say. "I have to tell you something, and I want you to brace yourself. I'm not doing this movie with you."

He clambers up from the floor, Joseph's check in his hand. "Flip," he says. "Don't even joke about things like that, Flip."

"I'm not joking. Where did you get 'Flip,' by the way?"

"It just came to me," Gunther says. "But I like it. That's you from now on. Flip, my man Flip."

"It's not bad," I say. "But you'll have to find somebody else." 150

"There is nobody else! Nobody like you! Nobody with your talent! Hey! A third of this money's yours! Half of it's yours! It's all yours, Flip!"

"I already have to go to a marriage counselor on account of you," I say. "If I throw in on this movie, Tina divorces me."

"She won't!" Gunther says. "Not when she hears about the money! I'll talk to her. Call her right now, I'll talk to her. No! We'll bring her in! Can she write? Can she act? Can she sing?"

"No, Gunther. She can't do anything. She's a vegetable now. The only thing she can do is say the word *quit*, over and over. If you ask me again I'm leaving, and I still have most of a drink here." I raise my glass. "Congratulations, pal."

"Thanks, Flip. Flip! We have to celebrate somehow! We have to do something fun together!" 155

"I can't think of anything, Gunther."

"It's hot out. It's muggy. Flip! You've never been in my pool!"

"I didn't bring my suit today, Gunther."

"You can use one of my suits."

"Really, Gunther." 160

He pounds upstairs. When he comes back down, he's in his trunks, a total embodiment of what it is to be flesh. He tosses me an extra pair. They're like a hot-air balloon or a parachute. I put them on in the bathroom and come out holding a yard of excess suit behind me. Gunther has the stapler from his desk. He staples the trunks until they stay up by themselves.

We go out the back door and into the yard. Gunther's pool is a big one, with all the fixtures: three ladders, two diving boards, ropes with colorful floats. The blue water sparkles with points of early evening light. "Just a quick dip in the low end here, Gunther," I say. "I have to get home for dinner."

"Flip," he says. "Did I tell you I started taking real scuba-diving lessons? From a registered diving teacher at the Y? He's been showing the class all this neat stuff, special things you have to do in case of emergencies. I have to show you a couple of these things. I can teach you the basics of diving in about two minutes."

"Gunther, no, really. I've always had a slight fear of the water, to tell you the truth. I was swept out into the ocean once when I was a kid, and lifeguards had to save me with a motorboat."

"You never told me that," he says. "That would make a great scene. You should be a little more forthcoming with your experiences. It would help you rise above them." He starts getting the scuba stuff out of the equipment shed. "Now look, these are what we call weight belts. They keep you from floating to the top." He hands me one and starts putting one on himself. 165

I drop it on the grass. "See you, Gunther. It's been, you know, nice."

He grabs my shoulder. "MaryLou goes diving with me, Flip, and she can't even drive a stick shift. Are you telling me you're afraid to do this? I know, you have to go home. Hey, it's been a special day. I'm asking you to take a little dive with me to celebrate. Ten lousy minutes for a little fun, and then you can go home."

I pick up the weight belt and put it on. Gunther is tying a heavy rope around his waist. About twenty feet of rope is left when he's finished, and he proceeds to tie the other end around me. "Like mountain climbers," he says.

"Divers don't do that, Gunther. No diver ties himself to another diver."

"Yes, they do, Flip. In certain kinds of salvage operations they do. It's a special knot that comes undone when you pull on it." He pulls on the knot and the rope drops off my waist onto the grass. "OK?" He reties the rope for me. "I have this neat maneuver I want to show you—what divers do when one diver for some reason loses his tank or runs out of air. We have to do this particular maneuver if we want to have some fun here today, because I only have one tank with air in it." 170

"Oh, Christ."

"Put on your flippers, Flip," he says, putting on the only tank with air in it.

I put on the flippers and we slap across the lawn to the concrete apron along the edge of the pool. Gunther explains that we're going to fall into the deep end on our backs, get ourselves oriented under water, and then start sharing the one mouthpiece. I'm going to love it, he says. It'll be much more interesting than simply having my own tank. He shows me how to put the mouthpiece in and out without swallowing water. "Granted, it's a little different up here on land," he says. "Ready? Lower your mask."

I lower my mask. Then, without even giving me a signal, Gunther topples backward like a bomb leaving a plane. The splash he makes comes right over my head like an ocean wave and then the rope runs out and snaps me into the vortex behind him.

Under water it's white and opaque, with millions of tiny bubbles, and I can't see anything. Then I make out Gunther, his legs and arms wafting gently like seaweed fronds. I watch him swim for a few seconds, fascinated by how graceful he is under water, the way whales are said to be. I can see him smiling around the mouthpiece. He waves goodbye to me as I sink. The weight belt is doing much more to me than to Gunther; soon I'm directly beneath him and panicking. I try to swim upward, but I don't know how to use the flippers and can't kick with them on. I pull on the special knot, but it doesn't work now that it's wet. I try to undo the weight belt, but it's jammed by the rope. I'm about to start crying, despite the unexpected thought that crying under water would be absurd.

Then I feel myself rising toward the surface. Arm over arm, Gunther is hauling me up by the umbilical rope. When he gets me to his level, he pushes the mouthpiece into my face. I'm afraid to breathe through it. *Breathe!* he says with his hands. I breathe. The air from the tank is the most wonderful thing I've ever known, physical ecstasy and my life to do over again. After a few breaths of it I'm all calmed down.

Gunther points to me and moves his arms and legs. *You're supposed to hold yourself up,* he's saying. I point to myself and make some gestures: *I can't.* He gestures, *Try,* takes the mouthpiece away, and lets go of the rope. I try again and sink stupidly, all the way down. He hauls me back up, collects the excess rope, and ties it all into one big bow between us, so that I can't sink too far away.

We fall into a rhythm with the tank, two breaths each time, passing the hose back and forth peace-pipe fashion. Peace is what it is, an amazing, liquid peace. Each sharing of the air is the deepest cooperation between comrades, something solid and good that would never be withheld. We hear nothing but the gurgling of the tank and somewhere, very distant, the persistent *om* of the pool filter. Random thoughts and memories bubble through me like Aqualung air, one notion after another in bubbly succession, each considered for a globular instant and then allowed to bubble away forever. I've never envied anything Gunther has, but maybe I've misunderstood it all, because I envy this. If I had a lot of money, a swimming pool and a scuba tank would be the first things I'd buy, so that I could leave the earth this way for an hour or two every evening.

A small kick or motion of the arm sends us orbiting slowly around each other in the water like space walkers. Behind Gunther's face mask his eyes are closed. He might almost be sleeping. I see that this is the essential Gunther—who he really is and who he'd be on land, too, if he didn't have to do what he does up there because of what his father did to him.

He opens his eyes and sees me staring at him. He smiles and gestures to the blueness around us as if to say, *Aren't you glad you stayed to check this out?* I nod and give him the OK sign. He points to the surface of the water, shrugs his shoulders, and flops his arms. He actually laughs and a bubble floats out of his mouth with the message, *You really saved me up there.*

I tap my chest, meaning, *I know I did, you huge oaf.*

But the rock-and-roll movie was my idea! he adds, slapping his own chest defiantly. *And I'm not a bad man!* he adds kicking his feet. *Not as bad as you make out, that's for sure. You're such a judgmental person. My tenants don't need to talk to me about every goddam leaky faucet.*

What about that Pakistani baby? I signal, imitating the mother's flowing robes and jutting out my chin self-righteously.

OK, he nods, *that was wrong, I admit it.*

I make a signal to my heart, meaning, *That really upset my wife. You almost destroyed my marriage.*

He shakes his head with great irritation and lashes his pink fists through the blue water. *Me destroy your marriage! Did you ever think that maybe you shouldn't com-*

plain to your wife so much? I'll bet she doesn't bring home every single stupid thing that happens to her every day and inflict it on you. You're such a baby!

I nod sadly. *OK, you have a point.*

He rolls onto his back and starts paddling both of us around the depths of the pool. I let myself be towed along, staring up at the silvery surface of the water, taking my turns on the scuba tank. The water's surface reminds me of the silver screen of a movie theater, and as a game I try to see a movie in it. At first I don't see anything, and then after a while I begin to see the rock-and-roll movie. I see precisely how it ought to go, what scenes it ought to have, all the things about life that you could make people understand while you had their attention with the music. I see that the world really needs this great, honest, full-of-heart movie about an American band, and that if I don't do it with Gunther he'll screw it up and it won't be the movie I'm seeing. Or Joseph will bring in somebody else to take my place. Somebody else will get to give the world all the pleasure and instruction of the great rock-and-roll movie, and then the world will give that person the swimming pool and scuba tank in return. Why shouldn't it be me?

Reginald McKnight (1956–   )

Reginald McKnight won the prestigious Drue Heinz Literature Prize in 1988 for his collection *Moustapha's Eclipse*. McKnight currently teaches at the University of Pittsburgh and at the low-residency MFA program at Bennington College. His other works include the novel *I Get on the Bus* (1990) and the story collection *The Kind of Light That Shines on Texas* (1991).

PEACHES

J.C. crosses the sun-faded carpet looking truculent and surly. He looks at me with his woman-get-out-my-seat face. His tail points straight up to the ceiling. He lets out with his most irate meow, stomps back and forth in front of me in that stiff-legged strut that drives me crazy. He always does this when I sit in "his" chair. "Looks like everybody's mad at me today," I say, crossing my arms and legs at the same time. Momma doesn't say a word so I know what's up with her. Daddy drops the paper to his lap, and sits up in his chair. Its old, arthritic wood creaks. "Ain't nobody mad, Baby Sister," he says, removing his glasses. "Ain't nobody disappointed, hurt, upset—'cept that little pea-brain cat of yours. Mystery to me why you even sit in that chair after he done rubbed all his hair off in it."

"Have you heard from Marc lately, Rita?" asks Momma, not looking up from her puzzle.

"Good Lord Almighty have I heard from him. Tuesday I got four letters. Four separate letters. In four separate envelopes."

"What's all this 'Lord Almighty' business, girl," says Daddy. "I ain't sending you to no twenty-thousand-dollar-a-year college to hear you talk like a imitation me. You gonna be a scientist. Let me hear my money's worth."

"Your money?" Momma says, "You mean Uncle Sam's money."

"I'll take his money too if it help put Baby Sis through school. I ain't proud."

"You ain't rich neither," Momma says, snapping a puzzle piece into place.

J.C. leaps up into my lap. His purring irritates me so I get up and move to the other side of the room.

"We got a postcard from him a couple of days before you got here, Rita," my mother says, still not looking up from the table. "Didn't say much though."

"Why didn't you tell me when I got home, Momma?"

"Moody as you was? No ma'am. I got better things to do than listen to you bawl from sunup to sundown. Anyway, we already talked about your plans before you got here. Now if I'd been bringing up his name all the time you might have thought I was trying to push you into sending him that . . . the—"

"How 'bout 'Dear John,' Lucille."

"James!"

"Daddy—"

"Well, that's the truth. I'm calling a spade a spade. Just like he did."

"James! Now I am not going to have you—"

"All right now, I'm just playing. But I don't care how much ass that boy kiss. And I don't care how long he stay in Africa to sensitivize hisself. Cain't no rich white boy call my child no nigger and—"

"Maybe not, but she grown, James. It's her life. Her decision. You and I got nothing to say whatsoever about what Rita decide. Now you promised me you'd leave the poor girl alone. Can't you see she upset as it is?" Momma snaps another piece into the puzzle, pushes her glasses up on her nose and looks up at Daddy. Daddy picks up the newspaper, crosses his legs, clears his throat. "You right," he grunts, then clears his throat again. "Yeah, you right. But if you ask me, you an apple, he an orange." I can tell from his eyes that he is staring at but not reading the paper. The room is as silent as the moon. Dust motes swim through the lamplight around Daddy's head. He looks hurt and I'd like to tell him he needn't be, because I myself am not hurting. I am numb. I don't know what to think or feel or do. I veer toward anger, then careen toward love, then roll toward regret and guilt. But as has been the case since the fight, I end up weightless and static like one of those motes around Daddy's head.

Daddy tosses the paper to the floor and in the silence it sounds like firecrackers. J.C. springs up from the chair and scoots under the couch. The room again falls silent, the brief flurry of sound and action is swallowed up like stones tossed into the ocean.

After awhile Daddy's chair squeaks and cracks. He inhales deep and slow, then slips on his glasses. "I believe," he says, "I could use a little help outside picking some peaches for old Mrs. Li's sweet and sour sauce. She says she gonna make some extry for you to take back to school with you. Come on."

The fog has not yet lifted, but the air feels dryer than usual. Mr. Givens's dog yaps at us from behind the gray cedar fence. In the thirteen years my parents and I and my two sisters have lived here, I've never seen the old dog and I don't know its name. Each evening, when chastising the dog, when telling it to shut up, when calling it in, Mr. Givens calls it, "Git-yer-dumb-ass-outta-that-garden, Shut-the-hell-up-ya-stupid-mutt, and Giddin-here-ya-damn-dog." As far as I can tell the dog seldom obeys. In the evenings Mr. Givens can often be heard bellowing, "OK, then don't eat, ya stupid!"

When the dog has barked long enough, my father picks up the usual peach pit, zings it in the area of Mr. Givens's garden, and finally we hear: "How many times I gotta tell ya to keep yer dumb ass outta that garden?" Silence. My father and I are alone in the backyard which is redolent with the smell of peaches, the sight of peaches. We feel peach pits beneath our feet.

"Grab that raggedy-looking box over next to the fence, Baby Sis," Daddy says. "Half them bushel baskets old Givens give me cain't hold air."

"This one?"

"Um hmm."

"Do we need a stepladder?"

"Well, they should be plenty of good ones on the ground. And if we shake us a branch or two we won't need a ladder." He kneels and begins sorting peaches, asks me a few questions about how school is going. I answer him in monosyllables, hoping the conversation won't drift toward anything that will upset us both. The afternoon air becomes cool all of a sudden. Goosebumps erupt on my arms and neck. "Daddy, I'll be right back," I say, "I need a jacket."

In my room I stand before the closet door, looking at my reflection in the full-length mirror. I look at myself, forgetting for several moments why I have come into the room. There I stand in baggy white pants and what Marcus calls my "favorite Dinty Moore shirt." He never told me he disliked the way I dress, but when I was clad in my flannels and baggies his eyes often glanced around—toward the bookshelf, "Hey, a new one by Mishima?" or my stereo, "Let's listen to some Marvin Gaye," or the Dali prints, "When did you say that one was painted?" He, like most men, wants to see women dress in anything tight enough to keep the blood static. He always told me he wasn't particularly a breast man, or a leg man—"I'm not an anything man," he'd say. "I'm an everything man. Legs, ass, brains, conscience." But he only seemed to tell me that kind of thing when I was wearing flannels and baggies.

"What does he see in me?" I think as I peruse the frizzy, uncombable black hair, the burdensome breasts, the face that he insisted no guy on campus could forget, the legs he insisted are not birdlike. "And look at my legs," he'd say, indicating with both hands, "They look like a couple of Venus number twos." He told me never to change a thing about myself. "I'm the one who needs to change," he'd say. And I'd tell him, in the beginning, he didn't need to change. That he was fine the way he was. But he would always sneer, "Simmons, you don't know the half of it." He kept saying things like that, becoming more strident, histrionic, and distant. "I'm no goddamned good," he'd say over and over. And soon enough, I began to feel as though his kisses were trying to smother something, that the walls of his apartment enfolded secret passages and chambers, that his conversation, numinous and trivial, full of New Age jargon, spoke around rather than of something. There was always something fleeting about him. Something just out the corner of my eye, something just out of reach. I imagined that an invisible incubus paced between us when we were together, thumbing its invisible nose at us, flipping us the invisible finger. I felt its presence so acutely sometimes, that I could almost see it burst forth in hyperactive, muscled flesh. Sometimes it made me fear him. Sometimes I think it made me love him more.

The more I loved him, the less I understood him, the farther I slipped from him. And when he started punching walls, calling me at two in the morning to apologize for no reason at all, threatening to slash his wrists every time I told him I was busy, I sensed how ripe he was for procreation. 30

"You never have time anymore, Rita. What's the matter, you mad at me?"

"Why should I be mad at you? I'm mad at me. I've got to really get going on my thesis."

"I know, I understand. I just want to see you. Why are you hiding from me all of a sudden?"

I'd say nothing.

"What's wrong, Rita? I just want to see you for one hour." 35

"Marc, I just haven't got the time."

He never let up. He'd set his heels and push. And push.

"Is it something I said to you? Is it my beliefs? When we first met you always said I was too rarified for you. You said I strut around 'up there' acting fey while you're 'down here' accepting life for what it is. 'Fey,' you said. Jesus Christ, Rita, I got no problem with your science. Why can't you give me what's mine?"

"I know, Marc. I know. I should. I do. It's got nothing to do with your beliefs. Really. I'm just preoccupied. I've got two midterms tomorrow. I've got that lousy seminar. We can talk about this tomorrow, at dinner."

And push. 40

"It's because you think I got no soul or some crap like that, isn't it? I just can't give you what a black guy can give you, right? That's what you think, isn't it? Well if it is, Rita, then you're wrong. It's all an illusion. It's maya. If anything, I can give you more because my world is so different from yours."

"Marc, there's only this world—"

"Look, Rita, I've been through this before. I've had relationships with Black women and Hispanic women, and Asian women. You can tell me. I think I'd understand. You probably think I don't take you seriously. You think I'm just using you."

He'd ask me if it was his disapproving family, his derisive friends, his age, his intellect, or that he was an undergraduate English major and I was a semester away from a master's degree in chemistry. It often left us very little to talk about at dinner. He's ask if his beard looked silly, or if he dressed poorly, or if my family really hadn't liked him but had simply been Oscarwinning polite, or if he was too easily depressed, irascible, antisocial, untruthful, or was I-sure-really-sure "it's not because I'm white?" I'd always say no.

I'd say no because it was easy to say no. Easier than unleashing untenable fears, easier, after awhile, than holding him close, feeling his diffuse heat. He'd push, and it was if he'd started pushing too deeply inside himself, rummaging and scraping, uncovering things that I'm not sure were ever there. "What's wrong with me?" he'd demand. "Tell me. Just tell me something. Do you still love me? Do I offend you in some way?" I couldn't tell him. I knew I'd just have to wait, then I'd see, he'd know. I'd tried to tell him once or twice, but everything would lock up inside me when I'd try to explain. And then it finally just slid out from him, loud and ugly. The word. The beast-incubus word, the inevitable issue of the "yin-yan" relationship. His phrase, "yin-yan relationship." Had I drawn it from him, headfirst screaming, kicking into the world? Or did he plant it in me, water it with his tears, incubate it in the heat of my womblike reticence? I don't know. 45

All I could say that night was, "That, Marc. That's just what I was afraid of. Wasn't but a matter of time, was it?"

How would things have gone if I had just told him of my fears and talked it out with him? I never did because to do so would have implied that he had transcended nothing. I flat would have been calling him a liar, or blind. And he was neither. He had transcended something, somehow. Or what if I had just buried myself in his auburn beard, his ginseng breath, the bend and curve of his body, and listened to his nonsense about the Ghosts of Lemuria, the Light of Atlantis, the Race of Tan just for the sake of hearing his voice. His voice was so nice to listen to, a little raspy, a little flutelike. Sometimes it seemed he told his stories in song. Sweet nonsense. And when I actually heard him say the word I was so sure he would eventually say, I was shocked. Shocked both because it always shocks you when someone calls you nigger and because the word fell from his mouth so awkwardly—as if he had never heard it before, said it before, imagined saying it before.

So he bought a ticket to Liberia. I didn't know what to feel. He told me he wouldn't come back till he knew, till he really, really understood what blackness was. I didn't know what to say. He hugged me, kissed me longer than I could stand, said goodbye, promised he'd change, we'd get it straight, he'd return reborn, we'd marry and raise fat, tan, unrarified babies. He got on the plane. He called me from Denver. He called me from New York. He called me from Dakar. He called me from Monrovia. I got his first letter in two weeks. By six weeks I'd received eight more. In three months over forty letters. Bombarded by missives of love, the seed of self-discovery. They came daily, weekly. Tidings of hope, love, joy. Peace Profound. Images of beautiful babies, beautiful ocean, sleek, cat-black men, women in rich Day-Glo rags. The taste of this. The smell of that. The size, shape, volume of his ever-expanding, ever-pregnant African love. But I just didn't. His seed fell on unsettled dust, a haze of motes never coming to rest.

"It won't lie still," I say aloud, suddenly remembering why I've come up to my room. I grab something warm-looking and bluish, then run back outside.

I stand on the stoop and watch Daddy kneeling in the grass, peach in hand. He sniffs, squeezes, removes his glasses and inspects it, then tosses it aside. His face is grave, almost sullen. I cross the yard and kneel beside him, trying to imitate the way he inspects the peaches, but I'm not really sure what he's looking for.

I've always loved the way my father throws himself into the task at hand. Whether it be selecting peaches for Mrs. Li's sauce, adjusting a bicycle seat, or expounding to three enraptured daughters at the dinner table just what it is that makes a grocery clerk's job so much more dangerous than a San Francisco cop's, there is no one I know with the intensity, the undivided surrender to the action, the moment.

While we sort through hard, woody peaches and soft, muddy peaches, peaches bruised and scarred, peaches clear-complected, he tells me the secret of Mrs. Li's sauce: "She take a whisk broom to J.C.'s chair and use all them cat hairs and cookie crumbs y'all leave in it." And he hints at the secret secret to his peach cobbler, which he says he extracted, through torture, from a Japanese POW. "If I told you, you wouldn't eat it." He tells me it once rained peaches in San Francisco when I was "just a baby, and couldn't possibly remember." And that old Moses told God that no way on earth would he sign those "commandoes or commandants, or whatever you call em, till you take peaches off the list." He tells me he never would have looked twice at Momma had she never stuffed peaches under her sweater back in '47, that peaches, at one time, contained an explosive substance instead of sugar, and the last

50

A Fiction Anthology

recorded use of the exploding peach was in the Boer War. "That was before your time," he is quick to add. He tells me about the Peach Bowl of 1968 (LSU won because they ate more peaches. "Well, why you think they call it Peach Bowl?").

"Paul Robeson couldn't sing note one 'less he had two, three quarts of peach wine in him," he says. And he tells me about all the peachy-keen people he had ever known (me, Juanita, and Theresa May, "and sometimes that hard-head mother of yours"). He tells me how Big Daddy used to push his cart around the streets of Alabaster, Alabama, hollering, "Waaaatermelon? Strawberries and Peeeeachez! Cold, sweet Peeeeachez!" Peaches and cream, peach ice cream, peacherinoes and peacherines, peach yogurt, peach popsicles, peach lipstick, peach pie, jam, and jelly. "Cold, sweet peeeeachez!"

The box is full of what he assures me are the finest peaches that soil could possibly produce. I offer him a peach from the brimming box; he frowns and says, "Shooot, naw, Baby Sister, I cain't eat them things." We laugh for a long time, leaning away from each other, folding toward each other, like jazz dancers. And then I start to cry. I cry so hard I can scarcely breathe. Daddy holds me, saying nothing. He doesn't even try to shush me, just holds me till I stop. Then he reaches in the box, takes out a peach, examines it, sniffs it, throws it aside. He takes another one and does the same thing. Then another, and another, and another.

Finally, he turns the whole box over. Peaches tumble across the lawn. He inspects every last one. His long fingers caress each, every one. His nose and eye, inspecting, seed-deep, each, every one. And then he finds what he is looking for. It is very large, the color of a sunrise, flows into a sunset, flows into the color of Mrs. Li's blush. He rubs it on his sleeve, holds it out to me in the palm of his hand. I wipe my nose with a finger, regard the peach for a long, long time. Till Daddy's arm trembles a bit. "Naw," I say, "I can't eat em." He drops the fruit and it cracks on the green grass. He takes my hand, and we walk inside.   55

14 Responding to Stories

This chapter presents you with four opportunities to observe how previous readers have responded differently to particular stories, and to compare these with your own responses. The responses take the form of essays—and, in one case, a story—presenting distinctive readings of the author's work being critiqued. As you read and reread each story, concentrate on developing your own interpretations and on thinking about how you might communicate those to another reader. You can then compare your ideas with those of another writer or critic and contemplate shared views as well as differences. After reading the responses, consider the questions that follow each section and decide how you might enter a dialogue with the writer. What issues strike you as most pressing? How would you integrate these views in producing an interpretation of your own?

At the end of this chapter is a unit on James Joyce's long story "The Dead" (which appears in Chapter 13), accompanied by two interpretive essays. These are followed by an example of how the essay material can be used by a student as a writing resource in the development of an interpretive paper. As you observe how a student source paper takes shape in response to statements by other critics, consider how you could develop your own interpretation of a story by quoting and responding to other writers' ideas.

Note: Should you wish to use any of the response essays in this chapter as sources in interpretive essays you may be writing, you can either track down the original source at the library and cite the actual pages in standard MLA form (see Appendix B), or you can cite the work as reprinted in *Literature: The Evolving Canon* and refer to the pages of this book. Your notation on your Works Cited page might read as follows:

Basler, Roy P. "The Interpretation of 'Ligeia.' " *Literature: The Evolving Canon.* 2nd ed. Ed. Sven P. Birkerts. Boston: Allyn and Bacon, 1996. pp. 469–477.

RESPONDING TO POE'S "LIGEIA"

Edgar Allan Poe (1809–1849)

Poe has the reputation—not unjustified—of being one of the "damned." Certainly, the subject matter of most of his writing supports this contention—it is dark and demon-haunted.

Like so many writers of his day, Poe struggled to make a living with his pen. He wrote journalism and reviews for hire and had some success selling his stories to magazines. The stories captured the attention of readers, and for a period Poe was selling work as fast as he could produce it (he was remarkably prolific). But Poe squandered his earnings in gambling dens and drinking establishments. He was only forty when he was found unconscious on a street in Baltimore; he died several days later.

LIGEIA

And the will therein lieth, which dieth not. Who knoweth, the mysteries of the will, with its vigor? For God is but a great will pervading all things by nature of its intentness. Man doth not yield himself to the angels, nor unto death utterly, save only through the weakness of his feeble will.

JOSEPH GLANVILLE

I cannot, for my soul, remember how, when, or even precisely where, I first became acquainted with the lady Ligeia. Long years have since elapsed, and my memory is feeble through much suffering. Or, perhaps, I cannot *now* bring these points to mind, because, in truth, the character of my beloved, her rare learning, her singular, yet placid cast of beauty, and the thrilling and enthralling eloquence of her low musical language, made their way into my heart by paces so steadily and stealthily progressive, that they have been unnoticed and unknown. Yet I believe that I met her first and most frequently in some large, old, decaying city near the Rhine. Of her family—I have surely heard her speak. That it is of a remotely ancient date cannot be doubted. Ligeia! Ligeia! Buried in studies of a nature more than all else adapted to deaden impressions of the outward world, it is by that sweet word alone—by Ligeia—that I bring before mine eyes in fancy the image of her who is no more. And now, while I write, a recollection flashes upon me that I have *never known* the paternal name of her who was my friend and my betrothed, and who became the partner of my studies, and finally the wife of my bosom. Was it a playful charge on the part of my Ligeia? or was it a test of my strength of affection, that I should institute no inquiries upon this point? or was it rather a caprice of my own—a wildly romantic offering on the shrine of the most passionate devotion? I but indistinctly recall the fact itself—what wonder that I have utterly forgotten the circumstances which originated or attended it? And, indeed, if ever that spirit which is entitled *Romance*—if ever she, the wan and the misty-winged *Ashtophet°* of idolatrous° Egypt, presided, as they tell, over marriages ill-omened, then most surely she presided over mine.

There is one dear topic, however, on which my memory fails me not. It is the *person* of Ligeia. In stature she was tall, somewhat slender, and, in her latter days,

---

Ashtophet: ancient Egyptian diety.
idolatrous: idol-worshipping.

even emaciated. I would in vain attempt to portray the majesty, the quiet ease of her demeanor, or the incomprehensible lightness and elasticity of her footfall. She came and departed as a shadow. I was never made aware of her entrance into my closed study, save by the dear music of her low sweet voice, as she placed her marble hand upon my shoulder. In beauty of face no maiden ever equalled her. It was the radiance of an opium-dream—an airy and spirit-lifting vision more wildly divine than the phantasies which hovered about the slumbering souls of the daughters of Delos.° Yet her features were not of that regular mold which we have been falsely taught to worship in the classical labors of the heathen. "There is no exquisite beauty," says Bacon, Lord Verulam,° speaking truly of all the forms and *genera*° of beauty, "without some *strangeness* in the proportion." Yet, although I saw that the features of Ligeia were not of a classic regularity—although I perceived that her loveliness was indeed "exquisite," and felt that there was much of "strangeness" pervading it, yet I have tried in vain to detect the irregularity and to trace home my own perception of "the strange." I examined the contour of the lofty and pale forehead—it was faultless—how cold indeed that word when applied to a majesty so divine!—the skin rivalling the purest ivory, the commanding extent and repose, the gentle prominence of the regions above the temples; and then the raven-black, the glossy, the luxuriant, and naturally-curling tresses, setting forth the full force of the Homeric epithet, "hyacinthine!"° I looked at the delicate outlines of the nose—and nowhere but in the graceful medallions of the Hebrews had I beheld a similar perfection. There were the same luxurious smoothness of surface, the same scarcely perceptible tendency to the aquiline, the same harmoniously curved nostrils speaking the free spirit. I regarded the sweet mouth. Here was indeed the triumph of all things heavenly—the magnificent turn of the short upper lip—the soft, voluptuous slumber of the under—the dimples which sported, and the color which spoke—the teeth glancing back, with a brilliancy almost startling, every ray of the holy light which fell upon them in her serene and placid yet most exultingly radiant of all smiles. I scrutinized the formation of the chin—and, here too, I found the gentleness of breadth, the softness and the majesty, the fulness and the spirituality, of the Greek—the contour which the god Apollo revealed but in a dream, to Cleomenes, the son of the Athenian. And then I peered into the large eyes of Ligeia.

For eyes we have no models in the remotely antique. It might have been, too, that in these eyes of my beloved lay the secret to which Lord Verulam alludes. They were, I must believe, far larger than the ordinary eyes of our own race. They were even fuller than the fullest of the gazelle eyes of the tribe of the valley of Nourjahad.° Yet it was only at intervals—in moments of intense excitement—that this peculiarity became more than slightly noticeable in Ligeia. And at such moments was her beauty—in my heated fancy thus it appeared perhaps—the beauty of beings either above or apart from the earth—the beauty of the fabulous Houri of the Turk.° The hue of the orbs was the most brilliant of black, and far over them, hung jetty° lashes of great length. The

---

Delos: island of Greece.
Bacon, Lord Verulam: English philosopher and essayist (1561–1626).
genera: kinds.
hyacinthine: pertaining to the hyacinth, a fragrant, intricately-shaped flower.
Nourjahad: region in the Near East.
Houri of the Turk: The *Houri* are the virgins found in the paradise of the Koran, the holy book of Islam.
jetty: jet black.

Responding to Stories

brows, slightly irregular in outline, had the same tint. The "strangeness," however, which I found in the eyes was of a nature distinct from the formation, or the color, or the brilliancy of the features, and must, after all, be referred to the *expression*. Ah, word of no meaning! behind whose vast latitude of mere sound we intrench our ignorance of so much of the spiritual. The expression of the eyes of Ligeia! How for long hours have I pondered upon it! How have I, through the whole of a midsummer night, struggled to fathom it! What was it—that something more profound than the well of Democritus°—which lay far within the pupils of my beloved. What *was* it? I was possessed with a passion to discover. Those eyes! those large, those shining, those divine orbs! they became to me twin stars of Leda, and I to them devoutest of astrologers.

There is no point, among the many incomprehensible anomalies of the science of mind, more thrillingly exciting than the fact—never, I believe, noticed in the schools—that in our endeavors to recall to memory something long forgotten, we often find ourselves *upon the very verge* of remembrance, without being able, in the end, to remember. And thus how frequently, in my intense scrutiny of Ligeia's eyes, have I felt approaching the full knowledge of their expression—felt it approaching—yet not quite be mine—and so at length entirely depart! And (strange, oh, strangest mystery of all!) I found, in the commonest objects of the universe, a circle of analogies to that expression. I mean to say that subsequently to the period when Ligeia's beauty passed into my spirit, there dwelling as in a shrine, I derived, from many existences in the material world, a sentiment such as I felt always aroused within me by her large and luminous orbs. Yet not the more could I define that sentiment, or analyze, or even steadily view it. I recognized it, let me repeat, sometimes in the survey of a rapidly growing vine—in the contemplation of a moth, a butterfly, a chrysalis, a stream of running water. I have felt it in the ocean—in the falling of a meteor. I have felt it in the glances of unusually aged people. And there are one or two stars in heaven (one especially, a star of the sixth magnitude, double and changeable, to be found near the large star in Lyra°) in a telescopic scrutiny of which I have been made aware of the feeling. I have been filled with it by certain sounds from stringed instruments, and not unfrequently by passages from books. Among innumerable other instances, I well remember something in a volume of Joseph Glanvill, which (perhaps merely from its quaintness—who shall say?) never failed to inspire me with the sentiment: "And the will therein lieth, which dieth not. Who knoweth the mysteries of the will, with its vigor? For God is but a great will pervading all things by nature of its intentness. Man doth not yield him to the angels, nor onto death utterly, save only through the weakness of his feeble will."

Length of years and subsequent reflection have enabled me to trace, indeed, some remote connection between this passage in the English moralist and a portion of the character of Ligeia. An *intensity* in thought, action, or speech was possibly, in her, a result, or at least an index, of that gigantic volition which, during our long intercourse, failed to give other and more immediate evidence of its existence. Of all the women whom I have ever known, she, the outwardly calm, the ever-placid Ligeia, was the most violently a prey to the tumultuous vultures of stern passion. And of such passion I could form no estimate, save by the miraculous expansion of those eyes which at once so delighted and appalled me—by the almost magical

---

Democritus: one of the first Greek philosophers.
Lyra: a constellation in the northern hemisphere.

melody, modulation, distinctness, and placidity of her very low voice—and by the fierce energy (rendered doubly effective by contrast with her manner of utterance) of the wild words which she habitually uttered. 5

I have spoken of the learning of Ligeia: it was immense—such as I have never known in woman. In the classical tongues was she deeply proficient, and as far as my own acquaintance extended in regard to the modern dialects of Europe, I have never known her at fault. Indeed upon any theme of the most admired because simply the most abstruse of the boasted erudition of the Academy, have I *ever* found Ligeia at fault? How singularly—how thrillingly, this one point in the nature of my wife has forced itself, at this late period only, upon my attention! I said her knowledge was such as I have never known in woman—but where breathes the man who has traversed, and successfully, *all* the wide areas of moral, physical, and mathematical science? I saw not then what I now clearly perceive that the acquisitions of Ligeia were gigantic, were astounding; yet I was sufficiently aware of her infinite supremacy to resign myself, with a child like confidence, to her guidance through the chaotic world of metaphysical investigation at which I was most busily occupied during the earlier years of our marriage. With how vast a triumph—with how vivid a delight—with how much of all that is ethereal in hope did I *feel*, as she bent over me in studies but little sought—but less known—that delicious vista by slow degrees expanding before me, down whose long, gorgeous, and all untrodden path, I might at length pass onward to the goal of a wisdom too divinely precious not to be forbidden.

How poignant, then, must have been the grief with which, after some years, I beheld my well-grounded expectations take wings to themselves and fly away! Without Ligeia I was but as a child groping benighted. Her presence, her readings alone, rendered vividly luminous the many mysteries of the transcendentalism in which we were immersed. Wanting the radiant lustre of her eyes, letters, lambent and golden, grew duller than Saturnian lead.° And now those eyes shone less and less frequently upon the pages over which I pored. Ligeia grew ill. The wild eyes blazed with a too—too glorious effulgence; the pale fingers became of the transparent waxen hue of the grave; and the blue veins upon the lofty forehead swelled and sank impetuously with the tides of the most gentle emotion. I saw that she must die—and I struggled desperately in spirit with the grim Azrael.° And the struggles of the passionate wife were, to my astonishment, even more energetic than my own. There has been much in her stern nature to impress me with the belief that, to her, death would have come without its terrors; but not so. Words are impotent to convey any just idea of the fierceness of resistance with which she wrestled with the Shadow. I groaned in anguish at the pitiable spectacle. I would have soothed—I would have reasoned; but in the intensity of her wild desire for life—for life—*but* for life—solace and reason were alike the uttermost of folly. Yet not until the last instance, amid the most convulsive writhings of her fierce spirit, was shaken the external placidity of her demeanor. Her voice grew more gentle—grew more low—yet I would not wish to dwell upon the wild meaning of the quietly uttered words. My brain reeled as I hearkened, entranced to a melody more than mortal—to assumptions and aspirations which mortality had never before known.

That she loved me I should not have doubted; and I might have been easily aware that, in a bosom such as hers, love would have reigned no ordinary passion. But in

---

Saturnian lead: Saturnian means "pertaining to lead" and is derived from the Roman god Saturn.
Azrael: in Moslem and Jewish legend, the angel who separates the soul from the body at death.

Responding to Stories

death only was I fully impressed with the strength of her affection. For long hours, detaining my hand, would she pour out before me the overflowing of a heart whose more than passionate devotion amounted to idolatry. How had I deserved to be so blessed by such confessions?—how had I deserved to be so cursed with the removal of my beloved in the hour of her making them? But upon this subject I cannot bear to dilate. Let me say only, that in Ligeia's more than womanly abandonment to a love, alas! all unmerited, all unworthily bestowed, I at length recognized the principle of her longing, with so wildly earnest a desire, for the life which was now fleeing so rapidly away. It is this wild longing—it is this eager vehemence of desire for life—*but* for life—that I have no power to portray—no utterance capable of expressing.

At high noon of the night on which she departed, beckoning me, peremptorily, to her side, she bade me repeat certain verses composed by herself not many days before. I obeyed her. They were these:—

> Lo! 'tis a gala night
>   Within the lonesome latter years!
> An angel throng, bewinged, bedight
>   In veils, and drowned in tears,
> Sit in a theatre, to see
>   A play of hopes and fears,
> While the orchestra breathes fitfully
>   The music of the spheres.
>
> Mimes, in the form of God on high,
>   Mutter and mumble low,
> And hither and thither fly;
>   Mere puppets they, who come and go
> At bidding of vast formless things
>   That shift the scenery to and fro,
> Flapping from out their Condor wings
>   Invisible Wo!
>
> That motley drama!—oh, be sure,
>   It shall not be forgot!
> With its Phantom chased for evermore,
>   By a crowd that seize it not,
> Through a circle that ever returneth in
>   To the self-same spot;
> And much of Madness, and more of Sin
>   And Horror, the soul of the plot!
>
> But see, amid the mimic rout
>   A crawling shape intrude!
> A blood-red thing that writhes from out
>   The scenic solitude!
> It writhes!—it writhes!—with mortal pangs
>   The mimes become its food,
> And the seraphs° sob at vermin fangs
>   In human gore imbued.

---

seraphs: celestial beings having three pairs of wings; one of the nine orders of angels.

Out—out are the lights—out all!
  And over each quivering form,
The curtain, a funeral pall,
  Comes down with the rush of a storm—
And the angels, all pallid and wan,
  Uprising, unveiling, affirm
That the play is the tragedy, "Man,"
  And its hero, the Conqueror Worm.

"O God!" half shrieked Ligeia, leaping to her feet and extending her arms aloft with a spasmodic movement, as I made an end of these lines—"O God! O Divine Father!—shall these things be undeviatingly so?—shall this Conqueror be not once conquered? Are we not part and parcel in Thee? Who—who knoweth the mysteries of the will with its vigor? Man doth not yield him to the angels, *nor unto death utterly*, save only through the weakness of his feeble will."

And now, as if exhausted with emotion, she suffered her white arms to fall, and returned solemnly to her bed of death. And as she breathed her last sighs, there came mingled with them a low murmur from her lips. I bent to them my ear, and distinguished, again, the concluding words of the passage in Glanvill: "*Man doth not yield him to the angels, nor unto death utterly, save only through the weakness of his feeble will.*"

She died: and I, crushed into the very dust with sorrow, could no longer endure the lonely desolation of my dwelling in the dim and decaying city by the Rhine. I had no lack of what the world calls wealth, Ligeia had brought me far more, very far more, than ordinarily falls to the lot of mortals. After a few months, therefore, of weary and aimless wandering, I purchased and put in some repair, an abbey, which I shall not name, in one of the wildest and least frequented portions of fair England. The gloomy and dreary grandeur of the building, the almost savage aspect of the domain, the many melancholy and time-honored memories connected with both, had much in unison with the feelings of utter abandonment which had driven me into that remote and unsocial region of the country. Yet although the external abbey, with its verdant decay hanging about it, suffered but little alteration, I gave way, with a child-like perversity, and perchance with a faint hope of alleviating my sorrows, to a display of more than regal magnificence within. For such follies, even in childhood, I had imbibed a taste, and now they came back to me as if in the dotage of grief. Alas, I feel how much even of incipient madness might have been discovered in the gorgeous and fantastic draperies, in the solemn carvings of Egypt, in the wild cornices and furniture, in the Bedlam° patterns of the carpets of tufted gold! I had become a bounden slave in the trammels of opium, and my labors and my orders had taken a coloring from my dreams. But these absurdities I must not pause to detail. Let me speak only of that one chamber, ever accursed, whither, in a moment of mental alienation, I led from the altar as my bride—as the successor of the unforgotten Ligeia— the fair-haired and blue-eyed Lady Rowena Trevanion, of Tremaine.

There is no individual portion of the architecture and decoration of that bridal chamber which is not now visibly before me. Where were the souls of the haughty family of the bride, when, through thirst of gold, they permitted to pass the threshold of an apartment *so* bedecked, a maiden and a daughter so beloved? I have said,

10

Bedlam: lunatic asylum.

that I minutely remember the details of the chamber—yet I am sadly forgetful on the topics of deep moment; and here there was no system, no keeping, in the fantastic display, to take hold upon the memory. The room lay in a high turret of the castellated abbey, was pentagonal in shape, and of capacious size. Occupying the whole southern face of the pentagon was the sole window—an immense sheet of unbroken glass from Venice—a single pane, and tinted of a leaden hue, so that the rays of either the sun or moon passing through it, fell with a ghastly lustre on the objects within. Over the upper portion of this huge window, extended the trelliswork of an aged vine, which clambered up the massy walls of the turret. The ceiling of gloomy-looking oak, was excessively lofty, vaulted, and elaborately fretted with the wildest and most grotesque specimens of a semi-Gothic,° semi-Druidical° device. From out the most central recess of this melancholy vaulting, depended, by a single chain of gold with long links, a huge censer of the same metals, Saracenic in pattern, and with many perforations so contrived that there writhed in and out of them, as if endued with a serpent vitality, a continual succession of parti-colored fires.

Some few ottomans and golden candelabra, of Eastern figure, were in various stations about; and there was the couch, too—the bridal couch—of an Indian model, and low, and sculptured of solid ebony, with a pall-like canopy above. In each of the angles of the chamber stood on end a gigantic sarcophagus of black granite, from the tombs of the kings over against Luxor,° with their aged lids full of immemorial sculpture. But in the draping of the apartment lay, alas! the chief phantasy of all. The lofty walls, gigantic in height—even unproportionably so—were hung from summit to foot, in vast folds, with a heavy and massive-looking tapestry—tapestry of a material which was found alike as a carpet on the floor, as a covering for the ottomans and the ebony bed, as a canopy for the bed and as the gorgeous volutes of the curtains which partially shaded the window. The material was the richest cloth of gold. It was spotted all over, at irregular intervals, with arabesque figures, about a foot in diameter, and wrought upon the cloth in patterns of the most jetty black. But these figures partook of the true character of the arabesque only when regarded from a single point of view. By a contrivance now common, and indeed traceable to a very remote period of antiquity, they were made changeable in aspect. To one entering the room, they bore the appearance of simple monstrosities; but upon a farther advance, this appearance gradually departed; and, step by step, as the visitor moved his station in the chamber, he saw himself surrounded by an endless succession of the ghastly forms which belong to the superstition of the Norman, or arise in the guilty slumbers of the monk. The phantasmagoric effect was vastly heightened by the artificial introduction of a strong continual current of wind behind the draperies—giving a hideous and uneasy animation to the whole.

In halls such as these—in a bridal chamber such as this—I passed, with the Lady of Tremaine, the unhallowed hours of the first month of our marriage—passed them with but little disquietude. That my wife dreaded the fierce moodiness of my temper—that she shunned me, and loved me but little—I could not help perceiving; but it gave me rather pleasure than otherwise. I loathed her with a hatred belong-

---

Gothic: Medieval German architecture style.
Druidical: pertaining to the ancient order of priests in Great Britain.
Luxor: city in Central Egypt, on the Nile.

ing more to demon than to man. My memory flew back (oh, with what intensity of regret!) to Ligeia, the beloved, the august, the beautiful, the entombed. I revelled in recollections of her purity, of her wisdom, of her lofty—her ethereal nature, of her passionate, her idolatrous love. Now, then, did my spirit fully and freely burn with more than all the fires of her own. In the excitement of my opium dreams (for I was habitually fettered in the shackles of the drug), I would call aloud upon her name, during the silence of the night, or among the sheltered recesses of the glens by day, as if, through the wild eagerness, the solemn passion, the consuming ardor of my longing for the departed, I could restore her to the pathways she had abandoned—ah, *could* it be forever?—upon the earth. 15

About the commencement of the second month of the marriage, the Lady Rowena was attacked with sudden illness, from which her recovery was slow. The fever which consumed her rendered her nights uneasy; and in her perturbed state of half-slumber, she spoke of sounds, and of motions, in and about the chamber of the turret, which I concluded had no origin save in the distemper of her fancy, or perhaps in the phantasmagoric influences of the chamber itself. She became at length convalescent—finally, well. Yet but a brief period elapsed, ere a second more violent disorder again threw her upon a bed of suffering; and from this attack her frame, at all times feeble, never altogether recovered. Her illnesses were, after this epoch, of alarming character, and of more alarming recurrence, defying alike the knowledge and the great exertions of her physicians. With the increase of the chronic disease, which had thus, apparently, taken too sure hold upon her constitution to be eradicated by human means, I could not fail to observe a similiar increase in the nervous irritation of her temperament, and in her excitability by trivial causes of fear. She spoke again, and now more frequently and pertinaciously, of the sounds—of the slight sounds—and of the unusual motions among the tapestries, to which she had formerly alluded.

One night, near the closing in of September, she pressed this distressing subject with more than usual emphasis upon my attention. She had just awakened from an unquiet slumber, and I had been watching, with feelings half of anxiety, half of vague terror, the workings of her emaciated countenance. I sat by the side of her ebony bed, upon one of the ottomans of India. She partly arose, and spoke, in an earnest low whisper, of sounds which she *then* heard, but which I could not hear—of motions which she *then* saw, but which I could not perceive. The wind was rushing hurriedly behind the tapestries, and I wished to show her (what, let me confess it, I could not *all* believe) that those almost inarticulate breathings, and those very gentle variations of the figures upon the wall, were but the natural effects of that customary rushing of the wind. But a deadly pallor, over-spreading her face, had proved to me that my exertions to reassure her would be fruitless. She appeared to be fainting, and no attendants were within call. I remembered where was deposited a decanter of light wine which had been ordered by her physicians, and hastened across the chamber to procure it. But, as I stepped beneath the light of the censer, two circumstances of a startling nature attracted my attention. I had felt that some palpable although invisible object had passed lightly by my person; and I saw that there lay upon the gold carpet, in the very middle of the rich lustre thrown from the censer, a shadow—a faint, indefinite shadow of angelic aspect—such as might be fancied for the shadow of a shade. But I was wild with the excitement of an immoderate dose of opium, and heeded these things but little, nor spoke of them to Rowena. Having found the wine, I recrossed the chamber, and poured out a gobletful, which I held to the lips of the fainting lady. She had now partially recovered, however, and took the vessel herself, while I sank upon an ottoman° near me, with my eyes fastened upon her person. It was then that I became distinctly aware of a gentle foot-fall upon the carpet, and near the couch; and in a second thereafter, as Rowena was in the act of raising the wine to her lips, I saw, or may have dreamed that I saw, fall within the goblet, as if from some invisible spring in the atmosphere of the room, three or four large drops of a brilliant and ruby-colored fluid. If this I saw—not so Rowena. She swallowed the wine unhesitatingly, and I forebore to speak to her of a circumstance which must, after all, I considered, have been but the suggestion of a vivid imagination, rendered morbidly active by the terror of the lady, by the opium, and by the hour.

Yet I cannot conceal it from my own perception that, immediately subsequent to the fall of the ruby-drops, a rapid change for the worse took place in the disorder of my wife; so that, on the third subsequent night, the hands of her menials prepared her for the tomb, and on the fourth, I sat alone with her shrouded body, in that fantastic chamber which had received her as my bride. Wild visions, opium-engendered, flitted, shadow-like, before me. I gazed with unquiet eye upon the sarcophagi in the angles of the room, upon the varying figures of the drapery, and upon the writhing of the parti-colored fires in the censer overhead. My eyes then fell, as I called to mind the circumstances of a former night, to the spot beneath the glare of the censer where I had seen the faint traces of the shadow. It was there, however, no longer; and breathing with greater freedom, I turned my glances to the pallid and rigid figure upon the bed. Then rushed upon me a thousand memories of Ligeia— and then came back upon my heart, with the turbulent violence of a flood, the whole of that unutterable woe with which I had regarded *her* thus enshrouded. The night waned; and still, with a bosom full of bitter thoughts of the one only and supremely beloved, I remained gazing upon the body of Rowena.

It might have been midnight, or perhaps earlier, or later, for I had taken no note of time, when a sob, low, gentle, but very distinct, startled me from my revery. I *felt* that it came from the bed of ebony—the bed of death. I listened in an agony of superstitious terror—but there was no repetition of the sound. I strained my vision to detect any motion in the corpse but there was not the slightest perceptible. Yet I could not have been deceived. I *had* heard the noise, however faint, and my soul was awakened within me. I resolutely and perseveringly kept my attention riveted upon the body. Many minutes elapsed before any circumstance occurred tending to throw light upon the mystery. At length it became evident that a slight, a very feeble, a barely noticeable tinge of color had flushed up within the cheeks, and along the sunken small veins of the eyelids. Through a species of unutterable horror and awe, for which the language of mortality has no sufficiently energetic expression, I felt my heart cease to beat, my limbs grow rigid where I sat. Yet a sense of duty finally operated to restore my self-possession. I could no longer doubt that we had been precipitate in our preparations—that Rowena still lived. It was necessary that some immediate exertion be made; yet the turret was altogether apart from the portion of the abbey tenanted by the servants—there were none within call—I had no means of summoning them to my aid without leaving the room for many minutes—and this I could not venture to do. I therefore struggled alone in my endeavors to call back the spirit still hovering. In a short period it was certain, however, that a relapse had

---

°*ottoman:* couch without arms or back.

taken place; the color disappeared from both eyelid and cheek, leaving a wanness even more than that of marble; the lips became doubly shrivelled and pinched up in the ghastly expression of death; a repulsive clamminess and coldness overspread rapidly the surface of the body; and all the usual rigorous stiffness immediately supervened. I fell back with a shudder upon the couch from which I had been so startlingly aroused, and again gave myself up to passionate waking visions of Ligeia.

An hour thus elapsed, when (could it be possible?) I was a second time aware of some vague sound issuing from the region of the bed. I listened—in extremity of horror. The sound came again—it was a sigh. Rushing to the corpse, I saw—distinctly saw—a tremor upon the lips. In a minute afterward they relaxed, disclosing a bright line of the pearly teeth. Amazement now struggled in my bosom with the profound awe which had hitherto reigned there alone. I felt that my vision grew dim, that my reason wandered; and it was only by a violent effort that I at length succeeded in nerving myself to the task which duty thus once more had pointed out. There was now a partial glow upon the forehead and upon the cheek and throat; a perceptible warmth pervaded the whole frame; there was even a slight pulsation at the heart. The lady *lived;* and with redoubled ardor I betook myself to the task of restoration. I chafed and bathed the temples and the hands, and used every exertion which experience, and no little medical reading, could suggest. But in vain. Suddenly, the color fled, the pulsation ceased, the lips resumed the expression of the dead, and, in an instant afterward, the whole body took upon itself the icy chilliness, the livid hue, the intense rigidity, the sunken outline, and all the loathsome peculiarities of that which has been, for many days, a tenant of the tomb.   20

And again I sunk into visions of Ligeia—and again (what marvel that I shudder while I write?) *again* there reached my ears a low sob from the region of the ebony bed. But why shall I minutely detail the unspeakable horrors of that night? Why shall I pause to relate how, time after time, until near the period of the gray dawn, this hideous drama of revivification was repeated; how each terrific relapse was only into a sterner and apparently more irredeemable death; how each agony wore the aspect of a struggle with some invisible foe; and how each struggle was succeeded by I know not what of wild change in the personal appearance of the corpse? Let me hurry to a conclusion.

The greater part of the fearful night had worn away, and she who had been dead once again stirred—and now more vigorously than hitherto, although arousing from a dissolution more appalling in its utter hopelessness than any. I had long ceased to struggle or to move, and remained sitting rigidly upon the ottoman, a helpless prey to a whirl of violent emotions, of which extreme awe was perhaps the least terrible, the least consuming. The corpse, I repeat, stirred, and now more vigorously than before. The hues of life flushed tip with unwonted energy into the countenance—the limbs relaxed—and, save that the eyelids were yet pressed heavily together, and that the bandages and draperies of the grave still imparted their charnel character to the figure, I might have dreamed that Rowena had indeed shaken off, utterly, the fetters of Death. But if this idea was not, even then, altogether adopted, I could at least doubt no longer, when, arising from the bed, tottering, with feeble steps, with closed eyes, and with the manner of one bewildered in a dream, the thing that was enshrouded advanced boldly and palpably into the middle of the apartment.

I trembled not—I stirred not—for a crowd of unutterable fancies connected with the air, the stature, the demeanor, of the figure, rushing hurriedly through my brain, had paralyzed—had chilled me into stone. I stirred not—but gazed upon the apparition. There was a mad disorder in my thoughts—a tumult unappeasable. Could it, indeed, be the *living* Rowena who confronted me? Could it, indeed, be Rowena *at all*—the fair-haired, the blue-eyed Lady Rowena Trevanion of Tremaine? Why, *why* should I doubt it? The bandage lay heavily about the mouth—but then might it not be the mouth of the breathing Lady of Tremaine? And the cheeks—there were the roses as in her noon of life—yes, these might indeed be the fair cheeks of the living Lady of Tremaine. And the chin, with its dimples, as in health, might it not be hers?—but *had she then grown taller since her malady?* What inexpressible madness seized me with that thought? One bound, and I had reached her feet! Shrinking from my touch, she let fall from her head, unloosened, the ghastly cerements° which had confined it, and there streamed forth into the rushing atmosphere of the chamber huge masses of long and dishevelled hair; *it was blacker than the raven wings of the midnight!* And now slowly opened *the eyes* of the figure which stood before me. "Here then, at least," I shrieked aloud, "can I never—can I never be mistaken—these are the full, and the black, and the wild eyes—of my lost love—of the Lady—of the Lady Ligeia."

Roy P. Basler

THE INTERPRETATION OF "LIGEIA"

Although a number of biographers, psychoanalytical and otherwise, have employed the data and theories of several schools of thought in nonrational psychology in attempting to interpret the personality of Poe, and have indicated the need for such an approach in the interpretation of much of his writing, no one, as far as I am aware, has undertaken to point out the specific bearing of nonrational psychology on the critical interpretation of a number of Poe's stories which in their entire context seem to indicate that Poe dealt deliberately with the psychological themes of obsession and madness. Such a story is "Ligeia," the most important of a group of stories, generally but inadequately classified as "impressionistic," which includes the kindred pieces "Morella" and "Berenice." Each of these three tales shows a similar preoccupation with the *idée fixe* or obsession in an extreme form of monomania° which seems intended by Poe to be the psychological key to its plot. Even a casual comparison of these stories will reveal not merely the similar theme of obsession but also the dominant concepts which provide the motivation in all three: the power of the psychical over the physical and the power of frustrate love to create an erotic symbolism and mythology in compensation for sensual disappointment. Although Poe grinds them differently in each story, they are the same grist to his mill.

In the interpretation of "Ligeia" particularly, an understanding of the nonrational makes necessary an almost complete reversal of certain critical opinions and

---

cerements: grave clothes.
monomania: obsession with one thing.

explanations which assume that the story is a tale of the supernatural. Clayton Hamilton's analysis of "Ligeia" in his *Manual of the Art of Fiction* (1918) is a rationalization which outdoes Poe's rationalization of "The Raven" in its attempt to show how Poe chose with mathematical accuracy just the effect and just the word which would make the perfect story of the supernatural. Unfortunately, Hamilton's basic assumptions seem obviously erroneous when he takes for granted that Ligeia is the main character, that the action of the story is concerned primarily with her struggle to overcome death, that the hero (the narrator) is "an ordinary character" who functions merely as an "eyewitness" and as a "standard by which the unusual capabilities of the central figure may be measured," and that Ligeia is "a woman of superhuman will, and her husband, a man of ordinary powers." These assumptions ignore the obvious context with its emphasis on the hero's obsession, madness, and hallucination. Actually, the story seems both aesthetically and psychologically more intelligible as a tale, not of supernatural, but rather of entirely natural, though highly phrenetic, psychological phenomena.

Perhaps the naïveté and excesses of certain psychoanalytical biographies of Poe have militated against the recognition of the value of nonrational psychology in the study of Poe. At any rate, scholarly critical biographers have hesitated to credit the indubitable data of the science; and even recent critical studies following the traditional interpretation, ignore the most obvious evidence of the nonrational theme and motivation of "Ligeia" and undertake to analyze the story again as a tale of the supernatural. Although we need not consider here either the value of nonrational psychology as a means of understanding Poe's personality or the mistakes of broad assumption and overconfidence which the analysts of Poe have made, it must be recognized that, if nonrational psychology provides a better means of understanding the structure and effect of a tale like "Ligeia" and enables the reader to appreciate better what Poe accomplished as an artist, then the critic who refuses to accept nonrational psychology does so at the risk of his entire critical principle.

Let us examine the personality of the hero of "Ligeia," the narrator whose psycho-emotional experience weaves the plot. He is presented in the first paragraph as a man with an erotic obsession of long standing; his wife is presumably dead, but his idolatrous devotion to her has kept her physical beauty and her personality painfully alive in his every thought. That this devotion approaches monomania becomes more clear with every statement he makes about her. She is the acme of womanly beauty and spiritual perfection. From the time of his first acquaintance with her he has been oblivious of all but her beauty and her power over him: "I cannot, for my soul, remember how, when, or even precisely where, I first became acquainted with the lady Ligeia." Furthermore, there is his interesting admission that "I have *never known* the paternal name of her who was my friend and my betrothed, and who became the partner of my studies, and finally the wife of my bosom." In view of the fact that she was of an exceedingly ancient family and had brought him wealth "very far more, than ordinarily falls to the lot of mortals," these admissions are more than strange. Though the hero half recognizes the incongruity of his unbelievable ignorance, he dismisses it as evidence of a lover's devotion—a "wildly romantic offering on the shrine of the most passionate devotion."

Beginning with the second paragraph, we see more clearly the degree of his obsession. Although he makes much of the power of Ligeia's intellect, his imaginative preoccupation with her physical beauty is highly sensuous, even voluptuous, in its

intensity. He seems to be a psychopath who has failed to find the last, final meaning of life in the coils of Ligeia's raven hair, her ivory skin, her "jetty lashes of great
length," and, above all, in her eyes, "those shining, those divine orbs!" But his imaginative desire has outrun his capabilities. Though his senses have never revealed the
final meaning of the mystery which has enthralled him, his imagination refuses to
accept defeat. The key to his failure is hinted in the paragraph which reveals his
symbolic deification of Ligeia as a sort of personal Venus Aphrodite° who personifies the dynamic urge of life itself but who, because of the hero's psychic incapacity,
cannot reveal to him the "forbidden knowledge":   5

> There is no point, among the many incomprehensible anomalies of the science
> of mind, more thrillingly exciting than the fact—never, I believe, noticed in the
> schools—that in our endeavors to recall to memory something long forgotten, we
> often find ourselves *upon the very verge* of remembrance, without being able, in
> the end, to remember. And thus how frequently, in my intense scrutiny of Ligeia's
> eyes, have I felt approaching the full knowledge of their expression—felt it ap-
> proaching—yet not quite be mine—and so at length entirely depart! And
> (strange, oh, strangest mystery of all!) I found, in the commonest objects of the
> universe, a circle of analogies to that expression. I mean to say that, subsequently
> to the period when Ligeia's beauty passed into my spirit, there dwelling as in a
> shrine, I derived, from many existences in the material world, a sentiment such
> as I felt always aroused within me by her large and luminous orbs. Yet not the
> more could I define that sentiment, or analyze, or even steadily view it. I recog-
> nized it, let me repeat, sometimes in the survey of a rapidly-growing vine—in the
> contemplation of a moth, a butterfly, a chrysalis, a stream of running water. I have
> felt it in the ocean; in the falling of a meteor. I have felt it in the glances of un-
> usually aged people. And there are one or two stars in heaven (one especially, a
> star of the sixth magnitude, double and changeable, to be found near the large
> star in Lyra) in a telescopic scrutiny of which I have been made aware of the feel-
> ing. I have been filled with it by certain sounds from stringed instruments, and
> not unfrequently by passages from books. Among innumerable other instances, I
> well remember something in a volume of Joseph Glanvill, which (perhaps merely
> from its quaintness—who shall say?) never failed to inspire me with the senti-
> ment;—"And the will therein lieth, which dieth not. Who knoweth the myster-
> ies of the will, with its vigor? For God is but a great will pervading all things by
> nature of its intentness. Man doth not yield him to the angels, nor unto death
> utterly, save only through the weakness of his feeble will."

In this passage it is not difficult to perceive the oblique confession of inadequacy
and to trace the psychological process of symbolism, which compensates for the failure of sense by apotheosis of the object of desire. Although sensuous delight leads the
hero to "the very verge" of a "wisdom too divinely precious not to be forbidden," final
knowledge of the secret of Ligeia's eyes is blocked by an obstacle deep within the
hero's own psyche, and the insatiable imagination seeks for a realm of experience not
sensual and mortal and identifies Ligeia with the dynamic power and mystery of the
entire universe. She becomes not merely a woman but a goddess, through the worship of whom he "feels" that he may "pass onward to the goal of a wisdom too di-

---

Venus Aphrodite: goddess of love in classical mythology.

vinely precious not to be forbidden." There is for him, however, no possibility of fathoming the mystery which she symbolizes, though in the height of passionate adoration he feels himself to be *"upon the very verge,"* which experience he likens to that of almost but not quite recalling something from the depths of his unconscious.

This analogy of the will's inability to dictate to the unconscious and its inability to dictate to love reveals something more than the hero's vague awareness of a psychic flaw which thwarts his desire; it reveals the source of the obsession which dominates in a compensatory process his struggle to achieve by power of mind what he cannot achieve through love. The passage from Glanvill is the key, the psychic formula, which he hopes may open to him the very mystery of being, his own as well as Ligeia's, in which as he conceives lies the source of the dark failure and frustration of his senses. From this psychic formula derives, then, the megalomania that he can by power of will become godlike, blending his spirit with the universal spirit of deity symbolized in the divine Ligeia, who possesses in apotheosis all the attributes of his own wish, extended in a symbolic ideal beyond the touch of mortality and raised to the absoluteness of deity—intensity in thought, passion, and sensibility; perfection in wisdom, beauty, and power of mind. It is worth noting that Poe had earlier used the name Ligeia in *Al Aaraaf*° for a divinity representing much the same dynamic beauty in all nature.

But the hero's approach to power is thwarted by Ligeia's death. Just at the point when triumph seems imminent, when he feels "that delicious vista by slow degrees expanding before me, down whose long, gorgeous, and all untrodden path, I might at length pass onward to the goal of a wisdom too divinely precious not to be forbidden"—just then Ligeia dies, because of the weakness of her own mortal will and in spite of the fervor with which the hero himself "struggled desperately in spirit with the grim Azrael."

At this point it may be noted that the obsession with the *idée fixe* expressed in the passage from Glanvill begins with the hero himself and does not express Ligeia's belief. It is his will to conquer death that motivates the rest of the story, not hers. Even when she recites the formula on her deathbed, the lines are but the echo of his wish, given in antiphonal response to the materialistic creed which she has avowed in her poem "The Conqueror Worm," which represents her philosophy and is read by the hero merely at her peremptory request. This fact is always overlooked in the rational interpretations of the story, which assume that Ligeia's struggle is the primary motivating action of the tale. Thus, in spite of her power and beauty and her passionate desire for life, *"but* for life," the earthly body of Ligeia dies—perhaps, as the obsessed hero conceives, because she has not believed in her power to conquer death. Her failure of spirit, however, is not the end. Nor is the hero's failure as he "struggled desperately in spirit with the grim Azrael" the end, but rather the beginning of the grim mania in which he is resolved to bring her back to life.

In following all that the hero says, the reader must keep constantly in mind that, if the hero is suffering from obsession, his narrative cannot be accepted merely at its face value as authentic of all the facts; and he must remember that incidents and circumstances have a primary significance in terms of the hero's mania which is often at variance with the significance which the hero believes and means to convey. This

---

Al Aaraaf: a long poem by Poe rich in symbolism.

Responding to Stories

is to say that Poe's psychological effect in "Ligeia" is similar to that of later delvers in psychological complexity like Henry James, whose stories told by a narrator move on two planes. There is the story which the narrator means to tell, and there is the story which he tells without meaning to, as he unconsciously reveals himself.

Hence, the important elements in the hero's description of Ligeia are of primary significance as they reveal his feeling of psychic inadequacy, his voluptuous imagination, and his megalomania and fierce obsession with the idea that by power of will man may thwart death through spiritual love. Likewise, the narrative of the circumstances of Ligeia's death is of significance, not merely as it reveals her love of life and her struggle to live, but as it reveals the psychological crisis in which the hero's psychic shock and frustration bring on final and complete mania, the diagnostic fallacy of which is that his will is omnipotent and can bring Ligeia back to life. Up to the point of her death the hero's obsession has taken the form of adoration and worship of her person in an erotomania primarily sensual (though frustrated by a psychic flaw which he is aware of but does not understand) and hence projected into a symbolic realm of deity and forbidden wisdom. Following her death, however, his obsession becomes an intense megalomania motivated by his will to restore her to life in another body through a process of metempsychosis.°

It is of particular importance that, with the beginning of the second half of the story, the reader keep in mind these two planes of meaning, for the primary significance of what the hero tells in this part is never in any circumstance the plain truth. It is rather an entirely, and obviously, fantastic representation of the facts, which justifies his obsessed psyche and proves that he has been right and Ligeia (and perhaps the gentle reader) wrong in the assumption that mortality is the common human fate—the old story of the madman who knows that he is right and the rest of the world wrong.

Thus even the hero's admission of his "incipient madness" must be recognized as the cunning condescension of the megalomaniac to the normal mind, which would not otherwise understand the excesses of his peculiar "childlike perversity" in choosing such macabre furnishings for his bridal chamber or in debauching his senses with opium—both of which "perversities" he dismisses with pseudo-naïveté as minor "absurdities." The contempt which he feels for people of normal mentality almost leads him to give himself away in his blistering question: "Where were the souls of the haughty family of the bride, when, through thirst of gold, they permitted to pass the threshold of an apartment so bedecked, a maiden and a daughter so beloved?" In other words, why could not the parents of Rowena perceive in the macabre furnishings—the "ebony couch" with draperies of gold "spotted all over, at regular intervals, with arabesque figures . . . of the most jetty black," the "sarcophagus of black granite," and the "endless succession of the ghastly forms which belong to the superstition of the Norman, or arise in the guilty slumbers of the monk"—why could they not perceive the obvious death chamber which he intended the bridal room to be? Likewise, one must recognize the maniacal condescension which prompts the hardly disarming naïveté with which he confesses the pleasure he derived from Rowena's dread avoidance of him in the "unhallowed hours of the first month of our marriage" and with which he testifies, "I loathed her with a hatred belonging more to demon than to man."

---

metempsychosis: process similar to reincarnation whereby a spirit returns in another body.

Perhaps he relies on this impercipiency of the normal mind to befuddle also the moral equilibrium of his audience into a sentimental acceptance of the phrenetic° devotion of his spirit to the memory of Ligeia, which in his madness justifies, of course, his ghastly treatment of Rowena in terms of a pure, ethereal love for Ligeia. Thus he concludes his introductory statement in the second half of the story on a plane which, while utterly sincere in its obsessional idealism, is highly equivocal in its moral and psychological implications and reveals the fact that underlying his mad persecution of Rowena lies his frustrate desire for and worship of the lost Ligeia:

> ... My memory flew back (oh, with what intensity of regret!) to Ligeia, the beloved, the august, the beautiful, the entombed. I revelled in recollections of her purity, of her wisdom, of her lofty—her ethereal nature, of her passionate, her idolatrous love. Now, then, did my spirit fully and freely burn with more than all the fires of her own. In the excitement of my opium dreams (for I was habitually fettered in the shackles of the drug), I would call aloud upon her name, during the silence of the night, or among the sheltered recesses of the glens by day, as if, through the wild eagerness, the solemn passion, the consuming ardor of my longing for the departed, I could restore her to the pathways she had abandoned— ah, *could* it be forever?—upon the earth.

Up to this point in the second half of the story, the hero has unintentionally mixed a generous amount of obliquely truthful interpretation with the facts of his story; but from this point to the end he narrates events with a pseudo-objectivity that wholly, though not necessarily intentionally, falsifies their significance. He tells what he saw and heard and felt, but these things must be understood as the hallucinations of his mania, as wish-projections which arise from his obsession with the idea of resurrecting Ligeia in the body of Rowena. He tells the effects but ignores or misrepresents the causes: he wants his audience to believe that the power of Ligeia's will effected her resurrection in the body of Rowena but does not want his audience to recognize (what he himself would not) that he was the actual agent of Rowena's death and his perceptions mere hallucinations produced by obsessional desire.   15

In brief, it must be recognized that the hero has murdered Rowena in his maniacal attempt to restore Ligeia to life. Although his narrative of the "sudden illness" which seized Rowena "about the second month of the marriage" avoids anything which suggests a physical attempt at murder, there are unintentional confessions of deliberate psychological cruelty in the macabre furnishings of the apartment and in the weird sounds and movements designed to produce ghostly effects. The hero mentions with apparent casualness and objectivity that, "in her perturbed state of half-slumber, she spoke of sounds, and of motions, in and about the chamber of the turret, which I concluded had no origin save in the distemper of her fancy, or perhaps in the phantasmagoric° influences of the chamber itself." But by his earlier confession he had calculated these "sounds" and "motions" in advance, as instruments of mental torture for the young bride, by so arranging the figured draperies as to produce optical illusions of motion and by introducing "a strong current of wind behind the draperies." He further confesses that as her dread and fear began to produce symptoms of hysteria and physical collapse he "wished to show her (what, let me confess it, I could not *all* believe) that those almost inarticulate breathings,

---

phrenetic: frenetic, frenzied.
phantasmagoric: characterized by fantastical imagery.

and those very gentle variations of the figures upon the wall, were but the natural effects of that customary rushing of the wind." But he did not tell her!

At this point he narrates how he became aware of a "presence" in the chamber, a supernatural agency at work. This is the wish-illusion that not he but the ghost of Ligeia, vampire-like, is preying upon the distraught and febrile body of Rowena. The details of resuscitation and relapse he wishes to believe evidence of the struggle of Ligeia's spirit to drive Rowena's spirit out of the body and to reanimate it herself. Hence arises the hallucination of the shadow on the carpet—"a faint, indefinite shadow of angelic aspect—such as might be fancied for the shadow of a shade." But, as he admits immediately, he had indulged in "an immoderate dose of opium, and heeded these things but little, nor spoke of them to Rowena." Such deprecation of his own perception is again the cunning of the maniac who must tell his story and must equally not tell it wholly, lest he spoil it by supplying evidence of a sort likely to encourage suspicion that there is something more than opiumism in his madness.

Then comes the crux of the death scene. Here, in the mélange of fact and hallucination, is *the fact* which betrays him: "I saw, or may have dreamed that I saw, fall within the goblet, as if from some invisible spring in the atmosphere of the room, three or four large drops of a brilliant and ruby colored fluid." Impatient for results and fearful that the apparent progress of Rowena's hysteria and physical collapse will not suffice, doubting the power of his will alone to effect his purpose, he has resorted to actual poison, which, however, his obsession adapts into the pattern of hallucination by perceiving that it is distilled from the atmosphere rather than dropped from a bottle held in his own hand. He cannot in his obsession recognize the bottle or the poison as physical facts, for then the power of the spirit must bow to the greater power of a merely physical drug.

The deed is accomplished, and the remainder of the narrative reveals the final stage of his mania. As the body of Rowena writhes in the throes of death, his wish takes complete command of his brain. As he watches, his mind is filled with "a thousand memories of Ligeia." The shadow on the carpet disappears, and he hears "a sob, low, gentle, but very distinct," which he "*felt* . . . came from the bed of ebony." As evidence of returning life appears in the corpse, he feels it necessary that "some immediate exertion be made; yet the turret was altogether apart from the portion of the abbey tenanted by the servants—there were none within call—I had no means of summoning them to my aid without leaving the room for many minutes—and this I could not venture to do." With this obviously satisfactory explanation made, he relates how he struggled alone to call back "the spirit still hovering," only to fall back with a shudder and resume his "passionate waking visions of Ligeia."

Again and again the symptoms of life appear and diminish, and each time the hero testifies that he "sunk into visions of Ligeia," with the result that each period of struggle "was succeeded by I know not what of wild change in the personal appearance of the corpse," until finally his obsessed brain and senses perceive their desire-wish accomplished. The phrenetic tension of hallucination mounts in the concluding paragraph to an orgasm of psychopathic horror and wish-fulfilment in the final sentence: " 'Here, then, at least,' I shrieked aloud, 'can I never—can I never be mistaken—these are the full, and the black, and the wild eyes—of my lost love—of the Lady—of the Lady Ligeia!' " [20]

This conclusion is artistically perfect and unassailable if the story is understood to be that of a megalomaniac, a revelation of obsessional psychology and mania. If, however, the story is taken to be a rational narrative of the quasi-supernatural told by a man in his right mind, the conclusion is not a conclusion but a climax, the proper denouement of which would be the corpse's reassumption of Rowena's lineaments and its final lapse into certain death, recognized this time as complete and final by the mind of the hero. Philip Pendleton Cooke, presuming the entirely rational interpretation to be the one Poe intended, called Poe's attention to this supposed weakness of the ending in a letter otherwise filled with large praise for the story's effect. Cooke's comment is as follows:

> There I was shocked by a violation of the ghostly proprieties—so to speak—and wondered how the Lady Ligeia—a wandering essence—could, in quickening *the body of the Lady Rowena* (such is the idea) become suddenly the visible, bodily Ligeia.

Poe's answer takes full cognizance of the justice of Cooke's criticism and tacitly admits the rational interpretation to be the one he intended, making the somewhat lame excuse that

> . . . it was necessary, since "Morella" was written, to modify "Ligeia." I was forced to be content with a sudden half-consciousness, on the part of the narrator, that Ligeia stood before him. One point I have not fully carried out—I should have intimated that the *will* did not perfect its intention—there should have been a relapse—a final one—and Ligeia (who had only succeeded in so much as to convey an idea of the truth to the narrator) should be at length entombed as Rowena—the bodily alterations having gradually faded away.

It is possible that Poe meant in this statement merely to bow to Cooke's praise and accept a criticism which completely misses the primary significance of the entire story, in order to avoid the necessity of explaining to an admirer the painful truth that he had missed the point. Poe was avid for the praise that came all too seldom, and he may have avoided controversy with his appreciative correspondent somewhat out of gratitude. That he could not have held seriously or for long the opinion that the story needed an added denouement seems obvious from the fact that, although he made careful and detailed revisions of the story afterward, he did not alter the nature of the conclusion. That he would have done so without hesitation had he actually believed the conclusion defective, we may be sure from his indefatigable practice of revising his favorite pieces even in the minor details which did not fulfil his wishes.

There seem to be two alternatives here: either Poe meant the story to be read as Cooke read it, and failed to provide the sort of conclusion which he admitted to be necessary, or he meant it to be read approximately as we have analyzed it, and merely bowed to Cooke's criticism out of gratitude for appreciation. Possibly there is a third alternative, however, which is not incompatible with Poe's genius. Perhaps the intention in the story was not entirely clear and rationalized in Poe's own mind, preoccupied as he was with the very ideas and obsessions which motivate the hero of the story. Anyone who has studied Poe's rationalization of "The Raven" in "The Philosophy of Composition" must recognize that in its *post hoc°* reasoning Poe largely ignores the obvious psycho-emotional motivation of his own creative process. In his offhand and casual comments on his writings, however, he sometimes

---

post hoc: after the fact.

Responding to Stories

admitted the essentially "unconscious" source of his compositions. An example of this admission is his comment written in a copy of the *Broadway Journal* which he sent to Mrs. Sarah Helen Whitman:

> The poem ["To Helen"—of 1848] which I sent you contained all the events of a *dream* which occurred to me soon after I knew you. Ligeia was also suggested by a *dream*—observe the *eyes* in both tale and poem.

As an artist Poe depicted the functioning of both rational and nonrational processes in a character obsessed by a psychopathic desire. But, since Poe was not entirely clear in his own mind concerning the nonrational logic of the unconscious which he used as an artist, he accepted Cooke's criticism as justified, even though he felt the "truth" and appropriateness of the conclusion as he had written it, in part, at least, out of his own unconscious. Poe's penciled comment on the manuscript copy of one of his later poems, as quoted by Mrs. Whitman, is again indicative of the source of his artistic if not of his critical certainty:

> "All that I have here expressed was actually present to me. Remember the mental condition which gave rise to 'Ligeia'—recall the passage of which I spoke, and observe the coincidence . . . I regard these visions," he says, "even as they arise, with an awe which in some measure moderates or tranquillizes the ecstasy— I so regard them through a conviction that this ecstasy, in itself, is of a character supernal to the human nature—*is a glimpse of the spirit's outer world*."

Thus, when he came to revise the story, his artistic sense, rooted deeply in his own unconscious processes (or, if one chooses, in "the spirit's outer world"), did not permit the alteration of the conclusion to fit an interpretation essentially superficial and incomplete in its perception of the psychological origin of the story. Had Poe been able to understand the nonrational processes of the psyche as fully as Freud did later, he might have written a reply to Cooke that would have outdone "The Philosophy of Composition" in logical analysis of the creation of a work of art out of both rational and nonrational mental processes, but it is not likely that he could have written as an artist a more effective psychological story than "Ligeia."

The merits of this analysis must, of course, stand or be dismissed on the evidence within the context of the story itself, and the evidence in this case is—what it is not in the case of Poe's personality—complete. The hero of the story either is or is not to be completely trusted as a rational narrator whose account can be accepted with the meaning which he wishes it to have, and Poe either does or does not give the reader to understand which point of view he must take. To me, at least, Poe makes obvious the fact of the hero's original obsession in the first half of the story and his megalomania in the second half. The concluding paragraph remains aesthetically as utterly incomprehensible to me as it was to Philip Pendleton Cooke, if the story is merely a story of the supernatural designed to produce an impression. And I cannot think that Poe, fully aware of the justice of Cooke's criticism in that view, would have left the denouement as it was originally written unless he believed that there was more artistic verisimilitude° in the story as he had created it than there was in the story as Cooke had interpreted it.

[1948]

---

verisimilitude: appearing to be real.

1. How does Basler establish his interpretation as diverging from that of his predecessor, Clayton Hamilton?

2. How does Basler distinguish "nonrational" explanations from "supernatural" ones, and how does he use this distinction to build his interpretation?

3. Summarize in a single paragraph Basler's basic interpretation of "Ligeia." Do you share, or disagree with, his views? Explain.

4. According to Basler, what was Philip Pendleton Cooke's problem with the story? What was Poe's response? How do Poe's stated views find accord with Basler's?

TWO METHODS OF RESPONDING TO CHEKHOV'S "THE LADY WITH THE LITTLE DOG"

Anton Chekhov (1860–1904)

Writers, like all craftspeople, have their own pantheon of cherished heroes, and their lists of masters are not always in accord with the judgments of scholars and critics. Anton Chekhov, the great favorite among generations of writers, is a case in point. His continuing popularity is almost solely the consequence of the passion he has inspired in writers and lay readers. The critics, while willing to regard him seriously, have never quite known what to make of his genius—it is fresh and distinct, and it defies every effort to place it in a critical category.

Chekhov, still another in the ranks of the short-lived, was the son of a failed grocer. He studied medicine at Moscow University but at a very young age began to write stories and sketches for newspapers in order to support his family. His gift for imbuing the slightest cluster of impressions with life was immediately obvious, and he never lacked for markets for his work.

Chekhov published two collections of stories in rapid succession—in 1886 and 1887—and their reception encouraged him to put his medical practice to the side. (But while he gave up the profession, he never stopped ministering to the sick; for years he treated peasants who lived near his estate outside Moscow.)

In 1890, determined to face for himself the extremities of human suffering, Chekhov journeyed overland to the distant penal island of Sakhalin. At the time of the trip he was already

suffering from the tuberculosis that would finally
kill him, but he bore the arduous miles
cheerfully—one might even say with a
masochistic cheerfulness.

By the time of his thirties, Chekhov had
already achieved renown throughout Russia. He
befriended Tolstoy and exerted great influence
on the literary life of his times. He also turned
his hand to play writing, in a few years writing
some of the great plays of the world stage.
(*The Seagull, Uncle Vanya, The Cherry Orchard,*
and *The Three Sisters* were all penned between
1896 and 1904.) In 1901, in failing health, he
married the celebrated actress Olga Knipper. He
died three years later in Yalta° from tuberculosis.

THE LADY WITH THE
LITTLE DOG

I

It was said that a new person had appeared on the sea-front: a lady with a little dog.
Dmitri Dmitrich Gurov, who had by then been a fortnight at Yalta, and so was fairly
at home there, had begun to take an interest in new arrivals. Sitting in Verney's
pavilion, he saw, walking on the sea-front, a fair-haired young lady of medium
height, wearing a *béret*; a white Pomeranian dog was running behind her.

And afterwards he met her in the public gardens and in the square several times
a day. She was walking alone, always wearing the same *béret*, and always with the
same white dog; no one knew who she was, and every one called her simply "the
lady with the dog."

"If she is here alone without a husband or friends, it wouldn't be amiss to make
her acquaintance," Gurov reflected.

He was under forty, but he had a daughter already twelve years old, and two sons
at school. He had been married young, when he was a student in his second year, and
by now his wife seemed half as old again as he. She was a tall, erect woman with dark
eyebrows, staid and dignified, and, as she said of herself, intellectual. She read a great
deal, used phonetic spelling, called her husband, not Dmitri, but Dimitri, and he secretly considered her unintelligent, narrow, inelegant, was afraid of her, and did not
like to be at home. He had begun being unfaithful to her long ago—had been unfaithful to her often, and, probably on that account, almost always spoke ill of women,
and when they were talked about in his presence, used to call them "the lower race."

It seemed to him that he had been so schooled by bitter experience that he
might call them what he liked, and yet he could not get on for two days together
without "the lower race." In the society of men he was bored and not himself, with

---

°*Yalta:* a resort city on the Crimean Sea where Chekhov lived.

them he was cold and uncommunicative; but when he was in the company of women he felt free, and knew what to say to them and how to behave; and he was at ease with them even when he was silent. In his appearance, in his character, in his whole nature, there was something attractive and elusive which allured women and disposed them in his favour; he knew that, and some force seemed to draw him, too, to them.

Experience often repeated, truly bitter experience, had taught him long ago that with decent people, especially Moscow people—always slow to move and irresolute—every intimacy, which at first so agreeably diversifies life and appears a light and charming adventure, inevitably grows into a regular problem of extreme intricacy, and that in the long run the situation becomes unbearable. But at every fresh meeting with an interesting woman this experience seemed to slip out of his memory, and he was eager for life, and everything seemed simple and amusing.

One evening he was dining in the gardens, and the lady in the *béret* came up slowly to take the next table. Her expression, her gait, her dress, and the way she did her hair told him that she was a lady, that she was married, that she was in Yalta for the first time and alone, and that she was dull there. . . . The stories told of the immorality in such places as Yalta are to a great extent untrue; he despised them, and knew that such stories were for the most part made up by persons who would themselves have been glad to sin if they had been able; but when the lady sat down at the next table three paces from him, he remembered these tales of easy conquests, of trips to the mountains, and the tempting thought of a swift, fleeting love affair, a romance with an unknown woman, whose name he did not know, suddenly took possession of him.

He beckoned coaxingly to the Pomeranian, and when the dog came up to him he shook his finger at it. The Pomeranian growled: Gurov shook his finger at it again.

The lady looked at him and at once dropped her eyes.

"He doesn't bite," she said, and blushed.

"May I give him a bone?" he asked; and when she nodded he asked courteously, "Have you been long in Yalta?"

"Five days."

"And I have already dragged out a fortnight here."

There was a brief silence.

"Time goes fast, and yet it is so dull here!" she said, not looking at him.

"That's only the fashion to say it is dull here. A provincial will live in Belyov or Zhidra and not be dull, and when he comes here it's 'Oh, the dullness! Oh, the dust!' One would think he came from Grenada."

She laughed. Then both continued eating in silence, like strangers, but after dinner they walked side by side; and there sprang up between them the light jesting conversation of people who are free and satisfied, to whom it does not matter where they go or what they talk about. They walked and talked of the strange light on the sea: the water was of a soft warm lilac hue, and there was a golden streak from the moon upon it. They talked of how sultry it was after a hot day. Gurov told her that he came from Moscow, that he had taken his degree in Arts, but had a post in a bank; that he had trained as an opera-singer, but had given it up, that he owned two houses in Moscow. . . . And from her he learnt that she had grown up in Petersburg, but had lived in S—— since her marriage two years before, and that her husband, who needed a holiday too, might perhaps come and fetch her. She was not sure

5

10

15

whether her husband had a post in a Crown Department or under the Provincial Council—and was amused by her own ignorance. And Gurov learnt, too, that she was called Anna Sergeyevna.

Afterwards he thought about her in his room at the hotel—thought she would surely meet him next day; it would be sure to happen. As he got into bed he thought how lately she had been a girl at school, doing lessons like his own daughter; he recalled the diffidence, the angularity, that was still manifest in her laugh and her manner of talking with a stranger. This must have been the first time in her life she had been alone in surroundings in which she was followed, looked at, and spoken to merely from a secret motive which she could hardly fail to guess. He recalled her slender, delicate neck, her lovely grey eyes.

"There's something pathetic about her, anyway," he thought, and fell asleep.

II

A week had passed since they had made acquaintance. It was a holiday. It was sultry indoors, while in the street the wind whirled the dust round and round, and blew people's hats off. It was a thirsty day, and Gurov often went into the pavillion, and pressed Anna Sergeyevna to have syrup and water or an ice. One did not know what to do with oneself. 20

In the evening when the wind had dropped a little, they went out on the groyne° to see the steamer come in. There were a great many people walking about the harbour; they had gathered to welcome some one, bringing bouquets. And two peculiarities of a well-dressed Yalta crowd were very conspicuous: the elderly ladies were dressed like young ones, and there were great numbers of generals.

Owing to the roughness of the sea, the steamer arrived late, after the sun had set, and it was a long time turning about before it reached the groyne. Anna Sergeyevna looked through her lorgnette° at the steamer and the passengers as though looking for acquaintances, and when she turned to Gurov her eyes were shining. She talked a great deal and asked disconnected questions, forgetting next moment what she had asked; then she dropped her lorgnette in the crush.

The festive crowd began to disperse; it was too dark to see people's faces. The wind had completely dropped, but Gurov and Anna Sergeyevna still stood as though waiting to see some one else come from the steamer. Anna Sergeyevna was silent now, and sniffed the flowers without looking at Gurov.

"The weather is better this evening," he said. "Where shall we go now? Shall we drive somewhere?"

She made no answer. 25

Then he looked at her intently, and all at once put his arm around her and kissed her on the lips, and breathed in the moisture and the fragrance of the flowers; and he immediately looked round him, anxiously wondering whether any one had seen them.

"Let us go to your hotel," he said softly. And both walked quickly.

The room was close and smelt of the scent she had bought at the Japanese shop. Gurov looked at her and thought: "What different people one meets in the world!" From the past he preserved memories of careless, good-natured women, who loved

---

groyne: pier.
lorgnette: opera glasses with a short handle.

cheerfully and were grateful to him for the happiness he gave them, however brief it might be; and of women like his wife who loved without any genuine feeling, with superfluous phrases, affectedly, hysterically, with an expression that suggested that it was not love nor passion, but something more significant; and of two or three others, very beautiful, cold women, on whose faces he had caught a glimpse of a rapacious expression—an obstinate desire to snatch from life more than it could give, and these were capricious, unreflecting, domineering, unintelligent women not in their first youth, and when Gurov grew cold to them their beauty excited his hatred, and the lace on their linen seemed to him like scales.

But in this case there was still the diffidence, the angularity of inexperienced youth, an awkward feeling; and there was a sense of consternation as though some one had suddenly knocked at the door. The attitude of Anna Sergeyevna—"the lady with the dog"—to what happened was somehow peculiar, very grave, as though it were her fall—so it seemed, and it was strange and inappropriate. Her face dropped and faded, and on both sides of it her hair hung down mournfully; she mused in a dejected attitude like "the woman who was a sinner" in an old-fashioned picture.

"It's wrong," she said. "You will be the first to despise me now." 30

There was a water-melon on the table. Gurov cut himself a slice and began eating it without haste. There followed at least half an hour of silence.

Anna Sergeyevna was touching; there was about her the purity of a good, simple woman who had seen little of life. The solitary candle burning on the table threw a faint light on her face, yet it was clear that she was very unhappy.

"How could I despise you?" asked Gurov. "You don't know what you are saying."

"God forgive me," she said, and her eyes filled with tears. "It's awful."

"You seem to feel you need to be forgiven." 35

"Forgiven? No. I am a bad, low woman; I despise myself and don't attempt to justify myself. It's not my husband but myself I have deceived. And not only just now; I have been deceiving myself for a long time. My husband may be a good, honest man, but he is a flunkey! I don't know what he does there, what his work is, but I know he is a flunkey! I was twenty when I was married to him. I have been tormented by curiosity; I wanted something better. 'There must be a different sort of life,' I said to myself. I wanted to live! To live, to live! . . . I was fired by curiosity . . . you don't understand it, but, I swear to God, I could not control myself; something happened to me: I could not be restrained. I told my husband I was ill, and came here. . . . And here I have been walking about as though I were dazed, like a mad creature; . . . and now I have become a vulgar, contemptible woman whom any one may despise."

Gurov felt bored already, listening to her. He was irritated by the naïve tone, by this remorse, so unexpected and inopportune; but for the tears in her eyes, he might have thought she was jesting or playing a part.

"I don't understand," he said softly. "What is it you want?"

She hid her face on his breast and pressed close to him.

"Believe me, believe me, I beseech you . . . " she said. "I love a pure, honest life, and sin is loathsome to me. I don't know what I am doing. Simple people say: 'The Evil One has beguiled me.' And I may say of myself now that the Evil One has beguiled me." 40

"Hush, hush! . . ." he muttered.

He looked at her fixed, scared eyes, kissed her, talked softly and affectionately, and by degrees she was comforted, and her gaiety returned; they both began laughing.

Afterwards when they went out there was not a soul on the sea-front. The town with its cypresses had quite a deathlike air, but the sea still broke noisily on the shore; a single barge was rocking on the waves, and a lantern was blinking sleepily on it.

They found a cab and drove to Oreanda.

"I found out your surname in the hall just now: it was written on the board—Von Diderits," said Gurov. "Is your husband a German?"

"No; I believe his grandfather was a German, but he is an Orthodox° Russian himself."

At Oreanda they sat on a seat not far from the church, looked down at the sea, and were silent. Yalta was hardly visible through the morning mist; white clouds stood motionless on the mountain-tops. The leaves did not stir on the trees, grasshoppers chirruped, and the monotonous hollow sound of the sea rising up from below, spoke of the peace, of the eternal sleep awaiting us. So it must have sounded when there was no Yalta, only Oreanda here; so it sounds now, and will sound as indifferently and monotonously when we are all no more. And in this constancy, in this complete indifference to the life and death of each of us, there lies hid, perhaps, a pledge of our eternal salvation, of the unceasing movement of life upon earth, of unceasing progress towards perfection. Sitting beside a young woman who in the dawn seemed so lovely, soothed and spellbound in these magical surroundings—the sea, mountains, clouds, the open sky—Gurov thought how in reality everything is beautiful in this world when one reflects: everything except what we think or do ourselves when we forget our human dignity and the higher aims of our existence.

A man walked up to them—probably a keeper—looked at them and walked away. And this detail seemed mysterious and beautiful, too. They saw a steamer come from Theodosia, with its lights out in the glow of dawn.

"There is dew on the grass," said Anna Sergeyevna, after a silence.

"Yes. It's time to go home."

They went back to the town.

Then they met every day at twelve o'clock on the sea-front, lunched and dined together, went for walks, admired the sea. She complained that she slept badly, that her heart throbbed violently; asked the same questions, troubled now by jealousy and now by the fear that he did not respect her sufficiently. And often in the square or gardens, when there was no one near them, he suddenly drew her to him and kissed her passionately. Complete idleness, these kisses in broad daylight while he looked round in dread of some one's seeing them, the heat, the smell of the sea, and the continual passing to and fro before him of idle, well-dressed, well-fed people, made a new man of him; he told Anna Sergeyevna how beautiful she was, how fascinating. He was impatiently passionate, he would not move a step away from her, while she was often pensive and continually urged him to confess that he did not respect her, did not love her in the least, and thought of her as nothing but a common woman. Rather late almost every evening they drove somewhere out of town, to Oreanda or to the waterfall; and the expedition was always a success, the scenery invariably impressed them as grand and beautiful.

They were expecting her husband to come, but a letter came from him, saying that there was something wrong with his eyes, and he entreated his wife to come home as quickly as possible. Anna Sergeyevna made haste to go.

Orthodox: the Eastern Orthodox Church, Russia's major religion.

"It's a good thing I am going away," she said to Gurov. "It's the finger of destiny."

She went by coach and he went with her. They were driving the whole day. When she had got into a compartment of the express, and when the second bell had rung, she said:

55

"Let me look at you once more . . . look at you once again. That's right."

She did not shed tears, but was so sad that she seemed ill, and her face was quivering.

"I shall remember you . . . think of you," she said. "God be with you; be happy. Don't remember evil against me. We are parting forever—it must be so, for we ought never to have met. Well, God be with you."

The train moved off rapidly, its lights soon vanished from sight, and a minute later there was no sound of it, as though everything had conspired to end as quickly as possible that sweet delirium, that madness. Left alone on the platform, and gazing into the dark distance, Gurov listened to the chirrup of the grasshoppers and the hum of the telegraph wires, feeling as though he had only just waked up. And he thought, musing, that there had been another episode or adventure in his life, and it, too, was at an end, and nothing was left of it but a memory. . . . He was moved, sad, and conscious of a slight remorse. This young woman whom he would never meet again had not been happy with him; he was genuinely warm and affectionate with her, but yet in his manner, his tone, and his caresses there had been a shade of light irony, the coarse condescension of a happy man who was, besides, almost twice her age. All the time she had called him kind, exceptional, lofty; obviously he had seemed to her different from what he really was, so he had unintentionally deceived her. . . .

Here at the station was already a scent of autumn; it was a cold evening. 60

"It's time for me to go north," thought Gurov as he left the platform. "High time!"

III

At home in Moscow everything was in its winter routine; the stoves were heated, and in the morning it was still dark when the children were having breakfast and getting ready for school, and the nurse would light the lamp for a short time. The frosts had begun already. When the first snow has fallen, on the first day of sledge-driving it is pleasant to see the white earth, the white roofs, to draw soft, delicious breath, and the season brings back the days of one's youth. The old limes and birches, white with hoarfrost, have a good-natured expression; they are nearer to one's heart than cypresses and palms, and near them one doesn't want to be thinking of the sea and the mountains.

Gurov was Moscow born; he arrived in Moscow on a fine frosty day, and when he put on his fur coat and warm gloves, and walked along Petrovka, and when on Saturday evening he heard the ringing of the bells, his recent trip and the places he had seen lost all charm for him. Little by little he became absorbed in Moscow life, greedily read three newspapers a day, and declared he did not read the Moscow papers on principle! He already felt a longing to go to restaurants, clubs, dinner-parties, anniversary celebrations, and he felt flattered at entertaining distinguished lawyers and artists, and at playing cards with a professor at the doctors' club. He could already eat a whole plateful of salt fish and cabbage. . . .

In another month, he fancied, the image of Anna Sergeyevna would be shrouded in a mist in his memory, and only from time to time would visit him in his dreams with a touching smile as others did. But more than a month passed, real winter had come, and everything was still clear in his memory as though he had parted with Anna Sergeyevna only the day before. And his memories glowed more and more vividly. When in the evening stillness he heard from his study the voices of his children, preparing their lessons, or when he listened to a song or the organ at the restaurant, or the storm howled in the chimney, suddenly everything would rise up in his memory: what had happened on the groyne, and the early morning with the mist on the mountains, and the steamer coming from Theodosia, and the kisses. He would pace a long time about his room, remembering it all and smiling; then his memories passed into dreams, and in his fancy the past was mingled with what was to come. Anna Sergeyevna did not visit him in dreams, but followed him everywhere like a shadow and haunted him. When he shut his eyes he saw her as though she were living before him, and she seemed to him lovelier, younger, tenderer than she was; and he imagined himself finer than he had been in Yalta. In the evenings she peeped out at him from the bookcase, from the fireplace, from the corner—he heard her breathing, the caressing rustle of her dress. In the street he watched the women, looking for some one like her.

He was tormented by an intense desire to confide his memories to some one. But in his home it was impossible to talk of his love, and he had no one outside; he could not talk to his tenants nor to any one at the bank. And what had he to talk of? Had he been in love, then? Had there been anything beautiful, poetical, or edifying or simply interesting in his relations with Anna Sergeyevna? And there was nothing for him but to talk vaguely of love, of woman, and no one guessed what it meant; only his wife twitched her black eyebrows, and said: "The part of a lady-killer does not suit you at all, Dimitri."   65

One evening, coming out of the doctors' club with an official with whom he had been playing cards, he could not resist saying:

"If only you knew what a fascinating woman I made the acquaintance of in Yalta!"

The official got into his sledge and was driving away, but turned suddenly and shouted:

"Dmitri Dmitritch!"

"What?"   70

"You were right this evening: the sturgeon was a bit too strong!"

These words, so ordinary, for some reason moved Gurov to indignation, and struck him as degrading and unclean. What savage manners, what people! What senseless nights, what uninteresting, uneventful days! The rage for card-playing, the gluttony, the drunkenness, the continual talk always about the same thing. Useless pursuits and conversations always about the same things absorb the better part of one's time, the better part of one's strength, and in the end there is left a life grovelling and curtailed, worthless and trivial, and there is no escaping or getting away from it—just as though one were in a madhouse or a prison.

Gurov did not sleep all night, and was filled with indignation. And he had a headache all next day. And the next night he slept badly; he sat up in bed, thinking, or paced up and down his room. He was sick of his children, sick of the bank; he had no desire to go anywhere or to talk of anything.

In the holidays in December he prepared for a journey, and told his wife he was going to Petersburg to do something in the interests of a young friend—and he set off for S——. What for? He did not very well know himself. He wanted to see Anna Sergeyevna and to talk with her—to arrange a meeting, if possible.

He reached S—— in the morning, and took the best room at the hotel, in which the floor was covered with grey army cloth, and on the table was an inkstand, grey with dust and adorned with a figure on horseback, with its hat in its hand and its head broken off. The hotel porter gave him the necessary information; Von Diderits lived in a house of his own in Old Gontcharny Street—it was not far from the hotel: he was rich and lived in good style, and had his own horses; every one in the town knew him. The porter pronounced the name "Dridirits." 75

Gurov went without haste to Old Gontcharny Street and found the house. Just opposite the house stretched a long grey fence adorned with nails.

"One would run away from a fence like that," thought Gurov, looking from the fence to the windows of the house and back again.

He considered: to-day was a holiday, and the husband would probably be at home. And in any case it would be tactless to go into the house and upset her. If he were to send a note it might fall into her husband's hands, and then it might ruin everything. The best thing was to trust to chance. And he kept walking up and down the street by the fence, waiting for the chance. He saw a beggar go in at the gate and dogs fly at him; then an hour later he heard a piano, and the sounds were faint and indistinct. Probably it was Anna Sergeyevna playing. The front door suddenly opened, and an old woman came out, followed by the familiar white Pomeranian. Gurov was on the point of calling to the dog, but his heart began beating violently, and in his excitement he could not remember the dog's name.

He walked up and down, and loathed the grey fence more and more, and by now he thought irritably that Anna Sergeyevna had forgotten him, and was perhaps already amusing herself with someone else, and that was very natural in a young woman who had nothing to look at from morning till night but that confounded fence. He went back to his hotel room and sat for a long while on the sofa, not knowing what to do, then he had dinner and a long nap.

"How stupid and worrying it is!" he thought when he woke and looked at the dark windows: it was already evening. "Here I've had a good sleep for some reason. What shall I do in the night?" 80

He sat on the bed, which was covered by a cheap grey blanket, such as one sees in hospitals, and he taunted himself in his vexation:

"So much for the lady with the dog . . . so much for the adventure. . . . You're in a nice fix. . . ."

That morning at the station a poster in large letters had caught his eye. "The Geisha" was to be performed for the first time. He thought of this and went to the theatre.

"It's quite possible she may go to the first performance," he thought.

The theatre was full. As in all provincial theatres, there was a fog above the chandelier, the gallery was noisy and restless; in the front row the local dandies were standing up before the beginning of the performance, with their hands behind them; in the Governor's box the Governor's daughter, wearing a boa, was sitting in the front seat, while the Governor himself lurked modestly behind the curtain with only his hands visible; the orchestra was a long time tuning up; the stage curtain swayed. All the time the audience were coming in and taking their seats. Gurov looked at them eagerly. 85

Anna Sergeyevna, too, came in. She sat down in the third row, and when Gurov looked at her his heart contracted, and he understood clearly that for him there was in the whole world no creature so near, so precious, and so important to him; she, this little woman, in no way remarkable, lost in a provincial crowd, with a vulgar lorgnette in her hand, filled his whole life now, was his sorrow and his joy, the one happiness that he now desired for himself, and to the sounds of the inferior orchestra, of the wretched principal violins, he thought how lovely she was. He thought and dreamed.

A young man with small side-whiskers, tall and stooping, came in with Anna Sergeyevna and sat down beside her; he bent his head at every step and seemed to be continually bowing. Most likely this was the husband whom at Yalta, in a rush of bitter feeling, she had called a flunkey. And there really was in his long figure, his side-whiskers, and the small bald patch on his head, something of the flunkey's obsequiousness; his smile was sugary, and in his buttonhole there was some badge of distinction like the number on a waiter.

During the first interval the husband went away to smoke; she remained alone in her stall. Gurov, who was sitting in the stalls, too, went up to her and said in a trembling voice, with a forced smile:

"Good-evening."

She glanced at him and turned pale, then glanced again with horror, unable to believe her eyes, and tightly gripped the fan and the lorgnette in her hands, evidently struggling with herself not to faint. Both were silent. She was sitting, he was standing, frightened by her confusion and not venturing to sit down beside her. The violins and the flute began tuning up. He felt suddenly frightened; it seemed as though all the people in the boxes were looking at them. She got up and went quickly to the door; he followed her, and both walked senselessly along passages, and up and down stairs, and figures in legal, scholastic, and civil service uniforms, all wearing badges, flitted before their eyes. They caught glimpses of ladies, of fur coats hanging on pegs; the draughts blew on them, bringing a smell of stale tobacco. And Gurov, whose heart was beating violently, thought:

"Oh, heavens! Why are these people here and this orchestra! . . ."

And at that instant he recalled how when he had seen Anna Sergeyevna off at the station he had thought that everything was over and they would never meet again. But how far they were still from the end!

On the narrow, gloomy staircase over which was written "To the Amphitheatre," she stopped.

"How you have frightened me!" she said, breathing hard, still pale and overwhelmed. "Oh, how you have frightened me! I am half dead. Why have you come? Why?"

"But do understand, Anna, do understand . . ." he said hastily in a low voice. "I entreat you to understand. . . ."

She looked at him with dread, with entreaty, with love; she looked at him intently, to keep his features more distinctly in her memory.

"I am so unhappy," she went on, not heeding him. "I have thought of nothing but you all the time; I live only in the thought of you. And I wanted to forget, to forget you; but why, oh, why, have you come?"

On the landing above them two schoolboys were smoking and looking down, but that was nothing to Gurov; he drew Anna Sergeyevna to him, and began kissing her face, her cheeks, and her hands.

"What are you doing, what are you doing!" she cried in horror, pushing him away. "We are mad. Go away to-day; go away at once. . . . I beseech you by all that is sacred, I implore you. . . . There are people coming this way!"

Some one was coming up the stairs.

"You must go away," Anna Sergeyevna went on in a whisper. "Do you hear me, Dmitri Dmitritch? I will come and see you in Moscow. I have never been happy; I am miserable now, and I never, never shall be happy, never! Don't make me suffer still more! I swear I'll come to Moscow. But now let us part. My precious, good, dear one, we must part!"

She pressed his hand and began rapidly going downstairs, looking round at him, and from her eyes he could see that she really was unhappy. Gurov stood for a little while, listened, then, when all sound had died away, he found his coat and left the theatre.

IV

And Anna Sergeyevna began coming to see him in Moscow. Once in two or three months she left S——, telling her husband that she was going to consult a doctor about an internal complaint—and her husband believed her, and did not believe her. In Moscow she stayed at the Slaviansky Bazaar hotel, and at once sent a man in a red cap to Gurov. Gurov went to see her, and no one in Moscow knew of it.

Once he was going to see her in this way on a winter morning (the messenger had come the evening before when he was out). With him walked his daughter, whom he wanted to take to school: it was on the way. Snow was falling in big wet flakes.

"It's three degrees above freezing-point, and yet it is snowing," said Gurov to his daughter. "The thaw is only on the surface of the earth; there is quite a different temperature at a greater height in the atmosphere."

"And why are there no thunderstorms in the winter, father?"

He explained that, too. He talked, thinking all the while that he was going to see *her*, and no living soul knew of it, and probably never would know. He had two lives: one, open, seen and known by all who cared to know, full of relative truth and of relative falsehood, exactly like the lives of his friends and acquaintances; and another life running its course in secret. And through some strange, perhaps accidental, conjunction of circumstances, everything that was essential, of interest and of value to him, everything in which he was sincere and did not deceive himself, everything that made the kernel of his life, was hidden from other people; and all that was false in him, the sheath in which he hid himself to conceal the truth—such, for instance, as his work in the bank, his discussions at the club, his "lower race," his presence with his wife at anniversary festivities—all that was open. And he judged of others by himself, not believing in what he saw, and always believing that every man had his real, most interesting life under the cover of secrecy and under the cover of night. All personal life rested on secrecy, and possibly it was partly on that account that civilised man was so nervously anxious that personal privacy should be respected.

After leaving his daughter at school, Gurov went on to the Slaviansky Bazaar. He took off his fur coat below, went upstairs, and softly knocked at the door. Anna Sergeyevna, wearing his favorite grey dress, exhausted by the journey and the suspense, had been expecting him since the evening before. She was pale; she looked at him, and did not smile, and he had hardly come in when she fell on his breast. Their kiss was slow and prolonged, as though they had not met for two years.

"Well, how are you getting on there?" he asked. "What news?"

"Wait; I'll tell you directly. . . . I can't talk."

She could not speak; she was crying. She turned away from him, and pressed her handkerchief to her eyes.

"Let her have her cry out. I'll sit down and wait," he thought, and he sat down in an arm-chair.

Then he rang and asked for tea to be brought him, and while he drank his tea she remained standing at the window with her back to him. She was crying from emotion, from the miserable consciousness that their life was so hard for them; they could only meet in secret, hiding themselves from people, like thieves! Was not their life shattered?

"Come, do stop!" he said.

It was evident to him that this love of theirs would not soon be over, that he could not see the end of it. Anna Sergeyevna grew more and more attached to him. She adored him, and it was unthinkable to say to her that it was bound to have an end some day; besides, she would not have believed it!

He went up to her and took her by the shoulders to say something affectionate and cheering, and at that moment he saw himself in the looking-glass.

His hair was beginning to turn grey. And it seemed strange to him that he had grown so much older, so much plainer during the last few years. The shoulders on which his hands rested were warm and quivering. He felt compassion for this life, still so warm and lovely, but probably already not far from beginning to fade and wither like his own. Why did she love him so much? He always seemed to women different from what he was, and they loved in him not himself, but the man created by their imagination, whom they had been eagerly seeking all their lives; and afterwards, when they noticed their mistake, they loved him all the same. And not one of them had been happy with him. Time passed, he had made their acquaintance, got on with them, parted, but he had never once loved; it was anything you like, but not love.

And only now when his head was grey he had fallen properly, really in love—for the first time in his life.

Anna Sergeyevna and he loved each other like people very close and akin, like husband and wife, like tender friends; it seemed to them that fate itself had meant them for one another, and they could not understand why he had a wife and she a husband; and it was as though they were a pair of birds of passage, caught and forced to live in different cages. They forgave each other for what they were ashamed of in their past, they forgave everything in the present, and felt that this love of theirs had changed them both.

In moments of depression in the past he had comforted himself with any arguments that came into his mind, but now he no longer cared for arguments; he felt profound compassion, he wanted to be sincere and tender. . . .

"Don't cry, my darling," he said. "You've had your cry; that's enough. . . . Let us talk now, let us think of some plan."

Then they spent a long while taking counsel together, talked of how to avoid the necessity for secrecy, for deception, for living in different towns and not seeing each other for long at a time. How could they be free from this intolerable bondage?

"How? How?" he asked, clutching his head. "How?"

And it seemed as though in a little while the solution would be found, and then a new and splendid life would begin; and it was clear to both of them that they still had a long, long road before them, and that the most complicated and difficult part of it was only the beginning.

[1899]

Translated by Constance Garnett

Vladimir Nabokov's discussion of "The Lady with the Little Dog" is one of the many written lectures prepared by the author for his course on Russian literature at Cornell University in the 1950s. Nabokov himself, while Russian born, lived from late adolescence in England, Berlin, Paris, and the United States. He established his chief reputation as a novelist and short-story writer (some of his better known works include *Lolita, Pnin, Laughter in the Dark,* and *Ada*), but was also celebrated as a translator and as an essayist (and lecturer) on literary subjects.

Nabokov is a subtle reader and an ironic commentator. He loves the patient untangling of complexities as well as lingering over what may seem to other readers to be the slightest of details. As much as it is possible to do so, he views a particular work of art from within. That is, he views it from the perspective of a maker, one who understands that the work of art is always the sum of innumerable strategies by the author.

Vladimir Nabokov (1899–1977)

"THE LADY WITH THE LITTLE DOG"

Chekhov comes into the story "The Lady with the Little Dog" without knocking. There is no dilly-dallying. The very first paragraph reveals the main character, the young fair-haired lady followed by her white Spitz dog on the waterfront of a Crimean resort, Yalta, on the Black Sea. And immediately after, the male character Gurov appears. His wife, whom he has left with the children in Moscow, is vividly depicted: her solid frame, her thick black eyebrows, and the way she had of calling herself "a woman who thinks." One notes the magic of the trifles the author collects—the wife's manner of dropping a certain mute letter in spelling and her calling her husband by the longest and fullest form of his name, both traits in combination with the impressive dignity of her beetle-browed face and rigid poise forming exactly the necessary impression. A hard woman with the strong feminist and social ideas of her time, but one whom her husband finds in his heart of hearts to be narrow, dull-minded and devoid of grace. The natural transition is to Gurov's constant unfaithfulness to her, to his general attitude toward women—"that inferior race" is what he calls them, but without that inferior race he could not exist. It is hinted that these Russian romances were not altogether as light-winged as in the Paris of Maupassant.° Complications and problems are unavoidable with those decent hesitating people of Moscow who are slow heavy starters but plunge into tedious difficulties when once they start going.

Then with the same neat and direct method of attack, with the bridging formula, "and so . . . ,"[1] we slide back to the lady with the dog. Everything about her,

---

°*Maupassant:* Guy de Maupassant (1850–1893), a celebrated French author (see Chapter 3).

[1]VN follows with the deleted "or perhaps still better rendered in English by that 'Now' which begins a new paragraph in straightforward fairy tales." [Editor's note]

even the way her hair was done, told him that she was bored. The spirit of adventure—though he realized perfectly well that his attitude toward a lone woman in a fashionable sea town was based on vulgar stories, generally false—this spirit of adventure prompts him to call the little dog, which thus becomes a link between her and him. They are both in a public restaurant.

"He beckoned invitingly to the Spitz, and when the dog approached him, shook his finger at it. The Spitz growled; Gurov threatened it again.

"The lady glanced at him and at once dropped her eyes.

" 'He doesn't bite,' she said and blushed.   5

" 'May I give him a bone?' he asked; and when she nodded he inquired affably, 'Have you been in Yalta long?'

" 'About five days.' "

They talk. The author has hinted already that Gurov was witty in the company of women; and instead of having the reader take it for granted (you know the old method of describing the talk as "brilliant" but giving no samples of the conversation), Chekhov makes him joke in a really attractive, winning way. "Bored, are you? An average citizen lives in . . . (here Chekhov lists the names of beautifully chosen, super-provincial towns) and is not bored, but when he arrives here on his vacation it is all boredom and dust. One could think he came from Grenada" (a name particularly appealing to the Russian imagination). The rest of their talk, for which this sidelight is richly sufficient, is conveyed indirectly. Now comes a first glimpse of Chekhov's own system of suggesting atmosphere by the most concise details of nature, "the sea was of a warm lilac hue with a golden path for the moon"; whoever has lived in Yalta knows how exactly this conveys the impression of a summer evening there. The first movement of the story ends with Gurov alone in his hotel room thinking of her as he goes to sleep and imagining her delicate weak-looking neck and her pretty gray eyes. It is to be noted that only now, through the medium of the hero's imagination, does Chekhov give a visible and definite form to the lady, features that fit in perfectly with her listless manner and expression of boredom already known to us.

"Getting into bed he recalled that she had been a schoolgirl only recently, doing lessons like his own daughter; he thought how much timidity and angularity there was still in her laugh and her manner of talking with a stranger. It must have been the first time in her life that she was alone in a setting in which she was followed, looked at, and spoken to for one secret purpose alone, which she could hardly fail to guess. He thought of her slim, delicate throat, her lovely gray eyes.

" 'There's something pathetic about her, though,' he thought, and dropped off."   10

The next movement (each of the four diminutive chapters or movements of which the story is composed is not more than four or five pages long), the next movement starts a week later with Gurov going to the pavillion and bringing the lady iced lemonade on a hot windy day, with the dust flying; and then in the evening when the scirocco subsides, they go on the pier to watch the incoming steamer. "The lady lost her lorgnette in the crowd," Chekhov notes shortly, and this being so casually worded, without any direct influence on the story—just a passing statement—somehow fits in with that helpless pathos already alluded to.

Then in her hotel room her awkwardness and tender angularity are delicately conveyed. They have become lovers. She was now sitting with her long hair hanging down on both sides of her face in the dejected pose of a sinner in some old picture. There was a watermelon on the table. Gurov cut himself a piece and began to eat unhurriedly. This realistic touch is again a typical Chekhov device.

She tells him about her existence in the remote town she comes from and Gurov is slightly bored by her naiveté, confusion, and tears. It is only now that we learn her husband's name: von Dideritz—probably of German descent.

They roam about Yalta in the early morning mist. "At Oreanda they sat on a bench not far from the church, looked down at the sea, and were silent. Yalta was barely visible through the morning mist; white clouds rested motionlessly on the mountaintops. The leaves did not stir on the trees, the crickets chirped, and the monotonous muffled sound of the sea that rose from below spoke of the peace, the eternal sleep awaiting us. So it rumbled below when there was no Yalta, no Oreanda here; so it rumbles now, and it will rumble as indifferently and hollowly when we are no more. . . . Sitting beside a young woman who in the dawn seemed so lovely, Gurov, soothed and spellbound by these magical surroundings—the sea, the mountains, the clouds, the wide sky—thought how everything is really beautiful in this world when one reflects: everything except what we think or do ourselves when we forget the higher aim of life and our own human dignity.

"A man strolled up to them—probably a watchman—looked at them and walked away. And this detail, too, seemed so mysterious and beautiful. They saw a steamer arrive from Feodosia, its light extinguished in the glow of the dawn.   15

" 'There is dew on the grass,' said Anna Sergeievna, after a silence.

" 'Yes, it's time to go home.' Then several days pass and then she has to go back to her home town.

" 'Time for me, too, to go North,' thought Gurov as he returned after seeing her off."[2] And there the chapter ends.

The third movement plunges us straight into Gurov's life in Moscow. The richness of a gay Russian winter, his family affairs, the dinners at clubs and restaurants, all this is swiftly and vividly suggested. Then a page is devoted to a queer thing that happened to him: he cannot forget the lady with the little dog. He has many friends, but the curious longing he has for talking about his adventures finds no outlet. When he happens to speak in a very general way of love and women, nobody guesses what he means, and only his wife moves her dark eyebrows and says: "Stop that fatuous posing; it does not suit you."

And now comes what in Chekhov's quiet stories may be called the climax. There is something that your average citizen calls romance and something he calls prose—though both are the meat of poetry for the artist. Such a contrast has already been hinted at by the slice of watermelon which Gurov crunched in a Yalta hotel room at a most romantic moment, sitting heavily and munching away. This contrast is beautifully followed up when at last Gurov blurts out to a friend late at night as they come out of the club: If you knew what a delightful woman I met in Yalta! His friend, a bureaucratic civil servant, got into his sleigh, the horses moved, but suddenly he turned and called back to Gurov. Yes? asked Gurov, evidently expecting some reaction to what he had just mentioned. By the way, said the man, you were quite right. That fish at the club was decidedly smelly.   20

This is a natural transition to the description of Gurov's new mood, his feeling that he lives among savages where cards and food are life. His family, his bank, the whole trend of his existence, everything seems futile, dull, and senseless. About

---

[2]In the margin VN adds for the benefit of his Cornell class, "From Florida back to Ithaca." [Editor's note]

Christmas, he tells his wife he is going on a business trip to St. Petersburg, instead of which he travels to the remote Volga town where the lady lives.

Critics of Chekhov in the good old days when the mania for the civic problem flourished in Russia were incensed with his way of describing what they considered to be trivial unnecessary matters instead of thoroughly examining and solving the problems of bourgeois marriage. For as soon as Gurov arrives in the early hours to that town and takes the best room at the local hotel, Chekhov, instead of describing his mood or intensifying his difficult moral position, gives what is artistic in the highest sense of the word: he notes the gray carpet, made of military cloth, and the inkstand, also gray with dust, with a horseman whose hand waves a hat and whose head is gone. That is all: it is nothing but it is everything in authentic literature. A feature in the same line is the phonetic transformation which the hotel porter imposes on the German name von Dideritz. Having learned the address Gurov goes there and looks at the house. Opposite was a long gray fence with nails sticking out. An unescapable fence, Gurov says to himself, and here we get the concluding note in the rhythm of drabness and grayness already suggested by the carpet, the inkstand, the illiterate accent of the porter. The unexpected little turns and the lightness of the touches are what places Chekhov, above all Russian writers of fiction, on the level of Gogol and Tolstoy.

Presently he saw an old servant coming out with the familiar little white dog. He wanted to call it (by a kind of conditional reflex), but suddenly his heart began beating fast and in his excitement he could not remember the dog's name—another delightful touch. Later on he decides to go to the local theatre, where for the first time the operetta *The Geisha* is being given. In sixty words Chekhov paints a complete picture of the provincial theatre, not forgetting the town-governor who modestly hid in his box behind a plush curtain so that only his hands were visible. Then the lady appeared. And he realized quite clearly that now in the whole world there was none nearer and dearer and more important to him than this slight woman, lost in a small-town crowd, a woman perfectly unremarkable, with a vulgar lorgnette in her hand. He saw her husband and remembered her qualifying him as a flunkey—he distinctly resembled one.

A remarkably fine scene follows when Gurov manages to talk to her, and then their mad swift walk up all kinds of staircases and corridors, and down again, and up again, amid people in the various uniforms of provincial officials. Neither does Chekhov forget "two schoolboys who smoked on the stairs and looked down at him and her."

" 'You must leave,' Anna Sergeievna went on in a whisper. 'Do you hear, Dmitri Dmitrich? I will come and see you in Moscow. I have never been happy; I am unhappy now, and I never, never shall be happy, never! So don't make me suffer still more! I swear I'll come to Moscow. But now let us part. My dear, good, precious one, let us part!'"

"She pressed his hand and walked rapidly downstairs, turning to look round at him, and from her eyes he could see that she really was unhappy. Gurov stood for a while, listening, then when all grew quiet, he found his coat and left the theatre."

The fourth and last chapter gives the atmosphere of their secret meetings in Moscow. As soon as she would arrive she used to send a red-capped messenger to Gurov. One day he was on his way to her and his daughter was with him. She was going to school, in the same direction as he. Big damp snowflakes were slowly coming down.

The thermometer, Gurov was saying to his daughter, shows a few degrees above freezing point (actually 37° above, fahrenheit), but nevertheless snow is falling. The explanation is that this warmth applies only to the surface of the earth, while in the higher layers of the atmosphere the temperature is quite different.

And as he spoke and walked, he kept thinking that not a soul knew or would ever know about these secret meetings.

What puzzled him was that all the false part of his life, his bank, his club, his conversations, his social obligations—all this happened openly, while the real and interesting part was hidden.

"He had two lives: an open one, seen and known by all who needed to know it, full of conventional truth and conventional falsehood, exactly like the lives of his friends and acquaintances; and another life that went on in secret. And through some strange, perhaps accidental, combinations of circumstances, everything that was of interest and importance to him, everything that was essential to him, everything about which he felt sincerely and did not deceive himself, everything that constituted the core of his life, was going on concealed from others; while all that was false, the shell in which he hid to cover the truth—his work at the bank for instance, his discussions at the club, his references to the 'inferior race,' his appearances at anniversary celebrations with his wife—all that went on in the open. Judging others by himself, he did not believe what he saw, and always fancied that every man led his real, most interesting life under cover of secrecy as under cover of night. The personal life of every individual is based on secrecy, and perhaps it is partly for that reason that civilized man is so nervously anxious that personal privacy should be respected."

The final scene is full of that pathos which has been suggested in the very beginning. They meet, she sobs, they feel that they are the closest of couples, the tenderest of friends, and he sees that his hair is getting a little gray and knows that only death will end their love.

"The shoulders on which his hands rested were warm and quivering. He felt compassion for this life, still so warm and lovely, but probably already about to fade and wither like his own. Why did she love him so much? He always seemed to women different from what he was, and they loved in him not himself, but the man whom their imagination had created and whom they had been eagerly seeking all their lives; and afterwards, when they saw their mistake, they loved him nevertheless. And not one of them had been happy with him. In the past he had met women, come together with them, parted from them, but he had never once loved; it was anything you please, but not love. And only now when his head was gray he had fallen in love, really, truly—for the first time in his life."

They talk, they discuss their position, how to get rid of the necessity of this sordid secrecy, how to be together always. They find no solution and in the typical Chekhov way the tale fades out with no definite full-stop but with the natural motion of life.

"And it seemed as though in a little while the solution would be found, and then a new and glorious life would begin; and it was clear to both of them that the end was still far off, and that what was to be most complicated and difficult for them was only just beginning."

All the traditional rules of story telling have been broken in this wonderful short story of twenty pages or so. There is no problem, no regular climax, no point at the end. And it is one of the greatest stories ever written.

We will now repeat the different features that are typical for this and other Chekhov tales.

First: The story is told in the most natural way possible, not beside the after-dinner fireplace as with Turgenev or Maupassant but in the way one person relates to another the most important things in his life, slowly and yet without a break, in a slightly subdued voice.

Second: Exact and rich characterization is attained by a careful selection and careful distribution of minute but striking features, with perfect contempt for the sustained description, repetition, and strong emphasis of ordinary authors. In this or that description one detail is chosen to illume the whole setting.

Third: There is no special moral to be drawn and no special message to be received. Compare this to the special delivery stories of Gorki or Thomas Mann.° 40

Fourth: The story is based on a system of waves, on the shades of this or that mood. If in Gorki's world the molecules forming it are matter, here, in Chekhov, we get a world of waves instead of particles of matter, which, incidentally, is a nearer approach to the modern scientific understanding of the universe.

Fifth: The contrast of poetry and prose stressed here and there with such insight and humor is, in the long run, a contrast only for the heroes; in reality we feel, and this is again typical of authentic genius, that for Chekhov the lofty and the base are *not* different, that the slice of watermelon and the violet sea, and the hands of the town-governor, are essential points of the "beauty plus pity" of the world.

Sixth: The story does not really end, for as long as people are alive, there is no possible and definite conclusion to their troubles or hopes or dreams.

Seventh: The storyteller seems to keep going out of his way to allude to trifles, every one of which in another type of story would mean a signpost denoting a turn in the action—for instance, the two boys at the theatre would be eavesdroppers, and rumors would spread, or the inkstand would mean a letter changing the course of the story; but just because these trifles are meaningless, they are all-important in giving the real atmosphere of this particular story.

A Fiction Writer's Creative Response

Joyce Carol Oates (1938–   )

Joyce Carol Oates was born in Lockport, New York. From earliest childhood she manifested a desire to get words onto paper. Indeed, she has been writing continually since she was fourteen. To date, she has published over fifty books, including novels, story collections, essays, mysteries, and poetry. Oates's concern is with the tensions in the societal fabric and the way those tensions erupt within family systems. She has a ready perception of how individuals move in crises; her gift is for setting these characters

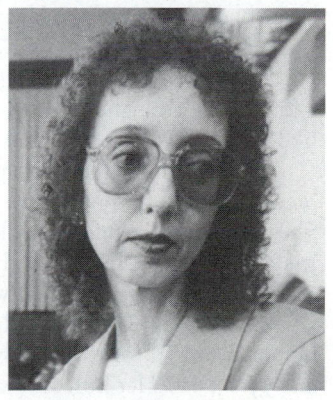

Gorki; Mann: Maxim Gorki (1868–1936), Russian author; Thomas Mann (1875–1955), German-born author, winner of 1929 Nobel Prize.

in credible dramatic situations and bringing them to moments of self-recognition. Oates has won many awards and honors for her work. Her novels include *With Shuddering Fall, Them, Do With Me What You Will, Bellefleur,* and *You Must Remember This,* and among her story collections are *By the North Gate, Upon the Sweeping Flood,* and *Raven's Wing.* Oates currently teaches at Princeton University.

THE LADY WITH THE PET DOG

I

Strangers parted as if to make way for him.

There he stood. He was there in the aisle, a few yards away, watching her.

She leaned forward at once in her seat, her hand jerked up to her face as if to ward off a blow—but then the crowd in the aisle hid him, he was gone. She pressed both hands against her cheeks. He was not there, she had imagined him.

"My God," she whispered.

She was alone. Her husband had gone out to the foyer to make a telephone call; it was intermission at the concert, a Thursday evening.

Now she saw him again, clearly. He was standing there. He was staring at her. Her blood rocked in her body, draining out of her head . . . she was going to faint. . . . They stared at each other. They gave no sign of recognition. Only when he took a step forward did she shake her head *no—no—keep away.* It was not possible.

When her husband returned, she was staring at the place in the aisle where her lover had been standing. Her husband leaned forward to interrupt that stare.

"What's wrong?" he said. "Are you sick?"

Panic rose in her in long shuddering waves. She tried to get to her feet, panicked at the thought of fainting here, and her husband took hold of her. She stood like an aged woman, clutching the seat before her.

At home he helped her up the stairs and she lay down. Her head was like a large piece of crockery that had to be held still, it was so heavy. She was still panicked. She felt it in the shallows of her face, behind her knees, in the pit of her stomach. It sickened her, it made her think of mucus, of something thick and gray congested inside her, stuck to her, that was herself and yet not herself—a poison.   \

She lay with her knees drawn up toward her chest, her eyes hotly open, while her husband spoke to her. She imagined that other man saying, *Why did you run away from me?* Her husband was saying other words. She tried to listen to them. He was going to call the doctor, he said, and she tried to sit up. "No, I'm all right now," she said quickly. The panic was like lead inside her, so thickly congested. How slow love was to drain out of her, how fluid and sticky it was inside her head!

Her husband believed her. No doctor. No threat. Grateful, she drew her husband down to her. They embraced, not comfortably. For years now they had not been comfortable together, in their intimacy and at a distance, and now they struggled gently as if the paces of this dance were too rigorous for them. It was something they might have known once, but had now outgrown. The panic in her thickened at this double betrayal: she drew her husband to her, she caressed him wildly, she shut her eyes to think about that other man.

A crowd of men and women parting, unexpectedly, and there he stood—there he stood—she kept seeing him, and yet her vision blotched at the memory. It had been finished between them, six months before, but he had come out here . . . and she had escaped him, now she was lying in her husband's arms, in his embrace, her face pressed against his. It was a kind of sleep, this love-making. She felt herself falling asleep, her body falling from her. Her eyes shut.

"I love you," her husband said fiercely, angrily.

She shut her eyes and thought of that other man, as if betraying him would give her life a center. 15

"Did I hurt you? Are you—?" her husband whispered.

Always this hot flashing of shame between them, the shame of her husband's near failure, the clumsiness of his love—

"You didn't hurt me," she said.

II

They had said good-by six months before. He drove her from Nantucket, where they had met, to Albany, New York, where she visited her sister. The hours of intimacy in the car had sealed something between them, a vow of silence and impersonality: she recalled the movement of the highways, the passing of other cars, the natural rhythms of the day hypnotizing her toward sleep while he drove. She trusted him, she could sleep in his presence. Yet she could not really fall asleep in spite of her exhaustion, and she kept jerking awake, frightened, to discover that nothing had changed—still the stranger who was driving her to Albany, still the highway, the sky, the antiseptic odor of the rented car, the sense of a rhythm behind the rhythm of the air that might unleash itself at any second. Everywhere on this highway, at this moment, there were men and women driving together, bonded together—what did that mean, to be together? What did it mean to enter into a bond with another person?

No, she did not really trust him; she did not really trust men. He would glance at her with his small cautious smile and she felt a declaration of shame between them. 20

Shame.

In her head she rehearsed conversations. She said bitterly, "You'll be relieved when we get to Albany. Relieved to get rid of me." They had spent so many days talking, confessing too much, driven to a pitch of childish excitement, laughing together on the beach, breaking into that pose of laughter that seems to eradicate the soul, so many days of this that the silence of the trip was like the silence of a hospital—all these surface noises, these rattles and hums, but an interior silence, a befuddlement. She said to him in her imagination, "One of us should die." Then she leaned over to touch him. She caressed the back of his neck. She said, aloud, "Would you like me to drive for a while?"

They stopped at a picnic area where other cars were stopped—couples, families—and walked together, smiling at their good luck. He put his arm around her shoulders and she sensed how they were in a posture together, a man and a woman forming a posture, a figure, that someone might sketch and show to them. She said slowly, "I don't want to go back. . . ."

Silence. She looked up at him. His face was heavy with her words, as if she had pulled at his skin with her fingers. Children ran nearby and distracted him—yes, he was a father too, his children ran like that, they tugged at his skin with their light, busy fingers.

"Are you so unhappy?" he said.

"I'm not unhappy, back there. I'm nothing. There's nothing to me," she said.

They stared at each other. The sensation between them was intense, exhausting. She thought that this man was her savior, that he had come to her at a time in her life when her life demanded completion, an end, a permanent fixing of all that was troubled and shifting and deadly. And yet it was absurd to think this. No person could save another. So she drew back from him and released him.

A few hours later they stopped at a gas station in a small city. She went to the women's rest room, having to ask the attendant for a key, and when she came back her eye jumped nervously onto the rented car—why? did she think he might have driven off without her?—onto the man, her friend, standing in conversation with the young attendant. Her friend was as old as her husband, over forty, with lanky, sloping shoulders, a full body, his hair thick, a dark, burnished brown, a festive color that made her eye twitch a little—and his hands were always moving, always those rapid conversational circles, going nowhere, gestures that were at once a little aggressive and apologetic.

She put her hand on his arm, a claim. He turned to her and smiled and she felt that she loved him, that everything in her life had forced her to this moment and that she had no choice about it.

They sat in the car for two hours, in Albany, in the parking lot of a Howard Johnson's restaurant, talking, trying to figure out their past. There was no future. They concentrated on the past, the several days behind them, lit up with a hot, dazzling August sun, like explosions that already belonged to other people, to strangers. Her face was faintly reflected in the green-tinted curve of the windshield, but she could not have recognized that face. She began to cry; she told herself: *I am not here, this will pass, this is nothing.* Still, she could not stop crying. The muscles of her face were springy, like a child's unpredictable muscles. He stroked her arms, her shoulders, trying to comfort her. "This is so hard . . . this is impossible . . ." he said. She felt panic for the world outside this car, all that was not herself and this man, and at the same time she understood that she was free of him, as people are free of other people, she would leave him soon, safely, and within a few days he would have fallen into the past, the impersonal past. . . .

"I'm so ashamed of myself!" she said finally.

She returned to her husband and saw that another woman, a shadow-woman, had taken her place—noiseless and convincing, like a dancer performing certain difficult steps. Her husband folded her in his arms and talked to her of his own loneliness, his worries about his business, his health, his mother, kept tranquillized and mute in a nursing home, and her spirit detached itself from her and drifted about the rooms of the large house she lived in with her husband, a shadow-woman delicate and imprecise. There was no boundary to her, no edge. Alone, she took hot baths and sat exhausted in the steaming water, wondering at her perpetual exhaustion. All that winter she noticed the limp, languid weight of her arms, her veins bulging slightly with the pressure of her extreme weariness. *This is fate,* she

25

30

thought, to be here and not there, to be one person and not another, a certain man's wife and not the wife of another man. The long, slow pain of this certainty rose in her, but it never became clear, it was baffling and imprecise. She could not be serious about it; she kept congratulating herself on her own good luck, to have escaped so easily, to have freed herself. So much love had gone into the first several years of her marriage that there wasn't much left, now, for another man. . . . She was certain of that. But the bath water made her dizzy, all that perpetual heat, and one day in January she drew a razor blade lightly across the inside of her arm, near the elbow, to see what would happen.

Afterward she wrapped a small towel around it, to stop the bleeding. The towel soaked through. She wrapped a bath towel around that and walked through the empty rooms of her home, lightheaded, hardly aware of the stubborn seeping of blood. There was no boundary to her in this house, no precise limit. She could flow out like her own blood and come to no end.

She sat for a while on a blue love seat, her mind empty. Her husband telephoned her when he would be staying late at the plant. He talked to her always about his plans, his problems, his business friends, his future. It was obvious that he had a future. As he spoke she nodded to encourage him, and her heartbeat quickened with the memory of her own, personal shame, the shame of this man's particular, private wife. One evening at dinner he leaned forward and put his head in his arms and fell asleep, like a child. She sat at the table with him for a while watching him. His hair had gone gray, almost white, at the temples—no one would guess that he was so quick, so careful a man, still fairly young about the eyes. She put her hand on his head, lightly, as if to prove to herself that he was real. He slept, exhausted.

One evening they went to a concert and she looked up to see her lover there, in the crowded aisle, in this city, watching her. He was standing there, with his overcoat on, watching her. She went cold. That morning the telephone had rung while her husband was still home, and she had heard him answer it, heard him hang up— it must have been a wrong number—and when the telephone rang again, at 9:30, she had been afraid to answer it. She had left home to be out of the range of that ringing, but now, in this public place, in this busy auditorium, she found herself staring at that man, unable to make any sign to him, any gesture of recognition. . . . 35

He would have come to her but she shook her head. *No. Stay away.*

Her husband helped her out of the row of seats, saying, "Excuse us, please. Excuse us," so that strangers got to their feet, quickly, alarmed, to let them pass. Was that woman about to faint? What was wrong?

At home she felt the blood drain slowly back into her head. Her husband embraced her hips, pressing his face against her, in that silence that belonged to the earliest days of their marriage. She thought, *He will drive it out of me.* He made love to her and she was back in the auditorium again, sitting alone, now that the concert was over. The stage was empty; the heavy velvet curtains had not been drawn; the musicians' chairs were empty, everything was silent and expectant; in the aisle her lover stood and smiled at her—Her husband was impatient. He was apart from her, working on her, operating on her; and then, stricken, he whispered, "Did I hurt you?"

The telephone rang the next morning. Dully, sluggishly, she answered it. She recognized his voice at once—that "Anna?" with its lifting of the second syllable, questioning and apologetic and making its claim—"Yes, what do you want?" she said.

"Just to see you. Please—" 40

"I can't."

"Anna, I'm sorry, I didn't mean to upset you—"

"I can't see you."

"Just for a few minutes—I have to talk to you—"

"But why, why now? Why now?" she said.

She heard her voice rising, but she could not stop it. He began to talk again, drowning her out. She remembered his rapid conversation. She remembered his gestures, the witty energetic circling of his hands.

"Please don't hang up!" he cried.

"I can't—I don't want to go through it again—"

"I'm not going to hurt you. Just tell me how you are."

"Everything is the same."

"Everything is the same with me."

She looked up at the ceiling, shyly. "Your wife? Your children?"

"The same."

"Your son?"

"He's fine—"

"I'm glad to hear that. I—"

"Is it still the same with you, your marriage? Tell me what you feel. What are you thinking?"

"I don't know. . . ."

She remembered his intense, eager words, the movement of his hands, that impatient precise fixing of the air by his hands, the jabbing of his fingers.

"Do you love me?" he said.

She could not answer.

"I'll come over to see you," he said.

"No," she said.

What will come next, what will happen?

Flesh hardening on his body, aging. Shrinking. He will grow old, but not soft like her husband. They are two different types: he is nervous, lean energetic, wise. She will grow thinner, as the tension radiates out from her backbone, wearing down her flesh. Her collarbones will jut out of her skin. Her husband, caressing her in their bed, will discover that she is another woman—she is not there with him—instead she is rising in an elevator in a downtown hotel, carrying a book as a prop, or walking quickly away from that hotel, her head bent and filled with secrets. Love, what to do with it? . . . Useless as moths' wings, as moths' fluttering. . . . She feels the flutterings of silky, crazy wings in her chest.

He flew out to visit her every several weeks, staying at a different hotel each time. He telephoned her, and she drove down to park in an underground garage at the very center of the city.

She lay in his arms while her husband talked to her, miles away, one body fading into another. He will grow old, his body will change, she thought, pressing her cheek against the back of one of these men. If it was her lover, they were in a hotel room: always the propped-up little booklet describing the hotel's many services, with color photographs of its cocktail lounge and dining room and coffee shop. Grow old, leave me, die, go back to your neurotic wife and your sad, ordinary children, she thought, but still her eyes closed gratefully against his skin and she felt how complete their silence was, how they had come to rest in each other.

"Tell me about your life here. The people who love you," he said, as he always did.

One afternoon they lay together for four hours. It was her birthday and she was intoxicated with her good fortune, this prize of the afternoon, this man in her arms! She was a little giddy, she talked too much. She told him about her parents, about her husband. . . . "They were all people I believed in, but it turned out wrong. Now, I believe in you. . . ." He laughed as if shocked by her words. She did not understand. Then she understood. "But I believe truly in you. I can't think of myself without you," she said. . . . He spoke of his wife, her ambitions, her intelligence, her use of the children against him, her use of his younger son's blindness, all of his words gentle and hypnotic and convincing in the late afternoon peace of this hotel room . . . and she felt the terror of laughter, threatening laughter. Their words, like their bodies, were aging.

She dressed quickly in the bathroom, drawing her long hair up around the back of her head, fixing it as always, anxious that everything be the same. Her face was slightly raw, from his face. The rubbing of his skin. Her eyes were too bright, wearily bright. Her hair was blond but not so blond as it had been that summer in the white Nantucket air.

She ran water and splashed it on her face. She blinked at the water. Blind. Drowning. She thought with satisfaction that soon, soon, he would be back home, in that house on Long Island she had never seen, with that woman she had never seen, sitting on the edge of another bed, putting on his shoes. She wanted nothing except to be free of him. Why not be free? *Oh*, she thought suddenly, *I will follow you back and kill you. You and her and the little boy. What is there to stop me?*

She left him. Everyone on the street pitied her, that look of absolute zero.

III

A man and a child, approaching her. The sharp acrid smell of fish. The crashing of waves. Anna pretended not to notice the father with his son—there was something strange about them. That frank, silent intimacy, too gentle, the man's bare feet in the water and the boy a few feet away, leaning away from his father. He was about nine years old and still his father held his hand.

A small yipping dog, a golden dog, bounded near them.

Anna turned shyly back to her reading; she did not want to have to speak to these neighbors. She saw the man's shadow falling over her legs, then over the pages of her book, and she had the idea that he wanted to see what she was reading. The dog nuzzled her; the man called him away.

She watched them walk down the beach. She was relieved that the man had not spoken to her.

She saw them in town later that day, the two of them brown-haired and patient, now wearing sandals, walking with that same look of care. The man's white shorts were soiled and a little baggy. His pullover shirt was a faded green. His face was broad, the cheekbones wide, spaced widely apart, the eyes stark in their sockets, as if they fastened onto objects for no reason, ponderous and edgy. The little boy's face was pale and sharp; his lips were perpetually parted.

Anna realized that the child was blind.

The next morning, early, she caught sight of them again. For some reason she went to the back door of her cottage. She faced the sea breeze eagerly. Her heart hammered. . . . She had been here, in her family's old house, for three days, alone, bitterly satisfied at being alone, and now it was a puzzle to her how her soul strained to fly outward, to meet with another person. She watched the man with his son, his cautious, rather stooped shoulders above the child's small shoulders.

The man was carrying something, it looked like a notebook. He sat on the sand, not far from Anna's spot of the day before, and the dog rushed up to them. The child approached the edge of the ocean, timidly. He moved in short jerky steps, his legs stiff. The dog ran around him. Anna heard the child crying out a word that sounded like "Ty"—it must have been the dog's name—and then the man joined in, his voice heavy and firm.

"Ty—"

Anna tied her hair back with a yellow scarf and went down to the beach.

The man glanced around at her. He smiled. She stared past him at the waves. To talk to him or not to talk—she had the freedom of that choice. For a moment she felt that she had made a mistake, that the child and the dog would not protect her, that behind this man's ordinary, friendly face there was a certain arrogant maleness—then she relented, she smiled shyly.

"A nice house you've got there," the man said.

She nodded her thanks.

The man pushed his sunglasses up on his forehead. Yes, she recognized the eyes of the day before—intelligent and nervous, the sockets pale, untanned.

"Is that your telephone ringing?" he said.

She did not bother to listen. "It's a wrong number," she said.

Her husband calling: she had left home for a few days, to be alone.

But the man, setting himself on the sand, seemed to misinterpret this.

He smiled in surprise, one corner of his mouth higher than the other. He said nothing. Anna wondered: *What is he thinking?* The dog was leaping about her, panting against her legs, and she laughed in embarrassment. She bent to pet it, grateful for its busyness. "Don't let him jump up on you," the man said. "He's a nuisance."

The dog was a small golden retriever, a young dog. The blind child, standing now in the water, turned to call the dog to him. His voice was shrill and impatient.

"Our house is the third one down—the white one," the man said.

She turned, startled. "Oh, did you buy it from Dr. Patrick? Did he die?"

"Yes, finally. . . ."

Her eyes wandered nervously over the child and the dog. She felt the nervous beat of her heart out to the very tips of her fingers, the fleshy tips of her fingers: little hearts were there, pulsing. *What is he thinking?* The man had opened his notebook. He had a piece of charcoal and he began to sketch something.

Anna looked down at him. She saw the top of his head, his thick brown hair, the freckles on his shoulders, the quick, deft movement of his hand. Upside down, Anna herself being drawn. She smiled in surprise.

"Let me draw you. Sit down," he said.

She knelt awkwardly a few yards away. He turned the page of the sketch pad. The dog ran to her and she sat, straightening out her skirt beneath her, flinching from the dog's tongue. "Ty!" cried the child. Anna sat, and slowly the pleasure of the moment began to glow in her; her skin flushed with gratitude.

She sat there for nearly an hour. The man did not talk much. Back and forth the dog bounded, shaking itself. The child came to sit near them, in silence. Anna felt that she was drifting into a kind of trance while the man sketched her, half a dozen rapid sketches, the surface of her face given up to him. "Where are you from?" the man asked.

"Ohio. My husband lives in Ohio."

She wore no wedding band.

"Your wife—" Anna began.

"Yes?"

"Is she here?"

"Not right now."

She was silent, ashamed. She had asked an improper question. But the man did not seem to notice. He continued drawing her, bent over the sketch pad. When Anna said she had to go, he showed her the drawings—one after another of her, Anna, recognizably Anna, a woman in her early thirties, her hair smooth and flat across the top of her head, tied behind by a scarf. "Take the one you like best," he said, and she picked one of her with the dog in her lap, sitting very straight, her brows and eyes clearly defined, her lips girlishly pursed, the dog and her dress suggested by a few quick irregular lines.

"Lady with pet dog," the man said.

She spent the rest of the day reading, nearer her cottage. It was not really a cottage—it was a two-story house, large and ungainly and weathered. It was mixed up in her mind with her family, her own childhood, and she glanced up from her book, perplexed, as if waiting for one of her parents or her sister to come up to her. Then she thought of the man, the man with the blind child, the man with the dog, and she could not concentrate on her reading. Someone—probably her father—had marked a passage that must be important, but she kept reading and rereading it: *We try to discover in things, endeared to us on that account, the spiritual glamour which we ourselves have cast upon them; we are disillusioned, and learn that they are in themselves barren and devoid of the charm that they owed, in our minds, to the association of certain ideas. . . ."*

She thought again of the man on the beach. She lay the book aside and thought of him: his eyes, his aloneness, his drawings of her.

They began seeing each other after that. He came to her front door in the evening, without the child; he drove her into town for dinner. She was shy and extremely pleased. The darkness of the expensive restaurant released her; she heard herself chatter; she leaned forward and seemed to be offering her face up to him, listening to him. He talked about his work on a Long Island newspaper and she seemed to be listening to him, as she stared at his face, arranging her own face into the expression she had seen in that charcoal drawing. Did he see her like that, then?—girlish and withdrawn and patrician? She felt the weight of his interest in her, a force that fell upon her like a blow. A repeated blow. Of course he was married, he had children—of course she was married, permanently married. This flight from her husband was not important. She had left him before, to be alone, it was not important. Everything in her was slender and delicate and not important.

They walked for hours after dinner, looking at the other strollers, the weekend visitors, the tourists, the couples like themselves. Surely they were mistaken for a couple, a married couple. *This is the hour in which everything is decided,* Anna thought. They had both had several drinks and they talked a great deal. Anna found herself saying too much, stopping and starting giddily. She put her hand to her forehead, feeling faint.

"It's from the sun—you've had too much sun—" he said.

At the door to her cottage, on the front porch, she heard herself asking him if he would like to come in. She allowed him to lead her inside, to close the door. *This is not important*, she thought clearly, *he doesn't mean it, he doesn't love me, nothing will come of it.* She was frightened, yet it seemed to her necessary to give in; she had to leave Nantucket with that act completed, an act of adultery, an accomplishment she would take back to Ohio and to her marriage.

Later, incredibly, she heard herself asking: "Do you . . . do you love me?"   115

"You're so beautiful!" he said, amazed.

She felt this beauty, shy and glowing and centered in her eyes. He stared at her. In this large, drafty house, alone together, they were like accomplices, conspirators. She could not think: how old was she? which year was this? They had done something unforgivable together, and the knowledge of it was tugging at their faces. A cloud seemed to pass over her. She felt herself smiling shrilly.

Afterward, a peculiar raspiness, a dryness of breath. He was silent. She felt a strange, idle fear, a sense of the danger outside this room and this old, comfortable bed—a danger that would not recognize her as the lady in that drawing, the lady with the pet dog. There was nothing to say to this man, this stranger. She felt the beauty draining out of her face, her eyes fading.

"I've got to be alone," she told him.

He left, and she understood that she would not see him again. She stood by the window of the room, watching the ocean. A sense of shame overpowered her: it was smeared everywhere on her body, the smell of it, the richness of it. She tried to recall him, and his face was confused in her memory: she would have to shout to him across a jumbled space, she would have to wave her arms wildly. *You love me! You must love me!* But she knew he did not love her, and she did not love him; he was a man who drew everything up into himself, like all men, walking away, free to walk away, free to have his own thoughts, free to envision her body, all the secrets of her body. . . . And she lay down again in the bed, feeling how heavy this body had become, her insides heavy with shame, the very backs of her eyelids coated with shame.   120

"This is the end of one part of my life," she thought.

But in the morning the telephone rang. She answered it. It was her lover: they talked brightly and happily. She could hear the eagerness in his voice, the love in his voice, that same still, sad amazement—she understood how simple life was, there were no problems.

They spent most of their time on the beach, with the child and the dog. He joked and was serious at the same time. He said, once, "You have defined my soul for me," and she laughed to hide her alarm. In a few days it was time for her to leave. He got a sitter for the boy and took the ferry with her to the mainland, then rented a car to drive her up to Albany. She kept thinking: *Now something will happen. It will come to an end.* But most of the drive was silent and hypnotic. She wanted him to joke with her, to say again that she had defined his soul for him, but he drove fast, he was serious, she distrusted the hawkish look of his profile—she did not know him at all. At a gas station she splashed her face with cold water. Alone in the grubby little rest room, shaky and very much alone. In such places are women totally alone with their bodies. The body grows heavier, more evil, in such silence. . . . On the beach everything had been noisy with sunlight and gulls and waves; here, as if run to earth, everything was cramped and silent and dead.

She went outside, squinting. There he was, talking with the station attendant. She could not think as she returned to him whether she wanted to live or not.

504

She stayed in Albany for a few days, then flew home to her husband. He met her at the airport, near the luggage counter, where her three pieces of pale-brown luggage were brought to him on a conveyer belt, to be claimed by him. He kissed her on the cheek. They shook hands, a little embarrassed. She had come home again.

"How will I live out the rest of my life?" she wondered.

In January her lover spied on her: she glanced up and saw him, in a public place, in the DeRoy Symphony Hall. She was paralyzed with fear. She nearly fainted. In this faint she felt her husband's body, loving her, working its love upon her, and she shut her eyes harder to keep out the certainty of his love—sometimes he failed at loving her, sometimes he succeeded, it had nothing to do with her or her pity or her ten years of love for him, it had nothing to do with a woman at all. It was a private act accomplished by a man, a husband or a lover, in communion with his own soul, his manhood.

Her husband was forty-two years old now, growing slowly into middle age, getting heavier, softer. Her lover was about the same age, narrower in the shoulders, with a full, solid chest, yet lean, nervous. She thought, in her paralysis, of men and how they love freely and eagerly so long as their bodies are capable of love, love for a woman; and then, as love fades in their bodies, it fades from their souls and they become immune and immortal and ready to die.

Her husband was a little rough with her, as if impatient with himself. "I love you," he said fiercely, angrily. And then, ashamed, he said, "Did I hurt you? . . ."

"You didn't hurt me," she said.

Her voice was too shrill for their embrace.

While he was in the bathroom she went to her closet and took out that drawing of the summer before. There she was, on the beach at Nantucket, a lady with a pet dog, her eyes large and defined, the dog in her lap hardly more than a few snarls, a few coarse soft lines of charcoal . . . her dress smeared, her arms oddly limp . . . her hands not well drawn at all. . . . She tried to think: did she love the man who had drawn this? did he love her? The fever in her husband's body had touched her and driven her temperature up, and now she stared at the drawing with a kind of lust, fearful of seeing an ugly soul in that woman's face, fearful of seeing the face suddenly through her lover's eyes. She breathed quickly and harshly, staring at the drawing.

And so, the next day, she went to him at his hotel. She wept, pressing against him, demanding of him, "What do you want? Why are you here? Why don't you let me alone?" He told her that he wanted nothing. He expected nothing. He would not cause trouble.

"I want to talk about last August," he said.

"Don't—" she said.

She was hypnotized by his gesturing hands, his nervousness, his obvious agitation. He kept saying, "I understand. I'm making no claims upon you."

They became lovers again.

He called room service for something to drink and they sat side by side on his bed, looking through a copy of *The New Yorker,* laughing at the cartoons. It was so peaceful in this room, so complete. They were on a holiday. It was a secret holiday. Four-thirty in the afternoon, on a Friday, an ordinary Friday: a secret holiday.

"I won't bother you again," he said.

He flew back to see her again in March, and in late April. He telephoned her from his hotel—a different hotel each time—and she came down to him at once. She rose to him in various elevators, she knocked on the doors of various rooms, she stepped into his embrace, breathless and guilty and already angry with him, pleading with him. One morning in May, when he telephoned, she pressed her forehead against the doorframe and could not speak. He kept saying, "What's wrong? Can't you talk? Aren't you alone?" She felt that she was going insane. Her head would burst. Why, why did he love her, why did he pursue her? Why did he want her to die? 140

She went to him in the hotel room. A familiar room: had they been here before? "Everything is repeating itself. Everything is stuck," she said. He framed her face in his hands and said that she looked thinner—was she sick?—what was wrong? She shook herself free. He, her lover, looked about the same. There was a small, angry pimple on his neck. He stared at her, eagerly and suspiciously. Did she bring bad news?

"So you love me? You love me?" she asked.

"Why are you so angry?"

"I want to be free of you. The two of us free of each other."

"That isn't true—you don't want that—" 145

He embraced her. She was wild with that old, familiar passion for him, her body clinging to his, her arms not strong enough to hold him. Ah, what despair! —what bitter hatred she felt!—she needed this man for her salvation, he was all she had to live for, and yet she could not believe in him. He embraced her thighs, her hips, kissing her, pressing his warm face against her, and yet she could not believe in him, not really. She needed him in order to live, but he was not worth her love, he was not worth her dying. . . . She promised herself this: when she got back home, when she was alone, she would draw the razor more deeply across her arm.

The telephone rang and he answered it: a wrong number.

"Jesus," he said.

They lay together, still. She imagined their posture like this, the two of them one figure, one substance; and outside this room and this bed there was a universe of disjointed, separate things, blank things, that had nothing to do with them. She would not be Anna out there, the lady in the drawing. He would not be her lover.

"I love you so much. . . ." she whispered. 150

"Please don't cry! We have only a few hours, please. . . ."

It was absurd, their clinging together like this. She saw them as a single figure in a drawing, their arms and legs entwined, their heads pressing mutely together. Helpless substance, so heavy and warm and doomed. It was absurd that any human being should be so important to another human being. She wanted to laugh: a laugh might free them both.

She could not laugh.

Sometime later he said, as if they had been arguing, "Look. It's you. You're the one who doesn't want to get married. You lie to me—"

"Lie to you?" 155

"You love me but you won't marry me, because you want something left over—Something not finished—All your life you can attribute your misery to me, to our not being married—you are using me—"

"Stop it! You'll make me hate you!" she cried.

"You can say to yourself that you're miserable because of *me*. We will never be married, you will never be happy, neither one of us will ever be happy—"

"I don't want to hear this!" she said.

She pressed her hands flatly against her face. 160

She went to the bathroom to get dressed. She washed her face and part of her body, quickly. The fever was in her, in the pit of her belly. She would rush home and strike a razor across the inside of her arm and free the pressure, that fever.

The impatient bulging of the veins: an ordeal over.

The demand of the telephone's ringing: that ordeal over.

The nuisance of getting the car and driving home in all that five o'clock traffic: an ordeal too much for a woman.

The movement of this stranger's body in hers: over, finished. 165

Now, dressed, a little calmer, they held hands and talked. They had to talk swiftly, to get all their news in: he did not trust the people who worked for him, he had faith in no one, his wife had moved to a textbook publishing company and was doing well, she had inherited a Ben Shahn° painting from her father and wanted to "touch it up a little"—she was crazy!—his blind son was at another school, doing fairly well, in fact his children were all doing fairly well in spite of the stupid mistake of their parents' marriage—and what about her? what about her life? She told him in a rush the one thing he wanted to hear: that she lived with her husband lovelessly, the two of them polite strangers, sharing a bed, lying side by side in the night in that bed, bodies out of which souls had fled. There was no longer even any shame between them.

"And what about me? Do you feel shame with me still?" he asked.

She did not answer. She moved away from him and prepared to leave.

Then, a minute later, she happened to catch sight of his reflection in the bureau mirror—he was glancing down at himself, checking himself mechanically, impersonally, preparing also to leave. He too would leave this room: he too was headed somewhere else.

She stared at him. It seemed to her that in this instant he was breaking from her, the image of her lover fell free of her, breaking from her . . . and she realized that he existed in a dimension quite apart from her, a mysterious being. And suddenly, joyfully, she felt a miraculous calm. This man was her husband, truly—they were truly married, here in this room—they had been married haphazardly and accidentally for a long time. In another part of the city she had another husband, a "husband," but she had not betrayed that man, not really. This man, whom she loved above any other person in the world, above even her own self-pitying sorrow and her own life, was her truest lover, her destiny. And she did not hate him, she did not hate herself any longer; she did not wish to die; she was flooded with a strange certainty, a sense of gratitude, of pure selfless energy. It was obvious to her that she had, all along, been behaving correctly; out of instinct. 170

What triumph, to love like this in any room, anywhere, risking even the craziest of accidents!

"Why are you so happy? What's wrong?" he asked, startled. He stared at her. She felt the abrupt concentration in him, the focusing of his vision on her, almost a bitterness in his face, as if he feared her. What, was it beginning all over again? Their love beginning again, in spite of them? "How can you look so happy?" he asked. "We don't have any right to it. Is it because . . . ?"

"Yes," she said.

Shahn: Ben Shahn (1898–1969), a Russian-born American artist.

1. The following exercise should be worked through in sequence, as follows:
   a. Read Chekhov's "The Lady with the Little Dog" carefully, even if you have read it before.
   b. Read Nabokov's lecture on the story, noting each point where he gives you an insight you might have missed in your own reading.
   c. Keeping Nabokov's lecture in mind, reread the story and write a paragraph in which you characterized the differences between your two readings.

2. Read Joyce Carol Oates's "The Lady with the Pet Dog," a story that refers in many ways to Chekhov's. After making a careful study of Nabokov's list of seven "typical" features of a Chekhov story, write a short commentary on their applicability to the Oates story.

3. Nabokov was known to be an opinionated and idiosyncratic critic. Read his lecture with care and point out those places where personality and bias seem to overwhelm the objectivity expected of the critic/lecturer.

RESPONDING TO HEMINGWAY'S "THE KILLERS"

Ernest Hemingway (1898–1961)

Ernest Hemingway was born in Oak Park, Illinois. He passed his boyhood summers hunting and fishing in the wooded country of Northern Michigan, a setting that recurs throughout his early stories. After a few months as a reporter at the *Kansas City Star,* Hemingway enlisted in an ambulance unit and was sent to the French front. He was only eighteen. A shrapnel wound cut short his service; he returned home to his family.

But war and travel had infected his soul. After only a short stay with his family, Hemingway sailed for Paris. He was determined to make his way as a writer. And there, in the midst of a great many other expatriates— Gertrude Stein, F. Scott Fitzgerald, Ezra Pound, James Joyce, and others—he honed the style that would make his name.

Hemingway's career was tumultuous in the extreme. Apart from attaining world celebrity as a writer, he was constantly in the public eye for other exploits: he fished, hunted on safari, married and divorced, drank and fought; he served as a correspondent in the Spanish Civil War and World War II, survived spectacular accidents, traveled incessantly. . . . In short, he created a myth for his times. What almost no one realized was that there was a dark, depressed side to this most flamboyant man. His father had died a suicide, and he would, too. Hemingway shot himself at his hunting lodge in Ketchum, Idaho, in 1961 after a lingering period of mental distress.

Hemingway's many books include the story collection *In Our Time* (1925) and the novels *A Farewell to Arms* (1929), *The Sun Also Rises* (1926), and *For Whom the Bell Tolls* (1940).

THE KILLERS

The door of Henry's lunch-room opened and two men came in. They sat down at the counter.

"What's yours?" George asked them.

"I don't know," one of the men said. "What do you want to eat, Al?"

"I don't know," said Al. "I don't know what I want to eat."

Outside it was getting dark. The street-light came on outside the window. The two men at the counter read the menu. From the other end of the counter Nick Adams watched them. He had been talking to George when they came in. 5

"I'll have a roast pork tenderloin with apple sauce and mashed potatoes," the first man said.

"It isn't ready yet."

"What the hell do you put it on the card for?"

"That's the dinner," George explained. "You can get that at six o'clock."

George looked at the clock on the wall behind the counter. 10

"It's five o'clock."

"The clock says twenty minutes past five," the second man said.

"It's twenty minutes fast."

"Oh, to hell with the clock," the first man said. "What have you got to eat?"

"I can give you any kind of sandwiches," George said. "You can have ham and eggs, bacon and eggs, liver and bacon, or a steak." 15

"Give me chicken croquettes with green peas and cream sauce and mashed potatoes."

"That's the dinner."

"Everything we want's the dinner, eh? That's the way you work it."

"I can give you ham and eggs, bacon and eggs, liver——"

"I'll take ham and eggs," the man called Al said. He wore a derby hat and a black overcoat buttoned across the chest. His face was small and white and he had tight lips. He wore a silk muffler and gloves. 20

"Give me bacon and eggs," said the other man. He was about the same size as Al. Their faces were different, but they were dressed like twins. Both wore overcoats too tight for them. They sat leaning forward, their elbows on the counter.

"Got anything to drink?" Al asked.

"Silver beer, bevo, ginger-ale," George said.

"I mean you got anything to *drink?*"

"Just those I said." 25

"This is a hot town," said the other. "What do they call it?"

"Summit."

"Ever hear of it?" Al asked his friend.

"No," said the friend.

"What do you do here nights?" Al asked.   30

"They eat the dinner," his friend said. "They all come here and eat the big dinner."

"That's right," George said.

"So you think that's right?" Al asked George.

"Sure."

"You're a pretty bright boy, aren't you?"   35

"Sure," said George.

"Well, you're not," said the other little man. "Is he, Al?"

"He's dumb," said Al. He turned to Nick. "What's your name?"

"Adams."

"Another bright boy," Al said. "Ain't he a bright boy, Max?"   40

"The town's full of bright boys," Max said.

George put the two platters, one of ham and eggs, the other of bacon and eggs, on the counter. He set down two side-dishes of fried potatoes and closed the wicket into the kitchen.

"Which is yours?" he asked Al.

"Don't you remember?"

"Ham and eggs."   45

"Just a bright boy," Max said. He leaned forward and took the ham and eggs. Both men ate with their gloves on. George watched them eat.

"What are *you* looking at?" Max looked at George.

"Nothing."

"The hell you were. You were looking at me."

"Maybe the boy meant it for a joke, Max," Al said.   50

George laughed.

"*You* don't have to laugh," Max said to him. "*You* don't have to laugh at all, see?"

"All right," said George.

"So he thinks it's all right." Max turned to Al. "He thinks it's all right. That's a good one."

"Oh, he's a thinker," Al said. They went on eating.   55

"What's the bright boy's name down the counter?" Al asked Max.

"Hey, bright boy," Max said to Nick. "You go around on the other side of the counter with your boy friend."

"What's the idea?" Nick asked.

"There isn't any idea."

"You better go around, bright boy," Al said. Nick went around behind the counter.   60

"What's the idea?" George asked.

"None of your damn business," Al said. "Who's out in the kitchen?"

"The nigger."

"What do you mean the nigger?"   65

"The nigger that cooks."

"Tell him to come in."

"What's the idea?"

Responding to Stories

"Tell him to come in."

"Where do you think you are?"

"We know damn well where we are," the man called Max said. "Do we look silly?"

"You talk silly," Al said to him. "What the hell do you argue with this kid for? Listen," he said to George, "tell the nigger to come out here."

"What are you going to do to him?"

"Nothing. Use your head, bright boy. What would we do to a nigger?"

George opened the slit that opened back into the kitchen. "Sam," he called. "Come in here a minute."

The door to the kitchen opened and the nigger came in. "What was it?" he asked. The two men at the counter took a look at him.

"All right, nigger. You stand right there," Al said.

Sam, the nigger, standing in his apron, looked at the two men sitting at the counter. "Yes, sir," he said. Al got down from his stool.

"I'm going back to the kitchen with the nigger and bright boy," he said. "Go on back to the kitchen, nigger. You go with him, bright boy." The little man walked after Nick and Sam, the cook, back into the kitchen. The door shut after them. The man called Max sat at the counter opposite George. He didn't look at George but looked in the mirror that ran along back of the counter. Henry's had been made over from a saloon into a lunch-counter.

"Well, bright boy," Max said, looking into the mirror, "why don't you say something?"

"What's it all about?"

"Hey, Al," Max called, "bright boy wants to know what it's all about."

"Why don't you tell him?" Al's voice came from the kitchen.

"What do you think it's all about?"

"I don't know."

"What do you think?"

Max looked into the mirror all the time he was talking.

"I wouldn't say."

"Hey, Al, bright boy says he wouldn't say what he thinks it's all about."

"I can hear you, all right," Al said from the kitchen. He had propped open the slit that dishes passed through into the kitchen with a catsup bottle. "Listen, bright boy," he said from the kitchen to George. "Stand a little further along the bar. You move a little to the left, Max." He was like a photographer arranging for a group picture.

"Talk to me, bright boy," Max said. "What do you think's going to happen?"

George did not say anything.

"I'll tell you," Max said. "We're going to kill a Swede. Do you know a big Swede named Ole Andreson?"

"Yes."

"He comes here to eat every night, don't he?"

"Sometimes he comes here."

"He comes here at six o'clock, don't he?"

"If he comes."

"We know all that, bright boy," Max said. "Talk about something else. Ever go to the movies?"

"Once in a while."

"You ought to go to the movies more. The movies are fine for a bright boy like you." 100

"What are you going to kill Ole Andreson for? What did he ever do to you?"

"He never had a chance to do anything to us. He never even seen us."

"And he's only going to see us once," Al said from the kitchen.

"What are you going to kill him for, then?" George asked.

"We're killing him for a friend, just to oblige a friend, bright boy." 105

"Shut up," said Al from the kitchen. "You talk too goddam much."

"Well, I got to keep bright boy amused. Don't I, bright boy?"

"You talk too damn much," Al said. "The nigger and my bright boy are amused by themselves. I got them tied up like a couple of girl friends in the convent."

"I suppose you were in a convent?"

"You never know." 110

"You were in a kosher convent. That's where you were."

George looked up at the clock.

"If anybody comes in you tell them the cook is off, and if they keep after it, you tell them you'll go back and cook yourself. Do you get that, bright boy?"

"All right," George said. "What you going to do with us afterward?"

"That'll depend," Max said. "That's one of those things you never know at the time." 115

George looked up at the clock. It was a quarter past six. The door from the street opened. A street-car motorman came in.

"Hello, George," he said. "Can I get supper?"

"Sam's gone out," George said. "He'll be back in about half an hour."

"I'd better go up the street," the motorman said. George looked at the clock. It was twenty minutes past six.

"That was nice, bright boy," Max said. "You're a regular little gentleman." 120

"He knew I'd blow his head off," Al said from the kitchen.

"No," said Max. "It ain't that. Bright boy is nice. He's a nice boy. I like him."

At six-fifty-five George said: "He's not coming."

Two other people had been in the lunch-room. Once George had gone out to the kitchen and made a ham-and-egg sandwich "to go" that a man wanted to take with him. Inside the kitchen he saw Al, his derby hat tipped back, sitting on a stool beside the wicket with the muzzle of a sawed-off shotgun resting on the ledge. Nick and the cook were back to back in the corner, a towel tied in each of their mouths. George had cooked the sandwich, wrapped it up in oiled paper, put it in a bag, brought it in, and the man had paid for it and gone out.

"Bright boy can do everything," Max said. "He can cook and everything. You'd make some girl a nice wife, bright boy." 125

"Yes?" George said. "Your friend, Ole Andreson, isn't going to come."

"We'll give him ten minutes," Max said.

Max watched the mirror and the clock. The hands of the clock marked seven o'clock, and then five minutes past seven.

"Come on, Al," said Max. "We better go. He's not coming."

"Better give him five minutes," Al said from the kitchen. 130

In the five minutes a man came in, and George explained that the cook was sick.

"Why the hell don't you get another cook?" the man asked. "Aren't you running a lunch-counter?" He went out.

"Come on, Al," Max said.

"What about the two bright boys and the nigger?"

"They're all right."

"You think so?"

"Sure. We're through with it."

"I don't like it," said Al. "It's sloppy. You talk too much."

"Oh, what the hell," said Max. "We got to keep amused, haven't we?"

"You talk too much, all the same," Al said. He came out from the kitchen. The cut-off barrels of the shotgun made a slight bulge under the waist of his too tight-fitting overcoat. He straightened his coat with his gloved hands.

"So long, bright boy," he said to George. "You got a lot of luck."

"That's the truth," Max said. "You ought to play the races, bright boy."

The two of them went out the door. George watched them, through the window, pass under the arc-light and cross the street. In their tight overcoats and derby hats they looked like a vaudeville team. George went back through the swinging-door into the kitchen and untied Nick and the cook.

"I don't want any more of that," said Sam, the cook. "I don't want any more of that."

Nick stood up. He had never had a towel in his mouth before.

"Say," he said. "What the hell?" He was trying to swagger it off.

"They were going to kill Ole Andreson," George said. "They were going to shoot him when he came in to eat."

"Ole Andreson?"

"Sure."

The cook felt the corners of his mouth with his thumbs.

"They all gone?" he asked.

"Yeah," said George. "They're gone now."

"I don't like it," said the cook. "I don't like any of it at all."

"Listen," George said to Nick. "You better go see Ole Andreson."

"All right."

"You better not have anything to do with it at all," Sam, the cook, said. "You better stay way out of it."

"Don't go if you don't want to," George said.

"Mixing up in this ain't going to get you anywhere," the cook said. "You stay out of it."

"I'll go see him," Nick said to George. "Where does he live?"

The cook turned away.

"Little boys always know what they want to do," he said.

"He lives up at Hirsch's rooming-house," George said to Nick.

"I'll go up there."

Outside the arc-light shone through the bare branches of a tree. Nick walked up the street beside the car-tracks and turned at the next arc-light down a side-street. Three houses up the street was Hirsch's rooming-house. Nick walked up the two steps and pushed the bell. A woman came to the door.

"Is Ole Andreson here?"

"Do you want to see him?"

"Yes, if he's in."

Nick followed the woman up a flight of stairs and back to the end of a corridor. She knocked on the door.

The Killers   **513**

"Who is it?"

"It's somebody to see you, Mr. Andreson," the woman said. 170

"It's Nick Adams."

"Come in."

Nick opened the door and went into the room. Ole Andreson was lying on the bed with all his clothes on. He had been a heavyweight prizefighter and he was too long for the bed. He lay with his head on two pillows. He did not look at Nick.

"What was it?" he asked.

"I was up at Henry's," Nick said, "and two fellows came in and tied up me and the cook, and they said they were going to kill you." 175

It sounded silly when he said it. Ole Andreson said nothing.

"They put us out in the kitchen," Nick went on. "They were going to shoot you when you came in to supper."

Ole Andreson looked at the wall and did not say anything.

"George thought I better come and tell you about it."

"There isn't anything I can do about it," Ole Andreson said. 180

"I'll tell you what they were like."

"I don't want to know what they were like," Ole Andreson said. He looked at the wall. "Thanks for coming to tell me about it."

"That's all right."

Nick looked at the big man lying on the bed.

"Don't you want me to go and see the police?" 185

"No," Ole Andreson said. "That wouldn't do any good."

"Isn't there something I could do?"

"No. There ain't anything to do."

"Maybe it was just a bluff."

"No. It ain't just a bluff." 190

Ole Andreson rolled over toward the wall.

"The only thing is," he said, talking toward the wall, "I just can't make up my mind to go out. I been in here all day."

"Couldn't you get out of town?"

"No," Ole Andreson said. "I'm through with all that running around."

He looked at the wall. 195

"There ain't anything to do now."

"Couldn't you fix it up some way?"

"No. I got in wrong." He talked in the same flat voice. "There ain't anything to do. After a while I'll make up my mind to go out."

"I better go back and see George," Nick said.

"So long," said Ole Andreson. He did not look toward Nick. "Thanks for coming around." 200

Nick went out. As he shut the door he saw Ole Andreson with all his clothes on, lying on the bed looking at the wall.

"He's been in his room all day," the landlady said down-stairs. "I guess he don't feel well. I said to him: 'Mr. Andreson, you ought to go out and take a walk on a nice fall day like this,' but he didn't feel like it."

"He doesn't want to go out."

"I'm sorry he don't feel well," the woman said. "He's an awfully nice man. He was in the ring, you know."

"I know it." 205

"You'd never know it except from the way his face is," the woman said.

They stood talking just inside the street door. "He's just as gentle."

"Well, good-night, Mrs. Hirsch," Nick said.

"I'm not Mrs. Hirsch," the woman said. "She owns the place. I just look after it for her. I'm Mrs. Bell."

"Well, good-night, Mrs. Bell," Nick said. 210

"Good-night," the woman said.

Nick walked up the dark street to the corner under the arclight, and then along the car-tracks to Henry's eating-house. George was inside, back of the counter.

"Did you see Ole?"

"Yes," said Nick. "He's in his room and he won't go out."

The cook opened the door from the kitchen when he heard Nick's voice. 215

"I don't even listen to it," he said and shut the door.

"Did you tell him about it?" George asked.

"Sure. I told him but he knows what it's all about."

"What's he going to do?"

"Nothing." 220

"They'll kill him."

"I guess they will."

"He must have got mixed up in something in Chicago."

"I guess so," said Nick.

"It's a hell of a thing." 225

"It's an awful thing," Nick said.

They did not say anything. George reached down for a towel and wiped the counter.

"I wonder what he did?" Nick said.

"Double-crossed somebody. That's what they kill them for."

"I'm going to get out of this town," Nick said. 230

"Yes," said George. "That's a good thing to do."

"I can't stand to think about him waiting in the room and knowing he's going to get it. It's too damned awful."

"Well," said George, "you better not think about it."

The Critics' View

Cleanth Brooks (1906–1994) and Robert Penn Warren (1905–1989)

THE DISCOVERY OF EVIL: AN ANALYSIS OF "THE KILLERS"

There are certain fairly obvious points to be made about the technique of this story. It breaks up into one long scene and three short scenes. Indeed, the method is so thoroughly scenic that not over three or four sentences are required to make the transitions. The focus of the narration is objective throughout, practically all information being conveyed in simple realistic dialogue. In the first scene the revelation of the mission of the gangsters is accomplished through a few significant details—the fact that the gangsters eat with gloves (to avoid leaving fingerprints), the fact that they keep their eyes on the mirror behind the bar, the fact that, after Nick and the cook have been tied up, the gangster who has the shotgun at the service window stations his friend and George out front "like a photographer arranging for a group picture"—all of this before the specific nature of their mission is made clear.

Other observations concerning the technique of the story could be made—the cleverness of composition, the subtlety with which the suspense is maintained in the first scene by the banter of the gangsters, and then is transferred to another level in the second scene. But such observations, though they are worth making, do not answer the first question which, to the reader, usually presents itself, or should be allowed to present itself. That question is: what is the story about?

The importance of giving an early answer to this question is indicated by the fact that a certain kind of reader, upon first acquaintance with the story, is inclined to feel that the story is exhausted in the first scene, and in fact that the first scene itself does not come to focus—does not have a "point." Another kind of reader sees that the first scene, with its lack of resolution, is really being used to "charge" the second scene. He finds his point in Ole Andreson's decision not to try to escape the gangsters—to stop "all that running around." This reader feels that the story should end here. He sees no relevance in the last several pages of the story, and wonders why the author has flattened out his effect. The first reader, we may say, feels that "The Killers" is the gangsters' story—a story of action which does not come off. The second and more sophisticated reader interprets it as Andreson's story, though perhaps with some wonder that Andreson's story has been approached so indirectly and is allowed to trail off so irrelevantly. In other words, the reader is inclined to transpose the question, What is the story? into the question, Whose story is it? When he states the question in this way, he confronts the fact that Hemingway has left the story focused not on the gangsters, nor on Andreson, but on the boys at the lunchroom. Consider the last sentences of the story:

> "I'm going to get out of this town," Nick said.
> "Yes," said George. "That's a good thing to do."
> "I can't stand to think about him waiting in the room and knowing he's going to get it. It's too damned awful."
> "Well," said George, "you better not think about it."

So, of the two boys, it is obviously Nick on whom the impression has been made. George has managed to come to terms with the situation. By this line of reasoning, it is Nick's story. And the story is about the discovery of evil. The theme, in a sense, is the Hamlet theme, or the theme of Sherwood Anderson's "I Want to Know Why."

This definition of the theme of the story, even if it appears acceptable, must, of course, be tested against the detailed structure. In evaluating the story, as well as understanding it, the skill with which the theme has been assimilated must be taken into account. For instance, to put a concrete question: does the last paragraph of the story illuminate for the reader certain details which had, at their first appearance, seemed to be merely casual, realistic items? If we take the theme to be the boy's discovery of evil, several such details do find their fulfillment and meaning. Nick had been bound and gagged by the gangsters, and has been released by George. To quote: "Nick stood up. He had never had a towel in his mouth before. 'Say,' he said. 'What the hell?' He was trying to swagger it off." Being gagged was something you read about in a thriller and not something which happened to you; and the first effect is one of excitement, almost pleasurable, certainly an excuse for a manly pose. (It may be worth noting in this connection that Hemingway uses the specific word *towel* and not the general word *gag*. It is true that the word *towel* has a certain sensory advantage over the word *gag*—because it suggests the coarseness of the fabric and the unpleasant drying effect on the membranes of the mouth. But this advantage in immediacy is probably overshadowed by another: the towel is sanctified in the thriller as the gag, and here that cliché of the thriller has come true.) The way the whole incident is given—"He had *never* had a towel in his mouth *before*"—charges the apparently realistic detail as a pointer to the final discovery.   5

Another pointer appears in the gangster's wisecrack about the movies: "You ought to go to the movies more. The movies are fine for a bright boy like you." In one sense, of course, the iterated remarks about the movies, coming just after the gangsters have made their arrangements in the lunchroom, serve as a kind of indirect exposition: the reader knows the standard reason and procedure for gang killings. But at another level, these remarks emphasize the discovery that the unreal clichés of horror have a reality.

The boy to whom the gangster speaks understands the allusion to the movies, for he immediately asks: "What are you going to kill Ole Andreson for? What did he ever do to you?"

"He never had a chance to do anything to us. He never even seen us," the gangster replies. The gangster accepts, and even glories a little in, the terms by which he lives—terms which transcend the small-town world. He lives, as it were, by a code, which lifts him above questions of personal likes or personal animosities. This unreal code—unreal because it denies the ordinary personal elements of life—has, like the gag, suddenly been discovered as real. This unreal and theatrical quality is reflected in the description of the gangsters as, after leaving the lunchroom, they go out under the arc light and cross the street: "In their tight overcoats and derby hats they looked like a vaudeville team." It even permeates their dialogue. The dialogue itself has the sleazy quality of mechanized gag and wisecrack, a kind of inflexible and stereotyped banter that is always a priori to the situation and overrides the situation. On this level the comparison to the vaudeville team is a kind of explicit summary of details which have been presented more indirectly and dramatically. On another level, the weary and artificial quality of their wit has a grimmer implication. It is an index to the professional casualness with which they accept a situation which to the boys is shocking. They are contemptuous and even bored, with the contempt and boredom of the initiated when confronted by callow lay observers. This code, which has suddenly been transferred from the artificial world of the thriller and movie into reality, is shocking enough, but even more shocking to Nick is the fact that Ole Andreson, the hunted man, accepts the code, too. Confronted by the news which Nick brings, he rejects all the responses which the boy would have considered normal: he will not call the police; he will not regard the thing as a mere bluff; he will not leave town. "Couldn't you fix it up some way?" the boys asks. "No. I got in wrong."

As we observed earlier, for a certain type of reader this is the high point of the story, and the story should end here. If one is to convince such a reader that the author is right in proceeding, one is obligated to answer his question: What is the significance of the rather tame, and apparently irrelevant, little incident which follows, the conversation with Mrs. Bell? It is sometimes said that Mrs. Bell serves to give a bit of delayed exposition or even to point the story by gaining sympathy for Andreson, who is, to her, "an awfully nice man," not at all like her idea of a pugilist. But this is not enough to satisfy the keen reader, and he is right in refusing to be satisfied with this. Mrs. Bell is, really, the Porter at Hell's Gate in *Macbeth*. She is the world of normality, which is shocking now from the very fact that it continues to flow on in its usual course. To her, Ole Andreson is just a nice man, despite the fact that he has been in the ring; he ought to go out and take his walk on such a nice day. She points to his ordinary individuality, which is in contrast to the demands of the mechanical code. Even if the unreal horror of the movie thriller has become real, even if the hunted man lies upstairs on his bed trying to make up his mind to go out, Mrs. Bell is still Mrs. Bell. She is not Mrs. Hirsch. Mrs. Hirsch owns the place, she just looks after it for Mrs. Hirsch. She is Mrs. Bell.

At the door of the rooming house Nick has met Mrs. Bell—normality unconscious of the ironical contrast it presents. Back at the lunchroom, Nick returns to the normal scene, but the normal scene is conscious of the impingement of horror. It is the same old lunchroom, with George and the cook going about their business. But they, unlike Mrs. Bell, know what has happened. Yet even they are scarcely deflected from their ordinary routine. George and the cook represent two different levels of response to the situation. The cook, from the first, has wanted no part of it. When he hears Nick's voice, on his return, he says, "I don't even want to listen to it." And he shuts the door. But George had originally suggested that Nick go see Andreson, telling him, however, "Don't go if you don't want to." After Nick has told his story, George can comment, "It's a hell of a thing," but George, in one sense at least, has accepted the code, too. When Nick says: "I wonder what he did?" George replies, with an echo of the killer's own casualness: "Double-crossed somebody. That's what they kill them for." In other words, the situation is shocking to the cook only in so far as it involves his own safety. George is aware of other implications but can dismiss them. For neither of them, does the situation mean the discovery of evil. But for Nick, it is the discovery, for he has not yet learned to take George's adult advice: "Well, you better not think about it." 10

QUESTIONS

Cleanth Brooks Jr. and Robert Penn Warren, both highly influential Southern men of letters, were strong advocates of a critical mode that is often called "close reading." Close reading approaches a text with the assumption that is a self-contained world unto itself. The critic's, or reader's, task is to isolate the various moments of thematic and linguistic tension and to show how they contribute to the shaping of the overall effect. Close reading takes great care with the writer's language and manipulation of detail, with the assumption that the words on the page have all been placed for maximum effect.

1. Read Hemingway's story and the analysis carefully. Write a short commentary in which you discuss the overall strategy of Brooks's and Warren's reading. How do the critics use specific instances from the story to build their argument about Nick's discovery of evil?
2. Write a short paper (three or four paragraphs) in which you explore how the critics' reading of the story differs from your own. Can you find instances where they locate significance in a description or bit of conversation that you had not noticed? Has their analysis shown you levels of meaning of which you were unaware? Explain.

3. The critics make a great deal in their analysis about the influence of movie dialogue on the dialogue of the characters. Movies have obviously changed a great deal since Hemingway wrote his story. Do you find that this element of the story has dated, or is it still effective? Explain.

4. Rewrite the lunch-counter scene in a more up-to-date idiom without sacrificing any of the ominousness achieved by Hemingway. Write a short paragraph in which you comment on your attempt to update this part of the story.

T. G. Vaidyanathan

From "THE NICK ADAMS STORIES" AND THE MYTH OF INITIATION

'Initiation' was first employed by Philip Young in his early study in 1952 to describe the character of the Nick Adams stories in *In Our Time*, although Edmund Wilson, in his still useful 1939 essay had already laid the foundations. 'A typical Nick Adams Story,' writes Young, 'is of an initiation.' And later, more definitely, he observes: 'The pattern of Nick Adams' development . . . is of a boy who, while with his father up in Michigan, and without him on his own as a hobo or with friends, *has been learning some lessons about life*' (italics mine). This definition seems to have had a hypnotic influence on Hemingway criticism, for, with minor exceptions, many later writers on Hemingway have been under its spell. . . . Joseph De Falco's *The Hero in Hemingway's Short Stories* is written directly under the protective shadow of Young and although he is patently annoyed when the stories don't fit the master's categories, he consistently toes the line. And so does Earl Rovit in his 1963 study: 'For convenience' sake I will refer to the Nick Adams hero as the *tyro* and to the code-hero as the tutor: for it is basically an *educational relationship*, albeit a very one-sided one, which binds them together.'

In the face of this formidable array of Hemingway criticism it may seem a little presumptuous to ask whether the notion of 'initiation' is at all useful to an understanding of Hemingway's short fiction. Yet so pervasive has been its influence on criticism and so limiting its results when applied to the stories that it looks as if it is time to take stock again and ask some fundamental questions. To start with: What is initiation? . . . [We may] define an 'initiation' story as one which shows a significant change in its protagonist, either in his knowledge of the world or of himself or which shows a moral change directly in him or both and this/these change(s) must point to or lead him towards an acceptance of the world.

Obviously many so-called 'initiation' stories do not satisfy any of the above conditions. Most of Hemingway's early stories, for instance, merely bring their protagonist, Nick Adams, to the threshold of maturity without actually making him cross it.

To take the [favourite of Cleanth Brooks and Robert Penn Warren]: 'The Killers.' The authors concluded, in their now famous reading, that the story is 'a discovery of evil' by Nick the protagonist. Recent criticism . . . has cast doubts even on this foundational assumption and has put forward Ole Andreson as the real protagonist of the story. But we need not go so far. Assuming Nick to be the protagonist, can we say that at the end he gains in self-knowledge or knowledge of the world or that he is a thoroughly changed man, morally speaking? What we find in the story is that at the end he merely expresses an *intention* to leave town. As to self-knowledge, he merely states: 'I can't bear to think about him waiting in the room and knowing he's going to get it. It's too damned awful.' This is perhaps what any young man of his youth and inexperience would have felt. It hardly deserves the ennobling label of self-knowledge. And in what sense can we say with Brooks and Warren that it is 'a discovery of evil'? What evil? The evil of gangsterdom? Or the evil of indifference in Sam, the cook? Or the evil of apathy in Ole Andreson himself? All we know is that Nick can't bear to think about it. Yet [Adrian H. Jaffe and Virgil Scott], blind to the facts of the story, can confidently assert [in their *Studies in the Short Stories*] that the story shows 'a person who suddenly discovers the basic nature of existence'. Such is the power of the myth.

'The Killers' is an excellent short story but, unfortunately, it does not meet the requirements of either a *weak* or a *strong* initiation story. We cannot even confidently assert that its protagonist has been brought to the threshold of maturity because the 'episodic' nature of the story, which has been completely overlooked by the critics, does not permit of any such facile inferences. The plot is static and the feeling generated at the end is one of horror at the plight of Ole Andreson who is taking his imminent murder with an disquieting apathy. The focus is too little on Nick for us to expect any change in him. A careful examination of many of the early stories will similarly reveal Nick not at the centre of the experience described, but very likely at the periphery. He is mostly a spectator of the action and only occasionally moves to the centre. And even when he does so it is often (with important exceptions) not clear what kind of experience he has had and whether this will leave any permanent marks on him. 5

QUESTIONS

1. T. G. Vaidyanathan refers to Cleanth Brooks and Robert Penn Warren in his comment on "The Killers." How does his interpretation differ from theirs? What grounds does he find for disagreeing with their view?

2. Carefully consider both responses to Hemingway's story. Which position do you side with? Explain your choice.

RESPONDING TO JOYCE'S "THE DEAD"

Joyce's story appears in Chapter 13.

Walton Litz

ON JOYCE'S "THE DEAD"

Because of its position at the end of the collection, and at the end of Joyce's work on *Dubliners*, "The Dead" brings the themes of all the other stories into vital relationship with each other, while at the same time it traces a complex process of self-recognition which purges *Dubliners* of all vestiges of provincialism. The hero of "The Dead," Gabriel Conroy, bears the name of the archangel who will one day wake the dead. As the story opens, he and his wife, Gretta, come in from the snow and cold of a Dublin winter, into the warmth of the Misses Morkan's annual Christmas dance. Immediately Joyce focuses our attention on Gabriel and begins to characterize him, but not through direct comment; instead, Gabriel is rendered through dialogue and action. He damns himself before our eyes. His first encounter is with the caretaker's daughter, Lily; and his blunder with her reveals his self-centeredness and lack of communion with others. Instead of sympathizing with Lily, Gabriel makes the self-conscious, "generous" gesture: he gives her a coin. The incident has disturbed his pose of self-assurance, and he is convinced that his speech later in the evening will be a failure. Here again his thoughts are controlled by his ego; he feels that he will fail because of his superior education and taste: "He would only make himself ridiculous by quoting poetry to them which they could not understand."

Gabriel now is joined by his wife, and as they joke with the Misses Morkan over Gretta's goloshes, the latest Continental fashion, Gabriel's discontent with Ireland, his longing to escape, is epiphanized. Once he is caught up in the bustle of the dance, Gabriel's confidence begins to return; but again his self-assurance is broken, this time by an encounter with the patriotic Miss Ivors who goads him about his lack of national feeling and his secret intellectual life. She has touched the insecurity and pride revealed earlier in Gabriel's doubts about his speech, and she forces from him the petulant exclamation: "I'm sick of my own country, sick of it!" In contrast to Gabriel's attitude, Gretta longs to return to the west of Ireland where she was born:

> "You can go if you like," said Gabriel coldly.
> She looked at him for a moment, then turned to Mrs. Malins and said:
> "There's a nice husband for you, Mrs. Malins."

At this point in "The Dead" Gabriel, upset and unsure of himself, retires into the embrasure of a window:

> Gabriel's warm trembling fingers tapped the cold pane of the window. How cool it must be outside! How pleasant it would be to walk out alone, first along by the river and then through the park! The snow would be lying on the branches of the trees and forming a bright cap on the top of the Wellington Monument. How much more pleasant it would be there than at the supper-table!

At the beginning of "The Dead" the snow seemed to represent—in contrast to the warmth indoors—coldness, isolation, inhumanity. But here, midway through the story, it has been transformed in Gabriel's mind into a symbol of release, of escape and soothing anonymity. Gradually Joyce is preparing us for the complex symbolism of the closing passage.

Once Gabriel is at the dinner table, the conversation turns to great singers; and suddenly the emphasis of the story shifts from the present to the past, to those who are now gone, to the world of the dead. There is talk of monasteries and religious orders, and of monks who sleep in their coffins "to remind them of their last end." Dessert comes just in time, and the exotic fruits from foreign lands bring our thoughts back to the living; it is time for Gabriel to make his speech. Leaning with trembling fingers on the table, he makes a gracious if conventional speech, a speech about change and the inexorable movements of time. But his thoughts are all on his own performance, and signs of emotion in Aunt Kate cause him to hasten nervously to a close. The dinner is over; the guests are ready to depart. 5

Perhaps this would be an appropriate point at which to pause and review the movement of "The Dead" up to this scene. Gabriel has been placed in a number of revealing situations which emphasize his insecurity and self-love. The theme of change has been introduced, and the world of the dead has been invoked. But all these elements are still in suspension; the remaining action must draw them together and disclose them as aspects of a single, overriding theme.

Cabs come and go outside. Most of the guests are gone. Bartell D'Arcy is singing, and as Gabriel gazes up the staircase from the dark part of the hall he glimpses the still figure of a woman. It is his wife:

> She was leaning on the banisters, listening to something. Gabriel was surprised at her stillness and strained his ear to listen also. But he could hear little save the noise of laughter and dispute on the front steps, a few chords struck on the piano and a few notes of a man's voice singing.
>
> He stood still in the gloom of the hall, trying to catch the air that the voice was singing and gazing up at his wife. There was grace and mystery in her attitude as if she were a symbol of something. He asked himself what is a woman standing on the stairs in the shadow, listening to distant music, a symbol of. If he were a painter he would paint her in that attitude.

Gabriel thinks of the scene only as a subject for art. He even constructs a poetic title, "Distant Music," and the music *is* distant to him: it is the music of love and understanding that he has never heard. But for Gretta the music is immediate and overpowering, evoking the memory of Michael Furey, who died for love of her. All Gabriel can see of his wife are the terra-cotta and salmon-pink panels of her skirt. The scene is indeed a "symbol of something," a symbol of Gabriel's separation from Gretta's secret life.

As Gretta and Gabriel drive back to their hotel, Gabriel is inflamed by keen pangs of lust. He thinks of their life together in romantic terms, once more using the phrase "distant music." The imagery of his memories is explicitly sexual: "They were standing on the crowded platform and he was placing a ticket inside the warm palm of her glove. He was standing with her in the cold, looking in through a grated window at a man making bottles in a roaring furnace. It was very cold." Gabriel thinks complacently of the passionate scene he will soon enact, but once they are inside the hotel room Gretta is abstracted and distant. Gabriel, who longs "to be master of her strange mood," tries to impress her with the fact that he loaned a pound to Freddy Malins. She makes the conventional reply, "You are a very generous person, Gabriel," but we know that Gabriel was not generous; his action was a bid for admiration. In contrast to the generous tears he will soon shed, this praise by Gretta seems intensely ironic.

Gabriel judges that the moment is now propitious for making love, and he begins his advances; but Gretta runs from him and throws herself upon the bed, weeping. First in anger, then in bewilderment, then in humiliation, Gabriel elicits from her the story of Michael Furey. At the end of the confession, he is left alone to confront himself: "She stopped, choking with sobs, and, overcome by emotion, flung herself face downward on the bed, sobbing in the quilt. Gabriel held her hand for a moment longer, irresolutely, and then, shy of intruding on her grief, let it fall gently and walked quietly to the window." 10

The moment of self-realization, toward which the entire story has been tending, is now upon Gabriel. He suddenly realizes that the secret life he imagined be-

Responding to Stories

tween himself and Gretta was illusory, that his passion was merely self-love. He has never possessed Gretta's soul, never penetrated to the world of self-sacrifice represented by Michael Furey. Here, at the end of "The Dead," at the end of *Dubliners*, Gabriel is given that self-knowledge which is denied to all the other characters except the young boy in "Araby," who sees himself at the close of the tale as a "creature driven and derided by vanity."

But Gabriel's self-knowledge is not the sudden intuition of a child; it is the full experience of a sensitive and intelligent man. Conscious for the first time of his own paralysis, Gabriel rises above his personal limitations and enters into communion with all the living and the dead. For the first time in *Dubliners* there is a true communion, not of the Church but of humanity; and Joyce symbolizes this transformation through the snow, which has been an active agent in "The Dead" from the opening scene. At first the snow seemed to be an emblem of isolation and lack of human warmth; later it became for Gabriel a symbol of soothing, forgetful escape; but finally, at the close of "The Dead," it becomes a complex symbol of Gabriel's new awareness, the impetus which turns his mind away from himself and toward humanity. Tears of true generosity fill his eyes for the first time, and in rhythmic prose which soon takes on the order and intensity of poetry Joyce leaves us with an evocation which balances paralysis against liberation, criticism against sympathy.

> Generous tears filled Gabriel's eyes. He had never felt like that himself towards any woman but he knew that such a feeling must be love. The tears gathered more thickly in his eyes and in the partial darkness he imagined he saw the form of a young man standing under a dripping tree. Other forms were near. His soul had approached that region where dwell the vast hosts of the dead. He was conscious of, but could not apprehend, their wayward and flickering existence. His own identity was fading out into a grey impalpable world: the solid world itself, which these dead had one time reared and lived in, was dissolving and dwindling.
>
> A few light taps upon the pane made him turn to the window. It had begun to snow again. He watched sleepily the flakes, silver and dark, falling obliquely against the lamplight. The time had come for him to set out on his journey westward. Yes, the newspapers were right: snow was general all over Ireland. It was falling on every part of the dark central plain, on the treeless hills, falling softly upon the Bog of Allen and, farther westward, softly falling into the dark mutinous Shannon waves. It was falling, too, upon every part of the lonely churchyard on the hill where Michael Furey lay buried. It lay thickly drifted on the crooked crosses and headstones, on the spears of the little gate, on the barren thorns. His soul swooned slowly as he heard the snow falling faintly through the universe and faintly falling, like the descent of their last end, upon all the living and the dead.

C. C. Loomis Jr.

STRUCTURE AND SYMPATHY IN "THE DEAD"

James Joyce's "The Dead" culminates in Gabriel Conroy's timeless moment of almost supreme vision. The fragments of his life's experience, of the epitomizing experiences of one evening in particular, are fused together into a whole: "self-bounded and self-contained upon the immeasurable background of space and time."[1] Initiated by a moment of deep, if localized, sympathy, his vision and his sympathy expand together to include not only himself, Gretta, and his aunts, but all Ireland, and, with the words "all the living and all the dead," all humanity.

Gabriel's epiphany manifests Joyce's fundamental belief that true, objective perception will lead to true, objective sympathy; such perception and such sympathy, however, ultimately defy intellectual analysis. Joyce carefully avoids abstract definition of Gabriel's vision by embodying it within the story's central symbol: the snow, which becomes paradoxically warm in the moment of vision, through which Gabriel at long last feels the deeply unifying bond of common mortality.

Gabriel's experience is intellectual only at that level on which intellect and emotional intuition blend, and the full power of the story can be apprehended by the reader only if he sympathetically shares the experience with Gabriel. As understanding of himself, then of his world, then of humanity floods Gabriel, so understanding of Gabriel, his world, and humanity in terms of the story floods the reader. The understanding in both cases is largely emotional and intuitive; intellectual analysis of the snow symbol, however successful, leaves a large surplus of emotion unexplained.

Therefore, Joyce had to generate increasing reader-sympathy as he approached the vision, but this sympathy could not be generated by complete reader-identification with Gabriel. If the reader identifies himself unreservedly with Gabriel in the first ninety percent of the story, he will lose that critical insight into him which is necessary for full apprehension of his vision. It is, after all, Gabriel's vision, and there is no little irony in this fact. The vision is in sharp contrast with his previous view of the world: in fact, it literally opens a new world to him. If the reader identifies himself uncritically with Gabriel at any point in the story, he is liable to miss those very shortcomings which make the vision meaningful. Yet, in the actual moments of vision, the reader must share Gabriel's view; in a real sense, he must identify himself with Gabriel: "feel with" him.

Joyce, therefore, had to create sympathy without encouraging the reader to a blind, uncritical identification. One aspect of his solution to this problem is a monument to his genius. In the main body of the story, while he is constantly dropping meaningful, often semi-symbolic details which deepen the gulf between the reader and Gabriel, he is also generating what can best be called "aesthetic sympathy"; by the very structure of the story, he increasingly pulls the reader into the story. 5

"The Dead" can be divided, not arbitrarily, into five sections: the *musicale*, the dinner, the farewells and the drive to the hotel, the scene between Gabriel and Gretta in their room, and, finally, the vision itself. A few of these sections are separated by a time lapse, a few flow smoothly into one another; in all cases, however, the reader is aware of a slight "shifting of gears" between sections.

These sections become shorter as the story progresses. The effect of this constant shortening of scenes, together with a constant speeding up in the narrative line, is an almost constant increase of pace. Within each of the sections, Joyce care-

---

[1]James Joyce, *Portrait of the Artist as a Young Man* (New York, 1928), p. 249. See also Irene Hendry, "Joyce's Epiphanies" in *Critiques and Essays on Modern Fiction*, John W. Aldridge, ed. (New York, 1952), p. 129.

fully builds up to a climax, then slackens the pace slightly at the beginning of the next section as he begins to build up to a new climax. The pace in the sections is progressively more rapid, however, partially because of the cumulative effect of the narrative. As the story progresses, more things happen in less time.

The effect of increasing pace is complemented and strengthened by another structural aspect of the story. As the pace increases, the focus narrows. The constantly narrowing focus and the constantly increasing pace complement one another and act to pull the reader into the story. He is caught up in a whirlpool movement, ever-narrowing, ever-faster.

There is much activity in the first part of "The Dead," but the activity is diffuse and the effect is not of great pace. We are given a slightly confused, over-all picture of activity: dancing, drinking, singing, chatting. Characters are introduced one after another: Lily, Gabriel, Gretta, the Misses Morkan, Mary Jane, Mr. Browne, Freddy Malins and his mother, Miss Ivors, and so on. Our scope is broad and general. Increasingly, Gabriel becomes our mode of consciousness, but he himself cannot assimilate all the activity. He retreats, isolates himself within his deep but insecure egotism. Rationalizing that "their grade of culture differed from his," he bides his time until dinner, when he knows he will be the center of all eyes.

In this first section, it is interesting to note how Joyce gives us Gabriel's point of view without compromising his own fundamental objectivity; even though we see largely through Gabriel's "delicate and restless" eyes, we nevertheless become increasingly aware of his character, of his defensive feelings of intellectual and social superiority in particular. His eyes are offended by the glittering, waxed floors, his ears by the "indelicate clattering" of the dancers, his intellect by all those present, particularly Miss Ivors, who "has a crow to pluck" with him, and constitutes a threat to his shaky feelings of superiority. His attitude can best be summed up by his reflection, ironic and revealing in view of the toast to come, that his aunts are "only two ignorant old women." Such comments are introduced quietly, but they serve to keep the reader from identifying himself too wholeheartedly with Gabriel. We feel with him to a degree even in these early sections of the story, but our sympathy is seriously reserved and qualified.[2]

In the second section, our focus narrows to the dinner table, and to a few characters at it; the others are blurred in the background. Tension about Gabriel's toast has been built up in the first section; now the pace increases as this particular tension is relieved. The toast, hypocritical and condescending, makes us further aware of Gabriel's isolation from those around him.

The pace in this scene is considerably more rapid than in the first. It builds up to the climax, the toast, in a few brief pages; then there is a slackening with the applause and singing.

There is a time-lapse between the conclusion of the toast and the next section; Joyce seems to shift to a higher range. From this point to the moment of vision, the pace increases and the focus narrows almost geometrically.

The shouts and laughter of the departure signal the end of the party, but are counter-balanced by the fine, almost silent tableau of Gabriel watching Gretta on the

10

---

[2]For an enlightening discussion of the problem of reader-identification and "extraordinary perspective" in 19th- and 20th-century literature, see. R. W. Langbaum, *The Poetry of Experience* (New York, 1957).

staircase. Our focus is beginning to narrow down to these two main characters. Gretta has been deliberately held in the background until this moment; now she emerges.

The repeated goodnights and the noisy trip through silent, snow-blanketed Dublin are given increased pace through Gabriel's increasing lust; the pace becomes the pace of "the blood bounding along his veins" and the "thoughts rioting through his brain." The fires of their lust begin to thaw the almost life-deep frost of his self-consciousness. The superiority and self-delusion are still dominant: there is much irony in his remembering "their moments of ecstasy," for his lust is far from ecstatic love. It is, however, the first step toward the moment of objective vision.

15

We are now approaching the still center of the increasingly rapid, increasingly narrow whirlpool. The scene in the hotel room between Gabriel and Gretta takes up only a few brief minutes, but in these minutes much happens. Gabriel "discovers" Gretta: suddenly she becomes more than a mere appendage to his ego. He discovers himself in a mirror. His lust turns to anger, then his anger to humility. Gretta, caught up in her memories of the "boy in the gasworks," Michael Furey, is not even aware of his presence. "A shameful consciousness of his own person assailed him. He saw himself as a ludicrous figure, acting as a pennyboy for his aunts, a nervous, well-meaning sentimentalist, orating to vulgarians and idealising his own clownish lusts, the pitiable fatuous fellow he had caught a glimpse of in the mirror."

The peak of intensity is reached with Gretta's "Oh, the day I heard that, that he was dead." She collapses on the bed, sobbing, and Gabriel quietly, shyly, retires to the window. At this moment, Joyce creates another time-lapse to lead into the vision itself.

Until this moment, the pace has increased and the focus has narrowed almost constantly. Now Joyce does something remarkable and effective: he reverses the process. In doing so, he makes the structure of the story not only useful as a means of generating an "aesthetic sympathy" (perhaps "empathy" with its impersonal connotation would be a more accurate word), but also makes it reinforce the ultimate emotional-intellectual meaning of the vision itself.[3]

Pace simply ceases to exist in the vision, and, of course, this is fitting. We are in an essentially timeless world at this point; true, the vision involves time and mortality, but it is timeless time and eternal mortality, man's endless fate as man. The snow "falling faintly through the universe" measures absolute, not relative time. The impact of the sudden cessation of pace on the reader is great; in fact, it parallels the impact on Gabriel himself. With this sudden structural change, we share Gabriel's vision; we do not merely analyze it.

Gabriel's vision begins with Gretta; it is narrow in focus. The whole story has led us down to this narrow focus. Now, as he does with pace, Joyce reverses the process. As the vision progresses toward the ultimate image of the snow falling

---

[3]William T. Noon, S. J., in *Joyce and Aquinas* (New Haven, 1957), pp. 84–85, places Gabriel's epiphany at "the moment when the full impact of Gretta's disclosure of her secret strikes him": before the snow image of the closing paragraphs. Father Noon separates Gabriel's moment of vision from the reader's, and he seems to state that the snow image is for the reader's enlightenment, not Gabriel's. I agree with Father Noon that the reader cannot possibly apprehend the depth of Gabriel's sudden sympathy with Gretta until Joyce gives him the closing image, but I do not believe that Gabriel's own vision is complete until this final image; the epiphany begins with his sympathy for Gretta, but is not complete, because not universal, until he "heard the snow falling faintly through the universe."

through the universe, the focus broadens, from Gretta, to his aunts, to himself, to Ireland, to "the universe." Time and space are telescoped in the final words of the story: The snow falls on "all the living and all the dead." 20

"The Dead" follows a logical pattern; we move from the general to the particular, then to a final universal. We see Gabriel's world generally; then we focus down to the particular, and from the combination of the general and particular we are given a universal symbol in the vision itself.

The logic of "The Dead," however, is not the logic of mere intellect; it is the logic which exists on a plane where intellectual perception and emotional intuition, form and content, blend.

QUESTIONS

1. Read Joyce's "The Dead" (Chapter 13) and the responses of Litz and Loomis. Before reading Monica Betz's essay (following), write a paragraph in which you characterize the fundamental differences in the two readings of the story.
2. Read Betz's essay (following) and compare her findings with your own. Discuss the effectiveness of her presentation. How well does Betz use her two sources to create a sense of debate?

USING SOURCES WHEN WRITING ABOUT A STORY

In Chapter 10 we followed a student through the stages of conceiving and writing his own essay interpreting a story. The thinking processes described there are basic for developing ideas when writing about literature in any way. However, there are additional kinds of essays to be written and additional skills you need to practice.

Teachers very often require their literature students to practice finding and incorporating different critical perspectives into their writing. For the student, this means spending time at the library using databases to track down source materials. It also means reading critical works with an eye toward distilling which arguments might be useful to cite *and* which quotations to use in representing those arguments. Learning how to read and cite from sources is one of the most valuable aspects of literary study. No less important is testing your own insights and judgments against those of professional readers.

While there are many ways to make use of material from other sources, nearly all of them will require you to summarize a writer's views as well as illustrate them. Students should turn to Appendix B for more information on how to use and cite sources correctly.

The following paper, written by second-semester freshman Monica Betz, shows how a student can draw on sources to explore a particular literary work. The assignment was to compare or contrast two critical views of one story. Betz found two readings of James Joyce's "The Dead" that were mainly in agreement on the big picture but looked through very different lenses when accounting for effects. She found a way to present the views side by side, using the differences as a way of highlighting the complexity of the story. Joyce's story begins on page 288, and Betz's paper follows here.

Betz 1

Monica Betz
Professor Johnson
English 101
11 May 1995

Gabriel's Final Vision in James Joyce's "The Dead":
Two Critical Views

One of the marks of a great writer is that his or
her work can lend itself to various interpretations.
In other words, it is possible for a number of critics
to offer different readings, all of which can be defended as valid. Irish writer James Joyce (1882-1941)
is a case in point. Known for his subtle and often poetic language and his complex manipulation of symbol
and structure, Joyce lends himself especially well to
diverse readings. These may in some instances contradict each other, or disagree on which elements are the
most important, but often they can be placed side by
side, or even joined like pieces of a jigsaw puzzle,
to reveal more of the total picture.

Joyce's "The Dead" is the concluding story in his
collection <u>The Dead</u>--a collection Joyce intended
should be read in its entirety, almost like a novel.
"The Dead" is not only the longest story in the book
but, as critic Walton Litz has written, it "brings the
themes of all the other stories into vital relationship with each other . . . " (55). The story leads its
protagonist, Gabriel Conroy, to a moment of intense
self-realization, which then becomes, in a sense, the
concluding vision of the book. The scene is complex,
moving from a conversation between Gabriel and Gretta,
his wife, to a more poetically written inner monologue
in which Gabriel seems to experience his connection
with the rest of humanity. In its complexity the scene
provides an excellent opportunity for us to see how
two critics can discover differing but finally complementary interpretations of a single work.

Walton A. Litz in his book <u>James Joyce</u> discusses "The Dead" alongside the other stories in <u>Dubliners</u>. While he acknowledges that the final scene does bring together a number of important threads, his focus is much more upon character and symbolism than upon structure. Litz works through the story in some detail, mainly pointing out incidents that show Gabriel to be insecure and self-involved. This is evident from Gabriel's first encounter with Lily, the caretaker's daughter, where "Instead of sympathizing with Lily, Gabriel makes the self-conscious, 'generous' gesture: he gives her a coin" (57). And the characterization is carried on right up until the final scene. When Gabriel and Gretta return to the hotel after their evening out, "Gabriel thinks complacently of the passionate scene he will soon enact . . ." (57).

Litz makes Gabriel's change of heart, his final vision, depend almost completely on a moment of self-realization. When Gretta tells him about her girlhood love for Michael Furey, the young man who died after he came to see her, Gabriel feels angry at first, then bewildered, then humiliated (58). But as Litz describes the moment, his tangled emotions very quickly lead to self-knowledge, which is "not the sudden intuition of a child; it is the full experience of a sensitive and intelligent man" (58). Litz adds that "Joyce symbolizes this transformation through the snow, which has been an active agent in 'The Dead' from the opening scene" (58).

Though Litz is an eloquent critic, his account of Gabriel's transformation is not completely convincing. It seems unlikely, at least to this reader, that a man previously shown to be selfish could so suddenly respond fully and openly. Yet when we read the story from the beginning, the moment seems believable, maybe even inevitable. How do we explain this? Maybe we need to allow that Gabriel, for all of his self-involvement, was not finally as egotistical as Litz suggests. Maybe he was humane in ways that the critic chose not to see. And if we look back through the story for evi-

dence, we find many instances of Gabriel's feeling na-
ture--his treatment of Freddy Malins and the Morkan
sisters, for example. Maybe Litz was so set on making
his argument that he just overlooked aspects of the
protagonist that might not fit.

If we look to C. C. Loomis's "Structure and Sympathy in 'The Dead,'" we find a different interpretation. Loomis, like Litz, sees the final scene as a
vision in which Gabriel experiences sympathy with the
whole universe. But in Loomis's view, "we share
Gabriel's vision; we do not merely analyze it" (114).
And in this critic's interpretation we hear less about
the character of Gabriel, and the effect on him of
Gretta's story, and much more about the underlying
structure that makes the moment affect us as it does.

Loomis breaks the story into five sections. He
writes:

> Within each of the sections, Joyce carefully builds
> up to a climax, then slackens the pace slightly at
> the beginning of the next section as he begins to
> build up to a new climax. The pace in the sections
> is progressively more rapid, however, partially be-
> cause of the cumulative effect of the narrative....
>   As the pace increases, the focus narrows. The con-
> stantly narrowing focus and the constantly increas-
> ing pace complement one another and act to pull the
> reader into the story. (111)

Loomis spends a good part of his essay discussing
structural elements that most readers would probably
not notice. But as he documents his case with scenes
from the story, we begin to see that the structure is
very carefully controlled. The writer knows exactly
what he is doing. And when we reach the scene of
Gabriel's vision, we recognize that while part of its
effectiveness may come from Gabriel's self-awakening,
part also comes from the writer's manipulation of pace
and focus. As Loomis explains it, the increasing speed
of the story through its five sections suddenly stops.
"Pace simply ceases to exist in the vision," he explains. "We are in an essentially timeless world at
this point" (113).

This does not mean that Loomis ignores all the other thematic components of the story. He makes clear in his final sentences that the "logic of 'The Dead'...is not the logic of mere intellect; it is the logic which exists on a plane where intellectual perception and emotional intuition, form and content, blend" (114).

Neither Litz nor Loomis offer a completely satisfying reading. Both have valuable insights to contribute, but each, alone, gives what is at best a partial explanation. In addition, both leave certain mysterious things unexplained. Litz never tells us how the snow works to "symbolize" Gabriel's transformation, and Loomis leaves us wondering just how "perception and intuition, form and content, blend." Maybe if Litz's insights into character were combined with Loomis's theory of the story's structure we would have a more comprehensive account of why Joyce's ending, and story, is so powerful.

Works Cited

Litz, Walton A. James Joyce. Boston: Twayne, 1966.

Loomis Jr., C. C. "Structure and Sympathy in 'The Dead.'" Twentieth Century Interpretations of Dubliners: A Collection of Critical Essays. Ed. Peter K. Garrett. Englewood Cliffs: Prentice, 1968. 110-14.

Poetry

15 Reading Poetry

Although it is probably hard for most of us to believe it, poetry was once viewed as the most vital and important of the arts. The poet was a seer, a visionary, a keeper, and dispenser of the secret wisdom of a culture. Indeed, less than two hundred years ago, the English poet Shelley announced with some bravado that poets were the "unacknowledged legislators of the world." Shelley's was a telling phrase, for it captured both the sense of importance that the poet felt for the art and the poet's awareness that society did not value that importance as it may once have done.

The situation has not improved for the poet since Shelley's day. Catch any poet on a bad day and you are likely to get an earful of lament. Nobody publishes, nobody reads, nobody buys . . . none of which is really true. What the poet is actually complaining about is the feeling of being marginal in a world intent upon other things. Poet Donald Hall has wittily captured this perception of the poet's plight in "To a Waterfowl," where he mocks himself as one condemned to travel the circuit of women's self-improvement clubs (Hall is, of course, also poking fun at the sexist assumption that poetry is not somehow a "masculine" endeavor). He writes:

> These are the women whose husbands I meet on airplanes,
> who close their briefcases and ask, "What are *you* in?"
> I look in their eyes and tell them I am in poetry,
>
> and their eyes fill with anxiety, and with little tears.
> "Oh, yeah?" they say, developing an interest in clouds.
> "My wife, she likes that sort of thing? Hah-hah?
> I guess I'd maybe better watch my grammar, huh?"
> I leave them in the airports, watching their grammar.

Behind the humor, Hall is making a serious point: that in a culture devoted to business and conspicuous material success, the person who is given to arranging words into lines and lines into stanzas is an odd duck indeed (and maybe this is what he means by calling the poem "To a Waterfowl"). Yes, the poet is seen as the ineffectual dreamer, the scruffy misfit. And the drop in prestige suffered by the art has been immense. The poet writing in Shelley's day did not have to compete with a multi-billion-dollar entertainment industry—with movies, video games, television, and the like. People had more time to sit with themselves, and—some would argue—they had longer attention spans. In our day the poet's greatest obstacle is the attitude of the person who would say: "With so many things to see and do, and with so much information that I have to take in just to get through the day, why should I stare at a little cluster of words to find some meaning that I probably wouldn't understand anyway?"

But enough about the complaint side of the picture. The fact is that for all the laments that can be made about the state of poetry, Hall and thousands of other similarly inclined men and women continue to put their best energies into shaping lines, stanzas, and poems. And a small, but fervent, population of readers buys their books and flocks to readings and festivals. For all the changes our society has undergone, the poet remains the possessor of a peculiar magic. And the artifact—the poem itself—is still the site of profound enjoyment and self-discovery; it is still a place where ideas and verbal music combine to detonate surprise—even wisdom. Ultimately, poetry does not need to be argued for; when read with the right sort of attention, and with a certain confidence, it sells itself, handing over its concentrated pleasures. But poetry must be given a hearing. The reader needs to understand something about its aims and strategies and to cultivate a receptive attitude. It will be the work of the pages that follow to turn the nonreader into a reader, perhaps even a fan.

APPROACHES TO POETRY

There is no single door that one *must* go through to get to poetry. We see as many kinds of poems as kinds of poets, and as many kinds of poets as kinds of people. The art has been actively practiced as long as language has existed and in every country and culture. Poetic expressions have grown, evolved, and changed, but in some fundamental ways they have also stayed true to their origins. If we were to take a wide sample among poets writing today we would find the most challenging sorts of experimentalism as well as orderly verses obeying the strictest requirements of rhyme and meter. Where to begin?

Probably the first thing to say about poetry is that it has its roots in pleasure: the pleasure of rhythm and repetition, and of sounds arranged in patterns. The links to song and dance remain strong; in the tribal cultures of origin those links were absolute. Poetry was danced, clapped, chanted, and performed with the whole body.

To grasp this idea of origin we have only to look back into our own childhoods, to remember the compulsion with which we repeated rhymes and nonsense songs, and the delight these gave us. The child chanting a common ditty like

En-gine, en-gine, num-ber nine,
Go-ing down Chi-ca-go line;
If the train should jump the track,
Would you want your mo-ney back?

is not aware of mouthing a tetrameter verse built up of trochees (Én-gǐne / eń-gǐne / núm-běr / níne), nor does it much matter. The point is that the repeating rhythm soothes and gratifies. The words are fun to say, even now.

Of course, the comparison between the child singing rhymes and the ancients shaping poetry out of the language of their speech soon breaks down. For ancient poetry early on became the medium for the most significant sorts of tribal expression. Verses were made to honor gods and goddesses, cycles of nature, and important episodes in the collective history. Homer's *Iliad* and *Odyssey* were not merely epics that had acquired form over generations, they were also monuments of Greek tribal history, not to mention encyclopedias of preserved lore about sailing, warfare, geography, customs and rituals, and so on. These epics, not to mention the countless other odes of praise, elegies of mourning, and other expressions, took the form they did—rhythmic, repetitive, studded with formulaic figures of speech (like Homer's recurrently used "rosy fingers of dawn")—for a very obvious reason. Simply, these were oral cultures. The technology of writing had not yet been invented. Human memory had to do all the work of preservation, and rhythm and repetition were the most efficient ways to order material for recall. Whatever truths a culture wished to keep alive found their way into poetic form.

Poetry has changed a great deal since its earliest incarnations, but not beyond recognition. With the invention of writing—and, later, of print—lines of poetry no longer had to function as a memory machine. But from these earliest days until as recently as the beginning of our own century, poetry never strayed very far from its basis in rhythm and repetition. This is because poets recognized very early on that repeating sound patterns, and the beat of stresses that underlies the poetic line, are something more than just handy prods to memory. They are, in fact, universal echoes of the human organism. The primary functions of the body are grounded in rhythm— the beating of the heart, the steady drawing of the breath. We are creatures of rhythm. We walk to a beat and perform tasks to a beat. And we *love* to dance.

Not only dance rhythms are appealing; the natural and manmade worlds around us manifest recurrent patterns of differing tempos: the rising and setting of the sun, the returning seasons, the breaking of waves, the ticking of our clocks, the mechanical functioning of our machines. Poets over the centuries honored this fact. They devised a broad array of poetic forms and metric formulas. Each had a function; each had proven a specific kind of usefulness. It was widely believed that there was a natural accord, or "rightness," between certain forms and the feelings they sought to evoke.

The early decades of our century witnessed the great revolutions of modernism. The premises of poetry—indeed, of all the arts—were called into question. Leading modernist poets, like T. S. Eliot, Ezra Pound, H. D. (Hilda Doolittle), and others waged a sustained attack upon the ruling assumptions of poetry. Their argument, in essence, was that the traditional poetic patterns were no longer adequate to convey the meanings of modern experience. The farmstead of Wordsworth's day had become the choked urban center; natural cycles of agriculture were being pushed aside by the urgencies of industry; religious faith was giving way to fashionable skepticism; and, most importantly, the deaths of millions of soldiers in European trenches had destroyed any lingering optimism about our collective spiritual attainment. In short, a changed world required a changed poetry. Modernism was born, with its difficult, often jangling rhythms, its sudden line breaks, its intentionally disturbing images, and its deliberately obscure references (Eliot's "The Waste Land" carried a set of footnotes as long as the poem itself).

Many would-be readers have tried to find their way to poetry by turning first to the modernists, and many have turned away convinced that poetry is unreadable. This is unfortunate, for while much of the material *is* difficult, it can, when understood in its context, bring as much pleasure and provocation as poetry of the more accessible sort. But the reader must also remember that modernism was only one of the poetic developments in our epoch, and that much—even most—of the poetry of our time continues the traditions of earlier expression. It is a good idea to make a wide survey of the terrain before deciding that poetry is just too hard to read. It's not.

THE BEST WORDS IN THE BEST ORDER

Poet and critic Samuel Taylor Coleridge (1772–1834) once defined poetry as "the best words in the best order." It is an accessible definition, and it is as good a place as any from which to begin an exploration.

Coleridge's definition is useful because it highlights two of the most important aspects of the art. His "best words" point us toward the fusion of sound and sense that could be called the life-blood of poetry, while "best order" indicates the rhythm, or heartbeat, that sets that blood into circulation.

Here we need to slow down for a moment to give those common coins—our words—a closer inspection. Though we don't often think about them in these terms, our words can be seen to have several different properties. One is their *designation*, or meaning; a word both encodes and represents a concept—the concept of liberty, the concept of a fountain pen, and so on. Another, less commonly considered property, is its sound and appearance. Though we mainly take in the meaning of a given word, we are not unaware of what might be considered its physical body. We know what *squash* means, but we also register its softly collapsing sound. In addition, words have *connotations*—meanings and associations that they suggest indirectly. If I use the word *volume* for book, you might pick up connotations of weightiness or importance. These are not part of the dictionary definition, but they are values that the word has acquired through usage. No one would ever say, "I picked up a volume called *Secret Caresses* yesterday," though you still might catch someone referring to "a volume of Poe's work."

The poet works with words as a carpenter works with wood, considering every property and trying to get maximum use out of the materials. The overall word-choice is called *diction*, which comes from the Latin verb for "to say." The desired effect determines the means of saying. Consider, for instance, a word like *buzzing*. It has a *denotative*, or designatory, or dictionary, meaning. It indicates a specific kind of noise, as in "Exploring the attic, he heard a buzzing at the window." The word also has a specific sound value. In fact, it actually sounds like what it designates. To pronounce the word is to make a buzzing noise—it is an *onomato-poetic* word, one that suggests its meaning with its sound. Finally, it carries connotations: the reader may make associations to the insects or appliances that make buzzing sounds, or to a sense of active animation. We think of a bee, or the final seconds of a basketball game, or the barber giving us a haircut.

In any case, the poet chooses words for various reasons and has specific effects in mind. These effects can be regulated by context; that is, by the meanings, connotation, sound, and rhythm of the other words in the line. He or she may choose to emphasize the sound component by writing "the quizzical buzzing of the bees," allowing the echoing *z*'s to focus the attention. Or the poet may evoke a sense of noisy agitation by clustering together words that have a certain natural stress. By itself, *buzzing* is a trochee—a stressed syllable followed by an unstressed syllable, indicated thus: búz-zing. (Stress and meter will be discussed at length in a later section.) To achieve that noisy agitation, the poet could plant "buzzing" between two other trochaic words: Sud-den buz-zing rack-et. The reader encountering this phrase in a poem will not only absorb the meaning, but will also feel a strong rhythmic emphasis brought out by the combination of the words.

The poet, then, works with all the resources of language, including at times the visual. e. e. cummings, who was an artist as well as a poet, loved to play with the look of words. One of his better-known short poems bears the title "l(a" and looks like this:

```
l(a

le
af
fa

ll

s)
one
l

iness
```

A moment or two of staring will unravel his intent.

What all this means is that poetry can attain a density of meaning and suggestion that we seldom encounter in prose. We are simultaneously affected by meaning, word sound, rhythm, and word appearance. It should go without saying that since poetry is composed differently, it must be read differently. We cannot race through a poem the way we race through an article in the newspaper, skimming off the content and moving on. Different reading habits are required. To begin with, a poem should be read with great concentration, away from the competing distractions of music, television, or conversation. The sounds of the words must be heard clearly in what T. S. Eliot called our "auditory inwardness." Moreover, those words must be sounded out attentively and expressively in order to liberate the underlying rhythm. Finally, the reader will most likely need to read the poem several times, even if it appears to be simple. Unless we are very gifted as readers, odds are that we will not be able to grasp all at once the delicate interplay of elements. This prescription does go against our customary reading habits, and the procedure may seem difficult or unnecessarily time-consuming, but the payoff is worth the effort. Familiarity brings not contempt, but increased comprehension, and increased comprehension opens the way to the poetic experience.

READING A POEM

To illustrate some of these ideas, I have chosen a well-known poem by Robert Frost, entitled "Birches." The reader should try to work through the lines slowly and carefully, paying heed to every word. It may help to read the poem aloud, ideally twice: once to get a general sense of the motion and meaning, and a second time to pick out some of the nuances. A selective commentary follows.

Robert Frost

BIRCHES

When I see birches bend to left and right
Across the lines of straighter darker trees,
I like to think some boy's been swinging them.
But swinging doesn't bend them down to stay
As ice storms do. Often you must have seen them
Loaded with ice a sunny winter morning
After a rain. They click upon themselves,
As the breeze rises, and turn many-colored
As the stir cracks and crazes their enamel.
Soon the sun's warmth makes them shed crystal shells   10
Shattering and avalanching on the snow crust—
Such heaps of broken glass to sweep away
You'd think the inner dome of heaven had fallen.
They are dragged to the withered bracken by the load,
And they seem not to break; though once they are bowed   15
So low for long, they never right themselves:
You may see their trunks arching in the woods
Years afterwards, trailing their leaves on the ground
Like girls on hands and knees that throw their hair
Before them over their heads to dry in the sun.   20
But I was going to say when Truth broke in
With all her matter of fact about the ice storm,
I should prefer to have some boy bend them
As he went out and in to fetch the cows—
Some boy too far from town to learn baseball,   25
Whose only play was what he found himself,
Summer or winter, and could play alone.
One by one he subdued his father's trees
By riding them down over and over again
Until he took the stiffness out of them,   30
And not one but hung limp, not one was left
For him to conquer. He learned all there was
To learn about not launching out too soon
And so not carrying the tree away
Clear to the ground. He always kept his poise   35
To the top branches, climbing carefully
With the same pains you use to fill a cup
Up to the brim, and even above the brim.
Then he flung outward, feet first, with a swish,
Kicking his way down through the air to the ground.   40
So was I once myself a swinger of birches.
And so I dream of going back to be.

It's when I'm weary of considerations,
And life is too much like a pathless wood
Where your face burns and tickles with the cobwebs   45
Broken across it, and one eye is weeping
From a twig's having lashed across it open.
I'd like to get away from earth awhile
And then come back to it and begin over.
May no fate willfully misunderstand me   50
And half grant what I wish and snatch me away
Not to return. Earth's the right place for love:
I don't know where it's likely to go better.
I'd like to go by climbing a birch tree,
And climb black branches up a snow-white trunk   55
Toward heaven, till the tree could bear no more,
But dipped its top and set me down again.
That would be good both going and coming back.
One could do worse than be a swinger of birches.

As you read the following discussion, consider these questions:

1. Find three instances in the poem where the poet's use of language makes the sense of the words more vivid. Look at sounds, rhythms, and line endings. Be as specific as you can about how the poetic effect is achieved.

2. What lessons about life does Frost seek to impart? How does the swinging of birches reflect a larger philosophy?

3. Isolate the various concrete images Frost uses. Write a sentence for each, reflecting what suggestions it conveys to you.

Discussion. Robert Frost was one of the great poetic craftsmen of our age, and to do full justice to the subtleties of "Birches" would require a lengthy dissertation. What's more, this chapter is meant to be an introduction to the experience of poetry. Discussions of the various elements of poetry will come later, and some of the terminologies and approaches necessary for a more exhaustive reading may not yet be part of the reader's tool kit. Nevertheless, a sampling of a few of Frost's poetic strategies and specific technique may not be out of place. These are meant to provide a hint of what is involved in the process of poetic appreciation.

Even a cursory first reading will give a fairly clear picture of Frost's approach to his subject. "Birches" is at once a masterpiece of concrete description—of nature, and of a boy's solitary game of swinging on birches—and a more general meditation. Frost is not so much trying to drive home a single theme as suggesting a complex web of associations in a grown man's mind. The poem is descriptive, nostalgic, and philosophical all at the same time. We will get a clearer sense of how these concerns are woven together if we look at some of the nuts and bolts of the poem's construction.

To begin with, Frost makes it very clear from the opening line that he has a specific metrical pattern in mind.

When I see birches bend to left and right

is a perfect *iambic pentameter* line. That means that the pattern of stresses is uniformly short/long or unaccented/accented across the five *feet* of the line. The feet are the rhythmic units (see the extended discussion in the section on Rhythm in Chapter 18) that the line naturally breaks into. When we read the words naturally, we tend to organize the pronunciation thus: Whĕn Í / sĕe bír- / chĕs bénd / tŏ léft / ănd ríght. Iambic pentameter is the most common metric pattern in the English-language tradition. Scholars and poets have said that this is because our speech has a natural affinity for the basic iambic rhythm. This does not mean that we go around speaking in iambs or pentameters to each other, but that of all formal patterns it holds the most options for making word combinations that do not sound strained.

The fact that Frost begins "Birches" with a perfect iambic pentameter line does not mean that every following line will conform exactly to the pattern. That would be too predictable and limiting. Rather, the poet writes the first line that way to set up an expectation in the reader's mind. He is like the jazz musician who plays the traditional melody in the first chorus and then starts working out variations. Frost, too, will strike countless variations against the reader's expectation, each calculated to produce a different effect.

Frost sustains this even iambic pentameter, with a few subtle modulations, through the fourth line. By this point the reader has fallen in with the rhythm and has begun to expect it. Frost here delivers an abrupt shock. His fifth line greets the ear with four punchy syllables, all accented: Aś iće stórms dó. The poem now makes a turn, abandoning for a time the idea of a boy swinging—Frost will return to it— and focusing instead upon the sensual detailing of ice-covered branches. Now we have a chance to see how a master wordsmith contrives impressions using sounds, meanings, and rhythms:

> Often you must have seen them
>
> Loaded with ice a sunny winter morning
> After a rain. They click upon themselves
> As the breeze rises, and turn many-colored
> As the stir cracks and crazes their enamel.
> Soon the sun's warmth makes them shed crystal shells
> Shattering and avalanching on the snow crust—
> Such heaps of broken glass to sweep away
> You'd think the inner dome of heaven had fallen.

There are a great many striking manipulations of language in these lines, but we must content ourselves with noting just a few. We might remark, for instance, Frost's use of word-sounds to enhance the portrait of ice-covered trees. The third line of the passage introduces a pause following "After a rain." The reader is made to wait an extra beat before continuing, and this can be seen as marking the lapse between the falling rain and the discovery of ice in the morning. Such a pause within a line, here indicated by the period, is called a *caesura*, from the Latin word for "cut."

The next phrase introduces the onomato-poetic word "click," which strongly suggests the sound made by iced branches knocking against each other. That *k*-sound is then woven through the next lines, in "many-colored," "cracks," "crazes," and "crystal." As readers, we may be only half-consciously aware of these sounds, but they reach the inner ear, and they help to explain why we feel such a strong sensation of melting as soon as Frost speaks of "the sun's warmth." For what happens is that the *k*-sound gives way to the softer *s*-sounds of the next few lines: "sun's," "shed crystal shells," "Shattering," "snow crust," and so on. We experience through language the yielding of a crusty hardness.

While we are considering word choice—diction—we might also give a nod to Frost's playfulness in the fifth line, where the "stir cracks and crazes their enamel." The poet makes use of an unusual word here—"crazes"—but if we check the dictionary we find that it is the right one. Apart from the primary meaning of "to make insane," the verb also means "to make small cracks on a surface," as on a ceramic glaze. But Frost cannot have been unaware of the proximity of "stir" and "craze" in his line. Indeed, hunting for subtleties at this level can drive a person stir-crazy.

There is one more major poetic event in this passage, this one rhythmic. We may notice that after the iambic regularity of the phrase "They click / u-pon / themselves," the metric structure becomes highly irregular for four lines. Frost is not, however, dozing at the wheel. To the contrary, he is setting up yet another surprise for the ear. This happens on two levels. First, there is the build-up and release of tension in the lines

> Soon the sun's warmth makes them shed crystal shells
> Shattering and avalanching on the snow crust—

The irregular rhythm of the first line, combined with the relative difficulty of making so many consecutive s- sounds, tightens the spring. The next line releases it. It's hard to miss the sudden free-fall, achieved by chasing the stressed first syllables of "Shattering" and "avalanching" with long strings of unstressed syllables. Thus "Shăt-těr-ing ănd á-va-lăn-chǐng ŏn thĕ snŏw crúst." And then, after such a vivid crashing down, Frost restores order. The next line brings the satisfactions of return—it is another perfect iambic pentameter line: "Sŭch héaps / ŏf bró- / kĕn gláss / tŏ swéep / ă-wáy." The poem is ready to turn again.

A reader working closely with the poem could go on and on. I have said nothing, for instance, about Frost's inventive use of *metaphors* and *similes*. Both are operations of comparison. Metaphor functions directly, simply substituting the likeness—"Such heaps of broken glass"—while simile uses *like* or *as*. Frost uses the former to nice effect when he says of the birches that they are "Like girls on hands and knees that throw their hair/ Before them over their heads to dry in the sun." Such figures of speech will be treated at length in a later chapter.

Before moving on from Frost's poem, it is necessary to say a few words about the place of meaning in poetry. The matter is not clear cut. Meaning—capital M—is one of the things that students most fear about poetry. Many have bad memories of high-school teachers insisting that they explain what a certain poet *meant* by writing a given poem. And when that same teacher later suggested an acceptable answer, the inevitable question came up: "Well, why didn't he just *say* so?" Many poets, by contrast, would agree with Archibald MacLeish's dictum that "A poem should not mean but *be*." To put it another way: a poem does not deliver a simple meaning or message in wrapping paper and ribbons—it is, rather, an entire complex experience, all of which is meaningful. Nor do all poets set out to write with meaning as their goal. The accurate rendering of sensation or appearance in words is purpose enough for many.

The kinds of meanings that poems do have is to some extent determined by the kinds of poems they are. The chief division is between *narrative* poems, including epics like Homer's *Odyssey* and Milton's *Paradise Lost,* which tell a story of greater or lesser complexity, and *lyric* poems, which tend to make a more direct appeal to the emotions and senses and do not link their expression on the unfolding of an episodic sequence.

Frost's "Birches," though it does make use of narrative bits—mainly the speaker's imagining of the boy climbing the tree—is essentially in the lyric tradition. It is a meditation. We are to take the voice as belonging to the poet; the thoughts are his own. And the meaning—better, meanings—are given in layers.

The initial sight of the birch trees prompts the narrator to a series of linked reflections, all of which contribute resonance to the poem, none of which by itself could be said to be *the* meaning. In his imagining of the boy, who is clearly a kind of idealized younger self, Frost touches on the themes of growth and self-testing. The boy, solitary, has "subdued" his father's trees, thus staking out a certain independence for himself. He has learned some basic lessons, lessons that carry moral as well as practical consequence. He has picked up necessary insights about the importance of timing—in swinging, in life—and poise.

The next layer of meanings and suggestions is exposed when Frost writes: "So was I once myself a swinger of birches." From this point on the poem carries a strong flavor of nostalgia. Youth is seen as being in many ways a better time, more intense and less compromised than adulthood. There follows a moving plea by the poet for earthbound certainties, which he opposes to more abstract concerns. "Earth's the right place for love," he writes. "I don't know where it's likely to go better." At the same time, though, he appears to celebrate the middle way, the tension between the common and the elevated. His contemplation of the birches leads him to the thought that there should be an elasticity about our approach to life, and that we should make room for aspiration as well as concrete practicality.

Nor do the meanings end there. On yet another level the poem, through its sheer attentiveness to the details of nature, seems to argue for an attitude of reverence. Nature is beautiful, yes, but it also embodies the laws and principles that we need to understand if we are to live meaningful lives as individuals. The imagined "swinger of birches" represents a natural and innocent relation to nature—a relation we would do well to establish in our own lives.

Meaning in poetry, then, is not a simple affair. If the content of the poem could be restated in a few sentences there would be no reason to have the poem. We might say instead that a poem does not so much state a meaning or message as embody the *experience* of meaning. The progression of the whole poem is such that we are able to recreate in ourselves the perceptions, thoughts, and emotions of another person. This, perhaps more than any of the poet's stated observations, is what gives the work its value.

Obviously not every poem is as immediate and comprehensible as Frost's. And before moving on to more specific discussions of the various poetic elements, we might take a quick look at a somewhat different kind of expression.

Denise Levertov

THE DOG OF ART

That dog with daisies for eyes
who flashes forth
flame of his very self at every bark
is the Dog of Art.
Worked in wool, his blind eyes   5
look inward to caverns and jewels
which they see perfectly
and his voice
measures forth the treasure
in music sharp and loud,   10
sharp and bright,
bright flaming barks,
and growling smoky soft, the Dog
of Art turns to the world
the quietness of his eyes.   15

<table>
<tr><td>As you read the
following discussion,
consider these
questions:</td><td>1. Read the poem carefully and make a list of which words seem striking or surprising. Write a sentence for each word, explaining why.

2. How does Levertov make use of the various senses in her poem? Cite any unexpected or irrational images that pertain to the senses.

3. Write a short paragraph in which you explore how Levertov's "The Dog of Art" comments on creativity and the purposes of art.</td></tr>
</table>

Discussion. Though it is a lyric poem like "Birches," Levertov's "The Dog of Art" provides an entirely different poetic experience. For one thing, the poem is composed in irregular *free verse*—it follows no set metrical pattern. Two sentences are broken up over fifteen lines. They are not, however, sentences of the kind we generally encounter when we read prose. Though the words are common and the syntax is straightforward, we very likely find ourselves baffled as we read. Nor do several re-readings clear up all of the confusion. For Levertov, unlike Frost, is not writing a lyric that lends itself to complete logical comprehension. What we discover as we keep reading is that we must give up on certain expectations. We have to allow that a work may carry some strong associative resonances without ever resolving into a content, or message, that can be paraphrased.

Nevertheless, it is possible to speak about certain features of the poem and to track its suggestions. Reading the first four lines we are simultaneously mystified and enlightened. We cannot say for sure why a dog should be described as having "daisies for eyes," or why that dog should be the "Dog of Art." We either have to accept the uncertain terms or give up. If we accept, then we find that a strand of sense does emerge. Levertov seems to be using her unusual *image* (an image in poetry is any depiction that appeals to one of the senses) to characterize the quality of true art; that is, that it "flashes forth" its authenticity at every moment and does so expressively, as a dog might bark. The reader may well ask: "Why doesn't she just say *that?*" To which the answer might be that such a direct statement might not capture our attention. We are much more responsive when a writer finds a way to arrest our interest with a surprising use of language. And that we are often more readily drawn to reflection when we are asked to lend a hand in the making of meaning.

The poem continues in this vein of tantalizing obscurity:

> Worked in wool, his blind eyes
> look inward to caverns and jewels
> which they see perfectly,

Pondering these words, the reader might surmise that Levertov is in fact describing a made thing, a woolen dog with daisies stitched over its eyes. The poem does not supply enough information to confirm such a guess. But perhaps it doesn't matter. What does matter is what she attributes to the creature in her imagination—that it is outwardly blind, but possessed of perfect inward vision. Here is another kind of characterization of the artist—that he or she is one so taken up with the splendor of the inner vision as to be blind to the outer world. Levertov may well be speaking *figuratively*—suggestively, but not literally—implying that the blindness is not physical, but symbolic. She may also have in mind the age-old lore of the blind seer. The great epic bard Homer was said to be blind, as was the poet John Milton. One tradition, admittedly a romantic one, holds that the physical blindness was actually an incentive and enhancement to the writing of poetry—that Homer and Milton did not need to see outwardly because they possessed such powerful inner vision.

The rest of the poem makes use of strong opposition. What the dog sees within are "caverns and jewels" but what he barks forth is "sharp and loud." His barks, as in earlier lines, are "flaming." Here Levertov is making use of the intensifying device of *synaesthesia;* she is expressing one sensory image in terms of another sense. The sound is featured as a visual (and, in a sense, tactile) thing. The static jewels are transformed into sudden and vibrant noises.

But then the poet contradicts the contradiction. The "bright flaming barks" give way to a growling that is "smoky soft," and the sharpness of the barks is set off against the "quietness of his eyes." We could mull over these lines for a long time and still not be able to give a clear report about what Levertov intends. It is not that kind of poem. But after several readings we most certainly carry away a distinct impression about the nature of art; that it is born of a tension between the inner life and the outer world; that it strives to resolve this tension; and that it finally achieves—or may achieve—the kind of peace that is won from struggle.

These are, obviously, one reader's reactions. They may have little bearing on what Levertov intended—that we cannot know. Nor are they in any way exclusive responses. Other readers will find other associations and possibly draw other conclusions. This openness to interpretation is the hallmark, not just of poetry, but of all art. The reader is an active participant in the making of meaning and the discovery of beauty.

The chapters that follow will include poems of all descriptions. Some are more formal, observing traditional metric patterns and yielding to logic. Others, and this is especially true of certain poems from the modern period, will leave the reader grasping, or in John Keats's words, irritably "reaching after fact and reason." When this happens, the best thing to do is to try to enjoy the ride. Avoid getting angry or frustrated and let the words work their mysterious way. Indeed, one of the special pleasures of poetry comes when we find that words have somehow grown into sense: we suddenly know exactly what the writer means.

In the following chapters we will look at the basic elements of poetry in isolation. Various terms will be introduced and explained, and various poetic procedures will be explored. In one way, such a focus is a falsification, for the poet never thinks simply in terms of meter, or diction, or imagery, but juggles all the options at once. Therefore, I add to these discussions a chapter devoted to writing about poetry. It is an attempt to put Humpty-Dumpty back together again.

16 Sound and Sense in Poetry

If painting is finally a matter of color, shape and line, and sculpture a matter of mass and surface, then poetry can be broken down into its two basic components, sound and sense. Poetry is made out of language, and language is made out of sounds that signify. So is all writing, of course. But poetry is a special case. The poet seeks out ways to give sound a meaning and meaning a sound. Language is condensed and charged with rhythm. The poet recognizes that words have sounds *and* meanings, and that the sounds can be orchestrated in ways that intensify the meanings.

SOUND AND SENSE

Reading poetry can be an uncanny experience. The sounds and rhythms affect the reader in an almost bodily way; the contents, meanwhile, reach the mental and emotional self. At certain lucky moments, the poet is able to bring sound and meaning into a relation that sends a shiver up the reader's spine. This is what Emily Dickinson meant when she said a real poem made her feel as though the top of her head were coming off. This is the reason that a poem cannot be validly summarized—the meaning may be noted, but not the experience of the meaning.

The connections between sound and meaning in poetry can be elusive. Sounds can, for example, be combined in ways that simulate meaning, as in these lines from Lewis Carroll's well-known "Jabberwocky":

> 'Twas brillig, and the slithy toves
> Did gyre and gimble in the wabe:
> All mimsy were the borogroves,
> And the mome raths outgrabe.

The pleasure in Carroll's poem is found on two levels. There is the delight in sounds and rhythms—which must remind all of us, even if unconsciously, of our own early efforts to master language. Second, and no less important, there is the ticklish tension that results from the resemblance between this nonsense and that which we call sense. "Did gyre and gimble in the wabe" very nearly *means*. We make associations to the sounds: "gyre" has to do with turning, "gimble" sounds like "gambol," and "wabe" is very close to "wave." Carroll has given us an image of something— "slithy toves"?—frolicking in water. He has done so by way of nonsense.

On the other extreme, where sound can intensify sense, we may find lines like these from West Indian poet Derek Walcott:

White sanderlings race the withdrawing surf to pick,
with wink-quick stabs, shellfish between the pebbles.

Here is an instance of a poet tuning his ear to the subtlest suggestions of the sound values—so subtle, in fact, that readers may dispute whether the hints are even there. Does "withdrawing surf" not create the sensation of hissing waves? And "pick" and "wink-quick"—do they not give the impression of the rapid strokes of a sea-bird's beak?

Or how about these lines from John Keats's justly celebrated "To Autumn"? Don't the word sounds make a texture that is like the essence of autumn itself?

Season of mists and mellow fruitfulness,
    Close bosom-friend of the maturing sun;
Conspiring with him how to load and bless
    With fruit the vines that round the thatch-eves run;
To bend with apples the moss'd cottage-trees,
    And fill all fruit with ripeness to the core;
    To swell the gourd, and plump the hazel shells
With a sweet kernel; to set budding more,
And still more, later flowers for the bees,
Until they think warm days will never cease,
    For Summer has o'er-brimm'd their clammy cells.

What a feast for the ear! The slow, languorous unfolding of "mellow fruitfulness," the density of "moss'd cottage trees," the sweet explosion of "plump," and the sticky sensation of excess in "o'er-brimm'd their clammy cells." These are not poetic accidents, but the hard-won "fruits" of the poet's wrestle with the language.

One could go on and on, culling passages from the poetry of the ages and pointing up moments where the language exceeds its traditional function of simply conveying sense; moments when the sounds become a part of the sense. But for the present it might be more useful to look at some of the special ways that the poet can create effects with words in combination.

ALLITERATION: Alliteration is the technique of repeating consonant sounds, most commonly at the beginnings of words that are in proximity. "Peter Piper picked a peck of pickled peppers" is alliteration taken to humorous extremes. When Keats writes "Season of mists and mellow fruitfulness," he is alliterating the *m* sounds. He picks up an alliterative echo in the next line with "bosom-friend of the maturing sun." English poetry, which grew out of the strongly consonantal Anglo-Saxon tradition, is deeply alliterative, though there are examples in the poetry of every culture.

The effects of alliteration are various. Often a poet will use it to create a desired emphasis, or *euphony*—a pleasing music (literally a "pleasant sound"); "mists and mellow" is certainly euphonious. But alliteration can also bring tension, or even a jarring sense of collision—or *cacaphony*—into a line. Gerard Manley Hopkins, for instance, uses alliteration to work a sense of power and rough vigor into the beginning of his poem "God's Grandeur":

The world is charged with the grandeur of God.
    It will flame out, like *shining* from *shook* foil;

It gathers to greatness, like the ooze of oil
Crushed. Why do men then now not reck his rod?

Alliteration can also result from the echoing of consonants within words: re-peated arpeggios, regurgitating engine noises, and so on. The consonants don't have to be the same, they only have to sound the same: citing severe stress, kicking the cat, and so on.

ASSONANCE: An assonance is a repetition of the same vowel sound in nearby words. Derek Walcott's lines cited above are an excellent example: the sanderlings that "pick" with "wink-quick" stabs. As with alliteration, the effects of assonance are various. They can tend toward euphony or cacophony; they can ei-ther speed the reader's progress or deliberately slow it down. Indeed, these very words—"speeding the reader's progress"—have a swiftness to them that derives from the sequence of *ee* sounds. Hopkins, meanwhile, writing "Why do men then now not reck his rod," gets a halting effect by distributing assonant sounds through a series of single syllable words.

CONSONANCE: A consonance, which is often used as a kind of indirect, or *slant*, rhyme, involves a substitution of vowels within words that have the same con-sonant sounds, like "litter" and "letter," or "tick" and "tock."

ONOMATOPOEIA: A number of words sound like what they mean. The ex-ample of "buzzing" was used in Chapter 15. Others are "ooze," "gong," "click," "whis-per," "splatter." In some cases the line is hard to draw. Does "slap" sound like a slap? Or does "crush" somehow carry the idea of flattening in its sounds, the hard *c* be-coming the softer *sh*?

RHYME: Rhyme, one of the poet's basic tools, is another way that sound can function in a poem. Rhymes are words that repeat the same sounds, often—but not always—coming at the end of a line:

I don't know, but I've been told
Streets up in heaven are paved with gold.

But rhymes come in many forms and are not always simple. In the Keats pas-sage, for instance, we can locate several types. The poet uses *exact* rhymes, like "sun" and "run" (which are also known as *perfect* rhymes); *partial*, or *near*, or *imperfect* rhymes, such as we find between "bees" and "cease"; and *internal* rhymes, where words within a line, or in adjacent lines, match up. Keats's "To *swell* the gourd, and plump the hazel *shells*," strikes an internal rhyme between the second and last words in the line. Poets may also on occasion make use of *visual* or *eye* rhymes, where the words look as though they rhyme but in fact do not. Words like "enough" and "cough" are eye rhymes.

The uses of rhyme are many. They can make for solemnity and order, and a sense of inevitability, as they do in the first stanza of William Cowper's "Light Shin-ing Out of Darkness":

God moves in a mysterious way,
    His wonders to perform;
He plants his footstep in the sea,
    And rides upon the storm.

Or they can bring levity, even absurdity, as they do in these lines from Gjertrud Schnackenberg's "Two Tales of Clumsy":

When Clumsy harks the gladsome ting-a-lings
Of dinner chimes that Mrs. Clumsy rings,
His two hands winglike at his most bald head,
Then clumsy readies Clumsy to be fed.
He pulls from satchel huge a tiny chair,
And waggling his pillowed derriere,

He hitches up his pants to gently sit.
Like two ecstatic doves his white hands flit

In this excerpt, Schnackenberg relies mainly on *masculine rhymes*. These are rhymes based on the correspondence of single syllables, like "head" and "fed." A *feminine rhyme* is slightly more complex (though this is not necessarily a reflection of gender differences). In a feminine rhyme it is the first syllables of two-syllable words (or any syllable other than the last of a word of more than two syllables) that correspond: *dinner* and *thinner*, pre*posterous* and rhi*nocerous*.

Whatever rhyme contributes to the sense of a poem—adding to the solemnity or humor, say—it also gives shape to the whole. The reader notes the recurrence of sounds (poets generally rhyme in some pattern) and reads with a certain expectation. When the rhyme clicks into place, it brings a sense of rightness to the expression. When various rhymes are worked in a pattern of some intricacy, the reader responds as if to a musical structure. Rhymes send signals of connection; they establish relationships among key words. They can also nudge a poem closer to music, marking off a sharp distinction from the nonrecurrent structure of most prose.

Rhyme patterns will be discussed more fully in Chapter 19, but here, as an illustration, is a lyric that makes generous use of some of the possibilities offered by rhyme. The letters to the right indicate the pattern of recurrences:

Ruth Stone

I HAVE THREE DAUGHTERS

I have three daughters	A
Like greengage plums.	B
They sat all day	C
Sucking their thumbs.	B
And more's the pity,	D
They cried all day,	C
Why doesn't our mother's brown hair	E
Turn gray?	C
I have three daughters	A
Like three cherries.	F
They sat at the window	G

The boys to please.	F
And they couldn't wait	H
For their mother to grow old.	G
Why doesn't our mother's brown hair	E
Turn to snow?	I (H)
I have three daughters	A
In the apple tree	J (F)
Singing Mama send Daddy	J
With three young lovers	A
To take them away from me.	J
I have three daughters	A
Like greengage plums,	B
Sitting all day	C
And sighing all day	C
And sucking their thumbs.	B
Singing, Mama won't you fetch and carry,	K
And Daddy, won't you let us marry,	K
Singing, sprinkle snow down on Mama's hair	E
And lordy, give us our share.	E

As you read the following discussion, consider these questions:

1. What is the attitude of the speaker toward her three daughters? What images and expressions create this attitude?

2. What is the function of the repetitions in the poem? Is this poem different from a nursery rhyme? Explain your answer.

3. Read the poem aloud and concentrate on the rhymes. How does the last stanza differ from the previous stanzas? What effect do the changes have?

Discussion. Stone's poem is clearly built around rhymes, yet an inspection of the different sound correspondences reveals no pattern. (Where a second letter is marked in parentheses, we generally have a half rhyme, such as that of "day" and "wait".) The rhymes function in two ways. Stone's overall strategy seems to be to strike echoes of nursery rhymes or children's songs (especially in the first and last stanzas) and then to counter the expectation of lilting innocence with a much harsher content. We quickly realize that these girls are not sitting idly in the garden waiting for three nice men to come along. No, they are wishing age—and, ultimately, death—on their mother so that they can get a share of her money.

The poet accentuates the tension between the pleasant convention of the nursery rhyme and the real facts of the matter by using exact rhymes to frame the scene and set the reader up ("plums" and "thumbs"), and then using slant or half rhymes to pull the poem away from calm predictability. Thus, in the second stanza, she rhymes "cherries" with "please" (not the nicest fit) and "window" and "old." The final stanza, interestingly, is once again solidly rhymed. But now, knowing the scenario, we read a certain ominousness into the fact. The lilt of the rhymes is anything but cheery.

SOUND AND SENSE: SELECTIONS WITH COMMENTS

In the following poem Amy Clampitt makes exceedingly skillful use of word sounds to conjure up the impression of a fog stealing in from the ocean. Her poem achieves its particular delicacy by playing off the cloudy indistinctness of the fog against the precise articulation of certain physical details.

Amy Clampitt

FOG

A vagueness comes over everything,
as though proving color and contour
alike dispensable: the lighthouse
extinct, the islands' spruce-tips
drunk up like milk in the   5
universal emulsion; houses
reverting into the lost
and forgotten; granite
subsumed, a rumor
in a mumble of ocean.   10
                Tactile
definition, however, has not been
totally banished: hanging
tassel by tassel, panicled°
foxtail and needlegrass,   15
dropseed, furred hawkweed,
and last season's rose-hips
are vested in silenced
chimes of the finest,
clearest sea-crystal.   20
                Opacity
opens up rooms, a showcase
for the hueless moonflower
corolla, as Georgia
O'Keeffe° might have seen it,   25
of foghorns; the nodding
campanula of bell buoys;
the ticking, linear
filigree of bird voices.

FOG. 14 *panicled*: loosely branched flower cluster.   25 *Georgia O'Keeffe*: American painter who often depicted abstracted flower shapes.

1. Write a prose paragraph in which you attempt to evoke the same sensations as those found in Clampitt's poem.
2. Isolate the different senses that Clampitt appeals to. Which one is dominant?
3. Identify uses of alliteration, assonance, and consonance.

Discussion. The logic of Amy Clampitt's poem moves from blurriness to precision and back to blurriness, and this movement is at every point determined by the sounds. The first ten lines, which make a sentence, weave together a dense pattern of long vowel sounds (*vagueness* / *proving* / *lighthouse* / *islands'* / *universal*/ *houses*), combining them with alliterated *s* sounds (*vagueness comes . . . lighthouse*/ *extinct, the islands' spruce-tips*, etc.), *l* sounds (*alike, dispensible*, etc.), and *m* sounds (*subsumed, a rumor*/ in a *mumble* of ocean). Why these sounds should combine to intensify our impression of fog is the cook's secret—her ear has dictated them to her. But that they function in this way comes clear as soon as we read the next ten lines, which again make a sentence.

Here we meet with words that require an agile tongue. Just compare "mumble of ocean" from the preceding line and "Tactile/ definition." Likewise "hanging/ tassel by tassel" and "panicled/ foxtail." The quick short vowels (*definition*/*banished*/*tassel*/ *panicled*) gradually make way for lines governed by long vowel sounds and *s*'s:

> and last *s*eason's ro*s*e-hips
> are vested in *s*ilenced
> chimes of the fine*s*t,
> clea*r*est *s*ea-crystal.

The effect, interestingly, is of delicacy and precision, not in the least of murkiness. Which ought to tell us something: that context is everything in poetry. A set of sounds can make one suggestion in one cluster of lines, quite another elsewhere. There are few hard rules.

Clampitt's final stanza shifts from visual phenomena to sounds. The fog may obscure all but the most close-range detailing, but a range of noises will penetrate the density. The attentive reader will notice that the poet has selected three sounds, arranging them in sequence. We move from "foghorns" (an onomato-poetic word), their sound amplified by the assonance with "nodding," to the lighter "*bell buoys*"—an obvious alliteration of *b*'s—to the still lighter assonance of *i* sounds in "ticking, linear/ filagree of bird voices." The final sensation is of a crisp clarity cutting through the thick surrounding element.

Mary Oliver

THE HERMIT CRAB

> Once I looked inside
>   the darkness
>   of a shell folded like a pastry,
>   and there was a fancy face—

or almost a face—
   it turned away
      and frisked up its brawny forearms
         so quickly   5

against the light
   and my looking in   10
      I scarcely had time to see it,
         gleaming

under the pure white roof
   of old calcium.
      When I set it down, it hurried   15
         along the tideline

of the sea,
   which was slashing along as usual,
      shouting and hissing
         toward the future,   20

turning its back
   with every tide on the past,
      leaving the shore littered
         every morning

with more ornaments of death—   25
   what a pearly rubble
      from which to choose a house
         like a white flower—

and what a rebellion
   to leap into it   30
      and hold on,
         connecting everything,

the past to the future—
   which is of course the miracle—
      which is the only argument there is   35
         against the sea.

As you read the following discussion, consider these questions:

1. Read Oliver's poem carefully. Without looking at the commentary, try to identify places where the poet's use of certain word-sounds seems to amplify the meaning. Try to account for how these word-sounds create their effect.
2. Identify any alliterations, assonances, or consonances Oliver uses in the poem.

Discussion. Mary Oliver's "The Hermit Crab" is a good example of how word-sounds can weave a subtle accompaniment to the sense of a poem. There is nothing overt or dramatic in Oliver's presentation, just a sense of physical particulars being intensified or brought into sharper relief through the possibilities of sound.

In the first stanza Oliver makes use of the f-sound. The word "folded" in line 3 establishes an associational key, so when we encounter "fancy face" in the next line we automatically link it to the foldedness that the shape of the shell necessarily imposes. The repetition of long *a* sounds in "pastry," "face," and "away" (line 6) sets us up to register the abrupt switch to the quicker, more active short *i* sounds— "frisked" and "quickly"—that communicate the sudden retraction of the crab into its shell.

Oliver's third stanza builds elegantly to the last line in which the word "gleaming" is showcased. The predominantly short vowels and the slightly awkward diction pave the way for the smooth calm presence of the single word "gleaming"; its long *ea* sound in itself seems to shine.

The fifth and sixth stanzas make a fairly traditional play with *s*'s and *sh* sounds— poets can't resist the onomato-poetic possibilities. Oliver crowds the lines with surf and water sounds, using "sea," "slashing," "usual," "shouting," "hissing" in one stanza alone, and then creates an impression of withdrawal in the next stanza by reducing the explosion to a mere murmur with "its," "past," and "shore." The image of the exposed shore then accepts the tangible debris, the sense of clutter implicit in the word "littered" and the pairing of "pearly rubble." In both cases we get the effect through pronounciation—stumbling a beat over the doubled *t*'s and *d* in the first word, and the crowded mouth-movements forced on us by the *r*'s of the latter.

Interestingly, Oliver's reliance on word-sounds to emphasize physical particularity has no counterpart in her dealing with abstractions. The last two stanzas of the poem are about ideas, not things, and we look in vain for the skillful amplifications of sense by sound.

Wallace Stevens

BANTAMS IN PINE-WOODS

Chieftain Iffucan of Azcan in caftan°
Of tan with henna° hackles,° halt!

Damned universal cock, as if the sun
Was blackamoor° to bear your blazing tail.

Fat! Fat! Fat! Fat! I am the personal.
Your world is you. I am my world.

You ten-foot poet among inchlings. Fat!
Begone! An inchling bristles in these pines,

Bristles, and points their Appalachian tangs,
And fears not portly Azcan nor his hoos.

10

BANTAMS IN PINE-WOODS. 1 *caftan*: long gown like a nightshirt worn in the Near East. 2 *henna*: reddish color. 2 *hackles*: neckfeathers. 4 *blackamoor*: dark-skinned person.

1. Copy the poem and mark the dominant repeated sounds. How do these help to create the impression of bantams?

2. Read the lines aloud and try to emphasize the stressed syllables. How do the vocal emphases contribute to Stevens's sound portrait?

3. Try your hand at writing a short poem that uses unusual sounds and rhythms to evoke an animal.

Discussion. The reader's first response to Wallace Stevens's poem is likely to be complete bewilderment. The lines seem pure nonsense, or very close to it. Clearly the logical interpretation is not going to yield much. But if we change our approach, allowing ourselves to be relaxed and playful, and if we are willing to consult the dictionary from time to time, a kind of impression emerges.

Stevens's poem depends almost exclusively on sound. The ten lines create an aural portrait of bantams in a natural setting. Bantams are small chickens known to be quarrelsome. The poem, made up in part of interesting but obscure words, in part of fanciful coinages, seems to be about a standoff between two birds—a boastful challenge from one to the other. The energy is that of a street-fight, fast and mocking.

"Chieftain Iffucan of Azcan" is pure invention, employed for its colorful sound values—the alliterated *f*'s and the assonant *can*s. The rest of the sentence is, in fact, highly precise description, a "caftan" being a kind of tunic, "henna" being a color, and "hackles" referring to the delicate neckfeathers of a bird. The "*henna hackles, halt!*" is an excessive alliteration meant to convey not only enraged breathlessness on the part of the one bird, but also to suggest ruffling feathers.

The second pair of lines extends an insult. The third pair is more ambiguous. The "Fat! Fat! Fat! Fat!" could either represent a continuation of the insult, or else mimic the sound of small wings beating. Most likely Stevens intended both.

The rest of the poem carries on the threats and simultaneous self-preening. "Bristles," repeated in the ninth line, gives off an angry hiss. The weave of sounds in the last two lines is intricate, set down more for musical value than meaning. "Appalachian tangs" refers to the protruding needles on the pine trees. The bantam may be asserting a special skill at pecking, adding one last time that he has no reason to be afraid of the large strutting bird or its "hoos."

The poem is pure play, finally. Stevens wants the reader to have the pleasures of the mouth and ear. It resembles Lewis Carroll's "Jabberwocky," but with this one difference—that beneath the turbulence of its colliding syllables is an actual subject.

William Carlos Williams

THE COD HEAD

Miscellaneous weed
strands, stems, debris—
firmament

to fishes—
where the yellow feet
of gulls dabble

oars whip
ships churn to bubbles—
at night wildly

agitate phosphores-
cent midges°—but day by day
flaccid

moons in whose
discs sometimes a red cross
lives—four

fathom°—the bottom skids
a mottle of green
sands backward—

amorphous waver-
ing rocks—three fathom
the vitreous°

body through which—
small scudding fish deep
down—and

now a lulling lift
and fall—
red stars—a severed cod—

head between two
green stones—lifting
falling

5

10

15

20

25

30

THE COD HEAD.   11 *midges*: gnat-like flies.   16 *fathom*: six feet (of sea depth).   21 *vitreous*: glassy.

As you read the following discussion, consider these questions:

1. Look carefully at Williams's line endings. Find two instances where the break intensifies the sense of the poem.

2. Compare the sensory impression Williams achieves here with that created by Clampitt in "Fog" (p. 552). Isolate differences in the poets' use of sound and imagery.

3. Notice Williams's many participial (*-ing*) endings. What effect do these have on the impression he wants to create?

Discussion. In "The Cod Head," William Carlos Williams, like Wallace Stevens in "Bantams in Pine-Woods," makes careful use of the evocative possibilities of word sounds. He goes to great lengths to describe his sea-side setting, the ultimate focus of which is the severed head of a cod. Like many of Williams's poems, this one argues for the surprise that can lurk within the commonplace. And what could be more commonplace—at least for the person who lives near water—than the sight of a fish-head washed to shore.

Williams begins by evoking an impression of clutter at seaside. The first stanza—he has written the poem in ten 3-line stanzas—bunches s sounds and r sounds close together, forcing the reader to pick along slowly. The break between the first and second stanza is initially confusing. The reader needs a moment to catch on to the fact that "firmament" and "to fishes" are set off between dashes, and to realize further that the "strands, stems, debris" are seen by the fishes as a kind of sky. The shift in perspective is important, for the following lines, describing the events on the water's surface, are meant to be seen as if from beneath.

The stanzas that follow are full of inventive uses of sound. Williams's "oars whip/ ships churn to bubbles" actively joins image to sound, while the "churn to bubbles" phrase makes a music very suggestive of churning. Similarly, the alliteration of "phospores-/ cent" and "flaccid" makes a momentary sparkle of s sounds.

A poet like Williams often uses alliterations, assonances, and various kinds of rhyme to stitch together a fabric from words and associations that might otherwise sprawl toward chaos. Though his poem is not regularly metered or rhymed, there are abundant links of this sort: the partially rhyming alliteration of "bottom" and "mottle" in the sixth stanza, for example, or the repetition of "fathom."

Williams also makes clever use of line breaks, at times cutting a word in two to underscore a particular facet of the description. In the seventh stanza, to cite one instance, he writes "amorphous waver-/ ing rocks. The breaking of the word not only gets us to see the word "wave" hidden within the longer word, but it also captures, with wonderful economy, the way that shifting water can break the image of something under the surface—in this case, rocks. A similar play, more obvious, comes with "cod-" and "head" between ninth and final stanzas.

While there are many such prizes to be found in the poem, let us finish by pointing out Williams's subtle use of l sounds in the last three stanzas: "small," "lulling lift," "fall," "lifting/falling" combine to generate something like the up and down movement—the lapping—made by waves as they undulate. It is difficult to read these last three stanzas out loud without feeling that sensation of rise and fall. We can be sure that Williams worked it into the poem with great care. He is celebrated by his fellow-poets for the great precision and inventiveness of his poetic "ear."

Robert Herrick

DELIGHT IN DISORDER

A sweet disorder in the dress
Kindles in clothes a wantonness:
A lawn about the shoulders thrown
Into a fine distraction,
An erring lace, which here and there   5
Enthralls the crimson stomacher,°
A cuff neglectful, and thereby
Ribbands° to flow confusedly,

DELIGHT IN DISORDER. 6 *stomacher*: stiff covering or bodice for the stomach. 8 *ribbands*: ribbons.

A winning wave (deserving note)
In the tempestuous petticoat,
A careless shoe-string, in whose tie
I see a wild civility,
Do more bewitch me, than when art
Is too precise in every part.

As you read the following discussion, consider these questions:	1. Read Herrick's poem aloud and find three instances where the word-sounds can be seen to augment the meaning. Find instances of consonance, assonance, and alliteration. 2. How might Herrick's fashion preferences be applied to art (and to poetry in particular)? Is there a philosophy of life lurking in these lines? Explain.

Discussion. Robert Herrick wrote in the early- to mid-seventeenth century, and some of the words he uses have become archaic. A "lawn" is a thin linen or cotton fabric; a "stomacher" is a stiff garment that covers the stomach; and "ribbands" is just an earlier version of ribbons. Once those references have been cleared up, the poem poses no particular problems.

The poem is written in the 14-line *sonnet* form (see Chapter 19), making use of exact rhymes (art/part) as well as numerous imperfect rhymes (there/stomacher, tie/civility, etc.). Indeed, here the rhymes and sounds are skillfully manipulated to enhance the sense of casual disorder, allowing Herrick to click his message home at the end with a neatly rhyming *couplet*, or line-pair.

Herrick is obviously mindful of the rustling suggestiveness of the s sounds, making use of them throughout: "A sweet disorder in the dress," "Ribbands to flow confusedly," and so on. In the fifth line, "An erring lace, which here and there" plays with the rhyme possibilities of *erring, here*, and *there*, thus accenting the impression that the lace is peeping out in several places. The alliterated t sounds in "tempestuous petticoat" add a starchy hardness to the softer s sounds. "A winning wave," in the previous line, uses the alliterated w's to hint at the up-and-down motion that a wave makes. The final effect is to win the reader over to the main point: that there is an energy and spontaneity in casual disorder that is not often found in the more premeditated approaches to fashion—or, perhaps, life itself.

SOUND AND SENSE: SELECTIONS WITH QUESTIONS

Dylan Thomas

AND DEATH SHALL HAVE NO DOMINION

And death shall have no dominion.
Dead men naked they shall be one

With the man in the wind and the west moon;
When their bones are picked clean and the clean bones gone,
They shall have stars at elbow and foot;   5
Though they go mad they shall be sane,
Though they sink through the sea they shall rise again;
Though lovers be lost love shall not;
And death shall have no dominion.

And death shall have no dominion.   10
Under the windings of the sea
They lying long shall not die windily;
Twisting on racks when sinews give way,
Strapped to a wheel, yet they shall not break;
Faith in their hands shall snap in two,   15
And the unicorn evils run them through;
Split all ends up they shan't crack;
And death shall have no dominion.

And death shall have no dominion.
No more may gulls cry at their ears   20
Or waves break loud on the seashores;
Where blew a flower may a flower no more
Lift its head to the blows of the rain;
Though they be mad and dead as nails,
Heads of the characters hammer through daisies;   25
Break in the sun till the sun breaks down,
And death shall have no dominion.

QUESTIONS

1. Pick one stanza and locate all instances of alliteration and assonance.

2. Select two examples of each and discuss how they function in the poem to intensify the effect.

3. Find three lines where Thomas uses word-sounds in a striking manner. Can you isolate how those sounds emphasize the sense of the lines?

4. Compose several lines of your own in imitation of Thomas. Try to find words that alliterate strongly as well as a rhythm that conveys a hammering effect. You may do this as a parody if you wish.

Jean Toomer

REAPERS

Black reapers with the sound of steel on stones
Are sharpening scythes. I see them place the hones
In their hip-pockets as a thing that's done,
And start their silent swinging, one by one.

Black horses drive a mower through the weeds,
And there, a field rat, startled, squealing bleeds,
His belly close to ground. I see the blade,
Blood-stained, continue cutting weeds and shade.

QUESTIONS

1. Copy this short poem on a separate sheet and leave space between lines and words. Using circles and connecting lines, map out the pattern of alliterations and assonances.

2. Find two instances where these effects heighten the poet's expression. Explain how the sounds relate to the sensation of impression that is being evoked.

3. Discuss the change that takes place between the first five lines and the sixth. How does Toomer create sudden tension? Explore alliteration, assonance, and rhythmic change.

4. Explain how Toomer creates tension by using an orderly rhyme sequence to depict an incident in the reapers' day. Does the regularity of the verse itself convey a message of sorts?

Alice Fulton

YOUR CARD READ "POET-MECHANIC"

the day you came   carrying a two-cylinder
slice of winter sun on your back,
toolcase with a greasy lock in
your spoon-shaped fingers
said you could do anything   5
with your hands &
went right to work, using
nouns as furniture, assembling
verbs into go-carts & motorcycles
till they roared off, followed by   10
a gang of sycophant° adverbs.
The few transitives° that remained
you turned into trampolines &
the expletives° jumped on them all day.
When I watched you build "vituperate"°   15
into a Harley-Davidson, I knew
it was goodbye.
Now there're just the adjectives
all day primping   singing choruses of popsongs.
I want to shake them & say   20
"Have you no respect
for the magnificent
lexicon you represent?" But "magnificent"
is in the bathroom
humming be-bop-a-lula.   25

YOUR CARD READ "POET-MECHANIC." 11 *sycophant:* slavishly following. 12 *transitives:* verbs with objects. 14 *expletives:* curses or filler-words. 15 *vituperate:* berate.

QUESTIONS

1. What is the relation between Fulton's title and the fantasy she weaves in the poem itself?

2. How does the poet use alliteration for comic effect in lines 12 and 13?

3. Why is "vituperate" (line 15) an excellent word choice for a Harley-Davidson? What is the meaning of the word, and what are its sound-associations? Can you think of any other words that would work in this context?

4. Find the alliteration in the last three lines of the poem.

5. Speculate on the significance of Fulton's ending her poem with "be-bop-a-lula."

6. Fulton creates a collision between what might be called "everyday words" and a more academic terminology. What is the effect of this? Do you take the poem seriously, or do you see it as a playful exercise?

7. Try your hand at writing a few lines on some commonplace subject in which you mix together levels of diction as Fulton has done.

8. Fulton intends this poem as a comment on poetry itself, comparing the poet's work with words to the mechanic's work with machine parts. Is this just an idle fancy, or is there some point to the comparison? Discuss.

William Shakespeare

SONNET LX

Like as the waves make towards the pebbled shore,	
So do our minutes hasten to their end;	
Each changing place with that which goes before,	
In sequent° toil all forwards do contend.	*sequential*
Nativity,° once in the main° of light,	*birth; center* 5
Crawls to maturity, wherewith being crown'd,	
Crooked eclipses 'gainst his glory fight,	
And Time that gave doth now his gift confound.	
Time doth transfix° the flourish set on youth	*pierce through*
And delves the parallels in beauty's brow,	10
Feeds on the rarities of nature's truth,	
And nothing stands but for his scythe to mow:	
And yet to times in hope my verse shall stand,	
Praising thy worth, despite his cruel hand.	

QUESTIONS

1. Find the alliteration in the first two lines and comment upon its connection to the sense of the words.

2. How does the word "pebbled" in the first line help to enact the sensation appropriate to the description? Substitute the words "rocky" and "sandy" and explain what difference the word choice makes.

3. What function do the alliterations in lines 6 and 7 have in the sonnet?

4. Comment on the particular appropriateness of the alliteration in line 10. Does it have any visual suggestion? If so, what? Also, what is the internal rhyme in line 10? And how does it serve the meaning of the line?

5. Trace the various assonances that are woven through the last three lines of the sonnet.

6. Write as close a paraphrase as you can of this sonnet, following the logic of its "argument." Write a short paragraph detailing the differences you feel reading the poem and the paraphrase. What has been lost?

7. Compare this sonnet to another by Shakespeare (see Chapter 27). How does he use different kinds of sounds to make a verbal music, and how does that music relate to his thematic concerns?

Lucie Brock-Broido

AUTOBIOGRAPHY

It is only three o'clock & already I'm alone
Listening to the lovers next door
Like Patsy Cline° & her Man
Throwing barebacked wooden furniture
Like the real life bicker of true love.   5
I love that hands-on
Die-while-you're-dark-haired-still
& young, fists curled to desire,
Take Me kind of love.
They'll make love without apology   10
& I'll be left to the afternoon
& the autoerotic sounds of my American voice
Getting it all down.

AUTOBIOGRAPHY. 3 *Patsy Cline:* hard-living country singer of the 1950s.

QUESTIONS

1. Copy the poem out as three consecutive prose sentences. Read it over several times and try to determine what qualities of language make it poetry rather than prose.

2. How is Brock-Broido using sound combinations—alliterations, assonances, and repeated words—to create a heightened picture of her subject? Look in particular at lines 4 and 5, and lines 6, 7, and 8.

3. How does Brock-Broido create intensity in the middle lines of the poem, and how does she then release that intensity? Does the shift in tone between the middle and end have any parallels in the subject itself?

4. Write several lines of poetry in which you attempt to create the sensations of action and then the feeling of the aftermath. Look back at your attempt and explain whether there were any significant differences in your use of language.

17 Voice in Poetry

A few decades ago it was very fashionable for writers and would-be writers to speak in terms of "finding a voice." It was not enough to have a subject and a skill with words. What mattered was finding the right personal expression. The underlying assumption was that each person has a unique way of seeing and articulating the world, and that success in writing depended upon discovering these.

This is a very personalized idea of voice—voice seen as the unique sound-print of the self—and the commotion surrounding the topic almost made it seem that this was something new to poetry. It was not, of course. Voice has always, in one way or another, been an implicit part of literary expression, reflected in the writer's style, tone, choice of subject, and angle of presentation. Readers of novels can quickly identify Jane Austen's voice, or Ernest Hemingway's, just as the poetry lover can pick out the differences between John Donne, Thomas Hardy, Elizabeth Barrett Browning, and several dozen other masters of the art. The recent buzzing about voice had more to do with a development known as "Confessionalism," which was the unprecedented injection of formerly private subject matter into the practice of poetry. This will be discussed shortly.

VOICE

Voice in a more general sense, then, has been an attribute of all poetry—indeed, all literature—from the very beginning. Simply put, every poem is the product of some speaker. That speaker can present himself or herself in the first person as the poet, or can adopt a *persona*, or mask, speaking as "I" out of an invented identity. A young poet can speak as an old king; a woman can speak as a man, and vice versa. Or else the poet can choose the stance of anonymity, eliminating the personal presence and writing in the neutral third person that is the closest one can come to the appearance of objectivity. The options are many and various, and poets have made use of so many of them that any charting of rules is pointless. Still, a few rough generalizations are necessary.

To begin with, poetry has always spanned the full gamut between impersonal and intimate modes of address. We can look back at the great tradition of the epic narrative as represented by Homer, Virgil, Milton, and others, and see vast panoramas set forth as if seen from the lofty and removed vantage of the gods. There is no fiddling about with the first-person "I" in these works. On the other hand, we have the long history of more intimate lyrics: Sappho mourning her lost loves from her island of Lesbos, the Roman poet Catullus sniping at the fickle character of his mistress, Cynthia, and Shakespeare forging sonnets to his unnamed beloved: "Shall I compare thee to a summer's day. . . ."

But even when the poets of the past were writing in the first person, they did so by and large within certain formalized conventions. Shakespeare was speaking as a Shakespeare who attempted to universalize himself into the type of all ardent lovers, not as the man who may have suffered from rotting teeth or fallen arches. The revolution fought by the Confessional poets was, as we shall see, to bring the real life of the warts-and-all individual into poetic focus. And once the taboo of the personal had been shattered completely, it was possible to say that there were no more limits on the use of voice in poetry. Every stance and tone was available to the poet.

What follows here is a survey of just some of the options open to the poet. There are, of course, others, but the reader will get at least a sense of some of the possibilities the poet can choose from.

Third-Person Voice

In poetry, as in fiction, the third-person address is very common. This is probably because it is so flexible. Hiding behind a mask of impersonality, the poet can approach the subject at different degrees of intimacy. John Keats's sonnet, "On the Grasshopper and the Cricket," is fairly representative of the norm. The poet adopts a detached vantage, speaking with the calm omniscience (all-knowingness) of a god:

John Keats

ON THE GRASSHOPPER AND THE CRICKET

The poetry of earth is never dead:
When all the birds are faint with the hot sun,
And hide in cooling trees, a voice will run
From hedge to hedge about the new-mown mead;°   *meadow*
That is the Grasshopper's—he takes the lead   5
In summer luxury,—he has never done
With his delights; for when tired out with fun
He rests at ease beneath some pleasant weed.
The poetry of earth is ceasing never:
On a lone winter evening, when the frost   10
Has wrought a silence, from the stove there shrills
The Cricket's song, in warmth increasing ever,
And seems to one in drowsiness half lost
The Grasshopper's among some grassy hills.

As you read the following discussion, consider this question:

1. Keats wrote his sonnet in the third-person voice. How would the poem change if the "one" in line 13 were to be changed to "me"? Would the poem sacrifice any of its philosophical authority? Explain.

Discussion. Not limited to inhabiting one human perspective, the voice can take on a generality that strikes the reader as very nearly objective: *This must be the voice of truth*.

In instances like the above, where the poet uses the third person to make pronouncements ("The poetry of earth is never dead"), the effect can be prophetic; it is as if the poet is drawing on deep wells of collective knowledge. But some poets, like William Carlos Williams in "The Cod Head" (Chapter 16), use third-person vantage much more strictly. For them it is, in a sense, the equivalent of the impersonal camera eye, and they keep all suggestions of the inner life *off* the page. A good example of this enforced neutrality can be seen in A. R. Ammons's poem "Bonus":

A. R. Ammons

BONUS

The hemlocks slumped
already as if bewailing
the branch-loading

shales of ice, the rain
changes and a snow   5
sifty as fog

begins to fall, brightening
the ice's bruise-glimmer
with white holdings:

the hemlocks, muffled,   10
deepened to the grim
taking of a further beauty on.

As you read the following discussion, consider these questions:

1. Imagine that Ammons's poem began "I saw." How would the introduction of the first-person voice change the poem's effect?

2. Compare the impersonal voice in Ammons's poem with that of the preceding Keats sonnet. Compare the impressions of nature you get from each poem. To what degree are these determined by the address? How do you imagine Ammons would write of the grasshopper and the cricket, and Keats of the hemlock?

Discussion. One of the charms of a poem like this is that it is purely about its subject. We are not asked to interpret any human motivations or to draw any deep conclusions about existence. Rather, we admire the view, the clean lines of the composition, as if we were admiring a photograph. We do not think of the poet because nothing asks us to. Only at a closer second look do we see that slight traces of the human, if not the personal, are present. The poet's description of the hemlocks slumped "as if bewailing" in the second line, and the introduction of the idea of beauty in the last line, tell us that human emotions and value-judgments are not entirely absent from the composition.

But as Stuart Dischell's poem "Cheats" shows, the third-person voice can also allow the poet a high degree of involvement with the inner realm. Dischell's voice, comic but also open to more serious concerns, is one of enfolding intimacy. The poet hovers over the scene as an all-knowing presence, finding a bitter humor in his knowledge of what goes on in the private life behind the manager's facade of public responsibility.

Stuart Dischell

CHEATS

When the girls at the register cheat her, when they bag
the can of lentil soup on top of her bread and fruit,
When the prices on the packages don't match up,
Rotten berries buried in the center of the pint,
The chopped meat brown on the side that faces down,   5
The frankfurters green below their plastic wrapping,
In a rage she circles the items on the receipt
And packs them up to take them back. At the market
She shouts for the manager, a man used to complaints.
He answers her in a booming vice, thinking she can't   10
Hear him as he goes over each of the products and shakes
His head, disgusted with her or the moldy fruit.
"Good for you," says a man who is cutting coupons
At the courtesy booth and pats her on the shoulder.
"They're all a bunch of crooks." But the fellow behind her,   15
Waiting for his check to be approved, clucks his tongue.
"It's not just the money it's the principle of the thing,"
She says as she carefully counts the coins and bills.
"You should pay me for my time." The manager smiles
Down on her, an old lady with a blue cloud of hair.   20
From behind the high booth he is a giant, a sun,
A Supreme Court Justice, all the occupations
He might have been. He'd like to tell this lady
And the whole store about his wife's medical bills,
The problems with his car, his daughter's drug habit.   25
He'd like to shout it over the loud speaker
As if he were announcing a special on Fig Newtons.
He'd like to rip off his apron and leap into the clouds
Like Superman. He'd like to get into the pants

Of the punked-out stock boy. Then just punch 30
The time clock once and for all. Punch it for real
Like they do in cartoons. "Have a good day," he says
Because it is Wednesday. "Have a safe weekend," he'd say
If today were Friday. The woman sighs and says nothing.
She walks past the bag boys and gum machines, the rubber 35
Hen on a nest of prizes, the wooden pony, and the bottle
Redemption center. She steps toward the doors and they open
For her in an instant; they open as if by magic.

As you read the
following discussion,
consider these
questions:

1. Dischell's "Cheats" is in the third person, yet the voice is very different from the detached voice in Ammons's "Bonus" (see above). How does Dischell convey a sense of wry intimacy?

2. Pick out phrases that give this poem a sense of natural ease. Are there others that strike you as more "poetic"? What is the effect of their juxtaposition?

3. Try to write your own version of a supermarket poem—first in imitation of Dischell, then in the first person (see Ginsberg's "Supermarket in California" in Chapter 27). What difference do you find in the approaches?

Discussion: First-Person Voice. The first-person voice likewise offers a fairly diverse menu of options for the poet. As I noted earlier, the use of the "I" has been a staple of lyric poetry from the very beginnings of the art. Most commonly, though, the poet would attempt to universalize the "I." When Wordsworth writes

> A slumber did my spirit seal;
>   I had no human fears:
> She seem'd a thing that could not feel
>   The touch of earthly years.
>   *From "A Slumber Did My Spirit Seal"*

he is using the first person as a pivot-point, as a place to speak from. We do not feel that we are getting a privileged look into the life of the man that was William Wordsworth.

The same is true to an even greater degree in the work of a poet like Walt Whitman, who uses the "I" with hammering intensity. But Whitman, for all his openness about the body and sexuality, moves in the opposite direction from intimacy. When he writes

> I am the poet of the Body and I am the poet of the Soul,
>   The pleasures of heaven are with me and the pains of hell are
>   with me,
> The fist I graft and increase upon myself, the latter I translate
>   into a new tongue.

he is wearing the mantle of the *bard*. Bards were the epic poets in the Celtic tradition who declaimed before the tribal group, often accompanying themselves on the harp. The poet who speaks as a bard is taking on a role, casting himself not so much as a singular individual as a representative figure—a spokesperson.

Then, in the 1950s, the movement that would come to be known as "Confessionalism" began in American poetry. Poets like Robert Lowell, W. D. Snodgrass, Anne Sexton, and others opened a whole new frontier; the first-person "I" would never be the same. In essence, these poets began to write a poetry that refused to use the "I" in a representative way. They focused, instead, on the particulars of the private self. And the voice in their poems was open, starkly direct, and very often gave expression to the darker fears and longings (hence "Confessional").

The effect of this new mode upon American poetry was tremendously liberating, for it not only opened up whole new areas of subject matter—the previously hidden personal life of the poet—but it also expanded the possibilities of voice. A whole range of new tonalities became available. The community of readers felt the wind of revelation blowing through the pages of their books. Reading the works of these poets often felt like eavesdropping on a person's innermost thoughts. Now that the mode has become a norm of its own, it's hard to imagine that a poem like this one by Robert Lowell once struck readers as radical, even shocking.

Robert Lowell

THE OLD FLAME

My old flame, my wife!
Remember our lists of birds?
One morning last summer, I drove
by our house in Maine. It was still
on top of its hill—   5

Now a red ear of Indian maize
was splashed on the door.
Old Glory with thirteen stars
hung on a pole. The clapboard
was old-red schoolhouse red.   10

Inside, a new landlord,
a new wife, a new broom!
Atlantic seaboard antique shop
pewter and plunder
shone in each room.   15

A new frontier!
No running next door
now to phone the sheriff
for his taxi to Bath
and the State Liquor Store!   20

No one saw your ghostly
imaginary lover
stare through the window,
and tighten
the scarf at his throat.   25

Health to the new people,
health to their flag, to their old
restored house on the hill!
Everything had been swept bare,
furnished, garnished, and aired.   30

Everything's changed for the best—
how quivering and fierce we were,
there snowbound together,
simmering like wasps
in our tent of books!   35

Poor ghost, old love, speak
with your old voice
of flaming insight
that kept us awake all night.
In one bed and apart,   40

we heard the plow
groaning up hill—
a red light, then a blue,
as it tossed off the snow
to the side of the road.   45

As you read the following discussion, consider these questions:	1. Lowell uses the first-person voice. Read the poem carefully and speculate on the character of the speaker. What is his attitude toward his past?
	2. Do you feel included or excluded by Lowell's intimacy in this poem? Explain. Imagine you are the person addressed in the first line. How would your reaction be different?
	3. What descriptive details does Lowell use, and what do these suggest about the life the poet shared with his wife?

Discussion. In this poem, Lowell takes the great liberty of presenting the details of his life directly, without generalizing or explaining. As readers, we must imagine the relationship of husband and wife, as well as the circumstances of their parting. We are not always sure how to interpret the information. Does the reference to the State Liquor Store imply that husband and wife drank to excess, or is it a passing mention and nothing more? There are mysteries and blank patches. But by the same token, the straightforward tone and the selection of detail establish strong credibility. We trust the voice, believe what it tells us. And when we experience the unexpected force of the final image—the plow pushing the snow to the side of the road—we feel that we know something about the inner life of the poet.

A far more dramatic, and controversial, instance of a poet venting her private feelings is found in Sylvia Plath's well-known poem "Daddy." But in this case, even though the poet makes use of the "I," we are not reading a simple transcription of the private life. Rather, Plath has projected her powerful emotions—rage mixed with love—through an alter ego, or persona. Though she is declaring what must be real feelings, she has given the father–daughter conflict the shape of a fictitious dramatic situation. When the poem first appeared, the head-on frankness of the voice, coupled with the specificity of the details, convinced many readers that Plath's father had been a Nazi. He had not. But Plath was intent upon capturing a truth of a different kind.

Sylvia Plath

DADDY

You do not do, you do not do
Any more, black shoe
In which I have lived like a foot
For thirty years, poor and white,
Barely daring to breathe or Achoo.

Daddy, I have had to kill you.
You died before I had time—
Marble-heavy, a bag full of God,
Ghastly statue with one gray toe
Big as a Frisco seal   10

And a head in the freakish Atlantic
Where it pours bean green over blue
In the waters off beautiful Nauset.°
I used to pray to recover you.
Ach, du.   15

In the German tongue, in the Polish town
Scraped flat by the roller
Of wars, wars, wars.
But the name of the town is common.
My Polack friend   20

Says there are a dozen or two.
So I never could tell where you
Put your foot, your root,
I never could talk to you.
The tongue stuck in my jaw.   25

DADDY. 13 *Nauset:* beach on Cape Cod, Mass.

It stuck in a barb wire snare.
Ich, ich, ich, ich,
I could hardly speak.
I thought every German was you.
And the language obscene   30

An engine, an engine
Chuffing me off like a Jew.
A Jew to Dachau,° Auschwitz,° Belsen.°
I began to talk like a Jew.
I think I may well be a Jew.   35

The snows of the Tyrol,° the clear beer of Vienna
Are not very pure or true.
With my gipsy ancestress and my weird luck
And my Taroc° pack and my Taroc pack
I may be a bit of a Jew.   40

I have always been scared of *you*,
With your Luftwaffe,° your gobbledygoo.
And your neat mustache
And your Aryan eye, bright blue.
Panzer°-man, panzer-man, O You—   45

Not God but a swastika
So black no sky could squeak through.
Every woman adores a Fascist,
The boot in the face, the brute
Brute heart of a brute like you.   50

You stand at the blackboard, daddy,
In the picture I have of you,
A cleft in your chin instead of your foot
But no less a devil for that, no not
Any less the black man who   55

Bit my pretty red heart in two.
I was ten when they buried you.
At twenty I tried to die
And get back, back, back to you.
I thought even the bones would do.   60

But they pulled me out of the sack,
And they stuck me together with glue.
And then I knew what to do.
I made a model of you,
A man in black with a Meinkampf° look   65

And a love of the rack and the screw.
And I said I do, I do.

---

33 *Dachau; Auschwitz; Belsen:* Nazi death camps.   36 *Tyrol:* region of the Austrian/Italian Alps.
39 *Taroc:* cards used for fortune-telling.   42 *Luftwaffe:* WW II German air force.   45 *Panzer:* WW II
German armor and tanks.   65 *Meinkampf:* Hitler's autobiography.

Voice in Poetry

So daddy, I'm finally through.
The black telephone's off at the root,
The voices just can't worm through.

70

If I've killed one man, I've killed two—
The vampire who said he was you
And drank my blood for a year,
Seven years, if you want to know.
Daddy, you can lie back now.

75

There's a stake in your fat black heart
And the villagers never liked you.
They are dancing and stamping on you.
They always *knew* it was you.
Daddy, daddy, you bastard, I'm through.

80

As you read the following discussion, consider these questions:

1. Like Lowell's "The Old Flame" (preceding), Plath's "Daddy" uses direct address. Compare the emotions of the speakers. Which is the more intimate poem? Explain your answer.

2. As we see from her title, Plath speaks—at least in part—from the vantage of a child. How does this add power to the poem? Find the places where she departs from the believable tone of a young girl. What is the effect of the different voices juxtaposed?

3. Do you imagine Plath is addressing her real father? In what ways do you imagine "Daddy" is autobiographical? Explain.

Discussion. The difference between "Daddy" and "The Old Flame" is worth noting. Lowell's poem is no less carefully written than Plath's, yet it conveys the casualness of a letter or a conversation between people who know each other very well. Both poems are addressed in the second-person singular, to a "you," but the voice in "Daddy" is charged and dramatic. Plath achieves tremendous power not only through her selective use of charged imagery, but also through the thudding recurrence of simple rhyme sounds and a *diction*, or word use, that is simultaneously sophisticated and childlike. It is as if the "I" who has "lived like a foot/ For thirty years" supplies the contents and references ("The snows of the Tyrol, the clear beer of Vienna") while the child inside comes up with expressions very near to jingles in their simplicity: "Panzer-man, panzer-man; O You—".

The territory of self-as-subject has now been fully colonized. Indeed, it is safe to say that the great majority of poems written in our time are to greater or lesser degree personal. Some are funny, others quite serious or dramatic, and the approaches vary considerably. Certain poets choose to be straightforwardly autobiographical, presenting episodes from their lives very much as they happened. Others use the "I," but find ways to universalize, or perhaps mute, the intimacy of their material.

Rita Dove, an African American poet, has found an affecting way to approach private subject matter—a girl's arrival at puberty—in symbolic terms. The poem is at once urgent and mysterious. As with so many first-person poems, it is not entirely clear whether the speaker is using the confessional "I" and telling about her own experience, or whether she has imagined herself into the persona of a young girl.

Rita Dove

ADOLESCENCE—II

Although it is night, I sit in the bathroom, waiting.
Sweat prickles behind my knees, the baby-breasts are alert.
Venetian blinds slice up the moon; the tiles quiver in pale strips.

Then they come, the three seal men with eyes as round
As dinner plates and eyelashes like sharpened tines.   5
They bring the scent of licorice. One sits in the washbowl,

One on the bathtub edge; one leans against the door.
"Can you feel it yet?" they whisper.
I don't know what to say, again. They chuckle,

Patting their sleek bodies with their hands.   10
"Well, maybe next time." And they rise,
Glittering like pools of ink under moonlight,

And vanish. I clutch at the ragged holes
They leave behind, here at the edge of darkness.
Night rests like a ball of fur on my tongue.   15

Read the discussion preceding the poem and consider these questions:

1. Dove's poem, like Plath's "Daddy," is in the first person. Compare the two poets' use of imagery to express feelings. How does the imagery reflect the vantage of the speaker?
2. How does Dove's use of imagery suggest the anxieties of adolescence? Cite two specific images and explain their effect.

With most persona poems, however, it is quite clear that the poet has picked an identity to inhabit. Whether it is Robert Browning writing a dramatic monologue in the voice of some historical personage, or a young contemporary, like Puerto Rico–born poet Martín Espada, assuming the voice of a poor janitor, the reader knows full well to whom the "I" belongs.

Martín Espada

JORGE THE CHURCH JANITOR FINALLY QUITS

No one asks
where I am from,
I must be
from the country of janitors,
I have always mopped this floor.
Honduras, you are a squatter's camp

outside the city
of their understanding.

No one can speak
my name,
I host the fiesta
of the bathroom,
stirring the toilet
like a punchbowl.
The Spanish music of my name
is lost
when the guests complain
about toilet paper.

What they say
must be true:
I am smart,
but I have a bad attitude.

No one knows
that I quit tonight,
maybe the mop
will push on without me,
sniffing along the floor
like a crazy squid
with stringy gray tentacles.
They will call it Jorge.

10

15

20

25

30

As you read the
following discussion,
consider these
questions:

1. How does Espada's "I" differ from that of Lowell's (p. 569) and Plath's (p. 571)?

2. Compare Jorge's imagining in the last stanza with Dove's (see above) in her last two stanzas. How do these imaginings help you to understand the state of the "I"?

3. What is Jorge's attitude toward his surroundings, his world? Do you trust his voice? Explain your answer.

Discussion. The voice, then, can be pitched with the most detached neutrality or with extraordinary intimacy. The poet must choose the vantage by determining the effect desired. Once that choice has been made, then it is a matter of deciding what *tone* to take. Should the voice be direct, or understated, or playful, or emotional, or ironic? The poem sets the agenda; the poet must trust that the reader will know how to read the tone. There is no mystery about this. We make the same decisions in our daily communication with others, and we ask the same questions when we are being addressed. Who is speaking? What is being said? What is the speaker's attitude about what is being said? The big difference is that as readers we cannot monitor facial expressions or interpret the intonations of the voice. We have only the words on the page to guide our reactions. But common sense will carry us most of the way. When we read a poem like "Jorge the Church Janitor Finally Quits," we are reasonably sure that the speaker is serious. We proceed as we do in most social contexts. That is, we take the communication at face value until something alerts us not to. And while Jorge does lapse into darkly humorous imaginings ("No one knows/ that I quit tonight,/ maybe the mop/ will push on without me,"), we know that he is voicing real feelings.

When we are given no reason to question the speaker's attitude, we measure the meaning accordingly. We trust that Robert Lowell, in "The Old Flame," is confiding actual thoughts and responses; we take him literally. When we read Sylvia Plath's "Daddy," on the other hand, we might find ourselves making certain adjustments. While we trust that the speaker is sincere in the expression of rage, we may also allow that she is exaggerating her assertions for greater effect—that she is using *hyperbole*, or overstatement.

Sometimes, however, we find that there is a sizable gulf between *what* is being said and *how* it is conveyed in the poem. Here is a case in point:

Robert Frost

FIRE AND ICE

Some say the world will end in fire,
Some say in ice.
From what I've tasted of desire
I hold with those who favor fire.
But if I had to perish twice,   5
I think I know enough of hate
To say that for destruction ice
Is also great
And would suffice.

As you read the following discussion, consider these questions:

1. Here is a first-person poem with no autobiographical elements. Compare Frost's philosophizing with that of Keats in "On the Grasshopper and the Cricket" (p. 565). Explain how each manifests a different authority.

2. What would you say has been the life experience of Frost's speaker? Explain your answer.

Discussion. Frost is making a serious point about human nature here, but his understated tone is completely at odds with his message. The discrepancy gives a chilling effect, and it makes us think more deeply about the statement than we might if it were hedged around with exclamation points.

Frost's understatement comes very close to being *irony*, but it stops short. True irony uses words to convey the opposite of their intended meaning. Frost's expression hovers at the borderline. If he had written, in the final line, "and would be nice," then we could identify the poem as overtly ironical.

IRONY

In poetry, as in other literary genres, there are three major kinds of irony—*dramatic, situational,* and *verbal.* Dramatic irony depends upon the contrast between the speaker's perception of a situation and the perception held by the reader. It is more commonly found in longer dramatic works than in short lyrics, for the obvious reason that it requires a developed context. A speaks of B in tones of trust, while we know that B has been unfaithful; C carries on about future plans, unaware that she has taken poison and will soon die. The mode is most commonly found in dramas written for the stage—hence the name.

Situational irony, on the other hand, involves a confounding of the reader's expectations. Led to expect or believe one thing, we suddenly confront a different outcome. Percy Bysshe Shelley's sonnet "Ozymandias" is often cited for its masterful use of situational irony.

Percy Bysshe Shelley

OZYMANDIAS

I met a traveler from an antique land
Who said: Two vast and trunkless legs of stone
Stand in the desert. Near them, on the sand,
Half sunk, a shattered visage lies, whose frown,
And wrinkled lip, and sneer of cold command,   5
Tell that its sculptor well those passions read
Which yet survive, stamped on these lifeless things,
The hand that mocked them, and the heart that fed;
And on the pedestal these words appear:
"My name is Ozymandias, king of kings: 10
Look on my works, ye Mighty, and despair!"
Nothing beside remains. Round the decay
Of that colossal wreck, boundless and bare
The lone and level sands stretch far away.

As you read the following discussion, consider these questions:

1. Shelley has enclosed one speaker's voice (the traveler's) inside another's. And Ozymandias's words are embedded in the traveler's. How do these voices differ? Why do we need the first-person "I"? Would the poem work if it began with the traveler's account?

2. What is the worldview (the life philosophy) of the traveler? How is his tone (his address) suited to the subject of his report?

3. What is the traveler's response to the ruins and the words of Ozymandias? What is yours?

Discussion. As the poet leads us through the desert landscape of ruins, we accept a large view of time and reckon the folly of human pretensions. We are then startled by the ancient boast that survives on the vacant pedestal. The context renders the proclamation ironic in the extreme, and our understanding of the vanity of human deeds is intensified all the more.

Verbal irony, by contrast, does not arise so much from the presentation of situation as from variations struck from the expected uses of words. The most common kind of verbal irony is simple reversal. The speaker says one thing and means another, perhaps the very opposite. We look out at the rain and remark to a friend, "Nice day, huh?"

But verbal irony need not necessarily turn the meaning on its head. Poets will often create ironic effects by playing against the reader's expectations. Consider these lines from Philip Larkin's poem, "Love":

> The difficult part of love
> Is being selfish enough,
> Is having the blind persistence
> To upset an existence
> Just for your own sake.
> What cheek it must take.

As any reader familiar with Larkin will tell you, the poet does not hold a high opinion of love. There may indeed be no irony in his words. Nevertheless, the poem depends upon verbal irony for its effect. Cynic though he may be, Larkin also knows that his statements run exactly counter to the popularly held beliefs about love.

VOICE: EXAMPLES AND QUESTIONS

William Wordsworth

THREE YEARS SHE GREW

Three years she grew in sun and shower,
Then Nature said, "A lovelier flower
On earth was never sown;
This child I to myself will take:
She shall be mine, and I will make   5
A lady of my own.

"Myself will to my darling be
Both law and impulse: and with me
The girl, in rock and plain,
In earth and heaven, in glade and bower,°   *a shaded garden retreat* 10

Shall feel an overseeing power
To kindle or restrain.

"She shall be sportive as the fawn
That wild with glee across the lawn
Or up the mountain springs;
And hers shall be the breathing balm,
And hers the silence and the calm
Of mute insensate things.

"The floating clouds their state shall lend
To her; for her the willow bend;
Nor shall she fail to see
Even in the motions of the storm
Grace that shall mold the maiden's form
By silent sympathy.

"The stars of midnight shall be dear
To her; and she shall lean her ear
In many a secret place
Where rivulets dance their wayward round,
And beauty born of murmuring sound
Shall pass into her face.

"And vital feelings of delight
Shall rear her form to stately height,
Her virgin bosom swell;
Such thoughts to Lucy I will give
While she and I together live
Here in this happy dell."

Thus Nature spake.—The work was done.—
How soon my Lucy's race was run!
She died, and left to me
This heath, this calm and quiet scene;
The memory of what has been,
And never more will be.

QUESTIONS

1. Identify the two voices in this poem and characterize both.
2. Nature is usually conceived as an indifferent force moving through all things. How does Wordsworth's treatment differ?
3. What is the attitude expressed by the voice of Nature toward Lucy? Is she being granted eternal life in the familiar Christian sense? If not, then explain the sort of transformation that is described.
4. Do you think that the speaker really believes that this is the voice of Nature? What other interpretation could be offered for this lofty speech?
5. Do Nature's words, or the speaker's imagining of them, finally reconcile him to the loss of Lucy? How does the tone of the final stanza differ from that of the preceding stanzas?

Ellen Bryant Voigt

QUARREL

Since morning they have been quarreling—
the sun pouring its implacable white bath
over the birches, each one undressing
slyly, from the top down—and they hammer
at each other with their knives, nailfiles,   5
graters of complaint as the day unwinds,
the plush clouds lowering a gray matte°   *a dull surface finish*
for the red barn. Lunch, the soup
like batting in their mouths, last week,
last year, they're moving on to always   10
and never, their shrill pitiful children
crowd around but they see the top of this
particular mountain, its glacial headwall,
the pitch is terrific all through dinner,
and they are committed, the sun long gone,   15
the two of them back to back in the blank
constricting bed, like marbles on aluminum—
O this fierce love
that needs to reproduce in one another
wounds inflicted by the world.   20

QUESTIONS

1. Here is a poem in the third person. What is the attitude of the voice that narrates to the couple?

2. How does the image of the sun "pouring its implacable white bath over the birches" correlate to the perspective of the poem? How do we see the struggles of the couple within that perspective?

3. How does the chronology of the day's events intensify the impression of distance?

4. Characterize the tone of the poem. Is Voigt compassionate, pitying, judgmental, or neutral in her presentation? Explain.

5. When Voigt writes "O this fierce love," do you imaging that she is speaking ironically? How does Voigt create the impression that this quarrel is like a force of nature, that it is greater than either husband or wife?

6. Do you believe that the fight is just part of a familiar cycle in the emotional life of the couple? Or is it the blow that will part them? Cite evidence from the poem to explain your answer.

7. How do the last three lines change the focus of the poem and shift the sense of blame? Do the lines change your attitude toward the situation described? How so?

Wislawa Szymborska

THE TERRORIST, HE WATCHES

The bomb will go off in the bar at one twenty p.m.
Now it's only one sixteen p.m.

580

Some will still have time to get in,
some to get out.

The terrorist has already crossed to the other side of the street.   5
The distance protects him from any danger,
and what a sight for sore eyes:

A woman in a yellow jacket, she goes in.
A man in dark glasses, he comes out.
Guys in jeans, they are talking.   10
One seventeen and four seconds.
That shorter guy's really got it made, and gets on a scooter,
and that taller one, he goes in.

One seventeen and forty seconds.
That girl there, she's got a green ribbon in her hair.   15
Too bad that bus just cut her off.
One eighteen p.m.
The girl's not there any more.
Was she dumb enough to go in, or wasn't she?
That we'll see when they carry them out.   20

One nineteen p.m.
No one seems to be going in.
Instead a fat baldy's coming out.
Like he's looking for something in his pockets and
at one nineteen and fifty seconds   25
he goes back for those lousy gloves of his.

It's one twenty p.m.
The time, how it drags.
Should be any moment now.
Not yet.   30
Yes, this is it.
The bomb, it goes off.

QUESTIONS

1. Explain, briefly, the narrative logic of the poem.

2. Isolate the two voices and locate the point at which the switch takes place.

3. Characterize the terrorist's voice, the tone of the comments?

4. How does Szymborska link the voice of the opening stanzas and the voice of the terrorist?

5. Find several instances of the terrorist's casual diction. How does the informality play against the larger reality of the situation?

6. What is the effect of the understatement of the last few lines? Does it heighten or lessen the impact of the event? Explain.

7. What do you imagine is Szymborska's intention in writing this poem? What comment is she making upon events of this kind?

Robert Browning

MY LAST DUCHESS

FERRARA°

That's my last Duchess painted on the wall,
Looking as if she were alive. I call
That piece a wonder, now: Frà° Pandolf's hands
Worked busily a day, and there she stands
Will't please you sit and look at her? I said   5
"Frà Pandolf" by design, for never read
Strangers like you that pictured countenance,
The depth and passion of its earnest glance,
But to myself they turned (since none puts by
The curtain I have drawn for you, but I)   10
And seemed as they would ask me, if they durst,
How such a glance came there; so, not the first
Are you to turn and ask thus. Sir, 'twas not
Her husband's presence only, called that spot
Of joy into the Duchess' cheek; perhaps   15
Frà Pandolf chanced to say, "Her mantle laps
Over my lady's wrist too much," or "Paint
Must never hope to reproduce the faint
Half-flush that dies along her throat": such stuff
Was courtesy, she thought, and cause enough   20
For calling up that spot of joy. She had
A heart—how shall I say?—too soon made glad,
Too easily impressed; she liked whate'er
She looked on, and her looks went everywhere.
Sir, 'twas all one! My favour at her breast,   25
The dropping of the daylight in the West,
The bough of cherries some officious fool
Broke in the orchard for her, the white mule
She rode with round the terrace—all and each
Would draw from her alike the approving speech,   30
Or blush, at least. She thanked men,—good! but thanked
Somehow—I know now how—as if she ranked
My gift of a nine-hundred-years-old name
With anybody's gift. Who'd stoop to blame
This sort of trifling? Even had you skill   35
In speech—(which I have not)—to make your will
Quite clear to such an one, and say, "Just this
Or that in you disgusts me; here you miss,
Or there exceed the mark"—and if she let
Herself be lessoned so, nor plainly set   40
Her wits to yours, forsooth,° and made excuse,

MY LAST DUCHESS. *Ferrara:* a city in Northern Italy. 3 *Frà:* Brother—a friar's title. 41 *forsooth:* in truth (archaic).

—E'en then would be some stooping; and I choose
Never to stoop. Oh sir, she smiled, no doubt,
Whene'er I passed her; but who passed without
Much the same smile? This grew; I gave commands;   45
Then all smiles stopped together. There she stands
As if alive. Will't please you rise? We'll meet
The company below, then, I repeat,
The Count your master's known munificence
Is ample warrant that no just pretence   50
Of mine for dowry will be disallowed;
Though his fair daughter's self, as I avowed
At starting, is my object. Nay, we'll go
Together down, sir. Notice Neptune, though,
Taming a sea-horse, thought a rarity   55
Which Claus of Innsbruck cast in bronze for me!

QUESTIONS

Robert Browning has written a dramatic monologue—a poem which is the speech of a single character, usually a historical figure.

1. What can you determine about the speaker of "My Last Duchess"? What is the "last Duchess" of the title? Who is the speaker addressing?

2. What is the narrative that emerges from the speaker's comments? How does his tone change as he explains the character of the woman in the painting?

3. What was it, finally, that the speaker held against the woman?

4. How does your sense of his true character change?

5. What does he mean when he says, "I gave commands"?

6. What is the effect of the speaker's changing the subject after this terse explanation? Comment on Browning's use of irony in the last three lines.

7. What did Browning finally want his reader to believe about the speaker?

SUGGESTION FOR WRITING

Imagine an analogous situation in modern dress—a lover commenting upon his or her absent mate. Write a monologue—in prose, if you prefer—in which the comments of the speaker allow the reader to build up a full picture of the situation between the two. Remember, the whole piece must be written to be spoken.

Ezra Pound

THE RIVER-MERCHANT'S WIFE: A LETTER

While my hair was still cut straight across my forehead
I played about the front gate, pulling flowers.
You came by on bamboo stilts, playing horse,
You walked about my seat, playing with blue plums.
And we went on living in the village of Chokan: 5
Two small people, without dislike or suspicion.

At fourteen I married My Lord you.
I never laughed, being bashful.
Lowering my head, I looked at the wall.
Called to, a thousand times, I never looked back.   10

At fifteen I stopped scowling,
I desired my dust to be mingled with yours
Forever and forever and forever.
Why should I climb the look out?

At sixteen you departed,   15
You went into far Ku-to-yen,° by the river of swirling eddies,
And you have been gone five months.
The monkeys make sorrowful noise overhead.

You dragged your feet when you went out.
By the gate now, the moss is grown, the different mosses,   20
Too deep to clear them away!
The leaves fall early this autumn, in wind.
The paired butterflies are already yellow with August
Over the grass in the West garden;
They hurt me. I grow older.   25
If you are coming down through the narrows of the river Kiang,
Please let me know beforehand,
And I will come out to meet you
                    As far as Cho-fu-Sa.

Translated by Rihaku

_____

    THE RIVER-MERCHANT'S WIFE: A LETTER. 16 *Ku-to-yen:* all the names refer to ancient regions of
China.

QUESTIONS

Ezra Pound claimed that this work was a translation from the poet Rihaku, but in fact it was
as much free creation as transcription.

1. Who is the speaker? What do you learn about her upbringing and her personality from the
images and explanations in her letter? How would you describe her tone? Does it fit what you
imagine to be the tone of a young wife writing to her husband? Explain your answer.

2. What is your sense of the "you" to whom the poem is addressed? What kind of relationship do you imagine the merchant's wife shared with her husband?

3. Can you find variations in the voice, suggestions that there might be strong emotions behind the reserve of the letter?

4. Look at Pound's use of various natural images, especially in the second half of the poem.
How do they contribute to the overall tone?

SUGGESTION FOR WRITING

Imagine a historical situation and write a letter from husband to wife or wife to husband. Try
to convey the state of feelings indirectly, through details and images.

Randall Jarrell

NEXT DAY

Moving from Cheer° to Joy,° from Joy to All,°
I take a box
And add it to my wild rice, my Cornish game hens.
The slacked or shorted, basketed, identical
Food-gathering flocks   5
Are selves I overlook. Wisdom, said William James,°

Is learning what to overlook. And I am wise
If that is wisdom.
Yet somehow, as I buy All from these shelves
And the boy takes it to my station wagon,   10
What I've become
Troubles me even if I shut my eyes.

When I was young and miserable and pretty
And poor, I'd wish
What all girls wish: to have a husband,   15
A house and children. Now that I'm old, my wish
Is womanish:
That the boy putting groceries in my car

See me. It bewilders me he doesn't see me.
For so many years   20
I was good enough to eat: the world looked at me
And its mouth watered. How often they have undressed me,
The eyes of strangers!
And, holding their flesh within my flesh, their vile

Imaginings within my imagining,   25
I too have taken
The chance of life. Now the boy pats my dog
And we start home. Now I am good.
The last mistaken,
Ecstatic, accidental bliss, the blind   30

Happiness that, bursting, leaves upon the palm
Some soap and water—
It was so long ago, back in some Gay
Twenties, Nineties, I don't know . . . Today I miss
My lovely daughter   35
Away at school, my sons away at school,

NEXT DAY. 1 *Cheer; Joy; All:* names of detergents, used punningly.   6 *William James:* American philosopher.

My husband away at work—I wish for them.
The dog, the maid,
And I go through the sure unvarying days
At home in them. As I look at my life,   40
I am afraid
Only that it will change, as I am changing:

I am afraid, this morning, of my face.
It looks at me
From the rear-view mirror, with the eyes I hate,   45
The smile I hate. Its plain, lined look
Of gray discovery
Repeats to me: "You're old." That's all, I'm old.

And yet I'm afraid, as I was at the funeral
I went to yesterday.   50
My friend's cold made-up face, granite among its flowers,
Her undressed, operated-on, dressed body
Were my face and body.
As I think of her I hear her telling me

How young I seem; I *am* exceptional;   55
I think of all I have.
But really no one is exceptional,
No one has anything, I'm anybody,
I stand beside my grave
Confused with my life, that is commonplace and solitary.   60

[1963]

QUESTIONS

1. The speaker in Randall Jarrell's poem is a woman. Describe her situation in life. What is she doing in the course of the poem? How does she present a self-portrait through memories?

2. What is the woman's attitude toward her life? How has she changed over the years?

3. What is the source of her regret? What triggers her emotions?

4. How does the woman's tone shift as she goes through different memories?

5. What recollection leads her to her last sad observation? What is the significance of the title?

6. Discuss how the poem's first line is ironic within the context of the whole.

C. P. Cavafy

THE GOD ABANDONS ANTONY

At midnight, when suddenly you hear
an invisible procession going by
with exquisite music, voices,

don't mourn your luck that's failing now,
work gone wrong, your plans   5
all proving deceptive—don't mourn them uselessly:
as one long prepared, and full of courage,
say goodbye to her, to Alexandria who is leaving.
Above all, don't fool yourself, don't say
it was a dream, your ears deceived you: 10
don't degrade yourself with empty hopes like these.
As one long prepared, and full of courage,
as is right for you who were given this kind of city,
go firmly to the window
and listen with deep emotion,   15
but not with the whining, the pleas of a coward;
listen—your final pleasure—to the voices,
to the exquisite music of that strange procession,
and say goodbye to her, to the Alexandria you are losing.

QUESTIONS

1. What is the effect of the second-person ("you") address? Do you feel that it invites you into the poem?
2. Read the poem aloud to yourself. What is Cavafy writing about? Write a short interpretation. How would the poem change if it were written in the first person? the third person?

Stephen Dobyns

HOW TO LIKE IT

These are the first days of fall. The wind
at evening smells of roads still to be traveled,
while the sound of leaves blowing across the lawns
is like an unsettled feeling in the blood,
the desire to get in a car and just keep driving.   5
A man and a dog descend their front steps.
The dog says, Let's go downtown and get crazy drunk.
Let's tip over all the trash cans we can find.
This is how dogs deal with the prospect of change.
But in his sense of the season, the man is struck   10
by the oppressiveness of his past, how his memories
which were shifting and fluid have grown more solid
until it seems he can see remembered faces
caught up among the dark places in the trees.
The dog says, Let's pick up some girls and just   15
rip off their clothes. Let's dig holes everywhere.
Above his house, the man notices wisps of cloud
crossing the face of the moon. Like in a movie,
he says to himself, a movie about a person

leaving on a journey. He looks down the street 20
to the hills outside of town and finds the cut
where the road heads north. He thinks of driving
on that road and the dusty smell of the car
heater, which hasn't been used since last winter.
The dog says, Let's go down to the diner and sniff 25
people's legs. Let's stuff ourselves on burgers.
In the man's mind, the road is empty and dark.
Pine trees press down to the edge of the shoulder,
where the eyes of animals, fixed in his headlights,
shine like small cautions against the night. 30
Sometimes a passing truck makes his whole car shake.
The dog says, Let's go to sleep. Let's lie down
by the fire and put our tails over our noses.
But the man wants to drive all night, crossing
one state line after another, and never stop 35
until the sun creeps into his rearview mirror.
Then he'll pull over and rest awhile before
starting again, and at dusk he'll crest a hill
and there, filling a valley, will be the lights
of a city entirely new to him. 40
But the dog says, Let's just go back inside.
Let's not do anything tonight. So they
walk back up the sidewalk to the front steps.
How is it possible to want so many things
and still want nothing? The man wants to sleep 45
and wants to hit his head again and again
against a wall. Why is it all so difficult?
But the dog says, Let's go make a sandwich.
Let's make the tallest sandwich anyone's ever seen.
And that's what they do and that's where the man's 50
wife finds him, staring into the refrigerator
as if into the place where the answers are kept—
the ones telling why you get up in the morning
and how it is possible to sleep at night,
answers to what comes next and how to like it. 55

QUESTIONS

1. Describe the narrative situation that Dobyns presents. In what ways is it preposterous?

2. What are the man's feelings and thoughts? What is his psychological crisis?

3. How do the suggestions of the dog counterpoint the man's thoughts? What is it that the dog seems to represent? Is there any wisdom in the dog's reactions? Do they add up to a kind of philosophy of life?

4. What is the effect of the two perspectives, the man's and the dog's, in combination?

5. Read the last five lines of the poem and explain how they relate to what the dog has been saying.

6. What is Dobyns's purpose in creating this uncanny scenario?

Write a version of this poem in which it is the man who speaks and the dog who thinks. Vary the situation as you see fit.

Robert Bly

THE EXECUTIVE'S DEATH

Merchants have multiplied more than the stars of heaven.
Half the population are like the long grasshoppers
That sleep in the bushes in the cool of the day:
The sound of their wings is heard at noon, muffled, near the
    earth.
The crane handler dies, the taxi driver dies, slumped over   5
In his taxi. Meanwhile, high in the air, executives
Walk on cool floors, and suddenly fall:
Dying, they dream they are lost in a snowstorm in mountains,
On which they crashed, carried at night by great machines.
As he lies on the wintry slope, cut off and dying,   10
A pine stump talks to him of Goethe and Jesus.
Commuters arrive in Hartford at dusk like moles
Or hares flying from a fire behind them,
And the dusk in Hartford is full of their sighs;
Their trains come through the air like a dark music,   15
Like the sound of horns, the sound of thousands of small wings.

QUESTIONS

1. What sort of vision does Bly depict by using the third person? Imagine that Bly has begun the poem with the words "I have seen." How does this change the effect of his words?
2. Read the poem carefully. How do the words relate to the title? Write a short paragraph explaining what you think the poem is about.

18 Rhythm and Meter in Poetry

All good writing is characterized by rhythm, but nowhere is it so pronounced and deliberate as in poetry. Rhythm is a natural holdover from poetry's origins in tribal song and chant. For most of the long history of the art, particularly in the West, the rhythms have been organized more or less strictly into patterns, or *meters*. Meters are sequences of stressed and unstressed syllables, which are customarily divided into *feet*. We will examine what these are and how they function shortly, but first a few reflections are in order.

RHYTHM

To begin with, it is important to understand that rhythms and meters are not artificial, but natural. All speech is rhythmic, though all speech is not necessarily effectively rhythmic. Rhythm is a direct consequence of the fact that words are made up of syllables that are both stressed and unstressed. We don't say *syl-la-bles* with equal weight on each part of the word. We tend to pronounce the word with a strong stress on the first syllable, and lesser emphasis on the second and third. Thus: sýl-lă-blĕs. If we combine this word with others we get different rhythmic results. The phrase "effortless speaking of syllables"—éf-fŏrt-lĕss spéak-ĭng ŏf sýl-lă-blĕs—makes a pattern that a poet would identify as a *dactylic trimeter*, or a line in three *feet* with a recurrent ´ ˘ ˘ meter. But, as indicated, every sentence has an underlying rhythm:

é-vĕr-ў sén-tĕnce hăs ăn ún-dĕr-lý-ĭng *rhýthm*.

The one I have just written is irregular.

Metered poetry (free verse, which does not make use of metric patterns, will be treated later) is not sing-song poetry—unless, of course, it is badly written, or unless the poet deliberately seeks the effect of a lulling monotony. Poets recognized millenia ago that language could be arranged into patterns that would both captivate the ear and intensify the emotion or meaning to be expressed by way of emphasis. They discovered that between the tendencies of natural pronunciation and the discipline of pattern there existed an exciting tension that could activate the speaker's sense of the language. Recall the first two lines of Robert Frost's "The Birches," which were discussed earlier. Though the meter of the lines is a perfectly regular iambic pentameter (five feet in a uniform pattern of short/long, or ˘ ´),

Whĕn Í sĕe bír-chĕs bénd tŏ léft ănd ríght

Ă-cróss thĕ línes ŏf stráight-ĕr dárk-ĕr trées

we do not naturally speak them with unwavering repetition. Certainly not the second line. The meter is regular, but tension arises when we give the words *straighter* and *darker* their natural beat. That tension, when combined with our sense of the underlying meter, heightens our impression of straightness and darkness. Poets who write in meter, as we will soon see, spend as much time deviating from their patterns as adhering to them. They recognize what a dulling effect a perfectly regular singsong would have.

Regular meter, then, is a device for enhancing emphasis—and memorability. It is not so much imposed straitjacket-like on the language as discovered there. If he were writing casual prose, or speaking to a neighbor, Frost might have phrased his perception thus: "When I see those birch trees bending to the left and to the right across the lines made by the straighter and darker trees . . ." the sense would have been quite the same. What he did, in effect, was to prune the bush, revealing a regularity that gives the statement an added weight. A rightness. The iambic pattern—the possibility of it—was already there in the phrasing. He did with words what any good photographer would do with a subject: he framed the composition to bring out a stronger form.

METER

Meters are sequences of stressed and unstressed syllables. They are divided into *feet*, or units, because in normal speech we tend to pronounce strings of sounds in clusters. Meter is a slight formalization of a natural tendency.

The most common meter in poetry—and speech—is *iambic*; that is, a short syllable followed by a long syllable:

> Thĕre wás ă fár-mĕr hád ă dóg, ănd Bín-gŏ wás hĭs náme-ŏ.

The opposite of an iambic meter is *trochaic*, where a long, or stressed, syllable precedes a short (´ ˘):

> Óld Măc-Dón-aĭd hád ă fárm—é-ĭ-é-ĭ-ó.

A foot with three beats can either be *anapestic*, or unstressed/unstressed/stressed (˘ ˘ ´), as in

> Bў thĕ séa, bў thĕ séa, bў thĕ béau-tĭ-fŭl séa

or *dactylic:* stressed/unstressed/unstressed (´ ˘ ˘), as in

> Híck-ŏrў díck-ŏrў dóck.

The feet are called, respectively, *iambs*, *trochees*, *anapests*, and *dactyls*.

To achieve some particular effect or emphasis, poets will often make use of a *spondaic* foot (a *spondee*), made up of two stressed syllables (´ ´)—

> I told the child "Stóp thát!"

—or a *pyrrhic* (˘ ˘), which is much less common.

The different metric patterns are found in lines of varying length. These are named according to the number of feet they contain, as follows:

monometer: one foot
dimeter: two feet
trimeter: three feet
tetrameter: four feet
pentameter: five feet
hexameter (or Alexandrine): six feet
heptameter: seven feet

Lines of poetry seldom get any longer than a heptameter; metered verse is most commonly tetrameter, pentameter, or hexameter. The lines are generally arranged by the poet in groupings called *stanzas*, which will be taken up in a later section.

The formal process of counting out and marking feet is known as *scansion*. The usual procedure is to break the feet with a vertical mark, and to indicate stressed and unstressed syllables with markings:

Shĕ walks / ĭn béau- / tў líke / thĕ níght   (Byron)

or

Frŏm lów / tŏ hígh / dŏth dís- / sŏ-lú / tiŏn clímb   (Wordsworth)

So far, because I have picked simple and regular lines, the business of scansion appears almost mechanical. Actually, however, few lines, even in the most meter-conscious poets, are perfectly regular, and a great many are marked by pauses. These are found wherever the poet has placed a comma, or a period, or if we are more exacting, wherever one naturally might break for breath. The pause is called a *caesura* (from the Latin for "cut") and is marked with a double slash: //.

The Wordsworth line should actually be scanned like this:

Frŏm lów / tŏ hígh // dŏth dís- / sŏ-lú / tiŏn clímb

for there is a slight natural pause after "high." A more obvious caesura, also from Wordsworth, is found in the line

Sŭr-prísed / bў jóy— // ĭm-pá- / tiĕnt ás / thĕ wínd—

By now it must be more clear that the poet has a number of linguistic and poetic resources to make use of to achieve specific effects. The choice of a kind of meter and a length of line are important. Anapests and dactyls make for speed and lightness, as do shorter line lengths. By contrast, an iambic hexameter can create a sense of slow muscularity, as in

Thăt líke / ă woúnd- / ĕd snáke / drágs ĭts / slów léngth / ă-lóng.

(Note that the fifth foot is a spondee, deliberately placed to emphasize the slowness of movement.)

Another option for the poet is the line ending. This can take the form of a full stop—a period—or a significant pause, as indicated by a comma, or a natural breathing pause, as when a cluster of words ends with an emphasis. The first stanza of Emily Dickinson's "A Narrow Fellow in the Grass" illustrates all three:

A narrow fellow in the grass	**Natural pause**
Occasionally rides;	**Significant pause**
You may have met him,—did you not?	**Full stop**
His notice sudden is.	**Full stop**

Each one of these lines is *end-stopped*.

The poet can also use *run-on* or *enjambed* lines to orchestrate other effects, either of conversational casualness, or, as in this first stanza of W. H. Auden's Preface to *The Sea and the Mirror*, specific sensation:

> The aged catch their breath,
> For the nonchalant couple go
> Waltzing across the tightrope
> As if there were no death
> Or hope of falling down;   5
> The wounded cry as the clown
> Doubles his meaning, and O
> How the dear little children laugh
> When the drums roll and the lovely
> Lady is sawn in half.   10

The enjambment in line two heightens the sense of the perilous, forcing the reader to make a slight wobble of transition. In the sixth line, the pause after *clown*, slight as it is, stresses the suddenness of the clown's contortion. The slight hesitation in the shift in the ninth line from *lovely* to *lady* underscores the sundering action of the saw.

Finally, there is the all-important matter of *substitution*. In the earlier discussion of Frost's "The Birches," I emphasized that poet's skill at setting up a rhythmic expectation (in that case of iambic pentameter) and then surprising the reader's ear with variations. The poet's job is to hold the attention and to use the myriad expressive possibilities of language. Substitution, or variation, is the most common and adaptable of all techniques. The possible applications are infinite.

Shakespeare, from "Sonnet LXXIII":

> That time of year thou mayst in me behold
> When yellow leaves, or none, or few, do hang
> Upon those boughs which shake against the cold,
> Bare ruin'd choirs, where late the sweet birds sang.

In these four lines, Shakespeare builds carefully toward the surprise of the fourth line. He lulls the reader's ear with three lines of perfectly regular iambic pentameter; his strategy is to shock the reader with the stark spondee substitution (in fact, he has three successive stresses) of Báre ruín'd chóirs. We feel the speaker's own sense of devastation at the works of time.

William Butler Yeats, from "Leda and the Swan":

> A sudden blow: the great wings beating still
> Above the staggering girl, her thighs caressed
> By the dark webs, her nape caught in his bill,
> He holds her helpless breast upon his breast.

The subject in these opening lines of Yeats's poem is the myth of the rape of Leda by Zeus disguised as a swan. The poet uses his meters and variations to enact a vividly rhythmic version of the event. The lines scan thus:

> Ă súd- / děn blów: // the greát / wings beát- / ing stíll
> Ă-bóve / the stág- / ger-ing / gírl, // her thíghs / car-essed

Bў the / dárk webs, // her nápe / caúght in / his bíll,
He hólds / her hélp- / less breást / u-pón / his breást.

The lines begin in iambs, and the basic pattern is that of iambic pentameter. The spondee in the fourth foot on line 1 emphasizes the greatness of the wings. The next line poses scansion problems, for Yeats has taken the liberty of adding an extra syllable. The reason is obvious: he wants the rhythmic impression of Leda staggering, and the placement of "staggering girl" achieves it. The third line is the most irregular, beginning with a pyrrhic foot, following that with a spondee, then adding a trochaic substitution in the fourth foot to intensify the effect of violence. The fourth line marks a significant use of regular iambic pentameter. After the disruptions of the first three lines, we read the regular rise and fall of stresses as suggesting the return to normal breathing after the violent act is over. Yeats has, in a sense, done the opposite of Shakespeare, finding regularity rather than breaking against it.

The readings that follow, which will concentrate on rhythm and meter almost exclusively, will illustrate a number of other possibilities that can result from artful variation.

Alexander Pope

ODE ON SOLITUDE

Happy the man whose wish and care
    A few paternal acres bound,
Content to breathe his native air,
      In his own ground.

Whose herds with milk, whose fields with bread,
    Whose flocks supply him with attire,   5
Whose trees in summer yield him shade,
      In winter fire.

Blest, who can unconcern'dly find
    Hours, days, and years slide soft away,   10
In health of body, peace of mind,
      Quiet by day,

Sound sleep by night; study and ease,
    Together mixt; sweet recreation;
And Innocence, which most does please   15
      With meditation.

Thus let me live, unseen, unknown,
    Thus unlamented let me die,
Steal from the world, and not a stone
      Tell where I lie.   20

"Ode on Solitude"—Scansion and Commentary

Háp-py̆/ thĕ mán / whŏse wísh / añd cáre
Ă féw / pă-tér / năl ác- / rĕs boúnd,
Cŏn-tént / tŏ breáthe / hĭs ná- / tĭve aír
Ín his / own groúnd.

Whŏse hérds / wĭth mílk, // whŏse fíelds / wĭth bréad,
Whŏse flócks / sŭp-ply̆ / hĭm wíth / ăt-tíre,
Whŏse trées / ĭn súm- / mĕr yíeld / hĭm sháde,
Ĭn wín- / tĕr fíre.

Blést, // whŏ/ căn ún- / cŏn-cern'd / ly̆ fínd
Hoúrs, // dáys, // añd yéars / slĭde sóft / ă-wáy.
Ĭn héalth / ŏf bó- / dy̆, // peáce / ŏf mínd,
Qúi-ĕt / by̆ dáy,

Soúnd sléep / by̆ níght; // stŭ-dy̆ / añd eáse,
Tŏ-gé / thĕr míxt; // swéet ré- / crĕ-á- / tión;
Añd Ín- / nŏ cénce, // whĭch móst / dŏĕs pléase
Wĭth mé- / dĭ-tá / tión.

Thús lét / mĕ líve, // uń-séen, // ún-knówn,
Thús ún- / lă-mén / tĕd lét / mĕ díe,
Stéal frŏm / thĕ wórld, // añd nót / ă stóne
Téll whére / Í líe.

As you read the following discussion, consider these questions:

1. Study the scanned version of the poem, and find three instances where the departure from the expected meter creates a special emphasis. Try to explain just what the variation accomplishes.

2. Look at the caesuras in the poem (marked as / /) and try to explain why the extra pause is appropriate to the development of the poem.

Discussion. Alexander Pope's "Ode on Solitude" is composed in five stanzas, with an A-B-A-B rhyme pattern. The first three lines of every stanza are in iambic tetrameter, with substitutions, while the fourth line is in dimeter.

The first stanza begins with a trochee, which creates a sense of exclamation, and then falls into a regular pattern of iambs. There are no caesuras. The fourth line, the dimeter, I have scanned with four stresses, though the first foot could be pronounced without stress, as Ĭn hís. The solid and even stresses of the fourth line confer emphasis; they are like upright boundary posts.

The second stanza is completely regular. The one caesura, directly in the middle of the first line, simply supports the general impression of balance.

The third stanza departs from regularity with a number of variations. The caesura after the first syllable isolates the word "Blest," which gets further emphasis by being a stressed syllable. Pope wants the reader to pause and to savor what an exceptional thing such a life would be. The double caesura in the next line, setting off "Hours," and "days," which are both stressed, lends weight to these measures of time.

The fourth stanza has several interesting variations. The spondee in the first foot enforces the soundness of the sleep, while the caesura in mid-line again creates balance. But in the next line Pope takes a liberty, adding a syllable and violating the strict regularity. This is because he is introducing the idea of recreation, which is itself a departure from the orderly rhythms of work. "Meditation" in the fourth line adds an extra syllable to maintain the overall symmetry.

Pope's final stanza is emphatic, loaded with extra stresses. The two caesuras in the first line mark out the speaker's solitariness. The strong stresses in the first foot of each line drive the decisiveness home. The two spondees in the very last line echo the two at the end of the first stanza, thus carrying a link between the ground that a person lives on and the ground that the person is buried in.

George Herbert

THE PULLEY

When God at first made man,
Having a glass of blessings standing by—
Let us (said he) pour on him all we can;
Let the world's riches, which dispersed lie,
    Contract into a span.°   5

So strength first made a way,
Then beauty flow'd, then wisdom, honour, pleasure:
When almost all was out, God made a stay,
Perceiving that, alone of all His treasure,
    Rest in the bottom lay.   10

  For if I should (said he)
Bestow this jewel also on My creature,
He would adore My gifts instead of Me,
And rest in Nature, not the God of Nature:
    So both should losers be.   15

  Yet let him keep the rest,
But keep them with repining° restlessness;
Let him be rich and weary, that at least,
If goodness lead him not, yet weariness
    May toss him to My breast.   20

THE PULLEY. 5 *span*: measure determined by a person's fully outstretched hands.   17 *repining*: disconnected.

"The Pulley"—Scansion and Commentary

When Gŏd / ăt first / măde mán,

Háv-ĭng / ă gláss / ŏf blés- / sĭngs stánd / ĭng bý—

Lĕt ús / (saĭd hé) / póur ŏn / hĭm áll / wĕ cán;

Lét thĕ / wórld's rĭ- / chĕs, // whĭch / dĭs-pér / sĕd líe,

    Cŏn-tráct / ĭn-tó / ă spán.

    Só strength / fírst máde / ăwáy,

Thĕn beáu- / tў flów'd, // thĕn wís- / dŏm, // hón- / ŏur, // pléa- / sŭre:

Whĕn ál- / mŏst áll / wăs oút, // Gód máde / ă stáy,

Pĕr-céi- / vĭng thát, // ă-lóne / ŏf áll / Hĭs tréa- / sŭre,

    Rést ĭn / thĕ bót- / tŏm láy.

    Fŏr íf / Ĭ shóuld / (saĭd hé)

Bĕ-stów / thĭs jéw- / ĕl ál- / sŏ ón / Mў Créa- / tŭre,

Hĕ woúld / ă-dóre / Mў gífts / ĭn-stéad / ŏf mé,

Ănd rést / ĭn Ná- / tŭre, // nót / thĕ Gód / ŏf Ná- / tŭre:

    Só bóth / shŏuld ló- / sĕrs bé.

    Yĕt lét / hĭm kéep / thĕ rést,

Bŭt kéep / thĕm wíth / rĕ-pín— / ĭng rést- / lĕss-néss;

Lĕt hím / bĕ rích / ănd wéa- / rў, // thát / ăt leást,

Ĭf góod- / nĕss léad / hĭm nót, // yĕt wéar- / ĭ-néss

    Măy tóss / hĭm tó / Mў bréast.

As you read the following discussion, consider these questions:

1. Copy the poem without looking at the scansion, then try to scan it yourself. Check your version against the printed scansion.

2. Find three variations in the meter, and try to explain what effect they create. Do this without referring to the commentary.

Discussion. English poet George Herbert was ordained as a priest in 1630. "The Pulley," one of his best-known poems, uses a strong and steady meter to dramatize the relation of God to his created creatures.

The poem is in four stanzas of five lines each. The first and fifth lines are in iambic trimeter, the middle three lines in iambic pentameter.

The first stanza uses several strategic substitutions to heighten effect. The third foot in line 1 is a spondee, adding a suggestion of purposeful vigor. This suggestion recurs in line 3 with the spondees in the third and fourth foot—again, Herbert is accentuating the strength of God's intention. The fourth line is broken by a caesura right at the mid-point, sustaining balance, while the even iambic beat of the last line seems to confirm the rightness of that intention.

The four strong stresses that open stanza 2 confirm the power of God's action. The three caesuras in the second line underscore the idea that other attributes were added in increments, in each case after a certain deliberation. The caesura in the third line dramatizes the pause that the line itself describes. In the fourth line, Herbert adds an extra beat to balance off the beat in the second line. And the trochaic substitution in the first foot of line 5 brings extra focus to bear on the word "Rest," allowing the reader to understand that he means it in the sense of "repose."

The third stanza, like the second, carries an extra syllable in lines 2 and 4. The one caesura, in line 4, is perfectly placed to force us to heed the crucial distinction: that God wants man to worship Him, not the world he has created.

The final stanza makes a subtle and crucial play with the two senses of the word "rest." Herbert has God saying, in effect, that man should keep all the gifts He has given, except that of rest. In other words, let him keep everything else—all the rest. The first line of the stanza is slightly confusing in this respect, but Herbert solves the confusion in the next line with his use of "restlessness." The last foot of the line is pyrrhic, and we cannot read it without feeling the lack of resolution that lies at the heart of the idea of restlessness. We ourselves are restless, expecting a stress where none was given.

Except for the spondee at the beginning of the third line, the last three lines are regular, emblematic of rightness and necessity. Herbert breaks the monotony of a too-regular iambic pentameter with carefully placed caesuras. These we find, if we read carefully, are meant to keep us slightly off-center—until Herbert can deliver the solid comfort of:

yĕt wéar- / ĭ -néss / Măy tóss / hĭm tó / Mў bréast."

As these scansion samples suggest, metered poetry in English is dominated by the iambic rhythm. Trochaic feet are most commonly used in substitutions to create certain kinds of emphasis, though a significant number of poems are based around a trochaic pattern. Dactylic meter is uncommon, except in lighter verse, though nineteenth-century poets like Robert Browning and Charles Algernon Swinburne made some effort at bringing that rhythm into their work. Likewise, anapestic meters are rarely found.

A few excerpts in these various meters follow.

Trochaic

From "Song" by John Donne

Gó aňd / catch ǎ / fál-lĭng / stár,
   Gét wĭth / chíld ǎ / mán-drăke / róot,
Téll mĕ / whére aˇll / pást yéars / aˇre,
   Ŏr who / cléft thĕ / Dé-vĭl's / fóot,
Teách mĕ / tŏ héar / mér-maĭds / síng-ĭng   5

Ŏr tŏ / kéep óff eń-vў's / stíngĭng,

    Ănd fińd

        Whăt wínd

Sérves tŏ / ăd-vańce / ăn hón- / ĕst mínd.

QUESTIONS

1. Read the Donne excerpt aloud. Why do you suppose that the poet chose a sing-song meter?

2. Try to cast Donne's lines into a different meter while keeping the sense intact. Comment on the effect of the change.

Dactylic

"Errand" by George Starbuck

Búck-ĕ-tў- / búck-ĕ-tў

Sú-săn B̆. / Ań-thŏn-ў

Stróde tŏ the / beńch tŏ bĕ

Chárged bў the / Júdge:

"Hý-pĕr-aĕs- / the-nĭ-ă!

Flí-bĕr-tĭ- / gíb-bĕt-rў!

Hóg-wăsh! Hўs- / tér-ĭ-căl

Fém-ĭ-nĭst / fúdge!"

QUESTIONS

1. Write a short humorous poem in dactyls following Starbuck's rhyme scheme.

2. Try to write a serious poem using the same pattern; comment on the result.

Anapestic

From "Summum Bonum" by Robert Browning

Ăll thĕ bréath / ănd thĕ blóom / ŏf thĕ yéar / ĭn thĕ bág / ŏf ŏne bée:

Ăll thĕ wón- / dĕr ănd weálth / ŏf thĕ míne / ĭn thĕ heárt / ŏf ŏne gém:

Ĭn thĕ córe / ŏf ŏne peárl / ăll thĕ sháde / ănd thĕ shíne / ŏf thĕ séa:

1. What is the effect of Browning's anapestic meter in this fragment?
2. Try to simplify these lines into iambic pentameter (˘ ´ ˘ ´ ˘ ´ ˘ ´ ˘ ´). What is the difference in effect?

RHYTHM AND METER—EXERCISES IN SCANSION

Write out each of the following poems and scan them to find the meter. Follow the natural stresses of the speaking voice—do not try to force the lines to conform to regularity. Mark the caesuras. In each case, find several places in the poem where the meter deviates from the expected pattern, and explain how the deviation adds emphasis to the expression.

William Wordsworth

THE DAFFODILS

I wandered lonely as a cloud
That floats on high o'er vales° and hills,   *valleys*
When all at once I saw a crowd,
A host of golden daffodils;
Beside the lake, beneath the trees,   5
Fluttering and dancing in the breeze.

Continuous as the stars that shine
And twinkle on the milky way,
They stretched in never-ending line
Along the margin of a bay: 10
Ten thousand saw I at a glance,
Tossing their heads in sprightly dance.

The waves beside them danced; but they
Out-did the sparkling waves in glee.
A poet could not but be gay,   15
In such a jocund° company: *jolly*
I gazed—and gazed—but little thought
What wealth the show to me had brought:

For oft, when on my couch I lie
In vacant or in pensive mood,   20
They flash upon that inward eye
Which is the bliss of solitude;
And then my heart with pleasure fills,
And dances with the daffodils.

1. Identify the meter of "The Daffodils."
2. How does the meter change in lines 6 and 12? What is the effect of the deviation in each case?

Robert Browning

MEETING AT NIGHT

The grey sea and the long black land;
And the yellow half-moon large and low;
And the startled little waves that leap
In fiery ringlets from their sleep,
As I gain the cove with pushing prow,   5
And quench its speed i' the slushy sand.

Then a mile of warm sea-scented beach;
Three fields to cross till a farm appears;
A tap at the pane, the quick sharp scratch
And blue spurt of a lighted match,   10
And a voice less loud, thro' its joys and fears,
Than the two hearts beating each to each!

QUESTIONS

Determine how Browning is using variations in meter to create specific effects. Consider
1. the clustered stresses in line 1,
2. the transition to iambic meter in the middle of line 3,
3. the three strong stresses at the end of line 9,
4. the double stresses of "blue spurt" in line 10, and
5. the return to a strong iambic rhythm in the last four syllables of the poem.

Theodore Roethke

MY PAPA'S WALTZ

The whiskey on your breath
Could make a small boy dizzy;
But I hung on like death:
Such waltzing was not easy.

We romped until the pans   5
Slid from the kitchen shelf;
My mother's countenance
Could not unfrown itself.

The hand that held my wrist
Was battered on one knuckle;
At every step you missed
My right ear scraped a buckle.

You beat time on my head
With a palm caked hard by dirt,
Then waltzed me off to bed
Still clinging to your shirt.

10

15

QUESTIONS:

1. After writing out a scansion, determine whether there is any way in which the rhythm of the poem mimics the bumbling waltz it depicts.

2. What is the effect of the alternation of regular and irregular lines throughout the poem (with a few exceptions)?

3. Pay special attention to Roethke's way of using meter to highlight his expression in lines 2, 6, 12, 13, and 16. In each case isolate the specific effect achieved.

June Jordan

THE RECEPTION

Doretha wore the short blue lace last night
and William watched her drinking so she fight
with him in flying collar slim-jim orange
tie and alligator belt below the navel pants uptight

"I flirt. You hear me? Yes I flirt.
Been on my pretty knees all week
to clean the rich white downtown dirt
the greedy garbage money reek.

5

I flirt. Damned right. You look at me."
But William watched her carefully
his mustache shaky she could see
him jealous, "which is how he always be

10

at parties." Clementine and Wilhelmina
looked at trouble in the light blue lace
and held to George while Roosevelt Senior
circled by the yella high and bitterly light blue face

15

he liked because she worked
the crowded room like clay like molding men
from dust to muscle jerked
and arms and shoulders moving when

20

she moved. The Lord Almighty Seagrams bless
Doretha in her short blue dress
and Roosevelt waiting for his chance:
a true gut-funky blues to make her really dance.

[1967]

June Jordan's poem seeks to capture the energy and tension of a particular social occasion. The poem is grounded in the rhythms of colloquial speech, but it returns from time to time to an identifiable iambic pattern. Pay special attention to the following lines and try to determine what effects Jordan is after and how she uses rhythmic variations, caesuras, and line and stanza breaks to attain each.

1. the tightly packed stresses in lines 3 and 4,
2. the caesuras in lines 5 and 9,
3. the clustered stresses in line 7,
4. the break between the third and fourth stanzas,
5. the packed together stresses in line 16,
6. the break between the fifth and sixth stanzas, and
7. the return to iambic regularity in the second half of the last line.

SYLLABICS

Thus far, the discussion of poetic rhythm has centered upon the more traditional strictly metered verse, also known as *accentual syllabic* because of the regular observance of syllable and stress counts. There are, of course, other ways to write poetry. Indeed, it could be argued that formal accentual syllabic verse now makes up but a small part of the poetry written in our age. The other options, at least in English-language poetry, are *syllabic verse* and *free verse*, which is also called *open form*. (Other approaches and variations, as practiced in different cultures, will be discussed later.)

Both syllabic and free verse represent attempts to break free of the confinements of conventional metric forms—attempts to bring new possibilities of expression, as well as a more natural sense of rhythm into poetry.

Syllabic verse does not depend upon the recurrence of stresses, but upon the number of syllables in a line. These may vary from line to line, but will be equivalent when stanzas are compared. One of the best known major works written in syllabics is Dylan Thomas's "Fern Hill," which achieves a powerful verbal momentum even as it conforms to a strict syllable count. A simple finger-count of syllables will confirm just how scrupulous Thomas was about his composition.

Dylan Thomas

FERN HILL

Now as I was young and easy under the apple boughs
About the lilting house and happy as the grass was green,
    The night above the dingle° starry,
      Time let me hail and climb
    Golden in the heydays of his eyes,   5

FERN HILL. 3 *dingle:* wooded valley.

And honoured among wagons I was prince of the apple towns
And once below a time I lordly had the trees and leaves
        Trail with daisies and barley
     Down the rivers of the windfall light.

And as I was green and carefree, famous among the barns   10
About the happy yard and singing as the farm was home,
    In the sun that is young once only,
        Time let me play and be
     Golden in the mercy of his means,
And green and golden I was huntsman and herdsman, the calves   15
Sang to my horn, the foxes on the hills barked clear and cold,
       And the sabbath rang slowly
    In the pebbles of the holy streams.

All the sun long it was running, it was lovely, the hay
Fields high as the house, the tunes from the chimneys, it was air   20
    And playing, lovely and watery
       And fire green as grass.
     And nightly under the simple stars
As I rode to sleep the owls were bearing the farm away,
All the moon long I heard, blessed among stables, the night-jars°   25
    Flying with the ricks,° and the horses
       Flashing into the dark.

And then to awake, and the farm, like a wanderer white
With the dew, come back, the cock on his shoulder: it was all
    Shining, it was Adam and maiden,   30
       The sky gathered again
     And the sun grew round that very day.
So it must have been after the birth of the simple light
In the first, spinning place, the spellbound horses walking warm
    Out of the whinnying green stable   35
       On to the fields of praise.

And honoured among foxes and pheasants by the gay house
Under the new made clouds and happy as the heart was long,
    In the sun born over and over,
       I ran my heedless ways,   40
     My wishes raced through the house high hay
And nothing I cared, at my sky blue trades, that time allows
In all his tuneful turning so few and such morning songs
    Before the children green and golden
       Follow him out of grace,   45

Nothing I cared, in the lamb white days, that time would take me
Up to the swallow thronged loft by the shadow of my hand,

---

25 *night-jars:* birds.   26 *ricks:* stacks of hay.

                                      Rhythm and Meter in Poetry

In the moon that is always rising,
　　　Nor that riding to sleep
I should hear him fly with the high fields   50
And wake to the farm forever fled from the childless land.
Oh as I was young and easy in the mercy of his means,
　　　Time held me green and dying
Though I sang in my chains like the sea.

QUESTIONS

1. Taking two stanzas of Thomas's poem, count the syllables in the lines.

2. Try your hand at scanning the same stanzas in question 1, and comment on what regularity or irregularity you find.

3. Why do you suppose that Thomas chose to write "Fern Hill" in syllabics instead of a regular meter?

FREE VERSE

Though what scholars sometimes call the "free verse revolution" took place in the early years of our century, pushed forward by the energetic example of poets like Ezra Pound, Marianne Moore, H. D. (Hilda Doolittle), William Carlos Williams, and others, the first major free versifier was probably Walt Whitman. In *Leaves of Grass*, his grand cycle of autobiographical poems, Whitman made use of a highly irregular poetic line. He claimed great liberties, abandoning regular metric schemes, exploring repetitions and recurrent rhythms, and taking off on idiosyncratic verbal flights that sent the more conventionally minded readers into apoplectic fits. Whitman's message was freedom, and the verse followed.

Nor was Whitman alone in his irregularity. His contemporary, Emily Dickinson, of Amherst, Massachusetts, was likewise laying siege to poetic convention, writing poems that broke against formal constraints through the sheer urgency of their expression.

These poets, however, did not theorize at any length about what they were doing and how poetic tradition might be affected. That work fell to the twentieth century advocates of the free-verse mode, who conducted lengthy debates about the formal and philosophical implications of departing from metric norms. More than poetry was at issue. Some of the early free versifiers went so far as to argue that closed forms were oppressive and elitist, and that to write in free verse was to be aligned with a more progressive political sensibility. (One might add, however, that both T. S. Eliot and Ezra Pound, while liberal in their poetics, were extreme conservatives politically.)

Free verse is not undisciplined verse—it is not arbitrariness and chaos cut up into lines. What Williams and others intended was that the customary foot—the iamb, trochee, anapest, and dactyl—be revised into something called the *variable foot*. The idea was that the poem would still retain some sense of measure, even as the tight weave of regular meter was loosened. The rhythmic pattern, or *prosody*, these poets believed, should emerge from the needs of the expression, not from some predetermined plan.

Free verse has become the dominant form of our age. In less capable hands it reads like prose cut up and arranged vertically on the page. But when written by a poet with a keen ear and a good sense of linguistic rhythm, the most supple kind of expression can result.

Here are some examples of poems that belong to the free-verse tradition.

Walt Whitman

SONG OF MYSELF— SECTION 21

I am the poet of the Body and I am the poet
    of the Soul,
The pleasures of heaven are with me and the
    pains of hell are with me,
The first I graft and increase upon myself,
    the latter I translate into a new tongue.

I am the poet of the woman the same as the man,
And I say it is as great to be a woman as to be a man,   5
And I say there is nothing greater than the mother of men.

I chant the chant of dilation or pride,
We have had ducking and deprecating about enough,
I show that size is only development.

Have you outstript the rest? are you the President?   10
It is a trifle, they will more than arrive there every one, and still pass on.

I am he that walks with the tender and growing night,
I call to the earth and sea half-held by the night.

Press close bare-bosom'd night—press close magnetic nourishing night!
Night of south winds—night of the large few stars!   15
Still nodding night—mad naked summer night.

Smile O voluptuous cool-breath'd earth!
Earth of the slumbering and liquid trees!
Earth of departed sunset—earth of the mountains misty-topt!
Earth of the vitreous° pour of the full moon just tinged with blue!   20
Earth of shine and dark mottling° the tide of the river!
Earth of the limpid° gray of clouds brighter and clearer for my sake!
Far-swooping elbow'd earth—rich apple-blossom'd earth!
Smile, for your lover comes.

Prodigal, you have given me love—therefore I to you give love!   25
O unspeakable passionate love.

SONG OF MYSELF—SECTION 21. 20 *vitreous*: glassy. 21 *mottling*: spotting. 22 *limpid*: transparent.

1. Scan the first sixteen lines of Whitman's poem; comment upon any metrical patterns or irregularities you find.
2. What elements give this passage a sense of measure?
3. Read the passage aloud and write a short comment on what you noticed in your reading.

Discussion. The reader of Walt Whitman quickly discovers that the conventions of traditional meter cannot be applied to this expression. Whitman felt the great call to declaim, and his verse, while strongly rhythmic, seems to ride the swell of his deep exhalations without obeying any strictures of regularity. Consider the scansion of the first three long lines:

Í am thĕ póĕt ŏf thĕ Bódy̆ and Í am thĕ póĕt ŏf thĕ Sóul,

Thĕ pléasŭrĕs ŏf héavĕn arĕ with mĕ and thĕ páins ŏf héll arĕ with mĕ,

Thĕ first Í graft and íncreásĕ upón mysélf, // thĕ láttĕr Í tránslătĕ íntŏ ă néw tónguĕ.

Scansion is a tricky business, with a certain amount of guesswork (would Whitman have said *ín-crease* or *in-créase?*). But even if I have misconstrued a syllable here or there, it is quite obvious that there is no overall pattern of recurrence. There are patches and clusters, yes—the third line slips into a regular iambic beat for a time—but variety rules. And why not? The force of Whitman's declaration is strong enough to hold the lines together. There is no danger of the language expiring from a lack of intensity. And the freedom of utterance gained more than compensates for the loss of formal compactness.

At the opposite end of the spectrum from Whitman's energetic expansiveness we find the slight grapevine verses of Emily Dickinson. But their visual slightness belies the urgent force of the address. So urgent is her voice, in fact, that Dickinson is forced time and again to leave the trodden ways of rhythmic convention and to create her own prosody. A poem like the following shows the sharp tension between the norm and the emotion that escapes it.

Emily Dickinson

THE SOUL SELECTS HER OWN SOCIETY

The Soul selects her own Society—
Then—shuts the Door—
To her divine Majority—
Present no more—

Unmoved—she notes the Chariots—pausing —
At her low Gate—

5

Unmoved—an Emperor be kneeling
Upon her Mat—

I've known her—from an ample nation—
Choose One—
Then—close the Valves of her attention—
Like Stone—

The Soul selects her own Society—

Then—shuts the Door—

To her divine Majority—

Present no more—

Unmoved—she notes the Chariots — pausing —

At her low Gate—

Unmoved—an Emperor be kneeling

Upon her mat—

I've known her—from an ample nation—

Choose One —

Then—close the Valves of her attention—

Like Stone—

As you read the following discussion, consider these questions:

1. Study Dickinson's poem; comment briefly on the effect of her use of dashes.

2. Read the poem aloud without pausing at the dashes. Now read it again making appropriate pauses. What differences do you find?

Discussion. As with the earlier Whitman passage, I have some doubts about my scansion. Dickinson's idiosyncratic use of dashes to separate clusters of words has a way of throwing the pronounciation into question. Had the poet written, in the second line, "Then shuts the door," one would tend to read the syllables as two iambs: ˘ ´ / ˘ ´. The dash changes the emphasis completely.

Though Dickinson does periodically return to the iambic rhythm of the first line, one could not really say that the poem was governed by an iambic pattern. There are too many departures and switches; each stanza maps its own rhythmic design, a design conforming to the needs of the voice. But do not suppose for a moment that Dickinson is not conscious of the placement of every syllable, every hesitation. The powerful effect of the last line is not a happy accident. The poet has prepared the way carefully, setting up the erratic rhythm of the preceding line (which itself seems to mimic the loosening of attention that it names).

Finally, here is a short poem by Robert Creeley, a poet believed by many of his fellow poets to have one of the most delicate ears in the business:

Robert Creeley

LIKE THEY SAY

Underneath the tree on some
soft grass I sat, I

watched two happy
woodpeckers be dis-

turbed by my presence. And
why not, I thought to

myself, why
not.

As you read the following discussion, consider these questions:

1. Read Creeley's poem aloud, paying close attention to the line breaks. What is the effect of the unusual pauses? How would the poem be different if arranged into, say, two long lines?

2. Try to explain why the poet chooses to end his poem with a single word.

3. Read Creeley's poem aloud a number of times and note how your sense of the poem changes. What argument could you make that this is *not* a poem? How would you defend yourself?

Discussion. With a poem like this, rhythmic pattern is not the point. Creeley is far more concerned to engage the reader's full attention, and he achieves his end with pauses and inventive line breaks. Disruptions of expected word arrangements set off small shocks, pulling the reader into the situation and the speaker's mind-state. The break between the second and third stanza, which divides the word "disturbed," conveys the sense of jarring and allows us to feel how the woodpeckers break off their pecking. Similarly, the enforced pause between the last two words "why / not" captures precisely that sudden break in the smooth flow of thought that signals realization. The first "why not," in the third stanza, is then seen to be a reflex thought, not genuine in the way of the second.

As the Creeley poem suggests, the ground rules of free verse are very different from those governing traditionally metered poetry. One could almost say that there are no ground rules, and that the success or failure of a poem depends entirely upon the poet's ability to find a compelling and vital way to arrange the words on the page. Poets of every stripe make use of the mode. Some sustain coherence through their use of imagery, others through narrative. It is up to the poet to capture and hold the reader's attention, but the reader needs to extend some benefit of the doubt to the poet as well. The poems that follow will give some hint of the approaches taken by poets using free verse.

William Carlos Williams

YOUNG SYCAMORE

I must tell you
this young tree
whose round and firm trunk
between the wet

pavement and the gutter
(where water
is trickling) rises
bodily

into the air with
one undulant
thrust half its height—
and then

dividing and waning
sending out
young branches on
all sides—

hung with cocoons
it thins
till nothing is left of it
but two

eccentric knotted
twigs
bending forward
hornlike at the top

5
10
15
20

QUESTIONS

Read Williams's poem carefully, paying attention to shifts in rhythm as well as line and stanza breaks.

1. How does the break between the first two stanzas help to enact the description?
2. How do the breaks between stanzas 2 and 3, and 3 and 4, help to establish a motion of growth?
3. Scan the third stanza and explain how Williams uses rhythm to intensify the sensation.
4. Scan the last two lines and explain the correlation between the rhythm and the sense.

Laura Mullen

THE LEASE

I dry my clothes in a dryer.

Fall comes, then winter, then spring.

I watch the spiders
Doing and undoing their elaborate
Theories about what it means to be 5
Cornered and to wait
To corner something smaller than yourself;
Dinner.

　　　All this happens a long way away from the place
I told you about before. 10

The ugly young man in the laundromat
Riffs his jacket zipper,

Stands up in front of the MTV and says
"I'm a drummer."

　　　Annoyed by the way 15
We girls are dying over Mick Jagger's tongue.

The clothes smell of nothing when I bring them home.

Why should I want them to take up the wind's
Imitations: cut grass, burning leaves, the scent
Of the river, 20

　　　Or see them on a line I put up myself,
Like pieces of myself—

Hacked up but struggling furiously
(Tonguing the air)—and maybe
Pulling it down. 25

In the dryer they go up
And they fall back down on each other
With a violent complacency, like slam dancers.
After spring, summer.

Hot and damp. When my tennis shoes 30

Kick their way out before it's over,
I stuff them back in, feed it another quarter.

When you say Whoops I know exactly what you mean.

QUESTIONS

Laura Mullen has used the looseness and variety of free verse to orchestrate a sequence of perceptions. Look carefully at the diction, rhythm, and line breaks and explain how she arrives at various effects. Consider the relation between these poetic techniques and the sense in line 2, lines 3 to 8, 21 to 22, 26 to 29, and 30 to 31.

Liam Rector

IN SNOW

With the window sitting with you,
and with glass, with air to see with,
there I came with you to be with,
asking *if* and *ever were*.

And with snow, with wet and moving,   5
there we brought the afternoon in.
Soon with gin we poured the ache down
and with window sitting with us

soon we felt the air we moved with.
Now in snow and later raining   10
we went out and moved the walking
and in snow resumed the drifting

of the past that we'd been speaking.
I was cold and you were raining—
I had stayed while you went leaving   15
and the life that I was walking

turned to air, and then went dark.
You now mentioned all your leaving
(now that afternoon had left us)
and you rained with need and grieving   20

for that staring boy you'd left.
I recalled the boy who saw you
as you moved through girl, through bleeding,
and I mentioned movement boyward

where in snow we'd lain all needing.   25
We lie down, within this window,
and in snow, in rain and moving,
we give back our time its longing

over field and snow and leaving.

QUESTIONS

1. Scan Rector's poem and comment on irregularities in meter. What do you notice about the final foot in each line?

2. Find, if you can, singer David Broza's recording of Rector's poem. How does the singer interpret the lines, and how does the interpretation differ from the strict scansion?

3. Rector's poem can be said to follow an emotional rather than a rational logic. Write a short paraphrase of the poem. Is there a central narrative?

Christopher Jane Corkery

DIVORCE

A small girl on a porch
left by her mother
while Mother drives Father
to the 8:02 train.

Father always goes   5
when the sun hits the porch.
It is June, those are lilacs,
she does not know the word

for what is hers,
what is his.   10
What is the thing
between them?

But she does feel something
pressing against her
as the Plymouths and Fords   15
bump along the road.

It is flying inside her,
trying to get out.
It is rising through her body,
beating in her hands.   20

She feels tears in her eyes
but they are not hers.
They belong to those stupid
girls in the stories.

Her legs are crossed   25
at the ankles. Her feet swing
above the grey boards
where six ants are running.

She knows that the birds
in the lilacs are warblers.   30
Her father told her that
but flicker is her favorite

word for a bird.
The white on his back
when he flies away   35
is how she remembers.

Flicker. Flicker.

The red on his head
means love forever.
He's a good bird, she says,   40
And he loves to fly.

QUESTIONS

Christopher Jane Corkery's "Divorce" is an example of tightly disciplined free verse. The
poem is built around four-line stanzas (quatrains) and carries a consecutive narrative.

1. What is the effect of the short lines and the simple diction? How would this poem change
if the lines were lengthened and the diction were complicated?

2. Look at the line breaks and determine which ones seem calculated to intensify the sense.
Look particularly at lines 6, 9 and 10, and 25.

3. How does the rhythm change in stanzas 4, 5, and 6? What is the purpose of the change?
How does the poem then return to its earlier rhythm?

4. Corkery only breaks her pattern of four-line stanzas once, when she sets line 37 off by itself. Speculate about why she might have done this? How does this one change alter the
poem?

19 Fixed Forms
in Poetry

As we saw in the previous chapter, most of the poetry in our time is being written in free (or sometimes called "open") form. This designation would almost seem to be a contradiction in terms, insofar as freedom and openness suggest the lack of constraint, while "form" carries the sense of rules and limitations. Maybe the best way to understand this joining of opposed terms is by widening our understanding of form. For isn't it finally true that all things, whatever their appearance and nature, have their own unique form? In poetry that form is determined by the expressive need, and in a period where the practice of free verse is dominant, variety is bound to be the law of the land.

In a climate of such democratic independence, it is sometimes hard to recall that things were ever any different. But in fact they were quite different. Poetry was an art with a past—a very long past—when the first gestures toward innovation were made. Since its earliest origins in the oral tradition, poetry has had a deep tendency toward formal regularity. Line lengths and meters were fitted to set patterns, and a number of fixed forms evolved; most required the poet to work within very strict parameters. Some of these forms will be discussed shortly.

First, though, we need to consider the origins and implications of this regularity, and to do so we must put away any prejudices we may have about form being necessarily stodgy or repressive. Fixed patterns took the shape they did for several very good reasons. To begin with, poetry originated in cultures that worshiped cycles and recurrence, seeing in them the hand of a deity. Oral poetry arose directly out of the song and dance that accompanied ritual observances, and retained their structural regularity. But in oral cultures there was an additional incentive for composing in fixed forms. In a word: memorability. Before the technology of writing was invented memory was the only tool of preservation. The epic poets who chanted the legends of the tribe, and who very likely entertained their listeners with recitations of hundreds upon hundreds of lines, needed strategies for recall. They found their answer in patterns: strict organizations of rhythmic lines and stanzas with familiar formulas of transition (like Homer's "When dawn once again with her rosy fingers . . .").

With the invention of writing, of course, the memorability factor became less important. But the fact that nearly all verse continued to observe the time-honored formulas was hardly a reflection of laziness or lack of imagination on the part of poets. There were better reasons. The primary one was that order and symmetry were deemed the very hallmarks of beauty. So far as we know, all early cultures were deeply religious, and most attributed the harmonies of nature to the perfected design of their deities. The artist—poet—could strive for nothing higher than emulation. The mirroring of natural order in a work of art was an act of worship.

The tendency toward fixed form, then, is deeply rooted. Nor could its persistence be explained solely on religious grounds. There was also the belief in the preordained rightness of certain modes of expression, that human truths—indeed perceptions in general—inevitably structured themselves into a handful of patterns. And these patterns were keyed, perhaps biologically, to the human makeup.

Finally, poets, like other artists, believed that the limitations of fixed structure intensified the transmission of the work. When the content had to press against the constraint, the resulting tension would animate the art. The supposition makes good sense. Imagine what basketball would be like without its myriad rules and time strictures. Or chess. Or just about any other game. Remove the built-in limits, and the tension and excitement all but evaporate.

Free verse, in this sense, took on a high challenge. By removing the traditional tensing devices—the expectations of regularity—poets took on for themselves the task of creating coherence and purpose in their poems. The gifted poets were up to it. They undertook more purposeful manipulations of line breaks; they exerted themselves to create interesting rhythms and sound patterns. They discovered that "free" was anything but easy, and in the process they brought new variety and vigor into poetry.

Even in our liberated artistic era, however, fixed forms are much more than historical curios. For one thing, a great many poets—a great many of our *best* poets— still use them. They love the formal problems that arise in fitting their expression into a ready frame—many claim that it stimulates their creativity. Moreover, more than a few believe that there *is* a rightness about these forms, that they are the best vehicles for carrying the messages and stirring the reader.

But fixed forms also hold the greater part of our poetic legacy. They are the tradition, the necessary past. For the poet—even the poet who champions open form— they represent a vast set of options to be learned from. Much of the greatest poetry ever written has been written in form, and a knowledge of that poetry is essential for any departure. What's more, by learning about form, a poet—and reader—inevitably learns about the possibilities of language, and about what can be done with rhythm, sound, and their variations.

SOME COMMON FORMS FOR GROUPING VERSE LINES

The various fixed forms of English-language poetry are essentially different arrangements of line and stanza and reflect the incorporation of specific rhyme schemes. Each form has its own uses and creates its own effects.

Before we inspect some of the different shapes of the containers—the forms themselves—some mention should be made of the basic poetic material that fills them. This, of course, varies with the poet and the purpose of the expression, particularly in the shorter forms (most fixed forms are short, using the stanza as their building block). The longer—unfixed—forms such as the epic, elegy, ode, pastoral, and dramatic monologue (see the Glossary for definitions of these terms) are not structured around repeated stanzas. Except for epic works, like Milton's *Paradise Lost*, which are divided into books, the long poems tend to unfold in great swatches of unbroken *blank verse*. Blank verse, essentially unrhymed iambic pentameter, is the basic bolt cloth of English poetry. Poets from Shakespeare to Milton to Dryden to Wordsworth to Browning have fashioned substantial works from it—it is the supplest and most adaptable of meters. Here is the blank verse opening of the first book of Milton's great epic, "Paradise Lost."

> Of Man's first disobedience, and the fruit
> Of that forbidden tree, whose mortal taste
> Brought death into the world, and all our woe,
> With loss of Eden, till one greater man
> Restore us, and regain the blissful seat,
> Sing Heav'nly Muse, that on the secret top
> of Oreb, or of Sinai, didst inspire
> That shepherd, who first taught the chosen seed,
> In the beginning how the Heav'ns and Earth
> Rose out of chaos:

In this section, however, we are primarily concerned with fixed forms based upon stanza length and rhyme patterns. A *stanza* is any grouping of lines that is set off from other groupings by white space. Stanzas within a poem need not be identical in length, though they usually are; nor need they share a common rhyme scheme, though they usually do. There is no simple charting of stanza forms, for poets are forever inventing, modifying, and otherwise putting their personal stamp on the stanza. But there are certain conventions and classic arrangements, and much of the poetry in the English-language tradition is based upon them.

Stanzas are customarily labeled by the number of their lines. Two-line stanzas (and also two-line groupings) are *couplets*, three-liners are *tercets*, and four-liners are *quatrains*. There are names for other line formations, but they need not concern us here. Far more important are their applications.

COUPLETS: A couplet is any pair of lines that make a single unit, or statement; quite often the lines rhyme. While the two lines can be isolated from other lines, in the manner of a small stanza, we also often identify couplets within some larger poetic body. Alexander Pope, the eighteenth-century English poet, was a master at composing lengthy, often witty poems in what are called *heroic couplets*, or rhyming pairs of iambic pentameter lines, as shown in this excerpt from "Essay on Man."

> God, in the nature of each being, founds
> Its proper bliss, and sets its proper bounds:
> But as he framed a whole, the whole to bless,
> Our mutual wants built mutual happiness:
> So from the first eternal Order ran,
> And creature link'd to creature, man to man.

Each pair of lines, we note, represents a thought, or a stage in a sequence of thoughts. Indeed, the couplet by its very nature encourages precision and the swift rounding out of a thought or observation. The problem with writing lengthier works built upon strings of couplets is that recurrence quickly leads to predictability. The poet must be especially inventive and agile in order to succeed—Pope was one of the few who did.

TERCETS: The three-line stanza, or tercet, is common in English-language poetry. Rhyming is less common, for while triple rhymes exist, the likelihood of finding three that make a natural fit is not especially great.

One special variation of the tercet is called the *terza rima*, a rhyme scheme that allows the poet to braid short stanzas together. The pattern is as follows: a-b-a, b-c-b, c-d-c, and so on; the middle line of any stanza supplies the rhyme for the first line of the next. The pattern was used with extraordinary skill by the Italian poet Dante in his *Divine Comedy*. The Italian language is rich in so-called "marriageable" endings, however; sustained ventures in terza rima are not often encountered in English. Robert Frost's "Acquainted with the Night" is a good example of a short poem built around a terza rima scheme. Note that Frost concludes the poem with a heroic couplet.

Robert Frost

ACQUAINTED WITH THE NIGHT

I have been one acquainted with the night.
I have walked out in rain—and back in rain.
I have outwalked the furthest city light.

I have looked down the saddest city lane.
I have passed by the watchman on his beat   5
And dropped my eyes, unwilling to explain.

I have stood still and stopped the sound of feet
When far away an interrupted cry
Came over houses from another street,

But not to call me back or say good-by;   10
And further still at an unearthly height
One luminary clock against the sky

Proclaimed the time was neither wrong nor right.
I have been one acquainted with the night.

As you read the poem, consider these questions:

1. Read Frost's poem aloud several times, noting the rhyme pattern. Why do you suppose the poet chose the *terza rima* scheme?

2. Copy the poem and scan it. What is the dominant meter? Explain any departures from the metrical norm.

THE QUATRAIN: The four-line stanza, or quatrain, is the most popular building block for the rhymed poem. It allows for some of the same compression found in the couplet, but affords the poet more flexibility and room for development. Examples, to pluck just two from the storehouse of English-language verse, are Ralph Waldo Emerson's "Concord Hymn" and William Blake's "The Sick Rose." The first holds strictly to a rhyme pattern of a-b-a-b, while the second is a-b-c-b.

Ralph Waldo Emerson

CONCORD HYMN

Sung at the Completion of the
Battle Monument, July 4, 1837

By the rude bridge that arched the flood,
　　Their flag to April's breeze unfurled,
Here once the embattled farmers stood
　　And fired the shot heard round the world.

The foe long since in silence slept;　　　　　　　　　　　　5
　　Alike the conqueror silent sleeps;
And Time the ruined bridge has swept
　　Down the dark stream which seaward creeps.

On this green bank, by this soft stream,
　　We set to-day a votive° stone;　　　　　　　　　　　　10
　　That memory may their deed redeem,
When, like our sires,° our sons are gone.

Spirit, that made those heroes dare
　　To die, and leave their children free,
Bid Time and Nature gently spare　　　　　　　　　　　　15
　　The shaft we raise to them and thee.

CONCORD HYMN.　10 *votive:* given in dedication.　12 *sires:* fathers.

William Blake

THE SICK ROSE

O Rose, thou art sick!
The invisible worm
That flies in the night,
In the howling storm,

Has found out thy bed　　　　　　　　　　　　5
Of crimson joy:
And his dark, secret love
Does thy life destroy.

Read the discussion preceding the poems and consider these questions:

1. Scan "Concord Hymn." What is the dominant meter? Look at departures from the metrical norm in lines 3 and 8, and try to explain Emerson's choice.

2. Blake rhymes only the *b* and *d* lines of each stanza. How would the poem be different if he had rhymed the *a* and *c* as well?

3. Read "The Sick Rose" aloud as if it were a single eight-line stanza. Do you detect any difference? Why did Blake use quatrains?

Discussion. Critic Paul Fussell, speculating about the popularity of the quatrain, has suggested that there may be "something in four-line stanzaic organization (or in the principle of alternate rhyming) that projects a deep and permanent appeal to human nature." He then adds: "If we destroyed all English poetry written in quatrains—as well as that written in blank verse and heroic couplets—what would remain would resemble the literary corpus of, say, Venezuela."

Indeed, it is the quatrain that can be seen to form the joining point of poetry and song. The vast majority of English and Scottish ballads, which date from the Middle Ages, are composed in four-line stanzas:

> There lived a wife at Usher's well,
> And a wealthy wife was she;
> She had three stout and stalwart sons,
> And sent them o'er the sea.
>
> They hadna been a week from her,   5
> A week but barely ane,
> When word came to the carline° wife   *Scots: young woman*
> That her three sons were gane.

From Anonymous, "The Wife of Usher's Well"

This mode of rhyming—a-b-c-b—which we also find in Blake's "The Sick Rose," identifies the *ballad stanza*. The other alternative is the a-b-b-a pattern, used by Alfred, Lord Tennyson in his long poem "In Memoriam":

> I held it truth, with him who sings
> To one clear harp in divers° tones,   *diverse*
> That men may rise on stepping stones
> Of their dead selves to higher things.
>
> But who shall so forecast the years   5
> And find in loss a gain to match?
> Or reach a hand thro' time to catch
> The far-off interest of tears?

Poet John Hollander has cleverly characterized this scheme by saying that the middle two lines are "holding hands as lovers do."

There are, of course, other patterns of stanza (and rhyme within stanza) available to the poet, but couplets, tercets, and qu rains are the main ones. Two of the more elaborate possibilities are the seven-line *rhyme royal* (a-b-a-b-b-c-c) and the eight-line *ottava rima* (a-b-a-b-a-b-c-c)—but these, and others still, are really the province of the connoisseur.

SOME EXAMPLES OF FIXED FORMS

The reader of poetry—even the beginning reader—ought to be aware of a few of the better-known fixed forms. Chief among these is the *sonnet* (from the Italian for "little song"). The sonnet is a poem in fourteen lines that follows one of two general patterns.

THE ITALIAN SONNET: The earliest form of the sonnet was brought to a high state of perfection by the Italian poet Petrarch, who used it for a cycle of poems that declared his love for a certain Laura. The Italian sonnet is structured in two parts. The first eight lines make up the *octave*, and follow an a-b-b-a, a-b-b-a rhyme scheme. The next six lines, the *sestet*, are usually separated from the octave; the rhymes can follow any number of patterns, so long as the poem does not end with a rhyming couplet. A famous sonnet by John Keats shows one variation: a-b-b-a, a-b-b-a, c-d-c-d-c-d.

John Keats

ON FIRST LOOKING INTO CHAPMAN'S HOMER

Much have I travell'd in the realms of gold;
And many goodly states and kingdoms seen;
Round many western islands have I been
Which bards° in fealty to Apollo° hold.
Oft of one wide expanse had I been told   5
That deep-brow'd Homer ruled as his demesne°;
Yet did I never breathe its pure serene
Till I heard Chapman° speak out loud and bold:
Then felt I like some watcher of the skies
When a new planet swims into his ken;   10
Or like stout Cortez° when with eagle eyes
He star'd at the Pacific—and all his men
Look'd at each other with a wild surmise —
Silent, upon a peak in Darien.°

ON FIRST LOOKING INTO CHAPMAN'S HOMER. 4 *bards*: poets; *Apollo*: Greek god of the sun, prophecy, music, medicine, and poetry. 6 *demesne*: realm. 8 *Chapman*: translator of Homer. 11 *Cortez*: Hernando Cortez, Spanish conquistador (of Mexico). 14 *Darien*: region of Panama.

Read the poem and consider this question:

1. Divide the sonnet into its octave and sestet. How is the presentation shaped by the break?

Discussion. Keats's sonnet, incidentally, contains one of the most famous "mistakes" in the history of the poet's art—it was not Cortez, but Balboa, who first discerned the Pacific Ocean from that mountain peak. But the power of the image has triumphed over factual accuracy, and the poem lives on.

THE SHAKESPEAREAN (ENGLISH) SONNET: The sonnet form was imported from Italy to England in the sixteenth century, just in time for Shakespeare and a succession of Elizabethan masters to leave their distinctive imprint on the format. The *English,* or *Shakespearean,* sonnet has a somewhat different shape, and allows a greater variety of rhymes. It also finishes with a rhyming couplet. Keats's "Bright Star!" shows the poet using the customary pattern of a-b-a-b, c-d-c-d, e-f-e-f, g-g.

John Keats

BRIGHT STAR! WOULD I WERE STEADFAST AS THOU ART

Bright Star! would I were steadfast as thou art—
Not in lone splendor hung aloft the night,
And watching, with eternal lids apart,
Like Nature's patient sleepless Eremite,°   hermit, recluse
The moving waters at their priestlike task   5
Of pure ablution round earth's human shores,
Or gazing on the new soft-fallen mask
Of snow upon the mountains and the moors—
No—yet still steadfast, still unchangeable,
Pillowed upon my fair love's ripening breast,   10
To feel for ever its soft fall and swell,
Awake for ever in a sweet unrest,
Still, still to hear her tender-taken breath,
    And so live ever—or else swoon to death.

        Another option—that of composing in couplets—is taken up by English poet
John Clare.

Read the
preceding
discussion and
consider these
questions:

1. Divide this sonnet into octave and sestet; comment on how the division reflects the logical progression of the poem.
2. Comparing this sonnet with "On First Looking into Chapman's Homer," what is the effect of the final rhyming couplets?

John Clare

THE FEAR OF FLOWERS

The nodding oxeye bends before the wind,
The woodbine quakes lest boys their flowers should find,
And prickly dog-rose, spite of its array,

Can't dare the blossom-seeking hand away,
While thistles wear their heavy knobs of bloom   5
Proud as a war-horse wears its haughty plume,
And by the roadside danger's self defy;
On commons where pined sheep and oxen lie,
In ruddy pomp and ever thronging mood
It stands and spreads like danger in a wood,   10
And in the village street, where meanest weeds
Can't stand untouched to fill their husks with seeds,
The haughty thistle o'er all danger towers,
In every place the very wasp of flowers.

Read the poem and consider this question:

1. Does Clare's sonnet warrant its packaging in sonnet form? How would the poem be different if presented as a set of seven couplets?

Discussion. Many poets and scholars have tried to account for the popularity of the 14-line poem. One argument that is often advanced is that our ideas tend to come in units, and that the closest approximation to an idea-unit is the 14-line sonnet format. Of course, this cannot be proven. But there must be some explanation for the enormous popularity of the sonnet among poets, practicing contemporaries included.

THE VILLANELLE: Another fixed form imported by the English is the *villanelle*. This one originated in France in the Middle Ages, and was favored by poets writing in the formal courtly tradition. The form requires five tercets in an a-b-a rhyme scheme, followed by a quatrain in a-b-a-b. Further, the first line is also repeated as the sixth, twelfth, and eighteenth, while line three recurs as the ninth, fifteenth, and nineteenth. This may strike the reader as unnecessarily arbitrary, and mechanical, but the result is the very opposite, at least when a skilled poet achieves it. Theodore Roethke's "The Waking" comes across as both necessary and fluently lyrical.

Theodore Roethke

THE WAKING

I wake to sleep, and take my waking slow.
I feel my fate in what I cannot fear.
I learn by going where I have to go.

We think by feeling. What is there to know?
I hear my being dance from ear to ear.   5
I wake to sleep, and take my waking slow.

Of those so close beside me, which are you?
God bless the Ground! I shall walk softly there,
And learn by going where I have to go.

Light takes the Tree; but who can tell us how?
The lowly worm climbs up a winding stair;
I wake to sleep, and take my waking slow.

Great Nature has another thing to do
To you and me; so take the lively air,
And, lovely, learn by going where to go.

This shaking keeps me steady. I should know.
What falls away is always. And is near.
I wake to sleep, and take my waking slow.
I learn by going where I have to go.

10

15

<table>
<tr><td>Read the poem
and consider these
questions:</td><td>1. Read "The Waking" aloud, then mark its rhyme scheme and scan its lines.
2. What does the structural formality, with its specific line repetitions, contribute to the effect?
3. Remove the repeated lines and try to compose a shorter poem. What is lost? Comment.</td></tr>
</table>

THE SESTINA: Still another form surviving from the Middle Ages is the *sestina* (or "song of sixes"), which was widely used by the wandering troubadour poets from what is now the Provence region of France. The poet uses six stanzas, each six lines long, that repeat six different end-words in a set order. The order varies from stanza to stanza. A final stanza, of three lines (a *tercet*), uses three of the end-words to make what is called a closing *envoy*. The other three end-words are incorporated into the lines. Here is an example of the sestina in contemporary dress.

Laura Mullen

SESTINA IN WHICH MY GRANDMOTHER IS GOING DEAF

It is dusk. Somewhere is the sound of water,
And our white chairs are drawn up to the edge
Of the lawn. In the trees above us large grey
Birds are shifting uneasily and a single leaf
Comes down, turning. What it suffers is release,
Scratch of its landing on stone, too small to hear.

So little we have to hold us. What you don't hear
Is distance blossoming; mooring lines snaking deep water
Beyond the embrace of the harbor. Call it release;
Say that you got what you wanted, here at the edge:
To be drifting lightly away like a leaf
On the quiet surface of water showing you grey.

5

10

624   Fixed Forms in Poetry

We sip coffee in very white cups and the sky is grey.
I tell you autumn is ending, and do you hear?
At the back of the soft cold wind we can smell leaves
Burning, past the sprinkler, through the veil of water.
I have to shout to be heard—as though, at the edge
Of a dock, I were flinging good-byes to a boat's release.

Branches rustle above us, is this release?
The trees returning a grey bird into a grey
Sky? The bird slipping over the edge
Of seeing, into the night where I can only hear
Its low cry, poured back like water
to the empty branches, to what doesn't leave . . .

Behind you, I thought, a fluttering leaf
Spun up, pale, inside a window; released.
It was a moth, coming back as though through water,
Dragged up again in the darker grey.
It is almost time to go in, I hear
You say, pushing your chair away from the edge

Of the wet lawn. Yes. The shining edge
Of moon sails into the sky like a silver leaf,
As though the dark branches were words it didn't hear.
Is it so simple? Not to listen, is that release?
To go into silence alone, becoming that color, grey,
The way the drowned leave their names above water.

15

20

25

30

35

As you read the following discussion, consider these questions:

1. Mark the word recurrences at line endings. Write casual notes as you reread Mullen's poem, commenting on what effect, if any, the repetitions have on you.

2. Pick six key words of your own and experiment with writing a sestina. What main difficulties do you encounter?

Discussion. It is not hard to see why Mullen should have adopted the sestina form—its cycle of repeated key words makes it particularly suitable for evoking the inwardness of the grandmother's state. The reader can feel the vast realm of conversation narrowing down. There is the suggestion of a mind slowly circling, weaving a pattern of sense, which chimes perfectly with the speaker's calm description of the surroundings.

SHORT FORMS—LIMERICKS, EPIGRAMS, HAIKUS: Almost everyone will be familiar with the *limerick,* a five-line comical rhyme. Five anapestic lines are rhymed a-a-b-b-a, with the a lines in trimeter and the b lines in dimeter, as in this example from Edward Lear:

There was an Old Man of the Dee,
Who was sadly annoyed by a Flea;
When he said, "I will scratch it,"
They gave him a hatchet,
Which grieved that Old Man of the Dee.

Another short form—its brevity is its point—is the *epigram*. An epigram is a sleek dart hurled with great precision. Generally two lines long, seldom more than four, it compresses volumes of implication into a few syllables. Though there is no required syllable count or rhyme, many epigrams do take the form of couplets. Not surprisingly, Alexander Pope, master of the couplet, was also master of the epigram, as shown in this example "Epigram from the French."

> Sir, I admit your general rule,
> That every poet is a fool:
> But you yourself may serve to show it
> That every fool is not a poet.

Finally, there is the well-known *haiku* form, adapted from the Japanese tradition. A haiku expresses a single flash of insight or impression in 17 syllables (though many poets are content with approximate syllable counts). These can be arranged in three lines (5-7-5), or else in a single line, as in the following haiku by John Ashbery:

> Old-fashioned shadows hanging down, that difficulty in love too soon

The customary three-line arrangement is exemplified by poet Raymond Roseliep:

> campfire extinguished
> the woman washing dishes
> in a pan of stars

Though the form of the haiku is fixed, the determinants are not line or meter, but syllable count; it is a fixed form in the *syllabic* tradition (see Chapter 18).

This survey does not begin to exhaust the archive of fixed forms that poets at times choose to write in, but for our purposes it will suffice. Students interested in exploring the menu of available possibilities might do well to consult the *Princeton Encyclopedia of Poetry and Poetics*, a standard reference volume available in any library.

POEMS IN STANZAS FOR EXERCISE AND ANALYSIS

The following poems are written in stanza form using the couplet, the tercet, and the quatrain. Experiment with different stanzaic organizations—turning couplets in some poems into quatrains, for example—and then look carefully at how the new arrangement affects the poem. Try to give a brief explanation of why the poets chose the stanza forms they did in each of these poems. Consider the effects of rhymes and rhyme patterns where they exist.

John Crowe Ransom

SURVEY OF LITERATURE°

In all the good Greek of Plato
I lack my roastbeef and potato.

SURVEY OF LITERATURE. The proper names in this poem identify ancient Greek philosophers (Plato, Aristotle) and the most venerable of the classic English poets.

A better man was Aristotle,
Pulling steady on the bottle.

I dip my hat to Chaucer,   5
Swilling soup from his saucer,

And to Master Shakespeare
Who wrote big on small beer.

The abstemious Wordsworth
Subsisted on a curd's-worth,   10

But a slick one was Tennyson,
Putting gravy on his venison.

What these men had to eat and drink
Is what we say and what we think.

The influence of Milton   15
Came wry out of Stilton.°

Sing a song for Percy Shelley,
Drowned in pale lemon jelly,

And for precious John Keats,
Dripping blood of pickled beets.   20

Then there was poor Willie Blake,
He foundered on too sweet cake.

God have mercy on the sinner
Who must write with no dinner,

No gravy and no grub,   25
No pewter and no pub,

No belly and no bowels,
Only consonants and vowels.

_____

16 *Stilton:* a strong cheese.

QUESTIONS

1. Scan Ransom's poem and compare the effect of different rhymes; for example, those falling
on a regular beat (like the second couplet) and others.
2. Is there a point to Ransom's witticisms? Do they add up to a view of poetry? Would there
be any difference if the couplets were presented as a long single stanza? Comment.

George Starbuck

INCIDENT OF THE BLIZZARD OF '81

*Note: The "vanishing hitchhiker" is well attested. Three incidents made the
national newswires in 1980, and in the fall of 1981 a book appeared, devoted to
him and his reappearances. Always, the hiker talks earnestly of religion. Always,
at highway speed, the car door opens, it must have opened, and the hiker is gone.*

I left Fat City,° toolin' my Coupe de Gras.°
I'm givin' them high-hatters the ha ha
Like J. Paul Getty° if Getty had been the Shah.

Man with the map of neon in his eyeballs.
Wigwaggin'° with a backpack full of Bibles   5
Next to the scorched blue chassis of a Ford.

Levels a sixpack at me. Swings aboard
And ballyhoos the good news of the Lord
From Cedar Rapids halfway to Grand Island.

Singin' his checkered pastureland is my land.   10
Settin' the Millers cans up single file and
Mowin' em down like Midianites.° Nebraska

Vanished without a trace. No road, no landscape,
Just Kellogg's famous featherweight white breakfast
Shot from the snub-nose silos of the plains.   15

Seventy per and a prayer in place of chains,
Opens the door and gets out. Shit for brains.
Stunt like that he could pass for Lyndon Baines.°

Before he left he spouted some damn doggerel°
And handed me six tickets to the Inaugural.   20
Balls and all. That's how I met Carl Sagan°

And got to shake the hand of Nancy Reagan
And heard that stuff about Menachem Begin°
I told you back there west of Wichita?

INCIDENT OF THE BLIZZARD OF '81. 1 *Fat City*: Washington, D.C. *coupe de gras*: twisted French for "finishing blow" and a play on Coupe de Ville, a fancy car name. 3 *J. Paul Getty*: billionaire founder of Getty Oil Company. 5 *wigwaggin'*: signaling. 12 *Midianites*: tribesmen of ancient Arabia. 18 *Lyndon Baines*: Lyndon Baines Johnson, U.S. President in the late 1960s. 19 *doggerel*: casual lines in rhyme. 21 *Carl Sagan*: popularizer of science in books and TV. 23 *Menachem Begin*: Israeli Prime Minister in the 1970s.

QUESTION

1. Pick some well-known contemporary names and write several triplets in imitation of Starbuck's. Write a short paragraph commenting on the difficulty or ease of the exercise.

Henry Vaughan

ASCENSION-HYMN

They are all gone into the world of light!
    And I alone sit lingring here;
Their very memory is fair and bright,
    And my sad thoughts doth clear.

It glows and glitters in my cloudy breast
    Like stars upon some gloomy grove,
Or those faint beams in which this hill is drest,
    After the Sun's remove.   5

I see them walking in a Air of glory,
    Whose light doth trample on my days: 10
My days, which are at best but dull and hoary,°
    Mere glimmering and decays.

O holy hope! and high humility,
    High as the Heavens above!
These are your walks, and you have shew'd them me   15
    To kindle my cold love.

Dear, beauteous death! the Jewel of the Just,
    Shining no where, but in the dark;
What mysteries do lie beyond thy dust;
    Could man outlook that mark!   20

He that hath found some fledg'd° birds nest, may know
    At first sight, if the bird be flown;
But that fair Well, or Grove he sings in now,
    That is to him unknown.

And yet, as Angels in some brighter dreams   25
    Call to the soul, when man doth sleep:
So some strange thoughts transcend our wonted° themes,
    And into glory peep.

If a star were confin'd into a Tomb
    Her captive flames must needs burn there;   30
But when the hand that lockt her up, gives room,
    She'll shine through all the sphere.

O Father of eternal life, and all
    Created glories under thee!
Resume thy spirit from this world of thrall   35
    Into true liberty.

Either disperse these mists, which blot and fill
    My perspective as they pass,
Or else remove me hence unto that hill,
    Where I shall need no glass.   40

ASCENSION-HYMN. 11 *hoary:* gray or white with age.   21 *fledg'd:* newly feathered.   27 *wonted:* usual.

QUESTIONS

1. What is it about Vaughan's poem that lends itself to presentation in quatrains?
2. Scan the first and last two stanzas. Identify the meter, then find two departures from meter to comment upon.

Vassar Miller

SPINSTER'S LULLABY

For Jeff

Clinging to my breast, no stronger
Than a small snail snugly curled,
Safe a moment from the world,
Lullaby a little longer.

Wondering how one tiny human   5
Resting so, on toothpick knees
In my scraggly lap, gets ease,
I rejoice, no less a woman

With my nipples pinched and dumb
To your need whose one word's sucking.   10
Never mind, though. To my rocking
Nap a minute, find your thumb

While I gnaw a dream and nod
To the gracious sway that settles
Both our hearts, imperiled petals   15
Trembling on the pulse of God.

                              [1960]

QUESTIONS

1. Note that Miller's poem is made up of four sentences. The first spans the opening quatrain and the second and third break in the third quatrain. How does Miller play off the sentence breaks and the stanza breaks? How do the stanzas confer unity upon the poem?

2. Scan the fourth quatrain. Explain the logic of the meter and how it reflects the sense of the lines.

FIXED-FORM POEMS WITH QUESTIONS

Dylan Thomas

DO NOT GO GENTLE INTO THAT GOOD NIGHT

Do not go gentle into that good night,
Old age should burn and rave at close of day;
Rage, rage against the dying of the light.

Though wise men at their end know dark is right,
Because their words had forked no lightning they   5
Do not go gentle into that good night.

Good men, the last wave by, crying how bright
Their frail deeds might have danced in a green bay,
Rage, rage against the dying of the light.

Wild men who caught and sang the sun in flight,   10
And learn, too late, they grieved it on its way,
Do not go gentle into that good night.

Grave men, near death, who see with blinding sight
Blind eyes could blaze like meteors and be gay,
Rage, rage against the dying of the light.   15

And you, my father, there on the sad height,
Curse, bless, me now with your fierce tears, I pray.
Do not go gentle into that good night.
Rage, rage against the dying of the light.

QUESTIONS

1. What fixed form is Dylan Thomas using? Mark out the rhyme scheme and identify the repeated lines.

2. Are the repeated lines in any way different from the others? Do they change their meaning or suggestion in different contexts?

3. Experiment with changing order. Try using different lines in the repetitions. Can you make a coherent poem out of a different pattern? Explain what changes you have made in the content of the poem.

4. Compare Thomas's poem with the poem by Donald Justice (p. 635). How have these two poets bent the form to very different uses?

James Weldon Johnson

MY CITY

When I come down to sleep death's endless night,
The threshold of the unknown dark to cross,
What to me then will be the keenest loss,
When this bright world blurs on my fading sight?
Will it be that no more I shall see the trees   5
Or smell the flowers or hear the singing birds
Or watch the flashing streams or patient herds?
No, I am sure it will be none of these.

But, ah! Manhattan's sights and sounds, her smells,
Her crowds, her throbbing force, the thrill that comes   10

From being of her a part, her subtle spells,
Her shining towers, her avenues, her slums —
O God! the stark, unutterable pity,
To be dead, and never again behold my city!

QUESTIONS

1. Identify the form of "My City." Write out a scansion of the first stanza, and mark the rhyme scheme of the whole.

2. How does the logic of Johnson's statement justify the use of the form? What is the difference between the statement made by the octave and that made by the sestet?

William Butler Yeats

LEDA AND THE SWAN°

A sudden blow: the great wings beating still
Above the staggering girl, her thighs caressed
By the dark webs, her nape caught in his bill,
He holds her helpless breast upon his breast.

How can those terrified vague fingers push
The feathered glory from her loosening thighs?

And how can body, laid in that white rush,
But feel the strange heart beating where it lies?

A shudder in the loins engenders there
The broken wall, the burning roof and tower   10
And Agamemnon° dead.
                         Being so caught up,
So mastered by the brute blood of the air,
Did she put on his knowledge with his power
Before the indifferent beak could let her drop?

LEDA AND THE SWAN. Yeats depicts the mythological rape of the mortal Leda by Zeus as transformed into a swan. 11 *Agamemnon:* Greek king who wed Leda's daughter Clytaemnestra and was killed by her on his return from conquering the city of Troy (as told in Homer's *Iliad*).

QUESTIONS

1. Identify the form, mark the rhyme scheme.

2. Does Yeats's expression divide into parts? What sort of change takes place between the octave and the sestet of the poem?

3. Why did Yeats break the 11th line as he did? What is the effect of the gap and how does it bear upon the meaning of the poem?

4. Speculate on what benefit Yeats might have derived by working in a strict form. Try your hand at rewriting the form in a loose free-verse pattern. What differences do you find?

Fixed Forms in Poetry

Percy Bysshe Shelley

ODE TO THE WEST WIND[1]

I

O wild West Wind, thou breath of Autumn's being,
Thou, from whose unseen presence the leaves dead
Are driven, like ghosts from an enchanter fleeing,

Yellow, and black, and pale, and hectic red,
Pestilence-stricken multitudes: O thou,   5
Who chariotest to their dark wintry bed

The wingeèd seeds, where they lie cold and low,
Each like a corpse within its grave, until
Thine azure sister of the Spring shall blow

Her clarion° o'er the dreaming earth, and fill   10
(Driving sweet buds like flocks to feed in air)
With living hues and odors plain and hill:

Wild Spirit, which art moving everywhere;
Destroyer and preserver; hear, oh, hear!

II

Thou on whose stream, mid the steep sky's commotion,   15
Loose clouds like earth's decaying leaves are shed,
Shook from the tangled boughs of Heaven and Ocean,

Angels of rain and lightning: there are spread
On the blue surface of thine aery surge,
Like the bright hair uplifted from the head   20

Of some fierce Maenad,° even from the dim verge
Of the horizon to the zenith's height,
The locks of the approaching storm. Thou dirge

Of the dying year, to which this closing night
Will be the dome of a vast sepulcher,   25
Vaulted with all thy congregated might

---

[1]This poem was conceived and chiefly written in a wood that skirts the Arno, near Florence, and on a day when that tempestuous wind, whose temperature is at once mild and animating, was collecting the vapors which pour down the autumnal rains. They began, as I foresaw, at sunset with a violent tempest of hail and rain, attended by that magnificent thunder and lightning peculiar to the Cisalpine regions.

The phenomenon alluded to at the conclusion of the third stanza is well known to naturalists. The vegetation at the bottom of the sea, of rivers, and of lakes, sympathizes with that of the land in the change of seasons, and is consequently influenced by the winds which announce it. [Shelley's note.]

ODE TO THE WEST WIND. 10 *clarion:* trumpet. 21 *Maenad:* a woman under the spell of the orgiastic cult of Dionysius (Greek god of wine).

Of vapors, from whose solid atmosphere
Black rain, and fire, and hail will burst: oh, hear!

III

Thou who didst waken from his summer dreams
The blue Mediterranean, where he lay,   30
Lulled by the coil of his crystàlline streams,

Beside a pumice isle° in Baiae's bay,
And saw in sleep old palaces and towers
Quivering within the wave's intenser day,

All overgrown with azure moss and flowers   35
So sweet, the sense faints picturing them! Thou
For whose path the Atlantic's level powers

Cleave themselves into chasms, while far below
The sea-blooms and the oozy woods which wear
The sapless foliage of the ocean, know   40

Thy voice, and suddenly grow gray with fear,
And tremble and despoil themselves: oh, hear!

IV

If I were a dead leaf thou mightest bear;
If I were a swift cloud to fly with thee;
A wave to pant beneath thy power, and share   45

The impulse of thy strength, only less free
Than thou, O uncontrollable! If even
I were as in my boyhood, and could be

The comrade of thy wanderings over Heaven,
As then, when to outstrip they skiey speed   50
Scarce seemed a vision; I would ne'er have striven

As thus with thee in prayer in my sore need.
Oh, lift me as a wave, a leaf, a cloud!
I fall upon the thorns of life! I bleed!

A heavy weight of hours has chained and bowed   55
One too like thee: tameless, and swift, and proud.

V

Make me thy lyre, even as the forest is:
What if my leaves are falling like its own!
The tumult of thy mighty harmonies

---

32 *pumice isle:* volcanic island.

Will take from both a deep, autumnal tone,
Sweet though in sadness. Be thou, Spirit fierce,
My spirit! Be thou me, impetuous one!   60

Drive my dead thoughts over the universe
Like withered leaves to quicken a new birth!
And, by the incantation of this verse,   65

Scatter, as from an unextinguished hearth
Ashes and sparks, my words among mankind!
Be through my lips to unawakened earth

The trumpet of a prophecy! O, Wind,
If Winter comes, can Spring be far behind?   70

QUESTIONS

1. Mark out the rhyme scheme of the first two sections and identify the form.
2. What is Shelley's subject and in what ways does it lend itself to treatment in this form?
3. Look closely at the different sections and at the development of the poem as a whole. What changes, if any, do you find between the first and final sections?
4. Mark the caesuras and full stops in the poem. How does Shelley change the momentum in strategic places and to what effect?
5. Try your hand at writing a short (9–12 line) poem using this rhyme pattern. Don't worry if your rhymes are simple.

Donald Justice

VILLANELLE AT SUNDOWN

Turn your head. Look. The light is turning yellow.
The river seems enriched thereby, not to say deepened.
Why this is, I'll never be able to tell you.

Or are Americans half in love with failure?
One used to say so, reading Fitzgerald,° as it happened.   5
(That Viking Portable,° all water-spotted and yellow—

Remember?) Or does mere distance lend a value
To things?—false, it may be, but the view is hardly cheapened.
Why this is, I'll never be able to tell you.

The smoke, those tiny cars, the whole urban milieu—   10
One can like *anything* diminishment has sharpened.
Our painter friend, Lang,° might show the whole thing yellow

VILLANELLE AT SUNDOWN.   5 *Fitzgerald:* F. Scott Fitzgerald, American novelist.   6 *Viking Portable:* popular anthology of literature.   12 *Lang:* American painter.

And not be much off. It's nuance that counts, not color —
As in some late James° novel, saved up for the long weekend,
And vivid with all the Master simply won't tell you.   15

How frail our generation has got, how sallow
And pinched with just surviving! We all go off the deep end
Finally, gold beaten thinly out to yellow.
And why this is, I'll never be able to tell you.

---

14 *James:* Henry James, whose late novels were known for their suggestive obscurity.

QUESTIONS

Justice has identified his poem as a villanelle.
1. Mark out the rhyme scheme and write down the rhymed words. Do these carry any suggestions of their own?
2. Mark all of the caesuras in this poem. What is the effect of so many pauses used in a form that usually has a smooth musical flow?
3. Justice repeats one line three times. How does the meaning change according to context? Why would the poet write this poem as a villanelle?

David Lehman

FIRST OFFENSE

I'm sorry, officer. I didn't see the sign
Because, in fact, there wasn't any. I tell you
The light was green. How much is the fine?

Will the tumor turn out malignant or benign?
Will the doctor tell us? He said he knew.   5
I'm sorry, officer. I didn't see the sign.

Not every madman is an agent of the divine,
Not all who pass are allowed to come through.
The light was green. How much is the fine?

Which is worse, the rush or the wait? The line   10
Interminable, or fear of coming late? His anxiety grew.
I'm sorry, officer. I didn't see the sign.

I'm cold sober. All I had was one glass of wine.
Was anyone hurt? Is there anything I can do?
The light was green. How much is the fine?   15

Will we make our excuses like so many clever lines,
Awkwardly delivered? Never to win, always to woo?
I'm sorry, officer. I didn't see the sign.
The light was green. How much is the fine?

1. Lehman's villanelle is also a first-person persona poem. The speaker is addressing a police officer. Can you think of any reasons why Lehman would have written the poem as a villanelle?

2. Mark the many caesuras in the poem. What is the effect of so many pauses? Try to read the poem in a natural conversational tone, and comment on the difficulties of staying with the scheme.

3. How does the meaning of repeated lines change in their different contexts? Write a short explication of Lehman's poem.

20 Imagery in Poetry

Though the word *image* generally means a visual likeness or representation, *imagery* in poetry may appeal to any of the bodily senses. Visual images are by far the most common, but poets often look for ways to evoke sound (*auditory imagery*), touch (*tactile imagery*), and even smell and taste. The imagery may occur in isolation—a poet may use strictly visual details, say—or it may be used in combinations to get the reader's senses working in concert. Consider, for instance, this poem.

Seamus Heaney

OYSTERS

Our shells clacked on the plates.
My tongue was a filling estuary,°
My palate hung with starlight:
As I tasted the salty Pleiades°
Orion dipped his foot into the water.   5

Alive and violated
They lay on their beds of ice:
Bivalves°: the split bulb
And philandering sigh of ocean.
Millions of them ripped and shucked and scattered.   10

We had driven to that coast
Through flowers and limestone
And there we were, toasting friendship,
Laying down a perfect memory
In the cool of thatch and crockery.   15

Over the Alps, packed deep in hay and snow,
The Romans hauled their oysters south to Rome:
I saw damp panniers° disgorge
The frond-lipped, brine stung
Glut of privilege   20

OYSTERS. *2 estuary:* ocean inlet.   *4 pleiades:* star cluster in the constellation Taurus.   *8 bivalve:* a mollusc with a hinged shell.   *18 panniers:* carrying baskets for horses or mules.

And was angry that my trust could not repose
In the clear light, like poetry or freedom
Leaning in from sea. I ate the day
Deliberately, that its tang
Might quicken me all into verb, pure verb.   25

As you read the following discussion, consider these questions:

1. Read through the poem carefully and note all of the images and which senses each appeals to.

2. Are the images linked in any way? Do they share thematic connection? Explain.

3. How do Heaney's images help pave the way for the powerful statement of the last three lines?

Discussion. In the first stanza alone we find images of sound ("clacked"), taste ("the salty Pleiades"), and sight ("hung with starlight"). Heaney further activates the senses in combination through his use of *synaesthesia*, which is the evocation of sensations proper to one sense by appealing to another sense. "My palate hung with starlight" is a fine instance—it is the poet's solution to one of the great difficulties that beset the descriptive writer, namely that of finding ways to represent taste. (Smell, incidentally, poses the same problem.)

The topics of *simile* and *metaphor* will be treated more fully in Chapter 21, but it is worth noting here that wherever we find imagery, there we will also find these important modes of comparison. *Simile* expresses the fact of likeness with a comparative link such as "like" or "as," and had Heaney written "My tongue was *like* a filling estuary," he would have been using a simile. Instead, he opted for the more compressed mode of *metaphor*. A metaphor omits the "like" or "as" from the equivalence: "My tongue was a filling estuary," or "the sun was a burning brand," or "the chapter on imagery was an obstacle course."

In a sense, imagery itself, even when no likeness is evoked, is a kind of metaphor. That is, the poet trusts in the power of the depicted things, that they can stand for, or suggest, moods and inner states. Indeed, poet Ezra Pound and some of his associates founded a short-lived movement called Imagism on just such a notion. *The Princeton Encyclopedia of Poetry and Poetics* characterizes Imagism thus: "A belief in the short poem, structured by the single image or metaphor and a rhythm of cadences, presenting for direct apprehension by the reader an object or scene from the external world, *and refusing to implicate the poem's effect in extended abstract meaning*" (italics mine). Here is one of the best-known examples of an Imagist poem.

Ezra Pound

IN A STATION OF THE METRO

The apparition of these faces in the crowd;
Petals on a wet, black bough.

As you read the
following discussion,
consider this
question:

1. Write an imitation of Pound's poem. Pick a common sight and then, using metaphor, transform the image into another. Strive for compression. Comment on the ease, or difficulty, of the exercise.

Discussion. The image of faces in the crowd is sharpened and intensified for the reader through the second—metaphoric—image, that of petals on a "wet, black bough." The intent of the two lines is not only to present a picture to the senses, but to recreate the dreamy sensation that attended the original perception.

The images in Pound's little poem are isolated and *static*. In longer poems, however, we often find the images in patterns or series. And while groupings of static images are often used to create a descriptive still-life effect, poets will also string together *kinetic*, or active, images to emphasize movement and change. "Spring Hail" by the Australian poet Les A. Murray shows how static and kinetic imagery can work together to bring a particular memory to life.

Les A. Murray

SPRING HAIL

This is for spring and hail, that you may remember:
for a boy long ago, and a pony that could fly.

We had huddled together a long time in the shed
in the scent of vanished corn and wild bush birds,
and then the hammering faltered, and the torn   5
cobwebs ceased their quivering and hung still
from the nested rafters. We became uneasy
at the silence that grew about us, and came out.

The beaded violence had ceased. Fresh-minted hills
smoked, and the heavens swirled and blew away.   10
The paddocks° were endless again, and all around
leaves lay beneath their trees, and cakes of moss.
Sheep trotted and propped, and shook out ice from their wool.
The hard blue highway that had carried us there
fumed as we crossed it, and the hail I scooped   15
from underfoot still bore the taste of sky
and hurt my teeth, and crackled as we walked.

This is for spring and hail, that you may remember
a boy long ago, and a pony that could fly.

With the creak and stop of a gate, we started to trespass: 20
my pony bent his head and drank up grass
while I ate ice, and wandered, and ate ice.

SPRING HAIL. 11 *paddocks:* fenced areas for animals.

Imagery in Poetry

There was a peach tree growing wild by a bank
and under it and round, sweet dented fruit
weeping pale juice amongst hail-shotten leaves,   25
and this I picked up and ate till I was filled.
I sat on a log then, listening with my skin
to the secret feast of the sun, to the long wet worms
at work in the earth, and, deeper down, the stones
beneath the earth, uneasy that their sleep   30
should be troubled by dreams of water soaking down,
and I heard with my ears the creek on its bed of mould
moving and passing with a mothering sound.

      This is for spring and hail, that you may remember
      a boy long ago on a pony that could fly.   35

My pony came up then and stood by me,
waiting to be gone. The sky was now
spotless from dome to earth, and balanced there
on the cutting-edge of mountains. It was time
to leap to the saddle and go, a thunderbolt whirling   40
sheep and saplings behind, and the rearing fence
that we took at a bound, and the old, abandoned shed
forgotten behind, and the paddock forgotten behind.
Time to shatter peace and lean into spring
as into a battering wind, and be rapidly gone.   45

It was time, high time, the highest and only time
to stand in the stirrups and shout out, blind with wind
for the height and clatter of ridges to be topped
and the racing downward after through the lands
of floating green and bridges and flickering trees.   50
It was time, as never again it was time
to pull the bridle up, so the racketing hooves
fell silent as we ascended from the hill
above the farms, far up to where the hail
formed and hung weightless in the upper air,   55
charting the birdless winds with silver roads
for us to follow and be utterly gone.

      This is for spring and hail, that you may remember
      a boy and a pony long ago who could fly.

As you read the following discussion, consider these questions:

1. Read the poem carefully and pick out four images that strike you particularly. Try to account for the effect of each.

2. Mark the images in the poem according to which sense they appeal to; comment on which senses are dominant.

3. Taking as your subject "spring rain," collect your own images—be as true to memory and as specific as you can be. Try to arrange your images into a short poem.

Discussion. Murray, an Australian, has written about the memory of a hailstorm in his native countryside. The first stanza describes the last moments of the storm, and moves from a more kinetic set of auditory and visual images ("the hammering faltered" and "the torn/ cobwebs ceased their quivering") to impressions of stillness, where the webs "hung still/ from the nested rafters." The rest of the poem moves from the silence of the storm's ending to the signs of stirring life ("Sheep trotted and propped, and shook out ice from their wool" and so on). "Spring Hail," like Heaney's "Oysters," is a banquet of sensory detailings. Murray, too, makes use of synaesthesia to render taste ("the hail I scooped/ from underfoot still bore the taste of sky") and tactile sensation ("I sat on a log then, listening with my skin"). The reader can learn a great deal about the language of imagery just by reading these two poems with care. Both draw from that original archive of sense images, the natural world.

James Schuyler

A STONE KNIFE

December 26, 1969

Dear Kenward,°
        What a pearl
of a letter knife. It's just
the thing I needed, something
to rest my eyes on, and always   5
wanted, which is to say
it's that of which I
felt the lack but
didn't know of, of no
real use and yet   10
essential as a button
box, or maps, green
morning skies, islands and
canals in oatmeal, the steam
off oyster stew. Brown   15
agate, veined as a woods
by smoke that has to it
the watery twist of eel grass
in a quick, rust-discolored
cove. Undulating lines of   20
northern evening—a Munch°
without the angst—a
hint of almost amber:°
to the nose, a resinous

A STONE KNIFE. 1 *Kenward:* Kenward Elmslie, artist friend of Schuyler. 21 *Munch:* Edvard Munch (1863–1944), Norwegian painter. 23 *amber:* fossilized resin.

thought, to the eye, a
lacquered needle green
where no green is, a
present after-image.
Sleek as an ax, bare
and elegant as a tarn,°

manly as a lingam°
November weather petrified,
it is just the thing
to do what with? To
open letters? No, it

is just the thing, an
object, dark, fierce
and beautiful in which
the surprise is that
the surprise, once

past, is always there:
which to enjoy is
not to consume. The un-
recapturable returns
in a brown world

made out of wood,
snow streaked, storm epi-
center still in stone.

---

30 *tarn:* small mountain lake. 31 *lingam:* stylized phallus worshipped as a symbol of the Hindu god Shiva.

As you read the following discussion, consider these questions:

1. Make a list of the images that the stone knife suggests to the poet. Pick three of the most unusual ones, and write a short paragraph tracing how Schuyler arrived at each.

2. Find Schuyler's various uses of color. Then reread the poem, trying hard to visualize each image. What is the final effect of so many different visualizations? Do you see the knife more or less clearly? Comment.

Discussion. Poet James Schuyler uses an array of different images in a tour de force to write a poem thanking his friend, Kenward Elmslie, for the gift of a stone knife. Schuyler is by turns wry, philosophical, and inventively descriptive. By the time he has finished it is clear that he has brought the object into the zone of cherished associations that composes this private poetic universe. The gift is much appreciated.

Shuyler begins in a relaxed and chatty fashion. In the second line he plays with the image of the knife as a "pearl." A pearl, of course, is a kind of deposit that gathers around a grain of sand in certain molluscs—something of value that grows from the merest of causes. Pearl and stone are different, but, as we shall see, the knife is acted upon by the poet's imagination until it becomes an object of considerable personal value.

The poet begins to characterize the knife in terms of images in line 11. He focuses first on its quality of essentialness, comparing it to five different things, and with each comparison adds a new dimension to his possession. It is as essential as a "button box" (humble), a "map" (practical), "green morning skies" (surreal and somewhat ominous), "islands and canals in oatmeal" (comic and child-like), and "the steam off oyster stew" (sensuous). In lines 15 and 16 he finally tells us what kind of stone it is—brown agate—and then immediately launches forth to capture its appearance by way of arresting analogies. Indeed, Schuyler presents us with a compound analogy (lines 16–20) that startles the senses even as it lures us away from the immediacy of the gift he so prizes: "veined as a woods / by smoke that has to it / the watery twist of eel grass / in a quick, rust-discolored / cove."

The poet does not let his reader pause to absorb the image, but introduces another straightaway, this time an abstraction; that is, understanding the image, getting a visual response, depends upon our knowing how the Norwegian painter Edvard Munch rendered lines. But again, no lingering. The invocation of Munch seems to have set Schuyler upon an associative track—he now cites amber (line 23), the yellow-colored petrified resin found in Scandinavian countries and used to make jewelry. You may recall the mention of "pearl" at the poem's beginning and establish a link.

The amber leads Schuyler to venture an interesting synaesthesia, or fusion of senses: the stone does not smell, but imparts to the nose "a resinous thought." And to the eye, curiously, it gives a "lacquered needle green / where no green is"—an image that is present through absence, "a present after-image." The poet understands the power of suggestion; that we try harder to establish the reality of what is missing than what is palpably present. A cloud of impressions has by now gathered around the artifact.

Shuyler cuts through the diffusion with a series of plain comparisons, each a simile. The knife is "Sleek as an ax, bare / and elegant as a tarn, / manly as a lingam," and as with the earlier string of comparisons, each one is a bit more outlandish. Then in line 32, the poet switches from simple similes to a more suggestive metaphor, calling the object "November weather petrified," with the word "petrified" triggering associations directly back to the amber, and indirectly to the pearl.

Having made all of these different imagistic attributions, Schuyler moves in line 36 back to origins; he suddenly insists the knife is "just the thing, an / object, dark, fierce / and beautiful." The simple power seems all the more evident to us now that its various poetic associations have been inventoried. But then, not quite content to end on the note of self-evident simplicity, Schuyler invokes one last string of images in line 45 to 49. Now there is confusion. Having spoken of a surprise which is there to be had and returned to, he refers to the "un-recapturable," saying that it returns "in a brown world / made out of wood, / snow streaked, storm epi- / center still in stone." What is the poet getting at? It would seem that if it is the "surprise" that *is* there to be recaptured, then the "unrecapturable" must be the origin of the stone itself, its ancient material beginnings in a world we can scarcely imagine, a world the poet must characterize in these obscure and primal terms. The final image is baffling, a cipher for some larger mystery, the double sense of the word "still" fixing both the stillness at the center of the storm (as in the eye of a hurricane) *and* the fact that the original conditions endure, are *still evident* in the stone.

Though figures of speech like *similes* and *metaphors* will be treated at greater length in the next chapter, they are so intimately bound up with images and image-making that they deserve mention here as well. Similes and metaphors are, to reiterate, figures of comparison. We describe one thing in terms of another. If we make the comparison explicit—"The bread was as hard as a rock"—then we are using simile. If we state the comparison directly, substituting one thing for another—"The bread was a rock"—we are using metaphor. Poets, in creating images to convey sensations of various kinds, are constantly searching our comparisons. "My mistress' eyes are nothing like the sun," writes Shakespeare, making a simile—rather, the reverse of a simile. "When I behold, upon the night's starred face,/ Huge cloudy symbols of a high romance," asserts John Keats; the implicit likening of the night sky to a face is a metaphor. It is virtually impossible to find any poems that make use of imagery that do not resort to strategies of simile or comparison. While reading the poems and questions that follow, try to monitor just how the poets achieve intensity in their imagistic effects.

IMAGERY: POEMS WITH QUESTIONS

T. E. Hulme

AUTUMN

A touch of cold in the Autumn night—
I walked abroad,
And saw the ruddy moon lean over a hedge
Like a red-faced farmer.
I did not stop to speak, but nodded,   5
And round about were the wistful stars
With white faces like town children.

QUESTIONS

T. E. Hulme was a gifted English critic and the author of a small handful of poems. When Ezra Pound was formulating his theories of Imagism, he seized upon Hulme's short poems, finding them exemplary.
1. What are the governing images in this seven-line poem? What is the relation between the images; what opposition do they suggest?
2. What is the overall effect of the two images in combination?

William Corbett

YELLOW

A gust shakes
dusty yellow pollen
off the pine trees
onto the lake

washed thickly
upon the shore.   5
The bumblebee works
his yellowblack head
into the baby blue
bell like comfrey° flower   *a hairy, bristly plant* 10
for a moment goes off
off like twilight's scatter
flicked from the young
banana green ferns.
The moon behind   15
blue and black clouds
the kitchen's bug lights
like buttercups spread
over the pine planks.

QUESTIONS

William Corbett's short poem is composed exclusively of images.

1. Isolate the images and discuss how they bring a world to life.

2. How does Corbett use color throughout the poem? What is the recurrent color and how does it knit the poem together?

3. Find the places where Corbett generates sensations of texture and explain how they have been achieved.

4. What overall impression emerges from this collection of impressions? What kind of atmosphere does Corbett evoke?

Jane Kenyon

CATCHING FROGS

I crouched beside the deepest pool,
and the smell of damp and moss
rose rich between my knees. Water-striders
creased the silver-black silky surface.
Rapt, I hardly breathed. Gnats   5
roiled in a shaft of sun.

Back again after supper I'd see
a nose poke up by the big flat stone
at the lip of the fall; then the humped
eyes and the slippery emerald head,   10
freckled brown. The buff membrane
pulsed under the jaw while
subtleties of timing played in my mind.

With a patience that came like grace
I waited. Mosquitoes moaned all
around. Better to wait. Better to reach
from behind. . . . It grew dark.

I came into the warm, bright room
where father held aloft the evening
paper, and there was talk, and maybe
laughter, though I don't remember laughter.

QUESTIONS

1. Isolate the different images Kenyon uses. Pay close attention to her adjectives, adverbs, and verbs, as well as to her detailing of colors.
2. How does Kenyon use these images to focus upon and enlarge a small part of a child's world?
3. Discuss the interplay in this poem between static and kinetic images. What is the atmosphere that Kenyon creates in the first three stanzas?
4. How does the final stanza "break the spell"? What is the effect of the last four lines? How does the transition establish the difference between the child's world and that of the adults?

SUGGESTION FOR WRITING

Recall some specific and absorbing activity from the time of your own childhood. Write a short paragraph in which you use images of different kinds to evoke sensations of that activity.

Elizabeth Spires

WHODUNIT

Like a photographer developing a photograph,
slipping the light-sensitive paper
into solution until the image rises,
clear as a piece of evidence,
day rises slowly out of dawn,
each tree dripping with mist, leaning
toward the house with mute, inarticulate
secrets, new leaves suffusing the rooms
with the green light of memory,
green's utter recall.

The day is a question mark,
unpredictable as the detective novel
you were reading last night:
a car on a hairpin curve skidding

toward a guardrail, a woman
pushed from a second-story window
who may be guilty or innocent.
The book lies facedown
on the table beside the glass of water
and the sleeping pills, open to the page
where you left off reading,
so that she falls and continues to fall
all night, silently screaming,
an unfinished, interrupted dream
with only one possible ending.

Below the yard is brightening,
long shadows lie like stains in the grass.
You sleep unaware I'm not beside you,
the sound of a pen scratching out
a message on paper, a car door slamming,
a shout, making their way
into your dreams, the first clues
that the day may or may not turn out
as you expected coming to you in sleep,
gentle, insistent, veiled.

QUESTIONS

1. Isolate the various images in the poem. What is the difference between the first and second stanza in terms of how the images are used.

2. What is the effect of the transitions between stanzas one and two, and two and three?

3. Spires uses the governing simile of a developing photograph in the first stanza. How does that simile return in different form in the third stanza?

4. What is Spires trying to express? What is the significance of the title?

Thomas Lux

THERE WERE SOME SUMMERS

There were some summers
like this: The blue barn steaming,
some cowbirds dozing with their heads
on each other's shoulders, the electric fences
humming low in the mid-August heat . . .
So calm the slow sweat existing
in half-fictive memory: a boy
wandering from house, to hayloft, to coop,
past a dump where a saddle rots
on a sawhorse, through the still forest

of a cornfield, to a pasture talking to himself
or the bored, baleful Holsteins° nodding
beneath the round shade of catalpa,° the boy
walking his trail toward the brook
in a deep but mediocre gully,   15
through skunk cabbage and popweed,
down sandbanks (a descending
quarter-acre Sahara), the boy wandering,
thinking nothing, thinking: *Sweatbox,*
sweatbox, the boy on his way   20
toward a minnow whose slight beard
tells the subtleties of the current, holding there,
in water cold enough to break your ankles.

THERE WERE SOME SUMMERS. 12 *Holsteins:* large black-and-white dairy cows.   13 *catalpa:* large-
leafed American tree.

QUESTIONS

1. Pick out the different kinds of images Lux uses, paying special attention to static and kinetic effects.
2. What kind of mood or atmosphere does Lux evoke, and how do the specific images contribute to the evocation?
3. How does Lux vary the scale of his descriptions to achieve a sense of surprise at the end
of the poem?

SUGGESTION FOR WRITING

On a separate sheet of paper write out a list, in sequence, of all of the nouns Lux uses. Without referring to the poem, write a short prose paragraph using the complete list.

Anthony Hecht

MESSAGE FROM THE CITY

It is raining here.
On my neighbor's fire escape
geraniums are set out
in their brick-clay pots,
along with the mop,   5
old dishrags, and a cracked
enamel bowl for the dog.

I think of you out there
on the sandy edge of things,
rain strafing the beach,   10
the white maturity

of bones and broken shells,
and little tin shovels and cars
rusting under the house.

And between us there is—what?
Love and constraint,
conditions, conditions,
and several hundred miles
of billboards, filling-stations,
and little dripping gardens.
The fir tree full of whispers,
trinkets of water,
the bob, duck, and release
of the weighted rose,
life in the freshened stones.
(They used to say that rain
is good for growing boys,
and once I stood out in it
hoping to rise a foot.
The biggest drops fattened
on the gutters under the eaves,
sidled along the slant,
picked up speed, let go,
and met their dooms in a "plock"
beside my gleaming shins.
I must have been near the size
of your older son.)

Yesterday was nice.
I took my boys to the park.
We played Ogre on the grass.
I am, of course, the Ogre,
and invariably get killed.
Merciless and barefooted,
they sneak up from behind
and they let me have it.

O my dear, my dear,
today the rain pummels
the sour geraniums
and darkens the grey pilings
of your house, built upon sand.
And both of us, full grown,
have weathered a long year.
Perhaps your casual glance
will settle from time to time
on the sea's travelling muscles
that flex and roll their strength
under its rain-pocked skin.

Imagery in Poetry

And you'll see where the salt winds
have blown bare the seaward side
of the berry bushes,
and will notice
the faint, fresh
smell of iodine.

60

QUESTIONS

1. How does Hecht collect images to suggest city life? Isolate those that seem especially effective, and explain why.
2. How do the urban images resonate against the images of the sea in the fifth stanza? Comment upon the difference in images and how they are used.
3. Look carefully at Hecht's use of water imagery, and write a short commentary on what you see as his poetic strategy.
4. Compare Hecht's poem to Lowell's "The Old Flame" (Chapter 17). Focus on tone and emotional content.

Mark Rudman

CHROME

On the late news I watch hundreds of helmeted riders
almost indecipherable in the dust
tearing up the holes of desert turtles in the Mojave°—
and I remember our bravura cycling:
the trick was to go as fast as you could   5
without being thrown by rock or incline.
Hills leeched of color,
the desert a kind of form,
with rimrock and succulents° and gulches
providing borders—boundaries.   10
Dust and desire.
I wanted to go down toward the desert floor,
where the spines of the saguaro cactus
guarded the sticky pulp I loved,
the sweet, incomparable, centerless center.   15
O sweet sixteen, to be sprung again and again against
the rock-studded sand, the danger not
in the desert but around it.
The body's oneness with the mind
on the lean machine seemed just right, the body   20
soaring while hovering close
to the sand as the Honda 125

CHROME. 3 *Mojave*: a Southwestern desert.   9 *succulents*: juicy plants like cactus.

jounced past yucca° and cactus and took
the long dip into the arroyo° where the ring
of distant chimney rocks and hills   25
like space stations receded, and I
twisted the handle-bars like the horns
of a steer to side-wind up and over the rim.
I was thrown only by breaks in the terrain,
grit and stones and dips in the sand,   30
or by sudden soft patches; or by swerving to avoid
a brush with tumbleweed or a mesquite bush.
Spills were rehearsals for free falling, a way to slow
time down, cease to feel your own weight,
achieve clarity and edge as if edging down   35
off the concrete onto the sand was the aim. . . .
Circling demoniacally, I didn't notice
the ferocious sun, a fusion of horizon and sky,
or the hawks stunned and motionless as clouds.
Each time, bloody but happy,   40
I eased back onto the highway,
and set off down the canyon road
into the sun, whitening as it hung
level with the cliff. Once I rode toward it
hearing only the hush of the tires,   45
the pure elation of it taking my head off as I took
a horseshoe curve at 50 and approached
an even sharper one—the slender cycle shaking apart—;
and I wondered *what to do*, like Porthos°
going back to the bomb he'd planted to make sure   50
he'd lit the fuse . . . when—BOOM!—;
I turned the accelerator handle all the way forward
to slow down—gunning the engine
by accident when the cycle bucked, reared,
and surged ahead—I rose, the cliff's gravel   55
gleamed, radiant, it was all over;
I could feel my soul leave my body and see my body flung out
over the canyon rim —
it looked as if I'd leap the cliff and fly
into the sun, time gone, space erased,   60
not a piñon in sight to break my fall, only the cliff
wall, studded with jagged stones.
And I knew if I braked abruptly on the gravel the bike
would catapult me headlong into the open,
so I let go of the throttle—threw up my hands—   65
and the bike went off the highway, keeled over
and died at the cliff's edge.
I owe my life to letting go.

---

    23 *yucca:* a tall, stout-stemmed plant.   24 *arroyo:* a gully, gulch, or stream-bed.   49 *Porthos:* one
of the three musketeers in a Dumas story.

QUESTIONS

1. Find the various images in Rudman's poem. What senses do they primarily appeal to?
2. How does Rudman build up his descriptions to give you the sense of riding a motorcycle?
3. Isolate and comment upon the verbs—how do they help to evoke sensation?
4. Locate Rudman's similes and metaphors. How do they intensify the impression of riding a motorcycle?
5. What is the message of Rudman's account? How does the last line convey a literal truth and a larger philosophical truth as well?

SUGGESTION FOR WRITING

Take an activity—perhaps a sport—that you know well and write a prose description that uses different kinds of images to bring it to life. Try to develop several similes or metaphors.

21 Figures of Speech in Poetry

Since poetry almost by definition uses language in a heightened way, it is natural to find that poems are crowded with *figures of speech*. While these figures come in various forms—we shall look at these shortly—they are all fundamentally ways of heightening and intensifying language.

On the most basic level, words *denote* and *connote*. The denotation of a word is its specific meaning, that which we would discover if we looked it up in the dictionary. The connotations are more elusive, for they comprise the various shades of suggestion and association that words inevitably carry. A "flash flood" is defined as "a sudden and destructive rush of water." But I cannot hear the word without picturing bursts of lightning—for me they are part of the connotation of the word "flash."

Figures of speech may be said to operate at the next level. They change, and generally amplify, the meaning of a statement in any one of a number of ways. They make free use of both denotations and connotations of words. Figures of speech include metaphor, simile, apostrophe, hyperbole, understatement, metonymy, synecdoche, personification, and oxymoron. Some are, naturally, more important—and more common—than others.

But these figures of speech are by no means exclusive to poetry. They turn up everywhere—in advertisements, speeches, and in our daily conversation. The person who says, "I was a complete mess yesterday," is speaking metaphorically. The mother rolling her eyes up at her teenage daughter and saying "Help me, God!" is using apostrophe. If we say of a linebacker that he is "as big as a barn" we are simultaneously calling on simile and hyperbole, or overstatement. A "hand offered in marriage" is a synecdoche. And so on. The point is just that in studying the literary process—in this case the poetic process—we give names to things we do naturally all the time.

METAPHOR AND SIMILE

Metaphor and simile have both been mentioned in earlier sections, but since they are such an integral part of poetry they deserve to be discussed at greater length. Both are forms of comparison and we resort to them naturally whenever we wish to give a special emphasis to our expression. Simply saying "He was tall" might not convey the desired effect. If we said, "He was as tall as a giraffe," we would be using *simile*, which is the direct correlation of two things—in this case, person and animal—by means of *like*, *as*, *than*, or some other word establishing direct relation. If we dropped the connective word and simply stated, "He was a giraffe," then we would be using a *metaphor*. A metaphor is literally a "carrying across," or substitution.

Metaphors and similes are used to add color to speech and to single out specific properties or attributes for special attention. Quite naturally, therefore, they partake of *hyperbole* (overstatement) or *understatement*. The comparison of a tall person with a giraffe is hyperbolic—he is not *really* that tall. When we use understatement, in contrast, we say less than we mean. "The dictator was not a nice person" readily suggests crimes and outrages that have not been stated. It likewise suggests an ironic attitude on the part of the speaker. *Irony* results when there is a discrepancy between what is stated and what is meant. Understatement is one of the most effective ways of creating irony.

Simile and metaphor function in various ways in a poem. They can be used as a singular instance, as in this selection from a poem called "Spring," where Robert Hass uses a double simile to make his point:

> A bearded bird-like man
> (He looked like a Russian priest
> with imperial bearing
> and a black ransacked raincoat)
> turned to us, cleared   5
> his cultural throat, and
> told us both interminably
> who Ugo Betti was.

In fact, Hass uses two similes. The man is "bird-like" and he "looked like a Russian priest." Neither comparison is mentioned again.

Quite often, however, a poet will use metaphors or similes in some sort of pattern, allowing one comparison to suggest others until a network of correspondences is created. When that network becomes part of the governing idea of the poem, as it does in so many of the sonnets of Shakespeare, it is called a *conceit*. The reader is called upon to recognize the logic of the comparison and to judge its applicability to the subject. Irish poet Eavan Boland's "Lace" is a good example of a contemporary usage of a conceit. The act of writing is not only likened to the ancient art of lace-making, but the comparisons are extended to make a moral: that both arts attain their highest beauty at a price. Makers of lace not infrequently lost their sight; it is for us to determine what may be the cost imposed upon the makers of sentences.

Eavan Boland

LACE

Bent over
the open notebook—

light fades out
making the trees stand out
and my room   5
at the back
of the house, dark.

In the dusk
I am still
looking for it —
the language that is   10

lace:

a baroque° obligation
at the wrist
of a prince   15
in a petty court.
Look, just look
at the way he shakes out

the thriftless phrases,
the crystal rhetoric   20
of bobbined° knots
and bosses:°
a vagrant drift
of emphasis
to wave away an argument   25
or frame the hand
he kisses;
which, for all that, is still

what someone
in the corner   30
of a room,
in the dusk,
bent over
as the light was fading

lost their sight for.   35

LACE. 13 *baroque:* ornamented European art style of the seventeenth century.   21 *bobbined:* knotted thread wrapped around pins or bobbins.   22 *bosses:* raised or knobbed patterns in fabric.

Read the preceding discussion and consider these questions:

1. Read Boland's poem carefully and identify any metaphors or similes.

2. Substitute the "like" and "as" of simile for Boland's metaphors. How do the substitutions change the poem?

3. How effective do you find Boland's conceit, likening writing to lacemaking? Does she make either art seem attractive or worth pursuing? Explain your answer.

SYNECDOCHE, METONYMY, AND OTHER FIGURES

Synecdoche and *metonymy* are two related figures of speech—so related, in fact, that it is often difficult to tell the difference between them. *Synecdoche* (si-néc-do-kee) makes use of a part to indicate a whole. The expression noted earlier—a "hand of-fered in marriage"—is a synecdoche, with the hand standing for the entire person. *Metonymy* (m'-táwn-ni-mee), meanwhile, replaces the thing intended with some other thing that is associated with it. To say, "Tell Robert I send my kisses," is to make a statement using metonymy, with the kisses representing love or fond greetings.

Robert Hass's poem "Spring" was cited earlier for its use of simile. The ending of the poem likewise supplies a fine illustration of the similarity of synecdoche and metonymy. Here is the complete poem.

Robert Hass

SPRING

We bought great ornamental oranges,
Mexican cookies, a fragrant yellow tea.
Browsed the bookstores. You
asked mildly, "Bob, who is Ugo Betti°?"   *Italian writer*
A bearded bird-like man   5
(he looked like a Russian priest
with imperial bearing
and a black ransacked raincoat)
turned to us, cleared
his cultural throat, and   10
told us both interminably
who Ugo Betti was. The slow
filtering of sun through windows
glazed to gold the silky hair
along your arms. Dusk was   15
a huge weird phosphorescent beast
dying slowly out across the bay.
Our house waited and our books,
the skinny little soldiers on the shelves.
After dinner I read one anyway.   20
You chanted, "Ugo Betti has no bones,"
and when I said, "The limits of my language
are the limits of my world," you laughed.
We spoke all night in tongues,
in fingertips, in teeth.   25

As you read the following discussion, consider these questions:

1. Pick out and identify Hass's various figures of speech.
2. Think of several interesting or unusual uses of synecdoche and metonymy, and use them to write an absurd or comic poem.

Discussion. The "tongues," "fingertips," and "teeth" are, on the one hand, exten-sions of the body that represent the whole; they are, on the other hand, specific nouns used to represent a general array of intimate contacts. They are, in this sense, both synecdoche and metonymy. The Hass poem also makes use of metaphor at several points. Dusk is "a huge weird phosphorescent beast" and books are "skinny little soldiers." The latter is a specific instance of metaphor known as *personification*, where a non-human thing or concept is given human attributes. Personification has been a common figure of speech from the very beginnings of the poetic art. Homer begins several of the books of his great epics, the *Iliad* and the *Odyssey*, with descriptions of the "rosy fingers of the dawn." Here is John Milton's sonnet "How Soon Hath Time," which personifies that most abstract of entities, time.

John Milton

HOW SOON HATH TIME

How soon hath Time, the subtle thief of youth,
   Stol'n on his wing my three-and-twentieth year!
   My hasting° days fly on with full career,°
   But my late spring no bud or blossom shew'th.
Perhaps my semblance° might deceive the truth,   5
   That I to manhood am arriv'd so near,
   And inward ripeness doth much less appear,
   That some more timely-happy spirits indu'th.°
Yet it be less or more, or soon or slow,
   It shall be still in strictest measure ev'n,   10
   To that same lot, however mean or high,
Toward which Time leads me, and the will of Heav'n;
   All is, if I have grace to use it so,
   As ever in my great Taskmaster's eye.

HOW SOON HATH TIME. 3 *hasting*: hurrying; *career*: momentum. 5 *semblance*: appearance. 8 *indu'th*: puts on (endure + -eth).

Read the poem and consider these questions:	1. In addition to personifying Time, Milton makes use of several figures of speech in this poem—identify the figures of speech. 2. What does Milton communicate by using these various figures of speech? Can you construct a short interpretation of his sonnet?

APOSTROPHE: An apostrophe is a figure of speech that literally means "a turning away." It occurs in poetry when the speaker addresses words to some person or thing, very often calling it to mind in its absence. Thus, Allen Ginsberg begins his poem "A Supermarket in California" by addressing his great—and long-dead—poetic predecessor:

> What thoughts I have of you tonight, Walt Whitman, for I
> walked down the sidestreets under the trees with a headache
> self-conscious looking at the full moon.

A poet will often use apostrophe as a way of giving direction and intensity to an interior meditation. The figure of speech allows what is essentially a monologue to take on some of the animation of a dialogue. It allows the poet, further, to carry on a private communion with some figure from the past and establishes a mood of intimacy.

OXYMORON: An oxymoron is a figure of speech that links together two terms which are customarily opposites. It is nearly always used to convey intensity—"burning ice" is more vivid than "freezing ice"—or to suggest complex emotional states: "He felt a fond anger toward the boy." An easy way to remember the term is to add an *f*. A "foxy moron" is an oxymoron.

FIGURES OF SPEECH: POEMS AND QUESTIONS

Carolyn Forché

DEPARTURE

We take it with us, the cry
of a train slicing a field
leaving its stiff suture, a distant
tenderness as when rails slip
behind us and our windows   5
touch the field, where it seems
the dead are awake and so reach
for each other. Your hand
cups the light of a match
to your mouth, to mine, and I want   10
to ask if the dead hold
their mouths in their hands like this
to know what is left of them.
Between us, a tissue of smoke,
a bundle of belongings, luggage   15
that will seem to float beside us,
the currency we will change
and change again. Here is the name
of a friend who will take you in,
the papers of a man who vanished,   20
the one you will become when
the man you have been disappears.
I am the woman whose photograph
you will not recognize, whose face
emptied your eyes, whose eyes   25
were brief, like the smallest
of cities we slipped through.

1. Locate the similes and metaphors in this poem.

2. Comment upon Forché's use of understatement at the end of the poem. What purpose does it serve?

3. Can you find an instance of synecdoche in the last five lines of the poem?

4. What is the situation suggested in the poem and how do the various images and figures of speech add their suggestions?

Matthew Arnold

DOVER BEACH

The sea is calm to-night.
The tide is full, the moon lies fair
Upon the straits;—on the French coast the light
Gleams and is gone; the cliffs of England stand,
Glimmering and vast, out in the tranquil bay.   5
Come to the window, sweet is the night air!
Only, from the long line of spray
Where the sea meets the moon-blanched° land,
Listen! you hear the grating roar
Of pebbles which the waves draw back, and fling,   10
At their return, up the high strand,°
Begin, and cease, and then again begin,
With tremulous cadence slow, and bring
The eternal note of sadness in.

Sophocles° long ago   15
Heard it on the Aegean,° and it brought
Into his mind the turbid ebb and flow
Of human misery; we
Find also in the sound a thought,
Hearing it by this distant northern sea.   20

The Sea of Faith
Was once, too, at the full, and round earth's shore
Lay like the folds of a bright girdle furled.
But now I only hear
Its melancholy, long, withdrawing roar,   25
Retreating, to the breath
Of the night wind, down the vast edges drear
And naked shingles° of the world.

DOVER BEACH. 8 *moon-blanched*: moon whitened.   11 *strand*: beach.   15 *Sophocles*: author of ancient Greek tragedies such as *Oedipus Rex* (Chapter 30).   16 *Aegean*: Grecian sea.   28 *shingles*: beachstones.

                      Figures of Speech in Poetry

Ah, love, let us be true
To one another! for the world, which seems
To lie before us like a land of dreams,
So various, so beautiful, so new,
Hath really neither joy, nor love, nor light,   35
Nor certitude, nor peace, nor help for pain;
And we are here as on a darkling° plain
Swept with confused alarms of struggle and flight
Where ignorant armies clash by night.

—————————
35 *darkling*: clouded, obscure, gloomy.

QUESTIONS

1. Arnold invokes the sea in all three stanzas of his poem. At what point does the sea become a metaphor? What does he seek to evoke with the metaphor; how does he use it to create a thematic core in the poem?

2. Find the similes used by Arnold. How do they add to and intensify the central metaphoric concept?

3. Who was Sophocles, and what is the poet's purpose in invoking his name?

4. Where does Arnold use apostrophe and how does it change the direction of the poem?

5. What message is Arnold finally giving to his love? What is his view of life and what kind of attitude does he advocate?

SUGGESTION FOR WRITING

Write a short prose paragraph in which you suggest how Arnold's wisdom does or does not apply to your experience.

Jorie Graham

I WATCHED A SNAKE

hard at work in the dry grass
        behind the house
catching flies. It kept on
        disappearing.
And though I know this has   5
        something to do

with lust, today it seemed
        to have to do
with work. It took it almost half
        an hour to thread   10
roughly ten feet of lawn,
        so slow

between the blades you couldn't see
        it move. I'd watch

its path of body in the grass go
    suddenly invisible
only to reappear a little
    further on

black knothead up, eyes on
    a butterfly.
This must be perfect progress where
    movement appears
to be a vanishing, a mending
    of the visible

by the invisible—just as we
    stitch the earth,
it seems to me, each time
    we die, going
back under, coming back up. . . .
    It is the simplest

stitch, this going where we must,
    leaving a not
unpretty pattern by default. But going
    out of hunger
for small things—flies, words—going
    because one's body

goes. And in this disconcerting creature
    a tiny hunger,
one that won't even press
    the dandelions down,
retrieves the necessary blue-
    black dragonfly

that has just landed on a pod . . .
    all this to say
I'm not afraid of them
    today, or anymore
I think. We are not, were not, ever
    wrong. Desire

is the honest work of the body,
    its engine, its wind.
It too must have its sails—wings
    in this tiny mouth, valves
in the human heart, meanings like sailboats
    setting out

over the mind. Passion is work
    that retrieves us,
lost stitches. It makes a pattern of us,
    it fastens us
to sturdier stuff
    no doubt.

15

20

25

30

35

40

45

50

55

60

1. Find the metaphors and similes in Graham's poem.

2. Trace the progression of the poem. Where does the image of stitching originate? How does the poet's central conceit hold together the various ideas? And what does Graham mean when she states in her last stanza that passion "fastens us/ to sturdier stuff"?

3. Is this in any sense a religious poem? If so, explain.

Askold Melnyczuk

YOUNG WOMAN IN THE PRADO°

"And Humanity is like a young girl
abounding with longing . . ."
Miguel de Unamuno°

My feet are sore, and so
is my spirit, from so
much to see. Like this Greco°
with his people braiding into

fire, the relentless
bodies stalks and nettles
or weird-colored flames, his
world far as Cadiz°

from the things I know.
This is not shopping. No
straw hats, flowers, or zapatos.°
What should I do

with what I see?
That boy near
the fat woman —
the dark one

in tight jeans,
black eyes, full lips:
I saw him before, at
the Garden of Earthly Delights°

where the Bosch-God, hidden
in the canvas, tortured sinners for their
indiscreet desires.

5

10

15

20

YOUNG WOMAN IN THE PRADO. The Prado is a famous art museum in Madrid, which the young woman is presumably visiting from her native Colombia. *Miguel de Unamuno:* a Spanish philosopher (1864–1936). 3 *Greco:* El Greco, seventeenth-century Spanish painter of passionate spiritual figures. 8 *Cadiz:* a Mediterranean port city in Spain. 11 *zapatos:* Spanish for "shoes." 20 *Garden of Earthly Delights:* allegorical fantasy painting by fifteenth-century Dutch artist Hieronymus Bosch.

Surrounded by saints, why   25
do I feel he's
asking me to choose?
My father, the minister,

told me I couldn't
keep "the ecstasy   30
of faith" alive
without prayer and good

works. He said the body
was like Chinese Mountains
lunging upward, to the sky.   35
I would like to be

seven again, and riding
bareback by the streams
on my grandfather's farm,
Medellín's° mountains drowsing   40

in twilight, and knowing
my sisters and mother
stood in the kitchen
preparing pescado, setting

plates, their laughter stirring   45
the air, drifting
through the farmhouse,
braiding with orchids and leaves

under the crowded sky.

———————————
   40 *Medellín:* provincial city in Colombia.

QUESTIONS

1. These are meant to be the thoughts of a young woman as she walks through the Prado Museum in Madrid. How does her thought process naturally make use of metaphor and simile?
2. Find the synaesthesia in the last lines of the poem and explain why the poet would use it.
3. How do the last lines echo the opening lines, and what is the effect of this?
4. How does the imagery of the last lines differ from that of the opening? How does the difference help to explain the poem?

22 Symbol, Allegory, Myth, and Allusion in Poetry

In the previous chapter we looked at various figures of speech, among them metaphor and simile, which find likeness and establish comparisons between disparate things. Of the two, metaphor is the more immediate; it omits the comparative terms, such as "like" or "as," and proposes a direct equivalence. A is not *like* B, A *is* B: *Robert is a giraffe*.

SYMBOL

A *symbol* may be viewed as a specific sort of metaphor, at least insofar as one thing is made to stand in for, or represent, another. Symbols differ from conventional metaphors, however, in that what is symbolized is generally a concept or an abstraction, and that the importance is more universalized. The purpose of a metaphor is to heighten some particular attribute—"Her eyes were burning coals" emphasizes the intensity of a gaze, for instance—while the purpose of a symbol is to point the reader toward a larger, and more generalized, order of significance. A wedding ring symbolizes union (as well as purity, true love, constancy, and so on), and a bird symbolizes freedom. A white dove, meanwhile, is a symbol for peace.

These are examples of universal or conventional symbols; they have been accepted as having specific public meanings throughout our culture. But symbols can also be *contextual*, depending for their meaning upon the conventions of a particular group. We have all seen enough westerns to know that when an Indian chief breaks an arrow it means that trust has been broken and war is nigh. But in another context the breaking of an arrow might represent the end of fighting. In the second instance, the arrow is a symbol for honor and integrity; in the first, it stands for conflict. The significance of the breaking depends upon the accepted meaning of the symbol.

Looking for symbols in poetry can be a tricky business. For one thing, it is seldom the case that A symbolizes B. Symbols are not so much indicators of equivalence as suggestive entities. The ring is a symbol for marriage, but what that symbolism involves is a rich array of ideals and values. The reader has to be very careful not to rush through a poem with a pointer saying "This symbolizes that." Not all poets use symbolism, and even in poetry that does use it, not every thing is a symbol. Most commonly, things are what they are: the rabbit is just a rabbit, the cherries are themselves. (But the apple . . . ?)

If the symbol-making process is so mysterious, and if there are no hard-and-fast rules, then how is a reader to know whether or not a poet is using symbolism in a poem? It comes down to a judgment call, finally. We should first attempt to read the poem on the literal level, accepting all denotations at face value. As we do so, we should pay close heed to our responses. Is the description of gathering clouds just that, or is there some reason—something in the logic of the poem as a whole—that leads us to think that the darkening sky may stand for something more? If so, then *what* does it stand for? Again, we have to trust our responses as readers. What does a darkening sky make us think of; what does it suggest? Is it prominent enough in the poem to warrant being called a symbol, or is it just the poet's way to add a certain tension to the atmosphere? Are we looking at a symbol of approaching death or just a natural atmospheric disturbance? Some examples and further discussion may bring some clarity to this elusive subject.

Here are two short poems that make obvious and intentional use of symbols. The first, by Langston Hughes, actually makes the symbolic connection explicit.

Langston Hughes

THE NEGRO SPEAKS OF RIVERS

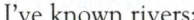

I've known rivers:
I've known rivers ancient as the world and older than the
    flow of human blood in human veins.

My soul has grown deep like the rivers.

I bathed in the Euphrates° when dawns were young.   5
I built my hut near the Congo° and it lulled me to sleep.
I looked upon the Nile° and raised the pyramids above it.
I heard the singing of the Mississippi when Abe Lincoln went down to New
    Orleans, and I've seen its muddy bosom turn all golden in the sunset.

I've known rivers:
Ancient, dusky rivers.

My soul has grown deep like rivers.   10

THE NEGRO SPEAKS OF RIVERS. 4 *Euphrates:* part of the Tigris-Euphrates river valley flowing from Turkey to the Persian Gulf; called the "cradle of civilization" for cultures developing there since 4000 B.C. 5 *Congo:* an African river in present-day Zaire. 6 *Nile:* a river central to ancient African and Egyptian cultures.

As you read the following discussion, consider the questions:

1. Study Hughes's various ways of speaking of rivers; write a short description of the different symbolic uses he makes of them.

2. How does Hughes use different rivers to encapsulate aspects of history? Explain his image of the Mississippi turning "all golden in the sunset."

Discussion. Hughes has taken a common feature of the natural world, a river, and has drawn strong connections to the historical experience of black people. In two instances he uses a simile likening the speaker's soul to rivers. But the final effect of the poem is such that the river is more than just an element in a comparison. We feel that Hughes is saying that the collective soul of the black race *is* a river, deep and enduring.

Alfred, Lord Tennyson's short poem, "The Eagle," can likewise be read as symbolic. But Tennyson makes no connection to the human sphere. Indeed, he does not mention humans at all. If we choose to regard his eagle as symbolic it is because we relate the images in the description to our own idealized conception of courageous independence. (In America, of course, the eagle *is* a public symbol of these very qualities. Readers in other parts of the world might not have identical associations.)

Alfred, Lord Tennyson

THE EAGLE

He clasps the crag with crooked hands;
Close to the sun in lonely lands;
Ring'd with the azure world, he stands.

The wrinkled sea beneath him crawls;
He watches from his mountain walls,   5
And like a thunderbolt he falls.

Read the preceding discussion and consider this question:

1. What symbolic suggestions do you get from Tennyson's eagle? How do you account for the impact of his last line? Look at his use of simile and his metrical technique.

Rivers and eagles are both universal kinds of symbols, and while the associations of different readers may vary to some degree, the general suggestions do not pose much of a problem. But sometimes poets find or create symbols, choosing to endow a particular thing with higher conceptual significance. Thus, Robert Pinsky writes of finding the mouthbones of a shark on the beach. His poem is a meditation upon the symbolic possibilities of the artifact; it hints at many things, but refuses to hand the reader any simple message. We might think of this as a poem about a symbol in search of a meaning.

Robert Pinsky

THE WANT BONE

The tongue of the waves tolled in the earth's bell.
Blue rippled and soaked in the fire of blue.
The dried mouthbones of a shark in the hot swale°
Gaped on nothing but sand on either side.

The bone tasted of nothing and smelled of nothing.   5
A scalded toothless harp, uncrushed, unstrung.
The joined arcs made the shape of birth and craving
And the welded-open shape kept mouthing O.

Ossified° cords held the corners together
In groined° spirals pleated like a summer dress.   10
But where was the limber grin, the gash of pleasure?
Infinitesimal mouths bore it away.

The beach scrubbed and etched and pickled it clean.
But O I love you it sings, my little my country
My food my parent my child I want you my own   15
My flower my fin my life my lightness my O.

THE WANT BONE. *3 swale:* low or marshy area.   *9 ossified:* turned to bone.   *10 groined:* curved edging joining two ceiling vaults.

Read the poem
and consider these
questions:

1. What associations do you have with the shark? Are these reflected in any way in the image of the shark's jawbone?

2. Isolate key words in Pinsky's poem. Do they guide you to some sense of how the poet wants you to view the bone?

3. How do the last three lines of the poem differ from the preceding ones? How do these lines connect with the title of the poem? Write a short paragraph in which you interpret the significance of the shark's jawbone.

ALLEGORY

An *allegory* is a carefully constructed system of equivalences. In an allegory each element matches to another, more universal element; a specific narrative matches, point by point, to a larger and more general narrative. Allegory has been commonly used to communicate religious instruction, as in John Bunyan's *Pilgrim's Progress*, a long prose work by a seventeenth-century English preacher, which featured the exploits of his hero, Christian, as he made his way toward salvation. Each episode and encounter was correlated to a specific point of Christian doctrine. Allegory of this type is sometimes called *didactic*—its primary functions are instruction and indoctrination.

Though allegory uses symbolic elements, it is different from symbolism in one crucial respect. The artistic use of symbol is usually suggestive, with the symbol opening out onto diverse possibilities of meaning. Allegory, by contrast, is fundamentally reductive. The system or correspondences requires that each thing match to another. An allegory has been grasped once the reader has drawn all of the connecting lines. A symbol works more mysteriously, resonating its meanings rather than indicating them.

Emily Dickinson's "We Grow Accustomed to the Dark" is an example of an allegorical poem. On the surface it relates, in very general terms, a narrative about walking at night. The reader quickly ascertains that Dickinson intends a larger message about living with an awareness of the unknown:

Emily Dickinson

WE GROW ACCUSTOMED TO THE DARK

We grow accustomed to the Dark—
When light is put away—
As when the neighbor holds the Lamp
To witness her Goodbye—

A Moment—We uncertain step   5
For newness of the night—
Then—fit our Vision to the Dark—
And meet the Road—erect—

And so of larger—Darknesses—
those Evenings of the Brain—   10
When not a Moon disclose a sign—
Or star—come out—within—

The Bravest—grope a little—
And sometimes hit a Tree
Directly in the Forehead—   15
But as they learn to see—

Either the Darkness alters—
Or something in the sight
Adjusts itself to Midnight—
And Life steps almost straight.   20

Read the discussion preceding the poem and consider these questions:

1. Isolate the abstract terms Dickinson uses in her poem. How does she allegorize light and dark?

2. What is the lesson, the wisdom, of Dickinson's poem?

3. Try your hand at writing a different allegory using the same key terms.

Another example might be George Herbert's "Love," in which the poet personifies love and imagines it as a host inviting a guest to a meal. The poem is, of course, a Christian allegory, carrying a message about sin and grace and the psychology of salvation.

George Herbert

LOVE

Love bade me welcome; yet my soul drew back,
    Guilty of dust and sin.
But quick-ey'd Love, observing me grow slack
    From my first entrance in,
Drew nearer to me, sweetly questioning   5
    If I lacked anything.

A guest, I answer'd, worthy to be here.
    Love said, You shall be he.
I, the unkind, ungrateful? Ah, my dear,
    I cannot look on Thee.   10
Love took my hand, and smiling, did reply,
    Who made the eyes but I?

Truth, Lord, but I have marred them: let my shame
    Go where it doth deserve.
And know you not, says Love, who bore the blame?   15
    My dear, then I will serve.
You must sit down, says Love, and taste my meat:
    So I did sit and eat.

Read the discussion preceding the poem and consider these questions:

1. In what ways does Herbert personify Love? What are its attributes? What is the relation of Love to the speaker?
2. How does the poem relate to Christian doctrine?
3. Write a short interpretation of Herbert's allegory.

MYTH

Myths are the tales and legends that grew up out of the earliest collective experience of various cultures. They were often narratives that invoked a higher order of gods or protective beings; their purpose, most often, was to give some account for elements of the unknown. Most cultures have creation myths that seek to explain how the world was brought into existence, as well as myths accounting for cycles of birth and death, fertility, and the various natural phenomena, like rain and snow.

The mythic traditions of the world are many and various. Anyone interested in getting a comprehensive overview might consult Joseph Cambell's four-volume collection entitled *The Masks of God*.

As cultures became more sophisticated and as word-of-mouth—or oral—transmission of information and lore spread, the myths themselves were refined and elaborated. In many cultures—the Greek, the Roman, and the Indian, for example—the legends attained great complexity, with many characters and subplots. As these myths comprised a culturally shared heritage, it was natural that poets and storytellers should draw extensively upon the lore. The early poetry of most cultures is closely allied to the dominant mythic tradition. Thus, Homer readily invoked the Greek gods and goddesses in his *Iliad* and *Odyssey*, and the Roman poet Ovid built the whole of his *Metamorphoses* around stories drawn from Roman mythology.

For the purposes of poetry—indeed, art in general—it is useful to consider the body of lore that is Christianity as a kind of mythology for European-influenced culture. This is not intended as a value judgment, and is not meant to suggest that the believing Christian is in any way primitive. It is merely an acknowledgement of the fact that the tales and parables of the Bible have entered our collective memory in much the same way that stories of gods and goddesses entered the memories of the early Greeks or Romans. And, further, poets draw upon the whole order of Christian references in much the same way as their predecessors drew upon the materials of their cultures.

Myths are not unrelated to symbols. In fact, at one level, myths *are* themselves symbolic narratives, with various mythic figures representing distinct attributes. Thus, Hermes, the messenger of the gods in Greek mythology, is not only swift, but is identified with cunning and theft. Athena, born from the head of Zeus, is the goddess of wisdom. Hercules represents physical strength. So, too, does Judas Iscariot stand for betrayal ("You are such a Judas," someone might say), Samson for strength, David for courage against overwhelming odds. . . .

If myths are themselves symbolic, then what is their place in poetry? Poets take advantage of the rich store of meanings and associations they contain, frequently invoking them, animating them, or otherwise making reference. The poet who uses the image of a cross in a poem is not creating a symbol, but is drawing upon the associations already present in an existing symbol.

The uses of myth in poetry are almost unlimited. Such uses can range from the direct appropriation of a mythic subject, as in Yeats's retelling of the story of Leda and the Swan (Chapter 19), to the most glancing of references, as when Sir Walter Raleigh invokes Philomel (the daughter of an Athenian king whose tongue was cut out by her abductor) in a single line of "The Nymph's Reply to the Shepherd":

> But time drives flocks from field to fold,
> When rivers rage and rocks grow cold,
> And Philomel becometh dumb;
> The rest complain of cares to come.

We will here take note of just three ways in which myth can be used to enrich poetry. The first, "Ulysses," by Alfred, Lord Tennyson, is a re-telling—and reimagining—of a part of the story of Odysseus, the hero of Homer's great epic. Tennyson takes his cue from the Italian poet Dante, who in his *Divine Comedy* told the story of Odysseus (Dante, like Tennyson after him, used "Ulysses," which was the hero's Roman name); the hero sailed forth in old age to discover what lay beyond the Pillars of Hercules, said to mark the edge of the world. Tennyson inhabits Ulysses directly, letting him speak of his plans in the first person. The result, a *dramatic monologue*—an extended speech spoken by a *persona*—is at once a variation on a mythic tale and a stirring meditation on old age.

Alfred, Lord Tennyson

ULYSSES

It little profits that an idle king,
By this still hearth, among these barren crags,
Matched with an aged wife, I mete and dole°
Unequal laws unto a savage race,
That hoard, and sleep, and feed, and know not me.   5
I cannot rest from travel: I will drink
Life to the lees°; all times I have enjoyed
Greatly, have suffered greatly, both with those
That loved me, and alone; on shore, and when
Through scudding drifts the rainy Hyades°   10
Vext° the dim sea: I am become a name;
For always roaming with a hungry heart
Much have I seen and known; cities of men
And manners, climates, councils, governments,
Myself not least, but honoured of them all;   15
And drunk delight of battle with my peers;
Far on the ringing plains of windy Troy.°
I am a part of all that I have met;
Yet all experience is an arch wherethrough
Gleams that untravelled world, whose margin fades   20
For ever and for ever when I move.
How dull it is to pause, to make an end,
To rust unburnished, not to shine in use!
As though to breathe were life. Life piled on life
Were all too little, and of one to me   25
Little remains; but every hour is saved
From that eternal silence, something more,
A bringer of new things; and vile it were
For some three suns to store and hoard myself,
And this grey spirit yearning in desire   30
To follow knowledge like a sinking star,

ULYSSES. *3 mete and dole:* hand down.   *7 lees:* dregs.   *10 Hyades:* rain-stars.   *11 Vext:* troubled.
17 Troy: site of the Trojan War.

Symbol, Allegory, Myth, and Allusion in Poetry

Beyond the utmost bound of human thought.

    This is my son, mine own Telemachus,°
To whom I leave the sceptre° and the isle°—
Well-loved of me, discerning to fulfil   35
This labour, by slow prudence to make mild
A rugged people, and through soft degrees
Subdue them to the useful and the good.
Most blameless is he, centered in the sphere
Of common duties, decent not to fail   40
In offices of tenderness, and pay
Meet° adoration to my household gods,
When I am gone. He works his work, I mine.

    There lies the port; the vessel puffs her sail:
There gloom the dark broad seas. My mariners,   45
Souls that have toiled, and wrought, and thought with me—
That ever with a frolic welcome took
The thunder and the sunshine, and opposed
Free hearts, free foreheads—you and I are old;
Old age hath yet his honour and his toil;   50
Death closes all; but something ere the end,
Some work of noble note, may yet be done,
Not unbecoming men that strove with Gods.
The lights begin to twinkle from the rocks:
The long day wanes: the slow moon climbs: the deep   55
Moans round with many voices. Come, my friends,
'Tis not too late to seek a newer world.
Push off, and sitting well in order smite°
The sounding furrows°; for my purpose holds
To sail beyond the sunset, and the baths   60
Of all the western stars, until I die.
It may be that the gulfs will wash down:
It may be we shall touch the Happy Isles,°
And see the great Achilles,° whom we knew.
Though much is taken, much abides; and though   65
We are not now that strength which in old days
Moved earth and heaven; that which we are, we are;
One equal temper of heroic hearts,
Made weak by time and fate, but strong in will
To strive, to seek, to find, and not to yield.   70

---

33 *Telemachus:* son of Ulysses (Odysseus).   34 *sceptre:* symbol of a king's power; *isle:* Ithaka—island home of Ulysses.   42 *Meet:* appropriate.   58 *smite:* hit, as with oars.   59 *furrows:* waves.   63 *Happy Isles:* afterlife.   *Achilles:* Greek hero.

Read the discussion preceding the poem and consider these questions:

1. Find out about Odysseus's travels as recounted in Homer's *Odyssey.* How does Tennyson adapt the story to his own needs?
2. What is Ulysses's character as Tennyson conceives it? What is the message he would have the reader carry away from the poem?

Discussion. A somewhat different application of myth is found in W. H. Auden's well-known poem, "Musée Des Beaux Arts." The title means "Museum of Fine Arts," and it clues us in to the fact that the poem is a meditation upon a painting—Breughel's *Icarus*, as we learn in line 14. The painting itself is a sixteenth-century interpretation of the myth of Icarus, the son of Daedalus, who ignored his father's warnings and flew too close to the sun (when the wax on his wings melted, he fell to his death in the sea). Thus, Auden is giving his reader a reflection upon the nature of suffering based upon a painted interpretation of a mythological subject.

W. H. Auden

MUSÉE DES BEAUX ARTS

About suffering they were never wrong,
The Old Masters: how well they understood
Its human position; how it takes place
While someone else is eating or opening a window or just walking dully along;
How, when the aged are reverently, passionately waiting   5
For the miraculous birth, there always must be
Children who did not specially want it to happen, skating
On a pond at the edge of the wood:
They never forgot
That even the dreadful martyrdom must run its course   10
Anyhow in a corner, some untidy spot
Where the dogs go on with their doggy life and the torturer's horse
Scratches its innocent behind on a tree.
In Brueghel's *Icarus*, for instance: how everything turns away
Quite leisurely from the disaster; the ploughman may   15
Have heard the splash, the forsaken cry,

But for him it was not an important failure; the sun shone
As it had to on the white legs disappearing into the green
Water; and the expensive delicate ship that must have seen
Something amazing, a boy falling out of the sky,   20
Had somewhere to get to and sailed calmly on.

Read the discussion preceding the poem and consider these questions:

1. Research the original myth of Icarus and Daedalus; write a short summary.

2. Find a print of Brueghel's "Icarus" and compare the painted rendition with Auden's narrative. Which tells more of a story? How does that story compare with your understanding of the myth?

3. How does Auden's poem subvert—or demythologize—the original myth? What is Auden telling us about the nature of life?

The third instance, the poem "Elk at Black Fork Canyon" by Tom Sleigh, is not overtly mythological at all. But insofar as the poem imagines a transformation—

from man to beast—that has many sources in (and associations to) Greek and Roman mythology, it may be said to derive its power from the mythic order.

Tom Sleigh

ELK AT BLACK FORK CANYON

Great furred noses nuzzling at hay bales.
Sidling jaws grinding the sweet
Green fodder, they looked up
To where I hunched, clutching

My coat tighter   5
As the cold like a mouth
Spoke promises.
Their eyes dark and wary

Stared through me as through crystal
And I dissolved into their looking   10
Like salt the long, liverish tongues
Licked from the block.

Staring from their eyes,
I bulked like a boulder,
A man-thing carved   15
Into the stone of the morning—

The mountain loomed into my eyes
Like a monstrous word
Pulverizing in its gutturals
The dwindling pebble   20

Of my name shouted down
The canyon. Trapped in the stillness,
The boulder-humped meadow, I heard
With more than, less than human ears

The cold mouth of the outdoors   25
Whisper me my wish:
Bone-trees sprouted
In mossy symmetry, skin

Coarsened with velvet fur,
And jaw and nose elongated   30
And snuffed the freezing air
With the cold scrutiny of a connoisseur.

My smell no longer wrinkled their nostrils
Or set their ears flapping, foolish,

But still lordly. Wholly animal, 35
My heart rose on knobbled

Legs lunging and stumbling
In the thicket of my chest
To the wild forebears, their heads lifting
Crowns of antlers— 40

Bursting in my ears, my name
Crashed back from the stillness
As beneath the unshod
Hooves the snow-crust

Cracked with frigid speed, 45
The wheeling, flicking tails
Unsheathed like skinning-knives.
They shied off down the canyon,

Disappeared into the beard
Of fog lengthening down the mountain, 50
The trampled snow spattered
Golden from their urine.

Read the poem
and consider these
questions:

1. Many of the world's mythologies feature tales of transformation. How does Sleigh use imagery to depict the stages of his own imagined metamorphosis?

2. Write a short interpretation of this poem. What do you think is the point of the poet's imagined transformation?

ALLUSION

An *allusion* is an indirect reference. It can be to almost anything: a living or histor-ical person, a place, an event, another work of literature, and so on. Allusions can be to something everyone knows—the Kennedy assassination, the space shuttle, Coca-Cola—or it can be obscure. T. S. Eliot's *Wasteland* and Ezra Pound's *Cantos* are so dense in allusions that tracking them all down becomes an education in itself. Sometimes, in reading poetry from earlier centuries, we encounter allusions that would have been commonplace for the poet's contemporaries, but need to be *glossed*, or explained, for us. Sir Walter Raleigh's citation of Philomel, for instance, was prob-ably familiar to the educated readers of his day. We are no longer as attuned to the lore of Greek and Roman mythology as were Raleigh's contemporaries. Most of us would need to check a dictionary or a guide to mythology before the meaning of the line was clear.

We need not look far to find a poem that will illustrate the uses of allusion—most of our tradition comprises such poems. John Keats's "Ode on Melancholy" is an excellent example.

John Keats

ODE ON MELANCHOLY

No, no, go not to Lethe, neither twist
    Wolf's-bane, tight-rooted, for its poisonous wine;
Nor suffer thy pale forehead to be kissed
    By nightshade, ruby grape of Proserpine;
Make not your rosary of yew-berries,   5
    Nor let the beetle, nor the death-moth be
        Your mournful Psyche, nor the downy owl
A partner in your sorrow's mysteries;
    For shade to shade will come too drowsily,
        And drown the wakeful anguish of the soul.   10

But when the melancholy fit shall fall
    Sudden from heaven like a weeping cloud,
That fosters the droop-headed flowers all,
    And hides the green hill in an April shroud;
Then glut thy sorrow on a morning rose,   15
    Or on the rainbow of the salt sand-wave,
        Or on the wealth of globèd peonies;
Or if thy mistress some rich anger shows,
    Emprison her soft hand, and let her rave,
        And feed deep, deep upon her peerless eyes.   20

She dwells with Beauty—Beauty that must die,
    And Joy, whose hand is ever at his lips
Bidding adieu; and aching Pleasure nigh,
    Turning to poison while the bee-mouth sips:
Ay, in the very temple of delight   25
    Veiled Melancholy has her sovran shrine,
        Though seen of none save him whose strenuous tongue
    Can burst Joy's grape against his palate fine;
His soul shall taste the sadness of her might,
    And be among her cloudy trophies hung.   30

As you read the
following discussion,
consider these
questions:

1. Use a dictionary or other reference work to clarify all of the allusions and references in Keats's poem. Write out a de-poeticized paraphrase.

2. What is the point of Keats's allusions? What is he saying about melancholy?

Discussion. A look at the first stanza will suffice. Here, Keats makes allusions to *Lethe,* the river of forgetfulness in Hades; *Wolf's-bane,* a plant said to carry poison; *Proserpine,* also known as Persephone, the daughter of Zeus who was abducted by Pluto to be his queen in the underworld; *Psyche,* the personification of the soul in the form of a beautiful girl in Greek mythology; and *owl,* the bird identified with Athena, goddess of wisdom. Again, what was familiar knowledge to the reader of an earlier day is now, for most, a body of material to be researched.

Countee Cullen

TABLEAU°

Locked arm in arm they cross the way,
   The black boy and the white,
The golden splendor of the day,
   The sable pride of night.

From lowered blinds the dark folk stare,   5
   And here the fair folk talk,
Indignant that these two should dare
   In unison to walk.

Oblivious to look and word
   They pass, and see no wonder   10
That lightning brilliant as a sword
   Should blaze the path of thunder.

TABLEAU. a scene showing actors in a picture.

QUESTIONS

Countee Cullen, a noted black poet and leading figure in the "Harlem Renaissance" movement of the 1930s, has written what might be called a short allegory.

1. Who are the figures and what about their presentation makes them representative?

2. What images does Cullen use and which senses does he appeal to? Why is there such lack
of specificity in his narration?

3. What is the situation described and how does it involve the two figures?

4. How does Cullen prepare you for the metaphor of the last two lines? What does he mean
when he writes that "lightning brilliant as a sword/Should blaze the path of thunder"?

5. Do you think that Cullen is giving expression to a truth or to an ideal? Explain. What is
his vision of the relation between black and white races?

Thomas Hardy

THE DARKLING THRUSH

DECEMBER 1900

I leant upon a coppice° gate   *thicket*
   When Frost was spectre-gray,
And Winter's dregs made desolate
   The weakening eye of day.
The tangled bine-stems° scored the sky   *flexible stems* 5
   Like strings of broken lyres,

And all mankind that haunted nigh
    Had sought their household fires.

The land's sharp features seemed to be
    The Century's corpse outleant,   10
His crypt the cloudy canopy,
    The wind his death lament.
The ancient pulse of germ and birth
    Was shrunken hard and dry,
And every spirit upon earth   15
    Seemed fervourless as I.

At once a voice arose among
    The bleak twigs overhead
In a full-hearted evensong
    Of joy illimited;   20
An aged thrush, frail, gaunt, and small,
    In blast-beruffled plume,
Had chosen thus to fling his soul
    Upon the growing gloom.

So little cause for carollings   25
    Of such ecstatic sound
Was written on terrestrial things
    Afar or nigh around,
That I could think there trembled through
    His happy good-night air   30
Some blessed Hope, whereof he knew
    And I was unaware.

QUESTIONS

1. What is the setting that Hardy depicts? How does he use simile and metaphor to intensify the atmosphere? Why would Hardy cite the date of the poem under the title?

2. What is the speaker's own attitude or emotion?

3. How does he introduce the thrush? How does his description of the bird play against expectation? Does this heighten or diminish your response?

4. What could the bird be said to symbolize? What is the message that you get from the description of such a bird singing in such a surrounding?

5. Is Hardy finally optimistic or pessimistic? Which view of life wins out? Explain your answer.

Mary Jo Salter
THE REBIRTH OF VENUS°

He's knelt to fish her face up from the sidewalk
all morning, and at last some shoppers gather

THE REBIRTH OF VENUS. The title refers to *The Birth of Venus*, a famous Renaissance painting by Sandro Botticelli.

to see it drawn—wide-eyed, and dry as chalk—
whole from the sea of dreams. It's she. None other

than the other one who's copied in the book   5
he copies from, that woman men divined
ages before a painter let them look
into the eyes their eyes had had in mind.

Love's called him too, today, though she has taught
him in her beauty to love best   10
the one who first had formed her from a thought.
One square of pavement, like a headstone (lest

anyone mistake where credit lies),
reads BOTTICELLI, but the long-closed dates
suggest, instead, a view of centuries   15
coming unbracketed, as if the gates

might swing wide to admit, here, in the sun,
one humble man into the pantheon
older and more exalted than her own.
    Slow gods of Art, late into afternoon   20

let there be light: a few of us drop the wish
into his glinting coinbox like a well,
remembering the forecast. Yet he won't rush
her finish, though it means she'll have no shell

to harbor in; it's clear enough the rain   25
will swamp her like a tide, and lion-hearted
he'll set off, black umbrella sprung again,
envisioning faces where the streets have parted.

QUESTIONS

Look in an art history book to find a reproduction of Botticelli's "The Birth of Venus."

1. What is the scenario that Salter depicts?

2. How does Salter use metaphor and simile to pave the way for her more philosophical speculations?

3. What is the contrast established between the painter and the thing painted?

4. What does Salter mean when she writes "Love's called him too, today" and how does this phrase bear upon the point she is making?

5. What does the poet mean in lines 15 to 19 with the image of centuries "coming unbracketed"?

6. What is the allusion in line 21? What are the literal and figurative meanings of the words?

7. If light is given a certain symbolic weight, then what about the rain mentioned in line 25?

8. What is Salter finally trying to communicate about art and its place in our lives?

Find a painting, preferably a painting with a mythological theme, and use it as the basis for a poem or prose piece set in the present. Try to allow the meanings of the work (or myth) play against the situation you depict.

Gjertrud Schnackenberg

SUPERNATURAL LOVE

My father at the dictionary-stand
Touches the page to fully understand
The lamplit answer, tilting in his hand

His slowly scanning magnifying lens,
A blurry, glistening circle he suspends   5
Above the word "Carnation." Then he bends

So near his eyes are magnified and blurred,
One finger on the miniature word,
As if he touched a single key and heard

A distant, plucked, infinitesimal string,   10
"The obligation due to every thing
That's smaller than the universe." I bring

My sewing needle close enough that I
Can watch my father through the needle's eye,
As through a lens ground for a butterfly   15

Who peers down flower-hallways toward a room
Shadowed and fathomed as this study's gloom
Where, as a scholar bends above a tomb

To read what's buried there, he bends to pore
Over the Latin blossom. I am four,   20
I spill my pins and needles on the floor

Trying to stitch "Beloved" X by X.
My dangerous, bright needle's point connects
Myself illiterate to this perfect text

I cannot read. My father puzzles why   25
It is my habit to identify
Carnations as "Christ's flowers," knowing I

Can give no explanation but "Because."
Word-roots blossom in speechless messages
The way the thread behind my sampler does   30

Where following each X I awkward move
My needle through the word whose root is love.
He reads, "A pink variety of Clove,°

Carnatio, the Latin, meaning flesh."
As if the bud's essential oils brush   35
Christ's fragrance through the room, the iron-fresh

Odor carnations have floats up to me,
A drifted, secret, bitter ecstasy,
The stems squeak in my scissors, *Child, it's me,*

He turns the page to "Clove" and reads aloud: 40
"The clove, a spice, dried from a flower-bud."
Then twice, as if he hasn't understood,

He reads, "From French, for *clou*, meaning a nail."
He gazes, motionless. "Meaning a nail."
The incarnation blossoms, flesh and nail,   45

I twist my threads like stems into a knot
And smooth "Beloved," but my needle caught
Within the threads, *Thy blood so dearly bought,*

The needle strikes my finger to the bone.
I lift my hand, it is myself I've sewn,   50
The flesh laid bare, the threads of blood my own,

I lift my hand in startled agony
And call upon his name, "Daddy daddy"—
My father's hand touches the injury

As lightly as he touched the page before,   55
Where incarnation bloomed from roots that bore
The flowers I called Christ's when I was four.

SUPERNATURAL LOVE. 33 *clove*: an East Indian evergreen tree and source of clove spice.

QUESTIONS

1. Describe the situation in the poem. How old is the girl? What is she doing? What is her father doing?

2. How does the father's search through the dictionary initiate one of the themes of the poem?

3. How does Schnackenberg dramatize the child's point of view? What similes and metaphors does she use to highlight the child's perceptions?

4. Look carefully at the poet's way of switching between the father's activity and the daughter's. How do the father's spoken words relate to the daughter's actions?

5. At what point does the situation start to take on symbolic overtones?

6. What is the climax moment of the poem? How does it connect with what the father has been saying?

7. How does this narrative relate to what you know of the Christ story? Do father and daughter take on a symbolic relation to one another? If so, what is that relation?

8. Speculate briefly about what Schnackenberg might be getting at in writing this poem. What is the connection of the title to the narrative?

Adrienne Rich

DIVING INTO THE WRECK

First having read the book of myths,
and loaded the camera,
and checked the edge of the knife-blade,
I put on
the body-armor of black rubber   5
the absurd flippers
the grave and awkward mask.
I am having to do this
not like Cousteau° with his
assiduous team   10
aboard the sun-flooded schooner
but here alone.

There is a ladder.
The ladder is always there
hanging innocently
close to the side of the schooner.
We know what it is for,   15
we who have used it.
Otherwise
it's a piece of maritime floss
some sundry equipment.   20

I go down.
Rung after rung and still
the oxygen immerses me
the blue light
the clear atoms   25
of our human air.
I go down.
My flippers cripple me,
I crawl like an insect down the ladder
and there is no one   30
to tell me when the ocean
will begin.

First the air is blue and then
it is bluer and then green and then   35
black I am blacking out and yet
my mask is powerful
it pumps my blood with power
the sea is another story
the sea is not a question of power   40

DIVING INTO THE WRECK. 10 *Cousteau:* Jacques Cousteau, celebrated French undersea explorer.

I have to learn alone
to turn my body without force
in the deep element.

And now: it is easy to forget
what I came for   45
among so many who have always
lived here
swaying their crenellated° fans
between the reefs
and besides   50
you breathe differently down here.

I came to explore the wreck.
The words are purposes.
The words are maps.
I came to see the damage that was done   55
and the treasures that prevail.
I stroke the beam of my lamp
slowly along the flank
of something more permanent
than fish or weed   60

the thing I came for:
the wreck and not the story of the wreck
the thing itself and not the myth
the drowned face always staring
toward the sun   65
the evidence of damage
worn by salt and sway into this threadbare beauty
the ribs of the disaster
curving their assertion
among the tentative haunters.   70

This is the place.
And I am here, the mermaid whose dark hair
streams black, the merman in his armored body
We circle silently
about the wreck   75
we dive into the hold.
I am she: I am he

whose drowned face sleeps with open eyes
whose breasts still bear the stress
whose silver, copper, vermeil cargo lies   80
obscurely inside barrels
half-wedged and left to rot
we are the half-destroyed instruments
that once held to a course

---

49 *crenellated:* notched in a row, as a castle battlement.

Symbol, Allegory, Myth, and Allusion in Poetry

the water-eaten log
the fouled compass

We are, I am, you are
by cowardice or courage
the one who find our way
back to this scene
carrying a knife, a camera
a book of myths
in which
our names do not appear.

QUESTIONS

Adrienne Rich has written a complex (and in some ways obscure) poem with allegorical overtones. You will need to follow her suggestions carefully to grasp what she is getting at.

1. What is the basic situation that Rich has outlined? How does the literal sense of her narration carry nonliteral suggestions?

2. What does the transition into the underwater realm convey?

3. How does Rich vary her description in order to capture the sense of entering depths? What similes and metaphors does she use to evoke the changes experienced by the speaker?

4. What does Rich mean when she writes: "The words are purposes. / The words are maps."?

5. What are your first impressions about the wreck, about what it might signify?

6. What does she mean by saying "I am she: I am he"?

7. If you allow the wreck to represent the wreck of a relationship, then what sense does her exploring have?

8. In what ways does this poem bear upon a woman's search for her female identity?

9. What might Rich mean by the "book of myths" referred to at the beginning and end of the poem?

10. When this poem first appeared, during the years of the women's movement, many readers found it to be a compelling description of their own inner circumstances. Write a short paragraph explaining what you think Rich was telling other women.

SUGGESTION FOR WRITING

Think of a situation that might lend itself to allegorical interpretation and try your hand at writing a short allegorical passage. Strike a balance, if you can, between the obvious statement and the suggestion. You may wish to re-read the paragraphs on allegory in this section.

Louise Glück

THE TRIUMPH OF ACHILLES

In the story of Patroclus
no one survives, not even Achilles

who was nearly a god.
Patroclus resembled him; they wore
the same armor.   5

Always in these friendships
one serves the other, one is less than the other:
the hierarchy
is always apparent, though the legends
cannot be trusted—   10
their source is the survivor,
the one who has been abandoned.

What were the Greek ships on fire
compared to this loss?

In his tent, Achilles   15
grieved with his whole being
and the gods saw

he was a man already dead, a victim
of the part that loved,
the part that was mortal.   20

QUESTIONS

Using sources in the library, research the story of Achilles and Patroclus, who were both figures in Homer's *Iliad*.

1. What was the story of Achilles's birth? Why was he not made fully immortal?
2. What was the relation between Achilles and Patroclus? Explain what Glück means in her second stanza. In this case, who was the survivor? What happened?
3. What does Glück mean when she writes "In the story of Patroclus/ no one survives"?
4. What are the loyalties that Achilles is torn between in the third stanza?
5. What is Glück saying about love? Is it a strength or a weakness? Explain the title of the poem.

SUGGESTION FOR WRITING

Consult a dictionary of mythology and find a short myth. Write a poem or a short piece of prose in which you use the myth as the basis of narration. Try adapting the mythic situation to a modern context.

23 Poetry in Translation

The reader will probably have noticed that nearly all the poems used in illustrations and exercises this far have been poems originally written in English. This should not be interpreted as any sign of bias against the poetry of other cultures. And, indeed, in the poems collected for further reading every effort has been made to restore a necessary sense of balance. But the fact remains that a poem in the original and the same poem in translation—no matter how accomplished the translation—are two different poems. The translated poem is inevitably something less than the original. Its rhythms have been altered, the subtle play of sounds and word-associations has been compromised, and shades of meaning have been eliminated. This is unfortunate, but there is nothing to be done. Poetry feeds on what poets throughout the ages have called the "soul of the language," and exact equivalences between languages cannot be found, no matter how similar the languages. For this reason, the discussions of the various elements of poetry have all referred to works in the original.

Robert Frost took an uncompromising position on this matter: "Poetry," he said, "is what gets lost in translation." We need not go quite so far. If we did, we would be narrowing our horizons considerably. Worse still, we would be missing out on countless experiences of beauty. To be sure, not everything about a poem can be carried over the threshold from one language to another (*translation* literally means "across the threshold"), but a great deal can. And many fine poets and translators have struggled mightily to render the sounds, images, and meanings in new versions. Though much is lost, much also does come through.

But there is another consideration, one that applies not just to poetry but to all works of literature. Simply, that we, as members of English-speaking cultures, are leaving behind our former provincialisms. Not only is our language spoken in perhaps hundreds of cultures and subcultures, but global communications and commerce are rapidly breaking down old barriers between speakers of different languages. We are all becoming multicultural and internationalized, and our concept of culture and literature is bound to reflect the change. We therefore owe it to ourselves to become susceptible to the voices—the attitudes and understandings—from "out there," from cultures different from ours. Contact with other literatures is a pleasurable way to begin.

TRANSLATION: A PROCESS OF MAKING CHOICES

Of the various literary forms, poetry is the most concentrated in its use of language. The poet simultaneously uses the sounds, meanings, associations, and rhythms of words, creating a densely woven verbal artifact. Different languages obviously offer different possibilities of sound and rhythm to the poet, not to mention unique patterns of association. The translator generally has several options, each of which entail certain sacrifices. One might concentrate upon reproducing the meaning as accurately as possible; another might strive for compromise by trying to get the gist of the meaning as well as some approximation of the rhyme scheme. A third may choose to take certain departures from the original in an effort to capture something of its "spirit." Robert Lowell, for example, published a book called *Imitations*, in which he freely added, deleted, and reinterpreted poems from a group of European masters. He was severely criticized by a number of scholars and translators, but others, some of his fellow poets among them, found that his versions had more poetic life than versions by more literal-minded translators. In any case, there are many approaches to this most demanding art.

As each language is different, with its own grammatical rules and deeply imbedded word-associations, the degree of difficulty facing the would-be translator will vary significantly. It is one thing to translate a poem from one of the Romance languages, quite another to work with a text in Chinese. There are structural kinships between Italian and English that simply do not exist between English and Chinese. For one thing, the latter language is written in characters—the symbols have sound values as well as visual suggestions. The character for our word "autumn," for instance, is made up of two signs—one signifying "grain" and the other "fire." The problem facing the translator is obvious. As the authors of the *Princeton Encyclopedia of Poetry and Poetics* write, "it is no less presumptuous to render it as 'season of grain and fire' than it would be for a Chinese to reverse the process and translate Keats's 'season of mists and mellow fruitfulness' merely as 'autumn.'" The translator must be tirelessly inventive, but also willing to strike compromises at every turn.

Rhythms and meters impose difficulties of another kind. Take the case of poetry from India, which is, to this day, deeply rooted in the now-extinct Sanskrit language. The foundation of Indian poetry, its dominant reference point, is the Sanskrit *Rigveda*, which is a collection of hymns to various deities. These hymns were composed in a number of meters, most of which are very different from meters in our tradition. To make matters still more complicated, these metrical formulas each carried their own set of religious associations. To bring the verses out of their original context would obviously result in a drastic loss of resonance—perhaps even to the point where losses would exceed gains. The translator could, of course, add abundant explanatory notes, but reading poetry that requires constant glossing is almost more of a chore than a pleasure.

SOME TRANSLATIONS AND THE TRANSLATION PROCESS

The reader might get a better sense of the range of options open to the translator, as well as of the diversity that exists among versions of certain poems, if a comparison is presented. Here, followed by two translations, is the French original of Baudelaire's "L'Albatros" (The Albatross), a poem about the capture of a large seagoing bird that spends most of its life aloft.

Charles Baudelaire

L'ALBATROS

Souvent, pour s'amuser, les hommes d'équipage
Prennent des albatros, vastes oiseaux des mers,
Qui suivent, indolents compagnons de voyage,
Le navire glissant sur les gouffres amers.

A peine les ont-ils déposés sur les planches,
Que ces rois de l'azur, maladroits et honteux,
Laissent piteusement leurs grandes ailes blanches
Comme des avirons traîner à côté d'eux.

Ce voyageur ailé, comme il est gauche et veule!
Lui, naguère si beau, qu'il est comique et laid!   10
L'un agace son bec avec un brûle-gueule,
L'autre mime, en boitant, l'infirme qui volait!

Le Poète est semblable au prince des nuées
   Qui hante la tempête et se rit de l'archer;
   Exilé sur le sol au milieu des huées,   15
   Ses ailes de géant l'empêchent de marcher.

THE ALBATROSS

Translated by Roy Campbell

Sometimes for sport the men of loafing crews
Snare the great albatrosses of the deep,
The indolent companions of their cruise
As through the bitter vastitudes they sweep.

Scarce have they fished aboard these airy kings   5
When helpless on such unaccustomed floors,
They piteously drop their huge white wings
And trail them at their sides like drifting oars.

How comical, how ugly, and how meek   10
Appears this soarer of celestial snows!
One, with his pipe, teases the golden beak,
One limping, mocks the cripple as he goes.

The Poet, like this monarch of the clouds,
Despising archers, rides the storm elate.   15
But, stranded on the earth to jeering crowds,
The great wings of the giant baulk his gait.

THE ALBATROSS

Translated by Richard Howard

Often, to pass the time on board, the crew
will catch an albatross, one of those big birds
which nonchalantly chaperone a ship
across the bitter fathoms of the sea.

Tied to the deck, this sovereign of space,   5
as if embarrassed by its clumsiness,
pitiably lets its great white wings
drag at its sides like a pair of unshipped oars.

How weak and awkward, even comical
this traveller but lately so adroit—   10
one deckhand sticks a pipestem in its beak,
another mocks the cripple that once flew!

The Poet is like this monarch of the clouds
riding the storm above the marksman's range;
exiled on the ground, hooted and jeered,   15
he cannot walk because of his great wings.

Baudelaire's original is composed in four quatrains and follows an a-b-a-b rhyme scheme. Roy Campbell has stayed with the formal indications of the scheme, matching his rhyme pattern to Baudelaire's. But he has also resorted to a basic iambic pentameter metric (a-cross/ the bit-/ ter fa-/ thoms of/ the sea) which is not a property of French poetry. The result is faithful to the meaning and basic form, but is somewhat stiff and tick-tock in its rhythm. Howard, by contrast, abandons any attempt to render the rhymes. His interest, clearly, lies in reproducing something of the subtle flow of the original. It is up to the reader to weigh the relative losses and gains.

While English and French are distinct languages, with deep syntactical and grammatical differences, they are not completely unrelated. Indeed, in the late Middle Ages, the dominant Anglo-Saxon core of the language was enriched by a great infusion of French words. (Geoffrey Chaucer, author of *Canterbury Tales*, was the first major poet to capitalize on the expanded verbal resources of English.) The transfer from French to English of a poem by Baudelaire, then, is a challenging but not unthinkable project. But what happens when the languages are entirely unrelated and do not even share an alphabet in common? The answer to this might give us another kind of understanding of what is involved not only in the making of a poem, but in the re-making of that poem in an utterly alien language.

Eliot Weinberger and Octavio Paz undertook to explore just this. Their book, *Nineteen Ways of Looking at Wang Wei*, takes a single short lyric by the great Chinese poet Wang Wei (700–761) and traces the various attempts in our century to capture its beauty in translation. There is not space, of course, to look at each and every version, nor to reproduce the commentaries comparing the pros and cons of different solutions. But a look at several different approaches is nonetheless illuminating.

Weinberger and Paz begin by showing the original text, composed in Chinese characters, or ideograms:

柴 鹿

空 山 不 見 人，
但 聞 人 語 響；
返 景 入 深 林，
復 照 青 苔 上。

They then supply a transliteration, transferring the ideograms into their modern Chinese sound equivalents:

Transliteration

LÙ ZHÁI

Kōng shān bù jiàn rén

Dàn wén rén yǔ xiǎng

Fǎn jǐng (yǐng) rù shēn lín

Fù zhào qīng tái shàng

From this, finally, they derive a character-by-character translation. The word order, as we see, bears no relation at all to the basic subject-verb-predicate pattern of English:

Empty	mountain(s) hill(s)	(negative)	to see	person people
But	to hear	person people	words conversation	sound to echo
To return	bright(ness) shadow(s)	to enter	deep	forest
To return Again	to shine to reflect	green blue black	moss lichen	above on (top of) top

These, then, are the basic ingredients that each of the translators worked with, the raw materials out of which a sensible, if not artistic, English version was to be made. The results show us a great deal about the range of approaches taken by different translators, as well as the divergent poetic ideals they espouse. The first version is by W. J. B. Fletcher and dates from 1919:

> So lone seem the hills; there is no one in sight there.
> > But whence is the echo of voices I hear?
> The rays of the sunset pierce slanting the forest,
> > And in their reflection green mosses appear.

The authors comment as follows: "Fletcher, like all early (and many later) translators, feels he must explain and 'improve' the original poem. Where Wang's sunlight *enters* the forest, Fletcher's rays *pierce slanting*; where Wang states simply that voices are heard, Fletcher invents a first-person narrator who asks where the sounds are coming from. (And if the hills are *there*, where is the narrator?) In line 4, ambiguity has been translated into confusion: Fletcher's line has no meaning. (What reflection where?)"

Another rendering, from 1958, is by Chang Yin-nan and Lewis C. Walmsley:

> Through the deep wood, the slanting sunlight
> Casts motley patterns on the jade-green mosses.
> No glimpse of man in this lonely mountain,
> Yet faint voices drift on the air.

As the commentary Weinberger points out, the two couplets "are reversed for no reason. The voices are *faint* and *drift on the air*. The mountain is *lonely* (surely a Western conceit, that empty = lonely!) but it's a decorator's delight: the moss is as green as jade and the sunlight "casts motley patterns." The translation is, like Fletcher's, an attempt to improve on the original. And Weinberger is unforgiving: "It never occurs to Chang and Walmsley that Wang could have written the equivalent of *casts motley patterns on the jade-green mosses* had he wanted to. He didn't."

Another effort, no more successful in their view, is G. W. Robinson's 1973 rendition:

> Hills empty, no one to be seen
> We hear only voices echoed—
> With light coming back into the deep wood
> The top of the green moss is lit again.

Here the authors are critical on several counts. For one thing, Robinson, like Fletcher, has created a narrator—indeed, "he makes it a group, as though it were a family outing. With that one word, *we*, he effectively scuttles the mood of the poem." They also object to the image of the last line: "Reading the last word of the poem as *top*, he offers an image that makes little sense on the forest floor: one would have to be small indeed to think of moss vertically."

The shadings, as we can see, are very fine, but the translator lives day in and day out among distinctions just like this, forever juggling the claims of accuracy and expressiveness.

But lest we think that Weinberger and Paz have nothing to offer but criticism, here is a translation they judge to be successful. It is by Gary Snyder (see Chapter 26) and was made in 1955:

Empty mountains:
    no one to be seen.
Yet—hear—
    human sounds and echoes.
Returning sunlight
    enters the dark woods;
Again shining
    on green moss, above.

The commentary, as ever, is instructive. Snyder, the authors agree, "can see the scene. Every word of Wang has been translated, and nothing added, yet the translation exists as an American poem."

Looking at the specific choices made by Snyder, they note: "Changing the passive *is heard* to the imperative *hear* is particularly beautiful, and not incorrect: it creates an exact moment, which is now. Giving us both meanings, *sounds and echoes*, for the last word of line 2 is, like most sensible ideas, revolutionary. Translators always assume that only one reading of a foreign word or phrase may be presented, despite the fact that perfect correspondence is rare."

Concluding their remarks, Weinberger and Paz make a statement that all of us as readers should keep in mind as we read poems that have been re-created into English from other languages: "The point is that translation is more than a leap from dictionary to dictionary; it is a reimagining of the poem. As such, every reading of every poem, regardless of language, is an act of translation: translation into the reader's intellectual and emotional life. As no individual reader remains the same, each reading becomes a different—not merely another—reading. The same poem cannot be read twice." The words repay thoughtful re-reading.

TRANSLATION—SOME EXERCISES

In each of the following exercises, the original poem has been included. Most of you, naturally, will not be able to read the original fluently, if at all. You should nevertheless spend some time looking back and forth between languages. English is enough related to these Romance languages that it is possible, not to mention interesting, to puzzle over the sense. There is really no other way to begin to get a grasp of what is involved in the act of translation.

A Chilean Poem Translated from Spanish

Read the following poem, "Walking Around," by the Chilean poet Pablo Neruda. Try to read some of the Spanish out loud so that you can get some feel for the rhythm and the word sounds. Then read both English versions.

Pablo Neruda

WALKING AROUND

Sucede que me canso de ser hombre.
Sucede que entro en las sastrerías y en los cines
marchito, impenetrable, como un cisne de fieltro
navegando en un agua de origen y ceniza.

El olor de las peluquerías me hace llorar a gritos.
Sólo quiero un descanso de piedras o de lana,
sólo quiero no ver establecimientos ni jardines,
ni mercaderías, ni anteojos, ni ascensores.

Sucede que me canso de mis pies y mis uñas
y mi pelo y mi sombra.
Sucede que me canso de ser hombre.   10

Sin embargo sería delicioso
asustar a un notario con un lirio cortado
o dar muerte a una monja con un golpe de oreja.
Sería bello   15
ir por las calles con un cuchillo verde
y dando gritos hasta morir de frío.

No quiero seguir siendo raíz en las tinieblas,
vacilante, extendido, tiritando de sueño,
hacia abajo, en las tapias mojadas de la tierra,   20
absorbiendo y pensando, comiendo cada día.

No quiero para mí tantas desgracias.
No quiero continuar de raíz y de tumba,
de subterráneo solo, de bodega con muertos,
aterido, muriéndome de pena.   25

Por eso el día lunes arde como el petróleo
cuando me ve llegar con mi cara de cárcel,
y aúlla en su transcurso como una rueda herida,
y da pasos de sangre caliente hacia la noche.

Y me empuja a ciertos rincones, a ciertas casas húmedas,   30
a hospitales donde los huesos salen por la ventana,
a ciertas zapaterías con olor a vinagre,
a calles espantosas como grietas.

Hay pàjoros de color de azufre y horribles intestinos
colgando de las puertas de las casas que odio,   35
hay dentaduras olvidadas en una cafetera,
hay espejos
que debieran haber llorado de vergüenza y espanto,
hay paraguas en todas partes, y venenos, y ombligos.

694

Yo paseo con calma, con ojos, con zapatos,   40
con furia, con olvido,
paso, cruzo oficinas y tiendas de ortopedia,
y patios donde hay ropas colgadas de un alambre:
calzoncillos, toallas y camisas que lloran
lentas lágrimas sucias.   45

WALKING AROUND

Translated by Robert Bly

It so happens I am sick of being a man.
And it happens that I walk into tailorshops and movie houses
dried up, waterproof, like a swan made of felt
steering my way in a water of wombs and ashes.

The smell of barbershops makes me break into hoarse sobs.   5
The only thing I want is to lie still like stones or wool.
The only thing I want is to see no more stores, no gardens,
no more goods, no spectacles, no elevators.

It so happens I am sick of my feet and my nails
and my hair and my shadow.   10
It so happens I am sick of being a man.

Still it would be marvelous
to terrify a law clerk with a cut lily,
or kill a nun with a blow on the ear.
It would be great   15
to go through the streets with a green knife
letting out yells until I died of the cold.

I don't want to go on being a root in the dark,
insecure, stretched out, shivering with sleep,
going on down, into the moist guts of the earth,   20
taking in and thinking, eating every day.

I don't want so much misery.
I don't want to go on as a root and a tomb,
alone under the ground, a warehouse with corpses,
half frozen, dying of grief.   25

That's why Monday, when it sees me coming
with my convict face, blazes up like gasoline,
and it howls on its way like a wounded wheel,
and leaves tracks full of warm blood leading toward the night.

And it pushes me into certain corners, into some moist houses,   30
into hospitals where the bones fly out the window,
into shoeshops that smell like vinegar,
and certain streets hideous as cracks in the skin.

There are sulphur-colored° birds, and hideous intestines
hanging over the doors of houses that I hate,   35
and there are false teeth forgotten in a coffeepot,
there are mirrors
that ought to have wept from shame and terror,
there are umbrellas everywhere, and venoms, and umbilical cords.

I stroll along serenely, with my eyes, my shoes,   40
my rage, forgetting everything,
I walk by, going through office buildings and orthopedic shops,
and courtyards with washing hanging from the line:
underwear, towels and shirts from which slow
dirty tears are falling.   45

_____

WALKING AROUND (Bly trans.). 34 *sulphur-colored:* yellow.

WALKING AROUND

Translated by Donald D. Walsh

I happen to be tired of being a man.
I happen to enter tailorshops and moviehouses
withered, impenetrable, like a felt swan
navigating in a water of sources and ashes.

The smell of barbershops makes me wail.   5
I want only respite of stones or wool,
I want only not to see establishments or gardens,
or merchandise, or eyeglasses, or elevators.

I happen to be tired of my feet and my nails
and my hair and my shadow.   10
I happen to be tired of being a man.

Nevertheless it would be delightful
to startle a notary with a cut lily
or slay a nun by striking her with an ear.
It would be lovely   15
to go through the streets with a sexy knife
and shouting until I froze to death.

I don't want to go on being a root in the dark,
vacillating, stretched out, shivering with sleep,
downward, in the soaked guts of the earth,   20
absorbing and thinking, eating each day.

I do not want for myself so many misfortunes.
I do not want to continue as root and tomb,

subterranean only, a vault with corpses,
stiff with cold, dying of distress.   25

That is why Monday day burns like petroleum
when it sees me coming with my prison face,
and it howls in its transit like a wounded wheel,
and it takes hot-blooded steps toward the night.

And it pushes me into certain corners, into certain moist houses,   30
into hospitals where the bones stick out the windows,
into certain shoestores with a smell of vinegar,
into streets as frightening as chasms.

There are brimstone-colored birds and horrible intestines
hanging from the doors of the houses that I hate,   35
there are dentures left forgotten in a coffeepot,
there are mirrors
that ought to have wept from shame and fright,
there are umbrellas everywhere, and poisons, and navels.

I walk around with calm, with eyes, with shoes,   40
with fury, with forgetfulness,
I pass, I cross by offices and orthopedic° shoestores,
and courtyards where clothes are hanging from a wire:
underdrawers, towels and shirts that weep
slow, dirty tears.   45

WALKING AROUND (Walsh trans.). 42 *orthopedic:* corrective.

QUESTIONS

1. What are the main differences in diction and use of imagery between the Bly and Walsh versions?

2. Isolate three passages of two lines or more where the difference is most striking. Set them side by side and characterize each translator's choices. Look back at the original and try to puzzle out which translator is more literally faithful to the text.

3. Which translation do you prefer as a poem in English? Explain your choice.

4. Characterize each translation with three adjectives (e.g., "surprising," "precious," "casual," etc.).

A Poem Translated from Italian

Eugenio Montale

L'ANGUILLA

L'anguilla, la sirena
dei mari freddi che lascia il Baltico
per giungere ai nostri mari,

ai nostri estuarî, ai fiumi
che risale in profondo, sotto la piena avversa,   5
di ramo in ramo e poi
di capello in capello, assottigliati,
sempre più addentro, sempre più nel cuore
del macigno, filtrando
tra gorielli di melma finché un giorno   10
una luce scoccata dai castagni
ne accende il guizzo in pozze d'acquamorta,
nei fossi che declinano
dai balzi d'Appennino alla Romagna;
l'anguilla, torcia, frusta,   15
freccia d'Amore in terra
che solo i nostri botri o i disseccati
ruscelli pirenaici riconducono
a paradisi di fecondazione;
l'anima verde che cerca   20
vita lá dove solo
morde l'arsura e la desolazione,
la scintilla che dice
tutto comincia quando tutto pare
incarbonirsi, bronco seppellito;   25
l'iride breve, gemella
di quella che incastonano i tuoi cigli
e fai brillare intatta in mezzo ai figli
dell'uomo, immersi nel tuo fango, puoi tu
non crederla sorella?   30

THE EEL

Translated by William Arrowsmith

The eel, coldwater
siren, who leaves the Baltic° behind her
to reach these shores of ours,
our wetlands and marshes, our rivers,
who struggles upstream hugging the bottom, under the flood of the
    downward torrent,   5
from branch to branch, thinning,
narrowing in, stem by stem,
snaking deeper and deeper into the rock core
of slab ledge, squirming through
stone interstices of slime until   10
one day, light,
exploding, blazes from the chestnut leaves,
ignites a wriggle in deadwater sumps

THE EEL (Arrowsmith trans.). 2 *Baltic:* the North European sea.

and run-off ditches of Apennine°
ravines spilling downhill toward the Romagna;°   15
eel, torchlight, lash,
arrow of Love on earth,
whom only these dry gulches of ours or burned-out
Pyrenean° gullies can draw back up
to Edens of generation;   20
the green soul seeking
life where there's nothing but stinging
drought, desolation;
spark that says
everything begins when everything seems   25
dead ashes, buried stump;
brief rainbow, twin
of that other iris shining between your lashes,
by which your virtue blazes out, unsullied among the sons
of men floundering in your mud, can you   30
deny a sister?

---

14 *Apennine:* central mountain range in Italy.   15 *Romagna:* Roman plain.   19 *Pyrenean:* of the
Pyrenees, mountains on the French–Spanish border.

THE EEL

Translated by John Frederick Nims

The eel, the
siren of sleety seas, abandoning
the Baltic for our waters,
our estuaries, our
freshets, to lash upcurrent under the brunt   5
of the flood, sunk deep, from brook to brook and then
trickle to trickle dwindling,
more inner always, always more in the heart
of the rock, thrusting
through ruts of the mud, until, one day,   10
explosion of splendor from the chestnut groves
kindles a flicker in deadwater sumps,
in ditches pitched
from the ramparts of the Apennine to Romagna;
eel: torch and whip,   15
arrow of love on earth,
which nothing but our gorges or bone-dry
gutters of the Pyrenees usher back
to edens of fertility;
green soul that probes   20
for life where only
fevering heat or devastation preys,

spark that says
the whole commences when the whole would seem
charred black, an old stick buried;   25
brief rainbow, twin
to that within your lashes' dazzle, that
you keep alive, inviolate,° among
the sons of men, steeped in your mire°—in this
not recognize a sister?   30

THE EEL (Nims trans.).   28 *inviolate:* untouched, undisturbed.   29 *mire:* mud.

QUESTIONS

Try to read some of the Italian out loud to hear the rhythms and word sounds. Then read both English versions carefully.

1. What are the main differences in terms of diction, presentation of images, and line breaks?

2. Find two passages of two or more lines where the difference in treatment is most striking. Set them side by side, then characterize the differences and comment. Look back at the original and see if you can guess which translator has come closer to the sense and expression.

3. Which version seems more effective to you? Why?

4. Can you find places where Montale appears to be using end-rhymes? Check both translations and determine if any effort was made to retain the rhymes.

5. Write a short paragraph in which you explain what "The Eel" is about.

A Mexican Poem Translated from Spanish

Here are two short and relatively simple poems by Mexican poet César Vallejo and the German poet Rainer Maria Rilke. Try your hand at the exercises that follow the English translations.

César Vallejo

LOS DADOS ETERNOS

*Para Manuel Gonzáles Prada, esta emoción
bravía y selecta, una de las que, con más
entusiasmo, me ha aplaudido el gran maestro.*

Dios mío, estoy llorando el ser que vivo;
me pesa haber tomádote tu pan;
pero este pobre barro pensativo
no es costra fermentada en tu costado:
tú no tienes Marías que se van!   5

Dios mío, si tú hubieras sido hombre,
hoy supieras ser Dios;

pero tú, que estuviste siempre bien,
no sientes nada de tu creación.
Y el hombre sí te sufre: el Dios es él!   10

Hoy que en mis ojos brujos hay candelas,
como en un condenado,
Dios mío, prenderás todas tus velas,
y jugaremos con el viejo dado . . .
Tal vez ¡oh jugador! al dar la suerte   15
del universo todo,
surgirán las ojeras de la Muerte,
como dos ases fúnebres de lodo.

Dios mío, y esta noche sorda oscura,
ya no podrás jugar, porque la Tierra   20
es un dado roído y ya redondo
a fuerza de rodar a la aventura,
que no puede parar si no en un hueco
en el hueco de inmensa sepultura.

THE ETERNAL DICE

Translated by James Wright

For Manuel González Prada, this wild and unique
feeling—one of those emotions which the great mas-
ter has admired most in my work.

God of mine, I am weeping for the life that I live;
I am sorry to have stolen your bread;
but this wretched, thinking piece of clay
is not a crust formed in your side:
you have no Marys that abandon you!   5

My god, if you had been man,
today you would know how to be God;
but you always lived so well,
that now you feel nothing of your own creation.
And the man who suffers you: he is God!   10

Today, when there are candles in my witch-like eyes,
as in the eyes of a condemned man,
God of mine, you will light all your lamps,
and we will play with the old dice . . .
Gambler, when the whole universe, perhaps,   15
is thrown down,
the circled eyes of Death will turn up,
like two final aces of clay.

My God, in this muffled, dark night,
you can't play any more, because the Earth
is already a die nicked and rounded
from rolling by chance;
and it can stop only in a hollow place,
in the hollow of the enormous grave.

20

QUESTIONS

1. Read the original Spanish of Vallejo's poem without looking at James Wright's translation. Try to establish the meaning of the lines. Then read the translation several times. Now return to the original and see how much you can understand. How would you describe your experience in this process?
2. Read both versions side by side, working slowly. Can you find places where Wright might have taken liberties with the syntax or literal sense of Vallejo's original? Be prepared to compare these findings in class.

Rainer Maria Rilke

DER PANTHER

Im Jardin des Plantes, Paris

Sein Blick ist vom Vorübergehn der Stäbe
so müd geworden, dass er nichts mehr hält.
Ihm ist, als ob es tausend Stäbe gäbe
und hinter tausend Stäben keine Welt.

Der weiche Gang geschmeidig starker Schritte,
der sich im allerkleinsten Kreise dreht,
ist wie ein Tanz von Kraft um eine Mitte,
in der betäubt ein grosser Wille steht.

Nur manchmal schiebt der Vorhang der Pupille
sich lautlos auf—. Dann geht ein Bild hinein,
geht durch der Glieder angespannte Stille—
und hört im Herzen auf zu sein.

5

10

THE PANTHER

In the Jardin des Plantes, Paris

Translated by Stephen Mitchell

His vision, from the constantly passing bars,
has grown so weary that it cannot hold

anything else. It seems to him there are
a thousand bars; and behind the bars, no world.

As he paces in cramped circles, over and over,
the movement of his powerful soft strides
is like a ritual dance around a center
in which a mighty will stands paralyzed.

Only at times, the curtain of the pupils
lifts, quietly—. An image enters in,
rushes down through the tensed, arrested muscles,
plunges into the heart and is gone.

5

10

THE PANTHER

Jardin des Plantes, Paris

Translated by J. B. Leishman

His gaze those bars keep passing is so misted
with tiredness, it can take in nothing more.
He feels as though a thousand bars existed,
and no more world beyond them than before.

Those supply-powerful paddings, turning there
in tiniest of circles, well might be
the dance of forces round a centre where
some mighty will stands paralyticly.

Just now and then the pupil's noiseless shutter
is lifted. —Then an image will indart,
down through the limbs' intensive stillness flutter,
and end its being in the heart.

5

10

QUESTIONS

1. Read both translations of Rilke's poem individually, without looking at the other. Decide which you think is the more successful translation and write down your reasons.
2. Read the poems side by side, comparing every line. Write a short characterizing description of each translator's style.
3. Reading both translations carefully, can you find differences important enough to change the overall meaning of the poem?
4. Look at the translations in terms of parts of speech. List in two columns the verbs, nouns, adjectives, and adverbs.

24 Writing about Poetry

In order to write about poetry with any comprehension you need to know how to read poetry. This reading will differ from other kinds—from reading the newspaper or a mystery novel, say—because poetry uses language at a much greater degree of concentration. As the preceding chapters have indicated, very specific skills are required. You need to grasp the poem on many different levels—hearing its sounds, registering its rhythms, and paying attention to the way that images and figures of speech enrich the meaning. You also need to think of meaning in a different way. It is not always a message that can be summarized. Indeed, a part of the pleasure of poetry is that it communicates the *experience* of meaning; it not only means, but *is*. To get at this experience you have to be very open and attentive. You have to be prepared, likewise, to read certain poems not once or twice, but many times. Reading poetry is in some ways like listening to a complex piece of music; many of the subtleties are not apparent until the work has become familiar.

The earlier chapters looked at the various elements of poetry in isolation. And while it is useful in studying a poem to be able to look at one component and then another, the goal of responsive reading—and responsive writing—is to appreciate how all the parts work together. This will take a certain amount of practice, but as you will see from the sample paper that follows, there are specific steps that can be taken to forge specific impressions into a more unified response.

THINKING INTERPRETIVELY

Many students are daunted by the prospect of having to interpret a poem. Some instructors, like the one in this particular Introduction to Literature course, choose to begin the study of poetry by assigning short in-class interpretation exercises. Before passing out the poem, she explains the purpose of the exercise. Poetry, she tells her students, is a mode of expression. Readers are supposed to "get it" and to enjoy it. There are difficult poems, true, but even these will seem less difficult once some of the rules of the game are clear. She then passes out her preliminary guidelines for interpretation, which are as follows:

1. A poem must be read not just once, but a number of times. It needs to be grasped on several different levels before it can be appreciated fully.

2. Read slowly and carefully. Use common sense and try to determine what the poet is intent upon saying.

3. Read with an alert ear and listen to the language. What is the poet doing with word sounds and rhythms?

4. Look for rhymes and patterns of rhyme. Pay close attention to line breaks and stanza breaks. Do these contribute to the sense of the poem in some way? Does the poem have a form you can identify?

5. What kinds of images does the poet use? Which senses do the images appeal to? How do the images relate to the thematic content of the poem?

6. What is the poet's tone and attitude? Is it whimsical, ironic, angry, sorrowful, and so on?

The instructor tells the students that if they can answer most of these questions, they are ready to write a short interpretation. Procedures for this vary, but she recommends these steps: (a) Briefly summarize the poem: what is it about? (b) Discuss *how* the poet communicates the *what*: look at tone, imagery, the use of language, the formal elements (rhyme scheme, stanza pattern), and then try to explain how these poetic elements enhance the meaning. "There are no right or wrong answers," she tells them, "only more and less convincing interpretations."

In one class session the instructor passed out a sheet with Shakespeare's Sonnet LXXIII.

SONNET LXXIII

That time of year thou mayst in me behold
When yellow leaves, or none, or few, do hang
Upon those boughs which shake against the cold,
Bare ruin'd choirs, where late the sweet birds sang.
In me thou see'st the twilight of such day   5
As after sunset fadeth in the west,
Which by and by black night doth take away,
Death's second self, that seals up all in rest.
In me thou see'st the glowing of such fire
That on the ashes of his youth doth lie,   10
As the death-bed whereon it must expire,
Consumed with that which it was nourished by.
    This thou perceiv'st, which makes thy love more strong,
    To love that well which thou must leave ere° long.

SONNET LXXIII. 14 *ere:* before.

She gave her students twenty minutes to ponder and write. Ryan Kelly's paper was fairly representative:

In William Shakespeare's sonnet LXXIII, the poet speaks in the voice of an older man who knows that death is near. He is addressing a loved one, possibly a younger ——— *do you have any reason for thinking it's a younger woman?* woman, and telling her quite frankly that he will soon be gone. He eases the pain of —— *he is also being dramatic* telling slightly by using poetic comparisons. First he compares his time of life to late autumn when the last leaves are falling from the trees, then to the twilight of the day, just before night (death) arrives. After he has pictured for her the "black night," he speaks of "the glowing of such fire / That on the ashes of his youth doth lie." The reader wonders why the speaker is giving such a depressing description of his state--until Shakespeare produces a kind of surprise. The final two lines, the only rhyming pair in ——— *called a "couplet"* the sonnet, introduce the idea that the woman's love will now be stronger. He tells her "To love that well which thou must leave ere long."

We see the poet's skill with language throughout. In the very beginning (line 2), he gives us the image "When yellow leaves, or none, or few, do hang." It is not a complex image, but Shakespeare has broken the line into phrases which, when we read them, give an impression of isolated leaves clinging to branches. The pauses we make somehow give the feeling of leaves coming loose and falling. In line 4, to take another example of his subtlety, he opposes the empty vowel sounds of "Bare ruin'd" to the softer "sweet birds sang"--the effect is to heighten the feeling of oncoming winter. Also, multiple *s* sounds in lines 8, 9, and 10 convey the atmosphere of a hissing fire.

is it the rhythm, his use of commas, or what?

can you pin down how this works?

But maybe the strongest thing about the sonnet is the way that Shakespeare lets everything die down by line 12 so that he can suddenly rise up with the final rhymed lines. The poem, so sad until then, lightens up and gives us a certain hope that the woman's love will grow stronger.

discuss those lines. Is their tone different? their rhythm?

Writing about Poetry

AN ASSIGNMENT

The same students were then asked by their teacher to pursue a project of independent reading that would culminate in a response essay to a poem of their own choosing. In giving the assignment, the instructor emphasized that students should feel free to look for poems outside the textbook anthology. She handed out a list of poets who she thought might be of interest. She further urged the class to root the writing process as much as possible in pleasure. "Find a poem that speaks to you," she suggested.

Ryan Kelly took his teacher's advice. Using the list, he combed the library shelves until he had a stack of books to look through. The hard part was finding something that connected. He felt that most of the poems he tried to read eluded him. Either the language was difficult or the images were confusing. He was at the point of going back to the textbook when he found a poem called "The Thought-Fox" by Ted Hughes. It appealed to him right away—it was tense, mysterious, and used images that he could understand. He felt a great sense of relief.

Ryan had not had much practice at writing about poetry. He decided that he would work slowly. His first step was to familiarize himself thoroughly with the poem. He read through silently a number of times, and then once out loud. Vocalizing the lines turned out to be so useful that he did it again. He noticed things about the rhythm—pauses and points of emphasis—and word-sounds that he had missed before. Ryan then reviewed his notes from class, highlighting various elements that the teacher had discussed. He was ready to write out the poem for closer inspection.

With the copied version in front of him, Ryan read and made markings. He consulted his notes and tried to focus. He looked for alliteration and assonance, important caesuras, enjambments, and images. He tried scanning the poem, counting off stresses. As far as he could tell the poem did not follow any strict metrical pattern. But he did find a few lines where the words seemed to carry a special emphasis, and he marked what he thought were the stresses. After a while he had covered the margin of his page with notes. Ryan stopped. He felt that he probably had enough material to build a paper around.

Ted Hughes

THE THOUGHT-FOX

I imagine this midnight moment's forest:
Something else is alive
Beside the clock's loneliness
And this blank page where my fingers move.

Through the window I see no star;   5
Something more near
Though deeper within darkness
Is entering the loneliness:

Cold, delicately as the dark snow
A fox's nose touches twig, leaf;
Two eyes serve a movement, that now
And again now, and now, and now   10

Sets neat prints into the snow
Between trees, and warily a lame
Shadow lags by stump and in hollow   15
Of a body that is bold to come

Across clearings, an eye,
A widening deepening greenness,
Brilliantly, concentratedly,
Coming about its own business   20

Till, with a sudden sharp hot stink of fox,
It enters the dark hole of the head.
The window is starless still; the clock ticks,
The page is printed.

The Thought-Fox— Worksheet

I imagine this midnight moment's forest: ——— Alliteration

Something else is alive

Beside the clock's (loneliness) —— personification—it is not the clock that is lonely

And this blank page where my fingers move. [?page is not really alive...]

Through the window I see no star;

Something more near —— repeated word—why loneliness, why not "solitude"?

Though deeper within darkness ——— why "deeper within darkness"?

Is entering the (loneliness:) —— Alliteration

Cold, delicately as the dark snow —— sense of delicacy here—why?

A fox's nose touches twig,‖ leaf;

Two eyes serve a movement, that now —— rhythm and words repeating make you feel the footprints/

And again now,‖ and now,‖ and now —— Also, use of caesuras to emphasize pauses

Sets neat prints into the snow —— Assonance in "ee" sound

Between trees, and warily a lame —— enjambments

Shadow lags by stump and in hollow

Of a body that is bold to come

Across clearings, an eye,

A widening deepening greenness, —— Assonances: T sound, ee sound

Brilliantly,‖ concentratedly, —————————— caesura emphasizes
                                          determination
Coming about its own business ————————— assonance/alliteration

Till,‖ with a sudden sharp hot stink of fox, ————
                                          metaphor
It enters the dark hole of the head. ◁——————— key line—what does poet mean?

The window is starless still;‖ the clock ticks, ——— caesura emphasizes stillness
                                          and pauses
The page is printed. ——————————————
                          alliteration

                          —————————— play on words, referring to
                                          footprints and writing

BRAINSTORMING: GETTING STARTED

When he had first read "The Thought-Fox" in the library, Ryan had enjoyed the poem. He had also understood it—more or less. But now, staring at his annotations and faced with the task of writing a coherent essay, he experienced confusion. He could not see what all of his notes and markings added up to. He could identify a few uses of alliteration, point out certain images, but that was hardly enough for what his teacher had called a "thoughtful response." Indeed, Ryan knew that if he simply worked his way through the poem, from start to finish, pointing out poetic elements and usages, he would have a boring and chaotic paper. But he also knew that a number of these elements were vital for any deeper discussion. He was at a loss.

After a certain amount of agonizing, Ryan made two decisions. First, he realized that it would not do to include all of the particular details he had noted. He would try to concentrate on what Hughes was getting at, and he would discuss only those elements that seemed to have a direct bearing on the meaning. The second decision was strategic, and was based on Ryan's experience with writing other kinds of papers. He would spend some time brainstorming—jotting down his responses and observations. The process usually worked. There would come a point when he would find some link or hit upon some organizing pattern. He put his annotation of the poem to one side and started in on a clean sheet of paper. Here are Ryan's brainstormed notes:

> "The Thought-Fox"—title gives first clue. This is not a real animal. The poem begins: "I imagine . . ."
> Obvious alliteration in first line—but why?
> Something mysterious is happening to the "I"
> He—Hughes?—feels that "Something else is alive"
> He is writing, probably composing a poem late at night

But he creates a sense of *life*, as if this is more than just an idea. Maybe this is what poets mean by inspiration.

H. uses loneliness twice—why? Is there something lonely about the act of writing? Or is it loneliness that makes a person write (probably irrelevant to this paper)

A sense of approach—something coming closer. Stanza 3 introduces the fox. Interesting idea: that a thought can get closer just like a real creature. The thought reaches him.

H. uses precise writing. Look closely at language in stanza 3. Important. So is the repetition of "now"—the word becomes the footprint of the fox.

Footprints in snow—marks on the page!!

Stanza 4 uses an enjambment. Break between "lame" and "shadow" somehow gets sense of fox's shadow lingering. Another enjambment to stanza 5. This time we feel how the fox breaks away from the cover and crosses the field.

Stanza 5 has odd words. Check rhythm. H. seems to be making it hard. Not easy to say out loud. Maybe builds tension.

Last stanza feels sudden. Both alliteration and assonance in the first line. Intensity. The fox—the *real* fox?—"enters the dark hole of the head." Strange image. How is the head a dark hole? A metaphor, but for what? First use of metaphor. After that line the rest feels abrupt, cold. The life goes out of the poem. The poem is suddenly done. And we are done reading it.

Important play on words in last line, with "printed" referring to the fox and the writing.

What is the poem *about?* H. maybe trying to give a sense of what it feels like to write a poem. We get the idea that it's somehow more than just thinking of a subject, that the thing is alive, that it needs be written. The ending is hard to pin down. Why does the fox enter the "dark hole of the head"? Is it like a den, a home? Not clear.

Strong sense of contrast between the mechanical ticking of the clock and the life of the imagination, the "sharp hot stink" of the fox. Maybe use this. Begin with clock, and end with clock. Oppose the ticking to the movements of nature. Emphasize the way that H. makes it seem that the thought is independent. The poet doesn't think it—more like it *comes* to the poet.

Ryan stopped. He did not have his essay clearly in mind from start to finish, but his brainstorming had led him to a few ideas he felt were promising. The most striking thing about the poem, for him, was the way that Hughes had made the fox seem real—more real than the actual clock or desk. It occurred to him that the poet was trying to say something about the act of creation, and the power—even necessity—of inspiration. Since the poem began and ended at the poet's desk, he could use the same cycle to begin and end his discussion. Though he was not sure of his whole argument, he knew he had enough in the way of ideas and documentation to write a first draft. He also knew that the paper would eventually be rewritten (after a conference with the teacher) and that additions and changes could be made.

"The Thought-Fox"--A Response

"The Thought-Fox" by Ted Hughes is a poem about a poet finding the inspiration to write a poem. It is written in the first person, beginning with the words "I imagine." The reader assumes that the voice belongs to the poet himself.

opening a bit flat—

The poem begins, as it will end, with the poet working alone in his room. Hughes creates a mood of silence and expectation. What he imagines is "this midnight moment's ———

why the alliteration?

Writing about Poetry

forest," and he emphasizes the solitude with a personification, referring to "the clock's loneliness." Of course, it is not the clock that is lonely. Probably it is the poet, waiting for his inspiration.

The coming of an idea is announced in the second line, where Hughes writes that "Something else is alive." We don't know what that might be and we feel a sense of mystery. In the second stanza, he repeats the word "something," now bringing it closer.

the setup feels thin

look closer

In the third stanza we meet the fox; rather, the "thought fox." Hughes uses his language carefully to give the reader the sensation of a fox's nose coming forward. He alliterates the d-sound in the first line, making the reader pronounce the words slowly and carefully. And his use of the caesura in the next line--"A fox's nose touches twig,// leaf;" makes us hesitate just like the fox. The last two lines of the third stanza repeat the word "now" four times. We picture the footprints of the fox in the snow.

use quote to illustrate

good

The fourth stanza has the fox coming closer. The animal is still wary, and Hughes suggests this with an enjambment at the end of the second line. He writes: "a lame/ shadow lags" and we pause, just long enough to feel the lagging. ——————— *excellent observation*

There is another enjambment, this time between the fourth and fifth stanzas. The fox is "bold to come// Across clearings." We sense something breaking loose from cover and hurrying.

expand—why do we sense this?

But after the brief rush, the poem slows down again. Hughes packs the fifth stanza with long words:

why?

A widening deepening greenness,

Brilliantly,// concentratedly,

The rhythm of the words is falling, mainly dactylic (´ ˘ ˘). Hughes even uses the word "concentratedly" to describe its movement. He develops a tension that he will release in the final stanza.

what is the effect of the rhythm?

The last stanza is a surprise. The first line is full of assonances and alliterations. The words "sharp," "hot," and "fox" are assonant, while "sudden," "sharp," "stink" and "fox" all alliterate the s-sound. After the big words in the previous stanza, these short words hit us like punches. It is the poem's moment of climax. Now the fox, which has been outside, moving through the snow, "enters the dark hole of the head." It is a strange image, for the head is a solid, not a hole. But Hughes is making a metaphor. The hole, which makes us think of a fox's burrow, is the inside of the head, maybe the imagination.

good examples

expand discussion

As soon as the fox has entered, the poem ends. We are back to the room, the window, and the clock. "The page is printed." The last word is a pun, with the print referring both to the fox's footprints and the printed letters of the poem.

interesting— develop further

Hughes's descriptions in the last two lines of the poem are cold, very different from the living words that he used when describing the fox. He seems to be saying to the reader that the imagination is what gives life to things. When the act of imagining ends we are left with just a room and a ticking clock.

ending feels anticlimactic

show the contrast

expand on imagination

Reading his essay over, Ryan was not sure that he had done justice to his experience of the poem. Though he thought that he had accounted for most of the important features, he was not sure if he had fully captured the thematic aspect. But he could not see how to improve upon what he had done. He decided to hand the draft in and talk to his teacher in conference.

Ryan's teacher began their session on a note of encouragement. She praised his choice—she had not known the poem—and remarked on the shrewdness of some

Writing about Poetry

of his observations. In particular, she said, she had liked Ryan's reading of the third and fourth stanzas, with the comments on alliteration and enjambment. But she admitted that there were several problems with the paper as a whole. Mainly, she found it a bit "thin." She echoed Ryan's own suspicion, remarking that the treatment of the theme needed expansion. She had several questions. Was Hughes just writing about a fox, or did he have something deeper in mind? And wasn't there something to be said about the poem's ending—the way that the fox entering the hole of the head coincided with the page being printed?

Ryan listened. Her questions reminded him of some of the ideas he had meant to include. He asked the teacher if she thought the fox might have been intended as a symbol—for thought, or inspiration. She looked doubtful. Here was a case, she said, of that fine line between a symbol and a suggestion that the class had talked about earlier. The fox was certainly presented in a significant way, and the final image was mysterious. But at the same time, Hughes was depicting it so precisely, making its movements so specifically fox-like, that reading it as a symbol did not seem quite right. Symbols, she reminded Ryan, were generally abstract. To turn the fox into a straight symbol would change the nature of the poem. Ryan had to agree.

After their conference, Ryan returned to his room and his desk. He took out the sheet on which he had typed the poem and spent a long time just staring at the lines. He was not really reading—he was thinking about how to approach his rewrite. He was, he realized, waiting for an idea just as the poet was waiting for the poem. He smiled to himself and wondered briefly if he couldn't get an idea from *that* comparison. He was just beginning to leaf through the pages of his draft when he had a thought that struck him as useful. He suddenly saw that there was a paradox in the presentation. The fox, which comes alive in the poet's imagination, is already *in* his head. How, then, could he have it *entering* the dark hole of the head at the poem's end? What did this mean? And there was another paradox as well. For in the poem that entering in some way marked the end rather than the beginning of the writing process. Something that had been away had come home, and the writing was the cause.

Ryan was not at all sure what to make of these thoughts, but he knew that he could touch upon them in the second part of his revision. The teacher had said that the thematic treatment could use some expansion. He noted the paradoxes on a sheet of paper and got ready to rework his paper.

The basic structure, he felt, was fine. And his teacher had liked some of his more technical observations. Ryan was sure he could single out a few more poetic details. What he needed most was a strong opening and some added reflections around the paradoxes that he had found. It was just a matter of finding an effective opening.

Ryan looked back at the first paragraph of his draft. It was flat. He had made a few obvious assertions and had done nothing to suggest the nature of the poem. What *was* the nature of the poem? He was just beginning to doodle on the margins of his draft when an image came to him: a mirror. The fox putting its tracks in the snow was a direct reflection of the poet printing the words on the page. The poem was in some strange way about its subject—the fox—and about the writing of itself. Everything depended on the poet's idea finding a home on the page.

Ryan felt the ideas start up. He was getting somewhere! He jotted the word "mirror" down right at the top of his sheet of notes, then added: "poem is about its own process." He decided to start right in. He knew that if he could get the right wording in the first few sentences, the rest would follow. And so, after a few false starts, it did. Ryan worked steadily for several hours, writing in longhand. Much of that time was taken up by active pauses—he stared, tried to isolate a detail. Finally, though, he was ready to sit down at the computer. Two hours later he was done.

"The Thought-Fox"--A Response (Revision)

Ted Hughes's "The Thought-Fox" is a poem watching itself in a mirror. That is, it is about how a poem--itself--gets written. To some extent, therefore, it is about the writing process in general, or even creativity in general.

> *Much livelier opening!*

The poem is written in the first-person, beginning with the words "I imagine." The reader may assume that the voice belongs to Hughes himself, though it very well may be spoken through a persona who happens to be a poet. There is no regular pattern of meter or rhyme. "The Thought-Fox" remains unpredictable, like its subject.

> *nice*

It is interesting that Hughes would have tipped the reader off with his title, for the first two stanzas try to create an air of mystery, as if some unknown thing were approaching.

The poem begins, as it will end, with the poet working alone in his room. Hughes suggests the focus and intensity of a poet at work right away by using a strongly alliterated line: "I imagine this midnight moment's forest." There is no apparent reason for the repetition of m-sounds, except that they capture the reader's attention.

> *doesn't it make a murmuring sound and give a sense of meditation?*

Hughes goes on to emphasize the solitude. He uses personification, pointing to the "clock's loneliness." He then repeats the word "loneliness" at the end of the next stanza. It is clear to the reader that

> *How does personification emphasize solitude?*

714

the process of composition must represent a genuine isolation for the poet.

But he also writes, as early as line 2, that "Something else is alive." The reader is confused and waits to find out. Hughes's repetition of the word "something" in the next stanza heightens the tension. Now it is something "more near" than the stars, but "deeper within darkness." The reader might pause here. It is easy to see how that something could be nearer than the stars, but less easy to grasp how it might lie "deeper within darkness." The answer, we later decide, is that the fox, since it is imaginary, does not belong to the physical world at all.

Hughes has done an excellent job of creating expectation and of giving the sense of some creature approaching. What is amazing is that the poet is referring to a mental event. We don't usually think of a thought drawing near as if it were coming from some other place. We don't, for that matter, think of thought as an independent thing, outside our control. We say that we have thoughts. In this poem, it is almost as if the thoughts live lives of their own, ——— *fascinating!* and as if they have us.

Hughes is not talking about abstract thought but something more along the lines of poetic inspiration. What comes to him as if from some other place is an <u>image,</u> a very concrete image of a fox.

Stanza three represents a dramatic change. The abstract words like "darkness" and "loneliness" suddenly yield to concrete descriptions. We meet the fox. Hughes uses his language to give the reader the impression of a fox's nose coming forward. He alliterates the d-sound in the first line—— "Cold, delicately as the dark snow"——making

the reader pronounce the words with great
care (you cannot say the line rapidly). And
his use of the caesura in the next line--
"nose touches twig,// leaf;"--makes us hesitate just like the fox.

Then, in an image that combines sound,
rhythm, and even the appearance of words,
Hughes writes

> Two eyes serve a movement, that now
> And again now, and now, and now
> Sets neat prints into the snow

The repetition of "now" four times
forces us to see the word as a footprint. ——————— *show the markings over the line*
And the rhythm, which is very nearly
iambic, has just the slightest jerky hesitation. By putting into our minds the picture of footprints in the snow, Hughes gets
us ready for the final line of the poem,
which will compare the printed page with
the prints in the snow.

you may be tipping off the reader too much—the reader gets distracted

The fourth stanza has the fox coming
closer. The animal is still wary, and
Hughes suggests this with an enjambment at
the end of the second line. He writes: "a
lame / shadow lags" and we have to pause
for a moment, just long enough to feel the
lagging.

Hughes uses another effective enjambment
between the end of the fourth and the beginning of the fifth stanza. The fox is
"bold to come// Across clearings." Here the
sensation is of something breaking loose
from cover and hurrying through the open.
This is especially apparent when the poem
is read aloud.

can you specify what creates this effect?

But after this brief rush, the poem
slows down again. The poet builds tension
through the fifth stanza. He does this in
several ways. On the one hand, he uses a
great many long vowel sounds, especially in
the first three lines. There are assonances

716

between "eye" and "widening" and between "deepening" and "greenness." Further, lines 2 and 3 seem to use a dactylic rhythm, which is supposed to bring speed into a poem. On the other hand, he does things to slow the reader down. He sets long, multi-syllable words alongside one another, which slows down pronunciation, and he fills the stanza full of caesuras so that the reader keeps pausing. Reading the stanza out loud, we feel frustrated, bottled-up.

show —quote a line and scan it.

this helps to clarify things!

The last stanza comes as a surprise. There is an immediate sense of release. The first line is packed with assonances ("sharp," "hot," and "fox") and alliterated word-sounds ("sudden," "sharp," "stink," and "fox"). After the long words in the previous stanza, these short words are like punches: "Till, with a sudden sharp hot stink of fox." It is the climax of the poem. The fox, which we have imagined to be outside in a snowfield, now "enters the dark hole of the head." It is a strange image, for the head is usually considered a solid, not a hole. But Hughes is making a metaphor. The hole is the inside of the head--that is, the imagination.

scan the line— it's loaded with stresses

I don't get it. How can the imagination be a place?

As soon as the fox has entered, the poem ends. And the end comes as a surprise. We are suddenly back in the room, with the window and the clock. "The page is printed." The last word is a pun, with the print referring both to the tracks in the snow and the letters put down on paper by the writer.

On one level the poem is about itself-- about a poet imagining a fox and writing of that experience. On another, "The Thought-Fox" suggests things about the nature of thought and inspiration in general. Hughes wants us to feel the process, and the para-

dox, how the thoughts and images may be inside us, but how they seem to come from
elsewhere. This inside/outside paradox may
explain why it is that the fox, which
Hughes tells us right away is part of what
he imagines, can also be described as mov-   *interesting*
ing toward him from someplace else.   *idea—well*
                                                     expressed

    Interestingly, Hughes's descriptions in
the last two lines of the poem are cold and
detached, much as they were before the fox
appeared. He seems to be suggesting, without ever saying so in words, that it is the
imagination that gives life to things. For
when the act of imagining--writing--ends,
we are left with a starless window and a
ticking clock--two bleak images.   ———— strong ending

OTHER APPROACHES TO WRITING ABOUT POETRY

The response paper that Ryan's class was asked to write is but one of several common approaches to a poem. Others you should be aware of include *explication, analysis*, and *comparison and contrast*.

Explication

An explication is literally an "unfolding." The reader is asked to dismantle a poem and account for every element of its making, line by line. The poem is generally of manageable length, for to do the job well requires great fastidiousness and concentration. Anything longer than a 14-line sonnet becomes a challenge of a high order.

    Working line by line, then, the reader lays out all that can be discovered—about diction, meter, imagery, allusion, figures of speech, and so on. The result may read more like a lab report than a creative essay, but this is fitting. For the ultimate point of the explication is to get you to know the poem down to its least detail—to understand it as well as the chemist understands a compound he is working with.

Analysis

A poetic analysis is in some ways the opposite of an explication. Instead of trying to grasp all the elements as they are woven together, the reader singles out one for sustained attention. He or she may choose to focus upon a poet's use of imagery, or symbol, or meter, or some other salient element. And where the explication tends to look at shorter poems or isolated passages, the analysis often approaches longer works. The sonnet by Shakespeare that looms like a mountain before the explicator may not carry enough of any one element to support a comprehensive analysis; one of the longer odes of Keats may better fit the bill.

The structure of the analysis paper, while not as limited as that of the explication, is nonetheless fairly predictable. The writer usually begins by establishing some reason for picking that particular approach to the poem, or poems ("Theodore Roethke's sequence of greenhouse poems in *The Lost Son* uses precisely orchestrated images of plants in manmade settings to express stages in the developing awareness of a young child . . ."), and then sets about proving the case with well-chosen examples and supporting discussions. The conclusion generally reframes the rationale of the opening in deeper and more philosophical terms. Ingenuity and inventiveness are not unwelcome, but the form tends to discourage them in favor of straightforward presentation. The more insightful the observations, naturally, the better.

Comparison and Contrast

With poetry, as with other genres, comparison and contrast assignments are a favored way to get the reader to look for connections outside the immediate orbit of the work. The poems themselves must be suitable—neither too much alike nor too different—and the reader needs to gain something from the exercise. Comparison and contrast assignments are very rarely explications—to follow two poems, no matter how short, on a line-by-line basis is tedious in the extreme. The common approach is to take an element—generally a nontechnical element like symbol or imagery—and to survey key similarities and differences in their application. The reader will seldom be working with more than two poems, though these may be poems by two poets from one historical period, or from different epochs; or else they may be two poems by the same poet.

The key to writing a comparison and contrast essay is to find two things that can be put into useful relation, and about which something can be said. This must be left to common sense. The practical strategy, however, deserves a few comments.

The most important thing about structuring a comparison and contrast paper is to find a viable way to treat both works. The hardest approach to sustain is the one that moves from A to B back to A back to B, and so on. The reader loses all sense of context, and the writer scrambles desperately to find new ways to say, "In Milton's sonnet, on the other hand . . ."

A more natural—and reader-friendly—approach is to begin by setting out the general basis of the comparison, then to look at one text in some depth, and *then* to take up the other. Where necessary, connecting lines can be established: "Though Eliot, like Milton, has a religious imagination, his attitude toward salvation is a good deal more skeptical . . ." The reader follows one track, then the other. At the end, the writer rears up to an altitude and points up the key commonalities and divergences.

Keep in mind that these short discussions are not recipes. They are only the most approximate sorts of indicators. The writer should do whatever is needed to best serve the argument or ideas, and if this means departing from the mold then so be it. Whatever restrictions are put on writing by common sense become apparent soon enough. What matters is finding subject or approach that engages the interest. When the engagement is there, the rest follows quite naturally, if not always easily.

QUOTING A POEM

If you are going to write about poetry, you have to be prepared to cite passages in the body of your paper. You will also be making frequent references to specific lines and words or phrases within lines. It is a good idea, therefore, to include the poem(s) you discuss with the paper and to number the lines. Usually it is enough to indicate every fifth line in the right hand margin with a small numeral. In places where the context does not make the line reference perfectly clear, you should indicate it in parentheses: "Hughes's later reference to a 'deepening greenness' (18) will add to the impression of solitude."

If you wish to quote a short passage from the poem—no more than two lines—in your paper without setting the lines off from the text, you may do so by using quotation marks and a slash to indicate the line division, thus:

> Hughes ends the poem with images of emptiness: "The window is starless still; the clock ticks, / The page is printed." It is as if the human concerns played no part once the poem was written.

If only part of a line is to be cited thus, an ellipsis (. . .) should be used:

> Hughes likes to set the active against the static: ". . . the clock ticks, / The page is printed."

When the passage is longer than two lines, it is best to set it off from the text as you would any quotation, arranging it just as it appears in the book:

> I imagine this midnight moment's forest:
> Something else is alive
> Beside the clock's loneliness
> And this blank page where my fingers move.

If the lines are staggered or set up in some particular arrangement, try to duplicate indentations and spacings between words.

Finally, if you are making references to other works, or quoting from different sources, make sure to follow the new MLA guidelines as described in Appendix B.

More extensive treatments of documentation are available in the *MLA Handbook*, 3rd ed., as well as in numerous style books. The reference librarian at your school or public library can show you where to look.

25 A Poet's Career: Adrienne Rich

It's hard to think of a contemporary poet who has gone through a more dynamic evolution than Adrienne Rich. Through enormous personal strength as well as her artistic talent, Rich has not only created herself as a woman and a poet, but she has done so in a way that a great many of her readers have found exemplary. On one level, her struggles for self-liberation coincided with the rise of the women's movement in the 1960s and 1970s; on another level, they helped give that movement direction and momentum. Rich has worked tirelessly for decades, not just as a poet and critic, but also as a spokesperson and organizer.

A survey of Rich's poetry over more than four decades illuminates the private and public faces of female self-definition. From book to book she has mapped a trajectory, beginning with the obediently traditional work of her younger years, moving through zones of intense self-questioning, into ever more intense social and political engagements. As Rich has moved in more recent years through a spectrum of feminist stances and, more lately, into what might be called a tough-minded self-assessment, her poetic voice and stylistic approaches have changed accordingly.

Behind the work, of course, are the changing circumstances of her private life, and much about these deserves to remain just that—private. But Rich has also written about certain relevant portions of her own history, and these shed a good deal of light on the changing shape of her career.

Adrienne Rich was born in Baltimore, Maryland, in 1929. Her father, a pathologist at Johns Hopkins University, was Jewish, and in those times that was enough to keep the family on the margins of the local society. The family was neither outcast nor fully accepted.

Rich's father tutored her in various subjects, including poetry, throughout her early childhood. Rich learned the arts of formal versification, and from a young age wrote poems. She wrote, in part, to please her father (and she will later make much of the connection between formal verse style and the great male tradition that it serves). Rich's mother, Helen Jones, had once studied to be a concert pianist, but had given over her career hopes for the responsibilities of motherhood. The daughter would have to realize later that she was part of the reason her mother abandoned her vocation.

Attending Radcliffe College in the late 1940s, Rich continued to work at her poetic craft. Her main influence (as she discusses in her essay, "When We Dead Awaken: Writing as Re-Vision") were male poets, and her earliest public work, including *A Change of World* (1951) reflects the influence of their technique. It is regulated, formal, and prizes intellectual and technical agility over emotional expressiveness. Rich's poem, "The Middle-aged," from the early 1950s, is a good example of her early mode. The reader should compare the staid diction and studious approach of this poem to some of the work from the 1970s.

THE MIDDLE-AGED

Their faces, safe as an interior
Of Holland tiles and Oriental carpet,
Where the fruit-bowl, always filled, stood in a light
Of placid afternoon—their voices' measure,
Their figures moving in the Sunday garden   5
To lay the tea outdoors or trim the borders,
Afflicted, haunted us. For to be young
Was always to live in other peoples' houses
Whose peace, if we sought it, had been made by others,
Was ours at second-hand and not for long.   10
The custom of the house, not ours, the sun
Fading the silver-blue Fortuny curtains,
The reminiscence of a Christmas party
Of fourteen years ago—all memory,
Signs of possession and of being possessed,   15
We tasted, tense with envy. They were so kind,
Would have given us anything; the bowl of fruit
Was filled for us, there was a room upstairs
We must call ours: but twenty years of living
They could not give. Nor did they ever speak   20
Of the coarse stain on that polished balustrade,°
The crack in the study window, or the letters
Locked in a drawer and the key destroyed.
All to be understood by us, returning
Late, in our own time—how that peace was made,   25
Upon what terms, with how much left unsaid.

THE MIDDLE-AGED. 21 *balustrade*: the rail at the edge of a staircase.

After traveling through Europe on a Guggenheim fellowship, Rich returned to Cambridge, Massachusetts. She married Alfred Conrad, a Harvard economist, in 1953. In 1955, a son, David, was born. Two other sons, Paul and Jacob, were born in 1957 and 1959. Though Rich continued to write poetry, she felt the strain of traditional expectations—the very ones that had pulled her mother away from a pianist's career. As Rich wrote in her book *Of Woman Born* about this period: "I understood that my struggles as a writer were a kind of luxury, a peculiarity of mine." And: "The child (or children) might be absorbed in busyness, in his own dreamworld; but as soon as he felt me gliding into a world which did not include him, he would come to pull at my hand. . . ." After the publication of her second book, *The Diamond Cutters*, in 1955, Rich did not publish another book for nearly a decade.

That next collection, *Snapshots of a Daughter-in-Law*, is a powerful record of Rich's anger and frustration. Rich is still fighting the internal war between what she has absorbed of the societal expectations about being a wife and mother, and the steady pressure of her creative drive. In the light of her later poetic and personal development, the poems of this period stand out as vitally transitional.

The title poem of that collection shows Rich turning away from the confining formalism of her early work. The poem is looser, and adopts the natural speaking voice of a woman in distress. Its ten sections—each a snapshot—project the stages of an inner argument. The speaker, "once a belle in Shreveport," confronts the male-imposed definitions of women, and ends with a prophetic vision of women taking up their cause. The poem is already quick with the energies and impulses that would shape the women's movement a few years later.

SNAPSHOTS OF A DAUGHTER-IN-LAW

1.

You, once a belle in Shreveport,°
with henna-colored hair, skin like a peachbud,
still have your dresses copied from that time,
and play a Chopin prelude
called by Cortot°: *"Delicious recollections*   5
float like perfume through the memory."

Your mind now, moldering like wedding-cake,
heavy with useless experience, rich
with suspicion, rumor, fantasy,
crumbling to pieces under the knife-edge   10
of mere fact. In the prime of your life.

Nervy, glowering, your daughter
wipes the teaspoons, grows another way.

2.

Banging the coffee-pot into the sink
she hears the angels chiding, and looks out   15
past the raked gardens to the sloppy sky.
Only a week since They said: *Have no patience.*

The next time it was: *Be insatiable.*
Then: *Save yourself; others you cannot save.*
Sometimes she's let the tapstream scald her arm,   20
a match burn to her thumbnail,

SNAPSHOTS OF A DAUGHTER-IN-LAW. 1 *Shreveport*: a Louisiana city.   5 *Cortot*: a French pianist and conductor.

or held her hand above the kettle's snout
right in the woolly steam. They are probably angels,
since nothing hurts her anymore, except
each morning's grit blowing into her eyes.   25

3.

A thinking woman sleeps with monsters.
The beak that grips her, she becomes. And Nature,
that sprung-lidded, still commodious
steamer-trunk of *tempora*° and *mores*°
gets stuffed with it all: the mildewed orange-flowers,   30
the female pills, the terrible breasts
of Boadicea° beneath flat foxes' heads and orchids.

Two handsome women, gripped in argument,
each proud, acute, subtle, I hear scream
across the cut glass and majolica°   35
like Furies° cornered from their prey:
The argument *ad feminam*,° all the old knives
that have rusted in my back, I drive in yours,
ma semblable, ma soeur!°

4.

Knowing themselves too well in one another: 40
their gifts no pure fruition, but a thorn,
the prick filed sharp against a hint of scorn . . .
Reading while waiting
for the iron to heat,
writing, *My Life had stood—a Loaded Gun—*°   45
in that Amherst° pantry while the jellies boil and scum,
or, more often,
iron-eyed and beaked and purposed as a bird,
dusting everything on the whatnot every day of life.

5.

Dulce ridens, dulce loquens,°   50
she shaves her legs until they gleam
like petrified mammoth-tusk.

6.

When to her lute Corinna sings°
neither words nor music are her own;
only the long hair dipping   55

---

29 *tempora; mores*: times, customs.   32 *Boadicea*: an ancient Celtic warrior-queen.   35 *majolica*:
colorful glazed ceramic.   36 *Furies*: female monsters of mythology.   37 *ad feminam*: against a woman—
echoes the traditional term *ad hominem*, a personal attack against a man.   39 *ma semblable, ma soeur*: "my
duplicate, my sister"—refers to the last line of a classic Baudelaire poem of dark self-discovery.   45 *My
Life . . . Gun*: a poem by Emily Dickinson.   46 *Amherst*: the town in Massachusetts where Emily Dickinson lived.   50 *Dulce . . . loquens*: "sweetly laughing, sweetly speaking."   53 *When to her lute Corinna
sings*: a verse by Renaissance poet and musician Thomas Campion.

over her cheek, only the song
of silk against her knees
and these
adjusted in reflections of an eye.

Poised, trembling and unsatisfied, before
an unlocked door, that cage of cages,
tell us, you bird, you tragical machine —
is this *fertilisante douleur?*° Pinned down
by love, for you the only natural action,
are you edged more keen
to prise the secrets of the vault? has Nature shown
her household books to you, daughter-in-law,
that her sons never saw?

7.

"To have in this uncertain world some stay
which cannot be undermined, is
of the utmost consequence."
                              Thus wrote
a woman, partly brave and partly good,
who fought with what she partly understood.
Few men about her would or could do more,
hence she was labeled harpy, shrew and whore.

8.

"You all die at fifteen," said Diderot,°
and turn part legend, part convention.
Still, eyes inaccurately dream
behind closed windows blankening with steam.
Deliciously, all that we might have been,
all that we were—fire, tears,
wit, taste, martyred ambition—
stirs like the memory of refused adultery
the drained and flagging bosom of our middle years.

9.

Not that it is done well, but
that it is done at all?° Yes, think
of the odds! or shrug them off forever.
This luxury of the precocious child,
Time's precious chronic invalid,—
would we, darlings, resign it if we could?
Our blight has been our sinecure:°
mere talent was enough for us—
glitter in fragments and rough drafts.

60

65

70

75

80

85

90

---

    63 *fertilisante douleur*: fertile or rich sorrow.   77 *Diderot*: Denis Diderot, French author and compiler of a famous encyclopedia.   87 *Not that . . . at all*: a negative comment by Samuel Johnson on women's writing.   92 *sinecure*: a salaried position with little or no work.

Snapshots of a Daughter-in-Law

Sigh no more, ladies.
                    Time is male   95
and in his cups drinks to the fair.
Bemused by gallantry, we hear
our mediocrities over-praised,
indolence read as abnegation,°   100
slattern thought styled intuition,
every lapse forgiven, our crime
only to cast too bold a shadow
or smash the mold straight off.

        For that, solitary confinement,   105
tear gas, attrition shelling.
Few applicants for that honor.

10.

                    Well,
she's long about her coming, who must be
more merciless to herself than history.
Her mind full to the wind, I see her plunge   110
breasted and glancing through the currents,
taking the light upon her
at least as beautiful as any boy
or helicopter,
                    poised, still coming,   115
her fine blades making the air wince

but her cargo
no promise then:
delivered
palpable   120
ours.
                            [1958–1960]

_____

    100 *abnegation*: self-denial.

In 1966, Rich published *Necessities of Life: Poems, 1962–65*; the book was nominated for the National Book Award. Critic Wendy Martin has described the work as follows:

> In this collection, Rich articulates her emerging awareness that individual experience cannot be separated from its historic context, and there is growing conviction that the tension she experiences between her personal values and larger social forms embodies the cultural schism between mind and body, nature and civilization, oppressor and oppressed, which she feels is the basis for patriarchal order. Many of the poems express an increasing despair with masculine territoriality as manifested in the French civil strife, the Vietnam War, and the Arab-Israeli conflicts that took place in the decade of the 1960s.

From An American Triptych: Anne Bradstreet,
Emily Dickinson, Adrienne Rich

In her poetry, as in her own life, Rich was moving rapidly toward a stance of active engagement with the social and political realities of the times. In 1966, she and her husband moved to New York City. Rich began teaching—which served her both as a job and a form for social interaction—and for the next ten years would hold positions at a number of colleges and universities. The publication of *Leaflets: Poems, 1965–1968* showed the poet ever more willing to declare stances and to speak in an open and non-"poetic" voice. The look of her poems began to change as well, as Rich experimented with the technique of leaving long gaps, or caesuras, in her lines. As her 1968 poem "Nightbreak" confirms, she was intent upon breaking with the conventions she had been raised with.

NIGHTBREAK

Something broken   Something
I need   By someone
I love   Next year
will I remember what
This anger   unreal   5
                         yet
has to be gone through
The sun to set
on this anger
                         I go on   10
head down   into it
The mountain pulsing
Into the oildrum   drops
the ball of fire.

Time is quiet   doesn't break things   15
or even wound   Things are in danger
from people   The frail clay lamps
of Mesopotamia
row on row under glass
in the ethnological section   20
little hollows for dried-
up oil   The refugees
with their identical
tales of escape   I don't
collect what I can't use   I need   25
what can be broken.
In the bed the pieces fly together
and the rifts fill   or else
my body is a list   of wounds
symmetrically placed   30
a village
blown open   by planes

that did not   finish the job
The enemy has   withdrawn
between raids   become invisible
there are   35
        no agencies
            of relief
the darkness becomes utter
Sleep   cracked and flaking
sifts over the shaken   target   40

What breaks   is night
not day   The white
scar   splitting
over the east
The crack weeping   45
Time for the pieces
            to move
dumbly back
        toward each other.

1970 was a watershed year for the poet. She published *The Will to Change: Poems, 1968–1970*, a collection overtly expressive of Rich's mounting rage against a patriarchal, or male-dominated, society. The title can be read as a call to women everywhere to declare their dissatisfactions and act upon them. But it also reflects Rich's own determination to liberate herself. That year, she left her husband and struck out on her own. Her 1971 poem, "Trying to Talk with a Man," can be seen as a direct reflection of her emotional condition. With an associative boldness that has always characterized her work, Rich invokes the backdrop of a bomb-testing site for her stark scenario:

TRYING TO TALK
WITH A MAN

Out in this desert we are testing bombs,

that's why we came here.

Sometimes I feel an underground river
forcing its way between deformed cliffs
an acute angle of understanding   5
moving itself like a locus° of the sun   *place, position*
into this condemned scenery.

What we've had to give up to get here—
whole LP collections, films we starred in
playing in the neighborhoods, bakery windows   10
full of dry, chocolate-filled Jewish cookies,

the language of love-letters, or suicide notes,
afternoons on the riverbank
pretending to be children

Coming out to this desert   15
we meant to change the face of
driving among dull green succulents°   *juicy plants, cacti*
walking at noon in the ghost town
surrounded by a silence

that sounds like the silence of the place   20
except that it came with us
and is familiar
and everything we were saying until now
was an effort to blot it out—
coming out here as we are up against it   25

Out here I feel more helpless
with you than without you
You mention the danger
and list the equipment
we talk of people caring for each other   30
in emergencies—laceration, thirst—
but you look at me like an emergency

Your dry heat feels like power
your eyes are stars of a different magnitude
they reflect lights that spell out: EXIT   35
when you get up and pace the floor

talking of the danger
as if it were not ourselves
as if we were testing anything else.

    Since that time, Rich has involved herself ever more deeply with the cause of
women's liberation. The focus of the poetry has shifted over the years. Where the
poems in *Diving into the Wreck: Poems, 1971–72* were still occupied with the problem, raising a fierce cry against the patriarchal order (the title poem appears in
Chapter 22), later collections, like *The Dream of a Common Language* (1978) and *A
Wild Patience Has Taken Me This Far* (1981) were more concerned with finding solutions. Rich looked for ways to foster a sense of autonomy in women. She turned
her attention increasingly to history, trying to undo misconceptions and to give
equal time to voices that have been suppressed or ignored. A number of her poems
feature women in their historical circumstances. Her subjects include Marie Curie,
the discoverer of radium, Elvira Shatayev, leader of a Russian mountain-climbing
expedition, artists Paula Becker and Clara Westhoff, and astronomer Caroline Herschel (see Rich's discussion in "When We Dead Awaken"). "Power," about Marie
Curie, is representative.

POWER

Living   in the earth-deposits   of our history

Today a backhoe divulged   out of a crumbling flank of earth
one bottle   amber   perfect   a hundred-year-old
cure for fever   or melancholy   a tonic
for living on this earth   in the winters of this climate   5

Today I was reading about Marie Curie°:
she must have known she suffered   from radiation sickness
her body bombarded for years   by the element
she had purified
It seems she denied to the end   10
the source of the cataracts on her eyes
the cracked and suppurating skin   of her finger-ends
till she could no longer hold   a test-tube or a pencil

She died   a famous woman   denying
her wounds   15
denying
her wounds   came   from the same source as her power
                                                             [1974]

POWER. 6 *Marie Curie (1867–1934)*: the scientist who discovered radium.

If we set "Power" alongside "Rape," another poem from the same period, we get a clear sense of the span of her work during these years:

RAPE

There is a cop who is both prowler and father:
he comes from your block, grew up with your brothers,
had certain ideals.
You hardly know him in his boots and silver badge,
on horseback, one hand touching his gun.   5

You hardly know him but you have to get to know him:
he has access to machinery that could kill you.
He and his stallion clop like warlords among the trash,
his ideals stand in the air, a frozen cloud
from between his unsmiling lips.   10

And so, when the time comes, you have to turn to him,
the maniac's sperm still greasing your thighs,
your mind whirling like crazy. You have to confess

to him, you are guilty of the crime
of having been forced.

And you see his blue eyes, the blue eyes of all the family
whom you used to know, grow narrow and glisten,
his hand types out the details
and he wants them all
but the hysteria in your voice pleases him best.   20

You hardly know him but now he thinks he knows you:
he has taken down your worst moment

on a machine and filed it in a file.
He knows, or thinks he knows, how much you imagined;
he knows, or thinks he knows, what you secretly wanted,   25

He has access to machinery that could get you put away;
and if, in the sickening light of the precinct,
and if, in the sickening light of the precinct,
your details sound like a portrait of your confessor,
will you swallow, will you deny them, will you lie your way home?

    Nor should Rich's more private voice be overlooked. Though her poem "After
Twenty Years" was written in 1971, when outrage and defiance were the dominant
impulses of the work, the tenderness and compassion belong to the complementary
side of Rich which emerged most fully in the late 1970s and after:

AFTER TWENTY YEARS

Two women sit at a table by a window. Light breaks
unevenly on both of them.
Their talk is a striking of sparks
which passers-by in the street observe
as a glitter in the glass of that window.   5
Two women in the prime of life.
Their babies are old enough to have babies.
Loneliness has been part of their story for twenty years,
the dark edge of the clever tongue,
the obscure underside of the imagination.   10
It is snow and thunder in the street.
While they speak the lightning flashes purple.
It is strange to be so many women,
eating and drinking at the same table,
those who bathed their children in the same basin   15
who kept their secrets from each other
walked the floors of their lives in separate rooms

and flow into history now as the woman of their time
living in the prime of life
as in a city where nothing is forbidden   20
and nothing permanent.

More recent work, as in the collection *Your Native Land, Your Life* (1986), reveals Rich casting a long look back over her own private life. These poems often
take the form of an inner dialogue—or, in some instances, a letter written to the
self—with different sides of the self staking their claim. Rich takes up the question
of her Jewish heritage, searching out her connection to her race and its history. She
also addresses herself to her father, as well as to the husband she left (who committed suicide that same year), looking to understand what happened in their marriage.
Finally, she turns again and again to the question of physical pain, writing with great
clarity about her own debilitating arthritis. No matter where she turns, or what she
takes as her subject, the reader hears in Rich's voice a unique blend of power and
vulnerability. We recognize a poet who long ago set herself a task—to stay true to
herself and her beliefs, damn the consequences.

XVI

from "Sources" in *Your Native Land, Your Life*

The Jews I've felt rooted among
are those who were turned to smoke

Reading of the chimneys against the blear air
I think I have seen them myself

the fog of northern Europe licking its way   5
along the railroad tracks

to the place where all tracks end
You told me not to look there

to become
a citizen of the world   10

bound by no tribe or clan
yet dying you followed the Six Day War°

with desperate attention
and this summer I lie awake at dawn

sweating the Middle East through my brain   15
wearing the star of David

on a thin chain at my breastbone

XVI. 12 *Six Day War*: 1967 war between Israel and Arab states.

7

from "Contradictions: Tracking Poems"
in *Your Native Land, Your Life*

Dear Adrienne,
          I feel signified by pain
from my breastbone through my left shoulder down
through my elbow into my wrist is a thread of pain
I am typing this instead of writing by hand   5
because my wrist on the right side
blooms and rushes with pain
like a neon bulb
You ask me how I'm going to live
the rest of my life   10
Well, nothing is predictable with pain
Did the old poets write of this?
—in its odd spaces, free,
many have sung and battled—
But I'm already living the rest of my life   15
not under conditions of my choosing
wired   into pain
          rider on the slow train
                    Yours, Adrienne

WHEN WE DEAD AWAKEN:
WRITING AS RE-VISION

Ibsen's *When We Dead Awaken* is a play
about the use that the male artist and thinker—in the process of creating culture as
we know it—has made of women, in his life and in his work; and about a woman's
slow struggling awakening to the use to which her life has been put. Bernard Shaw
wrote in 1900 of this play:

> [Ibsen] shows that no degradation ever devized or permitted is as disastrous as this
> degradation; that through it women can die into luxuries for men and yet can kill
> them; that men and women are becoming conscious of this; and that what re-
> mains to be seen as perhaps the most interesting of all imminent social develop-
> ments is what will happen "when we dead awaken."[1]

It's exhilarating to be alive in a time of awakening consciousness; it can also be
confusing, disorienting, and painful. This awakening of dead or sleeping consciousness has already affected the lives of millions of women, even those who don't know
it yet. It is also affecting the lives of men, even those who deny its claim upon them.

---

[1]G. B. Shaw, *The Quintessence of Ibsenism* (New York: Hill & Wang, 1922), p. 139.

The argument will go on whether an oppressive economic class system is responsible for the oppressive nature of male/female relations, or whether, in fact, patriarchy—the domination of males—is the original model of oppression on which all others are based. But in the last few years the women's movement has drawn inescapable and illuminating connections between our sexual lives and our political institutions. The sleepwalkers are coming awake, and for the first time this awakening has a collective reality; it is no longer such a lonely thing to open one's eyes.

Re-vision—the act of looking back, of seeing with fresh eyes, of entering an old text from a new critical direction—is for women more than a chapter in cultural history; it is an act of survival. Until we can understand the assumptions in which we are drenched we cannot know ourselves. And this drive to self-knowledge, for women, is more than a search for identity; it is part of our refusal of the self-destructiveness of male-dominated society. A radical critique of literature, feminist in its impulse, would take the work first of all as a clue to how we live, how we have been living, how we have been led to imagine ourselves, how our language has trapped as well as liberated us, how the very act of naming has been till now a male prerogative, and how we can begin to see and name—and therefore live—afresh. A change in the concept of sexual identity is essential if we are not going to see the old political order reassert itself in every new revolution. We need to know the writing of the past, and know it differently than we have ever known it; not to pass on a tradition but to break its hold over us.

For writers, and at this moment for women writers in particular, there is the challenge and promise of a whole new psychic geography to be explored. But there is also a difficult and dangerous walking on the ice, as we try to find language and images for a consciousness we are just coming into, and with little in the past to support us. I want to talk about some aspects of this difficulty and this danger.   5

Jane Harrison, the great classical anthropologist, wrote in 1914 in a letter to her friend Gilbert Murray:

> By the by, about "Women," it has bothered me often—why do women never want to write poetry about Man as a sex—why is Woman a dream and a terror to man and not the other way around? . . . Is it mere convention and propriety, or something deeper?[2]

I think Jane Harrison's question cuts deep into the myth-making tradition, the romantic tradition; deep into what women and men have been to each other; and deep into the psyche of the woman writer. Thinking about that question, I began thinking of the work of two twentieth-century women poets, Sylvia Plath and Diane Wakoski. It strikes me that in the work of both Man appears as, if not a dream, a fascination and a terror; and that the source of the fascination and the terror is, simply, Man's power—to dominate, tyrannize, choose, or reject the woman. The charisma of Man seems to come purely from his power over her and his control of the world by force, not from anything fertile or life-giving in him. And, in the work of both these poets, it is finally the woman's sense of *herself*—embattled, possessed—that gives the poetry its dynamic charge, its rhythm of struggle, need, will, and female energy. Until recently this female anger and this furious awareness of the Man's power over her were not available materials to the female poet, who tended to write of Love as the source of her suffering, and to view that victimization by Love as an

---

[2]G. Stewart, *Jane Ellen Harrison: A Portrait from Letters* (London: Merlin, 1939), p. 140.

almost inevitable fate. Or, like Marianne Moore and Elizabeth Bishop, she kept sexuality at a measured and chiseled distance in her poems.

One answer to Jane Harrison's question has to be that historically men and women have played very different parts in each others' lives. Where woman has been a luxury for man, and has served as the painter's model and the poet's muse, but also as comforter, nurse, cook, bearer of his seed, secretarial assistant, and copyist of manuscripts, man has played a quite different role for the female artist. Henry James repeats an incident which the writer Prosper Mérimée described, of how, while he was living with George Sand,

> he once opened his eyes, in the raw winter dawn, to see his companion, in a dressing-gown, on her knees before the domestic hearth, a candlestick beside her and a red *madras* round her head, making bravely, with her own hands the fire that was to enable her to sit down betimes to urgent pen and paper. The story represents him as having felt that the spectacle chilled his ardor and tried his taste; her appearance was unfortunate, her occupation an inconsequence, and her industry a reproof—the result of all of which was a lively irritation and an early rupture.[3]

The specter of this kind of male judgment, along with the misnaming and thwarting of her needs by a culture controlled by males, has created problems for the woman writer: problems of contact with herself, problems of language and style, problems of energy and survival.

In rereading Virginia Woolf's *A Room of One's Own* (1929) for the first time in some years, I was astonished at the sense of effort, of pains taken, of dogged tentativeness, in the tone of that essay. And I recognized that tone. I had heard it often enough, in myself and in other women. It is the tone of a woman almost in touch with her anger, who is determined not to appear angry, who is *willing* herself to be calm, detached, and even charming in a roomful of men where things have been said which are attacks on her very integrity. Virginia Woolf is addressing an audience of women, but she is acutely conscious—as she always was—of being overheard by men: by Morgan° and Lytton° and Maynard Keynes and for that matter by her father, Leslie Stephen.[4] She drew the language out into an exacerbated thread in her determination to have her own sensibility yet protect it from those masculine presences. Only at rare moments in that essay do you hear the passion in her voice; she was trying to sound as cool as Jane Austen, as Olympian as Shakespeare, because that is the way men of the culture thought a writer should sound.

No male writer has written primarily or even largely for women, or with the sense of women's criticism as a consideration when he chooses his materials, his theme, his language. But to a lesser or greater extent, every woman writer has written for men even when, like Virginia Woolf, she was supposed to be addressing women. If we have come to the point where this balance might begin to change,

---

[3]Henry James, "Notes on Novelists," in *Selected Literary Criticism of Henry James*, Morris Shapira, ed. (London: Heinemann, 1963), pp. 157–58.

[4]*A. R., 1978:* This intuition of mine was corroborated when, early in 1978, I read the correspondence between Woolf and Dame Ethel Smyth (Henry W. and Albert A. Berg Collection, The New York Public Library, Astor, Lenox, and Tilden Foundations); in a letter dated June 8, 1933, Woolf speaks of having kept her own personality out of *A Room of One's Own* lest she not be taken seriously: ". . . . how personal, so will they say, rubbing their hands with glee, women always are; *I even hear them as I write.*" (Italics mine.)

Morgan: writer E. M. Forster; *Lytton:* Woolf's friend, biographer Lytton Strachey.

when women can stop being haunted, not only by "convention and propriety" but by internalized fears of being and saying themselves, then it is an extraordinary moment for the woman writer—and reader.

I have hesitated to do what I am going to do now, which is to use myself as an illustration. For one thing, it's a lot easier and less dangerous to talk about other women writers. But there is something else. Like Virginia Woolf, I am aware of the women who are not with us here because they are washing the dishes and looking after the children. Nearly fifty years after she spoke, that fact remains largely unchanged. And I am thinking also of women whom she left out of the picture altogether—women who are washing other people's dishes and caring for other people's children, not to mention women who went on the streets last night in order to feed their children. We seem to be special women here, we have liked to think of ourselves as special, and we have known that men would tolerate, even romanticize us as special, as long as our words and actions didn't threaten their privilege of tolerating or rejecting us and our work according to *their* ideas of what a special woman ought to be. An important insight of the radical women's movement has been how divisive and how ultimately destructive is this myth of the special woman, who is also the token woman. Every one of us here in this room has had great luck—we are teachers, writers, academicians; our own gifts could not have been enough, for we all know women whose gifts are buried or aborted. Our struggles can have meaning and our privileges—however precarious under patriarchy—can be justified only if they can help to change the lives of women whose gifts—and whose very being— continue to be thwarted and silenced.

My own luck was being born white and middle-class into a house full of books, with a father who encouraged me to read and write. So for about twenty years I wrote for a particular man, who criticized and praised me and made me feel I was indeed "special." The obverse side of this, of course, was that I tried for a long time to please him, or rather, not to displease him. And then of course there were other men— writers, teachers—the Man, who was not a terror or a dream but a literary master and a master in other ways less easy to acknowledge. And there were all those poems about women, written by men: it seemed to be a given that men wrote poems and women frequently inhabited them. These women were almost always beautiful, but threatened with the loss of beauty, the loss of youth—the fate worse than death. Or, they were beautiful and died young, like Lucy° and Lenore.° Or, the woman was like Maud Gonne,° cruel and disastrously mistaken, and the poem reproached her because she had refused to become a luxury for the poet.

A lot is being said today about the influence that the myths and images of women have on all of us who are products of culture. I think it has been a peculiar confusion to the girl or woman who tries to write because she is peculiarly susceptible to language. She goes to poetry or fiction looking for *her* way of being in the world, since she too has been putting words and images together; she is looking eagerly for guides, maps, possibilities; and over and over in the "words' masculine persuasive force" of literature she comes up against something that negates everything she is about: she meets the image of Woman in books written by men. She finds a

10

Lucy: young woman in a series of poems by William Wordsworth; *Lenore:* subject of a poem by Edgar Allen Poe.

Maud Gonne: Irish actress, subject of love poems by William Butler Yeats.

A Poet's Career: Adrienne Rich

terror and a dream, she finds a beautiful pale face, she finds La Belle Dame Sans Merci,° she finds Juliet° or Tess° or Salome,° but precisely what she does not find is that absorbed, drudging, puzzled, sometimes inspired creature, herself, who sits at a desk trying to put words together.

So what does she do? What did I do? I read the older women poets with their peculiar keenness and ambivalence: Sappho, Christina Rossetti, Emily Dickinson, Elinor Wylie, Edna Millay, H. D. I discovered that the woman poet most admired at the time (by men) was Marianne Moore, who was maidenly, elegant, intellectual, discreet. But even in reading these women I was looking in them for the same things I had found in the poetry of men, because I wanted women poets to be the equals of men, and to be equal as still confused with sounding the same.

I know that my style was formed first by male poets: by the men I was reading as an undergraduate—Frost, Dylan Thomas, Donne, Auden, MacNiece, Stevens, Yeats. What I chiefly learned from them was craft.[5] But poems are like dreams: in them you put what you don't know you know. Looking back at poems I wrote before I was twenty-one, I'm startled because beneath the conscious craft are glimpses of the split I even then experienced between the girl who wrote poems, who defined herself in writing poems, and the girl who was to define herself by her relationship with men. "Aunt Jennifer's Tigers" (1951), written while I was a student, looks with deliberate detachment at this split.[6]

Aunt Jennifer's tigers stride across a screen,
Bright topaz denizens of a world of green.
They do not fear the men beneath the tree;
They pace in sleek chivalric certainty.

Aunt Jennifer's fingers fluttering through her wool
Find even the ivory needle hard to pull.
The massive weight of Uncle's wedding band
Sits heavily upon Aunt Jennifer's hand.

When Aunt is dead, her terrified hands will be
Still ringed with ordeals she was mastered by.
The tigers in the panel that she made
Will go on striding, proud and unafraid.

In writing this poem, composed and apparently cool as it is, I thought I was creating a portrait of an imaginary woman. But this woman suffers from the opposition of her imagination, worked out in tapestry, and her life-style, "ringed with ordeal she was mastered by." It was important to me that Aunt Jennifer was a person as distinct from myself as possible—distanced by the formalism of the poem, by its objective, observant tone—even by putting the woman in a different generation.

(par 11) *La Belle . . . Merci:* the beautiful lady without mercy—title of a poem by John Keats. *Juliet, Tess, Salome:* tragic heroines in literary works.

[5]*A. R., 1978:* Yet I spent months, at sixteen, memorizing and writing imitations of Millay's sonnets; and in notebooks of that period I find what are obviously attempts to imitate Dickinson's metrics and verbal compression. I knew H. D. only through anthologized lyrics; her epic poetry was not then available to me.

[6]*A. R., 1978:* Texts of poetry quoted herein can be found in A. R., *Poem Selected and New: 1950–1974* (New York: Norton, 1975).

In those years formalism was part of the strategy—like asbestos gloves, it allowed me to handle materials I couldn't pick up barehanded. A later strategy was to use the persona of a man, as I did in "The Loser" (1958):

A man thinks of the woman he once loved: first, after her
wedding, and then nearly a decade later.

I
I kissed you, bride and lost, and went
home from that bourgeois sacrament,
your cheek still tasting cold upon
my lips that gave you benison°   *blessing*
with all the swagger that they knew—
as losers somehow learn to do.

Your wedding made my eyes ache; soon
the world would be worse off for one
more golden apple dropped to the ground
without the least protesting sound,
and you would windfall° lie, and we   *apple blown from a tree*
forget your shimmer on the tree.

Beauty is always wasted: if
not Mignon's° song sung to the deaf,   *melodic singing role for*
at all events to the unmoved.   *an opera heroine*
A face like yours cannot be loved
long or seriously enough.
Almost, we seem to hold it off.

II
Well, you are tougher than I thought.
Now when the wash with ice hangs taut
this morning of St. Valentine,
I see you strip the squeaking line,
your body weighed against the load,
and all my groans can do no good.

Because you are still beautiful,
though squared and stiffened by the pull
of what nine windy years have done.
You have three daughters, lost a son.
I see all your intelligence
flung into that unwearied stance.

My envy is of no avail
I turn my head and wish him well
who chafed your beauty into use
and lives forever in a house
lit by the friction of your mind.
You stagger in against the wind.

I finished college, published my first book by a fluke, as it seemed to me, and broke off a love affair. I took a job, lived alone, went on writing, fell in love. I was young, full of energy, and the book seemed to mean that others agreed I was a poet.

Because I was also determined to prove that as a woman poet I could also have what was then defined as a "full" woman's life, I plunged in my early twenties into marriage and had three children before I was thirty. There was nothing overt in the environment to warn me: these were the fifties, and in reaction to the earlier wave of feminism, middle-class women were making careers of domestic perfection, working to send their husbands through professional schools, then retiring to raise large families. People were moving out to the suburbs, technology was going to be the answer to everything, even sex; the family was in its glory. Life was extremely private; women were isolated from each other by the loyalties of marriage. I have a sense that women didn't talk to each other much in the fifties—not about their secret emptinesses, their frustrations. I went on trying to write; my second book and first child appeared in the same month. But by the time that book came out I was already dissatisfied with those poems, which seemed to me mere exercises for poems I hadn't written. The book was praised, however, for its "gracefulness"; I had a marriage and a child. If there were doubts, if there were periods of null depression or active despairing, these could only mean that I was ungrateful, insatiable, perhaps a monster.   15

About the time my third child was born, I felt that I had either to consider myself a failed woman and a failed poet, or to try to find some synthesis by which to understand what was happening to me. What frightened me most was the sense of drift, of being pulled along on a current which called itself my destiny, but in which I seemed to be losing touch with whoever I had been, with the girl who had experienced her own will and energy almost ecstatically at times, walking around a city or riding a train at night or typing in a student room. In a poem about my grandmother I wrote (of myself): "A young girl, thought sleeping, is certified dead" ("Halfway"). I was writing very little, partly from fatigue, that female fatigue of suppressed anger and loss of contact with my own being; partly from the discontinuity of female life with its attention to small chores, errands, work that others constantly undo, small children's constant needs. What I did write was unconvincing to me; my anger and frustration were hard to acknowledge in or out of poems because in fact I cared a great deal about my husband and my children. Trying to look back and understand that time I have tried to analyze the real nature of the conflict. Most, if not all, human lives are full of fantasy—passive day-dreaming which need not be acted upon. But to write poetry or fiction, or even to think well, is not to fantasize, or to put fantasies on paper. For a poem to coalesce, for a character or an action to take shape, there has to be an imaginative transformation of reality which is in no way passive. And a certain freedom of the mind is needed—freedom to press on, to enter the currents of your thought like a glider pilot, knowing that your motion can be sustained, that the buoyancy of your attention will not suddenly be snatched away. Moreover, if the imagination is to transcend and transform experience it has to question, to challenge, to conceive of alternatives, perhaps to the very life you are living at that moment. You have to be free to play around with the notion that day might be night, love might be hate; nothing can be too sacred for the imagination to turn into its opposite or to call experimentally by another name. For writing is re-naming. Now, to be maternally with small children all day in the old way, to be with a man in the old way of marriage, requires a holding-back, a putting-aside of that imaginative activity, and demands instead a kind of conservatism. I want to make it clear that I am *not* saying that in order to write well, or think well, it is necessary to become unavailable to others, or to become a devouring ego. This has been the myth of the masculine artist and thinker; and I do not accept it. But to be a female human being trying to fulfill traditional female functions in a traditional way *is* in direct conflict with the subversive function of the imagination. The word traditional is important here. There must be ways, and we will be finding out more and more of them, in which the energy of creation and the energy of relation can be united. But in those years I always felt the conflict as a failure of love in myself. I had thought I was choosing a full life: the life available to most men, in which sexuality, work, and parenthood could coexist. But I felt, at twenty-nine, guilt toward the people closest to me, and guilty toward my own being.

I wanted, then, more than anything, the one thing of which there was never enough: time to think, time to write. The fifties and early sixties were years of rapid revelations: the sit-ins and marches in the South, the Bay of Pigs,° the early antiwar movement, raised large questions—questions for which the masculine world of the academy around me seemed to have expert and fluent answers. But I needed to think for myself—about pacifism and dissent and violence, about poetry and society, and about my own relationship to all these things. For about ten years I was reading in fierce snatches, scribbling in notebooks, writing poetry in fragments; I was looking desperately for clues, because if there were no clues then I thought I might be insane. I wrote in a notebook about this time:

> Paralyzed by the sense that there exists a mesh of relationships—e.g., between my anger at the children, my sensual life, pacifism, sex (I mean sex in its broadest significance, not merely sexual desire)—an interconnectedness which, if I could see it, make it valid, would give me back myself, make it possible to function lucidly and passionately. Yet I grope in and out among these dark webs.

I think I began at this point to feel that politics was not something "out there" but something "in here" and of the essence of my condition.

In the late fifties I was able to write, for the first time, directly about experiencing myself as a woman. The poem was jotted in fragments during children's naps, brief hours in a library, or at 3:00 A.M. after rising with a wakeful child. I despaired of doing any continuous work at this time. Yet I began to feel that my fragments and scraps had a common consciousness and a common theme, one which I would have been very unwilling to put on paper at an earlier time because I had been taught that poetry should be "universal," which meant, of course, nonfemale. Until then I had tried very much *not* to identify myself as a female poet. Over two years I wrote a ten-part poem called "Snapshots of a Daughter-in-Law" (1958–1960), in a longer looser mode than I'd ever trusted myself with before. It was an extraordinary relief to write that poem. It strikes me now as too literary, too dependent on allusion. I hadn't found the courage yet to do without authorities, or even to use the pronoun "I"—the woman in the poem is always "she." One section of it, No. 2, concerns a woman who thinks she is going mad; she is haunted by voices telling her to resist and rebel, voices which she can hear but not obey.

2.
Banging the coffee-pot into the sink
she hears the angels chiding, and looks out
past the raked gardens to the sloppy sky.
Only a week since They said: *Have no patience.*

Bay of Pigs: a failed invasion of Cuba during the Kennedy administration.

The next time it was: *Be insatiable.*
Then: *Save yourself; others you cannot save.*
Sometimes she's let the tapstream scald her arm,
a match burn to her thumbnail,

or held her hand above the kettle's snout
right in the woolly steam. They are probably angels,
since nothing hurts her anymore, except
each morning's grit blowing into her eyes.

The poem "Orion," written five years later, is a poem of reconnection with a part of myself I had felt I was losing—the active principle, the energetic imagination, the "half-brother" whom I projected, as I had for many years, into the constellation Orion. It's no accident that the words "cold and egotistical" appear in this poem, and are applied to myself.

Far back when I went zig-zagging
through tamarack pastures
you were my genius, you
my cast-iron Viking, my helmed
lion-heart king in prison.
Years later now you're young

my fierce half-brother, staring
down from that simplified west
your breast open, your belt dragged down
by an oldfashioned thing, a sword
the last bravado you won't give over
though it weighs you down as you stride

and the stars in it are dim
and maybe have stopped burning.
But you burn, and I know it;
as I throw back my head to take you in
an old transfusion happens again:
divine astronomy is nothing to it.

Indoors I bruise and blunder,
break faith, leave ill enough
alone, a dead child born in the dark.
Night cracks up over the chimney,
pieces of time, frozen geodes
come showering down in the grate.

A man reaches behind my eyes
and finds them empty
a woman's head turns away
from my head in the mirror
children are dying my death
and eating crumbs of my life.

Pity is not your forte.
Calmly you ache up there
pinned aloft in your crow's nest,
my speechless pirate!
You take it all for granted
and when I look you back

it's with a starlike eye
shooting its cold and egotistical spear
where it can do least damage.
Breathe deep! No hurt, no pardon
out here in the cold with you
you with your back to the wall.

The choice still seemed to be between "love"—womanly, maternal love, altruistic love—a love defined and ruled by the weight of an entire culture; and egotism—a force directed by men into creation, achievement, ambition, often at the expense of others, but justifiably so. For weren't they men, and wasn't that their destiny as womanly, selfless love was ours? We know now that the alternatives are false ones—that the word "love" is itself in need of re-vision.

There is a companion poem to "Orion," written three years later, in which at last the woman in the poem and the woman writing the poem become the same person. It is called "Planetarium," and it was written after a visit to a real planetarium, where I read an account of the work of Caroline Herschel, the astronomer, who worked with her brother William, but whose name remained obscure, as his did not.   20

Thinking of Caroline Herschel, 1750–1848, astronomer,
sister of William; and others

A woman in the shape of a monster
a monster in the shape of a woman
the skies are full of them

a woman   "in the snow
among the Clocks and instruments
or measuring the ground with poles"

in her 98 years to discover
8 comets

she whom the moon ruled
like us
levitating into the night sky
riding the polished lenses

Galaxies of women, there
doing penance for impetuousness
ribs chilled
in those spaces   of the mind

An eye,

        "virile, precise and absolutely certain"
        from the mad webs of Uranisborg

                        encountering the NOVA

every impulse of light exploding
from the core
as life flies out of us

    Tycho° whispering at last   *Tycho Brache,*
    "Let me not seem to have lived in vain"   *famous Danish astronomer*

What we see, we see
and seeing is changing

the light that shrivels a mountain
and leaves a man alive

Heartbeat of the pulsar
heart sweating through my body

The radio impulse
pouring in from Taurus°   *a constellation*

    I am bombarded yet   I stand
I have been standing all my life in the
direct path of a battery of signals
the most accurately transmitted most
untranslatable language in the universe
I am a galactic cloud so deep   so invo-
luted that a light wave could take 15
years to travel through me   And has
taken   I am an instrument in the shape
of a woman trying to translate pulsations
into images   for the relief of the body
and the reconstruction of the mind.

In closing I want to tell you about a dream I had last summer. I dreamed I was asked to read my poetry at a mass women's meeting, but when I began to read, what came out were the lyrics of a blues song. I share this dream with you because it seemed to me to say something about the problems and the future of the woman writer, and probably of women in general. The awakening of consciousness is not like the crossing of a frontier—one step and you are in another country. Much of woman's poetry has been of the nature of the blues song: a cry of pain, of victimization, or a lyric of seduction.[7] And today, much poetry by women—and prose for that matter—is charged with anger. I think we need to go through that anger, and we will betray our own reality if we try, as Virginia Woolf was trying, for an objectivity, a detachment, that would make us sound more like Jane Austen or Shakespeare. We know more than Jane Austen or Shakespeare knew: more than Jane Austen because our lives are more complex, more than Shakespeare because we know more about the lives of women—Jane Austen and Virginia Woolf included.

Both the victimization and the anger experienced by women are real, and have real sources, everywhere in the environment, built into society, language, the struc-

---

[7]*A. R., 1978:* When I dreamed that dream, was I wholly ignorant of the tradition of Bessie Smith and other women's blues lyrics which transcended victimization to sing of resistance and independence?

tures of thought. They will go on being tapped and explored by poets, among others. We can neither deny them, nor will we rest there. A new generation of women poets is already working out of the psychic energy released when women begin to move towards what the feminist philosopher Mary Daly has described as the "new space" on the boundaries of patriarchy.[8] Women are speaking to and of women in these poems, out of a newly released courage to name, to love each other, to share risk and grief and celebration.

To the eye of a feminist, the work of Western male poets now writing reveals a deep, fatalistic pessimism as to the possibilities of change, whether societal or personal, along with a familiar and threadbare use of women (and nature) as redemptive on the one hand, threatening on the other; and a new tide of phallocentric sadism and overt woman-hating which matches the sexual brutality of recent films. "Political" poetry by men remains stranded amid the struggles for power among male groups; in condemning U.S. imperialism of the Chilean junta the poet can claim to speak for the oppressed while remaining, as male, part of a system of sexual oppression. The enemy is always outside the self, the struggle somewhere else. The mood of isolation, self-pity, and self-imitation that pervades "nonpolitical" poetry suggests that a profound change in masculine consciousness will have to precede any new male poetic—or other—inspiration. The creative energy of patriarchy is fast running out; what remains is its self-generating energy for destruction. As women, we have our work cut out for us.

QUESTIONS

1. Read the poems by Rich, including those cited in her essay "When We Dead Awaken." Drawing upon lines you have excerpted, write a short descriptive commentary (2 to 3 paragraphs) in which you discuss the transformations in Rich's poetic style. Consider her diction, rhythms, line breaks, caesuras, and imagery.

2. Reading through the same poems, focus your attention on Rich's images, similes and metaphors. Discuss how these change and how the changes reflect Rich's growing involvement with the cause of women's liberation (2 paragraphs).

3. Using the evidence of the poems as well as Rich's essay, compose an open letter addressed to American women. Give an account, as Rich might see it, of the problems as well as the solutions. You may quote Rich's own words as needed.

4. Write a short thematic comparison of "Diving into the Wreck" (see Chapter 22) and "Trying to Talk with a Man." Discuss in particular how Rich uses imagined settings and scenarios to amplify her meanings.

5. Using two poems from each poet, compare the poetic voice and style of Rich and Elizabeth Bishop (see Chapter 27).

SUGGESTIONS FOR WRITING

1. Go to the library and find one collection of Rich's poetry. Write a short essay exploring how the poems work out a particular set of themes. Comment upon Rich's poetic style and its effectiveness. Try to place these poems in the line of development outlined by Rich in her essay "When We Dead Awaken."

---

[8]Mary Daly, *Beyond God the Father: Toward a Philosophy of Women's Liberation* (Boston: Beacon, 1973).

2. Find a historical figure and try your hand at writing a poem of your own. Use the figure, and information about him or her, to make a statement about some aspect of our present-day culture.

3. Using the *Readers' Guide to Periodical Literature* in your library, locate reviews of Rich's books in various newspapers and journals. Either (a) compare representative reviews of her first two books with reviews of her more outspokenly feminist collections, or (b) compare how different journals responded to the same book. Write a short paper in which you assess your findings and discuss the impact of Rich's work on the culture of her times.

26 A Poet's Career: Gary Snyder

The poetic careers of Gary Snyder and Adrienne Rich make an instructive comparison. They belong to the same generation—born in 1930 and 1929, respectively—and both are writers who have chosen to "live" their poetry. That is, they write their poetry out of the circumstances of their living and their beliefs. Neither has settled for the more popular option—the university teaching post and the orderly stream of publications in respected journals. For Rich this has meant the exhilarating but also painful exploration of female identity and what it means to be a woman in a world largely structured around male-imposed traditions. That exploration has led her over the course of four decades from a traditional and submissive formalism into increasingly personal and expressively open poetic styles. The *how* of her poetry has evolved right along with the *what* of her subject matter.

Gary Snyder's career presents a different picture. From his earliest work on, Snyder has sought to write with clarity and reverence of the natural world and the place of the human within that world. Indeed, the poet's essential reverence is communicated mainly through the clarity of the expression. The implicit message seems to be: If you learn to see the beauty and complexity of the world, you will be in the right alignment with it; if you are in the right alignment, you will see the beauty and complexity.

Snyder discovered his basic orientation early. Born in the rural country near Washington's Puget Sound in 1930, Snyder grew up on a farm. He took a strong interest in the cultures and myths of the Native Americans. His undergraduate thesis at Oregon's Reed College was a study of a Haida Indian version of a myth about a swan turning into a woman. Snyder's fascination with the lore of indigenous cultures of the East and West has continued undiminished. He finds in the myths and tales of humans and animals in interaction a store of archetypes, all of which are meant to instruct us about modes of relation and coexistence within the natural world.

In the early 1950s, Snyder worked a number of jobs in the wilds of the Northwest. He signed on to be a fire-watcher—possibly the loneliest and most meditative of all employments—and also served on trail crews in the Yosemite region. The latter experience led directly to the writing of his first book, *Riprap* (1959). This collection already bore the distinctive markings of what would become the Snyder style—a sharp eye for precise images (often, but not always, of nature), a clean and unadorned diction that owed as much to the minimal approach of the Eastern Zen poets as it did to the perception-based units of William Carlos Williams, and a personal restraint that kept the author's personal presence at a remove. Snyder would bring himself in as a participant, the person making the observations, but the poems were never really *about* him. The poem "Milton by Firelight" is representative of this period. The title captures nicely the grafting of bookish tradition and the immediate observation of the outdoors.

MILTON BY FIRELIGHT°

Piute Creek, August 1955

"O hell, what do mines eyes
    with grief behold?"°
Working with an old
Singlejack miner, who can sense
The vein and cleavage   5
In the very guts of rock, can
Blast granite, build
Switchbacks° that last for years
Under the beat of snow, thaw, mule-hooves.
What use, Milton, a silly story   10
Of our lost general parents,
        eaters of fruit?°

The Indian, the chainsaw boy,
And a string of six mules
Came riding down to camp   15
Hungry for tomatoes and green apples.
Sleeping in saddle-blankets
Under a bright night-sky
Han River slantwise by morning.
Jays squall   20
Coffee boils

In ten thousand years the Sierras
Will be dry and dead, home of the scorpion.
Ice-scratched slabs and bent trees.

No paradise, no fall,   25
Only the weathering land
The wheeling sky,
Man, with his Satan
Scouring the chaos of the mind.
Oh Hell!   30
Fire down

MILTON BY FIRELIGHT. The speaker, presumably the poet, is reading from the seventeenth-century poet John Milton, including from the epic poem *Paradise Lost*.   1–2 *"Oh hell . . . behold"*: line from *Paradise Lost*.   8 *switchbacks*: where hillside roads or paths make a U-turn to cut back across a slope.   11–12 *lost general parents . . . fruit*: reference to Adam and Eve, subjects of *Paradise Lost*.

Too dark to read, miles from a road
The bell-mare clangs in the meadow
That packed dirt for a fill-in
Scrambling through loose rocks
On an old trail
All of a summer's day.

                                                35

Later in the 1950s, while living in the San Francisco area (he entered the doctoral program in Japanese at Berkeley), Snyder became involved with many of the figures who would later be celebrated as founders of the Beat Movement—including Jack Kerouac, Allen Ginsberg, Philip Whalen, and others. Snyder read his poetry at the same reading at which Allen Ginsberg read his legendary poem "Howl" for the first time, an occasion that many regard as the explosive beginning of the Beat phenomenon. And Jack Kerouac made him the hero (under the pseudonym Japhy Ryder) of his novel *The Dharma Bums*. In the book, Snyder/Ryder is presented as a young man burning to attain spiritual enlightenment; he is a loner, with a rucksack full of books on Zen Buddhism.

In the mid-1950s, Snyder acted on his impulses, making his way to Japan on a tramp steamer. His poem "Nooksack Valley," written on the eve of departure, can be read as a pilgrim's farewell letter, an expectant summing up that successfully resists the temptations of bravado and sentimentalism.

NOOKSACK VALLEY

February 1956

At the far end of a trip north
In a berry-pickers cabin
At the edge of a wide muddy field
Stretching to the woods and cloudy mountains,
Feeding the stove all afternoon with cedar,
Watching the dark sky darken, a heron flap by,
A huge setter pup nap on the dusty cot.
High rotten stumps in the second-growth woods
Flat scattered farms in the bends of the Nooksack
River. Steelhead run now
           a week and I go back
Down 99, through towns, to San Francisco
                    and Japan.

All America south and east,
Twenty-five years in it brought to a trip-stop
Mind-point, where I turn
Caught more on this land—rock tree and man,
Awake, than ever before, yet ready to leave.
           damned memories,
Whole wasted theories, failures and worse success,

        5

        10

        15

        20

Schools, girls, deals, try to get in
To make this poem a froth, a pity,
A dead fiddle for lost good jobs.
     the cedar walls
Smell of our farm-house, half built in '35.   25
Clouds sink down the hills
Coffee is hot again. The dog
Turns and turns about, stops and sleeps.

Between 1956 and 1964, Snyder lived in Japan, studying Zen at a monastery near Kyoto. The poetry of this period remains watchful and precise, very much rooted in the world as it is known to the senses. As Snyder has said, quoting the Zen master Dogen, "We study the self to forget the self. And when you forget the self you become *one* with all things." Meditation, then, should not be seen as a path away from the world, but rather as a more direct path *to* it. Certainly Snyder's poems about his Japanese experience show the poet with both feet on the ground, and all five senses tuned to the subtlest impressions. Nor should the reader overlook Snyder's natural touch for the comic possibilities of a situation and his absolute lack of prudishness. As the second of the following poems reveals, Snyder married and fathered a child during his stay in Japan.

THE PUBLIC BATH

the bath-girl
    getting dressed, in the mirror,
      the bath-girl with a pretty mole and a
   red skirt is watching me:
      am I
        different?   5

the baby boy
    on his back, dashed with scalding water
    silent, moving eyes
    inscrutably
    pees.

the daughters
    gripping and scrubbing his two little daughters   10
     they squirm, shriek at
      soap-in-the-eye,
    wring out their own hair
     with grave wifely hands,
    peek at me, point, while he   15
    soaps up and washes their
     plump little tight-lip pussies

peers in their ears,
        & dunks them in hot tile tub.
        with a brown-burnt farmboy
     a shrivelled old man
and a student who sings *silent night*.   20

—we waver and float like seaweed
pink flesh in the steamy light.

the old woman
        too fat and too old to care   25
           she just stands there
               idly knocking dewy water off her
                  bush.

the young woman
        gazing vacant, drying her neck
           faint fuzz of hair   30
           little points of breasts
               —next year she'll be dressing
                  out of sight.

the men
        squatting soapy and limber
        smooth dense skin, long muscles—   35

        I see dead men naked
        tumbled on beaches
               newsreels, the
                war

THE BED IN THE SKY

Motorcycle strums   the empty streets
Heading home at one a.m.
      ice slicks shine in the moon
         I weave a safe path through

Naked shivering light flows down   5
Fills the basin over Kyoto°   *city in Japan*
      and the plain
         a ghost glacier dream

From here a hundred miles are clear
The cemetery behind   10
      Namu   Amida   Butsu°   *Japanese place-names*
         chiselled   ten thousand times

Tires crackle the mud-puddles
The northern hills gleam white

I ought to stay outside   alone
                    and watch the moon all night

But the bed is full and spread and dark
I hug you and sink in the warm
          my stomach against your big belly

                    feels our baby turn   20

Upon his return from Japan, Snyder became a visible presence in the counter-
culture of the late 1960s and early 1970s. He was one of the many who, as much out
of natural inclination as out of protest against what he saw as the growing evil of in-
dustrialization, returned to the land. Snyder built a house for himself and his family
in the wilds of the northern Sierra Nevada. He lives there to this day, working his
land, writing poetry and prose (much of which is about our relation to our remaining wildernesses), and traveling from time to time to read his work and to participate in conferences and workshops. The poems that follow show how his more
disengaged perceptions have become colored by a sense of urgency. There is a clear
identification of sides—us and them, good consciousness and bad consciousness—
as well as a consistent invocation of the Native American cultures that represent
for Snyder the right and natural relation to the earth.

I WENT INTO THE MAVERICK BAR

I went into the Maverick Bar
In Farmington, New Mexico.
And drank double shots of bourbon
                    backed with beer.
My long hair was tucked up under a cap   5
I'd left the earring in the car.

Two cowboys did horseplay
                    by the pool tables,
A waitress asked us
                    where are you from?   10
a country-and-western band began to play
"We don't smoke Marijuana in Muskokie"
And with the next song,
                    a couple began to dance.

They held each other like in High School dances   15
                    in the fifties;
I recalled when I worked in the woods
                    and the bars of Madras, Oregon.
That short-haired joy and roughness—
                    America—your stupidity.   20
I could almost love you again.

We left—onto the freeway shoulders—
                    under the tough old stars—
In the shadow of bluffs
                    I came back to myself,   25
To the real work, to
        "What is to be done."
                                    [1960s]

POKE HOLE FISHING AFTER THE MARCH°

"Those pine shingles—gunpowder dry.
        if you want to save money on shingles
        go up to Petaluma
        a place called Wicks"
on anything; handling; pre-finished plywood;   5
"I got a house with those kind of walls."

Eel-fishing, poke-holing for blinnies°
down cliffs through poison oak,
        a minus-two low tide.

        thirty thousand brothers and sisters   10
        bare-breasted girl on TV
        her braids whipping
        round about her haid,

"A hawk with a fish or a bird, up in the air,
        in his claws."   15

An older fatter short-haired man
Down fishing too—all catching nothing—
A roofing contractor.
Says "I'd like to stay down here all week."
11.30 AM now, tide's coming back in   20
        rusty wrecked car on the rocks

After the Peoples' Park march.
Monday, low tide.
        he sits with us down by the fire
        in the truck-high boulders, smoke   25
        stinging of salt
"Yeah I saw you guys on TV." Laugh, beer.
as the sea moves in
we all talk as friends;
as if America wasn't in a war—   30

POKE HOLE FISHING AFTER THE MARCH. Snyder is writing about the aftermath of the Peoples' Park
march in San Francisco, an early eruption of the protest movements of the late 1960s.   7 *blinnies*: fish.

A Poet's Career: Gary Snyder

(Gone to the mountains
    gathering herbs
       I do not know
            when he will return—)

High tide.   35
Where the rocks were
Now there are fish.

                  [N. of Slide Ranch late 1960s]

FRONT LINES

The edge of the cancer
Swells against the hill—we feel
      a foul breeze—
And it sinks back down.
The deer winter here   5
A chainsaw growls in the gorge.

Ten wet days and the log trucks stop,
The trees breathe.
Sunday the 4-wheel jeep of the
Realty Company brings in   10
Landseekers, lookers, they say
To the land,
Spread your legs.

The jet crack sound overhead, it's OK here;
Every pulse of the rot at the heart   15
In the sick fat veins of Amerika°
Pushes the edge up closer—

A bulldozer grinding and slobbering
Sideslipping and belching on top of
The skinned-up bodies of still-live bushes   20
In the pay of a man
From town.

Behind is a forest that goes to the Arctic
And a desert that still belongs to the Piute°
And here we must draw   25
Our line.

FRONT LINES. 16 *Amerika*: spelling reflecting an antigovernment sentiment. 26 *Piute*: Indian tribe of the far West.

TOMORROW'S SONG

The USA slowly lost its mandate
in the middle and later twentieth century
it never gave the mountains and rivers,
    trees and animals,
        a vote.   5
all the people turned away from it
      myths die; even continents are impermanent

    Turtle Island returned.
    my friend broke open a dried coyote-scat
    removed a ground squirrel tooth   10
    pierced it, hung it
    from the gold ring
    in his ear.

We look to the future with pleasure
we need no fossil fuel   15
get power within
grow strong on less.

Grasp the tools and move in rhythm side by side
    flash gleams of wit and silent knowledge
        eye to eye   20
sit still like cats or snakes or stones
    as whole and holding as
        the blue black sky.
gentle and innocent as wolves
        as tricky as a prince.   25

At work and in our place:
    in the service
    of the wilderness
    of life
    of death   30
    of the Mother's breasts!

    Gary Snyder has remained remarkably consistent in his craft and his subject matter. What has changed has been the world––that is, public consciousness about just the things he writes about. Since Snyder first began writing and publishing, Western and Eastern countries alike have begun to face the implications of indiscriminate industrial development. In the past twenty years, the collective level awareness about the environment and the need for sound ecological practices has risen dramatically. Without selling himself, and without changing anything about his fundamental vision, Snyder has become a central figure in the American imagination. His poems are no longer seen as being about isolated natural settings so much as about the integrity of living systems and living things. His audience, which has been growing steadily for years, is likely to keep growing. The greater the urgency we feel about our natural world, the more necessary will seem the wisdom and honesty of this man's work.

Here follow a short essay, "The Wilderness," by Snyder, and excerpts from a 1977 interview with Paul Geneson.

THE WILDERNESS[1]

I am a poet. My teachers are other poets, American Indians, and a few Buddhist priests in Japan. The reason I am here is because I wish to bring a voice from the wilderness, my constituency. I wish to be a spokesman for a realm that is not usually represented either in intellectual chambers or in the chambers of government.

I was climbing Glacier peak in the Cascades of Washington several years ago, on one of the clearest days I had ever seen. When we reached the summit of Glacier Peak we could see almost to the Selkirks in Canada. We could see south far beyond the Columbia River to Mount Hood and Mount Jefferson. And, of course, we could see Mount Adams and Mount Rainier. We could see across Puget Sound to the ranges of the Olympic Mountains. My companion, who is a poet, said: "You mean, there is a senator for all this?"

Unfortunately, there isn't a senator for all that. And I would like to think of a new definition of humanism and a new definition of democracy that would include the nonhuman, that would have representation from those spheres. This is what I think we mean by an ecological conscience.

I don't like Western culture because I think it has much in it that is inherently wrong and that is at the root of the environmental crisis that is not recent; it is very ancient; it has been building up for a millennium. There are many things in Western culture that are admirable. But a culture that alienates itself from the very ground of its own being—from the wilderness outside (that is to say, wild nature, the wild, self-contained, self-informing ecosystems) and from that other wilderness, the wilderness within—is doomed to a very destructive behavior, ultimately perhaps self-destructive behavior.

The west is not the only culture that carries these destructive seeds. China had effectively deforested itself by 1000 A.D. India had effectively deforested itself by 800 A.D. The soils of the Middle East were ruined even earlier. The forests that once covered the mountains of Yugoslavia were stripped to build the Roman fleet, and those mountains have looked like Utah ever since. The soils of southern Italy and Sicily were ruined by latifundia slave-labor farming in the Roman Empire. The soils of the Atlantic seaboard in the United States were effectively ruined before the American Revolution because of the one-crop (tobacco) farming. So the same forces have been at work in East and West.

5

---

[1]Transcript of a statement made at a seminar at The Center for the Study of Democratic Institutions, Santa Barbara, California.

You would not think a poet would get involved in these things. But the voice that speaks to me as a poet, what Westerners have called Muse, is the voice of nature herself, whom the ancient poets called the great goddess, the Magna Mater.° I regard that voice as a very real entity. At the root of the problem where our civilization goes wrong is the mistaken belief that nature is something less than authentic, that nature is not as alive as man is, or as intelligent, that in a sense it is dead, and that animals are of so low an order of intelligence and feeling, we need not take their feelings into account.

A line is drawn between primitive peoples and civilized peoples. I think there is a wisdom in the worldview of primitive peoples that we have to refer ourselves to, and learn from. If we are on the verge of postcivilization, then our next step must take account of the primitive worldview which has traditionally and intelligently tried to open and keep open lines of communication with the forces of nature. You cannot communicate with the forces of nature in the laboratory. One of the problems is that we simply do not know much about primitive people and primitive cultures. If we can tentatively accommodate the possibility that nature has a degree of authenticity and intelligence that requires that we look at it more sensitively, then we can move to the next step. "Intelligence" is not really the right word. The ecologist Eugene Odum uses the term "biomass."

Life-biomass, he says, is stored information; living matter is stored information in the cells and in the genes. He believes there is more information of a higher order of sophistication and complexity stored in a few square yards of forest than there is in all the libraries of mankind. Obviously, that is a different order of information. It is the information of the universe we live in. It is the information that has been flowing for millions of years. In this total information context, man may not be necessarily the highest or most interesting product.

Perhaps one of its most interesting experiments at the point of evolution, if we can talk about evolution in this way, is not man but a high degree of biological diversity and sophistication opening to more and more possibilities. Plants are at the bottom of the food chain; they do the primary energy transformation that makes all the life-forms possible. So perhaps plant-life is what the ancients meant by the great goddess. Since plants support the other life-forms, they become the "people" of the land. And the land—a country—is a region within which the interactions of water, air, and soil and the underlying geology and the overlying (maybe stratospheric) wind conditions all go to create both the microclimates and the large climatic patterns that make a whole sphere or realm of life possible. The people in that realm include animals, humans, and a variety of wild life.

What we must find a way to do, then, is incorporate the other people—what the Sioux Indians called the creeping people, and the standing people, and the flying people, and the swimming people—into the councils of government. This isn't as difficult as you might think. If we don't do it, they will revolt against us. They will submit non-negotiable demands about our stay on the earth. We are beginning to get non-negotiable demands right now from the air, the water, the soil. 10

I would like to expand on what I mean by representation here at the Center from these other fields, these other societies, these other communities. Ecologists talk about the ecology of oak communities, or pine communities. They *are* communities. This institute—this Center—is of the order of a kiva of elders. Its function is

---

THE WILDERNESS. (par. 6) *Magna Mater*: Great Mother (Latin).

A Poet's Career: Gary Snyder

to maintain and transmit the lore of the tribe on the highest levels. If it were doing its job completely, it would have a cycle of ceremonies geared to the seasons, geared perhaps to the migrations of the fish and to the phases of the moon. It would be able to instruct in what rituals you follow when a child is born, when someone reaches puberty, when someone gets married, when someone dies. But, as you know, in these fragmented times, one council cannot perform all these functions at one time. Still it would be understood that a council of elders, the caretakers of the lore of the culture, would open themselves to representation from other life-forms. Historically this has been done through art. The paintings of bison and bears in the caves of southern France were of that order. The animals were speaking through the people and making their point. And when, in the dances of the Pueblo Indians and other peoples, certain individuals became seized, as it were, by the spirit of the deer, and danced as a deer would dance, or danced the dance of the corn maidens, or impersonated the squash blossom, they were no longer speaking for humanity, they were taking it on themselves to interpret, through their humanity, what these other life-forms were. That is about all we know so far concerning the possibilities of incorporating spokesmanship for the rest of life in our democratic society.

Let me describe how a friend of mine from a Rio Grande pueblo hunts. He is twenty-seven years old. The Pueblo Indians, and I think probably most of the other Indians of the Southwest, begin their hunt, first by purifying themselves. They take emetics,° a sweat bath, and perhaps avoid their wife for a few days. They also try not to think certain thoughts. They go out hunting in an attitude of humility. They make sure that they need to hunt, that they are not hunting without necessity. Then they improvise a song while they are in the mountains. They sing aloud or hum to themselves while they are walking along. It is a song to the deer, asking the deer to be willing to die for them. They usually still-hunt, taking a place alongside a trail. The feeling is that you are not hunting the deer, the deer is coming to you; you make yourself available for the deer that will present itself to you, that has given itself to you. Then you shoot it. After you shoot it, you cut the head off and place the head facing east. You sprinkle corn meal in front of the mouth of the deer, and you pray to the deer, asking it to forgive you for having killed it, to understand that we all need to eat, and to please make a good report to the other deer spirits that he has been treated well. One finds this way of handling things and animals in all primitive cultures.

(par. 12) *emetics:* purgatives to induce vomiting.

THE REAL WORK (EXCERPTS FROM AN INTERVIEW)

INTERVIEWER: For you personally, what is the attraction of the rural life?

SNYDER: Well, apart from arguments about poetry, and *city* or *country*, it's obvious that city life has become difficult. It's *quite* obvious. And it's only natural that people should look for other ways to live. There is an implicit satisfaction in rural life, and in back-country life—at least for some people. The pleasures are numerous and the work is hard, and one is literally less alienated from one's water, one's fuel, one's vegetables, and so forth. Those are fundamentals, those are ancient human fundamentals.

And it wouldn't be going too far to say that human creativity and all of the arts will begin to wither if they are pulled too far away from fundamentals of how people really should and have had to live, over millennia. We are, after all, an animal that was brought into being on this biosphere by these processes of sun and water and leaf. And if we depart too far from them, we're departing too far from the mother, from our own heritage. But I've written some of my best poems working in the engine room of a tanker for months at a time where I didn't see a green leaf, or even a fly. That's not the problem. The problem is, where do you put your feet down, where do you raise your children, what do you do with your hands. Now, working in a tanker with my body and with my hands in the engine room of a ship is in some ways less alienated than it would be to sit and look at this beautiful view, talking constantly on the telephone, and typing on a typewriter and never *touching* it. It's the use of the *body* and the involvement of all the senses that is important at that point. . . .

INTERVIEWER: You mentioned Eliot°—don't you find Eliot . . . a *heady* poet?

SNYDER: What's really fun about Eliot is his intelligence, and his highly selective and charming use of Occidental° symbols which point you in a certain direction. I read *From Ritual to Romance*,° and went on to read *Prolegomena to Greek Religion*, Jane Ellen Harrison, and it just kept pushing me back. It takes you all the way back to the cave at Trois Frères in France, ultimately. If you follow anything that has any meat to it it'll take you back there. And so Eliot, without maybe even consciously being aware of it, points us in some profound directions. *Four Quartets* is my favorite Eliot work, and I think that it is a major work. He had the sense of the roots. He had the sense of the roots more deeply than Pound° did, actually. Pound was never able to get back to—you know, he could get back to the Early Bronze Age and his imagination couldn't go back any further than that. Olson° at least gets to the Neolithic.°

INTERVIEWER: What do you mean when you say modern poets can get back to the Neolithic?

SNYDER: I mean their imagination is able to encompass it, that they feel that it's part of their lives, that they feel comradeship in connection with it, that they feel that there is humanity in that that speaks to them. This is part of our history. . . .

INTERVIEWER: In the genesis of the poem as you write it: Do you take notes, or do these things just come to you? How does it arrive and what do you do first?

SNYDER: I listen to my own interior mind-music closely, and most of the time there's nothing particularly interesting happening. But once in a while I hear something which I recognize as belonging to the sphere of poetry. I listen very closely to that.

THE REAL WORK. (par. 4) *Eliot:* poet T. S. Eliot; see Chapter 28.   (par. 5) *Occidental:* Western. *From Ritual to Romance:* a study of cultural myths by Jessie Weston, which influenced Eliot in his poem *The Waste Land.*   *Pound:* American poet Ezra Pound; see Chapter 27.   *Olson:* American poet Charles Olson.   *neolithic:* late Stone Age from about 10,000 B.C.

A Poet's Career: Gary Snyder

INTERVIEWER: Inside?

SNYDER: Inside. But it's coming from outside, if you like. Maybe I have a radio receiver planted in my spinal cord.

INTERVIEWER: Are you talking about voices or ideas that are being directed at you? For example, your son might mention something about the creek that might trigger something—

SNYDER: I might hear that too, that's true. Prior to the writing of the poems I tend to have a sense of key areas that I'm watching that are beginning to evolve as points I must know about, that are beginning to evolve in my life. And poems will flow out of those in time. Now here's the list of things I want to watch right now. [He opens a file drawer and takes out several cards.] These three cards. That's how I identify things, by those little phrases. Part of my psychological and spiritual evolution is tied up with that. Out of that more precise language and symbol ultimately will come—more precise *music* will come. I tend to nourish poems in the mind for a long time before I actually sing them and write them down. So that when they're born they're generally about the right term, and they don't have to be corrected or re-tuned too much.

INTERVIEWER: You don't do much revising then?

SNYDER: Don't have to because I do it in my mind. I give them lots of time before they come out. That's short poems. On long poems like "Mountains and Rivers Without End," which I'm working on now, I have to be more organized. Because I'm doing a number of long poems simultaneously, writing them all simultaneously [He opens the various file cabinets and explains the use of the many folders, cards, and catalogs to the ongoing work of composing poetry.] So what I'm saying, I use a system of organization to keep on top of it. . . .

INTERVIEWER: Can you conceive of a person being a good teacher of poetry?

SNYDER: I like the apprentice relation as a way to go for that. I think that young people who want to have a teacher should not look at a university as a university, but look for the teacher. If the teacher happens to be a professor in the university, that's all right. But if not, not. In either case you go to that person directly, not to the administration building, and you say, "I want to be your student. What do I have to do?" And in doing that you expand the relationship into something more *personal*, more *menial*, more *direct*.

The model for that, for me, is the Japanese potters who take apprentices. And the thing that the apprentice first learns how to do is mix clay. Or Japanese carpentry apprentices who will spend months learning how to sharpen chisels and planes before they ever touch the tools to do work.

INTERVIEWER: And for poets: Is it to see, or to sharpen the language?

SNYDER: Depends on what they're studying at that time and what the teacher is. The teacher could be a car repair man. You could learn as much from a good mechanic and how parts go together, and how you move and what goes in what order—you learn craft from a craftsman, it doesn't matter which. You learn how to use your mind in the act of handling parts and working. You learn how to work. You learn how things go together.

INTERVIEWER: You're making an analogy here.

SNYDER: But it's a *true* analogy. A master is a master. If you saw a man who was a master mechanic you'd do better—say you wanted to be a poet, and you saw a man that you recognized is a master mechanic or a great cook. You would do better, for yourself as a poet, to study under that man than to study under another poet who was not a master, that you didn't recognize as a master.

INTERVIEWER: Who was not a true poet?

SNYDER: Not only a true poet but a master—a *real* craftsman. There are true poets who can't teach because they're hooked onto inspiration, spontaneity, voice, language—they do it but they're not grounded in details. They don't *really* know the materials. A carpenter, a builder knows what Ponderosa pine can do, what Douglas fir can do, what Incense cedar can do and builds accordingly. You can build some very elegant houses without knowing that, but some of them aren't going to work, ultimately.

And so, I'm saying that behind the scenes there is the structural and the fundamental knowledge of materials in poetry, and learning from a master mechanic would give you some of those fundamentals as well as studying from an academician, say.

INTERVIEWER: It sounds as if you're talking more about an Oriental or an eastern kind of mechanic, someone who is more sensitive, or *sensitized*.

SNYDER: No. I use the term "master mechanic" because I know a master mechanic. Whenever I spend any time with him, I learn something from him.

INTERVIEWER: About?

SNYDER: About *everything*. But I see it in terms of my craft as a poet. I learn about my craft as a poet. I learn about what it really takes to be a craftsman, what it really means to be committed, what it really means to work. What it means to be *serious* about your craft and no bullshit. . . . Not backing off any of the challenges that are offered to you. You know, like not being willing to read books, for Christ's sake. You run into people who want to write poetry, who don't want to read anything in the tradition. That's like wanting to be a builder but not finding out what different kinds of wood you use.

INTERVIEWER: When a person teaches poetry, ought he to talk about inspiration?

SNYDER: Inspiration is something that can be talked about, but can't be taught in the university context. What you *can* point out is that inspire has the word "spirit" in it, and is related to *expire*, *respire*, and *conspire*. And point out a few other connections like that. I would say, offhand, if you want inspiration, the two simplest and best ways to get it are to go on a long walking trip by yourself, or take a sweat bath. This will inspire you for poetry. Sweat baths, especially . . .

INTERVIEWER: Kerouac° talks a lot about the idea of spontaneity: the "spontaneous get with it," the "spontaneous recall of the unconscious." Do you also feel that way about composing poetry?

SNYDER: It's only part of it. The spontaneity is beautiful, and Jack's *haiku*, in *Mexico City Blues*, are some of the prettiest poems in the English language. But to complete the work of poetry as I see it in our time, here, I'd like to see some instantly apprehended because so-well-digested larger loopings of lore. Now, if you haven't digested it and it hasn't become part of you, then you are looking things up in your library books. Or, as Philip Whalen says, in your Handbook of Comparative Mythology—to look for the symbols to put in. That, of course, is wrong. But if you've absorbed and apprehended and digested it, why your apprehensive, prehensive mass that you can draw on is very large and very

---

(par. 32) *Kerouac:* Jack Kerouac, American "beat" novelist and friend of Snyder's.

beautiful. This is part of the training you come in there with. Your spontaneity, in other words, can be very rich.

INTERVIEWER: But it's a prior experience that makes it rich?

SNYDER: That's right. That's really what we mean by learning and by being cultured—that the time process really does enrich and deepen what you have at hand at any time. And there's a point where you have enough at hand at any time and you're so comfortable with it that you can really turn some very rich thing out. That's what a great potter is . . .

INTERVIEWER: Do you feel the university has a function beyond what Allen Ginsberg° feels is its importance—cataloguing?

SNYDER: Well, that's a great value of it. But in fact the university also has the function of reassessing our tradition, our body of lore, every generation. And in the process sometimes discovering things that were missed before and bringing them back to our attention—as Blake° was brought to us, or as Melville's° poetry was brought to us—that might have been lost otherwise. So the English department is a cardboard box that everybody throws every poetry magazine that comes in the mail into and says, "Well, we'll look at that later. I haven't got time to read it now." So it's a backward function in time. Like some kinds of academic and intellectual pursuits are forward-looking—most of the sciences are looking for new breakthroughs, new discoveries. An English department is looking backward in time, trying to understand what happened as they go—you know, looping backward as they go, and trying to connect.

So they're establishing the tradition and that is their value. And I respect that. I have great respect for that. I don't think that they *understand* their function enough to have enough pride or enough pleasure in their work, though. And that's what makes me sad. They don't have a *tribal* sense of their own work, and it is a truly tribal work.

INTERVIEWER: What would you suggest to them?

SNYDER: I suggest that they get an anthropological and a prehistoric perspective on these things and then they'll see where what they're doing fits into the picture. And how the professors in the English department are like *kiva* priests, priests of the *kiva* that we have to go to from time to time to say "Now why was it that there are three lines painted at the top of this eagle feather, with a little bit of red fluff on it. Now what was the reason for doing that?" Somebody who keeps that in mind for us.

It doesn't mean that they have to care a lot about it. But they do have to care about their role, about their function. And their function is maybe to tell some young guy who's going to be a beautiful poet or a beautiful dancer, to give him that one little extra bit of information to deepen what he's doing.

Because, you know, they carry the lore, they bear it. And they bear it for the benefit of the dancers who get inspired out there in the plaza.

In earlier times the English professor would have also been the *raconteur*, the storyteller who would, to a small select audience of students after the storytelling was over and the audience had gone home, tell them some of the

---

(par. 36) *Allen Ginsberg:* American "beat" poet.   (par. 37) *Blake; Melville:* English Romantic poet William Blake (see Chapter 19); and American novelist and poet Herman Melville; writers of outstanding work unearthed from obscurity by scholars.

inner meanings, some of the *background,* some of the *professional secrets* of what he had just recited. He doesn't have to be the poet who made it up necessarily, see? . . .

INTERVIEWER: Some people would say to a young poet, "Poetry is self-expression. Sit down and write what you can whenever you can." Would you say that?

SNYDER: No, I wouldn't say that. I don't think that's true. I think that poetry is a social and traditional art that is linked to its past and particularly its language, that *loops* and draws on its past and that serves as a vehicle for contact with the depths of our own unconscious—and that it gets better by practicing. And that the expression of self, although it's a nice kind of energy to start with, would not make any expression of poetry *per se.*

We all know that the power of a great poem is not that we felt that person expressed himself well. We don't think that. What we think is "How deeply *I* am touched." That's our level of response. And so a great poet does not express his or her self; he expresses *all* of our selves. And to express *all* of our selves you have to go beyond your own self. And when you forget the self, you become *one* with all things." And that's why poetry's not self-expression in those small self terms.

INTERVIEWER: Japan plays a considerable role in your poetry. Would you say to a young poet, "Go to Japan"?

SNYDER: Good heavens, no. What Japan as advice implies is: if there's a spiritual path that you feel is important to you, go out and study it, no matter where it leads. And the other thing that implies is: if you have the will and the energy and the opportunity, go live in an alien culture for a while. It really does, as they say, "broaden" you. [He laughs.]

INTERVIEWER: So a poet then, like a novelist, has to know human nature?

SNYDER: Well, I like the way Jack Spicer° saw it where all pure and true poetry is ultimately inspired in origin. It comes to us as a voice from outside. To even say that it comes from within is to mislead yourself. So we are the vehicle of that voice. However, if we are people who can hear that voice, then we should strive to be the best possible vehicle of that voice we can. Which means to learn other languages, to become as broadly human and as well informed and aware as we can because that will give strength to our handling and expressing the power of the voice. I think that's just right on the money.

INTERVIEWER: Including translations?

SNYDER: Yeah, including translations. Reading. Learning how to *do* translations.

INTERVIEWER: Wallace Stevens said that the translator is a parasite. Do you agree with that?

SNYDER: We need everyone who can do it. Any good translator is a great help to all of us. . . . A translator's no more a parasite than an interpreter standing at the edge of the creek helping a group of Crow and a group of Hunkpapa Sioux do some trading is a parasite—it's a valuable function. A translator is a valuable switch in an energy-exchange flow. . . .

You ask me what is the function of poetry so I think, "What is the function of poetry since forty thousand years ago?" In all cultures of the world—total planetary overview. And in that sense the function of poetry is not only the intensification and clarification of the implicit potentials of the language,

---

(par. 49) *Jack Spicer:* West Coast poet.

which we can hope means a sharpening, a bringing of more delight to the normal function of language and making maybe language even work better since communication is what it's about. But on another level, poetry is intimately linked to any culture's fundamental world view, body of lore, which is its myth-base, its symbol-base, and the source of much of its values—that myth-lore foundation that underlies any society. That foundation is most commonly expressed and transmitted in the culture by poems, which is to say *by songs*. By songs that are linked to a dramatic or ritual performance much of the time.

INTERVIEWER: Then it doesn't have to be poetry *per se*—it could be through the drama or novels—

SNYDER: But we haven't had novels for forty thousand years. We have had poems.

INTERVIEWER: No, but we've had tales. We've had *Gilgamesh,*° and that sort of thing.

SNYDER: All right. But those were in the oral tradition. What we're talking about there is the epic, and that is a variety of poetry because it is sung or chanted. The oral tradition almost always puts its transmission into a form of measured language, which is easier to remember and can be chanted. Much of the world's lore has been transmitted, in one form or another, via poetic forms, measured language or sung language.

INTERVIEWER: In terms of today's society, particularly the American, what forms would you see that might develop back into, or *forward* to, the mythic or oral tradition?

SNYDER: Well, we don't necessarily have to transmit a body of myth lore in only an oral mode. A key line of Occidental poetic Goethe, Milton, James Joyce, and William Blake. Now each one of those major poets has attempted in his own time, through a process of vision and meditation, so to speak, to assimilate, absorb and re-speak the fundamental myth-archetypal, world-view images of that whole world that they were in—to compress it and compact it and bring it back again into its own time. That's the ongoing work of major poets; to restate the society's whole body of world-view lore periodically. And, with the exception of Homer, all of the poets I've just mentioned were in writing. . . .

INTERVIEWER: W. H. Auden° said about poetry that it won't change anything. Is that how you see poetry?

SNYDER: Ezra Pound said, to quote an oft-quoted line, that artists are the antennae of the race. How that probably functions in practice is that some people's sensibilities, as well as maybe their lifestyles, are out at the very edge of the unraveling cause-and-effect network of a society in time. And also are, by virtue of the nature of their sensibilities, turned into other voices than simply the social or human voice. So they are like an early-warning system that hears the trees and the air and the clouds and the watersheds beginning to groan and complain a little bit. And so they try to send a little bit of a warning back, although they themselves may not know what it is they're hearing. They also can hear the stresses and the fault block slippage creaking in the social batholith and also begin to give out warnings.

What proceeds on that is, for the poet in particular, a sense of the need to look at the key archetype image and symbol blocks and see if the blocks are

---

(par. 57) *Gilgamesh:* Ancient Babylonian creation epic.   (par. 61) *W. H. Auden:* English poet.

working. Poetry effects change by fiddling with the archetypes and getting at people's dreams about a century before it actually effects historical change.

INTERVIEWER: I'm not too clear on the idea of the archetype blocks.

SNYDER: What I'm saying is we change the values of a society.

INTERVIEWER: Then the poet is essentially a pioneer?

SNYDER: No, I wouldn't say a pioneer. A pioneer clear-cuts an eco-system and sets the succession phase back to zero again. A poet would be, in terms of the ecology of symbols, noting the main structural connections and seeing which parts of the symbol system are no longer useful or applicable, though everyone is giving them credence. And out of his own vision and hearing of voices he seeks for his new paths for the mind energy to flow, which would be literally more creative directions, but directions which change politics. Poets are more like mushrooms or fungi—they can digest the symbol detritus. . . .

The value and function of poetry can be said in a very few words. One side of it is *in time*, the other is *out of time*. The in-time side of it is to tune us in to *mother* nature and *human* nature so that we live *in time*, in our societies in a way and on a path in which all things can come to fruition equally, and together in harmony. A path of beauty. And the out-of-time function of poetry is to return us to our own true original nature at this instant forever. And those two things happen, sometimes together, sometimes not, here and there all over the world, and always have.

Now whether or not that particular pattern of processes has had any great or small effects on the major flow of human social evolution is not something I can say. And yet if you look at a society that *sings* and that *dances* as a regular thing, it's not that it has an effect on their life—it *is* their life. It is their life: the lore of the culture is carried in the songs. And so poetry *is* our life. It's not that poetry has an effect on it, or a function in it, or a value for it. It *is* our life as much as eating and speaking is our life. It's like asking, "Well, what's the function of eating? What's the value of speaking?" . . .

INTERVIEWER: On a personal level, is the individual poet important? Does he need recognition?

SNYDER: Some do, some don't. I think for a lot of poets recognition from their peers is essentially what they need. You know, architects seldom get a lot of recognition from the public—the public doesn't see what's going on. An architect is pleased to have a fellow architect say, "I saw what you did there—that's really something." That's what you need, for the most part. People who crave recognition beyond that I tend to suspect a little bit as wanting some food for their ego, which won't do them any good. Excessive recognition—it does no harm to have lots of money, to be sure. That's not entirely true. But we can hope it doesn't do much harm to have lots of money. It may even be helpful. But *recognition* can really be detrimental to somebody who's interested in getting his or her work done and not in collecting Karma Cookies at testimonial dinners.

Even so young and little-known a poet as myself could fritter away a great deal of time going to testimonial dinners, so to speak, which would not write any more poems or give me any time to do all the work I want to do. So I need a certain level of anonymity, and I *am* that level of anonymity—I don't need it; I *make* it. I *live* that level of anonymity because I'm not interested in gaining social fruits from being a poet. I'm interested in writing my poems and finishing out the work that I envision for myself. . . .

INTERVIEWER: In your poem "The Real Work" you mention that the "real work" is

> washing and sighing,
> sliding by.

What exactly is "the real work"?

SNYDER: I've used that phrase, "the real work," a few times before. I used that term, "the real work," and then I asked myself a lot: What is the real work? I think it's important, first of all, because it's good to work—I love work; work and play are one. And that all of us will come back again to hoe in the ground, or gather wild potato bulbs and digging sticks, or hand-adze a beam, or skin a pole, or scrape a hive—we're never going to get away from that. We've been living a dream that we're going to get away from it, that we won't have to do it again. Put that out of our minds. We'll always do that work. That work is always going to be there. It might be stapling papers, it might be typing in the office. But we're never going to get away from that work, on one level or another. So that's real. The real work is what we really do. And what our lives are. And if we can live the work we have to do, knowing that we are real, and it's real, and that the work is real, then it becomes right. And that's the *real work:* to make the world as real as it is, and to find ourselves as real as we are within it.

I used that phrase again at the end of the poem "The Maverick Bar," where we go back out of that bar in Farmington, New Mexico, out onto the highway

> under the tough old stars . . .
> To the real work, to
> What is to be done.

The *real work* is to be the warriors that we have to be, to find the heart of the monster and kill it, whether we have any hope of actually winning or not. That's part of it. To take the struggle on without the *least* hope of doing any good. To check the destruction of the interesting and necessary diversity of life on the planet so that the dance can go on a little better for a little longer. The other part of it is that it is always here,

> washing and sighing,
> sliding by.

That was the wash of the waves on the island out in San Francisco Bay with the sea birds, and the feeding and schooling of the little fish—that's going on. The *real work* is eating each other, I suppose . . .

[Interviewed by Paul Geneson, 1977]

QUESTIONS

1. Compare "Reading Milton by Firelight," "The Public Bath," and "All the Spirit Powers Went to Their Dancing Place." Citing extracts from the poems, discuss the most obvious changes in Snyder's poetry. Look at his use of images and descriptions, the arrangement of lines, and the presence of the speaker. What elements appear to have remained constant in the poetry?

2. Pick two poems that seem particularly rich in detail. Look closely at Snyder's line breaks and his use of spacing. Try to isolate the places where you see the poet's eye and ear at work. Why do you think Snyder arranged these lines as he did?

The Real Work (Excerpts from an Interview)

3. Find three instances in the poems where a detail, or sequence of details, evokes a larger context. Try to explain what it is about the detail that allows this to happen.

4. Read Snyder's essay "The Wilderness" and relate his statements about nature to his depictions of nature in the poems. In what ways do Snyder's poems embody the philosophy he reveals in his essay?

SUGGESTIONS FOR WRITING

1. Read the statements on poetry by Wordsworth, Eliot, and Bly (see Chapter 28). Can you find a way to relate their views to those expressed by Snyder in his interview? Which of the poets would seem to hold beliefs closest to Snyder's? Explain. Write a short dialogue on the place of the poet in society between Snyder and any of the three poets.

2. Go to the library and do some research on the philosophy of Zen Buddhism. Based on your reading, discuss some of the ways that Zen Buddhist philosophy may have influenced Snyder's poetry.

3. Write a short essay comparing any of Snyder's poems to any of the poems by William Carlos Williams included in this anthology (see Chapter 27).

27 An Anthology of Poetry

Homer (c. 850 B.C.)

ODYSSEUS BATTLES THE WAVES°

Odyssey, Book v

Two nights, two days, in the solid deep-sea swell
he drifted, many times awaiting death,
until with shining ringlets in the East
the dawn confirmed a third day, breaking clear
over a high and windless sea; and mounting   5
a rolling wave he caught a glimpse of land.
What a dear welcome thing life seems to children
whose father, in the extremity, recovers
after some weakening and malignant illness:
his pangs have gone, the gods have delivered him.   10
So dear and welcome to Odysseus
the sight of land, of woodland, on that morning.
It made him swim again, to get a foothold
on solid ground. But when he came in earshot
he heard the trampling roar of sea on rock,   15
where combers,° rising shoreward, thudded down
on the sucking ebb—all sheeted with salt foam.
Here were no coves or harborage or shelter,
only steep headlands, rockfallen reefs and crags.
Odysseus' knees grew slack, his heart faint,   20
a heaviness came over him, and he said:
'A cruel turn, this. Never had I thought
to see this land, but Zeus° has let me see it—
and let me, too, traverse the Western Ocean—

ODYSSEUS BATTLES THE WAVES. In this episode, Odysseus has left the island nymph Calypso to continue his homeward journey to Ithaka. Poseidon, the god of the ocean, raises a storm and wrecks his craft. He comes to shore on the land of the peaceful Phaeacians, where the king's daughter, Nausicaa, rescues him.   16 *combers:* waves.   23 *Zeus:* chief among gods.

only to find no exit from these breakers. 25
Here are sharp rocks off shore, and the sea a smother
rushing around them; rock face rising sheer
from deep water; nowhere could I stand up
on my two feet and fight free of the welter.
No matter how I try it, the surf may throw me 30
against the cliffside; no good fighting there.
If I swim down the coast, outside the breakers,
I may find shelving shore and quiet water—
but what if another gale comes on to blow?
Then I go cursing out to sea once more. 35
Or then again, some shark of Amphitritê's°
may hunt me, sent by the genius of the deep.
I know how he who makes earth tremble hates me.'

During this meditation a heavy surge
was taking him, in fact, straight on the rocks. 40
He had been flayed there, and his bones broken,
had not grey-eyed Athena° instructed him:
he gripped a rock-ledge with both hands in passing
and held on, groaning, as the surge went by,
to keep clear of its breaking. Then the backwash 45
hit him, ripping him under and far out.
An octopus, when you drag one from his chamber,
comes up with suckers full of tiny stones:
Odysseus left the skin of his great hands
torn on that rock-ledge as the wave submerged him. 50
And now at last Odysseus would have perished,
battered inhumanly, but he had the gift
of self-possession from grey-eyed Athena.
So, when the backwash spewed him up again,
he swam out and along, and scanned the coast 55
for some landspit that made a breakwater.
Lo and behold, the mouth of a calm river
at length came into view, with level shores
unbroken, free from rock, shielded from wind—
by far the best place he had found. 60
But as he felt the current flowing seaward
he prayed in his heart:
'O hear me, lord of the stream:

how sorely I depend upon your mercy!
derelict as I am by the sea's anger. 65
Is he not sacred, even to the gods,
the wandering man who comes, as I have come,
in weariness before your knees, your waters?

---

36 *Amphitritê*: wife of Poseidon, queen of the sea.　42 *Athena*: daughter of Zeus, goddess of wisdom; protector of Odysseus.

Here is your servant; lord, have mercy on me.'
Now even as he prayed the tide at ebb
had turned, and the river god made quiet water,
drawing him in to safety in the shallows.
His knees buckled, his arms gave way beneath him,
all vital force now conquered by the sea.
Swollen from head to foot he was, and seawater
gushed from his mouth and nostrils. There he lay,
scarce drawing breath, unstirring, deathly spent.
In time, as air came back into his lungs
and warmth around his heart, he loosed the veil,
letting it drift away on the estuary
downstream to where a white wave took it under
and Ino's° hands received it. Then the man
crawled to the river bank among the reeds
where, face down, he could kiss the soil of earth,
in his exhaustion murmuring to himself:
'What more can this hulk suffer? What comes now?
In vigil through the night here by the river
how can I not succumb, being weak and sick,
to the night's damp and hoarfrost of the morning?
The air comes cold from rivers before dawn.
But if I climb the slope and fall asleep
in the dark forest's undergrowth—supposing
cold and fatigue will go, and sweet sleep come—
I fear I make the wild beasts easy prey.'

But this seemed best to him, as he thought it over.
He made his way to a grove above the water
on open ground, and crept under twin bushes
grown from the same spot—olive and wild olive—
a thicket proof against the stinging wind
or Sun's blaze, fine soever the needling sunlight;
nor could a downpour wet it through, so dense
those plants were interwoven. Here Odysseus
tunnelled, and raked together with his hands
a wide bed—for a fall of leaves was there,
enough to save two men or maybe three
on a winter night, a night of bitter cold.
Odysseus' heart laughed when he saw his leaf-bed,
and down he lay, heaping more leaves above him.

A man in a distant field, no hearthfires near,
will hide a fresh brand in his bed of embers
to keep a spark alive for the next day;
so in the leaves Odysseus hid himself,

70

75

80

85

90

95

100

105

110

---

82 *Ino*: sea deity.

while over him Athena showered sleep
that his distress should end, and soon, soon.
In quiet sleep she sealed his cherished eyes.

Translated by Robert Fitzgerald

115

Sappho (612–580 B.C.)

SOME THERE ARE WHO SAY . . .

Some there are who say that the fairest thing seen
on the black earth is an array of horsemen;
some, men marching; some would say ships; but I say
    she whom one loves best

is the loveliest. Light were the work to make this   5
plain to all, since she, who surpassed in beauty
all mortality, Helen,° once forsaking
    her lordly husband,

fled away to Troy-land across the water.
Not the thought of child nor beloved parents   10
was remembered, after the Queen of Cyprus°
    won her at first sight.

Since young brides have hearts that can be persuaded
easily, light things, palpitant to passion
as am I, remembering Anaktória°   15
    who has gone from me

and whose lovely walk and the shining pallor
of her face I would rather see before my
eyes than Lydia's° chariots in all their glory
    armored for battle.   20

SOME THERE ARE WHO SAY . . . 7 *Helen:* Helen of Troy, legendary beauty whose abduction started
the Trojan War.   11 *Cyprus:* Greek island.   15 *Anaktória:* woman loved by Sappho.   19 *Lydia:* present-
day Turkey.

TO A RIVAL

You will die and be still, never shall be memory left of you
after this, nor regret when you are gone. You have not touched the flowers

of the Muses, and thus, shadowy still in the domain of Death,
you must drift with a ghost's fluttering wings, one of the darkened dead.

Sappho poems translated by Richard Lattimore

Catullus (84–54 B.C.)

LESBIA'S SPARROW

Lesbia's° sparrow! the poet's love
          Lesbia's plaything!
in her lap or at her breast
when Catullus's desire
          gleams   5
and fancies playing at something,
                  perhaps precious,
a little solace for satiety
          when love has ebbed,
   you are invited to nip her finger   10
   you are coaxed into pecking sharply,
if I could play with you
          her sparrow
lifting like that my sorrow
          I should be eased   15
as the girl was of her virginity
when the miniature apple,
          gold/undid
her girl's girdle
       —too long tied.   20

WHO LOVES BEAUTY

Who loves beauty
          veil her statues
veil Venus°
          her attendant Cupids°
Lesbia's plaything   5
          Lesbia's sparrow
                is dead
dearer to her than her two eyes
sweeter than honey

WHO LOVES BEAUTY. 3 *Venus*: goddess of beauty.   4 *Cupids*: gods of love.

closer (even) than the young girl to her mother,   10
in her lap or at her breast
hopping from one shoulder to another
cheeping continually
                    to its mistress alone
. . . has now hopped solitarily   15
down that dark alleyway of no return
evil shadows of the underworld
                              Orcus°
who swallows up all beautiful things
needless act! a small bird!   20
to close in on Lesbia's sparrow,
and swelling my girl's veiled eyes
                         which redden with tears.

Catullus poems translated by Peter Whigham

18 *Orcus:* the world of the dead.

Virgil (70–19 B.C.)

THE SLEEP OF PALINURUS°

from *Aeneid*, Book V, lines
835–871

And now the dewy night had nearly come to its halfway
Mark in the heavens: the mariners, sprawled on the hard benches
Beside their oars, were all relaxed in solacing quiet.
Just then did Sleep come feathering down from the stars above,
Lightly displacing the shadowy air, parting the darkness,   5
In search of you, Palinurus, carrying death in a dream
To your staunch heart. Now, taking the shape of Phorbas, the Sleep-god
Perched up there in the stern-sheets and rapidly spoke these words—
    Palinurus, son of Iasus, the seas are bearing the ships on,
Steadily blows the breeze, and you have a chance to rest.   10
Lay your head down, and take a nap; your eyes are tired with
Watching. I will stand your trick at the helm for a little.
    Palinurus could hardly raise his eyes, but he answered—
    Are you asking me to forget what lies behind the pacific
Face of the sea and its sleeping waves? to trust this devil?   15
What? Shall I leave Aeneas to the mercy of tricky winds—
I who, time and again, have been taken in by a clear sky?

THE SLEEP OF PALINURUS. Palinurus was the helmsman of the hero Aeneas' ship. On the journey
from Sicily to Italy, the god of sleep caused Palinurus to fall asleep at his post and he was washed over-
board. He clung to an oar and after three days reached shore, where he was killed by natives.

While he spoke, Palinurus kept a good grip on the tiller—
By no means would he release it—and a steadfast gaze on the stars.
But look! over his temples the god is shaking a bough 20
That drips with the dew of Lethe,° the drowsy spell of Stygian°
Waters. And now, though he struggles, his swimming eyes are closing.
As soon as, taken off guard, he was relaxed in unconsciousness,
The god, leaning down over him, hurled him into the sea
Still gripping the tiller; a part of the taffrail° was torn away: 25
As he fell, he kept calling out to his friends, but they did not hear him.
Up and away skywards the Sleep-god now went winging.
Safe as before, the fleet was scudding upon its course—
Nothing to fear, for Neptune° had guaranteed a safe passage.
And now, racing on, they were near the rocky place of the Sirens,° 30
Dangerous once for mariners, white with the bones of many;
From afar the rasp of the ceaseless surf on those rocks could be heard.
Just then Aeneas became aware that his ship was yawing
Badly, her helmsman missing; he brought her back on to course
In the night sea, and deeply sighing, stunned by the loss of his friend, said— 35
    O Palinurus, too easily trusting clear sky and calm sea,
You will lie on a foreign strand, mere jetsam, none to bury you.

Translated by C. D. Lewis

---

21 *Lethe*: river of forgetfulness in the underworld. *Stygian*: from Styx, the river forming the
boundary of Hades, or hell. 25 *taffrail*: railing around the stern of a vessel. 29 *Neptune*: ocean god,
Roman equivalent for Poseidon. 30 *Sirens*: sea nymphs who lured sailors onto rocks with their beautiful singing.

Wang Wei (701–761)

from TWENTY VIEWS OF WANG-CH'UAN

Meng-ch'eng Hollow

A new home at the mouth of Meng-ch'eng;°
old trees—last of a stand of dying willows:
years to come, who will be its owner,
vainly pitying the one who had it before?

Deer Fence°

Empty hills, no one in sight,
only the sound of someone talking;
late sunlight enters the deep wood,
shining over the green moss again.

TWENTY VIEWS OF WANG-CH'UAN. 1 *Meng-ch'eng*: Meng-ch'eng is the name of a river in the area
depicted by Wang Wei. *Deer Fence*: See Chapter 23 for other translations.

Bamboo Mile Lodge

Alone I sit in dark bamboo,
strumming the lute, whistling away;
deep woods that no one knows,
where a bright moon comes to shine on me.

Li Po (701–762)

MOUNTAIN DRINKING SONG

To drown the ancient sorrows,
we drank a hundred jugs of wine
there in the beautiful night.
We couldn't go to bed with the moon so bright.

Then finally the wine overcame us   5
and we lay down on the empty mountain—
the earth for a pillow,
and a blanket made of heaven.

TO A FRIEND

Late autumn strips the distant hills
beyond the city gate.

A huge white cloud interrupts my dreams
and returns me to this world.

And you, old friend? Flown silent as a crane.   5
Will you ever come home again?

IN A VILLAGE BY THE RIVER

The rain stops in this river village.
The wine gone, you say goodby.

Comfortable in your little boat,
you ride your sails homeward on the water,

passing islands burning up with flowers,   5
passing slender river willows.

And what of the one you leave behind?
I return to my rock and my fishing line.

Li Po poems translated by Sam Hamill

Tu Fu (711–770)

DREAMING OF LI PO°

Parting from the dead, I've stifled my sobs,
but this parting from the living brings me constant pain.
South of the Yangtze° is a land of plague and fever;
no word comes from the exile.
Yet my old friend has entered my dreams,   5
proof of how long I've pined for him.
He didn't look the way he used to,
the road so far—farther than I can guess.
His spirit came from where the maple groves are green,
then went back, leaving me in borderland blackness.   10
Now you're caught in the meshes of the law—
how could you have wings to fly with?
The sinking moon floods the rafters of my room
and still I seem to see it lighting your face.
Where you go, waters are deep, the waves so wide—   15
don't let the dragons, the horned dragons harm you!

Translated by Burton Watson

DREAMING OF LI PO. Li Po (see previous selection) was the celebrated Chinese poet and friend of
Tu Fu.   3 *Yangtze*: major river in China; Li Po had been exiled to south of this river.

Jelaludin Rumi (Twelfth Century)

THAT SPIRIT WHICH DOES NOT WEAR

That spirit which does not wear
the inner garment of Love
should never have been.
Its being is just shame.

Be drunken with Love,   5
for Love is all that exists.
Where is intimacy found,
if not in the give and take of Love?

If they ask what Love is,
say, the sacrifice of will.
If you have not left will behind,
you have no will at all.

The lover is a king of kings
with both worlds beneath him;
and a king does not regard
what lies at his feet.

Only Love and the lover
can resurrect beyond time.
Give your heart to this—
the rest is second-hand.

How long will you embrace
a lifeless beloved?
Embrace that entity
to which nothing can cling.

What sprouts up every spring
will wither by autumn,
but the rose-garden of Love
needs no special season.

Both the rose and the thorn
appear together in spring,
and the wine of the grape
is not without its headaches.

Do not be an impatient
bystander on this path—
by God there is no death
worse than expectancy.

Set your heart on hard cash
if you are not counterfeit,
and listen to my advice
if you are not a slave:

Don't falter on the horse
of the body—go lighter on foot.
God gives wings to those
who are not content to ride an ass.

Let go of your worries
and be completely clear hearted,
Like the face of a mirror
that contains no images.

When it is empty of forms,
all forms are contained in it.

No face would be ashamed
to be so clear.

If you want a clear mirror,
behold yourself,
and see the shameless truth   55
which the mirror reflects.

If metal can be polished
to a mirror-like finish—
what polishing does the mirror
of the heart require?   60

Between the mirror and the heart
is this single difference:
the heart conceals secrets
while the mirror does not.

> *Translated by Edmund Helminski*

Peire Vidal (1175?–1205)

FOR A LONG TIME I WAS BITTER

For a long time I was bitter,
but now am happier than bird in rain or fish in water,
for my lady has sent me a note to tell me
        "Act like a man, a lover!"
        And I never thought to have her   5
        return me to hope again.

        God
        knows I can't be happy
unless I return quickly
to that soft cage her beauty
        has put me in.   10
There it's all softness, warm
joy, everything courteous.
Take everything I possess
        plow it under!
only to do her pleasure.   15

So good to look upon the way she's fashioned, her
        love-shooting eyes, I
        don't know what I'm doing, or
        where I am, she's got me
seized, won, conquered, taken, tied me down, that I   20
        cannot turn

left, right or away my love or eyes. All I
        have to do is see her—I
                sing, I'm
                    happy with everything.   25

From the thicket, a flushed bird:
the heart is open to the hunter's arrow.
But a thousand arrows!
and her eyes the bow
and the wound so soft!   30
Were I next God's throne, lady, and you called
            I'd run to you,
                willingly rendered and humble,
                  waiting your mercy and choice.
I live under heavy fear of being   35
enlaced by a desire for
someone I cannot have. But I
            see roses
                in ice-sheets on the roads,
clear weather   40
in a sky that's overcast.
Birds sing from the snowdrifts.

But I have a spiteful heart toward one
and wish she'd never lived
since, for a blond count,   45
she threw me in the road.
                Loba!°
I think she is a wolf—
she's been taken by a count and
dropped an emperor whose days   50
all were spent in spreading praise
of her for all the world to hear.
              Who lies
            does not tell the truth
A false love's done me in the eye but   55
I have gained a better lady that way.

      God save the illustrious marquis°
      and his lovely sister,
      who with her loyal love has known
      how to gently conquer me, and   60
      still more kindly, how to keep me.

      I have no walled castle
      and my land's not worth two gloves,
            but I am lover.   65

                Translated by Paul Blackburn

FOR A LONG TIME I WAS BITTER. **48** *Loba:* female wolf.   **58** *marquis:* titled gentleman.

Dante Alighieri (1265–1321)

THE HUNTER OF UGOLINO

from *The Inferno*,° Canto XXXIII, lines 38–78

'When I awoke dark on my stony bed
   I heard my children weeping in their sleep,
   Them who were with me, and they cried for bread.
Cruel art thou if thou from tears canst keep
   To think of what my heart misgave in fear.   5
   If thou weep not, at what then canst thou weep?
By now they were awake, and the hour drew near
   When food should be set by us on the floor.
   Still in the trouble of our dreams we were:
And down in the horrible tower I heard the door   10
   Locked up. Without a word I looked anew.
   Into my sons' faces, all the four.
I wept not, so to stone within I grew.
   They wept; and one, my little Anselm,° cried:
   "You look so, Father, what has come to you?"   15
But I shed not a tear, neither replied
   All that day nor the next night, until dawn
   Of a new day over the world rose wide.
A cranny of light crept in upon the stone
   Of that dungeon of woe; and I saw there   20
   On those four faces the aspect° of my own.
I bit upon both hands in my despair.
   And they supposing it was in the access
   Of hunger, rose up with a sudden prayer,
And said: "O Father, it will hurt much less   25
   If you of us eat: take what once you gave
   To clothe us, this flesh of our wretchedness."
Thereon I calmed myself, their grief to save.
   That day and the one after we were dumb.

   Hard earth, couldst thou not open for our grave?   30
But when to the fourth morning we were come,
   Gaddo° at my feet stretched himself with a cry:
   "Father, why won't you help me?" and lay numb
And there died. Ev'n as thou seest me, saw I,
   One after the other, the three fall. They drew,   35

THE HUNGER OF UGOLINO. 1 *Inferno:* "Hell," the title of the first volume of Dante's trilogy poem, *The Divine Comedy.* On his journey through hell, Dante the narrator meets various people who have been punished for their deeds in life; many tell him their story. This excerpt is from the account of one Ugolino, who had been imprisoned along with his sons.   14 *Anselm:* one of Ugolino's sons.   21 *aspect:* appearance.   32 *Gaddo:* another son.

Between the fifth and sixth day, their last sight.
I, blind now, groping arms about them threw,
  And still called on them that were two days dead.
  Then fasting did what anguish could not do.'
He ceased, and with eyes twisted in his head   40
  His teeth seized on the lamentable skull°
  Strong as a dog's upon a bony shred.

Translated by Laurence Binyon

---

41 *lamentable skull*: Ugolino's punishment in hell is to gnaw at a skull.

Geoffrey Chaucer (1340?–1400)

PROLOGUE TO THE CANTERBURY TALES

Whan that Aprille with his shoures soote°   *sweet*
The droghte of March hath perced to the roote,
And bathed every veyne in swich licour°   *such moisture*
Of which vertu engendred is the flour;
When Zephirus° eek° with his sweete breeth   *the west wind; also* 5

Inspired hath in every holt° and heeth   *woods*
The tendre croppes, and the yonge sonne
Hath in the Ram° his half cours yronne,°   *Aires; halfway run*
And smale foweles° maken melodye,   *birds*
That slepen al the nyght with open eye   10
(So priketh hem° nature in hir corages°):   *inspires them; hearts*
Than longen folk to goon on pilgrymages,
And palmeres° for to seken straunge strondes,°   *pilgrims; shores*
To ferne halwes°, kouthe° in sondry londes;   *distant shrines; known*
And specially from every shires ende   15
Of Engelond to Caunterbury they wende,
The holy blisful martir° for to seke,   *martyr (St. Thomas)*
That hem° hath holpen whan that they were seeke.°   *them; sick*

  Bifel that, in that sesoun on a day,
In Southwerk at the Tabard° as I lay   *(an inn)* 20
Redy to wenden on my pilgrymage
To Caunterbury with ful devout corage,
At nyght was come into that hostelrye
Wel nyne and twenty in a compaignye,
Of sondry folk, by aventure yfalle°   *chance befallen* 25
In felaweshipe, and pilgrymes were they alle
That toward Caunterbury wolden ryde.
The chambres and the stables weren wyde,°   *spacious*
And wel we weren esed° atte beste.   *entertained*
And shortly, whan the sonne was to reste,   30

So hadde I spoken with hem everichon,°   *every one*
That I was of hir felaweshipe anon,
And made forward erly for to ryse,
To take oure wey ther as I yow devyse.°   *am telling you*

But nathelees, whil I have tyme and space,   35
Er that I ferther in this tale pace,
Me thynketh it acordant to resoun
To telle yow al the condicioun
Of ech of hem, so as it semed me,
And whiche they weren, and of what degree,   40
And eek° in what array that they were inne: *also*
And at a Knyght than wol I first bigynne.

A Knyght ther was, and that a worthy man,
That fro the tyme that he first bigan
To riden out, he loved chivalrye   45
Trouthe and honour, fredom° and curteisye.   *generosity*
Ful worthy was he in his lordes werre,°   *war*
And ther-to hadde he riden, no man ferre,°   *farther*
As wel in Cristendom as in hethenesse,
And evere honoured for his worthynesse.   50
At Alisaundre° he was whan it was wonne.   *Alexandria (Egypt)*
Ful ofte tyme he hadde the bord bigonne°   *presided at table*
Aboven alle nacions in Pruce.°   *Prussia*
In Lettow hadde he reysed° and in Ruce,°   *campaigned; Russia*
No Cristen man so ofte of his degree   55
In Gernade° at the seege eek hadde he be°   *Grenada; been*
Of Algezir, and riden in Belmarye.
At Lyeys was he and at Satalye,
Whan they were wonne; and in the Grete See°   *Mediterranean*
At many a noble armee hadde he be.   60
At mortal batailles hadde he been fiftene,
And foghten for oure feith at Tramyssene
In lystes° thries, and ay slayn his foo.   *lists, tournaments*
This ilke° worthy knyght hadde been also   *same*
Som-tyme with the lord of Palatye,   65
Agayn another hethen in Turkye.
And evere-moore he hadde a sovereyn prys;°   *reputation*
And though that he were worthy, he was wys,
And of his port° as meke° as is a mayde.   *manners; meek*
He nevere yet no vileynye ne sayde   70
In al his lyf un-to no maner wight.°   *lowly person*
He was a verray,° parfit gentil knyght.   *true*
But for to tellen yow of his array,
Hise hors were goode, but he was nat gay.
Of fustian° he wered a gypoun°   *rough cotton; vest* 75
Al bismotered° with his habergeoun,°   *stained; chain mail*
For he was late ycome from his viage,°   *voyage*
And wente for to doon° his pilgrymage.   *do*

With hym ther was his sone, a young Squyer,
A lovere and a lusty bachelor,   80
With lokkes crulle,° as they were leyd in presse.   *curly locks*
Of twenty yeer of age he was, I gesse.

    Of his stature he was of evene lengthe,
And wonderly delyvere,° and of greet strengthe.   *agile*
And he hadde been som-tyme in chivachye°   *cavalry raids* 85
In Flaundres, in Artoys, and Picardye,°   *(Belgium; north France)*
And born° hym wel, as of so litel space,°   *behaved; short time*
In hope to stonden in his lady grace.

    Embrouded° was he, as it were a meede°   *embroidered; meadow*
Al ful of fresshe floures, white and reede.°   *red* 90
Syngynge he was, or floytynge,° al the day;   *fluting*
He was as fressh as is the monthe of May.
Short was his gowne, with sleves longe and wyde.
Wel koude he sitte on hors and faire ryde.
He koude songes make and wel endite,°   *make verse* 95
Juste° and eek daunce, and wel purtreye and write.   *joust*
So hoote he lovede, that by nyghtertale°   *night-time*
He slepte namoore than dooth a nyghtyngale.
    Curteys° he was, lowely, and servysable,   *courteous*
And carf° biforn his fader at the table.   *carved* 100

    A Yeman hadde he and servantz namo°   *no other*
At that tyme, for hym liste ryde so:
And he was clad in coote and hood of grene.
A sheef of pecok arwes bright and kene
Under his belt he bar ful thriftily,   105
(Wel koude he dresse his takel° yemanly: *tackle, gear*
His arwes drouped noght with fetheres lowe),
And in his hand he bar a myghty bowe.

Anonymous (c. 1400?)

LORD RANDAL

"O where ha you been, Lord Randal, my son?
And where ha you been, my handsome young man?"
"I ha been at the greenwood; mother, mak my bed soon,
For I'm wearied wi huntin, and fain° wad lie down."   *gladly*

"An wha° met ye there, Lord Randal, my son?   *whom* 5
An wha met you there, my handsome young man?"
"O I met wi my true-love; mother, mak my bed soon,
For I'm wearied wi huntin, and fain wad lie down."

"And what did she give you, Lord Randal, my son?
And what did she give you, my handsome young man?"   10

"Eels fried in a pan; mother, mak my bed soon,
For I'm wearied wi huntin, and fain wad lie down."

"And wha gat your leavins, Lord Randal, my son?
And wha gat your leavins, my handsome young man?"
"My hawks and my hounds; mother, mak my bed soon,   15
For I'm wearied wi huntin, and fain wad lie down."

"And what becam of them, Lord Randal, my son?
And what becam of them, my handsome young man?"
"They swelled and they died; mother, mak my bed soon,
For I'm wearied wi huntin, and fain wad lie down."   20
"O I fear you are poisoned, Lord Randal, my son!
I fear you are poisoned, my handsome young man!"
"O yes, I am poisoned, mother, mak my bed soon,
For I'm sick at the heart, and I fain wad lie down."

"What d' ye leave to your mother, Lord Randal, my son?   25
What d' ye leave to your mother, my handsome young man?"
"Four and twenty milk kye;° mother, mak my bed soon,   *cattle*
For I'm sick at the heart, and I fain wad lie down."

"What d' ye leave to your sister, Lord Randal, my son?
What d' ye leave to your sister, my handsome young man?"   30
"My gold and my silver; mother, mak my bed soon,
For I'm sick at the heart, and I fain wad lie down."

"What d' ye leave to your brother, Lord Randal, my son?
What d' ye leave to your brother, my handsome young man?"
"My houses and my lands; mother, mak my bed soon,   35
For I'm sick at the heart, and I fain wad lie down."

"What d' ye leave to your true-love, Lord Randal, my son?
What d' ye leave to your true-love, my handsome young man?"
"I leave her hell and fire; mother, mak my bed soon,
For I'm sick at the heart, and I fain wad lie down."   40

François Villon (1431–1463)

THE EPITAPH IN FORM OF A BALLAD

(Which Villon made for himself and his comrades,
expecting to be hanged along with them)

Men, brother men, that after us yet live,
    Let not your hearts too hard against us be;
For if some pity of us poor men ye give,
    The sooner God shall take of you pity.
    Here are we five or six strung up, you see,   5
And here the flesh that all too well we fed

Bit by bit eaten and rotten, rent° and shred,
 And we the bones grow dust and ash withal°;
Let no man laugh at us discomforted,
 But pray to God that he forgive us all.   10

If we call on you, brothers, to forgive,
 Ye should not hold our prayer in scorn, though we
Were slain by law; ye know that all alive
 Have no wit always to walk righteously;
 Make therefore intercession° heartily   15
With him° that of a virgin's womb was bred,
That his grace be not as a dry well-head
 For us, nor let hell's thunder on us fall;
We are dead, let no man harry° or vex us dead,
 But pray to God that he forgive us all.   20

The rain has washed and laundered us all five,
 And the sun dried and blackened; yea, perdie,°
Ravens and pies° with beaks that rend° and rive°
 Have dug our eyes out, and plucked off for fee
 Our beards and eyebrows; never are we free,   25
Not once, to rest; but here and there still sped,°
Drive at its wild will by the wind's change led,
 More pecked of birds than fruits on garden-wall;
Men, for God's love, let no gibe° here be said,
 But pray to God that he forgive us all.   30

Prince Jesus, that of all art Lord and head,
Keep us, that hell be not our bitter bed;
 We have nought to do in such a master's hall.
Be not ye therefore of our fellowhead,°
 But pray to God that he forgive us all.   35

Translated by Algernon Swinborne

BALLADE François Villon was known as a thief as well as a poet. Many of his poems depict his life as a criminal. In "Ballade" he writes from prison. 7 *rent:* torn. 8 *withal:* nevertheless. 15 *intercession:* plea on behalf of another. 16 *him:* Christ. 19 *harry:* disturb. 22 *perdie:* by God. 23 *pies:* magpie; *rend and rive:* tear and break open. 26 *sped:* moved along. 29 *gibe:* insult. 34 *Be . . . fellowhead:* Be not like the others.

Sir Thomas Wyatt (1503–1542)

THEY FLEE FROM ME . . .

They flee from me, that sometime did me seek,
With naked foot stalking° in my chamber.

THEY FLEE FROM ME . . . 2 *stalking:* walking softly.

I have seen them gentle, tame, and meek,
That now are wild, and do not remember
That sometime they put themselves in danger   5
To take bread at my hand; and now they range
Busily seeking with a continual change.

Thankèd be fortune it hath been otherwise
Twenty times better; but once, in special,
In thin array, after a pleasant guise,   10
When her loose gown from her shoulders did fall,
And she me caught in her arms long and small,°
Therewithal sweetly did me kiss,
And softly said, Dear heart, how like you this?

It was no dream; I lay broad waking: 15
But all is turnèd thorough my gentleness°
Into a strange fashion of forsaking;
And I have leave to go of her goodness,
And she also to use newfangleness.°
But since that I so kindely° am servèd,   20
How like you this, what hath she now deservèd?

_____

    12 *small*: slender. 16 *thorough my gentleness*: through my politeness. 19 *use newfangleness*: seek novelty. 20 *kindely*: kindly (usage is ironic).

Edmund Spenser (1552?–1599)

LXXV

from *Amoretti*

_____

One day I wrote her name upon the strand,°   beach
But came the waves and washed it away:
Agayne I wrote it with a second hand,
But came the tyde, and made my paynes his pray.
Vayne man, sayde she, that doest in vaine assay°   try   5
A mortal thing so to immortalize,
For I my selve shall lyke to this decay,
And eek° my name bee wyped out lykewize.   also
Not so, (quod I) let baser things devize
To dy in dust, but you shall live by fame: 10
My verse your vertues rare shall eternize,°   make eternal
And in the heavens wryte your glorious name.
Where whenas death shall al the world subdew,
Our love shall live, and later life renew.

Sir Walter Raleigh (1552–1618)

THE LIE

Go soul, the body's guest,
   Upon a thankless arrant:°
Fear not to touch the best;
   The truth shall be thy warrant.
     Go, since I needs must die,   5
     And give the world the lie.°

Say to the court, it glows
   And shines like rotten wood;
Say to the church, it shows
   What's good, and doth no good: 10
     If church and court reply,
     Then give them both the lie.

Tell potentates,° they live
   Acting by others' action,
Not loved unless they give,   15
   Not strong but by a faction:
     If potentates reply,
     Give potentates the lie.

Tell men of high condition
   That manage the estate,   20
Their purpose is ambition,
   Their practice only hate:
     And if they once reply,
     Then give them all the lie.

Tell them that brave it most,   25
   They beg for more by spending,
Who, in their greatest cost,
   Seek nothing but commending:
     And if they make reply,
     Then give them all the lie.   30

Tell zeal it wants devotion;
   Tell love it is but lust;
Tell time it is but motion;
   Tell flesh it is but dust;
     And wish them not reply   35
     For thou must give the lie.

THE LIE. 2 *arrant:* errand.   6 *give . . . the lie:* accuse of lying.   13 *potentates:* powers, rulers.

Tell age it daily wasteth;
 Tell honour how it alters;
Tell beauty how she blasteth;
 Tell favour how it falters: 40
  And as they shall reply,
  Give every one the lie.

Tell wit how much it wrangles
 In tickle° points of niceness;
Tell wisdom she entangles   45
 Herself in over-wiseness:
  And when they do reply,
  Straight give them both the lie.

Tell physic° of her boldness;
 Tell skill it is prevention;   50
Tell charity of coldness;
 Tell law it is contention:
  And as they do reply,
  So give them still the lie.

Tell fortune of her blindness;   55
 Tell nature of decay;
Tell friendship of unkindness;
 Tell justice of delay:
  And if they will reply,
  Then give them all the lie.   60

Tell arts they have no soundness,
 But vary by esteeming;
Tell schools they want profoundness,
 And stand too much on seeming:
  If arts and schools reply,   65
  Give arts and schools the lie.

Tell faith it's fled the city;
 Tell how the country erreth;
Tell, manhood shakes off pity;
 Tell, virtue least preferreth: 70
  And if they do reply
  Spare not to give the lie.

So when thou hast, as I
 Commanded thee, done blabbing,
Although to give the lie   75
 Deserves no less than stabbing,
  Stab at thee he that will,
  No stab the soul can kill.

---

44 *tickle:* sensitive.   49 *physic:* medicine (archaic).

Sir Philip Sidney (1554–1586)

WITH HOW SAD STEPS, O MOON...

With how sad steps, O Moon, thou climb'st the skies,
How silently, and with how wan° a face!
What! may it be that even in heav'nly place
That busy archer his sharp arrows tries?
Sure, if that long-with-love-acquainted eyes   5
Can judge of love, thou feel'st a lover's case.
I read it in thy looks; thy languisht° grace
To me, that feel the like, thy state descries.
Then, ev'n of fellowship, O Moon, tell me,
Is constant love deem'd there but want of wit?   10
Are beauties there as proud as here they be?
Do they above love to be lov'd, and yet
Those lovers scorn whom that love doth possess?
Do they call virtue there ungratefulness?

WITH HOW SAD STEPS, O MOON... 2 *wan*: pale.   7 *languisht*: weakened, languished.

Christopher Marlowe (1564–1593)

THE PASSIONATE SHEPHERD TO HIS LOVE

Come live with me and be my Love,
And we will all the pleasures prove
That valleys, groves, hills and fields,
Woods or steepy mountain yields.

And we will sit upon the rocks   5
Seeing the shepherds feed their flocks,
By shallow rivers, to whose falls
Melodious birds sing madrigals.°

And I will make thee beds of roses
And a thousand fragrant posies,   10
A cap of flowers, and a kirtle°
Embroidered all with leaves of myrtle.

A gown made of the finest wool,
Which from our pretty lambs we pull
Fair lined slippers for the cold,   15
With buckles of the purest gold.

THE PASSIONATE SHEPHERD TO HIS LOVE. 8 *madrigals*: songs, airs.   11 *kirtle*: knee-length tunic worn by men.

A belt of straw and ivy buds,
With coral clasps and amber studs:
And if these pleasures may thee move,
Come live with me and be my Love.   20

The shepherd swains° shall dance and sing
For thy delight each May-morning:
If these delights thy mind may move,
Then live with me and be my Love.

---

21 *swains*: lovers.

William Shakespeare (1564–1616)

SONNETS

XVIII

Shall I compare thee to a Summer's day?
Thou art more lovely and more temperate:
Rough winds do shake the darling buds of May,
And Summer's lease hath all too short a date:
Sometime too hot the eye of heaven shines,   5
And often is his gold complexion dimm'd;
And every fair from fair sometime declines,
By chance or nature's changing course untrimm'd:
But thy eternal Summer shall not fade
Nor lose possession of that fair thou ow'st;   10
Nor shall Death brag thou wander'st in his shade,
When in eternal lines to time thou grow'st:
    So long as men can breathe, or eyes can see,
    So long lives this, and this gives life to thee.

XXIX

When, in disgrace with Fortune and men's eyes,
I all alone beweep my outcast state,
And trouble deaf heaven with my bootless° cries,
And look upon myself, and curse my fate,
Wishing me like to one more rich in hope,   5
Featured like him, like him with friends possest,
Desiring this man's art and that man's scope,
With what I most enjoy contented least;
Yet in these thoughts myself almost despising-
Haply I think on thee: and then my state,   10
Like to the Lark at break of day arising

XXIX. 3 *bootless*: useless.

From sullen earth, sings hymns at Heaven's gate;
  For thy sweet love rememb'red such wealth brings
  That then I scorn to change my state with Kings.

XXX

When to the sessions of sweet silent thought
I summon up remembrance of things past,
I sigh the lack of many a thing I sought,
And with old woes new wail° my dear time's waste:
Then can I drown an eye, unused to flow,   5
For precious friends hid in death's dateless° night,
And weep afresh love's long-since-cancell'd woe,
And moan th' expense of many a vanish'd sight:
Then can I grieve at grievances foregone,
And heavily from woe to woe tell o'er   10
The sad account of fore-bemoaned moan,
Which I new pay as if not paid before.
  But if the while I think on thee, dear friend,
  All losses are restored and sorrows end.

XXX. 4 *wail*: bewail.   6 *dateless*: endless.

LXXI

No longer mourn for me when I am dead
Than you shall hear the surly sullen bell
Give warning to the world that I am fled
From this vile world, with vilest worms to dwell:
Nay, if you read this line, remember not   5
The hand that writ it; for I love you so
That I in your sweet thoughts would be forgot
If thinking on me then should make you woe.
O, if, I say, you look upon this verse
When I perhaps compounded° am with clay,   10
Do not so much as my poor name rehearse,°
But let your love even with my life decay,
  Lest the wise world should look into your moan
  And mock you with me after I am gone.

LXXI. 10 *compounded*: mixed.   11 *rehearse*: speak.

LXXIII

That time of year thou mayst in me behold
When yellow leaves, or none, or few, do hang
Upon those boughs which shake against the cold,
Bare ruin'd choirs, where late the sweet birds sang.
In me thou see'st the twilight of such day   5

        An Anthology of Poetry

As after sunset fadeth in the west,
Which by and by black night doth take away,
Death's second self, that seals up all in rest.
In me thou see'st the glowing of such fire
That on the ashes of his youth doth lie, 10
As the death-bed whereon it must expire,
Consumed with that which it was nourish'd by.
    This thou perceivest, which makes thy love more strong,
    To love that well which thou must leave ere° long.

_____

LXXIII. 14 *ere:* before.

CXVI

Let me not to the marriage of true minds
Admit impediments. Love is not love
Which alters when it alteration finds,
Or bends with the remover to remove:
O, no! it is an ever-fixèd mark, 5
That looks on tempests and is never shaken;
It is the star to every wand'ring bark,°
Whose worth's unknown, although his heighth be taken.
Love's not Time's fool, though rosy lips and cheeks
Within his bending sickle's compass come; 10
Love alters not with his brief hours and weeks,
But bears it out even to the edge of doom:—
    If this be error and upon me proved,
    I never writ, nor no man ever loved.

_____

CXVI. 7 *bark:* ship, craft.

CXXIX

Th' expense of spirit in a waste of shame
Is lust in action; and till action, lust
Is perjur'd,° murd'rous, bloody, full of blame,
Savage, extreme, rude, cruel, not to trust:
Enjoy'd no sooner but despised straight;° 5
Past reason hunted, and no sooner had,
Past reason hated, as a swallow'd bait
On purpose laid to make the taker mad:
Mad in pursuit and in possession so:
Had, having, and in quest to have, extreme; 10
A bliss in proof, and prov'd, a very woe;
Before, a joy propos'd; behind, a dream.
    All this the world well knows; yet none knows well
    To shun the heaven that leads men to this hell.

_____

CXXIX. 3 *perjur'd:* false.   5 *straight:* right away.

Thomas Campion (1567–1620)

CHERRY-RIPE

There is a garden in her face
   Where roses and white lilies grow;
A heavenly paradise is that place,
   Wherein all pleasant fruits do flow.
     There cherries grow which none may buy   5
     Till "Cherry-ripe" themselves do cry.

Those cherries fairly do inclose
   Of orient° pearl a double row,
Which when her lovely laughter shows,
   They look like rosebuds filled with snow;   10
     Yet them nor peer° nor prince can buy
     Till "Cherry-ripe" themselves do cry.

Her eyes like angels watch them still;
   Her brows like bended bows do stand,
Threat'ning with piercing frowns to kill   15
   All that attempt with eye or hand
     Those sacred cherries to come nigh,
     Till "Cherry-ripe" themselves do cry.

CHERRY-RIPE. 8 *orient:* luster characteristic of pearls. 11 *peer:* nobleman.

John Donne (1572–1631)

THE GOOD-MORROW

I wonder, by my troth, what thou and I
Did, till we loved? were we not wean'd till then?
But suck'd on country pleasures, childishly?
Or snorted° we in the Seven Sleepers' den?°
'Twas so; but this, all pleasures fancies be;   5
If ever any beauty I did see,
Which I desired, and got, 'twas but a dream of thee.

And now good-morrow to our waking souls,
Which watch not one another out of fear;
For love all love of other sights controls,   10
And makes one little room an everywhere.

THE GOOD-MORROW. 4 *snorted:* snored, slept; *Seven Sleepers' den:* refers to legendary Christians who fled the Romans and hid in a cave for two centuries.

Let sea-discoverers to new worlds have gone;
Let maps to other worlds on worlds have shown:
Let us possess one world; each hath one, and is one.

My face in thine eye, thine in mine appears,   15
And true plain hearts do in the faces rest;
Where can we find two better hemispheres
Without sharp north, without declining west?
Whatever dies, was not mix'd equally;°
If our two loves be one, or thou and I   20
Love so alike that none do slacken, none can die.

_____

19 *whatever . . . equally:* refers to belief of scholastic philosophers that death resulted from chemical imbalances.

THE ECSTACY

Where, like a pillow on a bed,
    A pregnant bank swell'd up, to rest
The violet's reclining head,
    Sat we two, one another's best.
Our hands were firmly cemented   5
    With a fast balm, which thence did spring;
Our eye-beams twisted, and did thread
    Our eyes upon one double string.

So to'entergraft our hands, as yet
    Was all the means to make us one;   10
And pictures in our eyes to get
    Was all our propagation.°
As, 'twixt two equal armies, Fate
    Suspends uncertain victory,
Our souls (which to advance their state,   15
    Were gone out) hung 'twixt her and me.

And whilst our souls negotiate there,
    We like sepulchral° statues lay;
All day, the same our postures were,
    And we said nothing, all the day.   20
If any, so by love refined,
    That he soul's language understood,
And by good love were grown all mind,
    Within convenient distance stood,
He (though he knew not which soul spake,   25
    Because both meant, both spake the same)

_____

THE ECSTACY.   12 *propagation:* mode of increase, production.   18 *sepulchral:* pertaining to tombs.

Might thence a new concoction° take,
    And part far purer than he came.
This ecstacy doth unperplex°
    (We said) and tell us what we love;   30
We see by this, it was not sex;
    We see, we saw not, what did move:
But as all several souls contain
    Mixture of things they know not what,
Love these mix'd souls doth mix again,   35
    And makes both one, each this, and that.
A single violet transplant,
    The strength, the colour, and the size,
(All which before was poor and scant)
    Redoubles still, and multiples.   40
When love with one another so
    Interinanimates° two souls,
That abler soul, which thence doth flow,
    Defects of loneliness controls.
We then, who are this new soul, know,   45
    Of what we are composed, and made,
For th' atomies° of which we grow
    Are souls, whom no change can invade.
But O alas! so long, so far,
    Our bodies why do we forbear?°   50
They are ours, though they are not we; we are
    Th' intelligences, they the spheres.
We owe them thanks, because they thus
    Did us, to us, at first convey,
Yielded their forces, sense, to us,   55
    Nor are dross° to us, but allay.°
On man heaven's influence works not so,
    But that it first imprints the air;
So soul into the soul may flow,
    Though it to body first repair.°   60
As our blood labours to beget
    Spirits, as like souls as it can;
Because such fingers need to knit
    That subtle knot, which makes us man;
So must pure lovers' souls descend
    T' affections, and to faculties,
Which sense may reach and apprehend,   65
    Else a great prince in prison lies.
To'our bodies turn we then, that so
    Weak men on love reveal'd may look;   70
Love's mysteries in souls do grow,

---

27 *concoction:* mixture.   29 *unperplex:* demystify.   42 *interinanimates:* fills with animation.   47 *atomies:* atomic structures.   50 *forbear:* refrain.   56 *dross:* waste left after alchemical process; *allay:* alloy, metal.   60 *repair:* to go to.

But yet the body is his book.
And if some lover, such as we,
  Have heard this dialogue of one,
Let him still mark us, he shall see
  Small change when we're to bodies gone.

Ben Jonson (1572–1637)

TO CELIA

Drink to me only with thine eyes,
  And I will pledge° with mine;
Or leave a kiss but in the cup,
  And I'll not look for wine.
The thirst that from the soul doth rise,
  Doth ask a drink divine:
But might I of Jove's° nectar° sup,
  I would not change for thine.

I sent thee late a rosy wreath,
  Not so much honouring thee
As giving it a hope that there
  It could not withered be.
But thou thereon didst only breathe,
  And sent'st° it back to me:
Since when it grows, and smells, I swear,
  Not of itself, but thee.

75

5

10

15

TO CELIA. *2 pledge:* raise a toast, offer up.   *7 Jove:* Jupiter, chief of the gods;   *nectar:* drink of the gods.   *14 sent'st:* sent (sent + est).

ON MY FIRST SONNE

Farewell, thou child of my right hand, and joy;
My sinne was too much hope of thee, lov'd boy,
Seven yeeres tho'wert lent to me, and I thee pay,
Exacted by thy fate, on the just day.
O, could I loose all father, now. For why
Will man lament the state he should envie?
To have so soone scap'd worlds, and fleshes rage,
And, if no other miserie, yet age?
Rest in soft peace, and, ask'd, say here doth lye
Ben. Jonson his best piece of poetrie.
For whose sake, hence-forth, all his vowes be such,
As what he loves may never like too much.

5

10

George Herbert (1593–1633)

THE COLLAR

I struck the board,° and cry'd, No more;
      I will abroad!
What? shall I ever sigh and pine?
My lines and life are free; free as the road,
   Loose as the winde, as large as store,°   5
     Shall I be still in suit?°
  Have I no harvest but a thorn
  To let me blood, and not restore
What I have lost with cordial° fruit?
     Sure there was wine   10
  Before my sighs did dry it: there was corn
   Before my tears did drown it.
  Is the year only lost to me?
   Have I no bays° to crown it?
No flowers, no garlands gay? all blasted?   15
     All wasted?
  Not so, my heart: but there is fruit,
    And thou hast hands.
  Recover all thy sigh-blown age
On double pleasures: leave thy cold dispute   20
Of what is fit, and not; forsake thy cage,
    Thy rope of sands,
Which petty thoughts have made, and made to thee
  Good cable, to enforce and draw
     And be thy law,   25
  While thou didst wink and wouldst not see.
     Away; take heed:
     I will abroad.
Call in thy death's head° there: tie up thy fears.
     He that forbears   30

     To suit and serve his need,
     Deserves his load.
But as I rav'd and grew more fierce and will
    At every word,
Me thought I heard one calling, *Child*:   35
    And I replied, *My Lord.*

THE COLLAR. 1 *board*: table.   5 *store*: warehouse.   6 *in suit*: serving or tending another.   9 *cordial*: restoring.   14 *bays*: wreaths (of bay leaf).   29 *death's head*: skull, also known as a "memento mori," or reminder of death.

                                       An Anthology of Poetry

LOVE

Love bade me welcome; yet my soul drew back,
    Guilty of dust and sin.
But quick-ey'd Love, observing me grow slack
    From my first entrance in,
Drew nearer to me, sweetly questioning   5
    If I lacked anything.

A guest, I answer'd, worthy to be here.
    Love said, You shall be he.
I, the unkind, ungrateful? Ah, my dear,
    I cannot look on Thee.   10
Love took my hand, and smiling, did reply,
    Who made the eyes but I?

Truth, Lord, but I have marred them: let my shame
    Go where it doth deserve.
And know you not, says Love, who bore the blame?   15
    My dear, then I will serve.
You must sit down, says Love, and taste my meat:
    So I did sit and eat.

John Milton (1608–1674)

LYCIDAS°

Yet once more, O ye laurels, and once more,
Ye myrtles brown, with ivy never sere,
I come to pluck your berries harsh and crude,°   *unripe*
And with forced fingers rude
Shatter your leaves before the mellowing year.   5

Bitter constraint and sad occasion dear
Compels me to disturb your season due:
For Lycidas is dead, dead ere his prime,
Young Lycidas, and hath not left his peer.
Who would not sing for Lycidas? he knew   10

LYCIDAS. Milton wrote "Lycidas" as a lament for a friend, a scholar, who drowned in the Irish Seas in 1637. Lycidas is a conventional name for a young shepherd in the pastoral tradition. Milton begins by invoking the materials—laurels, myrtles, and ivy—from which honorary garlands are woven.

Himself to sing, and build the lofty rhyme.
He must not float upon his watery bier°   *base for a coffin*
Unwept, and welter° to the parching wind,   *roll around*
Without the meed° of some melodious tear.   *recognition, reward*
   Begin then, Sisters of the sacred well°   *Muses* 15
That from beneath the seat of Jove° doth spring;   *Zeus (chief god)*
Begin, and somewhat loudly sweep the string;
Hence with denial vain and coy excuse:
So may some gentle Muse
With lucky words favor my destined urn;   20
And as he passes, turn
And bid fair peace be to my sable shroud.
   For we were nursed upon the self-same hill,
Fed the same flock by fountain, shade, and rill.
Together both, ere the high lawns appeared   25
Under the opening eye-lids of the Morn,
We drove a-field, and both together heard
What time the gray-fly winds° her sultry horn,   *blows, sounds*
Battening° our flocks with the fresh dews of night;   *nourishing*
Oft till the star, that rose at evening bright,   30
Toward heaven's descent had sloped his westering° wheel.   *west-turning*
Meanwhile the rural ditties° were not mute;   *simple songs*
Tempered to the oaten flute,
Rough Satyrs° danced, and Fauns° with cloven heel
From the glad sound would not be absent long;   35
And old Damoetas° loved to hear our song.
   But, O! the heavy change, now thou art gone,
Now thou art gone, and never must return!
Thee, Shepherd, thee the woods and desert caves,
With wild thyme and the gadding° vine o'ergrown,   *wandering* 40
And all their echoes, mourn:
The willows and the hazel copses green
Shall now no more be seen
Fanning their joyous leaves to thy soft lays.
As killing as the canker to the rose,   45
Or taint-worm to the weanling° herds that graze,   *just weaned*
Or frost to flowers, that their gay wardrobe wear
When first the white-thorn blows;°   *blooms*
Such, Lycidas, thy loss to shepherd's ear.
   Where were ye, Nymphs, when the remorseless deep   50
Closed o'er the head of your loved Lycidas?
For neither were ye playing on the steep°   *slope*
Where your old bards, the famous Druids,° lie,   *poet-priests*
Nor on the shaggy top of Mona° high,
Nor yet where Deva° spreads her wizard stream.   55
Ay me! I fondly° dream   *self-indulgently*

---

34 *Satyrs, Fauns*: mythic woodland creatures.   36 *Damoetas*: may refer to a Cambridge tutor. 54 *Mona*: island off Wales.   55 *Deva*: River Dee between England and Wales.

"Had ye been there,"—for what could that have done?
What could the Muse herself that Orpheus° bore,
The Muse herself, for her enchanting son,
Whom universal nature did lament,   60
When by the rout° that made the hideous roar   *mob*
His gory visage down the stream was sent,
Down the swift Hebrus° to the Lesbian° shore?
   Alas! what boots it° with uncessant care   *does it matter*
To tend the homely, slighted, shepherd's trade   65
And strictly meditate the thankless Muse?
Were it not better done, as others use,
To sport with Amaryllis° in the shade,
Or with the tangles of Neaera's° hair?
Fame is the spur that the clear spirit doth raise   70
(That last infirmity of noble mind)
To scorn delights, and live laborious days;
But the fair guerdon° when we hope to find,   *prize*
And think to burst out into sudden blaze,
Comes the blind Fury° with the abhorred shears   75
And slits the thin-spun life. "But not the praise,"
Phoebus° replied, and touched my trembling ears: *Apollo (sun god)*
"Fame is no plant that grows on mortal soil,
Nor in the glistering foil
Set off to the world, nor in broad rumor lies: 80
But lives and spreads aloft by those pure eyes
And perfect witness of all-judging Jove;
As he pronounces lastly on each deed,
Of so much fame in heaven expect thy meed."
   O fountain Arethuse,° and thou honored flood,   85
Smooth-sliding Mincius,° crowned with vocal reeds,
That strain I heard was of a higher mood.
But now my oat° proceeds,   *oaten pipe*
And listens to the herald of the sea
That came in Neptune's plea;°   90
He asked the waves, and asked the felon winds,
What hard mishap hath doomed this gentle swain?
And questioned every gust of rugged wings
That blows from off each beaked promontory:
They knew not of his story;   95
And safe Hippotades° their answer brings,
That not a blast was from his dungeon strayed;
The air was calm, and on the level brine

---

58 *Orpheus*: mythic figure famed for his musical gift; also a tragic figure.   63 *Hebrus . . . Lesbian*:
refers to Orpheus legend, in which women, angered by Orpheus' love for Euridice, dismembered him and
threw his head and lyre into the Hebrus River.   68–69 *Amaryllis . . . Neaera*: names for carefree pastoral shepherdesses.   75 *Fury*: avenging deity in myth.   85 *Arethuse*: Sicilian fountain near home of
Theocritus, Greek poet.   86 *Mincius*: river near Latin poet Virgil's birthplace.   89–90 *Herald . . . plea*:
Triton (the "herald") carried word that Neptune, the sea god, was innocent of Lycidas' death.   96 *Hip-
potades*: Aeolus, Greek wind god.

Sleek Panope° with all her sisters played.
It was that fatal and perfidous bark,
Built in the eclipse, and rigged with curses dark,   100
That sunk so low that sacred head of thine.
   Next Camus,° reverend sire, went footing slow,
His mantle hairy, and his bonnet sedge,
Inwrought with figures dim, and on the edge   105
Like to that sanguine flower° inscribed with woe.
"Ah! who hath reft," quoth he, "my dearest pledge?"
Last came, and last did go
The Pilot of the Galilean lake;°
Two massy keys° he bore of metals twain   110
(The golden opes, the iron shuts amain°);   *in haste*
He shook his mitred locks,° and stern bespake:
"How well could I have spared for thee, young swain,
Enow of such, as for their bellies' sake
Creep and intrude and climb into the fold!   115
Of other care they little reckoning make
Than how to scramble at the shearers' feast,
And shove away the worthy bidden guest.
Blind mouths! that scarce themselves know how to hold
A sheep-hook,° or have learned aught else the least   120
That to the faithful herdman's art belongs!
What recks it° them? What need they? They are sped;°   *matters; well off*
And when they list,° their lean and flashy songs   *wish*
Grate on their scrannel° pipes of wretched straw;   *harsh*
The hungry sheep look up, and are not fed,   125
But, swol'n with wind° and the rank mist they draw,   *stomach gas*
Rot inwardly, and foul contagion spread:
Besides what the grim wolf° with privy° paw   *stealthy*
Daily devours apace, and nothing said:
—But that two-handed engine° at the door   130
Stands ready to smite once, and smite no more."
   Return, Alpheus; the dread voice is past
That shrunk thy streams; return, Sicilian Muse,°
And call the vales, and bid them hither cast
Their bells and flowerets of a thousand hues.   135
Ye valleys low, where the mild whispers use
Of shades, and wanton winds, and gushing brooks
On whose fresh lap the swart star° sparely looks;
Throw hither all your quaint enameled eyes
That on the green turf suck the honeyed showers,   140

---

   99 *Panope:* sea nymph.   103 *Camus:* spirit of the Cam, river at Cambridge University.   106 *san-guine flower:* hyacinth, created in myth by the blood of the slain youth Hyacinthus.   109 *Pilot . . . lake:* St. Peter.   110 *keys:* St. Peter was promised keys to the Kingdom of Heaven.   112 *mitred locks:* St. Peter wears the bishop's miter as head of the church.   120 *sheep-hook:* symbol of the flock-leading, the priestly vocation.   128 *privy:* stealthy; *grim wolf:* refers to anti-Protestant forces in seventeenth-century religious wars.   130 *two-handed engine:* avenging sword of God.   133 *Sicilian Muse:* muse of pastoral poet Theocritus.   138 *swart star:* Sirius, a star thought to turn vegetation black.

And purple all the ground with vernal flowers.
Bring the rathe° primrose that forsaken dies,   *early*
The tufted crow-toe, and pale jessamine,
The white pink, and the pansy freaked° with jet,   *streaked*
The glowing violet,   145
The musk-rose, and the well-attired woodbine,
With cowslips wan that hang the pensive head,
And every flower that sad° embroidery wears;   *dull-colored*
Bid amaranthus all his beauty shed,
And daffadillies fill their cups with tears   150
To strew the laureate hearse where Lycid lies.
For so to interpose a little ease,
Let our frail thoughts dally with false surmise.°   *vain hope (of recovery)*
Ay me! whilst thee the shores and sounding seas
Wash far away, where'er thy bones are hurled;   155
Whether beyond the stormy Hebrides
Where thou, perhaps, under the whelming tide,
Visit'st the bottom of the monstrous world;
Or whether thou, to our moist vows° denied,   *tearful declarations*
Sleep'st by the fable of Bellerus° old,   160
Where the great Vision of the guarded mount°
Looks toward Namancos and Bayona's hold.°
Look homeward, Angel, now, and melt with ruth:°   *pity*
And, O ye dolphins, waft the hapless youth!
    Weep no more, woeful shepherds, weep no more,   165
For Lycidas, your sorrow, is not dead,
Sunk though he be beneath the watery floor;
So sinks the day-star in the ocean bed,
And yet anon repairs his drooping head,
And tricks° his beams, and with new-spangled ore°   *adorns; gold* 170
Flames in the forehead of the morning sky:
So Lycidas sunk low, but mounted high
Through the dear might of Him that walked the waves;
Where, other groves and other streams along,
With nectar pure his oozy locks he laves,°   *bathes* 175
And hears the unexpressive nuptial song°
In the blest kingdoms meek of joy and love.
There entertain him all the saints above
In solemn troops, and sweet societies,
That sing, and singing in their glory move,   180
And wipe the tears for ever from his eyes.
Now, Lycidas, the shepherds weep no more;
Henceforth thou art the Genius° of the shore   *presiding spirit*
In thy large recompense, and shalt be good
To all that wander in that perilous flood.   185

---

160 *Bellerus:* legendary giant buried in Cornwall.   161 *guarded mount:* mountain guarded by
Archangel Michael.   162 *Namancos and Bayona's hold:* area in Spain.   176 *unexpressive nuptial song:*
Biblical reference to song sung at "marriage supper of the lamb" (Rev. 19:9).

Thus sang the uncouth° swain to the oaks and rills,   *uneducated*
While the still morn went out with sandals gray;
He touched the tender stops of various quills,°   *tuned lyre-strings*
With eager thought warbling his Doric lay:°   *pastoral poem*
And now the sun had stretched out all the hills,   190
And now was dropt into the western bay.
At last he rose, and twitched° his mantle blue: *put on*
Tomorrow to fresh woods, and pastures new.

WHEN I CONSIDER HOW MY LIGHT IS SPENT°

When I consider how my light is spent
   Ere half my days in this dark world and wide,
   And that one talent° which is death to hide
   Lodged with me useless, though my soul more bent
To serve therewith my Maker, and present   5
   My true account, lest he returning chide,
   Doth God exact day-labor, light denied?
   I fondly° ask. But Patience, to prevent   *self-indulgently*
That murmur, soon replies, God doth not need
   Either man's work or his own gifts. Who best   10
   Bear his mild yoke, they serve him best. His state
Is kingly: Thousands at his bidding speed,
   And post o'er land and ocean without rest;
   They also serve who only stand and wait.

WHEN I CONSIDER HOW MY LIGHT IS SPENT. Milton lost his sight four years before this poem was written.   3 *that one talent*: reference to Biblical parable in which a servant entrusted with a talent (a coin) buries it instead of investing it and is punished by his master (Matt. 25:14–30). The word talent is used with a double meaning.

Anne Bradstreet (1612?–1672)

TO MY DEAR AND LOVING HUSBAND

If ever two were one, then surely we.
If ever man were lov'd by wife, then thee;
If ever wife was happy in a man,
Compare with me ye women if you can.
I prize thy love more than whole Mines of gold,   5
Or all the riches that the East doth hold.
My love is such that Rivers cannot quench,
Nor ought but love from thee, give recompence.
Thy love is such I can no way repay,
The heavens reward thee manifold I pray.   10

Then while we live, in love lets so persever,
That when we live no more, we may live ever.

[1678]

Andrew Marvell (1621–1678)

TO HIS COY MISTRESS

Had we but world enough, and time,
This coyness, lady, were no crime.
We would sit down, and think which way
To walk, and pass our long love's day.
Thou by the Indian Ganges° side   5
Shouldst rubies find; I by the tide
Of Humber° would complain.° I would
Love you ten years before the Flood
And you should, if you please, refuse
Till the conversion of the Jews.   10
My vegetable love should grow
Vaster than empires, and more slow;
An hundred years should go to praise
Thine eyes and on thy forehead gaze,
Two hundred to adore each breast,   15
But thirty thousand to the rest:
An age at least to every part,
And the last age should show your heart.
For, lady, you deserve this state,
Nor would I love at lower rate.   20
    But at my back I always hear
Time's winged chariot hurrying near;
And yonder all before us lie
Deserts of vast eternity.
Thy beauty shall no more be found,   25
Nor in thy marble vault shall sound
My echoing song; then worms shall try
That long preserved virginity,
And your quaint honor turn to dust,
And into ashes all my lust.   30
The grave's a fine and private place,
But none, I think, do there embrace.
    Now, therefore, while the youthful hue
Sits on thy skin like morning dew,
And while thy willing soul transpires°   35

TO HIS COY MISTRESS. 5 *Ganges:* river in India.   7 *Humber:* river in northeast England; *complain:*
write love lyrics.   35 *transpires:* breathes through.

At every pore with instant fires,
Now let us sport us while we may,
And now, like amorous birds of prey,
Rather at once our time devour
Than languish in his slow-chapped° power.   40
Let us roll all our strength and all
Our sweetness up into one ball,
And tear our pleasures with rough strife
Thorough° the iron gates of life.
Thus, though we cannot make our sun   45
Stand still, yet we will make him run.

---

40 *slow-chapped:* slow-jawed.   44 *thorough:* through.

Thomas Gray (1716–1771)

ELEGY

Written in a Country Churchyard

The Curfew° tolls the knell of parting day,
    The lowing herd wind slowly o'er the lea,
The plowman homeward plods his weary way,
    And leaves the world to darkness and to me.

Now fades the glimmering landscape on the sight,   5
    And all the air a solemn stillness holds,
Save where the beetle wheels his droning flight,
    And drowsy tinklings lull the distant folds;

Save that from yonder ivy-mantled tower
    The moping owl does to the moon complain   10
Of such, as wandering near her secret bower,
    Molest her ancient solitary reign.

Beneath those rugged elms, that yew-tree's shade,
    Where heaves the turf in many a mouldering heap,
Each in his narrow cell for ever laid,   15
    The rude° Forefathers of the hamlet sleep.

The breezy call of incense-breathing Morn,
    The swallow twittering from the straw-built shed,
The cock's shrill clarion, or the echoing horn,°
    No more shall rouse them from their lowly bed.   20

ELEGY.   1 *Curfew:* evening bell.   16 *rude:* simple.   19 *echoing horn:* hunters' horn.

For them no more the blazing hearth shall burn,
    Or busy housewife ply her evening care:
No children run to lisp their sire's return,
    Or climb his knees the envied kiss to share.

Oft did the harvest to their sickle yield,   25
    Their furrow oft the stubborn glebe° has broke;
How jocund did they drive their team afield!
    How bowed the woods beneath their sturdy stroke!

Let no Ambition mock their useful toil,
    Their homely joys, and destiny obscure;   30
Nor Grandeur hear with a disdainful smile
    The short and simple annals of the poor.

The boast of heraldry,° the pomp of power,
    And all that beauty, all that wealth e'er gave,
Awaits alike the inevitable hour.   35
    The paths of glory lead but to the grave.

Nor you, ye Proud, impute to These the fault,
    If Memory o'er their Tomb no Trophies raise,
Where through the long-drawn aisle and fretted° vault
    The pealing anthem swells the note of praise.   40

Can storied urn or animated bust
    Back to its mansion call the fleeting breath?
Can Honor's voice provoke the silent dust,
    Or Flattery sooth the dull cold ear of Death?

Perhaps in this neglected spot is laid   45
    Some heart once pregnant with celestial fire;
Hands, that the rod of empire might have swayed,
    Or waked to ecstasy the living lyre.

But Knowledge to their eyes her ample page
    Rich with the spoils of time did ne'er unroll;   50
Chill Penury° repressed their noble rage,
    And froze the genial current of the soul.

Full many a gem of purest ray serene,
    The dark unfathomed caves of ocean bear:
Full many a flower is born to blush unseen,   55
    And waste its sweetness on the desert air.

Some village-Hampden,° that with dauntless breast
    The little Tyrant of his fields withstood;
Some mute inglorious Milton here may rest,
    Some Cromwell guiltless of his country's blood.   60

---

26 *glebe:* sod, turf.   33 *heraldry:* noble birth.   39 *fretted:* ribbed.   51 *Penury:* poverty.   57 *Hampden:* name of a statesman.

The applause of listening senates to command,
    The threats of pain and ruin to despise,
To scatter plenty o'er a smiling land,
    And read their history in a nation's eyes,

Their lot forbad: nor circumscribed alone   65
    Their growing virtues, but their crimes confin'd;
Forbade to wade through slaughter to a throne,
    And shut the gates of mercy on mankind,

The struggling pangs of conscious truth to hide,
    To quench the blushes of ingenuous shame,   70
Or heap the shrine of Luxury and Pride
    With incense kindled at the Muse's flame.

Far from the madding crowd's ignoble strife,
    Their sober wishes never learned to stray;
Along the cool sequestered vale of life   75
    They kept the noiseless tenor° of their way.

Yet even these bones from insult to protect,
    Some frail memorial still erected nigh,
With uncouth rhymes and shapeless sculpture decked,
    Implores the passing tribute of a sigh.   80

Their name, their years, spelt by the unlettered muse,
    The place of fame and elegy supply:
And many a holy text around she strews,
    That teach the rustic moralist to die.

For who to dumb Forgetfulness a prey,   85
    This pleasing anxious being e'er resigned,
Left the warm precincts of the cheerful day,
    Nor cast one longing lingering look behind?

On some fond breast the parting soul relies,
    Some pious drops the closing eye requires;   90
Ev'n from the tomb the voice of Nature cries,
    Ev'n in our Ashes live their wonted° Fires.

For thee, who mindful of the unhonoured Dead
    Dost in these lines their artless tale relate,
If chance,° by lonely contemplation led,   95
    Some kindred Spirit shall inquire thy fate,

Haply° some hoary-headed Swain° may say,
    "Oft have we seen him at the peep of dawn
Brushing with hasty steps the dews away
    To meet the sun upon the upland lawn.   100

---

76 *noiseless tenor:* silent momentum.   93 *wonted:* customary.   95 *If chance:* if perchance.
97 *Haply:* perhaps; *hoary-headed Swain:* gray-haired shepherd.

"There at the foot of yonder nodding beech
   That wreathes its old fantastic roots so high,
His listless length at noontide would he stretch,
   And pore upon the brook that babbles by.

"Hard by yon wood, now smiling as in scorn,   105
   Muttering his wayward fancies he would rove,
Now drooping, woeful wan, like one forlorn,
   Or crazed with care, or crossed in hopeless love.

"One morn I missed him on the customed hill,
   Along the heath and near his favorite tree;   110
Another came; nor yet beside the rill,
   Nor up the lawn, nor at the wood was he;

"The next with dirges° due in sad array
   Slow through the church-way path we saw him borne.
Approach and read (for thou can'st read) the lay,°   115
   Graved on the stone beneath yon agèd thorn."

                    THE EPITAPH

Here rests his head upon the lap of earth
   A youth to fortune and to fame unknown.
Fair Science° frowned not on his humble birth,
   And Melancholy marked him for her own.   120

Large was his bounty, and his soul sincere,
   Heaven did a recompense as largely send:
He gave to Misery all he had, a tear,
   He gained from Heaven ('twas all he wished) a friend.

No farther seek his merits to disclose,   125
   Or draw his frailties from their dread abode,
(There they alike in trembling hope repose)
   The bosom of his Father and his God.

---

113 *dirges:* lamenting melodies.   115 *lay:* song.   119 *Science:* knowledge.

William Blake (1757–1827)

SONG

How sweet I roam'd from field to field,
   And tasted all the summer's pride,
Till I the Prince of Love beheld
   Who in the sunny beams did glide.

He show'd me lilies for my hair,   5
    And blushing roses for my brow;
He led me through his gardens fair,
    Where all his golden pleasures grow.

With sweet May-dews my wings were wet,
    And Phoebus° fir'd my vocal range;   sun 10
He caught me in his silken net,
    And shut me in his golden cage.

He loves to sit and hear me sing,
    Then, laughing, sports and plays with me;
Then stretches out my golden wing,   15
    And mocks my loss of liberty.

THE TYGER

Tyger! Tyger! burning bright
In the forests of the night,
What immortal hand or eye
Could frame thy fearful symmetry?

In what distant deeps or skies   5
Burnt the fire of thine eyes?
On what wings dare he aspire?
What the hand dare seize the fire?

And what shoulder, & what art,
Could twist the sinews of thy heart?   10
And when thy heart began to beat,
What dread hand? & what dread feet?

What the hammer? what the chain?
In what furnace was thy brain?
What the anvil? what dread grasp   15
Dare its deadly terrors clasp?

When the stars threw down their spears,
And water'd heaven with their tears,
Did he smile his work to see?
Did he who made the Lamb make thee?   20

Tyger! Tyger! burning bright
In the forests of the night,
What immortal hand or eye,
Dare frame thy fearful symmetry?

808

AH! SUN-FLOWER

Ah, Sun-flower! weary of time,
Who countest the steps of the Sun;
Seeking after that sweet golden clime
Where the traveller's journey is done;

Where the Youth pined away with desire,   5
And the pale Virgin shrouded in snow,
Arise from their graves, and aspire
Where my Sun-flower wishes to go.

LONDON

I wander thro' each charter'd° street,   *defined by law*
Near where the charter'd Thames does flow,
And mark in every face I meet
Marks of weakness, marks of woe.

In every cry of every Man,   5
In every Infant's cry of fear,
In every voice, in every ban,
The mind-forg'd manacles I hear.

How the Chimney-sweeper's cry
Every black'ning Church appalls;   10
And the hapless Soldier's sigh
Runs in blood down Palace walls.

But most thro' midnight streets I hear
How the youthful Harlot's curse
Blasts the new born Infant's tear,   15
And blights with plagues the Marriage hearse.

Robert Burns (1759–1796)

TO A MOUSE, ON TURNING UP HER NEST WITH THE PLOUGH, NOVEMBER 1785

Wee, sleekit, cow'rin', tim'rous beastie,°   *little beast*
O what a panic's in thy breastie!°   *little breast*
Thou need na start awa sae hasty,
       Wi' bickering brattle!°   *prattle, noise*

I wad be laith° to rin an' chase thee   *loath, reluctant* 5
      Wi' murd'ring pattle!°   *paddle*

I'm truly sorry man's dominion
Has broken Nature's social union,
An' justifies that ill opinion
      Which makes thee startle 10
At me, thy poor earth-born companion,
      An' fellow-mortal!

I doubt na, whiles,° but thou may thieve;   *meanwhile*
What then? poor beastie, thou maun° live!   *must*
A daimen-icker° in a thrave°   *few grains; sheaf* 15
      'S a sma' request:
I'll get a blessin' wi' the lave,°   *leavings*
      And never miss't!

Thy wee bit housie, too, in ruin!
Its silly wa's° the win's° are strewin'!   *walls, winds* 20
An' naething, now, to big° a new ane,   *make*
      O' foggage° green!   *forage*
An' bleak December's winds ensuin',
      Baith snell° an' keen!   *bitter*

Thou saw the fields laid bare and waste, 25
An' weary winter comin' fast,
An' cozie here, beneath the blast,
      Thou thought to dwell,
Till crash! the cruel coulter° past   *plow*
      Out-thro' thy cell. 30

That wee bit heap o'leaves an' stibble
Has cost thee mony a weary nibble!
Now thou's turn'd out, for a' thy trouble,
      But house or hald,
To thole° the winter's sleety dribble,   *endure* 35
      An' cranreuch° cauld!   *frost*

But, Mousie, thou art no thy lane,°   *not alone*
In proving foresight may be vain:
The best laid schemes o' mice an' men
      Gang aft a-gley,°   *askew* 40
An' lea'e° us nought but grief an' pain   *leave*
      For promis'd joy.

Still thou art blest compar'd wi' me!
The present only toucheth thee:
But oh! I backward cast my e'e 45
      On prospects drear!
An' forward tho' I canna see,
      I guess an' fear!

William Wordsworth (1770–1850)

UPON WESTMINSTER BRIDGE

Earth has not anything to show more fair:
Dull would he be of soul who could pass by
A sight so touching in its majesty:
This City now doth, like a garment, wear
The beauty of the morning; silent, bare,   5
Ships, towers, domes, theatres, and temples lie
Open unto the fields, and to the sky;
All bright and glittering in the smokeless air.
Never did sun more beautifully steep
In his first splendour valley, rock, or hill;   10
Ne'er saw I, never felt, a calm so deep!
The river glideth at his own sweet will:
Dear God! the very houses seem asleep;
And all that mighty heart is lying still!

LINES

Composed a few miles above Tintern Abbey,
on revisiting the banks of the Wye during a tour.
July 13, 1798.[1]

Five years have past; five summers, with the length
Of five long winters! and again I hear
These waters, rolling from their mountain-springs
With a soft inland murmur.[2]—Once again
Do I behold these steep and lofty cliffs,   5
That on a wild secluded scene impress
Thoughts of more deep seclusion; and connect
The landscape with the quiet of the sky.
The day is come when I again repose
Here, under this dark sycamore, and view,   10
These plots of cottage-ground, these orchard-tufts,
Which at this season, with their unripe fruits,
Are clad in one green hue, and lose themselves
'Mid groves and copses.   Once again I see

---

[1] No poem of mine was composed under circumstances more pleasant for me to remember than this. I began it upon leaving Tintern, after crossing the Wye, and concluded it just as I was entering Bristol in the evening, after a ramble of four or five days, with my Sister. Not a line of it was altered, and not any part of it written down till I reached Bristol. It was published almost immediately after in the Lyrical Ballads. [Wordsworth's note.]

[2] The river is not affected by the tides a few miles above Tintern. [Wordsworth's note.]

These hedge-rows, hardly hedge-rows, little lines   15
Of sportive wood run wild: these pastoral farms,
Green to the very door; and wreaths of smoke
Sent up, in silence, from among the trees !
With some uncertain notice, as might seem
Of vagrant dwellers in the houseless woods,   20
Or of some Hermit's cave, where by his fire
The Hermit sits alone.
                      These beauteous forms
Through a long absence, have not been to me
As is a landscape to a blind man's eye:
But oft, in lonely rooms, and 'mid the din   25
Of towns and cities, I have owed to them
In hours of weariness, sensations sweet,
Felt in the blood, and felt along the heart;
And passing even into my purer mind,
With tranquil restoration:—feelings too   30
Of unremembered pleasure: such, perhaps,
As have no slight or trivial influence
On that best portion of a good man's life,
His little, nameless, unremembered, acts
Of kindness and of love.   Nor less, I trust,   35
To them I may have owed another gift,
Of aspect more sublime; that blessed mood
In which the burthen of the mystery,
In which the heavy and the weary weight
Of all this unintelligible world,   40
Is lightened:—that serene and blessed mood,
In which the affections gently lead us on,—
Until, the breath of this corporeal frame
And even the motion of our human blood
Almost suspended, we are laid asleep   45
In body, and become a living soul:
While with an eye made quiet by the power
Of harmony, and the deep power of joy,
We see into the life of things.
                          If this
Be but a vain belief, yet, oh ! how oft—   50
In darkness and amid the many shapes
Of joyless daylight; when the fretful stir
Unprofitable, and the fever of the world,
Have hung upon the beatings of my heart—
How oft, in spirit, have I turned to thee,   55
O sylvan Wye ! thou wanderer thro' the woods,
How often has my spirit turned to thee !
    And now, with gleams of half-extinguished thought,
With many recognitions dim and faint,
And somewhat of a sad perplexity,   60
The picture of the mind revives again:

While here I stand, not only with the sense
Of present pleasure, but with pleasing thoughts
That in this moment there is life and food
For future years.   And so I dare to hope, 65
Though changed, no doubt, from what I was when first
I came among these hills; when like a roe
I bounded o'er the mountains, by the sides
Of the deep rivers, and the lonely streams,
Wherever nature led: more like a man 70
Flying from something that he dreads, than one
Who sought the thing he loved.   For nature then
(The coarser pleasures of my boyish days,
And their glad animal movements all gone by)
To me was all in all.—I cannot paint 75
What then I was.   The sounding cataract
Haunted me like a passion: the tall rock,
The mountain, and the deep and gloomy wood,
Their colours and their forms, were then to me
An appetite; a feeling and a love, 80
That had no need of a remoter charm,
By thought supplied, nor any interest
Unborrowed from the eye.—That time is past,
And all its aching joys are now no more,
And all its dizzy raptures.   Not for this 85
Faint I, nor mourn nor murmur; other gifts
Have followed; for such loss, I would believe,
Abundant recompence.   For I have learned
To look on nature, not as in the hour
Of thoughtless youth; but hearing oftentimes 90
The still, sad music of humanity,
Nor harsh nor grating, though of ample power
To chasten and subdue.   And I have felt
A presence that disturbs me with the joy
Of elevated thought; a sense sublime 95
Of something far more deeply interfused,
Whose dwelling is the light of setting suns,
And the round ocean and the living air,
And the blue sky, and in the mind of man;
A motion and a spirit, that impels 100
All thinking things, all objects of all thought,
And rolls through all things. Therefore am I still
A lover of the meadows and the woods,
And mountains; and of all that we behold
From this green earth; of all the mighty world 105
Of eye, and ear,—both what they half create,[3]
And what perceive; well pleased to recognise

---

[3] This line has a close resemblance to an admirable line of Young's the exact expression of which I
do not recollect. [Wordsworth's note.]

In nature and the language of the sense,
The anchor of my purest thoughts, the nurse,
The guide, the guardian of my heart, and soul   110
Of all my moral being.
                              Nor perchance,
If I were not thus taught, should I the more
Suffer my genial spirits to decay:
For thou art with me here upon the banks
Of this fair river; thou my dearest Friend,°   115
My dear, dear Friend; and in thy voice I catch
The language of my former heart, and read
My former pleasures in the shooting lights
Of thy wild eyes.   Oh ! yet a little while
May I behold in thee what I was once,   120
My dear, dear Sister !°and this prayer I make,
Knowing that nature never did betray
The heart that loved her; 'tis her privilege,
Through all the years of this our life, to lead
From joy to joy: for she can so inform   125
The mind that is within us, so impress
With quietness and beauty, and so feed
With lofty thoughts, that neither evil tongues,
Rash judgments, nor the sneers of selfish men,
Nor greetings where no kindness is, nor all   130
The dreary intercourse of daily life,
Shall e'er prevail against us, or disturb
Our cheerful faith, that all which we behold
Is full of blessings.   Therefore let the moon
Shine on thee in thy solitary walk;   135
And let the misty mountain-winds be free
To blow against thee: and, in after years,
When these wild ecstasies shall be matured
Into a sober pleasure; when thy mind
Shall be a mansion for all lovely forms,   140
Thy memory be as a dwelling-place
For all sweet sounds and harmonies; oh! then,
If solitude, or fear, or pain, or grief,
Should be thy portion, with what healing thoughts
Of tender joy wilt thou remember me,   145
And these my exhortations !   Nor, perchance—
If I should be where I no more can hear
Thy voice, nor catch from thy wild eyes these gleams
Of past existence—wilt thou then forget

---

115 *Friend:* apparently refers to Coleridge who, with Wordsworth's sister Dorothy, accompanied the poet on country hiking trips. Coleridge's work, "Kubla Khan" (following) and later "Frost at Midnight" (Chapter 28) was copublished with Wordsworth's work in a ground-breaking volume entitled *Lyrical Ballads.*   121 *Sister:* Wordsworth's sister Dorothy lived with him at this time and was his constant companion (along with Coleridge) on mountain hikes.

That on the banks of this delightful stream150
We stood together; and that I, so long
A worshipper of Nature, hither came
Unwearied in that service: rather say
With warmer love—oh ! with far deeper zeal
Of holier love.   Nor wilt thou then forget,155
That after many wanderings, many years
Of absence, these steep woods and lofty cliffs,
and this green pastoral landscape, were to me
More dear, both for themselves and for they sake !

Friedrich Hölderlin (1770–1843)

THE MIDDLE OF LIFE

With yellow pears the land
And full of wild roses
Hangs down into the lake,
You lovely swans,
And drunk with kisses5
You dip your heads
Into the hallowed, the sober water.

But oh, where shall I find
When winter comes, the flowers, and where
The sunshine10
And shade of the earth?
The walls loom
Speechless and cold, in the wind
Weathercocks° clatter.*weathervanes*

Translated by Michael Hamberger

Samuel Taylor Coleridge (1772–1834)

KUBLA KHAN°

In Xanadu did Kubla Khan°
A stately pleasure-dome decree:
Where Alph, the sacred river, ran

KUBLA KHAN. The poem sometimes carries the subtitle "Or, a Vision in a Dream," for Coleridge received his inspiration in an opium-induced dream. His composition was interrupted and permanently halted by a visitor, known to history as "the man from Porlock."   1 *Kubla Khan*: grandson of Ghengis Khan, who was the founder of China's Mongol dynasty.

Through caverns measureless to man

     Down to a sunless sea.   5
   So twice five miles of fertile ground
   With walls and towers were girdled round:
And here were gardens bright with sinuous rills
Where blossomed many an incense-bearing tree;
And here were forests ancient as the hills,   10
Enfolding sunny spots of greenery.
But oh! that deep romantic chasm which slanted
Down the green hill athwart a cedarn° cover!
A savage place! as holy and enchanted
As e'er beneath a waning moon was haunted   15
By woman wailing for her demon-lover!
And from this chasm, with ceaseless turmoil seething,
As if this earth in fast thick pants were breathing,
A mighty fountain momently was forced;
Amid whose swift half-intermitted burst   20
Huge fragments vaulted like rebounding hail,
Or chaffy grain beneath the thresher's flail:
And 'mid these dancing rocks at once and ever
It flung up momently the sacred river.
Five miles meandering with a mazy motion   25
Through wood and dale the sacred river ran,
Then reached the caverns measureless to man,
And sank in tumult to a lifeless ocean:
And 'mid this tumult Kubla heard from far
Ancestral voices prophesying war!   30

   The shadow of the dome of pleasure
     Floated midway on the waves;
   Where was heard the mingled measure
     From the fountain and the caves.
It was a miracle of rare device,°   35
A sunny pleasure-dome with caves of ice!

   A damsel with a dulcimer
   In a vision once I saw:
   It was an Abyssinian maid,
   And on her dulcimer she play'd,   40
   Singing of Mount Abora.
   Could I revive within me
   Her symphony and song,
To such a deep delight 'twould win me,
That with music loud and long,   45
I would build that dome in air,
That sunny dome! those caves of ice!
And all who heard should see them there,
And all should cry, Beware! Beware! His flashing eyes, his floating hair!   50

---

13 *cedarn*: cedar.   35 *device*: invention, devising.

Weave a circle round him thrice,
And close your eyes with holy dread,
For he on honey-dew hath fed,
And drunk the milk of Paradise.

George Gordon, Lord Byron (1788–1824)

SHE WALKS IN BEAUTY

She walks in beauty, like the night
   Of cloudless climes and starry skies;
And all that's best of dark and bright
   Meet in her aspect and her eyes:
Thus mellowed to that tender light   5
   Which heaven to gaudy day denies.

One shade the more, one day the less,
   Had half impaired the nameless grace
Which waves in every raven tress,
   Or softly lightens o'er her face;
Where thoughts serenely sweet express   10
   How pure, how dear, their dwelling-place.

And on that cheek, and o'er that brow,
   So soft, so calm, so eloquent,
The smiles that win, the tints that glow,   15
   But tell of days in goodness spent,
A mind at peace with all below,
   A heart whose love is innocent!

Percy Bysshe Shelley (1792–1822)

CHORUS FROM HELLAS

The world's great age begins anew,
   The golden years return,
The earth doth like a snake renew
   Her winter weeds outworn:
Heaven smiles, and faiths and empires gleam,   5
Like wrecks of a dissolving dream.

A brighter Hellas° rears its mountains
   From waves serener far:

CHORUS FROM *HELLAS*. 7 *Hellas*: Greece.

A new Peneus° rolls his fountains
    Against the morning star.
Where fairer Tempes bloom, there sleep
Young Cyclads on a sunnier deep.

A loftier Argo cleaves the main,
    Fraught with a later prize;
Another Orpheus sings again,
    And loves, and weeps, and dies.
A new Ulysses leaves once more
Calypso for his native shore.

Oh, write no more the tale of Troy,
    If Earth Death's scroll must be!
Nor mix with Laian rage the joy
    Which dawns upon the free:
Although a subtler Sphinx renew
Riddles of death Thebes never knew.°

Another Athens shall arise,
    And to remoter time
Bequeath, like sunset to the skies,
    The splendour of its prime;
And leave, if nought so bright may lie,
All earth can take or Heaven can give.

Saturn and Love their long repose
    Shall burst, more bright and good
Than all who fell, than One who rose,
    Than many unsubdued:
Not gold, not blood, their altar dowers,
But votive tears and symbol flowers.

Oh, cease! Must hate and death return?
    Cease! Must men kill and die?
Cease! drain not to its dregs the urn
    Of bitter prophecy.
The world is weary of the past,
Oh, might it die, or rest at last!

10

15

20

25

30

35

40

---

9 *Peneus:* a river god. The classical references that follow all point to a renewal of the powers of figures from the mythical age of the gods.   24 *Sphinx . . . Thebes:* refers to Oedipus's power to guess the Sphinx's riddle; see Chapter 30, *Oedipus Rex.*

John Keats (1795–1821)

ODE ON A GRECIAN URN

Thou still unravish'd bride of quietness,
    Thou foster-child of silence and slow time,

Sylvan° historian, who canst thus express
   A flowery tale more sweetly than our rhyme:
What leaf-fring'd legend haunts about thy shape
    Of deities or mortals, or of both,
      In Tempe° or the dales of Arcady?°   5
What men or gods are these? What maidens loth?
   What mad pursuit? What struggle to escape?
     What pipes and timbrels? What wild ecstasy?   10

Heard melodies are sweet, but those unheard
   Are sweeter; therefore, ye soft pipes, play on;
Not to the sensual ear, but, more endear'd,
   Pipe to the spirit ditties of no tone:
Fair youth, beneath the trees, thou canst not leave   15
   Thy song, nor ever can those trees be bare;
    Bold Lover, never, never canst thou kiss
Though winning near the goal—yet, do not grieve;
   She cannot fade, though thou hast not thy bliss,
     For ever wilt thou love, and she be fair!   20

Ah, happy, happy boughs! that cannot shed
   Your leaves, nor ever bid the Spring adieu;
And, happy melodist, unwearied,
   For ever piping songs for ever new;

More happy love! more happy, happy love!   25
   For ever warm and still to be enjoy'd,
    For ever panting, and for ever young;
All breathing human passion far above,
   That leaves a heart high-sorrowful and cloy'd,
    A burning forehead, and a parching tongue.   30

Who are these coming to the sacrifice?
   To what green altar, O mysterious priest,
Lead'st thou that heifer lowing at the skies,
   And all her silken flanks with garlands dressed?
What little town by river or sea shore,   35
   Or mountain-built with peaceful citadel,
    Is emptied of this folk, this pious morn?
And, little town, thy streets for evermore
   Will silent be; and not a soul to tell
    Why thou art desolate, can e'er return.   40

O Attic° shape! Fair attitude! with brede°
   Of marble men and maidens overwrought

ODE ON A GRECIAN URN. 3 *Sylvan:* rustic, the urn carries a pastoral scene.   7 *Tempe; Arcady:* valleys in Greece.   41 *Attic:* characteristic of ancient Attica, or Athens; *brede:* design.

With forest branches and the trodden weed;
   Thou, silent form, dost tease us out of thought
As doth eternity: Cold Pastoral!   45
   When old age shall this generation waste,
      Thou shalt remain, in midst of other woe
Than ours, a friend to man, to whom thou say'st,
   "Beauty is truth, truth beauty,"—that is all
      Ye know on earth, and all ye need to know.   50

TO AUTUMN

Season of mists and mellow fruitfulness,
   Close bosom-friend of the maturing sun;
Conspiring with him how to load and bless
   With fruit the vines that round the thatch-eaves run;
To bend with apples the moss'd cottage-trees,   5
   And fill all fruit with ripeness to the core;
      To swell the gourd, and plump the hazel shells
With a sweet kernel; to set budding more,
   And still more, later flowers for the bees,
      Until they think warm days will never cease,   10
      For Summer has o'er-brimmed their clammy cells.

Who hath not seen thee oft amid thy store?
   Sometimes whoever seeks abroad may find
Thee sitting careless on a granary floor,
   Thy hair soft-lifted by the winnowing wind;   15
Or on a half-reap'd furrow sound asleep,
   Drows'd with the fume of poppies, while thy hook
      Spares the next swath and all its twined flowers:
And sometimes like a gleaner thou does keep
   Steady thy laden head across a brook;   20
   Or by a cider-press, with patient look,
      Thou watchest the last oozings hours by hours.

Where are the songs of Spring? Ay, where are they?
   Think not of them, thou hast thy music too,—
While barred clouds bloom the soft-dying day,   25
   And touch the stubble-plains with rosy hue;
Then in a wailful choir the small gnats mourn
   Among the river sallows, borne aloft
      Or sinking as the light wind lives or dies;
And full-grown lambs loud bleat from hilly bourn;   30
   Hedge-crickets sing; and now with treble soft

The red-breast whistles from a garden-croft°;
  And gathering swallows twitter in the skies.

TO AUTUMN. 32 *garden-croft:* small enclosed field.

Elizabeth Barrett Browning (1806–1861)

HOW DO I LOVE THEE?

How do I love thee? Let me count the ways.
I love thee to the depth and breadth and height
My soul can reach, when feeling out of sight
For the ends of being and ideal grace.
I love thee to the level of every day's   5
Most quiet need, by sun and candle-light.

I love thee freely, as men strive for right.
I love thee purely, as they turn from praise.
I love thee with the passion put to use
In my old griefs, and with my childhood's faith.   10
I love thee with a love I seemed to lose
With my lost saints. I love thee with the breath,
Smiles, tears, of all my life; and, if God choose,
I shall but love thee better after death.

                        [1850]

GRIEF

I tell you, hopeless grief is passionless;
  That only men incredulous of despair,
  Half-taught in anguish, through the midnight air
Beat upward to God's throne in loud access
Of shrieking and reproach. Full desertness   5

  In souls, as countries, lieth silent-bare
  Under the blanching, vertical eye-glare
Of the absolute Heavens. Deep-hearted man, express
Grief for the Dead in silence like to death:
  Most like a monumental statue set   10
In everlasting watch and moveless woe
Till itself crumble to the dust beneath.
  Touch it: the marble eyelids are not wet—
If it could weep, it could arise and go.

Grief   **821**

Edgar Allan Poe (1809–1849)

TO HELEN

Helen, thy beauty is to me
  Like those Nicèan° barks of yore
That gently, o'er a perfumed sea,
  The weary way-worn wanderer bore
  To his own native shore.   5

On desperate seas long wont to roam,
  Thy hyacinth° hair, thy classic face,
Thy Naiad° airs have brought me home
  To the glory that was Greece
And the grandeur that was Rome.   10

Lo, in yon brilliant window-niche
  How statue-like I see thee stand,
The agate lamp within thy hand,
Ah! Psyche,° from the regions which
  Are holy land!   15

TO HELEN. 2 *Nicèan:* of Nicèa in Asia Minor. 7 *hyacinth:* curled, referring to Hyacinthus, a youth loved by the god Apollo. 8 *Naiad:* water nymph. 14 *Psyche:* personification of soul in Greek mythology.

ANNABEL LEE

It was many and many a year ago,
  In a kingdom by the sea,
That a maiden there lived whom you may know
  By the name of Annabel Lee;—
And this maiden she lived with no other thought   5
  Than to love and be loved by me.

I was a child and she was a child,
  In this kingdom by the sea,
But we loved with a love that was more than love—
  I and my Annabel Lee—   10
With a love that the wingèd seraphs° of Heaven   *angels*
  Coveted her and me.

And this was the reason that, long ago,
  In this kingdom by the sea,
A wind blew out of a cloud by night   15
  Chilling my Annabel Lee;
So that her highborn kinsman came
  And bore her away from me,

To shut her up in a sepulcher°   *tomb*
   In this kingdom by the sea.   20

The angels, not half so happy in heaven,
   Went envying her and me:—
Yes! that was the reason (as all men know,
   In this kingdom by the sea)
That the wind came out of the clouds, chilling   25
   And killing my Annabel Lee.

But our love it was stronger by far than the love
   Of those who were older than we—
   Of many far wiser than we—
And neither the angels in heaven above   30
   Nor the demons down under the sea
Can ever dissever my soul from the soul
   Of the beautiful Annabel Lee:—

For the moon never beams without bringing me dreams
   Of the beautiful Annabel Lee;   35
And the stars never rise but I feel the bright eyes
   Of the beautiful Annabel Lee;
And so, all the night-tide, I lie down by the side
Of my darling, my darling, my life and my bride,
   In her sepulcher there by the sea,   40
   In her tomb by the side of the sea.

Robert Browning (1812–1889)

PARTING AT MORNING

Round the cape of a sudden came the sea,
And the sun looked over the mountain's rim:
And straight was a path of gold for him,
And the need of a world of men for me.

Emily Brontë (1818–1848)

LOVE AND FRIENDSHIP

Love is like the wild rose-briar,
Friendship like the holly-tree—
The holly is dark when the rose-briar blooms
But which will bloom most constantly?

The wild rose-briar is sweet in spring,
Its summer blossoms scent the air;
Yet wait till winter comes again
And who will call the wild-briar fair?

Then scorn the silly rose-wreath now
And deck thee with the holly's sheen,
That when December blights thy brow
He still may leave thy garland green.

Walt Whitman (1819–1892)

CROSSING BROOKLYN FERRY

1. Flood-tide below me! I see you face to face!
   Clouds of the west—sun there half an hour high—I see you also
       face to face.
   Crowds of men and women attired in the usual costumes,
       how curious you are to me!
   On the ferry-boats the hundreds and hundreds that cross, returning
       home, are more curious to me than you suppose,
   And you that shall cross from shore to shore years hence are
       more to me, and more in my meditations,
       than you might suppose.

2. The impalpable sustenance of me from all things at all
       hours of the day,
   The simple, compact, well-join'd scheme, myself disintegrated,
       every one disintegrated yet part of the scheme,
   The similitudes of the past and those of the future,
   The glories strung like beads on my smallest sights and hearings,
       on the walk in the street and the passage over the river
   The current rushing so swiftly and swimming with me far away,
   The others that are to follow me, the ties between me and them,
   The certainty of others, the life, love, sight, hearing of others.

   Others will enter the gates of the ferry and cross from shore to shore,
   Others will watch the run of the flood-tide,
   Others will see the shipping of Manhattan north and west,
       and the heights of Brooklyn to the south and east,
   Others will see the islands large and small;
   Fifty years hence, others will see them as they cross, the sun
       half an hour high,
   A hundred years hence, or ever so many hundred years hence,
       others will see them,
   Will enjoy the sunset, the pouring-in of the flood-tide,
       the falling-back to the sea of the ebb-tide.

3. It avails not, time nor place—distance avails not,   20
    I am with you, you men and women of a generation,
        or ever so many generations hence,
    Just as you feel when you look on the river and sky, so I felt,
    Just as any of you is one of a living crowd, I was one of a crowd,
    Just as you are refresh'd by the gladness of the river and the bright
        flow, I was refresh'd,
    Just as you stand and lean on the rail, yet hurry with the swift current,
        I stood yet was hurried,   25
    Just as you look on the numberless masts of ships
        and the thick-stemm'd pipes of steamboats, I look'd.

    I too many and many a time cross'd the river of old,
    Watched the Twelfth-month sea-gulls, saw them high in the air
        floating with motionless wings, oscillating their bodies,
    Saw how the glistening yellow lit up parts of their bodies
        and left the rest in strong shadow,
    Saw the slow-wheeling circles and the gradual edging
        toward the south,   30
    Saw the reflection of the summer sky in the water,
    Had my eyes dazzled by the shimmering track of beams,
    Look'd at the find centrifugal spokes of light round the shape
        of my head in the sunlit water,
    Look'd on the haze on the hills southward and south-westward,
    Look'd on the vapor as it flew in fleeces tinged with violet,   35
    Look'd toward the lower bay to notice the vessels arriving,
    Saw their approach, saw aboard those that were near me,
    Saw the white sails of schooners and sloops, saw the ships at anchor,
    The sailors at work in the rigging or out astride the spars,
    The round masts, the swinging motion of the hulls,
        the slender serpentine pennants,   40
    The large and small steamers in motion, the pilots in their
        pilot-houses,
    The white wake left by the passage, the quick tremulous whirl
        of the wheel,
    The flags of all nations, the falling of them at sunset,
    The scallop-edged waves in the twilight, the ladled cups,
        the frolicsome crests and glistening,
    The stretch afar growing dimmer and dimmer,
        the gray walls of the granite storehouses by the docks,   45
    On the river the shadowy group, the big steam-tug closely flank'd
        on each side by the barges, the hay-boat, the belated lighter,
    On the neighboring shore the fires from the foundry chimneys
        burning high and glaringly into the night,
    Casting their flicker of black contrasted with wild red and yellow
        light over the tops of houses, and down into the clefts
        of streets.

4. These and all else were to me the same as they are to you,
    I loved well those cities, loved well the stately and rapid river,   50

The men and women I saw were all near to me,
Others the same—others who look back on me
    because I look'd forward to them,
(The time will come, though I stop here to-day and to-night.)

5. What is it then between us?
    What is the count of the scores or hundreds of years between us?   55

    Whatever it is, it avails not—distance avails not, and place avails not,
    I too lived, Brooklyn of ample hills was mine,
    I too walk'd the streets of Manhattan island,
        and bathed in the waters around it,
    I too felt the curious abrupt questionings stir within me,
    In the day among crowds of people sometimes they came upon me,   60
    In my walks home late at night or as I lay in my bed they came
        upon me,
    I too had been struck from the float forever held in solution,
    I too had receiv'd identity by my body,
    That I was I knew was of my body, and what I should be
        I knew I should be of my body.

6. It is not upon you alone the dark patches fall,   65
    The dark threw its patches down upon me also,
    The best I had done seem'd to me blank and suspicious,
    My great thoughts as I supposed them, were they not
        in reality meagre?
    Nor is it you alone who know what it is to be evil,
    I am he who knew what it was to be evil,   70
    I too knitted the old knot of contrariety,
    Blabb'd, blush'd, resented, lied, stole, grudg'd,
    Had guile, anger, lust, hot wishes I dared not speak,
    Was wayward, vain, greedy, shallow, sly, cowardly, malignant,
    The wolf, the snake, the hog, not wanting in me,   75
    The cheating look, the frivolous word, the adulterous wish,
        not wanting,
    Refusals, hates, postponements, meanness, laziness, none
        of these wanting,
    Was one with the rest, the days and haps of the rest,
    Was call'd by my nighest name by clear loud voices of young men
        as they saw me approaching or passing,
    Felt their arms on my neck as I stood, or the negligent leaning
        of their flesh against me as I sat,   80
    Saw many I loved in the street or ferry-boat or public assembly,
        yet never told them a word,
    Lived the same life with the rest, the same old laughing, gnawing,
        sleeping,
    Play'd the part that still looks back on the actor or actress,
    The same old role, the role that is what we make it, as great
        as we like,   85
    Or as small as we like, or both great and small.

7. Closer yet I approach you,
    What thought you have of me now, I had as much of you—
        I laid my stores in advance,
    I consider'd long and seriously of you before you were born.

    Who was to know what should come home to me?
    Who knows but I am enjoying this?   90
    Who knows, for all the distance, but I am as good as looking at you
        now, for all you cannot see me?

8. Ah, what can ever be more stately and admirable to me
        than mast-hemm'd Manhattan?
    River and sunset and scallop-edg'd waves of flood-tide?
    The sea-gulls oscillating their bodies, the hay-boat in the twilight,
        and the belated lighter?
    What gods can exceed these that clasp me by the hand, and with
        voices I love call me promptly and loudly by my nighest name
        as I approach?   95
    What is more subtle than this which ties me to the woman or man
        that looks in my face?
    Which fuses me into you now, and pours my meaning into you?

    We understand then do we not?
    What I promis'd without mentioning it, have you not accepted?
    What the study could not teach—what the preaching could not   100
        accomplish is accomplish'd, is it not?

9. Flow on, river! flow with the flood-tide, and ebb with the ebb-tide!
    Frolic on, crested and scallop-edg'd waves!
    Gorgeous clouds of the sunset! drench with your splendor me,
        or the men and women generations after me!
    Cross from shore to shore, countless crowds of passengers!
    Stand up, tall masts of Manhattan! stand up, beautiful hills   105
        of Brooklyn!
    Throb, baffled and curious brain! throw out questions and answers!
    Suspend here and everywhere, eternal float of solution!
    Gaze, loving and thirsting eyes, in the house or street or public
        assembly!
    Sound out, voices of young men! loudly and musically call me
        by my nighest name!   110
    Live, old life! play the part that looks back on the actor or actress!
    Play the old role, the role that is great or small according as one
        makes it!
    Consider, you who peruse me, whether I may not in unknown ways
        be looking upon you;
    Be firm, rail over the river, to support those who lean idly,
        yet haste with the hasting current;
    Fly on, sea-birds! fly sideways, or wheel in large circles high in the air;

Receive the summer sky, you water, and faithfully hold it   115
    till all downcast eyes have time to take it from you!
Diverge, fine spokes of light, from the shape of my head,
    or any one's head, in the sunlit water!
Come on, ships from the lower bay! pass up or down,
    white-sail'd schooners, sloops, lighters!
Flaunt away, flags of all nations! be duly lower'd at sunset!
Burn high your fires, foundry chimneys! cast black shadows
    at nightfall! cast red and yellow light over the tops of the houses!
Appearances, now or henceforth, indicate what you are,   120
You necessary film, continue to envelop the soul,
About my body for me, and your body for you, be hung our divinest
    aromas,
Thrive, cities—bring your freight, bring your shows, ample and
    sufficient rivers,
Expand, being than which none else is perhaps more spiritual,
Keep your places, objects than which none else is more lasting.   125

You have waited, you will always wait, you dumb, beautiful ministers.
We receive you with free sense at last, and are insatiate henceforward.
Not you any more shall be able to foil us, or withhold yourselves
    from us,
We use you and do not cast you aside—we plant you permanently
    within us,
We fathom you not—we love you—there is perfection in you also,   130
You furnish your parts toward eternity,
Great or small, your furnish your parts toward the soul.

Emily Dickinson (1830–1886)

A NARROW FELLOW IN THE GRASS

A narrow Fellow in the Grass
Occasionally rides—
You may have met Him—did you not
His notice sudden is—

The Grass divides as with a Comb—
A spotted shaft is seen—   5
And then it closes at your feet
And opens further on—

He likes a Boggy Acre
A Floor too cool for Corn—
Yet when a Boy, and Barefoot—   10
I more than once at Noon
Have passed, I thought, a Whip lash

Unbraiding in the Sun,
When, stooping to secure it,   15
It wrinkled, and was gone—

Several of Nature's People
I know, and they know me—
I feel for them a transport
Of cordiality—   20

But never met this Fellow,
Attended or alone,
Without a tighter breathing,
And Zero at the Bone—

BECAUSE I COULD NOT STOP FOR DEATH

Because I could not stop for Death—
He kindly stopped for me—
The carriage held but just Ourselves—
And Immortality.

We slowly drove—He knew no haste   5
And I had put away
My labor and my leisure too,
For His Civility—

We passed the School, where Children strove
At Recess—in the Ring—
We passed the Fields of Gazing Grain—   10
We passed the Setting Sun—

Or rather—He passed Us—
The Dews drew quivering and chill—
For only Gossamer, my Gown—   15
My Tippet—only Tulle—

We paused before a House that seemed
A Swelling of the Ground—
The Roof was scarcely visible—
The Cornice—in the Ground—   20

Since then—'tis Centuries—and yet
Feels shorter than the Day
I first surmised the Horses' Heads
Were toward Eternity—

I HEARD A FLY BUZZ WHEN I DIED

I heard a Fly buzz—when I died—
The Stillness in the Room
Was like the Stillness in the Air—
Between the Heaves of Storm—

The Eyes around—had wrung them dry—   5
And Breaths were gathering firm
For that last Onset—when the King
Be witnessed—in the Room—

I willed my Keepsakes—Signed away
What portion of me be   10
Assignable—and then it was
There interposed a Fly—

With Blue—uncertain, stumbling Buzz—
Between the light—and me—
And then the Windows failed—and then   15
I could not see to see—

THE LIGHTNING IS A YELLOW FORK

The Lightning is a yellow Fork
From Tables in the sky
By inadvertent fingers dropt
The awful Cutlery

Of mansions never quite disclosed   5
And never quite concealed
The Apparatus of the Dark
To ignorance revealed.

THE SOUL SELECTS HER OWN SOCIETY

The Soul selects her own Society—
Then—shuts the Door—
To her divine Majority—
Present no more—

Unmoved—she notes the Chariots—pausing—   5
At her low Gate—

Unmoved—an Emperor be kneeling
Upon her Mat—

I've known her—from an ample nation—
Choose One—   10
Then—close the Valves of her attention—
Like Stone—

WILD NIGHTS—WILD NIGHTS!

Wild Nights—Wild Nights!
Were I with thee
Wild Nights should be
Our luxury!

Futile—the Winds—   5
To a Heart in port—
Done with the Compass—
Done with the Chart!

Rowing in Eden—
Ah, in Sea!   10
Might I but moor—Tonight—
In Thee!

Thomas Hardy (1840–1928)

THE CONVERGENCE OF THE TWAIN

(Lines on the Loss of the "Titanic")

I

In a solitude of the sea
Deep from human vanity,
And the Pride of Life that planned her, stilly couches she.

II

Steel chambers, late the pyres
Of her salamandrine° fires,   5
Cold currents thrid,° and turn to rhythmic tidal lyres.

THE CONVERGENCE OF THE TWAIN. 5 *salamandrine:* the salamander was said to be able to live in fire.
6 *thrid:* thread.

III

Over the mirrors meant
To glass the opulent
The sea-worm crawls—grotesque, slimed, dumb, indifferent.

IV

Jewels in joy designed
To ravish the sensuous mind
Lie lightless, all their sparkles bleared and black and blind.

V

Dim moon-eyed fishes near
Gaze at the gilded gear
And query: "What does this vaingloriousness down here?"

VI

Well: while was fashioning
This creature of cleaving wing,
The Immanent° Will that stirs and urges everything

VII

Prepared a sinister mate
For her—so gaily great—
A Shape of Ice, for the time far and dissociate.

VIII

And as the smart ship grew
In stature, grace, and hue,
In shadowy silent distance grew the Iceberg too.

IX

Alien they seemed to be;
No mortal eye could see
The intimate welding of their later history,

X

Or sign that they were bent
By paths coincident
On being anon twin halves of one august event,

XI

Till the Spinner of the Years
Said "Now!" And each one hears,
And consummation comes, and jars two hemispheres.

---

18 *Immanent:* in-dwelling.

AFTERWARDS

When the Present has latched its postern° behind my tremulous stay,
   And the May month flaps its glad green leaves like wings,
Delicate-filmed as new-spun silk, will the neighbours say,
   "He was a man who used to notice such things"?

If it be in the dusk when, like an eyelid's soundless blink,   5
   The dewfall-hawk comes crossing the shades to alight
Upon the wind-warped upland thorn, a gazer may think,
   "To him this must have been a familiar sight."

If I pass during some nocturnal blackness, mothy, and warm,
   When the hedgehog travels furtively over the lawn,   10
One may say, "He strove that such innocent creatures should come to no harm,
   But he could do little for them; and now he is gone."

If, when hearing that I have been stilled at last, they stand at the door,
   Watching the full-starred heavens that winter sees,
Will this thought rise on those who will meet my face no more,   15
   "He was one who had an eye for such mysteries"?

And will any say when my bell of quittance° is heard in the gloom
   And a crossing breeze cuts a pause in its outrollings,
Till they rise again, as they were a new bell's boom,
   "He hears it not now, but used to notice such things"?   20

AFTERWARDS. 1 *postern:* gate.   17 *bell of quittance:* death bell.

Gerard Manley Hopkins (1844–1889)

GOD'S GRANDEUR

The world is charged with the grandeur of God.
   It will flame out, like shining from shook foil;
   It gathers to a greatness, like the ooze of oil
Crushed. Why do men then now not reck° his rod?
Generations have trod, have trod, have trod;   5
   And all is seared with trade; bleared, smeared with toil;
   And wears man's smudge and shares man's smell: the soil
Is bare now, nor can foot feel, being shod.

GOD'S GRANDEUR. 4 *reck:* consider.

And for all this, nature is never spent;
   There lives the dearest freshness deep down things;
And though the last lights off the black West went
   Oh, morning, at the brown brink eastward, springs—
Because the Holy Ghost over the bent
   World broods with warm breast and with ah! bright wings.

THE WINDHOVER°

To Christ Our Lord

I caught this morning morning's minion,° king-
    dom of daylight's dauphin, dapple-dawn-drawn Falcon, in his riding
    Of the rolling level underneath him steady air, and striding
High there, how he rung upon the rein° of a wimpling wing
In his ecstasy! then off, off forth on swing,
    As a skate's heel sweeps smooth on a bow-bend: the hurl and gliding
    Rebuffed the big wind. My heart in hiding
Stirred for a bird,—the achieve of, the mastery of the thing!

Brute beauty and valor and act, oh, air, pride, plume, here
    Buckle! AND the fire that breaks from thee then, a billion
Times told lovelier, more dangerous, O my chevalier!
    No wonder of it: shéer plód makes plow down sillion°
Shine, and blue-bleak embers, ah my dear,
    Fall, gall themselves, and gash gold-vermilion.

THE WINDHOVER. A kind of falcon whose shape in flight resembles a cross. 1 *minion*: favorite. 4 *rung upon the rein*: pivoted in a circle, guided as if by a rein. 12 *sillion*: ridge between plowed furrows.

Arthur Rimbaud (1854–1891)

YOUTH

from *Illuminations*

I. *Sunday*

When homework is done, the inevitable descent from heaven and the visitation of memories, and the session of rhythms invade the dwelling, the head and the world of the spirit.

   —A horse scampers off along the suburban turf and the gardens and the wood lots, besieged by the carbonic plague. Somewhere in the world, a wretched melodramatic woman is sighing for unlikely desertions. Desperadoes are languishing for storms, drunkenness, wounds. Little children are stifling curses along the rivers.

I must study some more to the sound of the consuming work which forms in all the people and rises up in them.

II. *Sonnet*

Man of usual constitution, wasn't the flesh a fruit hanging in the orchard?—O child-hood days!—wasn't the body a treasure to spend?—wasn't love the peril or the strength of Psyche?° The earth had slopes fertile in princes and artists, and your descendants and your race drove you to crime and mourning: the world, your fortune and your peril. But now that this work is done, you and your calculations, you and your impatience, are only your dance and your voice, not fixed and not forced, although they are the reason for a double event made up of invention and success, in brotherly and discreet humanity throughout the universe without pictures. Force and right reflect the dance and the voice which are only now appreciated . . .

III. *Twenty years Old*

The exiled voices teach . . . Physical candor bitterly put in its place . . . Adagio.° Oh! infinite egoism of adolescence, and studious optimism. How full of flowers was the world that summer! Melodies and forms dying . . . A choir, to pacify impotence and absence! A choir of glasses, of night tunes . . . Yes, and one's nerves go out quickly to hunt.

IV

You are still at the stage of the temptation of St. Anthony. The struggle with diminished zeal, grimacings of a child's insolence, collapse and fright. But you will begin this work. All the possibilities of harmony and architecture will rise up around your seat. Perfect and unpredictable beings will offer themselves for your experiments. Around you the curiosity of ancient crowds and idle luxuries will move in dreamily. Your memory and your senses will only serve to feed your creative urge. What will happen to the world when you leave it? Nothing, in any case, will remain of what is now visible.

YOUTH. *II. Psyche:* soul.   *III. Adagio:* slow, sad musical movement.

A. E. Housman (1859–1936)

TERENCE, THIS IS STUPID STUFF°

"Terence, this is stupid stuff;
You eat your victuals fast enough;
There can't be much amiss, 'tis clear,
To see the rate you drink your beer.

TERENCE, THIS IS STUPID STUFF. Terence, an early Roman author of classical, Greek-inspired verse comedy (see Chapter 32), was frequently assigned for translation by English schoolboys.

But oh, good Lord, the verse you make,   5
It gives a chap the belly-ache.
The cow, the old cow, she is dead;
It sleeps well, the horned head:
We poor lads, 'tis our turn now
To hear such tunes as killed the cow.   10
Pretty friendship 'tis to rhyme
Your friends to death before their time
Moping melancholy mad:
Come, pipe a tune to dance to, lad."

Why, if 'tis dancing you would be,   15
There's brisker pipes than poetry.
Say, for what were hop-yards° meant,
Or why was Burton built on Trent?
Oh, many a peer of England brews
Livelier liquor than the Muse,   20
And malt does more than Milton can
To justify God's ways to man.
Ale, man, ale's the stuff to drink
For fellows whom it hurts to think:
Look into the pewter pot   25
To see the world as the world's not.
And faith, 'tis pleasant till 'tis past:
The mischief is that 'twill not last.
Oh, I have been to Ludlow fair
And left my necktie God knows where,   30
And carried half way home, or near,
Pints and quarts of Ludlow beer:
Then the world seemed none so bad,
And I myself a sterling lad;
And down in lovely muck I've lain,   35
Happy til I woke again.
Then I saw the morning sky:
Heigho, the tale was all a lie;
The world, it was the old world yet,
I was I, my things were wet,   40
And nothing now remained to do
But begin the game anew.

Therefore, since the world has still
Much good, but much less good than ill,
And while the sun and moon endure   45
Luck's a chance, but trouble's sure,
I'd face it as a wise man would,
And train for ill and not for good.
'Tis true, the stuff I bring for sale

---

17 *hop-yards:* where hops are produced for flavoring ale or beer.

Is not so brisk a brew as ale:
Out of a stem that scored the hand
I wrung it in a weary land.
But take it: if the smack° is sour,   50
The better for the embittered hour;
It should do good to heart and head   55
When your soul is in my soul's stead;
And I will friend you, if I may,
In the dark and cloudy day.

There was a king reigned in the East:
There, when kings will sit to feast,   60
They get their fill before they think
With poisoned meat and poisoned drink.
He gathered all that springs to birth
From the many-venomed earth;
First a little, thence to more,   65
He sampled all her killing store;
And easy, smiling, seasoned sound,
Sate the king when healths went round.
They put arsenic in his meat
And stared aghast to watch him eat;   70
They poured strychnine in his cup
And shook to see him drink it up;
They shook, they stared as white's their shirt:
Them it was their poison hurt.
—I tell the tale that I heard told.   75
Mithridates,° he died old.

---

53 *smack*: taste.   76 *Mithridates*: legendary long-lived king.

W. B. Yeats (1865–1939)

TO A FRIEND WHOSE WORK HAS COME TO NOTHING

Now all the truth is out,
Be secret and take defeat
From any brazen throat,
For how can you compete,
Being honour bred, with one   5
Who, were it proved he lies,
Were neither shamed in his own
Nor in his neighbours' eyes?
Bred to a harder thing

Than Triumph, turn away
And like a laughing string
Whereon mad fingers play
Amid a place of stone,
Be secret and exult,
Because of all things known
That is most difficult.

AN IRISH AIRMAN FORSEES HIS DEATH

I know that I shall meet my fate
Somewhere among the clouds above;
Those that I fight I do not hate,°
Those that I guard I do not love;
My country is Kiltartan Cross,
My countrymen Kiltartan's poor,
No likely end could bring them loss
Or leave them happier than before.
Nor law, nor duty bade me fight,
Nor public men, nor cheering crowds,
A lonely impulse of delight
Drove to this tumult in the clouds;
I balanced all, brought all to mind,
The years to come seemed waste of breath,
A waste of breath the years behind
In balance with this life, this death.

AN IRISH AIRMAN FORESEES HIS DEATH. 3 *do not hate:* The Irish, rebelling against Britain during
World War I, were reluctant combatants in the British war against Germany.

THE FISHERMAN

Although I can see him still,
The freckled man who goes
To a grey place on a hill
In grey Connemara° clothes
At dawn to cast his flies,
It's long since I began
To call up to the eyes
This wise and simple man.
All day I'd looked in the face

THE FISHERMAN 4 *Connemara:* Hilly highland country of western Ireland.

What I had hoped 'twould be
To write for my own race
And the reality;
The living men that I hate,
The dead man that I loved,
The craven man in his seat,
The insolent unreproved,
And no knave brought to book
Who has won a drunken cheer,
The witty man and his joke
Aimed at the commonest ear,
The clever man who cries
The catch-cries of the clown,
The beating down of the wise
And great Art beaten down.

Maybe a twelvemonth since
Suddenly I began,
In scorn of this audience,
Imagining a man,
And his sun-freckled face,
And grey Connemara cloth,
Climbing up to a place
Where stone is dark under froth,
And the down-turn of his wrist
When the flies drop in the stream;
A man who does not exist,
A man who is but a dream;
And cried, 'Before I am old
I shall have written him one
Poem maybe as cold
And passionate as the dawn.'

THE SECOND COMING

Turning and turning in the widening gyre°
The falcon cannot hear the falconer;
Things fall apart; the center cannot hold;
Mere anarchy is loosed upon the world,
The blood-dimmed tide is loosed, and everywhere
The ceremony of innocence is drowned;
The best lack all conviction, while the worst
Are full of passionate intensity.

THE SECOND COMING. 1 *gyre:* spiral.

Surely some revelation is at hand;
Surely the Second Coming is at hand;   10
The Second Coming! Hardly are those words out
When a vast image out of *Spiritus Mundi*°
Troubles my sight: somewhere in sands of the desert
A shape with lion body and the head of a man,
A gaze blank and pitiless as the sun,   15
Is moving its slow thighs, while all about it
Reel shadows of the indignant desert birds.
The darkness drops again; but now I know
That twenty centuries of stony sleep
Were vexed to nightmare by a rocking cradle,   20
And what rough beast, its hour come round at last,
Slouches towards Bethlehem° to be born?

---

12 *Spiritus Mundi:* collective "world spirit." 22 *Bethlehem:* Christ's birthplace.

EASTER, 1916°

I have met them at close of day
Coming with vivid faces
From counter or desk among grey
Eighteenth-century houses.
I have passed with a nod of the head   5
Or polite meaningless words,
Or have lingered awhile and said
Polite meaningless words,
And thought before I had done
Of a mocking tale or a gibe   10
To please a companion
Around the fire at the club,
Being certain that they and I
But lived where motley° is worn:
All changed, changed utterly: 15
A terrible beauty is born.

That woman's days were spent
In ignorant good-will,
Her nights in argument
Until her voice grew shrill.   20
What voice more sweet than hers
When, young and beautiful,
She rode to harriers?

EASTER, 1916. Yeats is writing about the 1916 uprising of Irish nationalists against the British.
14 *motley:* many-colored cloth; Yeats refers to tolerance for diverse opinions and allegiances.

         An Anthology of Poetry

This man had kept a school
And rode our wingèd horse;
This other his helper and friend
Was coming into his force;
He might have won fame in the end,
So sensitive his nature seemed,
So daring and sweet his thought.
This other man I had dreamed
A drunken, vainglorious lout.
He had done most bitter wrong
To some who are near my heart,
Yet I number him in the song;
He, too, has resigned his part
In the casual comedy;
He, too, has been changed in his turn,
Transformed utterly:
A terrible beauty is born.

Hearts with one purpose alone
Through summer and winter seem
Enchanted to a stone
To trouble the living stream.
The horse that comes from the road,
The rider, the birds that range
From cloud to tumbling cloud,
Minute by minute they change;
A shadow of cloud on the stream
Changes minute by minute;
A horse-hoof slides on the brim,
And a horse plashes within it;
The long-legged moor-hens dive,
And hens to moor-cocks call;
Minute by minute they live:
The stone's in the midst of all.

Too long a sacrifice
Can make a stone of the heart.
O when may if suffice?
That is Heaven's part, our part
To murmur name upon name,
As a mother names her child
When sleep at last has come
On limbs that had run wild.
What is it but nightfall?
No, no, not night but death;
Was it needless death after all?
For England may keep faith
For all that is done and said.
We know their dream; enough

25

30

35

40

45

50

55

60

65

70

Easter, 1916

To know they dreamed and are dead;
And what if excess of love
Bewildered them till they died?
I write it out in a verse—
MacDonagh and MacBride   75
And Connolly and Pearse°
Now and in time to be,
Wherever green is worn,
Are changed, changed utterly:
A terrible beauty is born.   80
                   [*September 25, 1916*]

75–76 *MacDonagh . . . Pearse:* heroes of the Irish revolt.

AMONG SCHOOL CHILDREN

I walk through the long schoolroom questioning,
A kind old nun in a white hood replies;
The children learn to cipher and to sing,
To study reading-books and history,
To cut and sew, be neat in everything   5
In the best modern way—the children's eyes
In momentary wonder stare upon
A sixty year old smiling public man.

I dream of a Ledaean° body, bent
Above a sinking fire, a tale that she   10
Told of a harsh reproof, or trivial event
That changed some childish day to tragedy—
Told, and it seemed that our two natures blent
Into a sphere from youthful sympathy,
Or else, to alter Plato's parable,°   15
Into the yolk and white of the one shell.

And thinking of that fit of grief or rage
I look upon one child or t'other there
And wonder if she stood so at that age—
For even daughters of the swan can share   20
Something of every paddler's heritage—
And had that color upon cheek or hair;
And thereupon my heart is driven wild:
She stands before me as a living child.

AMONG SCHOOL CHILDREN. 9 *Ledaean:* refers to Leda, who was raped by Zeus in the guise of a swan (see Yeat's poem "Leda and the Swan," in Chapter 19). 15 *Plato's parable:* refers to Plato's belief, expressed in the *Symposium*, that male and female natures are halves of a former whole.

Her present image floats into the mind—
Did quattrocento° finger fashion it
Hollow of cheek as though it drank the wind
And took a mess of shadows for its meat?
And I though never of Ledaean kind
Had pretty plumage once—enough of that,
Better to smile on all that smile, and show
There is a comfortable kind of old scarecrow.

What youthful mother, a shape upon her lap
Honey of generation had betrayed,
And that must sleep, shriek, struggle to escape
As recollection or the drug decide,
Would think her son, did she but see that shape
With sixty or more winters on its head,
A compensation for the pang of his birth,
Or the uncertainty of his setting forth?

Plato thought nature but a spume that plays
Upon a ghostly paradigm of things;
Solider Aristotle played the taws°
Upon the bottom of a king of kings;°
World-famous golden-thighed Pythagoras°
Fingered upon a fiddle stick or strings
What a star sang and careless Muses heard:
Old clothes upon old sticks to scare a bird.

Both nuns and mothers worship images,
But those the candles light are not as those
That animate a mother's reveries,
But keep a marble or a bronze repose.
And yet they too break hearts—O Presences
That passion, piety or affection knows,
And that all heavenly glory symbolize—
O self-born mockers of man's enterprise;

Labor is blossoming or dancing where
The body is not bruised to pleasure soul,
Nor beauty born out of its own despair,
Nor blear-eyed wisdom out of midnight oil.
O chestnut tree, great rooted blossomer,
Are you the leaf, the blossom or the bole?
O body swayed to music, O brightening glance,
How can we know the dancer from the dance?

25

30

35

40

45

50

55

60

---

26 *quattrocento:* fifteenth century period of Italian Renaissance art.   43 *played the taws:* tanned the hides.   44 *king of kings:* Aristotle was the teacher of Alexander the Great.   45 *Pythagoras:* Greek mathematician who calculated the laws of harmony in nature.

SAILING TO BYZANTIUM°

That is no country for old men. The young
In one another's arms, birds in the trees
—Those dying generations—at their song,
The salmon-falls, the mackerel-crowded seas,
Fish, flesh, or fowl, commend all summer long   5
Whatever is begotten, born, and dies.
Caught in that sensual music all neglect
Monuments of unaging intellect.

An aged man is but a paltry thing,
A tattered coat upon a stick, unless   10
Soul clap its hands and sing, and louder sing
For every tatter in its mortal dress,
Nor is there singing school but studying
Monuments of its own magnificence;
And therefore I have sailed the seas and come   15
To the holy city of Byzantium.

O sages standing in God's holy fire
As in the gold mosaic of a wall,
Come from the holy fire, perne in a gyre,°
And be the singing-masters of my soul.   20
Consume my heart away; sick with desire
And fastened to a dying animal
It knows not what it is; and gather me
Into the artifice of eternity.

Once out of nature I shall never take   25
My bodily form from any natural thing,
But such a form as Grecian goldsmiths make
Of hammered gold and gold enameling
To keep a drowsy Emperor awake;
Or set upon a golden bough to sing   30
To lords and ladies of Byzantium
Of what is past, or passing, or to come.

SAILING TO BYZANTIUM. Byzantium is the ancient capital of the Byzantine Empire and the site of modern Istanbul, Turkey. For Yeats the city was an emblem of the spiritual life.   19 *perne in a gyre:* spin down a spiral.

FOR ANNE GREGORY

"Never shall a young man,
Thrown into despair
By those great honey-coloured

844   An Anthology of Poetry

Ramparts° at your ear,
Love you for yourself alone
And not your yellow hair."   5

"But I can get a hair-dye
And set such colour there,
Brown, or black, or carrot,
That young men in despair   10
May love me for myself alone
And not my yellow hair."

"I heard an old religious man
But yesternight declare
That he had found a text to prove   15
That only God, my dear,
Could love you for yourself alone
And not your yellow hair."

FOR ANNE GREGORY. 4 *ramparts*: literally "fortifications"; figurative for coils of hair.

James Weldon Johnson (1871–1938)

O BLACK AND UNKNOWN BARDS°

O black and unknown bards of long ago,
How came your lips to touch the sacred fire?
How, in your darkness, did you come to know
The power and beauty of the minstrel's lyre?
Who first from midst his bonds lifted his eyes?   5
Who first from out the still watch, lone and long,
Feeling the ancient faith of prophets rise
Within his dark-kept soul, burst into song?

Heart of what slave poured out such melody
As "Steal away to Jesus"? On its strains   10
His spirit must have nightly floated free,
Though still about his hands he felt his chains.
Who heard great "Jordan roll"? Whose starward eye
Saw chariot "swing low"? And who was he
That breathed that comforting, melodic sigh,   15
"Nobody knows de trouble I see"?

What merely living clod, what captive thing,
Could up toward God through all its darkness grope,
And find within its deadened heart to sing

O BLACK AND UNKNOWN BARDS. Johnson addresses the unknown composers of the great spirituals.

These songs of sorrow, love and faith, and hope? 20
How did it catch that subtle undertone,
That note in music heard not with the ears?
How sound the elusive reed so seldom blown,
Which stirs the soul or melts the heart to tears.

Not that great German master in his dream 25
Of harmonies that thundered amongst the stars
At the creation, ever heard a theme
Nobler than "Go down, Moses." Mark its bars
How like a mighty trumpet-call they stir
The blood. Such are the notes that men have sung 30
Going to valorous deeds; such tones there were
That helped make history when Time was young.

There is a wide, wide wonder in it all,
That from degraded rest and servile toil
The fiery spirit of the seer should call 35
These simple children of the sun and soil.
O black slave singers, gone, forgot, unfamed,
You—you alone, of all the long, long line
Of those who've sung untaught, unknown, unnamed,
Have stretched out upward, seeking the divine. 40

You sang not deeds of heroes or of kings;
No chant of bloody war, no exulting paean
Of arms-won triumphs; but your humble strings
You touched in chord with music empyrean.
You sang far better than you knew; the songs 45
That for your listeners' hungry hearts sufficed
Still live,—but more than this to you belongs:
You sang a race from wood and stone to Christ.

Robert Frost (1874–1963)

THE WOOD-PILE

Out walking in the frozen swamp one gray day
I paused and said, "I will turn back from here.
No, I will go on farther—and we shall see."
The hard snow held me, save where now and then
One foot went through. The view was all in lines 5
Straight up and down of tall slim trees
Too much alike to mark or name a place by
So as to say for certain I was here
Or somewhere else: I was just far from home.

A small bird flew before me. He was careful 10
To put a tree between us when he lighted,
And say no word to tell me who he was
Who was so foolish as to think what he thought.
He thought that I was after him for a feather—
The white one in his tail; like one who takes 15
Everything said as personal to himself.
One flight out sideways would have undeceived him.
And then there was a pile of wood for which
I forgot him and let his little fear
Carry him off the way I might have gone, 20
Without so much as wishing him good-night.
He went behind it to make his last stand.
It was a cord of maple, cut and split
And piled—and measured, four by four by eight.
And not another like it could I see. 25
No runner tracks in this year's snow looped near it.
And it was older sure than this year's cutting,
Or even last year's or the year's before.
The wood was gray and the bark warping off it
And the pile somewhat sunken. Clematis°   *a vine* 30
Had wound strings round and round it like a bundle.
What held it though on one side was a tree
Still growing, and on one a stake and prop,
These latter about to fall. I thought that only
Someone who lived in turning to fresh tasks 35
Could so forget his handiwork on which
He spent himself, the labour of his axe,
And leave it there far from a useful fireplace
To warm the frozen swamp as best it could
With the slow smokeless burning of decay. 40

MENDING WALL

Something there is that doesn't love a wall,
That sends the frozen-ground-swell under it,
And spills the upper boulders in the sun;
And makes gaps even two can pass abreast.
The work of hunters is another thing: 5
I have come after them and made repair
Where they have left not one stone on a stone,
But they would have the rabbit out of hiding,
To please the yelping dogs. The gaps I mean,
No one has seen them made or heard them made, 10
But at spring mending-time we find them there.
I let my neighbour know beyond the hill;
And on a day we meet to walk the line

And set the wall between us once again.
We keep the wall between us as we go.
To each the boulders that have fallen to each.
And some are loaves and some so nearly balls
We have to use a spell to make them balance:
"Stay where you are until our backs are turned!"
We wear our fingers rough with handling them.
Oh, just another kind of out-door game,
One on a side. It comes to little more:
There where it is we do not need the wall:
He is all pine and I am apple orchard.
My apple trees will never get across
And eat the cones under his pines, I tell him.
He only says, "Good fences make good neighbours."
Spring is the mischief in me, and I wonder
If I could put a notion in his head:
"Why do they make good neighbours? Isn't it

Where there are cows? But here there are no cows.
Before I built a wall I'd ask to know
What I was walling in or walling out,
And to whom I was like to give offence.
Something there is that doesn't love a wall,
That wants it down." I could say "Elves" to him,
But it's not elves exactly, and I'd rather
He said it for himself. I see him there
Bringing a stone grasped firmly by the top
In each hand, like an old-stone savage armed.
He moves in darkness as it seems to me,
Not of woods only and the shade of trees.
He will not go behind his father's saying,
And he likes having thought of it so well
He says again, "Good fences make good neighbours."

15

20

25

30

35

40

45

STOPPING BY WOODS ON A SNOWY EVENING

Whose woods these are I think I know.
His house is in the village, though;
He will not see me stopping here
To watch his woods fill up with snow.

My little horse must think it queer
To stop without a farmhouse near
Between the woods and frozen lake
The darkest evening of the year.

5

He gives his harness bells a shake
To ask if there is some mistake.
The only other sound's the sweep
Of easy wind and downy flake.
10

The woods are lovely, dark, and deep,
But I have promises to keep,
And miles to go before I sleep,
And miles to go before I sleep.
15

Rainer Maria Rilke (1875–1926)

THE SWAN

This laboring through what is still undone,
as though, legs bound, we hobbled along the way,
is like the awkward walking of the swan.
And dying—to let go, no longer feel
the solid ground we stand on every day—
is like his anxious letting himself fall

into the water, which receives him gently
and which, as though with reverence and joy,
draws back past him in streams on either side;
while, infinitely silent and aware,
in his full majesty and ever more
indifferent, he condescends to glide.
10

AUTUMN DAY

Lord: it is time. The huge summer has gone by.
Now overlap the sundials with your shadows,
and on the meadows let the wind go free.

Command the fruits to swell on tree and vine;
grant them a few more warm transparent days,
urge them on to fulfillment then, and press
the final sweetness into the heavy wine.
5

Whoever has no house now, will never have one.
Whoever is alone will stay alone,
will sit, read, write long letters through the evening,
and wander on the boulevards, up and down,
restlessly, while the dry leaves are blowing.
10

Rilke poems translated by Stephen Mitchell

Kotaro Takamura (1883–1956)

PLUM WINE

The bottle of plum wine made and left by dead Chieko,
dully stagnant with ten years' weight, holds the light,
and in the amber of a wine cup congeals like a jewel-ball.
When alone late at night in the cold time of early spring
please have this, she said.   5
I think of the one who left this after dying.
Being threatened with the anxiety of a broken mind,
with the distressing idea of ruin before long,
Chieko took care of things around her.
Seven years of madness finished with death.   10
The fragrant sweetness of this plum wine found in the kitchen
quietly, quietly, I appreciate.
Even the roar of the world of frenzied angry waves
can hardly violate this moment.
When one wretched life is looked straight at   15
the world just distantly surrounds it.
Now the night wind has stopped.
                    Translated by Edith Marcombe Shiffert and Yuki Sawa

William Carlos Williams (1883–1963)

THE RED WHEELBARROW

so much depends
upon

a red wheel
barrow

glazed with rain   5
water

beside the white
chickens.

Ezra Pound (1885–1972)

SONG OF THE BOWMEN OF SHU

HERE we are, picking the first fern-shoots
And saying: When shall we get back to our country?
Here we are because we have the Ken-nin for our foemen,

We have no comfort because of these Mongols.
We grub the soft fern-shoots,
When anyone says, "Return," the others are full of sorrow. 5
Sorrowful minds, sorrow is strong, we are hungry and thirsty.
Our defence is not yet made sure, no one can let his friend return.
We grub the old fern-stalks.
We say: Will we be let to go back in October? 10
There is no ease in royal affairs, we have no comfort.
Our sorrow is bitter, but we would not return to our country.
What flower has come into blossom?
Whose chariot? The General's.
Horses, his horses even, are tired. They were strong. 15
We have no rest, three battles a month.
By heaven, his horses are tired.
The generals are on them, the soldiers are by them.
The horses are well trained, the generals have ivory
      arrows and quivers ornamented with fish-skin. 20
The enemy is swift, we must be careful.
When we set out, the willows were drooping with spring,
We come back in the snow,
We go slowly, we are hungry and thirsty,
Our mind is full of sorrow, who will know of our grief? 25

                  [By Bunno, reputedly 1100 B.C.]

H. D. (Hilda Doolittle) (1886–1961)

HELEN

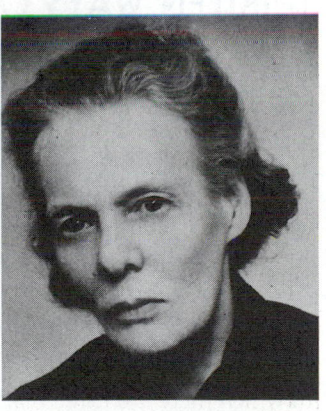

All Greece hates
the still eyes in the white face,
the lustre as of olives
where she stands,
and the white hands.

All Greece reviles
the wan face when she smiles,
hating it deeper still
when it grows wan and white,
remembering past enchantments 10
and past ills.

Greece sees unmoved,
God's daughter, born of love,
the beauty of cool feet
and slenderest knees, 15
could love indeed the maid,
only if she were laid,
white ash amid funereal cypresses.

Helen

Wallace Stevens (1887–1955)

THE EMPEROR OF ICE-CREAM

Call the roller of big cigars,
The muscular one, and bid him whip
In kitchen cups concupiscent° curds.   *lustful*
Let the wenches dawdle in such dress
As they are used to wear, and let the boys   5
Bring flowers in last month's newspapers.
Let be be finale of seem.
The only emperor is the emperor of ice-cream.

Take from the dresser of deal,°   *board*
Lacking the three glass knobs, that sheet   10
On which she embroidered fantails once
And spread it so as to cover her face.
If her bony feet protrude, they come
To show how cold she is, and dumb.
Let the lamp affix its beam.   15
The only emperor is the emperor of ice-cream.

THIRTEEN WAYS OF LOOKING AT A BLACKBIRD

I

Among twenty snowy mountains,
The only moving thing
Was the eye of the blackbird.

II

I was of three minds,
Like a tree   5
In which there are three blackbirds.

III

The blackbird whirled in the autumn winds.
It was a small part of the pantomime.

IV

A man and a woman
Are one.
A man and a woman and a blackbird   10
Are one.

V

I do not know which to prefer,
The beauty of inflections
Or the beauty of innuendoes,
The blackbird whistling
Or just after.

VI

Icicles filled the long window
With barbaric glass.
The shadow of the blackbird
Crossed it, to and fro.
The mood
Traced in the shadow
An indecipherable cause.

VII

O thin men of Haddam,°
Why do you imagine golden birds?
Do you not see how the blackbird
Walks around the feet
Of the women about you?

VIII

I know noble accents
And lucid, inescapable rhythms;
But I know, too,
That the blackbird is involved
In what I know.

IX

When the blackbird flew out of sight,
It marked the edge
Of one of many circles.

X

At the sight of blackbirds
Flying in a green light,
Even the bawds of euphony
Would cry out sharply.

15

20

25

30

35

40

THIRTEEN WAYS OF LOOKING AT A BLACKBIRD. 25 *Haddam:* suburban town in Connecticut, near Stevens's home.

He rode over Connecticut
In a glass coach.
Once, a fear pierced him,
In that he mistook   45
The shadow of his equipage
For blackbirds.

XII

The river is moving.
The blackbird must be flying.

XIII

It was evening all afternoon.   50
It was snowing
And it was going to snow.
The blackbird sat
In the cedar-limbs.

Marianne Moore (1887–1972)

THE STEEPLE-JACK

Dürer° would have seen a reason for living
        in a town like this, with eight stranded whales
to look at; with the sweet sea air coming into your house
on a fine day, from water etched
        with waves as formal as the scales   5
on a fish.

One by one in two's and three's, the seagulls keep
        flying back and forth over the town clock,
or sailing around the lighthouse without moving their wings—
rising steadily with a slight   10
        quiver of the body—or flock
mewing where

a sea the purple of the peacock's neck is
        paled to greenish azure as Dürer changed

THE STEEPLE-JACK. 1 *Dürer*: German Renaissance artist and etcher. 15 *Tyrol*: area of Austria;
shade of green.

the pine green of the Tyrol° to peacock blue and guinea 15
gray. You can see a twenty-five-
     pound lobster; and fish nets arranged
to dry. The

whirlwind fife-and-drum of the storm bends the salt
     marsh grass, disturbs stars in the sky and the 20
star on the steeple; it is a privilege to see so
much confusion. Disguised by what
     might seem the opposite, the sea-
side flowers and

trees are favored by the fog so that you have 25
     the tropics at first hand: the trumpet-vine,
fox-glove, giant snap-dragon, a salpiglossis that has
spots and stripes; morning-glories, gourds,
     or moon-vines trained on fishing-twine
at the back door; 30

cat-tails, flags, blueberries and spiderwort,
     striped grass, lichens, sunflowers, asters, daisies—
yellow and crab-claw ragged sailors with green bracts—toad-plant,
petunias, ferns; pink lilies, blue
     ones, tigers; poppies; black sweet-peas. 35
The climate

is not right for the banyan, frangipani, or
     jack-fruit trees; or for exotic serpent
life. Ring lizard and snake-skin for the foot, if you see fit;
but here they've cats, not cobras, to 40
     keep down the rats. The diffident
little newt°

with white pin-dots on black horizontal spaced-
     out bands lives here; yet there is nothing that
ambition can buy or take away. The college student 45
named Ambrose sits on the hillside
     with his not-native books and hat
and sees boats

at sea progress white and rigid as if in
     a groove. Liking an elegance of which 50
the source is not bravado, he knows by heart the antique
sugar-bowl shaped summer-house of
     interlacing slats, and the pitch
of the church

---

42 *newt*: small salamander.

spire, not true, from which a man in scarlet lets
    down a rope as a spider spins a thread;
he might be part of a novel, but on the sidewalk a
sign says C. J. Poole, Steeple-Jack,
    in black and white; and one in red
and white says

Danger. The church portico has four fluted
    columns, each a single piece of stone, made
modester by white-wash. This would be a fit haven for
waifs, children, animals, prisoners,
    and presidents who have repaid
sin-driven

senators by not thinking about them. The
    place has a school-house, a post-office in a
store, fish-houses, hen-houses, a three-masted
    schooner on
the stocks. The hero, the student,
    the steeple-jack, each in his way,
is at home.

It could not be dangerous to be living
    in a town like this, of simple people,
who have a steeple-jack placing danger-signs by the church
while he is gilding° the solid-
    pointed star, which on a steeple
stands for hope.

---

77 *gilding:* covering with thin layer of gold.

POETRY

I, too, dislike it: there are things that are important beyond all this fiddle.
    Reading it, however, with a perfect contempt for it, one discovers in
    it after all, a place for the genuine.
        Hands that can grasp, eyes
        that can dilate, hair that can rise
            if it must, these things are important not because a

high-sounding interpretation can be put upon them but because they are
    useful. When they become so derivative as to become unintelligible,
    the same thing may be said for all of us, that we
        do not admire what
        we cannot understand: the bat
            holding on upside down or in quest of something to

eat, elephants pushing, a wild horse taking a roll, a tireless wolf under

    a tree, the immovable critic, twitching his skin like a

        horse that feels a flea, the base-

    ball fan, the statistician—   15

        nor is it valid

            to discriminate against 'business documents and

school-books'; all these phenomena are important. One must make a distinction

    however: when dragged into prominence by half poets, the result is not poetry,   20

    nor till the poets among us can be

        'literalists of

        the imagination'—above

            insolence and triviality and can present

for inspection, imaginery gardens with real toads in them, shall we have   25

    it. In the meantime, if you demand on the one hand,

    the raw material of poetry in

        all its rawness and

        that which is on the other hand

            genuine, then you are interested in poetry.   30

[1921]

Robinson Jeffers (1887–1962)

BOATS IN A FOG

Sports and gallantries, the stage, the arts, the antics of dancers,
The exuberant voices of music,
Have charm for children but lack nobility; it is bitter
    earnestness
That makes beauty; the mind
Knows, grown adult.
                A sudden fog-drift muffled the ocean,   5
A throbbing of engines moved in it,
At length, a stone's throw out, between the rocks and the
    vapor,
One by one moved shadows
Out of the mystery, shadows, fishing-boats, trailing each other
Following the cliff for guidance,   10
Holding a difficult path between the peril of the sea-fog
And the foam on the shore granite.
One by one, trailing their leader, six crept by me,
Out of the vapor and into it,
The throb of their engines subdued by the fog, patient and
    cautious,   15

Coasting all around the peninsula
Back to the buoys in Monterey Harbor. A flight of pelicans
Is nothing lovelier to look at;
The flight of the planets is nothing nobler; all the arts lose
    virtue
Against the essential reality   20
Of creatures going about their business among the equally
Earnest elements of nature.

SALMON-FISHING

The days shorten, the south blows wide for showers now,
The south wind shouts to the rivers,
The rivers open their mouths and the salt salmon
Race up into the freshet.
In Christmas month against the smoulder and menace   5
Of a long angry sundown,
Red ash of the dark solstice, you see the anglers,
Pitiful, cruel, primeval,
Like the priests of the people that built Stonehenge,°
Dark silent forms, performing   10
Remote solemnities in the red shallows
Of the river's mouth at the year's turn,
Drawing landward their live bullion, the bloody mouths
And scales full of the sunset
Twitch on the rocks, no more to wander at will   15
The wild Pacific pasture nor wanton and spawning
Race up into fresh water.

SALMON-FISHING. 9 *Stonehenge:* Prehistoric circle, of what are believed to be sacred stones, in England.

T. S. Eliot (1888–1965)

PORTRAIT OF A LADY

Thou hast committed—
Fornication: but that was in another country,
And besides, the wench is dead.
                    THE JEW OF MALTA.°

PORTRAIT OF A LADY. The epigraph by Christopher Marlowe is from a melodramatic play involving multiple betrayals.

I

Among the smoke and fog of a December afternoon
You have the scene arrange itself—as it will seem to do—
With 'I have saved this afternoon for you';
And four wax candles in the darkened room,
Four rings of light upon the ceiling overhead,   5
An atmosphere of Juliet's tomb°
Prepared for all the things to be said, or left unsaid.
We have been, let us say, to hear the latest Pole
Transmit the Preludes,° through his hair and fingertips.
'So intimate, this Chopin, that I think his soul   10
Should be resurrected only among friends
Some two or three, who will not touch the bloom
That is rubbed and questioned in the concert room.'
—And so the conversation slips
Among velleities° and carefully caught regrets   15
Through attenuated tones of violins
Mingled with remote cornets
And begins.
'You do not know how much they mean to me, my friends,
And how, how rare and strange it is, to find   20
In a life composed so much, so much of odds and ends,
(For indeed I do not love it . . . you knew? you are not blind!
How keen you are!)
To find a friend who has these qualities,
Who has, and gives   25
Those qualities upon which friendship lives.
How much it means that I say this to you—
Without these friendships—life, what *cauchemar!*'°
Among the windings of the violins
And the ariettes°   30
Of cracked cornets
Inside my brain a dull tom-tom begins
Absurdly hammering a prelude of its own,
Capricious monotone
That is at least one definite 'false note.'   35
—Let us take the air, in a tobacco trance,
Admire the monuments,
Discuss the late events,
Correct our watches by the public clocks.
Then sit for half an hour and drink our bocks.°   40

---

6 *Juliet's tomb*: refers to Shakespeare's *Romeo and Juliet*.   9 *Preludes*: set of piano compositions by
Frédéric Chopin.   15 *velleities*: whims.   28 *cauchemar*: nightmare (French).   30 *ariettes*: short arias.
40 *bocks*: beers.

II

Now that lilacs are in bloom
She has a bowl of lilacs in her room
And twists one in her fingers while she talks.
'Ah, my friend, you do not know, you do not know
What life is, you should hold it in your hands';   45
(Slowly twisting the lilac stalks)
'You let it flow from you, you let it flow,
And youth is cruel, and has no remorse
And smiles at situations which it cannot see.'
I smile, of course,   50
And go on drinking tea.
'Yet with these April sunsets, that somehow recall
My buried life, and Paris in the Spring,
I feel immeasurably at peace, and find the world
To be wonderful and youthful, after all.'   55

The voice returns like the insistent out-of-tune
Of a broken violin on an August afternoon:
'I am always sure that you understand
My feelings, always sure that you feel,
Sure that across the gulf you reach your hand.   60

You are invulnerable, you have no Achilles' heel.
You will go on, and when you have prevailed
You can say: at this point many a one has failed.
But what have I, but what have I, my friend,
To give you, what can you receive from me?   65
Only the friendship and the sympathy
Of one about to reach her journey's end.

I shall sit here, serving tea to friends. . . .'

I take my hat: how can I make a cowardly amends
For what she has said to me?   70
You will see me any morning in the park
Reading the comics and the sporting page.
Particularly I remark
An English countess goes upon the stage.
A Greek was murdered at a Polish dance,   75
Another bank defaulter has confessed.
I keep my countenance,
I remain self-possessed
Except when a street piano, mechanical and tired
Reiterates some worn-out common song   80
With the smell of hyacinths across the garden
Recalling things that other people have desired.
Are these ideas right or wrong?

III

The October night comes down; returning as before
Except for a slight sensation of being ill at ease   85
I mount the stairs and turn the handle of the door
And feel as if I had mounted on my hands and knees.
'And so you are going abroad; and when do you return?
But that's a useless question.
You hardly know when you are coming back,   90
You will find so much to learn.'
My smile falls heavily among the bric-à-brac.°

'Perhaps you can write to me.'
My self-possession flares up for a second;
This is as I had reckoned.   95
'I have been wondering frequently of late
(But our beginnings never know our ends!)
Why we have not developed into friends.'
I feel like one who smiles, and turning shall remark
Suddenly, his expression in a glass.   100
My self-possession gutters;° we are really in the dark.

'For everybody said so, all our friends,
They all were sure our feelings would relate
So closely! I myself can hardly understand.
We must leave it now to fate.   105
You will write, at any rate.
Perhaps it is not too late.
I shall sit here, serving tea to friends.'

And I must borrow every changing shape
To find expression . . . dance, dance   110
Like a dancing bear,
Cry like a parrot, chatter like an ape.
Let us take the air, in a tobacco trance—

Well! and what if she should die some afternoon,
Afternoon grey and smoky, evening yellow and rose;   115
Should die and leave me sitting pen in hand
With the smoke coming down above the housetops;
Doubtful, for a while
Not knowing what to feel or if I understand
Or whether wise or foolish, tardy or too soon . . .   120
Would she not have the advantage, after all?
This music is successful with a 'dying fall'
Now that we talk of dying—
And should I have the right to smile?

---

92 *bric-à-brac:* miscellaneous furnishings.   101 *gutters:* sputters out.

LA FIGLIA CHE PIANGE°

O quan te memorem virgo . . .°

Stand on the highest pavement of the stair—
Lean on a garden urn—
Weave, weave the sunlight in your hair—
Clasp your flowers to you with a painted surprise—
Fling them to the ground and turn   5
With a fugitive resentment in your eyes:
But weave, weave the sunlight in your hair.

So I would have had him leave,
So I would have had her stand and grieve,
So he would have left   10
As the soul leaves the body torn and bruised,
As the mind deserts the body it has used.
I should find
Some way incomparably light and deft,
Some way we both should understand,   15
Simple and faithless as a smile and shake of the hand.

_____

LA FIGLIA CHE PIANGE. Literally "The girl who cries." *O quan . . . virgo:* "What memories of you, young girl . . ."

Federico García Lorca (1889–1936)

THE LITTLE MUTE BOY

The little boy was looking for his voice
(The king of the crickets had it.)
In a drop of water
the little boy was looking for his voice.

I do not want it for speaking with;   5
I will make a ring of it
that my silence may wear
on its little finger.

In a drop of water
the little boy was looking for his voice.   10

(The captive voice, far away,
put on a cricket's clothes.)

862   An Anthology of Poetry

SONG OF THE BARREN ORANGE TREE

Woodcutter.
Cut my shadow from me.
Free me from the torment
of seeing myself without fruit.

Why was I born among mirrors?   5
The day walks in circles around me,
and the night copies me
in all its stars.

I want to live without seeing myself.
And I will dream that ants   10
and thistleburrs are my
leaves and my birds

Woodcutter.
Cut my shadow from me.
Free me from the torment   15
of seeing myself without fruit.

García Lorca poems translated by W. S. Merwin

Anna Akhmatova (1889–1966)

THE SONG OF THE FINAL MEETING

My breast was bound with a cold band,
And still my steps were light.
The glove intended for my left hand,
I put upon my right.

At the thought of the stairs, I grew faint-hearted,   5
But I knew, there were only three!
An autumnal whisper in the maples started
Begging: "Die with me!

"Fate cheated me—fate, so abysmal,
So moody and full of spite . . . "   10
I answered: "My dear! I too am dismal.
I'll die with you tonight . . . "

The final meeting: I stood on the road.
The house was as dark as shame.

Only, in the bedroom, candles showed 15
An indifferent yellow flame.

[1911]

THE MUSE°

When at night I await the beloved guest,
Life seems to hang by a thread. "What is youth?" I demand
Of the room. "What is honor, freedom, the rest,
In the presence of her who holds the flute in her hand?"

But now she is here. Tossing aside her veil, 5
She considers me. "Are you the one who came
To Dante, who dictated the pages of Hell
To him?" I ask her. She replies, "I am."

[1924]

Akhmatova poems translated by Lyn Coffin

THE MUSE. The ancient poets believed in the Muse, the personified spirit of inspiration.

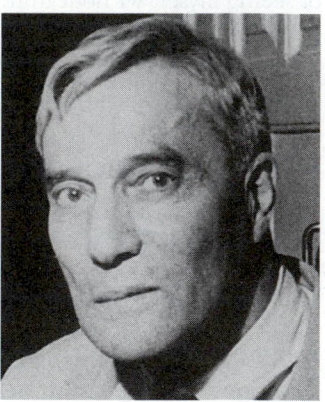

Boris Pasternak (1890–1960)

FEBRUARY

Black spring! Pick up your pen, and weeping,
Of February, in sobs and ink,
Write poems, while the slush in thunder
Is burning in the black of spring.

Through clanking wheels, through church bells ringing 5
A hired cab will take you where
The town has ended, where the showers
Are louder still than ink and tears.

Where rooks, like charred pears, from the branches
In thousands break away, and sweep 10
Into the melting snow, instilling
Dry sadness into eyes that weep.

Beneath—the earth is black in puddles,
The wind with croaking screeches throbs,
And—the more randomly, the surer 15
Poems are forming out of sobs.

Edna St. Vincent Millay
(1892–1950)

SONNET XVII

from "Sonnets from an Ungrafted Tree"

Gazing upon him now, severe and dead,
It seemed a curious thing that she had lain
Beside him many a night in that cold bed,
And that had been which would not be again.
From his desirous body the great heat
Was gone at last, it seemed, and the taut nerves
Loosened forever. Formally the sheet
Set forth for her today those heavy curves
And lengths familiar as the bedroom door.
She was as one who enters, sly, and proud,   10
To where her husband speaks before a crowd,
And sees a man she never saw before—
The man who eats his victuals at her side,
Small, and absurd, and hers: for once, not hers, unclassified.

[1923]

César Vallejo (1892–1938)

THE BLACK RIDERS

There are blows in life so violent—Don't ask me!
Blows as if from the hatred of God; as if before them,
the deep waters of everything lived through
were backed up in the soul . . . Don't ask me!

Not many; but they exist . . . They open dark ravines   5
in the most ferocious face in the most bull-like
        back.
Perhaps they are the horses of that heathen Attila,
or the black riders sent to us by Death.

They are the slips backward made by the Christs
        of the soul,
away from some holy faith that is sneered at by
                Events.   10
These blows that are bloody are the crackling sounds
from some bread that burns at the oven door.

And man ... poor man! ... poor man! He swings
    his eyes, as
when a man behind us calls us by clapping his hands;
swings his crazy eyes, and everything alive   15
is backed up, like a pool of guilt, in that glance.

There are blows in life so violent ... Don't ask me!

Translated by Robert Bly

DOWN TO THE DREGS

This afternoon it rains as never before; and I
don't feel like staying alive, heart.

The afternoon is pleasant. Why shouldn't it be?
It is wearing grace and pain; it is dressed like a
    woman.

This afternoon in Lima it is raining. And I remember   5
the cruel caverns of my ingratitude;
my block of ice laid on her poppy,
stronger than her crying "Don't be this way!"

My violent black flowers; and the barbarous
and staggering blow with a stone; and the glacial
    pause.   10
And the silence of her dignity will pour
scalding oils on the end of the sentence.

Therefore, this afternoon, as never before, I walk
with this owl, with this heart.

And other women go past; and seeing me sullen,   15
they sip a little of you
in the abrupt furrow of my deep grief.

This afternoon it rains, rains endlessly. And I
don't feel like staying alive, heart.

Translated by James Wright

Wilfred Owen (1893–1918)

DULCE ET DECORUM EST

Bent double, like old beggars under sacks,
Knock-kneed coughing like hags, we cursed through sludge,
Till on the haunting flares we turned our backs,

And towards our distant rest began to trudge.
Men marched asleep. Many had lost their boots,
But limped on, blood-shot. All went lame, all blind;
Drunk with fatigue; deaf even to the hoots
Of gas-shells dropping softly behind.   5

Gas! GAS! Quick boys!—An ecstasy of fumbling,
Fitting the clumsy helmets just in time,   10
But someone still was yelling out and stumbling
And flound'ring like a man in fire or lime.°—
Dim through the misty panes and thick green light,
As under a green sea, I saw him drowning.

In all my dreams before my helpless sight   15
He plunges at me, guttering, choking, drowning.

If in some smothering dreams, you too could pace
Behind the wagon that we flung him in,
And watch the white eyes writhing in his face,
His hanging face, like a devil's sick of sin,   20
If you could hear, at every jolt, the blood

Come gargling from the froth-corrupted lungs
Bitter as the cud°
Of vile, incurable sores on innocent tongues,—
My friend, you would not tell with such high zest   25
To children ardent for some desperate glory,
The old lie: *Dulce et decorum est*
Pro patria mori.°

DULCE ET DECORUM EST. 12 *lime*: sticky substance. 23 *cud*: something held in the mouth and
chewed. 27–28 *Dulce . . . mori*: old Latin slogan: "It is a sweet and fitting thing to die for one's country."

e. e. cummings (1894–1962)

ANYONE LIVED IN A PRETTY HOW TOWN

anyone lived in a pretty how town
(with up so floating many bells down)
spring summer autumn winter
he sang his didn't he danced his did.

Women and men(both little and small)   5
cared for anyone not at all
they sowed their isn't they reaped their same
sun moon stars rain

children guessed(but only a few
and down they forgot as up they grew
autumn winter spring summer)
that noone loved him more by more

when by now and tree by leaf
she laughed his joy she cried his grief
bird by snow and stir by still
anyone's any was all to her

someones married their everyones
laughed their cryings and did their dance
(sleep wake hope and then)they
said their nevers they slept their dream

stars rain sun moon
(and only the snow can begin to explain
how children are apt to forget to remember
with up so floating many bells down)

one day anyone died i guess
(and noone stooped to kiss his face)
busy folk buried them side by side
little by little and was by was

all by all and deep by deep
and more by more they dream their sleep
noone and anyone earth by april
wish by spirit and if by yes.

Women and men(both dong and ding)
summer autumn winter spring
reaped their sowing and went their came
sun moon stars rain

Bertolt Brecht (1898–1956)

BAD TIME FOR POETRY

Yes, I know: only the happy man
Is liked. His voice
Is good to hear. His face is handsome.

The crippled tree in the yard
Shows that the soil is poor, yet
The passers-by abuse it for being crippled
And rightly so.

868   An Anthology of Poetry

The green boats and the dancing sails on the Sound
Go unseen. Of it all
I see only the torn nets of the fishermen.   10
Why do I only record
That a village woman aged forty walks with a stoop?
The girls' breasts
Are as warm as ever.

In my poetry a rhyme   15
Would seem to me almost insolent.

Inside me contend
Delight at the apple tree in blossom
And horror at the house-painter's speeches.
But only the second   20
Drives me to my desk.

Hart Crane (1899–1932)

THE HARBOR DAWN

Insistently through sleep—a tide of voices—
They meet you listening midway in your dream,
The long, tired sounds, fog-insulated noises:
Gongs in white surplices,° beshrouded wails,
Far strum of fog horns . . . signals dispersed in veils.   5

And then a truck will lumber past the wharves
As winch engines begin throbbing on some deck;
Or a drunken stevedore's° howl and thud below
Comes echoing alley-upward through dim snow.

And if they take your sleep away sometimes   10
They give it back again. Soft sleeves of sound
Attend the darkling harbor, the pillowed bay;
Somewhere out there in blankless steam

Spills into steam, and wanders, washed away
—Flurried by keen fifings, eddied   15
Among distant chiming buoys—adrift. The sky,

Cool feathery fold, suspends, distills
This wavering slumber. . . . Slowly—
Immemorially the window, the half-covered chair
Ask nothing but this sheath of pallid air.   20

THE HARBOR DAWN. 4 *surplices:* loose-fitting gowns worn by some clergy. 8 *stevedore:* one who
loads and unloads ships.

And you beside me, blessèd now while sirens
Sing to us, stealthily weave us into day—
Serenely now, before day claims our eyes
Your cool arms murmurously about me lay.

While myriad snowy hands are clustering at the panes—   25

> your hands within my hands are deeds;
> my tongue upon your throat—singing
> arms close; eyes wide, undoubtful
>   dark
>   drink the dawn—   30
> a forest shudders in your hair!

The window goes blond slowly. Frostily clears,
From Cyclopean° towers across Manhattan waters
—Two—three bright window-eyes aglitter, disk
The sun, released—aloft with cold gulls hither.   35

The fog leans one last moment on the sill.
Under the mistletoe of dreams, a star—
As though to join us at some distant hill—
Turns in the waking west and goes to sleep.

33 *Cyclopean:* like Cyclops, a one-eyed giant in Greek mythology.

Takako Hashimoto (1899–1963)

All plucked off—
a chicken's feathers lying
under a winter moon.

Into a white peach
the edge of a blade is thrust—   5
the seed has been cut.

Translated by Edith Marcombe Shiffert and Yuki Sawa

Francis Ponge (1899–   )

RAIN

Rain, in the courtyard where I watch it fall, comes down at very different speeds. At the center it is a sheer uneven curtain (or net), an implacable but relatively slow descent of fairly light drops, an endless precipitation without vigor, a concentrated fraction of the total meteor. Not far from the walls to the right and left, heavier individuated drops fall more noisily. Here they seem the size of wheat kernels, there large as peas, elsewhere big as marbles. Along the window sills and mouldings the rain streaks horizontally, while on the underside of these obstacles it hangs suspended like lozenges. It ripples along, thinly coating the entire surface of a little zinc roof beneath my glance, moiréed° with the various currents caused by the imperceptible rises and falls of the covering. From the nearby gutter, where it flows with the effort of a shallow brook poorly sloped, it plummets sharply to the ground in a perfectly vertical, thickly corded trickle where it shatters and rebounds like glistening icicles.

Each of its forms has a particular speed, accompanied by a particular sound. All of it runs with the intensity of a complex mechanism, as precise as it is unpredictable, like a clockwork whose mainspring is the weight of a given mass of precipitating vapor.

The pealing of the vertical jets on the ground, the gurgling of the gutters, the tiny gong strokes, multiply and resound together in a concert neither monotonous nor unsubtle.

When the mainspring has unwound, some wheels go on turning for a while, more and more slowly, until the whole machinery stops. Should the sun then reappear, everything is soon effaced; the glimmering mechanism evaporates: it has rained.

Translated by Betty Archer

RAIN. (par. 1) *moiréed:* ripple-patterned, as on a watery-looking silk.

George Seferis (1900–1971)

THE HOUSE NEAR THE SEA

The houses I had they took away from me. The times
happened to be unpropitious: war, destruction, exile;
sometimes the hunter hits the migratory birds,
sometimes he doesn't hit them. Hunting
was good in my time, many felt the pellet;   5
the rest circle aimlessly or go mad in the shelters.
Don't talk to me about the nightingale or the lark
or the little wagtail
inscribing figures with his tail in the light;
I don't know much about houses   10
I know they have their own nature, nothing else.
Now at first, like babies
who play in gardens with the tassels of the sun,
they embroider colored shutters and shining doors
over the day.   15
When the architect's finished, they change,
they frown or smile or even grow stubborn
with those who stayed behind, with those who went away

with others who'd come back if they could
or others who disappeared, now that the world's become   20
an endless hotel.

I don't know much about houses,
I remember their joy and their sorrow
Sometimes, when I stop to think;

                              again   25
sometimes, near the sea, in naked rooms
with a single iron bed and nothing of my own,
watching the evening spider, I imagine
that someone is getting ready to come, that they dress him up
in white and black robes, with many-colored jewels,   30
and around him venerable ladies,
gray hair and dark lace shawls, talk softly,
that he is getting ready to come and say goodbye to me;
or that a woman—eyelashes quivering, slim-waisted,
returning from southern ports,   35
Smyrna Rhodes Syracuse Alexandria,
from cities closed like hot shutters,
with perfume of golden fruit and herbs—
climbs the stairs without seeing
those who've fallen asleep under the stairs.   40

Houses, you know, grow stubborn easily when you strip them bare.

Translated by Edmund Keeley and Philip Sherrard

Shinkichi Takahashi (1901–   )

THE OCEAN

The ocean was bottomlessly deep.
Standing at the edge of the ocean
I looked toward the bottom of the ocean.

Dangerously near tumbling off,
what I thought of was the things of my future.   5
Time was imagined like the legs of an infant who has not yet walked.

No matter what happens anywhere
there is nothing else to do
but stand on this steep cliff, clench my teeth, and close my eyes.

The unexperienced future   10
like fishermen's fires flickering past the horizon
has darkness around itself.

I seem to have thrown my body down into that ocean.

An Anthology of Poetry

THE FLY

I thought I would live forever.
Forever was inside a single fly.

When the fly was chased by a hand
he flew away gently.
Toward that attitude of composure   5
I felt friendliness.

Late at night
with the electric light shining,
listening to the sounds of rain outside,
I was reading a book.   10

On a page of the opened book
a single fly
cast a shadow of loneliness without realizing it.

Forever, like a fly's legs, is
thinly bending.

    Takahaski poems translated by Edith Marcombe Shiffert and Yuki Sawa

Nazim Hikmet (1902–1963)

LIFE, FRIENDS, ENEMIES, YOU AND THE EARTH

I am so happy to be alive!
I love the Earth, the Sun
        fighting for my bread.
Although I know the Earth's measurements
        down to the last centimetre,   5
although it looks tiny next to the Sun,
the Earth is incomprehensibly
            large for me.

I long to travel and see
fishes I have not seen
          fruits and stars.   10
But only through reading
have I made my journey across Europe,
and all my life I have waited
       for a letter with a blue stamp
          franked in Asia.   15

My local grocer and I
are physically unknown in America
but all the same
I have friends and enemies
         all the way
                 from China to Spain,
from the Cape of Good Hope
                      to Alaska,
at every knot at every kilometre.
Friends whose hands I have not shaken
but for whom and with whom
                 I am ready to die
in our struggle for Freedom.
And enemies whose blood I could drain
and who could drain my own blood.
My greatest point of strength
         is to know
                 that I am not alone
                 in this world.
The world and its multitudes
are not obscurities in my heart
nor mysteries in scientific books.

In our great struggle
I have chosen my rank
         openly, fearlessly
And outside this rank
         neither the soil nor you
             can be my completion.
And yet you are so incredibly beautiful
    the soil so warm
                 so lovable . . .
                 [1939]
             Translated by Taner Baybars

20

25

30

35

40

45

Langston Hughes (1902–1967)

HARLEM (A DREAM DEFERRED)

What happens to a dream deferred?

    Does it dry up
    like a raisin in the sun?
    Or fester like a sore—
    And then run?

5

Does it stink like rotten meat?
Or crust and sugar over—
like a syrupy sweet?

Maybe it just sags
like a heavy load.   10

Or does it explode?

THEME FOR ENGLISH B

The instructor said,

Go home and write
a page tonight.
And let that page come out of you—
Then, it will be true.   5

I wonder if it's that simple?

I am twenty-two, colored, born in Winston-Salem.
I went to school there, then Durham,° then here
to this college on the hill above Harlem.
I am the only colored student in my class.   10
The steps from the hill lead down into Harlem,
through a park, then I cross St. Nicholas,
Eighth Avenue, Seventh, and I come to the Y,
the Harlem Branch Y, where I take the elevator
up to my room, sit down, and write this page: 15

It's not easy to know what is true for you or me
at twenty-two, my age. But I guess I'm what
I feel and see and hear. Harlem, I hear you:
hear you, hear me—we two—you, me, talk on this page.
(I hear New York, too.) Me—who?   20

Well, I like to eat, sleep, drink, and be in love.
I like to work, read, learn, and understand life.
I like a pipe for a Christmas present,
or records—Bessie,° bop,° or Bach.
I guess being colored doesn't make me *not* like   25
the same things other folks like who are other races.

So will my page be colored that I write?
Being me, it will not be white.
But it will be

THEME FOR ENGLISH B. 7–8 *Winston-Salem, Durham:* cities in North Carolina.   24 *Bessie:* Bessie
Smith, black American jazz singer; *bop:* jazz style of the 1950s.

a part of you, instructor.
You are white—
yet a part of me, as I am a part of you.
That's American.
Sometimes perhaps you don't want to be a part of me. 30
Nor do I often want to be a part of you. 35
But we are, that's true!
As I learn from you,
I guess you learn from me—
although you're older—and white—
and somewhat more free. 40

This is my page for English B.

Pablo Neruda (1904–1973)

ALLIANCE (SONATA)

Of dusty glances fallen to the ground
or of soundless leaves burying themselves.
Of meals without light, with the emptiness,
with the absence of the suddenly dead day.
At the tip of the hands the dazzlement of butterflies, 5
the upflight of butterflies whose light has no end.

You kept the trail of light, of broken beings
that the abandoned sun, sinking, casts at the churches.
Stained with glances, dealing with bees,
your substance fleeing from unexpected flame 10
precedes and follows the day and its family of gold.

The spying days cross in secret
but they fall within your voice of light.
Oh mistress of love, in your rest
I established my dream, my silent attitude. 15

With your body of timid number, suddenly extended
to the quantities that define the earth,
behind the struggle of the days white with space
and cold with slow deaths and withered stimuli,
I feel your lap burn and your kisses travel 20
shaping fresh swallows in my sleep.

At times the destiny of your tears ascends
like age to my forehead, there
the waves are crashing, smashing themselves to death:
their movement is moist, drifting, ultimate. 25

Translated by Donald D. Walsh

W. H. Auden (1907–1973)

LAY YOUR SLEEPING HEAD, MY LOVE

Lay your sleeping head, my love,
Human on my faithless arm;
Time and fevers burn away
Individual beauty from
Thoughtful children, and the grave   5
Proves the child ephemeral:
But in my arms till break of day
Let the living creature lie,
Mortal, guilty, but to me
The entirely beautiful.   10

Soul and body have no bounds:
To lovers as they lie upon
Her tolerant enchanted slope
In their ordinary swoon,
Grave the vision Venus° sends   15
Of supernatural sympathy,
Universal love and hope;
While an abstract insight wakes
Among the glaciers and the rocks
The hermit's° sensual ecstasy.   20

Certainty, fidelity
On the stroke of midnight pass
Like vibrations of a bell,
And fashionable madmen raise
Their pedantic boring cry: 25
Every farthing of the cost,
All the dreaded cards foretell,
Shall be paid, but from this night
Not a whisper, not a thought,
Not a kiss nor look be lost.   30

Beauty, midnight, vision dies:
Let the winds of dawn that blow
Softly round your dreaming head
Such a day of sweetness show
Eye and knocking heart may bless,   35
Find the mortal world enough;
Noons of dryness see you fed

LAY YOUR SLEEPING HEAD, MY LOVE. 15 *Venus:* goddess of love in Roman mythology. 20 *hermit:* religious recluse.

By the involuntary powers,
Nights of insult let you pass
Watched by every human love.

[January 1937]

SEPTEMBER 1, 1939°

I sit in one of the dives
On Fifty-Second Street
Uncertain and afraid
As the clever hopes expire
Of a low dishonest decade: 5
Waves of anger and fear
Circulate over the bright
And darkened lands of the earth,
Obsessing our private lives;
The unmentionable odour of death   10
Offends the September night.

Accurate scholarship can
Unearth the whole offence
From Luther° until now
That has driven a culture mad,   15
Find what occurred at Linz,°
What huge imago° made
A psychopathic god:
I and the public know
What all schoolchildren learn   20
Those to whom evil is done
Do evil in return.

Exiled Thucydides° knew
All that a speech can say
About Democracy,   25
And what dictators do,
The elderly rubbish they talk
To an apathetic grave;
Analysed all in his book,
The enlightenment driven away,   30
The habit-forming pain,
Mismanagement and grief:
We must suffer them all again.

SEPTEMBER 1, 1939. Auden is writing right on the eve of World War II, which began on September 3 when the German command did not respond to a British ultimatum.   14 *Luther:* Martin Luther, German Protestant reformer (1483–1546).   16 *Linz:* birthplace of Adolf Hitler.   17 *imago:* psychoanalytic term for idealized image.   23 *Thucydides:* Greek historian.

Into this neutral air
Where blind skyscrapers use   35
Their full height to proclaim
The strength of Collective Man,
Each language pours its vain
Competitive excuse:
But who can live for long   40
In an euphoric dream;
Out of the mirror they stare,
Imperialism's face
And the international wrong.

The windiest militant trash   45
Important persons shout
Is not crude as our wish:
What mad Nijinsky° wrote
About Diaghilev°
Is true of the normal heart;   50
For the error bred in the bone
Of each woman and each man
Craves what it cannot have,
Not universal love
But to be loved alone.   55

From the conservative dark
Into the ethical life
The dense commuters come,
Repeating their morning vow,
"I *will* be true to the wife,   60
I'll concentrate more on my work,"
And helpless governors wake
To resume their compulsory game:
Who can release them now,
Who can reach the deaf,   65
Who can speak for the dumb?

All I have is a voice
To undo the folded lie,
The romantic lie in the brain
Of the sensual man-in-the-street   70
And the lie of Authority
Whose buildings grope the sky:
There is no such thing as the State
And no one exists alone;
Hunger allows no choice   75
To the citizen or the police;
We must love one another or die.

48–49 *Nijinsky:* celebrated Russian dancer who went insane; *Diaghilev* was his impresario.

Defenceless under the night
Our world in stupor lies;
Yet, dotted everywhere,
Ironic points of light
Flash out wherever the Just
Exchange their messages:
May I, composed like them
Of Eros° and of dust,
Beleaguered by the same
Negation and despair,
Show an affirming flame.
                    [September 1939]

80
85

---

85 *Eros:* love.

IN MEMORY OF W. B. YEATS°

(d. January 1939)

I

He disappeared in the dead of winter:
The brooks were frozen, the air-ports almost deserted,
And snow disfigured the public statues;
The mercury sank in the mouth of the dying day.
O all the instruments agree
The day of his death was a dark cold day.

Far from his illness
The wolves ran on through the evergreen forests,
The peasant river was untempted by the fashionable quays;°
By mourning tongues
The death of the poet was kept from his poems.

But for him it was his last afternoon as himself,
An afternoon of nurses and rumours;
The provinces of his body revolted,
The squares of his mind were empty,
Silence invaded the suburbs,
The current of his feeling failed: he became his admirers.

Now he is scattered among a hundred cities
And wholly given over to unfamiliar affections;
To find his happiness in another kind of wood
And be punished under a foreign code of conscience.

5
10
15
20

IN MEMORY OF W. B. YEATS. William Butler Yeats was the reknowned Irish poet (see Chapters 18 and 19).   9 *quays:* wharves, docks.

The words of a dead man
Are modified in the guts of the living.

But in the importance and noise of to-morrow
When the brokers are roaring like beasts on the
                        floor of the Bourse,°   25
And the poor have the sufferings to which
                      they are fairly accustomed,
And each in the cell of himself is almost
                      convinced of his freedom;
A few thousand will think of this day
As one thinks of a day when one did something
                      slightly unusual.

O all the instruments agree   30
The day of his death was a dark cold day.

II

You were silly like us: your gift survived it all;
The parish of rich women, physical decay,
Yourself; mad Ireland° hurt you into poetry.
Now Ireland has her madness and her weather still,   35
For poetry makes nothing happen: it survives
In the valley of its saying where executives
Would never want to tamper; it flows south
From ranches of isolation and the busy griefs,
Raw towns that we believe and die in; it survives,   40
A way of happening, a mouth.

III

    Earth, receive an honoured guest;
    William Yeats is laid to rest:
    Let the Irish vessel lie
    Emptied of its poetry.   45

    Time that is intolerant
    Of the brave and innocent,
    And indifferent in a week
    To a beautiful physique,

    Worships language and forgives   50
    Everyone by whom it lives;
    Pardons cowardice, conceit,
    Lays its honours at their feet.

    Time that with this strange excuse
    Pardoned Kipling° and his views,   55

---

    25 *Bourse:* stock exchange.   34 *mad Ireland:* reference to Ireland under British subjugation.
55 *Kipling:* Rudyard Kipling, British author known to hold right-wing views.

And will pardon Paul Claudel,°
Pardons him for writing well.

In the nightmare of the dark
All the dogs of Europe bark,
And the living nations wait,   60
Each sequestered in its hate;

Intellectual disgrace
Stares from every human face,
And the seas of pity lie
Locked and frozen in each eye.   65

Follow, poet, follow right
To the bottom of the night,
With your unconstraining voice
Still persuade us to rejoice;

With the farming of a verse   70
Make a vineyard of the curse,
Sing of human unsuccess
In a rapture of distress;

In the deserts of the heart
Let the healing fountain start,   75
In the prison of his days
Teach the free man how to praise.
             [*February 1939*]

_____

56 *Paul Claudel:* conservative French writer.

Cesare Pavese (1908–1950)

PASSION FOR SOLITUDE

I eat a bite of supper beside the open window.
The room is dark now, you can see the sky.
Step outside, and the quiet streets will take you
quickly, after a little walk, into open country.
I eat and look at the sky—think of all the women   5
eating suppers now!—and my body rests.
Drudgery deadens my body, it deadens women too.

Outside, after supper, the stars will appear,
touching the earth on the great plain. The stars are alive,
but are not worth these cherries which I eat alone. 10
I see the sky, but I know the lights are shining

among the reddish roofs, and there are sounds below.
A healthy gulp, and my body tastes the life
of trees and brooks, and feels cut off from everything.
A little silence, and everything is arrested 15
in its real place, the way my body rests.

Everything stands isolated before my senses,
which accept it calmly: a rustling of silence.
There's nothing in this darkness I couldn't know,
the way I know my blood is running through my veins. 20
The plain is a great running of water through the grass,
a supper of all things. Every plant, every stone
lives and rests. I hear my food nourishing my veins
with all the things that live upon this plain.

Night makes no difference. My square of sky 25
whispers to me of all the sounds, and a tiny star
is struggling in the sky, far from food and home:
a different thing from me. It isn't self-sufficient,
it needs too many companions. Here, in the dark, alone,
my body rests and feels it is the one master of itself. 30

Translated by William Arrowsmith

Theodore Roethke (1908–1963)

ROOT CELLAR

Nothing would sleep in that cellar, dank as a ditch,
Bulbs broke out of boxes hunting for chinks in the dark,
Shoots dangled and drooped,
Lolling obscenely from mildewed crates,
Hung down long yellow evil necks, like tropical snakes. 5
And what a congress of stinks!—
Roots ripe as old bait,
Pulpy stems, rank, silo-rich,
Leaf-mold, manure, lime, piled against slippery planks.
Nothing would give up life: 10
Even the dirt kept breathing a small breath.

CHILD ON TOP OF A GREENHOUSE

The wind billowing out the seat of my britches,
My feet crackling splinters of glass and dried putty,
The half-grown chrysanthemums staring up like accusers,

Up through the streaked glass, flashing with sunlight,
A few white clouds all rushing eastward,
A line of elms plunging and tossing like horses,
And everyone, everyone pointing up and shouting! 5

Elizabeth Bishop (1911–1979)

THE FISH

I caught a tremendous fish
and held him beside the boat
half out of water, with my hook
fast in a corner of his mouth.
He didn't fight. 5
He hadn't fought at all.
He hung a grunting weight,
battered and venerable
and homely. Here and there
his brown skin hung in strips 10
like ancient wallpaper,
and its pattern of darker brown
was like wallpaper:
shapes like full-blown roses
stained and lost through age. 15
He was speckled with barnacles,
fine rosettes of lime,
and infested
with tiny white sea-lice,
and underneath two or three 20
rags of green weed hung down.
While his gills were breathing in
the terrible oxygen
—the frightening gills,
fresh and crisp with blood, 25
that can cut so badly—
I thought of the coarse white flesh
packed in like feathers,
the big bones and the little bones,
the dramatic reds and blacks 30
of his shiny entrails,
and the pink swim-bladder
like a big peony.
I looked into his eyes
which were far larger than mine 35
but shallower, and yellowed,
the irises backed and packed

with tarnished tinfoil
seen through the lenses
of old scratched isinglass.
They shifted a little, but not   40
to return my stare.
—It was more like the tipping
of an object toward the light.
I admired his sullen face,   45
the mechanism of his jaw,
and then I saw
that from his lower lip
—if you could call it a lip—
grim, wet, and weaponlike,   50
hung five old pieces of fish-line,
or four and a wire leader
with the swivel still attached,
with all their five big hooks
grown firmly in his mouth.   55
A green line, frayed at the end
where he broke it, two heavier lines,
and a fine black thread
still crimped from the strain and snap
when it broke and he got away.   60
Like medals with their ribbons
frayed and wavering
a five-haired beard of wisdom
trailing from his aching jaw.
I stared and stared   65
and victory filled up
the little rented boat,
from the pool of bilge
where oil had spread a rainbow
around the rusted engine   70
to the bailer rusted orange,
the sun-cracked thwarts,
the oarlocks on their strings,
the gunnels—until everything
was rainbow, rainbow, rainbow!   75
And I let the fish go.

Czeslaw Milosz (1911–   )

RIVERS GROW SMALL

Rivers grow small. Cities grow small. And splendid gardens
show what we did not see there before: crippled leaves and dust.

When for the first time I swam across the lake
it seemed immense, had I gone there these days
it would have been a shaving bowl   5
between post-glacial rocks and junipers.
The forest near the village of Halina° once was for me primeval,
smelling of the last but recently killed bear,
though a ploughed field was visible through the pines.
What was individual becomes a variety of a general pattern.   10
Consciousness even in my sleep changes primary colors.
The features of my face melt like a wax doll in the fire.
And who can consent to see in the mirror the mere face of man?

[Berkeley, 1963]
Translated by Czeslaw Milosz

RIVERS GROW SMALL. *7 Halina:* village in Milosz's native Lithuania.

WINDOW

I looked out the window at dawn and saw a young apple tree translucent
in brightness.

And when I looked out at dawn once again, an apple tree laden with
fruit stood there.

Many years had probably gone by but I remember nothing of what
happened in my sleep.

[Berkeley, 1965]
Translated by Czeslaw Milosz and Lillian Vallee

Robert Hayden (1913–1980)

HOMAGE TO THE EMPRESS OF THE BLUES°

Because there was a man somewhere in a candystripe silk shirt,
gracile and dangerous as a jaguar and because a woman moaned
for him in sixty-watt gloom and mourned him Faithless Love
Twotiming Love Oh Love Oh Careless Aggravating Love,

    She came out on the stage in yards of pearls, emerging like   5
    a favorite scenic view, flashed her golden smile and sang.

HOMAGE TO THE EMPRESS OF THE BLUES. Legendary jazz singer Bessie Smith was known as "the Empress of the Blues."

Because grey laths began somewhere to show from underneath
torn hurdygurdy lithographs of dollfaced heaven;
and because there were those who feared alarming fists of snow
on the door and those who feared the riot-squad of statistics,   10

     She came out on the stage in ostrich feathers, beaded satin,
     and shone that smile on us and sang.

THOSE WINTER SUNDAYS

Sundays too my father got up early
and put his clothes on in the blueblack cold,
then with cracked hands that ached
from labor in the weekday weather made
banked fires blaze. No one ever thanked him.   5

I'd wake and hear the cold splintering, breaking.
When the rooms were warm, he'd call,
and slowly I would rise and dress,
fearing the chronic angers of that house,

Speaking indifferently to him,   10
who had driven out the cold
and polished my good shoes as well.
What did I know, what did I know
of love's austere and lonely offices?

William Stafford (1914–1993)

LISTENING

My father could hear a little animal step,
or a moth in the dark against the screen,
and every far sound called the listening out
into places where the rest of us had never been.

More spoke to him from the soft wild night   5
than came to our porch for us on the wind;
we would watch him look up and his face go keen
till the walls of the world flared, widened.

My father heard so much that we still stand
inviting the quiet by turning the face,   10
waiting for a time when something in the night
will touch us too from that other place.

AT THE UN-NATIONAL MONUMENT ALONG THE CANADIAN BORDER

This is the field where the battle did not happen,
where the unknown soldier did not die.
This is the field where grass joined hands,
where no monument stands,
and the only heroic thing is the sky.   5

Birds fly here without any sound,
unfolding their wings across the open.
No people killed—or were killed—on this ground
hallowed by neglect and an air so tame
that people celebrate it by forgetting its name.   10

Octavio Paz (1914–   )

HERE

My steps along this street
resound
            in another street
in which
            I hear my steps
passing along this street   5
in which

Only the mist is real
        Translated by Charles Tomlinson and Octavio Paz

TROWBRIDGE STREET

                            1
Sun throughout the day
                        Cold throughout the sun
Nobody on the streets
                        parked cars
Still no snow   5
            but wind wind
A red tree
            still burns
in the chilled air
Talking to it I talk to you   10

2

I am in a room abandoned by language
You are in another identical room
Or we both are
on a street your glance has depopulated
The world   15
imperceptibly comes apart
                              Memory
decayed beneath our feet
I am stopped in the middle of this
unwritten line   20

3

Doors open and close by themselves
                              Air
enters and leaves our house
                              Air
talks to itself talking to you   25
                              Air
nameless in the endless corridor
Who knows who is on the other side?
                              Air
turns and turns in my empty skull   30
                              Air
turns to air everything it touches
                              Air
with air-fingers scatters everything I say
I am the air you don't see   35
I can't open your eyes
                              I can't close the door
The air has turned solid

4

This hour has the shape of a pause
This pause has your shape   40
You have the shape of a fountain made
not of water but of time
My pieces bob
at the jet's tip
what I was   am   still am not   45
My life is weightless
                              The past thins out
The future   a little water in your eyes

5

Now you have a bridge-shape
Our room navigates beneath your arches   50

From your railing we watch us pass
You ripple with wind   more light than body
The sun on the other bank
                              grows upside down
Its roots buried deep in the sky   55
We could hide ourselves in its foliage
Build a bonfire with its branches
The day is habitable

                    6

The cold has immobilized the world
Space is made of glass   60
                  Glass made of air
The lightest sounds build
quick sculptures
Echoes multiply and scatter them
Maybe it will snow   65
The burning tree quivers
surrounded now by night
Talking to it I talk to you

                    Translated by Eliot Weinberger

Gwendolyn Brooks (1917–   )

MARTIN LUTHER KING JR.

A man went forth with gifts.

He was a prose poem.
He was a tragic grace.
He was a warm music.

He tried to heal the vivid volcanoes.
His ashes are
   reading the world.

His Dream still wishes to anoint
   the barricades of faith and of control.

His word still burns the center of the sun,
   above the thousands and the
   hundred thousands.

The word was Justice. It was spoken.

So it shall be spoken.   10
So it shall be done.

Robert Lowell (1917–1977)

TO SPEAK OF WOE
THAT IS IN MARRIAGE°

*"It is the future generation that presses into being by
means of these exuberant feelings and supersensible
soap bubbles of ours."*

SCHOPENHAUER°

"The hot night makes us keep our bedroom windows open.
Our magnolia blossoms. Life begins to happen.
My hopped up husband drops his home disputes,
and hits the streets to cruise for prostitutes,
free-lancing out along the razor's edge.   5
This screwball might kill his wife, then take the pledge.
Oh the monotonous meanness of his lust. . . .
It's the injustice . . . he is so unjust—
whiskey-blind, swaggering home at five.
My only thought is how to keep alive.   10
What makes him tick? Each night now I tie
ten dollars and his car key to my thigh. . . .
Gored by the climacteric° of his want,
he stalls above me like an elephant."

TO SPEAK OF WOE THAT IS IN MARRIAGE. The title quotation, from Chaucer's *Canterbury Tales*, is
spoken by his character, the Wife of Bath, as prelude to her litany of marital disasters. Schopenhauer, the
epigraph author, was a German pessimist philosopher who wrote books downgrading the role of women.
13 *climacteric:* male menopause.

Philip Larkin (1922–1985)

HOME IS SO SAD

Home is so sad. It stays as it was left,
Shaped to the comfort of the last to go
As if to win them back. Instead, bereft
Of anyone to please, it withers so,
Having no heart to put aside the theft   5

And turn again to what it started as,
A joyous shot at how things ought to be,
Long fallen wide. You can see how it was:
Look at the pictures and the cutlery.
The music in the piano stool. That vase.

Richard Wilbur (1922–   )

ADVICE TO A PROPHET

When you come, as you soon must, to the streets of our city,
Mad-eyed from stating the obvious,
Not proclaiming our fall but begging us
In God's name to have self-pity,

Spare us all word of the weapons, their force and range,   5
The long numbers that rocket the mind;
Our slow, unreckoning hearts will be left behind,
Unable to fear what is too strange.

Nor shall you scare us with talk of the death of the race.
How should we dream of this place without us?—   10
The sun mere fire, the leaves untroubled about us,
A stone look on the stone's face?

Speak of the world's own change. Though we cannot conceive
Of an undreamt thing, we know to our cost
How the dreamt cloud crumbles, the vines are blackened by frost,   15
How the view alters. We could believe,

If you told us so, that the white-tailed deer will slip
Into perfect shade, grown perfectly shy,
The lark avoid the reaches of our eye,
The jack-pine lose its knuckled grip   20

On the cold ledge, and every torrent burn
As Xanthus° once, its gliding trout
Stunned in a twinkling. What should we be without
The dolphin's arc, the dove's return,

These things in which we have seen ourselves and spoken?   25
Ask us, prophet, how we shall call
Our natures forth when that live tongue is all
Dispelled, that glass obscured or broken

In which we have said the rose of our love and the clean
Horse of our courage, in which beheld   30
The singing locust of the soul unshelled,
And all we mean or wish to mean.

Ask us, ask us whether with the worldless rose
Our hearts shall fail us; come demanding
Whether there shall be lofty or long standing   35
When the bronze annals of the oak-tree close.

ADVICE TO A PROPHET. 22 *Xanthus:* river near Troy, scene of Trojan War.

Amy Clampitt (1923–1994)

DANCERS EXERCISING

Frame within frame, the evolving conversation
is dancelike, as though two could play
at improvising snowflakes'
six-feather-vaned evanescence,
no two ever alike. All process   5
and no arrival: the happier we are,
the less there is for memory to take hold of,
or—memory being so largely a predilection
for the exceptional—come to a halt
in front of. But finding, one evening   10
on a street not quite familiar,
inside a gated
November-sodden garden, a building
of uncertain provenance,
peering into whose vestibule we were   15
arrested—a frame within a frame,
a lozenge of impeccable clarity—
by the reflection, no, not
of our two selves, but of
dancers exercising in a mirror   20
at the center
of that clarity, what we saw
was not stillness
but movement: the perfection
of memory consisting, it would seem,   25
in the never-to-be-completed.
We saw them mirroring themselves,
never guessing the vestibule
that defined them, frame within frame,
contained two other mirrors.   30

Denise Levertov (1923–   )

TO THE SNAKE

Green Snake, when I hung you round my neck
and stroked your cold, pulsing throat
          as you hissed to me, glinting
arrowy gold scales, and I felt
          the weight of you on my shoulders,   5

and the whispering silver of your dryness
        sounded close at my ears—

Green Snake—I swore to my companions that certainly
        you were harmless! But truly
I had no certainty, and no hope, only desiring   10
        to hold you, for that joy,
                which left
a long wake of pleasure, as the leaves moved
and you faded into the pattern
of grass and shadows, and I returned   15
smiling and haunted, to a dark morning.

Louis Simpson (1923–   )

AMERICAN CLASSIC

It's a classic American scene—
a car stopped off the road
and a man trying to repair it.

The woman who stays in the car
in the classic American scene
stares back at the freeway traffic.   5

They look surprised, and ashamed
to be so helpless . . .
let down in the middle of the road!

To think that their car would do this!
They look like mountain people   10
whose son has gone against the law.

But every night they set out food
and the robber goes skulking back to the trees.
That's how it is with the car . . .   15

it's theirs, they're stuck with it.
Now they know what it's like to sit
and see the world go whizzing by.

In the fume of carbon monoxide and dust
they are not such good Americans   20
as they thought they were.

The feeling of being left out
through no fault of your own, is common.
That's why I say, an American classic.

Yehuda Amichai (1924–   )

FLOWERS IN A ROOM

Flowers in a room are beautiful
Through their desire for the seed outside.
Even though they're cut from the earth,
And even though they're without hope,
Their useless desire adorns the room.   5
You too sit in my room, made beautiful
By your love for someone else.

I can't help you.
The happy ones wear a thin gold band in their black hair
And a mark of joy is on their forehead.   10
And a Greek looks with blue eyes
Into a dark thicket and is in the dream of a woman
Far away without his knowing.

I can't help you,
The way I can't help myself.   15

I also make square pictures
Out of round love that was without limit.

Translated by Glenda Abramson and Tudor Parfitt

Dennis Brutus (1924–   )

LETTERS TO MARTHA, 1 AND 2

1

After the sentence
mingled feelings:
sick relief,
the load of the approaching days
apprehension—   5
the hints of brutality
have a depth of personal meaning;

exultation—
the sense of challenge,
of confrontation,   10
vague heroism
mixed with self-pity

and tempered by the knowledge of those
who endure much more
and endure . . .   15

2

One learns quite soon
that nails and screws
and other sizeable bits of metal
must be handed in;

and seeing them shaped and sharpened   20
one is chilled, appalled
to see how vicious it can be
—this simple, useful bit of steel:

and when these knives suddenly flash
—produced perhaps from some disciplined anus—   25
one grasps at once the steel-bright horror
in the morning air
and how soft and vulnerable is naked flesh.

Zbigniew Herbert (1924–   )

ON TRANSLATING POETRY

Like an awkward bumble-bee
he sits on the flower
until the delicate stalk bends
he squeezes through rows of petals
like the pages of a dictionary   5
he tries to reach the centre
where the scent and sweetness are
and though he has a cold
and lacks any taste
still he perseveres   10
until he knocks his head
against the yellow pistil

and here already is the end
it is difficult to penetrate
from the cups of flowers   15
to their roots
so the bumble-bee goes out
very proud

and loudly buzzing;
I have been inside
and to those
who don't quite believe him
he shows his nose
yellow with pollen

Translated by John and Bogdana Carpenter

Gerald Stern (1925–   )

BEHAVING LIKE A JEW

When I got there the dead opossum looked like
an enormous baby sleeping on the road.
It took me only a few seconds—just
seeing him there—with the hole in his back
and the wind blowing through his hair   5
to get back again into my animal sorrow.
I am sick of the country, the bloodstained
bumpers, the stiff hairs sticking out of the grilles,
the slimy highways, the heavy birds
refusing to move: 10
I am sick of the spirit of Lindbergh° over everything,
that joy in death, that philosophical
understanding of carnage, that
concentration on the species.
—I am going to be unappeased at the opossum's death.   15
I am going to behave like a Jew
and touch his face, and stare into his eyes,
and pull him off the road.
I am not going to stand in a wet ditch
with the Toyotas and the Chevies passing over me   20
at sixty miles an hour
and praise the beauty and the balance
and lose myself in the immortal lifestream
when my hands are still a little shaky
from his stiffness and his bulk   25
and my eyes are still weak and misty
from his round belly and his curved fingers
and his black whiskers and his little dancing feet.

BEHAVING LIKE A JEW. 11 *Lindbergh:* Charles Lindbergh, the first pilot to cross the Atlantic Ocean, was idealized as an American hero in the 1920s and 1930s.

BURYING AN ANIMAL ON THE WAY TO NEW YORK

Don't flinch when you come across a dead animal lying on the road;
you are being shown the secret of life.
Drive slowly over the brown flesh;
you are helping to bury it.
If you are the last mourner there will be no cares   5
at all from the crushed limbs
and you will have to slide over the dark spot imagining
the first suffering all by yourself
Shreds of spirit and little ghost fragments will be spread out
for two miles above the white highway.   10
Slow down with your radio off and your window open
to hear the twittering as you go by.

Donald Justice (1925–   )

TRAIN

*(Heading north through Florida, late at night and long ago, and ending with a line
from Thomas Wolfe)°*

Midnight or after, and the little lights
Glitter like lost beads from a broken necklace
Beyond smudged windows, lost and irretrievable—
Some promise of romance these Southern nights
Never entirely keep—unless, sleepless,   5
We should pass down dim corridors again
To stand, braced in a swaying vestibule,
Alone with the darkness and the wind—out there
Nothing but pines and one new road perhaps,
Straight and white, aimed at the distant gulf—   10
And hear, from the smoking room, the sudden high-pitched
Whinny of laughter pass from throat to throat;
And the great wheels smash and pound beneath our feet.

TRAIN. epigraph: *Thomas Wolfe:* Romantic Southern novelist of the 1930s who wrote about life in
New York City.

ON THE DEATH OF FRIENDS IN CHILDHOOD

We shall not ever meet them bearded in heaven,
Nor sunning themselves among the bald of hell;

If anywhere, in the deserted schoolyard at twilight,
Forming a ring, perhaps, or joining hands
In games whose very names we have forgotten.   5
Come, memory, let us seek them there in the shadows.

Robert Creeley (1926–   )

I KNOW A MAN

As I sd to my
friend, because I am
always talking,—John, I

sd, which was not his
name, the darkness sur-   5
rounds us, what

can we do against
it, or else, shall we &
why not, buy a goddamn big car,

drive, he sd, for   10
christ's sake, look
out where yr going.

GOODBYE

She stood at the window. There was
a sound, a light.
She stood at the window. A face.

Was it that she was looking for,
he thought. Was it that   5
she was looking for. He said,

turn from it, turn
from it. The pain is
not unpainful. Turn from it.

The act of her anger, of   10
the anger she felt then,
not turning to him.

Allen Ginsberg (1926–   )

A SUPERMARKET IN CALIFORNIA

What thoughts I have of you tonight, Walt Whitman, for I walked down the sidestreets under the trees with a headache self-conscious looking at the full moon.

In my hungry fatigue, and shopping for images, I went into the neon fruit supermarket, dreaming of your enumerations!°

What peaches and what penumbras!° Whole families shopping at night! Aisles full of husbands! Wives in the avocados, babies in the tomatoes!—and you, García Lorca, what were you doing down by the watermelons?

I saw you, Walt Whitman, childless, lonely old grubber, poking among the meats in the refrigerator and eyeing the grocery boys.

I heard you asking questions of each: Who killed the pork chops? What price bananas? Are you my Angel?   5

I wandered in and out of the brilliant stacks of cans following you, and followed in my imagination by the store detective.

We strode down the open corridors together in our solitary fancy tasting artichokes, possessing every frozen delicacy, and never passing the cashier.

Where are we going, Walt Whitman? The doors close in an hour. Which way does your beard point tonight?

(I touch your book and dream of our odyssey in the supermarket and feel absurd.)

Will we walk all night through solitary streets? The trees add shade to shade, lights out in the houses, we'll both be lonely.   10

Will we stroll dreaming of the lost America of love past blue automobiles in driveways, home to our silent cottage?

Ah, dear father, graybeard, lonely old courage-teacher, what America did you have when Charon° quit poling his ferry and you got out on a smoking bank and stood watching the boat disappear on the black waters of Lethe?°

A SUPERMARKET IN CALIFORNIA. 2 *enumerations:* lists, catalogues. 3 *penumbras:* shadows. 12 *Charon:* ferryman of the underworld; *Lethe:* river of forgetfulness in underworld.

James Merrill (1926–1995)

THE BROKEN HOME

Crossing the street,
I saw the parents and the child

At their window, gleaming like fruit
With evening's mild gold leaf.

In a room on the floor below,   5
Sunless, cooler—a brimming
Saucer of wax, marbly and dim—
I have lit what's left of my life.

I have thrown out yesterday's milk
And opened a book of maxims.°   10
The flame quickens. The word stirs.

Tell me, tongue of fire,
That you and I are as real
At least as the people upstairs.

My father, who had flown in World War I,   15
Might have continued to invest his life
In cloud banks well above Wall Street and wife.
But the race was run below, and the point was to win.

Too late now, I make out in his blue gaze
(Through the smoked glass of being thirty-six)   20
The soul eclipsed by twin black pupils, sex
And business; time was money in those days.

Each thirteenth year he married. When he died
There were already several chilled wives
In sable orbit—rings, cars, permanent waves.   25
We'd felt him warming up for a green bride.

He could afford it. He was "in his prime"
At three score ten. But money was not time.

When my parents were younger this was a popular act:
A veiled woman would leap from an electric, wine-dark car   30
To the steps of no matter what—the Senate or the Ritz Bar—
And bodily, at newsreel speed, attack

No matter whom—Al Smith° or José Maria Sert°
Or Clemenceau°—veins standing out on her throat
As she yelled *War mongerer! Pig! Give us the vote!*,   35
And would have to be hauled away in her hobble skirt.

What had the man done? Oh, made history.
Her business (he had implied) was giving birth,
Tending the house, mending the socks.

THE BROKEN HOME. 10 *maxims:* wise sayings.   33 *Al Smith:* American politician; *José Maria Sert:*
South American–born architect.   34 *Clemenceau:* French statesman.

Always that same old story—
Father Time and Mother Earth,
A marriage on the rocks.

One afternoon, red, satyr°-thighed
Michael, the Irish setter, head
Passionately lowered, led
The child I was to a shut door. Inside,

Blinds beat sun from the bed.
The green-gold room throbbed like a bruise.
Under a sheet, clad in taboos
Lay whom we sought, her hair undone, outspread,

And of a blackness found, if ever now, in old
Engravings where the acid bit.
I must have needed to touch it
Or the whiteness—was she dead?
Her eyes flew open, startled strange and cold.
The dog slumped to the floor. She reached for me. I fled.

Tonight they have stepped out onto the gravel.
The party is over. It's the fall
Of 1931. They love each other still.

She: Charlie, I can't stand the pace.
He: Come on, honey—why, you'll bury us all!

A lead soldier guards my windowsill:
Khaki rifle, uniform, and face.
Something in me grows heavy, silvery, pliable.

How intensely people used to feel!
Like metal poured at the close of a proletarian novel,
Refined and glowing from the crucible,
I see those two hearts, I'm afraid,
Still. Cool here in the graveyard of good and evil,
They are even so to be honored and obeyed.

. . . Obeyed, at least, inversely. Thus
I rarely buy a newspaper, or vote.
To do so, I have learned, is to invite
The tread of a stone guest within my house.

Shooting this rusted bolt, though, against him,
I trust I am no less time's child than some
Who on the heath impersonate Poor Tom°
Or on the barricades risk life and limb.

40

45

50

55

60

65

70

75

---

43 *satyr:* woodland god with goat horns and hoofs.   77 *Poor Tom:* legendary mad wanderer on English heath.

Nor do I try to keep a garden, only
An avocado in a glass of water—
Roots pallid, gemmed with air. And later,   80

When the small gilt leaves have grown
Fleshy and green, I let them die, yes, yes,
And start another. I am earth's no less.

A child, a red dog roam the corridors,   85
Still, of the broken home. No sound. The brilliant
Rag runners halt before wide-open doors.
My old room! Its wallpaper—cream, medallioned
With pink and brown—brings back the first nightmares,
Long summer colds, and Emma, sepia-faced,   90
Perspiring over broth carried upstairs
Aswim with golden fats I could not taste.

The real house became a boarding-school.
Under the ballroom ceiling's allegory
Someone at last may actually be allowed   95
To learn something; or, from my window, cool
With the unstiflement of the entire story,
Watch a red setter stretch and sink in cloud.

Bohdan Boychuk (1927–   )

LATE SPRING

In 1980
spring was late
in Georgia.

Only one bare tree
that I passed
had some buds   5
pushing through the bark,
like white blisters
bursting on the wind.

On my way back,   10
I failed to notice
that tree.

And I realized
that I was late into my life,
walking out of the landscape   15
and entering myself.

    Translated by David Ignatow

John Ashbery (1927–   )

DOWN BY THE STATION,
EARLY IN THE MORNING

It all wears out. I keep telling myself this, but
I can never believe me, though others do. Even things do.
And the things they do. Like the rasp of silk, or a certain
Glottal stop in your voice as you are telling me how you
Didn't have time to brush your teeth but gargled with Listerine   5
Instead. Each is a base one might wish to touch once more

Before dying. There's the moment years ago in the station in Venice,
The dark rainy afternoon in fourth grade, and the shoes then,
Made of a dull crinkled brown leather that no longer exists.
And nothing does, until you name it, remembering, and even then   10
It may not have existed, or existed only as a result
Of the perceptual dysfunction you've been carrying around for years.
The result is magic, then terror, then pity at the emptiness,
Then air gradually bathing and filling the emptiness as it leaks,
Emoting all over something that is probably mere reportage   15
But nevertheless likes being emoted on. And so each day
Culminates in merriment as well as a deep shock like an electric one,

As the wrecking ball bursts through the wall with the bookshelves
Scattering the works of famous authors as well as those
Of more obscure ones, and books with no author, letting in   20
Space, and an extraneous babble from the street
Confirming the new value the hollow core has again, the light
From the lighthouse that protects as it pushes us away.

THE ONE THING THAT
CAN SAVE AMERICA

Is anything central?
Orchards flung out on the land,
Urban forests, rustic plantations, knee-high hills?
Are place names central?

Elm Grove, Adcock Corner, Story Book Farm?   5
As they concur with a rush at eye level
Beating themselves into eyes which have had enough
Thank you, no more thank you.
And they come on like scenery mingled with darkness
The damp plains, overgrown suburbs,   10
Places of known civic pride, of civil obscurity.

These are connected to my version of America
But the juice is elsewhere.
This morning as I walked out of your room
After breakfast crosshatched with   15
Backward and forward glances, backward into light,
Forward into unfamiliar light,
Was it our doing, and was it
The material, the lumber of life, or of lives
We were measuring, counting?   20
A mood soon to be forgotten
In crossed girders of light, cool downtown shadow
In this morning that has seized us again?

I know that I braid too much my own
Snapped-off perceptions of things as they come to me.   25
They are private and always will be.
Where then are the private turns of event
Destined to boom later like golden chimes
Released over a city from a highest tower?
The quirky things that happen to me, and I tell you,   30
And you instantly know what I mean?
What remote orchard reached by winding roads
Hides them? Where are these roots?

It is the lumps and trials
That tell us whether we shall be known   35
And whether our fate can be exemplary, like a star.
All the rest is waiting
For a letter that never arrives,
Day after day, the exasperation
Until finally you have ripped it open not knowing what it is,   40
The two envelope halves lying on a plate.
The message was wise, and seemingly
Dictated a long time ago.
Its truth is timeless, but its time has still
Not arrived, telling of danger, and the mostly limited   45
Steps that can be taken against danger
Now and in the future, in cool yards,
In quiet small houses in the country,
Our country, in fenced areas, in cool shady streets.
                                                            [1975]

Galway Kinnel (1927–   )

FIRST SONG

Then it was dusk in Illinois, the small boy
After an afternoon of carting dung

Hung on the rail fence, a sapped thing
Weary to crying. Dark was growing tall
And he began to hear the pond frogs all
Calling on his ear with what seemed their joy. 5

Soon their sound was pleasant for a boy
Listening in the smoky dusk and the nightfall
Of Illinois, and from the fields two small
Boys came bearing cornstalk violins 10
And they rubbed the cornstalk bows with resins
And the three sat there scraping of their joy.

It was now fine music the frogs and the boys
Did in the towering Illinois twilight make
And into dark in spite of a shoulder's ache 15
A boy's hunched body loved out of a stalk
The first song of his happiness, and the song woke
His heart to the darkness and into the sadness of joy.

James Wright (1927–1980)

AUTUMN BEGINS IN MARTINS FERRY, OHIO

In the Shreve High football stadium,
I think of Polacks nursing long beers in Tiltonsville,
And gray faces of Negroes in the blast furnace at Benwood,
And the ruptured night watchman of Wheeling Steel,
Dreaming of heroes. 5

All the proud fathers are ashamed to go home.
Their women cluck like starved pullets,
Dying for love.

Therefore,
Their sons grow suicidally beautiful 10
At the beginning of October,
And gallop terribly against each other's bodies.

OUTSIDE FARGO, NORTH DAKOTA

Along the sprawled body of the derailed
  Great Northern freight car,
I strike a match slowly and lift it slowly.
No wind.

Beyond town, three heavy white horses
Wade all the way to their shoulders
In a silo shadow.

Suddenly the freight car lurches.
The door slams back, a man with a flashlight
Calls me good evening.
I nod as I write good evening, lonely
And sick for home.

Maya Angelou (1928–   )

AFRICA

Thus she had lain
sugar cane sweet

deserts her hair
golden her feet
mountains her breasts
two Niles° her tears
Thus she has lain
Black through the years.

Over the white seas
rime white and cold
brigands ungentled
icicle bold
took her young daughters
sold her strong sons
churched her with Jesus
bled her with guns.
Thus she has lain.

Now she is rising
remember her pain
remember the losses
her screams loud and vain
remember her riches
her history slain
now she is striding
although she had lain.

10

15

20

25

AFRICA. *6 Niles:* The Nile, an ancient African river.

Philip Levine (1928–   )

COMING HOME

Detroit, 1968

A winter Tuesday, the city pouring fire,
Ford Rouge° sulfurs the sun, Cadillac, Lincoln,
Chevy gray. The fat stacks
of breweries hold their tongues. Rags,
papers, hands, the stems of birches   5
dirtied with words.
                      Near the freeway
you stop and wonder what came off,
recall the snowstorm where you lost it all,
the wolverine, the northern bear, the wolf   10
caught out, ice and steel raining
from the foundries in a shower
of human breath. On sleds in the false sun
the new material rests. One brown child
stares and stares into your frozen eyes   15
until the lights change and you go
forward to work. The charred faces, the eyes
boarded up, the rubble of innards, the cry
of wet smoke hanging in your throat,
the twisted river stopped at the color of iron.   20
We burn this city every day.

COMING HOME. 2 *Ford Rouge*, etc.: automotive plants in Detroit.

Donald Hall (1928–   )

NAMES OF HORSES

All winter your brute shoulders strained against collars, padding
and steerhide over the ash hames,° to haul
sledges of cordwood for drying through spring and summer,
for the Glenwood stove next winter, and for the simmering range.

In April you pulled cartloads of manure to spread on the fields,   5
dark manure of Holsteins,° and knobs of your own clustered with oats.

NAMES OF HORSES. 2 *hames*: parts of harness.   6 *Holsteins*: cattle.

All summer you mowed the grass in meadow and hayfield, the mowing machine
clacketing beside you, while the sun walked high in the morning;

and after noon's heat, you pulled a clawed rake through the same acres,
gathering stacks, and dragged the wagon from stack to stack,   10
and the built hayrack back, up hill to the chaffy barn,
three loads of hay a day, hanging wide from the hayrack.

Sundays you trotted the two miles to church with the light load
of a leather quartertop buggy, and grazed in the sound of hymns.
Generation on generation, your neck rubbed the window sill   15
of the stall, smoothing the wood as the sea smooths glass.

When you were old and lame, when your shoulders hurt bending to graze,
one October the man who fed you and kept you, and harnessed you
          every morning,
led you through corn stubble to sandy ground above Eagle Pond,
and dug a hole beside you where you stood shuddering in your skin,   20

and lay the shotgun's muzzle in the boneless hollow behind your ear,
and fired the slug into your brain, and felled you into your grave,
shoveling sand to cover you, setting goldenrod upright above you,
where by next summer a dent in the ground made your monument.

For a hundred and fifty years, in the pasture of dead horses,   25
roots of pine trees pushed through the pale curves of your ribs,
yellow blossoms flourished above you in autumn, and in winter
frost heaved your bones in the ground—old toilers, soil makers:

O Roger, Mackerel, Riley, Ned, Nellie, Chester, Lady Ghost.

Derek Walcott (1930–   )

THE SEASON OF PHANTASMAL PEACE

Then all the nations of birds lifted together
the huge net of the shadows of this earth
in multitudinous dialects, twittering tongues,
stitching and crossing it. They lifted up
the shadows of long pines down trackless slopes,
the shadows of glass-faced towers down evening streets,
the shadow of a frail plant on a city sill—
the net rising soundless as night, the birds' cries soundless, until

there was no longer dusk, or season, decline, or weather,
only this passage of phantasmal light 10
that not the narrowest shadow dared to sever.

And men could not see, looking up, what the wild geese drew,
what the ospreys trailed behind them in silvery ropes
that flashed in the icy sunlight; they could not hear
battalions of starlings waging peaceful cries, 15
bearing the net higher, covering this world
like the vines of an orchard, or a mother drawing
the trembling gauze over the trembling eyes
of a child fluttering to sleep;
                        it was the light 20
that you will see at evening on the side of a hill
in yellow October, and no one hearing knew
what change had brought into the raven's cawing,
the killdeer's screech, the ember-circling chough
such an immense, soundless, and high concern 25
for the fields and cities where the birds belong,
except it was their seasonal passing, Love,
made seasonless, or, from the high privilege of their birth,
something brighter than pity for the wingless ones
below them who shared dark holes in windows and in houses, 30
and higher they lifted the net with soundless voices
above all change, betrayals of falling suns,
and this season lasted one moment, like the pause
between dusk and darkness, between fury and peace,
but, for such as our earth is now, it lasted long. 35

Tomas Tranströmer (1931–   )

TRACKS

---

2 a.m.: moonlight. The train has stopped
out in the middle of the plain. Far away, points of light in a town,
flickering coldly at the horizon.

As when someone has gone into a dream so deep
he'll never remember having been there 5
when he comes back to his room.

As when someone has gone into an illness so deep
everything his days were becomes a few flickering points, a swarm,
cold and tiny at the horizon.

The train is standing quite still.
2 a.m.: bright moonlight, few stars.

10

UNDER PRESSURE

The roar of engines in the blue sky is deafening.
We're living here on a shuddering work-site
where the ocean depths can suddenly open up—
shells and telephones hiss.

Beauty you can see only hastily from the side.   5
The dense grain on the field, many colors in a yellow stream.
The restless shadows in my head are drawn there.
They want to creep into the grain and turn to gold.

Darkness falls. At midnight I go to bed.
The smaller boat puts out from the larger boat.   10
You are alone on the water.
Society's dark hull drifts further and further away.

Tranströmer poems translated by Robin Fulton

W. S. Merwin (1932–   )

LOOKING FOR MUSHROOMS AT SUNRISE

for Jean and Bill Arrowsmith

When it is not yet day
I am walking on centuries of dead chestnut leaves
In a place without grief
Though the oriole
Out of another life warns me   5
That I am awake

In the dark while the rain fell
The gold chanterelles pushed through a sleep that was not mine
Waking me
So that I came up the mountain to find them   10

Where they appear it seems I have been before
I recognize their haunts as though remembering
Another life

Where else am I walking even now
Looking for me   15

IN THE WINTER OF MY
THIRTY-EIGHTH YEAR

It sounds unconvincing to say *When I was young*
Though I have long wondered what it would be like
To be me now
No older at all it seems from here
As far from myself as ever   5

Waking in fog and rain and seeing nothing
I imagine all the clocks have died in the night
Now no one is looking I could choose my age
It would be younger I suppose so I am older
It is there at hand I could take it   10
Except for the things I think I would do differently
They keep coming between they are what I am
They have taught me little I did not know when I was young

There is nothing wrong with my age now probably
It is how I have come to it   15
Like a thing I kept putting off as I did my youth

There is nothing the matter with speech
Just because it lent itself
To my uses

Of course there is nothing the matter with the stars   20
It is my emptiness among them
While they drift farther away in the invisible morning

Allen Grossman (1932–   )

THE ROOM

A man is sitting in a room made quiet by him.
Outside, the August wind is turning the leaves of its book.
The door is open, everything is disclosed, each leaf, all the voices.

The man is resting from the making of the quiet in which he sits.
The floor is swept, his books are laid aside open, his eyes are open.   5
All the leaves and voices are outside in the restless wind.

Soon he will rise, or take up a book, or someone will enter;
Or, perhaps, a leaf will come in across the threshold, or a voice
Will blunder through the room, blind and unanswerable on its way elsewhere.

But now the room is quiet as the man has made it.   10
Everything in its place is at rest inside the room.
And the man is at rest, seeing each leaf, and hearing all the voices.

Sylvia Plath (1932–1963)

WINTERING

This is the easy time, there is nothing doing.
I have whirled the midwife's extractor,
I have my honey,
Six jars of it,
Six cat's eyes in the wine cellar,   5

Wintering in a dark without window
At the heart of the house
Next to the last tenant's rancid jam
And the bottles of empty glitters—
Sir So-and-so's gin.   10

This is the room I have never been in.
This is the room I could never breathe in.
The black bunched in there like a bat,
No light
But the torch and its faint   15

Chinese yellow on appalling objects—
Black asininity. Decay.
Possession.
It is they who own me.
Neither cruel nor indifferent,   20

Only ignorant.
This is the time of hanging on for the bees—the bees
So slow I hardly know them,
Filing like soldiers
To the syrup tin   25

To make up for the honey I've taken.
Tate and Lyle keeps them going,
The refined snow.
It is Tate and Lyle they live on, instead of flowers.
They take it. The cold sets in.   30

Now they ball in a mass,
Black

Mind against all that white.
The smile of the snow is white.
It spreads itself out, a mile-long body of Meissen,° 35

Into which, on warm days,
They can only carry their dead.
The bees are all women,
Maids and the long royal lady.
They have got rid of the men, 40

The blunt, clumsy stumblers, the boors.
Winter is for women—
The woman, still at her knitting,
At the cradle of Spanish walnut,
Her body a bulb in the cold and too dumb to think. 45

Will the hive survive, will the gladiolas
Succeed in banking their fires
To enter another year?
What will they taste of, the Christmas roses?
The bees are flying. They taste the spring. 50

WINTERING. 35 *Meissen:* a delicate porcelain.

WINTER TREES

The wet dawn inks are doing their blue dissolve.
On their blotter of fog the trees
Seem a botanical drawing—
Memories growing, ring on ring,
A series of weddings. 5

Knowing neither abortions nor bitchery,
Truer than women,
They seed so effortlessly!
Tasting the winds, that are footless,
Waist-deep in history— 10

Full of wings, otherworldliness.
In this, they are Ledas.°
O mother of leaves and sweetness
Who are these pietas?
The shadows of ringdoves chanting, but easing nothing. 15

WINTER TREES. 12 *Ledas:* Leda, the maiden who was raped by Zeus in the guise of a swan.

Imants Ziedonis (1933–   )

I LOVE A FLOATING APPLE

I love a floating apple in the night.
Treeless, twigless,
I love the floating apple tree in the night,
rootless, weighting down branches in the night.

And the whole earth, afloat in the night   5
neither borne nor braced by anyone
I love darkness—that doesn't disappear
as I wake again

But keeps a distance, unseen
and then, as the sun sets, draws near.   10
I see someone approaching:
emerging from the dark, merging into the dark again.

Translated by Barry Callagham

Etheridge Knight (1933–1990)

IT WAS A FUNKY DEAL

It was a funky deal.
The only thing real was red,
Red blood around his red, red beard.

It was a funky deal.

In the beginning was the word,   5

And in the end the deed.
Judas did it to Jesus
For the same Herd.   Same reason.
You made them mad, Malcolm.° Same reason.

It was a funky deal.   10

You rocked too many boats, man.
Pulled too many coats, man.
Saw through the jive.

IT WAS A FUNKY DEAL. 9 *Malcolm*: Malcolm X, civil rights leader, assassinated in 1965.

You reached the wild guys
Like me.   You and Bird.° (And that
Lil LeRoi° cat.)

It was a funky deal.

15 *Bird:* Charlie "Bird" Parker, legendary saxophonist.   16 *LeRoi:* LeRoi Jones, African American
writer who changed his name to Amiri Baraka.

Audre Lorde (1934–1992)

HANGING FIRE

I am fourteen
and my skin has betrayed me
the boy I cannot live without
still sucks his thumb
in secret   5
how come my knees are
always so ashy
what if I die
before morning
and momma's in the bedroom   10
with the door closed.

I have to learn how to dance
in time for the next party
my room is too small for me
suppose I die before graduation   15
they will sing sad melodies
but finally
tell the truth about me
There is nothing I want to do
and too much   20
that has to be done
and momma's in the bedroom
with the door closed.

Nobody even stops to think
about my side of it   25
I should have been on Math Team
my marks were better than his
why do I have to be
the one
wearing braces   30
I have nothing to wear tomorrow

will I live long enough
to grow up
and momma's in the bedroom
with the door closed.   35

N. Scott Momaday (1934–   )

THE DELIGHT SONG OF TSOAI-TALEE

I am a feather on the bright sky
I am the blue horse that runs in the plain
I am the fish that rolls, shining, in the water
I am the shadow that follows a child
I am the evening light, the lustre of meadows   5
I am an eagle playing with the wind
I am a cluster of bright beads
I am the farthest star
I am the cold of the dawn
I am the roaring of the rain   10
I am the glitter on the crust of the snow
I am the long track of the moon in a lake
I am a flame of four colors
I am a deer standing away in the dusk
I am a field of sumac and the pomme blanche   15
I am an angle of geese in the winter sky
I am the hunger of a young wolf
I am the whole dream of these things

You see, I am alive, I am alive
I stand in good relation to the earth   20
I stand in good relation to the gods
I stand in good relation to all that is beautiful
I stand in good relation to the daughter of Tsen-tainte
You see, I am alive, I am alive

Mark Strand (1934–   )

KEEPING THINGS WHOLE

In a field
I am the absence
of field.
This is
always the case.   5

Wherever I am
I am what is missing.

When I walk
I part the air
and always   10
the air moves in
to fill the spaces
where my body's been.

We all have reasons
for moving.   15
I move
to keep things whole.

Frank Bidart (1939–   )

TO THE DEAD

What I hope (when I hope) is that we'll
see each other again,—

. . . and again reach the VEIN

in which we loved each other . . .
It existed. *It existed.*   5

There is a NIGHT within the NIGHT,—

. . . for, like the detectives (the Ritz Brothers)
in *The Gorilla*,°

once we'd been battered by the gorilla

we searched the walls, the intricately carved   10
impenetrable panelling

for a button, lever, latch

that unlocks a secret door that
reveals at last the secret chambers,

CORRIDORS within WALLS,   15

(the disenthralling, necessary, dreamed structure
beneath the structure we see,)

TO THE DEAD. 8 *The Gorilla*: a film starring the Ritz Brothers, a comedy team.

that is the HOUSE within the HOUSE . . .

There is a NIGHT within the NIGHT,—

. . . there were (for example) months when I seemed only   20
to displease, frustrate,

disappoint you—; then, something triggered

a drunk lasting for days, and as you
slowly and shakily sobered up,

sick, throbbing with remorse and self-loathing,   25

insight like ashes: clung
to; useless; hated . . .

This was the viewing of the power of the waters

while the waters were asleep:—

secrets, histories of loves, betrayals, double-binds   30
not fit (you thought) for the light of day . . .

There is a NIGHT within the NIGHT,—

. . . for, there at times at night, still we
inhabit the secret place together . . .

Is this wisdom, or self-pity?—   35

The love I've known is the love of
two people staring

not at each other, but in the same direction.

Seamus Heaney (1939–   )

THE SKUNK

Up, black, striped and damasked° like the chasuble°
At a funeral Mass, the skunk's tail
Paraded the skunk. Night after night
I expected her like a visitor.

The refrigerator whinnied into silence.   5
My desk light softened beyond the verandah.

THE SKUNK. 1 *damasked:* richly patterned; *chasuble:* sleeveless garment worn by priest.

Small oranges loomed in the orange tree.
I began to be tense as a voyeur.

After eleven years I was composing
Love-letters again, broaching the word 'wife'   10
Like a stored cask, as if its slender vowel
Had mutated into the night earth and air

Of California. The beautiful, useless
Tang of eucalyptus spelt your absence.
The aftermath of a mouthful of wine   15
Was like inhaling you off a cold pillow.

And there she was, the intent and glamorous.
Ordinary, mysterious skunk,
Mythologized, demythologized,
Snuffing the boards five feet beyond me.   20

It all came back to me last night, stirred
By the sootfall of your things at bedtime.
Your head-down, tail-up hunt in a bottom drawer
For the black plunge-line nightdress.

Joseph Brodsky (1940–)

SIX YEARS LATER

So long had life together been that now
the second of January fell again
on Tuesday, making her astonished brow
lift like a windshield wiper in the rain,
  so that her misty sadness cleared, and showed   5
  a cloudless distance waiting up the road.

So long had life together been that once
the snow began to fall, it seemed unending;
that, lest the flakes should make her eyelids wince,
I'd shield them with my hand, and they, pretending   10
  not to believe that cherishing of eyes,
  would beat against my palm like butterflies.

So alien had all novelty become
that sleep's entanglements would put to shame
whatever depths the analysts might plumb;   15

that when my lips blew out the candle flame,
>   her lips, fluttering from my shoulder, sought
>   to join my own, without another thought.

So long had life together been that all
that tattered brood of papered roses went,
and a whole birch grove grew upon the wall,
and we had money, by some accident,
>   and tonguelike on the sea, for thirty days,
>   the sunset threatened Turkey with its blaze.

So long had life together been without
books, chairs, utensils—only that ancient bed—
that the triangle, before it came about,
had been a perpendicular, the head
>   of some acquaintance hovering above
>   two points which had been coalesced by love.

So long had life together been that she
and I, with our joint shadows, had composed
a double door, a door which, even if we
were lost in work or sleep, was always closed:
>   somehow its halves were split and we went right
>   through them into the future, into night.

[1969]

Translated by Richard Wilbur

Jaan Kaplinski (1941–   )

UNTITLED POEM

This summer is full of insects.
As soon as you go to the garden,
a cloud of flies buzzes around your head.
Bumblebees nest in the birdhouses,
wasps nest in the hazel,
and as I sit at the window
I hear a buzz I cannot name,
whether the voice of bumblebees, wasps,
or electric lines,
a plane in the sky, a car on the road,
or the voice of life itself that wants
to tell you something from the inside out.

Translated by Jaan Kaplinski with Sam Hamill and Riina Tamm

Mahmoud Darwish (1942–   )

PSALM 4

I left my face on my mother's handkerchief,
packed the mountains in my memory
and departed . . .
The city was slamming its doors
and moving onto ships, multiplying   5
the way weeds multiply in receding gardens . . .
I lean against the wind.
You, unbreakable figure—
why am I staggering? When you are my wall?

The distance hones me, the way   10
fresh death hones the faces of lovers.
The closer I get to the psalms,
the leaner I grow . . .
Oh, passageways busy with emptiness:
when will I arrive?   15

Blessed is he who cloaks himself in his own skin!
Blessed is he who remembers his first name without a mistake!
Blessed is he who eats an apple and does not become a tree!
Blessed is he who drinks from the waters of distant rivers
and does not turn into a cloud!   20
Blessed is the rock that worships its own captivity,
and does not choose the freedom of the wind!

Translated by Lena Jayyusi and Anselm Hollo

From "Poems, Essays, Documents," *Poetry East* #28, Spring 1989. Reprinted by permission.

Douglas Dunn (1942–   )

THE CLOTHES PIT

The young women are obsessed with beauty.
Their old fashioned sewing machines rattle in Terry Street.
They must keep up, they must keep up.

They wear teasing skirts and latest shoes,
Lush, impermanent coats, American cosmetics.   5
But they lack intellectual grooming.

In the culture of clothes and little philosophies,
They only have clothes. They do not need to be seen
Carrying a copy of *International Times*,

Or the Liverpool Poets, the wish to justify their looks   10
With things beyond themselves. They mix up colours,
And somehow they are often fat and unlovely.

They don't get high on pot, but get sick on cheap
Spanish Burgundy, or beer in rampant pubs,
And come home supported and kissed and bad-tempered.   15

But they have clothes, bright enough to show they dream
Of places other than this, an inarticulate paradise,
Eating exotic fowl in sunshine with courteous boys.

Three girls go down the street with the summer wind.
The litter of pop rhetoric blows down Terry Street,   20
Bounces past their feet, into their lives.

Sharon Olds (1942–   )

THE ELDER SISTER

When I look at my elder sister now
I think how she had to go first, down through the
birth canal, to force her way
head-first through the tiny channel,
the pressure of Mother's muscles on her brain,   5
the tight walls scraping her skin.
Her face is still narrow from it, the long
hollow cheeks of a Crusader on a tomb,
and her inky eyes have the look of someone who has
been in prison a long time and   10
knows they can send her back. I look at her
body and think how her breasts were the first to
rise, slowly, like swans on a pond.

By the time mine came along, they were just
two more birds on the flock, and when the hair   15
rose on the white mound of her flesh, like
threads of water out of the ground, it was the
first time, but when mine came
they knew about it. I used to think
only in terms of her harshness, sitting and   20
pissing on me in bed, but now I

see I had her before me always
like a shield. I look at her wrinkles, her clenched
jaws, her frown-lines—I see they are
the dents on my shield, the blows that did not reach me.   25
She protected me, not as a mother
protects a child, with love, but as a
hostage protects the one who makes her
escape as I made my escape, with my sister's
body held in front of me.

William Corbett (1942–   )

OUT THE WINDOW

After lunch I nap
sitting in a chair
and wake looking out
through the mess
of ailanthus branches   5
to lattice topped
decks until I stare
and all disappears.
I want to return
lean and wantless,   10
out from under
what crushes me,
but I never do.
What weighs
my heart is me.   15

Dave Smith (1942–   )

THE CHESAPEAKE AND OHIO CANAL

Thick now with sludge from the years of suburbs, with toys,
fenders, wine bottles, tampons, skeletons of possums,
edged by blankets of leaves, jellied wrappers unshakably
stuck to the scrub pines that somehow lift themselves
from the mossed wall of blockstone headlined a hundred   5
years back, this water is bruised as a shoe at Goodwill.
Its brown goes nowhere, neither does it remain, and elms
bend over its heavy back like patient fans, dreamlessly.
This is the death of hope's commerce, the death of cities

924

blank as winter light, the death of people who are gone 10
erratic and passive as summer's glittering water-skimmers.
Yet those two climbing that path like a single draft horse
saw the heart of the water break open only minutes ago,
and the rainbow trout walked its tail as if the evening
was only an offering in an unimaginable room where plans 15
inch ahead for the people, as if the trout always meant
to hang from their chain, to be borne through last shades
like a lure drawn carefully, deviously in the blue ache
of air that thickens still streets between brown walls.

Louise Glück (1943–   )

THE DROWNED CHILDREN

You see, they have no judgment.
So it is natural that they should drown,
first the ice taking them in
and then, all winter, their wool scarves
floating behind them as they sink 5
until at last they are quiet.
And the pond lifts them in its manifold dark arms.

But death must come to them differently,
so close to the beginning.
As though they had always been 10
blind and weightless. Therefore
the rest is dreamed, the lamp,
the good white cloth that covered the table,
their bodies.

And yet they hear the names they used 15
like lures slipping over the pond:
What are you waiting for
come home, come home, lost
in the waters, blue and permanent.

Mark Rudman (1948–   )

THE SHOEBOX

I finally broke down and opened the shoebox
which arrived just weeks after my father died.
All winter I had put it out of sight on top

of the bookshelves where I wouldn't be tempted.
The box was not, as I would have expected,
stuffed with photographs, but packets,

wallet-sized, each with a dozen
"snaps," each sequence a kind of story,
and I couldn't have predicted how they would spring out

once I removed the rubber bands
wound tight as bowstrings around the top—
too late now to put them back,

to stop what I had set in motion—
there is no love in them, only
a memorializing will.

A predictable cast, my father's five
older sisters, their several (only three
between them!) issue.

It wasn't that everyone looked demented,
those spinster aunts, those whiz kid cousins,
but that no one looked like they wanted

to be where they were, in that parking lot fronting the beach,
in front of that penny arcade or movie marquee,
clutching that bulging suitcase. . . .

Only one glossy found its way into the box,
the only shot not taken with my father's *Minolta:*
a puppet without strings, no,

a ventriloquist's dummy, all shocked innocence—
me, glassy-eyes, open-mouthed, plenty of space
between my teeth, dangling above

my father, a rotund, baby-faced, leering man,
and his mother, a slack-jawed, toothless old woman,
greedily gazing up at the child as if she were its mother. . . .

The passersby on Times Square look happy
in a miserable sort of way.
In the mid-fifties laissez-faire seems

to extend everywhere except the family.
I plucked the images I didn't like
but when, after a few hours,

I tried to stuff the slender packets back
and close the box, even with half
of the photographs smoking in the wood stove,

they wouldn't smash down, the rubber bands
would not stretch beyond the limit
they had held for a decade,

yet I felt if I was to sleep, to have peace,
the box had to be shut.
The top had to fit snug around the edges.

Jane Kenyon (1948–1995)

THE PEAR

There is a moment in middle age
when you grow bored, angered
by your middling mind,
afraid.

That day the sun
burns hot and bright,
making you more desolate.

It happens subtly, as when a pear
spoils from the inside out,
and you may not be aware
until things have gone too far. 10

SEPTEMBER GARDEN PARTY

We sit with friends at the round
glass table. The talk is clever;
everyone rises to it. Bees
come to the spiral pear peelings
on your plate.
From my lap or your hand
the spice of our morning's privacy
comes drifting up. Fall sun 5
passes through the wine.

THE POND AT DUSK

A fly wounds the water but the wound
soon heals. Swallows tilt and twitter
overhead, dropping now and then toward
the outward-radiating evidence of food.

The green haze on the trees changes   5
into leaves, and what looks like smoke
floating over the neighbor's barn
is only apple blossoms.

But sometimes what looks like disaster
is disaster: the day comes at last,   10
and the men struggle with the casket
just clearing the pews.

Leslie Marmon Silko (1948–   )

DEER SONG

Storm winds carry snow
to the mountain stream
clotted white in silence,
pale blue streak under ice
to the sea.   5

The ice shatters into glassy
bone splinters that tear deep into
soft parts of the hoof.
Swimming away from the wolves
before dawn   10
            choking back salt water
            the streaming red froth tide.

It is necessary.
Reflections that blind
from a thousand feet of   15
gray schist
            snow-covered in dying winter sunlight.
The pain is numbed by the freezing,
            the depths of the night sky,
            the distance beyond pale stars.   20

Do you think that I do not love you
if I scream
          while I die.
Antler and thin black hoof
smashed against dark rock—   25
          the struggle is the ritual
shining teeth tangled in
          sinew and flesh.

You see,
          I will go with you.   30
Because you call softly
because you are my brother
          and my sister
Because the mountain is
our mother.   35
I will go with you
because you love me
while I die.

Marie Howe (1950–   )

GUESTS

You are at a cocktail party, talking to someone who is skewering
a small hot dog with a toothpick when you see the dead peeking
out of the pantry, motioning to you.

Your partner, looking up, just misses your raised eyebrows and
the small wave that has ended in your hand pushing through your hair.   5
You say, "Suddenly, I have a headache. I need a glass of water,"

and head through the pantry door where the hostess emerges carrying a tray
and announcing a game of charades. You allow her to pass, then step
through the empty pantry to the kitchen where the cook and three

older uncles are sitting around the kitchen table talking.   10
They say, "Sit down, sit down, the party's in here." You laugh, but decline
and go to the kitchen door where you hear something scratching to get in.

You open it to admit the cat that walks in precise steps to its bowl and eats.
Outside, the snow is falling like teeming arrows to the pavement
and piling up. A sudden roar of laughter comes from the living room.   15

Many people are calling your name. They want you on their team.
The men at the table are rising. You join them, passing by the cook
and the cat that never looks up from its dinner.

Jorie Graham (1951–   )

SALMON

I watched them once, at dusk, on television, run,
in our motel room half-way through
Nebraska, quick, glittering, past beauty, past
the importance of beauty,
archaic,   5
not even hungry, not even endangered, driving deeper and deeper
into less. They leapt up falls, ladders,
and rock, tearing and leaping, a gold river
and a blue river traveling
in opposite directions.   10
They would not stop, resolution of will
and helplessness, as the eye
is helpless
when the image forms itself, upside-down, backward,
driving up into   15
the mind, and the world
unfastens itself
from the deep ocean of the given. . . . Justice, aspen
leaves, mother attempting
suicide, the white night-flying moth   20
the ants dismantled bit by bit and carried in
right through the crack
in my wall. . . . How helpless
the still pool is,
upstream,   25
awaiting the gold blade
of their hurry. Once, indoors, a child,
I watched, at noon, through slatted wooden blinds,
a man and woman, naked, eyes closed,
climb onto each other,   30
on the terrace floor,
and ride—two gold currents
wrapping round and round each other, fastening,
unfastening. I hardly knew
what I saw. Whatever shadow there was in that world   35
it was the one each cast
onto the other,
the thin black seam
they seemed to be trying to work away
between them. I held my breath.   40
As far as I could tell, the work they did
with sweat and light
was good. I'd say

they traveled far in opposite
directions. What is the light   45
at the end of the day, deep, reddish-gold, bathing the walls,
the corridors, light that is no longer light, no longer clarifies,
illuminates, antique, freed from the body of
the air that carries it. What is it
for the space of time   50
where it is useless, merely
beautiful? When they were done, they made a distance
one from the other
and slept, outstretched,
on the warm tile   55
of the terrace floor,
smiling, faces pressed against the stone.

Rita Dove (1952–   )

MOTHERHOOD

She dreams the baby's so small she keeps
misplacing it—it rolls from the hutch
and the mouse carries it home, it disappears
with his shirt in the wash.
Then she drops it and it explodes   5
like a watermelon, eyes spitting.

Finally they get to the countryside;
Thomas has it in a sling.
He's strewing rice along the road
while the trees chitter with tiny birds.   10
In the meadow to their right three men
are playing rough with a white wolf. She calls

warning but the wolf breaks free
and she runs, the rattle   15
rolls into the gully, then she's
there and tossing the baby behind her,
listening for its cry as she straddles
the wolf and circles its throat, counting

until her thumbs push through to the earth.   20
White fur seeps red. She is hardly breathing.
The small wild eyes
go opaque with confusion and shame, like a child's.

Alice Fulton (1952–   )

THE GONE YEARS

Night pockets the house
in a blue
muffle the color
of my father's Great Depression.
I see him move   5
over the snow, leaving
the snow unmoved.
The snow has no imagination.

My mother and I shuffle by
each other as if we were   10
the dead, speechless
breathers at windows done in black
oilcloth tacked down by stars.

"It's fair that his clothes be worn
out as he was." She irons them   15
for distant cousins, the tattersalls
sending up a hush
beneath her hands.

Through January's flannel
nights she turns old   20
stories over and over,
letting the gone
years hug her
with his long wool arms.

Alan Shapiro (1952–   )

ASTRONOMY LESSON

The two boys lean out on the railing
of the front porch, looking up.
Behind them they can hear their mother
in one room watching "Name That Tune,"
their father in another watching   5
a Walter Cronkite° Special, the TVs
turned up high and higher till they
each can't hear the other's show.

ASTRONOMY LESSON. 6 *Walter Cronkite*: well-known television newscaster.

The older boy is saying that no matter
how many stars you counted there were   10
always more stars beyond them
and beyond the stars black space
going on forever in all directions,
so that even if you flew up
millions and millions of years   15
you'd be no closer to the end
of it than they were now
here on the porch on Tuesday night
in the middle of summer.
The younger boy can think somehow   20
only of his mother's closet,
how he likes to crawl in back
behind the heavy drapery
of shirts, nightgowns and dresses,
into the sheer black where   25
no matter how close he holds
his hand up to his face
there's no hand ever, no
fact to hold it to.

A woman from another street   30
is calling to her stray cat or dog,
clapping and whistling it in,
and farther away deep in the city
sirens now and again
veer in and out of hearing.   35

The boys edge closer, shoulder
to shoulder now, sad Ptolemies,°
the older looking up, the younger
as he thinks back straight ahead
into the black leaves of the maple   40
where the street lights flicker
like another watery skein of stars.
"Name That Tune" and Walter Cronkite
struggle like rough water
to rise above each other.   45
And the woman now comes walking
in a nightgown down the middle
of the street, clapping and
whistling, while the older boy
goes on about what light years   50
are, and solar winds, black holes,
and how the sun is cooling
and what will happen to
them all when it is cold.

---

37 *Ptolemies:* Ptolemy, an ancient world astronomer.

Tom Sleigh (1953–   )

HOPE

for Aunt Hope

Overhung by evergreen, your house was cool
Those afternoons the sun's long ghost shimmered
in the fading curtains. The rocker's senile
Back and forth wore ruts in the floor, the boards'

Soft creaking wheezing in, out. It's seven years   5
Since I saw you last for the last time,
Your eyes molten with remembrance's flicker
As events like magma poured and cooled, time

Confounding my grown-up face with your image
Of the photogenic faded child.   10
Who was I to you?, your bed barred like a cage,
A stainless-steel cradle, as in your head

My name roamed connectionless. And you too
Were strange, your hip smashed, your legs drawn up
And shrunken like a cricket's, your eyes' blue   15
Like clouded water in which I saw trapped,

Lost in terminal helplessness, the eyes
Of my aunt of childhood, ironic, clear,
And merciless, their killing-with-kindness
Stare that sent me to the boneyard° hour after hour   20

Those endless afternoon wars at dominoes
Still lurking aloof from your stranger's face.
I held your hand and saw in the window
The two of us suspended beyond the glass

As through us waved a dusty branch, a rag   25
Of green wiping our smudge of color
From the air. . . . Seven years, and your name still drags
Its luminous syllable like a lure

My heart still swallows, open-mouthed and hungry,
Its barb of light irresistible: 30
"Go fish in the boneyard," I hear you say,
Your eyes poker-faced, impenetrable.

HOPE. 20 *to the boneyard:* penalty in dominoes.

SUNDAY DRIVE

Beyond the window fields of milkweed pass.
The engine's hum and the spinning wheels beneath
Are like the drone of far-off voices
In the front seat. He sees in the glass

The hover of the peaks and his own face   5
Skimming across the darkness. Shadows
Sliding off the slopes lift up the Queen Anne's lace
Buoyant as the stars above the meadows'

Rising mists. The face that speeds along beside
Meets his wide stare (eyes of a schoolteacher,   10
Eyes of a scientist?). The distant glide
Of all the stars is entrusted to his care

As he voyages out among them, connecting
Them like numbered dots in a puzzle book.
Those three stars make the belt of Orion,°   *constellation* 15
And sequestered over there in a nook

Next to the moon the Seven Sisters° shine.   *constellation*
He can almost hear them talk, their glimmering
Like whispers of what he will become
(Scientist like dad; schoolteacher like mom?).   20

The round world spinning spins beneath the tires
Till the dry fields borne along on rivers
Of white mist seem to float in a blur
Through the face looking in as if the fields were

Dreams dreamed till they came true. The road   25
Spinning faster catches up to the tires
That slow to a standstill beneath the turning stars.
His eyes slowly close on the eyes of the world.

Brad Leithauser (1953–   )

ANGEL

There between the riverbank
and half-submerged tree trunk
it's a kind of alleyway
inviting loiterers—
    in this case, water striders.   5

Their legs, twice body-length, dent
the surface, but why they don't
sink is a transparent riddle:
the springs of their trampoline
    are nowhere to be seen.   10

Inches and yet far below, thin
as compass needles, almost, minnows flicker through the sun's
tattered netting, circling past
    each other as if lost.   15

Enter an angel, in
the form of a dragon-
fly, an apparition whose
coloring, were it not real,
    would scarcely be possible: 20

see him, like a sparkler,
tossing lights upon the water,
surplus greens, reds, milky
blues, and violets blended
    with ebony. Suspended   25

like a conductor's baton,
he hovers, then goes the one
way no minnow points: straight
up, into that vast solution
    of which he's a concentrate.   30

Stuart Dischell (1954–   )

EVENING

For an hour or two the evening has no limits
Or so it seems to you as you walk the pavements
Of this, your adoptive city. Before you the sun
At play lights the windows of the office buildings
In the vault of the avenue, conveying odd images   5
Like the faces seen in the flames of the hearth.

For an hour or two the evening has no limits
And you are pedaling again your English Racer,
Riding double down the boardwalk along the sea,
Your girlfriend sideways on the bar, her legs   10
Dangling out of the way, the wind blowing the ironed

Length of her hair, the wind covering and revealing
The profile of her face. Her young body was snug
Between your arms when you steered the handlebars
Past all the frowning strollers. For awhile you forget   15
But always it comes back, your brother's cologne
You wore, the games you played in her parents' bed
Until the headlights on the wall drove you home
Naked inside your clothes. She is a mother now,
You suppose. It happens that people lose touch.   20

The evening has no limits and the streets go on
What could be forever, linking cities and outposts;
Suburbs that were villages separated by farms
Have merged the way they once were forested.
What it means to be alive has never troubled you.   25
Strange as you are you have always felt this welcome.

Louise Erdrich (1954–   )

WINDIGO

For Angela

*The Windigo is a flesh-eating, wintry demon with a man buried deep inside of it.
In some Chippewa stories, a young girl vanquishes this monster by forcing boiling
lard down its throat, thereby releasing the human at the core of ice.*

You knew I was coming for you, little one,
when the kettle jumped into the fire.
Towels flapped on the hooks,
and the dog crept off, groaning,
to the deepest part of the woods.   5

In the hackles of dry brush a thin laughter started up.
Mother scolded the food warm and smooth in the pot
and called you to eat.
But I spoke in the cold trees:
New one, I have come for you, child hide and lie still.   10

The sumac pushed sour red cones through the air.
Copper burned in the raw wood.
You saw me drag toward you.
Oh touch me. I murmured, and licked the soles of your feet.
You dug your hands into my pale, melting fur.   15

I stole you off, a huge thing in my bristling armor.
Steam rolled from my wintry arms, each leaf shivered

from the bushes we passed
until they stood, naked, spread like the cleaned spines of fish.

Then your warm hands hummed over and shoveled themselves full
of the ice and the snow. I would darken and spill
all night running, until at last morning broke the cold earth
and I carried you home,
a river shaking in the sun.

[1984]

Lorna Dee Cervantes (1954–)

POEM FOR THE YOUNG WHITE MAN

Who Asked Me How I, An Intelligent Well-Read Person
Could Believe in the War Between Races

In my land there are no distinctions.
The barbed wire politics of oppression
have been torn down long ago. The only reminder
of past battles, lost or won, is a slight
rutting in the fertile fields.   5

In my land
people write poems about love,
full of nothing but contented childlike syllables.
Everyone reads Russian short stories and weeps.
There are no boundaries.   10
There is no hunger, no
complicated famine or greed.

I am not a revolutionary.
I don't even like political poems.
Do you think I can believe in a war between races?   15
I can deny it. I can forget about it
when I'm safe,
living on my own continent of harmony
and home, but I am not
there.   20

I believe in revolution
because everywhere the crosses are burning,
sharp-shooting goose-steppers round every corner,
there are snipers in the schools . . .
(I know you don't believe this.   25
You think this is nothing

but faddish exaggeration. But they
are not shooting at you.)
I'm marked by the color of my skin.
The bullets are discrete and designed to kill slowly.   30
They are aiming at my children.
These are facts.
Let me show you my wounds: my stumbling mind, my
"excuse me" tongue, and this
nagging preoccupation   35
with the feeling of not being good enough.

These bullets bury deeper than logic.
Racism is not intellectual.
I cannot reason these scars away.

Outside my door   40
there is a real enemy
who hates me.
I am a poet
who yearns to dance on rooftops,
to whisper delicate lines about joy   45
and the blessings of human understanding.
I try. I go to my land, my tower of words and
bolt the door, but the typewriter doesn't fade out
the sounds of blasting and muffled outrage.
My own days bring me slaps on the face.   50
Every day I am deluged with reminders
that this is not
my land

and this is my land.

I do not believe in the war between races   55

but in this country
there is war.

Judith Ortiz Cofer (1955–   )

VIDA

My lover is the old poet, Gabriel,
who lives on a mountain, high above the rest of us—
in the place, he says, where sadness makes its nest,
where time is very long.

The day begins, Gabriel writes his ailments for an age,   5
then night comes like a thief dressed in black.

Sometimes, when the moon is bright enough,
I climb the rocky hill to his house.
He is always waiting at the window—for me or for daybreak;
I don't ask. He knows he has little time left,   10
and will not waste it on sleep.

When I hold this old man in my arms,
his thin body light as bird-bones, I feel
as if I were warming a wounded sparrow. From his gray eyes
little light comes. And I know   15
that he is now writing words for the stone carver.

Before autumn, I will be gathering flowers for his grave:
a basketful of Bird-of-Paradise,
the ones he once called in a poem
a flock of yellow-crested cockateels. I will pick   20
Flame-of-the-Forest, the burning orange blossom
he likes to see in my black hair.

I will spread them over the little square of earth
he has himself chosen: at the point where sky touches ground
and a Kapok tree has offered him shade   25
for half a century. There he has often rested his head
on the lap of its smooth trunk, to watch
the little wild parrots alight at dusk, greening the branches
like new leaves; there too he has listened
to their murmurings until darkness silenced them.   30

But on this night, he will welcome me with wine and flowers.
He will call me *mi vida*—his life.
I will keep him company until the sun rises over the mountain.

Ha Jin (1956–   )

MARCHING TOWARDS MARTYRDOM

The commander gave orders
and we started marching.
We swung our hands vigorously up to our second buttons,
and watched each other through the corners of our eyes
to keep our bodies in a straight line.   5
We marched as if we were on parade,
although we knew these were exercises.

But we stopped before a deep trash pit,
and kept marching in place on its edge.

"Go ahead! Who told you to stop?   10
If you kill yourselves
your families will know you are martyrs!"

We marched on.

It was so easy to become a martyr,
and there were so many ways.   15

Li-Young Lee (1957–   )

MNEMONIC°

I was tired. So I lay down.
My lids grew heavy. So I slept.
Slender memory, stay with me.

I was cold once. So my father took off his blue sweater.
He wrapped me in it, and I never gave it back.   5
It is the sweater he wore to America,
this one, which I've grown into, whose sleeves are too long,
whose elbows have thinned, who outlives its rightful owner.
Flamboyant blue in daylight, poor blue by daylight,
it is black in the folds.   10

A serious man who devised complex systems of numbers and rhymes
to aid him in remembering, a man who forgot nothing, my father
would be ashamed of me.
Not because I'm forgetful,
but because there is no order   15
to my memory, a heap
of details, uncatalogued, illogical.
For instance:
God was lonely. So he made me.
My father loved me. So he spanked me.   20
It hurt him to do so. He did it daily.

The earth is flat. Those who fall off don't return.
The earth is round. All things reveal themselves to men only gradually.

I won't last. Memory is sweet.
Even when it's painful, memory is sweet.   25

Once, I was cold. So my father took off his blue sweater.

MNEMONIC. A mnemonic is a memory aid, a way to recollect information.

THE GIFT

To pull the metal splinter from my palm
my father recited a story in a low voice.
I watched his lovely face and not the blade.
Before the story ended, he'd removed
the iron sliver I thought I'd die from.   5

I can't remember the tale,
but hear his voice still, a well
of dark water, a prayer.
And I recall his hands,
two measures of tenderness   10
he laid against my face,
the flames of discipline
he raised above my head.

Had you entered that afternoon
you would have thought you saw a man   15
planting something in a boy's palm,
a silver tear, a tiny flame.
Had you followed that boy
you would have arrived here,
where I bend over my wife's right hand.   20

Look how I shave her thumbnail down
so carefully she feels no pain.
Watch as I lift the splinter out.
I was seven when my father
took my hand like this,   25

and I did not hold that shard
between my fingers and think,
Metal that will bury me,
christen it Little Assassin,
Ore Going Deep for My Heart,   30
And I did not lift up my wound and cry,
Death visited here!
I did what a child does
when he's given something to keep.
I kissed my father.   35

Jimmy Santiago Baca (1958–   )

AT NIGHT

I lie in bed
and hear the soft throb of water

An Anthology of Poetry

surging through the ditch,
from extreme to extreme water bounds,
clumsy country boy,   5
stumbling over fallen logs and rubber tires
to meet a lover
who awaits in her parent's house, window open.

As I used to for love.

Now gray-black hair,   10
vigorous cheeks, weathered brow, chapped lips,
dismal thoughtful eyes,
I float in brown melancholy on the lazy currents
of memory, studying my reflection
on the water this night,   15
with distant devotion,
a swimmer who has forgotten how to swim.

E. Ethelbert Miller (1959–   )

BIGHEAD & SNOTNOSE

they come around
the corner speeding in their cars
their sirens panting and their guns
dangling as they step into our world
pushing us back into nowhere   5
and nowhere left to hide our faces
and now our names faceless as we stare
at their whiteness and dark blue mysteries
filled with law resting heavy in the air

bighead and snotnose   10
freeze like basketball stars
going to the hoop
their bodies suspending over history
as they pump and fake and double fake
and dare laws to stop their lives   15
on a corner where they lean
as cool as gravity
pulling their sneakers
back to earth

28 Responding to Poems

This chapter offers you the chance to see how readers (and the authors themselves) have responded to particular poems, or groups of poems, and the chance to compare these with your own responses. Each section offers one or two essays along with the poem (or poems) being critiqued in order to show you some distinctive readings of the author's work. In two cases the critiques are by fellow poets.

As you read and carefully observe the effects of each poem, first focus on developing your own interpretation of it, then think about how you might communicate this to another reader. You can compare your ideas with those of another writer or critic, considering the views you share as well as your points of difference. After reading the essays that respond to these poems, consider the questions that follow each section and decide how you might pose some questions to the essayist. What issues strike you as most pressing? How would you integrate these views into an interpretation of your own? In fact, the perception of a poem, not to mention the discussion of it, varies according to one's viewpoint, as shown in these commentaries. In one response, the more detached view of the scholar-critic Harold Bloom writes about a classic poem, Coleridge's "Frost at Midnight." In another kind, "On Writing 'First Death' " is from the horse's mouth—the poet describes the origin and composition of his own poem. In still another response, a poet discourses with casual directness on a poem by one of his peers. Robert Lowell's "On Stanley Kunitz's 'Father and Son' " gives vivid insight into the thoughts and associations a poet might have when reading the work of another poet.

At the end of this chapter is a unit on the poetry of Adrienne Rich (a generous selection of which appears in Chapter 25), along with two interpretive essays about several of those poems. These are followed by an example of how the essay material can be used by a student as a writing resource in the development of an interpretive paper. As you observe how a student source paper takes shape in response to statements by other critics, consider how you could develop your own interpretation of Rich's poems by quoting and responding to other writers' ideas.

Note: If you intend to use any of the response essays as sources in interpretive essays you may be writing, you can either track down the original source at the library and cite the actual pages in standard MLA form (see Appendix B), or you can cite the work as reprinted in *Literature: The Evolving Canon, Second Edition,* and refer to the pages of this book. Your notation on your Works Cited page might read as follows:

Estess, Sybil P. "Description and Imagination in Elizabeth Bishop's 'The Map.' "
  Literature: The Evolving Canon. 2nd ed. Ed. Sven P. Birkerts. Boston: Allyn
  and Bacon, 1996. p. 972.

RESPONDING TO DONNE'S "A VALEDICTION: FORBIDDING MOURNING"

John Donne (1572–1631)

The Renaissance poet John Donne was born in London and attended Oxford University. After converting from Roman Catholicism, Donne studied for the priesthood within the Anglican Church. He was ordained in 1614 and seven years later he became dean of St. Paul's Cathedral in London. Donne was known as a compelling preacher and had a large following. His poetry reflects his evolution. The love poems, written before his ordination, show a sensuous imagination. *Poems*, published in 1633, reveals an altogether more serious moral sensibility. Donne also wrote a series of essays called *Meditations* during a period of illness in 1623. The fortunes of the Metaphysical Poets have gone up and down in recent centuries. At the end of the Victorian period, for instance, Donne had almost no reputation. Poet and critic T. S. Eliot can be said to have rescued Donne from near oblivion, campaigning to bring the ironic complexity of Donne's work back into favor.

A VALEDICTION: FORBIDDING MOURNING

As virtuous men pass mildly away,
   And whisper to their souls to go,
Whilst some of their sad friends do say,
   The breath goes now, and some say, No:

So let us melt, and make no noise,   5
   No tear-floods, nor sigh-tempests move;
'Twere profanation of our joys
   To tell the laity° our love.

Moving of th' earth brings harms and fears,
   Men reckon what it did, and meant;   10

A VALEDICTION: FORBIDDING MOURNING. *8 laity:* uninitiated laymen, those who don't comprehend.

But trepidation° of the spheres,
　　Though greater far, is innocent.

Dull sublunary° lovers' love
　　(Whose soul is sense) cannot admit
Absence, because it doth remove　　　　　　　　　　　　　　　　15
　　Those things which elemented° it.

But we by a love so much refined
　　That ourselves know not what it is,
Inter-assurèd of the mind,
　　Care less eyes, lips and hands to miss.　　　　　　　　　　　20

Our two souls therefore, which are one,
　　Though I must go, endure not yet
A breach, but an expansion,
　　Like gold to airy thinness beat.

If they be two, they are two so　　　　　　　　　　　　　　　　25
　　As stiff twin compasses are two;
Thy soul, the fix'd foot, makes no show
　　To move, but doth, if th' other do.

And though it in the centre sit,
　　Yet, when the other far doth roam,　　　　　　　　　　　　30
It leans, and hearkens after it,
　　And grows erect, as that comes home.

Such wilt thou be to me, who must,
　　Like th' other foot, obliquely run;
Thy firmness makes my circle just,　　　　　　　　　　　　　　35
　　And makes me end where I begun.

---

　　11 *trepidation:* quivering movement.　13 *sublunary:* beneath the moon, earthly.　16 *elemented:* were composed of, made up of.

QUESTIONS

1. Read the poem carefully and locate Donne's various similes and metaphors. Explain how each contributes to the poem's meaning. How do they link up in the last three stanzas to become a governing conceit?

2. Explain the title of the poem (check a dictionary if you need to) and explain how it relates to the similes and metaphors the poet has developed. What is he finally saying to the person he addresses? How does Donne's message compare (or contrast) with that offered by Matthew Arnold in "Dover Beach"?

3. Write a short paragraph explaining Donne's conception of love. In what ways does this differ from what you understand to be the modern views of love?

Hugh Kenner

ON DONNE'S "A VALEDICTION"

from *Seventeenth Century Poetry*

But not only was the habit of elaborately justifying a comparison no innovation of Donne's but part of the tradition he inherited, the comparisons themselves are apt to be, if not traditional, secondhand, bits of machinery employed by a decadent poeticizing. Not even the famous comparison of lovers to compasses is necessarily original: we find it embedded in a madrigal by the Italian poet G. B. Guarini, published in 1598. Donne's poem is said to have been written thirteen years later. We may gather the content of Guarini's poem from Thomas Carew's translation:

> You'le aske perhaps wherefore I stay,
> Loving so much, so long away,
> O doe not thinke t'was I did part,
> It was my body, not my hearte,
> For like a Compasse in your love,
> One foote is fix'd and cannot moove,
> The other may follow her blinde guide
> Of giddy fortune, but not slide
> Beyond your service, nor dares venture
> To wander farre from you the Center.

Carew extracts from Guarini what Guarini extracted from the idea, a graceful singable compliment. If part of him (his body) moves, the other part (his heart) is fixed; and the fixed part controls the moving; and she is to take cheer, for what is fixed is fixed in her love.

Whether or not Donne borrowed the image from Italy, he means our attention to focus not on the image itself, where generations of commentary have tended to fix it, but rather on the details of his dramatic dealing with it. He articulates it into parts, as he does every other figure he employs, and puts it to a use from which irony is not absent. For beneath the graceful quatrains beats the insistent accent of a man talking, steadily talking, to keep the lady from bursting into tears. He is about to leave her and cross the seas; and as in another valediction he had suggested that her lamentations were competing with the tempests on the English Channel—

> Weepe me not dead, in thine armes, but forebeare
>   To teach the sea, what it may doe too soone;
> Let not the winde
> Example finde,
>   To doe me more harm, than it purposeth;

so in *A Valediction: Forbidding Mourning* he strives to head off 'tear-floods' and 'sigh-tempests' by fixing her essentially simple attention on all sorts of difficult things he is finding to say: on the death of virtuous men, the moving of the earth, the relation of sense and soul, the expansion of gold leaf; for so long as her mind is 'puzzled with metaphysics' she is likely to be quiet, more or less. And having posited that their two souls are one, which is enough of a poetic commonplace to be thin comfort, he quickens attention once more by introducing the famous simile:

> If they be two, they are two so
> As stiff twin compasses are two.

It is not really an image, but a puzzle: Why are our two souls like a pair of compasses? And he keeps her attention fixed on it, producing not one solution but three:

> Thy soul the fixed foot, makes no show
> To move, but doth, if the'other do.

[1. The centre does not turn.]

> And though it in the centre sit,
> Yet when the other far doth roam,
> It leans, and hearkens after it,
> And grows erect, as that comes home.

[2. If you close the compasses the spraddled legs grow upright.]

> Such wilt thou be to me, who must
> Like th'other foot, obliquely run;
> Thy firmness makes my circle just,
> And makes me end, where I begun.

[3. The moving foot, when you are drawing a circle, ends where it began, though not, he avoids pointing out, where the stationary foot is.]

'And makes me end, where I begun.' These are the words that ring in her grateful ears at the end. They contain scant comfort if she has been following the logic carefully, but she probably has not, and is unlikely to notice that the circle ends as far from its centre as it started. The poem is brilliant, tender in its tone and in its concern, casuistic, a little cynical in its methods, in those final stanzas more than a little meretricious. But there is something meretricious, the gravity of tone succeeds in reminding us, in all attempts at comfort which must seek to wave away some irremediable fact: a death, a parting.

[1964]

QUESTIONS

1. Kenner identifies a predecessor to Donne's "Valediction" in a poem by G. B. Guarini. Compare the translated excerpt to Donne's poem. How has Donne modified the central conceit in Guarini's poem?
2. Read Kenner's commentary carefully, and summarize. What is the critic's understanding of the poem? In what ways do you suppose that Kenner might be going against the conventional interpretations? What are your reasons for saying so?

RESPONDING TO COLERIDGE'S "FROST AT MIDNIGHT"

Samuel Taylor Coleridge (1772–1834)

The Romantic writer Coleridge was born in Devon, England. A radical young poet in the years following the French Revolution, he collaborated with poet William Wordsworth on the book *Lyrical Ballads* (1798). Coleridge's restless talent had him working in many directions—as poet, dramatist, political journalist, essayist, and public lecturer. He created a singular work of literary criticism, the *Biographia Literaria* (1817). Coleridge suffered from ill health in his later years and became addicted to opium. (His famous poem "Kubla Khan" was written under the influence of the drug—or so legend has it.) In 1816 he took up residence with a surgeon and was able to spend his last years productively. He published a periodical, and produced a volume of meditations, the *Aids to Reflection* (1825), and a treatise on political theory, *On the Constitution of the Church and State* (1829).

FROST AT MIDNIGHT

The frost performs its secret ministry,
Unhelped by any wind. The owlet's cry
Came loud—and hark, again! loud as before.
The inmates of my cottage, all at rest,
Have left me to that solitude, which suits   5
Abstruser musings: save that at my side
My cradled infant slumbers peacefully.
'Tis calm indeed! so calm, that it disturbs
And vexes meditation with its strange
And extreme silentness. Sea, hill, and wood,   10
This populous village! Sea, and hill, and wood,
With all the numberless goings on of life,
Inaudible as dreams! the thin blue flame
Lies on my low burnt fire, and quivers not;
Only that film, which fluttered on the grate,°   15

FROST AT MIDNIGHT. 15 *grate:* a frame inside a fireplace to hold fuel.

Still flutters there, the sole unquiet thing.
Methinks, its motion in this hush of nature
Gives it dim sympathies with me who live,
Making it a companionable form,
Whose puny flaps and freaks° the idling Spirit   20
By its own moods interprets, every where
Echo or mirror seeking of itself,
And makes a toy of Thought.
                              But O! how oft,
How oft, at school, with most believing mind,   25
Presageful,° have I gazed upon the bars,
To watch that fluttering stranger! and as oft
With unclosed lids, already had I dreamt
Of my sweet birth-place, and the old church-tower,
Whose bells, the poor man's only music, rang
From morn to evening, all the hot Fair-day,   30
So sweetly, that they stirred and haunted me
With a wild pleasure, falling on mine ear
 Most like articulate sounds of things to come!
So gazed I, till the soothing things I dreamt
Lulled me to sleep, and sleep prolonged my dreams!   35
And so I brooded all the following morn,
Awed by the stern preceptor's° face, mine eye
Fixed with mock study on my swimming book:
Save if the door half opened, and I snatched
A hasty glance, and still my heart leaped up,   40
For still I hoped to see the *stranger's* face,
Townsman, or aunt, or sister more beloved,
My play-mate when we both were clothed alike!

   Dear Babe, that sleepest cradled by my side,
Whose gentle breathings, heard in this deep calm,   45
Fill up the interspersed vacancies
And momentary pauses of the thought!
My babe so beautiful! it thrills my heart
With tender gladness, thus to look at thee,
And think that thou shalt learn far other lore   50
And in far other scenes! For I was reared
In the great city, pent 'mid cloisters° dim,
And saw nought lovely but the sky and stars.
But thou, my babe! shalt wander like a breeze
By lakes and sandy shores, beneath the crags   55
Of ancient mountain, and beneath the clouds,
Which image in their bulk both lakes and shores
And mountain crags: so shalt thou see and hear
The lovely shapes and sounds intelligible

---

    20 *freaks:* streaks of color.   26 *presageful:* having a presentiment or warning.   37 *preceptor:* in-
structor.   52 *cloisters:* confined places.

Of that eternal language, which thy God   60
Utters, who from eternity doth teach
Himself in all, and all things in himself.
Great universal Teacher! he shall mould
Thy spirit, and by giving make it ask.

  Therefore all seasons shall be sweet to thee,   65
Whether the summer clothe the general earth
With greenness, or the redbreast sit and sing
Betwixt the tufts of snow on the bare branch
Of mossy apple-tree, while the night thatch
Smokes in the sun-thaw; whether the eave-drops fall   70
Heard only in the trances of the blast
Or if the secret ministry of frost
Shall hang them up in silence icicles,
Quietly shining to the quiet Moon.

Harold Bloom (1930–   )

ON "FROST AT MIDNIGHT"

With *Dejection, The Ancient Mariner,* and
Kubla Khan,° *Frost at Midnight* shows Coleridge at his most impressive. *Frost at Midnight* is the masterpiece of the "conversation poems"; it gathers the virtues of the
group, without diffuseness, into one form, and it shares with *Tintern Abbey*° the distinction of inaugurating the major Wordsworthian myth of the memory as salvation.
Indeed, Coleridge precedes Wordsworth. *Frost at Midnight* is dated February 1798;
Tintern Abbey, we know from its title, was composed on July 13, 1798. The closing
paragraph of Coleridge's poem, directed to his infant son, beginning "Therefore all
seasons shall be sweet to thee," is a prelude to the closing lines of *Tintern Abbey,* addressed to Dorothy Wordsworth, where the poet asks nature's blessings on his sister:

> Therefore let the moon
> Shine on thee in thy solitary walk;
> And let the misty mountain-winds be free
> To blow against thee

Frost at Midnight begins with Coleridge addressing himself to "abstruser musings." His cradled infant slumbers near him. The calm around the poet is so profound that its silentness vexes meditation:

> the thin blue flame
> Lies on my low-burnt fire, and quivers not;

ON "FROST AT MIDNIGHT." (par 1) *Dejection . . . Kubla Khan:* other poems by Coleridge (see Chapter 27). *Tintern Abbey:* a poem by William Wordsworth (see Chapter 27).

Only that film, which fluttered on the grate
Still flutters there, the sole unquiet thing.

The film on the grate was called, in popular superstition, a *stranger,* and was supposed to portend° the arrival of some absent friend. The motion of the film makes it a companionable form to the poet, for only they stir in this hush of nature. The puny flaps of the film are like the motions of the poet's idling Spirit, which both deprecates itself and seeks fellowship by finding echo or mirror in the fluttering *stranger.* By doing so, the poet says of his abstracter musings that they are turned into a toy. Yet this playfulness becomes vital, for the mind travels back in memory as it idly broods on an identity with the film:

> But O! how oft,
> How oft, at school, with most believing mind,
> Presageful, have I gazed upon the bars,
> To watch that fluttering *stranger!*

One memory of school days leads to another in the same vein. The child watching the grate dreams of his birth place, and:

> the old church-tower,
> Whose bells, the poor man's only music, rang
> From morn to evening, all the hot Fair-day,
> So sweetly, that they stirred and haunted me
> With a wild pleasure, falling on mine ear
> Most like articulate sounds of things to come!

This is a memory within a memory, and the poem goes back to the initial recall. The child sleeps that night, dreaming of his sweet birth place. The next morning he broods, his eye fixed on his book but seeing nothing of it and looking up each time the door opens:

> For still I hoped to see the *stranger's* face,
> Townsman, or aunt, or sister more beloved

Carried back to his own childhood, the poet by an associative progression is prepared to brood on the future of his slumbering infant.

Coleridge, like Wordsworth, was country-born, but, unlike Wordsworth, he passed his school years in London. As he looks at the sleeping infant Hartley, he utters a wishful prophecy that was to find ironic fulfillment. His son, he hopes, will learn far other lore, and in more natural scenes:

> For I was reared
> In the great city, pent 'mid cloisters dim,
> And saw nought lovely but the sky and stars.
> But *thou,* my babe! shalt wander like a breeze
> By lakes and sandy shores

So Hartley was to wander, a vagrant in the Wordsworth country, a Solitary prematurely decayed. In a happier sense, as a Wordsworthian minor poet, he fulfilled the other half of the prophecy:

(par 3) *portend:* serve as an omen.

so shalt thou see and hear
The lovely shapes and sounds intelligible
Of that eternal language, which thy God
Utters, who from eternity doth teach
Himself in all, and all things in himself.
Great universal Teacher! he shall mould
Thy spirit, and by giving make it ask.

Again we recognize the doctrine and sound of *Tintern Abbey*,° anticipated but with a tremulous intensity, very unlike the primitive confidence Wordsworth at his best was to bring to the Coleridgean formulation of the religion of Nature. The fierce epiphanies° of Wordsworth are declared with the trumpetings of the prophets Amos,° for whom judgment could run down like waters, and righteousness as a mighty stream. But something of an eternal child is in Coleridge (and in Hartley Coleridge after him), and a naive sweetness graces *Frost at Midnight*. The end of *Tintern Abbey* has a deeper music than that of *Frost of Midnight*, but is not more moving than this:

Therefore all seasons shall be sweet to thee,
Whether the summer clothe the general earth
With greenness, or the redbreast sit and sing
Betwixt the tufts of snow on the bare branch
Of mossy apple-tree, while the night thatch
Smokes in the sun-thaw; whether the eave-drops fall
Heard only in the trances of the blast,
Or if the secret ministry of frost
Shall hang them up in silent icicles,
Quietly shining to the quiet Moon.

The poem comes full circle, back to its opening. The secret ministry of frost is analogous to the secret ministry of memory, for both bind together apparently disparate phenomena in an imaginative unity. The frost creates a surface to both receive and reflect the shining of the winter moon. Memory, moving by its overtly arbitrary but deeply designed associations, creates an identity between the mature poet and the child who is his ancestor, as well as his own child. In this identity the poem comes into full being, with its own receiving and reflecting surfaces that mold the poet's and (he hopes) his son's spirits, and, by giving, make them ask who is the author of the gift. Wordsworth, in his prime years, would have given a phenomenological° answer, and have been content to say Nature herself. In a more traditionally balanced *Frost at Midnight*, the answer is ontological,° but the eternal language the Great Being is compelled to use is that of Nature, with her "lovely shapes and sounds intelligible." 10

QUESTIONS

1. Read Coleridge's poem with care; then read Bloom's commentary with equal care. Note all of the places where the critic helped you to understand something new about the poem. Now reread the poem. Be prepared to compare notes in class.

(par 9) *Tintern Abbey:* See Wordsworth's poem in Chapter 27. *epiphanies:* recognitions. *Amos:* Biblical prophet.   (par 10) *phenomenological:* focused on immediate physical appearances. *ontological:* focused upon inner being.

2. Give a one paragraph account of Bloom's interpretation. Having read the poem closely, can you imagine a divergent interpretation? Try to formulate the main argument a critical adversary of Bloom's might take.

RESPONDING TO ELIOT'S "THE LOVE SONG OF J. ALFRED PRUFROCK"

T. S. Eliot (1888–1965)

Although he was born in St. Louis, Missouri, and educated at Harvard University, T. S. Eliot is often thought to be a British poet. Not only did the poet move to England and become a British subject, but he carried himself every much like the bowler-hatted and furled-umbrellaed Englishman of popular stereotype. Conservative though his appearance might have been, he was one of the revolutionists of modernism, publishing little but exerting tremendous influence. His first important poem was "The Love Song of J. Alfred Prufrock," published in 1915, in which he explored the instability of consciousness and the problems of identity in the modern age. More influential still was his long poem "The Waste Land" (1922), in which he used a wealth of historical and cultural reference in a strikingly unadorned, collage-like mode. The poem was widely read as a lament for a civilization in decline. Later Eliot published his deeply meditative *Four Quartets* (1944). He also wrote two poetic dramas, *Murder in the Cathedral* and *The Family Reunion* (1939), and several collections of important criticism. It is likely that Eliot will be remembered as much for his criticism of poetry as for his own poetry.

THE LOVE SONG OF J. ALFRED PRUFROCK°

S'io credesse che mia risposta fosse
A persona che mai tornasse al mondo,
Questa fiamma staria senza piu scosse.

THE LOVE SONG OF J. ALFRED PRUFROCK. Eliot takes his epigraph from Dante's *Inferno*. In this passage the speaker, one of the damned, believes that Dante will remain in hell and therefore can be told his story: "If I thought my reply would be made to someone who could return to the world, this flame would not waver. But as I've heard that no one ever escapes from this pit, I'll tell you without fear of an ill fame."

Ma perciocche giammai di questo fondo
Non torno vivo alcun, s'i'odo il vero,
Senza tema d'infamia ti rispondo.

Let us go then, you and I,
When the evening is spread out against the sky
Like a patient etherised upon a table;
Let us go, through certain half-deserted streets,
The muttering retreats   5
Of restless nights in one-night cheap hotels
And sawdust restaurants with oyster-shells:
Streets that follow like a tedious argument
Of insidious intent
To lead you to an overwhelming question . . .   10
Oh, do not ask, 'What is it?'
Let us go and make our visit.

In the room the women come and go
Talking of Michelangelo.

The yellow fog that rubs its back upon the window-panes,   15
The yellow smoke that rubs its muzzle on the window-panes
Licked its tongue into the corners of the evening,
Lingered upon the pools that stand in drains,
Let fall upon its back the soot that falls from chimneys,
Slipped by the terrace, made a sudden leap,   20
And seeing that it was a soft October night,
Curled once about the house, and fell asleep.

And indeed there will be time
For the yellow smoke that slides along the street
Rubbing its back upon the window-panes;   25
There will be time, there will be time
To prepare a face to meet the faces that you meet:
There will be time to murder and create,
And time for all the works and days° of hands
That lift and drop a question on your plate;   30
Time for you and time for me,
And time yet for a hundred indecisions,
And for a hundred visions and revisions,
Before the taking of a toast and tea.

In the room the women come and go   35
Talking of Michelangelo.

And indeed there will be time
To wonder, 'Do I dare?' and, 'Do I dare?'
Time to turn back and descend the stair,

---

29 *works and days:* title of a work by the Greek poet Hesiod.

With a bald spot in the middle of my hair—   40
(They will say: 'How his hair is growing thin!')
My morning coat, my collar mounting firmly to the chin,
My necktie rich and modest, but asserted by a simple pin—
(They will say: 'But how his arms and legs are thin!')
Do I dare   45
Disturb the universe?
In a minute there is time
For decisions and revisions which a minute will reverse

For I have known them all already, known them all:
Have known the evenings, mornings, afternoons,   50
I have measured out my life with coffee spoons;
I know the voices dying with a dying fall
Beneath the music from a farther room.
      So how should I presume?

And I have known the eyes already, known them all—   55
The eyes that fix you in a formulated phrase,
And when I am formulated, sprawling on a pin,
When I am pinned and wriggling on the wall,
Then how should I begin
To spit out all the butt-ends of my days and ways?   60
      And how should I presume?

And I have known the arms already, known them all—
Arms that are braceleted and white and bare
(But in the lamplight, downed with light brown hair!)
Is it perfume from a dress   65
That makes me so digress?
Arms that lie along a table, or wrap about a shawl.
      And should I then presume?
      And how should I begin?

                              *   *   *

Shall I say, I have gone at dusk through narrow streets   70
And watched the smoke that rises from the pipes
Of lonely men in shirt-sleeves, leaning out of windows? . . .
I should have been a pair of ragged claws
Scuttling across the floors of silent seas.

                              *   *   *

And the afternoon, the evening, sleeps so peacefully!   75
Smoothed by long fingers,
Asleep . . . tired . . . or it malingers,
Stretched on the floor, here beside you and me.
Should I, after tea and cakes and ices,
Have the strength to force the moment to its crisis?   80
But though I have wept and fasted, wept and prayed,

Though I have seen my head (grown slightly bald) brought in upon a platter,°
I am no prophet—and here's no great matter;
I have seen the moment of my greatness flicker,
And I have seen the eternal Footman hold my coat, and snicker,   85
And in short, I was afraid.

And would it have been worth it, after all,
After the cups, the marmalade, the tea,
Among the porcelain, among some talk of you and me,
Would it have been worth while,   90
To have bitten off the matter with a smile,
To have squeezed the universe into a ball
To roll it toward some overwhelming question,
To say: 'I am Lazarus,° come from the dead,
Come back to tell you all, I shall tell you all'—   95
If one, settling a pillow by her head,
    Should say: 'That is not what I meant at all;
    That is not it, at all.'

And would it have been worth it, after all,
Would it have been worth while,   100
After the sunsets and the dooryards and the sprinkled streets,
After the novels, after the teacups, after the skirts
that trail along the floor—
And this, and so much more?—
It is impossible to say just what I mean!   105
But as if a magic lantern threw the nerves in patterns on a screen:
Would it have been worth while
If one, settling a pillow or throwing off a shawl,
And turning toward the window, should say: 110
    'That is not it at all,
    That is not what I meant, at all.'

No! I am not Prince Hamlet, nor was meant to be;
Am an attendant lord, one that will do
To swell a progress,° start a scene or two,
Advise the prince; no doubt, an easy tool,   115
Deferential, glad to be of use,
Politic, cautious, and meticulous;
Full of high sentence,° but a bit obtuse;
At times, indeed, almost ridiculous—
Almost, at times, the Fool.   120

I grow old . . . I grow old . . .
I shall wear the bottoms of my trousers rolled.

---

82 *head . . . platter:* reference to John the Baptist, beheaded by King Herod at the request of his wife, Herodias.   94 *Lazarus:* man raised from the dead by Jesus.   114 *progress:* princely parade. 118 *full . . . sentence:* full of high-sounding phrases.

Shall I part my hair behind? Do I dare to eat a peach?
I shall wear white flannel trousers, and walk upon the beach.
I have heard the mermaids singing, each to each.

125

I do not think that they will sing to me.

I have seen them riding seaward on the waves
Combing the white hair of the waves blown back
When the wind blows the water white and black.

We have lingered in the chambers of the sea

130

By sea-girls wreathed with seaweed red and brown
Till human voices wake us, and we drown.

Joseph Margolis

ON "THE LOVE SONG OF J. ALFRED PRUFROCK"

We are, as readers, actually led to construct the poetry of the *Love Song*. It appears quite legible at first but becomes progressively disjointed. And as we sense its difficulty, seemingly contradictory features strike our attention. It has no obvious technical structure, it is in fact quite fragmentary; yet it obliges our wit to study the impression of a strong and apt order. The language is leisurely, sometimes merely repetitious, but ultimately we recognize its deliberate compression and great economy; and, though they are frequently diffused, the images convey the inexorable movement of the entire mood. The language is vernacular and superficial but suddenly it becomes dark and filled with savage expressions. It seems casual and ironic but we sense an underlying urgency. At first two persons seem to be involved but we discover there is only one; and he is J. Alfred Prufrock whose name is at once important and slightly absurd. Yet he is also unknown; we suspect he is Everyman. And his love song is uncertain too. We are led to believe it is concerned with a romantic coupling but it soon spreads into the more social themes of friendship and of the desperate need of sympathetic company. Dante is used to announce the song but at first we cannot see why. And its themes, which are remarkably diverse, are offered in contrary pairs: youth and old age, work and idleness, spiritual life and death, commitment and indecision, dreams and actuality, action and analysis, courage and fear, personal needs and social obligations, communion and loneliness, pride and disgust in the self, sincerity and hypocrisy, interest and boredom.

Even the casual invitation of the first lines is disjunctive and disturbed:

> Let us go then, you and I,
> When the evening is spread out against the sky
> Like a patient etherised upon a table

It is coupled with a simile as deliberate as itself which opposes an image of inertia to the intended activity. We cannot imagine that it is an actual invitation and we cannot help noticing a certain delicious lingering over the cadence and careful phrasing. We are inclined from the very start to diagnose Prufrock's remarks as symptoms of his own disorder. He is divided against himself; he suffers perhaps from a kind of anesthesia or wishes to possess it; he is preoccupied with inert bodies and has a strange habit of treating the atmosphere as an organic creature.

Yet, in a sense, we are only explicating Prufrock's self-analysis. For he quite obviously distinguishes 'you and I' and constructs his own simile. It is too early to know the meaning of the invitation, but as we follow his soliloquy we learn that each term and phrase has its own specific resonance and that our estimate of Prufrock must adjust constantly to new sets of overtones, It is as if we would attribute to Prufrock an interest in constructing not merely extravagant similes but an apt poetic form for his own probing and self-dissection.

He repeats his invitation and the romantic suggestions dissolve in an air of fatigue and surrender:

> Let us go, through certain half-deserted streets.
> The muttering retreats
> Of restless nights in one-night cheap hotels
> And sawdust restaurants with oyster shells;
> Streets that follow like a tedious argument
> Of insidious intent
> To lead you to an overwhelming question . . .
> Oh, do not ask, 'What is it?'
> Let us go and make our visit.

Prufrock's question is obviously idle and too familiar. He appears in an alien but attractive setting, a would-be tourist of the vulgar and the commonplace. And, as if in recognition, he steps out of his reveries:

> In the room the women come and go
> Talking of Michelangelo

Another disjunction! We are at once in a salon where the conversation is self-assured on difficult matters. It is a world which can be summarized in a jingle; we know it certainly to be the world Prufrock understands best, commonplace as well and perhaps hiding its own vulgarity. The invitation was a momentary dream Prufrock had permitted himself amid the busy movements of his own society.

But the couplet is a subtle contrivance; it is in fact the rule of Prufrock's life. We know he must select his companions from this company, ladies apparently impervious to reflection and uncertainty, who 'come and go' with an altogether different attitude. The couplet suggests an endless and familiar routine; and it serves as well as a refrain, repeated once again after another hint at the nature of Prufrock's sickly leisure. It intrudes, unspoken, with each successive exposure; it is presupposed everywhere, isolating Prufrock from the society of the salon as well as from the workmen's quarters of the city. We cannot even be certain where he is standing and dreaming at present, but the lines have confirmed his grooming and his longing. They are lines of sudden wit, almost improvisation, yet at the same time the outcome of a sustained and self-absorbed effort; Prufrock's reverie engages both worlds and he is quite alone.

5

He is at least a talented and self-conscious dabbler in language, an amateur of verse. We always observe a certain careful searching for the apt phrase and for nice modifiers; we are always met with gifted summaries of his own experience. He is aware of the efforts of others to 'fix you in a formulated phrase' but he cannot repress his own clever skill. He makes deliberate literary references, some quite indirect, almost puns on the language of other poets; other references are openly directed to the great literature of the world. And in the very last passages of the *Love Song* he actually composes a short set of verses which could readily be separated as a distinct lyric, an expression growing out of his preoccupied versifying and arranging itself almost automatically. It is as if his invitation were designed to 'invoke the Muse'.

The chatter of the salon is about art. The ladies are concerned with Michelangelo, a hero and an artist of heroes. And Prufrock, whose inspiration has broken down, speaks of himself in mock-heroic terms. The creative community has broken down; the ladies cannot understand him and he cannot express himself. The search through the 'half-deserted streets' is more than romantic, more than inspirational.

Suddenly Prufrock escapes again:

The yellow fog that rubs its back upon the window-panes,
The yellow smoke that rubs its muzzle on the window-panes
Licked its tongue into the corners of the evening,
Lingered upon the pools that stand in drains,
Let slip upon its back the soot that falls from chimneys,
Slipped by the terrace, made a sudden leap,
And seeing that it was a soft October night,
Curled once about the house, and fell asleep.

It is as if the casual jingle were too bold—as if, failing to deflect the question, it merely focussed it more precisely. So that Prufrock must attempt an evasion through some invented, noncommittal interest. He muses on the weather, he turns an eye to the street, he explores a conceit slowly and lovingly. The postponement is ineffectual. The yellow fog 'slides along the street' like an identifiably corrupting power that finally encircles the house; implicitly Prufrock admits his 'overwhelming question' to be the same for the waterfront and the salon.

We are tempted to regard the image as an unconscious disguise for Prufrock himself; we surely do not sense the passage as a digression. The fog is amorphous, solitary, leisurely, perversely curious, observed in autumn, and finally inert. There is an uncomfortable insistence in the repeated images and their morbid quality, which seems at first random and detached like the initial simile, is inevitably linked to Prufrock's own condition:

And indeed there will be time
For the yellow smoke that slides along the street
Rubbing its back upon the window-panes;
There will be time, there will be time
To prepare a face to meet the faces that you meet;
There will be time to murder and create,
And time for all the works and days of hands
That lift and drop a question on your plate;
Time for you and time for me,

And time yet for a hundred indecisions,
And for a hundred visions and revisions,
Before the taking of toast and tea.

All of the earlier themes resound through these lines, still vague and diffused but increasingly focused on the salon society of which Prufrock is a member. The progress of the fog parallels the progress of the poetic revelation of Prufrock's question as it 'slides along the street' and curls 'about the house'.

The persons of the invitation are informed that there is still 'time for you and time for me'. Prufrock cannot yet bring himself to speak directly of his own career; he hides his concern in polite advice. But in the following passage, beyond the refrain (which stresses now Prufrock's membership and isolation in the society of the salon), he turns abruptly to point the question at himself:

Do I dare
Disturb the universe?
In a minute there is time
For decisions and revisions which a minute will reverse.

Shortly thereafter he demands:

Then how should I begin
To spit out all the butt-ends of my days and ways?

We must associate the image of the question with the curbs and gutters of the city; still later the fog seems to have penetrated the salon itself, for Prufrock finds it 'stretched on the floor, here beside you and me'. The fog is a kind of hallucination present only to the divided souls of Prufrock, for we recall that the women 'come and go' freely; the 'street' and the 'floor' are continuous and reinforce, wherever they appear, our impression of Prufrock's spiritual disorder and isolation. The fog is a kind of Grail, ambiguously characterized as corrupting but actually providing the occasion and the test of spiritual regeneration.

So the question which he finally manages to express as his own deep concern permits us to view a heroic and admirable struggle in the very soul of Prufrock. He has discarded, at least momentarily, the 'you' of earlier reference; he has overcome in part his initial paralysis; he acknowledges frankly the triviality of his existence. We are face to face with a human being of considerable intelligence and humility who is attempting to decide in a serious way the significance of his own life. And, though we are inclined to generalize with Prufrock about the trivial condition of all of human life, we must admit the necessity of an answer to the question. There is a religious dimension here, and the collapse of Prufrock's would-be defence identifies the ultimate futility of arguments drawn to justify the positive commitment of one's own life.

There are, interestingly enough, three arguments offered to prove that he should not 'dare.' They begin and end in the same way; we learn that Prufrock knows the 'voices,' 'eyes' and 'arms' of the ladies of the salon. He emphasizes the acquaintance, so to speak, with their organs of communications. Yet we know there never has been a satisfactory communication between them; there is a strong impression of distance, disdain, possible conflict, that invades each of the arguments. It is however the deliberately versified monotony of his remarks that betrays his fatigue most clearly:

> For I have known them all already, known them all
> I know the voices dying with a dying fall
> And I have known the eyes already, known them all
> And I have known the arms already, known them all

But there is more than boredom here; Prufrock is fatigued by his own worldliness and his invitation sought to escape this condition.

If we ask what is this crucial commitment which he postpones and which saps all of his strength, what decision of his might 'disturb the universe,' we are met by another question—whether there is

> Time to turn back and descend the stair,
> With a bald spot in the middle of my hair

It is of course a piece of impertinence, a pompous and 'at times, indeed, almost ridiculous' mixture of the trivial and the cosmic. But we cannot dispel the impression of its high seriousness; it is a question whether Prufrock can accept the actual conditions of his existence, his own ageing and the discerning eye of his associates. Does he dare 'disturb the universe', affirm his life courageously amid all of his obvious decline? Ought he to 'descend' once again into the illusions of the salon, having finally pierced through to a clear vision of his career? Does he have a constant hold of that rare 'time' which could sustain him in the changing trivialities of his own world?

There is a pathetic note in his preoccupation with the parts of his own body:

> (They will say: 'How his hair is growing thin!')
> My morning coat, my collar mounting firmly to the chin,
> My necktie rich and modest, but asserted by a simple pin—
> (They will say: 'But how his arms and legs are thin!')

We recall the images of surgical dissection and amorphous living creatures and anticipate the 'voices,' 'eyes' amid 'arms' of the ladies. Prufrock is fascinated by his own torment. He turns the confident 'simple pin' into an instrument of torture:

> And when I am formulated, sprawling on a pin,
> When I am pinned and wriggling on the wall,
> Then how should I begin

and, as he comments on the ladies of the salon, his disgust in his own awkward and helpless condition secretly mounts; so that at length he bursts out in a savage and poetically isolated pair of lines:

> I should have been a pair of ragged claws
> Scuttling across the floors of silent seas.

The duality of his nature is implied by the image and by the lines themselves which are separated from the principal reverie by a brief digression. We cannot help contrasting his 'scuttling across the floors of silent seas' with the assured movement of the women of that other couplet who 'come and go' across the floors of the salon. It is in the spirit of this outburst perhaps that Eliot chose the passage from Dante (Inferno, Canto XXVII) to introduce the piece; Prufrock is in a sense unsuspectingly overheard by the living in an open rejection of himself in his own private Hell.

15

But his quite admirable analytic power, as Prufrock himself very well knows, can neither project him into a new life nor free him from the old. The tired and some-what bitter arguments against the salon relent and he observes rather humorously:

> Is it perfume from a dress
> That makes me so digress?

In fact, all three arguments end in questions and all three emphasize his essential passivity. Prufrock understands that he is activated chiefly by external forces and he suggests almost gravitational and mechanical models for his relation to the salon. His digression is a double movement away from a personally motivated and personally acceptable action; he is constantly attracted to the society pattern that he despises or side-tracked into a fruitless reverie about the world of the poorer classes. No sooner does he admit his tendency, than he is off on another digression:

> Shall I say, I have gone at dusk through narrow streets
> And watched the smoke that rises from the pipes
> Of lonely men in shirt-sleeves, leaning out of windows? . . .

There are surprising associations here that force all that has already passed to echo through these lines. The 'lonely men in shirt-sleeves' reminds us of the 'arms that are braceleted and white and bare,' the 'smoke that rises from the pipes' recalls the yellow smoke that 'let fall upon its back the soot that falls from chimneys.' The contrasts are superficial, the question remains always the same.

Nevertheless, in a later passage the two worlds are more deliberately contrasted and their relative merits implicitly compared:

> After the sunsets and the dooryards and the sprinkled streets,
> After the novels, after the teacups, after the skirts that trail along the floor

Prufrock's power of summary is nowhere more successful. It is not accidental that the lines end in 'streets' and 'floor.' They confirm the ultimate equality of the two worlds. But the first is somewhat larger, more open, stabler, more robust than the second; the second is fragile and artificial. The first gives an impression of a setting for human life; the second suggests the improbable instruments if a highly special-ized kind of life. It is to the first that Prufrock is somewhat romantically inclined, though it is for the second that he has been specifically trained. Prufrock is a spec-tator of both worlds who cannot participate fully and cordially in either.

His admirable clarity appears to be the outcome of a struggle against his own tendency toward mystification and digression. In a moment of complete openness he remarks:

> Should I, after tea and cakes and ices,
> Have the strength to force the moment to its crisis?
> But though I have wept and fasted, wept and prayed,
> Though I have seen my head (grown slightly bald) brought in
>   upon a platter,
> I am no prophet—and here's no great matter;
> And I have seen the eternal Footman hold my coat, and snicker,
> And in short, I was afraid.

All that has preceded this statement now appears as a prolonged hesitation; the violent pathetic outburst at the end of the digression now serves to dramatize the degrees of his final self-control. The trivial and the momentous are linked once again and Prufrock's mock-heroic self-estimate reveals a deeper humility. In fact, his curious habit of comparing himself with certain literary heroes—with John the Baptist, Lazarus, with Hamlet—seems quite proper now and not all as ludicrous as Prufrock would have us believe.

These may be fairly said to be partial aspects of his own nature. The reference to John is anticipated by his preoccupation with his own baldness and the exposure of his spiritual condition through images relating to dissected, impotent and deformed bodies. We must think of him also as Everyman and therefore as a prophet as well, discovering the disorder of modern man—his alienation and his anxiety. Similarly, he is the new Lazarus, overwhelmed by the revelation of his spiritual death and incapable of communicating his experience to his own society. The assertion

'I am Lazarus, come from the dead,
Come back to tell you all, I shall tell you all'

reminds us of his failure 'to turn back and descend the stair' and his oscillation between his reverie and the actual world of his society. He is baffled finally by the isolating power of his own experience:

'That is not what I meant at all.
That is not it, at all.'

And despite his denial: 'No! I am not Prince Hamlet, nor was meant to be', he is surely Hamlet as well, procrastinating yet moving skilfully among his own reflections. The phrasing here is appropriately clever; 'to be' takes on a peculiarly modern significance: man was not 'meant to be' but to become, to live and endure, to age, to end his career, and to accept these conditions as the boundaries of his existence.

We accept therefore the trivial and the solemn together. We accept the dignity and the power of Prufrock's careful estimate of his own role:

Am an attendant lord, one that will do
To swell a progress, start a scene or two,
Advise the prince; no doubt, an easy tool,
Deferential, glad to be of use,
Politic, cautious, and meticulous;
Full of high sentence, but a bit obtuse;
At times, indeed, almost ridiculous—
Almost, at times, the Fool.

This is the only occasion on which Prufrock has attempted to sustain an exact evaluation of his entire career, and the statement—including his denial of heroic pretensions—forms a part of a larger and most remarkable unity. It is a kind of poetic 'passage' from light to dark, from order to disorder. Prufrock begins modestly and with a sense of his own limitations, he defines his career as subsidiary but useful, he observes that it is perhaps also vain and somewhat stupid, he admits it may also be absurd; and in the movement of the lines we feel a growing panic and the impending disorganization of the perilously balanced confidence which could admit 'I was afraid'. The 'passage' is completed with the hysterical couplet

Responding to Poems

> I grow old . . . I grow old . . .
> I shall wear the bottoms of my trousers rolled.

and the bewildered questions and remarks that follow:

> Shall I part my hair behind? Do I dare to eat a peach?
> I shall wear white flannel trousers, and walk upon the beach.
> I have heard the mermaids singing, each to each. 20

He has made a complete circuit and returned to his original fantasies. And like the poem itself, these last outbursts are composed of individual, disjunctive items which do not follow each other in any obviously consecutive order. Yet the impression of their order is as strong as their random arrangement. Surprisingly enough, Prufrock had himself commented on this very feature:

> It is impossible to say just what I mean!
> But as if a magic lantern threw the nerves in patterns on a screen

These are the only lines which comment, as it were, on the very language of the poem. Nothing is to be taken quite literally. Prufrock's remarks are more deliberate observations; they are also symptoms of a deeper spiritual distress and Prufrock is not unaware of the presence of this level of meaning. We must try to discover, as if with some X-ray technique and as Prufrock himself has attempted, the spiritual pattern which hold all of these separate outbursts together in a convincing way. The requirement marks the *Love Song* as a peculiarly modern invention. The image itself suggests a sort of pschoanalytic technique and aptly recalls once again the Myth of the Cave.

The monologue closes with Prufrock's romantic fantasies about the sea:

> I have herd the mermaids singing, each to each.
> I do not think that they will sing to me.
> I have seen them riding seaward on the waves
> Combing the white hair of the waves blown back.
> When the wind blows the water white and black.
> We have lingered in the chambers of the sea
> By sea-girls wreathed with seaweed red and brown
> Till human voices wake us, and we drown.

This is finally Prufrock's song, mad and sweet, subdued and freed from his earlier hysteria as if his dreaming permitted him to collect himself for an acceptance of the unsatisfactory conditions of his life. There is always present however a constant, if unexpressed, reference to all of the features of his waking life and the fantasy is only a temporary respite. Much reminds us of the fog that 'lingered upon the pools, the music from a farther room'. Prufrock concludes 'we have lingered in the chambers of the sea'; the 'I' suddenly has become again the two persons of the original invitation. It is as if the song were actually composed in that first reverie, as if its fantasies expressed too nearly Prufrock's actual condition and could not be sustained. The final line 'till human voices wake us, and we drown' confuses and inverts the image of the sirens and we are obliged to hear again the labour of that implicit and endless refrain:

> In the room the women come and go
> Talking of Michelangelo.

[1955]

1. Read "The Love Song of J. Alfred Prufrock" and write an initial response to the poem. Now read Margolis's interpretation carefully, and note places where your comprehension is altered or deepened.

2. What does Margolis suggest are the features that make "Prufrock" a modern poem?

3. Do you find yourself persuaded by Margolis's interpretation? Are there places where you can imagine another critic disagreeing? Specify.

4. What does Margolis finally believe about the poem? How has he helped you in your understanding? Write a short account of the process of your making sense of "Prufrock."

RESPONDING TO WILLIAMS'S "THE YACHTS"

William Carlos Williams (1883–1963)

William Carlos Williams was born in Rutherford, New Jersey, and he died in the same city. Unlike so many of the other American modernists, Williams did not travel from place to place. He stayed close to his roots, and he anchored himself financially by becoming a general practitioner. His work, seen as experimentally spare in his day, is resolutely American, exploring the landscapes, traditions, and speech idioms in straightforward and unadorned lines. Williams's best known work is the long poem "Paterson," consisting of five books published between 1946 and 1958. His lyrics have been gathered in two volumes: *Collected Later Poems* (1950) and *Collected Earlier Poems* (1951). He also wrote novels and autobiographical prose. His most often repeated pronouncement, taken by many to be his credo, is "No ideas but in things." Poets have taken these words as endorsing a poetry of impressions and sensations.

THE YACHTS

contend in a sea which the land partly encloses
shielding them from the too-heavy blows
of an ungoverned ocean which when it chooses

tortures the biggest hulls, the best man knows
to pit against its beatings, and sinks them pitilessly.
Mothlike in mists, scintillant in the minute   5

966

brilliance of cloudless days, with broad bellying sails
they glide to the wind tossing green water
from their sharp prows while over them the crew crawls

ant-like, solicitously grooming them, releasing,
making fast as they turn, lean far over and having
caught the wind again, side by side, head for the mark.

In a well guarded arena of open water surrounded by
lesser and greater craft which, sycophant, lumbering
and flittering follow them, they appear youthful, rare

as the light of a happy eye, live with the grace
of all that in the mind is fleckless, free and
naturally to be desired. Now the sea which holds them

is moody, lapping their glossy sides, as if feeling
for some slightest flaw but fails completely.
Today no race. Then the wind comes again. The yachts

move jockeying for a start, the signal is set and they
are off. Now the waves strike at them but they are too
well made, they slip through, they take in canvas.

Arms with hands grasping seek to clutch at the prows.
Bodies thrown recklessly in the way are cut aside.
It is a sea of faces about them in agony, in despair

until the horror of the race dawns staggering the mind;
the whole sea become an entanglement of watery bodies
lost to the world bearing what they cannot hold. Broken,

beaten, desolate, reaching from the dead to be taken up
they cry out, failing failing! their cries rising
in waves still as the skillful yachts pass over.

Harvey Gross

SOUND AND FORM IN THE POETRY
OF WILLIAM CARLOS WILLIAMS

Our first contact with William Carlos
Williams' verse makes us jump; nothing, and certainly nothing in the way of a deliberate metric, seems to intervene between us and the sensibility of this extraordinary man. Our first example, a fragment Williams reprints from *Paterson*, delights
both ear and eye with its carefully spaced lines and young girl voice:

I bought a new
bathing suit

Just pants
and a brassiere—

I haven't shown
it

to my mother
yet.

As in Imagist poetry, the lines are arranged for a rhetorical emphasis; the half-
rhymes (*suit*/*it*/*yet*) mark slight hesitations in the young lady's brief and pithy
discourse. (We must sternly suppress, as being critically undemonstrable, our inclination to see in the shape of the poem an emblem of its subject: both poem and
bathing suit share a tantalizing brevity.) Williams was early associated with the
Imagists; his first literary friends were Pound and H. D., and Pound included a poem
by Williams in *Des Imagistes* (1914). But Williams never officially joined the Imagists nor signed their manifestos. He went to Europe on trips, preferring to remain
an American sightseer rather than take up the uncertain life of an expatriate. His
aggressive and positive Americanism resembles Pound's aggressive, *negative* Americanism.

Both Williams and Pound take an antihistorical stand. Williams shows his contempt for history simply by ignoring it; he tells us again and again he prefers direct
experience to the ash-heaps of the past. Pound's antihistoricism makes more devious but nevertheless followable tracks. He became a scholar, digested what he
needed, and rejected the rest. The "philosophy of history" informing the *Cantos*
retells history as Pound, from his odd angle of vision, sees it. We find no "history,"
of course: only mythology animated by demonology. Pound brought his American
brashness to Europe and started a poetic revolution; Williams stayed home, practiced medicine in Rutherford, and cultivated his sensibility.

We see a clue to Williams' position, both technical and spiritual, in his tirade
against Eliot. I quoted from *The Autobiography of William Carlos Williams:*

> . . . To me especially [*The Waste Land*] struck like a sardonic bullet. I felt at once
> that it had set me back twenty years, and I'm sure it did. Critically Eliot returned
> us to the classroom just at the moment when I felt that we were on the point of
> escape to matters much closer to the essence of a new art form itself—rooted in
> the locality which should give it fruit. . . .
>
> If with his skill he could have been kept here to be employed by our slowly
> shaping drive, what strides might we not have taken! We needed him in the
> scheme I was half-consciously forming. I needed him: he might have become our
> adviser, even our hero. By his walking out on us we were stopped, for the mo-
> ment, cold. It was a bad moment. Only now, as I predicted, have we begun to
> catch hold again and restarted to make the line over. This is not to say that Eliot
> has not, indirectly, contributed much to the emergence of the next step in met-
> rical construction, but if he had not turned away from the direct attack here, in
> the western dialect, we might have gone ahead much faster. . . .

After discounting Williams' considerable personal antipathy for Eliot, we understand his cry against the calculated craftsmanship, the dazzling metrical virtuosity of

Responding to Poems

The Waste Land. To Williams, *The Waste Land* seemed a step backward into the prosodical past; it returned the poet "to the classroom." Williams found no use for Eliot's meters: which scarcely demolishes Eliot but helps to explain Williams. We need not quarrel with Williams about Eliot's repudiation of America; Eliot *had* to go to Europe just as Williams *had* to remain in New Jersey. Matters of temperament determined their location as well as their style. Style is the man; and the man is the air he breathes, the food he eats, the ground on which his house is built.

Williams built his poetic line on "the western dialect" and on the idea that the poem assumes a rhythmic shape congruent to its shape as a presented *object*. The Objectivist theory

> ... argued the poem, like every other form of art, is an object, an object that
> in itself formally presents its case and its meaning by the very form it assumes.
> Therefore, being an object, it should be so treated and controlled—but not as
> in the past.

Williams did not make clear whether the poem-object existed in space or time; he implies the poem exists in time *and* space ("like a symphony or cubist painting"). Objectivist theory emphasized the concreteness of the poem, the "thingness" of its words; Williams discovered in the writings of Gertrude Stein " . . . [a] feeling of words themselves, a curious immediate quality quite apart from their meaning, much as in music different notes are dropped, so to speak, into a repeated chord one at a time, one after another—for itself alone." A word in a poem must function as a discrete perceptual entity; it must be given, with all its physical immediacy, to hearing, vision, or touch. The poet and his reader must revive their childhood belief that words are indeed the things and qualities they symbolize; words like *rough, smooth, round* possess for the mind perceptual roughness, smoothness, roundness.

Objectivist theory represents another variety of the spatial heresy and the attempts of modern poets to fight the medium. Language is stubbornly conceptual; poets must resist abstraction and struggle to make their words vivid to eye, ear, and touch. The objectivist poem achieves its vividness by stopping time; the poem sits on the page in its unmoving "thingness":

BETWEEN WALLS

the back wings
of the

hospital where
nothing

will grow lie
cinders

in which shine
the broken

pieces of a green
bottle

Nothing happens; the verbs (*lie, shine*) present little action and function nearly as copulas. The poem's significance is implied, not stated. We understand that the back of the hospital, the infertile cinders, and the shattered bottle, add up to a feeling of sudden desolation. The sun, catching the green glass, points up the bleak surroundings. ⁵

5

Such a poem requires a bare minimum of prosodic means. The lines are alternately long and short and hold two and one stress respectively. Important words stand by themselves or at the end of lines: *nothing, cinders, broken, green.* The poem is composed in space, and the eye comes to rest on *green.* Perhaps *green* suggests fertility in contrast to the barren back of the hospital. But Williams would probably snort at this "interpretation," and maintain ". . . The feeling is of words themselves, a curious immediate quality, quite apart from their meaning. . . ." As words detach themselves from their meanings, prosody becomes static. Rhythmic structure moves in time, but the Objectivist poem does not move; like the Gumbie Cat it "sits and sits and sits and sits," maintaining its inscrutability.

Not all of Williams' poems, however, sit motionless, pinned down by typography and visual form. "The Dance" has a boisterous, even catchy swing:

> In Breughel's great picture, The Kermess,
> the dancers go round, they go round and
> around, the squeal and the blare and the
> tweedle of bagpipes, a bugle and fiddles
> tipping their bellies (round as the thick-
> sided glasses whose wash they impound)
> their hips and bellies off balance
> to turn them. Kicking and rolling about
> the Fair Grounds, swinging their butts, those
> shanks must be sound to bear up under such
> rollicking measures, prance as they dance
> in Breughel's great picture, The Kermess.

The lines stomp along in heavily accented triple time: the German *Ländler* with its ONE-two-three, OOM-pah-pah. Interior rhyme and a firm anapestic meter hold the poem together:

> their híps | and their bél | lies off bál | ance
>
> to túrn | them.ˌ Kíck | ing and ról | ing a bóut |
>
> the Fair Gróunds, | ˌswíng | ing their bútts | those
>
> shánks | must be sóund . . .

We cannot miss the obvious music of "The Dance." Williams' eye is sharp but his ear is equally sharp. We hear finer, more intricate music in other poems. Hoagy Carmichael reads "Tract" (*I will teach you my townspeople / how to perform a funeral*) over a pulsing jazz accompaniment; his soft Southern voice gracefully picks out the rhythms and we know that Williams writes for the ear as well as the eye.

Most of Williams' poems are composed in characteristic short lines. However, he has written a number of poems using a longer and more conventional line. These are the concluding tercets from "The Yachts":

> Arms with hands grasping seek to clutch at the prows.
> Bodies thrown recklessly in the way are cut aside.
> It is a sea of faces about them in agony, in despair

until the horror of the race dawns staggering the mind,
the whole sea becomes an entanglement of watery bodies
lost to the world bearing what they cannot hold. Broken,

beaten, desolate, reaching from the dead to be taken up
they cry out, failing, failing! their cries rising
in waves still as the skillful yachts pass over.

The lines approximate blank verse—the modern, loosened kind with free use of substitution and hypermetrical effects. Rhythmic beauty is achieved by a long *rallentando*, a gradual slowing down of prosodic movement. The first tercet has the normal rising rhythm of blank verse, but beginning with the last line of the second tercet, the rhythm begins to shift. A pattern of trochaic words, *Broken, beaten, reaching, failing, rising*, crosses the rising iambic base; like the waves themselves, we have a rocking movement generated by the falling metrical units of trochee and dactyl:

béat en, | dé so late, | réach ing from | the déad | to be tá | ken úp

they crý | out, faíl | ing, faíl | ing! their críes | rí sing . . .

The final lines evoke a nearly unbearable pathos—nearly, but not quite; the passionately well-ordered metric keeps the feeling within bounds. "The Yachts" is among Williams' best poems; it ranks with the best poems of our age.

[1964]

QUESTIONS

1. What does Gross suggest is Williams's immediate attraction for a reader?

2. Williams and Eliot were very different kinds of poets. Read "The Love Song of J. Alfred Prufrock" and Margolis's interpretation, then "The Yachts" and Gross's commentary; explain what some of the differences between the poets may have been.

3. How does Gross characterize the difference between "The Dance" and "Between Walls"?

4. Taking your cue from Gross's comments on the final tercets of "The Yachts": (a) read the poem carefully, (b) scan the lines, and (c) comment further on what the scansion suggests about Williams's poetics.

5. Compare "The Yachts" with "The Cod Head" (p. 556) How are these two poems identifiably the work of the same poet?

RESPONDING TO BISHOP'S "THE MAP"

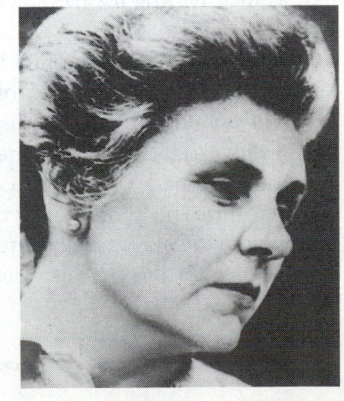

Elizabeth Bishop (1911–1979)

Although she was born in Worcester, Massachusetts, and died in Boston, Elizabeth Bishop spent most of her life outside the state of Massachusetts. After the death of her parents, she was raised in Nova Scotia. She spent much of her adult life traveling, particularly in the tropics. After 1951 she lived for many years in

Petropolis, Brazil. Bishop's travels fed her exacting and inquisitive eye and, in time, her poetry. Though her output was sparse, she was admired by readers and fellow poets the world over for her ability to render fresh sensation in natural-seeming lines of poetry. Bishop's first book, *North and South* (1945), opens with "The Map," a poem that suggests the power of her geographical imagination. Later collections include *Questions of Travel* (1965) and *Geography III* (1977).

THE MAP

Land lies in water; it is shadowed green.
Shadows, or are they shallows, at its edges
showing the line of long sea-weeded ledges
where weeds hang to the simple blue from green.
Or does the land lean down to lift the sea from under,   5
drawing it unperturbed around itself?
Along the fine tan sandy shelf
is the land tugging at the sea from under?

The shadow of Newfoundland lies flat and still.
Labrador's yellow, where the moony Eskimo   10
has oiled it. We can stroke these lovely bays,
under a glass as if they were expected to blossom,
or as if to provide a clean cage for invisible fish.
The names of seashore towns run out to sea,
the names of cities cross the neighboring mountains   15
—the printer here experiencing the same excitement
as when emotion too far exceeds its cause.
These peninsulas take the water between thumb and finger
like women feeling for the smoothness of yard-goods.

Mapped waters are more quiet than the land is.   20
lending the land their waves' own conformation:
and Norway's hare° runs south in agitation,
profiles investigate the sea, where land is.
Are they assigned, or can the countries pick their colors?
—What suits the character or the native waters best.   25
Topography displays no favorites: North's as near as West.
More delicate than the historians' are the map-makers' colors.

THE MAP. 22 *Norway's hare:* Norway on the map can be seen to resemble a hare.

Sybil P. Estess

DESCRIPTION AND IMAGINATION IN ELIZABETH BISHOP'S "THE MAP"

The filmmaker Michelangelo Antonioni maintains that he attempts in his movies to focus on details in order to emphasize his perceiving. He writes, "I am obliged to linger ad infinitum on the details, on the repetition of the most futile gestures, in order that what I show may assume a form and sense."[1] Joseph Conrad's statement in the preface to *The Nigger of the "Narcissus"* is now a classic one: "—My task which I am trying to achieve is, by the power of the written word, to make you hear, to make you feel—it is, before all, to make you *see*. That—and no more, and it is everything." Randall Jarrell commented on Elizabeth Bishop's first book, "All her poems have written underneath *I have seen it*."[2] Indeed the inclination of modern and postmodern literature has long been to communicate individual vision rather than abstract truth. Bishop, like Conrad, like Antonioni, like most modern and contemporary artists, takes as her task enabling us to see as she sees. She makes description the most salient characteristic of her poetry and prose. Poems such as "The Map," "The Fish," and "The Bight," though at first glance realistic descriptions of ordinary entities, are actually much more: they are guides to her own vision of those realities. Many Bishop poems evolve toward what James Joyce thought of as an epiphanic vision.

Elizabeth Bishop seldom violates objects by imposing on them preconceived definitions, a priori interpretations, or sentimental descriptions. But even though she may seem to look at things with the exactitude and tenacity of a naturalist, Bishop necessarily creates art out of her personal life experiences, and ultimately out of her synthesized vision of whatever she chooses to describe; her "empiricism" is not as unalloyed as it may first appear.

In the poem "The Map," Bishop offers a significant hint to her sense of how an "objective" work of art may embody the artist's subjective experience of a given reality. "The Map" embodies a way of understanding her work, for she placed it first in both *North & South* (1946) and in *The Complete Poems* (1969). On one level, the poem objectively describes an actual map: "Land lies in water; it is shadowed green." But beginning as early as the second line of the poem, Bishop's subjective kind of seeing becomes apparent. She starts to question what seem to her the nuances of the map's configurations.

Shadows, or are they shallows, at its edges
showing the line of long sea-weeded ledges
where weeds hang to the simple blue from green.

---

[1] Michel Mardore, "Antonioni, je suis an incurable optimiste," *Les lettres française*, No. 924 (Sept. 6, 1962), p. 6; cited and translated by Ted Perry in "A Contextual Study of M. Antonioni's Film *L'Eclisse*," *Speech Monographs 37*, no. 2 (June 1970) p. 92. [Estess's note.]

[2] *Poetry and the Age* (1953; reprint ed., New York: Farrar, Straus and Giroux/Noonday, 1972), p. 5. [Estess's note.]

On her first look at the map, she seems to see water as surrounding and supporting land. In the following lines, however, we see the possibility that sea and land form an alliance so complementary that it is difficult to determine the exact nature of their interdependence:

Or does the land lean down to lift the sea from under,
drawing it unperturbed around itself?
Along the fine tan sandy shelf
is the land tugging at the sea from under?

Bishop's map enables us to imagine myriad kinds of connections between land and sea. The land's peninsulas may seem to "take the water between thumb and finger / like women feeling for the smoothness of yard-goods." A configuration such as Norway's may appear a "hare" which "runs south in agitation." Bishop suggests in these lines that what one sees depends upon how one looks.

Is it not, then, our perspectives on the real which determine its very nature? The initial stanza of "The Map" seems to suggest that the essence of reality may be determined by our manner of seeing. Do "sea-weeded ledges . . . / hang to the simple blue from green?" "Or does the land lean down to lift the sea from under"? It all depends, Bishop first seems to say, on our chosen vantage point.

Yet reality is not merely relative to how we see it. As the poem progresses, we find that the imagination cannot create nor can it alter things as they are. A map's images can never be arbitrarily presented. As Wallace Stevens writes in what he calls an an *opusculum paedagogum*: "The pears are not seen / as the observer wills" ("Study of Two Pears"). On maps, the poet's interlocutor asks of her, are countries colored "what suits the character or the native waters best"? Must reality, then, always be scrupulously and unerringly presented?

The issue at stake is that the images on maps are by definition constructions of the mind, as the mind attempts to plot the landscape in order to find its way. Though such artifacts must be "accurate," must be faithful to things as we know them, they may still be imaginatively constructed or arranged. Bishop's kind of navigational description is an invention derived not only from her empirical eye but also from her mind, as it becomes the agent which charts the various depths of the waters of her personal imagination. Such compositions are, as A. D. Hope writes, "held between the intellectual eye and the landscape."[3] Bishop seems to make a judgement in "The Map" concerning the efficacy of all "maps," of all invented, artistic images. Though the shadows of their new-found-lands may (like those of Newfoundland appear to lie "flat and still" in comparison to real sea or land, their waters too have a strategic function: they lend the land "their waves' own conformation." No aesthetic images, even Bishop's verisimilar kind of description, should be taken as exhaustive of reality. The maps to experience which her art provides are the result of the constant intrusion of things-as-they-are upon her particular power to come to terms with them. Bishop attempts in descriptive poems to make form and imaginative sense of what she sees. It is through her personalized, imaginative perspective that she allows us, as Stevens would have it, to "see the earth again."

5

---

[3] "The Esthetic Theory of James Joyce," in *Joyce's Portrait: Criticisms and Critiques*, ed. Thomas E. Connolly (New York: Appleton-Century-Crofts Press, 1962), p. 200. [Estess's note.]

As in most Bishop poems, the meaning of "The Map" extends far beyond a mere realistic description of a literal object. This poem delineates the nature of a relationship between objective reality and one's subjective and imaginative assimilation of such "facts." Bishop suggests in "The Map" that an art work may be seen as a map to an artist's particular sense of things. The analogy, of course, can be drawn further: her works—cumulations of realistic details shaped into an imaginative form—are maps to and of her own sensibility.

"Mapped waters are more quiet than the land is," the poem says. It concludes, however, "More delicate than the historians' are the map-makers' colors." Here Bishop adds to the correlation between the task of the poet and the task of the historian an even subtler dimension than did Aristotle when he claimed that "poetry is higher than history." She implies that, like the historian, the map-maker should not distort "truth"; yet she seems to know too that it is impossible to be completely objective. For just as the individual sensibility of the historian informs what he records, the artist's particular vision (with all its peculiar slants) shapes what he or she creates. Thus any poet's images are the delicate result of the imagination lending its conformation to manifestations of the real. A fragile, perhaps, yet keen and subtle sense of discrimination—"the map-makers' colors"—comprises an artists way of seeing.

[1983]

QUESTIONS

1. How does Estess distinguish between simple visual "seeing" and the seeing that characterizes "epiphanic vision"? How does she suggest that Bishop's poem makes use of the latter?
2. What strategies did Bishop have for "The Map" when including it in a book? Explain what you imagine to have been her rationale.
3. Compare "The Map" with "The Fish" (p. 884). Find instances in each of Bishop's particular way of handling detail. Try to describe what makes her handling of detail unique.
4. How does Estess read "The Map" as a larger statement about mind and perception? Explain.

THE POET'S OWN RESPONSE: DONALD JUSTICE'S "FIRST DEATH"

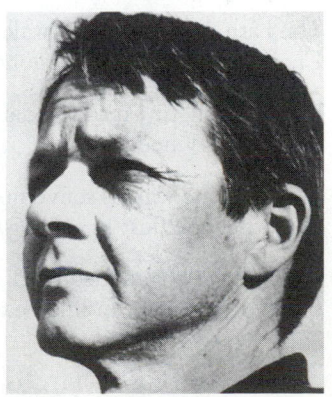

Donald Justice (1925–   )

Donald Justice grew up in rural Florida, taking in the atmosphere of places that would surface so distinctively in his poetry years later. Educated at the University of Miami, Stanford, and the University of Iowa, Justice has taught widely. His poetry has received numerous awards, and though his books—like the enormously influential *The Summer Anniversaries* (1960)—are slim, his reputation, particularly among his fellow poets, is enormous.

ON WRITING "FIRST DEATH"

First Death

June 12, 1933

I saw my grandmother grow weak.
When she died, I kissed her cheek.

I remember the new taste—
Powder mixed with a drying paste.

Down the hallway, on its table,   5
Lay the family's great Bible.

In the dark, by lamplight stirred,
The Void grew pregnant with the Word.

In black ink they wrote it down.
The other ink was turning brown.   10

From the woods there came a cry—
a hoot owl asking who, not why.

The men sat silent on the porch,
Each lighted pipe a friendly torch

Against the unknown and the known.   15
But the child knew himself alone.

June 13, 1933

The morning sun rose up and stuck.
Sunflower strove with hollyhock.°

I ran the worn path past the sty.
Nothing was hidden from God's eye.   20

The barn door creaked. I walked among
Chaff° and wrinkled cakes of dung.

In the dim light I read the dates
On the dusty license plates   25

Nailed to the wall as souvenirs.
I breathed the dust in of the years.

I circled the abandoned Ford
Before I tried the running board.

FIRST DEATH: JUNE 13, 1933. 18 *hollyhock*: a tall plant with a showy flower. 22 *chaff*: grain husks after seed is removed.

At the wheel I felt the heat   30
Press upwards through the springless seat.

And when I touched the silent horn,
Small mice scattered through the corn.

I remember the soprano
Fanning herself at the piano,

And the preacher looming large
Above me in his dark blue serge.°

My shoes brought in a smell of clay   5
To mingle with the faint sachet°

Of flowers sweating in their vases.
A stranger showed us to our places.

The stiff fan stirred in mother's hand.
Air moved, but only when she fanned.   10

I wondered how could all her grief
Be squeezed into one small handkerchief.

There was a buzzing on the sill.
It stopped, and everything was still.

We bowed our heads, we closed our eyes   15
To the mercy of the flies.

FIRST DEATH: JUNE 14, 1933. 4 *serge:* woolen suit cloth.   6 *sachet:* perfumed powders used to scent clothing.

"First Death" developed consciously, so far as the development was conscious, out of no more than a feeling many poets must have conditioned themselves to respond to—the generalized desire simply to be writing a poem, any poem.[1] Having been sick for some months, I had not been writing and was, perhaps, beginning to feel guilty. A first worksheet shows that I was typing out tetrameter couplets° about nothing in particular. Since it is not my usual

---

[1]To a questionnaire sent out by Alberta Turner, who was editing a book eventually to be published under the title *Fifty Contemporary Poets* (New York: David McKay, 1977), I wrote this response. Most of the points touched on and even the order in which they come up were determined by the questionnaire itself. [Justice's note.]

ON WRITING "FIRST DEATH."   (par 1) *tetrameter couplets:* couplets in joined pairs, forming four-line sequences.

practice to *type* a first draft, I suspect that I was merely practicing, trying to warm up, not feeling altogether responsible for what my fingers might find to say. Ultimately, about halfway down the first page, I typed a couplet or two *about* something, about something specific and real: raindrops caught in a spiderweb on a back porch. I knew which porch that was—my grandparents' porch, on a farm near Tifton, Georgia, some time in the early thirties. (The detail was not to survive in the poem.) I rationalized the process by supposing that, while my conscious mind was attending to details of rhyming and metering these couplets about nothing, my unconscious had been freed to rove and dive until it came up with a fragment of memory, entangled with associations rich, for me, in feeling and significance. Why I was writing couplets° at all I cannot remember. I had never published a poem in such couplets; indeed, I had not tried rhyme for years (except in a libretto° that year for which the composer had requested rhyme), and I had never rejoiced in rhyming, being less than adept at it. I do recall feeling then that most poets were tending to write more and more sloppily and that some attention to the strictest formal etiquette might check that inclination insofar as I shared it. Nor did I wish simply to repeat myself, to write on and on of the themes and in the manners of *Departures*, the book I had recently completed. I would try to be new, at least for myself, by returning to the old—old form, old subject.

It is rare for a poem of mine to go through an orderly succession of drafts, versions which begin at the beginning and go right through to the end. The four or five drafts usually required in such cases are quickly done, and with pleasure. A different pleasure comes from the kind of work this poem involved, the pleasure resulting from care and labor, as in making something with tools in a manual training class or putting up a house of cards. Each line and, in this poem, each couplet had, it seemed, to be shaped into something close to its final form, or at least made to fill up its imagined place with more or less the right meaning, before I was ready to continue. Although there are no drafts except for very late ones, I can count thirty-four worksheets. Unhappily, long periods elapsed between intervals of work. If I started the poem some time in the summer of 1973, as I believe I did, and made substantial progress on it then, getting through much of the first two sections, I did not resume serious work on it till June, 1975. I was not sure how long the poem would or should be—couplets have a way of running on and on—but I did see it early as falling into parts (if not pieces), and once I had more than enough for the first two sections down on paper, it seemed that one last section, something conclusive, should suffice. What—I must have asked myself, on coming back to it—what more conclusive than the funeral itself? (The first funeral I had ever attended.) In this sense the poem expanded, grew, was added on to. But in other ways it just as clearly shrank, the first section from twenty or more lines to an exact sixteen, and similarly throughout. And if I had vaguely imagined a poem that might re-create the Georgia summers I had passed as a child—a part of my own lesser *Prelude*, so to speak—a poem of no fewer surely, than two hundred lines; if, indeed, I must have written that many lines for it (though I do not wish to count the worksheets to verify the number), it nevertheless ended as a mere forty-eight, not a documentary of all that those Georgia summers had been, but an edited cinema of three days remembered from one summer only.

In the nature of the case, the structure, this once, did not much change, except for the fixing of the exact number of lines for each section. The theme changed only

---

(par 1) *couplets:* paired lines. *libretto:* text of an opera or musical drama.

Responding to Poems

in being narrowed down and focused on my grandmother's death and my reactions as a child to that shaking, though common, experience. The tone, unfortunately, did undergo some modification. I had wanted from the first something childlike, folklike, near-primitive, feeling the couplet to be a fit vehicle for such a tone, and that tone to be in keeping with both the subject and, as might be remarked of a fiction or memoir, the child's point of view. The first two lines, I felt, set the tone I wanted to maintain. But I could not maintain it, despite effort. In what follows there is a growing self-consciousness, perhaps some reminiscence even of the handling of this particular verse line from Milton's° great pair of poems, but I hope not so much as to spoil completely the innocence from which it started. The first two lines of the poem, then, are the unchanged lines, the model lines. Only slightly changed were the "witty" line about the Void, the lines about the hoot owl, and the final couplets of the first and last sections. Everything in the second section was considerably revised; signs of the trouble which that part gave me still seem visible. Most of the revisions seem to have been made for the sake of coherence—narrative, stylistic, and especially tonal.

The meters require little explanation and, in my view, no defense. The tetrameter couplet is a more flexible instrument than generally acknowledged, and the line itself may crop up anywhere from ballads to Milton. Its particular adaptation here is the one which allows you, depending on whether you regard the line as iambic or trochaic, to drop or to add a first syllable; in other words, the first foot is free. In "L'Allegro" and "Il Penseroso" this slight admixture of freedom opens the line to grace, beauty, and delight, and in this respect suggests the attractive waywardness with which the line is treated in certain ballads. Wishing to keep the tone casual and unsophisticated, in tension with the apparent severity of the couplet, I was happy to find a handful of inexact rhymes. The metaphor, what there may be of it, is conventional or so simple as to escape notice. It seems to have become virtually a principle with me—in practice if not yet in theory—to use literal details so that they imply metaphor. Summer heat is equivalent to intense misery: temperature becomes metaphor. When the child in the poem touches the dead horn of the old Ford and the mice scatter, the paradox of creatures responding to silence as if it were a sudden frightening noise is, I propose, metaphorical, an attempt to render the child's projection of his own terror onto his surroundings. As for language, anything that is not simple, not obviously rooted in the child's sensibility, is most likely to be traced to the oppressive influence of the religion which afflicted that sensibility (as in lines 8 and 20). Against custom, including my own, I was willing to admit here and there certain old-fashioned "poetic" devices, such as inversion ("by lamplight stirred"), easy enough otherwise to get around, on the grounds that they reinforced the tone I was after. I was trying to write a poem, not an exemplary text on how poetry ought to be written now or in the future.

The order of the poem is chronological, a narrative with a beginning, middle, and end, and with no more ellipsis° than common in narrative, yet selective rather than accumulative, more like a short story than a novel. I wanted a big ending, quietly done. The boy in the poem is myself, but myself at seven, which gives me the illusion of distance I prefer to work with. I had, as usual, no particular audience in

---

(par 3) *Milton's:* referring to English poet John Milton (see Chapter 27) and his companinon poems "L'Allegro" and "Il Penseroso."
(par 5) *ellipsis:* material left out.

mind, but readers certainly, nameless readers. And for once, this was a poem I would have been glad to have my mother read, but she died before I finished it. 5

The outline of the poem is easy enough to paraphrase, and paraphrases that do not wallow in prolixity° are of outlines only. Paraphrase: (1) A boy sees his grandmother die and is terrified by the mysteries and customs surrounding the death, feeling himself alone in a hostile world. (2) He hides himself away from others and attempts to know the past, to master it and escape from the present through an act of make-believe. (3) At the funeral he feels oppressed by the heat, the rituals, and the inefficacy of religious consolation. Such a paraphrase necessarily leaves out what I trust may seem the magical reality which comes about through the more detailed rendering and more substantial ordering required by the poem, though some of what is lost might be restored by expanding the prose commentary. (With a "creative" critic something might even be added.) What would be lost forever if only the prose commentary survived would be the pleasure (if any) of the meters and rhymes themselves and whatever effects of coherence, compression, and point their binding force had led to (or not prevented), all of which ought to have helped *fix* the poem, as the right solution fixes the snapshot. The reader would have lost the chance to experience the event for himself. I would have lost my own pleasure in having put the poem together in this way, in having made something, this.

The poem is not at all obscure, I think, and should give no one trouble on that score. How good or bad the poem may be is another question, one I cannot properly answer. I do like it. I like it because it records something otherwise lost.

[1975]

(par 6) *proxility:* wordiness.

QUESTIONS

1. Read "First Death" carefully, then read Justice's account of writing the poem. How does the intimate testimony of the poet change your sense of the poem? Specify.
2. Can you make an argument about why it is generally better for the reader *not* to know how a work has been conceived and written?

ANOTHER POET'S RESPONSE: STANLEY KUNITZ'S "FATHER AND SON"

Stanley Kunitz (1905–   )

As Robert Lowell observes in his essay, and as is reinforced by his poem, Kunitz grew up in a suburban setting around Worcester, Massachusetts, and lived much of his life "lost between two wars." He published his first book, *Intellectual Things,* in 1930. His *Selected Poems, 1928–1958,* followed other publications. Kunitz now lives in Provincetown, Massachusetts, where he continues to write and to serve as a much-loved mentor to a great many young American poets.

FATHER AND SON

Now in the suburbs and the falling light
I followed him, and now down sandy road
Whiter than bone-dust, through the sweet
Curdle of fields, where the plums
Dropped with their load of ripeness, one by one.   5
Mile after mile I followed, with skimming feet,
After the secret master of my blood,
Him, steeped in the odor of ponds, whose indomitable love
Kept me in chains. Strode years; stretched into bird;
Raced through the sleeping country where I was young,   10
The silence unrolling before me as I came,
The night nailed like an orange to my brow.

How should I tell him my fable and the fears,
How bridge the chasm in a casual tone,
Saying, "The house, the stucco one you built,   15
We lost. Sister married and went from home,
And nothing comes back, it's strange, from where she goes.
I lived on a hill that had too many rooms:
Light we could make, but not enough of warmth,
And when the light failed, I climbed under the hill.   20
The papers are delivered every day;
I am alone and never shed a tear."

At the water's edge, where the smothering ferns lifted
Their arms, "Father!" I cried, "Return! You know
The way. I'll wipe the mudstains from your clothes;   25
No trace, I promise, will remain. Instruct
Your son, whirling between two wars,
In the Gemara° of your gentleness,
For I would be a child to those who mourn
And brother to the foundlings° of the field   30
And friend of innocence and all bright eyes.
O teach me how to work and keep me kind."

Among the turtles and the lilies he turned to me
The white ignorant hollow of his face.

FATHER AND SON. 28 *Gemara*: second part of the Talmud, the Jewish book of ancient rabbinical writings. 30 *foundlings*: deserted children.

Robert Lowell (1917–1977)

Robert Lowell was born in Boston to a prominent
American family (which included poets James
Russell Lowell and Amy Lowell). His roots in the

Puritan past of New England converged with his conversion to Roman Catholicism in 1940 to produce the complex and religiously meditative poems of his first book, *Land of Unlikeliness* (1944). In the 1950s, however, Lowell transformed his poetry, leaving behind formal artifice and introducing a directness about private matters that was something new to American poetry. Lowell's book *Life Studies* (1959) is regarded by many as the book that instigated what became known as "Confessional Poetry." In later years, Lowell became an important public voice, protesting American involvement in Vietnam. He undertook the writing of hundreds of unrhymed sonnets which, taken together, can be seen as a kind of verse journal of a public and private man. Lowell suffered for much of his life from a depressive illness and was often hospitalized. He died unexpectedly in New York City in 1977 while riding in a taxi cab.

ON STANLEY KUNITZ'S "FATHER AND SON"

I suppose the fashion of looking very, very closely at poems began with *The Waste Land*.° This poem was widely attacked as immoral non-sense. Many who like it found it complex yet unintelligible. The author's footnotes had a breezy, pedantic dash to them that was in itself a warning. They assumed more knowledge than most readers had, yet everywhere in their inadequacy pointed to more work to be done: myths to be pondered, symbols to be harmonized, books to be read. Soon there was a crackling controversy among the admirers of *The Waste Land*, as to whether it was religious, anti-religious or without beliefs. Long analytical essays began to appear; soon this kind of writing spread, and everything, ancient and modern, was being explained.

Eliot seemed to gaze on this new industry from the background, a friendly god, silent and brooding. But when he broke silence, his remarks were far from helpful. The footnotes, faithfully reprinted according to the author's wishes in each new anthologizing of *The Waste Land*, turned out to be a publisher's afterthought, a trick to make a book out of a poem that was too short to be one. Far from being a devotee of analysis, it seemed that Eliot read it, if at all, with weary, incredulous amazement. Commenting on a book of close critical studies of "the poem," he had many doubts and ended by saying that such writings certainly didn't make for very interesting reading.

Analysis doesn't make for interesting reading. Few of us, I imagine, spend much time pouring over *The Explicator*, that solid, dull little publication, where poems are processed into monthly exegesis. Analysis is necessary for teaching poems, and for

---

ON STANLEY KUNITZ'S "FATHER AND SON." (par 1) *The Waste Land:* famous modernist poem into which T. S. Eliot (see above and Chapter 27) incorporated extensive footnotes.

student papers. Still, somehow, nothing very fresh or to the point is said. One knows ahead of time how the machine will grind. Conventionality has overtaken the industry; nothing new is set up, nothing bad is destroyed. There is even a kind of modern poem, now produced in bulk, that seems written to be explained. Training and labor are required for such efforts, but this can't be the way good poems are written. Inspiration, passions, originality and even technical assurance must be something that can't be produced in bulk, or merely by training and labor. Nor can good criticism be produced by training and labor and conventionality.

Dullness and the sad, universal air of the graduate schools have descended on close literary criticism. Once it was far otherwise. I can remember when the early essays on *The Waste Land*, the first editions of the Brooks and Warren° *Understanding Poetry*, and *Blackmur's*° pieces on Stevens° and Marianne Moore° came as a revelation. The world was being made anew. Nothing, it seemed, had ever really been read. Old writings, once either neglected or simplified and bowdlerized into triteness, were now for the first time seen as they were. New writing that met the new challenges was everywhere painfully wrestling itself into being. Poetry was still unpopular, but it seemed as though Arnold's° "immense future" for literature and particularly poetry was being realized. Here, for a few, was religion and reality.

Perhaps all this was only my adolescent fever. A glow seems to be gone, but perhaps this was just my illusion. Perhaps there never was a glow; more likely, it is still there and yearly seizes new writers and new critics. For me, anyways, the fever is a chronic malaria. I will never quite disbelieve that the world is being remade by the new ways of writing and careful reading. With this admission, I feel in the right mood of warmth and naiveness to start looking closely at Stanley Kunitz's poem, "Father and Son." However, I really doubt the possibilities of the method, and even more my own talents for it.   5

"Father and Son" is a modern poem, one that has obviously been through the new mill and the new training. Yet when read, say twice, there seems to be an embarrassing lack of difficulty. The theme, a son looking for his dead father, must have existed in the time of Cain.° The fact of the experience seems so closely joined and identical with its unavoidable symbolic reverberations that it would be banal and schoolteacherish to point them out. The pathos and dignity of expression are as open and apparent as such things are in ordinary conversation. The meter is a tolerably regular blank verse.

My first questions are cheating personal ones that mean much to me, but which are no doubt uncritical and unanswerable by careful reading. I want to know if Kunitz and his own father are the father and son. Is the countryside, the country around Worcester, Massachusetts, where Kunitz grew up and I went to boarding school? What happened to the sister? What's the point of the pond? Did the father drown himself, or was his favorite sport fishing or wading for water bugs? *Gemara* seems to be some Torah appendage to the Bible. Some sort of lonely pilgrimage? An experience of bitter purging? But I really don't know, and have no books or knowledge-

---

(par 4) *Brooks and Warren:* Cleanth Brooks and Robert Penn Warren, influential "New Critics" (see the Appendix: "Critical Perspectives.") *Blackmur:* R. P. Blackmur, American critic. *Stevens:* Wallace Stevens, American poet (see Chapter 27). *Marianne Moore:* American poet, see above. *Arnold:* Matthew Arnold, English critic and poet (see Chapter 27).   (par 6) *Cain:* Biblical figure, the son of Adam and Eve who slew his brother Abel.

able people to consult. The word *Gemara* and the poem's tone seem to say it is personal. So, I say yes to most of my questions except the suicide. The pond must somehow touch on the remembered father, and is a puff of blue smoke from everyone's childhood, when ponds, waterlilies and nature were closer and more demandingly mysterious. The sister is nowhere, an intentional question mark.

A few hard expressions stand out. "A sweet curdle of fields!" Fields don't curdle, curdle is somehow the opposite of sweet. Here is the journey in a phrase. The pathos is in its hard sterility, it's a curdle because no such journey can really be made. Finding the dead father is a pipe dream. Nothing could be more natural or idly futile. The only sand on such a road must be like "bone-dust." "The secret master of my blood" is a stern expression of filial piety. This too is hard, unconfessable, tyrannical, and in the terrible nature of things. And this particular father in life loved with a kind of love that was indomitable for him but "chains" for his son. Then several natural and impossible things happen: one strides down years, the fields are fields of childhood, the silence unrolls. Then comes an odd, violent phrase, the night nailed like an orange to the son's brow. Perhaps this is Baudelaire's° "old orange squeezed dry," but oranges can be squeezed, they are not nailed. I think of the kind of contradiction I am now familiar with, a mush of obscurity and impossibility nailed to one by necessity, the inescapably absent and unshakable father. Is the orange a sop° for a headache savagely nailed to the brow it is supposed to sooth? A grim, jocular reference to the Crucifixion, the torture that saves for believers, and here made low and foolish?

In the next section, three things stop me: the life that has become so unreal and meaningful that it is a *fable*, the hill so figuratively easy and literally impossible to climb *under* (Is it for warmth? Is it to get totally away from the light that is now gone, a kind of death for the son and one that has long been hinted at?) and the somehow reproachful, Stoical° hysteria of "I'm alone and never shed a tear."

In the last section, the son "whirling between two wars" reminds me of a remark made by Mary McCarthy° in an essay. She says that in our nuclear age it is impossible to write as Jane Austen and Tolstoy did about what we know. A house is no longer simply a house, a man is no longer simply a man in a town. The inhuman, unreal, smashing universal is always at our elbow. All must signify and ache with the unnatural and necessary nightmare. The "white ignorant hollow of his face" is the skull, the always known attainableness of the search and a kind of answer and reassurance. The search must be tried, though one knows that nothing solid can be touched.   10

Many of the things I like about this poem are simple things hardly worth remarking on but genuine and precious. They are the suburbs, the stucco house, the sister who marries as a matter of course and is not heard of as a matter of course. There's a curious distance, vagueness and dignity about the house on the hill with light but not enough warmth, and whose light fails—marriage in our wandering world perhaps and no doubt. This is our world, none of it can be put away or expunged any more than boyhood, the need to yearn, and the fact that we are all sons of someone, who is as he was. There's a boyish coziness, innocence and hopelessness to the turtles and water-lilies. The lines after *Gemara* have the vulnerable openness of a prayer. The poem is as much a struggle to recover childhood, or the prayer once held in childhood, as it is about the father.

(par 8) *Baudelaire:* French symbolist poet. *sop:* something given to placate.   (par 9) *Stoical:* not showing emotion, hard-bitten; refers to a school of ancient Greek philosophy.   (par 10) *Mary McCarthy:* American novelist and essayist.

Responding to Poems

The other things that make this poem are of a kind that take great art and passion to accomplish. They are matters of rhythm and syntax, all that is the life blood of a poem when we read it ourselves. These are what Paul Valéry° meant when he said a poem was some huge weight carried to some height or the top of a skyscraper and dropped on the reader. The reader feels the simple brute impact, but is ignorant of the sweat and science that carried the weight into position. In the working-out of a poem, I look for two things: a commanding, deadly effectiveness in the arrangement, and something that breathes and pauses and grunts and is rough and unpredictable to assure me that the journey is honest. In the first sentence, I like plums that actually do drop one by one in their ripeness, the way they round off the sentence and their good-natured illusory reference to the father's dropping off. There's a fine careless loosening-up of the rhythm in the "odor of ponds" line. The three verbs, "strode," "stretched," and "raced" are strong in their position, movement and pauses. The two principal lines at the end of the first section are authoritatively placed.

So is the last line of section two. So is the whole artful, broken simplicity of the speech in this section. Also the very different speech and prayer in section three. Just right is the confused rhythm describing the ferns, turtles and lilies.

Are there flaws and limitations? I am not sure. I blink a little at a certain over-resolute, petrified firmness here and there, in the "master of my blood," the nailed orange, the "never shed a tear," and the "white ignorant hollow of his face." Perhaps these are just characteristics of the experience, and the inking that makes the poem a poem and not an improvisation. Certainly there's authority and honesty, a noble hallucination.

I have written under disadvantages, far from books, and in a rush to make a deadline. I haven't Kunitz's *Selected Poems* at hand to refer to. He has never published an unfelt and unfinished poem. Each line shows his fine touch and noble carefulness.   15

(par 12) *Paul Valéry:* French poet and critic.

QUESTIONS

1. Read Kunitz's poem carefully without reading Lowell's commentary. Write a short interpretation of the poem. Now read Lowell's interpretation and comment on the differences. Do you feel you gained new insights from Lowell's response? Explain.

2. Here we see a poet writing a response to a fellow poet. Can you isolate any parts of the response that seem to reveal the insights that only another craftsman could offer? Specify.

RESPONSES TO THE POETRY OF ADRIENNE RICH

Adrienne Rich (1929–   )

Chapter 25, entitled "A Poet's Career," is devoted to the poetry and prose of Adrienne Rich. Students are referred to that chapter, as well as to Rich's long poem, "Diving into the Wreck" (included in Chapter 22). Rich's

autobiographical essay, "When We Dead
Awaken" (Chapter 25), also includes a number
of her poems in their entirety.

Alice Ostriker

from HER CARGO: ADRIENNE RICH
AND THE COMMON LANGUAGE

Adrienne Rich is a poet of ideas.

In most poetic circles, it is unfashionable to espouse ideas—except, of course,
for ideas about technique. (p. 102)[1]

[Rich's poems] depend on the assumption that the writer's mind exists to embody the implicit meaning of a culture at a moment in time, the place history has
marched to, intelligence at its keenest pitch; and to bring the reader there. They declare a state of awakened consciousness—the poet's—and claim that the present actual consciousness of the writer, and the latent consciousness of the reader, are
identical.

Whitman asks us to think that we are innocent and great. Baudelaire asks us to
think that we are guilty and wearily disgusted. Rich asks us to think that we need
to give birth to ourselves. (p. 103)

The poet springs from the soil of Modernism. Her youthful writing in *A Change
of World* (1951) and *The Diamond Cutters* (1955) reflects the ranking styles in postwar literary academe. From Frost and Auden in particular she inherits craftsmanly
formalism, an analytical rather than emotional treatment of material, and a resigned
sense of life as a diminished thing. (p. 104)

Failures of language, standing for failures of love, appear at key points in these
first two volumes. Superficially, the young poet's handling of this theme seems conventional enough. . . . Rich has "the unsaid word" of a wife in loyal stasis while her
husband ranges. There are uncommunicating parental figures in "The Middle-
Aged." A woman who "thought that life was different than it is" goes down to old
age mildly, unprotesting. "Living in Sin," a poem of Lowellian distaste for shabby
reality, depicts the tainting of romance by common grime; but the heroine says
nothing.

Some of these poems tremble on the brink of indignation. They seem about to
state explicitly the pattern they all share, of a connection between feminine subordination in male-dominated middle-class relationships, and emotionally lethal inar-

5

---

[1] When researching the work of authors, you may wish to make use of some of the volumes published by the Gale Research Company. These include *Contemporary Literary Criticism*, *Contemporary Authors*, *Twentieth Century Literary Critcism*, and *Nineteenth Century Literary Criticism*. The volumes usefully
collect major critical articles about important authors and present them in excerpted form. Ostriker's
essay, as well as the following selection by Willard Spiegelman, have been taken from Gale's literary
criticism series. The page numbers that appear in parentheses refer to the original publication of the
text.

ticulateness for both sexes. But the poetry in these two books is minor because it is polite. It illustrates symptoms but does not probe causes. There is no disputing the ideas of the predecessors, and Adrienne Rich at this point is a cautious good poet in the sense of being a good girl, a quality noted with approval by her early reviewers. (pp. 104–05)

Snapshots of a Daughter-in-Law (1963) [is] Rich's breakthrough volume.

The title poem of *Snapshots* was the first Rich wrote openly as "a female poet" although she had not found "the courage . . . to use the pronoun 'I'—the woman in the poem is always 'she.' " The young woman speaker sees all women as "pinned down by love," and thinks she is going mad. But her real subject is the woman of intellect. . . . "A thinking woman sleeps with monsters," Rich discovers. "The beak that grips her, she becomes." The culture of the past is a predator to a woman; an intellectual woman who absorbs it becomes her own enemy. Thus for the first time in this poem, Rich challenges the language of the past, quoting Cicero, Horace, Campion, Diderot, Johnson, Shakespeare—as the flattering, insulting, condescending enemies of women's intellect. . . . "Snapshots" consists of fragmentary and odd-shaped sections instead of stanzas, and has the immediacy and force Rich did not attempt earlier. (pp. 106–07)

After *Snapshots*, nothing inhibits Rich's intensity or integrity. The feeling of something inexplicably wrong has been transformed into cries that the house is on fire, and the mind of the poet is ablaze. . . . *Necessities of Life* (1966) concerns the necessity of personal withdrawal and reconstruction: "I used myself, let nothing use me," as a prerequisite for life in the world. . . . *Leaflets* (1969) and *The Will to Change* (1971) extend the field of struggle and intensify the sense of crisis. Confronting not only Vietnam but the barricades of class, race, sex, youth versus age, activist versus theorist, Rich cannot accept either a public or a private life not motivated by the will to change oneself, to change others, to change the world. . . . The tempo of the work speeds to reflect the speeding mind. Divesting herself of traditional formalities, the poet lets herself think in (apparently) disconnected streaks. "The notes for the poem are the only poem," she says. "The moment of change is the only poem." There are gestures in the direction of hope. . . . A few pieces—"Women," "The Observer," "Planetarium"—suggest strength through some connection between woman and the world of nature. But mostly the will is paralyzed by the monstrosity of evil it faces. Nothing seems alterable except by violence. (pp. 108–09)

By *Diving Into the Wreck* (1973), Rich's ideas have become systematically feminist, and she is assuming an influential position in an intellectual movement. . . . The constellation of institutions which comprise patriarchy is held responsible for all imperialisms, political and psychic. Our civilization's religion, philosophy, history, law and literature rest on the subordination of women and of the female principle in men, and our civilization is therefore finished:

> The tragedy of sex
> lies around us, a woodlot
> the axes are sharpened for.
> The old shelters and huts . . .
> scenes of masturbation
> and dirty jokes.
> A man's world. But finished.
> They themselves have sold it to the machines. . . .

The "compromised" woman who continues to live in this society finds herself envying

> the freedom of the wholly mad
> to smear & play with their madness
> write with her fingers dipped in it. . .

She nevertheless continues to take the risk and suffer the pain of self-knowledge. . . . She identifies with other women and attempts to understand their common history in order to organize a collective, not an individual, escape, in which the traditional dualisms of Western philosophy and literature will be transcended. (pp. 109–11)

The poet thinks in images, and Rich's gift for vivid and energetic imagery has been one of her chief strengths since the beginning. Her range includes astronomy, modern technology, natural history, movies . . . , historical records, as well as the contemporary urban scene and domestic setting. She uses dream and fantasy images extensively. Her primary subject is herself battling "the beak that grips her," which is the male culture's denial of her identity, and her language functions at a level where her life and the lives of others evidently coincide. (p. 111)

Throughout the period subsequent to *Snapshots*, Rich questions the idea of language and the value of poetry, exemplifying the conflicts "a thinking woman," whose tools are words, undergoes when she wants expression of personal truth and communication of realities hitherto unrecognized. (p. 112)

What Rich does with this problem comes in three stages, corresponding to her phases of self-reconstruction, political engagement, and feminism. In the first two, I think she hits dead ends. In the last, she begins to discover an alternative. . . . In *Leaflets* and *The Will to Change*, the poet reenters the world with the desire to use language for healing, but is repeatedly defeated. "Images for Godard" sees "language as city" surrounded by shockproof suburbs and squatters awaiting eviction—a place out of touch with reality. "A Valediction Forbidding Mourning" has "my swirling wants. Your frozen lips. / The grammar turned and attacked me." "The Burning Paper Instead of Children" juxtaposes the idea of book-burning by two schoolboys, which has shocked a liberal neighbor, against the literal burning of Jeanne d'Arc and the napalming of Vietnam. . . . Attacking not only the formal language of the past but that of the present—however well intentioned—Rich prefers a child's semi-literate composition on poverty, or Artaud's *burn the texts*. "This is the oppressor's language / yet I need it to talk to you. . . . I cannot touch you and this is the oppressor's language," she concludes in desperation. Two years later, in the title poem of *Diving into the Wreck*, a new possibility opens. There is a breakthrough comparable to that of "Snapshots."

The poet in "Diving" reads but cannot use "the book of myths" in which "our names do not appear." She seeks "the thing itself and not the myth," which sounds like an extension of the anti-intellectualism of the *Leaflets* and *Will to Change* period. But this is a different sort of poem from anything earlier. For one thing, it is narrative. The poet does not remain trapped in stasis and analysis, helplessly acted upon. She makes a move; she acts. For another, her language is revisionist. Out of the past, she invents an altered symbolism. (pp. 112–13)

If the source of an oppressor's language is a set of false perceptions of reality, it is necessary to begin at the beginning. The poem suggests a place, a scene, where

15

our iron distinctions between perceiver and perceived, subject and object, he and she, I and you, dissolve. There it leaves us. (p. 114)

Why, in Rich's writing, does one find so little joy, so little sense of the power of joy? Why does the work come from a sense of unrelieved crisis in which nothing can be celebrated, nothing savored? Rich is not, one feels, a poet to whom love—untheoretical, undoctrinal love—comes easily, either toward herself or toward others. . . . She does not construct desirable fantasies. There is suffering, and then there is more suffering, with "no imagination to forestall woe," almost as if suffering itself were a value. . . . [But] Rich's readers need to know about the female equivalent of the burning bush, the voice of the covenant, the promised land. They need to know about the goddess. Lacking the imagination's projection of a world without victims, a self unvictimized, unmastered, complete—and it is for the poets to give us this, to articulate the delight that is *there*, latently, as much as women's despair is *there*—lacking this, the will to change is helplessly fettered.

A more dismaying aspect of Rich's work to me is her partisanship. Explicitly or implicitly, since *Snapshots*, Rich's position has depended on the idea of an enemy. Her "I" affirms by excluding, her communal "we" implies a hostile "they." Of course "we" know who "they" are. For a period after *Snapshots* the poet uses male figures sympathetically; there are poems of kindness and hopefulness addressed to her husband; there is Orion, her brother-double; there are friend/lover figures in *Leaflets*, and the male artists Chekhov, Ghalib, Rodin, Berrigan, Artaud, Godard in *Leaflets* and *The Will to Change*. In *Diving* the poet defines herself as the androgyne, the being who is at once female and male. But men in this volume are depicted universally and exclusively as parasitic on women, emotionally threatened by them, brutal—the cop is identified with the rapist—and undeserving of pity. "His" mind is a nightmare of possessiveness, conquest, and misogyny. (pp. 116–17)

I hope not to oversimplify this issue. Women's anger is real, and it is legitimate. We see it surfacing everywhere in women's writing, the best and the worst (I suppose it is missing only from the mediocre), like a scream from a mouth that has just been ungagged. This anger needs acknowledgement. Unacknowledged, it poisons and cripples. But when an angry woman implies that she fantasizes punishing her enemy purely for his own good, she begins to resemble the officer who said he burned the village to save it. (p. 118)

These elements in Rich's work dismay me, I must add, for several reasons. First Rich is the strongest women poet in the country, and a major influence. If she is in error, her influence serves error. Second, whatever distresses me in Rich—the joylessness, the self-pity, the self-righteousness, exists also within myself and within others. She is a mirror in which multitudes are seen as one. Third, she may not be in error. If this is the case, we are emerging from the tangled growths of the past, only to enter a desert which appears to stretch indefinitely before us, arid and stony, and none of us will see the end of it in our lifetimes.

The Dream of a Common Language at last gives us Rich as visionary. "Dream" implies this. "Language" means not only words, poetry—several of the poems are about "a whole new poetry"—but any form of communication, including the touch of bodies, and including silence. It means the ability "to name the world" essential for gaining strength in the world; and "the drive / to connect," through symbols and in actuality, with each other, the world, and ourselves. "Common" language means a faith that attempts to communicate can succeed, that we can connect, not as privileged persons or under special circumstances, but in ordinary dailiness.

The core of the book is its exploration of loving woman-to-woman relationships. Rich speaks of mothers and daughters, literal and figurative sisters, cohorts in poetry, lovers, ancestresses. (pp. 119-20)

As a flute song of personal meditation, "Sibling Mysteries" is hauntingly lovely. As a myth of female sexuality, it is too narrow. Yes, women's initial erotic experiences are maternal-infantile. So are men's. Yes, perhaps mature sexuality attempts to recover and replay the blissful mother-child union. Perhaps all adult tenderness, all affection, finds its source and models itself on those memories. This idea could explain a great deal about human romance—not confined to love between women. For some women, the sterotypic dominant-father/subordinate-mother family pattern does not apply. For some, the physicality of our mothers never stopped being available. And for some, heterosexual experience has never meant terror or resignation. . . . (p. 121)

Three other poems in *Dream* excite my skepticism. The opening pieces on Marie Curie and Elvira Shatayev appear to romanticize feminine martyrdom; the latter is an all-female *liebestod*. Where is the portrait of a woman whose power kills neither others nor herself? "Hunger" seems marred by a naive belief that women's love, "hosed" on the world, would eliminate its literal and figurative famines. Those who believe in infallible feminine virtue may recall the comparable virtue of the American Worker in the 1930s. ²⁵

These are comparatively tangential matters, not vitiating this volume's courageous spirit, its transformations, the beauty of its poetry. The force of love, negligible in her earlier books, here brings Rich a resolution to trust, to move from victimization toward responsibility and choice, and to reject (not withstanding the aura of the first two poems) martyrdom. . . . (pp. 121–22)

The most important poems break new ground metaphorically. "Origins and History of Consciousness," opening in the poet's crisis-haunted room, moves to a dream of walking into water:

> My bare feet are numbed already by the snow
> but the water
> is mild, I sink and float
> like a warm, amphibious animal
> that has broken the net, has run
> through fields of snow leaving no print;
> this water washes off the scent—
> *you are clear now*
> *of the hunter, the trapper*
> *the wardens of the mind*—

This of course recalls "Diving into the Wreck," but the speaker of "Diving" needed props—rubber suit, knife, camera, book of myths, schooner, ladder—which this speaker, entering her animal nature, can discard. . . . Moreover, where "Diving" closes under water, "Origins and History of Consciousness" resurfaces. It returns from dream to reality. The pond in woods becomes the city of muggers. But the poet recapitulates her decision of risked love as a descent "in a darkness / which I remember as drenched with light," and resolves to move outward. The poem ends with a sense of introducing Eros into Civilization.

"Natural Resources," another poem of transformations, revives and synthesizes two metaphors from *Snapshots*: the aerial cargo of the new woman, and the "abandoned mineshaft of doubt" in "Double Monologue." (pp. 122-23)

The technique employed in these two poems is a kind of overlay of transparencies. Present and past, reality and imagination, the life of the self and the lives of other selves, the spatially enclosed and the spatially unenclosed, are held in a tenuous, luminous balance. . . . A philosophically developed feminism may mean an alternative idea of time and change, neither linear as in Hebrew tradition, cyclic as in classical philosophy, or juxtaposed against eternity as in Christianity. There is a flexing of the mind here, and no sense of an enemy. I am filled with curiosity to see more of what Rich can do along these lines, confident that whatever comes next will be an advance. What does not change is the pressure of Adrienne Rich's intelligence. . . . (p. 124)

[1983]

Willard Spiegelman

from VOICE OF THE SURVIVOR: THE POETRY OF ADRIENNE RICH

At first it would seem simple to chart the growth of Rich's poetry, away from the elegant and graceful work of her first two volumes to the more spare, jagged, and free forms of the past decade, and from poems about lovely things and scenes to those about war, torture, oppression, and rape. But with the omniscience of hindsight we can see how the beginning contained, organically and logically, all that followed. These poems that flow with the prosodic assurance of Auden or Wilbur give off the slightest aroma of stagnation and of discontent with the lives presented and the styles employed. The characteristic early themes are suffocation, alienation, and entombment, none particularly dangerous because each is viewed with a well-bred youthful skepticism that seems unwilling to take appearance for truth. They are poems in the conversational manner of Auden and Yeats, worldly and witty, polished and careful. But like the characters they present, these poems are crushed under the weight of the very tradition they parade. (pp. 370–71)

The people in *A Change of World* and *The Diamond Cutters* (1955) are elegant, passive, and will-less. . . . Alienation in these poems is neither painful nor merely fashionable; it is the precondition for creativity and for a certain set of attitudes about art and life: "Art requires a distance: let me be / Always the connoisseur of your perfection" ("Love in the Museum"); "Form is the ultimate gift that love can offer— / The vital union of necessity / With all that we desire, all that we suffer" ("At a Bach Concert"). "Proud restraining purity" is needed to repair the human heart in a world of inevitable imperfection and disappointment, and to construct art as defense against invasions or threats from without. This is the stoicism of the young, half-accepting the reality of human weakness, yet holding out for an ideal landscape, however distanced, artful or irrecoverable. This is the last infirmity of romantic mind which Rich begins to abandon later, as she increasingly refuses to take the world as it is given. . . . [In] Rich's later work hardness becomes stridency, seriousness polemic, and pride political awareness. The artist, "careful arriviste," is less important than the raw material she is given and the product she creates. Her task is unending: "Africa will yield you more to do."

What Auden praised in his 1951 introduction, "good manners," "modesty," "craftsmanship," "capacity for detachment," begins to give way to a terrible kind of beauty, new formal freedom, and the presentation of a major personal tone in Rich's third book, *Snapshots of a Daughter-in-Law* (1963). His estimate now seems inaccurate, precisely the condescension that Rich strove to escape and overwhelm: "These poems . . . are neatly and modestly dressed, speak quietly but do not mumble, respect their elders but are not cowed by them, and do not tell fibs: that, for a first volume, is a good deal." Perhaps Auden was correct. But what he heard in these poems was his own voice echoed back to him, imitated by a schoolgirl for the approval of pedagogic and paternal elders. (pp. 371-72)

"Snapshots of a Daughter-in-Law" is a major stylistic and thematic advance. First of all, it is a medley of lyrics, varying in length and form from a three-line epigram to an unpunctuated fade-out at the end. There is neither plot nor character; rather, the poem offers images of women throughout history, freely citing Horace, Dr. Johnson, Diderot, and Mary Wollstonecraft and the condition and nature of the sex, and suggesting as well versions of modern entrapment and repression. Second, the search for form is a search for an honest speaking voice (Keats's "true voice of feeling") and a true self: "What I know I know through making poems," Rich wrote in "Poetry and Experience" (1964). Still, "Snapshots" refrains from autobiography. The women in the poem, a Shreveport belle, a mad housewife, Horace's Lalage, Campion's Corrinna, Emily Dickinson, and others, are variations on a single theme. They are presented candidly and rapidly, and pasted down in the photo album of history.

Rich refuses to blame men or history completely for the suppression of women; it is they themselves who have enjoyed and tacitly approved the status quo. . . . (p. 373)

Edges, doorways, thresholds: these are central images in the books from *Snapshots* to *Diving into the Wreck* (1973). *Snapshots* is the liminal volume, attempting a journey from one self, world, poetic form, to another. The poet comes clear in one of her finest lyrics, "The Roof-walker," in which she sees herself as the double of the roof-builders, poised dangerously "on a listing deck" above her. . . . Earlier she was a tourist; now she's trying to be a builder, but firmness and sureness are still lacking. . . . The elegant skepticism of the first volumes now borders on despair. (pp. 374–75)

The next three books, *Necessities of Life* (1966), *Leaflets* (1969), and *The Will to Change* (1971) are Rich's most radical (pulling herself up by her own roots), most strident, and most original. Sometimes obscure, doctrinally unattractive, or badly prosaic, these poems are the necessary passage to the deeper humanism of Rich's more recent work. But they are also, especially on rereading, impressive in themselves. Anger and hatred are the most difficult emotions to express in poetry: they inhibit creativity and defy articulation. In the past two hundred years, only Blake and Pound have been great poetic haters, and they at least had the advantage of more capacious forms for their prophetic rage. Rich encloses her outrage within the lyric, an almost impossible task and one which proves the originality of her art. Moreover, her indignation is both righteous and generous. (p. 376)

The lucidity of Rich's later poetry shows how well she has understood Keats's dictum, "scenery is fine, human nature is finer." The starting point for an understanding of the world is the self, and the last four volumes are all joint explorations of the self and its political relationship to the world it inhabits.

5

Still, a tension exists between an attempt to define the self by withdrawing and fixing its limits, and a desire to push beyond the boundaries of the ego and contain, Whitman-like, multitudes. Keatsian empathy, the ability to participate in all forms of life and be affected by them, to transform the enemy for his rebirth and to identify the enemy within, triumphs in Rich's poetry, but with pain and struggle. In the title poem from *Necessities of Life* the conflict is clearly stated: either the self has a rigid identity, in which case it is "a small, fixed dot . . . a dark-blue thumbtack, pushed into the scene," or it loses itself under the onrush of other lives and influences. . . . What some readers will find appalling or offensive in these poems is only the necessary expression of the will—the tough, combative and intellectual strength—to change. A new galactic dimension in some of the poems, marked by images of chiseled coldness and those vast interstellar spaces which frightened Pascal, might be mistaken for an iciness in the woman herself. But it serves to identify foreign elements within her. (pp. 378–79)

The danger of empathy is Rich's stunningly original theme. She reaches beyond the sexes in an attempt to understand sexuality, and she plunges within herself to discover the perfect balance between *anima* and *animus*. Easy traditional dichotomies about the sexes will not bear the weight of her ideas or contain the explosion of her imagery. Her prose statements on this matter are more polemical and less persuasive than the poems, which urge us to accept the bisexual nature of the psyche; it is here that we see her moving into ever larger realms of selflessness and inclusiveness, in spite of the seeming exlusiveness of her political pronouncements. (pp. 384–85)   10

With the exception of Lowell, Rich is our only poet who understands heroism and grandeur as the other side of degradation and suffering, and who, even in her most personal lyrics, stretches all human activities on the frame of social and political consciousness. With stripped-down language, images shot out like bullets not always hitting the target, her movie scripts of the late sixties tried to capture the reckless daring and depression of a moment. In poems like "Diving into the Wreck," and the more meditative and generous new ones, Rich has begun to contemplate and to create a world worthy of her care. Her major long poem, "From an Old House in America" (1974), shows the newly achieved calm which nevertheless contains the spirited excitement of the time before. (p. 386)

[1975]

QUESTIONS

1. Without looking at "Writing a Source Paper on Poetry," read both the Ostriker and Spiegelman passages. What is the most striking difference between them? What similarities, if any, do you find?

2. What does Ostriker appear to believe about feminism and the responsibility of women to the cause of the women's movement?

3. Based on your reading of Rich's poetry and prose (Chapter 25), what do you think her response to Ostriker's critique might be?

USING SOURCES WHEN WRITING ABOUT A POEM

In Chapter 24 ("Writing about Poetry") we saw how one student worked with a single poem—Ted Hughes's "The Thought-Fox"—and developed his own interpretation. Now we need to consider the use of sources when writing about a poem. How do we incorporate the views of other critics when we are writing about a poet or a poem? Writers can follow much the same procedures as those found in Chapter 14 for writing a source paper on a work of fiction, with the difference being that there are specific rules of citation to follow when quoting lines of poetry. These are set out in the second section of Appendix B.

When you are writing a paper in which you draw upon the insights and opinions of others, you must very clearly identify not only the words or statements that belong to each critic, but also each critic's ideas and perspectives. The general rule—here as in all scholarly procedure—is that if you are in any doubt about which came first, your insight, or your reading of critic X who had a similar insight, give credit to critic X. This can either be done directly, by citing a passage and supplying references, or by including the author's last name and the relevant pages after the discussion. Thus, you might write: "Adrienne Rich's early poems owe a debt to worldly male poets like W. H. Auden and William Butler Yeats (Spiegelman, 370)." Though you have not quoted the author directly, you have acknowledged that you made use of his insight about influences.

Here is a long extract from "Anger in the Poetry of Adrienne Rich," by student writer Alexandra Johnson. Pay close attention to Johnson's acknowledgment of her critical sources, which are both included in this text (pp. 986 and 991):

Interestingly, critics are divided in their views of this phase of Rich's career, and it is the poet's anger that they focus on. In what is a reversal of expectations, we find a female critic, Alicia Ostriker, questioning the value of Rich's anger during a transitional phase of her career, while male critic Willard Spiegelman seems to celebrate its necessity.

In "Her Cargo: Adrienne Rich and The Common Language," Ostriker asks, "Why, in Rich's writing, does one find so little joy, so little sense of the power of joy?" (116). She suggests that we need the vision of a "world without victim, a self unvictimized" (117) in order to keep the determination to fight for change alive. Ostriker goes on to deplore Rich's reliance in her poetry of this period on the idea of men as enemies. Looking to the book Diving into the Wreck, she finds that "men in this volume are depicted universally and exclusively as parasitic on women" (116–17). She cites as evidence the policeman in Rich's poem "Rape," and turning to the last lines of that poem we can see what she means:

He has access to machinery that could get you put away;

and if, in the sickening light of the precinct,

and if, in the sickening light of the precinct,

your details sound like a portrait of your confessor,

will you swallow, will you deny them, will you lie

   your way home?

(<u>Fact</u>, 172)

Critic Willard Spiegelman, by contrast, sees the books of this period--from <u>Snapshots</u> <u>of</u> <u>a</u> <u>Daughter-in-Law</u> (1963) to <u>Diving</u> <u>into</u> <u>the</u> <u>Wreck</u> (1973)--as "the necessary passage to the humanism of Rich's more recent work" (376). He acknowledges that the poetry may be "obscure" or "badly prosaic" but praises the effort:

Anger and hatred are the most difficult emotions to express in poetry: they inhibit creativity and defy articulation. . . . Rich encloses her outrage within the lyric, an almost impossible task and one which proves the originality of her art. (376)

The critics appear deadlocked on this issue, Ostriker seeing the negativity as inhibiting what Rich has called, in the title of one of her books, "the will to change," and Spiegelman arguing that it is part of the passage to the greater acceptance found in the poet's later work.

When Johnson concluded her paper, she listed her sources as follows:

Works Cited

Ostriker, Alicia. <u>Writing</u> <u>Like</u> <u>a</u> <u>Woman</u>. Ann Arbor:
   U of Michigan, 1983.
Rich, Adrienne. <u>The</u> <u>Fact</u> <u>of</u> <u>a</u> <u>Doorframe:</u> <u>Poems</u> <u>Selected</u>
   <u>and</u> <u>New</u> <u>1950-1984</u>. New York: Norton, 1984.
Spiegelman, Willard. "Voice of the Survivor: The Poetry
   of Adrienne Rich." <u>Southwest</u> <u>Review</u> (1975): 370-88.

Drama

29 Reading Plays and Watching Theater

Among the literary genres, drama is a special case. Unlike poems or stories, plays are not written simply to be read. The playwright's aim is to have a play read, interpreted, acted on a stage, and experienced in all four dimensions. The written form is essential, of course, but it is essential in the way that a symphonic score is—as a starting place. Interpretability is figured into the words on the page. In one sense, then, when we speak of a given play, we refer not only to the written artifact, the copy of *Hamlet* that we hold in our hands, but also to the sum total of all the different interpretations the play has been given since the time of its first performance. Which is the *real Hamlet*? It's hard to say. The closest we might come—if we were ever able to make such a judgment—would be to isolate the best of its many performances. But even if we were able through some wave of the wand to see every single staging, how would we decide? Would it be the subtlest or the most moving performance we would honor? There is no answer.

From the perspective of the student in the classroom, the point may seem moot. The odds of seeing *any* of the assigned plays performed over the course of the semester may be slim. The plays are here to be read and discussed. Perhaps, if time allows, a scene may be acted or read aloud by volunteers. The question then becomes this: How is a play to be approached in a university classroom setting?

The best way to answer is by stressing the performative act of reading itself. When we read imaginative literature, especially stories and novels, we do not simply take in information. More often than not, we call upon our faculty of imagination to create the work in our minds. We read a description and conjure up a setting; we follow the actions of a character and we picture them. The story lies flat on the page in its words, but it also lives in ghostly animation behind the eyes. The more vivid that animation, the more memorable the reading experience.

The same holds true for reading a play, though with certain differences. A play is at once simpler and more difficult to read than most other kinds of artistic prose. It is simpler because all we are reading, apart from occasional brief cues for staging, is dialogue. It is more difficult because we must often exert our imagination more intensively to keep the work alive in our minds. We must create a sense of setting and supply what we suppose are the appropriate gestures and expressions. We must do the same thing that a director does—interpret.

In an ideal sense, then, when we read a play, we go through some of the steps intended by the playwright. In our own nonprofessional way, we stage and perform the work: inwardly and for no audience but ourselves.

THE CHALLENGE OF READING PLAYS

The history of drama is a long one, and the plays we might encounter are as varied as can be. Most college anthologies will span a range from Sophocles, who lived from 496 to 406 B.C., to contemporary work from the past few decades. How we read a play will necessarily depend upon what play we are reading. What we conjure up for a setting "in front of the royal palace in Thebes" will be very different from how we imagine a contemporary living room.

The other major variable is the language—or, if the play has been translated, the idiom—of the work. A reader encountering the Greek dramatists for the first time will have one kind of response working through the florid diction of a Victorian translation, and another response with one of the streamlined modernizations that are published every few years. But Shakespeare is, for the most part, still Shakespeare. Though there have been attempts to simplify the Bard to meet the needs of younger readers, most instructors prefer that the student come face to face with the difficult but beautiful language of the original.

Language and usage, of course, change. One way to measure our historical distance from the Elizabethan England of Shakespeare's time is by noting how the page ratio of text to *gloss* has changed. A gloss is an explanation or definition of a word. For example, a *doublet* is a "close-fitting sleeveless jacket worn by men." Every year, it seems, the bottom of the page gets more crowded with glosses—to the point that the reading of one of Shakespeare's plays becomes a kind of visual ping-pong game, with the eye moving from the line to the notes and back. But increased familiarity with the work brings greater ease, and a second or third reading is generally free of significant obstacles.

One piece of advice to the person reading any play is to vocalize the lines. They are, no matter who the playwright or what period, written to be spoken, and the language acquires a new life when it is sounded out. Suddenly it is possible to hear the cut and thrust of a particular passage of dialogue or to recognize the concealed puns. By the same token, even the most bumbling in-class performance will disclose aspects of the work that are not evident in a silent reading.

THE CONVENTIONS OF STAGING THAT SHAPE OUR READING

Even though the play-as-read and the play-as-staged are two different entities, they are obviously related, and we can learn things about reading by thinking about performance. The most important of these influences on our reading are the *conventions*, the implicit rules that can be said to underwrite the experience of theater. These may seem so basic that they don't need to be discussed, but they are the very heart of the art and a quick reminder will not hurt.

Staged drama is an illusion that we agree to participate in. The core convention is the viewer's acceptance of this fact. We need to suspend our natural disbelief and give ourselves over to the illusion. The actors are not actors but are the people they pretend to be. The situations exist; they are happening—now—right before our eyes. One measure of the abilities of a cast of performers is how readily they can help us forget that we are seated in a building and watching movements on a lighted stage.

Similarly, we must assent to certain representations of actions. The dagger used in Act III is not real, and the victim sheds no real blood. But we must set aside our craving for state-of-the-art special effects and grant the fact of the death. We will lose out on an important experience if we judge the effectiveness of an action by how lifelike (or cinemalike) it is.

A third and vital convention requires that we loosen our normal expectations relating to space and time. The playwright is ruled by an ideal of artistic economy; the director is ruled by economics. This may mean that the living room, represented by a couch and a lamp, occupies the left side of the stage, and the upstairs bedroom—a bed and dresser—is positioned right beside it. This is not reality, but it is the reality that confronts the set-designer on a budget. Convention demands that the viewer imagine the bedroom atop the living room and complete the furnishings in the mind's eye. The same applies to time. Theater time, like cinema time, is compressed. We are very often asked to cut from one important moment to the next, to do away with the dull clutter of intervening hours, days, or years. In the same way, the scene itself may exhibit greater compression than real life, with important revelations and arrivals coming one hard upon the next.

Finally, there are the conventions of speech and gesture. Actors may speak to one another just like normal people, whether formally or casually, but they may also do things that "real life" people never do. They may step forward and deliver a *monologue* or a *soliloquy*, leaving the other members of the cast either frozen or carrying on as if the speaker were not there. The soliloquy, a convention for presenting thought or internal debate, is a way of giving the audience access to a side of the character that would otherwise be unavailable. We must accept it as such, and not as an aberration.

The speech of characters, in dialogue or monologue, is generally a heightening of normal speech, though sometimes, as in plays by Molière, it is so stylized as to seem artificial. We rarely encounter stage dialogue that maps the actual track of human conversation. Even a playwright like David Mamet, who is renowned for his gritty and often profane realism, makes use of a much-heightened and intensified idiom. His characters speak as their real-life counterparts might if their utterances were stripped of all vagueness and redundancy and speeded-up by half. Alternatively, the extended poetic musings of a Tennessee Williams or Eugene O'Neill character belong in the halfway zone between what people really say and what they would say if they had a writer as verbally gifted as Williams or O'Neill saying it for them.

It should be clear from this listing of the dramatic conventions that plays ultimately do not echo reality so much as they produce a parallel reality that refers to the world we know. The magic of the theater-going experience depends upon this: that we enter wholeheartedly an order that is different from what we know in our day-to-day lives. The resemblances may be there. We may know, or have experienced, similar situations; we may recognize characters from our lives. But the atmosphere from the first raising of the curtain until the lights go out is more intense—more charged—than anything we know. Tensions are heightened, and emotions are amplified. Good actors can twist us one way and another until we are wrung dry. And when we walk out into the night, we feel—either with gratitude or with disappointment—how the world shrinks back into its familiar contours.

READING A PLAY

What follows here is Wendy Wasserstein's very short one-act play, "Tender Offer." It is a small play and makes no pretense to dramatic intensity. Indeed, Wasserstein has, on the surface, done little more than capture a moment in the domestic lives of a father and his daughter. There are no overt struggles; no one shouts or falls or even stalks away in anger. The whole exchange is conducted in the quieter part of the emotional spectrum. And yet, it is a play; it exposes a truth about adult–child relationships. And if we are willing to listen to the dialogue and heed the gestures and movements, we will very likely experience a jolt of recognition. The fact that it is so short and so economic in its means makes it a fine place for us to limber up for the more challenging plays that follow.

Wendy Wasserstein (1950–   )

Wendy Wasserstein won both the 1989 Pulitzer Prize and a Tony Award for Best Play for *The Heidi Chronicles*. Her plays include *Isn't It Romantic, Montpelier Pa-Zazz,* and *When Dinah Shore Ruled the Earth* (co-authored with Christopher Durang).

TENDER OFFER

A girl of around nine is alone in a dance studio. She is dressed in traditional leotards and tights. She begins singing to herself, "Nothing Could Be Finer Than to Be in Carolina." She maps out a dance routine, including parts for the chorus. She builds to a finale. A man, Paul, around thirty-five, walks in. He has a sweet, though distant, demeanor. As he walks in, Lisa notices him and stops.

PAUL. You don't have to stop, sweetheart.
LISA. That's okay.
PAUL. Looked very good.
LISA. Thanks.
PAUL. Don't I get a kiss hello?
LISA. Sure.
PAUL. [*Embraces her.*] Hi, Tiger.
LISA. Hi, Dad.
PAUL. I'm sorry I'm late.
LISA. That's okay.
PAUL. How'd it go?

LISA. Good.

PAUL. Just good?

LISA. Pretty good.

PAUL. "Pretty good." You mean you got a lot of applause or "pretty good" you could have done better.

LISA. Well, Courtney Palumbo's mother thought I was pretty good. But you know the part in the middle when everybody's supposed to freeze and the big girl comes out. Well, I think I moved a little bit.

PAUL. I thought what you were doing looked very good.

LISA. Daddy, that's not what I was doing. That was tap-dancing. I made that up.

PAUL. Oh. Well it looked good. Kind of sexy.

LISA. Yuch!

PAUL. What do you mean "yuch"?

LISA. Just yuch!

PAUL. You don't want to be sexy?

LISA. I don't care.

PAUL. Let's go, Tiger. I promised your mother I'd get you home in time for dinner.

LISA. I can't find my leg warmers.

PAUL. You can't find your what?

LISA. Leg warmers. I can't go home till I find my leg warmers.

PAUL. I don't see you looking for them.

LISA. I was waiting for you.

PAUL. Oh.

LISA. Daddy.

PAUL. What?

LISA. Nothing.

PAUL. Where do you think you left them?

LISA. Somewhere around here. I can't remember.

PAUL. Well, try to remember, Lisa. We don't have all night.

LISA. I told you. I think somewhere around here.

PAUL. I don't see them. Let's go home now. You'll call the dancing school tomorrow.

LISA. Daddy, I can't go home till I find them. Miss Judy says it's not professional to leave things.

PAUL. Who's Miss Judy?

LISA. She's my ballet teacher. She once danced the lead in *Swan Lake*, and she was a June Taylor dancer.

PAUL. Well, then, I'm sure she'll understand about the leg warmers.

LISA. Daddy, Miss Judy wanted to know why you were late today.

PAUL. Hmmmmmmmm?

LISA. Why were you late?

PAUL. I was in a meeting. Business. I'm sorry.

LISA. Why did you tell Mommy you'd come instead of her if you knew you had business?

PAUL. Honey, something just came up. I thought I'd be able to be here. I was looking forward to it.

LISA. I wish you wouldn't make appointments to see me.

PAUL. Hmmmmmmm.

LISA. You shouldn't make appointments to see me unless you know you're going to come.

PAUL. Of course I'm going to come.

LISA. No, you're not. Talia Robbins told me she's much happier living without her father in the house. Her father used to come home late and go to sleep early.

PAUL. Lisa, stop it. Let's go.

LISA. I can't find my leg warmers.

PAUL. Forget your leg warmers.

LISA. Daddy.

PAUL. What is it?

LISA. I saw this show on television, I think it was WPIX Channel 11. Well, the father was crying about his daughter.

PAUL. Why was he crying? Was she sick?

LISA. No. She was at school. And he was at business. And he just missed her, so he started to cry.

PAUL. What was the name of this show?

LISA. I don't know. I came in in the middle.

PAUL. Well, Lisa, I certainly would cry if you were sick or far away, but I know that you're well and you're home. So no reason to get maudlin.

LISA. What's maudlin?

PAUL. Sentimental, soppy. Frequently used by children who make things up to get attention.

LISA. I am sick! I am sick! I have Hodgkin's disease and a bad itch on my leg.

PAUL. What do you mean you have Hodgkin's disease? Don't say things like that.

LISA. Swoosie Kurtz, she had Hodgkin's disease on a TV movie last year, but she got better and now she's on *Love Sidney*.

PAUL. Who is Swoosie Kurtz?

LISA. She's an actress named after an airplane. I saw her on *Live at Five*.

PAUL. You watch too much television; you should do your homework. Now, put your coat on.

LISA. Daddy, I really do have a bad itch on my leg. Would you scratch it?

PAUL. Lisa, you're procrastinating.

LISA. Why do you use words I don't understand? I hate it. You're like Daria Feldman's mother. She always talks in Yiddish to her husband so Daria won't understand.

PAUL. Procrastinating is not Yiddish.

LISA. Well, I don't know what it is.

PAUL. Procrastinating means you don't want to go about your business.

LISA. I don't go to business. I go to school.

PAUL. What I mean is you want to hang around here until you and I are late for dinner and your mother's angry and it's too late for you to do your homework.

LISA. I do not.

PAUL. Well, it sure looks that way. Now put your coat on and let's go.

LISA. Daddy.

PAUL. Honey, I'm tired. Really, later.

LISA. Why don't you want to talk to me?

PAUL. I do want to talk to you. I promise when we get home we'll have a nice talk.

LISA. No, we won't. You'll read the paper and fall asleep in front of the news.

PAUL. Honey, we'll talk on the weekend, I promise. Aren't I taking you to the theater this weekend? Let me look. [*He takes out appointment book.*] Yes. Sunday. *Joseph and the Amazing Technicolor Raincoat* with Lisa. Okay, Tiger?

LISA. Sure. It's Dreamcoat.

PAUL. What?

LISA. Nothing. I think I see my leg warmers. [*She goes to pick them up, and an odd-looking trophy.*]

PAUL. What's that?

LISA. It's stupid. I was second best at the dance recital, so they gave me this thing. It's stupid.

PAUL. Lisa.

LISA. What?

PAUL. What did you want to talk about?

LISA. Nothing.

PAUL. Was it about my missing your recital? I'm really sorry, Tiger, I would have liked to have been here.

LISA. That's okay.

PAUL. Honest?

LISA. Daddy, you're prostrastinating.

PAUL. I'm procrastinating. Sit down. Let's talk. So. How's school?

LISA. Fine.

PAUL. You like it?

LISA. Yup.

PAUL. You looking forward to camp this summer?

LISA. Yup.

PAUL. Is Daria Feldman going back?

LISA. Nope.

PAUL. Why not?

LISA. I don't know. We can go home now. Honest, my foot doesn't itch anymore.

PAUL. Lisa, you know what you do in business when it seems like there's nothing left to say? That's when you really start talking. Put a bid on the table.

LISA. What's a bid?

PAUL. You tell me what you want and I'll tell you what I've got to offer. Like Monopoly. You want Boardwalk, but I'm only willing to give you the Railroads. Now, because you are my daughter I'd throw in Water Works and Electricity. Understand, Tiger?

LISA. No. I don't like board games. You know, Daddy, we could get Space Invaders for our home for thirty-five dollars. In fact, we could get an Osborne System for two thousand. Daria Feldman's parents . . .

PAUL. Daria Feldman's parents refuse to talk to Daria, so they bought a computer to keep Daria busy so they won't have to speak in Yiddish. Daria will probably grow up to be a homicidal maniac lesbian prostitute.

LISA. I know what that word prostitute means.

PAUL. Good. [*Pause.*] You still haven't told me about school. Do you still like your teacher?

LISA. She's okay.

PAUL. Lisa, if we're talking try to answer me.

LISA. I am answering you. Can we go home now, please?

PAUL. Damn it, Lisa, if you want to talk to me . . . Talk to me!

LISA. I can't wait till I'm old enough so I can make my own money and never have to see you again. Maybe I'll become a prostitute.

PAUL. Young lady, that's enough.

1004   Reading Plays and Watching Theater

LISA. I hate you, Daddy! I hate you! [*She throws her trophy into the trash bin.*]

PAUL. What'd you do that for?

LISA. It's stupid.

PAUL. Maybe I wanted it.

LISA. What for?

PAUL. Maybe I wanted to put it where I keep your dinosaur and the picture you made of Mrs. Kimbel with the chicken pox.

LISA. You got mad at me when I made that picture. You told me I had to respect Mrs. Kimbel because she was my teacher.

PAUL. That's true. But she wasn't my teacher. I liked her better with the chicken pox. [*Pause.*] Lisa, I'm sorry. I was very wrong to miss your recital, and you don't have to become a prostitute. That's not the type of profession Miss Judy has in mind for you.

LISA. [*Mumbles.*] No.

PAUL. No. [*Pause.*] So Talia Robbins is really happy her father moved out?

LISA. Talia Robbins picks open the eighth-grade lockers during gym period. But she did that before her father moved out.

PAUL. You can't always judge someone by what they do or what they don't do. Sometimes you come home from dancing school and run upstairs and shut the door, and when I finally get to talk to you, everything is "okay" or "fine." Yup or nope?

LISA. Yup.

PAUL. Sometimes, a lot of times, I come home and fall asleep in front of the television. So you and I spend a lot of time being a little scared of each other. Maybe?

LISA. Maybe.

PAUL. Tell you what. I'll make you a tender offer.

LISA. What?

PAUL. I'll make you a tender offer. That's when one company publishes in the newspaper that they want to buy another company. And the company that publishes is called the Black Knight because they want to gobble up the poor little company. So the poor little company needs to be rescued. And then a White Knight comes along and makes a bigger and better offer so the shareholders won't have to tender shares to the Big Black Knight. You with me?

LISA. Sort of.

PAUL. I'll make you a tender offer like the White Knight. But I don't want to own you. I just want to make a much better offer. Okay?

LISA. [*Sort of understanding.*] Okay. [*Pause. They sit for a moment.*] Sort of, Daddy, what do you think about? I mean, like when you're quiet what do you think about?

PAUL. Oh, business usually. If I think I made a mistake or if I think I'm doing okay. Sometimes I think about what I'll be doing five years from now and if it's what I hoped it would be five years ago. Sometimes I think about what your life will be like, if Mount Saint Helen's will erupt again. What you'll become if you'll study penmanship or word processing. If you'll speak kindly of me to your psychiatrist when you are in graduate school. And how the hell I'll pay for your graduate school. And sometimes I try and think what it was I thought about when I was your age.

LISA. Do you ever look out your window at the clouds and try to see which kinds of shapes they are? Like one time, honest, I saw the head of Walter Cronkite in a flower vase. Really! Like look don't those kinda look like if you turn it upside down, two big elbows or two elephant trunks dancing?

PAUL. Actually still looks like Walter Cronkite in a flower vase to me. But look up a little. See the one that's still moving? That sorta looks like a whale on a thimble.

LISA. Where?

PAUL. Look up. To your right.

LISA. I don't see it. Where?

PAUL. The other way.

LISA. Oh, yeah! There's the head and there's the stomach. Yeah! [LISA *picks up her trophy.*] Hey, Daddy.

PAUL. Hey, Lisa.

LISA. You can have this thing if you want it. But you have to put it like this, because if you put it like that it is gross.

PAUL. You know what I'd like? So I can tell people who come into my office why I have this gross stupid thing on my shelf, I'd like it if you could show me your dance recital.

LISA. Now?

PAUL. We've got time. Mother said she won't be home till late.

LISA. Well, Daddy, during a lot of it I freeze and the big girl in front dances.

PAUL. Well, how 'bout the number you were doing when I walked in?

LISA. Well, see, I have parts for a lot of people in that one, too.

PAUL. I'll dance the other parts.

LISA. You can't dance.

PAUL. Young lady, I played Yvette Mimimeux in a *Hasty Pudding Show.*

LISA. Who's Yvette Mimimeux?

PAUL. Watch more television. You'll find out. [PAUL *stands up.*] So I'm ready. [He *begins singing.*] "Nothing could be finer than to be in Carolina."

LISA. Now I go. In the morning. And now you go. Dum-da.

PAUL. [*Obviously not a tap dancer.*] Da-da-dum.

LISA. [*Whines.*] Daddy!

PAUL. [*Mimics her.*] Lisa! Nothing could be finer . . .

LISA. That looks dumb.

PAUL. Oh, yeah? You think they do this better in *The Amazing Minkcoat?* No way! Now you go—da da da dum.

LISA. Da da da dum.

PAUL. If I had Aladdin's lamp for only a day, I'd make a wish. . . .

LISA. Daddy, that's maudlin!

PAUL. I know it's maudlin. And here's what I'd say:

LISA and PAUL. I'd say that "nothing could be finer than to be in Carolina in the mooooooooooornin'."

Examining the Language of a Play

The first thing we need to remember when we read a play—any play—is that, while the dialogue is the most significant element, it is not the only element. Even though we are very likely encountering the work on the printed page and have no intention of staging it, the various notes, descriptions, and cues are also essential to our understanding. They aid and direct our imagination and often—as in this play—contain important material. Thus, it is vital for us to learn that Lisa is in a dance studio, that she is singing "Nothing Could Be Finer," which figures importantly at the end, and that Paul, the father, "has a sweet, though distant, demeanor." The last cue is especially important, for much of the play turns on the fact of his emotional distance from his daughter.

In the simplest possible terms, the play would appear to be about a misunderstanding, or failure to communicate, that leads to an outburst and then a reconciliation. A busy father has not paid enough attention to his daughter, and she communicates that message to him. He recognizes her pain and tries to make up for his distractedness. The fact that he asks to see her routine and that she lets him participate, however clumsily, signals that they have renewed their understanding, perhaps reached a new level.

Such a *précis*, or synopsis, catches the basic development, but it naturally leaves out a great deal. In drama, as in all literature, the true art lies in the accumulation of moments, the little surprises and twists that engage our attention and invite us into the experience. In the case of drama, which consists almost entirely of speech between characters, we need to become alert to the shifts and nuances that point us toward the underlying—and often unstated—situation.

Speech and gesture are the playwright's stock-in-trade. The challenge is to use these tools to maximum effect—to reveal not only the full dimensions of the outward reality, but to take the viewer (or reader) into the complex psychological reality behind the surface. Speech, therefore, has several functions. It can state, confess, and reveal, or else it can point in innumerable ways to what is going on in the realm of the unstated—which is, often as not, the reverse of what is overtly expressed.

Interpreting Dialogue

Interpreting dialogue is the main thing we do when we read a play. The process is really no different from what we do all the time in social contexts. We form an estimate of the person we are dealing with, and we weigh and measure that person's words to see how we should take them. Some people are inveterate kidders, and we take their every utterance with a grain of salt. Others use irony or understatement; still others are perfect literalists and say what they mean (or try to). We go through the same stages of interpretation when we read or watch drama. The speech and mannerisms of the characters give us a general sense of their personality structure. We then listen to their words within the context of what we assume about their characters. Shocks and revelations come when the playwright elicits an unexpected reaction, thereby changing our sense about the character. We modify and deepen our interpretation, and the process—which often takes place outside our conscious awareness—draws us further into the play.

If we pay close attention to the interchanges between Paul and Lisa, we quickly pick up how things are between them. Paul is late. He has missed Lisa's recital, though we do not know this fact yet, and even though his apology is skimpy ("I'm sorry I'm late"), he attempts to get on his daughter's good side with an easy compliment. He compliments what he saw of her solitary routine and addresses her with the familiar nickname of "Tiger." Lisa is upset, even though she makes no reproaches (she accepts his apology with a simple "That's okay"). We guess at her feelings through her refusal to answer her father in anything but monosyllables. She is determined to keep her world to herself, to refuse him admittance.

Paul, for his part, tries what must be proven ways of winning his daughter over. He offers further compliments, jokes with her about being "sexy," and tries to humor her.

The first overt hint we get about Lisa's inner world—about the fact that she has something on her mind—comes with this simple three-word interchange:

LISA. Daddy.
PAUL. What?
LISA. Nothing.

It is the merest hint, but it sets up a suspicion in the reader. We now know to watch her speech for cues. These come quickly. First, explaining why she must find her leg warmers, she says that "it's not professional to leave things." It is an innocent remark, except that it gathers weight a few lines on, when Lisa says, "You shouldn't make appointments to see me unless you know you're going to come." Both words, "professional" and "appointments," suggest that the girl is trying to reach her father in terms that he might understand—terms that belong to the adult order of things.

The gambit fails. Paul replies, simply: "Of course I'm going to come." His reply leads Lisa to up the ante. She now brings up a friend of hers whose parents are divorced, announcing that Talia Robbins is "much happier living without her father in the house." Paul still doesn't get it. He changes the subject back to leg warmers. And this act of avoidance prompts Lisa to her next observation, about a TV show where a father was crying about his daughter. Paul persists in not *hearing* her. Indeed, he belittles her point by invoking an adult perspective—and an adult word: "maudlin"—further frustrating her.

The to-and-fro skirmishing goes on for quite a while. Father and daughter have a psychological tug-of-war over finding the leg warmers, Paul's idea being that they must hurry home for dinner. Lisa continually dislodges him, returning to the underlying issue, which is his inattentiveness. Again she says: "Daddy." But this time she follows it up with a direct accusation: "Why don't you want to talk to me?"

The play makes a turn when Lisa suddenly spots her leg warmers. When she picks them up, she produces an "odd-looking" trophy as well. (This will become an important prop soon.) Her "finding" of the leg warmers is a way of acknowledging the pointlessness of their conversation. She had postponed finding them in the hope that they could communicate; she now clearly believes that they cannot, as her monosyllabic answers to his interrogations seem to confirm.

Now it's Paul's turn to give the situation a turn. He brings in an adult—business—analogy: "Lisa, you know what you do in business when it seems like there's nothing left to say? That's when you really start talking. Put a bid on the table." Lisa, of course, has no idea what he's talking about. Paul translates into the language of board games. Lisa changes the subject. She voices her anger more explicitly by telling Paul that she will "become a prostitute" when she grows up. And she brings this scene to a climax by blurting out "I hate you, Daddy! I hate you!" and throwing her trophy in the trash.

Reflecting on the Action of a Play

In dramatic terms, the *climax* is the culminating moment in the play—the end of the *rising action* (which comprises all action that leads to this explosion of tension). The climax is customarily followed by the *falling action* (which leads away), which includes the *resolution* (the outcome of the climactic explosion) and the *denouement* (the tying up of threads). (*Note:* please see the discussion of fictional elements as well as the Glossary for more on these terms.)

Wasserstein's play adheres to this basic dramatic convention. After Lisa's eruption, the emotional repair work can begin. Paul apologizes again, more sincerely. Lisa acknowledges that she won't very likely become a prostitute. The exchanges become longer, and there is the clear sense that father and daughter are at least listening to each other and trying to find a common language. Paul brings up the business concept of the "tender offer," from which the play takes its title. Lisa tries to grasp what he means. Paul and Lisa come still closer when she asks him what he thinks about and he tells her.

At last a deal has been struck. Paul has given Lisa something: he has told her honestly what his life is like. And now she makes a gift in return. She lets him into *her* world. Her observation about the clouds is a test. Had she ventured it earlier, Paul would very likely have disregarded or ridiculed it. But now he understands it as part of an exchange. He has given her the language—and thinking—of his world; now she is doing the same for him. And when he enters in, peace is attained. The cue [LISA *picks up her trophy.*] is significant.

The rest is obvious. Having finally met as equals of a sort, Paul and Lisa can begin to interact. He coaxes her into showing her routine and she allows him to take part. Singing "Nothing Could Be Finer" together they are literally, and figuratively, making harmony.

What Can a Play Accomplish?

Granted, "Tender Offers" is not a deep play. Unlike other works you will find here—by Sophocles, Shakespeare, Chekhov, and Wilson, among others—it does not try to plumb the ultimate sources of human behavior. Nor does it use language distinguished for its elegance—like Molière, say—or complex shifts in time, as in Arthur Miller's *Death of a Salesman*. No, it is a straightforward scene set forth with the simplest of means. And yet Wasserstein's play, like the others, was written for a reason. It has a message to communicate, a theme. The theme, in the simplest terms, is that the necessary basis for any true communication is empathy, and that one cannot simply take in another's words without making the effort to understand what those words *mean* to the person. The play suggests, further, that people have their own languages and frames of reference that are based on their experience of the world and that sometimes acts of translation are necessary. Paul cannot know what is bothering Lisa until he accepts her way of speaking and understands that her seemingly incidental observations ("Talia Robbins told me she's much happier living without her father in the house") are important communications. As Lisa tries to understand Paul's "business" frame of reference, so he needs to follow the very different kinds of hints she throws out.

The theme is simple enough, the reader might think—so why put it into a play? Why not just state the message and be done? Questions like these bring us back to the main point about drama—indeed, about all literature. That art does not merely put a fancy wrapping around some human meaning. Rather, it gives the reader—or viewer—the *experience* of meaning. Wasserstein's short play not only imparts what may be a familiar truth about communication, but also performs it. The play creates an involvement through characters and situation, and the involvement allows us to recognize the truths experientially. We are given instruction through a subtle play of theme and variation, and we receive it as much with our emotions as with our more analytic intelligence. Besides—and this is no small matter—we take pleasure in the process.

30 Greek Drama and the Origins of Tragedy

What we now know as Greek drama—mainly the corpus of surviving works by Aeschylus, Sophocles, Aristophanes, and Euripides—had its prehistoric origins in chants of praise offered up by choruses of men to the gods, mainly Dionysos. Dionysos was the god of wine and fertility, and he was honored at various religious festivals, especially at the period of the spring planting. According to legend, the first rudimentary drama took shape when Thespis, the leader of one such chorus, broke apart from the chant and called out questions. The others answered in unison, and the roots of Greek dramatic art were set down. To this day actors are sometimes known as "Thespians."

The original subject matter of the call-and-response enactments would most likely have been the legend of Dionysos, but as the art evolved to bring in more individual speakers and a broader array of themes, other parts of the Greek mythology were brought into play. Within a period of a century or so, major changes had been effected. The size and importance of the chorus were diminished; a second, then a third, actor was added. Over time the staging of these plays was formalized as a central part of Greek civic life.

THE SIGNIFICANCE OF DRAMA FOR THE ANCIENT GREEKS

The great yearly event for lovers of the drama was the Great Festival of Dionysos at Athens, which took place every spring. Up to 15,000 people took seats in the Theater of Dionysos, near the Acropolis, to watch the plays, which were usually given in cycles of three and lasted for long hours.

The theater itself was in the open air. Great concentric rings of benches rose up the slope of the hillside. In what we think of as the stage area was a long building called the *scene house,* which had several sets of doors in its facade. The chorus occupied the area between the scene house and the tiers of seats. The actors themselves—all male, all priests of Dionysos—performed in front of the scene house, which was more often than not understood to represent a palace.

The plays were staged in competition, generally on successive days, and the winners carried away significant prizes. As the subjects were nearly always drawn from common legend, most of the audience members knew the origins and outcomes of the plots. Involvement was intense. What mattered was how well the dramatist could manipulate the familiar material to evoke the emotions of pity and terror in the audience. According to the Greek view of life, pity and terror were the proper responses

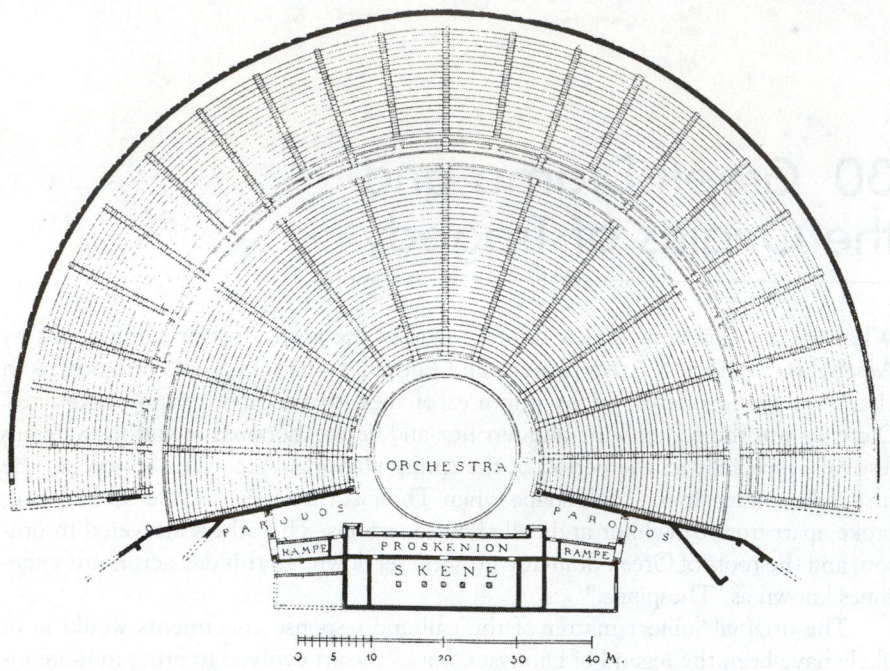

The plan of an ancient theater still used at Epidaurus, Greece, in a form that developed from the Theater of Dionysos at the Acropolis in Athens. The scene house (skene) stood behind the side corridors (parados) where the chorus entered the orchestra area. The scene house provided backing to the performing area (proskenion) that gradually developed into a stage. (From Dörpfeld, *Griechische Theater*, 1896.)

to a true recognition of the human condition. Once the spectators had been roused to these emotions, the playwright would effect a *katharsis*, or release. As often as not, this release was purchased by the tragic death of the protagonist, or leading actor.

Greek tragedy crystallized into a very specific and predictable form. The individual play begins with a *prologue*, which may be given as a monologue or dialogue and which informs the audience of the basic situation. The prologue is followed by the *parados* (from which we derive our word "parade")—the arrival of the chorus, its members singing and dancing as they enter. When their singing ends, the first *episode* (which is like an act) is presented. Then the chorus sings an ode, or *stasimon*. The pattern is repeated for four or five episodes, after which there is an *exodus*, or departure of actors from the stage.

Those of us who squirm while sitting through a three-hour movie would have a hard time at one of these festivals. It was common to have three tragedies, each 60 to 90 minutes long, presented in succession. At the end of the third, it was not time to leave—it was time for comedy. But first, as though to clear the air of too much brooding seriousness, the *satyr play* was performed. The satyr was a mythological creature—half-man and half-beast—said to be a companion to Dionysos. The satyr play was deliberate mocking of the preceding tragedy, an attempt to restore balance—a concept sacred to the Greeks—by giving expression to the opposite. Where there was solemnity before, whimsey and wildness now reigned.

This notion of balance—indeed, of balance achieved by bringing opposition to harmony—is central to an understanding of the Greek mind. The German philosopher Friedrich Nietzsche wrote a brilliant study, *The Birth of Tragedy*, in which he explored what he saw as the two sides of the Greek soul. The Apollonian (referring to the god Apollo) represented order and discipline—everything we associate with the classical ideal; the Dionysian was the formless release of drives and aggressions. The ideal, represented by the golden mean, was "nothing to excess"; after chaos must come order. And this was the idea behind the Dionysian festivals as well; that the dramas would show all manner of horror and excess, but that equilibrium would finally be established, and that law would prevail.

After the satyr play, once the spell of the tragic had been broken, the festival would generally feature a comedy performance. The comedies differed from tragedies in several crucial ways. Where the tragic chorus served as a kind of supplement to, or commentary upon, the actions depicted in the episodes, the comic chorus (which was generally larger) was divided into two groups. Their function was to give voice to both sides of any given issue, and the interplay of views was often comic itself. In addition, the comedies were inventive and unexpected. The audience had no idea of what might come next in any situation, except that—unlike in the tragic plays—the protagonist (or main actor) would most likely triumph over the obstacles placed in his path. If tragedy was the province of noble souls, kings and princes, then comedy belonged to the little man, the commoner with whom most audience members could identify.

THE NATURE OF GREEK TRAGEDY

The traditional emblem for Greek dramatic art is a pair of masks linked together, with one visage representing a grimace of pain, the other laughter. This emblem would seem to grant the two modes an equal status, fixing them as the extreme poles of the human emotional spectrum. Traditionally, however, the tragic mode has been given precedence—as more serious, more worthy. Perhaps no one is more responsible for the perpetuation of this view than the philosopher Aristotle (384–322 B.C.), whose treatise, the *Poetics*, remains the single most important study of Greek drama. His terms and discussions are still the touchstones for anyone who would study the art as the Greeks originated and perfected it.

Aristotle's View of Tragedy

The *Poetics* was written, it must be noted, nearly a century after the great dramatists had composed their works. It is not, therefore, prescriptive; it does not tell what the dramatic art ought to be. Rather, it describes and analyzes, attempting to determine the essence of that art.

According to Aristotle, who fixed his attention on tragedy and more or less ignored comedy, the tragedian worked with six essential elements, which he identified as Fable (or Plot), Characters, Thought (or Theme), Language, Melody, and *Mise en*

Scène (or Spectacle). And for all the changes that have befallen the dramatic arts over the centuries, those elements may still be the most useful way to approach a play.

Much of Aristotle's general discussion of these matters is common sense. Obviously there can be no Plot ("the imitation of the action; the whole structure of the incidents . . . ") without Character; and certainly, a few experimental modern plays notwithstanding, there is little use for Character without Plot. Thought, or Theme, is the governing idea or concept, that which motivates the playwright to create the work in the first place—it is the play's reason for being. Language we can think of as dialogue, the accompaniment to action and the basic medium of communication, while Melody is a somewhat more elusive ingredient, including the rhythms and sounds of the words as well as their voicing by the actors, and encompassing as well the incidental sounds (hoofbeats, doors closing, etc.) that are integral to any performance. *Mise en Scène*, or Spectacle, is an inclusive term for the entire visual impression, including all costumes, lighting effects, and movements, as it changes throughout the course of the play.

Every play, ancient or modern, will have these six elements in some form or another, although the proportions will naturally vary. For Aristotle, the criteria of excellence were the harmony and balance of parts, and the artistic subordination of all to the effect of the whole.

The Structure of Greek Tragedy

At the core of Greek tragedy, as Aristotle recognized, were deep tendencies toward unity and economy. These unities extended to *time* (the action of the play generally took place within a 24-hour period), *place* (the locale was usually confined to a single city, often to the environs of a palace), and *action* (the plot would focus upon the central conflict, avoiding subplots and extraneous episodes).

The main reason the Greek tragedies were able to succeed within these confining strictures is because they drew upon mythic lore familiar to the audience. The groundwork was, in effect, already laid, and the playwright could position the action very near to the point of *climax* (for maximum tension). We see a marked contrast in the Shakespearean tragedies of a later period, where the complications and tensions had to build from the ground up.

Greek tragedy was a compressed and powerful form of public expression. The playwright's aim was to fill his audiences with the emotions of pity and terror and to effect a cathartic purging. There were, as Aristotle noted, several premises shared by all the dramatists. First, it was essential that the *protagonist* (or "main actor") be a figure of lofty social position (a ruler, a member of the royal family) and evident nobility of soul. That protagonist would in the course of the tragedy be brought low (often to death) through the operation of implacable fate and, to some degree, through a tragic flaw in his or her character—most often it was *hubris*, or excessive pride before the gods.

The downfall was all the more terrible for being fated, and the protagonist was bound to endure extraordinary suffering with noble resignation. The effect of watching was the collective shudder, the emotional release. The sense of inevitability, of course, heightened the tension. The playwright could tighten the string even further by *foreshadowing*—hinting at what was to come, either by introducing a character with prophetic insight (like Teiresias in *Oedipus Rex*), or allowing the protagonist to voice forebodings. Or else the playwright would insert a plot reversal, teasing the viewer with the possibility that the inevitable may not have to be inevitable after all—just before setting events back on their appointed track.

The tragedy unfolds in four stages; the *exposition* (which sets out the situation), the *complication* (which ties the knot), the *climax* (which brings tensions to their highest pitch and leads up to the *turning point*), and finally the *denouement* (in which the knot is untied—the term literally means "unraveling"). The protagonist is brought low, and in the process the entire civic edifice is endangered. For in Greek drama the characters are never seen in isolation for their society. The tragedy of an Oedipus or Antigonê sends ripples through the whole *polis* (for "city"). But while the protagonist comes to grief, order must otherwise prevail once again. Though the chaotic forces of Dionysos have run riot, it is finally the balance represented by Apollo that must be restored. In this way, the protagonist serves the role of sacrificial victim; his or her tragedy is an expiation of sins that is necessary for the smooth running of society.

Oedipus Rex and *Antigonê*, which follow, are not only among the earliest and greatest of the Greek tragedies, but also offer a superb illustration of many of the ideas and principles discussed here. Questions follow the texts.

Sophocles (496?–406 B.C.)

Sophocles is, with Aeschylus and Euripides, one of the three great Greek tragedians. He wrote well over a hundred plays during his lifetime, most of which were performed at the Dionysian festivals in Athens. Only seven of these have survived complete; the best known are *Antigonê*, *Philoctetes*, *Oedipus at Colonus,* and *Oedipus Rex. Oedipus Rex* was first produced in 425 B.C., several years after a plague had devastated Athens. *Oedipus at Colonus,* Sophocles's last play, was written when the playwright was nearly ninety. It shows the king still wandering after twenty years of exile—an emblem, perhaps, of his once prosperous city-state, Athens, now in decline.

OEDIPUS REX

English Version
by Dudley Fitts and Robert Fitzgerald

PERSONS REPRESENTED

OEDIPUS	MESSENGER
A PRIEST	SHEPHERD OF LAÏOS
CREON	SECOND MESSENGER
TEIRESIAS	CHORUS OF THEBAN ELDERS
IOCASTÊ	

THE SCENE

Before the palace of Oedipus, King of Thebes. A central door and two lateral doors open into a platform which runs the length of the facade. On the platform, right and left, are altars; and three steps lead down into the "orchestra," or chorus-ground. At the beginning of the action these steps are crowded by suppliants who have brought branches and chaplets of olive leaves and who lie in various attitudes of despair. OEDIPUS *enters.*

PROLOGUE

OEDIPUS.

My children, generations of the living
In the line of Kadmos,° nursed at his ancient hearth:
Why have you strewn yourself before these altars
In supplication,° with your boughs and garlands?
The breath of incense rises from the city   5
With a sound of prayer and lamentation.

                                 Children,
I would not have you speak through messengers,
And therefore I have come myself to hear you—
I, Oedipus, who bear the famous name.
[*To a* PRIEST.] You, there, since you are eldest in the company,   10
Speak to them all, tell me what preys upon you,
Whether you come in dread, or crave some blessing:
Tell me, and never doubt that I will help you
In every way I can: I should be heartless
Were I not moved to find you suppliant here.   15

PRIEST. Great Oedipus, O powerful King of Thebes!
You see how all the ages of our people
Cling to your altar steps; here are boys
Who can barely stand alone, and here are priests
By weight of age, as I am a priest of God,   20
And young men chosen from those yet unmarried;
As for the others, all that multitude,
They wait with olive chaplets° in the squares,
At the two shrines of Pallas,° and where Apollo°
Speaks in the glowing embers.

                              Your own eyes   25
Must tell you: Thebes is in her extremity
And cannot lift her head from the surge of death.
A rust consumes the buds and fruits of the earth;
The herds are sick; children die unborn,
And labor is vain. The god of plague and pyre   30
Raids like detestable lighting through the city,
And all the house of Kadmos is laid waste,
All emptied, and all darkened: Death alone

---

2 *Kadmos:* ruling dynasty of Thebes.   4 *supplication:* beseeching, prayerful posture.   23 *chaplet:* wreath, garland.   24 *Pallas:* Pallas Athene, goddess;   *Apollo:* god of sun, prophecy, and song.

Battens upon the misery of Thebes.
You are not one of the immortal gods, we know;   35
Yet we have come to you to make our prayer
As to the men of all men best in adversity
And wisest in the ways of God. You saved us
From the Sphinx,° that flinty singer, and the tribute
We paid to her so long; yet you were never   40
Better informed than we, nor could we teach you:
It was some god breathed in you to set us free.

Therefore, O mighty King, we turn to you:
Find us our safety, find us a remedy,
Whether by counsel of the gods or the men.   45
A king of wisdom tested in the past
Can act in a time of troubles, and act well.
Noblest of men, restore
Life to your city! Think how all men call you
Liberator for your triumph long ago;   50
Ah, when your years of kingship are remembered,
Let them not say *We rose, but later fell*—
Keep the State from going down in the storm!
Once, years ago, with happy augury,
You brought us fortune; be the same again!   55
No man questions your power to rule the land:
But rule over men, not over a dead city!
Ships are only hulls, citadels are nothing,
When no life moves in the empty passageways.

OEDIPUS. Poor children! You may be sure I know   60
    All that you longed for in your coming here.
    I know that you are deathly sick; and yet,
    Sick as you are, not one is as sick as I.
    Each of you suffers in himself alone
    His anguish, not another's; but my spirit   65
    Groans for the city, for myself, for you.

    I was not sleeping, you are not waking me.
    No, I have been in tears for a long while
    And in my restless thought walked many ways.
    In all my search, I found one helpful course,   70
    And that I have taken: I have sent Creon,°
    Son of Menoikeus, brother of the Queen,
    To Delphi,° Apollo's place of revelation,
    To learn there, if he can,
    What act or pledge of mine may save the city.   75

-----

39 *Sphinx:* mythical monster with a lion's body and a woman's head, sent to Thebes as punishment
for the lust of King Laïos. Oedipus' answering the Sphinx's riddle saved the city from the curse.   71 *Creon:*
succeeded Laïos as King of Thebes, then abdicated in favor of Oedipus, who had saved the country from
the Sphinx.   73 *Delphi:* famous oracle, place where Apollo's prophecies foretold the future.

I have counted the days, and now, this very day,
I am troubled, for he has overstayed his time.
What is he doing? He has been gone too long.
Yet whenever he comes back, I should do ill
To scant whatever hint the god may give. 80

PRIEST. It is a timely promise. At this instant
They tell me Creon is here.

OEDIPUS.   O Lord Apollo!
May his news be fair as his face is radiant!

PRIEST. It could not be otherwise: he is crowned with bay,
The chaplet is thick with berries.

OEDIPUS.   We shall soon know; 85
He is near enough to hear us now.

Enter Creon.

O Prince:
Brother: son of Menoikeus:
What answer do you bring us from the god?

CREON. It is favorable. I can tell you, great afflictions
Will turn out well, if they are taken well. 90

OEDIPUS. What was the oracle? These vague words
Leave me still hanging between hope and fear.

CREON. Is it your pleasure to hear me with all these
Gathered around us? I am prepared to speak,
But should we not go in?

OEDIPUS.   Let them all hear it. 95
It is for them I suffer, more than myself.

CREON. Then I will tell you what I heard at Delphi.

In plain words
The god commands us to expel from the land of Thebes
An old defilement that it seems we shelter. 100
It is a deathly thing, beyond expiation.
We must not let it feed upon us longer.

OEDIPUS. What defilement? How shall we rid ourselves of it?

CREON. By exile or death, blood for blood. It was
Murder that brought the plague-wind on the city. 105

OEDIPUS. Murder of whom? Surely the god has named him?

CREON. My lord: long ago Laïos was our king,
Before you came to govern us.

OEDIPUS.   I know;
I learned of him from others, I never saw him.

CREON. He was murdered; and Apollo commanded us now 110
To take revenge upon whoever killed him.

OEDIPUS. Upon whom? Where are they? Where shall we find a clue
To solve that crime, after so many years?

CREON. Here in this land, he said.
If we make enquiry,

We may touch things that otherwise escape us.   115
OEDIPUS. Tell me: Was Laïos murdered in his house,
     Or in the fields, or in some foreign country?
CREON. He said he planned to make a pilgrimage.
     He did not come home again.
OEDIPUS.   And was there no one,
     No witness, no companion, to tell what happened?   120
CREON. They were all killed but one, and he got away
     So frightened that he could remember one thing only.
OEDIPUS. What was that one thing? One may be the key
     To everything, if we resolve to use it.
CREON. He said that a band of highwaymen attacked them,   125
     Outnumbered them, and overwhelmed the King.
OEDIPUS. Strange, that a highwayman should be so daring—
     Unless some faction here bribed him to do it.
CREON. We thought of that. But after Laïos' death
     New troubles arose and we have no avenger.   130
OEDIPUS. What troubles could prevent your hunting down the killers?
CREON. The riddling Sphinx's song
     Made us deaf to all mysteries but her own.
OEDIPUS. Then once more I must bring what is dark to light.
     It is most fitting that Apollo shows,   135
     As you do, this compunction for the dead.
     You shall see how I stand by you, as I should,
     To avenge the city and the city's god,
     And not as though it were for some distant friend,
     But for my own sake, to be rid of evil.   140
     Whoever killed King Laïos might—who knows?—
     Decide at any moment to kill me as well.
     By avenging the murdered king I protect myself.
     Come, then, my children; leave the altar steps,
     Lift up your olive boughs!
                                        One of you go   145
     And summon the people of Kadmos to gather here.
     I will do all that I can; you may tell them that.

                          Exit a Page.

     So, with the help of God,
     We shall be saved—or else indeed we are lost.
PRIEST. Let us rise, children. It was for this we came,   150
     And now the King has promised it himself.
     Phoibos° has sent us an oracle; may he descend
     Himself to save us and drive out the plague.

     *Exeunt Oedipus and Creon into the palace by the central door. The Priest and the
     Suppliants disperse right and left. After a short pause the Chorus enters the orchestra.*

---

152 *Phoibos:* name for Apollo, sun god.

PÁRADOS

Strophe 1

CHORUS. What is god singing in his profound
  Delphi of gold and shadow?
  What oracle for Thebes, the sunwhipped city?
  Fear unjoints me, the roots of my heart tremble.
  Now I remember, O Healer, your power, and wonder;   5
  Will you send doom like a sudden cloud, or weave it
  Like nightfall of the past?
  Speak, speak to us, issue of holy sound:
  Dearest to our expectancy: be tender!

Antistrophe 1

  Let me pray to Athenê, the immortal daughter of Zeus,   10
  And to Artemis her sister
  Who keeps her famous throne in the market ring,
  And to Apollo, bowman at the far butts of heaven—

  O gods, descend! Like three streams leap against
  The fires of our grief, the fires of darkness;   15
  Be swift to bring us rest!

  As in the old time from the brilliant house
  Of air you stepped to save us, come again!

Strophe 2

  Now our afflictions have no end,
  Now all our stricken host lies down   20
  And no man fights off death with his mind;

  The noble plowland bears no grain,
  And groaning mothers cannot bear—

  See, how our lives like birds take wing.
  Like sparks that fly when a fire soars,   25
  To the shore of the god of evening.

Antistrophe 2

  The plague burns on, it is pitiless,
  Though pallid children laden with death
  Lie unwept in the stony ways,
  And old gray women by every path   30
  Flock to the strand about the altars

  There to strike their breasts and cry
  Worship of Phoibos in wailing prayers:
  Be kind, God's golden child!

Strophe 3

  There are no swords in this attack by fire,   35
  No shields, but we are ringed with cries.
  Send the besieger plunging from our homes

Into the vast sea-room of the Atlantic
Or into the waves that foam eastward of Thrace°—
For the day ravages what the night spares—   40

Destroy our enemy, lord of the thunder!
Let him be riven by lightning from heaven!

Antistrophe 3

Phoibos Apollo, stretch the sun's bowstring,
That golden cord, until it sings for us,
Flashing arrows in heaven!

      Artemis, Huntress,   45
Race with flaring lights upon our mountains!
O scarlet god, O golden-banded brow,
O Theban Bacchos° in a storm of Maenads,°

    Enter Oedipus, center.

Whirl upon Death, that all the Undying hate!   50
Come with blinding cressets, come in joy!

SCENE I

OEDIPUS. Is this your prayer? It may be answered. Come,
Listen to me, act as the crisis demands,
And you shall have relief from all these evils.

Until now I was a stranger to this tale,
As I had been a stranger to the crime.   5
Could I track down the murderer without a clue?
But now, friends,
As one who became a citizen after the murder,
I make this proclamation to all Thebans:
If any man know by whose hand Laïos, son of Labdakos,   10
Met his death, I direct that man to tell me everything,
No matter what he fears for having so long withheld it.
Let it stand as promised that no further trouble
Will come to him, but he may leave the land in safety.

Moreover: If anyone knows the murderer to be foreign,   15
Let him not keep silent: he shall have his reward from me.
However, if he does conceal it; if any man
Fearing for his friend or for himself disobeys this edict,
Hear what I propose to do:

I solemnly forbid the people of this country,   20
Where power and throne are mine, ever to receive that man
Or speak to him, no matter who he is, or let him
Join in sacrifice, lustration,° or in prayer.
I decree that he be driven from every house,

---

39 *Thrace:* northern region of Greece. 48 *Bacchos:* Bacchus or Dionysos, god of wine; *Maenads:* frenzied women, followers of Dionysos. SCENE 1. 23 *lustration:* ritual washing.

Being, as he is, corruption itself to us: the Delphic   25
Voice of Zeus has pronounced this revelation.
Thus I associate myself with the oracle
And take the side of the murdered king.

As for the criminal, I pray to God—
Whether it be a lurking thief, or one of a number—   30
I pray that that man's life be consumed in evil and wretchedness.
And as for me, this curse applies no less
If it should turn out that the culprit is my guest here,
Sharing my hearth.
                You have heard the penalty.
I lay it on you now to attend to this   35
For my sake, for Apollo's, for the sick
Sterile city that heaven has abandoned.
Suppose the oracle had given you no command:
Should this defilement go uncleansed for ever?
You should have found the murderer: your king,   40
A noble king, had been destroyed!
               Now I,
Having the power that he held before me,
Having his bed, begetting children there
Upon his wife, as he would have, had he lived—
Their son would have been my children's brother,   45
If Laïos had had luck in fatherhood!
(But surely ill luck rushed upon his reign)—
I say I take the son's part, just as though
I were his son, to press the fight for him
And see it won! I'll find the hand that brought   50
Death to Labdakos'° and Polydoros'° child,
Heir of Kadmos' and Agenor's° line.
And as for those who fail me,
May the gods deny them the fruit of the earth,
Fruit of the womb, and may they rot utterly!   55
Let them be wretched as we are wretched, and worse!
For you, for loyal Thebans, and for all
Who find my actions right, I pray the favor
Of justice, and of all the immortal gods.
CHORAGOS. Since I am under oath, my lord, I swear   60
    I did not do the murder, I cannot name
    The murderer. Might not the oracle
    That has ordained the search tell where to find him?
OEDIPUS. An honest question. But no man in the world
    Can make the gods do more than the gods will.   65
CHORAGOS. There is one last expedient—
OEDIPUS.   Tell me what it is.
    Though it seem slight, you must not hold it back.

---

51 *Labdakos:* guardian of Laïos, King of Thebes and (not yet revealed) Oedipus' father; *Polydoros:* Labdakos' father.   52 *Agenor:* father of Kadmos and son of Poseidon, ocean god.

CHORAGOS. A lord clairvoyant to the lord Apollo,
    As we all know, is the skilled Teiresias.
    One might learn much about this from him, Oedipus.   70
OEDIPUS. I am not wasting time:
    Creon spoke of this, and I have sent for him—
    Twice, in fact; it is strange that he is not here.
CHORAGOS. The other matter—that old report—seems useless.
OEDIPUS. Tell me, I am interested in all reports.   75
CHORAGOS. The king was said to have been killed by highwaymen.
OEDIPUS. I know. But we have no witnesses to that.
CHORAGOS. If the killer can feel a particle of dread,
    Your curse will bring him out of hiding!
OEDIPUS.   No.
    The man who dared that act will fear no curse.   80

Enter the blind seer Teiresias, led by a Page.

CHORAGOS. But there is one man who may detect the criminal.
    This is Teiresias, this is the holy prophet
    In whom, alone of all men, truth was born.
OEDIPUS. Teiresias: seer: student of mysteries,
    Of all that's taught and all that no man tells,   85
    Secrets of Heaven and secrets of the earth:
    Blind though you are, you know the city lies
    Sick with plague; and from this plague, my lord,
    We find that you alone can guard or save us.

    Possibly you did not hear the messengers?   90
    Apollo, when we sent to him,
    Sent us back word that this pestilence
    Would lift, but only if we established clearly
    The identity of those who murdered Laïos.
    They must be killed or exiled.
                                    Can you use   95
    Birdflight or any art of divination
    To purify yourself, and Thebes, and me
    From this contagion? We are in your hands.
    There is no fairer duty
    Than that of helping others in distress.   100
TEIRESIAS. How dreadful knowledge of the truth can be
    When there's no help in truth! I knew this well,
    But did not act on it: else I should not have come.
OEDIPUS. What is troubling you? Why are your eyes so cold?
TEIRESIAS. Let me go home. Bear your own fate, and I'll   105
    Bear mine. It is better so: trust what I say.
OEDIPUS. What you say is ungracious and unhelpful
    To your native country. Do not refuse to speak.
TEIRESIAS. When it come to speech, your own is neither temperate
    Nor opportune. I wish to be more prudent.   110
OEDIPUS. In God's name, we all beg you—

TEIRESIAS.   You are all ignorant.
    No; I will never tell you what I know.
    Now it is my misery; then, it would be yours.
OEDIPUS. What! You do know something, and will not tell us?
    You will betray us all and wreck the State?   115
TEIRESIAS. I do not intend to torture myself, or you.
    Why persist in asking? You will not persuade me.
OEDIPUS. What a wicked old man you are! You'd try a stone's
    Patience! Out with it? Have you no feeling at all?
TEIRESIAS. You call me unfeeling. If you could only see   120
    The nature of your own feelings . . .
OEDIPUS.   Why,
    Who would not feel as I do? Who could endure
    Your arrogance toward the city?
TEIRESIAS.   What does it matter!
    Whether I speak or not, it is bound to come.
OEDIPUS. Then, if "it" is bound to come, you are bound to tell me.   125
TEIRESIAS. No, I will not go on. Rage as you please.
OEDIPUS. Rage? Why not!
                                        And I'll tell you what I think:
    You planned it, you had it done, you all but
    Killed him with your own hands: if you had eyes,
    I'd say the crime was yours, and yours alone.   130
TEIRESIAS. So? I charge you, then,
    Abide by the proclamation you have made:
    From this day forth
    Never speak again to these men or to me;
    You yourself are the pollution of this country.   135
OEDIPUS. You dare say that! Can you possibly think you have
    Some way of going free, after such insolence?
TEIRESIAS. I have gone free. It is the truth sustains me.
OEDIPUS. Who taught you shamelessness? It was not your craft.
TEIRESIAS. You did. You made me speak. I did not want to.   140
OEDIPUS. Speak what? Let me hear it again more clearly.
TEIRESIAS. Was it not clear before? Are you tempting me?
OEDIPUS. I did not understand it. Say it again.
TEIRESIAS. I say that you are the murderer whom you seek.
OEDIPUS. Now twice you have spat out infamy. You'll pay for it!   145
TEIRESIAS. Would you care for more? Do you wish to be really angry?
OEDIPUS. Say what you will. Whatever you say is worthless.
TEIRESIAS. I say you live in hideous shame with those
    Most dear to you. You cannot see the evil.
OEDIPUS. It seems you can go on mouthing like this forever.   150
TEIRESIAS. I can, if there is power in truth.
OEDIPUS.   There is:
    But not for you, not for you,
    You sightless, witless, senseless, mad old man!
TEIRESIAS. You are the madman. There is no one here
    Who will not curse you soon, as you curse me.   155

1024   Greek Drama and the Origins of Tragedy

OEDIPUS. You child of endless night! You cannot hurt me
  Or any other man who sees the sun.
TEIRESIAS. True: it is not from me your fate will come.
  That lies within Apollo's competence,
  As it is his concern.
OEDIPUS.   Tell me: 160
  Are you speaking for Creon, or for yourself?
TEIRESIAS. Creon is no threat. You weave your own doom.
OEDIPUS. Wealth, power, craft of statesmanship!
  Kingly position, everywhere admired!
  What savage envy is stored up against these,   165
  If Creon, whom I trusted, Creon my friend,
  For this great office which the city once
  Put in my hands unsought—if for this power
  Creon desires in secret to destroy me!

  He has brought this decrepit fortune-teller, this   170
  Collector of dirty pennies, this prophet fraud—
  Why, he is no more clairvoyant than I am!
                                    Tell us:
  Has your mystic mummery ever approached the truth?
  When that hellcat the Sphinx was performing here,
  What help were you to these people?   175
  Her magic was not for the first man who came along:
  It demanded a real exorcist.° Your birds—°
  What good were they? or the gods, for the matter of that?
  But I came by,
  Oedipus, the simple man who knows nothing—   180
  I thought it out for myself, no birds helped me!
  And this is the man you think you can destroy,
  That you may be close to Creon when he's king!
  Well you and your friend Creon, it seems to me,
  Will suffer most. If you were not an old man,   185
  You would have paid already for your plot.
CHORAGOS. We cannot see that his words or yours
  Have been spoken except in anger, Oedipus,
  And of anger we have no need. How can God's will
  Be accomplished best? That is what most concerns us.   190
TEIRESIAS. You are a king. But where argument's concerned
  I am your man, as much a king as you.
  I am not your servant, but Apollo's.
  I have no need of Creon to speak for me.

  Listen to me. You mock my blindness, do you?   195
  But I say that you, with both your eyes, are blind:
  You cannot see the wretchedness of your life,
  Nor in whose house you live, no, nor with whom.

---

177 *exorcist:* one who gets rid of evil; *birds:* their flight patterns were read by prophets to foretell
the future.

Who are your father and mother? Can you tell me?
You do not even know the blind wrongs
That you have done them, on earth and in the world below.
But the double lash of your parents' curse will whip you
Out of this land some day, with only night
Upon your precious eyes.
Your cries then—where will they not be heard?
What fastness of Kithairon° will not echo them?
And that bridal-descant of yours—you'll know it then,
The song they sang when you came here to Thebes
And found your misguided berthing.
All this, and more, that you cannot guess at now,
Will bring you to yourself among your children.
Be angry, then. Curse Creon. Curse my words.
I tell you, no man that walks upon the earth
Shall be rooted out more horribly than you.

OEDIPUS. Am I to hear this from him?—Damnation
     Take you! Out of this place! Out of my sight!
TEIRESIAS. I would not have come at all if you had not asked me.
OEDIPUS. Could I have told that you'd talk nonsense, that
     You'd come here to make a fool of yourself, and of me?
TEIRESIAS. A fool? Your parents thought me sane enough.
OEDIPUS. My parents again!—Wait: who were my parents?
TEIRESIAS. This day will give you a father, and break your heart.
OEDIPUS. Your infantile riddles! Your damned abracadabra!
TEIRESIAS. You were a great man once at solving riddles.
OEDIPUS. Mock me with that if you like; you will find it true.
TEIRESIAS. It was true enough. It brought about your ruin.
OEDIPUS. But it saved this town?
TEIRESIAS [to the Page]. Boy, give me your hand.
OEDIPUS. Yes, boy; lead him away.

               —While you are here
     We can do nothing. Go; leave us in peace.
TEIRESIAS. I will go when I have said what I have to say.
     How can you hurt me? And I tell you again:
     The man you have been looking for all this time,
     The damned man, the murderer of Laïos,
     That man is in Thebes. To your mind he is foreignborn,
     But it will soon be shown that he is a Theban,
     A revelation that will fail to please.

                         A blind man,
     Who has his eyes now; a penniless man, who is rich now;
     And he will go tapping the strange earth with his staff;
     To the children with whom he lives now he will be
     Brother and father—the very same; to her
     Who bore him, son and husband—the very same
     Who came to his father's bed, wet with his father's blood.

---

206 *Kithairon:* mountain dwelling of the goddesses of vengeance, called Erinyes.

Enough. Go think that over.
If later you find error in what I have said,
You may say that I have no skill in prophecy.   245

    Exit Teiresias, led by his Page; Oedipus goes into the palace.

ODE I

Strophe 1

CHORUS. The Delphic stone of prophecies
    Remembers ancient regicide
    And a still bloody hand.
    That killer's hour of flight has come.
    He must be stronger than riderless   5
    Coursers of untiring wind,
    For the son of Zeus° armed with his father's thunder
    Leaps in lightning after him;
    And the Furies follow him, the sad Furies.

Antistrophe 1

    Holy Parnassos'° peak of snow   10
    Flashes and blinds that secret man,
    That all shall hunt him down;
    Though he may roam the forest shade
    Like a bull gone wild from pasture
    To rage through glooms of stone.   15
    Doom comes down on him; flight will not avail him;
    For the world's heart calls him desolate,
    And the immortal Furies follow, for ever follow.

Strophe 2

    But now a wilder thing is heard
    From the old man skilled at hearing Fate in the wingbeat of a bird.   20
    Bewildered as a blown bird, my soul hovers and cannot find
    Foothold in this debate, or any reason or rest of mind.
    But no man ever brought—none can bring
    Proof of strife between Thebes' royal house,
    Labdakos' line, and the son of Polybos;°   25
    And never until now has any man brought word
    Of Laïos' dark death staining Oedipus the King.

Antistrophe 2

    Divine Zeus and Apollo hold
    Perfect intelligence alone of all tales ever told;
    And well though this diviner works, he works in his own night;   30
    No man can judge that rough unknown or trust in second sight,
    For wisdom changes hands among the wise.
    Shall I believe my great lord criminal

ODE 1. *7 son of Zeus:* Apollo.   *10 Parnassos:* Parnassus, sacred mountain of Apollo.   *25 Polybos:*
king who adopted the infant Oedipus.

At a raging word that a blind old man let fall?
I saw him, when the carrion woman faced him of old,   35
Prove his heroic mind! These evil words are lies.

SCENE II

CREON. Men of Thebes:
    I am told that heavy accusations
    Have been brought against me by King Oedipus.
    I am not the kind of man to bear this tamely.

    If in these present difficulties   5
    He holds me accountable for any harm to him
    Through anything I have said or done—why, then,
    I do not value life in this dishonor.
    It is not as though this rumor touched upon
    Some private indiscretion. The matter is grave.   10
    The fact is that I am being called disloyal
    To the State, to my fellow citizens, to my friends.
CHORAGOS. He may have spoken in anger, not from his mind.
CREON. But did you not hear him say I was the one
    Who seduced the old prophet into lying?   15
CHORAGOS. The thing was said; I do not know how seriously.
CREON. But you were watching him! Were his eyes steady?
    Did he look like a man in his right mind?
CHORAGOS.   I do not know.
    I cannot judge the behavior of great men.
    But here is the King himself.

                 Enter Oedipus.

OEDIPUS.   So you dared come back.   20
    Why? How brazen of you to come to my house,
    You murderer!
            Do you think I do not know
    That you plotted to kill me, plotted to steal my throne?
    Tell me, in God's name: am I coward, a fool,
    That you should dream you could accomplish this?   25
    A fool who could not see your slippery game?
    A coward, not to fight back when I saw it?
    You are the fool, Creon, are you not? hoping
    Without support or friends to get a throne?
    Thrones may be won or bought: you could do neither.   30
CREON. Now listen to me. You have talked; let me talk, too.
    You cannot judge unless you know the facts.
OEDIPUS. You speak well: there is one fact; but I find it hard
    To learn from the deadliest enemy I have.
CREON. That above all I must dispute with you.   35
OEDIPUS. That above all I will not hear you deny.
CREON. If you think there is anything good in being stubborn
    Against all reason, then I say you are wrong.
OEDIPUS. If you think a man can sin against his own kind

And not be punished for it, I say you are mad.   40
CREON. I agree. But tell me: what have I done to you?
OEDIPUS. You advised me to send for that wizard, did you not?
CREON. I did. I should do it again.
OEDIPUS.   Very well. Now tell me:
   How long has it been since Laïos—°
CREON.   What of Laïos?
OEDIPUS. Since he vanished in that onset by the road?   45
CREON. It was long ago, a long time.
OEDIPUS.   And this prophet,
   Was he practicing here then?
CREON.   He was; and with honor, as now.
OEDIPUS. Did he speak of me at that time?
CREON.   He never did;
   At least, not when I was present.
OEDIPUS.   But . . . the enquiry?
   I suppose you held one?
CREON.   We did, but we learned nothing.   50
OEDIPUS. Why did the prophet not speak against me then?
CREON. I do not know; and I am the kind of man
   Who holds his tongue when he has no facts to go on.
OEDIPUS. There's one fact that you know, and you could tell it.
CREON. What fact is that? If I know it, you shall have it.   55
OEDIPUS. If he were not involved with you, he could not say
   That it was I who murdered Laïos.
CREON. If he says that, you are the one that knows it!—
   But now it is my turn to question you.
OEDIPUS. Put your questions. I am no murderer.   60
CREON. First, then: You married my sister?
OEDIPUS.   I married your sister.
CREON. And you rule the kingdom equally with her?
OEDIPUS. Everything that she wants she has from me.
CREON. And I am the third, equal to both of you?
OEDIPUS. That is why I call you a bad friend.   65
CREON. No. Reason it out, as I have done.
   Think of this first. Would any sane man prefer
   Power, with all a king's anxieties,
   To that same power and the grace of sleep?
   Certainly not I.   70
   I have never longed for the king's power—only his rights.
   Would any wise man differ from me in this?
   As matters stand, I have my way in everything
   With your consent, and no responsibilities.
   If I were king, I should be a slave to policy.   75
   How could I desire a scepter° more
   Than what is now mine—untroubled influence?

---

44 *Laïos*: the former Theban king is not yet revealed to be Oedipus' father.   76 *scepter*: symbol of royal power.

No, I have not gone mad; I need no honors,
Except those with the perquisites I have now.
I am welcome everywhere; every man salutes me,   80
And those who want your favor seek my ear,
Since I know how to manage what they ask.
Should I exchange this ease for that anxiety?
Besides, no sober mind is treasonable.
I hate anarchy   85
And never would deal with any man who likes it.

Test what I have said. Go to the priestess
At Delphi, ask if I quoted her correctly.
And as for this other thing: if I am found
Guilty of treason with Teiresias,   90
Then sentence me to death! You have my word
It is a sentence I should cast my vote for—
But not without evidence!
                              You do wrong
When you take good men for bad, bad men for good.
A true friend thrown aside—why, life itself   95
Is not more precious!
                         In time you will know this well:
For time, and time alone, will show the just man,
Though scoundrels are discovered in a day.
CHORAGOS. This is well said, and a prudent man would ponder it.
    Judgments too quickly formed are dangerous.   100
OEDIPUS. But is he not quick in his duplicity?
    And shall I not be quick to parry him?
    Would you have me stand still, hold my peace, and let
    This man win everything, through my inaction?
CREON. And you want—what is it, then? To banish me?   105
OEDIPUS. No, not exile. It is your death I want,
    So that all the world may see what treason means.
CREON. You will persist, then? You will not believe me?
OEDIPUS. How can I believe you?
CREON.   Then you are a fool.
OEDIPUS. To save myself?
CREON.   In justice, think of me.   110
OEDIPUS. You are evil incarnate.
CREON.   But suppose that you are wrong?
OEDIPUS. Still I must rule.
CREON.   But not if you rule badly.
OEDIPUS. O city, city!
CREON.   It is my city, too!
CHORAGOS. Now, my lords, be still. I see the Queen,
    Iocastê,° coming from her palace chambers;   115

---

115 *Iocastê*: Queen of Thebes, widow of Laïos, wife to Oedipus, and—as yet unrevealed—also his mother.

And it is time she came, for the sake of you both.
This dreadful quarrel can be resolved through her.

Enter Iocastê.

IOCASTÊ. Poor foolish men, what wicked din is this?
With Thebes sick to death, is it not shameful
That you should rake some private quarrel up?   120

To Oedipus.

Come into the house.
—And you, Creon, go now:
Let us have no more of this tumult over nothing.
CREON. Nothing? No, sister: what your husband plans for me
Is one of two great evils: exile or death.
OEDIPUS. He is right.
Why, woman, I have caught him squarely   125
Plotting against my life.
CREON.   No! Let me die
Accurst if ever I have wished you harm!
IOCASTÊ. Ah, believe it, Oedipus!
In the name of the gods, respect this oath of his
For my sake, for the sake of these people here!   130

Strophe 1
CHORAGOS. Open your mind to her, my lord. Be ruled by her, I beg you!
OEDIPUS. What would you have me do?
CHORAGOS. Respect Creon's word. He has never spoken like a fool,
And now he has sworn an oath.
OEDIPUS. You know what you ask?
CHORAGOS.   I do.
OEDIPUS.   Speak on, then.
CHORAGOS. A friend so sworn should not be baited so,   135
In blind malice, and without final proof.
OEDIPUS. You are aware, I hope, that what you say
Means death for me, or exile at the least.

Strophe 2
CHORAGOS. No, I swear by Helios,° first in Heaven!
May I die friendless and accurst,   140
The worst of deaths, if ever I meant that!
It is the withering fields
That hurt my sick heart:
Must we bear all these ills,
And now your bad blood as well?   145
OEDIPUS. Then let him go. And let me die, if I must,
Or be driven by him in shame from the land of Thebes.
It is your unhappiness and not his talk,
That touches me.

----

139 *Helios:* the sun.

As for him—
    Wherever he is, I will hate him as long as I live.   150
CREON. Ugly in yielding, as you were ugly in rage!
    Natures like yours chiefly torment themselves.
OEDIPUS. Can you not go? Can you not leave me?
CREON.   I can.
    You do not know me; but the city knows me,
    And in its eyes I am just, if not in yours.   155

Exit Creon.

Antistrophe 1
CHORAGOS. Lady Iocastê, did you not ask the King
    to go to his chambers?
IOCASTÊ. First tell me what has happened.
CHORAGOS. There was suspicion without evidence; yet it rankled
    As even false charges will.
IOCASTÊ.   On both sides?
CHORAGOS.   On both.
IOCASTÊ.   But what was said?
CHORAGOS. Oh let it rest, let it be done with!   160
    Have we not suffered enough?
OEDIPUS. You see to what your decency has brought you:
    You have made difficulties where my heart saw none.

Antistrophe 2
CHORAGOS. Oedipus, it is not once only I have told you—
    You must know I should count myself unwise   165
    To the point of madness, should I now forsake you—
        You, under whose hand,
            In the storm of another time,
    Our dear land sailed out free.
        But now stand fast at the helm!   170
IOCASTÊ. In God's name, Oedipus, inform your wife as well:
    Why are you so set in this hard anger?
OEDIPUS. I will tell you, for none of these men deserves
    My confidence as you do. It is Creon's work,
    His treachery, his plotting against me.   175
IOCASTÊ. Go on, if you can make this clear to me.
OEDIPUS. He charges me with the murder of Laïos.
IOCASTÊ. He has some knowledge? Or does he speak from hearsay?
OEDIPUS. He would not commit himself to such a charge,
    But he has brought in that damnable soothsayer   180
    To tell his story.
IOCASTÊ.   Set your mind at rest.
    If it is a question of soothsayers, I will tell you
    That you will find no man whose craft gives knowledge
    Of the unknowable.
            Here is my proof:

An oracle was reported to Laïos once 185
(I will not say from Phoibos himself, but from
His appointed ministers, at any rate)
That his doom would be death at the hands of his own son—
His son, born of his flesh and of mine!
Now, you remember the story: Laïos was killed 190
By marauding strangers where three highways meet;
But his child had not been three days in this world
Before the King had pierced the baby's ankles
And left him to die on a lonely mountainside.

Thus, Apollo never caused that child 195
To kill his father, and it was not Laïos' fate
To die at the hands of his son, as he had feared.
This is what prophets and prophecies are worth!
Have no dread of them.
                              It is God himself
Who can show us what he wills, in his own way. 200
OEDIPUS. How strange a shadowy memory crossed my mind,
    Just now while you were speaking: it chilled my heart.
IOCASTÊ. What do you mean? What memory do you speak of?
OEDIPUS. If I understand you, Laïos was killed
    At a place where three roads meet.
IOCASTÊ.   So it was said; 205
    We have no later story.
OEDIPUS.   Where did it happen?
IOCASTÊ. Phokis, it is called: at a place where the Theban Way
    Divides into the roads towards Delphi and Daulia.
OEDIPUS. When?
IOCASTÊ.   We had the news not long before you came
    And proved the right to your succession here. 210
OEDIPUS. Ah, what net had God been weaving for me?
IOCASTÊ. Oedipus! Why does this trouble you?
OEDIPUS.   Do not ask me yet.
    First, Tell me how Laïos looked, and tell me
    How old he was.
IOCASTÊ.   He was tall, his hair just touched
    With white; his form was not unlike your own. 215
OEDIPUS. I think that I myself may be accurst
    By my own ignorant edict.
IOCASTÊ.   You speak strangely.
    It makes me tremble to look at you, my King.
OEDIPUS. I am not sure that the blind man cannot see.
    But I should know better if you were to tell me— 220
IOCASTÊ. Anything—though I dread to hear you ask it.
OEDIPUS. Was the King lightly escorted, or did he ride
    With a large company, as a ruler should?
IOCASTÊ. There were five men with him in all: one was a herald;
    And a single chariot, which he was driving. 225

OEDIPUS. Alas, that makes it plain enough!

But who—
Who told you how it happened?

IOCASTÊ. A household servant,
The only one to escape.

OEDIPUS. And is he still
A servant of ours?

IOCASTÊ. No; for when he came back at last
And found you enthroned at the place of the dead king,   230
He came to me, touched my hand with his, and begged
That I would send him away to the frontier district
Where only the shepherds go—
As far away from the city as I could send him.
I granted his prayer; for although the man was a slave,   235
He had earned more than this favor at my hands.

OEDIPUS. Can he be called back quickly?

IOCASTÊ. Easily.
But why?

OEDIPUS. I have taken too much upon myself
Without enquiry; therefore I wish to consult him.

IOCASTÊ. Then he shall come.

But am I not one also   240
To whom you might confide these fears of yours!

OEDIPUS. That is your right; it will not be denied you,
Now least of all; for I have reached a pitch
Of wild foreboding. Is there anyone
To whom I should sooner speak?   245
Polybos of Corinth is my father.
My mother is a Dorian: Meropê.
I grew up chief among the men of Corinth
Until a strange thing happened—
Not worth my passion, it may be, but strange.   250

At a feast, a drunken man maundering in his cups
Cries out that I am not my father's son!

I contained myself that night, though I felt anger
And a sinking heart. The next day I visited
My father and mother, and questioned them. They stormed,   255
Calling it all the slanderous rant of a fool;
And this relieved me. Yet the suspicion
Remained always aching in my mind;
I knew there was talk; I could not rest;
And finally, saying nothing to my parents,   260
I went to the shrine at Delphi.
The god dismissed my questions without reply;
He spoke of other things.

Some were clear,
Full of wretchedness, dreadful, unbearable:
As, that I should lie with my own mother, breed   265

1034   Greek Drama and the Origins of Tragedy

Children from whom all men would turn their eyes;
And that I should be my father's murderer.

I heard all this, and fled. And from that day
Corinth to me was only in the stars
Descending in that quarter of the sky,   270
As I wandered farther and farther on my way
To a land where I should never see the evil
Sung by the oracle. And I came to this country
Where, so you say, King Laïos was killed.
I will tell you all that happened there, my lady.   275

There were three highways
Coming together at a place I passed;
And there a herald came towards me, and a chariot
Drawn by horses, with a man such as you describe
Seated in it. The groom leading the horses   280
Forced me off the road at his lord's command;
But as this charioteer lurched over towards me
I struck him in my rage. The old man saw me
And brought his double goad° down upon my head
As I came abreast.
                        He was paid back, and more!   285
Swinging my club in this right hand I knocked him
Out of his car, and he rolled on the ground.
                                        I killed him.
I killed them all.
Now if that stranger and Laïos were—kin,
Where is a man more miserable than I?   290
More hated by the gods? Citizen and alien alike
Must never shelter me or speak to me—
I must be shunned by all.
                        And I myself
Pronounced this malediction upon myself!

Think of it: I have touched you with these hands,   295
These hands that killed your husband. What defilement!

Am I all evil, then? It must be so,
Since I must flee from Thebes, yet never again
See my own countrymen, my own country,
For fear of joining my mother in marriage   300
And killing Polybos, my father.
                        Ah,
If I was created so, born to this fate,
Who could deny the savagery of God?
O holy majesty of heavenly powers!
May I never see that day! Never!   305

---

284 *goad*: stick for prodding animals.

Rather let me vanish from the race of men
Than know the abomination destined me!
CHORAGOS. We too, my lord, have felt dismay at this.
    But there is hope: you have yet to hear the shepherd.
OEDIPUS. Indeed, I fear no other hope is left me.   310
IOCASTÊ. What do you hope from him when he comes?
OEDIPUS.   This much:
    If his account of the murder tallies with yours,
    Then I am cleared.
IOCASTÊ.   What was it that I said
    Of such importance?
OEDIPUS.   Why, "marauders," you said,
    Killed the King, according to this man's story.   315
    If he maintains that still, if there were several,
    Clearly the guilt was not mine: I was alone.
    But if he says one man, singlehanded, did it,
    Then the evidence all points to me.
IOCASTÊ. You may be sure that he said there were several;   320
    And can he call back that story now? He cannot.
    The whole city heard it as plainly as I.
    But suppose he alters some detail of it:
    He cannot ever show that Laïos' death
    Fulfilled the oracle: for Apollo said   325
    My child was doomed to kill him: and my child—
    Poor baby!—it was my child that died first.

    No. From now on, where oracles are concerned,
    I would not waste a second thought on any.
OEDIPUS. You may be right.
                      But come: let someone go   330
    For the shepherd at once. This matter must be settled.
IOCASTÊ. I will send for him.
    I would not wish to cross you in anything,
    And surely not in this.—Let us go in.

                 Exeunt into the palace.

ODE II
Strophe 1
CHORUS. Let me be reverent in the ways of right,
    Lowly the paths I journey on;
    Let all my words and actions keep
    The laws of the pure universe
    From highest Heaven handed down.   5
    For Heaven is their bright nurse,
    Those generations of the realms of light;
    Ah, never of mortal kind were they begot,
    Nor are they slaves of memory, lost in sleep:
    Their Father is greater than Time, and ages not.   10

Antistrophe 1

> The tyrant is a child of Pride
> Who drinks from his great sickening cup
> Recklessness and vanity,
> Until from his high crest headlong
> He plummets to the dust of hope.   15
> That strong man is not strong.
> But let no fair ambition be denied;
> May God protect the wrestler for the State
> In government, in comely policy,
> Who will fear God, and on His ordinance wait.   20

Strophe 2

> Haughtiness and the high hand of disdain
> Tempt and outrage God's holy law;
> And any mortal who dares hold
> No immortal Power in awe
> Will be caught up in a net of pain: 25
> The price for which his levity is sold.
> Let each man take due earnings, then,
> And keep his hands from holy things,
> And from blasphemy stand apart—
> Else the crackling blast of heaven   30
> Blows on his head, and on his desperate heart;
> Though fools will honor impious men,
> In their cities no tragic poet sings.

Antistrophe 2

> Shall we lose faith in Delphi's obscurities,
> We who have heard the world's core   35
> Discredited, and the sacred wood
> Of Zeus at Elis praised no more?
> The deeds and the strange prophecies
> Must make a pattern yet to be understood.
> Zeus, if indeed you are a lord of all,   40
> Throned in light over night and day,
> Mirror this in your endless mind:
> Our masters call the oracle
> Words on the wind, and the Delphic vision blind!
> Their hearts no longer know Apollo,   45
> And reverence for the gods has died away.

SCENE III

Enter Iocastê.

IOCASTÊ. Prince of Thebes, it has occurred to me
    To visit the altars of the gods, bearing
    These branches as a suppliant, and this incense.
    Our King is not himself: his noble soul

Is overwrought with fantasies of dread,   5
Else he would consider
The new prophecies in the light of the old.
He will listen to any voice that speaks disaster,
And my advice goes for nothing.

She approaches the altar, right.

                    To you, then, Apollo,
Lycean° lord, since you are nearest, I turn in prayer.   10
Receive these offerings, and grant us deliverance
From defilement. Our hearts are heavy with fear
When we see our leaders distracted, as helpless sailors
Are terrified by the confusion of their helmsman.

Enter Messenger.

MESSENGER. Friends, no doubt you can direct me: 15
    Where shall I find the house of Oedipus,
    Or, better still, where is the King himself?
CHORAGOS. It is this very place, stranger; he is inside.
    This is his wife and mother of his children.
MESSENGER. I wish her happiness in a happy house,   20
    Blest in all the fulfillment of her marriage.
IOCASTÊ. I wish as much for you: your courtesy
    Deserves a like good fortune. But now, tell me:
    Why have you come? What have you to say to us?
MESSENGER. Good news, my lady, for your house and your husband.   25
IOCASTÊ. What news? Who sent you here?
MESSENGER.   I am from Corinth.°
    The news I bring ought to mean joy for you,
    Though it may be you will find some grief in it.
IOCASTÊ. What is it? How can it touch us in both ways?
MESSENGER. The people of Corinth, they say,   30
    Intend to call Oedipus to be their king.
IOCASTÊ. But old Polybos—is he not reigning still?
MESSENGER. No. Death holds him in his sepulchre.
IOCASTÊ. What are you saying? Polybos is dead?
MESSENGER. If I am not telling the truth, may I die myself.   35
IOCASTÊ [*to a Maidservant*]. Go in, go quickly; tell this to your master.

O riddlers of God's will, where are you now!
    This was the man whom Oedipus, long ago,
    Feared so, fled so, in dread of destroying him—
    But it was another fate by which he died.   40

Enter Oedipus, center.

OEDIPUS. Dearest Iocastê, why have you sent for me?
IOCASTÊ. Listen to what this man says, and then tell me

SCENE III. 10 *Lycean:* Lyceaus was the surname for Zeus.   26 *Corinth:* another city-state of Greece.

What has become of the solemn prophecies.

OEDIPUS. Who is this man? What is his news for me?

IOCASTÊ. He has come from Corinth to announce your father's death! 45

OEDIPUS. Is it true, stranger? Tell me in your own words.

MESSENGER. I cannot say it more clearly: the King is dead.

OEDIPUS. Was it by treason? Or by an attack of illness?

MESSENGER. A little thing brings old men to their rest.

OEDIPUS. It was sickness, then?

MESSENGER.   Yes and his many years. 50

OEDIPUS. Ah!

    Why should a man respect the Pythian hearth,° or

    Give heed to the birds that jangle above his head?

    They prophesied that I should kill Polybos,

    Kill my own father; but he is dead and buried, 55

    And I am here—I never touched him, never,

    Unless he died in grief for my departure,

    And thus, in a sense, through me. No. Polybos

    Has packed the oracles off with him underground.

    They are empty words.

IOCASTÊ.   Had I not told you so? 60

OEDIPUS. You had; it was my faint heart that betrayed me.

IOCASTÊ. From now on never think of those things again.

OEDIPUS. And yet—must I not fear my mother's bed?

IOCASTÊ. Why should anyone in this world be afraid,

    Since Fate rules us and nothing can be foreseen? 65

    A man should live only for the present day.

    Have no more fear of sleeping with your mother:

    How many men, in dreams, have lain with their mothers!

    No reasonable man is troubled by such things.

OEDIPUS. That is true, only— 70

    If only my mother were not still alive!

    But she is alive. I cannot help my dread.

IOCASTÊ. Yet this news of your father's death is wonderful.

OEDIPUS. Wonderful. But I fear the living woman.

MESSENGER. Tell me, who is this woman that you fear? 75

OEDIPUS. It is Meropê, man; the wife of King Polybos.

MESSENGER. Meropê? Why should you be afraid of her?

OEDIPUS. An oracle of the gods, a dreadful saying.

MESSENGER. Can you tell me about it or are you sworn to silence?

OEDIPUS. I can tell you, and I will. 80

    Apollo said through his prophet that I was the man

    Who should marry his own mother, shed his father's blood

    With his own hands. And so, for all these years

    I have kept clear of Corinth, and no harm has come—

    Though it would have been sweet to see my parents again. 85

MESSENGER. And is this the fear that drove you out of Corinth?

---

52 *Pythian hearth:* the python, a giant serpent, guarded the Oracle at Delphi.

OEDIPUS. Would you have me kill my father?

MESSENGER.   As for that
　　You must be reassured by the news I gave you.

OEDIPUS. If you could reassure me, I would reward you.

MESSENGER. I had that in mind, I will confess: I thought   90
　　I could count on you when you returned to Corinth.

OEDIPUS. No: I will never go near my parents again.

MESSENGER. Ah, son, you still do not know what you are doing—

OEDIPUS. What do you mean? In the name of God tell me!

MESSENGER. —If these are the reasons for not going home.   95

OEDIPUS. I tell you, I fear the oracle may come true.

MESSENGER. And guilt may come upon you through your parents?

OEDIPUS. That is the dread that is always in my heart.

MESSENGER. Can you not see that all your fears are groundless?

OEDIPUS. How can you say that? They are my parents, surely?   100

MESSENGER. Polybos was not your father.

OEDIPUS.   Not my father?

MESSENGER. No more your father than the man speaking to you.

OEDIPUS. But you are nothing to me!

MESSENGER.   Neither was he.

OEDIPUS. Then why did he call me son?

MESSENGER.   I will tell you:
　　Long ago he had you from my hands, as a gift.   105

OEDIPUS. Then how could he love me so, if I was not his?

MESSENGER. He had no children, and his heart turned to you.

OEDIPUS. What of you? Did you buy me? Did you find me by chance?

MESSENGER. I came upon you in the crooked pass of Kithairon.

OEDIPUS. And what were you doing there?

MESSENGER.   Tending my flocks.   110

OEDIPUS. A wandering shepherd?

MESSENGER.   But your savior, son, that day.

OEDIPUS. From what did you save me?

MESSENGER.   Your ankles should tell you that.

OEDIPUS. Ah, stranger, why do you speak of that childhood pain?

MESSENGER. I cut the bonds that tied your ankles together.

OEDIPUS. I have had the mark as long as I can remember.   115

MESSENGER. That was why you were given the name you bear.°

OEDIPUS. God! Was it my father or my mother who did it?
　　Tell me!

MESSENGER. I do not know. The man who gave you to me
　　Can tell you better than I.   120

OEDIPUS. It was not you that found me, but another?

MESSENGER. It was another shepherd gave you to me.

OEDIPUS. Who was he? Can you tell me who he was?

MESSENGER. I think he was said to be one of Laïos' people.

OEDIPUS. You mean the Laïos who was king here years ago?   125

MESSENGER. Yes; King Laïos; and the man was one of his herdsmen.

---

116 *name you bear:* Oedipus in Greek means "swollen foot."

OEDIPUS. Is he still alive? Can I see him?
MESSENGER.   These men here
    Know best about such things.
OEDIPUS.   Does anyone here
    Know this shepherd that he is talking about?
    Have you seen him in the fields, or in the town?   130
    If you have, tell me. It is time things were made plain.
CHORAGOS. I think the man he means is that same shepherd
    You have already asked to see. Iocastê perhaps
    Could tell you something.
OEDIPUS.   Do you know anything
    About him, Lady? Is he the man we have summoned?   135
    Is that the man this shepherd means?
IOCASTÊ.   Why think of him?
    Forget this herdsman. Forget it all.
    This talk is a waste of time.
OEDIPUS.   How can you say that,
    When the clues to my true birth are in my hands?
IOCASTÊ. For God's love, let us have no more questioning!   140
    Is your life nothing to you?
    My own is pain enough for me to bear.
OEDIPUS. You need not worry. Suppose my mother a slave,
    And born of slaves; no baseness can touch you.
IOCASTÊ. Listen to me, I beg you: do not do this thing!   145
OEDIPUS. I will not listen; the truth must be made known.
IOCASTÊ. Everything that I say is for your own good!
OEDIPUS. My own good
    Snaps my patience, then: I want none of it.
IOCASTÊ. You are fatally wrong! May you never learn who you are!
OEDIPUS. Go, one of you, and bring the shepherd here.   150
    Let us leave this woman to brag of her royal name.
IOCASTÊ. Ah, miserable!
    That is the only word I have for you now.
    That is the only word I can ever have.

                    Exit into the palace.

CHORAGOS. Why has she left us, Oedipus? Why has she gone   155
    In such a passion of sorrow? I fear this silence:
    Something dreadful may come of it.
OEDIPUS.   Let it come!
    However base my birth, I must know about it.
    The Queen, like a woman, is perhaps ashamed
    To think of my low origin. But I   160
    Am a child of luck; I cannot be dishonored,
    Luck is my mother; the passing months, my brothers,
    Have seen me rich and poor.
                              If this is so,
    How could I wish that I were someone else?
    How could I not be glad to know my birth?   165

Oedipus Rex   **1041**

ODE III

Strophe

CHORUS. If ever the coming time were known
　　To my heart's pondering,
　　Kithairon, now by Heaven I see the torches
　　At the festival of the next full moon,
　　And see the dance, and hear the choir sing　　　　　　　5
　　A grace to your gentle shade:
　　Mountain where Oedipus was found,
　　O mountain guard of a noble race!
　　May the god who heals us lend us his aid,
　　And let that glory come to pass　　　　　　　　　　10
　　For our king's cradling-ground.

Antistrophe

　　Of the nymphs that flower beyond the years,
　　Who bore you, royal child,
　　To Pan° of the hills or the timberline Apollo,
　　Cold in delight where the upland clears,　　　　　　　15
　　Or Hermês° for whom Kyllenê's° heights are piled?
　　Or flushed as evening cloud,
　　Great Dionysos, roamer of mountains,
　　He—was it he who found you there,
　　And caught you up in his own proud　　　　　　　　　20
　　Arms from the sweet god-ravisher
　　Who laughed by the Muses' fountains?

SCENE IV

OEDIPUS. Sirs: though I do not know the man,
　　I think I see him coming, this shepherd we want:
　　He is old, like our friend here, and the men
　　Bringing him seem to be servants of my house.
　　But you can tell, if you have ever seen him.　　　　　　5

Enter Shepherd escorted by servants.

CHORAGOS. I know him, he was Laïos' man. You can trust him.
OEDIPUS. Tell me first, you from Corinth: is this the shepherd
　　We were discussing?
MESSENGER. 　　　　　　This is the very man.
OEDIPUS [*to Shepherd*]. Come here. No, look at me. You must answer
　　Everything I ask.—You belonged to Laïos?　　　　　　10
SHEPHERD. Yes: born his slave, brought up in his house.
OEDIPUS. Tell me: what kind of work did you do for him?
SHEPHERD. I was a shepherd of his, most of my life.
OEDIPUS. Where mainly did you go for pasturage?
SHEPHERD. Sometimes Kithairon, sometimes the hills near-by.　　15
OEDIPUS. Do you remember ever seeing this man out there?

ODE III. 14 *Pan:* son of Hermês and god of shepherds.　16 *Hermês:* messenger of the gods; *Kyllenê:* sacred mountain, Hermês' birthplace.

SHEPHERD. What would he be doing there? This man?

OEDIPUS. This man standing here. Have you ever seen him before?

SHEPHERD. No. At least, not to my recollection.

MESSENGER. And that is not strange, my lord. But I'll refresh   20
    His memory: he must remember when we two
    Spent three whole seasons together, March to September,
    On Kithairon or thereabouts. He had two flocks;
    I had one. Each autumn I'd drive mine home
    And he would go back with his to Laïos' sheepfold.—   25
    Is this not true, just as I have described it?

SHEPHERD. True, yes; but it was all so long ago.

MESSENGER. Well, then: do you remember, back in those days
    That you gave me a baby boy to bring up as my own?

SHEPHERD. What if I did? What are you trying to say?   30

MESSENGER. King Oedipus was once that little child.

SHEPHERD. Damn you, hold your tongue!

OEDIPUS.   No more of that!
    It is your tongue that needs watching, not this man's.

SHEPHERD. My King, my Master, what is it I have done wrong?

OEDIPUS. You have not answered his question about the boy.   35

SHEPHERD. He does not know . . . He is only making trouble . . .

OEDIPUS. Come, speak plainly, or it will go hard with you.

SHEPHERD. In God's name, do not torture an old man!

OEDIPUS. Come here, one of you; bind his arms behind him.

SHEPHERD. Unhappy king! What more do you wish to learn?   40

OEDIPUS. Did you give this man the child he speaks of?

SHEPHERD.   I did.
    And I would to God I had died that very day.

OEDIPUS. You will die now unless you speak the truth.

SHEPHERD. Yet if I speak the truth, I am worse than dead.

OEDIPUS. Very well; since you insist upon delaying—   45

SHEPHERD. No! I have told you already that I gave him the boy.

OEDIPUS. Where did you get him? From your house? From somewhere else?

SHEPHERD. Not from mine, no. A man gave him to me.

OEDIPUS. Is that man here? Do you know whose slave he was?

SHEPHERD. For God's love, my King, do not ask me any more!   50

OEDIPUS. You are a dead man if I have to ask you again.

SHEPHERD. Then . . . Then the child was from the palace of Laïos.

OEDIPUS. A slave child? or a child of his own line?

SHEPHERD. Ah, I am on the brink of dreadful speech!

OEDIPUS. And I of dreadful hearing. Yet I must hear.   55

SHEPHERD. If you must be told, then . . .
                         They said it was Laïos' child,
    But it is your wife who can tell you about that.

OEDIPUS. My wife!—Did she give it to you?

SHEPHERD.   My lord, she did.

OEDIPUS. Do you know why?

SHEPHERD.   I was told to get rid of it.

OEDIPUS. An unspeakable mother!

SHEPHERD.   There had been prophecies . . .   60

OEDIPUS. Tell me.

SHEPHERD.   It was said that the boy would kill his own father.

OEDIPUS. Then why did you give him over to this old man?

SHEPHERD. I pitied the baby, my King.

And I thought that this man would take him far away

To his own country.

                        He saved him—but for what a fate!   65

For if you are what this man says you are,

No man living is more wretched than Oedipus.

OEDIPUS. Ah God!

It was true!

                All the prophecies!

                                —Now,

O Light, may I look on you for the last time!   70

I, Oedipus,

Oedipus, damned in his birth, in his marriage damned,

Damned in the blood he shed with his own hand!

He rushes into the palace.

ODE IV

Strophe I

CHORUS. Alas for the seed of men.

What measure shall I give these generations

That breathe on the void and are void

And exist and do not exist?

Who bears more weight of joy   5

Than mass of sunlight shifting in images,

Or who shall make his thought stay on

That down time drifts away?

Your splendor is all fallen.

O naked brow of wrath and tears,   10

O change of Oedipus!

I who saw your days call no man blest—

Your great days like ghósts góne.

Antistrophe 1

That mind was a strong bow.

Deep, how deep you drew it then, hard archer,   15

At a dim fearful range,

And brought dear glory down!

You overcame the stranger—

The virgin with her hooking lion claws—

And though death sang, stood like a tower   20

To make pale Thebes take heart.

Fortress against our sorrow!

Divine king, giver of laws,
Majestic Oedipus!
No prince in Thebes had ever such renown,
No prince won such grace of power.

Strophe 2

And now of all men ever known
Most pitiful is this man's story:
His fortunes are most changed, his state
Fallen to a low slave's
Ground under bitter fate.

O Oedipus, most royal one!
The great door that expelled you to the light
Gave at night—ah, gave night to your glory:
As to the father, to the fathering son.

All understood too late.

How could that Queen whom Laïos won,
The garden that he harrowed at his height,
Be silent when that act was done?

Antistrophe 2

But all eyes fail before time's eye.
All actions come to justice there.
Though never willed, though far down the deep past,
Your bed, your dread sirings,
Are brought to book at last.
Child by Laïos doomed to die,
Then doomed to lose that fortunate little death,
Would God you never took breath in this air
That with my wailing lips I take to cry:

For I weep the world's outcast.

I was blind, and now I can tell why:
Asleep, for you had given ease of breath
To Thebes, while the false years went by.

EXODOS

Enter, from the palace, Second messenger.

SECOND MESSENGER. Elders of Thebes, most honored in this land,
What horrors are yours to see and hear, what weight
Of sorrow to be endured, if, true to your birth,
You venerate the line of Labdakos!
I think neither Istros nor Phasis, those great rivers,
Could purify this place of the corruption
It shelters now, or soon must bring to light—

25

30

35

40

45

50

5

Evil not done unconsciously, but willed.

The greatest griefs are those we cause ourselves.

CHORAGOS. Surely, friend, we have grief enough already: 10
What new sorrow do you mean?

SECOND MESSENGER.   The Queen is dead.

CHORAGOS. Iocastê? Dead? But at whose hand?

SECOND MESSENGER.   Her own.
The full horror of what happened you cannot know,
For you did not see it; but I, who did, will tell you
As clearly as I can how she met her death.   15

When she had left us,
In passionate silence, passing through the court,
She ran to her apartment in the house,
Her hair clutched by the fingers of both hands.
She closed the doors behind her; then, by that bed   20
Where long ago the fatal son was conceived—
That son who should bring about his father's death—
We heard her call upon Laïos, dead so many years,
And heard her wail for the double fruit of her marriage,
A husband by her husband, children by her child.   25

Exactly how she died I do not know:
For Oedipus burst in moaning and would not let us
Keep vigil to the end; it was by him
As he stormed about the room that our eyes were caught.
From one to another of us he went, begging a sword,   30
Cursing the wife who was not his wife, the mother
Whose womb had carried his own children and himself.
I do not know: it was none of us aided him,
But surely one of the gods was in control!   35
For with a dreadful cry
He hurled his weight, as though wrenched out of himself,
At the twin doors: the bolts gave, and he rushed in.
And there he saw her hanging, her body swaying
From the cruel cord she had noosed about her neck.
A great sob broke from him heartbreaking to hear,   40
As he loosed the rope and lowered her to the ground.

I would blot out from my mind what happened next!
For the King ripped from her gown the golden brooches
That were her ornament, and raised them, and plunged them down
Straight into his own eyeballs, crying, "No more,   45
No more shall you look on the misery about me,
The horrors of my own doing! Too long you have known
The faces of those whom I should never have seen,
Too long been blind to those for whom I was searching!
From this hour, go in darkness!" And as he spoke,   50
He struck at his eyes—not once, but many times;

And the blood spattered his beard,
Bursting from his ruined sockets like red hail.

So from the unhappiness of two this evil has sprung,
A curse on the man and woman alike. The old   55
Happiness of the house of Labdakos
Was happiness enough: where is it today?
It is all wailing and ruin, disgrace, death—all
The misery of mankind that has a name—
And it is wholly and for ever theirs.   60

CHORAGOS. Is he in agony still? Is there no rest for him?
SECOND MESSENGER. He is calling for someone to lead him to the gates
So that all the children of Kadmos may look upon
His father's murderer, his mother's—no,
I cannot say it!
　　　　　　　And then he will leave Thebes,   65
Self-exiled, in order that the curse
Which he himself pronounced may depart from the house.
He is weak, and there is none to lead him,
So terrible is his suffering.
　　　　　　　　　　　But you will see:
Look, the doors are opening; in a moment   70
You will see a thing that would crush a heart of stone.

　　　　The central door is opened; Oedipus, blinded, is led in.

CHORAGOS. Dreadful indeed for men to see.
Never have my own eyes
Looked on a sight so full of fear.

Oedipus!   75
What madness came upon you, what daemon
Leaped on your life with heavier
Punishment than a mortal man can bear?
No: I cannot even
Look at you, poor ruined one.   80
And I would speak, question, ponder,
If I were able. No.
You make me shudder.
OEDIPUS. God. God.
Is there a sorrow greater?   85
Where shall I find harbor in this world?
My voice is hurled far on a dark wind.
What has God done to me?
CHORAGOS. Too terrible to think of, or to see.

Strophe 1
OEDIPUS. O cloud of night,   90
Never to be turned away: night coming on,
I cannot tell how: night like a shroud!

My fair winds brought me here.
                                        Oh God. Again
The pain of the spikes where I had sight,
The flooding pain   95
Of memory, never to be gouged out.
CHORAGOS. This is not strange.
    You suffer it all twice over, remorse in pain,
    Pain in remorse.

Antistrophe 1
OEDIPUS. Ah dear friend   100
    Are you faithful even yet, you alone?
    Are you still standing near me, will you stay here,
    Patient, to care for the blind?
                                        The blind man!
    Yet even blind I know who it is attends me,
    By the voice's tone—   105
    Though my new darkness hide the comforter.
CHORAGOS. Oh fearful act!
    What god was it drove you to rake black
    Night across your eyes?

Strophe 2
OEDIPUS. Apollo. Apollo. Dear   110
    Children, the god was Apollo.
    He brought my sick, sick fate upon me.
    But the blinding hand was my own!
    How could I bear to see
    When all my sight was horror everywhere?   115
CHORAGOS. Everywhere; that is true.
OEDIPUS. And now what is left?
    Images? Love? A greeting even.
    Sweet to the senses? Is there anything?
    Ah, no, friends: lead me away.   120
    Lead me away from Thebes.
                                        Lead the great wreck
    And hell of Oedipus, whom the gods hate.
CHORAGOS. Your fate is clear, you are not blind to that.
    Would God you had never found it out!

Antistrophe 2
OEDIPUS. Death take the man who unbound   125
    My feet on that hillside
    And delivered me from death to life! What life?
    If only I had died,
    This weight of monstrous doom
    Could not have dragged me and my darlings down.   130
CHORAGOS. I would have wished the same.

OEDIPUS. Oh never to have come here
     With my father's blood upon me! Never
     To have been the man they call his mother's husband!
     Oh accurst! Oh child of evil,   135
     To have entered that wretched bed—
                              the selfsame one!
     More primal than sin itself, this fell to me.
CHORAGOS. I do not know how I can answer you.
     You were better dead than alive and blind.
OEDIPUS. Do not counsel me any more. This punishment   140
     That I have laid upon myself is just.
     If I had eyes,
     I do not know how I could bear the sight
     Of my father, when I came to the house of Death,
     Or my mother: for I have sinned against them both   145
     So vilely that I could not make my peace
     By strangling my own life.
                         Or do you think my children,
     Born as they were born, would be sweet to my eyes?
     Ah never, never! Nor this town with its high walls,
     Nor the holy images of the gods.
                         For I,   150
     Thrice miserable—Oedipus, noblest of all the line
     Of Kadmos, have condemned myself to enjoy
     These things no more, by my own malediction°
     Expelling that man whom the gods declared
     To be a defilement in the house of Laïos.   155
     After exposing the rankness of my own guilt,
     How could I look men frankly in the eyes?
     No, I swear it,
     If I could have stifled my hearing at its source,
     I would have done it and made all this body   160
     A tight cell of misery, blank to light and sound:
     So I should have been safe in a dark agony
     Beyond all recollection.
                         Ah Kithairon!
     Why did you shelter me? When I was cast upon you,
     Why did I not die? Then I should never   165
     Have shown the world my execrable birth.

     Ah Polybos! Corinth, city that I believed
     The ancient seat of my ancestor: how fair
     I seemed, your child! And all the while this evil
     Was cancerous within me!
                         For I am sick   170
     In my daily life, sick in my origin.

---

153 *malediction:* curse.

O three roads, dark ravine, woodland and way
Where three roads met you, drinking my father's blood,
My own blood, spilled by my own hand: can you remember
The unspeakable things I did there, and the things   175
I went on from there to do?
                                        O marriage, marriage!
The act that engendered me, and again the act
Performed by the son in the same bed—
                                        Ah, the net
Of incest, mingling fathers, brothers, sons
With brides, wives, mothers: the last evil   180
That can be known to men: no tongue can say
How evil!
                No. For the love of God, conceal me
Somewhere far from Thebes; or kill me; or hurl me
Into the sea, away from men's eyes for ever.
Come, lead me. You need not fear to touch me.   185
Of all men, I alone can bear this guilt.

Enter Creon.

CHORAGOS. We are not the ones to decide; but Creon here
    May fitly judge of what you ask. He only
    Is left to protect the city in your place.
OEDIPUS. Alas, how can I speak to him? What right have I   190
    To beg his courtesy whom I have deeply wronged?
CREON. I have not come to mock you, Oedipus,
    Or to reproach you, either.

To Attendants.

                                —You, standing there:
    If you have lost all respect for man's dignity,
    At least respect the flame of Lord Helios: 195
    Do not allow this pollution to show itself
    Openly here, an affront to the earth
    And Heaven's rain and the light of day. No, take him
    Into the house as quickly as you can.
    For it is proper   200
    That only the close kindred see his grief.
OEDIPUS. I pray you in God's name, since your courtesy
    Ignores my dark expectation, visiting
    With mercy this man of all men most execrable:
    Give me what I ask—for your good, not for mine.   205
CREON. And what is it that you would have me do?
OEDIPUS. Drive me out of this country as quickly as may be
    To a place where no human voice can ever greet me.
CREON. I should have done that before now—only,
    God's will had not been wholly revealed to me.   210

OEDIPUS. But his command is plain: the parricide°
    Must be destroyed. I am that evil man.
CREON. That is the sense of it, yes; but as things are,
    We had best discover clearly what is to be done.
OEDIPUS. You would learn more about a man like me?   215
CREON. You are ready now to listen to the god.
OEDIPUS. I will listen. But it is to you
    That I must turn for help. I beg you, hear me.

The woman in there—
Give her whatever funeral you think proper: 220
She is your sister.
            —But let me go, Creon!
Let me purge my father's Thebes of the pollution
Of my living here, and go out to the wild hills,
To Kithairon, that has won such fame with me,
The tomb my mother and father appointed for me,   225
And let me die there, as they willed I should.
And yet I know
Death will not ever come to me through sickness
Or in any natural way: I have been preserved
For some unthinkable fate. But let that be.   230
As for my sons, you need not care for them.
They are men, they will find some way to live.
But my poor daughters, who have shared my table,
 Who never before have been parted from their father—
Take care of them, Creon; do this for me.   235
And will you let me touch them with my hands
A last time, and let us weep together?
Be kind, my lord,
Great prince, be kind!
           Could I but touch them,
They would be mine again, as when I had my eyes.   240

       Enter Antigonê and Ismenê, attended.

Ah, God!
Is it my dearest children I hear weeping?
Has Creon pitied me and sent my daughters?
CREON. Yes, Oedipus: I knew that they were dear to you
    In the old days, and know you must love them still.   245
OEDIPUS. May God bless you for this—and be a friendlier
    Guardian to you than he has been to me!

Children, where are you?
Come quickly to my hands: they are your brother's—
Hands that have brought your father's once clear eyes   250

---

211 *parricide:* one who kills his or her father.

To this way of seeing—
                    Ah dearest ones,
I had neither sight nor knowledge then, your father
By the woman who was the source of his own life!
And I weep for you—having no strength to see you—,
I weep for you when I think of the bitterness   255
That men will visit upon you all your lives.
What homes, what festivals can you attend
Without being forced to depart again in tears?
And when you come to marriageable age,
Where is the man, my daughters, who would dare   260
Risk the bane° that lies on all my children?
Is there any evil wanting? Your father killed
His father; sowed the womb of her who bore him;
Engendered you at the fount of his own existence!
That is what they will say of you.
                         Then, whom   265
Can you ever marry? There are no bridegrooms for you,
And your lives must wither away in sterile dreaming.
O Creon, son of Menoikeus!
You are the only father my daughters have,
Since we, their parents, are both of us gone for ever.   270
They are your own blood: you will not let them
Fall into beggary and loneliness;
You will keep them from the miseries that are mine!
Take pity on them; see, they are only children,
Friendless except for you. Promise me this,   275
Great Prince, and give me your hand in token of it.

                Creon clasps his right hand.

Children:
I could say much, if you could understand me;
But as it is, I have only this prayer for you:
Live where you can, be as happy as you can—   280
Happier, please God, than God has made your father!
CREON. Enough. You have wept enough. Now go within.
OEDIPUS. I must; but it is hard.
CREON.   Time eases all things.
OEDIPUS. But you must promise—
CREON.   Say what you desire.
OEDIPUS. Send me from Thebes!
CREON.   God grant that I may!   285
OEDIPUS. But since God hates me . . .
CREON.   No, he will grant your wish.
OEDIPUS. You promise?
CREON.   I cannot speak beyond my knowledge.
OEDIPUS. Then lead me in.

---

261 *bane:* curse.

CREON.   Come now, and leave your children.

OEDIPUS. No! Do not take them from me!

CREON.   Think no longer

That you are in command here, but rather think   290
How, when you were, you served your own destruction.

*Exeunt into the house all but the Chorus; the Choragos chants directly to
the audience.*

CHORAGOS. Men of Thebes: look upon Oedipus.
This is the king who solved the famous riddle
And towered up, most powerful of men.
No mortal eyes but looked on him with envy   295
Yet in the end ruin swept over him.
Let every man in mankind's frailty
Consider his last day; and let none
Presume on his good fortune until he find
Life, at his death, a memory without pain.   300

QUESTIONS

1. What is the situation in Thebes as the play begins? How do we learn of it?

2. What is our first impression of Oedipus? Are we given any evidence of *hubris*, the sin of pride?

3. What is Oedipus's proclamation to his fellow Thebans and how does it prove to be his own eventual ruin?

4. Outline the stages whereby Oedipus comes to understand the truth of his situation.

5. Discuss the function of Teiresias. How does Oedipus react to his words? Why does he suspect Creon?

6. What is Creon's defense? How does he argue his innocence?

7. How does Iocastê's progress toward understanding parallel that of Oedipus's?

8. How does the chorus function in the play? Compare the perspectives offered by the chorus to those offered by the main players.

9. How does Sophocles create a moment of reversal, raising the hopes of the protagonist and the audience? What is the dramatic function of such a reversal?

10. How does Oedipus manifest nobility once he fully understands his situation?

11. Is there any symbolic function to Oedipus's self-blinding? Discuss how this might deepen the thematic power of the play.

12. Describe the effect of the play, the source of its power. How would the whole effect be different if the prophetic elements were removed—if the discoveries were made without any reference to fate?

ANTIGONÊ

*English Version
by Dudley Fitts and Robert Fitzgerald*

PERSONS REPRESENTED

ANTIGONÊ }
ISMENÊ   } daughters of Oedipus, former King of Thebes
EURYDICE, Queen of Thebes, wife of Creon

CREON, King of Thebes
HAIMON, Creon's son
TEIRESIAS, blind prophet
A SENTRY
A MESSENGER
CHORUS

SCENE

Before the palace of Creon, King of Thebes. A central double door, and two lateral doors. A platform extends the length of the facade, and from this platform three steps lead down into the "orchestra," or chorus-ground. TIME: *dawn of the day after the repulse of the Argive army from the assault on Thebes.*

PROLOGUE

Antigonê and Ismenê enter from the central door of the Palace.

ANTIGONÊ. Ismenê, dear sister,
        You would think that we had already suffered enough
        For the curse on Oedipus.°
        I cannot imagine any grief
        That you and I have not gone through. And now—   5
        Have they told you of the new decree of our King Creon?
ISMENÊ. I have heard nothing: I know
        That two sisters lost two brothers, a double death
        In a single hour; and I know that the Argive army
        Fled in the night; but beyond this, nothing.   10
ANTIGONÊ. I thought so. And that is why I wanted you
        To come out here with me. There is something we must do.
ISMENÊ. Why do you speak so strangely?
ANTIGONÊ. Listen, Ismenê:
        Creon buried our brother Eteoclês   15
        With military honors, gave him a soldier's funeral,
        And it was right that he should; but Polyneicês,
        Who fought as bravely and died as miserably,—
        They say that Creon has sworn
        No one shall bury him, no one mourn for him,   20
        But his body must lie in the fields, a sweet treasure
        For carrion birds to find as they search for food.
        That is what they say, and our good Creon is coming here
        To announce it publicly; and the penalty—
        Stoning to death in the public square!
                                        There it is,   25
        And now you can prove what you are:
        A true sister, or a traitor to your family.
ISMENÊ. Antigonê, you are mad! What could I possibly do?
ANTIGONÊ. You must decide whether you will help me or not.

PROLOGUE. 3 *Oedipus:* Son of Laïos and Iocastê, King of Thebes who fulfilled the prophecy that he would slay his father and marry his mother. His tragedy is set out in *Oedipus Rex.* Oedipus was the father of Antigonê and Ismenê.

ISMENÊ. I do not understand you. Help you in what?
ANTIGONÊ. Ismenê, I am going to bury him. Will you come?
ISMENÊ. Bury him! You have just said the new law forbids it.
ANTIGONÊ. He is my brother. And he is your brother, too.
ISMENÊ. But think of the danger! Think what Creon will do!
ANTIGONÊ. Creon is not strong enough to stand in my way.
ISMENÊ. Ah sister!

    Oedipus died, everyone hating him
For what his own search brought to light, his eyes
Ripped out by his own hand; and Iocastê died,
His mother and wife at once: she twisted the cords
That strangled her life; and our two brothers died,
Each killed by the other's sword. And we are left:
But oh, Antigonê,
Think how much more terrible than these
Our own death would be if we should go against Creon
And do what he has forbidden! We are only women,
We cannot fight with men, Antigonê!
The law is strong, we must give in to the law
In this thing, and in worse. I beg the Dead
To forgive me, but I am helpless: I must yield
To those in authority. And I think it is dangerous business
To be always meddling.

ANTIGONÊ.   If that is what you think,
I should not want you, even if you asked to come.
You have made your choice, you can be what you want to be.
But I will bury him; and if I must die,
I say that this crime is holy: I shall lie down
With him in death, and I shall be as dear
To him as he to me.

                  It is the dead,
Not the living who make the longest demands:
We die for ever . . .

                You may do as you like,
Since apparently the laws of the gods mean nothing to you.
ISMENÊ. They mean a great deal to me; but I have no strength
To break laws that were made for the public good.
ANTIGONÊ. That must be your excuse, I suppose. But as for me,
I will bury the brother I love.
ISMENÊ.   Antigonê,
I am so afraid for you!
ANTIGONÊ.   You need not be:
You have yourself to consider, after all.
ISMENÊ. But no one must hear of this, you must tell no one!
I will keep it a secret, I promise!
ANTIGONÊ.   O tell it! Tell everyone!
Think how they'll hate you when it all comes out
If they learn that you knew about it all the time!
ISMENÊ. So fiery! You should be cold with fear.

ANTIGONÊ. Perhaps. But I am doing only what I must.

ISMENÊ. But can you do it? I say that you cannot.

ANTIGONÊ. Very well: when my strength gives out,
    I shall do no more. 75

ISMENÊ. Impossible things should not be tried at all.

ANTIGONÊ. Go away, Ismenê:
    I shall be hating you soon, and the dead will too,
    For your words are hateful. Leave me my foolish plan:
    I am not afraid of the danger; if it means death, 80
    It will not be the worst of deaths—death without honor.

ISMENÊ. Go then, if you feel that you must.
    You are unwise,
    But a loyal friend indeed to those who love you.

       Exit into the palace. Antigonê goes off, left. Enter the Chorus.

PÁRADOS
Strophe 1

CHORUS. Now the long blade of the sun, lying
    Level east to west, touches with glory
    Thebes of the Seven Gates. Open, unlidded
    Eye of golden day! O marching light
    Across the eddy and rush of Dircê's stream,° 5
    Striking the white shields of the enemy
    Thrown headlong backward from the blaze of morning!

CHORAGOS. Polyneicês their commander
    Roused them with windy phrases,
    He the wild eagle screaming 10
    Insults above our land,
    His wings their shields of snow,
    His crest their marshalled helms.°

Antistrophe 1

CHORUS. Against our seven gates in a yawning ring
    The famished spears came onward in the night; 15
    But before his jaws were sated with our blood,
    Or pinefire took the garland of our towers,
    He was thrown back; and as he turned, great Thebes—
    No tender victim for his noisy power—
    Rose like a dragon behind him, shouting war. 20

CHORAGOS. For God hates utterly
    The bray of bragging tongues;
    And when he beheld their smiling,
    Their swagger of golden helms,
    The frown of his thunder blasted 25
    Their first man from our walls.

PARADOS. 5 *Dircê:* a spring near Thebes. 13 *helms:* helmets (archaic).

Strophe 2

CHORUS. We heard his shout of triumph high in the air
    Turn to a scream; far out in a flaming arc
    He fell with his windy torch, and the earth struck him.
    And others storming in fury no less than his   30
    Found shock of death in the dusty joy of battle.

CHORAGOS. Seven captains at seven gates
    Yielded their clanging arms to the god
    That bends the battle-line and breaks it.
    These two only, brothers in blood,   35
    Face to face in matchless rage,
    Mirroring each the other's death,
    Clashed in long combat.

Antistrophe 2

CHORUS. But now in the beautiful morning of victory
    Let Thebes of the many chariots sing for joy!   40
    With hearts for dancing we'll take leave of war:
    Our temples shall be sweet with hymns of praise,
    And the long nights shall echo with our chorus.

SCENE I

CHORAGOS. But now at last our new King is coming:
    Creon of Thebes, Menoikeus'° son.
    In this auspicious dawn of his reign
    What are the new complexities
    That shifting Fate has woven for him?   5
    What is his counsel? Why has he summoned
    The old men to hear him?

Enter Creon from the palace, center. He addresses the Chorus from the top step.

CREON. Gentlemen: I have the honor to inform you that our Ship of State,
    which recent storms have threatened to destroy, has come safely to harbor
    at last, guided by the merciful wisdom of Heaven. I have summoned you   10
    here this morning because I know that I can depend upon you: your
    devotion to King Laïos° was absolute; you never hesitated in your duty to
    our late ruler Oedipus; and when Oedipus died, your loyalty was trans-
    ferred to his children. Unfortunately, as you know, his two sons, the
    princes Eteoclês and Polyneicês, have killed each other in battle; and I, as   15
    the next in blood, have succeeded to the full power of the throne.

        I am aware, of course, that no Ruler can expect complete loyalty from
    his subjects until he has been tested in office. Nevertheless, I say to you at
    the very outset that I have nothing but contempt for the kind of Governor
    who is afraid, for whatever reason, to follow the course that he knows is   20
    best for the State; and as for the man who sets private friendship above
    the public welfare,—I have no use for him, either. I call God to witness
    that if I saw my country headed for ruin, I should not be afraid to speak

---

SCENE I. 2 *Menoikeus:* father of Creon and Iocastê.   12 *Laïos:* father of Oedipus.

out plainly; and I need hardly remind you that I would never have any
dealings with an enemy of the people. No one values friendship more   25
highly than I; but we must remember that friends made at the risk of
wrecking our Ship are not real friends at all.

 These are my principles, at any rate, and that is why I have made the
following decision concerning the sons of Oedipus: Eteoclês, who died as
a man should die, fighting for his country, is to be buried with full military   30
honors, with all the ceremony that is usual when the greatest heroes die;
but his brother Polyneicês, who broke his exile to come back with fire and
sword against his native city and the shrines of his fathers' gods, whose one
idea was to spill the blood of his blood and sell his own people into
slavery—Polyneicês, I say, is to have no burial: no man is to touch him   35
or say the least prayer for him; he shall lie on the plain, unburied; and the
birds and the scavenging dogs can do with him whatever they like.

 This is my command, and you can see the wisdom behind it. As long
as I am King, no traitor is going to be honored with the loyal man. But   40
whoever shows by word and deed that he is on the side of the State,—he
shall have my respect while he is living and my reverence when he is dead.

CHORAGOS. If that is your will, Creon son of Menoikeus,
 You have the right to enforce it: we are yours.   45
CREON. That is my will. Take care that you do your part.
CHORAGOS. We are old men: let the younger ones carry it out.
CREON. I do not mean that: the sentries have been appointed.
CHORAGOS. Then what is it that you would have us do?
CREON. You will give no support to whoever breaks this law.   50
CHORAGOS. Only a crazy man is in love with death!
CREON. And death it is; yet money talks, and the wisest
 Have sometimes been known to count a few coins too many.

Enter Sentry from left.

SENTRY. I'll not say that I'm out of breath from running, King, because every
 time I stopped to think about what I have to tell you, I felt like going   55
 back. And all the time a voice kept saying, "You fool, don't you know
 you're walking straight into trouble?"; and then another voice: "Yes, but
 if you let somebody else get the news to Creon first, it will be even worse
 than that for you!" But good sense won out, at least I hope it was good
 sense, and here I am with a story that makes no sense at all; but I'll tell it   60
 anyhow, because, as they say, what's going to happen's going to happen and—
CREON. Come to the point. What have you to say?
SENTRY. I did not do it. I did not see who did it. You must not punish me for what
 someone else has done.
CREON. A comprehensive defense! More effective, perhaps,   65
 If I knew its purpose. Come: what is it?
SENTRY. A dreadful thing . . . I don't know how to put it—
CREON. Out with it!
SENTRY.   Well, then;
 The dead man—
     Polyneicês—

Pause. The Sentry is overcome, fumbles for words. Creon waits impassively.

out there—
                        someone,—   70
New dust on the slimy flesh!

                    Pause. No sign from Creon.

Someone has given it burial that way, and
Gone . . .

            Long pause. Creon finally speaks with deadly control.

CREON. And the man who dared do this?
SENTRY.   I swear I
    Do not know! You must believe me!   75
      Listen:
    The ground was dry, not a sign of digging, no,
    Not a wheeltrack in the dust, no trace of anyone.
    It was when they relieved us this morning: and one of them
    The corporal, pointed to it.
                        There it was,
    The strangest—
                    Look: 80
    The body, just mounded over with light dust: you see?
    Not buried really, but as if they'd covered it
    Just enough for the ghost's peace. And no sign
    Of dogs or any wild animal that had been there.
    And then what a scene there was! Every man of us   85
    Accusing the other: we all proved the other man did it,
    We all had proof that we could not have done it.
    We were ready to take hot iron in our hands,
    Walk through fire, swear by all the gods,
    It was not I!   90
    I do not know who it was, but it was not I!

*Creon's rage has been mounting steadily, but the Sentry is too intent upon his story
to notice it.*

    And then, when this came to nothing, someone said
    A thing that silenced us and made us stare
    Down at the ground: you had to be told the news,
    And one of us had to do it! We threw the dice,   95
    And the bad luck fell to me. So here I am,
    No happier to be here than you are to have me:
    Nobody likes the man who brings bad news.
CHORAGOS. I have been wondering, King: can it be that the gods have done this?
CREON. [*furiously*] Stop!   100
    Must you doddering wrecks
    Go out of your heads entirely? "The gods"!
    Intolerable!
    The gods favor this corpse? Why? How had he served them?
    Tried to loot their temples, burn their images.   105
    Yes, and the whole State, and its laws with it!
    Is it your senile opinion that the gods love to honor bad men?

Antigonê   **1059**

A pious thought!—

No, from the very beginning
There have been those who have whispered together,
Stiff-necked anarchists, putting their heads together,   110
Scheming against me in alleys. These are the men,
And they have bribed my own guard to do this thing.
[*Sententiously.*] Money!
There's nothing in the world so demoralizing as money.
Down go your cities,   115
Homes gone, men gone, honest hearts corrupted,
Crookedness of all kinds, and all for money!

To Sentry.

But you—!

I swear by God and by the throne of God,
The man who has done this thing shall pay for it!
Find that man, bring him here to me, or your death   120
Will be the least of your problems: I'll string you up
Alive, and there will be certain ways to make you
Discover your employer before you die;
And the process may teach you a lesson you seem to have missed:
The dearest profit is sometimes all too dear: 125
That depends on the source. Do you understand me?
A fortune won is often misfortune.

SENTRY. King, may I speak?
CREON.   Your very voice distresses me.
SENTRY. Are you sure that it is my voice, and not your conscience?
CREON. By God, he wants to analyze me now!   130
SENTRY. It is not what I say, but what has been done, that hurts you.
CREON. You talk too much.
SENTRY.   Maybe; but I've done nothing.
CREON. Sold your soul for some silver: that's all you've done.
SENTRY. How dreadful it is when the right judge judges wrong!
CREON. Your figures of speech   135
   May entertain you now; but unless you bring me the man,
   You will get little profit from them in the end.

Exit Creon into the palace.

SENTRY. "Bring me the man"—!
   I'd like nothing better than bringing him the man!
   But bring him or not, you have seen the last of me here.   140
   At any rate, I am safe!

Exit Sentry.

ODE I
Strophe 1
CHORUS. Numberless are the world's wonders, but none
   More wonderful than man; the stormgray sea
   Yields to his prows, the huge crests bear him high;

Earth, holy and inexhaustible, is graven°
With shining furrows where his plows have gone   5
Year after year, the timeless labor of stallions.

Antistrophe 1

The lightboned birds and beasts that cling to cover,
The lithe fish lighting their reaches of dim water,
All are taken, tamed in the net of his mind;
The lion on the hill, the wild horse windy-maned,   10
Resign to him; and his blunt yoke has broken
The sultry shoulders of the mountain bull.

Strophe 2

Words also, and thought as rapid as air,
He fashions to his good use; statecraft is his,
And his the skill that deflects the arrows of snow,   15
The spears of winter rain: from every wind
He has made himself secure—from all but one:
In the late wind of death he cannot stand.

Antistrophe 2

O clear intelligence, force beyond all measure!
O fate of man, working both good and evil!   20
When the laws are kept, how proudly his city stands!
When the laws are broken, what of his city then?
Never may the anárchic° man find rest at my hearth,
Never be it said that my thoughts are his thoughts.

SCENE II

Reenter Sentry leading Antigonê.

CHORAGOS. What does this mean? Surely this captive woman
    Is the Princess, Antigonê. Why should she be taken?
SENTRY. Here is the one who did it! We caught her
    In the very act of burying him.—Where is Creon?
CHORAGOS. Just coming from the house.

Enter Creon, center.

CREON.   What has happened?   5
    Why have you come back so soon?
SENTRY [*expansively*].   O King,
    A man should never be too sure of anything:
    I would have sworn
    That you'd not see me here again: your anger
    Frightened me so, and the things you threatened me with; 10
    But how could I tell then
    That I'd be able to solve the case so soon?

ODE I. 4 *graven:* engraved.   23 *anárchic:* lawless.

No dice-throwing this time: I was only too glad to come!
Here is this woman. She is the guilty one:
We found her trying to bury him. 15
Take her, then; question her; judge her as you will.
I am through with the whole thing now, and glad of it.
CREON. But this is Antigonê! Why have you brought her here?
SENTRY. She was burying him, I tell you!
CREON [severely].   Is this the truth?
SENTRY. I saw her with my own eyes. Can I say more? 20
CREON. The details: come, tell me quickly!
SENTRY.   It was like this:
After those terrible threats of yours, King,
We went back and brushed the dust away from the body.
The flesh was soft by now, and stinking,
So we sat on a hill to windward and kept guard. 25
No napping this time! We kept each other awake.
But nothing happened until the white round sun
Whirled in the center of the round sky over us:
Then, suddenly,
A storm of dust roared up from the earth, and the sky 30
Went out, the plain vanished with all its trees
In the stinging dark. We closed our eyes and endured it.
The whirlwind lasted a long time, but it passed;
And then we looked, and there was Antigonê!
I have seen 35
A mother bird come back to a stripped nest, heard
Her crying bitterly a broken note or two
For the young ones stolen. Just so, when this girl
Found the bare corpse, and all her love's work wasted,
She wept, and cried on heaven to damn the hands 40
That had done this thing.
                              And then she brought more dust
And sprinkled wine three times for her brother's ghost.

We ran and took her at once. She was not afraid,
Not even when we charged her with what she had done.
She denied nothing.
                              And this was a comfort to me, 45
And some uneasiness: for it is a good thing
To escape from death, but it is no great pleasure
To bring death to a friend.
                              Yet I always say
There is nothing so comfortable as your own safe skin!
CREON [slowly, dangerously]. And you, Antigonê, 50
You with your head hanging,—do you confess this thing?
ANTIGONÊ. I do. I deny nothing.
CREON [to Sentry].   You may go.

                              Exit Sentry.

[*To Antigonê.*] Tell me, tell me briefly:
Had you heard my proclamation touching this matter?

ANTIGONÊ. It was public. Could I help hearing it? 55

CREON. And yet you dared defy the law.

ANTIGONÊ.   I dared.
It was not God's proclamation. That final Justice
That rules the world below makes no such laws.

Your edict, King, was strong,
But all your strength is weakness itself against 60
The immortal unrecorded laws of God.
They are not merely now: they were, and shall be,
Operative for ever, beyond man utterly.

I knew I must die, even without your decree:
I am only mortal. And if I must die 65
Now, before it is my time to die,
Surely this is no hardship: can anyone
Living, as I live, with evil all about me,
Think Death less than a friend? This death of mine
Is of no importance; but if I had left my brother 70
Lying in death unburied, I should have suffered.
Now I do not.
                    You smile at me. Ah Creon,
Think me a fool, if you like; but it may well be
That a fool convicts me of folly.

CHORAGOS. Like father, like daughter: both headstrong, deaf to reason! 75
She has never learned to yield:

CREON.   She has much to learn.
The inflexible heart breaks first, the toughest iron
Cracks first, and the wildest horses bend their necks
At the pull of the smallest curb.
                                        Pride? In a slave?
This girl is guilty of a double insolence, 80
Breaking the given laws and boasting of it.
Who is the man here,
She or I, if this crime goes unpunished?
Sister's child, or more than sister's child,
Or closer yet in blood—she and her sister 85
Win bitter death for this!

                    To Servants.

                    Go, some of you,
Arrest Ismenê. I accuse her equally.
Bring her: you will find her sniffling in the house there.

Her mind's a traitor: crimes kept in the dark
Cry for light, and the guardian brain shudders; 90
But how much worse than this
Is brazen boasting of barefaced anarchy!

ANTIGONÊ. Creon, what more do you want than my death?

CREON.   Nothing.

That gives me everything.

ANTIGONÊ.   Then I beg you: kill me.

This talking is a great weariness: your words   95
Are distasteful to me, and I am sure that mine
Seem so to you. And yet they should not seem so:
I should have praise and honor for what I have done.
All these men here would praise me
Were their lips not frozen shut with fear of you.   100
[Bitterly.] Ah the good fortune of kings,
Licensed to say and do whatever they please!

CREON. You are alone here in that opinion.

ANTIGONÊ. No, they are with me. But they keep their tongues in leash.

CREON. Maybe. But you are guilty, and they are not.   105

ANTIGONÊ. There is no guilt in reverence for the dead.

CREON. But Eteoclês—was he not your brother too?

ANTIGONÊ. My brother too.

CREON.   And you insult his memory?

ANTIGONÊ [softly]. The dead man would not say that I insult it.

CREON. He would: for you honor a traitor as much as him.   110

ANTIGONÊ. His own brother, traitor or not, and equal in blood.

CREON. He made war on his country. Eteoclês defended it.

ANTIGONÊ. Nevertheless, there are honors due all the dead.

CREON. But not the same for the wicked as for the just.

ANTIGONÊ. Ah Creon, Creon,   115
Which of us can say what the gods hold wicked?

CREON. An enemy is an enemy, even dead.

ANTIGONÊ. It is my nature to join in love, not hate.

CREON [finally losing patience]. Go join them then; if you must have your love,
Find it in hell!   120

CHORAGOS. But see, Ismenê comes:

Enter Ismenê, guarded.

Those tears are sisterly, the cloud
That shadows her eyes rains down gentle sorrow.

CREON. You too, Ismenê,
Snake in my ordered house, sucking my blood   125
Stealthily—and all the time I never knew
That these two sisters were aiming at my throne!

                                            Ismenê,
Do you confess your share in this crime, or deny it?
Answer me.

ISMENÊ. Yes, if she will let me say so. I am guilty.   130

ANTIGONÊ [coldly]. No, Ismenê. You have no right to say so.
You would not help me, and I will not have you help me.

ISMENÊ. But now I know what you meant; and I am here
To join you, to take my share of punishment.

ANTIGONÊ. The dead man and the gods who rule the dead   135
　　Know whose act this was. Words are not friends.
ISMENÊ. Do you refuse me, Antigonê? I want to die with you:
　　I too have a duty that I must discharge to the dead.
ANTIGONÊ. You shall not lessen my death by sharing it.
ISMENÊ. What do I care for life when you are dead?   140
ANTIGONÊ. Ask Creon. You're always hanging on his opinions.
ISMENÊ. You are laughing at me. Why, Antigonê?
ANTIGONÊ. It's a joyless laughter, Ismenê.
ISMENÊ.　　　　　　　　　　　　　　But can I do nothing?
ANTIGONÊ. Yes. Save yourself. I shall not envy you.
　　There are those who will praise you; I shall have honor, too.   145
ISMENÊ. But we are equally guilty!
ANTIGONÊ.　　　　　　　　　　　　No more, Ismenê.
　　You are alive, but I belong to Death.
CREON [to the Chorus]. Gentlemen, I beg you to observe these girls:
　　One has just now lost her mind; the other,
　　It seems, has never had a mind at all.   150
ISMENÊ. Grief teaches the steadiest minds to waver, King.
CREON. Yours certainly did, when you assumed guilt with the guilty!
ISMENÊ. But how could I go on living without her?
CREON.　　　　　　　　　　　　　　　You are.
　　She is already dead.
ISMENÊ.　　　　　　　　But your own son's bride!
CREON. There are places enough for him to push his plow.   155
　　I want no wicked women for my sons!
ISMENÊ. O dearest Haimon,° how your father wrongs you!
CREON. I've had enough of your childish talk of marriage!
CHORAGOS. Do you really intend to steal this girl from your son?
CREON. No; Death will do that for me.
CHORAGOS.　　　　　　　　　　　Then she must die?   160
CREON [ironically]. You dazzle me.
　　　　　　　　　　　　—But enough of this talk!
　　[To Guards.] You, there, take them away and guard them well:
　　For they are but women, and even brave men run
　　When they see Death coming.

　　　　　　　Exeunt Ismenê, Antigonê, and Guards.

ODE II
Strophe 1
CHORUS. Fortunate is the man who has never tasted God's vengeance!
　　Where once the anger of heaven has struck, that house is shaken
　　For ever: damnation rises behind each child
　　Like a wave cresting out of the black northeast,

SCENE II. 157 *Haimon:* Creon's son.

Antigonê   **1065**

When the long darkness under sea roars up   5
And bursts drumming death upon the windwhipped sand.

Antistrophe 1

    I have seen this gathering sorrow from time long past
    Loom upon Oedipus' children: generation from generation
    Takes the compulsive rage of the enemy god.
    So lately this last flower of Oedipus' line   10
    Drank the sunlight! but now a passionate word
    And a handful of dust have closed up all its beauty.

Strophe 2

        What mortal arrogance
        Transcends the wrath of Zeus?°
    Sleep cannot lull him nor the effortless long months   15
    Of the timeless gods: but he is young for ever,
    And his house is the shining day of high Olympos.°
        All that is and shall be,
        And all the past, is his.
    No pride on earth is free of the curse of heaven.   20

Antistrophe 2

    The straying dreams of men
        May bring them ghosts of joy:
    But as they drowse, the waking embers burn them;
    Or they walk with fixed eyes, as blind men walk.
    But the ancient wisdom speaks for our own time: 25
    Fate works most for woe
    With Folly's fairest show.
    Man's little pleasure is the spring of sorrow.

SCENE III

CHORAGOS. But here is Haimon, King, the last of all your sons.
    Is it grief for Antigonê that brings him here,
    And bitterness at being robbed of his bride?

                   Enter Haimon.

CREON. We shall soon see, and no need of diviners.

                                  —Son,
    You have heard my final judgment on that girl: 5
    Have you come here hating me, or have you come
    With deference and with love, whatever I do?
HAIMON. I am your son, father. You are my guide.
    You make things clear for me, and I obey you.
    No marriage means more to me than your continuing wisdom.   10
CREON. Good. That is the way to behave: subordinate
    Everything else, my son, to your father's will.

———————————

ODE II. **14** *Zeus:* king of the gods.   **17** *Olympos:* a mountain in Thessaly, home of the gods.

This is what a man prays for, that he may get
Sons attentive and dutiful in his house,
Each one hating his father's enemies,   15
Honoring his father's friends. But if his sons
Fail him, if they turn out unprofitably,
What has he fathered but trouble for himself
And amusement for the malicious?
                                            So you are right
Not to lose your head over this woman.   20
Your pleasure with her would soon grow cold, Haimon,
And then you'd have a hellcat in bed and elsewhere.
Let her find her husband in Hell!
Of all the people in this city, only she
Has had contempt for my law and broken it.   25

Do you want me to show myself weak before the people?
Or to break my sworn word? No, and I will not.
The woman dies.
I suppose she'll plead "family ties." Well, let her.
If I permit my own family to rebel,
How shall I earn the world's obedience?   30
Show me the man who keeps his house in hand,
He's fit for public authority.
                                            I'll have no dealings
With lawbreakers, critics of the government:
Whoever is chosen to govern should be obeyed—   35
Must be obeyed, in all things, great and small,
Just and unjust! O Haimon,
The man who knows how to obey, and that man only,
Knows how to give commands when the time comes.
You can depend on him, no matter how fast   40
The spears come: he's a good soldier, he'll stick it out.

Anarchy, anarchy! Show me a greater evil!
This is why cities tumble and the great houses rain down,
This is what scatters armies!
No, no: good lives are made so by discipline.   45
We keep the laws then, and the lawmakers,
And no woman shall seduce us. If we must lose,
Let's lose to a man, at least! Is a woman stronger than we?
CHORAGOS. Unless time has rusted my wits,
     What you say, King, is said with point and dignity.   50
HAIMON [boyishly earnest]. Father:
     Reason is God's crowning gift to man, and you are right
     To warn me against losing mine. I cannot say—
     I hope that I shall never want to say!—that you
     Have reasoned badly. Yet there are other men   55
     Who can reason, too; and their opinions might be helpful.
     You are not in a position to know everything
     That people say or do, or what they feel:

Your temper terrifies—everyone
Will tell you only what you like to hear.   60
But I, at any rate, can listen; and I have heard them
Muttering and whispering in the dark about this girl.
They say no woman has ever, so unreasonably,
Died so shameful a death for a generous act:
"She covered her brother's body. Is this indecent?   65
She kept him from dogs and vultures. Is this a crime?
Death?—She should have all the honor that we can give her!"

This is the way they talk out there in the city.

You must believe me:
Nothing is closer to me than your happiness.   70
What could be closer? Must not any son
Value his father's fortune as his father does his?
I beg you, do not be unchangeable:
Do not believe that you alone can be right.
The man who thinks that,   75
The man who maintains that only he has the power
To reason correctly, the gift to speak, the soul—
A man like that, when you know him, turns out empty.

It is not reason never to yield to reason!

In flood time you can see how some trees bend,   80
And because they bend, even their twigs are safe,
While stubborn trees are torn up, roots and all.
And the same thing happens in sailing:
Make your sheet fast, never slacken,—and over you go,
Head over heels and under: and there's your voyage.   85
Forget you are angry! Let yourself be moved!
I know I am young; but please let me say this:
The ideal condition
Would be, I admit, that men should be right by instinct;
But since we are all too likely to go astray,   90
The reasonable thing to do is to learn from those who can teach.
CHORAGOS. You will do well to listen to him, King,
     If what he says is sensible. And you, Haimon,
     Must listen to your father.—Both speak well.
CREON. You consider it right for a man of my years and experience   95
     To go to school to a boy?
HAIMON.   It is not right
     If I am wrong. But if I am young, and right,
     What does my age matter?
CREON. You think it right to stand up for an anarchist?
HAIMON. Not at all. I pay no respect to criminals.   100
CREON. Then she is not a criminal?
HAIMON. The City would deny it, to a man.
CREON. And the City proposes to teach me how to rule?
HAIMON. Ah. Who is it that's talking like a boy now?

CREON. My voice is the one voice giving orders in this City! 105
HAIMON. It is no City if it takes orders from one voice.
CREON. The State is the King!
HAIMON.   Yes, if the State is a desert.

Pause.

CREON. This boy, it seems, has sold out to a woman.
HAIMON. If you are a woman; my concern is only for you.
CREON. So? Your "concern"! In a public brawl with your father! 110
HAIMON. How about you, in a public brawl with justice?
CREON. With justice, when all that I do is within my rights?
HAIMON. You have no right to trample on God's right.
CREON [*completely out of control*]. Fool, adolescent fool! Taken in
    by a woman!
HAIMON. You'll never see me taken in by anything vile. 115
CREON. Every word you say is for her!
HAIMON [*quietly, darkly*].   And for you.
    And for me. And for the gods under the earth.
CREON. You'll never marry her while she lives.
HAIMON. Then she must die.—But her death will cause another.
CREON. Another? 120
    Have you lost your senses? Is this an open threat?
HAIMON. There is no threat in speaking to emptiness.
CREON. I swear you'll regret this superior tone of yours!
    You are the empty one!
HAIMON.   If you were not my father, I'd say you were
    perverse. 125
CREON. You girlstruck fool, don't play at words with me!
HAIMON. I am sorry. You prefer silence.
CREON.   Now, by God—!
    I swear, by all the gods in heaven above us,
    You'll watch it, I swear you shall!

To the Servants.

                    Bring her out!
Bring the woman out! Let her die before his eyes! 130
Here, this instant, with her bridegroom beside her!
HAIMON. Not here, no; she will not die here, King.
And you will never see my face again.
Go on raving as long as you've a friend to endure you.

Exit Haimon.

CHORAGOS. Gone, gone.
    Creon, a young man in a rage is dangerous! 135
CREON. Let him do, or dream to do, more than a man can.
    He shall not save these girls from death.
CHORAGOS.   These girls?
    You have sentenced them both?
CREON.   No, you are right.
    I will not kill the one whose hands are clean. 140

CHORAGOS. But Antigonê?

CREON [*somberly*].   I will carry her far away
  Out there in the wilderness, and lock her
  Living in a vault of stone. She shall have food,
  As the custom is, to absolve the State of her death.
  And there let her pray to the gods of hell: 145
  They are her only gods:
  Perhaps they will show her an escape from death,
  Or she may learn,
                  though late,
  That piety shown the dead is pity in vain.

                    Exit Creon.

ODE III

Strophe

CHORUS. Love, unconquerable
  Waster of rich men, keeper
  Of warm lights and all-night vigil
  In the soft face of a girl:
  Sea-wanderer, forest-visitor!   5
  Even the pure Immortals cannot escape you,
  And mortal man, in his one day's dusk,
  Trembles before your glory.

Antistrophe

  Surely you swerve upon ruin
  The just man's consenting heart,   10
  As here you have made bright anger
  Strike between father and son—
  And none has conquered but Love!
  A girl's glánce wórking the will of heaven:
  Pleasure to her alone who mocks us,   15
  Merciless Aphroditê.°

SCENE IV

CHORAGOS [*as Antigonê enters guarded*]. But I can no longer stand
    in awe of this,
  Nor, seeing what I see, keep back my tears.
  Here is Antigonê, passing to that chamber
  Where all find sleep at last.

Strophe 1

ANTIGONÊ. Look upon me, friends, and pity me   5
  Turning back at the night's edge to say
  Good-by to the sun that shines for me no longer;
  Now sleepy Death

ODE III. 16 *Aphroditê:* Greek goddess of love.

Summons me down to Acheron,° that cold shore:
    There is no bridesong there, nor any music.   10
CHORUS. Yet not unpraised, not without a kind of honor,
    You walk at last into the underworld;
    Untouched by sickness, broken by no sword.
    What woman has ever found your way to death?

Antistrophe 1
ANTIGONÊ. How often I have heard the story of Niobê,°   15
    Tantalos'° wretched daughter, how the stone
    Clung fast about her, ivy-close: and they say
    The rain falls endlessly
    And sifting soft snow; her tears are never done.
    I feel the loneliness of her death in mine.   20
CHORUS. But she was born of heaven, and you
    Are woman, woman-born. If her death is yours,
    A mortal woman's, is this not for you
    Glory in our world and in the world beyond?

Strophe 2
ANTIGONÊ. You laugh at me. Ah, friends, friends,   25
    Can you not wait until I am dead? O Thebes,
    O men many-charioted, in love with Fortune,
    Dead springs of Dircê, sacred Theban grove,
    Be witness for me, denied all pity,
    Unjustly judged! and think a word of love   30
    For her whose path turns
    Under dark earth, where there are no more tears.
CHORUS. You have passed beyond human daring and come at last
    Into a place of stone where Justice° sits.
    I cannot tell   35
    What shape of your father's guilt appears in this.

Antistrophe 2
ANTIGONÊ. You have touched it at last: that bridal bed
    Unspeakable, horror of son and mother mingling:
    Their crime, infection of all our family!
    O Oedipus, father and brother!   40
    Your marriage strikes from the grave to murder mine.
    I have been a stranger here in my own land:
    All my life
    The blasphemy of my birth has followed me.
CHORUS. Reverence is a virtue, but strength   45
    Lives in established law: that must prevail.

SCENE IV. 9 *Acheron:* a river of Hades.   15 *Niobê:* mother of fourteen children; killed by Apollo and Artemis—gods—because of her pride, transformed into a rock on Mt. Sipylos.   16 *Tantalos:* father of Niobê, a king of Phrygia.   34 *Justice:* personification of the idea of justice, depicted as blind and holding a measuring scale in her hands.

You have made your choice,
Your death is the doing of your conscious hand.

Epode
ANTIGONÊ. Then let me go, since all your words are bitter,
And the very light of the sun is cold to me.   50
Lead me to my vigil, where I must have
Neither love nor lamentation; no song, but silence.

> *Creon interrupts impatiently.*

CREON. If dirges and planned lamentations could put off death,
Men would be singing for ever.

> *To the Servants.*

> Take her, go!
You know your orders: take her to the vault   55
And leave her alone there. And if she lives or dies,
That's her affair, not ours: our hands are clean.
ANTIGONÊ. O tomb, vaulted bride-bed in eternal rock,
Soon I shall be with my own again
Where Persephonê° welcomes the thin ghosts underground: 60
And I shall see my father again, and you, mother,
And dearest Polyneicês—
> dearest indeed
To me, since it was my hand
That washed him clean and poured the ritual wine:
And my reward is death before my time!   65

And yet, as men's hearts know, I have done no wrong,
I have not sinned before God. Or if I have,
I shall know the truth in death. But if the guilt
Lies upon Creon who judged me, then, I pray,
May his punishment equal my own.
CHORAGOS.   O passionate heart,   70
Unyielding, tormented still by the same winds!
CREON. Her guards shall have good cause to regret their delaying.
ANTIGONÊ. Ah! That voice is like the voice of death!
CREON. I can give you no reason to think you are mistaken.
ANTIGONÊ. Thebes, and you my fathers' gods,   75
And rulers of Thebes, you see me now, the last
Unhappy daughter of a line of kings,
Your kings, led away to death. You will remember
What things I suffer, and at what men's hands,
Because I would not transgress the laws of heaven.   80
[*To the Guards, simply.*] Come: let us wait no longer.

> *Exit Antigonê, left, guarded.*

---

60 *Persephonê*: queen of Hades.

ODE IV

Strophe 1

CHORUS. All Danaê's° beauty was locked away
  In a brazen cell where the sunlight could not come:
  A small room still as any grave, enclosed her.
  Yet she was a princess too,
  And Zeus in a rain of gold poured love upon her.   5
  O child, child,
  No power in wealth or war
  Or tough sea-blackened ships
  Can prevail against untiring Destiny!

Antistrophe 1

  And Dryas'° son also, that furious king,   10
  Bore the god's prisoning anger for his pride:
  Sealed up by Dionysos° in deaf stone,
  His madness died among echoes.
  So at the last he learned what dreadful power
  His tongue had mocked: 15
  For he had profaned the revels,
  And fired the wrath of the nine
  Implacable Sisters° that love the sound of the flute.

Strophe 2

  And old men tell a half-remembered tale
  Of horror where a dark ledge splits the sea   20
  And a double surf beats on the gráy shóres:
  How a king's new woman,° sick
  With hatred for the queen he had imprisoned,
  Ripped out his two sons' eyes with her bloody hands
  While grinning Arês° watched the shuttle plunge   25
  Four times: four blind wounds crying for revenge.

Antistrophe 2

  Crying, tears and blood mingled.—Piteously born,
  Those sons whose mother was of heavenly birth!
  Her father was the god of the North Wind
  And she was cradled by gales,   30
  She raced with young colts on the glittering hills
  And walked untrammeled in the open light:
  But in her marriage deathless Fate found means
  To build a tomb like yours for all her joy.

ODE IV.   1 *Danaê*: princess confined by her father in a bronze chamber underground; Zeus came in the form of a golden rain and seduced her, and she gave birth to Perseus.   10 *Dryas*: king of Thrace, father of Lykurgos, who was driven mad by Dionysos.   12 *Dionysos*: the god of wine.   18 *Implacable Sisters*: the nine Muses who preside over the various arts.   22 *new woman*: refers to King Phineas' second wife Eidothea, who blinded her stepsons.   25 *Arês*: god of war.

SCENE V

Enter blind Teiresias,° led by a boy. The opening speeches of Teiresias should be in singsong contrast to the realistic lines of Creon.

TEIRESIAS. This is the way the blind man comes, Princes, Princes,
    Lock-step, two heads lit by the eyes of one.
CREON. What new thing have you to tell us, old Teiresias?
TEIRESIAS. I have much to tell you: listen to the prophet, Creon.
CREON. I am not aware that I have ever failed to listen.   5
TEIRESIAS. Then you have done wisely, King, and ruled well.
CREON. I admit my debt to you. But what have you to say?
TEIRESIAS. This, Creon: you stand once more on the edge of fate.
CREON. What do you mean? Your words are a kind of dread.
TEIRESIAS. Listen Creon: 10

    I was sitting in my chair of augury, at the place
    Where the birds gather about me. They were all a-chatter,
    As is their habit, when suddenly I heard
    A strange note in their jangling, a scream, a
    Whirring fury; I knew that they were fighting,   15
    Tearing each other, dying
    In a whirlwind of wings clashing. And I was afraid.
    I began the rites of burnt-offering° at the altar,
    But Hephaistos° failed me: instead of bright flame,
    There was only the sputtering slime of the fat thigh-flesh   20
    Melting: the entrails dissolved in gray smoke,
    The bare bone burst from the welter. And no blaze!

    There was a sign from heaven. My boy described it,
    Seeing for me as I see for others.

    I tell you, Creon, yourself have brought   25
    This new calamity upon us. Our hearths and altars
    Are stained with the corruption of dogs and carrion birds
    That glut themselves on the corpse of Oedipus' son.
    The gods are deaf when we pray to them, their fire
    Recoils from our offering, their birds of omen   30
    Have no cry of comfort, for they are gorged
    With the thick blood of the dead.
                    O my son,
    These are no trifles! Think: all men make mistakes,
    But a good man yields when he knows his course is wrong,
    And repairs the evil. The only crime is pride.   35

    Give in to the dead man, then: do not fight with a corpse—
    What glory is it to kill a man who is dead?
    Think, I beg you:
    It is for your own good that I speak as I do.
    You should be able to yield for your own good.   40

SCENE V. *Teiresias:* blind prophet of Thebes who gave counsel to Oedipus and Creon.   18 *burnt-offering:* animal sacrifice made to appease the gods.   19 *Hephaistos:* god of fire.

CREON. It seems that prophets have made me their especial province.
    All my life long
    I have been a kind of butt for the dull arrows
    Of doddering fortune-tellers!
                   No, Teiresias:
    If your birds—if the great eagles of God himself   45
    Should carry him stinking bit by bit to heaven,
    I would not yield. I am not afraid of pollution:
    No man can defile the gods.
                  Do you what you will,
    Go into business, make money, speculate
    In India gold or that synthetic gold from Sardis,°   50
    Get rich otherwise than by my consent to bury him.
    Teiresias, it is a sorry thing when a wise man
    Sells his wisdom, lets out his words for hire!
TEIRESIAS. Ah Creon! Is there no man left in the world—
CREON. To do what?—Come, let's have the aphorism!   55
TEIRESIAS. No man who knows that wisdom outweighs any wealth?
CREON. As surely as bribes are baser than any baseness.
TEIRESIAS. You are sick, Creon! You are deathly sick!
CREON. As you say: it is not my place to challenge a prophet.
TEIRESIAS. Yet you have said my prophecy is for sale.
CREON. The generation of prophets has always loved gold.   60
TEIRESIAS. The generation of kings has always loved brass.°
CREON. You forget yourself! You are speaking to your King.
TEIRESIAS. I know it. You are a king because of me.
CREON. You have a certain skill; but you have sold out.   65
TEIRESIAS. King, you will drive me to words that—
CREON.   Say them, say them!
    Only remember: I will not pay you for them.
TEIRESIAS. No, you will find them too costly.
CREON.   No doubt. Speak:
    Whatever you say, you will not change my will.
TEIRESIAS. Then take this, and take it to heart!   70
    The time is not far off when you shall pay back
    Corpse for corpse, flesh of your own flesh.
    You have thrust the child of this world into living night,
    You have kept from the gods below the child that is theirs:
    The one in a grave before her death, the other   75
    Dead, denied the grave. This is your crime:
    And the Furies° and the dark gods of Hell
    Are swift with terrible punishment for you.

    Do you want to buy me now, Creon?
    Not many days,
    And your house will be full of men and women weeping,   80

---

50 *Sardis:* ancient city in Asia Minor.   62 *brass:* metal deemed inferior to gold.   77 *Furies:* spirits of divine vengeance.

And curses will be hurled at you from far
Cities grieving for sons unburied, left to rot
Before the walls of Thebes.

These are my arrows, Creon: they are all for you.

[*To Boy.*] But come, child: lead me home.   85
Let him waste his fine anger upon younger men.
Maybe he will learn at last
To control a wiser tongue in a better head.

Exit Teiresias.

CHORAGOS. The old man has gone, King, but his words
Remain to plague us. I am old, too,   90
But I cannot remember that he was ever false.
CREON. That is true. . . . It troubles me.
Oh it is hard to give in! but it is worse
To risk everything for stubborn pride.
CHORAGOS. Creon: take my advice.
CREON.   What shall I do?   95
CHORAGOS. Go quickly: free Antigonê from her vault
And build a tomb for the body of Polyneicês.
CREON. You would have me do this!
CHORAGOS.   Creon, yes!
And it must be done at once: God moves
Swiftly to cancel the folly of stubborn men.   100
CREON. It is hard to deny the heart! But I
Will do it: I will not fight with destiny.
CHORAGOS. You must go yourself, you cannot leave it to others.
CREON. I will go.
          —Bring axes, servants:
Come with me to the tomb. I buried her. I   105
Will set her free.
               Oh quickly!
My mind misgives—
The laws of the gods are mighty, and a man must serve them
To the last day of his life!

Exit Creon.

PAEAN
Strophe 1
CHORAGOS. God of many names
CHORUS.   O Iacchos°
                              son
     of Kadmeian Sémelê°
               O born of the Thunder!
     Guardian of the West

     PAEAN. 1 *Iacchos:* name for Dionysos.   2 *Kadmeian Sémelê:* Sémelê of the house of Kadmos, leg-
endary founder of Thebes; Sémelê was the mother, by Zeus, of Dionysos.

Regent

of Eleusis'° plain

O Prince of Maenad° Thebes

and the Dragon Field by rippling Ismenós.°   5

Antistrophe 1

CHORAGOS. God of many names

CHORUS.   the flame of torches

  flares on our hills

the nymphs of Iacchos

dance at the spring of Castalia.°

from the vine-close mountain

come ah come in ivy:

Evohé evohé! sings through the streets of Thebes   10

Strophe 2

CHORAGOS. God of many names

CHORUS.   Iacchos of Thebes

  heavenly Child

of Sémelê bride of the Thunderer!

The shadow of plague is upon us:

come

with clement feet

oh come from Parnasos

down the long slopes

across the lamenting water   15

Antistrophe 2

CHORAGOS. Iô Fire! Chorister° of the throbbing stars!

  O purest among the voices of the night!

  Thou son of God, blaze for us!

CHORUS. Come with choric rapture of circling Maenads

  Who cry *Iô Iacche!*

God of many names!   20

EXODOS

Enter Messenger from left.

MESSENGER. Men of the line of Kadmos,° you who live

  Near Amphion's° citadel,

I cannot say

Of any condition of human life "This is fixed,

This is clearly good or bad." Fate raises up,

And Fate casts down the happy and unhappy alike: 5

No man can foretell his Fate.

---

4 *Eleusis:* a city in Attica, sacred to Demeter (goddess of agriculture) and Persephonê, her daughter; *Maenad:* a priestess of Dionysos.   5 *Ismenós:* a river of Thebes, sacred to the god Apollo.   8 *Castalia:* a spring sacred to the Muses, at their home on Mt. Parnassos.   16 *Iô Fire! Chorister:* names for Dionysos.   EXODOS.   1 *Kadmos:* founder of Thebes.   2 *Amphion:* prince who marries Niobê, and hence an ancestor of Oedipus.

Take the case of Creon:
Creon was happy once, as I count happiness:
Victorious in battle, sole governor of the land,
Fortunate father of children nobly born.
And now it has all gone from him! Who can say   10
That a man is still alive when his life's joy fails?
He is a walking dead man. Grant him rich,
Let him live like a king in his great house:
If his pleasure is gone, I would not give
So much as the shadow of smoke for all he owns.   15

CHORAGOS. Your words hint at sorrow: what is your news for us?
MESSENGER. They are dead. The living are guilty of their death.
CHORAGOS. Who is guilty? Who is dead? Speak!
MESSENGER.   Haimon.
Haimon is dead; and the hand that killed him
Is his own hand.
CHORAGOS. His father's? or his own?   20
MESSENGER. His own, driven mad by the murder his father had done.
CHORAGOS. Teiresias, Teiresias, how clearly you saw it all!
MESSENGER. This is my news: you must draw what conclusions you can from it.
CHORAGOS. But look: Eurydicê, our Queen:
Has she overheard us?   25

Enter Eurydicê from the palace, center.

EURYDICÊ. I have heard something, friends:
As I was unlocking the gate of Pallas'° shrine,
For I needed her help today, I heard a voice
Telling of some new sorrow. And I fainted
There at the temple with all my maidens about me.   30
But speak again: whatever it is, I can bear it:
Grief and I are no strangers.
MESSENGER.   Dearest Lady,
I will tell you plainly all that I have seen.
I shall not try to comfort you: what is the use,
Since comfort could lie only in what is not true?   35
The truth is always best.
                        I went with Creon
To the outer plain where Polyneicês was lying,
No friend to pity him, his body shredded by dogs.
We made our prayers in that place to Hecatê°
And Pluto,° that they would be merciful. And we bathed   40
The corpse with holy water, and we brought
Fresh-broken branches to burn what was left of it,
And upon the urn we heaped up a towering barrow
Of the earth of his own land.
                        When we were done, we ran

---

27 *Pallas:* a name for Athena, goddess of wisdom, and of Athens.   39 *Hecatê:* goddess of Titan race, identified with sorcery and witchcraft.   40 *Pluto:* king of Hades.

To the vault where Antigonê lay on her couch of stone.   45
One of the servants had gone ahead,
And while he was yet far off he heard a voice
Grieving within the chamber, and he came back
And told Creon. And as the King went closer,
The air was full of wailing, the words lost,   50
And he begged us to make all haste. "Am I a prophet?"
He said, weeping, "And must I walk this road,
The saddest of all that I have gone before?
My son's voice calls me on. Oh quickly, quickly!
Look through the crevice there, and tell me   55
If it is Haimon, or some deception of the gods!"

We obeyed; and in the cavern's farthest corner
We saw her lying:
She had made a noose of her fine linen veil
And hanged herself. Haimon lay beside her,   60
His arms about her waist, lamenting her,
His love lost under ground, crying out
That his father had stolen her away from him.

When Creon saw him the tears rushed to his eyes
And he called to him: "What have you done, child?
        Speak to me.   65
What are you thinking that makes your eyes so strange?
O my son, my son, I come to you on my knees!"
But Haimon spat in his face. He said not a word,
Staring—
        And suddenly drew his sword
And lunged. Creon shrank back, the blade missed; and the boy,   70
Desperate against himself, drove it half its length
Into his own side, and fell. And as he died
He gathered Antigonê close in his arms again,
Choking, his blood bright red on her white cheek.
And now he lies dead with the dead, and she is his   75
At last, his bride in the house of the dead.

Exit Eurydicê into the palace.

CHORAGOS. She has left us without a word. What can this mean?
MESSENGER. It troubles me, too; yet she knows what is best,
    Her grief is too great for public lamentation,
    And doubtless she has gone to her chamber to weep   80
    For her dead son, leading her maidens in his dirge.°

Pause.

CHORAGOS. It may be so: but I fear this deep silence.
MESSENGER. I will see what she is doing. I will go in.

Exit Messenger into the palace.

---

81 *dirge*: funereal lament.

Enter Creon with attendants, bearing Haimon's body.

CHORAGOS. But here is the king himself: oh look at him,
    Bearing his own damnation in his arms. 85
CREON. Nothing you say can touch me any more.
    My own blind heart has brought me
    From darkness to final darkness. Here you see
    The father murdering, the murdered son—
    And all my civic wisdom! 90

    Haimon my son, so young, so young to die,
    I was the fool, not you; and you died for me.
CHORAGOS. This is the truth; but you were late in learning it.
CREON. This truth is hard to bear. Surely a god
    Has crushed me beneath the hugest weight of heaven, 95
    And driven me headlong a barbaric way
    To trample out the thing I held most dear.

    The pains that men will take to come to pain!

Enter Messenger from the palace.

MESSENGER. The burden you carry in your hands is heavy,
    But it is not all: you will find more in your house. 100
CREON. What burden worse than this shall I find there?
MESSENGER. The Queen is dead.
CREON. O port of death, deaf world,
    Is there no pity for me? And you, Angel of evil,
    I was dead, and your words are death again. 105
    Is it true, boy? Can it be true?
    Is my wife dead? Has death bred death?
MESSENGER. You can see for yourself.

The doors are opened and the body of Eurydicê is disclosed within.

CREON. Oh pity!
    All true, all true, and more than I can bear! 110
    O my wife, my son!
MESSENGER. She stood before the altar, and her heart
    Welcomed the knife her own hand guided,
    And a great cry burst from her lips for Megareus° dead,
    And for Haimon dead, her sons; and her last breath 115
    Was a curse for their father, the murderer of her sons.
    And she fell, and the dark flowed in through her closing eyes.
CREON. O God, I am sick with fear.
    Are there no swords here? Has no one a blow for me?
MESSENGER. Her curse is upon you for the deaths of both. 120
CREON. It is right that it should be. I alone am guilty.
    I know it, and I say it. Lead me in,
    Quickly, friends.
    I have neither life nor substance. Lead me in.

---

114 *Megareus:* a son of Creon who died during the assault on Thebes.

CHORAGOS. You are right, if there can be right in so much wrong. 125
    The briefest way is best in a world of sorrow.
CREON. Let it come,
    Let death come quickly, and be kind to me.
    I would not ever see the sun again.
CHORAGOS. All that will come when it will; but we, meanwhile, 130
    Have much to do. Leave the fortune to itself.
CREON. All my heart was in that prayer!
CHORAGOS. Then do not pray any more: the sky is deaf.
CREON. Lead me away. I have been rash and foolish.
    I have killed my son and my wife. 135
    I look for comfort; my comfort lies here dead.
    Whatever my hands have touched has come to nothing.
    Fate has brought all my pride to a thought of dust.

As Creon is being led into the house, the Choragos advances and speaks directly to the audience.

CHORAGOS. There is no happiness where there is no wisdom;
    No wisdom but in submission to the gods. 140
    Big words are always punished,
    And proud men in old age learn to be wise.

QUESTIONS

1. What belief drives Antigonê to defy Creon? How does her belief differ from his? How do these beliefs express a central tension in the Greek culture of the time?

2. What did Antigonê's brother Polyneicês do to incur Creon's wrath?

3. What is Antigonê's first act of defiance? How does Creon respond?

4. What is Ismenê's role in the play? Why does she not follow Antigonê? What is her reaction when Creon sentences her as well?

5. In what ways are Creon and Antigonê similar in character?

6. What is Haimon's advice to Creon? Find evidence of his clever argumentation. Why does Creon ignore his words?

7. What is the function of the Chorus? Isolate a scene and compare Creon's words to those spoken by the Chorus.

8. What are the themes expressed by the Odes? Find several instances of effective use of analogies in the Odes.

9. What is the role of Teiresias? How is his speech different from that of Haimon? How does Creon respond?

10. Comment on the difference between Teiresias's mode of speech and Creon's. What does the difference signify?

11. In what ways do you think the tragic outcome is inevitable? What would have had to happen for tragedy to be averted?

12. Reflect upon the last words of the play, spoken by the Choragos. How do they summarize the central themes of *Antigonê*?

13. Compare *Antigonê* to *Oedipus Rex*. What is the source of tragedy in each play? Which play, in your view, is the more powerful? Explain your answer.

31 Shakespearean Drama

If we take a drastically simplified aerial view of the history of drama, the next momentous development after the great golden age of the Greek tragedians was the playwrighting career of William Shakespeare (1546–1616). Such a drastic simplification, of course, leaves out a great deal of history—the farces of the Roman Plautus (254–184 B.C.) and the tragedies of Seneca (4 B.C.–A.D. 65), as well as the cycles of *mystery* and *morality* plays that were written and performed in Europe in the late Middle Ages.

Though these latter developments share almost nothing in common with the plays of Shakespeare and his contemporaries (Ben Jonson and Christopher Marlowe, among others), they nevertheless deserve at least brief notice here.

Medieval Drama as Background to the Elizabethans

Mystery plays had their origins in the religious pageants of twelfth- and thirteenth-century Europe. They were acted at Christian festivals, generally by traveling groups of actors. The main purpose of these plays was to impart religious instruction, and the narratives were drawn almost exclusively from the Bible. Performances would take place in town squares, where symbolically costumed figures would play their roles either against a simple backdrop or else on a rudimentary stage raised up off the ground. Morality plays arose in the fourteenth and fifteenth centuries and were not only more elaborate in their staging, but also presented a greater diversity of material. Instead of simply rendering a scene from the Bible, the morality play—like *Everyman* (1500)—might be an *allegorical* enactment, in which a whole system of symbols was combined into a narrative meant to instruct the viewer about the Christian life. Indeed, in *Everyman* (the title is part of the allegory), the protagonist, Christian, undertakes an elaborate representative journey to reach the Heavenly City, encountering and resisting temptation at every stage.

What a change took place in drama between *Everyman* with its prudish moralizing and the turbulent and often bawdy plays of Shakespeare written less than a century later! Several factors account for it. First, the increasingly powerful Protestant clergy, which took a dim view of the Catholic tradition of the morality play, began to set restrictions on performances, and the influence of the mode began to wane. Second, and far more important, was the arrival in England of the great tide of the Renaissance—with it came the ideals of humanism (that man is the measure of all things) and the revival of classical learning. Countless texts from ancient Greece and the Roman Empire were translated and put into circulation. An extraordinary liberation was in the offing, and dramatists, no less than scholars and artists, responded. As much of this period of awakening coincided with the reign of Queen Elizabeth, which lasted from 1558 to 1603, the period is commonly known as the "Elizabethan" period. Its most celebrated representative is William Shakespeare.

Shakespeare the Playwright

Given his extraordinary fame, it is remarkable how little we know about Shakespeare's life. To crib a line from poet W. H. Auden, "A shilling life will give you all the facts." We know that the playwright was born to a relatively well-to-do family in the town of Stratford-on-Avon in 1564 and that the family suffered serious financial reverses when Shakespeare was a youth. He was given a thorough early education but left school at the age of eighteen to make his way in the world. He married a woman named Anne Hathaway almost immediately, and they had three children in the next few years.

By 1592, Shakespeare was achieving notoriety in London as both an actor and a playwright. Two years later he joined a theater company that was called Lord Chamberlain's Men, later changing its name to the King's Men (King James had extended his patronage to the group). He stayed with this group until his retirement. Shakespeare was prolific in the extreme: He wrote 36 plays for his company. In 1611 he retired to his place of birth, Stratford-on-Avon, where he died five years later.

By any reckoning, this is a thin account of a vital and productive figure. So thin, indeed, that various scholars over the years have subscribed to a conspiracy theory, which proposes—at least in one version—that Shakespeare did not exist at all and that his plays were in fact written by his contemporary, Ben Jonson. Other theories propose other candidates. Another option, of course, is that he was by nature a private individual and did not publicize his deeds; that he lived his real life in the imagination that spawned so many masterpieces. Whatever the explanation, the individual whom we call Shakespeare left to posterity the most remarkable body of works ever achieved by one person—not only the tragedies, comedies, and histories, but also some of the most beautiful sonnets in the language.

THE ELIZABETHANS INVENT A NEW KIND OF DRAMA

Though a vital part of the Renaissance humanism was bound up with the rediscovery of the classic writings of Greek and Roman authors, their influence was not always exerted in predictable ways. The great revival of drama in the Elizabethan Age did *not* represent a reemergence of classical artistic ideals. To the contrary. While the larger culture was invigorated by contact with the secular energies of the past and the works of former masters (Shakespeare, for example, drew a great deal of inspiration from his reading of the Greek historian Plutarch, incorporating materials from his *Lives of the Noble Greeks and Romans* into his plays), the plays of Shakespeare and his contemporaries were anything but "classical."

Indeed, it is much more useful to see them as representing tendencies opposed to the classical ideals of restraint, harmony, and economy. They are, by contrast, rich, profuse, and chaotic in their multiplicities of character and situation. Critics and historians have often called Shakespeare's plays "romantic" tragedies and comedies. The word "romantic" should not, however, be construed in its narrow sense as pertaining to the affections, but rather as indicating an artistic sensibility at the opposite end of the spectrum from the classical.

Contrasts with Greek Drama

Shakespearean drama is readily contrasted to Greek drama. Where the classical plays observed the basic unities (discussed by Aristotle in his *Poetics)* of plot, time, and place, the plays of Shakespeare exhibit great variety in their use of subplots, time perspectives, and settings. While King Oedipus never leaves the environs of the Theban palace, Shakespeare's *Hamlet* moves the viewer from the ramparts of the Castle of Elsinore to the house of Polonius to an open plain in Denmark to a churchyard cemetery.

Another major difference, mentioned earlier, has to do with plot construction. The Greek dramatists assumed that their audiences would be familiar with the myths and legends of the culture. As many aspects of the dramatic situation were givens, dramatists could position events very close to the point of climax. Shakespeare built his plots through accumulation, giving his audiences the information they needed in increments. The climax, carefully prepared for, would generally come late in the play. Moreover, the use of multiple plots allowed Shakespeare to use different levels of language and also to introduce comic elements into his tragedies; the Greek playwrights were pledged to a purity of idiom that allowed them no such options. Finally, Shakespeare availed himself of the crowd-pleasing effects of direct action, what in the so-called "revenge plays" of the Roman playwright Seneca was called "seeing on stage." Swords were drawn and used; characters were killed before the eyes of the spectator. In the plays of the Greeks, all such dramatic actions took place off-stage and were reported by others, usually messengers.

There are, to be sure, certain similarities between Greek and Shakespearean drama. Shakespearean tragedies, like those of the Greeks, featured noble protagonists—great-souled individuals who would endure epical calamities. And the course of action was still—though less conspicuously—ruled by a sense of tragic inevitability. We know that Julius Caesar will be betrayed by his friend Brutus, that Cleopatra will die from the bite of the poisonous snake, and so on.

The Staging of Shakespearean Drama

A few conventions were likewise observed with respect to production. The parts of women were, as in the Greek drama, played by men. Actors were often elaborately costumed, and the sets were graced with few props. It was up to the viewer to furnish the rooms of the palace or to imagine the first light of day greeting Hamlet on the castle rampart.

The theater itself—the site of the staging—was considerably more intimate than what the Greek spectators knew. Theaters in Shakespeare's day, the most fa-

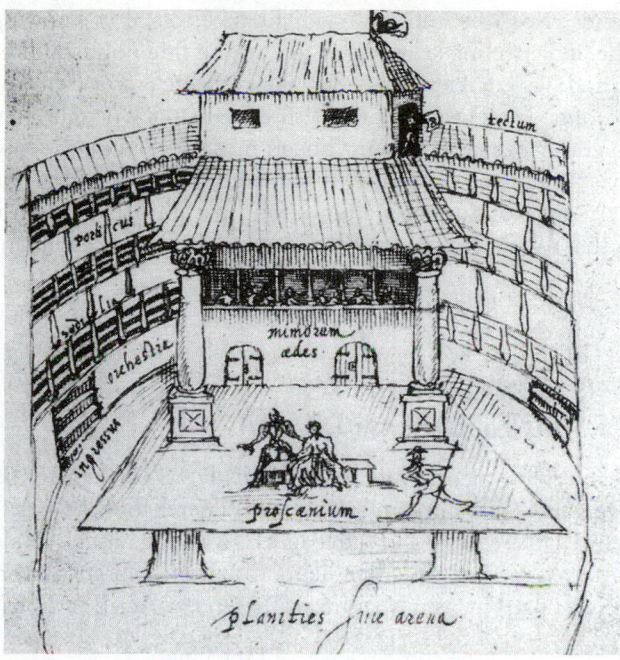

An early sketch of the Swan Theater, a competitor to Shakespeare's Globe. The viewing galleries for the upper classes surrounded a platform (with trapdoors) that stood shoulder-high, forming an outer stage (proscenium) extended into a yard for the standing audience. The theater building, with its columned portico, sheltered the entrance doors and upper levels of the inner stage. On occasion a temporary pavilion may have been set up between the doors to support a small interior curtained area or steps to upper levels. (From Bapst, *Essai sur l'Histoire du Théâtre*, 1893.)

mous of which was the Globe (built outside London to discourage rowdiness and petty crime), were generally constructed in the shape of an O (Shakespeare himself refers to the theater as "a wooden O"). An open stage—no curtains were used—was protected by an awning. It was surrounded on three sides by an open courtyard for standing patrons—the "groundlings" who could not afford the better seats. Around the courtyard ran the covered gallery, which provided seating and coverage against rain for the better class of patrons.

Compared with the amphitheaters of the Greeks, the Elizabethan playhouses were intimacy itself, holding only 2,500 spectators, as opposed to 15,000. The accessibility of the stage on three sides allowed the playwright certain artistic options. He could, for instance, make use of *asides* (comments supposedly outside the hearing of the other characters) and *soliloquies* (monologues representing a character's thoughts)—the relative proximity of the stage freed the actor from having to shout, thereby enhancing the believability of these more private modes of speech.

Like the drama of the Greeks, Shakespearean plays were public events staged for the enjoyment of spectators from all social levels. The student who balks at some of the more difficult passages—for Shakespeare wrote in a rich and elegantly patterned *pentameter* verse (see Glossary)—might take solace in knowing that many members of the audience missed out on some of the fine points of the diction, including puns and veiled references. But Shakespeare's crowd-pleasing instincts never betrayed him. The playwright made sure to include enough humor and gripping drama to gratify every play-goer. Though most of Shakespeare's plays contain difficult patches—and fresh difficulties throughout that result from changes in the language—every last work declares a power and passion that remain unsurpassed. The two plays that follow, *Hamlet* and *The Tempest*, show off the full range of Shakespeare's vision.

SOME USEFUL CONVENTIONS FOR DISCUSSING SHAKESPEAREAN DRAMA

BLANK VERSE: Shakespeare wrote many of his lines, particularly in longer passages of dialogue and soliloquies, in a loose pentameter form. A strict pentameter would have ten syllables, divided into five feet. Given the natural tendency of English speech patterns, the feet would be likely to fall into an *iambic* (or short/long–unstressed/stressed) pattern, as in the line at the end of Act II of *Hamlet*:

> Whĕre-ín / Ĭ'll cátch / thĕ cón- / sciĕnce óf / thĕ kíng.

A loose pentameter allows for frequent deviations from the norm, both in terms of syllable count and stress pattern, as in:

> Tŏ bé, ŏr nót tŏ bé: thăt ĭs thĕ quéstion.

which has 11 syllables and varies the metrical pattern throughout the second half of the line.

ALLUSION: Shakespeare makes incessant use of *allusion*. That is, he makes reference to mythology, history, and other spheres of knowledge. In the famous "O, that this too too sullied flesh would melt" soliloquy in Act I, Scene II, for instance, he makes a mythic allusion while setting up a comparison between Hamlet's real father and the man's brother (and murderer):

> So excellent a king, that was to this
> Hyperion to a satyr,

Hyperion was the sun god in ancient Greek mythology, while a satyr was a beast of lowly appetites.

SOLILOQUY: A monologue, meant to inform the audience of the character's thoughts, is generally given when that character is alone. Shakespeare uses soliloquy frequently as a way of breaking up the stage action with passages of poetic reflection. Hamlet's "To be, or not to be" soliloquy is probably the most famous in the whole dramatic repertory.

ASIDE: Words are spoken by one character in the presence of others, but are to be heard only by the audience. Asides frequently inform the viewer of a character's real motive or intention. In Act I, Scene II, Hamlet makes a punning aside when Claudius, murderer of his father, says, "But now, my cousin Hamlet, and my son—" Says Hamlet, to the audience: "A little more than kin, and less than kind!" The PUN is a play on the two different meanings of the word "kind." Shakespeare's plays abound in double and triple puns.

IRONY: Verbal irony, also common in Shakespeare's work, arises when a character states one thing and means another—indeed, very likely means the opposite. In Act III, Scene II, Hamlet speaks to Ophelia about the cheerful demeanors of his mother and Claudius so soon after his father's death. "O heavens! die two months ago, and not forgotten yet?" exclaims the Prince, professing shock at the fact that his father is still mentioned from time to time.

CRUX: A crux is a phrase or passage that scholars have not been able to elucidate—either because the usage is obscure or because of some undetected printer's mistake. In some versions of Act I, Scene IV, for example, we find in one of Hamlet's speeches to Horatio the phrase "the dram of eale." The word "eale" has no discoverable meaning, and the phrase is often construed as "the dram of evil."

FIGURES OF SPEECH (see also Chapter 21): One has to look long and hard to find a passage in Shakespeare that makes no use of *simile* or *metaphor*, the two most frequently used figures of speech. A simile is a comparison using *like* or *as*. In Act II, Scene II, Hamlet addresses Rosencrantz and Guildenstern on the supposed wonders of the human being: "in action how like an angel! in apprehension how like a god!" A few lines earlier, Rosencrantz uses metaphor, saying: " . . . and I hold ambition of so airy and light a quality that it is but a shadow's shadow." He does not say that it is *like* a "shadow's shadow"—he makes the comparison directly.

CONCEIT: A conceit is an extended figure of speech. An analogy, framed as either a simile or a metaphor, is pursued at some length. In Act III, Scene II, Hamlet and Guildenstern have a dialogue that makes elaborate play with the idea that a person is a kind of instrument that can be played upon. Says Hamlet:

> Why, look you now, how unworthy a thing you make of me! You would play upon me; you would seem to know my stops; you would pluck out the heart of my mystery; you would sound me from my lowest note to the top of my compass; and there is much music, excellent voice, in this little organ, yet cannot you make it speak. 'Sblood, do you think I am easier to be played on than a pipe? Call me what instrument you will, though you can fret me, you cannot play upon me.

We cannot help but notice the punning edge that Shakespeare imparts to Hamlet's words, the double meaning of "fret" being just one instance.

William Shakespeare (1564–1616)

Shakespeare was born in the town of Stratford-on-Avon, outside London, to which he retired after writing his last play, *The Tempest* (1611), and where he died. Shakespeare made his name as an actor and playwright in London, working for many years with one theatrical company, Lord Chamberlain's Men (which was later renamed The King's Men in recognition of the generous patronage of King James I).

Between 1594 and his retirement, Shakespeare wrote thirty-six plays, including Tragedies *Hamlet* and *Othello,* Comedies *A Midsummer Night's Dream* and *The Tempest,* and Histories *Henry V* and *Richard III.* In 1599 The King's Men moved into the Globe Theater outside London; it was the site of some of the playwright's greatest popular triumphs.

THE TRAGEDY OF HAMLET PRINCE OF DENMARK

Edited by Edward Hubler

DRAMATIS PERSONAE

CLAUDIUS, King of Denmark
HAMLET, son to the late, and
  nephew to the present, King
POLONIUS, Lord Chamberlain
HORATIO, friend to Hamlet
LAERTES, son to Polonius
VOLTEMAND ⎫
CORNELIUS ⎪
ROSENCRANTZ ⎪
GUILDENSTERN ⎬ courtiers
OSRIC ⎪
A GENTLEMAN ⎭
A PRIEST
MARCELLUS ⎫
BARNARDO ⎬ officers
FRANCISCO ⎭
REYNALDO, servant to Polonius

PLAYERS
TWO CLOWNS, gravediggers
FORTINBRAS, Prince of Norway
A NORWEGIAN CAPTAIN
ENGLISH AMBASSADORS
GERTRUDE, QUEEN OF DENMARK,
  mother to Hamlet
OPHELIA, daughter to Polonius
GHOST of Hamlet's father
LORDS
LADIES
OFFICERS
SOLDIERS
SAILORS
MESSENGERS
ATTENDANTS

SCENE
Elsinore

ACT I
Scene I
A guard platform of the castle.

   Enter Barnardo and Francisco, two sentinels.

BARNARDO. Who's there?
FRANCISCO. Nay, answer me. Stand and unfold° yourself.
BARNARDO. Long live the King!°
FRANCISCO. Barnardo?

SCENE I. 2 *unfold:* disclose.   3 *Long live the King:* (perhaps a password, perhaps a greeting).

BARNARDO. He.   5
FRANCISCO. You come most carefully upon your hour.
BARNARDO. 'Tis now struck twelve. Get thee to bed, Francisco.
FRANCISCO. For this relief much thanks. 'Tis bitter cold, And I am sick at heart.
BARNARDO. Have you had quiet guard?
FRANCISCO.   Not a mouse stirring.   10
BARNARDO. Well, good night.
    If you do meet Horatio and Marcellus,
    The rivals° of my watch, bid them make haste.

Enter Horatio and Marcellus.

FRANCISCO. I think I hear them. Stand, ho! Who is there?
HORATIO. Friends to this ground.
MARCELLUS.   And liegemen to the Dane.°   15
FRANCISCO. Give you° good night.
MARCELLUS.   O, farewell, honest soldier.
    Who hath relieved you?
FRANCISCO.   Barnardo hath my place.
    Give you good night.   *Exit Francisco.*
MARCELLUS.   Holla, Barnardo!
BARNARDO.   Say——
    What, is Horatio there?
HORATIO.   A piece of him.
BARNARDO. Welcome, Horatio. Welcome, good Marcellus.   20
MARCELLUS. What, has this thing appeared again tonight?
BARNARDO. I have seen nothing.
MARCELLUS. Horatio says 'tis but our fantasy,
    And will not let belief take hold of him
    Touching this dreaded sight twice seen of us;   25
    Therefore I have entreated him along
    With us to watch the minutes of this night,
    That, if again this apparition come,
    He may approve° our eyes and speak to it.
HORATIO. Tush, tush, 'twill not appear.
BARNARDO.   Sit down awhile,   30
    And let us once again assail your ears,
    That are so fortified against our story,
    What we have two nights seen.
HORATIO.   Well, sit we down,
    And let us hear Barnardo speak of this.   35
BARNARDO. Last night of all,
    When yond same star that's westward from the pole°
    Had made his course t' illume that part of heaven
    Where now it burns, Marcellus and myself,
    The bell then beating one——

Enter Ghost.

---

    13 *rivals:* partners.   15 *liegemen to the Dane:* loyal subjects to the King of Denmark.   16 *Give you:* God give you.   29 *approve:* confirm.   36 *pole:* polestar.

MARCELLUS. Peace, break thee off. Look where it comes again. 40
BARNARDO. In the same figure like the king that's dead.
MARCELLUS. Thou art a scholar; speak to it, Horatio.
BARNARDO. Looks 'a not like the king? Mark it, Horatio.
HORATIO. Most like: it harrows me with fear and wonder.
BARNARDO. It would be spoke to.
MARCELLUS.   Speak to it, Horatio. 45
HORATIO. What art thou that usurp'st this time of night,
    Together with that fair and warlike form
    In which the majesty of buried Denmark°
    Did sometimes march? By heaven I charge thee, speak.
MARCELLUS. It is offended.
BARNARDO.   See, it stalks away. 50
HORATIO. Stay! Speak, speak, I charge thee, speak.

Exit Ghost.

MARCELLUS. 'Tis gone and will not answer.
BARNARDO. How now, Horatio? You tremble and look pale.
    Is not this something more than fantasy?
    What think you on't? 55
HORATIO. Before my God, I might not this believe
    Without the sensible and true avouch°
    Of mine own eyes.
MARCELLUS.   Is it not like the King?
HORATIO. As thou art to thyself.
    Such was the very armor he had on. 60
    When he the ambitious Norway° combated:
    So frowned he once, when, in an angry parle,°
    He smote the sledded Polacks° on the ice.
    'Tis strange.
MARCELLUS. Thus twice before, and jump° at this dead hour, 65
    With martial stalk hath he gone by our watch.
HORATIO. In what particular thought to work I know not;
    But, in the gross and scope° of my opinion,
    This bodes some strange eruption to our state.
MARCELLUS. Good now, sit down, and tell me he that knows, 70
    Why this same strict and most observant watch
    So nightly toils the subject° of the land,
    And why such daily cast of brazen cannon
    And foreign mart° for implements of war,
    Why such impress° of shipwrights, whose sore task 75
    Does not divide the Sunday from the week,
    What might be toward° that this sweaty haste
    Doth make the night joint-laborer with the day?
    Who is't that can inform me?

---

48 *buried Denmark:* the buried King of Denmark.   57 *sensible and true avouch:* sensory and true
proof.   61 *Norway:* King of Norway.   62 *parle:* parley.   63 *sledded Polacks:* Poles in sledges.   65 *jump:*
just.   68 *gross and scope:* general drift.   72 *toils the subject:* makes the subjects toil.   74 *mart:* trading.
75 *impress:* forced service.   77 *toward:* in preparation.

HORATIO.   That can I.   80

     At least the whisper goes so: our last king,
     Whose image even but now appeared to us,
     Was, as you know, by Fortinbras of Norway,
     Thereto pricked on by a most emulate pride,
     Dared to the combat; in which our valiant Hamlet
     (For so this side of our known world esteemed him)   85
     Did slay this Fortinbras, who, by a sealed compact
     Well ratified by law and heraldry,°
     Did forfeit, with his life, all those his lands
     Which he stood seized° of, to the conqueror;
     Against the which a moiety competent°   90
     Was gagèd° by our King, which had returned
     To the inheritance of Fortinbras,
     Had he been vanquisher, as, by the same comart°
     And carriage of the article designed,°
     His fell to Hamlet. Now, sir, young Fortinbras,   95
     Of unimprovèd° mettle hot and full,
     Hath in the skirts° of Norway here and there
     Sharked up° a list of lawless resolutes,°
     For food and diet, to some enterprise
     That hath a stomach in't;° which is no other,   100
     As it doth well appear unto our state,
     But to recover of us by strong hand
     And terms compulsatory, those foresaid lands
     So by his father lost; and this, I take it,
     Is the main motive of our preparations,   105
     The source of this our watch, and the chief head°
     Of this posthaste and romage° in the land.
BARNARDO. I think it be no other but e'en so;
     Well may it sort° that this portentous figure
     Comes armèd through our watch so like the King   110
     That was and is the question of these wars.
HORATIO. A mote it is to trouble the mind's eye:
     In the most high and palmy state of Rome,
     A little ere the mightiest Julius fell,
     The graves stood tenantless, and the sheeted dead   115
     Did squeak and gibber in the Roman streets;°
     As stars with trains of fire and dews of blood,
     Disasters° in the sun; and the moist star,°
     Upon whose influence Neptune's empire stands,
     Was sick almost to doomsday with eclipse.   120

---

     87 *law and heraldry*: heraldic law (governing the combat).   89 *seized*: possessed.   90 *moiety competent*: equal portion.   91 *gagèd*: engaged, pledged.   93 *comart*: agreement.   94 *carriage of the article designed*: import of the agreement drawn up.   96 *unimprovèd*: untried.   97 *skirts*: borders.   98 *Sharked up*: collected indiscriminately (as a shark gulps its prey); *resolutes*: desperadoes.   100 *hath a stomach in't*: i.e., requires courage.   106 *head*: fountainhead, origin.   107 *romage*: bustle.   109 *sort*: befit. 116 *Did squeak . . . Roman streets*: (the break in the sense which follows this line suggests that a line has dropped out).   118 *Disasters*: threatening signs; *moist star*: moon.

And even the like precurse° of feared events,
As harbingers° preceding still° the fates
And prologue to the omen° coming on,
Have heaven and earth together demonstrated
Unto our climatures° and countrymen.   125

Enter Ghost.

But soft, behold, lo where it comes again!
I'll cross it,° though it blast me.—Stay, illusion.

It spreads his° arms.

If thou hast any sound or use of voice,
Speak to me.
If there be any good thing to be done   130
That may to thee do ease and grace to me,
Speak to me.
If thou art privy to thy country's fate,
Which happily° foreknowing may avoid,
O, speak!   135
Or if thou hast uphoarded in thy life
Extorted° treasure in the womb of earth,
For which, they say, you spirits oft walk in death,

The cock crows.

Speak of it. Stay and speak. Stop it, Marcellus.
MARCELLUS. Shall I strike at it with my partisan?°   140
HORATIO. Do, if it will not stand.
BARNARDO.   'Tis here.
HORATIO.   'Tis here.
MARCELLUS. 'Tis gone.   *Exit Ghost.*
We do it wrong, being so majestical,
To offer it the show of violence,
For it is as the air, invulnerable,   145
And our vain blows malicious mockery.
BARNARDO. It was about to speak when the cock crew.
HORATIO. And then it started, like a guilty thing
Upon a fearful summons. I have heard,
The cock, that is the trumpet to the morn,   150
Doth with his lofty and shrill-sounding throat
Awake the god of day, and at his warning,
Whether in sea or fire, in earth or air,
Th' extravagant and erring° spirit hies
To his confine; and of the truth herein   155
This present object made probation.°

---

121 *precurse:* precursor, foreshadowing. 122 *harbingers:* forerunners; *still:* always. 123 *omen:* calamity. 125 *climatures:* regions. 127 *cross it:* (1) cross its path, confront it (2) make the sign of the cross in front of it; s.d. *his:* i.e., its, the ghost's (though possibly what is meant is that Horatio spreads his own arms, making a cross of himself). 134 *happily:* haply, perhaps. 137 *Extorted:* ill-won. 140 *partisan:* pike (a long-handled weapon). 154 *extravagant and erring:* out of bounds and wandering. 156 *probation:* proof.

MARCELLUS. It faded on the crowing of the cock.
　　Some say that ever 'gainst° that season comes
　　Wherein our Savior's birth is celebrated,
　　This bird of dawning singeth all night long,　　　　　　　　　160
　　And then, they say, no spirit dare stir abroad,
　　The nights are wholesome, then no planets strike,°
　　No fairy takes,° nor witch hath power to charm:
　　So hallowed and so gracious is that time.
HORATIO. So have I heard and do in part believe it.　　　　　　165
　　But look, the morn in russet mantle clad
　　Walks o'er the dew of yon high eastward hill.
　　Break we our watch up, and by my advice
　　Let us impart what we have seen tonight
　　Unto young Hamlet, for upon my life　　　　　　　　　　　170
　　This spirit, dumb to us, will speak to him.
　　Do you consent we shall acquaint him with it,
　　As needful in our loves, fitting our duty?
MARCELLUS. Let's do't, I pray, and I this morning know
　　Where we shall find him most convenient.　　*Exeunt.*　　175

Scene II
The castle.

Flourish.° Enter Claudius, King of Denmark, Gertrude the Queen, Councilors,
Polonius and his son Laertes, Hamlet, cum aliis° [including Voltemand and
Cornelius].

KING. Though yet of Hamlet our dear brother's death
　　The memory be green, and that it us befitted
　　To bear our hearts in grief, and our whole kingdom
　　To be contracted in one brow of woe,
　　Yet so far hath discretion fought with nature　　　　　　　　5
　　That we with wisest sorrow think on him
　　Together with remembrance of ourselves.
　　Therefore our sometime sister,° now our Queen,
　　Th' imperial jointress° to this warlike state,
　　Have we, as 'twere, with a defeated joy,　　　　　　　　　10
　　With an auspicious° and a dropping eye,
　　With mirth in funeral, and with dirge in marriage,
　　In equal scale weighing delight and dole,
　　Taken to wife. Nor have we herein barred
　　Your better wisdoms, which have freely gone　　　　　　　　15
　　With this affair along. For all, our thanks.
　　Now follows that you know young Fortinbras,
　　Holding a weak supposal of our worth,
　　Or thinking by our late dear brother's death
　　Our state to be disjoint and out of frame,°　　　　　　　　20

---

158 *'gainst:* just before.　162 *strike:* exert an evil influence.　163 *takes:* bewitches.　SCENE II. s.d.
Flourish: fanfare of trumpets; *cum aliis:* with others (Latin).　8 *our sometime sister:* my (the royal "we")
former sister-in-law.　9 *jointress:* joint tenant, partner.　11 *auspicious:* joyful.　20 *frame:* order.

Colleaguèd with this dream of his advantage,°
He hath not failed to pester us with message,
Importing the surrender of those lands
Lost by his father, with all bands of law,
To our most valiant brother. So much for him.   25
Now for ourself and for this time of meeting.
Thus much the business is: we have here writ
To Norway, uncle of young Fortinbras—
Who, impotent and bedrid, scarcely hears
Of this his nephew's purpose—to suppress   30
His further gait° herein, in that the levies,
The lists, and full proportions° are all made
Out of his subject;° and we here dispatch
You, good Cornelius, and you, Voltemand,
For bearers of this greeting to old Norway,   35
Giving to you no further personal power
To business with the King, more than the scope
Of these delated articles° allow.
Farewell, and let your haste commend your duty.
CORNELIUS, VOLTEMAND. In that, and all things, will we show our duty.   40
KING. We doubt it nothing. Heartily farewell.

               Exit Voltemand and Cornelius.

And now, Laertes, what's the news with you?
You told us of some suit. What is't, Laertes?
You cannot speak of reason to the Dane
And lose your voice.° What wouldst thou beg, Laertes,   45
That shall not be my offer, not thy asking?
The head is not more native° to the heart,
The hand more instrumental to the mouth,
Than is the throne of Denmark to thy father.
What wouldst thou have, Laertes?
LAERTES.   My dread lord,   50
Your leave and favor to return to France,
From whence, though willingly I came to Denmark
To show my duty in your coronation,
Yet now I must confess, that duty done,
My thoughts and wishes bend again toward France   55
And bow them to your gracious leave and pardon.
KING. Have you your father's leave? What says Polonius?
POLONIUS. He hath, my lord, wrung from me my slow leave
By laborsome petition, and at last
Upon his will I sealed my hard consent.°   60
I do beseech you give him leave to go.

---

    21 *advantage:* superiority.   31 *gait:* proceeding.   32 *proportions:* supplies for war.   33 *Out of his sub-*
ject: i.e., out of old Norway's subjects and realm.   38 *delated articles:* detailed documents.   45 *lose your*
voice: waste your breath.   47 *native:* related.   60 *Upon his . . . hard consent:* to his desire I gave my reluctant consent.

KING. Take thy fair hour, Laertes. Time be thine,
  And thy best graces spend it at thy will.
  But now, my cousin° Hamlet, and my son——
HAMLET. [*Aside*] A little more than kin, and less than kind!°   65
KING. How is it that the clouds still hang on you?
HAMLET. No so, my lord. I am too much in the sun.°
QUEEN. Good Hamlet, cast thy nighted color off,
  And let thine eye look like a friend on Denmark.
  Do not forever with thy vailèd° lids   70
  Seek for thy noble father in the dust.
  Thou know'st 'tis common; all that lives must die,
  Passing through nature to eternity.
HAMLET. Ay, madam, it is common.°
QUEEN.   If it be,
  Why seems it so particular with thee?   75
HAMLET. Seems, madam? Nay, it is. I know not "seems."
  'Tis not alone my inky cloak, good mother,
  Nor customary suits of solemn black,
  Nor windy suspiration° of forced breath,
  No, nor the fruitful river in the eye,   80
  Nor the dejected havior of the visage,
  Together with all forms, moods, shapes of grief,
  That can denote me truly. These indeed seem,
  For they are actions that a man might play,
  But I have that within which passes show;   85
  These but the trappings and the suits of woe.
KING. 'Tis sweet and commendable in your nature, Hamlet,
  To give these mourning duties to your father,
  But you must know your father lost a father,
  That father lost, lost his, and the survivor bound   90
  In filial obligation for some term
  To do obsequious° sorrow. But to persever
  In obstinate condolement° is a course
  Of impious stubbornness. 'Tis unmanly grief.
  It shows a will most incorrect to heaven,   95
  A heart unfortified, a mind impatient,
  An understanding simple and unschooled.
  For what we know must be and is as common
  As any the most vulgar° thing to sense,
  Why should we in our peevish opposition   100
  Take it to heart? Fie, 'tis a fault to heaven,
  A fault against the dead, a fault to nature,
  To reason most absurd, whose common theme

---

  64 *cousin:* kinsman. 65 *kind:* (pun on the meanings "kindly" and "natural"; though doubly related—*more than kin*—Hamlet asserts that he neither resembles Claudius in nature nor feels kindly toward him). 67 *sun:* sunshine of royal favor (with a pun on "son"). 70 *vailèd:* lowered. 74 *common:*
(1) universal, (2) vulgar. 79 *windy suspiration:* heavy sighing. 92 *obsequious:* suitable to obsequies (fu-
nerals). 93 *condolement:* mourning. 99 *vulgar:* common.

Is death of fathers, and who still hath cried,
From the first corse° till he that died today,   105
"This must be so." We pray you throw to earth
This unprevailing° woe, and think of us
As of a father, for let the world take note
You are the most immediate to our throne,
And with no less nobility of love   110
Than that which dearest father bears his son
Do I impart toward you. For your intent
In going back to school in Wittenberg,
It is most retrograde° to our desire,
And we beseech you, bend you° to remain   115
Here in the cheer and comfort of our eye,
Our chiefest courtier, cousin, and our son.
QUEEN. Let not thy mother lose her prayers, Hamlet.
    I pray thee stay with us, go not to Wittenberg.
HAMLET. I shall in all my best obey you, madam.   120
KING. Why, 'tis a loving and a fair reply.
    Be as ourself in Denmark. Madam, come.
    This gentle and unforced accord of Hamlet
    Sits smiling to my heart, in grace whereof
    No jocund health that Denmark drinks today,   125
    But the great cannon to the clouds shall tell,
    And the King's rouse° the heaven shall bruit° again,
    Respeaking earthly thunder. Come away.

            Flourish. Exeunt all but Hamlet.

HAMLET. O that this too too sullied° flesh would melt,
    Thaw, and resolve itself into a dew,   130
    Or that the Everlasting had not fixed
    His canon° 'gainst self-slaughter. O God, God,
    How weary, stale, flat, and unprofitable
    Seem to me all the uses of this world!
    Fie on't, ah, fie, 'tis an unweeded garden   135
    That grows to seed. Things rank and gross in nature
    Possess it merely.° That it should come to this:
    But two months dead, nay, not so much, not two,
    So excellent a king, that was to this
    Hyperion° to a satyr, so loving to my mother   140
    That he might not beteem° the winds of heaven
    Visit her face too roughly. Heaven and earth,
    Must I remember? Why, she would hang on him
    As if increase of appetite had grown
    by what it fed on; and yet within a month—   145

---

105 *corse:* corpse.   107 *unprevailing:* unavailing.   114 *retrograde:* contrary.   115 *bend you:* incline.
127 *rouse:* deep drink; *bruit:* announce noisily.   129 *sullied:* (Q2 has *sallied,* here modernized to *sullied,*
which makes sense and is therefore given; but the Folio reading, *solid,* which fits better with *melt,* is quite
possibly correct).   132 *canon:* law.   137 *merely:* entirely.   140 *Hyperion:* the sun god, a model of beauty.
141 *beteem:* allow.

Shakespearean Drama

Let me not think on't; frailty, thy name is woman—
A little month, or ere those shoes were old
With which she followed my poor father's body
Like Niobe,° all tears, why she, even she—
O God, a beast that wants discourse of reason°   150
Would have mourned longer—married with my uncle,
My father's brother, but no more like my father
Than I to Hercules. Within a month,
Ere yet the salt of most unrighteous tears
Had left the flushing° in her gallèd eyes,   155
She married. O, most wicked speed, to post°
With such dexterity to incestuous° sheets!
It is not, nor it cannot come to good.
But break my heart, for I must hold my tongue.

Enter Horatio, Marcellus, and Barnardo.

HORATIO. Hail to your lordship!
HAMLET.   I am glad to see you well.   160
     Horatio—or I do forget myself.
HORATIO. The same, my lord, and your poor servant ever.
HAMLET. Sir, my good friend, I'll change° that name with you.
     And what make you from Wittenberg, Horatio?
     Marcellus.   165
MARCELLUS. My good lord!
HAMLET. I am very glad to see you. [*To Barnardo*]
     Good even, sir.
     But what, in faith, make you from Wittenberg?
HORATIO. A truant disposition, good my lord.
HAMLET. I would not hear your enemy say so,   170
     Nor shall you do my ear that violence
     To make it truster° of your own report
     Against yourself. I know you are no truant.
     But what is your affair in Elsinore?
     We'll teach you to drink deep ere you depart.   175
HORATIO. My lord, I came to see your father's funeral.
HAMLET. I prithee do not mock me, fellow student.
     I think it was to see my mother's wedding.
HORATIO. Indeed, my lord, it followed hard upon.
HAMLET. Thrift, thrift, Horatio. The funeral baked meats   180
     Did coldly furnish forth the marriage tables.
     Would I had met my dearest° foe in heaven
     Or ever I had seen that day, Horatio!
     My father, methinks I see my father.
HORATIO. Where, my lord?
HAMLET.   In my mind's eye, Horatio.   185

---

149 *Niobe:* (a mother who wept profusely at the death of her children).   150 *wants discourse of reason:* lacks reasoning power.   155 *left the flushing:* stopped reddening.   156 *post:* hasten.   157 *incestuous:* (canon law considered marriage with a deceased brother's widow to be incestuous).   163 *change:* exchange. 172 *truster:* believer.   182 *dearest:* most intensely felt.

HORATIO. I saw him once. 'A° was a goodly king.

HAMLET. 'A was a man, take him for all in all,
I shall not look upon his like again.

HORATIO. My lord, I think I saw him yesternight.

HAMLET. Saw? Who?   190

HORATIO. My lord, the King your father.

HAMLET.   The King my father?

HORATIO. Season your admiration° for a while
With an attent ear till I may deliver
Upon the witness of these gentlemen
This marvel to you.

HAMLET.   For God's love let me hear!   195

HORATIO. Two nights together had these gentlemen,
Marcellus and Barnardo, on their watch
In the dead waste and middle of the night
Been thus encountered. A figure like your father,
Armèd at point exactly, cap-a-pe,°   200
Appears before them, and with solemn march
Goes slow and stately by them. Thrice he walked
By their oppressed and fear-surprisèd eyes,
Within his truncheon's length,° whilst they, distilled°
Almost to jelly with the act° of fear,   205
Stand dumb and speak not to him. This to me
In dreadful° secrecy impart they did,
And I with them the third night kept the watch,
Where, as they had delivered, both in time,
Form of the thing, each word made true and good,   210
The apparition comes. I knew your father.
These hands are not more like.

HAMLET.   But where was this?

MARCELLUS. My lord, upon the platform where we watched.

HAMLET. Did you not speak to it?

HORATIO.   My lord, I did;   215
But answer made it none. Yet once methought
It lifted up it° head and did address
Itself to motion like as it would speak:
But even then the morning cock crew loud,
And at the sound it shrunk in haste away
And vanished from our sight.

HAMLET.   'Tis very strange.   220

HORATIO. As I do live, my honored lord, 'tis true,
And we did think it writ down in our duty
To let you know of it.

HAMLET. Indeed, indeed, sirs, but this troubles me.
Hold you the watch tonight?

---

186 'A: he. 192 *Season your admiration*: control your wonder. 200 *cap-a-pe*: head to foot.
204 *truncheon's length*: space of a short staff; *distilled*: reduced. 205 *act*: action. 207 *dreadful*: terrified.
216 *it*: its.

ALL.   We do, my lord.   225
HAMLET. Armed, say you?
ALL. Armed, my lord.
HAMLET. From top to toe?
ALL.   My lord, from head to foot.
HAMLET. Then saw you not his face.
HORATIO. O, yes, my lord. He wore his beaver° up.   230
HAMLET. What, looked he frowningly?
HORATIO. A countenance more in sorrow than in anger.
HAMLET. Pale or red?
HORATIO. Nay, very pale.
HAMLET.   And fixed his eyes upon you?
HORATIO. Most constantly.
HAMLET.   I would I had been there.   235
HORATIO. It would have much amazed you.
HAMLET. Very like, very like. Stayed it long?
HORATIO. While one with moderate haste might tell° a hundred.
BOTH. Longer, longer.
HORATIO. Not when I saw't.
HAMLET.   His beard was grizzled,° no?   240
HORATIO. It was as I have seen it in his life,
     A sable silvered.°
HAMLET.   I will watch tonight.
     Perchance 'twill walk again.
HORATIO.   I warr'nt it will.
HAMLET. If it assume my noble father's person,
     I'll speak to it though hell itself should gape   245
     And bid me hold my peace. I pray you all,
     If you have hitherto concealed this sight,
     Let it be tenable° in your silence still,
     And whatsoever else shall hap tonight,
     Give it an understanding but no tongue;   250
     I will requite your loves. So fare you well.
     Upon the platform 'twixt eleven and twelve
     I'll visit you.
ALL.   Our duty to your honor.
HAMLET. Your loves, as mine to you. Farewell.

                    Exeunt [all but Hamlet].

     My father's spirit—in arms? All is not well.   255
     I doubt° some foul play. Would the night were come!
     Till then sit still, my soul. Foul deeds will rise,
     Though all the earth o'erwhelm them, to men's eyes.

                                        Exit.

---

    230 *beaver:* visor, face guard.   238 *tell:* count.   240 *grizzled:* gray.   242 *sable silvered:* black min-
gled with white.   248 *tenable:* held.   256 *doubt:* suspect.

Scene III
A room.

     Enter Laertes and Ophelia, his sister.

LAERTES. My necessaries are embarked. Farewell.
  And, sister, as the winds give benefit
  And convoy° is assistant, do not sleep,
  But let me hear from you.
OPHELIA.   Do you doubt that?
LAERTES. For Hamlet, and the trifling of his favor,   5
  Hold it a fashion and a toy° in blood,
  A violet in the youth of primy° nature,
  Forward,° not permanent, sweet, not lasting,
  The perfume and suppliance° of a minute,
  No more.
OPHELIA.   No more but so?
LAERTES.   Think it no more.   10
  For nature crescent° does not grow alone
  In thews° and bulk, but as this temple° waxes,
  The inward service of the mind and soul
  Grows wide withal. Perhaps he loves you now,
  And now no soil nor cautel° doth besmirch   15
  The virtue of his will; but you must fear,
  His greatness weighed,° his will is not his own.
  For he himself is subject to his birth.
  He may not, as unvalued° persons do,
  Carve for himself; for on his choice depends   20
  The safety and health of this whole state;
  And therefore must his choice be circumscribed
  Unto the voice and yielding of that body
  Whereof he is the head. Then if he says he loves you,
  It fits your wisdom so far to believe it   25
  As he in his particular act and place
  May give his saying deed, which is no further
  Than the main voice of Denmark goes withal.
  Then weigh what loss your honor may sustain
  If with too credent° ear you list his songs,   30
  Or lose your heart, or your chaste treasure open
  To his unmastered importunity.
  Fear it, Ophelia, fear it, my dear sister,
  And keep you in the rear of your affection,
  Out of the shot and danger of desire.   35
  The chariest maid is prodigal enough
  If she unmask her beauty to the moon.
  Virtue itself scapes not calumnious strokes.

SCENE III. 3 *convoy*: conveyance. 6 *toy*: idle fancy. 7 *primy*: springlike. 8 *Forward*: premature.
9 *suppliance*: diversion. 11 *crescent*: growing. 12 *thews*: muscles and sinews; *temple*: i.e., the body. 15
cautel: deceit. 17 *greatness weighed*: high rank considered. 19 *unvalued*: of low rank. 30 *credent*: credulous.

                             Shakespearean Drama

The canker° galls the infants of the spring
Too oft before their buttons° be disclosed,   40
And in the morn and liquid dew of youth
Contagious blastments are most imminent.
Be wary then; best safety lies in fear;
Youth to itself rebels, though none else near.

OPHELIA. I shall the effect of this good lesson keep   45
As watchman to my heart, but, good my brother,
Do not, as some ungracious° pastors do,
Show me the steep and thorny way to heaven,
Whiles, like a puffed and reckless libertine,
Himself the primrose path of dalliance treads   50
And recks not his own rede.°

                    Enter Polonius.

LAERTES.   O, fear me not.
I stay too long. But here my father comes.
A double blessing is a double grace;
Occasion smiles upon a second leave.

POLONIUS. Yet here, Laertes? Aboard, aboard, for shame!   55
The wind sits in the shoulder of your sail,
And you are stayed for. There—my blessing with thee,
And these few precepts in thy memory
Look thou character.° Give thy thoughts no tongue,
Nor any unproportioned° thought his act.   60
Be thou familiar, but by no means vulgar.
Those friends thou hast, and their adoption tried,
Grapple them unto thy soul with hoops of steel,
But do not dull thy palm with entertainment
Of each new-hatched, unfledged courage.° Beware   65
Of entrance to a quarrel; but being in,
Bear't that th' opposèd may beware of thee.
Give every man thine ear, but few thy voice;
Take each man's censure,° but reserve thy judgment.
Costly thy habit as thy purse can buy,   70
But not expressed in fancy; rich, not gaudy,
For the apparel oft proclaims the man,
And they in France of the best rank and station
Are of a most select and generous, chief in that.°
Neither a borrower nor a lender be,   75
For loan oft loses both itself and friend,
And borrowing dulleth edge of husbandry.°
This above all, to thine own self be true,
And it must follow, as the night the day,

---

39 *canker:* cankerworm.   40 *buttons:* buds.   47 *ungracious:* lacking grace.   51 *recks not his own rede:*
does not heed his own advice.   59 *character:* inscribe.   60 *unproportioned:* unbalanced.   65 *courage:* gallant youth.   69 *censure:* opinion.   74 *Are of . . . in that:* show their fine taste and their gentlemanly instincts more in that than in any other point of manners (Kittredge).   77 *husbandry:* thrift.

Thou canst not then be false to any man.   80
    Farewell. My blessing season this° in thee!
LAERTES. Most humbly do I take my leave, my lord.
POLONIUS. The time invites you. Go, your servants tend.°
LAERTES. Farewell, Ophelia, and remember well
    What I have said to you.
OPHELIA.   'Tis in my memory locked,   85
    And you yourself shall keep the key of it.
LAERTES. Farewell.   *Exit Laertes.*
POLONIUS. What is't, Ophelia, he hath said to you?
OPHELIA. So please you, something touching the Lord Hamlet.
POLONIUS. Marry,° well bethought.   90
    'Tis told me he hath very oft of late
    Given private time to you, and you yourself
    Have of your audience been most free and bounteous.
    If it be so—as so 'tis put on me,
    And that in way of caution—I must tell you   95
    You do not understand yourself so clearly
    As it behooves my daughter and your honor.
    What is between you? Give me up the truth.
OPHELIA. He hath, my lord, of late made many tenders°
    Of his affection to me.   100
POLONIUS. Affection pooh! You speak like a green girl,
    Unsifted° in such perilous circumstance.
    Do you believe his tenders, as you call them?
OPHELIA. I do not know, my lord, what I should think.
POLONIUS. Marry, I will teach you. Think yourself a baby,   105
    That you have ta'en these tenders for true pay
    Which are not sterling. Tender yourself more dearly,
    Or (not to crack the wind of the poor phrase)
    Tend'ring it thus you'll tender me a fool.°
OPHELIA. My lord, he hath importuned me with love   110
    In honorable fashion.
POLONIUS. Ay, fashion you may call it. Go to, go to.
OPHELIA. And hath given countenance to his speech, my lord,
    With almost all the holy vows of heaven.
POLONIUS. Ay, springes to catch woodcocks.° I do know,   115
    When the blood burns, how prodigal the soul
    Lends the tongue vows. These blazes, daughter,
    Giving more light than heat, extinct in both,
    Even in their promise, as it is a-making,
    You must not take for fire. From this time   120
    Be something scanter of your maiden presence.

---

81 *season this:* make fruitful this (advice).   83 *tend:* attend.   90 *Marry:* (a light oath, from "By the
Virgin Mary").   99 *tenders:* offers (in line 103 it has the same meaning, but in line 106 Polonius speaks
of *tenders* in the sense of counters or chips; in line 109 *Tend'ring* means "holding," and *tender* means
"give," "present").   102 *Unsifted:* untried.   109 *tender me a fool:* (1) present me with a fool, (2) present
me with a baby.   115 *springes to catch woodcocks:* snares to catch stupid birds.

Set your entreatments° at a higher rate
Than a command to parley. For Lord Hamlet,
Believe so much in him that he is young,
And with a larger tether may he walk   125
Than may be given you. In few, Ophelia,
Do not believe his vows, for they are brokers,°
Not of that dye° which their investments° show,
But mere implorators° of unholy suits,
Breathing like sanctified and pious bonds,°   130
The better to beguile. This is for all:
I would not, in plain terms, from this time forth
Have you so slander° any moment leisure
As to give words or talk with the Lord Hamlet.
Look to't, I charge you. Come you ways.   135
OPHELIA. I shall obey, my lord.   *Exeunt.*

Scene IV
A guard platform.

    Enter Hamlet, Horatio, and Marcellus.

HAMLET. The air bites shrewdly;° it is very cold.
HORATIO. It is a nipping and an eager° air.
HAMLET. What hour now?
HORATIO.   I think it lacks of twelve.
MARCELLUS. No, it is struck.
HORATIO. Indeed? I heard it not. It then draws near the season   5
    Wherein the spirit held his wont to walk.

    A flourish of trumpets, and two pieces go off.

    What does this mean, my lord?
HAMLET. The King doth wake° tonight and takes his rouse,°
    Keeps wassail, and the swagg'ring upspring° reels,
    And as he drains his draughts of Rhenish° down   10
    The kettledrum and trumpet thus bray out
    The triumph of his pledge.°
HORATIO.   Is it a custom?
HAMLET. Ay, marry, is't,
    But to my mind, though I am native here
    And to the manner born, it is a custom   15
    More honored in the breach than the observance.
    This heavy-headed revel east and west
    Makes us traduced and taxed of° other nations.
    They clepe° us drunkards and with swinish phrase

---

122 *entreatments:* interviews.   127 *brokers:* procurers.   128 *dye:* i.e., kind; *investments:* garments.
129 *implorators:* solicitors.   130 *bonds:* pledges.   133 *slander:* disgrace.   SCENE IV. 1 *shrewdly:* bitterly.
2 *eager:* sharp.   8 *wake:* hold a revel by night; *takes his rouse:* carouses.   9 *upspring:* (a dance).   10
Rhenish: Rhine wine.   12 *The triumph of his pledge:* the achievement (of drinking a wine cup in one
draught) of his toast.   18 *taxed of:* blamed by.   19 *clepe:* call.

Soil our addition,° and indeed it takes   20
From our achievements, though performed at height,
The pith and marrow of our attribute.°
So oft it chances in particular men
That for some vicious mole° of nature in them,
As in their birth, wherein they are not guilty,   25
(Since nature cannot choose his origin)
By the o'ergrowth of some complexion,°
Oft breaking down the pales° and forts of reason,
Or by some habit that too much o'erleavens°
The form of plausive° manners, that (these men,   30
Carrying, I say, the stamp of one defect,
Being nature's livery, or fortune's star°)
Their virtues else, be they as pure as grace,
As infinite as man may undergo,
Shall in the general censure° take corruption   35
From that particular fault. The dram of evil
Doth all the noble substance of a doubt,
To his own scandal.°

                         Enter Ghost.

HORATIO.   Look, my lord, it comes.
HAMLET. Angels and ministers of grace defend us!
Be thou a spirit of health° or goblin damned,   40
Bring with thee airs from heaven or blasts from hell,
Be thy intents wicked or charitable,
Thou com'st in such a questionable° shape
That I will speak to thee. I'll call thee Hamlet,
King, father, royal Dane. O, answer me!   45
Let me not burst in ignorance, but tell
Why thy canonized° bones, hearsèd in death,
Have burst their cerements,° why the sepulcher
Wherein we saw thee quietly interred
Hath oped his ponderous and marble jaws   50
To cast thee up again. What may this mean
That thou, dead corse, again in complete steel,
Revisits thus the glimpses of the moon,
Making night hideous, and we fools of nature
So horridly to shake our disposition°   55
With thoughts beyond the reaches of our souls?
Say, why is this? Wherefore? What should we do?

---

20 *addition:* reputation (literally, "title of honor").   22 *attribute:* reputation.   24 *mole:* blemish.
27 *complexion:* natural disposition.   28 *pales:* enclosures.   29 *o'erleavens:* mixes with, corrupts.
30 *plausive:* pleasing.   32 *nature's livery, or fortune's star:* nature's equipment (i.e., "innate"), or a person's
destiny determined by the stars.   35 *general censure:* popular judgment.   36–38 *The dram . . . own scan-*
dal: (though the drift is clear, there is no agreement as to the exact meaning of these lines).   40 *spirit of*
health: good spirit.   43 *questionable:* (1) capable of discourse, (2) dubious.   47 *canonized:* buried according to the canon or ordinance of the church.   48 *cerements:* waxed linen shroud.   55 *shake our disposi-*
tion: disturb us.

Ghost beckons Hamlet.

HORATIO. It beckons you to go away with it,
    As if it some impartment° did desire
    To you alone.
MARCELLUS.   Look with what courteous action   60
    It waves you to a more removèd ground.
    But do not go with it.
HORATIO.   No, by no means.
HAMLET. It will not speak. Then I will follow it.
HORATIO. Do not, my lord.
HAMLET.   Why, what should be the fear?
    I do not set my life at a pin's fee,   65
    And for my soul, what can it do to that,
    Being a thing immortal as itself?
    It waves me forth again. I'll follow it.
HORATIO. What if it tempt you toward the flood, my lord,
    Or to the dreadful summit of the cliff   70
    That beetles° o'er his base into the sea,
    And there assume some other horrible form
    Which might deprive your sovereignty of reason°
    And draw you into madness? Think of it.
    The very place puts toys° of desperation,   75
    Without more motive, into every brain
    That looks so many fathoms to the sea
    And hears it roar beneath.
HAMLET.   It waves me still.
    Go on; I'll follow thee.
MARCELLUS. You shall not go, my lord.
HAMLET.   Hold off your hands.   80
HORATIO. Be ruled. You shall not go.
HAMLET.   My fate cries out
    And makes each petty artere° in this body
    As hardy as the Nemean lion's nerve.°
    Still am I called! Unhand me, gentlemen.
    By heaven, I'll make a ghost of him that lets° me!   85
    I say, away! Go on. I'll follow thee.

Exit Ghost and Hamlet.

HORATIO. He waxes desperate with imagination.
MARCELLUS. Let's follow. 'Tis not fit thus to obey him.
HORATIO. Have after! To what issue will this come?
MARCELLUS. Something is rotten in the state of Denmark.   90
HORATIO. Heaven will direct it.
MARCELLUS.   Nay, let's follow him.   *Exeunt.*

---

    59 *impartment:* communication.   71 *beetles:* juts out.   73 *deprive your sovereignty of reason:* destroy the sovereignty of your reason.   75 *toys:* whims, fancies.   82 *artere:* artery.   83 *Nemean lion's nerve:* sinews of the mythical lion slain by Hercules.   85 *lets:* hinders.

Scene V
The battlements.

> *Enter Ghost and Hamlet.*

HAMLET. Whither wilt thou lead me? Speak; I'll go no further.
GHOST. Mark me.
HAMLET.   I will.
GHOST.   My hour is almost come,
　　When I to sulf'rous and tormenting flames
　　Must render up myself.
HAMLET.   Alas, poor ghost.
GHOST. Pity me not, but lend thy serious hearing   5
　　To what I shall unfold.
HAMLET.   Speak. I am bound to hear.
GHOST. So art thou to revenge, when thou shalt hear.
HAMLET. What?
GHOST. I am thy father's spirit,
　　Doomed for a certain term to walk the night,   10
　　And for the day confined to fast in fires,
　　Till the foul crimes° done in my days of nature
　　Are burnt and purged away. But that I am forbid
　　To tell the secrets of my prison house,
　　I could a tale unfold whose lightest word   15
　　Would harrow up thy soul, freeze thy young blood,
　　Make thy two eyes like stars start from their spheres,°
　　Thy knotted and combinèd locks to part,
　　And each particular hair to stand an end
　　Like quills upon the fearful porpentine.°   20
　　But this eternal blazon° must not be
　　To ears of flesh and blood. List, list, O, list!
　　If thou didst ever thy dear father love——
HAMLET. O God!
GHOST. Revenge his foul and most unnatural murder.   25
HAMLET. Murder?
GHOST. Murder most foul, as in the best it is,
　　But this most foul, strange, and unnatural.
HAMLET. Haste me to know't, that I, with wings as swift
　　As meditation° or the thoughts of love,   30
　　May sweep to my revenge.
GHOST.   I find thee apt,
　　And duller shouldst thou be than the fat weed
　　That roots itself in ease on Lethe wharf,°
　　Wouldst thou not stir in this. Now, Hamlet, hear.
　　'Tis given out that, sleeping in my orchard,   35
　　A serpent stung me. So the whole ear of Denmark

SCENE V. 12 *crimes:* sins.　17 *spheres:* (in Ptolemaic astronomy, each planet was fixed in a hollow transparent shell concentric with the earth).　20 *fearful porpentine:* timid porcupine.　21 *eternal blazon:* revelation of eternity.　30 *meditation:* thought.　33 *Lethe wharf:* bank of the river of forgetfulness in Hades.

Is by a forgèd process° of my death
Rankly abused. But know, thou noble youth,
The serpent that did sting thy father's life
Now wears his crown.
HAMLET.   O my prophetic soul!   40
My uncle?
GHOST. Ay, that incestuous, that adulterate° beast,
With witchcraft of his wits, with traitorous gifts—
O wicked wit and gifts, that have the power
So to seduce!—won to his shameful lust   45
The will of my most seeming-virtuous queen.
O Hamlet, what a falling-off was there,
From me, whose love was of that dignity
That it went hand in hand even with the vow
I made to her in marriage, and to decline   50
Upon a wretch whose natural gifts were poor
To those of mine.
But virtue, as it never will be moved,
Though lewdness° court it in a shape of heaven,
So lust, though to a radiant angel linked,   55
Will sate itself in a celestial bed
And prey on garbage.
But soft, methinks I scent the morning air;
Brief let me be. Sleeping within my orchard,
My custom always of the afternoon,   60
Upon my secure° hour thy uncle stole
With juice of cursed hebona° in a vial,
And in the porches of my ears did pour
The leperous distillment, whose effect
Holds such an enmity with blood of man   65
That swift as quicksilver it courses through
The natural gates and alleys of the body,
And with a sudden vigor it doth posset°
And curd, like eager° droppings into milk,
The thin and wholesome blood. So did it mine,   70
And a most instant tetter° barked about
Most lazarlike° with vile and loathsome crust
All my smooth body.
Thus was I, sleeping, by a brother's hand
Of life, of crown, of queen at once dispatched,   75
Cut off even in the blossoms of my sin,
Unhouseled, disappointed, unaneled,°
No reck'ning made, but sent to my account
With all my imperfections on my head.

---

37 *forgèd process:* false account.   42 *adulterate:* adulterous.   54 *lewdness:* lust.   61 *secure:* unsuspecting.   62 *hebona:* a poisonous plant.   68 *posset:* curdle.   69 *eager:* acid.   71 *tetter:* scab.   72 *lazarlike:* leperlike.   77 *Unhouseled, disappointed, unaneled:* without the sacrament of communion, unabsolved, without extreme unction.

O, horrible! O, horrible! Most horrible!   80
If thou hast nature in thee, bear it not.
Let not the royal bed of Denmark be
A couch for luxury° and damnèd incest.
But howsomever thou pursuest this act,
Taint not thy mind, nor let thy soul contrive   85
Against thy mother aught. Leave her to heaven
And to those thorns that in her bosom lodge
To prick and sting her. Fare thee well at once.
The glowworm shows the matin° to be near
And 'gins to pale his uneffectual fire.   90
Adieu, adieu, adieu. Remember me.   *Exit.*
HAMLET. O all you host of heaven! O earth! What else?
And shall I couple hell? O fie! Hold, hold, my heart,
And you, my sinews, grow now instant old,
But bear me stiffly up. Remember thee?   95
Ay, thou poor ghost, whiles memory holds a seat
In this distracted globe.° Remember thee?
Yea, from the table° of my memory
I'll wipe away all trivial fond° records,
All saws° of books, all forms, all pressures° past   100
That youth and observation copied there,
And thy commandment all alone shall live
Within the book and volume of my brain,
Unmixed with baser matter. Yes, by heaven!
O most pernicious woman!   105
O villain, villain, smiling, damnèd villain!
My tables—meet it is I set it down
That one may smile, and smile, and be a villain.
At least I am sure it may be so in Denmark.   *[Writes.]*
So, uncle, there you are. Now to my word: 110
It is "Adieu, adieu, remember me."
I have sworn't.
HORATIO AND MARCELLUS. *[Within]* My lord, my lord!

         Enter Horatio and Marcellus.

MARCELLUS.   Lord Hamlet!
HORATIO.   Heavens secure him!
HAMLET. So be it!
MARCELLUS. Illo, ho, ho,° my lord!   115
HAMLET. Hillo, ho, ho, boy! Come, bird, come.
MARCELLUS. How is't, my noble lord?
HORATIO.   What news, my lord?
HAMLET. O, wonderful!
HORATIO. Good my lord, tell it.

---

     83 *luxury:* lust.   89 *matin:* morning.   97 *globe:* i.e., his head.   98 *table:* tablet, notebook.   99 *fond:* foolish.   100 *saws:* maxims; *pressures:* impressions.   115 *Illo, ho, ho:* (falconer's call to his hawk).

HAMLET.   No, you will reveal it.
HORATIO. Not I, my lord, by heaven.
MARCELLUS.   Nor I, my lord.   120
HAMLET. How say you then? Would heart of man once think it?
     But you'll be secret?
BOTH.   Ay, by heaven, my lord.
HAMLET. There's never a villain dwelling in all Denmark
     But he's an arrant knave.
HORATIO. There needs no ghost, my lord, come from the grave   125
     To tell us this.
HAMLET.   Why, right, you are in the right;
     And so, without more circumstance° at all,
     I hold it fit that we shake hands and part:
     You, as your business and desire shall point you,
     For every man hath business and desire   130
     Such as it is, and for my own poor part,
     Look you, I'll go pray.
HORATIO. These are but wild and whirling words, my lord.
HAMLET. I am sorry they offend you, heartily;
     Yes, faith, heartily.
HORATIO.   There's no offense, my lord.   135
HAMLET. Yes, by Saint Patrick, but there is, Horatio,
     And much offense too. Touching this vision here,
     It is an honest ghost,° that let me tell you.
     For your desire to know what is between us,
     O'ermaster't as you may. And now, good friends,   140
     As you are friends, scholars, and soldiers,
     Give me one poor request.
HORATIO. What is't, my lord? We will.
HAMLET. Never make known what you have seen tonight.
BOTH. My lord, we will not.
HAMLET.   Nay, but swear't.
HORATIO.   In faith,   145
     My lord, not I.
MARCELLUS.   Nor I, my lord—in faith.
HAMLET. Upon my sword.
MARCELLUS.   We have sworn, my lord, already.
HAMLET. Indeed, upon my sword, indeed.

                    Ghost cries under the stage.

GHOST. Swear.
HAMLET. Ha, ha, boy, say'st thou so? Art thou there, truepenny?°   150
     Come on. You hear this fellow in the cellarage.
     Consent to swear.
HORATIO.   Propose the oath, my lord.

---

     127 *circumstance:* details.   138 *honest ghost:* i.e., not a demon in his father's shape.   150 *truepenny:*
honest fellow.

HAMLET. Never to speak of this that you have seen.
    Swear by my sword.
GHOST. [*Beneath*] Swear.   155
HAMLET. *Hic et ubique?*° Then we'll shift our ground;
    Come hither, gentlemen,
    And lay your hands again upon my sword.
    Swear by my sword
    Never to speak of this that you have heard.   160
GHOST. [*Beneath*] Swear by his sword.
HAMLET. Well said, old mole! Canst work i' th' earth so fast?
    A worthy pioner!° Once more remove, good friends.
HORATIO. O day and night, but this is wondrous strange!
HAMLET. And therefore as a stranger give it welcome.   165
    There are more things in heaven and earth, Horatio,
    Than are dreamt of in your philosophy.
    But come:
    Here as before, never, so help you mercy,
    How strange or odd some'er I bear myself   170
    (As I perchance hereafter shall think meet
    To put an antic disposition° on),
    That you, at such times seeing me, never shall
    With arms encumb'red° thus, or this headshake,
    Or by pronouncing of some doubtful phrase,   175
    As "Well, well, we know," or "We could, an if we would,"
    Or "If we list to speak," or "There be, an if they might,"
    Or such ambiguous giving out, to note
    That you know aught of me—this do swear,
    So grace and mercy at your most need help you.   180
GHOST. [*Beneath*] Swear.   [*They swear.*]
HAMLET. Rest, rest, perturbèd spirit. So, gentlemen,
    With all my love I do commend me° to you,
    And what so poor a man as Hamlet is
    May do t' express his love and friending to you,   185
    God willing, shall not lack. Let us go in together,
    And still your fingers on your lips, I pray.
    The time is out of joint. O cursèd spite,
    That ever I was born to set it right!
    Nay, come, let's go together.   *Exeunt.*

ACT II
Scene I
A room.

    Enter old Polonius, with his man Reynaldo.

POLONIUS. Give him this money and these notes, Reynaldo.
REYNALDO. I will, my lord.

---

    156 *Hic et ubique:* here and everywhere (Latin).   163 *pioner:* digger of mines.   172 *antic disposition:* fantastic behavior.   174 *encumb'red:* folded.   183 *commend me:* entrust myself.

POLONIUS. You shall do marvell's° wisely, good Reynaldo,
    Before you visit him, to make inquire
    Of his behavior.
REYNALDO.   My lord, I did intend it.   5
POLONIUS. Marry, well said, very well said. Look you sir,
    Inquire me first what Danskers° are in Paris,
    And how, and who, what means, and where they keep,°
    What company, at what expense; and finding
    By this encompassment° and drift of question   10
    That they do know my son, come you more nearer
    Than your particular demands° will touch it.
    Take you as 'twere some distant knowledge of him,
    As thus, "I know his father and his friends,
    And in part him." Do you mark this, Reynaldo?   15
REYNALDO. Ay, very well, my lord.
POLONIUS. "And in part him, but," you may say, "not well,
    But if't be he I mean, he's very wild,
    Addicted so and so," And there put on him
    What forgeries° you please; marry, none so rank   20
    As may dishonor him—take heed of that—
    But, sir, such wanton, wild, and usual slips
    As are companions noted and most known
    To youth and liberty.
REYNALDO.   As gaming, my lord.
POLONIUS. Ay, or drinking, fencing, swearing, quarrelling,   25
    Drabbing.° You may go so far.
REYNALDO. My lord, that would dishonor him.
POLONIUS. Faith, no, as you may season it in the charge.
    You must not put another scandal on him,
    That he is open to incontinency.°   30
    That's not my meaning. But breathe his faults so quaintly°
    That they may seem the taints of liberty,
    The flash and outbreak of a fiery mind,
    A savageness in unreclaimèd blood,
    Of general assault.°
REYNALDO.   But, my good lord——   35
POLONIUS. Wherefore should you do this?
REYNALDO.   Ay, my lord,
I would know that.
POLONIUS.   Marry, sir, here's my drift,
    And I believe it is a fetch of warrant.°
    You laying these slight sullies on my son
    As 'twere a thing a little soiled i' th' working,
    Mark you,   40

SCENE 1. 3 *marvell's:* marvelous(ly).   7 *Danskers:* Danes.   8 *keep:* dwell.   10 *encompassment:* circling.   12 *demands:* questions.   20 *forgeries:* inventions.   26 *Drabbing:* wenching.   30 *incontinency:* habitual licentiousness.   31 *quaintly:* ingeniously, delicately.   35 *Of general assault:* common to all men.   38 *fetch of warrant:* justifiable device.

Your party in converse, him you would sound,
Having ever seen in the prenominate crimes°
The youth you breathe of guilty, be assured
He closes with you in this consequence:° 45
"Good sir," or so, or "friend," or "gentleman"—
According to the phrase or the addition°
Of man and country—

REYNALDO.   Very good, my lord.

POLONIUS. And then, sir, does 'a° this—'a does—
What was I about to say? By the mass, I was about 50
to say something! Where did I leave?

REYNALDO. At "closes in the consequence," at "friend
or so," and "gentleman."

POLONIUS. At "closes in the consequence"—Ay, marry!
He closes thus: "I know the gentleman; 55
I saw him yesterday, or t'other day,
Or then, or then, with such or such, and, as you say,
There was 'a gaming, there o'ertook in's rouse,
There falling out at tennis"; or perchance,
"I saw him enter such a house of sale," 60
Videlicet,° a brothel, or so forth.
See you now—
Your bait of falsehood take this carp of truth,
And thus do we of wisdom and of reach,°
With windlasses° and with assays of bias,° 65
By indirections find directions out.
So, by my former lecture and advice,
Shall you my son. You have me, have you not?

REYNALDO. My lord, I have.

POLONIUS.   God bye ye, fare ye well.

REYNALDO. Good my lord. 70

POLONIUS. Observe his inclination in yourself.°

REYNALDO. I shall, my lord.

POLONIUS. And let him ply his music.

REYNALDO.   Well, my lord.

POLONIUS. Farewell.   *Exit Reynaldo.*

            Enter Ophelia.

            How now, Ophelia, what's the matter?

OPHELIA. O my lord, my lord, I have been so affrighted! 75

POLONIUS. With what, i' th' name of God?

OPHELIA. My lord, as I was sewing in my closet,°
Lord Hamlet, with his doublet all unbraced,°
No hat upon his head, his stockings fouled,

_____

43 *Having . . . crimes:* if he has ever seen in the aforementioned crimes.   45 *He closes . . . this consequence:* he falls in with you in this conclusion.   47 *addition:* title.   49 *'a:* he.   61 *Videlicet:* namely.   64 *reach:* far-reaching awareness(?).   65 *windlasses:* circuitous courses; *assays of bias:* indirect attempts (metaphor from bowling; *bias* = curved course).   71 *in yourself:* for yourself.   77 *closet:* private room.   78 *doublet all unbraced:* jacket entirely unlaced.

Ungartered, and down-gyvèd° to his ankle,   80
Pale as his shirt, his knees knocking each other,
And with a look so piteous in purport,°
As if he had been loosèd out of hell
To speak of horrors—he comes before me.
POLONIUS. Mad for thy love?   85
OPHELIA.   My lord, I do not know,
     But truly I do fear it.
POLONIUS.   What said he?
OPHELIA. He took me by the wrist and held me hard;
     Then goes he to the length of all his arm,
     And with his other hand thus o'er his brow
     He falls to such perusal of my face   90
     As 'a would draw it. Long stayed he so.
     At last, a little shaking of mine arm,
     And thrice his head thus waving up and down,
     He raised a sigh so piteous and profound
     As it did seem to shatter all his bulk   95
     And end his being. That done, he lets me go,
     And, with his head over his shoulder turned,
     He seemed to find his way without his eyes,
     For out o' doors he went without their helps,
     And to the last bended their light on me.   100
POLONIUS. Come, go with me. I will go seek the King.
     This is the very ecstasy° of love,
     Whose violent property fordoes° itself
     And leads the will to desperate undertakings
     As oft as any passions under heaven   105
     That does afflict our natures. I am sorry.
     What, have you given him any hard words of late?
OPHELIA. No, my good lord; but as you did command,
     I did repel his letters and denied
     His access to me.
POLONIUS.   That hath made him mad.   110
     I am sorry that with better heed and judgment
     I had not quoted° him. I feared he did but trifle
     And meant to wrack thee; but beshrew my jealousy.°
     By heaven, it is as proper° to our age
     To cast beyond ourselves° in our opinions   115
     As it is common for the younger sort
     To lack discretion. Come, go we to the King.
     This must be known, which, being kept close, might move
     More grief to hide than hate to utter love.°
     Come.   *Exeunt.*   120

---

80 *down-gyvèd:* hanging down like fetters.   82 *purport:* expression.   102 *ecstasy:* madness.
103 *property fordoes:* quality destroys.   112 *quoted:* noted.   113 *beshrew my jealousy:* curse on my suspicions.   114 *proper:* natural.   115 *To cast beyond ourselves:* to be over-calculating.   117–119 *Come,
go . . . utter love:* (the general meaning is that while telling the King of Hamlet's love may anger the
King, more grief would come from keeping it secret).

Scene II
The castle.

Flourish. Enter King and Queen, Rosencrantz, and Guildenstern [with others].

KING. Welcome, dear Rosencrantz and Guildenstern.
   Moreover that° we much did long to see you,
   The need we have to use you did provoke
   Our hasty sending. Something have you heard
   Of Hamlet's transformation: so call it,   5
   Sith° nor th' exterior nor the inward man
   Resembles that it was. What it should be,
   More than his father's death, that thus hath put him
   So much from th' understanding of himself,
   I cannot dream of. I entreat you both   10
   That, being of so° young days brought up with him,
   And sith so neighbored to his youth and havior,°
   That you vouchsafe your rest° here in our court
   Some little time, so by your companies
   To draw him on to pleasures, and to gather   15
   So much as from occasion you may glean,
   Whether aught to us unknown afflicts him thus,
   That opened° lies within our remedy.
QUEEN. Good gentlemen, he hath much talked of you,
   And sure I am, two men there is not living   20
   To whom he more adheres. If it will please you
   To show us so much gentry° and good will
   As to expend your time with us awhile
   For the supply and profit of our hope,
   Your visitation shall receive such thanks   25
   As fits a king's remembrance.
ROSENCRANTZ.   Both your Majesties
   Might, by sovereign power you have of us,
   Put your dread pleasure more into command
   Than to entreaty.
GUILDENSTERN.   But we both obey,
   And here give up ourselves in the full bent°   30
   To lay our service freely at your feet,
   To be commanded.
KING. Thanks, Rosencrantz and gentle Guildenstern.
QUEEN. Thanks, Guildenstern and gentle Rosencrantz.
   And I beseech you instantly to visit   35
   My too much changèd son. Go, some of you,
   And bring these gentlemen where Hamlet is.
GUILDENSTERN. Heavens make our presence and our practices
   Pleasant and helpful to him!
QUEEN.   Ay, amen!

   SCENE II. 2 *Moreover that*: beside the fact that.   6 *Sith*: since.   11 *of so*: from such.   12 *youth and havior*: behavior in his youth.   13 *vouchsafe your rest*: consent to remain.   18 *opened*: revealed.   22 *gentry*: courtesy.   30 *in the full bent*: entirely (the figure is of a bow bent to its capacity).

Exeunt Rosencrantz and Guildenstern [with some Attendants].

Enter Polonius.

POLONIUS. Th' ambassadors from Norway, my good lord,   40
  Are joyfully returned.
KING. Thou still° hast been the father of good news.
POLONIUS. Have I, my lord? Assure you, my good liege,
  I hold my duty, as I hold my soul,
  Both to my God and to my gracious king;   45
  And I do think or else this brain of mine
  Hunts not the trail of policy so sure°
  As it hath used to do, that I have found
  The very cause of Hamlet's lunacy.
KING. O, speak of that! That do I long to hear.   50
POLONIUS. Give first admittance to th' ambassadors.
  My news shall be the fruit to that great feast.
KING. Thyself do grace to them and bring them in.

Exit Polonius.

  He tells me, my dear Gertrude, he hath found
  The head and source of all your son's distemper.   55
QUEEN. I doubt° it is no other but the main,°
  His father's death and our o'erhasty marriage.
KING. Well, we shall sift him.

Enter Polonius, Voltemand, and Cornelius.

                    Welcome, my good friends.
  Say, Voltemand, what from our brother Norway?
VOLTEMAND. Most fair return of greetings and desires.   60
  Upon our first,° he sent out to suppress
  His nephew's levies, which to him appeared
  To be a preparation 'gainst the Polack;
  But better looked into, he truly found
  It was against your Highness, whereat grieved,   65
  That so his sickness, age, and impotence
  Was falsely borne in hand,° sends out arrests
  On Fortinbras; which he, in brief, obeys,
  Receives rebuke from Norway, and in fine,°
  Makes vow before his uncle never more   70
  To give th' assay° of arms against your Majesty.
  Whereon old Norway, overcome with joy,
  Gives him threescore thousand crowns in annual fee
  And his commission to employ those soldiers,
  So levied as before, against the Polack,   75
  With an entreaty, herein further shown,

Gives a paper.

---

  42 *still:* always.   46 *Hunts not . . . so sure:* does not follow clues of political doings with such sureness.   56 *doubt:* suspect; *main:* principal point.   61 *first:* first audience.   67 *borne in hand:* deceived.
69 *in fine:* finally.   71 *assay:* trial.

That it might please you to give quiet pass
Through your dominions for this enterprise,
On such regards of safety and allowance°
As therein are set down.

KING.   It likes us well;   80
And at our more considered time° we'll read,
Answer, and think upon this business.
Meantime, we thank you for your well-took labor.
Go to your rest; at night we'll feast together.
Most welcome home!   *Exeunt Ambassadors.*

POLONIUS.   This business is well ended.   85
My liege and madam, to expostulate°
What majesty should be, what duty is,
Why day is day, night night, and time is time.
Were nothing but to waste night, day, and time.
Therefore, since brevity is the soul of wit,°   90
And tediousness the limbs and outward flourishes,
I will be brief. Your noble son is mad.
Mad call I it, for, to define true madness,
What is't but to be nothing else but mad?
But let that go.

QUEEN.   More matter, with less art.   95
POLONIUS. Madam, I swear I use no art at all.
That he's mad, 'tis true: 'tis true 'tis pity,
And pity 'tis 'tis true—a foolish figure.°
But farewell it, for I will use no art.
Mad let us grant him then; and now remains   100
That we find out the cause of this effect,
Or rather say, the cause of this defect,
For this effect defective comes by cause.
Thus it remains, and the remainder thus.
Perpend.°   105
I have a daughter: have, while she is mine,
Who in her duty and obedience, mark,
Hath given me this. Now gather, and surmise.

                    [*Reads*] *the letter.*

"To the celestial, and my soul's idol, the most
beautified Ophelia"—   110
That's an ill phrase, a vile phrase; "beautified" is a
vile phrase. But you shall hear. Thus:
"In her excellent white bosom, these, &c."
QUEEN. Came this from Hamlet to her?
POLONIUS. Good madam, stay awhile. I will be faithful.   115
          "Doubt thou the stars are fire,
                    Doubt that the sun doth move;

---

79 *regards of safety and allowance:* i.e., conditions.   81 *considered time:* time proper for considering.
86 *expostulate:* discuss.   90 *wit:* wisdom, understanding.   98 *figure:* figure of rhetoric.   105 *Perpend:*
consider carefully.

> Doubt° truth to be a liar,
>> But never doubt I love.
> O dear Ophelia, I am ill at these numbers.° I have
> not art to reckon my groans; but that I love thee
> best, O most best, believe it. Adieu.
>> Thine evermore, most dear lady, whilst this
>> machine° is to him, Hamlet."
> This in obedience hath my daughter shown me,   125
> And more above° hath his solicitings,
> As they fell out by time, by means, and place,
> All given to mine ear.

KING.   But how hath she
> Received his love?

POLONIUS.   What do you think of me?

KING. As of man faithful and honorable.   130

POLONIUS. I would fain prove so. But what might you think,
> When I had seen this hot love on the wing
> (As I perceived it, I must tell you that,
> Before my daughter told me), what might you,
> Or my dear Majesty your Queen here, think,   135
> If I had played the desk or table book,°
> Or given my heart a winking,° mute and dumb,
> Or looked upon this love with idle sight?
> What might you think? No, I went round to work
> And my young mistress thus I did bespeak: 140
> "Lord Hamlet is a prince, out of thy star.°
> This must not be." And then I prescripts gave her,
> That she should lock herself from his resort,
> Admit no messengers, receive no tokens.
> Which done, she took the fruits of my advice,   145
> And he, repellèd, a short tale to make,
> Fell into a sadness, then into a fast,
> Thence to a watch,° thence into a weakness,
> Thence to a lightness,° and, by this declension,
> Into the madness wherein now he raves,   150
> And all we mourn for.

KING.   Do you think 'tis this?

QUEEN. It may be, very like.

POLONIUS. Hath there been such a time, I would fain know that,
> That I have positively said " 'Tis so,"
> When it proved otherwise?

KING.   Not that I know.   155

POLONIUS. [Pointing to his head and shoulder] Take this from this, if this be otherwise.
> If circumstances lead me, I will find

---

118 *Doubt:* suspect.   120 *ill at these numbers:* unskilled in verses.   124 *machine:* complex device
(here, his body).   126 *more above:* in addition.   136 *played the desk or table book:* i.e., been a passive
recipient of secrets.   137 *winking:* closing of the eyes.   141 *star:* sphere.   148 *watch:* wakefulness.
149 *lightness:* mental derangement.

Where truth is hid, though it were hid indeed
Within the center.°
KING.   How may we try it further?
POLONIUS. You know sometimes he walks four hours together   160
Here in the lobby.
QUEEN.   So he does indeed.
POLONIUS. At such a time I'll loose my daughter to him.
Be you and I behind an arras° then.
Mark the encounter. If he love her not,
And be not from his reason fall'n thereon,   165
Let me be no assistant for a state
But keep a farm and carters.
KING.   We will try it.

Enter Hamlet reading on a book.

QUEEN. But look where sadly the poor wretch comes reading.
POLONIUS. Away, I do beseech you both, away.

Exit King and Queen.

I'll board him presently.° O, give me leave.   170
How does my good Lord Hamlet?
HAMLET. Well, God-a-mercy.
POLONIUS. Do you know me, my lord?
HAMLET. Excellent well. You are a fishmonger.°
POLONIUS. Not I, my lord.   175
HAMLET. Then I would you were so honest a man.
POLONIUS. Honest, my lord?
HAMLET. Ay, sir. To be honest, as this world goes, is to
be one man picked out of ten thousand.
POLONIUS. That's very true, my lord.   180
HAMLET. For if the sun breed maggots in a dead dog,
being a good kissing carrion°——Have you a
daughter?
POLONIUS. I have, my lord.
HAMLET. Let her not walk i' th' sun. Conception° is a   185
blessing, but as your daughter may conceive, friend,
look to't.
POLONIUS. [*Aside*] How say you by that? Still harping
on my daughter. Yet he knew me not at first. 'A said
I was a fishmonger. 'A is far gone, far gone. And   190
truly in my youth I suffered much extremity for
love, very near this. I'll speak to him again.—What
do you read, my lord?
HAMLET. Words, words, words.
POLONIUS. What is the matter, my lord?   195

---

159 *center:* center of the earth.   163 *arras:* tapestry hanging in front of a wall.   170 *board him presently:* accost him at once.   174 *fishmonger:* dealer in fish (slang for a procurer).   182 *a good kissing carrion:* (perhaps the meaning is "a good piece of flesh to kiss," but many editors emend *good* to *god*, taking the word to refer to the sun).   185 *Conception:* (1) understanding, (2) becoming pregnant.

HAMLET. Between who?

POLONIUS. I mean that matter° that you read, my lord.

HAMLET. Slanders, sir; for the satirical rogue says here
    that old men have gray beards, that their faces are
    wrinkled, their eyes purging thick amber and plum-   200
    tree gum, and that they have a plentiful lack of wit,
    together with most weak hams. All which, sir,
    though I most powerfully and potently believe, yet
    I hold it not honestly° to have it thus set down; for
    you yourself, sir, should be old as I am if, like a   205
    crab, you could go backward.

POLONIUS. [Aside] Though this be madness, yet there
    is method in't. Will you walk out of the air, my lord?

HAMLET. Into my grave.

POLONIUS. Indeed, that's out of the air. [Aside] How   210
    pregnant° sometimes his replies are! A happiness°
    that often madness hits on, which reason and sanity
    could not so prosperously be delivered of. I will
    leave him and suddenly contrive the means of
    meeting between him and my daughter.—My lord,   215
    I will take my leave of you.

HAMLET. You cannot take from me anything that I will
    more willingly part withal—except my life, except
    my life, except my life.

Enter Guildenstern and Rosencrantz.

POLONIUS. Fare you well, my lord.   220

HAMLET. These tedious old fools!

POLONIUS. You go to seek the Lord Hamlet? There he is.

ROSENCRANTZ. [To Polonius] God save you, sir!

Exit Polonius.

GUILDENSTERN. My honored lord!   225

ROSENCRANTZ. My most dear lord!

HAMLET. My excellent good friends! How dost thou,
    Guildenstern? Ah, Rosencrantz! Good lads, how do
    you both?

ROSENCRANTZ. As the indifferent° children of the earth.   230

GUILDENSTERN. Happy in that we are not overhappy.
    On Fortune's cap we are not the very button.

HAMLET. Nor the soles of her shoe?

ROSENCRANTZ. Neither, my lord.

HAMLET. Then you live about her waist, or in the middle
    of her favors?   235

GUILDENSTERN. Faith, her privates° we.

---

197 *matter:* (Polonius means "subject matter," but Hamlet pretends to take the word in the sense
of "quarrel").   204 *honesty:* decency.   211 *pregnant:* meaningful; *happiness:* apt turn of phrase.   230 *indifferent:* ordinary.   236 *privates:* ordinary men (with a pun on "private parts").

HAMLET. In the secret parts of Fortune? O, most true!
  She is a strumpet. What news?
ROSENCRANTZ. None, my lord, but that the world's
  grown honest. 240
HAMLET. Then is doomsday near. But your news is not
  true. Let me question more in particular. What
  have you, my good friends, deserved at the hands of
  Fortune that she sends you to prison hither? 245
GUILDENSTERN. Prison, my lord?
HAMLET. Denmark's a prison.
ROSENCRANTZ. Then is the world one.
HAMLET. A goodly one, in which there are many
  confines, wards,° and dungeons, Denmark being 250
  one o' th' worst.
ROSENCRANTZ. We think not so, my lord.
HAMLET. Why, then 'tis none to you, for there is nothing
  either good or bad but thinking makes it so. To me
  it is a prison. 255
ROSENCRANTZ. Why then your ambition makes it one.
  'Tis too narrow for your mind.
HAMLET. O God, I could be bounded in a nutshell and
  count myself a king of infinite space, were it not
  that I have bad dreams. 260
GUILDENSTERN. Which dreams indeed are ambition, for
  the very substance of the ambitious is merely the
  shadow of a dream.
HAMLET. A dream itself is but a shadow.
ROSENCRANTZ. Truly, and I hold ambition of so airy and 265
  light a quality that it is but a shadow's shadow.
HAMLET. Then are our beggars bodies, and our
  monarchs and outstretched heroes the beggars'
  shadows.° Shall we to th' court? For, by my fay,°
  I cannot reason. 270
BOTH. We'll wait upon you.
HAMLET. No such matter. I will not sort you with the
  rest of my servants, for, to speak to you like an
  honest man, I am most dreadfully attended. But in
  the beaten way of friendship, what make you at 275
  Elsinore?
ROSENCRANTZ. To visit you, my lord; no other occasion.
HAMLET. Beggar that I am, I am even poor in thanks,
  but I thank you; and sure, dear friends, my thanks
  are too dear a halfpenny.° Were you not sent for? 280
  Is it your own inclining? Is it a free visitation?

---

250 *wards:* cells.   267–269 *Then are . . . beggars' shadows:* i.e., by your logic, beggars (lacking ambition) are substantial, and great men are elongated shadows.   269 *fay:* faith.   280 *too dear a halfpenny:*
i.e., nor worth a halfpenny.

Come, come, deal justly with me. Come, come;
nay, speak.

GUILDENSTERN. What should we say, my lord?

HAMLET. Why anything—but to th' purpose. You were   285
sent for, and there is a kind of confession in your
looks, which your modesties have not craft enough
to color. I know the good King and Queen have
sent for you.

ROSENCRANTZ. To what end, my lord?   290

HAMLET. That you must teach me. But let me conjure
you by the rights of our fellowship, by the con-
sonancy of our youth, by the obligation of our ever-
preserved love, and by what more dear a better
proposer can charge you withal, be even and direct   295
with me, whether you were sent for or no.

ROSENCRANTZ. [Aside to Guildenstern] What say you?

HAMLET. [Aside] Nay then, I have an eye of you.—If
you love me, hold not off.

GUILDENSTERN. My lord, we were sent for.   300

HAMLET. I will tell you why; so shall my anticipation
prevent your discovery,° and your secrecy to the
King and Queen molt no feather. I have of late, but
wherefore I know not, lost all my mirth, forgone all
custom of exercises; and indeed, it goes so heavily   305
with my disposition that this goodly frame, the
earth, seems to me a sterile promontory; this most
excellent canopy, the air, look you, this brave
o'erhanging firmament, this majestical roof fretted°
with golden fire: why, it appeareth nothing to me   310
but a foul and pestilent congregation of vapors.
What a piece of work is a man, how noble in reason,
how infinite in faculties, in form and moving how
express° and admirable, in action how like an angel,
in apprehension how like a god: the beauty of the   315
world, the paragon of animals; and yet to me, what
is this quintessence of dust? Man delights not me;
nor woman neither, though by your smiling you
seem to say so.

ROSENCRANTZ. My lord, there was no such stuff in my thoughts.   320

HAMLET. Why did ye laugh then, when I said "Man
delights not me"?

ROSENCRANTZ. To think my lord, if you delight not in
man, what lenten° entertainment the players shall   325
receive from you. We coted° them on the way, and
hither are they coming to offer you service.

---

302 *prevent your discovery:* forestall your disclosure.   309 *fretted:* adorned.   314 *express:* exact.
325 *lenten:* meager.   326 *coted:* overtook.

HAMLET. He that plays the king shall be welcome; his
	Majesty shall have tribute of me; the adventurous
	knight shall use his foil and target;° the lover shall 330
	not sigh gratis; the humorous man° shall end his
	part in peace; the clown shall make those laugh
	whose lungs are tickle o' th' sere;° and the lady shall
	say her mind freely, or° the blank verse shall halt°
	for't. What players are they? 335
ROSENCRANTZ. Even those you were wont to take such
	delight in, the tragedians of the city.
HAMLET. How chances it they travel? Their residence,
	both in reputation and profit, was better both ways.
ROSENCRANTZ. I think their inhibition° comes by the   340
	means of the late innovation.°
HAMLET. Do they hold the same estimation they did
	when I was in the city? Are they so followed?
ROSENCRANTZ. No indeed, are they not.
HAMLET. How comes it? Do they grow rusty?   345
ROSENCRANTZ. Nay, their endeavor keeps in the wonted
	pace, but there is, sir, an eyrie° of children, little
	eyases, that cry out on the top of question° and are
	most tyrannically° clapped for't. These are now
	the fashion, and so berattle the common stages° (so 350
	they call them) that many wearing rapiers are afraid
	of goosequills° and dare scarce come thither.
HAMLET. What, are they children? Who maintains 'em?
	How are they escoted?° Will they pursue the
	quality° no longer than they can sing? Will they not 355
	say afterwards, if they should grow themselves to
	common players (as it is most like, if their means
	are no better), their writers do them wrong to make
	them exclaim against their own succession?°
ROSENCRANTZ. Faith, there has been much to-do on   360
	both sides, and the nation holds it no sin to tarre°
	them to controversy. There was, for a while, no
	money bid for argument° unless the poet and the
	player went to cuffs in the question.
HAMLET. Is't possible?   365
GUILDENSTERN. O, there has been much throwing about
	of brains.

---

330 *target:* shield.   331 *humorous man:* i.e., eccentric man (among stock characters in dramas were
men dominated by a "humor" or odd trait).   333 *tickle o' th' sere:* on hair trigger (*sere* = part of the gun-
lock).   334 *or:* else; *halt:* limp.   340 *inhibition:* hindrance.   341 *innovation:* (probably an allusion to the
companies of child actors that had become popular and were offering serious competition to the adult
actors).   347 *eyrie:* nest.   348 *eyases, that . . . of question:* unfledged hawks that cry shrilly above others in matters of debate.   349 *tyrannically:* violently.   350 *berattle the common stages:* cry down the public theaters (with the adult acting companies).   352 *goosequills:* pens (of satirists who ridicule the public
theaters and their audiences).   354 *escoted:* financially supported.   355 *quality:* profession of acting.
359 *succession:* future.   361 *tarre:* incite.   363 *argument:* plot of a play.

HAMLET. Do the boys carry it away?

ROSENCRANTZ. Ay, that they do, my lord—Hercules and
his load° too.

HAMLET. It is not very strange, for my uncle is King of
Denmark, and those that would make mouths at
him while my father lived give twenty, forty, fifty,
a hundred ducats apiece for his picture in little.
'Sblood,° there is something in this more than
natural, if philosophy could find it out.

A flourish.

GUILDENSTERN. There are the players.

HAMLET. Gentlemen, you are welcome to Elsinore.
Your hands, come then. Th' appurtenance of welcome is fashion and ceremony. Let me comply°
with you in this garb,° lest my extent° to the players
(which I tell you must show fairly outwards) should
more appear like entertainment than yours. You are
welcome. But my uncle-father and aunt-mother are
deceived.

GUILDENSTERN. In what, my dear lord?

HAMLET. I am but mad north-northwest:° when the
wind is southerly I know a hawk from a handsaw.°

Enter Polonius.

POLONIUS. Well be with you, gentlemen.

HAMLET. Hark you, Guildenstern, and you too; at each
ear a hearer. That great baby you see there is not
yet out of his swaddling clouts.

ROSENCRANTZ. Happily° he is the second time come to
them, for they say an old man is twice a child.

HAMLET. I will prophesy he comes to tell me of the
players. Mark it.—You say right, sir; a Monday
morning, 'twas then indeed.

POLONIUS. My lord, I have news to tell you.

HAMLET. My lord, I have news to tell you. When
Roscius° was an actor in Rome——

POLONIUS. The actors are come hither, my lord.

HAMLET. Buzz, buzz.°

POLONIUS. Upon my honor——

HAMLET. Then came each actor on his ass——

POLONIUS. The best actors in the world, either for
tragedy, comedy, history, pastoral, pastoral-comical,

369–370 *Hercules and his load:* i.e., the whole world (with a reference to the Globe Theater, which
had a sign that represented Hercules bearing the globe). 375 *'Sblood:* by God's blood. 380 *comply:* be
courteous. 381 *garb:* outward show; *extent:* behavior. 387 *north-northwest:* i.e., on one point of the
compass only. 388 *hawk from a handsaw* (*hawk* can refer not only to a bird but to a kind of pickax; *handsaw*—a carpenter's tool—may involve a similar pun on "hernshaw," a heron). 393 *Happily:* perhaps.
400 *Roscius:* (a famous Roman comic actor). 402 *Buzz, buzz:* (an interjection, perhaps indicating that
the news is old).

historical-pastoral, tragical-historical, tragical-comi-
cal-historical-pastoral; scene individable,° or poem
unlimited.° Seneca° cannot be too heavy, nor   410
Plautus° too light. For the law of writ and the
liberty,° these are the only men.

HAMLET. O Jeptha, judge of Israel,° what a treasure
    hadst thou!

POLONIUS. What a treasure had he, my lord?

HAMLET. Why,   415
      "One fair daughter, and no more,
        The which he lovèd passing well."

POLONIUS. [Aside] Still on my daughter.

HAMLET. Am I not i' th' right, old Jeptha?

POLONIUS. If you call me Jeptha, my lord, I have a   420
    daughter that I love passing well.

HAMLET. Nay, that follows not.

POLONIUS. What follows, then, my lord?

HAMLET. Why,
      "As by lot, God wot,"   425
    and then, you know,
      "It came to pass, as most like it was."
    The first row of the pious chanson° will show you
    more, for look where my abridgment° comes.

Enter the Players.

You are welcome, masters, welcome, all. I am glad   430
to see thee well. Welcome, good friend. O, old
friend, why, thy face is valanced° since I saw thee
last. Com'st thou to beard me in Denmark? What,
my young lady° and mistress? By'r Lady, your
ladyship is nearer to heaven than when I saw you   435
last by the altitude of a chopine.° Pray God your
voice, like a piece of uncurrent gold, be not cracked
within the ring.°—Masters, you are all welcome.
We'll e'en to't like French falconers, fly at any-
thing we see. We'll have a speech straight. Come,   440
give us a taste of your quality. Come, a passionate
speech.

PLAYER. What speech, my good lord?

---

    408 *scene individable:* plays observing the unities of time, place, and action.   408–409 *poem unlim-
ited:* plays not restricted by the tenets of criticism.   409 *Seneca:* (Roman tragic dramatist).   410 *Plautus:* (Roman comic dramatist).   410–411 *For the law of writ and the liberty:* (perhaps "for sticking to the
text and for improvising"; perhaps "for classical plays and for modern loosely written plays").   412 *Jeptha,
judge of Israel:* (the title of a ballad on the Hebrew judge who sacrificed his daughter; see Judges 11).
428 *row of the pious chanson:* stanza of the scriptural song.   429 *abridgment:* (1) i.e., entertainers, who
abridge the time, (2) interrupters.   432 *valanced:* fringed (with a beard).   434 *young lady:* i.e., boy for
female roles.   436 *chopine:* thick-soled shoe.   437–438 *like a piece . . . the ring:* (a coin was unfit for
legal tender if a crack extended from the edge through the ring enclosing the monarch's head. Hamlet,
punning on *ring,* refers to the change of voice that the boy actor will undergo).

HAMLET. I heard thee speak me a speech once, but it
was never acted, or if it was, not above once, for   445
the play, I remember, pleased not the million; 'twas
caviary to the general,° but it was (as I received it,
and others, whose judgments in such matters cried
in the top of° mine) an excellent play, well digested
in the scenes, set down with as much modesty as   450
cunning.° I remember one said there were no
sallets° in the lines to make the matter savory;
nor no matter in the phrase that might indict the
author of affectation, but called it an honest method,
as wholesome as sweet, and by very much more   455
handsome than fine.° One speech in't I chiefly loved.
'Twas Aeneas' tale to Dido, and thereabout of it
especially when he speaks of Priam's slaughter. If
it live in your memory, begin at this line—let me
see, let me see: 460
     "The rugged Pyrrhus, like th' Hyrcanian
          beast°——"
'Tis not so; it begins with Pyrrhus:
     "The rugged Pyrrhus, he whose sable° arms,
     Black as his purpose, did the night resemble
     When he lay couchèd in th' ominous horse,°   465
     Hath now this dread and black complexion
          smeared
     With heraldry more dismal.° Head to foot
     Now is he total gules, horridly tricked°
     With blood of father, mothers, daughters, sons,
     Baked and impasted° with the parching streets,   470
     Than lend a tyrannous and a damnèd light
     To their lord's murder. Roasted in wrath and fire,
     And thus o'ersizèd° with coagulate gore,
     With eyes like carbuncles, the hellish Pyrrhus
     Old grandsire Priam seeks."   475
     So, proceed you.
POLONIUS. Fore God, my lord, well spoken, with good
     accent and good discretion.
PLAYER.   "Anon he finds him,
     Striking too short at Greeks. His antique sword,   480
     Rebellious to his arm, lies where it falls,
     Repugnant to command.° Unequal matched,
     Pyrrhus at Priam drives, in rage strikes wide,

---

447 *caviary to the general*: i.e., too choice for the multitude.   449 *in the top of*: overtopping.
450–451 *modesty as cunning*: restraint as art.   452 *sallets*: salads, spicy jests.   455–456 *more handsome than
fine*: well-proportioned rather than ornamented.   461 *Hyrcanian beast*: i.e., tiger (Hyrcania was in Asia).
463 *sable*: black.   465 *ominous horse*: i.e., wooden horse at the siege of Troy.   467 *dismal*: ill-omened.
468 *total gules, horridly tricked*: all red, horridly adorned.   470 *impasted*: encrusted.   473 *o'ersizèd*: smeared
over.   482 *Repugnant to command*: disobedient.

But with the whiff and wind of his fell sword
Th' unnervèd father falls. Then senseless Ilium,° 485
Seeming to feel this blow, with flaming top
Stoops to his base,° and with a hideous crash
Takes prisoner Pyrrhus' ear. For lo, his sword,
Which was declining on the milky head
Of reverend Priam, seemed i' th' air to stick. 490
So as a painted tyrant° Pyrrhus stood,
And like a neutral to his will and matter°
Did nothing.
But as we often see, against° some storm,
A silence in the heavens, the rack° stand still, 495
The bold winds speechless, and the orb below
As hush as death, anon the dreadful thunder
Doth rend the region, so after Pyrrhus' pause,
A rousèd vengeance sets him new awork,
And never did the Cyclops' hammers fall 500
On Mars's armor, forged for proof eterne,°
With less remorse than Pyrrhus' bleeding sword
Now falls on Priam.
Out, out, thou strumpet Fortune! All you gods,
In general synod° take away her power, 505
Break all the spokes and fellies° from her wheel,
And bowl the round nave° down the hill of heaven,
As low as to the fiends."
POLONIUS. This is too long.
HAMLET. It shall to the barber's, with your beard.— 510
Prithee say on. He's for a jig or a tale of bawdry,
or he sleeps. Say on; come to Hecuba.
PLAYER. "But who (ah woe!) had seen the mobled° queen——"
HAMLET. "The mobled queen"?
POLONIUS. That's good. "Mobled queen" is good. 515
PLAYER. "Run barefoot up and down, threat'ning the flames
With bisson rheum;° a clout° upon that head
Where late the diadem stood, and for a robe,
About her lank and all o'erteemèd° loins,
A blanket in the alarm of fear caught up— 520
Who this had seen, with tongue in venom steeped
'Gainst Fortune's state would treason have pronounced.
But if the gods themselves did see her then,
When she saw Pyrrhus make malicious sport
In mincing with his sword her husband's limbs, 525
The instant burst of clamor that she made

---

485 *senseless Ilium:* insensate Troy.   487 *Stoops to his base:* collapses (*his* = its).   491 *painted tyrant:*
tyrant in a picture.   492 *matter:* task.   494 *against:* just before.   495 *rack:* clouds.   501 *proof eterne:* eternal endurance.   505 *synod:* council.   506 *fellies:* rims.   507 *nave:* hub.   513 *mobled:* muffled.   517 *bisson rheum:* blinding tears; *clout:* rag.   519 *o'erteemèd:* exhausted with childbearing.

(Unless things mortal move then not at all)
Would have made milch° the burning eyes of heaven
And passion in the gods."

POLONIUS. Look, whe'r° he has not turned his color,   530
    and has tears in's eyes. Prithee no more.

HAMLET. 'Tis well, I'll have thee speak out the rest of
    this soon. Good my lord, will you see the players
    well bestowed?° Do you hear? Let them be well
    used, for they are the abstract and brief chronicles   535
    of the time. After your death you were better have
    a bad epitaph than their ill report while you live.

POLONIUS. My lord, I will use them according to their desert.

HAMLET. God's bodkin,° man, much better! Use every   540
    man after his desert, and who shall scape whipping?
    Use them after your own honor and dignity. The
    less they deserve, the more merit is in your bounty.
    Take them in.

POLONIUS. Come, sirs.   545

HAMLET. Follow him, friends. We'll hear a play to-
    morrow. [Aside to Player] Dost thou hear me, old
    friend? Can you play The Murder of Gonzago?

PLAYER. Ay, my lord.

HAMLET. We'll ha't tomorrow night. You could for a   550
    need study a speech of some dozen or sixteen lines
    which I would set down and insert in't, could you
    not?

PLAYER. Ay, my lord.

HAMLET. Very well. Follow that lord, and look you   555
    mock him not. My good friends, I'll leave you till
    night. You are welcome to Elsinore.

Exeunt Polonius and Players.

ROSENCRANTZ. Good my lord.

Exeunt Rosencrantz and Guildenstern.

HAMLET. Ay, so, God bye to you.—Now I am alone.
    O, what a rogue and peasant slave am I!   560
    Is it not monstrous that this player here,
    But in a fiction, in a dream of passion,°
    Could force his soul so to his own conceit°
    That from her working all his visage wanned,
    Tears in his eyes, distraction in his aspect,   565
    A broken voice, and his whole function° suiting
    With forms° to his conceit? And all for nothing!
    For Hecuba!

---

528 *milch:* moist (literally, "milk-giving").   530 *whe'r:* whether.   534 *bestowed:* housed.   540 *God's bodkin:* by God's little body.   562 *dream of passion:* imaginary emotion.   563 *conceit:* imagination.   566 *function:* action.   567 *forms:* bodily expressions.

What's Hecuba to him, or he to Hecuba,
That he should weep for her? What would he do   570
Had he the motive and the cue for passion
That I have? He would drown the stage with tears
And cleave the general ear with horrid speech,
Make mad the guilty and appall the free,°
Confound the ignorant, and amaze indeed   575
The very faculties of eyes and ears.
Yet I,
A dull and muddy-mettled° rascal, peak
Like John-a-dreams,° unpregnant of° my cause,
And can say nothing. No, not for a king,   580
Upon whose property and most dear life
A damned defeat was made. Am I a coward?
Who calls me villain? Breaks my pate across?
Plucks off my beard and blows it in my face?
Tweaks me by the nose? Gives me the lie i' th' throat   585
As deep as to the lungs? Who does me this?
Ha, 'swounds,° I should take it, for it cannot be
But I am pigeon-livered° and lack gall
To make oppression bitter, or ere this
I should ha' fatted all the region kites°   590
With this slave's offal. Bloody, bawdy villain!
Remorseless, treacherous, lecherous, kindless° villain!
O, vengeance!
Why, what an ass am I! This is most brave,°
That I, the son of a dear father murdered,   595
Prompted to my revenge by heaven and hell,
Must, like a whore, unpack my heart with words
And fall a-cursing like a very drab,°
A scullion!° Fie upon't, foh! About,° my brains.
Hum——   600
I have heard that guilty creatures sitting at a play
Have by the very cunning of the scene
Been struck so to the soul that presently°
They have proclaimed their malefactions.
For murder, though it have no tongue, will speak   605
With most miraculous organ. I'll have these players
Play something like the murder of my father
Before mine uncle. I'll observe his looks,
I'll tent° him to the quick. If 'a do blench,°
I know my course. The spirit that I have seen   610
May be a devil, and the devil hath power

---

574 *appall the free:* terrify (make pale?) the guiltless.   578 *muddy-mettled:* weak-spirited.   578–579
peak/Like John-a-dreams: mope like a dreamer.   579 *unpregnant of:* unquickened by.   587 *'swounds:* by
God's wounds.   588 *pigeon-livered:* gentle as a dove.   590 *region kites:* kites (scavenger birds) of the sky.
592 *kindless:* unnatural.   594 *brave:* fine.   598 *drab:* prostitute.   599 *scullion:* kitchen wench; *About:* to
work.   603 *presently:* immediately.   609 *tent:* probe; *blench:* flinch.

T' assume a pleasing shape, yea, and perhaps
Out of my weakness and my melancholy,
As he is very potent with such spirits,
Abuses me to damn me. I'll have grounds   615
More relative° than this. The play's the thing
Wherein I'll catch the conscience of the King.   *Exit.*

ACT III
Scene I
The castle.

Enter King, Queen, Polonius, Ophelia, Rosencrantz, Guildenstern, Lords.

KING. And can you by no drift of conference°
  Get from him why he puts on this confusion,
  Grating so harshly all his days of quiet
  With turbulent and dangerous lunacy?
ROSENCRANTZ. He does confess he feels himself distracted,   5
  But from what cause 'a will by no means speak.
GUILDENSTERN. Nor do we find him forward to be sounded,°
  But with a crafty madness keeps aloof
  When we would bring him on to some confession
  Of his true state.
QUEEN.   Did he receive you well?   10
ROSENCRANTZ. Most like a gentleman.
GUILDENSTERN. But with much forcing of his disposition.°
ROSENCRANTZ. Niggard of question,° but of our demands
  Most free in his reply.
QUEEN.   Did you assay° him
  To any pastime?   15
ROSENCRANTZ. Madam, it so fell out that certain players
  We o'erraught° on the way; of these we told him,
  And there did seem in him a kind of joy
  To hear of it. They are here about the court,
  And, as I think, they have already order   20
  This night to play before him.
POLONIUS.   'Tis most true,
  And he beseeched me to entreat your Majesties
  To hear and see the matter.
KING. With all my heart, and it doth much content me
  To hear him so inclined.   25
  Good gentlemen, give him a further edge
  And drive his purpose into these delights.
ROSENCRANTZ. We shall, my lord.

        Exeunt Rosencrantz and Guildenstern.

---

616 *relative:* (probably "pertinent," but possibly "able to be related plausibly"). SCENE I. 1 *drift of conference:* management of conversation. 7 *forward to be sounded:* willing to be questioned. 12 *forcing of his disposition:* effort. 13 *Niggard of question:* uninclined to talk. 14 *assay:* tempt. 17 *o'erraught:* overtook.

KING.   Sweet Gertrude, leave us too,
          For we have closely° sent for Hamlet hither,
          That he, as 'twere by accident, may here
          Affront° Ophelia.   30
          Her father and myself (lawful espials°)
          Will so bestow ourselves that, seeing unseen,
          We may of their encounter frankly judge
          And gather by him, as he is behaved,
          If't be th' affliction of his love or no   35
          That thus he suffers for.
QUEEN.   I shall obey you.
          And for your part, Ophelia, I do wish
          That your good beauties be the happy cause
          Of Hamlet's wildness. So shall I hope your virtues   40
          Will bring him to his wonted way again,
          To both your honors.
OPHELIA.   Madam, I wish it may.

                         Exit Queen.

POLONIUS. Ophelia, walk you here.—Gracious, so please you,
          We will bestow ourselves. [*To Ophelia*] Read on this book,
          That show of such an exercise may color°   45
          Your loneliness. We are oft to blame in this,
          'Tis too much proved, that with devotion's visage
          And pious action we do sugar o'er
          The devil himself.
KING.   [*Aside*] O, 'tis too true.
          How smart a lash that speech doth give my conscience!   50
          The harlot's cheek, beautied with plast'ring art,
          Is not more ugly to the thing that helps it
          Than is my deed to my most painted word.
          O heavy burden!
POLONIUS. I hear him coming. Let's withdraw, my lord.   55

                    Exeunt King and Polonius.

                         Enter Hamlet.

HAMLET. To be, or not to be: that is the question:
          Whether 'tis nobler in the mind to suffer
          The slings and arrows of outrageous fortune,
          Or to take arms against a sea of troubles,
          And by opposing end them. To die, to sleep—   60
          No more—and by a sleep to say we end
          The heartache, and the thousand natural shocks
          That flesh is heir to! 'Tis a consummation
          Devoutly to be wished. To die, to sleep—
          To sleep—perchance to dream: ay, there's the rub,°   65

_____

29 *closely:* secretly.   31 *Affront:* meet face to face.   32 *espials:* spies.   45 *exercise may color:* act of
devotion may give a plausible hue to (the book is one of devotion).   65 *rub:* impediment (obstruction
to a bowler's ball).

For in that sleep of death what dreams may come
When we have shuffled off this mortal coil,°
Must give us pause. There's the respect°
That makes calamity of so long life:°
For who would bear the whips and scorns of time,   70
Th' oppressor's wrong, the proud man's contumely,
The pangs of despised love, the law's delay,
The insolence of office, and the spurns
That patient merit of th' unworthy takes,
When he himself might his quietus° make   75
With a bare bodkin?° Who would fardels° bear,
To grunt and swear under a weary life,
But that the dread of something after death,
The undiscovered country, from whose bourn°
No traveler returns, puzzles the will,   80
And makes us rather bear those ills we have,
Than fly to others that we know not of?
Thus conscience° does make cowards of us all,
And thus the native hue of resolution
Is sickled o'er with the pale cast° of thought,   85
And enterprises of great pitch° and moment,
With this regard° their current turn awry,
And lose the name of action.—Soft you now,
The fair Ophelia!—Nymph, in thy orisons°
Be all my sins remembered.
OPHELIA.   Good my lord,   90
        How does your honor for this many a day?
HAMLET. I humbly thank you; well, well, well.
OPHELIA. My lord, I have remembrances of yours
        That I have longèd long to redeliver.
        I pray you now, receive them.
HAMLET.   No, not I.   95
        I never gave you aught.
OPHELIA. My honored lord, you know right well you did,
        And with them words of so sweet breath composed
        As made these things more rich. Their perfume lost,
        Take these again, for to the noble mind   100
        Rich gifts wax poor when givers prove unkind.
        There, my lord.
HAMLET. Ha, ha! Are you honest?°
OPHELIA. My lord?
HAMLET. Are you fair?   105
OPHELIA. What means your lordship?

---

67 *coil*: (1) turmoil, (2) a ring of rope (here the flesh encircling the soul).   68 *respect*: consideration.   69 *makes calamity of so long life*: (1) makes calamity so long-lived, (2) makes living so long a
calamity.   75 *quietus*: full discharge (a legal term).   76 *bodkin*: dagger; *fardels*: burdens.   79 *bourn*: region.   83 *conscience*: self-consciousness, introspection.   85 *cast*: color.   86 *pitch*: height (a term from
falconry).   87 *regard*: consideration.   89 *orisons*: prayers.   103 *Are you honest*: (1) are you modest,
(2) are you chaste, (3) have you integrity.

HAMLET. That if you be honest and fair, your honesty
    should admit no discourse to your beauty.°
OPHELIA. Could beauty, my lord, have better commerce
    than with honesty?   110
HAMLET. Ay, truly; for the power of beauty will sooner
    transform honesty from what it is to a bawd° than
    the force of honesty can translate beauty into his
    likeness. This was sometime a paradox, but now
    the time gives it proof. I did love you once.   115
OPHELIA. Indeed, my lord, you made me believe so.
HAMLET. You should not have believed me, for virtue
    cannot so inoculate° our old stock but we shall relish
    of it.° I loved you not.
OPHELIA. I was the more deceived.   120
HAMLET. Get thee to a nunnery. Why wouldst thou be
    a breeder of sinners? I am myself indifferent honest,°
    but yet I could accuse me of such things that it were
    better my mother had not borne me: I am very
    proud, revengeful, ambitious, with more offenses at   125
    my beck° than I have thoughts to put them in,
    imagination to give them shape, or time to act them
    in. What should such fellows as I do crawling be-
    tween earth and heaven? We are arrant knaves all;
    believe none of us. Go thy ways to a nunnery.   130
    Where's your father?
OPHELIA. At home, my lord.
HAMLET. Let the doors be shut upon him, that he may
    play the fool nowhere but in's own house. Farewell.
OPHELIA. O help him, you sweet heavens!   135
HAMLET. If thou dost marry, I'll give thee this plague
    for thy dowry: be thou as chaste as ice, as pure as
    snow, thou shalt not escape calumny. Get thee to a
    nunnery. Go, farewell. Or if thou wilt needs marry,
    marry a fool, for wise men know well enough what   140
    monsters° you make of them. To a nunnery, go,
    and quickly too. Farewell.
OPHELIA. Heavenly powers, restore him!
HAMLET. I have heard of your paintings, well enough.
    God hath given you one face, and you make your-   145
    selves another. You jig and amble, and you lisp;
    you nickname God's creatures and make your
    wantonness your ignorance.° Go to, I'll no more
    on't; it hath made me mad. I say we will have no
    moe° marriage. Those that are married already—all   150
    but one—shall live. The rest shall keep as they are.

107–108 *your honesty . . . to your beauty:* your modesty should permit no approach to your beauty.   112
bawd: procurer.   118 *inoculate:* graft.   118–119 *relish of it:* smack of it (our old sinful nature).   122 *indifferent
honest:* moderately virtuous.   126 *beck:* call.   141 *monsters:* horned beasts, cuckolds.   147–148 *make your
wantonness your ignorance:* excuse your wanton speech by pretending ignorance.   150 *moe:* more.

To a nunnery, go.   *Exit.*

OPHELIA. O what a noble mind is here o'erthrown!
    The courtier's, soldier's, scholar's, eye, tongue, sword,
    Th' expectancy and rose° of the fair state,   155
    The glass of fashion, and the mold of form,°
    Th' observed of all observers, quite, quite down!
    And I, of ladies most deject and wretched,
    That sucked the honey of his musicked vows,
    Now see that noble and most sovereign reason   160
    Like sweet bells jangled, out of time and harsh,
    That unmatched form and feature of blown° youth
    Blasted with ecstasy.° O, woe is me
    T' have seen what I have seen, see what I see!

Enter King and Polonius.

KING. Love? His affections° do not that way tend,   165
    Nor what he spake, though it lacked form a little,
    Was not like madness. There's something in his soul
    O'er which his melancholy sits on brood,
    And I do doubt° the hatch and the disclose
    Will be some danger; which for to prevent,   170
    I have in quick determination
    Thus set it down: he shall with speed to England
    For the demand of our neglected tribute.
    Haply the seas, and countries different,
    With variable objects, shall expel   175
    This something-settled° matter in his heart,
    Whereon his brains still beating puts him thus
    From fashion of himself. What think you on't?
POLONIUS. It shall do well. But yet do I believe
    The origin and commencement of his grief   180
    Sprung from neglected love. How now, Ophelia?
    You need not tell us what Lord Hamlet said;
    We heard it all. My lord, do as you please,
    But if you hold it fit, after the play,
    Let his queen mother all alone entreat him   185
    To show his grief. Let her be round° with him,
    And I'll be placed, so please you, in the ear
    Of all their conference. If she find him not,°
    To England send him, or confine him where
    Your wisdom best shall think.
KING.   It shall be so.   190

    Madness in great ones must not unwatched go.

Exeunt.

---

    155 *expectancy and rose:* i.e., fair hope.   156 *The glass . . . of form:* the mirror of fashion, and the
pattern of excellent behavior.   162 *blown:* blooming.   163 *ecstasy:* madness.   165 *affections:* inclinations.   169 *doubt:* fear.   176 *something-settled:* somewhat settled.   186 *round:* blunt.   188 *find him not:*
does not find him out.

Scene II
The castle.

Enter Hamlet and three of the Players.

HAMLET. Speak the speech, I pray you, as I pronounced
it to you, trippingly on the tongue. But if you mouth
it, as many of our players do, I had as lief the town
crier spoke my lines. Nor do not saw the air too much
with your hand, thus, but use all gently, for in the   5
very torrent, tempest, and (as I may say) whirlwind
of your passion, you must acquire and beget a temperance that may give it smoothness. O, it offends
me to the soul to hear a robustious periwig-pated°
fellow tear a passion to tatters, to very rags, to split   10
the ears of the groundlings,° who for the most part
are capable of° nothing but inexplicable dumb
shows° and noise. I would have such a fellow
whipped for o'erdoing Termagant. It out-herods
Herod.° Pray you avoid it.   15
PLAYER. I warrant your honor.
HAMLET. Be not too tame neither, but let your own discretion be your tutor. Suit the action to the word, the
word to the action, with this special observance, that
you o'erstep not the modesty of nature. For anything   20
so o'erdone is from° the purpose of playing, whose
end, both at the first and now, was and is, to hold,
as 'twere, the mirror up to nature; to show virtue
her own feature, scorn her own image, and the very
age and body of the time his form and pressure.°   25
Now, this overdone, or come tardy off, though it
makes the unskillful laugh, cannot but make the
judicious grieve, the censure of the which one must
in your allowance o'erweigh a whole theater of
others. O, there be players that I have seen play,   30
and heard others praise, and that highly (not to
speak it profanely), that neither having th' accent of
Christians, nor the gait of Christian, pagan, nor
man, have so strutted and bellowed that I have
thought some of Nature's journeymen° had made   35
men, and not made them well, they imitated humanity so abominably.
PLAYER. I hope we have reformed that indifferently°
with us, sir.

SCENE II. 9 *robustious periwag-pated:* boisterous wig-headed.   11 *groundlings:* those who stood in the
pit of the theater (the poorest and presumably most ignorant of the audience).   12 *are capable of:* are
able to understand.   12–13 *dumb shows:* (it had been the fashion for actors to preface plays or parts of
plays with silent mime).   14–15 *Termagant . . . Herod:* (boisterous characters in the old mystery plays).
21 *from:* contrary to.   25 *pressure:* image, impress.   35 *journeymen:* workers not yet masters of their craft.
38 *indifferently:* tolerably.

HAMLET. O, reform it altogether! And let those that   40
   play your clowns speak no more than is set down
   for them, for there be of them that will themselves
   laugh, to set on some quantity of barren spectators to
   laugh too, though in the meantime some necessary
   question of the play be then to be considered. That's   45
   villainous and shows a most pitiful ambition in the
   fool that uses it. Go make you ready.

                              Exit Players.

Enter Polonius, Guildenstern, and Rosencrantz.

   How now, my lord? Will the King hear this piece of work?
POLONIUS. And the Queen too, and that presently.   50
HAMLET. Bid the players make haste.   *Exit Polonius.*
   Will you two help to hasten them?
ROSENCRANTZ. Ay, my lord.   *Exeunt they two.*
HAMLET. What, ho, Horatio!

                     Enter Horatio.

HORATIO. Here, sweet lord, at your service.   55
HAMLET. Horatio, thou art e'en as just a man
   As e'er my conversation coped withal.°
HORATIO. O, my dear lord——
HAMLET.   Nay, do you think I flatter.
   For what advancement° may I hope from thee,
   That no revenue hast but thy good spirits   60
   To feed and clothe thee? Why should the poor be flattered?
   No, let the candied° tongue lick absurd pomp,
   And crook the pregnant° hinges of the knee
   Where thrift° may follow fawning. Dost thou hear?
   Since my dear soul was mistress of her choice   65
   And could of men distinguish her election,
   S' hath sealed thee° for herself, for thou hast been
   As one, in suff'ring all, that suffers nothing,
   A man that Fortune's buffets and rewards
   Hast ta'en with equal thanks; and blest are those   70
   Whose blood° and judgment are so well commeddled°
   That they are not a pipe for Fortune's finger
   To sound what stop she please. Give me that man
   That is not passion's slave, and I will wear him
   In my heart's core, ay, in my heart of heart,   75
   As I do thee. Something too much of this—
   There is a play tonight before the King.
   One scene of it comes near the circumstance
   Which I have told thee, of my father's death.

---

   57 *coped withal:* met with.   59 *advancement:* promotion.   62 *candied:* sugared, flattering.   63 *pregnant:* (1) pliant, (2) full of promise of good fortune.   64 *thrift:* profit.   67 *S'hath sealed thee:* she (the soul) has set a mark on you.   71 *blood:* passion; *commeddled:* blended.

I prithee, when thou seest that act afoot,   80
Even with the very comment° of thy soul
Observe my uncle. If his occulted° guilt
Do not itself unkennel in one speech,
It is a damnèd ghost that we have seen,
And my imaginations are as foul   85
As Vulcan's stithy.° Give him heedful note,
For I mine eyes will rivet to his face,
And after we will both our judgments join
In censure of his seeming.°
HORATIO.   Well, my lord.
If 'a steal aught the whilst this play is playing,   90
And scape detecting, I will pay the theft.

*Enter Trumpets and Kettledrums, King, Queen, Polonius, Ophelia, Rosencrantz,
Guildenstern, and other Lords attendant with his Guard carrying torches. Danish
March. Sound a Flourish.*

HAMLET. They are coming to the play: I must be idle;°
Get you a place.
KING. How fares our cousin Hamlet?
HAMLET. Excellent, i' faith, of the chameleon's dish;°   95
I eat the air, promise-crammed; you cannot feed
capons so.
KING. I have nothing with this answer, Hamlet; these
words are not mine.
HAMLET. No, nor mine now. [*To Polonius*] My lord, you   100
played once i' th' university, you say?
POLONIUS. That did I, my lord, and was accounted a good
actor.
HAMLET. What did you enact?
POLONIUS. I did enact Julius Caesar. I was killed i' th'   105
Capitol; Brutus killed me.
HAMLET. It was a brute part of him to kill so capital a
calf there. Be the players ready?
ROSENCRANTZ. Ay, my lord they stay upon your patience.   110
QUEEN. Come hither, my dear Hamlet, sit by me.
HAMLET. No, good mother. Here's metal more attractive.°
POLONIUS. [*To the King*] O ho! Do you mark that?
HAMLET. Lady, shall I lie in your lap?   115

He lies at Ophelia's feet.

OPHELIA. No, my lord.
HAMLET. I mean, my head upon your lap?
OPHELIA. Ay, my lord.

---

81 *very comment*: deepest wisdom.   82 *occulted*: hidden.   86 *stithy*: forge, smithy.   89 *censure of
his seeming*: judgment on his looks.   92 *be idle*: play the fool.   95 *the chameleon's dish*: air (on which
chameleons were thought to live).   112 *attractive*: magnetic.

HAMLET. Do you think I meant country matters?°

OPHELIA. I think nothing, my lord.   120

HAMLET. That's a fair thought to lie between maids' legs.

OPHELIA. What is, my lord?

HAMLET. Nothing.

OPHELIA. You are merry, my lord.

HAMLET. Who, I?   125

OPHELIA. Ay, my lord.

HAMLET. O God, your only jig-maker!° What should a
man do but be merry? For look you how cheerfully
my mother looks, and my father died within's two   130
hours.

OPHELIA. Nay, 'tis twice two months, my lord.

HAMLET. So long? Nay then, let the devil wear black,
for I'll have a suit of sables.° O heavens! Die two
months ago, and not forgotten yet? Then there's   135
hope a great man's memory may outlive his life half
a year. But, by'r Lady, 'a must build churches then,
or else shall 'a suffer not thinking on, with the hobby-
horse,° whose epitaph is "For O, for O, the hobby-
horse is forgot!"   140

The trumpets sound. Dumb show follows:

*Enter a King and a Queen very lovingly, the Queen embracing him, and he her.
She kneels, and makes show of protestation unto him. He takes her up, and declines
his head upon her neck. He lies him down upon a bank of flowers. She, seeing him
asleep, leaves him. Anon come in another man: takes off his crown, kisses it, pours
poison in the sleeper's ears, and leaves him. The Queen returns, finds the King
dead, makes passionate action. The poisoner, with some three or four, come in
again, seem to condole with her. The dead body is carried away. The poisoner
woos the Queen with gifts; she seems harsh awhile, but in the end accepts love.*

Exeunt.

OPHELIA. What means this, my lord?

HAMLET. Marry, this is miching mallecho;° it means mischief.

OPHELIA. Belike this show imports the argument° of the play.   145

Enter Prologue.

HAMLET. We shall know by this fellow. The players
cannot keep counsel; they'll tell all.

OPHELIA. Will 'a tell us what this show meant?

HAMLET. Ay, or any show that you will show him. Be
not you ashamed to show, he'll not shame to tell you   150
what it means.

---

119 *country matters:* rustic doings (with a pun on the vulgar word for the pudendum).   127 *jig-maker:*
composer of songs and dances (often a Fool, who performed them).   134 *sables:* (pun on "black" and "luxurious furs").   138–139 *hobby-horse:* mock horse worn by a performer in the morris dance.   144 *miching
mallecho:* sneaking mischief.   145 *argument:* plot.

OPHELIA. You are naught,° you are naught; I'll mark the
   play.
PROLOGUE. For us, and for our tragedy,
      Here stooping to your clemency,
      We beg your hearing patiently.   [*Exit.*]   155
HAMLET. Is this a prologue, or the posy of a ring?°
OPHELIA. 'Tis brief, my lord.
HAMLET. As woman's love.

   Enter [two Players as] King and Queen.

PLAYER KING. Full thirty times hath Phoebus' cart° gone round   160
   Neptune's salt wash° and Tellus'° orbèd ground,
   And thirty dozen moons with borrowed sheen
   About the world have times twelve thirties been,
   Since love our hearts, and Hymen did our hands,
   Unite commutual in most sacred bands.   165
PLAYER QUEEN. So many journeys may the sun and moon
   Make us again count o'er ere love be done!
   But woe is me, you are so sick of late,
   So far from cheer and from your former state,
   That I distrust° you. Yet, though I distrust,   170
   Discomfort you, my lord, it nothing must.
   For women fear too much, even as they love,
   And women's fear and love hold quantity,
   In neither aught, or in extremity.°
   Now what my love is, proof° hath made you know,   175
   And as my love is sized, my fear is so.
   Where love is great, the littlest doubts are fear;
   Where little fears grow great, great love grows there.
PLAYER KING. Faith, I must leave thee, love, and shortly too;
   My operant° powers their functions leave to do: 180
   And thou shalt live in this fair world behind,
   Honored, beloved, and haply one as kind
   For husband shalt thou——
PLAYER QUEEN.   O, confound the rest!
   Such love must needs be treason in my breast.
   In second husband let me be accurst!   185
   None wed the second but who killed the first.
HAMLET. [*Aside*] That's wormwood.°
PLAYER QUEEN. The instances° that second marriage move°
   Are base respects of thrift,° but none of love.
   A second time I kill my husband dead   190
   When second husband kisses me in bed.

---

   152 *naught:* wicked, improper.   157 *posy of a ring:* motto inscribed in a ring.   160 *Phoebus' cart:* the
sun's chariot.   161 *Neptune's salt wash:* the sea; *Tellus:* Roman goddess of the earth.   170 *distrust:* am anxious about.   173–174 *And women's . . . in extremity:* (perhaps the idea is that women's anxiety is great or
little in proportion to their love. The previous line, unrhymed, may be a false start that Shakespeare neglected to delete).   175 *proof:* experience.   180 *operant:* active.   187 *wormwood:* a bitter herb.   188 *instances:* motives; *move:* induce.   189 *respects of thrift:* considerations of profit.

PLAYER KING. I do believe you think what now you speak,
    But what we do determine oft we break.
    Purpose is but the slave to memory,
    Of violent birth, but poor validity,°   195
    Which now like fruit unripe sticks on the tree,
    But fall unshaken when they mellow be.
    Most necessary 'tis that we forget
    To pay ourselves what to ourselves is debt.
    What to ourselves in passion we propose,   200
    The passion ending, doth the purpose lose.
    The violence of either grief or joy
    Their own enactures° with themselves destroy;
    Where joy most revels, grief doth most lament;
    Grief joys, joy grieves, on slender accident.   205
    This world is not for aye, nor 'tis not strange
    That even our loves should with our fortunes change,
    For tis a question left us yet to prove,
    Whether love lead fortune, or else fortune love.
    The great man down, you mark his favorite flies;   210
    The poor advanced makes friends of enemies;
    And hitherto doth love on fortune tend,
    For who not needs shall never lack a friend;
    And who in want a hollow friend doth try,
    Directly seasons him° his enemy.   215
    But, orderly to end where I begun,
    Our wills and fates do so contrary run
    That our devices still are overthrown;
    Our thoughts are ours, their ends none of our own.
    So think thou wilt no second husband wed,   220
    But die thy thoughts when thy first lord is dead.
PLAYER QUEEN. Nor earth to me give food, nor heaven light,
    Sport and repose lock from me day and night,
    To desperation turn my trust and hope,
    An anchor's° cheer in prison be my scope,   225
    Each opposite that blanks° the face of joy
    Meet what I would have well, and it destroy:
    Both here and hence pursue me lasting strife,
    If, once a widow, ever I be wife!
HAMLET. If she should break it now!   230
PLAYER KING. 'Tis deeply sworn. Sweet, leave me here awhile;
    My spirits grow dull, and fain I would beguile
    The tedious day with sleep.
PLAYER QUEEN.   Sleep rock thy brain,

                         [He] sleeps.

And never come mischance between us twain!   *Exit.*

---

   195 *validity:* strength.   203 *enactures:* acts.   215 *seasons him:* ripens him into.   225 *anchor's:* anchorite's, hermit's.   226 *opposite that blanks:* adverse thing that blanches.

HAMLET. Madam, how like you this play? 235
QUEEN. The lady doth protest too much, methinks.
HAMLET. O, but she'll keep her word.
KING. Have you heard the argument?° Is there no offense in't?
HAMLET. No, no, they do but jest, poison in jest; no 240
offense i' th' world.
KING. What do you call the play?
HAMLET. *The Mousetrap*. Marry, how? Tropically.°
This play is the image of a murder done in Vienna:
Gonzago is the Duke's name; his wife, Baptista. You 245
shall see anon. 'Tis a knavish piece of work, but
what of that? Your Majesty, and we that have free°
souls, it touches us not. Let the galled jade winch;°
our withers are unwrung.

Enter Lucianus.

This is one Lucianus, nephew to the King. 250
OPHELIA. You are as good as a chorus, my lord.
HAMLET. I could interpret° between you and your love,
if I could see the puppets dallying.
OPHELIA. You are keen,° my lord, you are keen.
HAMLET. It would cost you a groaning to take off mine edge. 255
OPHELIA. Still better, and worse.
HAMLET. So you mistake° your husbands.—Begin,
murderer. Leave thy damnable faces and begin.
Come, the croaking raven doth bellow for revenge.
LUCIANUS. Thoughts black, hands apt, drugs fit, and 260
time agreeing,
Confederate season,° else no creature seeing,
Thou mixture rank, of midnight weeds collected,
With Hecate's ban° thrice blasted, thrice infected,
Thy natural magic and dire property° 265
On wholesome life usurps immediately.

Pours the poison in his ears.

HAMLET. 'A poisons him i' th' garden for his estate. His
name's Gonzago. The story is extant, and written in
very choice Italian. You shall see anon how the mur-
derer gets the love of Gonzago's wife. 270
OPHELIA. The King rises.
HAMLET. What, frighted with false fire?°
QUEEN. How fares my lord?
POLONIUS. Give o'er the play.
KING. Give me some light. Away! 275

---

239 *argument*: plot.   243 *Tropically*: figuratively (with a pun on "trap").   247 *free*: innocent.
248 *galled jade winch*: chafed horse wince.   252 *interpret*: (like a showman explaining the action of puppets).   254 *keen*: (1) sharp, (2) sexually aroused.   257 *mistake*: err in taking.   262 *Confederate season*:
the opportunity allied with me.   264 *Hecate's ban*: the curse of the goddess of sorcery.   265 *property*:
nature.   272 *false fire*: blank discharge of firearms.

POLONIUS. Lights, lights, lights!

Exeunt all but Hamlet and Horatio.

HAMLET. Why, let the strucken deer go weep,
      The hart ungallèd play:
    For some must watch, while some must sleep;
      Thus runs the world away.   280
Would not this, sir, and a forest of feathers°—if the
rest of my fortunes turn Turk° with me—with two
Provincial roses° on my razed° shoes, get me a
fellowship in a cry° of players?

HORATIO. Half a share.   285

HAMLET. A whole one, I.
    For thou dost know, O Damon dear,
      This realm dismantled was
    Of Jove himself; and now reigns here
      A very, very—pajock.°   290

HORATIO. You might have rhymed.°

HAMLET. O good Horatio, I'll take the ghost's word for
a thousand pound. Didst perceive.

HORATIO. Very well, my lord.

HAMLET. Upon the talk of poisoning?   295

HORATIO. I did very well note him.

HAMLET. Ah ha! Come, some music! Come, the recorders!°
    For if the King like not the comedy,
    Why then, belike he likes it not, perdy.°
Come, some music!   300

Enter Rosencrantz and Guildenstern.

GUILDENSTERN. Good my lord, vouchsafe me a word
with you.

HAMLET. Sir, a whole history.

GUILDENSTERN. The King, sir——   305

HAMLET. Ay, sir, what of him?

GUILDENSTERN. Is in his retirement marvelous dis-
temp'red.

HAMLET. With drink, sir?

GUILDENSTERN. No, my lord, with choler.°   310

HAMLET. Your wisdom should show itself more richer
to signify this to the doctor, for, for me to put him to
his purgation would perhaps plunge him into more
choler.

GUILDENSTERN. Good my lord, put your discourse into   315
some frame,° and start not so wildly from my affair.

---

281 *feathers:* (plumes were sometimes part of a costume). 282 *turn Turk:* i.e., go bad, treat me
badly. 283 *Provincial roses:* rosettes like the roses of Provence (?); *razed:* ornamented with slashes. 284
cry: pack, company. 290 *pajock:* peacock. 291 *You might have rhymed:* i.e., rhymed "was" with "ass."
297 *recorders:* flutelike instruments. 299 *perdy:* by God (French: *par dieu*). 310 *choler:* anger (but
Hamlet pretends to take the word in its sense of "bilousness"). 316 *frame:* order, control.

HAMLET. I am tame, sir; pronounce.

GUILDENSTERN. The Queen, your mother, in most great
affliction of spirit hath sent me to you.

HAMLET. You are welcome. 320

GUILDENSTERN. Nay, good my lord, this courtesy is not
of the right breed. If it shall please you to make me
a wholesome answer, I will do your mother's commandment: if not, your pardon and my return shall
be the end of my business. 325

HAMLET. Sir, I cannot.

ROSENCRANTZ. What, my lord?

HAMLET. Make you a wholesome° answer; my wit's
diseased. But, sir, such answer as I can make, you
shall command, or rather, as you say, my mother. 330
Therefore no more, but to the matter. My mother,
you say——

ROSENCRANTZ. Then thus she says: your behavior hath
struck her into amazement and admiration.°

HAMLET. O wonderful son, that can so stonish a mother! 335
But is there no sequel at the heels of this mother's
admiration? Impart.

ROSENCRANTZ. She desires to speak with you in her
closet ere you go to bed.

HAMLET. We shall obey, were she ten times our mother. 340
Have you any further trade with us?

ROSENCRANTZ. My lord, you once did love me.

HAMLET. And do still, by these pickers and stealers.°

ROSENCRANTZ. Good my lord, what is your cause of distemper? You do surely bar the door upon your own 345
liberty, if you deny your griefs to your friend.

HAMLET. Sir, I lack advancement.°

ROSENCRANTZ. How can that be, when you have the
voice of the King himself for your succession in
Denmark? 350

Enter the Players with recorders.

HAMLET. Ay, sir, but "while the grass grows"—the
proverb° is something musty. O, the recorders. Let
me see one. To withdraw° with you—why do you
go about to recover the wind° of me as if you would
drive me into a toil?° 355

GUILDENSTERN. O my lord, if my duty be too bold, my
love is too unmannerly.°

---

328 *wholesome:* sane.   334 *admiration:* wonder.   343 *pickers and stealers:* i.e., hands (with reference
to the prayer; "Keep my hands from picking and stealing").   347 *advancement:* promotion.   352 *proverb:*
("While the grass groweth, the horse starveth").   353 *withdraw:* speak in private.   354 *recover the wind:*
get the windward side (as in hunting).   355 *toil:* snare.   356–357 *if my duty . . . too unmannerly:* i.e., if
these questions seem rude, it is because my love for you leads me beyond good manners.

HAMLET. I do not well understand that. Will you play
    upon this pipe?
GUILDENSTERN. My lord, I cannot.   360
HAMLET. I pray you.
GUILDENSTERN. Believe me, I cannot.
HAMLET. I pray you.
GUILDENSTERN. Believe me, I cannot.
HAMLET. I do beseech you.
GUILDENSTERN. I know no touch of it, my lord.
HAMLET. It is as easy as lying. Govern these ventages°   365
    with your fingers and thumb, give it breath with your
    mouth, and it will discourse most eloquent music.
    Look you, these are the stops.
GUILDENSTERN. But these cannot I command to any
    utt'rance of harmony; I have not the skill.   370
HAMLET. Why, look you now, how unworthy a thing
    you make of me! You would play upon me; you
    would seem to know my stops; you would pluck
    out the heart of my mystery; you would sound me
    from my lowest note to the top of my compass;°   375
    and there is much music, excellent voice, in this little
    organ,° yet cannot you make it speak. 'Sblood, do
    you think I am easier to be played on than a pipe?
    Call me what instrument you will, though you can
    fret° me, you cannot play upon me.   380

                    Enter Polonius.

    God bless you, sir!
POLONIUS. My lord, the Queen would speak with you,
    and presently.
HAMLET. Do you see yonder cloud that's almost in
    shape of a camel?   385
POLONIUS. By th' mass, and 'tis like a camel indeed.
HAMLET. Methinks it is like a weasel.
POLONIUS. It is backed like a weasel.
HAMLET. Or like a whale.
POLONIUS. Very like a whale.   390
HAMLET. Then I will come to my mother by and by.
    [*Aside*] They fool me to the top of my bent.°—I
    will come by and by.°
POLONIUS. I will say so.   *Exit.*
HAMLET. "By and by" is easily said. Leave me, friends.   395

                    Exeunt all but Hamlet.

    'Tis now the very witching time of night,

---

    365 *ventages:* vents, stops on a recorder.   375 *compass:* range of voice.   377 *organ:* i.e., the
recorder.   380 *fret:* vex (with a pun alluding to the frets, or ridges, that guide the fingering on some instruments).   392 *They fool . . . my bent:* they compel me to play the fool to the limit of my capacity.
393 *by and by:* very soon.

When churchyards yawn, and hell itself breathes out
Contagion to this world. Now could I drink hot blood
And do such bitter business as the day
Would quake to look on. Soft, now to my mother. 400
O heart, lose not thy nature; let not ever
The soul of Nero° enter this firm bosom.
Let me be cruel, not unnatural;
I will speak daggers to her, but use none.
My tongue and soul in this be hypocrites: 405
How in my words somever she be shent,°
To give them seals° never, my soul, consent! *Exit.*

Scene III
The castle.

Enter King, Rosencrantz, and Guildenstern.

KING. I like him not, nor stands it safe with us
To let his madness range. Therefore prepare you.
I your commission will forthwith dispatch,
And he to England shall along with you.
The terms° of our estate may not endure 5
Hazard so near's° as doth hourly grow
Out of his brows.
GUILDENSTERN.   We will ourselves provide.
Most holy and religious fear it is
To keep those many many bodies safe
That live and feed upon your Majesty. 10
ROSENCRANTZ. The single and peculiar° life is bound
With all the strength and armor of the mind
To keep itself from noyance,° but much more
That spirit upon whose weal depends and rests
The lives of many. The cess of majesty° 15
Dies not alone, but with a gulf° doth draw
What's near it with it; or it is a massy wheel
Fixed on the summit of the highest mount,
To whose huge spokes ten thousand lesser things
Are mortised and adjoined, which when it falls, 20
Each small annexment, petty consequence,
Attends° the boist'rous ruin. Never alone
Did the King sigh, but with a general groan.
KING. Arm° you, I pray you, to this speedy voyage,
For we will fetters put about this fear, 25
Which now goes too free-footed.
ROSENCRANTZ.   We will haste us.
                         Exeunt Gentlemen.

---

402 *Nero:* (Roman emperor who had his mother murdered).   406 *shent:* rebuked.   407 *give them*
seals: confirm them with deeds.   SCENE III.   5 *terms:* conditions.   6 *near's:* near us.   11 *peculiar:* individual, private.   13 *noyance:* injury.   15 *cess of majesty:* cessation (death) of a king.   16 *gulf:* whirlpool.
22 *Attends:* waits on, participates in.   24 *Arm:* prepare.

Enter Polonius.

POLONIUS. My lord, he's going to his mother's closet.°
    Behind the arras I'll convey myself
    To hear the process.° I'll warrant she'll tax him home,°
    And, as you said, and wisely was it said,   30
    'Tis meet that some more audience than a mother,
    Since nature makes them partial, should o'erhear
    The speech of vantage.° Fare you well, my liege.
    I'll call upon you ere you go to bed
    And tell you what I know.
KING.   Thanks, dear my lord.   35

Exit [Polonius].

    O, my offense is rank, it smells to heaven;
    It hath the primal eldest curse° upon't,
    A brother's murder. Pray can I not,
    Though inclination be as sharp as will.
    My stronger guilt defeats my strong intent,   40
    And like a man to double business bound
    I stand in pause where I shall first begin,
    And both neglect. What if this cursèd hand
    Were thicker than itself with brother's blood,
    Is there not rain enough in the sweet heavens   45
    To wash it white as snow? Whereto serves mercy
    But to confront° the visage of offense?
    And what's in prayer but this twofold force,
    To be forestallèd ere we come to fall,
    Or pardoned being down? Then I'll look up.   50
    My fault is past. But, O, what form of prayer
    Can serve my turn? "Forgive me my foul murder"?
    That cannot be, since I am still possessed
    Of those effects° for which I did the murder,
    My crown, mine own ambition, and my queen.   55
    May one be pardoned and retain th' offense?
    In the corrupted currents of this world
    Offense's gilded hand may shove my justice,
    And oft 'tis seen the wicked prize itself
    Buys out the law. But 'tis not so above.   60
    There is no shuffling;° there the action lies
    In his true nature, and we ourselves compelled,
    Even to the teeth and forehead of our faults,
    To give in evidence. What then? What rests?°
    Try what repentance can. What can it not?   65
    Yet what can it when one cannot repent?
    O wretched state! O bosom black as death!

---

    27 *closet:* private room.   **29** *process:* proceedings; *tax him home:* censure him sharply.   **33** *of vantage:* from an advantageous place.   **37** *primal eldest curse:* (curse of Cain, who killed Abel).   **47** *confront:* oppose.   **54** *effects:* things gained.   **61** *shuffling:* trickery.   **64** *rests:* remains.

O limèd° soul, that struggling to be free
Art more engaged!° Help, angels! Make assay.°
Bow, stubborn knees, and, heart with strings of steel,   70
Be soft as sinews of the newborn babe.
All may be well.   [He kneels.]

                            Enter Hamlet.

HAMLET. Now might I do it pat, now 'a is a-praying,
   And now I'll do't. And so 'a goes to heaven,
   And so am I revenged. That would be scanned.°   75
   A villain kills my father, and for that
   I, his sole son, do this same villain send
   To heaven.
   Why, this is hire and salary, not revenge.
   'A took my father grossly, full of bread,°   80
   With all his crimes broad blown,° as flush° as May;
   And how his audit° stands, who knows save heaven?
   But in our circumstance and course of thought,
   'Tis heavy with him; and am I then revenged,
   To take him in the purging of his soul,   85
   When he is fit and seasoned for his passage?
   No.
   Up, sword, and know thou a more horrid hent.°
   When he is drunk asleep, or in his rage,
   Or in th' incestuous pleasure of his bed,   90
   At game a-swearing, or about some act
   That has no relish° of salvation in't—
   Then trip him, that his heels may kick at heaven,
   And that his soul may be as damned and black
   As hell, whereto it goes. My mother stays.   95
   This physic° but prolongs thy sickly days.   Exit.
KING. [Rises] My words fly up, my thoughts remain below.
   Words without thoughts never to heaven go.   Exit.

Scene IV
The Queen's closet.

      Enter [Queen] Gertrude and Polonius.

POLONIUS. 'A will come straight. Look you lay home° to him.
   Tell him his pranks have been too broad° to bear with,
   And that your Grace hath screened and stood between
   Much heat and him. I'll silence me even here.
   Pray you be round with him.   5
HAMLET. [Within] Mother, Mother, Mother!

---

68 *limèd*: caught (as with birdlime, a sticky substance spread on boughs to snare birds).   69 *engaged*:
ensnared; *assay*: an attempt.   75 *would be scanned*: ought to be looked into.   80 *bread*: i.e., worldly gratification.   81 *crimes broad blown*: sins in full bloom; *flush*: vigorous.   82 *audit*: account.   88 *hent*: grasp
(here, occasion for seizing).   92 *relish*: flavor.   96 *physic*: (Claudius' purgation by prayer, as Hamlet thinks
in line 85).   SCENE IV.   1 *lay home*: thrust (rebuke) him sharply.   2 *broad*: unrestrained.

QUEEN. I'll warrant you; fear me not. Withdraw; I hear
   him coming.   [*Polonius hides behind the arras.*]

                   Enter Hamlet.

HAMLET. Now, Mother, what's the matter?
QUEEN. Hamlet, thou hast thy father much offended.   10
HAMLET. Mother, you have my father much offended.
QUEEN. Come, come, you answer with an idle° tongue.
HAMLET. Go, go, you question with a wicked tongue.
QUEEN. Why, how now, Hamlet?
HAMLET.   What's the matter now?
QUEEN. Have you forgot me?
HAMLET.   No, by the rood,° not so!   15
   You are the Queen, your husband's brother's wife,
   And, would it were not so, you are my mother.
QUEEN. Nay, then I'll set those to you that can speak.
HAMLET. Come, come, and sit you down. You shall not budge.
   You go not till I set you up a glass°   20
   Where you may see the inmost part of you!
QUEEN. What wilt thou do? Thou wilt not murder me?
   Help, ho!
POLONIUS. [*Behind*] What, ho! Help!
HAMLET. [*Draws*] How now? A rat? Dead for a ducat, dead!   25

   [*Makes a pass through the arras and*] *kills Polonius.*

POLONIUS. [*Behind*] O, I am slain!
QUEEN.   O me, what hast thou done?
HAMLET. Nay, I know not. Is it the King?
QUEEN. O, what a rash and bloody deed is this!
HAMLET. A bloody deed—almost as bad, good Mother,
   As kill a king, and marry with his brother.   30
QUEEN. As kill a king?
HAMLET.   Ay, lady, it was my word.

      Lifts up the arras and sees Polonius.

   Thou wretched, rash, intruding fool, farewell!
   I took thee for thy better. Take thy fortune.
   Thou find'st to be too busy is some danger.—
   Leave wringing of your hands. Peace, sit you down   35
   And let me wring your heart, for so I shall
   If it be made of penetrable stuff,
   If damnèd custom have not brazed° it so
   That it be proof° and bulwark against sense.°
QUEEN. What have I done that thou dar'st wag thy
     tongue   40
   In noise so rude against me?

---

   12 *idle:* foolish.   **15** *rood:* cross.   **20** *glass:* mirror.   **38** *brazed:* hardened like brass.   **39** *proof:*
armor; *sense:* feeling.

HAMLET.   Such an act
    That blurs the grace and blush of modesty,
    Calls virtue hypocrite, takes off the rose
    From the fair forehead of an innocent love,
    And sets a blister° there, makes marriage vows   45
    As false as dicers' oaths. O, such a deed
    As from the body of contraction° plucks
    The very soul, and sweet religion makes
    A rhapsody° of words! Heaven's face does glow
    O'er this solidity and compound mass   50
    With heated visage, as against the doom
    Is thoughtsick at the act.°
QUEEN.   Ay me, what act,
    That roars so loud and thunders in the index?°
HAMLET. Look here upon this picture, and on this,
    The counterfeit presentment° of two brothers.   55
    See what a grace was seated on this brow:
    Hyperion's curls, the front° of Jove himself,
    An eye like Mars, to threaten and command,
    A station° like the herald Mercury
    New lighted on a heaven-kissing hill—   60
    A combination and a form indeed
    Where every god did seem to set his seal
    To give the world assurance of a man.
    This was your husband. Look you now what follows.
    Here is your husband, like a mildewed ear   65
    Blasting his wholesome brother. Have you eyes?
    Could you on this fair mountain leave to feed,
    And batten° on this moor? Ha! Have you eyes?
    You cannot call it love, for at your age
    The heyday° in the blood is tame, it's humble,   70
    And waits upon the judgment, and what judgment
    Would step from this to this? Sense° sure you have,
    Else could you not have motion, but sure that sense
    Is apoplexed,° for madness would not err,
    Nor sense to ecstasy° was ne'er so thralled   75
    But it reserved some quantity of choice
    To serve in such a difference. What devil was't
    That thus hath cozened you at hoodman-blind?°
    Eyes without feeling, feeling without sight,
    Ears without hands or eyes, smelling sans° all,   80
    Or but a sickly part of one true sense

---

45 *sets a blister*: brands (as a harlot).   47 *contraction*: marriage contract.   49 *rhapsody*: senseless string.
49–52 *Heaven's face . . . the act*: i.e., the face of heaven blushes over this earth (compounded of four elements), the face hot, as if Judgment Day were near, and it is thoughtsick at the act.   53 *index*: prologue.
55 *counterfeit presentment*: represented image.   57 *front*: forehead.   59 *station*: bearing.   68 *batten*: feed
gluttonously.   70 *heyday*: excitement.   72 *Sense*: feeling.   74 *apoplexed*: paralyzed.   75 *ecstasy*: madness.
78 *cozened you at hoodman-blind*: cheated you at blindman's buff.   80 *sans*: without.

Could not so mope.°
O shame, where is thy blush? Rebellious hell,
If thou canst mutine in a matron's bones,
To flaming youth let virtue be as wax   85
And melt in her own fire. Proclaim no shame
When the compulsive ardor° gives the charge,
Since frost itself as actively doth burn,
And reason panders will.°

QUEEN.   O Hamlet, speak no more.
Thou turn'st mine eyes into my very soul,   90
And there I see such black and grainèd° spots
As will not leave their tinct.°

HAMLET.   Nay, but to live
In the rank sweat of an enseamèd° bed,
Stewed in corruption, honeying and making love
Over the nasty sty——

QUEEN.   O, speak to me no more.   95
These words like daggers enter in my ears.
No more, sweet Hamlet.

HAMLET.   A murderer and a villain,
A slave that is not twentieth part the tithe°
Of your precedent lord, a vice° of kings,
A cutpurse of the empire and the rule,   100
That from a shelf the precious diadem stole
And put it in his pocket——

QUEEN.   No more.

                    Enter Ghost.

HAMLET. A king of shreds and patches—
Save me and hover o'er me with your wings,
You heavenly guards! What would your gracious figure?   105

QUEEN. Alas, he's mad.

HAMLET. Do you not come your tardy son to chide,
That, lapsed in time and passion, lets go by
Th' important acting of your dread command?
O, say!   110

GHOST. Do not forget. This visitation
Is but to whet thy almost blunted purpose.
But look, amazement on thy mother sits.
O, step between her and her fighting soul!
Conceit° in weakest bodies strongest works.   115
Speak to her, Hamlet.

HAMLET.   How is it with you, lady?

_____

   82 *mope*: be stupid.   87 *compulsive ardor*: compelling passion.   89 *reason panders will*: reason acts
as a procurer for desire.   91 *grainèd*: dye in grain (fast dyed).   92 *tinct*: color.   93 *enseamèd*: (perhaps
"soaked in grease," i.e., sweaty; perhaps "much wrinkled").   98 *tithe*: tenth part.   99 *vice*: (like the Vice,
a fool and mischief-maker in the old morality plays).   115 *Conceit*: imagination.

QUEEN. Alas, how is't with you,
    That you do bend your eye on vacancy,
    And with th' incorporal° air do hold discourse?
    Forth at your eyes your spirits wildly peep, 120
    And as the sleeping soldiers in th' alarm
    Your bedded hair° like life in excrements°
    Start up and stand an end.° O gentle son,
    Upon the heat and flame of thy distemper
    Sprinkle cool patience. Whereon do you look? 125
HAMLET. On him, on him! Look you, how pale he glares!
    His form and cause conjoined, preaching to stones,
    Would make them capable.°—Do not look upon me,
    Lest with this piteous action you convert
    My stern effects.° Then what I have to do 130
    Will want true color; tears perchance for blood.
QUEEN. To whom do you speak this?
HAMLET.   Do you see nothing there?
QUEEN. Nothing at all; yet all that is I see.
HAMLET. Nor did you nothing hear?
QUEEN.   No, nothing but ourselves.
HAMLET. Why, look you there! Look how it steals away! 135
    My father, in his habit° as he lived!
    Look where he goes even now out at the portal!

Exit Ghost.

QUEEN. This is the very coinage of your brain.
    This bodiless creation ecstacy
    Is very cunning in.
HAMLET.   Ecstacy? 140
    My pulse as yours doth temperately keep time
    And makes as healthful music. It is not madness
    That I have uttered. Bring me to the test,
    And I the matter will reword, which madness
    Would gambol° from. Mother, for love of grace, 145
    Lay not that flattering unction° to your soul,
    That not your trespass but my madness speaks.
    It will but skin and film the ulcerous place
    Whiles rank corruption, mining° all within,
    Infects unseen. Confess yourself to heaven, 150
    Repent what's past, avoid what is to come,
    And do not spread the compost° on the weeds
    To make them ranker. Forgive me this my virtue.
    For in the fatness of these pursy° times

---

119 *incorporal:* bodiless.   122 *bedded hair:* hairs laid flat; *excrements:* outgrowths (here, the hair).
123 *an end:* on end.   128 *capable:* receptive.   129–130 *convert/ My stern effects:* divert my stern deeds.
136 *habit:* garment (Q1, though a "bad" quarto, is probably correct in saying that at line 102 the ghost
enters "in his nightgown," i.e., dressing gown).   145 *gambol:* start away.   146 *unction:* ointment.   149
mining: undermining.   152 *compost:* fertilizing substance.   154 *pursy:* bloated.

                    Shakespearean Drama

Virtue itself of vice must pardon beg,
Yea, curb° and woo for leave to do him good.   155
QUEEN. O Hamlet, thou hast cleft my heart in twain.
HAMLET. O, throw away the worser part of it,
    And live the purer with the other half.
    Good night—but go not to my uncle's bed.   160
    Assume a virtue, if you have it not.
    That monster custom, who all sense doth eat,
    Of habits devil, is angel yet in this,
    That to the use° of actions fair and good
    He likewise gives a frock or livery°   165
    That aptly is put on. Refrain tonight,
    And that shall lend a kind of easiness
    To the next abstinence; the next more easy;
    For use almost can change the stamp of nature,
    And either° the devil, or throw him out   170
    With wondrous potency. Once more, good night,
    And when you are desirous to be blest,
    I'll blessing beg of you.—For this same lord,
    I do repent; but heaven hath pleased it so,
    To punish me with this, and this with me,   175
    That I must be their° scourge and minister.
    I will bestow° him and will answer well
    The death I gave him. So again, good night.
    I must be cruel only to be kind.
    Thus bad begins, and worse remains behind.   180
    One word more, good lady.
QUEEN.   What shall I do?
HAMLET. Not this, by no means, that I bid you do:
    Let the bloat King tempt you again to bed,
    Pinch wanton on your cheek, call you his mouse,
    And let him, for a pair of reechy° kisses,   185
    Or paddling in your neck with his damned fingers,
    Make you to ravel° all this matter out,
    That I essentially am not in madness,
    But mad in craft. 'Twere good you let him know,
    For who that's but a queen, fair, sober, wise,   190
    Would from a paddock,° from a bat, a gib,°
    Such dear concernings hide? Who would do so?
    No, in despite of sense and secrecy,
    Unpeg the basket on the house's top,
    Let the birds fly, and like the famous ape,   195

---

156 *curb:* bow low.   164 *use:* practice.   165 *livery:* characteristic garment (punning on "habits"
in line 163).   170 *either* (probably a word is missing after *either;* among suggestions are "master,"
"curb," and "house"; but possibly *either* is a verb meaning "make easier").   176 *their:* i.e., the heavens'.
177 *bestow:* stow, lodge.   185 *reechy:* foul (literally "smoky").   187 *ravel:* unravel, reveal.   191 *paddock:* toad; *gib:* tomcat.

To try conclusions,° in the basket creep
And break your own neck down.
QUEEN. Be thou assured, if words be made of breath,
    And breath of life, I have no life to breathe
    What thou hast said to me.   200
HAMLET. I must to England; you know that?
QUEEN.   Alack,
    I had forgot. 'Tis so concluded on.
HAMLET. There's letters sealed, and my two school fellows,
    Whom I will trust as I will adders fanged,
    They bear the mandate;° they must sweep my way   205
    And marshall me to knavery. Let it work;
    For 'tis the sport to have the enginer
    Hoist with his own petar,° and 't shall go hard
    But I will delve one yard below their mines
    And blow them at the moon. O, 'tis most sweet   210
    When in one line two crafts° directly meet.
    This man shall set me packing:
    I'll lug the guts into the neighbor room.
    Mother, good night. Indeed, this counselor
    Is now most still, most secret, and most grave,   215
    Who was in life a foolish prating knave.
    Come, sir, to draw toward an end with you.
    Good night, Mother.

       [*Exit the Queen. Then*] *exit Hamlet, tugging in Polonius.*

ACT IV
Scene I
The castle.

    Enter King and Queen, with Rosencrantz and Guildenstern.

KING. There's a matter in these sighs. These profound heaves
    You must translate; 'tis fit we understand them.
    Where is your son?
QUEEN. Bestow this place on us a little while.

       Exeunt Rosencrantz and Guildenstern.

    Ah, mine own lord, what have I seen tonight!   5
KING. What, Gertrude? How does Hamlet?
QUEEN. Mad as the sea and wind when both contend
    Which is the mightier. In his lawless fit,
    Behind the arras hearing something stir,
    Whips out his rapier, cries, "A rat, a rat!"   10
    And in this brainish apprehension° kills
    The unseen good old man.

---

    196 *To try conclusions:* to make experiments.   205 *mandate:* command.   208 *petar:* bomb.   211 *crafts:*
(1) boats, (2) acts of guile, crafty schemes.   SCENE I. 11 *brainish apprehension:* mad imagination.

KING.   O heavy deed!
     It had been so with us, had we been there.
     His liberty is full of threats to all,
     To you yourself, to us, to every one.   15
     Alas, how shall this bloody deed be answered?
     It will be laid to us, whose providence°
     Should have kept short, restrained, and out of haunt°
     This mad young man. But so much was our love
     We would not understand what was most fit,   20
     But, like the owner of a foul disease,
     To keep it from divulging, let it feed
     Even on the pith of life. Where is he gone?
QUEEN. To draw apart the body he hath killed;
     O'er whom his very madness, like some ore   25
     Among a mineral° of metals base,
     Shows itself pure. 'A weeps for what is done.
KING. O Gertrude, come away!
     The sun no sooner shall the mountains touch
     But we will ship him hence, and this vile deed   30
     We must with all our majesty and skill
     Both countenance and excuse. Ho, Guildenstern!

               Enter Rosencrantz and Guildenstern.

     Friends both, go join you with some further aid:
     Hamlet in madness hath Polonius slain,
     And from his mother's closet hath he dragged him.   35
     Go seek him out; speak fair, and bring the body
     Into the chapel. I pray you haste in this.

               Exeunt Rosencrantz and Guildenstern.

     Come, Gertrude, we'll call up our wisest friends
     And let them know both what we mean to do
     And what's untimely done . . . °   40
     Whose whisper o'er the world's diameter,
     As level as the cannon to his blank°
     Transport his poisoned shot, may miss our name
     And hit the woundless° air. O, come away!
     My soul is full of discord and dismay.   *Exeunt.*   45

Scene II
The castle.

     Enter Hamlet.

HAMLET. Safely stowed.

---

     17 *providence:* foresight.   18 *out of haunt:* away from association with others.   25–26 *ore / Among a*
mineral: vein of gold in a mine.   40 *Done . . . :* (evidently something has dropped out of the text. Capell's
conjecture, "So, haply slander," is usually printed).   42 *Blank:* white center of a target.   44 *woundless:* invulnerable.

GENTLEMEN. [*Within*] Hamlet! Lord Hamlet!
HAMLET. But soft, what noise? Who calls on Hamlet?
    O, here they come.

        Enter Rosencrantz and Guildenstern.

ROSENCRANTZ. What have you done, my lord, with the dead body?   5
HAMLET. Compounded it with dust, whereto 'tis kin.
ROSENCRANTZ. Tell us where 'tis, that we may take it thence
    And bear it to the chapel.
HAMLET. Do not believe it.
ROSENCRANTZ. Believe what?   10
HAMLET. That I can keep your counsel and not mine
    own. Besides, to be demanded of° a sponge, what
    replication° should be made by the son of a king?
ROSENCRANTZ. Take you me for a sponge, my lord?
HAMLET. Ay, sir, that soaks up the King's countenance,°   15
    his rewards, his authorities. But such officers do the
    King best service in the end. He keeps them, like an
    ape, in the corner of his jaw, first mouthed, to be
    last swallowed. When he needs what you have
    gleaned, it is but squeezing you and, sponge, you   20
    shall be dry again.
ROSENCRANTZ. I understand you not, my lord.
HAMLET. I am glad of it: a knavish speech sleeps in a
    foolish ear.
ROSENCRANTZ. My lord, you must tell us where the body   25
    is and go with us to the King.
HAMLET. The body is with the King, but the King is not
    with the body. The King is a thing——
GUILDENSTERN. A thing, my lord?
HAMLET. Of nothing. Bring me to him. Hide fox, and   30
    all after.°   *Exeunt.*

Scene III
The castle.

        Enter King, and two or three.

KING. I have sent to seek him and to find the body:
    How dangerous is it that this man goes loose!
    Yet must not we put the strong law on him:
    He's loved of the distracted° multitude,
    Who like not in their judgment, but their eyes,   5
    And where 'tis so, th' offender's scourge is weighed,
    But never the offense. To bear° all smooth and even,
    This sudden sending him away must seem
    Deliberate pause.° Diseases desperate grown

SCENE II. 12 *demanded of:* questioned by. 13 *replication:* reply. 15 *countenance:* favor. 30–31 *Hide fox, and all after:* (a cry in a game such as hide-and-seek; Hamlet runs from the stage). SCENE III. 4 *distracted:* bewildered, senseless. 7 *bear:* carry out. 9 *pause:* planning.

By desperate appliance are relieved,   10
Or not at all.

Enter Rosencrantz, [Guildenstern,] and all the rest.

                How now? What hath befall'n?
ROSENCRANTZ. Where the dead body is bestowed, my
    lord,
We cannot get from him.
KING.   But where is he?
ROSENCRANTZ. Without, my lord; guarded, to know your
    pleasure.
KING. Bring him before us.
ROSENCRANTZ.   Ho! Bring in the lord.   15

They enter.

KING. Now, Hamlet, where's Polonius?
HAMLET. At supper.
KING. At supper? Where?
HAMLET. Not where he eats, but where 'a is eaten. A
    certain convocation of politic° worms are e'en at   20
    him. Your worm is your only emperor for diet. We
    fat all creatures else to fat us, and we fat ourselves
    for maggots. Your fat king and your lean beggar is
    but variable service°—two dishes, but to one table.
    That's the end.   25
KING. Alas, alas!
HAMLET. A man may fish with the worm that hath eat of
    a king, and eat of the fish that hath fed of that worm.
KING. What dost thou mean by this?
HAMLET. Nothing but to show you how a king may   30
    go a progress° through the guts of a beggar.
KING. Where is Polonius?
HAMLET. In heaven. Send thither to see. If your mes-
    senger find him not there, seek him i' th' other
    place yourself. But if indeed you find him not   35
    within this month, you shall nose him as you go
    up the stairs into the lobby.
KING. [*To Attendants*] Go seek him there.
HAMLET. 'A will stay till you come.

Exeunt Attendants.

KING. Hamlet, this deed, for thine especial safety,   40
    Which we do tender° as we dearly grieve
    For that which thou hast done, must send thee hence
    With fiery quickness. Therefore prepare thyself.
    The bark is ready and the wind at help,
    Th' associates tend,° and everything is bent   45

---

20 *politic:* statesmanlike, shrewd.   24 *variable service:* different courses.   31 *progress:* royal journey.
41 *tender:* hold dear.   45 *tend:* wait.

For England.

HAMLET.   For England?

KING.   Ay, Hamlet.

HAMLET.   Good.

KING. So is it, if thou knew'st our purposes.

HAMLET. I see a cherub° that sees them. But come, for
    England! Farewell, dear Mother.

KING. Thy loving father, Hamlet.   50

HAMLET. My mother—father and mother is man and
    wife, man and wife is one flesh, and so, my mother.
    Come, for England!   *Exit.*

KING. Follow him at foot;° tempt him with speed
      aboard.
    Delay it not; I'll have him hence tonight.   55
    Away! For everything is sealed and done
    That else leans° on th' affair. Pray you make haste.

                      Exeunt all but the King.

    And, England, if my love thou hold'st at aught—
    As my great power thereof may give thee sense,
    Since yet thy cicatrice° looks raw and red   60
    After the Danish sword, and thy free awe°
    Pays homage to us—thou mayst not coldly set
    Our sovereign process,° which imports at full
    By letters congruing to that effect
    The present° death of Hamlet. Do it, England,   65
    For like the hectic° in my blood he rages,
    And thou must cure me. Till I know 'tis done,
    Howe'er my haps,° my joys were ne'er begun.

                              Exit.

Scene IV
A plain in Denmark.

    Enter Fortinbras with his Army over the stage.

FORTINBRAS. Go, Captain, from me greet the Danish
      king.
    Tell him that by his license Fortinbras
    Craves the conveyance of° a promised march
    Over his kingdom. You know the rendezvous.
    If that his Majesty would aught with us,   5
    We shall express our duty in his eye;°
    And let him know so.

CAPTAIN.   I will do't, my lord.

---

    48 *cherub:* angel of knowledge.   54 *at foot:* closely.   57 *leans:* depends.   60 *cicatrice:* scar.   61 *free awe:* uncompelled submission.   62–63 *coldly set / Our sovereign process:* regard slightly our royal command. 65 *present:* instant.   66 *hectic:* fever.   68 *haps:* chances, fortunes.   SCENE IV. 3 *conveyance of:* escort for. 6 *in his eye:* before his eyes (i.e. in his presence).

FORTINBRAS. Go softly° on.

Exeunt all but the Captain.
Enter Hamlet, Rosencrantz, &c.

HAMLET. Good sir, whose powers° are these?
CAPTAIN. They are of Norway, sir.   10
HAMLET. How purposed, sir, I pray you?
CAPTAIN. Against some part of Poland.
HAMLET. Who commands them, sir?
CAPTAIN. The nephew to old Norway, Fortinbras.
HAMLET. Goes it against the main° of Poland, sir,   15
  Or for some frontier?
CAPTAIN. Truly to speak, and with no addition,°
  We go to gain a little patch of ground
  That hath in it no profit but the name.
  To pay five ducats, five, I would not farm it,   20
  Nor will it yield to Norway or the Pole
  A ranker° rate, should it be sold in fee.°
HAMLET. Why, then the Polack never will defend it.
CAPTAIN. Yes, it is already garrisoned.
HAMLET. Two thousand souls and twenty thousand
      ducats   25
  Will not debate° the question of this straw.
  This is the' imposthume° of much wealth and peace,
  That inward breaks, and shows no cause without
  Why the man dies. I humbly thank you, sir.
CAPTAIN. God bye you, sir.   [*Exit.*]
ROSENCRANTZ.   Will't please you go, my lord?   30
HAMLET. I'll be with you straight. Go a little before.

Exeunt all but Hamlet.

  How all occasions do inform against me
  And spur my dull revenge! What is a man,
  If his chief good and market° of his time
  Be but to sleep and feed? A beast, no more.   35
  Sure he that made us with such large discourse,°
  Looking before and after, gave us not
  That capability and godlike reason
  To fust° in us unused. Now, whether it be
  Bestial oblivion,° or some craven scruple   40
  Of thinking too precisely on th' event°—
  A thought which, quartered, hath but one part
      wisdom
  And ever three parts coward—I do not know
  Why yet I live to say, "This thing's to do,"

---

  8 *softly*: slowly.   9 *powers*: forces.   15 *main*: main part.   17 *with no addition*: plainly.   22 *ranker*:
higher; *in fee*: outright.   26 *debate*: settle.   27 *imposthume*: abscess, ulcer.   34 *market*: profits.   36
discourse: understanding.   39 *fust*: grow moldy.   40 *oblivion*: forgetfulness.   41 *event*: outcome.

Sith I have cause, and will, and strength, and means   45
To do't. Examples gross° as earth exhort me.
Witness this army of such mass and charge,°
Led by a delicate and tender prince,
Whose spirit, with divine ambition puffed,
Makes mouths at the invisible event,°   50
Exposing what is mortal and unsure
To all that fortune, death, and danger dare,
Even for an eggshell. Rightly to be great
Is not° to stir without great argument,°
But greatly° to find quarrel in a straw   55
When honor's at the stake. How stand I then,
That have a father killed, a mother stained,
Excitements° of my reason and my blood,
And let all sleep, while to my shame I see
The imminent death of twenty thousand men   60
That for a fantasy and trick of fame°
Go to their graves like beds, fight for a plot
Whereon the numbers cannot try the cause,
Which is not tomb enough and continent°
To hide the slain? O, from this time forth,   65
My thoughts be bloody, or be nothing worth!   *Exit.*

Scene V
The castle.

Enter Horatio, [Queen] Gertrude, and a Gentleman.

QUEEN. I will not speak with her.
GENTLEMAN. She is importunate, indeed distract.
    Her mood will needs be pitied.
QUEEN.   What would she have?
GENTLEMAN. She speaks much of her father, says she
        hears
    There's tricks i' th' world, and hems, and beats her
        heart,
    Spurns enviously at straws,° speaks things in doubt°   5
    That carry but half sense. Her speech is nothing,
    Yet the unshapèd use of it doth move
    The hearers to collection;° they yawn° at it,
    And botch the words up fit to their own thoughts,
    Which, as her winks and nods and gestures yield them,   10
    Indeed would make one think there might be thought,

---

46 *gross:* large, obvious.   47 *charge:* expense.   50 *Makes mouths at the invisible event:* makes scornful
faces (is contemptuous of) the unseen outcome.   54 *not:* (the sense seems to require "not not"); *argument:*
reason.   55 *greatly:* i.e., nobly.   58 *Excitements:* incentives.   61 *fantasy and trick of fame:* illusion and trifle of reputation.   64 *continent:* receptacle, container.   SCENE V.   6 *Spurns enviously at straws:* objects spite-
fully to insignificant matters; *in doubt:* uncertainly.   8–9 *Yet the . . . to collection:* i.e., yet the formless
manner of it moves her listeners to gather up some sort of meaning.   9 *yawn:* gape (?).

Though nothing sure, yet much unhappily.
HORATIO. 'Twere good she were spoken with, for she
    may strew
Dangerous conjectures in ill-breeding minds.   15
QUEEN. Let her come in.   [*Exit Gentleman.*]
    [*Aside*] To my sick soul (as sin's true nature is)
    Each toy seems prologue to some great amiss;°
    So full of artless jealousy° is guilt
    It spills° itself in fearing to be spilt.   20

          Enter Ophelia [*distracted.*]

OPHELIA. Where is the beauteous majesty of Denmark?
QUEEN. How now, Ophelia?
OPHELIA. [*She sings.*] How should I your truelove know
          From another one?
      By his cockle hat° and staff   25
      And his sandal shoon.°
QUEEN. Alas, sweet lady, what imports this song?
OPHELIA. Say you? Nay, pray you mark.
      He is dead and gone, lady,   [*Song*]
      He is dead and gone;   30
        At his head a grass-green turf,
        At his heels a stone,
  O, ho!
QUEEN. Nay, but Ophelia——
OPHELIA. Pray you mark.   35
    [*Sings.*] White his shroud as the mountain snow——

          Enter King.

QUEEN. Alas, look here, my lord.
OPHELIA.   Larded° all with sweet flowers [*Song*]
      Which bewept to the grave did not go
        With truelove showers.   40
KING. How do you, pretty lady?
OPHELIA. Well, God dild° you! They say the owl was a
    baker's daughter.° Lord, we know what we are, but
    know not what we may be. God be at your table!
KING. Conceit° upon her father.   45
OPHELIA. Pray let's have not words of this, but when
    they ask you what it means, say you this:
      Tomorrow is Saint Valentine's day.° [*Song*]

---

18 *amiss:* misfortune.   19 *artless jealousy:* crude suspicion.   20 *spills:* destroys.   25 *cockle hat:* (a cockleshell on the hat was the sign of a pilgrim who had journeyed to shrines overseas. The association of lovers and pilgrims was a common one).   26 *shoon:* shoes.   38 *Larded:* decorated.   42 *dild:* yield, i.e., reward.   43 *baker's daughter:* (an allusion to a tale of a baker's daughter who begrudged bread to Christ and was turned into an owl).   45 *Conceit:* brooding.   48 *Saint Valentine's day:* Feb. 14 (the notion was that a bachelor would become the truelove of the first girl he saw on this day).

All in the morning betime,
And I a maid at your window,
        To be your Valentine.   50

Then up he rose and donned his clothes
        And dupped° the chamber door,
Let in the maid, that out a maid
        Never departed more.   55

KING. Pretty Ophelia.

OPHELIA. Indeed, la, without an oath, I'll make an end
on't:
[Sings.] By Gis° and by Saint Charity,
        Alack, and fie for shame!
Young men will do't if they come to't,   60
        By Cock,° they are to blame.
Quoth she, "Before you tumbled me,
        You promised me to wed."

He answers:
        "So would I 'a' done, by yonder sun,   65
        An thou hadst not come to my bed."

KING. How long hath she been thus?

OPHELIA. I hope all will be well. We must be patient,
but I cannot choose but weep to think they would
lay him i' th' cold ground. My brother shall know   70
of it; and so I thank you for your good counsel.
Come, my coach! Good night, ladies, good night.
Sweet ladies, good night, good night.   Exit.

KING. Follow her close; give her a good watch, I pray
        you.   [Exit Horatio.]
O, this is the poison of deep grief; it springs   75
All from her father's death—and now behold!
O Gertrude, Gertrude,
When sorrows come, they come not single spies,
But in battalions: first, her father slain;
Next, your son gone, and he most violent author   80
Of his own just remove; the people muddied,°
Thick and unwholesome in their thoughts and
        whispers
For good Polonius' death, and we have done but
        greenly°
In huggermugger° to inter him; poor Ophelia
Divided from herself and her fair judgment,   85
Without the which we are pictures or mere beasts;
Last, and as much containing as all these,
Her brother is in secret come from France,
Feeds on his wonder,° keeps himself in clouds,

---

53 *dupped:* opened (did up).   58 *Gis:* (contraction of "Jesus").   61 *Cock:* (1) God, (2) phallus.
81 *muddied:* muddled.   83 *greenly:* foolishly.   84 *huggermugger:* secret haste.   89 *wonder:* suspicion.

And wants not buzzers° to infect his ear 90
With pestilent speeches of his father's death,
Wherein necessity, of matter beggared,°
Will nothing stick° our person to arraign
In ear and ear. O my dear Gertrude, this,
Like to a murd'ring piece,° in many places 95
Gives me a superfluous death.   *A noise within.*

                        Enter a Messenger.

QUEEN.   Alack, what noise is this?
KING. Attend, where are my Switzers?° Let them
          guard the door.
      What is the matter?
MESSENGER.   Save yourself, my lord.
      The ocean, overpeering of his list,°
      Eats not the flats with more impiteous haste 100
      Than your Laertes, in a riotous head,°
      O'erbears your officers. The rabble call him lord,
      And, as the world were now but to begin,
      Antiquity forgot, custom not known,
      The ratifiers and props of every word, 105
      They cry, "Choose we! Laertes shall be king!"
      Caps, hands, and tongues applaud it to the clouds,
      "Laertes shall be king! Laertes King!"   *A noise within.*
QUEEN. How cheerfully on the false trail they cry!
      O, this is counter,° you false Danish dogs! 110

                Enter Laertes with others.

KING. The doors are broke.
LAERTES. Where is this king?—Sirs, stand you all
          without.
ALL. No, let's come in.
LAERTES.   I pray you give me leave.
ALL. We will, we will.
LAERTES. I thank you. Keep the door. [*Exeunt his
          Followers.*] O thou vile King,
      Give me my father. 115
QUEEN.   Calmly, good Laertes.
LAERTES. That drop of blood that's calm proclaims me
          bastard,
      Cries cuckold° to my father, brands the harlot
      Even here between the chaste unsmirchèd brow
      Of my true mother.

---

      90 *wants not buzzers*: does not lack talebearers.   92 *of matter beggared*: unprovided with facts.
      93 *Will nothing stick*: will not hesitate.   95 *murd'ring piece*: (a cannon that shot a kind of shrapnel).
      97 *Switzers*: Swiss guards.   99 *list*: shore.   101 *in a riotous head*: with a rebellious force.   110 *counter*:
      (a hound runs counter when he follows the scent backward from the prey).   118 *cuckold*: man whose
      wife is unfaithful.

KING.   What is the cause, Laertes,   120
     That thy rebellion looks so giantlike?
     Let him go, Gertrude. Do not fear° our person.
     There's such divinity doth hedge a king
     That treason can but peep to° what it would,
     Acts little of his will. Tell me, Laertes,   125
     Why thou art thus incensed. Let him go, Gertrude.
     Speak, man.
LAERTES. Where is my father?
KING.   Dead.
QUEEN.   But not by him.
KING. Let him demand his fill.
LAERTES. How came he dead? I'll not be juggled with.   130
     To hell allegiance, vows to the blackest devil,
     Conscience and grace to the profoundest pit!
     I dare damnation. To this point I stand,
     That both the worlds I give to negligence,°
     Let come what comes, only I'll be revenged   135
     Most throughly for my father.
KING.   Who shall stay you?
LAERTES. My will, not all the world's.
     And for my means, I'll husband them° so well
     They shall go far with little.
KING.   Good Laertes,   140
     If you desire to know the certainty
     Of your dear father, is't writ in your revenge
     That swoopstake° you will draw both friend and foe,
     Winner and loser?
LAERTES. None but his enemies.
KING.   Will you know them then?
LAERTES. To his good friends thus wide I'll ope my
        arms   145
     And like the kind life-rend'ring pelican°
     Repast° them with my blood.
KING.   Why, now you speak
     Like a good child and a true gentleman.
     That I am guiltless of your father's death,
     And am most sensibly° in grief for it,   150
     It shall as level to your judgment 'pear
     As day does to your eye.

                A noise within: "Let her come in."

LAERTES. How now? What noise is that?

                Enter Ophelia.

_____

122 *fear:* fear for.   124 *peep to:* i.e., look at from a distance.   134 *That both . . . to negligence:* i.e.,
I care not what may happen (to me) in this world or the next.   138 *husband them:* use them economically.   143 *swoopstake:* in a clean sweep.   146 *pelican:* (thought to feed its young with its own blood).
147 *Repast:* feed.   150 *sensibly:* acutely.

O heat, dry up my brains; tears seven times salt
Burn out the sense and virtue° of mine eye!   155
By heaven, thy madness shall be paid with weight
Till our scale turn the beam.° O Rose of May,
Dear maid, kind sister, sweet Ophelia!
O heavens, is't possible a young maid's wits
Should be as mortal as an old man's life?   160
Nature is fine° in love, and where 'tis fine,
It sends some precious instance° of itself
After the thing it loves.

OPHELIA. They bore him barefaced on the bier [*Song*]
       Hey non nony, nony, hey nony   165
       And in his grave rained many a tear——
Fare you well, my dove!

LAERTES. Hadst thou thy wits, and didst persuade re-
       venge,
It could not move thus.

OPHELIA. You must sing "A-down a-down, and you call   170
him a-down-a." O, how the wheel° becomes it! It is
the false steward, that stole his master's daughter.

LAERTES. This nothing's more than matter.°

OPHELIA. There's rosemary, that's for remembrance.
Pray you, love, remember. And there is pansies,   175
that's for thoughts.

LAERTES. A document° in madness, thoughts and remembrance fitted.

OPHELIA. There's fennel° for you, and columbines.
There's rue for you, and here's some for me. We   180
may call it herb of grace o' Sundays. O, you must
wear your rue with a difference. There's a daisy. I
would give you some violets, but they withered all
when my father died. They say 'a made a good end.
[*Sings*]   For bonny sweet Robin is all my joy.   185

LAERTES. Thought and affliction, passion, hell itself,
She turns to favor° and to prettiness.

OPHELIA. And will 'a not come again?   [*Song*]
       And will 'a not come again?
          No, no, he is dead,   190
            Go to thy deathbed,
            He never will come again.

---

155 *virtue:* power.   157 *turn the beam:* weigh down the bar (of the balance).   161 *fine:* refined, delicate.   162 *instance:* sample.   171 *wheel:* (of uncertain meaning, but probably a turn or dance of Ophelia's, rather than Fortune's wheel).   173 *This nothing's more than matter:* this nonsense has more meaning than matters of consequence.   177 *document:* lesson.   179 *fennel:* (the distribution of flowers in the ensuing lines has symbolic meaning, but the meaning is disputed. Perhaps *fennel*, flattery; *columbines*, cuckoldry; *rue*, sorrow for Ophelia and repentance for the Queen; *daisy*, dissembling; *violets*, faithfulness. For other interpretations, see J. W. Lever in *Review of English Studies*, New Series 3 [1952], pp. 123–129). 187 *favor:* charm, beauty.

His beard was as white as snow,
All flaxen was his poll.°
   He is gone, he is gone,
   And we cast away moan.
God 'a' mercy on his soul!
And of all Christian souls, I pray God. God bye you.

Exit.

LAERTES. Do you see this, O God?

KING. Laertes, I must commune with your grief,
Or you deny me right. Go but apart,
Make choice of whom your wisest friends you will,
And they shall hear and judge 'twixt you and me.
If by direct or by collateral° hand
They find us touched,° we will our kingdom give,
Our crown, or life, and all that we call ours,
To you in satisfaction; but if not,
Be you content to lend your patience to us,
And we shall jointly labor with your soul
To give it due content.

LAERTES.   Let this be so.
His means of death, his obscure funeral—
No trophy, sword, nor hatchment° o'er his bones,
No noble rite nor formal ostentation°—
Cry to be heard, as 'twere from heaven to earth,
That I must call't in question.

KING.   So you shall;
And where th' offense is, let the great ax fall.
I pray you go with me.   *Exeunt.*

195

200

205

210

215

Scene VI
The castle.

Enter Horatio and others.

HORATIO. What are they that would speak with me?

GENTLEMEN. Seafaring men, sir. They say they have
letters for you.

HORATIO. Let them come in.   *[Exit Attendant.]*
I do not know from what part of the world
I should be greeted, if not from Lord Hamlet.

Enter Sailors.

SAILOR. God bless you, sir.

HORATIO. Let Him bless thee too.

SAILOR. 'A shall, sir, an't please Him. There's a letter
for you, sir—it came from th' ambassador that was
bound for England—if your name be Horatio, as
I am let to know it is.

5

10

---

   194 *All flaxen was his poll:* white as flax was his head.   204 *collateral:* indirect.   205 *touched:* implicated.   212 *hatchment:* tablet bearing the coat of arms of the dead.   213 *ostentation:* ceremony.

HORATIO. [*Reads the letter.*] "Horatio, when thou shalt
    have overlooked° this, give these fellows some
    means to the King. They have letters for him. Ere   15
    we were two days old at sea, a pirate of very warlike
    appointment° gave us chase. Finding ourselves too
    slow of sail, we put on a compelled valor, and in
    the grapple I boarded them. On the instant they
    got clear of our ship; so I alone became their   20
    prisoner. They have dealt with me like thieves of
    mercy, but they knew what they did: I am to do a
    good turn for them. Let the King have the letters
    I have sent, and repair thou to me with as much
    speed as thou wouldest fly death. I have words to   25
    speak in thine ear will make thee dumb; yet are they
    much too light for the bore° of the matter. These
    good fellows will bring thee where I am. Rosen-
    crantz and Guildenstern hold their course for Eng-
    land. Of them I have much to tell thee. Farewell.   30
                He that thou knowest thine, Hamlet."
    Come, I will give you way for these your letters,
    And do't the speedier that you may direct me
    To him from whom you brought them.   *Exeunt.*

Scene VII
The castle.

    Enter King and Laertes.

KING. Now must your conscience my acquittance seal,
    And you must put me in your heart for friend,
    Sith you have heard, and with a knowing ear,
    That he which hath your noble father slain
    Pursued my life.
LAERTES.   It well appears. But tell me   5
    Why you proceeded not against these feats
    So criminal and so capital° in nature,
    As by your safety, greatness, wisdom, all things else,
    You mainly° were stirred up.
KING.   O, for two special reasons,
    Which may to you perhaps seem much unsinewed,°   10
    But yet to me they're strong. The Queen his mother
    Lives almost by his looks, and for myself—
    My virtue or my plague, be it either which—
    She is so conjunctive° to my life and soul,
    That, as the star moves not but in his sphere,   15
    I could not but by her. The other motive

SCENE VI. 14 *overlooked*: surveyed. 17 *appointment*: equipment. 27 *bore*: caliber (here, "importance"). SCENE VII. 7 *capital*: deserving death. 9 *mainly*: powerfully. 10 *unsinewed*: weak. 14 *con-
junctive*: closely united.

Why to a public count° I might not go
Is the great love the general gender° bear him,
Who, dipping all his faults in their affection,
Would, like the spring that turneth wood to stone,° 20
Convert his gyves° to graces; so that my arrows,
Too slightly timbered° for so loud a wind,
Would have reverted to my bow again,
And not where I had aimed them.

LAERTES. And so have I a noble father lost, 25
A sister driven into desp'rate terms,°
Whose worth, if praises may go back again,°
Stood challenger on mount of all the age
For her perfections. But my revenge will come.

KING. Break not your sleeps for that. You must not
think 30
That we are made of stuff so flat and dull
That we can let our beard be shook with danger,
And think it pastime. You shortly shall hear more.
I loved your father, and we love ourself,
And that, I hope, will teach you to imagine—— 35

Enter a Messenger with letters.

How now? What news?

MESSENGER.   Letters, my lord, from Hamlet:
These to your Majesty; this to the Queen.

KING. From Hamlet? Who brought them?

MESSENGER. Sailors, my lord, they say; I saw them not.
They were given me by Claudio; he received them 40
Of him that brought them.

KING.   Laertes, you shall hear them.—
Leave us.   *Exit Messenger.*
[*Reads.*] "High and mighty, you shall know I am set
naked° on your kingdom. Tomorrow shall I beg
leave to see your kingly eyes; even when I shall (first 45
asking your pardon thereunto) recount the occasion
of my sudden and more strange return.

                              Hamlet."
What should this mean? Are all the rest come back?
Or is it some abuse,° and no such thing? 50

LAERTES. Know you the hand?

KING.   'Tis Hamlet's character.° "Naked"!
And in a postscript here, he says "alone."
Can you devise° me?

LAERTES. I am lost in it, my lord. But let him come.

---

17 *count:* reckoning.   18 *general gender:* common people.   20 *spring that turneth wood to stone:* (a
spring in Shakespeare's county was so charged with lime that it would petrify wood placed in it).   21 *gyves:*
fetters.   22 *timbered:* shafted.   26 *terms:* conditions.   27 *go back again:* revert to what is past.   44 *naked:*
destitute.   50 *abuse:* deception.   51 *character:* handwriting.   53 *devise:* advise.

It warms the very sickness in my heart   55
That I shall live and tell him to his teeth,
"Thus did'st thou."
KING.   If it be so, Laertes
(As how should it be so? How otherwise?),
Will you be ruled by me?
LAERTES.   Ay, my lord,
So you will not o'errule me to a peace.   60
KING. To thine own peace. If he be now returned,
As checking at° his voyage, and that he means
No more to undertake it, I will work him
To an exploit now ripe in my device,
Under the which he shall not choose but fall;   65
And for his death no wind of blame shall breathe,
But even his mother shall uncharge the practice°
And call it accident.
LAERTES.   My lord, I will be ruled;
The rather if you could devise it so
That I might be the organ.
KING.   It falls right.   70
You have been talked of since your travel much,
And that in Hamlet's hearing, for a quality
Wherein they say you shine. Your sum of parts
Did not together pluck such envy from him
As did that one, and that, in my regard,   75
Of the unworthiest siege.°
LAERTES.   What part is that, my lord?
KING. A very riband in the cap of youth,
Yet needful too, for youth no less becomes
The light and careless livery that it wears
Than settled age his sables and his weeds,°   80
Importing health and graveness. Two months since
Here was a gentlemen of Normandy.
I have seen myself, and served against, the French,
And they can° well on horseback, but this gallant
Had witchcraft in't. He grew unto his seat,   85
And to such wondrous doing brought his horse
As had he been incorpsed and deminatured
With the brave beast. So far he topped my thought
That I, in forgery° of shapes and tricks,
Come short of what he did.
LAERTES.   A Norman was't?   90
KING. A Norman.
LAERTES. Upon my life, Lamord.

---

    62 *checking at:* turning away from (a term in falconry).   67 *uncharge the practice:* not charge the de-
vice with treachery.   76 *siege:* rank.   80 *sables and his weeds:* i.e., sober attire.   84 *can:* do.   89 *forgery:* invention.

KING.   The very same.

LAERTES. I know him well. He is the brooch° indeed
    And gem of all the nation.

KING. He made confession° of you,   95
    And gave you such a masterly report,
    For art and exercise in your defense,
    And for your rapier most especial,
    That he cried out 'twould be a sight indeed
    If one could match you. The scrimers° of their
        nation   100
    He swore had neither motion, guard, nor eye,
    If you opposed them. Sir, this report of his
    Did Hamlet so envenom with his envy
    That he could nothing do but wish and beg
    Your sudden coming o'er to play with you.   105
    Now, out of this——

LAERTES.   What out of this, my lord?

KING. Laertes, was your father dear to you?
    Or are you like the painting of a sorrow,
    A face without a heart?

LAERTES.   Why ask you this?

KING. Not that I think you did not love your father,   110
    But that I know love is begun by time,
    And that I see, in passages of proof,°
    Time qualifies° the spark and fire of it.
    There lives within the very flame of love
    A kind of wick or snuff° that will abate it,   115
    And nothing is at a like goodness still,°
    For goodness, growing to a plurisy,°
    Dies in his own too-much. That we would do
    We would do when we would, for this "would"
        changes,
    And hath abatements and delays as many   120
    As there are tongues, are hands, are accidents,
    And then this "should" is like a spendthrift sigh,°
    That hurts by easing. But to the quick° of th' ulcer—
    Hamlet comes back; what would you undertake
    To show yourself in deed your father's son   125
    More than in words?

LAERTES.   To cut his throat i' th' church!

KING. No place indeed should murder sanctuarize;°
    Revenge should have no bounds. But, good Laertes,
    Will you do this? Keep close within your chamber.

---

93 *brooch*: ornament.   95 *confession*: report.   100 *scrimers*: fencers.   112 *passages of proof*: proved cases.   113 *qualifies*: diminishes.   115 *snuff*: residue of burnt wick (which dims the light).   116 *still*: always.   117 *plurisy*: fullness, excess.   122 *spendthrift sigh*: (sighing provides ease, but because it was thought to thin the blood and so shorten life it was spendthrift).   123 *quick*: sensitive flesh.   127 *sanctuarize*: protect.

Hamlet returned shall know you are come home. 130
We'll put on those° shall praise your excellence
And set a double varnish on the fame
The Frenchman gave you, bring you in fine°
    together
And wager on your heads. He, being remiss,
Most generous, and free from all contriving, 135
Will not peruse the foils, so that with ease,
Or with a little shuffling, you may choose
A sword unbated,° and, in a pass of practice,°
Requite him for your father.
LAERTES.   I will do't,
And for that purpose I'll anoint my sword. 140
I bought an unction of a mountebank,°
So mortal that, but dip a knife in it,
Where it draws blood, no cataplasm° so rare,
Collected from all simples° that have virtue°
Under the moon, can save the thing from death 145
That is but scratched withal. I'll touch my point
With this contagion, that, if I gall him slightly,
It may be death.
KING.   Let's further think of this,
Weigh what convenience both of time and means
May fit us to our shape.° If this should fail, 150
And that our drift look through° our bad per-
    formance.
'Twere better not assayed. Therefore this project
Should have a back or second, that might hold
If this did blast in proof.° Soft, let me see.
We'll make a solemn wager on our cunnings— 155
I ha't!
When in your motion you are hot and dry—
As make your bouts more violent to that end—
And that he calls for drink, I'll have prepared him
A chalice for the nonce,° whereon but sipping, 160
If he by chance escape your venomed stuck,°
Our purpose may hold there.—But stay, what noise?

Enter Queen.

QUEEN. One woe doth tread upon another's heel.
    So fast they follow. Your sister's drowned, Laertes.
LAERTES. Drowned! O, where? 165
QUEEN. There is a willow grows askant° the brook,
    That shows his hoar° leaves in the glassy stream:

---

131 *We'll put on those:* we'll incite persons who.   133 *in fine:* finally.   138 *unbated:* not blunted;
pass of practice: treacherous thrust.   141 *mountebank:* quack.   143 *cataplasm:* poultice.   144 *simples:*
medicinal herbs; *virtue:* (power to heal).   150 *shape:* role.   151 *drift look through:* purpose show
through.   154 *blast in proof:* burst (fail) in performance.   160 *nonce:* occasion.   161 *stuck:* thrust.
166 *askant:* aslant.   167 *hoar:* silver-gray.

Therewith° fantastic garlands did she make
Of crowflowers, nettles, daisies, and long purples,
That liberal° shepherds give a grosser name,   170
But our cold maids do dead men's fingers call them.
There on the pendent boughs her crownet° weeds
Clamb'ring to hang, an envious sliver° broke,
When down her weedy trophies and herself
Fell in the weeping brook. Her clothes spread wide,   175
And mermaidlike awhile they bore her up,
Which time she chanted snatches of old lauds,°
As one incapable° of her own distress,
Or like a creature native and indued°
Unto that element. But long it could not be   180
Till that her garments, heavy with their drink,
Pulled the poor wretch from her melodious lay
To muddy death.
LAERTES.   Alas, then she is drowned?
QUEEN. Drowned, drowned.
LAERTES. Too much of water hast thou, poor Ophelia,   185
And therefore I forbid my tears; but yet
It is our trick;° nature her custom holds,
Let shame say what it will: when these are gone,
The woman° will be out. Adieu, my lord.
I have a speech o'fire, that fain would blaze,   190
But that this folly drowns it.   *Exit.*
KING.   Let's follow, Gertrude.
How much I had to do to calm his rage!
Now fear I this will give it start again;
Therefore let's follow.   *Exeunt.*

ACT V
Scene I
A churchyard.

Enter two Clowns.°

CLOWN. Is she to be buried in Christian burial when she
willfully seeks her own salvation?
OTHER. I tell thee she is. Therefore make her grave
straight.° The crowner° hath sat on her, and finds
it Christian burial.   5
CLOWN. How can that be, unless she drowned herself
in her own defense?
OTHER. Why, 'tis found so.

---

    168 *Therewith:* i.e., with willow twigs.   170 *liberal:* free-spoken, coarse-mouthed.   172 *crownet:* coronet.   173 *envious silver:* malicious branch.   177 *lauds:* hymns.   178 *incapable:* unaware.   179 *indued:* in harmony with.   187 *trick:* trait, way.   189 *woman:* i.e., womanly part of me.   SCENE I. s.d. *Clowns:* rustics.   4 *straight:* straightway; *crowner:* coroner.

CLOWN. It must be *se offendendo*;° it cannot be else. 10
For here lies the point: if I drown myself wittingly,
it argues an act, and an act hath three branches—
it is to act, to do, to perform. Argal,° she drowned
herself wittingly.

OTHER. Nay, but hear you, Goodman Delver.

CLOWN. Give me leave. Here lies the water—good. 15
Here stands the man—good. If the man go to this
water and drown himself, it is, will he nill he,° he
goes; mark you that. But if the water come to him
and drown him, he drowns not himself. Argal, he
that is not guilty of his own death, shortens not his 20
own life.

OTHER. But is this law?

CLOWN. Ay marry, is't—crowner's quest° law.

OTHER. Will you ha' the truth on't? If this had not been
a gentlewoman, she should have been buried out 25
o' Christian burial.

CLOWN. Why, there, thou say'st. And the more pity
that great folk should have count'nance° in this
world to drown or hang themselves more than their
even-Christen.° Come, my spade. There is no an- 30
cient gentlemen but gard'ners, ditchers, and grave-
makers. They hold up° Adam's profession.

OTHER. Was he a gentleman?

CLOWN. 'A was the first ever bore arms.°

OTHER. Why, he had none. 35

CLOWN. What, art a heathen? How dost thou understand the Scripture? The Scripture says Adam
digged. Could he dig without arms? I'll put another
question to thee. If thou answerest me not to the
purpose, confess thyself—— 40

OTHER. Go to.

CLOWN. What is he that builds stronger than either the
mason, the shipwright, or the carpenter?

OTHER. The gallowsmaker, for that frame outlives a
thousand tenants. 45

CLOWN. I like thy wit well, in good faith. The gallows
does well. But how does it well? It does well to those
that do ill. Now thou dost ill to say the gallows
is built stronger than the church. Argal, the gallows
may do well to thee. To't again, come. 50

OTHER. Who builds stronger than a mason, a shipwright, or a carpenter?

---

9 *se offendendo:* (blunder for *se defendendo,* a legal term meaning "in self-defense"). 12 *Argal:* (blunder for Latin *ergo,* "therefore"). 17 *will he nill he:* will he or will he not (whether he will or will not). 23 *quest:* inquest. 28 *count'nance:* privilege. 30 *even-Christen:* fellow Christian. 32 *hold up:* keep up. 34 *bore arms:* had a coat of arms (the sign of a gentleman).

CLOWN. Ay, tell me that, and unyoke.°
OTHER. Marry, now I can tell.
CLOWN. To't.
OTHER. Mass,° I cannot tell.   55

        Enter Hamlet and Horatio afar off.

CLOWN. Cudgel thy brains no more about it, for your
    dull ass will not mend his pace with beating. And
    when you are asked this question next, say "grave-
    maker." The houses he makes lasts till doomsday.
    Go, get thee in, and fetch me a stoup° of liquor.   60

                      Exit Other Clown.

In youth when I did love, did love,   [*Song*]
    Methought it was very sweet
To contract—O—the time for—a—my behove,°
O, methought there—a—was nothing—a—meet.   65
HAMLET. Has this fellow no feeling of his business? 'A
    sings in gravemaking.
HORATIO. Custom hath made it in him a property of
    easiness.°
HAMLET. 'Tis e'en so. The hand of little employment   70
    hath the daintier sense.°
CLOWN. But age with his stealing steps   [*Song*]
    Hath clawed me in his clutch,
    And hath shipped me into the land,
    As if I had never been such.   75

               Throws up a skull.

HAMLET. That skull had a tongue in it, and could sing
    once. How the knave jowls° it to the ground, as if
    'twere Cain's jawbone, that did the first murder!
    This might be the pate of a politician, which this
    ass now o'erreaches,° one that would circumvent   80
    God, might it not?
HORATIO. It might, my lord.
HAMLET. Or, of a courtier, which could say "Good
    morrow, sweet lord! How dost thou, sweet lord?"
    This might be my Lord Such-a-one, that praised   85
    my Lord Such-a-one's horse when 'a went to beg
    it, might it not?
HORATIO. Ay, my lord.
HAMLET. Why, e'en so, and now my Lady Worm's,
    chapless,° and knocked about the mazzard° with a   90
    sexton's spade. Here's fine revolution, and we had

---

    53 *unyoke:* i.e., stop work for the day.   56 *Mass:* by the mass.   61 *stoup:* tankard.   64 *behove:* advantage.   68–69 *in him a property of easiness:* easy for him.   71 *hath the daintier sense:* is more sensitive (because it is not calloused).   77 *jowls:* hurls.   80 *o'erreaches:* (1) reaches over, (2) has the advantage over.   90 *chapless:* lacking the lower jaw; *mazzard:* head.

the trick to see't. Did these bones cost no more
the breeding but to play at loggets° with them?
Mine ache to think on't.

CLOWN. A pickax and a spade, a spade,   [Song]   95
     For and a shrouding sheet;
     O, a pit of clay for to be made
     For such a quest is meet.

Throws up another skull.

HAMLET. There's another. Why may not that be the
skull of a lawyer? Where be his quiddities° now, his   100
quillities,° his cases, his tenures,° and his tricks?
Why does he suffer this mad knave now to knock
him about the sconce° with a dirty shovel, and will
not tell him of his action of battery? Hum! This
fellow might be in's time a great buyer of land, with   105
his statutes, his recognizances, his fines,° his double
vouchers, his recoveries. Is this the fine° of his fines,
and the recovery of his recoveries, to have his fine
pate full of fine dirt? Will his vouchers vouch him
no more of his purchases, and double ones too, than   110
the length and breadth of a pair of indentures?°
The very conveyances° of his lands will scarcely
lie in this box, and must th' inheritor himself have no
more, ha?

HORATIO. Not a jot more, my lord.   115

HAMLET. Is not parchment made of sheepskins?

HORATIO. Ay, my lord, and of calveskins too.

HAMLET. They are sheep and calves which seek out
assurance° in that. I will speak to this fellow. Whose
grave's this, sirrah?   120

CLOWN. Mine, sir.
    [Sings.]   O, a pit of clay for to be made
                For such a guest is meet.

HAMLET. I think it be thine indeed, for thou liest in't.

CLOWN. You lie out on't, sir, and therefore 'tis not   125
yours. For my part, I do not lie in't, yet it is mine.

HAMLET. Thou dost lie in't, to be in't and say it is
thine. 'Tis for the dead, not for the quick;° therefore thou liest.

CLOWN. 'Tis a quick lie, sir; 'twill away again from   130
me to you.

HAMLET. What man dost thou dig it for?

---

    93 *loggets*: (a game in which small pieces of wood were thrown at an object). 100 *quiddities*: sub-
tle arguments (from Latin *quidditas*, "whatness"). 101 *quillities*: fine distinctions; *tenures*: legal means of
holding land. 103 *sconce*: head. 106 *his statutes, his recognizances, his fines*: his documents giving a
creditor control of a debtor's land, his bonds of surety, his documents changing an entailed estate into
fee simple (unrestricted ownership). 107 *fine*: end. 111 *indentures*: contracts. 112 *conveyances*: legal
documents for the transference of land. 119 *assurance*: safety. 128 *quick*: living.

CLOWN. For no man, sir.

HAMLET. What woman then?

CLOWN. For none neither. 135

HAMLET. Who is to be buried in't?

CLOWN. One that was a woman, sir: but, rest her soul, she's dead.

HAMLET. How absolute° the knave is! We must speak by the card,° or equivocation° will undo us. By the 140 Lord, Horatio, this three years I have took note of it, the age is grown so picked° that the toe of the peasant comes so near the heel of the courtier he galls his kibe.° How long hast thou been a grave- maker? 145

CLOWN. Of all the days i' th' year, I came to't that day that our last king Hamlet overcame Fortinbras.

HAMLET. How long is that since?

CLOWN. Cannot you tell that? Every fool can tell that. It was that very day that young Hamlet was born— 150 he that is mad, and sent into England.

HAMLET. Ay, marry, why was he sent into England?

CLOWN. Why, because 'a was mad. 'A shall recover his wits there; or, if 'a do not, 'tis no great matter there.

HAMLET. Why? 155

CLOWN. 'Twill not be seen in him there. There the men are as mad as he.

HAMLET. How came he mad?

CLOWN. Very strangely, they say.

HAMLET. How strangely? 160

CLOWN. Faith, e'en with losing his wits.

HAMLET. Upon what ground?

CLOWN. Why, here in Denmark. I have been sexton here, man and boy, thirty years.

HAMLET. How long will a man lie i' th' earth ere he rot? 165

CLOWN. Faith, if 'a be not rotten before 'a die (as we have many pocky corses° nowadays that will scarce hold the laying in), 'a will last you some eight year or nine year. A tanner will last you nine year.

HAMLET. Why he, more than another? 170

CLOWN. Why, sir, his hide is so tanned with his trade that 'a will keep out water a great while, and your water is a sore decayer of your whoreson dead body. Here's a skull now hath lien you i' th' earth three and twenty years. 175

HAMLET. Whose was it?

---

139 *absolute*: positive, decided.   139–140 *by the card*: by the compass card, i.e., exactly.   140 *equiv- ocation*: ambiguity.   142 *picked*: refined.   144 *kibe*: sore on the back of the heel.   167 *pocky corses*: bod- ies of persons who had been infected with the pox (syphilis).

CLOWN. A whoreson mad fellow's it was. Whose do you
    think it was?
HAMLET. Nay, I know not.
CLOWN. A pestilence on him for a mad rogue! 'A poured   180
    a flagon of Rhenish on my head once. This same
    skull, sir, was, sir, Yorick's skull, the King's jester.
HAMLET. This?
CLOWN. E'en that.
HAMLET. Let me see. [*Takes the skull.*] Alas, poor   185
    Yorick! I knew him, Horatio, a fellow of infinite
    jest, of most excellent fancy. He hath borne me on
    his back a thousand times. And now how abhorred
    in my imagination it is! My gorge rises at it. Here
    hung those lips that I have kissed I know not how   190
    oft. Where be your gibes now? Your gambols, your
    songs, your flashes of merriment that were wont to
    set the table on a roar? Not one now to mock your
    own grinning? Quite chapfall'n°? Now get you to my
    lady's chamber, and tell her, let her paint an inch   195
    thick, to this favor° she must come. Make her laugh
    at that. Prithee, Horatio, tell me one thing.
HORATIO. What's that, my lord?
HAMLET. Dost thou think Alexander looked o' this
    fashion i' th' earth?   200
HORATIO. E'en so.
HAMLET. And smelt so? Pah!   [*Puts down the skull.*]
HORATIO. E'en so, my lord.
HAMLET. To what base use we may return, Horatio!
    Why may not imagination trace the noble dust of   205
    Alexander till 'a find it stopping a bunghole?
HORATIO. 'Twere to consider too curiously,° to consider
    so.
HAMLET. No, faith, not a jot, but to follow him thither
    with modesty enough,° and likelihood to lead it; as   210
    thus: Alexander died, Alexander was buried, Alex-
    ander returneth to dust; the dust is earth; of earth
    we make loam; and why of that loam whereto he was
    converted might they not stop a beer barrel?
    Imperious Caesar, dead and turned to clay,   215
    Might stop a hole to keep the wind away.
    O, that that earth which kept the world in awe
    Should patch a wall t' expel th winter's flaw!°
    But soft, but soft awhile! Here comes the King.

*Enter King, Queen, Laertes, and a coffin, with Lords attendant [and a Doctor of
Divinity].*

---

194 *chapfall'n:* (1) down in the mouth, (2) jawless.   196 *favor:* facial appearance.   207 *curiously:*
minutely.   210 *with modesty enough:* without exaggeration.   218 *flaw:* gust.

The Queen, the courtiers. Who is this they follow?
And with such maimèd° rites? This doth betoken
The corse they follow did with desp'rate hand
Fordo it° own life. 'Twas of some estate.°
Couch° we awhile, and mark.   [*Retires with Horatio.*]

LAERTES. What ceremony else?

HAMLET.   That is Laertes,   225
A very noble youth. Mark.

LAERTES. What ceremony else?

DOCTOR. Her obsequies have been as far enlarged
As we have warranty. Her death was doubtful,°
And, but that great command o'ersways the order,   230
She should in ground unsanctified been lodged
Till the last trumpet. For charitable prayers,
Shards,° flints, and pebbles should be thrown on her.
Yet here she is allowed her virgin crants,°
Her maiden strewments,° and the bringing home   235
Of bell and burial.

LAERTES. Must there no more be done?

DOCTOR.   No more be done.
We should profane the service of the dead
To sing a requiem and such rest to her
As to peace-parted souls.

LAERTES.   Lay her i' th' earth,   240
And from her fair and unpolluted flesh
May violets spring! I tell thee, churlish priest,
A minist'ring angel shall my sister be
When thou liest howling!

HAMLET.   What, the fair Ophelia?   245

QUEEN. Sweets to the sweet! Farewell.

Scatters flowers.

I hoped thou shouldst have been my Hamlet's wife.
I thought thy bride-bed to have decked, sweet maid,
And not have strewed thy grave.

LAERTES.   O, treble woe
Fall ten times treble on that cursèd head
Whose wicked deed thy most ingenious sense°   250
Deprived thee of! Hold off the earth awhile,
Till I have caught her once more in mine arms.

Leaps in the grave.

Now pile your dust upon the quick and dead
Till of this flat a mountain you have made
T'o'ertop old Pelion° or the skyish head   255
Of blue Olympus.

---

221 *maimèd:* incomplete.   223 *Fordo it:* destroy its; *estate:* high rank.   224 *Couch:* hide.   229 *doubtful:* suspicious.   233 *Shards:* broken pieces of pottery.   234 *crants:* garlands.   235 *strewments:* i.e., of flowers.   250 *most ingenious sense:* finely endowed mind.   255 *Pelion:* (according to classical legend, giants in their fight with the gods sought to reach heaven by piling Mount Pelion and Mount Ossa on Mount Olympus).

HAMLET.   [*Coming forward*] What is he whose grief
    Bears such an emphasis, whose phrase of sorrow
    Conjures the wand'ring stars,° and makes them
        stand
    Like wonder-wounded hearers? This is I,
    Hamlet the Dane.
LAERTES.   The devil take thy soul!   260

Grapples with him.°

HAMLET. Thou pray'st not well.
    I prithee take thy fingers from my throat,
    For, though I am not splenitive° and rash,
    Yet have I in me something dangerous,
    Which let thy wisdom fear. Hold off thy hand.   265
KING. Pluck them asunder.
QUEEN.   Hamlet, Hamlet!
ALL. Gentlemen!
HORATIO.   Good my lord, be quiet.

Attendants part them.

HAMLET. Why, I will fight with them upon this theme
    Until my eyelids will no longer wag.
QUEEN. O my son, what theme?   270
HAMLET. I loved Ophelia. Forty thousand brothers
    Could not with all their quantity of love
    Make up my sum. What wilt thou do for her?
KING. O, he is mad, Laertes.
QUEEN. For love of God forbear him.   275
HAMLET. 'Swounds, show me what thou't do.
    Woo't weep? Woo't fight? Woo't fast? Woo't tear
        thyself?
    Woo't drink up eisel?° Eat a crocodile?
    I'll do't. Dost thou come here to whine?
    To outface me with leaping in her grave?   280
    Be buried quick with her, and so will I.
    And if thou prate of mountains, let them throw
    Millions of acres on us, till our ground,
    Singeing his pate against the burning zone,°
    Make Ossa like a wart! Nay, an thou'lt mouth,   285
    I'll rant as well as thou.
QUEEN.   This is mere madness;
    And thus a while the fit will work on him.
    Anon, as patient as the female dove

---

258 *wand'ring stars*: planets.   260 s.d. *Grapples with him*: (Q1, a bad quarto, presumably reporting a version that toured, has a previous direction saying "Hamlet leaps in after Laertes." Possibly he does so, somewhat hysterically. But such a direction—absent from the two good texts, Q2 and F—makes Hamlet the aggressor, somewhat contradicting his next speech. Perhaps Laertes leaps out of the grave to attack Hamlet).   263 *splenitive*: fiery (the spleen was thought to be the seat of anger).   278 *eisel*: vinegar. 284 *burning zone*: sun's orbit.

When that her golden couplets are disclosed,°
His silence will sit drooping.
HAMLET.   Hear you, sir.   290
What is the reason that you use me thus?
I loved you ever. But it is no matter.
Let Hercules himself do what he may,
The cat will mew, and the dog will have his day.
KING. I pray thee, good Horatio, wait upon him.   295

                    Exit Hamlet and Horatio.

[*To Laertes*] Strengthen your patience in our last
     night's speech.
We'll put the matter to the present push.°
Good Gertrude, set some watch over your son.
This grave shall have a living° monument.
An hour of quiet shortly shall we see;   300
Till then in patience our proceeding be.   *Exeunt.*

Scene II
The castle.

     Enter Hamlet and Horatio.

HAMLET. So much for this, sir; now shall you see the
     other.
     You do remember all the circumstance?
HORATIO. Remember it, my lord!
HAMLET. Sir, in my heart there was a kind of fighting
     That would not let me sleep. Methought I lay   5
     Worse than the mutines in the bilboes.° Rashly
     (And praised be rashness for it) let us know,
     Our indiscretion sometime serves us well
     When our deep plots do pall,° and that should learn
          us
     There's a divinity that shapes our ends,   10
     Rough-hew them how we will.
HORATIO.   That is most certain.
HAMLET. Up from my cabin,
     My sea gown scarfed about me, in the dark
     Groped I to find out them, had my desire,
     Fingered° their packet, and in fine° withdrew   15
     To mine own room again, making so bold,
     My fears forgetting manners, to unseal
     Their grand commission; where I found, Horatio—
     Ah, royal knavery!—an exact command,

---

289 *golden couplets are disclosed:* (the dove lays two eggs, and the newly hatched [disclosed] young are covered with golden down).   297 *present push:* immediate test.   299 *living:* lasting (with perhaps also a reference to the plot against Hamlet's life).   SCENE II.   6 *mutines in the bilboes:* mutineers in fetters.   9 *pall:* fail.   15 *Fingered:* stole; *in fine:* finally.

Larded° with many several sorts of reasons,   20
Importing Denmark's health, and England's too,
With, ho, such bugs and goblins in my life,°
That on the supervise,° no leisure bated,°
No, not to stay the grinding of the ax,
My head should be struck off.
HORATIO.   Is't possible?   25
HAMLET. Here's the commission; read it at more leisure,
But wilt thou hear now how I did proceed?
HORATIO. I beseech you.
HAMLET. Being thus benetted round with villains,
Or° I could make a prologue to my brains,   30
They had begun the play. I sat me down,
Devised a new commission, wrote it fair.
I once did hold it, as our statists° do,
A baseness to write fair,° and labored much
How to forget that learning, but, sir, now   35
It did me yeoman's service. Wilt thou know
Th' effect° of what I wrote?
HORATIO.   Ay, good my lord.
HAMLET. An earnest conjuration from the King,
As England was his faithful tributary,
As love between them like the palm might flourish,   40
As peace should still her wheaten garland wear
And stand a comma° 'tween their amities,
And many suchlike as's of great charge,°
That on the view and knowing of these contents,
Without debatement further, more or less,   45
He should those bearers put to sudden death,
Not shriving° time allowed.
HORATIO.   How was this sealed?
HAMLET. Why, even in that was heaven ordinant.°
I had my father's signet in my purse,
Which was the model° of that Danish seal,   50
Folded the writ up in the form of th' other,
Subscribed it, gave't th' impression, placed it safely,
The changeling never known. Now, the next day
Was our sea fight, and what to this was sequent
Thou knowest already.   55
HORATIO. So Guildenstern and Rosencrantz go to't.
HAMLET. Why, man, they did make love to this employment.
They are not near my conscience; their defeat
Does by their own insinuation° grow.

---

20 *Larded:* enriched.   22 *such bugs and goblins in my life:* such bugbears and imagined terrors if I
were allowed to live.   23 *supervise:* reading; *leisure bated:* delay allowed.   30 *Or:* ere.   33 *statists:*
statesmen.   34 *fair:* clearly.   37 *effect:* purport.   42 *comma:* link.   43 *great charge:* (1) serious exhor-
tation, (2) heavy burden (punning on *as's* and "asses").   47 *shriving:* absolution.   48 *ordinant:* ruling.
50 *model:* counterpart.   59 *insinuation:* meddling.

'Tis dangerous when the baser nature comes 60
    Between the pass° and fell° incensèd points
    Of might opposites.
HORATIO.   Why, what a king is this!
HAMLET. Does it not, think thee, stand me now upon°—
    He that hath killed my king, and whored my mother,
    Popped in between th' election° and my hopes, 65
    Thrown out his angle° for my proper life,°
    And with such coz'nage°—is't not perfect con-
       science
    To quit° him with this arm? And is't not to be
       damned
    To let this canker of our nature come
    In further evil? 70
HORATIO. It must be shortly known to him from England
    What is the issue of the business there.
HAMLET. It will be short; the interim's mine,
    And a man's life's no more than to say "one."
    But I am very sorry, good Horatio, 75
    That to Laertes I forgot myself,
    For by the image of my cause I see
    The portraiture of his. I'll court his favors.
    But sure the bravery° of his grief did put me
    Into a tow'ring passion.
HORATIO.   Peace, who comes here? 80

Enter young Osric, a courtier.

OSRIC. Your lordship is right welcome back to Den-
    mark.
HAMLET. I humbly thank you, sir. [*Aside to Horatio*]
    Dost know this waterfly?
HORATIO. [*Aside to Hamlet*] No, my good lord.
HAMLET. [*Aside to Horatio*] Thy state is the more gra- 85
    cious, for 'tis a vice to know him. He hath much
    land, and fertile. Let a beast be lord of beasts, and
    his crib shall stand at the king's mess.° 'Tis a
    chough,° but, as I say, spacious° in the possession
    of dirt. 90
OSRIC. Sweet lord, if your lordship were at leisure, I
    should impart a thing to you from his Majesty.
HAMLET. I will receive it, sir, with all diligence of spirit.
    Put your bonnet to his right use. 'Tis for the head.
OSRIC. I thank your lordship, it is very hot. 95
HAMLET. No, believe me, 'tis very cold; the wind is
    northerly.

---

    61 *pass:* thrust; *fell:* cruel.   63 *stand me now upon:* become incumbent upon me.   65 *election:* (the Danish monarchy was elective).   66 *angle:* fishing line; *my proper life:* my own life.   67 *coz'nage:* trickery.   68 *quit:* pay back.   79 *bravery:* bravado.   88 *mess:* table.   89 *chough:* jackdaw (here, chatterer); *spacious:* well off.

Osric. It is indifferent cold, my lord, indeed.
Hamlet. But yet methinks it is very sultry and hot for
  my complexion.°   100
Osric. Exceedingly, my lord; it is very sultry, as 'twere
  —I cannot tell how. But, my lord, his Majesty bade
  me signify to you that 'a has laid a great wager on
  your head. Sir, this is the matter——
Hamlet. I beseech you remember.   105

                Hamlet moves him to put on his hat.

Osric. Nay, good my lord; for ease, in good faith.
  Sir, here is newly come to court Laertes—believe
  me, an absolute gentleman, full of most excellent
  differences,° of very soft society and great showing.
  Indeed, to speak feelingly° of him, he is the card°   110
  or calendar of gentry; for you shall find in him the
  continent° of what part of a gentlemen would see.
Hamlet. Sir, his definement° suffers no perdition° in
  you, though, I know, to divide him inventorially
  would dozy° th' arithmetic of memory, and yet but   115
  yaw neither in respect of his quick sail.° But, in the
  verity of extolment, I take him to be a soul of great
  article,° and his infusion° of such dearth and rare-
  ness as, to make true diction° of him, his semblable°
  is his mirror, and who else would trace him, his um-   120
  brage,° nothing more.
Osric. Your lordship speaks most infallibly of him.
Hamlet. The concernancy,° sir? Why do we wrap the
  gentlemen in our more rawer breath?
Osric. Sir?   125
Horatio. Is't not possible to understand in another
  tongue? You will to't,° sir, really.
Hamlet. What imports the nomination of this gentle-
  man?
Osric. Of Laertes?   130
Horatio. [*Aside to Hamlet*] His purse is empty already.
  All's golden words are spent.
Hamlet. Of him, sir.
Osric. I know you are not ignorant——
Hamlet. I would you did, sir; yet, in faith, if you did, it   135
  would not much approve° me. Well, sir?
Osric. You are not ignorant of what excellence Laertes
  is——

---

  100 *complexion:* temperament.   109 *differences:* distinguishing characteristics.   110 *feelingly:*
justly; *card:* chart.   112 *continent:* summary.   113 *definement:* description; *perdition:* loss.   115 *dozy:*
dizzy.   115–116 *and yet . . . quick sail:* i.e., and yet only stagger despite all (*yaw neither*) in trying to over-
take his virtues.   118 *article:* (literally, "item," but here perhaps all "traits" or "importance"); *infusion:* essential quality.   119 *diction:* description; *semblable:* likeness.   120–121 *umbrage:* shadow.   123
concernancy: meaning.   127 *will to't:* will get there.   136 *approve:* commend.

HAMLET. I dare not confess that, lest I should compare
  with him in excellence; but to know a man well were   140
  to know himself.
OSRIC. I mean, sir, for his weapon; but in the imputa-
  tion° laid on him by them, in his meed° he's un-
  fellowed.
HAMLET. What's his weapon?   145
OSRIC. Rapier and dagger.
HAMLET. That's two of his weapons—but well.
OSRIC. The King, sir, hath wagered with him six Bar-
  bary horses, against the which he has impawned,° as
  I take it, six French rapiers and poniards, with their   150
  assigns,° as girdle, hangers,° and so. Three of the
  carriages,° in faith, are very dear to fancy, very re-
  sponsive° to the hilts, most delicate carriages, and
  of very liberal conceit.°
HAMLET. What call you the carriages?   155
HORATIO. [Aside to Hamlet] I knew you must be edified
  by the margent° ere you had done.
OSRIC. The carriages, sir, are the hangers.
HORATIO. The phrase would be more germane to the
  matter if we could carry a cannon by our sides. I   160
  would it might be hangers till then. But on! Six Bar-
  bary horses against six French swords, their assigns,
  and three liberal-conceited carriages—that's the
  French bet against the Danish. Why is this all im-
  pawned, as you call it?   165
OSRIC. The King, sir, hath laid, sir, that in a dozen
  passes between yourself and him he shall not exceed
  you three hits; he hath laid on twelve for nine, and
  it would come to immediate trial if your lordship
  would vouchsafe the answer.   170
HAMLET. How if I answer no?
OSRIC. I mean, my lord, the opposition of your person
  in trial.
HAMLET. Sir, I will walk here in the hall. If it please
  his Majesty, it is the breathing time of day with me.°   175
  Let the foils be brought, the gentleman willing, and
  the King hold his purpose. I will win for him an I
  can; if not, I will gain nothing but my shame and
  the odd hits.
OSRIC. Shall I deliver you e'en so?   180
HAMLET. To this effect, sir, after what flourish your
  nature will.

142–143 *imputation:* reputation.   143 *meed:* merit.   149 *impawned:* wagered.   151 *assigns:* ac-
companiments; *hangers:* straps hanging the sword to the belt.   152 *carriages:* (an affected word for hangers).   152–153 *responsive:* corresponding.   154 *liberal conceit:* elaborate design.   157 *margent:* i.e.,
marginal (explanatory) comment.   175 *breathing time of day with me:* time when I take exercise.

Shakespearean Drama

OSRIC. I commend my duty to your lordship.

HAMLET. Yours, yours. [*Exit Osric.*] He does well to
commend it himself; there are no tongues else for's 185
turn.

HORATIO. This lapwing° runs away with the shell on his
head.

HAMLET. 'A did comply, sir, with his dug° before 'a
sucked it. Thus has he, and many more of the 190
same breed that I know the drossy age dotes on,
only got the tune of the time and, out of an habit of
encounter,° a kind of yeasty° collection, which
carries them through and through the most fanned
and winnowed opinions; and do but blow them to 195
their trial, the bubbles are out.°

Enter a Lord.

LORD. My lord, his Majesty commended him to you by
young Osric, who brings back to him that you
attend him in the hall. He sends to know if your
pleasure hold to play with Laertes, or that you will 200
take longer time.

HAMLET. I am constant to my purposes; they follow the
King's pleasure. If his fitness speaks, mine is ready;
now or whensoever, provided I be so able as now.

LORD. The King and Queen and all are coming down. 205

HAMLET. In happy time.

LORD. The Queen desires you to use some gentle enter-
tainment° to Laertes before you fall to play.

HAMLET. She well instructs me. [*Exit Lord.*]

HORATIO. You will lose this wager, my lord. 210

HAMLET. I do not think so. Since he went into France
I have been in continual practice. I shall win at the
odds. But thou wouldst not think how ill all's here
about my heart. But it is no matter.

HORATIO. Nay, good my lord—— 215

HAMLET. It is but foolery, but it is such a kind of gain-
giving° as would perhaps trouble a woman.

HORATIO. If your mind dislike anything, obey it. I will
forestall their repair hither and say you are not fit.

HAMLET. Not a whit, we defy augury. There is a special 220
providence in the fall of a sparrow.° If it be now,
'tis not to come; if it be not to come, it will be now;

---

187 *lapwing:* (the new-hatched lapwing was thought to run around with half its shell on its head).
189 *'A did comply, sir, with his dug:* he was ceremoniously polite to his mother's breast. 192–193 *out of
an habit of encounter:* out of his own superficial way of meeting and conversing with people. 193 *yeasty:*
frothy. 196 *the bubbles are out:* i.e., they are blown away (the reference is to the "yeasty collection").
207–208 *to use some gentle entertainment:* to be courteous. 217 *gaingiving:* misgiving. 221 *the fall of a
sparrow:* (cf. Matthew 10:29 "Are not two sparrows sold for a farthing? and one of them shall not fall on
the ground without your Father").

if it be not now, yet it will come. The readiness is
all. Since no man of aught he leaves knows, what
is't to leave betimes?° Let be.   225

*A table prepared. [Enter] Trumpets, Drums, and Officers with cushions; King,
Queen, [Osric,] and all the State, [with] foils, daggers, [and stoups of wine borne
in]; and Laertes.*

KING. Come, Hamlet, come, and take this hand from
      me.

      The King puts Laertes' hand into Hamlet's.

HAMLET. Give me your pardon, sir. I have done you
            wrong,
      But pardon't, as you are a gentleman.
      This presence° knows, and you must needs have
            heard,
      How I am punished with a sore distraction.   230
      What I have done
      That might your nature, honor, and exception°
      Roughly awake, I here proclaim was madness.
      Was't Hamlet wronged Laertes? Never Hamlet.
      If Hamlet from himself be ta'en away,   235
      And when he's not himself does wrong Laertes,
      Then Hamlet does it not, Hamlet denies it.
      Who does it then? His madness. If't be so,
      Hamlet is of the faction° that is wronged;
      His madness is poor Hamlet's enemy.   240
      Sir, in this audience,
      Let my disclaiming from a purposed evil
      Free me so far in your most generous thoughts
      That I have shot my arrow o'er the house
      And hurt my brother.
LAERTES.   I am satisfied in nature,   245
      Whose motive in this case should stir me most
      To my revenge. But in my terms of honor
      I stand aloof, and will no reconcilement
      Till by some elder master of known honor
      I have a voice and precedent° of peace   250
      To keep my name ungored. But till that time
      I do receive your offered love like love,
      And will not wrong it.
HAMLET.   I embrace it freely,
      And will this brother's wager frankly play.
      Give us the foils. Come on.
LAERTES.   Come, one for me.   255

---

225 *betimes:* early.   229 *presence:* royal assembly.   232 *exception:* disapproval.   239 *faction:* party,
side.   250 *voice and precedent:* authoritative opinion justified by precedent.

HAMLET. I'll be your foil,° Laertes. In mine ignorance
    Your skill shall, like a star i' th' darkest night,
    Stick fiery off° indeed.
LAERTES.   You mock me, sir.
HAMLET. No, by this hand.
KING. Give me the foils, young Osric. Cousin Hamlet,   260
    You know the wager?
HAMLET.   Very well, my lord.
    Your grace has laid the odds o' th' weaker side.
KING. I do not fear it, I have seen you both;
    But since he is bettered,° we have therefore odds.
LAERTES. This is too heavy; let me see another.   265
HAMLET. This likes me well. These foils have all a
    length?

Prepare to play.

OSRIC. Ay, my good lord.
KING. Set me the stoups of wine upon that table.
    If Hamlet give the first or second hit,
    Or quit° in answer of the third exchange,   270
    Let all the battlements their ordnance fire.
    The King shall drink to Hamlet's better breath,
    And in the cup an union° shall he throw
    Richer than that which four successive kings
    In Denmark's crown have worn. Give me the cups,   275
    And let the kettle° to the trumpet speak,
    The trumpet to the cannoneer without,
    The cannons to the heavens, the heaven to earth,
    "Now the King drinks to Hamlet." Come, begin.

Trumpets the while.

    And you, the judges, bear a wary eye.   280
HAMLET. Come on, sir.
LAERTES.   Come, my lord.   *They play.*
HAMLET.   One.
LAERTES.   No.
HAMLET.   Judgment?
OSRIC. A hit, a very palpable hit.

Drum, trumpets, and shot. Flourish; a piece goes off.

LAERTES.   Well, again.
KING. Stay, give me drink. Hamlet, this pearl is thine.
    Here's to thy health. Give him the cup.

---

256 *foil*: (1) blunt sword, (2) background (of metallic leaf) for a jewel.   258 *Stick fiery off*: stand out brilliantly.   264 *bettered*: has improved (in France).   270 *quit*: repay, hit back.   273 *union*: pearl. 276 *kettle*: kettledrum.

HAMLET. I'll play this bout first; set it by awhile.   285
     Come. [*They play.*] Another hit. What say you?
LAERTES. A touch, a touch; I do confess't.
KING. Our son shall win.
QUEEN.   He's fat,° and scant of breath.
     Here, Hamlet, take my napkin, rub thy brows.
     The Queen carouses to thy fortune, Hamlet.   290
HAMLET. Good madam!
KING.   Gertrude, do not drink.
QUEEN. I will, my lord; I pray you pardon me. [*Drinks.*]
KING. [*Aside*] It is the poisoned cup; it is too late.
HAMLET. I dare not drink yet, madam—by and by.
QUEEN. Come, let me wipe thy face.   295
LAERTES. My lord, I'll hit him now.
KING.   I do not think't.
LAERTES. [*Aside*] And yet it is almost against my con-
     science.
HAMLET. Come for the third, Laertes. You do but dally.
     I pray you pass with your best violence;
     I am sure you make a wanton° of me.   300
LAERTES. Say you so? Come on.   [*They*] *play.*
OSRIC. Nothing neither way.
LAERTES. Have at you now!

          In scuffling they change rapiers [and both are wounded].

KING.   Part them. They are incensed.
HAMLET. Nay, come—again!   [*The Queen falls.*]
OSRIC.   Look to the Queen there, ho!
HORATIO. They bleed on both sides. How is it, my lord?   305
OSRIC. How is't, Laertes?
LAERTES. Why, as a woodcock to mine own springe,°
     Osric.
     I am justly killed with mine own treachery.
HAMLET. How does the Queen?
KING.   She sounds° to see them bleed.
QUEEN. No, no, the drink, the drink! O my dear
     Hamlet!   310
     The drink, the drink! I am poisoned.   [*Dies.*]
HAMLET. O villainy! Ho! Let the door be locked.
     Treachery! Seek it out.   [*Laertes falls.*]
LAERTES. It is here, Hamlet. Hamlet, thou art slain;
     No med'cine in the world can do thee good.   315
     In thee there is not half an hour's life.
     The treacherous instrument is in thy hand,
     Unbated and envenomed. The foul practice°
     Hath turned itself on me; Lo, here I lie,

----

     288 *fat:* (1) sweaty, (2) out of training.   300 *wanton:* spoiled child.   307 *springe:* snare.   309 *sounds:*
swoons.   318 *practice:* deception.

Never to rise again. Thy mother's poisoned.
I can no more. The King, the King's to blame.   320

HAMLET. The point envenomed too?
 Then, venom, to thy work.   *Hurts the King.*

ALL. Treason! Treason!

KING. O, yet defend me, friends, I am but hurt.   325

HAMLET. Here, thou incestuous, murd'rous, damnèd
  Dane,
 Drink off this potion. Is thy union here?
 Follow my mother.   *King dies.*

LAERTES.   He is justly served.
 It is a poison tempered° by himself,
 Exchange forgiveness with me, noble Hamlet.   330
 Mine and my father's death come not upon thee,
 Nor thine on me!   *Dies.*

HAMLET. Heaven made thee free of it! I follow thee.
 I am dead, Horatio. Wretched Queen, adieu!
 You that look pale and tremble at this chance,   335
 That are but mutes° or audience to this act,
 Had I but time (as this fell sergeant,° Death,
 Is strict in his arrest) O, I could tell you—
 But let it be. Horatio, I am dead;
 Thou livest; report me and my cause aright   340
 To the unsatisfied.°

HORATIO.   Never believe it.
 I am more an antique Roman° than a Dane.
 Here's yet some liquor left.

HAMLET.   As th' art a man,
 Give me the cup. Let go. By heaven, I'll ha't!
 O God, Horatio, what a wounded name,   345
 Things standing thus unknown, shall live behind me!
 If thou didst ever hold me in thy heart,
 Absent thee from felicity° awhile,
 And in this harsh world draw thy breath in pain,
 To tell my story. *A march afar off.* [*Exit Osric.*]
    What warlike noise is this?   350

       Enter Osric.

OSRIC. Young Fortinbras, with conquest come from
  Poland,
 To th' ambassadors of England gives
 This warlike volley.

HAMLET.   O, I die, Horatio!
 The potent poison quite o'ercrows° my spirit.
 I cannot live to hear the news from England,   355

---

129 *tempered:* mixed. 336 *mutes:* performers who have no words to speak. 337 *fell sergeant:* dread sheriff's officer. 341 *unsatisfied:* uniformed. 342 *antique Roman:* (with reference to the old Roman fashion of suicide). 348 *felicity:* i.e., the felicity of death. 354 *o'ercrows:* overpowers (as a triumphant cock crows over its weak opponent).

But I do prophesy th' election lights
On Fortinbras. He has my dying voice.
So tell him, with th' occurrents,° more and less,
Which have solicited°—the rest is silence.   *Dies*.

HORATIO. Now cracks a noble heart. Good night, sweet
    Prince,   360
And flights of angels sing thee to thy rest.

                           March within.

Why does the drum come hither?

Enter Fortinbras, with the Ambassadors with Drum, Colors, and Attendants.

FORTINBRAS. Where is this sight?
HORATIO.   What is it you would see?
If aught of woe or wonder, cease your search.
FORTINBRAS. This quarry° cries on havoc.° O proud
    Death,   365
What feast is toward° in thine eternal cell
That thou so many princes at a shot
So bloodily hast struck?
AMBASSADOR.   The sight is dismal;
And our affairs from England come too late.
The ears are senseless that should give us hearing   370
To tell him his commandment is fulfilled,
That Rosencrantz and Guildenstern are dead.
Where should we have our thanks?
HORATIO.   Not from his° mouth,
Had it th' ability of life to thank you.
He never gave commandment for their death.   375
But since, so jump° upon this bloody question,
You from the Polack wars, and you from England,
Are here arrived, give order that these bodies
High on a stage° be placèd to the view,
And let me speak to th' yet unknowing world   380
How these things came about. So shall you hear
Of carnal, bloody, and unnatural acts,
Of accidental judgments, casual° slaughters,
Of deaths put on by cunning and forced cause,
And, in this upshot, purposes mistook   385
Fall'n on th' inventors' heads. All this can I
Truly deliver.
FORTINBRAS.   Let us haste to hear it,
And call the noblest to the audience.
For me, with sorrow I embrace my fortune.

---

    358 *occurrents:* occurrences.   359 *solicited:* incited.   365 *quarry:* heap of slain bodies; *cries on havoc:* proclaims general slaughter.   366 *toward:* in preparation.   373 *his:* (Claudius').   376 *jump:* precisely.   379 *stage:* platform.   383 *casual:* not humanly planned, chance.

I have some rights of memory° in this kingdom,   390
Which now to claim my vantage doth invite me.
HORATIO. Of that I shall have also cause to speak,
And from his mouth whose voice will draw on°
      more.
But let this same be presently performed,
Even while men's minds are wild, lest more mis-
      chance   395
On° plots and errors happen.
FORTINBRAS.   Let four captains
Bear Hamlet like a soldier to the stage,
For he was likely, had he been put on,°
To have proved most royal; and for his passage°
The soldiers' music and the rite of war   400
Speak loudly for him.
Take up the bodies. Such a sight as this
Becomes the field,° but here shows much amiss.
Go, bid the soldiers shoot.

Exeunt marching; after the which a peal of ordnance are shot off.

FINIS

---

390 *rights of memory:* remembered claims.   393 *voice will draw on:* vote will influence.   396 *On:* on top of.   398 *put on:* advanced (to the throne).   399 *passage:* death.   403 *field:* battlefield.

QUESTIONS

1. Who is the ghost spotted by the guards? What does the ghost want from Hamlet? Does the ghost recognize different degrees of guilt in the actions of Claudius and Gertrude?

2. Examine Polonius's speech to Laertes (Act I, Scene III). What is the code of behavior advocated? Does anyone in the play actually act in accordance with Polonius's wisdom?

3. Single out one soliloquy of Hamlet's and discuss how it reveals his basic cast of character. What do you see as his strengths and virtues; as his flaws? Is his famous indecisiveness to be seen as strictly negative?

4. Is Hamlet's character fixed? Does he act in the same way throughout the play? If not, can you mark out points where he changes? Does he ever overcome his indecisiveness? If so, when?

5. Is the viewer to see Hamlet as heroic, or as victim of his own character flaws? Explain.

6. Explore the relationship between Hamlet and Ophelia. How do things stand with them at the beginning of the play? How does their relationship change? What is the nature of the misunderstanding that seems to divide them? Does it seem that they truly love one another? What motivates Ophelia's drowning of herself? Why was Hamlet so cruel to her in Act III, Scene I?

7. Find several passages where puns or figures of speech are dominant. Try to determine how the word play adds to the viewer's understanding of the situation.

8. How is the killing of Polonius essential to the development of the complications? What course of events does the death set into motion? What is Hamlet's response to his deed (the stabbing) and how does that reflect upon his character?

9. Reread the play within a play staged by Hamlet. What does Hamlet hope to accomplish? How do the events depicted reflect upon what actually happened? How do Gertrude and Claudius react?

10. Why is Hamlet being sent to England—ostensibly? What has Claudius really arranged? How does Hamlet find out, and what does he do?

11. What is the effect of the gravediggers' scene in Act V? Speculate on how it is that comic relief can actually intensify the tension within a play.

12. After Hamlet stabs Laertes in the final scene, why does Laertes forgive his friend? Why was he in league with Claudius in the first place? Do the deaths in the last scene fit the crimes?

13. What are we to understand by the arrival of Fortinbras at the very end of the play? Does Shakespeare have a message to impart about the health of countries and the fitness of the individuals who rule?

14. Isolate a passage that you found particularly difficult and work through it with great care. Make a list of the words and usages that give you trouble. Bring your clarified sense of the passage to class.

32 Comedy: From Greece to Shakespeare and Beyond

In his essay "The Idea of Comedy" (1877), English writer George Meredith distinguished between *high comedy*, which appeals to the intellect, and *low comedy*, which derives most of its effects from physical action as well as obvious jokes and misunderstandings. Though Meredith only codified his types in the late nineteenth century, these two basic modes have existed since the form originated with the Greek writer Aristophanes (448–380 B.C.).

As suggested earlier (see Chapter 30), comedy had its beginnings in the satyr plays that were staged between performances of the lengthier tragedies at the annual Dionysian festivals in Athens. The purpose of these often anarchic interludes was to restore a sense of balance to the audience after the intense emotional participation elicited by the tragedies. But with the satirist Aristophanes, comedy emerged as a distinct genre and a worthy counterpart to tragedy.

Aristophanes created what are sometimes called *Old Comedies*, works that took a sharply satirical attitude toward social issues of the day. (Where tragedy focuses upon the individual struggling with fate, comedy generally takes the broader societal vantage.) *Satire*, as practiced by Aristophanes and others through the ages, is an art of intense verbal ridicule; it holds its subject in a glaring light and is bent upon exposing lies and pretensions. Aristophanes's famous comedy *Lysistrata*, for example, takes as its premise the idea that the women of both Athens and Sparta decide to call a sexual strike until their men agree to stop waging war. The resulting situation allows the playwright to skewer the pomp and posturing of the militant Greek males.

Aristophanes's works provoke thoughtful response more than belly laughs, and thus conform to Meredith's strictures for high comedy. Meanwhile, the so-called *low comedies*, which followed in the fourth and third centuries B.C., were more on the order of farce, featuring mistaken identities, deceived lovers, and so on. Their humor was more of the "low" variety.

With Shakespeare, whose instinct for the comic was every bit as developed as his sense of the tragic, we encounter a hybrid mode that is often called *romantic comedy*. The high–low distinction is hard to apply, for Shakespeare was able to manipulate situational elements common to farce even as he assigned spirited and sophisticated lines to his characters. The physical buffoonery was usually accompanied by witty puns and intricate conceits (see Chapter 31). The Bard was an exception to the comedic norm, able to have it both ways. Indeed, even in his most wrenching tragedies, there is almost always a comic scene that brings relief from building tensions. One famous scene of comic relief is found at the opening of Act V of *Hamlet*, where two bantering gravediggers exchange quips for 65 lines before Hamlet and Laertes enter. Hamlet himself then enters into the wordplay, asking one of the gravedigger-clowns: "Whose grave's this, sirrah?"

CLOWN. Mine, sir.
   [*Sings.*]   O, a pit of clay for to be made
                  For such a guest is meet.
HAMLET. I think it be thine indeed, for thou liest in't.
CLOWN. You lie out on't, sir, and therefore 'tis not   125
   yours. For my part, I do not lie in't, yet it is mine.
HAMLET. Thou dost lie in't, to be in't and say it is
   thine. 'Tis for the dead, not for the quick;° there-   *quick: living.*
   fore thou liest.
CLOWN. 'Tis a quick lie, sir; 'twill away again from   130
   me to you.
HAMLET. What man dost thou dig it for?
CLOWN. For no man, sir.
HAMLET. What woman then?
CLOWN. For none neither.   135
HAMLET. Who is to be buried in't?
CLOWN. One that was a woman, sir: but, rest her soul,
   she's dead.

The *comedy of manners*, which also developed during Shakespeare's time and achieved its greatest popularity in the Restoration Comedy of the eighteenth century (in the work of playwrights such as William Congreve and Oliver Goldsmith), is a "high" mode. It derives its quick-paced verbal humor from the tensions and pretensions found in sharply stratified class societies. Both Molière's *The Misanthrope* (1666) and Oscar Wilde's *The Importance of Being Earnest* (1895) can be seen as examples (see Chapters 33 and 34).

THE MERGING OF COMEDY AND TRAGEDY

Over the centuries, high and low comedy have seen a greater divergence. As the former has come to dominate the theater stage, the latter carved out a niche in music halls and burlesque houses, and, more recently, in Hollywood films and on prime-time television.

What's more, our contemporary period seems to have occasioned a blurring of comic and tragic modes. In the tragedies of Shakespeare, like *Hamlet*, comedic scenes are sometimes introduced to provide comic relief, but they are clearly bounded and distinct. Many modern plays, in contrast, use both elements side by side to create the unsettling effect of *tragicomedy*. The viewer is suspended between laughter and despair and denied the solace of an unambivalent response.

The distinction is harder to make when we look at plays from the *Theater of the Absurd*, a dramatic movement that flourished in the decades after World War II. In the vision of playwrights like Eugene Ionesco, Edward Albee, Harold Pinter, and

Samuel Beckett (see Chapter 35), the human situation is understood to be without purpose. And where there is no ultimate sense of meaning in human affairs, notions like comedy and tragedy lose their distinctions. In plays like Albee's *The Sandbox* and Beckett's *Waiting for Godot*, the responses of characters to random-seeming events modulate incessantly between bleak humor, blank bewilderment, and the stark protestation of horror. Nor do endings bring the comfort of resolution. Viewers are left hanging in anxious, if sometimes laughable, uncertainty.

In Shakespeare's *The Tempest*, which here follows, we find the subtlest possible blending of elements. The play, said to be the last work of the Bard (see Chapter 31), combines the delightful comic touches we expect—the puns, misunderstandings, and so on—with more shadowy suggestions. The final effect is more of lightness than of laughter: we feel the buoyancy of spirit rising up above the gravity of matter.

William Shakespeare

THE TEMPEST

Edited by Northrup Frye

NAMES OF THE ACTORS

ALONSO, King of Naples
SEBASTIAN, his brother
PROSPERO, the right Duke of Milan
ANTONIO, his brother, the usurping
   Duke of Milan
FERDINAND, son to the King of Naples
GONZALO, an honest old councillor
ADRIAN and FRANCISCO, lords
CALIBAN, a savage and deformed
   slave
TRINCULO, a jester
STEPHANO, a drunken butler

MASTER OF A SHIP
MARINERS
BOATSWAIN
MIRANDA, daughter to Prospero
ARIEL, an airy spirit
IRIS
CERES
JUNO   } [presented by] spirits
NYMPHS
REAPERS
[OTHER SPIRITS ATTENDING
   ON PROSPERO]

THE SCENE
An uninhabited Island.

ACT I
Scene I

> *A tempestuous noise of thunder and lightning heard.*
> *Enter a Shipmaster and a Boatswain.*

MASTER. Boatswain!
BOATSWAIN. Here, master. What cheer?

MASTER. Good, speak to th' mariners; fall to't yarely,° or
we run ourselves aground. Bestir, bestir!   *Exit.*

Enter Mariners.

BOATSWAIN. Heigh, my hearts! Cheerly, cheerly, my   5
hearts! Yare, yare! Take in the topsail! Tend° to th'
master's whistle! Blow till thou burst thy wind,° if room
enough!°

Enter Alonso, Sebastian, Antonio, Ferdinand, Gonzalo and others.

ALONSO. Good boatswain, have care. Where's the master?
Play° the men.   10
BOATSWAIN. I pray now, keep below.
ANTONIO. Where is the master, bos'n?
BOATSWAIN. Do you not hear him? You mar our labor.
Keep your cabins: you do assist the storm.
GONZALO. Nay, good, be patient.
BOATSWAIN. When the sea is. Hence! What cares these   15
roarers° for the name of king? To cabin! Silence!
Trouble us not!
GONZALO. Good, yet remember whom thou hast aboard.
BOATSWAIN. None that I more love than myself. You are
a councillor: if you can command these elements to si-   20
lence and work the peace of the present, we will not hand°
a rope more; use your authority. If you cannot, give
thanks you have lived so long, and make yourself ready
in your cabin for the mischance of the hour, if it so hap.
—Cheerly, good hearts!—Out of our way, I say.   *Exit.*   25
GONZALO. I have great comfort from this fellow: me-
thinks he hath no drowning mark upon him; his com-
plexion° is perfect gallows.° Stand fast, good Fate, to his
hanging! Make the rope of his destiny our cable, for
our own doth little advantage.° If he be not born to be   30
hanged, our case is miserable.   *Exeunt.*

Enter Boatswain.

BOATSWAIN. Down with the topmast! Yare! Lower,
lower! Bring her to try with main-course!° [*A cry
within.*] A plague° upon this howling! They are louder
than the weather or our office.°   35

SCENE I. The deck of a ship.   3 *yarely*: briskly.   6 *Tend*: attend.   7 *Blow . . . wind*: (addressed to the
storm).   7–8 *if room enough*: i.e. so long as we have searoom.   9 *Play*: (perhaps 'ply,' keep the men busy).
16 *roarers*: (1) waves, (2) blusterers or bullies.   21 *hand*: handle.   28 *complexion*: indication of character
in appearance of face; *gallows*: (alluding to the proverb 'He that's born to be hanged need fear no drowning').   30 *doth little advantage*: doesn't help us much.   33 *try with main-course*: lie hove-to with only the
mainsail.   34 *plague*: (followed by a dash in F; possibly the boatswain's language was more profane than the
text indicates; cf. i, 38–39, and V, i, 218–19).   35 *our office*: (the noise we make at) our work.

Enter Sebastian, Antonio, and Gonzalo.

Yet again? What do you here? Shall we give o'er and
drown? Have you a mind to sink?

SEBASTIAN. A pox o' your throat, you bawling, blas-
phemous, incharitable dog!

BOATSWAIN. Work you, then.

ANTONIO. Hang, cur, hang, you whoreson, insolent noise-
maker! We are less afraid to be drowned than thou art.

GONZALO. I'll warrant him for drowning,° though the ship
were no stronger than a nutshell and as leaky as an
unstanched° wench.

BOATSWAIN. Lay her ahold, ahold!° Set her two courses!
Off to sea again! Lay her off!

Enter Mariners wet.

MARINERS. All lost! To prayers, to prayers! All lost!

Exeunt.

BOATSWAIN. What, must our mouths be cold?

GONZALO.
The King and Prince at prayers! Let's assist them,
For our case is as theirs.

SEBASTIAN.   I am out of patience.

ANTONIO.
We are merely° cheated of our lives by drunkards.
This wide-chopped° rascal—would thou mightst lie
drowning
The washing of ten tides!°

GONZALO.   He'll be hanged yet,
Though every drop of water swear against it
And gape at wid'st to glut° him.

A confused noise within:

'Mercy on us!—
We split, we split!—Farewell, my wife and children!—
Farewell, brother!—We split, we split, we split!'

Exit Boatswain.

ANTONIO.
Let's all sink with th' King.

SEBASTIAN.   Let's take leave of him.

Exit [with Antonio].

---

43 *warrant . . . for:* guarantee . . . against.   45 *unstanched:* i.e., loose.   46 *ahold:* (perhaps 'a-hull,'
without any sail. As the ship drifts to the rocks, the order is reversed and the *two courses,* foresail and mainsail, are set up again in an effort to clear the shore.)   52 *merely:* completely.   53 *wide-chopped:* wide-
jawed.   54 *ten tides:* (pirates were hanged on shore and left until three tides washed over them).   56 *glut:*
gobble.

GONZALO. Now would I give a thousand furlongs of sea   60
   for an acre of barren ground—long heath, brown furze,°
   anything. The wills above be done, but I would fain die
   a dry death.

      Exit.

Scene 2

   Enter Prospero and Miranda.

MIRANDA.
   If by your art, my dearest father, you have
   Put the wild waters in this roar, allay them.
   The sky, it seems, would pour down stinking pitch
   But that the sea, mounting to th' welkin's cheek,°
   Dashes the fire out. O, I have suffer<u>è</u>d   5
   With those that I saw suffer! a brave° vessel
   (Who had no doubt some noble creature in her)
   Dashed all to pieces! O, the cry did knock
   Against my very heart! Poor souls, they perished!
   Had I been any god of power, I would   10
   Have sunk the sea within the earth or ere°
   It should the good ship so have swallowed and
   The fraughting° souls within her.
PROSPERO.   Be collected.°
   No more amazement.° Tell your piteous° heart
   There's no harm done.   15
MIRANDA.   O, woe the day!
PROSPERO.   No harm.
   I have done nothing but in care of thee,
   Of thee my dear one, thee my daughter, who
   Art ignorant of what thou art, naught knowing
   Of whence I am; nor that I am more better
   Than Prospero, master of a full poor cell,   20
   And thy no greater father.
MIRANDA.   More to know
   Did never meddle° with my thoughts.
PROSPERO.   'Tis time
   I should inform thee farther. Lend thy hand
   And pluck my magic garment from me. So,
   Lie there, my art.° Wipe thou thine eyes; have comfort.   25
   The direful spectacle of the wrack, which touched
   The very virtue° of compassion in thee,

---

   61 *long heath, brown furze:* heather and gorse (sometimes emended to 'ling, heath, broom, furze').
SCENE 2. Before Prospero's cell.   4 *cheek:* face (with perhaps a secondary meaning of 'side of a grate').
6 *brave:* fine, handsome (and so elsewhere throughout the play).   11 *or ere:* before.   13 *fraughting:* forming the cargo; *collected:* composed.   14 *amazement:* distraction; *piteous:* pitying.   22 *meddle:* mingle.
25 *art:* i.e. his robe.   27 *virtue:* essence.

I have with such provision° in mine art
So safely orderèd that there is no soul—
No, not so much perdition° as an hair   30
Betid° to any creature in the vessel
Which thou heard'st cry, which thou saw'st sink. Sit
   down;
For thou must now know farther.

MIRANDA.   You have often
Begun to tell me what I am; but stopped
And left me to a bootless inquisition,°   35
Concluding, 'Stay: not yet.'

PROSPERO.   The hour's now come;
The very minute bids thee ope thine ear.
Obey,° and be attentive. Canst thou remember
A time before we came unto this cell?
I do not think thou canst, for then thou wast not   40
Out° three years old.

MIRANDA.   Certainly, sir, I can.

PROSPERO.
By what? By any other house or person?
Of any thing the image tell me° that
Hath kept with thy remembrance.

MIRANDA.   'Tis far off,
And rather like a dream than an assurance   45
That my remembrance warrants.° Had I not
Four or five women once that tended me?

PROSPERO.
Thou hadst, and more, Miranda. But how is it
That this lives in thy mind? What seest thou else
In the dark backward° and abysm° of time?   50
If thou rememb'rest aught ere thou cam'st here,
How thou cam'st here thou mayst.

MIRANDA.   But that I do not.

PROSPERO.
Twelve year since, Miranda, twelve year since,
Thy father was the Duke of Milan and
A prince of power.

MIRANDA.   Sir, are not you my father?   55

PROSPERO.
Thy mother was a piece° of virtue, and
She said thou wast my daughter; and thy father
Was Duke of Milan; and his only heir
A princess—no worse issuèd.°

---

28 *provision:* foresight.   30 *perdition:* loss.   31 *Betid:* happened.   35 *bootless inquisition:* fruitless inquiry.   38 *Obey:* listen.   41 *Out:* fully.   43 *tell me:* i.e. describe for me.   46 *remembrance warrants:* memory guarantees.   50 *backward:* past; *abysm:* abyss.   56 *piece:* masterpiece.   59 *no worse issuèd:* no meaner in descent.

MIRANDA.   O the heavens!
    What foul play had we that we came from thence?   60
    Or blessèd was't we did?
PROSPERO.   Both, both, my girl!
    By foul play, as thou say'st, were we heaved thence,
    But blessedly holp° hither.
MIRANDA.   O, my heart bleeds
    To think o' th' teen° that I have turned you° to,
    Which is from° my remembrance! Please you, farther.   65
PROSPERO.
    My brother and thy uncle, called Antonio—
    I pray thee mark me—that a brother should
    Be so perfidious!—he whom next thyself
    Of all the world I loved, and to him put
    The manage of my state,° as at that time   70
    Through all the signories° it was the first
    And Prospero the prime duke, being so reputed
    In dignity, and for the liberal arts
    Without a parallel; those being all my study,
    The government I cast upon my brother   75
    And to my state grew stranger, being transported
    And rapt in secret studies. Thy false uncle—
    Dost thou attend me?
MIRANDA.   Sir, most heedfully.
PROSPERO.
    Being once perfected° how to grant suits,
    How to deny them, who t' advance, and who   80
    To trash for over-topping,° new-created
    The creatures that were mine, I say, or° changed 'em,
    Or else new-formed 'em; having both the key°
    Of officer and office, set all hearts i' th' state
    To what tune pleased his ear, that now he was   85
    The ivy which had hid my princely trunk
    And sucked my verdure out on't. Thou attend'st not?
MIRANDA.
    O, good sir, I do.
PROSPERO.   I pray thee mark me.
    I thus neglecting worldly ends, all dedicated
    To closeness,° and the bettering of my mind   90
    With that which, but by being so retired,
    O'er-prized° all popular rate,° in my false brother

---

63 *blessedly holp*: providentially helped.   64 *teen*: trouble; *turned you to*: put you in mind of.   65 *from*: out of.   69–70 *put . . . state*: entrusted the control of my administration.   71 *signories*: states of northern Italy.   79 *perfected*: grown skillful.   81 *trash for over-topping*: (1) check, as hounds, for going too fast, (2) cut branches, as of over-tall trees.   82 *or*: either.   83 *key*: (used with pun on its musical sense, leading to the metaphor of tune).   90 *closeness*: seclusion (?), secret studies (?).   92 *O'er-prized*: outvalued; *rate*: estimation.

Awaked an evil nature, and my trust,
Like a good parent,° did beget of him
A falsehood in its contrary as great   95
As my trust was, which had indeed no limit,
A confidence sans bound.° He being thus lorded,
Not only with what my revenue° yielded
But what my power might else exact,° like one
Who having unto truth, by telling of it,°   100
Made such a sinner of his memory
To° credit his own lie, he did believe
He was indeed the Duke, out° o' th' substitution
And executing th' outward face of royalty
With all prerogative. Hence his ambition growing—   105
Dost thou hear?

MIRANDA.   Your tale, sir, would cure deafness.

PROSPERO.
To have no screen between this part he played
And him he played it for, he needs will be
Absolute Milan.° Me (poor man) my library
Was dukedom large enough. Of temporal royalties   110
He thinks me now incapable; confederates°
(So dry° he was for sway) with th' King of Naples
To give him annual tribute, do him homage,
Subject his coronet to his crown, and bend
The dukedom yet unbowed (alas, poor Milan!)   115
To most ignoble stooping.

MIRANDA.   O the heavens!

PROSPERO.
Mark his condition,° and th' event°; then tell me
If this might be a brother.

MIRANDA.   I should sin
To think but nobly of my grandmother.
Good wombs have borne bad sons.

PROSPERO.   Now the condition.   120
This King of Naples, being an enemy
To me inveterate, hearkens my brother's suit;
Which was, that he, in lieu o' th' premises°
Of homage and I know not how much tribute,
Should presently° extirpate° me and mine   125
Out of the dukedom and confer fair Milan,
With all the honors, on my brother. Whereon,

---

94 *good parent:* (alluding to the same proverb cited by Miranda in 1. 120).   97–99 *He . . . exact:*
(the sense is that Antonio had the prerogatives as well as the income of the Duke).   97 *sans bound:*
unlimited.   98 *revenue:* (accent second syllable).   100 *it:* i.e. the lie.   102 *To:* as to.   103 *out:* as a
result.   109 *Absolute Milan:* Duke of Milan in fact.   111 *confederates:* joins in league with.   112 *dry:*
thirsty, eager.   117 *condition:* pact; *event:* outcome.   123 *in lieu o' th' premises:* in return for the guarantees.   125 *presently:* immediately; *extirpate:* remove (accent second syllable).

A treacherous army levied, one midnight
Fated° to th' purpose, did Antonio open
The gates of Milan; and i' th' dead of darkness,   130
The ministers° for th' purpose hurrièd thence
Me and thy crying self.

MIRANDA.   Alack, for pity!
I, not rememb'ring how I cried out then,
Will cry it o'er again; it is a hint°
That wrings° mine eyes to't.   135

PROSPERO.   Hear a little further,
And then I'll bring thee to the present business
Which now's upon's; without the which this story
Were most impertinent.°

MIRANDA.   Wherefore did they not
That hour destroy us?

PROSPERO.   Well demanded, wench.
My tale provokes that question. Dear, they durst not,   140
So dear the love my people bore me; nor set
A mark so bloody on the business; but
With colors fairer painted their foul ends.
In few,° they hurried us aboard a bark,
Bore us some leagues to sea; where they prepared   145
A rotten carcass of a butt,° not rigged,
Nor tackle, sail, nor mast; the very rats
Instinctively have quit it. There they hoist us,
To cry to th' sea that roared to us; to sigh
To th' winds, whose pity, sighing back again,   150
Did us but loving wrong.

MIRANDA.   Alack, what trouble
Was I then to you!

PROSPERO.   O, a cherubim
Thou wast that did preserve me! Thou didst smile,
Infusèd with a fortitude from heaven,
When I have decked the sea with drops full salt,   155
Under my burden groaned: which raised in me
An undergoing stomach,° to bear up
Against what should ensue.

MIRANDA.   How came we ashore?

PROSPERO.
By providence divine.
Some food we had, and some fresh water, that   160
A noble Neapolitan, Gonzalo,
Out of his charity, who being then appointed
Master of this design, did give us, with

---

129 *Fated:* devoted.   131 *ministers:* agents.   134 *hint:* occasion.   135 *wrings:* constrains.   138 *impertinent:* irrelevant.   144 *few:* few words.   146 *butt:* tub.   157 *undergoing stomach:* resolution to endure.

Rich garments, linens, stuffs, and necessaries
Which since have steaded° much. So, of his gentleness,   165
Knowing I loved my books, he furnished me
From mine own library with volumes that
I prize above my dukedom.

MIRANDA.   Would I might
But ever see that man!

PROSPERO.   Now I arise.
Sit still, and hear the last of our sea-sorrow.   170
Here in this island we arrived; and here
Have I, thy schoolmaster, made thee more profit°
Than other princess° can, that have more time
For vainer hours, and tutors not so careful.

MIRANDA.
Heavens thank you for't! And now I pray you, sir,—   175
For still 'tis beating in my mind,—your reason
For raising this sea-storm?

PROSPERO.   Know thus far forth.
By accident most strange, bountiful Fortune
(Now, my dear lady) hath mine enemies
Brought to this shore; and by my prescience   180
I find my zenith° doth depend upon
A most auspicious star, whose influence
If now I court not, but omit,° my fortunes
Will ever after droop. Here cease more questions.
Thou art inclined to sleep. 'Tis a good dulness,   185
And give it way. I know thou canst not choose.

Miranda sleeps.

Come away,° servant, come! I am ready now.
Approach, my Ariel: come!

Enter Ariel.

ARIEL.
All hail, great master! Grave sir, hail! I come
To answer thy best pleasure; be't to fly,   190
To swim, to dive into the fire, to ride
On the curled clouds. To thy strong bidding task°
Ariel and all his quality.°

PROSPERO.   Hast thou, spirit,
Performed to point° the tempest that I bade thee?

ARIEL.
To every article.   195
I boarded the King's ship: now on the beak,°

---

165 *steaded:* been of use.   172 *more profit:* profit more.   173 *princess:* princesses.   181 *zenith:* apex
of fortune.   183 *omit:* neglect.   187 *come away:* come here.   192 *task:* (supply 'come').   193 *quality:*
cohorts (Ariel is leader of a band of elemental spirits).   194 *to point:* in detail.   196 *beak:* prow.

Now in the waist,° the deck,° in every cabin,
I flamed amazement°: sometime I'ld divide
And burn in many places; on the topmast,
The yards, and boresprit° would I flame distinctly,°   200
Then meet and join. Jove's lightnings, the precursors
O' th' dreadful thunderclaps, more momentary
And sight-outrunning were not. The fire and cracks
Of sulphurous roaring the most mighty Neptune
Seem to besiege and make his bold waves tremble;   205
Yea, his dread trident shake.

PROSPERO.   My brave spirit!
Who was so firm, so constant, that this coil°
Would not infect his reason?

ARIEL.   Not a soul
But felt a fever of the mad° and played
Some tricks of desperation. All but mariners   210
Plunged in the foaming brine and quit the vessel;
Then all afire with me° the King's son Ferdinand,
With hair up-staring° (then like reeds, not hair),
Was the first man that leapt; cried 'Hell is empty,
And all the devils are here!'   215

PROSPERO.   Why, that's my spirit!
But was not this nigh shore?

ARIEL.   Close by, my master.

PROSPERO.
But are they, Ariel, safe?

ARIEL.   Not a hair perished.
On their sustaining° garments not a blemish,
But fresher than before; and as thou bad'st me,
In troops I have dispersed them 'bout the isle.   220
The King's son have I landed by himself,
Whom I left cooling of the air with sighs
In an odd angle of the isle, and sitting,
His arms in this° sad knot.

PROSPERO.   Of the King's ship
The mariners say how thou hast disposed,   225
And all the rest o' th' fleet.

ARIEL.   Safely in harbor
Is the King's ship; in the deep nook where once
Thou call'dst me up at midnight to fetch dew
From the still-vexed Bermoothes,° there she's hid;
The mariners all under hatches stowed,   230

---

197 *waist*: middle; *deck*: poop.   198 *flamed amazement*: struck terror by appearing as (St Elmo's)
fire.   200 *boresprit*: bowsprit; *distinctly*: in different places.   207 *coil*: uproar.   209 *of the mad*: such as
madmen have.   212 *afire with me*: (refers either to the vessel or to Ferdinand, depending on the punctuation; F suggests the latter).   213 *up-staring*: standing on end.   218 *sustaining*: buoying them up in the
water.   224 *this*: (illustrated by a gesture).   229 *still-vexed Bermoothes*: constantly agitated Bermudas.

Who, with a charm joined to their suff'red° labor,
I have left asleep; and for the rest o' th' fleet,
Which I dispersed, they all have met again,
And are upon the Mediterranean flote°
Bound sadly home for Naples,   235
Supposing that they saw the King's ship wracked
And his great person perish.

PROSPERO.   Ariel, thy charge
Exactly is performed; but there's more work.
What is the time o' th' day?

ARIEL.   Past the mid season.°

PROSPERO.
At least two glasses.° The time 'twixt six and now   240
Must by us both be spent most preciously.

ARIEL.
Is there more toil? Since thou dost give me pains,
Let me remember° thee what thou hast promised,
Which is not yet performed me.

PROSPERO.   How now? moody?
What is't thou canst demand?   245

ARIEL.   My liberty.

PROSPERO.
Before the time° be out? No more!

ARIEL.   I prithee,
Remember I have done thee worthy service,
Told thee no lies, made no mistakings, served
Without or grudge or grumblings. Thou did promise
To bate me° a full year.   250

PROSPERO.   Dost thou forget
From what a torment I did free thee?

ARIEL.   No.

PROSPERO.
Thou dost; and think'st it much to tread the ooze
Of the salt deep,
To run upon the sharp wind of the North,
To do me business in the veins° o' th' earth   255
When it is baked° with frost.

ARIEL.   I do not, sir.

PROSPERO.
Thou liest, malignant thing! Hast thou forgot
The foul witch Sycorax,° who with age and envy°
Was grown into a hoop? Hast thou forgot her?

---

231 *suff'red:* undergone.   234 *flote:* sea.   239 *mid season:* noon.   240 *glasses:* hours.   243 *remember:* remind.   246 *time:* period of service.   250 *bate me:* shorten my term of service.   255 *veins:* streams.
256 *baked:* hardened.   258 *Sycorax:* (name not found elsewhere; usually connected with Greek 'sys', sow, and 'korax', which means both raven—cf. l. 322—and curved, hence perhaps *hoop*); *envy:* malice.

ARIEL.
    No, sir.

PROSPERO. Thou hast. Where was she born? Speak! 260
    Tell me!

ARIEL.
    Sir, in Argier.°

PROSPERO.   O, was she so? I must
    Once in a month recount what thou hast been,
    Which thou forget'st. This damned witch Sycorax,
    For mischiefs manifold, and sorceries terrible
    To enter human hearing, from Argier, 265
    Thou know'st, was banished. For one thing she did°
    They would not take her life. Is not this true?

ARIEL.
    Ay, sir.

PROSPERO.
    This blue-eyed hag was hither brought with child
    And here was left by th' sailors. Thou, my slave, 270
    As thou report'st thyself, was then her servant;
    And, for thou wast a spirit too delicate
    To act her earthly and abhorred commands,
    Refusing her grand hests,° she did confine thee,
    By help of her more potent ministers, 275
    And in her most unmitigable rage,
    Into a cloven pine; within which rift
    Imprisoned thou didst painfully remain
    A dozen years; within which space she died
    And left thee there, where thou didst vent thy groans 280
    As fast as millwheels° strike. Then was this island
    (Save for the son that she did litter here,
    A freckled whelp, hag-born) not honored with
    A human shape.

ARIEL.   Yes, Caliban her son.

PROSPERO.
    Dull thing, I say so: he, that Caliban 285
    Whom now I keep in service. Thou best know'st
    What torment I did find thee in: thy groans
    Did make wolves howl and penetrate the breasts
    Of ever-angry bears. It was a torment
    To lay upon the damned, which Sycorax 290
    Could not again undo. It was mine art,
    When I arrived and heard thee, that made gape
    The pine, and let thee out.

ARIEL.   I thank thee, master.

---

    261 *Argier*: Algiers.   266 *one thing she did*: (being pregnant, her sentence was commuted from death to exile).   274 *hests*: commands.   281 *millwheels*: i.e. the clappers on the millwheels.

PROSPERO.

    If thou more murmur'st, I will rend an oak

    And peg thee in his° knotty entrails till   295

    Thou hast howled away twelve° winters.

ARIEL.   Pardon, master.

    I will be correspondent° to command

    And do my spriting gently.°

PROSPERO.   Do so; and after two days

    I will discharge thee.

ARIEL.   That's my noble master!

    What shall I do? Say what? What shall I do?   300

PROSPERO.

    Go make thyself like a nymph o' th' sea. Be subject

    To no sight but thine and mine; invisible

    To every eyeball else. Go take this shape

    And hither come in't. Go! Hence with diligence!

                                        Exit [Ariel].

    Awake, dear heart, awake! Thou hast slept well.   305

    Awake!

MIRANDA. The strangeness of your story put

    Heaviness in me.

PROSPERO.   Shake it off. Come on.

    We'll visit Caliban, my slave, who never

    Yields us kind answer.

MIRANDA.   'Tis a villain, sir,

    I do not love to look on.   310

PROSPERO.   But as 'tis,

    We cannot miss° him: he does make our fire,

    Fetch in our wood, and serves in offices

    That profit us. What, ho! slave! Caliban!

    Thou earth, thou! Speak!

CALIBAN. *[within]*   There's wood enough within.

PROSPERO.

    Come forth, I say! There's other business for thee.   315

    Come, thou tortoise! When?°

    Enter Ariel like a water nymph.

    Fine apparition! My quaint° Ariel,

    Hark in thine ear.

ARIEL.   My lord, it shall be done.   *Exit.*

PROSPERO.

    Thou poisonous slave, got by the devil himself

    Upon thy wicked dam, come forth!   320

---

    295 *his:* its.   296 *twelve:* (the same length of time that Ariel has been released).   297 *correspondent:* obedient.   298 *spriting gently:* office as a spirit graciously.   311 *miss:* do without.   316 *When:* (expression of impatience).   317 *quaint:* ingenious.

Enter Caliban.

CALIBAN.
> As wicked dew as e'er my mother brushed
> With raven's feather from unwholesome fen
> Drop on you both! A south-west blow on ye
> And blister you all o'er!

PROSPERO.
> For this, be sure, to-night thou shalt have cramps,   325
> Side-stitches that shall pen thy breath up; urchins°
> Shall, for that vast° of night that they may work,°
> All exercise on thee; thou shalt be pinched
> As thick as honeycomb, each pinch more stinging
> Than bees that made 'em.

CALIBAN.   I must eat my dinner.   330
> This island's mine by Sycorax my mother,
> Which thou tak'st from me. When thou cam'st first,
> Thou strok'st me and made much of me; wouldst give me
> Water with berries in't; and teach me how
> To name the bigger light, and how the less,   335
> That burn by day and night; and then I loved thee
> And showed thee all the qualities° o' th' isle,
> The fresh springs, brine-pits, barren place and fertile.
> Cursed be I that did so! All the charms
> Of Sycorax—toads, beetles, bats, light on you!   340
> For I am all the subjects that you have,
> Which first was mine own king; and here you sty me
> In this hard rock, whiles you do keep from me
> The rest o' th' island.

PROSPERO.   Thou most lying slave,
> Whom stripes° may move, not kindness! I have used thee   345
> (Filth as thou art) with humane care, and lodged thee
> In mine own cell till thou didst seek to violate
> The honor of my child.

CALIBAN.
> O ho, O ho! Would't had been done!
> Thou didst prevent me; I had peopled else   350
> This isle with Calibans.

MIRANDA.°   Abhorrèd slave,
> Which any print of goodness will not take,
> Being capable of all ill! I pitied thee,
> Took pains to make thee speak, taught thee each hour
> One thing or other: when thou didst not, savage,   355
> Know thine own meaning, but wouldst gabble like

---

326 *urchins:* hedgehogs (i.e. goblins in that shape).   327 *vast:* void; *that they may work:* (referring to the belief that malignant spirits had power only during darkness).   337 *qualities:* resources.   345 *stripes:* lashes.   351 *Miranda:* (so F; some editors have given the speech to Prospero).

A thing most brutish, I endowed thy purposes°
With words that made them known. But thy vile race,°
Though thou didst learn, had that in't which good
    natures°
Could not abide to be with; therefore wast thou   360
Deservedly confined into this rock, who hadst
Deserved more than a prison.

CALIBAN.
You taught me language, and my profit on't
Is, I know how to curse. The red plague° rid° you
For learning me your language!

PROSPERO.   Hag-seed, hence!   365
Fetch us in fuel; and be quick, thou'rt best,°
To answer other business. Shrug'st thou, malice?
If thou neglect'st or dost unwillingly
What I command, I'll rack thee with old° cramps,
Fill all thy bones with aches,° make thee roar   370
That beasts shall tremble at thy din.

CALIBAN.   No, pray thee.

Aside.

I must obey. His art is of such pow'r
It would control my dam's god, Setebos,
And make a vassal of him.

PROSPERO.   So, slave; hence!

Exit Caliban.

Enter Ferdinand; and Ariel [invisible], playing and singing.

        Ariel's song.
    Come unto these yellow sands,   375
        And then take hands.
    Curtsied when you have and kissed,
        The wild waves whist,°
    Foot it featly° here and there;
        And, sweet sprites, the burden° bear.   380
        Hark, Hark!
Burden, dispersedly. Bowgh, wawgh!
        The watchdogs bark.
Burden, dispersedly. Bowgh, wawgh!
        Hark, hark! I hear   385
    The strain of strutting chanticleer
        Cry cock-a-diddle-dowe.

---

357 *purposes:* meanings. 358 *race:* nature. 359 *good natures:* natural virtues. 364 *red plague:*
bubonic plague; *rid:* destroy. 366 *thou'rt best:* you'd be well advised. 369 *old:* i.e., such as old people
have. 370 *aches:* (pronounced 'aitches'). 378 *whist:* being hushed. 379 *featly:* nimbly. 380 *burden:*
undersong, refrain.

FERDINAND.
> Where should this music be? I' th' air or th' earth?
> It sounds no more; and sure it waits upon
> Some god o' th' island. Sitting on a bank,   390
> Weeping again the King my father's wrack,
> This music crept by me upon the waters,
> Allaying both their fury and my passion°
> With its sweet air. Thence I have followed it,
> Or it hath drawn me rather; but 'tis gone.   395
> No, it begins again.

> > *Ariel's song.*
> > Full fathom five thy father lies;
> >   Of his bones are coral made;
> > Those are pearls that were his eyes;
> >   Nothing of him that doth fade   400
> > But doth suffer a sea-change
> > Into something rich and strange.
> > Sea nymphs hourly ring his knell:
> > *Burden.*   Ding-dong.
> > Hark! now I hear them—Ding-dong bell.   405

FERDINAND.
> The ditty does remember° my drowned father.
> This is no mortal business, nor no sound
> That the earth owes.° I hear it now above me.

PROSPERO.
> The fringèd curtains of thine eye advance°
> And say what thou seest yond.

MIRANDA.   What is't? a spirit?   410
> Lord, how it looks about! Believe me, sir,
> It carries a brave form. But 'tis a spirit.

PROSPERO.
> No, wench: it eats, and sleeps, and hath such senses
> As we have, such. This gallant which thou seest
> Was in the wrack; and, but he's something stained°   415
> With grief (that's beauty's canker), thou mightst call him
> A goodly person. He hath lost his fellows
> And strays about to find 'em.

MIRANDA.   I might call him
> A thing divine; for nothing natural
> I ever saw so noble.   420

PROSPERO. [*aside*] It goes on, I see,
> As my soul prompts° it. Spirit, fine spirit, I'll free thee
> Within two days for this.

---

393 *passion:* lamentation.   406 *remember:* allude to.   408 *owes:* owns.   409 *advance:* raise.
415 *stained:* disfigured.   421 *prompts:* would like.

FERDINAND.   Most sure,° the goddess
On whom these airs attend! Vouchsafe my prayer
May know if you remain° upon this island,
And that you will some good instruction give   425
How I may bear me° here. My prime request,
Which I do last pronounce, is (O you wonder!)
If you be maid or no?
MIRANDA.   No wonder, sir,
But certainly a maid.
FERDINAND.   My language? Heavens!
I am the best of them that speak this speech,   430
Were I but where 'tis spoken.
PROSPERO.   How? the best?
What wert thou if the King of Naples heard thee?
FERDINAND.
A single° thing, as I am now, that wonders
To hear thee speak of Naples. He does hear me;
And that he does I weep. Myself am Naples,°   435
Who with mine eyes, never since at ebb, beheld
The King my father wracked.
MIRANDA.   Alack, for mercy!
FERDINAND.
Yes, faith, and all his lords, the Duke of Milan
And his brave son° being twain.
PROSPERO. [aside]   The Duke of Milan
And his more braver daughter could control° thee,   440
If now 'twere fit to do't. At the first sight
They have changed eyes.° Delicate Ariel,
I'll set thee free for this.—A word, good sir.
I fear you have done yourself some wrong.° A word!
MIRANDA.
Why speaks my father so ungently? This   445
Is the third man that e'er I saw; the first
That e'er I sighed for. Pity move my father
To be inclined my way!
FERDINAND.   O, if a virgin,
And your affection not gone forth, I'll make you
The Queen of Naples.   450
PROSPERO.   Soft, sir! one word more.

Aside.

They are both in either's pow'rs. But this swift business
I must uneasy make, lest too light winning

_____

422 *Most sure:* this is certainly.   424 *remain:* dwell.   426 *bear me:* conduct myself.   433 *single:* (1)
solitary, (2) weak or helpless.   435 *Naples:* King of Naples.   439 *son:* (Antonio's son is not elsewhere mentioned).   440 *control:* refute.   442 *changed eyes:* exchanged love looks.   444 *done . . . wrong:* told a lie.

Make the prize light.—One word more! I charge thee
That thou attend me. Thou dost here usurp
The name thou ow'st° not, and hast put thyself   455
Upon this island as a spy, to win it
From me, the lord on't.

FERDINAND.   No, as I am a man!

MIRANDA.
There's nothing ill can dwell in such a temple.
If the ill spirit have so fair a house,
Good things will strive to dwell with't.   460

PROSPERO.   Follow me.—
Speak not you for him; he's a traitor.—Come!
I'll manacle thy neck and feet together;
Sea water shalt thou drink; thy food shall be
The fresh-brook mussels, withered roots, and husks
Wherein the acorn cradled. Follow!   465

FERDINAND.   No.
I will resist such entertainment° till
Mine enemy has more pow'r.

He draws, and is charmed from moving.

MIRANDA.   O dear father,
Make not too rash a trial° of him, for
He's gentle,° and not fearful.°

PROSPERO.   What, I say,
My foot my tutor?°—Put thy sword up, traitor!   470
Who mak'st a show but dar'st not strike, thy conscience
Is so possessed with guilt. Come, from thy ward!°
For I can here disarm thee with this stick
And make thy weapon drop.

MIRANDA.   Beseech you, father!

PROSPERO.
Hence! Hang not on my garments.   475

MIRANDA.   Sir, have pity.
I'll be his surety.

PROSPERO.   Silence! One word more
Shall make me chide thee, if not hate thee. What,
An advocate for an impostor? Hush!
Thou think'st there is no more such shapes as he,
Having seen but him and Caliban. Foolish wench?   480
To th' most of men this is a Caliban,
And they to him are angels.

MIRANDA.   My affections°

---

455 *ow'st:* ownest.   466 *entertainment:* treatment.   468 *trial:* judgment.   469 *gentle:* noble; *fearful:* cowardly.   470 *My . . . tutor:* i.e., instructed by my underling.   472 *ward:* fighting posture.   482 *affections:* inclinations.

Are then most humble. I have no ambition
  To see a goodlier man.

PROSPERO.   Come on, obey!°
  Thy nerves° are in their infancy again   485
  And have no vigor in them.

FERDINAND.   So they are.
  My spirits, as in a dream, are all bound up.
  My father's loss, the weakness which I feel,
  The wrack of all my friends, nor this man's threats
  To whom I am subdued, are but light to me,   490
  Might I but through my prison once a day
  Behold this maid. All corners else o' th' earth
  Let liberty make use of. Space enough
  Have I in such a prison.

PROSPERO. [aside]   It works.   [to Ferdinand] Come on.—
  Thou hast done well, fine Ariel!   495
  [To Ferdinand]   Follow me.
  [To Ariel]
  Hark what thou else shalt do me.

MIRANDA.   Be of comfort.
  My father's of a better nature, sir,
  Than he appears by speech. This is unwonted
  Which now came from him.

PROSPERO.   Thou shalt be as free
  As mountain winds; but then° exactly do   500
  All points of my command.

ARIEL.   To th' syllable.

PROSPERO.
  Come, follow.—Speak not for him.

  Exeunt.

ACT II
Scene 1

Enter Alonso, Sebastian, Antonio, Gonzalo, Adrian, Francisco, and others.

GONZALO.
  Beseech you, sir, be merry. You have cause
  (So have we all) of joy; for our escape
  Is much beyond our loss. Our hint° of woe
  Is common: every day some sailor's wife,
  The master of some merchant,° and the merchant,°   5
  Have just our theme of woe; but for the miracle,

---

484 *obey:* follow.   485 *nerves:* sinews, tendons.   500 *then:* till then.   SCENE 1. Another part of the island.   3 *hint:* occasion.   5 *master of some merchant:* master of a merchant ship; *the merchant:* the owner of the ship.

I mean our preservation, few in millions
Can speak like us. Then wisely, good sir, weigh
Our sorrow with our comfort.

ALONSO.   Prithee peace.

SEBASTIAN. He receives comfort like cold porridge.°   10

ANTONIO. The visitor° will not give him o'er° so.

SEBASTIAN. Look, he's winding up the watch of his wit;
      by and by it will strike.

GONZALO. Sir—

SEBASTIAN. One. Tell.°   15

GONZALO.
      When every grief is entertained, that's° offered
      Comes to th' entertainer°—

SEBASTIAN. A dollar.

GONZALO. Dolor° comes to him, indeed. You have spoken
      truer than you purposed.   20

SEBASTIAN. You have taken it wiselier than I meant you
      should.

GONZALO. Therefore, my lord—

ANTONIO. Fie, what a spendthrift° is he of his tongue!

ALONSO. I prithee spare.   25

GONZALO. Well, I have done. But yet—

SEBASTIAN. He will be talking.

ANTONIO. Which, of he or Adrian, for a good wager, first
      begins to crow?

SEBASTIAN. The old cock.°   30

ANTONIO. The cock'rel.°

SEBASTIAN. Done! The wager?

ANTONIO. A laughter.°

SEBASTIAN. A match!

ADRIAN. Though this island seem to be desert—   35

ANTONIO. Ha, ha, ha!

SEBASTIAN. So, you're paid.

ADRIAN. Uninhabitable and almost inaccessible—

SEBASTIAN. Yet—

ADRIAN. Yet—   40

ANTONIO. He could not miss't.

ADRIAN. It must needs be of subtle, tender, and delicate
      temperance.°

ANTONIO. Temperance° was a delicate wench.

SEBASTIAN. Ay, and a subtle, as he most learnedly delivered.   45

ADRIAN. The air breathes upon us here most sweetly.

SEBASTIAN. As if it had lungs, and rotten ones.

---

10 *porridge*: (pun on *peace*: [pease]).   11 *visitor*: spiritual adviser; *give him o'er*: let him alone.   15 *Tell*: count.   16 *that's*: that which is.   17 *entertainer*: (taken by Sebastian to mean 'innkeeper').   19 *Dolor*: grief (with pun on *dollar*, a continental coin).   24 *spendthrift*: (Antonio labors the pun).   30 *old cock*: i.e. Gonzalo.   31 *cock'rel*: i.e. Adrian.   33 *laughter*: the winner laughs.   43 *temperance*: climate.   44 *Temperance*: (a girl's name).

ANTONIO. Or as 'twere perfumed by a fen.

GONZALO. Here is everything advantageous to life.

ANTONIO. True; save means to live. 50

SEBASTIAN. Of that there's none, or little.

GONZALO. How lush and lusty the grass looks! how
    green!

ANTONIO. The ground indeed is tawny.

SEBASTIAN. With an eye° of green in't.

ANTONIO. He misses not much. 55

SEBASTIAN. No; he doth but mistake the truth totally.

GONZALO. But the rarity of it is—which is indeed almost
    beyond credit—

SEBASTIAN. As many vouched rarities° are.

GONZALO. That our garments, being, as they were, 60
    drenched in the sea, hold, notwithstanding, their fresh-
    ness and gloss, being rather new-dyed than stained with
    salt water.

ANTONIO. If but one of his pockets could speak, would it
    not say he lies?

SEBASTIAN. Ay, or very falsely pocket up his report. 65

GONZALO. Methinks our garments are now as fresh as
    when we put them on first in Afric, at the marriage of
    the King's fair daughter Claribel to the King of Tunis.

SEBASTIAN. 'Twas a sweet marriage, and we prosper
    well in our return. 70

ADRIAN. Tunis was never graced before with such a
    paragon to° their queen.

GONZALO. Not since widow Dido's° time.

ANTONIO. Widow? A pox o' that! How came that
    'widow' in? Widow Dido! 75

SEBASTIAN. What if he had said 'widower Aeneas' too?
    Good Lord, how you take it!

ADRIAN. 'Widow Dido,' said you? You make me study
    of that. She was of Carthage, not of Tunis.

GONZALO. This Tunis, sir, was Carthage. 80

ADRIAN. Carthage?

GONZALO. I assure you, Carthage.

ANTONIO. His word is more than the miraculous harp.°

SEBASTIAN. He hath raised the wall and houses too.

ANTONIO. What impossible matter will he make easy next? 85

SEBASTIAN. I think he will carry this island home in his
    pocket and give it his son for an apple.

---

54 *eye:* spot (or perhaps Gonzalo's eye).   59 *vouched rarities:* wonders guaranteed to be true.
72 *to:* for.   73 *widow Dido:* (Dido was the widow of Sychaeus; Aeneas was a widower, having lost his
wife in the fall of Troy. The reasons for Antonio's amusement, if that is what it is, have not been explained).   83 *miraculous harp:* (of Amphion, which raised the walls of Thebes; Tunis and Carthage
were near each other, but not the same city).

ANTONIO. And, sowing the kernels of it in the sea, bring
    forth more islands.

GONZALO. Ay!°   90

ANTONIO. Why, in good time.

GONZALO. Sir, we were talking that our garments seem
    now as fresh as when we were at Tunis at the marriage
    of your daughter, who is now Queen.

ANTONIO. And the rarest that e'er came there.   95

SEBASTIAN. Bate,° I beseech you, widow Dido.

ANTONIO. O, widow Dido? Ay, widow Dido!

GONZALO. Is not, sir, my doublet as fresh as the first day I
    wore it? I mean, in a sort.°

ANTONIO. That 'sort' was well fished for.   100

GONZALO. When I wore it at your daughter's marriage.

ALONSO.
    You cram these words into mine ears against
    The stomach of my sense.° Would I had never
    Married my daughter there! for, coming thence,
    My son is lost; and, in my rate,° she too,   105
    Who is so far from Italy removed
    I ne'er again shall see her. O thou mine heir
    Of Naples and of Milan, what strange fish
    Hath made his meal on thee?

FRANCISCO.   Sir, he may live.
    I saw him beat the surges under him   110
    And ride upon their backs. He trod the water,
    Whose enmity he flung aside, and breasted
    The surge most swol'n that met him. His bold head
    'Bove the contentious waves he kept, and oared
    Himself with his good arms in lusty stroke   115
    To th' shore, that o'er his° wave-worn basis° bowed,
    As stooping to relieve him. I not doubt
    He came alive to land.

ALONSO.   No, no, he's gone.

SEBASTIAN. Sir, you may thank yourself for this great loss,
    That would not bless our Europe with your daughter,   120
    But rather loose her to an African,
    Where she, at least, is banished from your eye
    Who hath cause to wet the grief on't.

ALONSO.   Prithee peace.

SEBASTIAN. You were kneeled to and importuned otherwise
    By all of us; and the fair soul herself   125
    Weighed, between loathness and obedience, at

---

90 *Ay:* (F reads "I"; this and Antonio's rejoinder have not been satisfactorily explained).   96 *Bate:*
except.   99 *in a sort:* i.e., comparatively.   103 *stomach . . . sense:* i.e., inclination of my mind.   105 *rate:*
opinion.   116 *his:* its; *basis:* i.e., the sand.

Which end o' th' beam should bow.° We have lost your son,
I fear, for ever. Milan and Naples have
Moe° widows in them of this business' making
Than we bring men to comfort them: 130
The fault's your own.

ALONSO.   So is the dear'st° o' th' loss.

GONZALO.
My Lord Sebastian,
The truth you speak doth lack some gentleness,
And time to speak it in. You rub the sore
When you should bring the plaster.

SEBASTIAN.   Very well.   135

ANTONIO.
And most chirurgeonly.°

GONZALO.
It is foul weather in us all, good sir,
When you are cloudy.

SEBASTIAN.   Foul weather?

ANTONIO.   Very foul.

GONZALO.
Had I plantation° of this isle, my lord—

ANTONIO.
He'd sow't with nettle seed.

SEBASTIAN.   Or docks, or mallows.   140

GONZALO.
And were the king on't, what would I do?

SEBASTIAN.
Scape being drunk for want of wine.

GONZALO.
I' th' commonwealth I would by contraries°
Execute all things; for no kind of traffic°
Would I admit; no name of magistrate;   145
Letters should not be known; riches, poverty,
And use of service,° none; contract, succession,°
Bourn,° bound of land, tilth, vineyard, none;
No use of metal, corn, or wine, or oil;
No occupation; all men idle, all;   150
And women too, but innocent and pure;
No sovereignty.

SEBASTIAN.   Yet he would be king on't.

ANTONIO. The latter end of his commonwealth forgets
the beginning.

125–27 *the fair . . . bow:* (the sense is that Claribel hated the marriage, and only obedience to her father turned the scale). 129 *Moe:* more. 131 *dear'st:* heaviest. 136 *chirurgeonly:* like a surgeon. 139 *plantation:* colonization (taken by Antonio in its other sense). 143 *by contraries:* in contrast to usual customs. 144 *traffic:* trade. 147 *use of service:* having a servant class; *succession:* inheritance. 148 *Bourn:* limits of private property.

GONZALO.

    All things in common nature should produce   155

    Without sweat or endeavor. Treason, felony,

    Sword, pike, knife, gun, or need of any engine°

    Would I not have; but nature should bring forth,

    Of it° own kind, all foison,° all abundance,

    To feed my innocent people.   160

SEBASTIAN. No marrying 'mong his subjects?

ANTONIO. None, man, all idle—whores and knaves.

GONZALO.

    I would with such perfection govern, sir,

    T'excel the golden age.

SEBASTIAN.   Save his Majesty!

ANTONIO.

    Long live Gonzalo!

GONZALO.   And—do you mark me, sir?   165

ALONSO.

    Prithee no more. Thou dost talk nothing to me.

GONZALO. I do well believe your Highness; and did it to

    minister occasion° to these gentlemen, who are of such

    sensible° and nimble lungs that they always use to laugh

    at nothing.   170

ANTONIO. 'Twas you we laughed at.

GONZALO. Who in this kind of merry fooling am nothing

    to you: so you may continue, and laugh at nothing still.

ANTONIO. What a blow was there given!

SEBASTIAN. An° it had not fall'n flatlong.°   175

GONZALO. You are gentlemen of brave mettle; you

    would lift the moon out of her sphere if she would con-

    tinue in it five weeks without changing.

Enter Ariel, [invisible,] playing solemn music.

SEBASTIAN. We would so, and then go a-batfowling.°

ANTONIO. Nay, good my lord, be not angry.   180

GONZALO. No, I warrant you: I will not adventure° my

    discretion so weakly. Will you laugh me asleep, for I am

    very heavy?

ANTONIO. Go sleep, and hear us.

All sleep except Alonso, Sebastian, and Antonio.

ALONSO. What, all so soon asleep? I wish mine eyes   185

    Would, with themselves, shut up my thoughts. I find

    They are inclined to do so.

---

157 *engine:* weapon. 159 *it:* its; *foison:* abundance. 168 *minister occasion:* afford opportunity.
169 *sensible:* sensitive. 175 *An:* if; *flatlong:* struck with the flat of a sword. 179 *a-batfowling:* hunting
birds with sticks ('bats') at night (using the moon for a lantern). 181 *adventure:* risk (Gonzalo is saying, very politely, that their wit is too feeble for him to take offense at it).

SEBASTIAN.   Please you, sir,
Do not omit° the heavy offer° of it.
It seldom visits sorrow; when it doth,
It is a comforter.
ANTONIO.   We two, my lord,   190
Will guard your person while you take your rest,
And watch your safety.
ALONSO.   Thank you. Wondrous heavy.

Alonso sleeps. Exit Ariel.

SEBASTIAN.
What a strange drowsiness possesses them!
ANTONIO.
It is the quality o' th' climate.
SEBASTIAN.   Why
Doth it not then our eyelids sink? I find not   195
myself disposed to sleep.
ANTONIO.   Nor I: my spirits are nimble.
They fell together all, as by consent.
They dropped as by a thunder-stroke. What might,
Worthy Sebastian—O, what might?—No more!
And yet methinks I see it in thy face,   200
What thou shouldst be. Th' occasion speaks° thee, and
My strong imagination sees a crown
Dropping upon thy head.
SEBASTIAN.   What? Art thou waking?
ANTONIO.
Do you not hear me speak?
SEBASTIAN.   I do; and surely
It is a sleepy language, and thou speak'st   205
Out of thy sleep. What is it thou didst say?
This is a strange repose, to be asleep
With eyes wide open; standing, speaking, moving,
And yet so fast asleep.
ANTONIO.   Noble Sebastian,
Thou let'st thy fortune sleep—die, rather; wink'st°   210
Whiles thou art waking.
SEBASTIAN.   Thou dost snore distinctly;
There's meaning in thy snores.
ANTONIO.
I am more serious than my custom. You
Must be so too, if heed me; which to do
Trebles° thee o'er.
SEBASTIAN.   Well, I am standing water.°   215

---

188 *omit:* neglect; *heavy offer:* opportunity its heaviness affords.   201 *speaks:* speaks to, summons.
210 *wink'st:* dost sleep.   215 *Trebles thee o'er:* increases thy status threefold; *standing water:* at slack tide.

ANTONIO.
    I'll teach you how to flow.

SEBASTIAN.   Do so. To ebb
    Hereditary sloth° instructs me.

ANTONIO.   O,
    If you but knew how you the purpose cherish°
    Whiles thus you mock it! how, in stripping it,
    You more invest° it! Ebbing men indeed   220
    (Most often) do so near the bottom run
    By their own fear or sloth.

SEBASTIAN.   Prithee say on.
    The setting of thine eye and cheek proclaim
    A matter from thee; and a birth, indeed,
    Which throes thee° much to yield.

ANTONIO.   Thus, sir: 225
    Although this lord of weak remembrance,° this
    Who shall be of as little memory°
    When he is earthed,° hath here almost persuaded
    (For he's a spirit of persuasion, only
    Professes° to persuade) the King his son's alive,   230
    'Tis as impossible that he's undrowned
    As he that sleeps here swims.

SEBASTIAN.   I have no hope
    That he's undrowned.

ANTONIO.   O, out of that no hope
    What great hope have you! No hope that way is
    Another way so high a hope that even   235
    Ambition cannot pierce a wink° beyond,
    But doubt discovery there.° Will you grant with me
    That Ferdinand is drowned?

SEBASTIAN.   He's gone.

ANTONIO.   Then tell me,
    Who's the next heir of Naples?

SEBASTIAN.   Claribel.

ANTONIO.
    She that is Queen of Tunis; she that dwells   240
    Ten leagues beyond man's life;° she that from Naples
    Can have no note,° unless the sun were post°—
    The man i' th' moon's too slow—till new-born chins
    Be rough and razorable; she that from whom
    We all were sea-swallowed, though some cast° again,   245

---

    217 *Hereditary sloth:* natural laziness.   218 *cherish:* enrich.   220 *invest:* clothe.   225 *throes thee much:* costs thee much pain, like a birth.   226 *remembrance:* memory.   227 *of . . . memory:* as little remembered. 228 *earthed:* buried.   230 *Professes:* has the function.   236 *wink:* glimpse.   237 *doubt discovery there:* is uncertain of seeing accurately.   241 *Ten . . . life:* i.e., thirty miles from nowhere.   242 *note:* communication; *post:* messenger.   245 *cast:* thrown up (with a suggestion of its theatrical meaning which introduces the next metaphor).

And, by that destiny, to perform an act
Whereof what's past is prologue, what to come,
In yours and my discharge.°
SEBASTIAN.   What stuff is this? How say you?
'Tis true my brother's daughter's Queen of Tunis;
So is she heir of Naples; 'twixt which regions   250
There is some space.
ANTONIO.   A space whose ev'ry cubit
Seems to cry out 'How shall that Claribel
Measure us° back to Naples? Keep in Tunis,
And let Sebastian wake!' Say this were death
That now hath seized them, why, they were no worse   255
Than now they are. There be that can rule Naples
As well as he that sleeps; lords that can prate
As amply and unnecessarily
As this Gonzalo; I myself could make
A chough° of as deep chat. O, that you bore   260
The mind that I do! What a sleep were this
For your advancement! Do you understand me?
SEBASTIAN.
    Methinks I do.
ANTONIO.   And how does your content
    Tender° your own good fortune?
SEBASTIAN.   I remember
    You did supplant your brother Prospero.
ANTONIO.   True.   265
    And look how well my garments sit upon me,
    Much feater° than before. My brother's servants
    Were then my fellows;° now they are my men.°
SEBASTIAN.
    But, for your conscience—
ANTONIO.
    Ay, sir, where lies that? If 'twere a kibe,°   270
    'Twould put me to° my slipper; but I feel not
    This deity in my bosom. Twenty consciences
    That stand 'twixt me and Milan, candied° be they
    And melt, ere they molest! Here lies your brother,
    No better than the earth he lies upon   275
    If he were that which now he's like—that's dead;
    Whom I with this obedient steel (three inches of it)
    Can lay to bed for ever; whiles you, doing thus,
    To the perpetual wink° for aye might put
    This ancient morsel, this Sir Prudence, who   280

---

248 *discharge*: business. 253 *us*: i.e., the cubits. 260 *chough*: jackdaw (a bird sometimes taught to speak). 263–264 *content Tender*: inclination estimate. 267 *feater*: more suitable. 268 *fellows*: equals; *men*: servants. 270 *kibe*: chilblain. 271 *put me to*: make me wear. 273 *candied*: frozen. 279 *wink*: sleep.

Should not upbraid our course. For all the rest,
They'll take suggestion as a cat laps milk;
They'll tell the clock° to any business that
We say befits the hour.
SEBASTIAN.   Thy case, dear friend,
Shall be my precedent. As thou got'st Milan,   285
I'll come by Naples. Draw thy sword. One stroke
Shall free thee from the tribute which thou payest,
And I the King shall love thee.
ANTONIO.   Draw together;
And when I rear my hand, do you the like,
To fall it° on Gonzalo.

They draw.

SEBASTIAN.   O, but one word!   290

Enter Ariel, [invisible,] with music and song.

ARIEL.
My master through his art foresees the danger
That you, his friend, are in, and sends me forth
(For else his project dies) to keep them living.

Sings in Gonzolo's ear.

While you here do snoring lie,
Open-eyed conspiracy   295
    His time doth take.
If of life you keep a care,
Shake off slumber and beware.
    Awake, awake!
ANTONIO.
Then let us both be sudden.
GONZALO. [*wakes*]   Now good angels   300
Preserve the King!
ALONSO.
Why, how now?—Ho, awake!—Why are you drawn?
Wherefore this ghastly looking?
GONZALO.   What's the matter?
SEBASTIAN.
Whiles we stood here securing° your repose,
Even now, we hear a hollow burst of bellowing   305
Like bulls, or rather lions. Did't not wake you?
It struck mine ear most terribly.
ALONSO.   I heard nothing.
ANTONIO.
O, 'twas a din to fright a monster's ear,
To make an earthquake! Sure it was the roar
Of a whole herd of lions.   310

---

283 *tell the clock:* answer appropriately.   290 *fall it:* let it fall.   304 *securing:* keeping watch over.

ALONSO.   Heard you this, Gonzalo?

GONZALO.

    Upon mine honor, sir, I heard a humming,

    And that a strange one too, which did awake me.

    I shaked you, sir, and cried. As mine eyes opened,

    I saw their weapons drawn. There was a noise,

    That's verily. 'Tis best we stand upon our guard,   315

    Or that we quit this place. Let's draw our weapons.

ALONSO.

    Lead off this ground, and let's make further search

    For my poor son.

GONZALO.   Heavens keep him from these beasts!

    For he is sure i' th' island.

ALONSO.   Lead away.

ARIEL.

    Prospero my lord shall know what I have done.   320

    So, King, go safely on to seek thy son.   *Exeunt.*

Scene 2

Enter Caliban with a burden of wood. A noise of thunder heard.

CALIBAN.

    All the infections that the sun sucks up

    From bogs, fens, flats, on Prosper fall, and make him

    By inchmeal° a disease! His spirits hear me,

    And yet I needs must curse. But they'll nor° pinch,

    Fright me with urchin-shows,° pitch me i' th' mire,   5

    Nor lead me, like a firebrand,° in the dark

    Out of my way, unless he bid 'em; but

    For every trifle are they set upon me;

    Sometime like apes that mow° and chatter at me,

    And after bite me; then like hedgehogs which   10

    Lie tumbling in my barefoot way and mount

    Their pricks at my footfall; sometime am I

    All wound with adders, who with cloven tongues

    Do hiss me into madness.

    Enter Trinculo.   Lo, now, lo!

    Here comes a spirit of his, and to torment me   15

    For bringing wood in slowly. I'll fall flat.

    Perchance he will not mind me.

    Lies down.

TRINCULO. Here's neither bush nor shrub to bear off° any

    weather at all, and another storm brewing: I hear it sing

---

SCENE 2. A place near Prospero's cell.   **3** *By inchmeal:* inch by inch.   **4** *nor:* neither.   **5** *urchin-shows:* apparitions in the form of hedgehogs.   **6** *like a firebrand:* in the form of a will-o'-the-wisp.   **9** *mow:* make faces.   **18** *bear off:* ward off.

i' th' wind. Yond same black cloud, yond huge one, 20
looks like a foul bombard° that would shed his° liquor.
If it should thunder as it did before, I know not where
to hide my head. Yond same cloud cannot choose but
fall by pailfuls. What have we here? a man or a fish?
dead or alive? A fish: he smells like a fish; a very ancient 25
and fishlike smell; a kind of not of the newest poor-John.°
A strange fish! Were I in England now, as once I was,
and had but this fish painted,° not a holiday fool there but
would give a piece of silver. There would this monster
make a man:° any strange beast there makes a man. When 30
they will not give a doit° to relieve a lame beggar, they
will lay out ten to see a dead Indian. Legged like a man!
and his fins like arms! Warm, o' my troth! I do now let
loose my opinion, hold it no longer: this is no fish, but
an islander, that hath lately suffered by a thunderbolt. 35
[*Thunder.*] Alas, the storm is come again! My best way
is to creep under his gaberdine°: there is no other shelter
hereabout. Misery acquaints a man with strange bed-
fellows. I will here shroud till the dregs of the storm be
past. 40

Creeps under Caliban's garment.
Enter Stephano, singing [with a bottle in his hand].

STEPHANO.   I shall no more to sea, to sea;
                    Here shall I die ashore.
This is a very scurvy tune to sing at a man's funeral.
Well, here's my comfort.

Drinks.

The master, the swabber, the boatswain, and I, 45
    The gunner, and his mate,
Loved Mall, Meg, and Marian, and Margery,
    But none of us cared for Kate.
    For she had a tongue with a tang,
    Would cry to a sailor 'Go hang!' 50
She loved not the savor of tar nor of pitch;
Yet a tailor might scratch her where'er she did itch.
    Then to sea, boys, and let her go hang!

This is a scurvy tune too; but here's my comfort.

Drinks.
55
CALIBAN. Do not torment me! O!
STEPHANO. What's the matter? Have we devils here? Do
    you put tricks upon's with savages and men of Inde, ha?

---

21 *bombard:* leather bottle; *his:* its.   26 *poor-John:* dried hake.   28 *painted:* i.e. as on a signboard
outside a booth at a fair.   30 *make a man:* also with a sense of "make a man's Fortune."   31 *doit:* small
coin.   37 *gaberdine:* cloak.

I have not scaped drowning to be afeard now of your
four legs; for it hath been said, 'As proper a man as ever
went on four legs cannot make him give ground'; and   60
it shall be said so again, while Stephano breathes at
nostrils.

CALIBAN. The spirit torments me. O!

STEPHANO. This is some monster of the isle, with four
legs, who hath got, as I take it, an ague. Where the devil   65
should he learn our language? I will give him some
relief, if it be but for that. If I can recover him, and keep
him tame, and get to Naples with him, he's a present
for any emperor that ever trod on neat's leather.°

CALIBAN. Do not torment me, prithee; I'll bring my   70
wood home faster.

STEPHANO. He's in his fit now and does not talk after the
wisest. He shall taste of my bottle: if he have never
drunk wine afore, it will go near to remove his fit. If I
can recover him and keep him tame, I will not take too   75
much° for him; he shall pay for him that hath him, and
that soundly.

CALIBAN.
Thou dost me yet but little hurt.
Thou wilt anon;° I know it by thy trembling.
Now Prosper works upon thee.   80

STEPHANO. Come on your ways: open your mouth: here
is that which will give language to you, cat.° Open your
mouth. This will shake your shaking, I can tell you, and
that soundly. [Gives Caliban drink.] You cannot tell
who's your friend. Open your chaps° again.   85

TRINCULO. I should know that voice. It should be—but
he is drowned; and these are devils. O, defend me!

STEPHANO. Four legs and two voices—a most delicate
monster! His forward voice now is to speak well of his
friend; his backward voice is to utter foul speeches and   90
to detract. If all the wine in my bottle will recover him,
I will help his ague. Come! [Gives drink.] Amen! I will
pour some in thy other mouth.

TRINCULO. Stephano!

STEPHANO. Doth thy other mouth call me? Mercy,   95
mercy! This is a devil, and no monster. I will leave
him; I have no long spoon.°

TRINCULO. Stephano! If thou beest Stephano, touch me
and speak to me; for I am Trinculo—be not afeard—thy
good friend Trinculo.   100

---

69 *neat's leather*: cowhide.   75–76 *not take too much*: i.e. take all I can get.   79 *anon*: soon.   82 *cat*:
(alluding to the proverb 'Liquor will make a cat talk').   85 *chaps*: jaws.   97 *spoon*: (alluding to the
proverb 'He who sups with the devil must have a long spoon').

STEPHANO. If thou beest Trinculo, come forth. I'll pull
thee by the lesser legs. If any be Trinculo's legs, these
are they. [*Draws him out from under Caliban's garment.*]
Thou art very Trinculo indeed: how cam'st thou to be
the siege° of this mooncalf?° Can he vent Trinculos?   105
TRINCULO. I took him to be killed with a thunder-stroke.
But art thou not drowned, Stephano? I hope now thou
art not drowned. Is the storm overblown? I hid me
under the dead mooncalf's gaberdine for fear of the
storm. And art thou living, Stephano? O Stephano,   110
two Neapolitans scaped?
STEPHANO. Prithee do not turn me about: my stomach is
not constant.
CALIBAN. [*aside*]
These be fine things, an if° they be not sprites.
That's a brave god and bears celestial liquor.   115
I will kneel to him.
STEPHANO. How didst thou scape? How cam'st thou
hither? Swear by this bottle how thou cam'st hither. I
escaped upon a butt of sack which the sailors heaved
o'erboard, by this bottle, which I made of the bark of a   120
tree with mine own hands since I was cast ashore.
CALIBAN. I'll swear upon that bottle to be thy true sub-
ject, for the liquor is not earthly.
STEPHANO. Here! Swear then how thou escapedst.
TRINCULO. Swum ashore, man, like a duck. I can swim   125
like a duck, I'll be sworn.
STEPHANO. Here, kiss the book.° [*Gives him drink.*] Though
thou canst swim like a duck, thou art made like a goose.°
TRINCULO. O Stephano, hast any more of this?
STEPHANO. The whole butt, man: my cellar is in a rock   130
by th' seaside, where my wine is hid. How now, moon-
calf? How does thine ague?
CALIBAN. Hast thou not dropped from heaven?
STEPHANO. Out o' th' moon, I do assure thee. I was the
Man i' th' Moon when time was.°   135
CALIBAN.
I have seen thee in her, and I do adore thee.
My mistress showed me thee, and thy dog, and thy bush.
STEPHANO. Come, swear to that; kiss the book. I will
furnish it anon with new contents. Swear.

Caliban drinks.

TRINCULO. By this good light, this is a very shallow mon-   140
ster! I afeard of him? A very weak monster! The Man

---

105 *siege:* excrement; *mooncalf:* monstrosity.   114 *an if:* if.   127 *book:* i.e., bottle.   128 *like a goose:*
i.e., with a long neck.   135 *when time was:* once upon a time.

i' th' Moon? A most poor credulous monster!—Well
drawn, monster, in good sooth!

CALIBAN.
I'll show thee every fertile inch o' th' island;
And I will kiss thy foot. I prithee be my god.   145

TRINCULO. By this light, a most perfidious and drunken
monster! When's god's asleep, he'll rob his bottle.

CALIBAN.
I'll kiss thy foot. I'll swear myself thy subject.

STEPHANO. Come on then. Down, and swear!

TRINCULO. I shall laugh myself to death at this puppy-   150
headed monster. A most scurvy monster! I could find
in my heart to beat him—

STEPHANO. Come, kiss.

TRINCULO. But that the poor monster 's in drink. An
abominable monster!   155

CALIBAN.
I'll show thee the best springs; I'll pluck thee berries;
I'll fish for thee, and get thee wood enough.
A plague upon the tyrant that I serve!
I'll bear him no more sticks, but follow thee,
Thou wondrous man.   160

TRINCULO. A most ridiculous monster, to make a wonder
of a poor drunkard!

CALIBAN.
I prithee let me bring thee where crabs° grow;
And I with my long nails will dig thee pignuts,°
Show thee a jay's nest, and instruct thee how   165
To snare the nimble marmoset; I'll bring thee
To clust'ring filberts, and sometimes I'll get thee
Young scamels° from the rock. Wilt thou go with me?

STEPHANO. I prithee now, lead the way without any more
talking. Trinculo, the King and all our company else   170
being drowned, we will inherit° here. Here, bear my
bottle. Fellow Trinculo, we'll fill him by and by° again.

Caliban sings drunkenly.

CALIBAN. Farewell, master; farewell, farewell!

TRINCULO. A howling monster! a drunken monster!

CALIBAN.
No more dams I'll make for fish,   175
Nor fetch in firing
At requiring,
Nor scrape trenchering,° nor wash dish.

---

163 *crabs:* crab apples.   164 *pignuts:* peanuts.   168 *scamels:* (unexplained, but clearly either a
shellfish or a rock-nesting bird; perhaps a misprint for 'seamels,' sea mews).   171 *inherit:* take possession.
172 *by and by:* soon.   178 *trenchering:* trenchers, wooden plates.

'Ban, 'Ban, Ca—Caliban
          Has a new master: get a new man.   180
    Freedom, high-day! high-day, freedom! freedom, high-
    day, freedom!
STEPHANO. O brave monster! lead the way.   *Exeunt.*

ACT III
Scene 1

    Enter Ferdinand, bearing a log.

FERDINAND. There be some sports are painful,° and their labor
          Delight in them sets off;° some kinds of baseness
          Are nobly undergone, and most poor matters°
          Point to rich ends. This my mean task
          Would be as heavy to me as odious, but   5
          The mistress which I serve quickens° what's dead
          And makes my labors pleasures. O, she is
          Ten times more gentle than her father's crabbèd;
          And he's composed of harshness! I must remove
          Some thousands of these logs and pile them up,   10
          Upon a sore injunction.° My sweet mistress
          Weeps when she sees me work, and says such baseness
          Had never like executor. I forget;
          But these sweet thoughts do even refresh my labors
          Most busy least,° when I do it.   15

    Enter Miranda; and Prospero [behind, unseen].

MIRANDA.   Alas, now pray you
          Work not so hard! I would the lightning had
          Burnt up those logs that you are enjoined to pile!
          Pray set it down and rest you. When this burns,
          'Twill weep° for having wearied you. My father
          Is hard at study: pray now rest yourself.   20
          He's safe for these three hours.
FERDINAND.   O most dear mistress,
          The sun will set before I shall discharge
          What I must strive to do.
MIRANDA.   If you'll sit down,
          I'll bear your logs the while. Pray give me that:
          I'll carry it to the pile.   25
FERDINAND.   No, precious creature:
          I had rather crack my sinews, break my back,
          Than you should such dishonor undergo

    SCENE 1. Before Prospero's cell.   1 *painful:* strenuous.   2 *sets off:* makes greater by contrast.   3 *mat-*
ters: affairs.   6 *quicken:* brings to life.   11 *sore injunction:* grievous command.   15 *least:* i.e. least conscious
of being busy (F reads 'lest').   19 *weep:* i.e. exude resin.

While I sit lazy by.

MIRANDA.   It would become me
As well as it does you; and I should do it
With much more ease; for my good will is to it,   30
And yours it is against.

PROSPERO. [aside]   Poor worm, thou art infected!
This visitation° shows it.

MIRANDA.   You look wearily.

FERDINAND.
No, noble mistress: 'tis fresh morning with me
When you are by at night. I do beseech you,
Chiefly that I might set it in my prayers,   35
What is your name?

MIRANDA.   Miranda. O my father,
I have broke your hest° to say so!

FERDINAND.   Admired Miranda!
Indeed the top of admiration,° worth
What's dearest to the world! Full many a lady
I have eyed with best regard,° and many a time   40
Th' harmony of their tongues hath into bondage
Brought my too diligent ear; for several° virtues
Have I liked several women; never any
With so full soul° but some defect in her
Did quarrel with the noblest grace she owed,°   45
And put it to the foil.° But you, O you,
So perfect and so peerless, are created
Of every creature's best.

MIRANDA.   I do not know
One of my sex; no woman's face remember,
Save, from my glass, mine own; nor have I seen   50
More that I may call men than you, good friend,
And my dear father. How features are abroad°
I am skilless° of; but, by my modesty
(The jewel in my dower), I would not wish
Any companion in the world but you;   55
Nor can imagination form a shape,
Besides yourself, to like of.° But I prattle
Something too wildly, and my father's precepts
I therein do forget.

FERDINAND.   I am, in my condition,°
A prince, Miranda; I do think a king   60
(I would not so), and would no more endure

---

32 *visitation:* (1) visit, (2) attack of plague (in the metaphor of *infected*).   37 *hest:* command.   38 *admiration:* wonder, astonishment (the name Miranda means wonderful woman; cf. I, ii, 427).   40 *best regard:* highest approval.   42 *several:* different.   44 *With . . . soul:* i.e. so wholeheartedly.   45 *owed:* owned.   46 *foil:* (1) overthrow, (2) contrast.   52 *abroad:* elsewhere.   53 *skilless:* ignorant.   57 *like of:* compare to.   59 *condition:* situation in the world.

This wooden slavery than to suffer
The fleshfly blow my mouth. Hear my soul speak!
The very instant that I saw you, did
My heart fly to your service; there resides,   65
To make me slave to it; and for your sake
Am I this patient log-man.

MIRANDA.   Do you love me?

FERDINAND.
O heaven, O earth, bear witness to this sound,
And crown what I profess with kind event°
If I speak true! if hollowly, invert   70
What best is boded me to mischief! I,
Beyond all limit of what else i' th' world,
Do love, prize, honor you.

MIRANDA.   I am a fool
To weep at what I am glad of.

PROSPERO. [aside]   Fair encounter
Of two most rare affections! Heavens rain grace   75
On that which breeds between 'em!

FERDINAND.   Wherefore weep you?

MIRANDA.
At mine unworthiness, that dare not offer
What I desire to give, and much less take
What I shall die to want.° But this is trifling;
And all the more it seeks to hide itself,   80
The bigger bulk it shows. Hence, bashful cunning,°
And prompt me, plain and holy innocence!
I am your wife, if you will marry me;
If not, I'll die your maid. To be your fellow°
You may deny me; but I'll be your servant,   85
Whether you will or no.

FERDINAND.   My mistress, dearest,
And I thus humble ever.

MIRANDA.   My husband then?

FERDINAND.
Ay, with a heart as willing
As bondage e'er of freedom.° Here's my hand.

MIRANDA.
And mine, with my heart in't; and now farewell
Till half an hour hence.   90

FERDINAND.   A thousand thousand!

Exeunt [Ferdinand and Miranda severally].

---

69 *kind event*: favorable outcome.   79 *want*: lack.   81 *bashful cunning*: i.e. coyness.   84 *fellow*:
equal.   89 *of freedom*: i.e. to win freedom.

PROSPERO.

    So glad of this as they I cannot be,

    Who are surprised withal°; but my rejoicing

    At nothing can be more. I'll to my book;

    For yet ere supper time must I perform   95

    Much business appertaining.°

Exit.

Scene 2

Enter Caliban, Stephano, and Trinculo.

STEPHANO. Tell not me! When the butt is out, we will

    drink water; not a drop before. Therefore bear up and

    board 'em!° Servant monster, drink to me.

TRINCULO. Servant monster? The folly of this island!

    They say there's but five upon this isle: we are three of   5

    them. If th' other two be brained like us, the state

    totters.

STEPHANO. Drink, servant monster, when I bid thee:

    thy eyes are almost set in thy head.

TRINCULO. Where should they be set else? He were a

    brave monster indeed if they were set in his tail.   10

STEPHANO. My man-monster hath drowned his tongue

    in sack. For my part, the sea cannot drown me. I swam,

    ere I could recover° the shore, five-and-thirty leagues off

    and on, by this light. Thou shalt be my lieutenant,

    monster, or my standard.°   15

TRINCULO. Your lieutenant, if you list; he's no standard.°

STEPHANO. We'll not run,° Monsieur Monster.

TRINCULO. Nor go° neither; but you'll lie° like dogs, and

    yet say nothing neither.

STEPHANO. Mooncalf, speak once in thy life, if thou beest   20

    a good mooncalf.

CALIBAN.

    How does thy honor? Let me lick thy shoe.

    I'll not serve him; he is not valiant.

TRINCULO. Thou liest, most ignorant monster: I am in

    case° to justle a constable. Why, thou deboshed° fish thou,   25

    was there ever man a coward that hath drunk so much

    sack as I to-day? Wilt thou tell a monstrous lie, being

    but half a fish and half a monster?

---

93 *surprised withal:* taken unaware by it.   96 *appertaining:* relevant.   SCENE 2. Another part of the island.   2–3 *bear . . . 'em:* i.e. drink up (Caliban has almost 'passed out').   13 *recover:* reach.   15 *standard:* ensign.   16 *no standard:* i.e. incapable of standing up.   17, 18 *run, lie:* (secondary meanings of) make water and excrete.   18 *go:* walk.   25 *case:* fit condition; *deboshed:* debauched.

CALIBAN. Lo, how he mocks me! Wilt thou let him, my
    lord? 30
TRINCULO. 'Lord' quoth he? That a monster should be
    such a natural!°
CALIBAN.
    Lo, lo, again! Bite him to death, I prithee.
STEPHANO. Trinculo, keep a good tongue in your head. If
    you prove a mutineer—the next tree! The poor mon- 35
    ster's my subject, and he shall not suffer indignity.
CALIBAN.
    I thank my noble lord. Wilt thou be pleased
    To hearken once again to the suit I made to thee?
STEPHANO. Marry, will I. Kneel and repeat it; I will
    stand, and so shall Trinculo. 40

    Enter Ariel, invisible.°

CALIBAN.
    As I told thee before, I am subject to a tyrant,
    A sorcerer, that by his cunning hath
    Cheated me of the island.
ARIEL.   Thou liest.
CALIBAN.
    Thou liest, thou jesting monkey thou!
    I would my valiant master would destroy thee. 45
    I do not lie.
STEPHANO. Trinculo, if you trouble him any more in's
    tale, by this hand, I will supplant some of your teeth.
TRINCULO. Why, I said nothing.
STEPHANO. Mum then, and no more.—Proceed. 50
CALIBAN.
    I say by sorcery he got this isle;
    From me he got it. If thy greatness will
    Revenge it on him—for I know thou dar'st,
    But this thing° dare not—
STEPHANO. That's most certain. 55
CALIBAN.
    Thou shalt be lord of it, and I'll serve thee.
STEPHANO.
    How now shall this be compassed?
    Canst thou bring me to the party?°
CALIBAN.
    Yea, yea, my lord! I'll yield him thee asleep,
    Where thou mayst knock a nail into his head. 60
ARIEL. Thou liest; thou canst not.

---

    32 *natural:* fool.   40 s.d. *invisible:* ('a robe for to go invisible' is listed in an Elizabethan stage ac-
count).   54 *this thing:* i.e., himself (or perhaps Trinculo).   58 *party:* person.

CALIBAN.
    What a pied ninny's° this! Thou scurvy patch!°
    I do beseech thy greatness give him blows
    And take his bottle from him. When that's gone,
    He shall drink naught but brine, for I'll not show him   65
    Where the quick freshes° are.
STEPHANO. Trinculo, run into no further danger: inter-
    rupt the monster one word further and, by this hand, I'll
    turn my mercy out o' doors and make a stockfish° of thee.
TRINCULO. Why, what did I? I did nothing. I'll go   70
    farther off.
STEPHANO. Didst thou not say he lied?
ARIEL. Thou liest.
STEPHANO. Do I so? Take thou that! [*Strikes Trinculo.*]
    As you like this, give me the lie another time.
TRINCULO. I did not give the lie. Out o' your wits, and   75
    hearing too? A pox o' your bottle! This can sack and
    drinking do. A murrain° on your monster, and the devil
    take your fingers!
CALIBAN. Ha, ha, ha!
STEPHANO. Now forward with your tale.—Prithee stand   80
    further off.
CALIBAN.
    Beat him enough. After a little time
    I'll beat him too.
STEPHANO.   Stand farther.—Come, proceed.
CALIBAN.
    Why, as I told thee, 'tis a custom with him
    I' th' afternoon to sleep; there thou mayst brain him,   85
    Having first seized his books, or with a log
    Batter his skull, or paunch° him with a stake,
    Or cut his wesand° with thy knife. Remember
    First to possess his books; for without them
    He's but a sot,° as I am, nor hath not   90
    One spirit to command. They all do hate him
    As rootedly as I. Burn but his books.
    He has brave utensils° (for so he calls them)
    Which, when he has a house, he'll deck withal.
    And that most deeply to consider is   95
    The beauty of his daughter. He himself
    Calls her a nonpareil. I never saw a woman
    But only Sycorax my dam and she;

---

    62 *pied ninny:* motley fool (Trinculo wears a jester's costume); *patch:* clown. 66 *quick freshes:* fresh-water springs. 69 *stockfish:* dried cod, prepared by beating. 77 *murrain:* cattle disease. 87 *paunch:* stab in the belly. 88 *wesand:* windpipe. 90 *sot:* fool. 93 *utensils:* furnishings.

But she as far surpasseth Sycorax
As great'st does least.   100
STEPHANO.   Is it so brave a lass?
CALIBAN.
    Ay, lord. She will become thy bed, I warrant,
    And bring thee forth brave brood.
STEPHANO. Monster, I will kill this man: his daughter
    and I will be king and queen, save our Graces! and
    Trinculo and thyself shall be viceroys. Dost thou like   105
    the plot, Trinculo?
TRINCULO. Excellent.
STEPHANO. Give my thy hand. I am sorry I beat thee; but
    while thou liv'st, keep a good tongue in thy head.
CALIBAN.
    Within this half hour will he be asleep.
    Wilt thou destroy him then?   110
STEPHANO. Ay, on mine honor.
ARIEL.
    This will I tell my master.
CALIBAN.
    Thou mak'st me merry; I am full of pleasure.
    Let us be jocund. Will you troll the catch°
    You taught me but whilere?°   115
STEPHANO. At thy request, monster, I will do reason, any
    reason. Come on, Trinculo, let us sing.

    Sings.

            Flout 'em and scout 'em
            And scout 'em and flout 'em!
            Thought is free.   120
CALIBAN.
    That's not the tune.

    Ariel plays the tune on a tabor° and pipe.

STEPHANO. What is this same?
TRINCULO. This is the tune of our catch, played by the
    picture of Nobody.°
STEPHANO. If thou beest a man, show thyself in thy like-   125
    ness. If thou beest a devil, take't as thou list.°
TRINCULO. O, forgive me my sins!
STEPHANO. He that dies pays all debts. I defy thee.
    Mercy upon us!
CALIBAN.
    Art thou afeard?   130

---

114 *troll the catch*: sing the part-song.   115 *whilere*: just now.   121 s.d. *tabor*: small drum worn at
the side.   124 *Nobody*: (referring to pictures of figures with arms and legs but no trunk, used on signs
and elsewhere).   126 *take't as thou list*: i.e. suit yourself.

STEPHANO. No, monster, not I.

CALIBAN.
    Be not afeard: the isle is full of noises,
    Sounds and sweet airs that give delight and hurt not.
    Sometimes a thousand twangling instruments
    Will hum about mine ears; and sometimes voices   135
    That, if I then had waked after long sleep,
    Will make me sleep again; and then, in dreaming,
    The clouds methought would open and show riches
    Ready to drop upon me, that, when I waked,
    I cried to dream again.   140

STEPHANO. This will prove a brave kingdom to me,
    where I shall have my music for nothing.

CALIBAN.
    When Prospero is destroyed.

STEPHANO. That shall be by and by°: I remember the story.

TRINCULO. The sound is going away: let's follow it, and   145
    after do our work.

STEPHANO. Lead, monster; we'll follow. I would I could
    see this taborer: he lays it on. Wilt come?

TRINCULO. I'll follow, Stephano.

    Exeunt.

Scene 3

    Enter Alonso, Sebastian, Antonio, Gonzalo, Adrian, Francisco, etc.

GONZALO.
    By'r Lakin,° I can go no further, sir:
    My old bones ache: here's a maze trod indeed
    Through forthrights° and meanders. By your patience,
    I needs must rest me.

ALONSO.   Old lord, I cannot blame thee,
    Who am myself attached° with weariness   5
    To th' dulling of my spirits. Sit down and rest.
    Even here I will put off my hope, and keep it
    No longer for my flatterer: he is drowned
    Whom thus we stray to find; and the sea mocks
    Our frustrate search on land. Well, let him go.   10

ANTONIO. [*aside to Sebastian*]
    I am right glad that he's so out of hope.
    Do not for one repulse forgo the purpose
    That you resolved t'effect.

SEBASTIAN. [*aside to Antonio*] The next advantage
    Will we take throughly.°

---

144 *by and by*: right away.   SCENE 3. Another part of the island.   1 *By'r Lakin*: by our Ladykin (Virgin Mary).   3 *forthrights*: straight paths.   5 *attached*: seized.   14 *throughly*: thoroughly.

ANTONIO. [*aside to Sebastian*] Let it be to-night;
    For, now they are oppressed with travel, they 15
    Will not nor cannot use such vigilance
    As when they are fresh.
SEBASTIAN. [*aside to Antonio*] I say to-night. No more.

Solemn and strange music; and Prospero on the top° [*invisible*]. *Enter several*
strange Shapes, bringing in a banquet; and dance about it with gentle actions of
salutations; and, inviting the King etc. to eat, they depart.

ALONSO.
    What harmony is this? My good friends, hark!
GONZALO.
    Marvellous sweet music!
ALONSO.
    Give us kind keepers,° heavens! What were these? 20
SEBASTIAN.
    A living drollery.° Now I will believe
    That there are unicorns; that in Arabia
    There is one tree, the phoenix' throne; one phoenix
    At this hour reigning there.
ANTONIO.   I'll believe both;
    And what does else want credit,° come to me, 25
    And I'll be sworn 'tis true. Travellers ne'er did lie,
    Though fools at home condemn 'em.
GONZALO.   If in Naples
    I should report this now, would they believe me
    If I should say I saw such islanders?
    (For certes these are people of the island) 30
    Who, though they are of monstrous shape, yet note,
    Their manners are more gentle, kind, than of
    Our human generation you shall find
    Many—nay, almost any.
PROSPERO. [*aside*]   Honest lord,
    Thou hast said well; for some of you there present 35
    Are worse than devils.
ALONSO.   I cannot too much muse°
    Such shapes, such gesture, and such sound, expressing
    (Although they want the use of tongue) a kind
    Of excellent dumb discourse.
PROSPERO. [*aside*]   Praise in departing.°
FRANCISCO.
    They vanished strangely.
SEBASTIAN.   No matter, since 40
    They have left their viands behind; for we have stomachs.

---

    17 s.d. *on the top:* (this may refer to an upper level of the tiring-house of the theater).   20 *kind keep-*
ers: guardian angels.   21 *living drollery:* puppet show with live figures.   25 *want credit:* lack credibility.
36 *muse:* wonder at.   39 *Praise in departing:* save your praise for the end.

Will't please you taste of what is here?

ALONSO.   Not I.

GONZALO.

Faith, sir, you need not fear. When we were boys,
Who would believe that there were mountaineers
Dewlapped° like bulls, whose throats had hanging at 'em   45
Wallets of flesh? or that there were such men
Whose heads stood in their breasts?° which now we find
Each putter-out of five for one° will bring us
Good warrant of.

ALONSO.   I will stand to, and feed;
Although my last, no matter, since I feel   50
The best is past. Brother, my lord the Duke,
Stand to, and do as we.

Thunder and lightning. Enter Ariel, like a harpy; claps his wings upon the table;
and with a quaint° device the banquet vanishes.

ARIEL.

You are three men of sin, whom destiny—
That hath to° instrument this lower world
And what is in't—the never-surfeited sea   55
Hath caused to belch up you, and on this island,
Where man doth not inhabit, you 'mongst men
Being most unfit to live, I have made you mad;
And even with such-like valor men hang and drown
Their proper selves.

Alonso, Sebastian, etc. draw their swords.

                        You fools: I and my fellows   60
Are ministers of Fate. The elements,
Of whom your swords are tempered, may as well
Wound the loud winds, or with bemocked-at stabs
Kill the still°-closing waters, as diminish
One dowle° that's in my plume. My fellow ministers   65
Are like° invulnerable. If you could hurt,
Your swords are now too massy° for your strengths
And will not be uplifted. But remember
(For that's my business to you) that you three
From Milan did supplant good Prospero;   70
Exposed unto the sea, which hath requit° it,°
Him and his innocent child; for which foul deed
The pow'rs, delaying, not forgetting, have

---

45 *Dewlapped:* with skin hanging from the neck (like the goitrous Swiss *mountaineers*).   47 *in their breasts:* (an ancient travellers' tale; cf. *Othello:* I, iii, 144–145).   48 *putter-out . . . one:* traveller depositing a sum for insurance in London, to be repaid fivefold if he returned safely and proved he had gone to his destination.   52 s.d. *quaint:* ingenious.   54 *to:* i.e., as its.   64 *still:* constantly.   65 *dowle:* fiber of feather-down.   66 *like:* also.   67 *massy:* massive.   71 *requit:* avenged; *it:* i.e., the usurpation.

Incensed the seas and shores, yea, all the creatures,
Against your peace. Thee of thy son, Alonso,   75
They have bereft; and do pronounce by me
Ling'ring perdition° (worse than any death
Can be at once) shall step by step attend
You and your ways; whose wraths to guard you from,
Which here, in this most desolate isle, else falls   80
Upon your heads, is nothing but heart's sorrow°
And a clear° life ensuing.

*He vanishes in thunder; then, to soft music, enter the Shapes again, and dance with
mocks and mows,° and carrying out the table.*

PROSPERO.
    Bravely the figure of this harpy hast thou
Performed, my Ariel; a grace it had, devouring.°
Of my instruction hast thou nothing bated°   85
In what thou hadst to say. So, with good life°
And observation strange,° my meaner ministers
Their several kinds° have done. My high charms work,
and these, mine enemies, are all knit up
In their distractions: they now are in my pow'r;   90
And in these fits I leave them, while I visit
Young Ferdinand, whom they suppose is drowned,
And his and mine loved darling.

    Exit above.

GONZALO.
    I' th' name of something holy, sir, why° stand you
In this strange stare?
ALONSO.   O, it° is monstrous, monstrous!   95
Methought the billows spoke and told me of it;
The winds did sing it to me; and the thunder,
That deep and dreadful organ pipe, pronounced
The name of Prosper; it did bass° my trespass.
Therefore My son i' th' ooze is bedded; and   100
I'll seek him deeper than e'er plummet sounded
And with him there lie mudded.

                                Exit.

SEBASTIAN.   But one fiend at a time,
    I'll fight their legions o'er!
ANTONIO.   I'll be thy second.

---

    77 *perdition:* ruin.   81 *heart's sorrow:* repentance.   82 *clear:* innocent; s.d. *mocks and mows:* gri-
maces and gestures.   84 *devouring:* i.e., making the banquet disappear.   85 *bated:* omitted.   86 *good life:*
realistic acting.   87 *observation strange:* wonderfully close attention.   88 *several kinds:* separate parts.
94 *why:* (Gonzalo has not heard Ariel's speech).   95 *it:* i.e., my sin.   99 *bass:* proclaim in deep tones
(literally, provide the bass part for).

Exeunt Sebastian and Antonio.

GONZALO.
    All three of them are desperate: their great guilt,
    Like poison given to work a great time after,   105
    Now gins to bite the spirits. I do beseech you,
    That are of suppler joints, follow them swiftly
    And hinder them from what this ecstasy°
    May now provoke them to.
ADRIAN.   Follow, I pray you.

                              Exeunt omnes.

ACT IV
Scene 1

Enter Prospero, Ferdinand, and Miranda.

PROSPERO.
    If I have too austerely punished you,
    Your compensation makes amends; for I
    Have given you here a third° of mine own life,
    Or that for which I live; who once again
    I tender to thy hand. All thy vexations   5
    Were but my trials of thy love, and thou
    Hast strangely° stood the test. Here, afore heaven,
    I ratify this my rich gift. O Ferdinand,
    Do not smile at me that I boast her off,°
    For thou shalt find she will outstrip all praise   10
    And make it halt° behind her.
FERDINAND.   I do believe it
    Against an oracle.°
PROSPERO.
    Then as my gift, and thine own acquisition
    Worthily purchased, take my daughter. But
    If thou dost break her virgin-knot before   15
    All sanctimonious° ceremonies may
    With full and holy rite be minist'red,
    No sweet aspersion° shall the heavens let fall
    To make this contract grow;° but barren hate,
    Sour-eyed disdain, and discord shall bestrew   20
    The union of your bed with weeds so loathly
    That you shall hate it both. Therefore take heed,
    As Hymen's lamp shall light you.

---

108 *ecstasy:* madness. SCENE 1. Before Prospero's cell. 3 *third:* (Prospero's love, his knowledge and his power being the other two-thirds?). 7 *strangely:* in a rare fashion. 9 *boast her off:* boast about her. 11 *halt:* limp. 12 *Against an oracle:* even if an oracle denied it. 16 *sanctimonious:* holy. 18 *aspersion:* blessing, like rain on crops. 19 *grow:* become fruitful.

FERDINAND.   As I hope
    For quiet days, fair issue, and long life,
    With such love as 'tis now, the murkiest den,   25
    The most opportune° place, the strong'st suggestion
    Our worser genius can,° shall never melt
    Mine honor into lust, to take away
    The edge of that day's celebration
    When I shall think or Phoebus' steeds are foundered°   30
    Or Night kept chained below.
PROSPERO.   Fairly spoke.
    Sit then and talk with her; she is thine own.
    What, Ariel! My industrious servant, Ariel!

    Enter Ariel.

ARIEL.
    What would my potent master? Here I am.
PROSPERO.
    Thou and thy meaner fellows your last service   35
    Did worthily perform; and I must use you
    In such another trick. Go bring the rabble,°
    O'er whom I give thee pow'r, here to this place.
    Incite them to quick motion; for I must
    Bestow upon the eyes of this young couple   40
    Some vanity° of mine art; it is my promise,
    And they expect it from me.
ARIEL.   Presently?
PROSPERO.
    Ay, with a twink.
ARIEL.
    Before you can say 'Come' and 'Go,'
    And breathe twice and cry, 'So, so,'   45
    Each one, tripping on his toe,
    Will be here with mop and mow.°
    Do you love me, master? No?
PROSPERO.
    Dearly, my delicate Ariel. Do not approach
    Till thou dost hear me call.
ARIEL.   Well: I conceive.°   50

                                Exit.

PROSPERO.
    Look thou be true°: do not give dalliance
    Too much the rein: the strongest oaths are straw
    To th' fire i' th' blood. Be more abstemious,

---

    26 *opportune:* (accent second syllable).   27 *worser genius can:* bad angel can make.   30
or . . . foundered: either the sun-god's horses are lame.   37 *rabble:* rank and file.   41 *vanity:* show.   47 *mop
and mow:* antics and gestures.   50 *conceive:* understand.   51 *be true:* (Prospero appears to have caught the
lovers in an embrace).

Or else good night your vow!

FERDINAND.   I warrant you, sir.
The white cold virgin snow upon my heart   55
Abates the ardor of my liver.°

PROSPERO.   Well.
Now come, my Ariel: bring a corollary°
Rather than want° a spirit. Appear, and pertly!°
No tongue! All eyes! Be silent.

Soft music. Enter Iris.

IRIS.°
Ceres, most bounteous lady, thy rich leas   60
Of wheat, rye, barley, fetches,° oats, and pease;
Thy turfy mountains, where live nibbling sheep,
And flat meads thatched with stover,° them to keep;
Thy banks with pionèd and twillèd° brims,
Which spongy April at thy hest betrims   65
To make cold nymphs chaste crowns; and thy broom groves,°
Whose shadow the dismissèd bachelor loves,
Being lasslorn; thy pole-clipt° vineyard;°
And thy sea-marge,° sterile and rocky-hard,
Where thou thyself dost air—the queen° o' th' sky,   70
Whose wat'ry arch and messenger am I,
Bids thee leave these, and with her sovereign grace,
Here on this grass-plot, in this very place,°
To come and sport: her peacocks° fly amain.
Approach, rich Ceres, her to entertain.   75

Enter Ceres.

CERES.
Hail, many-colorèd messenger, that ne'er
Dost disobey the wife of Jupiter,
Who, with thy saffron wings, upon my flow'rs
Diffusest honey drops, refreshing show'rs,
And with each end of thy blue bow dost crown
My bosky° acres and my unshrubbed down,   80
Rich scarf to my proud earth—why hath thy queen
Summoned me hither to this short-grassed green?

IRIS.
A contract of true love to celebrate
And some donation freely to estate°   85
On the blessed lovers.

---

56 *liver:* (supposed seat of sexual passion).   57 *corollary:* surplus.   58 *want:* lack; *pertly:* briskly.
60 *Iris:* goddess of the rainbow and female messenger of the gods.   61 *fetches:* vetch.   63 *stover:* winter
food for stock.   64 *pionèd and twillèd:* dug under by the current and protected by woven layers of branches
(sometimes emended to 'peonied and lilied').   66 *broom groves:* clumps of gorse.   68 *pole-clipt:* pruned;
vineyard: (probably a trisyllable).   69 *sea-marge:* shore.   70 *queen:* i.e. Juno.   73 *Here . . . place:* (in F
a stage direction at this point reads 'Juno descends').   74 *peacocks:* (these were sacred to Juno, as doves
were to Venus [l. 94], and drew her chariot).   81 *bosky:* wooded.   85 *estate:* bestow.

CERES.   Tell me, heavenly bow,
  If Venus or her son,° as thou dost know,
  Do now attend the queen? Since they did plot
  The means° that dusky Dis my daughter got,
  Her and her blind boy's scandalled° company   90
  I have forsworn.

IRIS.   Of her society
  Be not afraid: I met her Deity°
  Cutting the clouds towards Paphos,° and her son
  Dove-drawn with her. Here thought they to have done
  Some wanton charm upon this man and maid,   95
  Whose vows are, that no bed-right shall be paid
  Till Hymen's torch be lighted; but in vain.
  Mars's hot minion is returned again;°
  Her waspish-headed° son has broke his arrows,
  Swears he will shoot no more, but play with sparrows   100
  And be a boy right out.°

  Enter Juno.

CERES.   Highest queen of state,
  Great Juno, comes; I know her by her gait.

JUNO.
  How does my bounteous sister? Go with me
  To bless this twain, that they may prosperous be
  And honored in their issue.   105
  They sing.

JUNO.   Honor, riches, marriage blessing,
        Long continuance, and increasing,
        Hourly joys be still° upon you!
        Juno sings her blessings on you.

[CERES]   Earth's increase, foison° plenty,   110
        Barns and garners never empty,
        Vines with clust'ring bunches growing,
        Plants with goodly burden bowing;
        Spring come to you at the farthest
        In the very end of harvest.   115
        Scarcity and want shall shun you,
        Ceres' blessing so is on you.

FERDINAND.
  This is a most majestic vision, and
  Harmonious charmingly. May I be bold
  To think these spirits?   120

---

    87 *her son:* Cupid, often represented as blind or blindfolded.   89 *means:* i.e., the abduction of Proserpine, Ceres' daughter, by Pluto (Dis), god of the lower (*dusky*) world.   90 *scandalled:* disgraceful.   92 *her Deity:* i.e., her Divine Majesty.   93 *Paphos:* (in Cyprus, center of Venus' cult).   98 *Mars's . . . again:* the lustful mistress of Mars (Venus) has gone back to where she came from.   99 *waspish-headed:* spiteful and inclined to sting (with his arrows).   101 *right out:* outright.   108 *still:* constantly.   110 *foison:* abundance.

PROSPERO.   Spirits, which by mine art
    I have from their confines called to enact
    My present fancies.
FERDINAND.   Let me live here ever!
    So rare a wond'red° father and a wise
    Makes this place Paradise.

Juno and Ceres whisper, and send Iris on employment.

PROSPERO.   Sweet now, silence!
    Juno and Ceres whisper seriously.   125
    There's something else to do. Hush and be mute,
    Or else our spell is marred.
IRIS.
    You nymphs, called Naiades, of the windring° brooks,
    With your sedged crowns and ever-harmless looks,
    Leave your crisp° channels, and on this green land   130
    Answer your summons; Juno does command.
    Come, temperate nymphs, and help to celebrate
    A contract of true love: be not too late.

Enter certain Nymphs.

    You sunburned sicklemen, of August weary,
    Come hither from the furrow and be merry.   135
    Make holiday: Your rye-straw hats put on,
    And these fresh nymphs encounter every one
    In country footing.

*Enter certain Reapers, properly habited. They join with the Nymphs in a graceful
dance; towards the end whereof Prospero starts suddenly and speaks°; after which,
to a strange, hollow, and confused noise, they heavily vanish.*

PROSPERO. [aside]
    I had forgot that foul conspiracy
    Of the beast Caliban and his confederates   140
    Against my life: the minute of their plot
    Is almost come.

[To the Spirits] Well done! Avoid!° No more!

FERDINAND.
    This is strange. Your father's in some passion
    That works him strongly.
MIRANDA.   Never till this day
    Saw I him touched with anger so distempered.   145
PROSPERO.
    You do look, my son, in a moved sort,°
    As if you were dismayed: be cheerful, sir.

---

123 *wond'red*: wonderful.   128 *windring*: winding and wandering.   130 *crisp*: rippling.   138 s.d.
speaks: (thereby dissolving the scene, which depended on silence).   142 *Avoid*: be off.   146 *moved sort*:
troubled state.

Our revels° now are ended. These our actors,
As I foretold you, were all spirits and
Are melted into air, into thin air;
And, like the baseless° fabric of this vision, 150
The cloud-capped tow'rs, the gorgeous palaces,
The solemn temples, the great globe itself,
Yea, all which it inherit,° shall dissolve,
And, like this insubstantial pageant faded, 155
Leave not a rack° behind. We are such stuff
As dreams are made on,° and our little life
Is rounded with a sleep. Sir, I am vexed.
Bear with my weakness: my old brain is troubled.
Be not disturbed with my infirmity. 160
If you be pleased, retire into my cell
And there repose. A turn or two I'll walk
To still my beating mind.
FERDINAND, MIRANDA. We wish your peace.

Exit Ferdinand with Miranda.

Enter Ariel.

PROSPERO.
Come with a thought! I thank thee, Ariel. Come.
ARIEL.
Thy thoughts I cleave to. What's thy pleasure?
PROSPERO.   Spirit, 165
We must prepare to meet with Caliban.
ARIEL.
Ay, my commander: when I presented° Ceres,
I thought to have told thee of it, but I feared
Lest I might anger thee.
PROSPERO.
Say again, where didst thou leave these varlets?° 170
ARIEL.
I told you, sir, they were redhot with drinking;
So full of valor that they smote the air
For breathing in their faces, beat the ground
For kissing of their feet; yet always bending
Towards their project. Then I beat my tabor; 175
At which like unbacked° colts they pricked their ears,
Advanced° their eyelids, lifted up their noses
As they smelt music. So I charmed their ears
That calf-like they my lowing followed through
Toothed briers, sharp furzes, pricking goss,° and thorns, 180

---

148 *revels:* pageants.   151 *baseless:* insubstantial, non-material.   154 *it inherit:* occupy it.   156 *rack:*
wisp of cloud.   157 *on:* of.   167 *presented:* acted the part of (?), introduced (?).   170 *varlets:* ruffians.
176 *unbacked:* unbroken.   177 *Advanced:* lifted up.   180 *goss:* gorse.

Which ent'red their frail shins. At last I left them
I' th' filthy mantled° pool beyond your cell,
There dancing up to th' chins, that the foul lake
O'erstunk their feet.
PROSPERO.   This was well done, my bird.   185
Thy shape invisible retain thou still.
The trumpery in my house, go bring it hither
For stale° to catch these thieves.
ARIEL.   I go, I go.

                                        Exit.

PROSPERO.
A devil, a born devil, on whose nature
Nurture can never stick: on whom my pains,
Humanely taken, all, all lost, quite lost!   190
And as with age his body uglier grows,
So his mind cankers.° I will plague them all,
Even to roaring.

Enter Ariel, loaden with glistering apparel, etc.

            Come, hang them on this line.°

[*Prospero and Ariel remain, invisible.*] *Enter Caliban, Stephano, and Trinculo, all
wet.*

CALIBAN.
Pray you tread softly, that the blind mole may not
Hear a foot fall. We now are near his cell.   195
STEPHANO. Monster, your fairy, which you say is a harm-
less fairy, has done little better than played the Jack°
with us.
TRINCULO. Monster, I do smell all horse-piss, at which
my nose is in great indignation.
STEPHANO. So is mine. Do you hear, monster? If I   200
should take a displeasure against you, look you—
TRINCULO. Thou wert but a lost monster.
CALIBAN.
Good my lord, give me thy favor still.
Be patient, for the prize I'll bring thee to
Shall hoodwink° this mischance. Therefore speak softly.   205
All's hushed as midnight yet.
TRINCULO. Ay, but to lose our bottles in the pool—
STEPHANO. There is not only disgrace and dishonor in
that, monster, but an infinite loss.
TRINCULO. That's more to me than my wetting. Yet this   210
is your harmless fairy, monster.

---

182 *mantled:* scummed.   187 *stale:* decoy.   192 *cankers:* festers.   193 *line:* lime or linden-tree, or
perhaps a clothesline made of hair.   197 *Jack:* (1) knave, (2) jack-o'-lantern, will-o'-the-wisp.   205 *hood-
wink:* cover over.

STEPHANO. I will fetch off my bottle, though I be o'er
    ears for my labor.
CALIBAN.
    Prithee, my king, be quiet. Seest thou here?
    This is the mouth o' th' cell. No noise, and enter.   215
    Do that good mischief which may make this island
    Thine own for ever, and I, thy Caliban,
    For aye thy foot-licker.
STEPHANO. Give me thy hand. I do begin to have bloody
    thoughts.   220
TRINCULO. O King Stephano! O peer!° O worth Ste-
    phano, look what a wardrobe here is for thee!
CALIBAN.
    Let it alone, thou fool! It is but trash.
TRINCULO. O, ho, monster! we know what belongs to a
    frippery.° O King Stephano!   225
STEPHANO. Put off that gown, Trinculo: by this hand,
    I'll have that gown!
TRINCULO. Thy Grace shall have it.
CALIBAN.
    The dropsy drown this fool! What do you mean
    To dote thus on such luggage!° Let't alone,   230
    And do the murder first. If he awake,
    From toe to crown he'll fill our skins with pinches,
    Make us strange stuff.
STEPHANO. °Be you quiet, monster. Mistress line, is not
    this my jerkin? [*Takes it down.*] Now is the jerkin under   235
    the line. Now, jerkin, you are like to lose your hair and
    prove a bald jerkin.
TRINCULO. Do, do! We steal by line and level,° an't like°
    your Grace.
STEPHANO. I thank thee for that jest. Here's a garment   240
    for't. Wit shall not go unrewarded while I am king of
    this country. 'Steal by line and level' is an excellent pass
    of pate.° There's another garment for't.
TRINCULO. Monster, come put some lime° upon your
    fingers, and away with the rest.   245
CALIBAN.
    I will have none on't. We shall lose our time
    And all be turned to barnacles,° or to apes
    With foreheads villainous low.
STEPHANO. Monster, lay-to your fingers: help to bear

---

    221 *peer:* (referring to the song 'King Stephen was a worthy peer,' quoted in *Othello:* II, iii, 84–91).
225 *frippery:* old-clothes shop.   230 *luggage:* junk.   234 ff. (the jokes are probably obscene, but their point
is lost; sailors crossing the *line* or equator proverbially lost their hair from scurvy).   238 *by line and level:*
according to rule (with pun on *line*); *an't like:* if it please.   242–243 *pass of pate:* sally of wit.   244 *lime:*
birdlime (sticky, hence appropriate for stealing).   247 *barnacles:* geese.

this away where my hogshead of wine is, or I'll turn   250
you out of my kingdom. Go to, carry this.

TRINCULO. And this.

STEPHANO. Ay, and this.

A noise of hunters heard. Enter divers Spirits in shape of dogs and hounds, hunting
them about, Prospero and Ariel setting them on.

PROSPERO. Hey, Mountain, hey!

ARIEL. Silver! there it goes, Silver!   255

PROSPERO. Fury, Fury! There, Tyrant, there! Hark,
  hark!

Caliban, Stephano, and Trinculo are driven out.

Go, charge my goblins that they grind their joints
With dry° convulsions, shorten up their sinews
With agèd° cramps, and more pinch-spotted make them   260
Than pard or cat o' mountain.°

ARIEL.   Hark, they roar!

PROSPERO.
Let them be hunted soundly. At this hour
Lie at my mercy all mine enemies.
Shortly shall all my labors end, and thou
Shalt have the air at freedom. For a little,   265
Follow, and do me service.

                              Exeunt.

ACT V

Scene 1

Enter Prospero in his magic robes, and Ariel.

PROSPERO.
Now does my project gather to a head.
My charms crack not, my spirits obey, and time
Goes upright with his carriage.° How's the day?

ARIEL.
On the sixth hour, at which time, my lord,
You said our work should cease.

PROSPERO.   I did say so   5
When first I raised the tempest. Say, my spirit,
How fares the King and's followers?

ARIEL.   Confined together
In the same fashion as you gave in charge,
Just as you left them—all prisoners, sir,
In the line grove which weather-fends° your cell.   10

---

139 *dry:* (resulting from deficiency of 'humors' or bodily liquids).   260 *agèd:* i.e. such as old people have.   261 *pard or cat o' mountain:* leopard or catamount.   SCENE 1. Before Prospero's cell.   2–3
time . . . carriage: time's burden is light.   10 *weather-fends:* protects from the weather.

They cannot budge till your release.° The King,
His brother, and yours abide all three distracted,
And the remainder mourning over them,
Brimful of sorrow and dismay; but chiefly
Him that you termed, sir, the good old Lord Gonzalo.   15
His tears run down his beard like winter's drops
From eaves of reeds.° Your charm so strongly works 'em,
That if you now beheld them, your affections
Would become tender.

PROSPERO.   Dost thou think so, spirit?

ARIEL.
Mine would, sir, were I human.

PROSPERO.   And mine shall.   20
Hast thou, which art but air, a touch, a feeling
Of their afflictions, and shall not myself,
One of their kind, that relish° all° as sharply
Passion as they, be kindlier moved than thou art?
Though with their high wrongs I am struck to th' quick,   25
Yet with my nobler reason 'gainst my fury
Do I take part. The rarer action is
In virtue than in vengeance. They being penitent,
The sole drift of my purpose doth extend
Not a frown further. Go, release them, Ariel.   30
My charms I'll break, their senses I'll restore,
And they shall be themselves.

ARIEL.   I'll fetch them, sir.   *Exit.*

PROSPERO.
Ye elves of hills, brooks, standing lakes, and groves,
And ye that on the sands with printless foot
Do chase the ebbing Neptune, and do fly him   35
When he comes back; you demi-puppets° that
By moonshine do the green sour ringlets make,
Whereof the ewe not bites; and you whose pastime
Is to make midnight mushrumps,° that rejoice
To hear the solemn curfew; by whose aid   40
(Weak masters° though ye be) I have bedimmed
The noontide sun, called forth the mutinous winds,
And 'twixt the green sea and the azured vault
Set roaring war; to the dread rattling thunder
Have I given fire and rifted° Jove's stout oak   45
With his own bolt; the strong-based promontory
Have I made shake and by the spurs° plucked up
The pine and cedar; graves at my command

---

11 *till your release:* until you release them.   17 *eaves of reeds:* i.e., a thatched roof.   23 *relish:* feel;
all: quite.   36 *demi-puppets:* i.e., fairies.   39 *mushrumps:* mushrooms.   41 *masters:* forces.   45 *rifted:*
split.   47 *spurs:* roots.

Have waked their sleepers, oped, and let 'em forth
By my so potent art. But this rough magic   50
I here abjure; and when I have required°
Some heavenly music (which even now I do)
To work mine end upon their senses that°
This airy charm is for, I'll break my staff,
Bury it certain fathoms in the earth,   55
And deeper than did ever plummet sound
I'll drown my book.

Solemn music. Here enters Ariel before; then Alonso, with a frantic gesture,
attended by Gonzalo; Sebastian and Antonio in like manner, attended by Adrian
and Francisco. They all enter the circle which Prospero had made, and there stand
charmed; which Prospero observing, speaks.

A solemn air, and° the best comforter
To an unsettled fancy, cure thy brains,
Now useless, boiled within they skull! There stand,   60
For you are spell-stopped.
Holy Gonzalo, honorable man,
Mine eyes, ev'n sociable° to the show° of thine,
Fall° fellowly drops. The charm dissolves apace;
And as the morning steals upon the night,   65
Melting the darkness, so their rising senses
Begin to chase the ignorant fumes that mantle
Their clearer reason. O good Gonzalo,
My true preserver, and a loyal sir
To him thou follow'st, I will pay thy graces°   70
Home both in word and deed. Most cruelly
Didst thou, Alonso, use me and my daughter.
Thy brother was a furtherer in the act.
Thou art pinched for't now, Sebastian. Flesh and blood,
You, brother mine, that entertained ambition,   75
Expelled remorse° and nature°; who, with Sebastian
(Whose inward pinches therefore are most strong),
Would here have killed your king, I do forgive thee,
Unnatural though thou art. Their understanding
Begins to swell, and the approaching tide   80
Will shortly fill the reasonable shore,
That now lies foul and muddy. Not one of them
That yet looks on me or would know me. Ariel,
Fetch me the hat and rapier in my cell.
I will discase° me, and myself present   85
As I was sometime Milan.° Quickly, spirit!
Thou shalt ere long be free.

---

51 *required:* asked for.   53 *their senses that:* the senses of those whom.   58 *and:* i.e., which is.   63 *so-*
ciable: sympathetic; *show:* sight.   64 *Fall:* let fall.   70 *graces:* favors.   76 *remorse:* pity; *nature:* natural feeling.   85 *discase:* undress.   86 *sometime Milan:* when I was Duke of Milan.

Exit Ariel and returns immediately.
Ariel sings and helps to attire him.

> Where the bee sucks, there suck I;
> In a cowslip's bell I lie;
> There I couch when owls do cry.   90
> On the bat's back I do fly
> After summer merrily.

Merrily, merrily shall I live now
Under the blossom that hangs on the bough.

PROSPERO.

Why, that's my dainty Ariel! I shall miss thee,   95
But yet thou shalt have freedom; so, so, so.
To the King's ship, invisible as thou art!
There shalt thou find the mariners asleep
Under the hatches. The master and the boatswain
Being awake, enforce them to this place,   100
And presently,° I prithee.

ARIEL.

I drink the air° before me, and return
Or ere your pulse twice beat.   *Exit.*

GONZALO.

All torment, trouble, wonder, and amazement
Inhabits here. Some heavenly power guide us   105
Out of this fearful country!

PROSPERO.   Behold, sir King,
The wrongèd Duke of Milan, Prospero.
For more assurance that a living prince
Does now speak to thee, I embrace thy body,
And to thee and thy company I bid   110
A hearty welcome.

ALONSO.   Whe'r thou be'st he or no,
Or some enchanted trifle° to abuse° me,
As late I have been, I not know. Thy pulse
Beats, as of flesh and blood; and, since I saw thee,
Th' affliction of my mind amends, with which,   115
I fear, a madness held me. This must crave°
(An if this be at all)° a most strange story.
Thy dukedom I resign and do entreat
Thou pardon me my wrongs. But how should Prospero
Be living and be here?

PROSPERO.   First, noble friend,   120
Let me embrace thine age, whose honor cannot
Be measured or confined.

---

101 *presently:* right away.   102 *drink the air:* i.e. consume space.   112 *trifle:* trick; *abuse:* deceive.
116 *crave:* require.   117 *An if . . . all:* if this is really happening.

GONZALO.   Whether this be
Or be not, I'll not swear.
PROSPERO.   You do yet taste
Some subtleties° o' th' isle, that will not let you
Believe things certain. Welcome, my friends all.   125

Aside to Sebastian and Antonio.

But you, my brace of lords, were I so minded,
I here could pluck° his Highness' frown upon you,
And justify° you traitors. At this time
I will tell no tales.
SEBASTIAN. *[aside]* The devil speaks in him.
PROSPERO.   No.
For you, most wicked sir, whom to call brother   130
Would even infect my mouth, I do forgive
Thy rankest fault—all of them; and require
My dukedom of thee, which perforce I know
Thou must restore.
ALONSO.   If thou beest Prospero,
Give us particulars of thy preservation;   135
How thou hast met us here, who three hours since
Were wracked upon this shore; where I have lost
(How sharp the point of this remembrance is!)
My dear son Ferdinand.
PROSPERO.   I am woe° for't, sir.
ALONSO.
Irreparable is the loss, and patience   140
Says it is past her cure.
PROSPERO.   I rather think
You have not sought her help, of whose soft grace
For the like loss I have her sovereign aid
And rest myself content.
ALONSO.   You the like loss?
PROSPERO.
As great to me as late°; and, supportable   145
To make the dear° loss, have I means much weaker
Than you may call to comfort you; for I
Have lost my daughter.
ALONSO.   A daughter?
O heavens, that they were living both in Naples,
The King and Queen there! That they were, I wish   150
Myself were mudded in that oozy bed
Where my son lies. When did you lose your daughter?

---

124 *subtleties:* (secondary meaning of) elaborate pastries representing allegorical figures, used in
banquets and pageants.   127 *pluck:* pull down.   128 *justify:* prove.   139 *woe:* sorry.   145 *late:* recent.
146 *dear:* grievous.

PROSPERO.
 In this last tempest. I perceive these lords
 At this encounter do so much admire°
 That they devour their reason, and scarce think   155
 Their eyes do offices° of truth, their words
 Are natural breath. But, howsoev'r you have
 Been justled from your senses, know for certain
 That I am Prospero, and that very duke
 Which was thrust forth of Milan, who most strangely   160
 Upon this shore, where you were wracked, was landed
 To be the lord on't. No more yet of this;
 For 'tis a chronicle of day by day,
 Not a relation for a breakfast, nor
 Befitting this first meeting. Welcome, sir;   165
 This cell's my court. Here have I few attendants,
 And subjects none abroad. Pray you look in.
 My dukedom since you have given me again,
 I will requite you with as good a thing,
 At least bring forth a wonder to content ye   170
 As much as me my dukedom.

 Here Prospero discovers° Ferdinand and Miranda playing at chess.

MIRANDA.
 Sweet lord, you play me false.
FERDINAND.   No, my dearest love,
 I would not for the world.
MIRANDA.
 Yes, for a score of kingdoms you should wrangle,°
 And I would call it fair play.
ALONSO.   If this prove   175
 A vision of the island, one dear son
 Shall I twice lose.
SEBASTIAN.   A most high miracle!
FERDINAND.
 Though the seas threaten, they are merciful.
 I have cursed them without cause.

 Kneels.

ALONSO.   Now all the blessings
 Of a glad father compass thee about!   180
 Arise, and say how thou cam'st here.
MIRANDA.   O, wonder!
 How many goodly creatures are there here!
 How beauteous mankind is! O brave new world
 That has such people in't!

---

 154 *admire:* wonder. 156 *do offices:* perform services. 171 s.d. *discovers:* discloses. 174 *should wrangle:* i.e., playing fair, as Ferdinand is doing, is not a test of Miranda's love for him.

PROSPERO.   'Tis new to thee.

ALONSO.

    What is this maid with whom thou wast at play?   185
    Your eld'st° acquaintance cannot be three hours.
    Is she the goddess that hath severed us
    And brought us thus together?

FERDINAND.   Sir, she is mortal;

    But by immortal providence she's mine.
    I chose her when I could not ask my father   190
    For his advice, nor thought I had one. She
    Is daughter to this famous Duke of Milan,
    Of whom so often I have heard renown
    But never saw before; of whom I have
    Received a second life; and second father   195
    This lady makes him to me.

ALONSO.   I am hers.

    But, O, how oddly will it sound that I
    Must ask my child forgiveness!

PROSPERO.   There, sir, stop.

    Let us not burden our remembrance with
    A heaviness that's gone.

GONZALO.   I have inly wept,   200

    Or should have spoke ere this. Look down, you gods,
    And on this couple drop a blessèd crown!
    For it is you that have chalked forth the way
    Which brought us hither.

ALONSO.   I say amen, Gonzalo.

GONZALO.

    Was Milan thrust from Milan that his issue   205
    Should become kings of Naples? O, rejoice
    Beyond a common joy, and set it down
    With gold on lasting pillars: in one voyage
    Did Claribel her husband find at Tunis,
    And Ferdinand her brother found a wife   210
    Where he himself was lost; Prospero his dukedom
    In a poor isle; and all of us ourselves
    When no man was his own.

ALONSO. [*to Ferdinand and Miranda*]

                   Give me your hands.
    Let grief and sorrow still° embrace his heart
    That doth not wish you joy.

GONZALO.   Be it so! Amen!   215

Enter Ariel, with the Master and Boatswain amazedly following.

    O, look, sir; look, sir! Here is more of us!
    I prophesied, if a gallows were on land,

---

186 *eld'st:* i.e., longest period of.   214 *still:* forever.

This fellow could not drown. Now, blasphemy,
That swear'st grace o'erboard, not an oath on shore?
Hast thou no mouth by land? What is the news?   220
BOATSWAIN.
    The best news is that we have safely found
    Our king and company; the next, our ship,
    Which, but three glasses since, we gave out split,
    Is tight and yare° and bravely rigged as when
    We first put out to sea.
ARIEL. [aside to Prospero] Sir, all this service   225
    Have I done since I went.
PROSPERO. [aside to Ariel] My tricksy° spirit!
ALONSO.
    These are not natural events; they strengthen
    From strange to stranger. Say, how came you hither?
BOATSWAIN.
    If I did think, sir, I were well awake,
    I'ld strive to tell you. We were dead of sleep   230
    And (how we know not) all clapped under hatches;
    Where, but even now, with strange and several° noises
    Of roaring, shrieking, howling, jingling chains,
    And moe° diversity of sounds, all horrible,
    We were awaked; straightway at liberty;   235
    Where we, in all her trim,° freshly beheld
    Our royal, good, and gallant ship, our master
    Cap'ring° to eye° her. On a trice, so please you,
    Even in a dream, were we divided from them
    And were brought moping° hither.
ARIEL. [aside to Prospero]   Was't well done?   240
PROSPERO. [aside to Ariel]
    Bravely, my diligence. Thou shalt be free.
ALONSO.
    This is as strange a maze as e'er men trod,
    And there is in this business more than nature
    Was ever conduct° of. Some oracle
    Must rectify our knowledge.
PROSPERO.   Sir, my liege,   245
    Do not infest° your mind with beating on
    The strangeness of this business: at picked leisure,
    Which shall be shortly, single° I'll resolve° you
    (Which to you shall seem probable) of every°
    These happened accidents;° till when, be cheerful   250
    And think of each thing well.

---

224 *yare*: shipshape.   226 *tricksy*: i.e., ingenious.   232 *several*: various.   234 *moe*: more.   236 *trim*:
sail.   238 *Cap'ring*: dancing for joy; *eye*: see   240 *moping*: in a daze.   244 *conduct*: conductor.   246 *in-fest*: tease.   248 *single*: privately; *resolve*: explain.   249 *every*: every one of.   250 *accidents*: incidents.

[*Aside to Ariel*]   Come hither, spirit.
Set Caliban and his companions free.
Untie the spell.   *Exit Ariel.*
              How fares my gracious sir?
There are yet missing of your company
Some few odd lads that you remember not.   255

Enter Ariel, driving in Caliban, Stephano, and Trinculo, in their stolen apparel.

STEPHANO. Every man shift for all the rest, and let no
    man take care for himself; for all is but fortune.
    Coragio, bully-monster, coragio!
TRINCULO. If these be true spies° which I wear in my
    head, here's a goodly sight.   260
CALIBAN.
    O Setebos, these be brave spirits indeed!
    How fine my master is! I am afraid
    He will chastise me.
SEBASTIAN.   Ha, ha!
    What things are these, my Lord Antonio?
    Will money buy 'em?   265
ANTONIO.   Very like. One of them
    Is a plain fish and no doubt marketable.
PROSPERO.
    Mark but the badges of these men,° my lords,
    Then say if they be true.° This misshapen knave,
    His mother was a witch, and one so strong
    That could control the moon, make flows and ebbs,   270
    And deal in her° command without° her power.
    These three have robbed me, and this demi-devil
    (For he's a bastard one) had plotted with them
    To take my life. Two of these fellows you
    Must know and own; this thing of darkness I   275
    Acknowledge mine.
CALIBAN.   I shall be pinched to death.
ALONSO.
    Is not this Stephano, my drunken butler?
SEBASTIAN.
    He is drunk now: where had he wine?
ALONSO.
    And Trinculo is reeling ripe: where should they
    Find this grand liquor that hath gilded 'em?   280
    How cam'st thou in this pickle?
TRINCULO. I have been in such a pickle,° since I saw you

---

    259 *spies:* eyes.   267 *badges of these men:* signs of these servants.   268 *true:* honest.   271 *her:* i.e.,
the moon's; *without:* beyond.   282 *pickle:* (1) predicament, (2) preservative (from the horse-pond; hence
insects will let him alone).

last, that I fear me will never out of my bones. I shall not
    fear fly-blowing.
SEBASTIAN. Why, how now, Stephano?   285
STEPHANO. O, touch me not! I am not Stephano,° but a
    cramp.
PROSPERO. You'ld be king o' the isle, sirrah?
STEPHANO. I should have been a sore° one then.
ALONSO.
    This is a strange thing as e'er I looked on.   290
PROSPERO.
    He is as disproportioned in his manners
    As in his shape. Go, sirrah, to my cell;
    Take with you your companions. As you look
    To have my pardon, trim it handsomely.
CALIBAN.
    Ay, that I will; and I'll be wise hereafter,   295
    And seek for grace. What a thrice-double ass
    Was I to take this drunkard for a god
    And worship this dull fool!
PROSPERO.   Go to! Away!
ALONSO.
    Hence, and bestow your luggage where you found it.
SEBASTIAN. Or stole it rather.   300

       Exeunt Caliban, Stephano, and Trinculo.

PROSPERO.
    Sir, I invite your Highness and your train
    To my poor cell, where you shall take your rest
    For this one night; which, part of it, I'll waste°
    With such discourse as, I not doubt, shall make it
    Go quick away—the story of my life,   305
    And the particular accidents gone by
    Since I came to this isle; and in the morn
    I'll bring you to your ship, and so to Naples,
    Where I have hope to see the nuptial
    Of these our dear beloved solemnizèd;°   310
    And thence retire me to my Milan, where
    Every third thought shall be my grave.
ALONSO.   I long
    To hear the story of your life, which must
    Take° the ear strangely.
PROSPERO.   I'll deliver° all;
    And promise you calm seas, auspicious gales,   315
    And sail° so expeditious that shall catch

---

    286 *Stephano:* (this name is said to be a slang Neapolitan term for stomach).   289 *sore:* (1) tyran-
nical, (2) aching.   303 *waste:* spend.   310 *solemnizèd:* (accent second syllable).   314 *Take:* captivate;
deliver: tell.   316 *sail:* sailing.

Your royal fleet far off.—My Ariel, chick,
That is thy charge. Then to the elements
Be free, and fare thou well!—Please you draw near.

Exeunt omnes.

EPILOGUE

Spoken by Prospero.

Now my charms are all o'erthrown,
And what strength I have's mine own,
Which is most faint. Now 'tis true
I must be here confined by you,
Or sent to Naples. Let me not,   5
Since I have my dukedom got
And pardoned the deceiver, dwell
In this bare island by your spell;°
But release me from my bands°
With the help of your good hands.°   10
Gentle breath of yours my sails
Must fill, or else my project fails,
Which was to please. Now I want°
Spirits to enforce, art to enchant;
And my ending is despair   15
Unless I be relieved by prayer,
Which pierces so that it assaults
Mercy itself and frees all faults.
As you from crimes would pardoned be,
Let your indulgence set me free.   *Exit.*   20

EPILOGUE. 8 *spell*: i.e., silence.   9 *bands*: bonds.   10 *hands*: i.e., applause to break the spell.
13 *want*: lack.

QUESTIONS

1. Explain the circumstance of the shipwreck. Who has caused it, and why? How do
the reactions of the various passengers give clues about their characters and allegiances?

2. What is Prospero's situation? Characterize the relationship between father and
daughter. What is Prospero's reaction when he sees Miranda's attraction to Ferdinand?
Find the quotation that explains his desire to place obstacles in their path.

3. In what ways is Miranda innocent of the world? Do you believe that she is attracted to Ferdinand only because he is the first man that she has ever set eyes upon
(apart from her father)? What is your first sense of Ferdinand's character?

4. Contrast your impressions of Ariel and Caliban. What can they be said to represent? How do their modes of speech reflect their essential natures? Are we to see Caliban as the incarnation of evil, or merely as the hapless victim of his appetites?

5. What is Prospero's attitude to power? How was he betrayed, and by whom? Why
was he not killed by his enemies? What are Prospero's consolations? How did he come
to gain the services of Ariel? Why did he turn against Caliban?

6. What is the reader's first sense about the character of Alonso? Is there anything revealed that mitigates your attitude toward his treachery? Explain.

7. What do Antonio and Sebastian plot during Alonso's sleep? How is their plan foiled? Does this situation further change your attitudes toward Alonso?

8. What is the role of Trinculo, of Stephano? What do *they* plot? How does their conspiracy echo the earlier conspiracy involving Antonio and Alonso? How does Ariel trick Trinculo?

9. Discuss the function of Iris, Ceres, and Juno. What is the sense of their speeches? How does it relate to Prospero's acceptance of Ferdinand?

10. How does Prospero punish Caliban, Trinculo, and Stephano? Why should the punishment be so slight considering the nature of their conspiracy?

11. In Act V, Scene I, Prospero says "The rarer action is/ In virtue than in vengeance." Relate this statement to Prospero's actions in the final act of the play.

12. Why does Prospero give up his magic? Is the reader to see him the happier for having done so?

13. The final act of the play dissolves all evil in an atmosphere of lightness. Prospero says: "Let us not burden our remembrance with/ A heaviness that's gone." How does this attitude differ from that which underlies tragedies? Is there any way in which such a resolution is more profound?

14. *The Tempest* was Shakespeare's last play. What kind of parting vision does he offer his audiences?

SUGGESTIONS FOR WRITING

1. Both *Hamlet* and *The Tempest* are built around betrayals, yet the former is a tragedy, the latter a comedy. Discuss the differences. Explore the ways that Shakespeare uses character in each. How is the presentation of Hamlet's dilemma utterly unlike the presentation of Prospero's? Which character can be said to act more wisely?

2. Compare the ways that Shakespeare treats love—between Hamlet and Ophelia, and between Miranda and Ferdinand. How do these treatments exemplify the differences between the plays?

3. Pick a monologue from each play and discuss Shakespeare's distinctive ways of using language. How does each passage reflect upon the larger sense of the scene and the play?

33 French Neoclassical Drama

French Neoclassical drama (from *neo* for "new") arose in the middle of the seventeenth century during the reign of Louis XIV. Louis, also known as the "Sun King," was an absolutist monarch, and his declaration "I am the State" has come down to posterity as evidence of just how unbounded kingly ambition can be. His period of rule was characterized by the sharpest possible separation between the privileged and highly artificial lives of the nobility (the finest flower of which made up his court at the royal palace of Versailles) and the labors and sufferings of the mere mortals he ruled. It would not be until the French Revolution of 1789 that the rule of caste and class was thrown down.

For all his absolutist excesses, the "Sun King" was a generous patron of the arts, and during his reign the French stage enjoyed a period of glory that in many ways rivaled the attainments of the Elizabethan stage a half century earlier. Three of the most gifted dramatists in Europe—Pierre Corneille (1606–1684), Jean Racine (1639–1699), and Jean-Baptiste Poquelin (1622–1673), who took the stage name Molière—were all working at the peak of their powers during this time. Corneille and Racine wrote tragedies, while Molière wrote comedies. Between them they created a theater of exceptional polish and sophistication.

French Neoclassical drama can be sharply differentiated from the comedies and tragedies that Shakespeare wrote. As the word "classical" suggests, this drama returned to the principles laid down by Aristotle in his *Poetics*. The unities of time, place, and action were strictly adhered to. Plays were to represent actions taking place within a 24-hour period, to occur in a single locale, and to develop only one line of action. There was, further, absolutely no mixing of comic and tragic modes. A play like *Hamlet*, with its sprawling action, its subplots, and its mixture of tragic scenes with scenes of comic relief, would have been unthinkable on the French stage.

Along with observing these strictures—which mirrored so well the fastidious decorum of societal rituals—the playwrights downplayed the elements of spectacle in favor of poetic dialogue. As in Greek tragedy, any killings or acts of violence happened off stage. What mattered was the verbal expression—its nobility, its wit, its epigrammatical rightness. To this end, the dialogues were composed in formal *alexandrine* meter (six iambic feet—see Chapter 18), generally in paired lines, or *couplets*. As the alexandrine sounds somewhat unwieldy in English, most translations of Neoclassical plays adapt a more natural sounding *iambic pentameter* rhythm.

The Neoclassical Stage

The staging of the French Neoclassical plays was also quite different from what we find in either Greek or Elizabethan drama. Instead of the amphitheater of the classical period or the modified wooden O of Shakespeare's day, French playgoers of the seventeenth century sat in the sort of rectangular auditorium that closely resembles today's theaters. The stage itself was at one end of the hall and was clearly marked off from the rest of the room. It was what is often called a "picture-frame stage," with a *proscenium arch* clearly marking the boundary at which the world of the play began. Unlike the Elizabethan theater, the French stage made use of a curtain that rose and fell to mark the different acts of the drama. (The curtain did not fall with every scene, since in neoclassic drama a "scene" occurs whenever an actor enters or exits the stage.) The intended effect was one of intimacy; the viewer was made to feel as if he or she was looking directly into the room of some privileged members of the court. Plays, needless to say, were not about the ordinary doings of ordinary people. Ordinary people did not wear costumes so elaborate as to make movement nearly impossible.

Action, then, in tragedies as well as in comedies, was largely verbal: costume *and* custom dictated that it be so. Trained actors representing the members of the nobility traded lines—lightly or in deadly earnest—about the matters that most concerned the audience: lineage, proper codes of behavior, the lofty matters of love and friendship, and so on. Scenes of love and romance were rendered somewhat more convincing by the presence of female actors—a milestone in the staging of drama.

Neoclassical Comedy

As one might imagine, so much pomp and artificiality must have whetted the appetite of many a would-be satirist, but it was in Molière, its most sophisticated and witty chronicler, that the age found its match. Molière was the son of a furniture-maker to the king. Though well educated in philosophy and law, he turned toward the somewhat less reputable acting profession. In 1643, when he was 21, he joined a traveling troupe known as The Illustrious Theater. The troupe had its ups and downs, flirting with bankruptcy before it was eventually rescued by the patronage of Louis XIV.

Like Shakespeare, Molière learned his craft from acting. Indeed, from when he first joined the troupe until the day of his death in 1673, he acted as well as wrote. The king's recognition, which came in 1658, did, however, free Molière to explore his writing talent. In all, he wrote some 30 plays, including the celebrated *The Misanthrope* (1666), *The Miser* (1668), and *Tartuffe* (1669). In addition to writing comedies in a classical mode, Molière also achieved great popularity as an author of a number of *farces*, a less constrained form incorporating variety-show elements. For the most part, however, he is remembered for his coolly elegant yet merciless depictions of the follies and vanities of the upper classes. They were so fascinated to see their mannerisms dissected that they forgave the playwright even as they writhed in their expensive seats.

Molière (1622–1673)

Molière was the stage name of Jean-Baptiste Poquelin. As a young man, he defied his father's entreaties to join the family upholstery business and instead founded his own theater troupe. He suffered the ups and downs of the touring life for many years, experiencing bankruptcy and debtor's prison, but also honing his skills as actor and playwright. In 1658, he performed one of his comedies before Louis XIV and his court and was awarded his own theater in Paris. He became one of the greatest legends of his day, writing and acting in a wide range of modes. Indeed, he acted on the very day of his death from a lung hemorrhage.

THE MISANTHROPE°

Translated by Richard Wilbur

CHARACTERS

ALCESTE, in love with Célimène
PHILINTE, Alceste's friend
ORONTE, in love with Célimène
CÉLIMÈNE, Alceste's beloved
ELIANTE, Célimène's cousin
ARSINOÉ, friend of Célimène

ACASTE
CLITANDRE } Marquesses°
BASQUE, Célimène's servant
A GUARD OF THE MARSHALSEA°
DUBOIS, Alceste's valet

THE SCENE

The scene throughout is in Célimène's house at Paris.

ACT I

Scene 1

    Enter Philinte and Alceste.

PHILINTE. Now, what's got into you?
ALCESTE. [*seated*]   Kindly leave me alone.
PHILINTE. Come, come, what is it? This lugubrious tone . . .
ALCESTE. Leave me, I said: you spoil my solitude.
PHILINTE. Oh, listen to me, now, and don't be rude.
ALCESTE. I choose to be rude, Sir, and to be hard of hearing.   5
PHILINTE. These ugly moods of yours are not endearing;
    Friends though we are, I really must insist . . .
ALCESTE. [*abruptly rising*] Friends? Friends, you say? Well, cross me off your list.
    I've been your friend till now, as you well know;

MISANTHROPE: One who scorns fellow humans.   *Marquesses:* noblemen.   *Guards of the Marshalsea:* guards for the royal Marshall's office, responsible for order in the king's court.

But after what I saw a moment ago   10
I tell you flatly that our ways must part.
I wish no place in a dishonest heart.
PHILINTE. Why, what have I done, Alceste? Is this quite just?
ALCESTE. My God, you ought to die of self-disgust.
    I call your conduct inexcusable, Sir.   15
    And every man of honor will concur.
    I see you almost hug a man to death,
    Exclaim for joy until you're out of breath,
    And supplement these loving demonstrations
    With endless offers, vows and protestations;   20
    Then when I ask you "Who was that?" I find
    That you can barely bring his name to mind!
    Once the man's back is turned, you cease to love him,
    And speak with absolute indifference of him!
    By God, I say it's base and scandalous   25
    To falsify the heart's affections thus;
    If I caught myself behaving in such a way,
    I'd hang myself for shame, without delay.
PHILINTE. It hardly seems a hanging matter to me;
    I hope that you take it graciously   30
    If I extend myself a slight reprieve,
    And live a little longer, by your leave.
ALCESTE. How dare you joke about a crime so grave?
PHILINTE. What crime? How else are people to behave?
ALCESTE. I'd have them be sincere, and never part   35
    With any word that isn't from the heart.
PHILINTE. When someone greets us with a show of pleasure,
    It's but polite to give him equal measure,
    Return his love the best that we know how,
    And trade him offer for offer, vow for vow.   40
ALCESTE. No, no, this formula you'd have me follow,
    However fashionable, is false and hollow,
    And I despise the frenzied operations
    Of all these barterers of protestations,
    These lavishers of meaningless embraces,   45
    These utterers of obliging commonplaces,
    Who court and flatter everyone on earth
    And praise the fool no less than the man of worth.
    Should you rejoice that someone fondles you,
    Offers his love and service, swears to be true,   50
    And fills your ears with praises of your name,
    When to the first damned fop° he'll say the same?
    No, no; no self-respecting heart would dream
    Of prizing so promiscuous an esteem;
    However high the praise, there's nothing worse   55
    Than sharing honors with the universe.

SCENE 1. 52 *fop:* dandy, creature of fashion.

Esteem is founded on comparison:
To honor all men is to honor none.
Since you embrace this indiscriminate vice,
Your friendship comes at far too cheap a price;   60
I spurn the easy tribute of a heart
Which will not set the worthy man apart:
I choose, Sir, to be chosen; and in fine,
The friend of mankind is no friend of mine.

PHILINTE. But in polite society, custom decrees   65
    That we show certain outward courtesies . . .

ALCESTE. Ah, no! we should condemn with all our force
    Such false and artificial intercourse.°
    Let men behave like men; let them display
    Their inmost hearts in everything they say;   70
    Let the heart speak, and let our sentiments
    Not mask themselves in silly compliments.

PHILINTE. In certain cases it would be uncouth
    And most absurd to speak the naked truth;
    With all respect for our exalted notions,   75
    It's often best to veil one's true emotions.
    Wouldn't the social fabric come undone
    If we were wholly frank with everyone?
    Suppose you met with someone you couldn't bear;
    Would you inform him of it then and there?   80

ALCESTE. Yes.

PHILINTE.   Then you'd tell old Emilie it's pathetic
    The way she daubs her features with cosmetic
    And plays the gay coquette at sixty-four?

ALCESTE. I would.

PHILINTE.   And you'd call Dorilas a bore,
    And tell him every ear at court is lame   85
    From hearing him brag about his noble name?

ALCESTE. Precisely.

PHILINTE.   Ah, you're joking.

ALCESTE.   Au contraire;°
    In this regard there's none I'd choose to spare.
    All are corrupt; there's nothing to be seen
    In court or town but aggravates my spleen.°   90
    I fall into deep gloom and melancholy
    When I survey the scene of human folly,
    Finding on every hand base flattery,
    Injustice, fraud, self-interest, treachery . . .
    Ah, it's too much; mankind has grown so base,   95
    I mean to break with the whole human race.

PHILINTE. This philosophic rage is a bit extreme;
    You've no idea how comical you seem;

---

68 *intercourse:* interaction.   87 *Au contraire:* on the contrary.   90 *spleen:* in archaic usage, the bodily part said to govern moods of ill-humor.

Indeed, we're like those brothers in the play
Called *School for Husbands*,° one of whom was prey . . .   100
ALCESTE. Enough, now! None of your stupid similes.
PHILINTE. Then let's have no more tirades, if you please.
The world won't change, whatever you say or do;
And since plain speaking means so much to you,
I'll tell you plainly that by being frank   105
You've earned the reputation of a crank,
And that you're thought ridiculous when you rage
And rant against the manners of the age.
ALCESTE. So much the better; just what I wish to hear.
No news could be more grateful to my ear.   110
All men are so detestable in my eyes,
I should be sorry if they thought me wise.
PHILINTE. Your hatred's very sweeping, is it not?
ALCESTE. Quite right: I hate the whole degraded lot.
PHILINTE. Must all poor human creatures be embraced,   115
Without distinction, by your vast distaste?
Even in these bad times, there are surely a few . . .
ALCESTE. No, I include all men in one dim view:
Some men I hate for being rogues; the others
I hate because they treat the rogues like brothers,   120
And, lacking a virtuous scorn for what is vile,
Receive the villain with a complaisant smile.
Notice how tolerant people choose to be
Toward that bold rascal who's at law with me.
His social polish can't conceal his nature;   125
One sees at once that he's a treacherous creature;
No one could possibly be taken in
By those soft speeches and that sugary grin.
The whole world knows the shady means by which
The low-brow's grown so powerful and rich,   130
And risen to a rank so bright and high
That virtue can but blush, and merit sigh.
Whenever his name comes up in conversation.
None will defend his wretched reputation;
Call him knave, liar, scoundrel, and all the rest,   135
Each head will nod, and no one will protest.
And yet his smirk is seen in every house,
He's greeted everywhere with smiles and bows,
And when there's any honor that can be got
By pulling strings, he'll get it, like as not.   140
My God! It chills my heart to see the ways
Men come to terms with evil nowadays;
Sometimes, I swear, I'm moved to flee and find
Some desert land unfouled by humankind.

---

100 *School for Husbands:* an earlier play of Molière's featuring two brothers with opposite temperaments resembling Alceste's and Philinte's.

PHILINTE. Come, let's forget the follies of the times   145
    And pardon mankind for its petty crimes;
    Let's have an end of ranting and of railings,
    And show some lenience toward human failings.
    This world requires a pliant rectitude;°
    Too stern a virtue makes one stiff and rude;   150
    Good sense views all extremes with detestation,
    And bids us to be noble in moderation.
    And rigid virtues of the ancient days
    Are not for us; they jar with all our ways
    And ask of us too lofty a perfection.   155
    Wise men accept their times without objection,
    And there's no greater folly, if you ask me,
    Than trying to reform society.
    Like you, I see each day a hundred and one
    Unhandsome deeds that might be better done,   160
    But still, for all the faults that meet my view,
    I'm never known to storm and rave like you.
    I take men as they are, or let them be,
    And teach my soul to bear their frailty;
    And whether in court or town, whatever the scene,   165
    My phlegm's° as philosophic as your spleen.
ALCESTE. This phlegm which you so eloquently commend,
    Does nothing ever rile it up, my friend?
    Suppose some man you trust should treacherously
    Conspire to rob you of your property,   170
    And to do his best to wreck your reputation?
    Wouldn't you feel a certain indignation?
PHILINTE. Why, no. These faults of which you so complain
    Are part of human nature, I maintain,
    And it's no more a matter for disgust   175
    That men are knavish, selfish and unjust,
    Than that the vulture dines upon the dead,
    And wolves are furious, and apes ill-bred.
ALCESTE. Shall I see myself betrayed, robbed, torn to bits,
    And not . . . Oh, let's be still and rest our wits.   180
    Enough of reasoning, now, I've had my fill.
PHILINTE. Indeed, you would do well, Sir, to be still.
    Rage less at your opponent, and give some thought
    To how you'll win this lawsuit that he's brought.
ALCESTE. I assure you I'll do nothing of the sort.   185
PHILINTE. Then who will plead your case before the court?
ALCESTE. Reason and right and justice will plead for me.
PHILINTE. Oh, Lord. What judges do you plan to see?
ALCESTE. Why, none. The justice of my cause is clear.
PHILINTE. Of course, man; but there's politics to fear . . .   190

---

149 *rectitude*: uprightness. 166 *phlegm*: bodily part said to produce deliberate, calm action.

ALCESTE. No, I refuse to lift a hand. That's flat.
    I'm either right, or wrong.
PHILINTE.   Don't count on that.
ALCESTE. No, I'll do nothing.
PHILINTE.   Your enemy's influence
    Is great, you know . . .
ALCESTE.   That makes no difference.
PHILINTE. It will; you'll see.
ALCESTE.   Must honor bow to guile?   195
    If so, I shall be proud to lose the trial.
PHILINTE. Oh, really . . .
ALCESTE.   I'll discover by this case
    Whether or not men are sufficiently base
    And impudent and villainous and perverse
    To do me wrong before the universe.   200
PHILINTE. What a man!
ALCESTE.   Oh, I could wish, whatever the cost,
    Just for the beauty of it, that my trial were lost.
PHILINTE. If people heard you talking so, Alceste.
    They'd split their sides. Your name would be a jest.
ALCESTE. So much the worse for jesters.
PHILINTE.   May I enquire   205
    Whether this rectitude you so admire,
    And these hard virtues you're enamored of
    Are qualities of the lady whom you love?
    It much surprises me that you, who seem
    To view mankind with furious disesteem,°   210
    Have yet found something to enchant your eyes
    Amidst a species which you so despise.
    And what is more amazing, I'm afraid,
    Is the most curious choice your heart has made.
    The honest Eliante is fond of you,   215
    Arsinoé, the prude, admires you too;
    And yet your spirit's been perversely led
    To choose the flighty Célimène instead,
    Whose brittle malice and coquettish ways
    So typify the manners of our days.   220
    How is it that the traits you most abhor
    Are bearable in this lady you adore?
    Are you so blind with love that you can't find them?
    Or do you contrive, in her case, not to mind them?
ALCESTE. My love for that young widow's not the kind   225
    That can't perceive defects; no, I'm not blind.
    I see her faults, despite my ardent love,
    And all I see I fervently reprove.
    And yet I'm weak; for all her falsity,
    That woman knows the art of pleasing me,   230

_____

210 *disesteem:* cynicism.

And though I never cease complaining of her,
I swear I cannot manage not to love her.
Her charm outweighs her faults; I can but aim
To cleanse her spirit in my love's pure flame.

PHILINTE. That's no small task; I wish you all success.   235
    You think then that she loves you?

ALCESTE.   Heavens, yes!
    I wouldn't love her did she not love me.

PHILINTE. Well, if her taste for you is plain to see,
    Why do these rivals cause you such despair?

ALCESTE. True love, Sir, is possessive, and cannot bear   240
    To share with all the world. I'm here today
    To tell her she must send that mob away.

PHILINTE. If I were you, and had your choice to make,
    Eliante, her cousin, would be the one I'd take;
    That honest heart, which cares for you alone,   245
    Would harmonize far better with your own.

ALCESTE. True, true: each day my reason tells me so;
    But reason doesn't rule in love, you know.

PHILINTE. I fear some bitter sorrow is in store;
    This love . . .

Scene 2

Enter Oronte.

ORONTE. [*to Alceste*] The servants told me at the door
    That Eliante and Célimène were out,
    But when I heard, dear Sir, that you were about,
    I came to say, without exaggeration.
    That I hold you in the vastest admiration,   5
    And that it's always been my dearest desire
    To be the friend of one I so admire.
    I hope to see my love of merit requited,
    And you and I in friendship's bond united.
    I'm sure you won't refuse—if I may be frank—   10
    A friend of my devotedness—and rank.

During this speech of Oronte's, Alceste is abstracted and seems unaware that he is being spoken to. He only breaks off his reverie when Oronte says

    It was for you, if you please, that my words were intended.

ALCESTE. For me. Sir?

ORONTE.   Yes, for you. You're not offended?

ALCESTE. By no means. But this much surprises me . . .
    The honor comes most unexpectedly . . .   15

ORONTE. My high regard should not astonish you;
    The whole world feels the same. It is your due.

ALCESTE. Sir . . .

ORONTE.   Why, in all the State there isn't one
    Can match your merits; they shine, Sir, like the sun.

ALCESTE. Sir . . .

ORONTE.   You are higher in my estimation   20
   Than all that's most illustrious in the nation.

ALCESTE. Sir . . .

ORONTE.   If I lie, may heaven strike me dead!
   To show you that I mean what I have said,
   Permit me, Sir, to embrace you most sincerely,
   And swear that I will prize our friendship dearly.   25
   Give me your hand. And now, Sir, if you choose,
   We'll make our vows.

ALCESTE.   Sir . . .

ORONTE.   What! You refuse?

ALCESTE. Sir, it's a very great honor you extend:
   But friendship is a sacred thing, my friend;
   It would be profanation° to bestow   30
   The name of friend on one you hardly know.
   All parts are better played when well-rehearsed;
   Let's put off friendship, and get acquainted first.
   We may discover it would be unwise
   To try to make our natures harmonize.   35

ORONTE. By heaven! You're sagacious° to the core;
   This speech has made me admire you even more.
   Let time, then, bring us closer day by day;
   Meanwhile, I shall be yours in every way.
   If, for example, there should be anything   40
   You wish at court, I'll mention it to the King.
   I have his ear, of course; it's quite well known
   That I am much in favor with the throne.
   In short, I am your servant. And now, dear friend,
   Since you have such fine judgment, I intend   45
   To please you, if I can, with a small sonnet
   I wrote not long ago. Please comment on it,
   And tell me whether I ought to publish it.

ALCESTE. You must excuse me, Sir; I am hardly fit
   To judge such matters.

ORONTE.   Why not?

ALCESTE.   I am, I fear,   50
   Inclined to be unfashionably sincere.

ORONTE. Just what I ask; I'd take no satisfaction
   In anything but your sincere reaction.
   I beg you not to dream of being kind.

ALCESTE. Since you desire it, Sir, I'll speak my mind.   55

ORONTE. *Sonnet*. It's a sonnet . . . *Hope* . . . The poem's addressed
   To a lady who wakened hopes within my breast.
   Hope . . . this is not the pompous sort of thing,
   Just modest little verses, with a tender ring.

ALCESTE. Well, we shall see.

SCENE 2. 30 *profanation:* insult.   36 *sagacious:* wise.

ORONTE.   Hope . . . I'm anxious to hear   60
   Whether the style seems properly smooth and clear.
   And whether the choice of words is good or bad.
ALCESTE. We'll see, we'll see.
ORONTE.   Perhaps I ought to add
   That it took me only a quarter-hour to write it.
ALCESTE. The time's irrelevant, Sir: kindly recite it.   65
ORONTE. [reading] Hope comforts us awhile, 'tis true,
              Lulling our cares with careless laughter,
              And yet such joy is full of rue,°
              My Phyllis, if nothing follows after.
PHILINTE. I'm charmed to this already; the style's delightful. 70
ALCESTE. [sotto voce°, to Philinte] How can you say that? Why, the thing is frightful.
ORONTE.   Your fair face smiled on me awhile,
              But was it kindness to enchant me?
              'Twould have been fairer not to smile,
              If hope was all you meant to grant me.   75
PHILINTE. What a clever thought! How handsomely you phrase it!
ALCESTE. [sotto voce, to Philinte] You know the thing is trash. How dare you praise it?
ORONTE.   If it's to be my passion's fate
              Thus everlasting to wait,
              Then death will come to set me free: 80
              For death is fairer than the fair;
              Phyllis, to hope is to despair
              When one must hope eternally.
PHILINTE. The close is exquisite—full of feeling and grace.
ALCESTE. [sotto voce, aside] Oh, blast the close; you'd better close your face 85
   Before you send your lying soul to hell.
PHILINTE. I can't remember a poem I've liked so well.
ALCESTE. [sotto voce, aside] Good Lord!
ORONTE. [to Philinte]   I fear you're flattering me a bit.
PHILINTE. Oh no!
ALCESTE. [sotto voce, aside] What else d'you call it, you hypocrite?
ORONTE. [to Alceste] But you, Sir, keep your promise now: don't shrink 90
   From telling me sincerely what you think.
ALCESTE. Sir, these are delicate matters; we all desire
   To be told that we've the true poetic fire.
   But once, to one whose name I shall not mention,
   I said, regarding some verse of his invention,   95
   That gentlemen should rigorously control
   That itch to write which often afflicts the soul;
   That one should curb the heady inclination
   To publicize one's little avocation;
   And that in showing off one's works of art   100
   One often plays a very clownish part.
ORONTE. Are you suggesting in a devious way
   That I ought not . . .

---

68 *rue*: remorse.   71 *sotto voce*: in a "stage whisper"; an aside spoken privately.

ALCESTE.   Oh, that I do not say.
    Further, I told him that no fault is worse
    Than that of writing frigid, lifeless verse,   105
    And that the merest whisper of such a shame
    Suffices to destroy a man's good name.
ORONTE. D'you mean to say my sonnet's dull and trite?
ALCESTE. I don't say that. But I went on to cite
    Numerous cases of once-respected men   110
    Who came to grief by taking up the pen.
ORONTE. And am I like them? Do I write so poorly?
ALCESTE. I don't say that. But I told this person, "Surely
    You're under no necessity to compose;
    Why you should wish to publish, heaven knows.   115
    There's no excuse for printing tedious rot
    Unless one writes for bread, as you do not.
    Resist temptation, then, I beg of you;
    Conceal your pastimes from the public view;
    And don't give up, on any provocation,   120
    Your present high and courtly reputation,
    To purchase at a greedy printer's shop
    The name of silly author and scribbling fop."
    These were the points I tried to make him see.
ORONTE. I sense that they are also aimed at me;   125
    But now—about my sonnet—I'd like to be told . . .
ALCESTE. Frankly, the sonnet should be pigeonholed.
    You've chosen the worst models to imitate.
    The style's unnatural. Let me illustrate:
    For example. Your fair face smiled on me awhile,   130
    Followed by, 'Twould have been fairer not to smile!
    Or this: Such joy is full of rue;
    Or this: For death is fairer than the fair;
    Or, Phyllis, to hope is to despair
      When one must hope eternally!   135
    This artificial style, that's all the fashion,
    Has neither taste, nor honesty, nor passion;
    It's nothing but a sort of wordy play,
    And nature never spoke in such a way.
    What, in this shallow age, is not debased?   140
    Our fathers, though less refined, had better taste;
    I'd barter all that men admire today
    For one old love-song I shall try to say:
      If the King had given me for my own
      Paris, his citadel,   145
      And I for that must leave alone
      Her whom I love so well,
      I'd say then to the Crown,
      Take back your glittering town;
      My darling is more fair, I swear,   150
      My darling is more fair.

The rhyme's not rich, the style is rough and old,
But don't you see that it's the purest gold
Beside the tinsel nonsense now preferred,
And that there's passion in its every word?   155

       If the King had given me for my own
       Paris, his citadel,
       And I for that must leave alone
       Her whom I love so well,
       I'd say then to the Crown,   160
       Take back your glittering town;
       My darling is more fair, I swear,
       My darling is more fair.

There speaks a loving heart. [*to Philinte*] You're laughing, eh?
Laugh on, my precious wit. Whatever you say,   165
I hold that song's worth all the bibelots°
That people hail today with ah's and oh's.

ORONTE. And I maintain my sonnet's very good.
ALCESTE. It's not at all surprising that you should
   You have your reasons; permit me to have mine   170
   For thinking that you cannot write a line.
ORONTE. Others have praised my sonnet's to the skies.
ALCESTE. I lack their art of telling pleasant lies.
ORONTE. You seem to think you've got no end of wit.
ALCESTE. To praise your verse, I'd need still more of it.   175
ORONTE. I'm not in need of your approval, Sir.
ALCESTE. That's good; you couldn't have it if you were.
ORONTE. Come now, I'll tend you the subject of my sonnet;
   I'd like to see you try to improve upon it.
ALCESTE. I might, by chance, write something just as shoddy;   180
   But then I wouldn't show it to everybody.
ORONTE. You're most opinionated and conceited.
ALCESTE. Go find your flatterers, and be better treated.
ORONTE. Look here, my little fellow, pray watch your tone.
ALCESTE. My great big fellow, you'd better watch your own.   185
PHILINTE. [*stepping between them*] Oh, please, please, gentlemen!
   This will never do.
ORONTE. The fault is mine, and I leave the field to you.
   I am your servant, Sir, in every way.
ALCESTE. And I, Sir, am your most abject valet.   190

   Exit Oronte.

Scene 3

PHILINTE. Well, as you see, sincerity in excess
   Can get you into a very pretty mess;
   Oronte was hungry for appreciation . . .

---

166 *bibelots*: expensive trifles.

ALCESTE. Don't speak to me.

PHILINTE.   What?

ALCESTE.   No more conversation.

PHILINTE. Really, now . . .

ALCESTE.   Leave me alone.

PHILINTE.   If I . . .

ALCESTE.   Out of my sight!   5

PHILINTE. But what . . .

ALCESTE.   I won't listen.

PHILINTE.   But . . .

ALCESTE.   Silence!

PHILINTE.   Now, is it polite . . .

ALCESTE. By heaven, I've had enough. Don't follow me.

PHILINTE. Ah, you're just joking. I'll keep you company.

   Exeunt.

ACT 2
Scene 1

   Enter Alceste and Célimène.

ALCESTE. Shall I speak plainly, Madam? I confess
   Your conduct gives me infinite distress,
   And my resentment's grown too hot to smother.
   Soon, I foresee, we'll break with one another.
   If I said otherwise, I should deceive you;   5
   Sooner or later, I shall be forced to leave you,
   And if I swore that we shall never part,
   I should misread the omens of my heart.

CÉLIMÈNE. You kindly saw me home, it would appear,
   So as to pour invectives in my ear.   10

ALCESTE. I've no desire to quarrel. But I deplore
   Your inability to shut the door
   On all these suitors who beset you so.
   There's what annoys me, if you care to know.

CÉLIMÈNE. Is it my fault that all these men pursue me?   15
   Am I to blame if they're attracted to me?
   And when they gently beg an audience,
   Ought I to take a stick and drive them hence?

ALCESTE. Madam, there's no necessity for a stick;
   A less responsive heart would do the trick.   20
   Of your attractiveness I don't complain;
   But those your charms attract, you then detain
   By a most melting and receptive manner,
   And so enlist their hearts beneath your banner.°
   It's the agreeable hopes which you excite   25
   That keep these lovers round you day and night;
   Were they less liberally smiled upon,

SCENE 1. *24 enlist their hearts beneath your banner:* win them to your side.

That sighing troop would very soon be gone.
But tell me, Madam, why it is that lately
This man Clitandre interests you so greatly? 30
Because of what high merits do you deem
Him worthy of the honor of your esteem?
Is it that your admiring glances linger
On the splendidly long nail of his little finger?
Or do you share the general deep respect 35
For the blond wig he chooses to affect?
Are you in love with his embroidered hose?
Do you adore his ribbons and his bows?
Or is it that this paragon bewitches
Your tasteful eye with his vast German breeches? 40
Perhaps his giggle, or his falsetto° voice,
Makes him the latest gallant of your choice?

CÉLIMÈNE. You're much mistaken to resent him so.
Why I put up with him you surely know:
My lawsuit's very shortly to be tried, 45
And I must have his influence on my side.

ALCESTE. Then lose your lawsuit, Madam, or let it drop;
Don't torture me by humoring such a fop.

CÉLIMÈNE. You're jealous of the whole world, Sir.

ALCESTE.   That's true,
Since the whole world is well-received by you. 50

CÉLIMÈNE. That my good nature is so unconfined
Should serve to pacify your jealous mind;
Were I to smile on one, and scorn the rest,
Then you might have some cause to be distressed.

ALCESTE. Well, if I mustn't be jealous, tell me, then, 55
Just how I'm better treated than other men.

CÉLIMÈNE. You know you have my love. Will that not do?

ALCESTE. What proof have I that what you say is true?

CÉLIMÈNE. I would expect, Sir, that my having said it
Might give the statement a sufficient credit. 60

ALCESTE. But how can I be sure that you don't tell
The selfsame thing to other men as well?

CÉLIMÈNE. What a gallant speech! How flattering to me!
What a sweet creature you make me out to be!
Well then, to save you from the pangs of doubt, 65
All that I've said I hereby cancel out;
Now, none but yourself shall make a monkey of you:
Are you content?

ALCESTE.   Why, why am I doomed to love you?
I swear that I shall bless the blissful hour
When this poor heart's no longer in your power! 70
I make no secret of it; I've done my best
To exorcise this passion from my breast;

_____

41 *falsetto:* unnaturally high-voiced.

But thus far all in vain, it will not go;
It's for my sins that I must love you so.
CÉLIMÈNE. Your love for me is matchless. Sir; that's clear. 75
ALCESTE. Indeed, in all the world it has no peer;
Words can't describe the nature of my passion,
And no man ever loved in such a fashion.
CÉLIMÈNE. Yes, it's a brand-new fashion, I agree:
You show your love by castigating° me, 80
And all your speeches are enraged and rude.
I've never been so furiously wooed.
ALCESTE. Yet you could calm that fury, if you chose.
Come, shall we bring our quarrels to a close?
Let's speak with open hearts, then, and begin . . . 85

Scene 2

Enter Basque.

CÉLIMÈNE. What is it?
BASQUE.   Acaste is here.
CÉLIMÈNE.   Well, send him in.   *Exit Basque.*

Scene 3

ALCESTE. What! Shall we never be alone at all?
You're always ready to receive a call,
And you can't bear, for ten ticks of the clock,
Not to keep open house for all who knock.
CÉLIMÈNE. I couldn't refuse him, he'd be most put out. 5
ALCESTE. Surely that's not worth worrying about.
CÉLIMÈNE. Acaste would never forgive me if he guessed
That I consider him a dreadful pest.
ALCESTE. If he's a pest, why bother with him then?
CÉLIMÈNE. Heavens! One can't antagonize such men; 10
Why, they're the chartered gossips of the court,
And have a say in things of every sort.
One must receive them, and be full of charm;
They're no great help, but they can do you harm,
And though your influence be ever so great, 15
They're hardly the best people to alienate.
ALCESTE. I see, dear lady, that you could make a case
For putting up with the whole human race;
These friendships that you calculate so nicely . . .

Scene 4

Enter Basque.

BASQUE. Madam, Clitandre is here as well.
ALCESTE.   Precisely.

---

80 *castigating:* censuring, punishing.

CÉLIMÈNE. Where are you going?

ALCESTE.   Elsewhere.

CÉLIMÈNE.   Stay.

ALCESTE.   No, no.

CÉLIMÈNE. Stay, Sir.

ALCESTE.   I can't.

CÉLIMÈNE.   I wish it.

ALCESTE.   No, I must go.

    I beg you, Madam, not to press the matter;

    You know I have no taste for idle chatter.   5

CÉLIMÈNE. Stay; I command you.

ALCESTE.   No, I cannot stay.

CÉLIMÈNE. Very well; you will have my leave to go away.

Scene 5

Enter Eliante, Philinte, Agaste, Clintandre, and Basque.

ELIANTE. [*to Célimène*] The Marquesses have kindly come to call.

    Were they announced?

CÉLIMÈNE.   Yes. Basque, bring chairs for all.

    Basque provides the chairs, and exits. To Alceste.

    You haven't gone?

ALCESTE.   No; and I shan't depart

    Till you decide who's foremost in your heart.

CÉLIMÈNE. Oh, hush.

ALCESTE.   It's time to choose; take them or me.   5

CÉLIMÈNE. You're mad.

ALCESTE.   I'm not, as you shall shortly see.

CÉLIMÈNE. Oh?

ALCESTE.   You'll decide.

CÉLIMÈNE.   You're joking now, dear friend.

ALCESTE. No, no; you'll choose; my patience is at an end.

CLITANDRE. Madam, I come from court, where poor Cléonte

    Behaved like a perfect fool, as is his wont.°   10

    Has he no friend to counsel him, I wonder,

    And teach him less unerringly to blunder?

CÉLIMÈNE. It's true, the man's a most accomplished dunce;

    His gauche behavior charms the eye at once;

    And every time one sees him, on my word,   15

    His manner's grown a trifle more absurd.

ACASTE. Speaking of dunces, I've just now conversed

    With old Damon, who's one of the very worst;

    I stood a lifetime in the broiling sun

    Before his dreary monologue was done.   20

CÉLIMÈNE. Oh, he's a wondrous talker, and has the power

    To tell you nothing hour after hour:

SCENE 5. 10 *wont:* habit, tendency.

If, by mistake, he ever came to the point,
The shock would put his jawbone out of joint.
ELIANTE. [*to Philinte*] The conversation takes its usual turn, 25
And all our dear friends' ears will shortly burn.
CLITANDRE. Timante's a character, Madam.
CÉLIMÈNE.   Isn't he, though?
A man of mystery from top to toe,
Who moves about in a romantic mist
On secret missions which do not exist. 30
His talk is full of eyebrows and grimaces;
How tired one gets of his momentous faces;
He's always whispering something confidential
Which turns out to be quite inconsequential;
Nothing's too slight for him to mystify; 35
He even whispers when he says "good-by."
ACASTE. Tell us about Géralde.
CÉLIMÈNE.   That tiresome ass.
He mixes only with the titled class,
And fawns on dukes and princes, and is bored
With anyone who's not at least a lord 40
The man's obsessed with rank, and his discourses
Are all of hounds and carriages and horses;
He uses Christian names with all the great,
And the word Milord,° with him, is out of date.
CLITANDRE. He's very taken with Bélise, I hear. 45
CÉLIMÈNE. She is the dreariest company, poor dear.
Whenever she comes to call, I grope about
To find some topic which will draw her out,
But, owing to her dry and faint replies,
The conversation wilts, and droops, and dies. 50
In vain one hopes to animate her face
By mentioning the ultimate commonplace;
But sun or shower, even hail or frost
Are matters she can instantly exhaust.
Meanwhile her visit, painful though it is, 55
Drags on and on through mute eternities,
And though you ask the time, and yawn, and yawn.
She sits there like a stone and won't be gone.
ACASTE. Now for Adraste.
CÉLIMÈNE.   Oh, that conceited elf
Has a gigantic passion for himself; 60
He rails against the court, and cannot bear it
That none will recognize his hidden merit;
All honors given to others give offense
To his imaginary excellence.
CLITANDRE. What about young Cléon? His house, they say 65
Is full of the best society, night and day.

_____
44 *Milord:* title of respect.

CÉLIMÈNE. His cook has made him popular, not he:
    It's Cléon's table that people come to see.
ELIANTE. He gives a splendid dinner, you must admit.
CÉLIMÈNE. But must he serve himself along with it?   70
    For my taste, he's a most insipid dish
    Whose presence sours the wine and spoils the fish.
PHILINTE. Damis, his uncle, is admired to no end.
    What's your opinion, Madam?
CÉLIMÈNE.   Why, he's my friend.
PHILINTE. He seems a decent fellow, and rather clever.   75
CÉLIMÈNE. He works too hard at cleverness, however.
    I hate to see him sweat and struggle so
      To fill his conversation with bons mots.°
    Since he's decided to become a wit
    His taste's so pure that nothing pleases it;   80
    He scolds at all the latest books and plays,
    Thinking that wit must never stoop to praise,
    That finding fault's a sign of intellect,
    That all appreciation is abject,
    And that by damning everything in sight   85
    One shows oneself in a distinguished light.
    He's scornful even of our conversations:
    Their trivial nature sorely tries his patience;
    He folds his arms, and stands above the battle,
    And listens sadly to our childish prattle.   90
ACASTE. Wonderful, Madam! You've hit him off precisely.
CLITANDRE. No one can sketch a character so nicely.
ALCESTE. How bravely, Sirs, you cut and thrust at all
    These absent fools, till one by one they fall:
    But let one come in sight, and you'll at once   95
    Embrace the man you lately called a dunce,
    Telling him in a tone sincere and fervent
    How proud you are to be his humble servant.
CLITANDRE. Why pick on us? Madame's been speaking, Sir.
    And you should quarrel, if you must, with her.   100
ALCESTE. No, no, by God, the fault is yours, because
    You lead her on with laughter and applause.
    And make her think that she's the more delightful
    The more her talk is scandalous and spiteful.
    Oh, she would stoop to malice far, far less   105
    If no such claque° approved her cleverness.
    It's flatterers like you whose foolish praise
    Nourishes all the vices of these days.
PHILINTE. But why protest when someone ridicules
    Those you'd condemn, yourself, as knaves or fools?   110
CÉLIMÈNE. Why, Sir? Because he loves to make a fuss.
    You don't expect him to agree with us

---

78 *bon mots:* "good words"; witty sayings or aphorisms.   106 *claque:* fawning audiences.

The Misanthrope   **1275**

When there's an opportunity to express
His heaven-sent spirit of contrariness?
What other people think, he can't abide; 115
Whatever they say, he's on the other side;
He lives in deadly terror of agreeing;
'Twould make him seem an ordinary being.
Indeed, he's so in love with contradiction,
He'll turn against his most profound conviction 120
And with a furious eloquence deplore it,
If only someone else is speaking for it.

ALCESTE. Go on, dear lady, mock me as you please;
You have your audience in ecstasies.

PHILINTE. But what she says is true; you have a way 125
Of bridling at whatever people say;
Whether they praise or blame, your angry spirit
Is equally unsatisfied to hear it.

ALCESTE. Men, Sir, are always wrong, and that's the reason
That righteous anger's never out of season; 130
All that I hear in all their conversation
Is flattering praise or reckless condemnation.

CÉLIMÈNE. But . . .

ALCESTE.   No, no, Madam, I am forced to state
That you have pleasures which I deprecate,
And that these others, here, are much to blame 135
For nourishing the faults which are your shame.

CLITANDRE. I shan't defend myself, Sir; but I vow
I'd thought this lady faultless until now.

ACASTE. I see her charms and graces, which are many;
But as for faults, I've never noticed any. 140

ALCESTE. I see them, Sir; and rather than ignore them,
I strenuously criticize her for them.
The more one loves, the more one should object
To every blemish, every least defect.
Were I this lady, I would soon get rid 145
Of lovers who approved of all I did,
And by their slack indulgence and applause
Endorsed my follies and excused my flaws.

CÉLIMÈNE. If all hearts beat according to your measure,
The dawn of love would be the end of pleasure; 150
And love would find its perfect consummation
In ecstasies of rage and reprobation.°

ELIANTE. Love, as rule, affects men otherwise,
And lovers rarely love to criticize.
They see their ladies as a charming blur, 155
And find all things commendable in her.
If she has any blemish, fault, or shame,
They will redeem it by a pleasing name.

---

152 *reprobation*: condemnation.

The pale-faced lady's lily-white, perforce;°
The swarthy° one's a sweet brunette, of course;   160
The spindly lady has a slender grace;
The fat one has a most majestic pace;
The plain one, with her dress in disarray,
They classify as *beauté négligée;*°
The hulking one's a goddess in their eyes,   165
The dwarf, a concentrate of Paradise;
The haughty lady has a noble mind;
The mean one's witty, and the dull one's kind;
The chatterbox has liveliness and verve,
The mute one has a virtuous reserve.   170
So lovers manage, in their passion's cause,
To love their ladies even for their flaws.

ALCESTE. But I still say . . .

CÉLIMÈNE.   I think it would be nice
To stroll around the gallery once or twice.
What! You're not going, Sirs?

CLITANDRE *and* ACASTE. No, Madam, no.   175

ALCESTE. You seem to be in terror lest they go.
Do what you will, Sirs; leave or linger on,
But I shan't go till after you are gone.

ACASTE. I'm free to linger, unless I should perceive
Madame is tired, and wishes me to leave.   180

CLITANDRE. And as for me, I needn't go today
Until the hour of the King's *coucher.*°

CÉLIMÈNE. [*to Alceste*] You're joking, surely?

ALCESTE.   Not in the least; we'll see
Whether you'd rather part with them, or me.

Scene 6

Enter Basque.

BASQUE. [*to Alceste*] Sir, there's a fellow here who bids me state
That he must see you, and that it can't wait.

ALCESTE. Tell him that I have no such pressing affairs.

BASQUE. It's a long tailcoat that this fellow wears,
With gold all over.

CÉLIMÈNE. [*to Alceste*] You'd best go down and see.   5
Or—have him enter.

Exit Basque.

Scene 7

Enter a Guard of the Marshalsea.

ALCESTE. [*confronting the guard*] Well, what do you want with me?

---

159 *perforce:* by necessity.   160 *swarthy:* dark.   164 *beauté négligée:* careless beauty.   182 *coucher:* a ruling lord's official bedding down for a nap or for the night; a ceremony to be attended by court officers.

Come in, Sir.

GUARD. I've a word, Sir, for your ear.

ALCESTE. Speak it aloud, Sir; I shall strive to hear.

GUARD. The Marshals have instructed me to say
    You must report to them without delay. 5

ALCESTE. Who? Me, Sir?

GUARD.   Yes, Sir; you.

ALCESTE.   But what do they want?

PHILINTE. [to Alceste] To scotch your silly quarrel with Oronte.

CÉLIMÈNE. [to Philinte] What quarrel?

PHILINTE.   Oronte and he have fallen out
    Over some verse he spoke his mind about;
    The Marshals wish to arbitrate° the matter. 10

ALCESTE. Never shall I equivocate or flatter!

PHILINTE. You'd best obey their summons; come, let's go.

ALCESTE. How can they mend our quarrel, I'd like to know?
    Am I to make a cowardly retraction,
    And praise those jingles to his satisfaction? 15
    I'll not recant; I've judged that sonnet rightly.
    It's bad.

PHILINTE. But you might say so more politely. . . .

ALCESTE. I'll not back down; his verses make me sick.

PHILINTE. If only you could be more politic!
    But come, let's go.

ALCESTE.   I'll go, but I won't unsay 20
    A single word.

PHILINTE.   Well, let's be on our way.

ALCESTE. Till I am ordered by my lord the King
    To praise that poem, I shall say the thing
    Is scandalous, by God, and that the poet
    Ought to be hanged for having the nerve to show it. 25
    [to Clintandre and Acaste, who are laughing]
    By heaven, Sirs, I really didn't know
    That I was being humorous.

CÉLIMÈNE.   Go, Sir, go;
    Settle your business.

ALCESTE. I shall, and when I'm through,
    I shall return to settle things with you.   *Exeunt*

ACT 3
Scene 1

    Enter Clitandre and Acaste.

CLITANDRE. Dear Marquess, how contented you appear;
    All things delight you, nothing mars your cheer.
    Can you, in perfect honesty, declare

SCENE 7. 10 *arbitrate:* in court life the Marshall's guards were responsible to judge disputes of honor and to prevent duels.

That you've a right to be so debonair?

ACASTE. By Jove, when I survey myself, I find 5
    No cause whatever for distress of mind.
    I'm young and rich; I can in modesty
    Lay claim to an exalted pedigree;°
    And owing to my name and my condition
    I shall not want for honors and position. 10
    Then as to courage, that most precious trait,
    I seem to have it, as was proved of late
    Upon the field of honor, where my bearing,
    They say, was very cool and rather daring.
    I've wit, of course; and taste in such perfection 15
    That I can judge without the least reflection,
    And at the theater, which is my delight,
    Can make or break a play on opening night,
    And lead the crowd in hisses or bravos,
    And generally be known as one who knows. 20
    I'm clever, handsome, gracefully polite;
    My waist is small, my teeth are strong and white;
    As for my dress, the world's astonished eyes
    Assure me that I bear away the prize.
    I find myself in favor everywhere, 25
    Honored by these men, and worshiped by the fair;
    And since these things are so, it seems to me
    I'm justified in my complacency.°

CLITANDRE. Well, if so many ladies hold you dear,
    Why do you press a hopeless courtship here? 30

ACASTE. Hopeless, you say? I'm not the sort of fool
    That likes his ladies difficult and cool.
    Men who are awkward, shy, and peasantish
    May pine for heartless beauties, if they wish,
    Grovel before them, bear their cruelties, 35
    Woo them with tears and sighs and bended knees,
    And hope by dogged faithfulness to gain
    What their poor merits never could obtain.
    For men, like me, however, it makes no sense
    To love on trust, and foot the whole expense. 40
    Whatever any lady's merits be,
    I think, thank God, that I'm as choice as she;
    That if my heart is kind enough to burn
    For her, she owes me something in return;
    And that in any proper love affair 45
    The partners must invest an equal share.

CLITANDRE. You think, then, that our hostess favors you?

ACASTE. I've reason to believe that that is true.

CLITANDRE. How did you come to such a mad conclusion?
    You're blind, dear fellow. This is sheer delusion. 50

SCENE 1. 8 *pedigree:* bloodline. 28 *complacency:* self-satisfaction.

ACASTE. All right, then: I'm deluded and I'm blind.
CLITANDRE. Whatever put the notion in your mind?
ACASTE. Delusion.
CLITANDRE.   Whatever persuades you that you're right?
ACASTE. I'm blind.
CLITANDRE.   But have you any proofs to cite?
ACASTE. I tell you I'm deluded.
CLITANDRE.   Have you, then,   55
    Received some secret pledge from Célimène?
ACASTE. Oh, no: she scorns me.
CLITANDRE.   Tell me the truth, I beg.
ACASTE. She just can't bear me.
CLITANDRE.   Ah, don't pull my leg.
    Tell me what hope she's given you, I pray.
ACASTE. I'm hopeless, and it's you who win the day.   60
    She hates me thoroughly, and I'm so vexed
    I mean to hang myself on Tuesday next.
CLITANDRE. Dear Marquess, let us have an armistice
    And make a treaty. What do you say to this?
    If ever one of us can plainly prove   65
    That Célimène encourages his love,
    The other must abandon hope, and yield,
    And leave him in possession of the field.
ACASTE. Now, there's a bargain that appeals to me;
    With all my heart, dear Marquess, I agree.   70
    But hush.

Scene 2

Enter Célimène.

CÉLIMÈNE. Still here?
CLITANDRE.   'Twas love that stayed our feet.
CÉLIMÈNE. I think I heard a carriage in the street.
    Whose is it? D'you know?

Scene 3

Enter Basque.

BASQUE.   Arsinoé is here,
    Madame.
CÉLIMÈNE. Arsinoé, you say? Oh, dear.
BASQUE. Eliante is entertaining her below.
CÉLIMÈNE. What brings the creature here, I'd like to know?
ACASTE. They say she's dreadfully prudish, but in fact
    I think her piety . . .
CÉLIMÈNE.   It's all an act.   5
    At heart she's worldly, and her poor success
    In snaring men explains her prudishness.
    It breaks her heart to see the beaux and gallants

Engrossed by other women's charms and talents,
And so she's always in a jealous rage   10
Against the faulty standards of the age.
She lets the world believe that she's a prude
To justify her loveless solitude,
And strive to put a brand of moral shame
On all the graces that she cannot claim.   15
But still she'd love a lover; and Alceste
Appears to be the one she'd love the best.
His visits here are poison to her pride;
She seems to think I've lured him from her side;
And everywhere, at court or in the town,   20
The spiteful, envious woman runs me down.
In short, she's just as stupid as can be,
Vicious and arrogant in the last degree,
And . . .

    Exit Basque.

Scene 4

    Enter Arsinoé.

CÉLIMÈNE. Ah! What happy chance has brought you here?
    I've thought about you ever so much, my dear.
ARSINOÉ. I've come to tell you something you should know.
CÉLIMÈNE. How good of you to think of doing so!

    Clitandre and Acaste go out, laughing.

Scene 5

ARSINOÉ. It's just as well those gentlemen didn't tarry.
CÉLIMÈNE. Shall we sit down?
ARSINOÉ.   That won't be necessary.
    Madam, the flame of friendship ought to burn
    Brightest in matters of the most concern,
    And as there's nothing which concerns us more
    Than honor, I have hastened to your door   5
    To bring you, as your friend, some information
    About the status of your reputation.
    I visited, last night, some virtuous folk,
    And, quite by chance, it was of you they spoke;   10
    There was, I fear, no tendency to praise
    Your light behavior and your dashing ways.
    The quantity of gentlemen you see
    And your by now notorious coquetry°
    Were both so vehemently criticized   15
    By everyone, that I was much surprised.
    Of course, I needn't tell you where I stood;

SCENE 5. 14 *coquetry:* flirting.

I came to your defense as best I could,
Assured them you were harmless, and declared
Your soul was absolutely unimpaired.   20
But there are some things, you must realize,
One can't excuse, however hard one tries,
And I was forced at last into conceding
That your behavior, Madam, is misleading.
That it makes a bad impression, giving rise   25
To ugly gossip and obscene surmise,
And that if you were more *overtly* good,
You wouldn't be so much misunderstood.
Not that I think you've been unchaste°—no! no!
The saints preserve me from a thought so low!   30
But mere good conscience never did suffice:
One must avoid the outward show of vice.
Madam, you're too intelligent, I'm sure,
To think my motives anything but pure
In offering you this counsel—which I do   35
Out of a zealous interest in you.

CÉLIMÈNE.   Madam, I haven't taken you amiss;
I'm very much obliged to you for this;
And I'll at once discharge the obligation
By telling you about *your* reputation.   40
You've been so friendly as to let me know
What certain people say of me, and so
I mean to follow your benign example
By offering you a somewhat similar sample.
The other day, I went to an affair   45
And found some most distinguished people there
Discussing piety, both false and true,
The conversation soon came round to you.
Alas! Your prudery and bustling zeal
Appeared to have a very slight appeal,   50
Your affectation of a grave demeanor,
Your endless talk of virtue and of honor,
The aptitude of your suspicious mind
For finding sin where there is none to find,
Your towering self-esteem, that pitying face   55
With which you contemplate the human race,
Your sermonizings and your sharp aspersions°
On people's pure and innocent diversions—
All these were mentioned, Madam, and, in fact,
Were roundly and concertedly attacked.   60
"What good," they said, "are all these outward shows,
When everything belies her pious pose?
She prays incessantly; but then, they say,
She beats her maids and cheats them of their pay;

---

29 *unchaste:* guilty of amorous indulgence.   57 *aspersions:* criticisms.

She shows her zeal in every holy place, 65
But still she's vain enough to paint her face;
She holds that naked statues are immoral,
But with a naked *man* she'd have no quarrel."
Of course, I said to everybody there
That they were being viciously unfair; 70
But still they were disposed to criticize you,
And all agreed that someone should advise you
To leave the morals of the world alone,
And worry rather more about your own.
They felt that one's self-knowledge should be great 75
Before one thinks of setting others straight;
That one should learn the art of living well
Before one threatens other men with hell,
And that the Church is best equipped, no doubt,
To guide our souls and root our vices out. 80
Madam, you're too intelligent, I'm sure,
To think my motives anything but pure
In offering you this counsel—which I do
Out of a zealous interest in you.

ARSINOÉ. I dared not hope for gratitude, but I 85
    Did not expect so acid a reply;
    I judge, since you've been so extremely tart,
    That my good counsel pierced you to the heart.

CÉLIMÈNE. Far from it, Madam. Indeed, it seems to me
    We ought to trade advice more frequently. 90
    One's vision of oneself is so defective
    That it would be an excellent corrective.
    If you are willing, Madam, let's arrange
    Shortly to have another frank exchange
    In which we'll tell each other, *entre nous*,° 95
    What you've heard tell of me, and I of you.

ARSINOÉ. Oh, people never censure you, my dear;
    It's me they criticize. Or so I hear.

CÉLIMÈNE. Madam, I think we either blame or praise
    According to our taste and length of days. 100
    There is a time of life for coquetry,
    And there's a season, too, for prudery.
    When all one's charms are gone, it is, I'm sure,
    Good strategy to be devout and pure:
    It makes one seem a little less forsaken. 105
    Some day, perhaps, I'll take the road you've taken:
    Time brings all things. But I have time aplenty,
    And see no cause to be a prude at twenty.

ARSINOÉ. You give your age in such a gloating tone
    That one would think I was an ancient crone°; 110
    We're not so far apart, in sober truth,

---

95 *entre nous*: between ourselves.　110 *crone*: old woman.

That you can mock me with a boast of youth!
Madam, you baffle me. I wish I knew
What moves you to provoke me as you do.

CÉLIMÈNE. For my part, Madam, I should like to know 115
Why you abuse me everywhere you go.
Is it my fault, dear lady, that your hand
Is not, alas, in very great demand?
If men admire me, if they pay me court
And daily make me offers of the sort 120
You'd dearly love to have them make to you,
How can I help it? What would you have me do?
If what you want is lovers, please feel free
To take as many as you can from me.

ARSINOÉ. Oh, come. D'you think the world is losing sleep 125
Over that flock of lovers which you keep,
Or that we find it difficult to guess
What price you pay for their devotedness?
Surely you don't expect us to suppose
Mere merit could attract so many beaux? 130
It's not your virtue that they're dazzled by;
Nor is it virtuous love for which they sigh.
You're fooling no one, Madam; the world's not blind;
There's many a lady heaven has designed
To call men's noblest, tenderest feelings out, 135
Who has no lovers dogging her about;
From which it's plain that lovers nowadays
Must be acquired in bold and shameless ways,
And only pay one court for such reward
As modesty and virtue can't afford. 140
Then don't be quite so puffed up, if you please,
About your tawdry little victories;
Try, if you can, to be a shade less vain,
And treat the world with somewhat less disdain.
If one were envious of your amours, 145
One soon could have a following like yours;
Lovers are no great trouble to collect
If one prefers them to one's self-respect.

CÉLIMÈNE. Collect them then, my dear; I'd love to see
You demonstrate that charming theory;
Who knows, you might . . . 150

ARSINOÉ.   Now Madam, that will do;
It's time to end this trying interview.
My coach is late in coming to your door,
Or I'd have taken leave of you before.

CÉLIMÈNE. Oh, please don't feel that you must rush away; 155
I'd be delighted, Madam, if you'd stay,
However, lest my conversation bore you,
Let me provide some better company for you;

This gentlemen, who comes most apropos,°
Will please you more than I could do, I know.   160

Scene 6

Enter Alceste.

CÉLIMÈNE. Alceste, I have a little note to write
Which simply must go out before tonight;
Please entertain Madame; I'm sure that she
Will overlook my incivility.

Exit Célimène.

Scene 7

ARSINOÉ. Well, Sir, our hostess graciously contrives
For us to chat until my coach arrives;
And I shall be forever in her debt
For granting me this little tête-à-tête.°
We women very rightly give our hearts   5
To men of noble character and parts,
And your special merits, dear Alceste,
Have roused the deepest sympathy in my breast.
Oh, how I wish they had sufficient sense
At court, to recognize your excellence!   10
They wrong you greatly, Sir. How it must hurt you
Never to be rewarded to your virtue!
ALCESTE. Why, Madam, what cause have I to feel aggrieved?
What great and brilliant thing have I achieved?
What service have I rendered to the King   15
That I should look to him for anything?
ARSINOÉ. Not everyone who's honored by the State
Has done great services. A man must wait
Till time and fortune offer him the chance.
Your merit, Sir, is obvious at a glance,
And . . .   20
ALCESTE. Ah, forget my merit; I'm not neglected.
The court, I think, can hardly be expected
To mine men's souls for merit, and unearth
Our hidden virtues and our secret worth.
ARSINOÉ. Some virtues, though, are far too bright to hide;   25
Yours are acknowledged, Sir, on every side.
Indeed, I've heard you warmly praised of late
By persons of considerable weight.
ALCESTE. This fawning age has praise for everyone,
And all distinctions, Madam, are undone.   30
All things have equal honor nowadays,
And no one should be gratified by praise.

---

159 apropos: timely.   SCENE 7. 4 tête-à-tête: conversation, "putting heads together."

To be admired, one only need exist,
And every lackey's° on the honors list.

ARSINOÉ. I only wish, Sir, that you had your eye   35
On some position at court, however high;
You'd only have to hint at such a notion
For me to set the proper wheels in motion;
I've certain friendships I'd be glad to use
To get you any office you might choose.   40

ALCESTE. Madam, I fear that any such ambition
Is wholly foreign to my disposition.
The soul God gave me isn't of the sort
That prospers in the weather of a court.
It's all too obvious that I don't possess   45
The virtues necessary for success.
My one great talent is for speaking plain;
I've never learned to flatter or to feign;
And anyone so stupidly sincere
Had best not seek a courtier's° career.   50
Outside the court, I know, one must dispense
With honors, privilege, and influence;
But still one gains the right, foregoing these.
Not to be tortured by the wish to please.
One needn't live in dread of snubs and slights,   55
Nor praise the verse that every idiot writes,
Nor humor silly Marquesses, nor bestow
Politic° sighs on Madam So-and-so.

ARSINOÉ. Forget the court, then; let the matter rest.
But I've another cause to be distressed   60
About your present situation, Sir.
It's to your love affair that I refer.
She whom you love, and who pretends to love you,
Is, I regret to say, unworthy of you.

ALCESTE. Why, Madam! Can you seriously intend   65
To make so grave a charge against your friend?

ARSINOÉ. Alas, I must. I've stood aside too long
And let that lady do you grievous wrong;
But now my debt to conscience shall be paid:
I tell you that your love has been betrayed.   70

ALCESTE. I thank you, Madam; you're extremely kind.
Such words are soothing to a lover's mind.

ARSINOÉ. Yes, though she *is* my friend, I say again
You're very much too good for Célimène.
She's wantonly misled you from the start.   75

ALCESTE. You may be right; who knows another's heart?
But ask yourself if it's the part of charity
To shake my soul with doubts of her sincerity.

---

34 *lackey:* underling.   50 *courtier:* one who makes a career in the royal courts.   58 *Politic:* politically advantageous.

French Neoclassical Drama

ARSINOÉ. Well if you'd rather be a dupe than doubt her,
       That's your affair, I'll say no more about her.   80
ALCESTE. Madam, you know that doubt and vague suspicion
       Are painful to a man in my position;
       It's most unkind to worry me this way
       Unless you've some real proof of what you say.
ARSINOÉ. Sir, say no more; all doubts shall be removed,   85
       And all that I've been saying shall be proved.
       You've only to escort me home, and there
       We'll look into the heart of this affair.
       I've ocular evidence which will persuade you
       Beyond a doubt, that Célimène's betrayed you.   90
       Then, if you're saddened by that revelation,
       Perhaps I can provide some consolation.

       Exeunt.

ACT 4

Scene 1

       Enter Eliante and Philinte.

PHILINTE. Madam, he acted like a stubborn child;
       I thought they never would be reconciled;
       In vain we reasoned, threatened, and appealed;
       He stood his ground and simply would not yield.
       The Marshals, I feel sure, have never heard   5
       An argument so splendidly absurd.
       "No, gentlemen," said he, "I'll not retract.
       His verse is bad; extremely bad, in fact.
       Surely it does the man no harm to know it.
       Does it disgrace him, not to be a poet?   10
       A gentleman may be respected still.
       Whether he writes a sonnet well or ill.
       That I dislike his verse should not offend him;
       In all that touches honor, I commend him;
       He's noble, brave, and virtuous—but I fear   15
       He can't in truth be called a sonneteer.
       I'll gladly praise his wardrobe; I'll endorse
       His dancing, or the way he sits a horse;
       But, gentlemen, I cannot praise his rhyme.
       In fact, it ought to be a capital crime   20
       For anyone so sadly unendowed
       To write a sonnet, and read the thing aloud."
       At length he fell into a gentler mood
       And, striking a concessive° attitude,
       He paid Oronte the following courtesies: 25
       "Sir, I regret that I'm so hard to please,
       And I'm profoundly sorry that your lyric

SCENE 1. 24 *concessive:* prepared to yield.

Failed to provoke me to a panegyric."°
After these curious words, the two embraced,
And then the hearing was adjourned—in haste.   30
ELIANTE. His conduct has been very singular lately;
    Still, I confess that I respect him greatly.
    The honesty in which he takes such pride
    Has—to mind—its noble, heroic side.
    In this false age, such candor seems outrageous;   35
    But I could wish that it were more contagious.
PHILINTE. What most intrigues me in our friend Alceste
    Is the grand passion that rages in his breast.
    The sullen humors he's compounded of
    Should not, I think, dispose his heart to love;   40
    But since they do, it puzzles me still more
    That he should choose your cousin to adore.
ELIANTE. It does, indeed, belie the theory
    That love is born of gentle sympathy,
    And that the tender passion must be based   45
    On sweet accords of temper and of taste.
PHILINTE. Does she return his love, do you suppose?
ELIANTE. Ah, that's a difficult question, Sir. Who knows?
    How can we judge the truth of her devotion?
    Her heart's a stranger to its own emotion.   50
    Sometimes it thinks it loves, when no love's there;
    At other times it loves quite unaware.
PHILINTE. I rather think Alceste is in for more
    Distress and sorrow that he's bargained for;
    Were he of my mind, Madam, his affection   55
    Would turn in quite a different direction,
    And we would see him more responsive to
    The kind regard which he receives from you.
ELIANTE. Sir, I believe in frankness, and I'm inclined,
    In matters of the heart, to speak my mind.   60
    I don't oppose his love for her; indeed,
    I hope with all my heart that he'll succeed,
    And were it in my power, I'd rejoice
    In giving him the lady of his choice.
    But if, as happens frequently enough   65
    In love affairs, he meets with a rebuff—
    If Célimène should grant some rival's suit—
    I'd gladly play the role of substitute;
    Nor would his tender speeches please me less
    Because they'd once been made without success.   70
PHILINTE. Well, Madam, as for me, I don't oppose
    Your hopes in this affair; and heaven knows
    That in my conversations with the man
    I plead your cause as often as I can.

---

28 *panegyric:* work of high praise.

But if those two should marry, and so remove   75
All chances that he will offer you his love,
Then I'll declare my own, and hope to see
Your gracious favor pass from him to me.
In short, should you be cheated of Alceste,
I'd be most happy to be second best.   80

ELIANTE. Philinte, you're teasing.
PHILINTE.   Ah, Madam, never fear;
No words of mine were ever so sincere,
And I shall live in fretful expectation
Till I can make a fuller declaration.

Scene 2

Enter Alceste.

ALCESTE. Avenge me, Madam! I must have satisfaction.
Or this great wrong will drive me to distraction!
ELIANTE. Why, what's the matter? What's upset you so?
ALCESTE. Madam, I've had a mortal, mortal blow.
If Chaos° repossessed the universe,   5
I swear I'd not be shaken any worse.
I'm ruined . . . I can say no more . . . My soul . . .
ELIANTE. Do try, Sir, to regain your self-control.
ALCESTE. Just heaven! Why were so much beauty and grace
Bestowed on one so vicious and so base?   10
ELIANTE. Once more, Sir, tell us . . .
ALCESTE.   My world has gone to wrack;
I'm—I'm betrayed; she's stabbed me in the back;
Yes, Célimène (who would have thought it of her?)
Is false to me, and has another lover.
ELIANTE. Are you quite certain? Can you prove these things?   15
PHILINTE. Lovers are prey to wild imaginings
And jealous fancies. No doubt there's some mistake . . .
ALCESTE. Mind your own business, Sir, for heaven's sake.
[*to Eliante*] Madam, I have the proof that you demand
Here in my pocket, penned by her own hand.   20
Yes, all the shameful evidence one could want
Lies in this letter written to Oronte—
Oronte! whom I felt sure she couldn't love,
And hardly bothered to be jealous of.
PHILINTE. Still, in a letter, appearances may deceive;   25
This may not be so bad as you believe.
ALCESTE. Once more I beg you, Sir, to let me be;
Tend to your own affairs; leave mine to me.
ELIANTE. Compose yourself; this anguish that you feel . . .
ALCESTE. Is something, Madam, you alone can heal.   30

SCENE 2. 5 *Chaos:* in classical mythology, the original disorganized state of the universe before the
birth of the gods.

My outraged heart, beside itself with grief,
Appeals to you for comfort and relief.
Avenge me on your cousin, whose unjust
And faithless nature has deceived my trust;
Avenge a crime your pure soul must detest.   35
ELIANTE. But how, Sir?
ALCESTE.   Madam, this heart within my breast
Is yours; pray take it; redeem my heart from her,
And so avenge me on my torturer.
Let her be punished by the fond emotion,
The ardent love, the bottomless devotion,   40
The faithful worship which this heart of mine
Will offer up to yours as to a shrine.
ELIANTE. You have my sympathy, Sir, in all you suffer;
Nor do I scorn the noble heart you offer;
But I suspect you'll soon be mollified,°   45
And this desire for vengeance will subside.
When some beloved hand has done us wrong
We thirst for retribution—but not for long;
However dark the deed that she's committed,
A lovely culprit's very soon acquitted.   50
Nothing's so stormy as an injured lover,
And yet no storm so quickly passes over.
ALCESTE. No, Madam, no—this is no lover's spat;
I'll not forgive her; it's gone too far for that;
My mind's made up; I'll kill myself before   55
I waste my hopes upon her any more.
Ah, here she is. My wrath intensifies.
I shall confront her with her tricks and lies,
And crush her utterly, and bring you then
A heart no longer slave to Célimène.   60

Scene 3

Enter Célimène, exit Eliante and Philinte.

ALCESTE. [*aside*] Sweet heaven, help me to control my passion.
CÉLIMÈNE. [*aside, to Alceste*] Oh, Lord, why stand there staring in that fashion?
And what d'you mean by those dramatic sighs,
And that malignant glitter in your eyes?   5
ALCESTE. I mean that sins which cause the blood to freeze
Look innocent beside your treacheries;
That nothing Hell's or Heaven's wrath could do
Ever produced so bad a thing as you.
CÉLIMÈNE. Your compliments were always sweet and pretty.   10
ALCESTE. Madam, it's not the moment to be witty.
No, blush and hang your head; you've ample reason.
Since I've the fullest evidence of your treason.

---

45 *mollified:* softened, eased.

Ah, this is what my sad heart prophesied;
Now all my anxious fears are verified; 15
My dark suspicion and my gloomy doubt
Divined the truth, and now the truth is out.
For all your trickery, I was not deceived;
It was my bitter stars that I believed.
But don't imagine that you'll go scot-free; 20
You shan't misuse me with impunity.
I know that love's irrational and blind;
I know the heart's not subject to the mind,
And can't be reasoned into beating faster;
I know each soul is free to choose its master; 25
Therefore had you but spoken from the heart,
Rejecting my attentions from the start,
I'd have no grievance, or at any rate
I could complain of nothing but my fate.
Ah, but so falsely to encourage me— 30
That was treason and a treachery
For which you cannot suffer too severely,
And you shall pay for that behavior dearly.
Yes, now I have no pity, not a shred;
My temper's out of hand; I've lost my head; 35
Shocked by the knowledge of your double-dealings,
My reason can't restrain my savage feelings;
A righteous wrath deprives me of my senses,
And I won't answer for the consequences.
CÉLIMÈNE. What does this outburst mean? Will you please explain? 40
Have you, by any chance, gone quite insane?
ALCESTE. Yes, yes, I went insane the day I fell
A victim to your black and fatal spell,
Thinking to meet with some sincerity
Among the treacherous charms that beckoned me. 45
CÉLIMÈNE. Pooh. Of what treachery can you complain?
ALCESTE. How sly you are, how cleverly you feign!
But you'll not victimize me any more.
Look: here's a document you've seen before.
This evidence, which I acquired today,
Leaves you, I think, without a thing to say. 50
CÉLIMÈNE. Is that what sent you into such a fit?
ALCESTE. You should be blushing at the sight of it.
CÉLIMÈNE. Ought I to blush? I truly don't see why.
ALCESTE. Ah, now you're being bold as well as sly;
Since there's no signature, perhaps you'll claim . . . 55
CÉLIMÈNE. I wrote it, whether or not it bears my name.
ALCESTE. And you can view with equanimity°
This proof of your disloyalty to me!
CÉLIMÈNE. Oh, don't be so outrageous and extreme.

SCENE 3. *57 with equanimity:* calmly.

ALCESTE. You take this matter lightly, it would seem.   60
      Was it no wrong to me, no shame to you,
      That you should send Oronte this billet-doux?°
CÉLIMÈNE. Oronte! Who said it was for him?
ALCESTE.   Why, those
      Who brought me this example of your prose.
      But what's the difference? If you wrote the letter   65
      To someone else, it pleases me no better.
      My grievance and your guilt remain the same.
CÉLIMÈNE. But need you rage, and need I blush for shame,
      If this was written to a *woman* friend?
ALCESTE. Ah! Most ingenious. I'm impressed no end;   70
      And after that incredible evasion
      Your guilt is clear. I need no more persuasion.
      How dare you try so clumsy a deception?
      D'you think I'm wholly wanting in perception?
      Come, come, let's see how brazenly you'll try   75
      To bolster up so palpable a lie:
      Kindly construe this ardent closing section
      As nothing more than sisterly affection!
      Here, let me read it. Tell me, if you dare to.
      That this is for a woman . . .
CÉLIMÈNE.   I don't care to.   80
      What right have you to badger and berate me,
      And so highhandedly interrogate me?
ALCESTE. Now, don't be angry; all I ask of you
      Is that you justify a phrase or two . . .
CÉLIMÈNE. No, I shall not. I utterly refuse,   85
      And you may take those phrases as you choose.
ALCESTE. Just show me how this letter could be meant
      For a woman's eyes, and I shall be content.
CÉLIMÈNE. No, no, it's for Oronte; you're perfectly right.
      I welcome his attentions with delight,
      I prize his character and his intellect,   90
      And everything is just as you suspect.
      Come, do your worst now; give your rage free rein;
      But kindly cease to bicker and complain.
ALCESTE. [*aside*] Good God! Could anything be more inhuman?   95
      Was ever a heart so mangled by a woman?
      When I complain of how she has betrayed me,
      She bridles, and commences to upbraid me!
      She tries my tortured patience to the limit;
      She won't deny her guilt; she glories in it!   100
      And yet my heart's too faint and cowardly
      To break these chains of passion, and be free,
      To scorn her as it should, and rise above
      This unrewarded, mad, and bitter love.

---

62 *billet-doux:* love letter.

[*to Célimène*] Ah, traitress, in how confident a fashion   105
You take advantage of my helpless passion,
And use my weakness for your faithless charms
To make me once again throw down my arms!
But do at least deny this black transgression;
Take back that mocking and perverse confession;   110
Defend this letter and your innocence,
And I, poor fool, will aid in your defense.
Pretend, pretend, that you are just and true,
And I shall make myself believe in you.

CÉLIMÈNE. Oh, stop it. Don't be such a jealous dunce,   115
　Or I shall leave off loving you at once.
　Just why should I *pretend?* What could impel me
　To stoop so low as that? And kindly tell me
　Why, if I loved another, I shouldn't merely
　Inform you of it, simply and sincerely!   120
　I've told you where you stand, and that admission
　Should altogether clear me of suspicion;
　After so generous a guarantee,
　What right have you to harbor doubts of me?
　Since women are (from natural reticence)   125
　Reluctant to declare their sentiments,
　And since the honor of our sex requires
　That we conceal our amorous desires,
　Ought any man for whom such laws are broken
　To question what the oracle has spoken?   130
　Should he not rather feel an obligation
　To trust that most obliging declaration?
　Enough, now. Your suspicions quite disgust me;
　Why should I love a man who doesn't trust me?
　I cannot understand why I continue,   135
　Fool that I am, to take an interest in you.
　I ought to choose a man less prone to doubt,
　And give you something to be vexed about.

ALCESTE. Ah, what a poor enchanted fool I am;
　These gentle words, no doubt, were all a sham;   140
　But destiny requires me to entrust
　My happiness to you, and so I must.
　I'll love you to the bitter end, and see
　How false and treacherous you dare to be.

CÉLIMÈNE. No, you don't really love me as you ought.   145

ALCESTE. I love you more than can be said or thought;
　Indeed, I wish you were in such distress
　That I might show my deep devotedness.
　Yes, I could wish that you were wretchedly poor,
　Unloved, uncherished, utterly obscure;   150
　That fate has set you down upon the earth
　Without possessions, rank or gentle birth;
　Then, by the offer of my heart, I might

The Misanthrope   **1293**

Repair the great injustice of your plight;
 I'd raise you from the dust, and proudly prove   155
 The purity and vastness of my love.
CÉLIMÈNE. This is a strange benevolence indeed!
 God grant that I may never be in need . . .
 Ah, here's Monsieur Dubois, in quaint disguise.

Scene 4

 Enter Dubois.

ALCESTE. Well, why this costume? Why those frightened eyes?
 What ails you?
DUBOIS.   Well, Sir, things are most mysterious.
ALCESTE. What do you mean?
DUBOIS.   I fear they're very serious.
ALCESTE. What?
DUBOIS.   Shall I speak more loudly?
ALCESTE.   Yes; speak out.
DUBOIS. Isn't there someone here, Sir?
ALCESTE.   Speak, you lout!   5
 Stop wasting time.
DUBOIS.   Sir, we must slip away.
ALCESTE. How's that?
DUBOIS.   We must decamp° without delay.
ALCESTE. Explain yourself.
DUBOIS.   I tell you we must fly.
ALCESTE. What for?
DUBOIS.   We mustn't pause to say good-by.
ALCESTE. Now what d'you mean by all of this, you clown?   10
DUBOIS. I mean, Sir, that we've got to leave this town.
ALCESTE. I'll tear you limb from limb and joint from joint
 If you don't come more quickly to the point.
DUBOIS. Well, Sir, today a man in a black suit,
 Who wore a black and ugly scowl to boot,   15
 Left a document scrawled in such a hand
 As even Satan couldn't understand.
 It bears upon your lawsuit, I don't doubt;
 But all hell's devils couldn't make it out.
ALCESTE. Well, well, go on. What then? I fail to see   20
 How this event obliges us to flee.
DUBOIS. Well, Sir: an hour later, hardly more,
 A gentlemen who's often called before
 Came looking for you in an anxious way.
 Not finding you, he asked me to convey   25
 (Knowing I could be trusted with the same)
 The following message . . . Now, what *was* his name?
ALCESTE. Forget his name, you idiot. What did he say?

SCENE 4. 7 *decamp:* take leave.

DUBOIS. Well, it was one of your friends, Sir, anyway.
   He warned you to begone, and he suggested   30
   That if you stay, you may well be arrested.
ALCESTE. What? Nothing more specific? Think, man, think!
DUBOIS. No, Sir. He had me bring him pen and ink,
   And dashed you off a letter which, I'm sure,
   Will render things distinctly less obscure.   35
ALCESTE. Well—let me have it!
CÉLIMÈNE.   What *is* this all about?
ALCESTE. God knows; but I have hopes of finding out.
   How long am I to wait, you blitherer?
DUBOIS. [*after a protracted search for the letter*] I must have left it on
   your table, Sir.
ALCESTE. I ought to . . .
CÉLIMÈNE.   No, no keep your self-control;   40
   Go find out what's behind his rigmarole.
ALCESTE. It seems that fate, no matter what I do,
   Has sworn that I may not converse with you;
   But, Madam, pray permit your faithful lover
   To try once more before the day is over.   45

   Exeunt.

ACT 5
Scene 1

   Enter Alceste and Philinte.

ALCESTE. No, it's too much. My mind's made up, I tell you.
PHILINTE. Why should this blow, however hard, compel you . . .
ALCESTE. No, no, don't waste your breath in argument;
   Nothing you say will alter my intent;
   This age is vile, and I've made up my mind   5
   To have no further commerce with mankind.
   Did not truth, honor, decency, and the laws
   Oppose my enemy and approve my cause?
   My claims were justified in all men's sight;
   I put my trust in equity and right;   10
   Yet, to my horror and the world's disgrace,
   Justice is mocked, and I have lost my case!
   A scoundrel whose dishonesty is notorious
   Emerges from another lie victorious!
   Honor and right condone his brazen fraud,   15
   While rectitude and decency applaud!
   Before his smirking face, the truth stands charmed,
   And virtue conquered, and the law disarmed!
   His crime is sanctioned by a court decree!
   And not content with what he's done to me,   20
   The dog now seeks to ruin me by stating
   That I compose a book now circulating,

A book so wholly criminal and vicious
That even to speak its title is seditious!
Meanwhile Oronte, my rival, lends his credit   25
To the same libelous tale, and helps to spread it!
Oronte! a man of honor and of rank,
With whom I've been entirely fair and frank;
Who sought me out and forced me, willy-nilly,
To judge some verse I found extremely silly;   30
And who, because I properly refused
To flatter him, or see the truth abused,
Abets my enemy in a rotten slander!
There's the reward of honesty and candor!
The man will hate me to the end of time   35
For failing to commend his wretched rhyme!
And not this man alone, but all humanity
Do what they do from interest and vanity;
They prate of honor, truth, and righteousness,
But lie, betray, and swindle nonetheless.   40
Come then: man's villainy is too much to bear;
Let's leave this jungle and this jackal's lair.
Yes! treacherous and savage race of men.
You shall not look upon my face again.

PHILINTE. Oh, don't rush into exile prematurely;   45
Things aren't as dreadful as you make them, surely.
It's rather obvious, since you're still at large,
That people don't believe our enemy's charge.
Indeed, his tale's so patently untrue
That it may do more harm to him than you.   50

ALCESTE. Nothing could do that scoundrel any harm:
His frank corruption is his greatest charm,
And, far from hurting him, a further shame
Would only serve to magnify his name.

PHILINTE. In any case, his bald prevarication   55
Has done no injury to your reputation,
And you may feel secure in that regard.
As for your lawsuit, it should not be hard
To have the case reopened, and contest
This judgment . . .

ALCESTE.   No, no, let the verdict rest.   60
Whatever cruel penalty it may bring,
I wouldn't have it changed for anything.
It shows the times' injustice with such clarity
That I shall pass it down to our posterity
As a great proof and signal demonstration   65
Of the black wickedness of this generation.
It may cost twenty thousand francs; but I
Shall pay their twenty thousand, and gain thereby
The right to storm and rage at human evil,
And send the race of mankind to the devil.   70

PHILINTE. Listen to me . . .

ALCESTE.   Why? What can you possibly say?
    Don't argue, Sir; your labor's thrown away.
    Do you propose to offer lame excuses
    For men's behavior and the times' abuses?

PHILINTE. No, all you say I'll readily concede: 75
    This is a low, dishonest age indeed;
    Nothing but trickery prospers nowadays,
    And people ought to mend their shabby ways.
    Yes, man's a beastly creature; but must we then
    Abandon the society of men?   80
    Here in the world, each human frailty
    Provides occasion for philosophy,
    And that is virtue's noblest exercise;
    If honesty shone forth from all men's eyes,
    If every heart were frank and kind and just,   85
    What could our virtues do but gather dust
    (Since their employment is to help us bear
    The villainies of men without despair)?
    A heart well-armed with virtue can endure . . .

ALCESTE. Sir, you're a matchless reasoner, to be sure;   90
    Your words are fine and full of cogency;°
    But don't waste time and eloquence on me.
    My reasons bids me go, for my own good.
    My tongue won't lie and flatter as it should;
    God knows what frankness it might next commit.   95
    And what I'd suffer on account of it.
    Pray let me wait for Célimène's return
    In peace and quiet. I shall shortly learn,
    By her response to what I have in view,
    Whether her love for me is feigned or true.   100

PHILINTE. Till then, let's visit Eliante upstairs.

ALCESTE. No, I am too weighed down with somber cares.
    Go to her, do; and leave me with my gloom
    Here in the darkened corner of this room.

PHILINTE. Why, that's no sort of company, my friend;   105
    I'll see if Eliante will not descend.

    Exit Philinte.

Scene 2

    Enter Oronte and Célimène. Alceste withdraws to the corner.

ORONTE. Yes, Madam, if you wish me to remain
    Your true and ardent lover, you must deign
    To give me some more positive assurance.
    All this suspense is quite beyond endurance.
    If your heart shares the sweet desires of mine,   5

SCENE 1. 91 *cogency:* clear thinking.

Show me as much by some convincing sign;
And here's the sign I urgently suggest:
That you no longer tolerate Alceste,
But sacrifice him to my love, and sever
All your relations with the man forever.   10

CÉLIMÈNE. Why do you suddenly dislike him so?
    You praised him to the skies not long ago.

ORONTE. Madam, that's not the point. I'm here to find
    Which way your tender feelings are inclined.
    Choose, if you please, between Alceste and me,   15
    And I shall stay or go accordingly.

ALCESTE. [*emerging from the corner*] Yes, Madam, choose; this
    gentleman's demand
    Is wholly just, and I support his stand.
    I too am true and ardent; I too am here
    To ask you that you make your feelings clear.   20
    No more delays, now; no equivocation;°
    The time has come to make your declaration.

ORONTE. Sir, I've no wish in any way to be
    An obstacle to your felicity.

ALCESTE. Sir, I've no wish to share her heart with you;   25
    That may sound jealous, but at least it's true.

ORONTE. If, weighing us, she leans in your direction . . .

ALCESTE. If she regards you with the least affection . . .

ORONTE. I swear I'll yield her to you there and then.

ALCESTE. I swear I'll never see her face again.   30

ORONTE. Now, Madam, tell us what you've come to hear.

ALCESTE. Madam, speak openly and have no fear.

ORONTE. Just say which one is to remain your lover.

ALCESTE. Just name one name, and it will all be over.

ORONTE. What! Is it possible that you're undecided?   35

ALCESTE. What! Can your feelings possibly be divided?

CÉLIMÈNE. Enough; this inquisition's gone too far:
    How utterly unreasonable you are!
    Not that I couldn't make the choice with ease;
    My heart has no conflicting sympathies;   40
    I know full well which one of you I favor,
    And you'd not see me hesitate or waver.
    But how can you expect me to reveal
    So cruelly and bluntly what I feel?
    I think it altogether too unpleasant   45
    To choose between two men when both are present;
    One's heart has means more subtle and more kind
    Of letting its affections be divined,
    Nor need one be uncharitably plain
    To let a lover know he loves in vain.   50

SCENE 2. 21 *equivocation*: evasiveness.

ORONTE. No, no speak plainly; I for one can stand it.
    I beg you to be frank.
ALCESTE.   And I demand it.
    The simple truth is what I wish to know,
    And there's no need for softening the blow.
    You've made an art of pleasing everyone,   55
    But now your days of coquetry are done:
    You have no choice now, Madam, but to choose,
    For I'll know what to think if you refuse;
    I'll take your silence for a clear admission
    That I'm entitled to my worst suspicion.   60
ORONTE. I thank you for this ultimatum, Sir,
    And I may say I heartily concur.
CÉLIMÈNE. Really, this foolishness is very wearing:
    Must you be so unjust and overbearing?
    Haven't I told you why I must demur?   65
    Oh, here's Eliante; I'll put the case to her.

Scene 3

Enter Eliante and Philinte.

CÉLIMÈNE. Cousin, I'm being persecuted here
    By these two persons, who, it would appear,
    Will not be satisfied till I confess
    Which one I love the more, and which the less,
    And tell the latter to his face that he   5
    Is henceforth banished from my company.
    Tell me, has ever such a thing been done?
ELIANTE. You'd best not turn to me; I'm not the one
    To back you in a matter of this kind:
    I'm all for those who frankly speak their mind.   10
ORONTE. Madam, you'll search in vain for a defender.
ALCESTE. You're beaten, Madam, and may as well surrender.
ORONTE. Speak, speak, you must; and end this awful strain.
ALCESTE. Or don't, and your position will be plain.
ORONTE. A single word will close this painful scene.   15
ALCESTE. But if you're silent, I'll know what you mean.

Scene 4

Enter Acaste, Clitandre, and Arsinoé.

ACASTE. [*to Célimène*] Madam, with all due deference, we two
    Have come to pick a little bone with you.
CLITANDRE. [*to Oronte and Alceste*] I'm glad you're present, Sirs; as
        you'll soon learn,
    Our business here is also your concern.
ARSINOÉ. [*to Célimène*] Madam, I visit you so soon again   5
    Only because of these two gentlemen,
    Who came to me indignant and aggrieved

About a crime too base to be believed.
Knowing your virtue, having such confidence in it,
I couldn't think you guilty for a minute, 10
In spite of all their telling evidence;
And, rising above our little difference,
I've hastened here in friendship's name to see
You clear yourself of this great calumny.°

ACASTE. Yes, Madam, let us see with what composure 15
You'll manage to respond to this disclosure.
You lately sent Clitandre this tender note.

CLITANDRE. And this one, for Acaste, you also wrote.

ACASTE. [to Oronte and Alceste] You'll recognize this writing, Sirs, I think;
The lady is so free with pen and ink 20
That you must know it all too well, I fear.
But listen; this is something you should hear.

"How absurd you are to condemn my lightheartedness in society, and to accuse
me of being happiest in the company of others. Nothing could be more
unjust; and if you do not come to me instantly and beg pardon for saying 25
such a thing, I shall never forgive you as long as I live. Our big bumbling
friend the Viscount . . . "
What a shame that he's not here.
"Our big bumbling friend the Viscount, whose name stands first in your complaint, is hardly a man to my taste; and ever since the day I watched 30
him spend three-quarters of an hour spitting into a well, so as to make
circles in the water, I have been unable to think highly of him. As for
the little Marquess . . . "
In all modesty, gentlemen, that is I.
"As for the little Marquess, who sat squeezing my hand for such a long while 35
yesterday, I find him in all respects the most trifling creature alive; and
the only thing of value about him are his cape and his sword. As for
the man with the green ribbons . . . "
[To Alceste] It's your turn now, Sir.
"As for the man with the green ribbons, he amuses me now and then with 40
his bluntness and his bearish ill-humor; but there are many times indeed
when I think him the greatest bore in the world. And as for the sonneteer . . . "
[to Oronte] Here's your helping.
"And as for the sonneteer, who has taken it into his head to be witty, and 45
insists on being an author in the teeth of opinion, I simply cannot be
bothered to listen to him, and his prose wearies me quite as much as
his poetry. Be assured that I am not always so well-entertained as you
suppose; that I long for your company, more than I dare to say, at all
these entertainments to which people drag me; and that the presence of 50
those one loves is the true and perfect seasoning to all one's pleasures."

CLITANDRE. And now for me.
"Clitandre, whom you mention, and who so pesters me with his saccharine
speeches, is the last man on earth for whom I could feel any affection.

SCENE 4. 14 *calumny:* slander.

He is quite mad to suppose that I love him, and so are you, to doubt   55
that you are loved. Do come to your senses; exchange your suppositions
for his; and visit me as often as possible, to help me bear the annoyance
of his unwelcome attentions."
    It's a sweet character that these letters show.
    And what to call it, Madam, you well know.   60
    Enough. We're off to make the world acquainted
    With this sublime self-portrait that you've painted.

ACASTE. Madam, I'll make you no farewell oration;
    No, you're not worthy of my indignation.
    Far choicer hearts that yours, as you'll discover,   65
    Would like this little Marquess for a lover.

Exit Clitandre and Acaste.

Scene 5
ORONTE. So! After all those loving letters you wrote,
    You turn on me like this, and cut my throat!
    And your dissembling, faithless heart, I find,
    Has pledged itself by turns to all mankind!
    How blind I've been! But now I clearly see;   5
    I thank you, Madam, for enlightening me.
    My heart is mine once more, and I'm content;
    The loss of it shall be your punishment.
    [*to Alceste*] Sir, she is yours; I'll seek no more to stand
    Between your wishes and this lady's hand.   10

Exit Oronte.

Scene 6
ARSINOÉ. [*to Célimène*] Madam, I'm forced to speak, I'm far too stirred
    To keep my counsel, after what I've heard,
    I'm shocked and staggered by your want of morals.
    It's not my way to mix in others' quarrels;
    But really, when this fine and noble spirit,   5
    This man of honor and surpassing merit,
    Laid down the offering of his heart before you,
    How *could* you . . .
ALCESTE.   Madam, permit me, I implore you,
    To represent myself in this debate.
    Don't bother, please, to be my advocate.   10
    My heart, in any case, could not afford
    To give your services their due reward;
    And if I choose, for consolation's sake,
    Some other lady, t'would not be you I'd take.
ARSINOÉ. What makes you think you could, Sir? And how dare you   15
    Imply that I've been trying to ensnare you?
    If you can for a moment entertain
    Such flattering fancies, you're extremely vain.

I'm not so interested as you suppose
In Célimène's discarded gigolos.   20
Get rid of that absurd illusion, do.
Women like me are not for such as you.
Stay with this creature, to whom you're so attached;
I've never seen two people better matched.

Exit Arsinoé.

Scene 7
ALCESTE. [*to Célimène*] Well, I've been still throughout this exposé,
    Till everyone but me has said his say.
    Come, have I shown self-restraint?
    And may I now . . .
CÉLIMÈNE.   Yes, make your just complaint.
    Reproach me freely, call me what you will;   5
    You're every right to say I've used you ill.
    I've wronged you, I confess it; and in my shame
    I'll make no effort to escape the blame.
    The anger of those others I could despise;
    My guilt toward you I sadly recognize.   10
    Your wrath is wholly justified, I fear;
    I know how culpable I must appear,
    I know all things bespeak my treachery,
    And that, in short, you've grounds for hating me.
    Do so; I give you leave.
ALCESTE.   Ah, traitress—how,   15
    How should I cease to love you, even now?
    Though mind and will were passionately bent
    On hating you, my heart would not consent.
    [*to Eliante and Philinte*] Be witness to my madness, both of you;
    See what infatuation drives one to;   20
    But wait; my folly's only just begun,
    And I shall prove to you before I'm done
    How strange the human heart is, and how far
    From rational we sorry creatures are.
    [*To Célimène*] Woman, I'm willing to forget your shame,   25
    And clothe your treacheries in a sweeter name;
    I'll call them youthful errors, instead of crimes,
    And lay the blame on these corrupting times.
    My one condition is that you agree
    To share my chosen fate, and fly with me   30
    To that wild, trackless solitary place
    In which I shall forget the human race.
    Only by such a course can you atone
    For those atrocious letters; by that alone
    Can you remove my present horror of you,   35
    And make it possible for me to love you.

CÉLIMÈNE. What! *I* renounce the world at my young age,
    And die of boredom in some hermitage?
ALCESTE. Ah, if you really loved me as you ought,
    You wouldn't give the world a moment's thought;   40
    Must you have me, and all the world beside?
CÉLIMÈNE. Alas, at twenty one is terrified
    Of solitude. I fear I lack the force
    And depth of soul to take so stern a course.
    But if my hand in marriage will content you,   45
    Why, there's a plan which I might well consent to,
    And . . .
ALCESTE.   No, I detest you now. I could excuse
    Everything else, but since you thus refuse
    To love me wholly, as a wife should do,
    And see the world in me, as I in you,   50
    Go! I reject your hand, and disenthrall
    My heart from your enchantment, once for all.

    Exit Célimène.

Scene 8
ALCESTE. [*to Eliante*] Madam, your virtuous beauty has no peer.
    Of all this world, you only are sincere;
    I've long esteemed you highly, as you know;
    Permit me ever to esteem you so,
    And if I do not request your hand,   5
    Forgive me, Madam, and try to understand.
    I feel unworthy of it; I sense that fate
    Does not intend me for the married state,
    That I should do you wrong by offering you
    My shattered heart's unhappy residue,   10
    And that in short . . .
ELIANTE.   Your argument's well taken:
    Nor need you fear that I shall feel forsaken.
    Were I to offer him this hand of mine,
    Your friend Philinte, I think, would not decline.
PHILINTE. Ah, Madam, that's my heart's most cherished goal,   15
    For which I'd gladly give my life and soul.
ALCESTE. [*to Eliante and Philinte*] May you be true to all you now profess,
    And so deserve unending happiness.
    Meanwhile, betrayed and wronged in everything,
    I'll flee this bitter world where vice is king,   20
    And seek some spot unpeopled and apart
    Where I'll be free to have an honest heart.
PHILINTE. Come, Madam, let's do everything we can
    To change the mind of this unhappy man.

    Exeunt.

QUESTIONS

1. A misanthrope is, literally, a person who scorns humankind. What views does Alceste express in the first scene that makes him seem misanthropic? What are his specific grievances and what segment of society are they aimed at?

2. Are we to admire Alceste or to see him as somewhat foolish? Does his character change over the course of the play? Why, for all of his noble principles, does he come across as a comic figure?

3. What role does Alceste's friend Philinte play? Can you summarize his position? Do you think Molière wants us to scorn or endorse his views about the necessity of falsehoods?

4. Molière has several ways of generating comedy through dialogue. Compare a passage of extended dialogue by one of the central characters with a passage of rapid fire and give-and-take. How does Molière's use of rhyming couplets work when the lines are broken by different speakers? What is the effect?

5. What do you make of Alceste's professed "love" for Célimène? Does her reputation for being an outrageous flirt make him appear to be a hypocrite, or does he seem more human for his flawed judgment? Do you believe his assertions of love? Explain.

6. Why should Oronte be so offended by Alceste's reaction to his sonnet? What is your reaction to the verse? Why should Alceste be more insistent about his judgment of the writing than about other aspects of characters' behavior? What kind of statement is Molière making about the place of truth in art?

7. What do we learn about Alceste's character from his refusal to answer Oronte directly about his poem?

8. What is the role of Eliante in the play? Does Molière create a certain expectation in the reader/viewer about Eliante and Alceste? What happens to this expectation at the end of the play?

9. Look closely at the conversation between Arsinoé and Célimène. Are they two sides of the same coin? Which of the two women comes off better in the exchange?

10. Look at the scene in Act V in which Célimène is confronted by her duped suitors. Is she not, in her way, as honest as Alceste would like to be? What does her letter say about Alceste? How does Alceste respond? What is it, finally, that causes him to "see the light" about Célimène?

11. What kind of picture does Molière draw of the aristocracy and its morality? Is Alceste to be seen as a redeeming figure? Is there a serious point to this comedy? If so, what?

12. Ask yourself how much you and the people around you depend on little lies and deceptions to keep social exchanges moving pleasantly. What would be the effect of being completely honest to each person? Is Molière, by the same token, advocating complete honesty, or is he identifying different levels of hypocrisy—some essential, others despicable?

13. What would Alceste have to say about himself if he lived up to his ideal of complete truthfulness?

14. Molière observed the Aristotilean unities—of time, place and action—in this play. How would *The Misanthrope* be different without them?

34 Realism in Drama

Literature, as we have seen throughout this anthology, does not arise in a vacuum, but is at every turn closely bound to the historical conditions that shape every culture. The dramatic arts are no exception. As Greek drama originated in a culture that worshipped a pantheon of gods and as Elizabethan drama expressed the energies and spirit of Renaissance humanism, so did Neoclassical plays reflect the rigidly stylized rituals of a society ruled by a monarch and a court of aristocrats.

The next great development in the history of drama—*Realism*—was similarly the product of specific historical changes affecting Europe and the West. The transformation began in the late eighteenth century. Revolutions in America, France, and elsewhere successfully overthrew oppressive systems of monarchic rule and cleared the way for the new. The same period also witnessed the great expansion of industry and commerce and the rapid rise to power of the middle class. The ascendancy of these merchants and tradesmen was marked by a great zeal to self-betterment; they wanted the fruits of education and culture that had been denied them previously. But they also wanted something else. They wanted an art and a literature that would show them something other than the triumphs and travails of the well-to-do. They wanted to look into the mirror of art and see themselves.

It was in this climate that Realism was born. Artists and writers responded to the needs of the new public, creating works that presented issues and situations familiar to the common person. In drama, as in other genres, this new approach would result in the radical overhaul of the form. One need only compare the Neoclassical stage with the Realist stage to appreciate the difference. Where the former featured elegantly attired aristocrats exchanging quips or high-flown sentiments, the drama of the Realists placed middle-class people in natural settings. When they spoke to one another, the language was appropriately natural—they talked the way people of their station would really talk. Nor did they deliver their lines out to the audience. Rather, they addressed one another directly. The whole effect was that here was a slice of life; that the audience was looking in on actual situations—spying and eavesdropping, if you will. To intensify this illusion, the stage designers favored the *box set*, which was usually a realistically appointed room with a ceiling tilted toward the rear of the stage to accentuate the perspective. *Props* (the furniture and decorations) were arranged to further simulate the impression of the real.

In the late nineteenth century, largely owing to the influence of the French writer Émile Zola (1840–1902), Realism spawned a movement known as *Naturalism*. Naturalists, like Maxim Gorky (1868–1936), author of the powerful play *The Lower Depths*, subscribed to the view that humankind was just another species in the natural order and that material circumstances were all-determining. In a God-less universe, they felt, a writer's job was to show the dynamism of societal forces as nakedly as possible. As Gorky's title suggests, the task very often involved representing the abject conditions that the masses had as their lot. Though the philosophy of Naturalism was influential, few works from the repertoire have retained currency.

REALISTIC DRAMA IN WESTERN EUROPE: HENRIK IBSEN

Probably the best known of the Realist dramatists is the Norwegian Henrik Ibsen. The playwright was born in 1828 in Skien, a seaport town. A drastic reversal of fortune reduced the family from comparative wealth to poverty when Henrik was six. As *A Doll's House* testifies, a deep sense of financial precariousness remained with him for life.

Ibsen abandoned his plans to study medicine in order to work as a stage manager in the provincial city of Bergen, an experience that stood him in good stead when he turned to writing plays. He served for a time as the artistic director of the National Theater in Oslo and there wrote his first serious plays. Professional frustrations, however, sent him into exile. In 1864, when he was thirty-six, Ibsen moved to Rome. He would remain abroad for the next twenty-seven years, writing the plays that have secured his reputation. These include *Peer Gynt* (1867), *The Pillars of Society* (1876), *A Doll's House* (1879), *Ghosts* (1881), *The Wild Duck* (1884), and *Hedda Gabler* (1890). In 1891, Ibsen returned to Norway, where he remained until his death in 1906.

Ibsen was no stranger to controversy. Though he lived most of his adult life in Italy and Germany, he kept a close watch on social developments in his native land. His plays were often rooted in the important issues of the day—they are sometimes called *problem plays*, because they aim to give dramatic shape to specific, often disturbing, topics. *A Doll's House*, as we will see, poses the problem of the woman's place in a male-dominated society, while *Ghosts* confronts the taboo subject of venereal disease. The latter play, written while Ibsen was in Italy, was refused by theaters and booksellers alike.

A Doll's House was based on a tragedy that befell a young Norwegian woman whom Ibsen had befriended abroad. Like Nora, Laura Petersen had arranged a secret loan to help her husband. When the truth came out, her husband turned against her, driving the woman to a nervous breakdown. Ibsen perceived that her unhappy fate had as much to do with the unjust distribution of social power as with the private relations between husband and wife. *A Doll's House*, written with great speed in 1879, became a sensation throughout Europe. But Ibsen persisted in viewing the work as a statement about the universal need for self-actualization. He would not let himself be canonized as a spokesman for female emancipation.

Before he undertook to write *A Doll's House*, after he had learned the full story about Laura Petersen (she was committed to an asylum), Ibsen wrote down these "Notes for a Modern Tragedy":

There are two kinds of moral laws, two kinds of conscience, one for men and one, quite different, for women. They don't understand each other; but in practical life, woman is judged by masculine law, as though she weren't a woman but a man.

The wife in the play ends by having no idea what is right and what is wrong; natural feelings on the one hand and belief in authority on the other lead her to utter distraction.

A woman cannot be herself in modern society. It is an exclusively male society, with laws made by men and with prosecutors and judges who assess female conduct from a male standpoint.

She has committed forgery, which is her pride; for she has done it out of love for her husband, to save his life. But this husband of hers takes his standpoint, conventionally honourable, on the side of the law, and sees the situation with male eyes.

Moral conflict. Weighted down and confused by her trust in authority, she loses faith in her own morality, and in her fitness to bring up her children. Bitterness. A mother in society, like certain insects, retires and dies once she has done her duty by propagating the race. Love of life, of home, of husband and children and family. Now and then, as women do, she shrugs off her thoughts. Suddenly anguish and fear return. Everything must be borne alone. The catastrophe approaches, mercilessly, inevitably. Despair, conflict and defeat.

Translated by Michael Meyer

As much as the situation of women has improved over the past century, readers of both sexes are bound to experience frequent shocks of recognition as Ibsen sets out the plight of Nora Helmer.

Henrik Ibsen (1826–1906)

Henrik Ibsen was born in Skien, Norway. His father's once prosperous business failed while Ibsen was young, and the boy was forced to work at an apothecary. While at the university, Ibsen was invited to join the National Theater. It was a period of rich apprenticeship, but when the theater failed, Ibsen emigrated to Italy. He gained his first recognition with the publication of *Brand* in 1866. His subsequent plays, many of them treating controversial social themes, gained him international notoriety. These included *A Doll's House* (1879) and *Ghosts* (1881), which addressed the taboo subject of venereal disease. His late plays, including *The Wild Duck* (1884) and *Hedda Gabler* (1890), were viewed by critics as obscure and unnecessarily bleak. Ibsen returned to Norway in 1891, where he lived until his death from a stroke in 1906.

A DOLL'S HOUSE

Translated from the Norwegian by James McFarlane

CHARACTERS

TORVALD HELMER, a lawyer
NORA, his wife
DR. RANK
MRS. KRISTINE LINDE
NILS KROGSTAD

ANNE MARIE, the nursemaid
HELENE, the maid
THE HELMERS' THREE CHILDREN
A PORTER

The action takes place in the Helmers' flat.

ACT I

A pleasant room, tastefully but not expensively furnished. On the back wall, one door on the right leads to the entrance hall, a second door on the left leads to Helmer's study. Between these two doors, a piano. In the middle of the left wall, a door; and downstage from it, a window. Near the window a round table with armchairs and a small sofa. In the right wall, upstage, a door; and on the same wall downstage, a porcelain stove with a couple of armchairs and a rocking-chair. Between the stove and the door a small table. Etchings on the walls. A whatnot with china and other small objets d'art; a small book-case with books in handsome bindings. Carpet on the floor; a fire burns in the stove. A winter's day.

The front door-bell rings in the hall; a moment later, there is the sound of the front door being opened. Nora comes into the room, happily humming to herself. She is dressed in her outdoor things, and is carrying lots of parcels which she then puts down on the table, right. She leaves the door into the hall standing open; a Porter can be seen outside holding a Christmas tree and a basket; he hands them to the Maid who has opened the door for them.

NORA. Hide the Christmas tree away carefully, Helene. The children mustn't see it till this evening when it's decorated. [*To the Porter, taking out her purse.*] How much?
PORTER. Fifty öre.
NORA. There's a crown. Keep the change.

The Porter thanks her and goes. Nora shuts the door. She continues to laugh quietly and happily to herself as she takes off her things. She takes a bag of macaroons out of her pocket and eats one or two; then she walks stealthily across and listens at her husband's door.

NORA. Yes, he's in.

She begins humming again as she walks over to the table, right.

HELMER. [*in his study*] Is that my little sky-lark chirruping out there?
NORA. [*busy opening some of the parcels*] Yes, it is.
HELMER. Is that my little squirrel frisking about?
NORA. Yes!
HELMER. When did my little squirrel get home?
NORA. Just this minute. [*She stuffs the bag of macaroons in her pocket and wipes her mouth.*] Come on out, Torvald, and see what I've bought.

1308

HELMER. I don't want to be disturbed! [*A moment later, he opens the door and looks out, his pen in his hand.*] 'Bought', did you say? All that? Has my little spendthrift been out squandering money again?

NORA. But, Torvald, surely this year we can spread ourselves just a little. This is the first Christmas we haven't had to go carefully.

HELMER. Ah, but that doesn't mean we can afford to be extravagant, you know.

NORA. Oh yes, Torvald, surely we can afford to be just a little bit extravagant now, can't we? Just a teeny-weeny bit. You are getting quite a good salary now, and you are going to earn lots and lots of money.

HELMER. Yes, after the New Year. But it's going to be three whole months before the first pay cheque comes in.

NORA. Pooh! We can always borrow in the meantime.

HELMER. Nora! [*Crosses to her and takes her playfully by the ear.*] Here we go again, you and your frivolous ideas! Suppose I went and borrowed a thousand crowns today, and you went and spent it all over Christmas, then on New Year's Eve a slate fell and hit me on the head and there I was. . . .

NORA. [*putting her hand over his mouth*] Sh! Don't say such horrid things.

HELMER. Yes, but supposing something like that did happen . . . what then?

NORA. If anything as awful as that did happen, I wouldn't care if I owed anybody anything or not.

HELMER. Yes, but what about the people I'd borrowed from?

NORA. Them? Who cares about them! They are only strangers!

HELMER. Nora, Nora! Just like a woman! Seriously though, Nora, you know what I think about these things. No debts! Never borrow! There's always something inhibited, something unpleasant, about a home built on credit and borrowed money. We two have managed to stick it out so far, and that's the way we'll go on for the little time that remains.

NORA. [*walks over to the stove*] Very well, just as you say, Torvald.

HELMER. [*following her*] There, there! My little singing bird mustn't go drooping her wings, eh? Has it got the sulks, that little squirrel of mine? [*Takes out his wallet.*] Nora, what do you think I've got here?

NORA. [*quickly turning round*] Money!

HELMER. There! [*He hands her some notes.*] Good heavens, I know only too well how Christmas runs away with the housekeeping.

NORA. [*counts*] Ten, twenty, thirty, forty. Oh, thank you, thank you, Torvald! This will see me quite a long way.

HELMER. Yes, it'll have to.

NORA. Yes, yes, I'll see that it does. But come over here, I want to show you all the things I've bought. And so cheap! Look, some new clothes for Ivar . . . and a little sword. There's a horse and a trumpet for Bob. And a doll and a doll's cot for Emmy. They are not very grand but she'll have them all broken before long anyway. And I've got some dress material and some handkerchiefs for the maids. Though, really, dear old Anne Marie should have had something better.

HELMER. And what's in this parcel here?

NORA. [*shrieking*] No, Torvald! You mustn't see that till tonight!

HELMER. All right. But tell me now, what did my little spendthrift fancy for herself?

NORA. For me? Puh, I don't really want anything.

HELMER. Of course you do. Anything reasonable that you think you might like, just tell me.

A Doll's House

NORA. Well, I don't really know. As a matter of fact, though, Torvald . . .

HELMER. Well?

NORA. [*toying with his coat buttons, and without looking at him*] If you did want to give me something, you could . . . you could always . . .

HELMER. Well, well, out with it!

NORA. [*quickly*] You could always give me money, Torvald. Only what you think you could spare. And then I could buy myself something with it later on.

HELMER. But Nora . . .

NORA. Oh, please, Torvald dear! Please! I beg you. Then I'd wrap the money up in some pretty gilt paper and hang it on the Christmas tree. Wouldn't that be fun?

HELMER. What do we call my pretty little pet when it runs away with all the money?

NORA. I know, I know, we call it a spendthrift. But please let's do what I said, Torvald. Then I'll have a bit of time to think about what I need most. Isn't that awfully sensible, now, eh?

HELMER. [*smiling*] Yes, it is indeed—that is, if only you really could hold on to the money I gave you, and really did buy something for yourself with it. But it just gets mixed up with the housekeeping and frittered away on all sorts of useless things, and then I have to dig into my pocket all over again.

NORA. Oh but, Torvald . . .

HELMER. You can't deny it, Nora dear. [*Puts his arm round her waist.*] My pretty little pet is very sweet, but it runs away with an awful lot of money. It's incredible how expensive it is for a man to keep such a pet.

NORA. For shame! How can you say such a thing? As a matter of fact I save everything I can.

HELMER. [*laughs*] Yes, you are right there. Everything you *can*. But you simply can't.

NORA. [*hums and smiles quietly and happily*] Ah, if you only knew how many expenses the likes of us sky-larks and squirrels have, Torvald!

HELMER. What a funny little one you are! Just like your father. Always on the look-out for money, wherever you can lay your hands on it; but as soon as you've got it, it just seems to slip through your fingers. You never seem to know what you've done with it. Well, one must accept you as you are. It's in the blood. Oh yes, it is, Nora. That sort of thing is hereditary.

NORA. Oh, I only wish I'd inherited a few more of Daddy's qualities.

HELMER. And I wouldn't want my pretty little song-bird to be the least bit different from what she is now. But come to think of it, you look rather . . . rather . . . how shall I put it? . . . rather guilty today. . . .

NORA. Do I?

HELMER. Yes, you do indeed. Look me straight in the eye.

NORA. [*looks at him*] Well?

HELMER. [*wagging his finger at her*] My little sweet-tooth surely didn't forget herself in town today?

NORA. No, whatever makes you think that?

HELMER. She didn't just pop into the confectioner's for a moment?

NORA. No, I assure you, Torvald . . . !

HELMER. Didn't try sampling the preserves?

NORA. No, really I didn't.

HELMER. Didn't go nibbling a macaroon or two?

NORA. No, Torvald, honestly, you must believe me . . . !

HELMER. All right then! It's really just my little joke. . . .

NORA. [crosses to the table] I would never dream of doing anything you didn't want me to.

HELMER. Of course not, I know that. And then you've given me your word. . . . [Crosses to her.] Well then, Nora dearest, you shall keep your little Christmas secrets. They'll all come out tonight, I dare say, when we light the tree.

NORA. Did you remember to invite Dr. Rank?

HELMER. No. But there's really no need. Of course he'll come and have dinner with us. Anyway, I can ask him when he looks in this morning. I've ordered some good wine. Nora, you can't imagine how I am looking forward to this evening.

NORA. So am I. And won't the children enjoy it, Torvald!

HELMER. Oh, what a glorious feeling it is, knowing you've got a nice, safe job, and a good fat income. Don't you agree? Isn't it wonderful, just thinking about it?

NORA. Oh, it's marvellous!

HELMER. Do you remember last Christmas? Three whole weeks beforehand you shut yourself up every evening till after midnight making flowers for the Christmas tree and all the other splendid things you wanted to surprise us with. Ugh, I never felt so bored in all my life.

NORA. I wasn't the least bit bored.

HELMER. [smiling] But it turned out a bit of an anticlimax, Nora.

NORA. Oh, you are not going to tease me about that again! How was I to know the cat would get in and pull everything to bits?

HELMER. No, of course you weren't. Poor little Nora! All you wanted was for us to have a nice time—and it's the thought behind it that counts, after all. All the same, it's a good thing we've seen the back of those lean times.

NORA. Yes, really it's marvellous.

HELMER. Now there's no need for me to sit here all on my own, bored to tears. And you don't have to strain your dear little eyes, and work those dainty little fingers to the bone. . . .

NORA. [clapping her hands] No, Torvald, I don't, do I? Not any more. Oh, how marvellous it is to hear that! [Takes his arm.] Now I want to tell you how I've been thinking we might arrange things, Torvald. As soon as Christmas is over. . . . [The door-bell rings in the hall.] Oh, there's the bell. [Tidies one or two things in the room.] It's probably a visitor. What a nuisance!

HELMER. Remember I'm not at home to callers.

MAID. [in the doorway] There's a lady to see you, ma'am.

NORA. Show her in, please.

MAID. [to Helmer] And the doctor's just arrived, too, sir.

HELMER. Did he go straight into my room?

MAID. Yes, he did, sir.

Helmer goes into his study. The Maid shows in Mrs. Linde, who is in travelling clothes, and closes the door after her.

MRS. LINDE. [subdued and rather hesitantly] How do you do, Nora?

NORA. [uncertainly] How do you do?

MRS. LINDE. I'm afraid you don't recognize me.

NORA. No, I don't think I . . . And yet I seem to . . . [Bursts out suddenly.] Why! Kristine! Is it really you?

MRS. LINDE. Yes, it's me.

NORA. Kristine! Fancy not recognizing you again! But how was I to, when . . . [Gently.] How you've changed, Kristine!

A Doll's House

MRS. LINDE. I dare say I have. In nine . . . ten years. . . .

NORA. Is it so long since we last saw each other? Yes, it must be. Oh, believe me these last eight years have been such a happy time. And now you've come up to town, too? All that long journey in wintertime. That took courage.

MRS. LINDE. I just arrived this morning on the steamer.

NORA. To enjoy yourself over Christmas, of course. How lovely! Oh, we'll have such fun, you'll see. Do take off your things. You are not cold, are you? [*Helps her.*] There now! Now let's sit down here in comfort beside the stove. No, here, you take the armchair, I'll sit here on the rockingchair. [*Takes her hands.*] Ah, now you look a bit more like your old self again. It was just that when I first saw you . . . But you are a little paler, Kristine . . . and perhaps even a bit thinner!

MRS. LINDE. And much, much older, Nora.

NORA. Yes, perhaps a little older . . . very, very little, not really very much. [*Stops suddenly and looks serious.*] Oh, what a thoughtless creature I am, sitting here chattering on like this! Dear, sweet Kristine, can you forgive me?

MRS. LINDE. What do you mean, Nora?

NORA. [*gently*] Poor Kristine, of course you're a widow now.

MRS. LINDE. Yes, my husband died three years ago.

NORA. Oh, I remember now. I read about it in the papers. Oh, Kristine, believe me I often thought at the time of writing to you. But I kept putting it off, something always seemed to crop up.

MRS. LINDE. My dear Nora, I understand so well.

NORA. No, it wasn't very nice of me, Kristine. Oh, you poor thing, what you must have gone through. And didn't he leave you anything?

MRS. LINDE. No.

NORA. And no children?

MRS. LINDE. No.

NORA. Absolutely nothing?

MRS. LINDE. Nothing at all . . . not even a broken heart to grieve over.

NORA. [*looks at her incredulously*] But, Kristine, is that possible?

MRS. LINDE. [*smiles sadly and strokes Nora's hair*] Oh, it sometimes happens, Nora.

NORA. So utterly alone. How terribly sad that must be for you. I have three lovely children. You can't see them for the moment, because they're out with their nanny. But now you must tell me all about yourself. . . .

MRS. LINDE. No, no, I want to hear about you.

NORA. No, you start. I won't be selfish today. I must think only about your affairs today. But there's just one thing I really must tell you. Have you heard about the great stroke of luck we've had in the last few days?

MRS. LINDE. No. What is it?

NORA. What do you think? My husband has just been made Bank Manager!

MRS. LINDE. Your husband? How splendid!

NORA. Isn't it tremendous! It's not a very steady way of making a living, you know, being a lawyer, especially if he refuses to take on anything that's the least bit shady—which of course is what Torvald does, and I think he's quite right. You can imagine how pleased we are! He starts at the Bank straight after New Year, and he's getting a big salary and lots of commission. From now on we'll be able to live quite differently . . . we'll do just what we want. Oh, Kristine, I'm so happy and relieved. I must say it's lovely to have plenty of money and not have to worry. Isn't it?

MRS. LINDE. Yes. It must be nice to have enough, at any rate.

NORA. No, not just enough, but pots and pots of money.

MRS. LINDE. [*smiles*] Nora, Nora, haven't you learned any sense yet? At school you used to be an awful spendthrift.

NORA. Yes, Torvald still says I am. [*Wags her finger.*] But little Nora isn't as stupid as everybody thinks. Oh, we haven't really been in a position where I could afford to spend a lot of money. We've both had to work.

MRS. LINDE. You too?

NORA. Yes, odd jobs—sewing, crochet-work, embroidery and things like that. [*Casually.*] And one or two other things, besides. I suppose you know that Torvald left the Ministry when we got married. There weren't any prospects of promotion in his department, and of course he needed to earn more money than he had before. But the first year he wore himself out completely. He had to take on all kinds of extra jobs, you know, and he found himself working all hours of the day and night. But he couldn't go on like that; and he became seriously ill. The doctors said it was essential for him to go South.

MRS. LINDE. Yes, I believe you spent a whole year in Italy, didn't you?

NORA. That's right. It wasn't easy to get away, I can tell you. It was just after I'd had Ivar. But of course we had to go. Oh, it was an absolutely marvellous trip. And it saved Torvald's life. But it cost an awful lot of money, Kristine.

MRS. LINDE. That I can well imagine.

NORA. Twelve hundred dollars. Four thousand eight hundred crowns. That's a lot of money, Kristine.

MRS. LINDE. Yes, but in such circumstances, one is very lucky if one has it.

NORA. Well, we got it from Daddy, you see.

MRS. LINDE. Ah, that was it. It was just about then your father died, I believe, wasn't it?

NORA. Yes, Kristine, just about then. And do you know, I couldn't even go and look after him. Here was I expecting Ivar any day. And I also had poor Torvald, gravely ill, on my hands. Dear, kind Daddy! I never saw him again, Kristine. Oh, that's the saddest thing that has happened to me in all my married life.

MRS. LINDE. I know you were very fond of him. But after that you left for Italy?

NORA. Yes, we had the money then, and the doctors said it was urgent. We left a month later.

MRS. LINDE. And your husband came back completely cured?

NORA. Fit as a fiddle!

MRS. LINDE. But . . . what about the doctor?

NORA. How do you mean?

MRS. LINDE. I thought the maid said something about the gentleman who came at the same time as me being a doctor.

NORA. Yes, that was Dr. Rank. But this isn't a professional visit. He's our best friend and he always looks in at least once a day. No, Torvald has never had a day's illness since. And the children are fit and healthy, and so am I. [*Jumps up and claps her hands.*] Oh God, oh God, isn't it marvellous to be alive, and to be happy, Kristine! . . . Oh, but I ought to be ashamed of myself . . . Here I go on talking about nothing but myself. [*She sits on a low stool near Mrs. Linde and lays her arms on her lap.*] Oh, please, you mustn't be angry with me! Tell me, is it really true that you didn't love your husband? What made you marry him, then?

MRS. LINDE. My mother was still alive; she was bedridden and helpless. And then I had my two young brothers to look after as well. I didn't think I would be justified in refusing him.

NORA. No, I dare say you are right. I suppose he was fairly wealthy then?

MRS. LINDE. He was quite well off, I believe. But the business was shaky. When he died, it went all to pieces, and there just wasn't anything left.

NORA. What then?

MRS. LINDE. Well, I had to fend for myself, opening a little shop, running a little school, anything I could turn my hand to. These last three years have been one long relentless drudge. But now it's finished, Nora. My poor dear mother doesn't need me any more, she's passed away. Nor the boys either; they're at work now, they can look after themselves.

NORA. What a relief you must find it. . . .

MRS. LINDE. No Nora! Just unutterably empty. Nobody to live for any more. [*Stands up restlessly.*] That's why I couldn't stand it any longer being cut off up there. Surely it must be a bit easier here to find something to occupy your mind. If only I could manage to find a steady job of some kind, in an office perhaps. . . .

NORA. But, Kristine, that's terribly exhausting; and you look so worn out even before you start. The best thing for you would be a little holiday at some quiet little resort.

MRS. LINDE. [*crosses to the window*] I haven't any father I can fall back on for the money, Nora.

NORA. [*rises*] Oh, please, you mustn't be angry with me!

MRS. LINDE. [*goes to her*] My dear Nora, you mustn't be angry with me either. That's the worst thing about people in my position, they become so bitter. One has nobody to work for, yet one has to be on the look-out all the time. Life has to go on, and one starts thinking only of oneself. Believe it or not, when you told me the good news about your step up, I was pleased not so much for your sake as for mine.

NORA. How do you mean? Ah, I see. You think Torvald might be able to do something for you.

MRS. LINDE. Yes, that's exactly what I thought.

NORA. And so he shall, Kristine. Just leave things to me. I'll bring it up so cleverly . . . I'll think up something to put him in a good mood. Oh, I do so much want to help you.

MRS. LINDE. It is awfully kind of you, Nora, offering to do all this for me, particularly in your case, where you haven't known much trouble or hardship in your own life.

NORA. When I . . . ? I haven't known much . . . ?

MRS. LINDE. [*smiling*] Well, good heavens, a little bit of sewing to do and a few things like that. What a child you are, Nora!

NORA. [*tosses her head and walks across the room*] I wouldn't be too sure of that, if I were you.

MRS. LINDE. Oh?

NORA. You're just like the rest of them. You all think I'm useless when it comes to anything really serious. . . .

MRS. LINDE. Come, come. . . .

NORA. You think I've never had anything much to contend with in this hard world.

MRS. LINDE. Nora dear, you've only just been telling me all the things you've had to put up with.

NORA. Pooh! They were just trivialities! [*Softly.*] I haven't told you about the really big thing.

MRS. LINDE. What big thing? What do you mean?

NORA. I know you rather tend to look down on me, Kristine. But you shouldn't, you know. You are proud of having worked so hard and so long for your mother.

MRS. LINDE. I'm sure I don't look down on anybody. But it's true what you say; I am both proud and happy when I think of how I was able to make Mother's life a little easier towards the end.

NORA. And you are proud when you think of what you have done for your brothers, too.

MRS. LINDE. I think I have every right to be.

NORA. I think so too. But now I'm going to tell you something, Kristine. I too have something to be proud and happy about.

MRS. LINDE. I don't doubt that. But what is it you mean?

NORA. Not so loud. Imagine if Torvald were to hear! He must never on any account . . . nobody must know about it, Kristine, nobody but you.

MRS. LINDE. But what is it?

NORA. Come over here. [*She pulls her down on the sofa beside her.*] Yes, Kristine, I too have something to be proud and happy about. I was the one who saved Torvald's life.

MRS. LINDE. Saved . . . ? How . . . ?

NORA. I told you about our trip to Italy. Torvald would never have recovered but for that. . . .

MRS. LINDE. Well? Your father gave you what money was necessary. . . .

NORA. [*smiles*] That's what Torvald thinks, and everybody else. But . . .

MRS. LINDE. But . . . ?

NORA. Daddy never gave us a penny. I was the one who raised the money.

MRS. LINDE. You? All that money?

NORA. Twelve hundred dollars. Four thousand eight hundred crowns. What do you say to that!

MRS. LINDE. But, Nora, how was it possible? Had you won a sweepstake or something?

NORA. [*contemptuously*] A sweepstake? Pooh! There would have been nothing to it then.

MRS. LINDE. Where did you get it from, then?

NORA. [*hums and smiles secretively*] H'm, tra-la-la!

MRS. LINDE. Because what you couldn't do was borrow it.

NORA. Oh? Why not?

MRS. LINDE. Well, a wife can't borrow without her husband's consent.

NORA. [*tossing her head*] Ah, but when it happens to be a wife with a bit of a sense for business . . . a wife who knows her way about things, then. . . .

MRS. LINDE. But, Nora, I just don't understand. . . .

NORA. You don't have to. I haven't said I did borrow the money. I might have got it some other way. [*Throws herself back on the sofa.*] I might even have got it from some admirer. Anyone as reasonably attractive as I am. . . .

MRS. LINDE. Don't be so silly!

NORA. Now you must be dying of curiosity, Kristine.

MRS. LINDE. Listen to me now, Nora dear—you haven't done anything rash, have you?

NORA. [*sitting up again*] Is it rash to save your husband's life?

MRS. LINDE. I think it was rash to do anything without telling him. . . .

NORA. But the whole point was that he mustn't know anything. Good heavens, can't you see! He wasn't even supposed to know how desperately ill he was. It was me the doctors came and told his life was in danger, that the only way to save him was to go South for a while. Do you think I didn't try talking him into it first? I began dropping hints about how nice it would be if I could be taken on a little trip abroad, like other young wives. I wept, I pleaded. I told him he ought to show some consideration for my condition, and let me have a bit of my own way. And then I suggested he might take out a loan. But at that he nearly lost his temper, Kristine. He said I was being frivolous, that it was his duty as a husband not to give in to all these whims and fancies of mine—as I do believe he called them. All right, I thought, somehow you've got to be saved. And it was then I found a way. . . .

MRS. LINDE. Did your husband never find out from your father that the money hadn't come from him?

NORA. No, never. It was just about the time Daddy died. I'd intended letting him into the secret and asking him not to give me away. But when he was so ill . . . I'm sorry to say it never became necessary.

MRS. LINDE. And you never confided in your husband?

NORA. Good heavens, how could you ever imagine such a thing! When he's so strict about such matters! Besides, Torvald is a man with a good deal of pride—it would be terribly embarrassing and humiliating for him if he thought he owed anything to me. It would spoil everything between us; this happy home of ours would never be the same again.

MRS. LINDE. Are you never going to tell him?

NORA. [*reflectively, half-smiling*] Oh yes, some day perhaps . . . in many years' time, when I'm no longer as pretty as I am now. You mustn't laugh! What I mean of course is when Torvald isn't quite so much in love with me as he is now, when he's lost interest in watching me dance, or get dressed up, or recite. Then it might be a good thing to have something in reserve. . . . [*Breaks off.*] What nonsense! That day will never come. Well, what have you got to say to my big secret, Kristine? Still think I'm not much good for anything? One thing, though, it's meant a lot of worry for me, I can tell you. It hasn't always been easy to meet my obligations when the time came. You know in business there is something called quarterly interest, and other things called installments, and these are always terribly difficult things to cope with. So what I've had to do is save a little here and there, you see, wherever I could. I couldn't really save anything out of the housekeeping, because Torvald has to live in decent style. I couldn't let the children go about badly dressed either—I felt any money I got for them had to go on them alone. Such sweet little things!

MRS. LINDE. Poor Nora! So it had to come out of your own allowance?

NORA. Of course. After all, I was the one it concerned most. Whenever Torvald gave me money for new clothes and such-like, I never spent more than half. And always I bought the simplest and cheapest things. It's a blessing most things look well on me, so Torvald never noticed anything. But sometimes I did feel it was a bit hard, Kristine, because it is nice to be well dressed, isn't it?

MRS. LINDE. Yes, I suppose it is.

NORA. I have had some other sources of income, of course. Last winter I was lucky enough to get quite a bit of copying to do. So I shut myself up every night and sat and wrote through to the small hours of the morning. Oh, sometimes I was so tired, so tired. But it was tremendous fun all the same, sitting there working and earning money like that. It was almost like being a man.

MRS. LINDE. And how much have you been able to pay off like this?

NORA. Well, I can't tell exactly. It's not easy to know where you are with transactions of this kind, you understand. All I know is I've paid off just as much as I could scrape together. Many's the time I was at my wit's end. [*Smiles.*] Then I used to sit here and pretend that some rich old gentleman had fallen in love with me. . . .

MRS. LINDE. What! What gentleman?

NORA. Oh, rubbish! . . . and that now he had died, and when they opened his will, there in big letters were the words: 'My entire fortune is to be paid over, immediately and in cash, to charming Mrs. Nora Helmer.'

MRS. LINDE. But my dear Nora—who *is* this man?

NORA. Good heavens, don't you understand? There never was any old gentleman; it was just something I used to sit here pretending, time and time again, when I didn't know where to turn next for money. But it doesn't make very much difference; as far as I'm concerned, the old boy can do what he likes, I'm tired of him; I can't be bothered any more with him or his will. Because now all my worries are over. [*Jumping up.*] Oh God, what a glorious thought, Kristine! No more worries! Just think of being without a care in the world . . . being able to romp with the children, and making the house nice and attractive, and having things just as Torvald likes to have them! And then spring will soon be here, and blue skies. And maybe we can go away somewhere. I might even see something of the sea again. Oh yes! When you're happy, life is a wonderful thing!

The door-bell is heard in the hall.

MRS. LINDE. [*gets up*] There's the bell. Perhaps I'd better go.

NORA. No, do stay, please. I don't suppose it's for me; it's probably somebody for Torvald. . . .

MAID. [*in the doorway*] Excuse me, ma'am, but there's a gentleman here wants to see Mr. Helmer, and I didn't quite know . . . because the Doctor is in there. . . .

NORA. Who is the gentleman?

KROGSTAD. [*in the doorway*] It's me, Mrs. Helmer.

Mrs. Linde starts, then turns away to the window.

NORA. [*tense, takes a step towards him and speaks in a low voice*] You? What is it? What do you want to talk to my husband about?

KROGSTAD. Bank matters . . . in a manner of speaking. I work at the bank, and I hear your husband is to be the new manager. . . .

NORA. So it's . . .

KROGSTAD. Just routine business matters, Mrs. Helmer. Absolutely nothing else.

NORA. Well then, please go into his study.

She nods impassively and shuts the hall door behind him; then she walks across and sees to the stove.

MRS. LINDE. Nora . . . who was that man?

NORA. His name is Krogstad.

MRS. LINDE. So it really was him.

NORA. Do you know the man?

MRS. LINDE. I used to know him . . . a good many years ago. He was a solicitor's clerk in our district for a while.

NORA. Yes, so he was.

MRS. LINDE. How he's changed!

NORA. His marriage wasn't a very happy one, I believe.

MRS. LINDE. He's a widower now, isn't he?

NORA. With a lot of children. There, it'll burn better now.

She closes the stove door and moves the rocking chair a little to one side.

MRS. LINDE. He does a certain amount of business on the side, they say?

NORA. Oh? Yes, it's always possible. I just don't know. . . . But let's not think about business . . . it's all so dull.

Dr. Rank comes in from Helmer's study.

DR. RANK. [*still in the doorway*] No, no, Torvald, I won't intrude. I'll just look in on your wife for a moment. [*Shuts the door and notices Mrs. Linde.*] Oh, I beg your pardon. I'm afraid I'm intruding here as well.

NORA. No, not at all! [*Introduces them.*] Dr. Rank . . . Mrs. Linde.

RANK. Ah! A name I've often heard mentioned in this house. I believe I came past you on the stairs as I came in.

MRS. LINDE. I have to take things slowly going upstairs. I find it rather a trial.

RANK. Ah, some little disability somewhere, eh?

MRS. LINDE. Just a bit run down, I think actually.

RANK. Is that all? Then I suppose you've come to town for a good rest—doing the rounds of the parties?

MRS. LINDE. I have come to look for work.

RANK. Is that supposed to be some kind of sovereign remedy for being run down?

MRS. LINDE. One must live, Doctor.

RANK. Yes, it's generally thought to be necessary.

NORA. Come, come, Dr. Rank. You are quite as keen to live as anybody.

RANK. Quite keen, yes. Miserable as I am, I'm quite ready to let things drag on as long as possible. All my patients are the same. Even those with a moral affliction are no different. As a matter of fact, there's a bad case of that kind in talking with Helmer at this very moment. . . .

MRS. LINDE. [*softly*] Ah!

NORA. Whom do you mean?

RANK. A person called Krogstad—nobody you would know. He's rotten to the core. But even he began talking about having to *live*, as though it were something terribly important.

NORA. Oh? And what did he want to talk to Torvald about?

RANK. I honestly don't know. All I heard was something about the Bank.

NORA. I didn't know that Krog . . . that this Mr. Krogstad had anything to do with the Bank.

RANK. Oh yes, he's got some kind of job down there. [*To Mrs. Linde.*] I wonder if you've got people in your part of the country too who go rushing round sniffing out cases of moral corruption, and then installing the individuals concerned in nice, well-paid jobs where they can keep them under observation. Sound, decent people have to be content to stay out in the cold.

MRS. LINDE. Yet surely it's the sick who most need to be brought in.

RANK. [*shrugs his shoulders*] Well, there we have it. It's that attitude that's turning society into a clinic.

Nora, lost in her own thoughts, breaks into smothered laughter and claps her hands.

RANK. Why are you laughing at that? Do you know in fact what society is?

NORA. What do I care about your silly old society? I was laughing about something quite different . . . something frightfully funny. Tell me, Dr. Rank, are all the people who work at the Bank dependent on Torvald now?

RANK. Is *that* what you find so frightfully funny?

NORA. [*smiles and hums*] Never you mind! Never you mind! [*Walks about the room.*] Yes, it really is terribly amusing to think that we . . . that Torvald now has power over so many people. [*She takes the bag out of her pocket.*] Dr. Rank, what about a little macaroon?

RANK. Look at this, eh? Macaroons. I thought they were forbidden here.

NORA. Yes, but these are some Kristine gave me.

MRS. LINDE. What? I . . . ?

NORA. Now, now, you needn't be alarmed. You weren't to know that Torvald had forbidden them. He's worried in case they ruin my teeth, you know. Still . . . what's it matter once in a while! Don't you think so, Dr. Rank? Here! [*She pops a macaroon into his mouth.*] And you too, Kristine. And I shall have one as well; just a little one . . . or two at the most. [*She walks about the room again.*] Really I am so happy. There's just one little thing I'd love to do now.

RANK. What's that?

NORA. Something I'd love to say in front of Torvald.

RANK. Then why can't you?

NORA. No, I daren't. It's not very nice.

MRS. LINDE. Not very nice?

RANK. Well, in that case it might not be wise. But to us, I don't see why. . . . What is this you would love to say in front of Helmer?

NORA. I would simply love to say: 'Damn'.

RANK. Are you mad!

MRS. LINDE. Good gracious, Nora . . . !

RANK. Say it! Here he is!

NORA. [*hiding the bag of macaroons*] Sh! Sh!

Helmer comes out of his room, his overcoat over his arm and his hat in his hand.

NORA. [*going over to him*] Well, Torvald dear, did you get rid of him?

HELMER. Yes, he's just gone.

NORA. Let me introduce you. This is Kristine, who has just arrived in town. . . .

HELMER. Kristine . . . ? You must forgive me, but I don't think I know . . .

NORA. Mrs. Linde, Torvald dear. Kristine Linde.

HELMER. Ah, indeed. A school-friend of my wife's, presumably.

MRS. LINDE. Yes, we were girls together.

NORA. Fancy, Torvald, she's come all this long way just to have a word with you.

HELMER. How is that?

MRS. LINDE. Well, it wasn't really. . . .

NORA. The thing is, Kristine is terribly clever at office work, and she's frightfully keen on finding a job with some efficient man, so that she can learn even more. . . .

HELMER. Very sensible, Mrs. Linde.

NORA. And then when she heard you'd been made Bank Manager—there was a bit in the paper about it—she set off at once. Torvald please! You *will* try and do something for Kristine, won't you? For my sake?

HELMER. Well, that's not altogether impossible. You are a widow, I presume?

MRS. LINDE. Yes.

HELMER. And you've had some experience in business?

MRS. LINDE. A fair amount.

HELMER. Well, it's quite probable I can find you a job, I think . . .

NORA. [*clapping her hands*] There, you see!

HELMER. You have come at a fortunate moment, Mrs. Linde. . . .

MRS. LINDE. Oh, how can I ever thank you . . . ?

HELMER. Not a bit. [*He puts on his overcoat.*] But for the present I must ask you to excuse me. . . .

RANK. Wait. I'm coming with you.

He fetches his fur coat from the hall and warms it at the stove.

NORA. Don't be long, Torvald dear.

HELMER. Not more than an hour, that's all.

NORA. Are you leaving too, Kristine?

MRS. LINDE. [*putting on her things*] Yes, I must go and see if I can't find myself a room.

HELMER. Perhaps we can all walk down the road together.

NORA. [*helping her*] What a nuisance we are so limited for space here. I'm afraid it just isn't possible. . . .

MRS. LINDE. Oh, you mustn't dream of it! Goodbye, Nora dear, and thanks for everything.

NORA. Goodbye for the present. But . . . you'll be coming back this evening, of course. And you too, Dr. Rank? What's that? If you are up to it? Of course you'll be up to it. Just wrap yourself up well.

They go out, talking, into the hall; children's voices can be heard on the stairs.

NORA. Here they are! Here they are! [*She runs to the front door and opens it. Anne Marie, the Nursemaid, enters with the children.*] Come in! Come in! [*She bends down and kisses them.*] Ah! my sweet little darlings. . . . You see them, Kristine? Aren't they lovely!

RANK. Don't stand here chattering in this draught!

HELMER. Come along, Mrs. Linde. The place now becomes unbearable for anybody except mothers.

Dr. Rank, Helmer and Mrs. Linde go down the stairs: the Nursemaid comes into the room with the children, then Nora, shutting the door behind her.

NORA. How fresh and bright you look! My, what red cheeks you've got! Like apples and roses. [*During the following, the children keep chattering away to her.*] Have you had a nice time? That's splendid. And you gave Emmy and Bob a ride on your sledge? Did you now! Both together! Fancy that! There's a clever boy, Ivar. Oh, let me take her a little while, Anne Marie. There's my sweet little baby-doll! [*She takes the youngest of the children from the Nursemaid and dances with her.*] All right, Mummy will dance with Bobby too. What? You've been throwing snow-balls? Oh, I wish I'd been there. No, don't bother, Anne Marie, I'll help them off with their things. No, please, let me—I like doing it. You go on in, you look frozen. You'll find some hot coffee on the stove. [*The Nursemaid goes into the room, left. Nora takes off the children's coats and hats and throws them down anywhere, while the children all talk at once.*] Really! A great big dog came running after you? But he didn't bite. No, the doggies wouldn't bite my pretty little dol-lies. You mustn't touch the parcels, Ivar! What are they? Wouldn't you like to know! No, no, that's nasty. Now? Shall we play something? What shall we play? Hide and seek? Yes, let's play hide and seek. Bob can hide first. Me first? All right, let me hide first.

She and the children play, laughing and shrieking, in this room and in the adjacent room on the right. Finally Nora hides under the table; the children come rushing in to look for her but cannot find her; they hear her stifled laughter, rush to the table, lift up the tablecloth and find her. Tremendous shouts of delight. She creeps out and pretends to frighten them. More shouts. Meanwhile there has been a knock at the front door, which nobody has heard. The door half opens, and Krogstad can be seen. He waits a little; the game continues.

KROGSTAD. I beg your pardon, Mrs. Helmer. . . .
NORA. [*turns with a stifled cry and half jumps up*] Ah! What do you want?
KROGSTAD. Excuse me. The front door was standing open. Somebody must have forgotten to shut it. . . .
NORA. [*standing up*] My husband isn't at home, Mr. Krogstad.
KROGSTAD. I know.
NORA. Well . . . what are you doing here?
KROGSTAD. I want a word with you.
NORA. With . . . ? [*Quietly, to the children.*] Go to Anne Marie. What? No, the strange man won't do anything to Mummy. When he's gone we'll have another game. [*She leads the children into the room, left, and shuts the door after them; tense and uneasy.*] You want to speak to me?
KROGSTAD. Yes, I do.
NORA. Today? But it isn't the first of the month yet. . . .
KROGSTAD. No, it's Christmas Eve. It depends entirely on you what sort of Christ-mas you have.
NORA. What do you want? Today I can't possibly . . .
KROGSTAD. Let's not talk about that for the moment. It's something else. You've got a moment to spare?
NORA. Yes, I suppose so, though . . .
KROGSTAD. Good. I was sitting in Olsen's café, and I saw your husband go down the road . . .
NORA. Did you?

KROGSTAD. . . . with a lady.

NORA. Well?

KROGSTAD. May I be so bold as to ask whether that lady was a Mrs. Linde?

NORA. Yes.

KROGSTAD. Just arrived in town?

NORA. Yes, today.

KROGSTAD. And she's a good friend of yours?

NORA. Yes, she is. But I can't see . . .

KROGSTAD. I also knew her once.

NORA. I know.

KROGSTAD. Oh? So you know all about it. I thought as much. Well, I want to ask you straight: is Mrs. Linde getting a job in the Bank?

NORA. How dare you cross-examine me like this, Mr. Krogstad? You, one of my husband's subordinates? But since you've asked me, I'll tell you. Yes, Mrs. Linde *has* got a job. And I'm the one who got it for her, Mr. Krogstad. Now you know.

KROGSTAD. So my guess was right.

NORA. [*walking up and down*] Oh, I think I can say that some of us have a little influence now and again. Just because one happens to be a woman, that doesn't mean. . . . People in subordinate positions ought to take care they don't offend anybody . . . who . . . hm . . .

KROGSTAD. . . . has influence?

NORA. Exactly.

KROGSTAD. [*changing his tone*] Mrs. Helmer, will you have the goodness to use your influence on my behalf?

NORA. What? What do you mean?

KROGSTAD. Will you be so good as to see that I keep my modest little job at the Bank?

NORA. What do you mean? Who wants to take it away from you?

KROGSTAD. Oh, you needn't try and pretend to me you don't know. I can quite see that this friend of yours isn't particularly anxious to bump up against me. And I can also see now whom I can thank for being given the sack.

NORA. But I assure you. . . .

KROGSTAD. All right, all right. But to come to the point: there's still time. And I advise you to use your influence to stop it.

NORA. But, Mr. Krogstad, I *have* no influence.

KROGSTAD. Haven't you? I thought just now you said yourself . . .

NORA. I didn't mean it that way, of course. Me? What makes you think I've got any influence of that kind over my husband?

KROGSTAD. I know your husband from our student days. I don't suppose he is any more steadfast than other married men.

NORA. You speak disrespectfully of my husband like that and I'll show you the door.

KROGSTAD. So the lady's got courage.

NORA. I'm not frightened of you any more. After New Year I'll soon be finished with the whole business.

KROGSTAD. [*controlling himself*] Listen to me, Mrs. Helmer. If necessary I shall fight for my little job in the Bank as if I were fighting for my life.

NORA. So it seems.

KROGSTAD. It's not just for the money, that's the last thing I care about. There's something else . . . well, I might as well out with it. You see it's like this. You

1322   Realism in Drama know as well as anybody that some years ago I got myself mixed up in a bit of trouble.

NORA. I believe I've heard something of the sort.

KROGSTAD. It never got as far as the courts; but immediately it was as if all paths were barred to me. So I started going in for the sort of business you know about. I had to do something, and I think I can say I haven't been one of the worst. But now I have to get out of it. My sons are growing up; for their sake I must try and win back what respectability I can. That job in the Bank was like the first step on the ladder for me. And now your husband wants to kick me off the ladder again, back into the mud.

NORA. But in God's name, Mr. Krogstad, it's quite beyond my power to help you.

KROGSTAD. That's because you haven't the will to help me. But I have ways of making you.

NORA. You wouldn't go and tell my husband I owe you money?

KROGSTAD. Suppose I did tell him?

NORA. It would be a rotten shame. [*Half choking with tears.*] That secret is all my pride and joy—why should he have to hear about it in this nasty, horrid way . . . hear about it from *you*. You would make things horribly unpleasant for. . . .

KROGSTAD. Merely unpleasant?

NORA. [*vehemently*] Go on, do it then! It'll be all the worse for you. Because then my husband will see for himself what a bad man you are, and then you certainly won't be able to keep your job.

KROGSTAD. I asked whether it was only a bit of domestic unpleasantness you were afraid of?

NORA. If my husband gets to know about it, he'll pay off what's owing at once. And then we'd have nothing more to do with you.

KROGSTAD. [*taking a pace towards her*] Listen, Mrs. Helmer, either you haven't a very good memory, or else you don't understand much about business. I'd better make the position a little bit clearer for you.

NORA. How do you mean?

KROGSTAD. When your husband was ill, you came to me for the loan of twelve hundred dollars.

NORA. I didn't know of anybody else.

KROGSTAD. I promised to find you the money. . . .

NORA. And you did find it.

KROGSTAD. I promised to find you the money on certain conditions. At the time you were so concerned about your husband's illness, and so anxious to get the money for going away with, that I don't think you paid very much attention to all the incidentals. So there is perhaps some point in reminding you of them. Well, I promised to find you the money against an IOU which I drew up for you.

NORA. Yes, and which I signed.

KROGSTAD. Very good. But below that I added a few lines, by which your father was to stand security. This your father was to sign.

NORA. Was to . . . ? He did sign it.

KROGSTAD. I had left the date blank. The idea was that your father was to add the date himself when he signed it. Remember?

NORA. Yes, I think. . . .

KROGSTAD. I then gave you the IOU to post to your father. Wasn't that so?

NORA. Yes.

KROGSTAD. Which of course you did at once. Because only about five or six days later you brought it back to me with your father's signature. I then paid out the money.

NORA. Well? Haven't I paid the installments regularly?

KROGSTAD. Yes, fairly, But . . . coming back to what we were talking about . . . that was a pretty bad period you were going through then, Mrs. Helmer.

NORA. Yes, it was.

KROGSTAD. Your father was seriously ill, I believe.

NORA. He was very near the end.

KROGSTAD. And died shortly afterwards?

NORA. Yes.

KROGSTAD. Tell me, Mrs. Helmer, do you happen to remember which day your father died? The exact date, I mean.

NORA. Daddy died on 29 September.

KROGSTAD. Quite correct. I made some inquiries. Which brings up a rather curious point [takes out a paper] which I simply cannot explain.

NORA. Curious . . . ? I don't know . . .

KROGSTAD. The curious thing is, Mrs. Helmer, that your father signed this document three days after his death.

NORA. What? I don't understand. . . .

KROGSTAD. Your father died on 29 September. But look here. Your father has dated his signature 2 October. Isn't that rather curious, Mrs. Helmer? [Nora remains silent.] It's also remarkable that the words '2 October' and the year are not in your father's handwriting, but in a handwriting I rather think I recognize. Well, perhaps that could be explained. Your father might have forgotten to date his signature, and then somebody else might have made a guess at the date later, before the fact of your father's death was known. There is nothing wrong in that. What really matters is the signature. And that is of course genuine, Mrs. Helmer? It really was your father who wrote his name here?

NORA. [after a moment's silence, throws her head back and looks at him defiantly] No, it wasn't. It was me who signed father's name.

KROGSTAD. Listen to me. I suppose you realize that that is a very dangerous confession?

NORA. Why? You'll soon have all your money back.

KROGSTAD. Let me ask you a question: why didn't you send that document to your father?

NORA. It was impossible. Daddy was ill. If I'd asked him for his signature, I'd have had to tell him what the money was for. Don't you see, when he was as ill as that I couldn't go and tell him that my husband's life was in danger. It was simply impossible.

KROGSTAD. It would have been better for you if you had abandoned the whole trip.

NORA. No, that was impossible. This was the thing that was to save my husband's life. I couldn't give it up.

KROGSTAD. But did it never strike you that this was fraudulent . . . ?

NORA. That wouldn't have meant anything to me. Why should I worry about you? I couldn't stand you, not when you insisted on going through with all those cold-blooded formalities, knowing all the time what a critical state my husband was in.

KROGSTAD. Mrs. Helmer, it's quite clear you still haven't the faintest idea what it is you've committed. But let me tell you, my own offence was no more and no worse than that, and it ruined my entire reputation.

NORA. You? Are you trying to tell me that you once risked everything to save your wife's life?

KROGSTAD. The law takes no account of motives.

NORA. Then they must be very bad laws.

KROGSTAD. Bad or not, if I produce this document in court, you'll be condemned according to them.

NORA. I don't believe it. Isn't a daughter entitled to try and save her father from worry and anxiety on his deathbed? Isn't a wife entitled to save her husband's life? I might not know very much about the law, but I feel sure of one thing: it must say somewhere that things like this are allowed. You mean to say you don't know that—you, when it's your job? You must be a rotten lawyer, Mr. Krogstad.

KROGSTAD. That may be. But when it comes to business transactions—like the sort between us two—perhaps you'll admit I know something about *them?* Good. Now you must please yourself. But I tell you this: if I'm pitched out a second time, you are going to keep me company.

He bows and goes out through the hall.

NORA. [*stands thoughtfully for a moment, then tosses her head*] Rubbish! He's just trying to scare me. I'm not such a fool as all that. [*Begins gathering up the children's clothes; after a moment she stops.*] Yet . . . ? No, it's impossible! I did it for love, didn't I?

THE CHILDREN. [*in the doorway, left*] Mummy, the gentleman's just gone out of the gate.

NORA. Yes, I know. But you mustn't say anything to anybody about that gentleman. You hear? Not even to Daddy!

THE CHILDREN. All right, Mummy. Are you going to play again?

NORA. No, not just now.

THE CHILDREN. But Mummy, you promised!

NORA. Yes, but I can't just now. Off you go now, I have a lot to do. Off you go, my darlings. [*She herds them carefully into the other room and shuts the door behind them. She sits down on the sofa, picks up her embroidery and works a few stitches, but soon stops.*] No! [*She flings her work down, stands up, goes to the hall door and calls out.*] Helene! Fetch the tree in for me, please. [*She walks across to the table, left, and opens the drawer; again pauses.*] No, really, it's quite impossible!

MAID. [*with the Christmas tree*] Where shall I put it, ma'am?

NORA. On the floor there, in the middle.

MAID. Anything else you want me to bring?

NORA. No, thank you. I've got what I want.

The Maid has put the tree down and goes out.

NORA. [*busy decorating the tree*] Candles here . . . and flowers here.—Revolting man! It's all nonsense! There's nothing to worry about. We'll have a lovely Christmas tree. And I'll do anything you want me to, Torvald; I'll sing for you, dance for you. . . .

Helmer, with a bundle of documents under his arm, comes in by the hall door.

NORA. Ah, back again already?

HELMER. Yes. Anybody been?

NORA. Here? No.

HELMER. That's funny. I just saw Krogstad leave the house.

NORA. Oh? O yes, that's right. Krogstad was here a minute.

HELMER. Nora, I can tell by your face he's been asking you to put a good word in for him.

NORA. Yes.

HELMER. And you were to pretend it was your own idea? You were to keep quiet about his having been here. He asked you to do that as well, didn't he?

NORA. Yes, Torvald. But . . .

HELMER. Nora, Nora, what possessed you to do a thing like that? Talking to a person like him, making him promises? And then on top of everything, to tell me a lie!

NORA. A lie . . . ?

HELMER. Didn't you say that nobody had been here? [*Wagging his finger at her.*] Never again must my little song-bird do a thing like that! Little song-birds must keep their pretty little beaks out of mischief; no chirruping out of tune! [*Puts his arm round her waist.*] Isn't that the way we want things to be? Yes, of course it is. [*Lets her go.*] So let's say no more about it. [*Sits down by the stove.*] Ah, nice and cosy here!

He glances through his papers.

NORA. [*busy with the Christmas tree, after a short pause*] Torvald!

HELMER. Yes.

NORA. I'm so looking forward to the fancy dress ball at the Stenborgs on Boxing Day.

HELMER. And I'm terribly curious to see what sort of surprise you've got for me.

NORA. Oh, it's too silly.

HELMER. Oh?

NORA. I just can't think of anything suitable. Everything seems so absurd, so pointless.

HELMER. Has my little Nora come to *that* conclusion?

NORA. [*behind his chair, her arms on the chairback*] Are you very busy, Torvald?

HELMER. Oh. . . .

NORA. What are all those papers?

HELMER. Bank matters.

NORA. Already?

HELMER. I have persuaded the retiring manager to give me authority to make any changes in organization or personnel I think necessary. I have to work on it over the Christmas week. I want everything straight by the New Year.

NORA. So that was why that poor Krogstad. . . .

HELMER. Hm!

NORA. [*still leaning against the back of the chair, running her fingers through his hair*] If you hadn't been so busy, Torvald, I'd have asked you to do me an awfully big favour.

HELMER. Let me hear it. What's it to be?

NORA. Nobody's got such good taste as you. And the thing is I do so want to look my best at the fancy dress ball. Torvald, couldn't you give me some advice and tell me what you think I ought to go as, and how I should arrange my costume?

HELMER. Aha! So my impulsive little woman is asking for somebody to come to her rescue, eh?

NORA. Please, Torvald, I never get anywhere without your help.

HELMER. Very well, I'll think about it. We'll find something.

NORA. That's sweet of you. [*She goes across to the tree again; pause.*] How pretty these red flowers look.—Tell me, was it really something terribly wrong this man Krogstad did?

HELMER. Forgery. Have you any idea what that means?

NORA. Perhaps circumstances left him no choice?

HELMER. Maybe. Or perhaps, like so many others, he just didn't think. I am not so heartless that I would necessarily want to condemn a man for a single mistake like that.

NORA. Oh no, Torvald, of course not!

HELMER. Many a man might be able to redeem himself, if he honestly confessed his guilt and took his punishment.

NORA. Punishment?

HELMER. But that wasn't the way Krogstad chose. He dodged what was due to him by a cunning trick. And that's what has been the cause of his corruption.

NORA. Do you think it would . . . ?

HELMER. Just think how a man with a thing like that on his conscience will always be having to lie and cheat and dissemble; he can never drop the mask, not even with his own wife and children. And the children—*that's* the most terrible part of it, Nora.

NORA. Why?

HELMER. A fog of lies like that in a household, and it spreads disease and infection to every part of it. Every breath the children take in that kind of house is reeking with evil germs.

NORA. [*closer behind him*] Are you sure of that?

HELMER. My dear Nora, as a lawyer I know what I'm talking about. Practically all juvenile delinquents come from homes where the mother is dishonest.

NORA. Why mothers particularly?

HELMER. It's generally traceable to the mothers, but of course fathers can have the same influence. Every lawyer knows that only too well. And yet there's Krogstad been poisoning his own children for years with lies and deceit. That's the reason I call him morally depraved. [*Holds out his hands to her.*] That's why my sweet little Nora must promise me not to try putting in any more good words for him. Shake hands on it. Well? What's this? Give me your hand. There now! That's settled. I assure you I would have found it impossible to work with him. I quite literally feel physically sick in the presence of such people.

NORA. [*draws her hand away and walks over to the other side of the Christmas tree*] How hot it is in here! And I still have such a lot to do.

HELMER. [*stands up and collects his papers together*] Yes, I'd better think of getting some of this read before dinner. I must also think about your costume. And I might even be able to lay my hands on something to wrap in gold paper and hang on the Christmas tree. [*He lays his hand on her head.*] My precious little singing bird.

He goes into his study and shuts the door behind him.

NORA. [*quietly, after a pause*] Nonsense! It can't be. It's impossible. It *must* be impossible.

NURSEMAID. [*in the doorway, left*] The children keep asking so nicely if they can come in and see Mummy.

NORA. No, no, don't let them in! You stay with them, Anne Marie.

NURSEMAID. Very well, ma'am.

She shuts the door.

NORA. [*pale with terror*] Corrupt my children . . . ! Poison my home? [*Short pause; she throws back her head.*] It's not true! It could never, never be true!

ACT II

The same room. In the corner beside the piano stands the Christmas tree, stripped, bedraggled and with its candles burnt out. Nora's outdoor things lie on the sofa. Nora, alone there, walks about restlessly; at last she stops by the sofa and picks up her coat.

NORA. [*putting her coat down again*] Somebody's coming! [*Crosses to the door, listens.*] No, it's nobody. Nobody will come today, of course, Christmas Day—nor tomorrow, either. But perhaps. . . . [*She opens the door and looks out.*] No, nothing in the letter box; quite empty. [*Comes forward.*] Oh, nonsense! He didn't mean it seriously. Things like that *can't* happen. It's impossible. Why, I have three small children.

The Nursemaid comes from the room, left, carrying a big cardboard box.

NURSEMAID. I finally found it, the box with the fancy dress costumes.

NORA. Thank you. Put it on the table, please.

NURSEMAID. [*does this*] But I'm afraid they are in an awful mess.

NORA. Oh, if only I could rip them up into a thousand pieces!

NURSEMAID. Good heavens, they can be mended all right, with a bit of patience.

NORA. Yes, I'll go over and get Mrs. Linde to help me.

NURSEMAID. Out again? In this terrible weather? You'll catch your death of cold, ma'am.

NORA. Oh, worse things might happen.—How are the children?

NURSEMAID. Playing with their Christmas presents, poor little things, but . . .

NORA. Do they keep asking for me?

NURSEMAID. They are so used to being with their Mummy.

NORA. Yes, Anne Marie, from now on I can't be with them as often as I was before.

NURSEMAID. Ah well, children get used to anything in time.

NORA. Do you think so? Do you think they would forget their Mummy if she went away for good?

NURSEMAID. Good gracious—for good?

NORA. Tell me, Anne Marie—I've often wondered—how on earth could you bear to hand your child over to strangers?

NURSEMAID. Well, there was nothing else for it when I had to come and nurse my little Nora.

NORA. Yes but . . . how could you *bring* yourself to do it?

NURSEMAID. When I had the chance of such a good place? When a poor girl's been in trouble she must make the best of things. Because *he* didn't help, the rotter.

NORA. But your daughter will have forgotten you.

NURSEMAID. Oh no, she hasn't. She wrote to me when she got confirmed, and again when she got married.

NORA. [putting her arms round her neck] Dear old Anne Marie, you were a good mother to me when I was little.

NURSEMAID. My poor little Nora never had any other mother but me.

NORA. And if my little ones only had you, I know you would. . . . Oh, what am I talking about! [She opens the box.] Go in to them. I must . . . Tomorrow I'll let you see how pretty I am going to look.

NURSEMAID. Ah, there'll be nobody at the ball as pretty as my Nora.

She goes into the room, left.

NORA. [begins unpacking the box, but soon throws it down] Oh, if only I dare go out. If only I could be sure nobody would come. And that nothing would happen in the meantime here at home. Rubbish—nobody's going to come. I mustn't think about it. Brush this muff. Pretty gloves, pretty gloves! I'll put it right out of my mind. One, two, three, four, five, six. . . . [Screams.] Ah, they are coming. . . . [She starts towards the door, but stops irresolute. Mrs. Linde comes from the hall, where she has taken off her things.] Oh, it's you, Kristine. There's nobody else out there, is there? I'm so glad you've come.

MRS. LINDE. I heard you'd been over looking for me.

NORA. Yes, I was just passing. There's something you must help me with. Come and sit beside me on the sofa here. You see, the Stenborgs are having a fancy dress party upstairs tomorrow evening, and now Torvald wants me to go as a Neapolitan fisher lass and dance the tarantella.° I learned it in Capri, you know.

MRS. LINDE. Well, well! So you are going to do a party piece?

NORA. Torvald says I should. Look, here's the costume, Torvald had it made for me down there. But it's got all torn and I simply don't know. . . .

MRS. LINDE. We'll soon have that put right. It's only the trimming come away here and there. Got a needle and thread? Ah, here's what we are after.

NORA. It's awfully kind of you.

MRS. LINDE. So you are going to be all dressed up tomorrow, Nora? Tell you what—I'll pop over for a minute to see you in all your finery. But I'm quite forgetting to thank you for the pleasant time we had last night.

NORA. [gets up and walks across the room] Somehow I didn't think yesterday was as nice as things generally are.—You should have come to town a little earlier, Kristine.—Yes, Torvald certainly knows how to make things pleasant about the place.

MRS. LINDE. You too, I should say. You are not your father's daughter for nothing. But tell me, is Dr. Rank always as depressed as he was last night?

NORA. No, last night it was rather obvious. He's got something seriously wrong with him, you know. Tuberculosis of the spine, poor fellow. His father was a horrible man, who used to have mistresses and things like that. That's why the son was always ailing, right from being a child.

MRS. LINDE. [lowering her sewing] But my dear Nora, how do you come to know about things like that?

_____

tarantella: a whirling dance from southern Italy.

NORA. [*walking about the room*] Huh! When you've got three children, you get these visits from . . . women who have had a certain amount of medical training. And you hear all sorts of things from them.

MRS. LINDE. [*begins sewing again; short silence*] Does Dr. Rank call in every day?

NORA. Every single day. He was Torvald's best friend as a boy, and he's a good friend of *mine*, too. Dr. Rank is almost like one of the family.

MRS. LINDE. But tell me—is he really genuine? What I mean is: doesn't he sometimes rather turn on the charm?

NORA. No, on the contrary. What makes you think that?

MRS. LINDE. When you introduced me yesterday, he claimed he'd often heard my name in this house. But afterwards I noticed your husband hadn't the faintest idea who I was. Then how is it that Dr. Rank should. . . .

NORA. Oh yes, it was quite right what he said, Kristine. You see Torvald is so terribly in love with me that he says he wants me all to himself. When we were first married, it even used to make him sort of jealous if I only as much as mentioned any of my old friends from back home. So of course I stopped doing it. But I often talk to Dr. Rank about such things. He likes hearing about them.

MRS. LINDE. Listen, Nora! In lots of ways you are still a child. Now, I'm a good deal older than you, and a bit more experienced. I'll tell you something: I think you ought to give up all this business with Dr. Rank.

NORA. Give up what business?

MRS. LINDE. The whole thing, I should say. Weren't you saying yesterday something about a rich admirer who was to provide you with money. . . .

NORA. One who's never existed, I regret to say. But what of it?

MRS. LINDE. Has Dr. Rank money?

NORA. Yes, he has.

MRS. LINDE. And no dependents?

NORA. No, nobody. But . . . ?

MRS. LINDE. And he comes to the house every day?

NORA. Yes, I told you.

MRS. LINDE. But how can a man of his position want to pester you like this?

NORA. I simply don't understand.

MRS. LINDE. Don't pretend, Nora. Do you think I don't see now who you borrowed the twelve hundred from?

NORA. Are you out of your mind? Do you really think that? A friend of ours who comes here every day? The whole situation would have been absolutely intolerable.

MRS. LINDE. It *really* isn't him?

NORA. No, I give you my word. It would never have occurred to me for one moment. . . . Anyway, he didn't have the money to lend then. He didn't inherit it till later.

MRS. LINDE. Just as well for you, I'd say, my dear Nora.

NORA. No, it would never have occurred to me to ask Dr. Rank. . . . All the same I'm pretty certain if I were to ask him . . .

MRS. LINDE. But of course you won't.

NORA. No, of course not. I can't ever imagine it being necessary. But I'm quite certain if ever I were to mention it to Dr. Rank. . . .

MRS. LINDE. Behind your husband's back?

NORA. I have to get myself out of that other business. That's also behind his back. I *must* get myself out of that.

MRS. LINDE. Yes, that's what I said yesterday. But . . .

NORA. [*walking up and down*] A man's better at coping with these things than a woman. . . .

MRS. LINDE. Your own husband, yes.

NORA. Nonsense! [*Stops.*] When you've paid everything you owe, you do get your IOU back again, don't you?

MRS. LINDE. Of course.

NORA. And you can tear it up into a thousand pieces and burn it—the nasty, filthy thing!

MRS. LINDE. [*looking fixedly at her, puts down her sewing and slowly rises*] Nora, you are hiding something from me.

NORA. Is it so obvious?

MRS. LINDE. Something has happened to you since yesterday morning. Nora, what is it?

NORA. [*going towards her*] Kristine! [*Listens.*] Hush! There's Torvald back. Look, you go and sit in there beside the children for the time being. Torvald can't stand the sight of mending lying about. Get Anne Marie to help you.

MRS. LINDE. [*gathering a lot of the things together*] All right, but I'm not leaving until we have thrashed this thing out.

She goes into the room, left; at the same time Helmer comes in from the hall.

NORA. [*goes to meet him*] I've been longing for you to be back, Torvald, dear.

HELMER. Was that the dressmaker . . . ?

NORA. No, it was Kristine; she's helping me with my costume. I think it's going to look very nice. . . .

HELMER. Wasn't that a good idea of mine, now?

NORA. Wonderful! But wasn't it also nice of me to let you have your way?

HELMER. [*taking her under the chin*] Nice of you—because you let your husband have his way? All right, you little rogue, I know you didn't mean it that way. But I don't want to disturb you. You'll be wanting to try the costume on, I suppose.

NORA. And I dare say you've got work to do?

HELMER. Yes. [*Shows her a bundle of papers.*] Look at this. I've been down at the Bank. . . .

He turns to go into his study.

NORA. Torvald!

HELMER. [*stopping*] Yes.

NORA. If a little squirrel were to ask ever so nicely . . . ?

HELMER. Well?

NORA. Would you do something for it?

HELMER. Naturally I would first have to know what it is.

NORA. Please, if only you would let it have its way, and do what it wants, it'd scamper about and do all sorts of marvellous tricks.

HELMER. What is it?

NORA. And the pretty little sky-lark would sing all day long. . . .

HELMER. Huh! It does that anyway.

NORA. I'd pretend I was an elfin child and dance a moonlight dance for you, Torvald.

HELMER. Nora—I hope it's not that business you started on this morning?

NORA. [coming closer] Yes, it is, Torvald. I implore you!

HELMER. You have the nerve to bring that up again?

NORA. Yes, yes, you *must* listen to me. You must let Krogstad keep his job at the Bank.

HELMER. My dear Nora, I'm giving his job to Mrs. Linde.

NORA. Yes, it's awfully sweet of you. But couldn't you get rid of somebody else in the office instead of Krogstad?

HELMER. This really is the most incredible obstinacy! Just because you go and make some thoughtless promise to put in a good word for him, you expect me . . .

NORA. It's not that, Torvald. It's for your own sake. That man writes in all the nastiest papers, you told me that yourself. He can do you no end of harm. He terrifies me to death. . . .

HELMER. Aha, now I see. It's your memories of what happened before that are frightening you.

NORA. What do you mean?

HELMER. It's your father you are thinking of.

NORA. Yes . . . yes, that's right. You remember all the nasty insinuations those wicked people put in the papers about Daddy? I honestly think they would have had him dismissed if the Ministry hadn't sent you down to investigate, and you hadn't been so kind and helpful.

HELMER. My dear little Nora, there is a considerable difference between your father and me. Your father's professional conduct was not entirely above suspicion. Mine is. And I hope it's going to stay that way as long as I hold this position.

NORA. But nobody knows what some of these evil people are capable of. Things could be so nice and pleasant for us here, in the peace and quiet of our home— you and me and the children, Torvald! That's why I implore you. . . .

HELMER. The more you plead for him, the more impossible you make it for me to keep him on. It's already known down at the Bank that I am going to give Krogstad his notice. If it ever got around that the new manager had been talked over by his wife. . . .

NORA. What of it?

HELMER. Oh, nothing! As long as the little woman gets her own stubborn way . . . ! Do you want me to make myself a laughing stock in the office? . . . Give people the idea that I am susceptible to any kind of outside pressure? You can imagine how soon I'd feel the consequences of that! Anyway, there's one other consideration that makes it impossible to have Krogstad in the Bank as long as I am manager.

NORA. What's that?

HELMER. At a pinch I might have overlooked his past lapses. . . .

NORA. Of course you could, Torvald!

HELMER. And I'm told he's not bad at his job, either. But we knew each other rather well when we were younger. It was one of those rather rash friendships that prove embarrassing in later life. There's no reason why you shouldn't know we were once on terms of some familiarity. And he, in his tactless way, makes no attempt to hide the fact, particularly when other people are present. On the contrary, he thinks he has every right to treat me as an equal, with his 'Torvald this' and 'Torvald that' every time he opens his mouth. I find it extremely irritating, I can tell you. He would make my position at the Bank absolutely intolerable.

NORA. Torvald, surely you aren't serious?

HELMER. Oh? Why not?

NORA. Well, it's all so petty.

HELMER. What's that you say? Petty? Do you think I'm petty?

NORA. No, not at all, Torvald dear! And that's why . . .

HELMER. Doesn't make any difference! . . . You call my motives petty; so I must be petty too. Petty! Indeed! Well, we'll put a stop to that, once and for all. [*He opens the hall door and calls.*] Helene!

NORA. What are you going to do?

HELMER. [*searching among his papers*] Settle things. [*The Maid comes in.*] See this letter? I want you to take it down at once. Get hold of a messenger and get him to deliver it. Quickly. The address is on the outside. There's the money.

MAID. Very good, sir.

She goes with the letter.

HELMER. [*putting his papers together*] There now, my stubborn little miss.

NORA. [*breathless*] Torvald . . . what was that letter?

HELMER. Krogstad's notice.

NORA. Get it back, Torvald! There's still time! Oh, Torvald, get it back! Please for my sake, for your sake, for the sake of the children! Listen, Torvald, please! You don't realize what it can do to us.

HELMER. Too late.

NORA. Yes, too late.

HELMER. My dear Nora, I forgive you this anxiety of yours, although it is actually a bit of an insult. Oh, but it is, I tell you! It's hardly flattering to suppose that anything this miserable pen-pusher wrote could frighten *me*! But I forgive you all the same, because it is rather a sweet way of showing how much you love me. [*He takes her in his arms.*] This is how things must be, my own darling Nora. When it comes to the point, I've enough strength and enough courage, believe me, for whatever happens. You'll find I'm man enough to take everything on myself.

NORA. [*terrified*] What do you mean?

HELMER. Everything, I said. . . .

NORA. [*in command of herself*] That is something you shall never, never do.

HELMER. All right, then we'll share it, Nora—as man and wife. That's what we'll do. [*Caressing her.*] Does that make you happy now? There, there, don't look at me with those eyes, like a little frightened dove. The whole thing is sheer imagination.—Why don't you run through the tarantella and try out the tambourine? I'll go into my study and shut both the doors, then I won't hear anything. You can make all the noise you want. [*Turns in the doorway.*] And when Rank comes, tell him where he can find me.

He nods to her, goes with his papers into his room, and shuts the door behind him.

NORA. [*wild-eyed with terror, stands as though transfixed*] He's quite capable of doing it! He would do it! No matter what, he'd do it.—No, never in this world! Anything but that! Help? Some way out . . . ? [*The door-bell rings in the hall.*] Dr.

Rank . . . ! Anything but that, *anything!* [*She brushes her hands over her face, pulls herself together and opens the door into the hall. Dr. Rank is standing outside hanging up his fur coat. During what follows it begins to grow dark.*] Hello, Dr. Rank. I recognized your ring. Do you mind not going in to Torvald just yet, I think he's busy.

RANK. And you?

Dr. Rank comes into the room and she closes the door behind him.

NORA. Oh, you know very well I've always got time for you.

RANK. Thank you. A privilege I shall take advantage of as long as I am able.

NORA. What do you mean—as long as you are able?

RANK. Does that frighten you?

NORA. Well, it's just that it sounds so strange. Is anything likely to happen?

RANK. Only what I have long expected. But I didn't think it would come quite so soon.

NORA. [*catching at his arm*] What have you found out? Dr. Rank, you must tell me!

RANK. I'm slowly sinking. There's nothing to be done about it.

NORA. [*with a sigh of relief*] Oh, its *you* you're . . . ?

RANK. Who else? No point in deceiving oneself. I am the most wretched of all my patients, Mrs. Helmer. These last few days I've made a careful analysis of my internal economy. Bankrupt! Within a month I shall probably be lying rotting up there in the churchyard.

NORA. Come now, what a ghastly thing to say!

RANK. The whole damned thing is ghastly. But the worst thing is all the ghastliness that has to be gone through first. I only have one more test to make; and when that's done I'll know pretty well when the final disintegration will start. There's something I want to ask you. Helmer is a sensitive soul; he loathes anything that's ugly. I don't want him visiting me. . . .

NORA. But Dr. Rank. . . .

RANK. On no account must he. I won't have it. I'll lock the door on him.—As soon as I'm absolutely certain of the worst, I'll send you my visiting card with a black cross on it. You'll know then the final horrible disintegration has begun.

NORA. Really, you are being quite absurd today. And here was I hoping you would be in a thoroughly good mood.

RANK. With death staring me in the face? Why should I suffer for another man's sins? What justice is there in that? Somewhere, somehow, every single family must be suffering some such cruel retribution. . . .

NORA. [*stopping up her ears*] Rubbish! Do cheer up!

RANK. Yes, really the whole thing's nothing but a huge joke. My poor innocent spine must do penance for my father's gay subaltern life.

NORA. [*by the table, left*] Wasn't he rather partial to asparagus and *pâté de foie gras?*

RANK. Yes, he was. And truffles.

NORA. Truffles, yes. And oysters, too, I believe?

RANK. Yes, oysters, oysters, of course.

NORA. And all the port and champagne that goes with them. It does seem a pity all these delicious things should attack the spine.

RANK. Especially when they attack a poor spine that never had any fun out of them.

NORA. Yes, that is an awful pity.

RANK. [*looks at her sharply*] Hm. . . .

NORA. [*after a pause*] Why did you smile?

RANK. No, it was you who laughed.

NORA. No, it was you who smiled, Dr. Rank!

RANK. [*getting up*] You are a bigger rascal than I thought you were.

NORA. I feel full of mischief today.

RANK. So it seems.

NORA. [*putting her hands on his shoulders*] Dear, dear Dr. Rank, you mustn't go and die on Torvald and me.

RANK. You wouldn't miss me for long. When you are gone, you are soon forgotten.

NORA. [*looking at him anxiously*] Do you think so?

RANK. People make new contacts, then . . .

NORA. Who make new contacts?

RANK. Both you and Helmer will, when I'm gone. You yourself are already well on the way, it seems to me. What was this Mrs. Linde doing here last night?

NORA. Surely you aren't jealous of poor Kristine?

RANK. Yes, I am. She'll be my successor in this house. When I'm done for, I can see this woman. . . .

NORA. Hush! Don't talk so loud, she's in there.

RANK. Today as well? There you are, you see!

NORA. Just to do some sewing on my dress. Good Lord, how absurd you are! [*She sits down on the sofa.*] Now Dr. Rank, cheer up. You'll see tomorrow how nicely I can dance. And you can pretend I'm doing it just for you—and for Torvald as well, of course. [*She takes various things out of the box.*] Come here, Dr. Rank. I want to show you something.

RANK. [*sits*] What is it?

NORA. Look!

RANK. Silk stockings.

NORA. Flesh-coloured! Aren't they lovely! Of course, it's dark here now, but to-morrow. . . . No, no, no, you can only look at the feet. Oh well, you might as well see a bit higher up, too.

RANK. Hm. . . .

NORA. Why are you looking so critical? Don't you think they'll fit?

RANK. I couldn't possibly offer any informed opinion about that.

NORA. [*looks at him for a moment*] Shame on you. [*Hits him lightly across the ear with the stockings.*] Take that! [*Folds them up again.*]

RANK. And what other delights am I to be allowed to see?

NORA. Not another thing. You are too naughty. [*She hums a little and searches among her things.*]

RANK. [*after a short pause*] Sitting here so intimately like this with you, I can't imagine . . . I simply cannot conceive what would have become of me if I had never come to this house.

NORA. [*smiles*] Yes, I rather think you do enjoy coming here.

RANK. [*in a low voice, looking fixedly ahead*] And the thought of having to leave it all . . .

NORA. Nonsense. You aren't leaving.

RANK. [*in the same tone*] . . . without being able to leave behind even the slightest token of gratitude, hardly a fleeting regret even . . . nothing but an empty place to be filled by the first person that comes along.

NORA. Supposing I were to ask you to . . . ? No . . .

RANK. What?

NORA. . . . to show me the extent of your friendship . . .

RANK. Yes?

NORA. I mean . . . to do me a tremendous favour. . . .

RANK. Would you really, for once, give me that pleasure?

NORA. You have no idea what it is.

RANK. All right, tell me.

NORA. No, really I can't, Dr. Rank. It's altogether too much to ask . . . because I need your advice and help as well. . . .

RANK. The more the better. I cannot imagine what you have in mind. But tell me anyway. You do trust me, don't you?

NORA. Yes, I trust you more than anybody I know. You are my best and my most faithful friend. I know that. So I will tell you. Well then, Dr. Rank, there is something you must help me to prevent. You know how deeply, how passionately Torvald is in love with me. He would never hesitate a moment to sacrifice his life for my sake.

RANK. [bending towards her] Nora . . . do you think he's the only one who . . . ?

NORA. [stiffening slightly] Who . . . ?

RANK. Who wouldn't gladly give his life for your sake.

NORA. [sadly] Oh!

RANK. I swore to myself you would know before I went. I'll never have a better opportunity. Well, Nora! Now you know. And now you know too that you can confide in me as in nobody else.

NORA. [rises and speaks evenly and calmly] Let me past.

RANK. [makes way for her, but remains seated] Nora. . . .

NORA. [in the hall doorway] Helene, bring the lamp in, please. [Walks over to the stove.] Oh, my dear Dr. Rank, that really was rather horrid of you.

RANK. [getting up] That I have loved you every bit as much as anybody? Is that horrid?

NORA. No, but that you had to go and tell me. When it was all so unnecessary. . . .

RANK. What do you mean? Did you know . . . ?

The Maid comes in with the lamp, puts it on the table, and goes out again.

RANK. Nora . . . Mrs. Helmer . . . I'm asking you if you knew?

NORA. How can I tell whether I did or didn't. I simply can't tell you. . . . Oh, how could you be so clumsy, Dr. Rank! When everything was so nice.

RANK. Anyway, you know now that I'm at your service, body and soul. So you can speak out.

NORA. [looking at him] After this?

RANK. I beg you to tell me what it is.

NORA. I can tell you nothing now.

RANK. You must. You can't torment me like this. Give me a chance—I'll do anything that's humanly possible.

NORA. You can do nothing for me now. Actually, I don't really need any help. It's all just my imagination, really it is. Of course! [She sits down in the rocking-chair, looks at him and smiles.] I must say, you are a nice one, Dr. Rank! Don't you feel ashamed of yourself, now the lamp's been brought in?

RANK. No, not exactly. But perhaps I ought to go—for good?

NORA. No, you mustn't do that. You must keep coming just as you've always done. You know very well Torvald would miss you terribly.

RANK. And *you?*

NORA. I always think it's tremendous fun having you.

RANK. That's exactly what gave me wrong ideas. I just can't puzzle you out. I often used to feel you'd just as soon be with me as with Helmer.

NORA. Well, you see, there are those people you love and those people you'd almost rather *be* with.

RANK. Yes, there's something in that.

NORA. When I was a girl at home, I loved Daddy best, of course. But I also thought it great fun if I could slip into the maids' room. For one thing they never preached at me. And they always talked about such exciting things.

RANK. Aha! So it's their role I've taken over!

NORA. [*jumps up and crosses to him*] Oh, my dear, kind Dr. Rank, I didn't mean that at all. But you can see how it's a bit with Torvald as it was with Daddy. . . .

The Maid comes in from the hall.

MAID. Please, ma'am . . . !

She whispers and hands her a card.

NORA. [*glances at the card*] Ah!

She puts it in her pocket.

RANK. Anything wrong?

NORA. No, no, not at all. It's just . . . it's my new costume. . . .

RANK. How is that? There's your costume in there.

NORA. That one, yes. But this is another one. I've ordered it. Torvald mustn't hear about it. . . .

RANK. Ah, so that's the big secret, is it!

NORA. Yes, that's right. Just go in and see him, will you? He's in the study. Keep him occupied for the time being. . . .

RANK. Don't worry. He shan't escape me.

He goes into Helmer's study.

NORA. [*to the Maid*] Is he waiting in the kitchen?

MAID. Yes, he came up the back stairs. . . .

NORA. But didn't you tell him somebody was here?

MAID. Yes, but it was no good.

NORA. Won't he go?

MAID. No, he won't till he's seen you.

NORA. Let him in, then. but quietly. Helene, you mustn't tell anybody about this. It's a surprise for my husband.

MAID. I understand, ma'am. . . .

She goes out.

NORA. Here it comes! What I've been dreading! No, no, it can't happen, it *can't* happen.

She walks over and bolts Helmer's door. The Maid opens the hall door for Krogstad and shuts it again behind him. He is wearing a fur coat, over-shoes, and a fur cap.

NORA. [goes towards him] Keep your voice down, my husband is at home.

KROGSTAD. What if he is?

NORA. What do you want with me?

KROGSTAD. To find out something.

NORA. Hurry, then. What is it?

KROGSTAD. You know I've been given notice.

NORA. I couldn't prevent it, Mr. Krogstad, I did my utmost for you, but it was no use.

KROGSTAD. Has your husband so little affection for you? He knows what I can do to you, yet he dares. . . .

NORA. You don't imagine he knows about it!

KROGSTAD. No, I didn't imagine he did. It didn't seem a bit like my good friend Torvald Helmer to show that much courage. . . .

NORA. Mr. Krogstad, I must ask you to show some respect for my husband.

KROGSTAD. Oh, sure! All due respect! But since you are so anxious to keep this business quiet, Mrs. Helmer, I take it you now have a rather clearer idea of just what it is you've done, than you had yesterday.

NORA. Clearer than *you* could ever have given me.

KROGSTAD. Yes, being as I am such a rotten lawyer. . . .

NORA. What do you want with me?

KROGSTAD. I just wanted to see how things stood, Mrs. Helmer. I've been thinking about you all day. Even a mere money-lender, a hack journalist, a—well, even somebody like me has a bit of what you might call feeling.

NORA. Show it then. Think of my little children.

KROGSTAD. Did you or your husband think of mine? But what does it matter now? There was just one thing I wanted to say: you needn't take this business too seriously. I shan't start any proceedings, for the present.

NORA. Ah, I knew you wouldn't.

KROGSTAD. The whole thing can be arranged quite amicably. Nobody need know. Just the three of us.

NORA. My husband must never know.

KROGSTAD. How can you prevent it? Can you pay off the balance?

NORA. No, not immediately.

KROGSTAD. Perhaps you've some way of getting hold of the money in the next few days.

NORA. None I want to make use of.

KROGSTAD. Well, it wouldn't have been very much help to you if you had. Even if you stood there with the cash in your hand and to spare, you still wouldn't get your IOU back from me now.

NORA. What are you going to do with it?

KROGSTAD. Just keep it—have it in my possession. Nobody who isn't implicated need know about it. So if you are thinking of trying any desperate remedies . . .

NORA. Which I am. . . .

KROGSTAD. . . . if you happen to be thinking of running away . . .

NORA. Which I am!

KROGSTAD. . . . or anything worse . . .

NORA. How did you know?

KROGSTAD. . . . forget it!

NORA. How did you know I was thinking of *that*?

KROGSTAD. Most of us think of *that*, to begin with. I did, too; but I didn't have the
courage. . . .

NORA. [*tonelessly*] I haven't either.

KROGSTAD. [*relieved*] So you haven't the courage either, eh?

NORA. No, I haven't! I haven't!

KROGSTAD. It would also be very stupid. There'd only be the first domestic storm to
get over. . . . I've got a letter to your husband in my pocket here. . . .

NORA. And it's all in there?

KROGSTAD. In as tactful a way as possible.

NORA. [*quickly*] He must never read the letter. Tear it up. I'll find the money somehow.

KROGSTAD. Excuse me, Mrs. Helmer, but I've just told you. . . .

NORA. I'm not talking about the money I owe you. I want to know how much you
are demanding from my husband, and I'll get the money.

KROGSTAD. I want no money from your husband.

NORA. What do you want?

KROGSTAD. I'll tell you. I want to get on my feet again, Mrs. Helmer; I want to get
to the top. And your husband is going to help me. For the last eighteen months
I've gone straight; all that time it's been hard going; I was content to work my
way up, step by step. Now I'm being kicked out, and I won't stand for being
taken back again as an act of charity. I'm going to get to the top, I tell you. I'm
going back into that Bank—with a better job. Your husband is going to create
a new vacancy, just for me. . . .

NORA. He'll never do that!

KROGSTAD. He will do it. I know him. He'll do it without so much as a whimper.
And once I'm in there with him, you'll see what's what. In less than a year I'll
be his right-hand man. It'll be Nils Krogstad, not Torvald Helmer, who'll be
running that Bank.

NORA. You'll never live to see that day!

KROGSTAD. You mean you . . . ?

NORA. Now I have the courage.

KROGSTAD. You can't frighten me! A precious pampered little thing like you. . . .

NORA. I'll show you! I'll show you!

KROGSTAD. Under the ice, maybe? Down in the cold, black water? Then being
washed up in the spring, bloated, hairless, unrecognizable. . . .

NORA. You can't frighten me.

KROGSTAD. You can't frighten me, either. People don't do that sort of thing, Mrs.
Helmer. There wouldn't be any point to it, anyway, I'd still have him right in
my pocket.

NORA. Afterwards? When I'm no longer . . .

KROGSTAD. Aren't you forgetting that your reputation would then be entirely in my
hands? [*Nora stands looking at him, speechless.*] Well, I've warned you. Don't do
anything silly. When Helmer gets my letter, I expect to hear from him. And
don't forget: it's him who is forcing me off the straight and narrow again, your
own husband! That's something I'll never forgive him for. Goodbye, Mrs.
Helmer.

He goes out through the hall. Nora crosses to the door, opens it slightly, and listens.

NORA. He's going. He hasn't left the letter. No, no, that would be impossible!
[*Opens the door further and further.*] What's he doing? He's stopped outside. He's

not going down the stairs. Has he changed his mind? Is he . . . ? [*A letter falls into the letter-box. Then Krogstad's footsteps are heard receding as he walks down-stairs. Nora gives a stifled cry, runs across the room to the sofa table; pause.*] In the letter-box! [*She creeps stealthily across to the hall door.*] There it is! Torvald, Torvald! It's hopeless now!

MRS. LINDE. [*comes into the room left, carrying the costume*] There, I think that's everything. Shall we try it on?

NORA. [*in a low, hoarse voice*] Kristine, come here.

MRS. LINDE. [*throws the dress down on the sofa*] What's wrong with you? You look upset.

NORA. Come here. Do you see that letter? *There,* look! Through the glass in the letter-box.

MRS. LINDE. Yes, yes, I can see it.

NORA. It's a letter from Krogstad.

MRS. LINDE. Nora! It was Krogstad who lent you the money!

NORA. Yes. And now Torvald will get to know everything.

MRS. LINDE. Believe me, Nora, it's best for you both.

NORA. But there's more to it than that. I forged a signature. . . .

MRS. LINDE. Heavens above!

NORA. Listen, I want to tell you something, Kristine, so you can be my witness.

MRS. LINDE. What do you mean 'witness'? What do you want me to . . . ?

NORA. If I should go mad . . . which might easily happen . . .

MRS. LINDE. Nora!

NORA. Or if anything happened to me . . . which meant I couldn't be here. . . .

MRS. LINDE. Nora, Nora! Are you out of your mind?

NORA. And if somebody else wanted to take it all upon himself, the whole blame, you understand. . . .

MRS. LINDE. Yes, yes. But what makes you think . . . ?

NORA. Then you must testify that it isn't true, Kristine. I'm not out of my mind; I'm quite sane now. And I tell you this: nobody else knew anything, I alone was responsible for the whole thing. Remember that!

MRS. LINDE. I will. But I don't understand a word of it.

NORA. Why should you? You see something miraculous is going to happen.

MRS. LINDE. Something miraculous?

NORA. Yes, a miracle. But something so terrible as well, Kristine—oh, it must *never* happen, not for anything.

MRS. LINDE. I'm going straight over to talk to Krogstad.

NORA. Don't go. He'll only do you harm.

MRS. LINDE. There was a time when he would have done anything for me.

NORA. Him!

MRS. LINDE. Where does he live?

NORA. How do I know . . . ? Wait a minute. [*She feels in her pocket.*] Here's his card. But the letter, the letter . . . !

HELMER. [*from his study, knocking on the door*] Nora!

NORA. [*cries out in terror*] What's that? What do you want?

HELMER. Don't be frightened. We're not coming in. You've locked the door. Are you trying on?

NORA. Yes, yes, I'm trying on. It looks so nice on me, Torvald.

MRS. LINDE. [*who has read the card*] He lives just round the corner.

NORA. It's no use. It's hopeless. The letter is there in the box.

MRS. LINDE. Your husband keeps the key?

NORA. Always.

MRS. LINDE. Krogstad must ask for his letter back unread, he must find some sort of excuse. . . .

NORA. But this is just the time that Torvald generally . . .

MRS. LINDE. Put him off! Go in and keep him busy. I'll be back as soon as I can.

She goes out hastily by the hall door. Nora walks over to Helmer's door, opens it and peeps in.

NORA. Torvald!

HELMER. [*in the study*] Well, can a man get into his own living-room again now? Come along, Rank, now we'll see . . . [*In the doorway.*] But what's this?

NORA. What, Torvald dear?

HELMER. Rank led me to expect some kind of marvellous transformation.

RANK. [*in the doorway*] That's what I thought too, but I must have been mistaken.

NORA. I'm not showing myself off to anybody before tomorrow.

HELMER. Nora dear, you look tired. You haven't been practising too hard?

NORA. No, I haven't practised at all yet.

HELMER. You'll have to, though.

NORA. Yes, I certainly must, Torvald. But I just can't get anywhere without your help: I've completely forgotten it.

HELMER. We'll soon polish it up.

NORA. Yes, do help me, Torvald. Promise? I'm so nervous. All those people. . . . You must devote yourself exclusively to me this evening. Pens away! Forget all about the office! Promise me, Torvald dear!

HELMER. I promise. This evening I am wholly and entirely at your service . . . helpless little thing that you are. Oh, but while I remember, I'll just look first . . .

He goes towards the hall door.

NORA. What do you want out there?

HELMER. Just want to see if there are any letters.

NORA. No, don't, Torvald!

HELMER. Why not?

NORA. Torvald, *please!* There aren't any.

HELMER. Just let me see.

He starts to go. Nora, at the piano, plays the opening bars of the tarantella.

HELMER. [*at the door, stops*] Aha!

NORA. I shan't be able to dance tomorrow if I don't rehearse it with you.

HELMER. [*walks to her*] Are you really so nervous, Nora dear?

NORA. Terribly nervous. Let me run through it now. There's still time before supper. Come and sit here and play for me, Torvald dear. Tell me what to do, keep me right—as you always do.

HELMER. Certainly, with pleasure, if that's what you want.

He sits at the piano. Nora snatches the tambourine out of the box, and also a long gaily-coloured shawl which she drapes round herself, then with a bound she leaps forward.

NORA. [*shouts*] Now play for me! Now I'll dance.

Helmer plays and Nora dances; Dr. Rank stands at the piano behind Helmer and looks on.

HELMER. [*playing*] Not so fast! Not so fast!

NORA. I can't help it.

HELMER. Not so wild, Nora!

NORA. This is how it has to be.

HELMER. [*stops*] No, no, that won't do at all.

NORA. [*laughs and swings the tambourine*] Didn't I tell you?

RANK. Let me play for her.

HELMER. [*gets up*] Yes, do. Then I'll be better able to tell her what to do.

Rank sits down at the piano and plays. Nora dances more and more wildly. Helmer stands by the stove giving her repeated directions as she dances; she does not seem to hear them. Her hair comes undone and falls about her shoulders; she pays no attention and goes on dancing. Mrs. Linde enters.

MRS. LINDE. [*standing as though spellbound in the doorway*] Ah . . . !

NORA. [*dancing*] See what fun we are having, Kristine.

HELMER. But my dear darling Nora, you are dancing as though your life depended on it.

NORA. It does.

HELMER. Stop, Rank! This is sheer madness. Stop, I say.

Rank stops play and Nora comes to a sudden halt.

HELMER. [*crosses to her*] I would never have believed it. You have forgotten everything I ever taught you.

NORA. [*throwing away the tambourine*] There you are, you see.

HELMER. Well, some more instruction is certainly needed there.

NORA. Yes, you see how necessary it is. You must go on coaching me right up to the last minute. Promise me, Torvald?

HELMER. You can rely on me.

NORA. You mustn't think about anything else but me until after tomorrow . . . mustn't open any letters . . . mustn't touch the letter-box.

HELMER. Ah, you are still frightened of what that man might . . .

NORA. Yes, yes, I am.

HELMER. I can see from your face there's already a letter there from him.

NORA. I don't know. I think so. But you mustn't read anything like that now. We don't want anything horrid coming between us until all this is over.

RANK. [*softly to Helmer*] I shouldn't cross her.

HELMER. [*puts his arm round her*] The child must have her way. But tomorrow night, when your dance is done. . . .

NORA. Then you are free.

MAID. [*in the doorway, right*] Dinner is served, madam.

NORA. We'll have champagne, Helene.

MAID. Very good, madam.

She goes.

HELMER. Aha! It's to be quite a banquet, eh?

NORA. With champagne flowing until dawn. [*Shouts.*] And some macaroons, Helene . . . lots of them, for once in a while.

HELMER. [*seizing her hands*] Now, now, not so wild and excitable! Let me see you being my own little singing bird again.

NORA. Oh yes, I will. And if you'll just go in . . . you, too, Dr. Rank. Kristine, you must help me to do my hair.

RANK. [*Softly, as they leave*] There isn't anything . . . anything as it were, impending, is there?

HELMER. No, not at all, my dear fellow. It's nothing but these childish fears I was telling you about.

They go out to the right.

NORA. Well?

MRS. LINDE. He's left town.

NORA. I saw it in your face.

MRS. LINDE. He's coming back tomorrow evening. I left a note for him.

NORA. You shouldn't have done that. You must let things take their course. Because really it's a case for rejoicing, waiting like this for the miracle.

MRS. LINDE. What is it you are waiting for?

NORA. Oh, you wouldn't understand. Go and join the other two. I'll be there in a minute.

Mrs. Linde goes into the dining-room. Nora stands for a moment as though to collect herself, then looks at her watch.

NORA. Five. Seven hours to midnight. Then twenty-four hours till the next midnight. Then the tarantella will be over. Twenty-four and seven? Thirty-one hours to live.

HELMER. [*in the doorway, right*] What's happened to our little sky-lark?

NORA. [*running towards him with open arms*] Here she is!

ACT III

The same room. The round table has been moved to the centre of the room, and the chairs placed round it. A lamp is burning on the table. The door to the hall stands open. Dance music can be heard coming from the floor above. Mrs. Linde is sitting by the table, idly turning over the pages of a book; she tries to read, but does not seem able to concentrate. Once or twice she listens, tensely, for a sound at the front door.

MRS. LINDE. [*looking at her watch*] Still not here. There isn't much time left. I only hope he hasn't . . . [*She listens again.*] Ah, there he is. [*She goes out into the hall, and cautiously opens the front door. Soft footsteps can be heard on the stairs. She whispers.*] Come in. There's nobody here.

KROGSTAD. [*in the doorway*] I found a note from you at home. What does it all mean?

MRS. LINDE. I had to talk to you.

KROGSTAD. Oh? And did it have to be here, in this house?

MRS. LINDE. It wasn't possible over at my place, it hasn't a separate entrance. Come in. We are quite alone. The maid's asleep and the Helmers are at a party upstairs.

KROGSTAD. [*comes into the room*] Well, well! So the Helmers are out dancing tonight! Really?

MRS. LINDE. Yes, why not?

KROGSTAD. Why not indeed!

MRS. LINDE. Well then, Nils. Let's talk.

KROGSTAD. Have we two anything more to talk about?

MRS. LINDE. We have a great deal to talk about.

KROGSTAD. I shouldn't have thought so.

MRS. LINDE. That's because you never really understood me.

KROGSTAD. What else was there to understand, apart from the old, old story? A heartless woman throws a man over the moment something more profitable offers itself.

MRS. LINDE. Do you really think I'm so heartless? Do you think I found it easy to break it off?

KROGSTAD. Didn't you?

MRS. LINDE. You didn't really believe that?

KROGSTAD. If that wasn't the case, why did you write to me as you did?

MRS. LINDE. There was nothing else I could do. If I had to make the break, I felt in duty bound to destroy any feeling that you had for me.

KROGSTAD. [clenching his hands] So that's how it was. And all that . . . was for money!

MRS. LINDE. You mustn't forget I had a helpless mother and two young brothers. We couldn't wait for you, Nils. At that time you hadn't much immediate prospect of anything.

KROGSTAD. That may be. But you had no right to throw me over for somebody else.

MRS. LINDE. Well, I don't know. Many's the time I've asked myself whether I was justified.

KROGSTAD. [more quietly] When I lost you, it was just as if the ground had slipped away from under my feet. Look at me now: a broken man clinging to the wreck of his life.

MRS. LINDE. Help might be near.

KROGSTAD. It was near. Then you came along and got in the way.

MRS. LINDE. Quite without knowing, Nils. I only heard today it's you I'm supposed to be replacing at the Bank.

KROGSTAD. If you say so, I believe you. But now you do know, aren't you going to withdraw?

MRS. LINDE. No, that wouldn't benefit you in the slightest.

KROGSTAD. Benefit, benefit . . . ! I would do it just the same.

MRS. LINDE. I have learned to go carefully. Life and hard, bitter necessity have taught me that.

KROGSTAD. And life has taught me not to believe in pretty speeches.

MRS. LINDE. Then life has taught you a very sensible thing. But deeds are something you surely must believe in?

KROGSTAD. How do you mean?

MRS. LINDE. You said you were like a broken man clinging to the wreck of his life.

KROGSTAD. And I said it with good reason.

MRS. LINDE. And I am like a broken woman clinging to the wreck of her life. Nobody to care about, and nobody to care for.

KROGSTAD. It was your own choice.

MRS. LINDE. At the time there was no other choice.

KROGSTAD. Well, what of it?

MRS. LINDE. Nils, what about us two castaways joining forces.

KROGSTAD. What's that you say?

MRS. LINDE. Two of us on *one* wreck surely stand a better chance than each on his own.

KROGSTAD. Kristine!

MRS. LINDE. Why do you suppose I came to town?

KROGSTAD. You mean, you thought of me?

MRS. LINDE. Without work I couldn't live. All my life I have worked, for as long as I can remember; that has always been my one great joy. But now I'm completely alone in the world, and feeling horribly empty and forlorn. There's no pleasure in working only for yourself. Nils, give me somebody and something to work for.

KROGSTAD. I don't believe all this. It's only a woman's hysteria, wanting to be all magnanimous and self-sacrificing.

MRS. LINDE. Have you ever known me hysterical before?

KROGSTAD. Would you really do this? Tell me—do you know all about my past?

MRS. LINDE. Yes.

KROGSTAD. And you know what people think about me?

MRS. LINDE. Just now you hinted you thought you might have been a different person with me.

KROGSTAD. I'm convinced I would.

MRS. LINDE. Couldn't it still happen?

KROGSTAD. Kristine! You know what you are saying, don't you? Yes, you do. I can see you do. Have you really the courage . . . ?

MRS. LINDE. I need someone to mother, and your children need a mother. We two need each other. Nils, I have faith in what, deep down, you are. With you I can face anything.

KROGSTAD. [seizing her hands] Thank you, thank you, Kristine. And I'll soon have everybody looking up to me, or I'll know the reason why. Ah, but I was forgetting. . . .

MRS. LINDE. Hush! The tarantella! You must go!

KROGSTAD. Why? What is it?

MRS. LINDE. You hear that dance upstairs? When it's finished they'll be coming.

KROGSTAD. Yes, I'll go. It's too late to do anything. Of course, you know nothing about what steps I've taken against the Helmers.

MRS. LINDE. Yes, Nils, I do know.

KROGSTAD. Yet you still want to go on. . . .

MRS. LINDE. I know how far a man like you can be driven by despair.

KROGSTAD. Oh, if only I could undo what I've done!

MRS. LINDE. You still can. Your letter is still there in the box.

KROGSTAD. Are you sure?

MRS. LINDE. Quite sure. But . . .

KROGSTAD. [regards her searchingly] Is that how things are? You want to save your friend at any price? Tell me straight. Is that it?

MRS. LINDE. When you've sold yourself once for other people's sake, you don't do it again.

KROGSTAD. I shall demand my letter back.

MRS. LINDE. No, no.

KROGSTAD. Of course I will, I'll wait here till Helmer comes. I'll tell him he has to give me my letter back . . . that it's only about my notice . . . that he mustn't read it. . . .

MRS. LINDE. No, Nils, don't ask for it back.

KROGSTAD. But wasn't that the very reason you got me here?

MRS. LINDE. Yes, that was my first terrified reaction. But that was yesterday, and it's quite incredible the things I've witnessed in this house in the last twenty-four hours. Helmer must know everything. This unhappy secret must come out. Those two must have the whole thing out between them. All this secrecy and deception, it just can't go on.

KROGSTAD. Well, if you want to risk it. . . . But one thing I can do, and I'll do it at once. . . .

MRS. LINDE. [*listening*] Hurry! Go, go! The dance has stopped. We aren't safe a moment longer.

KROGSTAD. I'll wait for you downstairs.

MRS. LINDE. Yes, do. You must see me home.

KROGSTAD. I've never been so incredibly happy before.

He goes out by the front door. The door out into the hall remains standing open.

MRS. LINDE. [*tidies the room a little and gets her hat and coat ready*] How things change! How things change! Somebody to work for . . . to live for. A home to bring happiness into. Just let me get down to it. . . . I wish they'd come. . . . [*Listens.*] Ah, there they are. . . . Get my things.

She takes her coat and hat. The voices of Helmer and Nora are heard outside. A key is turned and Helmer pushes Nora almost forcibly into the hall. She is dressed in the Italian costume, with a big black shawl over it. He is in evening dress, and over it a black cloak, open.

NORA. [*still in the doorway, reluctantly*] No, no, not in here! I want to go back up again. I don't want to leave so early.

HELMER. But my dearest Nora . . .

NORA. Oh, please, Torvald, I beg you. . . . *Please*, just for another hour.

HELMER. Not another minute, Nora my sweet. You remember what we agreed. There now, come along in. You'll catch cold standing there.

He leads her, in spite of her resistance, gently but firmly into the room.

MRS. LINDE. Good evening.

NORA. Kristine!

HELMER. Why, Mrs. Linde. You're here so late?

MRS. LINDE. Yes. You must forgive me but I did so want to see Nora all dressed up.

NORA. Have you been sitting here waiting for me?

MRS. LINDE. Yes, I'm afraid I wasn't in time to catch you before you went upstairs. And I felt I couldn't leave again without seeing you.

HELMER. [*removing Nora's shawl*] Well take a good look at her. I think I can say she's worth looking at. Isn't she lovely, Mrs. Linde?

MRS. LINDE. Yes, I must say. . . .

HELMER. Isn't she quite extraordinarily lovely? That's what everybody at the party thought, too. But she's dreadfully stubborn . . . the sweet little thing! And what shall we do about that? Would you believe it, I nearly had to use force to get her away.

NORA. Oh Torvald, you'll be sorry you didn't let me stay, even for half an hour.

HELMER. You hear that, Mrs. Linde? She dances her tarantella, there's wild applause—which was well deserved, although the performance was perhaps rather realistic . . . I mean, rather more so than was strictly necessary from the artistic point of view. But anyway! The main thing is she was a success, a tremendous

Realism in Drama

success. Was I supposed to let her stay after that? Spoil the effect? No thank you! I took my lovely little Capri girl—my capricious little Capri girl, I might say—by the arm, whisked her once round the room, a curtsey all round, and then— as they say in novels—the beautiful vision vanished. An exit should always be effective, Mrs. Linde. But I just can't get Nora to see that. Phew! It's warm in here. [He throws his cloak over a chair and opens the door to his study.] What? It's dark. Oh yes, of course, Excuse me. . . .

He goes in and lights a few candles.

NORA. [*quickly, in a breathless whisper*] Well?

MRS. LINDE. [*softly*] I've spoken to him.

NORA. And . . . ?

MRS. LINDE. Nora . . . you must tell your husband everything.

NORA. [*tonelessly*] I knew it.

MRS. LINDE. You've got nothing to fear from Krogstad. But you must speak.

NORA. I won't.

MRS. LINDE. Then the letter will.

NORA. Thank you, Kristine. Now I know what's to be done. Hush . . . !

HELMER. [*comes in again*] Well, Mrs. Linde, have you finished admiring her?

MRS. LINDE. Yes. And now I must say good night.

HELMER. Oh, already? Is this yours, this knitting?

MRS. LINDE. [*takes it*] Yes, thank you. I nearly forgot it.

HELMER. So you knit, eh?

MRS. LINDE. Yes.

HELMER. You should embroider instead, you know.

MRS. LINDE. Oh? Why?

HELMER. So much prettier. Watch! You hold the embroidery like this in the left hand, and then you take the needle in the right hand, like this, and you describe a long, graceful curve. Isn't that right?

MRS. LINDE. Yes, I suppose so. . . .

HELMER. Whereas knitting on the other hand just can't help being ugly. Look! Arms pressed into the sides, the knitting needles going up and down—there's something Chinese about it. . . . Ah, that was marvellous champagne they served tonight.

MRS. LINDE. Well, good night, Nora! And stop being so stubborn.

HELMER. Well said, Mrs. Linde!

MRS. LINDE. Good night, Mr. Helmer.

HELMER. [*accompanying her to the door*] Good night, good night! You'll get home all right, I hope? I'd be only too pleased to . . . But you haven't far to walk. Good night, good night! [*She goes; he shuts the door behind her and comes in again.*] There we are, got rid of her at last. She's a frightful bore, that woman.

NORA. Aren't you very tired, Torvald?

HELMER. Not in the least.

NORA. Not sleepy?

HELMER. Not at all. On the contrary, I feel extremely lively. What about you? Yes, you look quite tired and sleepy.

NORA. Yes, I'm very tired. I just want to fall straight off to sleep.

HELMER. There you are, you see! Wasn't I right in thinking we shouldn't stay any longer.

NORA. Oh, everything you do is right.

HELMER. [kissing her forehead] There's my little sky-lark talking common sense. Did you notice how gay Rank was this evening?

NORA. Oh, was he? I didn't get a chance to talk to him.

HELMER. I hardly did either. But it's a long time since I saw him in such a good mood. [Looks at Nora for a moment or two, then comes nearer her.] Ah, it's wonderful to be back in our own home again, and quite alone with you. How irresistibly lovely you are, Nora!

NORA. Don't look at me like that, Torvald!

HELMER. Can't I look at my most treasured possession? At all this loveliness that's mine and mine alone, completely and utterly mine.

NORA. [walks round to the other side of the table] You mustn't talk to me like that tonight.

HELMER. [following her] You still have the tarantella in your blood, I see. And that makes you even more desirable. Listen! The guests are beginning to leave now. [Softly.] Nora . . . soon the whole house will be silent.

NORA. I should hope so.

HELMER. Of course you do, don't you, Nora my darling? You know, whenever I'm out at a party with you . . . do you know why I never talk to you very much, why I always stand away from you and only steal a quick glance at you now and then . . . do you know why I do that? It's because I'm pretending we are secretly in love, secretly engaged and nobody suspects there is anything between us.

NORA. Yes, yes. I know your thoughts are always with me, of course.

HELMER. And when it's time to go, and I lay your shawl round those shapely, young shoulders, round the exquisite curve of your neck . . . I pretend that you are my young bride, that we are just leaving our wedding, that I am taking you to our new home for the first time . . . to be alone with you for the first time . . . quite alone with your young and trembling loveliness! All evening I've been longing for you, and nothing else. And as I watched you darting and swaying in the tarantella, my blood was on fire . . . I couldn't bear it any longer . . . and that's why I brought you down here with me so early. . . .

NORA. Go away, Torvald! Please leave me alone. I won't have it.

HELMER. What's this? It's just your little game isn't it, my little Nora. Won't! Won't! Am I not your husband . . . ?

There is a knock on the front door.

NORA. [startled] Listen . . . !

HELMER. [going towards the hall] Who's there?

RANK. [outside] It's me. Can I come in for a minute?

HELMER. [in a low voice, annoyed] Oh, what does he want now? [Aloud.] Wait a moment. [He walks across and opens the door.] How nice of you to look in on your way out.

RANK. I fancied I heard your voice and I thought I would just look in. [He takes a quick glance round.] Ah yes, this dear, familiar old place! How cosy and comfortable you've got things here, you two.

HELMER. You seemed to be having a pretty good time upstairs yourself.

RANK. Capital! Why shouldn't I? Why not make the most of things in this world? At least as much as one can, and for as long as one can. The wine was excellent. . . .

HELMER. Especially the champagne.

RANK. You noticed that too, did you? It's incredible the amount I was able to put away.

NORA. Torvald also drank a lot of champagne this evening.

RANK. Oh?

NORA. Yes, and that always makes him quite merry.

RANK. Well, why shouldn't a man allow himself a jolly evening after a day well spent?

HELMER. Well spent? I'm afraid I can't exactly claim that.

RANK. [clapping him on the shoulder] But I can, you see!

NORA. Dr. Rank, am I right in thinking you carried out a certain laboratory test today?

RANK. Exactly.

HELMER. Look at our little Nora talking about laboratory tests!

NORA. And may I congratulate you on the result?

RANK. You may indeed.

NORA. So it was good?

RANK. The best possible, for both doctor and patient—certainty!

NORA. [quickly and searchingly] Certainty?

RANK. Absolute certainty. So why shouldn't I allow myself a jolly evening after that?

NORA. Quite right, Dr. Rank.

HELMER. I quite agree. As long as you don't suffer for it in the morning.

RANK. Well, you never get anything for nothing in this life.

NORA. Dr. Rank . . . you are very fond of masquerades, aren't you?

RANK. Yes, when there are plenty of amusing disguises. . . .

NORA. Tell me, what shall we two go as next time?

HELMER. There's frivolity for you . . . thinking about the next time already!

RANK. We two? I'll tell you. You must go as Lady Luck. . . .

HELMER. Yes, but how do you find a costume to suggest *that*?

RANK. Your wife could simply go in her everyday clothes. . . .

HELMER. That was nicely said. But don't you know what you would be?

RANK. Yes, my dear friend, I know exactly what I shall be.

HELMER. Well?

RANK. At the next masquerade, I shall be invisible.

HELMER. That's a funny idea!

RANK. There's a big black cloak . . . haven't you heard of the cloak of invisibility? That comes right down over you, and then nobody can see you.

HELMER. [suppressing a smile] Of course, that's right.

RANK. But I'm clean forgetting what I came for. Helmer, give me a cigar, one of the dark Havanas.

HELMER. With the greatest of pleasure.

   He offers his case.

RANK. [takes one and cuts the end off] Thanks.

NORA. [strikes a match] Let me give you a light.

RANK. Thank you. [She holds out the match and he lights his cigar.] And now, goodbye!

HELMER. Goodbye, goodbye, my dear fellow!

NORA. Sleep well, Dr. Rank.

A Doll's House

RANK. Thank you for that wish.

NORA. Wish me the same.

RANK. You? All right, if you want me to. . . . Sleep well. And thanks for the light.

He nods to them both, and goes.

HELMER. [*subdued*] He's had a lot to drink.

NORA. [*absently*] Very likely.

Helmer takes a bunch of keys out of his pocket and goes out into the hall.

NORA. Torvald . . . what do you want there?

HELMER. I must empty the letter-box, it's quite full. There'll be no room for the papers in the morning. . . .

NORA. Are you going to work tonight?

HELMER. You know very well I'm not. Hello, what's this? Somebody's been at the lock.

NORA. At the lock?

HELMER. Yes, I'm sure of it. Why should that be? I'd hardly have thought the maids . . . ? Here's a broken hair-pin. Nora, it's one of yours. . . .

NORA. [*quickly*] It must have been the children. . . .

HELMER. Then you'd better tell them not to. Ah . . . there . . . I've managed to get it open. [*He takes the things out and shouts into the kitchen.*] Helene! . . . Helene, put the light out in the hall. [*He comes into the room again with the letters in his hand and shuts the hall door.*] Look how it all mounts up. [*Runs through them.*] What's this?

NORA. The letter! Oh no, Torvald, no!

HELMER. Two visiting cards . . . from Dr. Rank.

NORA. From Dr. Rank?

HELMER. [*looking at them*] Dr. Rank, Medical Practitioner. They were on top. He must have put them in as he left.

NORA. Is there anything on them?

HELMER. There's a black cross above his name. Look. What an uncanny idea. It's just as if he were announcing his own death.

NORA. He is.

HELMER. What? What do you know about it? Has he said anything to you?

NORA. Yes. He said when these cards came, he would have taken his last leave of us. He was going to shut himself up and die.

HELMER. Poor fellow! Of course I knew we couldn't keep him with us very long. But so soon. . . . And hiding himself away like a wounded animal.

NORA. When it has to happen, it's best that it should happen without words. Don't you think so, Torvald?

HELMER. [*walking up and down*] He had grown so close to us. I don't think I can imagine him gone. His suffering and his loneliness seemed almost to provide a background of dark cloud to the sunshine of our lives. Well, perhaps it's all for the best. For him at any rate. [*Pauses.*] And maybe for us as well, Nora. Now there's just the two of us. [*Puts his arms round her.*] Oh, my darling wife, I can't hold you close enough. You know, Nora . . . many's the time I wish you were threatened by some terrible danger so I could risk everything, body and soul, for your sake.

NORA. [*tears herself free and says firmly and decisively*] Now you must read your letters, Torvald.

HELMER. No, no not tonight. I want to be with you, my darling wife.

NORA. Knowing all the time your friend is dying . . . ?

HELMER. You are right. It's been a shock to both of us. This ugly thing has come between us . . . thoughts of death and decay. We must try to free ourselves from it. Until then . . . we shall go our separate ways.

NORA. [*her arms round his neck*] Torvald . . . good night! Good night!

HELMER. [*kisses her forehead*] Good night, my little singing bird. Sleep well, Nora, I'll just read through my letters.

He takes the letters into his room and shuts the door behind him.

NORA. [*gropes around her, wild-eyed, seizes Helmer's cloak, wraps it round herself, and whispers quickly, hoarsely, spasmodically*] Never see him again. Never, never, never. [*Throws her shawl over her head.*] And never see the children again either. Never, never. Oh, that black icy water. Oh, that bottomless . . . ! If only it were all over! He's got it now. Now he's reading it. Oh no, no! Not yet! Torvald, goodbye . . . and my children.

She rushes out in the direction of the hall; at the same moment Helmer flings open his door and stands there with an open letter in his hand.

HELMER. Nora!

NORA. [*shrieks*] Ah!

HELMER. What is this? Do you know what is in this letter?

NORA. Yes, I know. Let me go! Let me out!

HELMER. [*holds her back*] Where are you going?

NORA. [*trying to tear herself free*] You mustn't try to save me, Torvald!

HELMER. [*reels back*] True! Is it true what he writes? How dreadful! No, no, it can't possibly be true.

NORA. It *is* true. I loved you more than anything else in the world.

HELMER. Don't come to me with a lot of paltry excuses!

NORA. [*taking a step towards him*] Torvald . . . !

HELMER. Miserable woman . . . what is this you have done?

NORA. Let me go. I won't have you taking the blame for me. You mustn't take it on yourself.

HELMER. Stop play-acting! [*Locks the front door.*] You are staying here to give an account of yourself. Do you understand what you have done? Answer me! Do you understand?

NORA. [*looking fixedly at him, her face hardening*] Yes, now I'm really beginning to understand.

HELMER. [*walking up and down*] Oh, what a terrible awakening this is. All these eight years . . . this woman who was my pride and joy . . . a hypocrite, a liar, worse than that, a criminal! Oh, how utterly squalid it all is! Ugh! Ugh! [*Nora remains silent and looks fixedly at him.*] I should have realized something like this would happen. I should have seen it coming. All your father's irresponsible ways. . . . Quiet! All your father's irresponsible ways are coming out in you. No religion, no morals, no sense of duty. . . . Oh, this is my punishment for turning a blind eye to him. It was for your sake I did it, and this is what I get for it.

NORA. Yes, this.

HELMER. Now you have ruined my entire happiness, jeopardized my whole future. It's terrible to think of. Here I am, at the mercy of a thoroughly unscrupulous person; he can do whatever he likes with me, demand anything he wants, order me about just as he chooses . . . and I daren't even whimper. I'm done for, a miserable failure, and it's all the fault of a feather-brained woman!

NORA. When I've left this world behind, you will be free.

HELMER. Oh, stop pretending! Your father was just the same, always ready with fine phrases. What good would it do me if you left this world behind, as you put it? Not the slightest bit of good. He can still let it all come out, if he likes; and if he does, people might even suspect me of being an accomplice in these criminal acts of yours. They might even think I was the one behind it all, that it was I who pushed you into it! And it's you I have to thank for this . . . and when I've taken such good care of you, all our married life. Now do you understand what you have done to me?

NORA. [coldly and calmly] Yes.

HELMER. I just can't understand it, it's so incredible. But we must see about putting things right. Take that shawl off. Take it off, I tell you! I must see if I can't find some way or other of appeasing him. The thing must be hushed up at all costs. And as far as you and I are concerned, things must appear to go on exactly as before. But only in the eyes of the world, of course. In other words you'll go on living here; that's understood. But you will not be allowed to bring up the children, I can't trust you with them. . . . Oh, that I should have to say this to the woman I loved so dearly, the woman I still. . . . Well, that must be all over and done with. From now on, there can be no question of happiness. All we can do is save the bits and pieces from the wreck, preserve appearances . . . [The front door-bell rings. Helmer gives a start.] What's that? So late? How terrible, supposing . . . If he should . . . ? Hide, Nora! Say you are not well.

Nora stands motionless. Helmer walks across and opens the door into the hall.

MAID. [half dressed, in the hall] It's a note for Mrs. Helmer.

HELMER. Give it to me. [He snatches the note and shuts the door.] Yes it's from him. You can't have it. I want to read it myself.

NORA. You read it then.

HELMER. [by the lamp] I hardly dare. Perhaps this is the end, for both of us. Well, I must know. [He opens the note hurriedly, reads a few lines, looks at another enclosed sheet, and gives a cry of joy.] Nora! [Nora looks at him inquiringly.] Nora! I must read it again. Yes, yes, it's true! I am saved! Nora, I am saved!

NORA. And me?

HELMER. You too, of course, we are both saved, you as well as me. Look, he's sent your IOU back. He sends his regrets and apologies for what he has done. . . . His luck has changed. . . . Oh, what does it matter what he says. We are saved, Nora! Nobody can do anything to you now. Oh, Nora, Nora . . . but let's get rid of this disgusting thing first. Let me see. . . . [He glances at the IOU.] No, I don't want to see it. I don't want it to be anything but a dream. [He tears up the IOU and both letters, throws all the pieces into the stove and watches them burn.] Well, that's the end of that. He said in his note you'd known since Christmas Eve. . . . You must have had three terrible days of it, Nora.

NORA. These three days haven't been easy.

HELMER. The agonies you must have gone through! When the only way out seemed to be. . . . No, let's forget the whole ghastly thing. We can rejoice and say: It's all over! It's all over! Listen to me, Nora! You don't seem to understand: It's all

over! Why this grim look on your face? Oh, poor little Nora, of course I understand. You can't bring yourself to believe I've forgiven you. But I have, Nora, I
swear it. I forgive you everything. I know you did what you did because you
loved me.

NORA. That's true.

HELMER. You loved me as a wife should love her husband. It was simply that you
didn't have the experience to judge what was the best way of going about things.
But do you think I love you any the less for that; just because you don't know
how to act on your own responsibility? No, no, you just lean on me, I shall give
you all the advice and guidance you need. I wouldn't be a proper man if I didn't
find a woman doubly attractive for being so obviously helpless. You mustn't
dwell on the harsh things I said in that first moment of horror, when I thought
everything was going to come crashing down about my ears. I have forgiven
you, Nora, I swear it! I have forgiven you!

NORA. Thank you for your forgiveness.

She goes out through the door, right.

HELMER. No, don't go! [*He looks through the doorway.*] What are you doing in the
spare room?

NORA. Taking off this fancy dress.

HELMER. [*standing at the open door*] Yes, do. You try and get some rest, and set your
mind at peace again, my frightened little song-bird. Have a good long sleep; you
know you are safe and sound under my wing. [*Walks up and down near the door.*]
What a nice, cosy little home we have here, Nora! Here you can find refuge.
Here I shall hold you like a hunted dove I have rescued unscathed from the
cruel talons of the hawk, and calm your poor beating heart. And that will come,
gradually, Nora, believe me. Tomorrow you'll see everything quite differently.
Soon everything will be just as it was before. You won't need me to keep on
telling you I've forgiven you; you'll feel convinced of it in your own heart. You
don't really imagine me ever thinking of turning you out, or even of reproach-
ing you? Oh, a real man isn't made that way, you know, Nora. For a man, there's
something indescribably moving and very satisfying in knowing that he has forgiven his wife—forgiven her, completely and genuinely, from the depths of his
heart. It's as though it made her his property in a double sense: he has, as it were,
given her a new life, and she becomes in a way both his wife and at the same
time his child. That is how you will seem to me after today, helpless, perplexed
little thing that you are. Don't you worry your pretty little head about anything,
Nora. Just you be frank with me, and I'll make all the decisions for you. . . .
What's this? Not in bed? You've changed your things?

NORA. [*in her everyday dress*] Yes, Torvald, I've changed.

HELMER. What for? It's late.

NORA. I shan't sleep tonight.

HELMER. But my dear Nora. . . .

NORA. [*looks at her watch*] It's not so terribly late. Sit down, Torvald. We two have
a lot to talk about.

She sits down at one side of the table.

HELMER. Nora, what is all this? Why so grim?

NORA. Sit down. It'll take some time. I have a lot to say to you.

HELMER. [*sits down at the table opposite her*] You frighten me, Nora. I don't understand you.

NORA. Exactly. You don't understand me. And I have never understood you, either—until tonight. No don't interrupt. I just wanted you to listen to what I
have to say. We are going to have things out, Torvald.

HELMER. What do you mean?

NORA. Isn't there anything that strikes you about the way we two are sitting here?

HELMER. What's that?

NORA. We have now been married eight years. Hasn't it struck you this is the first
time you and I, man and wife, have had a serious talk together?

HELMER. Depends what you mean by 'serious'.

NORA. Eight whole years—no, more, ever since we first knew each other—and
never have we exchanged one serious word about serious things.

HELMER. What did you want me to do? Get you involved in worries that you
couldn't possibly help me to bear?

NORA. I'm not talking about worries. I say we've never once sat down together and
seriously tried to get to the bottom of anything.

HELMER. But, my dear Nora, would that have been a thing for you?

NORA. That's just it. You have never understood me . . . I've been greatly wronged,
Torvald. First by my father, and then by you.

HELMER. What! Us two! The two people who loved you more than anybody?

NORA. [*shakes her head*] You two never loved me. You only thought how nice it was
to be in love with me.

HELMER. But, Nora, what's this you are saying?

NORA. It's right, you know, Torvald. At home, Daddy used to tell me what he
thought, then I thought the same. And if I thought differently, I kept quiet
about it, because he wouldn't have liked it. He used to call me his baby doll,
and he played with me as I used to play with my dolls. Then I came to live in
your house. . . .

HELMER. What way is that to talk about our marriage?

NORA. [*imperturbably*] What I mean is: I passed out of Daddy's hands into yours. You
arranged everything to your tastes, and I acquired the same tastes. Or I pretended to . . . I don't really know . . . I think it was a bit of both, sometimes one
thing and sometimes the other. When I look back, it seems to me I have been
living here like a beggar, from hand to mouth. I lived by doing tricks for you,
Torvald. But that's the way you wanted it. You and Daddy did me a great wrong.
It's your fault that I've never made anything of my life.

HELMER. Nora, how unreasonable . . . how ungrateful you are! Haven't you been
happy here?

NORA. No, never. I thought I was, but I wasn't really.

HELMER. Not . . . not happy!

NORA. No, just gay. And you've always been so kind to me. But our house has never
been anything but a play-room. I have been your doll wife, just as at home I was
Daddy's doll child. And the children in turn have been my dolls. I thought it
was fun when you came and played with me, just as they thought it was fun
when I went and played with them. That's been our marriage, Torvald.

HELMER. There is some truth in what you say, exaggerated and hysterical though it
is. But from now on it will be different. Play-time is over; now comes the time
for lessons.

NORA. Whose lessons? Mine or the children's?

HELMER. Both yours and the children's, my dear Nora.

NORA. Ah, Torvald, you are not the man to teach me to be a good wife for you.

HELMER. How can you say that?

NORA. And what sort of qualifications have I to teach the children?

HELMER. Nora!

NORA. Didn't you say yourself, a minute or two ago, that you couldn't trust me with that job.

HELMER. In the heat of the moment! You shouldn't pay any attention to that.

NORA. On the contrary, you were quite right. I'm not up to it. There's another problem needs solving first. I must take steps to educate myself. You are not the man to help me there. That's something I must do on my own. That's why I'm leaving you.

HELMER. [*jumps up*] What did you say?

NORA. If I'm ever to reach any understanding of myself and the things around me, I must learn to stand alone. That's why I can't stay here with you any longer.

HELMER. Nora! Nora!

NORA. I'm leaving here at once. I dare say Kristine will put me up for tonight. . . .

HELMER. You are out of your mind! I won't let you! I forbid you!

NORA. It's no use forbidding me anything now. I'm taking with me my own personal belongings. I don't want anything of yours, either now or later.

HELMER. This is madness!

NORA. Tomorrow I'm going home—to what used to be my home, I mean. It will be easier for me to find something to do there.

HELMER. Oh, you blind, inexperienced . . .

NORA. I must set about *getting* experience, Torvald.

HELMER. And leave your home, your husband and your children? Don't you care what people will say?

NORA. That's no concern of mine. All I know is that this is necessary for *me*.

HELMER. This is outrageous! You are betraying your most sacred duty.

NORA. And what do you consider to be my most sacred duty?

HELMER. Does it take me to tell you that? Isn't it your duty to your husband and your children?

NORA. I have another duty equally sacred.

HELMER. You have not. What duty might *that* be?

NORA. My duty to myself.

HELMER. First and foremost, you are a wife and mother.

NORA. That I don't believe any more. I believe that first and foremost I am an individual, just as much as you are—or at least I'm going to try to be. I know most people agree with you, Torvald, and that's also what it says in books. But I'm not content any more with what most people say, or with what it says in books. I have to think things out for myself, and get things clear.

HELMER. Surely you are clear about your position in your own home? Haven't you an infallible guide in questions like these? Haven't you your religion?

NORA. Oh, Torvald, I don't really know what religion is.

HELMER. What do you say!

NORA. All I know is what Pastor Hansen said when I was confirmed. He said religion was this, that and the other. When I'm away from all this and on my own,

I'll go into that, too. I want to find out whether what Pastor Hansen told me was right—or at least whether it's right for *me*.

HELMER. This is incredible talk from a young woman! But if religion cannot keep you on the right path, let me at least stir your conscience. I suppose you do have some moral sense? Or tell me—perhaps you don't?

NORA. Well, Torvald, that's not easy to say. I simply don't know. I'm really very confused about such things. All I know is my ideas about such things are very different from yours. I've also learnt that the law is different from what I thought; but I simply can't get it into my head that that particular law is right. Apparently a woman has no right to spare her old father on his death-bed, or to save her husband's life, even. I just don't believe it.

HELMER. You are talking like a child. You understand nothing about the society you live in.

NORA. No, I don't. But I shall go into that too. I must try to discover who is right, society or me.

HELMER. You are ill, Nora. You are delirious. I'm half inclined to think you are out of your mind.

NORA. Never have I felt so calm and collected as I do tonight.

HELMER. Calm and collected enough to leave your husband and children?

NORA. Yes.

HELMER. Then only one explanation is possible.

NORA. And that is?

HELMER. You don't love me any more.

NORA. Exactly.

HELMER. Nora! Can you say that!

NORA. I'm desperately sorry, Torvald. Because you have always been so kind to me. But I can't help it. I don't love you any more.

HELMER. [*struggling to keep his composure*] Is that also a 'calm and collected' decision you've made?

NORA. Yes, absolutely calm and collected. That's why I don't want to stay here.

HELMER. And can you also account for how I forfeited your love?

NORA. Yes, very easily. It was tonight, when the miracle didn't happen. It was then I realized you weren't the man I thought you were.

HELMER. Explain yourself more clearly. I don't understand.

NORA. For eight years I have been patiently waiting. Because, heavens, I knew miracles didn't happen every day. Then this devastating business started, and I became absolutely convinced the miracle *would* happen. All the time Krogstad's letter lay there, it never so much as crossed my mind that you would ever submit to that man's conditions. I was absolutely convinced you would say to him: Tell the whole wide world if you like. And when that was done . . .

HELMER. Yes, then what? After I had exposed my own wife to dishonour and shame . . . !

NORA. When that was done, I was absolutely convinced you would come forward and take everything on yourself, and say: I am the guilty one.

HELMER. Nora!

NORA. You mean I'd never let you make such a sacrifice for my sake? Of course not. But what would my story have counted for against yours?—That was the miracle I went in hope and dread of. It was to prevent it that I was ready to end my life.

HELMER. I would gladly toil day and night for you, Nora, enduring all manner of sorrow and distress. But nobody sacrifices his *honour* for the one he loves.

NORA. Hundreds and thousands of women have.

HELMER. Oh, you think and talk like a stupid child.

NORA. All right. But you neither think nor talk like the man I would want to share my life with. When you had got over your fright—and you weren't concerned about me but only about what might happen to you—and when all danger was past, you acted as though nothing had happened. I was your little sky-lark again, your little doll, exactly as before; except you would have to protect it twice as carefully as before, now that it had shown itself to be so weak and fragile. [*Rises.*] Torvald, that was the moment I realised that for eight years I'd been living with a stranger, and had borne him three children. . . . Oh, I can't bear to think about it! I could tear myself to shreds.

HELMER. [*sadly*] I see. I see. There is a tremendous gulf dividing us. But, Nora, is there no way we might bridge it?

NORA. As I am now, I am no wife for you.

HELMER. I still have it in me to change.

NORA. Perhaps . . . if you have your doll taken away.

HELMER. And be separated from you! No, no, Nora, the very thought of it is inconceivable.

NORA. [*goes into the room, right*] All the more reason why it must be done.

She comes back with her outdoor things and a small travelling bag which she puts on the chair beside the table.

HELMER. Nora, Nora, not now! Wait till the morning.

NORA. [*putting on her coat*] I can't spend the night in a strange man's room.

HELMER. But couldn't we live here together like brother and sister—

NORA. You know very well that would not last. [*Puts her shawl around her.*] Good-bye, Torvald. I don't want to see the children. I know that they are in better hands than mine. In my present state, I'm no use to them.

HELMER. But someday, Nora—someday?

NORA. How can I tell? I cannot know what will become of me.

HELMER. But you are my wife, no matter what happens.

NORA. Listen, Torvald. I have heard that when a wife deserts her husband's house as I am doing, he is then free from all legal obligations toward her. In any case, I free you from all responsibility. Don't feel bound in any way, any more than I shall. There has to be perfect freedom for both of us. Here, take your ring back. And give me mine.

HELMER. That too?

NORA. That too.

HELMER. Here it is.

NORA. Good. Well, now it is all done with. I am putting the keys here. The maids know all about keeping the house—better than I do. Tomorrow, after I have left town, Kristine will come to pack everything that is mine from home. I would like the things shipped to me.

HELMER. All over! All over! Nora, will you ever think of me again?

NORA. I shall think of you often, and of the children and the house.

HELMER. May I write to you?

NORA. Not that—never. I won't let you.

HELMER. But at least let me send you—

NORA. Nothing. Nothing.

HELMER. Let me help you if you are in need.

NORA. No. I can take nothing from strangers.

HELMER. Nora, can I never be anything more than a stranger to you?

NORA. [picking up her bag] Oh Torvald, the miracle of miracles would have to happen—

HELMER. Name it, this miracle of miracles!

NORA. You and I would both have to be so changed—Oh, Torvald, I don't believe in miracles anymore.

HELMER. But I will believe. Tell me! So changed that—

NORA. That we could make a real marriage of our lives together. Goodbye. [She goes out through the hall.]

HELMER. [sinks down in a chair and covers his face with his hands] Nora! Nora! [He rises and looks around.] Empty! She's gone! [With sudden hope.] The miracle of miracles. . . .?

The heavy sound of a door being slammed is heard from below.

QUESTIONS

1. What are your first impressions about the relationship between Nora and Helmer? What are the first hints that Ibsen gives that Nora may be concealing something?

2. Who is Mrs. Linde? How does her arrival allow Ibsen to unfold the plot complications? How are Nora and Mrs. Linde different? And how do Nora's responses to Mrs. Linde begin to reveal Nora's character?

3. What was Nora doing while she was supposed to be making Christmas decorations? Why?

4. What is Nora's reaction upon the appearance of Krogstad? Why?

5. How soon do we discover that Nora has difficulty in telling Helmer the truth? Give examples of her duplicity. Once we learn of the reasons for her deceit, are we to admire or disapprove of her actions?

6. Comment upon Nora's admission of her desire to say the word *damn*. What is Ibsen really saying about expectations and codes of behavior among the bourgeoisie?

7. How has Nora deceived Krogstad about the I.O.U.? Why did she resort to the deception?

8. Discuss the two sets of moralities that Ibsen sets out in the first act. Which do you sense will be triumphant? Why?

9. Find two passages in the play where Ibsen focuses on the role of heredity in the transmission of characteristics. What do you surmise to be the source of Dr. Rank's illness?

10. What do you suspect that Nora is thinking about when Dr. Rank informs her that he is dying? Why is she so coy with him, alternately flattering and rejecting?

11. How does Helmer's sending off the letter dismissing Krogstad mark a significant turning point in the play?

12. How does Krogstad attempt to blackmail Nora? Why? What causes him to change his mind?

13. Discuss Nora's dancing of the tarantella. How does the dancing scene, which happens offstage, function in the play?

14. What does Nora mean about waiting for a miracle to happen? What miracle does she imagine?

15. At what point do we learn that Nora intends to commit suicide? Given her tendency to deceive herself and others, how much credence do you give her words?

Realism in Drama

16. What is the relationship between Krogstad and Mrs. Linde? Is Mrs. Linde sincere in her avowals to the man? How does he react, and how does his reaction prepare the final scene of the play?

17. What do we learn about Helmer through his response to the idea of Rank's imminent death? How does this foreshadow his reaction to Nora's admission?

18. Why is it that Helmer's apology cannot undo the effect of his initial reaction? What does Nora tell him about their marriage?

19. Do you believe that Nora will make a new life for herself, or is she, like Laura Petersen, doomed to a tragic end? Discuss.

20. What is the "miracle" that Nora tells Helmer about and that preoccupies him at the very end of the play?

21. Discuss Ibsen's vision in terms of its relevance to contemporary thinking about sex roles. In what ways do you feel that A Doll's House has something to offer?

ANTON CHEKHOV AND THE MOSCOW ARTS THEATER

Anton Chekhov (1860–1904) was the son of an unsuccessful shopkeeper. He grew up in the provincial Russian town of Taganrog, near the borders of the Caucasus, a place that he described in later years as "dirty and dull, with deserted streets and a lazy, ignorant population." Along with his schooling, Chekhov was apprenticed to a local tailor for a time. Then, when he was sixteen, his father went bankrupt and took his wife and younger children to Moscow (Chekhov's older brothers were already living there). Chekhov remained alone in Taganrog for a time, attending school and publishing his first short sketches in the student magazine.

In 1879, when he was nineteen, Chekhov moved to Moscow, where he not only studied medicine and became the principal support for his family but also turned his facility for prose sketches to good account by writing for newspapers. In 1883 he is said to have written well over a hundred short stories.

Though Chekhov completed his medical studies and began working as a general practitioner, the writing impulse consumed more and more of his energy. He tried to balance his life, but as he found growing popularity as a story-writer he abandoned his medical practice (except for some pro bono work among the poor).

Chekhov did not begin writing plays seriously until 1887, and in that year his first four-act play, Ivanov, was produced in Moscow. He expressed his dramatic philosophy, which would not change a great deal, to a group of friends: "Let the things that happen on stage be as complex and yet just as simple as they are in life. For instance, people are having a meal at a table, just having a meal, but at the same time their happiness is being created, or their lives are being smashed up."

Chekhov's first great dramatic success was The Seagull, written in the autumn of 1895 and directed in its Moscow performances by the celebrated Konstantin Stanislavski. It marked a revolution in the dramatic arts, for while Realistic, it achieved its effects not through tight dramatic plotting of the kind we find from a playwright like Ibsen, but through a diffuse, almost relaxed Impressionism. The play, in other words, gathers power through its lifelike rendering of moods and impressions, not through its actions. But as Stanislavski wrote in his memoirs, My Life in Art, "His plays are full of action, not in their external but in their internal development. In the very inactivity of his characters a complex inner activity is concealed."

Stanislavski also wrote:

> The poetic power of Chekhov's plays does not manifest itself at the first reading. After having read them, you say to yourself: This is good, but . . . it's nothing special, nothing to stun you with admiration. . . .
>
> Yet, as you recollect some phrases and scenes, you feel you want to think about them more, think about them longer. In your mind, you go over other phrases and scenes, over the whole of the play. . . . You want to re-read it—and then you realize the depths hidden under the surface. . . .

Stanislavski's characterization certainly applies to the three great plays of Chekhov's maturity—*Uncle Vanya* (1899), *The Three Sisters* (1901), and *The Cherry Orchard* (1903). Many critics regard this last play, a complex meditation on Russian attitudes in the face of large-scale social unrest (the first Russian revolution broke out in 1905), as the author's finest.

Anton Chekhov (1860–1904)

Anton Chekhov was born in the town of Taganrog near the Russian Caucasus. He studied medicine at Moscow University but at a very young age began to write stories and sketches for newspapers to help support his family. The reception of two early collections, published in 1886 and 1887, encouraged Chekhov to put his medical practice aside. By his thirties he had achieved renown throughout Russia. He was also suffering from the tuberculosis that would finally kill him. In Chekhov's last decade he turned to playwriting, and in a few years created some of the great plays of the world stage, including *The Seagull, Uncle Vanya, The Cherry Orchard,* and *The Three Sisters.*

THE CHERRY ORCHARD

Translated by Constance Garnett

CHARACTERS

MADAME RANEVSKY (LYUBOV ANDREYEVNA), the owner of the Cherry Orchard
ANYA, her daughter, aged seventeen
VARYA, her adopted daughter, aged twenty-four
GAEV (LEONID ANDREYEVITCH), brother of Madame Ranevsky
LOPAHIN (YERMOLAY ALEXEYEVITCH), a merchant
TROFIMOV (PYOTR SERGEYEVITCH), a student

SEMYONOV-PISHTCHIK, a landowner
CHARLOTTA IVANOVNA, a governess
EPIHODOV (SEMYON PANTALEYEVITCH), a clerk
DUNYASHA, a maid
FIRS, an old valet, aged eighty-seven
YASHA, a young valet
A WAYFARER
THE STATION MASTER
A POST OFFICE CLERK
VISITORS, SERVANTS

The action takes place on the estate of Madame Ranevsky.

ACT I

A room, which has always been called the nursery. One of the doors leads into Anya's room. Dawn, sun rises during the scene. May, the cherry trees in flower, but it is cold in the garden with the frost of early morning. Windows closed.

Enter Dunyasha with a candle and Lopahin with a book in his hand.

LOPAHIN. The train's in, thank God. What time is it?

DUNYASHA. Nearly two o'clock. [*Puts out the candle.*] It's daylight already.

LOPAHIN. The train's late! Two hours, at least. [*Yawns and stretches.*] I'm a pretty one; what a fool I've been. Came here on purpose to meet them at the station and dropped asleep. . . . Dozed off as I sat in the chair. It's annoying. . . . You might have waked me.

DUNYASHA. I thought you had gone. [*Listens.*] There, I do believe they're coming!

LOPAHIN. [*Listens.*] No, what with the luggage and one thing and another. [*A pause.*] Lyubov Andreyevna has been abroad five years; I don't know what she is like now. . . . She's a splendid woman. A good-natured, kind-hearted women. I remember when I was a lad of fifteen, my poor father—he used to keep a little shop here in the village in those days—gave me a punch in the face with his fist and made my nose bleed. We were in the yard here, I forget what we'd come about—he had had a drop. Lyubov Andreyevna—I can see her now—she was a slim young girl then—took me to wash my face, and then brought me into this very room, into the nursery. "Don't cry, little peasant," says she, "it will be well in time for your wedding day." . . . [*A pause.*] Little peasant. . . . My father was a peasant, it's true, but here am I in a white waist-coat and brown shoes, like a pig in a bun shop. Yes, I'm a rich man, but for all my money, come to think, a peasant I was, and a peasant I am. [*Turns over the pages of the book.*] I've been reading this book and I can't make head or tail of it. I fell asleep over it. [*A pause.*]

DUNYASHA. The dogs have been awake all night, they feel that the mistress is coming.

LOPAHIN. Why, what's the matter with you, Dunyasha?

DUNYASHA. My hands are all of a tremble. I feel as though I should faint.

LOPAHIN. You're a spoilt soft creature, Dunyasha. And dressed like a lady too, and your hair done up. That's not the thing. One must know one's place.

Enter Epihodov with a nosegay; he wears a pea jacket and highly polished creaking top boots; he drops the nosegay as he comes in.

EPIHODOV. [*Picking up the nosegay.*] Here! the gardener's sent this, says you're to put it in the dining room. [*Gives Dunyasha the nosegay.*]

LOPAHIN. And bring me some kvass.°

DUNYASHA. I will. [*Goes out.*]

EPIHODOV. It's chilly this morning, three degrees of frost, though the cherries are all in flower. I can't say much for our climate. [*Sighs.*] I can't. Our climate is not often propitious to the occasion. Yermolay Alexeyevitch, permit me to call your attention to the fact that I purchased myself a pair of boots the day before yes-

---

kvass: a fermented beverage.

terday, and they creak, I venture to assure you, so that there's no tolerating them. What ought I to grease them with?

LOPAHIN. Oh, shut up! Don't bother me.

EPIHODOV. Every day some misfortune befalls me. I don't complain, I'm used to it, and I wear a smiling face.

Dunyasha comes in, hands Lopahin the kvass.

EPIHODOV. I am going. [*Stumbles against a chair, which falls over.*] There! [*As though triumphant.*] There you see now, excuse the expression, an accident like that among others. . . .It's positively remarkable. [*Goes out.*]

DUNYASHA. Do you know, Yermolay Alexeyevitch, I must confess, Epihodov has made me a proposal.

LOPAHIN. Ah!

DUNYASHA. I'm sure I don't know. . . . He's a harmless fellow, but sometimes when he begins talking, there's no making anything of it. It's all very fine and expressive, only there's no understanding it. I've a sort of liking for him too. He loves me to distraction. He's an unfortunate man; every day there's something. They tease him about it—two and twenty misfortunes they call him.

LOPAHIN. [*Listening.*] There! I do believe they're coming.

DUNYASHA. They are coming! What's the matter with me? . . . I'm cold all over.

LOPAHIN. They really are coming. Let's go and meet them. Will she know me? It's five years since I saw her.

DUNYASHA. [*In a flutter.*] I shall drop this very minute. . . . Ah, I shall drop.

There is a sound of two carriages up to the house. Lopahin and Dunyasha go out quickly. The stage is left empty. A noise is heard in the adjoining rooms. Firs, who has driven to meet Madame Ranevsky, crosses the stage hurriedly leaning on a stick. He is wearing old-fashioned livery and a high hat. He says something to himself, but not a word can be distinguished. The noise behind the scenes goes on increasing. A voice: "Come, let's go in here." Enter Lyubov Andreyevna, Anya, and Charlotta Ivanovna with a pet dog on a chain, all in traveling dresses. Varya in an outdoor coat with a kerchief over her head, Gaev, Semyonov-Pishtchik, Lopahin, Dunyasha with bag and parasol, servants with other articles. All walk across the room.

ANYA. Let's come in here. Do you remember what room this is, mamma?

LYUBOV. [*Joyfully, through her tears.*] The nursery!

VARYA. How cold it is, my hands are numb. [*To Lyubov Andreyevna.*] Your rooms, the white room and the lavender one, are just the same as ever, mamma.

LYUBOV. My nursery, dear delightful room. . . . I used to sleep here when I was little. . . . [*Cries.*] And here I am, like a little child. . . . [*Kisses her brother and Varya, and then her brother again.*] Varya's just the same as ever, like a nun. And I knew Dunyasha. [*Kisses Dunyasha.*]

GAEV. The train was two hours late. What do you think of that? Is that the way to do things?

CHARLOTTA. [*To Pishtchik.*] My dog eats nuts, too.

PISHTCHIK. [*Wonderingly.*] Fancy that!

They all go out except Anya and Dunyasha.

DUNYASHA. We've been expecting you so long. [*Takes Anya's hat and coat.*]

ANYA. I haven't slept for four nights on the journey. I feel dreadfully cold.

DUNYASHA. You set out in Lent, there was snow and frost, and now? My darling! [*Laughs and kisses her.*] I *have* missed you, my precious, my joy. I must tell you . . . I can't put it off a minute. . . .

ANYA. [*Wearily.*] What now?

DUNYASHA. Epihodov, the clerk, made me a proposal just after Easter.

ANYA. It's always the same thing with you. . . . [*Straightening her hair.*] I've lost all my hairpins. [*She is staggering from exhaustion.*]

DUNYASHA. I don't know what to think, really. He does love me, he does love me so!

ANYA. [*Looking toward her door, tenderly.*] My own room, my windows just as though I had never gone away. I'm home! Tomorrow morning I shall get up and run into the garden. . . . Oh, if I could get to sleep! I haven't slept all the journey. I was so anxious and worried.

DUNYASHA. Pyotr Sergeyevitch came the day before yesterday.

ANYA. [*Joyfully.*] Petya!

DUNYASHA. He's asleep in the bath house, he has settled in there. I'm afraid of being in their way, says he. [*Glancing at her watch.*] I was to have waked him, but Varvara Mihalovna told me not to. Don't you wake him, says she.

Enter Varya with a bunch of keys at her waist.

VARYA. Dunyasha, coffee and make haste. . . . Mamma's asking for coffee.

DUNYASHA. This very minute. [*Goes out.*]

VARYA. Well, thank God, you've come. You're home again. [*Petting her.*] My little darling has come back! My precious beauty has come back again!

ANYA. I have had a time of it!

VARYA. I can fancy.

ANYA. We set off in Holy Week—it was so cold then, and all the way Charlotta would talk and show off her tricks. What did you want to burden me with Charlotta for?

VARYA. You couldn't have traveled all alone, darling. At seventeen.

ANYA. We got to Paris at last, it was cold there—snow. I speak French shockingly. Mamma lives on the fifth floor, I went up to her and there were a lot of French people, ladies, an old priest with a book. The place smelt of tobacco and so comfortless. I felt sorry, oh! so sorry for mamma all at once. I put my arms round her neck, and hugged her and wouldn't let her go. Mamma was as kind as she could be, and she cried. . . .

VARYA. [*Through her tears.*] Don't speak of it, don't speak of it!

ANYA. She had sold her villa at Mentone, she had nothing left, nothing. I hadn't a farthing left either, we only just had enough to get here. And mamma doesn't understand! When we had dinner at the stations, she always ordered the most expensive things and gave the waiters a whole ruble. Charlotta's just the same. Yasha too must have the same as we do; it's simply awful. You know Yasha is mamma's valet now, we brought him here with us.

VARYA. Yes, I've seen the young rascal.

ANYA. Well, tell me—have you paid the arrears on the mortgage?

VARYA. How could we get the money?

ANYA. Oh, dear! Oh, dear!

VARYA. In August the place will be sold.

ANYA. My goodness!

LOPAHIN. [*Peeps in at the door and moos like a cow.*] Moo! [*Disappears.*]

VARYA. [*Weeping.*] There, that's what I could do to him. [*Shakes her fist.*]

ANYA. [*Embracing Varya, softly.*] Varya, has he made you an offer? [*Varya shakes her head.*] Why, but he loves you. Why is it you don't come to an understanding? What are you waiting for?

VARYA. I believe that there never will be anything between us. He has a lot to do, he has not time for me . . . and takes no notice of me. Bless the man, it makes me miserable to see him. . . . Everyone's talking of our being married, everyone's congratulating me, and all the while there's really nothing in it; it's all like a dream. [*In another tone.*] You have a new brooch like a bee.

ANYA. [*Mournfully.*] Mamma bought it. [*Goes into her own room and in a lighthearted childish tone.*] And you know, in Paris I went up in a balloon!

VARYA. My darling's home again! My pretty is home again!

Dunyasha returns with the coffee pot and is making the coffee.

VARYA. [*Standing at the door.*] All day long, darling, as I go about looking after the house, I keep dreaming all the time. If only we could marry you to a rich man, then I should feel more at rest. Then I would go off by myself on a pilgrimage to Kiev, to Moscow . . . and so I would spend my life going from one holy place to another. . . . I would go on and on. . . . What bliss!

ANYA. The birds are singing in the garden. What time is it?

VARYA. It must be nearly three. It's time you were asleep, darling. [*Going into Anya's room.*] What bliss!

Yasha enters with a rug and a traveling bag.

YASHA. [*Crosses the stage, mincingly.*] May one come in here, pray?

DUNYASHA. I shouldn't have known you, Yasha. How you have changed abroad.

YASHA: H'm! . . . And who are you?

DUNYASHA: When you went away, I was that high. [*Shows distance from floor.*] Dunyasha, Fyodor's daughter. . . . You don't remember me!

YASHA: H'm! . . . You're a peach! [*Looks round and embraces her: she shrieks and drops a saucer. Yasha goes out hastily.*]

VARYA. [*In the doorway, in a tone of vexation.*] What now?

DUNYASHA. [*Through her tears.*] I have broken a saucer.

VARYA. Well, that brings good luck.

ANYA. [*Coming out of her room.*] We ought to prepare mamma: Petya is here.

VARYA. I told them not to wake him.

ANYA. [*Dreamily.*] It's six years since father died. Then only a month later little brother Grisha was drowned in the river, such a pretty boy he was, only seven. It was more than mamma could bear, so she went away, went away without looking back. [*Shuddering.*] . . . How well I understand her, if only she knew! [*A pause.*] And Petya Trofimov was Grisha's tutor, he may remind her.

Enter Firs: he is wearing a pea jacket and a white waistcoat.

FIRS. [*Goes up to the coffee pot, anxiously.*] The mistress will be served here. [*Puts on white gloves.*] Is the coffee ready? [*Sternly to Dunyasha.*] Girl! Where's the cream?

DUNYASHA. Ah, mercy on us! [*Goes out quickly.*]

FIRS. [*Fussing round the coffee pot.*] Ech! you good-for-nothing! [*Muttering to himself.*] Come back from Paris. And the old master used to go to Paris too . . . horses all the way. [*Laughs.*]

VARYA. What is it, Firs?

FIRS. What is your pleasure? [*Gleefully.*] My lady has come home! I have lived to see her again! Now I can die. [*Weeps with joy.*]

Enter Lyubov Andreyevna, Gaev, and Semyonov-Pishtchik; the latter is in a short-waisted full coat of fine cloth, and full trousers. Gaev, as he comes in, makes a gesture with his arms and his whole body, as though he were playing billiards.

LYUBOV. How does it go? Let me remember. Cannon off the red!

GAEV. That's it—in off the white! Why, once, sister, we used to sleep together in this very room, and now I'm fifty-one, strange as it seems.

LOPAHIN. Yes, time flies.

GAEV. What do you say?

LOPAHIN. Time, I say, flies.

GAEV. What a smell of patchouli!

ANYA. I'm going to bed. Good night, mamma. [*Kisses her mother.*]

LYUBOV. My precious darling. [*Kisses her hands.*] Are you glad to be home? I can't believe it.

ANYA. Good night, uncle.

GAEV. [*Kissing her face and hands.*] God bless you! How like you are to your mother! [*To his sister.*] At her age you were just the same, Lyuba.

Anya shakes hands with Lopahin and Pishtchik, then goes out, shutting the door after her.

LYUBOV. She's quite worn out.

PISHTCHIK. Aye, it's a long journey, to be sure.

VARYA. [*To Lopahin and Pishtchik.*] Well, gentlemen? It's three o'clock and time to say good-bye.

LYUBOV. [*Laughs.*] You're just the same as ever, Varya. [*Draws her to her and kisses her.*] I'll just drink my coffee and then we will all go and rest. [*Firs puts a cushion under her feet.*] Thanks, friend. I am so fond of coffee, I drink it day and night. Thanks, dear old man. [*Kisses Firs.*]

VARYA. I'll just see whether all the things have been brought in. [*Goes out.*]

LYUBOV. Can it really be me sitting here? [*Laughs.*] I want to dance about and clap my hands. [*Covers her face with her hands.*] And I could drop asleep in a moment! God knows I love my country, I love it tenderly; I couldn't look out of the window in the train, I kept crying so. [*Through her tears.*] But I must drink my coffee, though. Thank you, Firs, thanks, dear old man. I'm so glad to find you still alive.

FIRS. The day before yesterday.

GAEV. He's rather deaf.

LOPAHIN. I have to set off for Harkov directly, at five o'clock. . . . It is annoying! I wanted to have a look at you, and a little talk. . . . You are just as splendid as ever.

PISHTCHIK. [*Breathing heavily.*] Handsomer, indeed. . . . Dressed in Parisian style . . . completely bowled me over.

LOPAHIN. Your brother, Leonid Andreyevitch here, is always saying that I'm a low-born knave, that I'm a money grubber, but I don't care one straw for that. Let him talk. Only I do want you to believe in me as you used to. I do want your wonderful tender eyes to look at me as they used to in the old days. Merciful God! My father was a serf of your father and of your grandfather, but you—

you—did so much for me once, that I've forgotten all that; I love you as though you were my kin . . . more than my kin.

LYUBOV. I can't sit still, I simply can't. . . . [*Jumps up and walks about in violent agitation.*] This happiness is too much for me. . . . You may laugh at me, I know I'm silly. . . . My own bookcase. [*Kisses the bookcase.*] My little table.

GAEV. Nurse died while you were away.

LYUBOV. [*Sits down and drinks coffee.*] Yes, the Kingdom of Heaven be hers! You wrote me of her death.

GAEV. And Anastasy is dead. Squinting Petruchka has left me and is in service now with the police captain in the town. [*Takes a box of caramels out of his pocket and sucks one.*]

PISHTCHIK. My daughter, Dashenka, wishes to be remembered to you.

LOPAHIN. I want to tell you something very pleasant and cheering. [*Glancing at his watch.*] I'm going directly . . . there's no time to say much . . . well, I can say it in a couple of words. I needn't tell you your cherry orchard is to be sold to pay your debts; the twenty-second of August is the date fixed for the sale; but don't you worry, dearest lady, you may sleep in peace, there is a way of saving it. . . . This is what I propose. I beg your attention! Your estate is not twenty miles from the town, the railway runs close by it, and if the cherry orchard and the land along the river bank were cut up into building plots and then let on lease for summer villas, you would make an income of at least twenty-five thousand rubles a year out of it.

GAEV. That's all rot, if you'll excuse me.

LYUBOV. I don't quite understand you, Yermolay Alexeyevitch.

LOPAHIN. You will get a rent of at least twenty-five rubles a year for a three-acre plot from summer visitors, and if you say the word now, I'll bet you what you like there won't be one square foot of ground vacant by the autumn, all the plots will be taken up. I congratulate you; in fact, you are saved. It's a perfect situation with that deep river. Only, of course, it must be cleared—all the old buildings, for example, must be removed, this house too, which is really good for nothing and the old cherry orchard must be cut down.

LYUBOV. Cut down? My dear fellow, forgive me, but you don't know what you are talking about. If there is one thing interesting—remarkable indeed—in the whole province, it's just our cherry orchard.

LOPAHIN. The only thing remarkable about the orchard is that it's a very large one. There's a crop of cherries every alternate year, and then there's nothing to be done with them, no one buys them.

GAEV. This orchard is mentioned in the *Encyclopedia.*

LOPAHIN. [*Glancing at his watch.*] If we don't decide on something and don't take some steps, on the twenty-second of August the cherry orchard and the whole estate too will be sold by auction. Make up your minds! There is no other way of saving it, I'll take my oath on that. No, No!

FIRS. In old days, forty or fifty years ago, they used to dry the cherries, soak them, pickle them, make jam too, and they used—

GAEV. Be quiet, Firs.

FIRS. And they used to send the preserved cherries to Moscow and to Harkov by the wagon load. That brought the money in! And the preserved cherries in those days were soft and juicy, sweet and fragrant. . . . They knew the way to do them then. . . .

LYUBOV. And where is the recipe now?

FIRS. It's forgotten. Nobody remembers it.

PISHTCHIK. [*To Lyubov Andreyevna.*] What's it like in Paris? Did you eat frogs there?

LYUBOV. Oh, I ate crocodiles.

PISHTCHIK. Fancy that now!

LOPAHIN. There used to be only the gentlefolks and the peasants in the country, but now there are these summer visitors. All the towns, even the small ones, are surrounded nowadays by these summer villas. And one may say for sure that in another twenty years there'll be many more of these people and that they'll be everywhere. At present the summer visitor only drinks tea in his veranda, but maybe he'll take to working his bit of land too, and then your cherry orchard would become happy, rich, and prosperous. . . .

GAEV. [*Indignant.*] What rot!

Enter Varya and Yasha.

VARYA. There are two telegrams for you, mamma. [*Takes out keys and opens an old-fashioned bookcase with a loud crack.*] Here they are.

LYUBOV. From Paris. [*Tears the telegrams, without reading them.*] I have done with Paris.

GAEV. Do you know, Lyuba, how old that bookcase is? Last week I pulled out the bottom drawer and there I found the date branded on it. The bookcase was made just a hundred years ago. What do you say to that? We might have celebrated its jubilee. Though it's an inanimate object, still it is a *book case*.

PISHTCHIK. [*Amazed.*] A hundred years! Fancy that now.

GAEV. Yes. . . . It is a thing. . . . [*Feeling the bookcase.*] Dear, honored, bookcase! Hail to thee who for more than a hundred years hast served the pure ideals of good and justice; thy silent call to fruitful labor has never flagged in those hundred years, maintaining [*In tears.*] in the generations of man, courage and faith in a brighter future and fostering in us ideals of good and social consciousness. [*A pause.*]

LOPAHIN. Yes. . . .

LYUBOV. You are just the same as ever, Leonid.

GAEV. [*A little embarrassed.*] Cannon off the right into the pocket!

LOPAHIN. [*Looking at his watch.*] Well, it's time I was off.

YASHA. [*Handing Lyubov Andreyevna medicine.*] Perhaps you will take your pills now.

PISHTCHIK. You shouldn't take medicines, my dear madam . . . they do no harm and no good. Give them here . . . honored lady. [*Takes the pillbox, pours the pills into the hollow of his hand, blows on them, puts them in his mouth, and drinks off some kvass.*] There!

LYUBOV. [*In alarm.*] Why, you must be out of your mind!

PISHTCHIK. I have taken all the pills.

LOPAHIN. What a glutton! [*All laugh.*]

FIRS. His honor stayed with us in Easter week, ate a gallon and a half of cucumbers. . . . [*Mutters.*]

LYUBOV. What is he saying?

VARYA. He has taken to muttering like that for the last three years. We are used to it.

YASHA: His declining years!

Charlotta Ivanovna, a very thin, lanky figure in the white dress with a lorgnette in her belt, walks across the stage.

LOPAHIN. I beg your pardon, Charlotta Ivanovna, I have not had time to greet you. [*Tries to kiss her hand.*]

CHARLOTTA. [*Pulling away her hand.*] If I let you kiss my hand, you'll be wanting to kiss my elbow, and then my shoulder.

LOPAHIN. I've no luck today! [*All laugh.*] Charlotta Ivanovna, show us some tricks!

LYUBOV. Charlotta, do show us some tricks!

CHARLOTTA. I don't want to. I'm sleepy. [*Goes out.*]

LOPAHIN. In three weeks' time we shall meet again. (*Kisses Lyubov Andreyevna's hand.*) Good-bye till then—I must go. [*To Gaev.*] Good-bye. [*Kisses Pishtchik.*] Good-bye. [*Gives his hand to Varya, then to Firs and Yasha.*] I don't want to go. [*To Lyubov Andreyevna.*] If you think over my plan for the villas and make up your mind, then let me know; I will lend you fifty thousand rubles. Think of it seriously.

VARYA. [*Angrily.*] Well, do go, for goodness sake.

LOPAHIN. I'm going, I'm going. [*Goes out.*]

GAEV. Low-born knave! I beg pardon, though . . . Varya is going to marry him, he's Varya's fiancé.

VARYA. Don't talk nonsense, uncle.

LYUBOV. Well, Varya, I shall be delighted. He's a good man.

PISHTCHIK. He is, one must acknowledge, a most worthy man. And my Dashenka . . . says too that . . . she says . . . various things. [*Snores, but at once wakes up.*] But all the same, honored lady, could you oblige me . . . with a loan of two hundred forty rubles . . . to pay the interest on my mortgage tomorrow?

VARYA. [*Dismayed.*] No, no.

LYUBOV. I really haven't any money.

PISHTCHIK. It will turn up. [*Laughs.*] I never lose hope. I thought everything was over, I was a ruined man, and lo and behold—the railway passed through my land and . . . they paid me for it. And something else will turn up again, if not today, then tomorrow . . . Dashenka'll win two hundred thousand . . . she's got a lottery ticket.

LYUBOV. Well, we've finished our coffee, we can go to bed.

FIRS. [*Brushes Gaev, reprovingly.*] You have got on the wrong trousers again! What am I to do with you?

VARYA. [*Softly.*] Anya's asleep. [*Softly opens the window.*] Now the sun's risen, it's not a bit cold. Look, mamma, what exquisite trees! My goodness! And the air! The starlings are singing!

GAEV. [*Opens another window.*] The orchard is all white. You've not forgotten it, Lyuba? That long avenue that runs straight, straight as an arrow, how it shines on a moonlit night. You remember? You've not forgotten?

LYUBOV. [*Looking out of the window into the garden.*] Oh, my childhood, my innocence! it was in this nursery I used to sleep, from here I looked out into the orchard, happiness waked with me every morning and in those days the orchard was just the same, nothing has changed. [*Laughs with delight.*] All, all white! Oh, my orchard! After the dark gloomy autumn, and the cold winter; you are young again, and full of happiness, the heavenly angels have never left you. . . . If I could cast off the burden that weighs on my heart, if I could forget the past!

GAEV. Hm! and the orchard will be sold to pay our debts; it seems strange. . . .

LYUBOV. See, our mother walking . . . all in white, down the avenue! [*Laughs with delight.*] It is she!

GAEV. Where?

VARYA. Oh, don't, mamma!

LYUBOV. There is no one. It was my fancy. On the right there, by the path to the arbor, there is a white tree bending like a woman. . . .

Enter Trofimov wearing a shabby student's uniform and spectacles.

LYUBOV. What a ravishing orchard! White masses of blossom, blue sky. . . .

TROFIMOV. Lyubov Andreyevna! [*She looks round at him.*] I will just pay my respects to you and then leave you at once. [*Kisses her hand warmly.*] I was told to wait until morning, but I hadn't the patience to wait any longer. . . .

Lyubov Andreyevna looks at him in perplexity.

VARYA. [*Through her tears.*] This is Petya Trofimov.

TROFIMOV. Petya Trofimov, who was your Grisha's tutor. . . . Can I have changed so much?

Lyubov Andreyevna embraces him and weeps quietly.

GAEV. [*In confusion.*] There, there, Lyuba.

VARYA. [*Crying.*] I told you, Petya, to wait till tomorrow.

LYUBOV. My Grisha . . . my boy . . . Grisha . . . my son!

VARYA. We can't help it, mamma, it is God's will.

TROFIMOV. [*Softly through his tears.*] There . . . there.

LYUBOV. [*Weeping quietly.*] My boy was lost . . . drowned. Why? Oh, why, dear Petya? [*More quietly.*] Anya is asleep in there, and I'm talking loudly . . . making this noise. . . . But, Petya? Why have you grown so ugly? Why do you look so old?

TROFIMOV. A peasant woman in the train called me a mangy-looking gentleman.

LYUBOV. You were quite a boy then, a pretty little student, and now your hair's thin—and spectacles. Are you really a student still? [*Goes toward the door.*]

TROFIMOV. I seem likely to be a perpetual student.

LYUBOV. [*Kisses her brother, then Varya.*] Well, go to bed. . . . You are older too, Leonid.

PISHTCHIK. [*Follows her.*] I suppose it's time we were asleep. . . . Ugh! my gout. I'm staying the night! Lyubov Andreyevna, my dear soul, if you could . . . tomorrow morning . . . two hundred forty rubles.

GAEV. That's always his story.

PISHTCHIK. Two hundred forty rubles . . . to pay the interest on my mortgage.

LYUBOV. My dear man, I have no money.

PISHTCHIK. I'll pay it back, my dear . . . a trifling sum.

LYUBOV. Oh, well, Leonid will give it to you. . . . You give him the money, Leonid.

GAEV. Me give it to him! Let him wait till he gets it!

LYUBOV. It can't be helped, give it to him. He needs it. He'll pay it back.

Lyubov Andreyevna, Trofimov, Pishtchik, and Firs go out. Gaev, Varya, and Yasha remain.

GAEV. Sister hasn't got out of the habit of flinging away her money. [*To Yasha.*] Get away, my good fellow, you smell of the henhouse.

YASHA. [*With a grin.*] And you, Leonid Andreyevitch, are just the same as ever.

GAEV. What's that? [*To Varya.*] What did he say?

VARYA. [*To Yasha.*] Your mother has come from the village; she has been sitting in the servants' room since yesterday, waiting to see you.

YASHA: Oh, bother her!

VARYA. For shame!

YASHA: What's the hurry? She might just as well have come tomorrow. [*Goes out.*]

VARYA. Mamma's just the same as ever, she hasn't changed a bit. If she had her own way, she'd give away everything.

GAEV. Yes. [*A pause.*] If a great many remedies are suggested for some disease, it means that the disease is incurable. I keep thinking and racking my brains; I have many schemes, a great many, and that really means none. If we could only come in for a legacy from somebody, or marry our Anya to a very rich man, or we might go to Yaroslavl and try our luck with our old aunt, the Countess. She's very, very rich, you know.

VARYA. [*Weeps.*] If God would help us.

GAEV. Don't blubber. Aunt's very rich, but she doesn't like us. First, sister married a lawyer instead of a nobleman. . . .

Anya appears in the doorway.

GAEV. And then her conduct, one can't call it virtuous. She is good, and kind, and nice, and I love her, but, however one allows for extenuating circumstances, there's no denying that she's an immoral woman. One feels it in her slightest gesture.

VARYA. [*In a whisper.*] Anya's in the doorway.

GAEV. What do you say? [*A pause.*] It's queer, there seems to be something wrong with my right eye. I don't see as well as I did. And on Thursday when I was in the district court . . .

Enter Anya.

VARYA. Why aren't you asleep, Anya?

ANYA. I can't get to sleep.

GAEV. My pet. [*Kisses Anya's face and hands.*] My child. [*Weeps.*] You are not my niece, you are my angel, you are everything to me. Believe me, believe. . . .

ANYA. I believe you, uncle. Everyone loves you and respects you . . . but, uncle dear, you must be silent . . . simply be silent. What were you saying just now about my mother, about your own sister? What made you say that?

GAEV. Yes, yes. . . . [*Puts his hand over his face.*] Really, that was awful! My God, save me! And today I made a speech to the bookcase . . . so stupid! And only when I had finished, I saw how stupid it was.

VARYA. It's true, uncle, you ought to keep quiet. Don't talk, that's all.

ANYA. If you could keep from talking, it would make things easier for you, too.

GAEV. I won't speak. [*Kisses Anya's and Varya's hands.*] I'll be silent. Only this is about business. On Thursday I was in the district court; well, there was a large party of us there and we began talking of one thing and another, and this and that, and do you know, I believe that it will be possible to raise a loan on an I.O.U. to pay the arrears on the mortgage.

VARYA. If the Lord would help us!

GAEV. I'm going on Tuesday; I'll talk of it again. [*To Varya.*] Don't blubber. [*To Anya.*] Your mamma will talk to Lopahin; of course, he won't refuse her. And as soon as you're rested you shall go to Yaroslavl to the Countess, your great-aunt. So we shall all set to work in three directions at once, and the business is done. We shall pay off arrears, I'm convinced of it. [*Puts a caramel in his mouth.*] I swear on my honor, I swear by anything you like, the estate shan't be sold. [*Ex-*

citedly.] By my own happiness, I swear it! Here's my hand on it, call me the basest, vilest of men, if I let it come to an auction! Upon my soul I swear it!

ANYA. [*Here equanimity has returned, she is quite happy.*] How good you are, uncle, and how clever! [*Embraces her uncle.*] I'm at peace now! Quite at peace! I'm happy!

Enter Firs.

FIRS. [*Reproachfully.*] Leonid Andreyevitch, have you no fear of God? When are you going to bed?

GAEV. Directly, directly. You can go, Firs. I'll . . . yes, I will undress myself. Come, children, bye-bye. We'll go into details tomorrow, but now go to bed. [*Kisses Anya and Varya.*] I'm a man of the eighties.° They run down that period, but still I can say I have had to suffer not a little for my convictions in my life, it's not for nothing that the peasant loves me. One must know the peasant! One must know how. . . .

ANYA. At it again, uncle!

VARYA. Uncle dear, you'd better be quiet!

FIRS. [*Angrily.*] Leonid Andreyevitch!

GAEV. I'm coming. I'm coming. Go to bed. Potted the shot°—there's a shot for you! A beauty! [*Goes out, Firs hobbling after him.*]

ANYA. My mind's at rest now. I don't want to go to Yaroslavl, I don't like my great-aunt, but still my mind's at rest. Thanks to uncle. [*Sits down.*]

VARYA. We must go to bed. I'm going. Something unpleasant happened while you were away. In the old servants' quarters there are only the old servants, as you know—Efimyushka, Polya, and Yevstigney—and Karp too. They began letting stray people in to spend the night—I said nothing. But all at once I heard they had been spreading a report that I gave them nothing but pease pudding° to eat. Out of stinginess, you know. . . . And it was all Yevstigney's doing. . . . Very well, I said to myself. . . . If that's how it is, I thought, wait a bit. I sent for Yevstigney. . . . [*Yawns.*] He comes. . . . "How's this, Yevstigney," I said, "you could be such a fool as to? . . ." [*Looking at Anya.*] Anitchka! [*A pause.*] She's asleep. [*Puts her arm around Anya.*] Come to bed . . . come along! [*Leads her.*] My darling has fallen asleep! Come . . . [*They go.*]

Far away beyond the orchard a shepherd on a pipe. Trofimov crosses the stage and, seeing Varya and Anya, stands still.

VARYA. Sh! asleep, asleep. Come, my own.

ANYA. [*Softly, half-asleep.*] I'm so tired. Still those bells. Uncle . . . dear . . . mamma and uncle. . . .

VARYA. Come, my own, come along.

They go into Anya's room.

TROFIMOV. [*Tenderly.*] My sunshine! My spring.

ACT II

The open country. An old shrine, long abandoned and fallen out of the perpendicular; near it a well, large stones that have apparently once been tombstones, and an old gar-

---

eighties: the 1880s an older generation (when the role of Russia's peasantry was romanticized).
the shot: in the imaginary billiard game.
pease pudding: pea soup.

den seat. *The road to Gaev's house is seen. On one side rise dark poplars; and there the cherry orchard begins. In the distance a row of telegraph poles and far, far away on the horizon there is faintly outlined a great town, only visible in very fine clear weather. It is near sunset. Charlotta, Yasha, and Dunyasha are sitting on the seat. Epihodov is standing near, playing something mournful on a guitar. All sit plunged in thought. Charlotta wears an old forage cap; she has taken a gun from her shoulder and is tightening the buckle on the strap.*

CHARLOTTA. [*Musingly.*] I haven't a real passport of my own, and I don't know how old I am, and I always feel that I'm a young thing. When I was a little girl, my father and mother used to travel about to fairs and give performances—very good ones. And I used to dance *salto-mortale*° and all sorts of things. And when papa and mamma died, a German lady took me and had me educated. And so I grew up and became a governess. But where I came from, and who I am, I don't know. . . . Who my parents were, very likely they weren't married. . . . I don't know. [*Takes a cucumber out of her pocket and eats.*] I know nothing at all. [*A pause.*] One wants to talk and has no one to talk to . . . I have nobody.

EPIHODOV. [*Plays on the guitar and sings.*] "What care I for the noisy world! What care I for friends or foes!" How agreeable it is to play on the mandolin!

DUNYASHA. That's a guitar, not a mandolin. [*Looks in a hand mirror and powders herself.*]

EPIHODOV. To a man mad with love, it's a mandolin. [*Sings.*] "Were her heart but aglow with love's mutual flame."

Yasha joins in.

CHARLOTTA. How shockingly these people sing! Foo! Like jackals!

DUNYASHA. [*To Yasha.*] What happiness, though, to visit foreign lands.

YASHA: Ah, yes! I rather agree with you there. [*Yawns, then lights a cigar.*]

EPIHODOV. That's comprehensible. In foreign lands everything has long since reached full complexion.

YASHA: That's so, of course.

EPIHODOV. I'm a cultivated man, I read remarkable books of all sorts, but I can never make out the tendency I am myself precisely inclined for, whether to live or to shoot myself, speaking precisely, but nevertheless I always carry a revolver. Here it is. . . . [*Shows revolver.*]

CHARLOTTA. I've had enough, and now I'm going. [*Puts on the gun.*] Epihodov, you're a very clever fellow, and a very terrible one too, all the women must be wild about you. Br-r-r! [*Goes.*] These clever fellows are all so stupid; there's not a creature for me to speak to. . . . Always alone, alone, nobody belonging to me . . . and who I am, and why I'm on earth, I don't know. [*Walks away slowly.*]

EPIHODOV. Speaking precisely, not touching upon other subjects, I'm bound to admit about myself, that destiny behaves mercilessly to me, as a storm to a little boat. If, let us suppose, I am mistaken, then why did I wake up this morning, to quote an example, and look round, and there on my chest was a spider of fearful magnitude . . . like this. [*Shows with both hands.*] And then I take up a jug of kvass, to quench my thirst, and in it there is something in the highest degree unseemly

---

salto-mortale: "fateful leap"—a standing somersault.

of the nature of a cockroach. [*A pause.*] Have you read Buckle?° [*A pause.*] I am
desirous of troubling you, Dunyasha, with a couple of words.

DUNYASHA. Well, speak.

EPIHODOV. I should be desirous to speak with you alone. [*Sighs.*]

DUNYASHA. [*Embarrassed.*] Well—only bring me my mantle first. It's by the cupboard. It's rather damp here.

EPIHODOV. Certainly. I will fetch it. Now I know what I must do with my revolver.
[*Takes guitar and goes off playing on it.*]

YASHA: Two and twenty misfortunes! Between ourselves, he's a fool. [*Yawns.*]

DUNYASHA. God grant he doesn't shoot himself! [*A pause.*] I am so nervous, I'm always in a flutter. I was a little girl when I was taken into our lady's house, and
now I have quite grown out of peasant ways, and my hands are white, as white
as a lady's. I'm such a delicate, sensitive creature. I'm afraid of everything. I'm
so frightened. And if you deceive me, Yasha, I don't know what will become of
my nerves.

YASHA. [*Kisses her.*] You're a peach! Of course a girl must never forget herself; what
I dislike more than anything is a girl being flighty in her behavior.

DUNYASHA. I'm passionately in love with you, Yasha: you are a man of culture—
you can give your opinion about anything. [*A pause.*]

YASHA. [*Yawns.*] Yes, that's so. My opinion is this: if a girl loves anyone, that means
that she has no principles. [*A pause.*] It's pleasant smoking a cigar in the open
air. [*Listens.*] Someone's coming this way . . . it's the gentlefolk. [*Dunyasha embraces him impulsively.*] Go home, as though you had been to the river to bathe;
go by that path, or else they'll meet you and suppose I have made an appointment with you here. That I can't endure.

DUNYASHA. [*Coughing softly.*] The cigar has made my head ache. . . . [*Goes off.*]

Yasha remains sitting near the shrine. Enter Lyubov Andreyevna, Gaev, and Lopahin.

LOPAHIN. You must make up your mind once and for all—there's no time to lose.
It's quite a simple question, you know. Will you consent to letting the land for
building or not? One word in answer: Yes or no? Only one word!

LYUBOV. Who is smoking such horrible cigars here? [*Sits down.*]

GAEV. Now the railway line has been brought near, it's made things very convenient. [*Sits down.*] Here we have been over and lunched in town. Cannon off
the white! I should like to go home and have a game.

LYUBOV. You have plenty of time.

LOPAHIN. Only one word! [*Beseechingly.*] Give me an answer!

GAEV. [*Yawning.*] What do you say?

LYUBOV. [*Looks in her purse.*] I had quite a lot of money here yesterday, and there's
scarcely any left today. My poor Varya feeds us all on milk soup for the sake of
economy; and old folks in the kitchen get nothing but pease pudding, while I
waste my money in a senseless way. [*Drops purse, scattering gold pieces.*] There,
they have all fallen out! [*Annoyed.*]

YASHA: Allow me, I'll soon pick them up. [*Collects the coins.*]

LYUBOV. Pray do, Yasha. And what did I go off to the town to lunch for? Your
restaurant's a wretched place with its music and the tablecloth smelling of
soap. . . . Why drink so much, Leonid? And eat so much? And talk so much?

Buckle: H. T. Buckle, early-nineteenth-century theorist on economics and history.

Today you talked a great deal again in the restaurant, and all so inappropriately. About the era of the seventies, about the decadents.° And to whom? Talking to waiters about decadents!

LOPAHIN. Yes.

GAEV. [*Waving his hand.*] I'm incorrigible; that's evident. [*Irritably to Yasha.*] Why is it you keep fidgeting about in front of us!

YASHA. [*Laughs.*] I can't help laughing when I hear your voice.

GAEV. [*To his sister.*] Either I or he. . . .

LYUBOV. Get along! Go away, Yasha.

YASHA. [*Gives Lyubov Andreyevna her purse.*] Directly. [*Hardly able to suppress his laughter.*] This minute. . . . [*Goes off.*]

LOPAHIN. Deriganov, the millionaire, means to buy your estate. They say he is coming to the sale himself.

LYUBOV. Where did you hear that?

LOPAHIN. That's what they say in town.

GAEV. Our aunt in Yaroslavl has promised to send help; but when, and how much she will send, we don't know.

LOPAHIN. How much will she send? A hundred thousand? Two hundred?

LYUBOV. Oh, well! . . . Ten or fifteen thousand, and we must be thankful to get that.

LOPAHIN. Forgive me, but such reckless people as you are—such queer, unbusinesslike people—I never met in my life. One tells you in plain Russian your estate is going to be sold, and you seem not to understand it.

LYUBOV. What are we to do? Tell us what to do.

LOPAHIN. I do tell you every day. Every day I say the same thing. You absolutely must let the cherry orchard and the land on building leases; and do it at once, as quick as may be—the auction's close upon us! Do understand! Once make up your mind to build villas, and you can raise as much money as you like, and then you are saved.

LYUBOV. Villas and summer visitors—forgive me saying so—it's so vulgar.

GAEV. There I perfectly agree with you.

LOPAHIN. I shall sob, or scream, or fall into a fit. I can't stand it! You drive me mad! [*To Gaev.*] You're an old woman!

GAEV. What do you say?

LOPAHIN. An old woman! [*Gets up to go.*]

LYUBOV. [*In dismay.*] No, don't go! Do stay, my dear friend! Perhaps we shall think of something.

LOPAHIN. What is there to think of?

LYUBOV. Don't go, I entreat you! With you here it's more cheerful, anyway. [*A pause.*] I keep expecting something, as though the house were going to fall about our ears.

GAEV. [*In profound dejection.*] Potted the white! It fails—a kiss.

LYUBOV. We have been great sinners. . . .

LOPAHIN. You have no sins to repent of.

GAEV. [*Puts a caramel in his mouth.*] They say I've eaten up my property in caramels. [*Laughs.*]

LYUBOV. Oh, my sins! I've always thrown my money away recklessly like a lunatic. I married a man who made nothing but debts. My husband died of cham-

---

decants: a literary and philosophical movement.

Realism in Drama

pagne—he drank dreadfully. To my misery I loved another man, and immediately—it was my first punishment—the blow fell upon me, here, in the river . . . my boy drowned and I went abroad—went away forever, never to return, not to see that river again . . . I shut my eyes, and fled, distracted, and *he* after me . . . pitilessly, brutally. I bought a villa at Mentone, for *he* fell ill there, and for three years I had no rest day or night. His illness wore me out, my soul was dried up. And last year, when my villa was sold to pay my debts, I went to Paris and there he robbed me of everything and abandoned me for another woman; and I tried to poison myself. . . . So stupid, so shameful! . . . And suddenly I felt a yearning for Russia, for my country, for my little girl. . . . [*Dries her tears.*] Lord, Lord, be merciful! Forgive my sins! Do not chastise me more! [*Takes a telegram out of her pocket.*] I got this today from Paris. He implores forgiveness, entreats me to return. [*Tears up the telegram.*] I fancy there is music somewhere. [*Listens.*]

GAEV. That's our famous Jewish orchestra. You remember, four violins, a flute, and a double bass.

LYUBOV. That still in existence? We ought to send for them one evening and give a dance.

LOPAHIN. [*Listens.*] I can't hear. . . . [*Hums softly.*] "For money the Germans will turn a Russian into a Frenchman." [*Listens.*] I did see such a piece at the theatre yesterday! It was funny!

LYUBOV. And most likely there was nothing funny in it. You shouldn't look at plays, you should look at yourselves a little oftener. How gray your lives are! How much nonsense you talk.

LOPAHIN. That's true. One may say honestly, we live a fool's life. [*Pause.*] My father was a peasant, an idiot; he knew nothing and taught me nothing, only beat me when he was drunk, and always with his stick. In reality I am just such another blockhead and idiot. I've learnt nothing properly. I write a wretched hand. I write so that I feel ashamed before folks, like a pig.

LYUBOV. You ought to get married, my dear fellow.

LOPAHIN. Yes . . . that's true.

LYUBOV. You should marry our Varya, she's a good girl.

LOPAHIN. Yes.

LYUBOV. She's a good-natured girl, she's busy all day long, and what's more, she loves you. And you have liked her for ever so long.

LOPAHIN. Well? I'm not against it. . . . She's a good girl. [*Pause.*]

GAEV. I've been offered a place in the bank: six thousand rubles a year. Did you know?

LYUBOV. You would never do for that! You must stay as you are.

Enter Firs with overcoat.

FIRS. Put it on, sir, it's damp.

GAEV. [*Putting it on.*] You bother me, old fellow.

FIRS. You can't go on like this. You went away in the morning without leaving word. [*Looks him over.*]

LYUBOV. You look older, Firs!

FIRS. What is your pleasure?

LOPAHIN. You look older, she said.

FIRS. I've had a long life. They were arranging my wedding before your papa was born.... [*Laughs.*] I was the head footman before the emancipation° came. I wouldn't consent to be set free then; I stayed on with the old master.... [*A pause.*] I remember what rejoicings they made and didn't know themselves what they were rejoicing over.

LOPAHIN. Those were fine old times. There was flogging anyway.

FIRS. [*Not hearing.*] To be sure! The peasants knew their place, and the masters knew theirs; but now they're all at sixes and sevens,° there's no making it out.

GAEV. Hold your tongue, Firs. I must go to town tomorrow. I have been promised an introduction to a general, who might let us have a loan.

LOPAHIN. You won't bring that off. And you won't pay your arrears, you may rest assured of that.

LYUBOV. That's all his nonsense. There is no such general.

Enter Trofimov, Anya, and Varya.

GAEV. Here come our girls.

ANYA. That's mamma on the seat.

LYUBOV. [*Tenderly.*] Come here, come along. My darlings! [*Embraces Anya and Varya.*] If you only knew how I love you both. Sit beside me, there, like that. [*All sit down.*]

LOPAHIN. Our perpetual student is always with the young ladies.

TROFIMOV. That's not your business.

LOPAHIN. He'll soon be fifty, and he's still a student.

TROFIMOV. Drop your idiotic jokes.

LOPAHIN. Why are you so cross, you queer fish?

TROFIMOV. Oh, don't persist!

LOPAHIN. [*Laughs.*] Allow me to ask you what's your idea of me?

TROFIMOV. I'll tell you my idea of you, Yermolay Alexeyevitch: you are a rich man, you'll soon be a millionaire. Well, just as in the economy of nature a wild beast is of use, who devours everything that comes in his way, so you too have your use.

All laugh.

VARYA. Better tell us something about the planets, Petya.

LYUBOV. No, let us go on with the conversation we had yesterday.

TROFIMOV. What was it about?

GAEV. About pride.

TROFIMOV. We had a long conversation yesterday, but we came to no conclusion. In pride, in your sense of it, there is something mystical. Perhaps you are right from your point of view; but if one looks at it simply, without subtlety, what sort of pride can there be, what sense is there in it, if man in his physiological formation is very imperfect, if in the immense majority of cases he is coarse, dull-witted, profoundly unhappy? One must give up glorification of self. One should work, and nothing else.

GAEV. One must die in any case.

TROFIMOV. Who knows? And what does it mean—dying? Perhaps man has a hundred senses, and only the five we know are lost in death, while the other ninety-five remain alive.

LYUBOV. How clever you are, Petya!

---

before the emancipation: before the freeing of peasant serfs in 1861.
at sixes and sevens: confused.

Realism in Drama

LOPAHIN. [*Ironically.*] Fearfully clever!

TROFIMOV. Humanity progresses, perfecting its powers. Everything that is beyond its ken now will one day become familiar and comprehensible; only we must work, we must with all our powers aid the seeker after truth. Here among us in Russia the workers are few in number as yet. The vast majority of the intellectual people I know seek nothing, do nothing, are not fit as yet for work of any kind. They call themselves intellectual, but they treat their servants as inferiors, behave to the peasants as though they were animals, learn little, read nothing seriously, do practically nothing, only talk about science, and know very little about art. They are all serious people, they all have severe faces, they all talk of weighty matters and air their theories, and yet the vast majority of us—ninety-nine percent— live like savages, at the least thing fly to blows and abuse, eat piggishly, sleep in filth and stuffiness, bugs everywhere, stench and damp and moral impurity. And it's clear all our fine talk is only to divert our attention and other people's. Show me where to find the *crèches*° there's so much talk about, and the reading rooms? They only exist in novels: in real life there are none of them. There is nothing but filth and vulgarity and Asiatic apathy. I fear and dislike very serious faces. I'm afraid of serious conversation. We should do better to be silent.

LOPAHIN. You know, I get up at five o'clock in the morning, and I work from morning to night; and I've money, my own and other people's, always passing through my hands, and I see what people are made of all round me. One has only to begin to do anything to see how few honest decent people there are. Sometimes when I lie awake at night, I think: "Oh! Lord, thou hast given us immense forests, boundless plains, and widest horizons, and living here we ourselves ought really to be giants."

LYUBOV. You ask for giants! They are no good except in storybooks; in real life they frighten us.

Epihodov advances in the background, playing on the guitar.

LYUBOV. [*Dreamily.*] There goes Epihodov.

ANYA. [*Dreamily.*] There goes Epihodov.

GAEV. The sun has set, my friends.

TROFIMOV. Yes.

GAEV. [*Not loudly but, as it were, declaiming.*] O nature, divine nature, thou art bright with eternal luster, beautiful and indifferent! Thou, whom we call mother, thou dost unite within thee life and death! Thou dost give life and dost destroy!

VARYA. [*In a tone of supplication.*] Uncle!

ANYA. Uncle, you are at it again!

TROFIMOV. You'd much better be cannoning off the red!

GAEV. I'll hold my tongue, I will.

All sit plunged in thought. Perfect stillness. The only thing audible is the muttering of Firs. Suddenly there is a sound in the distance, as it were from the sky—the sound of a breaking harp string, mournfully dying away.

LYUBOV. What is that?

LOPAHIN. I don't know. Somewhere far away a bucket fallen and broken in the pits. But somewhere very far away.

---

crèches: day-care centers.

GAEV. It might be a bird of some sort—such as a heron.

TROFIMOV. Or an owl.

LYUBOV. [*Shudders.*] I don't know why, but it's horrid. [*A pause.*]

FIRS. It was the same before the calamity—the owl hooted and the samovar hissed all the time.

GAEV. Before what calamity?

FIRS. Before the emancipation. [*A pause.*]

LYUBOV. Come, my friends, let us be going; evening is falling. [*To Anya.*] There are tears in your eyes. What is it, darling? [*Embraces her.*]

ANYA. Nothing, mamma; it's nothing.

TROFIMOV. There is somebody coming.

The Wayfarer appears in a shabby white forage cap and an overcoat; he is slightly drunk.

WAYFARER. Allow me to inquire, can I get to the station this way?

GAEV. Yes. Go along that road.

WAYFARER. I thank you most feelingly. [*Coughing.*] The weather is superb. [*Declaims.*] My brother, my suffering brother! . . . Come out to the Volga! Whose groan do you hear? . . . [*To Varya.*] Mademoiselle, vouchsafe a hungry Russian thirty kopeks.

Varya utters a shriek of alarm.

LOPAHIN. [*Angrily.*] There's a right and a wrong way of doing everything!

LYUBOV. [*Hurriedly.*] There, take this. [*Looks in her purse.*] I've no silver. No matter—here's gold for you.

WAYFARER. I thank you most feelingly! [*Goes off.*]

Laughter.

VARYA. [*Frightened.*] I'm going home—I'm going. . . . Oh, mamma, the servants have nothing to eat, and you gave him gold!

LYUBOV. There's no doing anything with me. I'm so silly! When we get home, I'll give you all I possess. Yermolay Alexeyevitch, you will lend me some more! . . .

LOPAHIN. I will.

LYUBOV. Come, friends, it's time to be going. And Varya, we have made a match of it for you. I congratulate you.

VARYA. [*Through her tears.*] Mamma, that's not a joking matter.

LOPAHIN. "Ophelia, get thee to a nunnery!"°

GAEV. My hands are trembling; it's a long while since I had a game of billiards.

LOPAHIN. "Ophelia! Nymph, in thy orisons be all my sins remember'd."°

LYUBOV. Come, it will soon be suppertime.

VARYA. How he frightened me! My heart's simply throbbing.

LOPAHIN. Let me remind you, ladies and gentlemen: on the twenty-second of August the cherry orchard will be sold. Think about that! Think about it!

All go off, except Trofimov and Anya.

ANYA. [*Laughing.*] I'm grateful to the wayfarer! He frightened Varya and we are left alone.

---

nunnery: See *Hamlet* (III.1.136).
remember'd: See the same *Hamlet* scene, lines 89–90, ending the soliloquy.

TROFIMOV. Varya's afraid we shall fall in love with each other, and for days together she won't leave us. With her narrow brain she can't grasp that we are above love. To eliminate the petty and transitory which hinder us from being free and happy—that is the aim and meaning of our life. Forward! We go forward irresistibly toward the bright star that shines yonder in the distance. Forward! Do not lag behind, friends.

ANYA. [*Claps her hands.*] How well you speak! [*A pause.*] It is divine here today.

TROFIMOV. Yes, it's glorious weather.

ANYA. Somehow, Petya, you've made me so that I don't love the cherry orchard as I used to. I used to love it so dearly. I used to think that there was no spot on earth like our garden.

TROFIMOV. All Russia is our garden. The earth is great and beautiful—there are many beautiful places in it. [*A pause.*] Think only, Anya, your grandfather, and great-grandfather, and all your ancestors were slave owners—the owners of living souls—and from every cherry in the orchard, from every leaf, from every trunk there are human creatures looking at you. Cannot you hear their voices? Oh, it is awful! Your orchard is a fearful thing, and when in the evening or at night one walks about the orchard, the old bark on the trees glimmers dimly in the dusk, and the old cherry trees seem to be dreaming of centuries gone by and tortured by fearful visions. Yes! We are at least two hundred years behind, we have really gained nothing yet, we have no definite attitude to the past, we do nothing but theorize or complain of depression or drink vodka. It is clear that to begin to live in the present, we must first expiate our past; we must break with it; and we can expiate it only by suffering, by extraordinary unceasing labor. Understand that, Anya.

ANYA. The house we live in has long ceased to be our own, and I shall leave it, I give you my word.

TROFIMOV. If you have the house keys, fling them into the well and go away. Be free as the wind.

ANYA. [*In ecstasy.*] How beautifully you said that!

TROFIMOV. Believe me, Anya, believe me! I am not thirty yet, I am young, I am still a student, but I have gone through so much already! As soon as winter comes I am hungry, sick, careworn, poor as a beggar, and what ups and downs of fortune have I not known! And my soul was always, every minute, day and night, full of inexplicable forebodings. I have a foreboding of happiness, Anya. I see glimpses of it already.

ANYA. [*Pensively.*] The moon is rising.

Epihodov is heard playing still the same mournful song on the guitar. The moon rises. Somewhere near the poplars Varya is looking for Anya and calling "Anya! where are you?"

TROFIMOV. Yes, the moon is rising. [*A pause.*] Here is happiness—here it comes! It is coming nearer and nearer; already I can hear its footsteps. And if we never see it—if we may never know it—what does it matter? Others will see it after us.

VARYA'S VOICE. Anya! Where are you?

TROFIMOV. That Varya again! [*Angrily.*] It's revolting!

ANYA. Well, let's go down to the river. It's lovely there.

TROFIMOV. Yes, let's go. [*They go.*]

VARYA'S VOICE. Anya! Anya!

ACT III

A drawing room divided by an arch from a larger drawing room. A chandelier burning. The Jewish orchestra, the same that was mentioned in Act II, is heard playing in the anteroom. It is evening. In the larger drawing room they are dancing the grand chain. The voice of Semyonov-Pishtchik: "Promenade à une paire!"° Then enter the drawing room in couples, first Pishtchik and Charlotta Ivanovna, then Trofimov and Lyubov Andreyevna, thirdly Anya with the Post Office Clerk, fourthly Varya with the Station Master, and other guests. Varya is quietly weeping and wiping away her tears as she dances. In the last couple is Dunyasha. They move across the drawing room. Pishtchik shouts: "Grand rond, balancez!" and "Les Cavaliers à genou et remerciez vos dames."°

Firs in a swallowtail coat brings in seltzer water on a tray. Pishtchik and Trofimov enter the drawing room.

PISHTCHIK. I am a full-blooded man; I have already had two strokes. Dancing's hard work for me, but as they say, if you're in the pack, you must bark with the rest. I'm as strong, I may say, as a horse. My parent, who would have his joke—may the Kingdom of Heaven be his!—used to say about our origin that the ancient stock of the Semyonov-Pishtchiks was derived from the very horse that Caligula° made a member of the senate. [*Sits down.*] But I've no money, that's where the mischief is. A hungry dog believes in nothing but meat. [*Snores, but at once wakes up.*] That's like me . . . I can think of nothing but money.

TROFIMOV. There really is something horsy about your appearance.

PISHTCHIK. Well . . . a horse is a fine beast . . . a horse can be sold.

There is the sound of billiards being played in an adjoining room. Varya appears in the arch leading to the larger drawing room.

TROFIMOV. [*Teasing.*] Madame Lopahin! Madame Lopahin!

VARYA. [*Angrily.*] Mangy-looking gentleman!

TROFIMOV. Yes, I am a mangy-looking gentleman, and I'm proud of it!

VARYA. [*Pondering bitterly.*] Here we have hired musicians and nothing to pay them! [*Goes out.*]

TROFIMOV. [*To Pishtchik.*] If the energy you have wasted during your lifetime in trying to find the money to pay your interest had gone to something else, you might in the end have turned the world upside down.

PISHTCHIK. Nietzsche,° the philosopher, a very great and celebrated man . . . of enormous intellect . . . says in his works that one can make forged bank notes.

TROFIMOV. Why, have you read Nietzsche?

PISHTCHIK. What next . . . Dashenka told me. . . . And now I am in such a position, I might just as well forge bank notes. The day after tomorrow I must pay three hundred ten rubles—one hundred thirty I have procured. [*Feels in his pockets, in alarm.*] The money's gone! I have lost my money! [*Through his tears.*] Where's the money? [*Gleefully.*] Why, here it is behind the lining. . . . It has made me hot all over.

Enter Lyubov Andreyevna and Charlotta Ivanovna.

---

promenade . . . : French dance instructions: "walk in couples."
grand rond . . . dames: dance instructions: "circle around"; "gents kneel and thank the ladies."
Caligula: mad Roman emperor who appointed a horse as senator.
Nietzsche: philosopher Friedrich Nietzsche, who argued for a "superman" above traditional morality.

Realism in Drama

LYUBOV. [*Hums the Lezginka.°*] Why is Leonid so long? What can he be doing in town? [*To Dunyasha.*] Offer the musicians some tea.

TROFIMOV. The sale hasn't taken place, most likely.

LYUBOV. It's the wrong time to have the orchestra, and the wrong time to give a dance. Well, never mind. [*Sits down and hums softly.*]

CHARLOTTA. [*Gives Pishtchik a pack of cards.*] Here's a pack of cards. Think of any card you like.

PISHTCHIK. I've thought of one.

CHARLOTTA. Shuffle the pack now. That's right. Give it here, my dear Mr. Pishtchik. *Ein, zwei, drei°*—now look, it's in your breast pocket.

PISHTCHIK. [*Taking a card out of his breast pocket.*] The eight of spades! Perfectly right! [*Wonderingly.*] Fancy that now!

CHARLOTTA. [*Holding pack of cards in her hands, to Trofimov.*] Tell me quickly which is the top card.

TROFIMOV. Well, the queen of spades.

CHARLOTTA. It is! [*To Pishtchik.*] Well, which card is uppermost?

PISHTCHIK. The ace of hearts.

CHARLOTTA. It is! [*Claps her hands, pack of cards disappears.*] Ah! what lovely weather it is today!

A mysterious feminine voice which seems coming out of the floor answers her, "Oh, yes, it's magnificent weather, madam."

CHARLOTTA. You are my perfect ideal.

VOICE. And I greatly admire you too, madam.

STATION MASTER. [*Applauding.*] The lady ventriloquist—bravo!

PISHTCHIK. [*Wonderingly.*] Fancy that now! Most enchanting, Charlotta Ivanovna. I'm simply in love with you.

CHARLOTTA. In love? [*Shrugging shoulders.*] What do you know of love, *guter Mensch, aber schlechter Musikant?°*

TROFIMOV. [*Pats Pishtchik on the shoulder.*] You dear old horse. . . .

CHARLOTTA. Attention, please! Another trick! [*Takes a traveling rug from a chair.*] Here's a very good rug; I want to sell it. [*Shaking it out.*] Doesn't anyone want to buy it?

PISHTCHIK. [*Wonderingly.*] Fancy that!

CHARLOTTA. *Ein, zwei, drei!* [*Quickly picks up rug she has dropped; behind the rug stands Anya; she makes a curtsy, runs to her mother, embraces her, and runs back into the larger drawing room amidst general enthusiasm.*]

LYUBOV. [*Applauds.*] Bravo! Bravo!

CHARLOTTA. Now again! *Ein, zwei, drei!* [*Lifts up the rug; behind the rug stands Varya, bowing.*]

PISHTCHIK. [*Wonderingly.*] Fancy that now!

CHARLOTTA. That's the end. [*Throws the rug at Pishtchik, makes a curtsy, runs into the larger drawing room.*]

PISHTCHIK. [*Hurries after her.*] Mischievous creature! Fancy! [*Goes out.*]

Lezginka: vigorous Russian dance.
Ein, zwei, drei: German dance instructions: "One, two, three. . . ."
. . . Musikant: German: "Good man, bad musician."

LYUBOV. And still Leonid doesn't come. I can't understand what he's doing in the town so long! Why, everything must be over by now. The estate is sold, or the sale has not taken place. Why keep us so long in suspense?

VARYA. [*Trying to console her.*] Uncle's bought it. I feel sure of that.

TROFIMOV. [*Ironically.*] Oh, yes!

VARYA. Great-aunt sent him an authorization to buy it in her name and transfer the debt. She's doing it for Anya's sake, and I'm sure God will be merciful. Uncle will buy it.

LYUBOV. My aunt in Yaroslavl sent fifteen thousand to buy the estate in her name, she doesn't trust us—but that's not enough even to pay the arrears. [*Hides her face in her hands.*] My fate is being sealed today, my fate. . . .

TROFIMOV. [*Teasing Varya.*] Madame Lopahin.

VARYA. [*Angrily.*] Perpetual student! Twice already you've been sent down from the university.

LYUBOV. Why are you angry, Varya? He's teasing you about Lopahin. Well, what of that? Marry Lopahin if you like, he's a good man, and interesting; if you don't want to, don't! Nobody compels you, darling.

VARYA. I must tell you plainly, mamma, I look at the matter seriously; he's a good man, I like him.

LYUBOV. Well, marry him. I can't see what you're waiting for.

VARYA. Mamma. I can't make him an offer myself. For the last two years, everyone's been talking to me about him. Everyone talks; but he says nothing or else makes a joke. I see what it means. He's growing rich, he's absorbed in business, he has no thoughts for me. If I had money, were it ever so little, if I had only a hundred rubles, I'd throw everything up and go far away. I would go into a nunnery.

TROFIMOV. What bliss!

VARYA. [*To Trofimov.*] A student ought to have sense! [*In a soft tone with tears.*] How ugly you've grown, Petya! How old you look! [*To Lyubov Andreyevna, no longer crying.*] But I can't do without work, mamma; I must have something to do every minute.

Enter Yasha.

YASHA. [*Hardly restraining his laughter.*] Epihodov has broken a billiard cue! [*Goes out.*]

VARYA. What is Epihodov doing here? Who gave him leave to play billiards? I can't make these people out. [*Goes out.*]

LYUBOV. Don't tease her, Petya. You see she has grief enough without that.

TROFIMOV. She is so very officious, meddling in what's not her business. All the summer she's given Anya and me no peace. She's afraid of a love affair between us. What's it to do with her? Besides, I have given no grounds for it. Such triviality is not in my line. We are above love!

LYUBOV. And I suppose I am beneath love. [*Very uneasily.*] Why is it Leonid's not here? If only I could know whether the estate is sold or not! It seems such an incredible calamity that I really don't know what to think. I am distracted . . . I shall scream in a minute . . . I shall do something stupid. Save me, Petya, tell me something, talk to me!

TROFIMOV. What does it matter whether the estate is sold today or not? That's all done with long ago. There's no turning back, the path is overgrown. Don't worry yourself, dear Lyubov Andreyevna. You mustn't deceive yourself; for once in your life you must face the truth!

LYUBOV. What truth? You see where the truth lies, but I seem to have lost my sight, I see nothing. You settle every great problem so boldly, but tell me, my dear boy, isn't it because you're young—because you haven't yet understood one of your problems through suffering? You look forward boldly, and isn't it that you don't see and don't expect anything dreadful because life is still hidden from your young eyes? You're bolder, more honest, deeper than we are, but think, be just a little magnanimous, have pity on me. I was born here, you know, my father and mother lived here, my grandfather lived here, I love this house. I can't conceive of life without the cherry orchard, and if it really must be sold, then sell me with the orchard. [Embraces Trofimov, kisses him on the forehead.] My boy was drowned here. [Weeps.] Pity me, my dear kind fellow.

TROFIMOV. You know I feel for you with all my heart.

LYUBOV. But that should have been said differently, so differently. [Takes out her handkerchief, telegram falls on the floor.] My heart is so heavy today, it's so noisy here, my soul is quivering at every sound, I'm shuddering all over, but can't go away; I'm afraid to be quiet and alone. Don't be hard on me, Petya . . . I love you as though you were one of ourselves. I would gladly let you marry Anya—I swear I would—only, my dear boy, you must take your degree, you do nothing—you're simply tossed by fate from place to place. That's so strange. It is, isn't it? And you must do something with your beard to make it grow somehow. [Laughs.] You look so funny!

TROFIMOV. [Picks up the telegram.] I've no wish to be a beauty.

LYUBOV. That's a telegram from Paris. I get one every day. One yesterday and one today. That savage creature is ill again, he's in trouble again. He begs forgiveness, beseeches me to go, and really I ought to go to Paris to see him. You look shocked, Petya. What am I to do, my dear boy, what am I to do? He is ill, he is alone and unhappy, and who'll look after him, who'll keep him from doing the wrong thing, who'll give him his medicine at the right time? And why hide it or be silent? I love him, that's clear. I love him! I love him! He's a millstone about my neck, I'm going to the bottom with him, but I love that stone and can't live without it. [Presses Trofimov's hand.] Don't think ill of me, Petya, don't tell me anything, don't tell me. . . .

TROFIMOV. [Through his tears.] For God's sake forgive my frankness: why, he robbed you!

LYUBOV. No! No! No! You mustn't speak like that. [Covers her ears.]

TROFIMOV. He is a wretch! You're the only person that doesn't know it! He's a worthless creature! A despicable wretch!

LYUBOV. [Getting angry, but speaking with restraint.] You're twenty-six or twenty-seven years old, but you're still a schoolboy.

TROFIMOV. Possibly.

LYUBOV. You should be a man at your age! You should understand what love means! And you ought to be in love yourself. You ought to fall in love! [Angrily.] Yes, yes, and it's not purity in you, you're simply a prude, a comic fool, a freak.

TROFIMOV. [In horror.] The things she's saying!

LYUBOV. I am above love! You're not above love, but simply as our Firs here says, "You are a good-for-nothing." At your age not to have a mistress!

TROFIMOV. [In horror.] This is awful! The things she is saying! [Goes rapidly into the larger drawing room clutching his head.] This is awful! I can't stand it! I'm going. [Goes off, but at once returns.] All is over between us! [Goes off into the anteroom.]

LYUBOV. [*Shouts after him.*] Petya! Wait a minute! You funny creature! I was joking! Petya! [*There is a sound of somebody running quickly downstairs and suddenly falling with a crash. Anya and Varya scream, but there is a sound of laughter at once.*]

LYUBOV. What has happened?

Anya runs in.

ANYA. [*Laughing.*] Petya's fallen downstairs! [*Runs out.*]

LYUBOV. What a queer fellow that Petya is!

The Station Master stands in the middle of the larger room and reads The Magdalene, *by Alexey Tolstoy.° They listen to him, but before he has recited many lines strains of a waltz are heard from the anteroom and the reading is broken off. All dance. Trofimov, Anya, Varya, and Lyubov Andreyevna come in from the anteroom.*

LYUBOV. Come, Petya—come, pure heart! I beg your pardon. Let's have a dance! [*Dances with Petya.*]

Anya and Varya dance. Firs comes in, puts his stick down near the side door. Yasha also comes into the drawing room and looks on at the dancing.

YASHA. What is it, old man?

FIRS. I don't feel well. In old days we used to have generals, barons, and admirals dancing at our balls, and now we send for the post office clerk and the station master and even they're not overanxious to come. I am getting feeble. The old master, the grandfather, used to give sealing wax for all complaints. I have been taking sealing wax for twenty years or more. Perhaps that's what's kept me alive.

YASHA. You bore me, old man! [*Yawns.*] It's time you were done with.

FIRS. Ach, you're a good-for-nothing! [*Mutters.*]

Trofimov and Lyubov Andreyevna dance in larger room and then on to the stage.

LYUBOV. *Merci.* I'll sit down a little. [*Sits down.*] I'm tired.

Enter Anya.

ANYA. [*Excitedly.*] There's a man in the kitchen has been saying that the cherry orchard's been sold today.

LYUBOV. Sold to whom?

ANYA. He didn't say to whom. He's gone away.

She dances with Trofimov, and they go off into the larger room.

YASHA. There was an old man gossiping there, a stranger.

FIRS. Leonid Andreyevitch isn't here yet, he hasn't come back. He has his light overcoat on, *demi-saison,°* he'll catch cold for sure. Ach! Foolish young things!

LYUBOV. I feel as though I should die. Go, Yasha, find out to whom it has been sold.

YASHA. But he went away long ago, the old chap. [*Laughs.*]

LYUBOV. [*With slight vexation.*] What are you laughing at? What are you pleased at?

YASHA. Epihodov is so funny. He's a silly fellow, two and twenty misfortunes.

LYUBOV. Firs, if the estate is sold, where will you go?

FIRS. Where you bid me, there I'll go.

Tolstoy: mid-nineteenth-century Russian writer of melodramatic narrative poems; not the author of *War and Peace. demi-saison:* French: between seasons or off-season.

Realism in Drama

LYUBOV. Why do you look like that? Are you ill? You ought to be in bed.

FIRS. Yes. [*Ironically.*] Me go to bed and who's to wait here? Who's to see to things without me? I'm the only one in all the house.

YASHA. [*To Lyubov Andreyevna.*] Lyubov Andreyevna, permit me to make a request of you; if you go back to Paris again, be so kind as to take me with you. It's positively impossible for me to stay here. [*Looking about him; in an undertone.*] There's no need to say it, you see for yourself—an uncivilized country, the people have no morals, and then the dullness! The food in the kitchen's abominable, and then Firs runs after one muttering all sorts of unsuitable words. Take me with you, please do!

Enter Pishtchik.

PISHTCHIK. Allow me to ask you for a waltz, my dear lady. [*Lyubov Andreyevna goes with him.*] Enchanting lady, I really must borrow of you just one hundred eighty rubles, [*Dances.*] only one hundred eighty rubles. [*They pass into the larger room.*]

In the larger drawing room, a figure in a gray top hat and in checked trousers is gesticulating and jumping about. Shouts of "Bravo, Charlotta Ivanovna."

DUNYASHA. [*She has stopped to powder herself.*] My young lady tells me to dance. There are plenty of gentlemen and too few ladies, but dancing makes me giddy and makes my heart beat. Firs, the post office clerk said something to me just now that quite took my breath away.

Music becomes more subdued.

FIRS. What did he say to you?

DUNYASHA. He said I was like a flower.

YASHA. [*Yawns.*] What ignorance! [*Goes out.*]

DUNYASHA. Like a flower. I am a girl of such delicate feelings, I am awfully fond of soft speeches.

FIRS. Your head's being turned.

Enter Epihodov.

EPIHODOV. You have no desire to see me, Dunyasha. I might be an insect. [*Sighs.*] Ah! life!

DUNYASHA. What is it you want?

EPIHODOV. Undoubtedly you may be right. [*Sighs.*] But, of course, if one looks at it from that point of view, if I may so express myself, you have, excuse my plain speaking, reduced me to a complete state of mind. I know my destiny. Every day some misfortune befalls me and I have long ago grown accustomed to it, so that I look upon my fate with a smile. You gave me your word, and though I—

DUNYASHA. Let us have a talk later, I entreat you, but now leave me in peace, for I am lost in reverie. [*Plays with her fan.*]

EPIHODOV. I have a misfortune every day, and if I may venture to express myself, I merely smile at it, I even laugh.

Varya enters from the larger drawing room.

VARYA. You still have not gone, Epihodov. What a disrespectful creature you are, really! [*To Dunyasha.*] Go along, Dunyasha! [*To Epihodov.*] First you play billiards and break the cue, then you go wandering about the drawing room like a visitor!

EPIHODOV. You really cannot, if I may so express myself, call me to account like this.

VARYA. I'm not calling you to account, I'm speaking to you. You do nothing but wander from place to place and don't do your work. We keep you as a counting house clerk, but what use you are I can't say.

EPIHODOV. [*Offended.*] Where I work or whether I walk, whether I eat or whether I play billiards, is a matter to be judged by persons of understanding and my elders.

VARYA. You dare to tell me that! [*Firing up.*] You dare! You mean to say I've no understanding. Begone from here! This minute!

EPIHODOV [*Intimidated.*] I beg you to express yourself with delicacy.

VARYA. [*Beside herself with anger.*] This moment! get out! away! [*He goes toward the door, she following him.*] Two and twenty misfortunes! Take yourself off! Don't let me set eyes on you! [*Epihodov has gone out, behind the door his voice, "I shall lodge a complaint against you."*] What! You're coming back? [*Snatches up the stick Firs has put down near the door.*] Come! Come! I'll show you! What! you're coming? Then take that! [*She swings the stick, at the very moment that Lopahin comes in.*]

LOPAHIN. Very much obliged to you!

VARYA. [*Angrily and ironically.*] I beg your pardon!

LOPAHIN. Not at all! I humbly thank you for your kind reception!

VARYA. No need of thanks for it. [*Moves away, then looks round and asks softly.*] I haven't hurt you?

LOPAHIN. Oh, no! Not at all! There's an immense bump coming up, though!

VOICES FROM LARGER ROOM. Lopahin has come! Yermolay Alexeyevitch!

PISHTCHIK. What do I see and hear? [*Kisses Lopahin.*] There's a whiff of cognac about you, my dear soul, and we're making merry here too!

Enter Lyubov Andreyevna.

LYUBOV. Is it you, Yermolay Alexeyevitch? Why have you been so long? Where's Leonid?

LOPAHIN. Leonid Andreyevitch arrived with me. He is coming.

LYUBOV. [*In agitation.*] Well! Well! Was there a sale? Speak!

LOPAHIN [*Embarrassed, afraid of betraying his joy.*] The sale was over at four o'clock. We missed our train—had to wait till half-past nine. [*Sighing heavily.*] Ugh! I feel a little giddy.

Enter Gaev. In his right hand he has purchases, with his left hand he is wiping away his tears.

LYUBOV. Well, Leonid? What news? [*Impatiently, with tears.*] Make haste, for God's sake!

GAEV. [*Makes her no answer, simply waves his hand; to Firs, weeping.*] Here, take them; there's anchovies, Kertch herrings. I have eaten nothing all day. What I have been through! [*Door into the billiard room is open. There is heard a knocking of balls and the voice of Yasha saying "Eighty-seven." Gaev's expression changes, he leaves off weeping.*] I am fearfully tired. Firs, come and help me change my things. [*Goes to his own room across the larger drawing room.*]

PISHTCHIK. How about the sale? Tell us, do!

LYUBOV. Is the cherry orchard sold?

LOPAHIN. It is sold.

LYUBOV. Who has bought it?

LOPAHIN. I have bought it. [*A pause. Lyubov is crushed; she would fall down if she were not standing near a chair and table.*]

Varya takes keys from her waistband, flings them on the floor in middle of drawing room, and goes out.

LOPAHIN. I have bought it! Wait a bit, ladies and gentlemen, pray. My head's a bit muddled, I can't speak. [*Laughs.*] We came to the auction. Deriganov was there already. Leonid Andreyevitch only had fifteen thousand and Deriganov bid thirty thousand, besides the arrears, straight off. I saw how the land lay. I bid against him. I bid forty thousand, he bid forty-five thousand, I said fifty-five, and so he went on, adding five thousands and I adding ten. Well . . . So it ended. I bid ninety, and it was knocked down to me. Now the cherry orchard's mine! Mine! [*Chuckles.*] My God, the cherry orchard's mine! Tell me that I'm drunk, that I'm out of my mind, that it's all a dream. [*Stamps with his feet.*] Don't laugh at me! If my father and my grandfather could rise from their graves and see all that has happened! How their Yermolay, ignorant, beaten Yermolay, who used to run about barefoot in winter, how that very Yermolay has bought the finest estate in the world! I have bought the estate where my father and grandfather were slaves, where they weren't even admitted into the kitchen. I am asleep, I am dreaming! It is all fancy, it is the work of your imagination plunged in the darkness of ignorance. [*Picks up keys, smiling fondly.*] She threw away the keys; she means to show she's not the housewife now. [*Jingles the keys.*] Well, no matter. [*The orchestra is heard tuning up.*] Hey, musicians! Play! I want to hear you. Come, all of you, and look how Yermolay Lopahin will take the ax to the cherry orchard, how the trees will fall to the ground! We will build houses on it and our grandsons and great-grandsons will see a new life springing up there. Music! Play up!

Music begins to play. Lyubov Andreyevna has sunk into a chair and is weeping bitterly.

LOPAHIN. [*Reproachfully.*] Why, why didn't you listen to me? My poor friend! Dear lady, there's no turning back now. [*With tears.*] Oh, if all this could be over, oh, if our miserable disjointed life could somehow soon be changed!

PISHTCHIK. [*Takes him by the arm, in an undertone.*] She's weeping, let us go and leave her alone. Come. [*Takes him by the arm and leads him into the larger drawing room.*]

LOPAHIN. What's that? Musicians, play up! All must be as I wish it. [*With irony.*] Here comes the new master, the owner of the cherry orchard! [*Accidentally tips over a little table, almost upsetting the candelabra.*] I can pay for everything! [*Goes out with Pishtchik. No one remains on the stage or in the larger drawing room except Lyubov, who sits huddled up, weeping bitterly. The music plays softly. Anya and Trofimov come in quickly. Anya goes up to her mother and falls on her knees before her. Trofimov stands at the entrance to the larger drawing room.*]

ANYA. Mamma! Mamma, you're crying, dear, kind, good mamma! My precious! I love you! I bless you! The cherry orchard is sold, it is gone, that's true, that's true! But don't weep, mamma! Life is still before you, you have still your good, pure heart! Let us go, let us go, darling, away from here! We will make a new garden, more splendid than this one; you will see it, you will understand. And joy, quiet, deep joy, will sink into your soul like the sun at evening! And you will smile, mamma! Come, darling, let us go!

ACT IV

Same as in first act. There are neither curtains on the windows nor pictures on the walls: only a little furniture remains piled up in a corner as if for sale. There is a sense of desolation; near the outer door and in the background of the scene are packed trunks, traveling bags, etc. On the left the door is open, and from here the voices of Varya and Anya are audible. Lopahin is standing waiting. Yasha is holding a tray with glasses full of champagne. In front of the stage Epihodov is tying up a box. In the background behind the scene a hum of talk from the peasants who have come to say good-bye. The voice of Gaev: "Thanks, brothers, thanks!"

YASHA. The peasants have come to say good-bye. In my opinion, Yermolay Alexeyevitch, the peasants are good-natured, but they don't know much about things.

The hum of talk dies away. Enter across front of stage Lyubov Andreyevna and Gaev. She is not weeping, but is pale; her face is quivering—she cannot speak.

GAEV. You gave them your purse, Lyuba. That won't do—that won't do!

LYUBOV. I couldn't help it! I couldn't help it!

[*Both go out.*]

LOPAHIN. [*In the doorway, calls after them.*] You will take a glass at parting? Please do. I didn't think to bring any from the town, and at the station I could only get one bottle. Please take a glass. [*A pause.*] What? You don't care for any? [*Comes away from the door.*] If I'd known, I wouldn't have bought it. Well, and I'm not going to drink it. [*Yasha carefully sets the tray down on a chair.*] You have a glass, Yasha, anyway.

YASHA. Good luck to the travelers, and luck to those that stay behind! [*Drinks.*] This champagne isn't the real thing, I can assure you.

LOPAHIN. It cost eight rubles the bottle. [*A pause.*] It's devilish cold here.

YASHA. They haven't heated the stove today—it's all the same since we're going. [*Laughs.*]

LOPAHIN. What are you laughing for?

YASHA. For pleasure.

LOPAHIN. Though it's October, it's as still and sunny as though it were summer. It's just right for building! [*Looks at his watch; says in doorway.*] Take note, ladies and gentlemen, the train goes in forty-seven minutes; so you ought to start for the station in twenty minutes. You must hurry up!

Trofimov comes in from out of doors wearing a greatcoat.

TROFIMOV. I think it must be time to start, the horses are ready. The devil only knows what's become of my galoshes; they're lost. [*In the doorway.*] Anya! My galoshes aren't there, I can't find them.

LOPAHIN. And I'm getting off to Harkov. I am going in the same train with you. I'm spending all the winter at Harkov. I've been wasting my time gossiping with you and fretting with no work to do. I can't get on without work. I don't know what to do with my hands, they flap about so queerly, as if they didn't belong to me.

TROFIMOV. Well, we're just going away, and you will take up your profitable labors again.

LOPAHIN. Do take a glass.

TROFIMOV. No thanks.

LOPAHIN. Then you're going to Moscow now?

Realism in Drama

TROFIMOV. Yes. I shall see them as far as the town, and tomorrow I shall go on to Moscow.

LOPAHIN. Yes, I daresay, the professors aren't giving any lectures, they're waiting for your arrival.

TROFIMOV. That's not your business.

LOPAHIN. How many years have you been at the university?

TROFIMOV. Do think of something newer than that—that's stale and flat. [*Hunts for galoshes.*] You know we shall most likely never see each other again, so let me give you one piece of advice at parting: don't wave your arms about—get out of the habit. And another thing, building villas, reckoning up that the summer visitors will in time become independent farmers—reckoning like that, that's not the thing to do either. After all, I am fond of you: you have fine delicate fingers like an artist, you've a fine delicate soul.

LOPAHIN. [*Embraces him.*] Good-bye, my dear fellow. Thanks for everything. Let me give you money for the journey, if you need it.

TROFIMOV. What for? I don't need it.

LOPAHIN. Why, you haven't got a half-penny.

TROFIMOV. Yes, I have, thank you. I got some money for a translation. Here it is in my pocket, [*Anxiously.*] but where can my galoshes be!

VARYA. [*From the next room.*] Take the nasty things! [*Flings a pair of galoshes onto the stage.*]

TROFIMOV. Why are you so cross, Varya? hm! . . . but those aren't my galoshes.

LOPAHIN. I sowed three thousand acres with poppies in the spring, and now I have cleared forty thousand profit. And when my poppies were in flower, wasn't it a picture! So here, as I say, I made forty thousand, and I'm offering you a loan because I can afford to. Why turn up your nose? I am a peasant—I speak bluntly.

TROFIMOV. Your father was a peasant, mine was a chemist—and that proves absolutely nothing whatever. [*Lopahin takes out his pocketbook.*] Stop that—stop that. If you were to offer me two hundred thousand I wouldn't take it. I am an independent man, and everything that all of you, rich and poor alike, prize so highly and hold so dear hasn't the slightest power over me—it's like so much fluff fluttering in the air. I can get on without you. I can pass by you. I am strong and proud. Humanity is advancing towards the highest truth, the highest happiness, which is possible on earth, and I am in the front ranks.

LOPAHIN. Will you get there?

TROFIMOV. I shall get there. [*A pause.*] I shall get there, or I shall show others the way to get there.

In the distance is heard the stroke of an ax on a tree.

LOPAHIN. Good-bye, my dear fellow; it's time to be off. We turn up our noses at one another, but life is passing all the while. When I am working hard without resting, then my mind is more at ease, and it seems to me as though I too know what I exist for; but how many people are in Russia, my dear boy, who exist, one doesn't know what for. Well, it doesn't matter. That's not what keeps things spinning. They tell me Leonid Andreyevitch has taken a situation. He is going to be a clerk at the bank—six thousand rubles a year. Only, of course, he won't stick to it—he's too lazy.

ANYA. [*In the doorway.*] Mamma begs you not to let them chop down the orchard until she's gone.

TROFIMOV. Yes, really, you might have the tact. [*Walks out across the front of the stage.*]

LOPAHIN. I'll see to it! I'll see to it! Stupid fellows! [*Goes out after him.*]

ANYA. Has Firs been taken to the hospital?

YASHA. I told them this morning. No doubt they have taken him.

ANYA. [*To Epihodov, who passes across the drawing room.*] Semyon Pantaleyevitch, inquire, please, if Firs has been taken to the hospital.

YASHA. [*In a tone of offense.*] I told Yegor this morning—why ask a dozen times?

EPIHODOV. Firs is advanced in years. It's my conclusive opinion no treatment would do him good; it's time he was gathered to his fathers. And I can only envy him. [*Puts a trunk down on a cardboard hatbox and crushes it.*] There, now, of course— I knew it would be so.

YASHA. [*Jeeringly.*] Two and twenty misfortunes!

VARYA. [*Through the door.*] Has Firs been taken to the hospital?

ANYA. Yes.

VARYA. Why wasn't the note for the doctor taken too?

ANYA. Oh, then, we must send it after them. [*Goes out.*]

VARYA. [*From the adjoining room.*] Where's Yasha? Tell him his mother's come to say good-bye to him.

YASHA. [*Waves his hand.*] They put me out of all patience! [*Dunyasha has all this time been busy about the luggage. Now, when Yasha is left alone, she goes up to him.*]

DUNYASHA. You might just give me one look, Yasha. You're going away. You're leaving me. [*Weeps and throws herself on his neck.*]

YASHA. What are you crying for? [*Drinks the champagne.*] In six days I shall be in Paris again. Tomorrow we shall get into the express train and roll away in a flash. I can scarcely believe it! *Vive la France!* It doesn't suit me here—it's not the life for me; there's no doing anything. I have seen enough of the ignorance here. I have had enough of it. [*Drinks champagne.*] What are you crying for? Behave yourself properly, and then you won't cry.

DUNYASHA. [*Powders her face, looking in a pocket mirror.*] Do send me a letter from Paris. You know how I loved you, Yasha—how I loved you! I am a tender creature, Yasha.

YASHA. Here they are coming!

Busies himself about the trunks, humming softly. Enter Lyubov Andreyevna, Gaev, Anya, and Charlotta Ivanovna.

GAEV. We ought to be off. There's not much time now. [*Looking at Yasha.*] What a smell of herrings!

LYUBOV. In ten minutes we must get into the carriage. [*Casts a look about the room.*] Farewell, dear house, dear old home of our fathers! Winters will pass and spring will come, and then you will be no more; they will tear you down! How much those walls have seen! [*Kisses her daughter passionately.*] My treasure, how bright you look! Your eyes are sparkling like diamonds! Are you glad? Very glad?

ANYA. Very glad! A new life is beginning, mamma.

GAEV. Yes, really, everything is all right now. Before the cherry orchard was sold, we were all worried and wretched, but afterwards, when once the question was settled conclusively, irrevocably, we all felt calm and even cheerful. I am a bank clerk now—I am a financier—cannon off the red. And you, Lyuba, after all, you are looking better; there's no question of that.

LYUBOV. Yes. My nerves are better, that's true. [*Her hat and coat are handed to her.*] I'm sleeping well. Carry out my things, Yasha. It's time. [*To Anya.*] My darling, we shall soon see each other again. I am going to Paris. I can live there on the money your Yaroslavl auntie sent us to buy the estate with—hurrah for auntie!—but that money won't last long.

ANYA. You'll come back soon, mamma, won't you? I'll be working up for my examination in the high school, and when I have passed that, I shall set to work and be a help to you. We will read all sorts of things together, mamma, won't we? [*Kisses her mother's hands.*] We will read in the autumn evenings. We'll read lots of books, and a new wonderful world will open out before us. [*Dreamily.*] Mamma, come soon.

LYUBOV. I shall come, my precious treasure. [*Embraces her.*]

Enter Lopahin. Charlotta softly hums a song.

GAEV. Charlotta's happy; she's singing!

CHARLOTTA. [*Picks up a bundle like a swaddled baby.*] Bye, bye, my baby. [*A baby is heard crying; "Ooah! ooah!"*] Hush, hush, my pretty boy! ["*Ooah! ooah!*"] Poor little thing! [*Throws the bundle back.*] You must please find me a situation. I can't go on like this.

LOPAHIN. We'll find you one, Charlotta Ivanovna. Don't you worry yourself.

GAEV. Everyone's leaving us. Varya's going away. We have become of no use all at once.

CHARLOTTA. There's nowhere for me to be in the town. I must go away. [*Hums.*] What care I . . .

Enter Pishtchik.

LOPAHIN. The freak of nature.

PISHTCHIK. [*Gasping.*] Oh . . . let me get my breath. . . . I'm worn out . . . my most honored . . . Give me some water.

GAEV. Want some money, I suppose? Your humble servant! I'll go out of the way of temptation. [*Goes out.*]

PISHTCHIK. It's a long while since I have been to see you . . . dearest lady. [*To Lopahin.*] You are here . . . glad to see you . . . a man of immense intellect . . . take . . . here [*Gives Lopahin.*] four hundred rubles. That leaves me owing eight hundred forty.

LOPAHIN. [*Shrugging his shoulders in amazement.*] It's like a dream. Where did you get it?

PISHTCHIK. Wait a bit . . . I'm hot . . . a most extraordinary occurrence! Some Englishmen came along and found in my land some sort of white clay. [*To Lyubov Andreyevna.*] And four hundred for you . . . most lovely . . . wonderful. [*Gives money.*] The rest later. [*Sips water.*] A young man in the train was telling me just now that a great philosopher advises jumping off a housetop. "Jump!" says he; "the whole gist of the problem lies in that." [*Wonderingly.*] Fancy that, now! Water, please!

LOPAHIN. What Englishmen?

PISHTCHIK. I have made over to them the rights to dig the clay for twenty-four years . . . and now, excuse me . . . I can't stay . . . I must be trotting on. I'm going to Znoikovo . . . to Kardamanovo. . . . I'm in debt all round. [*Sips.*] . . . To your very good health! . . . I'll come in on Thursday.

LYUBOV. We are just off to the town, and tomorrow I start for abroad.

PISHTCHIK. What! [*In agitation.*] Why to the town? Oh, I see the furniture . . . the boxes. No matter . . . [*Through his tears.*] . . . no matter . . . men of enormous intellect . . . those Englishmen. . . . Never mind . . . be happy. God will succor you . . . no matter . . . everything in this world must have an end. [*Kisses Lyubov Andreyevna's hand.*] If the rumor reaches you that my end has come, think of this . . . old horse, and say: "There once was such a man in the world . . . Semyonov-Pishtchik . . . the Kingdom of Heaven be his!" . . . Most extraordinary weather . . . yes. [*Goes out in violent agitation, but at once returns and says in the doorway.*] Dashenka wishes to be remembered to you. [*Goes out.*]

LYUBOV. Now we can start. I leave with two cares in my heart. The first is leaving Firs ill. [*Looking at her watch.*] We have still five minutes.

ANYA. Mamma, Firs has been taken to the hospital. Yasha sent him off this morning.

LYUBOV. My other anxiety is Varya. She is used to getting up early and working; and now, without work, she's like a fish out of water. She is thin and pale, and she's crying, poor dear! [*A pause.*] You are well aware, Yermolay Alexeyevitch, I dreamed of marrying her to you, and everything seemed to show that you would get married. [*Whispers to Anya and motions to Charlotta and both go out.*] She loves you—she suits you. And I don't know—I don't know why it is you seem, as it were, to avoid each other. I can't understand it!

LOPAHIN. I don't understand it myself, I confess. It's queer somehow, altogether. If there's still time, I'm ready now at once. Let's settle it straight off, and go ahead; but without you, I feel I shan't make her an offer.

LYUBOV. That's excellent. Why, a single moment's all that's necessary. I'll call her at once.

LOPAHIN. And there's champagne all ready too. [*Looking into the glasses.*] Empty! Someone's emptied them already. [*Yasha coughs.*] I call that greedy.

LYUBOV. [*Eagerly.*] Capital! We will go out. Yasha, allez!° I'll call her in. [*At the door.*] Varya, leave all that; come here. Come along! [*Goes out with Yasha.*]

LOPAHIN. [*Looking at his watch.*] Yes.

A pause. Behind the door, smothered laughter and whispering, and, at last, enter Varya.

VARYA. [*Looking a long while over the things.*] It is strange, I can't find it anywhere.

LOPAHIN. What are you looking for?

VARYA. I packed it myself, and I can't remember. [*A pause.*]

LOPAHIN. Where are you going now, Varvara Mihailova?

VARYA. I? To the Ragulins. I have arranged to go to them to look after the house— as a housekeeper.

LOPAHIN. That's in Yashnovo? It'll be seventy miles away. [*A pause.*] So this is the end of life in this house!

VARYA. [*Looking among the things.*] Where is it? Perhaps I put it in the trunk. Yes, life in this house is over—there will be no more of it.

LOPAHIN. And I'm just off to Harkov—by this next train. I've a lot of business there. I'm leaving Epihodov here, and I've taken him on.

VARYA. Really!

LOPAHIN. This time last year we had snow already, if you remember; but now it's so fine and sunny. Though it's cold, to be sure—three degrees of frost.

———

allez: French: "Go!"

VARYA. I haven't looked. [*A pause.*] And besides, our thermometer's broken. [*A pause.*]

VOICE AT THE DOOR FROM THE YARD. *"Yermolay Alexeyevitch!"*

LOPAHIN. [*As though he had long been expecting this summons.*] This minute!

> *Lopahin goes out quickly, Varya sitting on the floor and laying her head on a bag full of clothes, sobs quietly. The door opens. Lyubov Andreyevna comes in cautiously.*

LYUBOV. Well? [*A pause.*] We must be going.

VARYA. [*Has wiped her eyes and is no longer crying.*] Yes, mamma, it's time to start. I shall have time to get to the Ragulins today, if only you're not late for the train.

LYUBOV. [*In the doorway.*] Anya, put your things on.

> *Enter Anya, then Gaev and Charlotta Ivanovna. Gaev has on a warm coat with a hood. Servants and cabmen come in. Epihodov bustles about the luggage.*

LYUBOV. Now we can start on our travels.

ANYA. [*Joyfully.*] On our travels!

GAEV. My friends—my dear, my precious friends! Leaving this house forever, can I be silent? Can I refrain from giving utterance at leave-taking to those emotions which now flood all my being?

ANYA. [*Supplicatingly.*] Uncle!

VARYA. Uncle, you mustn't!

GAEV. [*Dejectedly.*] Cannon and into the pocket . . . I'll be quiet. . . .

> *Enter Trofimov and afterward Lopahin.*

TROFIMOV. Well, ladies and gentlemen, we must start.

LOPAHIN. Epihodov, my coat!

LYUBOV. I'll stay just one minute. It seems as though I have never seen before what the walls, what the ceilings in this house were like, and now I look at them with greediness, with such tender love.

GAEV. I remember when I was six years old sitting in that window on Trinity Day watching my father going to church.

LYUBOV. Have all the things been taken?

LOPAHIN. I think all. [*Putting on overcoat, to Epihodov.*] You, Epihodov, mind you see everything is right.

EPIHODOV [*In a husky voice.*] Don't you trouble, Yermolay Alexeyevitch.

LOPAHIN. Why, what's wrong with your voice?

EPIHODOV. I've just had a drink of water, and I choked over something.

YASHA. [*Contemptuously.*] The ignorance!

LYUBOV. We are going—and not a soul will be left here.

LOPAHIN. Not till the spring.

VARYA. [*Pulls a parasol out of a bundle, as though about to hit someone with it; Lopahin makes a gesture as though alarmed.*] What is it? I didn't mean anything.

TROFIMOV. Ladies and gentlemen, let us get into the carriage. It's time. The train will be in directly.

VARYA. Petya, here they are, your galoshes, by that box. [*With tears.*] And what dirty old things they are!

TROFIMOV. [*Putting on his galoshes.*] Let us go, friends!

GAEV. [*Greatly agitated, afraid of weeping.*] The train—the station! Double balk,° ah!

---

balk: billiards term.

LYUBOV. Let us go!

LOPAHIN. Are we all here! [Locks the side door on left.] The things are all here. We must lock up. Let us go!

ANYA. Good-bye, home! Good-bye to the old life!

TROFIMOV. Welcome to the new life!

Trofimov goes out with Anya, Varya looks round the room and goes out slowly. Yasha and Charlotta Ivanovna, with her dog, go out.

LOPAHIN. Till the spring, then! Come, friends, till we meet! [Goes out.]

Lyubov Andreyevna and Gaev remain alone. As though they had been waiting for this, they throw themselves on each other's necks, and break into subdued smothered sobbing, afraid of being overheard.

GAEV. [In despair.] Sister, my sister!

LYUBOV. Oh, my orchard!—my sweet, beautiful orchard! My life, my youth, my happiness, good-bye! Good-bye!

VOICE OF ANYA. [Calling gaily.] Mamma!

VOICE OF TROFIMOV. [Gaily, excitedly.] Aa—oo!

LYUBOV. One last look at the walls, at the windows. My dear mother loved to walk about this room.

GAEV. Sister, sister!

VOICE OF ANYA. Mamma!

VOICE OF TROFIMOV. Aa—oo!

LYUBOV. We are coming. [They go out.]

The stage is empty. There is the sound of the doors being locked up, then of the carriages driving away. There is silence. In the stillness there is the dull stroke of an ax in a tree, clanging with a mournful, lonely sound. Footsteps are heard. Firs appears in the doorway on the right. He is dressed as always—in a pea jacket and white waistcoat, with slippers on his feet. He is ill.

FIRS. [Goes up to the door, and tries the handles.] Locked! They have gone . . . [Sits down on sofa.] They have forgotten me. . . . Never mind . . . I'll sit here a bit. . . . I'll be bound Leonid Andreyevitch hasn't put his fur coat on and has gone off in his thin overcoat. [Sighs anxiously.] I didn't see after him. . . . These young people . . . [Mutters something that can't be distinguished.] Life has slipped by as though I hadn't lived. [Lies down.] I'll lie down a bit. . . . There's no strength in you, nothing left you—all gone! Ech! I'm good for nothing. [Lies motionless.]

A sound is heard that seems to come from the sky, like a breaking harp string, dying away mournfully. All is still again, and there is heard nothing but the strokes of the ax far away in the orchard.

QUESTIONS

1. Chekhov likes to set characters with various outlooks together on a stage. What different views of life are represented by the key characters in this play?

2. Chekhov insisted to Stanislavski that *The Cherry Orchard* was a comic play. Stanislavski thought it was fundamentally tragic. Which view would you take and how would you argue your case?

3. Does the play have a "villain"? Who is it and what are the grounds of the villainy?

4. Characterize the half-sisters Anya and Varya. What is their relation to each other and to their mother? In what state does Chekhov leave each of them at the end of the play?

5. What are the views of the student, Trofimov? How might these be contrasted with those of Firs, the old valet? Firs speaks the last words of the play—does he also have the proverbial "last word"?

6. How do different characters see the cherry orchard differently? What does it represent to Lyubov? To Lopahin? What does the sound of the ax in the final scene suggest in the larger sense?

7. Divide the characters into two groups, based on whether they appear to be "for" or "against" the "New Order" Trofimov invokes. Does Chekhov appear to be evenhanded in the matter?

8. What is at the root of Lopahin's glee in Act IV? What does his acquisition of the cherry orchard mean to him?

9. Do you sense that Chekhov himself has a position to take? Explain your answer.

10. Read Chekhov's story "The Lady with the Little Dog" (Chapter 14). Compare the mood of the story's conclusion to that at the end of the play. What do these suggest about Chekhov's view of life and of human nature?

OSCAR WILDE AND THE COMEDY OF MANNERS IN BRITAIN

Even as the great tide of Realism and Naturalism was sweeping over European culture in the late nineteenth century, the play-going public was startled—and delighted, and outraged—by the staging in London of Oscar Wilde's *The Importance of Being Earnest* (1895). Wilde evidenced his contrariness in everything he did, and the play was no exception. Light, glittery, and absolutely frivolous, *The Importance of Being Earnest* seeks to win its audience over by sheer force of wit—or so it appears. A closer inspection, however, reveals an intricate and superbly balanced structure. Wilde manipulates his pairs of would-be lovers with the skill of a master choreographer. As for the cut-and-thrust of its humor, the play is packed with memorable one-liners that owe more than a little to the tradition of conversational repartee. This was a part of the English Restoration stage especially prevalent in the works of William Congreve (1670–1729) and Richard Brinsley Sheridan (1751–1816), and looks back to the cleverness of French Neoclassical comedy as well. We can be sure that Molière would have been delighted with the pace and quicksilver delivery of Wilde's play.

Wilde was born in Ireland in 1854. After studying at Dublin's Trinity College, he made his way to London, where he achieved a reputation not only as a writer of poems, fiction (*The Picture of Dorian Gray*), and plays (his other major success was *Lady Windermere's Fan*), but also as one of the most brilliant conversationalists of the salon circuit. Indeed, Wilde is as much remembered for his recorded witticisms as for his literary work.

Wilde's last years were marred by scandal. The Marquis of Queensbury sued Wilde for leading his son, Lord Alfred Douglas, into a homosexual liaison. The suit was successful, and the writer spent two years in prison, where he wrote his famous letter to Douglas, "De Profundis" ("From the Depths"). After his release, Wilde moved to France, where he died in 1900.

The Importance of Being Earnest is not a "profound" play, nor is it meant to be. It has none of the topicality we find in the works of his prolific countryman George Bernard Shaw. The observations made by Algernon, Jack, and the others strike us with their cleverness, but few of the witticisms withstand deeper scrutiny. Still, out of the swirl of quips and preposterous misunderstandings, there emerges a kind of portrait of the studied nonchalance of England's upper classes during their last phase of glory.

Oscar Wilde (1854–1900)

Oscar Wilde was born in Ireland and died in Paris after a scandal-ridden career. He attended Dublin's Trinity College and later Magdalen College at Oxford, where he made a reputation as a poet and a witty conversationalist. He wrote successfully in several genres, publishing: poetry; the stories in *The Happy Prince;* a novel, *The Picture of Dorian Gray;* as well as highly popular plays like *Lady Windermere's Fan* and *The Importance of Being Earnest.* He fell afoul of the authorities after a much-publicized homosexual liaison. His last years were spent in prison and exile.

THE IMPORTANCE OF BEING EARNEST

A Trivial Comedy for
Serious People

FIRST ACT

Scene

Morning-room in Algernon's flat in Half-Moon Street. The room is luxuriously and artistically furnished. The sound of a piano is heard in the adjoining room.

> *Lane is arranging afternoon tea on the table and, after the music has ceased, Algernon enters.*

ALGERNON. Did you hear what I was playing, Lane?

LANE. I didn't think it polite to listen, sir.

ALGERNON. I'm sorry for that, for your sake. I don't play accurately—anyone can play accurately—but I play with wonderful expression. As far as the piano is concerned, sentiment is my forte.° I keep science for Life.

LANE. Yes, sir.

ALGERNON. And, speaking of the science of Life, have you got the cucumber sandwiches cut for Lady Bracknell?

LANE. Yes, sir. [*Hands them on a salver.°*]

---

    forte: special talent.
    salver: small tray.

           Realism in Drama

ALGERNON. [*Inspects them, takes two, and sits down on the sofa.*] Oh! . . . by the way, Lane, I see from your book that on Thursday night, when Lord Shoreman and Mr Worthing were dining with me, eight bottles of champagne are entered as having been consumed.

LANE. Yes, sir; eight bottles and a pint.

ALGERNON. Why is it that at a bachelor's establishment the servants invariably drink the champagne? I ask merely for information.

LANE. I attribute it to the superior quality of the wine, sir. I have often observed that in married households the champagne is rarely of a first-rate brand.

ALGERNON. Good heavens! Is marriage so demoralizing as that?

LANE. I believe it *is* a very pleasant state, sir. I have had very little experience of it myself up to the present. I have only been married once. That was in consequence of a misunderstanding between myself and a young person.

ALGERNON. [*Languidly.*] I don't know that I am much interested in your family life, Lane.

LANE. No, sir; it is not a very interesting subject. I never think of it myself.

ALGERNON. Very natural, I am sure. That will do, Lane, thank you.

LANE. Thank you, sir.

Lane goes out.

ALGERNON. Lane's views on marriage seem somewhat lax. Really, if the lower orders don't set us a good example, what on earth is the use of them? They seem, as a class, to have absolutely no sense of moral responsibility.

Enter Lane.

LANE. Mr Ernest Worthing.

Enter Jack. Lane goes out.

ALGERNON. How are you, my dear Ernest? What brings you up to town?

JACK. Oh, pleasure, pleasure! What else should bring one anywhere? Eating as usual, I see, Algy!

ALGERNON. [*Stiffly.*] I believe it is customary in good society to take some slight refreshment at five o'clock. Where have you been since last Thursday?

JACK. [*Sitting down on the sofa.*] In the country.

ALGERNON. What on earth do you do there?

JACK. [*Pulling off his gloves.*] When one is in town one amuses oneself. When one is in the country one amuses other people. It is excessively boring.

ALGERNON. And who are the people you amuse?

JACK. [*Airily.*] Oh, neighbours, neighbours.

ALGERNON. Got nice neighbours in your part of Shropshire?

JACK. Perfectly horrid! Never speak to one of them.

ALGERNON. How immensely you must amuse them! [*Goes over and takes sandwiches.*] By the way, Shropshire is your county, is it not?

JACK. Eh? Shropshire? Yes, of course. Hallo! Why all these cups? Why cucumber sandwiches? Why such reckless extravagance in one so young? Who is coming to tea?

ALGERNON. Oh! merely Aunt Augusta and Gwendolen.

JACK. How perfectly delightful!

ALGERNON. Yes, that is all very well; but I am afraid Aunt Augusta won't quite approve of your being here.

JACK. May I ask why?

ALGERNON. My dear fellow, the way you flirt with Gwendolen is perfectly disgraceful. It is almost as bad as the way Gwendolen flirts with you.

JACK. I am in love with Gwendolen. I have come up to town expressly to propose to her.

ALGERNON. I thought you had come up for pleasure? . . . I call that business.

JACK. How utterly unromantic you are!

ALGERNON. I really don't see anything romantic in proposing. It is very romantic to be in love. But there is nothing romantic about a definite proposal. Why, one may be accepted. One usually is, I believe. Then the excitement is all over. The very essence of romance is uncertainty. If ever I get married, I'll certainly try to forget the fact.

JACK. I have no doubt about that, dear Algy. The Divorce Court was specially invented for people whose memories are so curiously constituted.

ALGERNON. Oh, there is no use speculating on that subject. Divorces are made in Heaven—[Jack puts out his hand to take a sandwich. Algernon at once interferes.] Please don't touch the cucumber sandwiches. They are ordered specially for Aunt Augusta. [Takes one and eats it.]

JACK. Well, you have been eating them all the time.

ALGERNON. That is quite a different matter. She is my aunt. [Takes plate from below.] Have some bread and butter. The bread and butter is for Gwendolen. Gwendolen is devoted to bread and butter.

JACK. [Advancing to table and helping himself.] And very good bread and butter it is too.

ALGERNON. Well, my dear fellow, you need not eat as if you were going to eat it all. You behave as if you were married to her already. You are not married to her already, and I don't think you ever will be.

JACK. Why on earth do you say that?

ALGERNON. Well, in the first place, girls never marry the men they flirt with. Girls don't think it right.

JACK. Oh, that is nonsense!

ALGERNON. It isn't. It is a great truth. It accounts for the extraordinary number of bachelors that one sees all over the place. In the second place, I don't give my consent.

JACK. Your consent!

ALGERNON. My dear fellow, Gwendolen is my first cousin. And before I allow you to marry her, you will have to clear up the whole question of Cecily. [Rings bell.]

JACK. Cecily! What on earth do you mean? What do you mean, Algy, by Cecily! I don't know any one of the name of Cecily.

Enter Lane.

ALGERNON. Bring me that cigarette case Mr Worthing left in the smoking-room the last time he dined here.

LANE. Yes, sir.

Lane goes out.

JACK. Do you mean to say you have had my cigarette case all this time? I wish to goodness you had let me know. I have been writing frantic letters to Scotland Yard about it. I was very nearly offering a large reward.

ALGERNON. Well, I wish you would offer one. I happen to be more than usually hard up.

JACK. There is no good offering a large reward now that the thing is found.

Enter Lane with the cigarette case on a salver. Algernon takes it at once. Lane goes out.

ALGERNON. I think that is rather mean of you, Ernest, I must say. [*Opens case and examines it.*] However, it makes no matter, for, now that I look at the inscription inside, I find that the thing isn't yours after all.

JACK. Of course it's mine. [*Moving to him.*] You have seen me with it a hundred times, and you have no right whatsoever to read what is written inside. It is a very ungentlemanly thing to read a private cigarette case.

ALGERNON. Oh! it is absurd to have a hard and fast rule about what one should read and what one shouldn't. More than half of modern culture depends on what one shouldn't read.

JACK. I am quite aware of the fact, and I don't propose to discuss modern culture. It isn't the sort of thing one should talk of in private. I simply want my cigarette case back.

ALGERNON. Yes; but this isn't your cigarette case. This cigarette case is a present from someone of the name of Cecily, and you said you didn't know anyone of that name.

JACK. Well, if you want to know, Cecily happens to be my aunt.

ALGERNON. Your aunt!

JACK. Yes. Charming old lady she is, too. Lives at Tunbridge Wells. Just give it back to me, Algy.

ALGERNON. [*Retreating to back of sofa.*] But why does she call herself little Cecily if she is your aunt and lives at Tunbridge Wells? [*Reading.*] 'From little Cecily with her fondest love.'

JACK. [*Moving to sofa and kneeling upon it.*] My dear fellow, what on earth is there in that? Some aunts are tall, some aunts are not tall. That is a matter that surely an aunt may be allowed to decide for herself. You seem to think that every aunt should be exactly like your aunt! That is absurd. For Heaven's sake give me back my cigarette case. [*Follows Algernon round the room.*]

ALGERNON. Yes. But why does your aunt call you her uncle? 'From little Cecily, with her fondest love to her dear Uncle Jack.' There is no objection, I admit, to an aunt being a small aunt, but why an aunt, no matter what her size may be, should call her own nephew her uncle, I can't quite make out. Besides, your name isn't Jack at all; it is Ernest.

JACK. It isn't Ernest; it's Jack.

ALGERNON. You have always told me it was Ernest. I have introduced you to every one as Ernest. You answer to the name of Ernest. You look as if your name was Ernest. You are the most earnest-looking person I ever saw in my life. It is perfectly absurd your saying that your name isn't Ernest. It's on your cards. Here is one of them. [*Taking it from case.*] 'Mr Ernest Worthing, B.4, The Albany.' I'll keep this as a proof that your name is Ernest if ever you attempt to deny it to me, or to Gwendolen, or to anyone else. [*Puts the card in his pocket.*]

JACK. Well, my name is Ernest in town and Jack in the country, and the cigarette case was given to me in the country.

ALGERNON. Yes, but that does not account for the fact that your small Aunt Cecily, who lives at Tunbridge Wells, calls you her dear uncle. Come, old boy, you had much better have the thing out at once.

JACK. My dear Algy, you talk exactly as if you were a dentist. It is very vulgar to talk like a dentist when one isn't a dentist. It produces a false impression.

ALGERNON. Well, that is exactly what dentists always do. Now, go on! Tell me the whole thing. I may mention that I have always suspected you of being a confirmed and secret Bunburyist; and I am quite sure of it now.

JACK. Bunburyist? What on earth do you mean by a Bunburyist?

ALGERNON. I'll reveal to you the meaning of that incomparable expression as soon as you are kind enough to inform me why you are Ernest in town and Jack in the country.

JACK. Well, produce my cigarette case first.

ALGERNON. Here it is. [*Hands cigarette case.*] Now produce your explanation, and pray make it improbable. [*Sits on sofa.*]

JACK. My dear fellow, there is nothing improbable about my explanation at all. In fact it's perfectly ordinary. Old Mr Thomas Cardew, who adopted me when I was a little boy, made me in his will guardian to his granddaughter, Miss Cecily Cardew. Cecily, who addresses me as her uncle from motives of respect that you could not possibly appreciate, lives at my place in the country under the charge of her admirable governess, Miss Prism.

ALGERNON. Where is that place in the country, by the way?

JACK. That is nothing to you, dear boy. You are not going to be invited. . . . I may tell you candidly that the place is not in Shropshire.

ALGERNON. I suspected that, my dear fellow! I have Bunburyed all over Shropshire on two separate occasions. Now, go on. Why are you Ernest in town and Jack in the country?

JACK. My dear Algy, I don't know whether you will be able to understand my real motives. You are hardly serious enough. When one is placed in the position of guardian, one has to adopt a very high moral tone on all subjects. It's one's duty to do so. And as a high moral tone can hardly be said to conduce very much to either one's health or one's happiness, in order to get up to town I have always pretended to have a younger brother of the name of Ernest, who lives in the Albany, and gets into the most dreadful scrapes. That, my dear Algy, is the whole truth pure and simple.

ALGERNON. The truth is rarely pure and never simple. Modern life would be very tedious if it were either, and modern literature a complete impossibility!

JACK. That wouldn't be at all a bad thing.

ALGERNON. Literary criticism is not your forte, my dear fellow. Don't try it. You should leave that to people who haven't been at a University. They do it so well in the daily papers. What you really are is a Bunburyist. I was quite right in saying you were a Bunburyist. You are one of the most advanced Bunburyists I know.

JACK. What on earth do you mean?

ALGERNON. You have invented a very useful younger brother called Ernest, in order that you may be able to come up to town as often as you like. I have invented an invaluable permanent invalid called Bunbury, in order that I may be able to go down into the country whenever I choose. Bunbury is perfectly invaluable. If it wasn't for Bunbury's extraordinary bad health, for instance, I wouldn't be able to dine with you at Willis's to-night, for I have been really engaged to Aunt Augusta for more than a week.

JACK. I haven't asked you to dine with me anywhere to-night.

ALGERNON. I know. You are absurdly careless about sending out invitations. It is very foolish of you. Nothing annoys people so much as not receiving invitations.

JACK. You had much better dine with your Aunt Augusta.

ALGERNON. I haven't the smallest intention of doing anything of the kind. To begin with, I dined there on Monday, and once a week is quite enough to dine with one's own relations. In the second place, whenever I do dine there I am always treated as a member of the family, and sent down with either no woman at all, or two. In the third place, I know perfectly well whom she will place me next to, to-night. She will place me next Mary Farquhar, who always flirts with her own husband across the dinner-table. That is not very pleasant. Indeed, it is not even decent . . . and that sort of thing is enormously on the increase. The amount of women in London who flirt with their own husbands is perfectly scandalous. It looks so bad. It is simply washing one's clean linen in public. Besides, now that I know you to be a confirmed Bunburyist I naturally want to talk to you about Bunburying. I want to tell you the rules.

JACK. I'm not a Bunburyist at all. If Gwendolen accepts me, I am going to kill my brother, indeed I think I'll kill him in any case. Cecily is a little too much interested in him. It is rather a bore. So I am going to get rid of Ernest. And I strongly advise you to do the same with Mr . . . with your invalid friend who has the absurd name.

ALGERNON. Nothing will induce me to part with Bunbury, and if you ever get married, which seems to me extremely problematic, you will be very glad to know Bunbury. A man who marries without knowing Bunbury has a very tedious time of it.

JACK. That is nonsense. If I marry a charming girl like Gwendolen, and she is the only girl I ever saw in my life that I would marry, I certainly won't want to know Bunbury.

ALGERNON. Then your wife will. You don't seem to realize, that in married life three is company and two is none.

JACK. [Sententiously.] That, my dear young friend, is the theory that the corrupt French Drama has been propounding for the last fifty years.

ALGERNON. Yes; and that the happy English home has proved in half the time.

JACK. For heaven's sake, don't try to be cynical. It's perfectly easy to be cynical.

ALGERNON. My dear fellow, it isn't easy to be anything nowadays. There's such a lot of beastly competition about. [The sound of an electric bell is heard.] Ah! that must be Aunt Augusta. Only relatives, or creditors, ever ring in that Wagnerian manner. Now, if I get her out of the way for ten minutes, so that you can have an opportunity for proposing to Gwendolen, may I dine with you tonight at Willis's?

JACK. I suppose so, if you want to.

ALGERNON. Yes, but you must be serious about it. I hate people who are not serious about meals. It is so shallow of them.

Enter Lane.

LANE. Lady Bracknell and Miss Fairfax.

Algernon goes forward to meet them. Enter Lady Bracknell and Gwendolen.

LADY BRACKNELL. Good afternoon, dear Algernon, I hope you are behaving very well.

ALGERNON. I'm feeling very well, Aunt Augusta.

LADY BRACKNELL. That's not quite the same thing. In fact the two things rarely go together. [*Sees Jack and bows to him with icy coldness.*]

ALGERNON. [*To Gwendolen.*] Dear me, you are smart!

GWENDOLEN. I am always smart! Am I not, Mr Worthing?

JACK. You're quite perfect, Miss Fairfax.

GWENDOLEN. Oh! I hope I am not that. It would leave no room for developments, and I intend to develop in many directions. [*Gwendolen and Jack sit down together in the corner.*]

LADY BRACKNELL. I'm sorry if we are a little late, Algernon, but I was obliged to call on dear Lady Harbury. I hadn't been there since her poor husband's death. I never saw a woman so altered; she looks quite twenty years younger. And now I'll have a cup of tea, and one of those nice cucumber sandwiches you promised me.

ALGERNON. Certainly, Aunt Augusta. [*Goes over to tea-table.*]

LADY BRACKNELL. Won't you come and sit here, Gwendolen?

GWENDOLEN. Thanks, mamma, I'm quite comfortable where I am.

ALGERNON. [*Picking up empty plate in horror.*] Good heavens! Lane! Why are there no cucumber sandwiches? I ordered them specially.

LANE. [*Gravely.*] There were no cucumbers in the market this morning, sir. I went down twice.

ALGERNON. No cucumbers!

LANE. No, sir. Not even for ready money.

ALGERNON. That will do, Lane, thank you.

LANE. Thank you, sir. [*Goes out.*]

ALGERNON. I am greatly distressed, Aunt Augusta, about there being no cucumbers, not even for ready money.

LADY BRACKNELL. It really makes no matter, Algernon. I had some crumpets with Lady Harbury, who seems to me to be living entirely for pleasure now.

ALGERNON. I hear her hair has turned quite gold from grief.

LADY BRACKNELL. It certainly has changed its colour. From what cause I, of course, cannot say. [*Algernon crosses and hands tea.*] Thank you, I've quite a treat for you to-night, Algernon. I am going to send you down with Mary Farquhar. She is such a nice woman, and so attentive to her husband. It's delightful to watch them.

ALGERNON. I am afraid, Aunt Augusta, I shall have to give up the pleasure of dining with you tonight after all.

LADY BRACKNELL. [*Frowning.*] I hope not, Algernon. It would put my table completely out. Your uncle would have to dine upstairs. Fortunately he is accustomed to that.

ALGERNON. It is a great bore, and, I need hardly say, a terrible disappointment to me, but the fact is I have just had a telegram to say that my poor friend Bunbury is very ill again. [*Exchanges glances with Jack.*] They seem to think I should be with him.

LADY BRACKNELL. It is very strange. This Mr Bunbury seems to suffer from curiously bad health.

ALGERNON. Yes; poor Bunbury is a dreadful invalid.

LADY BRACKNELL. Well, I must say, Algernon, that I think it is high time that Mr Bunbury made up his mind whether he was going to live or to die. This shilly-shallying with the question is absurd. Nor do I in any way approve of the modern sympathy with invalids. I consider it morbid. Illness of any kind is hardly a thing to be encouraged in others. Health is the primary duty of life. I am always telling that to your poor uncle, but he never seems to take much notice . . . as far as any improvement in his ailment goes. I should be much obliged if you would ask Mr Bunbury, from me, to be kind enough not to have a relapse on Saturday, for I rely on you to arrange my music for me. It is my last reception, and one wants something that will encourage conversation, particularly at the end of the season when everyone has practically said whatever they had to say, which, in most cases, was probably not much.

ALGERNON. I'll speak to Bunbury, Aunt Augusta, if he is still conscious, and I think I can promise you he'll be all right by Saturday. Of course the music is a great difficulty. You see, if one plays good music, people don't listen, and if one plays bad music people don't talk. But I'll run over the programme I've drawn out, if you will kindly come into the next room for a moment.

LADY BRACKNELL. Thank you, Algernon. It is very thoughtful of you. [*Rising, and following Algernon.*] I'm sure the programme will be delightful, after a few expurgations. French songs I cannot possibly allow. People always seem to think that they are improper, and either look shocked, which is vulgar, or laugh, which is worse. But German sounds a thoroughly respectable language, and, indeed I believe is so. Gwendolen, you will accompany me.

GWENDOLEN. Certainly, mamma.

Lady Bracknell and Algernon go into the music-room, Gwendolen remains behind.

JACK. Charming day it has been, Miss Fairfax.

GWENDOLEN. Pray don't talk to me about the weather, Mr Worthing. Whenever people talk to me about the weather, I always feel quite certain that they mean something else. And that makes me so nervous.

JACK. I do mean something else.

GWENDOLEN. I thought so. In fact, I am never wrong.

JACK. And I would like to be allowed to take advantage of Lady Bracknell's temporary absence. . . .

GWENDOLEN. I would certainly advise you to do so. Mamma has a way of coming back suddenly into a room that I have often had to speak to her about.

JACK. [*Nervously.*] Miss Fairfax, ever since I met you I have admired you more than any girl . . . I have ever met since . . . I met you.

GWENDOLEN. Yes, I am quite well aware of the fact. And I often wish that in public, at any rate, you had been more demonstrative. For me you have always had an irresistible fascination. Even before I met you I was far from indifferent to you. [*Jack looks at her in amazement.*] We live, as I hope you know, Mr Worthing, in an age of ideals. The fact is constantly mentioned in the more expensive monthly magazines, and has reached the provincial pulpits, I am told; and my ideal has always been to love someone of the name of Ernest. There is something in that name that inspires absolute confidence. The moment Algernon first mentioned to me that he had a friend called Ernest, I knew I was destined to love you.

JACK. You really love me, Gwendolen?

GWENDOLEN. Passionately!

JACK. Darling! You don't know how happy you've made me.

GWENDOLEN. My own Ernest!

JACK. But you don't really mean to say that you couldn't love me if my name wasn't Ernest?

GWENDOLEN. But your name is Ernest.

JACK. Yes, I know it is. But supposing it was something else? Do you mean to say you couldn't love me then?

GWENDOLEN. [*Glibly.*] Ah! that is clearly a metaphysical speculation, and like most metaphysical speculations has very little reference at all to the actual facts of real life, as we know them.

JACK. Personally, darling, to speak quite candidly, I don't much care about the name of Ernest. . . . I don't think the name suits me at all.

GWENDOLEN. It suits you perfectly. It is a divine name. It has music of its own. It produces vibrations.

JACK. Well, really, Gwendolen, I must say that I think there are lots of other much nicer names. I think Jack, for instance, a charming name.

GWENDOLEN. Jack? . . . No, there is very little music in the name Jack, if any at all, indeed. It does not thrill. It produces absolutely no vibrations. . . . I have known several Jacks, and they all, without exception, were more than usually plain. Besides, Jack is a notorious domesticity for John! And I pity any woman who is married to a man called John. She would probably never be allowed to know the entrancing pleasure of a single moment's solitude. The only really safe name is Ernest.

JACK. Gwendolen, I must get christened at once—I mean we must get married at once. There is no time to be lost.

GWENDOLEN. Married, Mr Worthing?

JACK. [*Astounded.*] Well . . . surely. You know that I love you, and you led me to believe, Miss Fairfax, that you were not absolutely indifferent to me.

GWENDOLEN. I adore you. But you haven't proposed to me yet. Nothing has been said at all about marriage. The subject has not ever been touched on.

JACK. Well . . . may I propose to you now?

GWENDOLEN. I think it would be an admirable opportunity. And to spare you any possible disappointment, Mr Worthing, I think it only fair to tell you quite frankly beforehand that I am fully determined to accept you.

JACK. Gwendolen!

GWENDOLEN. Yes, Mr Worthing, what have you got to say to me?

JACK. You know what I have got to say to you.

GWENDOLEN. Yes, but you don't say it.

JACK. Gwendolen, will you marry me? [*Goes on his knees.*]

GWENDOLEN. Of course I will, darling. How long you have been about it! I am afraid you have had very little experience in how to propose.

JACK. My own one, I have never loved any one in the world but you.

GWENDOLEN. Yes, but men often propose for practice. I know my brother Gerald does. All my girl-friends tell me so. What wonderfully blue eyes you have, Ernest! They are quite, quite blue. I hope you will always look at me just like that, especially when there are other people present.

Enter Lady Bracknell.

LADY BRACKNELL. Mr Worthing! Rise, sir, from this semirecumbent° posture. It is most indecorous.

GWENDOLEN. Mamma! [*He tries to rise; she restrains him.*] I must beg you to retire. This is no place for you. Besides, Mr Worthing has not quite finished yet.

LADY BRACKNELL. Finished what, may I ask?

GWENDOLEN. I am engaged to Mr Worthing, mamma. [*They rise together.*]

LADY BRACKNELL. Pardon me, you are not engaged to any one. When you do become engaged to some one, I, or your father, should his health permit him, will inform you of the fact. An engagement should come on a young girl as a surprise, pleasant or unpleasant, as the case may be. It is hardly a matter that she could be allowed to arrange for herself. . . . And now I have a few questions to put to you, Mr Worthing. While I am making these inquiries, you, Gwendolen, will wait for me below in the carriage.

GWENDOLEN. [*Reproachfully.*] Mamma!

LADY BRACKNELL. In the carriage, Gwendolen! [*Gwendolen goes to the door. She and Jack blow kisses to each other behind Lady Bracknell's back. Lady Bracknell looks vaguely about as if she could not understand what the noise was. Finally turns round.*] Gwendolen, the carriage!

GWENDOLEN. Yes, mamma. [*Goes out, looking back at Jack.*]

LADY BRACKNELL. [*Sitting down.*] You can take a seat, Mr Worthing.

Looks in her pocket for note-book and pencil.

JACK. Thank you, Lady Bracknell, I prefer standing.

LADY BRACKNELL. [*Pencil and note-book in hand.*] I feel bound to tell you that you are not down on my list of eligible young men, although I have the same list as the dear Duchess of Bolton has. We work together, in fact. However, I am quite ready to enter your name, should your answers be what a really affectionate mother requires. Do you smoke?

JACK. Well, yes, I must admit I smoke.

LADY BRACKNELL. I am glad to hear it. A man should always have an occupation of some kind. There are far too many idle men in London as it is. How old are you?

JACK. Twenty-nine.

LADY BRACKNELL. A very good age to be married at. I have always been of opinion that a man who desires to get married should know either everything or nothing. Which do you know?

JACK. [*After some hesitation.*] I know nothing, Lady Bracknell.

LADY BRACKNELL. I am pleased to hear it. I do not approve of anything that tampers with natural ignorance. Ignorance is like a delicate exotic fruit; touch it and the bloom is gone. The whole theory of modern education is radically unsound. Fortunately in England, at any rate, education produces no effect whatsoever. If it did, it would prove a serious danger to the upper classes, and probably lead to acts of violence in Grosvenor Square. What is your income?

JACK. Between seven and eight thousand a year.

LADY BRACKNELL. [*Makes a note in her book.*] In land, or in investments?

---

semirecumbent: partly reclining.

JACK. In investments, chiefly.

LADY BRACKNELL. That is satisfactory. What between the duties expected of one during one's lifetime, and the duties exacted from one after one's death, land has ceased to be either a profit or a pleasure. It gives one position, and prevents one from keeping it up. That's all that can be said about land.

JACK. I have a country house with some land, of course, attached to it, about fifteen hundred acres, I believe; but I don't depend on that for my real income. In fact, as far as I can make out, the poachers are the only people who make anything out of it.

LADY BRACKNELL. A country house! How many bedrooms? Well, that point can be cleared up afterwards. You have a town house, I hope? A girl with a simple, unspoiled nature, like Gwendolen, could hardly be expected to reside in the country.

JACK. Well, I own a house in Belgrave Square, but it is let by the year to Lady Bloxham. Of course, I can get it back whenever I like, at six months' notice.

LADY BRACKNELL. Lady Bloxham? I don't know her.

JACK. Oh, she goes about very little. She is a lady considerably advanced in years.

LADY BRACKNELL. Ah, nowadays that is no guarantee of respectability of character. What number in Belgrave Square?

JACK. 149.

LADY BRACKNELL. [Shaking her head.] The unfashionable side. I thought there was something. However, that could easily be altered.

JACK. Do you mean the fashion, or the side?

LADY BRACKNELL. [Sternly.] Both, if necessary, I presume. What are your politics?

JACK. Well, I am afraid I really have none. I am a Liberal Unionist.

LADY BRACKNELL. Oh, they count as Tories. They dine with us. Or come in the evening, at any rate. Now to minor matters. Are your parents living?

JACK. I have lost both my parents.

LADY BRACKNELL. To lose one parent, Mr Worthing, may be regarded as a misfortune; to lose both looks like carelessness. Who was your father? He was evidently a man of some wealth. Was he born in what the Radical papers call the purple of commerce, or did he rise from the ranks of the aristocracy?

JACK. I am afraid I really don't know. The fact is, Lady Bracknell, I said I had lost my parents. I would be nearer the truth to say that my parents seem to have lost me. . . . I don't actually know who I am by birth. I was . . . well, I was found.

LADY BRACKNELL. Found!

JACK. The late Mr Thomas Cardew, an old gentleman of a very charitable and kindly disposition, found me, and gave me the name of Worthing, because he happened to have a first-class ticket for Worthing in his pocket at the time. Worthing is a place in Sussex. It is a seaside resort.

LADY BRACKNELL. Where did the charitable gentleman who had a first-class ticket for this seaside resort find you?

JACK. [Gravely.] In a hand-bag.

LADY BRACKNELL. A hand-bag?

JACK. [Very seriously.] Yes, Lady Bracknell. I was in a hand-bag—a somewhat large, black leather hand-bag, with handles to it—an ordinary hand-bag in fact.

LADY BRACKNELL. In what locality did this Mr James, or Thomas, Cardew come across this ordinary hand-bag?

Realism in Drama

JACK. In the cloak-room at Victoria Station. It was given to him in mistake for his own.

LADY BRACKNELL. The cloak-room at Victoria Station?

JACK. Yes. The Brighton line.

LADY BRACKNELL. The line is immaterial. Mr Worthing, I confess I feel somewhat bewildered by what you have just told me. To be born, or at any rate bred, in a hand-bag, whether it had handles or not, seems to me to display a contempt for the ordinary decencies of family life that reminds one of the worst excesses of the French Revolution. And I presume you know what that unfortunate movement led to? As for the particular locality in which the hand-bag was found, a cloak-room at a railway station might serve to conceal a social indiscretion—has probably, indeed, been used for that purpose before now—but it could hardly be regarded as an assured basis for a recognized position in good society.

JACK. May I ask you then what you would advise me to do? I need hardly say I would do anything in the world to ensure Gwendolen's happiness.

LADY BRACKNELL. I would strongly advise you, Mr Worthing, to try and acquire some relations as soon as possible, and to make a definite effort to produce at any rate one parent, of either sex, before the season is quite over.

JACK. Well, I don't see how I could possibly manage to do that. I can produce the hand-bag at any moment. It is in my dressing-room at home. I really think that should satisfy you, Lady Bracknell.

LADY BRACKNELL. Me, sir! What has it to do with me? You can hardly imagine that I and Lord Bracknell would dream of allowing our only daughter—a girl brought up with the utmost care—to marry into a cloak-room, and form an alliance with a parcel. Good morning, Mr Worthing!

Lady Bracknell sweeps out in majestic indignation.

JACK. Good morning! [*Algernon, from the other room, strikes up the Wedding March. Jack looks perfectly furious, and goes to the door.*] For goodness' sake don't play that ghastly tune, Algy! How idiotic you are!

The music stops and Algernon enters cheerily.

ALGERNON. Didn't it go off all right, old boy? You don't mean to say Gwendolen refused you? I know it is a way she has. She is always refusing people. I think it is most ill-natured of her.

JACK. Oh, Gwendolen is as right as a trivet. As far as she is concerned, we are engaged. Her mother is perfectly unbearable. Never met such a Gorgon°. . . . I don't really know what a Gorgon is like, but I am quite sure that Lady Bracknell is one. In any case, she is a monster, without being a myth, which is rather unfair. . . . I beg your pardon, Algy, I suppose I shouldn't talk about your own aunt in that way before you.

ALGERNON. My dear boy, I love hearing my relations abused. It is the only thing that makes me put up with them at all. Relations are simply a tedious pack of people, who haven't got the remotest knowledge of how to live, nor the smallest instinct about when to die.

JACK. Oh, that is nonsense!

ALGERNON. It isn't!

Gorgon: mythic creature with snakes for hair.

JACK. Well, I won't argue about the matter. You always want to argue about things.

ALGERNON. That is exactly what things were originally made for.

JACK. Upon my word, if I thought that, I'd shoot myself. . . . [*A pause.*] You don't think there is any chance of Gwendolen becoming like her mother in about a hundred and fifty years, do you, Algy?

ALGERNON. All women become like their mothers. That is their tragedy. No man does. That's his.

JACK. Is that clever?

ALGERNON. It is perfectly phrased! and quite as true as any observation in civilized life should be.

JACK. I am sick to death of cleverness. Everybody is clever nowadays. You can't go anywhere without meeting clever people. The thing has become an absolute public nuisance. I wish to goodness we had a few fools left.

ALGERNON. We have.

JACK. I should extremely like to meet them. What do they talk about?

ALGERNON. The fools? Oh! about the clever people, of course.

JACK. What fools.

ALGERNON. By the way, did you tell Gwendolen the truth about your being Ernest in town, and Jack in the country?

JACK. [*In a very patronizing manner.*] My dear fellow, the truth isn't quite the sort of thing one tells to a nice, sweet, refined girl. What extraordinary ideas you have about the way to behave to a woman!

ALGERNON. The only way to behave to a woman is to make love to her, if she is pretty, and to someone else, if she is plain.

JACK. Oh, that is nonsense.

ALGERNON. What about your brother? What about the profligate Ernest?

JACK. Oh, before the end of the week I shall have got rid of him. I'll say he died in Paris of apoplexy.° Lots of people die of apoplexy, quite suddenly, don't they?

ALGERNON. Yes, but it's hereditary, my dear fellow. It's a sort of thing that runs in families. You had much better say a severe chill.

JACK. You are sure a severe chill isn't hereditary, or anything of that kind?

ALGERNON. Of course it isn't!

JACK. Very well, then. My poor brother Ernest is carried off suddenly, in Paris, by a severe chill. That gets rid of him.

ALGERNON. But I thought you said that . . . Miss Cardew was a little too much interested in your poor brother Ernest? Won't she feel his loss a good deal?

JACK. Oh, that is all right. Cecily is not a silly romantic girl, I am glad to say. She has got a capital° appetite, goes on long walks, and pays no attention at all to her lessons.

ALGERNON. I would rather like to see Cecily.

JACK. I will take very good care you never do. She is excessively pretty, and she is only just eighteen.

ALGERNON. Have you told Gwendolen yet that you have an excessively pretty ward who is only just eighteen?

JACK. Oh! one doesn't blurt these things out to people. Cecily and Gwendolen are perfectly certain to be extremely great friends. I'll bet you anything you

---

apoplexy: a stroke.
capital: excellent.

like that half an hour after they have met, they will be calling each other sister.

ALGERNON. Women only do that when they have called each other a lot of other things first. Now, my dear boy, if we want to get a good table at Willis's, we really must go and dress. Do you know it is nearly seven?

JACK. [Irritably.] Oh! it always is nearly seven.

ALGERNON. I'm hungry.

JACK. I never knew you when you weren't. . . .

ALGERNON. What shall we do after dinner? Go to a theatre?

JACK. Oh, no! I loathe listening.

ALGERNON. Well, let us go to the Club?

JACK. Oh, no! I hate talking.

ALGERNON. Well, we might trot round to the Empire at ten?

JACK. Oh, no! I can't bear looking at things. It is so silly.

ALGERNON. Well, what shall we do?

JACK. Nothing!

ALGERNON. It is awfully hard work doing nothing. However, I don't mind hard work where there is no definite object of any kind.

Enter Lane.

LANE. Miss Fairfax.

Enter Gwendolen. Lane goes out.

ALGERNON. Gwendolen, upon my word!

GWENDOLEN. Algy, kindly turn your back. I have something very particular to say to Mr Worthing.

ALGERNON. Really, Gwendolen, I don't think I can allow this at all.

GWENDOLEN. Algy, you always adopt a strictly immoral attitude towards life. You are not quite old enough to do that. [*Algernon retires to the fireplace.*]

JACK. My own darling!

GWENDOLEN. Ernest, we may never be married. From the expression on mamma's face I fear we never shall. Few parents nowadays pay any regard to what their children say to them. The old-fashioned respect for the young is fast dying out. Whatever influence I ever had over mamma, I lost at the age of three. But although she may prevent us from becoming man and wife, and I may marry someone else, and marry often, nothing that she can possibly do can alter my eternal devotion to you.

JACK. Dear Gwendolen!

GWENDOLEN. The story of your romantic origin, as related to me by mamma, with unpleasing comments, has naturally stirred the deeper fibres of my nature. Your Christian name has an irresistible fascination. The simplicity of your character makes you exquisitely incomprehensible to me. Your town address at the Albany I have. What is your address in the country?

JACK. The Manor House, Woolton, Hertfordshire.

Algernon who has been carefully listening, smiles to himself, and writes the address on his shirt-cuff. Then picks up the Railway Guide.

GWENDOLEN. There is a good postal service, I suppose? It may be necessary to do something desperate. That of course will require serious consideration. I will communicate with you daily.

JACK. My own one!

GWENDOLEN. How long do you remain in town?

JACK. Till Monday.

GWENDOLEN. Good! Algy, you may turn round now.

ALGERNON. Thanks, I've turned round already.

GWENDOLEN. You may also ring the bell.

JACK. You will let me see you to your carriage, my own darling?

GWENDOLEN. Certainly.

JACK. [*To Lane, who now enters.*] I will see Miss Fairfax out.

LANE. Yes, sir. [*Jack and Gwendolen go off.*]

> Lane presents several letters on a salver, to Algernon. It is to be surmised that they are bills, as Algernon, after looking at the envelopes, tears them up.

ALGERNON. A glass of sherry, Lane.

LANE. Yes, sir.

ALGERNON. Tomorrow, Lane, I'm going Bunburying.

LANE. Yes, sir.

ALGERNON. I shall probably not be back till Monday. You can put up my dress clothes, my smoking jacket, and all the Bunbury suits . . .

LANE. Yes, sir. [*Handing sherry.*]

ALGERNON. I hope tomorrow will be a fine day, Lane.

LANE. It never is, sir.

ALGERNON. Lane, you're a perfect pessimist.

LANE. I do my best to give satisfaction, sir.

> *Enter Jack. Lane goes off.*

JACK. There's a sensible, intellectual girl! the only girl I ever cared for in my life. [*Algernon is laughing immoderately.*] What on earth are you so amused at?

ALGERNON. Oh, I'm a little anxious about poor Bunbury, that is all.

JACK. If you don't take care, your friend Bunbury will get you into a serious scrape some day.

ALGERNON. I love scrapes. They are the only things that are never serious.

JACK. Oh, that's nonsense, Algy. You never talk anything but nonsense.

ALGERNON. Nobody ever does.

> Jack looks indignantly at him, and leaves the room. Algernon lights a cigarette, reads his shirt-cuff, and smiles.

Act Drop

SECOND ACT

Scene

Garden at the Manor House. A flight of grey stone steps leads up to the house. The garden, an old-fashioned one, full of roses. Time of year, July. Basket chairs, and a table covered with books, are set under a large yew-tree.

> Miss Prism discovered seated at the table. Cecily is at the back, watering flowers.

MISS PRISM. [*Calling.*] Cecily, Cecily! Surely such a utilitarian° occupation as the watering of flowers is rather Moulton's duty than yours? Especially at a moment

---

utilitarian: practical.

when intellectual pleasures await you. Your German grammar is on the table. Pray open it at page fifteen. We will repeat yesterday's lesson.

CECILY. [*Coming over very slowly.*] But I don't like German. It isn't at all a becoming language. I know perfectly well that I look quite plain after my German lesson.

MISS PRISM. Child, you know how anxious your guardian is that you should improve yourself in every way. He laid particular stress on your German, as he was leaving for town yesterday. Indeed, he always lays stress on your German when he is leaving for town.

CECILY. Dear Uncle Jack is so very serious! Sometimes he is so serious that I think he cannot be quite well.

MISS PRISM. [*Drawing herself up.*] Your guardian enjoys the best of health, and his gravity of demeanour is especially to be commended in one so comparatively young as he is. I know no one who has a higher sense of duty and responsibility.

CECILY. I suppose that is why he often looks a little bored when we three are together.

MISS PRISM. Cecily! I am surprised at you. Mr Worthing has many troubles in his life. Idle merriment and triviality would be out of place in his conversation. You must remember his constant anxiety about that unfortunate young man his brother.

CECILY. I wish Uncle Jack would allow that unfortunate young man, his brother, to come down here sometimes. We might have a good influence over him, Miss Prism. I am sure you certainly would. You know German, and geology, and things of that kind influence a man very much. [*Cecily begins to write in her diary.*]

MISS PRISM. [*Shaking her head.*] I do not think that even I could produce any effect on a character that according to his own brother's admission is irretrievably weak and vacillating. Indeed I am not sure that I would desire to reclaim him. I am not in favour of this modern mania for turning bad people into good people at a moment's notice. As a man sows so let him reap. You must put away your diary, Cecily. I really don't see why you should keep a diary at all.

CECILY. I keep a diary in order to enter the wonderful secrets of my life. If I didn't write them down, I should probably forget all about them.

MISS PRISM. Memory, my dear Cecily, is the diary that we all carry about with us.

CECILY. Yes, but it usually chronicles the things that have never happened, and couldn't possibly have happened. I believe that Memory is responsible for nearly all the three-volume novels that Mudie sends us.

MISS PRISM. Do not speak slightingly of the three-volume novel, Cecily. I wrote one myself in earlier days.

CECILY. Did you really, Miss Prism? How wonderfully clever you are! I hope it did not end happily? I don't like novels that end happily. They depress me so much.

MISS PRISM. The good ended happily, and the bad unhappily. That is what Fiction means.

CECILY. I suppose so. But it seems very unfair. And was your novel ever published?

MISS PRISM. Alas! no. The manuscript unfortunately was abandoned. [*Cecily starts.*] I used the word in the sense of lost or mislaid. To your work, child, these speculations are profitless.

CECILY. [*Smiling.*] But I see dear Dr Chasuble° coming up through the garden.

MISS PRISM. [*Rising and advancing.*] Dr Chasuble! This is indeed a pleasure.

Enter Canon Chasuble.

Chasuble: name of a ceremonial gown for Anglican and Catholic priests.

CHASUBLE. And how are we this morning? Miss Prism, you are, I trust, well?

CECILY. Miss Prism has just been complaining of a slight headache. I think it would do her so much good to have a short stroll with you in the Park, Dr Chasuble.

MISS PRISM. Cecily, I have not mentioned anything about a headache.

CECILY. No, dear Miss Prism, I know that, but I felt instinctively that you had a headache. Indeed I was thinking about that, and not about my German lesson, when the Rector came in.

CHASUBLE. I hope, Cecily, you are not inattentive.

CECILY. Oh, I am afraid I am.

CHASUBLE. That is strange. Were I fortunate enough to be Miss Prism's pupil, I would hang upon her lips. [*Miss Prism glares.*] I spoke metaphorically.—My metaphor was drawn from bees. Ahem! Mr Worthing, I suppose, has not returned from town yet?

MISS PRISM. We do not expect him till Monday afternoon.

CHASUBLE. Ah yes, he usually likes to spend his Sunday in London. He is not one of those whose sole aim is enjoyment, as, by all accounts, that unfortunate young man his brother seems to be. But I must not disturb Egeria and her pupil any longer.

MISS PRISM. Egeria? My name is Laetitia, Doctor.

CHASUBLE. [*Bowing.*] A classical allusion merely, drawn from the Pagan authors. I shall see you both no doubt at Evensong?°

MISS PRISM. I think, dear Doctor, I will have a stroll with you. I find I have a headache after all, and a walk might do it good.

CHASUBLE. With pleasure, Miss Prism, with pleasure. We might go as far as the schools and back.

MISS PRISM. That would be delightful. Cecily, you will read your Political Economy in my absence. The chapter on the Fall of the Rupee° you may omit. It is somewhat too sensational. Even these metallic problems have their melodramatic side.

Goes down the garden with Dr Chasuble.

CECILY. [*Picks up books and throws them back on table.*] Horrid Political Economy! Horrid Geography! Horrid, horrid German!

Enter Merriman with a card on a salver.

MERRIMAN. Mr Ernest Worthing has just driven over from the station. He has brought his luggage with him.

CECILY. [*Takes the card and reads it.*] 'Mr Ernest Worthing, B.4, The Albany, W.' Uncle Jack's brother! Did you tell him Mr Worthing was in town?

MERRIMAN. Yes, Miss. He seemed very much disappointed. I mentioned that you and Miss Prism were in the garden. He said he was anxious to speak to you privately for a moment.

CECILY. Ask Mr Ernest Worthing to come here. I suppose you had better talk to the housekeeper about a room for him.

MERRIMAN. Yes, Miss. [*Merriman goes off.*]

Evensong: Anglican evening prayer.
Rupee: unit of currency in India.

CECILY. I have never met any really wicked person before. I feel rather frightened. I am so afraid he will look just like every one else.

Enter Algernon, very gay and debonair.

He does!

ALGERNON. [*Raising his hat.*] You are my little cousin Cecily, I'm sure.

CECILY. You are under some strange mistake. I am not little. In fact, I believe I am more than usually tall for my age. [*Algernon is rather taken aback.*] But I am your cousin Cecily. You, I see from your card, are Uncle Jack's brother, my cousin Ernest, my wicked cousin Ernest.

ALGERNON. Oh! I am not really wicked at all, Cousin Cecily. You mustn't think that I am wicked.

CECILY. If you are not, then you have certainly been deceiving us all in a very inexcusable manner. I hope you have not been leading a double life, pretending to be wicked and being really good all the time. That would be hypocrisy.

ALGERNON. [*Looks at her in amazement.*] Oh! Of course I have been rather reckless.

CECILY. I am glad to hear it.

ALGERNON. In fact, now you mention the subject, I have been very bad in my own small way.

CECILY. I don't think you should be so proud of that, though I am sure it must have been very pleasant.

ALGERNON. It is much pleasanter being here with you.

CECILY. I can't understand how you are here at all. Uncle Jack won't be back till Monday afternoon.

ALGERNON. That is a great disappointment. I am obliged to go up by the first train on Monday morning. I have a business appointment that I am anxious . . . to miss!

CECILY. Couldn't you miss it anywhere but in London?

ALGERNON. No: the appointment is in London.

CECILY. Well, I know, of course, how important it is not to keep a business engagement, if one wants to retain any sense of the beauty of life, but still I think you had better wait till Uncle Jack arrives. I know he wants to speak to you about your emigrating.

ALGERNON. About my what?

CECILY. Your emigrating. He has gone up to buy your outfit.

ALGERNON. I certainly wouldn't let Jack buy my outfit. He has no taste in neckties at all.

CECILY. I don't think you will require neckties. Uncle Jack is sending you to Australia.

ALGERNON. Australia! I'd sooner die.

CECILY. Well, he said at dinner on Wednesday night, that you would have to choose between this world, the next world, and Australia.

ALGERNON. Oh, well! The accounts I have received of Australia and the next world are not particularly encouraging. This world is good enough for me, Cousin Cecily.

CECILY. Yes, but are you good enough for it?

ALGERNON. I'm afraid I'm not that. That is why I want you to reform me. You might make that your mission, if you don't mind, Cousin Cecily.

CECILY. I'm afraid I've no time, this afternoon.

ALGERNON. Well, would you mind my reforming myself this afternoon?

CECILY. It is rather Quixotic of you. But I think you should try.

ALGERNON. I will. I feel better already.

CECILY. You are looking a little worse.

ALGERNON. That is because I am hungry.

CECILY. How thoughtless of me. I should have remembered that when one is going to lead an entirely new life, one requires regular and wholesome meals. Won't you come in?

ALGERNON. Thank you. Might I have a buttonhole first? I have never any appetite unless I have a buttonhole first.

CECILY. A Maréchal Niel? [*Picks up scissors.*]

ALGERNON. No, I'd sooner have a pink rose.

CECILY. Why? [*Cuts a flower.*]

ALGERNON. Because you are like a pink rose, Cousin Cecily.

CECILY. I don't think it can be right for you to talk to me like that. Miss Prism never says such things to me.

ALGERNON. Then Miss Prism is a short-sighted old lady. [*Cecily puts the rose in his buttonhole.*] You are the prettiest girl I ever saw.

CECILY. Miss Prism says that all good looks are a snare.

ALGERNON. They are a snare that every sensible man would like to be caught in.

CECILY. Oh, I don't think I would care to catch a sensible man. I shouldn't know what to talk to him about.

They pass into the house. Miss Prism and Dr Chasuble return.

MISS PRISM. You are too much alone, dear Dr Chasuble. You should get married. A misanthrope° I can understand—a womanthrope, never!

CHASUBLE. [*With a scholar's shudder.*] Believe me, I do not deserve so neologistic a phrase. The precept as well as the practice of the Primitive Church was distinctly against matrimony.

MISS PRISM. [*Sententiously.*] That is obviously the reason why the Primitive Church has not lasted up to the present day. And you do not seem to realize, dear Doctor, that by persistently remaining single, a man converts himself into a permanent public temptation. Men should be more careful; this very celibacy leads weaker vessels astray.

CHASUBLE. But is a man not equally attractive when married?

MISS PRISM. No married man is ever attractive except to his wife.

CHASUBLE. And often, I've been told, not even to her.

MISS PRISM. That depends on the intellectual sympathies of the woman. Maturity can always be depended on. Ripeness can be trusted. Young women are green. [*Dr Chasuble starts.*] I spoke horticulturally. My metaphor was drawn from fruits. But where is Cecily?

CHASUBLE. Perhaps she followed us to the schools.

Enter Jack slowly from the back of the garden. He is dressed in the deepest mourning, with crepe hat-band and black gloves.

MISS PRISM. Mr Worthing!

CHASUBLE. Mr Worthing?

---

misanthrope: one who claims distaste for fellow humans—literally "against mankind."

MISS PRISM. This is indeed a surprise. We did not look for you till Monday afternoon.

JACK. [*Shakes Miss Prism's hand in a tragic manner.*] I have returned sooner than I expected. Dr Chasuble, I hope you are well?

CHASUBLE. Dear Mr Worthing, I trust this garb of woe does not betoken some terrible calamity?

JACK. My brother.

MISS PRISM. More shameful debts and extravagance?

CHASUBLE. Still leading his life of pleasure?

JACK. [*Shaking his head.*] Dead!

CHASUBLE. Your brother Ernest dead?

JACK. Quite dead.

MISS PRISM. What a lesson for him! I trust he will profit by it.

CHASUBLE. Mr Worthing, I offer you my sincere condolence. You have at least the consolation of knowing that you were always the most generous and forgiving of brothers.

JACK. Poor Ernest! He had many faults, but it is a sad, sad blow.

CHASUBLE. Very sad indeed. Were you with him at the end?

JACK. No. He died abroad; in Paris, in fact. I had a telegram last night from the manager of the Grand Hotel.

CHASUBLE. Was the cause of death mentioned?

JACK. A severe chill, it seems.

MISS PRISM. As a man sows, so shall he reap.

CHASUBLE. [*Raising his hand.*] Charity, dear Miss Prism, charity! None of us are perfect. I myself am peculiarly susceptible to draughts. Will the interment take place here?

JACK. No. He seems to have expressed a desire to be buried in Paris.

CHASUBLE. In Paris! [*Shakes his head.*] I fear that hardly points to any very serious state of mind at the last. You would no doubt wish me to make some slight allusion to this tragic domestic affliction next Sunday. [*Jack presses his hand convulsively.*] My sermon on the meaning of the manna in the wilderness can be adapted to almost any occasion, joyful, or, as in the present case, distressing. [*All sigh.*] I have preached it at harvest celebrations, christenings, confirmations, on days of humiliation and festal days. The last time I delivered it was in the Cathedral, as a charity sermon on behalf of the Society for the Prevention of Discontent among the Upper Orders. The Bishop, who was present, was much struck by some of the analogies I drew.

JACK. Ah! that reminds me, you mentioned christenings I think, Dr Chasuble? I suppose you know how to christen all right? [*Dr Chasuble looks astounded.*] I mean, of course, you are continually christening, aren't you?

MISS PRISM. It is, I regret to say, one of the Rector's most constant duties in this parish. I have often spoken to the poorer classes on the subject. But they don't seem to know what thrift is.

CHASUBLE. But is there any particular infant in whom you are interested, Mr Worthing? Your brother was, I believe, unmarried, was he not?

JACK. Oh Yes.

MISS PRISM. [*Bitterly.*] People who live entirely for pleasure usually are.

JACK. But it is not for any child, dear Doctor. I am very fond of children. No! the fact is, I would like to be christened myself, this afternoon, if you have nothing better to do.

CHASUBLE. But surely, Mr Worthing, you have been christened already?

JACK. I don't remember anything about it.

CHASUBLE. But have you any grave doubts on the subject?

JACK. I certainly intend to have. Of course I don't know if the thing would bother you in any way, or if you think I am a little too old now.

CHASUBLE. Not at all. The sprinkling, and, indeed, the immersion of adults is a perfectly canonical practice.

JACK. Immersion!

CHASUBLE. You need have no apprehensions. Sprinkling is all that is necessary, or indeed I think advisable. Our weather is so changeable. At what hour would you wish the ceremony performed?

JACK. Oh, I might trot round about five if that would suit you.

CHASUBLE. Perfectly, perfectly! In fact I have two similar ceremonies to perform at that time. A case of twins that occurred recently in one of the outlying cottages on your own estate. Poor Jenkins the carter, a most hard-working man.

JACK. Oh! I don't see much fun in being christened along with other babies. It would be childish. Would half-past five do?

CHASUBLE. Admirably! Admirably! [*Takes out watch.*] And now, dear Mr Worthing, I will not intrude any longer into a house of sorrow. I would merely beg you not to be too much bowed down by grief. What seem to us bitter trials are often blessings in disguise.

MISS PRISM. This seems to me a blessing of an extremely obvious kind.

Enter Cecily from the house.

CECILY. Uncle Jack! Oh, I am pleased to see you back. but what horrid clothes you have got on. Do go and change them.

MISS PRISM. Cecily!

CHASUBLE. My child! my child. [*Cecily goes towards Jack; he kisses her brow in a melancholy manner.*]

CECILY. What is the matter, Uncle Jack? Do look happy! You look as if you had toothache, and I have got such a surprise for you. Who do you think is in the dining-room? Your brother!

JACK. Who?

CECILY. Your brother Ernest. He arrived about half an hour ago.

JACK. What nonsense! I haven't got a brother.

CECILY. Oh, don't say that. However badly he may have behaved to you in the past he is still your brother. You couldn't be so heartless as to disown him. I'll tell him to come out. And you will shake hands with him, won't you, Uncle Jack? [*Runs back into the house.*]

CHASUBLE. These are very joyful tidings.

MISS PRISM. After we had all been resigned to his loss, his sudden return seems to me peculiarly distressing.

JACK. My brother is in the dining-room? I don't know what it all means. I think it is perfectly absurd.

Enter Algernon and Cecily hand in hand. They come slowly up to Jack.

JACK. Good heavens! [*Motions Algernon away.*]

ALGERNON. Brother John, I have come down from town to tell you that I am very sorry for all the trouble I have given you, and that I intend to lead a better life in the future. [*Jack glares at him and does not take his hand.*]

CECILY. Uncle Jack, you are not going to refuse your own brother's hand?

JACK. Nothing will induce me to take his hand. I think his coming down here disgraceful. He knows perfectly well why.

CECILY. Uncle Jack, do be nice. There is some good in everyone. Ernest has just been telling me about his poor invalid friend Mr Bunbury whom he goes to visit so often. And surely there must be much good in one who is kind to an invalid, and leaves the pleasures of London to sit by a bed of pain.

JACK. Oh! he has been talking about Bunbury, has he?

CECILY. Yes, he has told me all about poor Mr Bunbury, and his terrible state of health.

JACK. Bunbury! Well, I won't have him talk to you about Bunbury or about anything else. It is enough to drive one perfectly frantic.

ALGERNON. Of course I admit that the faults were all on my side. But I must say that I think that Brother John's coldness to me is peculiarly painful. I expected a more enthusiastic welcome especially considering it is the first time I have come here.

CECILY. Uncle Jack, if you don't shake hands with Ernest, I will never forgive you.

JACK. Never forgive me?

CECILY. Never, never, never!

JACK. Well, this is the last time I shall ever do it. [*Shakes hands with Algernon and glares.*]

CHASUBLE. It's pleasant, is it not, to see so perfect a reconciliation? I think we might leave the two brothers together.

MISS PRISM. Cecily, you will come with us.

CECILY. Certainly, Miss Prism. My little task of reconciliation is over.

CHASUBLE. You have done a beautiful action today, dear child.

MISS PRISM. We must not be premature in our judgements.

CECILY. I feel very happy. [*They all go off except Jack and Algernon.*]

JACK. You young scoundrel, Algy, you must get out of this place as soon as possible. I don't allow any Bunburying here.

Enter Merriman.

MERRIMAN. I have put Mr Ernest's things in the room next to yours, sir. I suppose that is all right?

JACK. What?

MERRIMAN. Mr Ernest's luggage, sir. I have unpacked it and put it in the room next to your own.

JACK. His luggage?

MERRIMAN. Yes, sir. Three portmanteaus,° a dressing-case, two hatboxes, and a large luncheon-basket.

ALGERNON. I am afraid I can't stay more than a week this time.

JACK. Merriman, order the dog-cart at once. Mr Ernest has been suddenly called back to town.

MERRIMAN. Yes, sir. [*Goes back into the house.*]

ALGERNON. What a fearful liar you are, Jack. I have not been called back to town at all.

JACK. Yes, you have.

---

portmanteau: large traveling bag.

ALGERNON. I haven't heard any one call me.

JACK. Your duty as a gentleman calls you back.

ALGERNON. My duty as a gentleman has never interfered with my pleasures in the smallest degree.

JACK. I can quite understand that.

ALGERNON. Well, Cecily is a darling.

JACK. You are not to talk to Miss Cardew like that. I don't like it.

ALGERNON. Well, I don't like your clothes. You look perfectly ridiculous in them. Why on earth don't you go up and change? It is perfectly childish to be in deep mourning for a man who is actually staying for a whole week with you in your house as a guest. I call it grotesque.

JACK. You are certainly not staying with me for a whole week as a guest or anything else. You have got to leave . . . by the four-five train.

ALGERNON. I certainly won't leave you so long as you are in mourning. It would be most unfriendly. If I were in mourning you would stay with me, I suppose. I should think it very unkind if you didn't.

JACK. Well, will you go if I change my clothes?

ALGERNON. Yes, if you are not too long. I never saw anybody take so long to dress, and with such little result.

JACK. Well, at any rate, that is better than being always over-dressed as you are.

ALGERNON. If I am occasionally a little over-dressed, I make up for it by being always immensely over-educated.

JACK. Your vanity is ridiculous, your conduct an outrage, and your presence in my garden utterly absurd. However, you have got to catch the four-five, and I hope you will have a pleasant journey back to town. This Bunburying, as you call it, has not been a great success for you.

Goes into the house.

ALGERNON. I think it has been a great success. I'm in love with Cecily, and that is everything.

Enter Cecily at the back of the garden. She picks up the can and begins to water the flowers.

But I must see her before I go, and make arrangements for another Bunbury. Ah, there she is.

CECILY. Oh, I merely came back to water the roses. I thought you were with Uncle Jack.

ALGERNON. He's gone to order the dog-cart for me.

CECILY. Oh, is he going to take you for a nice drive?

ALGERNON. He's going to send me away.

CECILY. Then have we got to part?

ALGERNON. I am afraid so. It's a very painful parting.

CECILY. It is always painful to part from people whom one has known for a very brief space of time. The absence of old friends one can endure with equanimity. But even a momentary separation from any one to whom one has just been introduced is almost unbearable.

ALGERNON. Thank you.

Enter Merriman.

MERRIMAN. The dog-cart is at the door, sir.

Algernon looks appealingly at Cecily.

CECILY. It can wait, Merriman . . . for . . . five minutes.

MERRIMAN. Yes, Miss.

Exit Merriman.

ALGERNON. I hope, Cecily, I shall not offend you if I state quite frankly and openly that you seem to me to be in every way the visible personification of absolute perfection.

CECILY. I think your frankness does you great credit, Ernest. If you will allow me, I will copy your remarks into my diary. [*Goes over to table and begins writing in diary.*]

ALGERNON. Do you really keep a diary? I'd give anything to look at it. May I?

CECILY. Oh no. [*Puts her hand over it.*] You see, it is simply a very young girl's record of her own thoughts and impressions, and consequently meant for publication. When it appears in volume form I hope you will order a copy. But pray, Ernest, don't stop. I delight in taking down from dictation. I have reached 'absolute perfection.' You can go on. I am quite ready for more.

ALGERNON. [*Somewhat taken aback.*] Ahem! Ahem!

CECILY. Oh, don't cough, Ernest. When one is dictating one should speak fluently and not cough. Besides, I don't know how to spell a cough. [*Writes as Algernon speaks.*]

ALGERNON. [*Speaking very rapidly.*] Cecily, ever since I first looked upon your wonderful and incomparable beauty, I have dared to love you wildly, passionately, devotedly, hopelessly.

CECILY. I don't think that you should tell me that you love me wildly, passionately, devotedly, hopelessly. Hopelessly doesn't seem to make much sense, does it?

ALGERNON. Cecily.

Enter Merriman.

MERRIMAN. The dog-cart is waiting, sir.

ALGERNON. Tell it to come round next week, at the same hour.

MERRIMAN. [*Looks at Cecily, who makes no sign.*] Yes, sir.

Merriman retires.

CECILY. Uncle Jack would be very much annoyed if he knew you were staying on till next week, at the same hour.

ALGERNON. Oh, I don't care about Jack. I don't care for anybody in the whole world but you. I love you, Cecily. You will marry me, won't you?

CECILY. You silly boy! Of course. Why, we have been engaged for the last three months.

ALGERNON. For the last three months?

CECILY. Yes, it will be exactly three months on Thursday.

ALGERNON. But how did we become engaged?

CECILY. Well, ever since dear Uncle Jack first confessed to us that he had a younger brother who was very wicked and bad, you of course have formed the chief topic of conversation between myself and Miss Prism. And of course a man who is much talked about is always very attractive. One feels there must be something in him, after all. I daresay it was foolish of me, but I fell in love with you, Ernest.

ALGERNON. Darling. And when was the engagement actually settled?

CECILY. On the 14th of February last. Worn out by your entire ignorance of my existence, I determined to end the matter one way to the other, and after a long struggle with myself I accepted you under this dear old tree here. The next day I bought this little ring in your name, and this is the little bangle with the true lover's knot I promised you always to wear.

ALGERNON. Did I give you this? It's very pretty, isn't it?

CECILY. Yes, you've wonderfully good taste, Ernest. It's the excuse I've always given for your leading such a bad life. And this is the box in which I keep all your dear letters. [Kneels at table, opens box, and produces letters tied up with blue ribbon.]

ALGERNON. My letters! But, my own sweet Cecily, I have never written you any letters.

CECILY. You need hardly remind me of that, Ernest. I remember only too well that I was forced to write your letters for you. I wrote always three times a week, and sometimes oftener.

ALGERNON. Oh, do let me read them, Cecily?

CECILY. Oh, I couldn't possibly. They would make you far too conceited. [Replaces box.] The three you wrote me after I had broken off the engagement are so beautiful, and so badly spelled, that even now I can hardly read them without crying a little.

ALGERNON. But was our engagement ever broken off?

CECILY. Of course it was. On the 22nd of last March. You can see the entry if you like. [Shows diary.] 'Today I broke off my engagement with Ernest. I feel it is better to do so. The weather still continues charming.'

ALGERNON. But why on earth did you break it off? What had I done? I had done nothing at all. Cecily, I am very much hurt indeed to hear you broke it off. Particularly when the weather was so charming.

CECILY. It would hardly have been a really serious engagement if it hadn't been broken off at least once. But I forgave you before the week was out.

ALGERNON. [Crossing to her, and kneeling.] What a perfect angel you are, Cecily.

CECILY. You dear romantic boy. [He kisses her, she puts her fingers through his hair.] I hope your hair curls naturally, does it?

ALGERNON. Yes, darling, with a little help from others.

CECILY. I am so glad.

ALGERNON. You'll never break off our engagement again, Cecily?

CECILY. I don't think I could break it off now that I have actually met you. Besides, of course, there is the question of your name.

ALGERNON. Yes, of course. [Nervously.]

CECILY. You must not laugh at me, darling, but it had always been a girlish dream of mine to love some one whose name was Ernest. [Algernon rises, Cecily also.] There is something in that name that seems to inspire absolute confidence. I pity any poor married woman whose husband is not called Ernest.

ALGERNON. But, My dear child, do you mean to say you could not love me if I had some other name?

CECILY. But what name?

ALGERNON. Oh, any name you like—Algernon—for instance . . .

CECILY. But I don't like the name of Algernon.

ALGERNON. Well, my own dear, sweet, loving little darling, I really can't see why you should object to the name of Algernon. It is not at all a bad name. In fact, it is rather an aristocratic name. Half of the chaps who get into the Bankruptcy

Court are called Algernon. But seriously, Cecily . . . [*Moving to her.*] if my name was Algy, couldn't you love me?

CECILY. [*Rising.*] I might respect you, Ernest, I might admire your character, but I fear that I should not be able to give you my undivided attention.

ALGERNON. Ahem! Cecily! [*Picking up hat.*] Your Rector here is, I suppose, thoroughly experienced in the practice of all the rites and ceremonials of the Church?

CECILY. Oh, yes. Dr Chasuble is a most learned man. He has never written a single book, so you can imagine how much he knows.

ALGERNON. I must see him at once on a most important christening—I mean on most important business.

CECILY. Oh!

ALGERNON. I shan't be away more than half an hour.

CECILY. Considering that we have been engaged since February the 14th, and that I only met you to-day for the first time, I think it is rather hard that you should leave me for so long a period as half an hour. Couldn't you make it twenty minutes?

ALGERNON. I'll be back in no time. [*Kisses her and rushes down the garden.*]

CECILY. What an impetuous boy he is! I like his hair so much. I must enter his proposal in my diary.

Enter Merriman.

MERRIMAN. A Miss Fairfax has just called to see Mr Worthing. On very important business, Miss Fairfax states.

CECILY. Isn't Mr Worthing in his library?

MERRIMAN. Mr Worthing went over in the direction of the Rectory some time ago.

CECILY. Pray ask the lady to come out here; Mr Worthing is sure to be back soon. And you can bring tea.

MERRIMAN. Yes, Miss.

Goes out.

CECILY. Miss Fairfax! I suppose one of the many good elderly women who are associated with Uncle Jack in some of his philanthropic work in London. I don't quite like women who are interested in philanthropic work. I think it is so forward of them.

Enter Merriman.

MERRIMAN. Miss Fairfax.

Enter Gwendolen. Exit Merriman.

CECILY. [*Advancing to meet her.*] Pray let me introduce myself to you. My name is Cecily Cardew.

GWENDOLEN. Cecily Cardew? [*Moving to her and shaking hands.*] What a very sweet name! Something tells me that we are going to be great friends. I like you already more than I can say. My first impressions of people are never wrong.

CECILY. How nice of you to like me so much after we have known each other such a comparatively short time. Pray sit down.

GWENDOLEN. [*Still standing up.*] I may call you Cecily, may I not?

CECILY. With pleasure!

GWENDOLEN. And you will always call me Gwendolen, won't you?

CECILY. If you wish.

GWENDOLEN. Then that is all quite settled, is it not?

CECILY. I hope so. [*A pause. They both sit down together.*]

GWENDOLEN. Perhaps this might be a favourable opportunity for my mentioning who I am. My father is Lord Bracknell. You have never heard of papa, I suppose?

CECILY. I don't think so.

GWENDOLEN. Outside the family circle, papa, I am glad to say, is entirely unknown. I think that is quite as it should be. The home seems to me to be the proper sphere for the man. And certainly once a man begins to neglect his domestic duties he becomes painfully effeminate, does he not? And I don't like that. It makes men so very attractive. Cecily, mamma, whose views on education are remarkably strict, has brought me up to be extremely short-sighted; it is part of her system; so do you mind my looking at you through my glasses?

CECILY. Oh! not at all, Gwendolen. I am very fond of being looked at.

GWENDOLEN. [*After examining Cecily carefully through a lorgnette.°*] You are here on a short visit, I suppose.

CECILY. Oh no! I live here.

GWENDOLEN. [*Severely.*] Really? Your mother, no doubt, or some female relative of advanced years, resides here also?

CECILY. Oh no! I have no mother, nor, in fact, any relations.

GWENDOLEN. Indeed?

CECILY. My dear guardian, with the assistance of Miss Prism, has the arduous task of looking after me.

GWENDOLEN. Your guardian?

CECILY. Yes, I am Mr Worthing's ward.

GWENDOLEN. Oh! It is strange he never mentioned to me that he had a ward. How secretive of him! He grows more interesting hourly. I am not sure, however, that the news inspires me with feelings of unmixed delight. [*Rising and going to her.*] I am very fond of you, Cecily; I have liked you ever since I met you! But I am bound to state that now that I know that you are Mr Worthing's ward, I cannot help expressing a wish you were—well, just a little older than you seem to be— and not quite so very alluring in appearance. In fact, if I may speak candidly—

CECILY. Pray do! I think that whenever one has anything unpleasant to say, one should always be quite candid.

GWENDOLEN. Well, to speak with perfect candour, Cecily, I wish that you were fully forty-two, and more than usually plain for your age. Ernest has a strong upright nature. He is the very soul of truth and honour. Disloyalty would be as impossible to him as deception. But even men of the noblest possible moral character are extremely susceptible to the influence of the physical charms of others. Modern, no less than Ancient History, supplies us with many most painful examples of what I refer to. If it were not so, indeed, History would be quite unreadable.

CECILY. I beg your pardon, Gwendolen, did you say Ernest?

GWENDOLEN. Yes.

CECILY. Oh, but it is not Mr Ernest Worthing who is my guardian. It is his brother— his elder brother.

GWENDOLEN. [*Sitting down again.*] Ernest never mentioned to me that he had a brother.

---

lorgnette: opera glass or lens worn on a ribbon.

Realism in Drama

CECILY. I am sorry to say they have not been on good terms for a long time.

GWENDOLEN. Ah! that accounts for it. And now that I think of it I have never heard any man mention his brother. The subject seems distasteful to most men. Cecily, you have lifted a load from my mind. I was growing almost anxious. It would have been terrible if any cloud had come across a friendship like ours, would it not? Of course you are quite, quite sure that it is not Mr Ernest Worthing who is your guardian?

CECILY. Quite sure. [*A pause.*] In fact, I am going to be his.

GWENDOLEN. [*Inquiringly.*] I beg your pardon?

CECILY. [*Rather shy and confidingly.*] Dearest Gwendolen, there is no reason why I should make a secret of it to you. Our little county newspaper is sure to chronicle the fact next week. Mr Ernest Worthing and I are engaged to be married.

GWENDOLEN. [*Quite politely, rising.*] My darling Cecily, I think there must be some slight error. Mr Ernest Worthing is engaged to me. The announcement will appear in the *Morning Post* on Saturday at the latest.

CECILY. [*Very politely, rising.*] I am afraid you must be under some misconception. Ernest proposed to me exactly ten minutes ago. [*Shows diary.*]

GWENDOLEN. [*Examines diary through her lorgnette carefully.*] It is very curious, for he asked me to be his wife yesterday afternoon at 5.30. If you would care to verify the incident, pray do so. [*Produces diary of her own.*] I never travel without my diary. One should always have something sensational to read in the train. I am so sorry, dear Cecily, if it is any disappointment to you, but I am afraid I have the prior claim.

CECILY. It would distress me more than I can tell you, dear Gwendolen, if it caused you any mental or physical anguish, but I feel bound to point out that since Ernest proposed to you he clearly has changed his mind.

GWENDOLEN. [*Meditatively.*] If the poor fellow has been entrapped into any foolish promise, I shall consider it my duty to rescue him at once, and with a firm hand.

CECILY. [*Thoughtfully and sadly.*] Whatever unfortunate entanglement my dear boy may have got into, I will never reproach him with it after we are married.

GWENDOLEN. Do you allude to me, Miss Cardew, as an entanglement? You are presumptuous. On an occasion of this kind it becomes more than a moral duty to speak one's mind. It becomes a pleasure.

CECILY. Do you suggest, Miss Fairfax, that I entrapped Ernest into an engagement? How dare you? This is no time for wearing the shallow mask of manners. When I see a spade I call it a spade.

GWENDOLEN. [*Satirically.*] I am glad to say that I have never seen a spade. It is obvious that our social spheres have been widely different.

Enter Merriman, followed by the footman. He carries a salver, table cloth, and plate stand. Cecily is about to retort. The presence of the servants exercises a restraining influence, under which both girls chafe.

MERRIMAN. Shall I lay tea here as usual, Miss?

CECILY. [*Sternly, in a calm voice.*] Yes, as usual. [*Merriman begins to clear table and lay cloth. A long pause. Cecily and Gwendolen glare at each other.*]

GWENDOLEN. Are there many interesting walks in the vicinity, Miss Cardew?

CECILY. Oh! yes! a great many. From the top of one of the hills quite close one can see five counties.

GWENDOLEN. Five counties! I don't think I should like that; I hate crowds.

CECILY. [*Sweetly.*] I suppose that is why you live in town? [*Gwendolen bites her lip, and beats her foot nervously with her parasol.*]

GWENDOLEN. [*Looking around.*] Quite a well-kept garden this is, Miss Cardew.

CECILY. So glad you like it, Miss Fairfax.

GWENDOLEN. I had no idea there were any flowers in the country.

CECILY. Oh, flowers are as common here, Miss Fairfax, as people are in London.

GWENDOLEN. Personally I cannot understand how anybody manages to exist in the country, if anybody who is anybody does. The country always bores me to death.

CECILY. Ah! This is what the newspapers call agricultural depression, is it not? I believe the aristocracy are suffering very much from it just at present. It is almost an epidemic amongst them, I have been told. May I offer you some tea, Miss Fairfax?

GWENDOLEN. [*With elaborate politeness.*] Thank you. [*Aside.*] Detestable girl! But I require tea!

CECILY. [*Sweetly.*] Sugar?

GWENDOLEN. [*Superciliously.*] No, thank you. Sugar is not fashionable any more. [*Cecily looks angrily at her, takes up the tongs and puts four lumps of sugar into the cup.*]

CECILY. [*Severely.*] Cake or bread and butter?

GWENDOLEN. [*In a bored manner.*] Bread and butter, please. Cake is rarely seen at the best houses nowadays.

CECILY. [*Cuts a very large slice of cake and puts it on the tray.*] Hand that to Miss Fairfax.

Merriman does so, and goes out with footman. Gwendolen drinks the tea and makes a grimace. Puts down cup at once, reaches out her hand to the bread and butter, looks at it, and finds it is cake. Rises in indignation.

GWENDOLEN. You have filled my tea with lumps of sugar, and though I asked most distinctly for bread and butter, you have given me cake. I am known for the gentleness of my disposition, and the extraordinary sweetness of my nature, but I warn you, Miss Cardew, you may go too far.

CECILY. [*Rising.*] To save my poor, innocent, trusting boy from the machinations of any other girl there are no lengths to which I would not go.

GWENDOLEN. From the moment I saw you I distrusted you. I felt that you were false and deceitful. I am never deceived in such matters. My first impressions of people are invariably right.

CECILY. It seems to me, Miss Fairfax, that I am trespassing on your valuable time. No doubt you have many other calls of a similar character to make in the neighbourhood.

Enter Jack.

GWENDOLEN. [*Catching sight of him.*] Ernest! My own Ernest!

JACK. Gwendolen! Darling! [*Offers to kiss her.*]

GWENDOLEN. [*Drawing back.*] A moment! May I ask if you are engaged to be married to this young lady? [*Points to Cecily.*]

JACK. [*Laughing.*] To dear little Cecily! Of course not! What could have put such an idea into your pretty little head?

GWENDOLEN. Thank you. You may! [*Offers her cheek.*]

CECILY. [*Very sweetly.*] I knew there must be some misunderstanding, Miss Fairfax. The gentleman whose arm is at present round your waist is my guardian, Mr John Worthing.

GWENDOLEN. I beg your pardon?

CECILY. This is Uncle Jack.

GWENDOLEN. [*Receding.*] Jack! Oh!

Enter Algernon.

CECILY. Here is Ernest.

ALGERNON. [*Goes straight over to Cecily without noticing anyone else.*] My own love! [*Offers to kiss her.*]

CECILY. [*Drawing back.*] A moment, Ernest! May I ask you—are you engaged to be married to this young lady?

ALGERNON. [*Looking round.*] To what young lady? Good heavens! Gwendolen!

CECILY. Yes: to good heavens, Gwendolen, I mean to Gwendolen.

ALGERNON. [*Laughing.*] Of course not! What could have put such an idea into your pretty little head?

CECILY. Thank you. [*Presenting her cheek to be kissed.*] You may. [*Algernon kisses her.*]

GWENDOLEN. I felt there was some slight error, Miss Cardew. The gentleman who is now embracing you is my cousin, Mr Algernon Moncrieff.

CECILY. [*Breaking away from Algernon.*] Algernon Moncrieff! Oh! [*The two girls move towards each other and put their arms round each other's waists as if for protection.*]

CECILY. Are you called Algernon?

ALGERNON. I cannot deny it.

CECILY. Oh!

GWENDOLEN. Is your name really John?

JACK. [*Standing rather proudly.*] I could deny it if I liked. I could deny anything if I liked. But my name certainly is John. It has been John for years.

CECILY. [*To Gwendolen.*] A gross deception has been practised on both of us.

GWENDOLEN. My poor wounded Cecily!

CECILY. My sweet wronged Gwendolen!

GWENDOLEN. [*Slowly and seriously.*] You will call me sister, will you not? [*They embrace. Jack and Algernon groan and walk up and down.*]

CECILY. [*Rather brightly.*] There is just one question I would like to be allowed to ask my guardian.

GWENDOLEN. An admirable idea! Mr Worthing, there is just one question I would like to be permitted to put to you. Where is your brother Ernest? We are both engaged to be married to your brother Ernest, so it is a matter of some importance to us to know where your brother Ernest is at present.

JACK. [*Slowly and hesitatingly.*] Gwendolen—Cecily—it is very painful for me to be forced to speak the truth. It is the first time in my life that I have ever been reduced to such a painful position, and I am really quite inexperienced in doing anything of the kind. However, I will tell you quite frankly that I have no brother Ernest. I have no brother at all. I never had a brother in my life, and I certainly have not the smallest intention of ever having one in the future.

CECILY. [*Surprised.*] No brother at all?

JACK. [*Cheerily.*] None!

GWENDOLEN. [*Severely.*] Had you never a brother of any kind?

JACK. [*Pleasantly.*] Never. Not even of any kind.

GWENDOLEN. I am afraid it is quite clear, Cecily, that neither of us is engaged to be married to anyone.

CECILY. It is not a very pleasant position for a young girl suddenly to find herself in. Is it?

GWENDOLEN. Let us go into the house. They will hardly venture to come after us there.

CECILY. No, men are so cowardly, aren't they?

They retire into the house with scornful looks.

JACK. This ghastly state of things is what you call Bunburying I suppose?

ALGERNON. Yes, and a perfectly wonderful Bunbury it is. The most wonderful Bunbury I have ever had in my life.

JACK. Well, you've no right whatsoever to Bunbury here.

ALGERNON. That is absurd. One has a right to Bunbury anywhere one chooses. Every serious Bunburyist knows that.

JACK. Serious Bunburyist? Good heavens!

ALGERNON. Well, one must be serious about something, if one wants to have any amusement in life. I happen to be serious about Bunburying. What on earth you are serious about I haven't got the remotest idea. About everything, I should fancy. You have such an absolutely trivial nature.

JACK. Well, the only small satisfaction I have in the whole of this wretched business is that your friend Bunbury is quite exploded. You won't be able to run down to the country quite so often as you used to do, dear Algy. And a very good thing too.

ALGERNON. Your brother is a little off colour, isn't he, dear Jack? You won't be able to disappear to London quite so frequently as your wicked custom was. And not a bad thing either.

JACK. As for your conduct towards Miss Cardew, I must say that your taking in a sweet, simple, innocent girl like that is quite inexcusable. To say nothing of the fact that she is my ward.

ALGERNON. I can see no possible defence at all for your deceiving a brilliant, clever, thoroughly experienced young lady like Miss Fairfax. To say nothing of the fact that she is my cousin.

JACK. I wanted to be engaged to Gwendolen, that is all, I love her.

ALGERNON. Well, I simply wanted to be engaged to Cecily. I adore her.

JACK. There is certainly no chance of your marrying Miss Cardew.

ALGERNON. I don't think there is much likelihood, Jack, of you and Miss Fairfax being united.

JACK. Well, that is no business of yours.

ALGERNON. If it was my business, I wouldn't talk about it. [*Begins to eat muffins.*] It is very vulgar to talk about one's business. Only people like stockbrokers do that, and then merely at dinner parties.

JACK. How you can sit there, calmly eating muffins when we are in this horrible trouble, I can't make out. You seem to me to be perfectly heartless.

ALGERNON. Well, I can't eat muffins in an agitated manner. The butter would probably get on my cuffs. One should always eat muffins quite calmly. It is the only way to eat them.

JACK. I say it's perfectly heartless your eating muffins at all, under the circumstances.

ALGERNON. When I am in trouble, eating is the only thing that consoles me. Indeed, when I am in really great trouble, as any one who knows me intimately will tell you, I refuse everything except food and drink. At the present moment I am eating muffins because I am unhappy. Besides, I am particularly fond of muffins. [*Rising.*]

JACK. [*Rising.*] Well, there is no reason why you should eat them all in that greedy way. [*Takes muffins from Algernon.*]

ALGERNON. [*Offering tea-cake.*] I wish you would have tea-cake instead. I don't like tea-cake.

JACK. Good heavens! I suppose a man may eat his own muffins in his own garden.

ALGERNON. But you have just said it was perfectly heartless to eat muffins.

JACK. I said it was perfectly heartless of you, under the circumstances. That is a very different thing.

ALGERNON. That may be. But the muffins are the same. [*He seizes the muffin-dish from Jack.*]

JACK. Algy, I wish to goodness you would go.

ALGERNON. You can't possibly ask me to go without having some dinner. It's absurd. I never go without my dinner. No one ever does, except vegetarians and people like that. Besides I have just made arrangements with Dr Chasuble to be christened at a quarter to six under the name of Ernest.

JACK. My dear fellow, the sooner you give up that nonsense the better. I made arrangements this morning with Dr Chasuble to be christened myself at 5.30, and I naturally will take the name of Ernest. Gwendolen would wish it. We can't both be christened Ernest. It's absurd. Besides, I have a perfect right to be christened if I like. There is no evidence at all that I have ever been christened by anybody. I should think it extremely probable I never was, and so does Dr Chasuble. It is entirely different in your case. You have been christened already.

ALGERNON. Yes, but I have not been christened for years.

JACK. Yes, but you have been christened. That is the important thing.

ALGERNON. Quite so. So I know my constitution can stand it. If you are not quite sure about your ever having been christened, I must say I think it rather dangerous your venturing on it now. It might make you very unwell. You can hardly have forgotten that someone very closely connected with you was very nearly carried off this week in Paris by a severe chill.

JACK. Yes, but you said yourself that a severe chill was not hereditary.

ALGERNON. It usen't to be, I know—but I daresay it is now. Science is always making wonderful improvements in things.

JACK. [*Picking up the muffin-dish.*] Oh, that is nonsense; you are always talking nonsense.

ALGERNON. Jack, you are at the muffins again! I wish you wouldn't. There are only two left. [*Takes them.*] I told you I was particularly fond of muffins.

JACK. But I hate tea-cake.

ALGERNON. Why on earth then do you allow tea-cake to be served up for your guests? What ideas you have of hospitality!

JACK. Algernon! I have already told you to go. I don't want you here. Why don't you go!

ALGERNON. I haven't quite finished my tea yet! and there is still one muffin left. [*Jack groans, and sinks into a chair. Algernon continues eating.*]

Act Drop

THIRD ACT
Scene
Drawing-room at the Manor House

  Gwendolen and Cecily are at the window, looking out into the garden.

GWENDOLEN. The fact that they did not follow us at once into the house, as anyone else would have done, seems to me to show that they have some sense of shame left.

CECILY. They have been eating muffins. That looks like repentance.

GWENDOLEN. [*After a pause.*] They don't seem to notice us at all. Couldn't you cough?

CECILY. But I haven't got a cough.

GWENDOLEN. They're looking at us. What effrontery!°

CECILY. They're approaching. That's very forward of them.

GWENDOLEN. Let us preserve a dignified silence.

CECILY. Certainly. It's the only thing to do now.

> *Enter Jack followed by Algernon. They whistle some dreadful popular air from a British Opera.*

GWENDOLEN. This dignified silence seems to produce an unpleasant effect.

CECILY. A most distasteful one.

GWENDOLEN. But we will not be the first to speak.

CECILY. Certainly not.

GWENDOLEN. Mr Worthing, I have something very particular to ask you. Much depends on your reply.

CECILY. Gwendolen, your common sense is invaluable. Mr Moncrieff, kindly answer me the following question. Why did you pretend to be my guardian's brother?

ALGERNON. In order that I might have an opportunity of meeting you.

CECILY. [*To Gwendolen.*] That certainly seems a satisfactory explanation, does it not?

GWENDOLEN. Yes, dear, if you can believe him.

CECILY. I don't. But that does not affect the wonderful beauty of his answer.

GWENDOLEN. True. In matters of grave importance, style, not sincerity, is the vital thing. Mr Worthing, what explanation can you offer to me for pretending to have a brother? Was it in order that you might have an opportunity of coming up to town to see me as often as possible?

JACK. Can you doubt it, Miss Fairfax?

GWENDOLEN. I have the gravest doubts upon the subject. But I intend to crush them. This is not the moment for German scepticism. [*Moving to Cecily.*] Their explanations appear to be quite satisfactory, especially Mr Worthing's. That seems to me to have the stamp of truth upon it.

CECILY. I am more than content with what Mr Moncrieff said. His voice alone inspires one with absolute credulity.

GWENDOLEN. Then you think we should forgive them?

CECILY. Yes. I mean no.

GWENDOLEN. True! I had forgotten. There are principles at stake that one cannot surrender. Which of us should tell them? The task is not a pleasant one.

CECILY. Could we not both speak at the same time?

GWENDOLEN. An excellent idea! I nearly always speak at the same time as other people. Will you take the time from me?

CECILY. Certainly. [*Gwendolen beats time with uplifted finger.*]

GWENDOLEN AND CECILY. [*Speaking together.*] Your Christian names are still an insuperable barrier. That is all!

---

effrontery: impudence, audacity.

JACK AND ALGERNON. [*Speaking together.*] Our christian names! Is that all? But we are going to be christened this afternoon.

GWENDOLEN. [*To Jack.*] For my sake you are prepared to do this terrible thing?

JACK. I am.

CECILY. [*To Algernon.*] To please me you are ready to face this fearful ordeal?

ALGERNON. I am!

GWENDOLEN. How absurd to talk of the equality of the sexes! Where questions of self-sacrifice are concerned, men are infinitely beyond us.

JACK. We are. [*Clasps hands with Algernon.*]

CECILY. They have moments of physical courage of which we women know absolutely nothing.

GWENDOLEN. [*To Jack.*] Darling!

ALGERNON. [*To Cecily.*] Darling! [*They fall into each other's arms.*]

Enter Merriman. When he enters he coughs loudly, seeing the situation.

MERRIMAN. Ahem! Ahem! Lady Bracknell.

JACK. Good heavens!

Enter Lady Bracknell. The couples separate in alarm. Exit Merriman.

LADY BRACKNELL. Gwendolen! What does this mean?

GWENDOLEN. Merely that I am engaged to be married to Mr Worthing, mamma.

LADY BRACKNELL. Come here. Sit down. Sit down immediately. Hesitation of any kind is a sign of mental decay in the young, of physical weakness in the old. [*Turns to Jack.*] Apprised,° sir, of my daughter's sudden flight by her trusty maid, whose confidence I purchased by means of a small coin, I followed her at once by a luggage train. Her unhappy father is, I am glad to say, under the impression that she is attending a more than usually lengthy lecture by the University Extension Scheme on the Influence of a Permanent Income on Thought. I do not propose to undeceive him. Indeed I have never undeceived him on any question. I would consider it wrong. But of course, you will clearly understand that all communication between yourself and my daughter must cease immediately from this moment. On this point, as indeed on all points, I am firm.

JACK. I am engaged to be married to Gwendolen, Lady Bracknell!

LADY BRACKNELL. You are nothing of the kind, sir. And now as regards Algernon! . . . Algernon!

ALGERNON. Yes, Aunt Augusta.

LADY BRACKNELL. May I ask if it is in this house that your invalid friend Mr Bunbury resides?

ALGERNON. [*Stammering.*] Oh! No! Bunbury doesn't live here. Bunbury is somewhere else at present. In fact, Bunbury is dead.

LADY BRACKNELL. Dead! When did Mr Bunbury die? His death must have been extremely sudden.

ALGERNON. [*Airily.*] Oh! I killed Bunbury this afternoon. I mean poor Bunbury died this afternoon.

LADY BRACKNELL. What did he die of?

ALGERNON. Bunbury? Oh, he was quite exploded.

---

apprised: informed.

LADY BRACKNELL. Exploded! Was he the victim of a revolutionary outrage? I was not aware that Mr Bunbury was interested in social legislation. If so, he is well punished for his morbidity.

ALGERNON. My dear Aunt Augusta, I mean he was found out! The doctors found out that Bunbury could not live, that is what I mean—so Bunbury died.

LADY BRACKNELL. He seems to have had great confidence in the opinion of his physicians. I am glad, however, that he made up his mind at the last to some definite course of action, and acted under proper medical advice. And now that we have finally got rid of this Mr Bunbury, may I ask, Mr Worthing, who is that young person whose hand my nephew Algernon is now holding in what seems to me a peculiarly unnecessary manner?

JACK. That lady is Miss Cecily Cardew, my ward. [*Lady Bracknell bows coldly to Cecily.*]

ALGERNON. I am engaged to be married to Cecily, Aunt Augusta.

LADY BRACKNELL. I beg your pardon?

CECILY. Mr Moncrieff and I are engaged to be married, Lady Bracknell.

LADY BRACKNELL. [*With a shiver, crossing to the sofa and sitting down.*] I do not know whether there is anything peculiarly exciting in the air of this particular part of Hertfordshire, but the number of engagements that go on seems to me considerably above the proper average that statistics have laid down for our guidance. I think some preliminary inquiry on my part would not be out of place. Mr Worthing, is Miss Cardew at all connected with any of the larger railway stations in London? I merely desire information. Until yesterday I had no idea that there were any families or persons whose origin was a Terminus. [*Jack looks perfectly furious, but restrains himself.*]

JACK. [*In a cold, clear voice.*] Miss Cardew is the granddaughter of the late Mr Thomas Cardew of 149 Belgrave Square, S.W.; Gervase Park, Dorking, Surrey; and the Sporran, Fifeshire, N.B.

LADY BRACKNELL. That sounds not unsatisfactory. Three addresses always inspire confidence, even in tradesmen. But what proof have I of their authenticity?

JACK. I have carefully preserved the Court Guides of the period. They are open to your inspection, Lady Bracknell.

LADY BRACKNELL. [*Grimly.*] I have known strange errors in that publication.

JACK. Miss Cardew's family solicitors are Messrs Markby, Markby, and Markby.

LADY BRACKNELL. Markby, Markby, and Markby? A firm of the very highest position in their profession. Indeed I am told that one of the Mr Markby's is occasionally to be seen at dinner parties. So far I am satisfied.

JACK. [*Very irritably.*] How extremely kind of you, Lady Bracknell! I have also in my possession, you will be pleased to hear, certificates of Miss Cardew's birth, baptism, whooping cough, registration, vaccination, confirmation, and the measles; both the German and the English variety.

LADY BRACKNELL. Ah! A life crowded with incident, I see; though perhaps somewhat too exciting for a young girl. I am not myself in favour of premature experiences. [*Rises, looks at her watch.*] Gwendolen! the time approaches for our departure. We have not a moment to lose. As a matter of form, Mr Worthing, I had better ask you if Miss Cardew has any little fortune?

JACK. Oh! about a hundred and thirty thousand pounds in the Funds. That is all. Good-bye, Lady Bracknell. So pleased to have seen you.

LADY BRACKNELL. [*Sitting down again.*] A moment, Mr Worthing. A hundred and thirty thousand pounds! And in the Funds! Miss Cardew seems to me a most attractive young lady, now that I look at her. Few girls of the present day have any really solid qualities, any of the qualities that last, and improve with time. We live, I regret to say, in an age of surfaces. [*To Cecily.*] Come over here, dear. [*Cecily goes across.*] Pretty child! your dress is sadly simple, and your hair seems almost as Nature might have left it. But we can soon alter all that. A thoroughly experienced French maid produces a really marvellous result in a very brief space of time. I remember recommending one to young Lady Lancing, and after three months her own husband did not know her.

JACK. And after six months nobody knew her.

LADY BRACKNELL. [*Glares at Jack for a few moments. Then bends, with a practised smile, to Cecily.*] Kindly turn round, sweet child. [*Cecily turns completely round.*] No, the side view is what I want. [*Cecily presents her profile.*] Yes, quite as I expected. There are distinct social possibilities in your profile. The two weak points in our age are its want of principle and its want of profile. The chin a little higher, dear. Style largely depends on the way the chin is worn. They are worn very high, just at present, Algernon!

ALGERNON. Yes, Aunt Augusta!

LADY BRACKNELL. There are distinct social possibilities in Miss Cardew's profile.

ALGERNON. Cecily is the sweetest, dearest, prettiest girl in the whole world. And I don't care twopence about social possibilities.

LADY BRACKNELL. Never speak disrespectfully of Society, Algernon. Only people who can't get into it do that. [*To Cecily.*] Dear child, of course you know that Algernon has nothing but his debts to depend upon. But I do not approve of mercenary marriages. When I married Lord Bracknell I had no fortune of any kind. But I never dreamed for a moment of allowing that to stand in my way. Well, I suppose I must give my consent.

ALGERNON. Thank you, Aunt Augusta.

LADY BRACKNELL. Cecily, you may kiss me!

CECILY. [*Kisses her.*] Thank you, Lady Bracknell.

LADY BRACKNELL. You may also address me as Aunt Augusta for the future.

CECILY. Thank you, Aunt Augusta.

LADY BRACKNELL. The marriage, I think, had better take place quite soon.

ALGERNON. Thank you, Aunt Augusta.

CECILY. Thank you, Aunt Augusta.

LADY BRACKNELL. To speak frankly, I am not in favour of long engagements. They give people the opportunity of finding out each other's character before marriage, which I think is never advisable.

JACK. I beg your pardon for interrupting you, Lady Bracknell, but this engagement is quite out of the question. I am Miss Cardew's guardian, and she cannot marry without my consent until she comes of age. That consent I absolute decline to give.

LADY BRACKNELL. Upon what grounds, may I ask? Algernon is an extremely, I may almost say an ostentatiously, eligible young man. He has nothing, but he looks everything. What more can one desire?

JACK. It pains me very much to have to speak frankly to you, Lady Bracknell, about your nephew, but the fact is that I do not approve at all of his moral character.

I suspect him of being untruthful. [*Algernon and Cecily look at him in indignant amazement.*]

LADY BRACKNELL. Untruthful! My nephew Algernon? Impossible! He is an Oxonian.

JACK. I fear there can be no possible doubt about the matter. This afternoon during my temporary absence in London on an important question of romance, he obtained admission to my house by means of the false pretence of being my brother. Under an assumed name he drank, I've just been informed by my butler, an entire pint bottle of my Perrier-Jouet, Brut, '89; wine I was specially reserving for myself. Continuing his disgraceful deception, he succeeded in the course of the afternoon in alienating the affections of my only ward. He subsequently stayed to tea, and devoured every single muffin. And what makes his conduct all the more heartless is, that he was perfectly well aware from the first that I have no brother, that I never had a brother, and that I don't intend to have a brother, not even of any kind. I distinctly told him so myself yesterday afternoon.

LADY BRACKNELL. Ahem! Mr Worthing, after careful consideration I have decided entirely to overlook my nephew's conduct to you.

JACK. That is very generous of you, Lady Bracknell. My own decision, however, is unalterable. I decline to give my consent.

LADY BRACKNELL. [*To Cecily.*] Come here, sweet child. [*Cecily goes over.*] How old are you, dear?

CECILY. Well, I am really only eighteen, but I always admit to twenty when I go to evening parties.

LADY BRACKNELL. You are perfectly right in making some slight alteration. Indeed, no woman should ever be quite accurate about her age. It looks so calculating. . . . [*In a meditative manner.*] Eighteen, but admitting to twenty at evening parties. Well, it will not be very long before you are of age and free from the restrains of tutelage. So I don't think your guardian's consent is, after all, a matter of any importance.

JACK. Pray excuse me, Lady Bracknell, for interrupting you again, but it is only fair to tell you that according to the terms of her grandfather's will Miss Cardew does not come legally of age till she is thirty-five.

LADY BRACKNELL. That does not seem to me to be a grave objection. Thirty-five is a very attractive age. London society is full of women of the very highest birth who have, of their own free choice, remained thirty-five for years. Lady Dumbleton is an instance in point. To my own knowledge she has been thirty-five ever since she arrived at the age of forty, which was many years ago now. I see no reason why our dear Cecily should not be even still more attractive at the age you mention than she is at present. There will be a large accumulation of property.

CECILY. Algy, could you wait for me till I was thirty-five?

ALGERNON. Of course I could, Cecily. You know I could.

CECILY. Yes, I felt it instinctively, but I couldn't wait all that time. I hate waiting even five minutes for anybody. It always makes me rather cross. I am not punctual myself, I know, but I do like punctuality in others, and waiting, even to be married, is quite out of the question.

ALGERNON. Then what is to be done, Cecily?

CECILY. I don't know, Mr Moncrieff.

LADY BRACKNELL. My dear Mr Worthing, as Miss Cardew states positively that she cannot wait till she is thirty-five—a remark which I am bound to say seems to me to show a somewhat impatient nature—I would beg of you to reconsider your decision.

JACK. But my dear Lady Bracknell, the matter is entirely in your own hands. The moment you consent to my marriage with Gwendolen, I will most gladly allow your nephew to form an alliance with my ward.

LADY BRACKNELL. [Rising and drawing herself up.] You must be quite aware that what you propose is out of the question.

JACK. Then a passionate celibacy is all that any of us can look forward to.

LADY BRACKNELL. That is not the destiny I propose for Gwendolen. Algernon, of course, can choose for himself. [Pulls out her watch.] Come, dear [Gwendolen rises.], we have already missed five, if not six, trains. To miss any more might expose us to comment on the platform.

Enter Dr Chasuble.

CHASUBLE. Everything is quite ready for the christenings.

LADY BRACKNELL. The christenings, sir! Is not that somewhat premature?

CHASUBLE. [Looking rather puzzled, and pointing to Jack and Algernon.] Both these gentlemen have expressed a desire for immediate baptism.

LADY BRACKNELL. At their age? The idea is grotesque and irreligious! Algernon, I forbid you to be baptized. I will not hear of such excesses. Lord Bracknell would be highly displeased if he learned that that was the way in which you wasted your time and money.

CHASUBLE. Am I to understand then that there are to be no christenings at all this afternoon?

JACK. I don't think that, as things are now, it would be of much practical value to either of us, Dr Chasuble.

CHASUBLE. I am grieved to hear such sentiments from you, Mr Worthing. They savour of the heretical views of the Anabaptists,° views that I have completely refuted in four of my unpublished sermons. However, as your present mood seems to be one peculiarly secular, I will return to the church at once. Indeed, I have just been informed by the pew-opener that for the last hour and a half Miss Prism has been waiting for me in the vestry.

LADY BRACKNELL. [Starting.] Miss Prism! Did I hear you mention a Miss Prism?

CHASUBLE. Yes, Lady Bracknell. I am on my way to join her.

LADY BRACKNELL. Pray allow me to detain you for a moment. This matter may prove to be one of vital importance to Lord Bracknell and myself. Is this Miss Prism a female of repellent aspect, remotely connected with education?

CHASUBLE. [Somewhat indignantly.] She is the most cultivated of ladies, and the very picture of respectability.

LADY BRACKNELL. It is obviously the same person. May I ask what position she holds in your household?

CHASUBLE. [Severely.] I am a celibate, madam.

JACK. [Interposing.] Miss Prism, Lady Bracknell, has been for the last three years Miss Cardew's esteemed governess and valued companion.

°*Anabaptists*: name for early Baptists who broke from orthodox churches.

LADY BRACKNELL. In spite of what I hear of her, I must see her at once. Let her be sent for.

CHASUBLE. [*Looking off.*] She approaches; she is nigh.

Enter Miss Prism hurriedly.

MISS PRISM. I was told you expected me in the vestry, dear Canon. I have been waiting for you there for an hour and three-quarters. [*Catches sight of Lady Bracknell, who has fixed her with a stony glare. Miss Prism grows pale and quails. She looks anxiously round as if desirous to escape.*]

LADY BRACKNELL. [*In a severe, judicial voice.*] Prism! [*Miss Prism bows her head in shame.*] Come here, Prism! [*Miss Prism approaches in a humble manner.*] Prism! Where is that baby? [*General consternation. The Canon starts back in horror. Algernon and Jack pretend to be anxious to shield Cecily and Gwendolen from hearing the details of a terrible public scandal.*] Twenty-eight years ago, Prism, you left Lord Bracknell's house, Number 104, Upper Grosvenor Street, in charge of a perambulator° that contained a baby of the male sex. You never returned. A few weeks later, through the elaborate investigations of the Metropolitan police, the perambulator was discovered at midnight standing by itself in a remote corner of Bayswater. It contained the manuscript of a three-volume novel of more than usually revolting sentimentality. [*Miss Prism starts in involuntary indignation.*] But the baby was not there. [*Every one looks at Miss Prism.*] Prism! Where is that baby? [*A pause.*]

MISS PRISM. Lady Bracknell, I admit with shame that I do not know. I only wish I did. The plain facts of the case are these. On the morning of the day you mention, a day that is for ever branded on my memory, I prepared as usual to take the baby out of its perambulator. I had also with me a somewhat old, but capacious hand-bag in which I had intended to place the manuscript of a work of fiction that I had written during my few unoccupied hours. In a moment of mental abstraction, for which I can never forgive myself, I deposited the manuscript in the bassinette and placed the baby in the hand-bag.

JACK. [*Who has been listening attentively.*] But where did you deposit the hand-bag?

MISS PRISM. Do not ask me, Mr Worthing.

JACK. Miss Prism, this is a matter of no small importance to me. I insist on knowing where you deposited the hand-bag that contained that infant.

MISS PRISM. I left it in the cloak-room of one of the larger railway stations in London.

JACK. What railway station?

MISS PRISM. [*Quite crushed.*] Victoria. The Brighton line. (*Sinks into a chair.*)

JACK. I must retire to my room for a moment. Gwendolen, wait here for me.

GWENDOLEN. If you are not too long, I will wait here for you all my life. [*Exit Jack in great excitement.*]

CHASUBLE. What do you think this means, Lady Bracknell?

LADY BRACKNELL. I dare not even suspect, Dr Chasuble. I need hardly tell you that in families of high position strange coincidences are not supposed to occur. They are hardly considered the thing.

Noises heard overhead as if some one was throwing trunks about. Every one looks up.

CECILY. Uncle Jack seems strangely agitated.

---

perambulator: baby carriage, stroller.

CHASUBLE. Your guardian has a very emotional nature.

LADY BRACKNELL. This noise is extremely unpleasant. It sounds as if he was having an argument. I dislike arguments of any kind. They are always vulgar, and often convincing.

CHASUBLE. [*Looking up.*] It has stopped now. [*The noise is redoubled.*]

LADY BRACKNELL. I wish he would arrive at some conclusion.

GWENDOLEN. This suspense is terrible. I hope it will last.

Enter Jack with a hand-bag of black leather in his hand.

JACK. [*Rushing over to Miss Prism.*] Is this the hand-bag, Miss Prism? Examine it carefully before you speak. The happiness of more than one life depends on your answer.

MISS PRISM. [*Calmly.*] It seems to be mine. Yes, here is the injury it received through the upsetting of a Gower Street omnibus in younger and happier days. Here is the stain on the lining caused by the explosion of a temperance beverage, an incident that occurred at Leamington. And here, on the lock, are my initials. I had forgotten that in an extravagant mood I had had them placed there. The bag is undoubtedly mine. I am delighted to have it so unexpectedly restored to me. It has been a great inconvenience being without it all these years.

JACK. [*In a pathetic voice.*] Miss Prism, more is restored to you than this hand-bag. I was the baby you placed in it.

MISS PRISM. [*Amazed.*] You?

JACK. [*Embracing her.*] Yes . . . mother!

MISS PRISM. [*Recoiling in indignant astonishment.*] Mr Worthing. I am unmarried!

JACK. Unmarried! I do not deny that is a serious blow. But after all, who has the right to cast a stone against one who has suffered? Cannot repentance wipe out an act of folly? Why should there be one law for men, and another for women? Mother, I forgive you. [*Tries to embrace her again.*]

MISS PRISM. [*Still more indignant.*] Mr Worthing, there is some error. [*Pointing to Lady Bracknell.*] There is the lady who can tell you who you really are.

JACK. [*After a pause.*] Lady Bracknell, I hate to seem inquisitive, but would you kindly inform me who I am?

LADY BRACKNELL. I am afraid that the news I have to give you will not altogether please you. You are the son of my poor sister, Mrs Moncrieff, and consequently Algernon's elder brother.

JACK. Algy's elder brother! Then I have a brother after all. I knew I had a brother! I always said I had a brother! Cecily—how could you have ever doubted that I had a brother? [*Seizes hold of Algernon.*] Dr Chasuble, my unfortunate brother. Miss Prism, my unfortunate brother. Gwendolen, my unfortunate brother. Algy, you young scoundrel, you will have to treat me with more respect in the future. You have never behaved to me like a brother in all your life.

ALGERNON. Well, not till to-day, old boy, I admit. I did my best, however, though I was out of practice.

Shakes hands.

GWENDOLEN. [*To Jack.*] My own! But what own are you? What is your Christian name, now that you have become some one else?

JACK. Good heavens! . . . I had quite forgotten that point. Your decision on the subject of my name is irrevocable, I suppose?

GWENDOLEN. I never change, except in my affections.

CECILY. What a noble nature you have, Gwendolen!

JACK. Then the question had better be cleared up at once. Aunt Augusta, a moment. At the time when Miss Prism left me in the hand-bag, had I been christened already?

LADY BRACKNELL. Every luxury that money could buy, including christening, had been lavished on you by your fond and doting parents.

JACK. Then I was christened! That is settled. Now, what name was I given? Let me know the worst.

LADY BRACKNELL. Being the eldest son you were naturally christened after your father.

JACK. [Irritably.] Yes, but what was my father's Christian name?

LADY BRACKNELL. [Meditatively.] I cannot at the present moment recall what the General's Christian name was. But I have no doubt he had one. He was eccentric, I admit. But only in later years. And that was the result of the Indian climate, and marriage, and indigestion, and other things of that kind.

JACK. Algy! Can't you recollect what our father's Christian name was?

ALGERNON. My dear boy, we were never even on speaking terms. He died before I was a year old.

JACK. His name would appear in the Army Lists of the period, I suppose, Aunt Augusta?

LADY BRACKNELL. The General was essentially a man of peace, except in his domestic life. But I have no doubt his name would appear in any military directory.

JACK. The Army Lists of the last forty years are here. These delightful records should have been my constant study. [Rushes to bookcase and tears the books out.] M. Generals . . . Mallam, Maxbohm, Magley—what ghastly names they have— Markby, Migsby, Mobbs, Moncrieff! Lieutenant 1840, Captain, Lieutenant-Colonel, Colonel, General 1869, Christian names, Ernest John. [Puts book very quietly down and speaks quite calmly.] I always told you, Gwendolen, my name was Ernest, didn't I? Well, it is Ernest after all. I mean it naturally is Ernest.

LADY BRACKNELL. Yes, I remember now that the General was called Ernest. I knew I had some particular reason for disliking the name.

GWENDOLEN. Ernest! My own Ernest! I felt from the first that you could have no other name!

JACK. Gwendolen, it is a terrible thing for a man to find out suddenly that all his life he has been speaking nothing but the truth. Can you forgive me?

GWENDOLEN. I can. For I feel that you are sure to change.

JACK. My own one!

CHASUBLE. [To Miss Prism.] Laetitia! [Embraces her.]

MISS PRISM. [Enthusiastically.] Frederick! At last!

ALGERNON. Cecily! [Embraces her.] At last!

JACK. Gwendolen! [Embraces her.] At last!

LADY BRACKNELL. My nephew, you seem to be displaying signs of triviality.

JACK. On the contrary, Aunt Augusta, I've now realized for the first time in my life the vital Importance of Being Earnest.

Tableau

Curtain

1. Comment on the relationship between Algernon and his butler, Lane. How does Wilde both confirm and undermine our traditional notions of the separation between classes?

2. What is "Bunburying" and what purpose does it serve Algernon? What is Jack's own version of "Bunburying"?

3. What is it that both Gwendolyn and Cecily "see" in the name Ernest?

4. What are some of the ways that Wilde sets the pairs of would-be lovers into parallel situations? What are some of the differences between Jack's and Algernon's situations?

5. Find three instances where Wilde advances a paradoxical assertion or a deliberately shocking statement (e.g., "Divorces are made in Heaven . . . "). Are these comments pure silliness, or do they hold a grain of truth? Discuss.

6. What does Lady Bracknell represent? How does Wilde use her interchanges with Jack to expose her true nature?

7. Locate several scenes in which Wilde satirizes some particular thing—scholarship, the church, the manners of the upper classes, and so on—and explore his technique.

8. Based upon your reading of this play, what would you say is Wilde's view of modern love and the rituals of courtship? Explain.

9. What is Miss Prism's role in the play? How did her mistake come to determine Jack's fate? What evidence does he produce and what does it prove?

10. In what ways is it fitting that Jack and Algernon should be brothers?

35 Drama in the Modern Age

Developments in the dramatic arts in our century in many ways parallel the developments in other literary genres. Playwrights, like poets and fiction writers, responded to the intense agitations that afflicted the political and cultural life of the times. Artists of every persuasion shared the recognition that, with the coming of the new century, the whole of civilization as they knew it was experiencing what Shakespeare in another context called a "sea-change." Acceleration and violence were in the air. It was clear that the new era would belong to the city, to the machine, and to radical social upheaval and war. Whether these were to be regarded as indications of imminent decline or as the pangs that heralded the birth of some new order was not clear. What was clear was that the old forms and habits would never do.

DEVELOPMENTS IN THE MODERN THEATER

In literature—in the arts in general—a search for new and more urgent ways of expression was needed. As the world no longer felt "real" in the old sense of the word, so the old modes of Realism were no longer adequate—at least in many quarters. As a consequence, many new theories and approaches were ventured. The history of drama in our age is alive with movements and *isms*, some of them influential, and others quite short-lived.

But experiment and artistic departure are only part of the picture. At the same time that playwrights were working with Symbolism, Expressionism, Epic Theater, Theater of the Absurd, Guerrilla Theater, and multimedia productions, the formerly dominant Realist tradition continued—not unaffected, of course. Every experiment and revolutionary manifesto in some way enriched the response of the traditionalist, with the result that nearly every Realistic play makes some use of techniques drawn from one or another of these dramatic modes. Tennessee Williams was deeply influenced by Symbolist tenets, Arthur Miller took ideas from Expressionist theater, and so on.

Symbolism

Symbolism, which flourished briefly around the turn of the century, has more in common with the spirit of the 1800s than with the modern period. It originated as a kind of counterthrust to Realism, seeking to give expression to the world of dreams and forebodings that many felt lay under the surfaces of daily life. The Symbolists, like Maurice Maeterlinck (1862–1949), William Butler Yeats (1865–1939),

Paul Claudel (1868–1955), and others, were ultimately committed to a belief in a spiritual order. Drawing inspiration from French Symbolist poets like Charles Baudelaire and Stéphane Mallarmé, they tried to embody their convictions that the things of this world were just emblems of a deeper reality. As a result, their plays were often dense with otherworldly atmospheres, with characters speaking less to communicate to one another than to stir the veils of appearances to reveal what might lie on the other side. Situations and objects were, naturally, invested with dense significance, and the viewer's task was to connect with the world suggested by the stage action. Though it never attained great popularity, Symbolism did exert a certain influence. Playwrights from Chekhov to Tennessee Williams appropriated Symbolic elements for their plays.

Expressionism

Like Symbolism, Expressionism was a nonrealistic mode of drama, a reaction to the dramatic reductionism brought on by too great a trust in surfaces. Unlike Symbolism, however, Expressionism was not especially concerned with the religious/mystical side of existence. Rather, it aimed to project intense states of emotion and to release pent-up energies. The logic, as opposed to the mirroring procedure of Realism, was to present life not as it is perceived outwardly, but as it is felt. One of the great pioneers of dramatic Expressionism was the Swedish playwright August Strindberg, who abandoned the Naturalism that had won him his reputation in order to stage his tormented and logically disconnected plays like *The Dream Play* (1902) and *The Ghost Sonata* (1907). Expressionist theater was at its peak of popularity during the period of the 1920s in Europe.

Epic Theater

The Epic Theater is mainly associated with the work of German playwright Bertolt Brecht. Brecht was a figure of great controversy in Germany in the period before World War II. Outspoken, uncompromising, and intensely committed to his left-wing politics, he created a theater experience that did not so much swamp the audience in illusion as expose and comment upon the illusion-making process. Actors reminded the audience that they were acting; scene changes were made in full view. Brecht called his procedure "baring the device," and it was his belief that if the audience could see how stage behavior is constructed, it might likewise see how its own social and political identities are constructed. The watcher was to leave the play reflecting upon the issues and philosophies presented. Coming during a period of intense political questioning in Europe and America, plays like *The Caucasian Chalk Circle*, *The City of Mahagony*, *The Good Woman of Szechuan*, and *Mother Courage* were a vital expression of the cultural life of pre–World War II Europe, and continued to be influential for postwar movements in theater.

Theater of the Absurd

After World War II, Europe was morally devastated. Philosophies such as *Existentialism*, which questioned the very premise of meaning in a Godless universe, were popular. Literature and the other arts took a somber turn. The widely shared sense of pointlessness was given its clearest and starkest expression in the plays of the post-war Theater of the Absurd. In the works of playwrights Samuel Beckett, Eugène Ionesco, Harold Pinter, Edward Albee, and others, the last pretenses to narrative continuity were abandoned. Characters like Beckett's Lucky and Pozzo, in *Waiting for Godot*, stalked about in empty or ruinous landscapes. Their dialogues were unlike anything the Realist theater had ever ventured. Dark, disconnected, often humorous, they captured how it felt to live in a world no longer anchored to systems of meaning. Stage props were usually simple—an ashcan, a sandbox—and conventional actions were missing entirely. Instead, the audience might watch strange routines that looked more like mime or music hall bits. The best of these plays—Beckett's *Waiting for Godot*, Ionesco's *The Bald Soprano*, Albee's *The Sandbox*—prove that in the hands of the right dramatist even meaninglessness can be woven into a spell. Samuel Beckett's one-act play *Krapp's Last Tape*, which follows, shows something of the haunting power of the Absurdist mode.

Experimental Theater

During the late 1960s and early 1970s, the theater was given a radical, if short-lived, overhaul. Directors and dramatists realized the enormous potential that theater had for liberation and education. The stage was a microcosm of society, and since society appeared to be coming asunder, it was up to the playwright to bring illumination. This was a confused, turbulent, and intensely energized period. Actors stepped forth to interrogate members of the audience; manifestos were read. The traditional notion of spectators watching dramatic scenes unfold was exploded entirely.

Needless to say, the value of the theater experience lay more in its immediacy and its improvisatory possibilities than in the words on the page. In many instances of *Guerrilla Theater* (one of its designations), there were no words on the page. Ensembles of actors would simply take a premise, or a cue thrown out by the director, and trust to chance.

After so many twists and turns—some more extreme than others—most theater today has returned to the more familiar premises and procedures of Realism. But as we will see in the plays that follow, the old Realism of the nineteenth century has absorbed a whole set of new techniques and possibilities.

Samuel Beckett (1906–1989)

Samuel Beckett was born outside Dublin to an Irish Protestant family. He attended Trinity College in Dublin. After graduating in 1927, he moved to Paris, where he established a close friendship with James Joyce. After a brief return to Ireland, Beckett traveled in Europe and then settled permanently in Paris. In addition to stories, collected in *More Pricks than Kicks* (1934), and poems, Beckett published the novel *Murphy* (1938). When the war came, Beckett worked for the French resistance. He was forced to leave Paris during the German occupation, but after the war he returned and began to write the works that made his international reputation. These included mainly novels such as *Molloy* (1951), *Malone Dies* (1951), *Watt* (1953), and *The Unnameable* (1953); and plays, including *Waiting for Godot* (1952) and *Endgame* (1957).

KRAPP'S LAST TAPE

A Play in One Act

SCENE

A late evening in the future. Krapp's den. Front centre a small table, the two drawers of which open towards audience.

Sitting at the table, facing front, i.e. across from the drawers, a bearish old man: Krapp.

Rusty black narrow trousers too short for him. Rusty black sleeveless waistcoat,° four capacious pockets. Heavy silver watch and chain. Grimy white shirt open at neck, no collar. Surprising pair of dirty white boots, size ten at least, very narrow and pointed.

White face. Purple nose. Disordered grey hair. Unshaven.

Very near-sighted (but unspectacled). Hard of hearing.

Cracked voice. Distinctive intonation.

Laborious walk.

On the table a tape-recorder with microphone and a number of cardboard boxes containing reels of recorded tapes.

Tables and immediately adjacent area in strong white light. Rest of stage in darkness.

Krapp remains a moment motionless, heaves a great sigh, looks at his watch, fumbles in his pockets, takes out an envelope, puts it back, fumbles, takes out a small bunch of keys, raises it to his eyes, chooses a key, gets up and moves to front of table. He stoops, unlocks first drawer, peers into it, feels about inside it, takes out a reel of tape, peers at it, puts it back, locks drawer, unlocks second drawer, peers into it, feels about inside it, takes out a

---

waistcoat: vest.

large banana, peers at it, locks drawer, puts keys back in his pocket. He turns, advances to edge of stage, halts, strokes banana, peels it, drops skin at his feet, puts end of banana in his mouth and remains motionless, staring vacuously° before him. Finally he bites off the end, turns aside and begins pacing to and fro at edge of stage, in the light, i.e. not more than four or five paces either way, meditatively eating banana. He treads on skin, slips, nearly falls, recovers himself, stoops and peers at skin and finally pushes it, still stooping, with his foot over the edge of stage into pit. He resumes his pacing, finishes banana, returns to table, sits down, remains a moment motionless, heaves a great sigh, takes keys from his pockets, raises them to his eyes, chooses key, gets up and moves to front of table, unlocks second drawer, takes out a second large banana, peers at it, locks drawer, puts back keys in his pocket, turns, advances to edge of stage, halts, strokes banana, peels it, tosses skin into pit, puts end of banana in his mouth and remains motionless, staring vacuously before him. Finally he has an idea, puts banana in his waistcoat pocket, the end emerging, and goes with all the speed he can muster backstage into darkness. Ten seconds. Loud pop of cork. Fifteen seconds. He comes back into light carrying an old ledger and sits down at table. He lays ledger on table, wipes his mouth, wipes his hands on the front of his waistcoat, brings them smartly together and rubs them.

KRAPP. [briskly.] Ah! [He bends over ledger, turns the pages, finds the entry he wants, reads.] Box . . . thrree . . . spool . . . five. [He raises his head and stares front. With relish.] Spool! [Pause.] Spooool! [Happy smile. Pause. He bends over table, starts peering and poking at the boxes.] Box . . . thrree . . . thrree . . . four . . . two . . . [with surprise] nine! good God! . . . seven . . . ah! the little rascal! [He takes up box, peers at it.] Box thrree. [He lays it on table, opens it and peers at spools inside.] Spool . . . [he peers at ledger] . . . five . . . [he peers at spools] . . . five . . . five . . . ah! the little scoundrel! [He takes out a spool, peers at it.] Spool five. [He lays it on table, closes box three, puts it back with the others, takes up the spool.] Box thrree, spool five. [He bends over the machine, looks up. With relish.] Spooool! [Happy smile. He bends, loads spool on machine, rubs his hands.] Ah! [He peers at ledger, reads entry at foot of page.] Mother at rest at last . . . Hm . . . The black ball . . . [He raises his head, stares blankly front. Puzzled.] Black ball? . . . [He peers again at ledger, reads.] The dark nurse . . . [He raises his head, broods, peers again at ledger, reads.] Slight improvement in bowel condition . . . Hm . . . Memorable . . . what? [He peers closer.] Equinox,° memorable equinox. [He raises his head, stares blankly front. Puzzled.] Memorable equinox? . . . [Pause. He shrugs his shoulders, peers again at ledger, reads.] Farewell to—[he turns the page]—love.

He raises his head, broods, bends over machine, switches on and assumes listening posture, i.e. leaning forward, elbows on table, hand cupping ear towards machine, face front.

TAPE. [strong voice, rather pompous, clearly Krapp's at a much earlier time.] Thirty-nine today, sound as a—[Settling himself more comfortably he knocks one of the boxes off the table, curses, switches off, sweeps boxes and ledger violently to the ground, winds tape back to beginning, switches on, resumes posture.] Thirty-nine today, sound as a bell, apart from my old weakness, and intellectually I have now every reason to suspect at the . . . [hesitates] . . . crest of the wave—or thereabouts. Cele-

---

vacuously: emptily. Equinox: beginning of fall or spring, when day and night are approximately of equal length.

brated the awful occasion, as in recent years, quietly at the Winehouse. Not a soul. Sat before the fire with closed eyes, separating the grain from the husks. Jotted down a few notes, on the back of an envelope. Good to be back in my den, in my old rags. Have just eaten I regret to say three bananas and only with difficulty refrained from a fourth. Fatal things for a man with my condition. [*Vehemently.*] Cut 'em out! [*Pause.*] The new light above my table is a great improvement. With all this darkness round me I feel less alone. [*Pause.*] In a way. [*Pause.*] I love to get up and move about in it, then back here to . . . [*hesitates*] . . . me. [*Pause.*] Krapp.

Pause.

The grain, now what I wonder do I mean by that, I mean . . . [*hesitates*] . . . I suppose I mean those things worth having when all the dust has—when all *my* dust has settled. I close my eyes and try and imagine them.

Pause.
Krapp closes his eyes briefly.

Extraordinary silence this evening, I strain my ears and do not hear a sound. Old Miss McGlome always sings at this hour. But not tonight. Songs of her girlhood, she says. Hard to think of her as a girl. Wonderful woman though. Connaught, I fancy. [*Pause.*] Shall I sing when I am her age, if I ever am? No. [*Pause.*] Did I sing as a boy? No. [*Pause*] Did I ever sing? No.

Pause.

Just been listening to an old year, passages at random. I did not check in the book, but it must be at least ten or twelve years ago. At that time I think I was still living on and off with Bianca in Kedar Street. Well out of that, Jesus yes! Hopeless business. [*Pause.*] Not much about her, apart from a tribute to her eyes. Very warm. I suddenly saw them again. [*Pause.*] Incomparable! [*Pause.*] Ah well . . . [*Pause.*] These old P.M.s° are gruesome, but I often find them— [*Krapp switches off, broods, switches on*]—a help before embarking on a new . . . [*hesitates*] . . . retrospect. Hard to believe I was ever that young whelp.° The voice! Jesus! And the aspirations! [*Brief laugh in which Krapp joins.*] And the resolutions! [*Brief laugh in which Krapp joins.*] To drink less, in particular. [*Brief laugh of Krapp alone.*] Statistics. Seventeen hundred hours, out of the preceding eight thousand odd, consumed on licensed premises° alone. More than 20%, say 40% of his waking life. [*Pause.*] Plans for a less . . . [*hesitates*] . . . engrossing sexual life. Last illness of his father. Flagging pursuit of happiness. Unattainable laxation.° Sneers at what he calls his youth and thanks to God that it's over. [*Pause.*] False ring there. [*Pause.*] Shadows of the opus . . . magnum.° Closing with a—[*brief laugh*]—yelp to Providence.° [*Prolonged laugh in which Krapp joins.*] What remains of all that misery? A girl in a shabby green coat, on a railway-station platform? No?

Pause.

When I look—

P.M.: [abbr.] post mortem; examination of the past.   *whelp:* young animal offspring.   *licensed premises:* taverns, pubs.   *laxation:* bowel movement.   *opus . . . magnum:* a "great work."   *Providence:* fate.

Krapp switches off, broods, looks at his watch, gets up, goes backstage into darkness. Ten seconds. Pop of cork. Ten seconds. Second cork. Ten seconds. Third cork. Ten seconds. Brief burst of quavering song.

KRAPP. [*sings*]. Now the day is over,
Night is drawing nigh-igh,
Shadows—°

Fit of coughing. He comes back into light, sits down, wipes his mouth, switches on, resumes his listening posture.

TAPE. —back on the year that is gone, with what I hope is perhaps a glint of the old eye to come, there is of course the house on the canal where mother lay a-dying, in the late autumn, after her long viduity° [*Krapp gives a start*], and the— [*Krapp switches off, winds back tape a little, bends his ear closer to machine, switches on*]—a-dying, after her long viduity, and the—

Krapp switches off, raises his head, stares blankly before him. His lips move in the syllables of "viduity." No sound. He gets up, goes backstage into darkness, comes back with an enormous dictionary, lays it on table, sits down and looks up the word.

KRAPP. [*reading from dictionary.*] State—or condition of being—or remaining—a widow—or widower. [*Looks up. Puzzled.*] Being—or remaining?... [*Pause. He peers again at dictionary. Reading.*] "Deep weeds of viduity" ... Also of an animal, especially a bird ... the vidua or weaver-bird ... Black plumage of male ... [*He looks up. With relish.*] The vidua-bird!

Pause. He closes dictionary, switches on, resumes listening posture.

TAPE. —bench by the weir from where I could see her window. There I sat, in the biting wind, wishing she were gone. [*Pause.*] Hardly a soul, just a few regulars, nursemaids, infants, old men, dogs. I got to know them quite well—oh by appearance of course I mean! One dark young beauty I recollect particularly, all white and starch, incomparable bosom, with a big black hooded perambulator, most funereal thing. Whenever I looked in her direction she had her eyes on me. And yet when I was bold enough to speak to her—not having been introduced—she threatened to call a policeman. As if I had designs on her virtue! [*Laugh. Pause.*] The face she had! The eyes! Like ... [*hesitates*] ... chrysolite!° [*Pause.*] Ah well ... [*Pause.*] I was there when—[*Krapp switches off, broods, switches on again*]—the blind went down, one of those dirty brown roller affairs, throwing a ball for a little white dog, as chance would have it. I happened to look up and there it was. All over and done with, at last. I sat on for a few moments with the ball in my hand and the dog yelping and pawing at me. [*Pause.*] Moments. Her moments, my moments. [*Pause.*] The dog's moments. [*Pause.*] In the end I held it out to him and he took it in his mouth, gently, gently. A small, old, black, hard, solid rubber ball. [*Pause.*] I might have kept it. [*Pause.*] But I gave it to the dog.

Pause.

---

now the day . . . Shadows . . . : lines from an old hymn.   *viduity:* widowhood.   *chrysolite:* a gold-colored stone.

Ah well . . .

Pause.

Spiritually a year of profound gloom and indigence until that memorable night in March, at the end of the jetty, in the howling wind, never to be forgotten, when suddenly I saw the whole thing. The vision, at last. This I fancy is what I have chiefly to record this evening, against the day when my work will be done and perhaps no place left in my memory, warm or cold, for the miracle that . . . [*hesitates*] . . . for the fire that set it alight. What I suddenly saw then was this, that the belief I had been going on all my life, namely—[*Krapp switches off impatiently, winds tape forward, switches on again*]—great granite rocks the foam flying up in the light of the lighthouse and the wind-gauge spinning like a propellor, clear to me at last that the dark I have always struggled to keep under is in reality my most—[*Krapp curses, switches off, winds tape forward, switches on again*]—unshatterable association until my dissolution of storm and night with the light of the understanding and the fire—[*Krapp curses louder, switches off, winds tape forward, switches on again*]—my face in her breasts and my hand on her. We lay there without moving. But under us all moved, and moved us, gently, up and down, and from side to side.

Pause.

Past midnight. Never knew such silence. The earth might be uninhabited.

Pause.

Here I end—

Krapp switches off, winds tape back, switches on again.

—upper lake, with the punt, bathed off the bank, then pushed out into the stream and drifted. She lay stretched out on the floorboards with her hands under her head and her eyes closed. Sun blazing down, bit of a breeze, water nice and lively. I noticed a scratch on her thigh and asked her how she came by it. Picking gooseberries, she said. I said again I thought it was hopeless and no good going on, and she agreed, without opening her eyes. [*Pause.*] I asked her to look at me and after a few moments—[*pause*]—after a few moments she did, but the eyes just slits, because of the glare. I bent over her to get them in the shadow and they opened. [*Pause. Low.*] Let me in. [*Pause.*] We drifted in among the flags and stuck. The way they went down, sighing, before the stem! [*Pause.*] I lay down across her with my face in her breasts and my hand on her. We lay there without moving. But under us all moved, and moved us, gently, up and down, and from side to side.

Pause.

Past midnight. Never knew—

Krapp switches off, broods. Finally he fumbles in his pockets, encounters the banana, takes it out, peers at it, puts it back, fumbles, brings out the envelope, fumbles, puts back envelope, looks at his watch, gets up and goes backstage into darkness. Ten seconds. Sound of bottle against glass, then brief siphon. Ten seconds. Bottle against glass alone. Ten seconds. He comes back a little unsteadily into light, goes to front table, takes out keys, raises them to his eyes, chooses key, unlocks first drawer, peers into it, feels about inside, takes out reel, peers at it, locks drawer, puts keys back in his pocket, goes and sits down, takes reel off machine, lays it on dictionary, loads virgin reel on machine, takes envelope from his pocket, consults back of it, lays it on table, switches on, clears his throat and begins to record.

KRAPP. Just been listening to that stupid bastard I took myself for thirty years ago, hard to believe I was ever as bad as that. Thank God that's all done with anyway. [*Pause.*] The eyes she had! [*Broods, realizes he is recording silence, switches off, broods. Finally.*] Everything there, everything, all the—[*Realizes this is not being recorded, switches on.*] Everything there, everything on this old muckball, all the light and dark and famine and feasting of . . . [*hesitates*] . . . the ages! [*In a shout.*] Yes! [*Pause.*] Let that go! Jesus! Take his mind off his homework! Jesus! [*Pause. Weary.*] Ah well, maybe he was right. [*Pause.*] Maybe he was right. [*Broods. Realizes. Switches off. Consults envelope.*] Pah! [*Crumples it and throws it away. Broods. Switches on.*] Nothing to say, not a squeak. What's a year now? The sour cud° and the iron stool.° [*Pause.*] Revelled in the word spool. [*With relish.*] Spooool! Happiest moment of the past half million. [*Pause.*] Seventeen copies sold, of which eleven at trade price to free circulating libraries beyond the seas. Getting known. [*Pause.*] One pound six and something, eight I have little doubt. [*Pause.*] Crawled out once or twice, before the summer was cold. Sat shivering in the park, drowned in dreams and burning to be gone. Not a soul. [*Pause.*] Last fancies. [*Vehemently.*] Keep 'em under! [*Pause.*] Scalded the eyes out of me reading *Effie* again, a page a day, with tears again. Effie . . . [*Pause.*] Could have been happy with her, up there on the Baltic, and the pines, and the dunes. [*Pause.*] Could I? [*Pause.*] And she? [*Pause.*] Pah! [*Pause.*] Fanny came in a couple of times. Bony old ghost of a whore. Couldn't do much, but I suppose better than a kick in the crutch. The last time wasn't so bad. How do you manage it, she said, at your age? I told her I'd been saving up for her all my life. [*Pause.*] Went to Vespers° once, like when I was in short trousers. [*Pause. Sings.*]

> Now the day is over,
> Night is drawing nigh-igh,
> Shadows—[*coughing, then almost inaudible*]—of the evening
> Steal across the sky.

[*Gasping.*] Went to sleep and fell off the pew. [*Pause.*] Sometimes wondered in the night if a last effort mightn't— [*Pause.*] Ah finish your booze now and get to your bed. Go on with this drivel in the morning. Or leave it at that. [*Pause.*] Leave it at that. [*Pause.*] Lie propped up in the dark—and wander. Be again in the dingle° on a Christmas Eve, gathering holly, the red-berried. [*Pause.*] Be again on Croghan on a Sunday morning, in the haze, with the bitch, stop and listen to the bells. [*Pause.*] And so on. [*Pause.*] Be again, be again. [*Pause.*] All that old misery. [*Pause.*] Once wasn't enough for you. [*Pause.*] Lie down across her.

---

cud: something held in the mouth and chewed. *iron stool:* toilet or bowel movement. *Vespers:* evening prayer service. *dingle:* small wooded valley.

Long pause. He suddenly bends over machine, switches off, wrenches off tape, throws it away, puts on the other, winds it forward to the passage he wants, switches on, listens staring front.

TAPE. —gooseberries, she said. I said again I thought it was hopeless and no good going on, and she agreed, without opening her eyes. [*Pause.*] I asked her to look at me and after a few moments—[*pause*]—after a few moments she did, but the eyes just slits, because of the glare. I bent over her to get them in the shadow and they opened. [*Pause. Low.*] Let me in. [*Pause.*] I lay down across her with my face in her breasts and my hand on her. We lay there without moving. But under us all moved, and moved us, gently, up and down, and from side to side.

Pause.
Krapp's lips move. No sound.

Past midnight. Never knew such silence. The earth might be uninhabited.

Pause.

Here I end this reel. Box—[*pause*]—three, spool— [*pause*]—five. [*Pause.*] Perhaps my best years are gone. When there was a chance of happiness. But I wouldn't want them back. Not with the fire in me now. No, I wouldn't want them back.

Krapp motionless staring before him. The tape runs on in silence.

CURTAIN

[1958]

QUESTIONS

1. Critics often speak of Beckett's work as darkly comic. Can you find any justification for such a description in *Krapp's Last Tape*?

2. What is the narrative that emerges when Krapp listens to the tape from his thirty-ninth year? What are the central events or situations and how do you guess they have affected the man over the years?

3. Would the play be different if Krapp were allowed to simply speak his memories? How so? What is the effect of the tape recorder and the fumbling stops and starts it requires?

4. Do you sense that Krapp was once a very different person? What do his facial expressions and interjected comments tell you about his relation to his own younger self?

5. Locate the most lyrical moment in the play. What does it suggest about Krapp's past? To what extent is his depressed condition connected to the outcome of that relationship?

6. What does Krapp mean by his reference to "separating the grain from the husks"?

7. What do you learn about Krapp's profession, or art? What has become of his ambitions?

8. How does the song Krapp sings relate to the play? What do the quoted lyrics tell you about his state of mind?

9. Why would Beckett choose to set the play in the future?

10. What is your response to Krapp's last words? Do you believe him when he states that he does not want the past back—or is he simply venting his present bitterness?

11. What elements of absurdity do you find in the stage action? In the taped voice? What picture of reality does Beckett leave the reader with?

Arthur Miller (1915–)

Arthur Miller was born in New York City. He attended the University of Michigan, where he first began to write plays. *All My Sons* (1947) was his first success, winning the New York Drama Critics' Circle Award. Two years later, he wrote *Death of a Salesman,* which has taken its place as one of the classics of the American stage. Miller's other plays include *The Crucible* (1953), *A View From the Bridge* (1955), and *After the Fall* (1955). He also wrote the screenplay for the film *The Misfits,* which starred Marilyn Monroe, to whom Miller was married for a time.

DEATH OF A SALESMAN

SCENE
The action takes place in Willy Loman's house and yard and in various places he visits in the New York and Boston of today.

Throughout the play, in the stage directions, left and right mean stage left and stage right.

ACT ONE
A melody is heard, played upon a flute. It is small and fine, telling of grass and trees and the horizon. The curtain rises.

Before us is the Salesman's house. We are aware of towering, angular shapes behind it, surrounding it on all sides. Only the blue light of the sky falls upon the house and forestage; the surrounding area shows an angry glow of orange. As more light appears, we see a solid vault of apartment houses around the small, fragile-seeming home. An air of the dream clings to the place, a dream rising out of reality. The kitchen at center seems actual enough, for there is a kitchen table with three chairs, and a refrigerator. But no other fixtures are seen. At the back of the kitchen there is a draped entrance, which leads to the living-room. To the right of the kitchen, on a level raised two feet, is a bedroom furnished only with a brass bedstead and a straight chair. On a shelf over the bed a silver athletic trophy stands. A window opens onto the apartment house at the side.

Behind the kitchen, on a level raised six and a half feet, is the boys' bedroom, at present barely visible. Two beds are dimly seen, and at the back of the room a dormer window. (This bedroom is above the unseen living-room.) At the left a stairway curves up to it from the kitchen.

The entire setting is wholly, or, in some places, partially transparent. The roof-line of the house is one-dimensional; under and over it we see the apartment buildings. Before the house lies an apron, curving beyond the forestage into the orchestra. This forward area serves as the back yard as well as the locale of all Willy's imaginings and of his city scenes. Whenever the action is in the present the actors observe the imaginary wall-lines, entering the house only through its door at the left. But in the scenes of the past these boundaries are broken, and characters enter or leave a room by stepping "through" a wall onto the forestage.

From the right, Willy Loman, the Salesman, enters, carrying two large sample cases. The flute plays on. He hears but is not aware of it. He is past sixty years of age, dressed quietly. Even as he crosses the stage to the doorway of the house, his exhaustion is apparent. He unlocks the door, comes into the kitchen, and thankfully lets his burden down, feeling the soreness of his palms. A word-sigh escapes his lips—it might be "Oh, boy, oh, boy." He closes the door, then carries his cases out into the living-room, through the draped kitchen doorway.

Linda, his wife, has stirred in her bed at the right. She gets out and puts on a robe, listening. Most often jovial, she has developed an iron repression of her exceptions to Willy's behavior—she more than loves him, she admires him, as though his mercurial° nature, his temper, his massive dreams and little cruelties, served her only as sharp reminders of the turbulent longings within him, longings which she shares but lacks the temperament to utter and follow to their end.

LINDA. [*hearing Willy outside the bedroom, calls with some trepidation*] Willy!
WILLY. It's all right. I came back.
LINDA. Why? What happened? [*Slight pause.*] Did something happen, Willy?
WILLY. No, nothing happened.
LINDA. You didn't smash the car, did you?
WILLY. [*with casual irritation*] I said nothing happened. Didn't you hear me?
LINDA. Don't you feel well?
WILLY. I'm tired to the death. [*The flute has faded away. He sits on the bed beside her, a little numb.*] I couldn't make it. I just couldn't make it, Linda.
LINDA. [*very carefully, delicately*] Where were you all day? You look terrible.
WILLY. I got as far as a little above Yonkers.° I stopped for a cup of coffee. Maybe it was the coffee.
LINDA. What?
WILLY. [*after a pause*] I suddenly couldn't drive any more. The car kept going off onto the shoulder, y'know?
LINDA. [*helpfully*] Oh. Maybe it was the steering again. I don't think Angelo knows the Studebaker.
WILLY. No, it's me, it's me. Suddenly I realize I'm goin' sixty miles an hour and I don't remember the last five minutes. I'm—I can't seem to—keep my mind to it.
LINDA. Maybe it's your glasses. You never went for your new glasses.
WILLY. No, I see everything. I came back ten miles an hour. It took me nearly four hours from Yonkers.
LINDA. [*resigned*] Well, you'll just have to take a rest, Willy, you can't continue this way.
WILLY. I just got back from Florida.
LINDA. But you didn't rest your mind. Your mind is over-active, and the mind is what counts, dear.
WILLY. I'll start out in the morning. Maybe I'll feel better in the morning. [*She is taking off his shoes.*] These goddam arch supports are killing me.
LINDA. Take an aspirin. Should I get you an aspirin? It'll soothe you.

---

mercurial: quickly changing.   *Yonkers:* city just north of New York City.

WILLY. [with wonder] I was driving along, you understand? And I was fine. I was even observing the scenery. You can imagine, me looking at scenery, on the road every week of my life. But it's so beautiful up there, Linda, the trees are so thick, and the sun is warm. I opened the windshield and just let the warm air bathe over me. And then all of a sudden I'm going' off the road! I'm tellin' ya, I absolutely forgot I was driving. If I'd've gone the other way over the white line I might've killed somebody. So I went on again—and five minutes later I'm dreamin' again, and I nearly—[He presses two fingers against his eyes.] I have such thoughts, I have such strange thoughts.

LINDA. Willy, dear. Talk to them again. There's no reason why you can't work in New York.

WILLY. They don't need me in New York. I'm the New England man. I'm vital in New England.

LINDA. But you're sixty years old. They can't expect you to keep traveling every week.

WILLY. I'll have to send a wire to Portland.° I'm supposed to see Brown and Morrison tomorrow morning at ten o'clock to show the line. Goddammit, I could sell them! [He starts putting on his jacket.]

LINDA. [taking the jacket from him] Why don't you go down to the place tomorrow and tell Howard you've simply got to work in New York? You're too accommodating, dear.

WILLY. If old man Wagner was alive I'd a been in charge of New York now! That man was a prince, he was a masterful man. But that boy of his, that Howard, he don't appreciate. When I went north the first time, the Wagner Company didn't know where New England was!

LINDA. Why don't you tell those things to Howard, dear?

WILLY. [encouraged] I will, I definitely will. Is there any cheese?

LINDA. I'll make you a sandwich.

WILLY. No, go to sleep. I'll take some milk. I'll be up right away. The boys in?

LINDA. They're sleeping. Happy took Biff on a date tonight.

WILLY. [interested] That so?

LINDA. It was so nice to see them shaving together, one behind the other, in the bathroom. And going out together. You notice? The whole house smells of shaving lotion.

WILLY. Figure it out. Work a lifetime to pay off a house. You finally own it, and there's nobody to live in it.

LINDA. Well, dear, life is a casting off. It's always that way.

WILLY. No, no, some people—some people accomplish something. Did Biff say anything after I went this morning?

LINDA. You shouldn't have criticized him, Willy, especially after he just got off the train. You mustn't lose your temper with him.

WILLY. When the hell did I lose my temper? I simply asked him if he was making any money. Is that a criticism?

LINDA. But, dear, how could he make any money?

WILLY. [worried and angered] There's such an undercurrent in him. He became a moody man. Did he apologize when I left this morning?

LINDA. He was crestfallen, Willy. You know how he admires you. I think if he finds himself, then you'll both be happier and not fight any more.

Portland: city in southern Maine.

WILLY. How can he find himself on a farm? Is that a life? A farmhand? In the beginning, when he was young, I thought, well, a young man, it's good for him to tramp around, take a lot of different jobs. But it's more than ten years now and he has yet to make thirty-five dollars a week!

LINDA. He's finding himself, Willy.

WILLY. Not finding yourself at the age of thirty-four is a disgrace!

LINDA. Shh!

WILLY. The trouble is he's lazy, goddammit!

LINDA. Willy, please!

WILLY. Biff is a lazy bum!

LINDA. They're sleeping. Get something to eat. Go on down.

WILLY. Why did he come home? I would like to know what brought him home.

LINDA. I don't know. I think he's still lost, Willy. I think he's very lost.

WILLY. Biff Loman is lost. In the greatest country in the world a young man with such—personal attractiveness, gets lost. And such a hard worker. There's one thing about Biff—he's not lazy.

LINDA. Never.

WILLY. [with pity and resolve] I'll see him in the morning; I'll have a nice talk with him. I'll get him a job selling. He could be big in no time. My God! Remember how they used to follow him around in high school? When he smiled at one of them their faces lit up. When he walked down the street . . . [He loses himself in reminiscences.]

LINDA. [trying to bring him out of it] Willy, dear, I got a new kind of American-type cheese today. It's whipped.

WILLY. Why do you get American when I like Swiss?

LINDA. I just thought you'd like a change—

WILLY. I don't want a change! I want Swiss cheese. Why am I always being contradicted?

LINDA. [with a covering laugh] I thought it would be a surprise.

WILLY. Why don't you open a window in here, for God's sake?

LINDA. [with infinite patience] They're all open, dear.

WILLY. The way they boxed us in here. Bricks and windows, windows and bricks.

LINDA. We should've bought the land next door.

WILLY. The street is lined with cars. There's not a breath of fresh air in the neighborhood. The grass don't grow any more, you can't raise a carrot in the back yard. They should've had a law against apartment houses. Remember those two beautiful elm trees out there? When I and Biff hung the swing between them?

LINDA. Yeah, like being a million miles from the city.

WILLY. They should've arrested the builder for cutting those down. They massacred the neighborhood. [Lost] More and more I think of those days, Linda. This time of year it was lilac and wisteria. And then the peonies would come out, and the daffodils. What fragrance in this room!

LINDA. Well, after all, people had to move somewhere.

WILLY. No, there's more people now.

LINDA. I don't think there's more people. I think—

WILLY. There's more people! That's what's ruining this country! Population is getting out of control. The competition is maddening! Smell the stink from that apartment house! And another one on the other side . . . How can they whip cheese?

On Willy's last line, Biff and Happy raise themselves up in their beds, listening.

LINDA. Go down, try it. And be quiet.

WILLY. [*turning to Linda, guiltily*] You're not worried about me, are you, sweetheart?

BIFF. What's the matter?

HAPPY. Listen!

LINDA. You've got too much on the ball to worry about.

WILLY. You're my foundation and my support, Linda.

LINDA. Just try to relax, dear. You make mountains out of molehills.

WILLY. I won't fight with him any more. If he wants to go back to Texas, let him go.

LINDA. He'll find his way.

WILLY. Sure. Certain men just don't get started till later in life. Like Thomas Edison,° I think. Or B. F. Goodrich.° One of them was deaf. [*He starts for the bedroom doorway.*] I'll put my money on Biff.

LINDA. And Willy—if it's warm Sunday we'll drive in the country. And we'll open the windshield, and take lunch.

WILLY. No, the windshields don't open on the new cars.

LINDA. But you opened it today.

WILLY. Me? I didn't. [*He stops.*] Now isn't that peculiar! Isn't that a remarkable— [*He breaks off in amazement and fright as the flute is heard distantly.*]

LINDA. What, darling?

WILLY. That is the most remarkable thing.

LINDA. What, dear?

WILLY. I was thinking of the Chevvy. [*Slight pause.*] Nineteen twenty-eight . . . when I had that red Chevvy— [*Breaks off.*] That funny? I coulda sworn I was driving that Chevvy today.

LINDA. Well, that's nothing. Something must've reminded you.

WILLY. Remarkable. Ts. Remember those days? The way Biff used to simonize° that car? The dealer refused to believe there was eighty thousand miles on it. [*He shakes his head.*] Heh! [*To Linda*] Close your eyes, I'll be right up. [*He walks out of the bedroom.*]

HAPPY. [*to Biff*] Jesus, maybe he smashed up the car again!

LINDA. [*calling after Willy*] Be careful on the stairs, dear! The cheese is on the middle shelf! [*She turns, goes over to the bed, takes his jacket, and goes out of the bedroom.*]

> Light has risen on the boys' room. Unseen, Willy is heard talking to himself, "Eighty thousand miles," and a little laugh. Biff gets out of bed, comes downstage a bit, and stands attentively. Biff is two years older than his brother Happy, well built, but in these days bears a worn air and seems less self-assured. He has succeeded less, and his dreams are stronger and less acceptable than Happy's. Happy is tall, powerfully made. Sexuality is like a visible color on him, or a scent that many women have discovered. He, like his brother, is lost, but in a different way, for he has never allowed himself to turn his face toward defeat and is thus more confused and hard-skinned, although seemingly more content.

HAPPY. [*getting out of bed*] He's going to get his license taken away if he keeps that up. I'm getting nervous about him, y'know, Biff?

BIFF. His eyes are going.

Thomas Edison; B. F. Goodrich: American inventors and businessmen.   *simonizing:* wax polishing.

HAPPY. No, I've driven with him. He sees all right. He just doesn't keep his mind on it. I drove into the city with him last week. He stops at a green light and then it turns red and he goes. [He laughs.]

BIFF. Maybe he's color-blind.

HAPPY. Pop? Why he's got the finest eye for color in the business. You know that.

BIFF. [sitting down on his bed] I'm going to sleep.

HAPPY. You're not still sour on Dad, are you, Biff?

BIFF. He's all right, I guess.

WILLY. [underneath them, in the living-room] Yes, sir, eighty thousand miles—eighty-two thousand!

BIFF. You smoking?

HAPPY. [holding out a pack of cigarettes] Want one?

BIFF. [taking a cigarette] I can never sleep when I smell it.

WILLY. What a simonizing job, heh!

HAPPY. [with deep sentiment] Funny, Biff, y'know? Us sleeping in here again? The old beds. [He pats his bed affectionately.] All the talk that went across those two beds, huh? Our whole lives.

BIFF. Yeah. Lotta dreams and plans.

HAPPY. [with a deep and masculine laugh] About five hundred women would like to know what was said in this room.

They share a soft laugh.

BIFF. Remember that big Betsy something—what the hell was her name—over on Bushwick Avenue?

HAPPY. [combing his hair] With the collie dog!

BIFF. That's the one. I got you in there, remember?

HAPPY. Yeah, that was my first time—I think. Boy, there was a pig! [They laugh, almost crudely.] You taught me everything I know about women. Don't forget that.

BIFF. I bet you forgot how bashful you used to be. Especially with girls.

HAPPY. Oh, I still am, Biff.

BIFF. Oh, go on.

HAPPY. I just control it, that's all. I think I got less bashful and you got more so. What happened, Biff? Where's the old humor, the old confidence? [He shakes Biff's knee. Biff gets up and moves restlessly about the room.] What's the matter?

BIFF. Why does Dad mock me all the time?

HAPPY. He's not mocking you, he—

BIFF. Everything I say there's a twist of mockery on his face. I can't get near him.

HAPPY. He just wants you to make good, that's all. I wanted to talk to you about Dad for a long time, Biff. Something's—happening to him. He—talks to himself.

BIFF. I noticed that this morning. But he always mumbled.

HAPPY. But not so noticeable. It got so embarrassing I sent him to Florida. And you know something? Most of the time he's talking to you.

BIFF. What's he say about me?

HAPPY. I can't make it out.

BIFF. What's he say about me?

HAPPY. I think the fact that you're not settled, that you're still kind of up in the air . . .

BIFF. There's one or two other things depressing him, Happy.

HAPPY. What do you mean?

BIFF. Never mind. Just don't lay it all to me.

HAPPY. But I think if you just got started—I mean—is there any future for you out there?

BIFF. I tell ya, Hap, I don't know what the future is. I don't know—what I'm supposed to want.

HAPPY. What do you mean?

BIFF. Well, I spent six or seven years after high school trying to work myself up. Shipping clerk, salesman, business of one kind or another. And it's a measly manner of existence. To get on that subway on the hot mornings in summer. To devote your whole life to keeping stock, or making phone calls, or selling or buying. To suffer fifty weeks of the year for the sake of a two-week vacation, when all you really desire is to be outdoors, with your shirt off. And always to have to get ahead of the next fella. And still—that's how you build a future.

HAPPY. Well, you really enjoy it on a farm? Are you content out there?

BIFF. [with rising agitation] Hap, I've had twenty or thirty different kinds of jobs since I left home before the war, and it always turns out the same. I just realized it lately. In Nebraska when I herded cattle, and the Dakotas, and Arizona, and now in Texas. It's why I came home now, I guess, because I realized it. This farm I work on, it's spring there now, see? And they've got about fifteen new colts. There's nothing more inspiring or—beautiful than the sight of a mare and a new colt. And it's cool there now, see? Texas is cool now, and it's spring. And whenever spring comes to where I am, I suddenly get the feeling, my God, I'm not gettin' anywhere! What the hell am I doing, playing around with horses, twenty-eight dollars a week! I'm thirty-four years old, I oughta be makin' my future. That's when I come running home. And now, I get here, and I don't know what to do with myself. [After a pause] I've always made a point of not wasting my life, and everytime I come back here I know that all I've done is to waste my life.

HAPPY. You're a poet, you know that, Biff? You're a—you're an idealist!

BIFF. No, I'm mixed up very bad. Maybe I oughta get married. Maybe I oughta get stuck into something. Maybe that's my trouble. I'm like a boy. I'm not married, I'm not in business, I just—I'm like a boy. Are you content, Hap? You're a success, aren't you? Are you content?

HAPPY. Hell, no!

BIFF. Why? You're making money, aren't you?

HAPPY. [moving about with energy, expressiveness] All I can do now is wait for the merchandise manager to die. And suppose I get to be merchandise manager? He's a good friend of mine, and he just built a terrific estate on Long Island. And he lived there about two months and sold it, and now he's building another one. He can't enjoy it once it's finished. And I know that's just what I would do. I don't know what the hell I'm workin' for. Sometimes I sit in my apartment—all alone. And I think of the rent I'm paying. And it's crazy. But then, it's what I always wanted. My own apartment, a car, and plenty of women. And still, goddammit, I'm lonely.

BIFF. [with enthusiasm] Listen, why don't you come out West with me?

HAPPY. You and I, heh?

BIFF. Sure, maybe we could buy a ranch. Raise cattle, use our muscles. Men built like we are should be working out in the open.

HAPPY. [avidly] The Loman Brothers, heh?

BIFF. [with vast affection] Sure, we'd be known all over the counties!

HAPPY. [enthralled] That's what I dream about, Biff. Sometimes I want to just rip my clothes off in the middle of the store and outbox that goddam merchandise manager. I mean I can outbox, outrun, and outlift anybody in that store, and I have to take orders from those common, petty sons-of-bitches till I can't stand it any more.

BIFF. I'm tellin' you, kid, if you were with me I'd be happy out there.

HAPPY. [enthused] See, Biff, everybody around me is so false that I'm constantly lowering my ideals . . .

BIFF. Baby, together we'd stand up for one another, we'd have someone to trust.

HAPPY. If I were around you—

BIFF. Hap, the trouble is we weren't brought up to grub for money. I don't know how to do it.

HAPPY. Neither can I!

BIFF. Then let's go!

HAPPY. The only thing is—what can you make out there?

BIFF. But look at your friend. Builds an estate and then hasn't the peace of mind to live in it.

HAPPY. Yeah, but when he walks into the store the waves part in front of him. That's fifty-two thousand dollars a year coming through the revolving door, and I got more in my pinky finger than he's got in his head.

BIFF. Yeah, but you just said—

HAPPY. I gotta show some of those pompous, self-important executives over there that Hap Loman can make the grade. I want to walk into the store the way he walks in. Then I'll go with you, Biff. We'll be together yet, I swear. But take those two we had tonight. Now weren't they gorgeous creatures?

BIFF. Yeah, yeah, most gorgeous I've had in years.

HAPPY. I get that any time I want, Biff. Whenever I feel disgusted. The only trouble is, it gets like bowling or something. I just keep knockin' them over and it doesn't mean anything. You still run around a lot?

BIFF. Naa. I'd like to find a girl—steady, somebody with substance.

HAPPY. That's what I long for.

BIFF. Go on! You'd never come home.

HAPPY. I would! Somebody with character, with resistance! Like Mom, y'know? You're gonna call me a bastard when I tell you this. That girl Charlotte I was with tonight is engaged to be married in five weeks. [He tries on his new hat.]

BIFF. No kiddin'!

HAPPY. Sure, the guy's in line for the vice-presidency of the store. I don't know what gets into me, maybe I just have an overdeveloped sense of competition or something, but I went and ruined her, and furthermore I can't get rid of her. And he's the third executive I've done that to. Isn't that a crummy characteristic? And to top it all, I go to their weddings! [Indignantly, but laughing] Like I'm not supposed to take bribes. Manufacturers offer me a hundred-dollar bill now and then to throw an order their way. You know how honest I am, but it's like this girl, see. I hate myself for it. Because I don't want the girl, and, still, I take it and—I love it!

BIFF. Let's go to sleep.

HAPPY. I guess we didn't settle anything, heh?

BIFF. I just got one idea that I think I'm going to try.

HAPPY. What's that?

BIFF. Remember Bill Oliver?

HAPPY. Sure, Oliver is very big now. You want to work for him again?

BIFF. No, but when I quit he said something to me. He put his arm on my shoulder, and he said, "Biff, if you ever need anything, come to me."

HAPPY. I remember that. That sounds good.

BIFF. I think I'll go to see him. If I could get ten thousand or even seven or eight thousand dollars I could buy a beautiful ranch.

HAPPY. I bet he'd back you. 'Cause he thought highly of you, Biff. I mean, they all do. You're well liked, Biff. That's why I say to come back here, and we both have the apartment. And I'm tellin' you, Biff, any babe you want . . .

BIFF. No, with a ranch I could do the work I like and still be something. I just wonder though. I wonder if Oliver still thinks I stole that carton of basketballs.

HAPPY. Oh, he probably forgot that long ago. It's almost ten years. You're too sensitive. Anyway, he didn't really fire you.

BIFF. Well, I think he was going to. I think that's why I quit. I was never sure whether he knew or not. I know he thought the world of me, though. I was the only one he'd let lock up the place.

WILLY. [below] You gonna wash the engine, Biff?

HAPPY. Shh!

Biff looks at Happy, who is gazing down, listening. Willy is mumbling in the parlor.

HAPPY. You hear that?

They listen. Willy laughs warmly.

BIFF. [growing angry] Doesn't he know Mom can hear that?

WILLY. Don't get your sweater dirty, Biff!

A look of pain crosses Biff's face.

HAPPY. Isn't that terrible? Don't leave again, will you? You'll find a job here. You gotta stick around. I don't know what to do about him, it's getting embarrassing.

WILLY. What a simonizing job!

BIFF. Mom's hearing that!

WILLY. No kiddin', Biff, you got a date? Wonderful!

HAPPY. Go on to sleep. But talk to him in the morning, will you?

BIFF. [reluctantly getting into bed] With her in the house. Brother!

HAPPY. [getting into bed] I wish you'd have a good talk with him.

The light on their room begins to fade.

BIFF. [to himself in bed] That selfish, stupid . . .

HAPPY. Sh . . . Sleep, Biff.

Their light is out. Well before they have finished speaking, Willy's form is dimly seen below in the darkened kitchen. He opens the refrigerator, searches in there, and takes out a bottle of milk. The apartment houses are fading out, and the entire house and surroundings become covered with leaves. Music insinuates itself as the leaves appear.

WILLY. Just wanna be careful with those girls, Biff, that's all. Don't make any promises. No promises of any kind. Because a girl, y'know, they always believe what you tell 'em, and you're very young, Biff, you're too young to be talking seriously to girls.

Light rises on the kitchen. Willy, talking, shuts the refrigerator door and comes downstage to the kitchen table. He pours milk into a glass. He is totally immersed in himself, smiling faintly.

WILLY. Too young entirely, Biff. You want to watch your schooling first. Then when you're all set, there'll be plenty of girls for a boy like you. [*He smiles broadly at a kitchen chair.*] That so? The girls pay for you? [*He laughs.*] Boy, you must really be makin' a hit.

Willy is gradually addressing—physically—a point offstage, speaking through the wall of the kitchen, and his voice has been rising in volume to that of a normal conversation.

WILLY. I been wondering why you polish the car so careful. Ha! Don't leave the hubcaps, boys. Get the chamois to the hubcaps. Happy, use newspaper on the windows, it's the easiest thing. Show him how to do it, Biff! You see, Happy? Pad it up, use it like a pad. That's it, that's it, good work. You're doin' all right, Hap. [*He pauses, then nods in approbation for a few seconds, then looks upward.*] Biff, first thing we gotta do when we get time is clip that big branch over the house. Afraid it's gonna fall in a storm and hit the roof. Tell you what. We get a rope and sling her around, and then we climb up there with a couple of saws and take her down. Soon as you finish the car, boys, I wanna see ya. I got a surprise for you, boys.

BIFF. [*offstage*] Whatta ya got, Dad?

WILLY. No, you finish first. Never leave a job till you're finished—remember that. [*Looking toward the "big trees"*] Biff, up in Albany I saw a beautiful hammock. I think I'll buy it next trip, and we'll hang it right between those two elms. Wouldn't that be something? Just swingin' there under those branches. Boy, that would be . . .

Young Biff and Young Happy appear from the direction Willy was addressing. Happy carries rags and a pail of water. Biff, wearing a sweater with a block "S," carries a football.

BIFF. [*pointing in the direction of the car offstage*] How's that, Pop, professional?

WILLY. Terrific. Terrific job, boys. Good work, Biff.

HAPPY. Where's the surprise, Pop?

WILLY. In the back seat of the car.

HAPPY. Boy! [*He runs off.*]

BIFF. What is it, Dad? Tell me, what'd you buy?

WILLY. [*laughing, cuffs him*] Never mind, something I want you to have.

BIFF. [*turns and starts off*] What is it, Hap?

HAPPY. [*offstage*] It's a punching bag!

BIFF. Oh, Pop!

WILLY. It's got Gene Tunney's° signature on it!

Happy runs onstage with a punching bag.

BIFF. Gee, how'd you know we wanted a punching bag?

WILLY. Well, it's the finest thing for the timing.

HAPPY. [*lies down on his back and pedals with his feet*] I'm losing weight, you notice, Pop?

WILLY. [*to Happy*] Jumping rope is good too.

BIFF. Did you see the new football I got?

WILLY. [*examining the ball*] Where'd you get a new ball?

BIFF. The coach told me to practice my passing.

WILLY. That so? And he gave you the ball, heh?

BIFF. Well, I borrowed it from the locker room. [*He laughs confidentially.*]

WILLY. [*laughing with him at the theft*] I want you to return that.

HAPPY. I told you he wouldn't like it!

BIFF. [*angrily*] Well, I'm bringing it back!

WILLY. [*stopping the incipient argument, to Happy*] Sure, he's gotta practice with a regulation ball, doesn't he? [*To Biff*] Coach'll probably congratulate you on your initiative!

BIFF. Oh, he keeps congratulating my initiative all the time, Pop.

WILLY. That's because he likes you. If somebody else took that ball there'd be an uproar. So what's the report, boys, what's the report?

BIFF. Where'd you go this time, Dad? Gee we were lonesome for you.

WILLY. [*pleased, puts an arm around each boy and they come down to the apron*] Lonesome, heh?

BIFF. Missed you every minute.

WILLY. Don't say? Tell you a secret, boys. Don't breathe it to a soul. Someday I'll have my own business, and I'll never have to leave home any more.

HAPPY. Like Uncle Charley, heh?

WILLY. Bigger than Uncle Charley! Because Charley is not—liked. He's liked, but he's not—well liked.

BIFF. Where'd you go this time, Dad?

WILLY. Well, I got on the road, and I went north to Providence.° Met the Mayor.

BIFF. The Mayor of Providence!

WILLY. He was sitting in the hotel lobby.

BIFF. What'd he say?

WILLY. He said, "Morning!" And I said, "You got a fine city here, Mayor." And then he had coffee with me. And then I went to Waterbury.° Waterbury is a fine city. Big clock city, the famous Waterbury clock. Sold a nice bill there. And then Boston—Boston is the cradle of the Revolution. A fine city. And a couple of other towns in Mass., and on to Portland and Bangor° and straight home!

BIFF. Gee, I'd love to go with you sometime, Dad.

WILLY. Soon as summer comes.

HAPPY. Promise?

WILLY. You and Hap and I, and I'll show you all the towns. America is full of beautiful towns and fine, upstanding people. And they know me, boys, they know

---

Gene Tunney: American boxing champion.   *Providence:* Rhode Island capital city.   *Waterbury:* city in western Connecticut.   *Bangor:* city in northern Maine.

me up and down New England. The finest people. And when I bring you fellas up, there'll be open sesame for all of us, 'cause one thing, boys: I have friends. I can park my car in any street in New England, and the cops protect it like their own. This summer, heh?

BIFF AND HAPPY. [*together*] Yeah! You bet!

WILLY. We'll take our bathing suits.

HAPPY. We'll carry your bags, Pop!

WILLY. Oh, won't that be something! Me comin' into the Boston stores with you boys carryin' my bags. What a sensation!

Biff is prancing around, practicing passing the ball.

WILLY. You nervous, Biff, about the game?

BIFF. Not if you're gonna be there.

WILLY. What do they say about you in school, now that they made you captain?

HAPPY. There's a crowd of girls behind him everytime the classes change.

BIFF. [*taking Willy's hand*] This Saturday, Pop, this Saturday—just for you, I'm going to break through for a touchdown.

HAPPY. You're supposed to pass.

BIFF. I'm takin' one play for Pop. You watch me, Pop, and when I take off my helmet, that means I'm breakin' out. Then you watch me crash through that line!

WILLY. [*kisses Biff*] Oh, wait'll I tell this in Boston!

Bernard enters in knickers. He is younger than Biff, earnest and loyal, a worried boy.

BERNARD. Biff, where are you? You're supposed to study with me today.

WILLY. Hey, looka Bernard. What're you lookin' so anemic° about, Bernard?

BERNARD. He's gotta study, Uncle Willy. He's got Regents next week.

HAPPY. [*tauntingly, spinning Bernard around*] Let's box, Bernard!

BERNARD. Biff! [*He gets away from Happy.*] Listen, Biff, I heard Mr. Birnbaum say that if you don't start studyin' math he's gonna flunk you, and you won't graduate. I heard him!

WILLY. You better study with him, Biff. Go ahead now.

BERNARD. I heard him!

BIFF. Oh, Pop, you didn't see my sneakers! [*He holds up a foot for Willy to look at.*]

WILLY. Hey, that's a beautiful job of printing!

BERNARD. [*wiping his glasses*] Just because he printed University of Virginia on his sneakers doesn't mean they've got to graduate him, Uncle Willy!

WILLY. [*angrily*] What're you talking about? With scholarships to three universities they're gonna flunk him?

BERNARD. But I heard Mr. Birnbaum say—

WILLY. Don't be a pest, Bernard! [*To his boys*] What an anemic!

BERNARD. Okay, I'm waiting for you in my house, Biff.

Bernard goes off. The Lomans laugh.

WILLY. Bernard is not well liked, is he?

BIFF. He's liked, but he's not well liked.

---

anemic: bloodless.

HAPPY. That's right, Pop.

WILLY. That's just what I mean. Bernard can get the best marks in school, y'understand, but when he gets out in the business world, y'understand, you are going to be five times ahead of him. That's why I thank Almighty God you're both built like Adonises.° Because the man who makes an appearance in the business world, the man who creates personal interest, is the man who gets ahead. Be liked and you will never want. You take me, for instance. I never have to wait in line to see a buyer. "Willy Loman is here!" That's all they have to know, and I go right through.

BIFF. Did you knock them dead, Pop?

WILLY. Knocked 'em cold in Providence, slaughtered 'em in Boston.

HAPPY. [on his back, pedaling again] I'm losing weight, you notice Pop?

Linda enters, as of old, a ribbon in her hair, carrying a basket of washing.

LINDA. [with youthful energy] Hello, dear!

WILLY. Sweetheart!

LINDA. How'd the Chevvy run?

WILLY. Chevrolet, Linda, is the greatest car ever built. [To the boys] Since when do you let your mother carry wash up the stairs?

BIFF. Grab hold there, boy!

HAPPY. Where to, Mom?

LINDA. Hang them up on the line. And you better go down to your friends, Biff. The cellar is full of boys. They don't know what to do with themselves.

BIFF. Ah, when Pop comes home they can wait!

WILLY. [laughs appreciatively] You better go down and tell them what to do, Biff.

BIFF. I think I'll have them sweep out the furnace room.

WILLY. Good work, Biff.

BIFF. [goes through wall-line of kitchen to doorway at back and calls down] Fellas! Everybody sweep out the furnace room! I'll be right down!

VOICES. All right! Okay, Biff.

BIFF. George and Sam and Frank, come out back! We're hangin' up the wash! Come on, Hap, on the double! [He and Happy carry out the basket.]

LINDA. The way they obey him!

WILLY. Well, that's training, the training. I'm tellin' you, I was sellin' thousands and thousands, but I had to come home.

LINDA. Oh, the whole block'll be at that game. Did you sell anything?

WILLY. I did five hundred gross in Providence and seven hundred gross in Boston.

LINDA. No! Wait a minute, I've got a pencil. [She pulls pencil and paper out of her apron pocket.] That makes your commission . . . Two hundred—my God! Two hundred and twelve dollars!

WILLY. Well, I didn't figure it yet, but . . .

LINDA. How much did you do?

WILLY. Well, I—I did—about a hundred and eighty gross in Providence. Well, no—it came to—roughly two hundred gross on the whole trip.

LINDA. [without hesitation] Two hundred gross. That's . . . [She figures.]

WILLY. The trouble was that three of the stores were half closed for inventory in Boston. Otherwise I woulda broke records.

°Adonises: like Adonis, classic Greek youth of statuesque beauty.

LINDA. Well, it makes seventy dollars and some pennies. That's very good.

WILLY. What do we owe?

LINDA. Well, on the first there's sixteen dollars on the refrigerator—

WILLY. Why sixteen?

LINDA. Well, the fan belt broke, so it was a dollar eighty.

WILLY. But it's brand new.

LINDA. Well, the man said that's the way it is. Till they work themselves in, y'know.

They move through the wall-line into the kitchen.

WILLY. I hope we didn't get stuck on that machine.

LINDA. They got the biggest ads of any of them!

WILLY. I know, it's a fine machine. What else?

LINDA. Well, there's nine-sixty for the washing machine. And for the vacuum cleaner there's three and a half due on the fifteenth. Then the roof, you got twenty-one dollars remaining.

WILLY. It don't leak, does it?

LINDA. No, they did a wonderful job. Then you owe Frank for the carburetor.

WILLY. I'm not going to pay that man! That goddam Chevrolet, they ought to prohibit the manufacture of that car!

LINDA. Well, you owe him three and a half. And odds and ends, comes to around a hundred and twenty dollars by the fifteenth.

WILLY. A hundred and twenty dollars! My God, if business don't pick up I don't know what I'm gonna do!

LINDA. Well, next week you'll do better.

WILLY. Oh, I'll knock 'em dead next week. I'll go to Hartford.° I'm very well liked in Hartford. You know, the trouble is, Linda, people don't seem to take to me.

They move onto the forestage.

LINDA. Oh, don't be foolish.

WILLY. I know it when I walk in. They seem to laugh at me.

LINDA. Why? Why would they laugh at you? Don't talk that way, Willy.

Willy moves to the edge of the stage. Linda goes into the kitchen and starts to darn stockings.

WILLY. I don't know the reason for it, but they just pass me by. I'm not noticed.

LINDA. But you're doing wonderful, dear. You're making seventy to a hundred dollars a week.

WILLY. But I gotta be at it ten, twelve hours a day. Other men—I don't know—they do it easier. I don't know why—I can't stop myself—I talk too much. A man oughta come in with a few words. One thing about Charley. He's a man of few words, and they respect him.

LINDA. You don't talk too much, you're just lively.

WILLY. [smiling] Well, I figure, what the hell, life is short, a couple of jokes. [To himself] I joke too much! [The smile goes.]

LINDA. Why? You're—

WILLY. I'm fat. I'm very—foolish to look at, Linda. I didn't tell you, but Christmas time I happened to be calling on F. H. Stewarts, and a salesman I know, as I was

_____

Hartford: capital city in central Connecticut.

going in to see the buyer I heard him say something about—walrus. And I—I cracked him right across the face. I won't take that. I simply will not take that. But they do laugh at me. I know that.

LINDA. Darling . . .

WILLY. I gotta overcome it. I know I gotta overcome it. I'm not dressing to advantage, maybe.

LINDA. Willy, darling, you're the handsomest man in the world—

WILLY. Oh, no, Linda.

LINDA. To me you are. [*Slight pause.*] The handsomest.

From the darkness is heard the laughter of a woman. Willy doesn't turn to it, but it continues through Linda's lines.

LINDA. And the boys, Willy. Few men are idolized by their children the way you are.

Music is heard as behind a scrim,° to the left of the house, The Woman, dimly seen, is dressing.

WILLY. [*with great feeling*] You're the best there is, Linda, you're a pal, you know that? On the road—on the road I want to grab you sometimes and just kiss the life outa you.

The laughter is loud now, and he moves into a brightening area at the left, where The Woman has come from behind the scrim and is standing, putting on her hat, looking into a "mirror" and laughing.

WILLY. 'Cause I get so lonely—especially when business is bad and there's nobody to talk to. I get the feeling that I'll never sell anything again, that I won't be making a living for you, or a business, a business for the boys. [*He talks through The Woman's subsiding laughter; The Woman primps at the "mirror."*] There's so much I want to make for—

THE WOMAN. Me? You didn't make me, Willy. I picked you.

WILLY. [*pleased*] You picked me?

THE WOMAN. [*who is quite proper-looking, Willy's age*] I did. I've been sitting at that desk watching all the salesmen go by, day in, day out. But you've got such a sense of humor, and we do have such a good time together, don't we?

WILLY. Sure, sure. [*He takes her in his arms.*] Why do you have to go now?

THE WOMAN. It's two o'clock . . .

WILLY. No, come on in! [*He pulls her.*]

THE WOMAN. . . . my sisters'll be scandalized. When'll you be back?

WILLY. Oh, two weeks about. Will you come up again?

THE WOMAN. Sure thing. You do make me laugh. It's good for me. [*She squeezes his arm, kisses him.*] And I think you're a wonderful man.

WILLY. You picked me, heh?

THE WOMAN. Sure. Because you're so sweet. And such a kidder.

WILLY. Well, I'll see you next time I'm in Boston.

THE WOMAN. I'll put you right through to the buyers.

WILLY. [*slapping her bottom*] Right. Well, bottoms up!

°*scrim:* thin cloth or veil often used on stage to screen off another set to the rear which, when lighted up, becomes visible to the audience through the veil.

THE WOMAN. [slaps him gently and laughs] You just kill me, Willy. [He suddenly grabs her and kisses her roughly.] You kill me. And thanks for the stockings. I love a lot of stockings. Well, good night.

WILLY. Good night. And keep your pores open!

THE WOMAN. Oh, Willy!

The Woman bursts out laughing, and Linda's laughter blends in. The Woman disappears into the dark. Now the area at the kitchen table brightens. Linda is sitting where she was at the kitchen table, but now is mending a pair of her silk stockings.

LINDA. You are, Willy. The handsomest man. You've got no reason to feel that—

WILLY. [coming out of The Woman's dimming area and going over to Linda] I'll make it all up to you, Linda, I'll—

LINDA. There's nothing to make up, dear. You're doing fine, better than—

WILLY. [noticing her mending] What's that?

LINDA. Just mending my stockings. They're so expensive—

WILLY. [angrily, taking them from her] I won't have you mending stockings in this house! Now throw them out!

Linda puts the stockings in her pocket.

BERNARD. [entering on the run] Where is he? If he doesn't study!

WILLY. [moving to the forestage, with great agitation] You'll give him the answers!

BERNARD. I do, but I can't on a Regents! That's a state exam! They're liable to arrest me!

WILLY. Where is he? I'll whip him, I'll whip him!

LINDA. And he'd better give back that football, Willy, it's not nice.

WILLY. Biff! Where is he? Why is he taking everything?

LINDA. He's too rough with the girls, Willy. All the mothers are afraid of him!

WILLY. I'll whip him!

BERNARD. He's driving the car without a license!

The Woman's laugh is heard.

WILLY. Shut up!

LINDA. All the mothers—

WILLY. Shut up!

BERNARD. [backing quietly away and out] Mr. Birnbaum says he's stuck up.

WILLY. Get outa here!

BERNARD. If he doesn't buckle down he'll flunk math! [He goes off.]

LINDA. He's right, Willy, you've gotta—

WILLY. [exploding at her] There's nothing the matter with him! You want him to be a worm like Bernard? He's got spirit, personality . . .

As he speaks, Linda, almost in tears, exits into the living-room. Willy is alone in the kitchen, wilting and staring. The leaves are gone. It is night again, and the apartment houses look down from behind.

WILLY. Loaded with it. Loaded! What is he stealing? He's giving it back, isn't he? Why is he stealing? What did I tell him? I never in my life told him anything but decent things.

Happy in pajamas has come down the stairs; Willy suddenly becomes aware of Happy's presence.

HAPPY. Let's go now, come on.

WILLY. [*sitting down at the kitchen table*] Huh! Why did she have to wax the floors herself? Everytime she waxes the floors she keels over. She knows that!

HAPPY. Shh! Take it easy. What brought you back tonight?

WILLY. I got an awful scare. Nearly hit a kid in Yonkers. God! Why didn't I go to Alaska with my brother Ben that time! Ben! That man was a genius, that man was success incarnate! What a mistake! He begged me to go.

HAPPY. Well, there's no use in—

WILLY. You guys! There was a man started with the clothes on his back and ended up with diamond mines!

HAPPY. Boy, someday I'd like to know how he did it.

WILLY. What's the mystery? The man knew what he wanted and went out and got it! Walked into a jungle, and comes out, the age of twenty-one, and he's rich! The world is an oyster, but you don't crack it open on a mattress!

HAPPY. Pop, I told you I'm gonna retire you for life.

WILLY. You'll retire me for life on seventy goddam dollars a week? And your women and your car and your apartment, and you'll retire me for life! Christ's sake, I couldn't get past Yonkers today! Where are you guys, where are you? The woods are burning! I can't drive a car!

Charley has appeared in the doorway. He is a large man, slow of speech, laconic,° immovable. In all he says, despite what he says, there is pity, and, now, trepidation. He has a robe over pajamas, slippers on his feet. He enters the kitchen.

CHARLEY. Everything all right?

HAPPY. Yeah, Charley, everything's . . .

WILLY. What's the matter?

CHARLEY. I heard some noise. I thought something happened. Can't we do something about the walls? You sneeze in here, and in my house hats blow off.

HAPPY. Let's go to bed, Dad. Come on.

Charley signals to Happy to go.

WILLY. You go ahead, I'm not tired at the moment.

HAPPY. [*to Willy*] Take it easy, huh? [*He exits.*]

WILLY. What're you doin' up?

CHARLEY. [*sitting down at the kitchen table opposite Willy*] Couldn't sleep good. I had a heartburn.

WILLY. Well, you don't know how to eat.

CHARLEY. I eat with my mouth.

WILLY. No, you're ignorant. You gotta know about vitamins and things like that.

CHARLEY. Come on, let's shoot. Tire you out a little.

WILLY. [*hesitantly*] All right. You got cards?

CHARLEY. [*taking a deck from his pocket*] Yeah, I got them. Someplace. What is it with those vitamins?

WILLY. [*dealing*] They build up your bones. Chemistry.

CHARLEY. Yeah, but there's no bones in a heartburn.

WILLY. What are you talkin' about? Do you know the first thing about it?

CHARLEY. Don't get insulted.

---

laconic: sparing of words.

WILLY. Don't talk about something you don't know anything about.

They are playing. Pause.

CHARLEY. What're you doin' home?

WILLY. A little trouble with the car.

CHARLEY. Oh. [*Pause*] I'd like to take a trip to California.

WILLY. Don't say.

CHARLEY. You want a job?

WILLY. I got a job, I told you that. [*After a slight pause*] What the hell are you offering me a job for?

CHARLEY. Don't get insulted.

WILLY. Don't insult me.

CHARLEY. I don't see no sense in it. You don't have to go on this way.

WILLY. I got a good job. [*Slight pause*] What do you keep comin' in here for?

CHARLEY. You want me to go?

WILLY. [*after a pause, withering*] I can't understand it. He's going back to Texas again. What the hell is that?

CHARLEY. Let him go.

WILLY. I got nothin' to give him, Charley, I'm clean, I'm clean.

CHARLEY. He won't starve. None a them starve. Forget about him.

WILLY. Then what have I got to remember?

CHARLEY. You take it too hard. To hell with it. When a deposit bottle is broken you don't get your nickel back.

WILLY. That's easy enough for you to say.

CHARLEY. That ain't easy for me to say.

WILLY. Did you see the ceiling I put up in the living-room?

CHARLEY. Yeah, that's a nice piece of work. To put up a ceiling is a mystery to me. How do you do it?

WILLY. What's the difference?

CHARLEY. Well, talk about it.

WILLY. You gonna put up a ceiling?

CHARLEY. How could I put up a ceiling?

WILLY. Then what the hell are you bothering me for?

CHARLEY. You're insulted again.

WILLY. A man who can't handle tools is not a man. You're disgusting.

CHARLEY. Don't call me disgusting, Willy.

Uncle Ben, carrying a valise and an umbrella, enters the forestage from around the right corner of the house. He is a stolid man, in his sixties, with a mustache and an authoritative air. He is utterly certain of his destiny, and there is an aura of far places about him. He enters exactly as Willy speaks.

WILLY. I'm getting awfully tired, Ben.

Ben's music is heard. Ben looks around at everything.

CHARLEY. Good, keep playing: you'll sleep better. Did you call me Ben?

Ben looks at his watch.

WILLY. That's funny. For a second there you reminded me of my brother Ben.

BEN. I only have a few minutes. [*He strolls, inspecting the place. Willy and Charley continue playing.*]

CHARLEY. You never heard from him again, heh? Since that time?

WILLY. Didn't Linda tell you? Couple of weeks ago we got a letter from his wife in Africa. He died.

CHARLEY. That so.

BEN. [chuckling] So this is Brooklyn eh?

CHARLEY. Maybe you're in for some of his money.

WILLY. Naa, he had seven sons. There's just one opportunity I had with that man . . .

BEN. I must make a train, William. There are several properties I'm looking at in Alaska.

WILLY. Sure, sure! If I'd gone with him to Alaska that time, everything would've been totally different.

CHARLEY. Go on, you'd froze to death up there.

WILLY. What're you talking about?

BEN. Opportunity is tremendous in Alaska, William. Surprised you're not up there.

WILLY. Sure, tremendous.

CHARLEY. Heh?

WILLY. There was the only man I ever met who knew the answers.

CHARLEY. Who?

BEN. How are you all?

WILLY. [taking a pot, smiling] Fine, fine.

CHARLEY. Pretty sharp tonight.

BEN. Is Mother living with you?

WILLY. No, she died a long time ago.

CHARLEY. Who?

BEN. That's too bad. Fine specimen of a lady, Mother.

WILLY. [to Charley] Heh?

BEN. I'd hoped to see the old girl.

CHARLEY. Who died?

BEN. Heard anything from Father, have you?

WILLY. [unnerved] What do you mean, who died?

CHARLEY. [taking a pot] What're you talkin' about?

BEN. [looking at his watch] William, it's half-past eight!

WILLY. [as though to dispel his confusion he angrily stops Charley's hand] That's my build!

CHARLEY. I put the ace—

WILLY. If you don't know how to play the game I'm not gonna throw my money away on you!

CHARLEY. [rising] It was my ace, for God's sake!

WILLY. I'm through, I'm through!

BEN. When did Mother die?

WILLY. Long ago. Since the beginning you never knew how to play cards.

CHARLEY. [picks up the cards and goes to the door] All right! Next time I'll bring a deck with five aces.

WILLY. I don't play that kind of game!

CHARLEY. [turning to him] You ought to be ashamed of yourself!

WILLY. Yeah?

CHARLEY. Yeah! [He goes out.]

WILLY. [slamming the door after him] Ignoramus!

BEN. [as Willy comes toward him through the wall-line of the kitchen] So you're William.

WILLY. [shaking Ben's hand] Ben! I've been waiting for you so long! What's the answer? How did you do it?

BEN. Oh, there's a story in that.

Linda enters the forestage, as of old, carrying the wash basket.

LINDA. Is this Ben?

BEN. [gallantly] How do you do, my dear.

LINDA. Where've you been all these years? Willy's always wondered why you—

WILLY. [pulling Ben away from her impatiently] Where is Dad? Didn't you follow him? How did you get started?

BEN. Well, I don't know how much you remember.

WILLY. Well, I was just a baby, of course, only three or four years old—

BEN. Three years and eleven months.

WILLY. What a memory, Ben!

BEN. I have many enterprises, William, and I have never kept books.

WILLY. I remember I was sitting under the wagon in—was it Nebraska?

BEN. It was South Dakota, and I gave you a bunch of wild flowers.

WILLY. I remember you walking away down some open road.

BEN. [laughing] I was going to find Father in Alaska.

WILLY. Where is he?

BEN. At that age I had a very faulty view of geography, William. I discovered after a few days that I was heading due south, so instead of Alaska, I ended up in Africa.

LINDA. Africa!

WILLY. The Gold Coast!

BEN. Principally diamond mines.

LINDA. Diamond mines!

BEN. Yes, my dear. But I've only a few minutes—

WILLY. No! Boys! Boys! [Young Biff and Happy appear.] Listen to this. This is your Uncle Ben, a great man! Tell my boys, Ben!

BEN. Why, boys, when I was seventeen I walked into the jungle, and when I was twenty-one I walked out. [He laughs.] And by God I was rich.

WILLY. [to the boys] You see what I been talking about? The greatest things can happen!

BEN. [glancing at his watch] I have an appointment in Ketchikan° Tuesday week.

WILLY. No, Ben! Please tell about Dad. I want my boys to hear. I want them to know the kind of stock they spring from. All I remember is a man with a big beard, and I was in Mamma's lap, sitting around a fire, and some kind of high music.

BEN. His flute. He played the flute.

WILLY. Sure, the flute, that's right!

New music is heard, a high, rollicking tune.

BEN. Father was a very great and a very wild-hearted man. We would start in Boston, and he'd toss the whole family into the wagon, and then he'd drive the team right across the country; through Ohio, and Indiana, Michigan, Illinois, and all the Western states. And we'd stop in the towns and sell flutes that he'd

---

Ketchikan: coastal city in Alaska.

made on the way. Great inventor, Father. With one gadget he made more in a week than a man like you could make in a lifetime.

WILLY. That's just the way I'm bringing them up, Ben—rugged, well liked, all-around.

BEN. Yeah? [To Biff] Hit that, boy—hard as you can. [He pounds his stomach.]

BIFF. Oh no, sir!

BEN. [taking boxing stance] Come on, get to me! [He laughs.]

WILLY. Go to it, Biff! Go ahead, show him!

BIFF. Okay! [He cocks his fists and starts in.]

LINDA. [to Willy] Why must he fight, dear?

BEN. [sparring with Biff] Good boy! Good boy!

WILLY. How's that, Ben, heh?

HAPPY. Give him the left, Biff!

LINDA. Why are you fighting?

BEN. Good boy! [Suddenly comes in, trips Biff, and stands over him, the point of his umbrella poised over Biff's eye.]

LINDA. Look out, Biff!

BIFF. Gee!

BEN. [patting Biff's knee] Never fight fair with a stranger, boy. You'll never get out of the jungle that way. [Taking Linda's hand and bowing] It was an honor and a pleasure to meet you, Linda.

LINDA. [withdrawing her hand coldly, frightened] Have a nice—trip.

BEN. [to Willy] And good luck with your—what do you do?

WILLY. Selling.

BEN. Yes. Well . . . [He raises his hand in farewell to all.]

WILLY. No, Ben, I don't want you to think . . . [He takes Ben's arm to show him.] It's Brooklyn, I know, but we hunt too.

BEN. Really, now.

WILLY. Oh, sure, there's snakes and rabbits and—that's why I moved out here. Why, Biff can fell any one of these trees in no time! Boys! Go right over to where they're building the apartment house and get some sand. We're gonna rebuild the entire front stoop right now! Watch this, Ben!

BIFF. Yes, sir! On the double, Hap!

HAPPY. [as he and Biff run off] I lost weight, Pop, you notice?

Charley enters in knickers, even before the boys are gone.

CHARLEY. Listen, if they steal any more from that building the watchman'll put the cops on them!

LINDA. [to Willy] Don't let Biff . . .

Ben laughs lustily.

WILLY. You shoulda seen the lumber they brought home last week. At least a dozen six-by-tens worth all kinds of money.

CHARLEY. Listen, if that watchman—

WILLY. I gave them hell, understand. But I got a couple of fearless characters there.

CHARLEY. Willy, the jails are full of fearless characters.

BEN. [clapping Willy on the back, with a laugh at Charley] And the stock exchange, friend!

WILLY. [joining in Ben's laughter] Where are the rest of your pants?

CHARLEY. My wife bought them.

WILLY. Now all you need is a golf club° and you can go upstairs and go to sleep. [*To Ben*] Great athlete! Between him and his son Bernard they can't hammer a nail!

BERNARD. [*rushing in*] The watchman's chasing Biff!

WILLY. [*angrily*] Shut up! He's not stealing anything!

LINDA. [*alarmed, hurrying off left*] Where is he? Biff, dear! [*She exits.*]

WILLY. [*moving toward the left, away from Ben*] There's nothing wrong. What's the matter with you?

BEN. Nervy boy. Good!

WILLY. [*laughing*] Oh, nerves of iron, that Biff!

CHARLEY. Don't know what it is. My New England man comes back and he's bleedin', they murdered him up there.

WILLY. It's contacts, Charley, I got important contacts!

CHARLEY. [*sarcastically*] Glad to hear it, Willy. Come in later, we'll shoot a little casino. I'll take some of your Portland money. [*He laughs at Willy and exits.*]

WILLY. [*turning to Ben*] Business is bad, it's murderous. But not for me, of course.

BEN. I'll stop by on my way back to Africa.

WILLY. [*longingly*] Can't you stay a few days? You're just what I need, Ben, because I—I have a fine position here, but I—well, Dad left when I was such a baby and I never had a chance to talk to him and I still feel—kind of temporary about myself.

BEN. I'll be late for my train.

They are at opposite ends of the stage.

WILLY. Ben, my boys—can't we talk? They'd go into the jaws of hell for me, see, but I—

BEN. William, you're being first-rate with your boys. Outstanding, manly chaps!

WILLY. [*hanging on to his words*] Oh, Ben, that's good to hear! Because sometimes I'm afraid that I'm not teaching them the right kind of—Ben, how should I teach them?

BEN. [*giving great weight to each word, and with a certain vicious audacity*] William, when I walked into the jungle, I was seventeen. When I walked out I was twenty-one. And, by God, I was rich! [*He goes off into the darkness around the right corner of the house.*]

WILLY. . . . was rich! That's just the spirit I want to imbue them with! To walk into a jungle! I was right! I was right! I was right!

Ben is gone, but Willy is still speaking to him as Linda, in nightgown and robe, enters the kitchen, glances around for Willy, then goes to the door of the house, looks out and sees him. Comes down to his left. He looks at her.

LINDA. Willy, dear? Willy?

WILLY. I was right!

LINDA. Did you have some cheese? [*He can't answer.*] It's very late, darling. Come to bed, heh?

WILLY. [*looking straight up*] Gotta break your neck to see a star in this yard.

LINDA. You coming in?

---

golf club: knickers were a traditional part of a golfing outfit.

WILLY. Whatever happened to that diamond watch fob? Remember? When Ben came from Africa that time? Didn't he give me a watch fob with a diamond in it?

LINDA. You pawned it, dear. Twelve, thirteen years ago. For Biff's radio correspondence course.

WILLY. Gee, that was a beautiful thing. I'll take a walk.

LINDA. But you're in your slippers.

WILLY. [starting to go around the house at the left] I was right! I was! [Half to Linda, as he goes, shaking his head] What a man! There was a man worth talking to. I was right!

LINDA. [calling after Willy] But in your slippers, Willy!

Willy is almost gone when Biff, in his pajamas, comes down the stairs and enters the kitchen.

BIFF. What is he doing out there?

LINDA. Sh!

BIFF. God Almighty, Mom, how long has he been doing this?

LINDA. Don't, he'll hear you.

BIFF. What the hell is the matter with him?

LINDA. It'll pass by morning.

BIFF. Shouldn't we do anything?

LINDA. Oh, my dear, you should do a lot of things, but there's nothing to do, so go to sleep.

Happy comes down the stair and sits on the steps.

HAPPY. I never heard him so loud, Mom.

LINDA. Well, come around more often; you'll hear him. [She sits down at the table and mends the lining of Willy's jacket.]

BIFF. Why didn't you ever write me about this, Mom?

LINDA. How would I write to you? For over three months you had no address.

BIFF. I was on the move. But you know I thought of you all the time. You know that, don't you, pal?

LINDA. I know, dear, I know. But he likes to have a letter. Just to know that there's still a possibility for better things.

BIFF. He's not like this all the time, is he?

LINDA. It's when you come home he's always the worst.

BIFF. When I come home?

LINDA. When you write you're coming, he's all smiles, and talks about the future, and—he's just wonderful. And then the closer you seem to come, the more shaky he gets, and then, by the time you get here, he's arguing, and he seems angry at you. I think it's just that maybe he can't bring himself to—to open up to you. Why are you so hateful to each other? Why is that?

BIFF. [evasively] I'm not hateful, Mom.

LINDA. But you no sooner come in the door than you're fighting!

BIFF. I don't know why. I mean to change. I'm tryin', Mom, you understand?

LINDA. Are you home to stay now?

BIFF. I don't know. I want to look around, see what's doin'.

LINDA. Biff, you can't look around all your life, can you?

BIFF. I just can't take hold, Mom. I can't take hold of some kind of a life.

LINDA. Biff, a man is not a bird, to come and go with the springtime.

BIFF. Your hair . . . [He touches her hair.] Your hair got so gray.

LINDA. Oh, it's been gray since you were in high school. I just stopped dyeing it, that's all.

BIFF. Dye it again, will ya? I don't want my pal looking old. [He smiles.]

LINDA. You're such a boy! You think you can go away for a year and . . . You've got to get it into your head now that one day you'll knock on this door and there'll be strange people here—

BIFF. What are you talking about? You're not even sixty, Mom.

LINDA. But what about your father?

BIFF. [lamely] Well, I meant him too.

HAPPY. He admires Pop.

LINDA. Biff, dear, if you don't have any feeling for him, then you can't have any feeling for me.

BIFF. Sure I can, Mom.

LINDA. No. You can't just come to see me, because I love him. [With a threat, but only a threat, of tears] He's the dearest man in the world to me, and I won't have anyone making him feel unwanted and low and blue. You've got to make up your mind now, darling, there's no leeway any more. Either he's your father and you pay him that respect, or else you're not to come here. I know he's not easy to get along with—nobody knows that better than me—but . . .

WILLY. [from the left, with a laugh] Hey, hey, Biffo!

BIFF. [starting to go out after Willy] What the hell is the matter with him? [Happy stops him.]

LINDA. Don't—don't go near him!

BIFF. Stop making excuses for him! He always, always wiped the floor with you. Never had an ounce of respect for you.

HAPPY. He's always had respect for—

BIFF. What the hell do you know about it?

HAPPY. [surlily] Just don't call him crazy!

BIFF. He's got no character—Charley wouldn't do this. Not in his own house— spewing out that vomit from his mind.

HAPPY. Charley never had to cope with what he's got to.

BIFF. People are worse off than Willy Loman. Believe me, I've seen them!

LINDA. Then make Charley your father, Biff. You can't do that, can you? I don't say he's a great man. Willy Loman never made a lot of money. His name was never in the paper. He's not the finest character that ever lived. But he's a human being, and a terrible thing is happening to him. So attention must be paid. He's not to be allowed to fall into his grave like an old dog. Attention, attention must be finally paid to such a person. You called him crazy—

BIFF. I didn't mean—

LINDA. No, a lot of people think he's lost his—balance. But you don't have to be very smart to know what his trouble is. The man is exhausted.

HAPPY. Sure!

LINDA. A small man can be just as exhausted as a great man. He works for a company thirty-six years this March, opens up unheard-of territories to their trademark, and now in his old age they take his salary away.

HAPPY. [indignantly] I didn't know that, Mom.

LINDA. You never asked, my dear! Now that you get your spending money someplace else you don't trouble your mind with him.

HAPPY. But I gave you money last—

LINDA. Christmas time, fifty dollars! To fix the hot water it cost ninety-seven fifty!
For five weeks he's been on straight commission, like a beginner, an unknown!

BIFF. Those ungrateful bastards!

LINDA. Are they any worse than his sons? When he brought them business, when
he was young, they were glad to see him. But now his old friends, the old buyers that loved him so and always found some order to hand him in a pinch—
they're all dead, retired. He used to be able to make six, seven calls a day in
Boston. Now he takes his valises out of the car and puts them back and takes
them out again and he's exhausted. Instead of walking he talks now. He drives
seven hundred miles, and when he gets there no one knows him any more, no
one welcomes him. And what goes through a man's mind, driving seven hundred miles home without having earned a cent? Why shouldn't he talk to himself? Why? When he has to go to Charley and borrow fifty dollars a week and
pretend to me that it's his pay? How long can that go on? How long? You see
what I'm sitting here and waiting for? And you tell me he has no character? The
man who never worked a day but for your benefit? When does he get the medal
for that? Is this his reward—to turn around at the age of sixty-three and find his
sons, who he loved better than his life, one a philandering bum—

HAPPY. Mom!

LINDA. That's all you are, my baby! [To Biff] And you! What happened to the love
you had for him? You were such pals! How you used to talk to him on the phone
every night! How lonely he was till he could come home to you!

BIFF. All right, Mom. I'll live here in my room, and I'll get a job. I'll keep away from
him, that's all.

LINDA. No, Biff. You can't stay here and fight all the time.

BIFF. He threw me out of this house, remember that.

LINDA. Why did he do that? I never knew why.

BIFF. Because I know he's a fake and he doesn't like anybody around who knows!

LINDA. Why a fake? In what way? What do you mean?

BIFF. Just don't lay it all at my feet. It's between me and him—that's all I have to
say. I'll chip in from now on. He'll settle for half my pay check. He'll be all right.
I'm going to bed. [He starts for the stairs.]

LINDA. He won't be all right.

BIFF. [turning on the stairs, furiously] I hate this city and I'll stay here. Now what do
you want?

LINDA. He's dying, Biff.

Happy turns quickly to her, shocked.

BIFF. [after a pause] Why is he dying?

LINDA. He's been trying to kill himself.

BIFF. [with great horror] How?

LINDA. I live from day to day.

BIFF. What're you talking about?

LINDA. Remember I wrote you that he smashed up the car again? In February?

BIFF. Well?

LINDA. The insurance inspector came. He said that they have evidence. That all these accidents in the last year—weren't—weren't—accidents.

HAPPY. How can they tell that? That's a lie.

LINDA. It seems there's a woman . . . [*She takes a breath as*]

BIFF. [*sharply but contained*] What woman?

LINDA. [*simultaneously*] . . . and this woman . . .

LINDA. What?

BIFF. Nothing. Go ahead.

LINDA. What did you say?

BIFF. Nothing. I just said what woman?

HAPPY. What about her?

LINDA. Well, it seems she was walking down the road and saw his car. She says that he wasn't driving fast at all, and that he didn't skid. She says he came to that little bridge, and then deliberately smashed into the railing, and it was only the shallowness of the water that saved him.

BIFF. Oh, no, he probably just fell asleep again.

LINDA. I don't think he fell asleep.

BIFF. Why not?

LINDA. Last month . . . [*With great difficulty*] Oh, boys, it's so hard to say a thing like this! He's just a big stupid man to you, but I tell you there's more good in him than in many other people. [*She chokes, wipes her eyes.*] I was looking for a fuse. The lights blew out, and I went down the cellar. And behind the fuse box—it happened to fall out—was a length of rubber pipe—just short.

HAPPY. No kidding?

LINDA. There's a little attachment on the end of it. I knew right away. And sure enough, on the bottom of the water heater there's a new little nipple on the gas pipe.

HAPPY. [*angrily*] That—jerk.

BIFF. Did you have it taken off?

LINDA. I'm—I'm ashamed to. How can I mention it to him? Every day I go down and take away that little rubber pipe. But, when he comes home, I put it back where it was. How can I insult him that way? I don't know what to do. I live from day to day, boys. I tell you, I know every thought in his mind. It sounds so old-fashioned and silly, but I tell you he put his whole life into you and you've turned your backs on him. [*She is bent over in the chair, weeping, her face in her hands.*] Biff, I swear to God! Biff, his life is in your hands!

HAPPY. [*to Biff*] How do you like that damned fool!

BIFF. [*kissing her*] All right, pal, all right. It's all settled now. I've been remiss. I know that, Mom. But now I'll stay, and I swear to you, I'll apply myself. [*Kneeling in front of her, in a fever of self-reproach*] It's just—you see, Mom, I don't fit in business. Not that I won't try. I'll try, and I'll make good.

HAPPY. Sure you will. The trouble with you in business was you never tried to please people.

BIFF. I know, I—

HAPPY. Like when you worked for Harrison's. Bob Harrison said you were tops, and then you go and do some damn fool thing like whistling whole songs in the elevator like a comedian.

BIFF. [*against Happy*] So what? I like to whistle sometimes.

HAPPY. You don't raise a guy to a responsible job who whistles in the elevator!

LINDA. Well, don't argue about it now.

HAPPY. Like when you'd go off and swim in the middle of the day instead of taking the line around.

BIFF. [*his resentment rising*] Well, don't you run off? You take off sometimes, don't you? On a nice summer day?

HAPPY. Yeah, but I cover myself!

LINDA. Boys!

HAPPY. If I'm going to take a fade the boss can call any number where I'm supposed to be and they'll swear to him that I just left. I'll tell you something that I hate to say, Biff, but in the business world some of them think you're crazy.

BIFF. [*angered*] Screw the business world!

HAPPY. All right, screw it! Great, but cover yourself!

LINDA. Hap, Hap!

BIFF. I don't care what they think! They've laughed at Dad for years, and you know why? Because we don't belong in this nuthouse of a city! We should be mixing cement on some open plain, or—or carpenters. A carpenter is allowed to whistle!

Willy walks in from the entrance of the house, at left.

WILLY. Even your grandfather was better than a carpenter. [*Pause. They watch him.*] You never grew up. Bernard does not whistle in the elevator, I assure you.

BIFF. [*as though to laugh Willy out of it*] Yeah, but you do, Pop.

WILLY. I never in my life whistled in an elevator! And who in the business world thinks I'm crazy?

BIFF. I didn't mean it like that, Pop. Now don't make a whole thing out of it, will ya?

WILLY. Go back to the West! Be a carpenter, a cowboy, enjoy yourself!

LINDA. Willy, he was just saying—

WILLY. I heard what he said!

HAPPY. [*trying to quiet Willy*] Hey, Pop, come on now . . .

WILLY. [*continuing over Happy's line*] They laugh at me, heh? Go to Filene's, go to the Hub, go to Slattery's, Boston. Call out the name Willy Loman and see what happens! Big shot!

BIFF. All right, Pop.

WILLY. Big!

BIFF. All right!

WILLY. Why do you always insult me?

BIFF. I didn't say a word. [*To Linda*] Did I say a word?

LINDA. He didn't say anything, Willy.

WILLY. [*going to the doorway of the living-room*] All right, good night, good night.

LINDA. Willy, dear, he just decided . . .

WILLY. [*to Biff*] If you get tired hanging around tomorrow, paint the ceiling I put up in the living-room.

BIFF. I'm leaving early tomorrow.

HAPPY. He's going to see Bill Oliver, Pop.

WILLY. [*interestedly*] Oliver? For what?

BIFF. [*with reserve, but trying, trying*] He always said he'd stake me. I'd like to go into business, so maybe I can take him up on it.

LINDA. Isn't that wonderful?

WILLY. Don't interrupt. What's wonderful about it? There's fifty men in the City of New York who'd stake him. [*To Biff*] Sporting goods?

BIFF. I guess so. I know something about it and—

WILLY. He knows something about it! You know sporting goods better than Spalding,° for God's sake! How much is he giving you?

BIFF. I don't know, I didn't even see him yet, but—

WILLY. Then what're you talkin' about?

BIFF. [getting angry] Well, all I said was I'm gonna see him, that's all!

WILLY. [turning away] Ah, you're counting your chickens again.

BIFF. [starting left for the stairs] Oh, Jesus, I'm going to sleep!

WILLY. [calling after him] Don't curse in this house!

BIFF. [turning] Since when did you get so clean?

HAPPY. [trying to stop them] Wait a . . .

WILLY. Don't use that language to me! I won't have it!

HAPPY. [grabbing Biff, shouts] Wait a minute! I got an idea. I got a feasible idea. Come here, Biff, let's talk this over now, let's talk some sense here. When I was down in Florida last time, I thought of a great idea to sell sporting goods. It just came back to me. You and I, Biff—we have a line, the Loman Line. We train a couple of weeks, and put on a couple of exhibitions, see?

WILLY. That's an idea!

HAPPY. Wait! We form two basketball teams, see? Two water-polo teams. We play each other. It's a million dollars' worth of publicity. Two brothers, see? The Loman Brothers. Displays in the Royal Palms—all the hotels. And banners over the ring and the basketball court: "Loman Brothers." Baby, we could sell sporting goods!

WILLY. That is a one-million-dollar idea!

LINDA. Marvelous!

BIFF. I'm in great shape as far as that's concerned.

HAPPY. And the beauty of it is, Biff, it wouldn't be like a business. We'd be out playin' ball again . . .

BIFF. [enthused] Yeah, that's . . .

WILLY. Million-dollar . . .

HAPPY. And you wouldn't get fed up with it, Biff. It'd be the family again. There'd be the old honor, and comradeship, and if you wanted to go off for a swim or somethin'—well, you'd do it! Without some smart cooky gettin' up ahead of you!

WILLY. Lick the world! You guys together could absolutely lick the civilized world.

BIFF. I'll see Oliver tomorrow. Hap, if we could work that out . . .

LINDA. Maybe things are beginning to—

WILLY. [wildly enthused, to Linda] Stop interrupting! [To Biff] But don't wear sport jacket and slacks when you see Oliver.

BIFF. No, I'll—

WILLY. A business suit, and talk as little as possible, and don't crack any jokes.

BIFF. He did like me. Always liked me.

LINDA. He loved you!

WILLY. [to Linda] Will you stop! [To Biff] Walk in very serious. You are not applying for a boy's job. Money is to pass. Be quiet, fine, and serious. Everybody likes a kidder, but nobody lends him money.

Spalding: founder of a well-known sporting goods business.

HAPPY. I'll try to get some myself, Biff. I'm sure I can.

WILLY. I see great things for you kids, I think your troubles are over. But remember, start big and you'll end big. Ask for fifteen. How much you gonna ask for?

BIFF. Gee, I don't know—

WILLY. And don't say "Gee." "Gee" is a boy's word. A man walking in for fifteen thousand dollars does not say "Gee!"

BIFF. Ten, I think, would be top though.

WILLY. Don't be so modest. You always started too low. Walk in with a big laugh. Don't look worried. Start off with a couple of your good stories to lighten things up. It's not what you say, it's how you say it—because personality always wins the day.

LINDA. Oliver always thought the highest of him—

WILLY. Will you let me talk?

BIFF. Don't yell at her, Pop, will ya?

WILLY. [angrily] I was talking, wasn't I?

BIFF. I don't like you yelling at her all the time, and I'm tellin' you, that's all.

WILLY. What're you, takin' over this house?

LINDA. Willy—

WILLY. [turning on her] Don't take his side all the time, goddammit!

BIFF. [furiously] Stop yelling at her!

WILLY. [suddenly pulling on his cheek, beaten down, guilt ridden] Give my best to Bill Oliver—he may remember me. [He exits through the living-room doorway.]

LINDA. [her voice subdued] What'd you have to start that for? [Biff turns away.] You see how sweet he was as soon as you talked hopefully? [She goes over to Biff.] Come up and say good night to him. Don't let him go to bed that way.

HAPPY. Come on, Biff, let's buck him up.

LINDA. Please, dear. Just say good night. It takes so little to make him happy. Come. [She goes through the living-room doorway, calling upstairs from within the living-room.] Your pajamas are hanging in the bathroom, Willy!

HAPPY. [looking toward where Linda went out] What a woman! They broke the mold when they made her. You know that, Biff?

BIFF. He's off salary. My God, working on commission!

HAPPY. Well, let's face it: he's no hot-shot selling man. Except that sometimes, you have to admit, he's a sweet personality.

BIFF. [deciding] Lend me ten bucks, will ya? I want to buy some new ties.

HAPPY. I'll take you to a place I know. Beautiful stuff. Wear one of my striped shirts tomorrow.

BIFF. She got gray. Mom got awful old. Gee, I'm gonna go in to Oliver tomorrow and knock him for a—

HAPPY. Come on up. Tell that to Dad. Let's give him a whirl. Come on.

BIFF. [steamed up] You know, with ten thousand bucks, boy!

HAPPY. [as they go into the living-room] That's the talk, Biff, that's the first time I've heard the old confidence out of you! [From within the living-room, fading off] You're gonna live with me, kid, and any babe you want just say the word . . . [The last lines are hardly heard. They are mounting the stairs to their parents' bedroom.]

LINDA. [entering her bedroom and addressing Willy, who is in the bathroom. She is straightening the bed for him] Can you do anything about the shower? It drips.

WILLY. [*from the bathroom*] All of a sudden everything falls to pieces! Goddam plumbing, oughta be sued, those people. I hardly finished putting it in and the thing . . . [*His words rumble off.*]

LINDA. I'm just wondering if Oliver will remember him. You think he might?

WILLY. [*coming out of the bathroom in his pajamas*] Remember him? What's the matter with you, you crazy? If he'd've stayed with Oliver he'd be on top by now! Wait'll Oliver gets a look at him. You don't know the average caliber any more. The average man today—[*he is getting into bed*]—is got a caliber of zero. Greatest thing in the world for him was to bum around.

Biff and Happy enter the bedroom. Slight pause.

WILLY. [*stops short, looking at Biff*] Glad to hear it, boy.

HAPPY. He wanted to say good night to you, sport.

WILLY. [*to Biff*] Yeah. Knock him dead, boy. What'd you want to tell me?

BIFF. Just take it easy, Pop. Good night. [*He turns to go.*]

WILLY. [*unable to resist*] And if anything falls off the desk while you're talking to him —like a package or something—don't pick it up. They have office boys for that.

LINDA. I'll make a big breakfast—

WILLY. Will you let me finish? [*To Biff*] Tell him you were in the business in the West. Not farm work.

BIFF. All right, Dad.

LINDA. I think everything—

WILLY. [*going right through her speech*] And don't undersell yourself. No less than fifteen thousand dollars.

BIFF. [*unable to bear him*] Okay. Good night, Mom. [*He starts moving.*]

WILLY. Because you got a greatness in you, Biff, remember that. You got all kinds a greatness . . . [*He lies back, exhausted. Biff walks out.*]

LINDA. [*calling after Biff*] Sleep well, darling!

HAPPY. I'm gonna get married, Mom. I wanted to tell you.

LINDA. Go to sleep, dear.

HAPPY. [*going*] I just wanted to tell you.

WILLY. Keep up the good work. [*Happy exits.*] God . . . remember that Ebbets Field game? The championship of the city?

LINDA. Just rest. Should I sing to you?

WILLY. Yeah. Sing to me. [*Linda hums a soft lullaby.*] When that team came out— he was the tallest, remember?

LINDA. Oh, yes. And in gold.

Biff enters the darkened kitchen, takes a cigarette, and leaves the house. He comes downstage into a golden pool of light. He smokes, staring at the night.

WILLY. Like a young god. Hercules°—something like that. And the sun, the sun all around him. Remember how he waved to me? Right up from the field, with the representatives of three colleges standing by? And the buyers I brought, and the cheers when he came out—Loman, Loman, Loman! God Almighty, he'll be great yet. A star like that, magnificent, can never really fade away!

Hercules: Greek god known for strength.

The light on Willy is fading. The gas heater begins to glow through the kitchen wall, near the stairs, a blue flame beneath red coils.

LINDA. [*timidly*] Willy dear, what has he got against you?

WILLY. I'm so tired. Don't talk any more.

Biff slowly returns to the kitchen. He stops, stares toward the heater.

LINDA. Will you ask Howard to let you work in New York?

WILLY. First thing in the morning. Everything'll be all right.

Biff reaches behind the heater and draws out a length of rubber tubing. He is horrified and turns his head toward Willy's room, still dimly lit, from which the strains of Linda's desperate but monotonous humming rise.

WILLY. [*staring through the window into the moonlight*] Gee, look at the moon moving between the buildings?

Biff wraps the tubing around his hand and quickly goes up the stairs.

Curtain

ACT TWO

Music is heard, gay and bright. The curtain rises as the music fades away. Willy, in shirt sleeves, is sitting at the kitchen table, sipping coffee, his hat in his lap. Linda is filling his cup when she can.

WILLY. Wonderful coffee. Meal in itself.

LINDA. Can I make you some eggs?

WILLY. No. Take a breath.

LINDA. You look so rested, dear.

WILLY. I slept like a dead one. First time in months. Imagine, sleeping till ten on a Tuesday morning. Boys left nice and early, heh?

LINDA. They were out of here by eight o'clock.

WILLY. Good work!

LINDA. It was so thrilling to see them leaving together. I can't get over the shaving lotion in this house!

WILLY. [*smiling*] Mmm—

LINDA. Biff was very changed this morning. His whole attitude seemed to be hopeful. He couldn't wait to get downtown to see Oliver.

WILLY. He's heading for a change. There's no question, there simply are certain men that take longer to get—solidified. How did he dress?

LINDA. His blue suit. He's so handsome in that suit. He could be a—anything in that suit!

Willy gets up from the table. Linda holds his jacket for him.

WILLY. There's no question, no question at all. Gee, on the way home tonight I'd like to buy some seeds.

LINDA. [*laughing*] That'd be wonderful. But not enough sun gets back there. Nothing'll grow any more.

WILLY. You wait, kid, before it's all over we're gonna get a little place out in the country, and I'll raise some vegetables, a couple of chickens . . .

LINDA. You'll do it yet, dear.

1478   Drama in the Modern Age

Willy walks out of his jacket. Linda follows him.

WILLY. And they'll get married, and come for a weekend. I'd build a little guest house. 'Cause I got so many fine tools, all I'd need would be a little lumber and some peace of mind.

LINDA. [*joyfully*] I sewed the lining . . .

WILLY. I could build two guest houses, so they'd both come. Did he decide how much he's going to ask Oliver for?

LINDA. [*getting him into the jacket*] He didn't mention it, but I imagine ten or fifteen thousand. You going to talk to Howard today?

WILLY. Yeah. I'll put it to him straight and simple. He'll just have to take me off the road.

LINDA. And Willy, don't forget to ask for a little advance, because we've got the insurance premium. It's the grace period now.

WILLY. That's a hundred . . . ?

LINDA. A hundred and eight, sixty-eight. Because we're a little short again.

WILLY. Why are we short?

LINDA. Well, you had the motor job on the car . . .

WILLY. That goddam Studebaker!

LINDA. And you got one more payment on the refrigerator . . .

WILLY. But it just broke again!

LINDA. Well, it's old, dear.

WILLY. I told you we should've bought a well-advertised machine. Charley bought a General Electric and it's twenty years old and it's still good, that son-of-a-bitch.

LINDA. But, Willy—

WILLY. Whoever heard of a Hastings refrigerator? Once in my life I would like to own something outright before it's broken! I'm always in a race with the junkyard! I just finished paying for the car and it's on its last legs. The refrigerator consumes belts like a goddam maniac. They time those things. They time them so when you finally paid for them, they're used up.

LINDA. [*buttoning up his jacket as he unbuttons it*] All told, about two hundred dollars would carry us, dear. But that includes the last payment on the mortgage. After this payment, Willy, the house belongs to us.

WILLY. It's twenty-five years!

LINDA. Biff was nine years old when we bought it.

WILLY. Well, that's a great thing. To weather a twenty-five year mortgage is—

LINDA. It's an accomplishment.

WILLY. All the cement, the lumber, the reconstruction I put in this house! There ain't a crack to be found in it any more.

LINDA. Well, it served its purpose.

WILLY. What purpose? Some stranger'll come along, move in, and that's that. If only Biff would take this house, and raise a family . . . [*He starts to go.*] Goodby, I'm late.

LINDA. [*suddenly remembering*] Oh, I forgot! You're supposed to meet them for dinner.

WILLY. Me?

LINDA. At Frank's Chop House on Forty-eighth near Sixth Avenue.

WILLY. Is that so! How about you?

LINDA. No, just the three of you. They're gonna blow you to a big meal!

WILLY. Don't say! Who thought of that?

LINDA. Biff came to me this morning, Willy, and he said, "Tell Dad, we want to blow him to a big meal." Be there six o'clock. You and your two boys are going to have dinner.

WILLY. Gee whiz! That's really somethin'. I'm gonna knock Howard for a loop, kid. I'll get an advance, and I'll come home with a New York job. Goddammit, now I'm gonna do it!

LINDA. Oh, that's the spirit, Willy!

WILLY. I will never get behind a wheel the rest of my life!

LINDA. It's changing, Willy, I can feel it changing!

WILLY. Beyond a question. G'by, I'm late. [*He starts to go again.*]

LINDA. [*calling after him as she runs to the kitchen table for a handkerchief*] You got your glasses?

WILLY. [*feels for them, then comes back in*] Yeah, yeah, got my glasses.

LINDA. [*giving him the handkerchief*] And a handkerchief.

WILLY. Yeah, handkerchief.

LINDA. And your saccharine?

WILLY. Yeah, my saccharine.

LINDA. Be careful on the subway stairs.

She kisses him, and a silk stocking is seen hanging from her hand. Willy notices it.

WILLY. Will you stop mending stockings? At least while I'm in the house. It gets me nervous. I can't tell you. Please.

Linda hides the stocking in her hand as she follows Willy across the forestage in front of the house.

LINDA. Remember, Frank's Chop House.

WILLY. [*passing the apron*] Maybe beets would grow out there.

LINDA. [*laughing*] But you tried so many times.

WILLY. Yeah. Well, don't work hard today. [*He disappears around the right corner of the house.*]

LINDA. Be careful!

As Willy vanishes, Linda waves to him. Suddenly the phone rings. She runs across the stage and into the kitchen and lifts it.

LINDA. Hello? Oh, Biff! I'm so glad you called, I just . . . Yes, sure, I just told him. Yes, he'll be there for dinner at six o'clock, I didn't forget. Listen, I was just dying to tell you. You know that little rubber pipe I told you about? That he connected to the gas heater? I finally decided to go down the cellar this morning and take it away and destroy it. But it's gone! Imagine? He took it away himself, it isn't there! [*She listens.*] When? Oh, then you took it. Oh—nothing, it's just that I'd hoped he'd taken it away himself. Oh, I'm not worried, darling, because this morning he left in such high spirits, it was like the old days! I'm not afraid any more. Did Mr. Oliver see you? . . . Well, you wait there then. And make a nice impression on him, darling. Just don't perspire too much before you see him. And have a nice time with Dad. He may have big news too! . . . That's right, a New York job. And be sweet to him tonight, dear. Be loving to him. Because he's only a little boat looking for a harbor. [*She is trembling with sorrow and joy.*] Oh, that's wonderful, Biff, you'll save his life. Thanks, darling. Just put your arm around him when he comes into the restaurant. Give him a smile. That's the boy . . . Good-by, dear . . . You got your comb? . . . That's fine. Good-by, Biff dear.

In the middle of her speech, Howard Wagner, thirty-six, wheels on a small typewriter table on which is a wire-recording machine and proceeds to plug it in. This is on the left forestage. Light slowly fades on Linda as it rises on Howard. Howard is intent on threading the machine and only glances over his shoulder as Willy appears.

WILLY. Pst! Pst!

HOWARD. Hello, Willy, come in.

WILLY. Like to have a little talk with you, Howard.

HOWARD. Sorry to keep you waiting. I'll be with you in a minute.

WILLY. What's that, Howard?

HOWARD. Didn't you ever see one of these? Wire recorder.

WILLY. Oh. Can we talk a minute?

HOWARD. Records things. Just got delivery yesterday. Been driving me crazy, the most terrific machine I ever saw in my life. I was up all night with it.

WILLY. What do you do with it?

HOWARD. I bought it for dictation, but you can do anything with it. Listen to this. I had it home last night. Listen to what I picked up. The first one is my daughter. Get this. [*He flicks the switch and "Roll out the Barrel" is heard being whistled.*] Listen to that kid whistle.

WILLY. That is lifelike, isn't it?

HOWARD. Seven years old. Get that tone.

WILLY. Ts, ts. Like to ask a little favor if you . . .

The whistling breaks off, and the voice of Howard's daughter is heard.

HIS DAUGHTER. "Now you, Daddy."

HOWARD. She's crazy for me! [*Again the same song is whistled.*] That's me! Ha! [*He winks.*]

WILLY. You're very good!

HOWARD. Sh! Get this now, this is my son.

HIS SON. "The capital of Alabama is Montgomery; the capital of Arizona is Phoenix; the capital of Arkansas is Little Rock; the capital of California is Sacramento . . ." [*and on, and on.*]

HOWARD. [*holding up five fingers*] Five years old, Willy!

WILLY. He'll make an announcer some day!

HIS SON. [*continuing*] "The capital . . ."

HOWARD. Get that—alphabetical order! [*The machine breaks off suddenly.*] Wait a minute. The maid kicked the plug out.

WILLY. It certainly is a—

HOWARD. Sh, for God's sake!

HIS SON. "It's nine o'clock, Bulova watch time. So I have to go to sleep."

WILLY. That really is—

HOWARD. Wait a minute! The next is my wife.

They wait.

HOWARD'S VOICE. "Go on, say something." [*Pause.*] "Well, you gonna talk?"

HIS WIFE. "I can't think of anything."

HOWARD'S VOICE. "Well, talk—it's turning."

HIS WIFE. [*shyly, beaten*] "Hello." [*Silence.*] "Oh, Howard, I can't talk into this . . ."

HOWARD. [*snapping the machine off*] That was my wife.

WILLY. I think I'll get one myself.

HOWARD. Sure, they're only a hundred and a half. You can't do without it. Supposing you wanna hear Jack Benny, see? But you can't be at home at that hour. So you tell the maid to turn the radio on when Jack Benny comes on, and this automatically goes on with the radio . . .

WILLY. And when you come home you . . .

HOWARD. You can come home twelve o'clock, one o'clock, any time you like, and you get yourself a Coke and sit yourself down, throw the switch, and there's Jack Benny's program in the middle of the night!

WILLY. I'm definitely going to get one. Because lots of time I'm on the road, and I think to myself, what I must be missing on the radio!

HOWARD. Don't you have a radio in the car?

WILLY. Well, yeah, but who ever thinks of turning it on?

HOWARD. Say, aren't you supposed to be in Boston?

WILLY. That's what I want to talk to you about, Howard. You got a minute? [*He draws a chair in from the wing.*]

HOWARD. What happened? What're you doing here?

WILLY. Well . . .

HOWARD. You didn't crack up again, did you?

WILLY. Oh, no. No . . .

HOWARD. Geez, you had me worried there for a minute. What's the trouble?

WILLY. Well, tell you the truth, Howard. I've come to the decision that I'd rather not travel any more.

HOWARD. Not travel! Well, what'll you do?

WILLY. Remember, Christmas time, when you had the party here? You said you'd try to think of some spot for me here in town.

HOWARD. With us?

WILLY. Well, sure.

HOWARD. Oh, yeah, yeah. I remember. Well, I couldn't think of anything for you, Willy.

WILLY. I tell ya, Howard. The kids are all grown up, y'know. I don't need much any more. If I could take home—well, sixty-five dollars a week, I could swing it.

HOWARD. Yeah, but Willy, see I—

WILLY. I tell ya why, Howard. Speaking frankly and between the two of us, y'know—I'm just a little tired.

HOWARD. Oh, I could understand that, Willy. But you're a road man, Willy, and we do a road business. We've only got a half-dozen salesmen on the floor here.

WILLY. God knows, Howard, I never asked a favor of any man. But I was with the firm when your father used to carry you in here in his arms.

HOWARD. I know that, Willy, but—

WILLY. Your father came to me the day you were born and asked me what I thought of the name of Howard, may he rest in peace.

HOWARD. I appreciate that, Willy, but there just is no spot here for you. If I had a spot I'd slam you right in, but I just don't have a single solitary spot.

He looks for his lighter. Willy has picked it up and gives it to him. Pause.

WILLY. [*with increasing anger*] Howard, all I need to set my table is fifty dollars a week.

HOWARD. But where am I going to put you, kid?

Drama in the Modern Age

WILLY. Look, it isn't a question of whether I can sell merchandise, is it?

HOWARD. No, but it's a business, kid, and everybody's gotta pull his own weight.

WILLY. [*desperately*] Just let me tell you a story, Howard—

HOWARD. 'Cause you gotta admit, business is business.

WILLY. [*angrily*] Business is definitely business, but just listen for a minute. You don't understand this. When I was a boy—eighteen, nineteen—I was already on the road. And there was a question in my mind as to whether selling had a future for me. Because in those days I had a yearning to go to Alaska. See, there were three gold strikes in one month in Alaska, and I felt like going out. Just for the ride, you might say.

HOWARD. [*barely interested*] Don't say.

WILLY. Oh, yeah, my father lived many years in Alaska. He was an adventurous man. We've got quite a little streak of self-reliance in our family. I thought I'd go out with my older brother and try to locate him, and maybe settle in the North with the old man. And I was almost decided to go, when I met a sales-man in the Parker House. His name was Dave Singleman. And he was eighty-four years old, and he'd drummed merchandise in thirty-one states. And old Dave, he'd go up to his room, y'understand, put on his green velvet slippers—I'll never forget—and pick up his phone and call the buyers, and without ever leaving his room, at the age of eighty-four, he made his living. And when I saw that, I realized that selling was the greatest career a man could want. 'Cause what could be more satisfying than to be able to go, at the age of eighty-four, into twenty or thirty different cities, and pick up a phone, and be remembered and loved and helped by so many different people? Do you know? when he died—and by the way he died the death of a salesman, in his green velvet slip-pers in the smoker of the New York, New Haven and Hartford, going into Boston—when he died, hundreds of salesmen and buyers were at his funeral. Things were sad on a lotta trains for months after that. [*He stands up. Howard has not looked at him.*] In those days there was personality in it, Howard. There was respect, and comradeship, and gratitude in it. Today, it's all cut and dried, and there's no chance for bringing friendship to bear—or personality. You see what I mean? They don't know me any more.

HOWARD. [*moving away, to the right*] That's just the thing, Willy.

WILLY. If I had forty dollars a week—that's all I'd need. Forty dollars, Howard.

HOWARD. Kid, I can't take blood from a stone, I—

WILLY. [*desperation is on him now*] Howard, the year Al Smith was nominated, your father came to me and—

HOWARD. [*starting to go off*] I've got to see some people, kid.

WILLY. [*stopping him*] I'm talking about your father! There were promises made across this desk! You mustn't tell me you've got people to see—I put thirty-four years into this firm, Howard, and now I can't pay my insurance! You can't eat the orange and throw the peel away—a man is not a piece of fruit! [*After a pause*] Now pay attention. Your father—in 1928 I had a big year. I averaged a hundred and seventy dollars a week in commissions.

HOWARD. [*impatiently*] Now, Willy, you never averaged—

WILLY. [*banging his hand on the desk*] I averaged a hundred and seventy dollars a week in the year of 1928! And your father came to me—or rather, I was in the office here—it was right over this desk—and he put his hand on my shoulder—

HOWARD. [*getting up*] You'll have to excuse me, Willy, I gotta see some people. Pull yourself together. [*Going out*] I'll be back in a little while.

On Howard's exit, the light on his chair grows very bright and strange.

WILLY. Pull myself together! What the hell did I say to him? My God, I was yelling at him! How could I! [*Willy breaks off, staring at the light, which occupies the chair, animating it. He approaches this chair, standing across the desk from it.*] Frank, Frank, don't you remember what you told me that time? How you put your hand on my shoulder, and Frank . . . [*He leans on the desk and as he speaks the dead man's name he accidentally switches on the recorder, and instantly*]

HOWARD'S SON. " . . . of New York is Albany. The capital of Ohio is Cincinnati, the capital of Rhode Island is . . . " [*The recitation continues.*]

WILLY. [*leaping away with fright, shouting*] Ha! Howard! Howard! Howard!

HOWARD. [*rushing in*] What happened?

WILLY. [*pointing at the machine, which continues nasally, childishly, with the capital cities*] Shut it off! Shut it off!

HOWARD. [*pulling the plug out*] Look, Willy . . .

WILLY. [*pressing his hands to his eyes*] I gotta get myself some coffee. I'll get some coffee . . .

Willy starts to walk out. Howard stops him.

HOWARD. [*rolling up the cord*] Willy, look . . .

WILLY. I'll go to Boston.

HOWARD. Willy, you can't go to Boston for us.

WILLY. Why can't I go?

HOWARD. I don't want you to represent us. I've been meaning to tell you for a long time now.

WILLY. Howard, are you firing me?

HOWARD. I think you need a good long rest, Willy.

WILLY. Howard—

HOWARD. And when you feel better, come back, and we'll see if we can work something out.

WILLY. But I gotta earn money, Howard. I'm in no position to—

HOWARD. Where are your sons? Why don't your sons give you a hand?

WILLY. They're working on a very big deal.

HOWARD. This is no time for false pride, Willy. You go to your sons and you tell them that you're tired. You've got two great boys, haven't you?

WILLY. Oh, no question, no question, but in the meantime . . .

HOWARD. Then that's that, heh?

WILLY. All right, I'll go to Boston tomorrow.

HOWARD. No, no.

WILLY. I can't throw myself on my sons. I'm not a cripple!

HOWARD. Look, kid, I'm busy this morning.

WILLY. [*grasping Howard's arm*] Howard, you've got to let me go to Boston!

HOWARD. [*hard, keeping himself under control*] I've got a line of people to see this morning. Sit down, take five minutes, and pull yourself together, and then go home, will ya? I need the office, Willy. [*He starts to go, turns, remembering the recorder, starts to push off the table holding the recorder.*] Oh, yeah. Whenever you can this week, stop by and drop off the samples. You'll feel better, Willy, and then come back and we'll talk. Pull yourself together, kid, there's people outside.

Howard exits, pushing the table off left. Willy stares into space, exhausted. Now the music is heard—Ben's music—first distantly, then closer, closer. As Willy speaks, Ben enters from the right. He carries valise and umbrella.

WILLY. Oh, Ben, how did you do it? What is the answer? Did you wind up the Alaska deal already?

BEN. Doesn't take much time if you know what you're doing. Just a short business trip. Boarding ship in an hour. Wanted to say good-by.

WILLY. Ben, I've got to talk to you.

BEN. [*glancing at his watch*] Haven't the time, William.

WILLY. [*crossing the apron to Ben*] Ben, nothing's working out. I don't know what to do.

BEN. Now, look here, William. I've bought timberland in Alaska and I need a man to look after things for me.

WILLY. God, timberland! Me and my boys in those grand outdoors!

BEN. You've a new continent at your doorstep, William. Get out of these cities, they're full of talk and time payments and courts of law. Screw on your fists and you can fight for a fortune up there.

WILLY. Yes, yes! Linda, Linda!

Linda enters as of old, with the wash.

LINDA. Oh, you're back?

BEN. I haven't much time.

WILLY. No, wait! Linda, he's got a proposition for me in Alaska.

LINDA. But you've got—[*To Ben*] He's got a beautiful job here.

WILLY. But in Alaska, kid, I could—

LINDA. You're doing well enough, Willy!

BEN. [*to Linda*] Enough for what, my dear?

LINDA. [*frightened of Ben and angry at him*] Don't say those things to him! Enough to be happy right here, right now. [*To Willy, while Ben laughs*] Why must everybody conquer the world? You're well liked, and the boys love you, and someday—[*to Ben*]—why, old man Wagner told him just the other day that if he keeps it up he'll be a member of the firm, didn't he, Willy?

WILLY. Sure, sure. I am building something with this firm, Ben, and if a man is building something he must be on the right track, mustn't he?

BEN. What are you building? Lay your hand on it. Where is it?

WILLY. [*hesitantly*] That's true, Linda, there's nothing.

LINDA. Why? [*To Ben*] There's a man eighty-four years old—

WILLY. That's right, Ben, that's right. When I look at that man I say, what is there to worry about?

BEN. Bah!

WILLY. It's true, Ben. All he has to do is go into any city, pick up the phone, and he's making his living and you know why?

BEN. [*picking up his valise*] I've got to go.

WILLY. [*holding Ben back*] Look at this boy!

Biff, in his high school sweater, enters carrying suitcase. Happy carries Biff's shoulder guards, gold helmet, and football pants.

WILLY. Without a penny to his name, three great universities are begging for him, and from there the sky's the limit, because it's not what you do, Ben. It's who you know and the smile on your face! It's contacts, Ben, contacts! The whole wealth of Alaska passes over the lunch table at the Commodore Hotel, and that's the wonder, the wonder of this country, that a man can end with diamonds here on the basis of being liked! [*He turns to Biff.*] And that's why when you get out on that field today it's important. Because thousands of people will be rooting for you and loving you. [*To Ben, who has again begun to leave*] And Ben! when he walks into a business office his name will sound out like a bell and all the doors will open to him! I've seen it, Ben, I've seen it a thousand times! You can't feel it with your hand like timber, but it's there!

BEN. Good-by, William.

WILLY. Ben, am I right? Don't you think I'm right? I value your advice.

BEN. There's a new continent at your doorstep, William. You could walk out rich. Rich! [*He is gone.*]

WILLY. We'll do it here, Ben! You hear me? We're gonna do it here!

Young Bernard rushes in. The gay music of the Boys is heard.

BERNARD. Oh, gee, I was afraid you left already!

WILLY. Why? What time is it?

BERNARD. It's half-past one!

WILLY. Well, come on, everybody! Ebbets Field next stop! Where's the pennants? [*He rushes through the wall-line of the kitchen and out into the living-room.*]

LINDA. [*to Biff*] Did you pack fresh underwear?

BIFF. [*who has been limbering up*] I want to go!

BERNARD. Biff, I'm carrying your helmet, ain't I?

HAPPY. No, I'm carrying the helmet.

BERNARD. Oh, Biff, you promised me.

HAPPY. I'm carrying the helmet.

BERNARD. How am I going to get in the locker room?

LINDA. Let him carry the shoulder guards. [*She puts her coat and hat on in the kitchen.*]

BERNARD. Can I, Biff? 'Cause I told everybody I'm going to be in the locker room.

HAPPY. In Ebbets Field it's the clubhouse.

BERNARD. I meant the clubhouse. Biff!

HAPPY. Biff!

BIFF. [*grandly, after a slight pause*] Let him carry the shoulder guards.

HAPPY. [*as he gives Bernard the shoulder guards*] Stay close to us now.

Willy rushes in with the pennants.

WILLY. [*handing them out*] Everybody wave when Biff comes out on the field. [*Happy and Bernard run off.*] You set now, boy?

The music has died away.

BIFF. Ready to go, Pop. Every muscle is ready.

WILLY. [*at the edge of the apron*] You realize what this means?

BIFF. That's right, Pop.

WILLY. [*feeling Biff's muscles*] You're comin' home this afternoon captain of the All-Scholastic Championship Team of the City of New York.

BIFF. I got it, Pop. And remember, pal, when I take off my helmet, that touchdown is for you.

WILLY. Let's go! [*He is starting out, with his arms around Biff, when Charley enters, as of old, in knickers.*] I got no room for you, Charley.

CHARLEY. Room? For what?

WILLY. In the car.

CHARLEY. You goin' for a ride? I wanted to shoot some casino.°

WILLY. [*furiously*] Casino! [*Incredulously*] Don't you realize what today is?

LINDA. Oh, he knows, Willy. He's just kidding you.

WILLY. That's nothing to kid about!

CHARLEY. No, Linda, what's goin' on?

LINDA. He's playing in Ebbets Field.

CHARLEY. Baseball in this weather?

WILLY. Don't talk to him. Come on, come on! [*He is pushing them out.*]

CHARLEY. Wait a minute, didn't you hear the news?

WILLY. What?

CHARLEY. Don't you listen to the radio? Ebbets Field just blew up.

WILLY. You go to hell! [*Charley laughs. Pushing them out*] Come on, come on! We're late.

CHARLEY. [*as they go*] Knock a homer, Biff, knock a homer!

WILLY. [*the last to leave, turning to Charley*] I don't think that was funny, Charley. This is the greatest day of his life.

CHARLEY. Willy, when are you going to grow up?

WILLY. Yeah, heh? When this game is over, Charley, you'll be laughing out of the other side of your face. They'll be calling him another Red Grange.° Twenty-five thousand a year.

CHARLEY. [*kidding*] Is that so?

WILLY. Yeah, that's so.

CHARLEY. Well, then, I'm sorry, Willy. But tell me something.

WILLY. What?

CHARLEY. Who is Red Grange?

WILLY. Put up your hands. Goddam you, put up your hands!

Charley, chuckling, shakes his head and walks away, around the left corner of the stage. Willy follows him. The music rises to a mocking frenzy.

WILLY. Who the hell do you think you are, better than everybody else? You don't know everything, you big, ignorant, stupid . . . Put up your hands!

Light rises, on the right side of the forestage, on a small table in the reception room of Charley's office. Traffic sounds are heard. Bernard, now mature, sits whistling to himself. A pair of tennis rackets and an overnight bag are on the floor beside him.

WILLY. [*offstage*] What are you walking away for? Don't walk away! If you're going to say something say it to my face! I know you laugh at me behind my back. You'll laugh out of the other side of your goddam face after this game. Touchdown! Touchdown! Eighty thousand people! Touchdown! Right between the goal posts.

Bernard is a quiet, earnest, but self-assured young man. Willy's voice is coming from right upstage now. Bernard lowers his feet off the table and listens. Jenny, his father's secretary, enters.

---

casino: a card game.   Red Grange: football hero.

JENNY. [*distressed*] Say, Bernard, will you go out in the hall?

BERNARD. What is that noise? Who is it?

JENNY. Mr. Loman. He just got off the elevator.

BERNARD. [*getting up*] Who's he arguing with?

JENNY. Nobody. There's nobody with him. I can't deal with him any more, and your father gets all upset everytime he comes. I've got a lot of typing to do, and your father's waiting to sign it. Will you see him?

WILLY. [*entering*] Touchdown! Touch—[*He sees Jenny.*] Jenny, Jenny, good to see you. How're ya? Workin'? Or still honest?

JENNY. Fine. How've you been feeling?

WILLY. Not much any more, Jenny. Ha, ha! [*He is surprised to see the rackets.*]

BERNARD. Hello, Uncle Willy.

WILLY. [*almost shocked*] Bernard! Well, look who's here! [*He comes quickly, guiltily, to Bernard and warmly shakes his hand.*]

BERNARD. How are you? Good to see you.

WILLY. What are you doing here?

BERNARD. Oh, just stopped by to see Pop. Get off my feet till my train leaves. I'm going to Washington in a few minutes.

WILLY. Is he in?

BERNARD. Yes, he's in his office with the accountant. Sit down.

WILLY. [*sitting down*] What're you going to do in Washington?

BERNARD. Oh, just a case I've got there, Willy.

WILLY. That so? [*Indicating the rackets*] You going to play tennis there?

BERNARD. I'm staying with a friend who's got a court.

WILLY. Don't say. His own tennis court. Must be fine people, I bet.

BERNARD. They are, very nice. Dad tells me Biff's in town.

WILLY. [*with a big smile*] Yeah, Biff's in. Working on a very big deal, Bernard.

BERNARD. What's Biff doing?

WILLY. Well, he's been doing very big things in the West. But he decided to establish himself here. Very big. We're having dinner. Did I hear your wife had a boy?

BERNARD. That's right. Our second.

WILLY. Two boys! What do you know!

BERNARD. What kind of a deal has Biff got?

WILLY. Well, Bill Oliver—very big sporting-goods man—he wants Biff very badly. Called him in from the West. Long distance, carte blanche, special deliveries. Your friends have their own private tennis court?

BERNARD. You still with the old firm, Willy?

WILLY. [*after a pause*] I'm—I'm overjoyed to see how you made the grade, Bernard, overjoyed. It's an encouraging thing to see a young man really—really—Looks very good for Biff—very—[*He breaks off, then*] Bernard—[*He is so full of emotion, he breaks off again.*]

BERNARD. What is it, Willy?

WILLY. [*small and alone*] What—what's the secret?

BERNARD. What secret?

WILLY. How—how did you? Why didn't he ever catch on?

BERNARD. I wouldn't know that, Willy.

WILLY. [*confidentially, desperately*] You were his friend, his boyhood friend. There's something I don't understand about it. His life ended after that Ebbets Field game. From the age of seventeen nothing good ever happened to him.

BERNARD. He never trained himself for anything.

WILLY. But he did, he did. After high school he took so many correspondence courses. Radio mechanics; television; God knows what, and never made the slightest mark.

BERNARD. [taking off his glasses] Willy, do you want to talk candidly?

WILLY. [rising, faces Bernard] I regard you as a very brilliant man, Bernard. I value your advice.

BERNARD. Oh, the hell with the advice, Willy. I couldn't advise you. There's just one thing I've always wanted to ask you. When he was supposed to graduate, and the math teacher flunked him—

WILLY. Oh, that son-of-a-bitch ruined his life.

BERNARD. Yeah, but, Willy, all he had to do was go to summer school and make up that subject.

WILLY. That's right, that's right.

BERNARD. Did you tell him not to go to summer school?

WILLY. Me? I begged him to go. I ordered him to go!

BERNARD. Then why wouldn't he go?

WILLY. Why? Why! Bernard, that question has been trailing me like a ghost for the last fifteen years. He flunked the subject, and laid down and died like a hammer hit him!

BERNARD. Take it easy, kid.

WILLY. Let me talk to you—I got nobody to talk to. Bernard, Bernard, was it my fault? Y'see? It keeps going around in my mind, maybe I did something to him. I got nothing to give him.

BERNARD. Don't take it so hard.

WILLY. Why did he lay down? What is the story there? You were his friend!

BERNARD. Willy, I remember, it was June, and our grades came out. And he'd flunked math.

WILLY. That son-of-a-bitch!

BERNARD. No, it wasn't right then. Biff just got very angry, I remember, and he was ready to enroll in summer school.

WILLY. [surprised] He was?

BERNARD. He wasn't beaten by it at all. But then, Willy, he disappeared from the block for almost a month. And I got the idea that he'd gone up to New England to see you. Did he have a talk with you then?

Willy stares in silence.

BERNARD. Willy?

WILLY. [with a strong edge of resentment in his voice] Yeah, he came to Boston. What about it?

BERNARD. Well, just that when he came back—I'll never forget this, it always mystifies me. Because I'd thought so well of Biff, even though he'd always taken advantage of me. I loved him, Willy, y'know? And he came back after that month and took his sneakers—remember those sneakers with "University of Virginia" printed on them? He was so proud of those, wore them every day. And he took them down in the cellar, and burned them up in the furnace. We had a fist fight. It lasted at least half an hour. Just the two of us, punching each other down the cellar, and crying right through it. I've often thought of how strange it was that I knew he'd given up his life. What happened in Boston, Willy?

Willy looks at him as at an intruder.

BERNARD. I just bring it up because you asked me.

WILLY. [*angrily*] Nothing. What do you mean, "What happened?" What's that got to do with anything?

BERNARD. Well, don't get sore.

WILLY. What are you trying to do, blame it on me? If a boy lays down is that my fault?

BERNARD. Now, Willy, don't get—

WILLY. Well, don't—don't talk to me that way! What does that mean, "What happened?"

Charley enters. He is in his vest, and he carries a bottle of bourbon.

CHARLEY. Hey, you're going to miss that train. [*He waves the bottle.*]

BERNARD. Yeah, I'm going. [*He takes the bottle.*] Thanks, Pop. [*He picks up his rackets and bag.*] Good-by, Willy, and don't worry about it. You know, "If at first you don't succeed . . ."

WILLY. Yes, I believe in that.

BERNARD. But sometimes, Willy, it's better for a man just to walk away.

WILLY. Walk away?

BERNARD. [*after a slight pause*] I guess that's when it's tough. [*Extending his hand*] Good-by, Willy.

WILLY. [*shaking Bernard's hand*] Good-by, boy.

CHARLEY. [*an arm on Bernard's shoulder*] How do you like this kid? Gonna argue a case in front of the Supreme Court.

BERNARD. [*protesting*] Pop!

WILLY. [*genuinely shocked, pained, and happy*] No! The Supreme Court!

BERNARD. I gotta run. 'By, Dad!

CHARLEY. Knock 'em dead, Bernard!

Bernard goes off.

WILLY. [*as Charley takes out his wallet*] The Supreme Court! And he didn't even mention it!

CHARLEY. [*counting out money on the desk*] He don't have to—he's gonna do it.

WILLY. And you never told him what to do, did you? You never took any interest in him.

CHARLEY. My salvation is that I never took any interest in anything. There's some money—fifty dollars. I got an accountant inside.

WILLY. Charley, look . . . [*With difficulty*] I got my insurance to pay. If you can manage it—I need a hundred and ten dollars.

Charley doesn't reply for a moment; merely stops moving.

WILLY. I'd draw it from my bank but Linda would know, and I . . .

CHARLEY. Sit down, Willy.

WILLY. [*moving toward the chair*] I'm keeping an account of everything, remember. I'll pay every penny back. [*He sits.*]

CHARLEY. Now listen to me, Willy.

WILLY. I want you to know I appreciate . . .

CHARLEY. [*sitting down on the table*] Willy, what're you doin'? What the hell is goin' on in your head?

WILLY. Why? I'm simply . . .

CHARLEY. I offered you a job. You can make fifty dollars a week. And I won't send you on the road.

WILLY. I've got a job.

CHARLEY. Without pay? What kind of a job is a job without pay? [*He rises.*] Now, look, kid, enough is enough. I'm no genius but I know when I'm being insulted.

WILLY. Insulted!

CHARLEY. Why don't you want to work for me?

WILLY. What's the matter with you? I've got a job.

CHARLEY. Then what're you walkin' in here every week for?

WILLY. [*getting up*] Well, if you don't want me to walk in here—

CHARLEY. I am offering you a job.

WILLY. I don't want your goddam job!

CHARLEY. When the hell are you going to grow up?

WILLY. [*furiously*] You big ignoramus, if you say that to me again I'll rap you one! I don't care how big you are! [*He's ready to fight.*]

Pause.

CHARLEY. [*kindly, going to him*] How much do you need, Willy?

WILLY. Charley, I'm strapped, I'm strapped. I don't know what to do. I was just fired.

CHARLEY. Howard fired you?

WILLY. That snotnose. Imagine that? I named him. I named him Howard.

CHARLEY. Willy, when're you gonna realize that them things don't mean anything? You named him Howard, but you can't sell that. The only thing you got in this world is what you can sell. And the funny thing is that you're a salesman, and you don't know that.

WILLY. I've always tried to think otherwise, I guess. I always felt that if a man was impressive, and well liked, that nothing—

CHARLEY. Why must everybody like you? Who liked J. P. Morgan?° Was he impressive? In a Turkish bath he'd look like a butcher. But with his pockets on he was very well liked. Now listen, Willy, I know you don't like me, and nobody can say I'm in love with you, but I'll give you a job because—just for the hell of it, put it that way. Now what do you say?

WILLY. I—I just can't work for you, Charley.

CHARLEY. What're you, jealous of me?

WILLY. I can't work for you, that's all, don't ask me why.

CHARLEY. [*angered, takes out more bills*] You been jealous of me all your life, you damned fool! Here, pay your insurance. [*He puts the money in Willy's hand.*]

WILLY. I'm keeping strict accounts.

CHARLEY. I've got some work to do. Take care of yourself. And pay your insurance.

WILLY. [*moving to the right*] Funny, y'know? After all the highways, and the trains, and the appointments, and the years, you end up worth more dead than alive.

CHARLEY. Willy, nobody's worth nothin' dead. [*After a slight pause*] Did you hear what I said?

Willy stands still, dreaming.

J. P. Morgan: aggressive American financier and multimillionaire.

CHARLEY. Willy!

WILLY. Apologize to Bernard for me when you see him. I didn't mean to argue with him. He's a fine boy. They're all fine boys, and they'll end up big—all of them. Someday they'll all play tennis together. Wish me luck, Charley. He saw Bill Oliver today.

CHARLEY. Good luck.

WILLY. [*on the verge of tears*] Charley, you're the only friend I got. Isn't that a remarkable thing? [*He goes out.*]

CHARLEY. Jesus!

> *Charley stares after him a moment and follows. All light blacks out. Suddenly raucous music is heard, and a red glow rises behind the screen at right. Stanley, a young waiter, appears, carrying a table, followed by Happy, who is carrying two chairs.*

STANLEY. [*putting the table down*] That's all right, Mr. Loman, I can handle it myself. [*He turns and takes the chairs from Happy and places them at the table.*]

HAPPY. [*glancing around*] Oh, this is better.

STANLEY. Sure, in the front there you're in the middle of all kinds of noise. Whenever you got a party, Mr. Loman, you just tell me and I'll put you back here. Y'know, there's a lotta people they don't like it private, because when they go out they like to see a lotta action around them because they're sick and tired to stay in the house by theirself. But I know you, you ain't from Hackensack.° You know what I mean?

HAPPY. [*sitting down*] So how's it coming, Stanley?

STANLEY. Ah, it's a dog's life. I only wish during the war they'd a took me in the Army. I coulda been dead by now.

HAPPY. My brother's back, Stanley.

STANLEY. Oh, he come back, heh? From the Far West.

HAPPY. Yeah, big cattle man, my brother, so treat him right. And my father's coming too.

STANLEY. Oh, your father too!

HAPPY. You got a couple of nice lobsters?

STANLEY. Hundred per cent, big.

HAPPY. I want them with the claws.

STANLEY. Don't worry, I don't give you no mice. [*Happy laughs.*] How about some wine? It'll put a head on the meal.

HAPPY. No. You remember, Stanley, that recipe I brought you from overseas? With the champagne in it?

STANLEY. Oh, yeah, sure. I still got it tacked up yet in the kitchen. But that'll have to cost a buck apiece anyways.

HAPPY. That's all right.

STANLEY. What'd you, hit a number or somethin'?

HAPPY. No, it's a little celebration. My brother is—I think he pulled off a big deal today. I think we're going into business together.

STANLEY. Great! That's the best for you. Because a family business, you know what I mean?—that's the best.

HAPPY. That's what I think.

Hackensack: small town in New Jersey.

STANLEY. 'Cause what's the difference? Somebody steals? It's in the family. Know
what I mean? [*Sotto voce°*] Like this bartender here. The boss is goin' crazy what
kinda leak he's got in the cash register. You put it in but it don't come out.

HAPPY. [*raising his head*] Sh!

STANLEY. What?

HAPPY. You notice I wasn't lookin' right or left, was I?

STANLEY. No.

HAPPY. And my eyes are closed.

STANLEY. So what's the—?

HAPPY. Strudel's comin'.

STANLEY. [*catching on, looks around*] Ah, no, there's no—

> *He breaks off as a furred, lavishly dressed girl enters and sits at the next table. Both*
> *follow her with their eyes.*

STANLEY. Geez, how'd ya know?

HAPPY. I got radar or something. [*Staring directly at her profile*] Oooooooo . . .
Stanley.

STANLEY. I think that's for you, Mr. Loman.

HAPPY. Look at that mouth. Oh, God. And the binoculars.

STANLEY. Geez, you got a life, Mr. Loman.

HAPPY. Wait on her.

STANLEY. [*going to the girl's table*] Would you like a menu, ma'am?

GIRL. I'm expecting someone, but I'd like a—

HAPPY. Why don't you bring her—excuse me, miss, do you mind? I sell champagne,
and I'd like you to try my brand. Bring her a champagne, Stanley.

GIRL. That's awfully nice of you.

HAPPY. Don't mention it. It's all company money. [*He laughs.*]

GIRL. That's a charming product to be selling, isn't it?

HAPPY. Oh, gets to be like everything else. Selling is selling, y'know.

GIRL. I suppose.

HAPPY. You don't happen to sell, do you?

GIRL. No, I don't sell.

HAPPY. Would you object to a compliment from a stranger? You ought to be on a
magazine cover.

GIRL. [*looking at him a little archly*] I have been.

> *Stanley comes in with a glass of champagne.*

HAPPY. What'd I say before, Stanley? You see? She's a cover girl.

STANLEY. Oh, I could see, I could see.

HAPPY. [*to the Girl*] What magazine?

GIRL. Oh, a lot of them. [*She takes the drink.*] Thank you.

HAPPY. You know what they say in France, don't you? "Champagne is the drink of
the complexion"—Hya, Biff!

> *Biff has entered and sits with Happy.*

BIFF. Hello, kid. Sorry I'm late.

HAPPY. I just got here. Uh, Miss—?

Sotto voce: softly, confidentially.

GIRL. Forsythe.

HAPPY. Miss Forsythe, this is my brother.

BIFF. Is Dad here?

HAPPY. His name is Biff. You might've heard of him. Great football player.

GIRL. Really? What team?

HAPPY. Are you familiar with football?

GIRL. No, I'm afraid I'm not.

HAPPY. Biff is quarterback with the New York Giants.

GIRL. Well, that is nice, isn't it? [*She drinks.*]

HAPPY. Good health.

GIRL. I'm happy to meet you.

HAPPY. That's my name. Hap. It's really Harold, but at West Point they called me Happy.

GIRL. [*now really impressed*] Oh, I see. How do you do? [*She turns her profile.*]

BIFF. Isn't Dad coming?

HAPPY. You want her?

BIFF. Oh, I could never make that.

HAPPY. I remember the time that idea would never come into your head. Where's the old confidence, Biff?

BIFF. I just saw Oliver—

HAPPY. Wait a minute. I've got to see that old confidence again. Do you want her? She's on call.

BIFF. Oh, no. [*He turns to look at the Girl.*]

HAPPY. I'm telling you. Watch this. [*Turning to the Girl*] Honey? [*She turns to him.*] Are you busy?

GIRL. Well, I am . . . but I could make a phone call.

HAPPY. Do that, will you, honey? And see if you can get a friend. We'll be here for a while. Biff is one of the greatest football players in the country.

GIRL. [*standing up*] Well, I'm certainly happy to meet you.

HAPPY. Come back soon.

GIRL. I'll try.

HAPPY. Don't try, honey, try hard.

The Girl exits. Stanley follows, shaking his head in bewildered admiration.

HAPPY. Isn't that a shame now? A beautiful girl like that? That's why I can't get married. There's not a good woman in a thousand. New York is loaded with them, kid!

BIFF. Hap, look—

HAPPY. I told you she was on call!

BIFF. [*strangely unnerved*] Cut it out, will ya? I want to say something to you.

HAPPY. Did you see Oliver?

BIFF. I saw him all right. Now look, I want to tell Dad a couple of things and I want you to help me.

HAPPY. What? Is he going to back you?

BIFF. Are you crazy? You're out of your goddam head, you know that?

HAPPY. Why? What happened?

BIFF. [*breathlessly*] I did a terrible thing today, Hap. It's been the strangest day I ever went through. I'm all numb, I swear.

HAPPY. You mean he wouldn't see you?

Drama in the Modern Age

BIFF. Well, I waited six hours for him, see? All day. Kept sending my name in. Even tried to date his secretary so she'd get me to him, but no soap.

HAPPY. Because you're not showin' the old confidence, Biff. He remembered you, didn't he?

BIFF. [*stopping Happy with a gesture*] Finally, about five o'clock, he comes out. Didn't remember who I was or anything. I felt like such an idiot, Hap.

HAPPY. Did you tell him my Florida idea?

BIFF. He walked away. I saw him for one minute. I got so mad I could've torn the walls down! How the hell did I ever get the idea I was a salesman there? I even believed myself that I'd been a salesman for him! And then he gave me one look and—I realized what a ridiculous lie my whole life has been! We've been talking in a dream for fifteen years. I was a shipping clerk.

HAPPY. What'd you do?

BIFF. [*with great tension and wonder*] Well, he left, see. And the secretary went out. I was all alone in the waiting-room. I don't know what came over me, Hap. The next thing I know I'm in his office—paneled walls, everything. I can't explain it. I—Hap, I took his fountain pen.

HAPPY. Geez, did he catch you?

BIFF. I ran out. I ran down all eleven flights. I ran and ran and ran.

HAPPY. That was an awful dumb—what'd you do that for?

BIFF. [*agonized*] I don't know, I just—wanted to take something, I don't know. You gotta help me, Hap, I'm gonna tell Pop.

HAPPY. You crazy? What for?

BIFF. Hap, he's got to understand that I'm not the man somebody lends that kind of money to. He thinks I've been spiting him all these years and it's eating him up.

HAPPY. That's just it. You tell him something nice.

BIFF. I can't.

HAPPY. Say you got a lunch date with Oliver tomorrow.

BIFF. So what do I do tomorrow?

HAPPY. You leave the house tomorrow and come back at night and say Oliver is thinking it over. And he thinks it over for a couple of weeks, and gradually it fades away and nobody's the worse.

BIFF. But it'll go on forever!

HAPPY. Dad is never so happy as when he's looking forward to something!

Willy enters.

HAPPY. Hello, scout!

WILLY. Gee, I haven't been here in years!

Stanley has followed Willy in and sets a chair for him. Stanley starts off but Happy stops him.

HAPPY. Stanley!

Stanley stands by, waiting for an order.

BIFF. [*going to Willy with guilt, as to an invalid*] Sit down, Pop. You want a drink?

WILLY. Sure, I don't mind.

BIFF. Let's get a load on.

WILLY. You look worried.

BIFF. N-no. [*To Stanley*] Scotch all around. Make it doubles.

STANLEY. Doubles, right. [*He goes.*]

WILLY. You had a couple already, didn't you?

BIFF. Just a couple, yeah.

WILLY. Well, what happened, boy? [*Nodding affirmatively, with a smile*] Everything go all right?

BIFF. [*takes a breath, then reaches out and grasps Willy's hand*] Pal . . . [*He is smiling bravely, and Willy is smiling too.*] I had an experience today.

HAPPY. Terrific, Pop.

WILLY. That so? What happened?

BIFF. [*high, slightly alcoholic, above the earth*] I'm going to tell you everything from first to last. It's been a strange day. [*Silence. He looks around, composes himself as best he can, but his breath keeps breaking the rhythm of his voice.*] I had to wait quite a while for him, and—

WILLY. Oliver?

BIFF. Yeah, Oliver. All day, as a matter of cold fact. And a lot of—instances—facts, Pop, facts about my life came back to me. Who was it, Pop? Who ever said I was a salesman with Oliver?

WILLY. Well, you were.

BIFF. No, Dad, I was a shipping clerk.

WILLY. But you were practically—

BIFF. [*with determination*] Dad, I don't know who said it first, but I was never a salesman for Bill Oliver.

WILLY. What're you talking about?

BIFF. Let's hold on to the facts tonight, Pop. We're not going to get anywhere bullin' around. I was a shipping clerk.

WILLY. [*angrily*] All right, now listen to me—

BIFF. Why don't you let me finish?

WILLY. I'm not interested in stories about the past or any crap of that kind because the woods are burning, boys, you understand? There's a big blaze going on all around. I was fired today.

BIFF. [*shocked*] How could you be?

WILLY. I was fired, and I'm looking for a little good news to tell your mother, because the woman has waited and the woman has suffered. The gist of it is that I haven't got a story left in my head, Biff. So don't give me a lecture about facts and aspects. I am not interested. Now what've you got to say to me?

Stanley enters with three drinks. They wait until he leaves.

WILLY. Did you see Oliver?

BIFF. Jesus, Dad!

WILLY. You mean you didn't go up there?

HAPPY. Sure he went up there.

BIFF. I did. I—saw him. How could they fire you?

WILLY. [*on the edge of his chair*] What kind of a welcome did he give you?

BIFF. He won't even let you work on commission?

WILLY. I'm out! [*Driving*] So tell me, he gave you a warm welcome?

HAPPY. Sure, Pop, sure!

BIFF. [*driven*] Well, it was kind of—

WILLY. I was wondering if he'd remember you. [*To Happy*] Imagine, man doesn't see him for ten, twelve years and gives him that kind of a welcome!

HAPPY. Damn right!

BIFF. [trying to return to the offensive] Pop, look—

WILLY. You know why he remembered you, don't you? Because you impressed him in those days.

BIFF. Let's talk quietly and get this down to the facts, huh?

WILLY. [as though Biff had been interrupting] Well, what happened? It's great news, Biff. Did he take you into his office or'd you talk in the waiting-room?

BIFF. Well, he came in, see, and—

WILLY. [with a big smile] What'd he say? Betcha he threw his arm around you.

BIFF. Well, he kinda—

WILLY. He's a fine man. [To Happy] Very hard man to see, y'know.

HAPPY. [agreeing] Oh, I know.

WILLY. [to Biff] Is that where you had the drinks?

BIFF. Yeah, he gave me a couple of—no, no!

HAPPY. [cutting in] He told him my Florida idea.

WILLY. Don't interrupt. [To Biff] How'd he react to the Florida idea?

BIFF. Dad, will you give me a minute to explain?

WILLY. I've been waiting for you to explain since I sat down here! What happened? He took you into his office and what?

BIFF. Well—I talked. And—and he listened, see.

WILLY. Famous for the way he listens, y'know. What was his answer?

BIFF. His answer was—[He breaks off, suddenly angry.] Dad, you're not letting me tell you what I want to tell you!

WILLY. [accusing, angered] You didn't see him, did you?

BIFF. I did see him!

WILLY. What'd you insult him or something? You insulted him, didn't you?

BIFF. Listen, will you let me out of it, will you just let me out of it!

HAPPY. What the hell!

WILLY. Tell me what happened!

BIFF. [to Happy] I can't talk to him!

A single trumpet note jars the ear. The light of green leaves stains the house, which holds the air of night and a dream. Young Bernard enters and knocks on the door of the house.

YOUNG BERNARD. [frantically] Mrs. Loman, Mrs. Loman!

HAPPY. Tell him what happened!

BIFF. [to Happy] Shut up and leave me alone!

WILLY. No, no! You had to go and flunk math!

BIFF. What math? What're you talking about?

YOUNG BERNARD. Mrs. Loman, Mrs. Loman!

Linda appears in the house, as of old.

WILLY. [wildly] Math, math, math!

BIFF. Take it easy, Pop!

YOUNG BERNARD. Mrs. Loman!

WILLY. [furiously] If you hadn't flunked you'd've been set by now!

BIFF. Now, look, I'm gonna tell you what happened, and you're going to listen to me.

YOUNG BERNARD. Mrs. Loman!

BIFF. I waited six hours—

HAPPY. What the hell are you saying?

BIFF. I kept sending in my name but he wouldn't see me. So finally he . . . [*He continues unheard as light fades low on the restaurant.*]

YOUNG BERNARD. Biff flunked math!

LINDA. No!

YOUNG BERNARD. Birnbaum flunked him! They won't graduate him!

LINDA. But they have to. He's gotta go to the university. Where is he? Biff! Biff!

YOUNG BERNARD. No, he left. He went to Grand Central.°

LINDA. Grand—You mean he went to Boston!

YOUNG BERNARD. Is Uncle Willy in Boston?

LINDA. Oh, maybe Willy can talk to the teacher. Oh, the poor, poor boy!

Light on house area snaps out.

BIFF. [*at the table, now audible, holding up a gold fountain pen*] . . . so I'm washed up with Oliver, you understand? Are you listening to me?

WILLY. [*at a loss*] Yeah, sure. If you hadn't flunked—

BIFF. Flunked what? What're you talking about?

WILLY. Don't blame everything on me! I didn't flunk math—you did! What pen?

HAPPY. That was awful dumb, Biff, a pen like that is worth—

WILLY. [*seeing the pen for the first time*] You took Oliver's pen?

BIFF. [*weakening*] Dad, I just explained it to you.

WILLY. You stole Bill Oliver's fountain pen!

BIFF. I didn't exactly steal it! That's just what I've been explaining to you!

HAPPY. He had it in his hand and just then Oliver walked in, so he got nervous and stuck it is his pocket!

WILLY. My God, Biff!

BIFF. I never intended to do it, Dad!

OPERATOR'S VOICE. Standish Arms, good evening!

WILLY. [*shouting*] I'm not in my room!

BIFF. [*frightened*] Dad, what's the matter? [*He and Happy stand up.*]

OPERATOR. Ringing Mr. Loman for you!

WILLY. I'm not there, stop it!

BIFF. [*horrified, gets down on one knee before Willy*] Dad, I'll make good, I'll make good. [*Willy tries to get to his feet. Biff holds him down.*] Sit down now.

WILLY. No, you're no good, you're no good for anything.

BIFF. I am, Dad, I'll find something else, you understand? Now don't worry about anything. [*He holds up Willy's face*] Talk to me, Dad.

OPERATOR. Mr. Loman does not answer. Shall I page him?

WILLY. [*attempting to stand, as though to rush and silence the Operator*] No, no, no!

HAPPY. He'll strike something, Pop.

WILLY. No, no . . .

BIFF. [*desperately, standing over Willy*] Pop, listen! Listen to me! I'm telling you something good. Oliver talked to his partner about the Florida idea. You listening? He—he talked to his partner, and he came to me . . . I'm going to be all right, you hear? Dad, listen to me, he said it was just a question of the amount!

WILLY. Then you . . . got it?

HAPPY. He's gonna be terrific, Pop!

Grand Central: Grand Central Station, major train depot in New York City.

WILLY. [*trying to stand*] Then you got it, haven't you? You got it! You got it!

BIFF. [*agonized, holds Willy down*] No, no. Look, Pop. I'm supposed to have lunch with them tomorrow. I'm just telling you this so you'll know that I can still make an impression, Pop. And I'll make good somewhere, but I can't go tomorrow, see?

WILLY. Why not? You simply—

BIFF. But the pen, Pop!

WILLY. You give it to him and tell him it was an oversight!

HAPPY. Sure, have lunch tomorrow!

BIFF. I can't say that—

WILLY. You were doing a crossword puzzle and accidentally used his pen!

BIFF. Listen, kid, I took those balls years ago, now I walk in with his fountain pen? That clinches it, don't you see? I can't face him like that! I'll try elsewhere.

PAGE'S VOICE. Paging Mr. Loman!

WILLY. Don't you want to be anything?

BIFF. Pop, how can I go back?

WILLY. You don't want to be anything, is that what's behind it?

BIFF. [*now angry at Willy for not crediting his sympathy*] Don't take it that way! You think it was easy walking into that office after what I'd done to him? A team of horses couldn't have dragged me back to Bill Oliver!

WILLY. Then why'd you go?

BIFF. Why did I go? Why did I go! Look at you! Look at what's become of you!

Off left, The Woman laughs.

WILLY. Biff, you're going to go to that lunch tomorrow, or—

BIFF. I can't go. I've got no appointment!

HAPPY. Biff, for . . . !

WILLY. Are you spiting me?

BIFF. Don't take it that way! Goddammit!

WILLY. [*strikes Biff and falters away from the table*] You rotten little louse! Are you spiting me?

THE WOMAN. Someone's at the door, Willy!

BIFF. I'm no good, can't you see what I am?

HAPPY. [*separating them*] Hey, you're in a restaurant! Now cut it out, both of you! [*The girls enter.*] Hello, girls, sit down.

The Woman laughs, off left.

MISS FORSYTHE. I guess we might as well. This is Letta.

THE WOMAN. Willy, are you going to wake up?

BIFF. [*ignoring Willy*] How're ya, miss, sit down. What do you drink?

MISS FORSYTHE. Letta might not be able to stay long.

LETTA. I gotta get up very early tomorrow. I got jury duty. I'm so excited! Were you fellows ever on a jury?

BIFF. No, but I been in front of them! [*The girls laugh.*] This is my father.

LETTA. Isn't he cute? Sit down with us, Pop.

HAPPY. Sit him down, Biff!

BIFF. [*going to him*] Come on, slugger, drink us under the table. To hell with it! Come on, sit down, pal.

On Biff's last insistence, Willy is about to sit.

Death of a Salesman

THE WOMAN. [*now urgently*] Willy, are you going to answer the door!

The Woman's call pulls Willy back. He starts right, befuddled.

BIFF. Hey, where are you going?

WILLY. Open the door.

BIFF. The door?

WILLY. The washroom . . . the door . . . where's the door?

BIFF. [*leading Willy to the left*] Just go straight down.

Willy moves left.

THE WOMAN. Willy, Willy, are you going to get up, get up, get up, get up?

Willy exits left.

LETTA. I think it's sweet you bring your daddy along.

MISS FORSYTHE. Oh, he isn't really your father!

BIFF. [*at left, turning to her resentfully*] Miss Forsythe, you've just seen a prince walk by. A fine, troubled prince. A hardworking, unappreciated prince. A pal, you understand? A good companion. Always for his boys.

LETTA. That's so sweet.

HAPPY. Well, girls, what's the program? We're wasting time. Come on, Biff. Gather round. Where would you like to go?

BIFF. Why don't you do something for him?

HAPPY. Me!

BIFF. Don't you give a damn for him, Hap?

HAPPY. What're you talking about? I'm the one who—

BIFF. I sense it, you don't give a good goddam about him. [*He takes the rolled-up hose from his pocket and puts in on the table in front of Happy.*] Look what I found in the cellar, for Christ's sake. How can you bear to let it go on?

HAPPY. Me? Who goes away? Who runs off and—

BIFF. Yeah, but he doesn't mean anything to you. You could help him—I can't! Don't you understand what I'm talking about? He's going to kill himself, don't you know that?

HAPPY. Don't I know it! Me!

BIFF. Hap, help him! Jesus . . . help him . . . Help me, help me, I can't bear to look at his face! [*Ready to weep, he hurries out, up right.*]

HAPPY. [*starting after him*] Where are you going?

MISS FORSYTHE. What's he so mad about?

HAPPY. Come on, girls, we'll catch up with him.

MISS FORSYTHE. [*as Happy pushes her out*] Say, I don't like that temper of his!

HAPPY. He's just a little overstrung, he'll be all right!

WILLY. [*off left, as The Woman laughs*] Don't answer! Don't answer!

LETTA. Don't you want to tell your father—

HAPPY. No, that's not my father. He's just a guy. Come on, we'll catch Biff, and, honey, we're going to paint this town! Stanley, where's the check! Hey, Stanley!

They exit. Stanley looks toward left.

STANLEY. [*calling to Happy indignantly*] Mr. Loman! Mr. Loman!

Stanley picks up a chair and follows them off. Knocking is heard off left. The Woman enters, laughing. Willy follows her. She is in a black slip; he is buttoning his shirt. Raw, sensuous music accompanies their speech.

WILLY. Will you stop laughing? Will you stop?

THE WOMAN. Aren't you going to answer the door? He'll wake the whole hotel.

WILLY. I'm not expecting anybody.

THE WOMAN. Whyn't you have another drink, honey, and stop being so damn self-centered?

WILLY. I'm so lonely.

THE WOMAN. You know you ruined me, Willy? From now on, whenever you come to the office, I'll see that you go right through to the buyers. No waiting at my desk any more, Willy. You ruined me.

WILLY. That's nice of you to say that.

THE WOMAN. Gee, you are self-centered! Why so sad? You are the saddest, self-centeredest soul I ever did see-saw. [*She laughs. He kisses her.*] Come on inside, drummer boy. It's silly to be dressing in the middle of the night. [*As knocking is heard*] Aren't you going to answer the door?

WILLY. They're knocking on the wrong door.

THE WOMAN. But I felt the knocking. And he heard us talking in here. Maybe the hotel's on fire!

WILLY. [*his terror rising*] It's a mistake.

THE WOMAN. Then tell him to go away!

WILLY. There's nobody there.

THE WOMAN. It's getting on my nerves, Willy. There's somebody standing out there and it's getting on my nerves!

WILLY. [*pushing her away from him*] All right, stay in the bathroom here, and don't come out. I think there's a law in Massachusetts about it, so don't come out. It may be that new room clerk. He looked very mean. So don't come out. It's a mistake, there's no fire.

The knocking is heard again. He takes a few steps away from her, and she vanishes into the wing. The light follows him, and now he is facing Young Biff, who carries a suitcase. Biff steps toward him. The music is gone.

BIFF. Why didn't you answer?

WILLY. Biff! What are you doing in Boston?

BIFF. Why didn't you answer? I've been knocking for five minutes, I called you on the phone—

WILLY. I just heard you. I was in the bathroom and had the door shut. Did anything happen at home?

BIFF. Dad—I let you down.

WILLY. What do you mean?

BIFF. Dad . . .

WILLY. Biffo, what's this about? [*Putting his arm around Biff*] Come on, let's go downstairs and get you a malted.

BIFF. Dad, I flunked math.

WILLY. Not for the term?

BIFF. The term. I haven't got enough credits to graduate.

WILLY. You mean to say Bernard wouldn't give you the answers?

BIFF. He did, he tried, but I only got a sixty-one.

WILLY. And they wouldn't give you four points?

BIFF. Birnbaum refused absolutely. I begged him, Pop, but he won't give me those points. You gotta talk to him before they close the school. Because if he saw the kind of man you are, and you just talked to him in your way, I'm sure he'd come through for me. The class came right before practice, see, and I didn't go enough. Would you talk to him? He'd like you, Pop. You know the way you could talk.

WILLY. You're on. We'll drive right back.

BIFF. Oh, Dad, good work! I'm sure he'll change it for you!

WILLY. Go downstairs and tell the clerk I'm checkin' out. Go right down.

BIFF. Yes, sir! See, the reason he hates me, Pop—one day he was late for class so I got up at the blackboard and imitated him. I crossed my eyes and talked with a lithp.

WILLY. [laughing] You did? The kids like it?

BIFF. They nearly died laughing!

WILLY. Yeah? What'd you do?

BIFF. The thquare root of thixthy twee is . . . [Willy bursts out laughing; Biff joins him.] And in the middle of it he walked in!

Willy laughs and The Woman joins in offstage.

WILLY. [without hesitation] Hurry downstairs and—

BIFF. Somebody in there?

WILLY. No, that was next door.

The Woman laughs offstage.

BIFF. Somebody got in your bathroom!

WILLY. No, it's the next room, there's a party—

THE WOMAN. [enters, laughing. She lisps this] Can I come in? There's something in the bathtub, Willy, and it's moving!

Willy looks at Biff, who is staring open-mouthed and horrified at The Woman.

WILLY. Ah—you better go back to your room. They must be finished painting by now. They're painting her room so I let her take a shower here. Go back, go back . . . [He pushes her.]

THE WOMAN. [resisting] But I've got to get dressed, Willy, I can't—

WILLY. Get out of here! Go back, go back . . . [Suddenly striving for the ordinary] This is Miss Francis, Biff, she's a buyer. They're painting her room. Go back, Miss Francis, go back . . .

THE WOMAN. But my clothes, I can't go out naked in the hall!

WILLY. [pushing her offstage] Get outa here! Go back, go back!

Biff slowly sits down on his suitcase as the argument continues offstage.

THE WOMAN. Where's my stockings? You promised me stockings, Willy!

WILLY. I have no stockings here!

THE WOMAN. You had two boxes of size nine sheers for me, and I want them!

WILLY. Here, for God's sake, will you get outa here!

THE WOMAN. [enters holding a box of stockings] I just hope there's nobody in the hall. That's all I hope. [To Biff] Are you football or baseball?

BIFF. Football.

THE WOMAN. [angry, humiliated] That's me too. G'night. [She snatches her clothes from Willy, and walks out.]

WILLY. [after a pause] Well, better get going. I want to get to the school first thing in the morning. Get my suits out of the closet. I'll get my valise. [Biff doesn't move.] What's the matter? [*Biff remains motionless, tears falling.*] She's a buyer. Buys for J. H. Simmons. She lives down the hall—they're painting. You don't imagine—[*He breaks off. After a pause*] Now listen, pal, she's just a buyer. She sees merchandise in her room and they have to keep it looking just so . . . [*Pause. Assuming command*] All right, get my suits. [*Biff doesn't move.*] Biff, I gave you an order! Is that what you do when I give you an order? How dare you cry! [*Putting his arm around Biff*] Now look, Biff, when you grow up you'll understand about these things. You mustn't—you mustn't overemphasize a thing like this. I'll see Birnbaum first thing in the morning.

BIFF. Never mind.

WILLY. [*getting down beside Biff*] Never mind! He's going to give you those points. I'll see to it.

BIFF. He wouldn't listen to you.

WILLY. He certainly will listen to me. You need those points for the U. of Virginia.

BIFF. I'm not going there.

WILLY. Heh? If I can't get him to change that mark you'll make it up in summer school. You've got all summer to—

BIFF. [*his weeping breaking from him*] Dad . . .

WILLY. [*infected by it*] Oh, my boy . . .

BIFF. Dad . . .

WILLY. She's nothing to me, Biff. I was lonely, I was terribly lonely.

BIFF. You—you gave her Mama's stockings! [*His tears break through and he rises to go.*]

WILLY. [*grabbing for Biff*] I gave you an order!

BIFF. Don't touch me, you—liar!

WILLY. Apologize for that!

BIFF. You fake! You phony little fake! You fake! [*Overcome, he turns quickly and weeping fully goes out with his suitcase. Willy is left on the floor on his knees.*]

WILLY. I gave you an order! Biff, come back here or I'll beat you! Come back here! I'll whip you!

Stanley comes quickly in from the right and stands in front of Willy.

WILLY. [*shouts at Stanley*] I gave you an order . . .

STANLEY. Hey, let's pick it up, pick it up, Mr. Loman. [*He helps Willy to his feet.*] Your boys left with the chippies.° They said they'll see you home.

A second waiter watches some distance away.

WILLY. But we were supposed to have dinner together.

Music is heard, Willy's theme.

STANLEY. Can you make it?

WILLY. I'll—sure, I can make it. [*Suddenly concerned about his clothes*] Do I—I look all right?

STANLEY. Sure, you look all right. [*He flicks a speck off Willy's lapel.*]

WILLY. Here—here's a dollar.

STANLEY. Oh, your son paid me. It's all right.

WILLY. [*putting it in Stanley's hand*] No, take it. You're a good boy.

°*chippies:* slang term for fast young women.

STANLEY. Oh, no, you don't have to . . .

WILLY. Here—here's some more, I don't need it any more. [*After a slight pause*] Tell me—is there a seed store in the neighborhood?

STANLEY. Seeds? You mean like to plant?

As Willy turns, Stanley slips the money back into his jacket pocket.

WILLY. Yes. Carrots, peas . . .

STANLEY. Well, there's hardware stores on Sixth Avenue, but it may be too late now.

WILLY. [*anxiously*] Oh, I'd better hurry. I've got to get some seeds. [*He starts off to the right.*] I've got to get some seeds, right away. Nothing's planted. I don't have a thing in the ground.

Willy hurries out as the light goes down. Stanley moves over to the right after him, watches him off. The other waiter has been staring at Willy.

STANLEY. [*to the waiter*] Well, whatta you looking at?

The waiter picks up the chairs and moves off right. Stanley takes the table and follows him. The light fades on this area. There is a long pause, the sound of the flute coming over. The light gradually rises on the kitchen, which is empty. Happy appears at the door of the house, followed by Biff. Happy is carrying a large bunch of long-stemmed roses. He enters the kitchen, looks around for Linda. Not seeing her, he turns to Biff, who is just outside the house door, and makes a gesture with his hands, indicating "Not here, I guess." He looks into the living-room and freezes. Inside, Linda, unseen, is seated, Willy's coat on her lap. She rises ominously and quietly and moves toward Happy, who backs up into the kitchen, afraid.

HAPPY. Hey, what're you doing up? [*Linda says nothing but moves toward him implacably.*] Where's Pop? [*He keeps backing to the right, and now Linda is in full view in the doorway to the living-room.*] Is he sleeping?

LINDA. Where were you?

HAPPY. [*trying to laugh it off*] We met two girls, Mom, very fine types. Here, we brought you some flowers. [*Offering them to her*] Put them in your room, Ma.

She knocks them to the floor at Biff's feet. He has now come inside and closed the door behind him. She stares at Biff, silent.

HAPPY. Now what'd you do that for? Mom, I want you to have some flowers—

LINDA. [*cutting Happy off, violently to Biff*] Don't you care whether he lives or dies?

HAPPY. [*going to the stairs*] Come upstairs, Biff.

BIFF. [*with a flare of disgust, to Happy*] Go away from me! [*To Linda*] What do you mean, lives or dies? Nobody's dying around here, pal.

LINDA. Get out of my sight! Get out of here!

BIFF. I wanna see the boss.

LINDA. You're not going near him!

BIFF. Where is he? [*He moves into the living-room and Linda follows.*]

LINDA. [*shouting after Biff*] You invite him for dinner. He looks forward to it all day—[*Biff appears in his parents' bedroom, looks around, and exits*]—and then you desert him there. There's no stranger you'd do that to!

HAPPY. Why? He had a swell time with us. Listen, when I—[*Linda comes back into the kitchen*]—desert him I hope I don't outlive the day!

LINDA. Get out of here!

HAPPY. Now look, Mom . . .

LINDA. Did you have to go to women tonight? You and your lousy rotten whores!

Biff re-enters the kitchen.

HAPPY. Mom, all we did was follow Biff around trying to cheer him up! [*To Biff*] Boy, what a night you gave me!

LINDA. Get out of here, both of you, and don't come back! I don't want you tormenting him any more. Go on now, get your things together! [*To Biff*] You can sleep in his apartment. [*She starts to pick up the flowers and stops herself.*] Pick up this stuff, I'm not your maid any more. Pick it up, you bum, you!

Happy turns his back to her in refusal. Biff slowly moves over and gets down on his knees, picking up the flowers.

LINDA. You're a pair of animals! Not one, not another living soul would have had the cruelty to walk out on that man in a restaurant!

BIFF. [*not looking at her*] Is that what he said?

LINDA. He didn't have to say anything. He was so humiliated he nearly limped when he came in.

HAPPY. But, Mom, he had a great time with us—

BIFF. [*cutting him off violently*] Shut up!

Without another word, Happy goes upstairs.

LINDA. You! You didn't even go in to see if he was all right!

BIFF. [*still on the floor in front of Linda, the flowers in his hand; with self-loathing*] No. Didn't. Didn't do a damned thing. How do you like that, heh? Left him babbling in a toilet.

LINDA. You louse. You . . .

BIFF. Now you hit it on the nose! [*He gets up, throws the flowers in the wastebasket.*] The scum of the earth, and you're looking at him!

LINDA. Get out of here!

BIFF. I gotta talk to the boss, Mom. Where is he?

LINDA. You're not going near him. Get out of this house!

BIFF. [*with absolute assurance, determination*] No. We're gonna have an abrupt conversation, him and me.

LINDA. You're not talking to him!

Hammering is heard from outside the house, off right. Biff turns toward the noise.

LINDA. [*suddenly pleading*] Will you please leave him alone?

BIFF. What's he doing out there?

LINDA. He's planting the garden!

BIFF. [*quietly*] Now? Oh, my God!

Biff moves outside, Linda following. The light dies down on them and comes up on the center of the apron as Willy walks into it. He is carrying a flashlight, a hoe, and a handful of seed packets. He raps the top of the hoe sharply to fix it firmly, and then moves to the left, measuring off the distance with his foot. He holds the flashlight to look at the seed packets, reading off the instructions. He is in the blue of night.

WILLY. Carrots . . . quarter-inch apart. Rows . . . one-foot rows. [*He measures it off.*] One foot. [*He puts down a package and measures off.*] Beets. [*He puts down another package and measures again.*] Lettuce: [*He reads the package, puts it down.*] One foot—[*He breaks off as Ben appears at the right and moves slowly down to him.*]

What a proposition, ts, ts. Terrific, terrific. 'Cause she's suffered, Ben, the woman has suffered. You understand me? A man can't go out the way he came in, Ben, a man has got to add up to something. You can't, you can't—[*Ben moves toward him as though to interrupt.*] You gotta consider, now. Don't answer so quick. Remember, it's a guaranteed twenty-thousand-dollar proposition. Now look, Ben, I want you to go through the ins and outs of this thing with me. I've got nobody to talk to, Ben, and the woman has suffered, you hear me?

BEN. [*standing still, considering*] What's the proposition?

WILLY. It's twenty thousand dollars on the barrelhead. Guaranteed, gilt-edged, you understand?

BEN. You don't want to make a fool of yourself. They might not honor the policy.

WILLY. How can they dare refuse? Didn't I work like a coolie to meet every premium on the nose? And now they don't pay off? Impossible!

BEN. It's called a cowardly thing, William.

WILLY. Why? Does it take more guts to stand here the rest of my life ringing up a zero?

BEN. [*yielding*] That's a point, William. [*He moves, thinking, turns.*] And twenty thousand—that *is* something one can feel with the hand, it is there.

WILLY. [*now assured, with rising power*] Oh, Ben, that's the whole beauty of it! I see it like a diamond, shining in the dark, hard and rough, that I can pick up and touch in my hand. Not like—like an appointment! This would not be another damned-fool appointment, Ben, and it changes all the aspects. Because he thinks I'm nothing, see, and so he spites me. But the funeral—[*Straightening up*] Ben, that funeral will be massive! They'll come from Maine, Massachusetts, Vermont, New Hampshire! All the old-timers with the strange license plates—that boy will be thunder-struck, Ben, because he never realized—I am known! Rhode Island, New York, New Jersey—I am known, Ben, and he'll see it with his eyes once and for all. He'll see what I am, Ben! He's in for a shock, that boy!

BEN. [*coming down to the edge of the garden*] He'll call you a coward.

WILLY. [*suddenly fearful*] No, that would be terrible.

BEN. Yes. And a damned fool.

WILLY. No, no, he mustn't, I won't have that! [*He is broken and desperate.*]

BEN. He'll hate you, William.

The gay music of the Boys is heard.

WILLY. Oh, Ben, how do we get back to all the great times? Used to be so full of light, and comradeship, the sleigh-riding in winter, and the ruddiness on his cheeks. And always some kind of good news coming up, always something nice coming up ahead. And never even let me carry the valises in the house, and si-monizing, simonizing that little red car! Why, why can't I give him something and not have him hate me?

BEN. Let me think about it. [*He glances at his watch.*] I still have a little time. Re-markable proposition, but you've got to be sure you're not making a fool of yourself.

Ben drifts off upstage and goes out of sight. Biff comes down from the left.

WILLY. [*suddenly conscious of Biff, turns and looks up at him, then begins picking up the packages of seeds in confusion*] Where the hell is that seed? [*Indignantly*] You can't see nothing out here! They boxed in the whole goddam neighborhood!

BIFF. There are people all around here. Don't you realize that?

WILLY. I'm busy. Don't bother me.

BIFF. [taking the hoe from Willy] I'm saying good-by to you, Pop. [Willy looks at him, silent, unable to move.] I'm not coming back any more.

WILLY. You're not going to see Oliver tomorrow?

BIFF. I've got no appointment, Dad.

WILLY. He put his arm around you, and you've got no appointment?

BIFF. Pop, get this now, will you? Everytime I've left it's been a fight that sent me out of here. Today I realized something about myself and I tried to explain it to you and I—I think I'm just not smart enough to make any sense out of it for you. To hell with whose fault it is or anything like that. [He takes Willy's arm.] Let's just wrap it up, heh? Come on in, we'll tell Mom. [He gently tries to pull Willy to left.]

WILLY. [frozen, immobile, with guilt in his voice] No, I don't want to see her.

BIFF. Come on! [He pulls again, and Willy tries to pull away.]

WILLY. [highly nervous] No, no, I don't want to see her.

BIFF. [tries to look into Willy's face, as if to find the answer there] Why don't you want to see her?

WILLY. [more harshly now] Don't bother me, will you?

BIFF. What do you mean, you don't want to see her? You don't want them calling you yellow, do you? This isn't your fault; it's me, I'm a bum. Now come inside! [Willy strains to get away.] Did you hear what I said to you?

Willy pulls away and quickly goes by himself into the house. Biff follows.

LINDA. [to Willy] Did you plant, dear?

BIFF. [at the door, to Linda] All right, we had it out. I'm going and I'm not writing any more.

LINDA. [going to Willy in the kitchen] I think that's the best way, dear. 'Cause there's no use drawing it out, you'll just never get along.

Willy doesn't respond.

BIFF. People ask where I am and what I'm doing, you don't know, and you don't care. That way it'll be off your mind and you can start brightening up again. All right? That clears it, doesn't it? [Willy is silent, and Biff goes to him.] You gonna wish me luck, scout? [He extends his hand.] What do you say?

LINDA. Shake his hand, Willy.

WILLY. [turning to her, seething with hurt] There's no necessity to mention the pen at all, y'know.

BIFF. [gently] I've got no appointment, Dad.

WILLY. [erupting fiercely] He put his arm around . . . ?

BIFF. Dad, you're never going to see what I am, so what's the use of arguing? If I strike oil I'll send you a check. Meantime forget I'm alive.

WILLY. [to Linda] Spite, see?

BIFF. Shake hands, Dad.

WILLY. Not my hand.

BIFF. I was hoping not to go this way.

WILLY. Well, this is the way you're going. Good-by.

Biff looks at him a moment, then turns sharply and goes to the stairs.

WILLY. [stops him with] May you rot in hell if you leave this house!

BIFF. [turning] Exactly what is it that you want from me?

WILLY. I want you to know, on the train, in the mountains, in the valleys, wherever you go, that you cut down your life for spite!

BIFF. No, no.

WILLY. Spite, spite, is the word of your undoing! And when you're down and out, remember what did it. When you're rotting somewhere beside the railroad tracks, remember, and don't you dare blame it on me!

BIFF. I'm not blaming it on you!

WILLY. I won't take the rap for this, you hear?

Happy comes down the stairs and stands on the bottom step, watching.

BIFF. That's just what I'm telling you!

WILLY. [*sinking into a chair at the table, with full accusation*] You're trying to put a knife in me—don't think I don't know what you're doing!

BIFF. All right, phony! Then let's lay it on the line. [*He whips the rubber tube out of his pocket and puts it on the table.*]

HAPPY. You crazy—

LINDA. Biff! [*She moves to grab the hose, but Biff holds it down with his hand.*]

BIFF. Leave it there! Don't move it!

WILLY. [*not looking at it*] What is that?

BIFF. You know goddam well what that is.

WILLY. [*caged, wanting to escape*] I never saw that.

BIFF. You saw it. The mice didn't bring it into the cellar! What is this supposed to do, make a hero out of you? This supposed to make me sorry for you?

WILLY. Never heard of it.

BIFF. There'll be no pity for you, you hear it? No pity!

WILLY. [*to Linda*] You hear the spite!

BIFF. No, you're going to hear the truth—what you are and what I am!

LINDA. Stop it!

WILLY. Spite!

HAPPY. [*coming down toward Biff*] You cut it now!

BIFF. [*to Happy*] The man don't know who we are! The man is gonna know! [*To Willy*] We never told the truth for ten minutes in this house!

HAPPY. We always told the truth!

BIFF. [*turning on him*] You big blow, are you the assistant buyer? You're one of the two assistants to the assistant, aren't you?

HAPPY. Well, I'm practically—

BIFF. You're practically full of it! We all are! And I'm through with it. [*To Willy*] Now hear this, Willy, this is me.

WILLY. I know you!

BIFF. You know why I had no address for three months? I stole a suit in Kansas City and I was in jail. [*To Linda, who is sobbing*] Stop crying. I'm through with it.

Linda turns away from them, her hands covering her face.

WILLY. I suppose that's my fault!

BIFF. I stole myself out of every good job since high school!

WILLY. And whose fault is that?

BIFF. And I never got anywhere because you blew me so full of hot air I could never stand taking orders from anybody! That's whose fault it is!

WILLY. I hear that!

LINDA. Don't Biff!

BIFF. It's goddam time you heard that! I had to be boss big shot in two weeks, and I'm through with it!

WILLY. Then hang yourself! For spite, hang yourself!

BIFF. No! Nobody's hanging himself, Willy! I ran down eleven flights with a pen in my hand today. And suddenly I stopped, you hear me? And in the middle of that office building, do you hear this? I stopped in the middle of that building and I saw—the sky. I saw the things that I love in this world. The work and the food and time to sit and smoke. And I looked at the pen and said to myself, what the hell am I grabbing this for? Why am I trying to become what I don't want to be? What am I doing in an office, making a contemptuous, begging fool of myself, when all I want is out there, waiting for me the minute I say I know who I am! Why can't I say that, Willy? [*He tries to make Willy face him, but Willy pulls away and moves to the left.*]

WILLY. [*with hatred, threateningly*] The door of your life is wide open!

BIFF. Pop! I'm a dime a dozen, and so are you!

WILLY. [*turning on him now in an uncontrolled outburst*] I am not a dime a dozen! I am Willy Loman, and you are Biff Loman!

Biff starts for Willy, but is blocked by Happy. In his fury, Biff seems on the verge of attacking his father.

BIFF. I am not a leader of men, Willy, and neither are you. You were never anything but a hard-working drummer who landed in the ash can like all the rest of them! I'm one dollar an hour, Willy! I tried seven states and couldn't raise it. A buck an hour! Do you gather my meaning? I'm not bringing home any prizes any more, and you're going to stop waiting for me to bring them home!

WILLY. [*directly to Biff*] You vengeful, spiteful mut!

Biff breaks from Happy. Willy, in fright, starts up the stairs. Biff grabs him.

BIFF. [*at the peak of his fury*] Pop, I'm nothing! I'm nothing, Pop. Can't you understand that? There's no spite in it any more. I'm just what I am, that's all.

Biff's fury has spent itself, and he breaks down, sobbing, holding on to Willy, who dumbly fumbles for Biff's face.

WILLY. [*astonished*] What're you doing? What're you doing? [*To Linda*] Why is he crying?

BIFF. [*crying, broken*] Will you let me go, for Christ's sake? Will you take that phony dream and burn it before something happens? [*Struggling to contain himself, he pulls away and moves to the stairs.*] I'll go in the morning. Put him—put him to bed. [*Exhausted, Biff moves up the stairs to his room.*]

WILLY. [*after a long pause, astonished, elevated*] Isn't that—isn't that remarkable? Biff—he likes me!

LINDA. He loves you, Willy!

HAPPY. [*deeply moved*] Always did, Pop.

WILLY. Oh, Biff! [*Staring wildly*] He cried! Cried to me. [*He is choking with his love, and now cries out his promise*] That boy—that boy is going to be magnificent!

Ben appears in the light just outside the kitchen.

BEN. Yes, outstanding, with twenty thousand behind him.

LINDA. [*sensing the racing of his mind, fearfully, carefully*] Now come to bed, Willy. It's all settled now.

WILLY. [*finding it difficult not to rush out of the house*] Yes, we'll sleep. Come on. Go to sleep, Hap.

BEN. And it does take a great kind of a man to crack the jungle.

In accents of dread, Ben's idyllic music starts up.

HAPPY. [*his arm around Linda*] I'm getting married, Pop, don't forget it. I'm changing everything. I'm gonna run that department before the year is up. You'll see, Mom. [*He kisses her.*]

BEN. The jungle is dark but full of diamonds, Willy.

Willy turns, moves, listening to Ben.

LINDA. Be good. You're both good boys, just act that way, that's all.

HAPPY. 'Night, Pop. [*He goes upstairs.*]

LINDA. [*to Willy*] Come, dear.

BEN. [*with greater force*] One must go in to fetch a diamond out.

WILLY. [*to Linda, as he moves slowly along the edge of the kitchen, toward the door*] I just want to get settled down, Linda. Let me sit alone for a little.

LINDA. [*almost uttering her fear*] I want you upstairs.

WILLY. [*taking her in his arms*] In a few minutes, Linda. I couldn't sleep right now. Go on, you look awful tired. [*He kisses her.*]

BEN. Not like an appointment at all. A diamond is rough and hard to the touch.

WILLY. Go on now. I'll be right up.

LINDA. I think this is the only way, Willy.

WILLY. Sure, it's the best thing.

BEN. Best thing!

WILLY. The only way. Everything is gonna be—go on, kid, get to bed. You look so tired.

LINDA. Come right up.

WILLY. Two minutes.

Linda goes into the living-room, then reappears in her bedroom. Willy moves just outside the kitchen door.

WILLY. Loves me. [*Wonderingly*] Always loved me. Isn't that a remarkable thing? Ben, he'll worship me for it!

BEN. [*with promise*] It's dark there, but full of diamonds.

WILLY. Can you imagine that magnificence with twenty thousand dollars in his pocket?

LINDA. [*calling from her room*] Willy! Come up!

WILLY. [*calling into the kitchen*] Yes! Yes. Coming! It's very smart, you realize that, don't you, sweetheart? Even Ben sees it. I gotta go, baby. 'By! 'By! [*Going over to Ben, almost dancing*] Imagine? When the mail comes he'll be ahead of Bernard again!

BEN. A perfect proposition all around.

WILLY. Did you see how he cried to me? Oh, if I could kiss him, Ben!

BEN. Time, William, time!

WILLY. Oh, Ben, I always knew one way or another we were gonna make it, Biff and I!

BEN. [*looking at his watch*] The boat. We'll be late. [*He moves slowly off into the darkness.*]

WILLY. [*elegiacally, turning to the house*] Now when you kick off, boy, I want a seventy-yard boot, and get right down the field under the ball, and when you hit,

hit low and hit hard, because it's important, boy. [*He swings around and faces the audience.*] There's all kinds of important people in the stands, and the first thing you know . . . [*Suddenly realizing he is alone*] Ben! Ben, where do I . . . ? [*He makes a sudden movement of search.*] Ben, how do I . . . ?

LINDA. [*calling*] Willy, you coming up?

WILLY. [*uttering a gasp of fear, whirling about as if to quiet her*] Sh! [*He turns around as if to find his way; sounds, faces, voices, seem to be swarming in upon him and he flicks at them, crying.*] Sh! Sh! [*Suddenly music, faint and high, stops him. It rises in intensity, almost to an unbearable scream. He goes up and down on his toes, and rushes off around the house.*] Shhh!

LINDA. Willy?

There is no answer. Linda waits. Biff gets up off his bed. He is still in his clothes. Happy sits up. Biff stands listening.

LINDA. [*with real fear*] Willy, answer me! Willy!

There is the sound of a car starting and moving away at full speed.

LINDA. No!

BIFF. [*rushing down the stairs*] Pop!

As the car speeds off, the music crashes down in a frenzy of sound, which becomes the soft pulsation of a single cello string. Biff slowly returns to his bedroom. He and Happy gravely don their jackets. Linda slowly walks out of her room. The music has developed into a dead march. The leaves of day are appearing over everything. Charley and Bernard, somberly dressed, appear and knock on the kitchen door. Biff and Happy slowly descend the stairs to the kitchen as Charley and Bernard enter. All stop a moment when Linda, in clothes of mourning, bearing a little bunch of roses, comes through the draped doorway into the kitchen. She goes to Charley and takes his arm. Now all move toward the audience, through the wall-line of the kitchen. At the limit of the apron, Linda lays down the flowers, kneels, and sits back on her heels. All stare down at the grave.

REQUIEM

CHARLEY. It's getting dark, Linda.

Linda doesn't react. She stares at the grave.

BIFF. How about it, Mom? Better get some rest, heh? They'll be closing the gate soon.

Linda makes no move. Pause.

HAPPY. [*deeply angered*] He had no right to do that. There was no necessity for it. We would've helped him.

CHARLEY. [*grunting*] Hmmm.

BIFF. Come along, Mom.

LINDA. Why didn't anybody come?

CHARLEY. It was a very nice funeral.

LINDA. But where are all the people he knew? Maybe they blame him.

CHARLEY. Naa. It's a rough world, Linda. They wouldn't blame him.

LINDA. I can't understand it. At this time especially. First time in thirty-five years we were just about free and clear. He only needed a little salary. He was even finished with the dentist.

CHARLEY. No man only needs a little salary.

LINDA. I can't understand it.

BIFF. There were a lot of nice days. When he'd come home from a trip; or on Sundays, making the stoop; finishing the cellar; putting on the new porch; when he built the extra bathroom; and put up the garage. You know something, Charley, there's more of him in that front stoop than in all the sales he ever made.

CHARLEY. Yeah. He was a happy man with a batch of cement.

LINDA. He was so wonderful with his hands.

BIFF. He had the wrong dreams. All, all, wrong.

HAPPY. [almost ready to fight Biff] Don't say that!

BIFF. He never knew who he was.

CHARLEY. [stopping Happy's movement and reply. To Biff] Nobody dast blame this man. You don't understand: Willy was a salesman. And for a salesman, there is no rock bottom to the life. He don't put a bolt to a nut, he don't tell you the law or give you medicine. He's a man way out there in the blue, riding on a smile and a shoeshine. And when they start not smiling back—that's an earthquake. And then you get yourself a couple of spots on your hat, and you're finished. Nobody dast blame this man. A salesman is got to dream, boy. It comes with the territory.

BIFF. Charley, the man didn't know who he was.

HAPPY. [infuriated] Don't say that!

BIFF. Why don't you come with me, Happy?

HAPPY. I'm not licked that easily. I'm staying right in this city, and I'm gonna beat this racket! [He looks at Biff, his chin set.] The Loman Brothers!

BIFF. I know who I am, kid.

HAPPY. All right, boy. I'm gonna show you and everybody else that Willy Loman did not die in vain. He had a good dream. It's the only dream you can have— to come out number-one man. He fought it out here, and this is where I'm gonna win it for him.

BIFF. [with a hopeless glance at Happy, bends toward his mother] Let's go, Mom.

LINDA. I'll be with you in a minute. Go on, Charley. [He hesitates.] I want to, just for a minute. I never had a chance to say good-by.

Charley moves away, followed by Happy. Biff remains a slight distance up and left of Linda. She sits there, summoning herself. The flute begins, not far away, playing behind her speech.

LINDA. Forgive me, dear. I can't cry. I don't know what it is, but I can't cry. I don't understand it. Why did you ever do that? Help me, Willy, I can't cry. It seems to me that you're just on another trip. I keep expecting you. Willy, dear, I can't cry. Why did you do it? I search and search and I search, and I can't understand it, Willy. I made the last payment on the house today. Today, dear. And there'll be nobody home. [A sob rises in her throat.] We're free and clear. [Sobbing more fully, released] We're free. [Biff comes slowly toward her.] We're free . . . We're free . . .

Biff lifts her to her feet and moves out up right with her in his arms. Linda sobs quietly. Bernard and Charley come together and follow them, followed by Happy. Only the music of the flute is left on the darkening stage as over the house the hard towers of the apartment buildings rise into sharp focus, and

The Curtain Falls

1. Reread Miller's opening directions and description. What hints are you given about Willy and his circumstances before the first words have been spoken?

2. What is your first impression of Willy? Does it change in any significant way as the play unfolds? What does he believe, and how has he raised his sons? How does he express and distribute his affections?

3. What is the relationship between Biff and Happy? How are they alike and how are they different?

4. What do you learn about Willy and the family from the flashback scenes? At what point do these scenes begin to skirt the irrational?

5. What does Willy hope for his sons? How have they gratified or disappointed him?

6. What is Biff's problem? In what ways could he be said to be his father's son?

7. Discuss the "stockings." Why should Willy be so upset to see Linda mending her old stockings?

8. What do you learn about Willy's life on the road? Is there any parallel between Willy's treatment of women and that of Happy and Biff?

9. What has Linda found in the basement? What does Willy plan?

10. What do Charlie and Bernard represent to Willy and Biff, respectively?

11. What happened to Biff? Why did he not return to summer school and finish his degree? What did he see, and how did it affect his relationship with Willy?

12. Consider Willy's scene with Howard and the recording machine. How have things changed since the old days? Do you believe that Willy is simply idealizing the past, or have things really changed?

13. What does Ben represent to Willy? What is the effect of his ghostly appearances? What do we learn about Willy's father?

14. Why do Biff and Happy leave Willy at the restaurant? What do they say to each other later that night? What does Biff reveal? Does this change your view of his character, or simply confirm it? What makes Biff's failure so poignant to the viewer?

15. In what way is the situation "too late" for Willy from the start? Can you imagine anything that his wife or sons could do or say that could alter the final outcome?

16. Discuss the character of Linda—her role as a wife and a mother. Do you end up admiring her or pitying her? Explain.

Cassandra Medley

Cassandra Medley received the 1984 Outer Drama Critics' Circle Award for her play *A . . . . My Name Is Alice.* Her other plays include *Terrain* and *Ma Rose.* She currently teaches playwriting at Sarah Lawrence College in New York.

WAKING WOMEN

The setting is a closed-in porch of a neat A-frame house in a working-class black neighborhood in a midwestern city. At rise the porch is empty. Sunshine streams through the screen windows, glistening on the potted and hanging plants that are placed on the banister in great profusion. Birds can be heard as well as the barking of unseen nearby dogs and the occasional passing of a car.

The sound of banging is heard as if someone is knocking on the screen door. Ms. Edie enters as if coming from the direction of the street. She is a black woman in her mid to late fifties, dressed in a plain housedress and slippers. She is carrying a rattan hand fan in one hand to beat off the heat and a potted plant tied with a white ribbon in the other. Her hair is done up in curlers with a hair net tied securely on her head. She has a sorrowful expression on her face as she addresses the unseen woman before her. Throughout the monologue she speaks to the audience as if speaking directly to her close friend and confidante, Lucille.

Ms. EDIE. Lucille! . . . I was *so* sorry to hear about it! Girl, you *know* I was gonna make it over soon as I could, you *know* I was gonna be over to see 'bout you just as soon as I was able . . . honey, I was so surprised! Gina Hawthorne just called me just now and *told* me! I said to her, I said, "*Passed?*" Whose husband done passed? . . . "Well, when did it happen?!"

My goodness. 'Cause seem to me that I saw Coleman out working in the yard just last week, seem to me, and he looked to be so *healthy,* and now you tell me he done passed! have mercy! and when's the funeral? [*Pauses.*] Oh, I see . . . [*Pauses, listening.*] Well, where your in-laws spring from? ah, so his people from Ohio! Ah-so . . . you don't say . . . and you gonna have the wake at night . . . [*Nods her approval.*] Well, that's good, that's good. Well, sir, I was *so* sorry to hear . . . [*Points to herself.*] Me? [*She leans back and fans herself vigorously.*] Aw, girl, I'm all right, I guess I'll do. [*She is frowning and scowling.*] Chile, it's just that I'm so outdone so, till I don't know *what* to do! [*Pauses.*] Hon-nee, I just can't tell you! [*Pauses.*] Well, what time is it . . . ? Okay, well, hon-nee, get ready for this . . . Pinkie's in labor! [*Fanning herself with indignation.*] that's *right!* Yeah, girl, Pinkie done been in labor since . . . well, she went in at four this morning and here it is what . . . ? Twelve-thirty? Okay, so she's still, yeah, chile . . . well, you know they say that first baby is always the hardest. So she's in there now and uh . . . took her down at four o'clock, her water broke at three-thirty . . . uh-hum . . . Oh, yeah, that's what they say . . . that first one . . . yep . . . count on that to be the hardest. Well, now, course with me, they just "dropped" . . . I was real lucky . . . 'cause I weren't in there *no* time and 'fore I knew nothing, I was just opening up m'legs and look like my boys just "dropped" out of the barrel, but hon-nee, poor Pinkie, she's up in there now and she's having a time of it . . . [*Pauses, then with disapproval as if answering a question.*] . . . "De-troit General." . . . Yeah, that's where . . . um-hum . . . yeah [*Fans vigorously.*]

She pauses abruptly and with scowling reacts to the unseen woman's question.

Girl, don't ask! and ain't no sense in me troubling you with *my* trouble in *your* time of trouble! I don't even want to bother you. Naw-naw, you just rest. Never mind 'bout Pinkie, you just take it easy yourself . . . Naw-naw, never mind . . . [*Suddenly.*] Well, chile, it's just a shame! Just a sin and a shame, and that's *all* I'm gonna say!

She seems to have closed the subject for a few beats; then she suddenly launches into a tirade.

Shooo! That silly sister-in-law of mine! that Gladys! best good common sense my brother every had was to *leave* that woman . . . girl, the way she brought up that poor Pinkie! [*Pause.*] Say what? Now, girl, you mean to tell me you been living in this neighborhood all this time and you *don't* know? Ha! "Paulette." yeah! "Paulette," but we been calling her Pinkie ever since she first drew breath, 'cause she was such a pretty lil "pink" thing when she come. [*Pause.*] Oh, chile, I just don't even wanna get into it 'cause you got *enough* on your mind as it is, but hon-nee, do you know, that Pinkie, that child ain't *never* been to a picture show in her *life!* Now you know that's a shame! That's the gospel truth! Fifteen years old and ain't never *ever* been to the movies in her life! I ain't telling no tale. Cause my damn sister-in-law, 'scuse my French, cause my sister-in-law Gladys just keeps Pinkie all locked up in the house *all* the time! Oh, I don't know *what* be going through Gladys's mind! She think she be sheltering Pinkie or "protecting" her or I don't know what. Keeps Pinkie in the house *all* the time! Don't let her go *nowhere*. Don't let her go out shopping with her little friends . . . *parties?* You better forget it! *Sleepovers?* Forget it! *Dances?* Forget it! Join a club? Forget it! After-school home games and whatnot? [*She waits for Lucille to silently answer back "forget it," and she nods "correct."*] You got it! And like I told Gladys, I said, "Gladys," we was sitting out on the porch and I said, "Gladys" . . . 'cause you know me, I speak my mind, if that's one thing about me, I'm gonna pull your coat from the jump. I said, "Gladys you just can't keep your daughter locked up under lock and key in the house like that," I said, "Gladys, that ain't right! 'cause *you* know and I know we was all young once, and Gladys, you just can't keep Pinkie under your nose all the damn time."

Now I know for myself, see I'm gonna tell ya, when I was young, see, I was "fast." I'm gonna tell you like it is; I was "fast." And here I was dark skinned and considered "ugly" and the boys was after me? And here Pinkie is, light skinned and with straight hair! Well, now, you *know* the boys gonna be after her! And here she can't even go to the picture show and ain't never been in her life! And I told Gladys, I said, "Gladys," "Gladys," I said, "You know that now we have got to face reality. It ain't like when we was coming up, no, it ain't. It ain't like back when they didn't talk about nothing and you weren't supposed to know nothing and when your first time of the month first come on you, you thought you was bleeding to death and all that, 'cause you didn't know no better and all, like y'know, when we come up. After all, this is 1991 and my goodness, and things have changed and you gotta face up to it!" And I told my ole silly sister-in-law, "Gladys, you just can't rule that girl like that!" I've told Gladys time and time again, "We have got to face re-ality here, and we have got to tell these kids 'bout birth control and whatnot," and hon-nee, ooohhh! What did I want to say that for? Chile, do you know she looked at me like I was the devil's own *slut?* Oh, yes, she did!

Pause. She studies Lucille, nodding as to answer a retort.

Well, now, I know, I *know* that, hon-nee, I know what you mean 'bout "sin," and I'm as religious as the next one, I'm as upstanding as any one of the rest of your friends, Lucille, but keeping these kids *ignorant* ain't keeping them from "sin." How's *that* s'pposed to "keep 'em from sin" . . . ? [*Pauses.*] See what I'm saying? [*Pauses.*] I mean, I mean, yeah, I see what *you* saying, but do you see what *I'm* saying? . . . So anyway, okay . . . so I said to myself right there and then, I said, *all right! so be it! lemme just shut up and back off, lemme just shut my mouth!* so I shut my mouth.

Yessir, here I am trying to plead with that ole sanctified heifer—'scuse my talk, Lucille, in your time of sorrow, but it just makes me so "outdone" and dang-blasted put-out so, till I don't know what! naw, naw, Gladys just gonna make Pinkie stay up in that house all the damn time; make her come home from school and lock her up in that house and not let her go *nowhere*.

Well, course, now, my brother? I blame him as much as anybody. He just *had* to go 'head and marry and father a child by that ole light-skinned dumb bunny—I mean y'know, hey . . . let's just admit it and call the card like it is—just 'cause he thought she was educated and pretty and proper and holy! Well! He left her and left poor Pinkie *with* her, and you see what happened, don't you? Gladys call herself keeping Pinkie pure, and Pinkie *still* ended up here with the big belly! In *my* family! a relative of *mine*, a relation to *me* with *my* family name and ending up out of wedlock and "big"!

See, 'cause these here kids these days, they gonna get out here, they are curious. And a young girl like that? Huh! Pretty as she is? You *know* she gonna be wanting to find out and to experiment and whatnot . . . with what it's like to have a boy kissing her and—and holding her and hon-nee, . . . humph! [*Fans herself vigorously.*] That's just nature, wanting somebody to be rubbing up 'gainst ya and thing. . . . Course, now that ole fool I married, well, *my* time is now dried up. . . .

Suddenly she stops, throws her hand to her mouth, gasps in embarrassment at running on in such a way.

Oh, my goodness, chile, listen to me carrying on at "this" time! Why didn't you stop me; oughta be 'shamed of myself . . . ! [*Pauses.*] Darlin', Lord ha-mercy, forgive me, pardon me, this ain't the time for none of this kinda talk. . . . Naw-naw, I ain't going no further. Let me stop, let me just stop. [*Pauses.*] Yeah, you may *think* you "okay" and that it "don't bother you," but I'm gonna just *stop*.

Silence for several beats; she folds her hands in her lap.

[*Unable to contain her frustration.*] But you *see* what I'm saying, though! I mean this chile is young, fine, "new minted" and shuuuu!! [*Nodding in agreement with Lucille.*] Who you telling? That age you be *wanting* to be held and have your toes curl up and . . . whew! yes ma'am! And see, when you raising these here kids nowadays, you got to face it! face that fact! things are *not* like when we was coming up. See and Gladys wanna get sour faced with me when I tell her like it is. See 'cause, I ain't gonna hold back, you know me girl, if it's gotta be *looked at* then I'm gonna make you lay it out flat in the sun and take a good look at it, yessir, whatever it is! I'm gonna get you told about it!

Well, now, I'll tell you how it went down, see . . . Here all these weeks and weeks and carrying on, see, and I'm steady coming over visiting Gladys, and here I'm noticing that Pinkie up here always got on the *same* top, day after day, week after week, the same kinda blouselike thing, like a navy blue, you know like them navy blue nylon button-down things, like a jacket, and she's wearing this thing day in and day out, from "can't see to can't see," and I'm steady coming over. Well, one day, Gladys is out of earshot, and I say to Pinkie, "Say, Pinkie? honey, you gotta change that top, girl, I think you gonna have to wash that blouse, 'cause you know how 'navy' is now, that 'navy' gets that funk in it, and you can't wash it out. . . . " I said, "Well, Pinkie, uh, you gotta change your blouse *sometime* uh . . . " and I'm thinking to myself, well what is going on? And Gladys ain't saying nothing, and I'm waiting for her to notice or say something or *something*. I guess she ain't seen it, 'cause she ain't said nothing. Gladys got her head so stuck in them prayer books—'scuse me for saying so, Lucille, on such a sad occasion—but she can't half see no way. I mean—I mean, the Lord said for us to "pray," well, okay, but not to go deaf, dumb, and blind in doing it! And then if I try and say, "Gladys, ain't Pinkie got another jacket or something to put on?" Then Gladys think I'm trying to talk bad about her, and she wanna rile up and jump up in *my* face and jump bad with me. And look like to me every time I turn round here come Pinkie in that same navy blouse, jacket-type blouse thing, so I'm thinking, *What is with this child?* and I said to Gladys finally, I said, "Gladys, Pinkie's wearing that thing out"! And Gladys come talking 'bout [*Imitating a high-pitched voice.*] "Well, if that's what she wants to wear, then that's what she wants, what you trying to make something of it? what you trying to start?" so I said to myself, "Well, hell, I'm gonna just let well enough alone then!" And what happened? The next thing I know Bernadette from 'cross the street come calling me, calling *my* house, talking 'bout how her daughter Carol, who's Pinkie's best friend, told *her* that Pinkie up at the school told *Carol* that she *may* be pregnant and that Pinkie told Carol "not to tell nobody," but that Carol just now *told* her! Well, I said, *"Whaaaaa?"* Say *what?!* Well, hon-nee, I said to myself, *Let me go down here to Gladys's* and see what is what, see just *what* is going on here!" Well, so, hon-nee . . . I couldn't get out m'house fast enough! My phone come ringing off the hook, and who's on it but Gladys, weeping and wailing and having conniptions and pleading with me as the "Auntie" to come over and "have a word with Pinkie." Uh-hum! See!? And far be it for me to say, "I told you so," far be it for me to say, "I told you the pony was gonna jump the stable!"

See, and she wanna jump all up in my face when I was trying to *tell* her something way back, but now, now when it come down to the get-go, you *see* who she called on, now don't you! [*Pauses in fury.*] I'm telling you, girl! see, now that the monkey's out the bag, now that she finds out the cards done *already* been shuffled, *then* she come calling on me "to deal!"

Hon-nee, I was so outdone! So I come over there to the house, I come over saying to myself, "Oh, Lord ha-mercy! Oh, Lord!" 'Cause you know, honey, I been *seeing* that navy blue top day in and day out. . . .

Well, honey! Get down to the house and what do I find? Gladys sitting up there with Pinkie looking all long face and looking like she been nailed to the cross and Pinkie's all wide-eyed and mystified! And Gladys acting like she ain't never left Sunday school, just hedging and swallowing and ducking and dodging! Don't know what's *with* that woman; act like she ain't never see the "wee–wee" on a dog! Don't know *how* my brother ever got a child with that woman, my goodness—that's that ole sanctified church mess. They ain't like *our* kind of Christian; them people crazy—way she act you'd think she ain't never seen herself "down there," I swear! You shoulda seen her, [*Imitating a high-pitched, awkward voice.*] "uh . . . uh, P-P-P-P-P-Pinkie? P-P-P-P-P-Pinkie?" She wanna beat round the bush and hesitate and germinate and I don't know what else. "P-P-P-P-P-Pinkie . . . have you—have you *done* . . . have you been doing anything?" And Pinkie she just stares at Gladys wide-eyed and shakes her head back and forth [*She shakes her head in no response.*] "Un-uh" . . . Shit, girl!!—'Scuse me, 'scuse me, Lucille, this is not the place and this is not the time, but I was so outdone, I said, Well, hell! I mean hell! later for all this! Let's get it all out here in front and the hell with beating round the bush and carrying on and acting all prettified and citified. I said, Well, hell, let's just get it out in the open. I said, "Pinkie have you *fucked?*!" I mean, you know, *Let's just get it out here!*

Well, her Mama wanted to have a seizure, but I ain't studyin' that woman. I said to Pinkie, I said, "Pinkie, well, when was your last time you had your period?" I mean, you know, let's call a "trump card" a "trump," let's say it like *is*, let's bring it all out here! Later for all this shucking and jiving and ducking and dodging and conniving and hiding and carrying on!

Well, hon-nee, I am here to tell you, Pinkie went up to that calendar and hon-nee, them pages of that calendar went to . . .

She illustrates with her hands flipping the air.

. . . flipping and ah flipping and ah flipping and ah flipping and ah flipping . . . [*Her voice trails off.*] And I said, uh-oh, oh, Lord! oh, Lord ha-mercy! well, well sir, I walked up to her and hon-nee, I lifted up that ole navy blue blouse, jacket, whatever the hell it was, and that belly was ah sitting up there just as pre-tee!

And see Gladys all this time wanna keep hiding Pinkie way from the world and keeping her at home and keeping her under lock and key and keeping her all closed up and keeping her way from the boys and what happened? You *see* what happened! And I said to her, "Pinkie, when did this happen?" Well, it turns out she was sneaking some little boy round here, right in the very house of her so sanctified mama! Honey, it's the gospel truth! [*She throws her hands in the air.*] If I'm lying, Lord choke me! Right there in the basement, right under own noses. I was probably sitting up there, too, with Gladys upstairs, probably watching tee-vee with her and here Pinkie supposed to be following Gladys's ole-timey rules and regulations, supposed to be "in the bed." Ha, she was "in the bed," all right, "in the bed" down in the basement with that boy!"

And Gladys wanna act all horrified and carrying on. She wanna come talking 'bout, "If your father was still living here, if your father was still right with the Lord, then this never would have happened." I said, "Gladys, Gladys, the Lord ain't got nothing to do with it! You can't keep locking the girl up under lock and key and anyway, 'The fox has got the hen' *now*, so what we carrying on about?" And I dunno what Gladys getting all upset for, anyway, 'cause see [*She whispers very low.*] girl, I had to bite my tongue, see 'cause Gladys don't know that I know, but I know, 'cause see my brother *let me* know, that 'fore she married my brother, the "stork had already given notice as to Pinkie," if you know what I mean . . .

So anyway . . . yeah . . . Pinkie's laying up there now, she's laying up there in labor, and I'll tell you one thing, my dear. . . . Now she's fifteen and having this baby. . . . Oh, Gladys is gonna help take care of it, and Gladys and me we gonna hog whip that chile if she don't *stay* in school. . . . But honey . . .

Her face is suddenly a portrait of sadness, foreboding, and old hidden recollections.

Her childhood is *over* . . . her childhood is up! Them days of being a little carefree little girl? She can just lock 'em up . . . !

She struggles to fight back tears.

. . . 'Cause raising up a baby and raising up a child and being a child your own self and with no man? Trying to raise yourself plus raise something all by yourself? [*Pause.*] Talk about being "grounded in the house"? Now she *really* gonna be "grounded"! [*Pauses.*] she's on the killing ground now . . . yes, Ma'am!! Pinkie's gonna be a mama! She's on the killing ground now . . . ! [*Pauses and recovers herself.*]

So anyways, Lucille, I was so, so sorry to hear that Coleman passed . . . and now what day is the viewing of the body? Oh, that's good. Let him be laid out for a couple days. That way everybody that wants to can pay they respects; that's good. . . .

Her voice trails off, she nods to Lucille's remarks as the lights fade.

That's good . . . right . . . right. . . . Amen. . . .

Fade out.

QUESTIONS

1. Ms. Edie is a woman with a story to tell. How does she move from commiserating with Lucille on the death of her husband to beginning her narrative? Though she promises time and again to stop, she invariably resumes. Find several instances of this. What is the effect of the stop/start narration? How does it establish Ms. Edie as a character?

2. Ms. Edie uses a great many analogies and figures of speech in her monologue. Find three and comment in general on her speaking style. Do you find it compelling? Explain your answer.

3. How do you interpret the events that Ms. Edie tells about? Do you find yourself siding with Gladys or Pinkie? Why?

4. What is Ms. Edie's view on human nature and, in particular, on the raising of children? How do you imagine she might have raised Pinkie differently?

5. Comment on Medley's use of profanity at a key moment of Ms. Edie's monologue.

6. What is the effect of Ms. Edie's telling her story to the unseen Lucille? How does the fact that Lucille has had her own tragedy contribute to the effect of the play? How would "Waking Women" be different if Edie just told her story directly to the audience?

7. Discuss the possible ways that Medley's title could be read.

8. Does this play have a message, a theme, to relate? What is it?

Maria Irene Fornes (1930–)

Maria Fornes was born in Havana, Cuba. After moving to New York in 1945, she worked in a factory, later studying painting with Hans Hoffman at the Provincetown School. Inspired by the work of Samuel Beckett, Fornes began writing plays on her own. Soon she was working actively in the Off-Off Broadway movement, writing, producing, and directing. Among Fornes's many plays are *Tango Palace* (1963), *Molly's Dream* (1968), *Mud* (1983), and *And What of the Night?* Fornes has in recent years directed Manhattan's INTAR Hispanic Playwrights in Residence Laboratory. *The Successful Life of 3* was first produced in 1965.

THE SUCCESSFUL LIFE OF 3

CHARACTERS

HE, a handsome young man
SHE, a sexy young lady
3, a plump, middle-aged man
BODYGUARDS
POLICEMEN

*** *following a character's name indicates:*

For SHE, *that* SHE *thinks with a stupid expression [the* OTHERS *watch her]*

For HE, *that* HE *looks disdainful [the* OTHERS *watch him]*

And for 3, *that 3 looks with intense curiosity [the* OTHERS *watch him]*

Very deadpan.

SCENE 1

The Doctor's Office. 3 and HE *sit.* HE *is combing his hair. 3 takes a shoe off and drops it. At the sound of the shoe,* HE *becomes motionless, his arms suspended in the air. 3 looks at* HE *and freezes for a moment.*

3. What are you doing?
HE. Waiting.
3. What for?
HE. For the other shoe to drop.
3. Ah, and I was wondering what you were doing. If I hadn't asked, we would have stayed like that forever. You waiting and me wondering . . . That's the kind of person I am. I ask . . . That's good, you know.
HE. Why?
3. ***
HE. Why?
3. It starts action.
HE. What action did you start?
3. We're talking.
HE. That's nothing. We could be waiting for the other shoe to drop.

> HE *suspends his arms in the air again. 3 stares at* HE. THEY *remain motionless for a while.*

3. Sorry . . . I'm going to do my sewing.
HE. First take the other shoe off. Get it over with.
3. [*Taking off his shoe*] I wasn't going to take it off. [*3 takes needle and thread and sews a button on his shirt*] You see? If I do it now I don't have to do it later.
HE. What?
3. The sewing.

HE. And what are you going to do later?

3. *** [*Puts the needle and thread away*] Look, there are advantages to being optimistic.

HE. Sure.

3. What are they?

HE. You tell me.

3. Well, it makes one feel happier.

HE. You don't look happy to me.

3. Oh, no?

HE. No.

3. Well, things are not what they appear to the eye.

HE. They aren't?

3. Are they?

HE. Sometimes . . . sometimes they are just what they appear to the eye . . . Don't generalize.

3. Why?

HE. Because there are always exceptions. There's always one that isn't like the others.

3. If it's just one, it can be thrown in with the rest. It doesn't matter.

HE. It matters.

3. Perhaps you can exclude it in your mind. Without mentioning it.

HE. You have to mention it . . . You're splitting hairs anyway.

3. I like splitting hairs.

HE. Well, do it when I'm not around.

3. I was just joking.

HE. [*Correcting him*] Being facetious.

3. [*Taking an apple from his pocket*] Want an apple?

HE. No.

3. An apple a day keeps the doctor away.

HE. I knew you were going to say that.

> SHE *enters wearing a nurse's uniform.*

Miss, you're a fine dish.

SHE. Thanks. [SHE *exits and re-enters*]

HE. Miss, I would like to bounce on you.

SHE. Thank you. [*To 3*] Come in please.

> 3 *and* SHE *exit.* SHE *re-enters.*

HE. Miss, I would like to bang you.

SHE. Your friend just did.

HE. Well, I'm next.

SHE. I only do it once a day.

HE. I get you all worked up and you do it with him instead?

SHE. ***

HE. I'm handsome and sexy and I get you all worked up, and you go and do it with him? Answer now.

SHE. What?

HE. Is that natural?

SHE. I don't know.

> *3 enters.*

HE. A moment ago I was thinking of marrying you.

SHE. You just saw me for the first time.

3. He figured he'd see you a few more times if he married you.

HE. Don't speak to me after you ruined everything . . . Let me try again. Miss, would you go to the movies with me after work?

SHE. Okay, I like the movies.

HE. Everybody likes the movies.

SHE. I never liked them until a few months ago.

HE. What made you like them then?

SHE. I saw a movie with the Lane sisters.

HE. You like them?

SHE. Yes, they're all right.

HE. What do they do?

SHE. Stupid things.

HE. Like what?

SHE. They cry and laugh.

HE. That doesn't sound so great.

SHE. I like it. It's all right if you like sisters.

3. I like movies about marriage, divorce and remarriage.

SHE. I like sisters.

HE. I don't have any particular preference. I just like good movies . . . with action and a lot of killing.

SHE. I couldn't go to the movies if I didn't have a preference.

3. Neither could I.

> *3 takes* SHE *by the hand and exits.* SHE *re-enters.*

HE. Did you make it with him again?

SHE. Yes.

HE. How long are you going to keep this up?

SHE. I don't know.

> *3 re-enters.*

HE. Listen, I was even thinking of marrying you.

SHE. You'd have to give me a ring for that. Two rings. An engagement ring and a wedding band.

3. I'll give the bride away.

HE. From the looks of it you're not leaving anything to give away.

3. And I'm not through yet.

HE. I didn't say you were.

3. You didn't say I was but you sure wish I were.

SHE. Me too.

HE. I never wish.

SHE. In my profession you have to wish.

3. For what?

SHE. ***

HE. I don't have a profession.

SHE. How are you going to support me?

HE. I'll find a way.

3. He sure does have to support you. Doesn't he?

SHE. Yeah, my parents pay for the wedding and he supports me.

3. I'll pay for the wedding.

HE. He doesn't have any money. Get your parents to pay for the wedding.

SHE. Weddings are a pain in the neck.

3. Why do you want one then?

SHE. ***

HE. Don't you see she doesn't know?

3. Yes, I see.

SHE. The Andrews sisters° are all married.

HE. Do you like brothers too?

SHE. Not so much.

HE. Did you see *The Corsican Brothers?*

SHE. That's not brothers. That's just Douglas Fairbanks° playing twins. It's not the same.

HE. What brothers do you like?

SHE. I don't know any.

HE. How do you know you like them?

SHE. ***

3. She didn't say she liked them.

HE. Didn't you say you like them?

SHE. No, I said, "Not so much" . . . I don't think I'm going to marry you.

3. Why?

HE. I can ask my own questions, if you please [*To* SHE] Why?

SHE. You're too picky.

HE. That's all right. Are we going to the movies or not?

SHE. Sure.

3. If you find a sister movie.

SHE. That's all right. I'll try another kind.

3. Let's go in for a quickie before you leave.

> *3 and* SHE *exit,* SHE *re-enters wearing a hat.*

HE. Ready?

SHE. Yes.

HE. Hey, didn't you say you only do it once a day?

SHE. Yes.

HE. How come you did it with him three times already?

SHE. ***

HE. You're not a liar are you?

SHE. No.

HE. You better not be, because I can't stand liars.

> *3 re-enters.* HE *and* SHE *exit.*

3. Wait for me. [*3 exits*]

Andrews sisters: popular sweet-singing "sister" group who performed harmonious pop tunes in the later 1940s and 1950s. *Fairbanks:* Douglas Fairbanks, Jr., swashbuckling romantic movie hero of the 1940s and 1950s; he played twin roles in *The Corsican Brothers.*

SCENE 2

The Movies. The lights go down and flicker. HE, 3 *and* SHE *enter.* THEY *sit*—3 *in the middle,* SHE *and* HE *at his sides.*

HE. Hey, what do you mean by sitting next to her? Change with me. She's my date.
3. I can't feel her up from there.
HE. You don't have to feel her up.

> 3 *and* HE *change seats.*

3. How about some popcorn?
SHE. I'll go.
3. Don't go. Let him go.
HE. You go.
3. I can't.

> HE *exits.* 3 *moves next to* SHE. HE *re-enters.*

HE. Move back to your seat.
3. I already moved once. I'm not moving twice. Let's have some popcorn.

> HE *offers popcorn to* 3.

I'll hold it because I'm in the middle.

> 3 *tries to hold the bag, eat popcorn, and feel* SHE *up.*

You hold the bag. I can't feel her up and eat at the same time if I hold the bag.

> HE *takes the bag.*

HE. At least wait till the feature starts.

SCENE 3

The Porch. Ten years later. HE *dozes.* SHE *peels potatoes.* 3 *sews.*

SHE. I'm going to divorce him.
3. Give him another chance.
SHE. Him?
3. He's not bad.
SHE. Yes, he is.
3. There are worse.
SHE. No, there aren't.
3. Wouldn't it be worse if you were married to me?
SHE. What difference would it make?
3. It would make a difference.
SHE. No, it wouldn't.
3. Yes, it would.
SHE. What difference?
3. ***
SHE. What difference?
3. I'll ask him.

> 3 *shakes* HE.

Hey, would it make any difference if she was married to me instead of you?

HE. Yeah.

3. What difference?

HE. Ask her. She ought to know.

3. She doesn't know.

HE. She never knows anything.

3. Actually, this time she knows. She said it wouldn't make any difference.

HE. She's probably right, because she usually doesn't know anything.

SHE. I'm going to divorce him whether I'm right or wrong.

3. Marry a worse one for a while . . . then remarry him and you'll be happier.

HE. That would be like wearing tight shoes so it feels better when you take them off.

3. That's the idea. Do it.

SHE. You can't do that.

3. Why not?

SHE. I don't know.

3. [To HE] Do you know why you can't wear tight shoes so it feels better when you take them off?

HE. No.

SHE. But isn't it true that you're not supposed to?

HE. Yeah.

SHE. I knew it.

3. Well, you'd be happier if you did it.

SHE. You're not supposed to.

HE. [To 3] Get off that chair. I want to put my feet up.

3 moves to another chair.

3. Rivalry.

SHE. What?

3. Rivalry.

SHE. ***

3. Masculine rivalry.

SHE. ***

3. Masculine rivalry. [3 *points to* HE *and to himself*]

SHE. Who ever heard of such a thing.

3. What?

SHE. What you said.

3. Rivalry?

SHE. Yeah.

3. You haven't heard of it?

SHE. No.

3. I bet you he has. [To HE] Have you heard of rivalry?

HE. Sure.

3. See?

SHE. I mean the other.

3. Masculine?

SHE. Both, both together.

3. [To HE] Have you heard of masculine rivalry?

HE. Yeah.

SHE. So he has.

3 looks SHE *over.*

3. I don't desire you any more.

SHE. Thank God.

3. Don't thank God. Thank me.

SHE. Stop picking on me.

HE. Are you picking on her again?

3. I can't help it.

HE. Stop picking on her.

3. Masculine rivalry.

HE. What are you talking about? There's no comparison. I'm sexy and you're slimy.

SHE. That's the only thing I like about him.

HE. You like *that?*

SHE. It's all right . . . But I'm tired of having children.

HE. That's not true. You told me you like children.

SHE. Not that many.

3. How many are there?

SHE. I don't know.

3. How do you know there are too many?

SHE. ***

3. I'll go count them. [*3 exits*]

HE. Listen, you can't one day say you like babies and the next day say you don't.

SHE. Why not?

HE. You have to make up your mind.

SHE. *** [SHE *doesn't answer*]

HE. Well?

SHE. I can't stand the twins.

HE. Why not?

SHE. They look too much alike.

HE. Twins always do.

SHE. I didn't say they didn't.

HE. You didn't say they did either.

SHE. No, all I said was that I didn't like them.

HE. Why?

SHE. I don't see why they have to dress alike.

HE. Twins always do.

SHE. I didn't say they didn't.

HE. Bring the food out.

SHE. There's no food.

HE. How come?

SHE. You know how come.

HE. No, I don't.

SHE. You're supposed to provide for me, but you don't.

HE. Don't I get you all the potatoes?

SHE. I'm going. I can't stand peeling potatoes all the time.

SHE *exits. 3 enters.*

HE. She left.

3. Oh.

HE. That's all right. I never want what I don't have.

3. I missed it.

HE. What?

3. Her leaving. I've been waiting around to see her leave, and now she does it when I'm not looking. How did she go?

HE. ***

SCENE 4

The porch. Three years later. HE *peels potatoes.* 3 *sews.*

3. I'm going into business. I can't stand this home life any longer.

HE. You wouldn't be any good at it.

3. I might as well try it.

HE. You would just lose all your money.

3. I don't have any money.

HE. How're you going to go into business?

3. I'll put a bid on some nylon rope, go south, convince the fishermen to use nylon ropes instead of whatever they use, and take them for all they've got.

HE. They probably use nylon.

3. Then I'll sell it to them cheap and still make a fortune.

HE. It wouldn't work.

3. No? . . . Well, I can make a sandwich with peanut butter and Ritz crackers, dip it in chocolate, call it Tootsie Tootsie, and sell it.

HE. You're better off with the nylon rope.

3. I thought so too. I'll go try it.

HE. Okay.

3. Good-bye. Give my love to Ruth if you see her. Have you seen her?

HE. Yes, she's happily married.

3. Who to?

HE. I don't know.

3. Well, if you see her, tell her I would still like a roll in the hay with her, even if she's getting old and decrepit.

HE. Okay, I'll tell her.

3. Good-bye. You do think it will work?

HE. Sure.

3. Good-bye then. [3 *exits*]

HE. Just said that to get rid of him.

3. [*Re-enters, wearing top hat and furs*] It worked.

HE. Don't tell me it worked.

3. [*Respectfully*] Oh, sorry.

HE. What do you mean it worked?

3. I put a bid on some nylon rope, went south, convinced them fishermen to use nylon instead of whatever they were using, and took them for all they had. D'you know rope is sold by the weight, not the measure?

HE. Don't get smart with me, Arthur. I'm very annoyed. I have all the brains and looks and it's you who goes south with your squeaky voice and sweaty hands and makes all the money.

3. And I'm not finished yet. I'm going to make that peanut butter sandwich and make another mint.

The Successful Life of 3

HE. You're making me sick.

3. Don't get sick yet. I'm just starting. You think Ruth likes money?

HE. Sure.

3. Perhaps she'll come live with us for the money. It'll be good for the children.

HE. I'm the husband and the father. I'll make my own decisions.

3. Yeah, but I do all the screwing and make all the money.

HE. Don't rub it in.

3. Sorry.

HE. You may make all the money and all that, but you have no manners.

3. Teach me manners.

> HE *puts on the top hat and furs.* SHE *enters.*

SHE. Okay, I came back.

HE. Because of the money.

SHE. I like money.

HE. Everybody likes money. You say it as if it was something special.

SHE. It is special. I like money very much.

HE. More than sisters?

SHE. ***

HE. Never mind.

3. I have a present for you.

> *3 gives* SHE *three men's hats.*

SHE. These are men's hats. What's the matter with you?

3. Nothing.

HE. He doesn't know his ass from his elbow.

3. I do. [3 *points to his buttocks and his elbow*] I only didn't know what kind of hat to buy.

SHE. Where's the money?

3. In the bank.

SHE. Oh, damn it. I came for the money and you put it away.

HE. You didn't come for that. You didn't come for that. You came for me and for the children.

SHE. You said I came for the money.

HE. I was just accusing you.

SHE. And what was I supposed to say?

HE. "I didn't. I didn't. I came for you and the children." Defend yourself.

SHE. Well, I didn't.

HE. I don't have to stay here while you come back for his money. I'm sexy and bright and you're a bunch of morons. I'm leaving.

> *3 puts his arm around* SHE.

HE. You don't have to jump on her the moment I turn my back.

> *3 lets go of* SHE.

SHE. I'm glad he caught you.

HE. You can do what you want. I'm leaving. Good-bye. [HE *exits*]

SHE. What are we going to do without him?

3. Wait for him.

SCENE 5

The Store. Three years later. HE *is standing.* 3 *steals a pipe.*

HE. Arthur!

3. What are you doing here?

HE. I'm a store detective.

3. How long have you been a store detective?

HE. Since I left the house.

3. Is the pay good?

HE. Not for the risk you take.

3. What risk?

HE. You might get hit or knifed.

3. Who would do that?

HE. The thief. You see, I grab him like this. I identify myself and I tell him to go with me to the office. Then he either becomes frightened and comes along quietly, or becomes violent and attacks me.

[3 *punches* HE *and runs*]

SCENE 6

The Porch. A few minutes later. SHE *peels potatoes.* 3 *enters smoking the pipe.*

3. I just saw him. He's a detective.

SHE. I don't like detectives.

3. Why?

SHE. I can't understand them.

3. Why not?

SHE. They talk too fast.

3. He's a store detective. They don't talk fast.

SHE. A store detective is not a real detective.

3. Someone stole something though.

SHE. Did he figure out who did it?

3. I don't know. I hit him and ran.

SHE. You didn't run so fast. You're late for dinner . . . Did you figure out who did it?

3. Yeah, I did it.

SHE. What did you do?

3. [*Showing her the pipe*] Stole it.

HE *enters.*

HE. Why did you hit me?

SHE. Is that a way to come in after you've been gone for three years? Can't you say hello?

HE. I don't feel like saying hello.

SHE. You could at least pretend.

HE. Why did you hit me?

3. Because I had to.

HE. Why?

3. Because I'm the thief and you're the detective.

HE. What did you steal?

3. Guess.

HE. I give up.

3. The pipe.

HE. Now I have to take you in.

3. You have to identify yourself.

HE. Don't be silly. You know me. Come on.

3. Good-bye, Ruth.

SHE. Good-bye.

SCENE 7

The Porch. Three days later. SHE *and* HE *are sitting.*

SHE. How come you came back now?

HE. Because he's away . . . Masculine rivalry.

SHE. That's what he always says.

HE. So what. It's true.

SHE. How come he was stealing?

HE. He didn't know he could take the money out of the bank.

SHE. Can he?

HE. Yeah.

3. [*Enters wearing a prisoner's uniform*] I organized a revolt and got out.

HE. Can't you stay put in one place?

3. Can't I?

HE. No, you're always jumping from place to place.

3. I'll stay put now. Ruth, even if you're getting old and decrepit, I still want you. Jail makes a man want a woman.

HE. You disgust me. You spend three days in jail and you don't learn anything.

3. I did so. I organized the prisoners and now I'm the head of the mob. If you want I'll make you my bodyguard.

HE. You call that a body?

3. I know. I have to do some exercise. But in the meantime it's all right to call it a body.

HE. It is not all right with me. I'm leaving.

SHE. He's always leaving.

3. Like Shane° . . . Stay and have some fun. The guys are coming presently.

HE. What kind of idiot are you that says presently?

3. No idiot. I'm the Alec Guinness° type gangster.

HE. God damn it. I'm getting fed up. You have no style, no looks, you act like an old housewife, and it's you who gets to go to jail and become the head of the mob.

SHE. Let's eat.

HE. Okay, but if you want me to be your bodyguard, you have to give me a good salary . . . No. I don't care if you get slugged. Good-bye. (HE exits)

3. You be my bodyguard, Ruth.

Shane: Western movie of the 1950s in which the title character (played by Alan Ladd) leaves town after doing various good deeds.   *Alec Guinness:* actor who played soft-spoken, sophisticated villains in the movies of the 1950s and early 1960s.

Drama in the Modern Age

SHE. Okay, but I don't move from this chair.

3. You have to move. You have to keep an eye on me.

SHE. Skip it. Who wants to look at you all the time.

3. Okay. Don't be my bodyguard. I'll get the guys to look after me.

SCENE 8

The Porch. Six months later. 3 and SHE *sit. 3 is armed to the teeth.* BODYGUARDS *surround him.*

3. I have a sweet streak in me.

SHE. Where?

3. ***

SHE. What did you say?

3. I have a sweet streak in me.

SHE. Me too.

3. I'm tired of the life of crime.

SHE. Why don't you stop stealing?

3. I like stealing.

SHE. I thought you said you were tired of crime.

3. Yes, but not of stealing.

SHE. You're not supposed to steal.

3. Says who?

SHE. ***

3. You don't know anything. I'm going to steal from the rich and give to the poor.

SHE. I came back for the money and you're going to give it to the poor? I'm leaving.

3. Where are you going?

SHE. I'll go find a Joan Fontaine° movie.

3. What good would that do you?

SHE. She's Olivia de Havilland's° sister.

3. No, she's not.

SHE. Yes, she is.

3. They don't look alike.

SHE. The Lane sisters don't look alike either.

3. No, but they act like sisters.

SHE. ***

> *3 exits.* SHE *stands puzzled.*

SCENE 9

The Store. A few minutes later. HE *is standing. 3 walks by surrounded by* BODYGUARDS.

HE. Come with me to the office. You penny-pinching sonofabitch hoodlum. I finally
  caught you.

3. What for? I just came to get a Zorro costume. [3 *puts on a Zorro° costume*]

HE. You look like an idiot, like you always did. Did you steal it?

Fontaine: romantic heroine of melodramatic movies of the 1950s and 1960s.   *de Havilland:* screen
actress most popular during the 1940s and 1950s.   *Zorro:* masked Latino cowboy hero of a TV adventure series of the late 1950s and early 1960s, in which Zorro's role is a combination of Robin Hood, a
Musketeer, and the Lone Ranger.

3. I bought it.

HE. Show me the sales slip.

3. I lost it.

HE. You stole it. [*To the* BODYGUARDS] Did he steal it?

BODYGUARDS. Yeah.

HE. Come with me.

3. Don't be silly. If I'm Zorro and the store is rich, I have to steal from it. Now I have to give something to the poor. Here's a penny.

HE. I'm turning you in anyway. I'll get fired if I don't catch someone soon . . . I haven't caught anyone since the last time I caught you. Get moving.

3. No, I won't. I have better things to do, like ride around the pampas with my mask on. Come with me and you can ride too.

HE. What kind of idiot d'you think I am. You'll make me do all the riding and cut all the Z's and you'll get all the credit. You do your own dirty work.

3. No, I won't . . . I'm getting too old to ride around like an idiot.

HE. You used to do your own dirty work.

3. Yeah. But now I'm rich and lazy. [*To a* BODYGUARD] Can you ride?

BODYGUARD *shakes his head.*

Can you ride?

BODYGUARD *shakes his head.*

Can you ride?

BODYGUARD *shakes his head.*

Get out of my way. I don't need you any more. [*To* HE] Can Ruth ride?

HE. No, she can't do anything.

3. That's all right. I'll go to some rodeo and get myself a double.

[*3 exits*]

SCENE 10

The Porch. Three days later. HE *sits.* 3 *enters panting.*

3. Hide me.

HE. What from?

3. I'm being followed.

HE. What did you do?

3. I got tired of stealing from the rich and giving to the poor and started stealing from the rich and the poor. Hide me.

HE. I won't hide you. I don't care if they catch you.

3. Hide my *antifaz* then.

HE. What's that?

3. My mask. Do you know that Zorro means fox in Spanish?

HE. Never mind. I don't care if Zorro means fox. I can't hide your *antifaz*. I'll lose my job if I get caught with stolen goods.

3. I thought they were going to fire you.

HE. I caught a girl who didn't do anything and they let me stay.

3. That's not nice. Where's Ruth?

HE. She went to see Joan Fontaine and never came back.

3. Did she take any money with her?

HE. She doesn't need any money. She married the guy who owns the movie.

3. How're the children?

HE. They're all right. They're always playing doctor.

3. Are they sick?

HE. No, they just play doctor.

> The POLICEMEN *enter and grab* 3.

3. Where're you taking me?

POLICEMEN. To the scaffold.

3. Oh! Merciful God.

> The POLICEMEN *take* 3 *away.* 3 *re-enters, carrying a bouquet.*

HE. I thought they were going to hang you.

3. I got out of it. Here's Ruth. She must have broken up with that movie man.

> SHE *enters.* 3 *gives her the flowers.*

SHE. How did you know I was coming?

3. I didn't.

HE. How did you get out?

3. I told them you did it.

HE. I'll lose my job at the store.

3. Don't let that worry you. You won't need a job any more. They're coming to get you any minute. [*To* SHE] What made you come back?

SHE. I'm old and tired and I've had too many men. I'm just going to sit here and rest for the rest of my life.

3. Oh no you won't. You have to work for your keep. Scrub the floor.

HE. I'm going to the store. I can't stand seeing my wife scrubbing floors.

SHE. Don't go. I'm not going to scrub no floors. You've become a mean old sonofabitch, Arthur.

3. I was always mean. I just didn't know it.

SHE. You're not supposed to be mean.

3. Why not?

SHE. ***

HE. She's right. You're not supposed to be mean.

SHE. I knew it.

3. Well, perhaps I just have a mean streak in me.

SHE. Yeah, like the Grand Canyon.

HE. The Grand Canyon is not a streak.

SHE. What is it?

3. It's a ditch.

SHE. Same thing.

3. Well, here are the cops anyway. They're coming to get you.

HE. You're disgusting. You go around being a sonofabitch and then you pin it on me. What am I going to do now?

3. ***

SHE. ***

HE. You're a bunch of morons.

> The POLICEMEN *enter.* THEY *grab* 3.

3. Where are you taking me?

POLICEMEN. To the scaffold.

3. I just came from there.

> The POLICEMEN *take* 3 *away.*

SHE. Are you going to miss him?

HE. No, he's a sonofabitch—are you?

SHE. What?

HE. Going to miss him?

SHE. ***

> 3 *enters with a bouquet of flowers and gives them to* SHE.

HE. How come you always come back with flowers?

3. They have them there.

SHE. What for?

3. For the grave.

HE. Did you steal them?

3. No, they give them to you.

SHE. They go bad if they don't use them.

HE. How did you get away this time?

3. They caught the real Zorro.

SHE. I thought you were the real Zorro.

3. No, I'm too young.

HE. Bring in the food, Ruth.

SHE. What food?

3. I have some Tootsie Tootsies.

> THEY *eat Tootsie Tootsies. A* POLICEMAN *enters.* 3 *shoots him dead.*

I'm not armed to the teeth for nothing.

> THEY *freeze for a moment. Then* THEY *sing the "Song to Ignorance."*

ALL.

> Let me be wrong.
> But also not know it.
> Be wrong,
> Be wrong,
> And, oh, not to know it.
> Oh! Let me be wrong.

3.

> One day while walking
> Down the street,
> I found a petunia
> And took it.
> I took it.
> Oh! Let me be wrong.

ALL.

> Let me be wrong.
> But also not know it.
> Be wrong,
> Be wrong,

And, oh, not to know it.
Oh! Let me be wrong.

SHE.

I went from here

HE.

To where?

SHE.

I don't know where.
I called a parasol an umbrella.
Yes, an umbrella.
Oh, let me be wrong.
I don't care.

ALL.

Let me be wrong.
But also not know it.
Be wrong,
Be wrong,
And, oh, not to know it.
Oh! Let me be wrong.

HE.

I sprechen sie dutch very well
I said to Herr Auber:
Herr Auber, I sprechen sie
Dutch very well, Herr Auber.
Oh! Let me be wrong.

ALL.

Let me be wrong.
But also not know it.
Be wrong,
Be wrong,
And, oh, not to know it.
Oh! Let me be wrong.
Oh! Let me be wrong.
Oh! Let me be wrong.
I want to be wrong!

THEY *repeat the song and walk down the aisles selling Tootsie Tootsies.*

QUESTIONS

The Successful Life of 3 is a light absurdist play that nonetheless has several coherent narrative strands.

1. Summarize the main action of the play.

2. Describe the basic characters—He, She, and 3. What are each of them like when we first meet them? In what ways is the first scene representative of those that follow?

3. How do the three characters relate to each other? Do their relations change over the course of the play? Do any of them appear to grow over the years?

4. How does Fornes handle time changes in the play? What is the effect of her treatment of time?

5. Which of the three main characters most compels the reader's/viewer's interest? Why?

6. Is Fornes making any statement about the relations between the sexes? Find examples to support your answer.

7. How does Fornes treat the theme of law and lawlessness? How do you interpret 3's taking on the role of Zorro?

8. What do you suppose Fornes means by calling the play *The Successful Life of 3?*

9. Does the song at the end have any meaning? What do you think Fornes wants us to think?

Athol Fugard (1932–   )

Athol Fugard, a white South African, was born to an Afrikaner mother and a father of English descent. He grew up in Port Elizabeth, South Africa, where he now lives with his wife and daughter. His plays, which include *Boesman & Lena* and *A Lesson from Aloes,* study the effects of the government's apartheid policies on the lives of ordinary people. *"Master Harold" . . . and the boys* was first produced at the Yale Repertory Theatre in 1982.

"MASTER HAROLD" . . . AND THE BOYS

The St. George's Park Tea Room on a wet and windy Port Elizabeth° afternoon.

Tables and chairs have been cleared and are stacked on one side except for one which stands apart with a single chair. On this table a knife, fork, spoon and side plate in anticipation of a simple meal, together with a pile of comic books.

Other elements: a serving counter with a few stale cakes under glass and a not very impressive display of sweets, cigarettes and cool drinks, etc.; a few cardboard advertising handouts—Cadbury's Chocolate, Coca-Cola—and a blackboard on which an untrained hand has chalked up the prices of Tea, Coffee, Scones, Milkshakes—all flavors—and Cool Drinks; a few sad ferns in pots; a telephone; an old-style jukebox.

There is an entrance on one side and an exit into a kitchen on the other.

Leaning on the solitary table, his head cupped in one hand as he pages through one of the comic books, is Sam. A black man in his mid-forties. He wears the white coat of a waiter. Behind him on his knees, mopping down the floor with a bucket of water and a rag, is Willie. Also black and about the same age as Sam. He has his sleeves and trousers rolled up.

The year: 1950

WILLIE. [*Singing as he works.*]
    "She was scandalizin' my name,
    She took my money
    She called me honey

Port Elizabeth: city in South Africa.

But she was scandalizin' my name.
Called it love but was playin' a game . . . "

He gets up and moves the bucket. Stands thinking for a moment, then, raising his arms to hold an imaginary partner, he launches into an intricate ballroom dance step. Although a mildly comic figure, he reveals a reasonable degree of accomplishment.

Hey, Sam.

Sam, absorbed in the comic book, does not respond.

Hey, Boet° Sam!

Sam looks up.

I'm getting it. The quickstep. Look now and tell me. [*He repeats the step.*] Well?

SAM. [*Encouragingly*] Show me again.

WILLIE. Okay, count for me.

SAM. Ready?

WILLIE. Ready.

SAM. Five, six, seven, eight . . . [*Willie starts to dance*] A-n-d one two three four . . . and one two three four. . . . [*Ad libbing as Willie dances.*] Your shoulders, Willie . . . your shoulders! Don't look down! Look happy, Willie! Relax, Willie!

WILLIE. [*Desperate but still dancing.*] I am relax.

SAM. No, you're not.

WILLIE. [*He falters.*] Ag no man, Sam! Mustn't talk. You make me make mistakes.

SAM. But you're too stiff.

WILLIE. Yesterday I'm not straight . . . today I'm too stiff!

SAM. Well, you are. You asked me and I'm telling you.

WILLIE. Where?

SAM. Everywhere. Try to glide through it.

WILLIE. Glide?

SAM. Ja, make it smooth. And give it more style. It must look like you're enjoying yourself.

WILLIE. [*Emphatically*] I wasn't.

SAM. Exactly.

WILLIE. How can I enjoy myself? Not straight, too stiff and now it's also glide, give it more style, make it smooth. . . . Haai! Is hard to remember all those things, Boet Sam.

SAM. That's your trouble. You're trying too hard.

WILLIE. I try hard because it *is* hard.

SAM. But don't let me see it. The secret is to make it look easy. Ballroom must look happy, Willie, not like hard work. It must . . . Ja! . . . it must look like romance.

WILLIE. Now another one! What's romance?

SAM. Love story with happy ending. A handsome man in tails, and in his arms, smiling at him, a beautiful lady in evening dress!

WILLIE. Fred Astaire,° Ginger Rogers.°

SAM. You got it. Tapdance or ballroom, it's the same. Romance. In two weeks' time when the judges look at you and Hilda, they must see a man and a woman who are dancing their way to a happy ending. What I saw was you holding her like you were frightened she was going to run away.

Boet: buddy.   *Fred Astaire, Ginger Rogers:* famous American dance team in the cinema.

WILLIE. Ja! Because that is what she wants to do! I got no romance left for Hilda anymore, Boet Sam.

SAM. Then pretend. When you put your arms around Hilda, imagine she is Ginger Rogers.

WILLIE. With no teeth? You try.

SAM. Well, just remember, there's only two weeks left.

WILLIE. I know, I know! [*To the jukebox*] I do it better with music. You got sixpence for Sarah Vaughan?°

SAM. That's a slow foxtrot. You're practicing the quickstep.

WILLIE. I'll practice slow foxtrot.

SAM. [*Shaking his head*] It's your turn to put money in the jukebox.

WILLIE. I only got bus fare to go home. [*He returns disconsolately to his work.*] Love story and happy ending! She's doing it all right, Boet Sam, but is not me she's giving happy endings. Fuckin' whore! Three nights now she doesn't come practice. I wind up gramophone, I get record ready and I sit and wait. What happens? Nothing. Ten o'clock I start dancing with my pillow. You try and practice romance by yourself, Boet Sam. Struesgod,° she doesn't come tonight I take back my dress and ballroom shoes and I find me new partner. Size twenty-six. Shoes size seven. And now she's also making trouble for me with the baby again. Reports me to Child Wellfed,° that I'm not giving her money. She lies! Every week I am giving her money for milk. And how do I know he is my baby? Only his hair looks like me. She's fucking around all the time I turn my back. Hilda Samuels is a bitch! [*Pause*] Hey, Sam!

SAM. Ja.

WILLIE. You listening?

SAM. Ja.

WILLIE. So what you say?

SAM. About Hilda?

WILLIE. Ja.

SAM. When did you last give her a hiding?

WILLIE. [*Reluctantly*] Sunday night.

SAM. And today is Thursday.

WILLIE. [*He knows what's coming.*] Okay.

SAM. Hiding on Sunday night, then Monday, Tuesday and Wednesday she doesn't come to practice . . . and you are asking me why?

WILLIE. I said okay, Boet Sam!

SAM. You hit her too much. One day she's going to leave you for good.

WILLIE. So? She makes me the hell-in too much.

SAM. [*Emphasizing his point*] *Too* much and *too* hard. You had the same trouble with Eunice.

WILLIE. Because she also make the hell-in, Boet Sam. She never got the steps right. Even the waltz.

SAM. Beating her up every time she makes a mistake in the waltz? [*Shaking his head*] No, Willie! That takes the pleasure out of ballroom dancing.

WILLIE. Hilda is not too bad with the waltz, Boet Sam. Is the quickstep where the trouble starts.

Sarah Vaughan: American jazz singer.   *Struesgod:* So help me, God.   *Child Wellfed:* child welfare agency.

SAM. [*Teasing him gently*] How's your pillow with the quickstep?

WILLIE. [*Ignoring the tease*] Good! And why? Because it got no legs. That's her trouble. She can't move them quick enough, Boet Sam. I start the record and before halfway Count Basie° is already winning. Only time we catch up with him is when gramophone runs down.

Sam laughs.

Haaikona,° Boet Sam, is not funny.

SAM. [*Snapping his fingers*] I got it! Give her a handicap.

WILLIE. What's that?

SAM. Give her a ten-second start and then let Count Basie go. Then I put my money on her. Hot favorite in the Ballroom Stakes: Hilda Samuels ridden by Willie Malopo.

WILLIE. [*Turning away*] I'm not talking to you no more.

SAM. [*Relenting*] Sorry, Willie . . .

WILLIE. It's finish between us.

SAM. Okay, okay . . . I'll stop.

WILLIE. You can also fuck off.

SAM. Willie, listen! I want to help you!

WILLIE. No more jokes?

SAM. I promise.

WILLIE. Okay. Help me.

SAM. [*His turn to hold an imaginary partner.*] Look and learn. Feet together. Back straight. Body relaxed. Right hand placed gently in the small of her back and wait for the music. Don't start worrying about making mistakes or the judges or the other competitors. It's just you, Hilda and the music, and you're going to have a good time. What Count Basie do you play?

WILLIE. "You the cream in my coffee, you the salt in my stew."

SAM. Right. Give it to me in strict tempo.

WILLIE. Ready?

SAM. Ready.

WILLIE. A-n-d . . . [*Singing*]
"You the cream in my coffee.
You the salt in my stew.
You will always be my
     necessity.
I'd be lost without
     you. . . . " [*etc.*]

Sam launches into the quickstep. He is obviously a much more accomplished dancer than Willie. Hally enters. A seventeen-year-old white boy. Wet raincoat and school case. He stops and watches Sam. The demonstration comes to an end with a flourish. Applause from Hally and Willie.

HALLY. Bravo! No question about it. First place goes to Mr. Sam Semela.

WILLIE. [*In total agreement*] You was gliding with style, Boet Sam.

HALLY. [*Cheerfully*] How's it, chaps?

SAM. Okay, Hally.

Count Basie: big jazz band leader.   Haaikona: an African exclamation.

WILLIE. [*Springing to attention like a soldier and saluting*] At your service, Master Harold!

HALLY. Not long to the big event, hey!

SAM. Two weeks.

HALLY. You nervous?

SAM. No.

HALLY. Think you stand a chance?

SAM. Let's just say I'm ready to go out there and dance.

HALLY. It looked like it. What about you, Willie?

Willie groans.

What's the matter?

SAM. He's got leg trouble.

HALLY. [*Innocently*] Oh, sorry to hear that, Willie.

WILLIE. Boet Sam! You promised. [*Willie returns to his work.*]

Hally deposits his school case and takes off his raincoat. His clothes are a little neglected and untidy: black blazer with school badge, gray flannel trousers in need of an ironing, khaki shirt and tie, black shoes. Sam has fetched a towel for Hally to dry his hair.

HALLY. God, what a lousy bloody day. It's coming down cats and dogs out there. Bad for business, chaps . . . [*Conspiratorial whisper*] . . . but it also means we're in for a nice quiet afternoon.

SAM. You can speak loud. Your Mom's not here.

HALLY. Out shopping?

SAM. No. The hospital.

HALLY. But it's Thursday. There's no visiting on Thursday afternoons. Is my Dad okay?

SAM. Sounds like it. In fact, I think he's going home.

HALLY. [*Stopped short by Sam's remark*] What do you mean?

SAM. The hospital phoned.

HALLY. To say what?

SAM. I don't know. I just heard your Mom talking.

HALLY. So what makes you say he's going home?

SAM. It sounded as if they were telling her to come and fetch him.

Hally thinks about what Sam has said for a few seconds.

HALLY. When did she leave?

SAM. About an hour ago. She said she would phone you. Want to eat?

Hally doesn't respond.

Hally, want your lunch?

HALLY. I suppose so. [*His mood has changed.*] What's on the menu? . . . as if I don't know.

SAM. Soup, followed by meat pie and gravy.

HALLY. Today's?

SAM. No.

HALLY. And the soup?

SAM. Nourishing pea soup.

Drama in the Modern Age

HALLY. Just the soup. [*The pile of comic books on the table*] And these?

SAM. For your Dad. Mr. Kempston brought them.

HALLY. You haven't been reading them, have you?

SAM. Just looking.

HALLY. [*Examining the comics*] Jungle Jim . . . Batman and Robin . . . Tarzan . . . God, what rubbish! Mental pollution. Take them away.

Sam exits waltzing into the kitchen. Hally turns to Willie.

HALLY. Did you hear my Mom talking on the telephone, Willie?

WILLIE. No, Master Hally. I was at the back.

HALLY. And she didn't say anything to you before she left?

WILLIE. She said I must clean the floors.

HALLY. I mean about my Dad.

WILLIE. She didn't say nothing to me about him, Master Hally.

HALLY. [*With conviction*] No! It can't be. They said he needed at least another three weeks of treatment. Sam's definitely made a mistake. [*Rummages through his school case, finds a book and settles down at the table to read*] So, Willie!

WILLIE. Yes, Master Hally! Schooling okay today?

HALLY. Yes, okay . . . [*He thinks about it*] . . . No, not really. Ag, what's the difference? I don't care. And Sam says you've got problems.

WILLIE. Big problems.

HALLY. Which leg is sore?

Willie groans.

Both legs.

WILLIE. There is nothing wrong with my legs. Sam is just making jokes.

HALLY. So then you *will* be in the competition.

WILLIE. Only if I can find me a partner.

HALLY. But what about Hilda?

SAM. [*Returning with a bowl of soup*] She's the one who's got trouble with her legs.

HALLY. What sort of trouble, Willie?

SAM. From the way he describes it, I think the lady has gone a bit lame.

HALLY. Good God! Have you taken her to see a doctor?

SAM. I think a vet would be better.

HALLY. What do you mean?

SAM. What do you call it again when a racehorse goes very fast?

HALLY. Gallop?

SAM. That's it!

WILLIE. Boet Sam!

HALLY. "A gallop down the homestretch to the winning post." But what's that got to do with Hilda?

SAM. Count Basie always gets there first.

Willie lets fly with his slop rag. It misses Sam and hits Hally.

HALLY. [*Furious*] For Christ's sake, Willie! What the hell do you think you're doing!

WILLIE. Sorry, Master Hally, but it's him . . .

HALLY. Act your bloody age! [*Hurls the rag back at Willie.*] Cut out the nonsense now and get on with your work. And you too, Sam. Stop fooling around.

Sam moves away.

No. Hang on. I haven't finished! Tell me exactly what my Mom said.

SAM. I have. "When Hally comes, tell him I've gone to the hospital and I'll phone him."

HALLY. She didn't say anything about taking my Dad home?

SAM. No. It's just that when she was talking on the phone . . .

HALLY. [*Interrupting him.*] No, Sam. They can't be discharging him. She would have said so if they were. In any case, we saw him last night and he wasn't in good shape at all. Staff nurse even said there was talk about taking more X-rays. And now suddenly today he's better? If anything, it sounds more like a bad turn to me . . . which I sincerely hope it isn't. Hang on . . . how long ago did you say she left?

SAM. Just before two . . . [*His wrist watch*] . . . hour and a half.

HALLY. I know how to settle it. [*Behind the counter to the telephone. Talking as he dials.*] Let's give her ten minutes to get to the hospital, ten minutes to load him up, another ten, at the most, to get home and another ten to get him inside. Forty minutes. They should have been home for at least half an hour already. [*Pause—he waits with the receiver to his ear.*] No reply, chaps. And you know why? Because she's at his bedside in hospital helping him pull through a bad turn. You definitely heard wrong.

SAM. Okay.

As far as Hally is concerned, the matter is settled. He returns to his table, sits down and divides his attention between the book and his soup. Sam is at his school case and picks up a textbook.

Modern Graded Mathematics for Standards Nine and Ten. [*Opens it at random and laughs at something he sees*] Who is this supposed to be?

HALLY. Old fart-face Prentice.

SAM. Teacher?

HALLY. Thinks he is. And believe me, that is not a bad likeness.

SAM. Has he seen it?

HALLY. Yes.

SAM. What did he say?

HALLY. Tried to be clever, as usual. Said I was no Leonardo da Vinci and that bad art had to be punished. So, six of the best, and his are bloody good.

SAM. On your bum?

HALLY. Where else? The days when I got them on my hands are gone forever, Sam.

SAM. With your trousers down!

HALLY. No. He's not quite that barbaric.

SAM. That's the way they do it in jail.

HALLY. [*Flicker of morbid interest*] Really?

SAM. Ja. When the magistrate sentences you to "strokes with a light cane."

HALLY. Go on.

SAM. They make you lie down on a bench. One policeman pulls down your trousers and holds your ankles, another one pulls your shirt over your head and holds your arms . . .

HALLY. Thank you! That's enough.

SAM. . . . and the one that gives you the strokes talks to you gently and for a long time between each one. [*He laughs*]

HALLY. I've heard enough, Sam! Jesus! It's a bloody awful world when you come to
    think of it. People can be real bastards.

SAM. That's the way it is, Hally.

HALLY. It doesn't *have* to be that way. There is something called progress, you know.
    We don't exactly burn people at the stake anymore.

SAM. Like Joan of Arc.°

HALLY. Correct. If she was captured today, she'd be given a fair trial.

SAM. And then the death sentence.

HALLY. [*A world-weary sigh*] I know, I know! I oscillate between hope and despair
    for this world as well, Sam. But things will change, you wait and see. One day
    somebody is going to get up and give history a kick up the backside and get it
    going again.

SAM. Like who?

HALLY. [*After thought*] They're called social reformers. Every age, Sam, has got its so-
    cial reformer. My history book is full of them.

SAM. So where's ours?

HALLY. Good question. And I hate to say it, but the answer is: I don't know. Maybe
    he hasn't even been born yet. Or is still only a babe in arms at his mother's
    breast. God, what a thought.

SAM. So we just go on waiting.

HALLY. Ja, looks like it. [*Back to his soup and the book*]

SAM. [*Reading from the textbook*] "Introduction: In some mathematical problems
    only the magnitude . . . " [*He mispronounces the word "magnitude"*]

HALLY. [*Correcting him without looking up*] Magnitude.

SAM. What's it mean?

HALLY. How big it is. The size of the thing.

SAM. [*Reading*] " . . . magnitude of the quantities is of importance. In other problems
    we need to know whether these quantities are negative or positive. For exam-
    ple, whether there is a debit or credit bank balance . . . "

HALLY. Whether you're broke or not.

SAM. " . . . whether the temperature is above or below Zero . . . "

HALLY. Naught degrees. Cheerful state of affairs! No cash and you're freezing to
    death. Mathematics won't get you out of that one.

SAM. "All these quantities are called . . . " [*Spelling the word*] . . . s-c-a-l . . .

HALLY. Scalars.

SAM. Scalars! [*Shaking his head with a laugh*] You understand all that?

HALLY. [*Turning a page*] No. And I don't intend to try.

SAM. So what happens when the exams come?

HALLY. Failing a maths exam isn't the end of the world, Sam. How many times have
    I told you that examination results don't measure intelligence?

SAM. I would say about as many times as you've failed one of them.

HALLY. [*Mirthlessly*] Ha, ha, ha.

SAM. [*Simultaneously*] Ha, ha, ha.

HALLY. Just remember Winston Churchill° didn't do particularly well at school.

SAM. You've also told me that one many times.

    Joan of Arc: medieval French heroine and martyr.   *Winston Churchill:* English wartime Prime
Minister.

HALLY. Well, it just so happens to be the truth.

SAM. [*Enjoying the word*] Magnitude! Magnitude! Show me how to use it.

HALLY. [*After thought*] An intrepid social reformer will not be daunted by the magnitude of the task he has undertaken.

SAM. [*Impressed*] Couple of jaw-breakers in there!

HALLY. I gave you three for the price of one. Intrepid, daunted and magnitude. I did that once in an exam. Put five of the words I had to explain in one sentence. It was half a page long.

SAM. Well, I'll put my money on you in the English exam.

HALLY. Piece of cake. Eighty percent without even trying.

SAM. [*Another textbook from Hally's case*] And history?

HALLY. So-so. I'll scrape through. In the fifties if I'm lucky.

SAM. You didn't do too badly last year.

HALLY. Because we had World War One. That at least had some action. You try to find that in the South African Parliamentary system.

SAM. [*Reading from the history textbook*] "Napoleon and the principle of equality." Hey! This sounds interesting. "After concluding peace with Britain in 1802, Napoleon used a brief period of calm to in-sti-tute . . . "

HALLY. Introduce.

SAM. " . . . many reforms. Napoleon regarded all people as equal before the law and wanted them to have equal opportunities for advancement. All ves-ti-ges of the feu-dal system with its oppression of the poor were abolished." Vestiges, feudal system and abolished. I'm all right on oppression.

HALLY. I'm thinking. He swept away . . . abolished . . . the last remains . . . vestiges . . . of the bad old days . . . feudal system.

SAM. Ha! There's the social reformer we're waiting for. He sounds like a man of some magnitude.

HALLY. I'm not so sure about that. It's a damn good title for a book, though. A man of magnitude!

SAM. He sounds pretty big to me, Hally.

HALLY. Don't confuse historical significance with greatness. But maybe I'm being a bit prejudiced. Have a look in there and you'll see he's two chapters long. And hell! . . . has he only got dates, Sam, all of which you've got to remember! This campaign and that campaign, and then, because of all the fighting, the next thing is we get Peace Treaties all over the place. And what's the end of the story? Battle of Waterloo,° which he loses. Wasn't worth it. No, I don't know about him as a man of magnitude.

SAM. Then who would you say was?

HALLY. To answer that, we need a definition of greatness, and I suppose that would be somebody who . . . somebody who benefited all mankind.

SAM. Right. But like who?

HALLY. [*He speaks with total conviction*] Charles Darwin.° Remember him? That big book from the library. *The Origin of the Species.*

SAM. Him?

HALLY. Yes. For his Theory of Evolution.

Battle of Waterloo: scene of Napoleon's defeat.   *Charles Darwin:* English naturalist credited with developing the theory of natural selection.

SAM. You didn't finish it.

HALLY. I ran out of time. I didn't finish it because my two weeks was up. But I'm going to take it out again after I've digested what I read. It's safe. I've hidden it away in the Theology section. Nobody ever goes in there. And anyway who are you to talk? You hardly even looked at it.

SAM. I tried. I looked at the chapters in the beginning and I saw one called "The Struggle for an Existence." Ah ha, I thought. At last! But what did I get? Something called the mistletoe which needs the apple tree and there's too many seeds and all are going to die except one . . . ! No, Hally.

HALLY. [*Intellectually outraged*] What do you mean, No! The poor man had to start somewhere. For God's sake, Sam, he revolutionized science. Now we know.

SAM. What?

HALLY. Where we come from and what it all means.

SAM. And that's a benefit to mankind? Anyway, I still don't believe it.

HALLY. God, you're impossible. I showed it to you in black and white.

SAM. Doesn't mean I got to believe it.

HALLY. It's the likes of you that kept the Inquisition in business. It's called bigotry. Anyway, that's my man of magnitude. Charles Darwin! Who's yours?

SAM. [*Without hesitation*] Abraham Lincoln.

HALLY. I might have guessed as much. Don't get sentimental, Sam. You've never been a slave, you know. And anyway we freed your ancestors here in South Africa long before the Americans. But if you want to thank somebody on their behalf, do it to Mr. William Wilberforce.° Come on. Try again. I want a real genius.

Now enjoying himself, and so is Sam. Hally goes behind the counter and helps himself to a chocolate.

SAM. William Shakespeare.

HALLY. [*No enthusiasm*] Oh. So you're also one of them, are you? You're basing that opinion on only one play, you know. You've only read my *Julius Caesar* and even I don't understand half of what they're talking about. They should do what they did with the old Bible: bring the language up to date.

SAM. That's all you've got. It's also the only one *you've* read.

HALLY. I know. I admit it. That's why I suggest we reserve our judgment until we've checked up on a few others. I've got a feeling, though, that by the end of this year one is going to be enough for me, and I can give you the names of twenty-nine other chaps in the Standard Nine class of the Port Elizabeth Technical College who feel the same. But if you want him, you can have him. My turn now. [*Pacing*] This is a damned good exercise, you know! It started off looking like a simple question and here it's got us really probing into the intellectual heritage of our civilization.

SAM. So who is it going to be?

HALLY. My next man . . . and he gets the title on two scores: social reform and literary genius . . . is Leo Nikolaevich Tolstoy.°

SAM. That Russian.

William Wilberforce: English politician and abolitionist.   *Leo N. Tolstoy:* Russian novelist, author of *War and Peace.*

HALLY. Correct. Remember the picture of him I showed you?

SAM. With the long beard.

HALLY. [*Trying to look like Tolstoy*] And those burning, visionary eyes. My God, the face of a social prophet if ever I saw one! And remember my words when I showed it to you? Here's a *man*, Sam!

SAM. Those were words, Hally.

HALLY. Not many intellectuals are prepared to shovel manure with the peasants and then go home and write a "little book" called *War and Peace*. Incidentally, Sam, he was somebody else who, to quote, " . . . did not distinguish himself scholastically."

SAM. Meaning?

HALLY. He was also no good at school.

SAM. Like you and Winston Churchill.

HALLY. [*Mirthlessly*] Ha, ha, ha.

SAM. [*Simultaneously*] Ha, ha, ha.

HALLY. Don't get clever, Sam. That man freed his serfs of his own free will.

SAM. No argument. He was a somebody, all right. I accept him.

HALLY. I'm sure Count Tolstoy will be very pleased to hear that. Your turn. Shoot. [*Another chocolate from behind the counter*] I'm waiting, Sam.

SAM. I've got him.

HALLY. Good. Submit your candidate for examination.

SAM. Jesus.

HALLY. [*Stopped dead in his tracks*] Who?

SAM. Jesus Christ.

HALLY. Oh, come on, Sam!

SAM. The Messiah.

HALLY. Ja, but still . . . No, Sam. Don't let's get started on religion. We'll just spend the whole afternoon arguing again. Suppose I turn around and say Mohammed?°

SAM. All right.

HALLY. You can't have them both on the same list!

SAM. Why not? You like Mohammed, I like Jesus.

HALLY. I *don't* like Mohammed. I never have. I was merely being hypothetical. As far as I'm concerned, the Koran is as bad as the Bible. No. Religion is out! I'm not going to waste my time again arguing with you about the existence of God. You know perfectly well I'm an atheist . . . and I've got homework to do.

SAM. Okay, I take him back.

HALLY. You've got time for one more name.

SAM. [*After thought*] I've got one I know we'll agree on. A simple straightforward great Man of Magnitude . . . and no arguments. And *he* really *did* benefit all mankind.

HALLY. I wonder. After your last contribution I'm beginning to doubt whether anything in the way of an intellectual agreement is possible between the two of us. Who is he?

SAM. Guess.

HALLY. Socrates?° Alexandre Dumas?° Karl Marx?° Dostoevsky?° Nietzsche?°

Mohammed: founder of Islam. *Socrates:* Greek philosopher; *Alexandre Dumas:* French novelist; *Karl Marx:* German economist, author of *Das Kapital*; *Dostoevsky:* Russian novelist; *Nietzsche:* German philosopher.

Sam shakes his head after each name.

Give me a clue.

SAM. The letter P is important . . .

HALLY. Plato!

SAM. . . . and his name begins with an F.

HALLY. I've got it. Freud° and Psychology.

SAM. No. I didn't understand him.

HALLY. That makes two of us.

SAM. Think of mouldy apricot jam.

HALLY. [*After a delighted laugh*] Penicillin and Sir Alexander Fleming! And the title of the book: *The Microbe Hunters*.° [*Delighted*] Splendid, Sam! Splendid. For once we are in total agreement. The major breakthrough in medical science in the Twentieth Century. If it wasn't for him, we might have lost the Second World War. It's deeply gratifying, Sam, to know that I haven't been wasting my time in talking to you. [*Strutting around proudly*] Tolstoy may have educated his peasants, but I've educated you.

SAM. Standard Four to Standard Nine.

HALLY. Have we been at it as long as that?

SAM. Yep. And my first lesson was geography.

HALLY. [*Intrigued*] Really? I don't remember.

SAM. My room there at the back of the old Jubilee Boarding House. I had just started working for your Mom. Little boy in short trousers walks in one afternoon and asks me seriously: "Sam, do you want to see South Africa?" Hey man! Sure I wanted to see South Africa!

HALLY. Was that me?

SAM. . . . So the next thing I'm looking at a map you had just done for homework. It was your first one and you were very proud of yourself.

HALLY. Go on.

SAM. Then came my first lesson. "Repeat after me, Sam: Gold in the Transvaal, mealies in the Free State, sugar in Natal and grapes in the Cape." I still know it!

HALLY. Well, I'll be buggered. So that's how it all started.

SAM. And your next map was one with all the rivers and the mountains they came from. The Orange, the Vaal, the Limpopo, the Zambezi° . . .

HALLY. You've got a phenomenal memory!

SAM. You should be grateful. That is why you started passing your exams. You tried to be better than me.

They laugh together. Willie is attracted by the laughter and joins them.

HALLY. The old Jubilee Boarding House. Sixteen rooms with board and lodging, rent in advance and one week's notice. I haven't thought about it for donkey's years . . . and I don't think that's an accident. God, was I glad when we sold it and moved out. Those years are not remembered as the happiest ones of an unhappy childhood.

WILLIE. [*Knocking on the table and trying to imitate a woman's voice*] "Hally, are you there?"

Freud: Sigmund Freud, Viennese psychologist.   *The Microbe Hunters*: book by Paul de Kruif about the discovery of penicillin.   *Orange . . . Zambezi*: African rivers.

HALLY. Who's that supposed to be?

WILLIE. "What you doing in there, Hally? Come out at once!"

HALLY. [*To Sam*] What's he talking about?

SAM. Don't you remember?

WILLIE. "Sam, Willie . . . is he in there with you boys?"

SAM. Hiding away in our room when your mother was looking for you.

HALLY. [*Another good laugh*] Of course! I used to crawl and hide under your bed! But finish the story, Willie. Then what used to happen? You chaps would give the game away by telling her I was in there with you. So much for friendship.

SAM. We couldn't lie to her. She knew.

HALLY. Which meant I got another rowing for hanging around the "servants' quarters." I think I spent more time in there with you chaps than anywhere else in that dump. And do you blame me? Nothing but bloody misery wherever you went. Somebody was always complaining about the food, or my mother was having a fight with Micky Nash because she'd caught her with a petty officer in her room. Maud Meiring was another one. Remember those two? They were prostitutes, you know. Soldiers and sailors from the troopships. Bottom fell out of the business when the war ended. God, the flotsam and jetsam that life washed up on our shores! No joking, if it wasn't for your room, I would have been the first certified ten-year-old in medical history. Ja, the memories are coming back now. Walking home from school and thinking: "What can I do this afternoon?" Try out a few ideas, but sooner or later I'd end up in there with you fellows. I bet you I could still find my way to your room with my eyes closed. [*He does exactly that*] Down the corridor . . . telephone on the right, which my Mom keeps locked because somebody is using it on the sly and not paying . . . past the kitchen and unappetizing cooking smells . . . around the corner into the backyard, hold my breath again because there are more smells coming when I pass your lavatory, then into that little passageway, first door on the right and into your room. How's that?

SAM. Good. But, as usual, you forgot to knock.

HALLY. Like that time I barged in and caught you and Cynthia . . . at it. Remember? God, was I embarrassed! I didn't know what was going on at first.

SAM. Ja, that taught you a lesson.

HALLY. And about a lot more than knocking on doors, I'll have you know, and I don't mean geography either. Hell, Sam, couldn't you have waited until it was dark?

SAM. No.

HALLY. Was it that urgent?

SAM. Yes, and if you don't believe me, wait until your time comes.

HALLY. No, thank you. I am not interested in girls. [*Back to his memories . . . Using a few chairs he recreates the room as he lists the items*] A gray little room with a cold cement floor. Your bed against that wall . . . and I now know why the mattress sags so much! . . . Willie's bed . . . it's propped up on bricks because one leg is broken . . . that wobbly little table with the washbasin and jug of water . . . Yes! . . . stuck to the wall above it are some pin-up pictures from magazines. Joe Louis° . . .

Joe Louis: American boxing champion.

WILLIE. Brown Bomber. World Title. [*Boxing pose*] Three rounds and knockout.

HALLY. Against who?

SAM. Max Schmeling.

HALLY. Correct. I can also remember Fred Astaire° and Ginger Rogers,° and Rita Hayworth° in a bathing costume which always made me hot and bothered when I looked at it. Under Willie's bed is an old suitcase with all his clothes in a mess, which is why I never hide there. Your things are neat and tidy in a trunk next to your bed, and on it there is a picture of you and Cynthia in your ballroom clothes, your first silver cup for third place in a competition and an old radio which doesn't work anymore. Have I left out anything?

SAM. No.

HALLY. Right, so much for the stage directions. Now the characters.

Sam and Willie move to their appropriate positions in the bedroom.

Willie is in bed, under his blankets with his clothes on, complaining nonstop about something, but we can't make out a word of what he's saying because he's got his head under the blankets as well. You're on your bed trimming your toenails with a knife—not a very edifying sight—and as for me . . . What am I doing?

SAM. You're sitting on the floor giving Willie a lecture about being a good loser while you get the checker board and pieces ready for a game. Then you go to Willie's bed, pull off the blankets and make him play with you first because you know you're going to win, and that gives you the second game with me.

HALLY. And you certainly were a bad loser, Willie!

WILLIE. Haai!

HALLY. Wasn't he, Sam? And so slow! A game with you almost took the whole afternoon. Thank God I gave up trying to teach you how to play chess.

WILLIE. You and Sam cheated.

HALLY. I never saw Sam cheat, and mine were mostly the mistakes of youth.

WILLIE. Then how is it you two was always winning?

HALLY. Have you ever considered the possibility, Willie, that it was because we were better than you?

WILLIE. Every time better?

HALLY. Not every time. There were occasions when we deliberately let you win a game so that you would stop sulking and go on playing with us. Sam used to wink at me when you weren't looking to show me it was time to let you win.

WILLIE. So then you two didn't play fair.

HALLY. It was for your benefit, Mr. Malopo, which is more than being fair. It was an act of self-sacrifice. [*To Sam*] But you know what my best memory is, don't you?

SAM. No.

HALLY. Come on, guess. If your memory is so good, you must remember it as well.

SAM. We got up to a lot of tricks in there, Hally.

HALLY. This one was special, Sam.

SAM. I'm listening.

HALLY. It started off looking like another of those useless nothing-to-do afternoons. I'd already been down to Main Street looking for adventure, but nothing had happened. I didn't feel like climbing trees in the Donkin Park or pretending I

Fred Astaire, Ginger Rogers, Rita Hayworth: Hollywood stars of the 1940s.

was a private eye and following a stranger . . . so as usual: See what's cooking in Sam's room. This time it was you on the floor. You had two thin pieces of wood and you were smoothing them down with a knife. It didn't look particularly interesting, but when I asked you what you were doing, you just said, "Wait and see, Hally. Wait . . . and see" . . . in that secret sort of way of yours, so I knew there was a surprise coming. You teased me, you bugger, by being deliberately slow and not answering my questions!

Sam laughs.

And whistling while you worked away! God, it was infuriating! I could have brained you! It was only when you tied them together in a cross and put that down on the brown paper that I realized what you were doing. "Sam is making a kite?" And when I asked you and you said "Yes" . . . ! [*Shaking his head with disbelief*] The sheer audacity of it took my breath away. I mean, seriously, what the hell does a black man know about flying a kite? I'll be honest with you, Sam, I had no hopes for it. If you think I was excited and happy, you got another guess coming. In fact, I was shit-scared that we were going to make fools of ourselves. When we left the boarding house to go up onto the hill, I was praying quietly that there wouldn't be any other kids around to laugh at us.

SAM. [*Enjoying the memory as much as Hally*] Ja, I could see that.

HALLY. I made it obvious, did I?

SAM. Ja. You refused to carry it.

HALLY. Do you blame me? Can you remember what the poor thing looked like? Tomato-box wood and brown paper! Flour and water for glue! Two of my mother's old stockings for a tail, and then all those bits and pieces of string you made me tie together so that we could fly it! Hell, no, that was now only asking for a miracle to happen.

SAM. Then the big argument when I told you to hold the string and run with it when I let go.

HALLY. I was prepared to run, all right, but straight back to the boarding house.

SAM. [*Knowing what's coming*] So what happened?

HALLY. Come on, Sam, you remember as well as I do.

SAM. I want to hear it from you.

Hally pauses. He wants to be as accurate as possible.

HALLY. You went a little distance from me down the hill, you held it up ready to let it go. . . . "This is it," I thought. "Like everything else in my life, here comes another fiasco." Then you shouted, "Go, Hally!" and I started to run. [*Another pause*] I don't know how to describe it, Sam. Ja! The miracle happened! I was running, waiting for it to crash to the ground, but instead suddenly there was something alive behind me at the end of the string, tugging at it as if it wanted to be free. I looked back . . . [*Shakes his head*] . . . I still can't believe my eyes. It was flying! Looping around and trying to climb even higher into the sky. You shouted to me to let it have more string. I did, until there was none left and I was just holding that piece of wood we had tied it to. You came up and joined me. You were laughing.

SAM. So were you. And shouting, "It works, Sam! We've done it!"

HALLY. And we had! I was so proud of us! It was the most splendid thing I had ever seen. I wished there were hundreds of kids around us to watch us. The part that scared me, though, was when you showed me how to make it dive down to the ground and then just when it was on the point of crashing, swoop up again!

SAM. You didn't want to try yourself.

HALLY. Of course not! I would have been suicidal if anything had happened to it. Watching you do it made me nervous enough. I was quite happy just to see it up there with its tail fluttering behind it. You left me after that, didn't you? You explained how to get it down, we tied it to the bench so that I could sit and watch it, and you went away. I wanted you to stay, you know. I was a little scared of having to look after it by myself.

SAM. [*Quietly*] I had work to do, Hally.

HALLY. It was sort of sad bringing it down, Sam. And it looked sad again when it was lying there on the ground. Like something that had lost its soul. Just tomato-box wood, brown paper and two of my mother's old stockings! But, hell, I'll never forget that first moment when I saw it up there. I had a stiff neck the next day from looking up so much.

Sam laughs. Hally turns to him with a question he never thought of asking before.

Why did you make that kite, Sam?

SAM. [*Evenly*] I can't remember.

HALLY. Truly?

SAM. Too long ago, Hally.

HALLY. Ja, I suppose it was. It's time for another one, you know.

SAM. Why do you say that?

HALLY. Because it feels like that. Wouldn't be a good day to fly it, though.

SAM. No. You can't fly kites on rainy days.

HALLY.

He studies Sam. Their memories have made him conscious of the man's presence in his life.

How old are you, Sam?

SAM. Two score and five.

HALLY. Strange, isn't it?

SAM. What?

HALLY. Me and you.

SAM. What's strange about it?

HALLY. Little white boy in short trousers and a black man old enough to be his father flying a kite. It's not every day you see that.

SAM. But why strange? Because the one is white and the other black?

HALLY. I don't know. Would have been just as strange, I suppose, if it had been me and my Dad . . . cripple man and a little boy! Nope! There's no chance of me flying a kite without it being strange. [*Simple statement of fact—no self-pity*] There's a nice little short story there. "The Kite-Flyers." But we'd have to find a twist in the ending.

SAM. Twist?

HALLY. Yes. Something unexpected. The way it ended with us was too straightforward . . . me on the bench and you going back to work. There's no drama in that.

WILLIE. And me?

HALLY. You?

WILLIE. Yes me.

HALLY. You want to get into the story as well, do you? I got it! Change the title: "Afternoons in Sam's Room" . . . expand it and tell all the stories. It's on its way to being a novel. Our days in the old Jubilee. Sad in a way that they're over. I almost wish we were still in that little room.

SAM. We're still together.

HALLY. That's true. It's just that life felt the right size in there . . . not too big and not too small. Wasn't so hard to work up a bit of courage. It's got so bloody complicated since then.

The telephone rings. Sam answers it.

SAM. St George's Park Tea Room . . . Hello, Madam . . . Yes, Madam, he's here. . . . Hally, it's your mother.

HALLY. Where is she phoning from?

SAM. Sounds like the hospital. It's a public telephone.

HALLY. [*Relieved*] You see! I told you. [*The telephone*] Hello, Mom . . . Yes . . . Yes no fine. Everything's under control here. How's things with poor old Dad? . . . Has he had a bad turn? . . . What? . . . Oh, God! . . . Yes, Sam told me, but I was sure he'd made a mistake. But what's this all about, Mom? He didn't look at all good last night. How can he get better so quickly? . . . Then very obviously you must say no. Be firm with him. You're the boss. . . . You know what it's going to be like if he comes home. . . . Well then, don't blame me when I fail my exams at the end of the year. . . . Yes! How am I expected to be fresh for school when I spend half the night massaging his gammy leg? . . . So am I! . . . So tell him a white lie. Say Dr. Colley wants more X-rays of his stump. Or bribe him. We'll sneak in double tots of brandy in future. . . . What? . . . Order him to get back into bed at once! If he's going to behave like a child, treat him like one. . . . All right, Mom! I was just trying to . . . I'm sorry. . . . I said I'm sorry. . . . Quick, give me your number. I'll phone you back.

He hangs up and waits a few seconds.

Here we go again!

He dials.

I'm sorry, Mom. . . . Okay . . . But now listen to me carefully. All it needs is for you to put your foot down. Don't take no for an answer. . . . Did you hear me? And whatever you do, don't discuss it with him. . . . Because I'm frightened you'll give in to him. . . . Yes, Sam gave me lunch. . . . I ate all of it! . . . No, Mom not a soul. It's still raining here. . . . Right, I'll tell them. I'll just do some homework and then lock up. . . . But remember now, Mom. Don't listen to anything he says. And phone me back and let me know what happens. . . . Okay. Bye, Mom.

He hangs up. The men are staring at him.

My Mom says that when you're finished with the floors you must do the windows. [*Pause*] Don't misunderstand me, chaps. All I want is for him to get better. And if he was, I'd be the first person to say: "Bring him home." But he's not, and we can't give him the medical care and attention he needs at home. That's what hospitals are there for. [*Brusquely*] So don't just stand there! Get on with it!

Sam clears Hally's table.

Drama in the Modern Age

You heard right. My Dad wants to go home.

SAM. Is he better?

HALLY. [*Sharply*] No! How the hell can he be better when last night he was groaning with pain? This is not an age of miracles!

SAM. Then he should stay in hospital.

HALLY. [*Seething with irritation and frustration*] Tell me something I don't know, Sam. What the hell do you think I was saying to my Mom? All I can say is fuck-it-all.

SAM. I'm sure he'll listen to your Mom.

HALLY. You don't know what she's up against. He's already packed his shaving kit and pajamas and is sitting on his bed with his crutches, dressed and ready to go. I know him when he gets in that mood. If she tries to reason with him, we've had it. She's no match for him when it comes to a battle of words. He'll tie her up in knots. [*Trying to hide his true feelings*]

SAM. I suppose it gets lonely for him in there.

HALLY. With all the patients and nurses around? Regular visits from the Salvation Army? Balls! It's ten times worse for him at home. I'm at school and my mother is here in the business all day.

SAM. He's at least got you at night.

HALLY. [*Before he can stop himself*] And we've got him! Please! I don't want to talk about it anymore.

Unpacks his school case, slamming down books on the table.

Life is just a plain bloody mess, that's all. And people are fools.

SAM. Come on, Hally.

HALLY. Yes, they are! They bloody well deserve what they get.

SAM. Then don't complain.

HALLY. Don't try to be clever, Sam. It doesn't suit you. Anybody who thinks there's nothing wrong with this world needs to have his head examined. Just when things are going along all right, without fail someone or something will come along and spoil everything. Somebody should write that down as a fundamental law of the Universe. The principle of perpetual disappointment. If there is a God who created this world, he should scrap it and try again.

SAM. All right, Hally, all right. What you got for homework?

HALLY. Bullshit, as usual. [*Opens an exercise book and reads*] "Write five hundred words describing an annual event of cultural or historical significance."

SAM. That should be easy enough for you.

HALLY. And also plain bloody boring. You know what he wants, don't you? One of their useless old ceremonies. The commemoration of the landing of the 1820 Settlers,° or if it's going to be culture, Carols by Candlelight every Christmas.

SAM. It's an impressive sight. Make a good description, Hally. All those candles glowing in the dark and the people singing hymns.

HALLY. And it's called religious hysteria. [*Intense irritation*] Please, Sam! Just leave me alone and let me get on with it. I'm not in the mood for games this afternoon. And remember my Mom's orders . . . you're to help Willie with the windows. Come on now, I don't want any more nonsense in here.

1820 Settlers: 4000 settlers of the Cape in South Africa, who in 1820 were allotted 100 acres each by the British government.

SAM. Okay, Hally, okay.

Hally settles down to his homework; determined preparations . . . pen, ruler, exercise book, dictionary, another cake . . . all of which will lead to nothing.

Sam waltzes over to Willie and starts to replace tables and chairs. He practices a ballroom step while doing so. Willie watches. When Sam is finished, Willie tries.

Good! But just a little bit quicker on the turn and only move in to her after she's crossed over. What about this one?

Another step. When Sam is finished, Willie again has a go.

Much better. See what happens when you just relax and enjoy yourself? Remember that in two weeks' time and you'll be all right.

WILLIE. But I haven't got partner, Boet Sam.

SAM. Maybe Hilda will turn up tonight.

WILLIE. No, Boet Sam. [*Reluctantly*] I gave her a good hiding.

SAM. You mean a bad one.

WILLIE. Good bad one.

SAM. Then you mustn't complain either. Now you pay the price for losing your temper.

WILLIE. I also pay two pounds ten shilling entrance fee.

SAM. They'll refund you if you withdraw now.

WILLIE. [*Appalled*] You mean, don't dance?

SAM. Yes.

WILLIE. No! I wait too long and I practice too hard. If I find me new partner, you think I can be ready in two weeks? I ask Madam for my leave now and we practice every day.

SAM. Quickstep non-stop for two weeks. World record, Willie, but you'll be mad at the end.

WILLIE. No jokes, Boet Sam.

SAM. I'm not joking.

WILLIE. So then what?

SAM. Find Hilda. Say you're sorry and promise you won't beat her again.

WILLIE. No.

SAM. Then withdraw. Try again next year.

WILLIE. No.

SAM. Then I give up.

WILLIE. Haaikona, Boet Sam, you can't.

SAM. What do you mean, I can't? I'm telling you: I give up.

WILLIE. [*Adamant*] No! [*Accusingly*] It was you who start me ballroom dancing.

SAM. So?

WILLIE. Before that I use to be happy. And is you and Miriam who bring me to Hilda and say here's partner for you.

SAM. What are you saying, Willie?

WILLIE. You!

SAM. But me what? To blame?

WILLIE. Yes.

SAM. Willie . . . ? [*Bursts into laughter*]

WILLIE. And now all you do is make jokes at me. You wait. When Miriam leaves you is my turn to laugh. Ha! Ha! Ha!

SAM. [*He can't take Willie seriously any longer*] She can leave me tonight! I know what to do. [*Bowing before an imaginary partner*] May I have the pleasure?

He dances and sings.

"Just a fellow with his pillow . . .
Dancin' like a willow . . .
In an autumn breeze . . ."

WILLIE. There you go again!

Sam goes on dancing and singing.

Boet Sam!

SAM. There's the answer to your problem! Judges' announcement in two weeks' time: "Ladies and gentlemen, the winner in the open section . . . Mr. Willie Malopo and his pillow!"

This is too much for a now really angry Willie. He goes for Sam, but the latter is too quick for him and puts Hally's table between the two of them.

HALLY. [*Exploding*] For Christ's sake, you two!

WILLIE. [*Still trying to get at Sam*] I donner you, Sam! Struesgod!

SAM. [*Still laughing*] Sorry, Willie . . . Sorry . . .

HALLY. Sam! Willie! [*Grabs his ruler and gives Willie a vicious whack on the bum*] How the hell am I supposed to concentrate with the two of you behaving like bloody children!

WILLIE. Hit him too!

HALLY. Shut up, Willie.

WILLIE. He started jokes again.

HALLY. Get back to your work. You too, Sam. [*His ruler*] Do you want another one, Willie?

Sam and Willie return to their work. Hally uses the opportunity to escape from his unsuccessful attempt at homework. He struts around like a little despot, ruler in hand, giving vent to his anger and frustration.

Suppose a customer had walked in then? Or the Park Superintendent. And seen the two of you behaving like a pair of hooligans. That would have been the end of my mother's license, you know. And your jobs! Well, this is the end of it. From now on there will be no more of your ballroom nonsense in here. This is a business establishment, not a bloody New Brighton dancing school. I've been far too lenient with the two of you. [*Behind the counter for a green cool drink and a dollop of ice cream. He keeps up his tirade as he prepares it*] But what really makes me bitter is that I allow you chaps a little freedom in here when business is bad and what do you do with it? The foxtrot! Specially you, Sam. There's more to life than trotting around a dance floor and I thought at least you knew it.

SAM. It's a harmless pleasure, Hally. It doesn't hurt anybody.

HALLY. It's also a rather simple one, you know.

SAM. You reckon so? Have you ever tried?

HALLY. Of course not.

SAM. Why don't you? Now.

HALLY. What do you mean? Me dance?

SAM. Yes. I'll show you a simple step—the waltz—then you try it.

HALLY. What will that prove?

SAM. That it might not be as easy as you think.

HALLY. I didn't say it was easy. I said it was simple—like in simple-minded, meaning mentally retarded. You can't exactly say it challenges the intellect.

SAM. It does other things.

HALLY. Such as?

SAM. Make people happy.

HALLY. [The glass in his hand] So do American cream sodas with ice cream. For God's sake, Sam, you're not asking me to take ballroom dancing serious, are you?

SAM. Yes.

HALLY. [Sigh of defeat] Oh, well, so much for trying to give you a decent education. I've obviously achieved nothing.

SAM. You still haven't told me what's wrong with admiring something that's beautiful and then trying to do it yourself.

HALLY. Nothing. But we happen to be talking about a foxtrot, not a thing of beauty.

SAM. But that is just what I'm saying. If you were to see two champions doing, two masters of the art . . . !

HALLY. Oh, God, I give up. So now it's also art!

SAM. Ja.

HALLY. There's a limit. Sam. Don't confuse art and entertainment.

SAM. So then what is art?

HALLY. You want a definition?

SAM. Ja.

HALLY. [He realizes he has got to be careful. He gives the matter a lot of thought before answering] Philosophers have been trying to do that for centuries. What is Art? What is Life? But basically I suppose it's . . . the giving of meaning to matter.

SAM. Nothing to do with beautiful?

HALLY. It goes beyond that. It's the giving of form to the formless.

SAM. Ja, well, maybe it's not art, then. But I still say it's beautiful.

HALLY. I'm sure the word you mean to use is entertaining.

SAM. [Adamant] No. Beautiful. And if you want proof, come along to the Centenary Hall in New Brighton in two weeks' time.

The mention of the Centenary Hall draws Willie over to them.

HALLY. What for? I've seen the two of you prancing around in here often enough.

SAM. [He laughs] This isn't the real thing, Hally. We're just playing around in here.

HALLY. So? I can use my imagination.

SAM. And what do you get?

HALLY. A lot of people dancing around and having a so-called good time.

SAM. That all?

HALLY. Well, basically it is that, surely.

SAM. No, it isn't. Your imagination hasn't helped you at all. There's a lot more to it than that. We're getting ready for the championships, Hally, not just another dance. There's going to be a lot of people, all right, and they're going to have a good time, but they'll only be spectators, sitting around and watching. It's just the competitors out there on the dance floor. Party decorations and fancy lights all around the walls! The ladies in beautiful evening dresses!

HALLY. My mother's got one of those, Sam, and, quite frankly, it's an embarrassment every time she wears it.

SAM. [*Undeterred*] Your imagination left out the excitement.

Hally scoffs.

Oh, yes. The finalists are not going to be out there just to have a good time. One of those couples will be the 1950 Eastern Province Champions. And your imagination left out the music.

WILLIE. Mr. Elijah Gladman Guzana and his Orchestral Jazzonions.

SAM. The sound of the big band, Hally. Trombone, trumpet, tenor and alto sax. And then, finally, your imagination also left out the climax of the evening when the dancing is finished, the judges have stopped whispering among themselves and the Master of Ceremonies collects their scorecards and goes up onto the stage to announce the winners.

HALLY. All right. So you make it sound like a bit of a do. It's an occasion. Satisfied?

SAM. [*Victory*] So you admit that!

HALLY. Emotionally yes, intellectually no.

SAM. Well, I don't know what you mean by that, all I'm telling you is that it is going to be *the* event of the year in New Brighton. It's been sold out for two weeks already. There's only standing room left. We've got competitors coming from Kingwilliamstown, East London, Port Alfred.

Hally starts pacing thoughtfully.

HALLY. Tell me a bit more.

SAM. I thought you weren't interested . . . intellectually.

HALLY. [*Mysteriously*] I've got my reasons.

SAM. What do you want to know?

HALLY. It takes place every year?

SAM. Yes. But only every third year in New Brighton. It's East London's turn to have the championships next year.

HALLY. Which, I suppose, makes it an even more significant event.

SAM. Ah ha! We're getting somewhere. Our "occasion" is now a "significant event."

HALLY. I wonder.

SAM. What?

HALLY. I wonder if I would get away with it.

SAM. But what?

HALLY. [*To the table and his exercise book*] "Write five hundred words describing an annual event of cultural or historical significance." Would I be stretching poetic license a little too far if I called your ballroom championships a cultural event?

SAM. You mean . . . ?

HALLY. You think we could get five hundred words out of it, Sam?

SAM. Victor Sylvester has written a whole book on ballroom dancing.

WILLIE. You going to write about it, Master Hally?

HALLY. Yes, gentlemen, that is precisely what I am considering doing. Old Doc Bromely—he's my English teacher—is going to argue with me, of course. He doesn't like natives. But I'll point out to him that in strict anthropological terms the culture of a primitive black society includes its dancing and singing. To put my thesis in a nutshell: The war-dance has been replaced by the waltz. But it still amounts to the same thing: the release of primitive emotions through movement. Shall we give it a go?

SAM. I'm ready.

WILLIE. Me also.

HALLY. Ha! This will teach the old bugger a lesson. [*Decision taken*] Right. Let's get ourselves organized. [*This means another cake on the table. He sits.*] I think you've given me enough general atmosphere, Sam, but to build the tension and suspense I need facts. [*Pencil poised*]

WILLIE. Give him facts, Boet Sam.

HALLY. What you called the climax . . . how many finalists?

SAM. Six couples.

HALLY. [*Making notes*] Go on. Give me the picture.

SAM. Spectators seated right around the hall.

Willie becomes a spectator.

HALLY. . . . and it's a full house.

SAM. At one end, on the stage, Gladman and his Orchestral Jazzonions. At the other end is a long table with the three judges. The six finalists go onto the dance floor and take up their positions. When they are ready and the spectators have settled down, the Master of Ceremonies goes to the microphone. To start with, he makes some jokes to get the people laughing . . .

HALLY. Good touch! [*As he writes*] " . . . creating a relaxed atmosphere which will change to one of tension and drama as the climax is approached."

SAM. [*Onto a chair to act out the M.C.*] "Ladies and gentlemen, we come now to the great moment you have all been waiting for this evening. . . . The finals of the 1950 Eastern Province Open Ballroom Dancing Championships. But first let me introduce the finalists! Mr. and Mrs. Welcome Tchabalala from Kingwilliamstown . . . "

WILLIE. [*He applauds after every name*] Is when the people clap their hands and whistle and make a lot of noise, Master Hally.

SAM. "Mr. Mulligan Njikelane and Miss Nomhle Nkonyeni of Grahamstown; Mr. and Mrs. Norman Nchinga from Port Alfred; Mr. Fats Bokolane and Miss Dina Plaatjies from East London; Mr. Sipho Dugu and Mrs. Mable Magada from Peddie; and from New Brighton our very own Mr. Willie Malopo and Miss Hilda Samuels."

Willie can't believe his ears. He abandons his role as spectator and scrambles into position as a finalist.

WILLIE. Relaxed and ready to romance!

SAM. The applause dies down. When everybody is silent, Gladman lifts up his sax, nods at the Orchestral Jazzonions . . .

WILLIE. Play the jukebox please, Boet Sam!

SAM. I also only got bus fare, Willie.

HALLY. Hold it, everybody. [*Heads for the cash register behind the counter*] How much is in the till, Sam?

SAM. Three shillings. Hally . . . your Mom counted it before she left.

Hally hesitates.

HALLY. Sorry, Willie. You know how she carried on the last time I did it. We'll just have to pool our combined imaginations and hope for the best. [*Returns to the table*] Back to work. How are the points scored, Sam?

SAM. Maximum of ten points each for individual style, deportment, rhythm and general appearance.

WILLIE. Must I start?

HALLY. Hold it for a second, Willie. And penalties?

SAM. For what?

HALLY. For doing something wrong. Say you stumble or bump into somebody . . . do they take off any points?

SAM. [Aghast] Hally . . . !

HALLY. When you're dancing. If you and your partner collide into another couple.

Hally can get no further, Sam has collapsed with laughter. He explains to Willie.

SAM. If me and Miriam bump into you and Hilda . . .

Willie joins him in another good laugh.

Hally, Hally . . . !

HALLY. [Perplexed] Why? What did I say?

SAM. There's no collisions out there, Hally. Nobody trips or stumbles or bumps into anybody else. That's what that moment is all about. To be one of those finalists on that dance floor is like . . . like being in a dream about a world in which accidents don't happen.

HALLY. [Genuinely moved by Sam's image] Jesus, Sam! That's beautiful!

WILLIE. [Can endure waiting no longer] I'm starting!

Willie dances while Sam talks.

SAM. Of course it is. That's what I've been trying to say to you all afternoon. And it's beautiful because that is what we want life to be like. But instead, like you said, Hally, we're bumping into each other all the time. Look at the three of us this afternoon: I've bumped into Willie, the two of us have bumped into you, you've bumped into your mother, she bumping into your Dad. . . . None of us knows the steps and there's no music playing. And it doesn't stop with us. The whole world is doing it all the time. Open a newspaper and what do you read? America has bumped into Russia, England is bumping into India, rich man bumps into poor man. Those are big collisions, Hally. They make for a lot of bruises. People get hurt in all that bumping, and we're sick and tired of it now. It's been going on for too long. Are we never going to get it right? . . . Learn to dance life like champions instead of always being just a bunch of beginners at it?

HALLY. [Deep and sincere admiration of the man] You've got a vision, Sam!

SAM. Not just me. What I'm saying to you is that everybody's got it. That's why there's only standing room left for the Centenary Hall in two weeks' time. For as long as the music lasts, we are going to see six couples get it right, the way we want life to be.

HALLY. But is that the best we can do, Sam . . . watch six finalists dreaming about the way it should be?

SAM. I don't know. But it starts with that. Without the dream we won't know what we're going for. And anyway I reckon there are a few people who have got past just dreaming about it and are trying for something real. Remember that thing we read once in the paper about the Mahatma Gandhi? Going without food to stop those riots in India?

HALLY. You're right. He certainly was trying to teach people to get the steps right.

SAM. And the Pope.

HALLY. Yes, he's another one. Our old General Smuts° as well, you know. He's also out there dancing. You know, Sam, when you come to think of it, that's what the United Nations boils down to . . . a dancing school for politicians!

SAM. And let's hope they learn.

HALLY. [*A little surge of hope*] You're right. We mustn't despair. Maybe there's some hope for mankind after all. Keep it up, Willie. [*Back to his table with determination*] This is a lot bigger than I thought. So what have we got? Yes, our title: "A World Without Collisions."

SAM. That sounds good! "A World Without Collisions."

HALLY. Subtitle: "Global Politics on the Dance Floor." No. A bit too heavy, hey? What about "Ballroom Dancing as a Political Vision"?

The telephone rings. Sam answers it.

SAM. St. George's Park Tea Room . . . Yes, Madam . . . Hally, it's your Mom.

HALLY. [*Back to reality*] Oh, God, yes! I'd forgotten all about that. Shit! Remember my words, Sam? Just when you're enjoying yourself, someone or something will come along and wreck everything.

SAM. You haven't heard what she's got to say yet.

HALLY. Public telephone?

SAM. No.

HALLY. Does she sound happy or unhappy?

SAM. I couldn't tell. [*Pause*] She's waiting, Hally.

HALLY. [*To the telephone*] Hello, Mom . . . No, everything is okay here. Just doing my homework. . . . What's your news? . . . You've what? . . .

Pause. He takes the receiver away from his ear for a few seconds. In the course of Hally's telephone conversation, Sam and Willie discretely position the stacked tables and chairs. Hally places the receiver back to his ear.

Yes, I'm still here. Oh, well, I give up now. Why did you do it, Mom? . . . Well, I just hope you know what you've let us in for. . . . [*Loudly*] I said I hope you know what you've let us in for! It's the end of the peace and quiet we've been having. [*Softly*] Where is he? [*Normal voice*] He can't hear us from in there. But for God's sake, Mom, what happened? I told you to be firm with him. . . . Then you and the nurses should have held him down, taken his crutches away. . . . I know only too well he's my father! . . . I'm not being disrespectful, but I'm sick and tired of emptying stinking chamber pots full of phlegm and piss. . . . Yes, I do! When you're not there, he asks *me* to do it. . . . If you really want to know the truth, that's why I've got no appetite for my food. . . . Yes! There's a lot of things you don't know about. For your information, I still haven't got that science textbook I need. And you know why? He borrowed the money you gave me for it. . . . Because I didn't want to start another fight between you two. . . . He says that every time. . . . All right, Mom! [*Viciously*] Then just remember to start hiding your bag away again, because he'll be at your purse before long for money for booze. And when he's well enough to come down here, you better keep an eye on the till as well, because that is also going to develop a leak. . . .

General Smuts: Jan Christian Smuts, South African military leader.

Then don't complain to me when he starts his old tricks. . . . Yes, you do. I get it from you on one side and from him on the other, and it makes life hell for me. I'm not going to be the peacemaker anymore. I'm warning you now: when the two of you start fighting again, I'm leaving home. . . . Mom, if you start crying, I'm going to put down the receiver. . . . Okay . . . [*Lowering his voice to a vicious whisper*] Okay, Mom. I heard you. [*Desperate*] No. . . . Because I don't want to. I'll see him when I get home! Mom! . . . [*Pause. When he speaks again, his tone changes completely. It is not simple pretense. We sense a genuine emotional conflict*] Welcome home, chum! . . . What's that? . . . Don't be silly, Dad. You being home is just about the best news in the world. . . . I bet you are. Bloody depressing there with everybody going on about their ailments, hey! . . . How you feeling? . . . Good . . . Here as well, pal. Coming down cats and dogs. . . . That's right. Just the day for a kip and a toss in your old Uncle Ned. . . . Everything's just hunky-dory on my side, Dad. . . . Well, to start with, there's a nice pile of comics for you on the counter. . . . Yes, old Kemple brought them in. *Batman and Robin, Submariner* . . . just your cup of tea . . . I will. . . . Yes, we'll spin a few yarns tonight. . . . Okay, chum, see you in a little while. . . . No, I promise. I'll come straight home. . . . [*Pause—his mother comes back on the phone*] Mom? Okay. I'll lock up now. . . . What! . . . Oh, the brandy . . . Yes, I'll remember! . . . I'll put it in my suitcase now, for God's sake. I know well enough what will happen if he doesn't get it. . . . [*Places a bottle of brandy on the counter*] I *was* kind to him, Mom. I didn't say anything nasty! . . . All right. Bye. [*End of telephone conversation. A desolate Hally doesn't move. A strained silence*]

SAM. [*Quietly*] That sounded like a bad bump, Hally.

HALLY. [*Having a hard time controlling his emotions. He speaks carefully*] Mind your own business, Sam.

SAM. Sorry. I wasn't trying to interfere. Shall we carry on? Hally? [*He indicates the exercise book. No response from Hally.*]

WILLIE. [*Also trying*] Tell him about when they give out the cups, Boet Sam.

SAM. Ja! That's another big moment. The presentation of the cups after the winners have been announced. You've got to put that in.

Still no response from Hally.

WILLIE. A big silver one, Master Hally, called floating trophy for the champions.

SAM. We always invite some big-shot personality to hand them over. Guest of honor this year is going to be His Holiness Bishop Jabulani of the All African Free Zionist Church.

Hally gets up abruptly, goes to his table and tears up the page he was writing on.

HALLY. So much for a bloody world without collisions.

SAM. Too bad. It was on its way to being a good composition.

HALLY. Let's stop bullshitting ourselves, Sam.

SAM. Have we been doing that?

HALLY. Yes! That's what all our talk about a decent world has been . . . just so much bullshit.

SAM. We did say it was still only a dream.

HALLY. And a bloody useless one at that. Life's a fuckup and it's never going to change.

SAM. Ja, maybe that's true.

HALLY. There's no maybe about it. It's a blunt and brutal fact. All we've done this afternoon is waste our time.

SAM. Not if we'd got your homework done.

HALLY. I don't give a shit about my homework, so, for Christ's sake, just shut up about it. [*Slamming books viciously into his school case*] Hurry up now and finish your work. I want to lock up and get out of here. [*Pause*] And then go where? Home-sweet-fucking-home. Jesus, I hate that word.

Hally goes to the counter to put the brandy bottle and comics in his school case. After a moment's hesitation, he smashes the bottle of brandy. He abandons all further attempts to hide his feelings, Sam and Willie work away as unobtrusively as possible.

Do you want to know what is really wrong with your lovely little dream, Sam? It's not just that we are all bad dancers. That does happen to be perfectly true, but there's more to it than just that. You left out the cripples.

SAM. Hally!

HALLY. [*Now totally reckless*] Ja! Can't leave them out, Sam. That's why we always end up on our backsides on the dance floor. They're also out there dancing . . . like a bunch of broken spiders trying to do the quickstep! [*An ugly attempt at laughter*] When you come to think of it, it's a bloody comical sight. I mean, it's bad enough on two legs . . . but one and a pair of crutches! Hell, no, Sam. That's guaranteed to turn that dance floor into a shambles. Why you shaking your head? Picture it, man. For once this afternoon let's use our imaginations sensibly.

SAM. Be careful, Hally.

HALLY. Of what? The truth? I seem to be the only one around here who is prepared to face it. We've had the pretty dream, it's time now to wake up and have a good long look at the way things really are. Nobody knows the steps, there's no music, the cripples are also out there tripping up everybody and trying to get into the act, and it's all called the All-Comers-How-to-Make-a-Fuckup-of-Life Championships. [*Another ugly laugh*] Hang on, Sam! The best bit is still coming. Do you know what the winner's trophy is? A beautiful big chamber pot with roses on the side, and it's full to the brim with piss. And guess who I think is going to be this year's winner.

SAM. [*Almost shouting*] Stop now!

HALLY. [*Suddenly appalled by how far he has gone*] Why?

SAM. Hally? It's your father you're talking about.

HALLY. So?

SAM. Do you know what you've been saying?

Hally can't answer. He is rigid with shame. Sam speaks to him sternly.

No, Hally, you mustn't do it. Take back those words and ask for forgiveness! It's a terrible sin for a son to mock his father with jokes like that. You'll be punished if you carry on. Your father is your father, even if he is a . . . cripple man.

WILLIE. Yes, Master Hally. Is true what Sam say.

SAM. I understand how you are feeling, Hally, but even so . . .

HALLY. No, you don't!

SAM. I think I do.

HALLY. And I'm telling you you don't. Nobody does. [*Speaking carefully as his shame turns to rage at Sam*] It's your turn to be careful, Sam. Very careful! You're treading on dangerous ground. Leave me and my father alone.

SAM. I'm not the one who's been saying things about him.

HALLY. What goes on between me and my Dad is none of your business!

SAM. Then don't tell me about it. If that's all you've got to say about him, I don't want to hear.

For a moment Hally is at loss for a response.

HALLY. Just get on with your bloody work and shut up.

SAM. Swearing at me won't help you.

HALLY. Yes, it does! Mind your own fucking business and shut up!

SAM. Okay. If that's the way you want it, I'll stop trying. [*He turns away. This infuriates Hally even more.*]

HALLY. Good. Because what you've been trying to do is meddle in something you know nothing about. All that concerns you in here, Sam, is to try and do what you get paid for—keep the place clean and serve the customers. In plain words, just get on with your job. My mother is right. She's always warning me about allowing you to get too familiar. Well, this time you've gone too far. It's going to stop right now.

No response from Sam.

You're only a servant in here, and don't forget it.

Still no response. Hally is trying hard to get one.

And as far as my father is concerned, all you need to remember is that he is your boss.

SAM. [*Needled at last*] No, he isn't. I get paid by your mother.

HALLY. Don't argue with me, Sam!

SAM. Then don't say he's my boss.

HALLY. He's a white man and that's good enough for you.

SAM. I'll try to forget you said that.

HALLY. Don't! Because you won't be doing me a favor if you do. I'm telling you to remember it.

A pause. Sam pulls himself together and makes one last effort.

SAM. Hally, Hally . . . ! Come on now. Let's stop before it's too late. You're right. We *are* on dangerous ground. If we're not careful, somebody is going to get hurt.

HALLY. It won't be me.

SAM. Don't be so sure.

HALLY. I don't know what you're talking about, Sam.

SAM. Yes, you do.

HALLY. [*Furious*] Jesus, I wish you would stop trying to tell me what I do and what I don't know.

Sam gives up. He turns to Willie.

SAM. Let's finish up.

HALLY. Don't turn your back on me! I haven't finished talking.

He grabs Sam by the arm and tries to make him turn around. Sam reacts with a flash of anger.

SAM. Don't do that, Hally! [*Facing the boy*] All right, I'm listening. Well? What do you want to say to me?

HALLY. [*Pause as Hally looks for something to say*] To begin with, why don't you also start calling me Master Harold, like Willie.

SAM. Do you mean that?

HALLY. Why the hell do you think I said it?

SAM. And if I don't?

HALLY. You might just lose your job.

SAM. [*Quietly and very carefully*] If you make me say it once, I'll never call you anything else again.

HALLY. So? [*The boy confronts the man*] Is that meant to be a threat?

SAM. Just telling you what will happen if you make me do that. You must decide what it means to you.

HALLY. Well, I have. It's good news. Because that is exactly what Master Harold wants from now on. Think of it as a little lesson in respect, Sam, that's long overdue, and I hope you remember it as well as you do your geography. I can tell you now that somebody who will be glad to hear I've finally given it to you will be my Dad. Yes! He agrees with my Mom. He's always going on about it as well. "You must teach the boys to show you more respect, my son."

SAM. So now you can stop complaining about going home. Everybody is going to be happy tonight.

HALLY. That's perfectly correct. You see, you mustn't get the wrong idea about me and my Dad, Sam. We also have our good times together. Some bloody good laughs. He's got a marvelous sense of humor. Want to know what our favorite joke is? He gives out a big groan, you see, and says: "It's not fair, is it, Hally?" Then I have to ask: "What, chum?" And then he says: "A nigger's arse" . . . and we both have a good laugh.

The men stare at him with disbelief.

What's the matter, Willie? Don't you catch the joke? You always were a bit slow on the uptake. It's what is called a pun. You see, fair means both light in color and to be just and decent. [*He turns to Sam*] I thought *you* would catch it, Sam.

SAM. Oh ja, I catch it all right.

HALLY. But it doesn't appeal to your sense of humor.

SAM. Do you really laugh?

HALLY. Of course.

SAM. To please him? Make him feel good?

HALLY. No, for heaven's sake! I laugh because I think it's a bloody good joke.

SAM. You're really trying hard to be ugly, aren't you? And why drag poor old Willie into it? He's done nothing to you except show you the respect you want so badly. That's also not being fair, you know . . . and *I* mean just or decent.

WILLIE. It's all right, Sam. Leave it now.

SAM. It's me you're after. You should just have said "Sam's arse" . . . because that's the one you're trying to kick. Anyway, how do you know it's not fair? You've never seen it. Do you want to?

He drops his trousers and underpants and presents his backside for Hally's inspection.

Have a good look. A real Basuto° arse . . . which is about as nigger as they can come. Satisfied? [*Trousers up*] Now you can make your Dad even happier when you go home tonight. Tell him I showed you my arse and he is quite right. It's not fair. And if it will give him an even better laugh next time, I'll also let *him* have a look. Come, Willie, let's finish up and go.

Sam and Willie start to tidy up the tea room. Hally doesn't move. He waits for a moment when Sam passes him.

HALLY. [*Quietly*] Sam . . .

Sam stops and looks expectantly at the boy. Hally spits in his face. A long and heartfelt groan from Willie. For a few seconds Sam doesn't move.

SAM. [*Taking out a handkerchief and wiping his face*] It's all right, Willie. [*To Hally*]
Ja, well, you've done it . . . Master Harold. Yes, I'll start calling you that from now on. It won't be difficult anymore. You've hurt yourself, Master Harold. I saw it coming. I warned you, but you wouldn't listen. You've just hurt yourself *bad.* And you're a coward, Master Harold. The face you should be spitting in is your father's . . . but you used mine, because you think you're safe inside your fair skin . . . and this time I don't mean just or decent [*Pause, then moving violently towards Hally*] Should I hit him, Willie?

WILLIE. [*Stopping Sam*] No, Boet Sam.

SAM. [*Violently*] Why not?

WILLIE. It won't help, Boet Sam.

SAM. I don't want to help! I want to hurt him.

WILLIE. You also hurt yourself.

SAM. And if he had done it to you, Willie?

WILLIE. Me? Spit at me like I was a dog? [*A thought that had not occurred to him before. He looks at Hally.*] Ja. Then I want to hit him. I want to hit him hard!

A dangerous few seconds as the men stand staring at the boy. Willie turns away, shaking his head.

But maybe all I do is go cry at the back. He's little boy, Boet Sam. Little *white* boy. Long trousers now, but he's still little boy.

SAM. [*His violence ebbing away into defeat as quickly as if flooded*] You're right. So go on, then: groan again, Willie. You do it better than me. [*To Hally*] You don't know all of what you've just done . . . Master Harold. It's not just that you've made me feel dirtier than I've ever been in my life . . . I mean, how do I wash off yours and your father's filth? . . . I've also failed. A long time ago I promised myself I was going to try and do something, but you've just shown me . . . Master Harold . . . that I've failed. [*Pause*] I've also got a memory of a little white boy when he was still wearing short trousers and a black man, but they're not flying a kite. It was the old Jubilee days, after dinner one night. I was in my room. You came in and just stood against the wall, looking down at the ground, and only after I'd asked you what you wanted, what was wrong, I don't know

---

Basuto: Bantu tribe living in Basutoland in southeast Africa.

"Master Harold" . . . and the boys

how many times, did you speak and even then so softly I almost didn't hear you. "Sam, please help me to go and fetch my Dad." Remember? He was dead drunk on the floor of the Central Hotel Bar. They'd phoned for your Mom, but you were the only one at home. And do you remember how we did it? You went in first by yourself to ask permission for me to go into the bar. Then I loaded him onto my back like a baby and carried him back to the boarding house with you following behind carrying his crutches. [*Shaking his head as he remembers*] A crowded Main Street with all the people watching a little white boy following his drunk father on a nigger's back! I felt for that little boy . . . Master Harold. I felt for him. After that we still had to clean him up, remember? He'd messed in his trousers, so we had to clean him up and get him into bed.

HALLY. [*Great pain*] I love him, Sam.

SAM. I know you do. That's why I tried to stop you from saying these things about him. It would have been so simple if you could have just despised him for being a weak man. But he's your father. You love him and you're ashamed of him. You're ashamed of so much! . . . And now that's going to include yourself. That was the promise I made to myself: try and stop that happening. [*Pause*] After we got him to bed you came back with me to my room and sat in a corner and carried on just looking down at the ground. And for days after that! You hadn't done anything wrong, but you went around as if you owed the world an apology for being alive. I didn't like seeing that! That's not the way a boy grows up to be a man! . . . But the one person who should have been teaching you what that means was the cause of your shame. If you really want to know, that's why I made you that kite. I wanted you to look up, be proud of something, of yourself . . . [*Bitter smile at the memory*] . . . and you certainly were that when I left you with it up there on the hill. Oh, ja . . . something else! . . . If you ever do write it as a short story, there *was* a twist in our ending. I couldn't sit down there and stay with you. It was a "Whites Only" bench. You were too young, too excited to notice then. But not anymore. If you're not careful . . . Master Harold . . . you're going to be sitting up there by yourself for a long time to come, and there won't be a kite in the sky.

Sam has got nothing more to say. He exits into the kitchen, taking off his waiter's jacket.

WILLIE. Is bad. Is all bad in here now.

HALLY. [*Books into his school case, raincoat on*] Willie . . . [*It is difficult to speak*] Will you lock up for me and look after the keys?

WILLIE. Okay.

Sam returns. Hally goes behind the counter and collects the few coins in the cash register. As he starts to leave . . .

SAM. Don't forget the comic books.

Hally returns to the counter and puts them in his case. He starts to leave again.

SAM. [*To the retreating back of the boy*] Stop . . . Hally . . .

Hally stops, but doesn't turn to face him.

Hally . . . I've got no right to tell you what being a man means if I don't behave like one myself, and I'm not doing so well at that this afternoon. Should we try again, Hally?

HALLY. Try what?

SAM. Fly another kite, I suppose. It worked once, and this time I need it as much as you do.

HALLY. It's still raining, Sam. You can't fly kites on rainy days, remember.

SAM. So what do we do? Hope for better weather tomorrow?

HALLY. [*Helpless gesture*] I don't know. I don't know anything anymore.

SAM. You sure of that, Hally? Because it would be pretty hopeless if that was true. It would mean nothing has been learnt in here this afternoon, and there was a hell of a lot of teaching going on . . . one way or the other. But anyway, I don't believe you. I reckon there's one thing you know. You don't *have* to sit up there by yourself. You know what that bench means now, and you can leave it any time you choose. All you've got to do is stand up and walk away from it.

Hally leaves. Willie goes up quietly to Sam.

WILLIE. Is okay, Boet Sam. You see. Is . . . [*He can't find any better words*] . . . is going to be okay tomorrow. [*Changing his tone*] Hey, Boet Sam! [*He is trying hard*] You right. I think about it and you right. Tonight I find Hilda and say sorry. And make promise I won't beat her no more. You hear me, Boet Sam?

SAM. I hear you, Willie.

WILLIE. And when we practice I relax and romance with her from beginning to end. Non-stop! You watch! Two weeks' time: "First prize for promising newcomers: Mr. Willie Malopo and Miss Hilda Samuels." [*Sudden impulse*] To hell with it! I walk home.

He goes to the jukebox, puts in a coin and selects a record. The machine comes to life in the gray twilight, blushing its way through a spectrum of soft, romantic colors.

How did you say it, Boet Sam? Let's dream.

Willie sways with the music and gestures for Sam to dance.

Sarah Vaughan sings.

"Little man you're crying,
I know why you're blue,
Someone took your kiddy car away;
Better go to sleep now,
Little man you've had a busy day." [*etc., etc.*]
    You lead. I follow.

The men dance together.

"Johnny won your marbles,
Tell you what we'll do;
Dad will get you new ones
    right away;
Better go to sleep now,
Little man you've had a
    busy day."

1. What is the relationship between Sam and Willie? Which of them is the "leader"? Why is Willie practicing his dancing? Why is Hilda not with Willie?

2. What connection do Sam and Willie have with Hally's family? What kind of memories does Hally have of his boyhood?

3. How does Hally react when he first hears that his father might be coming home from the hospital? What do you surmise about the father/son relationship?

4. How do their suggestions during the "man of magnitude" discussion reveal aspects of their respective characters? How would you characterize the relationship among Hally, Sam, and Willie?

5. How is Hally's view of dancing different from Sam's and Willie's? What do the differences suggest about their deeper cultural beliefs?

6. What is the function of the kite-flying memory? How does it figure later in the play? Why was Hally ashamed?

7. What creates the tension that precipitates the argument between Hally and Sam? What offends Sam? Why does Sam threaten to henceforth call Hally "Master Harold"? What are the implications of the changed address?

8. What memory does Sam recall for Hally? What is Hally's reaction?

9. How do Sam and Hally reconcile—if indeed they do? What does the kite symbolize?

10. What grounds for optimism does the play provide? What lessons does it teach about racial relations?

11. Why does Fugard choose to end the play with the sung lyrics about the "little man"? What is their significance?

36 Writing about Drama

The process of writing about drama is to a large degree similar to that of writing about fiction or poetry. Just as you need to have a grasp of the story or poem as a whole, so you need to know the entire play—the full context—in order to address some particular aspect. Finding a specific focus or problem to write about matters every bit as much as it does in writing about other genres. The stages themselves, moreover, are the same. You must read, make notes, and formulate; to find your thesis and the points to support it you will very likely need to outline, freewrite, or both. Finally, you will probably need to work your thoughts through in a rough draft before giving the essay its final shape. These steps will be reviewed here, but you may also wish to consult the discussions on writing in the "Writing about Fiction" and "Writing about Poetry" chapters (Chapters 10 and 24).

EVALUATING DRAMA: WEIGHING THE SPOKEN WORD

Each genre is, of course, different from the others and poses different challenges to the student who would write in response. Plays are in many ways easier to deal with, if only because the texts consist mainly of dialogue with a few notations about staging added on. What's more, the purpose, or "message," of a dramatic work is generally easier to catch hold of than what we find in a moderately difficult poem or story. But while the reader of a play has mainly dialogue to contend with, that dialogue may require proportionately more attention. We see this clearly with a playwright such as Shakespeare, who wrote in a dense and poetic idiom and loved to play with meanings of words. However, the reader should be no less attentive with a playwright like Arthur Miller or Athol Fugard. Though you can read the dialogue in their plays quickly—it feels modern, familiar—you will find as you look more closely that there is much to pause over. Words and statements can have very different meanings depending on who is speaking and in what context.

When people address each other, on-stage or off-, context is everything. The same words can have opposite meanings, depending upon whether the speaker intends them literally or ironically. Irony, of course, uses tone to reverse the sense of a message (see Chapters 8 and 17). Or the meaning could fall somewhere in the middle. When you say "I'll never speak to you again" to a friend who shows up late to an appointment, you probably don't plan to follow through on your vow of silence, but you are not making idle chatter, either. Given the situation, your friend can rightly assume a certain irritation. The degree depends upon the quality of the friendship as well as the extent of the lateness.

It is the same with dramatic dialogue. You would not get far in your understanding of a play like *The Importance of Being Earnest* if you read without your "irony-sensors" in constant movement. Consider the following exchange between Jack and Algernon in Act I:

JACK: Well, I won't argue about the matter. You always want to argue about things.
ALGERNON: That is exactly what things were originally made for.
JACK: Upon my word, if I thought that, I'd shoot myself. . . . [*A pause.*] You don't think there is any chance of Gwendolen becoming like her mother in about a hundred and fifty years, do you, Algy?
ALGERNON: All women become like their mothers. That is their tragedy. No man does. That's his.
JACK: Is that clever?
ALGERNON: It is perfectly phrased! and quite as true as any observation in civilized life should be.

You realize from the very beginning of the play that the context is one of manners and fashion and that all exchanges have been calculated to amuse the audience. Jack and Algernon are playing at clever banter, and they are every bit as insincere in stating their views as they will be, later, in swearing their love to the young women. If you are looking for heartfelt emotion, you are in the wrong play.

Context is no less crucial in a reading of Ibsen's *A Doll's House*. Here it is not irony at all, but a wrenching effort to speak a difficult truth that guides the dialogue. And this difference points to another consideration about context. You not only need to be alert to the context *within* the play—the situation between characters, and their respective personalities—but also you should have some awareness of the historical context of the work. Thus, you need to know that Nora's declaration of her independence is not voiced in a postliberation climate like our own; rather, Nora is voicing sentiments that run counter to the assumptions about sex roles in Ibsen's age. The final slamming of the door is not just a prelude to another unhappy divorce—it is a call to arms. And in the theaters of the late nineteenth century, it created a furor.

No matter what the play, you have to begin your assessment with a very careful weighing of the spoken word. You need to look not only at who is speaking, and what that person's conscious and unconscious motivation might be, but you also need to ask what those words might signify in their historical time and place. As it happens, these were the very concerns that Richard Case found himself dealing with when he got his writing assignment: write a thoughtful and focused response to this same Ibsen play.

PREPARING A RESPONSE: FINDING AN IDEA

Richard had read *A Doll's House* when it was first assigned and had participated in the one class discussion. He was confident that he understood what Ibsen was driving at and that with some thought he could find a suitable topic. Long before he ever put a word to the page, he had considered and rejected several options. They were, he felt, too obvious. He did not want to write about Nora's emancipation, nor was he interested in investigating Ibsen's use of the "doll house" image. He therefore turned his attention to some of the less obvious aspects of the play. Several possibilities came to mind. Perhaps he could write about the role of Dr. Rank or about the relationship between Nora's friend, Mrs. Linde, and her enemy, the lawyer Nils Krogstad.

Both possibilities had some appeal for Richard, and he took some time to skim through the play again, looking closer at the passages that involved these characters. Nothing special struck him. But as he was reading, he found himself thinking about Helmer. Is he just a self-absorbed and oppressive man, or is there something more to him? Does he "wake up" at the end of the play? How does Ibsen set him up as a foil to Nora's self-awareness? Richard noted the questions on a sheet of paper as they came to him, and before long he had decided to make Helmer his subject.

Once again Richard picked up the play, this time to mark all the scenes that feature Helmer. He wanted to track Ibsen's depiction of this character. Is he just a one-dimensional figure, Nora's jailer, or is he a complex, rounded individual with good as well as negative attributes? Richard kept his notebook by his side so that he could jot down any key lines. Though he did not have any kind of thesis in mind, he was sure that he would begin to formulate one as he read.

Making Notes

Working slowly, Richard wrote down what he felt were key moments in Ibsen's presentation of Helmer. Since the play is divided into only three acts, with no scene divisions, Richard set down the page reference alongside each note. After he had gone through the play once, his paper was covered with coded markings: " 'skylark' p. 1308; philosophy of the 'second chance' p. 1327; loves her, but as an object, p. 1310; reaction to news of Rank's dying, p. 1350," and so on.

As he was thus annotating the play, Richard was also jotting occasional notes on a second sheet. These were reminders of ideas and questions that came to him as he looked over the play. He did not make any effort to organize them yet—he would return to them once he was ready to start developing a thesis. He wrote:

```
Not so simple--H. may treat N. like his little
"skylark," but she encourages it--toys with his but-
tons, uses charms to get money. . . .

    H. claims to "love" N. but treats her as his
property--is it possible to call this love? Or is
this Ibsen's whole point?

    H.'s reaction to learning of Rank's dying is im-
portant. I feel much less sorry for him when I see
how easily he pushes emotions aside--all because he
is lusting after N.

    Paradox at the end--Use this: N. leaves H., in a
sense, because she sees that H. won't sacrifice him-
self, but puts his honor first. But isn't this a de-
nial of the very responsibility she wants to claim?
```

If he did sacrifice his honor for her it would be
the ultimate act of chivalry. Isn't the whole idea
of chivalry based on a view of women as incapable?

Remember: it was different then. H. looks like a
bad guy now, but he was acting like most men of his
time and class. How much is his fault, and how much
is the fault of society? Is H. paying for society's
"crime" against women? Focus on this.

Freewriting

Richard knew from experience that notes do not lead to ideas right away. Once he
had the play fresh in his mind and knew which passages were crucial to an understanding of Helmer, he took a break. And indeed, when he got back to his desk a
few hours later, he felt ready to start shaping a thesis. Opening his notebook, he
began to write in longhand. His high school writing teacher had called the process
"freewriting," and it had worked well enough in the past. After a few moments of
reviewing the play in his mind, he wrote:

The big thing about this play is supposed to be
Nora's waking up to the fact that she has been oppressed all her life. By trying to help her husband,
she has gotten herself in deep financial trouble. She
is being blackmailed by Krogstad, who threatens to
tell her husband everything. Because of this, and because Helmer is shown right away as being a patronizing husband--he calls her his "little skylark" and
so on--we are prepared to see him as a villain. In
some ways this is true. But it is also misleading--
doesn't show the whole truth. For one thing, Helmer
is only acting as he believes a husband and head of
household is <u>supposed</u> to act--it is his society that
is to blame (it encourages that side of his nature).
Secondly, he is not acting in isolation. Nora plays
up to him in kittenish ways, especially in Act 1
when she needs to get money. She allows Helmer to
believe that this is the norm--the way the relationship works--and how could he be anything but shocked
when she drops her news on him. Third, and this is
important, he does seem to be making a genuine effort to understand at the end. He is not a completely soulless creature, and though he has in some

ways wronged his wife, it could be argued that she has also wronged him.

Richard stopped. Though he had not set down all of his thoughts on Helmer or the play, he felt that he had the germ of an idea—or at least a way to structure his response paper. It was a simple form, but he thought it would work. He would begin by setting out the standard argument: Helmer patronized Nora, treated her like a possession, and refused to take her seriously. He would acknowledge the validity of these points, but then he would propose that the fault was not all Helmer's. His three points made for a fairly solid argument, he thought. But he also knew that he did not want to write a paper that would get Helmer "off the hook." There *were* definite charges that could be leveled against his treatment of Nora. The paper would, therefore, have to end with a careful sorting out of the levels of guilt and blame.

Constructing an Interpretation

Richard's page of freewriting had helped him to clarify his approach. He knew he was in that crucial "zone" that his teacher often talked about—he was between having some ideas and having a workable interpretation. He understood the difference: ideas could be specific, pertaining to some part of the work; an interpretation was, essentially, an understanding of the whole. An interpretation was an explanation of the author's intention. As such, it was necessarily subjective. Richard's interpretation was bound to be different from the interpretations of other class members. This did not worry him. "There is no right or wrong in this business," his teacher had said. "But your understanding—your version—has to cohere, and it has to fit the work." Richard thought that his ideas about Helmer were on the mark. What's more, he believed that they added up to an interpretation—a way of viewing the whole play. He was ready to make an outline of his main points and to return to his notes to find the specific quotes that would support his assertions. He started a new page, this time determined to find a clear and workable structure. Here is Richard's outline:

> I. Usual interpretation of "A Doll's House":
>   Helmer treats Nora like child (calls her
>   silly names, gives her money, isolates her
>   from his work, etc.).
>
>   Nora has deceived Helmer, but only to help
>   him and save his pride.
>
>   Helmer's reaction to the truth shows her
>   the true state of things--they can't change
>   except for miracle.
>
>   Nora leaves to find herself, and make a new
>   life, leaving Helmer to guilt.

II. Interpretation stresses Nora's awakening and
    Helmer's <u>fault</u>, but Ibsen not so simple. Be-
    neath black and white version is another:

> Helmer a man of his time, acting tradi-
> tional role.

> Nora has been playing along, acting like a
> child at times. Helmer has not had a chance
> to hear the truth. Nora's withholding of
> truth isolates him in his role.

> Helmer believes in giving a second chance
> (p. 1327--Krogstad), and though he acknowl-
> edges problem, promises change, Nora is set
> on her action.

III. Still, Helmer is at fault in various ways.
     But to appreciate the play in its full com-
     plexity, as more than a simple emancipation
     tract, we have to try to see both sides.

Richard's outline did not follow the more formal pattern he had been taught, but for him it served the main purpose: It allowed him to see his argument mapped out in a clear sequence. It gave him his cues for which quotes to select and what sequence to follow in making his points. The rest would be a matter of trial and error.

Rough Draft

Richard knew he would have to sweat his way through a rough draft—there was no other way to see whether the presentation would really work. And as soon as he had noted page numbers for supporting quotes in the margin of his outline, he was ready to start. Richard wrote the following rough draft without worrying too much about the fine points of expression. The main thing, he knew, was to get the whole paper onto the page where he could see it. He gathered his notes and switched on his computer.

ROUGH DRAFT

We live in an age that pays a great deal of
attention to equality among the sexes. Older patterns
and ways of doing things are now seen as wrong, and
many changes have been instituted in our public and
private lives. It is therefore very likely that
today's reader (or playgoer) would see Henrik Ibsen's
<u>A Doll's House</u>, written in 1879, as presenting a

Writing about Drama

clear case of a young woman waking up to the fact that she has been wronged and doing something about it. When the play begins she is unaware that she is a second-class citizen with no rights or power. When the door slams at the end, she has realized this truth.

The usual interpretation of A Doll's House is that Helmer, who comes across as smug and superior, is the villain. That he has kept Nora back because it suits him. He seems to like having a submissive wife and to play the powerful breadwinner. When the play opens, Helmer asks--it is his first line, delivered from off-stage--"Is that my little skylark chirruping out there?" (1308). He then hands Nora some banknotes, saying "I know only too well how Christmas runs away with the housekeeping" (1309). And throughout the play he persists in treating her like a helpless child.

What Helmer doesn't know is that Nora has got herself into serious trouble. Some time ago, when Helmer was sick, Nora borrowed money and did not tell him. The debt has come due, and a man named Krogstad, who works at Helmer's bank, threatens to tell everything if Nora does not help him get a better position from her husband. Nora has deceived Helmer, but only in order to save his pride.

When the truth emerges in Act III, however, Helmer reacts by blaming Nora. He puts his personal pride before his love. Nora suddenly sees the truth about their relationship. She sees that she is just a toy. And even though Helmer soon apologizes and takes his words back, he cannot unsay this truth. Nora tells him that she must leave and make her way alone, leaving him crushed. She claims that "the miracle of miracles would have to happen" (1358) in order for their marriage to be saved. She means that they would both have to change as people. Her departure, the slamming door, lets us know that this will not happen.

The obvious response to A Doll's House is that Nora has awakened and that Helmer is left to pay for his faults. And while there is some truth to this, the play is not so black and white. Helmer is not a true villain, just as Nora is not a blameless hero-ine. A deeper reading of the play, therefore, would look to see how much of the problem between Helmer and Nora is societal, and how much is a matter of personalities. Such a reading may lead us to see Helmer in a somewhat different light.

First of all, we need to remember that this is not America in the 1990s. Helmer is a man of his time, and he is acting in what he believes is the accepted way. He is not, we see, a bad man. He does have a great deal of affection for his wife. Is it his fault that the affection takes forms which now seem belittling to her? The man who says "Is that my squirrel frisking about?" (1308) is not evil, just misguided.

But we should not be too quick to point the fin-ger. After all, Nora's response to his question is "Yes!" (1308). And she plays the game of the coy and submissive wife willingly--or so it seems. When she wants money from Helmer, Ibsen has her playing with the buttons of his coat and acting flirtatious. In other words, she has not been sending Helmer any clear signals that she does not appreciate his treat-ment of her.

Helmer has been kept in the dark. He does not know the deal that Nora arranged with Krogstad. He has every reason to believe that his wife is happy with her life, and is all the more likely to be stunned and angered when he confronts her deed. From his point of view it must look like she has under-mined all of the security he has been working to provide for the family.

Finally, though Helmer himself claims to believe in giving a person a second chance--"I'm not so heartless that I would necessarily want to condemn a man for a single mistake like that" (1327)--Nora will not hear his apologies or his promises to change. Is Helmer really so stuck in his ways that he cannot learn to be different? Slamming the door closes off Nora's chances to find out.

These arguments are not meant to show Helmer as
an innocent. He has his flaws--he is condescending
and excessively proud--but he is a decent human
being. It may be that the marriage will not work,
but the reader should be willing to give Helmer the
second chance that Nora denies him. It is not
Helmer, but his class, his sex, and his whole culture that is on trial. Too great a focus on Helmer
simplifies the play and takes away from its meaning.

Richard read over what he had written. Though his expression seemed rough or wordy in places, he was fairly satisfied. He particularly liked the twist in his last paragraph: making Helmer the villain prevents the reader from seeing the real cul- prits. He also knew that he had not been able to fit in one of his more interesting arguments—the argument that the miracle Nora had awaited, that Helmer would sacrifice himself and take full blame, went against everything that her declaration of independence would stand for. The more he considered this, the more Richard saw that the middle part of the paper needed the strength of that insight. It was his clincher, and he looked at his argument to see how he could work it in.

Writing the final draft was, for Richard, very different from writing the first. He knew what he wanted to say, and he knew that his sequence of points held to- gether on the page. Now he could take out his fine chisels and try to get the paper to read smoothly: he could go over the details of presentation and look for ways to make them more interesting. This is the response paper he finally submitted to his teacher:

A Second Chance for Torvald Helmer

by Richard Case

Most readers and playgoers in our liberated age
would probably find Henrik Ibsen's A Doll's House
(written in 1879) to be a clear statement of the way
things used to be. The marriage of Torvald Helmer
and his wife, Nora, is the very picture of inequality. When the play opens, Nora, who is shown to be a
nervous and submissive young woman, is unaware that
she is a second-class citizen with no real rights or
powers. When she slams the door at the end of the
play, leaving her husband, she has realized this
truth and is determined to take action.

Though Ibsen has presented Helmer as a figure of
some complexity, there is a strong tendency to see
him as a figure of blame. He is smug and superior,

and he condescends to Nora. He likes having a childish wife and being the authority figure. Indeed,
Helmer's first line, delivered from off-stage, dis-
poses the reader against him. He hears Nora moving
around and asks, "Is that my skylark chirruping out
there?" (1308) Anyone with strong views on sexual
equality will immediately perceive him as a negative
character.

The characterization is soon fleshed out. Helmer
keeps treating Nora like a helpless child, lecturing
her about money, but then handing her money and saying: "I know only too well how Christmas runs away
with the housekeeping." (1309)

What Helmer does not know is that Nora has gotten
herself into a serious difficulty on his account. She
had borrowed money to help him when he was ill and
had not told him. The debt has come due, and
Krogstad, the lender, who now works at Helmer's bank,
threatens to reveal her secret unless she helps him
get a better position. Nora has deceived her husband,
but only in order to save his pride.

When the truth emerges in Act III, however, Helmer
reacts by blaming Nora. Whereas she had hoped that he
would accept the guilt and sacrifice himself, he does
the opposite. He attacks her: "Oh, what a terrible
awakening this is" says Helmer. "All these eight
years--this woman who was my pride and joy . . . a
hypocrite, a liar . . . worse than that, a criminal!"
(1351). He has put his personal pride before his
love. Nora sees the truth all at once. She has been
just a plaything, a toy, a doll. And even though
Helmer later apologizes and tries to take his words
back, he cannot erase this truth she has discovered.

Nora tells Helmer that she must leave and make
her way alone. Helmer is crushed and starts to beg.
But she claims that "the miracle of miracles would
have to happen" for their marriage to be saved
(1358). She means that they would both have to
change as people, and the slamming door at her departure signals that such changes will never happen.
Her exit is final.

Writing about Drama

The obvious interpretation of <u>A Doll's House</u> is that Nora has finally awakened and that Helmer has just begun to realize the extent to which he has denied her the necessary freedom and respect. In other words, the blame for the broken marriage belongs to Helmer. Naturally, there is some truth here, but to insist on it too much is to simplify the play. Things are not quite so black and white. Helmer is not a true villain and Nora is not a blameless heroine. A deeper reading of the play shows that a true assessment of Helmer shifts the focus of blame.

The first thing the reader needs to remember is that this is nineteenth-century Norway and not 1990s America. Helmer is a man of his time, and he acts as he believes he should--as he has <u>learned</u> to act. Nor, for all his trivializing of Nora, is he a bad man. In fact, it is quite obvious that he has affection for his wife and wants her to be happy. Is it Helmer's fault that his affection takes forms which now seem insulting? The man who says "Is that my squirrel frisking about" (1308) is not evil. He has simply not reflected on the implications of his words and actions.

But one should remember, also, that Nora's response to Helmer is "Yes, it is." (1308) That is, she plays the submissive role willingly, at least when the reader first sees her. And when she wants money from Helmer, she is not above playing with the buttons of his coat and acting flirtatiously. In other words, she has not been sending Helmer any signals that would help him to see how his treatment of her is wrong.

Further, Helmer has been kept in the dark about Nora's financial dealings. He has no reason to suspect that things are not as they seem or that Nora is in any way unhappy with her life. He is, therefore, all the more likely to be stunned by the revelation of her dealings with Krogstad and all the more likely to act harshly and irrationally. He claims, later, that he did not mean what he was saying. Why should the reader suppose that he did?

What's more, if one looks closely at the confession scene in Act III, one sees that Nora's expecta-
tion--that Helmer would take full responsibility and
save her--has put him in a corner. She says "I was
absolutely convinced you would come forward and take
everything on yourself, and say: 'I am the guilty
one' " (1356). She has wanted him to be the person
she accuses him of being.

Interestingly, it is Helmer who has stated that a
person should be given a second chance. Defending
his decision to keep Krogstad on at the bank, he
says to Nora, "I'm not so heartless that I would
necessarily want to condemn a man for a single mistake like that" (1327). His own isolated action, if
one doesn't count his typically male attitudes, has
been to lash out in a rage, and for this he stands
condemned. Nora will not hear his apologies or his
promises to change. Is Helmer really so stuck in his
ways that he cannot learn to be different? Nora will
never find out.

Helmer is not blameless, far from it. He is condescending and proud, and he has not tried to come
to terms with Nora as a human being. But neither is
he the ogre that some have made him out to be. To
single Helmer out as the villain is to risk missing
a large part of Ibsen's message: Helmer's sex and
class--his whole culture--are to blame for Nora's
situation. She is not slamming the door on her
husband alone, but also on the society that made
him what he is.

Different kinds of essays require different procedures. Richard's response assignment allowed him to concentrate more upon ideas. As a result, he used quotations only where he needed to illustrate an argument. Moreover, the Ibsen play
is not divided into scenes, as many plays are. Thus, Richard identified the excerpts
by referring to the page number of the edition he was using. Wherever possible,
you should identify citations by putting the act and scene numbers in parentheses
(use upper- and lower-case Roman numerals—II, iv); where lines are numbered,
as is often the case with Shakespeare's plays, indicate the specifics after the scene
numeral, thus: (II.iv.19–34).

Other kinds of assignments you may expect to get include *explication*, *analysis*,
and *comparison and contrast*. (See the discussions in the "Writing about Fiction" and
"Writing about Poetry" chapters.) An explication is a very detailed—often line by

line—discussion of an important speech or passage, such as Hamlet's "To be or not to be" soliloquy. You would approach this task as if you were close-reading a poem. The purpose of an explication is to isolate specific features of the playwright's use of language—his or her way of making meaning. The main focus, therefore, would be upon *diction, imagery, allusion*, and perhaps even *rhythm* (see Glossary).

An analysis might require that you select a scene or passage of dialogue in order to examine its function in the play as a whole. A typical analysis assignment, say for Arthur Miller's *Death of a Salesman*, would ask that you discuss the scene in Act II where Biff and Happy take their father out to dinner. You would have to isolate the dynamics of the scene—how the brothers relate to each other and to Willy—and show how the words and actions of the characters reflect the larger pattern of the play.

You may also be asked to write an analysis that concentrates upon a single element: a character, the plot structure, the setting, and so on. The important thing to remember when undertaking such an essay is to balance the big picture—the unfolding of the whole play—with the details. You must find those instances where the dialogue most clearly illustrates your point and avoid the great temptation to quote long passages that are only generally relevant. When quoting exchanges of dialogue, remember to include the names of the speakers as well as any stage directions that may be part of the passage:

CECILY: Uncle Jack, if you don't shake hands with Ernest, I will never forgive you.
JACK: Never forgive me?
CECILY: Never, never, never!
JACK: Well, this is the last time I shall ever do it. [*Shakes hands with Algernon and glares.*]

Comparison and contrast assignments enlarge the scope of discussion by asking you to look for similarities and differences among separate plays or scenes or characters in the same play. The great challenge, especially if you are looking at two plays, is to target a subject that lends itself to essay treatment. Whatever your topic, you will most likely want to center your treatment around specific scenes. Otherwise, the risk is great that you will find yourself adrift among loose generalities.

When you compare and contrast, no matter what two things, or elements, you are setting side by side, you need to decide on the logic of your procedure. It is often easiest to set out case A (all of your points about the character of Oedipus, say) before moving on to case B (Hamlet's character). In that way, A becomes a ground for comparison, and the reader has a point of anchor. The ping-pong approach, which would look at one feature of A, then one of B, and so on, is likely to leave the reader at sea.

Whatever the assignment, you will do well to lay out your materials—quotations and references—before you start writing. Nothing so breaks the momentum of composition as stopping every few minutes to thumb through a pile of texts to find the passage you need. But more important still, leave time for writing a complete rough draft before you undertake the final version. The longer you write and the more accomplished you get at expressing yourself, the more you will understand the importance of letting your ideas take on a preliminary shape before you refine them.

37 Responding to Plays

This chapter offers you five opportunities to see how other readers have responded to plays included in the preceding chapters, and to compare these readings with your own responses. The selections present one or two essays for each of five plays to show you some distinctive readings of the play and the author's work—including responses to the two plays by Shakespeare. As you read and respond to the interaction and dialogue in each play, you should first focus on developing your own interpretation of the play, thinking about how you might communicate this to another reader. You can then compare your ideas with those of another writer or critic and consider the views you share as well as your points of difference.

After reading the essays that respond to these plays, consider the questions that follow each section and decide how you might pose some questions to the critics. What issues strike you as most pressing? How would you integrate these views in producing an interpretation of your own?

At the end of this chapter is a unit on techniques for using critical sources in writing about a play, with several examples of how the essay material can be used by a student as a writing resource in the development of an interpretive paper. As you observe how a student source paper develops a response to statements by other critics, consider how your own interpretive paper on these plays would quote from and respond to other writers' ideas.

Note: Should you wish to use any of the response essays in this chapter as sources in interpretive essays you may be writing, you can either track down the original source at the library and cite the actual pages in standard MLA form (see Appendix B), or you can cite the work as reprinted in *Literature: The Evolving Canon* and refer to the pages of this book. Your notation on your Works Cited page might read as follows:

> Frye, Northrop. "Introduction to *The Tempest.*" *Literature: The Evolving Canon.* 2nd ed. Ed. Sven P. Birkerts. Boston: Allyn and Bacon, 1996. pp. 1596–1602.

RESPONDING TO SOPHOCLES' *OEDIPUS REX*

Freud, the famous founder of psychoanalysis, provided one of the modern world's best-known responses to the Sophocles play in his well-known coinage of the "Oedipus complex." You can judge his formulation of this and its link to the play by reading this section from his early book *The Interpretation of Dreams.* Another response comes from a scholar of the theater, Francis Fergusson.

Sigmund Freud (1856–1939)

from THE INTERPRETATION OF DREAMS

According to my already extensive experience, parents play a leading part in the infantile psychology of all persons who subsequently become psychoneurotics.° Falling in love with one parent and hating the other forms part of the permanent stock of the psychic impulses which arise in early childhood, and are of such importance as the material of the subsequent neurosis. But I do not believe that psychoneurotics are to be sharply distinguished in this respect from other persons who remain normal—that is, I do not believe that they are capable of creating something absolutely new and peculiar to themselves. It is far more probable—and this is confirmed by incidental observations of normal children—that in their amorous or hostile attitude toward their parents, psychoneurotics do no more than reveal to us, by magnification, something that occurs less markedly and intensively in the minds of the majority of children. Antiquity has furnished us with legendary matter which corroborates this belief, and the profound and universal validity of the old legends is explicable only by an equally universal validity of the above-mentioned hypothesis of infantile psychology.

I am referring to the legend of King Oedipus and the *Oedipus Rex* of Sophocles. Oedipus, the son of Laius, king of Thebes, and Jocasta, is exposed° as a suckling,° because an oracle° had informed the father that his son, who was still unborn, would be his murderer. He is rescued, and grows up as a king's son at a foreign court, until, being uncertain of his origin, he, too, consults the oracle, and is warned to avoid his native place, for he is destined to become the murderer of his father and the husband of his mother. On the road leading away from his supposed home he meets King Laius, and in a sudden quarrel strikes him dead. He comes to Thebes, where he solves the riddle of the Sphinx,° who is barring the way to the city, whereupon he is elected king by the grateful Thebans, and is rewarded with the hand of Jocasta. He reigns for many years in peace and honour, and begets two sons and two daughters upon his unknown mother, until at last a plague breaks out—which causes the Thebans to consult the oracle anew. Here Sophocles' tragedy begins. The messengers bring the reply that the plague will stop as soon as the murderer of Laius is driven from the country. But where is he?

> "Where shall be found,
> Faint, and hard to be known, the trace of the ancient guilt?"

The action of the play consists simply in the disclosure, approached step by step and artistically delayed (and comparable to the work of a psychoanalysis) that Oedipus himself is the murderer of Laius, and that he is the son of the murdered man and Jocasta. Shocked by the abominable crime which he has unwittingly committed,

---

psychoneurotics: a term indicating psychological disorder.
exposed . . . suckling: Oedipus was left out to die while still an infant at his mother's breast.
oracle: person who makes prophecies.
Sphinx: monstrous creature.

Oedipus blinds himself, and departs from his native city. The prophecy of the oracle has been fulfilled.

The *Oedipus Rex* is a tragedy of fate; its tragic effect depends on the conflict between the all-powerful will of the gods and the vain efforts of human beings threatened with disaster; resignation to the divine will, and the perception of one's own impotence is the lesson which the deeply moved spectator is supposed to learn from the tragedy. Modern authors have therefore sought to achieve a similar tragic effect by expressing the same conflict in stories of their own invention. But the playgoers have looked on unmoved at the unavailing efforts of guiltless men to avert the fulfilment of curse or oracle; the modern tragedies of destiny have failed of their effect.

If the *Oedipus Rex* is capable of moving a modern reader or playgoer no less powerfully than it moved the contemporary Greeks, the only possible explanation is that the effect of the Greek tragedy does not depend upon the conflict between fate and human will, but upon the peculiar nature of the material by which this conflict is revealed. There must be a voice within us which is prepared to acknowledge the compelling power of fate in the *Oedipus*, while we are able to condemn the situations occurring in *Die Ahnfrau*° or other tragedies of fate as arbitrary inventions. And there actually is a motive in the story of King Oedipus which explains the verdict of this inner voice. His fate moves us only because it might have been our own, because the oracle laid upon us before our birth the very curse which rested upon him. It may be that we were all destined to direct our first sexual impulses toward our mothers, and our first impulses of hatred and violence toward our fathers; our dreams convince us that we were. King Oedipus, who slew his father Laius and wedded his mother Jocasta, is nothing more or less than a wish-fulfilment—the fulfilment of the wish of our childhood. But we, more fortunate than he, in so far as we have not become psychoneurotics, have since our childhood succeeded in withdrawing our sexual impulses from our mothers, and in forgetting our jealousy of our fathers. We recoil from the person for whom this primitive wish of our childhood has been fulfilled with all the force of the repression which these wishes have undergone in our minds since childhood. As the poet brings the guilt of Oedipus to light by his investigation, he forces us to become aware of our own inner selves, in which the same impulses are still extant, even though they are suppressed. The antithesis with which the chorus departs:—

> " . . . Behold, this is Oedipus,
> Who unravelled the great riddle, and was first in power,
> Whose fortune all the townsmen praised and envied;
> See in what dread adversity he sank!"

—this admonition touches us and our own pride, us who since the years of our childhood have grown so wise and so powerful in our own estimation. Like Oedipus, we live in ignorance of the desires that offend morality, the desires that nature has forced upon us and after their unveiling we may well prefer to avert our gaze from the scenes of our childhood.

In the very text of Sophocles' tragedy there is an unmistakable reference to the fact that the Oedipus legend had its source in dream-material of immemorial antiquity, the content of which was the painful disturbance of the child's relations to its parents caused by the first impulses of sexuality. Jocasta comforts Oedipus—who

5

Die Ahnfrau: German tragedy.

is not yet enlightened, but is troubled by the recollection of the oracle—by an allusion to a dream which is often dreamed, though it cannot, in her opinion, mean anything:—

> "For many a man hath seen himself in dreams
> His mother's mate, but he who gives no heed
> To suchlike matters bears the easier life."

The dream of having sexual intercourse with one's mother was as common then as it is to-day with many people, who tell it with indignation and astonishment. As may well be imagined, it is the key to the tragedy and the complement to the dream of the death of the father. The Oedipus fable is the reaction of fantasy to these two typical dreams, and just as such a dream, when occurring to an adult, is experienced with feelings of aversion, so the content of the fable must include terror and self-chastisement. The form which it subsequently assumed was the result of an uncomprehending secondary elaboration of the material, which sought to make it serve a theological intention. The attempt to reconcile divine omnipotence with human responsibility must, of course, fail with this material as with any other.

QUESTIONS

One of the pillars of Freud's psychological theory was his formulation of the "Oedipus Complex." In this excerpt from *The Interpretation of Dreams*, Freud discusses Sophocles' play and shows how the plot reveals this central dynamic of the psychic life of the male. (His idea about the "Electra Complex," discussed elsewhere in his work, proposed a similar erotic bond between girls and their fathers.)

1. How does Freud see modern playwrights failing in their attempt to "achieve a similar tragic effect"? What is the recognition that, in his view, has the power to move the "innocent" playgoer?

2. How does Freud's theory of the Oedipal fantasy connect with Aristotle's assertion that tragedy effects a purging of the emotions through "pity and fear"? What does the "repression"—or unconscious denial—of these sexual fantasies have to do with the purging (also known as "katharsis")?

3. Can you find any traces of the basic Oedipal tension (or its counterpart, Electra tension) in any of the other plays you have read? Consider Wasserstein (Chapter 29), Shakespeare's *Hamlet* (Chapter 31) and *The Tempest* (Chapter 32), and Miller (Chapter 35) in particular.

Francis Fergusson

OEDIPUS: RITUAL AND PLAY

The Cambridge School of Classical Anthropologists has shown in great detail that the form of Greek tragedy follows the form of a very ancient ritual, that of the *Eniautos-Daimon*, or seasonal god.[1] This was one of the most influential discoveries of the last few generations, and it gives us new insights into Oedipus which I think are not yet completely explored. The clue to

---

[1] See especially Jane Ellen Harrison's *Ancient Art and Ritual*, and her *Themis*, which contains an "Excursus on the ritual forms preserved in Greek Tragedy" by Professor Gilbert Murray. [Editor's Note]

Sophocles' dramatizing of the myth of Oedipus is to be found in this ancient ritual, which had a similar form and meaning—that is, it also moved in the "tragic rhythm."[2]

Experts in classical anthropology, like experts in other fields, dispute innumerable questions of fact and of interpretation which the layman can only pass over in respectful silence. One of the thornier questions seems to be whether myth or ritual came first. Is the ancient ceremony merely an enactment of the Ur-Myth of the year-god—Attis, or Adonis, or Osiris, or the "Fisher-King"—in any case that Hero-King-Father-High-Priest who fights with his rival, is slain and dismembered, then rises anew with the spring season? Or did the innumerable myths of this kind arise to "explain" a ritual which was perhaps mimed or danced or sung to celebrate the annual change of season?

For the purpose of understanding the form and meaning of *Oedipus*, it is not necessary to worry about the answer to this question of historic fact. The figure of Oedipus himself fulfills all the requirements of the scapegoat, the dismembered king or god-figure. The situation in which Thebes is presented at the beginning of the play—in peril of its life; its crops, its herds, its women mysteriously infertile, signs of a mortal disease of the City, and the disfavor of the gods—is like the withering which winter brings, and calls, in the same way, for struggle, dismemberment, death, and renewal. And this tragic sequence is the substance of the play. It is enough to know that myth and ritual are close together in their genesis, two direct imitations of the perennial experience of the race.

But when one considers *Oedipus* as a ritual one understands it in ways which one cannot by thinking of it merely as a dramatization of a story, even that story. Harrison has shown that the festival of Dionysos, based ultimately upon the yearly vegetation ceremonies, included *rites of passage*, like that celebrating the assumption of adulthood—celebrations of the mystery of individual growth and development. At the same time, it was a prayer for the welfare of the whole City; and this welfare was understood not only as material prosperity, but also as the natural order of the family, the ancestors, the present members, and the generations still to come, and, by the same token, obedience to the gods who were jealous, each in his own province, of this natural and divinely sanctioned order and proportion.

We must suppose that Sophocles' audience (the whole population of the City) came early, prepared to spend the day in the bleachers. At their feet was the semi-circular dancing-ground for the chorus, and the thrones for the priests, and the altar. Behind that was the raised platform for the principal actors, backed by the all-purpose, emblematic façade, which would presently be taken to represent Oedipus' palace in Thebes. The actors were not professionals in our sense, but citizens selected for a religious office, and Sophocles himself had trained them and the chorus.

This crowd must have had as much appetite for thrills and diversion as the crowds who assemble in our day for football games and musical comedies, and Sophocles certainly holds the attention with an exciting show. At the same time his audience must have been alert for the fine points of poetry and dramaturgy, for *Oedipus* is being offered in competition with other plays on the same bill. But the element which distinguishes this theater, giving it its unique directness and depth, is the *ritual expectancy* which Sophocles assumed in his audience. The nearest thing we have to this ritual sense of theater is, I suppose, to be found at an Easter performance of the *Mat-*

5

---

[2]Elsewhere Fergusson defined "tragic rhythm" as the movement which constitutes the shape of the whole play and of each episode in the play. [Editor's Note]

tias Passion. We also can observe something similar in the dances and ritual mummery of the Pueblo Indians. Sophocles' audience must have been prepared, like the Indians standing around their plaza, to consider the playing, the make-believe it was about to see—the choral invocations, with dancing and chanting; the reasoned discourses and the terrible combats of the protagonists; the mourning, the rejoicing, and the contemplation of the final stage-picture or epiphany—as imitating and celebrating the mystery of human nature and destiny. And this mystery was at once that of individual growth and development, and that of the precarious life of the human City.

I have indicated how Sophocles presents the life of the mythic Oedipus in the tragic rhythm, the mysterious quest of life. Oedipus is shown seeking his own true being; but at the same time and by the same token, the welfare of the City. When one considers the ritual form of the whole play, it becomes evident that it presents the tragic but perennial, even normal, quest of the whole City for its well-being. In this larger action, Oedipus is only the protagonist, the first and most important champion. This tragic quest is realized by all the characters in their various ways; but in the development of the action as a whole it is the chorus alone that plays a part as important as that of Oedipus; its counterpart, in fact. The chorus holds the balance between Oedipus and his antagonists, marks the progress of their struggles, and restates the main theme, and its new variation, after each dialogue or agon. The ancient ritual was probably performed by a chorus alone without individual developments and variations, and the chorus, in *Oedipus*, is still the element that throws most light on the ritual form of the play as a whole.

The chorus consists of twelve or fifteen "Elders of Thebes." This group is not intended to represent literally all of the citizens either of Thebes or of Athens. The play opens with a large delegation of Theban citizens before Oedipus' palace, and the chorus proper does not enter until after the prologue. Nor does the chorus speak directly for the Athenian audience; we are asked throughout to make-believe that the theater is the agora at Thebes; and at the same time Sophocles' audience is witnessing a ritual. It would, I think, be more accurate to say that the chorus represents the point of view and the faith of Thebes as a whole, and, by analogy, of the Athenian audience. Their errand before Oedipus' palace is like that of Sophocles' audience in the theatre: they are watching a sacred combat, in the issue of which they have an all-important and official stake. Thus they represent the audience and the citizens in a particular way—not as a mob formed in response to some momentary feeling, but rather as an organ of a highly self-conscious community: something closer to the "conscience of the race" than to the overheated affectivity of a mob.

According to Aristotle, a Sophoclean chorus is a character that takes an important role in the action of the play, instead of merely making incidental music between the scenes, as in the plays of Euripides. The chorus may be described as a group personality, like an old Parliament. It has its own traditions, habits of thought and feeling, and mode of being. It exists, in a sense, as a living entity, but not with the sharp actuality of an individual. It perceives; but its perception is at once wider and vaguer than that of a single man. It shares, in its way, the seeking action of the play as a whole; but it cannot act in all the modes; it depends upon the chief agonists to invent and try out the detail of policy, just as a rather helpless but critical Parliament depends upon the Prime Minister to act but, in its less specific form of life, survives his destruction.

When the chorus enters after the prologue, with its questions, its invocation of the various gods, and its focus upon the hidden and jeopardized welfare of the

City—Athens or Thebes—the list of essential *dramatis personae*, as well as the elements needed to celebrate the ritual, is complete, and the main action can begin. It is the function of the chorus to mark the stages of this action, and to perform the suffering and perceiving part of the tragic rhythm. The protagonist and his antagonists develop the "purpose" with which the tragic sequence begins; the chorus, with its less than individual being, broods over the agons, marks their stages with a word (like that of the chorus leader in the middle of the Tiresias scene), and (expressing its emotions and visions in song and dance) suffers the results, and the new perception at the end of the fight. 10

The choral odes are lyrics but they are not to be understood as poetry, the art of words, only, for they are intended also to be danced and sung. And though each chorus has its own shape, like that of a discrete lyric—its beginning, middle, and end— it represents also one passion or pathos in the changing action of the whole. This passion, like the other moments in the tragic rhythm, is felt at so general or, rather, so deep a level that it seems to contain both the mob ferocity that Nietzsche felt in it and, at the other extreme, the patience of prayer. It is informed by faith in the unseen order of nature and the gods, and moves through a sequence of modes of suffering. This may be illustrated from the chorus I have quoted at the end of the Tiresias scene.

It begins (close to the savage emotion of the end of the fight) with images suggesting that cruel "Bacchic frenzy" which is supposed to be the common root of tragedy and of the "old" comedy: "In panoply of fire and lightning / The son of Zeus now springs upon him." In the first antistrophe these images come together more clearly as we relish the chase; and the fleeing culprit, as we imagine him, begins to resemble Oedipus, who is lame, and always associated with the rough wilderness of Kithairon. But in the second strophe, as though appalled by its ambivalent feelings and the imagined possibilities, the chorus sinks back into a more dark and patient posture of suffering, "in awe," "hovering in hope." In the second antistrophe this is developed into something like the orthodox Christian attitude of prayer, based on faith, and assuming the possibility of a hitherto unimaginable truth and answer: "Zeus and Apollo are wise," etc. The whole chorus then ends with a new vision of Oedipus, of the culprit, and of the direction in which the welfare of the City is to be sought. This vision is still colored by the chorus's human love of Oedipus as Hero, for the chorus has still its own purgation to complete, cannot as yet accept completely either the suffering in store for it, or Oedipus as scapegoat. But it marks the end of the first complete "purpose-passion-perception" unit, and lays the basis for the new purpose which will begin the next unit.

It is also to be noted that the chorus changes the scene which we, as audience, are to imagine. During the agon between Oedipus and Tiresias, our attention is fixed upon their clash, and the scene is literal, close, and immediate: before Oedipus' palace. When the fighters depart and the choral music starts, the focus suddenly widens, as though we had been removed to a distance. We become aware of the interested City around the bright arena; and beyond that, still more dimly, of Nature, sacred to the hidden gods. Mr. Burke has expounded the fertile notion that human action may be understood in terms of the scene in which it occurs, and vice versa: the scene is defined by the mode of action. The chorus's action is not limited by the sharp, rationalized purposes of the protagonist; its mode of action, more patient, less sharply realized, is cognate with a wider, if less accurate, awareness of the scene of human life. But the chorus's action, as I have remarked, is not that of passion itself (Nietzsche's cosmic void of night) but suffering informed by the faith of the tribe in

Responding to Plays

a human and a divinely sanctioned natural order: "If such deeds as these are honored," the chorus asks after Jocasta's impiety, "why should I dance and sing?" Thus it is one of the most important functions of the chorus to reveal, in its widest and most mysterious extent, the theater of human life which the play, and indeed the whole Festival of Dionysos, assumed. Even when the chorus does not speak, but only watches, it maintains this theme and this perspective—ready to take the whole stage when the fighters depart.

If one thinks of the movement of the play, it appears that the tragic rhythm analyzes human action temporally into successive modes, as a crystal analyzes a white beam of light spatially into the colored bands of the spectrum. The chorus, always present, represents one of these modes, and at the recurrent moments when reasoned purpose is gone, it takes the stage with its faith-informed passion, moving through an ordered succession of modes of suffering, to a new perception of the immediate situation.

QUESTIONS

1. Fergusson goes outside the literary sphere to provide background to *Oedipus*. How do Fergusson's explanations add to your understanding of the origins of drama?
2. What other ritual enactments does Fergusson mention? What point is he making about the place of ritual in human culture?
3. How does Fergusson connect King Oedipus to the city of Thebes?
4. Summarize Fergusson's account of the importance of the chorus in Greek tragedy.

RESPONDING TO SHAKESPEARE'S *HAMLET*

Hamlet has proved to be a testing ground for some of the world's most famous literary figures and critics. Dr. Samuel Johnson established his early reputation as a scholar not only with his ground-breaking dictionary but with his comprehensive work *Prefaces to Shakespeare*, one of the first works to provide a survey of the Bard's work based on systematic critical principles. Since Johnson's time many other notable literary artists have taken the measure of their ideas through a critique of *Hamlet* and other Shakespeare plays. Coleridge, the famous Romantic poet (see Chapter 28), was among the first to follow up on Johnson with a carefully considered critical response in a series of lectures.

Samuel Johnson (1709–1784)

from NOTES ON SHAKESPEARE

General Observation. If the dramas of Shakespeare were to be characterized each by the particular excellence which distinguishes it from the rest, we must allow to the tragedy of *Hamlet* the praise of variety. The incidents are so numerous that the argument of the play would make a long tale. The scenes are interchangeably diversified with merriment and solemnity; with merriment that includes judicious and instructive observations, and solemnity not strained by poetical violence above the natural sentiments of man. New characters appear from time to time in continual succession, exhibiting various forms of life and particular modes of conversation. The pretended madness of Hamlet causes much mirth, the mournful distraction of Ophelia° fills the heart with tenderness, and every personage produces the effect intended, from the apparition that in the first act chills the blood with horror to the fop in the last that exposes affectation to just contempt.

The conduct is perhaps not wholly secure against objections. The action is indeed for the most part in continual progression, but there are some scenes which neither forward nor retard it. Of the feigned madness of Hamlet there appears no adequate cause, for he does nothing which he might not have done with the reputation of sanity. He plays the madman most when he treats Ophelia with so much rudeness, which seems to be useless and wanton cruelty.

Hamlet is, through the whole play, rather an instrument than an agent. After he has, by the stratagem of the play, convicted the king, he makes no attempt to punish him, and his death is at last effected by an incident which Hamlet has no part in producing.

Ophelia: young woman who loves Hamlet who goes mad and kills herself in the course of the play.

Samuel Taylor Coleridge (1772–1834)

from LECTURES ON SHAKESPEARE

Hamlet
[From the twelfth lecture, 2 January 1812]

. . . We will now pass to 'Hamlet,' in order to obviate some of the general prejudices against the author in reference to the character of the hero. Much has been objected to, which ought to have been praised, and many beauties of the highest kind have been neglected, because they are somewhat hidden.

The first question we should ask ourselves is—What did Shakespeare mean when he drew the character of Hamlet? He never wrote anything without design, and what was his design when he sat down to produce this tragedy? My belief is that he always regarded his story, before he began to write, much in the same light as a painter regards his canvas, before he begins to paint—as a mere vehicle for his thoughts—as the ground upon which he was to work. What then was the point to which Shakespeare directed himself in Hamlet? He intended to portray a person in whose view the external world, and all its incidents and objects, were comparatively dim, and of no interest in themselves, and which began to interest only when they were reflected in the mirror of his mind. Hamlet beheld external things in the same

Responding to Plays

way that a man of vivid imagination, who shuts his eyes, sees what has previously made an impression on his organs.

The poet places him in the most stimulating circumstances that a human being can be placed in. He is the heir apparent of a throne; his father dies suspiciously; his mother excludes her son from his throne by marrying his uncle. This is not enough; but the ghost of the murdered father is introduced, to assure the son that he was put to death by his own brother. What is the effect upon the son?—instant action and pursuit of revenge? No: endless reasoning and hesitating—constant urging and solic-itation of the mind to act, and as constant an escape from action; ceaseless reproaches of himself for sloth and negligence, while the whole energy of his resolution evapo-rates in these reproaches. This, too, not from cowardice, for he is drawn as one of the bravest of his time—not from want of forethought or slowness of apprehension, for he sees through the very souls of all who surround him, but merely from that aver-sion to action, which prevails among such as have a world in themselves.

How admirable, too, is the judgement of the poet! Hamlet's own disordered fancy has not conjured up the spirit of his father; it has been seen by others: he is prepared by them to witness its reappearance, and when he does see it, Hamlet is not brought forward as having long brooded on the subject. The moment before the Ghost enters, Hamlet speaks of other matters: he mentions the coldness of the night, and observes that he has not heard the clock strike, adding, in reference to the custom of drinking, that it is

More honour'd in the breach than the observance.
Act I, Scene 4

Owing to the tranquil state of his mind, he indulges in some moral reflections. Afterwards, the Ghost suddenly enters.

HOR.   Look, my lord! it comes.
HAM. Angels and ministers of grace defend us!

The same thing occurs in 'Macbeth': in the dagger scene, the moment before the hero sees it, he has his mind applied to some indifferent matters; 'Go, tell thy mistress,' etc. Thus, in both cases, the preternatural° appearance has all the effect of abruptness, and the reader is totally divested of the notion that the figure is a vi-sion of a highly wrought imagination.

Here Shakespeare adapts himself so admirably to the situation—in other words, so puts himself into it—that, though poetry, his language is the very language of na-ture. No terms associated with such feelings can occur to us so proper as those which he has employed, especially on the highest, the most august, and the most awful sub-jects that can interest a human being in this sentient world. That this is no mere fancy, I can undertake to establish from hundreds, I might say thousands, of passages. No character he has drawn, in the whole list of his plays, could so well and fitly ex-press himself, as in the language Shakespeare has put into his mouth.

There is no indecision about Hamlet, as far as his own sense of duty is con-cerned; he knows well what he ought to do, and over and over again he makes up his mind to do it. The moment the players, and the two spies set upon him, have withdrawn, of whom he takes leave with a line so expressive of his contempt,

5

_____

preternatural: outside the laws of nature.

Ay so; good bye you.—Now I am alone,

he breaks out into a delirium of rage against himself for neglecting to perform the solemn duty he had undertaken, and contrasts the factitious° and artificial display of feeling by the player with his own apparent indifference;

> What's Hecuba to him, or he to Hecuba,
> That he should weep for her?

Yet the player did weep for her, and was in an agony of grief at her sufferings, while Hamlet is unable to rouse himself to action, in order that he may perform the command of his father, who had come from the grave to incite him to revenge:

> This is most brave!
> That I, the son of a dear father murder'd,
> Prompted to my revenge by heaven and hell,
> Must, like a whore, unpack my heart with words
> And fall a-cursing like a very drab,
> A scullion.
> Act II, Scene 2

It is the same feeling, the same conviction of what is his duty, that makes Hamlet exclaim in a subsequent part of the tragedy:

> How all occasions do inform against me,
> And spur my dull revenge! What is a man,
> If his chief good, and market of his time,
> Be but to sleep and feed? A beast, no more.

*   *   *   *   *

> I do not know
> Why yet I live to say—'this thing's to do,'
> Sith I have cause and will and strength and means
> To do't.
> Act IV, Scene 4

Yet with all this strong conviction of duty, and with all this resolution arising out of strong conviction, nothing is done. This admirable and consistent character, deeply acquainted with his own feelings, painting them with such wonderful power and accuracy, and firmly persuaded that a moment ought not to be lost in executing the solemn charge committed to him, still yields to the same retiring from reality, which is the result of having what we express by the terms, a world within himself.

Such a mind as Hamlet's is near akin to madness. Dryden has somewhere said, 10

> Great wit to madness nearly is allied,

and he was right; for he means by 'wit' that greatness of genius which led Hamlet to a perfect knowledge of his own character, which, with all strength of motive, was so weak as to be unable to carry into act his own most obvious duty.

With all this he has a sense of imperfectness, which becomes apparent when he is moralizing on the skull in the churchyard. Something is wanting to his completeness—something is deficient which remains to be supplied, and he is therefore

---

factitious: artificially produced.

described as attached to Ophelia. His madness is assumed, when he finds that witnesses have been placed behind the arras to listen to what passes, and when the heroine has been thrown in his way as a decoy.

Another objection has been taken by Dr Johnson, and Shakespeare has been taxed very severely. I refer to the scene where Hamlet enters and finds his uncle praying, and refuses to take his life, excepting when he is in the height of his iniquity. To assail him at such a moment of confession and repentance, Hamlet declares,

> Why, this is hire and salary, not revenge.
> Act III, Scene 4

He therefore forbears,° and postpones his uncle's death, until he can catch him in some act

> That has no relish of salvation in't.

This conduct, and this sentiment, Dr Johnson has pronounced to be so atrocious and horrible, as to be unfit to be put into the mouth of a human being. The fact, however, is that Dr Johnson did not understand the character of Hamlet, and censured accordingly: the determination to allow the guilty King to escape at such a moment is only part of the indecision and irresoluteness of the hero. Hamlet seizes hold of a pretext for not acting, when he might have acted so instantly and effectually: therefore, he again defers the revenge he was bound to seek, and declares his determination to accomplish it at some time,

> When he is drunk, asleep, or in his rage,
> Or in th' incestuous pleasures of his bed.

This, allow me to impress upon you most emphatically, was merely the excuse Hamlet made to himself for not taking advantage of this particular and favourable moment for doing justice upon his guilty uncle, at the urgent instance of the spirit of his father.

Dr Johnson farther states that in the voyage to England Shakespeare merely follows the novel as he found it, as if the poet had no other reason for adhering to his original; but Shakespeare never followed a novel because he found such and such an incident in it, but because he saw that the story, as he read it, contributed to enforce or to explain some great truth inherent in human nature. He never could lack invention to alter or improve a popular narrative; but he did not wantonly° vary from it when he knew that, as it was related, it would so well apply to his own great purpose. He saw at once how consistent it was with the character of Hamlet that after still resolving, and still deferring, still determining to execute, and still postponing execution, he should finally, in the infirmity of his disposition, give himself up to his destiny, and hopelessly place himself in the power and at the mercy of his enemies.   15

Even after the scene with Osrick, we see Hamlet still indulging in reflection, and hardly thinking of the task he has just undertaken: he is all dispatch and resolution, as far as words and present intentions are concerned, but all hesitation and irresolution, when called upon to carry his words and intentions into effect; so that, resolving to do everything, he does nothing. He is full of purpose, but void of that quality of mind which accomplishes purpose.

---

forbears: refrains.
wantonly: rebelliously.

Anything finer than this conception and working out of a great character is merely impossible. Shakespeare wished to impress upon us the truth that action is the chief end of existence—that no faculties of intellect, however brilliant, can be considered valuable, or indeed otherwise than as misfortunes, if they withdraw us from, or render us repugnant to action, and lead us to think and think of doing, until the time has elapsed when we can do anything effectually. In enforcing this moral truth, Shakespeare has shown the fullness and force of his powers: all that is amiable and excellent in nature is combined in Hamlet, with the exception of one quality. He is a man living in meditation, called upon to act by every motive human and divine, but the great object of his life is defeated by continually resolving to do, yet doing nothing but resolve.

QUESTIONS

1. Samuel Johnson wrote at some length of his criticisms of Shakespeare. In this brief excerpt, he states, as one of his chief objections to *Hamlet*, that "Hamlet is, through the whole play, rather an instrument than an agent." Drawing upon your own understanding of the character of Hamlet, what do you think Johnson means by this distinction?

2. Coleridge believes that Johnson has misunderstood Shakespeare. How does Coleridge's view of the character of Hamlet—and the dramatic function of his inability to act—differ from Johnson's?

3. What does Coleridge see as Shakespeare's central accomplishment in the creation of Hamlet? According to Coleridge, what does Johnson object to about Hamlet's voyage to England? How does Coleridge reply to that objection?

4. What is the final message, or philosophy, that Coleridge derives from Shakespeare's presentation of Hamlet? What, in his view, does Shakespeare uphold as the highest truth?

5. Referring to Johnson and Coleridge, explore your own understanding of Hamlet's character. Do you see his inability to act as a weakness or as evidence of his profound insight into the complexities of human nature? What would become of the play if Shakespeare had empowered Hamlet to act?

RESPONDING TO SHAKESPEARE'S
THE TEMPEST

Among modern critics of Shakespeare have been scholars such as the Bostonian Sylvan Barnet and the Canadian Northrup Frye. Frye has also become identified with a particular approach to psychological criticism that attaches great significance to cultural "archetypes" or clusters of psychological meaning that have become embodies in the best-known myths of our culture. (See Appendix A, "Psychoanalytic Criticism.")

Sylvan Barnet

from A SHORT GUIDE
TO SHAKESPEARE

Like some of the early comedies, which are ultimately indebted in varying degrees to late Greek and Roman comedy, *The Tem-*

pest has a shipwreck (compare *The Comedy of Errors* and *Twelfth Night*), an irritable father (compare Egeus in *A Midsummer Night's Dream*), and a character who more or less manipulates the plot (compare Rosalind in *As You Like It*). Like *The Comedy of Errors*, possibly Shakespeare's earliest comedy, it obeys the ancient traditions of unity of time and place: the play spans only a few hours and occurs in one locale. But despite these and other resemblances, the unusual amount of spectacle in *The Tempest* —and, more important, the serious tone—ties the play to Shakespeare's other last plays. The old conventions are here, but with new meanings: *The Tempest* is concerned with guilt and forgiveness, royal children, wonderful quasi-resurrections, and finally reunions. "These are not natural events, they strengthen/From strange, to stranger" (V.i.227–28). The pastoral° setting, implying the freshness and vitality of nature, prominent in parts of *Cymbeline* under the thin disguise of the Welsh countryside and in *The Winter's Tale* in the Bohemian shepherds' feast, is presented in *The Tempest* in the mysterious island—though this island means different things to different people: to one observer the grass looks "lush and lusty," but to another the grass is "indeed tawny." Pastoralism appears too in the masque° of Ceres and Juno and the dance of nymphs and harvesters. Again there is a shipwreck, and again the results prove beneficent. Those who are cast upon the island find, strangely, that their "garments, being, as they were, drenched in the sea, hold, notwithstanding, their freshness and glosses, being rather new-dyed than stained with salt water" (II.i.64–67). This note of renewal or regeneration is variously sounded throughout the play. Suffering brings renewal: "Some kinds of baseness/Are nobly undergone, and most poor matters/Point to rich ends" (III.i.2–4). Even Caliban, more a beast than a man, though acknowledged by Prospero as Prospero's educational failure, at last resolves to "seek for grace," thus suggesting that the most rudimentary kind of human being can make some moral progress. Not Caliban but Antonio, Prospero's brother, is the real failure, for Antonio's silence in the reconciliation scene suggests the limits of Prospero's power: the shipwreck manufactured by Prospero can only provide the opportunity for repentance, but it cannot force repentance, for a man has the freedom to remain recalcitrant if he wishes. Still, much goodness has been found:

> In one voyage
> Did Claribel her husband find at Tunis,
> And Ferdinand her brother found a wife
> Where he himself was lost; Prospero his dukedom
> In a poor isle; and all of us ourselves
> When no man was his own. (V.i.208–13)

The sense of providence,° strong in the last plays, is embodied in *The Tempest* chiefly by the magician Prospero, who raises and allays the storm that helps to regenerate and reconcile. (But Prospero, though in some ways godlike, is not God; before the play began he was so enraptured by "secret studies" that he shirked the cares of the state, and during the play he learns to pity and, apparently, to forego vengeance and to forgive—somewhat grudgingly—the wrongdoer.)

Because *The Tempest* is probably the last play that is entirely Shakespeare's (he seems to have had a collaborator for *Henry VIII* and *The Two Noble Kinsmen*), there is a tendency to see in Prospero, the magician who can call up visions but who at the

---

pastoral: natural.
masque: a dramatic entertainment.
providence: fate.

end breaks his staff and abjures his "potent art," a picture of Shakespeare putting down his pen and contemplating retirement to Stratford. There is no harm in such a reading as long as it does not reduce the play to an autobiographical scrap. It would be a pity to see in *The Tempest* only a farewell to the theater and to fail to notice that Prospero goes not to retirement but to the active role of ruling in Milan as the duke.

QUESTIONS

1. According to Barnet, what are the main features that *The Tempest* shares with Shakespeare's other late plays?
2. Barnet writes of the note of "renewal or regeneration" that is "variously sounded throughout the play," and suggests the link to the character of Prospero. What examples does Barnet give of the limits of Prospero's magic?
3. Compare the last paragraph of the Barnet excerpt to the last paragraph of Coleridge's lecture on *Hamlet*. What overall theme do both interpretations share in common? In what ways might one argue that Prospero and Hamlet represent two very different paths leading to the same final destination?

Northrop Frye

from INTRODUCTION TO *THE TEMPEST*

In the opening scene of *The Tempest* there is not only a sinking ship but a dissolving society. The storm, like the storm in *King Lear*, does not care that it is afflicting a king, and Gonzalo's protests about the deference due to royalty seem futile enough. But while everyone is unreasonable, we can distinguish Gonzalo, who is ready to meet his fate with some detachment and humor, from Antonio and Sebastian, who are merely screaming abuse at the sailors trying to save their lives. The boatswain, who comes so vividly to life in a few crisp lines, dominates this scene and leaves us with a strong sense of the superiority of personal character to social rank.

The shipwreck characters are then divided by Ariel into three main groups: Ferdinand; the Court Party proper; Stephano and Trinculo. Each goes through a pursuit of illusions, an ordeal, and a symbolic vision. The Court Party hunts for Ferdinand with strange shapes appearing and vanishing around them; their ordeal is a labyrinth of "forthrights and meanders" in which the founder with exhaustion, and to them is presented the vision of the disappearing banquet, symbolic of deceitful desires. There follows confinement and a madness which brings them to conviction of sin, self-knowledge, and repentance. Like Hamlet, Prospero delays revenge and sets up a dramatic action to catch the conscience of a king; like Lear on a small scale, Alonso is a king who gains in dignity by suffering. The search of Stephano and Trinculo for Prospero is also misled by illusions; their ordeal is a horse-pond and their symbolic vision the "trumpery" dangled in front of them. What happens to them is external and physical rather than internal and mental: they are hunted by hounds, filled with cramps, and finally reach what might be called a conviction of inadequacy. Probably they then settle into their old roles again: if a cold-blooded sneering assassin like Antonio can be forgiven, these amusing and fundamentally likeable rascals can be too. Ferdinand, being the hero, has a better time: he is led by Ariel's music to Miranda, undergoes the ordeal of the log pile, where he takes over Caliban's role as a bearer of wood, and his symbolic vision is that of the wedding masque.

The characters thus appear to be taking their appropriate places in a new kind of social order. We soon realize that the island looks different to different people— it is a pleasanter place to Gonzalo than to Antonio or Sebastian—and that each one is stimulated to exhibit his own ideal of society. At one end, Ferdinand unwillingly resigns himself to becoming King of Naples by the death of Alonso; at the other, Sebastian plots to become King of Naples by murdering Alonso. In between come Stephano, whose ambition to be king of the island is more ridiculous but somehow less despicable than Sebastian's, and Gonzalo, who dreams of a primitive golden age of equality and leisure, not very adequate as a social theory, but simple and honest, full of good nature and good will, like Gonzalo himself.

Into the midst of this society comes the islander Caliban, who is, on one level of nature, a natural man, a primitive whose name seems to echo the "cannibals" of Montaigne's famous essay.° He is not a cannibal, but his existence in the play forms an ironic comment on Gonzalo's reverie, which has been taken from a passage in the same essay. Caliban is a human being, as Ariel is not; and whatever he does, Prospero feels responsible for him: "this thing of darkness I/Acknowledge mine," Prospero says. Whether or not he is, as one hopeful critic suggested, an anticipation of Darwin's "missing link,"° he knows he is not like the apes "With foreheads villainous low"; his sensuality is haunted by troubled dreams of beauty; he is not taken in by the "trumpery," and we leave him with his mind on higher things. His ambitions are to kill Prospero and rape Miranda, both, considering his situation, eminently natural desires; and even these he resigns to Stephano, to whom he tries to be genuinely loyal. Nobody has a good word for Caliban: he is a born devil to Prospero, an abhorred slave to Miranda, and to others not obviously his superiors either in intelligence or virtue he is a puppy-headed monster, a mooncalf, and a plain fish. Yet he has his own dignity, and he is certainly no Yahoo, for all his ancient and fishlike smell. True, Shakespeare, like Swift, clearly does not assume that the natural man on Caliban's level is capable also of a reasonable life. But he has taken pains to make Caliban as memorable and vivid as any character in the play.

As a natural man, Caliban is *mere* nature, nature without nurture, as Prospero would say: the nature that manifests itself more as an instinctive propensity to evil than as the calculated criminality of Antonio and Sebastian, which is rationally corrupted nature. But to an Elizabethan poet "nature" had an upper level, a cosmic and moral order that may be entered through education, obedience to law, and the habit of virtue. In this expanded sense we may say that the whole society being formed on the island under Prospero's guidance is a natural society. Its top level is represented by Miranda, whose chastity and innocence put her, like her poetic descendant the Lady in *Comus*,° in tune with the harmony of a higher nature. The discipline necessary to live in this higher nature is imposed on the other characters

---

Montaigne: sixteenth-century French essayist, considered father of the essay form.

Darwin's "missing link": popular image of an ape-like evolutionary forebear to humankind.

Comus: Milton's poem in the *masque* genre, a pageant-like court drama of the Renaissance era, often in a fantasy or garden setting, and in Milton's case with a naive heroine.

by Prospero's magic. In Shakespeare's day the occult arts, especially alchemy, whose language Prospero is using at the beginning of the fifth act, were often employed as symbols of such discipline.

Shakespeare did not select Montaigne's essay on the cannibals as the basis for Gonzalo's "commonwealth" speech merely at random. Montaigne is no Rousseau: he is not talking about imaginary noble savages. He is saying that, despite their unconventional way of getting their proteins, cannibals have many virtues we have not, and if we pretend to greater virtues we ought to have at least theirs. They are not models for imitation; they are children of nature who can show us what is unnatural in our own lives. If we can understand that, we shall be wiser than the cannibals as well as wiser than our present selves. Prospero takes the society of Alonso's ship, immerses it in magic, and then sends it back to the world, its original ranks restored, but given a new wisdom in the light of which Antonio's previous behavior can be seen to be "unnatural." In the Epilogue Prospero hands over to the audience what his art has created, a vision of society permeated by the virtues of tolerance and forgiveness, in the form of one of the most beautiful plays in the world. And, adds Prospero, you might start practising those virtues by applauding the play.

The Tempest is not allegory, or a religious drama: if it were, Prospero's great "revels" speech would say, not merely that all earthly things will vanish, but that an eternal world will take their place. In a religious context, Prospero's renunciation of magic would represent the resigning of his will to a divine will, one that can do what the boatswain says Gonzalo cannot do, command the elements to silence and work the peace of the present. In Christianity the higher level of nature is God's original creation, from which man broke away with Adam's fall. It is usually symbolized by the music of the heavenly spheres, of which the one nearest us is the moon. The traditional conception of the magician was of one who could control the moon: this power is attributed to Sycorax, but it is a sinister power not associated with Prospero, whose magic and music belong to the sublunary world.

In the wedding masque of the fourth act and the recognition scene of the fifth, therefore, we find ourselves moving, not out of the world, but from an ordinary to a renewed and ennobled vision of nature. The masque shows the meeting of fertile earth and a gracious sky introduced the goddess of the rainbow, and leads up to a dance of nymphs representing the spring rains with reapers representing the autumnal harvest. The masque has about it the freshness of Noah's new world, after the tempest had receded and the rainbow promised that seedtime and harvest should not cease. There is thus a glimpse, as Ferdinand recognizes, of an Earthly Paradise, where, as in Milton's Eden,° there is no winter but spring and autumn "Danced hand in hand." In the last act, as in *The Winter's Tale*, there is a curious pretense that some of the characters have died and are brought back to life. The discovery of Ferdinand is greeted by Sebastian, of all people, as "A most high miracle." But the miracles are those of a natural, and therefore also a moral and intellectual, renewal of life. Some of Shakespeare's romances feature a final revelation through a goddess or oracle, both of which Alonso expects, but in *The Tempest* goddess and oracle are represented by Miranda and Ariel (in his speech at the banquet) respectively. Ariel is a spirit of nature, and Miranda is a natural spirit, in other words a human being, greeting the "brave new world" in all the good faith of innocence.

Milton's Eden: the Garden of Eden, setting for *Paradise Lost*, Milton's epic poem on the fall of humankind.

Hence, we distort the play if we think of Prospero as supernatural, just as we do if we think of Caliban as a devil. Prospero is a tempest-raiser like the witches in *Macbeth*, though morally at the opposite pole; he is a "white" magician. Anyone with Prospero's powers is an agent of fate, a cheating fate if evil, a benevolent fate or providence if motivated as he is. Great courage was required of all magicians, white or black, for the elemental spirits they controlled were both unwilling and malignant, and any sign of faltering meant terrible disaster. Ariel is loyal because of his debt of gratitude to Prospero, and because he is a very high-class spirit, too delicate to work for a black witch like Sycorax. But even he has a short memory, and has to be periodically reminded what his debt of gratitude is. Of the others Caliban says, probably with some truth, "They all do hate him / As rootedly as I." The nervous strain of dealing with such creatures shows up in Prospero's relations with human beings too; and in his tormenting of Caliban, in his lame excuse for making Ferdinand's wooing "uneasy," in his fussing over protecting Miranda from her obviously honorable lover, there is a touch of the busybody.

Still, his benevolence is genuine, and as far as the action of the play goes he seems an admirable ruler. Yet he appears to have been a remarkably incompetent Duke of Milan, and not to be promising much improvement after he returns. His talents are evidently dramatic rather than political, and he seems less of a practical magician plotting the discomfiture of his enemies than a creative artist calling spirits from their confines to enact his present fancies. It has often been thought that Prospero is a self-portrait of Shakespeare, and there may well be something in him of a harassed overworked actor-manager, scolding the lazy actors, praising the good ones in connoisseur's language, thinking up jobs for the idle, constantly aware of his limited time before his show goes on, his nerves tense and alert for breakdowns while it is going on, looking forward longingly to peaceful retirement, yet in the meantime having to go out and beg the audience for applause.

10

Prospero's magic, in any case, is an "art" which includes, in fact largely consists of, music and drama. Dramatists from Euripedes to Priandello have been fascinated by the paradox of reality and illusion in drama: the play is an illusion like the dream, and yet a focus of reality more intense than life affords. The action of *The Tempest* moves from sea to land, from chaos to new creation, from reality to realization. What seems at first illusory, the magic and music, becomes real, and the *Realpolitik°* of Antonio and Sebastian becomes illusion. In this island the quality of one's dreaming is an index of character. When Antonio and Sebastian remain awake plotting murder, they show that they are real dreamers, sunk in the hallucinations of greed. We find Stephano better company because his are the exuberant dreams of the stage boaster, and when he claims to have swum thirty-five leagues "off and on," when we know that he has floated to shore on a wine cask. Caliban's life is full of nightmare interspersed by strange gleams of ectasy. When the Court Party first came to the island "no man was his own"; they had not found their "proper selves." Through the mirages of Ariel, the mops and mows of the other spirits, the vanities of Prospero's art, and the fevers of madness, reality grows up in them from inside, in response to the fertilizing influence of illusion.

Few plays are so haunted by the passing of time as *The Tempest*: it has derived even its name from a word (*tempestas*) which means time as well as tempest. Tim-

---

Realpolitik: (German, after Bismarck) practical power politics.

ing was important to a magician: everything depended on it when the alchemist's project gathered to a head; astrologers were exact observers of time ("The very minute bids thee ope thine ear," Prospero says to Miranda), and the most famous of all stories about magicians, the story told in Greene's play *Friar Bacon and Friar Bungay*,° had the warning of "time is past" for its moral. The same preoccupation affects the other characters too, from the sailors in the storm to Ariel watching the clock for his freedom. The tide, which also waits for no man, ebbs and flow around this Mediterranean island in defiance of geography, and its imagery enters the plotting of Antonio and Sebastian and the grief of Ferdinand. When everyone is trying to make the most of his time, it seems strange that a melancholy elegy over the dissolving of all things in time should be the emotional crux of the play.

A very deliberate echo in the dialogue gives us the clue to this. Morally, *The Tempest* shows a range of will extending from Prospero's self-control, which includes his control of all the other characters, to the self-abandonment of Alonso's despair, when, crazed with guilt and grief, he resolves to drown himself "deeper than e'er plummet sounded." Intellectually, it shows a range of vision extending from the realizing of a moment in time, the zenith of Prospero's fortune, which becomes everyone else's zenith, too, to the sense of the nothingness of all temporal things. When Prospero renounces his magic, his "book" falls into the vanishing world, "deeper than did ever plummet sound." He has done what his art can do; he has held the mirror up to nature. Alonso and the rest are promised many explanations after the play is over, but we are left only with the darkening mirror, the visions fading and leaving not a rack behind. Once again the Epilogue reminds us that Prospero has used up all his magic in the play, and what more he can do depends on us.

It is not difficult to see, then, why so many students of Shakespeare, rightly or wrongly, have felt that *The Tempest* is in a peculiar sense Shakespeare's play, and that there is something in it of Shakespeare's farewell to his art. Two other features of it reinforce this feeling: the fact that no really convincing general source for the play has yet been discovered, and the fact that it is probably the last play wholly written by Shakespeare.

Whether a general source turns up or not, *The Tempest* is still erudite and allusive enough, full of echoes of literature, from the classics to the pamphlets of Shakespeare's own time. The scene of the play, an island somewhere between Tunis and Naples, suggests the journey of Aeneas from Carthage to Rome.° Gonzalo's identification of Tunis and Carthage, and the otherwise tedious business about "Widow Dido" in the second act, seems almost to be emphasizing the parallel. Like *The Tempest*, the *Aeneid* begins with a terrible storm and goes on to tell a story of wanderings in which a banquet with harpies figures prominently. Near the route of Aeneas' journey, according to Virgil, was the abode of Circe, of whom (at least in her Renaissance form) Sycorax is a close relative. Circe suggests Medea, whose speech in Ovid's *Metamorphoses* is the model for Prospero's renunciation speech. Echoes from the shipwreck of St. Paul (Ariel's phrase "Not a hair perished" recalls Acts xxvii, 34), from St Augustine, who also had associations with Carthage, and from Apuleius, with his interest in magic and initiation, are appropriate enough in

---

. . . *Bungay*: Renaissance drama about magicians and alchemists.
    Aeneas . . . Rome: References here are to *The Aeneid*, Virgil's Roman epic poem on the founding of Rome from mythic origins by the hero Aeneas, fleeing from fallen Troy.

such a play. Most of the traditional magical names of elemental spirits were of Hebrew origin, and "Ariel," a name occurring in the Bible (Isaiah xxix, I), was among them.° ¹⁵

The imagery of contemporary accounts of Atlantic voyages has also left strong traces in *The Tempest*, and seems almost to have been its immediate inspiration. One ship of a fleet that sailed across the ocean to reinforce Raleigh's Virginian colony in 1609 had an experience rather like that of Alonso's ship. It was driven aground on the Bermudas by a storm and given up for lost, but the passengers managed to survive the winter there and reached Virginia the following spring. William Strachey's account of this experience, *True Repertory of the Wracke*, dated July 15, 1610, was not published until after Shakespeare's death, and as Shakespeare certainly knew it, he must have read it in manuscript. Strachey's and a closely related pamphlet, Sylvester Jourdain's *Discovery of the Barmudas* (1610), lie behind Caliban's allusions to making dams for fish and to water with "berries" (i.e., cedar-berries) in it. Other details indicate Shakespeare's reading in similar accounts. Setebos is mentioned as a god ("divell") of the Patagonians in Richard Eden's *History of Travayle in the West and East Indies* (1577), and the curious "Bowgh, wawgh" refrain in Ariel's first song seems to be from a contemporary account of an Indian dance. It is a little puzzling why New World imagery should be so prominent in *The Tempest*, which really has nothing to do with the New World, beyond Ariel's reference to the "still-vexed Bermoothes" and a general, if vague, resemblance between the relations of Caliban to the other characters and that of the American Indians to the colonizers and drunken sailors who came to exterminate or enslave them.

However that may be, the dates of these pamphlets help to establish the fact that *The Tempest* is a very late play. A performance of it is recorded for November 1, 1611, in Whitehall, and it also formed part of the celebrations connected with the wedding of King James' daughter Elizabeth in the winter of 1612–13. The versification is also that of a late play, for *The Tempest* is written in the direct speaking style of Shakespeare's last period, the lines full of weak endings and so welded together that every speech is a verse paragraph itself, often very close in rhythm to prose, especially in the speeches of Caliban. One should read the verse as an actor would read it, attending to the natural stresses, of which there are usually four to a line, rather than the metre. Some critics have felt that a few lines are "unmetrical," but no line that can be easily spoken on the stage is unmetrical, and it is simple enough to find the four natural stresses in "You do *like*, my *son* in a *moved sort*," or (in octosyllabics) "*Earth's* increase, *foison plenty*." In such writing all the regular schematic forms of verse, rhyme, alliteration, assonance, and the like, fall into the background, peeping out irregularly through the texture:

> I will stand to, and feed;
> Although my last, no matter, since I feel
> The best is past. Brother, my lord the Duke,
> Stand to, and do as we.

In its genre, *The Tempest* shows a marked affinity with dramatic forms outside the normal range of tragedy and comedy. Among these is the masque: besides con-

---

Echoes . . . *Bible*: references to stories from various Roman and early Christian miraculous voyages and pilgrimages.

taining an actual masque, *The Tempest* is like the masque° in its use of elaborate stage machinery and music. The magician with his wand and mantle was a frequent figure in masques, and Caliban is like the "wild men" common in the farcical interludes known as antimasques. Another is the *commedia dell'arte*,° which was well known in England. Some of the sketchy plots of this half-improvised type of play have been preserved, and they show extraordinary similarities to *The Tempest*, especially in the Stephano-Trinculo scenes. *The Tempest* in short is a spectacular and operatic play, and when we thing of other plays like it, we are more apt to think of, say, Mozart's *Magic Flute* than of ordinary stage plays.

But more important than these affiliations is the position of *The Tempest* as the fourth and last of the great romances of Shakespeare's final period. In these plays Shakespeare seems to have distilled the essence of all his work in tragedy, comedy, and history, and to have reached the very bedrock of drama itself, with a romantic spectacle which is at once primitive and sophisticated, childlike and profound. In these plays the central structural principles of drama emerge with great clarity, and we become aware of the affinity between the happy endings of comedy and the rituals marking the great rising rhythms of life: marriage, springtime, harvest, dawn, and rebirth. In *The Tempest* there is also an emphasis on moral and spiritual rebirth which suggests rituals of initiation, like baptism or the ancient mystery dramas, as well as of festivity. And just as its poetic texture ranges from the simplicity of Ariel's incredibly beautiful songs to the haunting solemnity of Prospero's speeches, so we may come to the play on any level, as a fairy tale with unusually lifelike characters, or as an inexhaustibly profound drama that has influenced some of the most complex poems in the language, including Milton's *Comus* and Eliot's *The Waste Land*. However we take it, *The Tempest* is a play not simply to be read or seen or even studied, but possessed.

---

masque: a pageant-like court drama of the Renaissance era, as in Comus above.

commedia dell'arte: stylized popular Italian melodrama form, with stock fantasy characters, dating from the medieval era.

QUESTIONS

1. Frye argues against seeing Prospero as supernatural. What is the point he is trying to make?
2. What does Frye say about the role of Caliban in the play?
3. Find instances where Frye refers to prior works that may have influenced Shakespeare in the writing of *The Tempest*. Make a list. How does this affect your understanding of Shakespeare and his art?
4. How do Frye's conclusions about *The Tempest* differ from Sylvan Barnet's?

RESPONDING TO MOLIÈRE'S
THE MISANTHROPE

Joining the ranks of literary artists who have contributed to criticism of literature is the poet Richard Wilbur (see his poem in Chapter 27). In addition to his poetry and criticism, Wilbur has become known as a translator of plays, and his translation of Molière's play is the one included in Chapter 33.

Richard Wilbur

INTRODUCTION TO *THE MISANTHROPE*

The idea that comedy is a ritual in which society's laughter corrects individual extravagance is particularly inapplicable to *The Misanthrope*. In this play, society itself is indicted, and though Alceste's criticisms are indiscriminate, they are not unjustified. It is true that falseness and intrigue are everywhere on view; the conventions enforce a routine dishonesty, justice is subverted by influence, love is overwhelmed by calculation, and these things are accepted, even by the best, as "natural." The cold vanity of Oronte, Acaste, and Clitandre, the malignant hypocrisy of Arsinoé, the insincerity of Célimène, are to be taken as exemplary of the age, and Philinte's philosophic tolerance will not quite do in response to such a condition of things. The honest Éliante is the one we are most to trust, and this is partly because she sees that Alceste's intransigence A *quelque chose en soy de noble & d'héroïque.*

But *The Misanthrope* is not only a critique of society; it is also a study of impurity of motive in a critic of society. If Alceste has a rage for the genuine, and he truly has, it is unfortunately compromised and exploited by his vast, unconscious egotism. He is a jealous friend (*Je veux qu'on me distingue*), and it is Philinte's polite effusiveness toward another which prompts his attack on promiscuous civility. He is a jealous lover, and his "frankness" about Oronte's sonnet owes something to the fact that Oronte is his rival, and that the sonnet is addressed to Célimène. Like many humorless and indignant people, he is hard on everybody but himself, and does not perceive it when he fails his own ideal. In one aspect, Alceste seems a moral giant misplaced in a trivial society, having (in George Eliot's° phrase) "a certain spiritual grandeur ill-matched with the meanness of opportunity"; in another aspect, he seems an unconscious fraud who magnifies the petty faults of others in order to dramatize himself in his own eyes.

He is, of course, both at once: but the two impressions predominate by turns. A victim, like all around him, of the moral enervation of the times, he cannot consistently be the Man of Honor—simple, magnanimous, passionate, decisive, true. It is his distinction that he is aware of that ideal, and that he can fitfully embody it; his comic flaw consists in a Quixotic confusion of himself with the ideal, a willingness to distort the world for his own self-deceptive and histrionic purposes. Paradoxically, then, the advocate of true feeling and honest intercourse is the one character most artificial, most out-of-touch, most in danger of that nonentity and solitude which all, in the chattery, hollow world of this play, are fleeing. He must play-act continually in order to believe in his own existence, and he welcomes the fact or show of injustice as a dramatic cue. At the close of the play, when Alceste has refused to appeal his lawsuit and has spurned the hand of Célimène, one cannot escape the suspicion that his indignation is in great part instrumental, a desperate means of counterfeiting an identity.

George Eliot: pen name of Victorian novelist Mary Anne Evans.

Martin Turnell (whose book *The Classical Moment* contains a fine analysis of *The Misanthrope*) observes that those speeches of Alceste which ring most false are, as it were, parodies of "Cornelian *tirade*." To duplicate this parody-tragic effect in English it was clearly necessary to keep the play in verse, where it would be possible to control the tone more sharply, and to recall our own tragic tradition. There were other reasons, too, for approximating Molière's form. The constant of rhythm and thyme was needed, in the translation as in the original, for bridging great gaps between high comedy and farce, lofty diction and ordinary talk, deep character and shallow. Again, while prose might preserve the thematic structure of the play, other "musical" elements would be lost, in particular the frequently intricate arrangements of balancing half-lines, lines, couplets, quatrains, and sextets. There is no question that words, when dancing within such patterns, are not their prosaic selves, but have a wholly different mood and meaning.

Consider, finally, two peculiarities of the dialogue of the play: redundancy and logic. When Molière has a character repeat essentially the same thing in three successive couplets, it will sometimes have a very clear dramatic point; but it will always have the intention of stabilizing the idea against the movement of the verse, and of giving a specifically rhetorical pleasure. In a prose rendering, these latter effects are lost, and the passage tends to seem merely prolix. As for logic, it is a convention of *The Misanthrope* that its main characters can express themselves logically, and in the most complex grammar; Molière's dramatic verse, which is almost wholly free of metaphor, derives much of its richness from argumentative virtuosity. Here is a bit of logic from Arsinoé:

> Madame, l'Amitié doit sur tout éclater
> Aux choses qui le plus nous peuvent importer:
> Et comme il n'en est point de plus grande importance
> Que celles de l'Honneur et de la Bienséance,
> Je viens par un avis qui touche vostre honneur
> Témoigner l'amitié que pour vous a mon Coeur.° 5

In prose it might come out like this: "Madam, friendship should most display itself when truly vital matters are in question: and since there are no things more vital than decency and honor, I have come to prove my heartfelt friendship by giving you some advice which concerns your reputation." Even if that were better rendered, it would still be plain that Molière's logic loses all its baroque exuberance in prose; it sounds lawyerish; without rhyme and verse to phrase and emphasize the steps of its progression, the logic becomes obscure like Congreve's,° not crystalline and followable as it was meant to be.

For all these reasons, rhymed verse seemed to me obligatory. The choice did not preclude accuracy, and what follows is, I believe, a line-for-line verse translation quite as faithful as any which have been done in prose. I hasten to say that I am boasting only of patience; a translation may, alas, be faithful on all counts, and still lack quality.

One word about diction. This is a play in which French aristocrats of 1666 converse about their special concerns, and employ the moral and philosophical terms peculiar to their thought. Not all my words, therefore, are strictly modern; I had for

---

. . . *Coeur*: Compare with *The Misanthrope* III.v.4–9.
Congreve: eighteenth-century British playwright of elaborately plotted comedies of manners.

example to use "spleen" and "phlegm"; but I think that I have avoided the zounds sort of thing, and that at best the diction mediates between then and now, suggesting no one period. There are occasional vulgarities, but for these there is precedent in the original, Molière's people being aristocrats and therefore not genteel.

If this English version is played or read aloud, the names should be pronounced in a fashion *roughly* French, without nasal and uvular agonies. Damon should be *dah-MOAN*, and for rhythmic convenience Arsinoé should be *ar-SIN-oh-eh*.

QUESTIONS

1. What does Wilbur suggest undermines Alceste's criticism of the world around him? What is Wilbur's assessment of Alceste's character?
2. What decisions did Wilbur make as a translator and why did he make them?

RESPONDING TO CHEKHOV'S *THE CHERRY ORCHARD*

Chekhov as a founding figure in the development of Realistic drama has been translated into nearly every European language and has attracted an international following of drama critics. Here is a translated piece from the German critic Siegfried Melchinger.

Siegfried Melchinger

ON *THE CHERRY ORCHARD*

The time is that in which Chekhov is writing, 1903.

The cherry orchard is part of an estate of a member of the old aristocracy. For years, the lady who owns it has lived abroad. Now her return is awaited. She has used up the money on which she has lived since the death of her husband, who was an attorney, and of her little son—she lost them both in the same year. The estate, on which her brother lives, is overloaded with debts and is soon to be auctioned off. And now a practical man of the world of business, a peasant's son who has achieved some wealth and position, tells the noble masters how they can rescue themselves financially. He suggests that the land of the estate be parceled into lots, and that villas be built on them. Its position by the river and near the railroad station is favorable. If this is done, the rents would yield a good income. The old manor house, of course, would have to be torn down, and the cherry orchard felled.

But that very idea makes the proposal unbearable. There must be another way out! There is a rich aunt. Perhaps, the daughter will marry into money. But on the day of the auction all these bubbles burst. The estate is sold. After the debts are paid a little money is left over, but it will not last long.

The rich, new owner is the man who proposed the plan for putting the estate back on its feet: now he himself will realize it. While the old masters take farewell forever of the manor house and the cherry orchard, the first blows of the ax are falling.

Stage time can, to quote Chekhov, not feign real time. Stage time has its own reality; it changes the character of real time, its constant passing away, when it becomes material that is used in a play with a beginning and an end. And so the problem of time has to be dealt with anew in every play. The concept of time will change according to a play's theme. As the stage time in *The Sea Gull* was designed to flow from a particular event in a kind of progression, with increasing intervals between the acts, so the stage time in *The Three Sisters* relates to the transitory quality of life, to aging, to saying goodbye to youth, to the withering of hope. In *The Cherry Orchard* Chekhov attempts his most ambitious endeavor, for the concept of time is the concept of history. Here the theme is the end of an era and the beginning of a new one: the moment of changing epochs. In this moment which is today—that is, Chekhov's present—yesterday and tomorrow collide. The change is irrevocable, whatever it may be called: progress, destruction, fate, or history. 5

Just as the stage has its own stage time, so it also presents, of course, not real people but stage characters. Just as real life can only be used as material and theme in stage time, so stage characters can only reflect the effect that historical change has upon the people who live through it. Chekhov chooses the human beings from whom he models his characters from the wealth of his life's experiences. He himself is one of his sources, though that is never obvious in Chekhov's writing. He chooses people for their suitability to his theme, and he collects and sets them in a particular place that allows the theme—which is change in *The Cherry Orchard*—to best be presented.

The stage reality does not simply stand for reality. Rather, it has been chosen for its demonstration value, its applicable material, for real people can provide the characters only the texture of their lives. Chekhov's contemporaries were right when they (like Gorky) accused him of "flogging realism to death." But they were wrong when they interpreted his new method of presenting reality on the stage as "symbolistic." The Cherry Orchard was not a symbol to Chekhov. But it is a symbol to the characters in his play who have made it into one.

Twice in the play, in dramatically heightened moments, a mysterious sound is heard: "A distant tone, as if out of the sky, like the sound of a breaking string." Chekhov said that he had heard such a sound as a boy on the shores of the Don, and that it came from a pail falling to the ground in a coal mine. The sound in itself is not mystical; but its eeriness startles people who then make it into a mystery. Therefore Chekhov utilized, for his own ends, the possibility that such a sound can exist and have this effect.

The theme of *The Cherry Orchard* requires that the persons represented in it are characterized to reflect their attitudes toward the changing times. Yet, according to Chekhov himself, these attitudes only have validity when they truly express individual and societal limitations. Each of the characters is what his station of birth destined him to be and also what he himself has become. This truism cannot be ignored when we want to understand Chekhov's aim of presenting a theme on the stage in order to get the audience to perceive the truth. The spectator, of course, is supposed to seek for truth not only in the attitude of each of the characters toward the changing times, but also in the distinctive behavior which each character responds to the same event with. Chekhov's objectivity draws the audience's attention to the fact that an irrevocable process that cannot be stopped, regardless of one's positive or negative attitude toward it (depending on how oneself is being affected by it), has a different impact on different people. And this must be kept in mind if the whole truth is to be perceived. This means that it was Chekhov's intention not to represent the change from a particular old to a particular new time but rather to demonstrate how changing times in general affects people. This is how the Greeks and how Shakespeare understood the meaning of history. Chekhov's particular daring lies in his use of this own time, as material for projecting this theme.

A Soviet literary historian called *The Cherry Orchard* Chekhov's "most optimistic play." One could, however, just as well interpret it as his most pessimistic play, as Stanislavsky had done when Chekhov said that he "had ruined his play." One can sentimentalize the play by identifying with the mourning of some of the characters for the decline of their age. Or one can ideologize it through identification with the views of those characters who presage the new times. Both attitudes are wrong. It is clear that Chekhov himself shared neither the mourning of the first nor the hope of the second. Doubtless, in private he had his own definite views. (And it is certain that at the time when *The Cherry Orchard* was written, two years before the revolution of 1905, he considered revolution in Russia irrevocable and desirable.) 10

But as a dramatist Chekhov was faithful to his intention not of giving a solution to a question but rather of precisely formulating a question so that the audience, "the jurors," could make their own decisions. Whether this judgment was to be like that of Stanislavsky or like that of the quoted Soviet scholar was something Chekhov wished to leave open. He once said that a writer should not write for the future, for he does not know it, and that the truth can only be said about what one knows—the present. He insisted that only the case was to be presented on the stage, not the judgment.

The choice of the play's characters is proof of this objectivity. For not only is the change of a certain yesterday to a certain tomorrow brought before our eyes but also a change of day before yesterday to yesterday, and from tomorrow to day after tomorrow. Feers, the aged servant, looms like a fossil of the day before yesterday in the play's world of Chekhov's present day. No one but Chekhov could have created this character as he is—touching, despite his incredible narrow-mindedness. For Feers the days of feudalism were and are still the golden era. "Before the great misfortune came upon us, everything was better," he once says. And what is this "misfortune"? The abolition of serfdom, in 1861, is what Feers means, who had been a serf himself until that year. But what about Feers's counterpart, the manservant who represents the day after tomorrow? Uprightness here is mirrored in cynicism, and that perhaps again in uprightness. At the end of the play the aged Feers, the man of the day before yesterday, stays behind, forgotten by the people of yesterday as if he were a piece of the house that is about to be torn down.

The tomorrow of *The Cherry Orchard* is not the revolution but the era of capitalism: Lopahin, the new owner, is a bourgeois with the nature of a peasant. Part of the material out of which this figure is forged comes from Chekhov himself: "I still remember when I was a boy of fifteen, my father, who is now dead, he then had a small shop here in the village, hit me so hard in the face with his fist that the blood streamed from my nose." Chekhov wrote: "How can one be against progress if one lived through a time when people were flogged and is now experiencing the present time when the floggings have been stopped?"

Chekhov upbraided Stanislavsky for wanting to present Lopahin as a despicable person: "He is a decent man, in every sense of the word. He strives to behave well and he is intelligent. Don't forget that he is loved by Varya, who is a serious and religious girl." Only the people of yesterday and those who mourn with them for the passing of their time can think of him as brutal. His most individual attribute is shyness. He, the successful man, feels small, even paltry, when he faces a woman. Surely he feels, though he does not admit it to himself, something like love for the grand lady from whom he takes the estate. And there is a note of defiance in his conduct, although the project he will now undertake was originally conceived by him for her benefit: "I have bought the estate on which my father and my grandfather were slaves, and not even good enough to be let into the kitchen."

The characters who belong to the time of tomorrow are a mixed group. There is Varya, who must always have some work to do, who does not trust that she can take her fate into her own hands. She is, in Chekhov's words, a religious crybaby. Then there is the bookkeeper, who always stumbles over his own legs and allows his girl to be snatched away under his very nose. 15

The characters of the time of the day after tomorrow are similarly varied. Their main speaker is Trofimov, the perennial student. Those who look upon the play as optimistic claim that his lines reflect Chekhov's views. Surely there is truth in this position. "We must work" in order to reach the goal. That, in order to do so, the cherry orchard has to be sacrificed is of no importance to him. Surely it is not quite justified to accuse Trofimov of idleness. The reason that he has been twice expelled from the university is undoubtedly political. Yet his ideology seems curious when he maintains that he has no time for banalities: "We are above love!" For it is understood that Anya (the daughter of the lady who owns the estate), who repeats his ideas, is not in love with them but with Trofimov himself.

Yet Trofimov is the capitalist's true adversary, and he has his great scene when he refuses to accept money from him. "I am a free person. And everything you hold so high and dear, all of you, rich men and beggars alike, doesn't have the least bit of power over me. . . . Mankind is marching toward the most sublime truth, toward the most sublime happiness, and I am marching among its first columns!" Will mankind in its sublime happiness "be above love"? Anya, who wants to work toward this "new, marvelous world," proves the opposite.

There is also the young manservant Yasha, quite a man, who takes what he fancies and discards what he no longer wants—he too is a man of the day after tomorrow.

In the foreground, a soft light falls upon the people of yesterday, who veil themselves in their illusions. They gush enthusiastically and dream and float like ghosts through their lives. What are they to each other? What do they do for one another? How do they look when they take off their beautiful masks?

There is Gaev, the aristocratic brother of the lady who owns the estate, a charming, affable parasite, "a good-for-nothing" as the old servant calls him, a fifty-year-old who has never done any serious work until the estate's ruin forces him to take a job at a bank. As he says ironically, he now will become a capitalist. 20

Foremost among the people of yesterday is Ranevskaya herself, the owner of the cherry orchard, whom everyone, even Trofimov the revolutionary, idolizes. Wherever she appears, Ranevskaya is the central figure. It is as if Chekhov, feature by feature, slowly lets us perceive the truth about her. All our compassion turns to her when we hear that she had left the cherry orchard (and Russia) in utter despair after she lost, one after the other, her husband and her only son. Now she admits that she had been unfaithful to her husband, who had consequently become an alcoholic. She becomes convinced that the child's death was her punishment. But has she learned a lesson from this? Her brother speaks harshly of her, saying that she is depraved, that the life she has led in Paris and on the Riviera cannot be called anything but dissolute, however much she may sentimentalize it. There is no doubt—and Chekhov is discreet enough to communicate this by intimation—that the young manservant, whom she has brought home and who will accompany her when she returns to Paris, where she goes with her last bit of money, is more than just an attendant.

In the last act, Lopahin, the peasantlike bourgeois, says, "We play our parts before each other and life goes on." And so it always will be: one lives and one play-acts life. One is happy to see the cherry orchard again and one playacts this happiness. One sits and dreams on an evening in the garden and talks past the others. Each is talking of himself and, at bottom, for himself. And one plays the games at hand: the evening the estate is to be auctioned off, there is a ball! And so they dance atop their own ruin. Always they are at the border of the grotesque, yes, even the absurd. One of the characters has the habit of constantly marking billiard moves. Alongside the young manservant, who puffs on the biggest cigars, there goes the one who always stumbles over his own legs. And one of the women runs through the house carrying a big bunch of keys; she is so busy that she accomplishes nothing. And then there is the most peculiar of all the characters, the loneliest of them all, one who playacts to herself that she means something to each of the others when she entertains them with artistic magic tricks. During the ball, before the news that the estate has been auctioned off arrives, these scenes take on the character of the ghostly.

Mood and atmosphere never are indicated for their own sakes. It is not an atmospheric play, but a cool and cruel one (as Gorky has said of another Chekhov play). Nevertheless, despite this coolness and this cruelty, sympathy and laughter are aroused in the audience. Chekhov became irate when it was reported to him during rehearsals that the play aroused much weeping: "But where are these characters who are weeping? It is only Varya, who is by nature a crybaby."

In the first act, in the gray light of dawn, the windows are opened and we see the blossoming cherry orchard. When the sun rises, and we hear a shepherd's flute in the distance, nothing could be more deceptive than this idyllic scene, set up only to be destroyed. Similarly, in the second act, the characters "all meditative and thoughtful," enjoy the summer evening, while the dialogue makes it increasingly clear that most of them are estranged from each other, and that even those who have paired off know and want to know nothing about each other. In the third act—now fall has come—this double meaning of the scenic conception becomes quite clear: what a cruel invention is this ball at the abyss. In the fourth act the tempo of departure and breakup, blended with sounds backstage, drives the people, who are freezing in the bitter-cold winter (the house is not heated), off the stage. Finally only the aged, forgotten Feers is left behind.

And now is heard for the second time the sound of the snapping string. It recalls the eerie moment in which it was heard before, at the end of the second act, when all those who now are gone were daydreaming and pensive. In addition, in that earlier scene there suddenly popped up a figure who has no particular relevance to the play: a stranger, a tramp, a drunk, who asks for the way to the station, and begs for a small coin "for a hungry Russian." He receives a gold piece and goes off, humming a volga song.

There is nothing sinister or gruesome about this tramp. But at his appearance, the people are startled and frightened, just as they are by the strange sound that "came out of the sky."

Fearfulness and dread: this is the basic atmosphere of a *comédie humaine* set between two epochs in time.

The premiere of *The Cherry Orchard*, the only one Chekhov attended after the failure of *The Sea Gull* in Saint Petersburg, took place on January 17, 1904, six months before his death.

Translated by Edith Tarcov

QUESTIONS

1. What is Melchinger's explanation of Chekhov's use of "stage time"? How does he explain the playwright's understanding of destined "stations of birth"?
2. How does Melchinger position himself with regard to the question of whether Chekhov's play is optimistic or pessimistic?
3. Look carefully at Melchinger's discussion of capitalism and the revolution. Find out what was happening in Russia during the last years of Chekhov's life. How does Melchinger understand Chekhov's political position? Is there evidence to support a contrary interpretation? Explain.

USING SOURCES IN WRITING
ABOUT A PLAY

We have seen student Richard Case discover and present his own interpretation of Ibsen's *A Doll's House* in Chapter 36. In writing his paper, Richard relied on his own insights and cited lines from the play where he needed to support or illustrate his argument. His essay is an example of one kind of approach.

Interested as instructors are in developing skills of reading and independent analysis in their students, they are also interested in your response to other critics, and in your ability to make responsible use of sources to integrate the views of scholars and other readers into a presentation of your own.

Schemes for Integrating and Synthesizing Critics' Views with Yours

There are different ways to proceed. You can, for instance, locate an array of critical perspectives and use the essay as a way of sampling what different critics have to say about a work. The important thing to remember when writing an essay of this kind is that you need to find a frame that can accommodate the various views of others. You need a structure. One possible approach is the chronological, as in this example:

```
Looking at the public reception of Samuel Beckett's
plays, we find that in many cases a strong negative
prejudice had to be overcome before their dramatic
```

Responding to Plays

value could be acknowledged. The first
performances of <u>Waiting for Godot</u> were greeted on
many sides with outraged ridicule. Characteristic of
this response was Burnwood Greene's review of the
opening night: "Seldom in the colorful history of
theatrical disasters have we been forced to add the
insult of boredom to the injury of misshapen vision"
(<u>Cahiers</u>, 74). As theatergoers became accustomed to
Beckett's innovations, however, there was an increased recognition of the play's visionary qualities. Clare Quilty's important evaluation in the
<u>Spectator</u> shows a willingness to grant the playwright
a greater license. "Watching Beckett, even if we are
uncomfortable, we are forced to concede that here is
something new under the sun" (<u>Gatherings</u>, 15).

This writer might then go on to establish a kind of chronological survey of responses
to Beckett's revolutionary play, moving from the initial negative assessments to the
eventual proclamations of triumph and innovative importance. The reader would
be taken on a historical tour that would also represent a panorama of critical reactions to the dramatist's work.

A similar organizational mode, while not strictly chronological, might gather
views from different periods and then arrange them to reflect a comparable spectrum
of responses, as in this sample:

A great artist invariably pays for his innovations,
at least at first. Some continue to pay, even as
they also reap certain critical benefits. Samuel
Beckett is a case in point. From the first he has
been hounded by angry incomprehension. At the very
same time he has basked in the adoration of admiring
fans. Cedric Smelling's verdict of "rampant idiocy!"
(Smelling, 147) was counterbalanced by his co-editor
Simon Hedring's cry of "Halleluja!" (<u>Playdate</u>, 62). A
closer look will show that these responses are shaped
by conflicting beliefs about the rules of dramatic
art, and several more mixed evaluations make it clear
that the business is not as simple as an either/or.

Knowing and Showing Where You Stand

You may wish to present a far more focused approach, using one, possibly two, critical voices alongside your own. Essential, then, is that you have a clear idea where

you stand. Know your position before you begin, otherwise you face a great risk of slipping back and forth from one view to another without giving your reader any sense of center. You need not state your view directly, however. Often it is more effective to let your critics argue the sides and to establish your position through your way of presenting the debate:

> Thus, while Baker remains bound to the dark view,
> seeing Beckett as "a despairing soul with his eye
> on the inferno within" (62), Mellencamp finds a way
> both to incorporate Baker's position <u>and</u> transcend
> it. He finds evidence, especially in the later
> plays, of "a force that knows joy all the more pow-
> erfully for having tasted the fruit of meaningless-
> ness" (<u>Heroes</u>, 138). His case is the more convincing
> one for he is prepared to point out the very places
> in these plays where darkness is overcome by some
> unexpected recognition of relief.

Writing about drama using sources is finally no different from writing about other literary genres (see the discussions in Chapter 10 on "Writing about Fiction Using Sources," and in Chapter 24 on "Writing about Poetry Using Sources"). The procedures for documentation follow guidelines established by the Modern Language Association, with parenthetical citation and an alphabetical listing of works cited at the end of the paper (see Appendix B).

Referring to Lines from a Play

Classic and modern plays are available in many different editions, and international plays in different translations. When you are citing lines from a play—a play by Shakespeare, say—identify the edition you are using and indicate act, scene, and line either by using arabic numerals (2.2.45–62) or the more traditional large and small roman numerals for act and scene (II.ii.45–62) For less standardized classic or contemporary plays, identify the edition, the translator, and the act or scene along with the speaker of the lines you are referring to.

Casebook

The Evolving Canon
in a Video Age

The "canon debate," as most people are by now aware, is a major controversy in the education community. The question of what texts should constitute the basis of college and university curricula has sharply polarized administrators and professors. On one side are the conservatives and traditionalists who uphold the centrality of the so-called "great works" that have long formed the basis of the humanist curriculum. Arrayed against them are the reformers who contend that the traditional canon reflects the exclusive ideology of "dead white males," and no longer addresses the needs of a multiculturally diverse student population. They urge that the curricula be opened to more works by women, African Americans, Hispanics, gays, and other formerly marginalized constituencies. The traditional-canon faction protests that this would result in the hijacking of scholarship by the political agendas of special-interest groups.

The articles and excerpts that follow present a spectrum of views on the canon question. They range from the traditionalist positions voiced by T. S. Eliot and Irving Howe to the more reform-minded statements by writers like Henry Louis Gates, Jr. and Todd Gitlin. The reader is sure to be provoked as well as irritated—perhaps even driven to formulate a personal response.

The canon controversy is, in one sense, a consequence of great demographic shifts in American education. In the past few decades our colleges and universities have seen a tremendous influx of students from minority cultures. Alongside this influx has come the social empowerment of these groups—women, African Americans, Native Americans, gays, and so on. That this new student population should demand greater representation and relevance from curricula is inevitable. And that the powers that be should oppose such changes only testifies to the deep ideological differences that divide our melting-pot culture.

But ideology aside, the canon controversy can also be seen from another angle. For no less important than the demographic shifts in our culture is our wholesale transformation from a print-based to an electronics-based society. A generation of students is now growing up in video environments that have little or nothing to do with what their parents experienced. The power and importance of the book, the printed text, is being contested. Fewer and fewer students read books and magazines of their own accord. Their main contact with the printed page takes place in the classroom. More than ever, then, the works in the curriculum will prove formative—not only for the information they contain, but for the values and biases they promote. Seen in this light, the struggle over the canon is a struggle for the hearts and minds of the young. Small wonder that the debate is so intense.

I have included in this inventory of opinions and positions an excerpt from an article by critic Katha Pollitt. It seems to me that once the pros and cons have been set out—assented to, rebutted—there is room left over for a few pages of clear common sense. Pollitt understands to what extent the canon issue obscures what might be a larger issue still—the radically diminished place of reading in our culture. In a country of real readers, she writes, who are "voluntary, active, self-determined readers, a debate like the current one over the canon would not be taking place." Perhaps if more energy were devoted to fostering the reading art and less to squabbling over what should be read, we would all be better off.

I round out the section with a reflection of my own on the incursion of new technologies into the once stable order of the printed word. The essay is meant not as a last word, but as a provocation.

T. S. Eliot

from WHAT IS A CLASSIC?

If there is one word on which we can fix, which will suggest the maximum of what I mean by the term 'a classic', it is the word *maturity*. I shall distinguish between the universal classics like Virgil, and the classic which is only such in relation to the other literature in its own language, or according to the view of life of a particular period. A classic can only occur when a civilization is mature; when a language and a literature are mature; and it must be the work of a mature mind. It is the importance of that civilization and of that language, as well as the comprehensiveness of the mind of the individual poet which gives the universality. To define *maturity* without assuming that the hearer already knows what it means, is almost impossible: let us say then, that if we are properly mature, as well as educated persons, we can recognize maturity in a civilization and in a literature, as we do in the other human beings whom we encounter. To make the meaning of maturity really apprehensible—indeed, even to make it acceptable—to the immature, is perhaps impossible. But if we are mature we either recognize maturity immediately, or come to know it on more intimate acquaintance. No reader of Shakespeare, for instance, can fail to recognize, increasingly as he himself grows up, the gradual ripening of Shakespeare's mind: even a less developed reader can perceive the rapid development of Elizabethan literature and drama as a whole, from early Tudor° crudity to the plays of Shakespeare, and perceive a decline in the work of Shakespeare's successors. We can also observe, upon a little conversance, that the plays of Christopher Marlowe° exhibit a greater maturity of mind and of style than the plays which Shakespeare wrote at the same age: it is interesting to speculate whether, if Marlowe had lived as long as Shakespeare, his development

---

Tudor: the early English Renaissance era and its rough-hewn, robust style.
Christopher Marlowe: Tudor dramatist, contemporary of Shakespeare.

would have continued at the same pace. I doubt it: for we observe some minds maturing earlier than others, and we observe that those which mature very early do not always develop very far. I raise this point as a reminder, first that the value of maturity depends upon the value of that which matures, and second, that we should know when we are concerned with the maturity of individual writers, and when with the relative maturity of literary periods. A writer who individually has a more mature mind may belong to a less mature period than another, so that in that respect his work will be less mature. The maturity of a literature is the reflection of that of the society in which it is produced: an individual author—notably Shakespeare and Virgil—can do much to develop his language: but he cannot bring that language to maturity unless the work of his predecessors has prepared it for his final touch. A mature literature, therefore, has a history behind it: a history, that is not merely a chronicle, an accumulation of manuscripts and writings of this kind and that, but an ordered though unconscious progress of a language to realize its own potentialities within its own limitations.

It is to be observed, that a society, and a literature, like an individual human being, do not necessarily mature equally and concurrently in every respect. The precocious child is often, in some obvious ways, childish for his age in comparison with ordinary children. Is there any one period of English literature to which we can point as being fully mature, comprehensively and in equilibrium? I do not think so: and, as I shall repeat later, I hope it is not so. We cannot say that any individual poet in English has in the course of his life become a more mature man than Shakespeare: we cannot even say that any poet has done so much, to make the English language capable of expressing the most subtle thought or the most refined shades of feeling. Yet we cannot but feel that a play like Congreve's° *Way of the World* is in some way more mature than any play of Shakespeare's: but only in this respect, that it reflects a more mature society—that is, it reflects a greater maturity of *manners*. The society for which Congreve wrote was, from our point of view, coarse and brutal enough: yet it is nearer to ours than the society of the Tudors: perhaps for that reason we judge it the more severely. Nevertheless, it was a society more polished and less provincial: its mind was shallower, its sensibility more restricted; it has lost some promise of maturity but realized another. So to maturity of *mind* we must add maturity of *manners*.

The progress towards maturity of language is, I think, more easily recognized and more readily acknowledged in the development of prose, than in that of poetry. In considering prose we are less distracted by individual differences in greatness, and more inclined to demand approximation towards a common standard, a common vocabulary and a common sentence structure: it is often, in fact, the prose which departs the farthest from these common standards, which is individual to the extreme, that we are apt to denominate 'poetic prose'. At a time when England had already accomplished miracles in poetry, her prose was relatively immature, developed sufficiently for certain purposes but not for others: at that same time, when the French language had given little promise of poetry as great as that in English, French prose was much more mature than English prose. You have only to compare any Tudor writer with Montaigne°—and Montaigne himself, as a stylist, is only a precursor, his style not ripe enough to fulfil the French requirements for the classic.

William Congreve: English dramatist of the late seventeenth and early eighteenth centuries, writing comedy comparable with that of Molière (see Chapter 33).

Michel de Montaigne: early French essayist of the Renaissance era.

Our prose was ready for some tasks before it could cope with others: a Malory° could come long before a Hooker,° a Hooker before a Hobbes,° and a Hobbes before an Addison.° Whatever difficulties we have in applying this standard to poetry, it is possible to see that the development of a classic prose is the development towards a *common style*. By this I do not mean that the best writers are indistinguishable from each other. The essential and characteristic differences remain: it is not that the differences are less, but that they are more subtle and refined. To a sensitive palate the difference between the prose of Addison and that of Swift° will be as marked as the difference between two vintage wines to a connoisseur. What we find, in a period of classic prose, is not a mere common convention of writing, like the common style of newspaper leader writers, but a community of taste. The age which precedes a classic age, may exhibit both eccentricity and monotony: monotony because the resources of the language have not yet been explored, and eccentricity because there is yet no generally accepted standard—if, indeed, that can be called eccentric where there is no centre. Its writing may be at the same time pedantic and licentious. The age following a classic age, may also exhibit eccentricity and monotony: monotony because the resources of the language have, for the time at least, been exhausted, and eccentricity because originality comes to be more valued than correctness. But the age in which we find a common style, will be an age when society has achieved a moment of order and stability, of equilibrium and harmony; as the age which manifests the greatest extremes of individual style will be an age of immaturity or an age of senility.

Maturity of language may naturally be expected to accompany maturity of mind and manners. We may expect the language to approach maturity at the moment when men have a critical sense of the past, a confidence in the present, and no conscious doubt of the future. In literature, this means that the poet is aware of his predecessors, and that we are aware of the predecessors behind his work, as we may be aware of ancestral traits in a person who is at the same time individual and unique. The predecessors should be themselves great and honoured: but their accomplishment must be such as to suggest still undeveloped resources of the language, and not such as to oppress the younger writers with the fear that everything that can be done has been done, in their language. The poet, certainly, in a mature age, may still obtain stimulus from the hope of doing something that his predecessors have not done: he may even be in revolt against them, as a promising adolescent may revolt against the beliefs, the habits and the manners of his parents; but, in retrospect, we can see that he is also the continuer of their traditions, that he preserves essential family characteristics, and that his difference of behaviour is a difference in the circumstances of another age. And, on the other hand, just as we sometimes observe men whose lives are overshadowed by the fame of a father or grandfather, men of whom any achievement of which they are capable appears comparatively insignificant, so a late age of poetry may be consciously impotent to compete with its distinguished ancestry. We meet poets of this kind at the end of any age, poets with a sense of the past only, or alternatively, poets whose hope of

---

Thomas Malory: late medieval translator/composer of King Arthur stories.
Richard Hooker: Tudor theologian whose essay treatises were admired for their prose style.
Thomas Hobbes: seventeenth-century English philosopher known for a strong prose style.
Joseph Addison: eighteenth-century English essayist known for elegant wit.
Jonathan Swift: eighteenth-century English writer and satirist, author of *Gulliver's Travels*, contemporary of Addison.

the future is founded upon the attempt to renounce the past. The persistence of literary creativeness in any people, accordingly, consists in the maintenance of an unconscious balance between tradition in the larger sense—the collective personality, so to speak, realized in the literature of the past—and the originality of the living generation.

Irving Howe

from THE VALUE OF THE CANON

Let me now mention some of the objections one hears in academic circles to the views I have put down here, and then provide brief replies.

By requiring students to read what you call "classics" in introductory courses, you impose upon them a certain worldview—and that is an elitist act.

In some rudimentary but not very consequential sense, all education entails the "imposing" of values. There are people who say this is true even when children are taught to read and write, since it assumes that reading and writing are "good."

In its extreme version, this idea is not very interesting, since it is not clear how the human race could survive if there were not some "imposition" from one generation to the next. But in a more moderate version, it is an idea that touches upon genuine problems.

Much depends on the character of the individual teacher, the spirit in which he or she approaches a dialogue of Plato,° an essay by Mill,° a novel by D. H. Lawrence.° These can be, and have been used to pummel an ideological line into the heads of students (who often show a notable capacity for emptying them out again). Such pummeling is possible for all points of view but seems most likely in behalf of totalitarian politics and authoritarian theologies, which dispose their adherents to fanaticism. On the other hand, the texts I've mentioned, as well as many others, can be taught in a spirit of openness, so that students are trained to read carefully, think independently, and ask questions. Nor does this imply that the teacher hides his or her opinions. Being a teacher means having a certain authority, but the student should be able to confront that authority freely and critically. This is what we mean by liberal education—not that a teacher plumps for certain political programs, but that the teaching is done in a "liberal" (open, undogmatic) style.

I do not doubt that there are conservative and radical teachers who teach in this "liberal" spirit. When I was a student at City College in the late 1930s, I studied philosophy with a man who was either a member of the Communist Party or was "cheating it out of dues." Far from being the propagandist of the Party line, which

5

Plato: classic Greek philosopher.
John Stuart Mill: nineteenth-century English philosopher.
D. H. Lawrence: English novelist (see Chapter 13).

Sidney Hook kept insisting was the necessary role of Communist teachers, this man was decent, humane, and tolerant. Freedom of thought prevailed in his classroom. He had, you might say, a "liberal" character, and perhaps his commitment to teaching as a vocation was stronger than his loyalty to the Party. Were such things not to happen now and then, universities would be intolerable.

If, then, a university proposes a few required courses so that ill-read students may at least glance at what they do not know, that isn't (necessarily) "elitist." Different teachers will approach the agreed-upon texts in different ways, and that is as it should be. If a leftist student gets "stuck" with a conservative teacher, or a conservative student with a leftist teacher, that's part of what education should be. The university is saying to its incoming students: "Here are some sources of wisdom and beauty that have survived the centuries. In time you may choose to abandon them, but first learn something about them."

Your list of classics include only dead, white males, all tied in to notions and values of Western hegemony. Doesn't this narrow excessively the horizons of education?

All depends on how far forward you go to compose your list of classics. If you do not come closer to the present than the mid-eighteenth century, then of course there will not be many, or even any, women in your roster. If you go past the mid-eighteenth century to reach the present, it's not at all true that only "dead, white males" are to be included. For example—and this must hold for hundreds of other teachers also—I have taught and written about Jane Austen,° Emily Brontë,° Charlotte Brontë,° Elizabeth Gaskell,° George Eliot,° Emily Dickinson,° Edith Wharton,° Katherine Anne Porter,° Doris Lessing,° and Flannery O'Connor.° I could easily add a comparable list of black writers. Did this, in itself, make me a better teacher? I doubt it. Did it make me a better person? We still lack modes of evaluation subtle enough to say for sure.

The absence of women from the literature of earlier centuries is a result of historical inequities that have only partly been remedied in recent years. Virginia Woolf,° in a brilliant passage in *A Room of One's Own,* approaches this problem by imagining Judith, Shakespeare's sister, perhaps equally gifted but prevented by the circumstances of her time from developing her gifts:

> Any woman born with a great gift in the sixteenth century would certainly
> have gone crazed, shot herself, or ended her days in some lonely cottage outside
> the village, half witch, half wizard, feared and mocked at. . . . A highly gifted
> girl who had tried to use her gift of poetry would have been so thwarted and
> hindered by other people, so tortured and pulled asunder by her own contrary
> instincts, that she must have lost her health and sanity. . . . 10

The history that Virginia Woolf describes cannot be revoked. If we look at the great works of literature and thought through the centuries until about the mid-eighteenth century, we have to recognize that indeed they have been overwhelmingly the achievements of men. The circumstances in which these achievements occurred may be excoriated. The achievements remain precious.

Austen; Brontës; Gaskell, Eliot: famous women and novelists of nineteenth-century England.
Dickinson: American poet (see Chapters 18, 22, 27).
Wharton; Porter; O'Connor: famous American writers (see Chapter 13).
Lessing: modern English novelist.
Virginia Woolf: English novelist of the early twentieth century.

To isolate a group of texts as the canon is to establish a hierarchy of bias, in behalf of which there can be no certainty of judgment.

There is mischief or confusion in the frequent use of the term "hierarchy" by the academic insurgents, a conflation of social and intellectual uses. A social hierarchy may entail a (mal)distribution of income and power, open to the usual criticisms; a literary "hierarchy" signifies a judgment, often based on historical experience, that some works are of supreme or abiding value, while others are of lesser value, and still others quite without value. To prefer Elizabeth Bishop to Judith Krantz° is not of the same order as sanctioning the inequality of wealth in the United States. To prefer Shakespeare to Sidney Sheldon° is not of the same order as approving the hierarchy of the nomenklatura in Communist dictatorships.

As for the claim that there is no certainty of judgment, all tastes being historically molded or individually subjective, I simply do not believe that the people who make it live by it. This is an "egalitarianism" of valuation that people of even moderate literacy know to be false and unworkable—the making of judgments, even if provisional and historically modulated, is inescapable in the life of culture. And if we cannot make judgments or demonstrate the grounds for our preferences, then we have no business teaching literature—we might just as well be teaching advertising—and there is no reason to have departments of literature.   15

The claim that there can be value-free teaching is a liberal deception or self-deception; so too the claim that there can be texts untouched by social and political bias. Politics or ideology is everywhere, and it's the better part of honesty to admit this.

If you look hard (or foolishly) enough, you can find political and social traces everywhere. But to see politics or ideology in all texts is to scrutinize the riches of literature through a single lens. If you choose, you can read all or almost all literary works through the single lens of religion. But what a sad impoverishment of the imagination, and what a violation of our sense of reality, this represents. Politics may be "in" everything, but not everything is politics. A good social critic will know which texts are inviting to a given approach and which it would be wise to leave to others.

To see politics everywhere is to diminish the weight of politics. A serious politics recognizes the limits of its reach; it deals with public affairs while leaving alone large spheres of existence; it seeks not to "totalize" its range of interest. Some serious thinkers believe that the ultimate aim of politics should be to render itself superfluous. That may seem an unrealizable goal; meanwhile, a good part of the struggle for freedom in recent decades has been to draw a line beyond which politics must not tread. The same holds, more or less, for literary study and the teaching of literature.

Wittingly or not, the traditional literary and intellectual canon was based on received elitist ideologies, the values of Western imperialism, racism, sexism, etc., and the teaching of the humanities was marked by corresponding biases. It is now necessary to enlarge the canon so that voices from Africa, Asia, and Latin America can be heard. This is especially important for minority students so that they may learn about their origins and thereby gain in self-esteem.

It is true that over the decades some university teaching has reflected inherited social biases—how, for better or worse, could it not? Most often this was due to the fact that many teachers shared the common beliefs of American society. But not all teachers! As long as those with critical views were allowed to speak freely, the situ-

---

°*Judith Krantz; Sidney Sheldon:* popular contemporary American writers of romance and intrigue novels.

ation, if not ideal, was one that people holding minority opinions and devoted to democratic norms had to accept.

Yet the picture drawn by some academic insurgents—that most teachers, until quite recently, were in the grip of the worst values of Western society—is overdrawn. I can testify that some of my school and college teachers a few decades ago, far from upholding Western imperialism or white supremacy, were sharply critical of American society, in some instances from a boldly reformist outlook. They taught us to care about literature both for its own sake and because, as they felt, it often helped confirm their worldviews. (And to love it even if it didn't confirm their worldviews.) One high school teacher introduced me to Hardy's *Jude the Obscure* as a novel showing how cruel society can be to rebels, and up to a point, she was right. At college, as a fervent anti-Stalinist Marxist, I wrote a thoughtless "class analysis" of Edmund Spenser° poetry for an English class, and the kindly instructor, whose politics were probably not very far from mine, suggested that there were more things in the world, especially as Spenser had seen it, than I could yet recognize. I mention these instances to suggest that there has always been a range of opinion among teachers, and if anything, the American academy has tilted more to the left than most other segments of our society. There were of course right-wing professors too; I remember an economics teacher we called "Steamboat" Fulton, the object of amiable ridicule among the students who nonetheless learned something from him.

Proposals to enlarge the curriculum to include non-Western writings—if made in good faith and not in behalf of an ideological campaign—are in principle to be respected. A course in ancient thought might well include a selection from Confucius; a course in the modern novel might well include a work by Tanizaki° or García Márquez.°

There are practical difficulties. Due to the erosion of requirements in many universities, those courses that survive are usually no more than a year or a semester in duration, so that there is danger of a diffusion to the point of incoherence. Such courses, if they are to have any value, must focus primarily on the intellectual and cultural traditions of Western society. That, like it or not, is where we come from and that is where we are. All of us who live in America are, to some extent, Western: it gets to us in our deepest and also our most trivial habits of thought and speech, in our sense of right and wrong, in our idealism and our cynicism.

As for the argument that minority students will gain in self-esteem through being exposed to writings by Africans and black Americans, it is hard to know. Might not entering minority students, some of them ill-prepared, gain a stronger sense of self-esteem by mastering the arts of writing and reading than by being told, as some are these days, that Plato and Aristotle plagiarized from an African source? Might not some black students feel as strong a sense of self-esteem by reading, say, Dostoyevsky° and Malraux° (which Ralph Ellison° speaks of having done at a susceptible age) as by being confined to black writers? Is there not something grossly patronizing in the notion that while diverse literary studies are appropriate for middle-class white students, something else, racially determined, is required for the minorities? Richard

---

Edmund Spenser: English Tudor poet.
Tanizaki: Japanese fictionist (see Chapter 9).
Gabriel García Márquez: Colombian fictionist (see Chapter 4).
Fyodor Dostoyevsky: nineteenth-century classic Russian novelist.
André Malraux: twentieth-century French novelist.
Ralph Ellison: twentieth-century African American novelist, author of *Invisible Man*.

from The Value of the Canon

Wright° found sustenance in Dreiser,° Ralph Ellison in Hemingway, Chinua Achebe° in Eliot, Leopold Senghor° in the whole of French poetry. Are there not unknown young Wrights and Ellisons, Achebes, and Senghors in our universities who might also want to find their way to an individually achieved sense of culture?

In any case, is the main function of the humanities directly to inculcate self-esteem? Do we really know how this can be done? And if done by bounding the curriculum according to racial criteria, may that not perpetuate the very grounds for a lack of self-esteem? I do not know the answers to these questions, but do the advocates of multi-culturalism?

25

One serious objection to "multicultural studies" remains; that it tends to segregate students into categories fixed by birth, upbringing, and obvious environment. Had my teachers tried to lead me toward certain writers because they were Jewish, I would have balked—I wanted to find my own way to Proust,° Kafka,° and Pirandello,° writers who didn't need any racial credentials. Perhaps things are different with students today—we ought not to be dogmatic about these matters. But are there not shared norms of pride and independence among young people, whatever their race and color?

The jazz musician Wynton Marsalis testifies: "Everybody has two heritages, ethnic and human. The human aspects give art its real enduring power. . . . The racial aspect, that's a crutch so you don't have to go out into the world." David Bromwich raises an allied question: Should we wish "to legitimize the belief that the mind of a student deserves to survive in exactly the degree that it corresponds with one of the classes of socially constructed group minds? If I were a student today I would find this assumption frightening. It is, in truth, more than a license for conformity. It is a four-year sentence to conformity."

Richard Wright: twentieth-century African American novelist.
Theodore Dreiser: twentieth-century American Realist novelist.
Chinua Achebe: Nigerian novelist, author of *Things Fall Apart.*
Leopold Senghor: African poet.
Marcel Proust: twentieth-century French novelist.
Franz Kafka: twentieth-century Czech-born writer.
Pirandello: modern Italian dramatist.

Henry Louis Gates, Jr.

from WHOSE CANON IS IT, ANYWAY?

Obviously, some of what I'm saying is by way of *mea culpa*, because I'm speaking here as a participant in a moment of canon formation in a so-called marginal tradition. As it happens, W. W. Norton, the "canonical" anthology publisher, will be publishing *The Norton Anthology of Afro-American Literature*. The editing of this anthology has been a great dream of mine for a long time, and it represents, in the most concrete way, the project of black canon formation. But my pursuit of this project has required me to negotiate a position between those on the cultural right who claim that black literature can have no canon, no masterpieces, and those on the cultural left who wonder why anyone wants to establish the existence of a canon, any canon, in the first place.

We face the outraged reactions of those custodians of Western culture who protest that the canon, that transparent decanter of Western values, may become— breathe the word—*politicized*. That people can maintain a straight face while they protest the irruption of politics into something that has always been political—well, it says something about how remarkably successful official literary histories have been in presenting themselves as natural objects, untainted by worldly interests.

I agree with those conservatives who have raised the alarm about our students' ignorance of history. But part of the history we need to teach has to be the history of the very idea of the "canon," which involves the history both of literary pedagogy and the very institution of the school. One function of literary history is then to conceal all connections between institutionalized interests and the literature we remember. Pay no attention to the men behind the curtain, booms the Great Oz of literary history.

Cynthia Ozick° once chastised feminists by warning that strategies become institutions. But isn't that really another way of warning that their strategies, Heaven forfend, may *succeed*?

Here we approach the scruples of those on the cultural left who worry about, well, the price of success. "Who's co-opting whom?" might be their slogan. To them, the very idea of the canon is hierarchical, patriarchal and otherwise politically suspect. They'd like us to disavow it altogether.   5

But history and its institutions are not just something we study, they're also something we live, and live through. And how effective and how durable our inventions in contemporary cultural politics will be depends upon our ability to mobilize the institutions that buttress and reproduce that culture. We could seclude ourselves form the real world and keep our hands clean, free from the taint of history. But that is to pay obeisance to the status quo, to the entrenched arsenal of sexual and racial authority, to say that things shouldn't change, become something other and, let's hope, better.

Indeed, this is one case where we've got to borrow a leaf from the right, which is exemplarily aware of the role of education in the reproduction of values. We must engage in this sort of canon reformation precisely because Mr. Bennett° is correct: the teaching of literature *is* the teaching of values, not inherently, no, but contingently, yes; it is—it has become—the teaching of an esthetic and political order, in which no person of color, no woman, was ever able to discover the reflection or representation of his or her cultural image or voice. The return of "the" canon, the high canon of Western masterpieces, represents the return of an order in which my people were the subjugated, the voiceless, the invisible, the unrepresented and the unrepresentable.

Let me be specific. Those of us working in my own tradition confront the hegemony of the Western tradition, generally, and of the larger American tradition, more locally, as we theorize about our tradition and engage in canon formation. Long after white American literature has been anthologized and canonized, and recanonized, our efforts to define a black American canon are often decried as racist, separatist, nationalist, or "essentialist." Attempts to derive theories about our liter-

---

Cynthia Ozick: contemporary American novelist and essayist.
William Bennett: Reagan-era Secretary of Education and proponent of educational reforms.

ary tradition from the black tradition—a tradition, I might add, that must include black vernacular forms as well as written literary forms—are often greeted by our colleagues in traditional literature departments as a misguided desire to secede from a union that only recently, and with considerable kicking and screaming, has been forged. What is wrong with you people? our friends ask us in genuine passion and concern; after all, aren't we all just citizens of literature here?

Well, yes and no. Every black American text must confess to a complex ancestry, one high and low (that is, literary and vernacular) but also one white and black. There can be no doubt that white texts inform and influence black texts (and vice versa), so that a thoroughly integrated canon of American literature is not only politically sound, it is intellectually sound as well. But the attempts of black scholars to define a black American canon, and to derive indigenous theories of interpretation from within this canon, are not meant to refute the soundness of these gestures of integration. Rather, it is a question of perspective, a question of emphasis. Just as we can and must cite a black text within the larger American tradition, we can and must cite it within its own tradition, a tradition not defined by a pseudoscience of racial biology, or a mystically shared essence called blackness, but the repetition and revision of shared themes, topoi and tropes, the call and response of voices, their music and cacophony.

And this is our special legacy: what in 1849 Frederick Douglass° called the "live, calm, grave, clear, pointed, warm, sweet, melodious and powerful human voice." The presence of the past in the African-American tradition comes to us most powerfully as *voice*, a voice that is never quite our own—or *only* our own—however much we want it to be.   10

Frederick Douglass: famous nineteenth-century African American orator and abolitionist.

Harold Bloom

from THE WESTERN CANON

The silliest way to defend the Western Canon is to insist that it incarnates all of the seven deadly moral virtues that make up our supposed range of normative values and democratic principles. This is palpably untrue. The *Iliad* teaches the surpassing glory of armed victory, while Dante rejoices in the eternal torments he visits upon his very personal enemies. Tolstoy's private version of Christianity throws aside nearly everything that anyone among us retains, and Dostoevsky preaches anti-Semitism, obscurantism, and the necessity of human bondage. Shakespeare's politics, insofar as we can pin them down, do not appear to be very different from those of his Coriolanus,° and Milton's ideas of free speech and free press do not preclude the imposition of all manner of societal restraints. Spenser rejoices in the massacre of Irish rebels, while the egomania of Wordsworth exalts his own poetic mind over any other source of splendor.

Coriolanus: emperor protagonist of Shakespeare's tragedy, *Coriolanus*.

The West's greatest writers are subversive of all values, both ours and their own. Scholars who urge us to find the source of our morality and our politics in Plato, or in Isaiah, are out of touch with the social reality in which we live. If we read the Western Canon in order to form our social, political, or personal moral values, I firmly believe we will become monsters of selfishness and exploitation. To read in the service of any ideology is not, in my judgment, to read at all. The reception of aesthetic power enables us to learn how to talk to ourselves and how to endure ourselves. The true use of Shakespeare or of Cervantes, of Homer or of Dante, of Chaucer or of Rabelais, is to augment one's own growing inner self. Reading deeply in the Canon will not make one a better or a worse person, a more useful or more harmful citizen. The mind's dialogue with itself is not primarily a social reality. All that the Western Canon can bring one is the proper use of one's own solitude, that solitude whose final form is one's confrontation with one's own mortality.

We possess the Canon because we are mortal and also rather belated. There is only so much time, and time must have a stop, while there is more to read than ever was before. From the Yahwist and Homer to Freud, Kafka, and Beckett is a journey of nearly three millennia. Since that voyage goes past harbors as infinite as Dante, Chaucer, Montaigne, Shakespeare, and Tolstoy, all of whom amply compensate a lifetime's rereadings, we are in the pragmatic dilemma of excluding something else each time we read or reread extensively. One ancient test for the canonical remains fiercely valid: unless it demands rereading, the work does not qualify. The inevitable analogue is the erotic one. If you are Don Giovanni° and Leporello° keeps the list, one brief encounter will suffice.

Contra certain Parisians,° the text is there to give not pleasure but the high unpleasure or more difficult pleasure that a lesser text will not provide. I am not prepared to dispute admirers of Alice Walker's° *Meridian*, a novel I have compelled myself to read twice, but the second reading was one of my most remarkable literary experiences. It produced an epiphany in which I saw clearly the new principle implicit in the slogans of those who proclaim the opening-up of the Canon. The correct test for the new canonicity is simple, clear, and wonderfully conducive to social change: it must not and cannot be reread, because its contribution to societal progress is its generosity in offering itself up for rapid ingestion and discarding. From Pindar through Hölderlin to Yeats, the self-canonizing greater ode has proclaimed its agonistic immortality. The socially acceptable ode of the future will doubtless spare us such pretensions and instead address itself to the proper humility of shared sisterhood, the new sublimity of quilt making that is now the preferred trope of Feminist criticism.

Yet we must choose: As there is only so much time, do we reread Elizabeth Bishop or Adrienne Rich? Do I again go in search of lost time with Marcel Proust, or am I to attempt yet another rereading of Alice Walker's stirring denunciation of all males, black and white? My former students, many of them now stars of the School of Resentment, proclaim that they teach social selflessness, which begins in learning

---

Don Giovanni: legendary seducer—"Don Juan"—of Mozart's opera of the same name; *Leporello*: Don Giovanni's friend and follower.
certain Parisians: Bloom is referring to French critic Roland Barthes, who likened reading to eroticism in his book *The Pleasures of the Text*.
Alice Walker: African American woman novelist, author also of *The Color Purple*.

how to read selflessly. The author has no self, the literary character has no self, and the reader has no self. Shall we gather at the river with these generous ghosts, free of the guilt of past self-assertions, and be baptized in the waters of Lethe?° What shall we do to be saved?

The study of literature, however it is conducted, will not save any individual, any more than it will improve any society. Shakespeare will not make us better, and he will not make us worse, but he may teach us how to overhear ourselves when we talk to ourselves. Subsequently, he may teach us how to accept change, in ourselves as in others, and perhaps even the final form of change. Hamlet is death's ambassador to us, perhaps one of the few ambassadors ever sent out by death who does not lie to us about our inevitable relationship with that undiscovered country. The relationship is altogether solitary, despite all of tradition's obscene attempts to socialize it....

*　　*　　*

All canons, including our currently fashionable counter-canons, are elitist, and as no secular canon is ever closed, what is now acclaimed as "opening up the canon" is a strictly redundant operation. Although canons, like all lists and catalogs, have a tendency to be inclusive rather than exclusive, we have now reached the point at which a lifetime's reading and rereading can scarcely take one through the Western Canon. Indeed, it is now virtually impossible to master the Western Canon. Not only would it mean absorbing well over three thousand books, many, if not most, marked by authentic cognitive and imaginative difficulties, but the relations between these books grow more rather than less vexed as our perspectives lengthen. There are also the vast complexities and contradictions that constitute the essence of the Western Canon, which is anything but a unity or stable structure. No one has the authority to tell us what the Western Canon is, certainly not from about 1800 to the present day. It is not, cannot be precisely the list I give, or that anyone else might give. If it were, that would make such a list a mere fetish, just another commodity. But I am not prepared to agree with the Marxists that the Western Canon is another instance of what they call "cultural capital." It is not clear to me that a nation as contradictory as the United States of America could ever be the context for "cultural capital," except for those slivers of high culture that contribute to mass culture. We have not had an official high culture in this country since about 1800, a generation after the American Revolution. Cultural unity is a French phenomenon, and to some degree a German matter, but hardly an American reality in either the nineteenth century or the twentieth. In our context and from our perspective, the Western Canon is a kind of survivor's list. The central fact about America, according to the poet Charles Olson, is space, but Olson wrote that as the opening sentence of a book on Melville and thus on the nineteenth century. At the close of the twentieth century, our central fact is time, for the evening land is now in the West's evening time. Would one call the list of survivors of a three-thousand-year-old cosmological war a fetish?

The issue is the mortality or immortality of literary works. Where they have become canonical, they have survived an immense struggle in social relations, but those relations have very little to do with class struggle. Aesthetic value emanates from the struggle between texts: in the reader, in language, in the classroom, in arguments within a society. Very few working-class readers ever matter in determining the survival of texts, and left-wing critics cannot do the working class's reading for it. Aes-

---

Lethe: river of forgetfulness in the classical underworld.

thetic value rises out of memory, and so (as Nietzsche saw) out of pain, the pain of surrendering easier pleasures in favor of much more difficult ones. Workers have anxieties enough and turn to religion as one mode of relief. Their sure sense that the aesthetic is, for them, only another anxiety helps to teach us that successful literary works are achieved anxieties, not releases from anxieties. Canons, too, are achieved anxieties, not unified props of morality, Western or Eastern. If we could conceive of a universal canon, multicultural and multivalent, its one essential book would not be a scripture, whether Bible, Koran, or Eastern text, but rather Shakespeare, who is acted and read everywhere, in every language and circumstance. Whatever the convictions of our current New Historicists, for whom Shakespeare is only a signifier for the social energies of the English Renaissance, Shakespeare for hundreds of millions who are not white Europeans is a signifier of their own pathos, their own sense of identity with the characters that Shakespeare fleshed out by his language. For them his universality is not historical but fundamental; he puts their lives upon his stage. In his characters they behold and confront their own anguish and their own fantasies, not the manifested social energies of early mercantile London.

The art of memory, with its rhetorical antecedents and its magical burgeonings, is very much an affair of imaginary places, or of real places transmuted into visual images. Since childhood, I have enjoyed an uncanny memory for literature, but that memory is purely verbal, without anything in the way of a visual component. Only recently, past the age of sixty, have I come to understand that my literary memory has relied upon the Canon as a memory system. If I am a special case, it is only in the sense that my experience is a more extreme version of what I believe to be the principal pragmatic function of the Canon: the remembering and ordering of a lifetime's reading. The greatest authors take over the role of "places" in the Canon's theater of memory, and their masterworks occupy the position filled by "images" in the art of memory. Shakespeare and *Hamlet*, central author and universal drama, compel us to remember not only what happens in *Hamlet*, but more crucially what happens in literature that makes it memorable and thus prolongs the life of the author.

Todd Gitlin

from ON THE VIRTUES OF A LOOSE CANON

Let's face it: Some of the controversy over the canon and the new multiculturalism has to do with the fact that the complexion of the US—on its campuses and in the country as a whole—is getting darker. In 1960, 94 percent of college students were white. Today almost 20 percent are nonwhite or Hispanic and about 55 percent are women.

It is the confluence of these events—the end of the Cold War and the transformation of the "typical American"—that appears to have stirred up a particular vocal reaction at this time to the multicultural movement within the academy. Just note the degree of alarm, the alacrity with which the media have jumped on this issue. *Newsweek*, the *Atlantic Monthly*, the *New Republic* and *New York* jumped up with cover stories on race, multiculturalism and the politically correct movement on college campuses. The *New York Times* has given extensive coverage to the PC trend. And George Bush, knowing a no-risk issue when he sees it, recently gave the commencement address at the University of Michigan at Ann Arbor on "the new intolerance" of political correctness sweeping college campuses, what he called "the boring politics of division and derision"—an ironic comment coming from the man who elevated race baiting, through his Willie Horton commercials, to an art form.

In important ways, hysteria rules the response to multiculturalism. Academic conservatives who defend a canon, tight or loose, sometimes sound as if American universities were fully and finally canonized until the barbarians showed up to smash up the pantheon and install Alice Walker and Toni Morrison in place of the old white men. These conservatives act as if we were floating along in unadulterated canon until sixties radicals came along and muddied the waters. Moreover, the hysterics give the misleading impression that Plato and St. Augustine have been banned.

The tight canonists don't take account either, of the fact that the canon has always been in flux, constantly shifting under our feet. Literary historian Leo Marx made the point recently that when he was in school it was a fight to get good, gay Walt Whitman° into the canon, and to get John Greenleaf,° Henry Wadsworth Longfellow° and James Russell Lowell° out.

Still, without doubt there *has* been a dilution of essential modes of critical reasoning, the capacity to write, and a general knowledge of the contours of world history and thought. And this is to be deplored and resisted.   5

Indeed, there is a side of the academic conservatives' argument I agree with. There are a shocking number of students not only in run-of-the-mill segments of higher education but in elite institutions who are amazingly uneducated in history, literature and the fundamentals of logic, who don't know the difference between an argument and an assertion. There *is* a know-nothing mood in some quarters which refuses to understand that the ideas and practices of many a dead white male have been decisive in Western—and therefore world—history.

But the stupidification of our students cannot be blamed simply on shifts in the canon. Cultural illiteracy has crept into our educational process for a variety of reasons. In fact, America's higher illiteracy—to call it by a name Thorstein Veblen° might have appreciated—is largely a function of the so-far irresistible force of popular culture as the shaper of popular discourse. By popular discourse, I mean not only the way we speak on the street but the way we speak as presidents and presidential candidates. This is a culture in which "read my lips" or "make my day" constitutes powerful and persuasive speech.

We live in a sound-bite culture, one that has taken anti-elitism as its sacred principle. In the US, to master a vocabulary that is superior to the mediocre is to be guilty of disdain, of scorning democracy. Though conservatives will not be happy to hear about it, this leveling principle has the full force of market capitalism working for it, a force that insists the only standard of value is consumer sovereignty—what people will buy. Since what people will buy are slogans and feel-good pronouncements, it is not surprising that schools and universities have degraded themselves in a frantic pursuit of the lowest common denominator.

Walt Whitman: American poet (see Chapter 27).

John Greenleaf [Whittier]; Henry Wadsworth Longfellow; James Russell Lowell: traditional New England poets of the Victorian era.

Thorstein Veblen: nineteenth-century American economist and sociologist.

Katha Pollitt

from WHY DO WE READ?

For the past couple of years, we've all been witness to a furious debate about the literary canon. What books should be assigned to students? What books should critics discuss? What books should the rest of us read —and who are *we*, anyway? Like everyone else, I've given these questions some thought and, when an invitation came my way, leaped to produce my own manifesto. But to my surprise, when I sat down to write—in order to discover, as E. M. Forster once said, what I really think—I found that I agreed with all sides in the debate at once.

Take the conservatives. Now, this rather dour collection of scholars and diatribists—Allan Bloom, Hilton Kramer, John Silber, and so on—are not, to my mind, a particularly appealing group of people. They are arrogant, they are rude, they are gloomy, they do not suffer fools gladly—and everywhere they look, fools are what they see. All good reasons not to elect them to public office, as the voters of Massachusetts recently decided. But what is so terrible, really, about what they are saying? I too believe that some books are profounder, more complex, more essential to an understanding of our culture than others; I too am appalled to think of students graduating from college not having read Homer, Plato, Virgil, Milton, Tolstoy—all writers, dead white Western men though they be, whose works have meant a great deal to me. As a teacher of literature and of writing, I too have seen at first hand how ill-educated many students are and how little aware they are of this important fact about themselves. Last year, for instance, I taught a graduate seminar in the writing of poetry. None of my students had read more than a smattering of poems by anyone, male or female, published more than ten years ago. Robert Lowell° was as far outside their frame of reference as Alexander Pope.° When I gently suggested to one student that it might benefit her to read some poetry if she planned to spend her life writing it, she told me that yes, she knew she should read more, but when she encountered a really good poem it only made her depressed. That contemporary writing has a history which it profits us to know in some depth, that we ourselves were not born yesterday, seems too obvious even to argue.

But ah, say the liberals, the canon exalted by the conservatives is itself an artifact of history. Sure, some books are more rewarding than others, but why can't we revise the list of which books those are? The canon itself was not always the list we know today: Until the 1920s, *Moby-Dick* was shelved with the boys' adventure stories. If T. S. Eliot could singlehandedly dethrone the Romantic poets in favor of the neglected Metaphysicals and place John Webster alongside Shakespeare, why can't we dip into the sea of stories and pluck out Edith Wharton or Virginia Woolf? And this position too makes a great deal of sense to me. After all, alongside the many good reasons why a book might end up on the required reading shelf are some rather suspect reasons why it might be excluded—because it was written by a woman and therefore presumed to be too slight; because it was written by a black person and

---

Robert Lowell (1917–1977): American poet; *Alexander Pope (1688–1744):* British poet (see Chapter 27).

therefore presumed to be too unsophisticated or, in any case, to reflect too special an instance. By all means, say the liberals, let's have great books and a shared culture. But let's make sure that all the different kinds of greatness are represented and that the culture we share reflects the true range of human experience.

If we leave the broadening of the canon up to the conservatives, it will never happen because, to them, change only means defeat. Look at the recent fuss over the latest edition of the Great Books series published by the Encyclopedia Britannica, headed by that old snake-oil salesman Mortimer Adler. Four women have now been added to the series: Virginia Woolf, Willa Cather, Jane Austen, and George Eliot. That's nice, I suppose, but really! Jane Austen has been a certified great writer for a hundred years! Lionel Trilling said so! There's something truly absurd about the conservatives, earnestly sitting in judgment on the illustrious dead as though up in Writers' Heaven Jane and George and Willa and Virginia were breathlessly waiting to hear if they'd finally made it into the club, while Henry Fielding, newly dropped from the list, howls in outer darkness and the Brontës, presumably, stamp their feet in frustration and hope for better luck in twenty years, when *Jane Eyre* and *Wuthering Heights* will suddenly turn out to have qualities of greatness never before detected in their pages. It's like Poets' Corner over at Manhattan's Cathedral of St. John the Divine, where mortal men—and a woman or two—of letters actually vote on which immortals to put up a plaque to—complete, no doubt, with electoral campaigns, compromise candidates, and all the rest of the underside of the literary life. "No, I'm sorry, I just can't vote for Whitman. I'm a Washington Irving man myself."

Well, being a liberal is not a very exciting thing to be, and so we have the radicals, who attack the concepts of "greatness," "shared," "culture," and "lists." (I'm overlooking here the ultra-radicals, who attack the "privileging," horrible word, of "texts," as they insist on calling books, and think one might as well spend one's college years "deconstructing," i.e., watching reruns of *Leave It to Beaver*.) Who is to say, ask the radicals, what is a great book? What's so terrific about complexity, ambiguity, historical centrality, and high seriousness? If *The Color Purple*, say, gets students thinking about their own experience, maybe they ought to read it and forget about—and here you can fill in the name of whatever classic work you yourself found dry and tedious and never got around to finishing. For the radicals, the notion of a shared culture is a lie, because it means presenting as universally meaningful and politically neutral books that reflect the interests and experiences and values of privileged white men at the expense of those of others—women, blacks, Hispanics, Asians, the working class, whatever. Why not scrap the one-list-for-everyone idea and let people connect with books that are written by people like themselves about people like themselves? It will be a more accurate reflection of a multifaceted and conflict-ridden society and do wonders for everyone's self-esteem, except, of course, for living white men—but they have too much self-esteem already. 5

Now, I have to say that I dislike the radicals' vision intensely. How foolish to argue that Chekhov has nothing to say to a black woman—or, for that matter, myself—merely because he is Russian, long dead, a man. The notion that one reads to increase one's self-esteem sounds to me like more snake oil: literature is not a session at the therapist's. But then I think of myself as a child, leafing through anthologies of poetry for the names of women. I never would have admitted that I needed a role model, even if that awful term had existed back in the prehistory of which I speak, but why was I so excited to find a female name, even when, as was often the case, it was attached to a poem of no interest to me whatsoever? Anna Laetitia Barbauld, author of "Life! I know not what thou art/ But know that thou and I must part!," Lady Anne Lindsay, writer of languid ballads in incomprehensible Scots dialect, and the other minor female poets included by chivalrous Sir Arthur Quiller-Couch in the old Oxford Anthology of English Verse—I have to admit it, just by their presence in that august volume they did something for me. And although it had nothing to do with reading or writing, it was an important thing they did.

Now, what are we to make of this spluttering debate, in which charges of imperialism are met by equally passionate accusations of vandalism, in which each side hates the others, and yet each seems to have its share of reason? It occurs to me that perhaps what we have here is one of those debates in which the opposing sides, unbeknownst to themselves, share a myopia that will turn out to be the most interesting and important feature of the whole discussion, a debate, for instance, like that of our Founding Fathers over the nature of the franchise. Think of all the energy and passion spent debating the question of property qualifications, or direct versus legislative elections, while all along, unmentioned and unimagined, was the fact—to us so central—that women and slaves were never considered for any kind of vote.

While everyone is busy fighting over the canon, something is being overlooked. That is the state of reading, and books, and literature in our country, at this time. Why, ask yourself, is everyone so hot under the collar about what to put on the required-reading shelf? It is because, while we have been arguing so fiercely about which books make the best medicine, the patient has been slipping deeper and deeper into a coma.

Let us imagine a country in which reading was a popular voluntary activity. There, parents read books for their own edification and pleasure and are seen by their children at this silent and mysterious pastime. There parents also read to their children, give them books for presents, talk to them about books, and underwrite, with their taxes, a public library system that is open all day, every day. In school— where an attractive library is invariably to be found—the children study certain books together but also have an active reading life of their own. Years later, it may even be hard for them to remember if they read *Jane Eyre* at home and Judy Blume in class or the other way around. In college, young people continue to be assigned certain books, but far more important are the books they discover for themselves browsing in the library, in bookstores, on the shelves of friends, one book leading to another, back and forth in history and across languages and cultures. After graduation, they continue to read and in the fullness of time produce a new generation of readers. Oh happy land! I wish we all lived there.

In that other country of real readers, voluntary, active, self-determined readers, a debate like the current one over the canon would not be taking place. Or if it did, it would be as a kind of parlor game: What books would *you* take to a desert island? Everyone would know that the top-ten list was merely a tiny fraction of the books one would read in a lifetime. It would not seem racist or sexist or hopelessly hidebound to put Hawthorne on the list and not Toni Morrison. It would be more like putting oatmeal and not noodles on the breakfast menu—a choice part arbitrary, part a nod to the national past, part, dare one say it, a kind of reverse affirmative action: School might frankly *be* the place where one read the books that are a little off-putting, that have gone a little cold, that you might overlook because they do not address, in reader-friendly contemporary fashion, the issues most immediately at stake in modern life but that, with a little study, turn out to have a great deal to say. Being on the list wouldn't mean so much. It might even add to a writer's cachet *not* to be on the list, to be in one way or another too heady, too daring, too exciting to be ground up into institutional fodder for teenagers. Generations of high-school kids have been turned off to George Eliot by being forced to read *Silas Marner* at a tender age. One can imagine a whole new readership for her if grownups were left to approach *Middlemarch* and *Daniel Deronda* with open minds, at their leisure. 10

But, of course, they rarely do. In America today, the underlying assumption behind the canon debate is that the books on the list are the only books that are going to be read and if the list is dropped, *no* books are going to be read. Becoming a textbook is a book's only chance—all sides take that for granted. And so all sides agree not to mention certain things that they themselves, as highly educated people and, one assumes, devoted readers, know perfectly well. For example, that if you read only twenty-five, or fifty, or a hundred books, you can't understand them, however well-chosen they are. And that if you don't have an independent reading life—and very few students do—you won't *like* reading the books on the list and will forget them the minute you finish them. And that books have, or should have, other lives than as items in a syllabus—which is why there is now a totally misguided attempt to put current literature in the classroom. How strange to think that people need professorial help to read John Updike or Alice Walker, writers people actually *do* read for fun. But all sides agree, if it isn't taught, it doesn't count. What a peculiar notion!

Let's look at the canon question from another angle. Instead of asking what books do we want others to read, let's ask, why do we read books ourselves? I think it will become clear very quickly that the canon debaters are being a little disingenuous here, are suppressing, in the interest of their own positions, their own experience of reading. Sure, we read to understand our own American culture and history, and we also read to recover neglected masterpieces, and to learn more about the accomplishments of our subgroup and thereby, as I've admitted about myself, increase our self-esteem. But what about reading for the aesthetic pleasures of language, form, image? What about reading to learn something new, to have a vicarious adventure, to follow the workings of an interesting, if possibly skewed, narrow and ill-tempered, mind? What about reading for the story? For an expanded sense of sheer human variety? There are a thousand reasons why a book might have a claim on our time and attention, other than its canonization.

Sven Birkerts

PERSEUS UNBOUND

Like it or not, interactive video technologies have muscled their way into the formerly textbound precincts of education. The videodisc has mated with the microcomputer to produce a juggernaut: a flexible and encompassing teaching tool that threatens to overwhelm the linearity of print with any array of option-rich multimedia packages. And although we are only in the early stages of implementation—institutions are by nature conservative—an educational revolution seems inevitable.

Several years ago in *Harvard Magazine*, writer Craig Lambert sampled some of the innovative ways in which these technologies have already been applied at Harvard.

Interactive video programs at the Law School allow students to view simulated police busts or actual courtroom procedures. With a tap of a digit they can freeze images, call up case citations, and quickly zero-in on the relevant fine points of precedent. Medical simulations, offering the immediacy of video images and instant access to the mountains of data necessary for diagnostic assessment, can have the student all but performing surgery. And language classes now allow the learner to make an end run around tedious drill repetitions and engage in protoconversations with video partners.

The hot news in the classics world, meanwhile, is Perseus 1.0, an interactive database developed and edited by Harvard associate professor Gregory Crane. Published on CD-ROM and videodisc, the program holds, according to its publishers, "the equivalent of 25 volumes of ancient Greek literature by ten authors (1 million Greek words), roughly 4,000 glosses in the on-line classical encyclopedia, and a 35,000-word on-line Greek lexicon." Also included are an enormous photographic database (six thousand images), a short video with narration, and "hundreds of descriptions and drawings of art and archeological objects." The package is affordable, too: Perseus software can be purchased for about $350. Plugged in, the student can call up a text, read it side by side with its translation, and analyze any word using the Liddell-Scott lexicon; he can read a thumbnail sketch on any mythic figure cited in the text, or call up images from an atlas, or zoom in on color Landsat photos; he can even study a particular vase through innumerable angles of vantage. The dusty library stacks have never looked dustier.

Although skepticism abounds, most of it is institutional, bound up with established procedures and the proprietorship of scholarly bailiwicks. But there are grounds for other, more philosophic sorts of debate, and we can expect to see flare-ups of controversy for some time to come. For more than any other development in recent memory, these interactive technologies throw into relief the fundamental questions about knowledge and learning. Not only what are its ends, but what are its means? And how might the means be changing the ends?

From the threshold, I think, we need to distinguish between kinds of knowledge and kinds of study. Pertinent here is German philosopher Wilhelm Dilthey's distinction between the natural sciences (*Naturwissenschaften*), which seek to explain physical events by subsuming them under causal laws, and the so-called sciences of culture (*Geisteswissenschaften*), which can only understand events in terms of the intentions and meanings that individuals attach to them.

To the former, it would seem, belong the areas of study more hospitable to the new video and computer procedures. Expanded databases and interactive programs can be viewed as tools, pure and simple. They give access to more information, foster cross-referentiality, and by reducing time and labor allow for greater focus on the essentials of a problem. Indeed, any discipline where knowledge is sought for its application rather than for itself could only profit from the implementation of these technologies. To the natural sciences one might add the fields of language study and law.

But there is a danger with these sexy new options—and the rapture with which the believers speak warrants the adjective—that we will simply assume that their uses and potentials extend across the educational spectrum into realms where different kinds of knowledge, and hence learning, are at issue. The realms, that is, of *Geisteswissenschaften*, which have at their center the humanities.

In the humanities, knowledge is a means, yes, but it is a means less to instrumental application than to something more nebulous: understanding. We study history or literature or classics in order to compose and refine a narrative, or a set of narratives about what the human world used to be like, about how the world came to be as it is, and about what we have been—and are—like as psychological or spiritual creatures. The data—the facts, connections, the texts themselves—matter insofar as they help us to deepen and extend that narrative. In these disciplines the *process* of study may be as vital to the understanding as are the materials studied.

Given the great excitement generated by Perseus, it is easy to imagine that in the near future a whole range of innovative electronic-based learning packages will be available and, in many places, in use. These will surely include the manifold variations on the electronic book. Special new software texts are already being developed to bring us into the world of, say, Shakespeare, not only glossing the literature, but bathing the user in multimedia supplements. The would-be historian will step into an environment rich in choices, be they visual detailing, explanatory graphs, or suggested connections and sideroads. And so on. Moreover, once the price is right, who will be the curmudgeons who would deny their students access to the state-of-the-art?

Being a curmudgeon is a dirty job, but somebody has to do it. Someone has to hoist the warning flags and raise some issues that the fast-track proselytizers might overlook. Here are a few reservations worth pondering.   10

1. Knowledge, certainly in the humanities, is not a straightforward matter of access, of conquest via the ingestion of data. Part of any essential understanding of the world is that it is opaque, obdurate. To me, Wittgenstein's famous axiom, "The world is everything that is the case," translates into a recognition of otherness. The past is as much about the disappearance of things through time as it is about the recovery of traces and the reconstruction of vistas. Say what you will about books, they not only mark the backward trail, but they also encode this sense of obstacle, of otherness. The look of the printed page changes as we regress in time; under the orthographic changes are the changes in the language itself. Old-style textual research may feel like an unnecessarily slow burrowing, but it is itself an instruction: It confirms that time is a force as implacable as gravity.

Yet the multimedia packages would master this gravity. For opacity they substitute transparency, promoting the illusion of access. All that has been said, known, and done will yield to the dance of the fingertips on the terminal keys. Space becomes hyperspace, and time, hypertime ("hyper-" being the fashionable new prefix that invokes the nonlinear and nonsequential "space" made possible by computer technologies). One gathers the data of otherness, but through a medium which seems to level the feel—the truth—of that otherness. The field of knowledge is rendered as a lateral and synchronic enterprise susceptible to collage, not as a depth phenomenon. And if our media restructure our perceptions, as McLuhan and others have argued, then we may start producing generations who know a great deal of "information" about the past but who have no purchase on pastness itself.

Described in this way, the effects of interactive programs on users sound a good deal like the symptoms of postmodernism. And indeed, this recent cultural aesthetic, distinguished by its flat, bright, and often affectless assemblages of materials may be a consequence of a larger transformation of sensibility by information-processing technologies. After all, our arts do tend to mirror who we are and anticipate what we might be becoming. Changes of this magnitude are of course systemic, and their direction is not easily dictated. Whether the postmodern "vision" can be endorsed as a pedagogic platform, however, is another question.

2. Humanistic knowledge, as I suggested earlier, differs from the more instrumental kinds of knowledge in that it ultimately seeks to fashion a comprehensible narrative. It is, in other words, about the creation and expansion of meaningful contexts. Interactive media technologies are, at least in one sense, anticontextual. They open the field to new widths, constantly expanding relevance and reference, and they equip their user with a powerful grazing tool. One moves at great rates across subject terrains, crossing borders that were once closely guarded. The multimedia approach tends ineluctably to multidisciplinarianism. The positive effect, of course, is the creation of new levels of connection and integration; more and more variables are brought into the equation.

But the danger should be obvious: The horizon, the limit that gave definition to the parts of the narrative, will disappear. The equation itself will become nonsensical through the accumulation of variables. The context will widen until it becomes, in effect, everything. On the model of Chaos science, wherein the butterfly flapping its wings in China is seen to affect the weather system over Oklahoma, all data will impinge upon all other data. The technology may be able to handle it, but will the user? Will our narratives—historical, literary, classical—be able to withstand the data explosion? Or will the knowledge of the world become, perforce, a map as large and intricate as the world itself?

3. We might question, too, whether there is not in learning as in physical science a principle of energy conservation. Does a gain in one area depend upon a loss in another? My guess would be that every lateral attainment is purchased with a sacrifice of depth. The student may, through a program on Shakespeare, learn an immense amount about Elizabethan politics, the construction of the Globe theater, the origins of certain plays in the writings of Plutarch, the etymology of key terms, and so on, but will this dazzled student find the concentration, the will, to live with the often burred and prickly language of the plays themselves? The play's the thing—but will it be? Wouldn't the sustained exposure to a souped-up cognitive collage not begin to affect the attention span, the ability if not willingness to sit with one text for extended periods, butting up against its cruxes, trying to excavate meaning from the original rhythms and syntax? The gurus of interaction love to say that the student learns best by doing, but let's not forget that *reading* a work is also a kind of doing.

4. As a final reservation, what about the long-term cognitive effects of these new processes of data absorption? Isn't it possible that more may be less, and that the neural networks have one speed for taking in—a speed that can be increased—and quite another rate for retention? Again, it may be that our technologies will exceed us. They will make it not only possible but irresistible to consume data at what must strike people of the book as very high rates. But what then? What will happen as our neural systems, evolved through millennia to certain capacities, modify themselves to hold ever-expanding loads? Will we simply become smarter, able to hold and process more? Or do we have to reckon with some other gain/loss formula? One possible cognitive response—call it the "S.A.T. cram-course model"—might be an expansion of the short-term memory banks and a correlative atrophying of long-term memory.

But here our technology may well assume a new role. Once it dawns on us, as it must, that our software will hold all the information we need at ready access, we may very well let it. That is, we may choose to become the technicians of our auxiliary brains, mastering not the information but the retrieval and referencing functions. At a certain point, then, we could become the evolutionary opposites of our forebears, who, lacking external technology, committed everything to memory. If this were to happen, what would be the status of knowing, of being educated? The leader of the electronic tribe would not be the person who knew most, but the one who could execute the broadest range of technical functions. What, I hesitate to ask, would become of the already antiquated notion of wisdom?

I recently watched a public television special on the history of the computer. One of the many experts and enthusiasts interviewed took up the knowledge question. He explained how the formerly two-dimensional process of book-based learning is rapidly becoming three-dimensional. The day will come, he opined, when interactive and virtual technologies will allow us to more or less dispense with our reliance on the sequence-based print paradigm. Whatever the object of our study, our equipment will be able to get us there directly: inside the volcano or the violin-maker's studio, right up on the stage. I was enthralled, but I shuddered, too, for it struck me that when our technologies are all in place—when all databases have been refined and integrated—that will be the day when we stop living in the old hard world and take up residence in some bright new hyperworld, a kind of Disney-land of information. I have to wonder if this is what Perseus and its kindred programs might not be edging us toward. That program got its name, we learn from the brochure, from the Greek mythological hero Perseus, who was the explorer of the limits of the known world. I confess that I can't think of Perseus without also thinking of Icarus, heedless son of Daedalus, who allowed his wings to carry him over the invisible line that was inscribed across the skyway.

QUESTIONS

1. Isolate the passage in each selection that best sums up the writer's position on the place of the traditional canon. Using these passages as your basis, decide whose are the most and least conservative voices.

2. Compare the statements made by Henry Louis Gates, Jr., and Harold Bloom. Pick out the similarities and differences in their respective positions. Which writer is taking the most uncompromising stance? Who is the greater realist? Explain your answers.

3. Katha Pollitt and Todd Gitlin are both "leftist" thinkers. Compare their excerpts. Do you find common ground or evidence of possible disagreement? Explain your answer.

4. Imagine that you are going to debate the canon with Irving Howe. Try to formulate some arguments that would counter his assertions. Feel free to use points made by the other writers.

5. Write a short statement (two paragraphs) in which you formulate and justify your own position on the canon issue.

6. Birkerts's "Perseus Unbound" takes a fairly cautious and conservative position on interactive technologies as learning tools. What are his main reasons for opposing the wholesale implementation of CD–ROM? Do you agree or disagree? Explain your stance.

Appendices

A: Critical Perspectives

In his book *Literary Theory: An Introduction*, English critic Terry Eagleton wrote that "one might very roughly periodize the history of modern literary theory in three stages: a preoccupation with the author (Romanticism and the nineteenth century); an exclusive concern with the text (New Criticism); and a marked shift of attention to the reader over recent years." With a few adjustments and additions, this formulation can serve as a useful frame for a synopsis of major trends in critical thought.

Before the twentieth century there was no formally recognized discipline known as literary criticism. Most writing about literature came from the pens of educated amateurs or writers interested in exploring their own genres. Thus we find Samuel Taylor Coleridge discoursing on poetry in his *Biographia Literaria*, and Edgar Allen Poe developing his theories of poetry and the short story in essays written for journals. Otherwise, the literary dialogue was mainly centered upon the noble attributes of the work and the author's biography, which was felt to hold the explanation for his or her genius. What we now think of as criticism was then known as "belles lettres" (literally *fine letters*). Certainly there were no schools of critical thought.

The early decades of our century saw the birth of this major new discipline. As mathematics, sciences, and the other so-called "hard" disciplines acquired prestige and patronage in European and American universities, professors of literature saw that they would either have to ground their studies in a more rigorous methodology or else face a drastic loss of influence. This recognition helped to sponsor the emergence of *Formalism* in England and its American counterpart *New Criticism*. Once literature had established itself securely as an object of academic study, theoretical movements of all descriptions flourished.

The theory underlying these various movements is often difficult. The summaries that follow aim only to set out the salient features of each. The interested reader should consult the short bibliographies of key texts that are included with each description.

FORMALISM/NEW CRITICISM

Formalist criticism is readily identified as the second of Terry Eagleton's stages—it is concerned exclusively with the written text, or what practitioners often called "the words on the page." The founding work of English-language Formalism (there are other branches with different orientations and they need not concern us here) was I.A. Richards's *Practical Criticism*, published in 1929. Richards, an English critic and professor, developed his methods based upon a set of teaching exercises in which he gave students unidentified passages of poetry and asked them for analysis and evaluation. The object of the exercise was to break what Richards saw as the distracting reliance upon historical and biographical assumptions. The words on the page marked off their own horizon, and it was the reader's first obligation to assess the work strictly on the basis of the immediate evidence. Never mind that the author had succumbed to madness, or that the poem had been written during a period of social revolution. If these factors were relevant they could be located in the language.

Formalist criticism, which now survives less as a distinct movement and more as an influential method, proved most useful in the analysis of poetry and shorter works of fiction—longer works like novels were too unwieldy. For it was the Formalist procedure not only to look closely at isolated passages of the text, but also to relate the functioning of parts of the structure of the whole.

Having first quarantined the text, the Formalist critic would then place it on the operating table for close inspection. Assuming that the purpose of the work was the creation of a unified artistic whole, the critic would look to see how wholeness was achieved. He or she would consider the structural organization, searching for repetitions and patterns as well as tensions and oppositions. Rhythms, use of imagery, and figures of speech would likewise be assessed. Was the writer playing off oppositions of light and darkness? Were there perceptible changes in the rhythm of the poetry, or the language of the prose? The critic would evaluate the tone for irony, and look at the nuances of the verbal expression. Was the writer amplifying the meanings of the text with connotations and ambiguities?

Another name for this approach to the literary text is "close reading" (see Chapter 2). Close reading was the favored operating procedure for the New Critics, which is what the American formalists called themselves. Influential theorists such as Cleanth Brooks, Robert Penn Warren, and John Crowe Ransom taught generations of students their techniques for the exhaustive examination of literary works. The danger, of course, is a loss of perspective. The freshness and purpose of a poem or a story can vanish while the vigilant critic searches for ironies and ambiguities. But when used with restraint, the close-reading methods of the New Critics can bring the reader deep into the functioning core of the text.

For an example of the New Critical approach to a work of fiction, see "The Discovery of Evil: An Analysis of 'The Killers' " by Cleanth Brooks and Robert Penn Warren (Chapter 13). Examples of the close-reading approach are seen in the discussions of Louis Jenkins's "Fish Out of Water" (Chapter 1) and of the first paragraph of John Updike's "Separating" (p. 20).

A Sample Opening of a Student Paper Using a Formalist Approach

```
     Kate Chopin's "The Story of an Hour" is just
that--a private drama condensed into a very short
time period. The narrative is bare, with the key
triggering event--the supposed death of Mrs. Mal-
lard's husband in a train accident--taking place off-
stage. Whatever happens can be said to happen in
(and finally to) that woman's heart. This does not
```

sound like a recipe for high drama, yet the story,
short as it is, has a genuine power. This is because
within the tight confines of her narrative (what
Chopin has called "an hour"), the author has set up
a double irony. First, there is the situational
irony. The reader expects Mrs. Mallard to be grief-
stricken and discovers (as she does herself) something very different--she is feeling the exultation
of sudden freedom. Playing against this, strengthen-
ing its effect, is the larger dramatic irony: that
Mrs. Mallard should begin to live because she believes that her husband has died, and that she
should then die when she sees that he is alive. The
reversal is almost too pat. However . . .

Suggested Reading

Cleanth Brooks, *The Well Wrought Urn*, London, 1947
John Crowe Ransom, *The World's Body*, New York, 1938
Allen Tate, *Collected Essays*, Denver, 1959
W. K. Wimsatt and Monroe Beardsley, *The Verbal Icon*, New York, 1958
William Empson, *Seven Types of Ambiguity*, London, 1930

PSYCHOANALYTIC CRITICISM

Psychoanalytic criticism incorporates various approaches based on a large body of theory about our mental and emotional processes. What the theories of Karl Marx are to Marxist criticism, the theories of Sigmund Freud (1856–1936) are to Psychoanalytic criticism. That is, they represent a point of origin from which divergent modes of analysis have developed.

Very briefly, Freud proposed a three-part model of psychic functioning in which the *ego* (or "I" concept), *id* (or unconscious), and *superego* (or conscience) sought the equilibrium that we describe as "balance" in a personality. One of the salient elements of Freud's psychology—important for an understanding of artistic process— was the theory of *repression*. Repression is the means whereby socially unacceptable desires and wishes, manifested by the id, are held in check by the ego. When the forces grow too insistent they may (in a healthy person) discharge themselves in dreams. But even in dream narratives, these desires are seldom expressed directly. More commonly they are disguised; the so-called dream work makes use of *symbols* (where one thing stands for something else: a gun for a penis, etc.), *condensations* (where several messages are combined), and *displacements* (associative substitutions, as when a blond-haired woman stands in for one's blond-haired mother). For Freud, the artist served as a pressure valve of sorts for the larger society, producing works that expressed, in acceptable forms, the various human longings and conflicts.

One of Freud's followers, Carl Gustave Jung (1875–1961), developed a comprehensive theory of symbolic forms, or *archetypes,* that had a certain influence on critical thought, particularly through the work of Canadian critic Northrop Frye. The theory of archetypes proposes that we all have a share in a collective unconscious, and that all human expression grows out of certain enduring symbolic patterns (the hero's quest, the journey to the underworld, etc.). Frye, in his powerful study *Anatomy of Criticism,* sought to identify the fundamental *mythoi* (or "myth configurations") that underlie all works of literature. He likewise devised a complex set of symbolic relations and sequences, finally orchestrating a grand cyclical theory of literature in which "ironic" phases alternate with "mythic" phases (a model of recurrent loss and reattainment of innocence).

A more recent current of Psychoanalytic criticism has grown up out of the work of French theorist Jacques Lacan. Lacan recognized that the therapeutic process was deeply bound to language (Freudian psychoanalysis is sometimes called "the talking cure"), and by modifying some of the insights of Deconstructionist theoreticians he achieved his own unique approach to texts. For Lacan, the child's entry into the system of language plunges him or her into a circuit of endlessly ungratified desire, instigating a search for meanings that is doomed to frustration by the very nature of symbolic structures.

Psychoanalytic criticism, then, sees the text as an embodiment of complex mental and emotional processes. A strict Freudian reading might treat the work as an analyst would treat a dream—the critic would search out symbols, condensations, and displacements, and distinguish the *manifest* (or "surface") from the *latent* (or "hidden") contents. (The interested reader might look to the discussions of Frank O'Connor's "My Oedipus Complex" or Delmore Schwartz's "In Dreams Begin Responsibilities" (both in Chapter 13) to see how fundamental Freudian notions can be applied to literary works.)

Jungian theory takes a broader view, looking past the individual artist to see how the work expresses universal archetypes. Lacanian criticism, which is notoriously obscure, searches the language of the text to determine how the play of *signifiers* (words) at once suggests and eludes meaning.

Traditional Freudian and Jungian critical modes have waned in influence in recent years. The Freudian interpretation has come under attack from feminists, in part because of the problematic centrality of the Oedipus complex, a theory of psychological development that is strongly biased toward the male. The Jungian approach, meanwhile, with is implicit appeal to fixed patterns and collective functioning, has been undermined by disciplines such as Deconstruction, which go in suspicion of all such systematic certainties. Lacanian criticism, while retaining a certain currency, is so difficult to put into practice that it has remained a kind of minority sport.

If the various psychoanalytic approaches appear outmoded or otherwise problematic, great benefit is nevertheless to be derived from an acquaintance with the basic principles. Even if the reader does not apply any of the theories systematically, that reader's insight into the dynamics of textual meaning is bound to be sharpened considerably. What's more, the theories themselves are every bit as fascinating as the literature they would explain.

For additional backgrounds to Psychoanalytic criticism, see also the selection from Freud's *The Interpretation of Dreams* (Chapter 37).

A Sample Opening of a Student Paper Using a Psychoanalytic Approach

   Frank O'Connor's story "My Oedipus Complex" takes its title from Sigmund Freud's famous theory of the same name. Freud believed that young boys have a powerful emotional bond with their mothers and actually see their fathers as being their rivals in love. This psychological rite of passage (usually believed to take place from ages three to six) is not considered resolved until the boy has accepted the reality that he <u>cannot</u> marry his mother and must coexist with his father. Writing from the perspective of a boy--who does not know that he is working out a familiar psychological pattern--O'Connor has great fun with his premise. He has, in fact, set things up so that the boy very nearly believes he <u>is</u> married to his mother. Certainly he is, for a time, the lord of the manor. For as it happens the father is a soldier and is off at war, and it is not until he has returned to resume his rightful place in the home that the confusion builds to a climax.

Suggested Reading

Sigmund Freud, *The Standard Edition of the Complete Psychological Works of Sigmund Freud*, London, 1953 (Freud's individual works are widely available in paperback editions)
Norman Holland, *The Dynamics of Literary Response*, Oxford, 1968
Ernst Kris, *Psychoanalytic Explorations of Art*, New York, 1952
Harold Bloom, *The Anxiety of Influence*, London, 1975
Shoshana Felman (ed.), *Literature and Psychoanalysis*, Baltimore, 1982
Jacques Lacan, *Ecrits: A Selection*, London, 1977
Northrop Frye, *Anatomy of Criticism*, Princeton, NJ, 1957

STRUCTURALISM AND DECONSTRUCTION

Structuralism is, as the name suggests, a theory focused upon the structure of human expressions. The movement was in its heyday in the 1960s and 1970s and was by no means confined to the study of the literary work. Structuralists worked their particular reading strategy on everything from mythology to linguistics to anthropology. Indeed, French critic Roland Barthes went so far as to venture Structuralist readings of fashion magazines and wrestling matches. So long as the activity or work was generated by humans, so the assumption went, it could be decoded.

   The original premise underlying the Structuralist enterprise derives from the theories of the noted French linguist Ferdinand de Saussure. In his influential

Course in General Linguistics (1915), Saussure proposed an arresting new way to understand language. It was, he argued, an entirely arbitrary system. There was no reason why any combination of letters or sounds could not represent any given thing so long as the difference between one word and another was clearly given. In other words, language is a construct, a system based on the recognition of difference. By treating language as a code operating according to fixed rules, Saussure paved the way for other thinkers (like the anthropologist Claude Lévi-Strauss) to view various human disciplines as "languages" likewise governed by codes.

Claude Lévi-Strauss, for instance, made exhaustive studies of the myth systems of various cultures. Once he had gathered and studied all the myths of a given society, he would apply the Structuralist method, isolating elements, looking for patterns of recurrence, seeking after the key that would reveal the logic according to which the parts were all fitted together.

The core assumption of the Structuralist is that the human psyche itself is strictly patterned, and that, therefore, all human expression can be seen to embody those fundamental structures. The most obvious way in which we are ourselves patterned, according to the Structuralists, is in terms of our natural tendency to perceive and think in terms of "binary oppositions." We break things into opposites: up and down, in and out, light and dark, and so on. This universal tendency naturally manifests itself in our artistic and cultural products. When the Structuralist looks to break the code, he looks first to one or another set of polarized terms. Thus, when Lévi-Strauss inventoried the ritual practices of one isolated tribal culture, he found his master key in the symbolic opposition of "raw" and "cooked." He proposed that the entire tribal structure could be understood through an investigation of the complex associations and behaviors relating to the two ways of consuming food.

Structuralism as an approach to the literary work has certain affinities with Formalism. Here, too, the text is closed off, and stripped of all cultural, historical, or biographical trappings. But where the Formalist looks for the ways in which meaning is achieved through the complex interplay of tensions, ironies, and the like, the Structuralist goes further still. His purpose is to see through the particulars of the story or poem in order to expose the bare bones of design.

Consider, for example, the well-known tale of Cinderella. If a Structuralist critic were to read the work, she would not concern herself in the least with the folk origins of the tale, or its meanings or implicit values. Rather, she would attempt to reveal how the work orchestrates a series of oppositions. Her interest would not be to evaluate, but simply to describe. Thus, our critic would likely take note of the contrasting roles of the wicked stepmother and the fairy godmother; she would reveal how Cinderella's sooty rags are converted into sumptuous finery. She might, further, remark on the way that the tale begins with Cinderella in isolation, divorced from her true family, and how at the end she has married the prince and is set to begin a family of her own. She might find a symmetrical relation, too, between the punishments inflicted on Cinderella at the outset and the indignities that later befall the stepmother's two cruel daughters.

Given the essential assumption of the Structuralist—that all human expression is patterned—it would follow that any work can be explored in just this fashion. And, indeed, ingenious critics have come up with the most remarkable readings of some of the least likely of literary works. What's more, a number of Structuralists have made the assertion that the artistic quality of the work is irrelevant to the operation. One can just as readily deconstruct a Donald Duck comic as a story by Tolstoy. This fact alone suggests the limits of application. The Structuralist approach is an interesting and instructive approach, but as much as it discloses, it necessarily blinds the reader to what is ultimately the point of literature—it turns its back on meaning.

Structuralism does not have the currency it had a few decades ago. Its strongest legacy is that it gave rise to the far more influential—and still vital—practice of Deconstructionist criticism.

A Sample Opening of a Student Paper Using a Structuralist Approach

```
     If we consider light/dark and high/low to be im-
portant polar concepts in Sarah Orne Jewett's "A
White Heron" (others might be innocence/experience,
male/female, youth/age . . . ), then we can see how
the story ultimately moves from the low/dark pairing
to the high/light pairing and thus maps an awakening
in the life of young Sylvy. Consider the first sen-
tence, which describes "woods already filled with
shadows" and the last light of sunset "glimmering
faintly among the trunks of the trees." We see the
girl making her way home down among those shadows.
Bring in one young man, the first stirrings of ro-
mantic (though probably not yet sexual) interest, and
we will see Sylvy leave her bed in the darkest night
to seek out a tree she knows, the tallest in the
area. She wants to find the nest of the elusive
white heron in order to lead the young man to it.
There, in the closing part of the story, she will
climb branch by branch to the highest point. As the
sun rises, she looks out and spots the nest of the
bird. It is a symbol of change in her life, of at-
tainment. She has moved from the low of the path to
the high of the treetop, and from the near darkness
to the dawning light.
```

Deconstruction

The whole point of Deconstruction is to reveal the slipperiness and instability of meanings in literary texts—indeed, in all human systems of discourse. Deconstruction can be seen as evolving from the premises and practices of Structuralism. It takes as one of its points of departure the Saussurian notion of language as a system of differences (*différance*, a word coined by the French theoretician Jacques Derrida, one of the leading exponents of Deconstruction, is a key term used by critics).

If it is true, argue the Deconstructionists, that words are just arbitrary markers, each made distinct by its visual and phonic difference from all others, then it stands to reason that all words are in a sense equal. But what we find in all human communications is an implicit privileging of certain terms and values and, in the last analysis, ideologies. An ideology can be defined as the whole set of assumptions (that men are superior to women, that capitalism is superior to socialism, etc.) against which the specific utterances of a text acquire their meanings.

The Deconstructionists assume that these ideologies are often concealed in a text. The critic's job is not simply to unfold the patterns and oppositions as a Structuralist would, but to go further. The privileged terms or assumptions, such a critic might reason, exist at the expense of their opposites. There must be some way in which, say, a *phallocentric* (or male-biased) text suppresses the female perspective. If this suppression can be unmasked—shown at work—then the text can be deconstructed. It can, in other words, be exposed as resting upon unsecured assumptions of male superiority.

This sounds complicated and abstractly theoretical, and it is. Indeed, of all critical movements, Deconstruction is the hardest to explain clearly in a short account. For one thing, Deconstructionists themselves are seldom in agreement about the strategies and intents of their discipline. Deconstruction is not so much a theory that asserts something as it is a set of intricate maneuvers for taking a text apart. Moreover, each work is deconstructed in its own way, with the procedure guided at every point by the twists and turns of the text itself, by what practitioners call its ruling systems of logic.

To get just a taste of how the Deconstructionist might think about a problem, consider the well-known flip of the causality argument. If a pin pricks the flesh, we customarily say that the pin (A) is the cause of the pain (B). The Deconstructionist might assert, on the contrary, that the dominant rule of all causal sequences is that the cause precedes the effect. In this case, it is the pain (B) that makes the person aware of the pin (A). Logically, then, the pain can be seen as the cause, the pin the effect. And with this tricky wedge, the critic could begin to wage assault upon the ironclad assumptions of causal reasoning. Here again, however, the summary presentation must belie the complexity of the procedure. The student who is interested in learning more about how to apply this controversial and challenging discipline should refer to some of the works listed below.

A Sample Opening of a Student Paper Using a Deconstructionist Approach

```
    Nathaniel Hawthorne's "Wakefield" can be seen to
be a subversion of the traditional ideas of narra-
tion. Most stories proceed by way of gradual disclo-
sure, keeping the reader engaged with various
techniques of suspense. Each new passage carries a
promise of new information. Hawthorne deliberately
```

undermines this normal practice. He tells the whole
of the story in the first paragraph, leading the
reader to ask, "What will the rest of the story be
about?" As it turns out, the rest of the story is a
retelling of the first paragraph. But it doesn't resolve the mystery of Wakefield's disappearance--it
only narrates it at greater length. The first paragraph, then, mocks the idea of beginnings and it
mocks the reader who imagines that the rest of the
story will compensate her for giving everything away
at the outset. If we look closely at the first
paragraph and then at the rest of the story, we
will see that the latter is simply an enlargement
of the former . . .

Suggested Reading

Structuralism:

Roland Barthes, *Critical Essays*, London, 1964
                   Mythologies, London, 1972
Vladimir Propp, *The Morphology of the Folktale*, Austin, Texas, 1968
Jonathan Culler, *Structuralist Poetics*, London, 1975
Terence Hawkes, *Structuralism and Semiotics*, London, 1977
Ferdinand de Saussure, *Course in General Linguistics*, London, 1978

Deconstruction:

Johnathan Culler, *On Deconstruction: Theory and Criticism after Structuralism*, London, 1982
Terry Eagleton, *Literary Theory*, Minneapolis, 1983
Barbara Johnson, *The Critical Difference: Essays in the Contemporary Rhetoric of Reading*,
     Cambridge, MA, 1980
Christopher Norris, *Deconstruction: Theory and Practice*, London, 1982
Paul de Man, *Allegories of Reading*, New Haven, CN, 1979
Jacques Derrida, *Writing and Difference*, London, 1978

READER-RESPONSE CRITICISM

As was noted at the outset, literary theory in recent decades has seen a marked shift
of emphasis. Exclusive preoccupation with the text has given way, at least for some
critics, to a growing awareness of the reader's role in the literary transaction. Where
Formalism sought to sequester the text, purging all extraneous elements that might
interfere with a pure perception of the words on the page, a growing number of theoreticians now assert that there is no such thing as a pure, or neutral, encounter with
a text. Every work is read—or "constructed"—differently. The reader is always a
unique individual situated in a specific context, and the reading is necessarily the
product of a whole array of personal and cultural determinants. The influential

movement of Reader-Response criticism aims to account for the central role played by the reader in the interpretative act.

Reader-Response theory recognizes the engagement of the reader within several contexts. First, there is the immediate context of "concretization"—the sentence-by-sentence creation of text. When we read a work, especially for the first time, we do not simply move our eyes back and forth and wait for images and concepts to announce themselves. We exert great energy, making surmises, arranging details into pictures, venturing and revising predictions. We stitch the clues together, closing up "gaps" (logical and sequential holes that we must fill in) and contending with "indeterminacies" (or uncertainties). We follow the text as if it were a shooting script for a film, trying to represent the action for ourselves on our mental screens.

The larger context of Reader-Response criticism recognizes that readings of any given work are likely to differ from reader to reader, sometimes to an extraordinary extent. The reception is necessarily affected by the reader's gender, age, cultural background, personal life-experience, beliefs, and historical vantage. A high school student reading a story about adulterous passion will have one set of reactions, and a middle-aged man who has divorced over accusations of infidelity will have quite another.

To see these two contexts at work, consider the opening sentences of Joyce Carol Oates's "The Lady with the Pet Dog" (see Chapter 14):

> Strangers parted as if to make way for him.
> There he stood. He was there in the aisle, a few yards away, watching her.
> She leaned forward at once in her seat, her hand jerked up to her face as if to ward off a blow—but then the crowd in the aisle hid him, he was gone. She pressed both hands against her cheeks. He was not there, she had imagined him.

If we have not read the story before, then we begin in complete ignorance (though a reader who knows Anton Chekhov's story of similar title may find certain expectations aroused). We must turn ourselves into detectives, readers of clues. We must simultaneously comb the sentences carefully for information *and* allow our imaginations free play in conjuring up possibilities. What do we learn? That there is a he and a she; that they are in a public place (a cinema, a train, at a baseball game?); that she reacts with surprise (or alarm, or shock) when she catches sight of him. The suppositions we make depend in part upon logical deduction, and in part upon our own disposition as readers. One reader straightaway concludes that these are old lovers; another thinks it might be an estranged father and daughter. Most readers will probably assume that these are young or middle-aged adults, but there is no reason they could not be old people.

And on and on we go, noting cues, making guesses, modifying the scenario. Each new sentence curtails certain possibilities, and opens others. An ever more specific picture takes shape. But specificity notwithstanding, there will never be two readers who can be said to have had an identical literary experience. The human response mechanisms are too subtle and various.

The issues that arise are obvious. If readings of the same work vary according to the reader, on what grounds are interpretations to be judged? Can there be a "right" or "best" reading of a work? Or is it finally a matter of what you say versus what I say?

As may be expected, the literary community is hardly unanimous on this score. On one end of the spectrum is the position taken by critic E. D. Hirsch in his book *Validity in Interpretation*. Hirsch affirms that while we cannot know for certain what an author intended in the creation of a work, we are nonetheless constrained by our estimate of the probable intent. In other words, the reader who would argue that *Moby-Dick* is first and foremost a work of sexual symbolism would have to contend with the legacy of evidence (assembled by critics, biographers, and historians) that suggests that his motives had more to do with religious allegory and with philosophical considerations of good and evil.

Critic Stanley Fish, in his book *Is There a Text in This Class?*, offers the challenge of complete relativism. There is, Fish believes, no central or authorized reading of a text; there are only readings. The idea of constraining interpretation through an appeal to authorial intention is a chimera. The only way that anything approaching consensus can be reached is through the application of common "interpretative strategies," such as are likely to be found in academic communities where readers agree to certain premises and procedures.

In practical terms, the criticism that draws upon the ideas of the Reader-Response theories is especially attuned (a) to the ways that the author presents the work as an entity to be constructed (how are settings and descriptions handled, how is the passing of time handled, how are "gaps" and "indeterminacies" implemented?) and (b) to the ways that different readers are likely to filter the text through different contexts of response. Reader-Response criticism could be said to resemble close reading on some levels, but rather than looking closely at just the text, the critic is also studying the specific ways in which it enlists the reader in the process of making it concrete.

For examples of various readers' responses to texts, see Vladimir Nabokov on "The Lady with the Little Dog" (Chapter 14), Harold Bloom's reading of Coleridge's "Frost at Midnight" (Chapter 28), and Robert Lowell's interpretation of Stanley Kunitz's "Father and Son" (Chapter 28).

A Sample Opening of a Student Paper Using a Reader-Response Approach

Amy Hempel's short story "In the Cemetery Where Al Jolson Is Buried" requires the reader to pay very close attention in order to figure out the real situation that the two friends find themselves in. The story begins on a casual, offbeat note, with one friend saying to the other, "Tell me things I won't mind forgetting. . . . Make it useless stuff or skip it." The friend obliges with all kinds of trivia, like "no one in America owned a tape recorder before Bing Crosby did." It is not until the third paragraph that we learn that the two friends are in the intensive care unit of a hospital. As the story pro-

ceeds, section by short section, we begin to piece
together an understanding, one which, as will be
seen, grows more complex and revealing with every new
bit of information. The ultimate shock of the story
is our realization that the flip comments mask a
very frightening actuality: one of the friends is
dying.

Suggested Reading

Wolfgang Iser, *The Implied Reader,* Baltimore, 1974
      The Act of Reading, London, 1978
Stanley Fish, *Is There a Text in This Class?,* Cambridge, MA, 1980
Susan R. Suleiman and Inge Crosman (eds.), *The Reader in the Text,* Princeton, NJ, 1980
Jane Tompkins, *Reader-Response Criticism,* Baltimore, 1980

MARXIST AND FEMINIST CRITICISM

Marxist and Feminist criticism, which are sometimes subsumed under the heading of *sociological criticism,* represent powerful currents in the academic community. Both approaches aim to remove the text from the kind of isolation favored by Formalists and to read it as a product and expression of a range of societal forces. In this way, Marxist and Feminist criticism politicize a discipline that is generally thought to be removed from worldly concerns.

Marxist criticism takes its name from Karl Marx (1818–1883), who, in his monumental *Das Kapital,* analyzed the intricate social and economic dynamics that underlay class society. He exposed the mechanism whereby the capitalist class extracts surplus labor from the proletariat (or "working class") and prophesied that a condition conducive to worker revolution would inevitably be reached. Although Marxist theories were originally focused upon the importance of revolution, its practitioners today are not generally out leafleting for the overthrow of the government. More likely, they are pursuing their sophisticated textual analyses, intent upon revealing how the forces of the economy, social class, and power relationships impinge upon literary works.

For such a critic, the value systems of writer and reader alike have been shaped in myriad ways by the ideologies that are the product of these forces. The critic feels a responsibility to bring these often concealed ideologies into the foreground, and to discuss just how they form part of the fabric of the work.

A Marxist critic would, for example, delight in a work like D. H. Lawrence's "The Odour of Chrysanthemums" (Chapter 13), which tells the story of a coalminer's wife and her response to her husband's death by suffocation. Rather than focusing on the psychological interactions between the various characters (except insofar as they are determined by economic and class pressures), the critic would be likely to look at the conditions of mine labor, and the larger systems of capital that make those conditions inevitable. The death by suffocation would probably be read less as a circumstantial accident, and more as a symbolic depiction of what the capitalist class is doing to the laboring class.

Unlike some critical approaches, Marxist criticism cannot be applied with equal success to every work. For a Marxist reading to bear fruit, the text must have a certain societal component. Where the subject matter is resolutely personal or subjective, the critic is at a loss. Not surprisingly, the favored texts for Marxist literary analysis are the great nineteenth-century social novels by writers such as Jane Austen, Anthony Trollope, Charles Dickens, and others.

Though Soviet communism has recently collapsed, its ideology discredited, Marxist modes of sociological criticism are likely to remain popular in universities. No other approach proposes so comprehensive a connection between the literary text and the complex functioning of social systems.

A Sample Opening of a Student Paper Using a Marxist Approach

The Marxist approach to literary criticism depends upon an understanding of the conflict between classes as set out in the political philosophy of Karl Marx (1818–1883). According to Marx, the economic structure of a capitalist society puts those who own the means of production (the factories, etc.) at war with those who are enslaved by their reliance on the owners. Though William Faulkner might never have read or studied the works of Marx, his story "Wash" can be read as a perfect illustration of this struggle. Representing the owning class--at least originally, before the Civil War--is Colonel Sutpen. Wash, one of his hands, represents what Marx might have called the "proletariat." The whole story turns upon Wash's mistaken belief that he and Sutpen have a bond, that they are friends, even equals of a sort, and the climax comes when Wash overhears a remark by Sutpen that reveals that this is not at all the case.

Feminist Criticism

Feminist criticism bears a certain relation to Marxist criticism. Feminist critics, too, believe that a powerful dynamic underlies our social conditions. But where the Marxist critic focuses upon class-related forces, the Feminist critics look to the radically unequal distribution of power among genders. Our social institutions, they believe, are governed by *patriarchal* (or "male-biased") codes. Women are treated as second-class citizens both economically and socially. This treatment is underwritten, or supported, by powerful ideologies about male superiority.

The agenda of Feminist criticism is twofold. First, it is to expose and deconstruct the ideology as it manifests itself in literary works. That is, the Feminist critic attempts to show not only the gender assumptions that are written into a work, but also to reveal, often through careful deconstruction of the text, that they are simply assumed and rest on no foundation. A writer like Ernest Hemingway, with his well-known "macho" ethos, makes an obvious target. A Feminist critic would first read the work to identify its patriarchal assumptions and attitudes. He or she might then look closely at the grounds upon which the male superiority is assumed, and proceed to take them apart one by one, showing that they rest on little more than bravado.

The approach is not always so direct. But at the very least, Feminist criticism attempts to read literary works through a specific lens: the lens of a long history of unequal distribution of power among men and women. Where women are portrayed as tragic, or unhappy, or (as in *Macbeth*) evil, the critic seeks to understand the extent to which the portrayal may be a reflection of a male ideology.

The other part of the Feminist agenda involves the rewriting of history, literary and otherwise. The Feminists believe that the manifestations of patriarchal power extend right to the canon (see Casebook) itself. As principal writers of history, men have naturally given themselves starring roles. In the process they have suppressed any number of vital contributions by women. The Feminist critics would rewrite the tradition and make substantial additions to the canon.

The Feminists have had striking success in realizing their aims. Feminist criticism is one of the most vital currents on the contemporary academic scene. And our literary history is being substantially rewritten, not only through the presentation of neglected works by women (like the stories and novels of Kate Chopin, Charlotte Perkins Gilman, and others), but also by the inclusion of a growing body of important work by contemporary women writers.

For further insight on Feminist (and political) perspectives, see Adrienne Rich's essay "When We Dead Awaken: Writing as Re-vision" (Chapter 25).

A Sample Opening of a Student Paper Using a Feminist Approach

Anton Chekhov's story "The Lady with the Little Dog" while apparently about the unfolding of a love between two married strangers, can also be seen as a critique of the patriarchal attitudes prevalent in late-nineteenth-century Russia. When we first meet the protagonist, Gurov, he is a self-satisfied male of his class; Chekhov wants us to see him as typical. He is a married man who thinks nothing of having an affair if he can get away with it. It is not until he falls in love with Anna, a married woman he

meets at the resort of Yalta, that his attitude--his
fundamental belief system--begins to change.

Gurov does not believe in the equality of the
sexes, certainly not at first. Chekhov tells us this
directly, referring to Gurov's wife: "He had begun
being unfaithful to her long ago--had been unfaithful to her often, and, probably on that account, almost always spoke ill of women, and when they were
talked about in his presence, used to call them 'the
lower race.'" Anna Sergeyevna is no exception for
him--not at first . . .

Suggested Reading

Marxist Criticism:

Terry Eagleton, *Marxism and Literary Criticism*, London, 1976
Raymond Williams, *Marxism and Literature*, Oxford, 1977
Lee Baxandall and Stefan Morowski (eds.), *Marx and Engels on Literature and Art*,
    New York, 1973
Georg Lukacs, *The Historical Novel*, London, 1974
                Studies in European Realism, London, 1975
Frederic Jameson, *Marxism and Form*, Princeton, NJ, 1971

Feminist Criticism:

Mary Ellmann, *Thinking about Women*, New York, 1968
M. Z. Rosaldo and L. Lamphere (eds.), *Women, Culture and Society*, Stanford, 1974
Kate Millett, *Sexual Politics*, London, 1971
Juliet Mitchell, *Psychoanalysis and Feminism*, Harmondsworth, 1976
Elaine Showalter, *A Literature of Their Own: British Women Novelists from Brontë to Lessing*,
    Princeton, NJ, 1977
Sandra Gilbert and Susan Gubar, *The Madwoman in the Attic*, London, 1979
Virginia Woolf, *A Room of One's Own*, London, 1929

B: Researching and Documenting a Paper about Literature

LOCATING SOURCES

Though we are hearing increasingly grandiose accounts these days of the extraordinary access to data afforded by a computer and modem link-up, for most of us the library is still the first place to turn when there is research to be done. Its resources are many and various, including standard reference volumes, computerized search systems, and—perhaps most important—trained librarians who understand the many ways in which knowledge is formally organized. If you have a hard time navigating the various cataloging and indexing systems, present yourself to the reference librarian. He or she can direct you to the object of your search, or at least point you to some of the standard research guides and bibliographies that can suggest what books and articles might be available on your chosen topic. Here are a few standard works you should know about.

An Annotated List of Standard References

Baker, Nancy L. *A Research Guide for Undergraduate Students: English and American Literature.* 2nd ed. New York: MLA, 1985. As the title suggests, this is a very useful guide to various reference sources.

Corse, Larry B., and Sandra B. Corse. *Articles on American and British Literature: An Index to Selected Periodicals, 1950–1977.* Athens, OH: Swallow, 1981.

Elliot, Emory, et al. *Columbia Literary History of the United States.* New York: Columbia UP, 1988. Excellent survey of American literary history from its colonial origins to its recent expressions.

Harner, James L. *Literary Research Guide: A Guide to Reference Sources for the Study of Literature in English and Related Topics.* New York: MLA, 1989. A very handy reference tool that features important information on bibliographies, abstracts, databases, etc.

Holman, C. Hugh, and William Harmon. *A Handbook to Literature*. 6th ed. New York: Macmillan, 1992. An excellent dictionary of key literary terms and movements.

MLA International Bibliography of Books and Articles on Modern Language and Literature. New York: MLA, 1921–   . An annual compilation, with a comprehensive listing of articles and books.

The New Cambridge Bibliography of English Literature. 5 vols. Cambridge, Eng.: Cambridge, 1967–1977. A key guide to literature from its origins in England to 1950.

The Oxford History of English Literature. 13 vols. Oxford, Eng.: Oxford UP, 1945–   , in progress. The most authoritative guide to the history of English literature.

The Penguin Companion to World Literature. 4 vols. New York: McGraw-Hill, 1969–1971. Information on authors and literary movements of classical, Oriental, African, European, English, and American literature.

Preminger, Alex, ed. *Princeton Encyclopedia of Poetry and Poetics*. Princeton, N.J.: Princeton, 1975. Indispensible guide to poetic movement and developments in poetics.

In addition, students should be aware of the following multivolume publications by the Gale Research Company (Detroit): *Contemporary Literary Criticism, Contemporary Authors, Twentieth Century Literary Criticism*, and *Nineteenth Century Literary Criticism*. These are an invaluable reference source for author biographies, bibliographies, and digests of important reviews and scholarly discussions.

Computer Searches

Most libraries now not only have transferred their old card catalogs into updated computer databases, but offer an array of on-line search options. As with most developments involving computers, change is the only constant. The reference librarian will be happy to show you the latest modes of access and to assist you in your search process. Most library computers have printers and can print out references at a keystroke.

Notes, and Bibliographical Notes

Technology has streamlined much that used to be cumbersome about library research. But the standard 3 × 5 card is not yet extinct. There are any number of situations in which a standard card annotation is the fastest and most reliable way to go. As you can see from the sample bibliography card below, the key information is arranged for quick transcription. If you are making a card for an article, include author, complete title, name of periodical, volume number, and date of the issue, and inclusive page numbers.

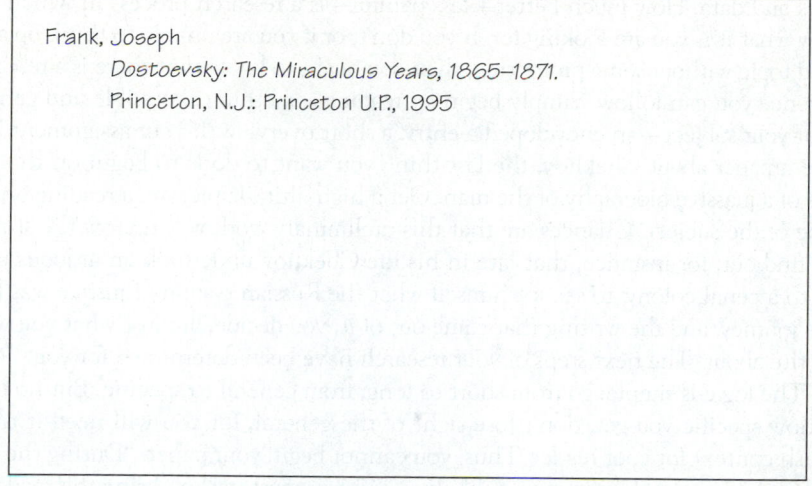

Frank, Joseph
   Dostoevsky: The Miraculous Years, 1865–1871.
   Princeton, N.J.: Princeton U.P., 1995

The same cards are also most handy for keeping notes, quotations, and so on. If you are keeping bibliographic cards, you need not duplicate the information on the note card. Simply make up a general heading and then copy out the important quotation or information. Make sure to cross-reference the note card to the bibliographic card.

Dostoevsky's gambling   Frank 19

Frank characterizes D's gambling behavior as "obsessive" and "in many ways worthy of one of his own characters."

                  [include in biography section]

ORGANIZING AND INCORPORATING SOURCES WITHIN YOUR PAPER

Researching a subject is very often the first step in writing a paper. Indeed, many students begin the research process before they know exactly what it is they want to write about. They hope that contact with scholars and critics will direct them to a topic. This can work, of course, and many fine papers have eventually resulted from such an approach. But it is inefficient, and it poses the real risk of drowning in unformulated views and data. How much better—less painful—is a research process in which you know what it is you are looking for. If you don't, or if you are unable to think up a focused topic without some prompting, then you ought to know that there is a research sequence you can follow. Simply begin by reading something accessible and general about your subject—an encyclopedia entry, a short overview. If your assignment is to write a paper about Chekhov, the last thing you want to do is to begin on the first page of a massive biography of the man. Get a high-altitude picture, a reading on the scope of the subject. Chances are that this preliminary work will narrow the search. You find out, for instance, that late in his life Chekhov undertook an arduous journey to a penal colony, to see for himself what the Russian system of justice was like. This journey, and the writing that came out of it, you decide, are just what you want to write about. The next steps of your research have been determined for you.

The logic is simple: go from short to long, from general to specific. But no matter how specific you get, don't lose sight of the general, for you will need it to establish context for your reader. Thus, you cannot begin your paper: "During the first week of his overland journey to Sakhalin. . . ." You must, rather, bring the reader in by stages: "Though he did not live to see old age, Anton Chekhov managed to compress the experience of several lifetimes into his forty-four years."

As you carry out your research, keep track of your progress. Use note cards, as suggested, and take great care to copy quotations accurately. Always indicate exactly where a given passage was found, and include the information in your paper using parenthetical citation and a "Works Cited" list at the end.

DOCUMENTING A PAPER ABOUT LITERATURE

Most kinds of academic and professional writing make some use of information and ideas belonging to others. It is therefore of the utmost importance that you learn to document your sources in the proper manner. This documentation is something more than simple politeness—it's the law. For in the world of information exchange certain ideas, insights, and pieces of information are protected by copyright and are regarded as private property. Their unattributed use is called *plagiarism*; it is a form of theft, and can bring severe penalties.

Plagiarism

The question of what belongs to whom is a complicated one. At what point is an idea the property of another? If you read F. Scott Fitzgerald's *The Great Gatsby*, and conclude on your own that it is a novel that deals with issues of class, should you worry that some critic may have voiced that theory before you? Obviously not. Indeed, so long as you are developing your own ideas without benefit of any secondary sources, you should not worry about whether or not you may have inadvertently duplicated anyone else's insights. Once you do begin consulting essays, articles, and critical studies by others, however, you cannot be too vigilant. That is, you must pay attention not only to your wording, making sure that you have not "borrowed" another writer's phrases, but you must also be on guard against appropriating specific observations, original theories, or sequences of argumentation. It is not enough to avoid using the other person's words, you must also avoid duplicating the structure of the presentation. The lines are fuzzy, and you must let common sense—if not your conscience—be your guide. If you have *any* doubt, document.

The situation is somewhat more straightforward with respect to facts. There are facts that can be said to belong in the public domain, which include anything that you could go to the library and look up in a reference work. Then there are the facts that are the fruit of some person's original scholarship. If you learn from a biography that a famous painter ate a mixture of kelp and raisins for breakfast, then you must annotate your source. The biographer herself could not have looked up that information, but had to discover it.

What *exactly* constitutes plagiarism? The short answer: using another person's ideas or words as if they were your own. Direct transcription is the obvious case. But there is also plagiarism wherein a writer has strategically modified another writer's wording to avoid the appearance of copying, as follows:

> Hardly more than a quarter-century after Henry Luce proclaimed "the American century," American confidence has fallen to a low ebb. Those who recently dreamed of world power now despair of governing the city of New York. Defeat in Vietnam, economic stagnation, and the impending exhaustion of natural resources have produced a mood of pessimism in higher circles, which spreads through the rest of society as people lose faith in their leaders.
>
> —from *The Culture of Narcissism* by Christopher Lasch

```
Though twenty-five years ago it was said that we
lived in "the American century," something seems to
have gone wrong. We cannot hope to rule the world--
we can barely rule our own cities. A whole series of
ills has befallen us and there is a spreading mood
of pessimism, which leads eventually to a loss of
faith in those who govern.
```

There is nothing shameful about quoting—and a skillfully placed quote can add a great deal to a presentation. The person who took so much trouble to avoid Lasch's phrasing—while keeping the central idea and the logic of the expression—would have done far better to quote the source entire, or to quote the telling phrases:

```
Citing Henry Luce's well-known proclamation of
this being "the American century," Christopher Lasch
goes on to remark the declines of recent years. "Those
who recently dreamed of world power," he writes,
"now despair of governing the city of New York"
(17). Among the causes, Lasch finds, are our defeat
in Southeast Asia, the slow-moving economy, and "the
impending exhaustion of natural resources" (17).
```

For further discussion of the incorporation and documentation of sources, refer to Chapters 10, 28, and 37.

All documentation of literary works follows the format recommended by the Modern Language Association (or MLA). The three-part procedure represents a great streamlining of the far more cumbersome system using numerical footnotes. The MLA documentation style uses *parenthetical citations* in the body of the text, a list of *works cited* after the text, and, where necessary, *explanatory notes*.

PARENTHETICAL CITATIONS IN THE TEXT OF YOUR PAPER

The object of the parenthetical citation is to convey the necessary source information as briefly and unobtrusively as possible. The information inside the parentheses refers the reader to the list of works cited at the end of the paper.

> Robert Alton's "Spiralsong" was originally conceived as a three-part reenactment of the Cinderella story (Miller 116).

If the list of works cited contains only one entry under Miller, then the author's last name and the page number are sufficient. But if there is another work by Miller, or another author named Miller, you must add a shortened title to the reference:

> Robert Alton's "Spiralsong" was originally conceived as a three-part reenactment of the Cinderella story (Miller, "Hoping Against Hope" 116).

If you have stated either the author's name or the title of the work as part of your sentence, a simple page reference will suffice in the citation:

> In his essay, "Hoping Against Hope: The Perils of Structure," Critic Bennett Miller points out that Alton had originally conceived his "Spiralsong" as a reenactment of the Cinderella story in three parts (116).

If your documented source is a work by *two or more authors*, give the citation as follows:

> (Hopspring and Gerstner 93) or (Melnick, Shulman, and Arp 40)

or, for works by more than three authors:

> (Arp et al. 88).

If the work is a *volume* in a larger set, indicate the volume number, then the page:

> (Smelton 3:66)

If you are citing from an *anthology*, indicate inclusive pagination:

> Alton took great pains to distinguish "mythic" from "natural" narrative techniques (Bendix 146–62).

If you are using an *indirect source*, use the abbreviation *qtd*. (quoted in):

> Alton often described himself as a "matchmaker made in heaven" (qtd. in Skillings 77).

When you are quoting an extended passage (four lines or more), separate the passage from the body of your text by indenting ten spaces. The parenthetical documentation should come at the end, two spaces after the final punctuation.

Hugh Kenner addresses this idea of Nick Carraway's naivete in his study *A Homemade World*:

> As a narrator, Nick has the deficiencies of the homemade. Henry James, more knowing, would have used him to locate a point of view without trying to pretend he wrote the book, and despite the technicalities of the first person, this is what he turns out to be: a point of view. (37)

If you are quoting from a poem or a play that has numbered lines, cite the inclusive lines or the act, and scene, and the lines:

"They made the coastline terrible to strangers," writes James Fenton in his poem "Chosun," "And in the interior whole forests were burned down" (21–22).

or:

"They made the coastline terrible to strangers / And in the interior whole forests were burned down" writes James Fenton in his "Chosun" (21–22).

The slash (/) is used to separate lines of poetry where they have not been set apart. A stanza break is indicated by a double slash (//).

When you quote four or more lines of poetry in the body of a critical paper, indent five spaces and reproduce the lines as they have been printed. Include line references in parentheses:

George Herbert concludes his poem "Love" with the following exchange between the "I" and the personified figure of Love:

> Truth, Lord, but I have marred them: let my shame
>   Go where it doth deserve.
> And know you not, says Love, who bore the blame?
>   My dear, then I will serve.
> You must sit down, says Love, and taste my meat:
>   So I did sit and eat. (13–18)

Documentation for lines quoted from a play is given thus:

Lysander speaks a lover's words in "A Midsummer Night's Dream": "How now my love? Why is your cheek so pale? / How chance the roses there do fade so fast?" (I.i.128–129).

The sequence is *act, scene,* and *lines.*

To cite more than three lines from a play—or even two, if they have different speakers—indent five spaces and present the dialogue as it appears in the text. Cite act, scene, and lines in parentheses after the quotation.

George Herbert concludes

> Philinte and Alceste have a fast-moving exchange, the speed of which is suggested by the staggering of lines on the page:

> PHILINTE. Well, as you see, sincerity in excess
>   Can get you into a very pretty mess;
>   Oronte was hungry for appreciation . . .
> ALCESTE. Don't speak to me.
> PHILINTE.   What?
> ALCESTE.   No more conversation.
> PHILINTE. Really, now.   (1.iii.1–5)

Note that the line count is done by syllable count when lines are staggered, with "Don't speak to me. / What? / No more conversation" counting as one line even though it represents an exchange between the two speakers.

THE "WORKS CITED" LISTING

The list of works cited always begins on a new page following the text of your paper. Alphabetize the works by the author's last name. Where the author is unknown, use the first word—not including articles *a*, *an*, and *the*—of the title. Publishers' names, if they are long, are given in shortened form. The format is as follows.

A Book by a Single Author

Boorstin, Daniel J. The Americans: The Democratic Experience. New York: Random House, 1973.

city of publication
publisher   *date of first publication*

A Book by Two or Three Authors

Berger, Peter L., and Thomas Luckmann. The Social Construction of Reality: A Treatise in the Sociology of Knowledge. New York: Doubleday, 1966.

Note that only the first author's name is listed last name first.

A Book by More Than Three Authors

Smithson, Thomas, et al., eds. Annals of the Perverse: The Literature of the Bedroom. Oslo: U. of Norway Pr., 1987.

Two or More Works by One Author

Workman, Allen. Torture Rack: A History of Editing. New York: Simon & Schuster, 1990.

---. Wombats in My Belfry: Further Accounts of Perfidy. New York: Simon & Schuster, 1992.

For every listing of the author's last name after the first, use three hyphens followed by a period. Order titles alphabetically.

A Book with an Editor

Cox, Harvey, ed. The Situation Ethics Debate. Philadelphia: Westminster, 1968.

A Book with a Volume Number

Eisenstein, Elizabeth L. The Printing Press as an Agent of Change: Communications and Cultural Transformation in Early Modern Europe. 2 vols. New York: Cambridge Univ. Press, 1979. Vol. 1.

A Literary Work from an Anthology

Bosco, Edward. "Terror in the Night." Stories of Fear. Ed. Benjamin H. D. Buchloh. Halifax: Arco Press, 1987. 46–68.

If you plan to list more than one work from an anthology, cite the anthology *and* give the individual selections separately under the author's last name, but supply only the author, title, editor's last name, and inclusive pages:

Sleigh, Tom. "My Love Affair with Poetry." Hall and Birkerts, 711–752.

A Translated Work

Marcos, Imogene. Shoes and Souls. Trans. Harris Footer. New York: Pendragon, 1989.

An Article from a Journal

Melnyczuk, Askold. "Masochistic Strains in Ukrainian Literature." Studies in Silence 3 (1989): 115–127.

A Magazine Article (No Author Listed)

"Seamus Heaney: The Irish Prankster." High Times 17 May 1977: 62+.

The "+" tells the reader that the magazine gapes are discontinuous. The article begins on page 62 and then continues in the back pages of the magazine.

A Newspaper Article

Dischell, Stuart. "New Jersey Is a State of Mind." Cambridge Tab 14 Feb. 1990, sec. 2: 1+.

An Essay in an Encyclopedia

"Symbolism." Encyclopaedia Britannica. 1985 ed.

Well-known reference works do not require full citation of publication information.

A Lecture or Speech

Pinsky, Robert. "The Saxophone Is a Poet's Friend." Talk given at Boston University. Boston, 1 April 1992.

EXPLANATORY NOTES

Explanatory notes use a superscript numeral ([1]) to indicate that additional information will be provided in another location—normally on the first numbered page following the last page of the essay (preceding the "Works Cited" list). These notes are to be used when you need to cite multiple sources for a given assertion:

Critics throughout the ages have wrestled with the legacy of Romanticism.[1]

NOTE: [1]Wilson 46; Pater 118; Diabelli 75; and Ornstein 190.

Notes are also useful when you wish to include more specific information that does not fit easily into your presentation:

Superstitions about the breaking of mirrors abounded during this period.[1]

NOTE: [1]King Osgood, for example, declared before the assembled court his conviction that the shattering of the looking glass prevented the escape of the soul from the body in the event of death (Baker 12).

C: Glossary

alexandrine Iambic hexameter ($\smallsmile\acute\smallsmile\smallsmile\acute\smallsmile$ $\smallsmile\acute\smallsmile\smallsmile\acute\smallsmile$), a form common in French poetry and drama, but thought to be unwieldy in English. See Chapter 33.

allegory A narrative in which characters and events represent larger ideas. The isolated elements function much like symbols, allowing the reader to make correspondences from the particular to the general. Allegory is often used to impart moral instruction. John Bunyan's *The Pilgrim's Progress* is a classic example. See Chapters 9, 22, and 37.

alliteration Repetition of initial sounds of words: "a lovely limber lass . . ." See Chapter 16.

allusion An author's indirect reference to something outside the work, often to another work with which the reader may be acquainted. Poets and fiction writers often allude to episodes in the Bible, or Shakespeare, or other writings they expect may be familiar to many. See Chapters 22 and 31.

ambiguity The quality in any situation or expression that allows for several possible interpretations. Since human actions are themselves often ambiguous, stemming from mixed motives, it is only natural that the interactions of characters should follow suit. Authors often use ambiguity to bring complexity to their portrayals and to deepen the thematic resonance of their work.

analysis The act of separating a work into its constituent elements. Analysis is often a preliminary step in finding a topic to write about. See Chapter 10.

anapestic meter A meter using feet of three syllables, the first two unstressed

and the third stressed ($\smallsmile\smallsmile\acute{}$). See Chapter 18.

antagonist The character in a work who opposes the *protagonist*—e.g., the wicked stepmother in the Cinderella story. See Chapter 3.

apostrophe A figure of speech common to poetry and drama, in which an absent character or force is addressed directly; e.g., in Matthew Arnold's "Dover Beach," the speaker suddenly says: "Ah, love, let us be true / To one another!" See Chapter 21.

archetypes Universal symbols, often felt to represent fundamental truths of the human spirit. The psychologist Jung believed that archetypes are an essential part of our psychic makeup and that when we encounter them in literature we feel a sense of deepened resonance. The hero-quest and the journey to the underworld are enduring literary archetypes. See "Psychoanalytic Criticism" in Appendix A.

aside A comment spoken by an actor to the audience; other characters on stage are assumed not to hear it. See Chapter 31.

assonance Repeated vowel sounds in a cluster of words: "He was tossed into the soft, mossy pile." See Chapter 16.

auditory image A way for a poet to evoke sound using an image, as in Seamus Heaney's line "Our shells *clacked* on the plates." See Chapter 20.

ballad stanza An arrangement of quatrains usually rhyming *abcb*—the basis of the ballad form. The ballad stanza is usually followed by a refrain, a stanza repeated at regular intervals throughout the poem. See "quatrain" and Chapter 19.

bard An epic poet from the times of the oral tradition. Usually male, he would declaim poems from memory at celebrations and important occasions. See Chapter 17.

binary oppositions Things—qualities—broken up into their opposing elements: light and dark, high and low, good and evil. Binary oppositions are part of the process whereby Structuralists break down and study a work of literature. See "Structuralism and Deconstruction" in Appendix A.

blank verse Lines of unrhymed iambic pentameter ($\smile´\smile´\smile´\smile´$) that are not usually set in any particular stanzaic form. Blank verse is used often because it is versatile and because it resembles the patterns of impassioned human speech. It is often found in Shakespeare's plays, especially in the mouths of his more noble characters. See Chapters 19 and 31.

box set A stage set meant to convey the impression of real life—e.g., a realistically appointed room with a ceiling tilted toward the rear of the stage to accentuate the sense of perspective. See Chapter 34.

cacophony Use of words to convey a jarring impression: "the clanging klaxons hooted. . . ." See Chapter 16.

caesura A strong pause in the middle of a line of poetry, created by punctuation or a natural shift of sense—marked // in scansion. See Chapter 18.

canon The group of works deemed to be central to the culture. Canons are usually devised and enforced by institutions—universities and academies. See Chapter 1 and Casebook.

catharsis The emotional purging that Aristotle saw as one of the dominant purposes of Greek tragedy. For Aristotle catharsis arose when the audience felt the mingling of pity and fear in the climactic moments of the play. See Chapter 30; *see also* "katharsis."

chorus A group of actors in Greek drama who comment in unison upon the actions on stage. They are led by a figure called the "Choragos." See Chapter 30.

climax The point of maximum tension in a play or a work of fiction. Events leading up to the climax are often called the "building action" or "rising action" and events that follow are the "falling action." See Chapters 4, 29, and 30.

close reading The technique of isolating a text or portion of a text and subjecting it to very careful inspection, looking at all of its literary elements and how they work in concert. A technique favored by the New Critics. See "Formalism/New Criticism" in Appendix A.

comedy of manners A theatrical style popular between the sixteenth and eighteenth centuries. Quick-paced humor grew up from the tensions and pretensions of the upper classes in highly stratified societies. See Chapter 32.

comparison and contrast An approach to writing about literary works that singles out one or more elements and discusses them in terms of their similarities and differences. See Chapter 10.

complication One of the four stages in tragic development. The complication follows the exposition and sets in motion the forces that lead to the climax. The complication is sometimes referred to as "tying the knot." See Chapter 30.

conceit The governing idea in a poem, as when a poet sets out to compare his love to a flower and develops a set of images that characterize ways in which his subject is flower-like. See Chapter 21 and 31.

concretization A term used in Reader-Response criticism (see Appendix A) which refers to the sentence-by-sentence construction of the fictional world.

condensation A psychological term referring to an author's compressing of several thematic strands into an image or episode—e.g., when a bird seems to represent both frailty and the desire for freedom. See "Psychoanalytic Criticism" in Appendix A.

confessional poetry A movement in American poetry that began in the 1950s in which poets began to use material from their own private experience in their poems. Confessional poetry tends to emphasize the dark, once "forbidden" subject matter—divorce, suicide, fears, and anxieties. See Chapter 17.

connotation The suggestion or implication of a particular expression. Words have specific denotative meanings, but they also carry strong associative charges; these are used by the author to bring subtlety and depth into the expression. See Chapters 2, 15, and 21.

consonance A poetic effect involving the substitution of vowels within words that have the same consonant sound, like "litter" and "letter." See Chapter 16.

conventional symbol Symbol that takes its meaning from universally agreed upon equivalences—e.g., a bird stands for freedom, a cross for suffering and redemption. See Chapter 9.

conventions A term used in theater to refer to the implicit rules of staging—that actors are not actors but are the people that they pretend to be, etc. See Chapter 29.

couplet A pair of lines in poetry, often connected by rhyming end words. See Chapters 16, 19, and 33.

crux A crucial or critical point, and often a difficult or obscure passage, in a literary work, one that scholars have not been able to elucidate satisfactorily. See Chapter 31.

dactylic meter Meter characterized by the use of feet with one stressed syllable followed by two unstressed syllables ($´\smile\smile$), often found in quick-moving humorous lyrics. See Chapter 18.

Deconstructionism A style of literary criticism that seeks to unravel the core premise of a work by turning its logic against itself. See "Deconstruction" in Appendix A.

denotation The explicit meaning of a word; the primary meaning identified in a dictionary. See Chapters 2, 15, and 21.

denouement A French term referring to the untying of knotted threads in a literary work after the climax. The denouement is part of the "falling action" of a work. See Chapters 4, 29, and 30.

diction The way in which a writer uses words. Diction determines the level of language in a literary work. Critics often distinguish between "formal" and "informal" diction. See Chapter 17.

dramatic irony Often used in classical tragedy, dramatic irony depends upon the audience knowing something that the protagonist is not yet aware of, as in *Oedipus Rex* where the viewer knows long before Oedipus that he is the guilty person he is searching for. See Chapters 17 and 21.

dynamic character A character in fiction who changes in some fundamental way over the course of the narrative. Dynamic characters are often opposed to "static" characters, who do not change. See Chapter 2.

end-stopped line A line of poetry that ends with a full stop—often punctuated with a period—and does not carry over into the next line. Lines that carry over are called "enjambed." See Chapter 18.

enjambment The poet's technique of carrying the sense over from line to line, using the line break as only a minimal pause.

envoy The three-line conclusion to a sestina which makes use of the poem's six key words. The envoy places three of the words at the ends of the lines and three within the lines. See Chapter 19.

epic theater A movement in twentieth-century theater associated with German playwright Bertolt Brecht. Epic theater sought to dispel the illusionism of the dramatic experience and to engage the audience directly in the issues and philosophies of the play. See Chapter 35.

epigram A short poem or a startling statement that uses keen wit to make its point. See Chapter 19.

episode A self-contained incident that is part of the larger narrative structure. In novels and more complex stories we often find several episodes in sequence, although a single episode—an event depicted from start to finish—is often suggestive enough to carry the work. See Chapters 4 and 30.

euphony Words used to make pleasing sounds—e.g., Keats's "Season of mists and mellow fruitfulness." See Chapter 16.

exact rhyme Also known as "perfect rhyme"—e.g., "sun" and "run." See Chapter 16.

Existentialism Post–World War II philosophical movement that sought to examine the condition of human beings in a godless world. See Chapter 35.

exodus Dramatic term, used especially in Greek tragedy, for the departure of actors from the stage. See Chapter 30.

explication A careful and detailed accounting of a passage or work. An explication looks closely at how the various elements work in concert. See Appendix A.

exposition The first stages of a narrative, wherein the author gives the reader information that will be needed to understand the subsequent developments. See Chapters 4 and 30.

Expressionism A twentieth-century artistic movement that sought the direct expression of powerful states of emotion, often involving the sacrifice of the tidier conventions of plot and character development. Expressionist theater, epitomized by the plays of the Swedish playwright August Strindberg, reached the peak of its popularity in the 1920s in Europe. See Chapter 35.

falling action The narrative that follows the climax in a play or a work of fiction. See Chapters 4 and 29.

feet (in poetry) The rhythmic units that a line of poetry naturally breaks into. The feet are usually either two or three syllables long and tend to fall into basic patterns—e.g., iambic pentameter, or five feet composed of unstressed/stressed (˘ ´) syllable groupings. See Chapter 15.

feminine rhyme The rhyming of the first syllables of two-syllable words in a poem, as in "*din*ner" and "*thin*ner." See Chapter 16.

Feminist criticism A movement in criticism that assesses the presentation of gender in literary works, with special attention given to the portrayal of women. See Appendix A.

fiction Invented accounts of the deeds and fates of people, most of them likewise invented. A major genre division in literary studies, along with poetry, drama, and nonfiction. See Chapter 2.

figurative language Language used in suggestive rather than literal ways. Figurative language in poetry includes simile, metaphor, personification and so on. See Chapters 15 and 21.

figures of speech Specific usages of figurative language, e.g., metaphor, simile, hyperbole, etc. See Chapters 17 and 21.

first-person voice The presentation of narrative in fiction in the voice of an "I." See Chapters 7 and 17.

fixed forms Generic term for an array of poetic forms that require the poet to conform to some exact specifications, whether of line length, meter, stanzaic construction, or rhyme scheme. Examples of fixed forms are the sonnet, the sestina, the haiku, and the villanelle. See Chapter 19.

flat characters Also known as "static" characters, flat characters don't change over the course of the narrative and are generally used as background figures. See Chapter 3.

foreshadowing A narrative device of planting hints and suggestions that anticipate significant upcoming developments. See Chapters 4 and 30.

Formalism A style of literary criticism that seeks to isolate the work from historical or biographical circumstance and to discuss its elements only as they relate to each other; emphasis is placed upon formal properties of the work, like structure, use of literary device, and so on. See Appendix A.

free verse Poetry that does not insist upon metrical regularity and allows the poet a greater range of rhythmic options for expression. Also called "open form." See Chapter 18.

freewriting A technique used to generate ideas, freewriting involves setting down ideas and connections with no advance sense of shape or structure. Freewriting seeks to liberate our associative powers to help us explore a range of possibilities in advance of the discipline of composition. See Chapter 10.

Freytag's triangle A mapping of the classic pattern of fiction and drama, where the rising action represents the side of a triangle, the climax represents its apex, and the falling action represents its other side; also known as "Freytag's pyramid." Gustav Freytag developed his idea in his *Technique of Drama* (1863). See Chapter 4.

gaps A term used in Reader-Response criticism (see Appendix A) to describe textual blanks that the reader fills in to actualize or "concretize" the text.

gloss The explanation or definition of a word in a text, often given in a footnote. See Chapter 29.

guerrilla theater A radical movement in theater during the late 1960s and early 1970s. Actors were encouraged to depart from scripts, to interact with audience members, and to subvert expectations on every front. See Chapter 35.

haiku A seventeen-syllable, three-line form of Japanese poetry. Most haiku draw upon imagery from the natural world. See Chapter 19.

heroic couplet Rhyming pairs of iambic pentameter lines ($\smile\acute{}\,\smile\acute{}\,\smile\acute{}$). The poet Alexander Pope was a master at composing lengthy, generally witty, poems using heroic couplets. See Chapter 19.

high comedy A term denoting comedy that appeals to the intellect, first introduced in 1877 by George Meredith. See Chapter 32.

hyperbole Intentional overstatement: "He was a giant of a man." One of the figures of speech often used by poets and fiction writers alike. See Chapters 17 and 21.

iambic meter A regular pattern of unstressed and stressed syllables ($\smile\acute{}$). Iambic meter is the closest formal approximation to spoken English and is thus the most common poetic meter. See Chapter 18.

iambic pentameter Five feet of iambs: $\smile\acute{}|\smile\acute{}|\smile\acute{}|\smile\acute{}|\smile\acute{}$. See Chapters 15, 18, and 31.

ideologies The systems of belief that underlie social or philosophical capitalism, democracy, liberalism, and so on. See Appendix A.

image An expression meant to appeal to the senses. What kind of image it is depends upon which sense it appeals to. Thus, auditory images, visual images, tactile images, etc. See Chapters 15 and 20.

indeterminacies Like "gaps," these are areas in a text that require the reader's collaboration to be actualized. The term is commonly used by Reader-Response critics. See Appendix A.

indirection Conveying information by suggestion rather than telling. See Chapter 4.

interior monologue The presentation of a character's thoughts in a work of fiction, generally in edited form. The reader is meant to listen in on the character's very thought process. See Chapter 7.

internal rhyme Rhymes occurring not at the ends of lines but between words within the lines of a poem. See Chapter 16.

irony The tension that arises from the discrepancy, either between what one says and what one means (verbal irony), or between what a character believes and what a reader knows (dramatic irony). See Chapters 7, 17, 21, and 31.

Italian sonnet The earliest form of the sonnet (or "little song"), brought to perfection by the Italian poet Petrarch. The Italian sonnet is structured in two parts. The first eight lines make up the "octave" and the remaining six lines are the "sestet." The rhyme pattern can vary, but the poem cannot end with a rhyming couplet. See Chapter 19.

katharsis A term used in discussions of Greek tragedy, referring to the release of emotions brought on by the explosion of tensions in the play's climax. See Chapter 30; *see also* "catharsis."

kinetic images Images emphasizing movement or change. See Chapter 20.

latent content A term used in Psychoanalytic criticism to refer to contents or messages hidden from the surface of the work. Latent contents are opposed to "manifest" or "surface" contents. See Appendix A.

limerick A five-line comical rhyme using anapestic (∪∪´) meter and rhyming in an *aabba* pattern. See Chapter 19.

limited omniscient point of view Narrative access to the inner processes of only a few characters. The thoughts and motives of the others are presumed to be unknowable. See Chapter 7.

line break The end of a line of poetry; can be "end-stopped" or "enjambed." See Chapter 18.

literary symbol Distinct from the natural symbol, which is a matter of general consensus, the literary symbol takes on meanings by virtue of its function in the text. See Chapters 9 and 22.

low comedy Comedy with little or no intellectual appeal—often used to supply comic relief. See Chapter 32.

lyric poem A poem that makes an appeal to the emotions or the senses and does not depend upon the unfolding of an episodic sequence. See Chapter 15.

manifest content Thematic content available on the surface of a text, as opposed to "latent content," which one must bring to the light. See "Psychoanalytic Criticism" in Appendix A.

Marxist criticism Criticism that depends upon Karl Marx's analysis of the class-based structure of society and the expropriation of the "have-nots" by the "haves." It is a criticism that focuses upon the social and historical dimensions of literary works. See Appendix A.

masculine rhyme In masculine rhyme single syllables correspond—"log" and "dog" make a masculine rhyme. See Chapter 16.

metaphor A comparison of two unrelated things which omits any specific word (*like, as*) serving as a likening term. Thus, "My love is a rose" is a metaphor, whereas "My love is like a rose" is a simile. See Chapter 17.

meter A regular pattern of stressed and unstressed syllables, each unit of which is called a "foot." See Chapter 18.

metonymy A figure of speech in which one term can stand for another with which it is closely associated. "He won her hand in marriage" is a metonymic figure of speech. See Chapter 21.

metric substitution The strategic reversal of stresses in an otherwise regular line of poetry—a means of emphasis. See Chapter 18.

mise-en-scène A term for the entire visual impression made by the various combined elements of a play—everything from lighting to the movements and costumes of characters. See Chapter 30.

monologue When a character talks to himself aloud or in thought, we call it a monologue. See Chapter 29; *see also* "interior monologue."

morality plays Cycles of religious plays written and performed in Europe in the late Middle Ages. Their main purpose was to offer moral instruction through the dramatization of religious themes. See Chapter 31.

moral tales Tales originating in the oral tradition that proposed to edify as well as entertain listeners. See Chapter 2.

mystery plays *See* "morality plays."

mythoi A term used by critic Northrop Frye to denote the myth configurations that he believed underlay all great works of literature. See "Psychoanalytic Criticism" in Appendix A.

narrative A sequence of events, often told as a story. See Chapter 4.

narrative poem A poem that tells a story of greater or lesser complexity, e.g., *The Iliad* or a traditional folk ballad. See Chapter 15.

naturalism Literary movement originating in the late nineteenth century. Naturalist writers like Émile Zola and Maxim Gorky subscribed to the view that people are just another species in the natural order and that material circumstances are all-determining. Naturalist works are often gritty and dark in their portrayals of human experience. See Chapter 34.

Neoclassical drama A dramatic movement arising in France in the middle of the seventeenth century, during the reign of Louis XIV. Neoclassical drama is characterized by its sophistication and wit as well as its observance of strict dramatic constraints. See Chapter 33.

New Criticism A mid-century critical movement that emphasized close attention to the text and its elements. New Criticism is also sometimes called Formalism. See Appendix A.

octave The first eight lines of a sonnet. The remaining six are called the "sestet." See Chapter 19.

Oedipus complex The Oedipus complex is part of Sigmund Freud's theory of human psychosexual development, a phase in the life of a young male during which he loves his mother possessively and wishes to triumph over his father in her affections. Frank O'Connor has written a short story called "My Oedipus Complex" (Chapter 13), in which he has a good deal of fun with the theory. See "Psychoanalytic Criticism" in Appendix A.

old comedies Greek comedies, mostly by Aristophanes, which take a sharply satirical attitude toward social issues of the day. See Chapter 32.

olfactory image An image in poetry that seeks to appeal to the sense of smell. See Chapter 20.

omniscient point of view Narrative access to the thoughts and feelings of all the characters. Omniscient means, literally, "all knowing." It is through omniscience that the reader becomes aware of what any given character is like behind his or her outward mannerisms. See Chapter 7.

onomatopoeia The poetic use of words that sound like what they denote, e.g., "buzzing." See Chapter 15.

open form *See* "free verse."

ottava rima An eight line stanza that is rhymed *abababcc* and is set in iambic pentameter. See Chapter 19.

oxymoron A phrase that brings together two incompatible elements for effect, e.g., "raging calm" or "deafening silence." See Chapter 21.

parados The arrival of the chorus in Greek tragedy, directly following the prologue. See Chapter 30.

parallel plot A narrative that tells two stories, often of equal importance, and shifts the telling back and forth from one to the other. See Chapter 4.

partial rhyme An inexact rhyme often used by poets, e.g., the rhyming of "bees" and "cease." See Chapter 16.

patriarchal codes The norms of behavior and thought that govern in a male-dominated society. See "Feminist Criticism" in Appendix A.

pause A break in the regular rhythm of a line of poetry, marked by a caesura (//). See Chapter 18.

persona The narrator or speaker of a poem or story, taken from the name of the mask worn by actors in Greek tragedy. See Chapter 17.

personification A figure of speech in which human attributes are conferred upon things that are not human, e.g., "The wind cried its grief." See Chapter 21.

phallocentrism A term used in Feminist criticism and referring to the primacy of the male principle. See "Feminist Criticism" in Appendix A.

plot The shaping of events into a story. See Chapter 4.

poetics (Aristotle's) A famous text by the philosopher Aristotle which is the basis for our understanding of the principles of Greek drama. See Chapter 30.

point of view The vantage from which a story is told—whether by a character or by an author with omniscient or limited omniscient perspective. See Chapter 7.

précis A short synopsis, or summing up, of a narrative. See Chapter 29.

problem plays Plays written to cast light on important issues of the day, such as those written by Henrik Ibsen in nineteenth-century Norway. See Chapter 34.

prologue The beginning portion of a Greek tragedy in which the audience is informed, either by monologue or dialogue, of the basic situation. See Chapter 30.

props The furniture, decorations, and other physical implements used on stage in a play. See Chapter 34.

prose poem A work of prose, often non-narrative, that makes use of many of the devices of poetry. See Chapter 1.

prosody The rhythmic pattern of a poem. See Chapter 18.

protagonist The main character and center of a story's psychological complications. The protagonist is sometimes called the "hero" or "heroine," although the attributes of the character need not be heroic. See Chapter 3.

Psychoanalytic criticism A critical approach to literature that draws upon the theories of psychologists, most commonly Sigmund Freud and C. G. Jung. See Appendix A.

pun A play on the double meanings of a word, generally made for comic effect. See Chapter 31.

pyrrhic foot A rarely used poetic foot consisting of two unstressed syllables (⌣⌣). A poet would never write a whole line using pyrrhic feet. See Chapter 18.

quatrain A four-line stanza in poetry. See Chapter 19.

Reader-Response criticism A movement in literary criticism that emphasizes the role of the reader in constructing the text and its meanings. See Appendix A.

Realism A way of presenting situations and characters that seeks to create the impression of real life. Realism steers clear of the miraculous and the fantastic. The larger movement of Realism in the arts followed on the heels of Romanticism and is often seen as a reaction to it. See Chapter 34.

repression (psychoanalytic) Repression involves not allowing undesired facts to intrude into conscious awareness. See "Psychoanalytic Criticism" in Appendix A.

resolution The part of the story that follows the climax; it is also called the "falling action." See Chapter 4.

rhyme The likeness of word sounds, used as a structural element by poets. See Chapter 16.

rhyme royal A seven-line stanza that is rhymed *ababbcc* and is set in iambic pentameter. See Chapter 19.

rhythm The regular recurrence and speed of sound and stresses in a poem or a work of prose. The writer uses the rhythm to intensify the meaning of the words, slowing it when the effect is to be meditative, hastening it when the climactic action breaks. See Chapter 18.

rising action The events that lead up to and bring about the climax or key turning point in a work of fiction or drama. The rising action generally involves the building up of the complication, or major conflict. See Chapter 4.

romantic comedy A dramatic mode used most expressively by Shakespeare. Romantic comedy combines comic features with the more serious expression generally belonging to tragedy. See Chapter 32.

rounded character A fictional character who has some complexity and independent stature, as opposed to a flat character who mainly serves a backdrop function. See Chapter 3.

satyr play A short, mocking play put on after the performance of a Greek tragedy, to clear the air and prepare audiences for the comedy to follow. See Chapter 30.

scene house A long building in the stage area of the Greek theatre. The actors themselves performed in front of the scene house, which was more often than not understood to represent a palace. See Chapter 30.

second-person point of view An uncommon vantage in fiction in which the narrative is addressed to a "you." See Chapter 7.

sestet The six lines following the octave—or first eight lines—in a sonnet. See Chapter 19.

sestina A poem composed of six six-line stanzas and a three-line envoy. Each line ends with one of six key words, but in each stanza the words are in different positions. The envoy uses all six words, but only three at the ends of the lines. See Chapter 19.

setting The time and place in which a fictional or dramatic narrative unfolds. See Chapter 5.

Shakespearean sonnet Also called the "English sonnet," it uses three quatrains rhymed *abab, cdcd, efef*, with a concluding couplet rhyming *gg*. See Chapter 19.

signifiers A term used in Structuralist criticism (see Appendix A) which refers to the capacity of language to denote. Words are signifiers, part of a signifying system, language.

simile A comparison commonly used in poetry. Unlike the metaphor, this figure of speech retains the "like" or "as": e.g., "My love is like a ray of light." See Chapter 15.

situational irony Situational irony results when the events in a story are suddenly at odds with the expectations created in the reader. See Chapter 7.

Sociological criticism Criticism that attempts to understand the text as a material entity that responds to and addresses specific historical circumstances. In spirit it runs directly counter to the kind of textual isolationism favored by the Formalists. See "Marxist and Feminist Criticism" in Appendix A.

soliloquy A monologue delivered by an actor, generally used to present thought or internal debate. See Chapter 29.

sonnet A fourteen-line poem, usually in iambic pentameter, which may follow several possible rhyme patterns. *See* "Italian sonnet" and "Shakespearean sonnet." See Chapter 19.

spondaic foot A poetic foot consisting of two stressed syllables ("). See Chapter 18.

sprinting The process of putting down words as quickly as possible in the effort to jump-start the composition process. See Chapter 10.

stanza A group of lines in a poem that are treated as a kind of unit. Stanzas can consist of two-line couplets, three-line tercets, four-line quatrains, six-line sestets, or eight-line octaves. See Chapter 18.

stasimon An ode sung by the chorus in Greek tragedy. See Chapter 30.

static character The opposite of a rounded character, a static character does not exhibit complexity or change over the course of the narrative. See Chapter 3; *see also* "flat character."

static image The opposite of a kinetic image, a static image is without motion, often part of a descriptive passage. See Chapter 20.

stereotype A flat character who is simplified into a common type—the shy clerk, the grasping landlord—often for comic effect. See Chapter 3.

stream of consciousness A technique used in fiction that seeks to render the flow of inner thought and sensation. Stream of consciousness is distinguished from interior monologue in that the author does not attempt to shape or heighten the thoughts and strives instead to give the impression of chaotic movement. See Chapter 7.

Structuralism A critical movement that looks to isolate the most fundamental component elements of a work's structure. See Appendix A.

subplot A story within a story. Subplots unfold alongside the main plot and often involve minor, or secondary, characters. They can serve to counterpoint the central events of the narrative. See Chapter 4.

substitution A term used in poetry when a poet deliberately breaks metrical pattern by inserting a different foot, such as a trochaic foot for an iambic foot. See Chapter 18.

suspense The holding over of actions or consequences by an author in order to arouse curiosity in the reader. The deliberate manipulation of the reader's natural desire to find out what happens next. See Chapter 4.

syllabic verse Poetry in which the lines are not structured according to metered feet but syllable count. See Chapter 18.

symbol An isolated thing, person, or situation that is used to represent a larger, thematic concern. A white bird may be a symbol of peace or innocence, but it may also be just a white bird. The reader needs to make a judgment about whether the context allows for symbolic interpretation. See Chapter 9.

Symbolism A turn-of-the-century literary movement that can be seen as a reaction to Realism. Symbolism emphasized the irrational and mysterious, often including dreams and mythic imagery. See Chapter 35.

synesthesia The expression of one sensory image in the terms of another sense, as when a dog's barks are called "bright flaming barks." See Chapter 15.

tactile images Images that appeal to the sense of touch. See Chapter 20.

tercet A three-line stanza in poetry. See Chapter 19.

terza rima A poetic form used first by Dante, terza rima has a rhyme scheme (*aba, bcb, cdc*) that links its tercets into a kind of braid. See Chapter 19.

theater of the absurd A movement of the post–World War II era that emphasizes the pointlessness of life in a godless universe. Samuel Beckett's *Waiting for Godot* is probably the most famous example of an absurdist play. See Chapter 35.

theme The central meaning, or idea, in a literary work. A theme is a generalized or abstract assertion of the work's message. See Chapter 6.

third-person point of view The projection of a narrative through a detached vantage that allows the narrator to refer to characters as "he," "she," or "they." The narrator may be, in effect, the author, claiming full or limited omniscience. See Chapter 7.

tone The attitude expressed by the style and overall presentation and reflected mainly through diction, or word choice. See Chapter 8.

tragicomedy A type of Elizabethan and Jacobean drama that used both comic and tragic elements. See Chapter 32.

trochaic meter A meter built up of feet of one stressed and one unstressed syllable (´˘). See Chapter 18.

turning point The change in the plot effected by the climax; the moment at which everything changes. See Chapter 30.

understatement The opposite of hyperbole. A figure of speech that creates its effect by declaring less than is the case, e.g., "Stalin was not a nice person." See Chapter 21.

unities (Aristotle's) Aristotle's prescription for Greek tragedy held that there were certain "unities": of time (the action should not take place over more than a twenty-four-hour time period), of place (the locale was usually confined to a single city), and of action (the plot would focus upon the central conflict and avoid confusing subplots). See Chapter 30.

variable foot A loosening of the strictures of poetic meter which recognized that a variety of feet could combine in a line—part of the development of free verse technique. See Chapter 18.

villanelle A nineteen-line poem composed of five tercets and a concluding quatrain. The rhyme scheme is *aba, aba, aba, aba, aba, abaa.* Two of the lines are repeated as follows: line 1 appears as lines 6, 12, and 18, and line 3 appears as lines 9, 15, and 19. The final quatrain concludes, by repeating both line 1 and line 3. See Chapter 19.

visual rhyme Use of words in a poem that look as if they should rhyme but in fact don't, e.g., "enough" and "cough." See Chapter 16.

voice The recognition that a literary work is a product of some speaker—either in the work or outside (the author). The voice is the way in which that speaker delivers the narrative. See Chapter 17.

Vladimir Nabokov. "The Lady with the Little Dog" from *Lectures on Russian Literature* by Vladimir Nabokov, edited by Fresdon Bowers, copyright © 1981 by the Estate of Vladimir Nabokov, reprinted by permission of Harcourt Brace & Company. Excerpts from "The Lady with the Pet Dog" from *The Portable Checkov* by Avrahm Yarmolinsky, editor. Copyright 1947, 1968 by Viking Penguin, Inc. Renewed copyright © 1975 by Avrahm Yarmolinsky. Used by permission of Viking Penguin, a division of Penguin Books USA Inc.

R. K. Narayan. "House Opposite" from *Under the Banyan Tree* by R. K. Narayan. Copyright © 1985 by R. K. Narayan. Used by permission of Viking Penguin, a division of Penguin Books USA Inc.

Joyce Carol Oates. "The Lady with the Pet Dog" from *Marriage and Infidelities*. Copyright © 1972 by Joyce Carol Oates. Reprinted by permission of John Hawkins & Associates, Inc.

Flannery O'Connor. "Everything That Rises Must Converge" from *Everything That Rises Must Converge* by Flannery O'Connor. Copyright © 1965 by the estate of Mary Flannery O'Connor. Copyright renewed © 1993 by Regina O'Connor. Reprinted by permission of Farrar, Straus & Giroux, Inc.

Frank O'Connor. "My Oedipus Complex" from *Collected Stories* by Frank O'Connor. Copyright 1950 by Frank O'Connor. Reprinted by permission of Alfred A. Knopf, Inc.

Delmore Schwartz. "In Dreams Begin Responsibilities" from *In Dreams Begin Responsibilities*. Copyright © 1948, 1961 by Delmore Schwartz. Reprinted by permission of New Directions Publishing Corporation.

Susan Sontag. "The Way We Live Now" by Susan Sontag. First appeared in *The New Yorker*, November 24, 1986. Copyright © 1986 by Susan Sontag. Reprinted by permission of Farrar, Straus & Giroux, Inc.

Junichiro Tanizaki. "Tattoo" from *Modern Japanese Stories: An Anthology*, translated by Ivan Morris. Copyright © 1962. Reprinted by permission of Charles E. Tuttle Co., Inc. of Tokyo, Japan.

Amos Tutuola. "Feather Woman of the Jungle" by Amos Tutuola from *Modern African Stories*, edited by Ellis Ayitey Komey and Ezekiel Mphahlele. Used by permission of Faber & Faber Ltd.

John Updike. "Separating" from *Problems and Other Stories* by John Updike. Copyright © 1975 by John Updike. Reprinted by permission of Alfred A. Knopf, Inc.

T. G. Vaidyanathan. Excerpt from " 'The Nick Adams Stories' and Myths of Imitation" from *Indian Studies in American Fiction*, M. K. Naik, S. K. Desai, S. Mokashi-Punekar, Editors, 1974. Reprinted by permission of Macmillan India Ltd.

Luisa Valenzuela. "I'm Your Horse in the Night" from *Cambio de Armas*. Reprinted by permission of Ediciones del Norte.

Eudora Welty. "A Worn Path" from *A Curtain of Green and Other Stories*, copyright 1941 and renewed 1969 by Eudora Welty, reprinted by permission of Harcourt Brace & Company.

Poetry Credits

Anna Akhmatova. "The Song of the Final Meeting" and "The Muse" are reprinted from *Poems* by Anna Akhmatova, translated by Lyn Coffin, with the permission of W. W. Norton & Company, Inc. Copyright © 1983 by Lyn Coffin.

Yehuda Amichai. "Flowers in a Room" from *Great Tranquillity* by Yehuda Amichai. Copyright © 1983 by Yehuda Amichai. Reprinted by permission of HarperCollins Publishers.

A. R. Ammons. "Bonus" is reprinted from *The Selected Poems 1951–1977* by A. R. Ammons, with the permission of W. W. Norton & Company, Inc. Copyright © 1977, 1975, 1974, 1972 by A. R. Ammons.

Maya Angelou. "Africa" from *Oh Pray My Wings Are Gonna Fit Me Well* by Maya Angelou. Copyright © 1975 by Maya Angelou. Reprinted by permission of Random House, Inc.

John Ashbery. Excerpt from "37 Haiku" and "Down by the Station, Early in the Morning" from *A Wave* by John Ashbery (New York: Viking, 1984). Reprinted by permission of Georges Borchardt, Inc., for the author. Copyright © 1984 by John Ashbery. "The One Thing That Can Save America" from *Self Portrait in a Convex Mirror*. Copyright © 1975 by John Ashbery. Reprinted by permission of Viking Penguin, a division of Penguin Books USA Inc.

W. H. Auden. "The Sea and the Mirror" from *W. H. Auden: Collected Poems* by W. H. Auden, edited by Edward Mendelson. Copyright 1944 by W. H. Auden. "Musee des Beaux Arts," "Lay your sleeping head, my love," "September 1, 1939," and "In Memory of W. B. Yeats" from *W. H. Auden: Collected Poems* by W. H. Auden, edited by Edward Mendelson. Copyright 1940 and renewed 1968 by W. H. Auden. Reprinted by permission of Random House, Inc.

Jimmy Santiago Baca. "At Night" from *Black Mesa Poems* by Jimmy Santiago Baca. Copyright © 1989 by Jimmy Santiago Baca. Reprinted by permission of New Directions Publishing Corporation. •

Charles Baudelaire. "The Albatross" translated by Roy Campbell from *Poems of Baudelaire*. Translation copyright © 1952 by Hughes Massey Ltd. for the estate of Roy Campbell. Used by permission of Aitken, Stone & Wylie. "The Albatross" from *Les Fleurs du Mal* by Charles Baudelaire, translated by Richard Howard. Translation copyrights © 1983 by Richard Howard. Reprinted by permission of David R. Godine, Publisher.

Frank Bidart. "To the Dead" from *In the Western Night: Collected Poems 1965–1990* by Frank Bidart. Copyright © 1990 by Frank Bidart.

Reprinted by permission of Farrar, Straus & Giroux, Inc.

Elizabeth Bishop. "The Map" and "The Fish" from *The Complete Poems 1927–1979* by Elizabeth Bishop. Copyright © 1979, 1983 by Alice Helen Methfessel. Reprinted by permission of Farrar, Straus & Giroux, Inc.

Harold Bloom. Excerpt by Harold Bloom from *The Visionary Company: A Reading of English Romantic Poetry,* published by Doubleday, a division of Bantam Doubleday Dell Publishing Group, Inc. Reprinted by permission of the author.

Robert Bly. "The Executive's Death" from *The Light Around the Body* by Robert Bly. Copyright © 1960 by Robert Bly. Reprinted by permission of HarperCollins Publishers, Inc.

Eavan Boland. "Lace" is reprinted from *Outside History: Selected Poems 1980–1990* by Eavan Boland, with the permission of W. W. Norton & Company, Inc. Copyright © 1990 by Eavan Boland.

Bohdan Boychuk. "Late Spring" by Bohdan Boychuk from *Memories of Love,* translated by David Ignatow and Mark Rudman, Sheep Meadow Press, © 1989, Bohdan Boychuk, © 1989 Ignatow and Rudman. Reprinted by permission of the translators.

Bertolt Brecht. "Bad Time for Poetry" is reprinted from *Bertolt Brecht Poems 1913–1956,* by permission of the publisher, Routledge, New York and the Brecht Estate.

Lucie Brock-Broido. "Autobiography" from *A Hunger* by Lucie Brock-Broido. Copyright © 1988 by Lucie Brock-Broido. Reprinted by permission of Alfred A. Knopf, Inc.

Joseph Brodsky. "Six Years Later" from *A Part of Speech* by Joseph Brodsky. Translation copyright © 1980 by Farrar, Straus & Giroux, Inc. Reprinted by permission of Farrar, Straus & Giroux, Inc.

Gwendolyn Brooks. "Martin Luther King Jr." from *Riot,* copyright 1970 by Gwendolyn Brooks Blakely. Permission to reprint granted by Broadside Press.

Dennis Brutus. "Letters to Martha, 1 and 2" from *Letters to Martha,* 1968, Heinemann Publishers (Oxford) Ltd. Reprinted by permission.

C. D. Cafavy. "The God Abandons Anthony" from *Collected Poems,* translated by Edmund Keeley and Philip Sherrard. Copyright © 1975 by Princeton University Press. Reprinted by permission of Princeton University Press.

Catullus. 2 untitled poems from *The Poems of Catullus* translated by Peter Whigham (Penguin Classics, 1966). Translation and Introduction copyright © Peter Whigham, 1966: Poem No. 2 (p. 51), Poem No. 3 (p. 52). Reprinted by permission of Penguin Books Ltd.

Lorna Dee Cervantes. "Poem for the Young White Man Who Asked Me How I, an Intelligent Well-Read Person Could Believe in the War Between Races" is reprinted from *Emplumada,* by Lorna Dee Cervantes, by permission of The University of Pittsburgh Press. © 1981 by Lorna Dee Cervantes.

Amy Clampitt. "Fog" and "Dancers Exercising" from *The Kingfisher* by Amy Clampitt. Copyright © 1983 by Amy Clampitt. Reprinted by permission of Alfred A. Knopf, Inc.

Judith Ortiz Cofer. "Vida" from *The Latin Deli: Prose & Poetry* by Judith Ortiz Cofer, © 1990 Judith Ortiz Cofer. Reprinted by permission of The University of Georgia Press.

William Corbett. "Out the Window" from *Don't Think: Look,* © 1991. Reprinted with permission of Zoland Books, Cambridge, MA. "Yellow" was previously published in *Collected Poems* by William Corbett (Orono, Maine: National Poetry Foundation, 1984). It is reprinted here with permission from The National Poetry Foundation.

Christopher Jane Corkery. "Divorce" from *Blessing.* Copyright © 1985 by Princeton University Press. Reprinted by permission of Princeton University Press.

Hart Crane. "The Harbour Dawn" is reprinted from *Complete Poems of Hart Crane,* edited by Marc Simon, with the permission of Liveright Publishing Corporation. Copyright 1933, © 1958, 1966 by Liveright Publishing Corporation. Copyright © 1986 by Marc Simon.

Robert Creeley. "Like They Say," "I Know a Man," and "Goodbye" from *Collected Poems of Robert Creeley, 1945–1975.* Copyright © 1983 The Regents of the University of California. Reprinted by permission.

Countee Cullen. "Tableau." Reprinted by permission of GRM Associates, Inc., Agents for the Estate of Ida M. Cullen. From the book *Color* by Countee Cullen. Copyright © 1925 by Harper & Brothers; copyright renewed 1953 by Ida M. Cullen.

e. e. cummings. "l(a" and "anyone lived in a pretty how town" are reprinted from *Complete Poems: 1904–1962* by e. e. cummings, edited by George J. Firmage, by permission of Liveright Publishing Corporation. Copyright © 1940, 1958, 1968, 1986, 1991 by the Trustees for the E. E. Cummings Trust.

Dante. Laurence Binyon translation: Extract from "Canto XXXIII" from *Inferno.* By permission of Mrs. Nicolete Gray and The Society of Authors, on behalf of the Laurence Binyon Estate.

Emily Dickinson. "The Soul Selects Her Own Society," "We Grow Accustomed to the Dark," "A Narrow Fellow in the Grass," "Because I Could Not Stop for Death," "I Heard a Fly Buzz When I Died," and "The Lightning Is a Yellow Fork." Reprinted by permission of the publishers and the Trustees of Amherst College from *The Poems of Emily Dickinson,* Thomas H. Johnson, ed., Cambridge, Mass.: The Belknap Press of Harvard University Press. Copyright © 1951, 1955, 1983 by the President and Fellows of Harvard College. "We Grow Accustomed to the Dark" also from

The Complete Poems of Emily Dickinson, edited by Thomas H. Johnson. Copyright 1935 by Martha Dickinson Bianchi; Copyright © renewed 1963 by Mary L. Hampson. By permission of Little, Brown and Company. "Wild Nights—Wild Nights!" from *The Complete Poems of Emily Dickinson*, edited by Thomas H. Johnson, Little, Brown and Company.

Stuart Dischell. "Evening," © Stuart Dischell 1994. "Cheats." Used by permission of the author.

Stephen Dobyns. "How to Like It" from *Cemetery Nights* by Stephen Dobyns. Copyright © 1987 by Stephen Dobyns. Used by permission of Viking Penguin, a division of Penguin Books USA Inc.

H. D. "Helen" from *H. D.: Collected Poems 1912–1944*. Copyright © 1982 by The Estate of Hilda Doolittle. Reprinted by permission of New Directions Publishing Corporation.

Rita Dove. "Adolescence—II." Reprinted from *The Yellow House on the Corner*. By permission of Carnegie Mellon University Press. © 1989 by Rita Dove. "Motherhood" is reprinted from *Thomas and Beula*. By permission of Carnegie Mellon University Press. © 1986 Rita Dove.

Douglas Dunn. "The Clothes Pit" from *Terry Street* by Douglas Dunn, © 1971. Used by permission of Faber and Faber, Ltd.

T. S. Eliot. "The Love Song of J. Alfred Prufrock," "Portrait of a Lady," and "La Figlia che Piange" from *Collected Poems 1909–1962* by T. S. Eliot, copyright 1936 by Harcourt Brace & Company, copyright © 1964, 1963 by T. S. Eliot, reprinted by permission of the publisher.

Louise Erdrich. "Windigo" from *Jacklight* by Louise Erdrich. Copyright © 1984 by Louise Erdrich. Reprinted by permission of Henry Holt & Co., Inc.

Martín Espada. "Jorge the Church Janitor Finally Quits" from *Rebellion Is the Circle of a Lover's Hands/Rebelion es el giro de manos del amante* by Martín Espada. (Curbstone, 1990) Distributed by InBook. Printed with permission of Curbstone Press.

Sybil P. Estess. "Description and Imagination in Bishop's 'The Map' " from *Elizabeth Bishop and Her Art*, Lloyd Schwartz and Sybil P. Estess, editors, © 1983, The University of Michigan Press. Part of this essay appeared, in a different form, in *Southern Review 13* (October 1977), pp. 705–727. Reprinted by permission.

Carolyn Forche. "Departure" from *The Country Between Us* by Carolyn Forche. Copyright © 1979 by Carolyn Forche. Reprinted by permission of HarperCollins Publishers.

Robert Frost. "Fire and Ice," "Acquainted with the Night," and "Stopping By Woods on a Snowy Evening" from *The Poetry of Robert Frost*, edited by Edward Connery Lathem. Copyright 1951, © 1956 by Robert Frost. Copyright 1923, 1928, © 1969 by Henry Holt & Co., Inc. Reprinted by permission of Henry Holt & Co., Inc. "The Woodpile" and "Mend-ing Wall" from *The Poetry of Robert Frost*, edited by Edward Connery Lathem, published by Holt Rinehart and Winston.

Tu Fu. "Dreaming of Li Po" from *The Columbia Book of Chinese Poetry*, edited by Burton Watson, copyright © 1984 by Columbia University Press. Reprinted with permission of the publisher.

Alice Fulton. "Your Card Read 'Poet-Mechanic' " from *Dance Script With Electric Ballerina*, published by University of Pennsylvania Press, copyright © 1976, 1983 by Alice Fulton. "The Gone Years" from *Dance Script With Electric Ballerina* (University of Pennsylvania Press), Copyright © 1979, 1983 by Alice Fulton. Reprinted by permission of the author.

Allen Ginsberg. "A Supermarket in California" from *Collected Poems 1947–1980* by Allen Ginsberg. Copyright © 1955 by Allen Ginsberg. Copyright renewed. Reprinted by permission of HarperCollins Publishers Inc.

Louise Glück. "The Triumph of Achilles" and "The Drowned Children" from *The Triumph of Achilles* by Louise Glück. © 1985 by Louise Glück. First published by The Ecco Press. Reprinted by permission.

Jorie Graham. "I Watched a Snake," and "Salmon" from *Erosion*, 1983, published by Princeton University Press. Used by permission of the author.

Harvey Gross. Excerpt from "Imagism and Visual Prosody: William Carlos Williams" from *Sound and Form in Modern Poetry* by Harvey Gross, © 1964, The University of Michigan Press. Reprinted by permission.

Allen Grossman. "The Room" from *The Woman on the Bridge Over the Chicago River*. Copyright © 1979 by Allen Grossman. Reprinted by permission of New Directions Publishing Corporation.

Thom Gunn. "Expression" from *Collected Poems*. Copyright © 1994 by Thom Gunn. Reprinted by permission of Farrar, Straus & Giroux, Inc.

Donald Hall. Excerpt from "To a Waterfowl" and "Names of Horses" from *Old and New Poems*. Copyright © 1990 by Donald Hall. First published in *The New Yorker*. Reprinted by permission of Houghton Mifflin Co. All rights reserved.

Takako Hashimoto. "All plucked off . . ." from *Anthology of Modern Japanese Poetry*, translated and compiled by Edith M. Shiffert and Yuki Sawa. Copyright © 1971. Reprinted by permission of Charles E. Tuttle Co., Inc., of Tokyo, Japan.

Robert Hass. "Spring" from *Field Guide* by Robert Hass. © 1973 Yale University Press. Reprinted by permission of Yale University Press.

Robert Hayden. "Homage to the Empress of the Blues" and "Those Winter Sundays" are reprinted from *Angle of Ascent: New and Selected Poems* by Robert Hayden, with the permission of Liveright Publishing Corporation. Copyright © 1966 by Robert Hayden.

sion of Boa Editions, Ltd., 92 Park Ave., Brockport, NY 14420.

David Lehman. "First Offense" from *An Alternative to Speech*. Copyright © 1986 by Princeton University Press. Reprinted by permission of Princeton University Press.

Brad Leithauser. "Angel" from *Hundreds of Fireflies* by Brad Leithauser. Copyright © 1981 by Brad Leithauser. Reprinted by permission of Alfred A. Knopf, Inc.

Denise Levertov. "The Dog of Art" and "To the Snake" from *Collected Earlier Poems, 1940–1960*. Copyright © 1959 by Denise Levertov. "To the Snake" was first printed in *Poetry*. Reprinted by permission of New Directions Publishing Corporation.

Philip Levine. "Coming Home" from *New Selected Poems* by Philip Levine. Copyright © 1991 by Philip Levine. Reprinted by permission of Alfred A. Knopf, Inc.

Federico García Lorca. "The Little Mute Boy" and "Song of Barren Orange Tree," translated by W. S. Merwin, from *Selected Poems*. Copyright 1955 by New Directions Publishing Corporation. Reprinted by permission of New Directions Publishing Corporation.

Audre Lorde. "Hanging Fire" is reprinted from *The Black Unicorn* by Audre Lorde, with the permission of W. W. Norton & Company, Inc. Copyright © 1978 by Audre Lorde.

Robert Lowell. "The Old Flame" and "To Speak of Woe That Is in Marriage" from *Selected Poems* by Robert Lowell. Copyright © 1976 by Robert Lowell. Reprinted by permission of Farrar, Straus & Giroux, Inc. "On Stanley Kunitz's 'Father and Son'" from *The Contemporary Poet as Artist and Critic*, edited by Anthony Ostroff. Published by Little, Brown and Company.

Thomas Lux. "There Were Some Summers" from *Half-Promised Land* by Thomas Lux. Copyright © 1986 by Thomas Lux. Reprinted by permission of Houghton Mifflin Company. All rights reserved.

Joseph Margolis, "On 'The Love Song of Alfred J. Prufrock'" in *Interpretations: Essays on 12 English Poets*, edited by John Wain (London: Routledge & Kegan Paul, 1972 and 1955). Reprinted by permission of Joseph Margolis.

Wendy Martin. Excerpt from *An American Triptych: Anne Bradstreet, Emily Dickinson, and Adrienne Rich*, by Wendy Martin. Chapel Hill: The University of North Carolina Press, 1983.

Askold Melnyczuk. "Young Woman in the Prado" first appeared in *The Nation*, June 17, 1991, page 826, © Askold Melnyczuk. Used by permission of the author and *The Nation*.

James Merrill. "The Broken Home" from *Selected Poems (1946–1985)* by James Merrill. Copyright © 1992 by James Merrill. Reprinted by permission of Alfred A. Knopf, Inc.

W. S. Merwin. "In the Winter of My Thirty-Eighth Year" and "Looking for Mushrooms at Sunrise" from *The Lice*, published by

Atheneum. Copyright © 1967 by W. S. Merwin. By permission of Georges Borchardt, Inc.

Edna St. Vincent Millay. 'Sonnet XVII' of "Sonnets from an Ungrafted Tree" by Edna St. Vincent Millay. From *Collected Poems*, HarperCollins. Copyright © 1923, 1951 by Edna St. Vincent Millay and Norma Millay Ellis. Reprinted with permission of Elizabeth Barnett, literary executor.

Ethelbert Miller. "Bighead and Snotnose" from *First Light,* © 1994 Ethelbert Miller. Reprinted by permission of the author.

Vassar Miller. "Spinster's Lullaby" from *My Bones Being Wiser,* © 1963 by Vassar Miller, Wesleyan University Press, by permission of the University Press of New England.

Czeslaw Milosz. "Rivers Grow Small" and "Window" from *The Collected Poems* by Czeslaw Milosz. © 1988 by Czeslaw Milosz Royalties, Inc. First published by The Ecco Press in 1988. Reprinted by permission.

N. Scott Momaday. "The Delight Song of Tsoai-Talee" from *The Gourd Dancer,* © 1975, published by HarperCollins Publishers. Reprinted by permission of the author.

Eugenio Montale. "L'anguilla." © 1957, Arnoldo Mondadori Editore Spa, Milano. Reprinted by permission. "The Eel" is reprinted from *The Storm and Other Things* by Eugenio Montale, translated by William Arrowsmith, with the permission of W. W. Norton & Company, Inc. English translation copyright © 1985 by William Arrowsmith. "The Eel," translated by John Frederick Nims, from *Selected Poems*. Copyright © 1961 by Robert Lowell. Reprinted by permission of New Directions Publishing Corporation.

Marianne Moore. "Poetry." Reprinted with permission of Simon & Schuster, Inc. from *Collected Poems of Marianne Moore*. Copyright 1935 by Marianne Moore, renewed 1963 by Marianne Moore and T. S. Eliot. "The Steeple-Jack," copyright 1951 © 1970 by Marianne Moore, © renewed 1979 by Lawrence E. Brinn and Louise Crane, Executors of the Estate of Marianne Moore, from *The Complete Poems of Marianne Moore* by Marianne Moore. Used by permission of Viking Penguin, a division of Penguin Books USA Inc.

Laura Mullen. "The Lease" and "Sestina in Which My Grandmother Is Going Deaf" from *The Surface,* © 1991 by The Board of Trustees of the University of Illinois. Used with permission of the author and the University of Illinois Press.

Les A. Murray. "Spring Hail" from *The Vernacular Republic: Selected Poems* by Les A. Murray, copyright © 1982 by Les A. Murray. Reprinted by permission of Persea Books.

Pablo Neruda. "Walking Around" (Spanish version) from *Residencia en la Tierra*. © Pablo Neruda, 1993 and Fundacion Pablo Neruda, Barcelona. Reprinted by permission. "Walking Around," translated by Robert Bly. Reprinted from *Neruda and Vallejo: Selected Poems* edited by Robert Bly, Beacon Press, Boston, 1976, with the permission of Robert Bly. "Walking Around" and "Alliance" from *Residence on Earth*. Copyright © 1973 by Pablo Neruda and Donald D. Walsh. Reprinted by permission of New Directions Publishing Corporation.

Sharon Olds. "The Elder Sister" from *The Dead and the Living* by Sharon Olds. Copyright © 1983 by Sharon Olds. Reprinted by permission of Alfred A. Knopf, Inc.

Mary Oliver. "The Hermit Crab." From *House of Light* by Mary Oliver. Copyright © 1990 by Mary Oliver. Reprinted by permission of Beacon Press.

Alicia Ostriker. Excerpt from "Her Cargo: Adrienne Rich and the Common Language" from *Writing Like a Woman* by Alicia Ostriker, The University of Michigan Press, 1983. First appeared in *American Poetry Review* 8, 4. Reprinted by permission.

Boris Pasternak. "February," translated by Lydia Pasternak Slater from *Second Nature: Forty Six Poems*, 1990. Reprinted by permission of Peter Owen Ltd. Publishers.

Cesare Pavese. "Passion for Solitude" from *Hard Labor* by Cesare Pavese, translated by William Arrowsmith, Translation copyright © 1976 by William Arrowsmith. LAVORARE STANCA Copyright © 1943 by Giulio Einaudi editore, Torino. Used by permission of Viking Penguin, a division of Penguin Books USA Inc.

Octavio Paz. "Here" and "Trowbridge Street" from *The Collected Poems of Octavio Paz 1957–1987*. Copyright © 1968, 1971 by Octavio Paz and Charles Tomlinson, 1986 by Octavio Paz and Eliot Weinberger. Reprinted by permission of New Directions Publishing Corporation.

Francis Petrarch. Untitled poem from *Songs and Sonnets from Laura's Lifetime* by Francis Petrarch, translated by Nicholas Kilmer, and published by Anvil Press Poetry in 1980. Reprinted by permission.

Robert Pinsky. "The Want Bone." From *The Want Bone* by Robert Pinsky. © 1990 by Robert Pinsky. First published by The Ecco Press in 1990. Reprinted by permission.

Sylvia Plath. "Daddy," "Wintering," and "Winter Trees" by Sylvia Plath. Copyright © 1963 by Ted Hughes. From *The Collected Poems of Sylvia Plath*, edited by Ted Hughes. Copyright © 1981 by Ted Hughes. Reprinted by permission of HarperCollins Publishers.

Li Po. "Mountain Drinking Song," "To a Friend," and "In a Village by the River" from *Banished Immortal*, translated by Sam Hamill, copyright 1987. Reprinted by permission of White Pine Press.

Francis Ponge. "Rain" from *The Voice of Things* (Translation by Betty Archer), translation copyright © 1972 by Herder & Herder. French copyright by Editions Gallimard. Reprinted by permission.

Ezra Pound. "The River-Merchant's Wife: A Letter," "In a Station of the Metro," "Autumn," and "Song of the Bowmen of Shu" from *Personae*. Copyright 1926 by Ezra Pound. Reprinted by permission of New Directions Publishing Corporation.

John Crowe Ransom. "Survey of Literature" from *Selected Poems* by John Crow Ransom. Copyright 1927 by Alfred A. Knopf, Inc. and renewed 1955 by John Crowe Ransom, Reprinted by permission of the publisher.

Liam Rector. "In Snow" from *The Sorrow of Architecture*, © 1984 by Liam Rector. Reprinted with permission of Dragon Gate, Inc., 508 Lincoln Street, Port Townsend, WA 98368.

Adrienne Rich. "Diving into the Wreck," "The Middle-aged," "Snapshots of a Daughter-in-Law," "Nightbreak," "Trying to Talk with a Man," "Power," "Rape," and "After Twenty Years" are reprinted from *The Fact of a Doorframe: Poems Selected and New, 1950–1984*, by Adrienne Rich by permission of W. W. Norton & Company, Inc. Copyright © 1984 by Adrienne Rich. Copyright © 1975, 1978 by W. W. Norton & Company, Inc. Copyright © 1981 by Adrienne Rich. 'XVI' from "Sources" and '#7' from "Contradictions: Tracking Poems" are reprinted from *Your Native Land: Your Life: Poems by Adrienne Rich*, by permission of W. W. Norton & Company, Inc. Copyright © 1986 by Adrienne Rich. "When We Dead Awaken: Writing as Re-vision" is reprinted from *On Lies, Secrets, and Silence: Selected Prose, 1966–1978* by Adrienne Rich, by permission of the author and W. W. Norton & Company, Inc. Copyright © 1979 by W. W. Norton & Company, Inc. Excerpt from "Origins and History of Consciousness" is reprinted from *The Dream of a Common Language: Poems 1974–1977* by Adrienne Rich, by permission of the author and W. W. Norton & Company, Inc. Copyright © 1978 by W. W. Norton & Company, Inc.

Rainer Maria Rilke. "The Panther," "The Swan," and "Autumn Day" from *The Selected Poetry of Rainer Maria Rilke* by Rainer Maria Rilke, translated by Stephen Mitchell. Copyright © 1982 by Stephen Mitchell. Reprinted by permission of Random House, Inc. "The Panther," translated by J. J. Leighman from *New Poems* by Rainer Maria Rilke. Copyright © 1964 by the Hogarth Press. Reprinted by permission of New Directions Publishing Corporation.

Arthur Rimbaud. Excerpt from "Illuminations" from *Complete Works, Selected Letters*, translated by Wallace Fowlie, © 1966. Reprinted by permission of The University of Chicago Press.

Theodore Roethke. "My Papa's Waltz," copyright 1942 by Hearst Magazines, Inc. "The Waking," copyright 1953 by Theodore Roethke. "Root Cellar," copyright 1943 by Modern Poetry Association, Inc. "Child on Top of a Green-

Imants Ziedonis. "I Love a Floating Apple" from *Flowers Of Ice*, translated by Barry Callaghan, © Barry Callaghan. Reprinted by permission of Exile Editions Ltd.

Drama Credits

Sylvan Barnet. Excerpt from *A Short Guide to Shakespeare* by Sylvan Barnet, copyright © 1974 by Harcourt, Brace & Company, reprinted by permission of the publisher.

Samuel Beckett. *Krapp's Last Tape.* Copyright © 1958 by Grove Press, Inc. Used by permission of Grove Press, Inc.

Francis Fergusson. "Oedipus: Ritual and Play" from *Idea of a Theater*, copyright © 1949 and renewed 1977 by Princeton University Press. Reprinted by permission of Princeton University Press.

Maria Irene Fornes. "The Successful Life of 3" from *Promenade & Other Plays*, © 1987. Reprinted by permission of The Johns Hopkins University Press.

Sigmund Freud. "The Interpretation of Dreams" by Sigmund Freud, translated by Dr. A. A. Brill from *The Basic Writings of Sigmund Freud*, Modern Library Edition, 1938, published by Random House. Copyright 1938, renewed 1966 by Gioia B. Bernheim and Edmund Brill. Reprinted by permission.

Northrop Frye, "Introduction" by Northrop Frye, from *The Tempest* by William Shakespeare; edited by Northrop Frye. Copyright © 1959, renewed 1987 by Northrop Frye on introduction and compilation. Used by permission of Penguin, a division of Penguin Books USA Inc.

Athol Fugard. From *"Master Harold" . . . and the boys.* Copyright © 1982 by Athol Fugard. Reprinted by permission of Alfred A. Knopf, Inc.

Henrik Ibsen. "A Doll's House," © Oxford University Press 1961. Reprinted from *The Oxford Ibsen*, vol. 5, translated and edited by J. W. McFarlane (1961) by permission of Oxford University Press.

Cassandra Medley. "Waking Women" from *Plays in One Act*, ANTAEUS #66, Spring, 1991, Daniel Halpern, Editor. Reprinted by permission of the author.

Siegfried Melchinger. "On 'The Cherry Orchard' " from *Anton Checkov*, translated by Edith Tarkov, 1972. Reprinted by permission of Ungar Press, an Imprint of Continuum Publishing Co.

Arthur Miller. From *Death of a Salesman* by Arthur Miller. Copyright 1949, renewed © 1977 by Arthur Miller. Used by permission of Viking Penguin, a division of Penguin Books USA Inc.

Molière. *The Misanthrope: Comedy in Five Acts* (including the Introduction), translation copyright © 1955, 1954 and renewed 1983, 1982 by Richard Wilbur, reprinted by permission of Harcourt Brace & Company. *Caution:* Professionals and amateurs are hereby warned that this translation, being fully protected under the copyright laws of the United States of America, the British Commonwealth, including the Dominion of Canada, and all other countries which are signatories to the Universal Copyright Convention and the International Copyright Convention, is subject to royalty. All rights, including professional, amateur, motion picture, recitation, lecturing, public reading, radio broadcasting, and television, are strictly reserved. Particular emphasis is laid on the question of readings, permission for which must be secured from the author's agent in writing. Inquiries on professional rights (except for amateur rights) should be addressed to Mr. Gilbert Parker, William Morris Agency, 1350 Avenue of the Americas, New York, NY 10019; inquiries on translation rights should be addressed to Permission Department, Harcourt Brace & Company, 6th Floor, Orlando, FL 32887–6777. The amateur acting rights of *The Misanthrope* are controlled exclusively by the Dramatists Play Service, Inc., 440 Park Avenue South, New York, NY 10016. No amateur performance of the play may be given without obtaining in advance the written permission of the Dramatists Play Service, Inc. and paying the requisite fee.

William Shakespeare. "The Tragedy of Hamlet, Prince of Denmark (text)," from *The Tragedy of Hamlet, Prince of Denmark* by William Shakespeare edited by Edward Hubler. Copyright © 1963 by Edward Hubler. Copyright © 1963, 1986, 1987 by Sylvan Barnet. Used by permission of New American Library, a division of Penguin Books USA, Inc.

Sophocles. "Oedipus Rex" and "Antigonê" from *Sophocles, The Oedipus Cycle: An English Version* by Dudley Fitts and Robert Fitzgerald, copyright 1939 by Harcourt Brace & Company and renewed 1967 by Dudley Fitts and Robert Fitzgerald, reprinted by permission of the publisher. *Caution:* All rights, including professional, amateur, motion picture, recitation, lecturing, performance, public reading, radio broadcasting, and television are strictly reserved. Inquiries on all rights should be addressed to Harcourt Brace & Company, Permissions Department, Orlando, FL 32887–6777.

Wendy Wasserstein. *Tender Offers* by Wendy Wasserstein, originally published in *Plays in One Act*, Antaeus #66, Spring, 1991, Daniel Halpern, Editor. Reprinted by permission of the author.

Casebook Credits

Sven Birkerts. "Perseus Unbound" from *The Gutenberg Elegies: The Fate of Reading in an Electronic Age* by Sven Birkerts. Copyright © 1994 by Sven Birkerts. Reprinted by permission of Faber & Faber, Inc.

Harold Bloom. Excerpts from *The Western Canon: The Books and School of the Ages*, copyright © 1994 by Harold Bloom, reprinted by permission of Harcourt Brace & Company.

T. S. Eliot. "What Is a Classic?" from *On Poetry and Poets* by T. S. Eliot. Copyright © 1957 by T. S. Eliot. Copyright renewed © 1985 by Valerie Eliot. Reprinted by permission of Farrar, Straus & Giroux, Inc.

Henry Louis Gates, Jr. "Whose Canon Is It Anyway?" by Henry Louis Gates, Jr. © 1989 Henry Louis Gates, Jr. First appeared in *The New York Times Book Review*. Reprinted by permission of Brandt & Brandt Literary Agents, Inc.

Todd Gitlin. "On the Virtues of a Loose Canon," NPQ, Summer, 1991, © Todd Gitlin 1991. Reprinted by permission of the author.

Irving Howe. "The Value of the Canon," © 1991, *The New Republic*. Reprinted by permission.

Katha Pollitt. "Why We Read," by Katha Pollitt, from the September 23, 1991 issue of *The Nation*. Reprinted with permission from *The Nation* magazine. © 1991 The Nation Company, Inc.

Photo Credits

Maya Angelou: AP/Wide World Photos; James Baldwin: UPI/Bettmann Newsphotos; Toni Cade Bambara: © Sandra L. Swans/Photographs and Prints Division, Schomburg Center for Research in Black Culture, New York Public Library, Astor, Lenox, and Tilden Foundations; Donald Charles Barthelme: AP/Wide World Photos; Charles Baudelaire: North Wind Picture Archives; Samuel Beckett: UPI/Bettmann; Elizabeth Bishop: AP/Wide World Photos; Gwendolyn Brooks: AP/Wide World Photos; Italo Calvino: AP/Wide World Photos; Raymond Carver: AP/Wide World Photos; Anton Chekov: Brown Brothers; Kate Chopin [photo has been cropped]: Holborn/Missouri Historical Society, St. Louis; Samuel Taylor Coleridge: North Wind Picture Archives; Emily Dickinson: The Bettmann Archive; Isak Dinesen: Culver Pictures, Inc.; John Donne: North Wind Picture Archives; Hilda Doolittle: AP/Wide World Photos; T. S. Eliot: Culver Pictures; Martín Espada: Courtesy of the author and Curbstone Press; William Faulkner: AP/Wide World Photos; Maria Irene Fornes: © Kim Zumwatt/Courtesy of Helen Merrill, Ltd.; Robert Frost: Brown Brothers; Athol Fugard: Ruphin Gaudyzer/SouthLight Photo Agency; Charlotte Perkins Gilman: Brown Brothers; Allen Ginsberg: AP/Wide World Photos; Nadine Gordimer: Gisele Wulfsohn/SouthLight Photo Agency; Nathaniel Hawthorne: North Wind Picture Archives; Bessie Head: George Hallett/SouthLight Photo Agency; Ernest Hemingway: Culver Pictures; Amy Hempel: © Jerry Bauer/Courtesy of Alfred A. Knopf, Inc.; Langston Hughes: AP/Wide World Photos; Zora Neale Hurston: The Granger Collection; Henrik Ibsen: North Wind Picture Archives; Washington Irving: North Wind Picture Archives; James Joyce: Culver Pictures; Sarah Orne Jewett: Brown Brothers; Donald Justice: UPI/Bettmann; Yasunari Kawabata: Burt Glinn/Magnum Photos; Jane Kenyon: Donald Hall/Courtesy of Graywolf Press; Milan Kundera: © A. Manheimer/Courtesy of HarperCollins Publishers; Stanley Kunitz: UPI/Bettmann; D. H. Lawrence: Brown Brothers; Ralph Lombreglia: © 1993, page 2 of 2 Mikki Ansin/Courtesy of Farrar, Straus & Giroux; Robert Lowell: AP/Wide World Photos; Edna St. Vincent Millay: Brown Brothers; Naguid Mahfouz: AP/Wide World Photos; Gabriel García Márquez: AP/Wide Word Photos; Guy de Maupassant: Culver Pictures; Reginald McKnight: Kimberly Pasko/Courtesy of University of Pittsburgh Press; Cassandra Medley: Anne Marsden/Courtesy of Cassandra Medley; Herman Melville: The Bettmann Archive; Arthur Miller: AP/Wide World Photos; Molière: North Wind Picture Archives; Alice Munro: © Marion Ettlinger/Courtesy of Alfred A. Knopf, Inc.; R. K. Narayan: AP/Wide World Photos; Pablo Neruda: UPI/Bettmann Newsphotos; Joyce Carol Oates: UPI/Bettmann; Flannery O'Connor: AP/Wide World Photos; Frank O'Connor: Brown Brothers; Boris Pasternak: AP/Wide World Photos; Sylvia Plath: UPI/Bettman; Edgar Allan Poe: North Wind Picture Archives; Adrienne Rich: AP/Wide World Photos; Rainier Maria Rilke: The Bettmann Archive; Olive Schreiner: Brown Brothers; Delmore Schwartz: Courtesy of New Directions; William Shakespeare: North Wind Picture Archives; Gary Snyder: AP/Wide World Photos; Susan Sontag: UPI/Bettmann Newsphotos; Sophocles: North Wind Picture Archives; Wallace Stevens: The Bettmann Archive; Junichiro Tanizaki: The Granger Collection; Jean Toomer: UPI/Bettmann; Amos Tutuola: Courtesy of Faber and Faber Limited; Mark Twain: North Wind Picture Archives; John Updike: AP/Wide World Photos; Luisa Valenzuela: Dorothy Alexander Photography/Courtesy of New York Institute for the Humanities; Derek Walcott: © 1989, Virginia Schendler/Courtesy of Farrar, Straus & Giroux, Inc.; Wendy Wasserstein: AP/Wide World Photos; Eudora Welty: AP/Wide World Photos; Oscar Wilde: North Wind Picture Archives; William Carlos Williams: Irving Wellcome/Courtesy of New Directions; Walt Whitman: North Wind Picture Archives; William Butler Yeats: North Wind Picture Archives.

Index of First Lines of Poetry

The tongue of the waves tolled in the earth's
    bell, 668
The two boys lean out on the railing, 932
The USA slowly lost its mandate, 754
The wet dawn inks are doing their blue dissolve,
    914
The whiskey on your breath, 601
The wind billowing out the seat of my britches,
    883
The world is charged with the grandeur of God,
    833
The world's great age begins anew, 817
The young women are obsessed with beauty, 922
Their faces, safe as an interior, 722
Then all the nations of birds lifted together, 909
Then it was dusk in Illinois, the small boy, 905
There are blows in life so violent—Don't ask me,
    865
There between the riverbank, 935
There is a cop who is both prowler and father,
    730
There is a garden in her face, 792
There is a moment in middle age, 927
There were some summers, 648
These are the first days of fall. The wind, 587
They are all gone into the world of light, 628
they come around, 943
They flee from me, that sometime did me seek,
    784
Thick now with sludge from the years of suburbs,
    with toys, 924
This afternoon it rains as never before; and I, 866
This is for spring and hail, that you may
    remember, 640
This is the easy time, there is nothing doing, 913
This is the field where the battle did not happen,
    888
This laboring through what is still undone, 849
This summer is full of insects, 921
"Those pine shingles—gunpowder dry, 752
Thou still unravish'd bride of quietness, 818
Three years she grew in sun and shower, 578
Thus she had lain, 907
To drown the ancient sorrows, 774
To pull the metal splinter from my palm, 942
Turn your head. Look. The light is turning
    yellow, 635
Turning and turning in the widening gyre, 839
2 a.m.: moonlight. The train has stopped, 779
Two nights, two days, in the solid deep-sea swell,
    767
Two women sit at a table by a window. Light
    breaks, 731
Tyger! Tyger! burning bright, 808

Underneath the tree on some, 609
Up, black, striped and damasked like the
    chasuble, 919

We bought great ornamental oranges, 657
We grow accustomed to the Dark—, 669
We shall not ever meet them bearded in heaven,
    898
We sit with friends at the round, 927
We take it with us, the cry, 659
Wee, sleekit, cow'rin', tim'rous beastie,
    809
Whan that Aprille with his shoures soote, 780
What happens to a dream deferred? 874
What I hope (when I hope) is that we'll, 918
What thoughts I have of you tonight, Walt
    Whitman, 900
When at night I await the beloved guest, 864
When God at first made man, 596
When homework is done, 834
"When I awoke dark on my stony bed, 779
When I come down to sleep death's endless
    night, 631
When I consider how my light is spent, 802
When I got there the dead opossum looked like,
    897
When I look at my elder sister now, 923
When I see birches bend to left and right, 539
When, in disgrace with Fortune and men's eyes,
    789
When it is not yet day, 911
When the girls at the register cheat her, when
    they bag, 567
When the Present has latched its postern behind
    my tremulous stay, 833
When to the sessions of sweet silent thought, 790
When you come, as you soon must, to the streets
    of our city, 892
Where, like a pillow on a bed, 793
While my hair was still cut straight across my
    forehead, 583
Who loves beauty, 771
Whose woods these are I think I know, 848
Wild Nights—Wild Nights! 831
With how sad steps, O Moon, thou climb'st the
    skies, 788
With the window sitting with you, 612
With yellow pears the land, 815
Woodcutter, 863

Yes, I know: only the happy man, 868
Yet once more, O ye laurels, and once more, 797
You are at a cocktail party, talking to someone
    who is skewering, 929
You do not do, you do not do, 571
You knew I was coming for you, little one, 937
You, once a belle in Shreveport, 723
You see, they have no judgment, 925
You will die and be still, never shall be memory
    left of you, 770

Index of Authors
and Titles

Index of Authors and Titles